THE NEW GROVE

DICTIONARY OF MUSIC AND MUSICIANS

Volume Two

THE NEW GROVE

Dictionary of Music and Musicians

SECOND EDITION

Edited by

Stanley Sadie

Executive Editor

John Tyrrell

VOLUME 2

Aristoxenus to Bax

GROVE

First Edition of *A Dictionary of Music and Musicians*, planned and edited by
SIR GEORGE GROVE, DCL, in four volumes, with an Appendix edited by J.A Fuller Maitland,
and an index by Mrs Edmond Wodehouse, 1878, 1880, 1883, 1889
Reprinted 1890, 1900

Second Edition, edited by J.A FULLER MAITLAND, in five volumes, 1904–10

Third Edition, edited by H.C. COLLES, in five volumes, 1927

Fourth Edition, edited by H.C. COLLES, in five volumes, with Supplementary Volume, 1940

Fifth Edition, edited by ERIC BLOM, in nine volumes, 1954; with Supplementary Volume 1961
Reprinted 1961, 1973, 1975

American Supplement, edited by WALDO SELDEN PRATT, in one volume, 1920
Reprinted with new material, 1928; many later reprints

The New Grove Dictionary of Music and Musicians ™ first edition
edited by STANLEY SADIE in twenty volumes, 1980
Reprinted 1981, 1984, 1985, 1986, 1987, 1988, 1989, 1990, 1991, 1992, 1993, 1994, 1995
Reprinted in paperback 1995, 1996, 1997, 1998

The New Grove Dictionary of Music and Musicians™ second edition
edited by STANLEY SADIE / executive editor JOHN TYRRELL,
published in twenty-nine volumes in the year 2001
Reprinted with minor corrections 2002

This edition is distributed within the United Kingdom and Europe by Macmillan Publishers Limited
London, and within the United States and Canada by Grove's Dictionaries Inc., New York

Text keyboarded by Alden Bookset, Oxford, England
Database management by Semantico, Brighton, England
Pagination by Clowes Group, Suffolk, England
Printed and bound by China Translation and Printing Services Ltd., China

---

British Library Cataloguing in Publication Data
The New Grove dictionary of music and musicians. – 2nd ed.
  1. Music – Dictionaries   2. Musicians – Dictionaries
  I. Sadie, Stanley, 1930–
ISBN 0-333-60800-3

Library of Congress Cataloging in Publication Data
The new Grove dictionary of music and musicians / edited by
Stanley Sadie; executive editor, John Tyrrell. – 2nd ed.
    p. cm.
  Includes bibliographical references and index.
  ISBN 1-56159-239-0 (cloth: alk.paper)
    1. Music—Encyclopedias. 2. Music—Bio-bibliography.
    I. Sadie, Stanley. II. Tyrrell, John.
ML100 .N48 2000
780'.3—dc21   00-0055156

Contents

General Abbreviations

A	alto, contralto [voice]
a	alto [instrument]
AA	Associate of the Arts
AB	Alberta; Bachelor of Arts
ABC	American Broadcasting Company; Australian Broadcasting Commission
Abt.	Abteilung [section]
ACA	American Composers Alliance
acc.	accompaniment, accompanied by
accdn	accordion
addl	additional
addn(s)	addition(s)
ad lib	ad libitum
aft(s)	afterpiece(s)
Ag	Agnus Dei
AGMA	American Guild of Musical Artists
AIDS	Acquired Immune Deficiency Syndrome
AK	Alaska
AL	Alabama
all(s)	alleluia(s)
AM	Master of Arts
a.m.	ante meridiem [before noon]
AMC	American Music Center
Amer.	American
amp	amplified
AMS	American Musicological Society
Anh.	Anhang [appendix]
anon.	anonymous(ly)
ant(s)	antiphon(s)
appx(s)	appendix(es)
AR	Arkansas
arr(s).	arrangement(s), arranged by/for
a-s	all-sung
ASCAP	American Society of Composers, Authors and Publishers
ASOL	American Symphony Orchestra League
attrib(s).	attribution(s), attributed to; ascription(s), ascribed to
Aug	August
aut.	autumn
AZ	Arizona
aztl	*azione teatrale*
B	bass [voice], bassus
B	Brainard catalogue [Tartini], Benton catalogue [Pleyel]
b	bass [instrument]
b	born
BA	Bachelor of Arts
bal(s)	ballad opera(s)
bap.	baptized
Bar	baritone [voice]
bar	baritone [instrument]
B-Bar	bass-baritone
BBC	British Broadcasting Corporation
BC	British Columbia
BCE	before Common Era [BC]
bc	basso continuo
Bd.	Band [volume]
BEd	Bachelor of Education
Beds.	Bedfordshire
Berks.	Berkshire
Berwicks.	Berwickshire

BFA	Bachelor of Fine Arts
BFE	British Forum for Ethnomusicology
bk(s)	book(s)
BLitt	Bachelor of Letters/Literature
blq(s)	burlesque(s)
blt(s)	burletta(s)
BM	Bachelor of Music
BME, BMEd	Bachelor of Music Education
BMI	Broadcast Music Inc.
BMus	Bachelor of Music
bn	bassoon
BRD	Federal Republic of Germany (Bundesrepublik Deutschland [West Germany])
Bros.	Brothers
BRTN	Belgische Radio en Televisie Nederlands
BS, BSc	Bachelor of Science
Bs	Benedictus
BSM	Bachelor of Sacred Music
Bte	Benedicite
Bucks.	Buckinghamshire
Bulg.	Bulgarian
bur.	buried
BVM	Blessed Virgin Mary
BWV	Bach-Werke-Verzeichnis [Schmieder, catalogue of J.S. Bach's works]
C	contralto
c	circa [about]
¢	cent
CA	California
Cambs.	Cambridgeshire
Can.	Canadian
CanD	Cantate Domino
cant(s).	cantata(s)
cap.	capacity
carn.	Carnival
cb	contrabass [instrument]
CBC	Canadian Broadcasting Corporation
CBE	Commander of the Order of the British Empire
CBS	Columbia Broadcasting System
CBSO	City of Birmingham Symphony Orchestra
CD(s)	compact disc(s)
CE	Common Era [AD]
CeBeDeM	Centre Belge de Documentation Musicale
cel	celesta
CEMA	Council for the Encouragement of Music and the Arts
cf	confer [compare]
c.f.	cantus firmus
CFE	Composers Facsimile Edition
CG	Covent Garden, London
CH	Companion of Honour
chap(s).	chapter(s)
chbr	chamber
Chin.	Chinese
chit	chitarrone
choreog(s).	choreography, choreographer(s), choreographed by
Cie	Compagnie
cimb	cimbalom
cl	clarinet
clvd	clavichord
cm	centimetre(s); *comédie en musique*
cmda	*comédie mêlée d'ariettes*

CNRS	Centre National de la Recherche Scientifique
CO	Colorado
Co.	Company; County
Cod.	Codex
col(s).	column(s)
coll.	collected by
collab.	in collaboration with
com	*componimento*
comm(s).	communion(s)
comp(s).	composer(s), composed (by)
conc(s).	concerto(s)
cond(s).	conductor(s), conducted by
cont	continuo
contrib(s).	contribution(s)
Corp.	Corporation
c.p.s.	cycles per second
cptr(s)	computer(s)
Cr	Credo, Creed
CRI	Composers Recordings, Inc.
CSc	Candidate of Historical Sciences
CT	Connecticut
Ct	Contratenor, countertenor
CUNY	City University of New York
CVO	Commander of the Royal Victorian Order
Cz.	Czech
D	Deutsch catalogue [Schubert]; Dounias catalogue [Tartini]
d.	denarius, denarii [penny, pence]
d	died
DA	Doctor of Arts
Dan.	Danish
db	double bass
DBE	Dame Commander of the Order of the British Empire
dbn	double bassoon
DC	District of Columbia
Dc	Discantus
DD	Doctor of Divinity
DDR	German Democratic Republic (Deutsche Demokratische Republik [East Germany])
DE	Delaware
Dec	December
ded(s).	dedication(s), dedicated to
DeM	Deus misereatur
Dept(s).	Department(s)
Derbys.	Derbyshire
DFA	Doctor of Fine Arts
dg	*dramma giocoso*
dir(s).	director(s), directed by
diss.	dissertation
dl	*drame lyrique*
DLitt	Doctor of Letters/Literature
DM	Doctor of Music
dm	*dramma per musica*
DMA	Doctor of Musical Arts
DME, DMEd	Doctor of Musical Education
DMus	Doctor of Music
DMusEd	Doctor of Music Education
DPhil	Doctor of Philosophy
Dr	Doctor
DSc	Doctor of Science/Historical Sciences
DSM	Doctor of Sacred Music
Dut.	Dutch
E.	East, Eastern
EBU	European Broadcasting Union
ed(s).	editor(s), edited (by)
EdD	Doctor of Education
edn(s)	edition(s)
EdS	Education Specialist
EEC	European Economic Community
e.g.	exempli gratia [for example]
el-ac	electro-acoustic
elec	electric, electronic
EMI	Electrical and Musical Industries
Eng.	English
eng hn	english horn
ENO	English National Opera

ens	ensemble
ENSA	Entertainments National Service Association
EP	extended-play (record)
esp.	especially
etc.	et cetera
EU	European Union
ex., exx.	example, examples
f, ff	following page, following pages
f., ff.	folio, folios
f	forte
fa(s)	farsa(s)
facs.	facsimile(s)
fasc(s).	fascicle(s)
Feb	February
ff	fortissimo
fff	fortississimo
fig(s).	figure(s) [illustration(s)]
FL	Florida
fl	flute
fl	floruit [he/she flourished]
Flem.	Flemish
fp	fortepiano [dynamic marking]
Fr.	French
frag(s).	fragment(s)
FRAM	Fellow of the Royal Academy of Music, London
FRCM	Fellow of the Royal College of Music, London
FRCO	Fellow of the Royal College of Organists, London
FRS	Fellow of the Royal Society, London
fs	full score
GA	Georgia
Gael.	Gaelic
GEDOK	Gemeinschaft Deutscher Organisationen von Künstlerinnen und Kunstfreundinnen
GEMA	Gesellschaft für Musikalische Aufführungs- und Mechanische Vervielfaltingungsrechte
Ger.	German
Gk.	Greek
Gl	Gloria
Glam.	Glamorgan
glock	glockenspiel
Glos.	Gloucestershire
GmbH	Gesellschaft mit Beschränkter Haftung [limited-liability company]
grad(s)	gradual(s)
GSM	Guildhall School of Music, London (to 1934)
GSMD	Guildhall School of Music and Drama, London (1935–)
gui	guitar
H	Hoboken catalogue [Haydn]; Helm catalogue [C.P.E. Bach]
Hants.	Hampshire
Heb.	Hebrew
Herts.	Hertfordshire
HI	Hawaii
hmn	harmonium
HMS	His/Her Majesty's Ship
HMV	His Master's Voice
hn	horn
Hon.	Honorary; Honourable
hp	harp
hpd	harpsichord
HRH	His/Her Royal Highness
Hung.	Hungarian
Hunts.	Huntingdonshire
Hz	Hertz [c.p.s.]
IA	Iowa
IAML	International Association of Music Libraries
IAWM	International Alliance for Women in Music
ibid.	ibidem [in the same place]
ICTM	International Council for Traditional Music
ID	Idaho
i.e.	id est [that is]
IFMC	International Folk Music Council
IL	Illinois
ILWC	International League of Women Composers

IMC	International Music Council		MEd	Master of Education
IMS	International Musicological Society		mel	*melodramma, mélodrame*
IN	Indiana		mels	*melodramma serio*
Inc.	Incorporated		melss	*melodramma semiserio*
inc.	incomplete		Met	Metropolitan Opera House, New York
incid	incidental		Mez	mezzo-soprano
incl.	includes, including		*mf*	mezzo-forte
inst(s)	instrument(s), instrumental		MFA	Master of Fine Arts
int(s)	intermezzo(s), introit(s)		MGM	Metro-Goldwyn-Mayer
IPEM	Instituut voor Psychoakoestiek en Elektronische Muziek, Ghent		MHz	megahertz [megacycles]
			MI	Michigan
IRCAM	Institut de Recherche et Coordination Acoustique/Musique		mic	microphone
			Middx	Middlesex
ISAM	Institute for Studies in American Music		MIDI	Musical Instrument Digital Interface
ISCM	International Society for Contemporary Music		MIT	Massachusetts Institute of Technology
ISDN	Integrated Services Digital Network		MLitt	Master of Letters/Literature
ISM	Incorporated Society of Musicians		Mlle, Mlles	Mademoiselle, Mesdemoiselles
ISME	International Society for Music Education		MM	Master of Music
It.	Italian		M.M.	Metronome Maelzel
			mm	millimetre(s)
Jan	January		MMA	Master of Musical Arts
Jap.	Japanese		MME, MMEd	Master of Music Education
Jb	Jahrbuch [yearbook]		Mme, Mmes	Madame, Mesdames
JD	Doctor of Jurisprudence		MMT	Master of Music in Teaching
Jg.	Jahrgang [year of publication/volume]		MMus	Master of Music
jr	junior		MN	Minnesota
Jub	Jubilate		MO	Missouri
			mod	modulator
K	Kirkpatrick catalogue [D. Scarlatti]; Köchel catalogue [Mozart: no. after '/' is from 6th edn; also Fux]		Mon.	Monmouthshire
			movt(s)	movement(s)
			MP(s)	Member(s) of Parliament
kbd	keyboard		*mp*	mezzo-piano
KBE	Knight Commander of the Order of the British Empire		MPhil	Master of Philosophy
			Mr	Mister
KCVO	Knight Commander of the Royal Victorian Order		Mrs	Mistress; Messieurs
			MS	Master of Science(s); Mississippi
kg	kilogram(s)		MS(S)	manuscript(s)
Kgl	Königlich(e, er, es) [Royal]		MSc	Master of Science(s)
kHz	kilohertz [1000 c.p.s.]		MSLS	Master of Science in Library and Information Science
km	kilometre(s)		MSM	Master of Sacred Music
KS	Kansas		MT	Montana
KY	Kentucky		Mt	Mount
Ky	Kyrie		mt(s)	music-theatre piece(s)
			MTNA	Music Teachers National Association
£	libra(e) [pound(s) sterling]		MusB, MusBac	Bachelor of Music
L.	no. of song in R.W. Linker: *A Bibliography of Old French Lyrics* (University, MS, 1979)			
			muscm(s)	musical comedy (comedies)
L	Longo catalogue [A. Scarlatti]		MusD, MusDoc	Doctor of Music
LA	Louisiana			
Lanarks.	Lanarkshire		musl(s)	musical(s)
Lancs.	Lancashire		MusM	Master of Music
Lat.	Latin			
Leics.	Leicestershire		N.	North, Northern
LH	left hand		n(n).	footnote(s)
lib(s)	libretto(s)		nar(s)	narrator(s)
Lincs.	Lincolnshire		NB	New Brunswick
lit(s)	litany (litanies)		NBC	National Broadcasting Company
Lith.	Lithuanian		NC	North Carolina
LittD	Doctor of Letters/Literature		ND	North Dakota
LLB	Bachelor of Laws		n.d.	no date of publication
LLD	Doctor of Laws		NDR	Norddeutscher Rundfunk
loc. cit.	loco citato [in the place cited]		NE	Nebraska
LP	long-playing record		NEA	National Endowment for the Arts
LPO	London Philharmonic Orchestra		NEH	National Endowment for the Humanities
LSO	London Symphony Orchestra		NET	National Educational Television
Ltd	Limited		NF	Newfoundland and Labrador
Ltée	Limitée		NH	New Hampshire
			NHK	Nippon Hōsō Kyōkai [Japanese broadcasting system]
M, MM.	Monsieur, Messieurs		NJ	New Jersey
m	metre(s)		NM	New Mexico
MA	Massachusetts; Master of Arts		no(s).	number(s)
Mag	Magnificat		Nor.	Norwegian
MALS	Master of Arts in Library Sciences		Northants.	Northamptonshire
mand	mandolin		Notts.	Nottinghamshire
mar	marimba		Nov	November
MAT	Master of Arts and Teaching		n.p.	no place of publication
MB	Bachelor of Music; Manitoba		nr	near
MBE	Member of the Order of the British Empire		NRK	Norsk Rikskringkasting [Norwegian broadcasting system]
MD	Maryland			
ME	Maine			

NS	Nova Scotia
NSW	New South Wales
NT	North West Territories
Nunc	Nunc dimittis
NV	Nevada
NY	New York [State]
NZ	New Zealand
ob	*opera buffa*; oboe
obbl	obbligato
OBE	Officer of the Order of the British Empire
obl	*opéra-ballet*
OC	Opéra-Comique, Paris [the company]
oc	*opéra comique* [genre]
Oct	October
off(s)	offertory (offertories)
OH	Ohio
OK	Oklahoma
OM	Order of Merit
ON	Ontario
op(s)	opera(s)
op., opp.	opus, opera [plural of opus]
op. cit.	opere citato [in the work cited]
opt.	optional
OR	Oregon
orat(s)	oratorio(s)
orch	orchestra(tion), orchestral
orchd	orchestrated (by)
org	organ
orig.	original(ly)
ORTF	Office de Radiodiffusion-Télévision Française
os	*opera seria*
oss	*opera semiseria*
OUP	Oxford University Press
ov(s).	overture(s)
Oxon.	Oxfordshire
P	Pincherle catalogue [Vivaldi]
p.	*pars*
p., pp.	page, pages
p	piano [dynamic marking]
PA	Pennsylvania
p.a.	per annum [annually]
pan(s)	pantomime(s)
PBS	Public Broadcasting System
PC	no. of chanson in A. Pillet and H. Carstens: *Bibliographie der Troubadours* (Halle, 1933)
PE	Prince Edward Island
perc	percussion
perf(s).	performance(s), performed (by)
pf	piano [instrument]
pfmr(s)	performer(s)
PhB	Bachelor of Philosophy
PhD	Doctor of Philosophy
PhDEd	Doctor of Philosophy in Education
pic	piccolo
pl(s).	plate(s); plural
p.m.	post meridiem [after noon]
PO	Philharmonic Orchestra
Pol.	Polish
pop.	population
Port.	Portuguese
posth.	posthumous(ly)
POW(s)	prisoner(s) of war
pp	pianissimo
ppp	pianississimo
PQ	Province of Quebec
PR	Puerto Rico
pr.	printed
prep pf	prepared piano
PRO	Public Record Office, London
prol(s)	prologue(s)
PRS	Performing Right Society
Ps(s)	Psalm(s)
ps(s)	psalm(s)
pseud(s).	pseudonym(s)
pt(s)	part(s)
ptbk(s)	partbook(s)
pubd	published

pubn(s)	publication(s)
PWM	Polskie Wydawnictwo Muzyczne
QC	Queen's Counsel
qnt(s)	quintet(s)
qt(s)	quartet(s)
R	[in signature] editorial revision
R	photographic reprint [edn of score or early printed source]
R.	no. of chanson in G. Raynaud, *Bibliographie des chansonniers français des XIIIe et XIVe siècles* (Paris, 1884)
ʀ	Ryom catalogue [Vivaldi]
r	recto
R	response
RAF	Royal Air Force
RAI	Radio Audizioni Italiane
RAM	Royal Academy of Music, London
RCA	Radio Corporation of America
RCM	Royal College of Music, London
re(s)	response(s) [type of piece]
rec	recorder
rec.	recorded [in discographic context]
recit(s)	recitative(s)
red(s).	reduction(s), reduced for
reorchd	reorchestrated (by)
repr.	reprinted
resp(s)	respond(s)
Rev.	Reverend
rev(s).	revision(s); revised (by/for)
RH	right hand
RI	Rhode Island
RIAS	Radio im Amerikanischen Sektor
RIdIM	Répertoire International d'Iconographie Musicale
RILM	Répertoire International de Littérature Musicale
RIPM	Répertoire International de la Presse Musicale
RISM	Répertoire International des Sources Musicales
RKO	Radio-Keith-Orpheum
RMCM	Royal Manchester College of Music
rms	root mean square
RNCM	Royal Northern College of Music, Manchester
RO	Radio Orchestra
Rom.	Romanian
r.p.m.	revolutions per minute
RPO	Royal Philharmonic Orchestra
RSFSR	Russian Soviet Federated Socialist Republic
RSO	Radio Symphony Orchestra
RTÉ	Radio Telefís Éireann
RTF	Radiodiffusion-Télévision Française
Rt Hon.	Right Honourable
RTVB	Radio-Télévision Belge de la Communauté Française
Russ.	Russian
ʀv	Ryom catalogue [Vivaldi]
S	San, Santa, Santo, São [Saint]; soprano [voice]
S	sound recording
S.	South, Southern
$	dollars
s	soprano [instrument]
s.	solidus, solidi [shilling, shillings]
SACEM	Société d'Auteurs, Compositeurs et Editeurs de Musique
San	Sanctus
sax	saxophone
SC	South Carolina
SD	South Dakota
sd	*scherzo drammatico*
SDR	Süddeutscher Rundfunk
Sept	September
seq(s)	sequence(s)
ser(s)	serenata(s)
ser.	series
Serb.	Serbian
sf, sfz	sforzando, sforzato
sing.	singular
SJ	Societas Jesu [Society of Jesus]
SK	Saskatchewan
SO	Symphony Orchestra

SOCAN	Society of Composers, Authors and Music Publishers of Canada
Sp.	Spanish
spkr(s)	speaker(s)
Spl	Singspiel
SPNM	Society for the Promotion of New Music
spr.	spring
sq	square
sr	senior
SS	Saints (It., Sp.); Santissima, Santissimo [Most Holy]
SS	steamship
SSR	Soviet Socialist Republic
St(s)	Saint(s)/Holy, Sankt, Sint, Szent
Staffs.	Staffordshire
STB	Bachelor of Sacred Theology
Ste	Sainte
str	string(s)
sum.	summer
SUNY	State University of New York
Sup	superius
suppl(s).	supplement(s), supplementary
Swed.	Swedish
SWF	Südwestfunk
sym(s).	symphony (symphonies), symphonic
synth	synthesizer, synthesized
T	tenor [voice]
t	tenor [instrument]
tc	*tragicommedia*
td(s)	*tonadilla*(s)
TeD	Te Deum
ThM	Master of Theology
timp	timpani
tm	*tragédie en musique*
TN	Tennessee
tpt	trumpet
Tr	treble [voice]
tr(s)	tract(s); treble [instrument]
trad.	traditional
trans.	translation, translated by
transcr(s).	transcription(s), transcribed by/for
trbn	trombone
TV	television
TWV	Menke catalogue [Telemann]
TX	Texas
U.	University
UCLA	University of California at Los Angeles
UHF	ultra-high frequency
UK	United Kingdom of Great Britain and Northern Ireland
Ukr.	Ukrainian
unacc.	unaccompanied
unattrib.	unattributed
UNESCO	United Nations Educational, Scientific and Cultural Organization
UNICEF	United Nations International Children's Emergency Fund
unorchd	unorchestrated

unperf.	unperformed
unpubd	unpublished
UP	University Press
US	United States [adjective]
USA	United States of America
USSR	Union of Soviet Socialist Republics
UT	Utah
v, vv	voice, voices
v., vv.	verse, verses
v	verso
v.	versus
V	versicle
VA	Virginia
va	viola
vc	cello
vcle(s)	versicle(s)
VEB	Volkseigener Betrieb [people's own industry]
Ven	Venite
VHF	very high frequency
VI	Virgin Islands
vib	vibraphone
viz	videlicet [namely]
vle	violone
vn	violin
vol(s).	volume(s)
vs	vocal score, piano-vocal score
VT	Vermont
W.	West, Western
WA	Washington [State]
Warwicks.	Warwickshire
WDR	Westdeutscher Rundfunk
WI	Wisconsin
Wilts.	Wiltshire
wint.	winter
WNO	Welsh National Opera
woo	Werke ohne Opuszahl
Worcs.	Worcestershire
WPA	Works Progress Administration
WQ	Wotquenne catalogue [C.P.E. Bach]
WV	West Virginia
ww	woodwind
WY	Wyoming
xyl	xylophone
YMCA	Young Men's Christian Association
Yorks.	Yorkshire
YT	Yukon Territory
YWCA	Young Women's Christian Association
YYS	(Zhongguo yishu yanjiuyuan) Yinyue yanjiusuo and variants (Music Research Institute (of the Chinese Academy of Arts))
z	Zimmermann catalogue [Purcell]
zar(s)	zarzuela(s)
zargc	*zarzuela género chico*

Bibliographical Abbreviations

All bibliographical abbreviations used in this dictionary are listed below, following the typography used in the text of the dictionary. Broadly, *italic* type is used for periodicals and for reference works; roman type is used for anthologies, series etc. (titles of individual volumes are italicized).

Full bibliographical information is not normally supplied in the list below if it is available elsewhere in the dictionary. Its availability is indicated as follows: D – in the list of 'Dictionaries and encyclopedias of music'; E – in the list of 'Editions, historical'; and P – in the list of 'Periodicals'; these lists are located in vol.28. For other items, in particular national (non-musical) biographical dictionaries, basic bibliographical information is given here; and in some cases extra information is supplied to clarify the abbreviation used.

Festschriften and congress reports are not generally covered in this list. Although Festschrift titles are sometimes shortened in the dictionary, sufficient information is always given for unambiguous identification (dedicatee; occasion, if the same person is dedicatee of more than one Festschrift; place and date of publication; and name(s) of editor(s) if known). For fuller information on musical Festschriften up to 1967 see W. Gerboth: *An Index to Musical Festschriften and Similar Publications* (New York, 1969). The published titles of congress reports are generally reduced to their essentials, but sufficient information is always given for purposes of identification (society or topic; place and date of occurrence; journal issue if published in a periodical; editor(s) and publication details in unfamiliar cases). A comprehensive list of musical and music-related 'Congress reports' appears in vol.28. Further information can be found in J. Tyrrell and R. Wise: *A Guide to International Congress Reports in Music, 1900–1975* (London, 1979).

19CM	*19th Century Music* P
ACAB	*American Composers Alliance Bulletin* P
AcM	*Acta musicologica* P
ADB	*Allgemeine deutsche Biographie* (Leipzig, 1875–1912)
AdlerHM	G. Adler, ed.: *Handbuch der Musikgeschichte* (Frankfurt, 1924, 2/1930/R)
AfM	*African Music* P
AH	Analecta hymnica medii aevi E
AllacciD	L. Allacci: *Drammaturgia* D
AM	Antiphonale monasticum pro diurnis horis (Tournai, 1934)
AmbrosGM	A.W. Ambros: *Geschichte der Musik* (Leipzig, 1862–82/R)
AMe, AMeS	*Algemene muziekencyclopedie* and suppl. D
AMf	*Archiv für Musikforschung* P
AMI	*L'arte musicale in Italia* E
AMMM	Archivium musices metropolitanum mediolanense E
AMP	Antiquitates musicae in Polonia E
AMw	*Archiv für Musikwissenschaft* P
AMZ	*Allgemeine musikalische Zeitung* (1798–1848, 1863–5, 1866–82) P
AMz	*Allgemeine (deutsche) Musik-Zeitung/Musikzeitung* (1874–1943) P
Anderson2	E.R. Anderson: *Contemporary American Composers: a Biographical Dictionary* D
AnM	*Anuario musical* P
AnMc, AnMc	*Analecta musicologica* P
AnnM	*Annales musicologiques* P
AnthonyFB	J.R. Anthony: *French Baroque Music from Beaujoyeulx to Rameau* (London, 1973, 3/1997)
AntMI	Antiquae musicae italicae E
AÖAW	*Anzeiger der Österreichischen Akademie der Wissenschaften, philosophisch-historische Klasse* (1948–)
ApelG	W. Apel: *Geschichte der Orgel- und Klaviermusik bis 1700* (Kassel, 1967; Eng. trans., rev., 1972)
AR	*Antiphonale sacrosanctae romanae ecclesiae pro diurnis horis* (Paris, Tournai and Rome, 1949)
AS	W.H. Frere, ed.: *Antiphonale sarisburiense* (London, 1901–25/R)
AshbeeR	A. Ashbee: *Records of English Court Music* (Snodland/Aldershot, 1986–95)
AsM	*Asian Music* P
AudaM	A. Auda: *La musique et les musiciens de l'ancien pays de Liège* D
AusDB	*Australian Dictionary of Biography* (Melbourne, 1966–96)
Baker5[–8]	*Baker's Biographical Dictionary of Musicians* D
BAMS	*Bulletin of the American Musicological Society* P
BDA	*A Biographical Dictionary of Actors, Actresses, Musicians, Dancers, Managers & Other Stage Personnel in London, 1660–1800* (Carbondale, IL, 1973–93)
BDECM	A. Ashbee and D. Lasocki, eds.: *A Biographical Dictionary of English Court Musicians, 1485–1714* (Aldershot, 1998)
BDRSC	A. Ho and D. Feofanov, eds.: *Biographical Dictionary of Russian/Soviet Composers* D
BeckEP	J.H. Beck: *Encyclopedia of Percussion* D
BeJb	*Beethoven-Jahrbuch* P
BenoitMC	M. Benoit: *Musiques de cour: chapelle, chambre, écurie, 1661–1733* (Paris, 1971)
BenzingB	J. Benzing: *Die Buchdrucker des 16. und 17. Jahrhunderts* (Wiesbaden, 1963, 2/1982)
BerliozM	H. Berlioz: *Mémoires* (Paris, 1870; ed. and trans. D. Cairns, 1969, 2/1970); ed. P. Citron (Paris, 1969, 2/1991)
BertolottiM	A. Bertolotti: *Musici alla corte dei Gonzaga in Mantova dal secolo XV al XVIII* (Milan, 1890/R)

BicknellH	S. Bicknell: *The History of the English Organ* (Cambridge, 1996)
BJb	*Bach-Jahrbuch* P
BladesPI	J. Blades: *Percussion Instruments and their History* (London, 1970, 2/1974)
BlumeEK	F. Blume: *Die evangelische Kirchenmusik* (Potsdam, 1931–4/R, enlarged 2/1965 as *Geschichte der evangelischen Kirchenmusik*; Eng. trans., enlarged, 1974, as *Protestant Church Music: a History*)
BMB	Bibliotheca musica bononiensis (Bologna, 1967–)
BMw	*Beiträge zur Musikwissenschaft*
BNB	*Biographie nationale [belge]* (Brussels, 1866–1986)
BoalchM	D.H. Boalch: *Makers of the Harpsichord and Clavichord 1440 to 1840* D
BoetticherOL	W. Boetticher: *Orlando di Lasso und seine Zeit* (Kassel, 1958)
Bouwsteenen: JVNM	*Bouwsteenen: jaarboek der Vereeniging voor Nederlandsche muziekgeschiedenis* P
BoydenH	D.D. Boyden: *A History of Violin Playing from its Origins to 1761* (London, 1965)
BPM	*Black Perspective in Music* P
BrenetC	M. Brenet: *Les concerts en France sous l'ancien régime* (Paris, 1900/R)
BrenetM	M. Brenet: *Les musiciens de la Sainte-Chapelle du Palais* (Paris, 1910/R)
BrookB	B.S. Brook, ed.: *The Breitkopf Thematic Catalogue, 1762–1787* (New York, 1966)
BrookSF	B.S. Brook: *La symphonie française dans la seconde moitié du XVIIIe siècle* (Paris, 1962)
BrownI	H.M. Brown: *Instrumental Music Printed Before 1600: a Bibliography* (Cambridge, MA, 1965)
Brown-Stratton BMB	J.D. Brown and S.S. Stratton: *British Musical Biography* D
BSIM	*Bulletin français de la S.I.M.* [also *Mercure musical* and other titles] P
BUCEM	E.B. Schnapper, ed.: *British Union-Catalogue of Early Music* (London, 1957)
BurneyFI	C. Burney: *The Present State of Music in France and Italy* (London, 1771, 2/1773)
BurneyGN	C. Burney: *The Present State of Music in Germany, the Netherlands, and the United Provinces* (London, 1773, 2/1775)
BurneyH	C. Burney: *A General History of Music from the Earliest Ages to the Present Period* (London, 1776–89); ed. F. Mercer (London, 1935/R) [p. nos. refer to this edn]
BWQ	*Brass and Woodwind Quarterly* P
CaffiS	F. Caffi: *Storia della musica sacra nella già cappella ducale di San Marco in Venezia dal 1318 al 1797* (Venice, 1854–5/R); ed. E. Surian (Florence, 1987)
CaM	Catalogus musicus (Kassel, 1963–)
CampbellGC	M. Campbell: *The Great Cellists* D
CampbellGV	M. Campbell: *The Great Violinists* D
CAO	Corpus antiphonalium officii (Rome, 1963–79)
CBY	*Current Biography Yearbook* (1955–)
CC	B. Morton and P. Collins, eds.: *Contemporary Composers*
CeBeDeM directory	*CeBeDeM et ses compositeurs affiliés*, ed. D. von Volborth-Danys (Brussels, 1977–80)
CEKM	Corpus of Early Keyboard Music E
CEMF	Corpus of Early Music (in Facsimile) (Brussels, 1970–72)
CHM	*Collectanea historiae musicae* (1953–66)
Choron-FayolleD	A.-E. Choron and F.J.M. Fayolle: *Dictionnaire historique des musiciens* D
ClinkscaleMP	M.N. Clinkscale: *Makers of the Piano* D
CM	Le choeur des muses E
CMc	*Current Musicology* P
CMI	I classici musicali italiani (Milan, 1941–56)
CMM	Corpus mensurabilis musicae E
ČMm	*Časopis Moravského musea [muzea, 1977–]* P
CMR	*Contemporary Music Review* P
CMz	*Cercetări de muzicologie* P
CohenE	A.I. Cohen: *International Encyclopedia of Women Composers* D
CohenWE	Y.W. Cohen: *Werden und Entwicklung der Musik in Israel* (Kassel, 1976)
COJ	*Cambridge Opera Journal* P
CooverMA	J.B. Coover: *Music at Auction: Puttick and Simpson* (Warren, MI, 1988)
CoussemakerS	C.-E.-H. de Coussemaker: *Scriptorum de musica medii aevi nova series* (Paris, 1864–76/R, 2/1908, ed. U. Moser)
CroceN	B. Croce: *I teatri di Napoli* (Naples, 1891/R, 5/1966)
ČSHS	*Československý hudební slovník* D
CSM	Corpus scriptorum de musica (Rome, later Stuttgart, 1950–)
CSPD	*Calendar of State Papers (Domestic)* (London, 1856–1972)
Cw	Das Chorwerk E
DAB	*Dictionary of American Biography* (New York, 1928–37, suppls., 1944–)
DAM	*Dansk aarbog for musikforskning* P
Day-Murrie ESB	C.L. Day and E.B. Murrie: *English Song-Books* (London, 1940)
DBF	*Dictionnaire de biographie française* (Paris, 1933–)
DBI	*Dizionario biografico degli italiani* (Rome, 1960–)
DBL, DBL2, DBL3	*Dansk biografisk leksikon* (Copenhagen, 1887–1905, 2/1933–45, 3/1979–84)
DBNM, DBNM	*Darmstädter Beiträge zur neuen Musik* P
DBP	E. Vieira, ed.: *Diccionário biográphico de musicos portuguezes* (Lisbon, 1900)
DČHP	*Dějiny české hudby v příkladech* (Prague, 1958)
DDT	Denkmäler deutscher Tonkunst E
DEMF	A. Devriès and F. Lesure: *Dictionnaire des éditeurs de musique français* D
DEUMM	*Dizionario enciclopedico universale della musica e dei musicisti* D
DeutschMPN	O.E. Deutsch: *Music Publishers' Numbers* (London, 1946)
DHM	Documenta historica musicae E
Dichter-ShapiroSM	H. Dichter and E. Shapiro: *Early American Sheet Music* D
DJbM	*Deutsches Jahrbuch der Musikwissenschaft* P
DlabaczKL	G.J. Dlabacž: *Allgemeines historisches Künstler-Lexikon* D
DM	Documenta musicologica (Kassel, 1951–)
DMt	*Dansk musiktidsskrift* P
DMV	*Drammaturgia musicale veneta* (Milan, 1983–)
DNB	*Dictionary of National Biography* (Oxford, 1885–1901, suppls., 1901–96)
DoddI	G. Dodd, ed.: *Thematic Index of Music for Viols* (London, 1980–)
DTB	Denkmäler der Tonkunst in Bayern E
DTÖ	Denkmäler der Tonkunst in Österreich E
DugganIMI	M.K. Duggan: *Italian Music Incunabula: Printers and Type* (Berkeley, 1991)
DVLG	*Deutsche Vierteljahrsschrift für Literaturwissenschaft und Geistesgeschichte* (1923–)
ECCS	The Eighteenth-Century Continuo Sonata E
ECFC	The Eighteenth-Century French Cantata E
EDM	Das Erbe deutscher Musik E
EECM	Early English Church Music E
EG	*Etudes grégoriennes*
EI	*The Encyclopaedia of Islam* (Leiden, 1928–38, 2/1960–)
EinsteinIM	A. Einstein: *The Italian Madrigal* (Princeton, NJ, 1949/R)
EIT	*Yezhegodnik imperatorskikh teatrov* P
EitnerQ	R. Eitner: *Biographisch-bibliographisches Quellen-Lexikon* D
EitnerS	R. Eitner: *Bibliographie der Musik-Sammelwerke des XVI. und XVII. Jahrhunderts* (Berlin, 1877/R)
EKM	Early Keyboard Music E
EL	The English School of Lutenist Songwriters, rev. as The English Lute-Songs E
EM	The English Madrigal School, rev. as The English Madrigalists E
EMc	*Early Music* P
EMC1, 2	*Encyclopedia of Music in Canada* (Toronto, 1981, 2/1992) D

EMDC	A. Lavignac and L. de La Laurencie, eds.: *Encyclopédie de la musique et dictionnaire du Conservatoire* D
EMH	*Early Music History* P
EMN	Exempla musica neerlandica E
EMS	see EM
EMuz	*Encyklopedia muzyczne* D
ERO	Early Romantic Opera E
ES	English Song 1600–1675 (New York, 1986–9)
ES	*Enciclopedia dello spettacolo* D
ESLS	see EL
EthM	*Ethnomusicology* P
EthM Newsletter	*Ethno[-]musicology Newsletter* P
EwenD	D. Ewen: *American Composers: a Biographical Dictionary* D
FAM	*Fontes artis musicae* P
FasquelleE	*Encyclopédie de la musique* D
FCVR	Florilège du concert vocal de la Renaissance E
FellererG	K.G. Fellerer: *Geschichte der katholischen Kirchenmusik* (Düsseldorf, 1939, enlarged 2/1949; Eng. trans., 1961/R)
FellererP	K.G. Fellerer: *Der Palestrinastil und seine Bedeutung in der vokalen Kirchenmusik des 18. Jahrhunderts* (Augsburg, 1929/R)
FenlonMM	I. Fenlon: *Music and Patronage in Sixteenth-Century Mantua* (Cambridge, 1980–82)
FétisB, FétisBS	F.-J. Fétis: *Biographie universelle des musiciens* and suppl. D
FisherMP	W.A. Fisher: *One Hundred and Fifty Years of Music Publishing in the United States* (Boston, 1933)
FiskeETM	R. Fiske: *English Theatre Music in the Eighteenth Century* (London, 1973, 2/1986)
FlorimoN	F. Florimo: *La scuola musicale di Napoli e i suoi conservatorii* (Naples, 1880–83/R)
FO	French Opera in the 17th and 18th Centuries (New York, 1983–)
FortuneISS	N. Fortune: *Italian Secular Song from 1600 to 1635: the Origins and Development of Accompanied Monody* (diss., U. of Cambridge, 1954)
Friedlaender DL	M. Friedlaender: *Das deutsche Lied im 18. Jahrhundert* (Stuttgart and Berlin, 1902/R)
FrotscherG	G. Frotscher: *Geschichte des Orgelspiels und der Orgelkomposition* (Berlin, 1935–6/R, music suppl. 1966)
FuldWFM	J.J. Fuld: *The Book of World-Famous Music* D
FullerPG	S. Fuller: *The Pandora Guide to Women Composers: Britain and the United States (1629 – Present)* D
FürstenauG	M. Fürstenau: *Zur Geschichte der Musik und des Theaters am Hofe zu Dresden* (Dresden, 1861–2/R)
GänzlBMT	K. Gänzl: *The British Musical Theatre* (London, 1986)
GänzlEMT	K. Gänzl and A. Lamb: *Encyclopedia of Musical Theatre* D
GaspariC	G. Gaspari: *Catalogo della Biblioteca del Liceo musicale di Bologna*, i–iv (Bologna, 1890–1905/R); v, ed. U. Sesini (Bologna, 1943/R)
GerberL	E.L. Gerber: *Historisch-biographisches Lexikon der Tonkünstler* D
GerberNL	E.L. Gerber: *Neues historisch-biographisches Lexikon der Tonkünstler* D
GerbertS	M. Gerbert: *Scriptores ecclesiastici de musica sacra potissimum* (St Blasien, 1784/R, 3/1931)
GEWM	*The Garland Encyclopedia of World Music* D
GfMKB	*Gesellschaft für Musikforschung: Kongress-Bericht* [1950–]
GiacomoC	S. di Giacomo: *I quattro antichi conservatorii musicali di Napoli* (Milan, 1924–8)
GLMT	Greek and Latin Music Theory (Lincoln, NE, 1984–)
GMB	Geschichte der Musik in Beispielen E
GMM	*Gazzetta musicale di Milano* P
GOB	German Opera 1770–1800, ed. T. Bauman (New York, 1985–6)
GöhlerV	A. Göhler: *Verzeichnis der in den Frankfurter und Leipziger Messkatalogen der Jahre 1564 bis 1759 angezeigten Musikalien* (Leipzig, 1902/R)

GoovaertsH	A. Goovaerts: *Histoire et bibliographie de la typographie musicale dans les Pays-Bas* (Antwerp, 1880/R)
GR	*Graduale sacrosanctae romanae ecclesiae* (Tournai, 1938)
Grove1[–5]	G. Grove, ed.: *A Dictionary of Music and Musicians* D
Grove6	*The New Grove Dictionary of Music and Musicians* D
GroveA	*The New Grove Dictionary of American Music* D
GroveI	*The New Grove Dictionary of Musical Instruments* D
GroveJ	*The New Grove Dictionary of Jazz* D
GroveJapan	*The New Grove Dictionary of Music and Musicians*, Jap. trans. D
GroveO	*The New Grove Dictionary of Opera* D
GroveW	*The New Grove Dictionary of Women Composers* D
GS	W.H. Frere, ed.: *Graduale sarisburiense* (London, 1894/R)
GSJ	*Galpin Society Journal* P
GSL	K.J. Kutsch and L. Riemann: *Grosses Sängerlexikon*
GV	R. Celletti: *Le grandi voci: dizionario critico-biografico dei cantanti* D
HAM	Historical Anthology of Music E
Harrison MMB	F.Ll. Harrison: *Music in Medieval Britain* (London, 1958, 4/1980)
HawkinsH	J. Hawkins: *A General History of the Science and Practice of Music* (London, 1776)
HBSJ	*Historical Brass Society Journal* P
HDM	W. Apel: *Harvard Dictionary of Music* D
HJb	*Händel-Jahrbuch* D
HJbMw	*Hamburger Jahrbuch für Musikwissenschaft* P
HM	Hortus musicus E
HMC	Historical Manuscripts Commission [Publications]
HMT	*Handwörterbuch der musikalischen Terminologie* D
HMw	Handbuch der Musikwissenschaft (Potsdam, 1927–34)
HMYB	*Hinrichsen's Musical Year Book* P
HoneggerD	M. Honegger: *Dictionnaire de la musique* D
HopkinsonD	C. Hopkinson: *A Dictionary of Parisian Music Publishers 1700–1950* D
Hopkins-RimbaultO	E.J. Hopkins and E.F. Rimbault: *The Organ: its History and Construction* (London, 1855, 3/1887/R)
HPM	Harvard Publications in Music E
HR	*Hudební revue* P
HRo	*Hudební rozhledy* P
Humphries-SmithMP	C. Humphries and W.C. Smith: *Music Publishing in the British Isles* D
HV	*Hudební věda* P
ICSC	The Italian Cantata in the Seventeenth Century (New York, 1985–6)
IIM	Italian Instrumental Music of the Sixteenth and Early Seventeenth Centuries E
IIM	*Izvestiya na Instituta za muzika* P
IMa	Instituta et monumenta
IMi	Istituzioni e monumenti dell'arte musicale italiana (Milan, 1931–9, new ser., 1956–64)
IMSCR	*International Musicological Society: Congress Report* [1930–]
IMusSCR	*International Musical Society: Congress Report* [II–IV, 1906–11]
IO	The Italian Oratorio 1650–1800 E
IOB	Italian Opera 1640–1770, ed. H.M. Brown E
IOG	Italian Opera 1810–1840, ed. P. Gossett E
IRASM	*International Review of the Aesthetics and Sociology of Music* P
IRMAS	*International Review of Music Aesthetics and Sociology* P
IRMO	S.L. Ginzburg: *Istoriya russkoy muzïki v notnïkh obraztsakh* (Leningrad, 1940–52, 2/1968–70)
ISS	Italian Secular Song 1606–1636 (New York, 1986)
IZ	*Instrumentenbau-Zeitschrift* P
JAMIS	*Journal of the American Musical Instrument Society* P
JAMS	*Journal of the American Musicological Society* P
JASA	*Journal of the Acoustical Society of America* P
JazzM	*Jazz Monthly* P
JBIOS	*Journal of the British Institute of Organ Studies* P

JbLH	*Jahrbuch für Liturgik und Hymnologie* P	
JbMP	*Jahrbuch der Musikbibliothek Peters* P	
JbO	*Jahrbuch für Opernforschung* P	
JbSIM	*Jahrbuch des Staatlichen Instituts für Musikforschung Preussischer Kulturbesitz* P	
JEFDSS	*Journal of the English Folk Dance and Song Society* P	
JFSS	*Journal of the Folk-Song Society* P	
JIFMC	*Journal of the International Folk Music Council* P	
JJ	*Jazz Journal* P	
JJI	*Jazz Journal International* P	
JJS	*Journal of Jazz Studies* P	
JLSA	*Journal of the Lute Society of America* P	
JM	*Journal of Musicology* P	
JMR	*Journal of Musicological Research* P	
JMT	*Journal of Music Theory* P	
JoãoIL	[João IV:] *Primeira parte do index da livraria de musica do muyto alto, e poderoso Rey Dom João o IV. nosso senhor* (Lisbon, 1649); ed. J. de Vasconcellos (Oporto, 1874–6)	
Johansson FMP	C. Johansson: *French Music Publishers' Catalogues* (Stockholm, 1955)	
JohanssonH	C. Johansson: *J.J. & B. Hummel: Music Publishing and Thematic Catalogues* (Stockholm, 1972)	
JR	*Jazz Review* P	
JRBM	*Journal of Renaissance and Baroque Music* P	
JRMA	*Journal of the Royal Musical Association* P	
JRME	*Journal of Research in Music Education* P	
JT	*Jazz Times* P	
JVdGSA	*Journal of the Viola da Gamba Society of America* P	
JVNM	see *Bouwsteenen: JVNM*	
KdG	*Komponisten der Gegenwart*, ed. H.-W. Heister and W.-W. Sparrer D	
KermanEM	J. Kerman: *The Elizabethan Madrigal: a Comparative Study* (New York, 1962)	
KidsonBMP	F. Kidson: *British Music Publishers, Printers and Engravers* D	
KingMP	A.H. King: *Four Hundred Years of Music Printing* (London, 1964)	
KJb	*Kirchenmusikalisches Jahrbuch* P	
KM	*Kwartalnik muzyczny* P	
KöchelKHM	L. von Köchel: *Die kaiserliche Hof-Musikkapelle in Wien von 1543 bis 1867* (Vienna, 1869/R)	
KretzschmarG	H. Kretzschmar: *Geschichte des neuen deutschen Liedes* (Leipzig, 1911/R)	
KrummelEMP	D.W. Krummel: *English Music Printing* (London, 1975)	
LaborD	*Diccionario de la música Labor* D	
La BordeE	J.-B. de La Borde: *Essai sur la musique ancienne et moderne* D	
LabordeMP	L.E.S.J. de Laborde: *Musiciens de Paris, 1535–1792* D	
LafontaineKM	H.C. de Lafontaine: *The King's Musick* (London, 1909/R)	
La Laurencie EF	L. de La Laurencie: *L'école française de violon de Lully à Viotti* (Paris, 1922–4/R)	
LAMR	*Latin American Music Review* P	
LaMusicaD	*La musica: dizionario* D	
LaMusicaE	*La musica: enciclopedia storica* D	
LangwillI7	see *Waterhouse-LangwillI*	
LedeburTLB	C. von Ledebur: *Tonkünstler-Lexicon Berlin's* (Berlin, 1861/R)	
Le HurayMR	P. Le Huray: *Music and the Reformation in England, 1549–1660* (London, 1967, 2/1978)	
LipowskyBL	F.J. Lipowsky: *Baierisches Musik-Lexikon* D	
LM	*Lucrări de muzicologie* P	
Lockwood MRF	L. Lockwood: *Music in Renaissance Ferrara* (Oxford, 1984)	
LoewenbergA	A. Loewenberg: *Annals of Opera, 1597–1940* D	
LPS	*The London Pianoforte School 1766–1860* E	
LS	*The London Stage, 1660–1800* (Carbondale, IL, 1960–68)	
LSJ	*Lute Society Journal* P	
LU	*Liber usualis missae et officii pro dominicis et festis duplicibus cum cantu gregoriano* (Solesmes, 1896, and later edns incl. Tournai, 1963)	
Lütgendorff GL	W.L. von Lütgendorff: *Die Geigen- und Lautenmacher vom Mittelalter bis zur Gegenwart* D	
LZMÖ	*Lexikon zeitgenössischer Musik aus Österreich* (Vienna, 1997)	

MA	*Musical Antiquary* P	
MAB	Musica antiqua bohemica E	
MAk	*Muzïkal'naya akademiya* P	
MAM	Musik alter Meister E	
MAMS	Monumenta artis musicae Sloveniae E	
MAn	*Music Analysis* P	
MAP	Musica antiqua polonica E	
MAS	Musical Antiquarian Society [Publications] E	
Mattheson GEP	J. Mattheson: *Grundlage einer Ehren-Pforte* (Hamburg, 1740); ed. Max Schneider (Berlin, 1910/R)	
MB	Musica britannica E	
MC	Musica da camera E	
McCarthyJR	A. McCarthy: *Jazz on Record* (London, 1968)	
MCL	H. Mendel and A. Reissmann, eds.: *Musikalisches Conversations-Lexikon* (Berlin, 1870–80, 3/1890–91/R)	
MD	*Musica disciplina* P	
ME	*Muzïkal'naya entsiklopediya* D	
MEM	Mestres de l'Escolanía de Montserrat E	
MersenneHU	M. Mersenne: *Harmonie universelle* D	
MeyerECM	E.H. Meyer: *English Chamber Music* (London, 1946/R, rev. 3/1982 with D. Poulton as *Early English Chamber Music*)	
MeyerMS	E.H. Meyer: *Die mehrstimmige Spielmusik des 17. Jahrhunderts* (Kassel, 1934)	
MF	Music in Facsimile (New York, 1983–91)	
Mf	*Die Musikforschung* P	
MG	*Musik und Gesellschaft* P	
MGG1, 2	*Die Musik in Geschichte und Gegenwart* D	
MGH	Monumenta Germaniae historica	
MH	Música hispana E	
MischiatiI	O. Mischiati: *Indici, cataloghi e avvisi degli editori e librai musicali italiani* (Florence, 1984)	
MISM	*Mitteilungen der Internationalen Stiftung Mozarteum*	
MJb	*Mozart-Jahrbuch* [Salzburg, 1950–] P	
ML	*Music & Letters* P	
MLE	Music for London Entertainment 1660–1800 E	
MLMI	Monumenta lyrica medii aevi italica E	
MM	*Modern Music* P	
MMA	*Miscellanea musicologica* [Australia] P	
MMB	Monumenta musicae byzantinae E	
MMBel	Monumenta musicae belgicae E	
MMC	*Miscellanea musicologica* [Czechoslovakia] P	
MME	Monumentos de la música española E	
MMFTR	Monuments de la musique française au temps de la Renaissance E	
MMg	*Monatshefte für Musikgeschichte* P	
MMI	Monumenti di musica italiana E	
MMMA	Monumenta monodica medii aevi E	
MMN	Monumenta musica neerlandica E	
MMP	Monumenta musicae in Polonia E	
MMR	*Monthly Musical Record* P	
MMRF	Les maîtres musiciens de la Renaissance française E	
MMS	Monumenta musicae svecicae E	
MNAN	Music of the New American Nation E	
MO	*Musical Opinion* P	
MooserA	R.-A. Mooser: *Annales de la musique et des musiciens en Russie au XVIIIme siècle* D	
MoserGV	A. Moser: *Geschichte des Violinspiels* (Berlin, 1923, rev. 2/1966–7 by H.J. Nösselt)	
MQ	*Musical Quarterly* P	
MR	*Music Review* P	
MRM	Monuments of Renaissance Music E	
MRS	Musiche rinascimentali siciliane E	
MS	*Muzïkal'nïy sovremennik* P	
MSD	Musicological Studies and Documents E	
MT	*Musical Times* P	
MusAm	*Musical America* P	
MVH	Musica viva historica E	
MVSSP	Musiche vocali e strumentali sacre e profane E	
Mw	Das Musikwerk E	
MZ	*Muzikološki zbornik* P	
NA	*Note d'archivio per la storia musicale* P	
NBeJb	*Neues Beethoven-Jahrbuch* P	
NBL	*Norsk biografisk leksikon* (Oslo, 1923–83)	
NDB	*Neue deutsche Biographie* (Berlin, 1953–)	

Neighbour-TysonPN	O.W. Neighbour and A. Tyson: *English Music Publishers' Plate Numbers* (London, 1965)	
NericiS	L. Nerici: *Storia della musica in Lucca* (Lucca, 1879/R)	
NewcombMF	A. Newcomb: *The Madrigal at Ferrara, 1579–1597* (Princeton, NJ, 1980)	
NewmanSBE	W.S. Newman: *The Sonata in the Baroque Era* (Chapel Hill, NC, 1959, 4/1983)	
NewmanSCE	W.S. Newman: *The Sonata in the Classic Era* (Chapel Hill, NC, 1963, 3/1983)	
NewmanSSB	W.S. Newman: *The Sonata since Beethoven* (Chapel Hill, NC, 1969, 3/1983)	
NicollH	A. Nicoll: *The History of English Drama, 1660–1900* (Cambridge, 1952–9)	
NM	Nagels Musik-Archiv E	
NMÅ	*Norsk musikkgranskning årbok* P	
NNBW	*Nieuw Nederlandsch biografisch woordenboek* (Leiden, 1911–37)	
NÖB	*Neue österreichische Biographie* (Vienna, 1923–35)	
NOHM, NOHM	*The New Oxford History of Music* (Oxford, 1954–90)	
NRMI	*Nuova rivista musicale italiana* P	
NZM	*Neue Zeitschrift für Musik* P	
OHM, OHM	*The Oxford History of Music* (Oxford, 1901–5, 2/1929–38)	
OM	*Opus musicum* P	
ÖMz	*Österreichische Musikzeitschrift* P	
ON	*Opera News* P	
OQ	*Opera Quarterly* P	
OW	*Opernwelt* P	
PalMus	Paléographie musicale E	
PAMS	*Papers of the American Musicological Society* P	
PÄMw	Publikation älterer praktischer und theoretischer Musikwerke E	
PazdírekH	B. Pazdírek: *Universal-Handbuch der Musikliteratur aller Zeiten und Völker* (Vienna, 1904–10/R)	
PBC	Publicaciones del departamento de música E	
PEM	C. Dahlhaus and S. Döhring, eds.: *Pipers Enzyklopädie des Musiktheaters* (Munich and Zürich, 1986–97)	
PG	*Patrologiae cursus completus*, ii: Series graeca, ed. J.-P. Migne (Paris, 1857–1912)	
PGfM	see PÄMw	
PierreH	C. Pierre: *Histoire du Concert spirituel 1725–1790* (Paris, 1975)	
PIISM	Pubblicazioni dell'Istituto italiano per la storia della musica E	
PirroHM	A. Pirro: *Histoire de la musique de la fin du XIVe siècle à la fin du XVIe* (Paris, 1940)	
PirrottaDO	N. Pirrotta and E. Povoledo: *Li due Orfei: da Poliziano a Monteverdi* (Turin, 1969, enlarged 2/1975; Eng. trans., 1982, as *Music and Theatre from Poliziano to Monteverdi*)	
PitoniN	G.O. Pitoni: *Notitia de contrapuntisti e de compositori di musica* (MS, c1725, I-Rvat C.G.I/1–2); ed. C. Ruini (Florence, 1988)	
PL	*Patrologiae cursus completus*, i: Series latina, ed. J.-P. Migne (Paris, 1844–64)	
PM	Portugaliae musica E	
PMA	*Proceedings of the Musical Association* P	
PMFC	Polyphonic Music of the Fourteenth Century E	
PMM	*Plainsong and Medieval Music* P	
PNM	*Perspectives of New Music* P	
PraetoriusSM	M. Praetorius: *Syntagma musicum*, i (Wittenberg and Wolfenbüttel, 1614–15, 2/1615/R); ii (Wolfenbüttel, 1618, 2/1619/R; Eng. trans., 1986, 2/1991); iii (Wolfenbüttel, 1618, 2/1619/R)	
PraetoriusTI	M. Praetorius: *Theatrum instrumentorum* [pt ii/2 of *PraetoriusSM*]	
PRM	*Polski rocznik muzykologiczny* P	
PRMA	*Proceedings of the Royal Musical Association* P	
Przywecka-SameckaDM	M. Przywecka-Samecka: *Drukarstwo muzyczne w Polsce do końca XVIII wieku* (Kraków, 1969)	
PSB	*Polskich słownik biograficzny* (Kraków, 1935)	
PSFM	Publications [Société française de musicologie] E	
Quaderni della RaM	*Quaderni della Rassegna musicale* P	

Rad JAZU	*Rad Jugoslavenske akademije znanosti i umjetnosti* P	
RaM	*Rassegna musicale* P	
RBM	*Revue belge de musicologie* P	
RdM	*Revue de musicologie* P	
RdMc	*Revista de musicología* P	
ReeseMMA	G. Reese: *Music in the Middle Ages* (New York, 1940)	
ReeseMR	G. Reese: *Music in the Renaissance* (New York, 1954, 2/1959)	
RefardtHBM	E. Refardt: *Historisch-biographisches Musikerlexikon der Schweiz* D	
ReM	*Revue musicale* P	
RFS	Romantic French Song 1830–1870 E	
RGMP	*Revue et gazette musicale de Paris* P	
RHCM	*Revue d'histoire et de critique musicales* P	
RicciTB	C. Ricci: *I teatri di Bologna nei secoli XVII e XVIII: storia aneddotica* (Bologna, 1888/R)	
RicordiE	C. Sartori and R. Allorto: *Enciclopedia della musica*	
RiemannG	H. Riemann: *Geschichte der Musiktheorie im IX.–XIX. Jahrhundert* (Berlin, 2/1921/R; Eng. trans. of pts i–ii, 1962/R, and pt iii, 1977)	
RiemannL11, 12	*Hugo Riemanns Musiklexikon* (11/1929, 12/1959–75) D	
RIM	*Rivista italiana di musicologia* P	
RIMS	*Rivista internazionale di musica sacra* P	
RM	*Ruch muzyczny* P	
RMARC	*R.M.A. [Royal Musical Association] Research Chronicle* P	
RMC	*Revista musical chilena* P	
RMF	Renaissance Music in Facsimile (New York, 1986–8)	
RMFC	*Recherches sur la musique française classique* P	
RMG	*Russkaya muzikal'naya gazeta* P	
RMI	*Rivista musicale italiana* P	
RMS	Renaissance Manuscript Studies (Stuttgart, 1975–)	
RN	*Renaissance News* P	
RosaM	C. de Rosa, Marchese di Villarosa: *Memorie dei compositori di musica del regno di Napoli* (Naples, 1840)	
RRAM	Recent Researches in American Music E	
RRMBE	Recent Researches in the Music of the Baroque Era E	
RRMCE	Recent Researches in the Music of the Classical Era E	
RRMMA	Recent Researches in the Music of the Middle Ages and Early Renaissance E	
RRMNETC	Recent Researches in the Music of the Nineteenth and Early Twentieth Centuries E	
RRMR	Recent Researches in the Music of the Renaissance E	
SachsH	C. Sachs: *The History of Musical Instruments* (New York, 1940)	
SainsburyD	J.H. Sainsbury: *A Dictionary of Musicians* D	
SartoriB	C. Sartori: *Bibliografia della musica strumentale italiana stampata in Italia fino al 1700* (Florence, 1952–68)	
SartoriD	C. Sartori: *Dizionario degli editori musicali italiani* D	
SartoriL	C. Sartori: *I libretti italiani a stampa dalle origini al 1800* (Cuneo, 1990–94)	
SBL	*Svenskt biografiskt lexikon* (Stockholm, 1918–)	
SCC	The Sixteenth-Century Chanson E	
ScheringGIK	A. Schering: *Geschichte des Instrumental-Konzerts* (Leipzig, 1905, 2/1927/R)	
ScheringGO	A. Schering: *Geschichte des Oratoriums* (Leipzig, 1911/R)	
SchillingE	G. Schilling: *Encyclopädie der gesammten musikalischen Wissenschaften, oder Universal-Lexicon der Tonkunst* D	
SČHK	*Slovník české hudební kultury* (Prague, 1997)	
SchmidlD, SchmidlDS	C. Schmidl: *Dizionario universale dei musicisti* and suppl. D	
SchmitzG	E. Schmitz: *Geschichte der weltlichen Solokantate* (Leipzig, 1914, 2/1955)	
SchullerEJ	G. Schuller: *Early Jazz* (New York, 1968/R)	
SchullerSE	G. Schuller: *The Swing Era* (New York, 1989)	
SchwarzGM	B. Schwarz: *Great Masters of the Violin* D	
SCISM	Seventeenth-Century Italian Sacred Music E	
SCKM	Seventeenth-Century Keyboard Music (New York, 1987–8)	
SCMA	Smith College Music Archives E	
SCMad	Sixteenth-Century Madrigal E	

SCMot	Sixteenth-Century Motet E
SeegerL	H. Seeger: *Musiklexikon* D
SEM	Series of Early Music [University of California] E
SennMT	W. Senn: *Musik und Theater am Hof zu Innsbruck* (Innsbruck, 1954)
SH	*Slovenská hudba* P
SIMG	*Sammelbände der Internationalen Musik-Gesellschaft* P
SKM	*Sovetskiye kompozitori i muzïkovedï* (Moscow, 1978–89)
SM	see *SMH*
SMA	*Studies in Music* [Australia] P
SMC	*Studies in Music from the University of Western Ontario* [Canada] P
SMd	Schweizerische Musikdenkmäler E
SMH	*Studia musicologica Academiae scientiarum hungaricae* P
SmitherHO	H. Smither: *A History of the Oratorio* (Chapel Hill, NC, 1977–)
SML	*Schweizer Musikerlexikon* D
SMM	Summa musicae medii aevi E
SMN	*Studia musicologica norvegica* P
SMP	*Słownik muzyków polskich* D
SMSC	Solo Motets from the Seventeenth Century (New York, 1987–8)
SMw	*Studien zur Musikwissenschaft* P
SMz	*Schweizerische Musikzeitung/Revue musicale suisse* P
SOB	Süddeutsche Orgelmeister des Barock E
SOI	L. Bianconi and G. Pestelli, eds.: *Storia dell'opera italiana* (Turin, 1987–; Eng. trans., 1998–)
SolertiMBD	A. Solerti: *Musica, ballo e drammatica alla corte medicea dal 1600 al 1637* (Florence, 1905/R)
SouthernB	E. Southern: *Biographical Dictionary of Afro-American and African Musicians* D
SovM	*Sovetskaya muzïka* P
SpataroC	B.J. Blackburn, E.E. Lowinsky and C.A. Miller: *A Correspondence of Renaissance Musicians* (Oxford, 1991)
SPFFBU	*Sborník prací filosofické [filozofické] fakulty brněnské university [univerzity]* P
SpinkES	I. Spink: *English Song: Dowland to Purcell* (London, 1974, repr. 1986 with corrections)
StevensonRB	R. Stevenson: *Renaissance and Baroque Musical Sources in the Americas* (Washington DC, 1970)
Stevenson SCM	R. Stevenson: *Spanish Cathedral Music in the Golden Age* (Berkeley, 1961/R)
StevensonSM	R. Stevenson: *Spanish Music in the Age of Columbus* (The Hague, 1960/R)
StiegerO	F. Stieger: *Opernlexikon* D
STMf	*Svensk tidskrift för musikforskning* P
StrohmM	R. Strohm: *Music in Late Medieval Bruges* (Oxford, 1985)
StrohmR	R. Strohm: *The Rise of European Music* (Cambridge, 1993)
StrunkSR1, 2	O. Strunk: *Source Readings in Music History* (New York, 1950/R, rev. 2/1998 by L. Treitler)
SubiráHME	J. Subirá: *Historia de la música española e hispanoamericana* (Barcelona, 1953)
TCM	Tudor Church Music E
TCMS	Three Centuries of Music in Score (New York, 1988–90)
Thompson1 [–11]	O. Thompson: *The International Cyclopedia of Music and Musicians*, 1st–11th edns D
TM	Thesauri musici E
TSM	*Tesoro sacro musical* P
TVNM	*Tijdschrift van de Vereniging voor Nederlandse muziekgeschiedenis* [and earlier variants] P
UVNM	Uitgave van oudere Noord-Nederlandsche Meesterwerken E
Vander Straeten MPB	E. Vander Straeten: *La musique aux Pays-Bas avant le XIXe siècle* D
VannesD	R. Vannes, with A. Souris: *Dictionnaire des musiciens (compositeurs)* D
VannesE	R. Vannes: *Essai d'un dictionnaire universel des luthiers* D
VintonD	J. Vinton: *Dictionary of Contemporary Music* D
VirdungMG	S. Virdung: *Musica getutscht* (Basle, 1511/R)
VMw	*Vierteljahrsschrift für Musikwissenschaft* P
VogelB	E. Vogel: *Bibliothek der gedruckten weltlichen Vocalmusik Italiens, aus den Jahren 1500 bis 1700* (Berlin, 1892/R)
WalterG	F. Walter: *Geschichte des Theaters und der Musik am kurpfälzischen Hofe* (Leipzig, 1898/R)
WaltherML	J.G. Walther: *Musicalisches Lexicon, oder Musicalische Bibliothec* D
Waterhouse-LangwillI	W. Waterhouse: *The New Langwill Index: a Dictionary of Musical Wind-Instrument Makers and Inventors* D
WDMP	Wydawnictwo dawnej muzyki polskiej E
WE	The Wellesley Edition E
WECIS	Wellesley Edition Cantata Index Series (Wellesley, MA, 1964–72)
Weinmann WM	A. Weinmann: *Wiener Musikverleger und Musikalienhändler von Mozarts Zeit bis gegen 1860* (Vienna, 1956)
WilliamsNH	P. Williams: *A New History of the Organ: from the Greeks to the Present Day* (London, 1980)
WinterfeldEK	C. von Winterfeld: *Der evangelische Kirchengesang und sein Verhältniss zur Kunst des Tonsatzes* (Leipzig, 1843–7/R)
WolfeMEP	R.J. Wolfe: *Early American Music Engraving and Printing* (Urbana, IL, 1980)
WolfH	J. Wolf: *Handbuch der Notationskunde* (Leipzig, 1913–19/R)
WurzbachL	C. von Wurzbach: *Biographisches Lexikon des Kaiserthums Oesterreich* (Vienna, 1856–91)
YIAMR	*Yearbook, Inter-American Institute for Musical Research*, later *Yearbook for Inter-American Musical Research* P
YIFMC	*Yearbook of the International Folk Music Council* P
YoungHI	P.T. Young: *4900 Historical Woodwind Instruments* (London, 1993) [enlarged 2nd edn of *Twenty Five Hundred Historical Woodwind Instruments* (New York, 1982)]
YTM	*Yearbook for Traditional Music* P
ZahnM	J. Zahn: *Die Melodien der deutschen evangelischen Kirchenlieder* (Gütersloh, 1889–93/R)
ZDADL	*Zeitschrift für deutsches Altertum und deutsche Literatur* (1876–)
ZfM	*Zeitschrift für Musik* P
ŹHMP	*Źródła do historii muzyki polskiej* E
ZI	*Zeitschrift für Instrumentenbau* P
ZIMG	*Zeitschrift der Internationalen Musik-Gesellschaft* P
ZL	*Zenei lexikon* D
ZMw	*Zeitschrift für Musikwissenschaft* P
ZT	*Zenetudományi tanulmányok* P

Discographical Abbreviations

20C	20th Century
20CF	20th Century-Fox
AAFS	Archive of American Folksong (Library of Congress)
A&M Hor.	A&M Horizon
ABC-Para.	ABC-Paramount
AH	Artists House
AIMP	Archives Internationales de Musique Populaire (Musée d'Ethnographie, Geneva), pubd by VDE-Gallo
Ala.	Aladdin
AM	American Music
Amer.	America
AN	Arista Novus
Ant.	Antilles
Ari.	Arista
Asy.	Asylum
Atl.	Atlantic
Aut.	Autograph
Bak.	Bakton
Ban.	Banner
Bay.	Baystate
BB	Black and Blue
Bb	Bluebird
Beth.	Bethlehem
BH	Bee Hive
BL	Black Lion
BN	Blue Note
Bruns.	Brunswick
BS	Black Saint
BStar	Blue Star
Cad.	Cadence
Can.	Canyon
Cand.	Candid
Cap.	Capitol
Car.	Caroline
Cas.	Casablanca
Cat.	Catalyst
Cen.	Century
Chi.	Chiaroscuro
Cir.	Circle
CJ	Classic Jazz
Cob.	Cobblestone
Col.	Columbia
Com.	Commodore
Conc.	Concord
Cont.	Contemporary
Contl	Continental
Cot.	Cotillion
CP	Charlie Parker
CW	Creative World
Del.	Delmark
DG	Deutsche Grammophon
Dis.	Discovery
Dra.	Dragon
EB	Electric Bird
Elec.	Electrola
Elek.	Elektra
Elek. Mus.	Elektra Musician
EmA	EmArcy
ES	Elite Special
Eso.	Esoteric
Ev.	Everest
EW	East Wind
Ewd	Eastworld
FaD	Famous Door
Fan.	Fantasy
FD	Flying Dutchman
FDisk	Flying Disk
Fel.	Felsted
Fon.	Fontana
Fre.	Freedom
FW	Folkways
Gal.	Galaxy
Gen.	Gennett
GM	Groove Merchant
Gram.	Gramavision
GTJ	Good Time Jazz
HA	Hat Art
Hal.	Halcyon
Har.	Harmony
Harl.	Harlequin
HH	Hat Hut
Hick.	Hickory
HM	Harmonia Mundi
Hor.	Horizon
Hyp.	Hyperion
IC	Inner City
IH	Indian House
ImA	Improvising Artists
Imp.	Impulse!
Imper.	Imperial
IndN	India Navigation
Isl.	Island
JAM	Jazz America Marketing
Jlgy	Jazzology
Jlnd	Jazzland
Jub.	Jubilee
Jwl	Jewell
Jzt.	Jazztone
Key.	Keynote
Kt.	Keytone
Lib.	Liberty
Lml.	Limelight
Lon.	London
Mdsv.	Moodsville
Mer.	Mercury
Met.	Metronome
Metro.	Metrojazz
MJR	Master Jazz Recordings
Mlst.	Milestone
Mlt.	Melotone
Moers	Moers Music
MonE	Monmouth-Evergreen
Mstr.	Mainstream
Musi.	Musicraft

Nat.	National		SE	Strata-East
NewJ	New Jazz		Sig.	Signature
Norg.	Norgran		Slnd	Southland
NW	New World		SN	Soul Note
			SolS	Solid State
OK	Okeh		Son.	Sonora
OL	Oiseau-Lyre		Spot.	Spotlite
Omni.	Omnisound		Ste.	Steeplechase
			Sto.	Storyville
PAct	Pathé Actuelle		Sup.	Supraphon
PAlt	Palo Alto			
Para.	Paramount		Tak.	Takoma
Parl.	Parlophone		Tan.	Tangent
Per.	Perfect		TE	Toshiba Express
Phi.	Philips		Tei.	Teichiku
Phon.	Phontastic		Tel.	Telefunken
PJ	Pacific Jazz		The.	Theresa
PL	Pablo Live		Tim.	Timeless
Pol.	Polydor		TL	Time-Life
Prog.	Progressive		Tran.	Transition
Prst.	Prestige			
PT	Pablo Today		UA	United Artists
PW	Paddle Wheel		Upt.	Uptown
Qual.	Qualiton		Van.	Vanguard
			Var.	Variety
Reg.	Regent		Vars.	Varsity
Rep.	Reprise		Vic.	Victor
Rev.	Revelation		VJ	Vee-Jay
Riv.	Riverside		Voc.	Vocalion
Roul.	Roulette			
RR	Red Records		WB	Warner Bros.
RT	Real Time		WP	World Pacific
Sack.	Sackville		Xan.	Xanadu
Sat.	Saturn			

Library Sigla

The system of library sigla in this dictionary follows that used by Répertoire International des Sources Musicales, Kassel, as listed in its publication *RISM-Bibliothekssigel* (Kassel, 1999). Below are listed the sigla to be found; a few of them are additional to those published in the RISM list, but have been established in consultation with the RISM organization. Some original RISM sigla that have now been changed are retained here.

More information on individual libraries is available in the libraries list in volume 28.

In the dictionary, sigla are always printed in *italic*. In any listing of sources a national sigillum applies without repetition until it is contradicted.

Within each national list, entries are alphabetized by sigillum, first by capital letters (showing the city or town) and then by lower-case ones (showing the institution or collection).

A: AUSTRIA

A	Admont, Benediktinerstift, Archiv und Bibliothek
DO	Dorfbeuren, Pfarramt
Ed	Eisenstadt, Domarchiv, Musikarchiv
Ee	——, Esterházy-Archiv
Eh	——, Haydn-Museum
Ek	——, Stadtpfarrkirche
El	——, Burgenländisches Landesmuseum
ETgoëss	Ebenthal (nr Klagenfurt), Goëss private collection
F	Fiecht, St Georgenberg, Benediktinerstift, Bibliothek
FB	Fischbach (Oststeiermark), Pfarrkirche
FK	Feldkirch, Domarchiv
Gd	Graz, Diözesanarchiv
Gk	——, Universität für Musik und Darstellende Kunst
Gl	——, Steiermärkische Landesbibliothek am Joanneum
Gmi	——, Institut für Musikwissenschaft
Gu	——, Universitätsbibliothek
GÖ	Göttweig, Benediktinerstift, Musikarchiv
GÜ	Güssing, Franziskaner Kloster
H	Herzogenburg, Augustiner-Chorherrenstift, Musikarchiv
HE	Heiligenkreuz, Zisterzienserkloster
Ik	Innsbruck, Tiroler Landeskonservatorium
Imf	——, Tiroler Landesmuseum Ferdinandeum
Imi	——, Musikwissenschaftliches Institut der Universität
Iu	——, Universitätsbibliothek
Kk	Klagenfurt, Kärntner Landeskonservatorium, Stiftsbibliothek
Kla	——, Landesarchiv
Kse	——, Schlossbibliothek Ebental
KN	Klosterneuburg, Augustiner-Chorherrenstift, Stiftsbibliothek
KR	Kremsmünster, Benediktinerstift, Musikarchiv
L	Lilienfeld, Zisterzienser-Stift, Musikarchiv und Bibliothek
LA	Lambach, Benediktinerstift
LIm	Linz, Oberösterreichisches Landesmuseum
LIs	——, Bundesstaatliche Studienbibliothek
M	Melk, Benediktiner-Superiorat Mariazell
MB	Michaelbeuern, Benediktinerabtei
MS	Mattsee, Stiftsarchiv
MT	Maria Taferl (Niederösterreich), Pfarre
MZ	Mariazell, Benediktiner-Priorat, Bibliothek und Archiv
N	Neuburg, Pfarrarchiv
R	Rein, Zisterzienserstift
RB	Reichersberg, Stift
Sca	Salzburg, Carolino Augusteum: Salzburger Museum für Kunst und Kulturgeschichte, Bibliothek
Sd	——, Dom, Konsistorialarchiv, Dommusikarchiv
Sk	——, Kapitelbibliothek
Sl	——, Landesarchiv
Sm	——, Internationale Stiftung Mozarteum, Bibliotheca Mozartiana
Smi	——, Universität Salzburg, Institut für Musikwissenschaft, Bibliothek
Sn	——, Nonnberg (Benediktiner-Frauenstift), Bibliothek
Sp	——, Bibliothek des Priesterseminars
Ssp	——, Erzabtei St Peter, Musikarchiv
Sst	——, Bundesstaatliche Studienbibliothek [in *Su*]
Su	——, Universitätsbibliothek
SB	Schlierbach, Stift
SCH	Schlägl, Prämonstratenser-Stift, Bibliothek
SE	Seckau, Benediktinerabtei
SEI	Seitenstetten, Benediktinerstift, Musikarchiv
SF	St Florian, Augustiner-Chorherrenstift, Stiftsbibliothek, Musikarchiv
SL	St Lambrecht, Benediktiner-Abtei, Bibliothek
SPL	St Paul, Benediktinerstift St Paul im Lavanttal
ST	Stams, Zisterzienserstift, Musikarchiv
STEp	Steyr, Stadtpfarre
TU	Tulln, Pfarrkirche St Stephan
VOR	Vorau, Stift
Wa	Vienna, St Augustin, Musikarchiv
Waf	——, Pfarrarchiv Altlerchenfeld
Wdo	——, Zentralarchiv des Deutschen Orden
Wdtö	——, Gesellschaft zur Herausgabe von Denkmälern der Tonkunst in Österreich
Wgm	——, Gesellschaft der Musikfreunde
Wh	——, Pfarrarchiv Hernals
Whh	——, Haus-, Hof- und Staatsarchiv
Whk	——, Hofburgkapelle [in *Wn*]
Wk	——, St Karl Borromäus
Wkm	——, Kunsthistorisches Museum
Wlic	——, Pfarrkirche Wien-Lichtental
Wm	——, Minoritenkonvent
Wmi	——, Institut für Musikwissenschaft der Universität
Wn	——, Österreichische Nationalbibliothek, Musiksammlung
Wp	——, Musikarchiv, Piaristenkirche Maria Treu
Ws	——, Schottenabtei, Musikarchiv
Wsa	——, Stadtarchiv
Wsfl	——, Schottenfeld, Pfarrarchiv St Laurenz

Wsp	——, St Peter, Musikarchiv
Wst	——, Stadt- und Landesbibliothek, Musiksammlung
Wu	——, Universitätsbibliothek
Wwessely	——, Othmar Wessely, private collection
WAIp	Waidhofen (Ybbs), Stadtpfarre
WIL	Wilhering, Zisterzienserstift, Bibliothek und Musikarchiv
Z	Zwettl, Zisterzienserstift, Stiftsbibliothek

AUS: AUSTRALIA

CAnl	Canberra, National Library of Australia
Msl	Melbourne, State Library of Victoria
Pml	Perth, Central Music Library
PVgm	Parkville, Grainger Museum, University of Melbourne
Sb	Sydney, Symphony Australia National Music Library
Scm	——, New South Wales State Conservatorium of Music
Sfl	——, University of Sydney, Fisher Library
Smc	——, Australia Music Centre Ltd, Library
Sml	——, Music Branch Library, University of Sydney
Sp	——, Public Library
Ssl	——, State Library of New South Wales, Mitchell Library

B: BELGIUM

Aa	Antwerp, Stadsarchief
Aac	——, Archief en Museum voor het Vlaamse Culturleven
Ac	——, Koninklijk Vlaams Muziekconservatorium
Ak	——, Onze-Lieve-Vrouw-Kathedraal, Archief
Amp	——, Museum Plantin-Moretus
As	——, Stadsbibliotheek
Asj	——, Collegiale en Parochiale Kerk St-Jacob, Bibliotheek en Archief
Ba	Brussels, Archives de la Ville
Bc	——, Conservatoire Royal, Bibliothèque, Koninklijk Conservatorium, Bibliotheek
Bcdm	——, Centre Belge de Documentation Musicale [CeBeDeM]
Bg	——, Cathédrale St-Michel et Ste-Gudule [in *Bc* and *Br*]
Bmichotte	——, Michotte private collection [in *Bc*]
Br	——, Bibliothèque Royale Albert 1er/Koninlijke Bibliotheek Albert I, Section de la Musique
Brtb	——, Radiodiffusion-Télévision Belge
Bsp	——, Société Philharmonique
BRc	Bruges, Stedelijk Muziekconservatorium, Bibliotheek
BRs	——, Stadsbibliotheek
D	Diest, St Sulpitiuskerk
Gc	Ghent, Koninklijk Muziekconservatorium, Bibliotheek
Gcd	——, Culturele Dienst Province Oost-Vlaanderen
Geb	——, St Baafsarchief
Gu	——, Universiteit, Centrale Bibliotheek, Handskriftenzaal
La	Liège, Archives de l'État, Fonds de la Cathédrale St Lambert
Lc	——, Conservatoire Royal de Musique, Bibliothèque
Lg	——, Musée Grétry
Lu	——, Université de Liège, Bibliothèque
LVu	Leuven, Katholieke Universiteit van Leuven
MA	Morlanwelz-Mariemont, Musée de Mariemont, Bibliothèque
MEa	Mechelen, Archief en Stadsbibliotheek
Tc	Tournai, Chapitre de la Cathédrale, Archives
Tv	——, Bibliothèque de la Ville

BR: BRAZIL

Rem	Rio de Janeiro, Universidade Federal do Rio de Janeiro, Escola de Música, Biblioteca Alberto Nepomuceno
Rn	——, Fundação Biblioteca Nacional, Divisão de Música e Arquivo Sonoro

BY: BELARUS

MI	Minsk, Biblioteka Belorusskoj Gosudarstvennoj Konservatorii

C: CUBA

HABn	Havana, Biblioteca Nacional José Martí

CDN: CANADA

Cu	Calgary, University of Calgary, Library
E	Edmonton (AB), University of Alberta
HNu	Hamilton (ON), McMaster University, Mills Memorial Library, Music Section
Lu	London (ON), University of Western Ontario, Music Library
Mc	Montreal, Conservatoire de Musique, Centre de Documentation
Mcm	——, Centre de Musique Canadienne
Mm	——, McGill University, Faculty and Conservatorium of Music Library
Mn	——, Bibliothèque Nationale
On	Ottawa, National Library of Canada, Music Division
Qmu	Quebec, Monastère des Ursulines, Archives
Qsl	——, Musée de l'Amérique Française
Qul	——, Université Laval, Bibliothèque des Sciences Humaines et Sociales
Tcm	Toronto, Canadian Music Centre
Tu	——, University of Toronto, Faculty of Music Library
Vcm	Vancouver, Canadian Music Centre
VIu	Victoria, University of Victoria

CH: SWITZERLAND

A	Aarau, Aargauische Kantonsbibliothek
Bab	Basle, Archiv der Evangelischen Brüdersoziät
Bps	——, Paul Sacher Stiftung, Bibliothek
Bu	——, Universität Basel, Öffentliche Bibliothek, Musikabteilung
BEb	Berne, Burgerbibliothek/Bibliothèque de la Bourgeoisie
BEl	——, Schweizerische Landesbibliothek/Bibliothèque Nationale Suisse/Biblioteca Nationale Svizzera/Biblioteca Naziunala Svizra
BEsu	——, Stadt- und Universitätsbibliothek
BM	Beromünster, Musikbibliothek des Stifts
BU	Burgdorf, Stadtbibliothek
CObodmer	Cologny-Geneva, Fondation Martin Bodmer, Bibliotheca Bodmeriana
D	Disentis, Stift, Musikbibliothek
E	Einsiedeln, Benedikterkloster, Musikbibliothek
EN	Engelberg, Kloster, Musikbibliothek
Fcu	Fribourg, Bibliothèque Cantonale et Universitaire
FF	Frauenfeld, Thurgauische Kantonsbibliothek
Gc	Geneva, Conservatoire de Musique, Bibliothèque
Gpu	——, Bibliothèque Publique et Universitaire
Lmg	Lucerne, Allgemeine Musikalische Gesellschaft
Lz	——, Zentralbibliothek
LAac	Lausanne, Archives Cantonales Vaudoises
LAcu	——, Bibliothèque Cantonale et Universitaire
LU	Lugano, Biblioteca Cantonale
MSbk	Mariastein, Benediktinerkloster
MÜ	Müstair, Frauenkloster St Johann
N	Neuchâtel, Bibliothèque Publique et Universitaire
OB	Oberbüren, Kloster Glattburg
P	Porrentruy, Bibliothèque Cantonale Jurasienne (incl. Bibliothèque du Lycée Cantonal)
R	Rheinfelden, Christkatholisches Pfarramt
S	Sion, Bibliothèque Cantonale du Valais
SAf	Sarnen, Benediktinerinnen-Abtei St Andreas
SAM	Samedan, Biblioteca Fundaziun Planta
SGd	St Gallen, Domchorarchiv
SGs	——, Stiftsbibliothek, Handschriftenabteilung
SGv	——, Kantonsbibliothek (Vadiana)
SH	Schaffhausen, Stadtbibliothek
SO	Solothurn, Zentralbibliothek, Musiksammlung
SObo	——, Bischöfliches Ordinariat der Diözese Basel, Diözesanarchiv des Bistums Basel
W	Winterthur, Stadtbibliothek
Zi	Zürich, Israelitische Kultusgemeinde
Zma	——, Schweizerisches Musik-Archiv [in *Nf*]
Zz	——, Zentralbibliothek
ZGm	Zug, Pfarrarchiv St Michael

	CO: COLOMBIA
B	Bogotá, Archivo de la Catedral
	CZ: CZECH REPUBLIC
Bam	Brno, Archiv města Brna
Bb	——, Klášter Milosrdných Bratří [in *Bm*]
Bm	——, Moravské Zemské Muzeum, Oddělení Dějin Hudby
Bsa	——, Státní Oblastní Archiv
Bu	——, Moravská Zemeská Knihovna, Hudební Oddělení
BER	Beroun, Statní Okresní Archiv
BROb	Broumov, Knihovna Benediktinů [in *HK*]
CH	Cheb, Okresní Archiv
CHRm	Chrudim, Okresní Muzeum
D	Dačice, Knihovna Františkánů [in *Bu*]
H	Hronov, Muzeum
HK	Hradec Králové, Státní Vědecká Knihovna
HKm	——, Muzeum Východních Čech
HR	Hradiště u Znojma, Knihovna Křižovníků[in *Bu*]
JIa	Jindřichův Hradec, Státní Oblastní Archív Třeboni
K	Český Krumlov, Státní Oblastní Archiv v Třeboni, Hudební Sbírka
KA	Kadaň, Děkansky Kostel
KL	Klatovy, Státní Oblastní Archiv v Plzni, Pobočka Klatovy
KR	Kroměříž, Knihovna Arcibiskupského Zámku
KRa	——, Státní y Zámek a Zahrady, Historicko-Umělecké Fondy, Hudební Archív
KRA	Králíky, Kostel Sv. Michala [in *UO*]
KU	Kutná Hora, Okresní Muzeum [in *Pnm*]
LIa	Česká Lípa, Okresní Archív
LIT	Litoměřice, Státní Oblastní Archiv
LO	Loukov, Farní Kostel
LUa	Louny, Okresní Archív
ME	Mělník, Okresní Muzeum [on loan to *Pnm*]
MH	Mnichovo Hradiště, Vlastivědné Muzeum
MHa	——, Státní Oblatní Archiv v Praze – Pobočka v Mnichověě Hradiští
MT	Moravská Třebová, Knihovna Františkánů [in *Bu*]
NR	Nová Říše, Klášter Premonstrátů, Knihovna a Hudební Sbírka
OLa	Olomouc, Zemeský Archiv Opava, Pracoviště Olomouc
OP	Opava, Slezské Muzeum
OS	Ostrava, Česky Rozhlas, Hudební Archiv
OSE	Osek, Knihovna Cisterciáků [in *Pnm*]
Pa	Prague, Státní Ústřední Archiv
Pak	——, Pražská Metropolitní Kapitula
Pdobrovského	——, Národní Muzeum, Dobrovského (Nostická) Knihovna
Pk	——, Konservatoř, Archiv a Knihovna
Pn	——, Knihovna Národního Muzea
Pnd	——, Národní Divadlo, Hudební Archiv
Pnm	——, Národní Muzeum
Pr	——, Česky Rozhlas, Archívní a Programové Fondy, Fond Hudebnin
Ps	——, Památník Národního Písemnictví, Knihovna
Psj	——, Kostel Sv. Jakuba, Farní Rad
Pst	——, Knihovna Kláštera Premonstrátů (Strahovská Knihovna) [in *Pnm*]
Pu	——, Národní Knihovna, Hudenbí Oddělení
Puk	——, Karlova Univerzita, Filozofická Fakulta, Ústav Hudební Vědy, Knihovna
PLa	Plzeň, Městský Archiv
PLm	——, Západočeské Muzeum, Uměleckoprůmyslové Oddělení
POa	Poděbrady, Okresní Archiv Nymburk, Pobočka Poděbrady
POm	——, Muzeum
R	Rajhrad, Knihovna Benediktinského Kláštera [in *Bm*]
RO	Rokycany, Okresní Muzeum
ROk	——, Děkansky Úřad, Kostel
SE	Semily, Okresní Archiv v Semilech se Sídlem v Bystré nad Jizerou
SO	Sokolov, Okresní Archiv se Sídlem Jindřchovice, Zámek
TC	Třebíč, Městsky Archiv

TU	Turnov, Muzeum, Hudební Sbírka [in *SE*]
VB	Vyšší Brod, Knihovna Cisterciáckého Kláštera
Z	Žatec, Muzeum
ZI	Žitenice, Státní Oblastní Archiv v Litoměřicích
ZL	Zlonice, Památník Antonína Dvořáka
	D: GERMANY
Aa	Augsburg, Kantoreiarchiv St Annen
Aab	——, Archiv des Bistums Augsburg
Af	——, Fuggersche Domänenkanzlei, Bibliothek
Ahk	——, Heilig-Kreuz-Kirche, Dominikanerkloster, Biliothek [in *Asa*]
As	——, Staats- und Stadtbibliothek
Asa	——, Stadtarchiv
Au	——, Universität Augsburg, Universitätsbibliothek
AAm	Aachen, Domarchiv (Stiftsarchiv)
AAst	——, Öffentliche Bibliothek, Musikbibliothek
AB	Amorbach, Fürstlich Leiningische Bibliothek
ABG	Annaberg-Buchholz, Kirchenbibliothek St Annen
ABGa	——, Kantoreiarchiv St Annen
AG	Augustusburg, Evangelisch-Lutherisches Pfarramt der Stadtkirche St Petri, Musiksammlung
AIC	Aichach, Stadtpfarrkirche [on loan to *FS*]
ALa	Altenburg, Thüringisches Hauptstaadtsarchiv Weimar, Aussenstelle Altenburg
AM	Amberg, Staatliche Bibliothek
AN	Ansbach, Staatliche Bibliothek
ANsv	——, Sing- und Orchesterverein (Ansbacher Kantorei), Archiv [in *AN*]
AÖhk	Altötting, Kapuziner-Kloster St Konrad, Bibliothek
ARk	Arnstadt, Evangelisch-Lutherisches Pfarramt, Bibliothek
ARsk	——, Stadt- und Kreisbibliothek
ASh	Aschaffenburg, Schloss Johannisburg, Hofbibliothek
ASsb	——, Schloss Johannisburg, Stiftsbibliothek
Ba	Berlin, Amerika-Gedenkbibliothek, Musikabteilung [in *Bz*]
Bda	——, Akademie der Künste, Stiftung Archiv
Bdhm	——, Hochschule für Musik Hanns Eisler
Bga	——, Geheimes Staatsarchiv, Stiftung Preussischer Kulturbesitz
Bgk	——, Bibliothek zum Grauen Kloster [in *Bs*]
Bhbk	——, Staatliche Hochschule für Bildende Kunst, Bibliothek
Bhm	——, Hochschule der Künste, Hochschulbibliothek, Abteilung Musik und Darstellende Kunst
Bim	——, Staatliches Institut für Musikforschung, Bibliothek
Bk	——, Staatliche Museen Preussischer Kulturbesitz, Kunstbibliothek
Bkk	——, Staatliche Museen Preussischer Kulturbesitz, Kupferstichkabinett
Br	——, Deutsches, Rundfunkarchiv Frankfurt am Main – Berlin, Historische Archive, Bibliothek
Bs	——, Stadtbibliothek, Musikabteilung [in *Bz*]
Bsb	——, Staatsbibliothek zu Berlin Preussischer Kulturbesitz
Bsommer	——, Sommer private collection
Bsp	——, Evangelische Kirche Berlin-Brandenburg, Sprachenkonvikt, Bibliothek
Bst	——, Stadtbücherei Wilmersdorf, Hauptstelle
BAa	Bamberg, Staatsarchiv
BAs	——, Staatsbibliothek
BAL	Ballenstedt, Stadtbibliothek
BAR	Bartenstein, Fürst zu Hohenlohe-Bartensteinsches Archiv [on loan to *NEhz*]
BAUd	Bautzen, Domstift und Bischöfliches Ordinariat, Bibliothek und Archiv
BAUk	Bautzen, Stadtbibliothek
BAUm	——, Stadtmuseum
BB	Benediktbeuern, Pfarrkirche, Bibliothek
BDk	Brandenburg, Dom St Peter und Paul, Domstiftsarchiv und -bibliothek
BDH	Bad Homburg vor der Höhe, Stadtbibliothek
BDS	Bad Schwalbach, Evangelisches Pfarrarchiv
BE	Bad Berleburg, Fürstlich Sayn-Wittgenstein-Berleburgsche Bibliothek

BEU	Beuron, Bibliothek der Benediktiner-Erzabtei
BFb	Burgsteinfurt, Fürst zu Bentheimsche Musikaliensammlung [on loan to *MÜu*]
BG	Beuerberg, Stiftskirche
BGD	Berchtesgaden, Stiftskirche, Bibliothek [on loan to *FS*]
BH	Bayreuth, Stadtbücherei
BIB	Bibra, Pfarrarchiv
BIT	Bitterfeld, Kreis-Museum
BKÖs	Bad Köstritz, Forschungs- und Gedenkstätte Heinrich-Schütz-Haus
BMs	Bremen, Staats- und Universitätsbibliothek
BNba	Bonn, Beethoven-Haus, Beethoven-Archiv
BNms	——, Musikwissenschaftliches Seminar der Rheinischen Friedrich-Wilhelm-Universität
BNsa	——, Stadtarchiv und Wissenschaftliche Stadtbibliothek
BNu	——, Universitäts- und Landesbibliothek
BO	Bollstedt, Evangelische Kirchengemeinde, Pfarrarchiv
BOCHmi	Bochum, Ruhr-Universität, Fakultät für Geschichtswissenschaft, Musikwissenschaftliches Institut
BS	Brunswick, Stadtarchiv und Stadtbibliothek
BUCH	Buchen (Odenwald), Bezirksmuseum, Kraus-Sammlung
Cl	Coburg, Landesbibliothek, Musiksammlung
Cs	——, Staatsarchiv
Cv	——, Kunstsammlung der Veste Coburg, Bibliothek
CEbm	Celle, Bomann-Museum, Museum für Volkskunde Landes- und Stadtgeschichte
CR	Crimmitschau, Stadtkirche St Laurentius, Notenarchiv
CZ	Clausthal-Zellerfeld, Kirchenbibliothek [in *CZu*]
CZu	——, Technische Universität, Universitätsbibliothek
Dhm	Dresden, Hochschule für Musik Carl Maria von Weber, Bibliothek [in *Dl*]
Dl	——, Sächsische Landesbibliothek – Staats- und Universitäts-Bibliothek, Musikabteilung
Dla	——, Sächsisches Hauptstaatsarchiv
Dmb	——, Städtische Bibliotheken, Haupt- und Musikbibliothek [in *Dl*]
Ds	——, Sächsische Staatsoper, Notenbibliothek [in *Dl*]
DB	Dettelbach, Franziskanerkloster, Bibliothek
DEl	Dessau, Anhaltische Landesbücherei
DEsa	——, Stadtarchiv
DGs	Duisburg, Stadtbibliothek, Musikbibliothek
DI	Dillingen an der Donau, Kreis- und Studienbibliothek
DL	Delitzsch, Museum, Bibliothek
DM	Dortmund, Stadt- und Landesbibliothek, Musikabteilung
DO	Donaueschingen, Fürstlich Fürstenbergische Hofbibliothek
DS	Darmstadt, Hessische Landes- und Hochschulbibliothek, Musikabteilung
DSim	——, Internationales Musikinstitut, Informationszentrum für Zeitgenössische Musik, Bibliothek
DSsa	Darmstadt, Hessisches Staatsarchiv
DT	Detmold, Lippische Landesbibliothek, Musikabteilung
DTF	Dietfurt, Franziskanerkloster [in *Ma*]
DÜha	——, Nordrhein-Westfälisches Hauptstaatsarchiv
DÜk	Düsseldorf, Goethe-Museum, Bibliothek
DÜl	——, Universitäts- und Landesbibliothek, Heinrich Heine Universität
DWc	Donauwörth, Cassianeum
Ed	Eichstätt, Dom [in *Eu*]
Es	——, Staats- und Seminarbibliothek [in *Eu*]
Eu	——, Katholische Universität, Universitätsbibliothek
Ew	——, Benediktinerinnen-Abtei St Walburg, Bibliothek
EB	Ebrach, Katholisches Pfarramt, Bibliothek
EC	Eckartsberga, Pfarrarchiv
EF	Erfurt, Statd- und Regionalbibliothek, Abteilung Wissenschaftliche Sondersammlungen
EIa	Eisenach, Stadtarchiv, Bibliothek
EIb	——, Bachmuseum
EN	Engelberg, Franziskanerkloster, Bibliothek
ERu	Erlangen, Universitätsbibliothek
ERP	Landesberg am Lech-Erpfting, Katholische Pfarrkirche [on loan to *Aab*]
EW	Ellwangen (Jagst), Stiftskirche
F	Frankfurt, Stadt- und Universitätsbibliothek
Ff	——, Freies Deutsches Hochstift, Frankfurter Goethe-Museum, Bibliothek
Frl	——, Musikverlag Robert Lienau
Fsa	——, Stadtarchiv
FBa	Freiberg (Lower Saxony), Stadtarchiv
FBo	——, Geschwister-Scholl-Gymnasium, Andreas-Möller-Bibliothek
FLa	Flensburg, Stadtarchiv
FLs	Flensburg, Landeszentralbibliothek Schleswig-Holstein
FRu	Freiburg, Albert-Ludwigs-Universität, Universitätsbibliothek, Abteilung Handschriften, Alte Drucke und Rara
FRva	——, Deutsches Volksliedarchiv
FRIts	Friedberg, Bibliothek des Theologischen Seminars der Evangelischen Kirche in Hessen und Nassau
FS	Freising, Erzbistum München und Freising, Dombibliothek
FUl	Fulda, Hessische Landesbibliothek
FÜS	Füssen, Katholisches Stadtpfarramt St Mang
FW	Frauenchiemsee, Benediktinerinnenabtei Frauenwörth, Archiv
Ga	Göttingen, Staatliches Archivlager
Gb	——, Johann-Sebastian-Bach-Institut
Gms	——, Musikwissenschaftliches Seminar der Georg-August-Universität
Gs	——, Niedersächsische Staats- und Universitätsbibliothek
GBR	Grossbreitenbach (nr Arnstadt), Pfarramt, Archiv
GD	Goch-Gaesdonck, Collegium Augustinianum
GI	Giessen, Justus-Liebig-Universität, Bibliothek
GLAU	Glauchau, St Georgen, Musikarchiv
GM	Grimma, Göschenhaus-Seume-Gedenkstätte
GMl	——, Landesschule [in *Dl*]
GOa	Gotha, Augustinerkirche, Notenbibliothek
GOl	——, Forschungs- und Landesbibliothek, Musiksammlung
GÖs	Görlitz, Oberlausitzische Bibliothek der Wissenschaften bei den Städtischen Sammlungen
GOL	Goldbach (nr Gotha), Pfarrbibliothek
GRu	Greifswald, Universitätsbibliothek
GRH	Gerolzhofen, Katholische Pfarrei [on loan to *WÜd*]
GÜ	Güstrow, Museum der Stadt
GZsa	Greiz, Thüringisches Staatsarchiv Rudolstadt, Aussenstelle Greiz
Ha	Hamburg, Staatsarchiv
Hkm	——, Kunstgewerbemuseum, Bibliothek
Hmb	——, Öffentlichen Bücherhallen, Musikbücherei
Hs	——, Staats- und Universitätsbibliothek Carl von Ossietzky, Musiksammlung
HAf	Halle, Hauptbibliothek und Archiv der Franckeschen Stiftungen
HAh	——, Händel-Haus
HAmi	——, Martin-Luther-Universität, Universitäts- und Landesbibliothek Sachsen-Anhalt, Institut für Musikwissenschaft, Bibliothek
HAmk	——, Marktkirche Unser Lieben Frauen, Marienbibliothek
HAu	——, Martin-Luther-Universität, Universitäts- und Landesbibliothek Sachsen-Anhalt
HAR	Hartha (Kurort), Kantoreiarchiv
HB	Heilbronn, Stadtarchiv
HEms	Heidelberg, Musikwissenschaftliches Seminar der Rupert-Karls-Universität
HEu	——, Ruprecht-Karls-Universität, Universitätsbibliothek, Abteilung Handschriften und Alte Drucke
HER	Herrnhut, Evangelische Brüder-Unität, Archiv
HGm	Havelberg, Prignitz-Museum, Bibliothek
HL	Haltenbergstetten, Schloss (über Niederstetten, Baden-Württemburg), Fürst zu Hohenlohe-Jagstberg'sche Bibliothek [in *Mbs*]

HOE	Hohenstein-Ernstthal, Kantoreiarchiv der Christophorikirche
HR	Harburg (nr Donauwörth), Fürstlich Oettingen-Wallerstein'sche Bibliothek Schloss Harburg [in *Au*]
HRD	Arnsberg-Herdringen, Schlossbibliothek (Bibliotheca Fürstenbergiana) [in *Au*]
HSj	Helmstedt, Ehemalige Universitätsbibliothek
HSk	——, Kantorat St Stephani [in *W*]
HVkm	Hanover, Bibliothek des Kestner-Museums
HVl	——, Niedersächsische Landesbibliothek
HVs	——, Stadtbibliothek, Musikbibliothek
HVsa	——, Staatsarchiv
IN	Markt Indersdorf, Katholisches Pfarramt, Bibliothek [on loan to *FS*]
ISL	Iserlohn, Evangelische Kirchengemeinde, Varnhagen-Bibliothek
Jmb	Jena, Ernst-Abbe-Bücherei und Lesehalle der Carl-Zeiss-Stiftung, Musikbibliothek
Jmi	Jena, Friedrich-Schiller-Universität, Sektion Literatur- und Kunstwissenschaften, Bibliothek des ehem. Musikwissenschaftlichen Instituts [in *Ju*]
Ju	——, Friedrich-Schiller-Universität, Thüringer Universitäts- und Landesbibliothek
JE	Jever, Marien-Gymnasium, Bibliothek
Kdma	Kassel, Deutsches Musikgeschichtliches Archiv
Kl	——, Gesamthochschul-Bibliothek, Landesbibliothek und Murhardsche Bibliothek, Musiksammlung
Km	——, Musikakademie, Bibliothek
Ksp	——, Louis Spohr-Gedenk- und Forschungsstätte, Archiv
KA	Karlsruhe, Badische Landesbibliothek
KAsp	——, Pfarramt St Peter
KAu	——, Universitätsbibliothek
KBs	Koblenz, Stadtbibliothek
KFp	Kaufbeuren, Protestantisches Kirchenarchiv
KIl	Kiel, Schleswig-Holsteinische Landesbibliothek
KIu	——, Universitätsbibliothek
KMs	Kamenz, Stadtarchiv
KNa	Cologne, Historisches Archiv der Stadt
KNd	——, Kölner Dom, Erzbischöfliche Diözesan- und Dombibliothek
KNh	——, Staatliche Hochschule für Musik, Bibliothek
KNmi	——, Musikwissenschaftliches Institut der Universität
KNu	——, Universitäts- und Stadtbibliothek
KPs	Kempten, Stadtbibliothek
KPsl	——, Stadtpfarrkirche St Lorenz, Musikarchiv
KR	Kleinröhrsdorf (nr Bischofswerda), Pfarrkirchenbibliothek
KZa	Konstanz, Stadtarchiv
Lm	Lüneburg, Michaelisschule
Lr	——, Ratsbücherei, Musikabteilung
LA	Landshut, Historischer Verein für Niederbayern, Bibliothek
LB	Langenburg, Fürstlich Hohenlohe-Langenburg'sche Schlossbibliothek [on loan to *NEhz*]
LEb	Leipzig, Bach-Archiv
LEbh	——, Breitkopf & Härtel, Verlagsarchiv
LEdb	——, Deutsche Bücherei, Musikaliensammlung
LEm	——, Leipziger Städtische Bibliotheken, Musikbibliothek
LEmi	——, Universität, Zweigbibliothek Musikwissenschaft und Musikpädagogik [in *LEu*]
LEsm	——, Stadtgeschichtliches Museum, Bibliothek, Musik- und Theatergeschichtliche Sammlungen
LEst	——, Stadtbibliothek [in *LEu* and *LEm*]
LEt	——, Thomanerchor, Bibliothek [in *LEb*]
LEu	——, Karl-Marx-Universität, Universitätsbibliothek, Bibliotheca Albertina
LFN	Laufen, Stiftsarchiv
LI	Lindau, Stadtbibliothek
LIM	Limbach am Main, Pfarrkirche Maria Limbach
LST	Lichtenstein, Stadtkirche St Laurentius, Kantoreiarchiv
LÜh	Lübeck, Bibliothek der Hansestadt, Musikabteilung
LUC	Luckau, Stadtkirche St Nikolai, Kantoreiarchiv
Ma	Munich, Franziskanerkloster St Anna, Bibliothek
Mb	——, Benediktinerabtei St Bonifaz, Bibliothek
Mbm	——, Bibliothek des Metropolitankapitels
Mbn	——, Bayerisches Nationalmuseum, Bibliothek
Mbs	——, Bayerische Staatsbibliothek
Mf	——, Frauenkirche [on loan to *FS*]
Mh	——, Staatliche Hochschule für Musik, Bibliothek
Mhsa	——, Bayerisches Hauptstaatsarchiv
Mk	——, Theatinerkirche St Kajetan
Mm	——, Bibliothek St Michael
Mo	——, Opernarchiv
Msa	——, Staatsarchiv
Mth	——, Theatermuseum der Clara-Ziegler-Stiftung
Mu	——, Ludwig-Maximilians-Universität, Universitätsbibliothek, Abteilung Handschriften, Nachlässe, Alte Drucke
MAl	Magdeburg, Landeshauptarchiv Sachsen-Anhalt [in *WERa*]
MAs	——, Stadtbibliothek Wilhelm Weitling, Musikabteilung
ME	Meissen, Stadt- und Kreisbibliothek
MEIk	Meiningen, Bibliothek der Evangelisch-Lutherischen Kirchengemeinde
MEIl	——, Thüringisches Staatsarchiv
MEIr	——, Meininger Museen, Abteilung Musikgeschichte/Max-Reger-Archiv
MERa	Merseburg, Domstift, Stiftsarchiv
MG	Marburg, Westdeutsche Bibliothek [in *Bsb*]
MGmi	——, Musikwissenschaftliches Institut der Philipps-Universität, Abteilung Hessisches Musikarchiv
MGs	——, Staatsarchiv und Archivschule
MGu	——, Philipps-Universität, Universitätsbibliothek
MGB	Mönchen-Gladbach, Bibliothek Wissenschaft und Weisheit, Johannes-Duns-Skotus-Akademie der Kölnischen Ordens-Provinz der Franziskaner
MH	Mannheim, Wissenschaftliche Stadtbibliothek
MHrm	——, Städtisches Reiss-Museum
MHst	——, Stadtbücherei, Musikbücherei
MLHb	Mühlhausen, Blasiuskirche, Pfarrarchiv Divi Blasii [on loan to *MLHm*]
MLHm	——, Marienkirche
MLHr	——, Stadtarchiv
MMm	Memmingen, Evangelisch-Lutherisches Pfarramt St Martin, Bibliothek
MR	Marienberg, Kirchenbibliothek
MT	Metten, Abtei, Bibliothek
MÜd	Münster, Bischöfliches Diözesanarchiv
MÜp	——, Bischöfliches Priesterseminar, Bibliothek
MÜs	——, Santini-Bibliothek [in *MÜp*]
MÜu	——, Westfälische Wilhelms-Universität, Universitäts- und Landesbibliothek, Musiksammlung
MÜG	Mügeln, Evangelisch-Lutherisches Pfarramt St Johannis, Musikarchiv
MY	Mylau, Kirchenbibliothek
MZmi	Mainz, Musikwissenschaftliches Institut der Johannes-Gutenberg-Universität
MZp	——, Bischöfliches Priesterseminar, Bibliothek
MZs	——, Stadtbibliothek
MZsch	——, Musikverlag B. Schott's Söhne, Verlagsarchiv
MZu	——, Johannes-Gutenberg-Universität, Universitätsbibliothek, Musikabteilung
Ngm	Nuremberg, Germanisches National-Museum, Bibliothek
Nla	——, Bibliothek beim Landeskirchlichen Archiv
Nst	——, Bibliothek Egidienplatz
NA	Neustadt an der Orla, Evangelisch-Lutherische Kirchengemeinde, Pfarrarchiv
NAUs	Naumburg, Stadtarchiv
NAUw	——, St Wenzel, Bibliothek
NEhz	Neuenstein, Hohenlohe-Zentralarchiv
NH	Neresheim, Bibliothek der Benediktinerabtei
NL	Nördlingen, Stadtarchiv, Stadtbibliothek und Volksbücherei
NLk	——, Evangelisch-Lutherisches Pfarramt St Georg, Musikarchiv
NM	Neumünster, Schleswig-Holsteinische Musiksammlung der Stadt Neumünster [in *KIl*]

NNFw	Neunhof (nr Nürnberg), Freiherrliche Welser'sche Familienstiftung
NO	Nordhausen, Wilhelm-von-Humboldt-Gymnasium, Bibliothek
NS	Neustadt an der Aisch, Evangelische Kirchenbibliothek
NT	Neumarkt-St Veit, Pfarrkirche
NTRE	Niedertrebra, Evangelisch-Lutherische Kirchgemeinde, Pfarrarchiv
OB	Ottobeuren, Benediktinerabtei
OBS	Gessertshausen-Oberschönenfeld, Abtei
OF	Offenbach am Main, Verlagsarchiv André
OLH	Olbernhau, Evangelisch-Lutherisches Pfarramt, Pfarrarchiv
ORB	Oranienbaum, Landesarchiv
Pg	Passau, Gymnasialbibliothek
Po	——, Bistum, Archiv
PA	Paderborn, Erzbischöfliche Akademische Bibliothek [in *HRD*]
PE	Perleberg, Pfarrbibliothek
PI	Pirna, Stadtarchiv
PL	Plauen, Stadtkirche St Johannis, Pfarrarchiv
PO	Pommersfelden, Graf von Schönbornsche Schlossbibliothek
POL	Polling, Katholisches Pfarramt
POTh	Potsdam, Fachhochschule Potsdam, Hochschulbibliothek
Rp	Regensburg, Bischöfliche Zentralbibliothek, Proske-Musikbibliothek
Rs	——, Staatliche Bibliothek
Rtt	——, Fürst Thurn und Taxis Hofbibliothek
Ru	——, Universität Regensburg, Universitätsbibliothek
RAd	Ratzeburg, Domarchiv
RB	Rothenburg ob der Tauber, Stadtarchiv und Rats- und Konsistorialbibliothek
RH	Rheda, Fürst zu Bentheim-Tecklenburgische Musikbibliothek [on loan to *MÜu*]
ROmi	Rostock, Universitätsbibliothek, Fachbibliothek Musikwissenschaften
ROs	——, Stadtbibliothek, Musikabteilung
ROu	——, Universität, Universitätsbibliothek
RT	Rastatt, Bibliothek des Friedrich-Wilhelm-Gymnasiums
RUh	Rudolstadt, Hofkapellarchiv [in *RUl*]
RUl	——, Thüringisches Staatsarchiv
Sl	Stuttgart, Württembergische Landesbibliothek
SBj	Straubing, Kirchenbibliothek St Jakob [in *Rp*]
SCHOT	Schotten, Liebfrauenkirche
SHk	Sondershausen, Stadtkirche/Superintendentur, Bibliothek
SHm	——, Schlossmuseum
SHs	——, Schlossmuseum, Bibliothek [in *SHm*]
SI	Sigmaringen, Fürstlich Hohenzollernsche Hofbibliothek
SNed	Schmalkalden, Evangelisches Dekanat, Bibliothek
SPlb	Speyer, Pfälzische Landesbibliothek, Musikabteilung
STBp	Steinbach (nr Bad Salzungen), Evangelische-Lutherisches Pfarramt, Pfarrarchiv
STOm	Stolberg (Harz), Pfarramt St Martini, Pfarrarchiv
SUH	Suhl, Wissenschaftliche Allgemeinbibliothek, Musikabteilung
SÜN	Sünching, Schloss
SWl	Schwerin, Landesbibliothek Mecklenburg-Vorpommern, Musiksammlung
SWs	——, Stadtbibliothek, Musikabteilung [in *SWl*]
SWth	——, Mecklenburgisches Staatstheater, Bibliothek
Tl	Tübingen, Schwäbisches Landesmusikarchiv [in *Tmi*]
Tmi	——, Bibliothek des Musikwissenschaftlichen Institut
Tu	——, Eberhard-Karls-Universität, Universitätsbibliothek
TEG	Tegernsee, Pfarrkirche
TEGha	——, Herzogliches Archiv
TEI	Teisendorf, Katholisches Pfarramt, Pfarrbibliothek
TIT	Tittmoning, Pfarrkirche [in *Fs*]
TO	Torgau, Evangelische Kirchengemeinde, Johann-Walter-Kantorei
TRb	Trier, Bistumarchiv

TRs	——, Stadtbibliothek
TZ	Bad Tölz, Katholisches Pfarramt Maria Himmelfahrt [in *FS*]
Us	Ulm, Stadtbibliothek
Usch	——, Von Schermar'sche Familienstiftung, Bibliothek
UDa	Udestedt, Evangelisch-Lutherisches Pfarramt [in *Dl*]
URS	Ursberg, St Josef-Kongregation, Orden der Franziskanerinnen
W	Wolfenbüttel, Herzog August Bibliothek, Handschriftensammlung
Wa	——, Niedersächsisches Staatsarchiv
WA	Waldheim, Stadtkirche St Nikolai, Bibliothek
WAB	Waldenburg, St Bartholomäus, Kantoreiarchiv
WD	Wiesentheid, Musiksammlung des Grafen von Schönborn-Wiesentheid
WERhb	Wernigerode, Harzmuseum, Harzbücherei
WEY	Weyarn, Pfarrkirche, Bibliothek [on loan to *FS*]
WF	Weissenfels, Schuh- und Stadtmuseum Weissenfels (mit Heinrich-Schütz-Gedenkstätte) [on loan to *BKÖs*]
WFe	——, Ephoralbibliothek
WFmk	——, Marienkirche, Pfarrarchiv [in *HAmk*]
WGl	Wittenberg, Lutherhalle, Reformationsgeschichtliches Museum
WGH	Waigolshausen, Katholische Pfarrei [on loan to *WÜd*]
WH	Bad Windsheim, Stadtbibliothek
WIl	Wiesbaden, Hessische Landesbibliothek
WINtj	Winhöring, Gräflich Toerring-Jettenbachsche Bibliothek [on loan to *Mbs*]
WO	Worms, Stadtbibliothek und Öffentliche Büchereien
WRdn	Weimar, Deutsches Nationaltheater und Staatskapelle, Archiv
WRgm	——, Goethe-National-Museum (Goethes Wohnhaus)
WRgs	——, Stiftung Weimarer Klassik, Goethe–Schiller-Archiv
WRh	——, Hochschule für Musik Franz Liszt
WRiv	——, Hochschule für Musik Franz Liszt, Institut für Volksmusikforschung
WRl	——, Thüringisches Hauptstaatsarchiv Weimar
WRtl	——, Thüringische Landesbibliothek, Musiksammlung [in *WRz*]
WRz	——, Stiftung Weimarer Klassik, Herzogin Anna Amalia Bibliothek
WS	Wasserburg am Inn, Chorarchiv St Jakob, Pfarramt [on loan to *FS*]
WÜd	Würzburg, Diözesanarchiv
WÜst	——, Staatsarchiv
WÜu	——, Bayerische Julius-Maximilians-Universität, Universitätsbibliothek
Z	Zwickau, Ratsschulbibliothek, Wissenschaftliche Bibliothek
Zsa	——, Stadtarchiv
Zsch	——, Robert-Schumann-Haus
ZE	Zerbst, Stadtarchiv
ZEo	——, Gymnasium Francisceum, Bibliothek
ZGh	Zörbig, Heimatmuseum
ZI	Zittau, Christian-Weise-Bibliothek, Altbestand [in *Dl*]
ZL	Zeil, Fürstlich Waldburg-Zeil'sches Archiv
ZZs	Zeitz, Stiftsbibliothek

DK: DENMARK

A	Århus, Statsbiblioteket
Ch	Christiansfeld, Brødremenigheden (Herrnhutgemeinde)
Kar	Copenhagen, Det Arnamagnaeanske Institut
Kc	——, Carl Claudius Musikhistoriske Samling [in *Km*]
Kk	——, Kongelige Bibliotek
Kmk	——, Kongelige Danske Musikkonservatorium
Ku	——, Det Kongelige Bibliotek Fiolstraede
Kv	——, Københavns Universitet, Musikvidenskabeligt Institut, Bibliotek
Ol	Odense, Landsarkivet for Fyen

Ou	——, Universitetsbibliotek, Musikafdelingen
Sa	Sorø, Sorø Akademi, Biblioteket
Tv	Tåsinge, Valdemars Slot

E: SPAIN

Ac	Avila, S Apostólica Iglesia Catedral de el Salvador, Archivo Catedralicio
Asa	——, Monasterio de S Ana
AL	Alquézar, Colegiata
ALB	Albarracín, Catedral, Archivo
AR	Aránzazu, Archivo Musical del Monasterio de Aránzazu
AS	Astorga, Catedral
Bac	Barcelona, Archivo de la Corona de Aragón/Arixiu de la Corona d'Aragó
Bbc	——, Biblioteca de Catalunya, Sección de Música
Bc	——, S.E. Catedra Basiclica, Arixiu
Bcd	——, Centro de Documentació Musical de la Generalitat de Catalunya 'El Jardi Dels Tarongers'
Bih	——, Arixiu Històric de la Ciutat
Bim	——, Consejo Superior de Investigaciones Científicas, Departamento de Musicología, Biblioteca
Bit	——, Institut del Teatre, Centre d'Investigació, Documentació i Difusió
Boc	——, Orfeó Catalá, Biblioteca
Bu	——, Universitat Autónoma
BA	Badajoz, Catedral, Archivo Capitular
BUa	Burgos, Catedral, Archivo
BUlh	——, Cistercian Monasterio de Las Huelgas
C	Córdoba, S Iglesia Catedral, Archivo de Música
CA	Calahorra, Catedral
CAL	Calatayud, Colegiata de S María
CU	Cuenca, Catedral, Archivo Capitular
CUi	——, Instituto de Música Religiosa
CZ	Cádiz, Archivo Capitular
E	San Lorenzo de El Escorial, Monasterio, Real Biblioteca
G	Gerona, Catedral, Archivo/Arxiu Capitular
Gp	——, Biblioteca Pública
GRc	Granada, Catedral Metropolitana, Archivo Capitular [in *GRcr*]
GRcr	——, Capilla Real, Archivo de Música
GRmf	——, Archivo Manuel de Falla
GU	Guadalupe, Real Monasterio de S María, Archivo de Música
H	Huesca, Catedral
J	Jaca, Catedral, Archivo Musical
JA	Jaén, Catedral, Archivo Capitular
JEc	Jerez de la Frontera, Colegiata
L	León, Catedral, Archivo Histórico
Lc	——, Real Basilica de S Isidoro
LEc	Lérida, Catedral
LPA	Las Palmas de Gran Canaria, Catedral de Canarias
Mah	Madrid, Archivo Histórico Nacional
Mba	——, Archivo de Música, Real Academia de Bellas Artes de S Fernando
Mc	——, Real Conservatorio Superior de Música, Biblioteca
Mca	——, Casa de Alba
Mcns	——, Congregación de Nuestra Señora
Md	——, Centro de Documentación Musical del Ministerio de Cultura
Mdr	——, Convento de las Descalzas Reales
Mm	——, Biblioteca Histórica Municipal
Mmc	——, Casa Ducal de Medinaceli, Biblioteca
Mn	——, Biblioteca Nacional
Mp	——, Patrimonio Nacional
Msa	——, Sociedad General de Autores y Editores
MA	Málaga, Catedral, Archivo Capitular
MO	Montserrat, Abadía
MON	Mondoñedo, Catedral, Archivo
OL	Olot, Biblioteca Popular
ORI	Orihuela, Catedral, Archivo
OV	Oviedo, Catedral Metropolitana, Archivo
P	Plasencia, Catedral, Archivo de Música
PAc	Palma de Mallorca, Catedral, Archivo

PAp	——, Biblioteca Provincial
PAL	Palencia, Catedral de S Antolín, Archivo de Música
PAMc	Pamplona, Catedral, Archivo
PAS	Pastrana, Museo Parroquial
RO	Roncesvalles, Monasterio S María, Biblioteca
Sc	Seville, Institución Colombina
SA	Salamanca, Catedral, Archivo Catedralicio
SAc	——, Conservatorio Superior de Música de Salamanca, Biblioteca
SAu	——, Biblioteca Universitaria
SAN	Santander, Biblioteca de la Universidad Menéndez, Sección de Música
SC	Santiago de Compostela, Catedral Metropolitana
SCu	——, Biblioteca de la Universidad
SD	Santo Domingo de la Calzada, Catedral Archivo
SE	Segovia, Catedral, Archivo Capitular
SEG	Segorbe, Archivo de la Catedral
SI	Silos, Abadía de S Domingo, Archivo
SU	Seo de Urgel, Catedral
Tc	Toledo, Catedral, Archivo y Biblioteca Capítulares
Tp	——, Biblioteca Pública Provincial y Museo de la S Cruz
TAc	Tarragona, Catedral
TE	Teruel, Catedral, Archivo Capitular
TO	Tortosa, Catedral
TUY	Tuy, Catedral
TZ	Tarazona, Catedral, Archivo Capitular
V	Valladolid, Catedral Metropolitana, Archivo de Música
Vp	——, Parroquia de Santiago
VAa	Valencia, Archivo Municipal
VAc	——, Catedral Metropolitana, Archivo y Biblioteca, Archivo de Música
VAcp	——, Real Colegio: Seminario de Corpus Christi, Archivo Musical del Patriarca
VAu	——, Biblioteca Universitaria
VI	Vich, Museu Episcopal
Zac	Zaragoza, Catedrale de La Seo y Basílica del Pilar, Archivo de Música de las Catedrales
Zcc	——, Colegio de las Escuelas Pías de S José de Calasanz, Biblioteca
Zs	——, La Seo, Biblioteca Capitular [in *Zac*]
Zvp	——, Iglesia Metropolitana [in *Zac*]
ZAc	Zamora, Catedral

ET: EGYPT

Cn	Cairo, National Library (Dar al-Kutub)
MSsc	Mount Sinai, St Catherine's Monastery

EV: ESTONIA

TALg	Tallinn, National Library of Estonia

F: FRANCE

A	Avignon, Médiathèque Ceccano
Ac	——, Bibliothèque du Conservatoire
AB	Abbeville, Bibliothèque Nationale
AG	Agen, Archives Départementales de Lot-et-Garonne
AI	Albi, Bibliothèque Municipale
AIXc	Aix-en-Provence, Bibliothèque du Conservatoire
AIXm	——, Bibliothèque Méjanes
AIXmc	——, Bibliothèque de la Maîtrise de la Cathédrale
AL	Alençon, Bibliothèque Municipale
AM	Amiens, Bibliothèque Municipale
AN	Angers, Bibliothèque Municipale
APT	Apt, Basilique Ste Anne
AS	Arras, Médiathèque Municipale
ASOlang	Asnières-sur-Oise, Collection François Lang
AUT	Autun, Bibliothèque Municipale
AVR	Avranches, Bibliothèque Nationale
B	Besançon, Bibliothèque Municipale
Ba	——, Bibliothèque de l'Archevêché
BE	Beauvais, Bibliothèque Municipale
BG	Bourg-en-Bresse, Bibliothèque Municipale
BO	Bordeaux, Bibliothèque Municipale
BS	Bourges, Bibliothèque Municipale
C	Carpentras, Bibliothèque Municipale (Inguimbertine)

CA	Cambrai, Médiathèque Municipale
CAc	——, Cathédrale
CC	Carcassonne, Bibliothèque Municipale
CF	Clermont-Ferrand, Bibliothèque Municipale et Interuniversitaire, Département Patrimoine
CH	Chantilly, Musée Condé
CHd	——, Musée Dobrie
CHRm	Chartres, Bibliothèque Municipale
CLO	Clermont-de-l'Oise, Bibliothèque
CO	Colmar, Bibliothèque de la Ville
COM	Compiègne, Bibliothèque Municipale
CSM	Châlons-en-Champagne, Bibliothèque Municipale
Dc	Dijon, Conservatoire Jean-Philippe Rameau, Bibliothèque
Dm	——, Bibliothèque Municipale
DI	Dieppe, Fonds Anciens et Local, Médiathèque Jean Renoir
DO	Dôle, Bibliothèque Municipale
DOU	Douai, Bibliothèque Nationale
E	Epinal, Bibliothèque Nationale
EMc	Embrun, Trésor de la Cathédrale
EV	Evreux, Bibliothèque Municipale
F	Foix, Bibliothèque Municipale
G	Grenoble, Bibliothèque Municipale
Lad	Lille, Archives Départementales du Nord
Lc	——, Bibliothèque du Conservatoire
Lm	——, Bibliothèque Municipale Jean Levy
LA	Laon, Bibliothèque Municipale
LG	Limoges, Bibliothèque Francophone Municipale
LH	Le Havre, Bibliothèque Municipale
LM	Le Mans, Bibliothèque Municipale Classée, Médiathèque Louis Aragon
LYc	Lyons, Conservatoire National de Musique
LYm	——, Bibliothèque Municipale
Mc	Marseilles, Conservatoire de Musique et de Déclamation
MD	Montbéliard, Bibliothèque Municipale
ME	Metz, Médiathèque
MH	Mulhouse, Bibliothèque Municipale
ML	Moulins, Bibliothèque Municipale
MO	Montpellier, Bibliothèque de l'Université
MOf	——, Bibliothèque Inter-Universitaire, Section Médecine
MON	Montauban, Bibliothèque Municipale Antonin Perbosc
Nm	Nantes, Bibliothèque Municipale, Médiathèque
NAc	Nancy, Bibliothèque du Conservatoire
O	Orléans, Médiathèque
Pa	Paris, Bibliothèque de l'Arsenal
Pan	——, Archives Nationales
Pc	——, Conservatoire [in *Pn*]
Pcf	——, Bibliothèque de la Comédie Française
Pcnrs	——, Centre National de la Recherche Scientifique, Bibliothèque
Pd	——, Centre de Documentation de la Musique Contemporaine
Pe	——, Schola Cantorum
Peb	——, Ecole Normale Supérieure des Beaux-Arts, Bibliothèque
Pgm	——, Gustav Mahler, Bibliothèque Musicale
Phanson	——, Collection Hanson
Pi	——, Bibliothèque de l'Institut de France
Pim	——, Bibliothèque Pierre Aubry
Pm	——, Bibliothèque Mazarine
Pmeyer	——, André Meyer, private collection
Pn	——, Bibliothèque Nationale de France
Po	——, Bibliothèque-Musée de l'Opéra
Ppincherle	——, Marc Pincherle, private collection
Ppo	——, Bibliothèque Polonaise de Paris
Prothschild	——, Germaine, Baronne Edouard de Rothschild, private collection
Prt	——, Radio France, Documentation Musicale
Ps	——, Bibliothèque de la Sorbonne
Psal	——, Editions Salabert
Pse	——, Société des Auteurs, Compositeurs et Editeurs de Musique
Psg	——, Bibliothèque Ste-Geneviève
Pshp	——, Société d'Histoire du Protestantisme Français, Bibliothèque

Pthibault	——, Geneviève Thibault, private collection [in *Pn*]
R	Rouen, Bibliothèque Municipale
Rc	——, Bibliothèque du Conservatoire
RS	Reims, Bibliothèque Municipale
RSc	——, Maîtrise de la Cathédrale
Sc	Strasbourg, Bibliothèque du Conservatoire
Sgs	——, Union Sainte Cécile, Bibliothéque Musicale du Grand Séminaire
Sim	——, Université des Sciences Humaines, Institut de Musicologie
Sm	——, Bibliothèque Municipale
Sn	——, Bibliothèque Nationale et Universitaire
Ssp	——, Bibliothèque du Séminaire Protestant
SDI	St Dié, Bibliothèque Municipale
SEm	Sens, Bibliothèque Municipale
SERc	Serrant, Château
SO	Solesmes, Abbaye de St-Pierre
SOM	St Omer, Bibliothèque Municipale
SQ	St Quentin, Bibliothèque Municipale
T	Troyes, Bibliothèque Municipale
TLm	Toulouse, Bibliothèque Municipale
TOm	Tours, Bibliothèque Municipale
V	Versailles, Bibliothèque
VA	Vannes, Bibliothèque Municipale
VAL	Valenciennes, Bibliothèque Municipale
VN	Verdun, Bibliothèque Municipale

FIN: FINLAND

A	Turku, Åbo Akademi, Sibelius Museum, Bibliotek ja Arkiv
Hy	Helsinki, Helsingin Yliopiston Kirjasto/Helsinki University Library/Suomen Kansalliskikjasto
Hyf	——, Helsingin Yliopiston Kirjasto, Department of Finnish Music

GB: GREAT BRITAIN

A	Aberdeen, University, Queen Mother Library
AB	Aberystwyth, Llyfryell Genedlaethol Cymru/National Library of Wales
ABu	——, University College of Wales
ALb	Aldeburgh, Britten-Pears Library
AM	Ampleforth, Abbey and College Library, St Lawrence Abbey
AR	Arundel Castle, Archive
Bp	Birmingham, Public Libraries
Bu	——, Birmingham University
BA	Bath, Municipal Library
BEcr	Bedford, Bedfordshire County Record Office
BEL	Belton (Lincs.), Belton House
BENcoke	Bentley (Hants.), Gerald Coke, private collection
BEV	Beverley, East Yorkshire County Record Office
BO	Bournemouth, Central Library
BRp	Bristol, Central Library
BRu	——, University of Bristol Library
Ccc	Cambridge, Corpus Christi College, Parker Library
Ccl	——, Central Library
Cclc	——, Clare College Archives
Ce	——, Emmanuel College
Cfm	——, Fitzwilliam Museum, Dept of Manuscripts and Printed Books
Cgc	——, Gonville and Caius College
Cjc	——, St John's College
Ckc	——, King's College, Rowe Music Library
Cmc	——, Magdalene College, Pepys Library
Cp	——, Peterhouse College Library
Cpc	——, Pembroke College Library
Cpl	——, Pendlebury Library of Music
Cssc	——, Sidney Sussex College
Ctc	——, Trinity College, Library
Cu	——, University Library
CA	Canterbury, Cathedral Library
CDp	Cardiff, Public Libraries, Central Library
CDu	——, University of Wales/Prifysgol Cymru
CF	Chelmsford, Essex County Record Office
CH	Chichester, Diocesan Record Office
CHc	——, Cathedral
CL	Carlisle, Cathedral Library
DRc	Durham, Cathedral Church, Dean and Chapter Library

DRu	——, University Library
DU	Dundee, Central Library
En	Edinburgh, National Library of Scotland, Music Dept
Ep	——, City Libraries, Music Library
Er	——, Reid Music Library of the University of Edinburgh
Es	——, Signet Library
Eu	——, University Library, Main Library
EL	Ely, Cathedral Library [in *Cu*]
EXcl	Exeter, Cathedral Library
Ge	Glasgow, Euing Music Library
Gm	——, Mitchell Library, Arts Dept
Gsma	——, Scottish Music Archive
Gu	——, University Library
GL	Gloucester, Cathedral Library
GLr	——, Record Office
H	Hereford, Cathedral Library
HAdolmetsch	Haslemere, Carl Dolmetsch, private collection
HFr	Hertford, Hertfordshire Record Office
Ir	Ipswich, Suffolk Record Office
KNt	Knutsford, Tatton Park (National Trust)
Lam	London, Royal Academy of Music, Library
Lbbc	——, British Broadcasting Corporation, Music Library
Lbc	——, British Council Music Library
Lbl	——, British Library
Lcm	——, Royal College of Music, Library
Lcml	——, Central Music Library
Lco	——, Royal College of Organists
Lcs	——, English Folk Dance and Song Society, Vaughan Williams Memorial Library
Ldc	——, Dulwich College Library
Lfm	——, Faber Music
Lgc	——, Guildhall Library
Lk	——, King's Music Library [in *Lbl*]
Lkc	——, King's College Library
Llp	——, Lambeth Palace Library
Lmic	——, British Music Information Centre
Lmt	——, Minet Library
Lpro	——, Public Record Office
Lrcp	——, Royal College of Physicians
Lsp	——, St Paul's Cathedral Library
Lspencer	——, Woodford Green: Robert Spencer, private collection
Lst	——, Savoy Theatre Collection
Lu	——, University of London Library, Music Collection
Lue	——, Universal Edition
Lv	——, Victoria and Albert Museum, Theatre Museum
Lwa	——, Westminster Abbey Library
Lwcm	——, Westminster Central Music Library
LA	Lancaster, District Central Library
LEbc	Leeds, University of Leeds, Brotherton Library
LEc	——, Leeds Central Library, Music and Audio Dept
LF	Lichfield, Cathedral Library
LI	Lincoln, Cathedral Library
LVp	Liverpool, Libraries and Information Services, Humanities Reference Library
LVu	——, University, Music Department
Mch	Manchester, Chetham's Library
Mp	——, Central Library, Henry Watson Music Library
Mr	——, John Rylands Library, Deansgate
MA	Maidstone, Kent County Record Office
NH	Northampton, Record Office
NO	Nottingham, University of Nottingham, Department of Music
NTp	Newcastle upon Tyne, Public Libraries
NW	Norwich, Central Library
NWhamond	——, Anthony Hamond, private collection
NWr	——, Record Office
Oas	Oxford, All Souls College Library
Ob	——, Bodleian Library
Oc	——, Coke Collection
Occc	——, Corpus Christi College Library
Och	——, Christ Church Library
Ojc	——, St John's College Library
Olc	——, Lincoln College Library

Omc	——, Magdalen College Library
Onc	——, New College Library
Ouf	——, Faculty of Music Library
Owc	——, Worcester College
P	Perth, Sandeman Public Library
PB	Peterborough, Cathedral Library
PM	Parkminster, St Hugh's Charterhouse
R	Reading, University, Music Library
SA	St Andrews, University of St Andrews Library
SB	Salisbury, Cathedral Library
SC	Sutton Coldfield, Oscott College, Old Library
SH	Sherborne, Sherborne School Library
SHR	Shrewsbury, Salop Record Office
SHRs	——, Library of Shrewsbury School
SOp	Southampton, Public Library
SRfa	Studley Royal, Fountains Abbey [in *LEc*]
STb	Stratford-on-Avon, Shakespeare's Birthplace Trust Library
STm	——, Shakespeare Memorial Library
T	Tenbury Wells, St Michael's College Library [in *Ob*]
W	Wells, Cathedral Library
WA	Whalley, Stonyhurst College Library
WB	Wimborne, Minster Chain Library
WC	Winchester, Chapter Library
WCc	——, Winchester College, Warden and Fellows' Library
WCr	——, Hampshire Record Office
WMl	Warminster, Longleat House Old Library
WO	Worcester, Cathedral Library
WOr	——, Record Office
WRch	Windsor, St George's Chapel Library
WRec	——, Eton College, College Library
Y	York, Minster Library
Ybi	——, Borthwick Institute of Historical Research

GCA: GUATEMALA

Gc	Guatemala City, Cathedral, Archivo Capitular

GR: GREECE

Aels	Athens, Ethniki Lyriki Skini
Akounadis	——, Panayis Kounadis, private collection
Aleotsakos	——, George Leotsakos, private collection
Am	——, Mousseio ke Kendro Meletis Ellinikou Theatrou
An	——, Ethnikē Bibliotēkē tēs Hellados
AOd	Mt Athos, Mone Dionysiou
AOdo	——, Mone Dohiariou
AOh	——, Mone Hilandariou
AOi	——, Mone ton Iveron
AOk	——, Mone Koutloumousi
AOml	——, Mone Megistis Lávras
AOpk	——, Mone Pantokrátoros
AOva	——, Vatopedi Monastery
P	Patmos
THpi	Thessaloniki, Patriarhikó Idryma Paterikon Meleton, Vivliotheke

H: HUNGARY

Ba	Budapest, Magyar Tudományos Akadémia Könytára
Bami	——, Magyar Tudományos Akadémia Zenetudományi Intézet, Könyvtár
Bb	——, Bartók Béla Zeneművészeti Szakközépiskola, Könyvtár [in *Bl*]
Bl	——, Liszt Ferenc Zeneművészeti Főiskola, Könyvtár
Bn	——, Országos Széchényi Könyvtár
Bo	——, Állami Operaház
Br	——, Ráday Gyűjtemény
Bs	——, Központi Szemináriumi Könyvtár
Bu	——, Eötvös Loránd Tudományegyetem, Egyetemi Könyvtár
BA	Bártfá, St Aegidius [in *Bn*]
Efko	Esztergom, Főszékesegyházi Kottatár
Efkö	——, Főszékesegyházi Könyvtár
Gc	Győr, Püspöki Papnevelő Intézet Könyvtára
Gk	——, Káptalan Magánlevéltár Kottatára
GYm	Gyula, Múzeum

K	Kalocsa, Érseki Könyvtár
KE	Keszthely, Helikon Kastélymúzeum, Könyvtár
P	Pécs, Székesegyházi Kottatár
PH	Pannonhalma, Főapátság, Könyvtár
Se	Sopron, Evangélikus Egyházközség Könyvtára
SFm	Székesfehérvár, István Király Múzeum
VEs	Veszprém, Székesegyházi Kottatár

HR: CROATIA

Dsmb	Dubrovnik, Franjevački Samostan Male Braće, Knjižnica
KIf	Kloštar Ivanić, Franjevački Samostan
OMf	Omiš, Franjevački Samostan
R	Rab, Župna Crkva
Sk	Split, Glazbeni Arhiv Katedrale Sv. Dujma
SMm	Samobor, Samoborski Muzej
Vu	Varaždin, Uršulinski Samostan
Zaa	Zagreb, Hrvatska Akademija Znanosti i Umjetnosti, Arhiv
Zh	——, Hrvatski Glazbeni Zavod, Knjižnica i Arhiv
Zha	——, Zbirka Don Nikole Udina-Algarotti [on loan to *Zh*]
Zhk	——, Arhiv Hrvatsko Pjevačko Društvo Kolo [in *Zh*]
Zs	——, Glazbeni Arhiv Nadbiskupskog Bogoslovnog Sjemeništa
Zu	——, Nacionalna i Sveučilišna Knjižnica, Zbirka Muzikalija i Audiomaterijala
ZAzk	Zadar, Znanstvena Knjižnica

I: ITALY

Ac	Assisi, Biblioteca Comunale [in *Af*]
Ad	——, Cattedrale S Rufino, Biblioteca dell'Archivio Capitolare
Af	——, Sacro Convento di S Francesco, Biblioteca-Centro di Documentazione Francescana
ALTsm	Altamura, Associazione Amici della Musica Saverio Mercadante, Biblioteca
AN	Ancona, Biblioteca Comunale Luciano Benincasa
AO	Aosta, Seminario Maggiore
AOc	——, Cattedrale, Biblioteca Capitolare
AP	Ascoli Piceno, Biblioteca Comunale Giulio Gabrielli
APa	——, Archivio di Stato
AT	Atri, Basilica Cattedrale di S Maria Assunta, Biblioteca Capitolare e Museo
Baf	Bologna, Accademia Filarmonica, Archivio
Bam	——, Collezioni d'Arte e di Storia della Casa di Risparmio (Biblioteca Ambrosini)
Bas	——, Archivio di Stato, Biblioteca
Bc	——, Civico Museo Bibliografico Musicale
Bca	——, Biblioteca Comunale dell'Archiginnasio
Bl	——, Conservatorio Statale di Musica G.B. Martini, Biblioteca
Bof	——, Congregazione dell'Oratorio (Padri Filippini), Biblioteca
Bpm	——, Università degli Studi, Facoltà di Magistero, Cattedra di Storia della Musica, Biblioteca
Bsf	——, Convento di S Francesco, Biblioteca
Bsm	——, Biblioteca del Convento di S Maria dei Servi e della Cappella Musicale Arcivescovile
Bsp	——, Basilica di S Petronio, Archivio Musicale
Bu	——, Biblioteca Universitaria, sezione Musicale
BAca	Bari, Biblioteca Capitolare
BAcp	——, Conservatorio di Musica Niccolò Piccinni, Biblioteca
BAn	——, Biblioteca Nazionale Sagarriga Visconti-Volpi
BAR	Barletta, Biblioteca Comunale Sabino Loffredo
BDG	Bassano del Grappa, Biblioteca Archivo Museo (Biblioteca Civica)
BE	Belluno, Biblioteche Lolliniana e Gregoriana
BGc	Bergamo, Biblioteca Civica Angelo Mai
BGi	——, Civico Istituto Musicale Gaetano Donizetti, Biblioteca
BI	Bitonto, Biblioteca Comunale E. Bogadeo (ex Vitale Giordano)
BRc	Brescia, Conservatorio Statale di Musica A. Venturi, Biblioteca
BRd	——, Archivio e Biblioteca Capitolari
BRq	——, Biblioteca Civica Queriniana

BRs	——, Seminario Vescovile Diocasano, Archivio Musicale
BRsmg	——, Chiesa della Madonna delle Grazie (S Maria), Archivio
BV	Benevento, Biblioteca Capitolare
BZa	Bolzano, Archivio di Stato, Biblioteca
BZf	——, Convento dei Minori Francescani, Biblioteca
BZtoggenburg	——, Count Toggenburg, private collection
CAcon	Cagliari, Conservatorio di Musica Giovanni Pierluigi da Palestrina, Biblioteca
CARc	Castell'Arquato, Archivio Capitolare (Parrocchiale)
CARcc	——, Chiesa Collegiata dell'Assunta, Archivio Musicale
CAS	Cascia, Monastero di S Rita, Archivio
CATa	Catania, Archivio di Stato
CATc	——, Biblioteche Riunite Civica e Antonio Ursino Recupero
CATm	——, Museo Civico Belliniano, Biblioteca
CATus	——, Università degli Studi di Catania, Facoltà di Lettere e Filosofia, Dipartimento di Scienze Storiche, Storia della Musica, Biblioteca
CC	Città di Castello, Duomo, Archivio Capitolare [in *CCsg*]
CCc	——, Biblioteca Comunale Giosuè Carducci
CCsg	——, Biblioteca Stori Guerri e Archivi Storico
CDO	Codogno, Biblioteca Civica Luigi Ricca
CEc	Cesena, Biblioteca Comunale Malatestiana
CF	Cividale del Friuli, Duomo (Parrocchia di S Maria Assunta), Archivio Capitolare
CFm	——, Museo Archeologico Nazionale, Biblioteca
CFVd	Castelfranco Veneto, Duomo, Archivio
CHc	Chioggia, Biblioteca Comunale Cristoforo Sabbadino
CHf	——, Archivio dei Padri Filippini [in *CHc*]
CHTd	Chieti, Biblioteca della Curia Arcivescovile e Archivio Capitolare
CMac	Casale Monferrato, Duomo di Sant'Evasio, Archivio Capitolare
CMbc	——, Biblioteca Civica Giovanni Canna
CMs	——, Seminario Vescovile, Biblioteca
COc	Como, Biblioteca Comunale
COd	——, Duomo, Archivio Musicale
CORc	Correggio, Biblioteca Comunale
CRas	Cremona, Archivio di Stato
CRd	——, Biblioteca Capitolare [in *CRsd*]
CRg	——, Biblioteca Statale
CRsd	——, Archivio Storico Diocesano
CRE	Crema, Biblioteca Comunale
CT	Cortona, Biblioteca Comunale e dell'Accademia Etrusca
DO	Domodossola, Biblioteca e Archivio dei Rosminiani di Monte Calvario [in *ST*]
E	Enna, Biblioteca e Discoteca Comunale
Fa	Florence, Ss Annunziata, Archivio
Fas	——, Archivio di Stato, Biblioteca
Fbecherini	——, Becherini private collection
Fc	——, Conservatorio Statale di Musica Luigi Cherubini
Fd	——, Opera del Duomo (S Maria del Fiore), Biblioteca e Archivio
Ffabbri	——, Mario Fabbri, private collection
Fl	——, Biblioteca Medicea Laurenziana
Fm	——, Biblioteca Marucelliana
Fn	——, Biblioteca Nazionale Centrale, Dipartimento Musica
Folschki	——, Olschki private collection
Fr	——, Biblioteca Riccardiana
Fs	——, Seminario Arcivescovile Maggiore, Biblioteca
Fsa	——, Biblioteca Domenicana di S Maria Novella
Fsl	——, Parrocchia di S Lorenzo, Biblioteca
Fsm	——, Convento di S Marco, Biblioteca
FA	Fabriano, Biblioteca Comunale
FAd	——, Duomo (S Venanzio), Biblioteca Capitolare
FAN	Fano, Biblioteca Comunale Federiciana
FBR	Fossombrone, Biblioteca Civica Passionei
FEc	Ferrara, Biblioteca Comunale Ariostea
FEd	——, Duomo, Archivio Capitolare
FELc	Feltre, Museo Civico, Biblioteca

FEM	Finale Emilia, Biblioteca Comunale
FERaa	Fermo, Archivio Storico Arcivescovile con Archivio della Pietà
FERas	——, Archivio di Stato di Ascoli Piceno, sezione di Fermo
FERc	——, Biblioteca Comunale
FERd	——, Metropolitana (Duomo), Archivio Capitolare [in *FERaa*]
FERvitali	——, Gualberto Vitali-Rosati, private collection
FOc	Forlì, Biblioteca Comunale Aurelio Saffi
FOLc	Foligno, Biblioteca Comunale
FOLd	——, Duomo, Archivio
FRa	Fara in Sabina, Monumento Nazionale di Farfa, Biblioteca
FZac	Faenza, Basilica Cattedrale, Archivio Capitolare
FZc	——, Biblioteca Comunale Manfrediana, Raccolte Musicali
Gc	Genoa, Biblioteca Civica Berio
Gim	——, Civico Istituto Mazziniano, Biblioteca
Gl	——, Conservatorio di Musica Nicolò Paganini, Biblioteca
Gremondini	——, P.C. Remondini, private collection
Gsl	——, S Lorenzo (Duomo), Archivio Capitolare
Gu	——, Biblioteca Universitaria
GO	Gorizia, Seminario Teologico Centrale, Biblioteca
GR	Grottaferrata, Biblioteca del Monumento Nazionale
GUBd	Gubbio, Biblioteca Vescovile Fonti e Archivio Diocesano (con Archivio del Capitolo della Cattedrale)
I	Imola, Biblioteca Comunale
IBborromeo	Isola Bella, Borromeo private collection
IE	Iesi, Biblioteca Comunale
IV	Ivrea, Cattedrale, Biblioteca Capitolare
La	Lucca, Archivio di Stato
Las	——, Biblioteca-Archivio Storico Comunale
Lc	——, Biblioteca Capitolare Feliniana e Biblioteca Arcivescovile
Lg	——, Biblioteca Statale
Li	——, Istituto Musicale L. Boccherini, Biblioteca
Ls	——, Seminario Arcivescovile, Biblioteca
LA	L'Aquila, Biblioteca Provinciale Salvatore Tommasi
LANc	Lanciano, Biblioteca Diocesano (con Archivio della Cattedrale)
LT	Loreto, Santuario della S Casa, Archivio Storico
LU	Lugo, Biblioteca Comunale Fabrizio Trisi
LUi	——, Istituto Musicale Pareggiato G.L. Malerbi
Ma	Milan, Biblioteca Ambrosiana
Malfieri	——, Familglia Trecani degli Alfieri, private collection
Mas	——, Archivio di Stato
Mb	——, Biblioteca Nazionale Braidense
Mc	——, Conservatorio di Musica Giuseppe Verdi, Biblioteca
Mcap	——, Archivio Capitolare di S Ambrogio, Biblioteca
Mcom	——, Biblioteca Comunale Sormani
Md	——, Capitolo Metropolitano, Biblioteca e Archivio
Mgallini	——, Natale Gallini, private collection
Mr	——, Biblioteca della Casa Ricordi
Ms	——, Biblioteca Teatrale Livia Simoni
Msartori	——, Claudio Sartori, private collection [in *Mc*]
Msc	——, Chiesa di S Maria presso S Celso, Archivio
Mt	——, Biblioteca Trivulziana e Archivio Storico Civico
Mu	——, Università degli Studi di Milano, Facoltà di Giurisprudenza, Biblioteca
Muc	——, Università Cattolica del Sacro Cuore, Biblioteca
MAa	Mantua, Archivio di Stato
MAad	——, Archivio Storico Diocesano
MAav	——, Accademia Nazionale Virgiliana di Scienze, Lettere ed Arti, Archivio Musicale
MAc	——, Biblioteca Comunale
MAC	Macerata, Biblioteca Comunale Mozzi-Borgetti
MC	Montecassino, Monumento Nazionale di Montecassino, Biblioteca
MDAegidi	Montefiore dell'Aso, Francesco Egidi, private collection
ME	Messina, Biblioteca Regionale Universitaria
MEs	——, Biblioteca Painiana (del Seminario Arcivescovile S Pio X)

MOd	Modena, Duomo, Biblioteca e Archivio Capitolare
MOe	——, Biblioteca Estense e Universitaria
MOs	——, Archivio di Stato [in *MOe*]
MTc	Montecatini Terme, Biblioteca Comunale
MTventuri	——, Antonio Venturi, private collection [in *MTc*]
MZ	Monza, Parrocchia di S Giovanni Battista, Biblioteca Capitolare
Na	Naples, Archivio di Stato
Nc	——, Conservatorio di Musica S Pietro a Majella, Biblioteca
Nf	——, Biblioteca Oratoriana dei Gerolamini (Filippini)
Ng	——, Monastero di S Gregorio Armeno, Archivio
Nlp	——, Biblioteca Lucchesi Palli [in *Nn*]
Nn	——, Biblioteca Nazionale Vittorio Emanuele III
NON	Nonantola, Seminario Abbaziale, Biblioteca
NOVd	Novara, S Maria (Duomo), Biblioteca Capitolare
NOVg	——, Seminario Teologico e Filosofico di S Gaudenzio, Biblioteca
NOVi	——, Istituto Civico Musicale Brera, Biblioteca
NT	Noto, Biblioteca Comunale Principe di Villadorata
Od	Orvieto, Opera del Duomo, Biblioteca
OFma	Offida, Parrocchia di Maria Ss Assunta, Archivio
OS	Ostiglia, Opera Pia G. Greggiati Biblioteca Musicale
Pas	Padua, Archivio di Stato
Pc	——, Duomo, Biblioteca Capitolare, Curia Vescovile
Pca	——, Basilica del Santo, Biblioteca Antoniana
Pci	——, Biblioteca Civica
Pl	——, Conservatorio Cesare Pollini
Ps	——, Seminario Vescovile, Biblioteca
Pu	——, Biblioteca Universitaria
PAac	Parma, Duomo, Archivio Capitolare con Archivio della Fabbriceria
PAas	——, Archivio di Stato
PAc	——, Biblioteca Palatina, sezione Musicale
PAcom	——, Biblioteca Comunale
PAp	——, Biblioteca Nazionale Palatina
PAt	——, Archivio Storico del Teatro Regio [in *PAcom*]
PAVc	Pavia, Chiesa di S Maria del Carmine, Archivio
PAVs	——, Seminario Vescovile, Biblioteca
PAVu	——, Biblioteca Universitaria
PCc	Piacenza, Biblioteca Comunale Passerini Landi
PCcon	——, Conservatorio di Musica G. Nicolini, Biblioteca
PCd	——, Duomo, Biblioteca e Archivio Capitolare
PCsa	——, Basilica di S Antonino, Biblioteca e Archivio Capitolari
PEas	Perugia, Archivio di Stato
PEc	——, Biblioteca Comunale Augusta
PEd	——, Biblioteca Domincini
PEl	——, Conservatorio di Musica Francesco Morlacchi, Biblioteca
PEsf	——, Congregazione dell' Oratorio di S Filippo Neri, Biblioteca e Archivio
PEsl	——, Duomo (S Lorenzo), Archivio
PEsp	——, Basilica Benedettina di S Pietro, Archivio e Museo della Badia
PEA	Pescia, Biblioteca Comunale Carlo Magnani
PESc	Pesaro, Conservatorio di Musica G. Rossini, Biblioteca
PESd	——, Duomo, Archivio Capitolare [in *PESdi*]
PESdi	——, Biblioteca Diocesana
PESo	——, Ente Olivieri, Biblioteca e Musei Oliveriana
PESr	——, Fondazione G. Rossini, Biblioteca
PIa	Pisa, Archivio di Stato
PIp	——, Opera della Primaziale Pisana, Archivio Musicale
PIraffaelli	——, Raffaelli private collection
PIst	——, Chiesa dei Cavalieri di S Stefano, Archivio
PIt	——, Teatro Verdi
PIu	——, Biblioteca Universitaria
PLa	Palermo, Archivio di Stato
PLcom	——, Biblioteca Comunale
PLcon	——, Conservatorio di Musica Vincenzo Bellini, Biblioteca

PLi	——, Università degli Studi, Facoltà di Lettere e Filosofia, Istituto di Storia della Musica, Biblioteca
PLn	——, Biblioteca Centrale della Regione Sicilia tex (Nazionale)
PLpagano	——, Roberto Pagano, private collection
PO	Potenza, Biblioteca Provinciale
PR	Prato, Archivio Storico Diocesano, Biblioteca (con Archivio del Duomo)
PS	Pistoia, Basilica di S Zeno, Archivio Capitolare
PSc	——, Biblioteca Comunale Forteguerriana
PSrospigliosi	——, Rospigliosi private collection
Ra	Rome, Biblioteca Angelica
Raf	——, Accademia Filarmonica Romana
Ras	——, Archivio di Stato, Biblioteca
Rbompiani	——, Bompiani private collection
Rc	——, Biblioteca Casanatense, sezione Musica
Rcg	——, Curia Generalizia dei Padre Gesuiti, Biblioteca
Rchg	——, Chiesa del Gesù, Archivio
Rcsg	——, Congregazione dell'Oratorio di S Girolamo della Carità, Archivio [in *Ras*]
Rdp	——, Archivio Doria Pamphili
Rf	——, Congregazione dell'Oratorio S Filippo Neri
Ria	——, Istituto di Archeologia e Storia dell'Arte, Biblioteca
Ribimus	——, Istituto di Bibliografia Musicale, Biblioteca [in *Rn*]
Rig	——, Istituto Storico Germanico di Roma, sezione Storia della Musica, Biblioteca
Rims	——, Pontificio Istituto di Musica Sacra, Biblioteca
Rli	——, Accademia Nazionale dei Lincei e Corsiniana, Biblioteca
Rlib	——, Basilica Liberiana, Archivio
Rmalvezzi	——, Lionello Malvezzi, private collection
Rmassimo	——, Massimo princes, private collection
Rn	——, Biblioteca Nazionale Centrale Vittorio Emanuele II
Rp	——, Biblioteca Pasqualini [in *Rsc*]
Rps	——, Chiesa di S Pantaleo (Padri Scolipi), Archivio
Rrai	——, RAI-Radiotelevisione Italiana, Archivio Musica
Rrostirolla	——, Giancarlo Rostirolla, private collection [in *Fn* and *Ribimus*]
Rsc	——, Conservatorio di Musica S Cecilia
Rscg	——, Abbazia di S Croce in Gerusalemme, Biblioteca
Rsg	——, Basilica di S Giovanni in Laterano, Archivio Musicale
Rslf	——, Chiesa di S Luigi dei Francesi, Archivio
Rsm	——, Basilica di S Maria Maggiore, Archivio Capitolare [in *Rvat*]
Rsmm	——, S Maria di Monserrato, Archivio
Rsmt	——, Basilica di S Maria in Trastevere, Archivio Capitolare [in *Rvic*]
Rsp	——, Chiesa di S Spirito in Sassia, Archivio
Rss	——, Curia Generalizia dei Domenicani (S Sabina), Biblioteca
Ru	——, Biblioteca Universitaria Alessandrina
Rv	——, Biblioteca Vallicelliana
Rvat	——, Biblioteca Apostolica Vaticana
Rvic	——, Vicariato, Archivio
RA	Ravenna, Duomo (Basilica Ursiana), Archivio Capitolare [in *RAs*]
RAc	——, Biblioteca Comunale Classense
RAs	——, Seminario Arcivescovile dei Ss Angeli Custodi, Biblioteca
REm	Reggio nell'Emilia, Biblioteca Panizzi
REsp	——, Basilica di S Prospero, Archivio Capitolare
RI	Rieti, Biblioteca Diocesana, sezione dell'Archivio Musicale del Duomo
RIM	Rimini, Biblioteca Civica Gambalunga
RPTd	Ripatransone, Duomo, Archivio
RVE	Rovereto, Biblioteca Civica Girolamo Tartarotti
RVI	Rovigo, Accademia dei Concordi, Biblioteca
Sac	Siena, Accademia Musicale Chigiana, Biblioteca
Sas	——, Archivio di Stato
Sc	——, Biblioteca Comunale degli Intronati
Sco	——, Convento dell'Osservanza, Biblioteca
Sd	——, Opera del Duomo, Archivio Musicale

Smo	Asciano (nr Siena), Abbazia Benedettina di Monte Oliveto Maggiore, Biblioteca
SA	Savona, Biblioteca Civica Anton Giulio Barrili
SAa	——, Seminario Vescovile, Biblioteca
SE	Senigallia, Biblioteca Comunale Antonelliana
SO	Sant'Oreste, Collegiata di S Lorenzo sul Monte Soratte, Biblioteca
SPc	Spoleto, Biblioteca Comunale Giosuè Carducci
SPd	——, Biblioteca Capitolare (Duomo di S Lorenzo)
SPE	Spello, Collegiata di S Maria Maggiore, Archivio
SPEbc	——, Biblioteca Comunale Giacomo Prampolini
ST	Stresa, Biblioteca Rosminiana
STE	Vipiteno, Convento dei Cappuccini (Kapuzinerkloster), Biblioteca
Ta	Turin, Archivio di Stato
Tci	——, Civica Biblioteca Musicale Andrea della Corte
Tco	——, Conservatorio di Musica Giuseppe Verdi, Biblioteca
Td	——, Cattedrale Metropolitana di S Giovanni Battista, Archivio Capitolare, Fondo Musicale della Cappella dei Cantori del Duomo e della Cappella Regia Sabauda
Tf	——, Accademia Filarmonica, Archivio
Tfanan	——, Giorgio Fanan, private collection
Tn	——, Biblioteca Nazionale Universitaria, sezione Musicale
Tr	——, Biblioteca Reale
Trt	——, RAI – Radiotelevisione Italiana, Biblioteca
TAc	Taranto, Biblioteca Civica Pietro Acclavio
TE	Terni, Istituto Musicale Pareggiato Giulio Briccialdi, Biblioteca
TEd	——, Duomo, Archivio Capitolare
TLp	Torre del Lago Puccini, Museo di Casa Puccini
TOL	Tolentino, Biblioteca Comunale Filelfica
TRa	Trent, Archivio di Stato
TRbc	——, Castello del Buon Consiglio, Biblioteca [in *TRmp*]
TRc	——, Biblioteca Comunale
TRcap	——, Biblioteca Capitolare con Annesso Archivio
TRfeininger	——, Biblioteca Musicale Laurence K.J. Feininger [in *TRmp*]
TRmd	——, Museo Diocesano, Biblioteca
TRmp	——, Castello del Buonconsiglio: Monumenti e Collezioni Provinciali, Biblioteca
TRmr	——, Museo Trentino del Risorgimento e della Lotta per la Libertà, Biblioteca
TRE	Tremezzo, Count Gian Ludovico Sola-Cabiati, private collection
TRP	Trapani, Biblioteca Fardelliana
TSci	Trieste, Biblioteca Comunale Attilio Hortis
TScon	——, Conservatorio di Musica Giuseppe Tartini, Biblioteca
TSmt	——, Civico Museo Teatrale di Fondazione Carlo Schmidl, Biblioteca
TVco	Treviso, Biblioteca Comunale
TVd	——, Biblioteca Capitolare della Cattedrale
Us	Urbino, Cappella del Ss Sacramento (Duomo), Archivio
UD	Udine, Duomo, Archivio Capitolare [in *UDs*]
UDa	——, Archivio di Stato
UDc	——, Biblioteca Comunale Vincenzo Joppi
UDs	——, Seminario Arcivescovile, Biblioteca
URBcap	Urbania, Biblioteca Capitolare [in *URBdi*]
URBdi	——, Biblioteca Diocesana
Vas	Venice, Archivio di Stato
Vc	——, Conservatorio di Musica Benedetto Marcello, Biblioteca
Vcg	——, Casa di Goldoni, Biblioteca
Vgc	——, Fondazione Giorgio Cini, Istituto per le Lettere, il Teatro ed il Melodramma, Biblioteca
Vlevi	——, Fondazione Ugo e Olga Levi, Biblioteca
Vmarcello	——, Andrighetti Marcello, private collection
Vmc	——, Museo Civico Correr, Biblioteca d'Arte e Storia Veneziana
Vnm	——, Biblioteca Nazionale Marciana
Vqs	——, Fondazione Querini-Stampalia, Biblioteca
Vs	——, Seminario Patriarcale, Archivio
Vsf	——, Biblioteca S Francesco della Vigna

Vsm	——, Procuratoria di S Marco [in *Vlevi*]
Vsmc	——, S Maria della Consolazione detta Della Fava
Vt	——, Teatro La Fenice, Archivio Storico-Musicale
VCd	Vercelli, Biblioteca Capitolare
VEaf	Verona, Accademia Filarmonica, Biblioteca e Archivio
VEas	——, Archivio di Stato
VEc	——, Biblioteca Civica
VEcap	——, Biblioteca Capitolare
VEss	——, Chiesa di S Stefano, Archivio
VIb	Vicenza, Biblioteca Civica Bertoliana
VId	——, Biblioteca Capitolare
VIs	——, Seminario Vescovile, Biblioteca
VIGsa	Vigévano, Biblioteca del Capitolo della Cattedrale
VRNs	Chiusi della Verna, Santuario della Verna, Biblioteca

IL: ISRAEL

J	Jerusalem, Jewish National and University Library, Music Dept
Jgp	——, Greek Orthodox Patriarchate, Library (Hierosolymitike Bibliotheke)
Jp	——, Patriarchal Library
Ta	Tel-Aviv, American for Music Library in Israel, Felicja Blumental Music Center and Library
Tmi	——, Israel Music Institute

IRL: IRELAND

C	Cork, Boole Library, University College
Da	Dublin, Royal Irish Academy Library
Dam	——, Royal Irish Academy of Music, Monteagle Library
Dc	——, Contemporary Music Centre
Dcb	——, Chester Beatty Library
Dcc	——, Christ Church Cathedral, Library
Dm	——, Archbishop Marsh's Library
Dmh	——, Mercer's Hospital [in *Dtc*]
Dn	——, National Library of Ireland
Dpc	——, St Patrick's Cathedral
Dtc	——, Trinity College Library, University of Dublin

J: JAPAN

Tma	Tokyo, Musashino Ongaku Daigaku, Ioshokan
Tn	——, Nanki Ongaku Bunko

LT: LITHUANIA

V	Vilnius, Lietuvos Muzikos Akademijos Biblioteka
Va	——, Lietuvos Moksly Akademijos Biblioteka

LV: LATVIA

J	Jelgava, Muzei
R	Riga, Latvijas Mūzikas Akademijas Biblioteka

M: MALTA

Vnl	Valletta, National Library

MD: MOLDOVA

KI	Chişinău, Biblioteca Gosudarstvennoj Konservatorii im. G. Muzyčesku

MEX: MEXICO

Mc	Mexico City, Catedral Metropolitana, Archivo Musical
Pc	Puebla, Catedral Metropolitana, Archivo del Cabildo

N: NORWAY

Bo	Bergen, Offentlige Bibliotek, Griegsamlingen
Ou	Oslo, Universitetsbiblioteket
Oum	——, Nasjonalbiblioteket, Avdeling Oslo, Norsk Musikksamling
T	Trondheim, Norges Teknisk-Naturvitenskapelige Universitet, Gunnerusbiblioteket

NL: THE NETHERLANDS

At	Amsterdam, Toonkunst-Bibliotheek
Au	——, Universiteitsbibliotheek
DEta	Delden, Huisarchief Twickel
DHa	The Hague, Koninklijk Huisarchief
DHgm	——, Haags Gemeentemuseum, Muziekafdeling
DHk	——, Koninklijke Bibliotheek
E	Enkhuizen, Archief Collegium Musicum
L	Leiden, Gemeentearchief
Lml	——, Museum Lakenhal
Lt	——, Bibliotheca Thysiana [in *Lu*]
Lu	——, Rijksuniversiteit, Bibliotheek
LE	Leeuwarden, Provinciale Bibliotheek van Friesland
R	Rotterdam, Gemeentebibliotheek
SH	's-Hertogenbosch, Illustre Lieve Vrouwe Broederschap
Uim	Utrecht, Letterenbibliotheek, Universiteit
Uu	——, Universiteit Utrecht, Universiteitsbibliotheek

NZ: NEW ZEALAND

Aua	Auckland, University of Auckland, Archive of Maori and Pacific Music
Wt	Wellington, Alexander Turnbull Library

P: PORTUGAL

AR	Arouca, Mosteirode de S Maria, Museu de Arte Sacra, Fundo Musical
BRp	Braga, Arquivo Distrital
BRs	——, Arquivo da Sé
Cmn	Coimbra, Museu Nacional de Machado de Castro
Cs	——, Arquivo da Sé Nova
Cug	——, Universidade de Coimbra, Biblioteca Geral, Impressos e Manuscritos Musicais
Cul	——, Faculdade de Letras da Universidade
Em	Elvas, Biblioteca Municipal
EVc	Évora, Arquivo da Sé, Museu Regional
EVp	——, Biblioteca Pública e Arquivo Distrital
F	Figueira da Foz, Biblioteca Pública Municipal Pedro Fernandes Tomás
G	Guimarães, Arquivo Municipal Alfredo Pimenta
La	Lisbon, Biblioteca da Ajuda
Lac	——, Academia das Ciências, Biblioteca
Lant	——, Arquivo Nacional da Torre do Tombo
Lc	——, Biblioteca do Conservatório Nacional
Lcg	——, Fundação Calouste Gulbenkian, Biblioteca Geral de Arte, Serviço de Música
Lf	——, Fabrica da Sé Patriarcal
Ln	——, Biblioteca Nacional, Centro de Estudos Musicológicos
Lt	——, Teatro Nacional de S Carlos
LA	Lamego, Arquivo da Sé
Mp	Mafra, Palácio Nacional, Biblioteca
Pm	Porto, Biblioteca Pública Municipal
Va	Viseu, Arquivo Distrital
Vs	——, Arquivo da Sé
VV	Vila Viçosa, Fundaçao da Casa de Bragança, Biblioteca do Paço Ducal, Arquivo Musical

PL: POLAND

B	Bydgoszcz, Wojewódzka i Miejska Biblioteka Publiczna, Dział Zbiórów Specjalnych
BA	Barczewo, Kościóła Parafialny, Archiwum
CZ	Częstochowa, Klasztor Ojców Paulinów: Jasna Góra Archiwum
GD	Gdańsk, Polska Akademia Nauk, Biblioteka Gdańska
GDp	——, Wojewódzka Biblioteka Publiczna
GNd	Gniezno, Archiwum Archidiecezjalne
GR	Grodzisk Wielkopolski, Kościół Parafialny św. Jadwigi [in *Pa*]
Kc	Kraków, Muzeum Narodowe, Biblioteka Czartoryskich
Kcz	——, Muzeum Narodowe, Biblioteka Czapskich
Kd	——, Biblioteka Studium OO. Dominikanów
Kj	——, Uniwersytet Jagielloński, Biblioteka Jagiellońska
Kk	——, Archiwum i Biblioteka Krakowskiej Kapituły Katedralnej
Kn	——, Muzeum Narodowe
Kp	——, Biblioteka Polskiej Akademii Nauk
Kpa	——, Archiwum Państwowe
Kz	——, Biblioteka Czartoryskich
KA	Katowice, Biblioteka Śląska

KO	Kórnik, Polska Akademia Nauk, Biblioteka Kórnicka
KRZ	Krzeszów, Cysterski Kościół Parafialny [in *KRZk*]
KRZk	——, Klasztor Ss Benedyktynek
Lw	Lublin, Wojewódzka Biblioteka Publiczna im. H. Lopacińskiego
LA	Łańcut, Biblioteka-Muzeum Zamku
LEtpn	Legnica, Towarzystwa Przyjaciół Nauk, Biblioteka
LZu	Łódź, Biblioteka Uniwersytecka
MO	Mogiła, Opactwo Cystersów, Archiwumi Biblioteka
OB	Obra, Klasztor OO. Cystersów
Pa	Poznań, Archiwum Archidiecezjalna
Pm	——, Biblioteka Zakładu Muzykologii Uniwersytetu Poznańskiego
Pr	——, Miejska Biblioteka Publiczna im. Edwarda Raczyńskiego
Pu	——, Uniwersytet im. Adama Mickiewicza, Biblioteka Uniwersytecka, Sekcja Zbiorów Muzycznych
PE	Pelplin, Wyższe Seminarium Duchowne, Biblioteka
R	Raków, Kościół Parafialny, Archiwum
SA	Sandomierz, Wyższe Seminarium Duchowne, Biblioteca
SZ	Szalowa, Archiwum Parafialne
Tm	Toruń, Ksiąznica Miejska im. M. Kopernika
Tu	——, Uniwersytet Mikołaja Kopernika, Biblioteka Głowna, Oddział Zbiorów Muzycznych
Wm	Warsaw, Muzeum Narodowe, Biblioteka
Wn	——, Biblioteka Narodowa
Wtm	——, Warszawskie Towarzystwo Muzyczne im Stanisława Moniuszki, Biblioteka, Muzeum i Archiwum
Wu	——, Uniwersytet Warszawski, Biblioteka Uniwersytecka, Gabinet Zbiorów Muzycznych
WL	Wilanów, Biblioteka [in *Wn* and *Wm*]
WRk	Wrocław, Biblioteka Kapitulna
WRu	——, Uniwersytet Wrocławski, Biblioteka Uniwersytecka
WRzno	——, Zakład Narodowy im. Ossolińskich, Biblioteka

RO: ROMANIA

Ba	Bucharest, Academiei Române, Biblioteca
BRm	Braşov, Biblioteca Judeteana
Cu	Cluj-Napoca, Universitatea Babes Bolyai, Biblioteca Centrală Universitară Lucian Blaga
J	Iaşi, Biblioteca Centrală Universitară Mihai Eminescu, Departmentul Colecţii Speciale
Sa	Sibiu, Direcţia Judeteană a Arhivelor Naţionale
Sb	——, Muzeul Naţional Bruckenthal, Biblioteca

RUS: RUSSIAN FEDERATION

KA	Kaliningrad, Oblastnaya Universal'naya Nauchnaya Biblioteka
KAg	——, Gosudarstvennaya Biblioteka
KAu	——, Nauchnaya Biblioteka Kalingradskogo Gosudarstvennogo Universiteta
Mcl	Moscow, Rossiyskiy Gosudarstvenniy Arkhiv Literaturï i Iskusstva (RGALI)
Mcm	——, Gosudarstvenniy Tsentral'niy Muzey Musïkal'noy Kul'turï imeni M.I. Glinki
Mim	——, Gosudarstvenniy Istoricheskïy Muzey
Mk	——, Moskovskaya Gosudarstvennaya Konservatoriya im. P.I. Chaykovskogo, Nauchnaya Muzïkal'naya Biblioteka imeni S.I. Taneyeva
Mm	——, Gosudarstvennaya Publichnaya Istoricheskaya Bibliotheka
Mrg	——, Rossiyskaya Gosudarstvennaya Biblioteka
Mt	——, Gosudarstvenniy Tsentral'nïy Teatral'nïy Musey im. A. Bakhrushina
SPan	St Petersburg, Rossiyskaya Akademiya Nauk, Biblioteka
SPia	——, Gosudarstvennïy Tsentral'nïy Istoricheskïy Arkhiv
SPil	——, Biblioteka Instituta Russkoy Literaturï Rossiyskoy Akademii Nauk (Pushkinskiy Dom)
SPit	——, Rossiyskiy Institut Istorii Iskusstv
SPk	——, Biblioteka Gosudarstvennoy Konservatorii im. N.A. Rimskogo-Korsakova
SPph	——, Gosurdarstvennaya Filarmoniya im D.D. Shostakovicha
SPsc	——, Rossiyskaya Natsional'naya Biblioteka
SPtob	——, Gosudarstvennïy Akademichesky Mariinsky Teatr, Tsentral'naya Muzïkal'naya Biblioteka

S: SWEDEN

A	Arvika, Ingesunds Musikhögskola
B	Bålsta, Skoklosters Slott
Gu	Göteborg, Universitetsbiblioteket
Hfryklund	Helsingborg, Daniel Fryklund, private collection [in *Skma*]
HÄ	Härnösand, Länsmuseet-Murberget
HÖ	Höör, Biblioteket
J	Jönköping, Per Brahegymnasiet
K	Kalmar, Stadsbibliotek, Stifts- och Gymnasiebiblioteket
Klm	——, Länsmuseet
L	Lund, Universitet, Universitetsbiblioteket, Handskriftsavdelningen
LB	Leufsta Bruk, De Geer private collection [in *Uu*]
Ll	Linköping, Linköpings Stadsbibliotek, Stiftsbiblioteket
N	Norrköping, Stadsbiblioteket
Sdt	Stockholm, Drottningholms Teatermuseum
Sfo	——, Frimurare Orden, Biblioteket
Sic	——, Svensk Musik
Sk	——, Kungliga Biblioteket: Sveriges Nationalbibliotek
Skma	——, Statens Musikbibliothek
Sm	——, Musikmuseet, Arkiv
Smf	——, Stiftelsen Musikkulturens Främjande
Sn	——, Nordiska Museet, Arkivet
Ssr	——, Sveriges Radio Förvaltning, Musikbiblioteket
St	——, Kung. Teatern [in *Skma*]
Sva	——, Svenskt Visarkiv
STr	Strängnäs, Roggebiblioteket
Uu	Uppsala, Universitetsbiblioteket
V	Västerås, Stadsbibliotek, Stiftsavdelningen
Vll	Visby, Landsarkivet
VX	Växjö, Landsbiblioteket

SI: SLOVENIA

Lf	Ljubljana, Frančiškanski Samostan, Knjižnica
Ln	——, Narodna in Univerzitetna Knjižnica, Glavni Knjižni Fond
Lna	——, Nadškofijski Arhiv
Lng	——, Narodna in Univerzitetna Knjižnica, Glasbena Zbirka
Lnr	——, Narodna in Univerzitetna Knjižnica, Rokopisna Zbirka
Ls	——, Katedral, Glazbeni Arhiv
Nf	Novo Mesto, Frančiškanski Samostan, Knjižnica
Nk	——, Kolegiatni Kapitelj, Knjižnica
Pk	Ptuj, Knjižnica Ivana Potrča

SK: SLOVAKIA

BRa	Bratislava, Štátny Oblastny Archív
BRhs	——, Knižnica Hudobného Seminára Filozofickej Fakulty Univerzity Komenského
BRm	——, Archív Mesta Bratislavy
BRmp	——, Miestne Pracovisko Matice Slovenskej [in *Mms*]
BRnm	——, Slovenské Národné Múzeum, Hudobné Múzeum
BRsa	——, Slovenský Národný Archív
BRsav	——, Ústav Hudobnej Vedy Slovenská Akadémia Vied
BRu	——, Univerzitná Knižnica, Narodné Knižničné Centrum, Hudobňý Kabinet
BSk	Banská Štiavnica, Farský Rímsko-Katolícky Kostol, Archív Chóru
J	Júr pri Bratislave, Okresny Archív, Bratislava-Vidiek [in *MO*]
KRE	Kremnica, Štátny Okresny Archív Žiar nad Hronom
Le	Levoča, Evanjelická a.v. Cirkevná Knižnica
Mms	Martin, Matica Slovenská
Mnm	——, Slovenské Národné Múzeum, Archív

MO	Modra, Štátny Okresny Archív Pezinok
NM	Nové Mesto nad Váhom, Rímskokatolícky Farsky Kostol
TN	Trenčín, Štátny Okresny Archív
TR	Trnava, Štátny Okresny Archív

TR: TURKEY

Ino	Istanbul, Nuruosmania Kütüphanesi
Itks	——, Topkapi Sarayi Müzesi
Iü	——, Üniversite Kütüphanesi

UA: UKRAINE

Kan	Kiev, Natsional'na Akademiya Nauk Ukraïni, Natsional'na Biblioteka Ukraïni im V.I. Vernads'kyy
Km	——, Spilka Kompozytoriv Ukrainy, Centr. 'Muz. Inform'
LV	L'viv, Biblioteka Vyshchoho Muzychnoho Instytutu im. M. Lyssenka

US: UNITED STATES OF AMERICA

AAu	Ann Arbor, University of Michigan, Music Library
AB	Albany (NY), New York State Library
AKu	Akron (OH), University of Akron, Bierce Library
ATet	Atlanta (GA), Emory University, Pitts Theology Library
ATu	——, Emory University Library
ATS	Athens (GA), University of Georgia Libraries
AU	Aurora (NY), Wells College Library
AUS	Austin, University of Texas at Austin, The Harry Ransom Humanities Research Center
AUSm	——, University of Texas at Austin, Fine Arts Library
Ba	Boston, Athenaeum Library
Bc	——, New England Conservatory of Music, Harriet M. Spaulding Library
Bfa	——, Museum of Fine Arts
Bgm	——, Isabella Stewart Gardner Museum, Library
Bh	——, Harvard Musical Association, Library
Bhs	——, Massachusetts Historical Society Library
Bp	——, Public Library, Music Department
Bu	——, Boston University, Mugar Memorial Library, Department of Special Collections
BAep	Baltimore, Enoch Pratt Free Library
BAhs	——, Maryland Historical Society Library
BApi	——, Arthur Friedheim Library, Johns Hopkins University
BAu	——, Johns Hopkins University Libraries
BAue	——, Milton S. Eisenhower Library, Johns Hopkins University
BAw	——, Walters Art Gallery Library
BAR	Baraboo (WI), Circus World Museum Library
BEm	Berkeley, University of California at Berkeley, Music Library
BER	Berea (OH), Riemenschneider Bach Institute Library
BETm	Bethlehem (PA), Moravian Archives
BL	Bloomington (IN), Indiana University Library
BLl	——, Indiana University, Lilly Library
BLu	——, Indiana University, Cook Music Library
BO	Boulder (CO), University of Colorado at Boulder, Music Library
BU	Buffalo (NY), Buffalo and Erie County Public Library
Cn	Chicago, Newberry Library
Cp	——, Chicago Public Library, Music Information Center
Cu	——, University, Joseph Regenstein Library, Music Collection
Cum	——, University of Chicago, Music Collection
CA	Cambridge (MA), Harvard University, Harvard College Library
CAe	——, Harvard University, Eda Kuhn Loeb Music Library
CAh	——, Harvard University, Houghton Library
CAt	——, Harvard University Library, Theatre Collection
CAward	——, John Milton Ward, private collection [on loan to *CA*]

CF	Cedar Falls (IA), University of Northern Iowa, Library
CHua	Charlottesville (VA), University of Virginia, Alderman Library
CHum	——, University of Virginia, Music Library
CHAhs	Charleston (SC), The South Carolina Historical Society
CHH	Chapel Hill (NC), University of North Carolina at Chapel Hill
CIhc	Cincinnati, Hebrew Union College Library: Jewish Institute of Religion, Klau Library
CIp	——, Public Library
CIu	——, University of Cincinnati College – Conservatory of Music, Music Library
CLp	Cleveland, Public Library, Fine Arts Department
CLwr	——, Western Reserve University, Freiberger Library and Music House Library
CLAc	Claremont (CA), Claremont College Libraries
COhs	Columbus (OH), Ohio Historical Society Library
COu	——, Ohio State University, Music Library
CP	College Park (MD), University of Maryland, McKeldin Library
CR	Cedar Rapids (IA), Iowa Masonic Library
Dp	Detroit, Public Library, Main Library, Music and Performing Arts Department
DAu	Dallas, Southern Methodist University, Music Library
DAVu	Davis (CA), University of California at Davis, Peter J. Shields Library
DMu	Durham (NC), Duke University Libraries
DN	Denton (TX), University of North Texas, Music Library
DO	Dover (NH), Public Library
E	Evanston (IL), Garrett Biblical Institute
Eu	——, Northwestern University
EDu	Edwardsville (IL), Southern Illinois University
EU	Eugene (OR), University of Oregon
FAy	Farmington (CT), Yale University, Lewis Walpole Library
FW	Fort Worth (TX), Southwestern Baptist Theological Seminary
G	Gainesville (FL), University of Florida Library, Music Library
GB	Gettysburg (PA), Lutheran Theological Seminary
GR	Granville (OH), Denison University Library
GRB	Greensboro (NC), University of North Carolina at Greensboro, Walter C. Jackson Library
Hhc	Hartford (CT), Hartt College of Music Library, The University of Hartford
Hm	——, Case Memorial Library, Hartford Seminary Foundation [in *ATet*]
Hs	——, Connecticut State Library
Hw	——, Trinity College, Watkinson Library
HA	Hanover (NH), Dartmouth College, Baker Library
HG	Harrisburg (PA), Pennsylvania State Library
HO	Hopkinton (NH), New Hampshire Antiquarian Society
I	Ithaca (NY), Cornell University
IDt	Independence (MO), Harry S. Truman Library
IO	Iowa City (IA), University of Iowa, Rita Benton Music Library
K	Kent (OH), Kent State University, Music Library
KC	Kansas City (MO), University of Missouri: Kansas City, Miller Nichols Library
KCm	——, Kansas City Museum, Library and Archives
KN	Knoxville (TN), University of Tennessee, Knoxville, Music Library
Lu	Lawrence (KS), University of Kansas Libraries
LAcs	Los Angeles, California State University, John F. Kennedy Memorial Library
LApiatigorsky	——, Gregor Piatigorsky, private collection [in *STEdrachman*]
LAs	——, The Arnold Schoenberg Institute Archives
LAuc	——, University of California at Los Angeles, William Andrews Clark Memorial Library
LAum	——, University of California at Los Angeles, Music Library

LAur	——, University of California at Los Angeles, Special Collections Dept, University Research Library
LAusc	——, University of Southern California, School of Music Library
LBH	Long Beach (CA), California State University
LEX	Lexington (KY), University of Kentucky, Margaret I. King Library
LOu	Louisville, University of Louisville, Dwight Anderson Music Library
LT	Latrobe (PA), St Vincent College Library
M	Milwaukee, Public Library, Art and Music Department
Mc	——, Wisconsin Conservatory of Music Library
MAhs	Madison (WI), Wisconsin Historical Society
MAu	——, University of Wisconsin
MB	Middlebury (VT), Middlebury College, Christian A. Johnson Memorial Music Library
MED	Medford (MA), Tufts University Library
MG	Montgomery (AL), Alabama State Department of Archives and History Library
MT	Morristown (NJ), National Historical Park Museum
Nf	Northampton (MA), Forbes Library
Nsc	——, Smith College, Werner Josten Library
NA	Nashville (TN), Fisk University Library
NAu	——, Vanderbilt University Library
NBu	New Brunswick (NJ), Rutgers – The State University of New Jersey, Music Library, Mabel Smith Douglass Library
NEij	Newark (NJ), Rutgers – The State University of New Jersey, Rutgers Institute of Jazz Studies Library
NH	New Haven (CT), Yale University, Irving S. Gilmore Music Library
NHoh	——, Yale University, Oral History Archive
NHub	——, Yale University, Beinecke Rare Book and Manuscript Library
NO	Normal (IL), Illinois State University, Milner Library, Humanities/Fine Arts Division
NORsm	New Orleans, Louisiana State Museum Library
NORtu	——, Tulane University, Howard Tilton Memorial Library
NYamc	New York, American Music Center Library
NYbroude	——, Broude private collection
NYcc	——, City College Library, Music Library
NYcu	——, Columbia University, Gabe M. Wiener Music & Arts Library
NYcub	——, Columbia University, Rare Book and Manuscript Library of Butler Memorial Library
NYgo	——, University, Gould Memorial Library [in *NYu*]
NYgr	——, The Grolier Club Library
NYgs	——, G. Schirmer, Inc.
NYhs	——, New York Historical Society Library
NYhsa	——, Hispanic Society of America, Library
NYj	——, The Juilliard School, Lila Acheson Wallace Library
NYkallir	——, Rudolf F. Kallir, private collection
NYlehman	——, Robert O. Lehman, private collection [in *NYpm*]
NYlibin	——, Laurence Libin, private collection
NYma	——, Mannes College of Music, Clara Damrosch Mannes Memorial Library
NYp	——, Public Library at Lincoln Center, Music Division
NYpl	——, Public Library, Center for the Humanities
NYpm	——, Pierpont Morgan Library
NYpsc	——, New York Public Library, Schomburg Center for Research in Black Culture in Harlem
NYq	——, Queens College of the City University, Paul Klapper Library, Music Library
NYu	——, University Bobst Library
NYw	——, Wildenstein Collection
NYyellin	——, Victor Yellin, private collection
OAm	Oakland (CA), Mills College, Margaret Prall Music Library
OB	Oberlin (OH), Oberlin College Conservatory of Music, Conservatory Library

OX	Oxford (OH), Miami University, Amos Music Library
Pc	Pittsburgh, Carnegie Library, Music and Art Dept
Ps	——, Theological Seminary, Clifford E. Barbour Library
Pu	——, University of Pittsburgh
Puf	——, University of Pittsburgh, Foster Hall Collection, Stephen Foster Memorial
PHci	Philadelphia, Curtis Institute of Music, Library
PHf	——, Free Library of Philadelphia, Music Dept
PHff	——, Free Library of Philadelphia, Edwin A. Fleisher Collection of Orchestral Music
PHgc	——, Gratz College
PHhs	——, Historical Society of Pennsylvania Library
PHlc	——, Library Company of Philadelphia
PHmf	——, Musical Fund Society [on loan to *PHf*]
PHphs	——, The Presbyterian Historical Society Library [in *PHlc*]
PHps	——, American Philosophical Society Library
PHu	——, University of Pennsylvania, Van Pelt-Dietrich Library Center
PO	Poughkeepsie (NY), Vassar College, George Sherman Dickinson Music Library
PRs	Princeton (NJ), Theological Seminary, Speer Library
PRu	——, Princeton University, Firestone Memorial Library
PRw	——, Westminster Choir College
PROhs	Providence (RI), Rhode Island Historical Society Library
PROu	——, Brown University
PRV	Provo (UT), Brigham Young University
R	Rochester (NY), Sibley Music Library, University of Rochester, Eastman School of Music
Su	Seattle, University of Washington, Music Library
SA	Salem (MA), Peabody and Essex Museums, James Duncan Phillips Library
SBm	Santa Barbara (CA), Mission Santa Barbara
SFp	San Francisco, Public Library, Fine Arts Department, Music Division
SFs	——, Sutro Library
SFsc	——, San Francisco State University, Frank V. de Bellis Collection
SJb	San Jose (CA), Ira F. Brilliant Center for Beethoven Studies, San José State University
SL	St Louis, St Louis University, Pius XII Memorial Library
SLug	——, Washington University, Gaylord Music Library
SLC	Salt Lake City, University of Utah Library
SM	San Marino (CA), Huntington Library
SPma	Spokane (WA), Moldenhauer Archives
SR	San Rafael (CA), American Music Research Center, Dominican College
STu	Palo Alto (CA), University, Memorial Library of Music, Department of Special Collections of the Cecil H. Green Library
STEdrachmann	Stevenson (MD), Mrs Jephta Drachman, private collection; Mrs P.C. Drachman, private collection
STO	Stony Brook (NY), State University of New York at Stony Brook, Frank Melville jr Memorial Library
SY	Syracuse (NY), University Music Library
SYkrasner	——, Louis Krasner, private collection [in *CAh* and *SY*]
TA	Tallahassee (FL), Florida State University, Robert Manning Strozier Library
U	Urbana (IL), University of Illinois, Music Library
Uplamenac	——, Dragan Plamenac, private collection [in *NH*]
V	Villanova (PA), Villanova University, Falvey Memorial Library
Wc	Washington, DC, Library of Congress, Music Division
Wca	——, Cathedral Library
Wcf	——, Library of Congress, American Folklife Center and the Archive of Folk Culture
Wcg	——, General Collections, Library of Congress
Wcm	——, Library of Congress, Motion Picture, Broadcasting and Recorded Sound Division
Wcu	——, Catholic University of America, Music Library

Wdo	——, Dumbarton Oaks
Wgu	——, Georgetown University Libraries
Whu	——, Howard University, College of Fine Arts Library
Ws	——, Folger Shakespeare Library
WB	Wilkes-Barre (PA), Wilkes College Library
WC	Waco (TX), Baylor University, Music Library
WGc	Williamsburg (VA), College of William and Mary, Earl Gregg Swenn Library
WI	Williamstown (MA), Williams College Library
WOa	Worcester (MA), American Antiquarian Society Library

WS	Winston-Salem (NC), Moravian Music Foundation, Peter Memorial Library
Y	York (PA), Historical Society of York County, Library and Archives

YU: YUGOSLAVIA (REPUBLICS OF MONTENEGRO AND SERBIA)

Bn	Belgrade, Narodna Biblioteka Srbije, Odelenje Posebnih Fondova

ZA: SOUTH AFRICA

Csa	Cape Town, South African Library

A Note on the Use of the Dictionary

This note is intended as a short guide to the basic procedures and organization of the dictionary. A fuller account will be found in the Introduction, vol. l, pp.xv–xxv.

Abbreviations in general use in the dictionary are listed on pp.vii–xi; bibliographical ones (periodicals, reference works, editions etc.) are listed on pp.xiii–xviii and discographical abbreviations on pp.xix–xx.

Alphabetization of headings is based on the principle that words are read continuously, ignoring spaces, hyphens, accents, bracketed matter etc., up to the first comma; the same principle applies thereafter. 'Mc' and 'M'' are listed as 'Mac', 'St' as 'Saint'.

Bibliographies are arranged chronologically (within section, where divided), in order of year of first publication, and alphabetically by author within years.

Cross-references are shown in small capitals, with a large capital at the beginning of the first word of the entry referred to. Thus 'The instrument is related to the BASS TUBA' would mean that the entry referred to is not 'Bass tuba' but 'Tuba, bass'.

Signatures where the article was compiled by the editors or in the few cases where an author has wished to remain anonymous are indicated by a square box (□).

Work-lists are normally arranged chronologically (within section, where divided). Italic symbols used in them (like *D-Dl* or *GB-Lbl*) refer to the libraries holding sources, and are explained on pp.xxi–xxxvii; each national sigillum stands until contradicted.

A

[continued]

Aristoxenus (*b* Tarentum, Magna Graecia, *c*375–360 BCE; *d* ?Athens). Greek music theorist, philosopher and writer. According to the *Suda* he was the son of a musician called Mnesias or Spintharus who gave him his early musical education. It is not known to which philosophical or musical school Mnesias belonged, but he may have been one of the Pythagoreans whose political influence had been dominant in Magna Graecia, particularly in Tarentum, with which Archytas had long been associated. Mnesias could have known a number of prominent figures both in Magna Graecia and in Athens: the musicians Archytas, Damon and Philoxenus, as well as Socrates and perhaps even the Theban general Epaminondas. Aristoxenus himself followed the teachings of Lampros of Erythrae, and then, in Athens, of Xenophilus the Pythagorean. He spent most of his life in Greece. A fragment of one of his works indicates that he lived for some time at Mantinea in Arcadia, where music, which was held in high esteem, was subject to the kind of conservative laws that appealed to his austerity and love of ancient traditions.

At some unspecified date Aristoxenus renounced Pythagorean doctrines, although he retained his admiration for Archytas, whose biography he wrote. He then followed the teachings of Aristotle and seems to have become one of the master's most eminent disciples, for Aristotle apparently considered appointing him his successor as head of the Lyceum. When Theophrastus gained the post instead, Aristoxenus broke with the school entirely and began teaching on his own account, concentrating mainly on music. However, he evidently did not reject the Aristotelian doctrines, because authors in antiquity consistently described him as a 'follower of Aristotle'. As a pure first-generation Peripatetic, Aristoxenus brought the new science of music into the Lyceum, the 'studio of all the arts'.

Aristoxenus was a prolific author with many interests: as well as writing on education and music he also produced biographies and histories of institutions. The *Suda* credits him with 453 works, although this is surely an exaggeration. Only 139 fragments of his memoranda, miscellanea and other small works have survived (ed. Wehrli); these reveal his interest not only in the theory of harmonics and rhythm, but also (unusually for a Greek theorist) in the history of music, musicians and musical institutions.

Aristoxenus's principal work, the one that gained him the reputation of supreme *mousikos* throughout antiquity, was the treatise *On Harmonics*, which has come down to us under the probably erroneous title *Harmonic Elements* (*Harmonika stoicheia*). It is the oldest work of music theory written in Greek to have been preserved in substantial fragments, and was the first part of a larger work *On Music*, in which the author studied the various branches of the subject, in particular rhythm. Only fragments of the *Rhythmic Elements* have survived, either through quotations by later authors (Aristides Quintilianus and more particularly Michael Psellus, an 11th-century Byzantine writer), or through papyri; it is possible that *POxy* 9 + 2687 contains part of the *Rhythmic Elements*.

In so far as the history of musical thought in ancient times is concerned, the doctrines of Aristoxenus represent an epistemological revolution whose importance was acknowledged by all later theorists, whether they agreed with him or not. Before him, the Pythagoreans (such as Philolaus and Archytas) and the Platonists had regarded the science of music as part of mathematics. Aristoxenus, on the other hand, believed that music should be an autonomous discipline, one entirely separate from arithmetic and astronomy. No longer could music be a matter of calculating intervals expressed by the relationship of two numbers, for its concern is not mathematical entities but sound, and musical sound as distinct from noise or the sounds of spoken language. Its tools are rational thought (*dianoia*) and auditory sensation (*akoē* and *aisthēsis*). Reason establishes musical principles through the investigation of theorems (*problēmata*), some of which are also the subject of demonstrations. As for auditory sensation, Aristoxenus was the first musical theorist to insist on the necessity of training the ear to make hearing more precise, and on the control to be exercised over it by rational thought. On this basis he constructed a science of music whose methods, terminology and principles derive directly from Aristotelian scientific doctrines.

The first part of the *Harmonic Elements* is an examination by Aristoxenus of the doctrines of his predecessors; he proves to be highly critical, less on points of detail than on the actual foundations of their teachings. He criticized the Pythagoreans (without naming them) for regarding intervals not as pure musical entities but as numerical ratios, which are superparticular when they 'define' consonant intervals: octave (2:1), 5th (3:2), 4th (4:3) and tone (9:8). For Aristoxenus, music consisted of sounds structurally organized within a sound-space, and the function of the science of harmonics was to describe and regulate their spatial and dynamic relations. Unlike the Pythagoreans, he postulated and demonstrated that the tone can be divided into two equal semitones, not a limma (*leimma*) in the ratio 256:243 and an *apotomē* in the ratio 2187:2048. He also took the exact semitone as the unit of measurement for all musical intervals, and he differed from the Harmonicists, whose diagrams exhibit 28 consecutive *dieses*, which are devoid of any musical reality since more than two quarter-tones are never heard in succession.

Aristoxenus himself endeavoured to describe the musical system in all its coherence and complexity, setting out from the simplest of entities (musical sound) and proceeding to increasingly complex combinations of intervals and 'systems', envisaged simultaneously according to their 'range', 'disposition' and 'function'. The last part of the treatise is a set of theorems setting out the laws of harmonics. Aristoxenus was the first to formulate the concept of the genus (*genos*), defined by the position of the two movable notes within a tetrachord (spanning the interval of a 4th), which divide it into three intervals of varying sizes. He described three genera: the enharmonic ('the oldest and finest'), the chromatic and the diatonic. The enharmonic tetrachord consists of a ditone followed by two quarter-tones, moving from top to bottom; the chromatic – a tone-and-a-half, a semitone and a semitone; and the diatonic – a tone, a tone and a semitone. The chromatic and diatonic genera permit 'coloration' or 'nuances' (*chroai*) in which the extent of the intervals varies within limits set out by Aristoxenus.

Finally Aristoxenus defined the *tonoi*, a term probably of his own coining and destined to replace the old concept of *harmonia*. On approaching this important subject he rejected all the classifications and dispositions advanced by his predecessors and proceeded 'from basics', with a view to bringing order to the confusion then prevalent in music. The *tonoi* are related to the positions of the voice 'in which each of the *systèmes* is placed in singing a melody'. In other words, the *tonoi* represent transpositions of the scales. Unfortunately the passage in which Aristoxenus enumerated the *tonoi* has not survived. Their names as given by Cleonides are: Hypermixolydian (also called Hyperphrygian), high and low Mixolydian (also respectively called Hyperiastian and Hyperdorian), high and low Lydian (the low also called Aeolian), high and low Phrygian (the low also called Iastian), Dorian, high and low Hypolydian (the low also called Hypoaeolian), high and low Hypophrygian (the low also called Hypoiastian) and Hypodorian. They are grouped on the principle of the 'affinity' of their tones, allowing modulation from one to the other with more or less ease. They are not, therefore, modes, as has so often been thought, but transposition scales rising from semitone to semitone.

Aristoxenus excluded musical practice and in particular musical composition from the science of harmonics, and consequently anything to do with musical notation, on the grounds that such subjects involve skill (*technē*) and not science (*epistēmē*).

Many Greek and Latin writers on music, including CLEONIDES and GAUDENTIUS, were directly inspired by the writings of Aristoxenus. Those theorists belonging to schools of philosophy opposed to the Aristoxenian musical doctrines tried either to refute them or, like THEON OF SMYRNA and PTOLEMY, to integrate certain of the demands of Aristoxenus into their own theories.

However, such a reconciliation of doctrines constructed on irreconcilable principles could never be entirely successful.

From what has survived of the *Rhythmic Elements*, it seems that Aristoxenus had adopted the same approach to rhythm as to harmonics: the determination of a small number of basic 'principles', the choice of a unit of measurement (the 'primary time' – *prōtos chronos*), the choice of criteria (hearing and judgment), and the articulation of the constituent elements of rhythm. Aristoxenus was the first to distinguish rhythmics from metrics, and he seems also to have been the first to write on the mutual relationship of musical durations, fundamentally distinct from words, melody or gesture, which were things that can be 'set in rhythm (*ta rhuthmizomena*)'.

See also GREECE, §I, 6(iii).

WRITINGS

H.S. Macran, ed. and trans.: *The Harmonics of Aristoxenus* (Oxford, 1902/R)

F. Wehrli, ed.: *Die Schule des Aristoteles: Texte und Kommentare*, ii (Basle, 1945, 2/1967)

R. da Rios, ed. and trans.: *Aristoxeni Elementa harmonica* (Rome, 1954)

G.B. Pighi, trans.: Aristoxenus: *Rhythmica* (Bologna, 1959)

A. Barker, ed.: *Greek Musical Writings*, ii: *Harmonic and Acoustic Theory* (Cambridge, 1989), 119–89

L. Pearson, ed. and trans.: *Elementa rhythmica: the Fragment of Book II and the Additional Evidence for Aristoxenian Rhythmic Theory* (Oxford, 1990)

A. Bélis, ed. and trans.: *Aristoxène de Tarente: le Traité d'harmonique* (forthcoming)

BIBLIOGRAPHY

R. Westphal: *Aristoxenus von Tarent: Melik und Rhythmik des classischen Hellenentums* (Leipzig, 1883–93/R)

R. Westphal: 'Die Aristoxenische Rhythmuslehre', *Vierteljahrsschrift für Musikwissenschaft*, vii (1891), 74–107

L. Laloy: *Aristoxène de Tarente, disciple d'Aristote et la musique d'antiquité* (Paris, 1904)

R.P. Winnington-Ingram: 'Aristoxenus and the Intervals of Greek Music', *Classical Quarterly*, xxvi (1932), 195–208

R.P. Winnington-Ingram: *Mode in Ancient Greek Music* (Cambridge, 1936/R)

M. Vogel: *Die Enharmonik der Griechen* (Düsseldorf, 1963)

F.R. Levin: 'Synesis in Aristoxenian Theory', *Transactions of the American Philological Association*, ciii (1972), 211–34

A. Barker: 'Music and Perception: a Study in Aristoxenus', *Journal of Hellenic Studies*, xlviii (1978), 9–16

A. Bélis: 'Les "nuances" dans le *Traité d'harmonique* d'Aristoxène de Tarente', *Revue des études grecques*, xcv (1982), 54–73

A. Barker: 'Aristoxenus' Theorems and the Foundations of Harmonic Science', *Ancient Philosophy*, iv (1984), 23–64

J. Solomon: 'Towards a History of *Tonoi*', *JM*, iii (1984), 242–51

A. Bélis: 'La théorie de l'âme chez Aristoxène de Tarente', *Revue de philologie*, lix (1985), 239–46

A. Bélis: *Aristoxène de Tarente et Aristote: le 'Traité d'harmonique'* (Paris, 1986)

L.E. Rossi: 'POxy9 + POxy 2687: trattato ritmico-metrico', *Aristoxenica, Menandrea, fragmenta philosophica*, ed. A. Brancacci and others (Florence, 1988), 11–30

A. Barker: 'Aristoxenus' Harmonics and Aristotle's Theory of Science', *Science and Philosophy in Classical Greece*, ed. A.C. Bowen (New York, 1991), 188–226

ANNIE BÉLIS

Arizaga, Rodolfo (*b* Buenos Aires, 11 July 1926; *d* Buenos Aires, 12 May 1985). Argentine composer and writer on music. He received his initial musical training at the National Conservatory in Buenos Aires, where his teachers were Alberto Williams, José Gil (harmony) and Luis Gianneo (composition). He also studied law at the National University and philosophy at the Free Institute of Higher Studies. In 1954 he settled in Paris, where he studied composition with Messiaen, Boulanger and Martenot. He later taught at the Higher Institute of Music of the National University in Rosario (1960–61) and at Buenos Aires University (1967–9). In his later compositions he employed 12-note serial technique, modal writing and notation providing performers with an element of choice. An active journalist, he served as critic for the daily *Clarín* (1946–64), wrote articles and reviews for numerous Argentine and foreign journals, and published the monographs *Manuel de Falla* (Buenos Aires, 1961) and *Juan José Castro* (Buenos Aires, 1963). His *Enciclopedia de la música argentina* (Buenos Aires, 1971) surveys 20th-century Argentine composers.

WORKS
(*selective list*)

Orch: Passacaglia, 1953; Delires, 1957; Pf Conc., 1963; Música para Cristóbal Colón, 1966; Hymnus, 1970

Chbr: Divertimento, 2 ob, cl, bn, 1945; Cantatas humanas, A, va, 1952, rev. 1961; Martirio de Santa Olalla, A, fl, cl, vn, vc, cel, hpd, 1950–52; 2 str qts, 1968, 1969

Pf: Suite, 1945; Sonata, 1946; Capricho, 1951; Serranillas del jaque, 1956; Piezas epigramáticas, 1961

Principal publisher: Editorial Argentina de Música

BIBLIOGRAPHY

Compositores de América/Composers of the Americas, ed. Pan American Union, v (Washington DC, 1959), 7ff

JOHN M. SCHECHTER

Arizmendi, Fermín de (*b* Puente La Reina, Navarra, bap. 11 June 1691; *d* Avila, 15 Dec 1733). Spanish composer. From 1705 to 1714 he was a *siese* in the choir of the church of the Primature of Toledo, where he was a pupil of Miguel de Ambiela. In July 1711, at the age of 20, he applied for the post of *maestro de capilla* at Jaén Cathedral, which fell vacant on the death of Pedro de Soto. However, the successful candidate for the position was Juan Manuel García de la Puente, like Arizmendi a *seise* at the cathedral of the Primature of Toledo. On 1 September 1714 he was appointed *maestro de capilla* of Avila Cathedral, succeeding Juan Cedazo, and remained there for the rest of his life. He was succeeded by Juan Oliac y Serra. A number of his religious works survive in manuscript (*E-Ac, E*).

BIBLIOGRAPHY

G. Bourligueux: 'Quelques aspects de la vie musicale à Avila: notes et documents (XVIIIe siècle)', *AnM*, xxv (1970), pp.169–209; esp. 173, 188, 196

J. López-Calo: *Catálogo del archivo de música de la catedral de Avila* (Santiago de Compostela, 1978), 140–42, 218–21, 255

P. Jiménez Cavallé: *La música en Jaén* (Jaén, 1991), 110

GUY BOURLIGUEUX

Arizo [Arizu, Arizcum], **Miguel de** (*b* ?Arizu or Arizcun, Navarra, *c*1593; *d* Madrid, 15 May 1648). Spanish composer and singer. Between 1601 and 1604 he entered the choir school of the Spanish royal chapel and studied with its *vicemaestro*, the composer Gabriel Díaz Bessón. On 1 January 1614, after his voice had broken, he was appointed alto in the same *capilla*. On 1 March 1629 his salary was doubled, and on 28 February 1642 he was granted an annual allowance of 350 ducats, followed by another of 250 ducats on 20 March 1645 (though his salary was no longer doubled). In addition to his duties in the *capilla* Arizo was responsible for the musical instruction of the Bourbon Queen Elisabeth's ladies-in-waiting for at least ten years (1618–28), during which period he must have been in touch with the queen's chamber musician, Álvaro de los Ríos.

Arizo's two extant secular compositions are a four-part canción, *Filis del alma mia*, and a three-part *romance*, *Vistióse el prado galán*, both in a cancionero assembled by Claudio de la Sablonara in 1624 or 1625 (*D-Mbs, E-Mn*; ed. J. Aroca, Madrid, 1918; ed. J. Etzion, London, 1996; the canción also ed. in MME, xxxii, 1970, and ed. M. Querol, *Cancionero musical de Lope de Vega*, ii, Barcelona, 1987). They exemplify the vocal chamber repertory of the Madrid court at that time. In both works a homophonic, declamatory style prevails over a pseudo-imitative one. Hemiola is used consistently in triple metre and there are chromatic false relations and unprepared dominant 7ths. A villancico, *Por coronar a Maria las flores se deojaron*, attributed to Arizo (*US-NYhsa*) consists of an introduction, *estribillo* (refrain) and *coplas* (verses). In the *coplas* solo vocal passages alternate with sections sung by the other three voices with instruments. The work is in triple time, with numerous hemiolas.

BIBLIOGRAPHY

N. Álvarez Solar-Quintes: 'Panorama musical desde Felipe III a Carlos II', *AnM*, xii (1957), 167–200, esp. 188

R.A. Pelinski: *Die weltliche Vokalmusik Spaniens am Anfang des 17. Jahrhunderts: der Cancionero Claudio de la Sablonara* (Tutzing, 1971), 31, 73–4

L. Robledo: *Juan Blas de Castro (ca. 1581–1631): vida y obra musical* (Zaragoza, 1989), 43–6

L. Robledo: 'El cantor y compositor Miguel de Arizu', *Musiker: cuadernos de música*, x (1998), 13–22

LUIS ROBLEDO

Arkad'yev, Mikhail Aleksandrovich (*b* Moscow, 15 March 1958). Russian musicologist, pianist and composer. In 1978 he entered the Gnesin Academy of Music, where he studied the piano with A.V. Aleksandrov and the theory of music with Yu.N. Kholopov, M.G. Kharlap and L.A. Mazel'. He completed his postgraduate studies there on the piano in 1988. In 1992 he began teaching at the Russian Academy of Choral Art in Moscow, becoming professor of the piano department in 1995. He is well known for his concert playing activities, as a soloist and ensemble player, and as an accompanist to the baritone Dmitry Hvorostovsky. His compositions include works for the piano, chamber and choral music, and a *Missa brevis* for mixed choir and organ, which is recorded on CD. He was made an Honoured Artist of Russia in 1995.

Arkad'yev's scholarly interests include the issues of time, rhythm and articulation in music. He gained the doctorate in 1993 with a dissertation on temporal structures in late 20th-century European music. His discussion relies on both the phenomenological and the hermeneutic traditions of Brentano, Husserl, Heidegger and Hadamer. The chief premise of his research is the existence of two modes for the structural organization of time: the 'sounding' and the 'non-sounding'. He demonstrates the fundamental difference in the relationships between these modes in music of the Baroque, Classical and Romantic periods and suggests that this difference is an important typological factor that characterizes each age.

WRITINGS

'Konflikt zhizni i noosferi' [The conflict of life and the noosphere], *Noosfera i khudozhestvennoye tvorchestvo*, ed. V.V. Ivanov (Moscow, 1991), 74–88

Vremennïye strukturï novoyevropeyskoy muzïki (opït fenomenologicheskogo issledovaniya) [Temporal structures in recent European music (an attempt at a phenomenological study)] (diss., Moscow State Institute of Art Studies, 1993; Moscow, 1993)

"'Kreativenoye vremiya", "arkhepis'mo" i opït Nichto' ['Creative time', 'arche-writing' and the experience of nothing], *Logos*, no.6 (1994), 164–78

"'Pikovaya dama" i mif ob Ėdipe' [*The Queen of Spades* and the myth of Oedipus], *Mizïkal'naya zhizn'* (1997), no.3, pp.34–6

'Liricheskaya vselennaya Sviridova' [The lyrical universe of Sviridov], *Russkaya muzïka i xx vek*, ed. M. Aranovsky (Moscow, 1997), 251–65

MARINA RAKU

Arkhangel'sky, Aleksandr Andreyevich (*b* Staroye Tezikovo, Penza, 11/23 Oct 1846; *d* Prague, 16 Nov 1924). Russian choral conductor and composer. He studied music theory while at the imperial chapel in St Petersburg, gaining also a wide knowledge of Russian church music. In 1880 he founded a mixed choir which soon won a reputation for high standards of performance. At first the choir comprised 20 voices but was later increased to 90; its repertory was extensive and included folksongs and pieces by Classical and contemporary composers. Arkhangel'sky took his choir on a tour of the major cities of Russia (1899–1900), and in 1907 and 1912 they went to western Europe, where their concerts of Russian church music were well received. He supported the movement to reform Russian church music, and his experiment of substituting women's for boys' voices in sacred music was widely adopted. He composed two masses, a requiem and many unaccompanied choral pieces. He also arranged folksongs for his choir and made transcriptions of Russian hymns and other liturgical pieces.

BIBLIOGRAPHY

'Peterburgskiye tserkovnïye khorï' [Petersburg church choirs], *Khorovoye i regentskoye delo*, no.1 (1910), 9–10

D. Yanchevetsky: 'Yubiley A.M. Arkhangel'skogo' [Arkhangel'sky's anniversary], *Khorovoye i regentskoye delo*, nos.5–6 (1912), 119–21

D. Lokshin: *Vïdayushchiyesya russkiye khorï i ikh dirizhyorï* [Outstanding Russian choirs and their conductors] (Moscow, 1953, 2/1963 as *Zamechatel'nïye russkiye khorï i ikh dirizhyorï: kratkiye ocherki* [Distinguished Russian choirs and their conductors: short essays])

D. Tkachov: '"Istoricheskiye kontsertï" khora A. Arkhangel'skogo' [Historical concerts given by Arkhangel'sky's choir], *Khorovoye iskusstvo*, ii (Leningrad, 1971)

D. Tkachov: *A.A. Arkhangel'sky: ocherk zhizni i tvorcheskoy deyatel'nosti* [Life and works] (Leningrad, 1974)

V. Il'in: *Ocherki istorii russkoy khorovoy kulturï vtoroy polovinï XVII – nachala XX veka* [Essays on Russian choral culture from the second half of the 17th century to the 20th] (Moscow, 1985)

JENNIFER SPENCER/MARINA FROLOVA-WALKER

Arkhipova, Irina (Konstantinovna) (*b* Moscow, 2 Dec 1925). Russian mezzo-soprano. She graduated in 1948 from the Moscow Institute of Architecture, where she learnt singing in N. Malïsheva's group, and in 1953 from L. Savransky's class at the Moscow Conservatory. She sang with the Sverdlovsk Opera (1954–6) and made her Bol'shoy début as Carmen in 1956. Her voice, of wide range, was remarkable for its emotional warmth and variety of tone-colour. Her roles included Lyubasha (*Tsar's Bride*), Pauline and Lyubov' (*Queen of Spades* and *Mazepa*), Amneris and Eboli, and Massenet's Charlotte. She participated in many Bol'shoy first performances, including Khrennikov's *Mat'* ('Mother'; Nilovna, 1957), Prokofiev's *Story of a Real Man* (Klavdiya, 1960), Shchedrin's *Ne tol'ko lyubov'* ('Not Love Alone'; Varvara, 1961) and Kholminov's *Optimisticheskaya tragediya* ('An Optimistic Tragedy'; Commissar, 1965). She sang throughout eastern Europe and in the USA, Japan, Austria and Scandinavia. After appearances in Naples in 1960, as Carmen, she sang Hélène with the Bol'shoy at La Scala in 1964, returning as Marfa (1967 and 1971) and Marina (1968). She scored a great success as Azucena at Orange in 1972, and this led to her Covent Garden début in the same role in 1975. She subsequently sang Ulrica at Covent Garden (1988), and appeared as the Countess (*Queen of Spades*) in performances by the Kirov Opera in New York in 1992.

I.M. YAMPOL'SKY/R

Arkor, André d' (*b* Liége, 23 Feb 1901; *d* Brussels, 19 Dec 1971). Belgian tenor and administrator. He was trained in Liége and made his début there as Gérald in *Lakmé* in 1924, moving then to Lyons and Ghent. In 1930 he became principal lyric tenor at La Monnaie, Brussels, and in his 17 years there sang more than 40 roles, taking part in several premières, including that of Lattuada's *Le preziose ridicole*. In 1937 he sang in Lehár's *Der Zarewitsch* and in 1940 in *Das Land des Lächelns*. He appeared at the Opéra-Comique, Paris, in 1931 as Des Grieux in *Manon*. He later became director of the Théâtre Royal de Liège; during his 20 years there more than 50 new productions were mounted. He was an accomplished singer with admirably even voice production and an extensive upper range, features well represented in his recordings.

J.B. STEANE

Arkwright, G(odfrey) E(dward) P(ellew) (*b* Norwich, 10 April 1864; *d* Highclere, Hants., 16 Aug 1944). English music scholar. He studied at Eton and Oxford, where he was subsequently editor of the *Musical Antiquary* (1909–13/R). He edited a large body of English vocal music of the 16th, 17th and 18th centuries – madrigals and songs by Weelkes, Ferrabosco and Blow, and sacred works by Tye and Milton – published in 25 volumes in the Old English Edition (London and Oxford, 1889–1902/R). For the Purcell Society he edited *Three Odes for St Cecilia's Day* (London, 1899) and *Birthday Odes for Queen Mary*, i (London, 1902). He also compiled a *Catalogue of Music in the Library of Christ Church, Oxford* (London, 1915/R). The composer Marian (Ursula) Arkwright was his sister.

BIBLIOGRAPHY

Collection of Old and Rare Music and Books on Music the Property of Godfrey E.P. Arkwright (London, 1939) [auction catalogue, 13 Feb 1939]

E. VAN DER STRAETEN/R

Arkwright, Marian (Ursula) (*b* Norwich, 25 Jan 1863; *d* Highclere, nr Newbury, 23 March 1922). English composer. She received both the MusB (1895) and MusD (1913) from Durham University. In 1893 she was one of the founders of the pioneering English Ladies' Orchestral Union, and was the orchestra's secretary as well as playing the double bass and timpani. She was the conductor of the Newbury Amateur Orchestral Union and was also involved in the Rural Music Schools movement. Arkwright was one of the few women members of the Society of British Composers (founded 1905) and her orchestral works, which do not appear to have survived, received critical acclaim. In 1906 her orchestral suite *Winds of the World*, inspired by the Kipling ballad 'The Flag of England', won *The Gentlewoman* prize for an orchestral work by a woman. It was first performed at Newbury in 1907 and repeated that year by the Bournemouth SO, conducted by Arkwright herself. Other works performed by the Bournemouth SO included the Variations on an Air of Handel (1897) and *Japanese Suite* (1911). Her

Suite for strings was written for the Australian Exhibition of Women's Work of 1907. The few works by Arkwright that have survived, such as the Requiem Mass and the Two Concert Pieces for viola and piano, show an assured and inventive style.

WORKS
(selective list)

printed works published in London

Stage: The Water-Babies (operetta, C. Kingsley)

Orch: The Blackbird's Matins, ov., 1900; Variations on an Air of Handel; Winds of the World, sym. suite; Suite, str, 1907; Japanese Suite

Chbr: 12 Duets, 2 vn, vc and pf ad lib (1896); 6 Duets, 2 vn, vc and pf ad lib (1896); 4 Duets, 2 vn, vc and pf ad lib (1896); 2 Concert Pieces, va, pf (1908); works for pf and ww

Vocal: Requiem Mass, S, Bar, chorus 8vv, orch (1914); The Dragon of Wantley, children's chorus, 3vv, pf (1915); Atalanta in Caledon, solo v, SATB, str; Hymn of Pan, Bar, orch; partsongs and songs

SOPHIE FULLER

Arlen, Harold [Arluck, Hyman] (*b* Buffalo, NY, 15 Feb 1905; *d* New York, 23 April 1986). American composer. The son of a cantor, he sang in the choir at his father's synagogue as a child, and at the age of 15 played the piano in local movie houses and on excursion boats on Lake Erie. Smitten by the new and distinctively American popular music of the post-World War I period, he organized his own band, the Snappy Trio, and later joined another which (as the Buffalodians) went to New York in the mid-1920s. He made some band arrangements for Fletcher Henderson but worked mostly as a pianist and singer on radio, in theatre pit orchestras and in dance bands; he recorded as a singer with Benny Goodman, Red Nichols and Joe Venuti. In 1929 he began a songwriting collaboration with the lyricist Ted Koehler and achieved his first success with the song 'Get Happy', which appeared in the *9:15 Revue* (1930). From 1930 to 1934 the two men went on to write several memorable songs for a series of revues at Harlem' Cotton Club, a cabaret that featured black entertainment for white audiences, including 'Between the Devil and the Deep Blue Sea' and 'Stormy Weather'. Such songs blended the forms and idioms of Tin Pan Alley with blues and jazz-based inflections, and through their commercial success helped to popularize the sounds of black music among a wider audience. During this period he also provided songs for numerous Broadway productions, including 'I Gotta Right to Sing the Blues' and 'It's Only a Paper Moon', and cemented his resolve to pursue a songwriting career.

In 1934 Arlen composed his last important Broadway revue, *Life Begins at 8:40*, and began to write for Hollywood films. During the next two decades he created a body of significant songs with the lyricists Johnny Mercer, Ira Gershwin and E.Y. Harburg, including 'Over the Rainbow' (1939; lyricist, Harburg) and 'The Man that Got Away' (1954; lyricist, Gershwin), both for the singer Judy Garland. Unlike many Hollywood composers in a period when the studio system prevailed, Arlen managed to preserve a strong musical identity. Many of his film songs also place an emphasis on the functions of narrative and character rather than on sheer spectacle and dance; *The Wizard of Oz* (1939; see illustration), the film for which Arlen's work is best remembered, is among the earliest film musicals to attempt to integrate the use of song into the development of character and plot.

From 1941 to 1945 in Hollywood, Arlen also worked closely with Mercer on developing such boldly jazz-influenced songs as 'Blues in the Night', 'That Old Black Magic', 'One for my Baby' and 'Ac-cent-tchu-ate the Positive'. In the mid-1940s he turned his attention to the theatre once again, this time providing songs for 'book' musicals. Of his five subsequent Broadway shows *House of Flowers* (1954), written with Truman Capote, is considered by many his most distinguished score. While Arlen's contributions remained of a consistently high level (for example 'Right as the Rain' and 'I Never has Seen Snow'), most of these shows were marred by serious weaknesses in their librettos or productions.

Arlen's style shows an affinity with African-American musical expression, and many of his shows were written

Harold Arlen (right) with E.Y. Harburg, who wrote the music and lyrics for 'The Wizard of Oz' (MGM, 1939)

directly for black performers (the Cotton Club revues, *St. Louis Woman* and its later expansion as the 'blues opera' *Free and Easy*, *House of Flowers*, and *Jamaica*), while others deal with themes relating to the lives and concerns of African Americans (*Bloomer Girl* and *Saratoga*). Much of his songwriting was influenced by the blues, most often in the form of blue melodic or harmonic inflections applied to the traditional song structure ('Stormy Weather'), but also more radically in an attempt to incorporate the blues structure itself into a new expanded form of popular song ('Blues in the Night'). Arlen frequently broke the mould of a 32-bar, *AABA* popular song form to write melodies both unconventional in length and asymmetrical in their phrase and sectional make-up. He extended the traditional eight-bar section of a song from ten bars ('Ill Wind') to 20 bars ('Out of this World').

As a songwriter, Arlen belongs with the handful of composers most responsible for the brilliant flowering of American popular song that occurred in the second quarter of the 20th century. Much in his output reflected the popular mood in America during the Great Depression and World War II; and, while most of his later songs did not have a similar cultural resonance, the best of them remain among the most exquisite examples of musical craft and invention within the popular domain.

WORKS

STAGE

all are musicals and all dates are those of first New York performance, unless otherwise stated

librettists and lyricists are listed in that order in parentheses

You Said It (J. Yellen, S. Silvers; Yellen, T. Koehler), orchd H. Jackson, 19 Jan 1931 [incl. Sweet and Hot, While You are Young, It's Different with Me, Learn to Croon, If He Really Loves Me]

Life Begins at 8:40 (revue, D. Freedman, H.I. Phillips, A. Baxter, H.C. Smith, F. Gabrielson; I. Gershwin, E.Y. Harburg), orchd H. Spialek, 27 Aug 1934 [incl. You're a Builder-Upper, Fun to be Fooled, Let's Take a Walk Around the Block, I Couldn't Hold My Man, What Can You Say in a Love Song?]

Hooray for What? (H. Lindsay, R. Crouse; Harburg), orchd D. Walker, 1 Dec 1937 [incl. God's Country, Moanin' in the Mornin', Down with Love, In the Shade of the New Apple Tree, Buds Won't Bud, I've Gone Romantic on You]

Bloomer Girl (F. Saidy, S. Herzig; Harburg), orchd R.R. Bennett, T. Royal, 5 Oct 1944 [incl. The Eagle and Me, Right as the Rain, It was Good Enough for Grandma, Evelina, Sunday in Cicero Falls]

St. Louis Woman (A. Bontemps, C.P. Cullen; J. Mercer), orchd Royal, A. Small, M. Salta, W. Paul, 30 March 1946; rev. as Free and Easy (addl lyrics, Koehler), orchd Q. Jones, B. Byers, Amsterdam, Netherlands, 17 Dec 1959 [incl. Come Rain or Come Shine, Any Place I Hang my Hat is Home, I had Myself a True Love, Legalize my Name, I Wonder what Became of Me]

House of Flowers (T. Capote; Capote, Arlen), orchd Royal, 30 Dec 1954 [incl. A Sleepin' Bee, Two Ladies in de Shade of de Banana Tree, Bamboo Cage, I'm Gonna Leave Off Wearin' my Shoes, I Never has Seen Snow, Don't like Goodbyes]

Jamaica (Harburg, Saidy; Harburg), orchd P.J. Lang, 31 Oct 1957 [incl. Pretty to Walk With, Push de Button, Cocoanut Sweet, Take it Slow Joe, Leave the Atom Alone]

Saratoga (M. DaCosta; Mercer), orchd Lang, 7 Dec 1959 [incl. Petticoat High, Love Held Lightly, Goose Never be a Peacock, You or No One]

FILMS

Let's Fall in Love (Koehler), 1934; Gold Diggers of 1937 (Harburg), 1936; The Singing Kid (Harburg), 1936; Stage Struck (Harburg), 1936; Strike me Pink (L. Brown), 1936; At the Circus (Harburg), 1939; The Wizard of Oz (Harburg), orchd H. Stothart, 1939 [incl. Over the Rainbow]; Blues in the Night (Mercer), 1941 [incl. Blues in the Night, This Time the Dream's on Me]; Star Spangled Rhythm (Mercer), 1942 [incl. That Old Black Magic]; The Sky's the Limit (Mercer), 1943 [incl. One for my Baby, My Shining Hour]

Here Come the Waves (Mercer), 1944 [incl. Ac-cent-tchu-ate the Positive]; Kismet (Harburg), 1944; Up in Arms (Koehler), 1944; Casbah (L. Robin), 1948 [incl. For Every Man there's a Woman, What's Good about Goodbye?]; My Blue Heaven (R. Blane, Arlen), 1950; The Petty Girl (Mercer), 1950; Mr. Imperium (D. Fields), 1951; Down Among the Sheltering Palms (Blane, Arlen), 1953; The Farmer Takes a Wife (Fields), 1953; The Country Girl (Gershwin), 1954; A Star is Born (Gershwin), 1954 [incl. The Man that Got Away]; Gay Purr-ee (Harburg), 1962; I Could Go on Singing (Harburg), 1963

SONGS
(*selective list*)

except for films, all dates are those of first New York performance

The Album of my Dreams (L. Davis), 1929; Get Happy (Koehler), in 9:15 Revue, 1930; Out of a Clear Blue Sky (Koehler), in Earl Carroll Vanities, 1930; Linda, Song of the Gigolo (Koehler), in Brown Sugar, 1930; I Love a Parade, Between the Devil and the Deep Blue Sea (Koehler), in Rhythmania, 1931; I Gotta Right to Sing the Blues (Koehler), in Earl Carroll Vanities, 1932; Satan's Li'l Lamb (Harburg, Mercer), in Americana, 1932; I've got the World on a String (Koehler), in Cotton Club Parade, 1932

Cabin in the Cotton (I. Caesar, G. White), Two Feet in Two Four Time (Caesar), in George White's Music Hall Varieties, 1932; It's Only a Paper Moon (B. Rose, Harburg), in The Great Magoo, 1932; Stormy Weather (Koehler), in Cotton Club Parade, 1933; Ill Wind (Koehler), in Cotton Club Parade, 1934; Last Night when We were Young (Harburg), 1935; How's by You?, Song of the Woodman (Harburg), in The Show is On, 1936; Happiness is a Thing Called Joe (Harburg), in Cabin in the Sky (film), 1943

INSTRUMENTAL
(*selective list*)

Minor Gaff, blues fantasy, pf, collab. D. George, 1926; Rhythmic Moments, pf, 1928; Mood in Six Minutes, orchd R.R. Bennett, 1935; American Minuet, orch, 1939; Americanegro Suite (Koehler), vv, pf, 1941

BIBLIOGRAPHY

'Arlen, Harold', *CBY 1955*

E. Jablonski: *Harold Arlen: Happy with the Blues* (Garden City, NY, 1961/R) [incl. list of works]

A. Wilder: *American Popular Song: the Great Innovators, 1900–1950* (New York, 1972)

A. Harmetz: *The Making of the Wizard of Oz* (New York, 1977)

J. Haskins: *The Cotton Club* (New York, 1977)

H. Meyerson and E.Harburg: *Who put the Rainbow in 'The Wizard of Oz'?* (Ann Arbor, 1993)

A. Forte: *The American Popular Ballad of the Golden Era, 1924–1950* (Princeton, NJ, 1995), 209–36

E. Jablonski: *Harold Arlen: Rhythm, Rainbows, and Blues* (Boston, 1996)

LARRY STEMPEL

Arles. City in Provence in France. Originally a Gallo-Greek settlement, it became a Roman colony in 46 BCE and prospered as a maritime trading centre. It soon had a theatre, an amphitheatre, arenas and a circus. Archaeological finds now in the Musée d'Archéologie show that there was a lively interest in music at the time: the sarcophagus of Julia Tyrannia is decorated with carvings of two hydraulic organs, panpipes and a three-string kithara, and other sarcophagi preserved in the Alyscamps Roman cemetery are ornamented with reliefs showing kitharas and depictions of the aulos, barbitos, syrinx and hydraulic organ.

1. Sacred music. 2. Secular music.

1. SACRED MUSIC. Christianity came early to Arles. In 314 the Emperor Constantine called the first of the 19 councils held in the city, and excommunicated the *theatrici*, actors and instrumentalists who were regarded as symbolic of paganism. Arles became the second city in the empire, and was designated the capital of the Gauls in 392, a title confirmed by Honorius in 418. During the 4th century it became a centre for Gallican chant.

St Caesarius, a monk from the abbey of Lérins and Bishop of Arles from 502 to 543, proposed the introduction of a repertory of hymns in the form of dialogues between the congregation and the clergy. In his sermons, he condemned his flock for preferring love songs to religious chant, thus anticipating later debates on the conflict between sacred and secular music. His *Vigiliae* were adopted for use in the monasteries of Arles (*Regula ad virgines*, c534) and introduced the regular daily singing of the canonical hours into the cathedral. The *Admonitio synodalis*, a text attributed to him, forbade dancing in or immediately outside churches and nocturnal incantations on the tombs in the Alyscamps cemetery. The cathedral chapter was founded in 796 and dedicated to St Etienne and St Trophime. It developed into a major centre for Gregorian chant. In 879 Arles became the capital of the kingdom founded by Boson, brother-in-law of Charles the Bald, and then in 1032 passed into the hands of the German emperors. Frederick Barbarossa was crowned King of Arles and Burgundy in the cathedral of St Trophime on 30th July 1178. On 29 April 1251, in the château of Tarascon, Charles I of Anjou signed the document whereby Provence annexed Arles. Contemporary accounts vouch for the existence and provenance of antiphoners, missals and choirbooks, and indicate the lively practice of religious music during the 12th and 13th centuries. Musical instruments became indispensable adjuncts to church festivals, and there is documentary evidence of their use during the procession of St Antoine on 17th January 1432. The first organ was installed in the cathedral of St Trophime by Jean Robelin in 1469. It was followed by other organs up to the time of the French Revolution, built in a style that synthesized the organ traditions of Provence and northern France.

When the city became part of France in 1481, ecclesiastical affairs were little affected. A chapter choir school was founded in 1493 at St Trophime, the only church in Arles permitted to have a *corps de musique*. In the early 17th century, post-Tridentine religious fervour in the aftermath of the Council of Trent breathed new life into the chapter, which added to the splendour of its ceremonies and enriched its musical repertory. Music was regularly performed on violins, cornetts and serpents as well as the organ, and a document of 1614 contains the first mention of bowed string instruments being played in French churches.

In the 17th and 18th centuries the choir school had six choirboys, and employed singers and instrumentalists recruited, like the *maîtres de chapelle*, from all over France. About 1650 there were two choristers, a baritone, a *concordant*, a tenor and an alto. Two additional singers make their appearance in 1785. Cornetts, a serpent and the organ were the basic instruments in regular use about 1650, with strings sometimes added. They became an established feature in the 18th century, and the cathedral had a permanent ensemble of four violins and three cellos in the 1770s. This instrumental ensemble, sometimes supplemented by musicians from the neighbouring towns of Avignon, Tarascon and Beaucaire, played for the Sunday services and church festivals and provided musical accompaniment for processions. As at court, Low Mass was accompanied by *grands motets*, which, unusually, were also inserted into the Ordinary sung during High Mass. The repertory was essentially French, and is known to us from three inventories of the chapter's collection of

musical material drawn up in 1736, 1749 and 1760. Works by the local *maîtres de chapelle* were performed along with those of such composers as M.-R. de Lalande, A.E. Blanchard, Desmarets, Campara, Mondonville and Nicolas Bernier.

Works by many of the musicians of St Trophime have been preserved. These include those of the *maîtres de chapelle* André Campra, Sauveur Intermet, Nicolas Saboly, Annibal Gantez, François Estienne, P.-C. Abeille, Alexandre de Villeneuve, Jean Audiffren, Jean Clavis, Joseph Boudou and Antoine Hugues, in addition to compositions by the organist J.-B. Vallière, the choristers Laurent Belissen and Vincent Archimbaud, and Guillaume Poitevin, formerly a choirboy at St Trophime, who became *maître de chapelle* at St Sauveur in Aix. The *grands motets concertants* of these Provençal musicians were strongly influenced by those of Lalande, Campra and other Versailles composers, although their choruses were usually in four rather than five parts. In the 18th century there were organs in Dominican and Carmelite monasteries, while there are records of the practice of plainchant by the Augustinians. In 1857 a large 16-foot organ by J.E. Isnard was installed at St Trophime. It was replaced in 1874 by a small Cavaillé-Coll instrument. Today four churches in Arles have organs: St Trophime, Notre Dame de la Major, St Césaire and St Julien.

2. SECULAR MUSIC. There is documentary evidence of the existence of two municipal trumpeters in the 15th century and in 1574 the city hired three violinists to play for the Carnival festivities. A group of four violinists was established in 1620 to play with the drummer Simon Rinqier, and until the Revolution there were bands of instrumentalists playing violins, oboes, trumpets, fifes and drums, to which the local Provençal *galoubet* (pipe and tabor) was sometimes added. From the end of the 16th century festivities with musical accompaniment were organized by the Jesuit college founded in 1636. *L'histoire de Jonas*, a tragedy by Father Verdier, was performed in 1600; *Le triomphe de la paix*, 'adorned with machinery and changes of scene', with music by Laurent Belissen, was staged in 1714; and in 1729 the ballet *La jalousie* by Father Marion was inserted into the tragedy of *Asdrubal* as an *intermède*. These spectacles continued even after the eviction of the Jesuits in 1762.

Major concerts were given at the Arles Académie, founded in 1668 and officially ratified by letters patent of Louis XIV. The festivities held on the occasion of the birth of Louis XIV's grandson at Versailles in 1682 included the performance of works (now lost) by Campra. In February 1687 rejoicings to celebrate the king's recovery from illness included pieces by Aubert, *maître de chapelle* at St Trophime. An Académie de Musique was founded in 1715, and although its activities were disrupted by the plague in 1721, it was revived in 1729. Its orchestra, conducted by Jean Clavis – who was also conductor of an ensemble of *bons vivants* called the Chambre Noire – took part in the festivities for the birth of Louis XV's son in October 1729.

In 1696 the Marseilles opera company conducted by Pierre Gautier gave performances of Lully's *Alceste*, *Atys*, *Bellérophon* and *Armide* on one of its many tours. The Lyons opera company, directed by Leguay, visited Arles in 1700. There was also a good deal of musical activity in the salons of the aristocracy; and the inventories of private libraries, containing scores and separate parts for *tragédies lyriques* and *opéras comiques*, suggest that performances were staged. Operas by Lully, Campra, Mouret, Destouches, François Rebel and Rameau featured in these libraries, together with *grands motets* by Lalande and Mondonville and cantatas by Bernier. The libraries also contained *opéras comiques* and operas by Gluck and Sacchini. The popularity of the violin is attested by works by Corelli, Mondonville, Leclair and Guillaume Navoigille. There was an equally lively interest in chamber and orchestral music, with works by Handel, Quantz, Wagenseil, Johann Stamitz, Haydn, Pleyel, J.C. Bach and others.

The municipal theatre, inaugurated in 1839, mounted performances by touring companies from Nîmes, Avignon and Marseilles, staging operas by Meyerbeer, Gounod, Verdi and Wagner. In the mid-19th century private libraries contained operas by Bellini, works by Clementi and trios and quartets by Beethoven. A string quartet led by Joseph Alavène was founded in the city in 1850 and the Quatuor Gallo-Romain was founded in 1897.

After 1860 open-air ensembles became very popular. The Arlésienne (a brass band), the Estudiantina (an orchestral ensemble) and the Société Philharmonique (a wind band) gave regular concerts consisting of dances, overtures and numbers from fashionable operas and operettas. In 1903 a new bandstand was inaugurated with lavish festivities. In the late 19th and early 20th centuries symphony concerts were given by the orchestra of the Marseilles Société Populaire des Concerts de Musique Classique.

In the 20th century the musical life of Arles went into decline: the city no longer has a conservatory, and there are no resident chamber ensembles or orchestras. However, concerts are sometimes given in the city's churches, while the St Trophime Cloister Concerts and other summer events are popular with tourists.

BIBLIOGRAPHY

MGG2 (M. Signorile)

A.-J. Rance: *L'Académie d'Arles au XVIe siècle*, ii–iii (Paris, 1887–90)

M. Signorile: *Musique et société: le modèle d'Arles à l'époque de l'absolutisme (1600–1789)* (Geneva, 1993)

M. Signorile: Introduction to A. Hugues, *Magnificat en symphonie* (Geneva, 1999) [facs. of F-C 1032]

M. Signorile: Introduction to J.-B Vallière, *Magnificat à 4* (Geneva, 1999) [facs. of F-C 1032]

MARC SIGNORILE

Arlt, Wulf (Friedrich) (*b* Breslau [now Wrocław], 5 March 1938). German musicologist. He studied musicology at the universities of Cologne (1958–60), and Basle (under Schrade), where he obtained the doctorate in 1966 with a dissertation on the Beauvais Office for the Feast of the Circumcision. As an assistant he maintained and expanded the Basle microfilm archives, and became editor of *Palaeographie der Musik*, prepared by Schrade. In 1965 he was appointed lecturer at Basle University, where he completed his *Habilitation* in musicology in 1970 with a work on the theory and practice of Ars Subtilior; he was appointed supernumerary professor in 1972. From 1971 to 1978 he was also director of the Schola Cantorum Basiliensis, the teaching and research institute for early music in Basle, and editor of the journal *Basler Jahrbuch für historische Musikpraxis*. He was made professor and chair of musicology at Basle in 1991.

In his research Arlt has concentrated on music of the Middle Ages. He is concerned with creating a productive relationship between the musicology of the past (in the tradition of Schrade and Handschin) and current approaches in the discipline. His writings focus on the genre, notation, analysis and interpretation of medieval, 17th- and 18th-century music, and he is particularly concerned with investigating the connections between music and text. Best known for his publications on medieval music, he has examined liturgical genres (particularly the trope and the lied), early polyphony, the motet, Machaut and the history of the chanson. In his work with the Schola Cantorum Basiliensis, he has successfully fused new findings in musicology with new standards of performance, assisted by international specialists in early music. His contribution in this area is exemplified by his collaboration with Dominique Vellard, whom he has advised on performing practice and style for a recording series which includes 11th-century polyphony, tropes from the St Gallen Codices 484 and 381, and the 'nova cantica' of the Engelberg Codex 314.

WRITINGS

Ein Festoffizium des Mittelalters aus Beauvais in seiner liturgischen und musikalischen Bedeutung (diss., U. of Basle, 1966; Cologne, 1970)

Praxis und Lehre der 'Ars subtilior': Studien zur Geschichte der Notation im Spätmittelalter (Habilitationsschrift, U. of Basle, 1970)

'Der *Tractatus figurarum*: ein Beitrag zur Musiklehre der "Ars subtilior"', *Schweizer Beiträge zur Musikwissenschaft*, i (1972), 35–53

ed.: *Palaeographie der Musik*, i: *Die einstimmige Musik des Mittelalters* (Cologne, 1973–9) [incl. introduction to vol. i/1]

'Gattung: Probleme mit einem Interpretationsmodell der Musikgeschichtsschreibung', *Gattung und Werk in der Musikgeschichte Norddeutschlands uns Skandinaviens: Kiel 1980*, 10–19

'Musik und Text im Liedsatz franko-flämischer Italienfahrer der ersten Hälfte des 15. Jahrhunderts', *Schweizer Jb für Musikwissenschaft*, i (1981), 23–69

'Anschaulichkeit und analytischer Charakter: Kriterien der Beschreibung und Analyse früher Neumenschriften', *Musicologie médiévale: Paris 1982*, 29–55

'Aspekte der Chronologie und des Stilwandels im französischen Lied des 14. Jahrhunderts', *Aktuelle Fragen der musikbezogenen Mittelalterforschung: Basle 1975* [*Forum musicologicum*, iii (1982)], 192–280

'Zur Handhabung der *inventio* in der deutschen Musiklehre des frühen achtzehnten Jahrhunderts', *New Mattheson Studies*, ed. G.J. Buelow and H.J. Marx (Cambridge, 1983), 371–91

'Instrumentalmusik im Mittelalter: Fragen der Rekonstruktion einer schriftlosen Praxis, mit einem Anhang: "Wiedergefunden?": zum kunstvollen Spiel mit dem Formablauf in einer Estampie des Robertsbridge-Kodex', *Basler Jb für historische Musikpraxis*, vii (1983), 32–64

'Der Beitrag der Chanson zu einer Problemgeschichte des Komponierens: "Las! j'ay perdu ..." und "Il m'est si grief ..." von Jacobus Vide', *Analysen: Beiträge zu einer Problemgeschichte des Komponierens: Festschrift für Hans Heinrich Eggebrecht*, ed. W. Breig, R. Brinkmann and E. Budde (Wiesbaden, 1984), 57–75

'Von der schriftlosen Praxis und Überlieferung zur Aufzeichnung: zu den Anfängen des Trecento im Stilwandel um 1300', *L'Europe e la musica del Trecento: Congresso IV: Certaldo 1984* [*L'Ars Nova italiana del Trecento*, vi (Certaldo, 1992)], 127–44

'Der Prolog des *Orfeo* als Lehrstück der Aufführungspraxis', *Claudio Monteverdi: Festschrift Reinhold Hammerstein*, ed. L. Finscher (Laaber, 1986), 35–51

'Musica e testo nel canto francese: dai primi trovatori al mutamento stilistico intorno al 1300', *La musica nel tempo da Dante: Ravenna 1986*, 175–97; see also round table discussion, 306–21

'*Nova cantica*: Grundsätzliches und Spezielles zur Interpretation Musikalischer Texte des Mittelalters', *Basler Jb für historische Musikpraxis*, x (1986), 13–62

'"Triginta denariis": Musik und Text in einer Motette des *Roman de Fauvel* über dem Tenor *Victimae paschali laudes*', *Pax et sapientia: Studies in Text and Music of Liturgical Tropes and Sequences in*

Memory of Gordon Anderson, ed. R. Jacobson (Stockholm, 1986), 97–112
'Vom Überlieferungsbefund zum Kompositionsprozess: Beobachtungen an den zwei Fassungen von Busnois' *Je ne puis vivre ainsy*', *Festschrift Arno Forchert*, ed. G. Allroggen and D. Altenburg (Kassel, 1986), 27–40
'A propos des notations pragmatiques: le cas du Codex Las Huelgas', *RdMc*, xiii (1990), 401–19
'Das eine Lied und die vielen Lieder: zur historischen Stellung der neuen Liedkunst des frühen 12. Jahrhunderts', *Festschrift Rudolf Bockholdt*, ed. N. Dubowy and S. Meyer-Eller (Pfaffenhofen, 1990), 113–27
'*Donnez signeurs*: zum Brückenschalg zwischen Ästhetik und Analyse bei Guillauem de Machaut', *Tradition und Innovation in der Musik: Festschrift für Ernst Lichtenhahn*, ed. C. Ballmer and T. Gartmann (Winterthur, 1993), 39–64
'Die Intervallnotation des Hermannus Contractus in Gradualien des 11. und 12. Jahrhunderts: das Basler Fragment N I 6 Nr.63 und der Engelberger Codex 1003', *De musica et cantu: Studien zur Geschichte der Kirchenmusik und der Oper: Helmut Hucke zum 60. Geburtstag*, ed. P. Cahn and A.-K. Heimer (Hildesheim, 1993), 243–56
Italien als produktive Erfahrung franko-flämischer Musiker im 15. Jahrhundert (Basle, 1993)
'Machaut, Senleches und der anonyme Liedsatz "Esperance qui en mon cuer s'embat"', *Musik als Text: Freiburg 1993*, 300–10
ed., with G. Björkvall: *Recherches nouvelles sur les tropes liturgiques* (Stockholm, 1993) [incl. 'Schichten und Wege in der Überlieferung der älteren Tropen zum Introitus *Nunc scio vere* des Petrus-Festes', 13–93]
'Stylistic Layers in Eleventh-Century Polyphony: How Can the Continental Sources Contribute to our Understanding of the Winchester Organa?', *Music in the Medieval English Liturgy: Plainsong & Mediaeval Music Society Centennial Essays*, ed. S. Rankin and D. Hiley (Oxford, 1993), 101–44
'Jehannot de Lescurel and the Function of Musical Language in the *Roman de Fauvel* as Presented in BN fr.146', *Fauvel Studies: Allegory, Chronicle, Music and Image in Paris, Bibliothèque Nationale de France, MS français 146*, ed. M. Bent and A. Wathey (Oxford, 1998), 25–34
'Liturgischer Gesang und gesungene Dichtung im Kloster St Gallen', *Das Kloster St Gallen im Mittelalter: die kulturelle Blüte vom 8. bis zum 12. Jahrhundert*, ed. P. Ochsenbein (Darmstadt, 1999), 137–65, 253–60
'Machauts Pygmalion Ballade, mit einem Anhang zur Ballade 27 "Une vipere en cuer"', *Musikalische Interpretation: Reflexionen im Spannungsfeld von Notentext, Werkcharakter und Aufführung*, ed. J. Willimann and D. Baumann (Berne, 1999), 23–57
'Hymnus und Ode: Horazvertonungen des Mittelalters', *Hymnen-Studien*, ed. A. Haug (Kassel, forthcoming)
ed., with G. Cattin: *Itinerari e stratificazioni dei tropi: San Marco, l'Italia settentrionale e le regioni transalpine* (Venice, forthcoming) [incl. 'Die Präsenz des St Galler Tropenrepertoires der Handschriften SG 484 und 381 in Italien bis ins frühe 12. Jahrhundert']
Lo Bozolari, i: *Ein Klerikerfest des Mittelalters aus Le Puy*, ii: *Lieder des 12. Jahrhunderts und Mehrstimmiges aus der Kathedrale des 16. Jahrhunderts* (forthcoming)

EDITIONS
with M. Stauffacher: *Engelberg Stiftsbibliothek Codex 314*, SMd, xi (1986) [in Eng., Ger.; incl. facs.]
with S. Rankin: *Stiftsbibliothek Sankt Gallen Codices 484 & 381* (Winterthur, 1996) [commentary in Eng., Ger.; incl. facs.]
JÜRG STENZL/R

Arma, Paul [Weisshaus, Imre] (*b* Budapest, 22 Oct 1905; *d* Paris, 28 Nov 1987). French composer, pianist and ethnomusicologist of Hungarian birth. He studied the piano at the Budapest Academy of Music with Bartók (1921–4), whose advice on composition he often sought in later years and who kindled his love for folksong and collection. (In a lecture given at Harvard in 1943, Bartók spoke of Arma's textless song for solo voice on one pitch with variations of vowel sound, dynamic and rhythm.) Arma began his career as a member of the Budapest Piano Trio (1925–6). Between 1924 and 1930 he gave many

recitals in Europe and the USA and lectured on contemporary music at American universities. He settled in Germany in 1931, and for a time he led the musical activities at the Dessau Bauhaus, lecturing on modern music and experimenting with electronic music produced on gramophone records. Later he lived in Berlin and Leipzig, where he conducted several smaller choirs and orchestras.

The advent of the Nazi regime in Germany forced Arma's move to Paris, where he made his permanent home. At first he was associated with the RTF, notably as founder-director of the Loisirs Musicaux de la Jeunesse (1936–40). He was a member of the Commission Interministrielle des Loisirs de l'Enfance (1936–8), he published the *Nouveau Dictionnaire de Musique* (1947) and he lectured at the Phonothèque Nationale and at the University of Paris (1949); from the 1950s he was associated with the RTF *musique concrète* group. In 1962 he was made a Chevalier de l'Ordre des Arts et des Lettres and a life member of the Institut International des Arts et des Lettres. He has been active in the collection of French folksongs, French Resistance songs (his material includes some 1600 such) and black American spirituals. As a composer he is known chiefly for his experimental work, though he has also published didactic pieces and folksong arrangements. He was made a member of the Légion d'Honneur in 1983.

WORKS
(*selective list*)

Orch: Pf Conc., 1939; Suite de danses, fl, str, 1940; Conc., str qt, str, 1949; Sym., 1950; 31 instantanés, ww, perc, cel, pf, xyl, 1951; Polydiaphonie, 1962; Structures variées, 1964; Divertimenti de concert, solo insts (fl/vn, cl/va etc.), orch; Résonances, sets of 6, 7, 8 and 5, 1971–2; 6 convergences, 1978
Vocal: Chant indien, chorus 4vv, gui, tambourine, 1937; Cantate du gai travail (A. Gerard), children's chorus 3vv, speaking chorus, orch, 1937; Gerbe hongroise, 7 folksong arrs., 1v, pf, 1943; Chants du silence, 11 songs, 1v, pf, 1942–4; Cant. de la terre, folksong arrs., 4 solo vv, chorus, 1952; Conc., Mez, T, chorus, 1954; Cant. da camera (J. Cassou), Bar, chorus, str, 1957; other songs, cants., choruses
Chbr: Recitativo nos.1–2, vn, 1925; 3 danses populaires russes, vn, pf, 1938; La fête au village, str qt for young people, 1938; Divertimenti: fl/vn, pf; cl/va, pf; 2 fl; 2 ob; 2 hn; 2 tpt etc.; Résonances: bn; 2 fl; Sonatas: vn; va; Sonatinas, solo insts (fl, ob, cl, bn etc.), str qt/str orch; Transparences: pf; 2 pf; fl, va; fl, cl; 2 cl; str qt; str, xyl, perc etc.; 3 mobiles, cl, 1971; Silences et emergences, str qt, 1979; 2 regards, vn, pf, 1984
Pf: Accelerando, 1925; 2 Pf Pieces, 1926–7; Images paysannes, 1939 [arr. Fr. folksongs]; Sonata da ballo, 1939 [arr. Fr. folksongs]; 5 esquisses, 1946 [arr. Hung. folksongs]; Le tour du monde en vingt minutes, 1951
Elec: Improvisation précédée et suivie de ses variations, orch, tape, 1954; Quand la mesure est pleine (M. Seuphor), cant. on tape, 1962; Convergence de mondes arrachés (J. Arp, B. Cendrars, E. Ionesco, St J. Perse, T. Tzara), spkr and orch on tape, 1968
Principal publishers: Billaudot, Editions Ouvrières, Editions Transatlantiques, Heugel, Lemoine, Salabert, Schott, Universal

BIBLIOGRAPHY
B. Bartók: 'Revolution and Evolution in Art', *Tempo*, no.103 (1972), 4–7
'Propos impromptu: Paul Arma', *Courrier musical de France*, no.45 (1974), 4
VERA LAMPERT

Armandine. A large gut-strung psaltery, resembling a harpsichord without a keyboard, invented by PASCAL TASKIN.

Armatrading, Joan (*b* 9 Dec, 1950, St Kitts, Leeward Islands). English singer-songwriter. One of five children, she spent the first few years of her life with her grandparents in the West Indies, following the rest of her family to Birmingham in 1958. An introverted youngster, she taught herself piano and guitar and as a teenager, inspired initially by Marianne Faithfull, she began writing and performing her own songs in clubs.

While singing in the touring production of *Hair*, Armatrading met Pam Nestor with whom she recorded an album, *Whatever's for Us* (Cube, 1972). Produced by Gus Dudgeon, who had also worked with David Bowie and Elton John, it was a critical success but a commercial failure. *Back to the Night* (A&M, 1975) established Armatrading as a solo artist. However, she gained both critical and popular acceptance with her next album, *Joan Armatrading* (A&M, 1976), which included her best-known hit single *Love and Affection*. She established her name in the USA in 1980 with the release of her fourth album for A&M, *Me, Myself, I* which featured Sly Dunbar and Robbie Shakespeare. Throughout the 1980s and 1990s Armatrading maintained a schedule of recording and touring, retreating from public view between outings. In 1996 an anthology was released entitled *Love and Affection* which contained her songs from the first twenty years of her career.

Armatrading has a rich, dark voice that carries her distinctive melodies well, framed by imaginative, uncluttered arrangements. Her disciplined, sophisticated and rather formal songs such as 'Down to zero', 'Willow', and 'Show some emotion' (*Show Some Emotion*, A&M, 1977) are good examples of her own blend of blues, jazz and reggae. She is significant as being the first black female singer-songwriter to achieve popular success in Britain.

BIBLIOGRAPHY

G.G. Gaar: *She's a Rebel: the History of Women in Rock & Roll* (London, 1993)

L. O'Brien: *She Bop: the Definitive History of Women in Rock, Pop and Soul* (London, 1995)

M. Cooper: 'Joan Armatrading: Love and Affection', *Q* no.126 (1997), 120–21 [review]

LIZ THOMSON

Armbruster, Reimundo. *See* BALLESTRA, REIMUNDO.

Armeeposaune (Ger.: 'army trombone'). A model of valve TROMBONE developed by V.F. Červený for use in bands.

Armenia, Republic of (Armenian Hayastan). Country in Transcaucasia. It borders Turkey, Georgia, Azerbaijan and Iran and covers approximately 29,800 km². At the end of the 20th century its population stood at just under four million, most of which is Christian and belongs to the Armenian Apostolic Church. Formerly a republic of the USSR, it became independent in 1991. Its capital is Yerevan.

Situated on the border between Europe and Asia, Armenia has a culture and history that spans more than a millennium. This is attested by archaeological finds that can be dated to the 5th and 4th millennia BCE as well as by numerous rock paintings and ancient written sources. Originating within the Armenian uplands, and assimilating in the course of its history several ancient peoples on the edges of Asia and in Anatolia (the Hurrians, the Assyrian-Aramaic and Urartian peoples), Armenia was already a slave-owning state with a single language and with its own distinctive culture by the 3rd millennium BCE. By then, the monodic character of Armenian vocal music had been fully formed, and lasted for an entire millennium. Armenian traditional instrumental music, however, contains elements of polyphony; the melody is often accompanied by a steady drone and the 'rhythmic' voice of a percussion instrument.

Armenian musics combine features of both Asian and European musics. They draw on traditions from the Middle East in that they are essentially monodic and modal with a strong tonal centre, and have auxiliary notes that provide an antithesis to the tonic assisting in the unfolding of the melody. At the same time, they share the dynamics and temporal organization of melodic development found to the West.

Characteristic Armenian melodies occur in traditional folk and art music, as well as in the music of the Armenian Church. They are used also in contemporary professional compositions, which developed from the mid-19th century in the mainstream of Western art music.

I. Folk music. II. Church music. III. Opera, ballet, orchestral and chamber music.

I. Folk music

1. Sources. 2. History. 3. Peasant song and instrumental music: (i) Work songs (ii) Ritual songs (iii) Lyrical and other songs (iv) Dance-songs (v) Instrumental music. 4. The *gusanner*. 5. Religious folksongs and secular *tagher*. 6. The *ashughner*. 7. Urban folksong and instrumental music. 8. Theoretical basis and structure. 9. Folk music during the 20th century.

1. SOURCES. The antiquity of Armenian folk music is attested by monuments of material and spiritual culture, including folksongs. In the high mountain areas of Armenia are thousands of rock paintings of the 3rd and 2nd millennia BCE. In the many hieroglyphs are detailed dance scenes, probably of ritual dances. They are important in that they depict a circle-dance and war dances that are still performed. No instrumentalists are shown, as most Armenian folkdances are accompanied only by the singing of the dancers themselves.

Archaeological excavations in Armenia have yielded relatively few musical artefacts, which can be explained by the fact that in ancient times instruments were made of highly perishable materials – reeds, wood or leather. But the findings include small bronze handballs, *bozhozh* (small oval-shaped bells) and clappers from the 2nd millennium BCE, these also having been used in rituals; a horn with a simple line ornament from the 1st millennium BCE, found on the south-east bank of Lake Sevan (the part preserved is 17 cm long, with a small diameter of 3 cm); and bronze cymbals from the 7th century BCE found in Karmir Blur (near Yerevan), which are not essentially different from the modern small cymbals. The bird-bone pipes found in Garni and Dvin date from the period between the 5th century BCE and the Middle Ages, and are similar in playing technique to the modern *blul* (end-blown flute). One of the better-preserved pipes has five finger-holes, producing a scale whose intervals, according to modern measurements, are a semitone above the open note, then another semitone, a whole tone, a semitone, and an interval of three semitones.

Early historians of Armenia paid considerable attention to manifestations of national music. Movses Khorenatsi and Faustus of Byzantium, for example, recorded in their 5th-century chronicles the names of song genres and of musical instruments, fragments of epic song texts, descriptions of their performance and of the performers themselves, and descriptions of some rituals accompanied by music. This relates to a period beginning in the pre-Christian era. Artistic miniatures, gravestone carvings and also old engravings provide early illustrations of the performance of folk music.

From the early Middle Ages the Armenians had an advanced musical aesthetic that included such concepts as the aim and calling of music, the relation of sacred and secular elements and nature as the source of art. They interpreted in their own way the ancient classical teachings on sound and harmony and they also created systems of musical notation. In the 8th century *khaz* notation, basically a type of neumatic notation, was devised; after the 10th century it entered its second period of development, when it was made more exact (see below, §II). Manuscripts of *khaz* notation from the 8th century to the 18th have survived, many of ritual and non-ritual church music, but secular music and folksongs are also found. After the 15th century *khaz* notation became so complex and awkward that it gradually fell into disuse, but the spiritual songs continued to be transmitted orally until they were eventually written down in an appropriate notation.

Copies of many poems on folk models from the 16th century to the 18th have survived, many of which must have been sung, judging by the structure of the poetry and the presence of refrains. But their melodies were not fixed, although some have survived orally. In 1813 Hambardzum Limondjian (1768–1839) created a simple and accessible modern Armenian music notation, which was useful for the transcription of medieval chants as well as for the notation of folksongs. Many handwritten song-books also contain a wealth of material for the study of Armenian folk music.

Armenian folk music began to be collected systematically in the last quarter of the 19th century. The most productive work among the many collectors was that of Komitas (1869–1935), a gifted ethnographer, scholar and composer. Other notable collectors, both pupils of Komitas, were Spiridon Melik'ian (1880–1933) and M. T'umadjian (1890–1973). Since the 1950s the Institute of Arts and the Institute of Archaeology and Ethnography of the Academy of Sciences and the department of folklore at the Yerevan Komitas State University have assembled over 30,000 examples of Armenian folk music. Further collections are found in the Institute of Archaeology and Ethnography of the Armenian Academy of Sciences and the State Museum of Literature and Art; many recordings are also housed in the archive of recorded sound at Pushkin House (the Institute of Russian Literature) in St Petersburg. The songs were notated only by ear until 1913, when Melik'ian first used the phonograph. From 1939 recordings were made by cutting discs on celluloid X-ray negative plates, using equipment designed by Djivan Kirakosian. Magnetic recording has been used exclusively since 1950. Scholarly study of Armenian folk music also began at the end of the 19th century, the most important studies again being by Komitas, who analysed several fundamental questions of peasant music. The work by K'ristofor K'ushnarian (1890–1960), investigating the problems of history and theory of Armenian folk and medieval professional vocal music, is also particularly significant.

2. HISTORY. The Armenian highland was one of the centres of ancient world civilization. In Armenian territory the first traces of man date from the Palaeolithic era. A highly developed copper metallurgy existed there in the 5th and 4th millennia BCE; in the 3rd and 2nd millennia agriculture and cattle-raising were advanced, as was a certain spiritual culture. The earliest ancestors of the Armenian people were the Urumeians, inhabitants of the north-eastern sector of Asia Minor, which was called Armatana from the 16th century BCE to the 14th according to Hittite inscriptions, and later, in the 14th and 13th centuries, Hayasa. From there they invaded Assyria, in the region of Shupra, which the Assyrians came to call Urme or Arme. In the 8th century BCE the land of Arme united with the increasingly powerful state of Urartu, but after the fall of this state it became independent and the Armenian state rose in power. Persian texts of the 6th century BCE mention the broad land of Armina. Thus from the most ancient times two names have been used for the people and the country: Armen and Armina (or Armenia), used by outsiders, and Hay and Hayk' (subsequently Hayastan), as the Armenians called it themselves. Over the years Armenian culture strengthened and developed through contact with that of other races of the ancient world, and as the language of the people evolved, so the national characteristics of folk music became established.

The Armenians adopted Christianity in 301. Comparison of historical records and old church music, which can be dated with reasonable accuracy, enabled K'ushnarian to give an approximate date of origin to the surviving folk music. With this chronological study he showed that the monodic form of Armenian music, as well as its basic means of expression, were fixed long before the modern era, and that its early categories were defined as peasant, *gusan* (a professional singer of epics) and religious. Traces of archaic modes, genres and forms of this prehistoric period are found in the exclamatory phrases of the *hòrovelner* (ploughing songs), in songs of work at home and in some dance-songs. Survivals of musical accompaniment of rites, described in the works of Movses Khorenatsi and Faustus of Byzantium, are found in wedding songs, laments and so on.

The Armenian people lived through countless wars and destruction, constantly struggling against foreign aggressors. In Armenian political, economic and spiritual life there were deep depressions and brilliant highpoints. Certain periods, and stages in Armenian culture generally, were reflected in the development of folk music. The period from the 5th century to the 7th is especially important from this point of view. At this time of struggle for liberation and of powerful peasant revolutionary movements there was an unprecedented upsurge in all Armenian culture, which began with the creation of the modern Armenian alphabet in 404. New forms and themes of folklore came into being; the modal basis of the music and the range of melodic structures was broadened; melodic singing (i.e. in a cantilena style) became more important. Evidence for this is found in certain surviving lyrical love-songs and work songs of the peasants, and in heroic dances. In the same period a similar upsurge took place in the art of the *gusanner* (see §4 below). This is confirmed not only by the chroniclers, who remarked upon the important place of *gusan* art in the life of various classes of people and described their singing and instrumental ensembles with their various tone qualities, but also by the menacing charge of the synod at Dvin of 649 levelled against the *gusanner*, and by some earlier authorities of the Armenian Church. In the struggle against the spread of *gusan* influence, the Church characterized it as 'the work of the Devil'.

Another important period was the 10th century to the 13th, when the Armenians expelled their aggressors, the Arabs and Seljuk Turks, and established their independence, achieving a new and important cultural advance. Almost every historian of this period referred to folk music, either to 'the muting of the sounds of singing and instruments' when describing the land laid in ruin by the invaders, or to 'the constant sounding of song and lyre' when discussing the new well-being of the people. The ideas of love of life and humanism which were characteristic of Armenian art in this period (in poetry, miniatures, architecture etc.), and which brought it close to the early Renaissance, were already evident in folk music in the epic *Sasuntsi Davit'* ('David of Sasun'). This epic took form under the influence of the Armenian struggle for freedom in the 8th and 9th centuries, and proclaims Mankind's right to freedom. The same trend of thought was characteristic of the peasant songs of that period, which are perfect models of harmony of form and content. Finally, in this period the rapid development of the *tagh* (a monophonic, aria-like vocal form of a lyrical, dramatic and laudatory character) took place (see §5 below). By contrast, in the mid-16th century, after the division of Armenia between Turkey and Persia, a particular type of 'natural selection' took place in folk music both in subject and in mood, and songs of anguish and sorrow predominated, with the rise of corresponding genres.

Among the interesting questions for the scholar in the history of Armenian folk music is that of Armenian contact with the cultures of the ancient world and the Middle Ages, the results of these mutual influences, and 'dialect' characteristics. The study of collateral data has led scholars to the conclusion that the early contiguity with Hittite and Assyrian-Aramaic cultures must have been important for Armenian music. Also important was the assimilation by the Armenians of the culture of Uranu, which was advanced for its time, as well as closer contact with the culture of ancient Persia and the exchange of creative experience with the cultures of the peoples included in the Seleucid Hellenistic kingdom.

A partial result of the creative intercourse which took place in the 12th and 13th centuries was the appearance of elements of the *mugamat* (Arabic *maqāmāt; see* MODE, §V, 2) in Armenian urban instrumental music. The *mugamat* – a genre found among many Middle Eastern peoples – was favoured in these centuries among the upper levels of the urban population, and until recent times Armenian instrumentalists were among the best performers of the Persian-Azerbaijani branch of *maqāmāt*, naturally leaving an impression on certain levels of urban music. In some Persian-Azerbaijani *maqāmāt*, however, especially in instrumental sections with a dance character, the influence of Armenian urban songs and dances can still be detected. The Armenian *ashughner* (professional folk poets: see §6 below) assimilated certain features relating to Middle Eastern *ashugh* poetics during the 17th and 18th centuries. In spite of these common cultural characteristics and mutual influences, the Armenians have retained a specific national culture.

The Armenian language encompasses about 60 clearly differentiated dialects. Analogous distinctions can also be observed in the traditional folk music styles of the speakers of these dialects, in the general character and features of timbre of their music, in the preferences for certain modal intonations and genres, and in the preference for certain instruments. The study of this subject, begun by Komitas (1907), still continues.

3. PEASANT SONG AND INSTRUMENTAL MUSIC. In enumerating stylistic subdivisions, Komitas divided Armenian peasant songs first of all geographically into songs from the mountains, and songs from the plains: the former are relatively harsh in sound, with greater importance given to recitative; the latter are softer, with a predominance of smooth cantilena style. He then divided them according to the larger regions of origin, that is, according to dialect: for example, songs from Shirak, Aparan, Alashkert (now Eleşkirt in Turkey), Van, Mokk, Mush (Muş in Turkey), Akn and Kharberd (places in historical Armenia). Next he divided them according to the most important centres of song creation within these regions.

The peasant song is generally monophonic (performed solo or by a unison chorus), but some types are performed antiphonally. Some peasant songs depend on conditions of place and time, and are linked with specific aspects of village life. Thus work songs and many everyday songs are performed only in appropriate situations. The ritual songs were created in ancient times but were performed and developed exclusively in the process of practising the rituals. The performance of very old epic-narrative and historical songs (which came to peasant life from the *gusanner*) is not linked with specific circumstances, however, nor is the creation and performance of songs about love and nature, those on social themes and certain others.

(i) Work songs. The most interesting work songs are the *hȯrovelner* (ploughing songs). The term *hȯrovel* derives from the joining of the exclamation 'ho' and the word 'aṙavel', which designates the unploughed strip between two fields. 'Hȯrovel' became a cry used by ploughmen. The words and music of *hȯrovelner* are improvised, and these songs consist of a main part, a refrain and many exclamations. Although the purpose is to stimulate work and enliven the ploughmen and the working animals, the singers also express personal feelings. The main subjects of the texts are work, grain and nature, but there are elements of prayer and thanksgiving, appeals and commands, complaints and expressions of satisfaction, and reflections of ancient customs and beliefs. The length of texts and melodies varies; one stanza of a *hȯrovel* from the Lori region, corresponding to ploughing one furrow, takes 90 lines of text and 301 bars of notation (see below, ex.13, transcr. Komitas). In all *hȯrovelner* powerful descending recitative phrases are followed by tranquil cantilena sections: the modal basis is rich (scales including an augmented 2nd predominate) and the rhythm and melodic phrases are varied. The *hȯrovel* is a consistent and common type of song for a large group of people; an especially beautiful exchange of calls results, giving rise to a natural form of polyphony.

Also important are bullock-cart songs, performed while wheat is transported from the field to the threshing floor, and threshing-floor songs, sung while the wheat is being threshed by a board drawn by oxen. This work does not demand great effort, so the texts consist almost entirely of affectionate words addressed to the animals, and the melodies are flowing and lyrical. Among the women's

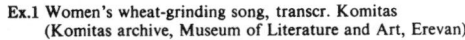

Ex.1 Women's wheat-grinding song, transcr. Komitas
(Komitas archive, Museum of Literature and Art, Erevan)

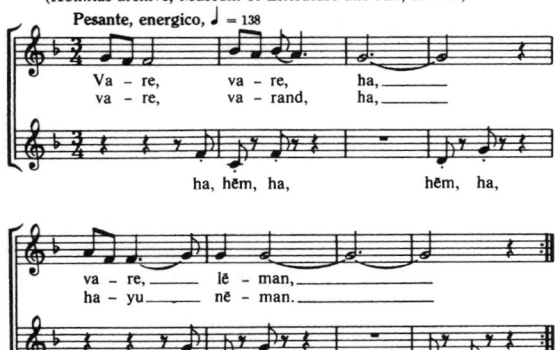

work songs in the field, the hoeing songs are outstanding for their supple melodies, which are in mixed metre.

Some women's domestic work songs are linked with the rhythm of the work, to make it easier: for example, a wheat-grinding song sung as a dialogue (ex.1). Others, though subject to the motor movement of the work, contain clearly-expressed emotional elements.

(ii) Ritual songs.   These can be subdivided into those of the calendar cycle, celebrated by everyone, and the ritual episodes of family life. Both generally consist of integral cycles. Little has survived from the first category because of the changes in the social conditions and customs of the people. The colourful songs of foretelling the maiden's future on the festival of Ascension and the songs of Shrovetide have proved especially persistent. Traces have also survived of songs of certain ancient pagan rituals, such as *tïndez*, the ritual of fire worship.

Among the family ritual songs is the wedding cycle, consisting of over 100 items, which must be sung at specific moments. These songs have many local variants. They are varied in poetic and musical themes, relating to the groom or bride, to their parents, friends and other participants in the wedding, or to special rituals such as the blessing of the wedding tree. A broad spectrum of emotions is portrayed, from the humble prayer to the sharp-witted joke, from deep sorrow to unconstrained hilarity. There are women's and men's recitative and melodic songs, solo and choral songs, dialogues between soloist and chorus, two soloists or two choruses and so on. The songs of praise and of consolation of the bride appear to be very old, as do those of the bride's leavetaking. There are solemn songs to the groom and to his parents, and humorous riddle songs. The wedding ritual also includes special dance-songs. Other family ritual songs are the *voghb*, or lament, the earliest examples of which were performed in pagan times by special women mourners and, according to the description by Faustus of Byzantium, were accompanied by funeral dances.

(iii) Lyrical and other songs.   A large proportion of peasant songs are lyrical love-songs. They are characterized by remarkable concentration of thought and feeling, strict definition of image and mood, laconic expression and depth of content. Their flowing cantilena style is developed within a narrow range, usually a 4th to a 7th, based on simple diatonic scales. Nature is always part of

the subject matter of love-songs. Expansion of the form of lyrical love-songs (although their brevity is unaltered) is effected in two ways: internally, when the question–response parts of one section are themselves expanded, resulting in a romance-like structure (ex.2); and externally, when one or two independent sections of a light, sometimes dance-like nature are added to the basic cantilena section (ex.3).

Among the everyday songs are those sung to and by children, and joking songs. There are songs for all the important events of the child's life: particularly beautiful, with the most interesting texts, are the lullabies, in which the mother often expressed her misery at oppression. The experiences of the peasant, oppressed by feudal lords, gave rise to songs with social themes. The hardest lot, however, is described in the *pandukht* songs, those of the

Ex.2 *I saw you*, love-song; transcr. Komitas (Komitas, 1931)

Ex.3 Love-song (Melik'yan and Ter-Ghevondyan, 1917)

Ex.4 *Pandukht* song, 'Song of the homeless'; transcr. Komitas (Komitas archive, Museum of Literature and Art, Erevan)

people who went abroad to work. In the late Middle Ages these folksongs constituted a special genre. A classic example of the heartbreaking sadness expressed in these songs is the 'Song of the homeless' (ex.4), in which the mode and the melodic structure are also of interest.

(iv) Dance-songs. By contrast, the *parerger* (dance-songs), the most widespread genre of peasant music, reflect optimism and enjoyment of life. Their melodic structure is based on the repetition of a rhythmic pattern. The rhythmic and metrical patterns of the different dances show endless variety; mixed metres are often found, with many variations of their internal division (ex.5). The dance-songs are also varied in tempo and emotional tone: they can be heavy or light, serene or energetic, slow or fast, lyrical or virile, joking or heroic. There is a further division into everyday and feasting dances, and ritual and epic dances (i.e. those danced to sung epics). In extant folklore lyrical dances predominate, performed chiefly by young people.

The dance movements have great variety: in the stance of the dancers, the frequency and direction of the movements, and the order and type of step – on the spot, walking and leaping. Dance-songs may be performed in various ways: with a soloist (who is also the director of the dance) and chorus; two soloists (question–response) and chorus (refrain); two soloists and two choruses; one or two choruses without soloists and so on. These all conform to the verse forms and the sequence pattern of the introduction, the refrain and

exclamations. The refrain may be at the beginning, middle or end of a stanza, and often appears in more than one position, interwoven with the basic text.

Circle-dances with instrumental accompaniment are also part of Armenian peasant life, although they are less important. They are danced to tunes of a chiefly ritual or epic-heroic character, which are always traditional. There are comparatively few peasant solo and couple-dances: they may be men's or women's dances, lyrical, humorous, pastoral or warlike. The last two types often use accessories such as a shepherd's crook, sabres or shields.

(v) Instrumental music. Peasant instrumental music is generally akin to song. It may be pastoral (ex.6) or epic-narrative in nature. Melodies may be performed on the *blul* (also called the *sring*), an end-blown flute of nasal tone quality, usually with seven finger-holes and one thumb-hole, or sometimes on the *t'ut'ak* (or *shvi*), a fipple flute. The *duduk* (or *nay*) is a cylindrical double-reed instrument with eight finger-holes and one thumb-hole, and a soft, slightly nasal timbre. Slow song-like melodies with lively dancing refrains are performed on two

Ex.5 Dance-songs showing mixed metre

(a) Komitas, 1931

(b) Melik'yan, 1949–52, vol. ii

Ex.6 Pastoral tune played on the *blul*: transcr. R. At'ayan

dudukner, the second *duduk* providing a tonic drone. Expansive ritual songs (which may be for weddings, funerals, pilgrimages, meeting the sunrise etc.) are performed on two or three *zuřna* (conical oboes with a pirouette, producing a sharp timbre) or on the *parkapzuk* (bagpipe with a double chanter but no drone), accompanied by a *dhol* (double-headed cylindrical drum, beaten with sticks). The dances mentioned above, and all kinds of song, are performed with such instruments. Often the music is improvised.

4. THE 'GUSANNER'.   The oldest evidence of this branch of folk music is found in 5th-century sources, which indicate that at that time the *gusanner* were already divided into several categories. These included tellers of tales, singers, instrumentalists, male and female dancers, comedians and tragic actors. They took part in theatrical performances, weddings, funerals and other rites, and always performed at feasts that were purely for entertainment. They appeared singly or in groups, at royal palaces and courts, and also among the common people. Apparently at that time the tellers of tales were considered most important and enjoyed special prestige, recalling in many ways the Greek rhapsodes. They presented the national myths and epics in word and song. The *gusanner* were professionals: their performances always involved an audience, demanding preparation and a ready repertory. Beginning probably in pagan times, the *gusanner* gradually developed a favourite set of themes, forms, devices and means of presentation. Characteristic features evolved which were handed down from master to disciple and acquired the force of tradition. Although the art of the *gusanner* did not sever its ties with real folk creativity (as is apparent from surviving examples), it took on distinctive professional characteristics.

Movses Khorenatsi wrote that he heard the singing of the *gusanner* who 'transmitted these tales singing, in songs of dances and performances, with the accompaniment of the *bambir*'. (Occasionally spelt *bambiřn*, this may have been a medieval plucked string instrument, although some scholars believe it was a kind of castanet.) Faustus of Byzantium, in a description of the royal feast at which King Pap (4th century) was murdered, also recalls 'the colourful throng of gusanner' who beat the drum, played the flute, the lyre and the horn, producing a diversity of sound'. The music of the *gusanner* presumably had artistic merit corresponding to the high quality of their poetry. An idea of the melodies of the oldest epic songs of the *gusanner* can be obtained from the fragments of the epic *Sasuntsi Davit'* that are sung (much of it is spoken). Although these have survived in village folk music, they still retain a style distinct from that of peasant music (ex.7). The 'angularity' of the melodic contours of the example, its diatonic scale (emphasis on the fourth degree in relation to the tonic is a basic characteristic of Armenian folk music) and the general character of the music convey the heroic spirit of the epos. Other examples of the epic have the same scale contours but a more developed melody: comparison of such examples suggests that the epic music of the *gusanner* developed in the direction of ever greater melodic complexity. It is also apparent from the many historical references to *gusanner* that from the 10th century to the 13th their art expanded increasingly, and that they played a leading role in all kinds of entertainment. During the next period (from the 13th century, according to M. Abeghian, 1951) the genre of

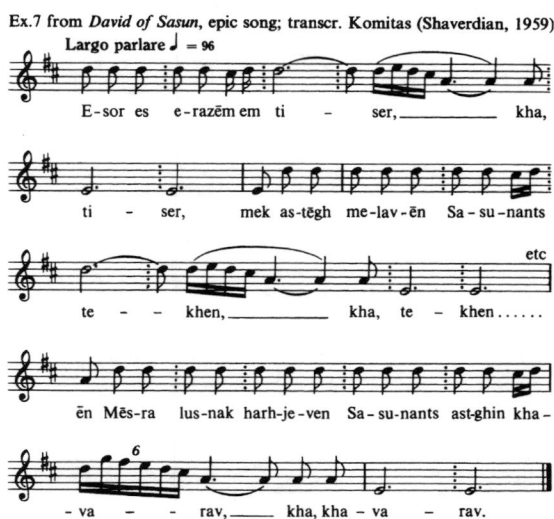

Ex.7 from *David of Sasun*, epic song; transcr. Komitas (Shaverdian, 1959)

the *gusan hayren* was created. The *hayren* form had existed for a long time in Armenian folk poetry and was taken over by professional poets, among whom Grigor Narekatsi (Gregory of Narek, 950–1003) used it with particular brilliance in his *tagher*. The *hayrenner* are verses composed in the 'Armenian' metre (*hayren*: 'in Armenian'): doubled seven- and eight-foot distichs, with dynamic displacement of accents.

When conditions once more became difficult, the *gusanner* drew closer to the people; there was more subjective lyricism in their works and the influence of folk music became more noticeable. *Hayrenner* are among the songs collected at the end of the 19th century in the town of Akn, where an abundant *gusan* tradition survived. The few surviving examples of *hayrenner* show the regard for tradition in *gusan* singing, which was accompanied by instruments, usually strings and percussion. In the 17th century the art of the *gusanner* merged with folk music, making way for the *ashughner* (see §6 below).

5. RELIGIOUS FOLKSONGS AND SECULAR 'TAGHER'.   Armenian folk and religious songs are closely related melodically. This reflects the early interchange between the two genres. From true religious songs there arose folk variants which were sung until modern times. There also exist independent religious songs, not intended for church use, which were composed in true folk style. These form a limited but characteristic genre in Armenian folklore; the rather short examples of songs for the Annunciation (close to village dance-songs) and the extended cantilena ones have an epic-narrative character.

At the point of convergence of Armenian folk and religious art there arose the secular and religious *tagher*. These were sung poems, lyrical, dramatic or solemnly laudatory, often with texts similar to the *hayrenner*, and dedicated to the lives of the Virgin Mary, Christ and the saints, but in essence reflecting the real life of human beings, expressing not ascetic but human feelings. The *tagher* were forerunners of the renaissance of Armenian art, and heralded the new humanistic trend in Armenian poetry and music of the 10th century. The earliest *tagher* (words and melodies) are by the 10th-century poet Grigor Narekatsi. The secular branch of the *tagher* developed somewhat later. From the 13th century to the 18th there

Ex.8 from *tagh Havik* ('The bird'), transcr. Komitas (Komitas, 1950)

songs, but are distinguished from these by greater melodic development and somewhat more open emotion. Ex.8 shows the *tagh Havik* ('The bird'), which is based on folk motifs but is elaborated in a religious spirit. Some sources ascribe this version to Narekatsi. A very simple example of a secular folk *tagh* – one of the most popular folksongs – is the song Krunk ('The crane'; ex.9), in which a *pandukht* (a man who must work abroad), bitterly complaining of his unhappy state, asks the crane for news of his home and family. In the 18th century the *tagher* merged partly with folksong, partly with the art of the *ashughner*.

6. THE 'ASHUGHNER'. The art of the *ashughner* spread in Armenia in the 17th and 18th centuries, although the term *ashugh* was found earlier in Armenian literature, in the 15th and 16th centuries. This art has some features in common with that of the *gusanner*, which it replaced. The name *ashugh*, which is found in many languages, is derived from Arabic and means 'in love'. Tradition has it that unhappy love turned three men into *ashughner*, who wandered the world seeking the meaning of life. Like the *taghergu* and *gusan*, the Armenian *ashugh* came mostly from a simple urban background, and performed for audiences of aristocrats and common folk alike. *Gusanner* and *ashughner* had the same social role and professional character, but the form and content of their music and certain features of performance differed.

The Armenian *ashughner* used personal and social themes. The subject of love was basic, sometimes expressed with touching directness or in striking imagery, always hyperbolic. In addition, prominence was given to social, philosophical and moralizing themes, to the celebration of human virtues and the censure of negative

was a large group of highly gifted secular poets to whom the people gave two names: *tagherguner* ('creators of *tagher*') and *taghasatsner* ('performers of *tagher*'), although in most cases composer and performer were one person. The chief representatives were Frik (13th century), Kostandin and Hovhannes Erznkatsi (13th–14th centuries), Mkrtich Nagharsh (15th century), Hovhannes T'lkurantsi and Grigons Aght'amartsi (15th–16th centuries), and Hovnat'an Naghash and Paghtasar Dpir (17th–18th centuries). Private and social feelings, for instance love, delight in nature and criticism of human life and morals, protest against social inequality and condemnation of foreign usurpation are reflected in the secular *tagher* of these authors, and in the many anonymous *tagher*.

The *khaz* notation of religious and secular *tagher* cannot yet be read. The *tagh* melodies which are now accessible were written down in the 1870s. From the time when *khaz* notation became unintelligible until their notation in the late 19th century the *tagher* were transmitted orally in the same way as genuine folksongs, thus losing some characteristics of professional compositions and almost becoming folksongs.

The religious *tagher* are extended, aria-like ornamented melodies, whose virtuoso structure shows the influence of urban folk music (possibly of *gusanner*); tense emotional passages are sometimes juxtaposed with meditative sections. The secular folk *tagher* are, however, lighter in form and more akin to arioso; feeling is expressed on one plane only. They show the influence of peasant lyrical

Ex.9 from *tagh Krunk* ('The crane'), transcr. Komitas (Komitas archive, Museum of Literature and Art, Erevan)

aspects of society or of the lives of individuals. There are also historical descriptions, jokes, riddles, Armenian versions of Middle Eastern *ashugh* tales and so on. In the course of time themes of public significance and themes of national liberation also entered their repertory, and new national *ashugh* tales arose. Armenian *ashughner* originally wrote in folk dialects, but later went over to the more generally accessible literary language. Some were fluent in many languages, wanting in Persian, Osmanli, Georgian and Azerbaijani as well as Armenian, and sometimes they composed macaronic verses. Classical versification was predominantly used by the *ashughner*, who developed it to a high standard. They adapted it to meet the demands of their language and ideas, creating new variants of classic forms of *ashugh* versification and even new forms. Especially prized is the medial 'complex rhyme' in each line. The *ashughner* often improvised (especially in competitions), employing a variety of technical devices.

Schools of *ashughner* with special traditions arose and were named after their centres: Vagharshapat (now Edjmiadsin), Alexandropol (now Gyumri), Tbilisi, and schools of Persian Armenians, Turkish Armenians and so on. They differed in dialect and manner of expression, in poetic subject and in details of musical style, both in composition and performance. The poems of distinguished *ashughner* were preserved in their authors' manuscript books, which were later printed. The melodies survived through oral transmission and from the end of the 19th century were also notated and later published.

In *ashugh* compositions the poetry was usually more important than the melody. Armenian *ashughner* used many traditional improvisatory motifs (there were up to 60), a general Middle Eastern feature. But alongside these they often composed original melodies. This was already a national feature, so that for the Armenian *ashugh* 'song' meant not only verses (as it often did among other *ashughner*) but a unified musical-poetic work. They maintained another Middle Eastern tradition, an *ashugh* pseudonym, which was always mentioned in the last couplet of each song, the aim being to preserve the knowledge of the song's authorship.

Compared with *gusan* melodies, those of the Armenian *ashughner* show more overt emotion, tension and pathos. The recitative, cantilena and dance character of the melodies is more apparent than in peasant folk music. Melodies are usually extended, mixed metres are widely used and ornamentation is relatively rich; they also have individual features that may reflect the creative personality of the *ashugh* and his folk music source. Like the *gusanner*, the *ashughner* used musical instruments, but only string ones: the *saz*, a lute with a long pear-shaped body and long neck, usually with six to eight metal strings and ten to thirteen frets; the *chunguṙ*, a four-string lute, one of the strings being shorter than the others with its peg halfway down the neck; the *t'aṙ*, a long-necked lute, with a body in the shape of a figure-of-eight, a skin soundboard and five to nine, 11 or 14 strings; the *k'anon*, a trapeziform zither with 24 triple courses (72 strings in all); the *sant'ur*, a trapeziform dulcimer; and the *k'yamancha*, a long spike fiddle with three or four strings and a round skin-covered body, often beautifully decorated. The *ashughner* appeared alone (singing and playing), or together with others who performed an instrumental or a vocal

accompaniment. Mimicry, movement and dramatization were not used by Armenian *ashughner*.

The first famous Armenian *ashughner* were the last *tagherguner*: Hovnat'an Naghash (1661–1722) and Paghtasar Dpir (1683–1768). Among the classical representatives of this art (one of the world's greatest masters of 'sound-painting' according to the poet Valery Bryusov) was Sayat'-Nova (Arut'in Sayadian, 1717–95), born in Aleppo, who served as court singer and musician to the Persian Nadir Shah, later to the Georgian ruler Iraklii II, and spent his last years in Sanahin (Armenia). He composed in Georgian and Azerbaijani as well as Armenian. Djivani (Serob Levonian, 1846–1909) was born in Akhalkalaki, lived and was active in Alexandropol and later in Tbilisi. His chief themes were social ones, notably the liberation of his people. The sources of his music were the songs of the Armenian peasants. Sheram (Grigor Talian, 1857–1938) of Alexandropol, was another famous *ashugh*, an ardent singer of happy love.

7. URBAN FOLKSONG AND INSTRUMENTAL MUSIC. Little of the music of the medieval Armenian cities has survived. The folk music now played and sung in the cities is the product of the last two or three hundred years. Melodic patterns from all branches of folk music, mixed with elements of *sazandar* music, which is found throughout Transcaucasia, together with some Slavonic and European elements, have been assimilated into a nationally unified and characteristic style. Urban folksongs, especially lyrical ones, are emotionally more intimate than the peasant songs; the modal basis is practically identical, but the development of the melodies is achieved by simpler means: there are elements of periodicity in their structure, and the rhythm is also simpler. In urban songs the local features can be heard more clearly, so that, for example, there are clear distinctions between the songs of Yerevan, Gyumri (formerly Alexandropol), Shush, Van and other towns. The texts, unlike those of peasant songs, are mostly by professional poets. The love-song is characteristic; there are also everyday, student, entertainment and table songs, songs for solo and couple-dancing and so on. Much urban folk music consists of national patriotic songs, which developed intensively from the 1860s. The theme of liberation appeared in slow songs, including romances and even lullabies, as well as in marches. Also widespread were translations and Armenian adaptations of the Marseillaise and of Russian revolutionary songs.

Urban instrumental music, used to accompany songs and a great variety of solo dances, some of which are found throughout the Caucasus, included ritual melodies, slow extended improvisatory pieces (usually with refrains in slow rhythm) and potpourris, in both solo and ensemble performance. Ensemble performance was in unison with elements of improvisatory heterophony, and a sustained part was widely used.

In the medieval cities of Armenia folk instruments were very widespread. This is known not only from chronicles, miniatures and archaeological findings, but also from manuscripts in the Matenadaran (the Institute of Ancient Manuscripts in Yerevan). Some of these instruments have disappeared and others have changed. The 10th-century poet Grigor Narekatsi referred to a string instrument called *djut'ak*, which is the modern Armenian word for violin. In the excavations of Dvin, one of the medieval capitals of Armenia, a vase from the 11th century shows a musician holding on his shoulder an instrument like the violin. The decrease in the number of folk instruments in the towns was also related to the introduction of European instruments.

The string instruments of the Armenian urban ensembles of later centuries have general Near Eastern distribution, and include the *k'yamancha* (fig.1) and the *k'amani* (the latter being a long rectangular three- or four-string fiddle); the *ud*, a short-necked unfretted lute, with 11 strings in six courses plucked with a plectrum; the *t'ar* (also plucked with a plectrum); and the *k'anon* and *sant'ur*. In the 1920s the musician and composer Vardan Buniyatian (1888–1960) constructed a family of *t'aryer* and *k'yamanchaner* of different pitches and timbres, from which an Middle Eastern symphony orchestra was created. These instruments have now spread to Dagestan and other Central Asian republics. Among the newer string instruments is a special type of folk cello in two sizes, which has been given the name of the old instrument *bambir*. The wind instruments used include the *duduk* and *zurna*; the percussion includes the *dhol* (double-headed drum), the *dap'* or *ghaval* (a single-headed frame drum, sometimes with rattles or rings inside the frame, played with the fingers), and the *naghara* (two single-headed drums of the kettledrum type). There are string and wind ensembles, and combinations of both. The most easily formed ensemble, consisting of a *t'ar* player, a *k'yamancha* player and a *ghaval* player (the latter is also the singer), is called a *nvagurd* in Armenian, while the general Transcaucasian word for it is *sazandar*. In all these ensembles the dynamic of the performance rests primarily on the percussion instrument, which varies and develops the rhythmic intensity.

8. THEORETICAL BASIS AND STRUCTURE.   The types of Armenian folk music described above and also the medieval religious music are monodic: they are formed exclusively from melodic elements. A basic diatonic scale gradually evolved, consisting of identical major tetrachords linked so that the highest note of one is the lowest

1. K'yamancha player

of the next tetrachord. The scale is not equal-tempered: in folk vocal and instrumental performing practice the third degree of each tetrachord is slightly flatter than the corresponding degree of the tempered scale. Thus there is a great variety of intervals. In addition to tempered major and minor 2nds, there are 'wide' minor 2nds and 'narrow' major 2nds. This applies also to 3rds and other intervals. The major 7th and augmented 4th do not appear as melodic intervals, and augmented intervals are absent. The diminished octave exists as a diatonic interval. The basic diatonic scale is shown in ex.10 with the slightly

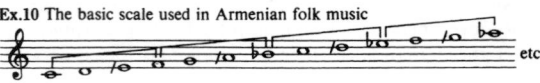

Ex.10 The basic scale used in Armenian folk music

flattened untempered degrees preceded by a small slanted line.

As the relations between the degrees are repeated after every fourth note, three types of mode can be formed naturally, corresponding to the G, A and B modes; these constituted the original basis of Armenian music. In the process of development of the melodic contours of the tunes, some degrees of the basic diatonic row were altered. These alterations may be divided into those of less than a semitone, when a partly raised variant occurs in the scale together with the original lower degree, and those of a semitone, which results in a new degree. Both types of alteration occurred from the earliest times and became increasingly frequent. Some modes formed with a semitone alteration (see ex.11*b* scales 1 and 2) appeared in simple forms in very early agricultural improvisations containing elements of pagan incantations to natural phenomena. Some (see ex.11*b*, scale 3) occurred with the development of the medieval *tagher* and the *gusan hayrenner* between the 10th and 13th centuries, while others (see ex.11*b* scales 6 and 7) occurred in the music of the *ashughner*; in the 17th and 18th centuries.

Chromaticism has no place in Armenian folk music. The basic degrees of the scale and their altered variants appear separately in practice as diatonic degrees. The scales are not confined to the octave and, in addition the notes of the mode above and below that octave are not automatically repeated; if a note is repeated an octave higher, it has a different melodic function in the mode. For example, if the final note occurs in the mode an octave above the actual *finalis*, the higher note will not be a final degree. As a result the mode has only one *finalis*: this usually appears in the middle of its scale, so that the modes are chiefly plagal. They are also centripetal in that the degrees below the *finalis* are raised notes and those above it are lowered: thus from both directions there is a tendency to move towards the *finalis*. The medians degrees also assume the role of leading notes.

The modes are made up of several joined segments which may be dichords, trichords, tetrachords or pentachords. A relatively full form of each mode usually consists of three segments, more rarely of four or five (see ex.11). The maximum range of a mode is generally a 10th or slightly more. The most important segment, defining its structure and expressive character, is the tonic segment, whose highest note (the beginning note of the segment above) has the role of a secondary tonal centre, slightly less stable than the tonic. In practice the complete stability of the tonic is felt most clearly when a folk melody is performed on two instruments (e.g. two *dudukner*), with

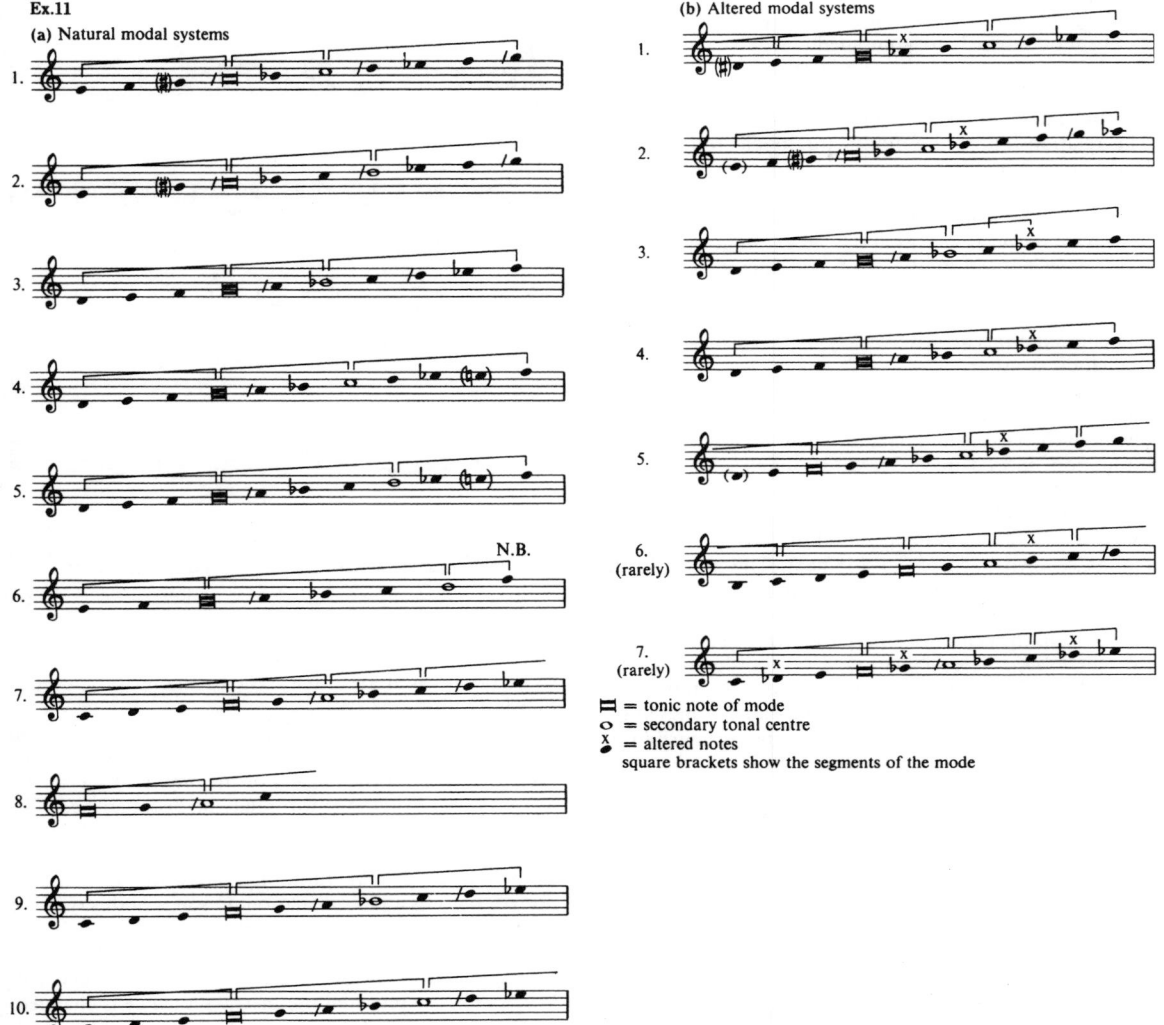

Ex.11

(a) Natural modal systems

(b) Altered modal systems

☐ = tonic note of mode
○ = secondary tonal centre
x = altered notes
square brackets show the segments of the mode

one holding the tonic throughout. Similarly the fair degree of stability of the secondary tonal centre is clear when three instruments are played and two hold the notes of the two tonal centres of the scale. At the end all come together on the *finalis*. The secondary tonal centre acts as the dominant note, from its frequent occurrence in the melody, its metrical emphasis and its more important role in the melodic contour in relation to the other degrees. It may be a 3rd, 4th or 5th above the tonic. In the closing part of the melody the secondary tonal centre usually relinquishes its role to the degrees immediately below, which then lead the melody in sequence to the *finalis*. In the process of melodic development each segment of the mode can serve as a new tonic segment, and if the melody is non-modulating the original tonic segment reestablishes its function later.

The *finalis* of each mode is linked with a certain degree of the basic diatonic scale and can be transposed only by a perfect 4th. For this reason the modal systems are in a sense also tonal systems. The scales of the chief modes are shown in ex.11 with their complete range of a 10th, to illustrate their differences fully.

In the old theory of Armenian music the concept of mode was part of a broader concept of *dzayn* ('voice'), which when used in relation to religious music implied specific melodic patterns and ways of developing the cantilena, to be linked with the various modes. The modes are all independent systems with a definite semantic character, and each of these is peculiar to a particular range of emotional expression. Within the limits of one cantilena they can occur in various combinations, as modal (sometimes also modal-tonal) modulation or deviation leading to an increase in melodic tension; in the old Armenian music theory such a modulation was called *zartughut'yun*. Possibilities include a combination of modes with various tonics (in the simplest cases with various secondary tonal centres) within the same scale; a combination of modes with various scales using the same tonic; and a combination of modes with various scales and various tonics. In the first and third cases the second (modulated) tonic is usually a major 2nd above or below the original or a major or minor 3rd or perfect 4th below it. The modes which are combined may have the same or different tendencies; when modulation occurs it is (in descending order of frequency) a transition from major to minor, from minor to minor or from minor to major. The relationship of the modes (or modal tonalities) is based on common traits.

The characteristics of the modal system apply to all branches of Armenian folk music with a slight reservation: in peasant music as well as in the old *gusan* music and the folk *tagher* natural modes are predominant, with fairly simple alterations and combinations, while in urban folk music and especially in *ashugh* songs complex alterations and combinations are also widely used. This also applies to melodic contour.

The melodic pattern ('intonation') of Armenian folk music is also diatonic. In the expressive sense it is distinctively natural and balanced, and is close to spoken intonation; indeed in village and *ashugh* songs certain musical phrases are often perceived as melodized speech. In spite of the close tie between the musical contour and the words (both in general mood and in details), each retains its own logic of development. The musical side dominates because melismatic development of the melody is often found alongside the syllabic principle. The melody also governs the general form; the text, which is expanded by repetition and exclamations, is subordinate to the musical form. Melodically, a flowing wave-like movement prevails, usually even but also with a short rising and a relatively long descending pattern. Skips (primarily upwards) occur, if at all, in opening structures, which are always completed with a wave-like movement.

One of the most typical forms of composition of the peasant melody is as follows: at the beginning the core motif appears, composed of the tonic or secondary modal centre (heard either at once or preceded by an upward skip) and the notes surrounding it. This motif (or part of it) is then varied rhythmically and melodically, constantly expanding horizontally or vertically, and a definite rhythmic-melodic structure develops; phrases and sections are usually unequal, and the melodic culmination stands out. A rapid opening is usually followed by a slow denouement. Ex.12a shows a song, ex.12b its motivic structure. It is this principle of varying the core motif that makes it possible to create an expanded and expressive melody from only four or five notes. Sometimes the basis of a melody is a complete phrase, and its relatively developed modal-melodic variant becomes an independent 'central section' (see above, ex.2), after which the first phrase is repeated in part or in full (reprise). In professional lyric monodies the form expanded by variation is still more highly developed Such devices of melodic structure are distinctive adaptations of motivic-thematic development. In one form or another they are characteristic of songs in all the branches of Armenian folk music. A second rule can also be discerned: these elementary melodic cells have their own characteristic melodic structure and modal features in the different song types, in accordance with the genre and emotional mood of the song. In this way the emotional mood, the modal-melodic features and the genre to which the cantilena belongs all have a determining effect on each other, and this interdetermination has traditional stable forms. The use of grace notes and mordents in Armenian melodies is

Ex.12 Lyric song, with its motivic structure; transcr. Komitas (Komitas, 1931)

rather limited, and they are more characteristic of *ashugh* songs. In peasant songs, however, the notes which appear to be ornamental are often basic to the melody, even if they are short.

The possibilities of rhythmic variation in Armenian folk music seem limitless, as may be seen in the improvisations of the players of the *dhol* and the *zurna*. Three types of rhythmic form may be distinguished. The first is the dance form in which relatively short rhythmic figures follow each other, repeated or slightly varied, with simple correlation of durations and with much use of dotted rhythms and syncopation. In songs of this type the number of rhythmic units usually equals the number of syllables. The second is the song form in which the rhythmic figures are quite broad and usually unrepeated. When they are repeated the metric sequence is changed; in any case the metric units do not correspond to each other. In songs in this form there is melismatic development, so that the number of rhythmic units is always greater than the number of syllables. The third is the recitative or improvisatory form in which the metre is free and the pulsation of time is produced not by metric but by separate rhythmic units, which can themselves change; the relation between the lengths is more marked and is irregular. In the songs with this rhythmic form a vocalization on one syllable follows every syllabic motif. These three rhythmic forms are characteristic in both vocal and instrumental music. Each may be said to be more characteristic of certain genres of song than others, but there is often a combination or interpenetration of two or all three forms. The special quality of rhythm in Armenian folk music is also emphasized by metric variety: along with the simple and compound metres many mixed metres are used (5/8, 7/8, 8/8, 9/8, 10/8, 11/8 etc.).

Polyphony has been little studied. Armenian folk music has traditionally been regarded as monophonic, although Komitas observed that in it 'one finds cases which show signs of true two-part singing'. A sustained part or drone, probably taken from folk instrumental music, was known in the Middle Ages in professional vocal monodic music (called *dzaynaṙut'yun* in old Armenian music theory). In folksinging with instrumental accompaniment and in ensemble playing this part is held by a single instrument or group of instruments. On a single instrument it may be played by one or two strings, or on a bagpipe by one pipe. The sustained pitch, usually the tonic, may be on the level of the melody or below or above it. It may be unbroken or interrupted; on percussion instruments it may be in the form of tremolo. It may consist of one note or of an ostinato phrase. The modal digressions of the melody can take place against the background of this part. Where a melody revolves directly around the sustained note and the untempered intervals (especially those smaller than a semitone) are more clearly perceived, sharp dissonances occur and the sustained note produces a remarkable artistic effect. In addition players of the *dhol* or *dap'* often strike various parts of the skin obtaining different pitches and timbres so that the instrument produces two-part music. Of general interest also is a polyphony of timbre in ensemble playing at the octave or in unison, when short phrases are added to the basic melody at its rhythmic pauses; heterophony also occurs. These are improvisatory devices, but they are linked with definite traditions.

Polyphonic elements are widely used in antiphonal vocal music: antiphony is divided into that arising spontaneously in natural conditions and that created deliberately. The former, like heterophony, is directly connected with improvisation and occurs in work songs, at home and in the field, performed by two or three people: ex.1 above is such a domestic work song, for grinding grain. Here the woman with the best voice or the leader of the work sings the main melodic line, and her co-worker performs the added phrases or exclamations. The antiphony during farm work, especially during ploughing, is more elaborate. Each member of the working group has his specific function in the work and in the singing. Ex.13 is an excerpt from a *hoṙovel* noted down by Komitas (for full version see Shaverdian, 1959, p.339).

What has been called a 'premeditated' type of antiphony is that found in ritual songs (wedding and carnival songs and songs of young girls foretelling the future), love-songs and other duets and dance-songs. This is basically traditional responsorial singing by a soloist and a chorus, or two soloists or two choruses: ex.14 shows a girls' lyrical dance-song. Komitas found an example of two-part singing during a circle-dance, in which the second part was in harmony with the first, an unusual feature: in songs with polyphonic features, one of the parts is almost always a continuation of the other.

The characteristics common to Armenian folk arts can be observed in the general 'emotional tone' and also in details of composition. The two most important of these are: the asymmetry of the component parts which form a balanced whole, a 'symmetry of asymmetry', while producing an internal dynamism; and the economy of expressive means and the avoidance of extremes, resulting in a particular restraint of expression, a concentration of thought and feeling. These characteristics are manifested in music and also in architecture, bas-reliefs, artistic miniatures, carpets and embroideries.

9. FOLK MUSIC DURING THE 20TH CENTURY. During the 20th century, especially since the beginning of Soviet rule in 1920, the life and ways of the Armenian people changed radically. The security of life, the decisive reconstruction and the swift development of the economy have brought

Ex.13 *Horhovel*, Vardablur, Lori region; transcr. Komitas (Shaverdian, 1959)

Ex.14 Girls' lyrical dance-song, transcr. Komitas (*Zeitschrift für armenische Philologie*, i/1, 1901)

in music in Armenia. The modern Armenian State Folk Song and Dance Ensemble was created and for a long time directed by the choral conductor T'atul Altiunian (1901–73); this group has gained recognition far beyond the borders of its own country. Old and new folksongs and *ashugh* songs are also performed on the stage, for radio and for television by folk musicians. Special organizations such as the House of Folk Creation and the Choral Society of Armenia arrange competitions for these musicians and for professional and amateur folk music ensembles, and organize song festivals for the entire country.

Folksong has played a great role in the development of Armenian composed music. In the 19th century the creative genre of folksong arrangement arose; it still retains its importance today. Folk music formed the basis of a significant part of the nationalistic compositions of Komitas, and such melodies or their stylistic features have been used in various forms in the works of Alexander Spendiarian, Romanos Melik'ian, Armen Tigranian, Aram Khachaturian and many other composers.

BIBLIOGRAPHY

COLLECTIONS

Komitas: *Shar Akna zhoghovrdakan ergeri* [Series of Akn folksongs] (Vagharshapat, 1895) [in Armenian notation]
S. Demurian: *K'nar*(St Petersburg, 1908) [in European notation]
S. Melik'ian and A.Ter-Ghevondian: *Shiraki erger* [Songs from Shirak] (Tbilisi, 1917)
S. Melik'ian and G.Gardashian: *Vana zhoghovrdakan erger* [Folksongs from Van] (Yerevan, 1927–8)
Komitas: *Zhoghovrdakan erger* [Folksongs] (Yerevan, 1931)
Sayat'-Nova: *Erger* [Songs] (Yerevan, 1946, 2/1963)
Sheram: *Erger* [Songs] (Yerevan, 1948, 2/1959)
S. Melik'ian: *Hay zhoghovrdakan erger ev parerger* [Armenian folksongs and dances] (Yerevan, 1949–52)
Komitas: *Hay zhoghovrdakan erger ev parerger* [Armenian folksongs and dances] (Yerevan, 1950)
Djivani: *Erger* [Songs] (Yerevan, 1955)
Gusan Ashot: *Erger* [Songs] (Yerevan, 1958)
H. Harut'unian: *Manyak: zhoghovadsu hay zhoghovrdakan ergeri* ['Manyak': a collection of Armenian folksongs] (Yerevan, 1958)
S. Lisitsian: *Starinnïye armianskiye plyaski i teatral'nïye predstavleniya* [Old Armenian dances and theatrical presentations] (Yerevan, 1958–72)
Gusan Havasi: *Erger* [Songs] (Yerevan, 1961)
Gusan Shahen: *Erger* [Songs] (Yerevan, 1964)
M. T'umadjian: *Hayreni erg u ban* [Folksongs] (Yerevan, 1972–86)
A. K'ocharian: *Hay gusanakan erger* [Armenian gusan songs] (Yerevan, 1976)
A. P'ahlevanian: *Hayreni erger* [Folksongs] (Yerevan, 1980)
N. T'ahmizian: *Voskepo'rik: Hay ergi goharner* [Voskeporik: selection of Armenian folksongs] (Yerevan, 1982)
A. P'ahlevanian and A. Sahakian: *T'alin: Haykakan zhoghovrdakan erger ev nvagner* [T'alin: Armenian folksongs and melodies] (Yerevan, 1984)
A. Brutian: *Ramkakan mrmundjner* [Peasant melodies], ed. M. Brutian (Yerevan, 1985)
M. Brutian and A.P'ahlevanian: *Hayrenakan meds paterazmë hay zhoghovrdakan ev gusanakan ergerum* [The Great Patriotic War (1941–5) in Armenain folksongs and the songs of the *gusanner*] (Yerevan, 1995)
A. Sahakian and A.P'ahlevanian: 'Sasna dsŕer' dyutsaznavep: aṙaspelakan ënderk', *Vipakan kaṙuyts, vipasanakan eghanak* [The heroic epic 'Sasun daredevils': the mythological roots, epic structure, method of delivery] (Pasadena, CA, 1996) [incl. musical exx.]
M. Manukian: *Martunu shrdjani zhoghovrdakan erger* [Songs of the Matuni region of Armenia] (Yerevan, 1997) [Eng. summary]

STUDIES

V. Korganov: *Kavkazskaya muzïka* [Caucasian music] (Tbilisi, 1900, 2/1908)
Komitas: *Zeitschrift für armenische Philologie*, i/1 (1901)

about new intellectual interests. These were also reflected in folk music, the chief genres of which have continued to exist. Those connected with the old way of life and old forms of work died out, some were modernized and some new ones arose. Themes acquired new elements: alongside the eternal personal motifs there were also contemporary social ones. Television and radio as well as the recording industry have also exerted an important influence over the development of Armenian music, especially in the urban centres where such technologies have increased enormously the interaction between the cultures of various nations.

The *ashugh* tradition continues, in spite of the fact that there are now many centres of professional training in literature and music, but with one important change: the *ashugh* songs are not only spread orally but also published. Contemporary *ashughner*, obviously wishing to emphasize their devotion to the ancient national art call themselves *gusanner*. The songs of these modern *gusanner*, while retaining traditional *ashugh* poetic and musical forms (especially the oratorical manner of expression) have also become relatively simple and clear optimistic subjects and views of life predominate. Among the many 20th-century *gusanner*, some of the most gifted were Gusan Sheram (1857–1938), Havasi (1896–1978), Ashot (1907–86), Shahen (1909–90), and Lgit' (1908–96).

Folksong and dance ensembles and orchestras of folk instruments were organized by professional musicians as early as the 1880s, and these brought folk music to the concert stage. A pioneer in this activity was the composer and choral conductor Khristofor Kara-Murza (1856–1902). The teaching of traditional instruments is now a professional activity and an integral part of the programme for all the educational establishments specializing

Komitas: 'La musique rustique arménienne', *BSIM*, iii (1907), 472–90

Komitas: *Hay geghdjuk erazhshtut'iwn* [Armenian peasant music] (Paris, 1938)

Komitas: *Hodvadsner ev usumnasirut'yunner* [Articles and Studies], ed. R. T'erlemezian (Yerevan, 1941)

M. Abeghian, ed.: *Sasna dsřer* [The heroes of Sasun], ii/2 (Yerevan, 1951) [epic song incl. transcr.]

Kh. Kushnarian: *Voprosï istorii i teorii armianskoy monodicheskoy muzïki* [Questions on the history and theory of Armenian monody] (Leningrad, 1958)

Ř. At'aian: *Haykakan khazayin notagrut'yune: usumnasirut'ian ev verdsanut'yan hartser* [Armenian khaz notation: questions of study and transcription (Yerevan, 1959)

E. Khanzadian: 'Haykakan hin erazhshtakan gordsik'neře' [Old Armenian musical instruments], *Hayastani Patmakan T'angarani ashkhatut'yunner*(1959), no.5, pp.63–93

A. Shahverdian: *Ocherki po ostorii armyanskoy muzïki XIX–XX vekov* [Sketches of the history of 19th- and 20th-century Armenian music] (Moscow, 1959)

Ř. At'aian: *Gusan Havasi* (Moscow, 1962)

V.M. Belyayev: 'Muzïkal'naya kul'tura Armenii', *Ocherki po istorii muzïki narodov SSSR* [The musical culture of Armenia: outline of the history of the music of the peoples of the USSR], ii, ed. G.A. Balter (Moscow, 1963), 82–204

A. K'och'arian: 'P'oghayin erazhshtakan gordsik'neře Hayastanum' [Armenian wind instruments], *Patma-banasirakan handes* (1963), no.3 p.163

G. Levonian: *Erker* [Collected works] (Yerevan, 1963)

M. Manukian: 'Sovetahay gusanakan arvestě' [Soviet Armenian gusan art], *Patma-banasirakan handes* (1963), no.2, p.117

A. T'adevosian: *S. Melik'ianě ev hay zhoghovrdakan ergě* [S. Melik'ian and Armenian folksong] (Yerevan, 1964)

Ř. At'aian: *Armyanskaya narodnaya pesnya* [Armenian folksong] (Moscow, 1965)

A. Tamburist: *Rukovodstvo po vostochnoy muzïke* [Handbook of oriental music], ed. N. T'ahmizian (Yerevan, 1968)

Komitasakan: Sbornik issledovaniy [Collection of studies], ed. Ř. At'aian (Yerevan, 1969–81)

G. Geodakian: *Komitas* (Yerevan, 1969)

M. Brutian: *Hay zhoghovrdakan eraszhshtakan steghdsagordut'yun: geghdjkakan erg* [Armenian folk music: peasant music] (Yerevan, 1971)

M. Brutian: 'Ladovaya sistema armyanskoy narodnoy (krest'yanskoy) muzïki' [Modal system of Armenian folk (peasant) music], *Problemï muzïkal'nogo fol'klora narodov SSSR*, iii, ed. I.I. Zemtsovsky (Moscow, 1973), 226

M. Brutian: *Hay zhoghovrdakan erazhshtakan steghdsagordsut'yun*, i: *Geghdjkakan erg* [Armenian folk music, i: Peasant songs] (Yerevan, 1971)

A. Sarian-Harut'unian: 'Hay k'aghak'ayin zhoghovrdakan ergarvestě' [Armenian urban folksong], *Hay azgagrut'yun ev banahyusut'yun*, iv (Yerevan, 1973), 83–174

A. P'ahlevanian: 'Printsipï notirovaniya armyanskikh narodnïkh pesen' [The principles of notating Armenian folksongs], *Haykakan SSH gitut'yunneri akademiayi teghekagir* (Yerevan, 1976), no.8, p.14

A. Tsistsikian: *Haykakan agheghnayin arvestě* [The instrumental art of the bow in Armenia] (Yerevan, 1977) [Eng. summary]

N. T'ahmizian: *Teoriya muzïki drevny Armenii* [Theory of music in ancient Armenia] (Yerevan, 1977) [Eng. summary]

A. P'ahlevanian: 'O roli narodnogo tvorchestva v muzïkal'hoy kul'ture sovetskoy Armenii' [On the role of folk art in the musical culture of Soviet Armenia], *Muzïkal'naya kul'tura Armyanskoy SR* (*Sbornik statey*), ed. M. Berko (Moscow, 1985), 367–95

G. Geodakian: 'Chertï ladovoy sistemï armyanskoy narodnoy muzïki' [Features of the modal system in Armenian folk music], *Traditsii i sovremennost'. Voprosï armyanskoy muzïki* (*Sbornik statey, kniga 1*), ed. G. Geodakian and M. Rukhkian (Yerevan, 1986), 7–40

A. Shahverdian: *Komitas*, ed. Ř. At'aian and N. T'ahmizian (Moscow, 1989)

N. T'ahmizian: *Komitasě ev hay zhoghovoordi erazhshtakan zhařangut'yuně* [Komitas and the musical legacy of Armenian notation] (Pasadena, CA, 1994)

H. Asadourian: *Komitas vardapeti het: Hay ergi arahetnerov* [With Komitas Vardapet: through Armenian song] (Tenafly, NJ, 1994)

N. T'ahmizian: *Sayat'-Novan ev hay gusana-ashughakan erg-erazhshtut'yuně* [Sayat'-Nova and the Armenian minstrel tradition] (Pasadena, CA, 1995)

G. Geodakian: 'Sistema khazovoy notopisi i vozmozhnosti yeyo rasshifrovki' [The *khaz* system of notation and the possibilities of deciphering it], *Traditsii i sovremennost'. Voprosï armyanskoy muzïki* (*Sbornik statey, kniga 2*), ed. G. Geodakian, M. Rukhkian and A. Sarian (Yerevan, 1996), 45–67

G. Geodakyan: 'Funktsional'nïye svyazi tonov v zvukovïsotnoy sisteme armyanskoy narodnoy muzïki' [The functional link between notes in the pitch system of Armenian folk music], ibid., 78–108

C. Dowsett: *Sayat'-Nova: an 18th-century Troubadour: a Literary and Biographical Study* (Leuven, 1997)

II. Church music

1. History. 2. Chant genres. 3. Notation. 4. Modal system and style.

1. HISTORY.   In 301 CE St Grigor the Illuminator converted King Trdat III (Tiridates) to Christianity; Armenia thus became the first officially Christian state. Having participated in the first three ecumenical councils only, the Church of Armenia belongs to the Lesser Eastern Orthodox group of churches. At the beginning of the 5th century, during the Catholicate of St Sahak Part'ew (387–436), St Mesrop Mashtots (*d* 440) devised the Armenian alphabet. The translation of the Bible into Armenian, which immediately followed, became the starting point for the development of a distinctive tradition of liturgical music. *Grabar*, the classical Armenian language, has remained the ritual language of the Armenian Church. The Divine Liturgy (*Patarag* is based on the liturgy of St Athanasius of Alexandria and the Alexandrian text of St Basil of Caesarea; it was reformed in the 12th century by Catholicos St Nerses IV Klayetsi, known as 'Shnorhali' ('Gracious').

Knowledge of the early periods of Armenian liturgical music is scarce and derives primarily from events and facts documented in medieval sources (information that was formerly transmitted orally). However, the historical development of the early rite and its music can be reconstructed from liturgical manuscripts, in which the archaic structure is largely preserved. During the first centuries of Christianity in Armenia, the greater part of the liturgy consisted of psalms and canticles whose chants were probably adapted from local melodies. Hymns such as *P'ark' i bardzuns* (Gloria in excelsis), *Luys zevart'* (*Phōs hilaron*) and *Surb Astuads* (Trisagion) were also gradually introduced. The organization of traditional melodic patterns into an eight-mode system is ascribed to the 8th-century theorist and hymnographer Step'anos Siwnetsi.

As the liturgy evolved, the number of chants increased and new forms appeared. Sacred song blossomed during the Armenian renaissance of the 10th–13th centuries, a period of political stability that favoured urban expansion and the flourishing of art and trade. By this time there was already a substantial repertory of liturgical chants whose music, with its diverse melodic turns and elaborate melismas, was often quite complex and ornate. A complete Proper repertory of the texts, of which there were regional melodic variants, was established by the 15th century, and many new chants continued to appear up to the 19th. The main melodic variants to have come down into the 20th century developed in diaspora centres such as Constantinople (where several schools existed), the Mekhitarist monastery in Venice, the Armenian monastery in Jerusalem and the Armenian communities of Egypt and

Iran. The origins of these variants derive from the musical traditions of the monasteries of Cilicia and Greater Armenia.

2. CHANT GENRES.   The Armenian liturgy is completely interwoven with music. Only the prayers and collects are spoken; the rest consists of three main forms of musical interpolation: (1) sung recitative, such as simple psalmody, introits and litanies, with a limited range; (2) chants, including the majority of *sharakan* (canonical hymns), based on traditional melodic patterns; and (3) chants with particular melodies, such as the *tagh*, *meghedi* and *erg*. The forms in all three categories are used for psalmody, for the chants of the Divine Liturgy and for the Office chants of the Book of Hours (*zhamagirkʿ*).

The substance of the Armenian Church's musical system is the *sharakan* repertory of more than 1300 cyclically organized chants contained in the Book of *Sharakan* (modern term *sharaknots*), which developed from the hymnbook compiled by Barsegh Tjon in the 7th century. In the earliest period these were sung during Offices, alternating with psalms and canticles; later, they replaced several psalms and canticles, the first verses of which were retained as introductions and intonations. Little is known about their early history: *sharakan* authors were listed only from the 13th century onwards, and their names reflect the hieratic character of the repertory. Thus, St Mesrop Mashtots and St Sahak Part'ew are traditionally considered to be the first composers of the genre, although the oldest attested chant of the present Book of *Sharakan* dates from the 7th century. Almost a fifth of all present canonical *sharakan* chants were composed by Catholicos St Nerses IV Klayetsi (1112–73). The melodic patterns of the *sharakan* have their own developed structure, but they are subordinate to the texts and are adapted according to the prosody of the words. Depending on the occasion, the same *sharakan* may be sung in its rapid, medium or slow variants, for which the melodic pattern is again adapted. (For a transcription of a *sharakan* for Resurrection Sundays see below, ex.15*b*.)

The *tagh* and the *meghedi*, which are no longer clearly distinct genres, are thought to have developed in about the 10th and 11th centuries. Their rich ornamentation and long phrases may have influenced some slow *sharakan* chants. The *gandz*, which have all but disappeared from the repertory, were originally litanies, usually in recitative style and of limited range; the handful that remain are no longer in litany form but have been transformed into chant-like melodies. The *erg* ('song'), the oldest of the genres, is the term used for the chants of the Book of Hours, most of which survive in numerous variants.

With the development of Armenian church ritual over the centuries, several liturgical books were compiled at different periods: the *zhamagirkʿ* (Book of Hours), *Pataragamatyuts* (Book of the Divine Liturgy) and the Book of *Sharakan* are for daily use; the *tagharan*, *gandzaran* and *ergaran* are specific collections of optional chants (the *zhamagirkʿ* also includes optional chants); and the *mashtots* contains canons for ordinations, baptisms and funerals, among other rites.

3. NOTATION.   An ekphonetic notation developed from prosodic accents was introduced into the Armenian Church in about the 9th century and was used primarily for the liturgical recitation of the Bible. During the same period a system of neumes, known as *khaz* notation, also

appeared (fig.2). The latter subsequently developed during the period of the Cilician kingdom (1187–1375) and was later adapted to the evolving traditional melodic patterns and new chant forms.

The most important reform of *khaz* notation and compiling of *khaz* transcriptions of the Book of *Sharakan* was undertaken by Grigor, nicknamed 'Khul' ('deaf'), during the reign of Levon II (1187–1219). Manuals called *manrusum*, in which chants notated in *khaz* are arranged according to the degree of difficulty, date from the Cilician period. The continuous contact of monks from Greater Armenia with the Cilician monasteries promoted musical exchange and evolution; it was through such interaction that the development of *khaz* notation was brought from the Cilician kingdom to Greater Armenia. Though highly elaborate, *khaz* notation remained a series of indications, valid only within the context of an orally transmitted, living tradition.

During the 16th century the teaching of *khaz* notation began to decline, and the transmission of liturgical chants was increasingly dependent on oral methods. In 1812 a modern system with diastematic characteristics, called 'church notation', was developed in Constantinople through the collective efforts of Baba Hambardzum Limondjian (1768–1839), Fr Minas Bejeshkian (1777–1851) of the Venice Mekhitarist congregation, Andon Duzian (1765–1814) and Hagop Duzian (1793–1847). Now known as 'Armenian modern musical notation', it was used to transcribe the canonical repertory of liturgical chant in different variants. (An example of this notation, together with a transcription into Western notation, is given in Ex.15.) The official publication of the transcriptions began in 1874 at the instigation of Catholicos Georg IV (1813–82), who had received his musical training at

Ex.15 *Sharakan* for Resurrection Sundays

(a) Armenian modern notation   (ed. Tashjian, 1875, p.671)

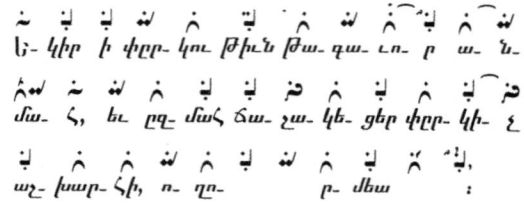

(b) Version of Mekhitarist Monastery, Venice (Dayan, 1960-76, v, 450)

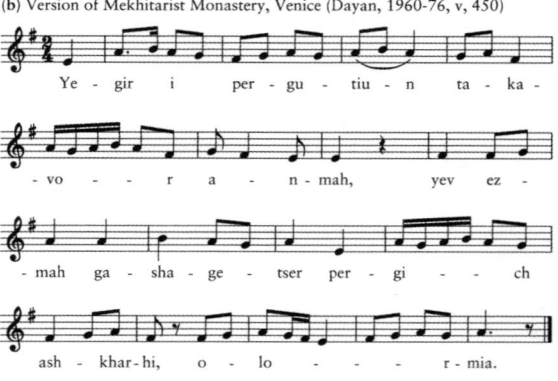

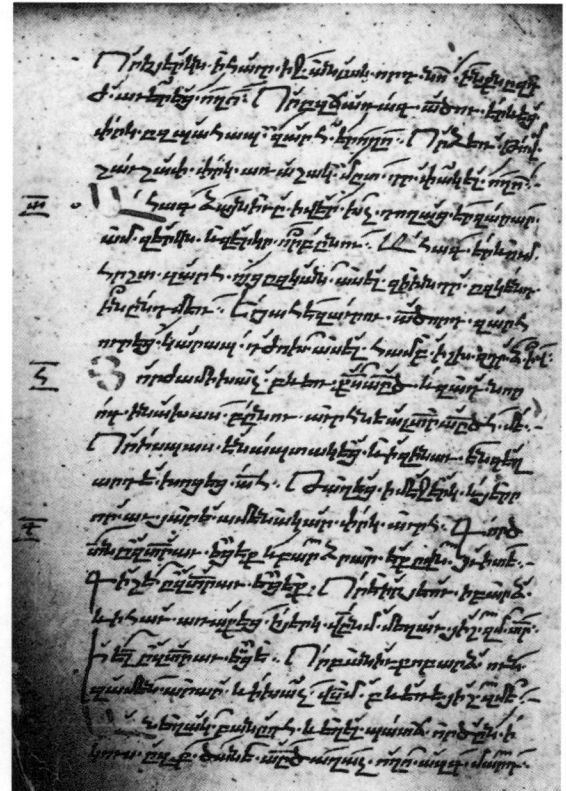 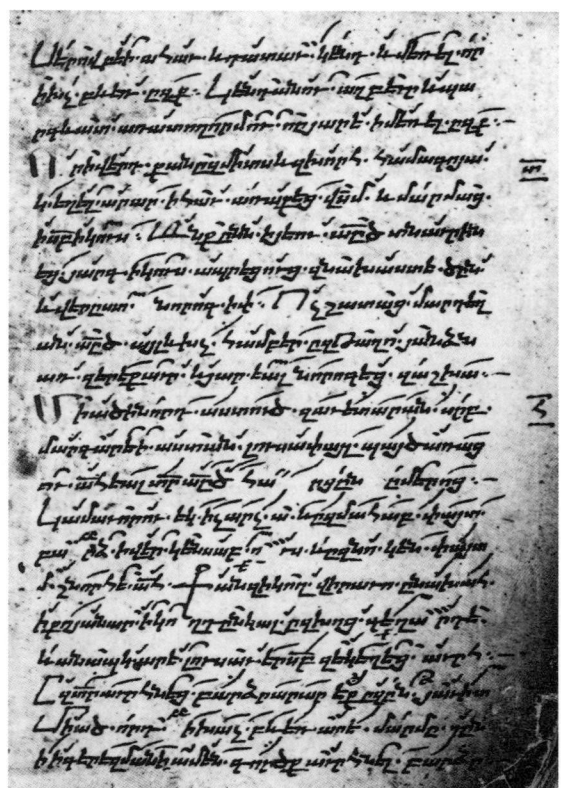

2. 'Khaz' notation in a 'Sharaknots' (Book of 'Sharakan'), 1312 (Vienna, Library of the Mekhitarist Monastery 202, ff.88v–89r)

Constantinople. When these transcriptions were begun, however, the elaborate melodies of numerous chants had already been forgotten; with the destruction of Armenian monasteries in 1915–16, further loss of the repertory occurred as many songs and variant traditions disappeared. Several books using Armenian modern musical notation have since been published, and manuscript notebooks belonging to ordained choristers remain in use or are preserved in libraries. Western notation has also been used since the early 20th century, especially for polyphonic versions of the Divine Liturgy and other frequently performed chants. Modern studies of *khaz* notation began with the work of Eghia Tntessian (1834–81) and Fr Komitas (1869–1935).

4. MODAL SYSTEM AND STYLE. Because no medieval Armenian music treatise has survived, information on chant theory must be sought in the repertory itself, especially from the *sharakan* chants, which are organized according to the system of the eight modes (*Ut' dzayn*). The Armenian *oktōēchos* is formally divided into four modes called *dzayn* ('voice'; equivalent to the Byzantine *ēchos*) and four termed *koghm* ('side'; the Byzantine *ēchos plagios*). There are also a number of modes called *dardzuatzk'* ('strophe'), ex.15 *steghi* ('branched') and *zartughi* ('deviated'), each classified under one or other of the eight modes. Approximately 20 modes are combined in the Armenian *oktōēchos*, each containing a number of different melodic patterns. The modes are defined by their characteristic melodic formulae and interval combinations. Pythagorean diatonic, natural diatonic and chromatic intervals are used with varying divisions. The definition also includes such characteristic features as the hierarchy of the fundamental, final, leading note and other degrees, as well as the interpretation required for each degree, for example, use of the full voice, vibrating the voice within a very small interval, or making minor pitch changes according to the upwards or downwards motion of the melody.

The main characteristics of melodic development in Armenian chant include movement within the natural 4th, direct passage between intervals of 3rds and 4ths, and slow upwards and rapid downwards (somewhat ornamental) progressions. A drone sung on the vowel '*u*', either on the fundamental degree or on the first degree of the basic interval (which in many cases is the same pitch) is frequently used to accompany solo singing and slow group songs such as processional chants.

In the 19th century, with the participation of polyphonic choirs and the organ in the celebration of the Divine Liturgy, equal temperament was introduced. Settings of the Divine Liturgy include those of Makar Ekmalian (1856–1905), Levon Chilingirian (1862–1932), Fr KOMITAS (1869–1935) and Khoren Mekhanedjian (*b* 1937). During the latter half of the 20th century the singing of traditional modal chant at the liturgy declined, and knowledge and teaching of the Armenian *oktōēchos* – still the musical basis of the Offices – has also diminished. The practice has nevertheless been kept alive by groups of ordained choristers led by precentors. Although notation is used to a certain extent, the musical training of such choristers relies mainly on oral transmission.

BIBLIOGRAPHY

EDITIONS

N. Tashjian, ed.: *Dzaynagreal ergetsoghut'iwnk' Srboy Pataragi* [Musical transcription of the chants of the Divine Liturgy] (Vagharshapat, 1874, 2/1878) [in Armenian modern notation]

N. Tashjian, ed.: *Dzaynagreal sharakan hogewor ergots* [Musical transcription of *sharakan* chants] (Vagharshapat, 1875) [in Armenian modern notation]; i (Yerevan, 1997) [in Western notation]

N. Tashjian, ed.: *Ergk' dzaynagrealk' i zhamagrots Hayastaneayts Surb Ekeghetswoy* [Musical transcription of the chants of the Armenian Church's Book of Hours] (Vagharshapat, 1877) [in Armenian modern notation]

M. Ekmalyan, ed.: *Die Gesänge der heiligen Messe der armenisch-apostolischen Kirche* (Leipzig and Vienna, 1896) [in Western notation]

A. Apkar, ed.: *Melodies of the Holy Apostolic Church of Armenia* (Calcutta, 1897, enlarged 2/1920) [in Western notation]

K. Mehterian, ed.: *Tonakarg dzaynagreal* [Ceremonial with musical transcriptions] (Constantinople, 1921, enlarged, Cairo, 1952) [in Armenian modern notation]

V. Sargsian, ed.: *Komitas Vardapet: Dashnaworeal ergetsoghut'iwnk' Srboy Pataragi* [Harmonized chants of the Divine Liturgy] (Paris, 1933/R)

Mayr Eghanak S. Pataragi [Mother-melody of the Divine Liturgy] (Istanbul, 1934) [in Armenian modern notation]

E. Tntesian, ed.: *Sharakan dzaynagreal* [Musical transcription of *sharakan* chants] (Istanbul, 1934) [in Armenian modern notation]

L.D. Daian, ed.: *Sharakan hayastaneayts ekeghetswoy/Les hymnes de l'église arménienne*, ii–viii (Venice, 1960–76) [in Western notation]

Arewagali ew hskumi erger [Sunrise Office and vigil chants] (Antelias, 1979) [in Western notation]

Meds Pahots Kirakiner [Canons for Lenten Sundays] (Antelias, 1981) [in Western notation]

Awag Shabat' [Canons for Holy Week] (Antelias, 1984) [in Western notation]

Awag Örhnut'iwnner [*Sharakan* chants for Resurrection Sundays] (Antelias, 1985) [in Western notation]

Meghediner, tagher ew gandzer [Melodies, odes and litanies] (Antelias, 1990) [in Western notation]

STUDIES

MGG2 (C. Hannick)

E. Tntesian: *Nkaragir ergots Hayastaneaytss ekeghetswoy* [Description of the hymns of the Armenian Church] (Constantinople, 1874/R)

Komitas Vardapet: 'Hayots ekeghetsakan eghanaknerě', *Ararat* (1894), no.7, pp.222–7; no.8, pp.256–60; Eng. trans. as 'The Church Melodies of the Armenians', in Nersession, 1998, pp.97–121

Komitas Vardapet: 'Hayots ekeghetsakan eghanaknerě 19. darum', *Ararat* (1897), no.5, pp.221–5; Fr. trans. as 'La musique religieuse arménienne au XIXe siècle', *Revue des études arméniennes*, new ser., xx (1986–7), 497–506; Eng. trans. as 'The Church music of the Armenians in the 19th century', in Nersession, 1998, pp.163–72

Komitas Vardapet: 'Die armenische Kirchenmusik, I: Das Interpunktionssystem des Armenier', *SIMG*, i (1899–1900), 54–64; Eng. trans. in Nersession, 1998, pp.143–56

N. Ter-Mikaëlian: *Das armenische Hymnarium: Studien zu seiner geschichtlichen Entwicklung* (Leipzig, 1905)

A. Hisarlian: *Patmut'iwn hay dzaynagrut'ean ew kensagrut'iwnk' erazhisht azganots, 1768–1909* [History of Armenian notation and biographies of Armenian musicians] (Constantinople, 1914)

Kh. S. Kushnarian: *Voprosi istorii i teorii armyanskoy monodicheskoy muziki* [Questions on the history and theory of Armenian monody] (Leningrad, 1958; Eng trans., ed. N.V. Nersession, 1998, as *Armenian Monodic Music: History and Theory*)

Ṙ.A. At'aian: *Haykakan khazayin notagrut'yuně: usumnasirutyan ev verdsanutian hartser* [Armenian *khaz* notation: questions of study and transcription] (Yerevan, 1959; Eng. trans., ed. N.V. Nersession, 1998, as *Armenian Neume System of Notation*)

R.A. Atajan: 'Armenische Chasen', *BMw*, x (1968), 65–82

N.K. T'ahmizian: 'Komitasě ev haykakan khazeri vertsanut'ean khndirě' [Komitas and the problem of deciphering Armenian neumes], *Patma-banasirakan handes*, iv (1969), 30–48

R.A. Atajan: 'Die armenische professionelle Liederkunst des Mittelalters', *Revue des études arméniennes*, new ser., vii (1970), 241–66; repr. in V. Nersession, ed.: *Essays on Armenian Music* (London, 1978)

N.K. T'ahmizian: 'Les anciens manuscrits musicaux arméniens et les questions relatives à leur déchiffrement', *Revue des études arméniennes*, new ser., vii (1970), 267–80; repr. in V. Nersession, ed.: *Essays on Armenian Music* (London, 1978)

B. Outtier: 'Recherches sur la genèse de l'octoéchos arménien', *EG*, xiv (1973), 129–211; repr. in V. Nersession, ed.: *Essays on Armenian Music* (London, 1978), 52–128

N.K. T'ahmizian: *Nerses Shnorhalin: ergahan ev erazhisht* [Nerses Shnorhali: composer and musician] (Yerevan, 1973)

V.N. Nersession, ed.: *Essays on Armenian Music* (London, 1978)

N.K. T'ahmizian: *Muzyka v drevnei i srednevekovoi Armenii* [Music in ancient and medieval Armenia] (Yerevan, 1982)

A. Ertlbauer: *Geschichte und Theorie der einstimmigen armenische Kirchenmusik: eine Kritik der bisherigen Forschung* (Vienna, 1985)

N.K. T'ahmizian: *Grigor Narekatsin ev hay erazhshtut'yuně, v–xv dd.* [Grigor Narekatsi and Armenian music, 5th–15th centuries] (Yerevan, 1985)

N.K. T'ahmizian: *Erazhshtut'yuně haykakan Kilikiayum* [Music in Cilician Armenia] (Yerevan, 1989)

A. Kerovpyan: 'Les *charakan* (*troparia*) et l'octoéchos arménien selon le *charaknots* (*tropologion* arménien) édité en 1875', *Aspects de la musique liturgique au Moyen-Age*, ed. C. Meyer (Paris, 1991) 93–123

A. Kerovpyan: 'Mündliche und schriftliche Überlieferung in der Musik der Armenier', *Armenien: Wiederentdeckung einer alten Kulturlandschaft*, ed. K. Platt (Bochum, 1995), 445–9 [exhibition catalogue]

A. Kerovpyan: 'Armenian Liturgical Chant; the System and Reflections on the Present Situation', *St Nersess Theological Review*, i (1996), 25–42

M. Bzheshkian: *Erazhshtut'iwn: or e hamaïot teghekut'iwn erazhshtakan skzbants elewejut'ean eghanakats ew nshanagrats khazits* [Music: a concise summary of musical principles, modal patterns and neumatic notation], ed. A. Kerovpian (Yerevan, 1997)

V.N. Nersession, ed.: *Armenian Sacred and Folk Music: Komitas* (Richmond, 1998)

A. Kerovpyan: *Manuel de notation musicale arménienne moderne* (Vienna, 1999)

V.N. Nersession: *The Armenian Neume System of Notation* (London, 1999)

SOUND RECORDINGS

Messe arménienne, Chorales réunies d'Istanbul, dir. J. Arslaniantz, ARAS 21003 (1966)

Chants de la liturgie arménienne, Choeurs Sipan-Komitas de Paris, dir. G. Aprikyan, Harmonia Mundi HM 5120 (1982) [originally issued in 1975]

Arménie: chants liturgique du Moyen-Age, dir. R. Atayan, Ocora–Radio France C559001 (1988) [originally issued in 1975]

Chants liturgiques arméniennes, Choir of the Mekhitarist Community of S Lazzaro, Venice, UNESCO: Anthologie des musiques traditionelles, Auvidis D8015 (1989) [chants for Lent and Easter; originally issued in 1975]

Chants liturgiques arméniennes, Ensemble Akn, dir. A. Kerovpyan, ALSUR CDAL274 (2000)

III. Opera, ballet, orchestral and chamber music

The growth of musics influenced by European art forms in the second half of the 19th century was brought about predominantly by the incorporation of two areas of eastern Armenia into Russia (one from Persia in 1828 and one from Turkey in 1878). Enforced emigration and the dispersal of Armenians in Europe and the East determined the development of Armenian culture; various Armenian societies, cultural and educational centres and publishing organizations sprang up, in Armenia as well as in Moscow, Tbilisi, St Petersburg, Baku, Constantinople, Paris, Venice and Vienna. Important roles were played by the Lazarian Institute (Moscow, 1815), the Nersessian College (Tbilisi,

1824), the Gevork'ian Theological Seminary (Vagharshapat [now Edjmiadsin], 1874) and by the K'nar musical society, set up in Constantinople on the initiative of G. Yeranian and Tigran Chukhajian, which published the periodicals *K'nar arevelian* ('Eastern lyre', 1857) and *K'nar Haykakan* ('Armenian lyre', from 1861). From the mid-19th century, arrangements of traditional and popular songs were made. Solo and choral performances became more frequent and the first small symphony orchestras were formed. Constantinople and Tbilisi became the biggest centres of musical culture for western and eastern Armenia; there were links with Western traditions in Constantinople and with Russia in Tbilisi. Various European genres, including opera, chamber music and romance, were adapted; Tigran Chukhajian, G. Yeranian and G. Korganian were the first composers of this trend. In 1868 Chukhajian composed the first Armenian opera, *Arshak Erkrord*, based on a historical patriotic theme. In the 1880s the systematic collection of folksongs and folkdances began. Khristofor Kara-Murza, Makar Yekmalian, Nikoghayos Tigranian, T'ashchian and Komitas laid the foundations of a new Armenian instrumental and choral culture, both secular and sacred, and were also associated with the nationalistic development of polyphony inspired by the harmonic style and tunes of folk music and by medieval Armenian church music. The central figure of the period was Komitas, who created a national compositional style and established Armenian musical scholarship.

In the early 20th century the first Armenian symphonic works were written, together with a new kind of national opera closely bound up with traditional music, for instance Armen Tigranian's lyrical opera *Anush* (1912). Armenian symphonic poems, overtures, suites, chamber music and vocal music were written by Aleksandr Spendiarian, Tigranian, Romanos Melik'ian, A. Ter-Ghevondian and Sarkis Barkhudarian. Spendiarian was the leading Armenian symphonic composer; his works, notable for their rich and expressive timbre, greatly influenced later Armenian composers. Skilful use of timbre and harmony is also characteristic of Melik'ian, the creator of a new style of romance (*Zmrukhti*, 1920). In the first few years after the establishment of the Soviet regime (1920–91) Yerevan, the capital of Armenia, became the centre of musical activity. In 1921 the Musical Studio was organized on the initiative of Melik'ian; in 1923 it was transformed into the conservatory (now the Komitas State Conservatory). Melik'ian also encouraged the formation of the first state choral ensemble. The opera and ballet theatre was opened in 1933; two years later it became the Spendiarian Armenian Theatre of Opera and Ballet. The Armenian PO, Choral Society and Composers' Union were founded in 1932, while the Komitas String Quartet was established in 1925. The highlights of native composition were the suite *Yerevan Sketches* (1925) and the opera *Almast* by Tumanian, as well as works by Ter-Ghevondian and Melik'ian, and organ music by K. K'ushnarian.

Armenian musicians were trained in the conservatories of Moscow and, particularly, Leningrad. Through the efforts of many composers over several decades, Armenian music developed a distinctive style that had reached maturity by the 1930s. Khachaturian laid down the principles of new symphonic thinking which, in addition to Spendiarian's idiom, became the determining factors for the development of Armenian music. He also influenced cultural development in Georgia, Azerbaijan and Soviet Central Asia.

In the 1930s Haro Stepan'ian composed several operas in a style novel for the period (including *Kaj Nazar*); operas and ballets were also written by A. Mailian, A. Ter-Ghevondian, A. Ayvazian, Sarkis Barkhudarian and Sergey Balasanian. Thematic versatility and associations with national literature, as well as the desire to depict contemporary events, were characteristic of the music of this period. There was also rapid development in choral music, romances, songs and arrangements of folktunes, which in turn influenced opera. The composers who became prominent in the 1940s and 1950s continued to base their work on Armenian heritage and to develop further the artistic principles of Spendiarian and Khachaturian. In this period the most important genre was the symphony, and works of the 1940s are notable for the increasing importance of patriotic themes, which determined the large scale and dramatic nature of the music. Khachaturian's Second Symphony (1943) is among the best-known wartime Soviet symphonies; other examples are Grigor Yeghiazarian's symphonic poem *Armenia* (1942) and Step'anian's two symphonies (1943–5). The patriotic theme was brilliantly expressed in Alexander Harut'unian's vocal symphony *Cantata on the Homeland* (1948). In the 1950s instrumental music flourished. The dramatic, epic and lyrical elements typical of Armenian music were integrated into a broader symphonic style, manifested in Khachaturian's ballet *Spartacus* (1954), the symphonies of Yeghiazarian, Harut'unian, Edgar Hovhanesian and Jivan Ter-Tatevosian, Harut'unian's Trumpet Concerto, A. Khudoian's Cello Concerto, the *Introduction and Perpetuum mobile* for violin and orchestra by Eduard Mirzoian, and Aṙno Babadjanian's *Herosakan Ballad*. Symphonic principles also found their way into chamber music.

A feature of Armenian music in the 1960s and 1970s has been the diversity and interaction of stylistic trends and genres: A. Adjemian's Symphony no.2 includes a solo voice; choral ballets have been written by K. Orbelian and Hovhanesian, and an opera-oratorio with pantomime by Avet Terterian; while Terterian's Symphony no.2 includes a solo tenor and choir. Composers have experimented with neo-Classical elements (e.g. Mirzoian in his Symphony, Mansurian in his Partita for orchestra, Harutunian in his Simphonietta, L. Sarian in his Violin Concerto and Gagik Hovunts in his orchestral Inventions); dodecaphony (in *Shest' kartin* (Six Pictures) for piano by Aṙno Babadjanian, Ter-Tatevosian's Second String Quartet, Mansurian's Piano Trio and E. Hayrapetian's oratorio *1915th*); and aleatory procedures (Terterian's second and third symphonies and Aristakesian's Simphonietta).

Since the 1970s Armenian composition has been characterized by the search for possibilities within the national style. Aram Khachaturian's music has been particularly influential on younger generations of composers, who increasingly regard Armenian music as part of the wider international culture. Within the stylistic variety, however, two main directions can be detected. Some composers have sought inspiration in the traditional monodic music. For example, E. Hovhannesian's opera-ballet *David of Sasun* is based on an Armenian epic and L. Astvatsatrian has used the modal structures of ancient Armenian music in his First Symphony. Other composers following a similar path include G. Hovunts (piano and violin concertos), S. Arghajanian (*Polymonodies* for strings), A. Voskanian (vocal works), Y. Erkanian (opera *St Shushanik*) and Hovhannesian. The other main direction has focussed on avant-garde techniques and the use of modern technology. Composers of such music include G. Eghiazarian, whose ballet *Ara Beautiful and Shamiram* uses both neo-impressionist and neo-expressionist styles, L. Sarian (Symphony and Passacaglia), Mansurian (*Preludes* for orchestra), Astvatsatrian (who uses spatial techniques and tape), and A. Zobrabian, whose chamber work *Elegy* employs microtonal heterophony.

BIBLIOGRAPHY

A. Hisarlian: *Patmut'yun hay dzaynargrut'ean ev kensagrutyunk' erazhisht azgaynots* [History of Armenian notation and biographies of musicians] (Constantinople, 1914)
M. Abeghian: 'Armianskaya dukhovnaya pesnya' [Armenian religious song], *Istoriya drevnearmianskoy literaturï*, i (Yerevan, 1948), 408
G. Tigranov: *Armianskiy muzikal'nïy teatr* [The Armenian music theatre] (Yerevan, 1956–60)
B. Asaf'yev: *Ocherki ob Armenii* [Sketches of Armenia] (Moscow, 1958)
K'. K'ushnarian: *Vosprosi istorii i teorii armianskoy monodicheskoy muziki*[Questions on the history and theory of Armenian monody] (Leningrad, 1958)
A. Shahverdian: *Ocherki po istorii armianskoy muziki XIX–XX vekov* [Sketches of the history of 19th- and 20th-century Armenian music] (Moscow, 1959; Armenian trans., 1959); Eng. trans. in N.V. Nersessian, ed., *Essays on Armenian Music* (London, 1978)
Muzika Sovetskoy Armenii (Moscow, 1960)
A. Barsamian and M.Harut'unian: *Hay erazhshtut'ean patmut'yun*[The history of Armenian music], i (Yerevan, 1968–96)
M. Muradian: *Hay erazhshtut'ean patmutyun'ë XIX darum ev XX dari skizbum*[The history of Armenian music in the 19th and early 20th centuries] (diss., U. of Yerevan, 1970)
M. Brutian: *Hay zhogkovodakan erazhshtakan steghdsegortsutyun'ë* [Armenian folk music works] (Yerevan, 1971, 2/1983)
M. Ter-Simonian: *Kamerno-instrumental'naya ansamblevaya muzika Armenii* [Chamber-instrumental ensemble music of Armenia] (Yerevan, 1974)
K. Khudabashian: *Armianskaya muzika na puti ot monodii k mnogogolosiyu* [Armenian music on the way from monody to polyphony] (Yerevan, 1977)
A. Tatevosian: *Edjer hay-rusakan erazhshtakan kaperi patmutyunits* [Pages from the history of musical links between Armenia and Russia] (Yerevan, 1977)
M. Rukhkian: *Armianskaya simfoniya* [The Armenian symphony] (Yerevan, 1980)
S. Sarkisian: *Voprosï sovremennoy armianskoy muzïki* [Problems in contemporary Armenian music] (Yerevan, 1983)
A. Grigorian: *Armianskaya kamerno-vokal'naya muzïka* [Armenian chamber vocal music] (Yerevan, 1982)
E. Pashinian: 'Superladovaya sistema armianskoy narodnoy muzïki i yeyo proyavleniye v tvorchestve sovremennïkh kompozitorov' [The super-modal tonal system of Armenian folk music and its appearance in the works of contemporary composers], *Theoretical Problems of non-European Musical Cultures* (Moscow, 1983), 104–54
M. Berko, K.Khudabashian and M. Ter-Simonian, eds.: *Muzikal'naya kul'tura Armianskoy SSR* [The musical culture of the Armenian SSR] (Moscow, 1985)
G. Geodakian and M.Rukhkian, eds.: *Traditsii i sovremennost'*[Traditions and the contemporary] (Yerevan, 1986, 2/1996)
R. Mazmanian: *Hay khorhrdayin erazhshtakan k'ianki taregrutyun'ë: 1946–60*[A chronicle of Soviet Armenian musical life, 1946–60] (Yerevan, 1986)
A. Arevshatian: 'Mashtots' zhoghovatsun vorpes hay midjnadarian erazhshtakan mshakuyti hushardzan [The 'Mashtots' collection as a monument of medieval Armenian musical culture] (Yerevan, 1991)
S. Koptev: *Muzikal'nye teroreticheskiye sistemy* [Theoretical systems in music] (Yerevan, 1992)
T. Brutian: *Hay erazhshtakan mshakuyti ashkharhaspyuř endjughner'ë* [The overseas sprouts of Armenian muic culture] (Yerevan, 1996)

ALINA PAHLEVANIAN (I), ARAM KEROVPYAN (II), SVETLANA SARKISYAN (III)

Armenreich, Bernhard. *See* AMENREICH, BERNHARD.

Armer, Elinor (*b* Oakland, CA, 6 Oct 1939). American composer and pianist. She studied composition at Mills College (BA 1961), the University of California, Berkeley (1966–8), and California State University, San Francisco (MA 1972). Her teachers included Milhaud and Leon Kirchner (composition), and Alexander Libermann (piano). In 1976 she was appointed to teach at San Francisco Conservatory of Music, where she was head of composition from 1985 to 1996. Eschewing such directions as serial writing and minimalism, she has developed an individual voice that draws together diverse materials through strong articulation of phrasing and gesture. Her compositions are often programmatic yet avoid musical literalism. Written in collaboration with the author Ursula K. Le Guin, *Uses of Music in Uttermost Parts* represents an imaginative cycle of eight separate works for various forces. In this fantasy journey through an archipelago each island puts music to extraordinary uses; for example as food, aphrodisiac, geology or as a means of survival. The first piece in this cycle, *The Great Instrument of the Geggerets*, employs a variety of styles, producing a wide range of expression: dense textures of sound mass occur alongside extended instrumental techniques, a tuneful waltz and allusions to ragtime. *Open and Shut*, the fifth work in the cycle, exemplifies her successful mix of playful and abstract elements. Her rich harmonic vocabulary is atonal – but not exclusively – and her scoring imaginative and vivid.

WORKS
(*selective list*)

Orch: Pearl, 1986; The Great Instrument of the Geggerets (U.K. Le Guin), nar, orch, 1988 [Uses of Music in Uttermost Parts no.1]
Chbr and solo inst: Thaw, pf, 1974; Recollections and Revel, vc, pf, 1978; Str Qt, 1983; The Seasons of Oling (Le Guin), nar, va, vc, pf, perc, 1987 [Uses of Music no.3]; Open and Shut (Le Guin), reader, ob/eng hn, cl/b cl, vn, vc, db, 1991 [Uses of Music no.5]; Sailing among the Pheromones, gui, mar, hp, tape, 1991 [Uses of Music no.6]; Mirror, Mirror, pf 4 hands, 1993; Oasis, hp, 1996
Vocal: Spin, Earth (J.R. Baughan), mixed vv, pf/org, 1970; Lockerbones/Airbones (Le Guin), Mez, fl, vn, pf, perc, 1983; Eating with the Hoi (Le Guin), S, nar, chorus, perc, 1986 [Uses of Music no.4]; A Season of Grief (A. Tennyson and W. Bynner), Mez/Bar, pf, 1987; Anithaca (Le Guin), girls' vv, 1990 [Uses of Music no.2]; Island Earth (Le Guin), chorus, orch, 1993 [Uses of Music no.8]

MSS in *US-BEm*

Principal publishers: J.B. Elkus & Sons, Fallen Leaf, Lawson-Gould, MMB, Peters

Principal recording Companies: Koch, Music and Arts

BIBLIOGRAPHY

E. Armer: 'A Conversation with Vivian Fine Two Composers Talk Shop', *Strings*, v/5 (1991), 73–8
P. Moor: 'Armer: Uses of Music in Uttermost Parts', *Audio*, lxxx/7 (1996), 75 only
A.P. Matson: *An Organic Program: Uses of Music in Uttermost Parts*, i (diss., UCLA, 1997)

J. MICHELE EDWARDS

Armes, Philip (*b* Norwich, 15 Aug 1836; *d* Durham, 10 Feb 1908). English cathedral organist, teacher and composer. After training as a chorister at Norwich Cathedral (1846–8) and at Rochester Cathedral (1848–

50) Armes became pupil-assistant to J.L. Hopkins at Rochester (1850–56). He was subsequently organist of Trinity Church, Gravesend (1855–7), St Andrew's, Wells Street, London (1857–61), Chichester Cathedral (1861–2) and Durham Cathedral (1862–1907). He took the Oxford BMus in 1858 and DMus in 1864. He was resident examiner in music at the University of Durham from 1890 and became its first professor in 1897; he was examiner at Oxford from 1894. During the 1880s Armes collated and indexed the four sets of manuscript partbooks surviving at Durham. These contained the service music together with separate organ parts of a wide repertory from Tallis to Purcell, formerly used in the cathedral. He composed three oratorios, various anthems, services and other church music.

BIBLIOGRAPHY

'Bibliographical Sketch of Dr Philip Armes', *MT*, xli (1900), 81–6

T.H. Collinson: *The Diary of an Organist's Apprentice: at Durham Cathedral 1871–1875*(Aberdeen, 1982)

BERNARR RAINBOW

Armingaud, Jules (*b* Bayonne, 3 May 1820; *d* Paris, 27 Feb 1900). French violinist and composer. A pupil of Alard, he attempted to enter the Paris Conservatoire in 1839 but was refused admission, according to Fétis, because of his advanced and individualistic talent. He played in the orchestra of the Opéra-Comique, and in the revolution of 1848 he was active, with Edouard Lalo, in the leftist Association des Artistes Musiciens. In 1855 he formed, with Lalo, Joseph Mas and Léon Jacquard, a string quartet in which he played first violin. The quartet enjoyed a great reputation for the works of Mendelssohn and Beethoven; many of their quartets had seldom been performed before. Clara Schumann apparently played with the Armingaud quartet during visits to Paris in 1862 and 1863. The ensemble was later transformed, by the addition of wind instruments, into the Société Classique. Armingaud was praised for his graceful but solid playing and his beautiful tone. His compositions, which run to at least op.53, are primarily light works for violin and piano, described by van der Straeten as 'florid [and] showy', but they also include a fantasy on themes from *Lohengrin* and a chorus with orchestra. He published two books of musical aphorisms, *Consonances et dissonances* (Paris, 1882) and *Modulations* (Paris, 1895).

BIBLIOGRAPHY

FétisB

A. P[?ougin].: Obituary, *Le ménestrel* (4 March 1900)

J. Tiersot: 'Edouard Lalo', *MQ*, xi (1925), 8–35

E. van der Straeten: *The History of the Violin* (London, 1933/R)

M. Kahane and N.Wild, eds.: *Wagner et la France* (Paris, 1983)

J.-M. Fauquet: *Les sociétés de musique de chambre à Paris de la Restauration à 1870* (Paris, 1986)

J.-M. Fauquet, ed.: *Edouard Lalo: correspondance* (Paris, 1989)

CORMAC NEWARK

Armitage, Reginald Moxon. *See* GAY, NOEL.

Armonia di flauto (It.). *See* TRIFLAUTO.

Armonica. A sophisticated form of MUSICAL GLASSES, invented by Benjamin Franklin in 1761, in which a row of glass bowls are nested within one another concentrically on a horizontal axle, which is turned with a pedal.

Armonica a bocca (It.). *See* HARMONICA (i).

Armonica a manticino (It.). *See* ACCORDION.

Armonioso (It.: 'harmonious'). An expression mark denoting a harmonious style. It was particularly favoured by Liszt, who used it in his piano music for long sections to be played under the sustaining pedal.

Armonipiano. *See* SOSTENENTE PIANO, §4.

Armsdorff, Andreas (*b* Mühlberg, nr Gotha, 9 Sept 1670; *d* Erfurt, 31 Dec 1699). German composer and organist. He studied law as well as music. He held organ posts at Erfurt, successively at the Reglerkirche, Andreaskirche and Kaufmannskirche. Although he wrote little because of his early death, his chorale-preludes were very popular in his day, judging from the numbers of manuscript copies of them circulating in Germany. *Allein Gott in der Höh' sei Ehr* is a charming trio, with the modified tune in the discant in canon with the real tune in the pedals, while *Allein zu dir, Herr Jesu Christ* exemplifies the ornamental discant chorale. Such pieces bear out Jakob Adlung's view in the following century that Armsdorff wrote music grateful to the ear.

WORKS

31 chorale-preludes [3 atrrib. Armsdorff by Beckmann], org; ed. K. Beckmann, *Samtliche Orgelwerke: Johann Friedrich Alberti, Andreas Armsdorff* (Messstetten, 1996); 4 ed. in EDM, 1st ser., ix (1937)

Fugue, org, lost, formerly Fürstliche Stolbergsche Bibliothek, Wernigerode

Other kbd works, lost (see Ritter)

Vocal works, lost, mentioned by Walker

BIBLIOGRAPHY

ApelG; *RiemannL12*

J. Adlung: *Anleitung zu der musikalischen Gelahrtheit* (Erfurt, 1758/ R, 2/1783)

A.G. Ritter: *Zur Geschichte des Orgelspiels, vornehmlich des deutschen, im 14. bis zum Anfange des 18. Jahrhunderts*, i (Leipzig, 1884/R), 173ff

G.B. SHARP

Armstrong, Frankie (*b* Workington, Cumbria, 13 Jan 1941). English traditional singer, writer and teacher. She began singing American songs in 1957 with a band, Skiffle Group, which eventually adopted a repertory of British traditional songs. From the early 1960s Armstrong, partially sighted, combined a singing career with that of social worker. Influenced by singer Louis Killen, she studied traditional singers and analysed the synthesis of content, style and form in traditional performance. In 1964, she joined Ewan MacColl and PEGGY SEEGER's Critics Group. In New York in 1973 she attended a Balkan singing class run by Ethel Raim, a meeting that had a long-term influence on her both as a singer and teacher and as an activist in the Women's Movement. In 1975, Armstrong began teaching Voice Workshops which aimed to help singers and non-singers to express themselves through voice and song. Since the late 1980s, she has run joint voice workshops with her husband, Darien Pritchard, a movement and relaxation specialist. A politically committed artist, who frequently performs for women's peace and environmental groups, Armstrong has one of the most distinctive and emotive voices of the Folk Revival.

BIBLIOGRAPHY

AND OTHER RESOURCES

K. Henderson, F. Armstrong and S. Kerr: *My Song is my Own: 100 Women's Songs* (London, 1979)

Let No One Deceive you: Songs of Bertolt Brecht, Flying Fish FF 70557 (1989)

F. Armstrong and J. Pearson: *As Far as the Eye can Sing* (London, 1992) [autobiography]
Til the Grass O'ergrew the Corn, Fellside FECD 116 (1997)
Ways of Seeing, Harbourtown HARCD 009 (1997)
The Garden of Love, Fellside, FECD 144 (1999)

DAVE ARTHUR

Armstrong, Louis [Dippermouth, Pops, Satchelmouth, Satchmo] (*b* New Orleans, 4 Aug 1901; *d* New York, 6 July 1971). American jazz trumpeter, singer and bandleader.

1. LIFE.   Armstrong's father abandoned his mother around the time of his birth, and the family lived in poverty in New Orleans, near the saloons and dance halls whose music, along with what he heard and sang in church, was his first musical influence. As a child he worked at odd jobs and began performing on the streets with a vocal quartet. In 1912 he was arrested for delinquency and sent to the Colored Waifs' Home in New Orleans, where he started to play the cornet and received his first formal musical tuition from Peter Davis, a member of the staff. After his release at the age of about 14, he again held various jobs and lived with his mother. He was befriended, taught and given his own cornet by his lifelong idol, the jazz cornettist Joe 'King' Oliver. Soon he began to play professionally, working with many New Orleans jazz musicians who later moved to the north, and in 1918 he joined Kid Ory's band, replacing Oliver himself, who had left for Chicago. At this time he also began working in Fate Marable's riverboat bands on excursions from New Orleans and St Louis.

In 1922 Oliver sent for Armstrong to join his successful Creole Jazz Band at Lincoln Gardens, Chicago. This offer was crucial for Armstrong, who maintained that he would have left New Orleans for no-one else; he now played with the finest and most influential New Orleans group in the north. He was recorded for the first time in Oliver's noteworthy 1923 series. The discipline and sensitivity of his improvised second cornet parts to Oliver's lead are specially apparent in the third chorus, first statement, of *Mabel's Dream*. While with Oliver's group Armstrong married the band's pianist, Lillian Hardin (they were divorced in 1938). Her influence and his own growing discontent with the band's restricting style led him reluctantly in 1924 to accept Fletcher Henderson's invitation to join his big band in New York. As a section player in a larger group, Armstrong made his ensemble playing conform to the stiff rhythms then favoured by Henderson (for example, *Copenhagen*, 1924, Voc.). His sophisticated, flowing solos, however, introduced a novel style into the city's jazz and dance music and exerted a wide influence on New York musicians, among them the band's arranger, Don Redman, who soon found orchestral counterparts for many of Armstrong's devices. While in New York, Armstrong made several recordings with other groups, including the striking *I ain't gonna play no second fiddle* (1925, Voc.) with Perry Bradford's Jazz Phools, a noteworthy series with Clarence Williams's groups (for example, *Texas Moaner Blues*, 1924, OK) and as an accompanist to such blues singers as Bessie Smith (*St Louis Blues*, 1925, Col.).

In 1925 Armstrong returned to Chicago, where he played with groups led by his wife, Carroll Dickerson and Erskine Tate and, for most of 1927, with his own ensemble. In 1925 he also began a series of recordings under his own name. His originality and range as an improviser and the power and beauty of his ideas, as revealed in these remarkable early recordings, established his international reputation as the greatest and most creative jazz musician. The series also traces the search for an accompaniment appropriate to his increasingly virtuoso solo manner. The earliest of these – the Hot Five and Hot Seven recordings with his wife, the Dodds brothers, Kid Ory and Johnny St Cyr – were modelled on New Orleans ensembles, leading to such masterpieces of the later New Orleans style as *Big Butter and Egg Man* (1926, OK), *Potato Head Blues* (1927, OK) and *Struttin' with some Barbecue* (1927, OK). Then in 1928 he turned to a more modern small band, which included the pianist Earl Hines, and made greater use of arranged material, as in the remarkable *Weather Bird*, a duet with Hines, *West End Blues* and *Beau Koo Jack* (all OK). Finally, in mid-1929 Armstrong adopted the format he was to use until 1947: a big band as a neutral accompaniment to his playing and singing, which by now was dominated by large-scale, virtuoso conceptions. At the same time he began to concentrate on a popular repertory.

There is controversy about Armstrong's big-band period. Although his technical innovations had ceased, his performing still had artistic merit, and he made recordings of great power, beauty and maturity, such as *Body and Soul* (1930, OK), *Star Dust* (1931, OK), *Sweethearts on Parade* (1930, Col.) and *I gotta right to sing the blues* (1933, Vic.). He toured and recorded with large groups, particularly that of Luis Russell (1935–44), in the USA and in Europe (1932–5). He made film appearances, the first in *Pennies from Heaven* with Bing Crosby (1936), and hundreds of recordings with his own and other groups, becoming increasingly influential as a singer of popular music and reaching a wider audience. The serious jazz content of his playing diminished, and he was criticized for the low quality of his bands, his

Louis Armstrong

repertory and his failure to live up to the promise of his earlier achievements.

After successful appearances with small groups in 1947, including one in the film *New Orleans*, Armstrong formed his All Stars, a sextet on the New Orleans model with which he worked until his death. Its personnel, but not its instrumentation, varied, and at times included the clarinettists Barney Bigard and Edmond Hall, the trombonists Jack Teagarden and Trummy Young, Armstrong's earlier associate Hines and the drummers Sid Catlett and Cozy Cole. With this group Armstrong again showed his superlative quality as a jazz musician, playing less elaborately than he had for some time. Among the best recordings from this period is a collection of new versions of his classic performances, *Satchmo: a Musical Autobiography* (1956–7, Decca). At the same time he continued to make popular recordings, such as *Mack the Knife* (1955, Col.), *Hello Dolly* (1963, Kapp) and *What a Wonderful World* (on the album *Louis Armstrong with his Friends*, 1970, Amsterdam). The All Stars toured with great success in the USA, Australia, East Asia, Europe and South America. In 1960 they toured Africa twice, and their international travelling in the 1960s earned Armstrong the nickname 'Ambassador Satch'. Illness incapacitated him several times in the late 1960s and took its toll on his playing. In public appearances from mid-1969 to September 1970 he was able only to sing; he then resumed playing, but he suffered a heart attack in March 1971.

2. WORK.   Armstrong's importance in the history of jazz is inestimable. The testimony of contemporary jazz musicians shows that his playing greatly impressed all who heard him. Much of his power lay in the grace, sensitivity and poise of his work, features not susceptible to imitation; but his concepts of tone and range, or rhythm and phrasing (both to some extent initially influenced by Oliver), and his sophisticated pitch choice were imitated. Almost all aspects of jazz technique and style, whether played or sung, were influenced directly by Armstrong's innovations of the 1920s.

Armstrong acquired a basic beauty and strength of sound early in his career, and it is apparent even in his work with Oliver and Henderson. His studies with Oliver and his New Orleans background had made him familiar with the expressive possibilities of timbre; but he developed still more expressive ways of attacking and sustaining notes, often, for example, increasing ambitus of vibrato after an attack to give an accumulating energy and a kind of interior rhythm to individual notes and an additional propulsion to entire phrases. Even in the relatively early *Potato Head Blues* (1927, OK) he showed a repertory of devices for varying timbre, including alternative fingerings for the same note (ex.1, bars 9–10). This was coupled with a dramatic expansion of his instrument's range: he had cultivated a solid low register as auxiliary cornettist with Oliver and Henderson, and he now gradually extended his range upwards to encompass an unprecedented three octaves, throughout which he could play with equal fluency and fullness of tone. His rhythms drew on the flowing New Orleans style and again on Oliver's example, but he was able to free his playing still further from the rhythmic predictability of early jazz by using short spans and later whole phrases that seemed at first to contradict the underlying pulse, only to merge with it again. This was a basic element in his lyricism that

Ex.1 Chorus from Armstrong's solo on *Potato Head Blues* (1927, OK) (rhythm section plays only on first beat of odd-numbered bars)

for a long time set him apart. Further, Armstrong was able to link phrases without the characteristic problem in early jazz of vacant or formulaic cadences. He had acquired from Oliver a dynamic ability to imply harmony through line and pitch, yet to this basic technique he added a harmonic awareness far in advance of his contemporaries, for example, the augmented passing harmonies in bars 6 and 22 of ex.1 and the implicit II^7–V^7 in bar 20. Further, although Armstrong did not introduce 9ths, 13ths and chromaticisms into jazz harmony, he used them so systematically and with such effective placing that his choice of pitch sounded completely fresh. The cogency of his technical innovations, each solving a particular problem faced by the jazz soloist, and his untiring wealth of lyric improvisation, enabled him to extend his solos for several choruses and to structure entire performances, another aspect of his originality.

Armstrong was equally noteworthy for his singing, particularly for his scat performances (see ex.1), some of which are among the earliest recorded examples (*Heebie Jeebies*, 1926, OK; *Gully Low Blues*, 1927, OK; *Hotter than that*, 1927, OK). His unique 'gravelly' voice, a mid-tenor but with an enlarged range, was a natural extension of his instrument: he elaborated a given melody or improvised new lines on the principles found in his trumpet playing. When applied to his singing his rhythmic subtleties were all the more striking, and he introduced a freedom and jazz sensibility that continue to be an important influence on popular singing.

Armstrong's publications for trumpet include *Fifty Hot Choruses* and *125 Hot Breaks* (both 1927), *Louis Satchmo Armstrong's Dixieland Trumpet Solos* (1947) and *Trumpet Method* (1961).

BIBLIOGRAPHY

L. Armstrong: *Swing that Music* (New York, 1936/R) [incl. transcrs.]
W. Russell: 'Louis Armstrong', *Jazzmen*, ed. F. Ramsey and C.E. Smith (New York, 1939/R), 119–42
R. Goffin: *Louis Armstrong: le roi du jazz* (Paris, 1947; Eng. trans., 1947/R1977, as *Horn of Plenty: the Story of Louis Armstrong*)
H. Panassié: *Louis Armstrong* (Paris, 1947)
J. Slawe: *Louis Armstrong: zehn monographische Studien* (Basle, 1953)
L. Armstrong: *Satchmo: my Life in New Orleans* (New York, 1954)
A. Hodeir: *Hommes et problèmes du jazz, suivi de La religion du jazz* (Paris, 1954; Eng. trans., rev., 1956/R, as *Jazz: its Evolution and Essence*)
M. Edey: 'Louis Armstrong', *Jazz Review*, ii (1959), Aug, 28
A. McCarthy: *Louis Armstrong* (London, 1960); repr. in *Kings of Jazz*, ed. S. Green (South Brunswick, NJ, 1978), 7–39
R. Hadlock: 'Louis Armstrong from 1924 to 1931', *Jazz Masters of the Twenties* (New York, 1965/R), 13–49
W. Austin: *Music in the 20th Century* (New York, 1966)
M. Williams: *Jazz Masters of New Orleans* (New York, 1967/R), 162–77
G. Schuller: 'The First Great Soloist', *Early Jazz: its Roots and Musical Development* (New York, 1968), 89–133
H. Panassié: *Louis Armstrong* (Paris, 1969; Eng. trans., 1971/R)
L. Armstrong: *A Self-portrait* (New York, 1971)
M. Jones and J.Chilton: *Louis: the Louis Armstrong Story, 1900–1971* (London, 1971/R)
L. Feather: 'With Louis: from London to Los Angeles', *From Satchmo to Miles* (New York, 1972/R), 13–42
H. Caffey: 'The Musical Style of Louis Armstrong, 1925–1929', *Journal of Jazz Studies*, iii/1 (1975), 72–96
R. Hoskins: *Louis Armstrong: Biography of a Musician* (Los Angeles, 1979) [incl. list of films and discography]
H. Westerberg: *Boy from New Orleans: Louis 'Satchmo' Armstrong, on Records, Films, Radio and Television* (Copenhagen, 1981) [incl. discography]
J.L. Collier: *Louis Armstrong: an American Genius* (New York, 1983), repr. as *Louis Armstrong: a Biography* (London, 1984)
G. Giddins, ed.: 'Armstrong at 85', *Village Voice* (27 Aug 1985) [special section]

JAMES DAPOGNY

Armstrong, Richard (*b* Leicester, 7 Jan 1943). English conductor. An organ scholar at Corpus Christi College, Cambridge, he joined the musical staff of Covent Garden in 1966, moving to the WNO in December 1968 as assistant musical director to James Lockhart. He made his conducting début with *Le nozze di Figaro* in 1969, and he was musical director from 1973 until 1986, when he became principal guest conductor at Frankfurt. This period covered the company's biggest expansion, including several foreign visits. His conducting repertory included an acclaimed cycle of five Janáček operas, the first Welsh *Ring* cycles, André Engel's production of *Salome*, and numerous Verdi productions, including the Peter Stein *Otello*.

Armstrong conducted two *Ring* cycles when the WNO became the first regional company to visit Covent Garden

in 1986, and took their *Falstaff* to New York and Milan in 1989. In May 1990 he conducted the première of John Metcalf's *Tornrak*, also for the WNO. In 1993 he became musical director of Scottish Opera, where he has conducted numerous operas, including *Tristan und Isolde* and Schnittke's *Life with an Idiot* (which he also conducted for the ENO). He has appeared with the leading British orchestras, the Japan Philharmonic and the Berlin Symphony Orchestra, and conducted operatic productions in Berlin, Geneva, Brussels and Amsterdam.

BIBLIOGRAPHY

K. Loveland: 'Richard Armstrong', *Opera*, xxxvii (1986), 1354–8

KENNETH LOVELAND

Armstrong, Sir Thomas (Henry Wait) (*b* Peterborough, 15 June 1898; *d* ? Olney, Bucks, 26 June 1994). English organist, conductor and educationist. He was trained by Haydn Keeton, organist of Peterborough Cathedral, where he was assistant organist, 1915–16. He then studied at the Royal College of Music and Keble College, Oxford. He became successively assistant organist of Manchester Cathedral (1921–2) and organist of St Peter's, Eaton Square, London (1922–8); during the later period he studied at the RCM with Holst and Vaughan Williams. He took the Oxford DMus in 1929. From 1928 to 1933 he was organist of Exeter Cathedral. In 1933 he was appointed organist of Christ Church, Oxford, and remained there until he was appointed principal of the Royal Academy of Music in 1955, a post from which he retired in 1968. He was knighted in 1958. While organist of Exeter Cathedral he was also director of music to the University College of the Southwest and this experience stood him in good stead at Oxford, where he achieved success as a tutor and lecturer and – in succession to Hugh Allen – as conductor of the Bach Choir and the Orchestral Society.

Armstrong was a sought-after adjudicator and an excellent music broadcaster to schools. Through these activities he reached a wide public. In his earlier days he was influenced by Hamilton Harty, for whom he worked at Manchester, and by his teachers Vaughan Williams and Holst but probably above all by Allen, director of the RCM and then professor of music at Oxford. As principal of the RAM he travelled abroad extensively, gathering ideas that would broaden the basis of the RAM and encourage an outward-looking attitude among its students. An extremely competent and versatile musician, he published two short books (on Mendelssohn's *Elijah* and Strauss's tone poems, both in 1931) and a few articles, and composed in the smaller choral forms.

BIBLIOGRAPHY

T. Armstrong: 'My First Year', *R.A.M. Magazine*, no.164 (1956), 30–35
R. Golding: Editorial, *Royal Academy of Music Magazine*, no.195 (1968), 2–6
K. Shenton: Obituary, *Organist's Review*, lxxx (1994), 325–7

BERNARD ROSE/R

Arnaoudov, Georgi (*b* Sofia, 18 March, 1957). Bulgarian composer. From 1978 to 1985 he attended the State Music Academy in Sofia, graduating from the composition classes of Bozhidar Spasov and Aleksandar Tanev; he also studied with Ton de Leeuw during international workshops in 1985 and 1991. From 1983 to 1989 he was secretary of the young composers' section of the Bulgarian Composers' Union. He was professor of composition and harmony at the State Academy (1985–95) and in 1993 became a leading representative of Musica Nova, the international music festival held in Sofia. In 1995 he was appointed associate professor in the New Bulgarian University's theatre department and has since become secretary-general of the Bulgarian section of the ISCM.

Arnaoudov is perhaps the most original of his generation of Bulgarian composers; he is also among the first to have embraced minimalism. In his musical style he deliberately eschews folksong as a source of inspiration turning instead to the mystical and ritualistic. His immediate antecedents are Crumb, Messiaen, Gorecki, Pärt, Kancheli and Korndorf. Arnaoudov employs a unique combination of minimalist devices, serial techniques, dynamic and registral extremities, silence and sonorous effects to forge a highly personal musical language. Favouring transparent textures and developmental stasis, his works are often built around a single musical element such as a pitch or interval. This is particularly apparent in his piano miniatures and *Footnote* (. . .*und Isoldens Winkfall lassen*) for voice and chamber orchestra (1991).

WORKS

Stage (ballets, choreog. M. Iskrenova): Offertorium I, 1988; Offertorium II, 1991; Choreordained, 1996; Transpatium, 1996

Orch: Sym. no.1, 1984; Conc. for Orch, 1986; Conc. Grosso, str, 1987; Kammerkonzert, pf, chbr orch, 1988; Sym. no.2, 1989; Laudes, 1996

Vocal-inst: Footnote (. . .und Isoldens Winkfall lassen) (after J. Joyce: A Prayer), S, chbr orch, 1991; Summe deus, S, chbr orch, 1993; The Circle of Rites (old Sanskrit text), S, chbr ens, 1993; The Way of the Birds, S, a fl, vn, 1995; Katawassi, Mez, str qt, 1996

Chbr and solo inst: Paysages sonores, pf, 1983; Ritual I, pf, 1988; Str Qt no.2, 1991; Incarnation dans la lumière (Ritual II), pf, 1992; Un pan de ciel au milieu du silence, 3 poems after R. Magrit, pf, 1991–4; Ritual III (Borges fragment), vc, 1993; Le temple du silence, 2 pf, 1996; Et iterum venturus est cum gloria, pf, 1997; Thyepolia, t rec, perc, vc, 1997

Principal publisher: Musica (Sofia)

BIBLIOGRAPHY

MGG2 (M. Kostakeva)

'Zadălbočeno, mnogoobrazno, iskreno: kompozitorăt G. Arnaudov' [Deep, multifaceted, sincere: the composer Arnaoudov], *Puls* (11 July 1989)

'Tvorčestvoto ne e stoka za prodan' [Composition is no commodity for sale], *Otečestven front* (26 June 1989) [interview]

'Georgi Arnaudov: rubrika na Maja Pramatarova', *Literaturen vesnik* (12 Feb 1997)

ANNA LEVY, GREGORY MYERS

Arnaud, François (*b* Aubignan, Carpentras, 27 July 1721; *d* Paris, 2 Dec 1784). French man of letters. As a boy he mixed with the many musicians in the service of the Italian prelates, attracted to Carpentras by generous stipends. Arnaud came to Paris from Provence in 1752 as attaché to Prince Louis of Würtemberg. He was Abbé de Grandchamp (1765), librarian to the Comte de Provence and historiographer to the order of St Lazare, and in 1771 became a member of the Académie Française. He was a classical scholar and accomplished linguist and translator, and collaborated with his close friend J.B.A. Suard (whose wife was said to be his mistress) on the *Journal étranger*, *Gazette littéraire de l'Europe*, *Variétés littéraires* and other writings. His humour, historical knowledge and vigorous polemical style make him stand out among the many literary writers on music of the second half of the 18th century.

Arnaud was a member of the Encyclopedist generation and deeply influenced by its ideas, but he did not share Marmontel's or Rousseau's exclusive admiration for Italian music. The *Lettre sur la musique* of 1754 sketches an unrealized plan for a major historical work; La Borde included it in his *Essai sur la musique*. In 1757 Arnaud also helped Rameau to write his *Code de musique pratique*. Arnaud was particularly interested in prosody, arguing that every language should have its own melody or 'déclamation lyrique'; his ideas had considerable influence on Grétry. Arnaud had long advocated operatic reform, and his fervent admiration for Gluck, who seemed to revive antique tragedy, led to his being nicknamed the 'St Paul of the Gluck religion'. He engaged in a duel of wits with Marmontel, in whose *Polymnie* he figures as Trigaut. He saw Gluck's synthesis of French and Italian elements as the logical outcome of Encyclopedist ideas, especially those of d'Alembert, and attacked the superficiality of Italian opera in his 'Profession de foi en musique' (*Journal de Paris*, 1777). The pamphlet *La soirée perdue à l'Opéra* is attributed to him in his posthumous *Oeuvres*, in the *Mémoires pour servir à l'histoire de la révolution opérée dans la musique par M. le Chevalier Gluck*, and by Bricqueville, but it may be the work of Pascal Boyer. When he died Arnaud was beginning work on the musical part of Panckoucke's *Encyclopédie méthodique*.

WRITINGS

Lettre sur la musique à Monsieur le comte de Caylus (Paris, 1754)

Réflexions sur la musique en général, et sur la musique française en particulier (Paris, 1754)

'Lettre sur un ouvrage italien intitulé Il Teatro alla Moda', *Oeuvres complètes*, ed. L. Boudon (Paris, 1808/R), i

'Essai sur le mélodrame ou drame lyrique', ibid., ii

The following are in *Oeuvres complètes*, ii, and in G.M. Le Blond, ed.: *Mémoires pour servir à l'histoire de la révolution opérée dans la musique par M. le Chevalier Gluck* (Naples, 1781): 'Lettre à Mme D'[Augny] et à la comtesse de B. ....sur l'Iphigénie de Gluck' (1774); 'La soirée perdue à l'opéra' (1776); 'Le souper des enthousiastes' (1776); 'Lettre au P. Martini' (1776); 'Lettre à l'ermite de la forêt de Sénart' (1777); 'Profession de foi en musique, d'un amateur des beaux-arts, à M. de La Harpe' (1777); 'Lettre sur l'Iphigénie en Tauride de M. le Chevalier Gluck' (1779)

BIBLIOGRAPHY

E. de Bricqueville: *L'Abbé Arnaud et la réforme de l'opéra au XVIIIe siècle* (Avignon, 1881)

E. de Bricqueville: *Deux abbés d'opéra au siècle dernier: J. Pellegrin, F. Arnaud* (Avignon, 1889)

J.M. Kaplan: *Marmontel et 'Polymnie'* (Oxford, 1984)

M. Couvreur: 'J.-Ph. Rameau, *Billet à l'abbé Arnaud*', *Diderot et son temps*, ed. R. Mortier and M. Mat (Brussels, 1985), 116–17

P. Vendrix: *Aux origines d'une discipline historique: la musique et son histoire en France aux XVIIe et XVIIIe siècles* (Liège, 1993)

JULIAN RUSHTON/MANUEL COUVREUR

Arnaut, Daniel. *See* DANIEL, ARNAUT.

Arnaut de Mareuil [Mareulh, Maroill] (*fl c*1170–1200). Provençal troubadour. He was apparently born at Mareuil-sur-Belle in the diocese of Périgord. According to his romanticized biography, he was by profession a scribe and notary, but abandoned his poorly paid duties in favour of a more enjoyable existence as troubadour; in the latter capacity he was first at the court of Roger II, Viscount of Béziers, and his wife Adelaide, and afterwards at the court of William VIII, Count of Montpellier. Of the 26 chansons attributed to him, six survive with music; 13 more works are ascribed to him in various sources, but are not likely to be his. In addition, he wrote both *saluts d'amours* (poetic love-letters), five of which survive, and an *ensenhamen*, a didactic, moralizing poem commenting on contemporary customs. He was among the first to cultivate these genres. His poetry was much appreciated by Petrarch. He preferred evolving tonalities and structures to centralized ones: only *La grans beutatz* is cast in bar form, the second *pes* recurring in varied form in the cauda and set off by new material, and only in this melody is the final predictable from the opening phrase. Although characteristic motifs may recur in other melodies in either symmetrical or irregular fashion, entire phrases are not repeated. For the most part the melodies progress in neumatic style, interspersed occasionally with largely syllabic phrases. Ranges between a 7th and a 9th are normal, although the unusual *Si·m destrenhetz* apparently has a range of an 11th. There is no strong evidence for regularity of rhythmic organization.

See also TROUBADOURS, TROUVÈRES.

WORKS

Editions: *Der musikalische Nachlass der Troubadours*, ed. F. Gennrich, iii–iv, xv (SMM, 1958–65) [G]
  Las cançons dels trobadors, ed. I. Fernandez de La Cuesta (Toulouse, 1979) [FC]
  The Extant Troubadour Melodies, ed. H. van der Werf (Rochester, NY, 1984) [W]

Aissi com cel qu'ama, e non es amatz, PC 30.3, G iii, 57, FC 236, W 15
La franca captenensa, PC 30.15, G iii, 58, and iv, 143, FC 238, W 16
La grans beutatz e·ls fis ensenhamens, PC 30.16, G iii, 58, and iv, 143, FC 240, W 17
L'ensenhamens e·l pretz e la valor, PC 30.17, G iii, 59, and iv, 144, FC 242, W 18
Molt era·m dolz mei conssir, PC 30.19, G iii, 60, FC 244, W 19
Si·m destrenhetz, dona, vos et amors, PC 30.23, G iii, 61, and iv, 144, FC 246, W 20

BIBLIOGRAPHY

H.J. Chaytor: *The Troubadours* (Cambridge, 1912/R)
R.C. Johnston, ed.: *Les poésies lyriques du troubadour Arnaut de Mareuil* (Paris, 1935/R)
P. Bec, ed.: *Les saluts d'amour du troubadour Arnaud de Mareuil* (Toulouse, 1961)
C. Page: *Voices and Instruments of the Middle Ages* (Berkeley, 1986)
E. Aubrey: *The Music of the Troubadours* (Bloomington, IN, 1996)

For further bibliography *see* TROUBADOURS, TROUVÈRES.

THEODORE KARP

Arnaut de Zwolle, Henri (*b* Zwolle, late 14th or early 15th century; *d* Paris, 6 Sept 1466). Franco-Flemish physician, astrologer, astronomer and author of a treatise on musical instruments, of which he was presumably also a maker. Even if he did not, as has been assumed, study at the University of Paris, he would have become familiar with much of its curriculum through Jean Fusoris, whom Arnaut called his master. Fusoris, who had received degrees in theology, arts and medicine at the University, was a physician, astrologer, astronomer and prolific maker of astronomical and horological devices. By 1432 Arnaut had entered the service of Philip the Good, Duke of Burgundy, as 'professeur en medecine', 'astronomien' and 'maistre . . . en astrologie'. Between 1454 and 1461 he left the Burgundian court in Dijon and entered the service of the French king in Paris (Charles VII, and later Louis XI), where he died of the plague.

Arnaut is known chiefly for a manuscript (*F-Pn* lat.7295), mostly autograph, which contains treatises in Latin, tables and technical drawings about subjects including astronomy, hydraulics and the construction of astronomical instruments. Other devices are described, including a folding ladder and a machine to polish gems. Of particular musical interest are a copy of Johannes de Muris's *Musica speculativa* and a treatise on the design of musical instruments, both in Arnaut's hand. The latter,

presumably of his own authorship (except for a brief section on clavichord scaling which he attributes to a certain Baudecetus), furnishes detailed information on the design and construction of the lute and various keyboard instruments, including the harpsichord, clavichord, *dulce melos* and organ (for his diagrams, *see* CLAVICHORD, fig. 2; DULCE MELOS, fig.1; HARPSICHORD, fig.2; and LUTE, fig.8). Also bound into the volume are notes written in several later 15th-century hands, mainly giving technical information about organs. Arnaut's manuscript probably existed as a collection of separate fascicles and sheets until they were bound together during the first half of the 16th century. The watermark in the paper used for the musical-instrument treatise suggests that it was written between about 1438 and 1446, whilst Arnaut was living in Dijon.

The treatise is an invaluable organological source: it gives the earliest known technical description of a large number of instruments. Often it documents earlier stages of development than can be observed in surviving examples, which, except for some fragments of organs, come from later periods. Arnaut's information about the portative and the dulce melos is especially significant, since no example of either instrument survives. Equally valuable is his unique record of the composition of the ranks in several *Blockwerk* organs.

Correspondences between Arnaut's designs and later 15th- and 16th-century organs, harpsichords, clavichords and lutes, as well as details known from other documentary and iconographical sources, demonstrate that he worked within the mainstream traditions of instrument making. His account of the harpsichord, which he called the *clavisimbalum*, is particularly interesting since it was written at a very early stage of the instrument's development. He explains that any one of four actions can be used; none is quite like the jack action that later became standard. One of these, a form of primitive hammer action not unlike that of a pianoforte, he associates particularly with the dulce melos, a rectangular keyed dulcimer which was probably his own invention. By suggesting that a plucking action could be applied to the clavichord, he also envisioned the virginal.

BIBLIOGRAPHY

G. Le Cerf and E.-R. Labande, eds.: *Instruments de musique du XVe siècle: les traités d'Henri-Arnaut de Zwolle et de divers anonymes* (Paris, 1932/R) [incl. facs., transcr. and Fr. trans.]
I. Harwood: 'A Fifteenth-Century Lute Design', *LSJ*, ii (1960), 3–8 [incl. partial facs., transcr. and Eng. trans.]
E. Poulle: *Un constructeur d'instruments astronomiques au XVe siècle: Jean Fusoris* (Paris, 1963)
K. Bormann: *Die gotische Orgel zu Halberstadt* (Berlin, 1966), 147–172 [incl. partial facs., transcr. and Ger. trans.]
E.M. Ripin: 'The Early Clavichord', *MQ*, liii (1967), 518–38
M.-K. Kaufmann: 'Le Clavier à balancier du clavisimbalum (XVe siècle): un moment exceptionnel de l'évolution des instruments à clavier', *La Facture de clavecin du XVe au XVIIIe siècle: Louvain-la-Neuve 1976*, 9–57 [incl. partial facs., transcr. and Fr. trans.]
P. Williams: *A New History of the Organ from the Greeks to the Present Day* (London, 1980), 59–63
H. Heyde: *Musikinstrumentenbau, 15.–19. Jahrhundert: Kunst-Handwerk-Entwurf* (Leipzig, 1986)
S. Howell: 'Medical Astrologers and the Invention of Stringed Keyboard Instruments', *JMR*, x († 1990), 1–17
S. Pollens: *The Early Pianoforte* (Cambridge, 1995), 7–26 [incl. partial facs., transcr. and Eng. trans.]
J. Koster: 'The Origins of Hans Ruckers's Craft', *Hans Ruckers* († 1598), *Stichter van een klavecimbelatelier van wereldformaat in Antwerpen*, ed. J. Lambrechts-Douillez (Peer, 1998), 53–64

JOHN KOSTER

Arndt, Felix (*b* New York, 20 May 1889; *d* Harmon, NY, 10 Oct 1918). American composer and pianist. After studying the piano at the National Conservatory of Music in America and taking private lessons with Alexander Lambert, he pursued a varied career in New York, writing material for vaudeville entertainers, serving as a staff pianist for various publishers and recording extensively both on piano rolls (Duo-Art, QRS) and discs (Victor). Arndt's compositions combine salon gentility with occasional ragtime syncopation, foreshadowing the novelty-piano works of the 1920s by such composers as Confrey and Bargy. They include *Clover Club, Desecration, Love in June, Marionette* and the well-known *Nola* (1916).

RONALD RIDDLE

Arndt, Günther (*b* Charlottenburg, Berlin, 1 April 1907; *d* Berlin, 25 Dec 1976). German choral conductor and radio producer. He studied at the Akademie für Kirchen- und Schulmusik in Berlin and at the university there. A choirmaster and lecturer in music at the Berlin Volkshochschule (1932–40), he also taught music at a secondary school (1932–4) and was co-founder and conductor of the Berlin Heinrich Schütz Chorale. With the resumption of postwar musical life in Berlin he was appointed head of Berlin radio's chamber music department and from 1949 was a specialist adviser on symphonic music for RIAS. He founded the Berlin Motet Choir in 1950 and was its conductor to 1960, and he was also conductor of the RIAS Chamber Choir (1955–72). From 1964 until his retirement in 1972 he was deputy head of music for RIAS, and from 1965 he was also music director at Berlin's Freie und Technische Hochschule. Arndt gave the RIAS Chamber Choir an international reputation through numerous broadcasts and concert tours; he did much to promote contemporary music, giving many first performances including works by Bialas, Henze, Krenek, Schoenberg, Genzmer, Milhaud, Reimann and Sakać. Arndt was awarded the Grosse Verdienstkreuz der Bundesrepublik Deutschland in 1971.

RUDOLF LÜCK/R

Arne, Michael (*b c*1740; *d* Lambeth, 14 Jan 1786). English composer. He was previously thought to be the 'natural son' of Thomas Arne mentioned by Burney. This comment, however, is now thought to refer to another son, Charles Arne, who was christened on 9 January 1734, before Thomas Arne's marriage to Cecilia Young. There is no record for Michael Arne at St Paul's, Covent Garden, where most of the Arne family were christened. His aunt, Mrs Susanna Cibber, was responsible for his upbringing. Under her guidance he is said to have made his stage début as the Page in Otway's tragedy *The Orphan*. He first appeared as a singer in Manfredini's concert on 20 February 1750, but his career as actor and vocalist was brief. Burney comments that 'his father tried to make him a singer, but he was naturally idle and not very quick. However, he acquired a powerful hand on the harpsichord'. He showed an early gift as a composer. *The Floweret*, his first collection of songs (1750), contains 'The Highland Laddie', a song in the Scottish style which became popular and as late as 1775 was adapted by Linley in *The Duenna*.

On 5 February 1751 he first played one of his father's organ concertos, of which he was the principal exponent for 30 years. Thereafter he found his true vocation as keyboard player and composer to the theatres and pleasure gardens. From 1756 onwards he contributed songs to various dramatic productions and in 1764 collaborated with Battishill in setting Richard Rolt's *Almena*, which enjoyed a limited success. His most famous song, *The Lass with the Delicate Air*, first appeared in 1762. He was elected to the Madrigal Society on 20 March 1765. On 5 November 1766 he married Elizabeth Wright, a young singer whom he had heard at Ranelagh in 1763. The marriage register indicates that he was a widower, though nothing is known of his first wife. His second wife sang the leading roles in many Drury Lane productions, including Arne's setting of Garrick's *Cymon* in 1767; this was his biggest success. In the same year he is reputed to have built a laboratory at Chelsea in order to study alchemy, which led him to a debtors' prison. When Mrs Arne died, on 1 May 1769, Burney bluntly placed the blame for her early death on the overwork to which her husband had subjected her.

In 1771–2 he toured Germany with a pupil, Ann Venables, and conducted the first public performance in Germany of Handel's *Messiah* on 21 May 1772 at Hamburg (preceded by a private performance on 15 April). On his return to England he married Miss Venables. In December 1776 he was engaged by Thomas Ryder to produce *Cymon* in Dublin, where his new wife was a popular attraction. But the lure of alchemy again prevailed; he took a house at Clontarf to resume the search for the philosopher's stone, which again drove him into debt. While confined to a Dublin sponging-house, he was assisted by Michael Kelly's father, who provided him with a piano in return for young Kelly's daily lesson. Returning to London, he was engaged as composer at Covent Garden for several seasons. One unusual engagement was to provide a harpsichord accompaniment for a display of moving pictures, *Eidophusikon*, in 1781. In 1784–5 he directed the Lenten Oratorios at the Haymarket. After his father's death he retained many of his unpublished manuscripts, including the organ concertos, and in 1784 announced his intention of publishing them. But he died, leaving his wife destitute, without having done so. The concertos were preserved and published in 1787 by John Groombridge.

His daughter Sarah was a leading singer at Drury Lane from 1795 to 1800. The daughter who nursed him in his last illness, however, was called Jemima. Whether they are one and the same person or whether he had two daughters is uncertain.

WORKS
DRAMATIC
LCG – London, Covent Garden
LDL – London, Drury Lane

Floritel and Perdita, or The Winter's Tale (D. Garrick, after W. Shakespeare)	LDL, 21 Jan 1756	by Boyce; 1 song by Arne
The Humorous Lieutenant (F. Beaumont and J. Fletcher)	LCG, 10 Dec 1756	
Harlequin Sorcerer (L. Theobald)	LCG, 1757	by T.A. Arne; 1 song by M. Arne
Harlequin's Invasion, or A Christmas Gambol (pantomime, Garrick)	LDL, 31 Dec 1759	by Boyce, Aylward and Arne
The Heiress, or the Antigallican (Mozeen)	LDL, 21 May 1759	

Edgar and Emmeline (entertainment, 2, J. Hawkesworth)	LDL, 31 Jan 1761	
A Midsummer Night's Dream: later renamed The Fairy Tale (Garrick and G. Colman, after Shakespeare)	LDL, 23 Nov 1763	by Burney; 3 songs by Arne
Hymen (interlude, Allen)	LDL, 23 Jan 1764	
Almena (op, 3, R. Rolt)	LDL, 2 Nov 1764	with Battishill
Cymon (dramatic romance, 5, Garrick, after J. Dryden: Cymon and Iphigenia)	LDL, 2 Jan 1767	revival, 17 Jan 1778, new ov., songs
Linco's Travels (interlude, Garrick)	LDL, 6 April 1767	with J. Vernon
Tom Jones (pasticcio)	LCG, 14 Jan 1769	1 song
The Maid of the Vale (T. Holcroft, after C. Goldoni: La buona figliuola)	Dublin, Smock Alley, 15 Feb 1775	
Emperor of the Moon (farce, after A. Behn)	London, Patagonian, 22 March 1777	
The Fairy Tale (2-act version of A Midsummer Night's Dream)	London, Haymarket, 18 July 1777	5 numbers
The Fathers, or the Good-natured Man (comedy, H. Fielding)	LCG, 30 Nov 1778	1 song
Love in a Village (comic op, I. Bickerstaff), revival	LCG, 13 Feb 1779	songs
The Comedy of Errors (comedy, 5, T. Hull, after Shakespeare)	LCG, ?1779–83	1 song
All alive at Jersey (pasticcio)	London, Sadler's Wells, 22 May 1779	songs
The Conscious Lovers (comedy, R. Steele), revival	LCG, 27 Sept 1779	1 song
The Belle's Stratagem (comedy, H. Cowley)	LCG, 22 Feb 1780	1 song, minuet
The Artifice (comic op, 2, W.A. Miles)	LDL, 14 April 1780	
The Choice of Harlequin, or the Indian Chief (pantomime, Messink)	LCG, 26 Dec 1781	
Vertumnus and Pomona (M. Feilde)	LCG, 21 Feb 1782	
The Positive Man (comedy, J. O'Keefe)	LCG, 16 March 1782	with S. Arnold
The Maid of the Mill (O'Keefe), revival	LCG, 25 Sept 1782	songs
The Capricious Lady (Beaumont, Fletcher and W. Cooke)	LCG, 17 Jan 1783	1 glee
Tristram Shandy (farce, L. McNally, after L. Sterne)	LCG, 26 April 1783	2 songs

SONG COLLECTIONS

The Floweret (London, 1750); The Violet (London, 1756); A Favourite Collection of English Songs (London, 1757); New Songs and Ballads (London, 1765); New Songs sung by Miss Wright at Vauxhall (London, c1765); A Collection of Favourite Songs sung by Mrs. Arne (London, 1773); Ranelagh Songs (London, 1780); c50 single songs for Vauxhall and Ranelagh

INSTRUMENTAL

Lesson, hpd (London, 1761)

BIBLIOGRAPHY

BDA; FiskeETM
C. Burney: 'M. Arne', Rees's Cyclopaedia (London, 1819–20)
M. Kelly: Reminiscences (London, 1826, 2/1826/R1968 with introduction by A.H. King); ed. R. Fiske (London, 1975)
W.H. Cummings: Dr. Arne and 'Rule, Britannia' (London, 1912)
M. Sands: Invitation to Ranelagh (London, 1946)
J.A. Parkinson: An Index to the Vocal Works of Thomas Augustine Arne and Michael Arne (Detroit, 1972)
T.J. Walsh: Opera in Dublin 1705–1797: the Social Scene (Dublin, 1973)
J. Kennedy: 'An Index to the Songs in The London Magazine (1732–1783)', MR, xlvi (1985), 83–92

JOHN A. PARKINSON/R

Arne, Mrs. English soprano, wife of Thomas Augustine Arne; see YOUNG family, (3).

Arne, Thomas Augustine (b London, 12 March 1710; d London, 5 March 1778). English composer, violinist and keyboard player. He was the most significant figure in 18th-century English theatre music.

1. LIFE. Arne inherited his first name from his grandfather and father, London upholsterers and undertakers and office holders in the London Company of Upholders. As a child he adopted the middle name Augustine, apparently to show his allegiance to the Roman Catholic faith of his mother, Anne. His father rented a large house in King Street, Covent Garden, where he ran a thriving business, the Two Crowns and Cushions, although he apparently allowed his own father and brother Edward to die in debtors' prisons. According to Charles Burney, who became his apprentice in 1744, Arne was sent to Eton, where a passion for music soon became evident: he tormented his fellow pupils 'night and day' by playing the recorder, practised the spinet secretly at night during the holidays, 'muffling the strings with a handkerchief', and studied composition on his own before taking violin lessons with Michael Christian Festing; Burney wrote that Arne and Festing were both present on 12 November 1725 to hear Thomas Roseingrave win the competition for the post of organist of St George's, Hanover Square.

The next year Arne was apprenticed for three years to a London attorney, Arthur Kynaston, but he soon abandoned the law for music. Burney wrote that Arne's father was reconciled to the change by the chance discovery of his son playing first violin in a concert at the house of a neighbour. The opposition cannot have been strong or prolonged, for Thomas Augustine was soon teaching his younger sister Susanna and his brother Richard to sing, and his father had some hand in the company formed in 1732 to put on English operas at the Little Theatre in the Haymarket; he sold tickets for the performances and probably provided financial backing. The company began in March with John Frederick Lampe's setting of Henry Carey's Amelia, and followed that with an unauthorized stage production of Handel's Acis and Galatea (17 May).

That autumn, however, the company split: Lampe remained at the Haymarket while Arne put on a production of Teraminta by Carey and John Stanley at Lincoln's Inn Fields (20 November) – the first definite record of his theatrical activities – and his own opera Rosamond (7 March 1733), a setting of Joseph Addison's 1707 libretto. The next season Arne put on his afterpiece setting of The Opera of Operas, or Tom Thumb the Great at the Little Theatre in the Haymarket in competition with a revival at Drury Lane of Lampe's full-length setting of the same text. Arne's setting ran for 15 nights and his masque *Dido and Aeneas* also did well, running for 17 performances.

Arne's position in the London theatre was strengthened by his sister Susanna's marriage in April 1734 to the actor and playwright Theophilus Cibber, whose company was in residence at Drury Lane. As a result he became house composer at Drury Lane, and wrote music for a number of plays and pantomimes over the next few years. Another profitable alliance was his own marriage to the soprano Cecilia Young on 15 March 1737, despite her father's objection to his Catholicism. He now had at his disposal the greatest tragedienne of her time (his sister) and the finest English female singer (his wife), and they contributed to his first enduring success, his setting of Milton's 1634 masque *Comus* as adapted by John Dalton (1738); it held the stage beyond the end of the century. *Comus* exploited the current fashion for old plays, the beginnings of a pre-Romantic interest in the past, though its success also had much to do with Arne's charming music; it was imitated by Handel in his Milton oratorio *L'Allegro, il Penseroso ed il Moderato*, written two years later.

By 1738 Arne was one of the leaders of musical life in London. That year he was one of the founder-members of the Society (later Royal Society) of Musicians, along with Handel, Boyce and Pepusch. In 1740 he was commissioned to set David Mallet and James Thomson's masque *Alfred* for performance in an entertainment given by the Prince of Wales in the gardens of Cliefden (Cliveden) House, near Maidenhead. The original work seems to have contained only seven musical numbers (including 'Rule, Britannia'), although Arne rewrote it a number of times, turning it in 1745 into an all-sung oratorio, and in 1753 into an all-sung opera. In the theatrical season

1. *Thomas Augustine Arne: caricature by Francesco Bartolozzi, etching with watercolour, c1770 (National Portrait Gallery, London)*

1740–41 he composed music for the Drury Lane productions of *The Tempest*, *As You Like It*, *Twelfth Night* and *The Merchant of Venice*, including songs such as 'Where the bee sucks' and 'Under the greenwood tree' that have never been surpassed or forgotten since they were written. Arne had another major success in spring 1742 with Congreve's 1700 masque *The Judgment of Paris*, presumably inspired by the unidentified setting performed with *Alfred* at Cliveden in 1740.

Up to this point, Arne had worked mostly in London. But his sister took refuge in Dublin in December 1741 from the scandal surrounding the failure of her marriage to Cibber, and sang there with Handel in spring 1742, notably in the first performance of *Messiah* on 13 April. Handel's success in Dublin presumably inspired Arne to try his luck there: he arrived with his wife and the tenor Thomas Lowe on 30 June and worked there for two seasons. He spent most of his time performing existing compositions, including a number of Handel oratorios, though his own oratorio *The Death of Abel* was first given at the Smock Alley Theatre on 18 February 1744. On his return journey in August he passed through Chester, where he met the young Charles Burney and agreed to take him to London as his apprentice without the usual fee.

Over the next few years Arne continued his work at Drury Lane, and had a hit with his setting of *God bless our noble king*, which was sung every night during the crisis caused by the Young Pretender's rebellion in September 1745. His long association with London's pleasure gardens also seems to have started that summer, when vocal music formed part of the entertainments at Vauxhall for the first time. According to Burney, Arne's dialogue *Colin and Phaebe* was 'constantly encored every night for more than three months', and was published in September in the first collection of Vauxhall songs, *Lyric Harmony*; Arne's later song collections, notably in the series *Vocal Melody* (1749–64), also contain many songs from the pleasure gardens.

The 1750s were not very fruitful years for Arne. David Garrick, joint patentee at Drury Lane from 1747, began to prefer other composers, and Arne had several flops, including the all-sung afterpieces *Henry and Emma* (1749) and *Don Saverio* (1750). Things came to a head when Susanna Cibber defected to Covent Garden with several other actors at the beginning of the 1750–51 season. Arne followed her and a battle ensued between the two theatres, beginning with competing productions of *Romeo and Juliet* put on on the same day, 28 September, with rival settings by Arne and Boyce of processional dirges at the end of the play. Arne's dirge continued to be performed long after Boyce's was forgotten, but in general he was no more successful at Covent Garden than at Drury Lane, and he had to put on his next major work, the all-sung opera *Eliza*, at the Little Theatre (1754); it was suppressed after one performance 'by an Order from a superior Power'. He returned to Drury Lane briefly with his setting of David Mallet's masque *Britannia* (1755), though in October that year he returned to Dublin with his wife, his pupil Charlotte Brent and his niece Polly Young.

It soon became apparent that Arne's marriage was in trouble. He attributed the situation to Cecilia's frequent illnesses, which he claimed resulted from her 'passions, equal to raving madness', while she complained of his repeated philandering. At the end of the season he

2. Scene from Arne's pasticcio 'Love in a Village' with Edward Shuter as Justice Woodcock (left), John Beard as Hawthorne (centre) and John Dunstall as Hodge: painting by Johan Zoffany, c1767 (Royal National Theatre, London)

returned to London with Charlotte Brent, now his mistress, while Cecilia remained in Dublin with Polly Young. He agreed to support her with £40 a year, though in 1758 Mrs Delany found her 'much humbled', teaching singing in Downpatrick: 'She has been severely used by a bad husband, and suffered to starve, if she had not met with charitable people'. However, he evidently attempted to raise money at this period by publishing collections of his music with John Walsh, including *Six Cantatas for a Voice and Instruments* (1755), *VIII Sonatas or Lessons for the Harpsichord* (1756), *VII Sonatas for Two Violins with a Thorough Bass* (1757) and the scores of *Britannia* (1755), *Alfred* (1757) and *Eliza* (1757).

With Charlotte Brent at his disposal, Arne's fortunes rapidly revived. After Garrick refused her services at Drury Lane, she scored major successes at Covent Garden in Arne's revision of *The Beggar's Opera* (1759), his comic operas *The Jovial Crew* and *Thomas and Sally* (both 1760), his Metastasio opera *Artaxerxes* and his comic opera *Love in a Village* (both 1762), as well as his oratorio *Judith*, given at Drury Lane on 27 February 1761. He finally achieved a measure of official recognition on 7 July 1759 with an Oxford doctorate. Arne could not sustain this level of success for long: his comic opera *The Guardian Out-Witted* only lasted for six performances in December 1764, while the lost *L'olimpiade*, an *opera seria* in Italian, failed after only two nights in April 1765.

Things were not helped in 1766 by the death of his sister and the marriage of Charlotte Brent to the violinist Thomas Pinto, and in the late 1760s he found little employment at either theatre. He found some compensation in his membership of the Noblemen and Gentlemen's Catch Club and the Madrigal Society, and in the profitable concerts of catches and glees he gave from 1767, although he was evidently in financial difficulty by 1770, when Cecilia's lawyer threatened legal action because he was £10 in arrears with his support payments.

Despite this, the last decade of Arne's life saw the production of some fine works, including *An Ode upon Dedicating a Building to Shakespeare* (7 September 1769), written for Garrick's Shakespeare festival at Stratford-upon-Avon, the masque *The Fairy Prince* (1771), the music for William Mason's Greek-style tragedy *Elfrida* (1772) and the lost music for Mason's tragedy *Caractacus* (1776), a score that according to Samuel Arnold contained 'some of the brightest and most vigorous emanations of our English 'Amphion''. In October 1777 Arne was reconciled with his wife, though two months later he fell ill and made his will. He died of a 'spasmodic complaint', and was buried in the churchyard of St Paul's, Covent Garden, on 15 March 1778; his effects, including 'a remarkably fine toned double key'd harpsichord, two guitars, a mandolin, a lute and other valuable effects', were disposed of on 8 April.

2. WORKS.   Arne was one of the most prolific composers of his day, though much of his output is lost, and the circumstances of his life restricted him to only a few genres. As a Catholic, he did not write anything for the Anglican liturgy or any organ voluntaries, and was denied the sort of official patronage given to his most important English contemporaries, William Boyce and John Stanley. Furthermore, he showed little interest in writing concert music: he did not contribute to the concerto grosso repertory, his symphonies or overtures mostly derive from stage works, and his keyboard concertos, like Handel's, also seem to have been mainly a by-product of his work in the theatre. For most of his life, Arne was essentially a theatre composer, and dominated the various genres of English theatre music.

It is unfortunate that most of Arne's stage works are, for one reason or another, unlikely to be revived in the modern theatre. Some of the best, such as *The Judgment of Paris* (1742), *Artaxerxes* (1762) and *The Fairy Prince* (1771), only survive incomplete; few of his manuscripts survive, and those works that were printed usually appeared without choruses, dances or recitatives, and often only in vocal score. Many works use spoken dialogue (the norm at the time in the two main London theatres) rather than recitative, he set a number of poor texts – some his own work – and he was surprisingly reluctant to abandon the outdated conventions of the heroic masque, even towards the end of his life. Nevertheless, he was a consistent and courageous theatrical innovator. He seems to have been largely responsible for the revival of English opera in the early 1730s, and for alerting Handel to the commercial possibilities of large-scale works in English. He was the first English composer to experiment with Italian-style all-sung comic opera, unsuccessfully in *The*

3. Autograph manuscript of the opening of the Adagio from Arne's Violin Sonata in E (GB-Lbl Add.39957, f.34)

Temple of Dullness (1745), *Henry and Emma* (1749) and *Don Saverio* (1750), but triumphantly in *Thomas and Sally* (1760). *Thomas and Sally* was the first of three highly successful works by Arne of the early 1760s that created

Ex.1 'O too lovely, too unkind' from Act 1 of *Artaxerxes*

new genres in English theatre music, and determined much of its subsequent development. *Artaxerxes* (1762) was the first attempt to set a full-blown *opera seria* in English; it held the stage until the 1830s. *Love in a Village* (1762) was equally novel (fig.2). It was a modernized ballad opera, with borrowed Italian arias and specially composed numbers as well as folk tunes, all orchestrated in an up-to-date manner. It began a vogue for pastiche opera that lasted well into the 19th century.

Arne was also an important musical innovator. Charles Burney wrote that he introduced into *Comus* 'a light, airy, original, and pleasing melody, wholly different from that of Purcell or Handel, whom all English composers had either pillaged or imitated'. He used this tuneful folklike style throughout his life, particularly in his songs for the pleasure gardens, though in his later stage works he began to develop a more advanced italianate style. Burney, who could never resist a sly dig at his former teacher, accused him of 'crowding the airs' of *Artaxerxes* with 'most of the Italian divisions and difficulties which had ever been heard at the opera', though in reality Arne was just the first English composer to go beyond the Baroque vocal technique established in England by Handel. His innovations, brilliantly demonstrated in performance by Charlotte Brent, were soon taken up by other English composers.

Similarly, Arne's orchestration developed greatly during his career. He wrote effectively for the orchestra in a Handelian idiom from the beginning of his career, but in the 1750s he began to be much more adventurous. He was the first English composer to use the clarinet (in *Thomas and Sally*), and in his later works he deployed wind instruments with verve and brilliance, though in such a way that the sound of a complete *galant* orchestra could be produced by about a dozen players: oboe, flute and clarinet parts normally alternate, so that they can be taken by the same players, while the occasional trumpet and timpani parts might have been taken by spare violinists. *Artaxerxes* is particularly imaginative in this respect: the opera opens with a striking evocation of the dawn, portrayed by a wind band with double bass and continuo, but without cellos, while the flowing river in 'Water parted from the sea' from Act 3 is beautifully rendered by dense writing for pairs of clarinets, horns, bassoons and strings. Arne could achieve equally striking effects just with strings, as in 'O too lovely, too unkind' from Act 1, where he muted the violins, divided the violas and mixed pizzicato and arco (ex.1).

Perhaps the most striking feature of Arne's music is its stylistic diversity. Even in *Comus* there is a distinction between his own tuneful folklike style and the numbers in a more elevated Handelian idiom, such as the beautiful air 'Nor on beds of fading flow'rs'. In his later works he began to use the *galant* idiom as well, often in order to aid characterization. In *Artaxerxes* he reserved the most advanced and richly scored airs for the main characters, mostly using the older idioms for the minor characters. 20th-century criticism, influenced by 19th-century notions of progress and stylistic unity, has tended to see this practice as a weakness, although Arne doubtless thought it made large-scale works agreeably varied, and it was taken up by his younger contemporaries, such as Thomas Linley (ii) and Samuel Wesley; it was the compositional equivalent of the retrospective concert repertory that was developing in England at the time.

Arne's sets of instrumental music are similarly diverse in style. In the *Eight Overtures in 8 Parts* (1751), nos.3 and 5 are italianate works in the fast–slow–fast pattern, while the others are broadly cast as French overtures, starting with an introduction in dotted rhythms and a fugue. Nos.3, 7 and 8 come from *Henry and Emma* (1749 setting), *Comus* and *The Judgment of Paris* respectively, though it is likely that they are all theatrical in origin. The *Four New Overtures or Symphonies* (1767), by contrast, are all in the modern three-movement pattern, and may have been composed as concert works. They suggest that Arne had been studying the *galant* symphonies of J.C. Bach and Abel as well as the series of Periodical Overtures published in London by Bremner from 1763, though they have a nervous brilliance in places that is closer to C.P.E. than J.C. Bach. Arne's *VIII Sonatas or Lessons for the Harpsichord* (1756) and *VII Sonatas for Two Violins with a Thorough Bass* (1757) are even more diverse in style and structure, and were probably hurriedly assembled for publication from works composed over a long period. Newspaper reports suggest that at least some of the *Six Favourite Concertos for the Organ, Harpsichord or Piano Forte* were written for Arne's son Michael in the 1750s, though they were not published until 1793, and there are signs of later revisions: an early variant of no.1 exists in manuscript, while the keyboard part of no.3 appears to have been modernized, presumably to make it more suitable for the pianoforte.

Arne's non-theatrical vocal works have generally been neglected, though the best of them deserve to be much better known. *Judith* (1761), with its lyrical airs and surprisingly un-Handelian, forward-looking choruses, is arguably the finest oratorio by an Englishman before *The Dream of Gerontius*. *An Ode upon Dedicating a Building to Shakespeare* (1769) unfortunately only survives in an incomplete vocal score, without the music that accompanied Garrick's melodramatic declamation of the text, although it does contain 'Thou soft flowing Avon', one of Arne's loveliest songs. *Whittington's Feast* (1776), his last major work apart from the lost *Caractacus*, survives complete in orchestral score and contains some fine, elaborate music, though its puerile text (a line-by-line parody of *Alexander's Feast*) has prevented modern revivals. *The Morning*, with its magical 'sunrise' opening, stands out among his smaller cantatas, as do *Cymon and Iphigenia* and *The Lover's Recantation*, witty explorations of rustic love.

Arne was undoubtedly an uneven composer. He was often hasty and slapdash, he was too easily satisfied by poor texts and he was content to use the language of the *galant* style without exploring its formal implications very far. Nevertheless, at his best he was capable of far outshining his more consistent contemporaries. He has been praised for his easy, natural sense of melody, though it is often his profound command of harmony and his simple yet highly effective orchestral writing that stays in the memory. As William Stafford put it in 1830:

Arne was neither so vigorous as Purcell, nor had he the magnificent simplicity, and lofty grandeur of Handel: but the ease and elegance of his melodies, and the variety of his harmony, render his compositions attractive in the highest degree: and we may justly be proud of his name, as an honour to English music.

WORKS
DRAMATIC

all printed works published in London

DBSA – *Dublin, Smock Alley Theatre*
LDL – *London, Drury Lane Theatre*
LLH – *London, Little or New Theatre, Haymarket*
LMG – *London, Marylebone Gardens*
LCG – *London, Covent Garden*
LKH – *London, Kings Theatre in the Haymarket*
LLF – *London, Lincoln's Inn Fields*
LSW – *London, Sadler's Wells Theatre*

Title	Genre, acts	Librettist	First performance	Sources, revivals, comments
Rosamond	Eng. serious op, 3	after J. Addison	LLF, 7 March 1733	rev. as afterpiece, LDL, 8 March 1740; 3 songs in The British Musical Miscellany, i (1734), iii (1735); 5 songs, 3 duets, 3 recits, GB-Lbl (full score, ?for afterpiece version); song pubd separately (c1770)
The Opera of Operas, or Tom Thumb the Great	burlesque op (afterpiece)	E. Haywood and W. Hatchett, after H. Fielding	LLH, 29 Oct 1733	song in The British Musical Miscellany, iii (1735), song in J. Markordt, Tom Thumb (1781), 16 others lost, listed in lib
Dido and Aeneas	masque	B. Booth	LLH, 12 Jan 1734	2 songs in The British Musical Miscellany, i (1734)
Love and Glory	masque, 2	T. Phillips	LDL, 21 March 1734	lib lists 14 nos., lost; revived as Britannia, LDL, 29 April 1734
Harlequin Orpheus, or The Magical Pipe	pantomime		LDL, 3 March 1735	lost
The Twin Rivals	play	G. Farquhar	LLH, 21 Aug 1735	act tunes, lost, medley ov., lost or same as one in Harlequin Restor'd
Harlequin Restor'd, or The Country Revels	pantomime		LDL, 18 Oct 1735	medley ov. (1736); comic tunes (1736), doubtful
Greenwich Park	play	W. Mountfort	LDL, 10 Nov 1735	act tunes, lost
The Miser	play	Fielding, after Molière: L'avare	LDL, 13 Nov 1735	act tunes, lost
Harlequin Restor'd, or Taste à la Mode	pantomime	R. Charke	LDL, 12 Jan 1736	lost
Zara	play	A. Hill, after Voltaire	LDL, 12 Jan 1736	march in The Compleat Tutor for the Hautboy (c1746)

Title	Genre, acts	Librettist	First performance	Sources, revivals, comments
The Fall of Phaeton	masque	W. Pritchard	LDL, 28 Feb 1736	song in The Songs in As You Like It and Twelfth Night (1741), 5 others lost, listed in lib
The Rival Queens, or The Death of Alexander the Great	play	N. Lee	LDL, 22 Nov 1736	duet in The Songs in As You Like It and Twelfth Night (1741)
The King and the Miller of Mansfield	play	R. Dodsley	LDL, 29 Jan 1737	song in The Musical Entertainer, i (1737/R)
Comus	masque, 3	J. Dalton, after J. Milton	LDL, 4 March 1738	score (1740), inc., Lbl (full score), ed. in MB, iii (1951, 2/1965); rev. as afterpiece (G. Colman the elder), LCG, 17 Oct 1772
The Tender Husband, or The Accomplish'd Fools	play	R. Steele	LDL, 25 Nov 1738	song in The Songs in As You Like It and Twelfth Nigfht (1741)
An Hospital for Fools	dramatic fable	J. Miller	LDL, 15 Nov 1739	4 songs pubd in lib, dance lost
Don John, or The Libertine Destroy'd	play	T. Shadwell	LDL, 13 Feb 1740	songs, dance of shepherds, dance of furies, lost
Lethe, or Esop in the Shades	play	D. Garrick	LDL, 1 April 1740	song in The Agreeable Musical Choice, vi (1754), other music by W. Boyce
Alfred	masque, 3	D. Mallet and J. Thomson	Cliveden House, Berks., 1 Aug 1740	revised as orat, LDL, 20 March 1745; revived as theatre masque, LDL, 23 Feb 1751, with music by Burney; revived as Alfred the Great (op), LCG, 12 May 1753; revived, LDL, 9 Oct 1773, with music by T. Smith score (1757), inc., ed. in MB, xlvii (1981)
Oepidius, King of Thebes	play	J. Dryden and N. Lee, after Sophocles	LDL, 19 Nov 1740	song, sacrificial scene, lost
The Tempest	play	Shadwell and Dryden, after W. Shakespeare	LDL, 28 Nov 1740	2 songs, unidentified; revived LDL, 31 Jan 1746, vocal music, incl. masques from acts 4 and 5, some in Lbl; revived LCG, 27 Dec 1776, song in The Syren (1777), 2 songs ed. P. Young, Nine Shakespeare Songs by Thomas Augustine Arne (London, 1963)
As You Like It	play	Shakespeare	LDL, 20 Dec 1740	3 songs in The Songs in … As You Like It and Twelfth Night (1741), ed. P. Young, Nine Shakespeare Songs by Thomas Augustine Arne (London, 1963)
Twelfth Night, or What You Will	play	Shakespeare	LDL, 15 Jan 1741	2 songs in The Songs in … As You Like It and Twelfth Night (1741), 2nd setting of Come away, Death in The Musick in the Comedy of Twelfth Night (c1785)
The Peasant's Triumph on the Death of the Wild Boar	ballet		LDL, 12 Feb 1741	The Comic Tunes … to the Celebrated Dances, i (1744)
The Merchant of Venice	play	Shakespeare	LDL, 14 Feb 1741	2 songs in The Songs and Duetto in the Blind Beggar of Bethnal Green (1741)
The Blind Beggar of Bethnal Green	ballad op, 2	Dodsley	LDL, 3 April 1741	lib lists 9 songs, 7 in The Songs and Duetto in the Blind Beggar of Bethnal Green (1741), others lost
The Rehearsal	play	G. Villiers	LDL, 21 Nov 1741	duet, Lcm
The Judgment of Paris	masque, 1	W. Congreve	LDL, 12 March 1742	rev. version, LCG, 3 April 1759; score (1745), inc., chorus, Lbl; ed. in MB, xlii (1978)
Miss Lucy in Town	ballad farce	Fielding	LDL, 6 May 1742	lib lists 10 songs, lost; revived as The Country Madcap in London, LDL, 7 June 1770
The Mock Doctor	farce	Addison	Dublin, Aungier St Theatre, 2 May 1743	lost, Arne's contrib. uncertain
Theodosius, or The Force of Love	play	Lee	DBSA, ?26 April 1744	5 nos., Lbl
Cymbeline	play	T. Cibber, after Shakespeare	LLH, 8 Nov 1744	dirge (text, W. Collins), probably for this production, in Lyric Harmony, ii (1746/R), ed. C. Bartlett (Wyton, 1991)
The Temple of Dullness	burlesque op	C. Cibber, after interludes in L. Theobald: The Happy Captive	LDL, 17 Jan 1745	lib lists 16 songs, incl. 3 from Miss Lucy in Town, lost; revived as Capochio and Dorinna, LMG, 28 July, 1768, music lost

Title	Genre, acts	Librettist	First performance	Sources, revivals, comments
The Picture, or The Cuckold in Conceit	play	Miller, after Molière: *Sganarelle*	LDL, 11 Feb 1745	song in Lyric Harmony, i (1745/R)
King Pepin's Campaign	burlesque op, 2	W. Shirley	LDL, 15 April 1745	lib lists 19 nos., lost
Harlequin Incendiary, or Colombine Cameron	pantomime		LDL, 3 March 1746	lib lists 14 nos., lost
The She-Gallants, or Once a Lover and Always a Lover	play	G. Granville	LDL, 13 March 1746	song in Lyric Harmony, ii (1746/R)
The Sheep-Shearing, or Florizel and Perdita	play	M. Morgan, after Shakespeare: *The Winter's Tale*	DBSA, 1747	songs, lost; revived LCG, 22 Dec 1760, with added song, in The Winter's Amusement (1761)
The Wild-Goose Chase	play	J. Fletcher	LDL, 7 March 1747	lib lists 1 song, lost
The Foundling	play	E. Moore	LDL, 13 Feb 1748	song in Amaryllis, ii (1748)
The Provok'd Wife	play	Garrick, after J. Vanbrugh	LDL, 21 March 1748	song in Vocal Melody, i (1749), 4 others, lost, listed in lib
Much Ado About Nothing	play	Shakespeare	LDL, 14 Nov 1748	song in Vocal Melody, i (1749)
The Triumph of Peace	masque	Dodsley	LDL, 21 Feb 1749	song in A Favourite Collection of English Songs (1757), 6 other nos. lost, listed in lib
The Muses' Looking Glass	play	T. Randolph	LCG, 9 March 1749	War, Peace and Plenty (? L. Ryan), lost
Henry and Emma, or The Nut-Brown Maid [1st setting]	musical drama	T. Holt, after M. Prior	LCG, 31 March 1749	ov. as no.3 of Eight Overtures (1751), song in The Masque of Alfred (1757), 13 other nos. lost, listed in lib
Don Saverio	comic op	Arne	LDL, 15 Feb 1750	song in London Magazine (1752), song in The Masque of Alfred (1757), 16 other nos. lost, listed in lib
Harlequin Mountebank, or The Squire Electrified	pantomime		London, New Wells, Clerkenwell, 16 April 1750	music lost
The Sacrifice of Iphigenia	entertainment		London, New Wells, Clerkenwell, 16 April 1750	song in London Magazine (1750)
Romeo and Juliet	play	Shakespeare	LCG, 28 Sept 1750	dirge (c1765)
The Country Lasses, or The Custom of the Manor	play	C. Johnson	LCG, 14 Dec 1751	song in Vocal Melody, iv (1752)
Harlequin Sorcerer	pantomime	after Theobald	LCG, 11 Feb 1752	4 songs in Vocal Melody, iv (1752), duet in The Agreeable Musical Choice, v (1753/R), Building Tune, *US-SFsc*, minuet, *BEm*; lib lists 6 other nos., lost
The Oracle	play	S.-M. Cibber, after Saint-Foix	LCG, 17 March 1752	song in Vocal Melody, iv (1752)
The Drummer, or The Haunted House	play	Addison	LCG, 8 Dec 1752	dialogue in The Agreeable Musical Choice, v (1753/R), later added to Harlequin Sorcerer
Eliza	op, 3	R. Rolt	LLH, 29 May 1754	score (1757), inc., complete score of Act 3, *CA*
Britannia	masque, 2	Mallet	LDL, 9 May 1755	score (1755), inc.
Injured Honour, or The Earl of Westmorland	play	H. Brooke	DBSA, 8 March 1756	anthem, dirge, triumphal hymn, lost
The Pincushion	farce	?Arne, attrib. J. Gay	DBSA, 20 March 1756	songs, duet, lost
The Painter's Breakfast	play		DBSA, 2 April 1756	duet, lost
Catherine and Petruchio	play	Garrick, after Shakespeare: *The Taming of the Shrew*	DBSA, 2 June 1756	lost, Arne's contrib. uncertain
Mercury Harlequin	pantomime	H. Woodward	LDL, 27 Dec 1756	song in The Literary Magazine (1757) and London Magazine (1757), song (1760)
The Fair Penitent	play	N. Rowe	LCG, 22 April 1757	song, lost
Isabella, or The Fatal Marriage	play	Garrick, after T. Southerne	LDL, 2 Dec 1757	2 songs in The Agreeable Musical Choice, viii (1758)
The Prophetess, or The History of Dioclesian	musical play	T. Betterton, after ?Fletcher and P. Massinger	LCG, 1 Feb 1758	song in A Collection of Songs, ix (c1760/R), 5 others lost
The Sultan, or Solyman and Zaida	masque		LCG, 23 Nov 1758	perf. with The Prophetess, rev., LCG, 30 Nov 1759; duet in A Choice Collection of Songs, xii (1761)
The Ambitious Stepmother	play	Rowe	LDL, 1 Feb 1759	Hymn to the Sun, lost
Cymbeline	play	W. Hawkins, after Shakespeare	LCG, 15 Feb 1759	Dirge, probably for this production, in The Winter's Amusement (1761)

Title	Genre, acts	Librettist	First performance	Sources, revivals, comments
The Beggar's Opera	ballad op, 3	Gay	LCG, 10 Oct 1759	vs (1769) with hornpipe and small revs. by Arne; revived 17 Oct 1777, with new song, in A Choice Collection of Favourite Hunting Songs (c1780)
The Desert Island	play	A. Murphy, after P. Metastasio	LDL, 24 Jan 1760	song in The Monthly Melody (1760), ed. P. Warlock, Songs of the Gardens (1925)
The Jovial Crew, or The Merry Beggars	comic op, 2	E. Roome, M. Concanen and W. Yonge, after R. Brome	LCG, 14 Feb 1760	7 songs in A Collection of Songs, ix (c1760/R); revived as The Ladies' Frolick, LDL, 7 May 1770
Thomas and Sally, or The Sailor's Return	comic op, 2	I. Bickerstaff	LCG, 28 Nov 1760	score (1761), ed. R. Fiske (London, 1977)
The Way to Keep Him	play	Murphy	LDL, 10 Jan 1761	song (1760), song (1763)
The Provok'd Husband, or A Journey to London	play	Vanbrugh and C. Cibber	LCG, 7 April 1761	2 songs in The Winter's Amusement, xiii (1761)
Artaxerxes	serious op, 3	?Rolt and Arne, after Metastasio	LCG, 2 Feb 1762	score without recits and final chorus (1762/R), addl recit and air in The Syren (1777); some recits by ?Arne in vs ed. J. Addison (c1820/R)
Beauty and Virtue Reconciled	serenata	Arne, after Metastasio	LDL, 26 Feb 1762	music lost
Love in a Village	pasticcio comic op, 3	Bickerstaff, after Johnson: The Village Opera	LCG, 8 Dec 1762	arr. Arne, incl. 19 songs by Arne; vs (1763), full score, GB-Lcm
The Arcadian Nuptials	masque	?Arne	LCG, 19 Jan 1764	dialogue in A Favourite Collection of Songs (1764/R)
The Guardian Out-witted	comic op, 3	Arne	LCG, 12 Dec 1764	vs (1764); ov. in Periodical Overtures, xxvii (1770), ed. G. Beechey (London, 1973)
L'olimpiade	os, 3	G.G. Bottarelli, after Metastasio	LKH, 27 April 1765	music lost
The Summer's Tale	pasticcio musical comedy	R. Cumberland	LCG, 6 Dec 1765	arr. S. Arnold; 2 new, 2 adapted songs, in vs (1765)
Miss in her Teens, or The Medley of Lovers	farce	Garrick, after Dancourt: La parisienne	LDL, 25 April 1766	song (1767)
Lionel and Clarissa	pasticcio comic op	Bickerstaff	LCG, 25 Feb 1768	arr. C. Dibdin; 1 new song in vs (1768)
King Arthur, or The British Worthy	masque, 3	Garrick, after Dryden	LDL, 13 Dec 1770	rev. of H. Purcell's semi-opera, incl. 10 new songs, vs (c1770); ov. (1770)
The Fairy Prince	masque, 3	Colman the elder, after B. Jonson: Oberon	LCG, 12 Nov 1771	score (1771/R), inc.; ov. (c1771)
Squire Badger	burletta, 2	Arne, after Fielding: Don Quixote in England	LLH, 16 March 1772	song in A Choice Collection of Favourite Hunting Songs (c1780), 14 other songs lost, listed in lib, medley ov., lost; revived as The Sot, LLH, 16 Feb 1775
The Cooper	musical entertainment, 2	Arne, after N.M. Audinot and A.F. Quétant: Le tonnelier	LLH, 10 June 1772	vs (1772); ed. J. Horovitz (London, 1956)
Elfrida	dramatic poem, 5	Colman the elder, after W. Mason	LCG, 21 Nov 1772	vs (1772), ov. pubd separately (1772)
The Rose	comic op, 3	?Arne	LDL, 2 Dec 1772	lib lists 19 songs, lost; ov. pubd separately (1773)
The Pigmy Revels, or Harlequin Foundling	pantomime	J. Messink	LDL, 26 Dec 1772	by Dibdin, Morris Dance by Arne, vs (1773)
The Golden Pippin	pasticcio comic op	K. O'Hara	LCG, 6 Feb 1773	arr. J.A. Fisher; 5 adapted songs by Arne, 2 of them unidentified, vs (1773)
Alzuma	play	Murphy, after Dryden and Voltaire	LCG, 23 Feb 1773	Procession of Virgins, Ode to the Sun, lost
The Trip to Portsmouth	comic op	G.A. Stevens	LLH, 11 Aug 1773	vocal music by Dibdin; ov. borrowed from The Rose, 2 dance tunes by Arne, vs (1773)
Achilles in Petticoats	burlesque op, 3	Colman the elder, after Gay	LCG, 16 Dec 1773	vs (1774)
Henry and Emma [2nd setting]	musical drama	H. Bate Dudley, after Prior	LCG, 13 April 1774	lib lists 4 songs, lost
May-Day, or The Little Gipsy	musical farce, 2	Garrick	LDL, 28 Oct 1775	vs (1776/R)
Phoebe at Court	operetta, 2	Arne, after R. Lloyd: The Capricious Lovers	LLH, 22 Feb 1776	music lost
The Seraglio	comic op	Dibdin and E. Thompson	LCG, 25 Nov 1776	by Dibdin and Arnold; song listed in lib. lost (not in vs 1776)
Caractacus	dramatic poem, 5	Mason	LCG, 6 Dec 1776	lib lists 21 nos., lost

Title	Genre, acts	Librettist	First performance	Sources, revivals, comments
Love Finds the Way	pasticcio comic op	T. Hull, after Murphy: *The School for Guardians*	LCG, 18 Nov 1777	arr. Fisher; new songs by Arne advertised, lost
The Nunnery Expedition				advertised for LDL, 20 April 1748, not perf., lost
Trick upon Trick	ballad op	R. Fabian		unknown production, 2 songs in The Winter's Amusement (1761), possibly perf. in The Comical Resentment, or Trick for Trick, LCG, 26 March 1759
The Birth of Hercules	masque	Shirley		rehearsed 1763, not perf.; lib (1765) lists 19 nos., lost

SACRED

The Death of Abel (orat, Arne, after P. Metastasio), 1744, lost except for Hymn of Eve (1756)

Judith (orat, I. Bickerstaff), 1761, score without recits and choruses (1761), complete score *GB-Lbl*

Mass, F, 3vv, org, lost or same as anon. Mass, Lulworth Castle, Dorset

Mass, G, 4vv, org, Lulworth Castle, Dorset (version for 2/3vv org)

Libera me, for the funeral of Francis Pemberton, 28 June 1770, dirge, S, T, B, SSATB, org, *Lbl*, ed. A. Lewis (London, 1950)

O salutaris hostia (motet), *Lbl*

1 song in Arnold's The Prodigal Son (orat, T. Hull), 1777, pubd in The Syren (1777)

ODES AND CANTATAS

A Grand Epithalamium, 1736, lost

Black-Ey'd Susan (cant., R. Leveridge), 1740, lost

God bless our noble king, A, T, B, ATB, 2 hn, 2 ob, str, bc, 1745, *GB-Lbl*, ed. C. Bartlett (Wyton, 1985)

Fair Celia love pretended (cant., W. Congreve), 1v, vns, bc, Vocal Melody, i (1749)

Chaucer's Recantation (cant.), 1v, str, bc, Vocal Melody, ii (1750)

Ode to Chearfulness, 1750, lost

Cymon and Iphigenia (cant., J. Dryden), 1v, str, bc, vs (1750), pts *Bu*

Six Cantatas, fs (1755): Bacchus and Ariadne, 1v, 2 fl, 2 ob, 2 hn, str, bc; Delia, 1v, str, bc; Frolick and Free (G. Granville), 1v, 2 ob, str, bc; Lydia (after Sappho), 1v, 2 bn, str, bc; The Morning, 1v, fl/rec, str, bc; The School of Anacreon, 1v, 2 hn, str, bc; Lydia and The Morning, both ed. R. Hufstader (New York, 1971)

5 odes in Del Canzionere d'Orazio (1757): Delle muse all'almo core, 1v, str, bc; Finche fedele il core, 2vv, 2 fl, str, bc; Finche fedele il core, 2vv, 2 vn, bc; Se vanti in Telefo, 1v, 2 hn, str, bc; Tu mi fuggi schizzinosa, 1v, 2 vn, bc [= Advice to Chloe]

The Spring (cant.), 1v, str, bc, British Melody (1760)

Love and Resentment (cant.), 1v, 2 cl, 2 vn, bc, Summer Amusement (1766)

The Lover's Recantation (cant.), 1v, 2 fl, 2 ob, str, bc; vs in The Winter's Amusement (1761), fs, *Lbl*, ed. P. Young (Leipzig, 1988)

Advice to Chloe (cant.), 1v, vns, bc, New Favourite Songs (1768)

An Ode upon Dedicating a Building to Shakespeare (D. Garrick), 1769, speaker, S, S, S, S, T, Bar, SATB, orch; 9 nos. in vs (1769)

Love and Resolution (musical dialogue), 1770, music lost

Reffley Spring (cant.), 2vv, 2 vn, bc, vs (1772)

Diana (cant.), 1v, 2 fl, 2 ob, 2 cl, 2 hn, 2 vn, bc; vs in The Vocal Grove (1774)

Whittington's Feast (secular orat, Arne, after Dryden: *Alexander's Feast*), 1776, S, S, T, B, SATB, 2 fl, 2 ob, 2bn, 2 tpt, 2 hn, timps, drum, str, bc, fs, *US-Wc*

A wretch long tortured with disdain (cant.), 1v, 2 fl, 2 ob, 2 hn, str, bc, full score *GB-Lbl*

SONGS
full list in Parkinson, 1972; number of songs by Arne in square brackets

The British Musical Miscellany, vi (1737) [1]

The Songs and Duetto in The Blind Beggar of Bethnal Green (1741) [1]

The British Orpheus, iii (1743) [1]

Universal Harmony (1743–5) [1]

Lyric Harmony, i (1745/R) [18]; Lyric Harmony, ii (1746/R) [18]

The Music in The Judgment of Paris (1745) [1]

Amaryllis, i (1746) [1]

Peter Prelleur, An Introduction to Singing (1747) [1]

Clio and Euterpe, i (1748) [1]

Vocal Melody, i (1749) [6]; ii (1750) [8]; iii (1751) [7]; iv (1752) [2]; v: The Agreeable Musical Choice (1753/R) [7]; vi: The Agreeable

Musical Choice (1754) [6]; vii: The Agreeable Musical Choice (1756/R) [8]; viii: The Agreeable Musical Choice (1758) [6]; xi: British Melody (1760) [4]; xii: A Choice Collection of Songs (1761/R) [3]; xiii: The Winter's Amusement (1761) [6]; xiv: A Favourite Collection of Songs (1764/R) [5]

Willem Defesch, Songs Sung at Mary-bon Gardens (1753) [2]

A Collection of Poems in Four Volumes by Several Hands (1755) [1]

A Favourite Collection of English Songs (1757–8) [6]

The Monthly Melody (1760) [22], mainly reissued as British Amusement (1762) [1]

The Royal Magazine, xi (1764) [1]

The New Songs Sung at Vauxhall (1765) [6]

Summer Amusement (1766) [8]

New Favourite Songs (1768) [4]

The Vocal Grove (1774) [7]

The Syren (1777) [7]

17 songs pubd separately

Chloe gives me pain, Those gaudy trinkets, *GB-Lbl*

CATCHES, CANONS, GLEES
number of songs by Arne in square brackets

A Collection of Catches, Canons and Glees, ed. E.T. Warren (1763–94), ii [4]; iii [5]; iv [2]; v [7]; vii [3]; viii [4]; xv [1]; xvi [1]; xx [1]

A Collection of Vocal Harmony, ed. E.T. Warren (c1775) [8]

Apollonian Harmony, iv (c1790) [2]

11 catches in Catch Club MSS, *GB-Lbl*

INSTRUMENTAL

Eight overtures in 8 parts, 2 fl, 2 ob, 2 tpt, 2 hn, str, bc (1751/R) [e/E, A, G (Henry and Emma), F, D, Bb, D (Comus), g (The Judgment of Paris)]; no.4, ed. A. Carse (London, 1935), no.6, ed. J. Herbage (London, 1937)

VIII Sonatas or Lessons, hpd (1756/R) [C, e, G, d, Bb, g, A, G], ed. C. Hogwood (London, 1983)

VII sonatas, 2 vn, vc/bc (1757/R) [A, G, Eb, f, D, b, e]; nos.2, 3, 4, 5, 7, ed. H. Murrill (London, 1939, 1951, 1960)

Four New Overtures or Symphonies in 8 and 10 Parts, 2 fl, 2 ob, bn, 2 hn, timp, str, bc (1767) [C, F, Eb, c], ed. R. Platt (London, 1973)

Six Favourite Concertos, org/hpd/pf, 2 tr, 2 hn, 2 ob, bn, str (1793/R) [C, G, A, Bb, g, Bb], ed. R. Langley (London, 1981); early version of no.1, kbd only, *GB-Lbl*

Solo, E, vn, b, *Lbl*, ed. J.A. Parkinson (London, 1978)

EDITIONS

J. Hartley: 6 Sonatas, 2 vn/fl, b (1758)

MISATTRIBUTED

The Most Celebrated Aires in the Opera of Tom Thumb (London, 1733), by J.F. Lampe

Ode upon St. Cecilia's Day (B. Thornton), lost, by C. Burney

Caractacus, vs (c1795), ?by C. Wesley

Epithalamium, At Cana's Feast, *US-Wc*, attrib. doubtful

Mass, D, *GB-Lbl, I-Rsc*, by A. d'Eve, see Grove5

WRITINGS

'The Compleat Musician', The Monthly Melody (1760), ?by Arne

'An Elegy on the Death of The Guardian Outwitted' (1765)

BIBLIOGRAPHY

BDA; BurneyH; FiskeETM; LS; SmitherHO, iii

T. Davies: *Memoirs of the Life of David Garrick* (London, 1780)

C. Dibdin: *The Musical Tour of Mr. Dibdin* (Sheffield, 1788)

C. Dibdin: *The Professional Life of Mr. Dibdin* (London, 1803)

Rees's Cyclopedia (London, 1819–20)

T. Busby: *Concert Room and Orchestra Anecdotes of Music and Musicians, Ancient and Modern* (London, 1825)

W.B. Squire: 'Dr Arne's Masses', *MT*, li (1910), 361–3, also 236, 511–12, 588, 647

W.H. Cummings: *Dr. Arne and 'Rule, Britannia'* (London, 1912)

H. Langley: *Dr Arne* (Cambridge, 1938)

R.C. Roscoe: 'Arne and *The Guardian Outwitted*', *ML*, xxiv (1943), 237–45

M. Sands: *Invitation to Ranelagh 1742–1803* (London, 1946)

H. Langley: 'The Newly Discovered Arne Mass', *MMR*, lxxxi (1951), 227–31

C. Cudworth: 'English Symphonists of the Eighteenth Century', *PRMA*, lxxviii (1951–2), 31–51; repr. in *English Eighteenth-Century Symphonies: Paper and Thematic Index* (London, 1952–3/R); index rev. J. LaRue in *Music in Eighteenth-Century England: Essays in Memory of Charles Cudworth*, ed. C. Hogwood and R. Luckett (Cambridge, 1983), 213–44

J. Herbage: 'The Vocal Style of Thomas Augustine Arne', *PRMA*, lxxviii (1951–2), 83–96

P. Scholes: *God Save the Queen! The History and Romance of the World's First National Anthem* (London, 1954)

A.E.F. Dickinson: 'Arne and the Keyboard Sonata', *MMR*, lxxxv (1955), 88–95

J. Herbage: 'Young Master Arne', *MMR*, xc (1960), 14–16

S. Sadie: 'The Chamber Music of Boyce and Arne', *MQ*, xlvi (1960), 425–36

H.W. Shaw: 'A Projected Arne Commemoration in 1802', *MMR*, xc (1960), 90–94

J. Herbage: 'Arne, his Character and Environment', *PRMA*, lxxxvii (1960–61), 15–29

S.T. Farish: *The Vauxhall Songs of Thomas Augustine Arne* (diss., U. of Illinois, 1962)

C. Cudworth: 'Song and Part-Song Settings of Shakespeare's Lyrics, 1660–1960', *Shakespeare in Music: a Collection of Essays*, ed. P. Hartnoll (London, 1964/R), 51–87

R. Lonsdale: *Dr Charles Burney: a Literary Biography* (Oxford, 1965/R)

W.C. Smith and C. Humphries: *A Bibliography of the Musical Works Published by the Firm of John Walsh during the Years 1721–1766* (London, 1968)

H.D. Johnstone: 'English Solo Song c1710–1760', *PRMA*, xcv (1968–9), 67–80

J.A. Parkinson: 'Garrick's Folly, or the Great Shakespeare Jubilee', *MT*, cx (1969), 922–6

J. Herbage: 'A Page from Arne's Draft Will', *MT*, cxii (1971), 126–7

P.A. Tasch: *The Dramatic Cobbler: the Life and Works of Isaac Bickerstaff* (Lewisburg, PA, 1971)

J.A. Parkinson: *An Index to the Vocal Works of Thomas Augustine Arne and Michael Arne* (Detroit, 1972)

J. Herbage: 'Arne's "Judith"', *Music and Musicians*, xxi/6 (1972–3), 8–10

P. Davies: *'Judith', an Oratorio by T.A. Arne: a Study and Performing Edition of Act I* (M. Mus. diss., King's College, U. of London, 1974)

A. Scott: 'Arne's "Alfred"', *ML*, 1v (1974), 385–97

P.T. Dircks: 'Thomas Arne to David Garrick: an Unrecorded Letter', *Theatre Notebook*, xxx (1975–6), 87–90

J.A. Parkinson: 'An Unknown Violin Solo by Arne', *MT*, cxvii (1976), 902 only

M. Nash: *The Provoked Wife: the Life and Times of Susannah Cibber* (London, 1977)

J.A. Parkinson: 'A-Hunting We Will Go', *MT*, cxviii (1977), 33–4

R. Langley: 'Arne's Keyboard Concertos', *MT*, cxix (1978), 233–6

D. Johnson: 'The Eighteenth-Century Glee' *MT*, cxx (1979), 200–02

G. Beechey: 'A Study of Thomas Arne (1710–1778): a Bibliography of Arne and his Time', *MO*, (1980), 429–31

J.P. Rowntree: 'Lulworth Chapel and a Missing Arne Mass', *MT*, cxxviii (1987), 347–9

M. Sands: *The Eighteenth-Century Pleasure Gardens of Marylebone 1737–1777* (London, 1987)

B. Boydell: *A Dublin Musical Calendar 1700–1760* (Dublin, 1988)

S. Klima, G.Bowers and K.S. Grant, eds.: *Memoirs of Dr Charles Burney* (Lincoln, NE, and London, 1988)

R.L. Neighbarger: *Music for London Shakespeare Productions 1660–1830* (diss., U. of Michigan, 1988)

R. Goodall: *Eighteenth-Century English Secular Cantatas* (New York and London, 1989)

M. Burden: *The British Masque 1690–1800* (diss., U. of Edinburgh, 1991)

B. Boydell: *Rotunda Music in Eighteenth-Century Dublin* (Dublin, 1992)

M. Argent, ed.: *Recollections of R.J.S. Stevens: an Organist in Georgian London* (London, 1992)

J. Adas: *Arne's Progress: an Eighteenth-Century Composer in London* (diss., Rutgers U., 1993)

G. Beechey: 'Songs and Cantatas in Eighteenth-Century England', *The Consort*, xlix (1993), 30–40

S. McVeigh: *Concert Life in London from Mozart to Haydn* (Cambridge, 1993)

M. Burden: *Garrick, Arne and the Masque of 'Alfred'* (Lewiston, NY, 1994)

M. Burden: 'The Independent Masque in Britain in the Eighteenth Century: a Catalogue', *RMARC*, xxviii (1995), 59–159

E.T. Harris: '*King Arthur*'s Journey into the Eighteenth Century', *Purcell Studies*, ed. C.A. Price (Cambridge, 1995), 257–95

R.J. Rabin and S.Zohn: 'Arne, Handel, Walsh and Music as Intellectual Property: Two Eighteenth-Century Lawsuits', *JRMA*, cxx (1995), 112–45

D.-J. Dugas: '"Such Heav'n: Taught Numbers should be More than Read": *Comus* and Milton's Reputation in Mid-Eighteenth-Century England', *Milton Studies*, xxxiv (1996), 137–57

J. Milhous and R.D.Hume: 'J.F. Lampe and English Opera at the Little Haymarket in 1732–3', *ML*, lxxviii (1997), 502–31

J. Milhous and R.D.Hume: 'Librettist versus Composer: the Property Rights to Arne's *Henry and Emma* and *Don Saverio*', *JRMA*, cxxii (1997), 52–67

J.A. Parkinson: *Thomas Arne: Master of a Scurvy Profession*, ed. S. Parkinson and T. Gilman (London, forthcoming)

PETER HOLMAN, TODD GILMAN

Arneiro, José Augusto da Ferreira Veiga, Visconde do. *See* VEIGA, JOSÉ AUGUSTO FERREIRA.

Arnell, Richard (Anthony Sayer) (*b* London, 15 Sept 1917). English composer and conductor. He studied at the RCM (1936–9) with Ireland (composition) and Dykes Bower (piano), winning the Farrar composition prize in 1938. He was music consultant to the North American service of the BBC (1939–45). In 1948 he became a professor of composition at Trinity College of Music. He made extended visits to the USA as a Fulbright Visiting Lecturer (1967–70). He was appointed music consultant to the London International Film School (1972) where he founded the course in music in film. He edited *Composer* magazine 1961–4 and served as chairman (1965–6 and 1974–5) and vice-president (from 1991) of the Composers' Guild.

Arnell's early works included three symphonies and concertos for violin and piano. His music was conducted by Stokowski, Herrmann and by Beecham, who conducted the première of the *Sinfonia quasi variazioni* at Carnegie Hall in 1942. In 1941 Arnell wrote his first film score for Robert Flaherty's documentary, *The Land*. Arnell's Second Symphony opens intensely, with a taughtly argued first movement. His *Canzona and Capriccio* (1943) is more restful, as is the Third String Quartet (1945), reflecting calm after the tensions of war. The ballet *Punch and the Child* (1947), for Balanchine's New York City Ballet, was also made into a suite. Arnell conducted its first concert performance during the Festival of Britain (1951). The American influence in Arnell's music has often been noted: the slow movement of his Fourth Symphony is reminiscent of Copland.

Arnell's 1953 *American Variations* for violin and piano are more stringent than earlier works: the neo-classical second movement recalls Prokofiev rather than Stravinsky. The unusual 1951 piano-duet *Sonatine* is also neo-classical. Several of Arnell's symphonies were first performed at Cheltenham in the 1950s.

Arnell's music has an immediately recognizable style. As a composer, he is known mainly for his instrumental music, including six symphonies: but he has also written distinctive stage and film music. Ireland's influence is largely absent from Arnell's music, except for an occasional burgeoning Romanticism, as in the Third String Quartet's second movement.

From boyhood Arnell made films, and later scored many documentary and feature films. Recalling his good fortune in having works performed by Beecham, Arnell's *Ode to Beecham* (1986) celebrated the RPO's 40th anniversary.

Arnell is an unusually effective conductor of his own works.

WORKS
(selective list)

Op: Moon Flowers, op.83 (Arnell), 1958

Ballets: Punch and the Child, op.49, 1947; Harlequin in April, op.63, 1951; The Angels, op.81, 1957

Orch: Classical Variations, op.1, str, 1939; Divertimento no.2, op.7, chbr orch, 1940; Vn Conc., op.9, 1940; Sinfonia quasi variazioni, op.13, 1941; Sonata, op.18, chbr orch, 1942; Sym. no.1, op.31, 1943; Pf Conc., op.44, 1946; Abstract Forms, op.50, str, 1947; Sym. no.4, op.52, 1948; Lord Byron, op.67, sym. portrait, 1952; Conc. capriccioso, op.71, vn, orch, 1954; Sym. no.5, 'The Gorilla', op.77, 1956–7; Landscape and Figures, op.78, 1956; Robert Flaherty Impression, op.87, 1960; Food of Love, op.112, ov., 1968; Ode to Beecham, spkr, orch, 1986

Choral: The War God, op.36, cant., chorus, orch, 1949; Ode to the West Wind, op.59, chorus, orch, 1949; Town Crier, op.118, spkr, chorus, orch, 1970; Xanadu, chorus, orch, 1993

Wind ens: Cassation, op.45, wind qnt, 1946; Serenade, op.57, wind, db, 1949; Brass Qnt, op.93, 1961; My Lady Greensleeves, op.119, band, 1965

Str qts: no.1, 1939; no.2, op.14, 1941; no.3, op.41, 1945; no.4, op.62, 1951; no.5, op.99, 1961

Solo inst: Org Sonata no.2, op.21, 1942; 22 Variations, op.24, pf, 1943; Partita, op.30, va, 1943; Pf Sonata, op.32, 1946; Sonata no.2, op.55, vn, pf, 1949; American Variations, vn, pf, 1953; Suite, d, op.73, 2 pf, 1955; Fox Variations, op.75, pf, 1956; Chorale Variations on 'Ein' feste' Burg', op.89, org, 1960

Songs, song cycles, film scores, mixed-media compositions

Principal publishers: Associated, Gray, Hinrichsen, Lorien, Mills, Peer, Robbins, Schott, Southern

BIBLIOGRAPHY

R. Arnell: '16 Years in the Electronic Maze', *Composer*, no.83 (1984), 8–9

M. Dawney: 'Richard Arnell at 75', *British Music*, xiv (1992), 3–6

CHRISTOPHER PALMER/MICHAEL DAWNEY

Arnestad, Finn (Oluf Bjaerke) (*b* Christiania, 23 Sept 1915; *d* Oslo, 30 Jan 1994). Norwegian composer. He took violin lessons with Eilif Gunstrøm (1930–34) and with Øivin Fjeldstad at the Oslo Conservatory, where he also studied the piano, the organ, harmony and theory. Apart from orchestration lessons with Bjarne Brustad, he was more or less self-taught as a composer. In 1952 he spent a year in Paris, studying Arab and East Asian folk music in particular and attending contemporary music festivals. In Norway he initially supported himself as a conductor.

In the late 1930s, looking for a theoretical basis for his composition, Arnestad began to develop what he called 'interference tonality', based on the phenomenon of COMBINATION TONES. These he regarded as consonant and irreducible harmonic products, and the insights he derived from studying them he developed into a compositional principle, though never a formal theory as such. The resulting music is neither tonal nor atonal; instead, it confidently walks a line between the two, using long, elegant melodies that sound essentially tonal but generally avoid committing themselves to a particular key. The orchestral music in particular has elements of Hindemith, coloured by the example of Fartein Valen, and often enlivened with a bluff, sprightly sense of humour. His relatively free treatment of rhythm, especially in his early music, occasionally recalls Stravinsky. In several pieces (not least *INRI* of 1954, perhaps his best-known piece), Arnestad develops another stylistic feature, a swift alternation between homophonic and polyphonic textures. From the late 1950s and early 60s onwards, he began to incorporate elements of dodecaphonic and serial practices into his music, but just as he had taken care not to elevate 'interference tonality' to a point of doctrine, so he felt free to incorporate those elements of modernism he felt useful to himself.

WORKS
(selective list)

Orch: Meditation, intermezzo, 1947; Constellation, intermezzo, 1948; Conversation, pf, orch, 1949; INRI, sym. mystery play, chorus, orch, 1954; Vn Conc., 1955–6; Aria appassionata, 1962; Cavatina cambiata, 1967; Arabesque, 1976; Pf Conc., 1976

Chbr and solo inst: Qt, fl, str, 1942; Berceuse, pf, 1946; Legend, vn, pf, 1946; Str Qt, 1947; Sextet, fl, cl, bn, va, vc, pf, 1959; Music for woodwind, fl, cl, bn, 1971; Sonata, trbn, pf, 1971; Sonata, db, 1980; Sonata, vn, 1980; Pf Trio, 1985

Choral: Missa brevis, SATB, fl, cl, bn, 2 hn, tpt, 1958

BIBLIOGRAPHY

MGG2 (H. Herresthal)

B. Kortsen: 'I.N.R.I.', *Contemporary Norwegian Orchestral Music* (Berlin, 1969)

H. Herresthal: *Norwegische Musik von den Anfangen bis zur Gegenwart* (Oslo, 2/1987)

N. Grinde: *A History of Norwegian Music* (Lincoln, NE, 3/1991)

MARTIN ANDERSON (with NIKOLAI PAULSEN)

Arnič, Blaž (*b* Luče, nr Kamnik, 31 Jan 1901; *d* Ljubljana, 1 Feb 1970). Slovenian composer. After studies at the Ljubljana Conservatory he was a pupil of Rudolf Nilius in Vienna (1930–32) and then studied composition in Warsaw (1938) and Paris (1939–40). He taught music at Bol on the island of Brač (1934–5) and at the Intermediate Music School of the Ljubljana Academy (1940–43) before his appointment in 1945 as composition teacher at the academy. Influenced at first by Bruckner and the Russian 'Five', he developed a neo-romantic style, deeply attached to the landscape and people of Slovenia. His music is essentially symphonic with a powerful dramatic touch.

WORKS
(selective list)

10 syms.: 1931–42, 1932, 1933, 1933, 1941, 1948, 1950, 1951, 1960

Other orch: Zapeljivec [The Seducer], sym. poem, 1937; Ples čarovnic [Witches's Dance], sym. poem, 1938, rev. 1955; Pesem planin [Song of the Mountains], sym. poem, 1940; Gozdovi pojo [The Forest Sings], sym. poem, 1945; Vn Conc. no.1, 1952; Vn Conc. no.2, 1954; Vc Conc., 1960; Cl Conc., 1963; Vn Conc. no.3, 1966

Other: Pf Trio no.1, 1929; Conc., org, perc, 1931; Str Qt, 1933; Pf Trio no.2, 1942; Z vlakom [With Train] (cant., O. Župančič), 1954; songs, choruses, pf pieces, film scores

Principal publisher: Društvo slovenskih skladateljev

ANDREJ RIJAVEC

Arnim, Bettine von [Elisabeth]. *See* BRENTANO, BETTINA.

Arnold, Denis (Midgley) (*b* Sheffield, 15 Dec 1926; *d* Budapest, 28 April 1986). English musicologist. He studied music with F.H. Shera at Sheffield University from 1944 to 1948 (BMus 1948). He was awarded the MA for a dissertation on Weelkes in 1950 and was appointed a lecturer at Queen's University, Belfast, in 1951. He became reader in music in 1960, and in 1964 went to Hull University as senior lecturer. In 1969 he became professor of music at Nottingham University, where he instituted a postgraduate course on the editing and interpretation of Renaissance and Baroque music, and in 1975 Heather Professor of Music at Oxford University. In 1976 he became joint editor of *Music and Letters*, in 1978 he was named president of the Royal Musical Association, and in 1982 he was elected to the directorium of the International Musicological Society. As a writer of criticism, he contributed regularly to *The Listener* and *Gramophone*. In 1980 he was awarded honorary degrees from Queen's University, Belfast (MMus), and Sheffield University (DMus).

Arnold was a lively and prolific writer, with a wider range of interests than his list of publications indicates. His research was predominantly concerned with Italian (most of all Venetian) music from the mid-16th century to the mid-17th, an interest that developed from his early work on the English madrigal. His archival studies cast light on performing styles and on educational methods at the Italian conservatories, while his critical work (exemplified by his Master Musicians study of Monteverdi and his volumes on Marenzio and Giovanni Gabrieli in the Oxford Studies of Composers series) has helped establish historical perspective in the study of style changes at the beginning of the Baroque period.

WRITINGS

'Thomas Weelkes and the Madrigal', *ML*, xxi (1950), 1–12
'Giovanni Croce and the Concertato Style', *MQ*, xxxix (1953), 37–48
'Ceremonial Music in Venice at the Time of the Gabrielis', *PRMA*, lxxxii (1955–6), 47–59
'Alessandro Grandi, a Disciple of Monteverdi', *MQ*, xliii (1957), 171–86
'Brass Instruments in Italian Church Music of the Sixteenth and Early Seventeenth Centuries', *Brass Quarterly*, i (1957–8), 81–98
'Con ogni sorte di stromenti: some Practical Suggestions', *Brass Quarterly*, ii (1958–9), 99–123
'Andrea Gabrieli und die Entwicklung der "cori-spezzati"-Technik', *Mf*, xii (1959), 258–74
'Music at the Scuola di San Rocco', *ML*, xl (1959), 229–41
'The Significance of "Cori spezzati"', *ML*, xl (1959), 4–14
'Orphans and Ladies: the Venetian Conservatoires (1690–1797)', *PRMA*, lxxxix (1962–3), 31–47
Monteverdi (London, 1963, rev. 3/1990 by T. Carter)
'Instruments and Instrumental Teaching elsewhere in the Early Italian Conservatoires', *GSJ*, xviii (1965), 72–81
Marenzio (London, 1965)
'Orchestras in Eighteenth-Century Venice', *GSJ*, xix (1966), 3–19
Monteverdi Madrigals (London, 1967)
'Charity Music in Eighteenth-Century Dublin', *GSJ*, xxi (1968), 162–74
'Formal Design in Monteverdi's Church Music', *Claudio Monteverdi e il suo tempo: Venice, Mantua and Cremona 1968*, 187–216
ed., with N. Fortune: *The Monteverdi Companion* (London, 1968, enlarged 2/1985 as *The New Monteverdi Companion*)
'Gli allievi di Giovanni Gabrieli', *NRMI*, v (1971), 943–72
ed., with N. Fortune: *The Beethoven Companion* (London, 1971/R)
'A Background Note to Monteverdi's Hymn Settings', *Scritti in onore di Luigi Ronga* (Milan, 1973), 33–44
Giovanni Gabrieli (London, 1974)
'Cavalli at St Mark's', *EMc*, iv (1976), 266–74
'The Corellian Cult in England', *Nuovi studi Corelliani* (Florence, 1978), 81–9
'The Grand Motets of Orlandus Lassus', *EMc*, vi (1978), 170–81
Giovanni Gabrieli and the Music of the Venetian High Renaissance (London, 1980)
'Vivaldi's Motets for Solo Voice', *Vivaldi veneziano europeo*, ed. F. Degrada (Florence, 1980), 37–48
Monteverdi Church Music (London, 1982)
ed.: *The New Oxford Companion to Music* (Oxford, 1983)
'Claudio Monteverdi', *The New Grove Italian Baroque Masters* (London, 1984), 1–79

'Music at the Mendicanti in the Eighteenth Century', *ML*, lxv (1984), 345–56
with E. Arnold: 'Russians in Venice: the Visit of the *Conti del Nord* in 1782', *Slavonic and Western Music: Essays for Gerald Abraham*, ed. M.H. Brown and R.J. Wiley (Ann Arbor and Oxford, 1985), 123–30
with E. Arnold: *The Oratorio in Venice* (London, 1986)
'Music at the Ospedali', *JRMA*, cxiii (1988), 156–67
'A Venetian Anthology of Sacred Monody', *Florilegium musicologicum: Hellmut Federhofer zum 75. Geburtstag*, ed. C.-H. Mahling (Tutzing, 1988), 25–35

EDITIONS

G. Gabrieli: Opera omnia, CMM, xii (1956–74)
Vier Madrigale von Mantuaner Komponisten zu 5 und 8 Stimmen, Cw, lxxx (1962)
A. Gabrieli: Drei Motetten zu 8 Stimmen, Cw, xcvi (1965)
L. Marenzio: Ten Madrigals (Oxford, 1966)
O. di Lasso: Ten Madrigals (London, 1977)
Ten Venetian Motets (Oxford, 1980)

DAVID SCOTT/ELIZABETH ROCHE

Arnold, F(rank) T(homas) (*b* Rugby, 6 Sept 1861; *d* Bath, 24 Sept 1940). English musical scholar. He was educated at Rugby and Trinity College, Cambridge, and in 1886 became a lecturer in German at the University College of South Wales and Monmouthshire (Cardiff), a post he held for 40 years until his retirement. His lifelong interest in music, particularly as an amateur cellist, led him to make an exhaustive study of the tradition of writing and playing from a figured bass, which culminated in his comprehensive treatise on *The Art of Accompaniment from a Thorough-Bass as Practised in the 17th and 18th Centuries* (London, 1931/R). He studied an enormous number of sources, both practical and theoretical, and produced his findings authoritatively in this book, which was declared by Newman 'the greatest work of musicography ever produced in this country' and is still of value. Arnold's collection of editions of contemporary treatises on figured bass was bequeathed to Cambridge University library.

BIBLIOGRAPHY

W.G. Whittaker: 'The Art of Accompaniment from a Thorough-Bass', *MT*, lxxiii (1932), 32–4, 123–5 [review]; 255 only [Arnold's reply]
E. Newman: 'A Job for a Dictator', *Sunday Times*, (2 July 1944)
M. Campbell: *Dolmetsch: the Man and his Work* (London, 1975)
MS catalogue of Arnold's collection, GB-Cu

H.C. COLLES/MALCOLM TURNER

Arnold, Georg (*b* Feldsberg, Lower Austria [now Valtice, Czech Republic], bap. 23 April 1621; *d* Bamberg, 16 Jan 1676). Austrian composer and organist, active in Germany. As early as 1640 he was organist of St Mark, Wolfsberg, formerly in the possession of the Franconian bishopric of Bamberg. After the end of the Thirty Years War, on 14 September 1649, he was appointed court organist at Bamberg through the influence of Prince-Bishop Melchior Otto Voit of Salzburg, who also began the Baroque restyling of the interior of Bamberg Cathedral and called on Arnold to provide a new repertory of masses, vespers and motets. The inclusion of a mass by Tobias Richter in Arnold's op.2 and a *Laudate pueri* by G.G. Porro in his *Psalmi vespertini* indicates that he had contacts with Mainz and Munich, while the presence of 22 of his motets in the Düben Collection and a canon in J.G. Fabricius's *Liber amicorum* testifies to his reputation outside the Bamberg area. As an organ expert he was connected with Spiridion and Matthias Tretzscher and helped with the reconstruction of the organs in Bamberg that had been destroyed in the war. He became Hofkapellmeister at Bamberg in 1667. A painting of 1675 by his son Georg Adam, who was appointed court organist in 1685, shows the interior of the restored cathedral with the splendid Baroque organ on the left wall; Arnold is seen standing next to it in court dress and wig.

There was a long tradition of polyphonic music in Bamberg, to which Arnold added the Venetian polychoral style, possibly to some extent inspired by the layout of the cathedral, with apses at either end of the nave. The use of the term 'sacrarum cantionum' in the titles of his 1651 volume and op.4 is indeed reminiscent of Giovanni Gabrieli and Schütz; intended as open-air music, their contents are well suited to the forces at his disposal. In his masses Arnold adopted the large-scale, south German concertante style: in the single choir works of 1665 the concertante principle is expressed in the alternation and different groupings of the obbligato instruments, while the parody masses of 1672 rely more on dynamic contrasts. In the double choir masses of 1656 Arnold introduced the spatial effects of polychoral writing into this style; his development is also marked by the integration of elements of contrapuntal settings. The marked antiphonal style of the psalms of 1662–3 owes something to Monteverdi and Viadana, in contrast to the more seamless polyphony of op.3, most of whose 47 pieces are canzonas. But it is in the more intimate concerted motets that Arnold is at his most inspired, particularly in the settings of non-liturgical mystical texts.

WORKS

Liber primus [21] sacrarum cantionum, 1–4vv, 2–3 vn/va, bc (Nuremberg, 1651)

Liber I, [4] missarum, [12] psalmorum et [2] magnificat, 5vv, 2 vn/tpt, va; 4vv, 3 trbns/viols ad lib, bc (org), op.2 (Innsbruck, 1656)

[45] Canzoni, ariae et sonatae, 1–4 vn/va, va/bn ad lib, bc (org), op.3 (Innsbruck, 1659)

Liber secundus [28] sacrarum cantionum , 1–5vv, 2–4 vn/va, bc, op.4 (Innsbruck, 1661); 10 ed. in DTB, new ser., x (1994)

Psalmi de BMV cum Salve regina, Ave regina, Alma Redemptoris mater, et Regina coeli, 3vv, 2 vn, va ad lib, bc (Innsbruck, 1662)

[16] Psalmi vespertini, 2vv, 2 vn, 5 vv/insts ad lib, bc (org) 1663²

3 missae pro defunctis et alia missa laudativa, 4–5vv, 2 vn, 1–4 va ad lib, bc (org), op.6 (Bamberg, 1665)

Motettae tredecim selectissime de nomine Jesu, ejusque SS Virgine Matre Maria, 1v, 2 vn/va, 4 vn/va ad lib, bc (Kempten, 1672)

Prima pars, 4 missae, 4vv, 2 vn, 3 va ad lib, bc (org) (Bamberg, 1672, some inst pts, 1673, with org, 1675, as Missarum quaternio); 1 ed. in DTB, new ser., x (1994)

22 concerted motets, 1–5vv, 2–5 vn/va, 1663–5, S-Uu [1 repr. from Liber primus (1651), 10 from Liber secundus (1661), 2 from 1663²]

Canon, 2vv, holograph entry of 18 Feb 1660 in J.G. Fabricius: Liber amicorum, D-Bsb, facs. in DTB, new ser., x (1994)

BIBLIOGRAPHY

M. Neumann: 'Frühe Musikkultur in Spittal und in der bambergischen Residenz Wolfsberg', Jb des Stadtmuseums, vi (Villach, 1969), 187ff

G. Weinzerl: 'Das Messenschaffen des fürstbischöflich-Bamberger Hoforganisten Georg Arnold', Bericht des Historischen Vereins Bamberg, cxix (1983), 151–286

G. Weinzierl: 'Repräsentant des Hochbarocks in Bamberg: der fürstbischöfliche Hoforganist Georg Arnold', Musik in Bayern, xxxvi (1988), 23–30

HANNS DENNERLEIN/GERHARD WEINZIERL

Arnold, Gustav (b Altdorf, canton of Uri, 1 Sept 1831; d Lucerne, 28 Sept 1900). Swiss conductor, organist and composer. After instruction in singing (with Aloys Zwyssig) and the piano, Arnold studied music in Engelberg (1842–4) and in Lucerne (1844–7), where he was active as a choral singer, organist and pianist and began to compose. In 1850 he went to England, where he was appointed organist and choirmaster at the Roman Catholic church in Lancaster and taught the piano and languages. Moving to Salford in 1854, he became organist and choral director at the cathedral. He studied with Charles Hallé, who greatly influenced him, and had singing lessons with Manuel García. From 1856 he took positions in Manchester, first at St Augustine's and subsequently at St Wilfrid's church.

Arnold returned to Switzerland permanently in 1865 to become musical director of Lucerne. His duties included conducting various choirs and an amateur orchestra for the performance of masses (at the cathedral), operas and oratorios. He founded an orchestra of professional musicians in 1875. Although he retired in 1883 he continued to adjudicate at singing festivals, worked to improve church music and became a music critic. He received honours from Lucerne and was elected president of the Schweizerischer Tonkünstlerverein in 1900.

Arnold's earliest publications include solo songs and piano music; later he wrote much sacred and secular music for male and mixed choruses, a mass, cantatas and incidental music for the theatre. He was best known for his works for male chorus, of which his cantatas Siegesfeier der Freiheit and Der Rütlischwur are particularly noteworthy.

BIBLIOGRAPHY

A. Portmann: 'Gustav Arnold, Musikdirektor', Katholische Schweizerblätter, new ser., xvi (1900), 504

A. Niggli: Obituary, Biographisches Jb und Deutscher Nekrolog, v (1900), 39–42

E. Refardt: 'Gustav Arnold', SMz, xc (1950), 473–81; repr. in Musik in der Schweiz, ed. H. Ehinger and E. Mohr (Berne, 1952), 33–46 [incl. list of works]

GAYNOR G. JONES

Arnold, György (b Paks, 6 June 1781; d Szabadka [now Subotica, Serbia], 25 Oct 1848). Hungarian composer and church musician. He studied music with his father József Arnold (1751–96), cantor of the Catholic church in Hajós, and Pál Pöhm, cathedral choirmaster in Kalocsa. In 1800 he was appointed music director of the town and regens chori of St Theresa's church in Szabadka, posts which he held until his death. In order to enlarge his establishment, which in 1803 consisted of only five musicians, he gave free musical tuition to 12 boys from 1805 to 1814. His first known compositions are offertories based on themes from fashionable operas (Grétry's Richard Coeur-de-lion, Don Giovanni and Weigl's Die Schweizerfamilie). In 1815, on the return of Pope Pius VII from captivity in France, he composed an offertory for which he received a letter of thanks from the pope, and in 1826 he was given a gold medal for an offertory composed for the coronation of Pope Leo XII; another papal breve (1831) thanked him for his offertory for the coronation of Gregory XVI. From 1836 he was an honorary member of the music society in Pressburg.

As well as church works, which were influenced by the Viennese Classical tradition, Arnold also composed secular music including stage works and dance music. As a stage composer experimenting with Hungarian themes, he was one of the pioneers of this art form in his country and is thus a predecessor of Ferenc Erkel. In his Hungarian dances, which were published in the largest collection of Hungarian dance music in the first three decades of the 19th century, Magyar táncok Veszprém vármegyéből

('Hungarian dances from County Veszprém'), Arnold expressed himself in the national musical idiom of the *verbunkos*. His other works include *Pismenik iliti skupljenje pisamâ razlicsitih za nadiljne, svetacsne i ostale dneve priko godine podobnih, za vechu slavu boxju i kriposli duhovne naroda Iliricskoju* (Eszék, 1819), a collection of religious songs in the Illyrian language, and an unpublished four-volume German dictionary of composers (1826).

WORKS

SINGSPIELE

Kemény Simon (after K. Kisfaludy), Szabadka, 1826
Mátyás királynak választása [The Election of Matthew as King] (after L. Szentjóbi Szabó), Kassa, 1830, collab. J. Heinisch
A gotthardhegyi boszorkány [The Witch of Mt Gotthard] (after A. Schuster), Debrecen, 1837

OTHER WORKS

Sacred choral: 13 offs, 11 hymns, 3 Libera me, 2 Tantum ergo, TeD, 3 masses (incl. Ger. mass, Hung. requiem), Regina coeli, Et incarnatus; religious songs to Illyrian texts
Inst.: 4 ovs., orch; numerous Hung. dances, pf

BIBLIOGRAPHY

ZL
K. Isoz: *Arnold György* (Budapest, 1908)
F. Brodszky: *A. Veszprémvármegyei Zenetársaság 1823–1832* [The music society in County Veszprém 1823–32] (Veszprém, 1941)
Z. Blažeković:: 'Due musicisti nella Pannonia del primo Ottocento: Ðuro Arnold e Petrus Jakob Haibel', iv: *Croazia, Serbia, Bulgaria, Romania*, ed. C. De Incontrera and A. Zanini

FERENC BÓNIS

Arnold, Johann Gottfried (*b* Niedernhall, Württemberg, 1 Feb 1773; *d* Frankfurt, 26 July 1806). German cellist. The son of a schoolmaster, who gave him preliminary musical training, he made local appearances with the cello when he was eight; in 1785 he was apprenticed to the town musician at Künzelsau, where he spent five years, followed by a period with his uncle, who held a similar position at Wertheim. But ensuing attempts to start a solo career, making short tours in southern Germany and Switzerland, proved abortive, hampered by the absence of proper training. Accordingly, he went first to Regensburg for some months' study with Max Willmann, the first cello teaching he had received. He proceeded to Hamburg in 1796; here, he profited greatly from the tuition and fine example of Romberg, who helped him to develop great technical ability and recommended his engagement, a year later, as solo cellist of the Frankfurt Opera. Arnold is said to have been described by his contemporaries as a great virtuoso, with a 'consistently enchanting' tone. He died of a lung infection at the age of 33 and was greatly mourned by the people of Frankfurt. His compositions include five cello concertos (published 1802–8), which became favourite items of Dotzauer's repertory; the third was republished by Karl Schröder (ii) in 1880. He also wrote a *Symphonie concertante* for two flutes and orchestra, and various works for piano, cello, guitar and chamber ensembles.

Arnold's son Carl (*b* Neukirchen, nr Mergentheim, 6 May 1794; *d* Christiania, 11 Nov 1877) studied the piano first at Frankfurt with C.A. Hoffmann and Aloys Schmitt, and then, after his father's death, at Offenbach with J.A. André and J.G. Vollweiler. After concert tours in Germany, Poland and Russia (where in 1820 he married the singer Henriette Kisting), he settled in Berlin in 1824. He spent 16 years composing but gave up after the failure of his opera *Irene* in 1832. In 1835 he became music director at Münster, and in 1847, director of the Philharmonic

Society at Christiania, where in 1857 he also became organist of the Trefoldighetskirke. His own son, Karl (*b* Berlin, 8 June 1824; *d* Christiania, 9 Aug 1867), studied the cello with Max Bohrer and became cellist of the court chapel at Stockholm. (*MGG1*, W. Matthäus)

LYNDA MacGREGOR

Arnold, John (*b* ?Essex, *c*1715; *d* Great Warley, Essex, March 1792). English psalmodist. He was a singing teacher, parish clerk and (at least in 1790) organist at Great Warley, Essex, and compiled several publications designed for country parish churches. The most important was *The Compleat Psalmodist* (seven editions, 1741–79) which was in general modelled on earlier books of the same kind, containing a didactic introduction, psalm tunes, hymns and anthems of the parochial kind. But it was unusually ambitious in including also a number of chants for the prose canticles and a complete setting of Morning and Evening Prayer (*see* ROBERT BARBER (i)). Many of the tunes and anthems were his own; others were supplied by members of his choir at Great Warley; the rest were taken from earlier collections.

Arnold published four other books of similar purpose and scope, and also *The Essex Harmony* (three editions, 1767–86) which contained songs, catches and glees from various sources. His prefaces give a colourful and informative picture of the musical life of an 18th-century village. The most expansive of these are in the fifth edition of *The Compleat Psalmodist* (1761) and in *Church Music Reformed* (1765).

BIBLIOGRAPHY

Bury and Norwich Post (14 March 1792)
A.H. Mann: *Essex Musical Events and Musicians* (MS, *GB-NW* 448), 91ff
R.T. Daniel: *The Anthem in New England before 1800* (Evanston, IL, 1966/R), 75–6
N. Temperley: *The Music of the English Parish Church* (Cambridge, 1979/R)
R.M. Wilson: *Anglican Chant and Chanting in England and America, 1660–1815* (Cambridge, 1996)

NICHOLAS TEMPERLEY

Arnol'd, Jurig (Karlovich) von. See ARNOL'D, YURY.

Arnold, Sir Malcolm (Henry) (*b* Northampton, 21 Oct 1921). English composer. He was descended on his mother's side from William Hawes. Arnold's musical gifts were soon apparent, and he began to receive private composition lessons. At the age of 16 he won a scholarship to the RCM, where he studied trumpet with Ernest Hall and composition briefly with Patrick Hadley, then with Gordon Jacob. The decimation of professional orchestras by the demands of World War II meant that Arnold regularly appeared in their ranks even before graduating, and he was acknowledged as a trumpeter of the first order. He played in the LPO (1941–2) and, after two unhappy years of war service (1944–5), which ended when he deliberately shot himself in the foot, and one season with the BBC SO, he returned to the LPO in 1946. However, the award of the Mendelssohn Scholarship (1948) changed his life and gave him the confidence to pursue a full-time composing career. For 20 years he maintained a double life of prodigious energy, writing up to six film scores a year as well as a full and varied list of concert works, from symphonies and concertos to highly idiomatic music for brass and woodwind, pieces for amateurs and children and for the famous Hoffnung humorous concerts. Eventually the strain told and he abandoned film; by this stage, though, he had already experienced recurrent bouts of illness. A further crisis in the early 1980s saw him in hospital for a long period, and after a noticeable decline in his powers he eventually abandoned composition altogether, soon after completing his last symphony. His achievements were recognized by the award of numerous honours, culminating in a knighthood (1993).

At the heart of Arnold's output stand nine symphonies. Completed at regular intervals over the length of his composing career, they stand like milestones definitive of particular periods – the London years, the Cornish period (1965–72), the move to Ireland (1972), breakdown (from 1979) and return home. They are the works by which Arnold himself preferred to be judged. They range from a First Symphony (1949) clearly intended as a calling-card and marking a rite of passage from player-composer to fully-fledged professional, to a valedictory Ninth (1986) clearly modelled on Tchaikovsky and Mahler. The Second (1953) follows in the line of English Pastorals that stretches back to Holst and Vaughan Williams and even earlier, and was and remains widely played; while the Third (1957), in somewhat similar vein, proved in places over-extended and was less successful. The Fourth and Fifth (both 1960) were conceived virtually as a pair, the latter, as Arnold acknowledged at its première, virtually the antithesis of its predecessor. The early influence of Sibelius, textural and emotional, is replaced by the more all-embracing aspirations and even the thematic contours of Mahler. Along with Berlioz, these composers were regularly described by Arnold as forming his private pantheon. The Seventh (1973), written in Dublin and seeming in its conflict-ridden outer movements to confront a personal drama in almost tragic terms, is the most Mahlerian of the canon; the Sixth (1967) and Eighth

Malcolm Arnold, 1986

(1978), while no less characteristic of Arnold's individual voice, add the virtues of discipline and conciseness.

Formally and stylistically the symphonies offer few surprises. Arnold's musical idiom is essentially conservative. His harmonies are seldom more adventurous than the conservative orthodoxies of Parry and Stanford a generation earlier, though making occasional use of bitonality to powerful expressive effect, as for example in the opening movement of the Seventh. Arnold also toyed with serial techniques from the Fifth Symphony onwards, but never obtrusively, and perhaps only out of characteristic bravado: they are never integral either to his melodic invention or his often modally-inflected harmonic schemes. Structurally his symphonies are all either in three or four movements, sometimes dispensing with a full-blown scherzo, sometimes integrating it into the middle movement, as in the Third Symphony; only the Ninth reverses the customary sequence and ends with an extended Adagio. First movements tend to be constructed in orthodox sonata form, with contrasts achieved not so much through key relationships as through thematic differentiation: Arnold's greatest strength was always as an endlessly inventive, fresh and memorable melodist. As a single instance, the return of the slow movement theme at the climax of the finale of the Fifth Symphony is overwhelming.

Further strength is sometimes added to his symphonic aspirations when there is a background agenda at work. The Notting Hill race riots of 1960 not only provoked the composer's outright public condemnation (his liberal credentials were always impeccable), but also prompted him to include an extensive Caribbean percussion section in his Fourth Symphony. In this work he also explores popular idioms of the 1960s in a manner calculated to provoke outraged criticism. Undaunted, Arnold included a homage to the saxophonist Charlie Parker in the Sixth, an imitation of an Irish folk band in the Seventh, and – with a nostalgia reminiscent of Vaughan Williams – an Irish marching-tune as the first subject of the opening Allegro of the Eighth. Prominent as these and other moments are, however, they remain incidental to the symphonic and emotional argument, which is always clear and properly proportioned. The two most prominent emotions in the later symphonies are anger and despair, but even the Ninth, almost as bleak as the violent Seventh, ends on a root-position D major triad.

In the remainder of Arnold's output the mood is generally more relaxed, though he continues to make occasional references outside his standard idiom, sometimes with startling effect. The superb Guitar Concerto, written for his longstanding friend Julian Bream, includes a blues that pays homage to Django Reinhardt. (Arnold's love of jazz, though strong, surfaces surprisingly seldom in his overall output.) A single-movement Fantasy for piano and orchestra, for John Lill, written in Dublin, is a concerto in all but name; it starts out innocently from a nocturne by the Irish composer John Field but develops into a heroic, even savage battle between soloist and orchestra that once again suggests a hidden agenda. Arnold described all his 20-odd concertos as portraits of the soloists to whom they are dedicated, the majority of whom were also close personal friends. The list is impressive, including Dennis Brain, Yehudi Menuhin, Leon Goossens, Richard Adeney, Benny Goodman, Larry Adler, Julian Lloyd Webber and Michala Petri, thus testifying to his generous and gregarious nature as a musician. Arnold was seldom if ever found in an ivory tower, and his work-list includes numerous occasional pieces that have outlasted their immediate purpose: the *Padstow Lifeboat March*, for the launch of a new lifeboat near the Cornish village where Arnold was then living, is a popular and typical example.

This virtuosity was sometimes held against him. An unashamed eclectic, Arnold was regularly accused in his symphonic as well as smaller works of allowing speed and sheer facility to get the better of his instinct for self-criticism. The occasional undeniable outbursts of vulgarity, as in the finale of the Second Clarinet Concerto, are in fact rare, but Arnold was an easy target, not only because he was prolific in so many areas of concert life, but also because he was a successful film composer who understood both the requirements and limitations of that medium, and refused to acknowledge any difference of aspiration in the music he wrote for different audiences. Like many extroverts, however, Arnold was also deeply sensitive, and like Britten (with whom he otherwise had little in common), he found criticism hard to bear. Seldom given to public utterances of any kind, least of all about his own music – he tended, rather, to throw out red herrings to put people off the scent – he was goaded more than once into attacking music critics as the scourge of musical life, and to see them as a contributory factor in his decline into alcoholism, illness and depression.

Because films can have only a short screen life, apart from their occasional revival on television, only a handful of Arnold's nearly 120 film scores are familiar: *Whistle Down the Wind*, *The Inn of the Sixth Happiness* and a trilogy for the director David Lean: *The Sound Barrier*, *Hobson's Choice* and *The Bridge on the River Kwai*, for which, incredibly, he was given a mere ten days' writing time. These are just the most famous, and the last deservedly won an Oscar. There are powerful and original moments in many of the other scores: for example, the integration of Indian modes, rhythms and instruments in *Nine Hours to Rama*, a film about the assassination of Gandhi, is strikingly assured. There is room for comprehensive research in this area.

Perhaps because of his long involvement in films, Arnold never wrote a full-length opera. He claimed never to have found the ideal subject or librettist. By all accounts, though, despite his lack of formal education, he was exceptionally well-read, and it is possible that far from being insensitive to words he was if anything over-responsive. Choosing texts for the *Five William Blake Songs*, he went to the early poems, claiming that good poetry had no need of music. Arnold's art was an abstract one, in which the play of sounds was the first consideration, and his strongest works – the later symphonies, the guitar, flute and horn concertos, the magnificent Symphony for Brass, the Second String Quartet – need no special pleading. They are easily recognizable for their individual voice, and their exceptional musical craftsmanship allied to emotional integrity of the highest order.

WORKS
(selective list)

for complete list see in Poulton (1986)

OPERAS

The Dancing Master (1, J. Mendoza, after W. Wycherley: *The Gentleman Dancing Master*), op.34, 1952, London, Barnes Music Club, 1 March 1962

The Open Window (1, S. Gilliat, after Saki), op.56, 1956, BBC TV, 14 Dec 1956; staged Horton-cum-Becking, Lincoln Opera Group, April 1958

Song of Simeon (nativity masque, 3 scenes, C. Hassall), op.69, 1959, London, Drury Lane, 5 Jan 1960

The Turtle Drum (children's TV play), op.92, 1967, BBC TV, 26 April 1967

OTHER DRAMATIC

Ballets: Homage to the Queen, op.42, 1953; Rinaldo and Armida, op.49, 1954, London, CG, 6 Jan 1955; Solitaire, 1956 [= English Dances, opp.27, 33 with added Sarabande and Polka]; Sweeney Todd, op.68, 1959, Stratford, Shakespeare Memorial Theatre, 10 Dec 1959; Electra, op.79, 1963, London, CG, 1946

Film scores (dirs. in parentheses): No Highway (H. Koster), 1951; It Started in Paradise (C. Bennett), 1952; The Sound Barrier (D. Lean), 1952; Albert RN (L. Gilbert), 1953; Hobson's Choice (Lean), 1953; The Belles of St Trinian's (F. Launder), 1954; The Sea Shall Not Have Them (Gilbert), 1954; 1984 (M. Radford), 1955; I am a Camera (H. Cornelius), 1955; The Deep Blue Sea (J. Hildyard), 1955; Tiger in the Smoke (R. Baker), 1956; The Bridge on the River Kwai (Lean), 1957; Dunkirk (L. Norman), 1957; Island in the Sun (R. Rossen), 1957; The Inn of the Sixth Happiness (M. Robson), 1958; The Key (C. Reed), 1958; The Roots of Heaven (J. Huston), 1958; Suddenly Last Summer (J.L. Mankiewicz), 1959; Whistle Down the Wind (B. Forbes), 1961

ORCHESTRA AND BAND

Syms.: Sym. for Str, op.13, 1947; Sym. no.1, op.22, 1949; Sym. no.2, op.40, 1953; 'Toy' Sym., op.62, 1957; Sym. no.3, op.63, 1957; Sym. no.4, op.71, 1960; Sym. no.5, op.74, 1960; Sym. no.6, op.95, 1967; Sym. no.7, op.113, 1973; Sym. for Brass, op.123, 1978; Sym. no.8, op.124, 1978; Sym. no.9, op.128, 1986

Concs.: Hn Conc., op.11, 1945; Cl Conc. [no.1], op.20, cl, str, 1948; Conc., op.32, pf 4 hands, str, 1951; Ob Conc., op.39, ob, str, 1952; Fl Conc. no.1, op.45, fl, str, 1954; Harmonica Conc., op.46, 1954; Conc., op.47, org, D-tpt, B♭-tpt, str, 1954; Serenade, op.50, gui, str, 1955; Hn Conc., hn, str, op.58, 1956; Gui Conc., gui, chbr orch, op.67, 1959; Grand Conc. Gastronomique for Eater, Waiter, Food and Orch., op.76, 1961; Conc., op.77, 2 vn, str, 1962; Conc., op.104, 2 pf (3 hands), orch, 1969; Conc. for 28 Players, op.105, 1970; Va Conc., op.108, va, chbr orch, 1971; Fl Conc. no.2, op.111, 1972; Cl Conc., op.115, 1974; Fantasy on a Theme of John Field, op.116, pf, orch, 1975; Philharmonic Conc., op.120, 1976; Tpt Conc., op.125, 1982; Conc., rec, chbr orch, op.133, 1988; Shakespearean Vc Conc., op.136, 1988

Other orch: Larch Trees, tone poem, op.3, 1943; Beckus the Dandipratt, comedy ov., op.5, 1943; Divertimento no.1, op.1, 1945, lost; Festival Ov., op.14, 1948; The Smoke, ov., op.21, 1948; Little Suite no.1, op.53, 1948; Divertimento no.2, op.24, 1950, rev. as op.75, 1961; Serenade, op.26, small orch, 1950; English Dances, set 1, op.27, 1950, set 2, op.33, 1951 [incl. in ballet Solitaire]; Machines, sym. study, op.30, 1951; A Sussex Ov., op.31, 1951; The Sound Barrier, rhapsody, op.38, 1952; Flourish for a 21st Birthday, op.44, 1953; Sinfonietta no.1, op.48, small orch, 1954; Tam o'Shanter, ov., op.51, 1955; A Grand Grand Ov., op.57, org, 3 vacuum cleaners, floor polisher, 4 rifles, orch, 1956; 4 Scottish Dances, op.59, 1957; Commonwealth Christmas Ov., op.64, 1957; Sinfonietta no.2, op.65, 1958; Overseas, march, op.70, 1960; Carnival of Animals, op.72, 1960; Divertimento no.2, op.75, 1961; Little Suite no.2, op.78, 1962; Sinfonietta no.3, op.81, 1964; Water Music, op.82, wind, perc, 1964; A Sunshine Ov., op.83, 1964, lost; Peterloo, ov., op.97, 1967; 4 Cornish Dances, op.91, 1968; Anniversary Ov., op.99, 1968; Fantasy for Audience and Orch, op.106, 1970; The Fair Field, ov., op.110, 1972; A Flourish, op.112, 1973; Variations on a Theme of Ruth Gipps, op.122, 1977; Salute to Thomas Merritt, op.98, 2 brass bands, orch, 1987; 4 Irish Dances, op.126, 1988; 4 Welsh Dances, op.138, 1989; Flourish for a Battle, op.139, ww, brass, 1990; Robert Kett Ov., op.141, 1990; Little Suite no.3 (A Manx Suite), op.142, 1990; Sym. Suite, op.12, lost

Brass band: 2 Little Suites, op.80, 1963, op.93, 1967; The Padstow Lifeboat, march, op.94, 1967; Fantasy, op.114a, 1974; Little Suite no.3, op.131, 1987

Military band: HRH the Duke of Cambridge, march, op.60, 1957

VOCAL

Vocal: 2 Songs, op.8, 1v, pf, 1947; Ps cl, op.25, chorus, org, 1950; 2 Ceremonial Pss, op.35, SSA, 1952; John Clare Cant., op.52, chorus, pf 4 hands, 1955; Song of Praise (J. Clare), op.55, unison vv, pf, 1956; 5 William Blake Songs, op.66, A, str, 1959; Song of Simeon (C. Hassall), op.69, mimes, solo vv, chbr orch, 1959; Song of Accounting Periods, op.103, 1v, pf, 1969; Song of Freedom, op.109, chorus, brass band, 1973; 2 John Donne Songs, op.114b, T, pf, 1974; The Return of Odysseus (cant., P. Dickinson), op.119, SATB, orch, 1976; Contrasts (Serenade), op.134, T, str, 1988

CHAMBER AND SOLO INSTRUMENTAL

3 or more insts: Wind Qnt, op.2, 1943, lost; 3 Shanties, op.4, wind qnt, 1943; Trio, op.6, fl, bn, va, 1943; Qnt, op.7, fl, bn, hn, vn, va, 1944; Str Qt no.1, op.23, 1949; Divertimento, op.37, fl, ob, cl, 1953; Pf Trio, op.54, 1956; Ob Qt, op.61, 1957; Qnt, op.73, 2 tpt, hn, trbn, tuba, 1961; Trevelyan Suite, op.96, 10 wind, 1967; Str Qt no.2, op.118, 1975; Brass Qnt no.2, op.132, 1988; Divertimento, op.137, wind octet, 1988; Fantasy, op.140, rec, str qt, 1990

1–2 insts: Duo, op.10, fl, va, 1945; Variations on a Ukrainian Folksong, op.9, pf, 1946; Sonatas no.1, op.15, vn, pf, 1947; Sonata, op.17, va, pf, 1947; 2 Bagatelles, op.18, pf, 1947; Children's Suite, op.16, pf, 1948; Sonatina, op.19, fl, pf, 1948; Sonatina, op.28, ob, pf, 1951; Sonatina, op.29, cl, pf, 1951; 8 Children's Pieces, op.36, pf, 1952; Sonatina, op.41, rec, pf, 1953; Sonata no.2, op.43, vn, pf, 1953; 5 Pieces, op.84, vn, pf, 1964; 6 Pieces, op.84, vn, pf, 1965; Duo, op.85, 2 vc, 1965; Fantasies: op.86, bn, 1966, op.87, cl, 1966, op.88, hn, 1966, op.89, fl, 1966, op.90, ob, 1966, op.100, tpt, 1969, op.101, trbn, 1969, op.102, tuba, 1969, op.107, gui, 1971, op.117, hp, 1975; Sonata, op.121, fl, pf, 1977; Fantasy, op.127, rec, 1986; Fantasy, op.130, vc, 1987; Duo, op.135, 2 cl; 3 Fantasies, op.129, pf

Principal publishers: Faher, Lengnick, Paterson

WRITINGS

'I Think of Music in Terms of Sound', *Music and Musicians*, iv/11 (1955–6), 9 only

'Don't Shoot the Pianist', *The Guardian* (3 June 1971)

'My Early Life', *Music and Musicians* (1986), Oct, 8–9

BIBLIOGRAPHY

W. Kallaway: *London Philharmonic: Music Makers Since 1932* (Havant, 1972) [incl. introduction by R. Baker]

P.J. Pirie: *The English Musical Renaissance* (London, 1979)

A. Poulton: *The Music of Malcolm Arnold: a Catalogue* (London, 1986)

H. Cole: *Malcolm Arnold: an Introduction to his Music* (London, 1989)

M. Kennedy: *Portrait of Walton* (Oxford, 1989)

P. Burton-Page: *Philharmonic Concerto: the Life and Music of Sir Malcolm Arnold* (London, 1994)

PIERS BURTON-PAGE

Arnold, Samuel (*b* London, 10 Aug 1740; *d* London, 22 Oct 1802). English composer, conductor, organist and editor. He was the son of Thomas Arnold, a commoner, and, according to some sources, the Princess Amelia. Arnold received his education as a Child of the Chapel Royal (*c*1750 to August 1758) and on leaving became known as an organist, conductor and teacher, and composed prolifically. In autumn 1764 he was engaged by John Beard as harpsichordist and composer to Covent Garden; there he compiled several pastiche operas, including the popular *The Maid of the Mill* (1765), which is among the supreme examples of the form. In 1769 Arnold bought Marylebone Gardens, and during the next six summers produced several short all-sung burlettas, composing or at least contributing to four new examples (now lost). These productions were simply written (from the literary point of view at least) and would have appealed to an audience with no previous experience of operatic music.

In 1771 Arnold married Mary Ann Napier, sometimes described as wealthy; but whatever the family fortune, the criminal activities of an employee at Marylebone lost Arnold most of his money and the Gardens were sold. The eldest of Arnold's four children, Samuel James, his only son, was the author of some weak opera librettos

which his father set; he became the first manager of the Lyceum Theatre. Unsurprisingly, Arnold pursued his early composing career with a sequence of oratorios on biblical subjects; *The Prodigal Son* (1773) was performed at Oxford at the installation of Lord North as Chancellor at the Encaenia of 1773. The university also offered Arnold the honorary degree of Doctor of Music, but he declined, preferring to take it in the ordinary manner. His other early compositions include songs for the London pleasure gardens and some keyboard sonatas.

Arnold resumed his professional association with the patent theatres when, in 1777, he was engaged by George Colman the elder as composer and music director for the Little Theatre in the Haymarket. As a result of an inheritance, Colman had just bought the theatre; he and Arnold had collaborated when they were on the Covent Garden staff in the 1760s, and were always close friends. Arnold composed for the Little Theatre for 25 years; from 1789 George Colman the younger was manager. There is little documentary material related to Arnold's residency at the theatre, except through evidence of the production and reception of his works performed there. With his afterpiece opera *Lilliput* (1777) and, in the same year, an arrangement of the full-length ballad opera *Polly* (text by Gay and original music attributed to Pepusch) – Arnold's only operatic material to survive orchestrally – was begun a successful series of his stage works, which achieved maturity in the full-length pasticcio 'comic opera' *The Castle of Andalusia* (1782). By that time Arnold was in a position to combine his summer directorship at the Little Theatre with several other posts in London, as organist and conductor. He was organist and composer to the Chapel Royal (from 1783) and organist to Westminster Abbey (from 1793). In 1786 Arnold (together with Thomas Linley (i)) succeeded John Stanley as manager of the Lenten oratorios at Drury Lane, and in 1787 he established the Glee Club with J.W. Callcott, who later helped him compile a large volume of psalm settings. In 1789 Arnold became official conductor of the Academy of Ancient Music, and in 1790 founded the Graduates' Meeting, a society of academic musicians which included Haydn among its associates; he was also an active member of the Anacreontic Society and appointed president in December 1791. Arnold's generous spirit is reflected in his continuous support for those in reduced circumstances, especially musicians; he established a Choral Fund in 1791, was for 40 years an active member of the Royal Society of Musicians and also, from 1796, conducted the annual performance at St Paul's for the benefit of the Sons of the Clergy. A long-standing freemason, Arnold, from 1795, conducted the societies' concerts in aid of the female orphans. Of importance to English musicology was the appearance in 1786 of Arnold's proposals for a complete Handel edition, 180 parts of which were published between 1787 and 1797. Other editorial enterprises by Arnold include *The New Musical Magazine*, together with Thomas Busby (*c*1783–6), *Harrison's New German-Flute Magazine* (1784–5) and a four-volume continuation of Boyce's *Cathedral Music* (1790). In autumn 1798 Arnold fell off his library steps, suffering injuries which eventually led to his death; he was buried on 29 October 1802 in Westminster Abbey. During his last three years he wrote three novel pantomimes and an oratorio, *The Hymn of Adam and Eve*, presumably composed for the Haymarket Lenten oratorio season.

Arnold's achievement was greatest as a dramatic composer who, besides pantomimes and incidental music, wrote, or contributed to, over 70 operas. Although some of his writing is lacking in compositional finesse, having been produced at great speed and with little thought, the number of editions and stage productions of his operas testifies to Arnold's popularity in the last quarter of the 18th century. Statistics show that Arnold's more successful operas, such as *The Agreeable Surprise* (1781) and *Inkle and Yarico* (1787), an early anti-slavery opera, were among the most frequently performed of all operas of the time.

No doubt Arnold's prominence as a musical figure and his position at the Little Theatre had something to do with the frequency of performances, but we can be sure that the operas found appreciative audiences. Arnold well knew the resources of his stage, the capabilities of his actor-singers and the taste of his audience, and in his best comic operas he managed to attain some individuality and to write dramatically vivid music. In his early works, Arnold closely adhered to the tradition of the Italian burletta, and in his first surviving all-sung opera, *The Portrait* (1770), he not only revealed an ability to write effective italianate ensembles full of bustling and amusing stage action, but also demonstrated how flexible the burletta form was and how easily it could be adapted to commentary on contemporary life.

For the Little Theatre Arnold wrote 'dialogue' operas, but whereas the operas of his middle creative period – for instance, *The Castle of Andalusia*, *The Spanish Barber* (1777), *Two to One* (1784) and *Turk and No Turk* (1785) – are bound to the conventions of English comic opera, with its mixture of serious and comic elements, Arnold attempted in his later works, such as *The Battle of Hexham* (1789), *The Surrender of Calais* (1791), *The Mountaineers* (1793) and *Zorinski* (1795), to develop a historical-hybrid form – a play for the chief characters but an opera for the subsidiary ones, set in the distant past – which released the romantic strain in his imagination. If the middle-period operas are principally successful in the portrayal of individual characters in music, for freely constructed ensembles as finales, for the frequent use of folktunes and for music composed in the folk idiom, the operas of Arnold's last period make greater dramatic use of the overture and chorus, and intermittently include instrumental music of an illustrative or 'programmatic' character and also ballet. Whereas the serious characters are generally allotted full-scale arias with florid vocal divisions, the comic characters sing mostly simple melodies in ballad style.

Of special importance are the ensembles, which often show that Arnold clearly understood the nature of music drama and was moved to match dramatic event with musical gesture. The tempo, the rhythm, the key, and the number of singers are constantly varied; duetting is mainly confined to 3rds and 6ths, and block chordal harmony predominates in the choruses. There is an excellent trio at the end of Act 1 of *The Siege of Curzola* (1786), and striking choral writing in *The Surrender of Calais* and in *The Shipwreck* (1796); the last was composed for Drury Lane and reveals how effectively Arnold could write for large instrumental and vocal resources.

Judging by the orchestral cues given in many of the published vocal scores, Arnold's instrumentation was remarkable for its variety and originality; wind cues abound, and there is occasional use of such instruments as the flageolet (in *The Children in the Wood*, 1793), harp (*Cambro-Britons*, 1798) and tubalcain, a glockenspiel in its original form of a miniature carillon (*The Veteran Tar*, 1801). Arnold showed his professionalism chiefly in his regard for singers – almost every aria is adapted to the special character and qualities of the person assigned to the role. Among his best are the coloratura arias with flute obbligato written for Elizabeth Bannister, such as 'The tuneful lark' in *The Agreeable Surprise* and 'Ah solitude' in *The Castle of Andalusia*. The use of English folksongs is one of the most important features of Arnold's operas, for example 'Peggy of Derby O' in *Two to One* and 'We go up Holborn Hill' in *Peeping Tom* (1784).

Arnold set a number of previously unrecorded songs; for instance, *The Children in the Wood* includes a version of 'The Truth sent from above' that in the 20th century has been associated with Vaughan Williams. Colourful Irish songs in Arnold's scores are the result of his successful collaboration with an Irish librettist, John O'Keeffe, who sometimes wrote lyrics to fit the tunes he remembered from his youth. Arnold's long theatrical experience gave him sufficient knowledge to borrow sensibly; an unusual number of citations from Haydn and Mozart occur in the Jamaican-outlaw pantomime *Obi, or Three-Finger'd Jack* (1800).

Samuel Arnold: portrait by George Dance, pencil, 1795 (National Portrait Gallery, London)

WORKS

LCG – *Covent Garden*
LDL – *Drury Lane*
LKH – *King's Theatre in the Haymarket*
LLH – *Little Theatre in the Haymarket*
LMG – *Marylebone Gardens*

all printed works published in London

STAGE

aft – *afterpiece*
a-s – *all-sung*
dialogue operas unless otherwise stated; vocal scores and librettos published in London soon after first performance, unless otherwise stated

The Maid of the Mill (pasticcio, 3, I. Bickerstaff, after S. Richardson: *Pamela*, and J. Fletcher and W. Rowley), LCG, 31 Jan 1765, 4 nos. by Arnold

Daphne and Amintor (aft, pasticcio, 1, Bickerstaff after G. de Saint-Foix and S.M. Cibber), LDL, 8 Oct 1765, music selected by author, collab. Arnold

The Summer's Tale (pasticcio, 3, R. Cumberland), LCG, 6 Dec 1765, 6 nos. by Arnold; rev. as Amelia (2), LDL, 14 Dec 1771, music unpubd

Harlequin Dr Faustus (pantomime, aft, 1, H. Woodward, after L. Theobald), LCG, 18 Nov 1766, music pubd

Rosamond (aft, a-s, 1, rev. of J. Addison), LCG, 21 April 1767, 1 song pubd

The Royal Garland (aft, a-s, 1, Bickerstaff), LCG, 10 Oct 1768, music unpubd

Tom Jones (pasticcio, 3, J. Reed and A.L.H. Poinsinet, after H. Fielding), LCG, 14 Jan 1769, 7 nos. by Arnold

The Rape of Proserpine (pantomime, aft, 1, L. Theobald, rev. ? F. Tenducci), LCG, 4 Nov 1769, music by J. Galliard, new music by Arnold unpubd

Amintas (aft, pasticcio, 3, Tenducci, after R. Rolt and P. Metastasio), LCG, 15 Dec 1769, 5 nos. by Arnold

The Servant Mistress (aft, a-s, 2, S. Storace, trans. of *La serva padrona*), LMG, 16 June 1770, Pergolesi's music arr. and airs added by Arnold, unpubd

The Madman (aft, pasticcio, 1), LMG, 28 Aug 1770, music unpubd

Apollo Turned Stroller (aft, a-s, 1), ?unperf., music and lib unpubd

True Blue (aft, a-s, 1, H. Carey), LCG, 12 Nov 1770, revival, new music by Arnold unpubd

The Portrait (aft, a-s, 3, G. Colman (i), after L. Anseaume: *Le tableau parlant*), LCG, 22 Nov 1770, vs lacks recits

Mother Shipton (pantomime, aft, 1, Colman (i)), 26 Dec 1770, music and song words pubd

The Magnet (aft, a-s, 1, D. Dubois), LMG, 27 June 1771, music unpubd

The Cure for Dotage (aft, a-s, 1), LMG, 3 Aug 1771, music and lib unpubd

Don Quixote (aft, a-s, 1, D.J. Piguenit, after M. de Cervantes), LMG, 30 June 1774, music unpubd

The Weathercock (aft, pasticcio, 2, T. Forrest), LCG, 17 Oct 1775; ov. by Arnold, music unpubd

The Seraglio (aft, 2, C. Dibdin and E. Thompson), LCG, 14 Nov 1776, music by Dibdin with 3 nos. by Arnold

Lilliput (aft, 1, D. Garrick, after J. Swift: *Gulliver's Travels*), LLH, 15 May 1777, revival, new music by Arnold

Polly (ballad op, 3, J. Gay, rev. Colman (i)), LLH, 19 June 1777, orch pts, *US-CA* (with Arnold's addns: ov. and 18 nos.), ed. R Hoskins (Wellington, forthcoming)

A Fairy Tale (aft, pasticcio, 2, D. Garrick, after W. Shakespeare, rev. Colman (i)), LLH, 18 July 1777, music by J.C. Smith and M. Arne with epilogue song by Arnold, unpubd

The Sheep Shearing (3, pasticcio, Colman (i), after Shakespeare), LLH, 18 July 1777, music by T. Arne with 2 airs by Arnold, music unpubd

April Day (a-s, 3, K. O'Hara, after G. Carey: *The Magic Girdle*), LLH, 22 Aug 1777, music unpubd

The Spanish Barber (3, Colman (i), after P.-A. Beaumarchais), op.17, LLH, 30 Aug 1777, music and song words pubd

Poor Vulcan (aft, a-s, 2, Dibdin, after P.A. Motteux), LCG, 4 Feb 1778, music by Dibdin with 2 nos. by Arnold

The Gipsies (aft, 2, Dibdin, after C.-S. Favart: *La Bohémienne*), LLH, 3 Aug 1778, music unpubd

Macbeth (tragedy, 5, Shakespeare), music by R. Leveridge with entr'actes by Arnold, LLH, 7 Sept 1778, ed. R Hoskins (Wellington, 1997)

Summer Amusement, or An Adventure at Margate (part pasticcio, 3, M.P. Andrews and W.A. Miles), LLH, 1 July 1779, 11 nos. by Arnold, vs (1779/R)

The Son in Law (aft, 2, J. O'Keeffe), op.14, LLH, 14 Aug 1779, only pirated lib extant

Fire and Water (aft, 2, Andrews), LLH, 8 July 1780, 2 songs and lib pubd

The Wedding Night (aft, part pasticcio, 1, J. Cobb), LLH, 12 Aug 1780, music and lib unpubd

The Genius of Nonsense op.27 (pantomime, aft, part pasticcio, 1, Colman (i)), op.27, LLH, 2 Sept 1780, music and song words pubd

The Dead Alive (aft, 2, O'Keeffe, after *The Thousand and One Nights*), op.18, LLH, 16 June 1781, only pirated lib extant

Baron Kinkvervankotsdorsprakingatchdern (part pasticcio, 3, Andrews, after Lady Craven), LLH, 9 July 1781, music unpubd

The Silver Tankard (aft, part pasticcio, 2, Lady Craven), LLH, 18 July 1781, music and lib unpubd, song words pubd, incl. music by T. Giordani, T. Arne and others

Hodge-podge (aft, Colman (i)), LLH, 28 Aug 1781, music and lib unpubd

The Agreeable Surprise, or The Secret Enlarged (aft, 2, O'Keeffe), op.16, LLH, 4 Sept 1781, only pirated lib extant

The Banditti (part pasticcio, 3, O'Keeffe), LCG, 28 Nov 1781, song words pubd; rev. as The Castle of Andalusia op.20 (part pasticcio, LCG, 2 Nov 1782, vs (1782/R 1991 in MLE, C5 with introduction by R. Hoskins) [incl. facs. of MS lib]

The Positive Man (farce, aft, 2, O'Keeffe), LCG, 16 March 1782, 1 incid song by Arnold

Fatal Curiosity (tragedy, 3, G. Lillo, rev. Colman (i)), LLH, 29 June 1782, 1 incid song by Arnold

The Tobacco Box (incid interlude), Fr. air, arr. Arnold, trans. Colman (i), LLH, 13 Aug 1782

None so blind as those who won't see (aft, 2, Dibdin, after L.-V. Dorvigny), LLH, 2 July 1782, music and lib unpubd

The Female Dramatist (aft, 2, Colman (i) after T. Smollett), LLH, 16 Aug 1782, only select words pubd

Harlequin Teague (pantomime, aft, part pasticcio, 1, Colman (i) and O'Keeffe), op.19, LLH, 17 Aug 1782, music and song words pubd

The Birth Day, or The Prince of Arragon (aft, 2, O'Keeffe, after Saint-Foix), op.21, LLH, 12 Aug 1783

Gretna Green (aft, pasticcio, 2, C. Stuart and O'Keeffe), op.22, LLH, 28 Aug 1783

Two to One (3, G. Colman (ii)), op.24, LLH, 19 June 1784

Hunt the Slipper (aft, 2, H. Knapp), op.26, LLH, 21 Aug 1784, only pirated lib extant (1792)

Peeping Tom (aft, part pasticcio, 2, O'Keeffe), op.25, LLH, 6 Sept 1784, only pirated lib extant

A Beggar on Horseback (farce, aft, 2, O'Keeffe), LLH, 16 June 1785, 1 incid song by Arnold

Turk and No Turk (3, Colman (ii)), op.28, LLH, 9 July 1785, music and song words pubd

Here and There and Everywhere (pantomime, aft, 1, C. Delpini), LLH, 31 Aug 1785, music and lib unpubd

The Siege of Curzola (3, O'Keeffe, after R. Knowles), op.29, LLH, 12 Aug 1786, music and song words pubd

Inkle and Yarico (comic dialogue op, 3, Colman (ii), after R. Steele and R. Ligon, also ?Weddell), op.30, LLH, 4 Aug 1787, vs (1787/R)

The Gnome (pantomime, aft ?2, R. Wewitzer and K. Invill), LLH, 5 Aug 1788, 1 song pubd, song words pubd

Ut Pictora Poesis!, or The Enraged Musician (aft, a-s, 1, Colman (i), based on W. Hogarth), op.31, LLH, 18 May 1789

The Battle of Hexham (3, Colman (ii), after Shakespeare), op.32, LLH, 11 Aug 1789

New Spain, or Love in Mexico (3, J. Scawen), op.33, LLH, 16 July 1790

The Basket Maker (aft, 2, O'Keeffe), LLH, 4 Sept 1790, music unpubd

The Surrender of Calais (3, Colman (ii)), op.33, LLH, 30 July 1791

The Enchanted Wood (3, W. Francis, after Shakespeare and T. Parnell), op.35, LLH, 25 July 1792

The Mountaineers (3, Colman (ii), after M. de Cervantes: *Don Quixote* and W. Hodson: *Zoraida*), op.34, LLH, 3 Aug 1793

The Children in the Wood (aft, 2, T. Morton), op.35, LLH, 1 Oct 1793, vs (1793/R1994 in *Nineteenth-Century American Musical Theater*, i, with introduction by S. Porter) [incl. facs. of published lib]

Harlequin Peasant (pantomime, aft, 1), LLH, 26 Dec 1793, music unpubd, song words pubd

Thomas and Sally (aft, a-s, 2, Bickerstaff), LLH, 24 Feb 1794, music by T. Arne with new finale by Arnold, music unpubd

Auld Robin Gray (aft, 2, part pasticcio, S.J. Arnold), op.36, LLH, 26 July 1794

How to be Happy (comedy, 5, G. Brewer), LLH, 9 Aug 1794, 1 song pubd, lib unpubd

Rule Britannia (aft, pasticcio, 2, J. Roberts), LLH, 18 Aug 1794, music unpubd

Britain's Glory (aft, part pasticcio, 1, R. Benson), LLH, 20 Aug 1794, 3 songs pubd

The Wedding Day (farce, aft, 2, E. Inchbald), LLH, 1 Nov 1794, 1 incid song by Arnold

The Death of Captain Faulknor (aft, part pasticcio, 1, W. Pearce), LCG, 6 May 1795, ov. by Arnold, music unpubd

Zorinski (3, Morton, after H. Brooke: *Gustavus Vasa*), op.37, LLH, 20 July 1795

Who Pays the Reckoning? (aft, 2, S.J. Arnold), LLH, 16 July 1795, 2 songs pubd, lib unpubd

Love and Money (aft, part pasticcio, 1, Benson), op.38, LLH, 29 Aug 1795

Love and Madness! (tragicomedy, 5, F. Waldron, after Shakespeare and J. Fletcher: *Two Noble Kinsmen*), LLH, 21 Sept 1795, music unpubd, song words pubd

Bannian Day (aft, 2, Brewer, after J. Cross: *The Apparition*), op.39, LLH, 11 June 1796

The Shipwreck (aft, 2, S.J. Arnold), op.40, LDL, 10 Dec 1796

The Hovel (aft, 2), LDL, 23 May 1797, music and lib unpubd

The Irish Legacy (aft, 2, S.J. Arnold), LLH, 26 June 1797, music and lib unpubd

The Italian Monk (3, J. Boaden, after A. Radcliffe), op.43, LLH, 15 Aug 1797, incid. only ov. and 4 songs

Throw Physic to the Dogs! (aft, 2, H. Lee), LLH, 6 July 1798, 1 song and song words pubd

Cambro-Britons (3, Boaden), op.45, LLH, 21 July 1798

False and True (3, G. Moultrie), op.46, LLH, 11 Aug 1798

Obi, or Three-Finger'd Jack (pantomime, aft, 2, J. Fawcett, after B. Moseley), op.48, LLH, 2 July 1800, vs (*c*1800/*R* 1996 in MLE, D4 with introduction by R. Hoskins and E. Southern) [incl. facs. of MS lib]

The Review (aft, 2, Colman (ii), after Lee and T. Dibdin), op.52, LLH, 1 Sept 1800

Virginia (3, D. Plowden, after M. Pix), LDL, 30 Oct 1800, ov. and songs accs. by Arnold, tunes by Plowden

Hamlet (tragedy, 5, Shakespeare), LDL, songs for Ophelia arr. Arnold (1801)

The Veteran Tar (aft, 2, S.J. Arnold, after C.-A. Pigault-Lebrun: *Le petit matelot*), op.50, LDL, 29 Jan 1801

The Corsair (pantomime, aft, 2, C. Farley, after M. Lewis: *The Castle Spectre*), op.51, LLH, 29 July 1801

The Sixty-third Letter (aft, 2, W.C. Oulton), LLH, 18 July 1802

Fairies' Revels, or Love in the Highlands (ballet-pantomime, aft, 1, Fawcett, after T. Moore: *The Ring*), LLH, 14 Aug 1802

Doubtful: The Revenge (aft, a-s, 1, T. Chatterton), unperf., music unpubd

ORATORIOS
not published unless otherwise stated

The Cure of Saul (J. Brown, after *1 Samuel* xvi.14–23), LKT, 23 Jan 1767, lib pubd, 2 nos., *US-Wc*

Abimelech (C. Smart, after *Genesis* xx, xi), LLH, 16 March 1768, lib pubd

The Resurrection (Arnold, various biblical texts), LCG, 9 March 1770, lib pubd

The Prodigal Son (T. Hull, after *Luke* xv.11–32), LLH, 5 March 1773, lib pubd

Omnipotence (pasticcio, Arnold and E. Toms), LLH, 25 Feb 1774, *GB-Lbl*, lib pubd [arr. from works by Handel]

Redemption (? W. Coxe, adapted by Arnold), LDL, 10 March 1786, lib and score (*c*1814), new recits by Arnold [arr. from works by Handel]

The Triumph of Truth (pasticcio, Arnold, after *Esdras* ii–iv, based on Toms: *Israel in Babylon*, 1764), LDL, 27 Feb 1789, lib pubd [arr. from works by Handel and others]

Elisha, or the Woman of Shunem (Hull, after *2 Kings* iv.8–37), LLH, 13 March 1801, lib pubd

The Hymn of Adam and Eve (J. Milton: *Paradise Lost*, book 5), not perf., *Lcm* [dated 28 Jan 1802]

OTHER SACRED

Psalms and Hymns for the Chapel of the Asylum, 3–4vv, ed. W. Riley (1767); collab. Battishill, Nares and others

The Psalms of David, 1–4vv, ed. Arnold and J.W. Callcott (1791)

Arnold's New Set of Hymn Tunes, 4vv (*c*1791)

A Collection of Hymn Tunes, 3–4vv (*c*1797); collab. G. Breillat and W. Dixon, vol.ii (*c*1815)

'Tis done, the Sovereign will's obey'd, 1774, *Lbl* [hymn on the death of J.F. Lampe]

6 Services: 5 for Morning, Communion and Evening, B♭ (*c*1840), C, D, F, G; 1 for Communion and Evening, A (*c*1860) [continuation of Boyce: Morning Service]

Anthems (4vv unless otherwise stated; MSS, *c*1783–1800): Have mercy upon me, A, T, B, SATB, 1783, *Ob**

   Hear O thou Shepherd, A, T, B, SATB, *Ob*

   Our Lord is risen from the dead, S, SATB (*c*1793) [for Easter]

   O be joyful, S, S, A, T, B, SSATB (*c*1795), arr. of Arne: Artaxerxes ov.

   Hallelujah, Salvation and Glory, [S, A,] T, B, [SA]TB, 29 Nov 1798, *Lwa*

   Who is that cometh from Edom?, A, T, B, SATB (1800), arr. of 'V'ardoro, pupille' from Handel: Giulio Cesare [for Palm Sunday]

   God in the great assembly, A, T, B, [SATB], frag., *Ob*

   I will magnify thee O God, ?S, S[AT]B, *Y*

   My song shall be always, A, B, SATB, *Ckc*, *Y*

   My song shall be of mercy, S, SATB, *Ob*

   O how amiable, S, S, T, B, ?SATB, frag., *Lbl*

   O praise the Lord, SATB, frag., *Lbl*

   O praise ye the Lord, A, T, B, SATB, *Y*

   Shepherds rejoice, SSATB, SSAB, 2 ob, 2 tpt, 2 hn, str, *US-BETm*

   The Lord is King, [A,T,] B, [SAT] B, *GB-Lbl*

   Wherewithal shall a young man, S, S, SATB, *Lbl*

   Who is the King of Glory?, SATB, SSAB, 2 ob, 2 tpt, 2 hn, str, *US-BETm*

ODES

Ode in Honour of the Prince of Wales's Birthday, 1769

Other royal odes, lost

Ode to the Haymakers (C. Smart), 1769

Ode to Shakespeare (F. Gentleman), 1769

Ode to the Jesuits (G. Marriott), 1773

The Power of Music (J. Hughes), 1773

Ode for the Anniversary of the London Hospital, 1785

Ode to Charity, 1798, *Ob*

Ode to Humanity, 1798, attrib. Arnold

Ode for the Sons of Clergy (N. Tew), 1799

OTHER SECULAR VOCAL

A Collection of the Favourite Songs sung at Vaux-Hall, i–ii (1767–8)

The New Songs sung at Marylebone (*c*1770)

A Collection of the Favourite Airs in Score sung at Haberdashers Hall (*c*1770)

A Third Collection of Songs sung at Vaux-Hall … with the Favourite Cantata call'd the Milk Maid, op.9 (1774)

6 Canzonets, pf/harp acc., op.12 (1778)

Elegy on the Death of Mr Shenstone (1778), *US-Wc* [Arne's glee scored by Arnold]

The Favorite Cantata and Songs sung this Season at Vaux-Hall (*c*1778)

From Earth to Heaven, 4vv (1784) [on the death of Paul Whitehead]

Anacreontic Songs, 1–4vv (1785)

The Prince of Arcadia, pastoral elegy (1788)

A Selection of … Favourite Scots Songs … By Eminent Masters (1790) [10 items arr. by Arnold]

Alcanzor: a Moorish Tale, 3vv (*c*1797)

The Hero's Return [Nelson's Return] (R. Whittington) (*c*1799)

Ireland's Defender, or Johnson Forever (Dr Felix) (*c*1800)

Songs with orch: If 'tis joy to wound a save (*c*1770); Hear me love (*c*1770); Come hope thou queen of endless smiles (*c*1779); No sport to the chace can compare (*c*1780); The Royal British Tar (1783); The Je ne sais quois (1787); Jockey was a braw young lad (*c*1788); Simplicity, thou fav'rite child (1789); What citadel so proud can see (1789); The Princess Elizabeth (*c*1790); When Jockey dances (*c*1790); O Phoebus (1793); Poor Little Gypsey (1795); Alley Croaker (1796); Little Bess (*c*1797)

32 songs, v, pf/hpd; 7 duets, some autograph

Catches, canons and glees incl. in: anthologies ed. Warren (1776–7), Clementi (*c*1790) and Sale (*c*1800); Amusement for the Ladies (*c*1785–93, *c*1800); Social Harmony (1818); *GB-Lcm* 15 (partly autograph); *Ckc* 199, 404

INSTRUMENTAL

A Favourite Lesson, hpd/pf (1768)

6 Sonatas, hpd/pf (*c*1769), collab. Galuppi and F. Mazzinghi

8 Lessons, hpd/pf, op.7 (*c*1771)

6 Overtures in 8 parts, op.8 (*c*1771/*R*), ed. R. Hoskins (Wellington, 1997) [also for hpd/pf]
15 Sonatas, hpd/pf, *c*1771, private collection, Dublin
Sonata, B♭, hpd/pf, *c*1773, *GB-Lbl*
12 Minuets, hpd, vn/fl (*c*1775)
8 Lessons, 2nd set, hpd/pf, op.10 (1775; 2/Paris, *c*1778)
8 Sonatas, 3rd set, hpd/pf, vn acc., op.11 (*c*1775–8)
A Set of Progressive Lessons I–II, hpd/pf, op.12 (*c*1777–9)

3 concs., hpd/pf, org, str, op.15 (1782)
Largo and Allegro, D, org, *c*1783, *Lbl*
3 Grand Sonatas, hpd/pf, op.23 (1784)
12 duets, 2 fl (1784); incl. works by Handel, Arne and others
Duettos on Scots songs, hpd, vn (*c*1785); collab. Barthélemon, Carter, Shield
New Instructions for the German Flute … with … a Variety of Favourite Tunes and Other Easy Lessons (1787)
La Chasse, or The Hunter's Medley, hpd/pf (*c*1793) [with words]
The New British Tar, medley sonata, hpd/pf (*c*1793) [with words]
The Princess of Wales; a Scots Minuet, hpd/pf, 1795, *Lbl*
Ally Croaker, with variations, hpd/pf (*c*1796)

EDITIONS AND ARRANGEMENTS

The New Musical Magazine or Compleat Library of Vocal and Instrumental Music … with an Universal Dictionary … and General History of Music [by T. Busby] (1783–6) [compiled by Arnold], 197 nos.
Harrison's New German-Flute Magazine, 60 nos., ed. Arnold (1784–5)
Convivial Harmony, ed. Arnold (1786)
The Songs of Handel, 4 vols (1786–7) [Harrison's edn corrected by Arnold]
12 English Ballads, pf acc. (1787) [adapted to music by Haydn]
The Works of Handel, 180 nos., ed. Arnold (1787–97)
Cathedral Music, 4 vols., ed. and rev. Arnold (1790) [orig. by Boyce]
Juvenile Amusement, 1–3vv (1797) [nursery songs arr. by Arnold]
Writings by Arnold incl.: Lesson on Thorough-bass (MS, 1798, *GB-Lbl*) [?pt. of treatise]; Exercise Book for Realization of Figured basses, Exercises and Examples for Teaching Purposes (MSS, 1790s, *US-Wc*); chapter on music in D. Fenning: The Young Man's Book of Knowledge (1786)

BIBLIOGRAPHY

FiskeETM; LS
W.C. Oulton: The History of the Theatres of London … from 1771 to 1795 (London, 1796)
'Biographical Sketch of the Late Dr. Arnold', The Monthly Mirror, x (1803), 147–52, 225–6
T. Busby: Concert Room and Orchestra Anecdotes (London, 1825), iii, 148ff
J. O'Keeffe: Recollections of the Life of John O'Keeffe (London, 1826/R), ii
G. Colman jr: Random Records (London, 1830), i
'Memoir of Samuel Arnold, Mus. Doc.', The Harmonicon, viii (1830), 137–9 [probably by William Ayrton, Arnold's son-in-law]
W.S. Ayrton: Memoir [1876] and Correspondence of Marianne Ayrton, c1793–1834 (MS, US-Wc)
J.M. Coopersmith: 'The First Gesamtausgabe: Dr. Arnold's Edition of Handel's Works', Notes, iv (1946–7), 277–92, 438–49
P. Hirsch: 'Dr. Arnold's Handel Edition', MR, viii (1947), 106–16
C. Cudworth: 'The English Symphonists of the Eighteenth Century', PRMA, lxxviii (1951–2), 31–51
F. Link, ed.: The Plays of John O'Keeffe (New York, 1981)
R. Hoskins: Dr Samuel Arnold (1740–1802): an Historical Assessment (diss., U. of Auckland, 1984), ii
R. Hoskins: 'The Pantomimes and Ballets of Samuel Arnold', Studies in Music, xix (1985), 80–93
R. Hoskins: 'Theatre Music II', Music in Britain: the Eighteenth Century, ed. H.D. Johnstone and R. Fiske (Oxford, 1990), 26–312
R. Hoskins: 'Samuel Arnold's Keyboard Sonatas: a Commentary and Index', Studies in Music, xxv (1991), 53–72
R. Hoskins: 'A Checklist of Samuel Arnold's Extant Songs, Vocal Ensembles and Odes', Research Chronicle [New Zealand Musicological Society], v (1995), 27–31
E. Zöllner: 'Israel in Babylon or the Triumph of Truth? A Late Eighteenth-Century Pasticcio Oratorio', The Consort, li (1995), 103–17
P.J. Rogers: 'A Bibliographic Survey of Arnold's Handel Edition, the First Gesamtausgabe', Music in Performance and Society: Essays

in Honor of Roland Jackson, ed. M. Cole and J. Koegel (Warren, MI, 1997), 165–75
R. Hoskins: The Theater Music of Samuel Arnold: a Thematic Index (Warren, MI, 1998)

ROBERT HOSKINS

Arnold, Samuel James (bap. London, 28 Dec 1774; *d* Walton upon Thames, 16 Aug 1852). English librettist and impresario, son of SAMUEL ARNOLD. Though trained as an artist, from the mid-1790s he worked with his father at the Little Theatre in the Haymarket, writing afterpieces set by the elder Arnold. He himself wrote the words and music for one such work there, *Foul Deeds Will Rise* (18 July 1804). In 1809, when Drury Lane burnt down and its company moved to the Lyceum in Wellington Street off the Strand, Arnold then became associated with that theatre and began to stage his own plays with music. The Drury Lane company left in 1812 and Arnold retained the Lyceum, naming it the English Opera House during summer seasons. In 1815 he obtained the lease and had the theatre almost completely rebuilt; it was formally opened as the English Opera House on 15 June 1816, presenting original works, many to Arnold's own texts, as well as adaptations of foreign pieces. Until his productions of *Der Freischütz* in 1824 and *Tarare* in 1825 (the earliest of those works in England), such adaptations had mostly been revivals of popular English plays with borrowed music, especially Mozart or Rossini, rather than versions of genuine continental operas. The Lyceum (uninsured) burnt down in February 1830, but after a successful public subscription it reopened in July 1834 as the English Opera House, Royal Lyceum, for 'the presentation of English operas and the encouragement of indigenous musical talent'. From this period dates the first real flowering of authentic English Romantic operas, by Loder (notably *Nourjahad*, to an S.J. Arnold libretto), Barnett, Thomson, and later Balfe and Macfarren. Arnold retired in the mid-1840s.

For a complete list of his librettos see *GroveO*.

BIBLIOGRAPHY

DNB (E.D. Cook); NicollH
'Rebuilding of the English Opera House', The Times (23 March 1830)
F. Boase: 'Arnold, Samuel James', Modern English Biography (London, 2/1965)

LEANNE LANGLEY

Arnol'd, Yury (Karlovich) [Jurig von] (*b* St Petersburg, 1/13 Nov 1811; *d* Karakesh, nr Simferopol', Crimea, 8/20 July 1898). Russian writer on music, teacher and composer. His father was a state councillor. After studying political economy at the German University of Dorpat in Estonia, he served in the army during the Polish campaign (1831–8). On resigning his commission he decided to make a career in music, studying harmony with Johann Leopold Fuchs and counterpoint with Joseph Hunke. In 1839 his cantata *Svetlana*, to words by Vasily Zhukovsky, was awarded a Philharmonic Society prize and subsequently performed in *tableaux vivants* in both St Petersburg and Moscow. He was a friend of the leading Russian musicians of his day, and his memoirs, published in three volumes in 1892–3, are a valuable record of 60 years of Russian musical life. From 1841 he contributed criticisms and reviews to a number of journals (the *S.-Peterburgskiye vedomosti*, *Biblioteka dlya chteniya*, *Literaturnaya gazeta*, *Severnaya pchela*, *Panteon* and others) under a variety of pseudonyms, including Meloman, Karl Karlovich, A. Yu., Harmonin and Karl Smeliy.

From 1863 to 1871 Arnol'd was in Leipzig, where he contributed to *Signal* and the *Neue Zeitschrift für Musik* (1863–5) and edited the *Neue allgemeine Zeitschrift für Theater und Musik* (1867–8). It is likely that at this time he was employed as an espionage agent by the tsarist police, and it is possible that the articles which appeared above his name were in fact written by a certain Peshenin who was handsomely rewarded for his silence. From 1871 to 1894 Arnol'd taught music privately in Moscow. He was an external lecturer in 'musical science' at Moscow Conservatory in 1888 and was invited to speak on Russian music in Leipzig the next year. From 1894 to his death he taught singing in St Petersburg. He published several useful monographs on the history of Russian church music, but his views on the origins of Russian folksong are now generally discredited. His most ambitious theoretical work, *Nauka 0 muzïke na osnovanii èsteticheskikh i fiziologicheskikh zakonov* ('The science of music on the basis of aesthetic and physiological laws') (Moscow, 1875), is praised as an original (if flawed) early monument of Russian speculative theory.

Arnol'd's compositions are mainly of academic interest. They include the operas *Tsïganka* ('Gypsy Girl', completed 1836) and *Posledniy den' Pompei* ('The Last Day of Pompeii', completed 1860); the operettas *Der Invalide* (completed and performed 1852) and *Za Bogom molitva, a za tsaryom sluzhba ne propadayut, ili Noch' pod Ivana Kupala* ('Prayer to God and Service to the Tsar are never wasted, or St John the Baptist's Night', performed 1853); sacred choral music; over 50 songs to words by Koltsov, Mey and others; and an orchestral overture to Pushkin's *Boris Godunov* (1861) – in his day the best-known and most frequently performed of all his works.

WRITINGS

Lyubov' muzïkal'nogo uchitelya [A music teacher's love] (St Petersburg, 1836) [fantasy-tale, pubd under pseud. Carlo Carlini]

Betrachtungen über die Kunst der Darstellung in Musikdrama (Leipzig, 1867)

Der Einfluss des Zeitgeistes auf die Entwicklung der Tonkunst (Leipzig, 1867)

Die Tonkunst in Russland bis zur Einführung des abendländischen Musik- und Notensystems (Leipzig, 1867)

Über Schulen für dramatische und musikalische Kunst (Leipzig, 1867)

24 auserlesene Opern-Charaktere im Berug auf deren musikalischdeclamatorische, wie dramatisch-mimische Darstellung, analysirt und beleuchtet, i–xii (Leipzig, 1867)

Über Franz Liszt's oratorium 'Die Heilige Elisabeth' (Leipzig, 1868)

Nauka o muzïke na osnovanii èsteticheskikh i fiziologicheskikh zakonov [The science of music on the basis of aesthetic and physiological laws] (Moscow, 1875)

Teoriya drevnerusskogo tserkovnogo i narodnogo peniya na osnovanii avtenticheskikh traktatov i akusticheskogo analiza [The theory of old Russian church and folk singing on the basis of authentic treatises and acoustic analysis], i (Moscow, 1880)

Garmonizatsiya drevnerusskogo tserkovnogo peniya po èllinskoy i vizantiyskoy teorii i akusticheskomu analizu [The harmonization of old Russian church singing based on ancient Greek and Byzantine theory and acoustic analysis] (Moscow, 1886)

Vospominaniye [Memoirs] (St Petersburg, 1892–3)

Die alten Kirchenmelodien historisch und akustisch entwickelt (Leipzig, 1898)

Teoriya postanovki golosa po metodu staroy ital'yanskoy shkolï i primeneniye teorii k prakticheskomu obucheniyu krasivomu obrazovaniyu pevcheskikh zvukov [The theory of voice training based on the old Italian school method and its practical application for good voice production], i–iii (St Petersburg, 1898)

BIBLIOGRAPHY

L.: 'Yury Arnol'd: ocherk yego muzïkal'noy deyatel'nosti' [A sketch of his musical activity], *RMG* (1896), no.12, cols. 1563–70

Ye. Ignat'yev: 'Pamyati Yuriya Karlovicha Arnol'da' [In memoriam Yu.K. Arnol'd], *Illyustrirovanniy sbornik Kiyevskogo literaturno-artisticheskogo obshchestva* [Illustrated collection of the Kiev literary/artistic society] (Kiev, 1900), 24–30

G.B. Bernandt and I.M.Yampol'sky: *Kto pisal o muzïke* [Writers on music], i (Moscow, 1971) [incl. list of writings]

E. Carpenter: *The Theory of Music in Russia and the Soviet Union ca.1650–1950* (diss., U. of Pennslyvania, 1988)

JENNIFER SPENCER/ROBERT W. OLDANI

Arnold de Lantins. *See* LANTINS, DE.

Arnoldo Fiamengo [Arnoldus Flandrus]. *See* FLANDRUS, ARNOLDUS.

Arnold of St Emmeram (*b* *c*1000; *d* before 1050). Benedictine writer and composer. He was a monk, and later prior, of St Emmeram in Regensburg and the author of a new plainchant Office for the patron saint of his monastery; he also wrote extensively about St Emmeram and on other matters. The Office, which survives in *D-Mbs* Clm 14870 (Arnold's autograph or at least a contemporary source) and in a number of later manuscripts, includes over 40 antiphons and 20 responsories arranged in numerical order of mode. According to Arnold, the Office was first celebrated while he was visiting Hungary, by the cathedral clergy at Esztergom.

BIBLIOGRAPHY

K. Langosch: 'Arnold von St. Emmeram', *Die deutsche Literatur des Mittelalters: Verfasserlexikon*, i (2/1978), 464–70

D. Hiley: 'Musik im mittelalterlichen Regensburg', *Regensburg im Mittelalter*, i: *Beiträge zur Stadtgeschichte vom frühen Mittelalter bis zum Beginn der Neuzeit*, ed. M. Angerer and H. Wanderwitz (Regensburg, 1995), 311–22

D. Hiley: *Historia Sancti Emmerammi Arnoldi Vohburgensis circa 1030* (Ottawa, 1996)

Arnold Schoenberg Choir. Austrian choir. It was founded in 1972 by Erwin Ortner, who in 1996 was appointed rector of the Hochschule für Musik in Vienna. The choir's name reflects three of its main emphases: Austrian music, new music, and a commitment to the works of Arnold Schoenberg. The choir is made up largely of students and former students of the Hochschule für Musik and expands or contracts according to the works it performs. For example, the choir was reduced to 12 voices for Messiaen's *Cinq rechants* and was augmented to 120 for his opera *Saint François d'Assise* (1992 and 1998, Salzburg Festival). Whatever the numbers, the Arnold Schoenberg Choir always aims for a chamber musical transparency of texture. The choir has recorded Schubert's complete choral music under Ortner and Harnoncourt, and has toured the USA with Harnoncourt (1997); it has recorded the major choral music of Mozart, Haydn and Beethoven under Harnoncourt. It has also given broadcasts of contemporary Austrian music. In 1993 it began giving an annual concert series for the Gesellschaft der Musikfreunde in Vienna. In the 1990s it performed at the Salzburg Festival giving the first performance of Berio's *Cronaco del Luogo* in 1999. The choir has also collaborated with the Berlin PO (1998) and the Vienna PO (1999) in performances at the festival.

HARALD GOERTZ

Arnold von Bruck. *See* BRUCK, ARNOLD VON.

Arnolfo da Francia. *See* GILIARDI, ARNOLFO.

Arnone [Arnoni], **Guglielmo** (*b* Milan, *c*1570; *d* Milan, 1630). Italian composer and organist. We know from the dedication of his *Partitura del 2° libro delli motetti* (1599) that he was Milanese and a pupil of Claudio Merulo, with whom he probably studied between 1584 and 1586 in Mantua. On 12 December 1591 he was appointed organist of Milan Cathedral at a salary of 400 imperial lire, and he kept this post until his death. The influence of Merulo is recognizable in his works 'in the clarity of the counterpoint and the nature of the invention' (to quote his own words). Banchieri numbered him among the most celebrated organists of his time.

WORKS

Partitura del 2° libro delli motetti, 5–8vv (Milan, 1599)
Il 1° libro de madrigali, 6vv (Venice, 1600); 4 repr. in 1613[10]
Sacrarum modulationum, 6vv, liber tertius (Venice, 1602), lost
Missa una, motecta, Magnificat, Litaniae B. Maria Virginis, falsis bordonis et Gloria Patri, 8vv, bc (org), op.6 (Venice, 1625)
Motets in 1608[13], 1610[1], 1611[1], 1612[3], 1615[13], 1617[1], 1619[4], 1622[5], 1626[6]
Pieces in 1605[6], 1610[10]; 2 pieces in L. Beretta I° libro delle canzoni (Milan, 1604)
Pater noster, 5vv, *I-Md*, also in 1619[4]

BIBLIOGRAPHY

A. Banchieri: *Conclusioni nel suono dell'organo* (Bologna, 1609/*R*, 2/1626 as Armoniche conclusioni nel suona dell'organo; Eng. trans., 1982), 12
P. Morigi: *La nobiltà di Milano* (Milan, 1619), 303
F. Mompellio: 'La musica a Milano nell'età moderna', *Storia di Milano*, xvi (Milan, 1962), 518

MARIANGELA DONÀ

Arnot, Robert. *See* CARVOR, ROBERT.

Arnould [Arnoult], (**Magdeleine**) [Madeleine] **Sophie** (*b* Paris, 13 Feb 1740; *d* Paris, 22 Oct 1802). French soprano. A precocious child, she studied Latin and Italian and received a solid general education. Her performance in sacred music impressed the royal family and Mme de Pompadour, and she was appointed to the Opéra, studying declamation with Clairon and singing with Marie Fel. Her voice was sweet and expressive, not powerful, supported by fine diction and acting. She was the leading Opéra soprano from 1757 (début in Mouret's *Les amours des dieux*) to 1778. She sang over 30 roles, by Lully, Rameau, Rousseau (*Le devin du village*) and others; several she created, but her greatest was Telaira in Rameau's *Castor et Pollux*. She adapted to Italian-influenced music such as Monsigny's *Aline*, and the climax of her career was in *Iphigénie en Aulide* (1774, at Fontainebleau as late as 1777; see illustration). Less successful as Eurydice, she was mortified by Gluck's choice of Rosalie Levasseur for *Alceste*. The Dorothy Parker of her day, she entertained the *philosophes* while alienating colleagues; she bore three illegitimate children to the Count of Lauraguais. Her colourful career inspired several biographies, two comedies, and an opera by Pierné.

BIBLIOGRAPHY

ES (E. Zanetti)
C.Y. Cousin d'Avalon: *Grimmiana* (Paris, 1813)
A. Deville: *Arnoldiana, ou Sophie Arnould et ses contemporaines* (Paris, 1813)
F. Fayolle: *L'esprit de Sophie Arnould* (Paris, 1813)
E.-L. Lamothe-Langon, ed.: *Mémoires de mademoiselle Sophie Arnoult* (Paris, 1837)
E. and J. de Goncourt: *Sophie Arnould d'après sa correspondance et ses mémoires inédits* (Paris, 1857, 2/1859)
H. Sutherland Edwards: *Idols of the French Stage* (London, 1889)
R.B. Douglas: *Sophie Arnould Actress and Wit* (Paris, 1898)
F. Rogers: 'Sophie Arnould', *MQ*, vi (1920), 57–61

Sophie Arnould as Iphigenia in Gluck's 'Iphigénie en Aulide': bust by Jean-Antoine Houdon, marble, c1777 (Musée du Louvre, Paris)

B. Dussanc: *Sophie Arnould: la plus spirituelle des bacchantes* (Paris, 1938)

JULIAN RUSHTON

Arnschwanger, Johann Christoph (*b* Nuremberg, 28 Dec 1625; *d* Nuremberg, 10 Dec 1696). German poet and theologian. He spent virtually his entire life at Nuremberg. He was educated at the St Egidien Gymnasium (whose director from 1642 was J.M. Dilherr), and from 1644 at Altdorf University. He gained the master's degree at Jena in 1647. In 1648 he went to Leipzig and then travelled to Hamburg but arrived completely destitute after risking his life in an escape from marauding soldiers. During 1649 he participated in a disputation at Helmstedt on Original Sin chaired by the controversial syncretist G.C. Calixtus. In 1650 he returned to Nuremberg and in 1651 was appointed curate, and in 1652 deacon, of the Egidienkirche. He officiated as Monday preacher at St Salvator and, after being ordained at Altdorf on 14 May 1653, was from 1654 morning preacher at St Walpurg auf der Vesten. In 1659 he became deacon of St Lorenz, the leading church in Nuremberg, where in 1679 he was promoted to senior rank and in 1690 to chief minister.

From 1675 until its dissolution in 1680, Arnschwanger was a member of the Fruchtbringende Gesellschaft, the oldest language society in Germany. He published two collections of sacred poems, with melodies, and included others in his various theological writings. The two collections are: *Neue geistliche Lieder* (Nuremberg, 1659) and *Heilige Palmen, und christliche Psalmen, das ist Unterschiedliche neue geistliche Lieder und Gesänge* (RISM, 1680[1]) (32 poems from both volumes in Fischer and Tümpel, nine melodies in Zahn). It may be noted that the second collection coincided with the dissolution of the Fruchtbringende Gesellschaft, that its title refers to the society's emblem, a palm tree, and that Arnschwanger signed it with his name in the society, 'Der Unschuldige' ('The Innocent'). In the preface to the 1659 volume he stated that its artistry 'does not aspire to individual treatment of the words nor to the exceedingly high standard of contemporary German poetry' but that 'music lovers are amply compensated for shortcomings in the texts by the beautifully worked settings of Nuremberg's leading organists and directors of music'. The poems in both volumes in fact were written to familiar melodies and newly set to music for solo voice and continuo by Nuremberg musicians. The composers of the 1659 collection are Paul Hainlein, A.M. Lundsdörffer, David Schedlich, Heinrich Schwemmer and G.C. Wecker. Johann Löhner replaced Schedlich in the 1680 volume, which also includes a melody by an otherwise unknown musician, A.C. Hültz, the only one Arnschwanger did not mention in his preface. Unlike the poets of another leading Nuremberg literary society, the Pegnesische Blumenorden, he used popular diction in his verses. The musical settings offer a good cross-section of German continuo song of the period. 23 items were taken into the *Nürnberger Gesangbuch* (1690), though divorced from their new settings, and only the chorale *Merk, Seele, was du dir hast vorgenommen* (1680) appears with its new melody (by Wecker) among the 42 texts reappearing in J.B. König's *Harmonischer Lieder-Schatz* (Frankfurt, 1738).

BIBLIOGRAPHY

*Winterfeld*EK; *Zahn*M

G.A. Will: *Nürnbergisches Gelehrten-Lexikon*, i (Nuremberg, 1755), 42ff

E.E. Koch: *Geschichte des Kirchenlieds und Kirchengesangs*, iii (Stuttgart, 3/1866–77/R), 517ff

A. Fischer and W. Tümpel: *Das deutsche evangelische Kirchenlied des 17. Jahrhunderts*, v (Gütersloh, 1911/R)

LINI HÜBSCH-PFLEGER

Arnt von Aich. *See* AICH, ARNT VON.

Arnulf of St Ghislain [Arnulphus de Sancto Gilleno] (*fl* ?*c*1400). Writer on music. He was presumably from St Ghislain in Hainaut and was possibly a member of its Benedictine community. One work by him is known, the *Tractatulus de differentiis et gradibus cantorum*, found only in St Paul im Lavanttal (*A-SPL* 264/4). Using highly coloured language, it surveys various kinds of musician. These comprise, firstly, those who know nothing about music, and who sing their parts in the reverse of the way they should; secondly, laymen, often ignorant of the art, who cultivate trained musicians so that natural industriousness and practice makes good their deficiencies, including certain clerics who compose difficult pieces for instruments; thirdly, those whose voices are defective but who study music and teach their pupils what they cannot perform themselves; and fourthly, those with fine voices and a knowledge of musical art, singing according to rule with *modus, mensura, numerus* and *color*. Among this latter group are female musicians who divide semitones into indivisible microtones. Medieval music theory does not lack passages that categorize musicians, usually according to the place of *ars* and *usus* in what they do, but Arnulf's treatise is exceptional for being devoted entirely to this subject.

The date of his treatise is hard to discern, and it could perhaps be substantially later. If so, there is a distinct possibility that Arnulf is to be identified with the Florentine singer and composer ARNOLFO GILIARDI and/or the writer and musician ARNOUL GREBAN.

BIBLIOGRAPHY

MGG1 (H. Hüschen); *Riemann*G

C. Page: 'A Treatise on Musicians from ?c.1400: the *Tractatulus de differentiis et gradibus cantorum* by Arnulf de St Ghislain', *JRMA*, cvii (1992), 1–21

CHRISTOPHER PAGE

Arom, Simha (*b* Düsseldorf, 16 Aug 1930). Israeli and French ethnomusicologist. After studying the french horn with Jean Devémy at the Paris Conservatoire (1951–4), he was first horn in the Israel Broadcasting Authority SO in Jerusalem (1958–63). In 1963 he founded the Musée National Boganda at Bangui in the Central African Republic, and was its director until 1967, and on returning to Paris he undertook musicological studies with Chailley at the Sorbonne (1968–73). He entered the CNRS in 1968 and his subsequent career has been with that institution. In 1993 he was appointed lecturer at the Ecole des Hautes Etudes en Sciences Sociales, Paris. He was an associate professor at Tel-Aviv University (1979–83) and music director of the Israel Broadcasting Authority (1980–82). He has been awarded the Grand Prix International du Disque de l'Académie Charles Cros (1971, 1978 and 1985), and the silver medal of the CNRS (1984). In 1992 he won the ASCAP Deems Taylor Award for excellence in music literature.

Simha Arom has devoted himself chiefly to the systematic study of oral traditional music, particularly the polyphonic and polyrhythmic music of Central Africa. He has devised new methodological procedures including a process, first used in 1972, for the analytical recording of polyphony and polyrhythm, enabling such music to be transcribed and analysed, and an interactive experimental method, introduced in 1989, for the perception of the organization of musical scales in cultures of oral tradition. His theoretical works concentrate on the structuring of time in music, particularly the relationship between metre and rhythm, on the modelling of orally transmitted music and on the cognitive aspects of musical practice in such cultures.

WRITINGS

'Essai d'une notation des monodies à des fins d'analyse', *RdM*, lv (1969), 172–216

Conte et chantefables ngbaka-ma'bo (République centrafricaine) (Paris, 1970)

'Eléments pour une analyse opérationnelle des monodies vocales dans les sociétés de tradition orale', *Les langues sans tradition écrite: Nice 1971*, 391–415 [with Eng. summary]

'De la chasse au piège considérée comme une liturgie', *The World of Music*, xiv/4 (1974), 3–19

with J.M.C. Thomas: *Les mimbo, génies du piégeage, et le monde surnaturel des Ngbaka-Ma'bo (République centrafricaine)* (Paris, 1974)

'The Use of Play-Back Techniques in the Study of Oral Polyphonies', *EthM*, xx (1976), 483–519

with F. Cloarec-Heiss: 'Le langage tambouriné des Banda-Linda: phonologie, morphologie, syntaxe', *Théories et méthodes en linguistique africaine: Yaoundé 1974*, ed. L. Bouquiaux (Paris, 1976), 113–69

'New Perspectives for the Description of Orally Transmitted Music', *The World of Music*, xxiii/2 (1981), 40–60

'The Music of the Banda-Linda Horn Ensembles: Form and Structure', *Selected Reports in Ethnomusicology*, v (1984), 173–93

Polyphonies et polyrythmies instrumentales d'Afrique Centrale: structure et méthodologie (Paris, 1985; Eng. trans., 1991)

with F. Alvarez-Pereyre: 'The Holistic Approach to Ethnomusicological Studies', *The World of Music*, xxviii/2 (1986), 3–13

'Systèmes musicaux en Afrique subsaharienne', *Canadian University Music Review/Revue de musique des universités canadiennes*, ix (1988), 1–18

'Une parenté inattendue: polyphonies médiévales et polyphonies africaines', *Polyphonies de tradition orale: Royaumont 1990*, 133–48

'A Synthesizer in the Central African Bush: a Method of Interactive Exploration of Musical Scales', *Für György Ligeti: Hamburg 1988* [*HJbMw*, xi (1991)], 163–78

'A la recherche du 'temps' perdu: métrique et rythme en musique', *Les rythmes: Cerisy-la-Salle 1989*, ed. J.-J. Wunenburger (Paris, 1992), 195–205

'Une voix multiple: entretien avec S. Pahaut', *Cahiers de musiques traditionnelles*, vi (1993), 184–96

with F. Alvarez-Pereyre: 'Ethnomusicology and the Emic/etic Issue', *The World of Music*, xxxv/1 (1993), 7–33

'Intelligence in Traditional Music', *What is Intelligence?*, ed. J. Khalfa (Cambridge, 1994), 137–60

with U. Sharvit: 'Plurivocality in the Liturgical Music of the Jews of San'a (Yemen)', *Jewish Oral Traditions: an Interdisciplinary Approach*, Yuval, vi, ed. I. Adler (Jerusalem, 1994), 34–67

'Su alcune impreviste parentele fra le polifonie medievali e africane', *Polifonie: procedimenti, tassonomie e forme: Venice 1995*, 163–79

with G. Léothaud and F. Voisin: 'Experimental Ethnomusicology: an Interactive Approach to the Study of Musical Scales', *Perception and Cognition of Music*, ed. I. Deliège and J. Sloboda (Hove, 1997), 3–30

BIBLIOGRAPHY

Ndroje Balendro: musiques, terrains et disciplines: textes offerts à Simha Arom, ed. V. Dehoux and others (Paris, 1995) [incl. full list of writings]

JEAN GRIBENSKI

Aron, Pietro *See* AARON, PIETRO.

Aronowitz, Cecil (*b* King William's Town, South Africa, 4 March 1916; *d* Ipswich, 7 Sept 1978). British viola player of Russian-Lithuanian parentage. He studied the violin with Achille Rivarde at the RCM, London, and played in the major London orchestras until the war, after which he changed to the viola. He became principal viola with the Goldsbrough Orchestra (later the English Chamber Orchestra) in 1949 and with the London Mozart Players from 1952 to 1964. In the English Opera Group orchestra he played in the early performances of Britten's church parables. However, it was chiefly in chamber music that he achieved distinction; he was a founder-member of Musica da Camera (1946), the Melos Ensemble (1950) and the Pro Arte Piano Quartet (1965). He had a particularly polished technique and an easy manner of integration, qualities very evident when he played as extra viola with the Amadeus String Quartet in quintets, blending with those players to produce performances of outstanding merit. He married the pianist Nicola Grunberg, with whom he formed a duo ensemble. He was professor of the viola and chamber music at the RCM from 1948, head of strings at the RNCM from 1973 to 1977 and director of studies in strings at Snape Maltings from 1977.

WATSON FORBES/R

ARP. American company of SYNTHESIZER manufacturers. It was founded as ARP Instruments by Alan R. Pearlman (and named from his initials) in Newton Highlands, near Boston, in 1970; it later moved to nearby Newton and Lexington. Models included the modular ARP 2500 (1970; for illustration *see* SYNTHESIZER, fig.1), the Odyssey (1971) and the digital Chroma (*c*1980; developed though not manufactured by ARP). The firm ceased to operate in 1981. *See also* ELECTRONIC INSTRUMENTS, §IV, 5(ii).

HUGH DAVIES

Arpa (It., Sp.). *See* HARP.

Arpa, Giovanni Leonardo dell' [dall']. *See* DELL'ARPA, GIOVANNI LEONARDO.

Arpa, Orazio dell'. *See* MICHI, ORAZIO.

Arpa, Rinaldo dall'. *See* RINALDO DALL'ARPA.

Arpa-citara (Sp.). *See* ARPANETTA.

Arpa d'Eolo [arpa ʾeolia] (It.). *See* AEOLIAN HARP.

Arpanetta (It.; Fr. *Arpanette, harpe pointue*; Ger. *Spitzharfe, Harfenett*; Sp. *Arpaneta, arpa-citara*). An upright double psaltery, with each main side of the trapezial box acting as a soundboard; it is classified as a box zither. In Germany the instrument was sometimes known as the *italienische Harfe* ('Italian harp'; e.g. Brockhaus; Welcker von Gontershausen). As shown in Renaissance and Baroque paintings, the instrument was placed on a table or on the seated player's lap, with the shortest strings at closest reach. Those associated with the right-hand soundboard (see illustration) were of case-hardened iron and were used for the melody; those at the left were of brass (or some similar copper alloy heavier than iron) and, with their curved bridge quite near to the upper edge of the box, provided a bass accompaniment.

A height of some 90 cm was common, but instruments between perhaps 60 and 150 cm tall were also made. The total range might vary between two-and-a-half and four octaves. Majer (1732) gave a range of only two octaves and a third (*C–e'* for the left hand side and a range of two octaves and a fifth (*b–f'''*; chromatically *f–d'''*) for the right hand side); Eisel (1738) gave a range from *f* to *d'''*, chromatic except for the lowest 5th. The seven diatonic notes in each octave were each supplied with double courses while the five chromatic notes were single-strung.

Surviving instruments date from 1621 to about 1730. The arpanetta's first appearance in the West may have been in Italy, but it had its greatest popularity in Germany (an example, made by J.H. Appel and dated 1713, survives in Hamburg) and the Netherlands after 1650. J.G. Walther's *Musicalisches Lexicon* of 1732 refers to three types of *Harfe*, the first of which was the 'common one, known everywhere, strung with wire and called *harpanetta*'. On account of its shape the instrument is occasionally referred to as a harp-psaltery, or psaltery-harp (e.g. Norlind, 1936).

Whilst the arpanetta enjoyed great popularity with amateur (especially female) players until the second half of the 18th century it is not known whether the instrument ever had a repertory of its own (the question is explored in Wackernagel, 1997). A modern revival of the instrument may be attributed in part to the English harpist Andrew Lawrence King, who played an arpanetta (and a harp of David) in public for the first time at the Berlin Bachtage festival in 1991.

BIBLIOGRAPHY

WaltherML

J.F.B.C. Majer: *Museum musicum theoretico practicum* (Schwäbisch Hall, 1732, 2/1741)

J.P. Eisel: *Musicus autodidactus* (Erfurt, 1738/R)

F.A. Brockhaus: *Konversations-Lexikon*(Altenburg and Leipzig, 4/1817–22)

H. Welcker von Gontershausen: *Neu eröffnetes Magazin musikalischer Tonwerkzeuge* (Frankfurt, 1855)

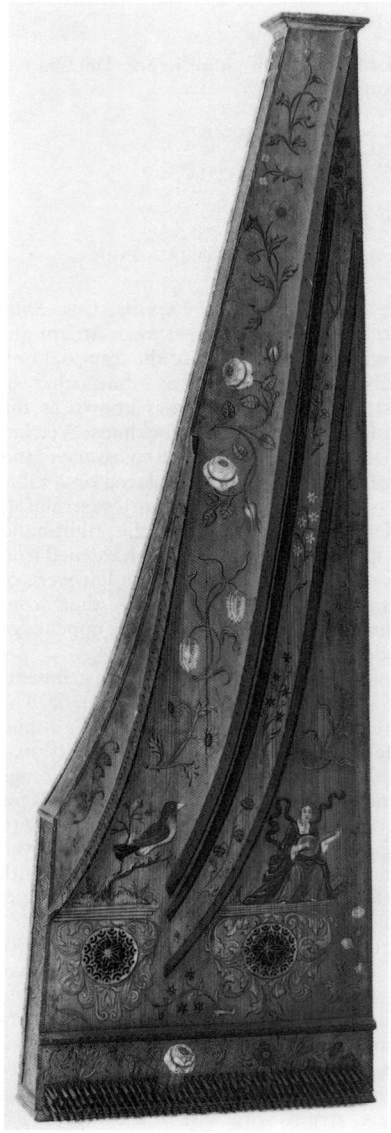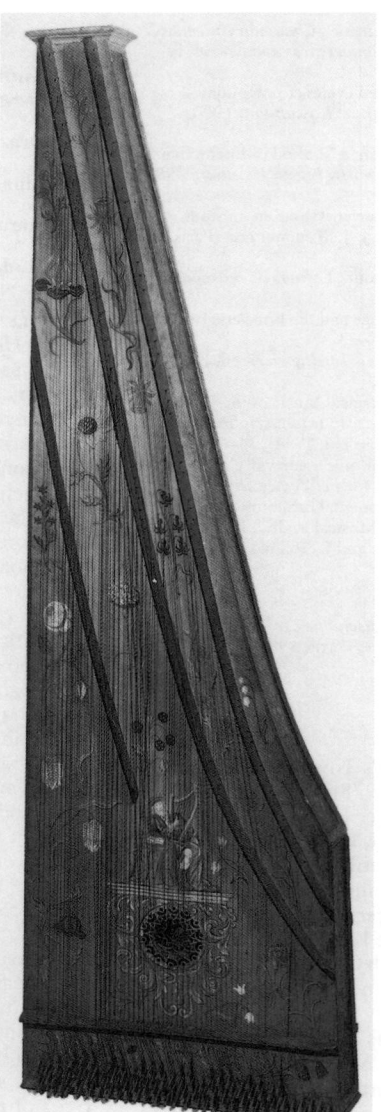

Right-hand and left-hand views of an arpanetta, ?Flemish, c1700 (Royal College of Music, London)

T. Norlind, ed.: *Systematik der Saiteninstrumente*, i: *Geschichte der Zither* (Stockholm, 1936)

S. Marcuse: *A Survey of Musical Instruments* (Newton Abbot and London, 1975)

B. Wackernagel: *Europäische Zupf- und Streichinstrumente, Hackbretter und Äolsharfen* (Frankfurt am Main, 1997)

ALEXANDER PILIPCZUK

Arpeado (Sp.). *See* ORNAMENTS, §2.

Arpeggiation (i). Use of arpeggio patterns. Arpeggiation as a regular feature of accompaniment in keyboard music dates from the mid-18th century (*see* ALBERTI BASS); earlier examples exist, for instance in Bach's Violin Sonata in C minor BWV1017. Such passages are normally written out in full, but even earlier than this the term 'arpeggio' ('arpeggiato', 'arpeggiando') may be found to indicate that a player is to interpret a series of chords by playing them in arpeggiated fashion, as shown in ex.1; sometimes the arpeggiation of the first chord in such a sequence is

Ex.1 J. S. Bach: Violin Sonata in A BWV1015

written out in full to indicate the required manner of performance for the entire passage.

The arpeggiation of a single chord (*see also* ORNAMENTS) may be notated in a number of ways. The commonest method in present-day notation is shown in ex.2*a*; ex.2*b* shows the notation generally used by Mozart,

Hummel and others of the late 18th and early 19th centuries. Ex.2*c* and *d* show Türk's notation for upwards

Ex.2

and downwards arpeggios respectively (*Clavierschule*, 1789). Ex.3 shows notations used when certain of the arpeggiated notes are not to be held for the full duration

Ex.3

of the main note, and ex.4 shows notations and interpretations of arpeggiated chords with acciaccaturas or

Ex.4

appoggiaturas. A distinction should properly be made between arpeggiation in the two hands separately and the two together (ex.5).

Ex.5

See also Bow, §II, 2(ix) and 3(xi).

FRANKLIN TAYLOR/R

Arpeggiation (ii) (Ger. *Brechung*). In Schenkerian analysis (*see* ANALYSIS, §II), the movement of the bass from the root of the tonic to its fifth (the dominant) and back again as an encapsulation of the basic harmonic plan of a piece; the lower part of the URSATZ. Also a method of PROLONGATION by which any part is elaborated in the form of a broken chord. In both cases, a vertical configuration (an interval or a chord) is made linear or 'horizontalized' (Ger. *horizontalisiert*). The arpeggiation of the bass I–V–I, which Schenker specifically referred to as *Bassbrechung*, brings the tonic chord to life, and represents the three elements essential for a piece to have tonal shape: establishment of tonic, move to a dominant

Ex.1

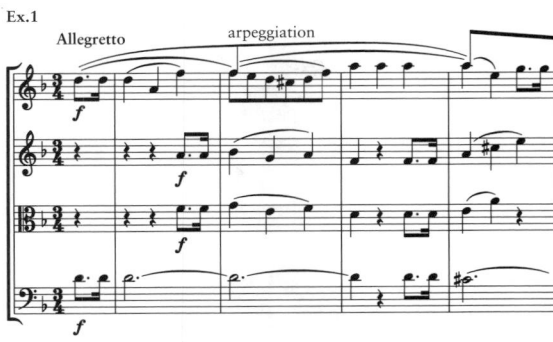

preparation, return of the tonic. Its fundamental importance in this respect led Schenker to give it the epithet of 'the sacred triangle' (*Der freie Satz*, 1935 §19).

As a method of prolongation, arpeggiation is used frequently in the service of a structurally important note in the upper voice; for example, in the Minuet from Mozart's String Quartet in D minor K421/417*b* the first violin part rises from *d″* through *f″* to *a″* (as indicated by the slurs in ex.1); *a″* is also the first note of a linear progression (ZUG (i)) through a fifth, *a″–g″–f″–e″–d″*, in bars 3–10.

Arpeggiation may similarly be used to serve a harmony of structural importance (STUFE), as illustrated by the arpeggiation *e′–c–A* at the opening of Chopin's Etude in A minor op.25 no.11 (ex.2; after *Der freie Satz*,

Ex.2

fig.100/3*c*). Sometimes an arpeggiation appears in conjunction with another method of prolongation (especially REACHING OVER), and often it effects an ascending or descending REGISTER TRANSFER.

It is not necessary for the arpeggiated chord to be a triad; Schenker illustrated the use of arpeggiation of a diminished chord at the start of Chopin's 'Revolutionary Etude', in his *Fünf Urlinie-Tafeln* (1932); for a reproduction of these graphs, see ANALYSIS, figs.20. Nor does it have to be modally 'pure' at a middleground level: in his analysis of *Auf dem Flusse* from Schubert's *Winterreise* (*Der freie Satz*, fig.40/2), the first note of the fundamental upper voice (URLINIE) is approached by the arpeggiation *e′–g♯′–b′–e″–g♮″*.

WILLIAM DRABKIN

Arpeggio (It. from *arpeggiare*: 'to play the harp'). The sounding of the notes of a chord in succession rather than simultaneously; also, especially in keyboard music, the breaking or spreading of a chord. The ability to play (or sing) arpeggio figuration fluently has traditionally been counted an important part of instrumental (or vocal) technique.

See also ARPEGGIATION (i).

Arpeggione [guitar violoncello, bowed guitar] (Fr. *guitarre d'amour*; Ger. *Sentiment*, *Bogenguitar*, *Violoncellguitarre*). A bowed string instrument. Both J.G. Staufer

Ex.1

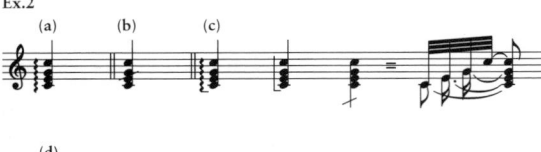

Arpeggione by Johann Georg Staufer, Vienna, 1824
(Musikinstrumenten-Museum, University of Leipzig)

(Stauffer) of Vienna and Peter Teufelsdorfer of Pest claimed to be inventors of what came to be known as the arpeggione. Both built a new instrument they called a 'bowed guitar', and both introduced their respective instruments in the spring of 1823. The violin maker Johann Ertl of Vienna might also have contributed to the arpeggione's invention. The concept of the instrument possibly originated with J.G. Leeb of Pressburg, who may have experimented with the construction of a bowed guitar 20 years earlier.

The instrument was essentially a bass viol with a guitar-type tuning, $E–A–d–g–b–e'$ (see illustration). The body was coarser in structure and the frets, 24 in number, were, guitar fashion, metal strips fixed to the fingerboard. It was bowed like a cello. The body was smooth-waisted, in imitation of the guitar rather than as a revival of the early viol form. The arpeggione was especially suited to playing runs in 3rds, double stops and arpeggios. Virtuosos of the instrument included Heinrich August Birnbach (1782–1848) and Vincenz Schuster.

A number of Staufer's instruments have survived, along with some unsigned instruments built after his model. Instruments signed by J.G. Leeb, Anton Mitteis of Leitmeritz and Tomasz Pasamoński of Kraków have also survived. It was not until the 1870s that the instrument came to be called the arpeggione, after Schubert's famous sonata (D821) of the same name, written in November 1824.

BIBLIOGRAPHY

V. Schuster: *Anleitung zur Erlernung des von G. Staufer neuerfundenen Guitarre-Violoncells* (Vienna, 1823)

E.K. Blüml: 'Johann Georg Stauffer', *Zeitschrift für die Gitarre*, iv (1923–4)

V. Gutmann: 'Arpeggione: Begriff oder Instrument?', *Schubert Congress: Vienna 1978*, 233–48

E. Gát Fontana: 'Teufelsdorfer contra Stauffer', *Gitarre & Laute*, viii/2 (1991), 15–19

GERALD HAYES/ESZTER FONTANA

Arpicembalo [arpi cimbalo] (It.). Term used in a Medici inventory of 1700 and by Frederigo Meccoli, a musician in the Medici court, to describe Bartolomeo Cristofori's newly invented piano. The prefix 'arpi' suggests either a harp-shaped case (a long-cased instrument with bentside) or a keyboard instrument producing a harp-like sound. Meccoli wrote that Cristofori's piano could imitate the sound of the harp.

For bibliography *see* GRAVICEMBALO. *See also* PIANOFORTE, §I, 2.

STEWART POLLENS

Arpichordum [arpichordium, harpichordium] **stop.** A device most commonly found on Flemish virginals of the (MUSELAR) type, but also mentioned in connection with German harpsichords, in which a sliding batten brings a series of metal hooks or wires close to the strings at one end. When the strings are plucked, they jar against the hooks or wires, producing a buzzing sound. On muselars, the arpichordum is normally provided only for the strings passing over the straight portion of the right-hand bridge, i.e. from C/E to f'.

O'Brien suggests that only muselars, which pluck the strings in the middle rather than close to the left-hand bridge, provide sufficient amplitude of motion of the strings to make reliable contact with the hooks. Praetorius (*Syntagma musicum*, ii, 1618) describes the stop as giving a 'harp-like resonance', apparently likening it to the 'bray pins' commonly found on Renaissance harps (*see* HARP, §V, 1). The term *arpichordum* is not used to define a type of instrument, and should not be confused with ARPICORDO.

For discussion of the use of such effects on plucked keyboard instruments, *see* REGISTRATION, §II.

BIBLIOGRAPHY

G. Leonhardt: 'In Praise of Flemish Virginals of the Seventeenth Century', *Keyboard Instruments*, ed. E.M. Ripin (Edinburgh, 1971), 43–8

G.G. O'Brien: *Ruckers: a Harpsichord and Virginal Building Tradition* (Cambridge, 1990), 77–8

EDWIN M. RIPIN/DENZIL WRAIGHT

Arpicordo [alpichordo, ampichordo, harpichordo] (It.). Term most commonly used in 15th- and 16th-century Italy for a polygonal VIRGINAL (see Cervelli). Other, less popular, names at this time for the same instrument were *clavicordio* and *spinetta*. Despite the etymological similarity, it is not to be confused with the harpsichord or the ARPICHORDUM stop. The name probably derives from the layout on a polygonal virginal of the bridges and strings, which resemble the shape of a harp (It. *arpa*). Some early instruments were made with curved case sides also suggesting a harp shape (see Winternitz, pl.50*a*). It is unclear whether a rectangular-cased virginal would have been called an arpicordo, but in any case, these were not common in the 16th century. The term *arpicordo leutato* was coined by Adriano Banchieri (*L'organo suonarino*, 2/1611) to describe several instruments he had seen with a sound between a harpsichord and a lute (*see* LUTE-HARPSICHORD).

BIBLIOGRAPHY

E. Winternitz: *Musical Instruments and their Symbolism in Western Art* (New York, 1967, 2/1979)

L. Cervelli: 'Arpicordo: mito di un nome e realtà di uno strumento', *Quadrivium*, xiv (1973), 187–95

D.J. Hamoen: 'The Arpicordo Problem: Armand Neven's Solution Reconsidered', *AcM*, xlviii (1976), 181–4

J.H. Van der Meer: 'Das Arpicordo-Problem nochmals erörtert', *AcM*, xlix (1977), 275–9

DENZIL WRAIGHT

Arpicordo leutato (It.). A gut-strung ARPICORDO that sounded like a lute. *See* LUTE-HARPSICHORD.

Arpitarrone. A keyboard instrument designed by Adriano Banchieri and described in the 1611 edition of his *L'organo suonarino*, pp.3–4. Banchieri mentions having seen 21 instruments he called 'arpicordo leutato' in Milan, which had a sound between that of an arpicordo (i.e. a polygonal, wire-strung virginal) and a lute (*see* LUTE-HARPSICHORD). Inspired by the chitarrone, he added more notes to the bass end of the *arpicordo* and gave the new instrument a name derived from both instruments, saying also that it had the quality of a chitarrone in the bass and a harp (It. *arpa*) in the treble. As harps and chitarroni often used gut strings (although wire strings were sometimes used) it seems most likely that the arpitarrone was a gut-strung instrument. An arpitarrone was made for Banchieri by a Milanese instrument maker (of French origin) named Michel de Hodes (who had also made an *arpicordo leutato*), with the unusual compass of *CD–e″* (i.e. lacking C♯).

DENZIL WRAIGHT

Arquier [D'Arquier], **Joseph** (*b* Toulon, 1763; *d* Bordeaux, Oct 1816). French composer. He went to Paris in 1790 or 1791, attracted by the proliferation of theatres following the abolition of the privilege system. The impresario and founder of the Théâtre Molière, Boursault-Malherbe, engaged him first as a cellist and then, after Scio left for the Théâtre Feydeau in 1792, as orchestral conductor. Arquier was subsequently appointed conductor at the Théâtre de la Gaîté (1793) and, with some periods of absence, at the Théâtre des Jeunes-Elèves between 1800 and 1807. When Napoleon closed that theatre he moved back to the south of France, where he had begun his career as a composer. His most notable work is probably *Marie-Christine* (1793), a trenchant satire on the aristocratic society of the Austrian Netherlands at the time of the French army's invasion; its music was judged to be 'pleasant'.

WORKS

OPERAS

L'Indienne, Carcassonne, 1788

Le pot au noir et le pot aux roses, ou Daphnis et Hortense (pastorale mêlée d'ariettes, 1, Saint-Priest), Marseilles, Elèves Privilégiés de Mgr le duc d'Orléans, 16 Feb 1789

Le pirate (3), Toulon, 1789, or Marseilles, 1790

Le mari corrigé (2), Paris, Français Comique et Lyrique, 21 Feb 1791

La peau de l'ours (oc, 1), Paris, Molière, 1791

Le congé des volontaires (oc, 1), Paris, Montansier, 1792 or 1793

Le bon hermite (opéra-vaudeville, 1, Provost-Montfort), Paris, Palais-Variétés, 2 May 1793

L'hôtellerie de Fontainebleau, Paris, Montansier, 18 May 1793

Marie-Christine, ou La tigresse du Nord (oc, 2, P. Desriaux), Paris, Lycée des Arts, 12 Nov 1793

Les Péruviens, Tours, 1798

Les deux petits troubadours (oc, 1), Paris, Jeunes-Elèves, 1800

L'hôtellerie de Sarzanno (1, Desriaux, after C. Goldoni), Paris, Jeunes-Elèves, 22 April 1802

Le désert, ou L'oasis, New Orleans, ?1802

La fée Urgèle (4, C.-S. Favart), Brest, 1804

L'hermitage des Pyrénées (comédie mêlée de chant, 1, Périn), Paris, Jeunes-Elèves, 5 March 1805

Montrose et Zisac (3), Marseilles, Pavillon, 1810

La suite du médecin turc, Marseilles, 1811

Zipéa et Adèle, ou La fuite précipitée (3), Perpignan, Dec 1812

BIBLIOGRAPHY

H. Duval: *Dictionnaire des ouvrages dramatiques* (MS, *c*1850, *F-Pn*)

MICHEL NOIRAY

Arquimbau, Domingo (*b* 1760; *d* Seville, 26 Jan 1829). Spanish composer. After having served as *maestro de capilla* at Tortosa Cathedral and sub-*maestro* at Barcelona, on 4 July 1785, although not yet ordained a priest, he won the post of *maestro de capilla* at Gerona Cathedral, beating six competitors. On 1 November 1790, he became substitute *maestro de capilla* at Seville Cathedral with the right of succession. When Ripa died he took the post on 6 November 1795, occupying it until his death. In 1815, on submitting as a test piece his Maundy Thursday *Lamentación primera* for chorus, soloists and full orchestra, he was admitted to the Accademia Filarmonica at Bologna and on 23 November given the title *dottore*. Of his many sacred works in Seville listed by Rosa y López (1904), Anglès in 1928 encountered only the three *Magnificat* settings, three hymns, a *Pange lingua* and a four-voice mass concordant with a much used *Misa Semi Festiva* at Santiago, Chile. Arquimbau refrained from writing jaunty Spanish-text villancicos of Ripa's piquant type, confining himself, instead, to noble, fully orchestrated liturgical expressions in the vein popularized by his older contemporary, Francisco Javier García Fajer ('Il Spagnoletto').

WORKS

26 masses, 29 motets, 11 Lamentations, 11 hymns, 5 TeD, 3 Salve, 22 vesper psalms, 10 Mag, 2 Miserere with orch, 8 Miserere a cappella, 4 villancicos: all *E-Sc* (see Ayarra Jarne)

2 masses, Santiago Cathedral, Chile; mass, with orch, 1807, Sucre Cathedral, Bolivia; Dixit Dominus, 8vv, *E-E*; other sacred works *CZ, SC*

Que ynstante dichoso, villancico, 4vv, orch, Archivo Arzobispal, Lima, Peru

La tigre ircana, rondo, 1v, wind insts, bc, *E-Bc*

2 solo Sp. arias, orch acc., PAL

BIBLIOGRAPHY

S. de la Rosa y López: *Los seises de la Catedral de Sevilla* (Seville, 1904), 328ff

H. Anglès: 'La música conservada en la Biblioteca Colombina y en la Catedral de Sevilla', *AnM*, ii (1947), 3–39, esp. 34

R. Stevenson: *Renaissance and Baroque Musical Sources in the Americas* (Washington DC, 1970), 117, 235, 320

J.E. Ayarra Jarne: *La música en la Catedral de Sevilla* (Seville, 1976), 65

R. Stevenson: 'Sixteenth- through Eighteenth-Century Resources in Mexico', *FAM* (1978), 156–87, esp. 162

ROBERT STEVENSON

Arrangement (Ger. *Bearbeitung*). The reworking of a musical composition, usually for a different medium from that of the original.

1. Definition and scope. 2. History to 1600. 3. 1600–1800. 4. 19th and 20th centuries. 5. Conclusion.

1. DEFINITION AND SCOPE. The word 'arrangement' might be applied to any piece of music based on or incorporating pre-existing material: variation form, the contrafactum, the parody mass, the pasticcio, and liturgical works based on a cantus firmus all involve some measure of arrangement. In the sense in which it is commonly used among musicians, however, the word

may be taken to mean either the transference of a composition from one medium to another or the elaboration (or simplification) of a piece, with or without a change of medium. In either case some degree of recomposition is usually involved, and the result may vary from a straightforward, almost literal, transcription to a paraphrase which is more the work of the arranger than of the original composer. It should be added, though, that the distinction implicit here between an arrangement and a TRANSCRIPTION is by no means universally accepted (cf the article 'Arrangement' in *Grove 5* and the title-pages of Liszt's piano 'transcriptions').

Arrangements exist in large numbers from all periods of musical history, and though external factors have influenced their character the reasons for their existence cut across stylistic and historical boundaries. Commercial interest has played an important part, especially since the invention of music printing. Opportunist publishers from Petrucci onwards have looked for financial reward either from arrangements of established works or from the simultaneous publication of music in different forms. English madrigals were advertised as being 'apt for voices as for viols'; Dowland's songs were published in a form which allowed for performance either as a solo with lute accompaniment or as a partsong; in the 18th century the English market was flooded with arrangements of vocal and other music for the popular and ubiquitous flute; and ever since their composition popular 'classics' such as Rachmaninoff's C♯ minor Prelude and Rimsky-Korsakov's *Flight of the Bumble Bee* have been arranged for almost every conceivable instrument and instrumental combination. Practical considerations of a different kind govern the preparation of vocal scores of operas and choral works, in which the orchestral part is reduced and printed, usually on two staves, in a form more or less playable at the keyboard. Such arrangements require little more than technical competence on the part of the arranger, though creative artists of the first rank have occasionally undertaken the task, often in a spirit of homage to the composer. Bülow prepared the vocal scores of some of Wagner's music dramas, and Berg did a similar service for Schoenberg's *Gurrelieder*. Several composers have arranged the music of others as a means of perfecting themselves in a particular form, technique or medium. Bach and Mozart, for example, both made arrangements of other composers' concertos before writing any of their own.

A large number of arrangements originate because performers want to extend the repertory of instruments which, for one reason or another, have not been favoured with a large or rewarding corpus of original solo compositions. Until such players as Segovia and Tertis improved the status of their instruments, guitarists and viola players had to rely to a considerable extent on arrangements, and this is still the case with brass bands and (in so far as they exist) salon orchestras. Arrangements of this kind necessarily involve a transference from one instrumental medium to another, but there are also numerous examples of arrangements which alter the layout but not the instrumentation of the original. Virtuoso piano pieces have often been published in arrangements which place them within the scope of the amateur; others, such as Chopin's *Etudes* in Godowsky's arrangements, have been made even more difficult as a challenge to professional keyboard technique. Orchestral

works have sometimes been reorchestrated, either to take advantage of improvements in the design of instruments (the brass parts of Beethoven's Third Symphony, for example, are not always heard as the composer wrote them) or because the original is considered to be in some respect deficient. Mahler's reorchestration of Schumann's symphonies and Rimsky-Korsakov's of Musorgsky's operas come into this category. There is also a relatively small group of arrangements made to accommodate a player's physical disability, for example those for the one-handed pianist Paul Wittgenstein, and those for the three-handed piano duo, Cyril Smith and Phyllis Sellick.

In considering all these and other categories of arrangements, any attempt to equate the motives of the arranger with the artistic merits of the result would be misleading. It is, however, possible to distinguish between the purely practical arrangement, in which there is little or no artistic involvement on the arranger's part, and the more creative arrangement, in which the original composition is, as it were, filtered through the musical imagination of the arranger. Arrangements by creative musicians are clearly the more important kind, both on account of their intrinsic merits and because they often serve to illuminate the musical personality of the composer-arranger; it is therefore towards this second type of arrangement that attention will be mainly directed in the historical conspectus that follows.

2. HISTORY TO 1600.   Some element of arrangement is present in the medieval trope and clausula, as well as in those early motets where a vocal part is replaced by an instrumental one (or vice versa), but the most important type of arrangement in the period up to 1600 is the keyboard or lute intabulation of vocal polyphony. The earliest examples of such keyboard arrangements (indeed the earliest extant keyboard pieces of any kind) are in the early 14th-century Robertsbridge Manuscript (*GB-Lbl* Add.28550), whose contents include intabulations of two motets from the musical appendix to the contemporary *Roman de Fauvel* (*F-Pn* fr.146). Far from being simple transcriptions of the vocal originals, these intabulations feature a florid elaboration of the upper part which is unmistakably instrumental in conception, and this is something which remains characteristic of all later keyboard intabulations. Ex.1a shows the beginning of the motet *Adesta–Firmissime–Alleluya Benedictus*, and ex.1b the keyboard version of the same passage. Also from the 14th century are some of the keyboard arrangements in the important Faenza Manuscript 117 (*I-FZc*), which includes intabulations of vocal music by Jacopo da Bologna, Machaut, Landini and others. The principles governing these arrangements are similar to those of the

Ex.1

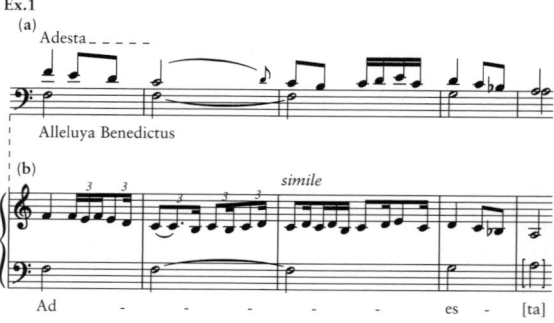

Ex.2

(a) Tenor

(b)

(c)

Ex.3

(a) Josquin

Mil — — le re — — gretz

Mil — — le re — gretz

Mil — — — le re — gretz

Mil — — le re — gretz

(b) L. de Narváez

Robertsbridge Manuscript, but the finger technique required of the performer is more advanced.

Intabulations are also to be found in the Buxheimer Orgelbuch (*D-Mbs* Cim.352*b*), which dates from about 1470, as well as examples of a rather different type of arrangement (if it can be called that) which occurs in several other German organ books of the 15th century, including Conrad Paumann's *Fundamentum organisandi* (*D-Bsb* 40613) (1452). Where the original vocal source is a monody, this is often made to serve as cantus firmus in the left hand, supporting what is presumably a free and often very florid part in the right. The technique had been applied in the Faenza Manuscript to plainsong Kyries and Glorias, but is here used for secular melodies also. Ex.2 shows the opening of the song *Ellend du hast*: (*a*) from the Lochamer Liederbuch (*c*1450, *D-Bsb* 40613); (*b*) from Paumann's *Fundamentum*, with the melody in the left hand; and (*c*) from one of the six versions in the Buxheimer Orgelbuch (no.50). Clearly such pieces and similar ones based on basse danse melodies should be regarded as variations rather than as arrangements.

With the introduction of music printing and the wider dissemination of instruments in the 16th century, intabulations proliferated not only in Germany but in Italy, Spain and France as well (see *BrownI* for a list of all printed arrangements with their sources). To those for keyboard must be added a vast literature of similar pieces for lute and vihuela, beginning with Francesco Spinacino's first book of *Intabulatura de lauto*, published by Petrucci in 1507.

Lute intabulations have a particular interest for the scholar since the tablature does not directly indicate pitch but tells the player which fret to use for each note; consequently lute arrangements can assist in determining the application of *musica ficta* to 16th-century vocal polyphony. Among the most famous examples is the arrangement for vihuela by Luys de Narváez of Josquin's motet *Mille regretz* as *Canción del emperador*. Here melodic elaboration is not confined to the top part (ex.3). The lute's function as an accompanying instrument is exemplified in numerous arrangements of polyphonic music in which all voice parts but the top one are transcribed for the instrument, resulting in a solo song with lute accompaniment. Such arrangements were important in preparing for the new monodic style that emerged towards the end of the 16th century.

3. 1600–1800. The practice of transferring vocal music to instruments continued during the next two centuries and beyond. Among the many keyboard arrangements of vocal pieces in the Fitzwilliam Virginal Book (*GB-Cfm*) is one by Peter Philips of Caccini's well-known song *Amarilli mia bella*. Philips repeated the first part of the song as printed in Caccini's *Le nuove musiche* (Florence, 1601–2) and gave a different version each time, so that the result is both an arrangement and a variation of the original (ex.4). Arrangements of this kind are to be found throughout the Baroque period; the six 'Schübler' organ chorales by Bach (BWV645–50), at least five of which are transcriptions of movements from the cantatas, are much later examples in the same tradition.

Ex.4

(a) Caccini

(b) Philips

(c) Philips

However, the surge of interest in instrumental music of all kinds that characterizes the Baroque period brought with it a new type of arrangement in which vocal music was for the first time not involved. Transcriptions from one instrumental medium to another were particularly cultivated in the period (late 17th century and early 18th) which saw the rise and dissemination of the concerto. Francesco Geminiani, as well as arranging his own music for the harpsichord, adapted Corelli's opp.3 and 5 violin sonatas as concerti grossi, and some of Domenico Scarlatti's harpsichord sonatas were turned into highly successful string concertos by Charles Avison. At Weimar J.G. Walther and J.S. Bach adapted concertos by Albinoni, Torelli, Telemann, Vivaldi and others for the organ and for the harpsichord, almost certainly at the behest of their patron Prince Johann Ernst. In many cases Bach made an almost literal transcription of the original, but often he subtly altered the harmony or filled out the texture with new counterpoints. In ex.5b, from the slow movement of BWV975 (arranged from Vivaldi's op.4 no.6), he elaborated Vivaldi's straightforward violin melody (ex.5a) and enriched the harmony with a totally chromatic bass line, while replacing the original bass suspensions with others

in the middle of the harmony. Bach's later arrangements include one of Vivaldi's Concerto for four violins and strings op.3 no.10 as a concerto for four harpsichords (BWV1065), and most of his other keyboard concertos with accompaniment are similarly arrangements of earlier works by himself or others.

Another aspect of Bach as arranger is his practice of reusing material from earlier, and sometimes quite different, works; the Mass in B minor furnishes several familiar examples. This practice, usually referred to as 'parody' (see PARODY (i)), was fairly widespread in a period when themes were largely fashioned on prototypes and when originality was measured as much in terms of craftsmanship as of melodic invention. Schütz incorporated music by Andrea Gabrieli, Alessandro Grandi and Monteverdi into his own compositions, and Francesco Durante transformed recitatives from Alessandro Scarlatti's secular cantatas into chamber duets; Handel's habit of re-using old music of his own, as well as appropriating music by other composers that suited his needs, is well known. The practice was justified by the extent to which the 'borrowed' material was refashioned. In the case of Handel this

Ex.5

(a) Vivaldi

(b) J. S. Bach

amounted often to a complete recomposition which entirely transformed the original.

Haydn's three different versions of *Die sieben letzten Worte unserers Erlösers am Kreuze* (as an orchestral piece, 1786; for string quartet, 1787; and as an oratorio, *c*1796) provide a locus classicus in the history of arrangement. But the key figure of the late 18th century is Mozart. Mozart is important less for the number than for the nature of his arrangements. His piano concertos K37, 39–41 and 107, based on movements from sonatas by Raupach, Honauer, J.C. Bach and others, are not without interest, but of more far-reaching importance is the rescoring for string trio and quartet of fugues by J.S. Bach (including some from *Das wohltemperirte Klavier*) and the reorchestration of Handel's *Acis and Galatea*, *Messiah*, *Alexander's Feast* and *Ode for St Cecilia's Day*. These arrangements, all done for Baron van Swieten, an enthusiast for Baroque music, are significant in representing the attitudes of their time to earlier music; together with the works heard at the Handel commemoration of 1784, they stand at the head of a long line of Bach transcriptions and Handel reorchestrations which continued throughout the 19th and early 20th centuries, only to be discredited afterwards.

4. 19TH AND 20TH CENTURIES. The nature of arrangements during the 19th century was largely determined by two important developments. One was a new interest (already evident to some extent in the late 18th century) in instrumental colour for its own sake; the other was the rise of the piano as both concert and domestic instrument *par excellence*. The first of these developments brought with it the concept of the composer's creation as an inviolable entity, so that, while the 19th-century arranger would happily reorchestrate the music of the past, the 19th-century composer would go to considerable trouble to ensure that his own music was played only on those instruments for which it was conceived. It is difficult to find a Romantic counterpart to the Corelli–Geminiani or Vivaldi–Bach concerto. One result of this was that most creative arrangements of contemporary instrumental music were made by the original composer himself. Examples include Beethoven's arrangements of the Violin Concerto as a piano concerto and of the Second Symphony as a piano trio, and the various versions of Brahms's Piano Quintet.

The exception to most of these remarks is the piano arrangement, probably the most interesting and the most widely cultivated type of arrangement in the 19th century. Innumerable transcriptions brought the orchestral and chamber repertory into the homes of domestic pianists (or piano-duettists), but more interesting are those with which the travelling virtuoso dazzled and delighted his audiences. Pre-eminent are those of Liszt, whose operatic arrangements range from straightforward transcriptions (the Prelude to Wagner's *Tristan und Isolde*, for instance, presents fewer problems to the pianist than does Bülow's version in the vocal score) to elaborate paraphrases of enormous technical difficulty, such as those based on Mozart's *Don Giovanni*, Verdi's *Rigoletto* and several of Wagner's music dramas. Liszt's voluminous arrangements also include many Schubert songs, all the Beethoven symphonies and Berlioz's *Symphonie fantastique*; further, he was the first important Romantic pianist-composer to reflect the spirit of the Bach revival in arrangements of the organ music (six fugues), a tradition continued later in the century by Tausig, Busoni and others.

Arrangements of piano music for orchestra have usually been either by the composer himself, or by others working after his death. An example of the former is Brahms's orchestration of his Variations for two pianos on a theme of Haydn (1873); almost as well known (if less often played) is Joachim's orchestral version of Schubert's Sonata in C for piano duet D812 ('Grand Duo'). Similar orchestral arrangements exist in great numbers in the 20th century. In most cases some attempt is made to match the orchestration to the style of the music (provided this is later than Bach and Handel), but that is less often the case when the arranger was himself a real composer. In Ravel's orchestral version (1922) of *Pictures at an Exhibition*, for example, the black-and-white originals of Musorgsky are filled out with colours which are very much Ravel's own. It is interesting to observe how later composer-arrangers have crossed the stylistic divide between their own work and that of the past. Schoenberg's arrangement of Brahms's G minor Piano Quartet op.25 (1937), even more than his earlier ones of pieces by Monn, Bach and Handel, seems to constitute a conscious act of identification with (perhaps even nostalgia for) the past. Schoenberg uses a slightly expanded Brahmsian orchestra in a more or less Brahmsian way. Webern's orchestral version of the six-part ricercare from Bach's *Musical Offering* (1935), on the other hand, sets out with the opposite intention of adapting the past to the language of the present (ex.6). It is instructive to compare it with the version by Igor Markevich (published 1952), who aimed (but failed) 'to delve into and absorb as faithfully as possible Bach's own sonorities'. The parodic element in Webern's fragmented instrumentation is pursued to the point of distortion in the several arrangements and 'realizations' of Peter Maxwell Davies.

A number of external factors have affected 20th-century practice in the making of arrangements. The implementation of copyright agreements has made it illegal to adapt and arrange musical works which are the property of a copyright holder without prior permission. Radio and the gramophone have largely replaced the piano transcription as a disseminator of the chamber, orchestral and operatic repertory, and the Lisztian paraphrase now exists only in isolated examples such as Ronald Stevenson's Fantasy on themes from Britten's *Peter Grimes*. The harmonic crisis of the 1920s led many composers to delve into the past for the seeds of a new musical language, which they did by collecting and arranging earlier music. J.C. Bach, Haydn and Beethoven had responded to a vogue for folksong arrangements in Britain during the late 18th and early 19th centuries, but the folksong arrangements of Bartók and Vaughan Williams were directed towards quite different ends. They were a means by which both composers achieved a musical style which was at the same time nationalistic and intensely individual. Similarly, Stravinsky's move in an opposite direction (away from a recognizably Russian style and towards neo-classicism) was effected with *Pulcinella* (1920), a ballet based on music by Pergolesi and others. Stravinsky's lasting obsession with the past was evident in his arrangements of composers as diverse as Gesualdo, Bach, Beethoven, Grieg and Tchaikovsky.

The late 18th-century practice of reorchestrating choral masterpieces of the Baroque period, especially those of

Ex.6

(a) Bach, arr. Markevich

(b) Bach, arr. Webern

Handel and Bach, was referred to above (see §3), and the provision of such 'additional accompaniments', as they are sometimes called, became still more widespread in the 19th and early 20th centuries. Arrangers were motivated no doubt by the practical requirements of large, well-established choral and orchestral societies – there were advantages in adapting the orchestration to the orchestra rather than the orchestra to the orchestration – and perhaps, in the case of mammoth performances, by a desire to magnify the original composer's reputation; but there was also often a genuine conviction that they were making positive improvements on the 'primitive' originals. Mozart's versions of Handel's oratorios gained currency (and were further 'improved') despite objections from some quarters. Among the objectors was Mendelssohn, who in his young days had provided additional accompaniments for Handel's 'Dettingen' *Te Deum* and *Acis and Galatea* and revised Bach's orchestration for a famous revival of the *St Matthew Passion*, but who later declined to do the same for Handel's *Israel in Egypt*.

I.F. von Mosel, C.F.G. Schwencke, Robert Franz, George Macfarren and Arthur Sullivan were among other 19th-century musicians engaged to provide new orchestrations for choral works by Bach, Handel and others, and their editions continued in use during the early part of the 20th century. However, the concern for historical accuracy in the performance of older music, which has gradually gained ground since about 1950, has profoundly influenced attitudes towards arrangements in general. Both the additional accompaniments of the 19th century and inflated orchestral versions of Baroque instrumental pieces, such as those by Elgar, Beecham, Harty and Stokowski, have been discredited. The 'edition' has replaced the 'arrangement', in critical esteem at least. Usually the distinction between one and the other is quite clear, but this is dependent to some extent on interpretation of the historical evidence. Raymond Leppard's versions of 17th-century Venetian opera, for example, purport to be editions, though many musicologists would class them as arrangements.

5. CONCLUSION.   Few areas of musical activity involve the aesthetic (and even the ethical) judgment of the musician as much as does the practice of arrangement. This involvement is at its most intense in the case of those arrangements which set out to popularize an acknowl-

edged masterpiece, either by adapting it for the stage or film (or, worse still, for the television advertisement), or by 'jazzing up' its rhythms and instrumentation. In either case the arrangement will often earn the musician's disapproval, and even his or her resentment. However, it is clearly inconsistent to deplore solely on aesthetic grounds the arrangements of Borodin's music in the musical *Kismet*, or the Bach arrangements made for the Swingle Singers, while using lack of 'historical authenticity' as the only stick to beat other, more seriously intentioned arrangements. Every arrangement creates its own historical authenticity, and Mozart's version of Handel's *Messiah* has been accorded the distinction of two scholarly editions and at least one complete, carefully prepared recording. Perhaps one day there will be 'historically accurate' performances of Ebenezer Prout's version (1902), with ornamentation restricted to frequent use of the portamento.

It would be unrealistic to propose that arrangements should be judged without reference to the original, but it is perhaps only by regarding the arrangement and the original as two different versions of the same piece that a solution to the aesthetic dilemma they so often create will be found.

BIBLIOGRAPHY

Grove6 ('Additional accompaniments'; J.A. Westrup); *La MusicaE* ('Trascrizione'; G. Dardo)

R. Franz: *Offener Brief an Eduard Hanslick, über Bearbeitungen älterer Tonwerke* (Leipzig, 1871)

S. Taylor: *The Indebtedness of Handel to Works by Other Composers* (Cambridge, 1906/R)

E. Friedländer: *Wagner, Liszt und die Kunst der Klavier-Bearbeitung* (Detmold, 1922)

O.A. Baumann: *Das deutsche Lied und seine Bearbeitungen in den frühen Orgeltabulaturen* (Kassel, 1934)

A. Mantelli: 'Compositore e trascrittore', *RaM*, vii (1934), 97–102

E. Howard-Jones: 'Arrangements and Transcriptions', *ML*, xvi (1935), 305–11

F. Munter: 'Beethovens Bearbeitung eigener Werke', *NBeJb 1935*, 159–73

F. Ballo: 'Interpretazione e trascrizione', *RaM*, ix (1936), 190–94

V. Gui: 'Sull'uso di trascrivere per orchestra', *RaM*, xiii (1940), 353

G. Tagliapietra: 'Ferruccio Busoni trascrittore e revisore', *RaM*, xiii (1940), 12–18

V. Terenzio: 'La trascrizione musicale come arte', *RaM*, xxi (1951), 130–33

A. Briskier: 'Piano Transcriptions of J.S. Bach', *MR*, xv (1954), 191–202

G. Feder: *Bachs Werke in die Bearbeitung 1750–1950*, i: *Die Vokalwerke* (diss., U. of Kiel, 1955)

C. Marinelli: 'La trascrizione come opera d'arte', *RaM*, xxvi (1956), 40–43

R. Craft: 'Strawinsky komponiert Bach', *Melos*, xxiv (1957), 35–9

H.L. Schilling: 'Igor Strawinskys Erweiterung und Instrumentation der Canonischen Orgelvariationen *Vom Himmel hoch, da komm ich her* von J.S. Bach', *Musik und Kirche*, xxvii (1957), 257–75

F. Giegling: 'Geminiani's Harpsichord Transcriptions', *ML*, xl (1959), 350–52

E.J. Simon: 'Sonata into Concerto', *AcM*, xxxi (1959), 170–85

A. Holschneider: *Händel's 'Messiah' in Mozarts Bearbeitung* (diss., U. of Tübingen, 1960)

H.J. Marx: 'Von der Gegenwärtigkeit historicher Musik: Zu Arnold Schönbergs Bach-Instrumentation', *NZM*, Jg.122 (1961), 49–51

B. Disertori, ed.: *Le frottole per canto e liuto intabulate da Franciscus Bossinensis*, IMi, new ser., iii (1964)

S. Scionti: 'Trascrizioni (Sono le trascrizioni un'offesa all'arte?)', *Rassegna musicale Curci* xix/2 (1965), 18–20

N. Carrell: *Bach the Borrower* (London, 1967/R)

J.T. Igoe: *J.S. Bach's Transcriptions for Solo Keyboard* (diss., U. of North Carolina, 1967)

K. Morawska: 'Kompozycje Orlando di Lasso w repertuarze instrumentalnym', *Muzyka*, xiii/3 (1968), 3–21

H. Keller: 'Arrangement For or Against?', *MT*, cx (1969), 22–5

T. Göllner: 'J.S. Bach and the Tradition of Keyboard Transcriptions', *Studies in Eighteenth-Century Music: a Tribute to Karl Geiringer*, ed. H.C.R. Landon and R.E. Chapman (London, 1970), 253–60

H.-J. Schulze: 'J.S. Bach's Concerto-Arrangements for Organ: Studies or Commissioned Works?', *Organ Yearbook*, iii (1972), 4–13

H.M. Brown: 'Embellishment in Early Sixteenth-Century Intabulations', *PRMA*, c (1973–4), 49–83

U. Siegele: *Kompositionsweise und Bearbeitungstechnik in der Instrumentalmusik Johann Sebastian Bachs* (Neuhausen-Stuttgart, 1975)

T. Hirsbrunner: 'Bearbeitungen, Fassungen von Strawinskys Hand', *Schweizer Jb für Musikwissenschaft*, iii (1983), 97–104

H. Loos: *Zur Klavierübertragung von Werken für und mit Orchester des 19. und 20. Jahrhunderts* (Munich, 1983)

S. Leopold, ed.: *Musikalische Metamorphosen: Formen und Geschichten der Bearbeitung* (Kassel, 1992)

MALCOLM BOYD

Arras. City in northern France, capital of the modern département of Pas-de-Calais, formerly the province of Artois. From the 12th century Arras was an important commercial centre and, increasingly in the 13th century, a bastion of the urban middle class. Much of its activity as a literary and musical centre originated with the Confrérie des Jongleurs et des Bourgeois d'Arras, a lay religious guild whose existence is documented from the last decade of the 12th century to about the mid-14th. During a plague in Arras (according to local legend) the Virgin Mary appeared separately to two *jongleurs*, Pierre Normand and Itier of Brabant, telling them to go to Arras and there reconcile their differences before Bishop Lambert. When they did this in the church of Notre Dame in Arras the Virgin appeared again and gave them a candle (the *sainte chandelle*); its wax was poured into the water used to treat the wounds of the plague-stricken, and they were miraculously healed. This prompted the Confrérie; and although written accounts of the miracle in both Latin and French place it at the beginning of the 12th century, the Confrérie was more probably founded nearer the end of the century.

The *Nécrologe* which records the deaths of the members extends from 1194 to 1361, and while the number of trouvère poets and composers it includes is considerably smaller than the figure of 180 found in many reference works, it nonetheless shows a considerable group to have come from or been active in Arras during the 13th century. A conservative list of these follows, many of them recorded in the *Nécrologe*: Adam de Givenchi,

Adam de la Halle, Andrieu Contredit, Andrieu Douchet, Andrieu de Paris, Audefroi le Bastart, Gautier de Dargies, Gilles le Vinier, Gillebert de Berneville, Henri d'Amion, Hue, chastellain d'Arras, Jaques le Vinier, Jehan Bodel, Jehan Bretel, Jehan le Cuvelier d'Arras, Jehan Erart, Jehan Fontainnes, Jehan de Grieviler, Jehan de Neuville, Lambert Ferri, Moniot d'Arras, Oede de la Couroierie, Robert de Castel, Robert de la Piere, Sauvage d'Arras, Sauvale Cosset, Simon d'Authie, Villain d'Arras. As the names indicate many of these trouvères were probably tradesmen, and most were of the middle class. The two outstanding names are Jehan Bretel (*d* 1272), a prolific poet and the principal exponent of the jeu-parti, a genre cultivated extensively in Arras, and Adam de la Halle (*d* 1285–8), the only trouvère known to have composed polyphonic music and the author of the *Jeu de Robin et de Marion*.

With the decline of secular monophony in the 14th century musical activity was concentrated in the churches, and Arras became an important centre for the training of singers until the 17th century. During the late 15th century and the 16th Arras produced a number of composers, the best known of whom were (probably born there) Antoine de Févin, Philippe Rogier and Valérian Gonet. Musicians and composers from the area were to be found all over Europe during this period, and the Ste Chapelle in Paris regularly sought singers in Arras.

With the incorporation of Artois into France in 1659 Arras lost most of its former importance as a musical centre. Despite municipal subsidies for visiting opera and operetta troupes Arras remained a musical backwater throughout the 18th century. In the 19th century musical activity centred on a number of amateur societies and a municipal music school.

BIBLIOGRAPHY

MGG1 (F. Lesure); Vander StraetenMPB

A. de Cardevacque: *La musique à Arras depuis les temps les plus reculés jusqu'à nos jours* (Arras, 1885)

A. Guesnon: *La Confrérie des jongleurs d'Arras et le tombeau de l'évêque Lambert* (Arras, 1913)

A. Jeanroy, ed.: *Le chansonnier d'Arras* (Paris, 1925) [facs. of F-AS 657]

A. Långfors, A. Jeanroy and L. Brandin, eds.: *Recueil général des jeux-partis*, i (Paris, 1926)

L. Petitot: *La musique à Arras au XIXe siècle* (Arras, 1942)

R. Berger: *La nécrologie de la Confrérie des jongleurs et des bourgeois d'Arras* (Arras, 1963–70)

M. Everist: 'The Rondeau Motet: Paris and Artois in the Thirteenth Century', *ML*, lxix (1988), 1–22

ROBERT FALCK

Arras, Chansonnier d' (*F-AS* 657). *See* SOURCES, MS, §III, 4.

Arras, Jean d' [Renverset, Jean] (*b* Arras; *d* ?Madrid, 1582). Flemish organist, active in Italy and Spain. On 1 January 1556 he was engaged at the ducal chapel of Parma. In 1580 he was organist in the chapel of Philip II of Spain, as is shown by a receipt that he signed for wages. His tenure there continued until his death. A madrigal by him, *Due rose*, is found in Josquino Persoens's first book of madrigals (RISM, 1570[28]). A chanson by him was published by Phalèse (RISM, 1575[4]).

Jean d'Arras should not be confused with a younger man of the same name who was listed in 1596 as a *mozzo de capilla* ('youth in the chapel') to Philip II, and to whom further references occur in listings of chapel personnel in 1598, 1599 and 1608.

BIBLIOGRAPHY

Vander Straeten MPB

P. Becquart: *Musiciens néerlandais à la cour de Madrid: Philippe Rogier et son école 1560–1647* (Brussels, 1967)

LAVERN J. WAGNER

Arrau, Claudio (*b* Chillán, 6 Feb 1903; *d* Mürzzuschlag, Austria, 9 June 1991). Chilean pianist, naturalized American. A child prodigy, he gave his first public recital at the age of five in Santiago. After studying with Paoli for two years, he was sent, with the support of the Chilean government, to study at the Stern Conservatory in Berlin, where he was a pupil of Martin Krause from 1912 to 1918. He never went to another teacher. During this period he won many awards including the Ibach Prize and the Gustav Holländer Medal. He gave his first recital in Berlin in 1914, followed by extensive tours of Germany and Scandinavia, and a European tour in 1918. At this time he played with many of the leading orchestras of Europe under conductors including Nikisch, Muck, Mengelberg and Furtwängler. In 1921 he returned for the first time to South America, where he gave successful concerts in Argentina and Chile. He first played in London in 1922, in a concert shared with Melba and Huberman, and this was followed a year later by a tour of the USA, where he made his Carnegie Hall début and appeared with the Boston SO and the Chicago SO.

In 1924 Arrau joined the staff of the Stern Conservatory, where he taught until 1940, and in 1927 he further enhanced his international reputation by winning the Grand Prix International des Pianistes in Geneva. Notable among his European concerts before World War II was a series of 12 recitals in Berlin in 1935, in which he played the entire keyboard works of Bach. However, he gave up playing Bach in public, after deciding that his music could not be performed satisfactorily on the piano. In 1940 he left Berlin, returning to Chile to found a piano school in Santiago. A year later, after a further tour of the USA (which was greeted with the highest critical acclaim), he and his family settled in New York. Highlights of his subsequent international career included complete performances of Beethoven's piano sonatas in London, New York and elsewhere, including a broadcast of the cycle by the BBC in 1952, and world tours in 1968 and 1974–5.

Reducing the number of concerts he gave annually (from as many as 100 to about 70) as he approached his ninth decade, he toured Europe, North America, Brazil and Japan in 1981–2. After a 17-year absence he made an emotional tour of Chile in May 1984, having been awarded the Chilean National Arts Prize the previous year.

Arrau acquired a special reputation for his interpretations of Brahms, Schumann, Liszt, Chopin and, above all, Beethoven, a reputation which is reflected by his many recordings. He had the technique of a virtuoso, but was one of the least ostentatious of pianists. His tempos were sometimes unusually broad, and even when they were not he gave the impression of having considered deeply the character and shape of each phrase. He could give performances so thorough in their consideration of detail that they seemed lacking in spontaneity and momentum. However, at its best his grand, rich-toned and thoughtful playing conveyed exceptional intellectual power and depth of feeling.

BIBLIOGRAPHY

N. Boyle: 'Claudio Arrau', *Gramophone Record Review*, nos.73–84 (1959–60), 195–6 [with discography by F.F. Clough and G.J. Cuming]

J. Kaiser: *Grosse Pianisten in unserer Zeit* (Munich, 1965, 5/1982; Eng. trans., 1971)

C. Arrau: 'A Performer Looks at Psychoanalysis', *High Fidelity/Musical America*, xvii/2 (1967), 50–54

R. Osborne: 'Keyboard Oracle: Claudio Arrau in Conversation', *Records and Recording*, xvi/1 (1972–3), 26–9

B. Morrison: 'Arrau at 75', *Music and Musicians*, xxvi/8 (1977–8), 32–4

R. Osborne: 'Claudio Arrau at 75', *Gramophone*, lv (1977–8), 1385–6

J. Horowitz: *Conversations with Arrau* (New York, 1982)

ROBERT PHILIP/R

Arraujo, Pedro de. *See* ARAÚJO, PEDRO DE.

Arregui, José Maria (*b* Villardo, *c*1875; *d* Aránzazu, 5 May 1955). Spanish composer. At the age of ten he entered the Franciscan college at Arántzazu, Guipúzcoa; he became a Franciscan in 1895 and then continued his music studies. After a missionary journey to Peru, he returned to Spain in 1912, completing his music education with Goberna and Borges. In addition to touring as a pianist, he became in 1918 conductor at the Capilla del Santuario, Arántzazu, which he reorganized. He also founded the Orfeon Caspolina in Caspe, Aragon, and conducted the Orquesta Seráfica Antoniana of Barcelona. Like other Spanish composer-priests, Arregui followed the directives of Pope Pius X's 1903 *moto proprio* on church music, sacrificing his personal voice and artistic concerns for an ecclesiastical style far removed from 20th-century aesthetics. His compositions, most of them sacred choral pieces, include *Himno a Bilbao* (1935), designated the official hymn of the Bilbao municipal government in 1936.

WORKS
(*selective list*)

Missa Sanctus Franciscus, 4vv; Ave Maria, 8vv; Benedicion de San Francisco, 6–7vv; Miserere, 8vv; Tota pulchra, 6–8vv; psalms, motets, responsories

Folksong arrs. for chorus

BIBLIOGRAPHY

MGG2 (C. Heine)

T. Marco: *Historia de la musica española*, ed. P. López de Osaba, vi: *Siglo XX* (Madrid, 1983; Eng. trans. as *Spanish Music in the Twentieth Century*, 1993)

ANTONIO RUIZ-PIPÓ

Claudio Arrau, 1961

Arregui Garay, Vicente (*b* Madrid, 3 July 1871; *d* Madrid, 2 Dec 1925). Spanish composer. He studied at the Madrid Conservatory, where he won first prizes in piano and composition and the Spanish Rome Prize (1899). In 1910 he received the National Music Prize for the orchestral *Historia de una madre*. With the exception of the *Sinfonía sobre temas vascos* his works do not reflect the nationalist trends of the time. Rather, together with Monrique de Lara, Fecundo de la Viña and del Campo, he was a leading exponent of the German Romantic aesthetic in Spain, and his music shows the strong influence of Wagner, Richard Strauss and Franck. For many years up to his death he was music critic for the Madrid daily paper *El debate*.

WORKS
(*selective list*)

Stage: Yolanda (op, 1), 1911, Madrid, Real, 1923; Chao, Tatin y la sombra de Mariani (comic op for children); El cuento de Barba Azul (op, 3), unperf.; La madona (op, 2), unperf.; La maja (op, 2), unperf.
Orch: Oración y escena de los angeles (1907) [from San Francisco]; Historia de una madre, sym. poem, after H.C. Anderson, 1910; Melodia religiosa, 1917; Sinfonia sobre temas vascos, 1922; Impresiones populares, 1924; Calipso
Choral: San Francisco, orat, 1907–8; El lobo ciego, cant, 1917; Mass, 3vv, org; motets
Inst: Str Qt, 1913; Pf Sonata, 1916

Principal publisher: Unión Musical Española

BIBLIOGRAPHY
RiemannL12
H. Collet: *L'essor de la musique espagnole au XXe siècle* (Paris, 1929)
M. Valls Gorina, ed.: *Enciclopedia de la musica* (Barcelona, 1967) [Sp. edn of *FasquelleE*]
T. Marco: *Historia de la musica española: siglo XX* (Madrid, 1983; Eng. trans., 1993)
ANTONIO RUIZ-PIPÓ

Arrested Development. American rap group. Formed in 1987 by 'Speech' (Todd Jenkins; *b* Milwaukee; rapper), they combined social comment and sampled beats with a non-aggressive stance. Other members included Rasa Don (drums), DJ Kermit (vocals), Nadirah Shakoor (lead vocals), Aerle Teree (poetry and vocals), the dancers Ajile and Montsho Eshe, and Speech's 60-year-old 'spiritual adviser', Baba Oje. They achieved US and European fame with their first album, *3 Years, 5 Months and 2 Days in the Life of* . . . (Chrysalis, 1992), which won two Grammy awards. Tracks such as 'Mr. Wendal' and 'People Everyday' combined the social comment of Speech's slow conversational rap with mellow funk samples and grooves. This continued the intelligent, gentle and commercially palatable rap begun by De La Soul and A Tribe Called Quest among others, and developed by the Fugees. Their appeal in live performance was proved with the live album *Unplugged* (Chrysalis, 1993). Speech adopted a different formula for the next album, *Zingalamaduni* (Chrysalis, 1994); named after the Swahili word for 'beehive of culture', it increased their earlier use of African vocals. In 1994 they performed in South Africa before Nelson Mandela but by the next year had split up. In 1996 Speech released an eponymous solo album, but did not achieve his earlier success.

IAN PEEL

Arresti [Aresti], Floriano (*b* Bologna, 15 Dec 1667; *d* Bologna, 1717). Italian organist and composer. The son of Giulio Cesare Arresti, on 6 April 1684 he became a member of the Accademia Filarmonica, Bologna; his musical attainments were sufficiently distinguished for him to serve there as its *principe* in 1715. In 1689 he studied keyboard and composition in Rome with Bernardo Pasquini, and was organist of S Maria in Trastevere for a time. He was *maestro di cappella* of S Lorenzo Martire in Sant'Oreste, to the north of Rome, until 1691. By 1703 he had returned to Bologna and was organist of the cathedral, a post he held until his death. He composed a quantity of music for both the church and the stage, but all his major works are lost.

WORKS
ORATORIOS

Abigail (J. Sanctorius), Rome, Oratorio del Crocifisso, 1701, lib *I-Lg*, *Rc*, *Rli*, *Rvat*
Mater Machabeorum, Rome, Oratorio del Crocifisso, 1704
La decollazione del S Precursore Giovanni Battista (G.B. Grappelli), Bologna, Casa Orsi, 1708
Zoe e Nicostrato convertiti da S Sebastiano martire (D.G.B. Taroni), Bologna, 1708, lib *F-Pn*, *I-Bl*, *Rn*, *Rsc*
Il zelo trionfante di S Filippo, Bologna, Oratorio of the Madonna di Galliera, 1710, lib *I-Bl*, Ravenna, Seminario Arcivescovile, *US-Wc*
Giuditta, Bologna, S Maria della Morte, 1717, perhaps also at Teatro Marsigli-Rossi, lib *I-Bl*
Jezabelle (G.B. Neri), with G.C. Predieri, Bologna, Madonna di Galliera, 1719, lib *B-Bc*

OPERAS

L'enigma disciolto (trattenimento pastorale, Neri), Bologna, Formagliari, carn. 1710, lib *I-Bl*, *Bu*, *IE*, *MOe*, *Rn*
Crisippo (os, G. Braccioli), Ferrara, Bonacossi, May 1710, lib *Bl*, *Fm*, *MOe*, *Vnm*, *US-Wc*; perf. with puppets, Bologna, Angelelli, 1710
Con l'inganno si vince l'inganno (divertimento per musica, F.M. Farné), perf. with puppets, Bologna, Angelelli, Dec 1710, lib *I-Bl*, *MOe*, *Vgc*
La costanza in cimento con la crudeltà (os, Braccioli), Venice, S Angelo, carn. 1712, lib *Bl*, *Bu*, *Fm*, *MOe*, *Nc*, *Pci*, *Rc*, *Rsc*, *Vcg*, *Vnm*, *US-Ba*, *LAum*, *Wc*; as La costanza in cimento, ossia Il Radamisto, Bologna, Marsigli-Rossi, carn. 1715
Il trionfo di Pallade in Arcadia (dramma pastorale), Bologna, Marsigli-Rossi, 1716

MISCELLANEOUS

3 cants.: Cieli! che cara pena; Sdegno ed amor in me, *I-Bc*, *Pca*; Vaghe luci amorose, *D-MÜs*
3 arias, *GB-Lbl*
Ky-Gl, *Lbl*; Ky-Gl, *F-Pn*
Sonata (?by G.C. Arresti) in XVII sonate da organo o cimbalo (Amsterdam, n.d.)
Elevazione, org, *I-Bc* (facs. AMI, iii, 1899/R)

Other works for vv alone and vv and insts, *D-MÜs*, *I-BGi*

BIBLIOGRAPHY
D. Alaleona: *Storia dell'oratorio musicale in Italia* (Milan, 1945), 356
G. Staffieri: *Colligite fragmenta: la vita musicale romana negli 'Avvisi Marescotti' (1683–1707)* (Lucca, 1991), 270–279
O. Gambassi: *L'Accademia Filarmonica di Bologna: fondazione, statuti, e aggregazioni* (Florence, 1992), 342, 419
JAMES L. JACKMAN/ANGELA LEPORE

Arresti, Giulio Cesare (*b* Bologna, 26 Feb 1619; *d* Bologna, 17 July 1701). Italian organist and composer. He spent his entire life in Bologna. He was a pupil of Ottavio Vernizzi whom he succeeded as second organist at S Petronio in 1649, being promoted to first organist ten years later. In December 1661 he was summarily dismissed following a vitriolic attack on the *maestro di cappella* MAURIZIO CAZZATI, circulated anonymously as the *Dialogo fatto tra un maestro ed un discepolo desideroso d'approfittare nel contrappunto*. While Gaspari attributed this work to Arresti, it is now considered unlikely that it is by him. Matters came to a head when Arresti published his *Messa e Vespro dell Beata Virgine* (1663), including the Kyrie of Cazzati's *Messe e salmi a 5 voci* (1655) liberally marked with alleged errors. Cazzati was forced to reply in the lengthy *Risposta alle opposizoni fatte dal Signor Giulio Cesare Arresti nella Lettera al Lettore posta nell'opera sua musicale* (1663). After Cazzati's own dismissal in 1671, Arresti was reinstated as first organist, being pensioned in 1696. He also served at S Salvatore in 1668 and 1680 and at the Cappella del Rosario, S Domenico. He played a major part in the foundation (1666) of the Accademia Filarmonica di Bologna, which apparently originated in some highly successful concerts of his given at the home of its founder Count Vincenzo Carrati. Arresti became president of the academy in 1671. He had previously been a member of the Accademia dei Filomusi, with the name 'Il Sollevato'.

The pedantic dispute over the proprieties of the *a cappella* style have coloured later perceptions of Arresti's music. His *Sonate* (1665), however, are novel in their inclusion of *arie* obviously indebted to contemporary secular vocal music, and his *Sonate da organo di varii autori* (?1697), containing three of his own compositions, is an important anthology of late 17th-century Italian organ music. His contribution to the oratorio appears to have been significant but cannot be assessed in the absence of surviving scores.

WORKS

Messa e Vespro della Beata Virgine con l'inno, reali composte di 3 figure cantandosi senza battuta, 8vv, org ad lib, op.1 (Venice, 1663)

Messe, 3vv, bc (org), con sinfonie, e ripieni ad lib [2 vn], … motetti, e concerti, op.2 (Venice, 1663; 2/1664 as Gare musicali, i)

[12] Sonate a 2, 3, vc ad lib, bc, op.4 (Venice, 1665)

Partitura di modulationi precettive sopra gl'hinni del canto fermo gregoriano con le riposte intavolate in 7 righe, org, op.7 (Bologna, after 1665; probably after 1685, according to Apel)

1 cant., 1685[1]

3 sonatas, org, c1697[8], ed. A.G. Ritter, *Geschichte des Orgelspiels* (Berlin, 1884)

Orats: L'orto di Getsemani, Bologna, 1661; Licenza di Gesù da Maria, Bologna, 1661; Lo sposalizio di Rebecca, Bologna, 1675; La decollazione di S Giovanni, Bologna, 1708: all lost

WRITINGS

Dialogo fatto tra un maestro ed un discepolo desideroso d'approfittare nel contrappunto (MS, 1659, *I-Bc* C.55), attrib. now thought doubtful

BIBLIOGRAPHY

ApelG; FrotscherG; NewmanSBE; ScheringGO

K.G. Fellerer: 'Zur italienischen Orgelmusik des 17./18. Jahrhunderts', *JbMP 1938*, 70–83

A. Schnoebelen: 'Cazzati vs. Bologna: 1657–1671', *MQ*, lvii (1971), 26–39

P.C. Allsop: 'Secular Influences in the Bolognese Sonata da chiesa', *PRMA*, civ (1977–8), 89–100

U. Brett: *Music and Ideas in Seventeenth-Century Italy: the Arresti–Cazzati Polemic* (diss., U. of London, 1986)

P.C. Allsop: *The Italian 'Trio' Sonata from its Origins until Corelli* (Oxford, 1992)

O. Gambassi: *L'Accademia Filarmonica di Bologna* (Florence, 1992)

PETER ALLSOP (text, bibliography),
NONA PYRON (work-list, bibliography)

Arriaga (y Balzola), Juan Crisóstomo (Jacobo Antonio) de (*b* Bilbao, 27 Jan 1806; *d* Paris, 12/17 Jan 1826, bur. 17 Jan 1826). Basque composer. His father, Juan Simón Arriaga, had been organist, royal clerk and schoolteacher at Guernica, and had become associated with members of the Real Sociedad Bascongada de los Amigos del Pais, a society upholding the ideals of the Enlightenment, before moving to Bilbao in 1804 to become a merchant and shipowner. Arriaga's brother Ramón Prudencio, his senior

by 14 years, played the violin and guitar. Both father and brother seem to have groomed the child for a musical career. They established contacts with musical amateurs and professionals, such as the aficionado José Luis Torres and José Sobejano, sometime organist and *maestro de capilla* at Santiago, Bilbao; with influential men of letters and musicians from Madrid court circles, such as the poet Alberto Lista and the violinist Francesco Maria Vaccari; and with the famous singer Manuel García. Reports on Arriaga's opera in the Spanish press presumably appeared on the initiative of his father and brother. The choice of texts for two patriotic hymns and the idea to set a Spanish opera also reflect the influence the family had on the boy.

By September 1821 Arriaga had produced about 20 works, only some of which are now extant. According to his father, Arriaga wrote his first piece at the age of 11, and the autograph of *Nada y mucho* seems to confirm this. Originally a trio for violins, the piece was revised by the addition of a bass and a text to the upper part. In 1818 he composed an overture (op.1) for nonet which, surprisingly, already shows many of the characteristic compositional strategies used in later works. In 1819 he wrote his opera *Los esclavos felices*, of which only the overture and fragments of several arias remain. A *romanza* for piano (published in Sobejano's *El Adam español*) may have been written when Sobejano was director of the Santiago *capilla* (1815–20). The motets *Stabat mater* and *O salutaris hostia* were probably composed for the *capilla*. The texts of the patriotic hymns *Ya luce en este hemisferio* and *Cantabros nobles* fit the political situation of the *trienio liberal* (1820–23). Variations are an important part of Arriaga's output. Op.17 for string quartet is a densely textured, heavily chromatic set of variations on a very simple diatonic melody; op.22 is a virtuoso set for violin with a very simple added bass.

In September 1821 (not 1822 as usually stated) Arriaga went abroad. He was introduced by García and Justo de Machado (the Spanish ambassador in Paris) to Cherubini, who was at that time one of the inspectors of the Paris Conservatoire. Arriaga was admitted to Fétis's newly created class of counterpoint and fugue and to the violin class of Pierre Baillot and his assistants. He won prizes for counterpoint and fugue in 1823 and 1824, and in the latter year Fétis made him teaching assistant.

Arriaga continued to be very industrious as a composer. In the course of revising some of his earlier works, he may have disowned some of them. At the request of Vaccari, the variations op.22 for violin and bass were arranged for string quartet in order to introduce them at court in Madrid. The overture to *Los esclavos felices* was revised: the form of the second version is more academic and Arriaga had some difficulty in cutting it down. A comparison of the two versions shows the composer's progress in orchestration.

His new compositions exhibit a continuing strength of invention. The prizes for counterpoint and fugue were not undeserved, as the *Canon perpétuel* for the album of Monsieur d'Henneville shows. Likewise, *Et vitam venturi*, a fugue for eight voices inspired by the corresponding section of Cherubini's C minor Requiem, 1816, was praised by Fétis. For all of his vocal works Arriaga chose texts that were well known in earlier settings. The three arias (*Hélas, hélas, d'une si pure flamme*, *Hymen, viens dissiper une vaine frayeur* and *Douce magie des lieux chéris*) had been set before by Sacchini, Cherubini and

Boieldieu in 1785, 1797 and 1803 respectively, and Arriaga certainly knew their settings. The texts of the cantata *Herminie* and the scena *Agar dans le désert* had been used already in the competition for the Prix de Rome. Three string quartets were published in 1824 by Philippe Petit, whom Arriaga probably knew through García. A symphony, showing the influence of Beethoven and uncannily reminiscent of Schubert's Fourth Symphony, was one of Arriaga's last works. Separate parts of both the symphony and the revised version of the overture to *Los esclavos felices* were copied, probably for professional performance in public. According to Fétis, some pieces of liturgical music and several romances, presumably for voice and piano or guitar, have been lost.

Arriaga's short career was heavily marked by a strong sense of competition. A dramatic impetus coupled with a flair for finding remarkably well-poised musical structures pervades all of his works, both vocal and instrumental. Melodies always seem to have come easily to him; a remarkable progression in the handling of accompaniment and orchestration can be seen. In his Parisian period Arriaga discovered a technique of continuous transformation of musical material. He was always fond of chromaticisms and used a chromatic *idée fixe* in most of his works from the very beginning.

Pedro Albéniz's letter to Arriaga's father and Fétis's report lead to the conclusion that Arriaga died from exhaustion and a pulmonary infection. After his death his belongings were sent to Bilbao and on the death of his father in 1836 his papers were divided between the five heirs. In 1868 Emiliano de Arriaga acquired what was believed to be the composer's violin and during the early 1880s he started gathering the documents concerning his ancestor. The present-day image of the composer has been created almost single-handedly by him. The nickname 'the Spanish Mozart', suggested by him and coined by Pascual Emilio Arrieta, stuck. The composer became an important symbol within the budding movement of Basque nationalism and thus was soon styled 'the Basque Mozart'.

Emiliano de Arriaga's son José continued his father's politics of divulgation. He had many of the works published before 1930, though in adulterated versions, and set up an international network for the propagation of Arriaga's music that was active from the 1920s to the 1950s. On José de Arriaga's instigation many of the works were published in arrangements.

WORKS

VOCAL

Los esclavos felices (op semiseria, 2, after L.F. Comella y Comella), 1819, Bilbao, 1820, mostly lost; 14 nos., inc.; ov., 2nd version, ed. (Bilbao, 1950)

Ya luce en este hemisferio la constitucion mas sabia, patriotic hymn, 1v, orch, ?1820–21

Cantabros nobles, la Patria a nuestras filas os llama, patriotic hymn, ?1820–21, mostly lost; T, B pts in *E-Bilbao*

Stabat mater dolorosa, motet, 3vv, orch, before July 1821, ed. (Bilbao)

Agar dans le désert (V.-J.E. de Jouy), scena, S, S/?T, orch; romanza, S, pf, ed. (Barcelona), finale, S, orch, ed. (Madrid)

Canon perpétuel à la quinte et à l'octave inférieure, 4vv, mainly lost; bars 1–13 in *S-Smf* (Nydahl collection)

Et vitam venturi, fugue, 8vv, mentioned in *FétisB*

Herminie (cant., J.-A. Vinaty, after T. Tasso: *La Gerusalemme liberata*), S, orch, ed. (Madrid)

Hymen, viens dissiper une vaine frayeur (from F.-B. Hoffman: *Médée*), aria, S, orch; arr. S, pf (Barcelona, *c*1920)

Malgré de trop justes allarmes . . . Douce magie des lieux chéris (from C. de Longchamps: *Ma tante Aurore*), recit and aria, duet, T, B, orch; arr. pf, mainly lost, 5 bars in *E-Bilbao*

Mass, 4vv, mentioned in *FétisB*

O salutaris hostia, motet, 3vv, str qnt, ed. (Bilbao)

Où vais-je, malheureux . . . Hélas, hélas, d'une si pure flamme (from N.-F. Guillard: *Oedipe à Colonne*), recit and aria, T, orch; arr. T, pf (Madrid)

Salve regina, mentioned in *FétisB*

Other frags. and lost works: melody, 8 bars, *Bilbao*; romances, mentioned in *FétisB*

INSTRUMENTAL

Nada y mucho, 3 vn (1 pt with added text), 'basso', 1817, ed. (Bilbao, 1929)

Overture, fl, 2 cl, 2 hn, 2 vn, va, vc, op.1, 1818, ed. (Madrid)

Romanza, pf, ?before 1820, lesson 38 in J. Sobejano Ayala: El Adam español (Madrid, 1826)

March, military band, ?1820–21

Tema variado en cuarteto, str qt, op.17, ed. (Bilbao)

La Húngara, variations, vn, pf, op.22, 1821; arr. str qt, with addl introduction, op.23, 1822

3 string quartets, d, A, E♭ (Paris, 1824)

Symphony, d, ed. (Bilbao, 1950)

3 études ou caprices, pf, ed. (Bilbao)

Frags.: sketches of 2 fugues, 4vv, *Bilbao*; 1 movt and Adagio, 1st vn pt *Bilbao*

BIBLIOGRAPHY

FétisB; *FétisBS*

I. Echazarra [Echezarra]: 'Análisis crítico de las obras del Maestro Arriaga', *Euzkadi*, iii (1906), 40–61

J. de Eresalde [J. de Arriaga]: '*Los esclavos felices*' ópera de J.C. de Arriaga: antecendentes, comentarios, argumento y algunas noticias bio-bibliográficas (Bilbao, 1935)

S.K. Hoke: *Juan Crisóstomo de Arriaga: a Historical and Analytical Study* (Ann Arbor, 1984)

B. Rosen: *Arriaga, the Forgotten Genius: the Short Life of a Basque Composer* (Reno, NV, 1988)

WILLEM DE WAAL

Arrieta (y Corera), Pascual (Juan) Emilio (*b* Puente de la Reina, 21 Oct 1823; *d* Madrid, 11 Feb 1894). Spanish composer. Born to a family of poor labourers, he was orphaned as a child and raised by a sister in Madrid, who arranged for his first solfège lessons. She also took him on his first journey to Italy in 1838, where he returned on his own the following year aboard a smuggler's ship. He travelled to Milan under the name of Juan, but once there began using Emilio. He studied piano with Perelli and harmony with Mandacini before entering the Milan Conservatory, where he studied composition with Nicola Vaccai and became a good friend of his fellow student, Ponchielli. Extreme poverty and malnourishment did not prevent him from excelling in his courses, and his talent attracted the patronage of Count Litta, to whom he dedicated his first opera, *Ildegonda*, to a libretto by Temistocle Solera. Upon completing his studies in Milan, he returned to Madrid in 1846, where *Ildegonda* was produced in the theatre of the royal palace in October 1849. He was appointed singing teacher and court composer to Isabel II, who encouraged him to write another opera with Solera; the resultant work, *La conquista di Granata*, was first performed at the Teatro del Real Palacio in October 1850. After a year's stay in Italy supervising performances of his works, he returned to Spain to find the zarzuela in the ascendant. He collaborated with the dramatist Francisco Camprodón in the zarzuela *El dominó azul*, first performed at the Teatro del Circo in February 1853 to enthusiastic notices.

His most famous work, *Marina*, was first given as a zarzuela in September 1855, but without success. In 1871 he converted it to an opera through the addition of recitatives, winning over both critics and public at the Teatro Real in March 1871. Of his dozens of theatrical works, it alone holds a place on the stage today. In 1857 he became a professor of composition at the Madrid Conservatory, where he counted Chapí and Bretón among his students. From 1868 to his death he served as director of the conservatory and made many important improvements. In addition to operas, he composed occasional pieces such as hymns and cantatas, often with political overtones. Though Arrieta's style was conservative and remained rooted in Italian opera, his zarzuelas employ folkloric references, and his stage works, especially *Marina*, were milestones in the development of Spanish musical theatre.

WORKS
(selective list)

for additional details see GroveO

Ops: Ildegonda (2, T. Solera), Milan, Conservatory, 1845; La conquista di Granata [La conquista de Granada; Isabel la Católica] (3, Solera), Madrid, Palacio, 10 Feb 1850; Marina (3, M. Ramos Carrión), Madrid, Real, 6 March 1871 [rev. of zar of 1855]

Zars (in order of first performance; all first performed in Madrid): Al amanecer, 1851; El dominó azul, 1853; El grumete, 1853; La estrella de Madrid, 1853; La cacería real, 1854; La dama del rey, 1855; Guerra a muerte, 1855; Marina, 1855; La zarzuela, 1856, collab. F.A. Barbieri and J.R. Gaztambide; La hija de la Providencia, 1856; El sonámbulo, 1856; El planeta Venus, 1858; Azón Visconti, 1858; Quien manda, manda, 1859; Los Circasianos [El caudillo de Baza], 1860; Llamada y tropa, 1861; El hombre feliz, 1861; Un ayo para el niño, 1861; Dos coronas, 1861; El agente de matrimonios, 1862

La tabernera de Londres, 1862; Un trono y un desengaño, 1862; La vuelta del corsario, 1863; Cadenas de oro, 1864; De tal palo tal astilla, 1864; El toque de ánimas, 1864; La ínsula Barataria, 1864; El capitán negrero, 1865; El conjuro, 1866; Un sarao y una soirée, 1866; La suegra del diablo, 1867; Los enemigos domésticos, 1867; El figle enamorado, 1867; Los novios de Teruel, 1867; A la humanidad doliente, 1868; Los misterios del Parnaso, 1868; Los progresos del amor, 1868; Las fuentes del Prado, 1870; El potosí submarino, 1870

De Madrid a Biarritz, 1870; El motín contra Esquilache, 1871; La sota de espadas, 1871; Las manzanas de oro, 1873; Un viaje a Cochinchina, 1875; Entre el alcalde y el rey, 1875, collab. M.F. Caballero; La guerra santa, 1879; El amor enamorado [Heliodora], 1880; San Franco de Sena, 1883; El guerrillero, 1885, collab. Caballero and Chapí

BIBLIOGRAPHY

GroveO (L. Salter)

A. Peña y Goñi: *La ópera española y la música dramática en España en el siglo XIX* (Madrid, 1881)

F. de Arteaga: *Celebridades musicales* (Barcelona, 1887)

E. Cotarelo y Mori: *Historia de la zarzuela* (Madrid, 1934)

J. Subirá: *El teatro del Real Palacio* (Madrid, 1950)

C. Gómez Amat: *Historia de la música española en el siglo XIX* (Madrid, 1984)

A. Sagardía: *Gaztambide y Arrieta* (Pamplona, 1986)

WALTER AARON CLARK

Arrieu, Claude [Simon, Anne Marie] (*b* Paris, 30 Nov 1903; *d* Paris, 7 March 1990). French composer. She received a *premier prix* in composition in 1932 at the Paris Conservatoire, having studied with Dukas, Roger-Ducasse, Nöel Gallon, Georges Caussade and Marguerite Long. She established a career in teaching and at French Radio, where she worked as a producer and assistant head of sound effects.

Much of Arrieu's output consists of dramatic works ranging from opera and incidental music to her farce for children *La tête du dragon* (1946). At least 30 film scores and 40 radio scores are also to her credit. Among her instrumental works, such finely wrought duos as the

Impromptu II for oboe and piano and the *Sonatine* for flute and piano, composed in the spirit of *Gebrauchsmusik*, are characterized by the style of Les Six, but take a strongly individual direction in their harmonic and metrical shifts. Her music's wit, charm and harmonically adventurous qualities places her in a line of musical descent from Chabrier. She took a direct interest in electro-acoustics, and was one of the first to work with Pierre Schaeffer. Even so, excepting the *Fantaisie lyrique* for ondes martenot and piano, her concert works do not make use of electronic instruments or resources.

WORKS
(selective list)

STAGE

Noé (imagerie musicale, 3, A. Obey), 1932–4, Strasbourg, Théâtre Municipal, 29 Jan 1950

Cadet-Roussel (ob, 5, A. de la Tourrasse, after J. Limozin), 1938–9, Marseilles, Opéra, 2 Oct 1953

La tête du dragon (R.M. de Valle-Inclán), 1946

Fête galante (ballet, B. Kochno), 1947, Berne, 1947

Les deux rendez-vous (oc, 1, P. Bertin, after G. de Nerval), 1948, RTF, 22 June 1951

Le chapeau à musique (opérette enfantine, 2, Tourrasse and P. Dumaine), 1953, RTF, 1953

La princesse de Babylone (ob, 3, P. Dominique, after Voltaire), 1953–5, Reims, Opéra, 3 March 1960

La cabine téléphonique (ob, 1, M. Vaucaire), 1958, RTF, 15 March 1959

Cymbeline (2, J. Tournier and M. Jacquemont, after W. Shakespeare), 1958–63, Quimper, 1971

Commedia umana (ballet, after G. Boccaccio), 1960, Nervi, 1960

Le marchand de Venise (incid music, W. Shakespeare), 1961

Balthazar, ou Le mort-vivant (ob, 1, Dominique), 1966, unperf.

La statue (ballet, J. Provins), 1968

Le bourgeois gentilhomme (incid music, Molière), 1969

Un clavier pour un autre (ob, 1, J. Tardieu), 1969–70, Avignon, Opéra, 3 April 1971

Barberine (3, after A. de Musset), 1972, inc.

Les amours de Don Perlimpin et Belise en son jardin (imagerie lyrique, 4 tableaux, after F. García Lorca), Tours, Grand Théâtre, 1 March 1980

Many scores for the theatre, cinema and broadcasting

OTHER WORKS

Vocal-orch: Cantate des sept poèmes d'amour en guerre (P. Eluard), S, Bar, orch, RTF, 1946; Mystère de Noël (L. Masson), 10 solo vv, chorus, orch, RTF, 1951

Orch: Pf. Conc., 1932; Partita, 1934; Vn Conc., 1938; Conc. for 2 pf, 1938; Petite Suite, 1945; Fl Conc., 1946; Vn Conc. 1949; Suite, str, 1959; Tpt Conc., 1965; Variations classiques, str, 1970

Chbr: Trio d'anches, ob, cl, bn, 1936; Sonatine, fl, pf, 1943; Histoires de Paris, str qt, db, perc, 1947; Vn Sonata, 1948; Wind Qnt, 1955; Pf Trio, 1957; Fantaisie lyrique, ondes martenot, pf, 1959; Cl Qt no.1, 1964; 5 mouvements, 4 cl, 1964; 2 pièces, str qnt, hp, hn, perc, 1966; Wind Dixtuor, 1967; Capriccio, cl, pf, 1970; Suite, ob, cl, bn, 1980; Suite, fl, ob, cl, bn, 1980; Cl Qt no.2, 1984; Impromptu II, ob, pf, 1985

Songs: Chansons bas (S. Mallarmé), 1933; Poèmes de Louis de Vilmorin, 1944; many other settings of poems by F. Jammes, L. Aragon, J. Cocteau and J. Tardieu

Radio scores incl. La coquille à planètes (P. Schaeffer), RTF, 1943–4; Candide (J. Tardieu, after Voltaire); Histoires de Paris; 7 poèmes de guerre (P. Eluard); pf and unacc. choral works

Principal publishers: Amphion, Billaudot, Editions Français de Musique, Heugel, Leduc, Ricordi

BIBLIOGRAPHY

K. Pendle, ed: *Women and Music: a History* (Bloomington, IN, 1991)

FRANÇOISE ANDRIEUX/JAMES R. BRISCOE

Arrigo [Henricus] (*fl* 2nd half of the 14th century). Italian composer. He is known only from a two-voice ballata, *Il capo biondo* (ed. in PMFC, x, 1977, p.71), which is transmitted *F-Pn* 568 (ff.96*v*–97; added to fill unused space in the manuscript) under the name Arrigo, and in

F-Pn 6771 (f.25*v*), ascribed to 'Henricus'. The piece combines elements of style both conservative and new for Italian music in the second half of the 14th century. Since, from the musical style, the composer was evidently Italian, he may not be identified with other known composers named Henricus.

BIBLIOGRAPHY

J. Wolf: *Geschichte der Mensural-Notation von 1250–1460* (Leipzig, 1904/*R*), ii, no.57*a*/*b*

N. Pirrotta: 'Rhapsodic Elements in North-Italian Polyphony of the 14th Century', *MD*, xxxvii (1983), 983–99

J. Nadas: *The Transmission of Trecento Polyphony: Manuscript Production and Scribal Practices in Italy at the End of the Middle Ages* (diss., New York U., 1985), 193, 207–8

KURT VON FISCHER/GIANLUCA D'AGOSTINO

Arrigo, Girolamo (*b* Palermo, 2 April 1930). Italian composer. He studied at the Palermo Conservatory, receiving diplomas in horn playing and (under the tutelage of Turi Belfiore) composition; in 1952 he went to Paris to study with Deutsch. He later spent time in New York (1964–5) and Berlin (1967) on grants from the Ford Foundation and the Deutscher Akademischer Austauschdienst. He won second prize in the third ISCM composition competition (1963), and first prize in the Pour que l'Esprit Vive Award (1957) and at the 1965 Paris Biennale.

Among Arrigo's first significant compositions, *Due melodie* for soprano and orchestra and *Due epigrammi* for five voices, both from 1956, betray the influence of the linear writing of the Schoenberg school and, in the choral work, elements of the Italian madrigal tradition. Neo-madrigalian writing, along with hints of late-Romantic orchestral writing, is also evident in *Epitaffi* (1963), one of a number of his works to set the poetry of Michelangelo. While the impact of both the Parisian avant garde and the 'informal' tendencies of the early 1960s is clear in such works as *Shadows* (1964) and *Infrarosso* (1967), such influences have contributed relatively little to Arrigo's personal stylistic synthesis.

Arrigo's activity in the theatre began in 1969 with *Orden*, a dramatic oratorio in which, against the background of the Parisian cultural upheavals of 1968, the composer voiced his political and social commitment in a denunciation of the atrocities commited by Franco in the Spanish Civil War. His 'musical epic' *Addio Garibaldi* (1972) signalled a return to more traditional dramaturgy, a move confirmed in his opera *Il ritorno di Casanova* of 1984, which can be viewed as a synthesis of his compositional concerns up to that point.

WORKS
(*selective list*)

Stage: Orden (oratorio drammatico, 3 pts, P. Bourgeade, after R. Alberti and others), Avignon, 2 Aug 1969; Addio Garibaldi (epopea musicale, 2, Arrigo, after U. Foscolo and G. Garibaldi), Paris, OC, 18 Oct 1972; Rorogigasos (ballet, A. Poliziano), S, orch, 1973; Palermo, 26 Feb 1977; Lo schiavo morente (ballet, Michelangelo), T, hn, 1973, Venice, 1975; Il ritorno di Casanova (op, 2, G. di Leva, after A. Schnitzler), Geneva, Grand, 18 April 1985

Vocal: 2 melodie, S, orch, 1956; 2 epigrammi (G. and C. Strozzi, Michelangelo), 5vv, 1956; 3 occasioni (E. Montale), S, orch, 1959; Quarta occasioni (Montale), T, 7 solo vv, 5 insts, 1961; Epitaffi (Michelangelo), chorus, orch, 1963; La cantata Hurbinek (P. Levi), 6vv, 12 inst, 1970; . . . E ciascuno salutò nell'altro la vita (Levi), 1v, 1972; 3 madrigali (Michelangelo), 5vv, 1973; Organum Jeronimus (textless), book 1, 8 solo vv, 14 insts, 1973; Tardi conosco (Michelangelo), 12vv, 1974; 4 pezzi (R. Guiducci), vv, 1981; O notte, o dolce tempo (Michelangelo), 12vv, chbr orch, 1987

Inst: Str Trio, 1956; Fluxus, 9 insts, 1961; Serenata, gui, 1962; Shadows, orch, 1964; Thumos, orch, 1964; Infrarosso, 19 insts, 1967; Solarium, 1976; Probabile, fl, 1978; Serenata per Andromeda, cl, va, pf, str, 1988; Fantasia, vc, 1991; Post-Scriptum, 10 insts, 1991

Principal publishers: Bruzzichelli, Heugel, Ricordi

RAFFAELE POZZI

Arrigo d'Ugo. *See* ISAAC, HENRICUS.

Arrigoni, Carlo (*b* Florence, 5 Dec 1697; *d* Florence, 18 Aug 1744). Italian lutenist, theorbo player and composer. Although he may have directed music for the Prince of Carignan in his early years, his name is principally associated with Florence. By at least 1718 he was a member of the musicians' company there. He is listed as a theorbo player at an oratorio performance on 31 March 1720 and as a violinist at a private concert on 30 July 1724, both in Florence. In 1721 he was elected a member of the Accademia Filarmonica of Bologna. His presence in London between 1731 and 1736 coincided with the lifespan of the Opera of the Nobility, rival to Handel's company, which presented four performances of his *Fernando* beginning on 5 February 1734. In the 1732–3 season he directed concerts at Hickford's Rooms, together with Giuseppe Sammartini, according to a newspaper announcement quoted by Burney. Other announcements mention his participation in London concerts on 20 April and 7 May 1733, 27 March and 11 April 1735, and 21 January, 5 March and 8 March 1736, either at Hickford's Rooms or Lincoln's Inn Fields. Arrigoni also sang and played his own music in Dublin on 20 October 1733. He sang the tenor part in Handel's cantata *Cecilia, volgi un sguardo* and played the lute in Handel's concerto op.4, no.6, both at original performances of Handel's *Alexander's Feast* at Covent Garden in February and March 1736 (see Dean). Later in 1736 he was made *aiutante di camera* by Grand Duke Giovanni Gastone of Tuscany, and in 1737 the new Grand Duke, Franz II, named him chamber composer. Performances of Arrigoni's music in Vienna in 1737 and 1738 reflect the fact that the new Tuscan grand duke was the husband of Maria Theresia, and do not necessarily place the composer in that city. After 1740 Arrigoni played his theorbo several times in Lucca at the festivals of the Holy Cross (13–14 September). In a letter of 12 August 1742, Horace Mann mentioned him as an arranger of private concerts in Florence. A fellow lutenist at the court, Nicolò Susier, reported that he was survived by a wife and four sons, one of whom may be the 'signor Arrigoni' mentioned in connection with performances in England, Scotland and Ireland, 1756–63.

In his surviving music Arrigoni is revealed as a composer of modest ability. His instrumental music is saturated with conventional figuration and organized into shortwinded periods of sequences, voice-exchanges, frequent cadences and literal repetitions of small units. His arias often seem to be constructed of brief, unrelated phrases, which awkwardly return to a few pitches and thus lack directional flow. Perhaps his relative success as a composer was due to his mastery of fashionable stylistic conventions rather than to the real worth of his music.

WORKS
OPERAS

La vedova (G.A. Moniglia), Foligno, carn. 1722, music lost
Fernando (Ferdinando) (melodrama, P.A. Rolli, after G. Gigli), London, Lincoln's Inn Fields, 5 Feb 1734, 8 arias, *GB-Lbl*

Scipione nella Spagne (A. Zeno) Florence, Cocomero, carn. 1739, music lost

Sirbace (C.N. Stampa), Florence, Cocomero, carn. 1739, music lost

ORATORIOS

L'innocenza di S Eugenia scoperta nel tradimento, Florence, S Filippo Neri, 1719, lost

Il pentimento d'Acabbo doppo il rimprovero della strage di Nabot (G.G. Arrigoni), Florence, 1722, music lost

Ester (P. Metastasio), Vienna, 1738, *A-Wgm*

OTHER WORKS

[10] Cantate da camera, S, bc (London, 1732)

3 arias, Raccolta di varie canzoni (Florence, 1739, 1740)

Menuet, D, vn, in the Compleat Tutor for the violin (London, *c*1750)

Sonata, A, hpd, before 1729, *US-Bfa*

Festa da camera, SATB, insts, 1732, *A-Wn*

Cants. for the namedays of the emperor and empress, 1737, *Wn*

Componimento da cantarsi, 1741, music lost

Componimento da cantarsi, 1743, music lost

Cants., *Wgm, Wn, B-Bc, D-DÜl, GB-Lbl*

Aria, *B-Bc*

3 sonatas, conc., mand, *US-Wc*; minuet, *NYp*

Vocal works in *B-Lc, CH-Gc, F-Pn, GB-Lam*

BIBLIOGRAPHY

W. Dean: 'An Unrecognized Handel Singer: Carlo Arrigoni', *MT*, cxviii (1977), 556–8

J.W. Hill: 'Oratory Music in Florence, III: the Confraternities from 1655 to 1785', *AcM*, lviii (1986), 129–79

W. Kirkendale: *The Court Musicians in Florence during the Principate of the Medici* (Florence, 1993)

JOHN WALTER HILL

Arrigoni [Arigoni], **Giovanni Giacomo** (*b* S Vito al Tagliamento, 10 March 1597; *d* S Vito al Tagliamento, 8 June 1675). Italian composer and organist. There is no evidence that he was related to Carlo Arrigoni. From 1632 to 1638 he is recorded as an organist in the Hofkapelle, Vienna. After 1638 he does not seem to have been active in Vienna, although his link with the Viennese imperial court continued: Leopold I was the dedicatee of his three-act *festa teatrale*, Gli amori di Alessandro Magno e di Rosane. From 1638 he was in his home town of S Vito al Tagliamento and in Venice, and from 1652 to 1655 he directed an opera company in Udine. According to Gerber he was a member of the Accademia Fileleutera in Venice, with the academic name of 'L'Affettuoso', although that need not signify that he lived there. He may also have had connections with the court of Duke Carlo II of Mantua, since he dedicated his volume of 1663 to him. Arrigoni's three surviving collections show that he favoured the concertato style. Their contents include independent instrumental parts, and the 1635 book contains four sonatas, two in six parts and two in eight. The vocal works in this book embrace a wide variety of forms – chamber duet, madrigal, dialogue and chaconne among them – and show that Arrigoni was a fluent, competent composer. His *festa teatrale* is also very varied in its forms and textures and includes comic scenes.

WORKS

Madrigals, 2, 3vv (Venice, 1623), lost, cited in Walther

Sacrae cantiones … liber secundus, 2–5vv, bc (org) (Venice, 1632)

Concerti di camera, 2–9vv, insts, bc (Venice, 1635)

[8] Salmi concertate et alquanti con li ripieni, 3vv … con 1 Magnificat, 5vv, 2 vn, op.9 (Venice, 1663)

Works in 1624³, 1624¹¹, 1625², 1641³, 1649⁶

Gli amori di Alessandro Magno e di Rosane (festa teatrale, 3, G.A. Cicognini), ?1657–8, *A-Wn* (prol, Act 1 and Ger. trans. of lib)

BIBLIOGRAPHY

GerberL; WaltherML

F. Caffi: *Storia della musica sacra nella già cappella ducale di San Marco in Venezia dal 1318 al 1797* (Venice, 1854–5/R, repr. 1931); ed. E. Surian (Florence, 1987)

L. von Köchel: *Die kaiserliche Hof-Musikkapelle in Wien von 1543 bis 1867* (Vienna, 1869/R)

G. and C. Salvioli: *Bibliografia universale del teatro drammatico italiano*, i (Venice, 1903), 260

R. Haas: *Die Musik des Barocks* (Potsdam, 1928), 175–6

A. Bauer: *Opern und Operetten in Wien: Verzeichnis ihrer Erstaufführungen in der Zeit von 1629 bis zur Gegenwart* (Graz and Cologne, 1955), 5

H. Knaus: *Die Musiker im Archivbestand des Kaiserlichen Obersthofmeisteramtes 1637–1705*, i (Vienna, 1967)

F. Metz: 'Notizie storiche sugli organi, gli organisti e i maestri di cappella della terra di S. Vito al Tagliamento', *Studi sanvitesi* [San Vito 1978], ed. M.M. Roberti, Antichità altoadriatiche, xvi (Udine, 1980), 105–34

T. Morsanuto: *Giovanni Giacomo Arrigoni (1597–1675): un compositore seicentesco fra Venezia, Vienna ed Udine* (diss., U. of Pavia, 1989–90)

JOSEF-HORST LEDERER

Arrigo Tedesco. *See* ISAAC, HENRICUS.

Arro, Elmar (*b* Riga, 2 July 1899; *d* Vienna, 14 Dec 1985). Estonian musicologist. He studied musicology in Vienna, where he took the doctorate in 1928 with a dissertation on music in Estonia in the 19th century. In 1933 he was appointed to a chair of musicology and also taught Slavonic studies at the German Luther Academy in Tartu, Estonia. He moved to Germany in 1939; in 1955 he was teaching at Heidelberg and after 1968 in Kiel. From 1959 he was involved in establishing the Ost-Europa Institut, first at Freiburg and later in Kiel, where it was renamed J.G. Herder Forschungsstelle für Musikgeschichte. Subsequently he moved to Vienna where he founded the periodical *Musica slavica*, of which only one volume appeared in 1977. Arro was one of the finest and most erudite scholars of Russian music history and musical life. Before he moved to Germany he published a number of studies on the history of music in the Baltic countries; while in Kiel, he established a superb collection of publications dealing with the history of music in eastern Europe, particularly the history of Russian chant. He was the founder and editor of the first four volumes of *Musik des Ostens* (until 1967).

WRITINGS

Über das Musikleben in Estland im 19. Jahrhundert (diss., U. of Vienna, 1928)

'Zum Problem der Kannel', *Sitzungsberichte der Gelehrten Estnischen Gesellschaft* (1929), 158–90

'Baltische Choralbücher und ihre Verfasser', *AcM*, iii (1931), 112–19, 166–70

'Die Dorpater Stadt-Musici, 1587–1809', *Sitzungsberichte der Gelehrten Estnischen Gesellschaft* (1931)

Geschichte der estnischen Musik, i (Tartu, 1933)

'Das estnische Musikschaffen der Gegenwart', *Baltische Revue* (1935)

'F. David und das Liphart-Quartet in Dorpat', *Baltische Revue* (1935)

ed., with others: *Musika sovetskoy Estonii* (Tallinn, 1956)

'Hauptprobleme der osteuropäischen Musikgeschichte', *Musik des Ostens*, i (1962), 9–48

'Über einige neuere deutsche Publikationen zur russischen Musikgeschichte', *Musik des Ostens*, i (1962), 122–40

'Das Ost-West-Schisma in der Kirchenmusik: über die Wesensverschiedenheit der Grundlagen kultischer Musik in Ost und West', *Musik des Ostens*, ii (1963), 7–83

'Die deutschbaltische Liedschule: Versuch einer nachträglichen musikhistorischen Rekonstruktion', *Musik des Ostens*, iii (1965), 175–239

'Richard Wagners Rigaer Wanderjahre: über einige baltische Züge im Schaffen Wagners', *Musik des Ostens*, iii (1965), 123–68

'Die russische Literatur-Oper, eine musikslawistische Studie', *ÖMz*, xxvi (1971), 538–77

'Die Frage der Existenz einer lokalen Dialekt: Variante des
gregorianischen chorals im Baltikum des 13.–15. Jahrhunderts',
Musica antiqua IV: Bydgoszcz 1975, 7–44
'Die altrussische Glockenmusik: eine musikslavistische
Untersuchung', *Musica slavica* (Wiesbaden, 1977), 77–159
'Sergej Prokofjews "Iwan der Schreckliche"', *ÖMz*, xxxvi (1981),
573–7

BIBLIOGRAPHY
Yu.V. Keldïsh: Obituary, *SovM* (1986), no.4, 115 only

MILOŠ VELIMIROVIĆ

Arroio [Arroyo], João Marcelino (*b* Oporto, 4 Oct 1861;
d Colares, 18 May 1930). Portuguese composer of Spanish
descent. A politician and member of the Coimbra
University law faculty, he practised music as an amateur.
His most significant work, the *drama lírico* in three acts
Amore e Perdizione, is based on Camilo Castelo Branco's
Portuguese novel *Amor de Perdição*. First performed at
the S Carlos, Lisbon, in 1907, it was later translated into
German as *Liebe und Verderben* for a Hamburg performance of 1910. The second act of Arroio's second *drama
lírico*, the four-act *Leonora Telles* to his own libretto, was
performed posthumously in 1941 and four years later the
entire opera was staged, in a Portuguese version. Dramatically, Arroio's operas are similar to the nationalist operas
of his compatriots Keil and Ferreira Veiga. At a stylistic
level, however, they attempt to escape from the Italian
style prevalent in Portugal through an intensive use of
chromaticism (particularly in *Leonora Telles*) more akin
to that of Wagner. Arroio's non-stage works include short
piano pieces, some of which were published in Leipzig
(1908–9), and a symphonic poem *Amor*, first performed
in 1913 in Lisbon.

WORKS
(selective list)

Stage: Amore e Perdizione (drama lírico, 3, F. Braga, after C. Castelo
Branco), *c*1907 (Mainz, 1909); Leonora Telles (drama lírico, 4,
Arroio), *c*1910, vs (Leipzig, 1910)
Other: Amor, sym. poem, orch, perf. 1913; Inez de Castro (cant.); pf
pieces, some pubd (Leipzig, 1908, 1909); songs

BIBLIOGRAPHY
F. Lisboa: 'Amor de Perdição', *A arte musical*, no.197 (1907), 56–61
A. Pinto Sacavém: *Camilo na música* (Lisbon, 1926)
'Arroio, João Marcelino', *Grande enciclopédia portuguesa e
brasileira* (Lisbon and Rio de Janeiro, 1936–60)
'Arroio, 2. João Marcelino', *Dicionário de música*, ed. T. Borba and
F.L. Graça (Lisbon, 1962)
R.V. Nery and P.F. Castro: *História da música: sínteses da cultura
portuguesa* (Lisbon, 1991)
M.C. Brito and L. Cymbron: *História da música portuguesa* (Lisbon,
1992)

LUISA CYMBRON

Arrow Music Press. American music publishing firm which
from 1938 leased the catalogue of the Cos Cob Press.

Arroyo, João Marcelino. *See* Arroio, João Marcelino.

Arroyo, Martina (*b* New York, 2 Feb 1937). American
soprano. She studied at Hunter College, New York, and
(with Grace Bumbry) won the 1958 Metropolitan Opera
Auditions. That year she sang in the American première
of Pizzetti's *L'assassinio nella cattedrale* at Carnegie Hall.
After taking minor roles at the Metropolitan, she went to
Europe, for major roles at Vienna, Düsseldorf, Berlin,
Frankfurt and Zürich (where she was under contract from
1963 to 1968). In 1965 she was a substitute Aida for
Birgit Nilsson at the Metropolitan; she played there all
the major Verdi parts that formed the basis of her

repertory, as well as Donna Anna, Cio-Cio-San, Liù,
Santuzza, Gioconda and Elsa. She made her London
début as Valentine at a concert performance of *Les
Huguenots* in 1968 – the year of her first Covent Garden
appearance, as Aida. Her rich, powerfully projected voice,
heard to greatest advantage in the Verdi *spinto* roles, was
flexible enough for Mozart (she recorded Donna Elvira
with Böhm and Donna Anna with Colin Davis). In the
USA she has often sung in oratorio and recital – she was
the first performer of Barber's concert scena, *Andromache's Farewell* (April 1963). Arroyo's most admired
recordings include Hélène (*Les vêpres siciliennes*), Amelia
(*Un ballo in maschera*), Leonora (*La forza del destino*)
and Aida.

BIBLIOGRAPHY
J.B. Steane: *The Grand Tradition* (London, 1974/R), 413ff

ALAN BLYTH

Ars Antiqua [Ars Veterum, Ars Vetus] (Lat.: 'old art'). A
term used by a group of writers, mostly active in Paris in
the early 14th century, to distinguish the polyphony and
notation of the immediate past from the new practice of
their own time, the Ars Nova (Ars Modernorum),
especially that associated with Philippe de Vitry, Johannes
de Muris and their circle in the 1310s and 20s. (The word
'ars', as understood in the Middle Ages, translates the
Greek word *technē*, a 'technique' or 'craft', and has no
aesthetic connotations.)

Among music theorists, the champion of the Ars
Antiqua was Jacobus of Liège, who in his encyclopedic
Speculum musice (1320s) upheld the authority of Franco
of Cologne, Magister Lambertus (whom he called 'Aristotle') and Petrus de Cruce, and while criticizing the
moderns defined the main virtues of the old practice: (1)
modern composers wrote only motets and chansons,
neglecting other genres such as organum, conductus and
hocket (CSM, iii/7, p.89); (2) modern composers used a
multiplicity of imperfect mensurations alongside perfect
ones in their work, whereas the old practice, following
Franco and Lambertus, adhered exclusively to perfection
(CSM, iii/7, pp.86–8); (3) the moderns divided semibreves
into smaller values, perfect and imperfect groups of
minims and semiminims, whereas the followers of the Ars
Antiqua divided breves only into semibreves in perfect
mensuration, holding that the semibreve was indivisible
(CSM, iii/7, pp.35–6, 51–3); (4) as a consequence,
paradoxically, the rhythmic language used by the moderns
was much more limited and inflexible than that of the
adherents to the old practice (CSM, iii/7, pp.38–9); (5)
the moderns engaged in a great deal of experimentation
with notation, resulting in an inconsistent practice,
whereas the followers of Franco had a clear and
established tradition for notating their music (CSM, iii/7,
pp.51–3); (6) the moderns indulged too much in quirky
and capricious rhythmic movement, *musica lasciva*, while
the followers of the old practice kept within the confines
of a more restrained *musica modesta* (CSM, iii/1, p.60).
From this it is evident that the Ars Antiqua is the musical
practice of the latter half of the 13th century, preserved
most comprehensively in manuscripts such as *F-MOf*
H196, *D-BAs* Lit.115, and *I-Tr* Vari 42, and described
by the theorists mentioned above, the many commentaries, *abbreviationes*, and *compendia* based on Franco's *Ars
cantus mensurabilis*, and the *De musica* of Johannes de
Grocheio. Such manuscripts as *B-Br* 19606 and *F-Pn*
fr.146 (the *Roman de Fauvel*), both from the second

decade of the 14th century, are transitional in a sense, containing works in both Ars Antiqua and Ars Nova.

The definition of the term 'Ars Antiqua' is often extended now to include the music of the Notre Dame period and its main composers, Leoninus and Perotinus. The genres that Jacobus praised and the rhythmic idiom he discussed developed from this earlier tradition; and indeed, the repertories of organum and conductus belong properly to that tradition rather than to the period with which he was concerned. In this more comprehensive definition, then, the Ars Antiqua includes two large historical periods, the Notre Dame school, dating from about 1160 to about 1250 and preserved in manuscripts such as *I-Fl* Plut.29.1, *D-W* 628, *D-W* 1099, and *E-Mn* 20486, and the period from about 1250 to about 1320, specifically referred to by Jacobus. The former is characterized by liturgical polyphony with Latin texts and by modal rhythm and an emerging mensural notation; the latter is dominated by controlled mensural rhythm and a developed notation, and by the genre of the motet, above all the French motet, but it also saw the beginning of a written tradition of instrumental music and secular polyphonic song. The earlier genres of conductus and organum were extensively reworked in the light of the changed aesthetic that came with mensural rhythm; it is undoubtedly through such modernized versions that Jacobus knew the earlier repertory. Whatever merits the expanded definition of the Ars Antiqua may have, a distinctly new period, an Ars Nova, did emerge in the 1310s and 20s. While many of the innovations of the Ars Nova were indeed radical, many others represent extensions of the earlier practice; thus Philippe de Vitry expressly based his rhythmic system on the Ars Vetus of Franco. Sensitivity to these changes and expansions of Ars Antiqua practices on the part of modern and more conservative musicians alike doubtless moulded the rather polemical distinction Jacobus drew between the two *artes*.

See also ARS NOVA; SOURCES, MS, §§IV, V, VII; and THEORY, THEORISTS, §6–7.

BIBLIOGRAPHY

MGG1 (H. Besseler); *MGG1* ('Notre-Dame-Epoche', H. Husmann); *MGG2* (W. Frobenius)

R. Bragard, ed.: *Jacobi leodiensis speculum musicae*, CSM, iii (1955–73)

L. Schrade: 'The Chronology of the Ars nova in France', *L'Ars Nova: Wégimont 1955*, 37–62

F.J. Smith: *Jacobi leodiensis speculum musicae: a Commentary* (Brooklyn, NY, 1966–83)

M. Huglo: 'De Francon de Cologne à Jacques de Liège', *RBM*, xxxiv–xxxv (1980–81), 44–60

M. Haas: 'Studien zur mittelalterlichen Musiklehre I: eine Übersicht über die Musiklehre im Kontext der Philosophie des 13. und frühen 14. Jahrhunderts', *Forum musicologicum*, iii (1982), 323–456

R. Eberlein: 'Ars antiqua: Harmonik und Datierung', *AMw*, xliii (1986), 1–16

S. Pinegar: *Textual and Contextual Relationships among Theoretical Writings on Measurable Music of the Thirteenth and Early Fourteenth Centuries* (diss., Columbia U., 1991)

GORDON A. ANDERSON/EDWARD H. ROESNER

ARSC. *See* ASSOCIATION FOR RECORDED SOUND COLLECTIONS.

Arsenal, Chansonnier de l' (*F-Pa* 5198). *See* SOURCES, MS, §III, 4.

Arsis, thesis (Gk.: 'raising', 'lowering'). In measured music, the terms used respectively for unstressed and stressed beats or other equidistant subdivisions of the bar. Originally they referred to raising and lowering the foot in ancient Greek dance. Later they were applied to the unaccented and accented parts of a poetic foot, and hence acquired their association with weak and strong beats. For music since the 17th century they mean much the same as, respectively, UPBEAT (or OFF-BEAT) and DOWNBEAT; the directions 'up' and 'down' remain associated with them by their respective functions in conducting.

In 1558 Zarlino coined the expression *fuga per arsin et thesin* to refer to imitative counterpoint in which the answering voice inverted the theme stated by the leading voice. Although this is in reality a misapplication of the original Greek terms, most musicians of the late Renaissance and Baroque who were familiar with Zarlino's work, including Morley and J.G. Walther, accepted the association with imitation by inversion. Marpurg (*Abhandlung von der Fuge*, 1753–4) reconciled the two conflicting traditions by redefining 'per arsin et thesin' to refer to the entrance of a theme (usually a fugue subject) with displaced accents, former strong beats becoming weak and vice versa. Entries in stretto (*see* STRETTO (i)) may well be 'per arsin et thesin' but are not usually referred to as such because the 'strong' and 'weak' beats of the subject are superimposed. Displacement of the subject by half a bar in 4/4 time, common in Baroque fugue, does not constitute an example of the device.

PAUL WALKER

Ars Nova (Lat.: 'new art'). In the most general terms Ars Nova is used as a synonym for '14th-century polyphony' just as Ars Antiqua stands for '13th-century polyphony'. The concept of Ars Nova is based on the enormous new range of musical expression made possible by the notational techniques explained in Philippe de Vitry's treatise *Ars nova* (c1322). The term was first used as a historical slogan by Johannes Wolf in his *Geschichte der Mensural-Notation* (1904) in which the treatise was seen as one of the major turning-points in the history of notation; and it was perhaps the chapter titles rather than the specific content of Wolf's work that brought about the use of 'Ars Nova' to include all 14th-century French music in the work of subsequent scholars.

Several early 14th-century theorists referred to the idea of an ARS ANTIQUA, represented primarily by Franco, and an Ars Nova instituted by Philippe de Vitry (see, for instance, *CoussemakerS*, iii, 371, 408); but in historical terms the usefulness of the idea is supported more by the treatise *Ars novae musicae* (c1320) of Johannes de Muris, the 1324–5 bull of Pope John XXII decrying the musicians who were 'novellae scholae discipuli' and the reference in Jacobus of Liège's *Speculum musice* to 'moderni cantores' and to 'aliqui nunc novi'. That there was some awareness of a change in musical techniques and outlook in the years around 1320 is suggested also by the earliest music to exemplify the notation described in Philippe de Vitry's treatise, the motets for the ROMAN DE FAUVEL copied into manuscript *F-Pn* fr.146 in 1316, some of them extensive works several times longer than the motets of the previous generation and displaying a range of notational values far greater than it was possible to notate with the previous Franconian and post-Franconian techniques.

Relatively few French musical sources survive from the years immediately following the *Roman de Fauvel* manuscript, and those few are fragments whose dating and provenance are subject to substantial disagreement, so there remain very few sources in the purest Ars Nova notation as described by PHILIPPE DE VITRY. The term was therefore almost inevitably applied (by Wolf and many later scholars) to the work of Machaut and, since several Machaut manuscripts are from the early 15th century, to all French 14th-century music in spite of Schrade's insistence that after 1330 the style was no longer new. Indeed, so convenient was the label that it came to stand for all music between the *Roman de Fauvel* and the Renaissance: thus volume iii of the New Oxford History of Music is entitled *Ars Nova and the Renaissance, 1300–1540* (London, 1960) and the major historical surveys in *MGG* follow the sequence 'Ars Antiqua', 'Ars Nova', 'Renaissance'. In such surveys Ars Nova can include music from all parts of Europe and stretch to about 1420 (*see* MEDIEVAL).

Italian music of the 14th century is now more often separated off with the name 'trecento'; but there is a reasonable (and strong) school of opinion that since the surviving repertory stretches from about 1325 to 1425 it is historically misleading to call it by a name that implies a division at the year 1400, and geographically separatist to use such an exclusively Italian name. Major considerations in support of excluding Italy from the idea of Ars Nova are: that Italian music until about 1370 was stylistically and notationally entirely different from French music; and that Italian notation evolved more gradually and a precise demarcation point between an Ars Antiqua and an Ars Nova in Italy cannot be established in any historically useful sense (see Clercx).

On the other hand it is hard to resist the claims of Nino Pirrotta (1966) that the fundamental change in both France and Italy in the years around 1320 was the same: that for the first time 'it required that the length of every sound be precisely determined so that the different voices could proceed on schedule and fall precisely into the combinations of sound and rhythm determined by the composer'. While that was just the culmination of processes that had been in hand for the preceding half-century, it remains one of the most startling and important moments in the history of music. No historian has ever denied that French and Italian music in the first half of the 14th century are, in general, stylistically quite different; but it is too easy to overlook the range of styles within each tradition, to impose facile boundaries. Moreover, Pirrotta's analysis allows room for seeing the undeniable links between musical evolution in all parts of Europe, including England and the eastern parts of the empire.

A further narrowing down of the terminology has been effected by Günther who formulated the term ARS SUBTILIOR to designate music of the post-Machaut generation of composers, those musicians of an International Gothic who fused the styles of France and Italy, paving the way for the simpler styles of the 15th century. In a sense this terminology is again an attempt to transfer a description of a notational style (called by Apel 'manneristic notation') to denote a musical style. The difficulty in this analysis is that many simpler styles in French music co-existed with the intricate music of the Ars Subtilior; that is, the Ars Subtilior did not replace existing styles, and its techniques were not fundamentally different from what had existed before, merely more elaborate. But since this distinction has been generally accepted and has led to the French Ars Nova being considered to end about 1370,

at a time when French and Italian styles were still clearly separated, there has been subsequently less force of opinion to support any references to an Italian Ars Nova.

It is therefore customary to use 'Ars Nova' to refer to French music from the *Roman de Fauvel* to the death of Machaut, for though this is not historically the most precise way of using the term, it is historiographically the most useful. At the same time it is worth observing that 'Ars Nova', like 'Renaissance', is a term found at many times in the course of history (see Schrade). Perhaps the most famous use outside the 14th century is that of Tinctoris (*CoussemakerS*, iv, 154), who described Dunstaple (*d* 1453) as 'ut ita dicam, novae artis fons et origo'.

BIBLIOGRAPHY

DEUMM (N. Pirrotta); *LaMusicaE* (N. Pirrotta); *MGG1* (H. Besseler); *MGG2* (K. Kügle)

J. Wolf: *Geschichte der Mensural-Notation von 1250–1460* (Leipzig, 1904/*R*)

H. Riemann: *Handbuch der Musikgeschichte*, i/2 (Leipzig, 1905/*R*)

S. Clercx: 'Propos sur l'Ars Nova', *RBM*, x (1956), 154–62

C. van den Borren: 'L'Ars Nova', *L'Ars Nova: Wégimont II 1955*, 17–26

E. Perroy: 'Le point de vue de l'historien', ibid., 261–9

N. Pirrotta: 'Cronologia e denominazione dell'Ars Nova italiana', ibid., 93–109

L. Schrade: 'The Chronology of the Ars Nova in France', ibid., 37–62

U. Günther: 'Das Ende der Ars Nova', *Mf*, xvi (1963), 105–20

F.J. Smith: 'Ars Nova: a Re-Definition?', *MD*, xviii (1964), 19–35; xix (1965), 83–97

N. Pirrotta: 'Ars Nova e stil novo', *RIM*, i (1966), 3–19

S. Fuller: 'A Phantom Treatise of the Fourteenth Century? Ars Nova', *JM*, iv (1985–6), 23–50

D. Leech-Wilkinson: 'Ars Antiqua – Ars Nova – Ars Subtilior', *Antiquity and the Middle Ages*, ed. J. McKinnon (London, 1990), 218–40

DAVID FALLOWS

Ars Subtilior (Lat.: 'more subtle art'). The highly refined musical style of the late 14th century, centred primarily on the secular courts of southern France, Aragon and Cyprus. The term was introduced to musicological vocabulary by Ursula Günther and derives from references in (?)Philippus de Caserta's *Tractatus de diversis figuris* to composers moving away from the style of the ARS NOVA motets 'post modum subtiliorem comparantes' and developing an 'artem magis subtiliter' as exemplified in the motet *Apta caro* (*CoussemakerS*, iii, 118); similarly Egidius de Murino referred to composition 'per viam subtilitatis' in his *Tractatus cantus mensurabilis* (*CoussemakerS*, iii, 127). The development of the idiom (chiefly encountered in *grandes ballades*) may be traced in successive, roughly chronological stages. Of these, the post-Machaut generation – De Landes, Franciscus, Grimace, Pierre de Molins, Solage, Susay (*A l'arbre sec*) and Vaillant – was largely engaged in developing the classical ballade style of Machaut.

There is a more florid extension in the works of Matheus de Sancto Johanne, Goscalch, Hasprois and Olivier. Aside from the growing contrapuntal independence of the contratenor, their works are notable for an admirable tonal and motivic cohesion. That Hasprois' *Ma doulce amour* is found in *GB-Ob* Can.misc.213 (after 1428) illustrates the underlying link between the early Ars Subtilior and the subsequent 15th-century chanson. The final disruption of the traditional Machaut style occurs in the compositions of Cuvelier, Egidius, Johannes de Alte Curie, Philippus de Caserta and Trebor. Their music is permeated with lavish minim displacements and italianate sequential patterns. Yet more advanced was a final group of composers (Rodericus, Zacharia and

Jaquemin de Senleches), who used elaborate rhythmic subdivisions, displacements (using split colorations), proportional, motet-like devices and multiple tonal layers. On occasion, even the less radical composers (such as Solage and Galiot in *S'aincy estoit* and *Le sault perilleux*) adopted this style, which ultimately spread to the French cultural outpost of Cyprus (anonymous ballade *Sur toute fleur, c*1410).

BIBLIOGRAPHY

U. Günther: 'Die Anwendung der Diminution in der Handschrift Chantilly 1047', *AMw*, xvii (1960), 1–21

U. Günther: 'Der Gebrauch des tempus perfectum diminutum in der Handschrift Chantilly 1047', *AMw*, xvii (1960), 277–97

J. Hirshberg: *The Music of the Late Fourteenth Century: a Study in Musical Style* (diss., U. of Pennsylvania, 1971)

G. Greene, ed.: *French Secular Music*, PMFC, xviii–xx (Monaco, 1981–2)

N. Josephson: 'Intersectional Relationships in the French *grande ballade*', *MD*, xl (1986), 79–97

NORS S. JOSEPHSON

Ars Veterum. *See* ARS ANTIQUA.

Ars Viva. German firm of music publishers. It was founded in Zürich in 1950 by Hermann Scherchen (1891–1966) to publish music by postwar avant-garde composers. The future of the Ars Viva catalogue was assured when in 1953 it was incorporated into the catalogue of B. Schott's Söhne, Mainz (*see* SCHOTT). Since then the Ars Viva list has gradually increased, its scores being mostly by such contemporary German and Swiss composers as Holliger, Klaus Huber, Klebe, Rolf Liebermann and Aribert Reimann, as well as including important compositions by Dallapiccola and Castiglioni and most of the early works of Nono. In addition, the firm has published a few relatively unknown works by earlier composers, including Beethoven, Cavalieri and Pergolesi, some in editions by Scherchen himself. (A. Melichar: *Musik in der Zwangsjacke: die deutsche Musik zwischen Orff und Schönberg*, Vienna and Stuttgart, 2/1959)

ALAN POPE

Artaria. Austrian firm of music publishers. It was founded in Mainz in 1765 and by 1768 was operating in Vienna, where it became the first important music publishing firm in the city.

1. History. 2. Publications.

1. HISTORY.   The Artaria family originated in Blevio on Lake Como, Italy. On 15 January 1759 the brothers Cesare Timoteo (1706–85), Domenico (i) (1715–84) and Giovanni Casimiro Artaria (1725–97) obtained passes to visit the fairs in Frankfurt, Leipzig and Würzburg; Carlo (1747–1808), son of Cesare, and Francesco (1744–1808), son of Domenico (i), accompanied them as *giovini* (commercial assistants). Cesare and Domenico (i) returned to their own country; Carlo and Francesco founded with their uncle Giovanni Casimiro the firm Giovanni Artaria & Co. in Mainz in 1765. By 1768, however, the cousins had moved to Vienna, where they at first carried on business without their own premises. According to the *Wienerisches Diarium* of 25 July 1770, Carlo owned a shop in the Kleine Dorotheergasse until that date, but there is no further evidence to support this. On 31 October 1770 the shop later known as 'Zum König von Dänemark' was opened in a house owned by Josef Christoph von Zorn, a civil servant. The firm was called Cugini Artaria, becoming Artaria & Comp. in 1771; the licence granted to Carlo Artaria dated 23 February 1770 covered only

dealings in copper engravings. In 1774 connections with the firm in Mainz were re-established. The businesses developed so favourably that on 28 January 1775 the Vienna firm was able to open a shop near the Kohlmarkt, which also bore the name 'Zum König von Dänemark'.

Giovanni Casimiro's son Pasquale (1755–8) entered the business as his father's successor and from 19 October 1776 (*Wienerisches Diarium*, no.84) trade in printed music began with the import of works from London, Amsterdam and particularly Paris (no first stock catalogue is extant). With the new dealing in printed music, plans for a music publishing business were also developed; the rise of the Viennese Classical period provided an encouraging context. The Paris music publisher Anton Huberty offered a stimulus to the business side of the undertaking. He had been selling his publications on the Viennese market since 1770 through various booksellers; at the beginning of 1777 he moved to Vienna with his family and established himself very successfully with a music engraving shop, but, owing to his failure to obtain a licence for exclusive protection, his undertaking was short-lived (he subsequently worked as an engraver for Artaria). The Artarias took the opportunity to issue their first publication, six trios by Paolo Bonaga, on 12 August 1778 (the plate numbers 1 and 2 of these minor works were later reassigned to Pleyel's quartets op.1); the firm's first extant music catalogue was published in 1779.

In 1780 Ignazio Artaria (1757–1820), brother of Francesco, was appointed a partner in the business. Artaria was granted a ten-year printing privilege on 28 January 1782 by the *Reichshofsrat* of Emperor Joseph II: published pieces from this time bear the mark C.P.S.C.M. ('cum privilegio Suae Caesareae Majestatis'). After the death of Pasquale Artaria in 1786, Ignazio's brother Domenico (ii) (1765–1823) became a partner in the business, and in the same year the firm set up its own music engraving workshop, using pewter plates. The firm expanded dramatically during the late 1780s with the acquisition of new printing presses. Another publisher, Christoph Torricella, a competitor in the Viennese market since 31 January 1781, and now in his 70s, was soon outstripped: on 12 August 1786 Artaria bought 980 of his engraving plates at a public auction, together with all his publishing rights.

In 1789 the flourishing business was transferred to the house 'Zum englischen Gruss', in the Kohlmarkt. In the early 1790s the firm began experimenting with new printing techniques, notably the fashionable *à la poupée* method of printing in colour from a single multi-coloured plate. A new cylinder press, designed in London, was acquired to increase productivity. Domenico (ii), who with his brother Giovanni Maria (1771–1835) had carried on the Mainz branch of the firm, becoming a partner in 1787, resigned in 1793, bringing about the final division of the firm, until then known as 'Artaria & Comp., Wien und Mainz'. The Mainz branch moved to Mannheim and combined with the firm of Fontaine to form an art bookshop and publishing business which existed until 1867.

Giovanni CAPPI (1765–1815, whose sister, Maria, Carlo Artaria subsequently married) became an apprentice in the firm in 1773, then an employee, and finally a partner in 1793. Another employee, TRANQUILLO MOLLO (1767–1837), from Bellinzona, also became a partner, in 1793. Finally Pietro Cappi (*fl c*1790–1830), a nephew of

Giovanni, was employed in the firm. During these years an increasing number of music publications were transferred from the publisher FRANZ ANTON HOFFMEISTER to Artaria. Between 1793 and 1798 the Artaria firm had five partners: Carlo, Francesco and Ignazio Artaria, as well as Cappi and Mollo. The war years and disagreements within the firm brought about a crisis which lasted until 1804 and had an extremely detrimental effect on the business. Ignazio and Mollo left the firm in 1798; the former returned to Italy while Mollo established his own shop in partnership with Domenico (iii) (1775–1842), son of Francesco. Although Francesco and Carlo signed a new three-year contract on 9 March 1801, a further division was agreed two months later when Francesco's capital was transferred to Domenico (iii). Carlo, who had continued as sole owner of the Artaria & Co. shop on the Kohlmarkt, sold the remaining stock to Mollo on 27 August 1802. Domenico (iii) then moved to the Kohlmarkt and for a time the two shops were run in association, although each mantained separate accounts. A final split occurred in 1805, when Pietro Cappi, a nephew of Giovanni, became Domenico's junior partner. Pietro remained in the firm until 1816; from 1807 until 1824 Carlo Boldroni was a third partner. In about 1830 the firm opened an auction room. After the death of Domenico (iii) on 5 June 1842, his son August (1807–93), who had entered the firm in 1833, became sole owner. The music publications of the house became fewer; new publishers were appearing and capturing the market, in particular Haslinger, Diabelli and Mechetti. In February 1858 the *Wiener Zeitung* carried the last announcement of an Artaria music publication (although the *Denkmäler der Tonkunst in Österreich* bears the Artaria imprint between 1894 and 1918). August's sons Karl August (1855–1919) and Dominik (1858–1936) entered the firm in 1881 and 1890 respectively, and after their father's death in 1893 became sole owners.

Mathias Artaria (1793–1835), son of Domenico (ii), was involved in music publishing independently of the family firm. He took over Daniel Sprenger's arts shop in 1818; his firm (which issued some Schubert first editions) was continued after his death (in 1835) by his widow (*see* MAISCH, LUDWIG).

2. PUBLICATIONS. The Artaria firm's activities began in the art trade and expanded into geography and iconography. In these areas it achieved world-wide importance, and the art and map publishing business was carried on as an integral branch of the firm into the 20th century. The arts shop offered paintings, foreign art journals, engravings, lithographs, contemporary portraits of famous men (from its own press) and numerous pictorial views; the house of Artaria gained international recognition and established itself as a cultural focus of the Viennese nobility and upper middle classes.

It was in music publishing however that the firm revealed a particularly felicitous touch (although its first owners apparently had no musical education). As early as 1779 they established contact with Joseph Haydn and on 12 April 1780 they published a set of his piano sonatas (HXVI:20, 35–9) with plate no.7; this inaugurated a series of over 300 editions of Haydn's compositions (see illustration). Composer and publisher enjoyed a warm relationship, reflected in their lively correspondence. The firm's first Mozart editon, consisting of the six sonatas for piano and violin K296 and K376–380, appeared on 8

Title-page of the first edition of Haydn's Six Quartets op.33 (Vienna: Artaria, 1782)

December 1781. Artaria subsequently became Mozart's chief publisher and issued 83 first editions and 36 early editions of his music before 1800, in addition to publications taken over from Hoffmeister. The young Beethoven, on arriving in Vienna, was also quickly drawn to Artaria; his first published work, a set of piano variations, appeared on 31 July 1793, followed by first editions of his works up to op.8. Despite subsequent disagreements, the firm continued to receive new works from Beethoven, and by 1858 editions of his works – including arrangements and reprints – numbered over 100. The numerous surviving catalogues from this early period reveal many other well-known names, including Boccherini, Clementi, Gluck, Leopold Kozeluch, Pleyel, Salieri and Vanhal.

A unique business relationship developed between Artaria and the composer and music publisher F.A. Hoffmeister, who until the turn of the century several times simply surrendered portions of his publishing business to Artaria. In 1802 production had reached publication no.906, almost entirely works of fine quality. Then came the interregnum of co-production with T. Mollo & Co., which embraces publication nos.907–1000 as well as 1501–1692 and which ended by 25 August 1804. Nos.1001–1500 are found in the firm's main ledger reserved for a series with the title *Raccolta d'arie*, but in fact were used for the publication of piano reductions from current operas and of individual arias (the pieces appeared between 1787 and 1804 with the special 'Raccolta' number, as distinguished from the plate number, on the bottom left margin). While at first using several independent music engravers, Artaria later employed its own engravers and also established its own press. Ferdinand Kauer is known to have been employed as a publisher's reader, and according to his own records carried out his duties for 17 years. Beyond its encouragement of Classical composers, the firm was committed to a demanding publishing programme; an impressive list of other composers, represented by numerous works, included Cramer, Hummel, Moscheles, Rossini, Sarti and Sterkel (Schubert, however, published only three works with Artaria).

Towards the middle of the 19th century publishing activities waned and works of poor quality began to be accepted; in 1858, under August Artaria, the music publishing house closed down. In 1894 the remaining assets were sold to the Viennese music publisher Josef Weinberger. The important collection of autographs which the family had accumulated over the years, partly through publishing activities and partly through subsequent independent purchases by Domenico Artaria (iii), was later transferred to the Preussische Staatsbibliothek. A large portion of the firm's administrative archive was acquired by the Stadt- und Landesbibliothek, Vienna, in 1936.

BIBLIOGRAPHY

L. von Köchel: *Chronologisch-thematisches Verzeichnis sämtlicher Tonwerke Wolfgang Amadé Mozarts* (Leipzig, 1862, rev. 6/1964 by F. Giegling, A. Weinmann and G. Sievers)

G. Adler, ed.: *Verzeichniss der musikalischen Autographe von Ludwig van Beethoven … im Besitze von A. Artaria in Wien* (Vienna, 1890)

A. Artaria: *Verzeichnis von musikalischen Autographen revidirten Abschriften und einigen seltenen gedruckten Original-Ausgaben … im Besitze von Artaria in Wien* (Vienna, 1893)

F. Artaria and H.Botstiber: *Joseph Haydn und das Verlagshaus Artaria* (Vienna, 1909)

J.P. Larsen: *Die Haydn-Überlieferung* (Copenhagen, 1939/R)

P. Arrigoni: *Gli Artaria di Milano: contributo alla storia editoriale cittadina dell'Ottocento* (Milan, 1952)

A. Weinmann: *Vollständiges Verlagsverzeichnis Artaria & Comp.* (Vienna, 1952, suppl. *Verzeichnis der Musikalien des Verlages Maisch, Sprenger, Artaria*, 1970; 2/1978)

G. Kinsky and H.Halm: *Das Werk Beethovens: thematisch-bibliographisches Verzeichnis seiner sämtlichen vollendeten Kompositionen* (Munich, 1955)

A. van Hoboken: *Joseph Haydn: thematisch-bibliographisches Werkverzeichnis* (Mainz, 1957–78)

A. Weinmann: *Verlagsverzeichnis Tranquillo Mollo* (Vienna, 1964, suppl. 1972)

A. Weinmann: *Verlagsverzeichnis Giovanni Cappi bis A.O. Witzendorf* (Vienna, 1967)

Geschichte der Firmen Artaria & Compagnie und Freytag-Berndt und Artaria (Vienna, 1970)

D. Johnson: 'The Artaria Collection of Beethoven Manuscripts: a New Source', *Beethoven Studies*, ed. A. Tyson (New York and London, 1973–4), 174–236

F. Slezak: 'Zur Firmengeschichte von Artaria & Compagnie', *BeJb 1973–7*, 453–68

R. Hilmar: *Der Musikverlag Artaria & Comp.: Geschichte und Probleme der Druckproduktion* (Tutzing, 1977)

G. Feder and F.H.Franken: 'Ein wiedergefundener Brief Haydns an Artaria & Co.', *Haydn-Studien*, v (1982), 55–9

G. Haberkamp: *Die Erstdrucke der Werke von Wolfgang Amadeus Mozart* (Tutzing, 1986)

G. Renner: *Die Nachlässe in der Wiener Stadt- und Landesbibliothek: ein Verzeichnis* (Vienna, 1993)

L. Weinhold and A.Weinmann: *Kataloge von Musikverlegern und Musikalienhändlern im deutschsprachigen Raum 1700–1850: Verzeichnis mit Fundortnachweisen* (Kassel, 1995)

D. Wyn Jones: 'From Artaria to Longman & Broderip: Mozart's Music on Sale in London', *Studies in Msuic History presented to H.C. Robbins Landon on his Seventieth Birthday*, ed. O. Biba and D. Wyn Jones (London, 1996), 105–14

R.M. Ridgewell: *Mozart and the Artaria Publishing House: Studies in the Inventory Ledgers, 1784–1793* (diss., U. of London, 1999)

ALEXANDER WEINMANN/RUPERT RIDGEWELL

Arteaga, Esteban de [Arteaga, Stefano] (*b* Moraleja de Coca, nr Segovia, 26 Dec 1747; *d* Paris, 30 Oct 1799). Spanish aesthetician and opera historian. After entering the Society of Jesus (1763) he studied in Madrid, Corsica and Italy, after which he abandoned the Society (1769) and attended Bologna University (1773–8). There at Padre Martini's behest he wrote the first critical history of opera, *Le rivoluzioni del teatro musicale italiano dalla sua origine fino al presente* (Bologna, 1783–8/R, 2/1785), which met with immediate success and was translated into German (1789) and French (1802). He moved to Venice and to Rome, where he prepared works on ideal beauty (1789) and ancient and modern rhythm. His last years were spent in travel.

The original edition of *Le rivoluzioni* began with chapters on opera aesthetics and on the suitability of Italian as a language for music. His somewhat muddled history did not get beyond the advent of Metastasio: he viewed the early 18th century as the Golden Age of Music, singling out the composers Vinci and Jommelli as exemplary and crediting Metastasio with having raised opera to the greatest perfection possible. The second, 'enlarged, varied and corrected' edition of 1785 acquired a detailed critique of the decadence into which opera had fallen since that time. Much of his criticism centres on the failure of composers to set the words in a natural way that conveyed the meaning and moved the listener. He deplored accompaniments that obscured the words, distorted the meaning, and were too noisy and heavily orchestrated, especially with winds. On the other hand, he praised Gluck for his sensitive text settings and the unity he achieved by means of continuous string accompaniments for recitative, credited Piccinni with having substituted the rondò for the distortions of da capo form, and cited other composers (Traetta, Paisiello, Sacchini and Sarti) and performers (Ferrari, Jarnovich, Lolli, Somis and Chiabrano, among others) whose work he believed had merit. Calzabigi countered with a sarcastic *Risposta* (Venice, 1790).

WRITINGS

Le rivoluzioni del teatro musicale italiano dalla sua origine fino al presente (Bologna, 1783–8/R, 2/1785; Ger. trans., 1789/R as *Geschichte der italiänischen Oper*; Fr. trans., 1802)

Investigaciones filosoficas sobre la belleza ideal, considerada como objeto de todas las artes de imitacion (Madrid, 1789), ed. A. Izquierdo (Madrid, 1993)

Della influenza degli arabi sull'origine della poesia moderna in Europa (Rome, 1791)

Del ritmo sonoro e del ritmo muto nella musica degli antichi (MS, c1796, *E-Mah*) [ed. in Batllori]

Lettere musico-filologiche (MS, c1796, *Mah*) [ed. in Batllori]

BIBLIOGRAPHY

M. Batllori: Introduction to Esteban de Arteaga: *Lettere musico-filologiche: II. Del ritmo sonoro* (Madrid, 1944)

R. Allorto: 'Stefano Arteaga e "Le rivoluzioni del teatro musicale italiano"', *RMI*, lii (1950), 124–7

V. Borghini: *Problemi d'estetica e di cultura nel Settecento spagnolo: Feijóo – Luzán – Arteaga* (Genoa, 1958)

E.M. Rudat: *The Aesthetic Ideas of Esteban de Arteaga: Origin, Meaning and Current Value* (diss., UCLA, 1969; pubd as *Las ideas estéticas de Esteban de Arteaga: origenes, significado y actualidad*, Madrid, 1971)

R. Freeman: *Opera without Drama: Currents of Change in Italian Opera, 1675–1725* (Ann Arbor, 1981), 93–6

G. Mangini: 'Le passioni, la virtù e la morale nella concezione tardo-settecentesca dell'opera a metastasiana', *RIM*, xxii (1987), 131–4

P. Pinamonti: 'Il ver si cerchi/non la vittoria: implicazioni filosofiche nel testo della Betulia metastasiana', *Mozart, Padova e la 'Betulia liberata': Padua 1989*, 73–86

MARITA P. McCLYMONDS

Arteaga, Manuel González Gaytán y. *See* GONZÁLEZ GAYTÁN Y ARTEAGA, MANUEL.

Artem′yev, Eduard Nikolayevich (*b* Novosibirsk, 30 November 1937). Russian composer. He attended the Moscow Conservatory (1955–60) where he studied composition under Shaporin and Sidel′nikov, polyphony under S.S. Bogatïryov and orchestration under Rakov. Later (1960–62), he studied general and musical acoustics and the theory and practice of electronic music under the guidance of Ye.A. Murzin (the engineer and mathematician who produced the first Soviet electronic ANS synthesiser). He worked as an engineer at the Institute for Electronic Research (1960–64), and then taught at the Institute of Culture (1964–86). In 1989 he became president of the Russian Association for electro-acoustic music, and in 1993 a member of the executive committee of ICEM (International Confederation for Electro-Acoustic Music). He is a laureate of the State Prize of the Russian Federation (1988, 1993, 1996), and a laureate of the 'Nika' Prize awarded by the Russian Academy for the art of cinematography.

Artem′yev is a unique figure among Russian composers. Having gained a formal conservatory education, he turned to electronic music, which at that time hardly existed at all in the USSR; in time he became a major Russian composer in this field. The study of the nature of sound and its capabilities in terms of timbre and dynamics was the basis of the works of the 1960s, especially the *Dvenadtsat′ vzglyadov na mir zvuka: variatsii na odin tembr* ('Twelve Views on the World of Sound: Variations on a Single Timbre'), where his starting point was the sound of the Yakut instrument, the temir-komuz, which is very rich in harmonics. The scores for Andrey Tarkovsky's films are also basically avant-garde; as a composer of film music Artem′yev has gained international recognition and has worked in Russia, the USA and in France.

In the mid-1970s the style of Artem′yev's music changed: the avant-garde use of sonoristic techniques was enriched by traditional elements (melody, tonality, fixed metre), initially via rock music. The combination of tradition, the avant garde and rock culture represents for Artem′yev a broader process of assimilation of styles and genres of earlier and contemporary music which itself is combined with a command of all existing acoustic space as a musical phenomenon. The grandest expression of this idea is to be found in the cantata *Ritual* ('Ritual'), written for the Olympic Games in Moscow (1980). The cantata is based on a symbiosis of styles and genres on the broadest possible scale to which electronic music lends a general coherence. The principle of symbiosis is equally important for Aterm′yev's later compositions.

WORKS

Stage: Za myortvïmi dushami [In Search of Dead Souls] (ballet-pantomime, after N. Gogol), S, orch, 1966; Raskol′nikov (op, A. Konchalovsky, M. Rozovsky, Yu. Ryashentsev, after F. Dostoyevsky: *Prestupleniye i nakazaniye* [Crime and Punishment], 1987, rev. 1996; Teplo zemli [The Heat of the Earth] (op, Ye. Kompanyets), 1988

Choral orch: Ya ubit podo Rzhevom [I was Killed near Rzhevo] (orat, A. Tvardovsky), Bar, chorus, orch, 1960; Lubki [Woodcuts], suite, chorus, orch, 1962; Vol′nïye pesni [Free Songs] (cant., trad.), chorus, orch, 1968; Ritual (cant., P. de Coubertain), T, choruses, rock group, orch, elecs, 1980, rev. as Oda dobromu vestniku [Ode to a Good Messenger], 1987; Tam i zdes′ [There and Here] (Ryashentsev), S, T, rock singer, orch 1996

Orch: Poëma, va, orch, 1958; Khorovodï [Round Dances], suite, orch, 1959; Okean [The Ocean], sym. poem, 1972; Pf Conc., 1994

Vocal: Romansï, 1v, pf, 1955–60; Teplo zemli [The Heat of the Earth] (song cycle, Yu. Rïtkheu), Mez, rock group, electronics, 1981; 4 poëmï (P. Celan, V. Dagurov, S. Geda), S, insts, electronics, 1982; Leto [Summer] (Geda), S, vn, synths, 1989; Fantom iz Mongolii [A Phantom from Mongolia], female v, synths, 1991

Pf: preludes, pf, 1956–9; Sonatina, pf, 1957

Numerous elec compositions, over 30 incid scores for the theatre, over 50 film scores, incl. Solaris (A. Tarkovsky), 1972

WRITINGS

'Slovo molodyozhi: E. Artem′yev [A word to young people], *SovM* (1968), no.5, 20 only

'God minuvshiy, god nïneshniy' [The year gone by and the current year], *Muzïkal′naya zhizn′* (1985), no.1 pp.2–3

'Nas svyazïvayet chuvstvo dukhovnogo rodstva' [We are bound together by a feeling of spiritual kinship], *Muzïkal′naya zhizn′* (1987), no.16, 22–3

'On bïl i vsegda ostanetsya tvortsom' [He was and will always remain a creative artist], *Muzïkal′naya zhizn′* (1988), no.17, 12–14 [on A. Tarkovsky]

'Sokhranit′ sebya' [Preserving oneself], *Muzïkal′naya zhizn′* (1994), no.4

BIBLIOGRAPHY

A. Petrov: 'Kompozitor Ēduard Artem′yev: mag sintezatora' [The composer Artem′yev: the wizard of the synthesiser], *Kul′tura i zhizn′* (1982), no.4

T. Yegorova: 'Muzïka seriala', *SovM* (1985), no.4, 98–102

G. Drubachevskaya: 'Ubezhdyon: budet tvorcheskiy vzrïv' [I am convinced: there will be an explosion of creative work], *MAk* (1993), no.2, pp.14–20 [interview]

L. Suslova: 'Prorïv v novïye zvukovïye mirï' [Breaking into new sound worlds], *MAk* (1995), no.2, pp.33–42

M. Katunyan: 'Ēduard Artem′yev: arkhitektor i poēt zvuka' [Artem′yev: architect and poet of sound], *Muzïka iz bïvshego SSSR*, ed. V. Tsenova and V. Barsky, ii (Moscow, 1996), 272–82

SVETLANA SAVENKO

Art Ensemble of Chicago [AEC]. Free-jazz quintet. Its members were Roscoe Mitchell and Joseph Jarman (reed instruments, vibraphone, marimba and unusual winds such as whistles and conch shells), Lester Bowie (brass instruments, harmonica, celeste, kelp horn, etc.), Malachi Favors (double bass, zither, melodica, banjo) and Don Moye ('sun percussion'). All vocalized and all played percussion instruments, including drums from several continents (especially Africa), cymbals, gongs, bells, woodblocks, sirens, bicycle horns, etc. The ensemble evolved from Chicago's Association for the Advancement of Creative Musicians. It was formed in Paris in 1969 as a 'drummerless' (but not percussionless) quartet consisting of Mitchell, Jarman, Bowie and Favors; Moye joined in 1970. While based in France the ensemble performed on television and radio, recorded extensively (including *A Jackson in your House*, 1969, BYG) and presented concerts throughout Western Europe. On returning to the USA in 1971 the members restricted their performances to profitable events such as large concerts, jazz festivals and university workshops. Their popularity grew in the late 1970s and early 1980s with the release of four albums, beginning with *Nice Guys* (1978, ECM). In the 1980s they performed on occasion in France, and in 1980 and 1984 made extensive tours of the USA. The group toured until Bowie's death in November, 1999 and, after the Modern Jazz Quartet, was the longest-lived small group in jazz.

The Art Ensemble of Chicago developed within the free-jazz tradition, the principal instruments being trumpet, alto saxophone, double bass and drums. Its members were virtuoso, experimental improvisers in this tradition who liberally used dissonance, non-tempered intonation, noise, fast flurries of saxophone melody, dense textures and irregular rhythms. However, their motto, 'Great Black Music – Ancient to Modern' more accurately described the breadth of their music than the term 'free jazz'. Their performances combined theatricality – costumes, make-up, dance, pantomime, comedy, parody, absurd dialogue, playlets – with musics from Africa (drum choirs), black America (blues, gospel, pop, jazz) and Europe (waltzes, marches). This diversity was further magnified by an economical, sensitive use of the tone colours of several hundred standard, exotic and invented instruments, and by an ever-changing melange of original compositions, individual features and collective improvisation.

BIBLIOGRAPHY

E. Jost: *Free Jazz* (Graz, 1974)

L. Birnbaum: 'Art Ensemble of Chicago: 15 Years of Great Black Music', *Down Beat*, xlvi/9 (1979), 15–17, 39–40, 42

P. Kemper: 'Zur Funktion des Mythos im Jazz der 70er Jahre: soziokulturelle Aspekte eines musikalisches Phänomens dargestellt an der ästhetischen Konzeption des "Art Ensemble of Chicago"', *Jazzforschung/Jazz Research*, xiii (1981), 45–78

J. Litweiler: 'The Art Ensemble of Chicago: Adventures in the Urban Bush', *Down Beat*, xlix/6 (1982), 19–22, 60 [incl. discography]

E. Janssens and H. de Craen: *Art Ensemble of Chicago Discography: Unit and Members* (Brussels, 1983) [incl. list of compositions]

J. Rockwell: 'The Art Ensemble of Chicago: Jazz, Group Improvisation, Race and Racism', *All American Music: Composition in the Late Twentieth Century* (New York, 1983), 164–75

BARRY KERNFELD

Arthopius [Artocopus, Artopaeus], **Balthasar** (*b* end of the 15th century; *d* Speyer, late July 1534). German organist and composer. There is no evidence to support Jauernig's assumption that he was the Balthasar Pistorius from Besike who matriculated at Heidelberg University on 12 April 1498. Arthopius was organist in Weissenburg (now Wissembourg), Alsace, around 1527. In 1527 he applied for the post of organist at Speyer Cathedral, but was not appointed because the cathedral chapter at Speyer wanted to fill the vacant organist's post with a cleric. At the end of July 1530 he again offered his services to the chapter, and after some negotiation he was installed as cathedral organist on 17 August 1530 for a period of four years. The humanist Theodor Reyssmann visited Speyer in 1531 and praised Arthopius's organ playing, comparing it with the ability of his predecessor, Conrad Bruman, a pupil of Hofhaimer's. The chapter archives report that Arthopius composed some pieces for Christmas 1533 and that for them he received a gift of 4 guilders. After Arthopius's death, the Heidelberg professor and humanist Jacob Micyllus dedicated an epitaph to him, which was set to music by Johannes Heugel (*D-Kl* Mus 4°118).

Arthopius used the elements of the later Netherlandish style in his sacred compositions; his technical skill, however, lacks the perfection of a master. For him the tenor settings of Netherlandish choral polyphony were compulsory, but he treated the cantus firmus in a fairly original manner. Imitation and the use of motifs are found throughout the pieces, and their rhythmic and harmonic flexibility is characteristic. Arthopius's German secular songs show clearly the tendency towards simplification and conciseness. He made frequent use of imitation but

subordinated it to harmonic considerations. As a rule the melody is in the tenor part, from which the other parts usually derive their melodic substance. The canonic setting of the melody in the tenor and alto of *Es fiel ein Baur* is unusual. The texts of the songs are often satirical and blunt.

WORKS

SACRED

Beatus qui intelligit, 5vv, *D-Z* 4; Cogniscimus Domine, 4vv, 1537[1]; Jubilate Deo omnis terra, 5vv, *Z* 4; Nisi Dominus aedificaverit domum, 4vv, 1542[6]

SECULAR

Die Brinlein, 4vv, 1535[10]; Es fiel ein Baur, 5vv, 1536[8]; Frawe, liebste Frawe, 5vv, 1536[8]; Wer Hoffart treibt, 4vv, 1536[8], ed. in *MMg*, xxvi (1894), 35–8

BIBLIOGRAPHY

R. Jauernig: 'Berichtigungen und Ergänzungen zu Eitners Quellenlexikon für Musiker und Musikgelehrte des 16. Jahrhunderts', *Mf*, vi (1953), 39–46, esp. 39–40

G. Pietzsch: 'Orgelbauer, Organisten und Orgelspiel in Deutschland bis zum Ende des 16. Jahrhunderts', *Mf*, xi (1958), 307–15, esp. 311

MANFRED SCHULER

Artia. The name of the imprint under which SUPRAPHON exports.

Articulation and phrasing. The separation of successive notes from one another, singly or in groups, by a performer, and the manner in which this is done. The term 'phrasing' implies a linguistic or syntactic analogy, and since the 18th century this analogy has constantly been invoked in discussing the grouping of successive notes, especially in melodies; the term 'articulation' refers primarily to the degree to which a performer detaches individual notes from one another in practice (e.g. in staccato and legato). This distinction between the two terms was recommended by Keller (1955); but articulation in a broader sense is sometimes taken to mean the ways in which sections of a work – of whatever dimensions – are divided from (or, from another point of view, joined to) one another.

1. General. 2. History.

1. GENERAL.   Articulation and phrasing represent some of the chief ways in which performers, and consequently listeners, may make 'sense' of a flux of otherwise undifferentiated sound, and convert clock time into musical time. In tonal music in the narrower sense, they are (with tonality and thematic organization) two of the chief elements contributing to diversity within organic unity; and they are the elements for which the performer bears the most direct responsibility. Clearly, they are important to the analysis of music. Yet phrasing theory is a relative newcomer to music theory, and still occupies a somewhat peripheral and problematic position within it. This may be because the intricacies of articulation are difficult to notate and are generally transmitted orally rather than in comprehensive notated form; they ought, perhaps, to be as amenable to ethnomusicological analysis as to the document-based methods usually employed. Moreover, there is scarcely any consideration of small-scale articulation in traditional theory, except insofar as this contributes to phrasing; only recently have analysts and those in the field of performance studies begun a belated exploration of its role in musical expression. Consequently phrasing theory has been formulated largely in terms of the linguistic analogy implicit in its terminology

(phrase, sentence, period), rather than in terms of the vocal and instrumental techniques, such as bowing and tonguing, that shape small-scale articulation.

The means of articulation, and hence of phrasing too, vary widely. Single notes may be articulated and phrases begun by the 'placing' of notes (their being played or sung a fraction late, separated from the preceding note by a brief silence or other agogic device), by an accent (or conversely by an unexpected unaccented note in a loud passage) or other dynamic device, or by nuances of timbre or intonation.

Resources of articulation also differ with the performing medium and acoustic surroundings. To achieve clarity in a hall with abundant reverberation generally requires energetic articulation, as well as a relatively slow tempo. The articulative characteristics of instruments are an important element in their musical capacities. Apart from vibrato the main differences in timbre of the violin, trumpet and oboe, for instance, lie in their different means of articulation: their sound becomes virtually identical if the initial and terminal articulation of each note is excised from a recording. A distinct feature of bagpipe music is the use of grace notes, mordents and other embellishments to compensate for the unavailability of silence as an articulative resource. Ornaments are also a characteristic means of articulating notes on the organ or harpsichord when they might otherwise be submerged in the texture. Techniques of articulation in most wind instruments include various patterns of TONGUING: equivalent aspects of technique of instruments of the violin family involve the handling of the BOW (and the occasional use of pizzicato). In vocal music the resources of articulation, apart from grace notes and the like, portamentos, and such slivers of silence between notes as are available to most performers, are the consonants and the glottal or smooth beginnings and endings of vowel sounds. Most keyboard instruments can achieve an almost perfect melodic legato, even in a small room, when the terminal articulation of one note is produced after the initial articulation of the succeeding one.

The attack (initial articulation) of a note will most often occupy between 0·01 and 0·1 seconds. Bass notes are relatively slow in articulation, however, partly because more time is required to perceive waveforms of slower frequency and partly because more time is required to put into regular motion the larger masses of air, string and so forth that are likely to be involved in producing bass notes. Hence the trombone, bassoon and double bass are generally less incisive than the trumpet, oboe and violin.

Incisive articulation (as well as bright tone) assists the ear in sensing the location of an instrument. In this regard a Romantic inclination to diffuseness might be seen in music from the late 18th century onwards, for example in the vogue for the glass harmonica, where crisp articulation is virtually impossible, and later in the increased orchestral prominence of horns and trombones, the use of ever more heavily padded hammers on the piano, the elimination of 'chiff' in the pipe organ and the popularity of the reed organ. Yet the resources of phrasing and articulation came under special scrutiny in the 19th century, and they are no less essential to Romantic music than to Renaissance or Baroque music.

Technological developments since World War II have permitted the detailed study of the transient acoustical phenomena of articulation. In electronic music since the mid-1960s, moreover, commercially available synthesizers have been capable of governing not only the duration of the attack or decay of a note, but also certain aspects of its internal shape. But the variety of transient waveforms in 'natural' articulation as wielded intuitively by singers and instrumentalists has remained greater than that of most synthetic music.

Although Western notators (especially before the 18th century) have generally relied on the stylistic intuition of performers to achieve correct articulation, an exceptionally elaborate method of specifying qualities of articulation can be found in the *jianzi* notation of the Chinese zither (Chou, 1969), in which:

a combination symbol for both hands would usually specify how a certain right-hand finger is to pluck the string, inward or outward, with the flesh or the nail, or how two or more right-hand fingers are to be used simultaneously or in succession, how a left-hand finger stops the string, or how a left-hand finger is to tap the string or to pluck it, upward or sideways, how the pitch is altered or inflected by means of glissando or portamento after the excitation of the string, and how the timbre is varied by the addition of a certain type of vibrato or by changing from one type of vibrato to another during the decay.

Phrasing, just as much as articulation, is an aspect of Western music essential to its stylish performance. Riemann (1884), like others before him, compared it to punctuation in prose or verse: an inappropriate punctuation (i.e. articulation) of the sentence 'Er verlor sein Leben, nicht nur sein Vermögen' as 'Er verlor sein Leben nicht, nur sein Vermögen' almost reverses its meaning, rather as in the sentence 'King Charles walked and talked; half an hour after, his head was cut off' with or without its punctuation. But, as writers had long before recognized, musical phrasing requires more subtlety and ambiguity than is implied by this simple analogy. The articulation implicit at a phrase-end, through tonality, cadence and so on, may for example be deliberately suppressed in order to maintain or increase momentum (see ex.1, in which

Ex.1 Square brackets show conventional phrasing; the slurs are in the original manuscript (Mozart: Rondo in A minor K511)

square brackets show a conventional phrase structure, but the slurs and other articulation signs are Mozart's own). Riemann was one of the first to attempt to catalogue these subtleties; of more modern writers, Cooper and Meyer (1960) and (from a different point of view) Keller (1955) may be found useful in this regard.

2. HISTORY. In the earliest notation of Gregorian chant, there are numerous subtle indications of agogics, lost in succeeding centuries; but in medieval and Renaissance music one does not expect to find any evidence of articulation, let alone phrasing, other than in the use of rests and fermatas (e.g. in the setting of some proper names in late medieval motets) and in the evidence of the joining together of successive notes provided by liquescent neumes, ligatures and plicas. Rests and fermatas have continued to be used as a means of notating articulation. Other early evidence of articulation is found mostly in writings about instrumental techniques, but specific

evidence of phrases in the usual sense (groups of notes to be performed in a single breath) may plausibly be sought in the special signs used by Cavalieri in his *Rappresentatione di Anima, et di Corpo* (1600: see NOTATION, fig.86). At the same period, the special signs for staccatos (dots and strokes) were introduced into string music, as was the bowing slur, the latter soon imitated in keyboard music such as Scheidt's *Tabulatura nova* (1624). Earlier string music was bowed with a single note to each bow, though separate bowing does not always necessarily imply strong articulation.

Phrasing theory developed out of 17th-century rhythmic theory which was conceived in terms of poetic metrical theory. The 18th century, however, introduced into it the rhetorical analogy of punctuation: Couperin drew on this notion in the foreword to his *Pièces de clavecin*, iii (1722), to justify his use of a comma in the notation of his pieces; and in Mattheson (1737) the idea of phrasing explicitly appeared. These and later writers show the modern reader that various different degrees of articulation were required (even at this date) to make phrases, sentences and so on perceptible: least for the 'comma', more for the 'colon' and still more for the 'period'. And they show that articulation was now linked to new expressive ideals. Later composers, notably Mozart, continued to show interest in the precise notation of articulation (see Badura-Skoda, 1957; Albrecht, 1957; Keller, 1955) and attempts were made to refine this notation (*see* NOTATION, fig.83); but well into the 19th century, performers were expected to have direct access to teachers able to instruct them in good taste, and hence both theory and notational practice remained far from rigorous, with no precise distinctions being made, for example, between wedges or strokes and dots to notate various degrees of articulation and of accentuation.

In the second half of the 19th century Lussy attempted to tackle the issue of 'expression' in a new way: to commit to writing the aspects of good taste in performance, especially in matters of accentuation and phrasing, which had hitherto been left mainly to oral tradition. As Riemann (1903) pointed out, Lussy's theory is far from rigorous, representing a reworking of various rules of thumb derived from early 19th-century sources. But, like Riemann's own theory, it grew from the conviction that 18th- and early 19th-century notation, by the second half of the 19th century, no longer provided an adequate representation of the expressive requirements of the classical repertory; and indeed (for performers used to the careful notation of composers like Wagner and Liszt and their contemporaries) this must have been true. Riemann believed also that phrase structure is generated ultimately by processes of linear growth rather than by abstract patterns of stressed and unstressed units; he developed a precise notation for phrasing (*see* NOTATION, fig.84) in which the course of a piece of music is related to a theoretical eight-bar structure (the numbers below the music indicate the 'punctuation' appropriate to the bars 2, 4, 6 and 8 in this structure), but with a fairly sophisticated apparatus to show the modifications to this sytem in practice.

Though Riemann's influence was strong, his views were not unchallenged. In Britain, an influential critic was Macpherson (1911), whose own theory is far less radical than Riemann's. The Urtext movement, however, may have represented the most thorough-going alternative to

Riemann; an articulate statement of the virtues of an Urtext against 'phrasing editions' was produced by Schenker (1925). It is clear from this essay that Schenker saw no difference in principle between legato (articulation) slurs in conventional notation, properly employed, and the slurs he used in his own mature analytical graphs, which were conceived in terms of performance of the works, and which repay study by performers; and it is true, as Schenker and several other writers of the late 19th and early 20th century point out, that the phrasing editions sometimes falsify and trivialize perfectly unambiguous indications of articulation in the music of composers like Mozart. Nevertheless, in the 20th century the pendulum swung so far in favour of Urtext editions that one is in some danger of neglecting the evidence of earlier practice which is undeniably offered by some phrasing editions.

Despite Schenker's clear interest in performance and, in particular, in articulation and phrasing, the subject remains undeveloped in his theory, and has not even yet been fully integrated into theory.

See also ACCENTUATION; ARTICULATION MARKS; LEGATO; SLUR; and STACCATO.

BIBLIOGRAPHY

J. Mattheson: *Kern melodischer Wissenschaft* (Hamburg, 1737/R)

M. Lussy: *Traité de l'expression musicale* (Paris, 1874, 8/1904; Eng. trans., 1885)

K. Fuchs: *Die Freiheit des musikalischen Vortrags* (Danzig, 1884)

H. Riemann: *Musikalische Dynamik und Agogik: Lehrbuch der musikalischen Phrasierung* (Hamburg, 1884)

O. Tiersch: *Rhythmik, Dynamik und Phrasierungslehre* (Berlin, 1886)

F. Kullak: *Der Vortrag in der Musik am Ende des 19. Jahrhunderts* (Leipzig, 1898)

M. Lussy: *L'anacrouse dans la musique moderne* (Paris, 1903)

H. Riemann: *System der musikalischen Rhythmik und Metrik* (Leipzig, 1903)

S. Macpherson: *Studies in Phrasing and Form* (London, 1911/R)

A. Dolmetsch: *The Interpretation of the Music of the 17th and 18th Centuries* (London, 1915, 2/1946/R)

H. Schenker: 'Weg mit dem Phrasierungsbogen', *Das Meisterwerk in der Musik: ein Jahrbuch*, i (Munich, 1925), 41–60

T. Matthay: *The Slur or Couplet of Notes* (London, 1928)

K. Speer: 'Die Artikulation in den Orgelwerken J.S. Bachs', *BJb 1954*, 66

H. Keller: *Phrasierung und Artikulation* (Kassel, 1955; Eng. trans., 1965)

H. Albrecht, ed.: *Die Bedeutung der Zeichen Keil, Strich und Punkt bei Mozart* (Kassel, 1957) [see also P. Mies, Mf, xi (1958), 428]

E. Badura-Skoda and P.Badura-Skoda: *Mozart-Interpretation* (Vienna, 1957; Eng. trans., 1962/R, as *Interpreting Mozart on the Keyboard*)

G.W. Cooper and L.B.Meyer: *The Rhythmic Structure of Music* (Chicago, 1960, 3/1966)

R. Donington: *The Interpretation of Early Music* (London, 1963)

C.A. Taylor: *The Physics of Musical Sounds* (London, 1965)

Chou Wen-chung: 'East and West, Old and New', *Asian Music*, i (1969), 19

B. Ganz: 'Von den geschleiften und den gestossenen Tönen in der Claviermusik des 18. Jahrhunderts', *SMz*, cxiv (1974), 205–14

D. Barnett: 'Non-Uniform Slurring in 18th-Century Music: Accident or Design?', *Haydn Yearbook 1978*, 179–99

L. Lohmann: *Studien zu Artikulationsproblemen bei den Tasteninstrumenten des 16.–18. Jahrhunderts*, Kölner Beiträge zur Musikforschung, cxxv (Regensburg, 1982)

M. Belotti: 'Das Problem der Überbindung am Beispiel der Orgelwerke Buxtehudes', *Acta organologica*, xvii (1984), 380–85

B. Gustafson: 'Shapes and Meanings of Slurs in Unmeasured Harpsichord Preludes', *French Baroque Music*, ii (1984), 20–22

H. Grüss: 'Über Stricharten und Artikulation in Streichinstrumentenstimmen Johann Sebastian Bachs', *Johann Sebastian Bach: Leipzig 1985*, 331–41

K. Kroeger: 'Slur and Tie in Anglo-American Psalmody', *American Choral Review*, xxviii/2 (1986), 17–29

C. Beck: 'Use of the Dot for Articulation and Accent in Orchestral Repertoire (1880–1920)', *Journal of the Conductors' Guild*, x (1989), 12–23

C. Beck: 'The Dot as a Nondurational Sign of Articulation and Accent', *Music Research Forum*, v (1990), 63–78

J. Butt: *Bach Interpretation: Articulation Marks in Primary Sources of J.S. Bach*(Cambridge, 1990)

L.G. Davenport: 'Slurring versus Tonguing: Questionable Articulation Practices in the Mozart Clarinet Concerto', *Quarterly Journal of Music Teaching and Learning*, ii/4 (1991), 38–41

D.O. Franklin: 'Die Artikulation in den Cembalowerken J.S. Bachs: eine Notationsstudie', *Johann Sebastian Bachs historischer Ort*, ed. R. Szeskus (Wiesbaden, 1991), 280–301

C. Schachter: '20th-Century Analysis and Mozart Performance', *EMc*, xix (1991), 620–24

P. Reichert: 'Refinement in Performance: Relationships Between Fingering and Articulation in Playing Historic Keyboard Instruments', *Acta organologica*, xxiii (1992), 297–318

C. Drake and C.Palmer: 'Accent Structures in Music Performance', *Music Perception*, x (1993), 343–78

B. Billeter: 'Verzierungs-und Artikulationszeichen in Johann Sebastian Bachs Triosonaten für Orgel', *Max Lütolf zum 60. Geburtstag: Festschrift*, ed. B. Hangartner and U. Fischer (Basle, 1994), 235

D. Heuchemer: 'Articulative Consistency and Change: a Study of Historical Articulation for Wind Instruments', *Music Research Forum*, ix (1994), 83–107

R. Toft: 'The Expressive Pause: Punctuation, Rests, and Breathing in England, 1770–1850', *Performance Practice Review*, vii (1994), 1–32, 199–232

V. Fischer: 'Articulation Notation in the Piano Music of Béla Bartók', *SMH*, xxxvi (1995), 285–301

GEOFFREY CHEW

Articulation marks. Symbols appended to musical notation which indicate to the performer the manner in which particular notes and phrases should be played.

1. Introduction. 2. The slur. 3. Treatment of unmarked notes. 4. The staccato mark. 5. Other markings. 6. Increasing systemization.

1. INTRODUCTION.   Until the late 18th century the only signs commonly used to indicate distinctions of articulation were the slur and the staccato mark (a dot, a vertical stroke, or a wedge) placed above or below the note head. In the 19th century composers became concerned to specify their requirements with ever greater precision, and other forms of articulation mark were introduced, though only a few of these were widely adopted. The principal meaning of the slur has remained relatively constant, though the manner of its employment has varied greatly over the centuries. Except where slurs are written over a succession of notes on the same pitch to indicate portato, they specify that notes of different pitches should be performed without separation, that is, legato. There is, strictly speaking, no greater or lesser degree of connectedness; terms such as *molto legato* in slurred passages cannot affect the degree of connection between notes within a slur, they can only mean that there should be the minimum possible separation between slurred groups. Staccato marks, on the other hand, either alone or in combination with a slur, have been employed to indicate every type and degree of separation, from the barely articulated to the very sharply detached, and have sometimes had implications of accent as well as of separation. The interpretation of these marks in specific instances will be dependent on such factors as period, nationality, musical context, and the known or inferred practices of individual composers. Other forms of articulation and accent marks (the two functions are seldom entirely discrete) have also varied considerably in their meaning between different composers and traditions.

2. THE SLUR.   From the 16th century slurs were used with growing frequency to specify legato, especially in the context of notes sung to a single syllable; slurs in instrumental music were slower to appear, and in 17th- and 18th-century music many passages of unslurred notes were undoubtedly intended to be performed with slurred bowstrokes or in single unarticulated breaths. The inclusion of slurs became more common during the 18th century, and some composers, notably J.S. Bach, used them extensively to indicate subtle and varied patterns of legato groups. But many composers seem not to have been particularly conscientious about marking slurs consistently; in most cases it was the responsibility of the performer, if the composer was not available to determine the matter in person, to decide firstly whether unslurred notes should, in fact, be played legato, and, if not, what degree and style of articulation to apply. The most careful composers of the later 18th century became increasingly punctilious in marking slurs. Until the early 19th century, however, it was rare for slurs to encompass more notes than could be performed in a single bowstroke or breath, and composers seem to have felt some degree of inhibition about extending them over bar lines; this was the case even in keyboard music where longer passages of continuous legato would have been practicable.

The question of whether slurs, in addition to specifying legato, required that the group of notes over which they stood should be performed in a particular manner has been a subject of much discussion. Slurred groups such as those in much of J.S. Bach's music, where there is a clear intention to elicit particular patterns of phrasing, were evidently intended to be made audible to the listener, and there are many references in theoretical writing to a manner of performance in which the first note under the slur would receive an accent (sometimes agogic) and the final note would be shortened. This mode of execution seems more likely to have been regarded as normal in the 18th century than in the 19th century; but even at the earlier period not all slurs may have been intended to be performed in this manner, as Türk pointed out. A number of 19th-century writers, including Czerny, limited this type of performance to groups of two or three notes, and it is clear that many slurs, particularly successions of longer slurs beginning on metrically strong beats, were intended merely to indicate a general legato. But other information (for instance Mendelssohn's reference to the distinct phrasing of slurred pairs as a practice of Handel's period that was not now widely understood) suggests that many 19th-century composers did not expect even short slurs to receive a particularly distinctive style of performance. Nevertheless, Brahms's correspondence with Joachim makes clear that, in keyboard playing at any rate, Brahms regarded a shortening of the second note in slurred pairs as obligatory, and a similar treatment of longer groups as 'a freedom and refinement in performance, which, to be sure, is generally appropriate'.

3. TREATMENT OF UNMARKED NOTES.   The style of performance envisaged for notes that have neither slurs nor any other kind of articulation mark has also been variable. In the 18th century many composers intended, and musicians inferred, a clearly detached execution of such notes. Some theorists suggested that unmarked notes were to be less detached (or accented) than those with staccato marks. This may have been common practice in the earlier part of the century, when staccato marks were

used chiefly in special cases, but even at that time some composers seem to have used staccato marks without implying a more detached or accented execution than normal unslurred notes, simply to ensure that the previous pattern of slurring would be discontinued or that slurs would not be added where they were not wanted; several of these uses of staccato marks appear to be represented in Bach's autographs. The use of the staccato mark to ensure that notes are not slurred (but not apparently to indicate a degree of separation greater than normal unslurred notes) may account for a considerable proportion of the staccato marks encountered in late 18th-century scores. Despite the frequently quoted instruction of some influential theorists that unslurred notes (with or without staccato marks) should, in general, be well separated, it would be rash to apply this rule universally even in moderate or fast music. There were certainly some schools in which a less detached style was cultivated. This may have been especially the case in Italian performance, while the French represented the opposite pole: hence Quantz's comment on the short bowstroke of the French and the 'long dragging stroke' of the Italians. The so-called *détaché*, or *grand détaché* bowstroke of the late-18th- and early-19th-century school of French string players (the Viotti school), which is actually as connected a stroke as can be obtained with separate bows, undoubtedly had its roots in the schools of Tartini and Pugnani, and such tendencies seem also to have been reflected in Leopold Mozart's treatise and in the Mannheim style. There is some evidence that a similar approach to unslurred notes was adopted in some schools of 18th-century keyboard playing, especially the Italian, and that Clementi's often cited instruction, to give preference to the legato over the staccato where nothing was indicated, was by no means an innovation. By the 1830s, conceivably, many passages of notes with staccato marks were intended to be played without either physical separation or particular accent, as indicated by the instruction in Spohr's *Violinschule* to play a succession of notes marked with staccato strokes 'in such a manner that in changing from the down- to the up-bow or the reverse no break or chasm may be observed'.

4. THE STACCATO MARK.   By the late Baroque period the dot, stroke and wedge (the latter largely confined to printed music) were widely used to indicate the physical separation of one note from the next by means of the replacement of part of its written value with a rest, or sometimes (though the implication of shortening the marked note seems seldom to have been entirely absent) to indicate accents. A few composers, for instance Veracini in his *Sonate accademiche*, devised and employed their own vocabulary of signs, but for the most part there is little evidence to suggest that composers utilized distinct signs for distinct purposes systematically, if at all. In the generation of Bach and Handel staccato marks were very rarely used, and the appropriate articulation for unslurred notes would generally have been determined by the performer on the basis of musical context, taking into account such factors as the type of piece and any terms of tempo or expression supplied by the composer. From the mid-18th century however, authors of tutors and theory books began increasingly to discuss and describe a variety of staccato marks. Writers were divided between those who employed a single staccato mark and those who advocated a distinction between the dot and the stroke.

C.P.E. Bach considered only one mark for unslurred staccato necessary; however, in his *Versuch*, stressing that one mark did not mean one kind of execution, he observed that the performer must execute the staccato in different ways according to the length of note, the tempo, and the dynamic. Bach's preference for a single staccato mark for unslurred notes was echoed by, among others, Leopold Mozart (1756), Reichardt (1776), Türk (1789), J.A. Hiller (1792), A.E. Müller (1804) and Spohr (1832). Others, including Quantz (1752), Riepel (1757), Löhlein (1774), G.J. Vogler (1778), H.C. Koch (1802), J.H. Knecht (1803) and J.L. Adam (1804) utilized two signs with different meanings in their instruction books. Importantly, such distinctions seem essentially to have been intended as a means of instruction within the context of a theoretical study; this was explicitly recognized by Joseph Riepel in his *Gründliche Erklärung der Tonordnung* (1757) where, after describing a sophisticated range of articulation marks that signified various kinds of bowstroke, he remarked: 'I have included the strokes and dots again only for the sake of explanation; for one does not see them in pieces of music except perhaps sometimes when it is necessary on account of clarity'.

Despite the extensive literature on Mozart's articulation marks, much of which concerns itself with a supposed distinction between dots and strokes, there is no compelling evidence that classical composers were conscientiously employing two forms of staccato mark with differentiated meaning on unslurred notes; no such distinctions are apparent, even in the music of composers who advocated two forms in their theoretical writing. Nevertheless, composers of Mozart's generation employed staccato marks much more extensively than their predecessors. In manuscript sources of the late 18th and early 19th century these appear as dots or strokes of various sizes over detached notes, and in combination with slurs primarily as dots, though strokes under slurs are occasionally encountered. All these have their counterparts in printed editions, yet consistent relationships between composers' autographs and printed editions are rare; sometimes in sets of orchestral parts, as in a number of Beethoven first editions, dots are used in one part throughout and strokes in another, apparently depending on the engraver's preferred or available punch for making staccato marks.

A special use of the staccato mark, mentioned in C.P.E. Bach's *Versuch*, can be found in the second movement of Beethoven's Violin Sonata op.30 no.3 in G. In the autograph score, throughout this movement Beethoven consistently placed a staccato stroke not over the first or second note on each appearance of a dotted figure first heard in the opening bars, but over the dot of prolongation; the placement is so careful and consistent in each case that it would seem to be deliberate, for such a consistent positioning of the staccato mark after the note head is not typical of Beethoven. The meaning is almost certainly that shown in ex.1, and Beethoven may possibly

Ex.1

have derived this notation directly from the passage in C.P.E. Bach's *Versuch*, where Bach suggests precisely this relationship of staccato mark and dot of prolongation to signify a rest in such figures.

5. OTHER MARKINGS.   Another sign, quite commonly encountered in music of this period, is the wavy line, occasionally under a slur, but normally on its own. Like all these signs it could have a number of meanings. Employed over a succession of notes at the same pitch it seems to have been synonymous with the portato notation of dots under a slur or a slur alone, and this is its probable meaning in the majority of cases during the 18th century. Over single notes, when it was not simply an instruction to divide the note into repeated portato notes, it usually implied some other form of trembling motion, either a vibrato or a tremolo with separately articulated repeated notes; it is frequently found with the latter meaning in string parts in Rossini's scores. In some piano reductions of orchestral parts of that period the wavy line seems to have been used as the equivalent of the modern abbreviation with white notes joined by multiple beams.

6. INCREASING SYSTEMIZATION.   From the late 18th century an increasing number of authorities advocated or acknowledged two signs, the dot and the stroke, for staccato on unslurred notes. But there was still no general agreement about precisely what these should signify. The majority of late 18th- and early 19th-century German authors who described both signs favoured the stroke as the sharper ('schärfer') of the two: in about 1810 F.J. Fröhlich referred, in the *Violinschule* of his *Vollständige ... Musikschule*, to the stroke as the more powerful staccato ('der kräftigere Stoss') and the dot as the gentler one ('der gelindere'). Yet some authors, for instance G.J. Vogler and his admirer J.H. Knecht seem to have wanted the stroke sharper and longer than the dot: in his *Allgemeiner musikalischer Katechismus* Knecht described the stroke as indicating that one should give the notes a 'somewhat sharp and long staccato' while the dot indicated a short and dainty execution. Schubert, among early 19th-century composers, may have intended a difference. In some of his autographs the distinctions between staccato dots (which match his dots of prolongation) and long narrow staccato strokes is pronounced. As late as the 1830s however the article 'Abstossen' in Gustav Schilling's *Encyclopädie der gesammten musikalischen Wissenschaften* still expressed uncertainty about the significance of the two types of staccato mark. By the second half of the 19th century the recognition of two signs with different implications was more or less universal and many major composers undoubtedly employed them in practice. The principal disagreements at this stage were between string players and keyboard players, and between composers in the German and French traditions. In string playing different forms of staccato mark became increasingly linked to specific types of bowing (*martelé, spiccato* etc.) and, partly because of the varying practices of French and German violinists, these signs acquired conflicting meanings in the two traditions. For Baillot strokes were associated with *martelé* and dots with *sautillé* or *spiccato*, while for Ferdinand David the reverse was the case. Thus German musicians continued to associate the stroke with accented staccato and the dot with lighter staccato, while the French appear, on the whole, to have associated the stroke with a shorter and usually lighter staccato and the dot with a less short and weightier staccato. Although the definition of the shortening effect of staccato marks propounded in J.L. Adam's *Méthode du piano du Conservatoire* of 1804, whereby a stroke shortened the note by three quarters, a dot by half and a dot under a slur by one quarter, was repeated in German, English, Italian and other theory books during the 19th century, it cannot be regarded as a reliable guide to the practices of many composers of the period. In any case, as many theorists continued to point out, the degree and type of articulation applied in particular cases was conditioned by many external factors, such as the size of the ensemble, the qualities of the instrument, or the space in which the performance took place.

The ambiguity in the meaning of staccato marks, particularly the question of whether they carried any implications of accent, induced some late 18th- and early 19th-century theorists, for instance Türk and Corri, to propose other symbols to indicate articulation, but these signs remained confined largely to the realm of theory. Interestingly, the uncertainty over the meaning of staccato dots and strokes was still sufficiently strong in the early 20th century for Schoenberg to consider it necessary to explain in the preface to his Serenade op.24 that wedges indicated 'hard, heavy, staccatoed' notes and dots 'light, elastic, thrown (spiccato) ones'.

The inclusion of other articulation marks in manuscript and printed music was relatively uncommon before the 19th century, but by the middle of that century additional signs had been proposed by theorists, and several were beginning to be adopted by composers. This process was encouraged by the growing concern of composers with details of articulation as an essential element in their music and by their determination to exercise greater control over the performer's interpretation. One consequence was a gradual, but by no means consistent, refinement and narrowing of the meaning of staccato marks, as other signs began to assume some of the functions previously subsumed in those signs. The horizontal line came gradually to be seen as a replacement for the old portato marking, though some conservative musicians, including Brahms, resisted using it in this sense. But initially the line seems to have been regarded rather as an accent marking, indicating a moderately weighty but not sharp execution, and it continued to be used by some composers with this meaning. Sometimes composers seem simply to have regarded it as a method of showing that a note should be held for its full value; however, that meaning may not be as common as is generally believed. By mid-century a number of composers, including Schumann, in line with the suggestions of contemporary theorists, began to use signs that explicitly indicated both accent and articulation (ex.2). Many later

Ex.2

19th-century composers, including Wagner, Verdi, Bruckner and Dvořák, availed themselves of these and other signs to prescribe their articulation and accentuation with ever greater precision. A sophisticated system of articulation marks was proposed by Hugo Riemann and employed in his editions of Classical piano music, specifying articulation and phrasing to a remarkable degree of nicety. Like those of earlier theorists, however, his markings were not generally adopted by composers, though Mahler among others did occasionally utilize the comma (which had periodically been proposed as a music symbol) in Riemann's sense, to indicate a short articulation. Some 20th-century composers, for example Bartók, used a very wide range of articulation and accent markings, while others, such as Shostakovich, contented themselves with a much more limited vocabulary of basic signs.

For further information and bibliography *see also* ARTICULATION AND PHRASING.

BIBLIOGRAPHY

P. Mies: 'Die Artikulationzeichen Strich und Punkt bei Wolfgang Amadeus Mozart', *DMf*, xi (1958), 428–55

H.J. Macdonald: 'Two Peculiarities of Berlioz's Notation', *ML*, l (1969), 25–36

N. Temperley: 'Berlioz and the Slur', *ML*, l (1969), 388–92

C. Brown: 'Bowing Styles, Vibrato and Portamento in Nineteenth-Century Violin Playing', *JRMA*, cxiii (1988), 97–128

P. Badura-Skoda: 'A Tie is a Tie is a Tie', *EMc*, xvi (1988), 84–8

S. Rosenblum: *Performance Practices in Classical Piano Music* (Bloomington, 1988)

S. Carter: 'The String Tremolo in the 17th Century', *EMc*, xix (1991), 49–60

F. Neumann: 'Dots and Strokes in Mozart', *EMc*, xxi (1993), 429–35

C. Brown: 'Dots and Strokes in Late 18th- and 19th-Century Music', *EMc*, xxi (1993), 593–60

C. Brown: 'Ferdinand David's Editions of Beethoven', *Performing Beethoven*, ed. R. Stowell (Cambridge, 1994), 117–49

C. Brown: 'String Playing Practices in the Classical Orchestra', *Basler Jb für historische Musikpraxis*, Jg.17 (1984), 41–64

C. Brown: *Classical and Romantic Performing Practice* (Oxford, 1999)

CLIVE BROWN

ARTISJUS. *See* COPYRIGHT, §VI (under Hungary).

Artis Quartet. Austrian string quartet. It was founded in 1980 by Peter Schuhmayer and Manfred Honeck, violins, Herbert Kefer, viola, and Othmar Müller, cello, all of whom studied at the Vienna Musikhochschule with Hatto Beyerle and Alfred Staar. Johannes Meissl replaced Honeck in 1982. In 1984–5 the group studied with the La Salle Quartet in Cincinnati, after which they quickly established an international reputation with débuts in Paris (1985), Berlin (1987), Tokyo (1987), London (Wigmore Hall, 1988), New York (1988) and Amsterdam (1989). The Artis has also appeared at major international festivals, and since 1988 has given an annual concert series in the Vienna Musikverein.

The quartet has given the premières of several works, including Eder's Quartet no.4 (1991) and von Einem's Quartet no.5 (1992), and is the dedicatee of Richard Dünser's Quartet no.2 and Thomas Pernes's Quartet no.4. The intensity and imagination of the Artis's playing, founded on a warm, characteristically Viennese sonority, can be heard on numerous recordings, ranging from Mozart, Schubert and a complete Mendelssohn cycle to the quartets of Magnard and Zemlinsky. Schuhmayer plays a Domenico Montagnana violin dated 1727, Meissl an Andrea Guarneri instrument of about 1690 and Kefer a J.B. Guadagnini viola of 1784. All four players are also active as teachers, Schuhmayer and Meissl at the Vienna Musikhochschule, and Kefer and Müller at the Graz Musikhochschule.

RICHARD WIGMORE

Artisticheskiy Kruzhok (Russ.: 'Artistic circle'). Moscow society active from 1865 to 1883. *See* MOSCOW, §3.

Artocopus, Balthasar. *See* ARTHOPIUS, BALTHASAR.

Artomius [Artomiusz, Krzesichleb, Artomius Grodicensis], **Piotr** (*b* Grodzisk, nr Poznań, 26 July 1552; *d* Toruń, 2 Aug 1609). Polish clergyman and hymnbook compiler. He first studied at Grodzisk, was then, from 1573, a private tutor at Ostroróg and in 1577–8 attended the University of Wittenberg. An outstanding Protestant divine, he spent his whole career as a preacher – in Warsaw from 1578, at Węgrów from 1581, at Kryłów (in the Małopolska district) from 1584 and at Toruń from 1586 until his death. He was the editor of the most popular Polish Protestant hymnbook, *Cantional, albo pieśni duchowne* ('Cantionale, or Spiritual songs'; Toruń, 1587 or ?1578). It was enlarged and reprinted many times as *Cantional, to iest pieśni krześcijańskie* ('Cantionale, or Christian songs') at Toruń in 1596, 1601, 1620, 1638, 1648, 1672 and 1697, at Gdańsk in 1640 and 1646 and at Leipzig as late as 1728. The biggest edition, that of 1601, contains 333 songs, 106 of which were set by Adam Freytag for three to five voices (the number of these settings was reduced in later editions). The melodies were taken from traditional Catholic sources and Czech and German hymnals, and some were native Polish tunes; some of the texts were adapted, presumably by Artomius himself, to fit the traditional melodies.

BIBLIOGRAPHY

MGG1 suppl. (J. Morawski); *PSB* (M. Sipayłłówna)

L. Witkowski: *Piotr Artomiusz: przycznek do historii polskich kancjonałów ewangielickich* [Piotr Artomius: contributions to the history of the Polish evangelical hymnals] (Poznań, 1933)

K. Budzyk, ed.: *Bibliografia literatury polskiej 'Nowy Korbut'*, ii, v (Warsaw, 1964)

G. Kratzel: 'Die altpolnischen protestantischen Kantionalfrühdrucke', *Mf*, xviii (1965), 253–67

M. Przywecka-Samecka: *Drukarstwo muzyczne w Polsce do końca XVIII wieku* [Music printing in Poland up to the end of the 18th century] (Kraków, 1969, 2/1987)

K. Hławiczka: 'Sprawa kancjonału Artomiusza z roku 1578' [The hymnal of Artomius from the year 1578], *Musica antiqua Europae orientalis II* [Bydgoszcz 1969], ed. J. Wiśniowski (Bydgoszcz, 1969), 141–73 [with Fr. summary]

ZYGMUNT M. SZWEYKOWSKI

Artopaeus, Balthasar. *See* ARTHOPIUS, BALTHASAR.

Artôt, Alexandre [Montagney, Joseph] (*b* Brussels, 25 Jan 1815; *d* Ville d'Avray, nr Paris, 20 July 1845). Belgian violinist. He was the son of Maurice Artôt (1772–1829), first horn player at the Théâtre de la Monnaie, and Theresa Eva Ries, cousin of Ferdinand Ries. Maurice Artôt's real name was Montagney. At the age of five Alexandre began studying the violin with his father and within 18 months played a Viotti concerto at the theatre. He received further instruction from Snel, principal first violin at the theatre, who advised him to study in Paris. There he was admitted as a page at the Chapelle Royale and continued his studies at the Conservatoire first with Rodolphe and later with Auguste Kreutzer, gaining the second and first prizes in 1827 and 1828. According to Fétis, Artôt then performed successfully in Brussels and London and toured Belgium, Holland, Italy, Germany and other European countries. At the Philharmonic on 3 June 1839 Artôt played a fantasy of his own for violin and orchestra; this was well received because of the delicacy of his playing and his remarkable execution rather than his tone, which, according to the *Athenaeum* (8 June 1839), was small. Berlioz's *Rêverie et caprice* (op.8) was written for Artôt.

In 1843 Artôt went on a concert tour of America and Cuba with the soprano Cinti-Damoreau. He was one of the first violin virtuosos to visit America, the others being Vieuxtemps and Ole Bull; they vied with each other for the admiration of the American public, the French elements preferring Artôt's Parisian elegance to the awkward but modest stage presence of Ole Bull. While in

America Artôt showed the first symptoms of the lung disease from which he died. His compositions include a Concerto in A minor (1845), fantasies and airs with variations and, in manuscript, string quartets and a Quintet for strings and piano.

BIBLIOGRAPHY

J. Quitin: 'Un grand violiniste belge injustement oublié: Alexandre-Joseph Artôt', *Bulletin de la société liégeoise de musicologie*, xliv (1984), 1–21

ALEXIS CHITTY/MANOUG PARIKIAN

Artôt, (Marguerite-Joséphine) Désirée (Montagney) (*b* Paris, 21 July 1835; *d* Berlin, 3 April 1907). Belgian mezzo-soprano, later soprano. She was the daughter of Jean Désiré Montagney Artôt, horn player and professor at the Brussels Conservatory. She studied with Pauline Viardot in London and Paris, making her first concert appearances in Brussels and London in 1857. On Meyerbeer's recommendation she was engaged for the Paris Opéra in 1858, making her début as Fidès in *Le prophète*. In spite of the praise lavished on her by many critics, she asked to be released from her contract following some intrigues and, deciding to concentrate on the Italian repertory, she toured the south of France and Belgium. Her vocal range had extended itself in both directions, allowing her to add soprano roles to her repertory. In 1859 she sang in Italy, and at the end of the year in Berlin, with Lorini's Italian company at the opening of the Victoria-Theater, where she won great acclaim as Rosina, Angelina (*La Cenerentola*), Leonora (*Il trovatore*) and even as Maddalena (*Rigoletto*). Thereafter the greater part of her career was spent in Germany, both in Italian and German opera.

During the 1859–60 season she appeared with great success in concerts in London, and in 1863 she sang with the Royal Italian Opera as Maria in *La figlia del reggimento*. In the same year she sang Adalgisa to the Norma of Tietjens and Violetta. In spite of the great impression she invariably made in London, her appearances at Covent Garden in 1864 and 1866 were her last in England. In 1868 she went to Russia where, after a brief friendship, Tchaikovsky proposed marriage to her. Without a word of explanation, however, she married the Spanish baritone Mariano Padilla y Ramos at Sèvres in September 1869; she sang with him in Italian opera in Germany, Austria and Russia until her retirement. On 22 March 1887 they appeared together in a scene from *Don Giovanni*, performed for the kaiser's birthday at the Imperial Palace in Berlin. She taught singing in that city until 1889, when she and her husband went to live in Paris.

Their daughter, Lola Artôt de Padilla (*b* Sèvres, 5 Oct 1876; *d* Berlin, 12 April 1933), made her début in Paris in 1904 and subsequently sang in Berlin at the Komische Oper (1905–8) and at the Hofoper (1909–27), where in 1911 she was the first Octavian heard in Berlin. Her other successful roles included Zerlina, Countess Almaviva and Oscar and Micaëla.

BIBLIOGRAPHY

ES (B. Horowicz)

M. Lipsius [La Mara]: *Musikalische Studienköpfe*, v (Leipzig, 1882)

HAROLD ROSENTHAL

Art Rock. A style of rock that overtly displays musical influences from Western classical styles or otherwise seeks to expand rock's stylistic and conceptual boundaries through exceptional technical prowess or fusion with prestigious or exotic styles. The Beatles' *Sgt Pepper's Lonely Hearts Club Band* (1967) was its founding document, both in its incorporation of classical referents such as orchestral instruments and in the implicit claims it made for the seriousness and complexity of popular music. The Moody Blues established a model for 'symphonic rock' when they collaborated with the London Festival Orchestra to produce *Days of Future Past* (1967). A group of mostly British bands continued to develop PROGRESSIVE ROCK through the late 1960s and 70s, including the Nice, Emerson, Lake and Palmer, Deep Purple, Yes, Procol Harum and Pink Floyd. Further experimentation and eclectic fusions arose through the work of Genesis, King Crimson, Jethro Tull and, in the United States, Styx, Kansas and Boston.

In a broader sense, the term is often used to describe musicians such as Roxy Music, Brian Eno, Frank Zappa, David Bowie, the Velvet Underground, Steely Dan, Rush and Laurie Anderson, who in various ways absorbed influences from classical music, although an ironic stance differentiated most of them from the progressive rockers. Art rock might properly include the classically influenced HEAVY METAL of the 1980s, yet the very fact of its popular success seems to have disqualified heavy metal as art, so demonstrating the ideological implications of such cultural categories. Apart from heavy metal, the audience for art rock has been comparatively small since the genre's heyday in the 1970s.

BIBLIOGRAPHY

J. Rockwell: 'Art Rock', *The Rolling Stone Illustrated History of Rock & Roll*, ed. J. Miller (New York, 1976, 2/1980), 347–52; rev. as 'The Emergence of Art Rock', ibid. (rev. 3/1992 by A. DeCurtis, J. Henke and H. George-Warren), 492–9

B. Martin: *Music of Yes: Structure and Vision in Progressive Rock* (Chicago, 1996)

E. Macan: *Rocking the Classics: English Progressive Rock and the Counterculture* (New York, 1997)

ROBERT WALSER

Arts Council of Great Britain. British organization, incorporated by royal charter in 1948 to take the place of the wartime Council for the Encouragement of Music and the Arts and to administer the subsidies granted by the state to artistic enterprises.

The Arts Council worked through panels, musical, literary, dramatic etc., independently of the government, though the government supplied its funds. It was not intended to represent an 'establishment' view of the arts and their place in society, and aimed for 'patronage without control'. Regional arts associations working under its aegis and partly supported by the council, were free to form their own policies. The council's care for music extended beyond professional orchestras and opera companies to amateur groups. London organizations (especially the Royal Opera House) took the greatest share of subsidies, but the policy from the 1960s and 1970s was to foster the arts in the regions by its support of small touring companies.

In 1994 the Arts Council's responsibilities and functions were transferred to three new bodies: the Arts Council of England, the Scottish Arts Council and the Arts Council of Wales. The Arts Council of Northern Ireland was already established as a separate body. Each of these organizations supports, in addition to orchestras and opera companies, a range of ensembles in the fields of jazz, music theatre, improvised music, early music and Asian, African, Caribbean and other non-European music.

They also actively encourage the works of living composers and have commissioned many new works.

HENRY RAYNOR/R

Arts Council of Ireland. Organization founded in 1951 in Dublin. *See* DUBLIN, §11.

Arts Florissants, Les. French Baroque vocal and instrumental ensemble. It was founded in Paris in 1979 by WILLIAM CHRISTIE.

Art song. A song intended for the concert repertory, as opposed to a traditional or popular song. The term is more often applied to solo than to polyphonic songs. *See* SONG.

Artufel, Dámaso (*b* southern France; *fl* 1609–14). Spanish liturgist of French birth. A Dominican friar, educated at the monastery at Saint-Maximin-la-Sainte-Baume, Provence, he served as *cantor* in a number of houses of his order in France, Aragon and Castile, including S Pablo at Valladolid and finally S María de Atocha in Madrid. He was commissioned to prepare a new simplified processional for the Spanish Dominicans, *Processionarium secundum morem almi ordinis Praedicatorum S.P.N. Dominici* (Madrid, 1609), which contains information on past chant manuals of the order, and the rubrics and music for the special services involving processions. Its music was badly garbled by the printer. Artufel's second work, *Modo de rezar las horas canónicas conforme al rezo de los Frayles Predicadores … con un Arte de canto llano y con la entonación de los hymnos y sus rúbricas* (Valladolid, 1614), is in three parts with separate paginations. The first, a ceremonial for the Office, is chiefly an extract in translation from the Dominican Ordinary but with some interesting added material on the use of the organ; the second part contains the hymn intonations; the third is a manual on chant consisting of 23 chapters on the rudiments of music (notation, solmization, intervals, modes) and a collection of examples. The bulk of the technical material is taken verbatim from the *Arte de tañer fantasía* (Valladolid, 1565) of Artufel's great predecessor at S Pablo, Tomás de Santa María.

BIBLIOGRAPHY

H. Anglés and J. Subirá: *Catálogo musical de la Biblioteca nacional de Madrid*, ii (Barcelona, 1949)

ALMONTE HOWELL

Artusi, Giovanni Maria (*b* *c*1540; *d* Bologna, 18 Aug 1613). Italian theorist, polemicist and composer. He was one of the leading Italian theorists in the years around 1600, specially notable for his criticisms from a traditional viewpoint of certain modern tendencies in the music of his day.

1. Life and polemics. 2. Principal theoretical works.

1. LIFE AND POLEMICS.   Except for becoming embroiled in several musical polemics, Artusi led a quiet, studious life as a canon regular in the Congregation of S Salvatore at Bologna, where there was an important and sumptuous library of Greek and Latin manuscripts and books. He entered the order on 14 February 1562 and professed on 21 February 1563. He studied for a time in Venice with Zarlino, to whom he always remained devoted, honouring him during his lifetime with a compendium of *Le istitutioni harmoniche* and after his death with a learned eulogy by way of an explication of his teacher's emblem or device, *Impresa del molto rev. Gioseffo Zarlino* (1604).

It was as a defender of Zarlino's theories that he entered two famous controversies.

Some years after Vincenzo Galilei had published *Dialogo della musica antica et della moderna* (1581), much of which is directed against the teachings of Zarlino, Artusi rose to the latter's defence in several pamphlets known only through quotations in Ercole Bottrigari's *Aletelogia di Leonardo Gallucio*. In *Lettera apologetica* (1588) he urged composers to imitate the works of Willaert, Rore, Merulo and Costanzo Porta rather than the 'bagatelles of certain modern composers'. After Zarlino's *Sopplimenti* (1588) and Galilei's *Discorso* (1589) in reply to it, Artusi issued a *Trattato apologetico* (1590). Galilei's final reply to Artusi and Zarlino remains in manuscript (*I-Fn* Gal.5).

The controversy that developed between Artusi and Bottrigari is not unrelated to that between Zarlino and Galilei. In *Il Desiderio* (1594) Bottrigari drew attention to some of the imperfections that arose in performance when instruments tuned to different standards were mixed in ensembles (*concerti*). The dialogue appeared under the name of one of the interlocutors, Alemanno Benelli; this is an anagram of Annibale Melone, a prominent Bolognese musician and teacher whom Bottrigari chose to honour. Melone greatly admired Bottrigari and used to spend hours each day studying theory with him and copying his works. When Melone died in April 1598, his widow Luccia handed over to Artusi at his request all of Melone's manuscripts, or so states an affidavit signed by her two years later when Bottrigari thought he recognized in Artusi's book, *L'Artusi*, published in December 1600, material from his own unfinished dialogue *Il Trimerone*. Artusi allowed his quarters to be searched, but nothing was found; then Bottrigari collected witnesses for the authorship of his own unpublished works (10 December 1600 to 15 July 1601, in *I-Bc* B.44 and B.46). Actually, although Artusi covered some of the same ground as Bottrigari and was probably stimulated by *Il Trimerone*, there is no evidence of plagiarism. Rather, Bottrigari's jealousy may have been aroused by Artusi's superior scholarship and theoretical acumen and by the understanding and detachment with which he dealt with the history of Greek theory on the basis of careful reading of Aristoxenus, Ptolemy and other ancient writers.

Meanwhile in 1599 Bottrigari had issued a new edition of *Il Desiderio* under his own name. This prompted Artusi to have it reprinted in Milan in 1601 under Melone's name, with a dedication to the senate of Bologna and a letter to the reader in which Artusi claimed that Bottrigari had stolen Melone's work. Bottrigari reacted with understandable indignation in *Lettera di Federico Verdicelli* (1602). Annoyed also by the fact that Artusi criticized his *Desiderio* without naming the author, Bottrigari answered in a dialogue, *Ant-Artusi*, which has not survived. To this Artusi replied in *Considerationi musicali*, printed in *Seconda parte dell'Artusi* (1603), mockingly dedicated to Bottrigari. It is devoted in large part to a refutation of *Il Patricio* (1593), in which Bottrigari had taken friendly issue with his old mentor, the philosopher Francesco Patrizi, on some points regarding the ancient Greek tuning systems. Bottrigari replied with *Aletelogia di Leonardo Gallucio* (1604), which apparently terminated the exchange.

2. PRINCIPAL THEORETICAL WORKS.   Artusi's first book, *L'arte del contraponto ridotta in tavole* (1586), mainly

outlines in tabular form Zarlino's *Le istitutioni harmoniche* (1558), including some of books 1, 2 and 4, but the core of it is a simplification of book 3, on counterpoint. Although these tables show remarkable synthetic powers and an occasional flash of original thought, it is only with the *Seconda parte dell'arte del contraponto* (1589) that Artusi emerged as an independent theorist of the first rank. It is the first published book devoted entirely to the use of dissonances. (Galilei completed in 1588 a draft of a book on dissonances, which was never published; Artusi knew of it but did not see it.) He noted that there are more dissonances in counterpoint than consonances and that they are particularly useful for setting words expressing sorrow, tears and pain. Artusi made a primary contribution to the understanding of the suspension when he distinguished the note that moves to cause the dissonance as the *agente* and the note that is held over from the previous beat as the *patiente*. He stated the rule that the *patiente* must descend a step to a perfect or imperfect consonance or occasionally to a dissonance. The *agente*, on the other hand, is free to move anywhere (Zarlino obliged it to remain still by requiring the dissonant interval to be followed by the consonance closest to it). Artusi permitted the 4th to be resolved by a diminished 5th and the 2nd by a unison (p.29): see ex.1.

Ex.1

He also recognized that certain dissonances arise from diminution, as in the occurrence in ex.2 of parallel 2nds, which otherwise would not be permissible.

Ex.2

L'arte del contraponto (1598) united the two previous books while replacing much of the material deriving from Zarlino with a broader-based theory to bring it into line with contemporary composition. He urged composers not to imitate those who obstinately remained within the strictures of the rules and forced fugues and clever subtleties into their counterpoint, missing opportunities for more pleasing passages. Rather he would have them imitate works by Andrea Gabrieli, Palestrina and Clemens non Papa, 'who, having avoided obstinacy, have given so much pleasure to all' (p.38).

Artusi is rightly famous, though unjustly maligned, for criticizing in his books of 1600 and 1603 certain contrapuntal licences taken by an unnamed composer (later identified as Monteverdi) in four madrigals not published until 1603 and 1605. This stimulated Monteverdi's famous reply in *Il quinto libro de' madrigali* (1605) and a gloss on this letter by his brother Giulio Cesare in *Scherzi musicali* (1607). The debate is important because it brought into focus the ideals of the new style, the *seconda pratica*, as Monteverdi called it. Through the interlocutor Vario in the 1600 dialogue Artusi accused the composer of improprieties in the use of dissonances and accidentals, in the coordination of parts and in mixing modes. Meanwhile through the interlocutor Luca, who defended Monteverdi, we learn that some of the free

dissonances could be justified as arising from *accenti* (ornamental figures) and diminutions, others as written examples of improvised counterpoint and still others as modelled on the freer part movement used in instrumental performance. Through the defence of Monteverdi by an unidentified composer who wrote under the academic name of L'Ottuso quoted in Artusi's 1603 book, we learn of some of the precedents and pretexts for the expressive use of harmonic and melodic dissonances that were recognized in the works of Rore, Wert and Marenzio, and also about the metaphoric use of dissonances as 'suppositions' or 'substitutions' for consonances. Artusi replied to Monteverdi's letter under the pseudonym 'Antonio Braccino da Todi' in a discourse of 1605 which is not extant, and to Giulio Cesare's *Dichiaratione* through a second discourse under that name in 1608. In the latter he answered point for point the letters of the Monteverdi brothers and added to his other criticisms the allegation that Monteverdi did not use time signatures correctly. His most interesting retort is that it is not the text that should be mistress of the harmony and rhythm, as Monteverdi, following Plato, believed, but that rhythm ought to be the master of the other two.

Although the quarrel with Monteverdi has attracted the most attention, in both *L'Artusi* volumes it is almost a side issue. Central to the first is the subject of the imperfection of modern *concerti*, which he had first broached in chapter 16 of the counterpoint treatise of 1589 and which received a long commentary by Bottrigari in *Il Desiderio*. Now he showed that the criteria for a good ensemble are more complex than the question of tuning raised by Bottrigari. He also rejected Bottrigari's classification of instruments as 'altogether stable' in tuning, 'altogether alterable' and 'stable-alterable' and proposed instead the following three categories: with equal tones and unequal semitones; completely flexible; with both equal tones and equal semitones. The main conclusion of Artusi's dialogue was that a major imperfection of modern music stemmed from the fact that musicians had not yet calculated a way to tune instruments so that they could all play together and that any melody could be transposed to any key. Denouncing the syntonic diatonic of Ptolemy supported by Zarlino and Bottrigari as opening the way to a flood of difficulties, the interlocutors agreed that only the equal tones and equal semitones of Aristoxenus could satisfy the needs of modern music (f.34*r*).

WORKS

Canzonette, 4vv, libro I (Venice, 1598)
Cantate Domino, 8vv, in 1599[2]

WRITINGS

L'arte del contraponto ridotta in tavole (Venice, 1586)
Lettera apologetica del Burla academico Burlesco al R.D. Vincentio Spada da Faenza, 14 Jan 1588; lost, except for excerpts in Bottrigari
Seconda parte dell'arte del contraponto, nella quale si tratta dell'utile et uso delle dissonanze (Venice, 1589)
Trattato apologetico in difesa dell'opere del ... Zarlino da Chioggia, giuditio musicale del S. Cabalao Nobile di Pocceia, academico Infarinato intorno alle differenze note frà il Dottissimo Zarlino, et ... Vincenzo Galilej nobile Fiorentino, 8 April 1590; lost, except for excerpts in Bottrigari
L'arte del contraponto (Venice, 1598)
L'Artusi, overo Delle imperfettioni della moderna musica ragionamenti dui (Venice, 1600/R)
Letter of dedication and preface to E. Bottrigari: *Il Desiderio, dialogo di Annibale Melone* (Milan, 1601)

Seconda parte dell'Artusi, overo Delle imperfettioni della moderna musica (Venice, 1603/R) [with appx: *Considerationi musicali*]

Impresa del molto Rev. M. Gioseffo Zarlino da Chioggia ... dichiarata (Bologna, 1604)

Discorso secondo musicale di Antonio Braccino da Todi per la dichiaratione della lettera posta ne' Scherzi musicali del sig. Claudio Monteverdi (Venice, 1608/R)

BIBLIOGRAPHY

E. Bottrigari: *Lettera di Federico Verdicelli ... in difesa del Sig. Cav. Hercole Bottrigaro, contro quanto ... di lui ha scritto un certo Artusi* (Milan, 1601; MS copy, *I-Bc* I.68)

Aletelogia di Leonardo Galluccio ... per la difesa del M.I. sig. Cav. Hercole Bottrigaro, contra a quanto ha scritto lo autore delle Inconsiderationi musicali (26 Feb 1604; MSS, *I-Bc* B.43, *Bu* 345 Busta III no.4)

G.C. Trombelli: *Memorie istoriche concernenti le due canoniche di S. Maria di Reno et di S. Salvatore* (Bologna, 1752)

G. Gaspari: 'Dei musicisti bolognesi al XVI secolo e delle loro opere a stampa: ragguagli biografici e bibliografici', *Atti e memorie della R. Deputazione di storia patria per le provincie di Romagna*, 2nd ser., ii (1876), 3–84, esp. 55

D. Arnold: '"Seconda pratica": a Background to Monteverdi's Madrigals', *ML*, xxxviii (1957), 341–52

C. Dahlhaus: 'Zur Theorie des klassischen Kontrapunkts', *KJb*, xlv (1961), 47–57

D. Arnold: *Monteverdi* (London, 1963, rev. 3/1990 by T. Carter)

A. Damerini: 'Giovanni Maria Artusi e alcune sue opere teoriche', *Le celebrazioni del 1963 e alcune nuove indagini sulla musica italiana del XIII e XIX secolo*, ed. M. Fabbri, A. Damerini and G. Roncaglia, Chigiana, xx (1963), 9–14

C.V. Palisca: 'The Artusi–Monteverdi Controversy', *The Monteverdi Companion*, ed. D. Arnold and N. Fortune (London, 1968, 2/1985 as *The New Monteverdi Companion*), 127–58

T. Carter: 'Artusi, Monteverdi, and the Poetics of Modern Music', *Musical Humanism and its Legacy: Essays in Honor of C.V. Palisca*, ed. N.K. Baker and B.R. Hanning (Stuyvesant, NY, 1992), 171–94

S.G. Cusick: 'Gendering Modern Music: Thoughts on the Monteverdi–Artusi Controversy', *JAMS*, xlvi (1993), 1–25

CLAUDE V. PALISCA

Artusini, Antonio (*b* Ravenna, bap. 2 Oct 1554; *d* Ravenna, before 6 May 1604). Italian composer, lawyer, poet and orator. According to Mazzuchelli, he was born in Forlì. His only known musical work is *Il primo libro de madrigali a cinque voci* (Venice, 1598), dedicated to Paolo Savelli, which contains 23 madrigals, including a setting of Guarini's popular *Ah dolente partita* and another, based on the scale ut, re, mi, fa, sol, la. His poetic writings include a canzonetta on the death of Cristina Racchi Lunardi.

BIBLIOGRAPHY

S. Pasolini: *Huomini illustri di Ravenna antica* (Bologna, 1703), 99

P.P. Ginanni, ed.: *Rime scelte de' poeti ravennati antichi, e moderni defunti* (Ravenna, 1739), 61–2, 413

G.M. Mazzuchelli: *Gli scrittori d'Italia*, i (Brescia, 1753), 1146 only

P.P. Ginanni: *Memorie storico-critiche degli scrittori ravennati*, i (Faenza, 1769), 58–9

L. Bianconi: 'Ah dolente partita: Espressione ed artificio', *Studi musicali*, iii (1974), 105–30

PIER PAOLO SCATTOLIN

Artyomov, Vyacheslav Petrovich (*b* Moscow, 29 June 1940). Russian composer. He attended the Moscow Conservatory where he studied composition with Sidel'nikov and the piano with Logovinsky (1962–8) although since 1957 he had already been engaged in various professional musical activities (teaching, working as a pianist at the Moscow Choreography, as a musical director with the Moscow theatres of drama, and as an editor for Muzïka publishers). Since 1977 Artyomov has concentrated wholly on creative work. In 1975, along with Gubaidulina and Suslin, Artyomov organised the

group Astrea, which performed improvisations on unusual and exotic instruments. In 1990 Artyomov was composer-in-residence at the University of Nevada and in 1992 he organized the *Fund dukhovnogo tvorchestva* (The fund for spiritual art) in Russia.

Artyomov's early works were written in a neo-folkloric style, a trend that was popular in Russian music during the 1960s. By the mid 1970s he had become more independent and his music became shaped by two spheres of interest that were important too in his later works. The first of these is associated with a striving for a characteristic sound, above all in the brass and percussion. In percussion writing Artyomov emphasizes ritualistic while his brass writing is characterized by a concerto style with freely composed solo parts. The other aspect of Artyomov's art veers towards neo-Romanticism, a trend which by the mid 1970s had acquired great importance in Russia. Tonal structures and melodic lines began to appear in Artyomov's music – not in pure form, but employing the more complex timbres and polyphonic textures that are generally typical of his style. By the end of the 1970s the mastery of his orchestration had become one of the strongest aspects of his style, even though sound colour in itself was not of primary importance to Artyomov; he strives to subordinate his art to higher spiritual goals that in time become more and more grandiose. This aspect of his work and the titles of two major instrumental works of the 1970s – *Girlyanda rechitatsiy* ('A Garland of Recitations') and *Simfoniya èlegiy* ('A Symphony of Elegies') – link his work to the Symbolism of the Russian Silver Age and more specifically to Skryabin, to whose style direct references are made. The title of a work becomes a distinctive, programmatic commentary, in most cases filled out by Artyomov himself or by his wife, the poet Valeriya Lyubetskaya; these commentaries accompany the performance in the form of printed texts.

In the 1980s Artyomov wrote chiefly instrumental music for non-standard forces but also applied himself to the writing of symphonic works in the spirit of late romanticism. These works, grandiose in their concept and in the scale of their realization, again demonstrate a direct link with the traditions of Skryabin. The first composition of this type to appear was the symphony *Put' k Olimpu* ('The Pathway to Olympus'), the first in the tetralogy *Simfoniya puti* ('The Symphony of a Pathway'), which was continued and completed in the 1990s. Conceptually, *Put' k Olimpu* follows in the footsteps of Skryabin's *Poèma èkstaza* ('The Poem of Ecstasy') and *Prometey*: central to the work is the idea of ascending from a primary static state towards the final moment of lucidity embodied in a 'chord of unity'. This prophetic grandiosity is characteristic of the remaining parts of the tetralogy: the symphonies *Na poroge svetlogo mira* ('On the Threshold of a Radiant World'), *Tikhoye veyaniye* ('Gentle Emanation') and *Dennitsa vossiyayet* ('The Morning Star Shines Forth').

Artyomov's musical language of the 1990s is synthetic, combining elements of a traditional melodic and harmonic style with sonoristic effects and a dramatic plan based on timbre and texture. In its most transparent form this synthetic quality manifests itself in the Requiem dedicated *Muchenikam mnogostradal'noy Rossii* ('To the Martyrs of Long-Suffering Russia'), the performance of which generated great public interest. Although the Requiem is written to canonical Latin texts, his interpretation follows not the liturgical but the concert hall tradition. His Requiem is an ecumenical mass, grandiose in terms of the forces required to play it and in its scale.

WORKS

Stage: Ozhidaniye [Expectation] (ballet-nostalgia), 1984; Sola Fide [By Faith Alone] (ballet, after A. Tolstoy: *The Road to Calvary*), 1987

Orch: Kontsert trinadtsati [Conc. of 13], 1967; Vn Conc. 'In memoriam', 1968, rev. 1984; Tempo costante, 1970, rev. 1980; Girlyand rechitatsiy [A Garland of Recitations], ob, cl/sax, bn, orch, 1975–81; Simfoniya élegiy [A Symphony of Elegies], 2 vn, orch, 1977; Simfoniya puti [Sym. of the Way]: Put' k Olimpu [The Way to Olympus], 1978–84, Na poroge svetlogo mira [On the Threshold of a Radiant World], 1990, Tikhoye veyaniye [Gentle Emanation], 1991, Dennitsa vossiyayet [The Morning Star Arises], 1993; Tristia I, pf, tpt, orch, 1983; Plachi [Lamentations], 1985; Guriyskiy gimn [Gurian Hymn], 3 vn, orch, 1986; Pietà, vc, orch, 1992–6; Russkiy gimn [Russian Hymn], 1994; Ave atque vale, 2 solo perc, orch, 1996; Tristia II, 1996; In Spe, sym., vc, orch, 1997

Choral orch: Plachi [Lamentations], 1986 [version of orch work]; Scenes from the ballet Tol'ko veroy, 1987; Requiem, solo descant, 3 S, T, Bar, 1985–8; Ave Maria, S, chorus/str, 1989

Choral: Plachi [Lamentations], version of orch work, 1986

Vocal-inst: Poteshki [Song-Amusements], S, pf, 1964, arr. S, ens, 1993; 4 dueta [4 Duets] (A. Grashi), S, Mez, pf, 1966; Severniye pesni [Northern Songs] (Russ. folk texts), Mez, perc, pf, 1966; Gimn zhasminovïm nocham [A Hymn to Jasmine Nights], S, pf, 1979; Mattinati [Mattinates], S, fl, gui, vn, 1981; Zaklinaniya [Invocations] (Artyomov), S, 4 perc, 1981; Snï pri lunnom svetye [Moonlight Dreams] (Wan Wei, Li Po, Ssu-K'ung Shu), S/Mez, a fl, pf, vc, 1982; Ave Maria, S, str qt, 1989

Chbr: Stsenï [Scenes], cl, perc, pf, vn, db, 1970; Ptenets Antsali [The Fledgling Antsali], variations, fl, pf, 1974; 5 p'yes [5 Pieces], cl, pf, 1975; Osennyaya sonatina [Autumn Sonatina], fl/ob/cl/sax, pf, 1975; Kaprichchio pod Noviy '75 god [Capriccio for the New Year in 1975], s sax, bar sax, vib, 1975; Romanticheskoye kaprichchio [Romantic capriccio], hn, pf/hn, pf, str qt, 1975; Totem, 6 perc, 1976; Litaniya I, sax qt, 1977; Voskresnaya sonata [A Sunday Sonata], bn, pf, 1977; Lesniye eskizï [Woodland Sketches], 2 pf, 1978; Probuzhdeniye [Awakening], 2 vn, 1978; Sonata razmïshleniya [A Sonata of Meditations], 4 perc, 1978; All' Rondo, a sax, pf, 1981; Litaniya II, fl, qt, 1981; Zvyozdnïy veter [Celestial Wind], fl, hn, bells, pf, vn, vc, 1983; Gimnï vnezapnïkh dunoveniy [Hymns of Sudden Waftings], sax, hpd, pf, 1985; Gimnï ognennïkh kasaniy [Hymns of Fiery Touches], vn, vc, hpd, pf, glockenspiel, plate bells, 1994

Solo inst: Sonata, cl, 1966; Ispoved' [Confession], cl, 1971; Rechitatsiya I [Recitation I], cl/sax, 1975; Rechitatsiya III, fl, 1977; Rechitatsiya IV, fl/ob/cl/sax, 1977; Rechitatsiya V, bn, 1977; Sonata Ricercata, perc, 1978; Rechitatsiya IX, fl/ob/cl/sax, 1980; Rechitatsiya X, fl/ob/cl/sax, 1980; Preludes to Sonnets, pf, 1981; Rechitatsiya II, fl, 1981; Litany III, org, 1986; Ave Atque Vale, perc, 1989

BIBLIOGRAPHY

N. Surkova: 'Vyacheslav Artyomov', *Kompozitorï Moskvï* (Moscow, 1976)

S. Savenko: 'Rekviem s "khoroshim kontsom"?' [A requiem with a 'happy ending'?], *SovM* (1989), no.5, pp.25–6

M. Tarakanov: *Artyomov: ocherk tvorchestva* [An essay on his creative work] (Moscow, 1994)

M. Tarakanov: 'Vyacheslav Artyomov: v poiskakh khudozhestvennoy istinï [In search of artistic truth], *Muzïka iz bïvshego SSSR* (Moscow, 1994; Eng. trans. 1997)

SVETLANA SAVENKO

Arundell [Arundel], **Dennis (Drew)** (*b* Finchley, London, 22 July 1898; *d* London, 10 Dec 1988). English opera producer, writer and composer. He studied the piano under his mother (both his parents were musicians) from the age of six, and was educated at Tonbridge School (1912–17) and St John's College, Cambridge (1919–29), where he read classics and music and became a Fellow. His musical studies were under C.B. Rootham, Henry Moule and Stanford and he was also influenced by E.J. Dent and Maynard Keynes. He made appearances as an actor and singer, from 1926, and from 1929 was a professional actor and producer. An influential figure in English musical-theatrical life for many years, his opera and masque productions cover a remarkably wide historical range: from Locke, Purcell and Handel (*Semele*, stage première, Cambridge, 1925) to Delius, Janáček (*Kaťá Kabanová*, British première, London, 1950), Britten, Honegger and Stravinsky (*Soldier's Tale*, British première, Cambridge, 1928); he also produced many works in the standard repertory, including several Mozart operas, as well as Balfe's *Bohemian Girl* at Covent Garden under Sir Thomas Beecham. His productions were noted for their sense of style, their dramatic vigour and their stage mastery. He believed in total fidelity to the score and stage directions, supported by a scholarly understanding of the social and historical background, and was intolerant of more freely interpreted productions.

Arundell wrote many articles, in *Opera* and elsewhere, mostly on matters concerning musical drama, as well as several books. He was a prolific composer of theatre music, including operas (*Ghost of Abel* and *A Midsummer Night's Dream*) and incidental music for plays, films, radio and television, mostly unpublished. He co-edited Purcell's *Miscellaneous Odes and Cantatas* for the Purcell Society (1957). He was appointed to the staff of the Royal College of Music Opera School in 1956, and was Crees lecturer at the college in 1971; he was made FRCM in that year. From 1974 for a brief period he was appointed opera producer and coach at the Royal Northern College of Music, Manchester, and in 1975–6 he produced *Hänsel und Gretel* and *Don Pasquale* in Melbourne. He was awarded the OBE in 1978.

WRITINGS

'Operatic Ignorance', *PMA*, li (1924–5), 73–96

Henry Purcell (London, 1927/R)

The Critic at the Opera (London, 1957/R)

The Story of Sadler's Wells (London, 1965, enlarged 2/1978)

Introduction to *Le nozze di Figaro and Così fan tutte* (London, 1971)

ERIC BLOM/ROSEMARY WILLIAMSON

Arutiunian, Alexander Grigoriyevich (*b* Yerevan, 23 Sept 1920). Armenian composer and pianist. At the Komitas Conservatory in Yerevan he studied composition (with Barkhudarian and Tal'ian) and the piano (with O. Babasian), graduating in 1941. He continued his studies at the Moscow Conservatory with Litinsky, Peyko and Zuckermann (1946–8). He was artistic director of the Armenian Philharmonic Society between 1954 and 1990. He began to teach composition at the Yerevan Conservatory in 1965, and was appointed to a professorship in 1977. He joined the Union of Composers in 1939 and the Union of Cinematographers of Armenia in 1975. He was awarded the State Prize of the USSR in 1949 for his graduation work *Kantat hayreinki masin* ('Cantata on the Homeland'), and was made a People's Artist of Armenia in 1960. Since then he has received numerous awards in Armenia, the USA and elsewhere.

The development in the late 1940s of Arutiunian's artistic perception, with its dualism between Classical and Romantic elements, coincided with the development of vitalist trends in Soviet art of the postwar period. Arutiunian's individual response to vitalism involved a spontaneous and improvisatory approach which drew on Armenia's cultural heritage, revealing the immanent potential of the national melodic style and the energy of its rhythms. Elements of vitalism also conditioned other aspects of Arutiunian's music: his preservation of Classical sequences of contrasting movements and his use of Baroque forms and genres, especially suites and concertos. The concertante principle influences not only his concertos and other orchestral and chamber works, but also the opera *Sayat-Nova* (1967), in which the *ashug*, an 18th-century Armenian minstrel comparable to the Western Meistersinger, is made to symbolize the originality of the national poet-musician. The *ashug* tradition, based on freely varied development, has been important to Arutiunian's work in general. His lyrical idiom is rooted in a specific national melodic character, while the Romantic side of his sensibility finds expression in an emotional radicalism and a predominantly lyrical impulse, producing music that is at once expressive, sentimental, nostalgic and ironic.

Although Arutiunian's style has evolved smoothly and continuously, distinct periods are discernible in his music. The works of the 1940s and 50s are characterized by thematic development and the sequential combination of large structures which creates a high degree of emotional intensity. These works, including the Festive Overture, the Symphony and the Piano Concertino, continue the tradition of Khachaturian in their combination of a highly colourful, decorative style with a tragic sense of pathos. The 1960s and 70s saw an abandonment of dramatic elements in favour of diatonic clarity and an orientation towards Classical forms. Alongside *Sayat-Nova*, his major achievement of this period, are a number of works written in the neo-classical style, such as the sinfoniettas, the Horn Concerto and the Variations for trumpet and orchestra. Stylistic synthesis characterizes his works of the 1980s and 90s, such as the concertos for trombone and tuba (like the earlier Horn Concerto the first Armenian concertos for their respective instruments), and the Violin Concerto 'Armenia – 88', considered by many his masterpiece, in which a rhetorical Baroque style, Classical form and a Romantic harmonic palette are employed in balanced combination. A number of Arutiunian's works for wind, notably the concertos for trumpet (1950) and tuba and the brass quintet *Armenian Scenes* (1984), have entered the international repertory.

WORKS
(*selective list*)

Stage: Sayat-Nova (op, 3, A. Khanjan), 1967, Yerevan, A. Spendiarian Theatre, 1969; Medsapativ muratskanner [Honourable Beggars] (musical comedy), 1972, unfinished
Vocal: Kantat hayreniki masin [Cant. on the Homeland] (Sarmen, A. Grashi), Mez, Bar, mixed chorus, orch, 1948; Conc., S, orch, 1950; 5 Capriccios, S, pf, 1959; Ask hayots zhogovurdi masin [The Tale of the Armenian People] (Grashi), T, Bar, spkr, chorus, orch, 1960; Requiem (Armenian sacred text), mixed chorus, 1965; S otchiznoy moyey [From my Fatherland] (Hov. Tumanian), solo vv, chorus, orch, 1969; Hushardzan mayrikis [Mother Memorial] (Hov. Shiraz), Ten, pf, 1970; Poem on a Song (trad.), S, chorus, orch, 1980; Triptych (vocalise), mixed chorus, pf, perc, 1982
Orch: Pf Conc., 1940; Torzhestvennaya oda [Ceremonial Ode], 1947; Prazdnichnaya uvertyura [Festive Ov.], 1949; Tpt Conc., 1950; Concertino, pf, orch, 1951; Tantseval'naya suita [Dance Suite], 1952; Concert Scherzo, tpt, orch, 1954; Sym., 1957; Hn Conc., 1962; Sinfonietta, str orch, 1966; Theme and Variations, tpt, orch, 1972; Our Old Songs, rhapsody, pf, perc, str, 1974; Poem, vc, orch, 1974; Ob Conc., 1977; Fl Conc., 1980; Armenia – 88, conc., vn, str, 1989; Rhapsody, tpt, wind, 1990; Trbn Conc., 1991; Tuba Conc., 1992
Chbr and solo inst: Polyphonic Sonata, pf, 1946; Haykakan rapsodia [Armenian Rhapsody], 2 pf, 1950, collab. A. Babadjanian; Concert Scherzo, tpt, pf, 1955; Festive, 2 pf, perc, 1961, collab. Babadjanian; 3 Musical Pictures, pf, 1961; Aria and Scherzo, tpt, pf, 1983; Retro-Sonata, va, pf, 1983; Suite, ww qnt, 1983;

Armenian Scenes, brass qnt, 1984; Piece, 4 trbn, 1985; 2 Pieces, tpt, pf, 1985; Poem-Sonata, vn, pf, 1985; Dance, 4 trbn, 1989; 2 pieces, 4 trbn, 1989; Trio, cl, vn, pf, 1992
Film scores, incid music

Principal publishers: Sovetskiy Kompozitor, Muzïka, Haypetrat

BIBLIOGRAPHY
S. Koptev: 'Simfoniya Arutiunyana', *50 sovetskikh simfoniy* (Leningrad, 1961), 11–17
I. Yeolian: *A. Arutiunyan* (Moscow, 1962)
R. Atayan, M. Harutyunyan and G. Budaghyan, eds.: *Muzïka sovetskoy Armeni* [The music of Soviet Armenia] (Moscow, 1967), 158–64, 195–203
Sh. Apoian: *Fortepiannaya muzïka sovetskoy Armenii* [The piano music of Soviet Armenia] (Yerevan, 1968), 142–9, 198–201
M. Berko: 'A. Arutiunian', *Muzikalnaya zhizn'*, no.22 (1970), 20–23
G. Tigranov: 'O prem'yere operï Arutiunyana', *SovM* (1970), no.1, pp.29–33
G. Tigranov: *Armianskiy muzïkal'nïy teatr* [Armenian music theatre], iii (Yerevany, 1975), 130–43
M. Rukhkyan: *Armianskaya simfoniya* [The Armenian symphony] (Yerevan, 1980), 40–45
R. Stepanian: 'Neutmoimii energichnii, karkii khoudozhnik' [Tireless, energetic artist], *SovM*, no.12 (1980), 34–7
S. Sarkisyan: 'Novïye puti kamerno-vokal'nogo zhanra' [New directions in chamber vocal music], *Sovetskaya muzïka na sovremennom etape*, ed. G.L. Golovinsky and N.G. Shakhnazarova (Mosocw, 1981), 238–78
M. Rukhkyan: 'The Colours of Life', *Music in the USSR* (1986), April–June, 10–12
S. Sarkisyan: 'Arouig vocku cannonerov' [The principles of the awakened spirit], *Havastan* [Yerevan] (25 Sept 1990)
N. Tahmizian: 'Kerckot hairenaser' [The passionate patriot], *Yerekoyan Yerevan* (22 Sept 1990)
M. Rukhkyan: 'Klassik armyanskoy muzïki' [A classic of Armenian music], *Azd* (23 Sept 1995)
M. Arutyunian and A. Barsamian: *Hay yerazhshtutian patmutian* [The history of Armenian music] (Yerevan, 1996), 319–22
SVETLANA SARKISIAN

Arzumanov, Valery Grantovich (*b* nr Vorkuta, Russia, 3 Aug 1944). Russian composer. He trained as a violinist and composer at the Special Music School attached to the Conservatory (1958–63) and then at the Conservatory itself (1963–8; postgraduate studies 1968–71) in the composition class of V. Salmanov. He has taught in both establishments. In 1974 he moved to France where he studied composition with Messiaen at the Paris Conservatoire (1974–8), and at the musicology faculty of the Sorbonne (1984–5). Since 1991 he has been *Professeur-animateur* of the national music school at Notre Dame de Gravenchon and since 1994 he has also taught analysis at the Rouen Conservatoire.

A prolific composer, Arzumanov's moral and religious quests are reflected in his continuous search for new styles and genres. He has studied the music of Mahler, Shostakovich and the Second Viennese School, the music of ancient civilizations, pop music, and the church canticles of the Orthodox tradition, and willingly uses their forms and devices in his works in his efforts to find a spiritual kinship with distant epochs and peoples. The piano cycle *Fortepiannïy mir* 'Piano World' which he wrote at the end of the 1980s includes more than 400 pieces and is a unique and resonant diary of the composer's life; in it he captured the vicissitudes of life through the most varied musical impressions retained by his memory. Themes of childhood are frequently encountered in Arzumanov's work; they are sometimes associated with recollections of his own dramatic childhood spent in the far north of Russia in the Stalinist Gulag where his parents met. They had been exiled there in 1936 as 'enemies of the people'; in works such as *Pamyati V.T. Shalamov* 'In memory of Varlam Tikhonovich Shalamov' and *Babushka Khava* 'Grandmother Khava' the composer expresses a thought which is dear to him – that of suffering as a means to penitence and purification. Another large cycle, having an autobiographical and deeply lyrical character, are the songs which Arzumanov set to his own words and which he himself performed with a guitar accompaniment. Many of his earliest works are orchestral, but he has since written works for soloists, ensemble (often of an unusual make-up) and choir. He has published six volumes of poetry (in Russian) and has written articles on many of his contemporaries including Butsko, Karamanov and Golovin.

WORKS

STAGE

Dvoye [The Two] (chbr op, S. Volkov), 1966; Babushka Khava [Grandmother Khava] (op-monologue, Arzumanov), 1952–90; Pamyati V.T. Shalamova [In Memory of Varlam Tikhonovich Shalamov] (mini-op, Arzumanov), 1956–88; Ikar [Icarus] (ballet, B. Eyfman, collab. A. Chernov), 1970; Pis'mo [The Letter] (op-monologue, I. Okunev), 1991

VOCAL

Cants.: Osennyaya pesnya [Autumn Song] (F. García Lorca), 1964; Veter voynï [The Wind of War] (A. Akhmatova), 1967; Vesyolaya kantata dlya detey [A Jolly Cant. for Children] (Arzumanov), 1972; Iz nagornoy propovedi [From the Sermon on the Mount] (Bible), 1989; Bratoubiystvo [Fratricide] (Arzumanov), 1993

Other choral (all to texts by Arzumanov unless otherwise stated): Moleniye [Praying] (choral conc.), 1990; Pokayaniye [Repentance] (choral conc.), 1990; Malen'kiy rozhdestvenskiy kontsert [A Little Christmas Conc.], 1991; Ivanushka [Little Ivan], 3 songs, 1992; 3 pesni [3 Songs] (A. Kol'tsov), 1992; Proshcheniye [Forgiveness], 1994; Vospominaniye o Vorkute [Reminiscences of Vorkuta], 1995

11 works for 1v, ens after Armenian epic poetry, Jap. poems of the Middle Ages, Arzumanov, M. Lermontov, F. García Lorca

39 works for 1v, pf, after Arzumanov, A. Blok, I. Bunin, O. Driz, M. Lermontov, V. Levin, F. García Lorca, O. Mandel'shtam, S. Marshak, B. Pasternak, A.S. Pushkin, N. Oleynikov, R.M. Rilke, I. Severyanin, W. Shakespeare, F. Tyutchev, V. Zhukovsky

for 1v, gui: Prosti nas greshnïkh! [Forgive us Sinners!], improvisation, 1976; Melodicheskiy svod [Melodic Collection], 200 songs, 1979–86

INSTRUMENTAL

Orch: Sinfonietta, 1965; Sym., str, 1966–91; Sym., 1968; Pamyati A. Berga [To the Memory of Alban Berg], 2 pieces, 1970; Vn Conc., 1967; Mir [Peace], va, str, church bell, 1991; Iz detstva [From Childhood], 10 pieces, 14 ww insts, perc, 1992; Conc. solo vc, 15 vc, perc, 1993; Davay potantsuyem! [Let's Dance], 8 dances, str, 1995

Chbr inst: 3 str qts: 1962, 1963, 1966; Pf Qt, 1993; Pf Trio, 1996, Sonata, vn, vc, 1996; Sonata, vn, 1997

Pf: Sonata, 1964; Prostaya sonata [Simple Sonata], 1986; Sonatina, 1988; 24 dvukhgolosnïye inventsii [24 2-Part Inventions], 1988; Fortepiannïy mir [Piano World], 13 vols., each containing from 27 to 40 pieces

Incid music

WRITINGS

'Dva pis'ma i tri portreta (o tvorchestve molodïkh kompozitorov)' [Two letters and three portraits (on the work of young composers)], SovM (1973), no.12, pp.22–8

'Nezrimïy svet vekov (traditsii mirovoy kul'turï i muzïka)' [The unseen light of centuries (the traditions of world culture and music)] Rossiyskaya muzïkal'naya gazeta (1990) March

BIBLIOGRAPHY

S. Volkov: 'Poznavaya mir' [Getting to know the world], Molodïye kompozitorï Leningrada [The young composers of Leningrad] (Leningrad, 1971)

M. Rakhmanova: 'Vozvrashcheniye v svoyu kul'turu' [Going back to one's culture], SovM (1989), no.4, pp.35–8 [incl. interview with Arzumanov]

A. Gerard: 'Otkrïtiye Arzumanova' [Arzumanov's discovery], Intemporel(1994), nos.11–12

MIKHAIL GRIGOR'YEVICH BYALIK

As (Ger.). A♭. *See* PITCH NOMENCLATURE.

Aṣ, Jamīl al- (*b* 17 Jan 1929). Jordanian traditional composer, singer and *buzuq* player of Palestinian Gypsy origin. At an early age he joined a group of Gypsy musicians as a singer and player of the *'ūd* (short-necked lute) and the *buzuq* (long-necked lute), and performed at weddings and other celebrations in Jerusalem and the neighbouring villages. He began to learn religious chants and Qur'anic recitation at the age of nine. In 1949 he joined the choir of the broadcasting service in Ramallah, and in 1959 he joined the music section of the newly established radio station in Amman. In 1963 he was appointed leader of the radio station's music ensemble; he held this position for several years, during which he performed many of his songs and also had the opportunity to join a group of researchers making a field survey of folk heritage including Jordanian folk singing and music in an area covering both banks of the river Jordan. As a *buzuq* player he participated in several national and international festivals and competitions, winning first prize in a competition in Tunisia in 1974. In 1976 he was appointed consultant for the radio and television stations in Amman and still held this position in 1999.

His vocal style reflects elements of east Jordanian and Palestinian heritage as well as influences from Iraq and Syria. Many of his songs have been performed by his second wife, the Palestinian singer Salwā, and by several Jordanian and Arab singers including Ismā'īl Khaḍr, Shukrī 'Ayyād, Sihām al-Ṣafadī, and Sāmī al-Shāyib; the songs of al-Aṣ have become widely known in Jordan and the Arab world through the performances of the Lebanese singer Samīra Tawfīq. Jamīl al-Aṣ received the Badge of Independence for his contribution to the development of Jordanian song.

ABDEL-HAMID HAMAM

Asaf'yev, Boris Vladimirovich [Glebov, Igor'] (*b* St Petersburg, 17/29 July 1884; *d* Moscow, 27 Jan 1949). Russian musicologist, composer and critic. He studied at the St Petersburg Conservatory from 1904 to 1910 with Rimsky-Korsakov and Lyadov, and graduated in 1908 from the faculty of history and philology of the University of St Petersburg. From 1910 he worked as a repetiteur; from 1916 edited and composed ballet music and from 1919 was a member of the board of directors and repertory consultant at the Mariinsky and Mikhaylovsky Theatres. In 1919 he became head of the Central Library for State Musical Theatres. In the same year, in association with Lyapunov and Bulich, he organized the music department at the Petrograd Institute for the History of the Arts (now the Zubov Institute for the History of the Arts); he was its director from 1921. Between 1922 and 1925 he was responsible for the organization there of concerts of contemporary music. He was made a professor at the Leningrad Conservatory in 1925, and established its music department as well as devising a programme of studies that aimed to unite a university education with a fundamental preparation in the techniques of musicianship. He also taught and administered at the Leningrad Music Technical School.

In 1926 Asaf'yev was one of the founders of the Leningrad branch of the Association for Contemporary

Music. He simultaneously set up and led the New Music Society; the two groups amalgamated a year later. Concerts were given of music by Les Six and other Western composers, as well as contemporary Leningrad composers; unfamiliar works by Prokofiev and Stravinsky were also heard. As a result of this he produced the first Russian book on Stravinsky, *Kniga o Stravinskom* (1929). He also had an active influence on the renewal of the repertory of the Leningrad opera houses. Between 1924 and 1928 more than ten new foreign operas were staged, including *Salome*, *Wozzeck*, Schreker's *Der ferne Klang* and Krenek's *Der Sprung über den Schatten* and *Jonny spielt auf*.

From 1914 Asaf'yev wrote regularly under the pseudonym Igor' Glebov in the journals *Muzïka*, *Muzïkal'nïy sovremennik*, *Zhizn' iskusstva* and *Krasnaya gazeta*. During his most prolific period as a writer (1919–28), he formulated his interests in the study of the classical legacy of Russian music and in contemporary music, consolidated through contact with Berg, Hindemith, Schoenberg, Milhaud, Honegger and Bartók. During the 1930s his academic work was pushed into the background by composition. He wrote an outstanding trio of ballets – *Plamya Parizha* ('The Fire of Paris', 1932), *Bakhchisarayskiy fontan* ('The Fountain of Bakhchisaray', 1933) and *Utrachennïye illyuzii* ('Lost Illusions', 1934) – as well as five symphonies and numerous other works. He returned to rigorous academic work at the start of the 1940s, even continuing to write prolifically during the Siege of Leningrad, and devised a cycle of research and writings called *Mïsli i duma* [Thoughts and reflections]. A significant aim was realized in 1947 with the publication of *Intonatsiya*, the second volume of his book *Muzïkal'naya forma kak protsess*. In this, he expounded his influential theories of music 'intonation', a term which, in Russian, has broader implications than in English, embracing the diverse expressive aspects of musical form. In addition to further writings on Russian subjects, he completed his fundamental monograph on Glinka (1947) and wrote a major article on the revival of Czech music in the decades preceding World War II (intended for the *Mïsli i duma* cycle, a fragment of the essay was published in *Izbrannïye trudï* (1952–7) iv, pp.357–68.

In 1943 he moved to Moscow, where he headed the research office at the Conservatory and the music department of the Institute of Art History of the USSR Academy of Sciences. He was also a consultant to the Bol'shoy Theatre. He was made a National Artist of the USSR in 1946, and was president of the Union of Composers from 1948 to 1949. His book on Russian paintings, *Russkaya zhivopis'*, was published posthumously in 1966.

WORKS
(selective list)

For complete list see *B.V. Asaf'yev: Izbrannïye trudï*, v (Moscow, 1957), 295–380

STAGE

Ops: Zolushka [Cinderella] (children's op, 2, L.A. Levandovskaya, after C. Perrault), 1906, private perf., St Petersburg, wint. 1906–7; Snezhnaya koroleva [The Snow Queen] (4, S.M. and V.M. Mart'yanov, after H.C. Andersen), 1907, private perf., St Petersburg, 20 Jan/2 Feb 1908; Kaznacheysha [The Treasurer's Wife] (6 scenes, prol and epilogue, A.A. Matveyev, after M.Yu. Lermontov: *Tambovskaya kaznacheysha*), 1935–6, Leningrad, Pakhomov Sailors' Club, 1 April 1937; Mednïy vsadnik [The Bronze Horseman] (sym.-monodrama, 8 episodes, prol and epilogue, after A.S. Pushkin), 1939–40; 7 others unperf.

Ballets: Belaya liliya/Gryozï poèta [The White Lily/Daydreams of a Poet] (3 scenes, N.M. Leont'yeva), 1910; Ledyanaya deva/Sol'veyg [The Ice Maiden/Solveig] (3, B.G. Romanov), 1918 [after E. Grieg]; Plamya Parizha [The Fire of Paris] (4, N.D. Volkov, V.V. Dmitriyev, choreog. V. Vaynonen), 1932; Bakhchisarayskiy fontan [The Fountain of Bakhchisaray] (4, Volkov, after Pushkin, choreog. P. Zakharov), 1933; Utrachyonnïye illyuzii [Lost Illusions] (3, Dmitriyev, after H. de Balzac, choreog. Zakharov), 1934; Partizanskiye dni [Partisan Days] (4, Dmitriyev, after V.I. Baynonen, choreog. Vaynonen), 1935; Kavkazskiy plennik [The Prisoner of the Caucasus] (3, Volkov, after Pushkin, choreog. L. Lavrovsky), 1936; Noch' pered rozhdestvom [The Night before Christmas] (3, Y.O. Slonimsky, after N.V. Gogol'), 1937; Ashik-Kerib (4, A.A. d'Actille and M.D. Volobrinsky, after Lermontov; choreog. B. Fenster), 1939; Barïshnya krest'yanka [The Peasant Princess] (6 scenes, Volkov, after Pushkin, choreog. Zakharov), 1945; 18 others

INSTRUMENTAL AND VOCAL

Sym. no.1 'Pamyati Lermontova' [In Memory of Lermontov], b, orch, 1938; Sym. no.2 'Iz èpokhi krest'yanskikh vosstaniy' [From the Age of the Peasant Uprisings], f♯, orch, 1938; Sym. no.3 'Rodina' [Homeland], C, orch, 1938–42; Sym. no.4 'Privestvennaya' [Welcome], B♭, orch, 1938–42; 2 Suites, wind band, 1940; March, wind band, 1941; Suite, folk orch, 1941; Sym. no.5 'Vremena goda' [The Seasons], orch, 1942, unfinished
Chbr music, pf pieces, songs etc.

WRITINGS

Items marked with a dagger written under the name Asaf'yev; all others written under the pseudonym Igor' Glebov

'Obzor khudozhestvennoy deyatel'nosti Mariinskogo teatra (sezon 1913–1914)' [Review of the 1913–14 season of the Mariinsky Theatre], *Muzïka*, no.173 (1914), 232–7; no.174 (1915), 251–6
'''Oresteya'': muzïkal'naya trilogiya S. Taneyeva' [*The Oresteia*: a musical trilogy by Taneyev], *Muzïka* (1915), no.233, pp.492–503; no.235, pp. 539–48, no.236, pp.555–72, no.237, pp. 579–87; pubd separately as *Oresteya …: analiza muzïkal'nogo soderzhaniya* [Analysis of the musical content] (Moscow, 1916)
'Romansï S.I. Taneyeva' [Taneyev's Romances], *Muzïkal'nïy sovremennik* (1915–16), no.8; pubd separately (Petrograd, 1916)
Putevoditel' po kontsertam: slovar' naiboleye neobkhodimïkh muzïkal'no-tekhnicheskikh oboznacheniy [Guide to concert-going: dictionary of principal musical and technical symbols] (Petrograd, 1919, 2/1978)
Russkaya poèziya v russkoy muzïke [Russian poetry in Russian music] (Petrograd, 1921, enlarged 2/1922)
Skryabin: opït kharakteristiki [A descriptive essay] (Petrograd, 1921, 2/1923)
Frants List: opït kharakeristiki (Petrograd, 1922)
Instrumental'noye tvorchestvo Chaykovskogo [Tchaikovsky's instrumental works] (Petrograd, 1922)
Pyotr Il'ich Chaykovsky: yego zhizn' i tvorchestvo [Life and works] (Petrograd, 1922)
Shopen: opït kharakteristiki (Petrograd, 1922)
Simfonicheskiye ètyudï [Symphonic studies] (Petrograd, 1922, rev. 2/1970 by E.M. Orlova) [collection of articles on Russian music]
Musorgsky: opït kharakteristiki (Moscow, 1923)
Glazunov: opït kharakteristiki (Leningrad, 1924)
'O politonal'nosti' [Polytonality], *Sovremennaya muzïka* (1925), no.7, pp.9–11
Rechevaya intonatsiya [Vocal intonation] (Moscow and Leningrad, 1925/R)
'Stroitel'stvo sovremennoy simfonii' [The structure of the contemporary symphony], *Sovremennaya muzïka* (1925), no.8, pp.29–32
'Frantsuzskaya muzïka i yeyo sovremennïye predstaviteli' [French music and its contemporary exponents], *Shest'* (Leningrad, 1926), 25–51
'Opera kak bïtovoye yavleniye' [Opera as everyday music], *Muzïka i revolyutsiya* (1926), no.11, pp.7–11.
'O polifonicheskom iskusstve, ob organnoy kul'ture i iskusstve sovremennosti' [On polyphonic art, the culture of the organ and the art of the present time], *Polifoniya i organ v sovremmenosti* (Leningrad, 1926)
'Simfonizm kak problema sovremennogo muzïkoznaniya' [The symphony: a problem for contemporary theoretical musical study], *Simfoniya ot Bètkhovena do Malera*, ed. P. Bekker (Leningrad, 1926),3–10
Bètkhoven (1827–1927) (Leningrad, 1927)

'Bïtovaya muzïka posle Oktyabrya' [Everyday music since Red October], *Novaya muzïka*, ii (1927), 17–32

Kazella [Casella] (Leningrad, 1927) [on the composer's 1926–7 visit to Leningrad]

Sergey Prokof'yeve (Leningrad, 1927)

Anton Grigor'yevich Rubinshteyn v yego muzïkal'noy deyatel'nosti i otzïvakh sovremennikov [Rubinstein, his musical activities and the opinions of his contemporaries] (Moscow, 1929)

Istoriya muzïki i muzïkal'noy kul'turï (vazhneyshiye ètapï): kratki konspekt lektsï [A history of music and musical culture (the principal stages): brief notes from the lectures] (Leningrad, 1929)

Kniga o Stravinskom [A book about Stravinsky] (Leningrad, 1929, 2/1977; Eng. trans., 1982)

†*Muzïkal'naya forma kak protsess* [Musical form as a process], i (Moscow, 1930–4, rev. 2/1963 by Ye.M. Orlova, 3/1971; Cz. trans., 1965, Ger. trans., 1976)

†*Russkaya muzïka ot nachala XIX stoletiya* [Russian music from the beginning of the 19th century] (Moscow and Leningrad, 1930, rev. 2/1968 by Ye.M. Orlova as *Russkaya muzïka: XIX i nachala XX veka* [Russian music: the 19th and early 20th centuries]; Eng. trans., 1953)

'O tvorchestve D. Shostakovicha i yego opere "Lèdi Makbet Mtsenskogo uyezda"' [On Shostakovich's composition and his opera *Lady Macbeth of the Mtsensk District*], *Lèdi Makbet Mtsenskogo uyezda*, ed. S.N. Gisin (Leningrad, 1934), 27–31; repr. in *D. Shostakovich: stat'i i materialï*, ed. G. Shneerson (Moscow, 1976), 150–59

Pamyati Petra Il'icha Chaykovskogo, 1840–1940 [In honour of Tchaikovsky] (Moscow and Leningrad, 1940)

†*M.I. Glinka: k 100-letiyu so dnya pervogo predstavleniya operï Ruslan i Lyudmila* [Glinka: on the centenary of the first performance of *Ruslan and Lyudmila*] (Leningrad, 1942)

'Cherez proshloye k budushchemu' [Through the past to the future], *SovM sbornik*, i (1943), 26–30

†*Yevgeniy Onegin, liricheskiye stsenï P.I. Chaykovskogo: opït intonatsionnogo analiza stilya i muzïkal'noy dramaturgii* [*Eugene Onegin*, Tchaikovsky's lyric scenes: an attempt at intonation analysis of style and musical dramaturgy] (Moscow and Leningrad, 1944; Ger. trans, 1949)

†*Nikolay Andreyevich Rimsky-Korsakov (1844–1944): k 100-letiyu so dnya rozhdeniya* [Rimsky-Korsakov: on the centenary of his birth] (Moscow and Leningrad, 1944)

†*Kompozitorï pervoy polovinï XIX veka: russkaya klassicheskaya muzïka* [Composers of the first half of the 19th century: Russian classical music] (Moscow, 1945)

S.V. Rakhmaninov (Moscow, 1945)

'Sovetskaya muzïka i muzïkal'naya kul'tura: opït vïvedeniya osnovnïkh printsipov' [Soviet music and musical culture: an attempt to find its basic principles], *SovM sbornik*, v (1946), 3–20

†*Charodeyka, opera P.I. Chaykovskogo: opït raskrïtiya intonatsionnogo soderzhaniya* [Tchaikovsky's opera *The Sorceress*: an attempt to reveal its tonal content] (Moscow and Leningrad, 1947)

†*Glinka* (Moscow, 1947, 3/1978 as *M.I. Glinka*)

†*Grig (1843–1907): issledovaniye* [Grieg: research] (Moscow and Leningrad, 1948, 4/1986)

'Iz moikh zapisok o Stasove, slushatele russkoy muzïki (Glinka i Borodin)' [From my notes on Stasov, listener to Russian music (Glinka and Borodin)], *V.V. Stasov, 1824–1906: k 125-letiyu so dnya rozhdeniya* (Moscow and Leningrad, 1949, 4/61)

'Pushkin v russkoy muzïke', *SovM* (1949), no.6, pp.7–13

B.V. Asaf'yev: Izbrannïye stat'i o russkoy muzïke [Selected articles on Russian music], i, ed. N. Braudo (Moscow, 1952)

Izbrannïye trudï [Selected works], ed. T.N. Livanova and others (Moscow, 1952–7) [incl. complete list of works, v, 295–380]

'Mïsli o sovetskoy muzïke' [Thoughts on Soviet music], *SovM* (1952), no.11, pp.12–14

Izbrannïye stat'i o muzïkal'nom prosveshchenii i obrazovanii [Selected articles on musical training and education], ed. Ye.M. Orlova (Leningrad, 1965)

Kriticheskiye stat'i, ocherki i retsenzii [Critical articles, essays and reviews], ed. I.V. Beletsky (Moscow, 1967)

O muzïke Chaykovskogo: izbrannoye [On the music of Tchaikovsky: a selection] (Leningrad, 1972)

O balete: stat'i – retsenzii – vospominaniya [Ballet: articles – reviews – memoirs] (Leningrad, 1974)

Ob opere: izbrannïye stat'i [Collected opera criticism] (Leningrad, 1976, 2/1985)

O khorovom iskusstve [The choral art] (Leningrad, 1980)

O simfonicheskoy i kamernoy muzïke: poyasneniya i prilozheniya k programmam simfonicheskikh i kamernïkh kontsertov [Symphonic and chamber music: explanations and appendices for programmes for symphony and chamber concerts] (Leningrad, 1981)

O muzïke XX veka: poyasneniya i prilozheniya k programmam simfonicheskikh i kamernykh kontsertov [20th-century music: explanations and appendices for programmes for symphony and chamber concerts] (Leningrad, 1982)

BIBLIOGRAPHY

GroveO (G. Norris)

B.V. Asaf'yeve: 'Moy put'' [Autobiography], *SovM* (1934), no.8, pp.47–50

V.M. Bogdanov-Berezovsky: *B.V. Asaf'yev* (Leningrad, 1937)

A.V. Ossovsky: *B.V. Asaf'yev: sovetskaya muzïka* (Moscow, 1945)

B.V. Asaf'yev: 'Moya tvorcheskaya rabota v Leningrade v pervïye godï Velikoy Otechestvennoy voynï' [My creative work in Leningrad during the early years of World War II], *SovM* (1946), no. 10, pp.90–96

D.B. Kabalevsky, ed.: *Pamyati akademika Borisa Vladimirovicha Asaf'yeva* [In memory of academician Asaf'yev] (Moscow, 1951)

B.V. Asaf'yev: Izbrannïye trudï [Selected works] (Leningrad, 1952–7) [incl. complete lists of writings and works, v, 295–380]

D.B. Kabalevsky: *B.V. Asaf'yev – Igor' Glebov* (Moscow, 1954)

M.A. Rïbnikova: *Baletï Asaf'yeva* (Asaf'yev's ballets) (Moscow, 1956)

L.A. Mazel: 'O muzïkal'no-teoreticheskoy kontseptsii B. Asaf'yeva' [Asaf'yev's concepts of music theory], *SovM* (1957), no.3, pp.73–82

Vospominaniya o B.V. Asaf'yeve [Recollections of Asaf'yev] (Leningrad, 1964)

Ye.M. Orlova: *B.V. Asaf'yeve: put' issledovatel'ya i publitsista* [Asaf'yev's development as a researcher and writer] (Leningrad, 1964)

J. Jiránek: *Asafjevova teorie intonace: její geneze a význam* [Asaf'yev's intonation theory: its origins and significance] (Prague, 1967)

J. Jiránek: 'Assafjews Intonationslehre und ihre Perspektiven', *De musica disputationes pragensis*, i (1972), 13–45

M. Druskin: 'Uchitel'' [A teacher], *Issledovaniya – vospominaniya* (Leningrad and Moscow, 1977), 170–224

A. Kryukov, ed.: *Materialï k biografii B. Asaf'yeva* [Material for a biography of Asaf'yev] (Leningrad, 1981)

B.V. Asaf'yev i sovetskaya muzïkal'naya kul'tura: Moscow 1984

Ye.M. Orlova and A. Kryukov: *Akademik Boris Vladimirovich Asaf'yev* (Leningrad, 1984)

Ye.M. Orlova: *Intonatsionnaya teoriya Asaf'yeva kak ucheniye o spetsifike muzïkal'nogo mïshleniya* [Asaf'yev's intonation theory as a comment on the special character of musical thinking] (Moscow, 1984)

LARISA GEORGIEVNA DAN'KO

Asante [Ashanti] **music.** The music of one of the dominant and culturally important ethnic groups in GHANA. The Asante number about 1,500,000 and are grouped politically into large territorial units, each of which is headed by a paramount chief under whom there are district chiefs of different ranks. The constitutional head of the Asante is the Asantehene, to whom all paramount chiefs owe allegiance. In the pre-colonial period, the Asante sphere of influence spread over many parts of Ghana and extended westwards to the borders of Côte d'Ivoire and eastwards across the Volta.

1. Musical organization. 2. Musical instruments. 3. Vocal music.

1. MUSICAL ORGANIZATION.   The traditional political structure of the Asante is reflected in the organization of their music. Firstly, the music of the court is separated from that of the community, while the hierarchical ordering of chiefs under the Asantehene is reflected in the number and types of instruments and ensembles that each royal court can have. Secondly, court music is performed on state occasions and festivals, whereas community music is performed on all other social occasions. Thirdly,

as the practice of music in community life is organized on the basis of the social groups within it, the inventory of musical types and songs of the community is much larger than that of the court. Fourthly, although there is no idiomatic differentiation between court music and the music of the community, the music of the court tends to be more sophisticated or elaborate in organization, or more complex in structure. Accordingly, the training and recruitment of court musicians is institutionalized.

2. MUSICAL INSTRUMENTS.   Asante music lays more emphasis on the use of idiophones and membranophones than on other instrumental types. Idiophones include *dawuro* and *nnawuta* (single and double clapperless bells); *firikyiwa* (castanets made of iron); *torowa* (vessel rattles); *astratoa* (concussion rattles); *mmaa* (stick clappers); *sraka* (scraped idiophones); and *prempensua* (large *sausa*s). The flat board *sausa* with five wooden lamellae is no longer widely used.

Membranophones are generally open and single-headed. They fall into three groups: *twenesin* (signal drums), *akukuadwo* and *atumpan*, which are the principal talking drums of the court, and those drums played in ensembles as basic supporting drums or those played as master drums. A few closed or double-headed membranophones, such as the *donno* (hourglass drum; see DRUM, fig.1*f*) and *gyamadudu* (large cylindrical drum), as well as some frame drums, are also used.

Aerophones include two varieties of flute: the *aten teben* (bamboo flute) and the *odurugya* (cane flute) played at the court of the Asantehene. Court trumpets are made from animal horns or elephant tusks and are played in hocket fashion in ensembles of five or seven instruments. Chordophones are rare, and only the *benta* (mouth bow) and the *seperewa* (bridge-harp) are found.

3. VOCAL MUSIC.   With the exception of the *kwadwom* historical chant and the song preludes of *kete* drum music and dance, the music of the court is almost entirely instrumental, while that of the community lays stress on vocal music. Asante songs are based on a seven-tone scale. They have a general descending trend. Melodic movement within the phrase is limited to 2nds, 3rds and 4ths and may be stepwise, interlocking or pendular. The singing of simultaneous melodies in parallel 3rds and the use of leader-chorus forms in alternating or overlapping sections are dominant characteristics of Asante vocal style.

As Asante is a tonal language, the melodic contour follows the intonation contour of speech. The rhythm of songs similarly follows speech rhythm closely. Hence spoken verse, declamations and other styles which treat song as a form of speech utterance are exploited.

BIBLIOGRAPHY

J.H.K. Nketia: *African Music in Ghana* (Accra, 1962)

J.H.K. Nketia: *Drumming in Akan Communities of Ghana* (Edinburgh, 1963)

J.H.K. Nketia: *Folk Songs of Ghana* (Legon, 1963)

J.T. Koetting: *An Analytical Study of Ashanti Kete Drumming* (thesis, UCLA, 1970)

C.D. Woodson: *The Atumpan Drum in Asante* (diss., UCLA, 1983)

W.G. Carter: *Asante Music in Old and New Juaben: a Comparative Study* (diss., UCLA, 1984)

J.H.K. Nketia: 'Asante Court Music', *Golden Stool: Studies of the Asante Center and Periphery*, ed. E. Schildkrout (New York, 1987), 200–208

P. Sarpong: *The Ceremonial Horns of the Ashanti* (Accra, 1990)

J.H. KWABENA NKETIA

Asas (Ger.). A♭♭. *See* PITCH NOMENCLATURE.

ASCAP [American Society of Composers, Authors and Publishers]. *See* COPYRIGHT, §V, 14(i).

Ascent, initial. *See* INITIAL ASCENT.

Asch, Moe [Moses] (*b* Warsaw, 1905; *d* New York, 19 Oct 1986). American record producer and co-founder of Folkways Records. The son of the Yiddish writer Sholem Asch, he was an electronics technician and an enthusiast for American folk music when he began to produce recordings in 1939. He released albums compiled from 78 r.p.m. discs on the Disc and Asch labels before founding Folkways in 1947 with Marian Distler. Over the next 40 years, Asch issued what he called a 'public archive of world sounds', including animal noises and steam engines as well as traditional music and song from the USA and many other countries. The largest part of the Folkways catalogue of 2200 albums consists of recordings of the major figures in American traditional music in the 1940s and 50s. Asch recorded over 900 songs from Leadbelly and more than 200 from Woody Guthrie, and he issued over 60 albums by Pete Seeger. He also issued albums by Doc Watson and Blind Willie Johnson and recordings of children's music by Ella Jenkins. After his death, Folkways was sold to the Smithsonian Institute, Washington, DC, which guaranteed to keep all the recordings in print. Smithsonian Folkways has reissued much of the catalogue on CD.

For more information see P.D. Goldsmith: *Making People's Music: Moe Asch and Folkways Records* (Washington DC, 1998).

DAVE LAING

Aschenbrenner, Christian Heinrich (*b* Stettin [now Szczecin], 29 Dec 1654; *d* Jena, 13 Dec 1732). German composer and violinist. He was taught the violin by his father, a Stettin town musician, and in 1668 he received composition lessons from Johann Theile. He studied with J.H. Schmelzer in Vienna in 1676 and 1677 and in the latter year became a violinist in the Hofkapelle at Zeitz, where he remained until the Kapelle was disbanded in 1682. In the following year he became Konzertmeister in the Hofkapelle at Merseburg. There he enjoyed friendly relations with the Hofkapellmeister, David Pohle, whom he had known when he held a similar position at Zeitz from 1680 to 1682. In 1695 Aschenbrenner returned to Zeitz, where he was director of music until, in 1713, he went back to Merseburg as Hofkapellmeister. He still, however, retained an honorary title from Zeitz as 'Kapellmeister von Haus aus', though this cannot have continued beyond 1718, when the death of the reigning duke at Zeitz put an end to musical life at the court there. He retired from Merseburg in 1719 and from then until his death lived at Jena on a small pension provided by Duke Moritz Wilhelm of Merseburg. He twice went to Vienna as a performer – in 1692, when he dedicated six violin sonatas to the Emperor Leopold I, and in 1703. His compositions, of which only three pieces survive, were known throughout Saxony and Thuringia, as is evident from their inclusion in inventories and catalogues of the time, such as the dictionaries of Walther and Gerber.

WORKS

Gast- und Hochzeit-Freude, bestehend in Sonaten, Präludien, Allemanden, Curanten, Balletten, Arien, Sarabanten, 3–6vv, bc (Leipzig, 1673), lost

Sonaten, Praeludien … etc., 3–6vv, bc (Leipzig, 1675), lost

Die Seele Christi heilige mich, 4vv, 4 insts, *S-Uu*

O Jesu süss, wer dein gedenkt, 3vv, 3 insts, bc, *D-Bsb*

Ländlicher Festtag, ed. W. Lott, *Platzmusik*, no.12 (Lippstadt, n.d.)
2 masses, 10vv, lost
14 motets, 1–16vv, 1–8 insts, lost
5 secular songs, 1–3vv, 1, 2 insts, lost
6 sonatas for Viennese court, 1692, lost
18 sonatas, insts, lost
1 sonata, b viol, lost, mentioned in Rudolstadt inventory (see Baselt)

BIBLIOGRAPHY

EitnerQ; FétisB; GerberNL; GöhlerV; WaltherML
M. Seiffert: 'Die Chorbibliothek der St. Michaelisschule in Lüneburg zu Seb. Bach's Zeit', *SIMG*, ix (1907–8), 593–620
A. Werner: *Städtische und fürstliche Musikpflege in Zeitz bis zum Anfang des 19. Jahrhunderts* (Bückeburg and Leipzig, 1922)
O. Dörfer: 'Chr.H. Aschenbrenner, gestorben 1732 in Jena: wo sind seine Notenhandschriften?', *Thüringer Fähnlein*, v (1936)
E. Wennig: *Chronik des musikalischen Lebens der Stadt Jena: Von den Anfängen bis zum Jahre 1750* (Jena, 1937)
W. Serauky: *Musikgeschichte der Stadt Halle*, ii/1 (Halle and Berlin, 1939/R)
B. Baselt: 'Die Musikaliensammlung der Schwarzburg-Rudolstädtischen Hofkapelle unter Philipp Heinrich Erlebach', *Traditionen und Aufgaben der hallischen Musikwissenschaft*, ed. W. Siegmund-Schultze (Halle, 1963), 105–34
F. Krummacher: *Die Überlieferung der Choralbearbeitungen in der frühen evangelischen Kantate* (Berlin, 1965)
H. Engel: *Musik in Thüringen* (Cologne and Graz, 1966), 198
A. Schmiedecke: 'Aufführungen von Opern, Operetten, Serenaden und Kantaten am Zeitzer Herzogshof', *Mf*, xxv (1972), 168–74, esp. 169

KARL-ERNST BERGUNDER

Ascher, Leo (*b* Vienna, 17 Aug 1880; *d* New York, 25 Feb 1942). Austrian composer. He studied law and music at Vienna University, the piano with Hugo Reinhold and L. Thern (1898–1904) and composition with Robert Fuchs and Franz Schmidt. By 1905 he had decided to devote his time to composition, and by 1932 had composed 32 operettas. His first, *Vergeltsgott* (1905), was produced at the Theater an der Wien and had 69 performances, while one of his greatest successes was *Hoheit tanzt Walzer* (1912), first produced at the Raimundtheater and performed more than 2500 times over the next ten years. Characteristically Ascher's music was in a strong local Viennese idiom, and he created a perfect example of the so-called Wienerlied with *S'Lercherl von Hernals* (1911). He also wrote lieder and film music. Ascher was arrested during the Reichskristallnacht, and upon his release emigrated to the USA (1939), where he worked as a lawyer, specializing successfully in law suits regarding plagiarism and royalties. The Leo Ascher Centre of Operetta Music at Millersville University, Pennsylvania contains hundreds of scores, sheet music and ephemera; upon the death of Ascher's daughter Franzi Ascher-Nash, her papers were also added to the library. (*GänzlEMT*, incl. complete list of stage works)

WORKS
(selective list)

Operettas: Die arme Lori, 1909; Die keusche Susanne, 1910; Eine fidele Nacht, 1911; Hoheit tanzt Walzer, 1912, rev. as Hochzeitswalzer, 1937; Die goldene Hanna, 1913; Der Soldat der Marie, 1917; Ein Jahr ohne Liebe, 1923; La Barberina, 1928; Sonja, 1925; Frühling im Wienerwald, 1930; Bravo Peggy, 1932; Um ein bisschen Liebe, 1937
Film scores: Ihre Durchlaucht, die Wäscherin, 1931; Mein Leopold, 1931; Purpur und waschblau 1931 (incl. Irgendeinmal kommt irgendwer von irgendwo her [Somewhere about someone is out looking for you])
Lieder: S'Lercherl von Hernals (1911); Hinaus (P. Cornelius); Es war ein braunes Maidelein (O.J. Bierbaum); Vom Scheiden (E. zu Schoenaich-Carolat); Diebstahl (R. Reinick); In Heiligenstadt steht ein Bankerl am Bach

Principal publisher: Doblinger

THOMAS L. GAYDA

Ascherberg, Hopwood & Crew. English music publishers. Eugene Ascherberg (*b* Dresden, 1843; *d* London, 28 May 1908) arrived in England after a period in Australia, and set up in London as E. Ascherberg & Co. by 1879, initially as a piano importer. The firm gradually moved over to music publishing and took over Duncan Davison & Co. in 1886. The firm of Hopwood & Crew (founded in 1860) published popular dance music by Charles d'Albert, Charles Coote (father and son), Waldteufel and others, as well as countless music-hall songs, and it absorbed the firms of Howard & Co. (1899) and Orsborn & Co. (1901) who had similar catalogues. An amalgamation in 1906 led to the formation of Ascherberg, Hopwood & Crew, and in the same year the firm of John Blockley was also acquired. Ascherberg, Hopwood & Crew's substantial catalogue covered music of every description, but was based mainly on light music. Among its successful stage works were the operettas *The Geisha* and *The Belle of New York*, and later musical comedies such as *The Maid of the Mountains* and Straus's *The Last Waltz*. The firm also held the British copyrights for Mascagni's *Cavalleria rusticana* and Leoncavallo's *Pagliacci*. Its many instrumental and choral series included works by Elgar, Reger and Coleridge-Taylor. In 1969 the firm was taken over by CHAPPELL.

BIBLIOGRAPHY

Obituary, MO, xxi (1907–8), 792 [for E. Ascherberg]
'The Music Publisher of Tradition: Ascherberg and his Amalgamations', *MO*, lxiv (1940–41), 508–9

J.A. FULLER MAITLAND/PETER WARD JONES

Aschpellmayr, Franz. *See* ASPLMAYR, FRANZ.

Asciolla, Dino [Edoardo] (*b* Rome, 9 June 1920; *d* Siena, 9 Sept 1994). Italian viola player and violinist. He studied the violin and viola at the Rome Conservatory and later attended masterclasses at the Accademia di S Cecilia, Rome, and at the Accademia Musicale Chigiana, Siena. He began his career as a violinist and won the 1950 Vivaldi Competition at Venice. For a time he was leader of the Alessandro Scarlatti Orchestra and the Salzburg Mozarteum Orchestra, but he later concentrated on the viola and became one of its best-known exponents. Firmino Sifonia, Ennio Morricone, Domenico Guaccero and Manuel De Sica are among the composers who wrote works for him. He had an international reputation as a soloist and chamber player, having toured widely with various ensembles such as the Virtuosi di Roma, I Musici, the Boccherini Quintet, Chigi Quintet, Rome Quartet and Quartetto Italiano. He played a Maggini viola, a rare instrument from the 17th-century Brescia school. His recordings included Paganini's Sonata for viola and orchestra, in which his performance is distinguished by richness of tone and flexibility of technique. He taught at the conservatory in L'Aquila.

PIERO RATTALINO/R

Ascone, Vicente (*b* Siderno, Calabria, 16 Aug 1897; *d* Montevideo, 5 March 1979). Uruguayan composer of Italian birth. Early in life he moved with his family to Montevideo, where he studied harmony and composition with Luis Sambucetti, and the trumpet with Aquiles Gubitosi. He was for several years first trumpet and soloist with the Montevideo Radio SO, which he conducted occasionally, and from 1940 to 1954 he directed the municipal band of Montevideo. He has also taught harmony at the Montevideo Instituto Verdi, and wind and percussion instruments at the Municipal School of Music, where he was later appointed director and professor of harmony. In 1938 the Venezuelan government asked him to establish a course for teaching choral music at the experimental music schools in Caracas; during his stay he composed *Venezuela*, a book of school songs. A prolific composer whose music has a nationalist character, he has received various national awards and his works have been favourably received outside Uruguay. Among his later compositions, the Trumpet Concerto (1969) places strongly rhythmic outer movements, in unstable harmonies and with reminiscences of military music, against a tonal, lyrical second movement consisting primarily of an extended melody by the trumpet soloist.

WORKS
(*selective list*)

Stage: Paraná Guazú (op, 4), 1930; Santos Vega (incid music), 1953
Orch: Suite uruguaya, 1926; Preludio y marcha de los bramines, 1926; 3 syms., 1948, 1955, 1964; Politonal, pf, orch, 1967; Tpt Conc., 1969; Vn Conc., 1970

Principal publishers: Andebu (Montevideo), Ricordi Americana

BIBLIOGRAPHY
Compositores de América/Composers of the Americas, ed. Pan American Union, xvi (Washington DC, 1970), 23ff

JOHN M. SCHECHTER

Ascot, Rosa García. Pianist and composer, wife of JESÚS BAL Y GAY.

'Asei beroshim (Heb.). Ancient Jewish instrument, possibly a cypress-wood clapper. *See* BIBLICAL INSTRUMENTS, §3(i).

Asenjo Barbieri, Francisco. *See* BARBIERI, FRANCISCO ASENJO.

Ásgeirsson, Jón (*b* Ísafjörður, 11 Oct 1928). Icelandic composer, teacher and critic. He graduated in 1955 from the Reykjavík College of Music, where he studied the piano with Árni Kristjánsson and theory with Victor Urbancic. Further composition studies were undertaken at the RSAMD in Glasgow (1955–6) and at the Guildhall School of Music in London (1965). In 1961 he received a teacher's diploma from the Reykjavík College of Music. Ásgeirsson has conducted various choirs, and became the principal music critic of *Morgunblaðið* in 1970. Formerly president of the Icelandic Composers' Society, he has taught at various institutions and is currently professor at the Icelandic Teachers' College.

His works are mainly traditional in style though he has written a few serial compositions. He is particularly interested in reviving Icelandic folksongs and dances and has set related folk poetry found without music; he has also served as music director for productions of the ancient dances by the National Dance Company. In 1974 his opera *Thrymskviða* ('The Lay of Thrym') was the first full-scale Icelandic opera to be staged in Iceland.

WORKS
(*selective list*)

Stage: Thrymskviða [The Lay of Thrym] (op, 5, after Elder Edda), Reykjavík, National, 1974; Blindisleikur [Blindman's Buff], ballet, perf. 1981; Galdra Loftur [Loftur the Magician] (op, 3), 1995, perf. 1996
Orch: Lilja, sym. poem, 1970; Vc Conc., 1984; Conc., 1999
Chbr: Sjöstrengjaljóð [A Poem of 7 Strings], 1968; Qnt no.1, ww, 1971; Octet, ww, 1977; Qnt no.2, ww, 1999
Choral pieces, 1968–77, incl. Timinn og vatnið [Time and the Water] (S. Steinarr), 7 songs, 1977 (1971, Burt)

BIBLIOGRAPHY
A. Burt: *Iceland's Twentieth-Century Composers and a Listing of their Works* (Annandale, VA, 1975, 2/1977)
G. Bergendal: *New Music in Iceland* (Reykjavík, 1991)
M. Podhajski: *Dictionary of Icelandic Composers* (Warsaw, 1997)
AMANDA M. BURT/THORKELL SIGURBJÖRNSSON

Ashbourne(-Firman), Peter (Thomas) (*b* 14 July 1950). Jamaican composer, violinist and keyboard player. He came from a musical family, and his talent for the piano and the violin revealed itself early on, with improvisation skills developing soon afterwards. His first musical lessons were given by his aunt, after which he was taught by other Jamaican teachers. He studied at the Berklee College of Music, Boston gaining the BM in 1976. His studies focussed mainly on composition and improvisation in modern, black American (including Jamaican) popular styles. He taught in the African-American department of the Jamaica School of Music (1976–9), then, as a freelancer, conducted workshops (including one at the Musikhochschule, Graz), judged festivals and directed theatre productions in the Caribbean.

Ashbourne is a leading violinist and keyboard performer in the Caribbean region, with styles ranging from religious to theatrical, classical, folk and popular. His compositions are equally wide-ranging: he has written and arranged music for theatrical productions, dance, recordings, commercials and documentaries. He has raised the technical and artistic standards of the composition and performance of commercial and popular music through his numerous works for soloists and for chamber, orchestral and vocal ensembles. He has successfully fulfilled commissions from the American Wind SO, the Graz Musikhochschule, the Jamaican-Canadian Chamber Music Festival and the National Dance Theatre Company of Jamaica.

WORKS
(*selective list*)

Choral: Alleluia, 2 choirs, drums, after 1994, unperf.
Dance theatre: Two Drums for Babylon, drums, pf, synth, perf. 1980
Sym. wind ens: Jamaican Suite (Fantasy on Jamaican Folk Tunes), perf. 1981; Avia (Fantasy), perf. 1986
Str qt: Jamaica Folk (Medley of Jamaican Folk Tunes), perf. 1985; Folk Suite (Fantasy on Jamaican Folk Tunes), perf. 1996
Other chbr; music for commercials, documentaries and TV; jazz compositions for special occasions

OLIVE LEWIN

Ashbrook, William (Sinclair) (*b* Philadelphia, 28 Jan 1922). American scholar and musicologist. He received the BA from the University of Pennsylvania in 1946 and the MA from Harvard University in 1947. He taught humanities at Stephens College (1949–55) and was a member of the English department at Indiana State University (1955–74). From 1974 to 1984 he was professor of opera at the Philadelphia College of the Performing Arts. Although trained as a teacher of English literature, Ashbrook also has a lively interest in Italian opera and has contributed numerous articles on the subject to numerous periodicals. He was editor of the *Opera Quarterly* from 1992. His books on Donizetti (1965, 1982) and Puccini (1968, 1991) are particularly valuable for the careful presentation of biographical material, the discussion of the literary and dramatic aspects of the operas and the description of the various revisions.

WRITINGS
'Anna Bolena', *MT*, cvi (1965), 432–6
Donizetti (London, 1965)
The Operas of Puccini (New York, 1968, 2/1985)

Donizetti and his Operas (Cambridge, 1982)

'La struttura drammatica nella produzione musicale di Donizetti dopo il 1838', *Studi donizettiani I: Bergamo 1975*, 721–40

'The First Singers of Tristan und Isolde', *OQ*, iii (1985), 11–23

'A Brief Stage History', *Giacomo Puccini: La bohème*, ed. A. Groos and R. Parker (Cambridge, 1986), 115–28

'Donizetti and Romani', *Italica*, lxiv (1987), 606–31

'Boito and the 1868 Mefistofele Libretto as a Reform Text', *Reading Opera*, ed. A. Groos and R. Parker (Princeton, NJ, 1988), 268–87

'Popular Success, the Critics and Fame: the Early Careers of Lucia di Lammermoor and Belisario', *COJ*, ii (1990), 65–81

with H. Powers: *Puccini's Turandot: the End of the Great Tradition* (Princeton, NJ, 1991)

'La rondine', *The Puccini Companion*, ed. W. Weaver and S. Puccini (New York, 1994), 244–64

'Nelson Eddy's Career in Opera', *OQ*, xiii (1996–7), 7–18

PAULA MORGAN

Ashdown, Edwin (*b* 1826; *d* 26 Nov 1912). English music publisher. He and Henry John Parry were employed by Wessel & Co. and took over the business on the retirement of CHRISTIAN RUDOLPH WESSEL in 1860; the firm then became known as Ashdown & Parry. Parry retired in 1882 and the firm's name changed to Edwin Ashdown, becoming a limited company in 1891. The firm's publications included much new English music and the short-lived periodical *Hanover Square* (1867–9), edited by the pianist Lindsay Sloper, which consisted largely of new music. Composers in the catalogue included G.A. Macfarren, Sullivan, Elgar and Vaughan Williams, and for many years the firm was also the English agent for BOTE & BOCK of Berlin. Piano and choral music and solo songs came to form the core of its publishing activities. Ashdown also took over the music publishing firms of Hatzfeld & Co. (1903), Enoch & Co. (1927) and J.H. Larway (1929). In its turn it was absorbed by Music Sales in 1982.

BIBLIOGRAPHY

CooverMA

'Mr. Edwin Ashdown', *Musical Herald*, no. 661 (1903), 99–101

'The House of Ashdown', *The Windmill*, i/13 (1958), 9–11

J.A. Parkinson: *Victorian Music Publishers: an Annotated List* (Warren, MI, 1990)

PETER WARD JONES

Ashe, Andrew (*b* Lisburn, Co. Antrim, *c*1759; *d* Dublin, 1838). Irish flautist and composer. When 12 he was adopted by Count Bentinck, a British naval captain, and travelled widely with him in Europe. He quickly learnt the flute but abandoned it because of his dissatisfaction with the contemporary one-keyed instrument. He returned to the flute in 1774 at The Hague, after hearing the flautist Vanhamme (or Vanham) play a six-keyed instrument by Richard Potter and purchasing it from him. Around 1778 Ashe was appointed first flute at the Brussels Opera, having beaten Vanhamme, the incumbent, in a public audition. After settling in Dublin in 1782, he was engaged by Saloman in 1791 for the Haydn concerts in London, where he made his solo début the following year. He succeeded Monzani at the King's Theatre in 1805, and in 1810 also became director of the Bath concerts on the death of Rauzzini, whose pupil, Miss Comer, he had married in 1799. In 1813 he was the founding first flute of the Philharmonic Society, serving until replaced by Charles Nicholson in 1816. Four years of losses led him to resign his position in Bath in the winter of 1821–2. After years of private teaching, he was appointed professor (with Nicholson) when the RAM opened in 1823, but the initial lack of flute students may have been a factor in his return to Dublin the same year. Ashe's tone, intonation and expressive playing made him an influential advocate of the flute with 'the extra keys' when it was still opposed by older players. His flute concertos, the novelty of which excited admiration, were never published and are now lost.

BIBLIOGRAPHY

BDA; SainsburyD

W.N. James: *A Word or Two on the Flute* (Edinburgh, 1826/R, 2/1836), 217–20

D.W. Eagle: 'Andrew Ashe: a Nearly Forgotten Master', *Flutist Quarterly*, xii/4 (1987), 60–63

PHILIP BATE, DAVID LASOCKI

Asheim, Nils Henrik (*b* Oslo, 20 Jan 1960). Norwegian organist and composer. He graduated as an organist in 1981 and after studying with Olav Anton Thommesen at the Norwegian Academy of Music he gained a graduate degree in composition (1987). He also spent a year with Ton de Leeuw at the Sweelinck Conservatory in Amsterdam. Asheim teaches at the Rogaland Conservatory in Stavanger. Between 1988 and 1991 he was chairman of the Norwegian Society of Composers.

An important part of his output is connected with his work as an organist and church musician. His largest work in this genre is the dramatic oratorio *The Ascension of Martin Luther King* (1990). He has also won acclaim for his chamber music and orchestral works, and has twice been awarded the Work of the Year prize in Norway, and as early as 1978 he received the UNESCO/EBU Rostrum prize for *Ensemble Music for Five*. Several of his compositions incorporate electro-acoustic elements. The installation *Axis* was realized through real time output from a computer.

WORKS

Orch: Opening, 1983; Mirrors, 1987; Don Giovanni Metamorphosis, 1991, rev. 1996

Chbr: Ensemble Music for Five, 1977; Window, vn, pf, 1979; Genesis, str qt, 1982; Like Rings in Water, perc, tape, 1984; Water Mirror, pf trio, 1985; In between, ob, elecs, 1996; Medusa's Head, ob, bn, va, vc, 1991; Summer's Play, vn, pf, 1992; Fanfare for the XVII Olympic Winter Games, 12 tpt, 1994

Org: Orgeleik, 1979; Christ lag in Todesbanden, chorale fantasy, 1983; Blowout, harbour music, wind band, steel perc, ship horns, 1996

Vocal: Ps xc, chorus, vns, perc, org, 1983; The Ascension of Martin Luther King (dramatic orat, A. Hague), chorus, brass, str, perc, org, actors, dancers, 1990; Proud Music of the Storm (W. Whitman), chorus, trbns, 1992; Obstfelder's Night, S, vc, 1993; The Book of Psalms, chorus, org, 1994; Turba (Lucretius), chorus, orch, 1997; Kyrie and Sanctus, 1997

Principal publisher: Norsk musikforlag/NMIC

ARVID O. VOLLSNES

Ashewell, Thomas. *See* ASHWELL, THOMAS.

Ashforth, Alden (Banning) (*b* New York, 13 May 1933). American composer, jazz researcher and teacher. He studied composition with E.B. Hill and Richard Hoffmann at Oberlin College (BA 1958, BM 1958) and with Sessions, Earl Kim and Babbitt at Princeton University (MFA 1960, PhD 1971). He began his teaching career at Princeton (1961) and held positions at Oberlin (1961–5) and several other schools before joining the faculty of UCLA in 1967. In 1969 he became coordinator of the UCLA electronic music studio and in 1980 he was made a full professor. Since 1952 he has been active as a producer of New Orleans jazz recordings. His writings include contributions to *Perspectives of New Music* (on Schoenberg), *The Music Review* (on Beethoven) and *The New Grove Dictionary of Jazz*. Ashforth has received particular notice for his electronic works. *Byzantia: Two Journeys after Yeats* (1971–3) is panoramic in dramatic effect, with mosaic-like juxtapositions of electronic, acoustic (voice, traditional instruments) and natural (flowing water, bird calls) sounds.

WORKS

Inst: Pf Sonata, 1955; Sonata, fl, hpd, 1956; 2 Pf Pieces, 1957; Variations, orch, 1958; Fantasy-variations, vn, pf, 1959; Episodes, chbr conc., 8 insts, 1962–8; Big Bang, pf 4 hands, 1970; Pas seul, fl, 1974; The Flowers of Orcus (Intavolatura), gui, 1976; Sentimental Waltz, pf, 1977; St Bride's Suite, hpd, 1983; The Miraculous Bugle, flugelhorn, perc, 1989; Palimpsests, org, 1997

Vocal: The Unquiet Heart (Tanka Songs), S, chbr orch/pf, 1959–68; 4 Lyric Songs, high v, pf, 1961; Our Lady's Song, A, va, hpd, 1961; Aspects of Love, T/S, pf, 1978; Christmas Motets, chorus, 1980

Elec: Vocalise, 1965; Cycles, 1965; Mixed Brew, 1968; Byzantia: Two Journeys after Yeats, tape/(org, tape), 1971–3

Principal publishers: E.C. Schirmer, C.F. Peters

KATHERINE K. PRESTON/BARRY SCHRADER

Ashkenazi music. *See* JEWISH MUSIC, §III, 3.

Ashkenazy, Vladimir (Davidovich) (*b* Gor'kiy [now Nizhniy Novgorod], 6 July 1937). Russian pianist and conductor, naturalized Icelandic. He was born into a musical Jewish family and entered the Moscow Central School of Music in 1945; his teacher there for the next ten years was Anaida Sumbatyan. His first major recital, devoted entirely to Chopin, was in the Great Hall of the Moscow Conservatory in April 1955, and later that year he gained second prize at the fifth Warsaw International Chopin Competition. In 1956, now a pupil of Lev Oborin at the Moscow Conservatory, he was awarded first prize at the Queen Elisabeth Competition in Brussels. While still a student he made his first tour outside the USSR the following year, to East and West Germany. After graduating, it was inescapable that he should be groomed for the second International Tchaikovsky Competition in Moscow in 1962 (the American Van Cliburn having won the first), and he duly restored national honour by carrying off a shared first prize (with John Ogdon). His London début followed in 1963, and in that year he defected and settled in London with his Icelandic wife and son. In 1969 the family moved to Iceland, where he started to conduct, away from the glare of publicity and the pressures of international concert life. He has subsequently made his home in Switzerland.

For many years Ashkenazy was considered the finest of the young Russian players: for the 1960s, a once-in-a-generation virtuoso, such as Kissin was in the 1990s. Establishing his career with Chopin, he was recognized early on as having all the virtues of a great performer: musicianship, intellectual perception, technical perfection and musical instincts that never failed to make his fingers say something. In his first recording of Chopin's Etudes, completed in 1960 (Melodiya), he matched to perfection Chopin's inspiration, which took off from an exploration of the resources of the piano and the potentialities of timbre to be exploited by a new keyboard technique. Although Ashkenazy went on to record the complete piano works of Chopin, he never surpassed these early Etudes. After settling in the West he began an association with Decca, for which he has recorded virtually all the major works of the piano repertory. The achievement, inevitably, has been variable; it includes a complete set of the Mozart concertos, in which he directed the Philharmonia from the keyboard, two widely admired sets of the

Vladimir Ashkenazy, 1986

four Rachmaninoff concertos and the Paganini Variations (first with the LSO and Previn, then with the Royal Concertgebouw and Haitink), all the Prokofiev concertos and much of Prokofiev's solo music, and sets of distinction of the ten Skryabin sonatas and Shostakovich's 24 Preludes and Fugues op.87.

As his conducting activities grew, so Ashkenazy's solo career was reduced in proportion. He has an individual but expressive conducting technique, forged in the 1970s during his early years in Iceland; but he made the transition to the podium with complete success and his orchestral recordings are now as numerous as his others and the best of them as masterly. His orchestral début on disc was in Prokofiev's Classical Symphony in 1974; he went on to record all the Prokofiev symphonies, all the Sibelius (he is a dedicated Sibelian), and the three Rachmaninoff symphonies, in addition to other large-scale works of Rachmaninoff. Having made a triumphant return to his homeland in 1989, after an absence of 26 years, now as pianist and conductor, he has been free to work there again and has recorded most of the Shostakovich symphonies with the St Petersburg PO. He was music director of the RPO in London from 1987 to 1994, and since 1988 has held the same post with the Deutsches Sinfonie-Orchester, Berlin (the former Berlin RSO), with which he has recorded a fine Skryabin series. In 1998 he was appointed music director of the Czech PO. He describes his favoured repertory as Beethoven, Sibelius and Rachmaninoff. As a chamber music player and partner to singers, his recordings include sets of the Rachmaninoff songs with Elisabeth Söderström, lieder with Matthias Goerne and the Beethoven violin sonatas with Itzhak Perlman. His autobiography, *Beyond Frontiers*, co-written with Jasper Parrott, was published in London in 1984.

STEPHEN PLAISTOW

Ashley. English family of musicians. They were active in London and the provinces c1780–1830.

(1) John Ashley   (*b* ?London, ?1734; *d* London, 14 March 1805). Bassoonist and conductor. He was first bassoon at Covent Garden Theatre, and became more widely known after his success as assistant conductor to Joah Bates at the 1784 Commemoration of Handel in Westminster Abbey. Charles Burney (*An Account of the Musical Performances … in Commemoration of Handel*; London, 1785) records that the 'unwearied zeal and diligence' of 'Mr John Ashly of the Guards … were constantly employed with such intelligence and success, as greatly facilitated the advancement of the plan'. According to Burney he was also the 'Mr Ashley' who played the then novel double bassoon at these celebrations. Ashley's four sons (see below) also took part in the commemoration and later in 1784 the whole family first appeared in the provinces at the Hereford meeting of the Three Choirs; they took part in subsequent Handel commemorations and from 1789 were regularly billed at Ranelagh Gardens.

With this experience, and sometimes working in conjunction with a local musician, Ashley promoted some 13 two-, three- and four-day 'Grand Musical Festivals' in provincial towns from Portsmouth to Newcastle upon Tyne in the summers between 1788 and 1793. His sons led various sections of the orchestra and he engaged professional singers from the London theatres together with leading chorus singers from the Ancient Concerts and, occasionally, boys from the Chapel Royal. Local rank-and-file singers and instrumentalists augmented the touring troupe. His interest in such ventures waned when he became director of the Lenten Oratorios at Covent Garden in 1793, a position he held until his death, although in 1801 he arranged an impressive five-town festival tour through East Anglia.

Ashley's enterprises have been doubly criticized. Edward F. Rimbault's suggestion (*Grove1*) that unscrupulous profiteering lay behind the festival schemes cannot be substantiated. Ashley, and later his sons, consistently featured eminent performers of the day at places otherwise bereft of metropolitan talent and the programmes always provided substantial, and at times novel, musical fare, such as performances of *The Creation* at Hull in 1801, Norwich in 1802 and Stamford in 1803. Ashley has also been condemned for changing the character of the Lenten Oratorios by replacing performances of complete works with miscellaneous selections of sacred and secular music. In fact complete performances did not entirely disappear. In a typical season of 11 concerts any three of *Messiah*, *Judas Maccabaeus*, *Acis and Galatea*, *L'Allegro* and *Alexander's Feast* received at least one airing. The miscellaneous selections, already introduced into the Oratorios before Ashley's directorship, reflect a public taste nurtured on the Commemoration programmes and their imitations at all important musical festivals. No doubt Ashley exploited this fashion. His programmes, an adroit mix of conservatism, patriotism and novelty, well suited the temper of the times. His particular achievements at the Oratorios are too frequently overlooked: the first performances in England of *The Creation* (28 March 1800, a month before Salomon) and Mozart's *Requiem* (27 February 1801), for which Ashley prepared a special biographical note.

Ashley was also briefly a publisher, bringing out a second edition of Boyce's *Cathedral Music* in 1788 and Boyce's anthem *Lord, thou hast been our refuge* (1755) in 1802. From 1765 he was a member of the Royal Society of Musicians and was Master of the Worshipful Company of Musicians, 1803–4.

The Jane Ashley (1740–1809) whom W. Barclay Squire (*DNB*) and *Grove2* and *3* describe as a brother of John Ashley, and the double bassoonist at the 1784 Commemoration, is a confusion of two surnames arising from a misinterpretation of the notice of death (9 April 1809) of Ashley's brother-in-law Richard Jane ('… aged 69, Mr Jane, uncle of the Messrs Ashley'; *Gentleman's Magazine*, lxxix (1809), 478).

(2) General Christopher Ashley   (*b* London, 6 Nov 1769; *d* London, 21 Aug 1818). Violinist, son of (1) John Ashley. He studied the violin with Felice Giardini and F.-H. Barthélemon and was apprentice to his father from 1784 to 1791. A second violin player at the 1784 Handel Commemoration, he led the orchestra at his father's musical festivals, first appearing in that role at Derby in 1790. His 25-year tenure as leader at the Covent Garden Oratorios began that same year. After his father's death he jointly managed that enterprise with (3) John James Ashley. These two brothers were also the mainstays of the festivals the family continued to promote in the provinces between 1806 and 1815.

Ashley was elected to the Royal Society of Musicians in 1791 and was engaged at Ranelagh and the Concerts of Ancient Music. He gained a considerable reputation in the performance of 'ancient and sacred music'. His concerto repertory, regularly aired at the Oratorios, was conservative. It included works by Geminiani, Giardini, Avison and Giornovichi and, occasionally, works of his own composition.

(3) John James Ashley   (*b* London, 6 March 1771; *d* London, 5 Jan 1815). Organist, pianist and singing master, son of (1) John Ashley. He and his two younger brothers were trebles in the chorus at the 1784 Handel Commemoration. Although noted as both organist (at Tavistock Chapel and subsequently at Covent Garden Theatre) and pianist, being a pupil of the celebrated J.S. Schroeter, he was even more famed as a singing teacher. His pupils included Eliza Salmon (née Munday), Mrs Vaughan (Miss Tennant), Master (James) Elliot and Charles Smith, all of whom performed in the Covent Garden Oratorios and further afield in the family's festivals. After his father's death, Ashley continued to preside at the organ for the Oratorios until 1813 and assisted his brother (2) General Christopher Ashley in their management.

Ashley was also a composer; his published works include three sonatas for piano and violin op.1 (London, c1790), a sonata for piano op.2 (London, c1790), and three vocal canzonets for one and two voices op.5 (London, c1795). The sonatas are substantial two-movement affairs with florid piano parts. The more attractive songs (again with bravura accompaniments) may have been written for his pupils. Curiously, two piano compositions *Arabella: Introduction with Theme and Variations* and *La fete heureuse* appeared in 1824. Both were disparaged by *The Harmonicon* but it recalled Ashley as 'a good conductor and an able organist'.

(4) Charles Jane Ashley   (*b* London, 30 Dec 1772; *d* Margate, 28 Aug 1843). Cellist, son of (1) John Ashley. He appeared as soloist at Ranelagh, in his father's and brother's festivals and at major music meetings throughout the country. He was one of the founders of the Glee Club (1793), a member of the Royal Society of Musicians from 1794 and its secretary during the period 1811–19, and an original member of the Philharmonic Society (1813). He performed at the Concerts of Ancient Music and belonged to the orchestra at the King's Theatre. He was sole manager of the Covent Garden Oratorios from 1816 to 1819 when the family's long connection ended, and continued promoting festivals in the provinces after the deaths of his elder brothers, running a particularly extensive series late in 1818. As a cellist he was often considered second only to Robert Lindley and was renowned for his playing of obbligatos in arias such as 'O liberty' (*Judas Maccabaeus*) and 'Gentle airs' (*Athalia*). Unfortunately Ashley's concerto repertory, a feature of the Oratorios, is unspecified. Apparently his own compositions loomed large and he was noted for including popular airs in the final movements.

Court proceedings in 1820 and 1822 saw Ashley confined in the King's Bench prison for debts of over £300. Discharged in August 1834, his health and career ruined, he moved to Margate where he was variously named as manager and proprietor of the Tivoli Gardens until his death.

(5) Richard Godfrey Ashley   (*b* London, 8 Sept 1774; *d* London, 11 Oct 1836). Violinist, viola player and timpanist, son of (1) John Ashley. He appeared in his father's undertakings and his brothers' provincial ventures, including the swansong 1818 festival series. However, from about 1805 his regular connection with the Covent Garden Oratorios is less certain. He was usually listed as performing on the 'Double Drums' but also led the second violins and violas on occasion. He performed at Ranelagh from an early age and was in demand at major festivals, being principal viola at the Three Choirs Festival of 1811 and leader of the section at festivals at York (1823), Chester (1829) and Ware (1829). He was also principal viola in the orchestra at the King's Theatre, London. Samuel Wesley thought him 'a most capital performer … laudable for his rigid observance of Time; moreover his Tone was universally steady, full and rich' (*GB-Lbl* Add.27593, 105f). Ashley was made a member of the Royal Society of Musicians in 1796 and the Worshipful Company of Musicians in 1800.

BIBLIOGRAPHY

SainsburyD

H. Saxe Wyndham: *The Annals of Covent Garden Theatre from 1732 to 1897* (London, 1906)

B.W. Pritchard: 'The Provincial Festivals of the Ashley Family', *GSJ*, xxii (1969), 58–77

BRIAN W. PRITCHARD

Ashley [of Bath], John (*b* Bath; *d* Bath, after 1834). English singer, composer and bassoonist. He was called John Ashley of Bath to distinguish him from his London namesake. He received his musical training from his elder brother Josiah, who was a well-known flautist and oboist. From about 1780 to 1830 he was active in Bath both as a bassoonist and singer. He wrote words and music to a number of songs and ballads, many of which acquired considerable popularity. He also published two pamphlets on *God save the King*, in which he refuted the since disproved theories of Richard Clark.

WRITINGS

Reminiscences and Observations respecting the Origin of God Save the King (Bath, 1827)

A Letter to the Rev. W.L. Bowles, supplementary to the 'Observations' (Bath, 1828)

WILLIAM WATERHOUSE

Ashley, Robert (Reynolds) (*b* Ann Arbor, 28 March 1930). American composer and performer. He studied music theory at the University of Michigan (1948–52) and piano and composition at the Manhattan School of Music (MS 1953); he then returned to Ann Arbor to study acoustics and composition (1957–60). His teachers in composition included Riegger, Finney, Bassett and Gerhard. As a composer and performer Ashley was active in Milton Cohen's Space Theater (1957–64), the ONCE Festivals and ONCE Group (*c*1958–69), and the Sonic Arts Union (1966–76); with each of these groups he toured the Americas and Europe. From 1969 to 1981 he directed the Center for Contemporary Music at Mills College, Oakland, California, where he organized an important public-access music and media facility. Subsequently he moved to New York, where he has become best known for a complex, interlocking series of highly unconventional operas for television, including *Perfect Lives*, *Atalanta* and the tetralogy *Now Eleanor's Idea*.

Ashley realized his early electro-acoustic pieces while working with Cohen, a painter and sculptor. Like the other Sonic Arts Union composers, Mumma, Lucier and Behrman, he invented electronic devices for the live generation, manipulation and deployment of sounds. The group was less interested in polished electronic compositions, however, than in conceptual processes whose details were often left to chance. Unlike the others, Ashley was inexorably drawn towards the theatre, and his works rarely had as much to do with sounds as with theatrical situations. In this he was also influenced by filmmaker George Manupelli, the artist Mary Ashley (Ashley's wife), and the pianist 'Blue' Gene Tyranny, who has had a major presence in Ashley's works.

From 1959 to 1963 Ashley wrote instrumental works, such as *Fives* (1962), which explore a jazz-like, improvisatory freedom. A 1963 quartet of *In memoriam* pieces – *In memoriam … Crazy Horse (Symphony)*, *In memoriam … Esteban Gomez (Quartet)*, *In memoriam … John Smith (Concerto)*, and *In memoriam … Kit Carson (Opera)* – apply the widest possible latitude to the genres parenthesized in their titles and provide the performers with graphics that allow for a variety of potential definitions. In *Kit Carson*, for example, the performers use geometric symbols to chart the nature of and relations between groups, events and time.

Soon, however, working with Manupelli on multiple-projection films, Ashley moved in the direction of mixed-media performance art. In 1964 he took a provocative move into his own personal theatre with *The Wolfman*. In this seminal work of the 1960s, Ashley played as background a tape collage of sounds recorded in a restaurant. He then walked onto the stage and began to project long vocal sounds, each duration consisting of one full breath. As one review (*Source*, no.3) described it:

Gradually the relatively articulate collage is transformed into an inchoate mass of electronic sound, the voice overcoming the holocaust of feedback in the circuit and becoming more and more indistinguishable from the tape. The volume level is extremely high; the audience is literally surrounded by a wall of sound that is comparable to and even surpassing that of today's rock music.

In another, equally provocative nightclub-ambience piece, *Purposeful Lady Slow Afternoon* (1968), a woman hesitantly describes a sexual act over an accompaniment of bells.

About 1978 Ashley came to much wider public attention with his opera *Perfect Lives* (originally entitled *Private Parts*) (1977–83). Convinced that he suffered a mild form of Tourette's syndrome, which can compel automatic speech, he began to record his spells of compulsive speaking, and to use the results in electronic collage works such as *Automatic Writing* (1979). Employing similar methods, he also generated texts that have eventually grown into a series of operatic works, in which one opera derives from the plot and characters of another. The first, *Perfect Lives*, was developed in stages, the composer originally performing it as a solo text with piano and tape, and later with other singers and video. In this, as in subsequent operas, the work is created by slowly piling layer upon layer of text and music, sometimes achieving indecipherability and information overload.

In addition to internal interrelation, the operas draw on a wide range of literary sources: *Perfect Lives* is structured after the *Tibetan Book of the Dead*; *Improvement* is based on Frances Yates's books on Neoplatonism; *Now Eleanor's Idea* draws letters from *Low Rider* magazine (about customized cars); *The Immortality Songs* (a series derived from *Now Eleanor's Idea*) uses material from *Forbes* magazine and the business section of the *New York Times*.

All Ashley's operas are collaborative, the composer's contribution consisting largely of the text and the rhythmic structure. Others who have provided elements of the music and video images include the singers Thomas Buckner, Jacqueline Humbert, Sam Ashley (the composer's son) and Joan La Barbara, the video producer John Sanborn, the rock musicians Peter Gordon and Jill Kroesen, the percussionist and performance artist David Van Tiegham and the sound designer Tom Hamilton.

Despite this multiple input and an overriding sense of freedom the operas remain highly structured. *Improvement*, for example, for its 88-minute length, is a passacaglia based on a 24-note row over two chords, b minor resolving to F minor; the length to which each central pitch is sustained varies with the intensity of the main character's situation at the moment in question. Likewise, *eL/Aficionado* is structured over a 16-note ostinato, and each scene is defined by a modal structure within which the soloist improvises on the text. Though intended for television, the daring and unconventional nature of Ashley's operas has meant that, with the exception of *Perfect Lives*, none has yet been broadcast.

WORKS
OPERAS
all composed for television and unless otherwise stated with librettos by Ashley

That Morning Thing (stage op), 1967, Ann Arbor, 8 Feb 1968
Music with Roots in the Aether, 1976, Paris, 1976
Perfect Lives (Private Parts), 1977–83, Channel 4 TV, 1984
The Lessons, 1981, New York, 1981 [may be perf. as part of Perfect Lives (Private Parts)]
Music Word Fire and I would Do it Again Coo Coo, 1981
Atalanta (Acts of God), 1982, Paris, 1982
Atalanta Strategy, 1984
Improvement (Don Leaves Linda), 1984–5

eL/Aficionado, 1987
Yellow Man with Heart with Wings, 1990
Now Eleanor's Idea, 1993
Foreign Experiences, 1994
The Immortality Songs, 1994–8
Balseros (M. Fornes), 1997
Many other works derived from the operas

ELECTRONIC MUSIC THEATRE
#+ Heat, pfmr, tape, 1961, Ann Arbor, Dec 1962
Public Opinion Descends upon the Demonstrators (Ashley), 1961, Ann Arbor, 18 Feb 1962
Boxing, sound-producing dance, 1963, Detroit, 9 April 1964
Combination Wedding and Funeral (Ashley), 1964, New York, 9 May 1965
Interludes for the Space Theater, sound-producing dance, 1964, Cleveland, 4 May 1965
Kittyhawk (An Antigravity Piece) (Ashley), 1964, St. Louis, 21 March 1965
The Lecture Series (Ashley), 1964, collab. M. Ashley, New York, 9 May 1965
The Wolfman, 1964
The Wolfman Motorcity Revue (Ashley), 1964
Morton Feldman Says, 1965, rev. 1970
Night Train (Ashley), 1966, collab. M. Ashley, Brandeis U., Waltham, MA, 7 Jan 1967
Orange Dessert (Ashley), 1965, Ann Arbor, 9 April 1966
Unmarked Interchange (Ashley), 1965, collab. ONCE Group, Ann Arbor, 17 Sept 1965
Four Ways, 1967 [from op That Morning Thing]
Frogs, 1967 [from op That Morning Thing]
Purposeful Lady Slow Afternoon, 1967, New York, 1968 [from op That Morning Thing]
She was a Visitor, 1967 [from op That Morning Thing]
The Trial of Anne Opie Wehrer and Unknown Accomplices for Crimes against Humanity (Ashley), 1968, Sheboygan, WI, 30 April 1968
Fancy Free (It's There) (Ashley), 1970, Brussels, April 1970
Illusion Models, hypothetical computer tasks, 1970
Night Sport, simultaneous monologues, 1975, L'Aquila, Italy, April 1975
Over the Telephone, remote/live audio installations, 1975, New York, March 1975
Automatic Writing, 1979
Tap Dancing in the Sand, 1982
Genezzano, 1983
The City of Kleist (Berlin), 1984
Susie Visits Arlington (Paris), 1985

INSTRUMENTAL AND VOCAL
Pf Sonata (Christopher Columbus crosses to the New World in the Niña, the Pinta and the Santa Maria using only dead reckoning and a crude astrolabe), pf, 1959, rev. pf, elecs, 1979; Maneuvers for Small Hands, pf, 1961; Fives, 2 pf, 2 perc, str qnt, 1962; Details, pf 4-hands, 1962; In memoriam … Crazy Horse (Sym.), 20 or more str/wind/other sustaining insts, 1963; In memoriam … Esteban Gomez (Quartet), 4 players, 1963; In memoriam … John Smith (Conc.), 3 players, assistants, 1963; In memoriam … Kit Carson (Opera), 8-part ens, 1963; Trios (White on White), any sustaining insts, 1963; Waiting Room (Quartet), any wind/str, 1965, rev. 1978; The Entrance, elec org, 1965; Revised, Finally, for Gordon Mumma, gong-like insts in pairs, 1973; Odalisque, 1v, chorus, 24 insts, 1985; Basic 10, snare drum, 1988; Superior Seven, fl, chorus, orch insts, 1988; Outcome Inevitable (8 or more insts), 1991; Van Cao's Meditation, pf, 1991; Tract, (1v, 4 str/str orch)/(1v, 2 kbd), 1992

OTHER ELECTRONIC
The 4th of July, tape, 1960; Something for Clarinet, Pianos and Tape, 1961; Complete with Heat, orch insts, tape, 1962; Detroit Divided, tape, 1962; Heat, tape, 1962; Big Danger in 5 Parts, tape, 1962; The Wolfman Tape, 1964 [with opt. amp v as The Wolfman]; Untitled Mixes, jazz trio, tape, 1965, collab. Bob Jones Trio; Str Qt Describing the Motions of Large Real Bodies, str qt, elecs, 1972; How can I Tell the Difference, vn/va, elecs, tape, 1974; Interiors without Flash, tape, 1979; Factory Preset, tape, 1993; Late at Night the Artist Works on his Piano Concerto, Oblivious of the Noise, tape, 1994

Discs: In Sate, Mencken, Christ, and Beethoven these were Men and Women (J.B. Wolgamot), 1v, elecs, 1972 (Cramps 6103, 1974); Automatic Writing, 1v, elecs, 1979 (Vital 1002, 1979)

FILMS AND VIDEOTAPES

Films (collab. G. Manupelli unless otherwise stated): The Image in Time, 1957; Bottleman, 1960; The House, 1961; Jenny and the Poet, 1964; My May, 1965; Overdrive, 1967; Dr. Chicago, 1968–70; Portraits, Selfportraits, and Still Lifes, 1969, collab. Manupelli and 'Blue' Gene Tyranny; Battery Davis, 1970, collab. P. Makanna
Videotapes: The Great Northern Automobile Presence, lighting accompaniments for other people's music, 1975; What she Thinks, 1976

recorded interview in US-NHoh

Principal publisher: Visibility

WRITINGS

'The ONCE Group', Arts in Society, v (1968), 86–9
'The ONCE Group', Source, no.3 (1968), 19–22
'And So it Goes, Depending (1980): About Perfect Lives, an Opera for Television (1983)', Words and Spaces: an Anthology of Twentieth Century Musical Experiments in Language and Sonic Environments, ed. S.S. Smith and T. DeLio (Lanham, MD, 1989), 3–32
'The ONCE Group: Three Pieces', Happenings and Other Acts, ed. M.B. Sandford (New York, 1995), 182–94
"From Foreign Experience", Conjunctions, no.28, ed. T. Field (New York, 1997), 144–79

BIBLIOGRAPHY

H.W. Hitchcock: 'Current Chronicle', MQ, xlviii (1962), 245–8
G. Mumma: 'The ONCE Festival and How it Happened', Arts in Society, iv (1967), 381–98
W. Zimmermann: Desert Plants: Conversations with 23 American Musicians(Vancouver, BC, 1976), 121–35
N. Osterreich: 'Music with Roots in the Aether', PNM, xvi/1 (1977), 214–28
J. Howell: 'Robert Ashley's Perfect Lives (Private Parts)', Live: Performance Art, iii (1980), 3–7
C. Gagne and T.Crass: 'Robert Ashley', Soundpieces: Interviews with American Composers (Metuchen, NJ, 1982), 15–34
J. Rockwell: 'Post-Cageian Experimentation and New Kinds of Collaboration: Robert Ashley', All American Music: Composition in the Late Twentieth Century (New York, 1983), 96–108
T. DeLio: 'Structural Pluralism', Circumscribing the Open Universe: Essays on Cage, Feldman, Wolff, Ashley and Lucier (Lanham, MD, 1984), 69–88
M. Sumner, K.Burch and M. Sumner, eds.: The Guests Go In to Supper: Texts, Scores and Ideas of Seven American Composers: Ashley, Ono, Gage, Anderson, Amirkhanian, Peppe, Atchley (Oakland, CA, 1986)
G. Smith and N.W.Smith: American Originals: Interviews with 25 Contemporary Composers (London, 1994)
K. Gann: American Music in the 20th Century (New York, 1997)
C. Herold: 'The Other Side of Echo: the Adventures of a Dyke-Mestiza-Chicana-Marimacha Ranchera Singer in (Robert) Ashleyland', Women & Performance, xviii (1998)

RICHARD S. JAMES/KYLE GANN

Ashrafi, Muhtar (b Bukhara, 29 May/11 June 1912; d Tashkent, 10 Dec 1975). Uzbek composer. He studied at the Samarkand Institute of Music, Theatre and Choreography (1929–31), then at the Moscow Conservatory with B. Shekhter and S. Vasilenko (1934–7) and the Leningrad Conservatory with M. Steinberg (1941–3). He joined the staff of the Tashkent Conservatory in 1944 and was later its director (1947–62) and rector (1971–5). He is regarded as one of the founders of new Uzbek music and was a leading public figure in the country: he was the director of the Navoi Theatre of Opera and Ballet (1943–7) and both founder and director of the Samarkand Theatre of Opera and Ballet (1964–6). He received a large number of honours and prizes in his lifetime, including the title of People's Artist of the USSR (1951). The renaming of the

Tashkent Conservatory after him in 1976 bears witness to his status both within and outside Uzbekistan.

WORKS
(selective list)

Buran (op, 5, K. Yashen), 1939, collab. S. Vasilenko, Tashkent, 12 June 1939; Velikiy kanal [The Great Canal] (op, 5, M. Rakhmanov and K. Yashen), 1941, collab. Vasilenko, Tashkent, 19 Jan 1941; Sym. no.1 (Geroicheskaya) [Heroic], 1942; Sym. no.2 (Slava pobeditelyam) [Glory to the Winners], 1944; Dilorom (op, 4, K. Yashen and M. Mukhamedov, after A. Navoi: Sem' planet [Seven Planets]), 1958, Tashkent, 5 Feb 1958; Serdtse poèta [Heart of the Poet] (op, 3, I. Sultan), 1962; Amulet lyubvi [Amulet of Love] (ballet), 1969; Timur Malik (ballet), 1970; Stoykost' [Fortitude] (ballet), 1971; Lyubov' i mech [Love and the Sword] (ballet), 1973; Skazaniye o Rustame [Legend about Rustam] (orat), 1974; film scores, incid music and works for chbr orch

WRITINGS

Muzïka v moyey zhizni [Music in My Life] (Tashkent, 1975)

BIBLIOGRAPHY

R. Moisenko: Realist Music: 25 Soviet Composers (London, 1949)
G.B. Bernandt: Slovar' oper [Dictionary of Opera] (Moscow, 1962)
J.R. Bennett: Melodiya: a Soviet Russian LP Discography (Westport, CT, 1981)

RAZIA SULTANOVA

Ashton, Algernon (Bennet Langton) (b Durham, 9 Dec 1859; d London, 10 April 1937). English composer and teacher. He spent his childhood in Leipzig. Ashton studied music under Franz Heinig and Iwan Knorr, and subsequently at the Leipzig Conservatory, with Jadassohn, Richter and Reinecke (theory and composition) and with Papperitz and Coccius (piano). In 1879, having won the Helbig composition prize, he briefly returned to England. He became a pupil of Raff. In 1885 he was appointed to teach the piano at the RCM, where he remained for 25 years.

Ashton's compositions cover most conventional forms except for opera, but he was best known for his piano and chamber works; they include a series of 24 string quartets (now lost) in all the major and minor keys. His published music exceeds 160 works. In 1898 Hofbauer issued a catalogue of the first 100 opus numbers (published by a variety of German and British publishers); they include works for solo piano, piano trio, piano quartet and quintet, short choral works and songs. Ashton's orchestral music, which includes five symphonies, overtures, an orchestral suite, a Turkish March, and violin and piano concertos, made no impression. They are believed to have been lost in World War II.

Truscott claimed Ashton's style was English, but the surviving piano works show a minor 19th-century composer influenced by Raff, Brahms and Schumann. The sonatas show considerable personality and are well worth investigation, the early ones in particular being memorable in invention and vigorous in execution.

Late in his life Ashton became something of a musical reactionary, underlining a natural pomposity evinced particularly in the hobby that obscured his merits as a teacher and composer: his passion for writing letters to the newspapers. His hobby-horses included the neglect of the graves of famous men, although his subjects were often musical, and the letters include much useful information. He published them in two collections: Truth, Wit and Wisdom (London, 1905) and More Truth, Wit and Wisdom (London, 1908).

BIBLIOGRAPHY

Obituary, *MT*, lxxviii (1937), 464

H. Truscott: 'Algernon Ashton, 1859–1937', *MMR*, lxxxix (1959), 142–61

P. Webb: 'Algernon Ashton 1859–1937', *British Music*, xiv (1992), 26–34

LEWIS FOREMAN

Ashton, Sir Frederick (William Malandaine) (*b* Guayaquil, Ecuador, 17 Sept 1904; *d* Eye, Suffolk, 19 Aug 1988). English dancer and choreographer. See BALLET, §3(ii).

Ashton, Hugh. *See* ASTON, HUGH.

Ashwell [Ashewell, Asshwell, Aswell, Hashewell], **Thomas** (*b c*1478; *d* after 1513). English composer. He was admitted as a chorister to St George's Chapel, Windsor, on 29 October 1491 and remained there until 14 January 1493. The roll of accounts of the stewards of Tattershall College, Lincolnshire, for Michaelmas 1502 to Michaelmas 1503 lists him as one of the singing clerks (*clerici conducticii*). An entry dated 29 January 1508 in the chapter acts of Lincoln Cathedral shows that at that time he was *informator choristarum* there but the date of his appointment is unknown. In 1513 he was cantor at Durham Cathedral. The inclusion of his song *She may be callyd a sovrant lady* in a collection printed in 1530 cannot be taken as evidence that he was still alive then, for Fayrfax (*d* 1521) and Cornysh (*d* 1523) are also represented. Ashwell is one of the English authorities listed by Morley at the end of his *Plaine and Easie Introduction to Practicall Musicke* (1597).

Ashwell's admission as a chorister at St George's Chapel in 1491 (see Bergsagel, 1976) suggests he was born about 1478, which would dispose of the unsubstantiated claim by Flood that Ashwell had composed an anthem *God Save King Harry* for the wedding of King Henry VII and Elizabeth of York on 17 January 1487. This assertion was apparently based on a curious statement by Strickland (*Lives of the Queens of England*, London, 1840–48) referring to the chance discovery of the piece in an old church chest and its recognition as a precursor of the British national anthem. There may have been some confusion with the Mass 'God Save King Harry' by Ashwell, two vocal parts of which have survived in Cambridge libraries.

Ashwell's presence at Tattershall College is particularly interesting for its support of a suspected teacher–pupil relationship between him and Taverner, who is supposed to have been a chorister at Tattershall at about this time. The only two works by Ashwell surviving complete are the six-voice *Missa 'Ave Maria'* and *Missa 'Jesu Christe'* in the Forrest-Heyther Partbooks copied by or for Taverner when he assumed his duties as choirmaster at the new Cardinal College, Oxford, in 1526. According to the indenture of Ashwell's appointment at Durham Cathedral (printed in Harrison, 1958) he was expected to teach 'planesong, priknott, faburden, dischant, swarenote et countre', to play the organ, to sing and to compose each year a four- or five-voice mass or equivalent work to the glory of God, the Blessed Virgin Mary, or St Cuthbert. A mass by Ashwell to each of these dedications has survived, but though it is reasonable to suppose that his mass to St Cuthbert was composed for Durham it cannot be automatically assumed that the other two were also written after his appointment there in 1513.

WORKS

Missa 'Ave Maria', 6vv, *GB-Ob*; ed. in EECM, i (1963)

Mass 'God Save King Harry', inc., *Cjc* 234 (B), *Cu* Dd.13.27 (Ct)

Missa 'Jesu Christe', 6vv, *Ob*; ed. in EECM, xvi (1976), facs. of T in *MD*, xvi (1962), pls.iv–vi; *Eu* (T only)

Missa Sancte Cuthberte, *Lbl* Add.30520 (frag.)

Sancta Maria, *Lbl* Add.34191 (B only), *Cu* Peterhouse 471–4, attrib. Pasche

Stabat mater, *Lbl* Harl.1709 (mean only)

She may be callyd a sovrant lady, inc., 1530⁶ (B); facs. in R. Steele, *The Earliest English Music Printing* (London, 1903), pl.vi

Te matrem Dei laudamus, 5vv, *Lbl* Harl.1709, 1v only; *Ob* Mus.Sch.E.1–5 attrib. Hugh Aston (ed. in TCM, x, 1929); *Lbl* Roy.24.d.2, 2 sections only, attrib. Taverner (ed. in TCM, iii, 1924); probably by Aston

BIBLIOGRAPHY

HarrisonMMB

W.H.G. Flood: *Early Tudor Composers* (London, 1925/R)

F.Ll. Harrison: 'English Polyphony (*c*1470–1540)', *Ars Nova and the Renaissance, 1300–1540*, NOHM, iii (1960), 303–48

J.D. Bergsagel: Introductionto *Early Tudor Masses*, i EECM, i (1963)

J.D. Bergsagel: 'The Date and Provenance of the Forrest-Heyther Collection of Tudor Masses', *ML*, xliv (1963), 240–48

R. Bowers: *Choral Institutions within the English Church: their Constitution and Development, 1340–1500* (diss., U. of East Anglia, 1975)

J.D. Bergsagel: Introductionto *Early Tudor Masses*, ii EECM, xvi (1976)

M. Hofman and J.Morehen: *Latin Music in British Sources, c.1485–c. 1610*, EECM, suppl. ii (1987)

J. Caldwell: *The Oxford History of English Music*, i (Oxford, 1991)

JOHN BERGSAGEL

Asia, Daniel (Issac) (*b* Seattle, 27 June 1953). American composer and conductor. He studied composition with Stephen Albert, Ronald Perera and Randall McClellan at Hampshire College (BA 1975). His teachers at Yale University (MM 1977) included Druckman and MacCombie (composition), and Arthur Weisberg (conducting). He also studied composition with Schuller at the Berkshire Music Center (1979) and with Yun at the Berlin Hochschule für Musik (1980). He served on the faculty of the Oberlin Conservatory from 1980 to 1986. A UK Fulbright Arts Fellowship and a Guggenheim Fellowship (1987–8) enabled him to work in London from 1986 to 1988, where he was a visiting lecturer at City University. He joined the faculty of the University of Arizona in 1988. He has conducted the university-based Arizona Contemporary Ensemble, founded and co-directed the New York contemporary music ensemble Musical Elements (1977–) and served as composer-in-residence for the Phoenix SO (1991–4). His awards include grants from the NEA (1978, 1985, 1993), the Fromm Foundation (1986), the Koussevitzky Foundation (1989), Meet the Composer (1994) and the Aaron Copland Fund (1994). His works have been commissioned by the Seattle SO (Symphony no.1, 1987), the American Composers Orchestra (*Black Light*, 1990) and the Cincinnati SO (*Gateways*, 1993) among others.

Asia's music of the 1970s, particularly *Miles Mix* (1976) and *Sand II* (1978), experiments with vernacular influences. Later works, especially the symphonies and the Piano Concerto, are more indebted to the music of Barber, Bernstein and Copland.

WORKS

Orch: Rivalries, chbr orch, 1980–81; 3 Movts, tpt, orch, 1984; Sym. no.1, 1987; Black Light, 1990; Sym. no.2 'Celebration' (Khagiga: In Memoriam Leonard Bernstein), 1988–90; At the Far Edge, 1991; Sym. no.3, 1992; Gateways, 1993; Sym. no.4, 1993; Pf Conc., 1994; Vc Conc., 1997

Vocal: Sound Shapes, SSAATTBB, pitch pipes, 1973; On the Surface, S, pf, hp, vc, perc, 1974–5; Sand II (G. Snyder), Mez, chbr ens,

1978; Why Jacob? (D. Asia), SSAATTBB, pf, 1979; Ossabaw Island Dream (P. Pines), Mez, chbr orch, 1981–2, reorchd 1986; She (Pines), SATB, 1981–2; Pines Songs (Pines), S, pf, 1983, arr. S, ww qnt, pf, 1983–4, arr. Bar, ob, pf, 1985; V'shamru, Bar, chbr orch, 1985; Ps xxx, Bar, vn, pf, 1986; Songs from the Page of Swords (Pines), Bar, ob, pf/chbr ens, 1986; Celebration, Bar, SATB, brass qnt, org, 1988; 2 Sacred Songs (*Kaddish*, Ps xcvi), S, fl, gui, vc, 1989; Fanfare, 1991; Abraham's Horn (Pines), S, pf, 1995; Purer than the Purest Pure, SATB, 1996; My Father's Name Was (Pines), S, db, pf

Chbr and solo inst: Dream Sequence I, amp trbn, 1975; Pf Set I, 1975; Pf Set II, 1976; Str Qt no.1, 1976; Plum-Ds II, fl, tape, 1977; Sand I, fl, hn, db, 1977; Line Images, ww ens, 1978; Orange, va, 1979; Mar music, 1983; Music for tpt and org, 1983; Why Jacob?, pf, Amherst, 1983; Str Qt no.2, 1985; Scherzo Sonata, pf, 1987; B for J, fl, b cl, trbn, vib, elec org, vn, va, vc, 1988; Pf Qt, 1989; Your Cry will be a Whisper, gui, 1992; 5 Designs, fl, bn, 1993; Summer Haze, gui, 1994; The Alex Set, ob, 1995; Embers, fl, gui, 1995

Tape: Shtay, 1975; Miles Mix, 1976; As Above (film score), 1977

Principal publisher: Presser

JAMES CHUTE

Asian Music Forum. Congress instituted in 1969 by the INTERNATIONAL MUSIC COUNCIL.

Asioli, Bonifazio (*b* Correggio, nr Reggio nell'Emilia, 30 Aug 1769; *d* Correggio, 18 May 1832). Italian composer and theorist. Born into a family of musicians, he was essentially self-taught although he studied briefly with Giovanni Battista Lanfranchi, the assistant *maestro di cappella* in the basilica. At the age of eight he had already written complex sacred pieces and chamber music. He studied in Parma with Angelo Morigi (called 'Il Merighi') during 1780–81 and in 1782 stayed for a time in Bologna (where he visited Paudre Martini) and Venice, where he had great success as a harpsichordist and improviser. Having returned to Correggio, at the age of 14 he taught the harpsichord, flute and cello at the Collegio Civico and in 1786 was appointed *maestro di cappella. La volubile*, performed in Correggio in 1785 with the intermezzo *Il ratto di Proserpina*, marked the beginning of his career as an opera composer. In the retinue of the Marchese Gherardini, he moved to Turin (1787), then to Venice (1796–9) and finally to Milan, where his opera *Cinna* had already been staged at La Scala (1792). In 1805 he was appointed *maestro di camera* and music director at the royal chapel of the viceroy Eugène Beauharnais; the appointment involved the composition of both sacred and secular music for the *accademie* held at the royal palace. In 1808, at the suggestion of Mayr, who had refused the post, he became the first director of the newly founded Milan Conservatory, and held the chair of composition. The second part of his life was devoted to teaching by the production of a series of theoretical works. He was responsible for the first performance in Italy of Haydn's *Creation* and *Seasons*. During his Milanese period he was in touch with Weigl, Clementi and Haydn, who, in a letter in 1806, recommended Karl Mozart to him as a pupil. Apart from a journey to Paris in Beauharnais' retinue in 1810, he remained in Milan until 1814, when he was compelled to leave the conservatory as a 'foreigner' after the fall of the Kingdom of Italy. Because of his exceptional merits he was allowed to retain his post at court but in October he was again in Correggio, where he remained until his death.

In Correggio in 1815 he established a music school, in which he was joined by his brother Giovanni Asioli (1767–1831), who, during a life spent entirely in Correggio, was municipal *maestro di cappella* (from 1755),

organist at the basilica, a pianist and composer. In this final period of his life, Bonifazio composed mostly sacred music and continued his theoretical writings. In 1826 he supplied the statutes for the Reggio music school of which, having refused the directorship, he was made honorary president.

Asioli's music is now forgotten, although the brilliance of his talent was widely acknowledged by his contemporaries. His idiom, pleasant and at times sentimental, is at its best in his vocal chamber music, which in style recalls Haydn and Mozart, without showing many traces of the stylistic crisis undergone by music at the beginning of the 19th century. His *sinfonie* have been compared to those by the young Beethoven, and his theatrical music was written in the style of Paisiello and Cimarosa. His didactic work survived longer, and it is to him that the Milan Conservatory owes the foundation of its library.

His brother Luigi Asioli (1778–1815) was a tenor, pianist and composer. A pupil of his brother Giovanni Asioli, he worked first in Naples and Palermo, and from 1804 in London, where he became a fashionable singing teacher. He composed a large amount of music in all forms, much of which, particularly vocal and instrumental chamber pieces, was published in London.

WORKS

VOCAL

Ops: La volubile (ob), Correggio, Oct 1785; Il ratto di Prosperina (int, G. Martinelli), Correggio, Oct 1795; La contadina vivace (ob), Parma, 1785; La gabbia de' pazzi (int), Venice, 1785; La discsordia teatrale (ob), Milan, 1786; Le nozze in ville (ob), Correggio, 1786; Cinna (dramma serio, 2, A. Anelli), Milan, Scala, 26 Dec 1792, *I-CORc**; *Mr**, *Fc*, *PAc*; Pigmalione (azione teatrale), 1796, *F-Pn*, *I-Bc*, *BGc*, *CORc**, *Fc*, *Gl*, *Mc*, *PAc*, vs (London, ?1800); Gustava al Malabar (dramma serio), Turin, 1802, *CORc**, *Tn*

Orats: Giuseppe in Galaad, 1785

Sacred: 10 masses, 1 pubd: TTB, orch, 1820 (Milan, ?1827); mass movts; Vesper service, 3vv, orch (Milan, ?1829); 5 Mag; 4 TeD; 7 Tantum ergo, incl. 1 for B, vv, orch (Milan, ?1827); numerous pss, hymns, motets; others

Chbr: numerous cants, incl. Il ciclope, 1787, *Mr**; Il nome (P. Metastasio) (London, ?1795); 3 cantate (?London, 1808): Il consiglio, La scusa, La primavera; scene liriche; duets; trios; qts; qnts; nocturnes, 2–5vv; arias; canzonettas; sonnets; canons; cavatinas; stanzas; divertimentos; odes; dialogues

INSTRUMENTAL

Orch: 9 sinfonie, incl. Sinfonia campestre, arr. pf (Milan, *c*1815), Sinfonia, f, *I-Mc**; Hpd Conc., *MOe*; 2 fl concs.; Vn Conc.; Act 5 of La Galzenna, ballet; ovs.; divertimentos

Band Suonate; Marcia funebre

Chbr: serenatas; Sextet, cl, 2 vn, vc, hn, bn, 1817; Sextet, cl, va, vc, 2 hn, bn, 1817 (Milan, *c*1820); 16 qts in 16 keys, cl, vc, 2 hn, bn, 1817; Qt, vn, fl, hn, b, 1782; Str Qt, 1785; Trio, mand, vn, b; divertimentos; Sonata, pf, vc acc., *c*1801 (Milan, *c*1817); Sonata, hp, 1800; Sonata, vn, pf, ?1783; db pieces; others

Pf: numerous sonatas, incl. 3 Sonatas op.8 (London, 1803), Sonata (Milan, *c*1816); sonatinas; sinfonie; variations; studies; divertimentos

THEORETICAL WRITINGS AND METHODS

Primi elementi di canto (Milan, 1809)

Principj elementari di musica (Milan, 1809)

Trattato d'armonia e d'accompagnamento (Milan, 1813)

Corso di modulazioni classificate a 4 e più parti (Milan, ?1814)

Dialoghi sul Trattato d'armonia (Milan, 1814)

Osservazioni sul temperamento proprio degl'istromenti stabili: dirette agli accordatori di pianoforte ed organo (Milan, 1816)

I. Scale e salti per il solfeggio, II. Preparazione al canto ed ariette (Milan, 1816)

L'allievo al clavicembalo (Milan, 1819)

Elementi di contrabbasso con una nuova maniera di digitare (Milan, 1823)

Disinganno sulle osservazioni fatte sul temperamento proprio degli istromenti stabili (Milan, 1833)

Elementi di contrappunto (Florence, 1836)

Il maestro di composizione, ossia Seguito al Trattato d'armonia (Milan, 1836)

BIBLIOGRAPHY

DBI (R. Nielson; also 'Asioli, Luigi', R. Nielson); *EitnerQ; FétisB*

G. Bertini: *Dizionario storico-critico degli scrittori di musica* (Palermo, 1814)

'Verzeichniss sämmtlicher Compositionen nebst einer kurzen Biographie des Herrn Bonifacio Asioli', *AMZ*, xxii (1820), 667–70

A. Coli: *Vita di Bonifazio Asioli da Correggio* (Milan, 1834) [incl. detailed list of works]

I. Saccozzi: 'Di Bonifazio Asioli', *Notizie biografiche e letterarie in continuazione della Biblioteca Modenese del Cavalier Abate G° Tiraboschi*, ii (Reggio nell'Emilia, 1834) [incl. letters and Asioli's *Riflessioni sopra l'opera del Signor di Momigni intitolata 'La sola e vera teorica della musica'*]

O.S. Ancarani: *Sopra alcune parole di Carlo Botta intorno al metodo musicale di Bonifazio Asioli* (1836)

G. Vitali: *Della necessità di riformare i 'Principi elementari di musica' di Bonifazio Asioli* (Milan, 1850)

G.C. Marchi Castellini: *Luigi Asioli: vita e lavori* (Correggio, 1880)

O. Chilesotti: *I nostri maestsri del passato* (Milan, 1882), 305–12

R. Finzi: *Asoliana: catalogo di quante opere di Bonifazio Asioli sono esistenti nella Civica biblioteca di Correggio preceduto dalla biografia del maestro* (Correggio, 1930)

F. Mompellio: *Il R. Conservatorio di musica 'Giuseppe Verdi' di Milano* (Florence, 1941)

G. Roncaglia: 'Bonifazio Asioli', *Atti e memorie della Deputazioni di storia patria per le antiche provincie modenesi*, 8th ser., ix (1956), 202–13

R. Finzi: *Celebrazione del musicista Bonifazio Asioli (1769–1832) nel secondo centenario della nascita* (Reggio nell'Emilia, 1969)

A. Zecca Laterza: 'Bonifacio Asioli maestro e direttore della Real scuola di musica', *Chigiana*, xxvi–xxvii, new ser. vi–vii (1969–70), 61–76 [with chronological list of church works perf. in Milan 1805–13 and sources]

C. Gallico: *Bonifazio Asioli musicista e didatta* (Correggio, 1970)

M. Gallarani: *Sinfonia a grand'orchestra (Milano 1801)* (Cremona, 1973)

C. Gallico: 'Scene nel *Saul*', *Il melodramma italiano dell'Ottocento: studi e ricerche per M. Mila* (Turin, 1977)

SERGIO LATTES/ROBERTA MONTEMORRA MARVIN

Asioli, Francesco (*b* probably in Reggio nell'Emilia, *fl* 1674–6). Italian composer and guitarist, ancestor of Bonifazio Asioli. He is known by two collections of guitar music, both printed by Giacomo Monti: *Primi scherzi di chitarra* (Bologna, 1674/R) and *Concerti armonici per la chitarra spagnuola* op.3 (Bologna, 1676; 3 ed. in Chilesotti, 1886; 1 also ed. in Chilesotti, 1921). The second book is more varied in content than the first, containing, besides the typical dances, two arias, two capriccios, a prelude and a sonata with fugue. Each piece is dedicated to a member of the Parma Collegio dei Nobili, where Asioli apparently served as guitar instructor. There are four pieces that spell out the dedicatees' names in *alfabeto* chords (where letters of the alphabet designate fingering positions), a device first used by Corbetta. Asioli's music combines strummed chords and pizzicato notes in a competent, if rather conservative style, with little use of *campanelas* (the playing of as many open strings as possible in the notes of scale passages so that the notes ring on) or the complex rhythms and textures of the contemporary works of, for example, Granata.

BIBLIOGRAPHY

MGG1 (G. Dardo)

O. Chilesotti: 'Fasolo-Asioli', *Gazzetta musicale di Milano*, xli (1886), 349–50, 354

O. Chilesotti: 'Notes sur les tablatures de luth et de guitare, XVIe et XVIIe siècles', *EMDC*, I/ii (1921), 636–84, esp. 679

G.R. Boye: *Giovanni Battista Granata and the Development of Printed Guitar Music in Seventeenth-Century Italy* (diss., Duke U., 1995), 173–6

G.R. Boye: 'Performing Seventeenth-Century Italian Guitar Music: the Question of an Appropriate Stringing', *Performance on Lute, Guitar, and Vihuela: Historical Practice and Modern Interpretation*, ed. V.A. Coelho (Cambridge, 1997), 180–94

GARY R. BOYE

Askenase, Stefan (*b* Lemberg, 10 July 1896; *d* Cologne, 18 Oct 1985). Belgian pianist and teacher of Polish birth. His first lessons were with his mother, who had studied with Chopin's pupil, Mikuli, after which his teacher was Mme Zacharjasiewicz, a former pupil of Mozart's son, Franz Xaver. Another teacher was Teodor Pollak. In 1914–15 he was a pupil of Sauer at the Vienna Music Academy, and he resumed studies with him in 1919 after serving in the Austrian army. Askenase made his début in Vienna in 1919. He moved to Cairo in 1922 to take up a post at the conservatory, but three years later returned to Europe, settling in Brussels and later becoming a Belgian citizen. Askenase toured widely during a career that spanned six decades. Although chiefly remembered for his elegant and poetic interpretations of Chopin, many of which were recorded, the priorities of clarity and simplicity in his approach were equally well suited to the sonatas of Mozart and Haydn.

JAMES METHUEN-CAMPBELL

Askew [Ascue, Askue], **R.** (*fl c*1595). Nothing is known of his identity. His extant compositions for lute are mostly in the University Library of Cambridge: they comprise a Jigg (Dd.2.11, f.100 and Dd.5.78, f.32*v*); Askewes Galliarde (Dd.2.11, f.80); R. Askue (one part of a duet; Dd.9.33, f.88*v*); and (in *GB-Ge*) Robin hoode (Euing 25, OLim R.d.43, f.46*v*). One piece for cittern – a Conceipte – is in *Cu* Dd.4.23, f.6*v*.

DIANA POULTON

Aslanishvili, Shalva (*b* Artanuji, nr Artvini, 10/23 March 1896; *d* Tbilisi, 13 Dec 1981). Georgian musicologist. After graduating from the Tbilisi State Conservatory (1927), he studied at the Leningrad Conservatory with Yury Tyulin and Khristofor Kushnaryov (1927–30). He taught music theory at the Tbilisi College of Music (1924–7) and at the Conservatory (from 1930). He established and headed the department of music theory at the Conservatory (1937–73), and was head of the ethnomusicology section of the Institute of History, Archaeology and Ethnography in Tbilisi (1946–50). He conducted fieldwork expeditions throughout Georgia (1927–50), on the basis of which he introduced a course in Georgian harmony at the Conservatory. His work formed the basis for further theoretical studies in Georgian musicology, both concerning folk music and Western music. He was awarded the doctorate (1964) for his book on Georgian folksong, and was the recipient of the Z. Paliashvili award (1972).

WRITINGS

Chaikovski sakartveloshi [Tchaikovsky in Georgia] (Tbilisi, 1940)

Kartl-Kakhuri khalkhuri sagundo simgerebis harmonia [Harmony of the Kartli-Kakhetian choral folksongs] (Tbilisi, 1950, 2/1970; Russ. trans., 1978)

Narkvevebi kartuli khalkhuri simgeris shesakheb [Essays on Georgian folksong] (Tbilisi, 1954–6; diss., Moscow Conservatory, 1964)

Printsipi formoobrazovaniya v fugah I.S. Bakha [Principles of form in the fugues of J.S. Bach] (Tbilisi, 1975)

BIBLIOGRAPHY

K. Tumanishvili: 'Shalva Aslanishvili', *Musikis teoriis sakitkhebi*, ed. A. Shaverzashvili (Tbilisi, 1982), 3–9

L. Kakuliia and S. Chkoniia: *Kompozitorï i muzïkovedï Gruzii* (Tbilisi, 1985), 24–5

E. Meskhishvili: *S. Aslanishvili: muzïkant, ucheni, pedagog* [Musician, scholar, teacher] (Moscow, 1983)

JOSEPH JORDANIA

Asmahān (*b* during a voyage from Turkey to Syria, 1917; *d* Egypt, 14 July 1944). Syrian singer. Born to a well-known Syrian family, she moved to Cairo with her family in 1924 and made some commercial recordings while still a teenager. In 1932 she married her cousin Prince Ḥasan al-Aṭrash and returned to Syria. After giving birth to a daughter she was pronounced unable to produce any more children (and therefore not a son and heir). She left her husband to give him the chance of having an heir, and thereafter deep sadness marked her life and the romantic meanings in her songs.

Staying in Cairo with her mother, she made singing her profession. She sang compositions by her brother, AṬRASH, FARĪD AL-, and later co-starred in his film *Intiṣār al-shabāb* ('Triumph of youth'). The greatest composers wrote for her: Midhat Assem, Zakariyyā Aḥmad, Muḥammad al-Qasabjī and Riyāḍ al-Sunbaṭī. She sang in Muḥammed 'Abdal-Wahhāb's film *Yom sa'eid* ('A happy day') (1939), and co-starred in his operetta *Qais and Laila*. Her rendition of Muḥammad al-Qasabjī's monologue *Yā ṭuyūr* ('O birds') put her at the peak of modernization in Arabic singing, acclaimed for the rare qualities of her voice and unique performance style.

Her repeated successes, carefree lifestyle and relationships with top Egyptian politicians made her many enemies. In 1941 she returned to her husband in Syria, but was caught up in political trickery and accused of treason. Subsequently she undertook a new film, *Gharām wa intiqām* ('Love and revenge'), in Cairo, receiving the highest payment yet known in Egyptian cinema. While filming she died in a mysterious car accident which may have been staged to kill her.

BIBLIOGRAPHY

S. Zuhur: 'Asmahan: Arab Musical Performance and Musicianship under the Myth', *Images of Enchantment* (Cairo, 1998), 81–107

SAADALLA AGHA AL-KALAA

Asmatikē akolouthia (Gk.: 'chanted service'). The urban or 'cathedral' Office of the Byzantine rite, performed at the Great Church of Hagia Sophia in Constantinople. In its complete form it is preserved in liturgical manuscripts copied between the 8th and the 12th centuries. *The asmatikē akolouthia* originally differed from the monastic Office celebrated in Palestine: the cathedral rite used music in the performance of its fixed psalms (psalms appropriate to the hour of the day) as well as responsorial chants and sung refrains; in monasteries, however, there was little or no singing, merely the verse by verse recitation of the complete Psalter throughout each week. (*See* PSALM, §III, 1.)

By the 11th century, the two traditions had gradually merged into a new, hybrid rite, although a strong element of the monastic *ordo* of Constantinople remained. Monasteries absorbed the fixed psalmody, ceremonial and the melodious chanting of the urban Office, while the presence of urban monks affected the shape of the cathedral rite. By 1200 the *asmatikē akolouthia* had been displaced by the new rite in almost all the main Byzantine cities.

However, it remained in occasional use at the cathedral of Thessaloniki, under the conservative Archbishop Symeon (1416–29).

The best musical sources for the *asmatikē akolouthia* are *GR-An* 2062 (late 14th century) and 2061 (early 15th century), which, despite their late date, preserve the service unadulterated by monastic elements.

BIBLIOGRAPHY

O. Strunk: 'The Byzantine Office at Hagia Sophia', *Dumbarton Oaks Papers*, ix–x (1956), 175–202

R. Taft: *The Liturgy of the Hours in East and West* (Collegeville, MN, 1986)

DIMITRI CONOMOS

ASOL. *See* AMERICAN SYMPHONY ORCHESTRA LEAGUE.

Asola [Asula, Asulae], **Giammateo** [Giovanni Matteo] (*b* Verona, ?1532 or earlier; *d* Venice, 1 Oct 1609). Italian composer. On 7 May 1546 he entered the congregation of secular canons of S Giorgio in Alga. After this he probably studied with Vincenzo Ruffo in Verona. From 1566 until his death he held benefices at S Stefano, Verona. After 1569, not wishing to take monastic vows, he left the congregation, became a secular priest and on 1 June 1571 went to work in the parish of S Maria in Organo, Verona. In 1577 he was appointed *maestro di cappella* at Treviso Cathedral but after a year accepted a better position at Vicenza Cathedral. In 1582 he probably went to Venice and in 1588 was appointed one of four chaplains at S Severo, a church under the jurisdiction of the monks of S Lorenzo. In 1590–91 he was again in Verona but otherwise probably remained at S Severo until his death. His most notable pupils were Leone Leoni and Amadio Freddi.

Asola's large body of sacred music is close in style to that exemplified by the late works of Palestrina, whom, in a dedication, he called the greatest musician of the period. Like Palestrina's his music is based essentially on the polyphonic combination of flowing, balanced melodic lines. There are no chromaticisms, disjunct dissonant intervals or extreme contrasts. Homophonic and canonic passages appear, but most of his music is in a freely imitative contrapuntal style balanced occasionally by brief sections of non-imitative texture. Some of the less spectacular innovations of the Venetian school, particularly in the treatment of *cori spezzati*, can be found in the eight-part works and to a lesser extent in those for six voices. Too much has been made of the dubious assertion that Asola was one of the first composers to write an independent continuo part.

WORKS

Editions: Musica divina, ed. K. Proske, i/1–2, ii (Regensburg, 1853–4)
　Composizioni sacre e profane a più voci secolo XVI, ed. L. Torchi, AMI, ii (1897/R)
　Iohannes Mathaei Asulae opera omnia, ed. G. Vecchi, AntMI, 6th ser., *Monumenta veronensia*, ii (1963–) [only vol. of madrigals has appeared]
　G. Asola: Sixteen Liturgical Works, ed. D.M. Fouse, RRMR, i (1964)

published in Venice unless otherwise noted

MASSES

Missae tres, 5vv … liber I (1570) [Dum complerentur, Reveillez, Standomi un giorno]
Missae tres, 6vv … liber II (1570) [Primi toni, Andreas Christi famulus, Escontez]
Le messe, 4vv pari … sovra li 8 toni … insieme con dui altre, l'una de S Maria a voce piena, l'altra pro defunctis … libro primo (1574); Il secondo libro delle messe, 4vv pari … sopra li toni rimanenti al

primo libro insieme con una messa pro defunctis accomodata per cantar à 2 chori (si placet) (1580)

Messa pro defunctis, 4vv pari (1576)

Secondus liber in quo reliquae missae, 4vv, compositae [5–8] tonis … ad facilitatem, brevitatem, mentemque sanctorum tridentini Concilij patrum accommodatae (1581)

Missae octonis compositae [1–4] tonis … continentur, facilitati, brevitate mentique sanctorum Concilii tridentini patrum accomodatae … 4vv (1586)

Missae tres, 8vv … liber I (1588); Liber II missas tres, duasque sacras cantiones continens, 8vv (1588); 1 mass ed. S. Cisilino (Venice, 1963)

Missae quatuor, 5vv (1588)

Missae duo decemque sacrae laudes, 3vv (2/1588; 3/with bc (org), 1620)

Missae tres totidiemque sacrae laudes, 5vv … liber II (1591)

Missae tres sacraque ex canticis canticorum cantio, 6vv (1591)

Missa defunctorum, 3vv (?1600)

OTHER SACRED

Completorium per totum annum quatuorque illae beatae virginis antiphonae, 6vv (1573)

Psalmodia ad vespertinas, 8vv, canticaeque duo BVM (1574)

Falsi bordoni per cantar salmi in 4 ordini divisi, sopra gli 8 tuoni … del … Asola et alcuni di M. Vincenzo Ruffo. Et anco per cantar gli hymni secondo il suo canto fermo, 4vv (1575[1]; enlarged 3/1584 as Falsi bordoni … aggiontovi ancora il modo di cantar letanie communi, e della beata vergine, et Lauda Sion Salvatorem … con alcuni versi a choro spezzato)

Vespertina majorum solemnitatum psalmodia, 6vv (1576)

Vespertina omnium solemnitatum psalmodia, juxta decretum sacrosancti tridentini Concilii, duoque beatae virginis cantica primi toni, 8vv (1578); Secundus chorus vespertinae omnium solemnitatum psalmodiae, 4vv (1578)

Duplex completorium romanum … quibus etiam adjunximus quatuor illas antiphonas … chorus primus, 4vv (1583); Secundus chorus duplicis completorii romani (1587)

In passionibus quatuor evangelistarum Christi locutio, 3vv (1583)

Introitus, missarum omnium solemnitatum … et alleluia ac musica super cantu plano … psalmi immutatis, 4vv (Brescia, 1583)

Prima pars musices continens officium Hebdomadae sanctae, videlicet benedictionem palmarum et alia missarum solemnis, 4vv (1583); Secunda pars continens officium Hebdomadae sanctae, id est lamentationes, responsoria, 4vv (1584)

Madrigali, 2vv, accomodati da cantar in fuga (1584, 2/1587), ed. M. Giuliani (Cles, 1993)

Sacrae cantiones in totius anni solennitatibus, 4vv (1584); some ed. in RRMR, i (1964)

Secundi chori quibusdam, respondens cantilenis, quae in secunda parte musicis maioris Hebdomadae … cantico Benedictus … et psalmo Miserere mei Deus, atque versiculis Heu heu domine, 4vv (1584)

Completorium romanum duae beatae virginis antiphonae, scilicet Salve regina et Regina coeli quatuorque alia motetta, 8vv (1585)

Hymni ad vespertinas omnium solemnitatum horas decantandi. Ad breviarii cantique plani formam restituti. Pars prima, 4vv (1585); Secunda pars hymnorum vespertinis omnium solennitatum horis deservientium, 4vv (1585); some ed. in RRMR, i (1964)

Officium defunctorum, 4vv (1586)

Psalmi ad tertiam … cum hymno Te Deum laudamus. Chorus primus, 4vv … chorus secundus ad 4vv pares (1586)

Nova vespertina omnium solemnitatum psalmodia, cum cantico beatae virginis, 8vv (1587)

Lamentationes improperia et aliae sacrae laudes, 3vv (1588)

Officium defunctorum, 4vv (1588)

Vespertina omnium solemnitatum psalmodia, canticum beata virginis duplici modulatione, primi videlicet, et 8 toni. Salve regina, missa, et 5 divinae laudes, 12vv, ternis variata choris, ac omni instrumentorum genere modulanda (1590)

Sacra omnium solemnitatum psalmodia vespertina cum cantico beatae virginis, 5vv (1592)

Officium defunctorum addito cantico Zachariae, 4vv (1593)

Sacra omnium solemnitatum vespertina psalmodia cum beatae virginis cantico, 6vv (1593)

Officium maioris Hebdomadae, videlicet benedictio palmarum atque missarum solemnia; et que in 4 evangelistarum passiones concinuntur, 4vv, et in eisdem passionibus, 3vv (1595)

Vespertina omnium solemnitatum psalmodia, 4vv pares (1597)

Completorium romanum primus et secundus chorus, Alma Redemptoris mater, Ave regina coelorum, 3vv (1598)

In omnibus totius anni solemnitatibus introitus et alleluia ad missalis romani formam ordinati, musica super cantu planu restituto, 4vv (1598)

Introitus in dominicis diebus totius anni, et ad aspersionem aque benedicte … musica super cantu plano restituto, 4vv (1598)

Nova omnium solemnitatum vespertina psalmodia, 6vv (1599)

Divinae Dei laudes, 2vv (1600)

Sacro sanctae Dei laudes, 8vv (1600[3])

Hymnodia vespertina in maioribus anni solemnitatibus, 8vv, org (1602)

Lamentationes Jeremiae prophetae … nec non et Zachariae canticum, BVM planctus, 6vv (1602)

Psalmi ad vespertinas omnium solemnitatum horas. Una cum cantico beatae virginis, Salve regina, et Regina coeli, 3vv (1602); Secundi chori vespertinae omnium solemnitatum psalmodiae, 3vv (1599)

Various works in 1586[1], 1588[6], 1590[7], 1591[1], 1592[3], 1598[6], 1599[1], 1606[6], 1612[13], 1613[2]

Canto fermo sopra messe, hinni, et altre cose ecclesiastiche appartenenti à sonatori d'organo per giustamente rispondere al choro (1592), ed. M. Casadei Turroni Motti (Verona, 1993), is a publication of chant in mensural notation edited by Asola, not a work of his own.

SECULAR

Le vergini, 3vv … libro I (1571)

[Le] Vergini, 3vv … libro II (1587)

Madrigali, 6vv (1605)

Madrigalii spirituali, 5vv (n.d.), lost; cited in MischiatiI

Various works in 1584[4], 1587[6], 1588[19], 1588[20], 1590[19], 1591[26], 1592[11], 1613[10]

BIBLIOGRAPHY

F. Caffi: Della vita e delle opere di Giammateo Asola (Padua, 1862)

G. d'Alessi: La cappella musicale del duomo di Treviso (1300–1633) (Vedelago, 1954), 127ff, 146, 182, 186 [includes edn of 3 motets]

D.M. Fouse: The Sacred Music of Giammatteo Asola (with) Musical Supplement (Ann Arbor, 1960)

E. Paganuzzi: 'Notizie biografiche sul primo periodo veronese di Giovan Matteo Asola', Vita veronese, xxi (1968), 91–3

B. Meier: 'Zur Modalität der ad aequales disponierten Werke Klassischer Vokalpolyphonie', Festschrift Georg von Dadelsen, ed. T. Kohlhase and V. Scherliess (Stuttgart, 1978), 230–39

R. Tibaldi: L'Ufficio e la Messa dei Defunti di Lodovico Viadana (diss., U. of Pavia, 1988)

DONALD FOUSE

Aspen Music Festival and School. An annual programme held in Aspen, Colorado, a major skiing resort during the winter. The summer festival, which developed from the 1949 Goethe Bicentennial Convocation and Music Festival, has since 1950 included lectures, discussions and concerts of vocal, chamber and orchestral music and jazz performed by faculty, guest artists and students. The Conference on Contemporary Music was founded by Milhaud in 1951. The music school comprises the Aspen Opera Theater Center, the Edgar Stanton Audio Recording Institute and the Center for Advanced Quartet Studies.

RITA H. MEAD/R

Asperen, Bob (Jan Gerard) van (b Amsterdam, 8 Oct 1947). Dutch harpsichordist, clavichordist, organist and conductor. After a classical education, he studied the harpsichord with Gustav Leonhardt and the organ with Albert de Klerk at the Amsterdam Conservatory, graduating in 1971. Since his début in Haarlem in 1968, van Asperen has performed as recitalist and occasionally as conductor in Europe, the USA and Australia. His repertory ranges from the keyboard music of the late 16th century to that of the late 18th, with emphasis on the works of the English virginalists, Frescobaldi, the French clavecinistes, Soler, and J.S. and C.P.E. Bach. From 1968 to 1984 he performed with the ensemble Quadro Hotteterre, with whom he made several recordings. In addition to the principal harpsichord works of J.S. Bach and the organ concertos of Handel, van Asperen has also recorded the complete printed keyboard works of C.P.E. Bach and the complete sonatas of Soler.

After serving as harpsichord professor at the Royal Conservatory in The Hague (1973–88), he succeeded Gustav Leonhardt as professor of harpsichord at the Sweelinck Conservatory in Amsterdam. He has also given masterclasses and has been a visiting professor at leading institutions in Europe, Canada and Australia. Van Asperen has researched extensively into the life and works of the 17th-century Dutch composer Cornelis Thymanszoon Padbrué, and into aspects of 18th-century performance practice.

HOWARD SCHOTT

Aspiration (Fr.). *See* ORNAMENTS, §7.

Asplmayr [Aspelmayr, Aspelmeier, Aschpellmayr, Appelmeyer etc.], **Franz** (*b* Linz, bap. 2 April 1728; *d* Vienna, 29 July 1786). Austrian composer and violinist. He probably received his first musical instruction from his father, a dancing-master. After his father's death he found employment by 1759 as *secretarius* and violinist to Count Morzin during Haydn's tenure as music director. He was by then an established composer, with works published in Paris perhaps as early as 1757. He married in 1760, and after the disbanding of Morzin's musical establishment in 1761 he worked as ballet composer for the Kärntnertortheater in Vienna, succeeding Gluck. There is no primary evidence that he was an imperial court composer and member of the Hofkapelle, as often reported. When Gassmann replaced him as ballet composer Asplmayr continued as a professional violinist, meanwhile composing substantial quantities of instrumental music. His activities as a composer of dance music led to a collaboration with the choreographer J.-G. Noverre (from 1768) and Noverre's successor Gaspero Angiolini, resulting in his writing music during the 1770s for at least ten major dramatic ballets, nine of which survive; also extant are scenebooks of *Iphigénie en Tauride* and *Alexandre et Campaspe de Larisse* (*A-Ws*) and a scene synopsis of *Acis et Galathée* (*Wn*). The most famous of these ballets, *Agamemnon vengé*, achieved international acclaim. Asplmayr also composed the music for the first German-language melodrama in 1772 (on a translation of Rousseau's *Pygmalion*) and a Singspiel, *Die Kinder der Natur*, for the first season of the German Nationaltheater at the Burgtheater. He was a founding member of the Tonkünstler-Societät, serving as an elected officer, and was a member of the quartet, also including Alois Luigi Tomasini, Pancrazio Huber and Joseph Weigl, that first performed Haydn's op.33 in 1781. His career then began to decline, and after an illness he died in poverty.

Asplmayr was an innovative composer, even an experimental one. His principal fame came as the result of his collaboration with Noverre. *Agamemnon vengé*, based on characters from Greek antiquity, contains 39 numbers as well as symphonies before each act. In addition to the usual set pieces there are passages of highly programmatic music to accompany mimed episodes. Asplmayr's *Die Kinder der Natur* was the most substantial of the earliest Viennese Singspiele. Although the music is excellent, the work suffered from an exceptionally bad libretto and disappeared from the repertory. Asplmayr's instrumental music is equally interesting. He composed more than 40

string quartets and over 40 symphonies. Several of the string quartets look forward to the style of Haydn's op.9. The symphonies, two of which appeared under Haydn's name, represent the Viennese mainstream styles of the 1760s and 70s. They are particularly advanced with respect to harmony and developmental techniques. Asplmayr also composed string trios, of which two were attributed by Hoboken to Haydn, as well as a great many divertimentos for strings, wind partitas, sonatas, concertinos and pieces of dance music. He has yet to find his place in the history of the Viennese Classical period.

WORKS

BALLETS

Les faucheurs (C. Bernardi), Vienna, 9 May 1761, *CZ-K*; Les noces japonoises (Ballo japonese) (Bernardi), Vienna, 16 June 1761; Ballo Stattgutti (La promenade du Stadtgut; ?Le divertissement dans le Stadt-Gutt) (Bernardi), Vienna, 16 June 1761, *K*; L'Egyptienne rusée (Les voleurs, ou La Bohemienne adroite; I Ladri) (Bernardi), Vienna, 9 Sept 1761, *K*; Les paisans, les païsannes, et les mineurs (De mineurs et paisans; Les mineurs) (Bernardi), Vienna, 1 Dec 1761, *K*; Le pére de famille, ou La feinte malade (La finta ammalata) (Bernardi), Vienna, 26 Dec 1761, *K*; Le prince jardiner (Il principe persiano) (Bernardi), Vienna, 4 Feb 1762, *K*; La mascarade (Une masquerade) (Bernardi), Vienna, 13 Feb 1762, *K*; Les montagnards (I montanari) (G. Salamone), Vienna, 2 July 1762, *K*; L'heureuse bergere, ou L'amant magicien (Les bergers) (Salamone), Vienna, 21 Nov 1762, *K*; La fête moresque (Ballo moresco) (Salamone), Vienna, 21 Nov 1762, *K*; La lotterie (F. Calzavara), Vienna, 15 Jan 1763, *K*; L'arrivé des charettiers dans un paisage de la Styrie, ou La noble pelerine (La pellegrine noble) (Salamone), Vienna, 23 Jan 1763, *K*; Flora (J.-G. Noverre), Vienna, 1766, *K*; Die Wäscherinnen von Cythere (La Lavandare di citere; Les blanchisseuses de Cythère; Le lavandage di Cittera) (Noverre), Vienna, 1770, *Pnm*; Agamemnon vengé (Der gerächte Agamemnon; La mort d'Agamemnon) (Noverre), Vienna, 1771, *A-Wgm, Wn*; *CZ-K, Pnm*; *D-Bs, Rtt*; Iphigénie en Tauride (Iphigenie in Tauris) (Noverre), Vienna, 1772, *CZ-K, D-Bs, I-MOe*; Acis et Galathée (Noverre), Vienna, 1773, *CZ-K, I-MOe*; Alexandre et Campaspe de Larisse, ou Le triomphe d'Alexandre sur soi-même (Alexander und Kampaspe, oder Der Sieg Alexanders über sich selbst) (Noverre), Vienna, 1773, *A-Wn, CZ-K, Pnm*; L'espiègle du village (Der Dorfeulenspiegel) (G. Angiolini), Vienna, 1774, *K*; Sidney e Silly (Angiolini), Vienna, 1774, *K*; Il sacrafizio al dio Pan (Le sacrifice de dieu Pan; ?Des Opfer des Gottes Pan), 1775, *K*; La nova sposa Persiana (La nouvelle épouse persane; Die persische Braut) (Noverre), Vienna, 1776, *K*

Undated: L'aventure alla campagne (Angiolini), Vienna, *CZ-K*; Ballo del Sign., *K*; Il contratempo, ossia Il ritorno opportuno (Die Wiederkehr zur rechten Zeit), *K*; La fête Cloris, *A-Wn*; Paride ed Elena, *CZ-Pnm*; A quelque chose malheur est bon (Noverre), Vienna, *K*; Die Wein Loese, *K*; Ballo, *K*

Doubtful: ?Il mori, espagnuoli, 1770s; Montgolfier, oder Der Luftkugel, ?1780s

Lost: La caravanne turque (Bernardi), Vienna, 23 March 1761; Une suite de plusieurs incidents qui arrivent parmi les païsans (Bernardi), Vienna, 23 March 1761; La foire (Bernardi), Vienna, 2 May 1761; La promenade des Quackers ou Le focsal à London (L'inglese; Englese; Theatre allemande) (Bernardi), 1 Aug 1761; Les tailleurs (Bernardi), Vienna, 9 Aug 1761; La querelle au cabaret, ou La jalouse apaisée (Bernardi), Vienna, 2 Dec 1761; Le sabbat des sorciers, et sorcieres (Bernardi), Vienna, 2 Dec 1761; Le repos des païsans (Bernardi), Vienna, 24 Jan 1762; La querelle appaisée (Salamone), Vienna, 19 April 1762; La retour de la chasse (Salamone), Vienna, 1 May 1762; L'algerien, ou Le capitain genereux (L'algerine captive et deliverée, ou Le capitain genereux) (Salamone), Vienna, 11 July 1762; Le suisse affamé (Salamone), Vienna, 7 Aug 1762; Les jardiniers (Salamone), Vienna, 21 Aug 1762; Les vendanges (Salamone), Vienna, 4 Oct 1762; L'avare trompé par les fourberies de sa fulle pour avoir le consentiment dans son mariage (L'avare corrigé) (Calzavara), Vienna, 6 Dec 1762; Les petit riens (Les Baget) (Noverre), Vienna, 1767; Die ländlichen Unterhaltungen (Angiolini), Vienna, 1775; Die unnütze Vorsicht, ? 1775

OTHER DRAMATIC

Makbeth der Hexenkönig (Leben und Tod des Königs Makbeth) (pantomime, H. Moll, after W. Shakespeare), Vienna, ?1771, lost; Pygmalion (melodrama/scene lyrique, J.J. Rousseau, trans. J.G. von Laudes), Vienna, 1772, pubd, *A-Wn*, music lost; Die Kinder der Natur (Spl, 2, J.F. von Kurz, after J.F. Hoffmann: *Wer is in der Liebe unbeständig*, after P.C. Chamberlain de Marivaux: *La dispute*), Vienna, 1778, *Wn*; Frühling und Liebe (Spl), Vienna, 1778, lost; ?La ressource comique (oc, 1), pubd lib, *Ws*, music lost; Der Sturm (incid music, J.J. Schink, after Shakespeare), Vienna, 1779, music lost; Orpheus und Euridice (melodrama, L. Bursay, trans. von Laudes), Vienna, 1779, pubd lib, *Ws*

INSTRUMENTAL

principal sources: A-GÖ, LA, ST, Wn, Wgm; B-Bc; CZ-K, Pnm; D-Mbs, Rtt

41 syms.: 3 ed. in The Symphony 1720–1840, ser. B, vii (New York 1984); 7 listed in Breitkopf catalogues, 1766, 1769; 5 doubtful; 2 formerly attrib. J. Haydn (H I: Es6, Es7)
43 str qts: 6 as op.6 (Paris, 1765); 6 as op.2 (Paris, 1769), ed. in RRMCE, lviii (forthcoming), no.2 ed. in Collegium musicum, xl (Leipzig, 1906); 13 listed in Breitkopf catalogues, 1768, 1769, 1779–80; 2 doubtful
61 str trios, 2 vn, b (some also 2 vn/va, b or 2 vn/pardessus de viole, b): 6 trio modernes, op.1 (Paris, 1761), no.4 ed. in Hausmusik, clxii (Vienna, 1970), no.455; 6 trio, op.5 (Paris, 1765), no.1 ed. in Collegium musicum, xxxix (Leipzig, 1906); 6 sonate o sia dilettamenti, op.7 (Paris, n.d.); 12 ed. in Henrotte; 12 listed in Breitkopf catalogues, 1767, 1774; 2 formerly attrib. J. Haydn (H V:F3, Es10)
*c*70 wind partitas, most for 2 ob (and/or 2 fl and/or 2 cl), 2 hn, b/bn; 6 listed in Leduc catalogue
Other works: 6 duos, 2vn/pardessus de viole, op.2 (Paris, Lyons and Dunkirk, n.d.); 6 duos, vn, vc, op.3 (Paris, n.d.); 6 duos, vn, vc (London, n.d.); 6 serenades, listed in Breitkopf catalogue, 1778; 6 sonatas, vn, b; Concerto, vn, str; 3 concertinos; 22 ballet music arrs., str qt; numerous minuets and other dances

BIBLIOGRAPHY

StiegerO
H. Riessberger: *Franz Asplmayr* (diss., U. of Innsbruck, 1954)
G.A. Henrotte: *The Ensemble Divertimento in Pre-Classic Vienna* (diss., U. of North Carolina, 1967)
G. Zechmeister: *Die Wiener Theater nächst der Burg und nächst dem Kärntnerthor von 1747 bis 1776* (Vienna, 1971)
B. Brown: *Gluck and the French Theatre in Vienna* (Oxford, 1991)
D. Heartz: *Haydn, Mozart and the Viennese School* (New York, 1995)
                                                   DENNIS C. MONK

Aspull, George (*b* bap. Bolton, 4 Sept 1814; *d* Leamington, 19 Aug 1832). English pianist and composer. He was the ninth of ten sons of Thomas and Martha Aspull, another of whom, William (1798–1875), was organist of St Mary's Church, Nottingham, in 1830–35. He first appeared as a pianist in 1823. Being very short, he stood at the piano, and his hand could barely stretch an octave; yet this did not prevent him from 'conquering the most complex and rapid passages that have ever appeared', including difficult works by Czerny, Moscheles and Kalkbrenner. He received unbounded admiration from leading musicians, and on 20 February 1824 played to George IV. After performing in Paris in April 1825, where he was praised by Rossini, George undertook a number of concert tours with his brothers William and Joseph (*b* 1812) throughout Great Britain and Ireland. By the time of his death (from tuberculosis) at the age of 19, he was extraordinarily famous. He is credited with having given the first performance in England of Weber's *Konzertstück*, in 1824. His compositions for the piano were edited by his father and published under the title *George Aspull's Posthumous Works for the Pianoforte* (London, 1837), with a portrait and a prefatory memoir. They are showy but musically undistinguished.

BIBLIOGRAPHY

DNB (W.B. Squire); *Grove1* (J.A. Fuller Maitland)
'Musical Phenomenon', *The Harmonicon*, ii (1824), 42–3
E. Taylor: 'Aspull, George', *Biographical Dictionary of the Society for the Diffusion of Useful Knowledge* (London, 1842)
[J.E. Cox]: *Musical Recollections of the Last Half-Century* (London, 1872), i, 206–7
M. Silburn: 'The Most Extraordinary Creature in Europe', *ML*, iii (1922), 200–05
                                               NICHOLAS TEMPERLEY

Asriel, Andre (*b* Vienna, 22 Feb 1922). German composer of Austrian birth. He studied the piano at the Vienna Music Academy from the age of 13. After the annexation of Austria by the Third Reich in 1938, he emigrated to London, where he studied as a licentiate at the RAM (1939–40). While in England he became interested in art of the political left, particularly Soviet music, songs of the Spanish Civil War and the compositions of Hanns Eisler. He forged personal contacts with communist artists such as the Cuban poet Kurt Barthel and Ernst Hermann Meyer, with whom he had occasional composition lessons. He continued his piano study with Franz Osborn (1944–5). In 1946 he moved to East Germany, where he studied at the Berlin-Charlottenburg Musikhochschule (1947–9) with Reinhard Schwarz-Schilling, Hermann Wunsch and others, and in Eisler's masterclass at the Akademie der Künste (1950–51). During this period he worked on a project entitled 'Unser Lied – unser Leben' for East German radio. In 1951 he was appointed to a lectureship at the newly founded Hanns Eisler Musikhochschule, where he served as a professor of composition from 1967 to 1981. His honours include the National Prize of the DDR (1951).

Much of Asriel's compositional output consists of documentary and feature film scores, incidental music for stage and radio plays, and choral songs intended for mass performance. He is the author of *Jazz: Analysen und Aspekte* (Berlin, 1966, enlarged 4/1985).

WORKS
(*selective list*)

Film scores: Auf der Sonnenseite, 1961; Der Schwur des Sergeanten Pooley, 1961; Der Dieb von San Marengo, 1963; Mir nach, Canaillen!, 1964; Der verlorene Engel, 1966; Der Lotterieschwede; Elixiere des Teufels; music for short films and TV
Incid music: Der Frieden (P. Hacks, after Aristophanes), 1962; Polly (Hacks, after J. Gay), 1965; Faust I, 1968
Vocal: Mahle, Mühle, mahle (W. Dehmel), mixed chorus, 1951; 6 Lieder (B. Brecht), 1v, pf, 1954; 8 Liebeslieder (J. Gerlach), 1v, pf, 1955; Suite in Scat, mixed chorus, rhythm ens, 1965; 6 Fabeln nach Äsop, mixed chorus, 1967; Baumlige Lieder (H. Stöhr), 1v, pf, 1971; Drei Kommentare zu Moro lasso, chbr chorus, 6 insts, 1971 [after C. Gesualdo]; 3 ernste Gesänge (Brecht), men's vv, 1977; 3 Chöre (Latin texts), mixed chorus, 1983; many other choral works, incl. canons, folksong arrangements and political songs; other songs, 1v, pf
Inst: Rondo, orch, 1952; 4 Inventionen, tpt, trbn, orch, 1963; Shakespeare-Suite, 2 tpt, 2 trbn, 1963; 20 Variationen, fl, gui, 1964; Volksliedersuite, orch, 1964; Metamorphosen, orch, 1968; Serenade, 9 insts, 1969; Toccata und Fuge, org, 1973

Principal publishers: Verlag Neue Musik, Litolff, Lied der Zeit
                                      BEATE SCHRÖDER-NAUENBURG

Assai (It.: 'very'). A word often used in tempo designations (like the approximately equivalent adjective *molto*) to indicate the superlative. *Allegro assai* ('very fast') is its commonest use, and is found particularly in 19th-century scores. *Allegro assai moderato*, 'a very moderate *allegro*', appears characteristically at the opening of Act 2 of Verdi's *Otello*. The Marcia funebre of Beethoven's Third Symphony is marked *adagio assai*.

But the meaning of the word for Beethoven may not have been consistent. Brossard in his *Dictionaire* (1703) gave the usual meaning and added that *assai* could also mean 'rather' or 'moderately'; and although Rousseau roundly chastised him for his ignorant interpretation of the word in terms of the cognate (*assez*) in his mother tongue, there is considerable evidence that most early uses of the word should be taken in that sense. The anonymous *A Short Explication* (London, 1724) gives only the meaning 'moderately'; J.G. Walther (1732) translated *allegro assai* as *ziemlich geschwind* ('fairly fast'); and late in the 19th century Stainer and Barrett's *Dictionary* translated *allegro assai* as '(lit.) Fast enough. A quicker motion than simple *allegro*'. Herrmann-Bengen (*Tempobezeichnungen*, 1959) drew attention to works by R.I. Mayr (1677) and Gottlieb Muffat (1735–9) which may well use *assai* in this more moderate sense; and Brossard himself is witness that he used it thus in his own first book of motets (1695). Stewart Deas ('Beethoven's "Allegro assai"', *ML*, xxxi, 1950, pp.333–6) argued plausibly that Beethoven also sometimes understood *assai* to mean 'moderately': of his copious evidence perhaps the most striking concerns the main theme's first entry in the finale of the Ninth Symphony, marked *moderato* in a late sketch but *allegro assai* in the finished product.

For bibliography see TEMPO AND EXPRESSION MARKS.

DAVID FALLOWS

Assandra, Caterina [Agata] (*b* ?Pavia, *c*1590; *d* Lomello, after 1618). Italian composer and nun. Assandra alluded to Pavia as her birthplace in the dedication of her surviving motet book, *Motetti à due, & tre voci*, op.2 (Milan, 1609³, 1 ed. in Bowers, 1996), which is dedicated to G.B. Biglia, the Bishop of Pavia. Her musical talents were noted early by the publisher Lomazzo in the dedication to G.P. Cima's *Partito de ricercari, e canzoni alla francese* (RISM 1606¹⁵). She received instruction from the German Catholic exile Benedetto Re (or Reggio), *maestro* at Pavia Cathedral, who dedicated a piece to her in 1607. Her op.1 (probably before 1608) is lost, but two motets, *Ave verum corpus* and *Ego flos campi*, which survive untexted in a German organ tablature, are probably from that volume (*D-Rtt*; ed. C. Johnson: *Organ music by Women Composers before 1800*, Pullman, WA, 1993). According to her 1609 dedication to Biglia, she took vows, in an ancient but isolated rural Benedictine monastery, shortly after the volume's publication (taking 'Agata' as her religious name). She seems to have continued to compose after her profession: an imitative eight-voice *Salve regina* appeared in Re's Vespers collection of 1611, and a motet, *Audite verbum Dominum*, for four voices was included in his motet book of 1618.

Borsieri characterized Assandra's motets as among the first in the Roman style to be published in Milan; he must have heard in her music the influence of Agazzari, whose small-scale works had recently been published in the city. The 18 small-scale motets (plus two works by Re) include both highly traditional pieces (e.g. *O salutaris hostia*, a reduction for two voices and two instruments of a simple double-choir motet) and more innovatory works. Among the latter is *Duo seraphim* (ed. B.G. Jackson, Fayetteville, AK, 1990), in which a change in modus reflects the Apocalyptic text; some of the features of this piece anticipate Monteverdi's setting of the same text in 1610.

BIBLIOGRAPHY

G. Borsieri: *Il sopplimento della Nobiltà di Milano* (Milan, 1619), 56
C. Gianturco: 'Caterina Assandra, suora compositrice', *La musica sacra in Lombardia nella prima metà del Seicento: Como 1985*, 117–27
J. Bowers: 'The Emergence of Women Composers in Italy, 1566–1700', *Women Making Music: the Western Art Tradition, 1150–1959*, ed. J. Bowers and J. Tick (Urbana, 1986), 116–67
J. Bowers: 'Caterina Assandra', *Women Composers: Music through the Ages*, ed. S. Glickman and M.F. Schleifer, i (New York, 1996), 330–40 [incl. edn of *O dulcis amor Jesu*]
R.L. Kendrick: *Celestial Sirens: Nuns and their Music in Early Modern Milan* (Oxford, 1996)

ROBERT L. KENDRICK

Assez (Fr.). *See* ASSAI.

Assisi. City in Italy, situated in the Umbria region. The earliest evidence of a flourishing musical activity in Assisi is given by a Franciscan breviary and two fragments with neumatic notation from the 13th century (*I-Ac* 683, 694 and 696). Another source from the same century (*Ac* 695), including nine compositions in early polyphonic style and probably originating at Reims, provides a link between Assisi's musical life and the prevailing polyphonic practice of the time. Giuliano da Spira (*d c*1250) was at Assisi (1227–30) after having served at the court of Louis VIII in Paris; he was delegated to compose the first rhythmical Office of the Franciscan Order. Troubadour songs were cultivated by several secular societies (the most famous being the Del Monte) and were heard on 1 May each year when the town's districts competed in a musical contest called the Calendimaggio.

The community of the Friars Minor, founded by St Francis (*c*1181–1226) at Assisi, promoted the singing of *laude* during sermons and religious services. In the 13th and 14th centuries the singing of *laude* was also practised in Assisi by 12 religious confraternities. The statutes of the Confraternita di S Stefano, compiled in 1327, report that meetings were held at least twice weekly, when *laude* were sung to stir the hearts of the brothers to lamentation and tears.

From its construction in the last quarter of the 13th century the Basilica di S Francesco was the centre of the city's musical activities. In 1363 a new organ was installed by Francesco di Santa Colomba of Rimini. The most noted *maestro di cappella* in the 15th century was Lorenzo Panconi of Arezzo (1489–94). Venanzio da Alessandria filled the post in 1503, probably preceded by Ruffino Bartolucci, who subsequently returned there (1534–9) and who organized the installation of a new organ in the lower church in 1537. Among the composers who held posts at the basilica in the 16th century were Ludovico Balbi (a pupil of Costanzo Porta), Lorenzo da Porciano (1563), Nicolò d'Assisi (1587) and Silvestro d'Assisi (*c*1599).

In the cathedral of S Rufino a *cappella musicale* was officially instituted in 1525 and organized on the model of the Roman papal chapel, after a new organ had been constructed in 1516 by Maestro Andrea da Firenze. The cathedral's *Atti capitolari* cite the appointments as organists and *maestri di cappella* of Ambrogino da Spello (1551), Matteo Rocchichiola (1561), Camillo da Frascati (1562), Gaetano Gabrat (1570), Francescantonio Contolini (1571), Camillo Lameto (1573), Giuseppe da Gubbio (1577), the Flemish Giovanni Tollio (1584) and Camillo Mattlem (1592).

In the 17th century *maestri di cappella* at S Francesco were Bartolomeo Agricola (*c*1622), Francesco Targhetti da Brescia (intermittently from 1614 to 1641), Claudio Cocchi (1632), Giovanni Battistini (1642), Antonio Cossando (1639–53) and Felice Arconati. From 1649 at least 40 singers were employed, and the *cappella* reached its greatest splendour under the direction of Francesco Maria Angeli in the second half of the century.

The theorist and singer Giovanni Battista Bovicelli (*d c*1627) was active in Assisi from 1592 to 1627, singing at S Rufino from 1622 to 1627. Giacomo Carissimi also served the cathedral from 1628 to 1630, and G.O. Pitoni from 1674 to 1676. Outside the churches, music was promoted by the Accademia dei Disiosi (founded 1554) which later (1656) changed its name to Accademia degli Eccitati. In 1657 the academy presented a *dramma per musica*, *Dafne*, with players and singers from the basilica. The printer Giacomo Salvi published Antonio Cifra's *Psalmi sacrique concentus* (1620) and *Psalmorum sacorumque concentuum liber secundus* (1621), motets by A. Perconti and E. Jarram and madrigals by G. Bovicelli.

Maestri di cappella at S Rufino included Democrito Vicomanni (1602), Vincenzo Pace (1620) and Timotello Timotelli (1643). At S Francesco were F.M. Benedetti (1711–15, 1716–46), Francesco Zuccari (1725–6, 1750–88), Clemente Mattei (1781–3) and Luigi Vantaggi (1798–1800), while the cathedral was served by Pietro Sabbatini (intermittently, 1705–43). Pietro Serafini (1745–55) and Giovanni Ricci (after 1750) were *maestri* at both S Rufino and S Francesco.

During the 18th century a music school was run by the Sacro Convento. Notably among its pupils, who were mostly castratos, were the sopranos Felice Fabiani, who later sang in Rome and Loreto, and G.B. Velluti. In 1750 the Accademia degli Eccitati was renamed Accademia dei Rinati; in 1754, Colonia Arcadica Properziana; and in 1810, Accademia Properziana del Subasio. Under its sponsorship, the architect Lorenzo Carpinelli began in 1836 the construction of the Teatro Metastasio, which was inaugurated in autumn 1840 with Mercadante's *Emma d'Antiochia*. Verdi was a member of the academy from 1874.

From 1858 to his death in 1896 Alessandro Borroni, a pupil of Rossini, directed the *cappella* at S Francesco. During this period, the cathedral frequently drew on the basilica for its singers and directors. During the first half of the 20th century Domenico Stella reorganized and catalogued the musical archives at the basilica, partly stored at the Biblioteca Comunale di Assisi, and directed its *cappella* (1919–56). The première of Licinio Recife's *Trittico Francescano* (1926) took place there; Lorenzo Perosi directed the première of his *Transitus animae Sancti Patris Nostri Francisci* there on 4 October 1937.

In 1927 the Accademia Properziana began to revive the tradition of the Calendimaggio, and each September since 1946 some of the musical productions of the Sagra Musicale Umbra have also taken place at Assisi. The Cantori di Assisi, directed by Evangelista Nicolini, was founded in 1960 and performs early music and traditional music.

BIBLIOGRAPHY

DEUMM (B.M. Brumana); *GroveO* (G. Ciliberti); *MGG2* (G. Ciliberti); *RicordiE*

Notizie relative al Teatro Metastasio di Assisi (Assisi, 1881)

G. Fratini: *Storia della Basilica e del Convento di S. Francesco d'Assisi* (Prato, 1882)

G. Mazzatinti and L.Alessandri: 'Assisi: Biblioteca del Convento di S. Francesco', *Inventari dei manoscritti delle biblioteche d'Italia*, iv (Forlì, 1894), 21–141

D. Stella: 'Serie dei maestri di cappella minori conventuali di San Francesco: compilata dal Padre Stanislao Mattei [1800]', *Miscellanea francescana*, xxi (1920), 42; xxii (1921), 44, 134; xxiii (1922), 122

F. Pennacchi: 'Città di Assisi: Biblioteca comunale', *Bollettino dell'Associazione dei musicologi italiani: catalogo generale*, xi (Parma, 1921)

A. Fortini: 'La tradizione musicale della Basilica di Assisi', *Perusia: rassegna del Comune di Perugia*, ix (1937), 14–23

A. Seay: 'Le manuscrit 695 de la Bibliothèque communale d'Assise', *RdM*, xxxix–xl (1957), 10–35

A. Fortini: *La lauda in Assisi e le origini del teatro italiano* (Assisi, 1961)

C. Sartori, ed.: *Assisi: la cappella della Basilica di San Francesco*, i: *Catalogo del fondo musicale nella Biblioteca comunale di Assisi* (Milan, 1962)

G. Zaccaria: 'Il principale fondo musicale della Cappella di S. Francesco', *Miscellanea francescana*, lxii (1962), 155ff

A. Varotti: *La cappella musicale di San Rufino in Assisi: contributo per una storia* (Assisi, 1967)

C. Pampaloni: 'Giovani castrati nell'Assisi del Settecento', *Musica/Realtà*, viii (1987), 133–54

C. Pampaloni: 'Musici invitati alla festa di San Francesco nella Sacra Basilica d'Assisi negli anni 1700–1750', *Studi in onore di Giulio Cattin* (Rome, 1990), 267–305

ELVIDIO SURIAN/CATERINA PAMPALONI

Assisi, Ruffino d'. *See* RUFFINO D'ASSISI.

Associated Board of the Royal Schools of Music. British institution which conducts examinations in practical and theoretical musical subjects; it is also a significant publisher of music and related pedagogical materials. The Associated Board is a London-based charitable company, established in 1889 by the Royal Academy of Music and the Royal College of Music, later joined by the other two 'royal' conservatories, the Royal Northern College of Music (Manchester) and the Royal Scottish Academy of Music and Drama (Glasgow). A.C. Mackenzie, the then Principal of the Royal Academy, provided a colourful account of the circumstances surrounding the foundation of the Associated Board in *A Musician's Narrative* (London, 1927). Its central activity is the provision of a scheme of graded practical examinations for instrumentalists and singers: candidates at each of the eight ascending levels of difficulty must perform set pieces, play scales and arpeggios and pass sight-reading and aural tests. The examinations are held at local centres in Britain and in about 85 other countries, with a high proportion of overseas candidates living in the countries of the Commonwealth, especially New Zealand, South Africa, Hong Kong, Malaysia and Singapore. During the late 1990s about 570,000 candidates were examined annually, 350,000 of these in Britain. The assessments are administered by a pool of about 530 touring examiners, almost all of whom are based in Britain. They are subject to regular compulsory training and elaborate moderation procedures.

The board's publishing activities are undertaken by a non-charitable limited company. This firm exists principally to supply teachers and pupils with the materials required for the board's examinations; consequently a high proportion of its output consists of specimen examination papers, books of exercises and albums of graded instrumental pieces. However, the Associated Board has for many years also produced authoritative editions of classical works, with a particular strength in the piano repertories of the 18th and 19th centuries (for example, the Beethoven Sonatas edited by Donald Tovey and Harold Craxton). Its editions tend to be didactic, offering worked-out fingerings and phrasings along with editorial suggestions for performance ranging from the choice of tempo to the realization of ornaments. Towards the end of the 1990s the firm's output diversified somewhat, notably with the publication of two volumes called *Spectrum*, containing newly commissioned piano pieces and an edition of a recently discovered manuscript of keyboard works by Purcell.

In recent years the Associated Board has sought to consolidate its position as the world's largest music examining body by reforming and extending its traditional activities. Thus the syllabus for graded examinations now includes jazz piano, jazz ensembles and choral singing; ungraded tests are offered for young children just beginning to learn an instrument and for adults. At post-Grade 8 level, a new syllabus and three levels of diploma were introduced in 2000. The Associated Board has also established a Professional Development department, which has operated courses for instrumental and singing teachers at regional centres in Britain since 1995; centres offering the same course have since opened in Singapore and Hong Kong.

DAVID ALLINSON

Associated Music Publishers [AMP]. American firm of music publishers, active in New York. It was founded in 1927 by Paul Heinicke, originally as the sole American agency for leading European music publishing houses, including Bote & Bock, Breitkopf & Härtel, Doblinger, Eschig, Schott, Simrock, Union Musical Español and Universal Edition. The firm began publishing in its own right and has built up an important catalogue of American composers, including John Adams, Elliott Carter, Cowell, Dello Joio, John Harbison, Harris, Husa, Ives, Kirchner, Peter Lieberson, Piston, Riegger, Schuller, Surinach, Tower and Wilder. In 1964 it was acquired by G. Schirmer, which in turn was acquired by Music Sales in 1986; as a BMI affiliate it has retained an interdependent publishing programme complementing Schirmer's affiliation with ASCAP.

ALAN PAGE

Association for Recorded Sound Collections [ARSC]. American organization, founded in 1966 to promote the preservation and study of historic recordings in all areas of music and the spoken word. Its membership, drawn from 23 countries, numbers over 1000 and includes private collectors as well as sound archivists, librarians, media producers, record dealers, discographers, recording engineers, musicians and record reviewers. The ARSC holds an annual conference each year to disseminate discographic information and to provide a forum for presentations and panel discussions in all aspects of recorded sound research. The ARSC also publishes a biannual journal which includes major research articles, technical developments, discographies, record and book reviews and bibliographies; a quarterly newsletter which contains information about member activities, meetings and events, and a membership directory, updated every two years, which lists all ARSC members, their collecting interests and research projects. Other special publications include major archival projects undertaken by an ARSC committee, the Associated Audio Archives, including *Rules for Archival Cataloging of Sound Recordings* (Albuquerque, 1980, 2/1995), *Audio Preservation: a*

Planning Study (Silver Spring, MD, 1988), and the *Rigler and Deutsch Record Index* (Syracuse, NY and Rochester, NY, 1983–6) which inventories all the 78 r.p.m. holdings of five major sound archives at the following institutions: Library of Congress, New York Public Library, Syracuse University, Yale University and Stanford University. The ARSC annually awards grants for researchers in the field of recorded sound as well as awards for excellence in historical sound research.

See also SOUND ARCHIVES.

BIBLIOGRAPHY
T. Brooks: 'Association for Recorded Sound Collections: an Unusual Organization', *Goldmine*, no.81 (1983), 22–3
E. McKee: 'ARSC/AAA: Fifteen Years of Cooperative Research', *ARSC Journal*, no.1 (1988–9), 3–13
< www.arsc-audio.org>

SARA VELEZ

Association Internationale d'Archives Sonores et Audiovisuelles. *See* INTERNATIONAL ASSOCIATION OF SOUND AND AUDIOVISUAL ARCHIVES.

Association Internationale des Bibliothèques Musicales (Fr.). *See* INTERNATIONAL ASSOCIATION OF MUSIC LIBRARIES, ARCHIVES AND DOCUMENTATION CENTRES.

Associazione Toscana per la Ricerca delle Fonti Musicali. Research centre founded in PISA in 1987.

Assoucy, Charles d'. *See* DASSOUCY, CHARLES.

Assyria. *See* MESOPOTAMIA.

Assyrian church music. *See* SYRIAN CHURCH MUSIC.

Ast, Dietmar von. *See* DIETMAR VON AIST.

Astaire, Fred [Austerlitz, Frederick] (*b* Omaha, NE, 10 May 1899; *d* Los Angeles, 22 June 1987). American dancer and singer. His early career was in partnership with his sister Adele (*b* Omaha, 10 Sept 1898; *d* Phoenix, AZ, 25 Jan 1981). They danced on the vaudeville circuit from 1905 until 1917, performing comedy and ballroom dances. Their Broadway début in Sigmund Romberg's revue *Over the Top* (1917) led to appearances of increasing length and variety, as their roles began to include singing and comedic acting. In the *Passing Show of 1918*, *Apple Blossoms* (1919) and *The Love Letter* (1921), they won praise for their loose-limbed, nonchalant agility, and in the last of these they introduced their trademark 'runaround' dance.

Their first starring roles were in Jerome Kern's *The Bunch and Judy* (1922), but it was their performances in *For Goodness Sake* (1923, with three songs by George and Ira Gershwin), and its West End version, *Stop Flirting* (1923), that made them transatlantic celebrities. Thus the Gershwins agreed to write their next two shows, *Lady, Be Good* (New York, 1924; London, 1926) and *Funny Face* (New York, 1927; London, 1928). After *Smiles* (1930), their unsuccessful collaboration with Marilyn Miller, and the hit revue *The Band Wagon* (1931), Adele retired to become the wife of Lord Charles Cavendish. Astaire's last stage musical was Cole Porter's *The Gay Divorcee* (New York, 1932; London, 1933), in which he was partnered by Claire Luce.

Astaire's Hollywood career began in 1933 with *Dancing Lady* and *Flying Down to Rio*, the first of ten collaborations with Ginger Rogers that reorientated cinematic dance away from the chorus lines of Busby

Berkeley towards romantic solos and duets. In films such as *The Gay Divorcee* (1934), *Top Hat* (1935), *Swing Time* (1936) and *Shall We Dance* (1937), he introduced many classic songs by Porter, Berlin, Kern and Gershwin. The dazzling choreography and debonair settings of these tended, however, to distract audiences and critics from his very real vocal talents. These talents were underplayed in his subsequent films, which used him primarily as a dancer; exceptions were *Easter Parade* (1948), *Funny Face* (1957) and *Silk Stockings* (1957). Astaire was given a special Academy Award in 1949. Although his last screen musical was *Finian's Rainbow* (1968), he had already begun a career as a dramatic actor (*On the Beach*, 1958) which continued until *Ghost Story* in 1981.

Astaire's light baritone was controlled by a highly refined stylistic sensibility; he was, after all, an accomplished pianist and songwriter ('I'm Building Up to an Awful Letdown', 1936). On his 1924 recording of 'Fascinatin' Rhythm', partnered by Adele Astaire and accompanied by Gershwin, one hears Astaire's nascent jazz rubato colliding with his sister's literalist approach to the printed rhythms. As might be expected from a dancer, his ability to relate rhythmic freedom to an unerring sense of pulse was paramount; his crisp yet relaxed enunciation, slightly nasal pronunciation, almost vibrato-less tone, and judicious use of portamento and ornaments created a conversational style as affably personable as it was immediately recognizable.

BIBLIOGRAPHY
F. Astaire: *Steps in Time* (New York, 1959/*R*)
A. Croce: *The Fred Astaire and Ginger Rogers Book* (New York, 1972/*R*)
S. Green and B. Goldberg: *Starring Fred Astaire* (New York, 1973/*R*)
B. Thomas: *Astaire: the Man, the Dancer* (New York, 1984/*R*)
J. Mueller: *Astaire Dancing* (New York, 1985)
L. Billman: *Fred Astaire: a Bio-Bibliography* (Westport, CT, 1997)

HOWARD GOLDSTEIN

Astarita [Astaritta], **Gennaro** (*b* ?Naples, *c*1745–9; *d* Rovereto, 18 Dec 1805). Italian composer. He has been called a Neapolitan, but his surname is very common on the Sorrento peninsula. He is first heard of in summer 1765, when he contributed some music to Piccinni's comic opera *L'orfana insidiata* at the Teatro dei Fiorentini, Naples, suggesting that he may have been Piccinni's pupil. He left Naples after producing two operas at the Fiorentini (1765–6); in 1768 an *azione drammatica* by him was performed in Palermo, and in 1770–71 he had at least two comic operas performed in Turin. From Carnival 1772 to autumn 1779 he produced a series of operas in Venice and other northern and central Italian cities, including Florence (1773) and Bologna (1778). In 1779 he completed his friend Traetta's last opera and in 1780 was at Pressburg (now Bratislava) where he produced three operas. After a long gap in his output he went to Moscow as music director of the Petrovsky Theatre (1784), producing a ballet there in January 1785; he then moved to St Petersburg (1786), where he may have had an opera performed in 1787 (according to a score with that date in St Petersburg). He evidently spent the rest of his life working in Italy and Russia: several new operas were performed in Venice and Florence between 1789 and 1793, and in 1794 he was sent by the director of the imperial theatres to engage an Italian opera company. He returned to St Petersburg in 1795 as its *maestro compositore*, and in 1796 he composed for it a comic opera, *Rinaldo d'Asti*; in 1799 the company was taken into the imperial service. In July 1803 he announced his departure from Russia and returned to Italy, stopping in Rovereto where he died on 18 December 1805.

Astarita wrote close to 40 operas, almost all of which are comic. La Borde called him a 'very pleasant modern composer' who appealed more to the general public than to connoisseurs; he singled out the rondò 'Come lasciar poss'io l'anima mia che adoro' as one of the best known.

WORKS

OPERAS

Il corsaro algerino (ob, G. Palomba), Naples, Fiorentini, aut. 1765
L'astuta cameriera (dg), Turin, Carignano, aut. 1770
Gli amanti perseguitati (semi-seria, P. Donzel), Turin, 1770
? Il re alla caccia, Turin, 1770, ov. *D-Bsb**
La critica teatrale, Turin, Carignano, aut. 1771
La contessa di Bimbimpoli (Il divertimento in campagna) (dg, 3, G. Bertati), Venice, S Moisè, carn. 1772, *Dl*
I visionari (dg, Bertati), Venice, S Moisè, aut. 1772, *I-Mr, Tf, P-La* (as I filosofi immaginari), *RUS-SPit, US-Wc*
L'avaro in campagna (dg, Donzel), Turin, Carignano, sum. 1772
La contessina (dg, M. Coltellini, after C. Goldoni), Livorno, S Sebastiano, aut. 1772
L'isola disabitata e Le cinesi (drammi per musica, 2, P. Metastasio), Florence, Accademia degl'Ingegnosi, sum. 1773, *A-Wn* (as perf. Pressburg, 1780)
Le finezze d'amore, o sia La farsa non si fa, ma si prova (farsa, 2, ?Bertati), Venice, S Cassiano, 1773; rev. Milan, 1791, *I-Mr* (as Non si fa ma si prova)
Li astrologi immaginari (dg), Lugo, Unione, fair 1774
Il marito che non ha moglie (dg, Bertati), Venice, S Moisè, aut. 1774
Il principe ipocondriaco (dg, 3, Bertati), Venice, S Moisè, carn. 1774, *P-La* (Act 3 missing)
La villanella incostante (dg), Cortona, Nuovo, spr. 1774
Il mondo della luna (dg, Goldoni), Venice, S Moisè, carn. 1775
Li sapienti ridicoli, ovvero Un pazzo ne fa cento (Bertati), Prague, Regio, 1775
L'avaro (dg, Bertati), Ferrara, Bonacossi, carn. 1776
Armida (2, Migliavacca), Venice, S Moisè, Ascension 1777, *I-Fc, Gl* (as Armida e Rinaldo), *P-La* (as Rinaldo)
La dama immaginaria (dg, P.A. Bagliacca), Venice, S Moisè, carn. 1777
L'isola del Bengodi (dg, 2, Goldoni), Venice, S Moisè, aut. 1777, *I-Fc**
Il marito indolente (dg), Bologna, Zagnoni, aut. 1778
Le discordie teatrali (dg), Florence, Borgo Ognissanti, aut. 1779
Il francese bizzarro (dg, 2), Milan, Regio Ducal, spr. 1779, *D-Dl, F-Pn, H-Bn* (with addns by Haydn)
Nicoletto bellavita (ob), Treviso, Onigo, 1779, *I-Mr*
La Didone abbandonata (os, 3, Metastasio), Pressburg, 1780, *A-Wn**
Il diavolo a quattro (farsa), Naples, S Carlino, 1785
I capricci in amore (dg, 2), ?St Petersburg, ?1787, *RUS-SPit**; Venice, S Cassiano, aut. 1791
Il curioso accidente (dg, 2, Bertati), Venice, S Moisè, aut. 1789, *I-Fc*
Ipermestra (os, Metastasio), Venice, Venier, 1789
L'inganno del ritratto (dg), Florence, Risoluti, 1791
La nobiltà immaginaria (int), Florence, Intrepidi, carn. 1791
Il medico parigino o sia L'amalato per amore (dg, 2, Palomba), Venice, carn. 1792, *RUS-SPit*
Le fallaci apparenze (dg, G.B. Lorenzi), Venice, S Samuele, aut. 1793
Rinaldo d'Asti (ob, 1, G. Carpani), St Petersburg, 30 June 1796, *P-La, RUS-SPit*
Gl'intrighi per amore, *SPit*
Music in: L'orfana insidiata, 1765; Gli eroi dei campi elisi, 1779

OTHER WORKS

Sacred: Laudate pueri, B, insts, 1784, *I-Gl*; Messa (1805); Credo; Les portes de la misericorde, 4vv (Moscow); Alma redemptoris mater, T, orch, *A-Wgm*; Tantum ergo, S, insts, *I-Nc*; Salve tu Domine, S, orch, *E-Mp*
Vocal: Cantata villareccia, 4vv, chorus, Verona, 12 May 1776; Il trionfo della pietà (?orat), Pressburg, 1780, *A-Wn**; Cantata, S, bc, *D-Dl*
Ballets: Olimpiade (choreog. G. Banti), with Telemaco nell'isola di Calipso, Florence, 1773; La vengeance de Cupidon, ou La fête offerte per Vénus à Adonis (M. Maddox), Moscow, Petrovsky, 20 Jan 1785 [Mooser, i, 483]

BIBLIOGRAPHY

La BordeE; MooserA

S. di Giacomo: 'Paisiello e i suoi contemporanei', Musica e musicisti, lx (1905), 762–8; repr. in Napoli: figure e paesi (Naples, 1909), 211–26, and Opere, ii (Milan, 1946), 532–9

C. Lunelli: 'Le ultime composizioni e la morte del musicista Gennaro Astarita', Civis [Trento], no.9 (1979), 304–12

DENNIS LIBBY (text), MARITA P. McCLYMONDS (work-list)

Aston [Asseton, Assheton, Ashton, Haston], **Hugh** [Hugo] (b c1485; bur. Leicester, 17 Nov 1558). English composer. On 20 November 1510 he supplicated at Oxford University for the degree of BMus, stating that he had spent eight years in the study of music and submitting a mass and an antiphon as his exercise. He apparently lived in Coventry in about 1520 when the dean and chapter of the collegiate church of St Mary at Warwick paid his expenses to come from there to advise them on the purchase of a new organ (see Bowers). In 1525 he was magister choristarum and keeper of the organs at St Mary Newarke Hospital and College in Leicester where he apparently remained until its dissolution in 1548. He was thus presumably the master of the choristers whom Bishop Langland proposed to send from Newarke College to Wolsey's new Cardinal College, Oxford, in 1526, a position ultimately filled by Taverner. In 1548 Aston was awarded an annual pension of £12, paid up to 17 November 1558, on which date he was buried in St Margaret's parish, Leicester.

The beginnings of the Gloria, Credo and Agnus Dei of the Missa 'Te Deum' refer to the opening duet of the antiphon Te Deum laudamus; this relationship suggests that these works may have been those Aston submitted for his degree in 1510. In the earlier sources (GB-Cjc 234, Cu Dd.13.27 and Lbl Harl.1709) the antiphon appears with the text Te matrem Dei laudamus, a Marian imitation of Te Deum laudamus and probably Aston's original text. The latter text is not the same as the hymn but an adaptation, making it an antiphon of the Trinity (the texts are given in TCM, x). The relationship is not so close that the mass can be said to be derived from the antiphon, however, and it also uses phrases of the plainsong Te Deum for its cantus firmus.

The virtues of Aston's vocal music have been overshadowed by the remarkable quality of his one surviving composition for the virginal. His 'Hornepype' shows an early grasp of idiomatic keyboard writing which is in advance of continental practice of the time. On stylistic grounds My Lady Careys Dompe and The Short Mesure off my Lady Wynkfelds Rounde have been attributed to Aston but there is no manuscript evidence for this. The references to Carew and Wyngfeld indicate that this music was associated with the court of Henry VIII and possibly that Aston was in London during the period 1510–20.

Hugh Ashton's Maske is a four-part untexted piece of which three parts survive in the late Elizabethan Christ Church partbooks (GB-Och), two ascribed to 'Mr. Hugh Ashton' and the third (possibly added later) to 'Mr. Whytbroke'. Like the keyboard pieces, it is built on an ostinato pattern; the ground, presumably in the missing bass book, is known from Byrd's Hugh Aston's Ground. The existence of a bass part of an anonymous mass constructed on this ground (GB-Lbl Add.34191) suggests that the mass may be by Aston (see Sandon, 1981) and that the piece in the Christ Church partbooks could be an extract from it (and 'Maske' a corruption of 'Mass').

WORKS

Editions: Hugh Aston, John Merbecke, Osbert Parsley, ed. P.C. Buck and others, TCM, x (1929) [contains all the vocal music except Ave domina]

Schott's Anthology of Early Keyboard Music, ed. F. Dawes, i (London, 1951) [S]

Gaude mater matris Christi, ed. N. Sandon (London, Mapa Mundi)

VOCAL

Missa 'Te Deum', 5vv, GB-Ob Mus.Sch.E.376–81; inc. in Cjc 234, Cu Dd.13.27, Cu Peterhouse 471–4 (471 contains beginning of another copy with heading Te matrem)

Missa 'Videte manus meas', 6vv, Ob Mus. Sch.E.376–81

Gaude mater matris Christe, 5vv, Ob Mus. Sch.E.1–5; inc. in Cu Peterhouse 471–4, Lbl Harl.1709, Add.34191 as Gaude virgo mater Christi; ed. N. Sandon (London, 1980)

Te Deum laudamus, 5vv, Ob Mus. Sch.E.1–5; inc. in Cjc 234, Cu Dd.13.27, Lbl Harl.1709 (attrib. T. Ashwell) as Te matrem Dei laudamus; two passages for 3vv, Tu ad liberandum and Tu angelorum domina, in Lbl Roy.24.D.2 (attrib. Taverner)

Ave domina, inc., Lbl Harl.7578 (triplex)

Ave Maria ancilla, inc., Cu Peterhouse 472–4

Ave Maria divae matris, inc., Cu Peterhouse 471–4

O baptista, inc., Cu Peterhouse 472–4

Hugh Ashton's Maske, 4vv, inc., Och 979, 981–2 (2vv attrib. 'Mr. Hugh Ashton', 1v attrib. 'Mr. Whytbroke'); inc. without attrib. in En Panmure 10 and Lbl Add.60577

KEYBOARD

A Hornepype, Lbl Roy.App.58, ed. in S

Attributed to Aston on stylistic grounds (but possibly not by him): My Lady Careys Dompe, Lbl Roy.App.58; The Short Mesure off my Lady Wynkfelds Rownde, Lbl Roy.App.58; both ed. in S

BIBLIOGRAPHY

HarrisonMMB

R. Bray: 'The Part-Books Oxford, Christ Church MSS 979–83: an Index and Commentary', MD, xxv (1971), 179–98, esp. 188

J. Caldwell: English Keyboard Music Before the Nineteenth Century (Oxford, 1973)

W. Edwards: The Sources of Elizabethan Consort Music (diss., U. of Cambridge, 1974)

R. Bowers: Choral Institutions within the English Church: their Constitution and Development, 1340–1500 (diss., U. of East Anglia, 1975)

N. Sandon: 'The Henrician Partbooks at Peterhouse, Cambridge', PRMA, ciii (1976–7), 106–40

H. Benham: Latin Church Music in England c1460–1575 (London, 1977)

J. Blezzard: 'A New Source of Tudor Secular Music', MT, cxxii (1981), 532–5

N. Sandon: 'Another Mass by Hugh Aston?', EMc, ix (1981), 184–91 [see also J. Blezzard, 'Hugh Ashton's Maske', 519]

O. Neighbour: 'Hugh Aston's Variations on a Ground', EMc, x (1982), 215–16

M. Hofman and J.Morehen: Latin Music in British Sources, c.1485–c.1610, EECM, suppl. ii (1987)

J. Caldwell: The Oxford History of English Music, i (Oxford, 1991)

JOHN BERGSAGEL

Aston, Peter (George) (b Birmingham, 5 Oct 1938). English composer and teacher. He studied at the Birmingham School of Music, at the University of York as a postgraduate, and privately with Mellers for composition. He was appointed lecturer in music at York in 1964 and became professor of music at the University of East Anglia in 1974. While pursuing his academic career he has directed the Tudor Consort (which he founded), the English Baroque Ensemble, the York University Choir and Chamber Choir, and the Aldeburgh Festival Singers (1975–88). He has appeared as a guest conductor at several choral festivals in the USA and Italy.

Aston's compositional output is dominated by his church music. However, it was with Five Songs of Crazy Jane (1960) that he first attracted attention. During the following decade he set secular texts for chorus and composed a children's opera, *Sacrapant the Sorcerer* (1967). In his church music, his preoccupations with music of the Baroque era (he has edited the works of George Jeffreys) and with 20th-century British music, in particular Britten, fuse naturally with his well-shaped vocal lines supported by transparent textures. The chromaticism of *God be merciful unto us* (1967) arises from close-weaved contrapuntal lines and extensive use of false relations. Aston retains a distinctive modern style in his writing for choirs of modest ability, for instance in *For I went with the multitude* (1970) and *The True Glory* (1976). A richer harmonic style is evident in some of his works of the 1980s, though a more contemplative note can be heard in the sustained harmonies and arabesques of *How lovely is your dwelling-place* (1996). Both in his distinctive voice and in the quantity of his works, Aston has made one of the most remarkable contributions to English church music of the late 20th century.

WORKS

Sacred: 3 Hymns to the Virgin, SATB, 1962; There is no Rose, S, SATB, org, 1965; Balulalow (J., J. and R. Wedderburn), SATB, org, 1966; God be merciful unto us, SSATB, org, 1967; Alleluya psallat I, 6 solo vv, 1967; And I saw a new heaven, S, SATB, org, 1969; For I went with the multitude, SATB, org, 1970; Divine Image (W. Blake), SATB, 1970; Praise ye the Lord, SSAATTBB, brass, 1970; Alleluya psallat II, SATB, 1971; Mag and Nunc, F, SSAATTBB, org, 1972; Communion Service, F, SATB, org, 1973; Make we Joye, 4 carols, SATB, 1973; Hosanna to the Son of David, SATB, org, 1974; Hodie Christus natus est, SATB, org, 1974; 14 Short Introits, SATB, org, 1974; So they gave their bodies (A. Zimmern), SATB, org, 1976; O sing unto the Lord a new song, SATB, org, 1976; Lift up your heads, O ye gates, SATB, org, 1979; God be in my head, SATB, 1979; Yuletide Carol, Tr, pf/org, 1979; Beloved, let us love (H. Bonar), SATB, 1979; Author of life divine (C. Wesley), SATB, org, 1981; Come, my Way, my Truth, my Life (G. Herbert), SATB, 1982; Welcome Yule!, SATB, org, 1984; Great is the Lord, SATB, org, 1986; Lord, make me an instrument of your peace, SATB, org, 1987; A Mass for All Saints, SSAATTBB, org, 1987; Where shall wisdom be found?, SATB, 1989; The King of Love (H.W. Baker), S, SATB, org, 1991; Ps cl, SATB, org, 1993; Eternal Grace (H. Bonar), SATB, org, 1993; I give you a new commandment, SA, org, 1995; You are Peter, SA, org, 1996; How lovely is your dwelling-place, 2 choirs (SS, SATB), 1996; Holy Spirit, truth divine (S. Longfellow), SATB, 1997; O be joyful in the Lord, SATB, org, 1999; I am the true vine, SATB, org, 1999

Other choral: Chbr Cant. (Pss xxxviii, xiii, cxvii, xxiii, lxvii), A, Bar, chorus, small orch, 1960; 3 Shakespeare Songs, S, SSA, 1964; There was a Boy (J. Short), SATB, 1964; 2 Choruses (K. Raine), SATB, 1965; Love Song (Raine), SATB, 1966; Illuminatio (cant., L.P. Wilkinson), SATB, wind qnt, 1969; Haec dies (cant.), T, B, SSAATTBB, org, 1971; Carmen lumenis (Bible: *Ecclesiastes*, J.J. Rousseau, Alcuin, Plato), chorus, wind, 1975; The True Glory (F. Drake, R. Hakluyt), SATB, orch, 1976; A Song of the Lord, thy Keeper, chorus, str orch, pf, perc, 1983

Solo vocal: 5 Songs of Crazy Jane (W.B. Yeats), S, 1960; A Northumbrian Sequence (Raine), Mez, pf, 1964; My Dancing Day (cant.), S, T, fl, cl, str qt, 1966; Lullay, my child, S, A, 1966; From the Book of Thel (W. Blake), 5 solo vv, 1983

Inst: Nocturne, fl, perc, 1965; 3 Pieces, ob, 1968

Children's op: Sacrapant the Sorcerer (P. Morgan), 1967

WRITINGS

'George Jeffreys', *MT*, cx (1969), 772–6

with J. Paynter: *Sound and Silence* (London, 1970)

The Music of York Minster (London, 1972)

'Tradition and Experiment in the Devotional Music of George Jeffreys', *PRMA*, xcix (1972–3), 105–15

with J. Webb: *Music Theory in Practice* (London, 1992–3)

'Benjamin Britten's *Hymn to St Cecilia*', *Chormusik und Analyse*, i (Mainz, 1997), 259–72

BIBLIOGRAPHY

W. Mellers: 'Peter Aston', *MT*, civ (1963), 115 only

M. Humphreys and R. Evans: *Dictionary of Composers for the Church in Great Britain and Ireland* (London, 1997)

M. Nicholas: 'Peter Aston at 60', *Cathedral Music* (1998), no.1, pp.8–9

MICHAEL NICHOLAS

Aston, A. William. Pseudonym of KETÈLBEY, ALBERT W.

Aston Magna Foundation for Music and the Humanities. American musical organization founded in 1972 by the harpsichordist Albert Fuller and Lee Elman. In September of that year the foundation initiated the Aston Magna Festival, the first professional summer festival of music on period instruments in the United States. The foundation's early educational activities took place on Elman's estate 'Aston Magna' in Great Barrington, Massachusetts. In 1973 the summer festival under artistic director Albert Fuller found a permanent home at St James's Church in Great Barrington, after initial misgivings by the local townspeople. Additional summer concerts are held annually at Bard College in Annandale-on-Hudson, New York.

Aston Magna quickly became a leading force of the early music movement in the USA, presenting concerts on instruments played with techniques known to the composers and offering educational programmes on music and its relation to the other arts and society. In 1977 Aston Magna gave the first US public performances in modern times of the complete Bach Brandenburg Concertos on period instruments, and in 1978 presented the first American performances of Mozart symphonies on original instruments. The same year, with funding from the NEH, Aston Magna launched its cross-disciplinary academy programme under the direction of harpsichordist and musicologist Raymond Erickson. The three-week academy was originally held at Simon's Rock of Bard College in Great Barrington. Subsequent academies have been held at Rutgers University in New Brunswick, New Jersey and at Yale University. The academy brings together scholars in the humanities and musicians to explore particular moments in Western culture, from the end of the Renaissance to the early Romantic period. In 1997 the academy initiated a publication series beginning with *Schubert's Vienna* (New Haven, CT, 1997), a volume of essays by the academy's faculty edited by Raymond Erickson and published by Yale University Press.

A dispute with the foundation board led to Fuller's resignation as artistic director in 1983. He was succeeded by the viola da gamba player John Hsu, who served as artistic director from 1984 to 1990. The violinist Daniel Stepner was appointed artistic director in 1990. The executive offices of the foundation are located in Danbury, Connecticut.

SALLY SANFORD

Astor. English and American firm of instrument makers, publishers and dealers. The two founders were the sons of Jacob Astor, a merchant of Mannheim. George [Georg] (Peter) Astor (*b* Waldorf [now Walldorf], nr Heidelberg, 28 April 1752; *d* London, Dec 1813), after an initial visit to London, decided to establish a business there with his brother John [Johann] Jacob Astor (*b* Waldorf, 17 July 1763; *d* New York, 29/30 March 1848). This operated as George & John Astor at 26 Wych Street *c*1778–83. In 1783 John left for the USA to sell flutes. He rapidly also became involved in the fur trade and built up a highly profitable business exporting furs to England and importing musical instruments for sale in the USA. In 1809 he established a fur trading company; this and the purchase of land in the Bowery laid the foundations of the Astor wealth.

George took sole charge of the London business at the Wych Street premises. He may have worked with George Miller (*fl c*1765–90), who made the earliest surviving English clarinets (one is dated 1770); a clarinet by Miller bears the address 26 Wych Street and he marked his instruments with a unicorn's head, as did Astor and his successors. In 1797 or 1798 the business moved to 79 Cornhill, where Astor made numerous woodwind instruments and pianos. During the period 1784–1826 the firm was known as either George Astor or Astor & Co.; it also operated at 27 Tottenham Street. By 1800 the firm's activities had extended to publishing, including sheet music and instruction manuals for the flute. In 1801 the firm styled itself 'organ builders'. On his death in 1813 George Astor was succeeded by his widow. From 1815 to 1819 the business at 79 Cornhill was known as Astor & Horwood, from 1824 to 1831 as Gerock, Astor & Co., and from 1831 to 1836 as Gerock & Wolf.

Surviving Astor instruments include numerous flutes, oboes, clarinets, bassoons and pianos (see *ClinkscaleMP*), mostly from the early 19th century. A one-key flute (Horniman Museum, London) marked 'Jacob, London' may have been made by the younger Astor. An interesting early clarinet by George Astor (pre-1796) in boxwood and ivory (Bate Collection, Oxford) is an extendable instrument playable in C, B♭ and probably A (one section is missing). George was the maker in 1800 of the bass-horn originally designed by Frichot of Paris. The firm published an annual collection of country dances (from 1815 under the Astor & Horwood imprint); two collections of 24 for violin survive from 1803 and 1818.

BIBLIOGRAPHY

Humphries-SmithMP; *KidsonBMP*

J. Parton: *Life of John Jacob Astor, to which is Appended a Copy of his Last Will* (New York, 1865)

C. Pierre: *La facture instrumentale à l'Exposition universelle de 1889* (Paris, 1890)

'Astor: Musical Instrument Maker', *Musical Courier* [New York] (9 Aug 1899)

A.D.H. Smith: *John Jacob Astor, Landlord of New York* (Philadelphia and London, 1929)

K.W. Porter: *John Jacob Astor, Business Man* (Cambridge, MA., 1931/*R*)

A. Baines: *The Bate Collection of Historical Wind Instruments* (Oxford, 1976)

NIALL O'LOUGHLIN

Astorga, Baron **Emanuele (Gioacchino Cesare Rincón)** d' (*b* Augusta, Sicily, 20 March 1680; *d* ?Madrid, ?1757). Italian composer. Before Volkmann's research his biography (as given by Fétis, for example) was largely a tissue of colourful legend. Over the last 50 years, sparked by Volkmann's work, other important contributions have been made by Frank Walker, Ottavio Tiby and Roberto Pagano which have brought some clarity to many events in Astorga's life, including some completely unknown to Volkmann. It still remains the case, however, that little or nothing is known of the final part of his life.

Astorga came from a family of Spanish origin, and he himself recognized this when he indicated his homeland as 'non sol l'Italia' but 'anco la Spagna'. The family became rich after purchasing in 1624 the appointment of *Regio Secreto* in the city of Augusta, and then joined the aristocracy after acquiring land linked to a baronial title: Ogliastro and Millaina in 1633, Mortiletto five years later. 'Don Emmanuello' gave himself these titles in the frontispiece of his *Cantadas* (1726). After the earthquake which destroyed half the cities of Sicily in January 1693, the family left Augusta for Palermo. Before they had time to join the capital's high society they found themselves at the centre of a scandal involving the composer's father Francesco, who, in autumn 1693 tried to kill his wife Giovanna Bongiovanni and daughter Tommasa 'cum ictu carrabinae' (with a rifle shot). For this he was banished from Palermo, losing his civil and political rights, and on 21 June 1694 his title and lands passed to his son Francesco, Emanuele's elder brother. It was not until January 1709 that the violent father regained his title and land, and resumed his place at the head of the family. For this reason, Roberto Pagano has suggested, while Francesco senior is likely to have been the 'barone d'Astorga' who was 'capo di squadra' of the company of nobles which manned the watch-tower during the people's uprising in 1708, it was undoubtedly Francesco junior who was a member of the Palermo senate between 1705 and 1706, since, before regaining his title, the father 'would not have been able to boast the title of baron, which however appears in all the Senate's official documents'. When he was still young, and for reasons that are still not completely clear, Emanuele left Palermo to travel across half of Europe, leading a fairly nomadic and adventurous life until the middle of 1714. His father's difficult and violent character was no doubt a factor in this, but there were perhaps other reasons, not least the fact that a man of his social standing was prevented from practising freely as a professional musician, although this was how he was to earn his living for a large part of his life.

Astorga's musical education probably began when he was a small child, and his studies continued in Palermo, a city which at the time was home to Francesco Scarlatti (according to Molitor, the young baron's personal tutor) and host to Francesco Gasparini. In 1698 he was ready to display his musical gifts, with a performance in the domestic theatre of Antonio Lucchese, the future Duke of Grazia, of his opera *La moglie nemica*, to a libretto by Francesco Silvani; he and his brother Francisco took the two principal female roles. Obviously this was a highly refined theatrical display, the reflection and product of an equally refined and exclusive society, and the composer felt it appropriate to stress his personal involvement, as was later the case in 1702 when 'D. Eman[uele] Rincon de Astorga, barone dell'Agliastro' composed the music for a *dialogo* by Francesco Maria Landolina, performed when Vincenzo Paternò Asmundo was enrolled in the prestigious military order of the Apostolo S Giacomo. In later years he gave salon performances of his own cantatas, which make up the bulk of his compositions and are mostly for solo voice and continuo.

It is not known exactly when Astorga left Sicily for Rome; it was certainly after 1702 but (as suggested by Pagano) some years before 1708, the date proposal by Tiby and Walker on the basis of Volkmann's supposition that two cantatas with orchestral accompaniment–really two lengthy monologues in the form of a short *opera seria* with an opening sinfonia–dated January 1708 were composed for Cardinal Ottoboni, with whom Astorga seems to have been in contact. Once in Rome, Astorga became part of the circle of the Duke of Uzeda, Spain's papal ambassador; there he made friends with the Neapolitan poet Sebastiano Biancardi, who provided the texts for some of his cantatas. The 1732 Venice edition of Biancardi's poems is prefaced by an account which is an important (if not always reliable) source of information about Astorga at this period. The two friends went to Genoa, where they were robbed by their servant, and to raise money Astorga wrote an opera, *Dafni*, performed there on 21 April 1709. Under the assumed names Giuseppe del Chiaro and Domenico Lalli, they then visited Tortona, Mantua and Venice, where, in autumn 1710, their second operatic collaboration, *L'amor tirannico*, was performed at the Teatro S Cassiano.

The precise date of Astorga's arrival in Barcelona, where he was summoned by the Habsburg claimont Charles III, is not known; probably, as Tiby indicated, it was before *L'amor tirannico* was performed in Venice. It is known, however, that in June 1709 *Dafni* was performed there 'before their Catholic majesties'. The opera was so well received that it was given several performances that summer at the express command of Charles III, who, wishing to retain the services of such a capable musician, assigned him a generous salary while also exempting him from various duties normally required of the other, non-aristocratic *maestros de capilla* in his service. As Pagano rightly observes, it was actually Emperor Joseph II who granted the salary (2000 florins per annum), but Astorga only began to receive it in 1712 when his protector Charles, who in 1711 had become emperor as Karl VI, confirmed it. By 9 May 1712 Astorga was in Vienna, where on that date he stood godfather to a daughter of Antonio Caldara, in place of his friend the Dutch ambassador Hamel von Bruynings, and he may have composed the anonymous one-act *Zenobia*, produced in Vienna a few weeks later. He left Vienna (and a number of debts) in spring 1714, and by September he was in Palermo, occupied with inheriting the family title and estates after the deaths of both his elder brother and his elderly father in 1712. This was possibly after prompt and decisive intervention by his mother and sister Tommasa, who, with a series of astute legal actions, prevented the exchequer from taking possession of the barony on the grounds that the succession had to be claimed within six months of the holder's death. In October 1717 Astorga married the 15-year-old Emanuela Guzzardi e Nicolaci, daughter of the Baron of S Giorgio, who bore him three daughters. From May 1717 to June 1718 he was a senator of Palermo and from 1718 to 1720 a governor of the hospital for incurables there. He was also, on 18 August 1718, one of the founders of the Accademia del Buon Gusto, an offshoot of the Arcadian Academy, and he may have played a part in developing music education at the old Casa degli Spersi, renamed the Conservatorio del Buon Pastore, helping to turn it into a genuine musical institution. In 1721, however, he restored his wife's dowry and made over to her the income from his estates in return for an annuity; he then left Sicily for Lisbon, and never returned home.

Manuscript cantatas (in *GB-Lcm*) are dated Lisbon 1721 and 1722; other works from the same years are the serenata *Aci e Galatea*, performed in Barcelona on 27 December 1721 and *Il Sacrifizio di Diana*, a *componimento musicale* (26 July 1722). The latter was performed in Lisbon, as noticed in the *Gazeta de Lisboa*, where the composer is indicated unambiguously as the 'Barone d'Astorga ao presente nesta Corte' (see M.C. de Brito: *Opera in Portugal in the Eighteenth Century* (Cambridge, 1989), 125). Two villancicos by him in honour of St Vincent were sung at the cathedral there on 21 June 1723, and in 1726 he published there a volume of 12 *Cantadas humanas a solo* with Spanish and Italian words, his only works to be printed in his lifetime.

Hawkins relates that Astorga 'was at Lisbon some time, and after that at Leghorn, where being exceedingly caressed by the English merchants there he was induced to visit England, and passed a winter or two in London, from where he went to Bohemia'. The London visit is not supported by documentary evidence, but Hawkin's details (for example that Astorga was very shortsighted) suggest that his information came from someone who had known the composer. Nothing certain is known about the final years of his life. The latest manuscript date is 1731, and in October 1739 a serenata by him was performed at the Buen Retiro palace in Madrid to celebrate the wedding of the infante Don Filippo (later Duke of Parma) to Louise Elisabeth, eldest daughter of Louis XV. Astorgas Sicilian estates were sold in 1744 by his deserted wife and sister, who were heavily in debt. The date and place given for his death are highly doubtful, being known only from a notation on a manuscript in the Santini collection (*D-MUs*).

The opera *Dafni* was revived at Parma in 1715 and Breslau in 1726. Only the first act is extant (in *A-Wn* and *D-DI*); the overture and some arias were published by Carreras y Bulbena in 1902. In his own day Astorga was best known for his chamber cantatas, which exist in numerous manuscripts. These fluently written and agreeable works move within the same general formal and stylistic bounds as Scarlatti's cantatas without attaining the degree of musical invention or sensitivity towards the joining of words and music displayed by Scarlatti at his best. One of Astorga's best-known compositions is the *Stabat mater* in C minor for solo voices, mixed chorus, strings and continuo, thought until recently to be his only extant sacred work. Beside it must now be placed another sacred work, the hymn *Ave maris stella* in G for soprano, alto, two violins and continuo (the same forces as Alessandro Scarlatti used in his *Stabat mater*), which is in the archive of the Chiesa Madre (now the cathedral) in Piazza Armerina, Sicily. This is probably a youthful work, as is suggested by the inscription 'del Sig. Astorga' on the title-page. Unlike the *Stabat mater*, which concentrates more on choral writing (only two of its nine movements are solo arias), the *Ave maris stella* is modelled on the style of a chamber cantata. Also unlike the *Stabat mater*, which is permeated by complex contrapuntal procedures, it is in a simple, fluent musical style, close to the 'modern' style which was forming in Naples after the first decade of the 18th century in the work of such composers as Domenico Sarro, Nicola Porpora and Leonardo Leo. The *Stabat mater* was dated about 1707–8 by Volkmann on purely stylistic grounds; no performances are known before the middle of the century. Its first known performance outside the liturgy took place in Oxford where, according to William Hayes, 'in 1753 it featured in the musical entertainments which the Academy of Ancient Music gave on Thursday evenings'. From that time until 1840 it enjoyed great popularity. It is thus quite revealing to record what Franz Grillparzer noted in his diary on the occasion of a private performance of the *Stabat mater* organized by the Viennese musicologist Kiesewetter: 'I had not been so profoundly moved for a considerable time; what type of men have come into the world, if not even the name is known today of such an example of the human race!' The *Stabat mater* appeared in print several times during the 19th century and took a permanent place in the European repertory from the beginning of the 20th.

WORKS
† – doubtful

OPERAS
music lost unless otherwise stated

La moglie nemica (melodrama, F. Silvani), Palermo, Casa Lucchese, 1698
Dafni (dramma pastorale, D. Lalli), Genoa, S. Agostino, 21 April 1709, *A-Wn* (Act 1 only), *D-Dl* (Act 1 only); ov. and some arias ed. in Carreras y Bulbena
L'amor tirannico (drama per musica, Lalli), Venice, S Cassiano, 1710
†Zenobia, Vienna, 1712
Il Coro (int a due voci), listed in Farinelli inventory (see Cappelletto)
Riccardo Negoziante (int a due voci), listed in Farinelli inventory (see Cappelletto)

CANTATAS AND ARIAS
for 1 voice and continuo unless otherwise stated

cantatas: printed

[12] Cantadas humanos a solo (Lisbon, 1726): Belando con placer/Saltando mostra ognor la gioia; Bellissima prision de mi alvedrio/Bellissima cagion de' miei voleri; Cristallina dulce fuente/Chiaro fonte cristallino; De contento està arrullando/Or su l'olmo et or sul faggio; Escucha dueño mio/Ascolta o bella ingrata; Filis, que abrigas en tu pecho hermoso/Filli che ascondi dentro al tuo bel seno; Fuera amor un gran contento/Gran piacer saria l'amore; Mira como el arroyuela/Come lieto il ruscelletto; Obedeciendo a leyes del destino/Per conformarmi al mio destin fatale; Respirad ma sea quedito/Venticel che sussurrando; Sean Filis de mi llanto/Da te lungi qual martire; Siempre in busca el alma mia/Vò cercando al monte al piano

cantatas: manuscript
dates are of the earliest dated source: for sources see Ladd

†A Clorinda, al suo bene; Ah Filli, troppo il pianto amor, 1707; All'or che Tirsi ingrato, 1722; †Al primo albero; Amami quant'io t'amo; Amo, ne ancor poss'io; Amor, amor hai vinto; Amor, amor vincesti; Amorosa contesa; Antri amici, a voi ritorno; Antri, spelonche, S, vc, bc; Ardo ma chiudo in seno; A Rosalba la bella; Ascolta o bella ingrata; A te bell'idol mio; Augellin, che tra le frondi; Augellin ch'imprigionato; Aure dolci che spirate; Aurette grate, S, S, bc; Aurora, idol mio; Barbara lontananza; Bella Irene, S, S, 2vv, bc; Bella madre d'erbe e fiori; Bell'idol mio, più d'un tormento; Benchè viva sempre in pena adorendo una belta, S, S, bc; Bench'io vissi sempre in pene, S, S, bc; Bocca vezzosa vega, S, S, bc; Brema d'esser amante il mio core; Cangio loco e cangio sorte (2 settings); Cara leggiadra Clori; Cara Lidia adorata; Care pupille amate; Che Dorinda mi sprezzi; Che dura pena è questa (inc.); Che mi e mieni usu vorrei (printed in 1826); Che Sisifo infelice; Che ti giova, amor crudele; Chiedo al sonno; Ch'io mi scordi d'amarti; Ch'io t'adori ingrata; Chiudetevi per sempre

Clori, bell'idol mio, di quest'amante; Clori che ardea d'amore; Clori che un dì vantava; Clorinda anima mia; Clorinda, s'io t'amai, 1711; Clori nel tuo bel viso; Clori, vorrei narrarti; Cogliea rose Amarilli, ed. K. Jeppesen, *La Flora* (Copenhagen, 1949); Col flebile lamento, 1722, facs. in Ladd; Col sen di gigli adorno, 1714; Come di vaghi fiori, 1724; Come il ciel ti formò; Come sei, tu mia Clori; Come talor in sul meriggio ardente, 1731; Come vago augellino; Così mesta ho l'alma in seno; Crudel del mio gran foco; Crudo spietato amore, facs. in Ladd; Da che due neri lumi; Da quel fatal momento; Da quel giorno che cinto; Deh, dimmi amor; †Deh, per merce (probably by A. Scarlatti); †Deh volate all'idol mio (probably by B. Marcello); Dell'umor di mie pupille; Del più chiaro e lieto dì, S, S, bc; Del sol cocente per fuggir; Dentro ameno giardino; Dentro fiorita selva; Di foco, o bella ingrata; Dissi t'amo, o bella Irene; †Doppo l'orrido verno; Doppo tante e tante pene; †Dormiva in grembo ai fiori; Dunque è pur ver, 1727; Dunque tu parti, o cara

Ecco a voi, cari sassi, A, bc; E puo dolce aurora, B, bc; Ecco l'ora fatal; Ecco perfida Irene; E come, e dove, e quando, facs. in Ladd; E mari e monti e selve, 1721; È possibile, oh Dio, 1722; E pur Cesare ha vinto, S, orch, bc, Genoa, 1708; E pur dolce amare; E quando o cieco nume; Era poco un laccio al core; È si vago il mio tesoro; Fedeltà sè tanto bella; Fermate il piede; Fè sette volte il maggio; Filli, già volge l'anno; Forza d'ingiusto fato; Fra solitarie balze; Giunto è l'aspro momento, 1722, facs. in Ladd; †Godea già fuor d'impaccio; Il doloroso Tirsi; Infelice mio core (inc.); Innocente sospiro; In qual parte del cielo; In queste amene selve, facs. in Ladd; In questo core più va crescendo, 1726, ed. in Volkmann; Io parto e teco resta; Io parto o mio bel sole; Io parto o mio tesoro; Io più quella non son; Io sarei pur fortunato; Io son povera pellegrina; Là dove alto e fastoso; L'aggiunger nuove pene; Lascia di tormentarmi; Lidia, tornami il core; Lontananza trafigge il mio core, 1722; Luci del mio bel sole; Lungi dalla sua Clori

Miei lumi tutti in lagrime; Ne soligni recessi; Neve al sole e cera al foco, B, bc; Nice e Clori, da me imparate; Non degg'io lagnarmi; Non è sol la lontananza, facs. in Ladd; Non è solo un tormento; Non ho più pace al core; Non lasciarmi o bella speme; Non più guerra; Non può dir qual pena sia; Non so d'Irene mia; Non vo più pene al cor; Non vuò mirarvi più fabri; Nuovo dardo il sen m'impiaga, 1713; O dolce mia speranza; O d'un nume ch'è cieco; †Ogni sospiro ch'esce dal core; Oh, come mi tormenti, S, S, bc; Oh Dio? Come in un punto; Oh insoffribil tormento; †Ora poco un laccio; †Or che Febo già scorre; Ove d'antica selva; Ove raggiri al piede; Palpitar già sento il core, ed. H. Riemann, *Ausgewählte Kammer-Kantaten der Seit um 1700* (Leipzig, 1911); Pasatorelle per pietà, S, vc, obbl, bc; Pensando a te, mio bene; †Pensier, che insidioso; Pensier che con l'imago, 1707; Pensier di gelosia; Perché mai, bell'idol mio

Piacque un tempo al mio core; Piange la tortorella; Piangi, deh, piangi; Piango, sospiro e peno, 1707; Più che porto il piè lontano; Poiché deggio partire; Poiché partir tu vuoi; Preparati a penar; Presso i momenti estremi, S, orch, bc, Genoa, 1708; †Prima del morir mio; Pupille serene; Qual da rupe scoscesa, facs. in Ladd; Quall'or bella fissate; Qual più fiero martire; Qual ruscello che il prato circonda, 1722, facs. in Ladd; Qual sia dentro al tuo core, facs. in Ladd; Quando ad altrui favella; Quando mai tiranno amore; Quando penso agl'affanni, 1712; Quando penso a quell'ore; Quando penso esser disciolto; Quante sian le mie pene; Quanto care mi siete, luci vezzose; Quanto piece ogli occhi miei, B, bc; Quella fè, che promettesti; Quella, Fileno, quella ch'un tempo; Questa, dunque, Amarilli; Qui dove il mar tranquillo, 1721; Qui nell'orror che arreca spavento, 1722, facs. in Ladd; Regio fior, pompa d'Aprile; Rideva in bel giardino; Ritorna il vago Aprile (in *I-Nc* attrib. to Morcella); Ruscelletto che ristretto; Ruscelletto che vai scherzando

Saria pur dolce amor; Scorso è gran tempo; Scrivo alla bella mia; Se del duol che m'affligge; Se de'miei fieri ardori; Se in remote contrade; Sei pur bella e in sol mirarti; Se l'amarti è diletto; Selve adorate e care; Sento là che ristretto; Sento nel seno il core; Sen va volando l'ape vezzosa; Se sia ninfa, non so; Se tu, bell'idol mio; Se volesti, ò Rosaura; Si, bellissima Clori; S'io ti mancai di fede; Solo, mesto e pensoso; Son più dì che sospirando, 1709; Son questi i dolci sguardi; Sopra d'un verde prato; Sovra letto d'erbette; Sovra poggietto ameno; Sovra una bella rosa; Stelle chiare e lucenti; Striugesi empie e crudele, B, bc; Su la nascente erbetta, 1718; T'ho perduto, e pur non moro; Ti lascio anima mia; Ti parlo, e non mi ascolti, 1712, ed. in Echoc d'Italie (arias, n.d.); Tirsi, da ch'io t'amai, facs. in Ladd; Tirsi partì d'unico; Tirsi partir dovea; Tormentosa partenza; Torna aprile, e l'aure; Tra solitarie balze; Trattar tutti egualmente; Tu parti amato bene; Usignol ch'or al bosco; Vezzosi rai, se un dì fedele, 1722; Vicino ad un ruscelletto, 1722; Vilipeso abborrito; Vo cercando fra le ombre, S, S, bc; Voi credete o molli erbette; Vola da questo seno; Vorrei per lusingarmi; Zeffiretto arresta il volo

Cantata, 3vv, listed without title in Farinelli inventory (see Cappelletto)

ARIAS
for sources see Volkmann

†Ah Filli, troppo; Alfin sei pur felice; Bocca vezzosa, 2vv, bc; †Che Dorinda mi sprezzi; †Conservati fedele; Ella parer mi fa; È ver ch'io ti lasciai; †Fra dubbii penosi; Giunto del mio morire; Limpido ruscelletto, S, ob, bc; Nel core scolpito, S, mandola, bc; Ogni sospiro; Or non giova più; Perché amor, A, 2 vn, bc; †Sceglier fra mille; †Sola mi lasci

OTHER WORKS

music lost unless otherwise stated

Dialogo (F.M. Landolina), 1702

Dialogo, 4vv, Sirecuse 1728

Aci e Galatea (serenata), Barcelona, 27 Dec 1721

Il Sacrifizio di Diana (componimento musicale), Lisbon, 26 July 1722

Serenata (title unknown), Lisbon, 7 Sept 1722

2 villancicos, 1723, 1726

Serenata (title unknown), Madrid, Buen Retiro, Oct 1739

Le nozze di Bacco (?serenata); other serenatas, 2, 3, 5, 6vv, listed without titles in Farinelli inventory (see Cappelletto)

Ave maris stella, S, A, 2 vn, bc, Piazza Armerina, Cathedral; ed. in Maccavino

Stabat mater, 4 solo vv, chorus, str, bc, *D-MÜs, GB-Lbl, Lcm, Ob*

BIBLIOGRAPHY

FétisB; HawkinsH

S. Biancardi: *Rime* (Venice, 1732)

S. Molitor: 'Bemerkungen zur Lebensgeschichte Emanuels, genannt der Baron d'Astorga', *AMZ*, xli (1839), 198–202, 226–30

H. Volkmann: *Emanuel d'Astorga* (Leipzig, 1911–19)

J.R. Carreras y Bulbena: *Carlos d'Austria i Elisabeth de Brunswick Wolfenbüttel a Barcelona y Gerona* (Barcelona, 1902)

L. Genuardi: 'Emmanuele Rincon d'Astorga, musicista siciliano del secolo XVIII', *Archivio storico siciliano*, new ser., xxxvi (1912), 488–92

G. Sorge: *I teatri di Palermo nei secoli XVI, XVII, XVIII* (Palermo, 1926), 207ff, 383

F. Walker: 'Emanuele d'Astorga and a Neapolitan Librettist', *MMR*, lxxxi (1951), 90–96

O. Tiby: 'Emanuele d'Astorga: aggiunte e correzioni da apportare alle ricerche del prof. Hans Volkmann', *IMSCR V: Utrecht 1952*, 398–403

K.S. Ladd: *The Solo Cantatas of Emanuele d'Astorga* (Ann Arbor, 1982)

R. Pagano: *Scarlatti Alessandro e Domenico: due vite in una* (Milan, 1985)

S. Cappelletto: *La voce perduta: vita di Farinelli, evirato cantore* (Turin, 1995), 70, 211–21

N. Maccavino: 'Una sconosciuta composizione sacra di Emanuel Rincon barone d'Astorga: Ave maris stella', *Studi musicali*, xxvii (1998), 89–122

ALFRED LOEWENBERG, FRANK WALKER/NICOLÒ MACCAVINO

Astorga, Jean Oliver. *See* OLIVER Y ASTORGA, JUAN.

Astor Place Opera House. New York theatre opened in 1847. *See* NEW YORK, §4.

Astrakhan. Town in Russia. Located near the mouth of the Volga, it became famous at the end of the 19th century as a centre of music in the south of Russia. Opera troupes and soloists came on tour, especially after the opening of the Winter Theatre (with seating for 700) in 1884 and the Summer Theatre (with seating for 1200) in 1892.

The Society for Music and Drama, which had been founded in 1885, began music classes in 1889 and taught singing and instruction on a number of instruments. In 1891 the society was reorganized into the Astrakhan division of the Imperial Russian Music Society; it remained active until 1920. The classes had been headed in 1897–9 by Fyodor Keneman, who introduced permanent symphony concerts. Four programmes per season were given and, with the participation of teachers, students and military musicians, the symphonies of Haydn and Beethoven, and later of Mozart and Tchaikovsky, were performed.

In September 1900 the classes were turned into a music school with a seven-year course of training. The first director was Aleksandr Gorelov (1900–03), who continued the concerts and also staged operas each year (*Rigoletto*, *La traviata*, Rubinstein's *Demon*, *Yevgeny Onegin*) with local amateur performers. He was succeeded by Artur Kapp (1903–20), who introduced performances of organ music and oratorios in the Lutheran church. The music society and Kapp personally assisted Chaliapin, Landowska, Artur Rubinstein and others to arrange their concert tours.

The social upheavals of 1917 and the ensuing Civil War combined at first to bring about an advance. For about five years an opera troupe in Astrakhan (directed by M. Maksakov 1920–23) managed to put on 20 productions or so. Alongside the first music school another three opened, but after a few years they closed due to financial collapse. Musical life remained stagnant for many years. A public Philharmonia was briefly active (1926–7), organizing tours. Amateur ensembles appeared in a number of clubs, including the Tatar Music and Drama Group. In the mid-1930s a symphony orchestra made up of teachers and students of the fishing industry institute played for several years. But the most significant feature of these times was the staging of opera by professionals and amateurs grouped around the music school. During World War II 12 productions were put on, organized by the Bol'shoy singer M. Maksakova. Immediately after the war a fishermen's song and dance ensemble called 'Moryana' was set up, as well as a theatre of musical comedy, which was active until 1948.

A notable revival of musical life began in the mid-1960s. In 1965 a concert hall for the Philharmonia was constructed with a seating capacity of 700, and this allowed musicians such as Richter, Rostropovich and Vishnevskaya to be invited to play. The music school moved into a renovated building, and in all the regions of the town children's music schools were founded. In 1969 the Astrakhan State Conservatory opened; six years later it gained a concert hall with an organ and a seating capacity of 400. Opera was given again under the auspices of the House of Culture attached to the fish-canning and refrigeration group (1958–69) and of the fishing industry institute. In May 1996 the Astrakhan State Music Theatre opened to present opera, ballet and operetta.

BIBLIOGRAPHY

M. Etinger: *Muzikal'naya kul'tura Astrakhana* [The musical culture of Astrakhan] (Volgograd, 1987)

Astrakhan Muzikal'naya [Musical Astrakhan] (Astrakhan, 1994) [incl. M. Etinger: 'Astrakhanskoye muzikal'noye uchilische' [The Astrakhan music school]; M. Etinger: 'Vchera, segodnya, zavtra . . .' [Yesterday, today, tomorrow . . .]; G. Slavnikov: 'Astrakhanskaya gosudarstvennaya konservatoriya' [The Astrakhan State Conservatory]; L. Vinogradova and E. Nemirova: 'Budni filarmonii' [The Philharmonia at work]]

MARK ARONOVICH ETINGER

Åstrand, (Karl) Hans (Vilhelm) (*b* Bredaryd, 5 Feb 1925). Swedish music administrator, writer and lexicographer. He studied the double bass, cello, organ and music theory privately and romance languages at Lund University (graduated 1958). He taught French and Spanish at the Malmö Gymnasium (1959–74), and has pursued various musical activities, including posts as music critic of the Malmö newspaper *Kvällsposten* (1950–80), founder and leader of Chamber Choir '53 (1953–62), founder (1960) and director (1965–71) of the Ars Nova society for new music and programme director of Sal. Smith Chamber Music Society (1966–73). He has also taught music history at the Malmö National School of Drama (1963–71), and served as a board member of the Malmö Musikhögskola (from 1964) and the Swedish Royal Academy of Music (1966–73; general secretary from 1973–90), and as vice-chairman of the board of the

Stockholm Elektronmusikstudion (1974–89), the Opera High School in Stockholm (1982–8) and the international J.M. Kraus-Gesellschaft (from 1982). In 1972 he was appointed editor-in-chief of the second edition of *Sohlmans musiklexikon* (Stockholm, 1975–9). Apart from his work for this, Åstrand has written much about the musical life of Skåne, the south-western province of Sweden, in which he himself has played a particularly active role; he has contributed several chapters to *Musik i Skåne* (Malmö, 1971) and to *Svenska musikperspektiv* (Stockholm, 1971). He was awarded the title of professor by the government in 1983, and the honorary doctorate from Lund University in 1985. He was appointed vice-chairman of the IMC project, *The Universe of Music: a History* in 1996.

WRITINGS

Louis van Beethoven: 'Wegen der schwedischen Histoire': Dokumente der Beziehungen Ludwig van Beethovens zu Schweden (Stockholm, 1977)

'Gedanken zur Wiederaufnahme von zwei Kraus-Opern', *Joseph Martin Kraus in seiner Zeit: Buchen 1980*, 170–80

ed., with G. Larsson: *Kraus und das gustavianische Stockholm: Stockholm 1982* [incl. 'Kraus im gustavianischen Stockholm: Arbeit und Freizeit', 55–66]

ed., with G. Schönfelder: *Prinzip Wahrheit, Prinzip Schönheit: Beiträge zur Ästhetik der neueren schwedischen Musik* (Stockholm, 1984) [incl. 'Prinzip Wahrheit', 9–26]

ed., with E. Broman: *Sten Broman: en man med kontrapunkter* (Stockholm, 1984) [incl. 'Upplevelser av Sten Bromans musik: tredje kvartseklet', 185–237]

'Pocket zarzuela: opereta de bolsillo', *Escritos sobre Luis de Pablo*, ed. J.L. García del Busto (Madrid, 1987), 23–41

with H.-G. Ottenberg and G. Schönfelder: *'Zur Tonsezzung vom Gustaf Wasa': Beiträge zur Biographie J.G. Naumann's* (Stockholm, 1991) [incl. 'Johann Gottlieb Naumann als Opernkomponist: heute', 5–24]

Joseph Martin Kraus, det stora undantaget (Stockholm, 1992)

with G. Schönfelder: *Contemporary Swedish Music Through the Telescopic Sight* (Stockholm, 1993) [incl. 'The Truth Principle', 7–27]

ed., with L. Jonsson: *Musiken i Sverige, iv: Konstmusik, folkmusik, popularmusik, 1920–1990* (Stockholm, 1994) [incl. 'Konstmusiken 1920–45', 'Konstmusik för vår egen tid', 'Musiken i Sverige och framtiden', 311–65, 395–6, 428–44, 477–529]

BIBLIOGRAPHY

B.H. van Boer, ed.: *Gustav III and the Swedish Stage: Opera, Theatre, and other Foibles: Essays in Honor of Hans Åstrand* (Lewiston, NY, 1993) [incl. list of writings]

JOHN BERGSAGEL/HENRIK KARLSSON

Astvatsatrian, Levon Arami (*b* Constantinople, 3 Jan 1922). Armenian composer. During his early life in France (1923–47) he attended the Collège Parc Impérial in Nice and studied composition with Eleuthier Lovreglio at the conservatoire there (1940–45). He moved to Yerevan in 1947 and worked as a music editor for the publishers *Sovetakan grokh* (1950–91) and joined the Armenian Composers' Union in 1949. His First Symphony (1970) was commissioned by the Armenian Ministry of Culture and the *Chorale and Queen of Kilikia* was written to mark the inauguration of an international symposium on the ancient Armenian kingdom of Kilikia, held in New York in 1993. His works have been heard at festivals in Vilnius (1972), Los Angeles (1980), Buenos Aires (1986) and Lille (1995). As a composer, Astvatsatrian is primarily concerned with rationalization of the creative process. Even the neo-classical works of the late 1950s and early 60s, such as the *Sonata-Breve* and *Havik*, are notable for their architectural proportions; in the later serial works, structural systematization is sometimes achieved by means

of computer analysis (as in the first and second symphonies). These works are frequently conceived in terms of what the composer has called 'melogenesis', in which the character of the source material – which includes medieval Armenian songs and Gregorian chant – directly informs the type of internal transformation applied to it. His own historical and conceptual views on not only the genesis of sound but also the unity of physical, acoustical and mathematical laws shape the spatial aspects of his music, which are an important feature of *Intégrales* and *Spatial Structures*.

WORKS
(selective list)

Inst: Havik, str orch, 1959; Sonata-Breve, pf, 1960; Partita, pf, 1964; Prologue and Motet, pf, 1970; Sym. no.1, 1970; Byurakan, 2 pf, 1981; Melogonie, tpt, orch, tape, 1983; Spatial Structures (In memory of A. Babajanian), 2 pf, 1983, arr. vv, insts, 1992; Isomorphic Structures, 2 pf, 1985 [from Partita, 1964]; Intégrales, 2 pf, 1989; Sym. no.2 'Tuba mirum', tpt, orch, 1990; Chorale and Queen of Kilikia, pf, 1993; Digitales rouges, cl, 3 pf, bongos, 1995; Holographiques et boucles étranges, pf, tape, 1998

Vocal: Le pivert et le coucou (V. Vardanian, Fr. trans. Astvatsatrian), children's chorus, orch, 1962, arr. chorus, pf, 1994; Ballade biblique (A. Manukian, Fr. trans. Astvatsatrian), S, T, chbr ens, 1994; Lacrymosa maggiore (Astvatsatrian), 12 solo vv, 9 insts, 1995; Miséricorde (orat, Astvatsatrian), spkr, chorus, orch, 1997

BIBLIOGRAPHY

M. Aranosky: *Simfonicheskiye iskaniya: problema zanra simfonii v sovetskoy muzike 1960–75 godov* [Symphonic investigations: studies on the symphonic genre in Soviet music 1960–75] (Leningrad, 1979), 133–8

K. Meyer: 'Hayastani zhamanakakits yerazhshtutyanmasin' [On contemporary Armenian music], *Sovetakan arvest* (1980), no.8, pp.39–42

S. Sarkisova: 'Bartók Béla es az uj ormeny zene' [Béla Bartók and the new Armenian music], *Magyar zene*, xxvi/3 (1985), 271–84

L. Astvatsatrian: 'Analiticheskiy ocherk o Simfonii' [An analytic essay on the symphony], *Fortepiannïye i simfonicheskiye proizvedeniya* (Yerevan, 1987), 207–231

SVETLANA SARKYSIAN

Asuar, José Vicente (*b* Santiago, 20 July 1933). Chilean composer and electro-acoustic engineer. He studied at the National Conservatory in Santiago with Urrutia-Blondel (1947–56), at the Berlin Hochschule für Musik with Blacher (1959–60) and at the Badische Hochschule für Musik with Wildberger. Simultaneously he studied engineering at the Catholic University in Santiago (1953–9). As part of his dissertation, in 1959 he assembled the first electro-acoustic music laboratory in Latin America, and composed the region's first electronic composition, *Variaciones espectrales*.

Asuar was the Chilean delegate to the 1960 ISCM Festival in Cologne. In 1962 he directed a seminar of electro-acoustic music in Salvador, Brazil. He was Professor of Acoustics and Contemporary Music at the National Conservatory in Santiago (1963–5). In 1964 he taught a seminar in electronic music at the di Tella Institute in Buenos Aires. From 1965 to 1968, at the invitation of the Instituto Nacional de Cultura y Bellas Artes of Venezuela, he established and directed the Instituto de Fonología, the country's first electro-acoustic music centre.

On his return to Chile he conceived and directed a course in sound technology at the University of Chile (1968–72). He became interested in the potential of computer music, and in 1970 he travelled to the USA with a Fulbright Grant to develop new techniques in that field with Lejaren Hiller at SUNY in Buffalo. He later worked at the Institut International de Musique Electroacoustique of Bourges, where he composed *Affaire des oiseaux*

(1976). He later returned as a special guest and participant at this institute's symposium 'Inventions et creation musicales: refus de l'Utopie', bringing together the world's pioneering figures of electro-acoustic and computer music (1989, 1990, 1991).

In 1978 Asuar developed a musical instrument based on the Intel 8080 microprocessor, called COMDASUAR (Computador Musical Digital Analogico Asuar). This was the first music computer of its type in the world, and the first overall in Latin America, bringing computer applications and music together. Since the mid-1990s Asuar has led a reclusive life, reportedly travelling extensively and occasionally making Málaga in Spain his base of operations.

Asuar has published several articles and a book, and has been the recipient of several awards for his work, from the University of Chile (1959, 1969), the Interamerican Festival Jury in Caracas (1966), the Dartmouth Arts Council (for his *Divertimento*, 1970) and the Bourges International Competition of Electro-Acoustic Music (for *Guararía repano*, 1975).

His pioneering career and ideas have been extremely influential in the development of Latin American electro-acoustic and computer music. He often uses traditional and popular melodies from Chile and Venezuela as source material. Works like *Guararía repano* and *Divertimento* have been praised for their technical achievement, evocative lyricism, colourful imagination and witty elegance, often inspired by natural and even cosmological imagery.

WORKS
(selective list)

El-ac and mixed media: Variaciones espectrales, 1959; Preludio para la noche, 1961; Serenata para mi voz, 1962; Estudio aleatorio, 1962; La noche II, 1966; Catedral, 1967; Caleidoscopio, 1967; Imagen de Caracas, 1968; Divertimento, 1968; Guararía repano, Venezuelan Indian insts, tape, 1968; Formas I, orch, elecs, 1970; Buffalo 71, tape, 1971; Formas II, orch, elecs, 1972; Partita electrónica, 1974; Affaire des oiseaux, 1976

Acoustic: Partita, pf, 1952; Fantasía, pf, 1954; Astarís, 1v, pf, 1954; Lamentos haitianos, 1v, pf, 1954; Funerales, chbr ens, 1954; Encadenamientos, fl, bn, vn, vc, 1956; 3 ejercicios, str qt, 1960; Heterofonías, orch, 1964; Octet, 4 fl, 4 perc, 1966

MSS in Latin American Music Center, Indiana University, Bloomington

Principal publishers: Instituto de Extensión Musical, Universidad de Chile-Santiago

WRITINGS

Generación mecánica y electrónica del sonido musical (Santiago, 1959)
'En el umbral de una nueva era musical', *RMC*, no.64 (1959), 11–32
'Y... sigamos componiendo', *RMC*, no.83 (1963), 55–100
'Música electrónica: poética músical de nuestros días', *RMC*, no.86 (1963), 12–20
'Música con computadores: ¿cómo hacerlo?', *RMC*, no.118 (1972), 36–66
'Haciendo música con un computador', *RMC*, nos.123–4 (1973), 81–3
'Recuerdos', *RMC*, no.132 (1975), 5–22
'La segunda generación de música electrónica', *RMC*, no.134 (1976), 75–110
'Un sistema para hacer música con un microcomputador', *RMC*, no.151 (1980), 5–28

BIBLIOGRAPHY

R. Dal Farra: 'Some Comments about Electro-Acoustic Music and Life in Latin America', *Leonardo Music Journal*, iv (1994), 91–8 [incl. CD with disc notes]
'Electroacoustic and Computer Music in Latin America', *International Computer Music Conference, XXII: Hong Kong 1996*, 165–8

M.A. Fumarola: 'Electroacoustic Music Practice in Latin America: an Interview with Juan Amenábar', *Computer Music Journal*, xxiii/1 (1999), 41–8
'Report on the COMDASUAR: a Significant and Unknown Chilean Contribution in the History of Computer Music', *International Computer Music Conference, XXIV: Ann Arbor 1998* (forthcoming)

CARMEN HELENA TÉLLEZ/JUAN ORREGO-SALAS

Asula [Asulae], **Giammateo.** *See* ASOLA, GIAMMATEO.

Atabekian, Angela (*b* 11 April 1938). Armenian *k'anon* player. She graduated from the Melikian Music College, Yerevan, in 1955. In the same year she joined the Ensemble of Folk Instruments of Armenian Radio and Television, performing as a soloist and as a member of the ensemble; many of the group's performances were recorded by the Melodiya company. In 1957 she received four gold medals and a finalist's diploma in performers' competitions held at the 6th World Festival of Youth and Students in Moscow. She began to teach at the Melikian Music College in 1959. In 1972 she created an ensemble of *k'anon* players with her sisters Apolina, Eghisabet, Anahit and Dsovinar; they performed in Armenia, Russia, Belarus, Ukraine, Moldavia, Germany and Hungary, and the group subsequently developed into a larger vocal and instrumental ensemble in which the children and grandchildren of the Atabekian sisters participated. In 1983 Angela Atabekian joined the staff of the Komitas State Conservatory, Yerevan where she graduated in 1985; she was named People's Artist of Armenia in 1986, and in 1994 she was appointed professor of *k'anon* at the Conservatory.

Her repertory has included Armenian traditional melodies, original works by Armenian composers, and extracts of western European music in idiomatic arrangements for the *k'anon*; she has been noted for her virtuoso technique. She has toured Europe, the Middle East, South Asia, Australia and the Americas, and was awarded a gold medal by the Hungarian government for her participation in concerts held during a festival of Armenian art and literature in Hungary.

BIBLIOGRAPHY

N. Polynina: 'The Five Sisters of Yerevan were a Great Success', *Soviet Woman* (1974), no. 3
A. Pahlevanian: 'Priznaniye' [Confession], *Armenia segodniya* [Armenia today] (1975), no.1
'Diskografiya armyanskoy monodicheskoy muziki, 1916–89' [Discography of Armenian monodic music], *Traditzionii fol'klor i sovremenniye narodnïye khori i ansambli* [Traditional folklore and contemporary folk choirs and ensembles], ed. V. Lapin (Leningrad, 1989), 175–246

ALINA PAHLEVANIAN

Atanacković, Slobodan (*b* Idvor, 23 Sept 1937). Serbian composer. He graduated from the composition classes of Živković and Josif at the Belgrade Academy of Music (1956) before becoming editor-in-chief of the music programme at Radio Belgrade; later, he became the programme's adviser. While his early works betray the influence of Bartók, the soundscapes of Atanackovi's later works resemble music of the postwar Polish school; the polyrhythms, heterophony and dense canonic writing – interspersed with folk elements – create clusters across instrumental groupings. Particularly well known among his works are *Akathist*, an oratorio inspired by the heroism and tragedy of war, and the *Sinfonia eterofonica*, which was placed among the top ten compositions at the 1987 UNESCO International Rostrum in Paris. The former work features antiphonal writing, rhythmic choral declamation and aleatory structures, while the *Sinfonia*, in an attempt to unify past, present and future, begins in the style of archaic folk music yet ends with electronic sounds. The orchestral diptych *Ad vivum* (1975) was inspired by unmeasured and non-tempered folk melodies. He has received more than 20 awards from competitions organized by the Association of Serbian Composers, and in 1981 he was presented with the October Prize of the City of Belgrade.

WORKS
(*selective list*)

Orch: Sinfonia da festa in modo eterofonico, 1973; Ad vivum, 2 sym. frescoes, 1975; Basso e contra, db, orch, 1975; Sym. diptych, perf. 1989; Variazioni seriosi, fl, ob, cl, str, 1981

Vocal: Mali vokalni triptih [Little Vocal Triptych] (song, M. Nastasijević), 1963; Canto eroico (cant., B. Miljković), chorus, orch, 1965; Uspavanke bola [Ache's Lullaby] (song, Nastasijević), 1969; Poema eterico (cant., M. Dizdar), chorus, orch, 1973; Incanto a due, song, S, db, 1974; Dies gloriae (orat, after D. Matić), chorus, orch, 1975; Akathist (orat) chorus, orch, 1977; Consecutio temporum (orat) chorus, orch, 1982; Sinfonia eterofonica, chorus, orch, 1986; Polijelej (orat, Polyélaion), folk vv, chorus, orch, 1989; Suguba jektenija [Double Ekténia] (orat), 1990; sacred works for unacc. chorus, incl. Minejsko pevanje (Meniaios), Dveri nebesne [The Door of the Sky] (orthodox prayers), Praznici Gospodnji [God's Holidays] (orthodox prayers)

Chbr and solo inst: Allio modo, vn, pf, 1963; Str Qt Fatalnost [Fatality], 1964; Figurazioni innocenti su una musica appassionata, pf trio, 1975; Pomana, fls, db, tape, 1980; Variazioni seriosi su un thema imperituro, 1981

Principal publishers: Udruženje Kompozitora Srbije

ROKSANDA PEJOVIĆ

Atanasov, [Athanassov] **Georgi** (*b* Plovdiv, 6/18 May 1882; *d* Fasana, Lake Garda, 17 Nov 1931). Bulgarian composer and conductor. At the age of 14 he began formal music studies in Bucharest. He studied composition with Mascagni at the Pesaro Conservatory (1901–3), then returned to Bulgaria, where he became well known as a military bandmaster. In 1922–3 he conducted the Sofia National Opera, and over a period of many years directed more than 90 orchestral concerts in the capital; these were the first regular symphony concerts in Bulgaria since the liberation of 1878.

Atanasov was the first Bulgarian professional opera composer. His lyrical, Romantic style shows the influence of late 19th-century Italian opera, but is primarily melodic and also bears traces of folk idioms. He achieved dramatic effects by the alternation of contrasting numbers. His most frequently performed opera is *Gergana*, the first Bulgarian opera to make an individual character the centre of the plot. The opera *Tsveta* is similar in its clearly expressed dramatic conflict. In *Kosara* (1924) Atanasov used a mystical-romantic style and a leitmotif technique, while *Altzec* developed features using ancient Slav motifs.

WORKS

Stage: (all first perf. in Sofia): Borislav (op, N. Popov, after I. Vasov), Bulg. Opera Society, 4 March 1911; Gergana (op, P. Bobevski, after P.R. Slaveykov: *Izvorat na Belonogata*), Bulg. Opera Society, 6 June 1917; Zapustyalata vodenitsa [The Abandoned Mill] (op, A. Morfov), National Opera, 31 March 1923; Tsveta (op, V. Chernodrinski), Cooperative Operetta, 31 Oct 1925; Kosara (op, B. Danovsky), National Opera, 20 Nov 1929; Altzec (op, P. Karapetrov), National Opera, 15 Sept 1930; Moralisti (comic operetta, A. Milenkov), Jan 1916; children's operettas

Many military marches, 25 children's songs, 10 songs, pf pieces

BIBLIOGRAPHY

V. Krastev: *Ocherki varkhu razvitiyeto na balgarskata muzika* [Essays on the Development of Bulgarian Music] (Sofia, 1954)

L. Sagayev: *Mayestro Georgi Atanasov* (Sofia, 1960)

R. Lazorova-Karakostova: 'Parvi balgarski opereti: profesionalen opit : istorichesko nasledstvo' [The first Bulgarian operettas: a historical account], *Balgarsko muzikoznanye*, xix/3 (1995), 76–90

MAGDALENA MANOLOVA

Atanasov, Nikola (*b* Kyustendil, 13/25 Oct 1886; *d* 30 Sept 1969). Bulgarian composer. From 1906 he studied in Zagreb with F. Dugan, V. Hummel, K. Junek and V. Ruzic, gaining his diploma in 1912 for the first three movements of his First Symphony (the fourth movement, a rondo, was completed on his return to Bulgaria). He then taught at grammar schools in Stara Zagora, Pleven and Sofia before joining the newly established Music Academy as a teacher of theory, later serving as professor (1929–58). During the early stages of Bulgarian concert music when most composers contented themselves with smaller genres, Atanasov stood alone in tackling large forms – he wrote the first Bulgarian symphony and piano sonato. With his first essays in the genre he took the first steps in Bulgarian symphonism. His thinking proceeded from purely instrumental lines, and he endeavoured to combine an accessible language with a national character with dynamic Classical form. The influences of Classical and Romantic music intertwine with Bulgarian folk sources.

WORKS

3 syms.: g, 1912; d, 1922; e, 1950

Ovs.: Khristo Botev, 1928; Ston"t na gorata [The Groan of the Forest], 1931

Other: Pf Sonata; Trio, vn, bn, pf; choruses incl. Tsone, milo chedo [Tsone, Dear Child]; marches; inst arrs. for amateur orch

BIBLIOGRAPHY

S. Petrov: 'Kompozitorat Nikola Atanasov na 70 godini' [The composer Atanasov is 70], *Balgarska muzika* (1956), no.9

P. Lyondev: *Nikola Atanasov* (Sofia, 1963)

M. Nikoforova: 'Kompozitor, pedagog, muzikalen obshchestvenik' [Composer, teacher and musical public figure], *Balgarska muzika* (1986), no.9

ANDA PALIYEVA

Atayan, Robert Arshaki (*b* Tehran, 7 Nov 1915; *d* Los Angeles, 5 March 1994). Armenian musicologist, folklorist and composer. After moving to Yerevan in 1923 he studied composition at the Yerevan Conservatory. From 1944 he taught harmony at the conservatory and completed a second degree at the Institute of Art of the Armenian Academy of Sciences with Kushnaryov, 1945–8. In 1951 he began taking part in folklore expeditions around Armenia and in 1955 he completed his dissertation at the conservatory on Armenian neumatic (*khazer*) notation. He joined the staff of the Institute of Arts in 1956 and was appointed professor in 1962 at the conservatory, where he also served intermittently as head of the music theory department until 1991. He was made an Honoured Representative of the Arts of Armenia in 1961. He participated in many congresses both within and outside the former Soviet Union, and was highly regarded as a teacher.

As a leading Armenian musicologist, Atayan had broad interests which included Armenian peasant and urban folklore, medieval monody and the music of Komitas, for which he compiled and edited the complete works in eight volumes (Yerevan, 1960–98). In the course of his work, Atayan systematized folklore elements (such as typology, genre, mode and dialect); he also examined the stylistic evolution, the structure and the issue of 'authenticity' of Komitas's compositions. Atayan's belief in the unity of the theory, history and ethnology of Armenian culture has informed his research into the legacy of Ekmalian and Tigranyan, whose works were published under Atayan's guidance. As a composer, Atayan showed a preference for vocal genres, including solo and choral songs, based on national themes and rhythms and arrangements of medieval monody.

WRITINGS

with T. Ter-Martirosyan: *Yerazhshtutian tarrakan tesutyun* [A textbook of elementary music theory] (Yerevan, 1949/R)
Haykakan nor notagrutian usumnasirhtian dzernark [A guide to Armenian new notation] (Yerevan, 1950)
with M. Muradyan and A. Tatevosyan: *Armyanskiye kompozitori* (Yerevan, 1956)
Haykakan khazayin notagrutyun (usumnasirutyan ev veradsanutyan hartser) [Armenian khaz notation: questions of study and transcription] (diss., Yerevan Conservatory, 1955; Yerevan, 1959)
Gusan Avasi (Moscow, 1962), (Yerevan, 1963)
Armyanskaya narodnaya pesnya [The Armenian folksong] (Moscow, 1965)
Armen Tigranyan (Moscow, 1966/R)
'Armenische Chasen', *BMw*, x (1968), 65–82; repr. in (1978), 129–48
Komitas (New York, 1969) [in Eng.]
ed., with others: *Komitasakan* (Yerevan, 1969–81) [vol.i incl. *Komitasi yerazhshtakan zharangutyune* [The musical legacy of Komitas], 7–83; vol.ii incl. *Komitasi 'Anush' anavart operayi urvagrere* [Sketches from the unfinished opera 'Anush' by Komitas], 42–82
'Die Armenische professionelle Liederkunst des Mittelalters', *Revue des études armèniennes*, new. ser., vii (1970), 241–66; repr. in *Essays on Armenian Music*, ed. V. Nersessian (London, 1978), 149–78
'Armyanskaya srednevekovaya notopis' [Armenian notation of the Middle Ages], *Muzika narodov Azii i Afriki*, ii, ed. V.S. Vinogradova (Moscow, 1973), 168–86
'Elemente der Mehrstimmigkeit in der Armenischen Volksmusik', *Beiträge zur Musikwissenschaft Österopas*, ed. E. Arro (Wiesbaden, 1977); repr. in *Essays on Armenian Music*, ed. V. Nersessian (London, 1978), 177–88
'Makar Yekmalyan', *The Journal of History and Philology, Armenian Academy of Sciences* (1981), no.1, pp.75–83; no.2, pp.89–105
'O tagakh i analogiyakh mezhdu muzikoy i drugimi iskusstvami v srednevekovoy Armenii' [On the tagh and analogies between music and other art forms in Armenia during the Middle Ages], *Musica antiqua VI: Bydgoszcz 1982*, 739–49
'Die altepische Lieder Armenias', *Musica antiqua VII: Bydgoszcz 1985*, 601–10

SVETLANA SARKISYAN

Atehortúa (Amaya), Blas Emilio (*b* Santa Helena, Antioquia, 22 Oct 1933). Colombian composer. In 1956 he entered the Escuela de Bellas Artes in Medellín and joined the Medellín SO as a violinist. In 1959 he moved to Bogotá to study at the Conservatory of the National University with Olav Roots (conducting), Fabio González Zuleta (composition) and José Rozo Contreras (orchestration). He studied composition at the di Tella Institute, Buenos Aires (1966–8), where he was influenced by Ginastera, Xenakis, Nono and others. On returning to Colombia (1969) he taught in Tunja, Popayán, Medellín and Ibagué and directed the Conservatory in Bogotá (1973–8). In 1992 he went to teach at Duchesne University, returning to Bogotá in 1994. In 1995 he settled in Bucaramanga. He teaches at the Universidad Industrial de Santander.

Atehortúa's compositions, some of which were commissioned or have won national and international prizes, amount to over 190 opus numbers. From his time at the di Tella Institute he experimented with serialism and electronic music while conserving neo-Classical tendencies. At the same time his music acquired a strong regional feeling, helping to create a Colombian musical identity. Although his traditional counterpoint can resemble Vivaldi, Mozart or Haydn, he comments on rather than imitates European culture. His intensely lyrical chromaticism and rhythmic complexity reveal that the main influence in his music, besides Ginastera, is Bartók.

WORKS
(selective list)

VOCAL

Choral: Cantico delle creature (St Francis), op.29, Bar, double chorus, wind, perc, 1965; Apu Inka Atawalpaman (Elegía americana), op.50, S, T, B, chorus, orch, 1971; Elegía para un adios en enero (R. Groot), op.73 no.1, SATB, 1978; Tiempo-Americandina (cant., A. Bello, M.A. Asturias, R. Gallegos and others), op.69, S, nar, chorus, orch, 1978; Simón Bolívar (P. Neruda, J. Martí, S. Bolívar and others), op.95, T, actors, children's vv, SATB, orch, 1980; Kadish, op.107, male chorus, winds, timp, str, 1981; Elegía de septiembre (P. Barba Jacob, M. Meijía Vallejo), op.121, nar, SATB, orch, 1983; Requiem del silencio (G. Cano, R. Lara Bonilla), op.143, SATB, orch, 1987; Cristoforo Colombo, T, boys' chorus, SATB, orch, 1991
Songs (1v, pf): 2 canciones (Barba Jacob), op.11, 1961; Canción del viento (L. de Greiff), op.148 no.1, 1988; Canción de Sergio Stepansky (de Greiff), op.18 no.2, 1988

INSTRUMENTAL

Orch: Tríptico, op.6, 1960; Conc., op.12, timp, orch, 1963; Obertura simétrica, op.17, 1962; Estudio sinfónico, op.36, 1968; Cántico y cántico funebre, op.48, 1971; Soggetto da Vivaldi, op.71, 1977; Brachot, op.109, 1982; Elegía sinfónica para Ginastera, op.125, 1983; Musica d'orchestra para Béla Bartók, op.135, 1985; Concertante antifonal, op.182, 1996
Chbr: Wind Qnt no.1, op.2, 1959; Str Qt no.2, op.9, 1961; Camara musica, vn, hn, vc, perc, pf, 1964; 3 preludios, op.44 no.1, gui, 1970; Str Qt no.4, op.87, 1979; Septimino, fl, ob, cl, vn, vc, pf, perc, op.93, 1980
Pf: Suite no.2, op.19, 1963; Fantasía y toccata op.41 no.1, 1970; 4 piezas líricas, op.148 no.3, 1988
El-ac: Sonocromías op.31, 1966; Syrigma 1, op.30, 1966; 4 danzas para una leyenda quajira, op.45, 1970

BIBLIOGRAPHY

G. Béhague: *Music in Latin America: an Introduction* (Englewood Cliffs, NJ 1979)
E. Bermúdez: *Compositores colombianos*, i (Bogotá, 1988)

ELLIE ANNE DUQUE

Atempause (Ger.: 'breath-break'). Usually a breathing-pause indicated by a superscript comma. *See* LUFTPAUSE.

A tempo (It.: 'in time'). An instruction to return to the previous tempo after a deliberate deviation.

Ath, Andreas d' (*fl* 1622–30). Flemish composer and organist. The title-page of his first publication shows that in 1622 he was chaplain and organist of the collegiate church of St Paul, Liège. From 17 October 1623 he held a benefice at Liège Cathedral. On the title-page of his volume of 1626 he is described as chaplain of the cathedral, and he is mentioned in documents in the cathedral archives dated 4 August 1628 and 20 April 1630. He was replaced as beneficiary before 1639. As a composer he is known by two books of motets, *Prolusiones musicae*, for two to five voices and continuo (Douai, 1622, incomplete), and *Tomus secundus Prolusionum musicarum*, for three to six voices and continuo (Douai, 1626). They are similar on all counts. Ath was brought up in the polyphonic tradition, but he included continuo parts and made each voice equally important. The motets begin with strict imitation and continue with freer imitative textures. The motifs are generally short, and there are some roulades, often in dotted rhythm. As a disciple of the Jesuits he took special care over the correct accentuation of the words. His works most probably influenced those of Hodemont and the young Du Mont.

BIBLIOGRAPHY
AudaM; Vander StraetenMPB, viii

JOSÉ QUITIN

Athanasian Creed. *See* CREDO.

Athanasiu-Gardeev, Esmeralda (*b* Galaţi, 1834; *d* Bucharest, 1917). Romanian composer and pianist. She studied in Bucharest, then in Paris with Julius Schulhoff (piano and composition) and in St Petersburg with Anton Rubinstein (composition). She was married briefly to Vasile Hermeziu, then to the Russian General Gardeev, who introduced her to European aristocratic circles (many of her works are dedicated to King Charles I of Romania and members of the aristocracy) and, in particular, to the salons of George Sand, Nicolò Rubini, Sophie Menter, Camillo Sivori, Vasile Alecsandri, Grigore Ventura, Dumitru Kiriac-Georgescu, Anton Rubinstein and others. At the end of the Romanian War of Independence (1877–8), she settled in Bucharest, teaching the piano, singing and the guitar. Her music was inspired by Romanian folklore, which in turn influenced Rubinstein (*The Demon* and *Sulamith*); her *Rumänisches Charakterstück* op.44 is dedicated to him.

WORKS
(selective list)
Choral: Imn [Hymn], mixed chorus
Songs: 3 Lieder, op.33 (J. von Eichendorff, O. Roquette, A. Wernherr); Collection de chansons, 7 bks, opp.35–41: op.35 (F. von Schiller, H. Heine), op.36 (Heine), op.37 (J.W. von Goethe), op.38 (Heine, Goethe, N. Lenau), op.39 (V. Alecsandri, D. Bolintineanu), op.40 (J.-J. Rousseau, Athanasiu-Gardeev, V. Alecsandri), op.41 (V. Alecsandri); Si tu m'aimais, op.46 (Athanasiu-Gardeev)
Pf: Marş român [Romanian March], op.1; Alboum collectif, 4 bks: op.18, op.30, op.31, op.32; Rumänisches Charakterstück, op.44; 2 mazurkas; Myosotis, Souvenir de Odessa; Polca capridoasa; Romanţă fără cuvinte [Wordless Romance]; Scherzo

BIBLIOGRAPHY
O.L. Cosma: *Hronicul muzicii româneşti* [Chronicle of Romanian music], vii–viii (Bucharest, 1986–8)

VIOREL COSMA

Athenaeus (*b* Naucratis, Egypt; *fl c*200 CE). Greek grammarian and encyclopedist. He settled in Rome at the beginning of the 3rd century CE. None of his works has survived except the *Deipnosophistai*, a vast compendium in 15 extant books, probably written after 192 CE. Its generic form is that of the literary symposium; as a species, it deals with antiquarian lore rather than such 'higher themes' as philosophy. Its main topic is food; the mock-academic title, often translated as 'The Sophists at Dinner', properly describes specialists whose learning centres tirelessly upon the joys of the kitchen. The work is not, however, a cookery book.

Many characters engage in this marathon after-dinner conversation; they include representatives of every profession thought to be consequential, among them musicians, both professional and amateur. It has been rightly noted that the diverse themes are related to the banquet itself with but indifferent success. The unified structure of Plato's *Symposium*, like its wit, has no parallel in the miscellaneous learning of Athenaeus. When his speakers turn their attention to music, what they say has frequent,

and sometimes unique, value for the historian of ancient music (especially in books i, iv, xiv and xv).

Almost at the outset (14b–d), Athenaeus interprets the function of bards in Homer as didactic: for him they are sober teachers of morality, not entertainers. A long section on instruments (174a–185a) contains valuable information: after a description of the hydraulis or water-organ (174a–e), the author considers the varieties of aulos and its popularity among the Greeks 'of the olden time' (176f–182e, 184d–f). The aulos is discussed further in a much later passage (616e–618c) containing especially valuable literary quotations. There follows an extensive and highly important section on the ethical and educational aspects of music (623f–638e). It embodies long passages (624c–625e) taken from the writings of an anonymous Academic theoretician from Heraclea in Pontus, a figure of the 4th century BCE usually given the name 'Heraclides Ponticus'. Most notably, he maintains that there were only three modes, corresponding to the broad national characteristics of the Dorians, Aeolians and Ionians. The claim at the end of this section that 'a mode must have a specific character (*ēthos*) or feeling (*pathos*)' sounds like a distorted version of Aristotle's comment in the opening passages of the *Poetics* (1447a28), perhaps including also the favourite *ethos–pathos* distinction made by later rhetoricians. A notable reference follows (628c) to the Damonian theory of singing and dancing as consequences of the soul's motion. He also mentions Pythagoras's belief in music as the binding principle of the cosmos (632b–c).

Athenaeus's claim to literary eminence is that of a compiler. He salvaged from oblivion more than 10,000 lines of Greek verse, including some of the finest surviving fragments of the lyrics of Sappho and Alcaeus. The great number of citations and comments concerning Hellenic and Hellenistic music has secured for him an unquestioned place among the valued later sources.

WRITINGS
G. Kaibel, ed.: *Athenaei Naucratitae: Deipnosophistarum libri XV* (Leipzig, 1887–90/R)
G.B. Gulick, ed. and trans.: *Athenaeus: The Deipnosophists* (London and Cambridge, MA, 1927–41/R)
A.M. Desrousseaux, ed. and trans.: *Athénée de Naucratis: Les deipnosophistes* (Paris, 1956)
G. Turturro, ed. and trans.: *Ateneo: I deipnosofisti, o Sofisti a banchetto* (Bari, 1961)

BIBLIOGRAPHY
C.A. Bapp: *De fontibus quibus Athenaeus in rebus musicis lyricisque enarrandis usus sit*(Leipzig, 1885)
A. Barker, ed.: *Greek Musical Writings*, i: *The Musician and his Art* (Cambridge, 1984), 258–303 [translated excerpts referring to musical subjects]

WARREN ANDERSON/THOMAS J. MATHIESEN

Athens (Gk. Athínai). Capital of Greece. It is the country's main musical centre. Its role in the overall development of Greek music is discussed in GREECE, §III.

1. Musical education. 2. Concert halls. 3. Orchestras, choirs and chamber music. 4. Opera.

1. MUSICAL EDUCATION. The 1994 *Panellinios odhigos odheion* lists 156 private conservatories, conservatory branches and music schools in Athens and its suburbs. The most important ones, in chronological order, are: the Odheion Athinon (Athens Conservatory), established in 1871 and the oldest institution of its kind in mainland Greece. Since 1979 it has been partly funded by the government. It contains a small concert hall; the Odheion Peiraïkou Syndesmou (Piraeus League Conservatory),

founded in 1904; the Ellinikon Odheion (Hellenic Conservatory), founded in 1919 by Kalomiris, which has 16 branches in Athens; the Ethnikon Odheion (National Conservatory), founded in 1926, also by Kalomiris, with 34 branches in Attica; the Athens Orpheion, founded in 1962 as a music school and a conservatory since 1967; the Attikon Odheion (Attica Conservatory), founded in 1967 as the Athens Music School and a conservatory since 1976; the Apolloneion Odheion (Apollonian Conservatory), founded in 1972; the Athenaeum Conservatory, founded in 1974. Since 1975 it has organized the annual the Maria Callas International Competition. It contains a small concert hall; the Nikos Skalkottas Conservatory, founded in 1981; the Philippos Nakas Conservatory, founded in 1981, and containing a small concert hall and a recording studio; and the Moussiki Etaeria Athinon (Athens Musical Society), founded in 1993 under the composer Yannis Ioannidis. The music department of Athens University, founded in 1991, is rather orientated towards Orthodox church music and ethnomusicology.

2. CONCERT HALLS.   The largest auditoriums in Athens are the ancient Odheion Herodou tou Attikou (Theatre of Herodes Atticus), constructed in AD 160–70 with a capacity of 5000 and since 1955 associated with the Athens Festival; and the modern amphitheatre on Lycabettus Hill, constructed in 1965 (cap. 4000) and in recent years used mainly for pop concerts. A third open-air theatre in Piraeus, Veakeion (cap. 1986), inaugurated in 1969, is used for opera, theatre, ballet, concerts and folk ensembles. Since 1991 the Megaro Moussikis Athinon (Athens Concert Hall) has either promoted or housed most of the city's winter concert activity. The other Athenian concert halls are, in order of capacity: the Pallas auditorium, (cap. 1750), which houses some of the concerts of the Athens State Orchestra; the Olympia Theatre, formerly an open-air theatre, which houses the Ethniki Lyriki Skini (National State Opera), with a seating capacity of 952; the Athens College auditorium in Psychiko (cap. 830), inaugurated in 1982; the Piraeus Dhimotikon Theatron (city Theatre) (cap. 700), inaugurated in 1895 for concerts, theatre and occasional opera performances; the Parnassus Hall (cap. 600), founded in 1865 and used for recitals and chamber concerts; the hall of the Ethniki Pinakothiki (National Gallery), completed in 1976 and, until the construction of the Athens Concert Hall, used for radio concerts and other events. It is still occasionally used as a concert venue; the new Athinaïko Dhimotiko Theatro (Athens City Theatre), near Nea Smyrni, inaugurated in 1989 with a capacity of 470; the auditorium of the Athens French Institute (cap. 437), opened in 1976; the auditorium of the Athens Goethe Institut (cap. 350); the auditorium of the Hellenic-American Union (cap. 200); and the auditorium of the Istituto Italiano di Cultura (cap. c150).

3. ORCHESTRAS, CHOIRS AND CHAMBER MUSIC.   The city's oldest established orchestras are the Athens State Orchestra (1942), which grew out of the Athens Conservatory RSO (1894), and the Athens SO (1938). More recent orchestras include the Orchistra ton Chromaton ('Orchestra of Colours'), founded in 1989 by Manos Hadjidakis; the Camerata of the 'Friends of Music' Society, founded in 1991 by the conductor Alexandros Myrat and based in the Athens Concert Hall; and the

Athens City SO, founded in 1996 under the conductor Eleftherios Kalkanis and based at the new Athens City Theatre.

The three principal choirs in Athens are the chorus of the National Opera, the Radio Chorus and Fons Musicalis, founded in 1989, which performs mainly at the Athens Concert Hall. Chamber music has always been a marginal feature of Athens musical life. Ensembles based in the city have included the Athens Trio (1933–55), the Hellenic String Quartet, later named the Georgios Lycoudis Quartet (founded 1952), the Athens String Octet (1961–9), the Hellenic Woodwind Quintet (1963–80), the Nikolaos Mantzaros Wind Ensemble (founded 1978), the sextet Symmolpa (1985–8) and the Skalkottas String Quartet (founded 1989), later the New Hellenic Quartet. The last three groups have been especially active in the promotion of contemporary Greek music.

4. OPERA.   It is difficult not to consider the foundation of the Ethniki Lyriki Skini (National Opera) as a branch of the National Theatre during Metaxas's dictatorship (1936–41) as one aspect of an attempt to control the artistic and mass media. It was inaugurated in 1940 at the Olympia Theatre with *Die Fledermaus*; four years later it became independent, under Kalomiris's directorship. It now has a virtual monopoly of opera production in Greece and operates as part of the ministry of culture. Promising young singers have often preferred to make their careers abroad, mainly in Germany; many return as guests. The Olympia Theatre, rebuilt several times, has traditionally been the company's home; its main season runs from November to May. The repertory is restricted by the dimensions of the building, with its narrow stage and small pit; there are 433 stalls seats, with a further 519 in two tiers of boxes and galleries. By the late 1990s the company had staged over 170 works. The average season consists of six operas and two operettas (usually including a popular Greek one). The repertory is conservative, with the emphasis on Verdi and Puccini, although contemporary Greek works have been increasingly performed since the early 1990s.

For bibliography *see* GREECE, §III.

GEORGE LEOTSAKOS

Atherton, David (*b* Blackpool, 3 Jan 1944). English conductor. After studying at Cambridge (1962–6), the RAM and the GSMD, he was appointed by Solti to the staff of Covent Garden in 1967. A year later he made his début there in *Il trovatore*, and served as resident conductor until 1980. He made his début at La Scala in 1976 and at the San Francisco Opera in 1978. From 1968 to 1973 and from 1989 to 1991 he was music director of the London Sinfonietta. Atherton was music director of the Royal Liverpool PO from 1980 to 1983 and from 1983 to 1986 its principal guest conductor. From 1980 to 1987 he was music director of the San Diego SO, a tenure marred by controversy. He became principal guest conductor of the BBC National Orchestra of Wales in 1984, and was principal guest conductor of the BBC SO from 1985 to 1989, when he was appointed music director of the Hong Kong PO and also founded the Mainly Mozart Festival in San Diego. In 1991 he conducted at Covent Garden the first London staged performance since World War II of Meyerbeer's *Les Huguenots*.

Atherton's early career, in particular, was marked by an enthusiastic commitment to new music. Notable first performances include Tavener's *The Whale* (1968), Birtwistle's *Punch and Judy* (1968), Crosse's *Grace of Todd* (1969), Iain Hamilton's *Voyage* (1971) and Henze's *We Come to the River* (1976). He has edited and recorded Schoenberg's complete works for chamber ensemble, and has recorded works by Janáček, Mozart, Schubert, Stravinsky, Weill and others with the Hong Kong PO, Berlin RSO and major British orchestras. Among Atherton's finest achievements on disc are his powerful, cogent readings of *Punch and Judy* and Tippett's *The Ice Break* and *King Priam*, the latter drawing particular praise from the composer.

CHARLES BARBER, JOSÉ BOWEN

Atherton, Michael (Jeffrey) (*b* Liverpool, 17 Feb 1950). Australian performer and composer, of English birth. After studying English at the University of New South Wales (1969–77) he worked as a solo and ensemble player on a wide range of medieval, Renaissance and Baroque string, wind and percussion instruments; he also specialized in folk instruments from a variety of countries. This instrumental ability led him to work with cross-cultural groups such as Sirocco, Southern Crossings (a world music quartet founded by Atherton in 1986), and Ariel (a quartet founded in 1995 to explore new music for shakuhachi, didjeridu, percussion and electronics); he has toured and lectured widely with these groups in Australia and abroad. He has also worked as a music therapist, and was curator of instruments at the Australian Museum in Sydney (1993 and 1998). In 1993 he was appointed foundation professor of music at the University of Western Sydney, Nepean. His interests include urban ethnomusicology, organology and Korean music. His work as a composer, arranger and improviser includes film scores, and choral and chamber works.

WRITINGS

Australian Made, Australian Played (Sydney, 1991)
The ABC Book of Musical Instruments (Sydney, 2/1992)
Self Promotion for the Professional Musician (Sydney, 1996)

PATRICIA BROWN

Athesinus, Leonardus. *See* LECHNER, LEONHARD.

Athos, Mount. Semi-autonomous monastic 'republic' comprising numerous Greek and other Christian monastic communities. It is located on a peninsula of the same name, east of Thessaloniki in northern Greece; the peninsula is also known as the 'Holy Mountain' (*Hagion oros*) or the 'Garden of the All-Holy Virgin'. Since the Middle Ages, and especially since the fall of Constantinople in 1453, Athos has been an important centre for Byzantine chant. A number of notable musicians and composers worked there, including Joannes Koukouzeles, who lived near Lavra in the 14th century, and many important manuscripts were produced in its monasteries. The Athonite monastic communities are now unusual in their adherence to the regular recitation of the Byzantine Offices.

1. History. 2. Organization. 3. Manuscripts.

1. HISTORY.   Because of its isolation and semi-desert nature, Athos is an ideal monastic site. Monasteries were first established there in the 9th century (references to earlier foundations are unsubstantiated). Great Lavra, the oldest continuously inhabited monastery, was founded in 963 by St Athanasius of Athos with the support of the Byzantine Emperor Nicephorus Phocas. The number of subsequent foundations grew rapidly; there are references (perhaps exaggerated) to some 180 monastic settlements in the 11th century and close to 300 by the early 13th century. Later, however, the number of monasteries diminished. In the early 13th century crusaders conquered Constantinople and many monasteries lost their property and suffered economic decline. In the early 14th century Athos was ravaged by Catalan soldiers, and for over 20 years in the middle of the century it was a part of the Serbian Empire. During this century, too, the monks were sharply divided by the theological controversy over the views of Gregory Palamas.

From about 1430 Athos submitted to the Turks, who granted the area internal autonomy but taxed it heavily. By the end of the 16th century the number of 'ruling' monasteries had been established at 20 (see §2 below). In 1783 Athos obtained its sixth constitution which, with some minor modifications, is still in effect. With the disintegration of the Ottoman Empire in the Balkan War of 1912, Greece assumed the responsibility for maintaining the traditions of Mount Athos.

A Greek Academy (school for monks) was established under the Turks in about 1749 but abolished after barely ten years; it reopened only in 1953 (an earlier attempt in 1930 failed), and besides the monks, orphans are educated there, in the hope that some may later become monks themselves. The Athos monks have never been exclusively Greek: at one time there was a Latin monastery of Amalfitans; the monastery of Iviron was founded by Georgians from the Caucasus; and there are Russian, Bulgarian, Serbian and Romanian monks. Since the mid-17th century the monastic population of Mount Athos, which once probably exceeded 12,000, has diminished considerably: in 1905 there were about 7500 monks (Russians constituting almost half, with slightly fewer Greeks, and the rest made up of other nationalities), but fewer than 1300 in 1968, of an average age between 55 and 60.

2. ORGANIZATION.   Athos resembles a confederation: each monastery sends a delegate to the 'Holy Community' (*hiera koinotēs*), the highest ruling body, which acts like a parliament. Daily affairs are administered by an executive 'Holy Epistasia' (*hiera epistasia*) of four members; each monastery is represented in the Epistasia one year in five, and the *prōtepistatēs* or head of the Epistasia must come from one of the five 'great' monasteries, Lavra, Vatopedi (Batopediou), Iviron (Ibērōn), Chilandari(ou) and Dionysiou.

Besides these five monasteries, the 'ruling' monasteries are, in order of rank rather than age, Koutloumousi(ou), Pantocrator (Pantokratōr or Pantokratōros), Xiropotamou (Xēropotamou), Zografou (Zōgraphou), Dochiariou (Docheiariou), Karakalou, Philotheou, Simonopetras, Agiou Pavlou (Hagiou Paulou, St Paul), Stavronikita (Stauronikēta), Xenofontou (Xenophōntos), Grigoriou (Grēgoriou), Esfigmenou (Esphigmenou), Agiou Panteleimonos (Hagiou Panteleēmonos, Panteleimonos, Rossikon) and Ko(n)stamonitou. These monasteries comprise at least a *katholikon* (main church), additional chapels and quarters for monks and servants. Besides the ruling monasteries there are communities termed *skētes* and *kellia*, and solitary hermitages. A *skētē*, juridically a dependency of a monastery, lacks the rank of the latter but is for practical purposes identical to it; it may, indeed, be more populated than the monastery to which it 'belongs'. A *kellia* (cell) is a small settlement with a chapel or chapels. Some monasteries have a cenobitic organization, where no monk has personal property and meals are taken communally; others are idiorhythmic (a system introduced in the 14th century), where monks may even receive salaries and eat mostly in their own quarters.

The Offices are recited in full: an Athonite monk spends eight hours daily in their recitation, eight hours at work and eight hours at rest. In this and other ways Mount Athos is a relic of the Middle Ages. Time is reckoned in the ancient way: the day begins at sunset, with midnight regarded as the sixth hour of the day; all the monasteries except Vatopedi adhere to the Julian ('old style') calendar, rejecting the Gregorian calendar as an innovation of Rome. The custom, attested since the 10th century, of refusing any female (even female animals) access to Athos is still maintained.

3. MANUSCRIPTS. Approximately 12,000 manuscripts survive in the Athonite monasteries. Catalogues (see Stathēs) and recent research suggest that approximately 2000 are music manuscripts, most of which date from the 16th century and later, but about 200 are from the period between the 10th century and the 15th and constitute an important source of evidence for the evolution of Byzantine musical style and notation as well as that of the liturgy (see Stathēs). The present manuscript holdings do not represent the entire corpus of those written at Mount Athos, however. There have been losses: the library of Simonopetras was completely destroyed by fire in 1891, and that of the *skētē* of St Andrew in 1958 (the fire of 1966 at Vatopedi spared the library). 50 manuscripts originally from Lavra are now in the Biblioteca Laurenziana, Florence, and 70 others in the *fonds Coislin* of the Bibliothèque nationale, Paris. Maxim the Greek took many Athonite manuscripts to Russia; in 1654 A. Sukhanov, a Russian merchant, bought 504 manuscripts from Athos, and of these some 400 came into the possession of the Synodal Library in Moscow (148 of them in Iviron). Further Athonite manuscripts are now in the British Library, London, and among the manuscripts of the Bibliothèque nationale, Paris (suppl.gr.). The Russian archimandrite Porphyry Uspensky (later Metropolitan of Kiev) not only stole complete manuscripts but also cut initials and miniatures from others.

The largest library is that of Lavra, with approximately 2000 manuscripts, of which about 600 were written before 1500. They include some of the earliest Byzantine music manuscripts, the well-known heirmologion B32, and two triōdia, Γ12 and Γ67, all of which date from the 10th century. 11th-century manuscripts include Γ72 and Γ74, and a partly notated fragment from the euchologion, Δ11. There is a late 13th-century heirmologion, Δ35, and a large group of akolouthiai anthologies of the 14th and 15th centuries, of which the most complete and sumptuous is E173, written in the 1430s by Raidestinos. Most of these manuscripts appear to have been written on Athos. A few leaves from Γ67, one bearing a 10th-century list of neumes, were torn off and taken to Chartres in 1840 (see Strunk, 1955). Two folios from the heirmologion B32 are in St Petersburg (Thibaut, no.371).

The triōdion 1488 of Vatopedi is published in facsimile in the series Monumenta musicae byzantinae (*Principale*, ix, 1975). Vatopedi has several beautiful and well-notated 13th-century stichēraria and at least three interesting heirmologia (1531, 1532 and 1529), as well as an

unknown number of akolouthiai. A late 12th-century heirmologion from Iviron (470), was the first of its type to be published in facsimile in Monumenta musicae byzantinae (*Principale*, ii, 1938). Other heirmologia from Iviron include 1101 and 1259; there are numerous stichēraria and akolouthiai (as in nearly every other library) awaiting investigation. Of the akolouthiai at Iviron, the most interesting is perhaps the voluminous autograph of Manuel Chrysaphes (1120) dating from 1458. Esfigmenou has an 11th-century heirmologion (54) and an 11th-century triōdion (53). Pantocrator has several manuscripts deserving study (208, 214 etc.). Dionysiou has at least one curious heirmologion (95); the Serbian monastery of Chilandari has two early Slavic manuscripts (307 and 308; facs. in MMB, *Principale*, v, 1957). The collections in Philotheou, Karakalou and Koutloumousi are known only in part.

Manuscripts outside Athos of Athonite origin include the collection of Uspensky, described by Thibaut, and the *fonds Coislin*, briefly described by Gastoué. The latter includes the well-known 12th-century heirmologion Coislin 220.

BIBLIOGRAPHY

A. Gastoué: *Introduction à la paléographie musicale byzantine: catalogue des manuscrits de musique byzantine de la Bibliothèque nationale de Paris et des bibliothèques publiques de France* (Paris, 1907)

J.-B. Thibaut: *Monuments de la notation ekphonétique et hagiopolite de l'église grecque* (St Petersburg, 1913/R)

C. Korolevskij: 'Athos', *Dictionnaire d'histoire et de géographie ecclésiastique*, v (1931), 54–124

E. Amand de Mendieta: *La presqu'île des caloyers: le Mont Athos* (Bruges, 1955; Eng. trans., 1972, as *Mount Athos: the Garden of the Panhagia*)

O. Strunk: 'The Notation of the Chartres Fragment', *AnnM*, iii (1955), 7–37

P. Sherrard: *Athos: the Mountain of Silence* (London, 1960)

P. Davos: 'Athos', *Thrēskeutikē kai ēthikē enkyklopaideia*, i (Athens, 1962), 855–9

I. Doens: 'Bibliographie de la sainte montagne de l'Athos', *Le millénaire du mont Athos 963–1963*, ii: *Convegno internazionale di studio: Venice 1963* (Chevetogne and Venice, 1964), 337–495; pubd separately (Chevetogne, 1965) [comprehensive bibliography for Athos and individual monasteries and libraries]

O. Strunk: *Specimina notationum antiquiorum*, MMB, *Principale*, vii (1966), pls.1–32

G. Stathēs: *Ta cheirographa buzantinēs mousikēs: Hagion Oros* [Byzantine music MSS: Mt Athos], i–iii (Athens, 1975–93) [catalogue of music MSS in the Mount Athos monastic libraries; vols.iv–vii, forthcoming]

D. Touliatos: 'State of the Discipline of Byzantine Music', *AcM*, l (1978), 181–92 [incl. list of microfilms of MSS in *GR-THpi*]

S. Kadas: *To Hagion Oros: ta monastēria kai hoi thēsauroi* [The Holy Mountain: the monasteries and treasures] (Athens, 1979; Eng. trans., 1979, as *Mount Athos: an Illustrated Guide to the Monasteries and their History*)

P.K. Chrēstou: *To Hagion Oros: athonikē politeia: historia, technē, zoē* [The Holy Mountain: the Athonite community: history, art, life] (Athens, 1987)

D. Touliatos: 'Research in Byzantine Music since 1975', *AcM*, lx (1988), 205–28 [incl. list of microfilms of MSS in *GR-THpi*]

MILOŠ VELIMIROVIĆ

Atienza y Pineda, Francisco de (*b* ?*c*1657; *d* Puebla, Mexico, March 1726). Mexican composer, probably of Spanish birth. He became a priest, and by 1695 ranked among the leading musicians at Mexico City Cathedral. In 1710 he officially protested against the selection of Zumaya as substitute for the ailing choirmaster Salazar, noting that he himself was considerably older than Zumaya, and indeed had substituted for Salazar in 1703. He departed soon after for Puebla, where he won the post of *maestro de capilla* on 15 January 1712, serving until his death. The Biblioteca Palafoxiana there contains texts of 12 sets of villancicos printed between 1715 and 1722 (and an undated one) and sung at Puebla Cathedral with music composed by Atienza. His surviving liturgical compositions reveal a skilled composer with a fluent command of polyphonic techniques. He adhered to the Spanish tradition in generally employing the *prima pratica*.

WORKS

Missa, 5vv, Archivo del Colegio de Santa Rosa, Morelia, Mexico

Missa, 4vv, vns, Archivo del Colegio de Santa Rosa, Morelia

Missa quinto tono, 5vv, Colección Jesús Sánchez Garza, Instituto Nacional de Bellas Artes, Mexico City

2 vesper pss, 6–7vv; 4 motets, 4–7vv (incl. 1 dated 'año de 706'); 2 hymns, for Feast of St Joseph, 4–5vv: Cathedral Archive, Puebla

Villancico, Colección Jesús Sánchez Garza, Instituto Nacional de Bellas Artes, Mexico City

BIBLIOGRAPHY

J.T. Medina: *La imprenta en la Puebla de los Angeles 1640–1821* (Santiago de Chile, 1908/R)

M. Bernal Jiménez: *El archivo musical del Colegio de Santa Rosa de Santa María de Valladolid, siglo XVIII, Morelia colonial* (Mexico City, 1939)

R. Stevenson: 'Mexico City Cathedral Music: 1600–1750', *The Americas*, xxi (1964), 111–35; pubd separately (Washington DC, 1964)

A.R. Catalyne: 'Music of the Sixteenth through the Eighteenth Centuries in the Cathedral of Puebla, Mexico', *YIAMR*, ii (1966), 75–90

R. Stevenson: 'Colonial Treasure in the Puebla Cathedral Music Archive', *Inter-American Music Review*, xv/1 (1996), 39–51

R. Stevenson: 'Sor Juana's Mexico City Musical Coadjutors', *Inter-American Music Review*, xv/1 (1996), 23–37

ALICE RAY CATALYNE

Atis. *See* ATYS.

Atkins, Sir Ivor (Algernon) (*b* Llandaff, 29 Nov 1869; *d* Worcester, 26 Nov 1953). English organist, composer and editor. After instruction from his father and C. Lee Williams, Atkins became a pupil and assistant of G.R. Sinclair at Truro and Hereford, and was appointed organist of Ludlow parish church in 1893. In 1897 he became organist of Worcester Cathedral, retiring in 1950, having directed the Worcester Three Choirs Festivals from 1898 to 1948. He revived the festivals after World War I and was knighted in 1921. Though he was not a gifted conductor, the programmes of the Worcester Festivals under him showed considerable breadth of taste, and it was at his insistence that Elgar's *The Dream of Gerontius* was performed in 1902. His own *Hymn of Faith* was given in 1905 and revived in 1993.

Atkins produced (with Elgar) an English-language edition of Bach's *St Matthew Passion*, and (alone) of Bach's *St John Passion*, Brahms's *German Requiem* and Debussy's *La demoiselle élue*. Though no longer acceptable, the treatment of Bach's recitative in relation to the English Bible marked an important stage in the appreciation of Bach's Passion settings in England. Atkins also edited Bach's *Orgelbüchlein* and Mendelssohn's organ sonatas. He took the Oxford DMus in 1920, was elected a Fellow of the Society of Antiquaries in 1921 and was Worcester Cathedral librarian from 1933 to 1953.

WRITINGS

The Early Occupants of the Office of Organist and Master of the Choristers of the Cathedral Church of Christ and the Blessed Virgin Mary, Worcester (Worcester, 1918)

ed., with N. Ker: *Catalogus librorum manuscriptorum Bibliothecae Wigorniensis, made in 1622–1623 by Patrick Young* (Cambridge, 1944)

BIBLIOGRAPHY

DNB

W. Shaw: *The Three Choirs Festival ... c.1713–1953* (Worcester and London, 1954)

WATKINS SHAW

Atkins [Atkinson], John (*d* London, bur. 12 Feb 1671). English violinist and composer. He became one of the king's band of violins in 1660 and served until his death early in 1671. His widow Sarah (whom he had married in 1639) was in receipt of his back pay for several years thereafter. Although John Playford did not publish any of his songs, several, mostly drinking-songs, survive (in *GB-Lbl* Add.29396, *F-Pn* Rés.2489, *US-NYp* Drexel 4275 and particularly Drexel 4041). One source, Drexel 4041, may have originated close to the composer as one of a circle of musicians having connections with the City of London. The fact that it is an important source of pre-Commonwealth playsongs could indicate that the composer was a theatre musician; his settings of Davenant's *This lady ripe and fair and fresh* may have been made for the original production of *The Just Italian* (1629; one of four songs by Atkins in *English Songs, 1625–1660*, MB, xxxiii, 1971). Possibly he was the principal copyist of two collections of consort music: the manuscripts *F-Pn* Rés.F.770 and *US-R* ML96 L814f which is signed 'J.A. 1661 Octo: ye 11th'. Some instrumental pieces attributed to him also survive (*Ob* Mus.Sch.D.220, 1654).

BIBLIOGRAPHY

AshbeeR, i, v, vii; *BDECM*; *SpinkES*

P. Holman: *Four and Twenty Fiddlers: the Violin at the English Court, 1540–1690* (Oxford, 1993), 275–6

IAN SPINK

Atlanta. American city, capital of Georgia. Concert life in Atlanta probably began in February 1858 when Sigismond Thalberg, assisted by Henry Vieuxtemps, brought his Grand Concert to the recently completed Athaeneum Theater. Opera appeared for the first time in October 1866 when Max Strakosch and the Ghioni and Sussini Grand Italian Opera company opened the Bell-Johnson Hall (cap. 600) with *Il trovatore*, *Norma*, and *Il barbiere di Siviglia*. The next month the Grover Opera Troupe staged an operatic concert, and in 1868 Grau's German Opera Company presented excerpts from various operas, followed by the McCulloch Opera Troupe with performances of *Il barbiere di Siviglia* and *Don Pasquale*. Demand for a better theatre prompted the Belgian Consul Laurent DeGive to build DeGive's Opera House (cap. 1200); in 1873 he increased the seating to 2000. During the 1870s Italian opera performances dwindled, supplanted by a succession of British opera companies, who presented a few of the stock Italian favourites in English. English operetta appeared in 1879 with *HMS Pinafore*. Several concert organizations were founded during this period, most importantly the Mozart Club (1867), the Beethoven Society (1872) and the Rossini Club (1876). The city gained its first professional musician when Alfredo Barili moved there in 1880. Barili organized Atlanta's first music festival in the autumn of 1883, when he oversaw the première of five major symphonic works in the city during the three-day festival. The first week of February 1889 saw Atlanta's first week-long operatic festival when the Emma Abbott Company staged eight operas, including *Faust*, *Norma*, *Il trovatore* and *Martha*. Increasingly frequent visits by major companies and concert artists continued throughout the final years of the century.

The year 1901 brought the first visit by singers from the Metropolitan Opera House under Maurice Grau, which included conductor Walter Damrosch, soprano Emma Eames and contralto Ernestine Schumann-Heink. The Atlanta Music Festival Association was established in 1905. It organized music festivals in 1907 and 1909, and supported the construction of a city auditorium and the installation of a 77-stop Austin organ, which was inaugurated under Percy Starnes for an audience of 7000. Enthusiasm for the highly successful music festivals finally resulted in annual tours by the Metropolitan Opera, beginning in 1910 and featuring such stars as Caruso, Geraldine Farrar and Louise Homer. From 1911 to 1923 Atlanta was the only city outside the North-east to which the Metropolitan toured. The annual visits continued, with a few interruptions, until the company ceased national tours after the 1986 season.

The Atlanta Music Club was formed in 1915 to enrich the city's musical life by sponsoring noted artists in recitals. Primarily a women's organization, the club continues its vital role of supporting the community's artistic life. It was instrumental in the establishment of the Atlanta SO, the Choral Guild of Atlanta (1940) and other groups, as well as providing music scholarships for talented young people.

Early attempts to establish a symphony orchestra proved frustrating. In 1923 the first organization to bear the title the Atlanta SO was formed, with 60 players drawn from the Howard and Metropolitan theatre orchestras under the direction of Enrico Leide. In 1944 the Atlanta Music Club founded the Atlanta Youth SO by the merging of two school orchestras, under the Chicago conductor Henry Sopkin. Two years later the group began adding professional players and changed its name to the Atlanta SO. Sopkin gradually built the group into a competent semi-professional ensemble until his retirement in 1966.

An air crash in Paris on 3 June 1962 took the lives of more than 100 leading Atlanta art patrons, who were commemorated with the construction of the Memorial Arts Center (later renamed the Robert W. Woodruff Memorial Arts Center). The largest of its four performance halls is Symphony Hall (cap. 1762), the first permanent home of the Atlanta SO; the complex also houses an art school and the professional Alliance Theater. A decision was made to upgrade the orchestra to full professional status and Robert Shaw was engaged as music director. For his first season in 1967 the orchestra numbered 87 musicians. Shaw founded the Atlanta SO Chorus and under his direction the orchestra and chorus grew into one of the nation's finest. When Shaw retired in 1988 he was succeeded by Yoel Levi.

Atlanta continues its thriving choral and organ tradition, mainly in its many churches, which contain some notable organs, especially the magnificent Flentrop organ at St Ann's Episcopal and the large Aeolian-Skinner at St Philip's Cathedral. Virtually all of the universities, colleges and junior colleges provide some musical instruction. The most important is Georgia State University (24,000 students), where the School of Music has 450 music majors taught by a staff of nearly 70 faculty members. Its new Rialto Theater (cap. 1200) has become the finest medium-sized concert hall in the area. Emory University also contributes to Atlanta's concert life with its Flora Glenn Candler concert series. Two predominantly black colleges, Spelman and Morehouse, also provide advanced music training programmes. The Georgia Academy of Music, a private institution, has enjoyed noteworthy success in teaching music to children. Other prominent musical groups include the Atlanta Boy Choir, the Pro-Mozart Society and the Atlanta Festival Singers, the finest small ensemble in the region. Several chamber groups enjoy widespread recognition, notably the Atlanta Chamber Players and Thamyris, which specializes in contemporary music.

Opera in Atlanta experienced the same difficulty as the Atlanta SO in establishing itself. Productions in the Memorial Arts Center began in 1968 with the American première of Purcell's *King Arthur*. Two ambitious professional companies emerged in the mid-1970s: the Atlanta Lyric Opera (1976) and the Music Theater Guild of Atlanta (1974), which became Georgia Opera in 1977, when it moved to the Woodruff Arts Center and added an orchestra. In 1979 the two companies merged to form the Atlanta Civic Opera. Financial problems plagued the company and both directors left by 1984. The following year the company was reorganized with William Fred Scott as conductor and artistic director, under whom Atlanta Opera has become the largest operatic organization in the South-east.

BIBLIOGRAPHY

N.L. Orr: *Alfredo Barili and the Rise of Classical Music in Atlanta* (Atlanta, 1996)

N. LEE ORR

Atlantic. American record company. It was founded in New York by Herb Abramson and Ahmet Ertegun (*b* 1923), both jazz and blues enthusiasts, in 1947, primarily to issue African American music; it achieved considerable commercial success with recordings of musicians whose work encompassed jazz, blues, and rhythm-and-blues. Ertegun's brother Nesuhi (1917–89) joined the organization in 1955, and supervised artists and repertory for the LP catalogue; around the same time the company established a new label, Atco, which was chiefly devoted to popular music. During the late 1950s and early 1960s the company made significant recordings marking the emergence of the free jazz style, but by the middle of the decade it was primarily known for soul music; in 1966, at the height of the company's success in this field, it founded the Vortex label for the release of jazz records. During this period Atlantic and its subsidiaries recorded many significant artists: the singers Lavern Baker, Ray Charles, Ben E. King, Esther Phillips, Wilson Pickett and Otis Redding; the vocal groups the Coasters, and the Drifters; and the jazz musicians Lennie Tristano, Lee Konitz, Charles Mingus, the Modern Jazz Quartet, John Coltrane, Ornette Coleman, Keith Jarrett and Chick Corea. It also presented gospel groups and important white popular musicians, including Bobby Darin and Sonny and Cher.

In 1967 the company was bought by Warner Bros., which in turn was purchased two years later by the Kinney Corp.; Ahmet and Nesuhi Ertegun, however, continued to direct Atlantic. With the emergence of Aretha Franklin, further recordings by Redding and Pickett and such new artists as King Curtis, Roberta Flack and the Temptations, Atlantic became one of the most significant labels in soul music. It also gained a huge presence in rock with recordings by international groups including the Bee Gees, Buffalo Springfield, Cream, Crosby, Stills and Nash (and Young), Led Zeppelin, the Rolling Stones, Yes, Genesis and AC/DC. Its prominent jazz artists included Keith Jarrett, the Modern Jazz Quartet and Manhattan Transfer. While Ahmet Ertegun remained directly in charge of Atlantic, Nesuhi moved in 1971 into the position of president and chief executive officer of the conglomerate WEA (Warner Brothers-Elektra-Atlantic); in 1985 he became its chairman and co-chief executive.

Atlantic remained a leading popular music label in the 1990s through such singer-songwriters as Tori Amos and Jewel and rock groups including Stone Temple Pilots and Hootie & the Blowfish. Corporate reorganization also gave Atlantic a presence in classical music when it took over US distribution of the European labels Teldec, Erato and Finlandia with recordings by Nikolaus Harnoncourt, Daniel Barenboim and others. In country music, an Atlantic Nashville division was set up in 1991 with a roster including Rickie Skaggs and John Michael Montgomery. The label was now less prominent in black music, although it issued recordings by Anita Baker and the gospel star Bebe Winans.

BIBLIOGRAPHY

C. Gillett: *Making Tracks: Atlantic Records and the Growth of a Multi-Billion-Dollar Industry* (London, 1975)
M. Ruppli: *Atlantic Records: a Discography* (Westport, CT, and London, 1979)
J. Picardie and D. Wade: *Atlantic and the Godfathers of Rock 'n Roll* (London, 1993)
G. Marsh and G. Callingham, eds.: *East Coasting: the Cover Art of New York's Prestige, Riverside and Atlantic Records* (Zürich, 1993)

BARRY KERNFELD, HOWARD RYE, DAVE LAING

Atlantic Symphony Orchestra. Orchestra based in HALIFAX (ii), formed in 1968 as a merger between the Halifax SO and the New Brunswick SO.

Atlantov, Vladimir (Andreyevich) (*b* Leningrad [now St Petersburg], 19 Feb 1939). Russian tenor. The son of an opera singer, he graduated from Bolotina's class at the Leningrad Conservatory in 1963, and had further training as a student-artist (1963–5) at La Scala opera school. He won the 1966 Tchaikovsky and the 1967 Sofia international competitions. In 1963 he made his début at the Kirov Theatre, and in 1967 he joined the Bol'shoy. His voice is full and ample, but capable of great beauty and delicacy; he has a strong temperament and a gift for character portrayal. His roles include Hermann, Vladimir (*Prince Igor*), Alfredo and Don José. He has toured in Europe, Canada and Japan, and was made People's Artist of the RSFSR in 1972. He made his Covent Garden début in *Otello*, one of his most famous roles, in 1987, and sang Canio there in 1989. Atlantov made his US début, as Canio, at San Francisco in 1990. He has also toured extensively as a concert singer. His recordings include Hermann, Lensky, Andrey Khovansky (*Khovanshchina*) and Canio.

I.M. YAMPOL'SKY/R

Atlas, Dalia (*b* Haifa, 17 Nov 1933). Israeli conductor. She studied the piano at the Rubin Academy of Music in Jerusalem, and subsequently studied conducting in Europe and the USA with Franco Ferrara, Celibidache, Hans Swarowsky and Boulez. From 1954 to 1960 she taught piano at the Rubin Academy of Music. Atlas won several international conducting awards, including the Dimitri Mitropoulos Competition (1964), the Leopold Stokowski Prize (1978) and the Eugene Ormandy Award (1980). In 1981 she was appointed associate professor and director of musical studies at the Technion in Haifa. She is the founder and principal conductor of the symphony orchestra and choir of Technion, the Israel Pro Musica Orchestra and the Atlas Camerata. She has also appeared as a guest conductor with the RPO in London, the Royal Liverpool PO and the Stockholm PO, among others. Atlas has given the first performances of works by the Israeli composers Amy Maayany and Zvi Avni, and has recorded Stravinsky's *The Firebird* and Symphony in E♭, works by Vaughan Williams, Bloch and Josef Suk, as well as her own orchestral arrangements of Schubert's String Quintet and Mendelssohn's Octet.

MICHAL BEN-ZUR

Atnah. Cantillation sign marking the end of a half-verse in Hebrew EKPHONETIC NOTATION. *See also* JEWISH MUSIC, §III, 2(ii).

Ato [Hatto] episcopus Trecensis (*fl* 1123–45). Ecclesiastic and composer. He was Bishop of Troyes from 1123 to 1145. He is credited with the composition of six polyphonic pieces for two voices in the Codex Calixtinus (*E-SC; see* SOURCES, MS, §IV). They are a versus, *Nostra phalanx plaudat leta*, the soloists' portion of four responsories from the Matins and 2nd Vespers of St James's Day and Translation (with a *prosa* for the *neuma* or melisma of the last one), and the soloists' portions of the gradual from Mass on that day.

DAVID HILEY

Atonality. A term that may be used in three senses: first, to describe all music which is not tonal; second, to describe all music which is neither tonal nor serial; and third, to describe specifically the post-tonal and pre-12-note music of Berg, Webern and Schoenberg. (While serial music is, by the first definition, atonal, it differs in essential respects from other atonal music and is discussed in the articles SERIALISM and TWELVE-NOTE COMPOSITION; it is, therefore, not considered here.)

1. Relations between tonality and atonality. 2. Differences between tonality and atonality. 3. The atonality of Schoenberg, Berg and Webern. 4. Theoretical issues: (i) Symmetry (ii) Pitch class set theory (iii) Transformational networks. 5. Conclusion.

1. RELATIONS BETWEEN TONALITY AND ATONALITY. An important aspect of tonality is the way in which pitches are contextually defined so that each particular definition of a given pitch yields a different tonal function. A G which is the root of a G major triad, for example, has a different function or meaning from that of a G which is the 3rd of an E♭ major triad. Such a definition is, in turn, further refined by larger musical contexts, and the roles of rhythm, register, dynamics and timbre in tonal music are closely related to, and interactive with, the definition of tonal functions.

Atonality may be seen roughly to delimit two kinds of music: (1) That in which there is no such contextual definition with reference to triads, diatonic scales or keys, but in which there are, nonetheless, hierarchical distinctions among pitches. This category would include some of the works of Schoenberg, Stravinsky and Hindemith. The inadequacy of theories of tonality in dealing with this music lends support to such a classification. (2) That in which such hierarchical distinctions are not so explicit, though sometimes present. This includes some of the pre-serial music of Webern, Schoenberg and, to a lesser extent, Berg.

The usual attitudes concerning atonality and its development are vague and misleading. It is often said that tonality developed to a point of complexity where it was no longer possible to determine contextual definition as described, and tonal functions were therefore abandoned. This attitude has a basis in reality but is a simplification which obscures essential issues. Two compositions near either side of the imagined border between tonality and atonality, Liszt's *Sonetto del Petrarca no.104* from the second book of *Années de pèlerinage*, and Skryabin's Prelude op.74 no.3, shed light on this question.

It is not difficult to determine tonal contextual definition in the opening measures of the *Sonetto* (ex.1). The F♯ dominant 7th chord at the downbeats of bars 1, 4 and 5 serves as a dominant to the B dominant 7th in bar 5, which is in turn the dominant of E in bar 7. In the opening bars of this composition, however, the diminished 7th chord plays a fundamental role as a referential collection through the use of different interpretations of that chord. The chords at the upbeats to bars 1, 2, 3, 4 and 5, and at the fourth quaver beats of bars 3 and 4, are all enharmonically equivalent forms of the initial diminished 7th collection B♯, D♯, F♯, A, which is transformed into the dominant 7th chord C♯, E, F♯, A♯ on the downbeat of bar 1. In that bar the F♯ octave moves to G as an upper neighbour, at which point another diminished collection is implied: C♯, E, G, (B♭). The sequence is repeated at successive minor 3rd transpositions until in bar 4 an octave transposition of the F♯ dominant 7th chord of bar 1 is reached. All pitches in bars 1–4 are thus enharmonically equivalent members of one of two diminished 7th collections. While it is useful to observe that these measures prolong the dominant of the dominant of E major, the actual method of prolongation is most easily understood in relation to the enharmonically undefined diminished 7th collections 0, 3, 6, 9 and 1, 4, 7, 10 (with 0 denoting C or B♯, 1 denoting C♯ or D♭, etc.). The absence of a key signature further emphasizes the non-diatonic nature of the passage.

The opening of Skryabin's Prelude op.74 no.3 provides an interesting counter-example (ex.2). The music is not tonal in the senses described above or in the sense of the Liszt composition. It is not clear that any note is defined as a member of a major or minor triad, or that the passage is using notes of some major or minor scale. There is a 'dominant 7th chord' embedded in bar 2, but this does not seem to function as a dominant of D major or minor. On the other hand a special aspect of this passage is that all notes except G♯ in bar 1 and D in bar 3 belong to one of the diminished 7th collections A♯, C♯, E, G and B♯, D♯, F♯, A; and Skryabin's spelling is consistent with this view. The 'dominant 7th chord' in bar 2 is thus understood as a conjunction of members of these two collections. In bar 3 the tritone transposition of the right hand of bar 1, against the untransposed bass, results in the appearance of the same collection as in bar 1 since the diminished 7th collection is invariant under transposition by a tritone, The G–A♯ succession in the middle register in bars 2–3 also emphasizes the unfolding of a diminished 7th collection.

In response to the above attitude concerning the development of atonality, it would seem safe to say, rather,

Ex.1

Agitato assai

Adagio

molto espress.

that tonality developed new ideas, which then lost some of their association with older concepts, and in doing so gained more independent status as compositional determinants. The diminished 7th chord in the music of Mozart, for example, most often acts as a tonicizing agent, with the two tritones resolving in contrary motion to a major or minor triad, but in the Liszt piece this is not

Ex.2

Allegro drammatico

so clearly the case, in that the chord seems to have some significance as a referential collection, and in the Skryabin it certainly functions in a completely different way.

In as much as notation reflects compositional thinking, it is interesting to observe the expanded denoting of key signatures in the late 19th and early 20th centuries as a kind of musical barometer. The point of a key signature in the music of Debussy, for example, is often only to delimit a pitch-class collection – usually the whole or part of a diatonic scale – rather than to prescribe a diatonic scale with the implied functional associations of tonic and dominant triads, consonance and dissonance, and so on, as in the notation and music of Liszt. On the other hand, the key signature of four sharps in Schoenberg's Chamber Symphony op.9 serves more to indicate that an E major triad will function in some hierarchically significant way than to delimit a scale. The first pages of the composition are, in fact, so full of symmetrical collections, such as the whole-tone scale and the augmented triad, that the key signature serves virtually no practical purpose. In the fourth movement of Schoenberg's Second Quartet op.10 the convention of a key signature is abandoned. Schoenberg commented upon this work as follows (as quoted by W. Reich in *Schoenberg*, London, 1971, p.31):

there are many sections in which the individual parts proceed regardless of whether or not their meeting results in codified harmonies …. The key is presented distinctly at all the main dividing points of the formal organization. Yet the overwhelming multitude of dissonances cannot be balanced any longer by occasional returns to such triads as represent a key.

The concept of atonality thus evolved as various components of tonality lost the high degree of interdependence they had formerly possessed.

An important aspect of late 19th-century music lies in a set of relatively abstract ideas about what music is and can be: a referential sonority (the triad) as the basis of a musical language; a motif as a compositional tool; the progress and unfolding of a musical composition as something defined by the transformation and development of motivic, contrapuntal and harmonic ideas; the concept of closure; significant relations between discrete parts of a musical composition; and the hierarchic superiority of certain specific pitches or configurations of pitches in a given composition.

The first composers whose music might be defined as atonal were trained in the traditions of 19th-century tonality, and their music reveals, in one way or another, the profound influence of these concepts, as may be exemplified by the opening of the second of Schoenberg's Five Orchestral Pieces op.16 (ex.3 is taken from Webern's two-piano reduction).

A succession of simultaneities between the two right hands unfolds transpositions and inversions (of interval content) of the same referential sonority: in bar 1, (A, D, G♯), (F, C, G♭); in bar 2, (A♭, D♭, G), (G, C, G♭), (E, B, F). The significance of the D–A dyad is emphasized by its role in the first movement, where the trichord D, A, C♯ is sustained as a pedal for most of the movement, and by the octave doubling in bar 1 of ex.3 and the retention of the D–A dyad for the first three bars. An important motivic idea here is a three-note melodic cell consisting of some kind of 2nd and some kind of 3rd. (In the opening of the first movement the cellos play the line (E, F, A, G♯, A, C♯) which consists of several interlocking versions of this cell.) The first three bars form a phrase unit defined by the new rhythmic and registral placement of the

Ex.3

descending minor 3rd (G♯–F in bar 1; A♭–F in bar 3), and the rest on the first beat of bar 4. The concept of a musical language as inferred from tonality thus extends deeply into atonality and forms a significant basis for the development of new ideas.

2. DIFFERENCES BETWEEN TONALITY AND ATONALITY. Although an attempt has been made to indicate the ways in which tonality developed into atonality and the similarities between the two, there are also significant differences. As has been noted, one of the remarkable aspects of tonality is the high degree of interdependence between the various dimensions of a composition, such as pitch, rhythm, dynamics, timbre and form. In atonality the functional relations between these dimensions are not clearly defined. The concept of a suspension in tonality, for example, embodies a conjunction of rhythmic and harmonic ideas, but the body of atonal works offers no similar operation as a general procedure. Comparisons of this sort have given rise to a second prevalent attitude concerning atonality: that its processes do not extend beyond the boundaries of a given composition. Again, this attitude is not entirely without basis but is highly oversimplified. As understanding of tonality is aided by the existence of a relatively highly developed theory, while no such assistance exists for atonality, the former is perceived as a more highly unified musical language than the latter. Atonal works do, however, have properties in common, but the manifestations of these properties are very different. Examples may be taken from two compositions in which, as in exx.1 and 2, the diminished 7th collection has some structural significance: the first movement of Bartók's Music for Strings, Percussion and Celesta, and the opening of Varèse's *Density 21·5* for solo flute.

Ex.4 is the theme of the 'fugue' that opens the Bartók work. The voices of the fugue make their entries at successive perfect 5ths alternately above and below the original entry until, in bars 26 and 27, F♯ and C are

Ex.4

reached, a major 13th above and below the original entry. The F♯ and C are members of the same diminished 7th collection as the initial A. They are doubled at the octave to emphasize their structural significance, and they initiate a more complex process of development which culminates in bar 56 where an E♭ (the pitch class at which the two diverging cycles of 5ths meet, and the remaining member of the diminished 7th collection A, C, E♭, F♯) is reached. The linear structure of the theme is relevant to the large-scale structure of the movement. The first two phrases span A–E♭, an interval of the diminished 7th collection; the third and fourth phrases span B–E and B♭–E♭, respectively. Thus a tritone, an interval which figures in the large-scale structure, is outlined by the first and second phrases, and also by the third and fourth phrases together. The span of the entire theme is a perfect 5th, anticipating the second statement on E. At bar 65, after E♭ is stated in several octaves, the literal inversion of the theme is introduced, and at the end of the movement (ex.5) a

Ex.5

simultaneous statement of the second phrase of the theme and of its inversion, both beginning on A, telescopes structural aspects of the movement in the unison A and octave E♭, and in the statement of all 12 pitch classes, a totality implied by the succession of fugal transpositional levels, and created by any two adjacent fugal entries.

Ex.6 contains the first large phrase of Varèse's *Density 21·5*. The number 0, 1, or 2, inserted below each note, shows the diminished 7th collection to which that note belongs: 0 denotes the collection on C, 1 that on C♯ and 2 that on D. Except for the Fs in bars 1 and 3, all notes in bars 1–10 belong to the 0 and 1 collections. These bars seem, in addition, to prolong the 1 collection since the 0 collection appears less frequently and with less rhythmic emphasis. The opening F–E–F♯ motif is special in that it contains one member of each collection. Bar 9 represents an important structural point: it is the loudest moment in the piece so far; the initial rhythmic figure returns, but with new and more emphatic articulation; an octave has been spanned from the lowest note so far and, since the 1 collection is now represented on the first semiquaver of this figure, a kind of 'modulation' occurs. The repetition of D♭–C in bars 9 and 10 delays the arrival of D (dynamically emphasized) until the downbeat of bar 11, thus prolonging a transposition of the initial motif. In bars 11–13 there are successive prolongations of the 2 and 0 collections, and a final return to the initial 1 collection. The B♭–E dyad in bars 13–14 contains the remaining members of the 1 collection as it appeared in its first salient statement in bar 2.

Ex.6

In both the Bartók and the Varèse a governing structural principle is the symmetrical partition of the octave through the diminished 7th collection. But the compositional procedures are very different and the respective results could hardly be more dissimilar.

3. THE ATONALITY OF SCHOENBERG, BERG AND WEBERN. Many of the atonal compositions of Berg, Webern and Schoenberg use procedures and concepts such as those discussed in relation to Schoenberg's op.16 no.2. Just as tonality yielded concepts which were reinterpreted for use in atonality, so the interactions between the various aspects of the atonality of Berg, Webern and Schoenberg yielded new concepts which eventually became relevant to serialism. A fundamental development was the elimination of hierarchical pitch-class distinctions, typified in tonality by entities such as the major scale. This led to the use of all 12 pitch classes within smaller time spans. Webern's Bagatelles for string quartet, for example, emphasize the unfolding of 12-note collections through a reduction of pitch and pitch-class repetition, and by very careful and precise attention to the articulation and orchestration of individual pitch classes (ex.7). The extreme brevity of each of the Bagatelles is a consequence of this approach.

The sense of octave relations as manifested in tonality undergoes a radical transformation in a composition such as the Bagatelles. Clearly defined octave relations would shift the focus away from an unfolding of the 12 pitch classes. This thinking strongly influenced the development

Ex.7

of the 12-note system where the collection of 12 pitch classes plays a fundamental role. (The meaning of an octave relation in this music differs profoundly from that in the Bartók and Varèse examples quoted above. In the latter compositions the octave has significance as a boundary, framing its symmetrical divisions – the whole-tone scale, the diminished 7th collection, the augmented triad, the tritone and the cycles of 5ths and semitones – and octave intervals may thus signify the culmination of a process of development or a common feature of different subdivisions.) In this sense one motivic idea of the Bagatelles is a tendency towards the unfolding of 12-note collections. In general the concept of a motif in this music merges into a much broader background encompassing the rhythmic and instrumental textures.

The atonal works of Berg, Webern and Schoenberg employ a wide variety of procedures and techniques for securing musical coherence. It is only necessary to compare Schoenberg's *Erwartung* with his Six Little Piano Pieces op.19, for example, to see, on the one hand, a large-scale unfolding of complex and varied pitch relations, and on the other, a small, detailed and precise expression of specific and simple musical ideas. The evolution to the 12-note system and serialism was guided mainly by a tendency to subdue traditional hierarchical pitch distinctions and to emphasize the use of ordered, or partially ordered, collections of pitch classes, or motifs, to generate chords and lines. Eventually the former tendency, in its encouragement of the use of 12-note collections, merged with the latter to become Schoenberg's 12-note system.

4. THEORETICAL ISSUES. In the latter half of the 20th century, three theories of organizational structures in atonal music emerged and became influential in musicians' perceptions and understanding: (1) normative structures based on symmetry, from George Perle; (2) pitch class set theory, from Allen Forte; and (3) transformational networks, from David Lewin. The last two are influenced by the premises of twelve-note theory given by Schoenberg and later expanded on by Babbitt. Each theory, while decidedly non-tonal in approach, defines relationships that have priority over others and govern successions of notes, in ways that are at least remotely analogous to the hierarchies of tonality.

These three theories share some general principles; in particular, two interpretations of melodic and harmonic events in atonal music have proven seminal. The first stems from the recognition that the referential sonorities in atonal music are not triads and that the organization is no longer based on tonal function and the hierarchical organization of key centres. Notes freed from tonal obligations have come to be regarded as enharmonically equivalent and functionally indistinguishable, and generalized into 12 pitch classes. In principle, any group of pitch classes can occur in a chord, melody or combination, and these note-groups may succeed each other without the dependent relationships of tonality. The second interpretation in atonal music is a focus on intervals rather than pitches for relating note-groups. With this change in orientation have come changes in the way intervals are described: they are no longer divided into 'consonant' and 'dissonant' categories; intervals are named by the number of semitones they contain, rather than by their tonal names; and equivalences of intervals related by octaves (defined as 12 'pitch class intervals'), and even by octave complements (those that add up to an

octave, defined as six 'interval classes'), are asserted. Thus, rather than talking about pieces being in keys, writers describe pieces as having intervallic tendencies among non-triad note-groups.

Without the organizing force of a tonic key note and hierarchical grouping and voice-leading between triads, new criteria for classification and relationships among note-groups have also developed: (1) collectional or order equivalence, where a note-group is recognizable as a categorized 'collection' when presented in any order, which may include horizontal or vertical; (2) transpositional equivalence, where a note-group is not differentiated functionally from transpositions of itself; (3) inversional equivalence, where a note-group is not differentiated functionally from inversions of itself; and (4) symmetry as a structural property, with mirror symmetry, symmetrical collections (those in which inversions are equivalent to transpositions) and interval cycles acting as alternatives to the chord progressions and voice-leading of tonality. All these criteria relate to 'invariance', a central concept in which some aspect of a note-group – either pitch, pitch class, interval or interval class – is retained following some operation.

Many writers have codified the possible collections available by various intervallic successions, initially as 'scales' for compositional resources and later as lists of equivalent note-groups. The traditional equivalence operations are transposition and inversion, where, for instance, the note-groups C–E♭–G and A–C–E (transposition) and C–E♭–G and C–E–G (inversion) are considered equivalent. A later addition is equivalence under 'M' or multiplicative operations, where 'M5'- or 'M7'-related collections – for example C–C♯–D and C–F–B♭ at M5, with exchanged interval class 1 and 5 values – are considered equivalent. Such lists and criteria are often defined using numbers and mathematical relationships, with C = 0, C♯/D♭ = 1, ... A♯/B♭ = 10, B = 11 (10 and 11 are also notated variously as 't', 'e'), with transposition expressed as addition and inversion as subtraction, and even with geometrical shapes and equations (see O'Connell, 1962, and Roeder, 1987). Some notational conventions are: (1) {x, y, z} ({C, E♭, G}) for unordered collections of pitches or pitch classes, that is, those in which order is not considered an identifying feature; (2) <x–y–z> (<C–E♭–G>) for ordered collections of pitches or pitch classes, that is, those in which order is an identifying feature; and (3) [xyz] ([037]) for a set class, an equivalence class of all unordered pitch class collections related by transposition or inversion to a representative note-group, here {C, E♭, G}.

(i) Symmetry. A letter from Berg to Schoenberg (27 July 1920), in which Berg outlined his interest in interval cycles and symmetry, is the strongest source evidence for symmetry being an organizing force in atonal music (as asserted by Perle). Perle has described symmetrical procedures in tonal music as 'windows of disorder' which become 'windows of order' in atonal music.

In reference to music principally by Berg and Bartók, but also by Schoenberg, Webern, Stravinsky, Skryabin and others, Perle describes 'normative' elements that underlie the surface in similar ways, stemming from the symmetry of the 12-note equal-tempered collection, which act as priority elements among other 'reflexive' or local elements in pieces. This symmetry is manifested as interval cycles (e.g. '3-cycles' of <C–E♭–F♯–A>, <C♯–E–G–B♭>

and <D–F–Ab–B>) and cyclic collections (e.g. {C, E, F♯, Ab} as a collection from the complete whole-tone collection {C, D, E, F♯, G♯, A♯}), and in inversional complementation (e.g. <c′–e′> as the complement or mirror pair to <d–f♯> around axis note a: <d–f♯–[a]–c′–e′>).

Symmetry results not only from the division of musical space into equal-division pitch space, resulting in 'mirror symmetry' and an 'axis' of symmetry, but in a more general sense from relationships among collections of pitch classes (e.g. <C–E> and <D–F♯> expressed numerically as <0–4> and <2–6>, then related by the sum of complementation 6, from 0+6 [C+F♯] and 4+2 [E+D]: Babbitt's term for this sum is 'index number'). Different symmetrical bases can combine, with pitches or pitch classes lying both inside and outside the prevailing symmetrical system(s), or acting as transitions to some new cyclic aspect of the system, allowing for a hierarchy of symmetrical and non-symmetrical notes. Where it occurs, symmetry is thus in a constant state of interruption and regeneration, tension and release, somewhat analogously to tonal stability and instability by motion away from and back to a tonic key.

The principal elements of symmetry are: (1) voice-leading and registral motion by interval cycles, where composition can be motivated to fill gaps within cycles, span cyclic intervals, transpose or invert cycles, or change to different cycles; (2) cyclic collections as a harmonic basis, either from pure cycles or cycles with added 'dissonant' notes (e.g. a whole-tone collection plus an added note C, <F–Eb–Db–A–C–B>, from the beginning of Berg's String Quartet op.3), with procedures such as transposition to different cycle forms, changes or reinterpretation in cyclic basis (e.g. <C–C♯–D–E> as a 1-cycle <C–C♯–D> collection plus E reinterpreted as a 2-cycle <C–D–E> collection plus C♯), and opposition and reconciliation of cyclic bases; (3) embedded cyclic collections functioning within larger note-groups, which are influenced by the intervallic properties of the interval cycle; and (4) a structural role for symmetrical note-groups, with their transpositional or inversional invariances, and axes of symmetry or pitch class sums of complementation. Such sums are identified by Perle as 'keys' and used to relate different pieces, such as the sum 9 relationship pairing E/F, Eb/F♯, D/G, Db/G♯, C/A and B/Bb (in numbers, 4/5, 3/6, 2/7, 1/8, 0/9, 11/10 (mod 12)) between the first movements of Berg's Lyric Suite and Bartók's Fourth String Quartet.

(ii) Pitch class set theory. Pitch class set theory, as set out principally by Forte, establishes a theoretical context in which pitches are grouped into pitch class sets, which are then further categorized into set classes equivalent under transposition and inversion. Set classes are labelled by cardinality, placement within a list ordered by interval class content and prime form (e.g. set class 4–1 [0123] indicates four notes, e.g. {C, C♯, D, D♯}, with its interval class 'vector' of <321000> identifying three interval class 1s, two interval class 2s etc., placed first in the list of four-note set classes, and with a prime or most compact form [0123]). Set classes grouped or 'segmented' in analyses of pieces are related to each other in several ways: in 'literal' relationships two sets share pitch classes; in 'abstract' relationships two sets share interval classes. Two other relationships are the 'complement' of a set, which may be a literal complement consisting of the remaining pitch classes or the abstract complement consisting of the set

class of the remaining pitch classes, and a 'Z-relation', in which two set classes of the same cardinality have the same interval class vector but not the same prime form (e.g. [0137] and [0146], both with vector <111111>).

The organization of atonal pieces is interpreted by a hierarchical network relating as many set classes as possible to a central 'nexus' set – a set, usually a hexachord, that shares the greatest number of interval class relationships with surrounding sets and their complement sets. Two types of network exist: (1) a 'K' network, which results when, among two set classes of different cardinalities, S and T, and their complements S′ and T′, S is a subset or superset of either T or T′; and (2) a more exclusive 'Kh' network, yielding a smaller number of related sets, which results when set class S is a subset or superset of both set classes T and T′.

Many writers have expanded on pitch class set theory to show the 'normative' elements that result from the 12-note equal-tempered system: (1) the equivalent invariance properties and intervallic structures of complementary sets, where interval class vector entries differ by the difference in cardinalities (e.g. given set class 3–1 {C, C♯, D} vector <210000> and complement 9–1 {D♯, E, F, F♯, G, G♯, A, A♯, B} vector <876663>, 876663 – 210000 = 666663, with the interval class 6 entry halved due to its invariance); (2) the tendency of hexachords to be nexus sets; (3) the presence of Z-related pairs of sets; and (4) the similarity of relationships, sharing pitch class and interval class content, between pitch class sets, usually expressed as percentages in a scale of 0 to 1. These 'normative' structures provide a context for the 'reflexive' elements of individual pieces. *See also* SET.

(iii) Transformational networks. Lewin's focus has been on the spans between musical events rather than on the events themselves – durations rather than attacks, intervals rather than pitches. These spans, called 'intervals' in a more generalized sense, are regarded as active rather than passive, transformational rather than simply measurable or classifiable, ordered in time and space, and interpretable according to relative, rather than absolute, criteria. By combining defined musical spaces ('S', e.g. pitch), a group of mathematical operations (IVLS, e.g. the addition of semitones), and defined mappings of objects on to one another by specific *intervals* (a function 'int' mapping s on to t, e.g. transposition), Lewin's analytical apparatus, the Generalized Interval System (GIS), can encompass aspects of many existing theories of atonal and tonal music. The successive *intervals* transforming one object through a succession of other objects are displayed in transformational networks, which are internally ordered and logical, and to varying extents independent of the objects being transformed.

In practice, Lewin's analyses are governed by several premises. Like Perle, Lewin defines intervals both as differences (transpositions) and sums (inversions). Inversion is described in terms of inversional 'balance', manifested as either pitch axes or pitch class sums that group surrounding notes (e.g. the axis A/Bb groups note pairs A/Bb, G♯/B, G/C, F♯/C♯, F/D and E/Eb. The completion of either a pitch-inversional dyad in register or of a pitch class-inversional pair is often a compositional premise. Intervals are regarded as having tendencies to propagate themselves as transpositional or inversional levels. Lewin allows for the equivalences of pitch class set theory, and combines transposition and inversion within the same set as 'Klumpenhouwer networks' (e.g. <A–F♯–B> with interval 2 <A–B> transposed to <A♭–B♭>, and interval <A–F♯> symmetrically expanded at sum 3 to <A♭–G> to yield <A♭–G–B♭>), analogous to Perle's combinations of sum and difference relationships in the 'cyclic sets' that are the basis of his 12-note tonality. Analytically, Lewin stresses pitch relationships with registral extremes or boundary notes as significant elements.

Noteworthy in analytical commentary from Lewin's approach are the following: aggregates and aggregate completion; instances of symmetrical pitch inversion as more 'audible' realizations of pitch class inversional complementation; axis notes of inversion occurring as adjacent notes in a series; and ordered relations among symmetrically related notes. The point of the analysis is often to relate as many collections as possible by a similar set of transformations – particularly to show that different collections, whether symmetrical or asymmetrical, adjacent or divided on the surface by register, have similar transformational relationships – and in this way to demonstrate the underlying unifying principles that connect the first note to the last in a passage. A transformational scheme is valued for including virtually every note, and is validated by recurring 'motivic' pitch registral connections on the surface and in relation to other movements.

5. CONCLUSION.   Atonality thus roughly delimits a wide range of compositional practices whose only features are the absence of the normative and interrelated procedures of tonality and of the basic concept of serialism. It remains to be seen to what extent atonality is a useful or relevant musical category. The tendency of historical criticism to construct systems of classification which attempt to index individual entries as neatly and unambiguously as possible has certainly been frustrated so far. The individuality of the contributions of Schoenberg, Stravinsky, Bartók, Webern, Berg and others ultimately transcends and trivializes such attempts, if it does not contradict them.

BIBLIOGRAPHY

B. Ziehn: Harmonie- und Modulationslehre (Berlin, 1887–8; Eng. trans., 1907)
A. Schoenberg: Harmonielehre (1911, 3/1922; Eng. trans., 1978)
B. Ziehn: Five- and Six-Part Harmonies and How to Use Them (Milwaukee, 1911)
E. Bacon: 'Our Musical Idiom', The Monist, xxvii (1917), 560–607
H. Eimert: Atonale Musiklehre (Leipzig, 1924)
F.H. Klein: 'Die Grenze der Halbtonwelt', Die Musik, xvii/4 (1925), 281–6
A. Hába: Neue Harmonielehre des diatonischen, chromatischen, Viertel-, Drittel-, Sechstel-, und Zwölftel-Tonsystems (Leipzig, 1927)
H. Cowell: New Musical Resources (1930/R)
A. Schoenberg: 'Analysis of the Four Orchestral Songs Opus 22' [1932], PNM, iii/2 (1964–5), 1–21; repr. in B. Boretz and E.T. Cone, eds.: Perspectives on Schoenberg and Stravinsky (Princeton, NJ, 1968, 2/1972), 25–45
A. Schoenberg: 'Problems of Harmony', MM, xxi (1934), 167; repr. in Style and Idea (New York, 1950, 3/1984), 268–87
A. Berg: 'Was Ist atonal?', 23: eine wiener Musikzeitschrift, vi–vii (1936), 1–11; Eng. trans. in N. Slonimsky: Music since 1900 (New York, 1938, 5/1994), 1027–9
P. Hindemith: Unterweisung im Tonsatz (Mainz, 1937–9, 2/1940; Eng trans., 1941–2, 2/1948)
J. Schillinger: Kaleidophone: New Resources of Melody and Harmony (New York, 1940)
O. Messiaen: Technique de mon langage musical (Paris, 1944; Eng. trans., 1956)
F. Salzer: Structural Hearing: Tonal Coherence in Music (New York, 1952)

D. Lewin: 'Intervallic Relations between Two Collections of Notes', JMT, iii (1959), 298–301
R. Travis: 'Toward a New Concept of Tonality?', JMT, iii (1959), 257–84
H. Hanson: Harmonic Materials of Twentieth-Century Music (New York, 1960)
W. O'Connell: 'Der Ton-Raum', Die Reihe, viii (1962), 35–61; Eng. trans. in Die Reihe, vii (1968), 34–67
G. Perle: Serial Composition and Atonality (Berkeley, 1962, 6/1991)
A. Berger: 'Problems of Pitch Organization in Stravinsky', PNM, ii/1 (1963–4), 11–42
A. Forte: 'A Theory of Set-Complexes for Music', JMT, viii (1964), 136–83
J. Tenney: Meta/Hodos and META Meta/Hodos (New Orleans, 1964)
J. Clough: 'Pitch-Set Equivalence and Inclusion (A Comment on Forte's Theory of Set-Complexes)', JMT, ix (1965), 163–71
R. Teitelbaum: 'Intervallic Relations in Atonal Music', JMT, ix (1965), 72–127
E. Carter: 'Expressionism and American Music', PNM, iv/1 (1965–6), 1–13
R. Travis: 'Directed Motion in Schoenberg and Webern', PNM, iv/2 (1965–6), 85–9
G. Perle: 'The Musical Language of Wozzeck', Music Forum, i (1967), 204–59
D. Lewin: 'Inversional Balance as an Organizing Force in Schoenberg's Music and Thought', PNM, vi/2 (1967–8), 1–21
R. Craft: 'Schoenberg's Five Pieces for Orchestra', Perspectives on Schoenberg and Stravinsky, ed. B. Boretz and E.T. Cone (Princeton, NJ, 1968, 2/1972), 3–24
B. Boretz: 'Meta-Variations: Studies in the Foundation of Musical Thought', PNM, viii/1 (1969–70), 1–74; viii/2 (1969–70), 49–111; xi/1 (1972–3), 146–233; xi/2 (1972–3), 156–203
B. Boretz: 'The Construction of Musical Syntax (I)', PNM, ix/1 (1970–71), 23–42
J. Maegaard: Studien zur Entwicklung des Dodekaphonene Satzes bei Arnold Schönberg (Copenhagen, 1972) [review in MQ, lxiii (1977), 273]
A. Forte: 'Sets and Nonsets in Schoenberg's Atonal Music', PNM, xi/1 (1972–3), 43–64
A. Forte: The Structure of Atonal Music (New Haven, CT, 1973)
B. Alphonse: The Invariance Matrix (diss., Yale U., 1974)
E. Cone: 'Sound and Syntax: an Introduction to Schoenberg's Harmony', PNM, xiii/1 (1974–5), 21–40
E. Regener: 'On Allen Forte's Theory of Chords', PNM, xiii/1 (1974–5), 191–212
P. Lansky: 'Pitch-Class Consciousness', PNM, xiii/2 (1974–5), 30–56
C. Gamer and P. Lansky: 'Fanfare for the Common Tone', PNM, xiv/2–xv/1 (1976), 229–35
R. Chrisman: 'Describing Structural Aspects of Pitch-Sets using Successive-Interval Arrays', JMT, xxi (1977), 1–28
D. Lewin: 'Forte's Interval Vector, My Interval Function, and Regener's Common-Note Function', JMT, xxi (1977), 194–237
G. Perle: 'Berg's Master Array of the Interval Cycles', MQ, lxiii (1977), 1–30
A. Chapman: A Theory of Harmonic Structure for Nontonal Music (diss., Yale U., 1978)
D. Starr: 'Sets, Invariance, and Partitions', JMT, xxii (1978), 1–42
D. Beach: 'Pitch Structure and the Analytic Process in Atonal Music: an Interpretation of the Theory of Sets', Music Theory Spectrum, i (1979), 7–22
D. Lewin: 'A Response to a Response: on Pcset Relatedness', PNM, xviii (1979–80), 498–502
R. Morris: 'A Similarity Index for Pitch-Class Sets', PNM, xviii (1979–80), 445–60
J. Rahn: 'Relating Sets', PNM, xviii (1979–80), 483–98
G. Perle: The Operas of Alban Berg, i: Wozzeck (Berkeley, 1980)
J. Rahn: Basic Atonal Theory (New York, 1980)
J. Tenney and L. Polansky: 'Temporal Gestalt Perception in Music', JMT, xxiv (1980), 205–41
A. Forte: 'The Magical Kaleidoscope: Schoenberg's First Atonal Masterwork, opus 11, no.1', Journal of the Arnold Schoenberg Institute, v (1981), 127–68
C. Hasty: 'Segmentation and Process in Post-Tonal Music', Music Theory Spectrum, iii (1981), 54–73
C. Lord: 'Intervallic Similarity Relations in Atonal Set Analysis', JMT, xxv (1981), 91–111
R. Morris: 'Review of John Rahn's Basic Atonal Theory', Music Theory Spectrum, iv (1982), 138–54

R. Morris: 'Set Groups, Complementation, and Mappings among Pitch-Class Sets', *JMT*, xxvi/1 (1982), 101–44

M. Kielian-Gilbert: 'Relationships of Symmetrical Pitch-Class Sets and Stravinsky's Metaphor of Polarity', *PNM*, xxi (1982–3), 209–40

D. Lewin: 'Transformational Techniques in Atonal and Other Music Theories', *PNM*, xxi (1982–3), 312–71

R. Morris: 'Combinatoriality without the Aggregate', *PNM*, xxi (1982–3), 432–86

J. Baker: 'Schenkerian Analysis and Post-Tonal Music', *Aspects of Schenkerian Theory*, ed. D. Beach (New Haven, CT, 1983)

J. Clough: 'Use of the Exclusion Relation to Profile Pitch-Class Sets', *JMT*, xxvii (1983), 181–201

J. Schmalfeldt: *Berg's 'Wozzeck': Harmonic Language and Dramatic Design* (New Haven, CT, 1983)

E. Antokoletz: *The Music of Béla Bartók* (Berkeley, 1984)

C. Hasty: 'Phrase Formation in Post-Tonal Music', *JMT*, xxviii (1984), 167–90

G. Perle: 'Scriabin's Self-Analyses', *MAn*, iii (1984), 101–22

A. Forte: 'Pitch-Class Set Analysis Today', *MAn*, iv (1985), 29–58

J. Bernard: *The Music of Edgard Varèse* (New Haven, CT, 1987)

D. Lewin: *Generalized Musical Intervals and Transformations* (New Haven, CT, 1987)

R.D. Morris: *Composition with Pitch-Classes: a Theory of Compositional Design* (New Haven, CT, 1987)

J. Roeder: 'A Geometric Representation of Pitch-Class Series', *PNM*, xxv (1987), 362–409

J. Straus: 'The Problem of Prolongation in Post-Tonal Music', *JMT*, xxxi (1987), 1–21

A. Forte: 'New Approaches to the Linear Analysis of Music', *JAMS*, xli (1988), 315–48

A. Forte: 'Pitch-Class Set Genera and the Origin of Modern Harmonic Species', *JMT*, xxxii (1988), 187–270

R. Wason: 'Tonality and Atonality in Frederick Rzewski's Variations on "The People United Will Never Be Defeated"', *PNM*, xxvi/1 (1988), 108–43

A. Mead: 'The State of Research in Twelve-Tone and Atonal Theory', *Music Theory Spectrum*, xi (1989), 40–48

J. Roeder: 'Harmonic Implications of Schoenberg's Observations of Atonal Voice Leading', *JMT*, xxxiii (1989), 27–62

J. Baker: 'Voice Leading in Post-Tonal Music: Suggestions for Extending Schenker's Theory', *MAn*, ix (1990), 177–200

D. Lewin: 'Klumpenhouwer Networks and Some Isographies that Involve Them', *Music Theory Spectrum*, xii (1990), 83–120

G. Perle: *The Listening Composer* (Berkeley, 1990)

G. Perle: 'Pitch-Class Set Analysis: an Evaluation', *JM*, viii (1990), 151–72

J. Straus: *Introduction to Post-Tonal Theory* (Englewood Cliffs, NJ, 1990)

J. Straus: *Remaking the Past: Musical Modernism and the Influence of the Tonal Tradition* (Cambridge, MA, 1990)

E.W. Marvin: 'The Perception of Rhythm in Non-Tonal Music: Rhythmic Contours in the Music of Edgard Varèse', *Music Theory Spectrum*, xiii (1991), 61–78

S. Neff: 'An American Precursor of Non-Tonal Theory: Ernst Bacon (1898–1990)', *CMc*, no.48 (1991), 5–26

D. Headlam: 'Fritz Heinrich Klein's "Die Grenze der Halbtonwelt" and *Die Maschine*', *Theoria*, vi (1992), 54–96

D.W. Bernstein: 'Symmetry and Symmetrical Inversion in Turn-of-the-Century Theory and Practice', *Music Theory and the Exploration of the Past*, ed. C. Hatch and D.W. Bernstein (Chicago, 1993), 377–407

R. Morris: 'New Directions in the Theory and Analysis of Musical Contour', *Music Theory Spectrum*, xv (1993), 205–28

G. Perle: 'Communication (Re: Lewin, "Klumpenhouwer Networks")', *Music Theory Spectrum*, xv (1993), 300–03

R. Morris: 'Recommendations for Atonal Music Pedagogy in General; Recognizing and Hearing Set-Classes in Particular', *Journal of Music Theory Pedagogy*, viii (1994), 75–134

G. Perle: *The Right Notes* (Stuyvesant, NY, 1995)

E. Haimo: 'Atonality, Analysis, and the Intentional Fallacy', *Music Theory Spectrum*, xviii (1996), 167–99

J.W. Bernard: 'Chord, Collection, and Set in Twentieth-Century Theory', *Music Theory in Concept and Practice*, ed. J.W. Baker, D.W. Beach and J.W. Bernard (Rochester, NY, 1997), 11–51

G. Perle: 'Berg's Style of Freedom', *MT*, cxxxix (1998), 12–31

PAUL LANSKY, GEORGE PERLE (1–3, 5),
DAVE HEADLAM (4, bibliography)

Atrash, Farīd al- (*b* al-Qrayya, Syria, 18 Oct 1915; *d* Beirut, 26 Dec 1974). Syrian singer, composer, *'ud* player and film actor and producer. In 1924 political circumstances forced his family to move to Egypt. His mother, the noted singer 'Aliyya al-Munther, taught him singing in the Syrian style. He studied the *'ud* (lute) at the Cairo Institute for Arab Music. His professional work began as an *'ud* player and singer at the national radio station and in Badi 'a Maṣabnī's variety show saloon.

In 1941, through his sister ASMAHĀN, he entered the cinema industry, and for the rest of his life was involved in films as a composer, singer actor, and producer. His singing of Syrian *mawwāl* (popular songs), tangos and rumbas achieved great popularity, and his work laid the foundations for Arab variety show films, cinematic operetta, orchestral musical overtures and comic and sad songs. His 31 films are mostly autobiographical and provide valuable insight into the role of the musician in society.

His skilful solo *'ud* playing moved listeners to ecstasy. He combined abstract conceptualism with a deep understanding of the instrument's artistic traditions, and was widely imitated. In 1962 he received a prestigious Turkish award for his playing.

He composed songs many of which were inspired by the emotional difficulties and health problems which he suffered, and instrumental pieces (some for dance performances by his lover Sāmīa Gamāl). Influences were his mother's Syrian songs, the Lebanese composer Farīd Ghuson, and the Egyptian composers Zakariyyā Aḥmad, Muḥammad al-Qaṣabjī and Muḥammad 'Abd al-Wahhāb (the latter also being a rival). He wrote for famous female singers (Asmahān and others) and some songs achieved fame in Europe. He headed the Association of Egyptian Songwriters and Composers for many years, and received numerous medals from all over the Arab world.

He promoted Arab nationalism and held Syrian, Lebanese, Egyptian and Sudanese nationalities. He suffered several strokes (the first aged 37) and eventually died from a heart attack.

SAADALLA AGHA AL-KALAA

Atrio, Hermanus de. *See* HERMANUS DE ATRIO.

Attacca (It.: 'attack', 'begin'; imperative of *attaccare*). A direction, usually found at the end of a movement, signifying that the next movement is to be joined to the preceding without a pause. The term also appears in the form *attacca subito*, 'begin immediately'. In Baroque music a movement without a normal cadence on the tonic at the end implied an *attacca*.

GEORGE GROVE/R

Attacco (It.: 'attack'). An extremely brief fugue subject. The word was apparently first so defined by G.B. Martini in volume ii of *Esemplare, ossia Saggio fondamentale pratico di contrappunto* (1775), where it is contrasted with SOGGETTO, a fugue subject of medium or average length, and ANDAMENTO, a fugue subject of extended length. For an example of *attacco*, Martini offered a theme of only three crotchets and a quaver, and he suggested that contrapuntal treatment of such a subject might be freer than that of other, longer fugue subjects. Indeed, because few fugue subjects are this brief some later writers have employed the term principally in the context of point-of-imitation technique rather than of fugue itself. Martini's three terms found only limited use outside Italy, but they have been included in every edition of *Grove's Dictionary* beginning with the supplement to the first edition, where they were treated at length by W.S. Rockstro.

PAUL WALKER

Attaingnant, Pierre (*b* probably in or nr Douai, *c*1494; *d* Paris, late 1551 or 1552). French music printer, publisher, bookseller, punchcutter and typecaster.

1. Life. 2. Publications.

1. LIFE.   By a document notarized 13 January 1513/14 Attaingnant, described as a 'bookseller, living in Paris', leased a press to Jean de la Roche, reserving the right to print ecclesiastical pardons and the like, should he receive commissions. He may have gone from Douai to Paris originally with a chorister's scholarship for the Collège de Dainville, which was subject to the cathedral chapters of Arras and Noyon. This institution leased the part of its buildings on the rue de la Harpe to Philippe Pigouchet (*fl* 1490–1514), the printer-engraver famous for his Hours and the master to whom Attaingnant was probably apprenticed. Marriage to one of Pigouchet's daughters, Claude, made Attaingnant his heir. Another of Pigouchet's daughters, Germaine, was married to Poncet le Preux (1481–1559), one of the four 'grands libraires jurés' of the university, Master of the Printers' Guild and a prolific publisher of scholarly texts.

The earliest surviving book to bear Attaingnant's name is a Noyon breviary of 1525, the only book that he is known to have published in conjunction with Le Preux.

Attaingnant continued to publish liturgical books for Noyon throughout his life as well as syllabuses for schoolboys. After experimenting with music types for several years he brought out the *Chansons nouvelles*, dated 4 April 1527/8. Within a year they were followed by at least seven other books in the same format. At this time he sought and obtained royal protection in the form of a privilege preventing others from copying the contents of his books for three years after printing. It specifically mentioned books 'tant en musique, jeux de Lutz, Orgues, et semblables instruments' which he had printed or at least planned. (These intentions were realized with the lute tablatures of 1529 and 1530 and the keyboard scores of 1531.)

When the protection covering his earliest music books began to run out in spring 1531, he sought a wider, six-year privilege covering 'messes, motetz, hymnes, chansons que desditz jeux de Lutz, Flustes et Orgues, en grans et petitz volumes'. The royal decree of 18 June 1531 granting this is printed in the first volume of folio masses (1532). Also in this volume is Attaingnant's dedicatory address to the Cardinal of Tournon, who was praised in a Latin poem, written by Nicolas Bourbon for the occasion. Each of the seven mass volumes was illustrated with a woodcut of the court hearing Mass by Oronce Finé, royal mathematician and cosmographer (fig.1). Further royal preferment was natural after the achievement represented by the folio masses – Tournon was a powerful statesman as well as titular head of the royal chapel. Hopes mentioned in the second privilege were also realized by

1. *French court at Mass: woodcut by Oronce Finé from 'Primus liber tres missas continens' (Paris: Attaingnant, 1532)*

the imposing 13-volume set of motets in quarto format brought out in 1534 and 1535. A 14th volume devoted to Manchicourt appeared in 1539 (fig.2).

In 1537, in addition to a renewal of his privilege, Attaingnant received the unprecedented appointment of 'imprimeur et libraire du Roy en musique'. The other royal printers were men of learning such as Robert Estienne. About the time of Attaingnant's nomination, he began to abandon the older text types for the italics and romans more in keeping with humanist tastes. In 1538 he took a partner, Hubert Jullet, husband of his daughter Germaine, with whom he jointly signed a portion of the firm's output from then until Jullet's death in 1545. After his wife's death in 1543, an inventory of the firm's extensive stock and equipment was made. Two years later Attaingnant married Marie Lescallopier. He witnessed a contract as late as 3 October 1551 but died before the end of 1552. His widow printed a few music books between 1553 and 1557, then restricted her publications almost exclusively to the scholarly commentaries of Léger du Chesne, the last of which appeared in 1567. In the general tax of 1571 she was levied 6 livres on the considerable fortune of 300,000 livres.

2. PUBLICATIONS.   In Attaingnant's method of printing music the staff-segments and notes were combined, so that both could be printed in a single impression (fig.2;

see also PRINTING AND PUBLISHING OF MUSIC, fig.8a). This process superseded the double- or triple-impression techniques required to produce Petrucci's expensive quartos and became the first international method of music printing. The reason was primarily economic, for it allowed the time and cost of production to be reduced by half, or more. The five music types Attaingnant used in his workshop (four for mensural notation, one for French lute tablature) seem to have been cut for his own use, since no other editions show them. A similar but more primitive method produced the music types used by John Rastell in his Interlude, which likely antedates the Chansons nouvelles. We may never know which of these two printers first thought of the new technique, but it is clear that Rastell's trials reached nothing like the scale of Attaingnant's production. An altogether different method that it gradually displaced was the printing of music from engraved woodblocks. This method, of which Andrea Antico was the foremost craftsman, had been mostly used in Italy (in Rome and Venice), but was also used in Lyons from about 1525 to 1528. Attaingnant at first followed the small oblong octavo format made popular by Antico in the 1520s, but from the mid-1530s oblong quarto became the norm for all his music publications.

The commercial success of the new method coincided with the flowering of the so-called Parisian chanson. The

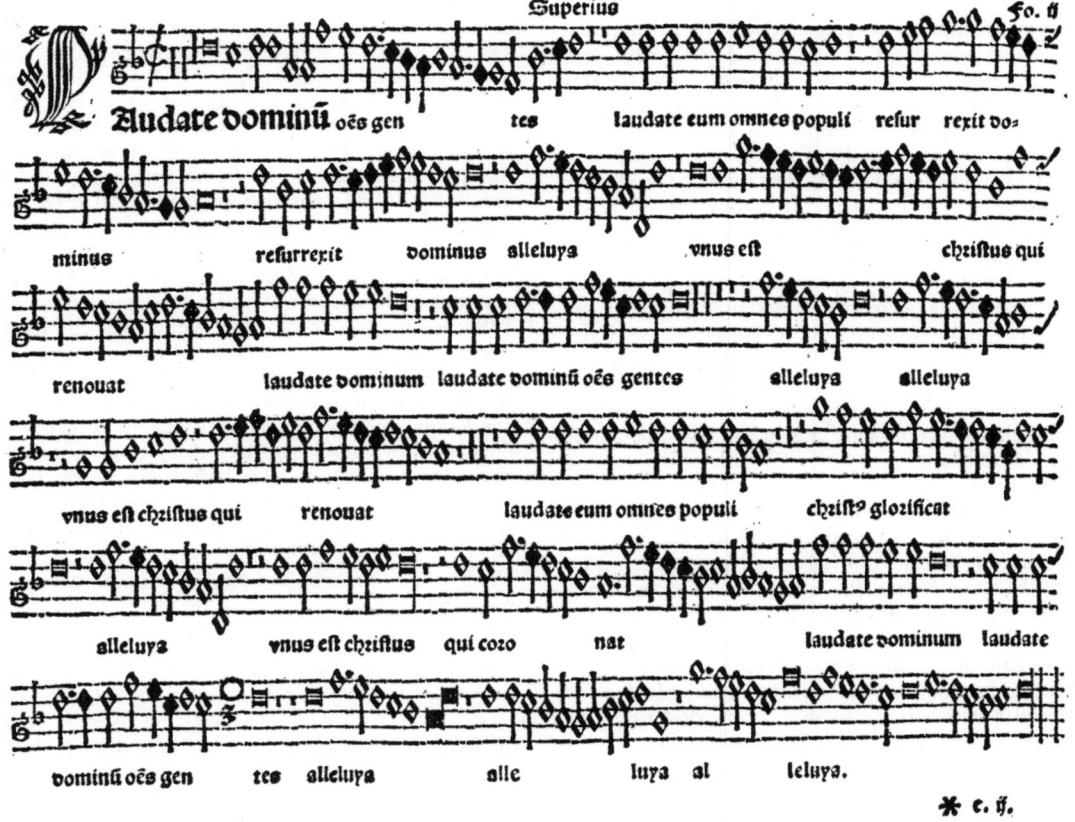

2. Superius voice of Manchicourt's 'Laudate Dominum' from 'Liber decimus quartus XIX musicus cantiones' (Paris: Attaingnant, 1539), printed from type by single impression

leading chanson composers, Claudin de Sermisy, Clément Janequin and Pierre Certon, all in royal service of one kind or another, are very well represented in Attaingnant's collections, which diffused their works widely. The tastes and liberality of Francis I were decisive: his patronage effectively made Attaingnant the official printer of the king's music. With this development a major step was taken towards the highly centralized establishment that has characterized French musical life ever since. In compiling his extensive catalogue of sacred and secular publications Attaingnant opened the way, showing others not only how to print, but also what to print; for example, his 1546 publication of settings by Certon and Mornable of the psalms in Marot's translations, the first books of their kind, were harbingers of a wave of similar settings.

Attaingnant was the first music publisher to achieve a true mass production. The numbered series of chansons from his later years, for instance, ran to 36 volumes and many of these went through two or three editions. With press runs conservatively estimated at 1000 copies, the total number of chansons put on the market by Attaingnant alone reached a staggering figure. To sell in such quantity required outlets on an international level. These were facilitated through the publishing business of Le Preux, who had dealings with some of the large German syndicates and maintained depots in various centres. He is known to have held stocks of Attaingnant's music books and may have been responsible for their foreign distribution.

As far as is known, Attaingnant was not a composer; yet he must have been skilled enough to do his own editing. At least, no house editor was named until the very last years, when Claude Gervaise (fl 1540–60) was given credit for revising and correcting some books of ensemble dances (Gervaise continued to give editiorial assistance to Marie Lescallopier until 1558). The lutenist Pierre Blondeau may have had a hand in editing an early lute tablature (1529/30), in which some pieces bear his initials. The accuracy of editing was generally high, with the exception of the earliest works and some from 1550. Verbal corrigenda were sometimes used to point out errors, but more frequently cancel slips were pasted over the original to correct passages or even single notes. Concern for utility and practical convenience are evident in the listing of voice combinations in the index for the six- and eight-voice motets, and in the instrumentation indications for flutes or recorders or both in two chanson books of 1533.

For the most part, Attaingnant offered the public new and original works of French composers. The music of the generation before Francis I found scant place in his books; the same is true for composers outside France, with the exception of certain Franco-Flemish masters working in the Low Countries (such as Gombert, Lupi and Richafort) or in Italy (Arcadelt, Verdelot and Willaert). Although he pirated Antico's canonic duets of 1520 and borrowed occasionally from Moderne, later from Susato and even from Du Chemin, he was by contemporary standards quite scrupulous. Certainly he was more imitated by other printers than imitative of them. He was chiefly responsible for starting the vogue for printing two- and three-voice arrangements of four-voice chansons – one of the clearest examples of a vast repertory created at the behest of the publishing business.

With the accession of Henri II in 1547, Attaingnant's special position soon vanished. Several other printers also received royal privileges, a fact which may explain Attaingnant's frenetic burst of activity at the end, with its concomitant lowering of standards in printing and proofreading. After Attaingnant's death, the appointment of 'King's Music Printers' was granted to Le Roy & Ballard, who gradually re-established the near monopoly first held by Attaingnant.

BIBLIOGRAPHY

F. Lesure: 'Pierre Attaingnant: notes et documents', MD, iii (1949), 34–40
D. Heartz: 'Parisian Music Publishing under Henry II: a Propos of Four Recently Discovered Guitar Books', MQ, xxxxvi (1960), 448–67
D. Heartz: Pierre Attaingnant, Royal Printer of Music: a Historical Study and Bibliographical Catalogue (Berkeley, 1969) [lists contents of all music books, with citation of modern edns]
D. Heartz: 'Au pres de vous – Claudin's Chanson and the Commerce of Publishers' Arrangements', JAMS, xxiv (1971), 193–225
A.H. King: 'The Significance of John Rastell in Early Music Printing', The Library, 5th ser., xxvi/3 (1971), 197–214
G.G. Allaire: 'L'apport de la typographie et de la musique à la poésie française du début du seizième siècle', Renaissance and Reformation/Renaissance et Réforme, vii (1978), 127–41
L.F. Bernstein: 'The "Parisian chanson": Problems of Style and Terminology', JAMS, xxxi (1978), 193–240
C.S. Courtney: 'The Early Chanson Anthologies Published by Pierre Attaingnant (1528–1530)', JM, v (1987), 526–48
L. Guillo: Les éditions musicales de la Renaissance lyonnaise (Paris, 1991)

DANIEL HEARTZ/LAURENT GUILLO

Attenhofer, Carl (b Wettingen, canton of Aargau, 5 May 1837; d Zürich, 22 May 1914). Swiss choral conductor and composer. He was a pupil of D. Elster and studied at the Leipzig Conservatory (1857–8) where E.F. Richter was among his teachers. After holding several minor teaching posts at Muri (1859), in 1863 he became director of music at Rapperswil, where his excellence as a choral conductor during a national singing festival in 1866 soon made his name known throughout the country. In the same year he moved to Zürich and fulfilled a number of important choral conducting engagements. In 1870 he was appointed director of music at the university, and in 1896 became second director, with Friedrich Hegar, of the conservatory. Together with the painter Arnold Böcklin and Hegar, he was given an honorary doctorate by the university in 1889. In addition to his various conducting duties he was an active composer; he wrote a great deal of church and chamber music, but excelled primarily in vocal music. His best works are, perhaps, his accompanied and a cappella compositions for male voices which have been printed in numerous collections and are still popular in Switzerland.

BIBLIOGRAPHY

RefardtHBM; SML
A. Glück: Karl Attenhofer (Zürich, 1888)
E. Isler: 'Karl Attenhofer', Neujahrsblatt der Allgemeine Musikgeschichte in Zürich, ciii (1915)

F.R. BOSONNET

Atterberg, Kurt (Magnus) (b Göteborg, 12 Dec 1887; d Stockholm, 15 Feb 1974). Swedish composer, administrator, conductor and critic. He studied the cello at school in Göteborg and then entered the Stockholm College of Technology. Having passed the examination in civil engineering in 1911, he spent his working life (1912–68) in the patent office. He was largely self-taught although he studied composition and instrumentation with Hallén at the Swedish Royal Academy of Music (1910–11), and partly used the state composer's scholarships he received between 1911 and 1915 to study in Germany (1911 and 1913). He made his début as a conductor at Göteborg in 1912, when the programme included his First Symphony; thereafter (particularly during the 1920s) he often conducted his own music and that of contemporaries, both at home and abroad (where he promoted Swedish music). From 1916 to 1922 he was *kapellmästare* at the Royal Dramatic Theatre, Stockholm; he also worked enthusiastically as co-founder and president (1924–47) of the Society of Swedish Composers, and as co-founder, president (1924–43) and vice-president (1943–62) of the Swedish Performing Rights Society (STIM). He was secretary to the Swedish Royal Academy of Music from 1940 to 1953 (he had been made a member in 1926), and was music critic of the *Stockholms-tidningen* from 1919 to 1957, gradually tending to dislike younger composers and new techniques.

Atterberg's manifold activities have diluted appreciation of his music, and in later years he met with less response than at the beginning of his career. Nevertheless, with Rangström, he was one of the leading Swedish composers in the generation after Peterson-Berger, Stenhammar and Alfvén, producing his best work in symphonies and stage music. The point of departure for his first two symphonies was German and Scandinavian Romanticism (Brahms and Alfvén), though he inclined less to detailed thematic working than to a kind of al fresco technique, with melodic lines – often cantilenas in an assimilated folk style – set off against colourful backgrounds. Having added an impressionist touch in the Third Symphony (arguably his best) and realistic effects in the symphonic poem *Älven* ('The River', 1929), he completed his repertory of symphonic procedures with polytonal elements, which he used in varying degrees up to his last symphony, the Ninth (1955–6). His Sixth Symphony won the prize awarded by the Columbia Graphophone Company for the Schubert centenary (1928). Some of his five operas and his two best ballets had many performances in Europe during the 1920s and 1930s, particularly in Germany. Best known of these was the ballet *De fåvitska jungfrurna* ('The Foolish Virgins', 1920), written for the Ballets Suédois of Paris. *Bäckahästen* ('The White Horse', 1923–4), with its naive folkloristic tone and Singspiel character, also met with success, and *Fanal* (1929–32) is an effective, ballad-style drama of freedom in 16th-century Germany. All Atterberg's stage works rely on decorative effect rather than psychological profundity. His music for Maeterlinck's *Soeur Béatrice* is typical in its lyrical-elegiac, slightly Impressionist treatment of sentiment; the suite drawn from it is one of his most frequently performed works.

WORKS
(selective list)

STAGE

op.
–	Jefta (incid music, Didring), 1913; used in Suite no.1	
9	Per Svinaherde (ballet), 1914–15; Stockholm, 1921	
–	Mats och Petter (incid music, J. Bauer), 1915; used in Suite no.2	
12	Härvard harpolekare [Härvard the Harpist] (op, K. Atterberg), 1916–18, Stockholm, 1919; rev. 1934–5; rev. 1952 as Härvards hemkomst [Härvard's Homecoming], Stockholm, 1954	
–	Syster Beatrice (incid music, M. Maeterlinck), 1917; used in Suite no.3	
13	Perseus och vidundret (incid music, T. Hedberg), 1918	
–	Balettskizzer, 1919; Stockholm, 1920	
17	De fåvitska jungfrurna [The Foolish Virgins] (ballet), 1920; Paris, 1920	
–	Turandot (incid music, C. Gozzi), 1920; used in Suite no.4	
18	Stormen (incid music, W. Shakespeare), 1921; orch suite	
–	De tre mostrarna (incid music, G. Holmgren), 1923	
–	En vintersaga (incid music, Shakespeare), 1923; used in Suite no.5	
24	Bäckahästen [The White Horse] (op, A. Österling), 1923–4; Stockholm, 1925	
–	Hassan (incid music, J.E. Flecker), 1925; used in Suite no.6	
–	Antonius och Kleopatra (incid music, Shakespeare), 1926	
35	Fanal (op), 1929–32; Stockholm, 1934	
43	Aladdin (op), 1936–41; Stockholm, 1941; ov., op.44, 1941	
49	Stormen (op), 1946–7; Stockholm, 1948	

ORCHESTRAL

Syms.: no.1, b, op.3, 1909–11; no.2, F, op.6, 1911–13; no.3 (Västkustbilder), op.10, 1914–16; no.4 (Sinfonia piccola), g, op.14, 1918; no.5 (Sinfonia funebre), d, op.20, 1919–22; no.6, C, op.31, 1927–8; no.7 (Sinfonia romantica), op.45, 1942; no.8, e, op.48, 1944; no.9 (Sinfonia visionaria), op.54, solo vv, chorus, orch, 1955–6 [after Voluspa]

Concertante works: Rhapsody, op.1, pf, orch, 1909; Vn Conc., e, op.7, 1913; Vc Conc., c, op.21, 1922; Hn Conc., A, op.28, 1926; Pf Conc., b♭, op.37, 1935; Double Conc., g–C, vn, vc/va, str, 1959–60

Suites: no.1 (Orientalisk svit), 1913; no.2, 1915; no.3, op.19/1, vn, va, str, 1917; Stormen, op.18, 1921; no.4 (Turandot), op.19/2, 1920; no.5 (Suite barocco), op.23, 1923; no.6 (Orientalisk legend), op.30, 1925; no.7, op.29, str/str qnt, 1926; no.8 (Suite pastorale in modo antico), op.34, 1931; no.9 (Suite drammatica), op.47, 1944

Other works: Concert Ov., a, op.4, 1910; Rondeau rétrospectif, op.26, 1925; Älven [The River], sym. poem, op.33, 1929; Ballad och passacaglia, op.38, 1935; Concert Ov., op.41, 1940; Rondeau caractéristique, op.42, 1940; Indian Tunes, sym. movt, op.51, 1950; Svensk sommarfest, 1957

VOCAL

Requiem, op.8, solo vv, chorus, orch, 1914; Järnbäraland, op.16, solo vv, chorus, orch, 1919; Sången, op.25, solo vv, chorus ad lib, orch, 1925; Sångens land, op.32, solo vv, chorus ad lib, orch, 1928

CHAMBER AND INSTRUMENTAL

Str Qt no.1, D, op.2, 1909; Str Qt no.2, op.11, 1918; 2 Höstballader, op.15, pf, 1918; Sonata, b, op.27, vc, pf, 1925; Pf Qnt, op.31 bis [arr. of Sym. no.6]; Str Qt no.3, D, op.39, 1937; Variations and Fugue, op.46, str qt, 1944

Principal publishers: Breitkopf & Härtel, Eulenburg, Leuckart, Musikaliska Konstföreningen

WRITINGS

ed.: *Föreningen svenska tonsättare 25 år* (Stockholm, 1943)
Med notpenna och taktpinne: ett och annat om partiturskrivning och taktslagning (Stockholm, 1946)
'In- och utländska musikminnen från tidigt 1900-tal', *Musikrevy*, xii (1967), 322–6

BIBLIOGRAPHY

E.M. Stuart: *Kurt Atterberg* (Stockholm, 1925)
G. Bergendal: 'Atterberg, vad vill du mig?', *Musikrevy*, xxii (1967), 331–2
I. Liljefors: 'Femtio år med Atterberg', *Musikrevy*, xxii (1967), 327–8
G. Percy: 'Kurt Atterberg 85 år', *Musikrevy*, xxviii (1973), 1–3 [incl. list of works]
S. Kruckenberg: 'Om Kurt Atterberg', *Konsertnytt*, xviii/4 (1982–3), 19–23
S. Jacobsson: *Kurt Atterberg* (Borås, 1985)
H. Åstrand: 'Perioden 1920–45 i backspegeln', *Musiken i Sverige*, iv: *Konstmusik, folkmusik, populärmusik 1920–1990*, ed. L. Jonsson (Stockholm, 1994), 346ff

HANS ÅSTRAND, BO WALLNER

Atterbury, Luffmann (bap. London, 5 Jan 1740; *d* London, 11 June 1796). English glee composer. He was apparently a builder or carpenter by trade, but later developed a second career as a composer and singer. In 1773 he was recommended by the renowned organist John Stanley to the Foundling Hospital as a singing master. Although appointed he was soon dismissed, as the General Court decided that the newly appointed organist, Thomas Grenville, needed no assistance in teaching the children. Two years later Atterbury became a musician-in-ordinary to George III. He sang in the Handel Commemoration of 1784. He composed about 50 glees and catches, the great majority for male voices. Many of them first appeared in Warren's *Collection of Catches Canons and Glees* (London, 1763–93) and in Atterbury's three collections of his own music (1777, c1790, c1797). The glee *Come let us all a-maying* and the catch *Hot cross buns* long remained popular. He also composed an oratorio *Goliath*, performed at the Haymarket Theatre on 5 May 1773, and two years later, at the church of St Lawrence at West Wycombe, Buckinghamshire, as part of the elaborate ceremonies accompanying the inurnment of the heart of the politician and satirical poet Paul Whitehead. He provided airs for a pasticcio, *Mago and Dago* (1794), and in the same year contributed 12 pieces to William Tattersall's *Improved Psalmody*. In September 1790 he married Elizabeth Ancell. Doane's *Musical Directory* of 1794 lists him as a member of the King's Band, composer and organist.

BIBLIOGRAPHY

BDA; *DNB* (W.B. Squire)
Foundling Hospital: General Court Minutes (30 June 1773, Greater London Record Office)
J. Doane: *A Musical Directory for the Year 1794* (London, 1794)
T. Busby: *Concert Room and Orchestra Anecdotes* (London, 1825)
D. Baptie: *A Handbook of Musical Biography* (London, 1889)
A.G. Williams: *The Life and Works of John Stanley* (diss., U. of Reading, 1977)

NICHOLAS TEMPERLEY, EVA ZÖLLNER

Attey, John (*fl* 1622; *d* ?Ross, Herefordshire, c1640). English lutenist and composer. In his book of ayres Attey described himself as 'Gentleman, and Practitioner in Musicke', while in the dedication to the Earl and Countess of Bridgwater he wrote that his songs were for 'the best part composed under your roofe while I had the happiness to attend the service of those worthy and incomparable young Ladies your daughters'. John Egerton (1579–1649), Earl of Bridgwater and his wife Frances, daughter of Ferdinando, Earl of Derby, lived at Ashridge, in the parish of Little Gaddesden, Hertfordshire. Fellowes (1921) gave Attey's death date as above but the source for his statement is not known: Ross parish registers do not survive from before 1662.

Attey's only publication, *The First Booke of Ayres* for four voices and lute (London, 1622/R; ed. in EL, 2nd ser., ix, 1967 and MB, liv, 1989), was the last of its kind to be printed in England. The songs appear to have been composed originally for four voices: *The Gordian knot*, for example, begins with the alto and tenor unaccompanied, implying that Attey considered the alternative lutesong arrangement for cantus, lute and bass viol his second choice of performance. The title-page suggestion that 'all the parts may be plaide together with the Lute' implies instrumental performance not suggested in any other book of ayres. The four lowest courses of Attey's ten-course lute were presumably off the finger-board: when F♯ is required (*In a grove of trees*) the tablature shows that this one note was to be played an octave

higher. These musical hiccups, together with Attey's idiosyncratic use of the basses, indicate the necessity of the bass viol when singing the ayres as solo songs. Attey had a pleasant talent for melody, but his songs have, as Warlock wrote, 'no outstanding qualities save for the last song in the book, *Sweet was the song the Virgin sung*, a flawless work of serene beauty which forms a fitting conclusion to this golden period of English song'.

BIBLIOGRAPHY

SpinkES
E.H. Fellowes: *English Madrigal Verse, 1588–1632* (Oxford, 1920, enlarged 3/1967 by F.W. Sternfeld and D. Greer)
E.H. Fellowes: *The English Madrigal Composers* (Oxford, 1921, 2/1948/R), 324
P. Warlock: *The English Ayre* (London, 1926)
E. Doughtie: *Lyrics from English Airs, 1596–1622* (Cambridge, MA, 1970)

DIANA POULTON/ROBERT SPENCER

Attwood, Thomas (*b* London, bap. 23 Nov 1765; *d* London, 24 March 1838). English composer and organist. His father, also called Thomas Attwood, was an under-page to George III, and a viola player and trumpeter in the King's Band. Throughout his life Attwood benefited from royal patronage. At the age of nine he became a chorister in the Chapel Royal. When he left the choir in 1781 he became one of the Pages of the Presence to the Prince of Wales, who was so impressed by his musical ability that he sent him abroad to study. From 1783 to 1785 he lived in Naples, studying with Felipe Cinque and Gaetano Latilla. He then travelled to Vienna, where he lived from August 1785 until February 1787, still apparently supported by the Prince of Wales, and taking lessons in composition from Mozart. His exercises, with Mozart's corrections, are extant and have been printed. In Oldman's words, they 'are valuable not only for the light they throw on the prentice years of a notable English composer, but as evidence that Mozart, given an apt and congenial pupil, took his duties as a teacher with the utmost seriousness'. Mozart became much attached to Attwood: according to Kelly (who is not always reliable) Mozart said of him, 'He partakes more of my style than any scholar I ever had; and I predict, that he will prove a sound musician'. He also played a large part in introducing Mozart's music to the British public.

Attwood returned to his court position in England, and began to publish some of his instrumental compositions. In December 1791 he was appointed music teacher to the Duchess of York, and in April 1795 to the Princess of Wales. More important appointments followed in 1796, when he was made organist of St Paul's Cathedral and, later in the year, composer to the Chapel Royal. Meanwhile he had become a successful composer for the stage. Beginning with *The Prisoner* (1792), for the next ten years he provided music in whole or in part for well over 30 productions. The great majority of these were afterpieces of slight musical substance, and many were pasticcios; but in Attwood's original contributions it is easy to see the polish and grace that distinguish him from such contemporaries as Arnold and Kelly, and which evidently derive from Mozart's teaching. In many of these pieces, particularly the earlier ones, he adapted Mozart's own music to the English texts.

After 1801 there were only five more dramatic pieces, spread over the next quarter of a century, as Attwood was increasingly occupied with other kinds of music. He was one of the 30 original members of the Philharmonic

Society on its foundation in 1813 and one of its directors in 1816–20 and 1824–32, and he conducted one concert almost every year, usually including one of Mozart's symphonies. He was also concerned with several vocal societies, for which he composed a number of glees. In 1821 he composed an anthem *I was glad* for the coronation of his former patron, now George IV, and shortly afterwards was appointed organist of the king's newly built private chapel at Brighton, a sinecure position. He was one of the founding professors of the RAM in 1823. He succeeded his father as musician-in-ordinary to the king in 1825; finally, in 1836, he was appointed organist of the Chapel Royal in succession to Stafford Smith. During all this time the emphasis in his composition moved steadily in the direction of church and organ music. In 1831 he was again called upon for a coronation anthem, this time for the 65-year-old William IV (*O Lord, grant the king a long life*), and on his death he is said to have left behind a third which had been commissioned for the coronation of Victoria. He was buried beneath the organ in St Paul's Cathedral.

Attwood was a man of kind and genial disposition, and had many friends in the musical world. In his later years he had the pleasure of a close friendship with Mendelssohn, who stayed with him at his house on Beulah Hill, Norwood, on several occasions: the Fantasia op.16 no.2 was composed there in 1829. Mendelssohn dedicated to him his Three Preludes and Fugues op.37, and the autograph of a Kyrie eleison in A minor is inscribed 'For Mr. Attwood, Berlin, 24th March 1833'. Attwood was a great admirer of Mendelssohn's brilliant performances on the organ of St Paul's Cathedral, and was converted by them to a tardy recognition of the genius of Bach. He was not himself a great executant on the organ.

Attwood's compositions, whether for the stage, the church or the home, were profoundly affected by his intense experience as Mozart's pupil. But the influence did not take the form of direct imitation except in some of the earliest stage pieces; it is found rather in the feeling for melodic shape and the beautifully tasteful organization of harmony that distinguish him from his English contemporaries. His style is recognizably English, as much as it is Mozartian, and he had a particularly sensitive feeling for verbal accent: this is noticeable in the songs, including *The cold wave my love lies under*, in glees like *The Curfew*, and in the many treble solos in his longer anthems. The dramatic works are collections of songs and choruses in the manner of their time, offering little opportunity for imitation of Mozart's operatic methods. The early instrumental trios, like Mozart's but unlike most English 'accompanied sonatas' of the time, treat the string instruments on equal terms with the piano. Attwood's most ambitious music is in his great coronation anthems with orchestral accompaniment, containing elaborate counterpoint (but also unfortunately introducing patriotic airs), and in the Service in F, with its 'Gloria Patri' in strict canon. However, his slender reputation now rests not on these large-scale works, but on intimate, exquisitely polished pieces such as *Turn thy face from my sins* and the hymn *Come, Holy Ghost*. They are in direct line from the Mozart of *Ave verum corpus* and the Andante section of the Fantasia K608. To him they owe their balance and serenity, their melodic grace, and the sweetness of their full four-part harmony.

Thomas Attwood: portrait by an unknown artist (Royal College of Music, London)

In 1793 Attwood married Mary Denton, who bore him five sons and a daughter. Some of his most distinguished pupils were Thomas Attwood Walmisley (who was also his godson), John Goss, George Bridgetower and Cipriani Potter. Walmisley inherited or acquired many of his manuscript compositions; he published a selection of the church music in 1852, but many other compositions, including most of the organ music, passed from the Walmisley family to Frederick Fertel, organist of Bromley, and were dispersed after his death.

WORKS
all printed works published in London

all first performed in London; published in vocal score in same year unless otherwise stated; Mss of most librettos in US-SM, Larpent Collection

LCG – *Covent Garden*
LDL – *Drury Lane*
LLH – *Theatre Royal, Haymarket*

The Prisoner (musical romance, 3, J. Rose, after J.M. Boutet de Monvel), LLH, 18 Oct 1792, finale by G.M. Giornovichi, incl. music by Mozart

Ozmyn and Daraxa (musical romance, 2, J. Boaden), LLH, 7 March 1793, incl. music by Mozart and Giornovichi, only songs and choruses pubd

The Mariners (musical entertainment, 2, S. Birch), LLH, 10 May 1793, incl. music by T. Shaw, J.P.A. Martini, B. Ferrari, Mozart, 'Miss Bannister' and Dittersdorf

Caernarvon Castle, or The Birth of the Prince of Wales (entertainment, 2, Rose), LLH, 12 Aug 1793, incl. music by Mozart

The Packet Boat, or A Peep behind the Veil (musical farce, 2, Birch), LCG, 13 May 1794, unpubd

The Adopted Child (musical farce, 2, Birch), LDL, 1 May 1795

The Poor Sailor, or Little Ben and Little Bob (musical drama, 2, J. Bernard), LCG, 29 May 1795

The Smugglers (musical drama, 2, Birch), LDL, 13 April 1796, incl. music by R. Suett and J.G. Distler

The Fairy Festival (masque, 1, Rose), LDL, 13 May 1797, only 4
   songs pubd
The Irish Tar, or Which is the Girl? (musical piece, 1, W.C. Oulton),
   LLH, 24 Aug 1797, unpubd
Fast Asleep (farce, 2, Birch, after J. Powell), LDL, 28 Oct 1797, only
   2 songs pubd
Britain's Brave Tars!! or All for St Paul's (musical farce, 1, J.
   O'Keeffe), LCG, 19 Dec 1797, only 1 song pubd
The Devil of a Lover (musical farce, 2, G. Moultrie), LCG, 17 March
   1798, unpubd
Reform'd in Time (comic opera, 2, H. Heartwell), LCG, 23 May
   1798, unpubd
A Day at Rome (musical farce, 2, C. Smith), LCG, 17 Oct 1798,
   unpubd
The Mouth of the Nile, or The Glorious First of August (musical
   entertainment, 1, T.J. Dibdin), LCG, 25 Oct 1798, incl. music by
   Dibdin and J. Mazzinghi
Albert and Adelaide, or The Victim of Constancy (grand heroic
   romance, 3, Birch, after B.J. Marsollier and Boutet de Monvel),
   LCG, 11 Dec 1798, pf score of ov. (Paris, n.d.), collab. D. Steibelt,
   incl. music by Cherubini
The Magic Oak, or Harlequin Woodcutter (pantomime, 2, Dibdin),
   LCG, 29 Jan 1799, collab. F. Attwood
The Old Clothesman (comic op, 3, T. Holcroft), LCG, 2 April 1799,
   ov. by ?W. Parke
The Castle of Sorrento (comic op, 2, Heartwell and G. Colman (ii),
   after A.V.P. Duval), LLH, 13 July 1799, incl. music by Paisiello
The Red Cross Knights (play, 5, J.G. Holman, after F. von Schiller),
   LLH, 21 Aug 1799, incl. music by S. Arnold, J.W. Calcott and
   Mozart
True Friends (musical farce, 2, Dibdin), LCG, 19 Feb 1800
St David's Day (musical piece, 2, Dibdin), LCG, 25 March 1800
The Hermione, or Valour's Triumph (musical piece, 1, Dibdin),
   LCG, 5 April 1800, unpubd
Il Bondocani, or The Caliph Robber (serio-comic musical drama, 3,
   Dibdin), LCG, 15 Nov 1800; collab. J. Moorehead, incl. music by
   Mozart
Harlequin's Tour, or The Dominion of Fancy (pantomime, 1,
   Dibdin), LCG, 22 Dec 1800, collab. Moorehead
The Sea-side Story (operatic drama, 2, W. Dimond), LCG, 12 May
   1801, unpubd
The Escapes, or The Water Carrier (musical entertainment, 2,
   Holcroft, after J.N. Bouilly), LCG, 14 Oct 1801, incl. music by
   Cherubini
Adrian and Orilla, or A Mother's Vengeance (play, 5, Dimond),
   LCG, 15 Nov 1801, only 2 songs by Attwood pubd, collab. M.
   Kelly
The Curfew (farce, S, J. Tobin), LDL, 19 Feb 1807, only 1 song pubd
Guy Mannering, or The Gipsey's Prophecy (musical play, 3, D.
   Terry, after W. Scott), LCG, 12 March 1816, collab. H.R. Bishop
Elphi Bey, or The Arab's Faith (musical drama, 3, R. Hamilton),
   LDL, 17 April 1817, only 3 songs by Attwood pubd, collab. C.E.
   Horn and H. Smart, incl. music by Mozart
David Rizzio (serious opera, 3, Hamilton), LDL, 17 June 1820, only
   1 song by Attwood pubd, collab. J. Braham, T.S. Cooke and W.
   Reeve
The Hebrew Family or A Traveller's Adventures (play, 3), LCG, 8
   April 1825, collab. P. Cianchettini, J. Whitaker and J. Watson

VOCAL

Editions: *Services and Anthems Composed by Thomas Attwood*, ed.
   T.A. Walmisley (London, 1852) [W]
English Songs 1800–1860, ed. G. Bush and N. Temperley, MB, xliii
   (1979) [B]

sacred

4 morning and evening services, W: F, 1796; A, 1825; D, orch,
   1831–2; C, 1832
Morning and Evening Service, Bb (c1837)
4 Kyrie and Sanctus: E (1816), F (c1817), C (1828), G (c1833)
18 anthems (unacc. unless otherwise stated; all pubd): Teach me, O
   Lord, 1797, W; Be thou my judge, 1800; Blessed is he that
   considereth, 1804; Grant, we beseech thee, 1814, W; O God, who
   by the leading of a star, 1814, W; O Lord, we beseech thee, 1814,
   W; Teach me thy way, 1817, W; Turn thee again, O Lord, 1817; I
   was glad, with orch, 1821; Let thy hand be strengthened, 1821;
   My soul truly waiteth, 1823; Withdraw not thy mercy, 1827,
   W; O Lord, grant the king a long life, with orch, 1831; Bow down
   thine ear, c1833; Enter not into judgment, 1834; Let the words of

my mouth, 1835, W; Turn thy face from my sins, 1835; They that
   go down to the sea, 1837, W
Kyrie, Gloria (Lat.), Naples, 1784
Come, Holy Ghost, hymn, 1831 (1851)
God, that madest earth and heaven, vesper hymn (1835)
Psalm tunes, chants, responses, 9 sacred songs, 2 duets, some in *GB-
   Lbl*

secular

c50 songs pubd singly, including Coronach (W. Scott), Mez/Bar, pf
   (1810), B; The cold wave my love lies under (T. Moore), S/T, pf
   (1817), B; Go, lovely rose (E. Waller, H. Kirke White), T, pf
   (1835), B; 5 duets pubd singly; 9 Glees, 3-bvv (1828); c50 glees
   pubd singly

INSTRUMENTAL

Chbr: 3 Pf Trios, op.1 (?1787); Pf Trio, in Storace's Collection of
   Original Harpsichord Music (1789); 3 Pf Sonatas, ad lib vn, vc,
   op.2 (1791); Marches, pf
Wind insts: Royal Exchange March, 2 cl, 2 fl, hn, tpt, bn, serpent
   (?1803), pf score (?1803); Piece, 3 cl, 2 hn, bn, *GB-Lbl*;
   Divertimento, 2 basset hn, 2 ob, 2 hn, 2 bn, serpent, collab. Pleyel,
   Storace, *Lbl*
Org: March, Piece (1797); Dirge for Lord Nelson, d (1805);
   Cathedral Fugue, Eb
Pedagogical: Easy Progressive Lessons for Young Beginners, pf/hpd
   (c1795); A Short Introduction to the Pianoforte (?1805)
Arrs. of works by Beethoven, Hummel, Mayseder, Meyerbeer,
   Mozart, Spontini, Weber, Winter, mostly pf, other insts

OTHER WORKS

Exercises, ed. E. Hertzmann, C.B. Oldman, D. Heartz and A. Mann
   as *Thomas Attwoods Theorie- und Kompositionsstudien bei
   Mozart*, Wolfgang Amadeus Mozart: Neue Ausgabe sämtlicher
   Werke, X:30/i (Kassel, 1965)

BIBLIOGRAPHY

M. Kelly: *Reminiscences* (London, 1826, 2/1826/R1968 with
   introduction by A.H. King); ed. R. Fiske (London, 1975), 116
Obituaries, *Musical World*, viii (1838), 220–21, 227–8
D. Baptie: *Sketches of the English Glee Composers* (London, 1896),
   58ff
J.S. Bumpus: *A History of English Cathedral Music 1549–1889*
   (London, 1908/R), 400–25
F.G. Edwards: 'Thomas Attwood (1765–1838)', *MT*, xli (1900),
   788–94 [with letters between Attwood and Mendelssohn]
E. Hertzmann: 'Mozart and Attwood', *JAMS*, xii (1959), 178–84
C.B. Oldman: 'Thomas Attwood, 1765–1838', *MT*, cvi (1965),
   844–5
C.B. Oldman: 'Attwood's Dramatic Works', *MT*, cvii (1966), 23–7
R. Fiske: *English Theatre Music in the Eighteenth Century* (London,
   1973)
D. Heartz: 'Thomas Attwood's Lessons in Composition with
   Mozart', *PRMA* (1973–4), 175–83
N. Temperley, ed.: *Music in Britain: the Romantic Age 1800–1914*
   (London, 1981/R)
M. Argent, ed.: *Recollections of R.J.S. Stevens* (London, 1992)
W.J. Gatens: 'Thomas Attwood (1765–1838), forefather of Victorian
   Cathedral Music', Victorian Cathedral Music in Theory and
   Practice (Cambridge, 1986), 84–102

NICHOLAS TEMPERLEY

Atumpan. Goblet-shaped TALKING DRUM (membrano-
phone) of Ghana. *See also* DRUM, §I, 2(ii)(d).

Atys [Atis; first name unknown] (*b* St Domingue [now
Haiti], 18 April 1715; *d* Paris, 8 Aug 1784). French creole
flautist, composer and teacher. His skill as a flute virtuoso
and teacher made him renowned in Paris and Vienna, but
his concert career was cut short by a chin wound received
in a pistol duel. He was among the first flautists to use
crescendo and diminuendo instead of simple echo contrasts. His compositions, all published in Paris, are
primarily intended for amateur flautists: they include duos
'en forme de conversation' op.1 (1754), sonatas 'dans le
goût italien' op.2 (1756, lost), further duos and quartets,
a *Feste concertante* (1775, lost) and minuets for orchestra.

He also published two flute methods. (*Choron-FayolleD*; *FétisB*; *La BordeE*)

ROGER J.V. COTTE

Atzmon [Groszberger], Moshe (*b* Budapest, 30 July 1931). Israeli conductor. His family settled in British-mandated Palestine in 1944 and he followed Israeli custom in changing his original surname to the present Hebrew form. Having studied the piano and horn, he graduated from the Tel-Aviv Academy of Music in composition and conducting (1962) and was encouraged by Antal Dorati to pursue a conducting career. In London, where he studied at the GSM, he won the school's conducting prize in 1963, followed in 1964 by the first prize at the international conducting competition sponsored by the Royal Liverpool PO. In 1967 he conducted the Vienna PO at the Salzburg Festival. From 1969 to 1971 he was chief conductor of the Sydney SO, and in 1972 he became chief conductor of the NDR SO and of the Basle SO. After a spell in Tokyo as musical adviser for the Tokyo Metropolitan SO (1978–82), he served as principal conductor of the American SO (1982–4) and permanent conductor of the Nagoya PO, Japan (1986–92). His operatic début was in October 1969 with Rossini's *La Cenerentola* at the Deutsche Oper, Berlin, and he first appeared on record conducting the New Philharmonia Orchestra in 1968, having already brought a skilled baton technique and a lively personality to concerts in Britain, the USA and Israel. In 1991 he was appointed Generalmusikdirektor at Dortmund.

ARTHUR JACOBS

Aubade [aube] (Fr.: 'dawn song'). A term originally applied to music intended for performance in the morning. It has now become simply a generic title. In the 17th and 18th centuries, aubades were played at court by military bands in honour of French sovereigns, and in provincial towns to celebrate the election of municipal officials. The Provençal ALBA is a distant antecedent. In the 19th and 20th centuries the term and its Spanish equivalent, ALBORADA, came into use as the title of a characteristic piece, for example the *Aubade* for piano by Bizet and the *Aubade et allegretto* for strings and wind by Lalo (1872). Poulenc used it as the title of a more extended work, his 'choreographic concerto' for piano and 18 instruments (1929).

□

Auber, Daniel-François-Esprit (*b* Caen, 29 Jan 1782; *d* Paris, 12 May 1871). French composer. He composed mostly *opéras comiques*, and the foremost representative of this genre in 19th-century France.

1. Early life and works. 2. Collaboration with Scribe. 3. Style and influence.

1. EARLY LIFE AND WORKS.   He was the son of a royal huntsman, who became a dealer in art materials after the Revolution. He showed an early talent for the piano, studying with Ignace Antoine Ladurner; he also learnt to play the violin and cello, and had a fine baritone voice. He took part in chamber music recitals and was admitted into the Société Académique des Enfants d'Apollon as a composer in 1806. Among his earliest compositions were several *romances*, at least one string quartet, a piano trio and a concerto for violin, viola, cello and piano. At first he was expected to go into his father's business, and after the Peace of Amiens in 1802 he went to London to study commerce and learn English. He seems to have had some

success in London as a performer and as a composer of *romances* and quartets, and Malherbe ascribes his self-discipline and understatement to this stay (1911, p.3). The resumption of Anglo-French hostilities in 1803 was presumably the reason for his return to Paris, where he remained for the rest of his life.

On his return to the capital he composed a violin concerto and five cello concertos (at least three of which were published under the name of Lamarre). His first stage work, *Julie*, was composed in 1805 for an amateur society that met in the Salle Doyen. Here Auber met the artist Ingres (they remained friends until the latter's death in 1867). At the same time Auber began taking private lessons from Cherubini, with whom he studied composition for three years; he subsequently composed a fugue on a theme from Cherubini's *Faniska*. During this period Auber attended the salon of the Prince of Caraman (later the Prince of Chimay) in the Rue de Babylone as an *accompagnateur*, where musicians such as Rudolphe Kreutzer, Rode, Baillot and Duchambge performed alongside amateurs. He twice went to the prince's Belgian château to perform in comedies and operas in a fully equipped theatre that still survives. Auber composed a mass for three voices (1812) for the chapel of this chateau; the theme of the Prière in *La muette de Portici* is taken from its 'Dona nobis pacem'. In 1812 he wrote his second opera, *Jean de Chimay*, for the prince's theatre. In the same year, encouraged by his parents and by Cherubini, Auber decided to compose a one-act opera, *Le séjour militaire*, for the Salle Feydeau; it had a satisfactory 16 performances, and was revived in 1826 and staged in the provinces. For the next seven years, until his father's death, he led a carefree life. His decision to devote himself seriously to opera composition arose from the bankruptcy of his father, which forced Auber to provide for his family.

His next opera, *Le testament et les billets doux*, to a libretto by François-Antoine-Eugène de Planard, was staged on 18 September 1819. It was dropped from the repertory after 11 performances, but Auber achieved greater success with *La bergère châtelaine* (1820) and *Emma* (1821), both to librettos by Planard; they were also successful in their first performances in Germany.

2. COLLABORATION WITH SCRIBE.   At this time he entered upon what soon became a very close collaboration with Eugène Scribe. With five *opéras comiques* and the *drame lyrique Léocadie*, Scribe and Auber became the leading exponents of *opéra comique* in France, enjoying success in the German-speaking states, Denmark and England as well – reflected in the numbers of vocal scores, piano arrangements and translations of the librettos.

Germain Delavigne had written a libretto for a three-act opera on a revolutionary subject, entitled *Masaniello, ou La muette de Portici*, in 1825. After several reworkings by Scribe it emerged as the first grand opera. The production realized a new quality of historical and geographical realism, as well as social verisimilitude in the depiction of the relationships between the characters. Solomé as director and Pierre Cicéri as designer created a sensation with their use of the very latest stage techniques. Although the chorus for the Neapolitan insurgents ('Grâce pour notre crime') at the end of the opera, inserted at the insistence of the censors, makes them descredit their own rebellion, *La muette* made its mark as an opera of revolution. Thanks to its association with the Belgian revolution of 22 August 1830 it became widely regarded as a symbol of revolutionary sentiment, to which Auber's music made a decisive contribution. Throughout the opera reminiscences are used to create a network of musico-dramatic relationships, supported by a scheme of tonalities. The build-up of tension towards the last act-finale, where the D minor harmony suggests the second finale of *Don Giovanni*, is particularly compelling. Its most important dramaturgical innovation was the frequent alternation between crowd scenes and intimate encounters of individuals. With the five-act structure and the tragic ending its authors turned away from the traditional aesthetics of *tragédie lyrique*.

Wagner regarded it as 'something quite new' because of its 'unusual concision and drastic concentration of form'. Besides being the first grand opera, *La muette de Portici* was one of the great operatic successes of the 19th century. By 1882 it had had 505 performances in Paris, and it was performed in translated versions throughout Europe. Auber consolidated his international reputation with *La fiancée* and *Fra Diavolo*; the latter is still performed, though predominantly in Germany.

From 1830 to 1840 he wrote at least one new opera a year, mostly *opéras comiques*, but he also composed more serious works for the Paris Opéra: *Le dieu et la bayadère*, *Le philtre*, *Le serment*, *Gustave III*, *Le cheval de bronze* and *Le lac des fées*. For *Gustave II*, great attention was lavished on production, scenery and costumes, especially in the ball scene, which brought about 300 people onto the stage, more than 100 of whom took part in the sensational Galop. The turbulent circumstances of the work's genesis are also reflected in a score which is convincing in its overall conception but suffers from the very variable quality of individual numbers. The importance attached to the visual aspects of *grand opéra* is demonstrated by Louis Véron's assertion that *Gustave III* was spoilt by the false conception of costumes and scenery

Daniel-François-Esprit Auber: caricature by André Gill from the cover of 'L'éclipse' (1 March 1868)

in the first four acts; in Véron's view, the Louis XV costumes inhibited the performers from freely expressing their passions. The opera had a long-lived success in Germany, Austria and England. The ball act, often performed on its own in Paris, had a strong influence on similar tableaux in other operas, and it served Auber himself as the model for other, mostly shorter, parlante scenes in later operas (*Le domino noir*, for example).

As the extant correspondence between Auber and Scribe shows, their conception of characters and musical numbers in their comic operas depended a good deal on the performers available to them, and was not determined solely by aesthetic criteria. Scribe's letter of 25 August 1843 describes the casting of *La sirène*:

> I have managed to arrange for Roger to play the lead. This will mean a good deal of work for me, but none for you, because – and this is what made the problem difficult to solve – I have not changed anything affecting the music, except in the finale of the first act which you have not written.
>
> When I wrote the part for Chollet, having no alternative, I was very uneasy about it. Though he can still be good in big parts which are not naturalistic, Chollet is terrible when verisimilitude, animation and above all interest are required. It is impossible for him to be interesting, but now, with Roger, I shall have animation, interest and comedy. Moreover, I have placed the little aria of which you gave me the rough sketch for Mlle Lavoye, and I may add a little smuggler's song for Roger, which will not detract from his second-act aria.

Scribe's reference to a rough sketch (*monstre*) denotes a procedure known to have been employed in French opera since its early days, and Scribe and Auber frequently adopted it. Auber often composed solo arias before he received Scribe's verses; next the composer gave his librettist a 'rough sketch' with the metre and sometimes certain key words, and Scribe would use this sketch to write the text to be sung. Study of Scribe's autographs has shown that when he first provided Auber with a text he used isometrical verses with regular rhyme-schemes for solo arias; however, when fitting his verses to Auber's music, they were generally heterometrical with no regular rhyme-scheme at all.

Rossini had taken the opera-going public by storm with the Paris première of *Il barbiere di Siviglia* on 26 October 1819. In his early comic operas Auber was accused of falling under Rossini's influence, not only in the coloratura passages of his arias, but also in the number of ensembles, many more than in the works of his predecessors and having considerable dramatic and musical weight. However, with *Léocadie*, set in Portugal but evincing musical coloration closer to Spain, he soon developed his own style, which was regarded throughout Europe as typically French and typically Parisian.

3. STYLE AND INFLUENCE. In Auber's *opéras comiques*, the introductions to the first acts are generally comparable in importance to the finales. As a rule, the climax is reached at the latest with the finale of the second act, in a manner similar to Verdi's. Only in *Fra Diavolo* is the climax delayed until the finale of the third act, as in Auber's grand operas. By the early 1840s the Opéra-Comique was staging works of more demanding musical aspirations, including Donizetti's *La fille du régiment* and Halévy's *Guitarréro*, which rivalled the Opéra and Théâtre-Italien. Correspondingly, in the important and more serious works of his middle creative period (*L'ambassadrice*, 1836; *Le domino noir*, 1837; *Les diamants de la couronne*, 1841; *La part du diable*, 1843; and *Haydée*, 1847) the solo arias gain in individuality,

musical expressiveness and harmonic depth, influenced by the *drame lyrique*. On the whole, however, the ensemble is also pre-eminent in these works. The first-act, or more rarely the second-act, finale is the richest in action and musical content. In these mature works and in his last creative period Auber usually opens the first act with an aria (only *Le premier jour de bonheur*, 1868, and *Rêve d'amour*, 1869, begin with introductions).

Scribe and Auber broke more new ground in their five-act biblical opera *L'enfant prodigue* (1850), which is almost without action, and contrasts markedly with the ideas of Berlioz. No other work that Auber composed for the Opéra matches it in musical depth or stylistic aspiration. The character of the patriarch Ruben, who dominates the entire work, and the magnificent final scene of forgiveness are among the opera's outstanding features. In *Manon Lescaut* (1856), the café-scene in Act 2 paints a multi-faceted picture of contemporary society in a manner close to Offenbach; the culmination of the action in a dramatic, half-hour-long death-scene is still more astonishing, anticipating, within the *opéra comique* genre, the fatal outcome of *Carmen* by 19 years. At the age of 86, only three years before his death and at a time when the repertory in Paris was dominated by Offenbach's *opéras bouffes* and the operas of Verdi, Auber had another great success in France and Germany with *Le premier jour de bonheur*. The first performance of his last *opéra comique*, *Rêve d'amour*, took place in December 1869, but the orchestral score is now lost.

Unlike many of his Romantic contemporaries, Auber did not seem to have any lofty sense of mission. He was inclined to express himself ironically. Throughout his career he introduced into his operas easily accessible melodies that lodged in the memory after a single hearing and became popular in all classes of society. In this he was following a typically French tradition, dating back to the *airs de vaudeville* Lully used in his *tragédies*. Besides the various types of aria, Auber made use of such vocal genres as the *couplet*, barcarolle, ballade, nocturne, rondeau, chanson, *valse chantée*, tyrolienne, bolero, canon and *mélodie*, both as solo numbers and within the ensembles. He was first and foremost a melodist and avoided profound emotions and all emphatic and extreme forms of expression; his (frequently criticized) rhythmic style was influenced strongly by contemporary dance. In spite of the almost invariable dominance of melody, his ensembles are often the most interesting and best-constructed pieces in his operas. His ideals were those of the French tradition in general and *opéra comique* in particular: the greatest possible simplicity, clear lines and transparent structures, lightness of spirit and coloration, elegance, esprit and moderation in expression.

Few if any remarks by Auber about composers he admired have survived, but his library gives some clues as to his preferences. The scores he owned include the operas of Gluck, Piccinni, Sacchini, Cherubini, Rossini, Grétry, Dalayrac, Monsigny and, especially, Mozart, whom Auber admired above all others.

Although Auber lived in Paris almost uninterruptedly, the popularity of his operas led to a flood of publication of his works throughout Europe and in America. Editions of the individual opera librettos and piano arrangements were printed in immense quantities, and particularly successful numbers gave rise to more than 400 transcriptions and free instrumental arrangements – sonatinas, fantasias, potpourris and *mélanges* – ranging from the piano to military bands and salon orchestras. The overtures of most of his operas were among the most popular items played at concerts, as well as in salons and private homes. Berlioz was among his sternest critics in France, while the hostile attitudes of Schumann and Mendelssohn in Germany were in marked contrast to the enthusiastic views of Wagner.

In addition to his activities as an opera composer, Auber was appointed director of the Paris Conservatoire in February 1842. His term of office was marked by special emphasis on vocal tuition, the separation of classes for male and female singers, provision of boarding accommodation for students, performances of opera in costume, and performances in the Conservatoire of music-theatre works by winners of the Prix de Rome. He was also appointed *maître de chapelle* by Napoleon III, and composed a substantial quantity of music for the royal chapel in the Louvre, the great majority of which remains unpublished. He had 40 choristers and 40 instrumentalists at his disposal, who performed under the direction of conductors from the Opéra. The most frequently performed of his sacred works was *Domine salvum fac*, first heard in Ste Marie-Madeleine in about 1849. Most of the pieces Auber wrote for the royal chapel are plain in style, homophonic and melody-led, and nearly all of them survive in two versions: one with orchestral accompaniment, and one with organ, with or without harp. The string quartets Auber composed in 1870 have long been lost; like other lost works they once belonged to Malherbe.

Auber was the recipient of numerous honours and orders, and a member of various institutions: he rose through the degrees of the Légion d'Honneur (from 1825); he was elected to the Académie des Beaux-Arts of the Institut de France in succession to Gossec (1829); he was also director of the Concerts de la Cour (1839) and a member of several European orders.

WORKS

unless otherwise stated, works were first performed in Paris and published in Paris in the year of first performance

For fuller list see H. Schneider: *Chronologisch-thematisches Verzeichnis sämtlicher Werke von D.F.E. Auber: AWK* (Hildesheim, 1994) [S]

STAGE

S
1	Julie [L'erreur d'un moment] (comédie, 1, J.-M. Boutet de Monvel), Salle Doyen, 1805, unpubd
2	Jean de Chimay [Le château de Couvain] (oc, 3, N. Lemercier), Belgium, Château de Chimay, Sept 1812, unpubd
3	Le séjour militaire (oc, 1, J.-N. Bouilly and E. Mercier-Dupaty), OC (Feydeau), 17 Feb 1813
4	Le testament et les billets doux (comédie mêlée de chant, 1, F.-A.-E. de Planard), OC (Feydeau), 18 Sept 1819
5	La bergère châtelaine (oc, 3, Planard), OC (Feydeau), 27 Jan 1820
6	Emma, ou La promesse imprudente (oc, 3, Planard), OC (Feydeau), 7 July 1821
7	Leicester, ou Le château de Kenilworth (oc, 3, E. Scribe and Mélesville [A.-H.-J. Duveyrier], after W. Scott: *Kenilworth*), OC (Feydeau), 25 Jan 1823
8	La neige, ou Le nouvel Eginhard (oc, 4, Scribe and G. Delavigne), OC (Feydeau), 9 Oct 1823
9	Vendôme en Espagne (drame lyrique, 1, A.-J.-S. d'Empis and E. Mennechet), Opéra, 5 Dec 1823, collab. Hérold
10	Les trois genres (prologue, Scribe, Dupaty and M. Pichat), Odéon, 27 April 1824, collab. A. Boieldieu
11	Le concert à la cour, ou La débutante (oc, 1, Scribe and Mélesville), OC (Feydeau), 5 May 1824

12 Léocadie (drame lyrique, 3, Scribe and Mélesville, after
    M. de Cervantes: *La fuerza de la sangre*), OC (Feydeau), 4
    Nov 1824

13 Le maçon (oc, 3, Scribe and Delavigne), OC (Feydeau), 3
    May 1825

14 Le timide, ou Le nouveau séducteur (oc, 3, Scribe and
    Saintine [X. Boniface]), OC (Feydeau), 2 June 1826

15 Fiorella (oc, 3, Scribe), OC (Feydeau), 28 Nov 1826

16 La muette de Portici [Masaniello] (op, 5, Scribe and
    Delavigne), Opéra, 29 Feb 1828

17 La fiancée (oc, 3, Scribe, after M. Mason and R. Brucker:
    Les contes de l'atelier), OC (Feydeau), 10 Jan 1829

18 Fra Diavolo, ou L'hôtellerie de Terracine (oc, 3, Scribe),
    OC (Ventadour), 28 Jan 1830

19 Le dieu et la bayadère, ou La courtisane amoureuse (op, 2,
    Scribe), Opéra, 13 Oct 1830

20 Le philtre (op, 2, Scribe), Opéra, 15 June 1831

21 La marquise de Brinvilliers (drame lyrique, 3, Scribe and
    Castil-Blaze [F.-H.-J. Blaze]), OC (Ventadour), 31 Oct
    1831, collab. Batton, H.-M. Berton, Blangini, A.
    Boieldieu, Carafa, Cherubini, Hérold and Paer

22 Le serment (ou Les faux monnoyeurs) (op, 3, Scribe and
    E.-J.-E. Mazères), Opéra, 1 Oct 1832

23 Gustave III, ou Le bal masqué (op historique, 5, Scribe),
    Opéra, 27 Feb 1833

24 Lestocq, ou L'Intrigue et l'Amour (oc, 4, Scribe), OC
    (Bourse), 24 May 1834

25 Le cheval de bronze (opéra-féerie, 3, Scribe), Opéra, 28
    March 1835; rev. as opéra-ballet, Opéra, 21 Sept 1857

26 Actéon (oc, 1, Scribe), OC (Bourse), 23 Jan 1836

27 Les chaperons blancs (oc, 3, Scribe), OC (Bourse), 26
    March 1836

28 L'ambassadrice (oc, 3, Scribe), OC (Bourse), 21 Dec 1836

29 La fête de Versailles (intermède en deux parties, Scribe),
    Versailles, 10 June 1837

30 Le domino noir (oc, 3, Scribe), OC (Bourse), 2 Dec 1837

31 Le bourgeois gentilhomme (comédie-ballet, Molière),
    1838, Turkish scene

32 Le lac des fées (op, 5, Scribe and Mélesville), Opéra, 1
    April 1839

33 Zanetta, ou Jouer avec le feu (oc, 3, Scribe and J.-H.
    Vernoy de Saint-Georges), OC (Favart), 18 May 1840

34 Les diamants de la couronne (oc, 3, Scribe and Saint-
    Georges), OC (Favart), 6 March 1841

35 Le duc d'Olonne (oc, 3, Scribe and Saintine), OC (Favart),
    4 Feb 1842

36 La part du diable (oc, 3, Scribe), OC (Favart), 16 Jan
    1843

37 La sirène (oc, 3, Scribe), OC (Favart), 26 March 1844

38 La barcarole, ou L'Amour et la Musique (oc, 3, Scribe),
    OC (Favart), 22 April 1845

39 Les premiers pas (oc, 1, A. Royer and G. Vaez), Opéra-
    National, 15 Nov 1847, collab. A. Adam, Carafa, Halévy

40 Haydée, ou Le secret (oc, 3, Scribe, after P. Mérimée: *Six
    et quatre*), OC (Favart), 28 Dec 1847

41 L'enfant prodigue (op, 5, Scribe), Opéra, 6 Dec 1850

42 Zerline, ou La corbeille d'oranges (op, 3, Scribe), Opéra,
    16 May 1851

43 Marco Spada (oc, 3, Scribe and Delavigne, final scene
    after H. Vernet: *La confession du bandit*), OC (Favart),
    21 Dec 1852; rev. as (46) Marco Spada, ou Le bandit
    (ballet, 3, J. Mazilier), Opéra, 1 April 1857

44 Jenny Bell (oc, 3, Scribe), OC (Favart), 2 June 1855

45 Manon Lescaut (oc, 3, Scribe, after A.-F. Prévost), OC
    (Favart), 23 Feb 1856

47 Le cheval de bronze (op ballet, 3, Scribe), Opéra, 21 Sept
    1857

48 La circassienne (oc, 3, Scribe), OC (Favart), 2 Feb 1861

49 La fiancée du Roi de Garbe (oc, 3, Scribe and Saint-
    Georges), OC (Favart), 11 Jan 1864

50 Le premier jour de bonheur (oc, 3, A.-P. Dennery and E.
    Cormon), OC (Favart), 15 Feb 1868

51 Rêve d'amour (oc, 3, Dennery and Cormon), OC (Favart),
    20 Dec 1869

?music in La gitana (ballet, 3, Taglioni), St Petersburg, Bol'shoy, 23
Nov 1838, collab. Schmidt

SACRED

52 Messe solennelle, 3vv, orch, 1812; Dona nobis later used
    in La muette de Portici (O dieu puissant), 1828

53 Litanie de la Sainte Vierge, 4vv, orch, *c*1815

54 Hymne à Sainte Cécile, *c*1840

55 Domine salvum fac rem publicam, 4vv, orch, *c*1849

67 O crux ave, 4vv, hp, pf, 1854

71 Parce Domine, 4vv, org, 1854

72 Sub tuum praesisium, 4vv, org, 1854

91 Ecce panis angelorum, 4vv, org, 1860

92 Pie Jesu, S, org, 1861

95 Veni creator, 4vv, org, 1864

98 Ave Maria, S, org, 1865

103 O quam tristis, 3vv, hp, hmn, org

104 Stabat mater/Virgo virginem, chorus, hmn, hp, org

107 O Dieu puisant, chorus, 2 cl, 2 bn

11 Ky, S56, 57, 58, 59, 73, 88, 90, 96, 97, 99 (1854–70); 2
    Ky and Cr, S60, 61 (1854); 3 Gl S62, 75, 94 (1854–63); 7
    Bs, S63, 77, 78, 79, 80, 83, 84 (1854–9); 7 Ag, S64, 65,
    66, 81, 93, 101, 102 (1854–*c*1870); 12 O salutaris, S68,
    69, 70, 74, 85, 86, 87, 89, 105, 106, 108 (1854–*c*1870)

SECULAR VOCAL

109 Non s'è più barbaro, T, orch, 1798

110 Ridotto a questo segno/Rendi mi figlio mio, T, orch, 1799

111 Tu t'éloignes de moi (scene from Procris), S, str orch,
     *c*1800

113 Quel ta page (finale of Act 3, Judith Arthur), frag.

114 Chasseur, qui parcourez la plaine, *c*1800

116 Je suis cette cousine, S, orch

117 Fêtez par vos chants, choeur chinois, *c*1834

140 Sauve, ô mon Dieu, le roi, *c*1843; later used in Jenny Bell,
     1855

118–49 Romances and chansonettes, *c*1783–1869

150 Chant des polonais (cant.), 1830; also known as La
     varsovienne

151 Cantate por le dîner du roi, 1837

152 Cantate pour l'inauguration du statue de Henri IV, 1843

153 Cantate pour le mariage de Napoléon III, 1853

155 Cantate pour la prise de Sébastopol, 1855

154 Cantate pour le baptême du Prince Impérial, 1856

156 Cantate pour la distribution des prix de la Société des
     Gens de Lettres, 1856

157 Magenta (cant.), 1859

INSTRUMENTAL

158 Sonata, C, pf, 1794/5

159 String Quartet, C, 1799

160 String Quartet, 1800, lost

162 Trio, D, pf, vn, vc, op.1 (Paris, *c*1806)

163 Piano Quartet, e, *c*1808

164 Fugue on a theme from Cherubini's Faniska, *c*1808

165 Violin Concerto, D, 1808, ed. S. Beck (New York, 1938)

166 Cello Concerto, no.1, a, *c*1809

167 Cello Concerto, no.2, D, solo part only, *c*1809

168 Cello Concerto, no.3, B♭, *c*1809

169 Cello Concerto, no.4, lost, mentioned by Fétis

170 Cello Concerto, no.5, D, *c*1809 [two mvts only]

171 Air varié, vc, orch/pf, *c*1807, lost, mentioned by Fétis

172 8 pieces, 2 vc, 1808

173 Air de danse, for Gluck's Iphigénie, 1811, lost

174 Overture

175 Overture

176 Variations on a theme by Handel, 1817: 1 Variations, 2
     Variations, 3 Dans le style de Handel, 4 Allegro maestoso,
     5 Andante con moto

177–200 Pieces for orch/pf, *c*1834–62

THEORETICAL WORKS

Règles de contrepoint, 1808

Quelques sujets de fugue

*Fugues et contrepoints, sujets de fugues pour les concours, datés de
    1833 à 1870, esquisses et réalisations*

Leçons de solfège à changements de clef, 1842–69

Leçons pour la lecture à première vue, 1844–70

*Observations … sur la méthode de musique de M. le docteur Emile
    Chevé* (Paris, 1860)

Recueil des leçons de solfège à changements de clef, 1842–69 (Paris,
    1886)

BIBLIOGRAPHY

X. Eyma and A. de Lucy: *Auber* (Paris, 1841)

L. de Loménie: *Auber* (Paris, 1842)

V. Véron: *Mémoires d'un bourgeois de Paris*, iii (Paris, 1854)

E. de Mirécourt: *Auber* (Paris, 1857)

B. Jouvin: *Auber: sa vie et ses oeuvres* (Paris, 1864)

E. Hanslick: *Geschichte des Concertwesens in Wien* (Vienna, 1869) [incl. 'Ein Besuch bei Auber', ii, 479–82, and 'Auber', ii, 530–34]

R. Wagner: 'Erinnerungen an Auber', *Gesammelte Schriften und Dichtungen* (Leipzig, 1871–3), ix (1873), 51–73; Eng. trans., ed. W.A. Ellis (London, 1892–9/R), v, 35–55

V. Massé: *Notice sur la vie et les travaux de D.F.E. Auber* (Paris, 1873)

A. Pougin: *Auber: ses commencements, les origines de sa carrière* (Paris, 1873)

J. Carlez: *L'oeuvre d'Auber* (Caen, 1874)

E. Hanslick: 'Auber', *Die moderne Oper*, ix: *Aus neuer und neuester Zeit* (Berlin, 1875, 3/1911), 123–37

H. Blaze de Bury: 'Scribe et Auber', *Revue des deux mondes*, xxxv (1879), 43–75

A. Kohut: *Auber*(Leipzig, 1895)

L. Dauriac: *La psychologie dans l'opéra français: Auber, Rossini, Meyerbeer* (Paris, 1897)

E. Prout: 'Auber's Le philtre and Donizetti's L'elisir d'amore: a Comparison', *MMR*, xxx (1900), 25–8, 49–53, 73–8

J. Chantavoine: 'Quelques lettres inédites d'Auber', *RHCM*, iii (1903), 161ff

C. Malherbe: *Auber* (Paris, 1911)

H. Grierson: 'My Visit to Auber', *English Review*, xviii (1914), 173–86

J. Tiersot: 'Auber', *ReM*, no.140 (1933), 265–78

A.B. Benson: 'Gustavus III in the Librettos of Foreign Operas', *Scandinavian Studies Presented to George T. Flom* (Urbana, IL, 1942), 92–105

A. Ringer: 'Fra Diavolo', *MQ*, xxxviii (1952), 642–4

R. Longyear: *D.F.E. Auber (1782–1871): a Chapter in the History of the Opéra Comique, 1800–1870* (diss., Cornell U., 1957)

R. Longyear: 'La muette de Portici', *MR*, xix (1958), 37–46

F. D'Amico: 'Il Ballo in maschera prima di Verdi', *Bollettino quadrimestrale dell'Istituto di Studi Verdiani*, i (1960), 1251–1328

W. Börner: *Die Opern von Daniel-François-Esprit Auber* (diss., Leipzig U., 1962)

R. Longyear: 'Le livret bien fait: the Opéra Comique Librettos of Eugène Scribe', *Southern Quarterly*, ii (1962–3), 169–92

C. Casini: 'Tre Manon', *Chigiana*, xxviii (1973), 171–217

K. Pendle: 'Scribe, Auber and the Count of Monte Cristo', *MR*, xxxiv (1973), 210–20

K. Pendle: *Eugène Scribe and the French Opera of the Nineteenth Century* (Ann Arbor, 1979)

S. Slatin: 'Opera and Revolution: La muette de Portici and the Belgian Revolution of 1830 Revisited', *JMR*, iii (1979), 45–62

Auber et l'opéra romantique(Paris, 1982) [exhibition catalogue]

L. Finscher: 'Aubers La muette de Portici und die Anfänge der Grand opéra', *Festschrift Heinz Becker*, ed. J. Schläder and R. Quandt (Laaber, 1982), 87–105

A. Gier: 'Manon Lescaut als Fabel von der Grille und der Ameise: D.F.E. Auber (1856)', *JbO*, i (1985), 73–89

J. Mongrédien: 'Variations sur un thème, Masaniello: du héros de l'histoire à celui de La muette de Portici', *JbO*, i (1985), 90–121

D. Kämper and P.-E. Knabe: 'Un requiem pour Manon', *Les écrivains français et l'opéra*: Cologne, 1986, 185–95

D. Rieger: 'La Muette de Portici von Auber/Scribe: eine Revolutionsoper mit antirevolutionärem Libretto', *Romanistische Zeitschrift für Literaturgeschichte*, x (1986), 349–59

J. Fulcher: *The Nation's Image: French Grand Opera as Politics and Politicized Art* (Cambridge, 1987)

H. Schneider: 'Die Barkarole und Venedig', *L'opera tra Venezia e Parigi*, ed. M.T. Muraro (Florence, 1988), 11–56

H.R. Cohen, ed.: *The Original Staging Manuals for Twelve Parisian Operatic Premières*(Stuyvesant, NY, 1991) [incl. production books for Fra Diavolo and La muette de Portici]

P. Vendrix, ed.: *Grétry et l'Europe de l'opéra-comique: Liège, 1991*

A. Gerhard: *Die Verstädterung der Oper* (Stuttgart, 1992)

H. Schneider and N. Wild: *La Muette de Portici: kritische Ausgabe des Librettos und Dokumentation ihrer ersten Inszenierung* (Tübingen, 1993)

H. Schneider: 'Wie komponierten Scribe und Auber eine Opéra comique, oder Was lehrt uns die Entstehungsgeschichte des Fra Diavolo', *Die Opéra comique und ihr Einfluss auf das europaische Musiktheater im 19. Jahrhundert: Frankfurt 1994*, 235–269

H. Schneider: 'Zur Entstehung und Gestalt des Domino noir', *D'un opéra à l'autre: hommage à Jean Mongrédien*, ed. J. Gribenski (Paris, 1996), 295–302

H. Schneider: 'Verdis Parlante und seine französischen Vorbilder', *Traditionen, Neuansätze: für Anna Amalie Abert*, ed. K. Hortschansky (Tutzing, 1997), 519–40

H. Schneider: *Correspondance d'Eugène Scribe et de D.F.E. Auber* (Liège, 1998)

H. Schneider: *Cavatine, Cantabile et Cabaletta cher Scribe et Auber* (forthcoming)

HERBERT SCHNEIDER

Aubert. French family of violinists and composers. They were active in Paris during the 18th century.

(1) Jacques Aubert [*le vieux, le père*]   (*b* Paris, 30 Sept 1689; *d* Belleville, nr Paris, 17/18 May 1753). He was probably a son of Jean Aubert, a member of the 24 Violons du Roi until his death in 1710. By 1717 Jacques Aubert was known as a dancing-master, violinist and composer, working at the Théâtres de la Foire, and had written the music for at least five ballets and comedies. In 1719, the year in which he married Marie Louise Lecat and published his first book of violin sonatas, Aubert was appointed to the service of Louis-Henri, Duke of Bourbon and Prince of Condé. In this capacity he composed a *Fête royale* and a *Ballet des XXIV heures* for the duke's entertainment when the young Louis XV passed through Chantilly to Reims in 1722; Aubert played the violin in the role of Orpheus in the latter work.

In 1727 Aubert succeeded Noël Converset in the 24 Violons du Roi, remaining a member until 1746, and in the next year he accepted a position with the Académie Royale de Musique and was named first violinist of the Opéra orchestra, with which he performed for the next 24 years. He made his début at the Concert Spirituel in 1729, and often played there until 1740.

Like many of his contemporaries, Aubert was greatly influenced by the Italian style. At the Concert Spirituel he must have heard and possibly played concertos and sonatas by Vivaldi and Corelli. Jean Baptiste Senaillé, Aubert's teacher (with whom he played a sonata for two violins at the Concert Spirituel in 1730), may have stimulated his growing interest in Italian music, and he was encouraged too by Madame de Prie, a friend of Aubert's patron, the Duke of Bourbon, and an adherent of the Italian style.

Aubert's large output as a composer includes ballet and dance music, *opéras comiques*, concertos, sonatas for violin and continuo and what he called 'concerts de simphonie' (pieces in suite form for trio, to which different sonorities could be added). He wrote the first violin concertos to be printed in France; whether they are the first concertos by a Frenchman is questionable (see Paillard and Brofsky). Of the stage works, *La reine des Péris* is perhaps the most interesting. In keeping with its more serious tone it was staged at the Opéra. Called a *comédie persane*, the work has a continuous plot and is fully sung. It is thus one of the earliest examples of French comic opera with sung dialogue.

Aubert was more than a composer of salon music or an imitator of the Italian style. While he accepted the basic concerto and sonata form from the Italian school, and their belief that the violin should be more than an instrument *pour faire danser*, he retained many French elements in his music, the most characteristic being the use of the gavotte, menuet, or other dance form as the slow middle movement and the fully written-out melodic embellishment of the solo pieces.

WORKS
(printed works published in Paris; op. nos. from Nouvelle edition,
op.1 (1794))

STAGE
(opéras comiques unless otherwise stated)

La paix triomphante (ballet), 1713, lost

Arlequin gentilhomme malgré lui, ou L'amant supposé (3, A.-R. Lesage and d'Orneval), Paris, Foire St Germain, 3 Feb/27 March 1716; Act 3 perf. as Les arrêts de l'amour (1), Paris, Foire St Germain, 17 July 1716, music in Le Théâtre de la Foire, ii (1721)

Arlequin Hulla, ou La femme répudiée (1, Lesage and d'Orneval), Paris, Foire St Laurent, 24 July 1716, music in Le Théâtre de la Foire, ii (1721)

La fête champêtre et guérrière (ballet), 1716; as op.30 (c1746)

Les animaux raisonnables (1, L. Fuzelier and M.-A. Legrand), Paris, Foire St Germain, 25/27 Feb 1718; collab. Gillier; airs in Le Théâtre de la Foire, iii (1721)

Diane (divertissement, A. Danchet), Chantilly, 8 Sept 1721; sym. only; vocal music by L.T. Bourgeois pubd (1721)

Le regiment de la calotte (1, Fuzelier, Lesage and d'Orneval), Paris, Foire St Laurent, 1 Sept 1721; airs in Le Théâtre de la Foire, v (1724)

Fête royale (divertissement), Chantilly, 4–8 Nov 1722; pubd (1722), see La Laurencie, i (1922), 203

Le ballet de 24 heures (comédie, prol, 4, Legrand), Chantilly, 5 Nov 1722; as op.6 (1723); music possibly known as Le ballet de Chantilly (1723)

La reine des Péris (comédie persane, prol, 5, Fuzelier), Paris, Opéra, 10 April 1725; as op.5 (1725)

La reine des Péris (parody and vaudeville, 1, Lesage and d'Orneval), n.d.; parody of the above, F-Pn

La triple Hécate (ballet, 2 scenes, C.-J.-F. Hénault), n.d., lib in Oeuvres inédites (1806)

Symphonie for T.-L. Bourgeois' Diane, 1721

Numerous airs and dances pubd in 18th-century anthologies

INSTRUMENTAL

Premier (–IVᵉ) livre de [10] sonates, vn, bc: op.1 (1719); op.2 (1721); op.3 (1723); op.4 (1731); Vᵉ livre de [6] sonates, vn, bc, op.25 (1738)

Pièces, 2 fl/vn, première suite (1723)

Concert de simphonies, suite première (–XIIᵉ), vns/fls/obs, bc: op.8 (1730); opp.9–12 (1731); op.13, also for viols/musettes (1733); opp. 18–23 (1735–7)

Les amuzettes, vielles/musettes/vns/fls/obs, op.14 (c1733)

Pièces, 2 vn/fl, op.15 (c1734); ed. H. Ruf (Mainz, 1984)

Les petits concerts, musettes/vielles/vns/fls/obs, op.16 (1734); ed. J. Harf (Wilhelmshaven, 1975)

[6] Concerto, 4 vn, vc, bc, op.17 (1734); 2 ed. R. Blanchard (Paris, 1973)

Sonates, 2 vn, op.24 (1738)

[4] Concerto, 4 vn, vc, bc, op.26 (1739); no.4 as Le carillon (n.d.); 2 ed. R. Blanchard (Paris, 1973)

Les jolis airs, vn, premier (–VIᵉ) livre: opp.27–9 (c1740–45); op.31 (1749); opp.32–3 (c1750)

Menuets nouveaux avec la basse (n.d.)

Various pieces pubd in 18th-century anthologies

(2) Louis Aubert [*le jeune, le fils*] **(i)** (*b* Paris, 15 May 1720; *d* after 1783). Eldest son of (1) Jacques Aubert. Taught by his father and hailed as a child prodigy, he was a back-desk violinist at the Opéra by the time he was 11 and perhaps even when he was only eight. In 1732 Joseph Francoeur nominated him to the 24 Violons du Roi, although he was not officially appointed until 1746. In 1753 he offered his father's violin for sale: it was a 17th-century instrument designed by Nicoló Amati. By 1756 he was first violinist and one of the principal conductors of the Opéra orchestra. He retired from these duties in 1774 with a pension and special gratuities 'in consideration of 43 years of service'; his name can be found on lists of patrons as late as 1783. Considering that he was active at a later time, Louis was a more conservative composer

than his father; his sonatas, each of which is really a series of dances, reflect the French early 18th-century style. He is remembered more for his *simphonies*, which have been mentioned among the precursors of the French symphony; but his works seem to look backward rather than forward. In four of the six *simphonies*, for example, all the movements are in the same key, and in orchestrating them he used three violins and bass without a viola as intermediate voice, the combination that his father had used in the concertos of the 1730s.

An Etienne-Louis Aubert, presumably distinct from Louis (and probably a younger brother), took (1) Jacques Aubert's place in the 24 Violons in 1746 and was relieved of his position on Jacques' death in 1753; no compositions survive in his name.

WORKS
all published in Paris

[6] Sonates, vn, bc, op.1 (1750); some for fl
6 simphonies à quatre, 3 vn, bc, op.2 (1755)
6 trio, 2 vn, vc (n.d.)

(3) Jean-Louis Aubert (*b* Paris, 15 Dec 1732; *d* c1810). Writer, dramatist and abbé, son of (1) Jacques Aubert. He may have composed some of the music to his own plays (*Jephté ou le voeu*, 1765; and *La mort d'Abel*, 1765), but he is remembered more for his essays on music, the most famous being his reply to J.-J. Rousseau's controversial *Lettre sur la musique françoise*. In his *Refutation suivie et détaillée des principes de M. Rousseau de Genève touchant la musique françoise* (1754) (taking up arms in the Querelle des Bouffons) Aubert met Rousseau on his own ground and, in language often sarcastic and witty, stressed the genius of French composers such as Rameau, Leclair and Mondonville.

BIBLIOGRAPHY
BenoitMC; BrookSF; LabordeMP; La LaurencieEF; NewmanSBE

L. de La Laurencie: 'Jacques Aubert et les premiers concertos français de violon', *BSIM*, ii/1 (1906), 441–53

L. de La Laurencie and G. de Saint-Foix: 'Contribution à l'histoire de la symphonie française vers 1750', *Année musicale* (1911), 1–123

C.D. Brenner: *A Bibliographical List of Plays in the French Language, 1700–1789* (Berkeley, 1947, 2/1979)

J.-F. Paillard: 'Les premiers concertos français pour instruments à vent', *ReM*, no.226 (1955), 144–62

H. Brofsky: 'Notes on the Early French Concerto', *JAMS*, xix (1966), 87–91

M. Landowski and G. Morançon: *Louis Aubert, musicien français* (Paris, 1967)

M. Benoit: *Versailles et les musiciens du roi, 1661–1733* (Paris, 1971)

D. Launay, ed.: *La Querelle des Bouffons* (Geneva, 1973) [repr., with introduction and index of 61 pamphlets pubd Paris, 1752–4]

H. Charnassé: 'Le commerce des instruments au XVIIIe siècle, d'après les annonces, affiches et avis divers, i (1751–1754)', *Instruments et musique instrumentale*, ed. H. Charnassé (Paris, 1986), 161–223

ELIZABETH KEITEL/M. SIGNORILE

Aubert, Louis(-François-Marie) (ii) (*b* Paramé, Ille-et-Vilaine, 19 Feb 1877; *d* Paris, 9 Jan 1968). French composer. Something of a child prodigy, Aubert sang with Fauré at the Madeleine, and as a boy treble took the solo part in the first performance of his Requiem. He entered the Paris Conservatoire in 1887 and became a pupil of Marmontel, Lavignac and Diémer and subsequently of Fauré. Aubert wrote songs and piano music as well as several ballets and incidental music but left only one opera, *La forêt bleue*, a fairy-tale piece with a happy ending that engagingly depicts the original characters of Pérrault.

While his early songs are little more than salon pieces, his mature language was influenced by Fauré, in its turns of harmony, and later by Ravel. He became a masterly orchestrator and employed modes extensively. *Dryade*, a programmatic work dating from the time of *La forêt bleue*, is typical of a style which uses Ravelian harmony and exotic arabesques. The successful *Habanera* for orchestra marked a distinct change of approach to a more dissonant style. The influence of jazz emerges in the ballet *Cinéma*, a series of pastiche pieces on various film stars, while the orchestral *Offrande*, a tribute to the victims of war, leaves behind the Ravelian style in favour of an elegiac language which uses dissonant added notes and octatonic devices. The several orchestrations he made of his songs made a significant contribution to this repertory. As a pianist, Aubert gave the first performance in 1911 of Ravel's *Valses nobles et sentimentales*, a work which is dedicated to him. His writings include *Notice sur la vie et les travaux de Gustave Charpentier* (Paris, 1956) and *L'orchestre* (Paris, 1951), the latter written in collaboration with Landowski.

WORKS
(selective list)

VOCAL

Songs (1v, pf, unless otherwise stated): Sous bois (L. Tiercelin) (1892); Vieille chanson espagnole (A. Houssaye) (1892); Rimes tendres (A. Silvestre), 1v, orch, 1896–8, arr. 1v, pf (1900); Fatum (A. Oeris), 1897; Melancholia (A.L. Hettich), 1897; L'inconnu (M. de Tonquedec) (1899); Légende (R. de Marès) (1899); Noël pastorale (Hettich) (1899); Péché véniel (Ludana) (1899); Sur le bord (Oeris) (1899); Chanson de mer (Sully-Prudhomme), 1900; La lampe du ciel (C.M.R. Leconte de Lisle), Mez, T, 1900; La lettre (H. Barbusse), 1900, orchd (1914); D'un berceau (Hettich), 1900; Les yeux (Sully-Prudhomme), 1900, orchd (1909); Déclaration (H. Giraud), 1901; Hélène (A. de Bengy-Puyvallée), 1901, also orchd; Secret aveu (E. Haraucourt), 1901; Les cloches (Ludana), 1902, arr. 1v, female vv, chorus, orch; Nocturne (P. Verlaine), Mez, Bar/T, 1902; Cache-cache (de Bengy-Puyvallée), Mez, Bar, (1903), arr. S, chorus; Sérénade (H. Vacaresco), 1906, orchd (1919); Première (de Bengy-Puyvallée) (1907); Crépuscules d'Automne (F. Hérold and others), 1908, 2 also orchd; Odelette (H. de Régnier), 1910; Roses du soir (R. Vivien), 1910, orchd (1910); Nuit mauresque (Vivien), 1911, orchd (1911); 2 poèmes (J. Chenevière) (1913), also orchd; 6 poèmes arabes (F. Toussaint), 1915–17, orchd 1919; Aigues marines (Vivien), 1918; Au pays (L.-P. Fargue), orchd, 1920; De Ceylan (R. Chalupt), 1920; Sérénade mélancolique (G. Jean-Aubry), 1923, also orchd; La fontaine d'Hélène (P. Ronsard), 1924; 3 chants hébraïques (T. Klingsor), 1925, orchd (1926); Le pays sans nom (E. Schneider), 1926, also orchd; L'heure captive (R. Dommange), 1v, pf, vn obbl (1928); La mauvaise prière (Chalupt) (1932), also orchd; La berceuse du marin (R. Champlay), 1933, orchd 1933; Tendresse (Champlay) (1933)

Other: Sagesse (J. Autran), 3 female vv, 1879; Matin de Pâques (G. Ardant), légende sacrée , S, Mez, Bar, pf, 1898; Invocation à Odin (de Bengy-Puyvallée), Bar, male vv, 1901, also orchd; O Salutaris, S/T, chorus, vn, org (1903); Pie Jesu, 1v, org (1903); Tu es petrus, ?chorus, 1917; Saisons (sym. poem, ?Aubert), Mez, chorus, (org, orch)/(4 sax, d bn), 1937; Incantation, chorus, jazz orch, orch, first perf. 1943; Ave Maria, chorus (1956)

OTHER WORKS

Dramatic: Chrysothemis (ballet-pantomime, 1, H. Ferrare), Vichy, Casino, 28 July 1904; La forêt bleue (op, 3, J. Chenevière, after C. Perrault), 1904–10, Geneva, Opera, 7 Jan 1913; Cinéma (ballet, R. Jeanne), Paris, Opéra, 13 March 1953
Inst: Berceuse, pf (1895); Romance, op.2, pf, 1897; Fantaisie, op.8, pf, orch, 1899; 3 esquisses, pf, 1900; Suite brève, op.6, 2 pf, 1900; Madrigal, op.9, fl, pf (1901); Valse caprice, op.10, pf, 1902; Lutins, op.11, pf, 1903; 2 pièces en forme de Mazurka, op.12, pf (1907); Sillages, op.27, pf, 1908–13; Habanera, orch, 1917–18, also pf 4 hands; Esquisse sur le nom de Fauré, pf, 1922; Introduction et allegro, fl, pf (1922); Caprice, vn, orch, 1924; Dryade, tableau musical, orch, 1924; Sonata, vn, pf (1927); Feuille

d'images, pièces enfantines, pf 4 hands (1930), also orchd; Offrande, orch, 1947; Aubade, vn, pf (1948); Tombeau de Chateaubriand, op.44, orch, 1948; Improvisation, 2 gui, 1959–60; Tableaux symphonique, orch [concert version of Cinéma, ballet, 1953]
Many song arrs. and ballet orchestrations

BIBLIOGRAPHY

L. Vuillemin: *Louis Aubert: son oeuvre* (Paris, 1921)
E. Vuillermoz: *Musiques d'aujourd'hui* (Paris, 1923), 33–42
J.-G. Prod'homme: 'Gustave Doret, Paul Ladmirault, Louis Aubert, Jacques Ibert', *Le théâtre lyrique en France* (Paris, 1937–9) [pubn of Poste National/Radio Paris], iii, 172–81
P. Landormy: *La musique française après Debussy* (Paris, 1943)
R. Dumesnil: *La musique française entre les deux guerres 1919–1939* (Geneva, 1946)
M. Landowski and G. Morançon: *Louis Aubert* (Paris, 1967)
V. Jankélévitch: 'Louis Aubert', *Scherzo*, no.6 (1971), 17–20; repr. in *Écrits sur la musique* (Paris, 1994)

RICHARD LANGHAM SMITH

Aubert, (Pierre-François-)Olivier (*b* Amiens, 1763; *d* Paris, *c*1830). French cellist and guitarist. He studied music at the *maîtrise* of his home town but was self-taught at his principal instrument, the cello. In 1787 he was established as a cello teacher in Paris, and he played for 25 years in the orchestra of the Opéra-Comique. Aubert also took up the guitar after Ferdinando Carulli's famous appearance in Paris in 1808, and later taught the guitar in the rue du Faubourg-Montmartre, where he also published music. He wrote important methods for the cello (1802) and the guitar, and one book of solfège. His published compositions, which show him to have been a cellist of considerable ability and to have enjoyed favour in Vienna, Zürich and Milan as well as Paris, begin with three sets of string quartets opp.1, 2 and 4, but consist mainly of duets for two cellos of which one, op.13, is based on Paris street cries: *Les marchandes de plaisirs d'artichauds, de pommes de terre et de gateaux de Nanterre*. There are five books of potpourris for guitar and some sets of guitar duets. In 1827 Aubert published his 44-page *Histoire abrégée de la musique ancienne et moderne, ou Réflexions sur ce qu'il y a de plus probable dans les écrits qui ont traité ce sujet*, the fruit of 25 years' reflection – a long time, as Fétis observed, devoted to very little. (*FétisB*; *MGG1*, K. Stephenson)

HUGH MACDONALD

Aubéry du Boulley, Prudent-Louis (*b* Verneuil, 9 Dec 1796; *d* Verneuil, 28 Jan 1870). French composer and teacher. His later achievements in the encouragement of amateur music-making in the provinces were foreshadowed in his youth when, at the age of 11, he wrote some marches for the local wind band at Verneuil. He played the flute and the horn, and in 1808 went to Paris to study composition with Momigny and later with Méhul and Cherubini at the Conservatoire. He returned to Verneuil in 1815 and divided his life between music and the management of his estate in the village of Grosbois nearby. He composed an opera *Les amants querelleurs*, accepted by the Opéra-Comique but played at the Théâtre du Gymnase in 1824. He was prolific in the popular genres of the time and devoted much attention to the guitar, for which he wrote a tutor. Many of his chamber works combine the guitar with strings or wind. He also supplied several books of wind music for the newly reorganized National Guard. In 1830 he published his *Grammaire musicale*, an introduction to musical theory, presented in dialogue form, which ran to three editions. Thereafter his main preoccupation was the coordination of music in his local region, especially music for wind band. In 1835 he formed a society of wind bands drawn from Evreux, Nonancourt, Dreux, Vernon, Alençon, Chartres and other towns of the area west of Paris, which came together twice a year to form a massed band of several hundred players. Despite ill-health du Boulley travelled from village to village providing instruments and instruction and recruiting players. His own village had a band of over 20. He published an account of the society in 1839 with a list of his own works. His opus numbers exceed 170 and include, besides much music for brass and wind band and guitar, a symphony for full orchestra (1847).

WORKS

Les amants querelleurs (oc, 1), Paris, Gymnase, 1824
Sym., orch, 1847
Works for military band: Marche funèbre; Collection of military music, 1830–32; Collection of fanfares, 1835–6; Cantata in honour of St Cecilia, 3vv, band, 1836; Collection of music for brass, 1858–9; Collection of syms., ovs., fantasias; Les échos des rives de l'Eure, op.152
Chbr and inst (most mentioned by Fétis): Septet, fl, cl, hn, gui, vn, vc, b; Qnt, fl, pf, vn, vc, gui; 7 qts, pf, vn, fl, gui; many trios and duos; Contredanses and waltzes, op.2, 2 gui; 3 sonates faciles, pf, op.1; La bataille de Montmirail, pf, 1814; romances, quadrilles, waltzes, polkas, gui; others
Méthode complète et simplifiée pour la guitare, op.42 (Paris, n.d.)

WRITINGS

Grammaire musicale (Paris, 1830, 3/after 1834)
Des associations musicales en France et de la Société philharmonique de l'Eure, de l'Orne et d'Eure-et-Loir (Verneuil, 1839)

BIBLIOGRAPHY

H. Berlioz: 'Des progrès de l'enseignement musical en France', Journal des débats (18 Sept 1836)
De Jémonville: 'Aubéry de Boulley', Revue des sciences, des lettres et des arts (15 Dec 1858)
F.-J. Fétis: La Société philharmonique de l'Eure, de l'Orne et d'Eure-et-Loir (L'Aigle, 1859, 2/1866)
J. de l'Avre: Notice sur Aubéry du Boulley (Verneuil, 1895)

HUGH MACDONALD

Aubin, Tony (Louis Alexandre) (b Paris, 8 Dec 1907; d Paris, 21 Sept 1981). French composer and conductor. He studied at the Paris Conservatoire (1925–30) with Samuel-Rousseau (harmony), Noël Gallon (counterpoint) and Dukas (composition), winning the Prix de Rome in 1930 with Actéon. Having studied conducting with Gaubert (1934–5) he took up the artistic direction of the RTF station Paris Mondial (1937–44) and then served as a conductor for French radio (1945–60), for whom his work included a recording of Ariane et Barbe-Bleue. In 1945 he was appointed professor of composition at the Conservatoire, and in 1969 he was elected to the Institut. In 1979 he became president of the Académie des Beaux-Arts and was made a Commandeur of the Légion d'Honneur. His compositions pursue the more harmonically rich and colourful aspects of the music of Ravel and Dukas. In Actéon (1930) he achieves a sense of mystery by combining dissonant clusters with a repeated motif. His only opera Goya is notable for its jocular inclusion of pastiche Spanish and folk elements.

WORKS
(selective list)

Op: Goya (5, 4 tableaux, R. Escholier), 1968–73, Lille, Opéra, 28 Nov 1974
Ballets: Fourberies [after G. Rossini] (after Molière), 1950; Variations [after F. Schubert], Paris, 1953; Grand pas [after J. Brahms], Paris, 1953; Périls, 1958; Au fil de l'eau, 1964
Vocal orch: Actéon (cant., P. Arosa), S, T, B, orch, 1930; Cressida (A. Suarès), spkr, S, T, chorus, orch, 1935; Jeanne d'Arc à Orléans,

1943; Chant d'amour, chant de mort de Troilus (A. Suarès), T, orch, 1962
Orch: Sym. romantique, 1937; Le chevalier Pécopin, after V. Hugo, 1942; Suite danoise, 1945; Sym. no.2, F, 1951; Suite éolienne, fl, cl, str, 1958; La joconde, after L. da Vinci: La gioconda, 1961; Concertino dell'amicizia, fl, str, 1964; Divertimento dell'incertezza, cl, str, 1967; Concertino delle scoiattolo, ob, pf, str, 1970; Concertino della brughiera, bn, str, 1975
Chbr and solo inst: Prélude, recitatif et final, pf, 1930; Str Qt, 1930; Pf Sonata, b, 1933; Le sommeil d'Iskender [for Le Tombeau de Paul Dukas], pf, 1936; Cantilène variée, vc, pf, 1937, orchd 1944; Toccatrotta, hpd, 1972; Hidalgoyas, gui, 1975
Songs: 6 poèmes de Verlaine, 1v, pf, 1932
Incid music, incl. Athalie (J. Racine), 1943; film scores

Principal publishers: Editions françaises de musique, Leduc, Billaudot

BIBLIOGRAPHY

A. Machabey: Portraits de trente musiciens français (Paris, 1949)
'Propus impromptu: Tony Aubin', Courrier musical de France, no.23 (1968), 154–63
E. Bondeville: Funerailles de Tony Aubin (Paris, 1981)
Daniel-Lesur: Notice sur la vie et les travaux de Tony Aubin (Paris, 1982)

PAUL GRIFFITHS/ANDREA MUSK

Aubry, Georges Jean. See JEAN-AUBRY, GEORGES.

Aubry, Marie (b c1656; d Paris, 1704). French singer. She first appeared on stage as Diana in Les amours de Diane et d'Endymion by Sablières at Versailles (1671). Her performance impressed Robert Cambert, who cast her as Phyllis in his pastorale Les peines et les plaisirs de l'amour (1671). She created six leading roles in Lully's operas: Aeglé in Thésée (1675), Sangaride in Atys (1676), Io in Isis (1677), Philonoé in Bellérophon (1679), the title role in Proserpine (1680) and Andromeda in Persée (1682). She assumed such a 'prodigious size' that she retired in 1684 because 'she could not walk and appeared toute ronde' (F. Parfaict: Histoire de l'Academie royale de musique, MS, 7741, F-Pn).

Aubry fanned the antagonism between Lully and Guichard, her former lover. She told Lully that Guichard plotted his murder by asking her brother to mix arsenic in Lully's tobacco. There followed a bitter trial lasting nearly three years.

JAMES R. ANTHONY

Aubry, Pierre (b Paris, 14 Feb 1874; d Dieppe, 31 Aug 1910). French musicologist and philologist. He graduated in philology (1892) and law (1894), and subsequently became archiviste paléographe at the Ecole des Chartes in Paris (1898). He took a diploma in Armenian (1900), and after travelling in Central Asia published articles on Armenian church music and on music of the Tajiks and Sarts in Turkestan. He later taught in Paris at the Institut Catholique, the Ecole des Hautes Etudes Sociales and at the Schola Cantorum, through whose Bureau d'Edition he issued his early articles.

Aubry brought to bear on musical problems the skills of the philologist (comparing concordant sources and establishing the best reading for a text) and of the palaeographer. In this he resembled his contemporary Friedrich Ludwig and others of the senior generation of 20th-century music scholars. He continued the work of Coussemaker and Riemann in the field of 13th-century French music, making texts available in edition and facsimile: his name is closely associated with three major sources, the Roman de Fauvel, the Chansonnier de l'Arsenal and the Bamberg manuscript. He produced much textual criticism in article form, and two series of larger studies, many of them in collaboration with literary scholars.

Aubry is known particularly for his work on the sources of troubadour and trouvère song. His rhythmic interpretations of monophonic song were largely based on the application of Franconian rules to the ligatures of the notation. In 1907 (with *La rhythmique musicale* and the recast form of 'Iter hispanicum') he adopted the modal interpretation (*see* RHYTHMIC MODES) evidently developed by Ludwig and J.B. Beck. A dispute arose between Aubry and Beck in 1909 as to which of them was the originator of modal theory; the result was Aubry's death from a foil wound, apparently while preparing for a duel.

WRITINGS

Huit chants héroïques de l'ancienne France, XIIe – XVIIIe siècle: poèmes et musique (Paris, 1896, 2/1896) [music in 2nd edn only]

'L'idée religieuse dans la poésie lyrique et la musique française au moyen âge', *Tribune de Saint-Gervais*, iii (1897), 37–40, 52–5, 84–8; iv (1898), 150–54, 202–7, 248–55, 286–8; also pubd separately (Paris, 1897)

'L'inspiration religieuse dans la poésie musicale en France', *Tribune de Saint-Gervais*, v (1899) 16–20, 40–43; also pubd separately (Paris, 1899)

Mélanges de musicologie critique: i *La musicologie médiévale: histoire et méthodes* (Paris, 1900/*R*); ii *Les proses d'Adam de Saint-Victor*(Paris, 1900) [with E. Misset]; iii *Lais et descorts français du XIIIe siècle* (Paris, 1901) [with A. Jeanroy and L. Brandin]; iv *Les plus anciens monuments de la musique française* (Paris, 1905)

'Le système musical de l'église arménienne', *Tribune de Saint-Gervais*, vii (1901), 325–32; viii (1902), 23–38, 72–85, 110–13, 320–27; ix (1903), 136–46, 287–8

Souvenir d'une mission d'études musicales en Arménie (Paris, 1902)

Essais de musicologie comparée: i *Le rhythme tonique dans la poésie liturgique et dans le chant des églises chrétiennes au moyen-âge* (Paris, 1903), ii *Esquisse d'une bibliographie de la chanson populaire en Europe* (Paris, 1905)

with R. Meyer and J.Bédier: 'La chanson de "Bele Aelis" par le trouvère Baude de la Quarière', *Tribune de Saint-Gervais*, x (1904), 151–6; also pubd separately (Paris, 1904)

'La chanson populaire dans les textes musicaux du moyen âge', *RHCM*, iv (1904), 594–604; also pubd separately (Paris, 1905)

'La musique de danse au moyen âge: une "estampida" de Rambaut de Vaqueiras', *RHCM*, iv (1904), 305–11; also pubd separately (Paris, 1904)

with A. Jeanroy and DrDejeanne: 'Quatre poésies de Marcabru, troubadour gascon du XIIe siècle', *Tribune de Saint-Gervais*, x (1904), 107–18; also pubd separately (Paris, 1904)

'Au Turkestan: note sur quelques habitudes musicales chez les Tadjiks et chez les Sartes', *BSIM*, i (1905), 97–108; also pubd separately (Paris, 1905)

with E. Dacier: *Les caractères de la danse: histoire d'un divertissement pendant la première moitié du XVIIIe siècle* (Paris, 1905)

'Estampies et danses royales: les plus anciens textes de musique instrumentale au moyen-âge', *BSIM*, ii/2 (1906), 169–201; also pubd separately (Paris, 1907/*R*)

'Un "explicit" en musique du roman de Fauvel', *BSIM*, ii/2 (1906), 118–26; also pubd separately (Paris, 1906)

'La musique et les musiciens d'église en Normandie au XIIIe siècle d'après le "Journal des visites pastorales" d'Odon Rigaud', *BSIM*, ii/1 (1906), 337–47, 455–62, 505–12, 556–68; also pubd separately (Paris, 1906/*R*)

'Iter hispanicum: notices et extraits de manuscrits de musique ancienne conservés dans les bibliothèques d'Espagne', *SIMG*, viii (1906–7), 337–55, 517–34; ix (1907–8), 32–51; x (1908–9), 157–83; also pubd separately (Paris, 1908)

'L'oeuvre mélodique des troubadours et des trouvères', *RHCM*, vii (1907), 317–33, 347–60, 389–95; pubd separately as *La rhythmique musicale des troubadours et des trouvères* (Paris, 1907)

Le roman de Fauvel: reproduction photographique du manuscrit français 146 de la Bibliothèque Nationale de Paris (Paris, 1907)

with A. Gastoué: 'Recherches sur les "tenors" latins dans les motets du XIIIe siècle d'après le manuscrit de Montpellier', *Tribune de Saint-Gervais*, xiii (1907), 145–51, 169–79; also pubd separately (Paris, 1907)

Cent motets du XIIIe siècle, publiés d'après le manuscrit Ed.IV.6 de Bamberg (Paris, 1908/*R*) [facs., transcr. and commentary]

with A. Jeanroy: 'Huit chansons de Bérenger de Palazol', *Anuari de l'institut d'estudis Catalans*, i (1908), 520–40

with J. Bédier: *Les chansons de croisade* (Paris, 1909/*R*)

'Refrains et rondeaux du XIIIe siècle', *Riemann-Festschrift* (Leipzig, 1909/*R*), 213–29

with A. Jeanroy: *Le chansonnier de l'Arsenal* (Paris, 1910) [inc.]

Trouvères et troubadours (Paris, 1909, 2/1910/*R*; Eng. trans., 1914/*R*)

BIBLIOGRAPHY

J.-B. Beck: 'Die modale Interpretation der mittelalterlichen Melodien, besonders der Troubadours und Trouvères', *Caecilia* [Strasbourg], xxiv (1907), 97–105

J.-B. Beck: 'Zur Aufstellung der modalen Interpretation der Troubadourmelodien', *SIMG*, xii (1910–11), 316–24 [contains full text of judicial tribunal; also a response by J. Wolf]

Obituaries: *Bibliothèque de l'Ecole des chartes*, lxxi (1910), 701–4 (E. Dacier); *ZIMG*, xii (1910–11), 13–15 (J. Wolf); *BSIM*, vii (1911), 41–5 (J. Écorcheville)

J. Ecorcheville: 'Bibliographie des ouvrages de Pierre Aubry', *BSIM*, vii/1 (1911), 45–8

H. Anglès: 'Les melodies del trobador Guiraut Riquier', *Estudis Universitaris Catalans*, xi (1926), 1–78

F. Gennrich: 'Wer ist der Initiator der "Modaltheorie"?', *Miscelánea en homenaje a Monseñor Higinio Anglés*, i (Barcelona, 1958–61), 315–30

J. Haines: 'The "modal theory", fencing and the death of Aubry', *PMM*, vi (1997), 143–50

IAN D. BENT

Aucassin et Nicolette. A French 13th-century *chante-fable*. The only surviving example of the genre, its sole source is *F-Pn* fr.2168. It tells, in prose, the romantic story of the love of a count's son for a foreign girl-captive. Interspersed in the narrative are verse sections (laisses) written in lines with equal numbers of syllables, all sung to the same double phrase of melody (a relic of narrative singing; *see* CHANSON DE GESTE), concluding with a single four-syllable line, which forms a musical coda. The melody is published in the standard edition by Roques and in the translation by Matarasso.

See also MEDIEVAL DRAMA.

BIBLIOGRAPHY

J. Stevens: *Words and Music in the Middle Ages* (Cambridge, 1986)

JOHN STEVENS

Auckland. City in New Zealand. Located in the north of the North Island, it is the country's largest city, with a population of approximately one million. European settlement dates from 1840; organized musical activities from 1845 featured the bands of the 58th and, later, 65th Regiments of the Imperial Forces. They supplied the music not only for military events but also for balls, soirées, outdoor concerts and church occasions. The Auckland Choral Society, founded in 1855, continues to the present day; other notable choirs have been the Auckland Liedertafel (later Royal Auckland Choir), the Albyn Singers and the choirs of Holy Trinity and St Patrick's cathedrals. The Dorian Choir, formed in 1935, established an international reputation under the direction of Peter Godfrey. The Primary School Choral Festival is well established after 50 years.

Opera has had a chequered life in Auckland since the 1860s, with a heavy dependence on touring groups such as the Lyster, Simonsen, Musgrave, Williamson and Pollard companies. The National Opera Company was short-lived (1979–83), but the merger of Mercury Opera with the Metropolitan Opera in 1992 to form Auckland

Opera (now Opera New Zealand) marked a resurgence of interest and success, helped by the opening of the Aotea Centre in 1989. With its 2256-seat auditorium, it is the first venue in Auckland with the facilities for a full operatic production. Operetta has been well served by the Auckland Light Opera Club, founded in 1919.

The role of the enthusiastic amateur has been central to Auckland's active musical life, supported by societies, schools, church and community choirs, brass bands and retailers. Maughan Barnett, the city organist, and the Municipal Band performed free concerts in the Town Hall for many years. The Bohemian Orchestra (1914–36) and the Auckland SO (1939–47) attempted to provide a range of orchestral works. The professional Auckland Philharmonia Orchestra was established in 1986, preceded by the Auckland String Orchestra (1940), later the Symphonia of Auckland and Auckland Regional Orchestra. It maintains a busy concert schedule across a broad repertory. The Town Hall and the Aotea Centre are the main musical venues; smaller ones include the Maidment Theatre (opened 1975), the University of Auckland Musical Theatre (1986) and the Bruce Mason Centre (1996).

The School of Music (from 1970 to 1981 called the Conservatorium) at the University of Auckland provides performers, composers, teaching and a wide range of musical activities. A chair in music was established in 1888. Composers attached to the university have included Douglas Mews and John Rimmer. The university also houses the Archive of Maori and Pacific Music. Music education in secondary schools is starting to reflect the strong Maori and Polynesian influences in the city, which have also affected emerging styles of popular music in the Auckland area. As the country's largest population base, Auckland has had a pivotal role in establishing and maintaining the national reputations of those working in popular music and jazz.

BIBLIOGRAPHY
Centennial Music Festival, Auckland, 1940 [programme book]

A. Annabel: *Music in Auckland 1840–55* (thesis, U. of Auckland, 1968)

S.P. Newcomb: *Challenging Brass* (Auckland, 1980)

C. Nalden: *A History of the Conservatorium of Music, University of Auckland, 1888–1981* (Auckland, 1981)

J.M. Thomson: *The Oxford History of New Zealand Music* (Auckland, 1991)

R. Watkins: *Hostage to the Beat: the Auckland Scene 1955–1970* (Auckland, 1995)

LIBBY NICHOL

Auda, Antoine (*b* St-Julien-en-Loiret, 28 Oct 1879; *d* Brussels, 19 Aug 1964). Belgian musicologist of French birth. He was a choirboy in the Maîtrise de St Joseph, Marseilles, where he experienced a large repertory of plainsong and 16th-century polyphony, under the direction of J.-B. Grosso. He became a lay brother of the Salesian order, and (after a year in Paris) taught in Liège from 1905 to 1925. Following a year in Tournai he settled in Brussels, where he lived until his death. Among his many interests was a far-sighted fascination with colour photography; he also first demonstrated the use of microfilms as aids to scholarship at a congress of archaeology at Mons in 1928.

Auda's chief work centred on plainsong, the music of Liège, scales and modes and the concept of *tactus* in music before 1650. In his *tactus* work, he gave pride of place to A. Tirabassi, whose doctoral dissertation (1925) prepared much of the ground that the two men were later to explore with a zeal and devotion fostered partly by the general opposition which met their conclusions. This resistance led Auda into several protracted scholarly disputes (carried out in articles and published letters) notably with Casimiri and Van den Borren. His last publication (finished a month before he died) was a complete survey of musical examples and theory clarifying the concept of *tactus*. This volume is an impressive testament to his logical scholarship; however, as it was privately printed, delayed by his death, and very difficult to obtain, it has been generally neglected. Apart from his major researches, Auda published studies of two neglected musicians with whom he felt a personal connection: the 19th-century Belgian organist and composer P.-L.-B. Thielemans, born at Woluwé-Saint-Pierre (the part of Brussels in which Auda lived), and the 16th-century adolescent prodigy Barthélemy Beaulaigue, poet and composer from Marseilles (the town where Auda himself had spent his adolescence singing polyphony). Auda dedicated this second study to the memory of his former teacher J.-B. Grosso.

WRITINGS
'L'école liégeoise au XIIe siècle: l'office de Saint Trudon', *Tribune de Saint-Gervais*, xvi (1910), 273–9; xvii (1911), 11–19, 33–7, 63–6, 88–92, 147–55

L'école musicale liégeoise au Xe siècle: Etienne de Liège (Brussels, 1923)

Manuel de chant à l'usage des paroisses et des maisons d'éducation (Liège, *c*1924)

La musique et les musiciens de l'ancien pays de Liège (Brussels, 1930)

'Léonard Terry, professeur, compositeur, chef d'orchestre et musicologue liégeois', *IMSCR I: Liège 1930*, 73–5

Les modes et les tons de la musique et specialement de la musique médiévale (Brussels, 1930/R)

'Contribution à l'histoire de l'origine des modes et des tons grégoriens', *Revue du chant grégorien*, xxxvi (1932), 33–9, 72–7, 105–11, 130–32

'Le tactus ou théorie de la transcription de la musique proportionnelle', *Musica sacra* [Bruges], xl (1933), 147–66

'La mesure dans la messe "L'homme armé" de Palestrina', *AcM*, xiii (1941), 39–59

'Le "tactus" dans la messe "L'homme armé" de Palestrina', *AcM*, xiv (1942), 27–73

'Pierre-Léon-Benoît Thielemans, organiste et compositeur, 1825–1898', *Hommage à Charles van den Borren*, ed. S. Clercx and A. vander Linden (Antwerp, 1945), 54–71

'La transcription en notation moderne du "Liber missarum" de Pierre de la Rue', *Scriptorium*, i (1946–7), 119–28

Les gammes musicales: essai historique sur les modes et sur les tons de la musique, depuis l'antiquité jusqu'à l'époque moderne (Brussels, 1947) [printed privately]

'Antonio Tirabassi', *Scriptorium*, ii (1948), 321–5

'La prolation dans l'édition princeps de la messe "L'homme armé" de Palestrina et sa *résolution* dans l'édition de 1559', *Scriptorium*, ii (1948), 85–102

'Le tactus, clef de la paléographie musicale des XVe et XVIe siècles', *Scriptorium*, ii (1948), 257–74

'Le tactus, principe générateur de l'interprétation de la musique polyphonique classique', *Scriptorium*, iv (1950), 44–66

Les 'motets wallons' du manuscrit de Turin: Vari 42 (Brussels, 1953) [printed privately]

'La théorie du tactus explique tous les faits paléographiques de la notation musicale des XVe et XVIe siècles', *Scriptorium*, x (1956), 65–82

ed., with A. Goosse: *Barthélemy Beaulaigue, poète et musicien prodige (1544–?)* (Brussels, *c*1957) [printed privately]

Théorie et pratique du tactus: transcription et exécution de la musique antérieure aux environs de 1650 (Brussels, 1965) [printed privately]

BIBLIOGRAPHY

[A. Gillet]: 'Notice biographique', in A. Auda: *Théorie et pratique du tactus* (Brussels, 1965)

B. Huys: 'Bibliografie van de werken van Antoine Auda (1879–1964)', *Archives et bibliothèques de Belgique*, xxxviii (1967), 197–201

DAVITT MORONEY

Audefroi le Bastart (*fl* 1190–1230). French trouvère. The dedication of two chansons (*Amours, de cui j'esmuef* and *Pour travail*) to Jehan de Nesle, castellan of Bruges, suggests that they were written before 1200, when Jehan joined the Fourth Crusade with Conon de Béthune. The interpolation of the first strophe of *Destrois, pensis* into Gerbert de Montreuil's *Roman de la violette* (1225 or slightly later) indicates that Audefroi belonged to one of the earlier generations of trouvères. He was probably a native of Picardy, perhaps of the area near the Artois border. He may have been associated with the Arras *puy*; the *Registre* records the death of his wife in 1259.

Although he was the creator of ten *chansons courtoises*, Audefroi did not achieve the recognition that such early trouvères as Gace Brulé or the Chastelain de Couci achieved. His works are to be found chiefly in the Noailles Chansonnier and the Manuscrit du Roi (*F-Pn* fr.12615 and 844), and appear only rarely in as many as four sources. His six romances (*Bele Emmelos*; *Bele Idoine*; *Bele Ysabiaus*; *En chambre a or*; *En l'ombre*; *En nouvel tens*), however, are an important contribution to the genre, elaborating on the older, popular tradition of the *chanson de toile*. The freshness of these works, their use of monologue and dialogue, and their expansive length (9–25 strophes) are distinguishing traits. Half of them open with a series of dodecasyllabic lines on a single rhyme, closing with octosyllabic refrains. The use of the hexasyllabic line as the main or sole structural unit of one romance and two *chansons courtoises* is also distinctive, and *Com esbahis* is one of a group of only 14 works in the repertory that open with a four-syllable line.

All of the romances except *En l'ombre* open with the characteristic repeat of the first phrase (two of them employing a varied repeat). Half employ no further repetition, but the rest exhibit either motivic quotation or varied repetition of some kind. The *chansons courtoises* employ bar form, except for *Pour travail*, which is non-repetitive. Several melodies are characterized by a comparatively small range. *Bele Emmelos* – with nine strophes – spans only a 5th, including a whole step below the final; two other works remain within the compass of a 6th. Of the two melodies that range widely, one involves a probable error of clef, whereas the other is a late setting. Most melodies are at least moderately florid. None survives in mensural notation, although there are brief suggestions of regular patterns of rhythmic organization in *Destrois, pensis*, *Fine amour* and *Onques ne seu chanter*.

WORKS

Editions: *Trouvères-Melodien*, ed. H. van der Werf, MMMA, xi–xii (1977–9), ii *Trouvere Lyrics with Melodies: Complete Comparative Edition*, ed. H. Tischler, CMM, cvii (1997–)

Abbreviations: (V) etc. indicates a MS (using Schwan sigla; *see* SOURCES, MS) containing a late setting of a poem. When the letter appears in italics, the original setting cannot be identified with certainty.

Amours, de cui j'esmuef mon chant, R.311
Bele Emmelos es prés desous l'arbroie, R.1688 (V)
Bele Idoine se siet desous la verde olive, R.1654
Bele Ysabiaus, pucele bien aprise, R.1616
Bien doi faire mon chant öir, R.1436 (R)
Com esbahis, R.1534a (=729) (*M, T*)
Destrois, pensis, en esmai, R.77
En chambre a or se siet la bele Beatris, R.1525
En l'ombre d'un vergier, R.1320
En nouvel tens Pascour que florist l'aubespine, R.1378
Fine amour et esperance, R.223
Ne sai mès en quel guise, R.1628 (R)
Onques ne seu chanter, R.831
Pour travail ne pour paine, R.139
Quant voi le tens verdir et blanchoier, R.1260
Tant ai esté pensis ireement, R.688

BIBLIOGRAPHY

G. Schlager: 'Über Musik und Strophenbau der französischen Romanzen', *Forschungen zur romanischen Philologie: Festgabe für Hermann Suchier* (Halle, 1900/R), 115–60

A. Cullman, ed.: *Die Lieder und Romanzen des Audefroi le Bastard* (Halle, 1914)

T. Gérold: *La musique au moyen âge* (Paris, 1932/R)

T. Gérold: *Histoire de la musique des origines à la fin du XIVe siècle* (Paris, 1936/R)

F. Gennrich, ed.: *Troubadours, Trouvères, Minne- und Meistergesang*, Mw, ii (1951; Eng. trans., 1960)

H. van der Werf: *The Chansons of the Troubadours and Trouvères: a Study of the Melodies and their Relation to the Poems* (Utrecht, 1972)

M. Zink: *Belle: essai sur les chansons de toile* (Paris, 1978) [incl. edn and trans., music ed. G. Le Vot]

For further bibliography *see* TROUBADOURS, TROUVÈRES.

THEODORE KARP

Auden, W(ystan) H(ugh) (*b* York, 21 Feb 1907; *d* Vienna, 29 Sept 1973). English poet, naturalized American. Of all the mid-20th-century poets, Auden was the most actively concerned with music. The third part of his *Collected Poems* (New York, 1945) consists of 38 'songs and other musical pieces', including the five lyrics set in Britten's cycle *On this Island* (1938), his *Song for St Cecilia's Day* (1941) and arias from his 'choral operetta' *Paul Bunyan* (1941). With Britten he collaborated on films (*Coal Face*, 1935; *Night Mail*, 1936), broadcasts (*Hadrian's Wall*, 1937; *The Dark Valley*, 1940), plays (*The Ascent of F.6*, 1937; *On the Frontier*, 1938), on the 'symphonic cycle' *Our Hunting Fathers* (1936) and on cabaret songs for Hedli Anderson (1938). Two quotations from the *St Cecilia* poem show how well Auden wrote words for music. The opening lines:

> In a garden shady this holy lady
> With reverent cadence and subtle psalm,
> Like a black swan as death came on
> Poured forth her song in perfect calm

demonstrate his command of cantabile, of rhythm and of vowel pattern, while the subsequent scherzo section is prompted by the lilt of:

> I cannot grow;
> I have no shadow
> To run away from,
> I only play.

In 1948, Auden declared himself an 'opera addict'; his friend Chester Kallman 'was the person who was responsible for arousing my interest in opera, about which previously, as you can see from *Paul Bunyan*, I knew little or nothing'. In that year Kallman and Auden collaborated on the libretto for Stravinsky's *The Rake's Progress*. In 1953 they published *Delia*, a delicate masque, written for Stravinsky but unset. Thereafter for Henze they produced two librettos, *Elegy for Young Lovers* and *The Bassarids*, and for Nabokov adapted *Love's Labour's Lost*. Their last libretto, *The Entertainment of the Senses*, was an antimasque for insertion into the Gibbons-Locke *Cupid and Death* (1653, 1659). It was posted to its composer, John Gardner, a few days before Auden's death. About half of *The Rake's Progress* and, by Auden, 'about 75%' of *Elegy* has been credited to Kallman – though, in a joint essay, the collaborators described themselves as a 'corporate personality'. Auden's theories about opera (among them: 'a good libretto plot is a melodrama in both the strict and the conventional sense of the word; it offers as many opportunities as possible for the characters to be swept off their feet by placing them in situations which are too tragic or too fantastic for "words"') were set out in several essays; his practice produced the most elegantly wrought librettos of the day. *Elegy*, for example, opens with full-voiced pentameters, linked by patterns of alliteration and internal rhyme:

> At dawn by the window in the wan light of today
> My bridegroom of the night, nude as the sun,
> with a brave
> Open sweep of his wonderful Samson-like
> hand

and, among its variety of carefully planned forms, includes simple songs:

> On yonder lofty mountain
> a lofty castle stands
> where dwell three lovely maidens,
> the fairest in the land

and scherzo patter:

> Blood-pressure drops,
> Invention stops;
> Upset tum,
> No images come

as well as conversational exchanges for recitative, conventional declarations of love, and a chorale. Despite his preference for opera in the original, Auden was also drawn to fit words to existing scores, and with Kallman he made translations of operas by Mozart (*Die Zauberflöte*, 1956; *Don Giovanni*, 1960), Weill (*Die sieben Todsünden*, 1958; *Aufstieg und Fall der Stadt Mahagonny*, 1960) and Dittersdorf (*Arcifanfano*, 1965). These are mellifluous, elegant, and better poetry than anything else of the kind, but on occasion they stray far from the original – quite deliberately so, since 'a too-literal translation of the original text may sometimes prove to be a falsification'.

Many composers have been attracted to set Auden's poetry, among them Berkeley (*Night covers up the rigid land* and *Five Poems*) and Maw (in his *Nocturne*); the 'Christmas Oratorio' *For the Time Being* attracted settings from both Marvin David Levy and (of the first section, 'Advent') Thea Musgrave. His poetry has also inspired purely instrumental works such as Berio's orchestral *Nones* (1954) and Bernstein's Symphony no.2, subtitled 'The Age of Anxiety' (1949). Later poems written specifically for musical setting include two translations in Barber's *Hermit Songs* (1953), Stravinsky's *Elegy for J.F.K.* (1964) and Walton's *The Twelve* (1965). Auden and Kallman were the text editors of *An Elizabethan Song Book* (Garden City, NY, 1955), whose music editor was Noah Greenberg, and in 1957 Auden wrote the narratives for Greenberg's performing edition of *The Play of Daniel*.

WRITINGS

Librettos: *Paul Bunyan*, Britten, 1941; *Moralities*, Henze, 1969
with C. Kallman: *The Rake's Progress*, Stravinsky, 1951; *Elegy for Young Lovers*, Henze, 1961; *The Bassarids*, Henze, 1966; *Love's Labour's Lost*, Nabokov, 1973; *The Entertainment of the Senses*, John Gardner, 1974

Essays: 'Opera on an American Legend: Problems of Putting the Story of Paul Bunyan on the Stage', *New York Times* (4 May 1941); Introduction to *An Elizabethan Song Book* (Garden City, NY, 1955); 'A Public Art', *Opera*, xii (1961), 12–15; [with C. Kallman] 'Genesis of a Libretto', *Elegy for Young Lovers* (Mainz, 1961); *The Dyer's Hand* (New York, 1962), 463–527 ('Notes on Music and Opera', 'Cav & Pag', 'Translating Opera Libretti' (with Kallman), 'Music in Shakespeare'); 'The World of Opera', *Secondary Worlds* (London, 1969); *Forewords and Afterwords* (New York, 1973), 244–55, 256–61, 345–50, 432–5 ['The Greatest of Monsters' (Gutman's *Wagner*), 'A Genius and a Gentleman' (Verdi's letters), 'A Marriage of True Minds' (the Strauss-Hofmannsthal correspondence) and 'A Tribute' (to Stravinsky)]

BIBLIOGRAPHY

J. Kerman: 'Opera à la mode', *Hudson Review*, vi (1954), 560–77; rev. in *Opera as Drama* (New York, 1956, 2/1988), 190–202
J.W. Beach: *The Making of the Auden Canon* (Minneapolis, 1957), 190ff
J. Kerman: 'Auden's Magic Flute', *Hudson Review*, x (1957), 309–16
I. Stravinsky and R. Craft: *Memories and Commentaries* (New York, 1960), 144ff
M.K. Spears: *The Poetry of W.H. Auden: the Disenchanted Island* (New York, 1963), 105ff, 262ff
I. Stravinsky and R. Craft: *Dialogues and a Diary* (New York, 1963)
J.C. Blair: *The Poetic Art of W.H. Auden* (Princeton, 1965), 163ff
I. Stravinsky and R. Craft: *Themes and Episodes* (New York, 1966), 56ff
I. Stravinsky and R. Craft: *Retrospectives and Conclusions* (New York, 1969), 145ff, 160ff, 173ff
U. Weisstein: 'Reflections on a Golden Style: W.H. Auden's Theory of Opera', *Comparative Literature*, xxii (1970), 108–24
B.C. Bloomfield and E. Mendelson: *W.H. Auden: a Bibliography* (Charlottesville, VA, 2/1972) [incl. complete list of musical settings up to 1969]
H.W. Henze: *Musik und Politik: Schriften und Gespräche 1955–1975*, ed. J. Brockmeier (Munich, 1976, enlarged 2/1984, 82–9, 114–16; Eng. trans. (London, 1982)
D. Mitchell: *Britten and Auden in the Thirties: the year 1936* (London, 1981)
B. Engelbert: *Wystan Hugh Auden, 1907–1973: seine opernästhetische Anschauung und seine Tätigkeit als Librettist* (Regensburg, 1983)
N. Miller: 'Prosperos Insel: W.H. Auden und die Musik', *Beziehungszauber: Musik in der modernen Dichtung* (Munich and Vienna, 1988), 105–28
P. Reed: 'A Rejected Love Song from Paul Bunyan', *MT*, cxxix (1988), 283–8
G. Chew: 'Pastoral and Neoclassicism: a Reinterpretation of Auden's and Stravinsky's *Rake's Progress*', *COJ*, v (1993), 239–63
E. Mendelson, ed.: *W.H. Auden and Chester Kallman: Libretti and Other Dramatic Writings, 1939–1973* (Princeton, 1993) [incl. critical texts of all libretti and of trans. of *Die Zauberflöte*]
W. Bernhart: 'Prekäre angewandte Opernästhetik: Audens "sekundäre Welt" und Hans Werner Henzes *Elegie für junge Liebende*', *Die Semantik der musiko-literarischen Gattungen: Methodik und Analyse: ein Festgabe für Ulrich Weisstein* (Tübingen, 1994), 233–46

ANDREW PORTER/R

Audiffren, Jean (*b* Barjols, Provence, bap. 24 Sept 1680; *d* Marseilles, 8 Aug 1762). French composer and priest. The son of Jean-Baptiste Audiffren and Marguerite Fabre, he presumably received his initial musical training as a choirboy at Barjols church; in 1694 he entered the service of the chapter of the Old Cathedral in Marseilles, where he was taught by the precentor, Melchior Barrachin. In 1696 he received the tonsure, and about the turn of the century began to show his talents. In 1702 he became deputy precentor at Marseilles Cathedral; from 1716 to 1720 he was precentor of the primate's church of St Trophime at Arles and subsequently held the same office at Marseilles Cathedral until his retirement in August 1758. He was the teacher of Charles Levens. Audiffren's masses, although of unequal merit, contain some fine movements, and attest to the existence in southern France at this period of a concertante style of *missa brevis* with instruments or continuo.

His nephew, Joseph-Lazare Audiffren (*b* Marseilles, 21 Oct 1736; *d* Marseilles, 17 June 1804), was organist at the royal abbey of St Victor in Marseilles from 1771 to 1786, and at the cathedral until 1790, when the chapter was dispersed in accordance with the decree of the Civil Constitution of the Clergy. His only known work is the *Premier recueil d'ariettes* with keyboard and violin accompaniment (Paris, 1773).

WORKS

Mass, C, 4vv, 2 vn, bc; 3 masses, a, d, g, 4vv, bc; Requiem, F, 4vv, bc: all *F-C*
Magnificat, d, 4vv, bc, *C*
2 Magnificat, B♭, lost

BIBLIOGRAPHY

MGG1 (H.A. Durand)
F. Raugel: 'La maîtrise et les orgues de la primatiale Saint-Trophime d'Arles', *RMFC*, ii (1961–2), 99–115, esp. 107
M. Signorile: *La vie musicale à Arles, du début du XVIIe siècle à la veille de la Révolution* (Geneva, 1992)

GUY BOURLIGUEUX

Audinot [Odinot, Oudinot], **Nicolas-Médard** (*b* Bourmont-en-Bassigny, Haute-Marne, 7 June 1732; *d* Paris, 21 May 1801). French impresario, singer and dramatist. He first made his name as a singer with the Opéra-Comique (after about 1758), chiefly in artisan roles; no doubt it was to exploit this special talent that he was allowed to put on an *opéra comique* of his own, *Le tonnelier*, after La Fontaine's *Le cuvier* (Foire St Laurent, 28 September 1761). The work failed but Audinot nevertheless joined the Comédie-Italienne when that company merged with the Opéra-Comique in 1762. Audinot revised the libretto of *Le tonnelier* with A.-F. Quétant, and the work was revived on 16 March 1765 at the Comédie-Italienne with new *ariettes* and ensembles by various composers. In this new version it had considerable success in France, Holland and Germany alike. Audinot left the Comédie-Italienne in 1767 and soon became one of the principal impresarios of the Paris stage. After attracting crowds to his puppet show at the Foire St Germain, he opened the Théâtre de l'Ambigu-Comique on 9 July 1769, remaining its owner-manager until 1796 (for his many disputes with the political authorities see Isherwood, 187–91). The Ambigu-Comique used child actors at first; Audinot then employed adolescents, whom he exploited in morally dubious circumstances. On the other hand, the repertory of his theatre, initially dominated by skits and coarse farces, was enriched during the 1780s by moral plays and heroic and romantic pantomimes. It is difficult to evaluate the place of music at the Ambigu-Comique, but such composers as Botson, André-Jean Rigade and Papavoine were regularly employed there in the 1770s.

BIBLIOGRAPHY

DBF (M. Prévost); *ES* (R, Averini and E. Zanetti)
Les spectacles des foires et des boulevards de Paris, vi (1778)
[Mayeur de Saint Paul]: *Le désoeuvré ou L'espion du boulevard du Temple* (London, 1781)
Almanach général de tous les spectacles de Paris, i (1791), 172–81, 244; ii (1792), 291–3
N. Brazier: *Histoire des petits théâtres de Paris depuis leur origine* (Paris, 1838), 28–37
E. Campardon: *Les spectacles des Foires depuis 1595 jusqu'à 1791* (Paris, 1877), i, 29–74
C.D. Brenner: *A Bibliographical List of Plays in the French Language, 1700–1789* (Ann Arbor, 1947, 2/1979)

R.M. Isherwood: *Farce and Fantasy: Popular Entertainment in Eighteenth-Century Paris* (New York and Oxford, 1986)
N. Wild: *Dictionnaire des théâtres parisiens au XIXe siècle* (Paris, 1989)

MICHEL NOIRAY

Auditory streaming. *See* HEARING AND PSYCHOACOUSTICS; PSYCHOLOGY OF MUSIC, §§II, 3; and VIII and RHYTHM.

Audran, Edmond (*b* Lyons, 12 April 1840; *d* Tierceville, nr Gisors, Oise, 17 Aug 1901). French composer. Son of Marius-Pierre Audran (1816–87), at one time tenor at the Opéra-Comique, Audran studied under Jules-Laurent Duprato at the Ecole Niedermeyer, where he won the composition prize in 1859. In 1861 he moved with his family to Marseilles, where his father became a singing teacher and later director of the conservatory. He himself became organist at the church of St Joseph, for which he wrote religious music including a mass (1873) which was also performed at St Eustache in Paris. His other compositions included a funeral march on the death of Meyerbeer and some songs in Provençal dialect. His early attempts at *opéra bouffe* brought an invitation from Cantin, director of the Bouffes-Parisiens and himself a native of Marseilles, and with *Les noces d'Olivette* (1879) and *La mascotte* (1880) Audran established himself in Paris as a rival to Lecocq and gained international fame. He was the most successful French operetta composer of the 1880s, but apart from *La poupée* (1896) his later works were less successful. During his last years he suffered a mental and physical breakdown which caused his withdrawal from Paris society and eventually led to his death. Audran's scores show a considerable talent for comedy and have great melodic appeal and rhythmic variety.

WORKS
(*selective list*)

OPERETTAS

first performed in Paris unless otherwise stated; publication dates are of vocal scores published in Paris; for complete list see GroveO
PBP – Paris, Bouffes-Parisiens

Le grand mogol (ob, 3, H. Chivot and A. Duru), Marseilles, Gymnase, 24 Feb 1877; rev. in 4 acts, Paris, Gaîté, 19 Sept 1884 (1884)
Les noces d'Olivette (opérette, 3, Chivot and Duru), PBP, 13 Nov 1879 (1880)
La mascotte (oc, 3, Chivot and Duru), PBP, 29 Dec 1880 (1881)
Gillette de Narbonne (oc, 3, Chivot and Duru), PBP, 11 Nov 1882 (1883)
Les pommes d'or (opérette, 3, Chivot, Duru, Blondeau and Monréal), Menus-Plaisirs, 12 Feb 1883 (1883)
La dormeuse éveillée (oc, 3, Chivot and Duru), PBP, 27 Dec 1883 (1884)
Serment d'amour (oc, 3, M. Ordonneau), Nouveautés, 19 Feb 1886 (1886)
La cigale et la fourmi (oc, 3, Chivot and Duru), Gaîté, 30 Oct 1886 (1887)
Miss Helyett (opérette, 3, M. Boucheron), PBP, 12 Nov 1890 (1890)
L'enlèvement de la Toledad (opérette, 3, F. Carré), PBP, 17 Oct 1894 (1894)
La poupée (oc, 4, Ordonneau, after E.T.A. Hoffmann: *Der Sandmann*), Gaîté, 21 Oct 1896 (1896)
Over 20 other operettas

MISCELLANEOUS

Sacred music, incl. Mass, 1873; La sulamite, orat, 1876; Adoro te, motet (Paris, 1882)
Songs, incl. La cour d'amour (in Provençal dialect) (Marseilles, 1881)
Funeral march on the death of Meyerbeer, salon pieces, dances etc.

BIBLIOGRAPHY

GänzlBMT; *GänzlEMT*
J. Bindejont-Offenbach: 'L'opérette', *Cinquante ans de musique Française* (Paris, 1925)

F. Bruyas: *Histoire de l'opérette en France* (Lyons, 1974)
R. Traubner: *Operetta: a Theatrical History* (New York, 1983)

ANDREW LAMB

Aue, Hartmann von. *See* HARTMANN VON AUE.

Auenbrugger [D'Auenbrugg], **Marianna von** (*fl* Vienna; *d* 1786). Austrian keyboard player and composer. The daughter of Leopold von Auenbrugger, a well-known Austrian physician who wrote the German libretto for Antonio Salieri's comic opera *Der Rauchfangkehrer*, she studied composition with Salieri and published her only known work together with two of his odes. Marianna and her sister Katharina, both distinguished keyboard players, were known to Haydn and to the Mozart family. Haydn dedicated six of his piano sonatas to them (H XVI: 3–59 and 20). In a letter of 25 February 1780 to his publisher Artaria, Haydn wrote that, 'the approval of the *Demoiselles* von Auenbrugger … is most important to me, for their way of playing and genuine insight into music equal those of the greatest masters. Both deserve to be known throughout Europe through the public newspapers'. Leopold Mozart, in a letter to his wife (12 August 1773), also refers to 'the daughter of Dr Auenbrugger … who … play[s] extraordinarily well and [is] thoroughly musical'. Her *Sonata per il clavicembalo o forte piano*, a three-movement Classical sonata of great charm and feeling, was published in Vienna by Artaria in about 1781. It has recently been edited by B. Harbach, *Women Composers for the Harpsichord* (Bryn Mawr, PA, 1986) and S. Glickman (Bryn Mawr, PA, 1990).

BIBLIOGRAPHY
GerberL; *Newman SCE*
S. Stern: *Women Composers: a Handbook* (Metuchen, NJ, 1978)
J. Meggett: *Keyboard Music by Women Composers* (Westport, CT, 1981)

SYLVIA GLICKMAN

Auer, Leopold (von) (*b* Veszprém, 7 June 1845; *d* Loschwitz, nr Dresden, 15 July 1930). Hungarian violinist and teacher. He began his studies at the age of eight at the Budapest Conservatory with Ridley Kohne, continued them at the Vienna Conservatory with Jakob Dont (1857–8), and, after concert tours in the provinces, completed them with Joachim in Hanover (1863–4). After a successful début at the Leipzig Gewandhaus, he was engaged as orchestral leader at Düsseldorf (1864–6) and then at Hamburg where he also led a string quartet. Visiting London in 1868, he played Beethoven's Trio op.97 at the Musical Union with Anton Rubinstein and Piatti. On Rubinstein's recommendation, Auer was appointed to succeed Wieniawski as violin professor at the St Petersburg Conservatory in 1868; he remained there until 1917. He also taught outside Russia: in London during the summers of 1906–11 and in Loschwitz (Dresden) in 1912–14. In June 1917 he left strife-torn Russia for Norway, ostensibly on a holiday, and sailed for New York in February 1918. Despite his age, Auer still gave concerts and taught, both in New York and at the Curtis Institute in Philadelphia.

Auer spent half a century in St Petersburg, during which time he exerted a decisive influence on the Russian violin school. As court violinist, one of his functions was to play the solos at the Imperial Ballet. Traditionally, these were entrusted to famous violinists (among Auer's predecessors were Vieuxtemps and Wieniawski), which stimulated Tchaikovsky and other composers to write attractive solos for them. From 1868 to 1906 Auer led the string

quartet of the Russian Musical Society; he also conducted the society's orchestra in 1883 and from 1887 to 1892.

Auer's technique lacked a certain virtuoso flair – perhaps because of the poor physical structure of his hand – and in the early years some Russian critics compared him unfavourably to Wieniawski; yet his noble and fine-grained interpretations of the great concertos succeeded in convincing the sceptics. Tchaikovsky (*Sérénade mélancolique*), Glazunov, Arensky and Taneyev all dedicated works to him. Yet he declined the dedication of Tchaikovsky's Violin Concerto, declaring it technically awkward and too long. Tchaikovsky rededicated it to Adolph Brodsky who gave the première in 1881. Auer later made some revisions in the violin part and played the concerto in 1893, shortly before the composer's death.

Auer's influence as a teacher grew slowly. His first students to arouse world-wide attention were Elman in 1905 and Zimbalist in 1907, followed by Heifetz, Polyakin and many others. Most of his students came to him as finished technicians so that he could develop their taste and interpretative powers. His approach was geared to the temperament of each. It is more appropriate to speak of an Auer style than of a school: virtuosity controlled by fine taste, classical purity without dryness, intensity without sentimentality. The so-called 'Russian' bow grip (ascribed to Auer by Flesch in his *Kunst des Violin-Spiels*) consists of pressing the bow stick with the centre joint of the index finger; the result is a richer tone, though at the expense of some flexibility. The heritage of the Auer style can still be felt in today's Russian school.

Auer's transcriptions and arrangements are tasteful but largely forgotten. His editions of the Classics are still useful, as are his *Violin Playing as I Teach it* (New York, 1921/R) and *Violin Masterworks and their Interpretation* (New York, 1925/R). He also published *My Long Life in Music* (New York, 1923).

BIBLIOGRAPHY
L.N. Raaben: *Leopol'd Semenovich Auer* (Leningrad, 1962)
J.W. Hartnack: *Grosse Geiger unserer Zeit* (Munich, 1967, 4/1993)
J. Creighton: *Discopaedia of the Violin, 1889–1971* (Toronto, 1974)
G. Kosloski: *The Teaching and Influence of Leopold Auer* (diss., Indiana U., 1977)
B. Schwarz: 'The Russian Violin School Transplanted to America', *Journal of the Violin Society of America*, iii/1 (1977), 27–33

BORIS SCHWARZ

Auerhan, Chrétien. *See* URHAN, CHRÉTIEN.

Auernhammer [Aurnhammer, Aurenhammer], **Josepha Barbara** (bap. Vienna, 25 Sept 1758; *d* Vienna, 30 Jan 1820). Austrian pianist and composer. She was the 11th child of Johann Michael Auernhammer and Elisabeth Auernhammer, née Timmer. She studied with Georg Friedrich Richter, Leopold Kozeluch and, from 1781, with W.A. Mozart, with whom she fell in love. On 27 June 1781 Mozart wrote of her: 'I dine almost daily with H. v. Auernhammer; the young lady is a fright, but plays enchantingly, though in cantabile playing she has not got the real delicate singing style. She clips everything'. In the same year Mozart dedicated his sonatas for piano and violin K296 and K376–80/374d-f, 317d, 373a to her. (The dedication to Auernhammer on the edition of the piano variations *Ah, vous dirai-je, maman* K265/300e was added in 1785 by the publisher Christoph Torricella.) Auernhammer corrected the proofs of several of Mozart's sonatas, and her performances with him were enthusiastically described by Abbé Stadler. At a private concert in the Passauerhof in Vienna on 23 November 1781, she and Mozart played the sonata for two pianos K448/375a and the double concerto K365/316a. They also appeared together in concerts in January 1782 and on 26 May 1782. After her father's death, Mozart found lodgings for Auernhammer with Countess Waldstätten in the Leopold-stadt area. A legacy of almost 20,000 gulden from her great-uncle Karl Timmer on his death in 1785 was probably the basis of Auernhammer's decision to continue devoting herself to her career as a pianist. In 1786 she married a civil servant, Johann Bessenig (c1752–1837), with whom she had four children. She continued to appear regularly in concerts at the Burgtheater and privately, amd gave her last public concert on 21 March 1813 with her daughter Marianna, who also made a name for herself as a singing teacher and pianist. Auernhammer composed mainly piano music, particularly variations, which are marked by a comprehensive knowledge of pianistic technique and an artistic use of the instrument.

WORKS
printed works published in Vienna unless otherwise stated

Kbd variations: 6 on Nel cor più non mi sento [G. Paisiello: La Molinara] (Speyer, 1791); 6 on Der Vogelfänger bin ich ja [Mozart: Die Zauberflöte] (Offenbach, 1792; 1793); 8 on contredanse [S. Viganò: La figlia mal custodita] (1794); 6 on La stessa, la stessissima [A. Salieri] (1799); 6 variazioni per il pianoforte (1801); 6 on march [L. Cherubini: Les deux journées] (1803); 6 variations sur un thème hongrois (1810); 10 on theme from ballet Les folies amoureuses (n.d.); 10 variations dédiées a Madame de Brown, op.63 (n.d.)
Other works incl. 6 German lieder (1790), 2 kbd sonatas, vn sonata, 6 minuets for kbd

BIBLIOGRAPHY
GroveW (R. Marciano and J. Sanchez-Chiong) [incl. further bibliography]
O.E. Deutsch: 'Das Fräulein von Auernhammer', MJb 1958, 17–19
A. Weinmann: Verlagsverzeichnis Giovanni Cappi bis A.O. Witzendorf (Vienna, 1967), 157
R. Angermüller: 'An die Auerhamer bitte kein Kompliment', MISM, xxx/3–4 (1982), 8–14
D. Link: The National Court Theatre in Mozart's Vienna: Sources and Documents 1783–1792 (Oxford, 1998)

RUDOLPH ANGERMÜLLER/MICHAEL LORENZ

Auffmann [Aufmann], Joseph Anton Xaver (b c1720; d after 1773). German composer and organist. Shortly before 1759 he succeeded F.X. Richter as Kapellmeister to the Prince-Abbot of Kempten-Allgäu, holding the post until 1756. He published *Triplex concentus organicus, seu III. concerti organici a octo instrumentis* as his op.1 (Augsburg, 1754). On leaving Kempten he worked for a time in Straubing, where he composed the incidental music for two plays, *Hirlanda* (1756) and *Pompejus Magnus* (only text material is extant, D-MT). The survival of several works – an organ concerto in F, organ preludes and a concerto in D – at Donaueschingen (D-DO) suggests that he held a post at the court there. In 1773, when Auffmann was organist and composer to the Bishop of Pruntrut, Switzerland, he dedicated two symphonies to the Zürich Musiksaalgesellschaft.

BIBLIOGRAPHY
GerberL; RefardtHBM
A. Layer: Musikgeschichte der Fürstabtei Kempten (Kempten, 1975), 50

ADOLF LAYER/PETER JANSON

Aufheben (Ger.: 'to lift up'). The term was used, together with closely related words such as the synonym *erheben*, as well as *heben* ('to lift'), *abheben* ('to lift off') and

ABSETZEN ('to take off'), by many 18th-century writers in connection with string bowing. The manner in which the term was employed implies that the bow should be raised clear of the string to produce an articulation. However, the technical means for doing this, and the extent to which the bow was expected to be raised, are generally unspecified; though in relation to specific contexts some writers clarified their meaning with expressions like *ein klein wenig gehoben* ('raised a little bit'; G.S. Löhlein: *Anweisung zum Violinspielen*, 1774, p.80), or *ganz von den Saiten abgehoben* ('completely lifted off the string'; J.F. Reichardt: *Ueber die Pflichten des Ripien-Violinisten*, 1776, p.24). It seems clear that whenever such terms were used there was no suggestion of the employment of a springing bowstroke.

See also BOW, §II, 2(vii)

CLIVE BROWN

Aufklärung (Ger.). See ENLIGHTENMENT.

Auflösungszeichen (Ger.). See NATURAL.

Aufreri, Damasceno. See UFFERERII, GIOVANNI DAMASCENI.

Aufschnaiter [Aufschneider, Auffschnaidter], Benedict Anton (b Kitzbühel, bap. 21 Feb 1665; d Passau, bur. 24 Jan 1742). Austrian composer. His main appointment was in Passau, where he succeeded Georg Muffat as court Kapellmeister in 1705. He spent his early years in Vienna, where he may have been a pupil of Johannes Ebner (a member of the well-known family of organ players and son of Wolfgang Ebner) whom he declared his model. Apparently he came into contact with members of the Viennese nobility, and he may have been employed at a court. In a letter of 1724 to Prince-Bishop Lamberg, while complaining about the quality of the violinists in Passau, Aufschnaiter claimed to have had in Vienna, where he spent many years, '16–18 excellent musicians' at his disposal. His op.1 (of which no copy is extant) was dedicated to Count Ferdinand Ernst von Trautmannsdorf, who may have been his employer. In 1695 his op.2 appeared in Nuremberg with a dedication to Archduke Joseph (later Emperor Joseph I). Under the title *Concors discordia* it contains six orchestral suites which show Italian concerto grosso structure but also an apparent French influence; they probably followed the example of Georg Muffat. All that is known of op.3 is that it was dedicated to Emperor Leopold I; no copy is extant. Op.4 consists of eight church sonatas published under the title *Dulcis fidium harmonia symphoniis ecclesiasticis concinnata*, which appeared in 1703 and were dedicated to the four early fathers of the church and the four evangelists. These are orchestral sonatas for two solo violins (which have complicated double stops), two violins ad libitum, viola, violone and organ; they may have been inspired by Heinrich Biber's works. From 1705, when he became Kapellmeister at Passau, Aufschnaiter was active as a composer of church music (although he was not officially appointed cathedral Kapellmeister as Muffat had been). His opp.5 and 8 comprise vespers for four voices, strings and continuo instruments (1709, 1728), his op.6 five masses (1712) and his op.7 offertories with two solo violas (1719). In all his church works Aufschnaiter favours a more traditional style similar to the Roman cantata style; there are fewer demanding violin passages and double stops than in his earlier works, and he prefers to please with melodic charm. In his theoretical writings he emphasizes the difference between church, chamber and theatre music.

WORKS

Concors discordia, 2 vn, 2 va, vc, op.2 (Nuremberg, 1695)

Dulcis fidium harmonia symphoniis ecclesiasticis concinnata, 2 vn solo, 2 vn, va, vle, org, op.4 (Augsburg, 1703)

Memnon sacer ab oriente animatus, seu Vesperae solemnissimae, 4vv, str, 2 bc, op.5 (Augsburg, 1709)

Alaudae V ad aram purpurati honoris victimae sive Sacra V [5 masses], 4vv, vn, 2 va, 3 tpt, 3 trbn, ?org, op.6 (n.p., 1712)

Aquila clangens, exaltata supra domum Domini, sive 12 offertoria, 4vv, 2 vn, 2 va solo, 2 bc, 2 trbn ad lib, op.7 (Passau, 1719)

Cymbalum Davidis vespertinum seu Vesperae pro festivitatibus, 4vv, 2 vn, 2 va, 2 bc, op.8 (Passau, 1728), 2 with 2 tpt and 2 ob ad lib

Miserere pro tempore quadragesimae, op.9, c1724, unpubd, ?lost Opp.1 and 3 lost

6 Miserere, A-KR [4 also in D-OB], ?orig. intended as part of op.9

Numerous other works, incl. masses, requiems, responses for Holy Week, grads/offs, A-KR, D-Bsb, Dkh, Mf, OB, Po, Rp, S-Uu

Praeludien, Fugen à 4, formerly A-GÖ, lost

WRITINGS

Regulae compositionis fundamentales Musurgiae (MS, D-Po)

Anweisung oder Fundamentalregeln um eine gute Musik zu componieren (MS, D-Po)

BIBLIOGRAPHY

MGG1 (E.F. Schmid)

F. Lehrndorfer: B.A. Aufschnaiter, Domkomponist in Passau (diss., U. of Munich, 1920; pubd in Die ostbairischen Grenzmarken, Jg.xix/11–12 (1930)

W.M. Schmid: 'Zur Passauer Musikgeschichte', ZMw, xiii (1930–31), 289–308, esp. 303

EVA BADURA-SKODA

Aufstrich (Ger.). In string playing, denotes 'up-bow'. See ABSTRICH. See also BOW, §II, 2(i).

Auftakt (Ger.). See UPBEAT.

Aufzug (i) (Ger.). See ACT.

Aufzug (ii) (Ger.). A type of trumpet ensemble music performed at German-speaking and associated courts for ceremonial processions, entrances and exits, at festive mealtimes and on other special occasions, also termed 'Einzug', 'Intrada', and (after 1740) 'Marsch' or 'Fanfare'. It first appeared about 1570, apparently in Dresden; it is related to the older, longer SONATA for five or six trumpets with timpani, which it had replaced at other German courts by about 1660, and to the INTRADA for other instruments. The Aufzug contrasts CLARINO melody (notated for the first time in this genre) with rhythmically active lower parts. The trumpet music in Praetorius's In dulci jubilo … cum Tubis (1619) is modelled on the early Aufzug. By the 18th century the ensemble included three to six trumpets, normally with timpani; the repertory of the Portuguese Charamela Real from the 1760s for one to four choirs, each of six trumpets with timpani, marks the musical highpoint. Composers of Aufzüge include Schmelzer, Speer, Zelenka, C.P.E. Bach, Altenburg and Diabelli.

PETER DOWNEY

Augener. English music publishers. The firm originated in 1853, when Charles Louis Graue, formerly employed by Ewer & Co., set up as a foreign music importer in London with the assistance of George Augener (b Hessen-Fechenheim, 1830; d London, 25 Aug 1915), who had come to England in 1852 from employment in the firm of André in Offenbach. Graue was succeeded by Gustav Scheuermann in 1854, and in 1857 Augener left to set up on his own. The following year he bought the Scheuer-

mann business at public auction and took over its premises, trading as Augener & Co., and opening a branch in Brighton in 1860. Scheuermann set up briefly elsewhere in 1859 for a couple of years. In November 1898 the firm acquired the trade name and goodwill of ROBERT COCKS, and the two businesses were fully amalgamated as Augener Ltd in 1904. With George Augener's retirement in 1910, Willy Strecker purchased full control of the concern; through him it reverted to B. Schotts Söhne of Mainz in 1913, though with the outset of the war Schott forfeited its ownership. About 1960 Augener acquired the firm of Joseph Weekes, and in 1961 that of JOSEPH WILLIAMS. In May 1962 the firm, together with its various concert and wholesale concerns, was purchased by Galaxy Music Corporation (New York) and made part of GALLIARD LTD; this firm was subsequently absorbed by STAINER AND BELL, in whose catalogue the Augener titles now appear.

The firm began mainly as importers of foreign music, and from 1873 to 1937 held the sole agency for Peters Edition. As a publisher it was notable for the adoption of lithographic methods, and active from 1867 in producing cheap editions of the classics as well as modern works in their extensive Augener Edition. In 1878, under the direction of William Augener (b ?1854–5; d Tunbridge Wells, 19 June 1904), George's eldest son, it began printing its own publications, achieving a high standard of production; from 1871 to 1960 it published the Monthly Musical Record, with Ebenezer Prout (whose theoretical works it also published) as its first editor, followed by J.S. Shedlock, Richard Capell, J.A. Westrup and Gerald Abraham. The firm was particularly identified with educational music, especially piano works, and published many volumes of music for examining bodies.

BIBLIOGRAPHY

'Mr. George Augener', Musical Herald, no.631, (1900), 291–4

'The Music Publisher of Tradition: George Augener and the Augener Edition', MO, lxiv (1940–41), 428 only

J.A. Parkinson: Victorian Music Publishers: an Annotated List (Warren, MI, 1990)

PETER WARD JONES

Augenmusik (Ger.). See EYE MUSIC.

Augér, Arleen (b Long Beach, CA, 13 Sept 1939; d Leusden, Netherlands, 10 June 1993). American soprano. As a girl she sang in a church choir and studied the piano and violin. She studied singing and the violin at the University of California, later took singing lessons in Chicago with Ralph Errolle, and won a scholarship to Vienna in 1967. At her audition she so impressed the conductor Josef Krips that he engaged her for the Staatsoper, with the role of the Queen of Night in Die Zauberflöte for her début. Another powerful admirer at this time was Böhm, with whom she sang, and also recorded, a notable Konstanze in Die Entführung aus dem Serail. Appearances at the Vienna Volksoper included Marie in Donizetti's La fille du régiment. Her reputation as a coloratura soprano grew with débuts at the New York City Opera (1969) and Salzburg (1970), both as the Queen of Night.

With her move to Frankfurt in 1974 Augér turned more to lyric roles in opera and to the development of her career as a concert singer. She toured Japan in programmes of Bach and Handel, and worked extensively with the pianist Irwin Gage in the lieder repertory. In 1975 she sang as Fire in L'enfant et les sortilèges at La Scala, and in 1978 made her début at the Metropolitan Opera as

Marzelline in *Fidelio*. She was greatly admired in Britain, where she gave many recitals and sang in memorable performances of *Alcina* and *L'incoronazione di Poppea* (both of which she recorded) at Spitalfields in the City of London Festival. In 1986 her singing of Mozart's *Exsultate, jubilate* at the wedding of Prince Andrew and Sarah Ferguson in Westminster Abbey was heard by millions worldwide on television. Augér's many recordings show her as a delightful singer of Bach, Haydn, Mozart, Schubert and Richard Strauss, to whose *Vier letzte Lieder* she brought a fresh voice and mature understanding in a performance with Previn. Among her last recordings were a distinguished contribution to Graham Johnson's Complete Schubert Song Edition and *Sonnets from the Portuguese*, written for her by Libby Larsen. Her voice was of a gentle character with impressive reserves of power: her singing was unfailingly musical, and her death, after operations for a brain tumour, was deeply mourned.

BIBLIOGRAPHY

J.B. Steane: *Singers of the Century* (London, 1996), 181–5

J.B. STEANE

Auget [Auger], Paul (*b* Pontoise [now Cergy-Pontoise], *c*1592; *d* Paris, 22 March 1660). French composer. The son of a wine merchant, Auget had the money and social connections to obtain quickly a musical position worthy of his talents. He found favour with Jean-François de Gondi, Abbé of St Autin and *doyen* of Notre Dame, and through him began his career at court. He served as master of the abbé's music and at various times as singer and master to the queen, the queen mother and the king. On 13 January 1625 he became *surintendant de la musique de la chambre du roi*, a post he shared with Antoine and, later, J.B. Boësset. By 1638 he was enobled and living on a comfortable pension, but he still held his position as *surintendant* in 1654 when he participated in the coronation of Louis XIV. Contrary to statements by Prunières and others his daughter did not marry Jean de Cambefort, his successor as *surintendant* – it was one of his nieces who did so.

Only 14 compositions by Auget, all songs, survive, and it is likely that he wrote them for his own performance. Most were originally sung in *ballets de cour*: *Ballet de la folie*, *Ballet royal du grand bal de Douairiere de Billebahaut* (1626) and *Ballet du sérieux et de grotesque* (1627). All but two were published twice in versions for voice alone and for voice accompanied by lute. They are typical *airs de cour*: strophic, in binary or bar forms, syllabic, simple in harmony and rhythm and restricted in tessitura. The lute part in *Les charmants attraits de vos yeux* is slightly more interesting than in most accompanied *airs* in that it is rhythmically independent of the voice and introduces the song with a motif derived from the opening vocal phrase.

WORKS

13 airs, 1v: 6 in 1617[9], 4 in 1619[10], 1 in 1621[13] [sometimes wrongly listed 1619[10]], 2 in 1628[9]

13 airs, 1v, lute: 6 in 1617[8]/R, 4 in 1618[9]/R, 1 in 1626[12]/R, 2 in 1628[11]/R; 1 ed. A. Verchaly, *Airs de cour pour voix et luth (1603–1643)* (Paris, 1961)

BIBLIOGRAPHY

M. Jurgens: *Documents du minutier central concernant l'histoire de la musique, 1600–1650* (Paris, 1967–74)

M. Le Moël: 'Paul Auget, Surintendant de la musique du roi (1592–1660)', *RMFC*, viii (1968), 5–14

M. Benoit: *Dictionnaire de la musique en France aux XVIIe et XVIIIe siècles* (Paris, 1992)

JOHN H. BARON

Augmentation (i). In PROPORTIONAL NOTATION, the process whereby note shapes acquire additional value in a simple mathematical ratio. The process is the opposite of diminution, and was normally used in Renaissance polyphony to restore to note shapes their original value after a period of diminution.

ROGER BULLIVANT

Augmentation (ii). The term describes the restatement of a cantus firmus in note values longer than when it was first sounded in a composition, a device found, for example, in a number of motets of the late Middle Ages and many masses and motets of the Renaissance. From its application to the cantus firmus, augmentation passed into the repertory of technical devices of early ricercares and fantasias, by such composers as Sweelinck and Frescobaldi (e.g. Sweelinck: *Fantasia chromatica*, bars 119–26, bass), and of contrapuntal, canonic and fugal technique generally (*see* FUGUE). It became less common in the later Baroque and subsequent periods. Since augmentation makes the theme longer in time and more noticeable, it is effective as a climax device, particularly when its first appearance is delayed until near the end of the fugue. A well-known example is Bach's C major organ fugue BWV547 where the entry of the pedals is delayed: they eventually enter at bar 49 with the subject heard for the first time in augmentation (this point also represents a prominent return to the tonic key prepared by minor-key harmonies).

In non-fugal music augmentation is also occasionally used. In Beethoven's Pastoral Symphony the hymn-like figure at bars 146–50 of the 'Storm' movement originates from augmentation of the initial motif of bar 3; and the recapitulation of the first movement of Brahms's Fourth Symphony augments the opening figure of the first subject (compare bars 1–4, violins, with 246–58, wind).

See also AUGMENTED INTERVAL.

ROGER BULLIVANT

Augmented interval. A perfect or major INTERVAL that has been increased by a chromatic semitone. The perfect 4th C–F is made into an augmented 4th by raising F or lowering C (i.e. C–F♯ or C♭–F). A doubly augmented interval has been increased by two chromatic semitones: for example, C–D✕, C♭–D♯ and C♭♭–D are all doubly augmented 2nds derived from the major 2nd C–D.

Augmented sixth chord. A chord built normally on the flattened submediant and containing the note an augmented 6th above (i.e. the raised subdominant): in C major, A♭–F♯. The normal resolution of this interval is outwards to the octave; thus an augmented 6th chord characteristically resolves to the chord of the dominant or to a I6-4 chord. The character of an augmented 6th chord is largely determined by the other notes it contains. The simplest type, commonly (but arbitrarily) called the Italian 6th chord, has a major 3rd above the flattened submediant and resolves more easily to the dominant (ex.1a). The so-called French 6th chord has both a major

Ex.1 Augmented 6th chords and their resolutions

3rd and an augmented 4th and therefore also resolves more easily to the dominant (ex.1*b*); it also contains more of the flavour of the whole-tone scale. The so-called German 6th chord has a major 3rd and a doubly augmented 4th or a perfect 5th and naturally resolves to I6-4 or V, being spelt accordingly (ex.1*c–d*); the latter resolution creates a type of consecutive 5ths called 'Mozart' 5ths (*see* CONSECUTIVE FIFTHS, CONSECUTIVE OCTAVES). In equal temperament the German 6th sounds like a dominant 7th chord, and therefore it can resolve 'deceptively' on to the chord of the flattened supertonic, or 'Neapolitan sixth' chord (ex.1*e*).

See also HARMONY.

WILLIAM DRABKIN

Augmented triad. A chord built of two superimposed major 3rds, e.g. C–E–G♯, D–F♯–A♯.

Augsburg. City in Bavaria, Germany. It was founded on the Lech, Wertach and Singold rivers by Augustus in 14 BCE and was the seat of a bishopric from the 8th century. Throughout its long history the city had several periods of economic expansion which generally led to a flowering of cultural activities, particularly music. A conspicuous rivalry developed from the 12th century between the prince-bishop, who ruled the city, and the increasingly independent imperial city, which led to denominational schisms at the time of the Reformation.

1. To 1600. 2. 17th and 18th centuries. 3. 19th and 20th centuries. 4. Printing and instrument making.

1. TO 1600.   In the high and late Middle Ages the principal centres of sacred music in Augsburg were the cathedral and the Benedictine abbey of St Ulrich and St Afra. These two churches cultivated liturgical music, particularly Gregorian chant, and contained the city's first organs. Hermannus Contractus (*d* 1054), the author of several treatises on music and a composer of hymns, studied at the cathedral school, and the poet and composer Abbot Udalscalcus of Maisach (*d* 1151) lived at the abbey. The cathedral received a bequest from the bishop in 1313 to promote choral singing. In the 14th century a middle-class musical culture arose, fostered by trumpeters, minstrels, lied composers and, at the end of the 15th century, the Meistersinger, and quite distinct from the courtly art of the Minnesinger. Musicians with municipal salaries were incorporated into the *Stadtpfeiferei*, and lutenists, representatives of the so-called 'stille Musik' (quiet music), also flourished in the city. Several ornate manuscripts attest to the rich musical life of Augsburg's middle class during the late Middle Ages: the Augsburger Liederbuch (1454), containing love songs and student songs, the Liederbuch of Clara Hätzerlin (1470–71), and an anthology of lieder found among the possessions of the patrician family Hörwart (1458–1513).

During the Renaissance Augsburg became a leading centre of music in Europe. The city owed much of its importance to the presence of Maximilian I, whose Kapelle included Isaac, Senfl and Hofhaimer. In the 16th century many prominent musicians, such as Virdung and Luscinius in 1510, gathered at the Augsburg Imperial Diet. Johannes Frosch, the prior of the Carmelite convent of St Anna and a close friend of Luther, helped to establish the practice of Lutheran sacred music in the city. After the Peace of Augsburg (1555) Catholics and Protestants competed to increase the role of music in their services, and the schools of St Anna (Lutheran) and St Salvator

(Jesuit) vied to improve the quality of their musical education.

Soon after its founding in 1561 the cathedral Kapelle went through its first period of brilliance, performing polychoral music in Venetian style. Among the most notable members of the Kapelle about 1600 were the organists Kerle and Christian Erbach, the Kapellmeister Klingenstein (a pupil of Johannes de Cleve), and the *chorvicar* Aichinger. Lassus and Giovanni Gabrieli were on friendly terms with the abbey of St Ulrich and St Afra, where music was reorganized by F.A. Dreer after the Counter-Reformation. The leading Lutheran composer and teacher about 1600 was Gumpelzhaimer.

The FUGGER family, wealthy Augsburg merchants, endowed organs at St Anna, St Ulrich, St Moritz, St Salvator and the church of the Dominicans, paid part of the organists' salaries, established valuable music libraries and instrument collections, and engaged such prominent musicians as Melchior Neusidler, Eccard and Hans Leo Hassler. The Kollegium der Stadtpfeifer, which had a fine reputation during the 16th and 17th centuries, employed not only members of Augsburg's established families of musicians such as Schubinger, Hurlacher and Rauh, but also newly arrived virtuosos such as Jakob Baumann and Philipp Zindelin. Many Renaissance musicians born in Augsburg achieved fame abroad as composers: the Kugelmann brothers in Innsbruck and Königsberg, Sixt Dietrich in Constance, Brayssing in Paris, Jakob Paix in Lauingen and Neuberg-an-der-Donau, and Zängel in Hechingen and Sigmaringen.

2. 17TH AND 18TH CENTURIES.   In the Thirty Years War (1618–48) Augsburg lost two thirds of its population, and its cultural life suffered for decades. Musical activity first revived at the Lutheran Barfüsserkirche and the cathedral, where the Kapellmeister Baudrexel and Gletle restored the concertato style introduced by Aichinger. These Kapellmeister and their successors (Johann Michael Caesar, J.M. Galley and others) were expected to be able to compose, but few of their compositions appeared in print and most of the manuscripts used by the cathedral Kapelle have been destroyed. Several of the cathedral organists were also composers, including Speth, Nauss and J.M. Demmler. Most young Catholic musicians received basic schooling at the cathedral choir school and at the Seminary of St Joseph. In addition to the cathedral, Catholic sacred music was outstanding at St Ulrich and St Afra, the Augustine monastery of the Holy Cross, the collegiate chapter of St Moritz and the Jesuit church of St Salvator. Two provosts of the Holy Cross were composers – Vitalis Mozart (a student of Christian Erbach) and Ludwig Zöschinger – and the monastery also employed the composers P.L. Hözl and P.O. Panzau.

A succession of composers began at the Lutheran Kantorei of St Anna with Tobias Kriegsdorfer and his pupils Schmezer and Merck. Their successors, P. Kräuter, Johann Caspar Seyfert and F.H. Graf, because of their educational or hereditary backgrounds, modelled their works on the compositions of north German composers, including Bach and Telemann. The choir of the Barfüsser-kirche was directed by Jakob Scheiffelhut, a master of the instrumental suite; this popular form was also cultivated by Johann Fischer, son of a Stadtpfeifer and a pupil of Lully, and by Schmierer, director of the Fuggersche Stiftung. The *Gesellschaftslied* and quodlibet, favourite forms of Baroque light music, were cultivated by such

Interior of Augsburg Cathedral: painting by Tobias Maurer, 1616 (Augsburg Cathedral); the organist is believed to be Christian Erbach, and the Kapellmeister (in front of the trombonist, wearing a white surplice) is possibly Bernhard Klingenstein

notable composers as the cathedral Kapellmeister Gletle and Caesar, the government official Matthias Kelz (ii) (who also wrote sonatas and dance pieces) and, later, Rathgeber.

Middle-class amateurs met regularly in the collegium musicum (founded 1713). Talented young composers were able to compose for the frequent theatrical productions at the schools of St Salvator and St Anna, and occasionally at those of St Ulrich, the Holy Cross and the Carmelites. Music at the court of the prince-bishop reached a peak between 1740 and 1770; during this period the Kapelle included J.A. Meichelbeck, J.M. Schmid and P.P. Sales as Kapellmeister and J.G. Lang, J.B. Baumgartner and Joseph Almerigi as resident virtuosos who were also capable composers. Several musicians born in Augsburg in the 17th and 18th centuries achieved prominence elsewhere: Wolfgang and Markus Ebner in

Vienna, T. Eisenhut in Kempten, Johann Fischer at northern German and Scandinavian courts, Motz in Tilsit and Leopold Mozart in Salzburg. The Mozart family had been associated with Augsburg for several centuries, and W.A. Mozart visited the city several times.

3. 19TH AND 20TH CENTURIES.   The secularization of the religious chapters and the decline of the imperial city at first brought a decrease of musical activity in Augsburg. However, it was revived through the efforts of middle-class amateurs, who organized musical societies, many of which were run by teachers. These societies included the Harmoniegesellschaft, founded in 1816, the Frohsinn (1824), the male-voice choirs Liederkranz (1830) and Liedertafel (1843), the Schwäbisch-Bayerischer Sängerbund (1862) and the Oratorienverein (1866). The idea of popular education also gained ground, and found expression in such new musical institutions as the public singing

school founded by Donat Müller in 1849, the Städtisches Orchester of 1865 and the Stadttheater of 1877, and in concerts, including amateur and charity concerts (such as those given by Liszt in 1843 and by the Liedertafel in 1844), as well as festivals. The first Schwäbisch-Bayerisches Sängerbundesfest was held in 1863, and the first Schwäbisches Musikfest in 1886. Such developments were influenced by patriotic, even nationalistic sentiments, as was the repertory of the male-voice choirs, which took part in German song festivals from 1844. Much of this repertory was published in the Augsburg Liedertafel collections that began to appear about 1847.

A bridge between court and civic music had been built early in the century by the Protestant music director Ernst Häussler, C.B. Witzka, later to be cathedral Kapellmeister, and J.C. von Ahorner, when they took part in Prince-Bishop Clemens Wenzeslaus's court concerts. Protestant church music, in which C.L. Drobisch was the leading figure, took its guidelines from Catholic church music. The Catholic churches themselves were already performing works by Lassus about 1820, and thereby paved the way for Cecilianism (the annual congress of the Cäcilienverein was held in Augsburg in 1880). The city was also a centre for the performance of oratorios and cantatas, in particular Haydn's *The Creation* and *The Seasons*, Drobisch's *Johannes Guttenberg* and *Frühlings-Feier* and Mendelssohn's *Antigone*. From 1866 H.M. Schletterer introduced performances of oratorios on a regular basis. Opera also rapidly became a major aspect of musical life in Augsburg; notable productions included Rossini's *Tancredi* in 1818, Weber's *Peter Schmoll* in 1803 and *Der Freischütz* in 1822 and Wagner's *Tannhäuser* in 1854, *Lohengrin* in 1855 and the *Ring* in 1890. In addition, concert life was enhanced by touring virtuosos who included Paganini in 1829 and Liszt in 1823 and 1843. These activities were reflected in journals such as the *Allgemeine Zeitung*, to which Stephen Heller, one of Schumann's 'Davidsbündler' musicians, and Heinrich Heine contributed.

These developments made Augsburg the musical centre of Bavarian Swabia in the second half of the 19th century. Large sections of the population of the industrial city itself now took an active part in musical life; the Arbeiter-Sängerbund Augsburg was founded in 1875, and the first Südbayerisches Arbeiter-Sängerbundesfest was held in 1926. The amateur choral movement as a whole reached a peak before World War I, with some 30 male-voice choirs and around 1500 active singers. In 1936 the festival of German choral music of the Reich Association of Mixed-Voice Choirs was held in Augsburg, with performances of works by contemporary composers including H.F. Michaelsen, Heinrich Kaminski, Armin Knab, Kurt Thomas and Hugo Distler. Under Schletterer's successors W. Weber and H.K. Schmid the Oratorienverein also performed the contemporary music of the day, including works by Brahms, Mahler and Pfitzner. In 1945 A. Piechler conducted Handel's *Judas Maccabaeus* in Augsburg and Brahms's *German Requiem* in Dachau. Carl Orff, Werner Egk, Gottfried von Einem and Otto Jochum came to the city for performances of their works. In 1970 the Oratorienverein merged with the Liedertafel to form the Philharmonischer Chor, which in 1987 gave the first performance in Germany of Andrew Lloyd Webber's Requiem). While the Musica Suevica choir founded in 1983 performs forgotten works of the 18th century, the

University choir gives performances of modern choral music. Contemporary operas were also performed at the Stadttheater from the beginning of the 20th century, including works by Hindemith, Weill, Krenek, Pfitzner, Weinberger and Schreker. Richard Strauss conducted *Arabella* there in 1933 and *Elektra* in 1936. The theatre building, destroyed in 1944, was reopened in 1956; it now concentrates primarily on 20th-century works. Its music directors have included István Kertész, Hans Zanotelli, Bruno Weil and, since 1995, Peter Leonard. The open-air theatre at the Rotes Tor, founded in 1929, stages a four-week opera festival in June and July.

The private music school founded in 1873 by H.M. Schletterer became a conservatory in 1925; it was given the name of the Leopold-Mozart-Konservatorium in 1948, and in 1973 became the Fachakademie für Musik. In 1998 the Fachakademie was incorporated into the new Musikhochschule Nürnberg-Augsburg. In 1905 Albert Greiner founded a singing school which in 1935 introduced a course for singing teachers; it was named the Albert-Greiner-Sing- und Musikschule in 1978. The Amt für Kirchenmusik of the diocesan authority of Augsburg, established in 1970, is responsible for all church music in the diocese. After World War II Augsburg, together with Salzburg and Vienna, became a centre for Mozart studies, and until 1995 was one of the headquarters of the Neue Mozart Ausgabe. The Deutsche Mozart-Gesellschaft was founded in the city in 1951; its journal *Acta mozartiana* has been published since 1969. The International Leopold Mozart Society was inaugurated in Augsburg in 1992. The training of music teachers acquired a new centre with the Pädagogische Hochschule of the University of Munich, founded in 1958 and later affiliated to the University of Augsburg. A chair of musicology was set up in 1980. The Oettingen-Wallerstein Hofmusik, housed in the Augsburg University library, is one of the richest musical collections from the period of Haydn and Mozart in southern Germany.

4. PRINTING AND INSTRUMENT MAKING. The achievements of Augsburg's music scribes, engravers, printers and publishers are among the finest in southern Germany. Outstanding music calligraphers, including Leonhard Wagner, wrote splendid manuscripts at the abbey of St Ulrich and St Afra during the 15th and 16th centuries, and at approximately the same time early German music printing culminated in the magnificent choral incunabula of Ratdolt. Music printing with movable type was introduced to Germany by Oeglin, who printed the earliest odes of the German Humanists; Johann Miller, Sigmund Grimm and Marx Wirsung similarly served the Humanist movement. In the mid-16th century Melchior Kriesstein and Philipp Ulhart printed anthologies edited by Salminger. The first large retail stock of printed music in southern Germany was established in Augsburg (with affiliated branches in Vienna and Tübingen) by Georg Willer, who published his first catalogue for the Frankfurt Fair of 1564. The printing houses established by Valentin Schönig and Johannes Praetorius were continued after the Thirty Years War by Andreas Erfurt, J.J. Schönig, J.C. Wagner, Jakob Koppmayer and Andreas Maschenbauer. The booksellers Goebel, Kroniger, Schlüter and Happach and printers Simon Utzschneider, J.M. Labhart, August Sturm and J.K. Bencard further contributed to Augsburg's active trade in music selling. In the 18th century the Lotter firm assumed a leading role in music publishing as did the

music engravers J.F. and J.C. Leopold and the publishers Matthäus Rieger and J.K. Gombart. In 1803 the *Stadtmusikant* Andreas Böhm founded the music publishing house Anton Böhm & Sohn, which is still active. The publishing house of Bärenreiter, established by Karl Vötterle of Augsburg, set up business there in 1923.

Augsburg was an important centre of instrument building during the 17th and 18th centuries. About 1600 the Bildermann family and others worked on the development of early mechanical instruments, while many lute, violin, organ and piano manufacturers were also active there, most notably J.A. Stein in the late 18th century, whose pianos were highly regarded by Mozart.

BIBLIOGRAPHY

MGG1 (E.F. Schmid); *MGG2* (F. Brusniak, J. Mančal)

E.F. Schmid: *Das goldene Zeitalter der Musik in Augsburg, Augusta 955–1955* (Munich, 1955)

A. Layer: *Musik und Musiker der Fuggerzeit: Begleitheft zur Ausstellung der Stadt Augsburg*(Augsburg, 1959)

A. Layer: 'Augsburger Musikdrucker der frühen Renaissancezeit', *Gutenberg-Jb 1965*, 124–9

L. Wegele, ed.: *Musik in der Reichsstadt Augsburg* (Augsburg, 1965)

L.E. Cuyler: 'Musical Activity in Augsburg and its *Annakirche*, ca. 1470–1630', *Cantors at the Crossroads: Essays on Church Music in Honor of Walter E. Buszin*, ed. J. Riedel (St Louis, 1967), 33–43

A. Layer: 'Augsburger Musik im Barock', *Augsburger Barock*, ed. C. Thon, Rathaus and Holbeinhaus, 15 June – 13 Oct 1968 (Augsburg, 1968), 453–8 [exhibition catalogue]

A. Layer: 'Augsburger Notendrucker und Musikverleger der Barockzeit', *Gutenberg-Jb 1969*, 150–53

A. Layer: 'Musikpflege am Hofe der Fürstbischöfe von Augsburg in der Renaissancezeit', *Jb des Vereins für Augsburger Bistumsgeschichte*, x (1976), 199–211

R. Micus: 'Augsburger Handschriftenproduktion im 15. Jahrhundert', *Zeitschrift für deutsche Philologie*, civ (1985), 411–24

H. Fischer and T.Wohnhaas: 'Die Fugger-Orgel von St Anna in Augsburg: ein Strukturmodell schwäbischer Renaissanceprospekte', *Der Meer Festschrift* (Tutzing, 1987), 127–41

H. Gier: *450 Jahre Staats- und Stadtbibliothek Augsburg: kostbare Handschriften und Drucke*, Augsburg, 15 May – 21 June 1987 (Augsburg, 1987) [exhibition catalogue]

Die Augsburg Pop-Geschichte (Augsburg, 1988)

F. Krautwurst and W.Zorn: *Bibliographie des Schrifttums zur Musikgeschichte der Stadt Augsburg* (Tutzing, 1989)

M. Schmidmüller: 'Die Augsburger Domkapellmeister seit dem Tridentinum bis zur Säkularisation', *Jb des Vereins für Augsburger Bistumsgeschichte*, xxiii (1989), 69–107

T. Wohnhaas: 'Marginalien zur Augsburger Dommusik im 19. Jahrhundert', ibid., 108–21

C. Petzsch: 'Augsburger Meistersingerschule von 1534', *Zeitschrift des Historisches Vereins für Schwaben*, lxxxiii (1990), 31–42

T. Wohnhaas: 'Die Augsburger Domorganisten im 19. und 20. Jahrhundert', *Jb des Vereins für Augsburger Bistumsgeschichte*, xxiv (1990), 115–30

H. Brunner and others, eds.: *Die Schulordnung und das Gemerkbuch der Augsburger Meistersinger* (Tübingen, 1991)

H. Fischer and T.Wohnhaas: *Die Augsburger Domorgeln*(Sigmaringen, 1991)

S. Gmeinwieser and T.Wohnhaas: 'Zur Geschichte der Augsburger Dommusik im 19. Jahrhundert', *Studien zur Kirchenmusik im 19. Jahrhundert: Friedrich Wilhelm Riedel zum 60. Geburtstag*, ed. C.-H. Mahling (Tutzing, 1994)

F.R. Miller: *Vom Ideal der Harmonie: Augsburgs philharmonische Gesellschaften* (Augsburg, 1994)

M. Rogall: 'Die Augsburger Musikbücherei', *Forum Musikbibliothek: Beiträge und Informationen aus der musikbibliothekarischen Praxis*, no.1 (1994), 35–41

R. Charteris: 'A Rediscovered Collection of Music Purchased for St. Anna, Augsburg, in June 1618', *ML*, lxxviii (1997), 487–501

For further bibliography *see* FUGGER.

ADOLF LAYER (1–2, 4), FRIEDHELM BRUSNIAK(3)

August, Peter (*b* ?Warsaw, 1726; *d* Dresden, 16 Feb 1787). German composer. He received a thorough musical grounding before becoming chamber musician and organist at the Dresden court in 1745. In the early 1750s he became first organist at the Catholic court chapel, a position he held until his death. He was responsible for the musical education of the elector's children, including the electoral prince. When the latter ascended to the throne in 1768 as Friedrich August III, August remained his musical adviser, Musizierpartner and librarian, with the tasks of procuring and copying church and chamber music for the court. As a harpsichordist he alternated with C.S. Binder at Dresden public concerts, and also took part in opera performances.

August's extant works, all in manuscript (*D-Dl*), comprise six harpsichord concertos with orchestra, two divertimentos for harpsichord and one for two harpsichords, 48 keyboard sonatas and a lute sonatina. All reflect their origins as pieces for the entertainment or instruction of the royal family. They represent the *galant* style, combining thematic development of the sequential spun-out type with clear periodization and transparent accompaniment. August also made arrangements for two harpsichords of a large number of orchestral and chamber works.

BIBLIOGRAPHY

EitnerQ; *MGG1* (J. Gress)

O. Schmid: 'Peter August', *Die Musik-Woche*, xxv (1901), 196

H. Fleischer: *Christlieb Siegmund Binder (1723–1789)* (Regensburg, 1941)

R. Engländer: *Die Dresdner Instrumentalmusik in der Zeit der Wiener Klassik* (Uppsala, 1956)

A. Rosenmüller: *Die Überlieferung der Clavierkonzerte in der Königlichen Privatmusikaliensammlung zu Dresden im letzten Drittel des 18. Jahrhunderts* (diss., forthcoming)

DIETER HÄRTWIG/ANNEGRET ROSENMÜLLER

Augustine of Hippo [Aurelius Augustinus] (*b* Thagaste, 13 Nov 354; *d* Hippo, 28 Aug 430). Saint, churchman and scholar. He was perhaps the most influential figure in the history of Christian thought, rivalled only by Thomas Aquinas and possibly Origen. Born in North Africa to a pagan father and Christian mother, the sainted Monica, he studied rhetoric in Carthage where he lost his boyhood Christian faith. In 373 his reading of Cicero's *Hortensius* inspired him to pursue the life of a philosopher, which he experienced first as a devotee of Manicheism. He served as professor of liberal arts for several years in his native Thagaste, moving in 383 to Rome and then in 384 to Milan, as professor of rhetoric. In Milan he came under the influence of the Christian Neoplatonist Simplicianus and St Ambrose. He was led gradually through Neoplatonism to Christianity and, after a period of retreat at Cassiacum, was baptized on Easter Eve of 387. He returned to Thagaste in 388 to form a monastic community along with a number of friends. On a visit to Hippo in 391 he was acclaimed by the people and persuaded to accept ordination. He became bishop in 395 and spent the remainder of his life administering to the needs of his diocese, preaching and writing. He died at Hippo in 430 as the city was under siege by the Vandals.

With the exception of Nicetas of Remesiana's *De bono psalmodiae*, the only patristic work devoted entirely to the subject of music is Augustine's *De musica*, a treatise on music as a liberal art. It was originally intended as one of a series of works on the liberal arts; he completed a book on grammar and began studies on dialectic, rhetoric, geometry, arithmetic and philosophy, but only *De musica* survives. The treatise is confined to two of the three branches of ancient musical theory – metrics and rhythmics; he announced his intention at one point to compose a treatise '*de melo*', that is, the third of the musical sub-disciplines, the daunting mathematical science of harmonics. It is doubtful, however, that the philosophically inclined Augustine, even if he had possessed the mathematical expertise, would have had the patience to persevere in this effort. The *De musica* as it stands is a treatise in six books, the first five of which were completed in 387. These show far more of a preference for rhythmics than metrics, exploiting and even distorting the details of classical metrical theory in an effort to display the omnipresence of the basic temporal proportions. The sixth book, written in 391 after Augustine's conversion, is more frankly philosophical; it is a cosmology of sounding number in the tradition of Plato's *Timaeus*, and a Christian theology, ethics and aesthetics of number as well.

Of at least equal significance to music history as the *De musica* are Augustine's numerous remarks about music that are scattered throughout his vast literary output. There are, for example, approving references to music as a liberal art and stern animadversions against contemporary musical practice. But of greatest interest are the many references in his sermons, of which more than 700 are preserved (including the *Enarrationes in psalmos*), to the liturgical singing of psalms; on more than 150 occasions explicit mention is made of a particular psalm or psalm verse that had been sung in the service at which the sermon was preached. A wealth of detail about the psalmodic practice of Hippo and Carthage in the late 4th and early 5th centuries can be extracted from these remarks. Finally there is the famous passage in the *Confessions* where Augustine recalls how he was moved by the psalmody of Ambrose's Milanese church, but felt remorse over the pleasure he had experienced in hearing it. The passage is utterly unique for its time in its quasi-romantic psychological penetration, yet conventional in its ultimate endorsement of the orthodox patristic position that melodious psalmody is acceptable to the Christian church.

BIBLIOGRAPHY

J. Quasten: *Musik und Gesang in den Kulten der heidnischen Antike und christlichen Frühzeit* (Münster, 1930/R; Eng. trans., 1983, as *Music and Worship in Pagan and Christian Antiquity*)

W. Roetzer: *Des heiligen Augustinus Schriften als liturgiegeschichtliche Quelle* (Munich, 1930)

T. Gerold: *Les pères de l'église et la musique* (Strasbourg, 1931/R)

G. Pietzsch: *Die Musik in Erziehungs- und Bildungsideal des ausgehenden Altertums und frühen Mittelalters* (Halle, 1932/R)

E. de Bruyne: *Études d'esthétique médiévale* (Bruges, 1946)

R.C. Taliaferro, ed.: 'De musica', *Writings of Saint Augustine*, Fathers of the Church, ii (New York, 1947)

F. van der Meer: *Augustinus de zielzorger* (Utrecht, 1947; Eng. trans., 1961, as *Augustine the Bishop*)

W.G. Waite: *The Rhythm of Twelfth-Century Polyphony* (New Haven, CT, 1954/R)

G.G. Willis: *St Augustine's Lectionary* (London, 1962)

G. Bonner: *St Augustine of Hippo: Life and Controversies* (London, 1963, 2/1986)

L. Verheijen: *La régle de saint Augustin* (Paris, 1967)

A. Zwinggi: 'Der Wortgottesdienst bei Augustinus', *Liturgisches Jb*, xx (1970), 92–113, 129–40, 250–53

A. Nowak: 'Die "numeri judicales" des Augustinus', *AMw*, xxxii (1975), 196–207

P.-P. Verbraken: *Etudes critiques sur les sermons authentiques de Saint Augustin* (The Hague, 1976)

R.J. O'Connell: *Art and the Christian Intelligence in St Augustine* (Cambridge, MA, 1978)

J. Dyer: 'Augustine and the "Hymni ante oblatium": the Earliest Offertory Chants?', *Revue des études augustiniennes*, xxvii (1981), 85–99

J. McKinnon: 'The Fourth-Century Origins of the Gradual', *EMH*, vii (1987), 91–106

J. McKinnon: *Music in Early Christian Literature* (Cambridge, 1987)

J. McKinnon: 'Desert Monasticism and the Fourth-Century Psalmodic Movement', *ML*, lxxv (1994), 505–21

J. McKinnon: 'Liturgical Psalmody in the Sermons of St Augustine', *Three Worlds of Medieval Chant: Comparative Studies in Greek, Latin and Slavonic Liturgical Music for Kenneth Levy*, ed. P. Jeffrey (forthcoming)

JAMES W. McKINNON

Augustini, Pietro Simone. *See* AGOSTINI, PIETRO SIMONE.

Augustinian canons. Augustinian canons, also known as Austin canons, or canons regular of St Augustine, are an order of priests living the full common life, as distinct from secular canons supported by prebends. The ideal of the canons regular was to imitate the 'apostolic life' of the first Christians. The most celebrated early attempt to follow this ideal was the community life established by AUGUSTINE OF HIPPO and his clergy.

It was not until the mid-11th century that the order emerged as an organized body, its rapid expansion being intimately connected with the Gregorian reform. Officially recognized by the Lateran Synods of 1059 and 1063, the revitalized order spread quickly over the whole of western Europe. In England it increased rapidly under the patronage of Henry I (1100–35). A century later it was the most numerous order in England, counting some 228 houses. Most were small priories, but the order also possessed some famous abbeys, including Waltham and Osney.

The tautological title 'Canonici regulares' was in common use by the early 12th century, by which time most houses of the order had adopted the Rule of St Augustine. This rule's complex historical and textual problems are being gradually elucidated. Existing in two versions, one for men and one for women, it is built up of several elements, notably St Augustine's Letter 211 to his sister. The rule's characteristic qualities are its fundamental sanity, flexibility and insistence on brotherly love, making it suitable for widely differing forms of apostolic or contemplative life. Besides their normal pastoral duties, the canons have undertaken the care of travellers (Great St Bernard) and of the sick (St Bartholomew's and St Thomas's hospitals in London) and the promotion of learning (Abbey of St Victor, Paris). The celebrated Hugh of St Victor contributed his *Didascalion* to the study of music in his day.

A fully developed liturgical life characterizes the order. St Chrodegang (*d* 766) strove to introduce the Roman chant and liturgy. Some independent congregations (Victorines, Premonstratensians) had their own Use. Augustinian canons have also contributed to the development of the liturgy, one of the most celebrated sequence writers being the poet Adam of St Victor. After a lapse of centuries, the Consilium ad Exsequendam Constitutionem de Sacra Liturgia recommended the adoption into the new Roman Breviary of five poems ascribed to him, among them the famous *Salve mater Salvatoris*.

Some houses appear to have had a strong tradition of polyphonic music. St Andrew's Priory in Scotland possessed the rich collection of 13th-century music now in *D-W 677*. It includes a large proportion of the Notre

Dame repertory but none of the motets. The Abbey of St Victor owned the equally famous collection *F-Pn* lat.15139 and the anonymous French *Tractatus de discantu*. It is known from archival documents that the choir of Notre Dame in later centuries paid regular annual visits to the abbey and that polyphony was sung.

Although Wolsey's Statutes of 1519 forbade the use of polyphony and excluded secular singers from conventual choirs, polyphony was undoubtedly practised in English houses of the order. Wolsey himself made provision for polyphony and organ playing by seculars during the Lady Mass and the Mass of the Name of Jesus. Thomas Tallis probably took charge of the 12 'singing-men' and five choristers employed by Waltham Abbey. Finally, at least three Augustinian canons were themselves composers of polyphony: T. Preston and W. Charite of St Mary de Pratis, Leicester, and Robert Carver of Scone Abbey in Scotland.

BIBLIOGRAPHY

HarrisonMMB

C. Dereine: 'Vie commune, Règle de St Augustin et chanoines réguliers au XIe siècle', *Revue d'histoire ecclésiastique*, xli (1946), 365–406

J.C. Dickinson: *The Origins of the Austin Canons and their Introduction into England* (London, 1950)

P. Brown: *Augustine of Hippo: a Biography* (London, 1967/R)

L. Verheijen: *La Règle de Saint-Augustin* (Paris, 1967)

Hymni instaurandi Breviarii romani (Rome, 1968)

L. Verheijen: 'Eléments d'un commentaire de la Règle de Saint Augustin', *Augustiniana*, xxi (1971), 5–23, 357–404

L. Verheijen: *Nouvelle approche de la Regule de Saint Augustin*, i (Begrolles-en-Mauges, 1980); ii (Leuven, 1988)

J. Harper: *The Forms and Orders of Western Liturgy from the Tenth to the Eighteenth Century* (Oxford, 1991)

MARY BERRY

Augustyn, Rafał (*b* Wrocław, 28 Aug 1951). Polish composer. After reading Polish philology at Wrocław University, he studied composition with R. Bukowski at the State Higher School of Music in Wrocław (1971–4) and with Górecki at the Katowice Academy (1975–8); in 1979–80 he attended the State University of New York at Stony Brook. In 1973 he was appointed lecturer at Wrocław University, where he gained the doctorate in 1982. A broadcaster and promoter of contemporary music, especially in connection with the Warsaw Autumn, he was artistic director of the Musica Polonica Nova festival in Wrocław from 1984 to 1994. In 1990 he co-founded the music publishers Brevis.

Characterized by its lyrical expressivity, Augustyn's vocal music draws on a wide range of literary sources, from 16th-century Polish poetry (in *Carmina de tempore*) to words by Apollinaire and Gerard Manley Hopkins. Uninfluenced by sonorism, as found in the work of older Polish composers, he has preferred to establish links, for example, with early 20th-century Austrian and French music; this is particularly true of the vocal-orchestral *A Life's Parallels*. The pieces with orchestra are especially resonant and sensuous. His rhapsodic episodes are as likely to be underpinned by tonal centres or canonic writing (for example in the Second String Quartet) as they are by inventive harmonic-motivic transformations. Several works, including the 'cyclic pieces', explore different aspects of the perception of time.

WORKS
(*selective list*)

Stage: Figle szatana [The Devil's Pranks] (ballet, 1, after A. Müncheimer and S. Moniuszko), 1985; Król siedmiodniowy [Seven-Day King] (ballet-pantomime, 2, H. Tomaszewski), 1988; Cantus puerorum (sacra rappresentazione, Tomaszewski, after Bible: *Daniel*), 1993

Vocal: Carmina de tempore (D. Naborowski and others), S, pf, va, 1981; Atlantyda II (Plato), chorus, orch, 1983; A Life's Parallels (G.M. Hopkins, W. Whitman, E. Pound, C. Rosetti), S, orch, 1983; 3 nokturny rzymskie [3 Roman Nocturnes] (Ennius, Catullus, Seneca), chorus, 1986–90; 5 kaligramów Apollinaire'a, S, pf, 1990; Deutsche fragment, chorus, 1994; In partibus, male vv, pf, 1995

Inst: A Welcome-Farewell Chorale-Like Tune, pf, 1971; Str Qt no.1, 1972; Monosonata, pf, 1976; Ballada, str, 1977; Capriccio sopra la lontananza di Gasparo a Leningrado, pf, 1978; Atlantyda I, orch, 1979; En blanc et noir, hpd, 1979, rev. for hpd, chbr orch, 1987; C.E.I w M. S-S, pf, 1981; Str Qt no.2, opt. fl, 1981; Long Island Rail Road, vn, accompanying objects, 1984; Sny [Dreams], pf, 1986; Utwór cykliczny nr 1 [Cyclic Piece no.1], vn/vn ens, 1986; Stela, vn, 1987, rev. str, 1991; Varesiana, fl, 1987; Wariacje na temat Paganiniego, pf, 1987–9; Auftakt, orch, 1989; Utwór cykliczny nr 2, db, opt. live elecs, 1990; SPHAE. RA (Utwór cykliczny nr 3), ens, tape, 1992; A linea, vc, str, 1995; 5 róznych utworów [5 Sundry Pieces], vn, pf, 1996; Miroirs, 5 pfmrs, 1997; Do ut des, str qt, 1998

Principal publishers: Brevis, PWM

BIBLIOGRAPHY

EMus (M. Zduniak)

K. Baculewski: 'The New Generation of Polish Composers: II', *Polish Music* (1978), no.1, pp.28–32

K. Meyer: 'Il kwartet smyczkowy Rafała Augustyna', *RM*, xxxv/10 (1991), 4 only

ADRIAN THOMAS

Aulen (*fl* late 15th century). German composer. His name may refer to the German city, Aalen, then called Aulen. Nothing is known of his biography, although Martin Just has drawn attention to two men named Johannes, from Aulen, who were at Vienna University in the middle of the century. A three-voice mass apparently by an 'Aulen' exists in several sources (*D-Bsb* 40021, *LEu* 1494, *Mbs* Mus.ms.3154, *Rp* B216–19; *E-Bbc* 454 ascribed to Cuvenor, *SE* ascribed to Agricola; *PL-WRu* Mf2016; ed. in Cw, xxxi, 1934/R, and EDM, 1st ser., xxxiii, 1960); although the earliest source dates from the end of the century the work appears to have been composed some decades earlier. It is written in a relatively homophonic, treble-dominated manner, showing the influence of the Netherlandish chanson style, and each movement has a three-voice head-motif. A four-voice motet, *Salve virgo virginum*, attributed to 'Joannes Aulen' in one of Petrucci's collections (RISM 1505², ed. in SCMot, iii, 1987), is probably not by the same composer. The motet is in a later style, more typical of the works of Josquin's generation.

BIBLIOGRAPHY

MGG1 (H. Besseler); *StrohmR*

M. Just: *Der Mensuralkodex Mus. ms. 40021 der Staatsbibliothek Preussischer Kulturbesitz Berlin: Untersuchungen zum Repertoire einer deutschen Quellen des 15. Jahrhunderts* (Tutzing, 1975), i, 82; ii, 89

A. Kirkman: *The Three-Voice Mass in the Later Fifteenth and Early Sixteenth Centuries: Style, Distribution, and Case Studies* (New York, 1995)

STANLEY BOORMAN/ERIC JAS

Auletta, Domenico (*b* Naples, 1723; *d* Naples, 1753). Italian composer and organist, son of PIETRO AULETTA. He was active in Naples as a composer of sacred music, but nothing is known of any appointments he may have held. Domenico's three sons were also musicians: Raffaele (*b* Naples, 1742; *d* Naples, 18 Feb 1768), composer of a motet *Alto Olimpo triumfate* (*GB-Lbl*), of whose life nothing is known; Ferdinando, a singer, who studied at the Conservatorio della Pietà dei Turchini, 1759–69, with Fago and Cafaro; and the younger Domenico (*d* Naples, 16 Nov 1796), who was appointed in November 1779, with Cimarosa, 'supernumerary' organist without salary in the royal chapel in Naples and in 1796 second organist (Cimarosa having been promoted to first). The homonymy between father and son poses problems of attribution, especially as regards undated works.

WORKS

Ammiro quel volto, aria (G), S, bc, *I-Mc*
Psalms, vv, insts: 5 salmi brevij (Dixit, Laudate pueri, Laetatus sum, Nisi Dominus, Magnificat), SATB, 2 vn, org; 3 Salve regina, 5vv, str, org; 2 De profundis, S, 2 hn, str, org; Dixit Dominus, SATB, 2 vn, 2 ob, 2 tpt, org; Requiem aeternam, S, 2 hn, str, org: all *GB-Lbl* Add.14162
3 concs., hpd, vns, bc, *I-Nc*

BIBLIOGRAPHY
H.-B. Dietz: 'A Chronology of Maestri and Organisti at the Cappella Reale in Naples 1745–1800', *JAMS*, xxv (1972), 379–406, esp. 396, 403

RENATO BOSSA

Auletta, Pietro (*b* Sant'Angelo, nr Avellino, *c*1698; *d* Naples, Sept 1771). Italian composer. He completed his musical training at the Neapolitan conservatory S Onofrio. Some time before 1724 (according to Prota-Giurleo) he was appointed *maestro di cappella* of S Maria la Nova, an important Neapolitan church. In 1725 he composed his first comic opera, *Il trionfo dell'amore, ovvero Le nozze tra amici*, for production at the Teatro Nuovo in Naples. His second comic opera, *La Carlotta*, appeared in Naples in 1726, and his first heroic opera, *Ezio*, in Rome in 1728. At Carnival 1737 he re-emerged as a dramatic composer with the first production in Naples of his comic opera *Orazio*. This work, which was extremely popular, had a long subsequent history; it was continually modified as it was performed in city after city and quickly turned into a pasticcio. In that form it was sometimes ascribed to Auletta and sometimes to other composers. One famous production, a much-shortened version of the original *Orazio*, took place in Paris in 1752 under the title *Il maestro di musica*. The score printed in Paris in 1753 attributed the music to Pergolesi, but in fact it was by several composers including Auletta, who was represented by four items from his original opera. As a pasticcio it was also known as *Le maître de musique*, *La scolara alla moda*, and perhaps *El maestro de capilla*. An anonymous *Impresario abbandonato* (*D-Dl*) is identified in the library catalogue as a revised version of *Orazio* and was probably performed at Munich in 1749 and 1758.

For a few years after the first production of *Orazio* Auletta was much in favour among the Neapolitans. Between 1738 and 1740 he wrote no fewer than four comic operas for Naples, as well as an intermezzo for the marriage of the Infante Felipe in Madrid. After 1740, for a reason as yet unknown, his operatic output fell sharply. In the librettos of some of his operas, including *Il trionfo dell'amore* (1725), *La Carlotta* (1726), *Ezio*(1728), *Il Marchese Sgrana* (1738) and *L'impostore* (1740), Auletta is called *maestro di cappella* to the Prince of Belvedere.

The small amount of Auletta's surviving music contains much that is of high quality. The two arias of his earliest surviving composition, the cantata *Sulla nascente herbetta* (1718), may be criticized for some awkward harmonies; their melodies, however, are most attractive. The melodic styles are surprisingly modern for a Neapolitan composition of 1718, exhibiting the lilting, buoyant qualities that

are commonly associated with Neapolitan music of the late 1720s and 30s. Ex.1, from the vocal line of the second

Ex.1

aria, typifies the style. Of Auletta's extant operas the short, two-act *La locandiera* is probably the most appealing. Written in 1738 to celebrate the marriage of Queen Maria Amalia to King Carlo III of Naples that year, it rivals Pergolesi's comic operas of the same period in its subtle musical characterization, its grotesque humour (especially in the parts for the elderly characters) and its portrayal of the playful yet tender feelings of youth – all achieved with the utmost economy of technical means. Once again, Auletta's attractive melodies are a crucial factor in the success of the work. His accompaniments are discreet and his orchestration never overbearing.

WORKS

DRAMATIC

Il trionfo dell'amore, ovvero Le nozze tra amici (op comica, 3, C. de Palma), Naples, Nuovo, aut. 1725, *D-MÜs*
La Carlotta (op comica, 3, B. Saddumene), Naples, Fiorentini, spr. 1726
Ezio (op eroica, 3, P. Metastasio), Rome, Dame, 26 Dec 1728, excerpts *I-Rc*
Orazio (commedia per musica, 3, A. Palomba), Naples, Nuovo, carn. 1737; as pasticcio Il maestro di musica, Paris, 1752 (Paris, 1753), trio *GB-Lbl*; as Impresario abbandonato, ? Munich, 1749, excerpts *CH-Bu*, *D-Dl*; as L'impressario, Verona, Filarmonico, carn. 1748; as L'impresario, Turin, Carignano, spr. 1748; as Orazio, Turin, 1748, *Dl*, *Wa*, *I-Fc*; as El maestro de capilla (2), Barcelona, 1750
Il Marchese Sgrana (drama per musica, Palomba), Naples, Nuovo, spr. 1738, *Tf*
Demetrio (Metastasio), ? Città, 1738, aria *Nc*
La locandiera (scherzo comico per musica, 2, G.A. Federico), Naples, S Carlo, 10 July 1738, *Nc*
Don Chichibio (op comica, 3), Naples, Nuovo, carn. 1739
L'amor costante (commedia per musica, 3, Palomba), Naples, Fiorentini, Spr. 1739, *Nn*
Intermezzo for the marriage of the Infante Felipe, Madrid, 1739
L'impostore (commedia per musica, 3, C. Fabozzi), Naples, Fiorentini, aut. 1740
Zenobia, ? Città, excerpts *Tf*
Caio Fabricio (drama per musica, 3, A. Zeno), Turin, Regio, carn. 1742, excerpts *Tf*
Il Marchese di Spartivento, ovvero Il cabalista ne sa' men del caso (farsetta), Rome, Valle, carn. 1747, addns B. Micheli
Il conte immaginario (intermezzo), Venice, S Cassiano, aut. 1748, aria *Mc*
Didone abbandonata (drama per musica, 3, Metastasio), Florence, Pergola, aut. 1759, *Fc*
Conte Schizza (int per musica), Brunswick, 4vv, orch, *A-KR*
1 aria in Venetian Ballads (London, *c*1748); arias in *KR*, *CH-EN*, *D-MÜs*, *F-Pn*, *I-BGi*, *Mc*, *Nc*, *Rc*

SACRED

Il martirio di S Ferma Vergine (orat), Civitavecchia, 25 April 1722
Oratorio sacro, Naples, 1745
Ave maris stella, 5vv, str, org, *GB-Lbl*; Christus factus est, 4vv, ob, 2 vn, va, bc, *D-MÜs*; De profundis, S, 2 vn, bc, *MÜs*

Duetto ... ad laudem et honorem B. Mariae, 2vv, 2 vn, 2 ob, 2 hn, bc, *I-Nc*

Salve regina, 3vv, org, *Vnm*; De profundis, S, orch, *Mc*

Omnes gentes (motet), S, str, org, *H-P*

OTHER SECULAR

Sinfonia, 3 movts, 2 ob, 2 hn, 2 vn, va, *I-Gl*

Sulla nascente erbetta (secular cant.), 1718, *GB-Lbl*

BIBLIOGRAPHY

DBI (U. Prota-Giurleo); *SartoriL*

F. Walker: 'Two Centuries of Pergolesi Forgeries and Misattributions', *ML*, xxx (1949), 297–320

F. Walker: 'Orazio: the History of a Pasticcio', *MQ*, xxxviii (1952), 369–83

M.F. Robinson: *Naples and Neapolitan Opera* (Oxford, 1972/R)

G. Hardie: 'Neapolitan Comic Opera, 1707–1750: Some Addenda and Corrigenda for *The New Grove*', *JAMS*, xxxvi (1983), 124–7

MICHAEL F. ROBINSON (WITH ROSA LEONETTI)

Aulí, Juan (*b* Felanitx, Mallorca, 19 Dec 1796; *d* Felanitx, 10 Jan 1869). Spanish organist and composer. He had a precocious musical talent and was already an organist when he entered the Dominican order in 1814. On the dissolution of the Spanish monasteries in 1823, he wandered over Spain for several months, but in November of the same year he was allowed to return to Mallorca. In 1825 he went back to Madrid to complete his theological education, playing the organ for a time at the church of S María de Atocha and being introduced to King Ferdinand VII. In 1828 he returned to Mallorca, living a very active musical life at the convent of S Domingo. The Mendizábal law of 1835 forced him to abandon his orders and to leave his native Mallorca. Shortly afterwards he became an organist at Gibraltar. In 1836 he returned to the Balearic Isles, where he settled in Felanitx and spent the rest of his life composing, serving occasionally as an organist and producing his own operas at the local theatres. His *Misa de coro*, with organ accompaniment by Antonio Noguera (Palma de Mallorca, 1887), is severe in style and frankly monastic in feeling. Other sacred works include a *Missa del santísimo sacramento*, *Te Deum*, *Stabat mater* and hymns. Only a few fragments survive from his operas *Norma* and *La doncella de Misolongi*; other stage works are *El sepultero* and *Grecia*. He also composed some piano pieces, including a set of variations. His extant manuscripts are in the Arxiu de Música Histórica de Sant Felip Neri, Palma de Mallorca and the Arxiu de la Parròquia de Sant Miguel, Felanitx.

BIBLIOGRAPHY

A. Pizà: *El músic Joan Aulí* (Felanitx, 1996)

X. Carbonell, ed: *VII nit bielenca: homenatge al compositor Joan Aulí* (Búger, 1997) [with CD]

J.B. TREND/ANTONI PIZÀ

Aulin, Tor (Bernhard Vilhelm) (*b* Stockholm, 10 Sept 1866; *d* Saltsjöbaden, 1 March 1914). Swedish violinist, composer and conductor, brother of VALBORG AULIN. He studied from 1877 to 1883 with J. Lindberg (violin) and C. Nordqvist (theory) at the Swedish Royal Academy of Music and in Berlin from 1884 to 1886 with E. Sauret (violin) and P. Scharwenka (composition). He was active as an orchestral musician in the early years of his career and served as leader of the Swedish Hovkapell from 1889 to 1902. In 1887 he founded the Aulin Quartet, which made annual tours of Sweden and other northern European countries until it was disbanded in 1912; it specialized not only in the Classical repertory, particularly Beethoven, but in a wide-ranging representation of the works of Scandinavian composers, above all Berwald,

Grieg, E. Sjögren and W. Stenhammar. From 1890 Aulin worked closely with Stenhammar, who also took part in most of the Aulin Quartet's tours as pianist. His circle of friends also included Grieg and Sjögren.

From 1900 Aulin devoted his time increasingly to conducting: until 1902 he directed the Svenska Musiker-förbundets Orkester, from 1902 to 1909 the Stockholm Concert Society (founded largely through his initiative) and from 1909 to 1912 the Göteborg Orchestral Society. He conducted the first performance of Berwald's *Sinfonie singulière*, which he subsequently edited for publication. In 1895 he was elected a member of the Royal Academy of Music.

As a composer Aulin was stylistically as close to German Romanticism as to the Scandinavians. He is best remembered for the last of his three violin concertos, op.14 in C minor, a highly accomplished work reflecting the influence of Bruch and Schumann as well as that of Grieg. He also composed numerous songs and chamber works, wrote incidental music to the play *Mäster Olof* by his friend Strindberg, and made transcriptions for violin and piano of some of Sjögren's songs.

WORKS

ORCHESTRAL

3 vn concs., incl. no.3, c, op.14 (Leipzig, n.d.)

Mäster Olof, suite (incid music for A. Strindberg's play), op.22 (Leipzig, n.d.)

3 gottländische Tänze, op.28 (Leipzig, n.d.); arr. vn, pf, op.23 (Leipzig, n.d.)

4 schwedische Tänze, op.32 (Leipzig, n.d.); arr. vn, pf, op.30 (Leipzig, n.d.)

OTHER WORKS

String quartet, op.1

Numerous works for vn, pf, incl. Sonata, d, op.12; 4 Stücke in Form einer Suite, op.15 (Leipzig, 1914); 4 Stücke, op.16 (Leipzig, n.d.); Midsommar-dans, op.18 (Leipzig, n.d.); Albumblatt, op.20 (Leipzig, n.d.); Lyrische Gedicht, op.21 (Leipzig, 1908); Fyra violinstycken, op.27 (Stockholm, 1912); 4 Kinderstücke, op.33 (Leipzig, n.d.); 2 karakterstycken (Stockholm, 1892); Minnesblad [Albumleaf] (Stockholm, 1898); Fyra akvareller [Four Watercolours] (Stockholm, 1899)

Songs, 1v, incl. Tre dikter af Tor Hedberg, op.24 (Copenhagen and Leipzig, n.d.); Två dikter af August Strindberg, op.31 (Stockholm, 1913); Trenne sånger (Stockholm, 1899); Vier serbische Volkslieder nach J. Runeberg (Strasbourg, 1903); Drei Lieder aus Tannhäuser von Julius Wolff, Bar, orch (Leipzig, n.d.)

Works for pf, incl. Tre albumblad, op.5 (Copenhagen, n.d.); Kleine Suite (Strasbourg, 1903); Valse caprice, pf 4 hands (Stockholm, 1887)

Studies for violin, incl. Violinskola (Stockholm, 1903)

Cadenzas for Mozart: Vn Conc. no.5, A, op.17 (Leipzig, n.d.); Vn Conc. no.3, G, op.29 (Leipzig, n.d.)

Arrs., incl. Lyriska dikter (E. Sjögren), vn, pf (Stockholm, 1903); Etüden für Violine (H.E. Kayser) (Stockholm, 1902)

For complete list see *SBL*

BIBLIOGRAPHY

SBL (O. Morales)

A. Aulin: 'En fyrväppling av svenska tonsättare', *Musikmänniskor*, ed. F.H. Törnblom (Uppsala, 1943)

M. Pergament: 'August Strindberg och Tor Aulin', *Svenska tonsättare* (Stockholm, 1943)

T. Rangström: 'De tystlåtna – och en stridsman!', *Musikmänniskor*, ed. F.H. Törnblom (Uppsala, 1943)

G. Törnbom: 'Aulin, Tor', *Sohlmans musiklexikon* (Stockholm, 1948–52, rev. 2/1975–9 by H. Åstrand)

B. Wallner, ed.: 'Edvard Griegs brev till Tor Aulin', *Ord och bild*, lxi (1952)

B. Wallner: 'Wilhelm Stenhammar och kammarmusiken', *STMf*, xxxiv (1952), 28–59; xxxv (1953), 5–73

B. Wallner, ed.: 'Tor Aulins brev till Edvard Grieg', *Ord och bild*, lxiv (1955)

ROBERT LAYTON

Aulin, (Laura) Valborg (*b* Gävle, 9 Jan 1860; *d* Örebro, 11 Jan 1928). Swedish pianist and composer, elder sister of TOR AULIN. After studying at the Swedish Royal Academy of Music (1877–82), where she was encouraged in composition by Ludvig Norman and Albert Rubenson, she was awarded a Jenny Lind grant (1885), which enabled her to study composition for a short time with Gade in Copenhagen and then to spend two years in Paris studying with Massenet and Godard. She was admired as a pianist and became sought after as a piano teacher. In 1903 she settled in Örebro where she remained until her death. Her works show harmonic refinement and a powerful temperament, while her tone poems for piano are written in a more lyrical style. The *Tre damkörer* were awarded a prize in Copenhagen in 1895. She ceased composing around the turn of the century.

WORKS

Orch: Suite, op.15, 1886
Vocal: Herr Olof, ballad, T, chorus, orch, op.3, 1880; Julsång, chorus 8vv, org, op.23; Två körer, unacc. mixed chorus, op.24, 1898; Procul este (C.D. Wirsén), S, chorus, str orch, harp, op.28, 1886; Tre damkörer, women's choir, pf, 1895; Veni sancte spiritus, mixed chorus, pf, op.31, 1898; 11 songs, 1v, pf, 1881–1900
Chamber: 2 str qts, F, 1884, e, op.17, 1889; pieces for vn, pf
Kbd (for pf unless otherwise stated): 5 tondikter, op.7, 1882; 7 pieces, op.8, 1884; Sonata, f, op.14, 1885; Valse élégiaque, 1892; Albumblad, op.29, 1898; Fantasistycken, op.30, 1898; Meditation, org

Principal publishers: Elkan & Schildknecht

BIBLIOGRAPHY

SBL (O. Morales)
E. Öhrström: *Borgerliga kvinnors musicerande i 1800-talets Sverige* (diss., U. of Göteborg, 1987), 145–55, 198–9
L. Johnsson and M.Tegen, eds.: *Musiken i Sverige: den nationella identiteten 1810–1920* (Stockholm, 1992), 419, 427–8

ROBERT LAYTON

Aulos (Gk.; Lat. *tibia*). A Greek reed instrument. It was the most important of the ancient Greek wind instruments. (The term has often been mistranslated 'flute' by modern scholars.)

I. The instrument. II. The performers: auletes and auletrides.

I. The instrument

1. Sources. 2. Description. 3. Origins. 4. Terminology and classification. 5. Construction: (i) Materials (ii) Pipes and assembly (iii) Holes (iv) Reeds (v) Mechanisms.

1. SOURCES.   The aulos occupied an important place in Greek civilization. Information about the instrument and its use is to be found in many and varied sources extending over a period of some ten centuries. The sources fall into three main categories: texts and written records, iconographic sources and archaeological sources.

Numerous references to the aulos exist throughout Greek literature, but several works (or parts of works) contain information of a more technical nature: for example, books iv and xiv of Athenaeus's *Sophists at Dinner*; Pseudo-Plutarch's *On Music*; fragments of treatises with remarks about the instrument's bore; notes by lexicographers; and scholia to tragic and comic writers and lyric poets. No works specifically devoted to the aulos appear to have survived: only the titles of works and the names of certain authors are known, for example, the treatises *On Auloi* by Aristoxenus of Tarentum and by the Pythagorean Euphranor. Several inscriptions and various papyri (musicians' contracts etc.) contain technical terms designating auloi.

Iconographic records, which extend uninterruptedly from the earliest times (the Cycladic and Minoan periods) to the 4th and 5th centuries CE, are numerous and range from Greek ceramics to mosaics, reliefs and wall paintings. After the 1st century BCE and most notably during the Roman period, relief techniques and the quality of depictions are such that a 'realistic' view of the instruments and especially their mechanisms, which are never shown on Attic ceramics, becomes possible.

Several hundred (maybe as many as a thousand) auloi, many of them fragmentary but some almost complete, have come to light during archaeological investigations. Often capable of being dated accurately, these remains provide direct evidence of what auloi were like in a given place at a given time. Instruments dating from the 6th century BCE to late antiquity have been discovered in countries as far afield as Greece, Italy, France, the Low Countries, Egypt, Sudan, Israel, Turkey and Tajikistan. Systematic study of this evidence is yet to be made, although work has begun on the tibiae of the Roman world (see Péché).

2. DESCRIPTION.   The Greek word *aulos*, even when used in the singular, usually denotes a wind instrument consisting of two pipes and two (probably double) reeds. However, since the word was also applied to any hollow, elongated tube, *aulos* may refer to any wind instrument consisting of a single pipe with or without a reed, including (occasionally) the trumpet. When qualified by the term *polukalamos*, the aulos is an instrument with several pipes of unequal length, otherwise called *surinx*, the ancient equivalent of modern pan-pipes (see SYRINX). The pipes of Greek auloi were always cylindrical. Instruments with a conical bore first appeared among the Etruscans and then in the Roman world. A very slightly flared bell at the end of the pipe occurs in a few specimens from the end of the Hellenistic and imperial periods.

To play the double aulos, instrumentalists placed the two double reeds between their lips. Their embouchure was sometimes sealed by a PHORBEIA (mouthband) perforated by two small holes to take the reeds; the pipes could be held either close together or further apart. On many Attic vases the little fingers are placed under the pipes, probably to give a better grip when the instrument was made of a heavy material such as ivory or metal.

3. ORIGINS.   The Greeks never regarded themselves as the inventors of the aulos: they saw it as an instrument of foreign origin (Aristoxenus classed it among the *ekphula organa*). Some writers considered it to have come from Libya, but most thought it was from Phrygia. If the lexicographers are to be believed, some of the instrument's indigenous names passed into Greek (i.e. *phōtinx*, *elumos*). In line with the typically Greek habit of identifying a 'first inventor' (*prōtos heuretēs*), authors invariably attributed the aulos's invention to one or another personnage, including Seirites, a Libyan 'of the people of the Numidians' (Athenaeus, *Sophists at Dinner*, xiv.9, citing the historian Douris of Samos, an attribution taken up by Pollux, *Dictionary*, iv.174), the semi-legendary auletes Olympus and Hyagnis, and even the Phrygian satyr Marsyas. Beginning in the the first half of the 5th century BCE, however, there were attempts to 'Hellenize' the origins of the aulos, a trend that became particularly

dominant at the end of the 4th century BCE. The instrument's invention was no longer ascribed to some barbarian character but to a Greek divinity, either Apollo himself (Anticleides and Istrus, as quoted in Pseudo-Plutarch, *On Music*, 1136a–b) or Athena, who is described as immediately rejecting it (Pindar, *Pythian*, xii.7ff; Epicharmus as quoted by Athenaeus, op. cit., ii.84; and many Latin texts referring to the tradition).

The true origins of the aulos remain obscure, even though Mesopotamian, Cypriot, Egyptian and Anatolian iconographic records attest the existence of the double aulos at very early periods around the Mediterranean basin as well as in Cycladic culture (Minoan marble statuettes dating from *c*2200 BCE). Nonetheless, the Hellenic aulos with two straight pipes of equal length always remained distinct from its supposed ancestor the Phrygian aulos, one of whose pipes ended in a joint that was either curved or made of horn, hence its Greek and, later, Latin name *keras* ('horn'; fig.1).

4. TERMINOLOGY AND CLASSIFICATION. The generic term *aulos* embraces a wide variety of instruments. As early as the 4th century BCE Greek authors endeavoured to draw up analytical classifications, of which the clearest are found in the Aristotelian *On Things Heard* (804a) and Aristoxenus's *Harmonic Elements* (ed. Meibom, 21). According to Aristoxenus (in Athenaeus, *Sophists at Dinner*, xiv.36) there were four categories covering 'more than three octaves'; from the highest to the lowest auloi they are the parthenian ('of young girls'), the 'childlike' (*paidikoi*), auloi to accompany the kithara (*kithariatērioi*), the 'perfect' (*teleioi*) and the 'more than perfect' (*huperteleioi*), the two last-named being also grouped under the term 'masculine' (*andreioi*). This classification by range has no bearing upon the practical use, material, origin or form of the instrument. Yet, its terminology goes hand in hand with certain terms known from other sources in connection with musical practice: 'Pythian aulos', suitable for playing the *nomos* of the same name and described as 'virile' (thus placing it among the *auloi teleioi*); 'kitharist auloi', that is, auloi played with the kithara or an instrument of the same register; and the much-discussed *aulos magadis*, about which Greek scholars cannot agree, although it is likely that it had qualities similar to the magadis, a kind of harp capable of playing octaves (see A. Barker: 'Che cos'era la "mágadis"?', *La musica in Grecia*, ed. B. Gentili and R. Pretagostini, Rome, 1988, pp.96–107). This points to the simultaneous existence, if not of several coherent classifications, at least of a variety of terminology, for which evidence may be found in the works of non-specialist and specialist authors alike, both Greek and Latin.

Some terms used for the instruments were derived from the materials of construction: *lōtos* (the wood of the nettle-tree), *buxus* (a Latin term that came to be used for the box-wood tibia), *kalamos* and *donax* (used for rustic instruments made of reeds), and *ebur* (Lat. 'ivory'). In addition there are several terms which came to be used typologically but whose original usage was related to geographical provenance: the *hellenikos aulos* ('Greek aulos'), which embraced all auloi with straight pipes, as distinct from the *elumos*, thought to be an indigenous name for the *phrugiaulos* ('Phrygian aulos'); the *gingras*, a small, very high-pitched instrument of Phoenician origin; and the *phōtinx*, an Egyptian aulos with a single pipe and

1. *Phrygian aulos (or Berecyntian tibiae) with kerata: detail of a relief from a marble sarcophagus, mid-3rd century CE (Catacombs of Praetextatus, Rome)*

possibly no reed. The term *plagiaulos* (literally 'oblique aulos') was used for the transverse flute with no reed.

No doubt the authors of the works *On Auloi* endeavoured to bring some kind of order into the terminology. A papyrus containing a young aulete's contract of apprenticeship (see Bélis and Delattre) shows that the terms used in everyday language and by scholars were not those employed by professionals: instrumentalists, teachers of the aulos, and probably the instrument makers, too, had a kind of jargon of their own.

5. CONSTRUCTION.

(i) Materials. While amateur musicians and particularly shepherds made their own auloi from reeds, using fire to bore the holes, professional musicians always turned to

specialist craftsmen (*aulopoiai*) to provide them with more durable, more attractive and, above all, more sophisticated instruments. Materials of a less perishable nature and more suitable for working were used for this purpose: ivory, bone, wood and metal, as the written sources and the remains of instruments show.

Makers of bone instruments used animals with long bones capable of providing sections measuring some 15 cm when worked, for instance, the legs of stags and the front legs of donkeys, which were much valued by Greek and Roman craftsmen alike. If Plutarch is to be believed, Theban craftsmen were the first to use the legs of stags, deer and fawns, which made the 'most sonorous' kinds of instruments (*Banquet of Seven Sages*, 150e–f). Latin authors provide evidence that donkey and deer bones continued in use throughout antiquity (Callimachus, *Hymn to Artemis*; Pliny the Elder, *Naturalis historia*, xvi.172; Antipater of Sidon, *Anthologia palatina*, 305, etc.); excavated auloi fragments confirm this, although examples made of the bones of sheep or cattle, materials not mentioned by classical authors, have also been discovered. A good many almost intact instruments, or sections of instruments, made of bone and ivory have survived (Alexandria, Tarento and Delos).

For wooden instruments, tree species with dense fibres (and therefore resistant to humidity) and long, thick, straight branches were chosen. Box (the Libyan *lōtos*, identified as the jujube tree of today) and nettle-tree – woods, as Pliny pointed out (xvi.212), that do not crack or split, are durable and not inclined to rot – were also popular with makers. A single text (Pollux, *Dictionary*, iv.71) mentions laurel 'with the pith removed'. The only wooden auloi to have come down to us are a few complete instruments from Ptolemaic Egypt, now in the Louvre, and the famous Elgin Pipes in the British Museum, which appear to be made of sycamore. Metal seems not to have been used for the body of auloi, but only as a covering for a bone or ivory tube. References to bronze, orichalc or silver auloi are therefore probably not to be taken literally. However, some specimens discovered during excavations do have coverings or rings made of these costly, precious metals; archaeology thus complements the accounts of the written sources and corrects the details.

(ii) Pipes and assembly. All the sources – written, pictorial and archaeological – show that the bore of the Greek aulos was strictly cylindrical, that is, of constant diameter. This is the characteristic of what the Greeks called the 'Hellenic aulos' (Aelian, quoted by Porphyry in his commentary on Ptolemy's *Harmonics*, i.3). Only the Etruscans and then the Romans made instruments with a conical bore (see Jannot). All the remains of instruments conform to this rule, including the upper joints with their bulbous outer shape into which the reed was inserted (the auloi of Delos, the Agora of Athens, and Corinth, the Elgin Pipes in the British Museum, and the double aulos in the Louvre, made of a single piece of wood including a bulbous swelling, also have a constant internal bore). The diameter varies from one specimen to another. Among the 30 or so sections found on the island of Delos, internal diameters range from 7·7 mm to 15 mm; five fragments have a bore of 10·5 mm, and three a bore of 12 mm. The average is an internal diameter of about 10 mm, which in today's terms seems very narrow, certainly much narrower than the bore of the modern clarinet or flute. However, there are notable and wide-ranging disparities, which

must correspond to the different kinds of instrument, from the small *auloi paidikoi*, very narrow and with a high range, to the *auloi huperteleioi*, with large-bore pipes to produce a deeper sound. The walls of the *huperteleioi* are usually 1·5 mm thick, whether the instrument is made of wood, bone or metal, giving an external diameter of some 15 mm. To judge by the surviving complete instruments, each pipe might consist of five or six joints, each about 15 cm long, assembled on the tenon and mortise principle, with the tenon always at the lower end. The entire pipe might therefore reach a length of 60–70 cm. Since the maximum reach of the players' fingers would not be greater than about 20 cm, it is evident that the holes arranged along these very long pipes could be stopped only with the aid of mechanical devices.

(iii) Holes. As a rule the holes (*trupēmata, trēmata*) are never shown on Attic or Apulian ceramics, even by a talented painter who would otherwise depict every detail (fig.2). This seems to have been a convention of stylization. The only exceptions are a few vases showing auletes holding pipes in their hands (the fragments of a red-figure Attic cup in the severe style of *c*490 BCE in the Musée du Cinquantenaire, Brussels, Inv. A 1331; the bottom of the Marsyas Cup, 4th century BCE, in Berkeley, University of California, Inv. 8.935). In the literature, too, authors show little concern for the practical aspects of instrument making; the most that can be learnt is that the holes were bored with a drill. Those passages in works of the Pythagorean school concerning the number and arrangement of the holes of auloi should not be taken as accurate

2. *Aulos player wearing a phorbeia, or mouthband: detail from a Greek amphora, Attic Red-figure style, c480* BCE *(British Museum, London)*

descriptions but rather as ideas put forward by theorists anxious to give proof of their calculations of musical intervals. The only reliable evidence for this aspect of construction is archaeological.

It is likely that instruments made during the Archaic period, as with rustic instruments made of reeds, had only a few holes, four or five to each pipe, capable of being stopped by the fingers alone. A commentator on Horace quotes a passage from Varro's *De lingua latina*, to the effect that tibiae in former times had only four holes; Varro claims to have seen such instruments in a temple of Marsyas. Sometime after the beginning of the 5th century BCE the instrument played by professional auletes seems to have merited the description *polutrētos* ('with many holes') and *poluphthongos* ('with many sounds'), much to the displeasure of thinkers such as Plato, a declared opponent of the virtuoso style and a champion of the (lost) cause of asceticism and simplicity in music. During the last quarter of the 4th century BCE Aristotle alluded to 'those who see an analogy' between the 24 letters of the Greek alphabet and the interval separating the *bombux* (the lowest note of the aulos) from its highest note (*Metaphysics*, 1093a29–b4).

The holes were mostly on the upper surface of the pipe, but there were also holes underneath to be stopped by the thumb, as found in a number of joints made of bone, wood and ivory. Usually the thumb-hole was placed between two holes on the opposite surface, calling for the hand position frequently shown by painters of red-figure Attic ceramics, with the aulete's thumb placed between his index and middle fingers, as on the Kleophrades amphora (fig.2). Such an arrangement probably avoided boring three holes dangerously close together on the same side of the pipe, especially in the upper joints of the instrument. The majority of holes are perfectly circular, with impeccably trimmed edges and no sign of repairs or errors; they are usually 6–7 mm in diameter, capable of being stopped with the finger-tips. There are also non-circular holes: those of an oval shape were probably intended to be partially stopped in order to produce intervals smaller than a semitone; others, in the shape of a cat's eye (in tibiae from Pompeii), perhaps resulted from corrections to the tuning.

Certain sections of auloi discovered at Delos, in Athens, and near Dushanbe in Tajikistan, have rectangular holes along the length of the pipe. These were obviously too far apart to be stopped manually, and it is likely that they were operated by some form of mechanism (see §I, 5(v) below). Although the holes are usually strictly aligned along the pipe, the lowest hole in a joint is sometimes set slightly to one side so that it could easily be stopped by the shorter little finger. Holes arranged all over the surface of the pipe, as in the large Pompeian tibiae, were obviously stopped by mechanical devices: the player's fingers would not have been adequate, especially to reach the most distant holes. However, there is no reason to believe that the side holes were always meant to be stopped by the little finger; as vase painters often showed, this finger could be placed under the pipe, no doubt to provide better support, particularly when an instrument might be weighed down by bronze or silver rings or coverings.

(iv) Reeds.   Probably because it functioned as the organ of sound production, the reed was called 'tongue' (Gk. *glōtta*, *glōttis*; Lat. *ligula* or *lingula*: 'little tongue').

Partially split straws were used for rustic instruments, but there is overwhelming evidence in the sources that a special kind of reed, known as *zeugitēs* ('musical reeds'), was used throughout antiquity for most auloi and tibiae. The most sought-after reeds came from the floating islands of Lake Copais in Boeotia, north-west of Thebes (Theophrastus, *Enquiry into Plants*, iv.11; Pliny the Elder, *Naturalis historia*, xvi.168–72), where the best workshops specializing in double reed manufacture were located. The marshes of the Celenes region of Phrygia also provided material for high-quality reeds (Strabo, *Geography*, xii.8.15).

It is clear from Greek and Latin texts that makers took particular care over the harvesting and manufacture of their reeds (see Bélis and Péché, 1996). The plants were required to be of at least two years' growth, and specimens described as 'eunuchs' (without plumes) were preferred. Until the middle of the 4th century BCE the reeds were gathered in mid-September, but after the great floods of the lake in 338 BCE the date was brought forward by three months to 'a little before the solstice, or at the time of the solstice'. After harvesting, the reeds were bunched together and left to dry for several years; during the first winter they were wrapped and left out of doors. When spring came the reeds were cleaned and cut into sections at the internodes; only the middle part of a section, of a length no less than two palms (14·8 cm), was retained. After a final drying, the manufacture of the reed began.

A section was split in half lengthways to provide two symmetrical blades that would form the double reeds fitted to each of the two pipes of a single instrument in the hope that they would be perfectly 'in tune'. Each blade was then folded in half, split, and one of the ends tied by thread wound around several times; the vibrating end was called the 'mouth' (*stoma*). The reed was inserted into the mouthpiece so that the bottom of the mouth was level with the olive-shaped swelling of the bulb (*holmos*) that fitted into the upper joint of the instrument (*hupholmion*). According to Theophrastus, the manufacturing process did not always go smoothly, many reeds being spoilt despite the craftsmen's best efforts. Theophrastus emphasized the important point that 'until the time of Antigenidas', a virtuoso aulete active between 392 and 353 BCE, reeds were rather hard; the maker would season them before use, and players would moisten them with saliva or even grease before playing. When the instruments were not being used, auletes would place the reeds in a small ivory box with a lid (a *glōttokomeion*), and this was attached to the case in which the pipes were kept.

(v) Mechanisms.   As with the holes, the mechanisms are by convention never shown on Attic and Italic ceramics; certain polychrome items, for example, a small votive plaque from Pitsa, show joints in different colours, no doubt to illustrate the difference between bone and bronze (as Pindar confirms). Funnel-shaped projections do not appear until the Roman period; so far as can be determined, their function was to increase the length of the air column, by plugging the holes, in order to obtain chromatic notes. They are most frequently found on Phrygian auloi after the 2nd century BCE. Although the name of these particular devices is not known, it appears that *kerata* was the term for the large horn-shaped mechanisms (see fig.1) which allowed the player to stop holes; a lever would cause a ring perforated by a hole of the same dimensions to slide around or up and down the

tube, thus opening or closing the hole. The function of the *kerata* was also to increase the length of the air column, perhaps to obtain chromatic degrees.

From the 5th century BCE onwards, written sources mention progress in the manufacture of auloi; it seems that during the course of the century the aulete Pronomus invented a means of modulating, but no further details of this technique are known. Other authors give the names of certain mechanisms but do not describe them in sufficient detail to permit definite identification; for instance, Aristotle explained how *suringes* allowed the aulos to play in octaves, and at the time of Demosthenes a famous aulete called Telephanes of Megara refused to fit his auloi with these devices, preferring to use a less virtuoso instrument, one in keeping with the musical style he favoured. It is possible that the *suringes* were slides, and although texts referring to them remain obscure, future examination of surviving instruments in a good state of preservation (e.g. an aulos from Pergamon and others from Tajikistan) may help to clarify this question.

It is worth emphasizing that the virtuoso players of antiquity never had to make do with rudimentary wind instruments of only approximate accuracy. Their instruments always issued from specialist workshops, some of which were extremely famous and attracted the custom of the best musicians of the time. So far, the only workshop to have been located precisely is that near the Temple of Apollo on Delos (see Bélis, 1988). Worked with great precision by highly qualified craftsmen using rare and valuable materials, fitted with ingenious mechanical devices and individually made to order to the detailed specification of instrumentalists, the Greek auloi and Roman tibiae were high-performance, powerful and precise instruments, evidence of the degree of perfection that could be attained by the technology of the ancient world.

II. The performers: auletes and auletrides

1. The aulete: definition and related terminology. 2. Social status of auletes. 3. Virtuoso auletes: training and career. 4. Auletrides.

1. THE AULETE: DEFINITION AND RELATED TERMINOLOGY. An 'aulete' (Gk. *aulētēs*; Lat. *tibicen*) was a male player, either amateur or professional, of the aulos; 'auletride' (*aulētris*) was the name for a female player of the instrument. These terms should not be confused with 'aulode' (*aulōdos*), the singer accompanied by an aulete. The generic term *aulētēs* gave rise to a number of more specific (though often quite obscure) terms. They fall into three distinct categories, according to whether they denote (*i*) the kind of instrument played by the aulete, (*ii*) his function or employment, or (*iii*) his repertory.

(*i*) *Kalamaulēs* or, less commonly, *kalamaulētēs*, is literally 'an aulete who plays a reed aulos' with a single pipe (Athenaeus, *Sophists at Dinner*, iv.78, quoting the *Dialectics* of Amerias of Macedonia). These two words were taken over directly into Latin, as seen for instance in the funerary inscription of the 'calamaula' Eutychianus and in the *Notae Tironianae* (107.2). *Monaulos* designates an aulos with a single pipe, but in an epigram of Hedylus quoted by Athenaeus (op. cit.) the word appears to be used poetically to refer to the player (i.e. Theon) accompanying mime. *Ascaules*, the Latinized form of *askaulēs* (a hybrid Greek term formed from *askos*, 'beyond', and *aul[ēt]ēs*), signifying a player of the bagpipes, is found in a poem by Martial (*Epigrams*, x.3.6–

8); the true Latin equivalent, *utricularius* (deriving from *uter*, 'beyond'), was applied to Nero, who towards the end of his life planned not only to play the lyre on stage but to perform on the hydraulis, as a *choraulēs* (see §1(iii) below) and as an *utricularius* (Suetonius, *De vita Caesarum*, vi [Nero], 54.1). *Keraulēs* or *kerataulēs* means, strictly, a player of the *keras*, a short trumpet made of horn but also, as mentioned above, the name for the Phrygian aulos, one pipe of which had a strongly curved end (*keras*). A very ancient term, *keraulēs* occurs in a fragment by Archilochus (*c*650 BCE). A *tumbaulēs*, who played the *aulos keras* at funerals, was a kind of *keraulēs*. All the terms in this group are of infrequent occurrence.

(*ii*) A *trieraulēs* was an aulete on board a trireme of the Athenian war fleet who played the instrument to encourage the oarsmen and to set the stroke rate. In an inscription of the early 4th century BCE (*Inscriptiones graecae*, ii, 2), the list of sailors on the warships includes a certain Sogenes of Siphnos, 'aulētēs', who is mentioned just after the three chief officers. The word *trieraulēs* is found in other, more literary texts, as in Demosthenes' oration *On the Crown* (referring to Phormion, 'slave of Dion of Phrearres' and lover of the wife of Demosthenes' rival Aeschines) and in Philodemus (*On Music*, iv.72). *Spondaulēs*, an 'aulete of libation', is found during the Roman period in inscriptions at Olympia though not elsewhere; however, other temples did recruit auletes annually for cult purposes, for example, at Delos, where the players were women.

(*iii*) The single, generic term *aulētēs* was used for the highly esteemed virtuoso players who gave recitals and also competed against each other, especially at sacred festivals. However, at the beginning of the Hellenistic period (the last quarter of the 4th century BCE), other, more specific terms began to appear in connection with two musical genres – the solo *aulos* and the *aulos* with chorus, both of which were originally performed by auletes until they decided to specialize in one or the other category.

Reflecting this specialization, the periphrases *aulētēs puthikos* ('aulete [playing] the Pythian [*nomos*]'), *kuklios aulētēs* ('cyclical aulete') and *aulētēs meta chorou* ('aulete with chorus') were replaced by the simpler terms *puthaulēs* and *choraulēs*, which became current during the 1st century BCE in literary texts as well as inscriptions. Latin either took over these Greek terms or adapted them slightly (*puthaula* and *choraula*). From the 1st century CE, a further distinction seems to have applied to those auletes who were employed in hierarchic companies of professional musicians: the *prōtaulēs* (*prōtaulos* is also found) was the 'first aulete', or head of the company, as distinct from the *hupaulēs*, the 'second aulete'.

2. SOCIAL STATUS OF AULETES.   In both Greece and Rome, auletes might occupy very different places on the social scale, depending on the circumstances of their employment and their musical competence. In general, the profession was not highly esteemed; in fact 'to lead an aulete's life' had a distinctly pejorative meaning. A number of proverbs and sayings depict auletes as unscrupulous, grasping, self-interested, vain and mindless; one lexicographer likened them to the parasites who played during sacrifices. Most were of humble origin or of very low rank and led a frugal existence; those like Phormion who served on the triremes were slaves; some were part of rich men's households, and it was said that 'whenever the cook does

something wrong, the aulete gets the beating' (Athenaeus, *Sophists at Dinner*, ix.26, quoting *The Islands* by the comic writer Philyllius).

By contrast, the most prominent auletes had brilliant careers, which brought them great popularity and, according to Lucian (*Harmonides*), ensured their 'fame and fortune'. They were recognized in the street; rich men or princes would offer them colossal fees to give private recitals or play in musical competitions; and various rulers, beginning with Philip of Macedonia and after him Alexander and all the Hellenistic monarchs, sought to attach them exclusively to their courts. Living on intimate terms with the rich and powerful, auletes would sometimes neglect their art in favour of a life of debauchery. Comic poets and satirists often ridiculed their jealousy, impertinence, profligacy, gluttony and heavy drinking; and various works tell of their eccentricities and love of luxury, their collections of precious stones, the price of the fabrics used for their costumes, and their efforts to acquire instruments made from the finest materials. Plutarch mentioned the famously wealthy aulete Ismenias of Thebes, who in about 350 BCE paid the huge sum of seven talents for the auloi of a Corinthian instrument maker. The demand for instruments of high quality increased during the Hellenistic period and seems to have been particularly marked during the Roman empire, to judge by the splendour of the tibiae found at Pompeii, some of which are covered with silver, or have sections covered with bronze decorated to the highest degree of workmanship.

Earlier, in 5th-century Greece, virtuoso auletes, whatever their fame, apparently led more moderate lives and were less open to criticism. There are two possible explanations: first, in classical tragedies the aulete was less important than the poet and chorus; second, in the early pan-Hellenic competitions held every four years (the Pythian Games at Delphi and the Isthmian and Nemean festivals) the victor was rewarded by a simple wreath, whereas after the 3rd century BCE it became customary to bestow in addition an increasingly large sum of money. Greek moralists lamented this change as marking the decline of art for art's sake.

3. VIRTUOSO AULETES: TRAINING AND CAREER. Young auletes ambitious for a professional career at the highest level were trained by experienced virtuosos, men who themselves might have been victors at the great competitions or else had acquired a sound reputation at the religious festivals organized by important cities such as Athens, Sparta, Thebes and Delos. From the end of the 5th century BCE Thebes was predominant in both the number and excellence of its auletes, among whom were Pronomus, Ismenias, Antigenidas, Timotheus and Caphisias; representatives of the Theban school, acknowledged by all Greeks to be the best, were paid high fees to pass on their art to young men of means.

First, however, a prospective aulete had to persuade his chosen master to accept him. A truly demanding teacher would have only three or four pupils at a time, who, like pupils of the various philosophical schools, would usually live with him for several years. Fees were completely at the master's discretion and were undoubtedly very high. Timotheus of Thebes, a famous aulete of the last quarter of the 4th century BCE, charged double any instrumentalist who came to him from another school, on the grounds that he would have twice the amount of work to do, first

ridding the newcomer of his bad habits and then teaching him better ones. Greek and Latin authors stress the time and effort necessary to acquire perfect mastery of the instrument, and there is much evidence of the toughness of the great teachers: a pupil found at fault would be ridiculed in front of the others and might well have his ears boxed or even be beaten; errors of style were punished particularly severely by purist teachers. There was great competition between the schools. Some famous auletes would take their pupils to hear their rivals' followers to show them 'the wrong way to do it'. Vehement criticisms of technique and style were often voiced publicly: 'You played a wrong note, just like all the pupils of Timotheus', a member of the audience shouted at one aulete during a concert.

Because of the intense competition to reach the top rank of players, a newly formed virtuoso would have a fierce struggle ahead of him, particularly in the early stages. Unless he managed to perform brilliantly in a competition or gain public approval by some other means, he would have little hope of making his name. Honorific and funerary inscriptions show that a musical career could begin very early; child auletes took part in special competitions before going on to compete against adults. Greek writers mention several exceptional careers, including that of Sacadas of Argos, whose six successive victories at the quadrennial Pythian festival placed him in the unrivalled position of 'best musician' for a period of 24 years. Many virtuoso auletes, like their singer or kithara-playing colleagues, were constantly travelling, and most took part in the regular or occasional competitions organized by great cities or rulers throughout the Mediterranean basin.

Less technically accomplished auletes, who were unable to enter the most prestigious competitions, might belong to the companies of musicians and actors known as *dionusiakoi technitai*; those of lesser ability still could join smaller troupes (*sumphōniakoi*), working within a limited geographical area for lower fees. During the Hellenistic period, the three most important groups of *technitai* were based in Attica (at Teos in Ionia and at Isthmia and Nemea) and were granted financial and diplomatic privileges; participation in the musical festivals of the most famous temples was shared out among them. Various inscriptions relating to the powerful *technitai* companies and a number of papyri from Egypt provide limited information about the circumstances of engagement of these musicians. The evidence, in the form of contracts containing different types of clause, not only indicates the level of professionalism attained by the musicians, but also includes details about payment – whether in money or in kind (bread, oil, wine), the content and duration of programmes, the instruments required, the penalty for breaking a contract, and the means of conveying the musicians' most valuable possessions (instruments and clothing).

In post-Republic Rome tibia players, except for those soloists who managed their own careers, were grouped into colleges (*collegia*) or corporations, which were genuinely professional institutions. Like their Greek predecessors, the members took part in public ceremonies, particularly divine worship (no sacrifice in the ancient world conformed to the prescribed ritual without musical accompaniment on an aulos). The auletes who led troops into battle in Sparta and Crete belonged to a rather different category from the rest, one about which little is known.

4. AULETRIDES. Women musicians were not allowed to perform in public in ancient Greece, either at the competitions or in recitals. However, like the *psaltriai* (women string instrument players), the *aulētrides* and the Roman *tibicinae* might sometimes be both excellent musicians and women of very easy virtue, hired to enliven banquets and all-male parties. Aristotle's *The Constitution of the Athenians* (50.2) explains that the ten city *astunomoi* prohibited their being paid more than the legally fixed tariff of two drachmas, and that the *proxenoi* would institute criminal proceedings should that sum be exceeded (Hyperides, *For Euxenippus*, 3). If several people wanted to hire the same musician, the *astunomoi* decided the matter by lot.

A great many auletrides came from Aegion and Piraeus and were the most sought after. The names of some have come down to us, either because a painter wrote a woman's name on a vase (e.g. Helike, on a stamnos painted by Smikros; and Syko, 'the Fig', on a krater painted by Euphronios), or because they became high-class prostitutes or the mistresses of historically important men. One of these musicians was Lamia, the mistress of Demetrius Poliorcetes (*c*300 BCE), who scandalized all Greece by aspiring to take part in the aulos competition in the Pythian festival at Delphi; another was Bromias, whose lover Phayllus, tyrant of Phocis, stole offerings for her from the temple of Delphi (*c*355 BCE). In general, however, the ambition of such a girl was to escape the wretchedness of her life by winning the love of a young man of good family who would buy her from her pimp and marry her: this is the subject of a number of Greek and Latin comedies (*comoediae togatae*). Among the least fortunate of the *tibicinae* were the *ambubaiae*, generally of Syrian origin, who were brought to Rome to play in the streets or taverns.

BIBLIOGRAPHY

A.A. Howard: 'The *Aulos* or *Tibia*', *Harvard Studies in Classical Philology*, iv (1893), 1–60
T. Reinach: 'Tibia', *Dictionnaire des antiquités grecques et romaines d'après les textes et les documents*, ed. C. Daremberg and E Saglio, v (Paris, 1919/R), 300–32
L. Robert: 'Inscriptions agonistiques de Delphes', *Revue de philologie*, iv (1930), 54–5
K. Schlesinger: *The Greek Aulos* (London, 1939/R)
N. Bodley: 'The *Auloi* of Meroe: a Study of the Greek-Egyptian *Auloi* Found at Meroe, Egypt', *American Journal of Archaeology*, l (1946), 217–40
J.-G. Landels: 'The Brauron Aulos', *Annual of the British School at Athens*, lviii (1963), 116–19
J.-G. Landels: 'Fragments of *Auloi* Found in the Athenian Agora', *Hesperia*, xxxiii (1964), 392–400
J.R. Jannot: 'L'aulos étrusque', *Antiquité classique*, xliii (1974), 118–42
C. Ziegler: *Catalogue des instruments de musique égyptiens du Musée du Louvre* (Paris, 1979)
J.-G. Landels: 'The Reconstruction of Ancient Greek *Auloi*', *World Archaeology*, xii (1981), 298–302
A. Baudot: *Musiciens romains de l'antiquité* (Montreal and Paris, 1982)
C. Salles: *Les bas-fonds de l'antiquité* (Paris, 1982)
A. Barker, ed.: *Greek Musical Writings*, i: *The Musician and his Art* (Cambridge, 1984)
A. Bélis: '*Auloi* grecs du Louvre', *Bulletin de correspondance héllenique*, cviii (1984), 111–22
A. Bélis: 'L'aulos phrygien', *Revue archéologique*, xlviii (1986), 21–40
A. Bélis: 'Charnières ou auloi?', *Revue archéologique*, l (1988), 109–18
A. Bélis: 'Studying and Dating Ancient Greek *Auloi* and Roman *Tibiae*', *The Archaeology of Early Music Cultures [II]: Berlin 1988*, 233–48
A. Bélis: 'Les termes grecs et latins désignant des spécialités musicales', *Revue de philologie*, lxii (1988), 227–50
I.E. Stefanis: *Dionusiakoi technitai* (Heraklion, 1988)
A. Bélis and D.Delattre: 'A propos d'un contrat d'apprentissage d'aulète', *Papiri documentari greci*, ed. M. Capasso (Galatina, 1993), 105–64
A. Bélis: 'Du bon usage du roseau: Théophraste, *Recherches sur les plantes* (IV, 11, 1–9)' *L'homme, le végétal et la musique*, ed. J. Coget (Parthenay, 1996), 10–18
V. Péché: 'Pline l'Ancien: *Histoire naturelle* (XVI, 168–172)', ibid., 18–29
A. Bélis: 'Timothée de Thèbes', *Latomus* (forthcoming)

ANNIE BÉLIS

Aumann [Aumonn, Aumon, Auman], **Franz Josef** [Franz-Seraph, Johann, Leopold] (*b* Traismauer, 24 Feb 1728; *d* St Florian, 30 March 1797). Austrian composer. He was a choirboy in the Vienna Jesuit hostel, where he befriended Michael Haydn and J.G. Albrechtsberger. In 1753 he entered the Augustinian monastery of St Florian; in the following year he took vows there, in 1757 was ordained a priest and from 1755 until his death served as *regens chori*. His works, circulated only in manuscript, show the influence of the Neapolitan and Venetian schools, although the local traditions of Vienna and Salzburg as well as the particular performance requirements of his monastery also affected his style. His early masses and requiem settings are in a strong, cantata-like idiom with many sectional divisions, although the later through-composed *Missa brevis* shows a preference for simpler settings (two *missae brevissimae* are accompanied only by continuo). He wrote two secular Singspiele which contributed to the development of the Austrian dialect farce. His contemporaries commented particularly on his command of counterpoint, and his colourful harmony and delight in formal experimentation impressed the young Bruckner. A *Missa profana*, sub-titled 'a mass to satirize stuttering, bad singing and the onerous office of a schoolmaster', is attributed to Mozart and to Florian Gassmann in two Viennese copies, but a manuscript of the work in Göttweig and a notice in the Vienna Nationalbibliothek show it to be Aumann's.

WORKS

Lat. sacred: 37 masses with orch, 4 lost; 12 requiems, 1 lost; Gradual; 22 offertories, 3 lost; 7 Vespers; 29 psalms; 25 Magnificat; 10 litanies; 4 Te Deum; 8 responsories; In exequiis; hymns; sequences; duet cants.
Ger. sacred: Missa germanica (Wir werfen uns darnieder); 4 Passion orats, 2 lost; arias and songs with orch
Secular vocal: 2 Spl; Missa profana (Missa parodica, Faschingsmesse); couplets; lieder, canons
Inst: 3 syms., 2 doubtful; 9 divertimentos; 9 cassations; 7 parthias; Serenata, str, wind insts
MSS mainly in *A-GÖ, H, LA, SF, SEI, Wn*

BIBLIOGRAPHY

EitnerQ
F. Kurz: 'Bericht über den Musikzustand des oberennsischen Stiftes Sanct Florian', *Allgemeine musikalische Zeitung* [Vienna], i (1817), 128–31, esp. 129–30
G. Huemer: *Die Pflege der Musik im Stift Kremsmünster bis 1877* (Wels, 1877)
B.O. Cernik: *Die Schriftsteller der noch bestehenden Augustiner-Chorherrenstifte von 1600 bis auf den heutigen Tag* (Vienna, 1905)
J. Hollnsteiner: *Das Chorherrenstift Sankt Florian: Bilder zur Kultur- und Kunstgeschichte* (Steyr, 1923)
A. Kellner: *Musikgeschichte des Stiftes Kremsmünster* (Kassel, 1956)

P. Dormann: *Franz Joseph Aumann (1728–1797): ein Meister in St. Florian vor Anton Bruckner* (Munich, 1985) [incl. thematic catalogue]

PETER DORMANN

Aumerus. *See* AMERUS.

Aura (from Lat. *aura*: 'breath'). An instrument consisting of several heteroglot Jew's harps, invented by J.H. Scheibler and described in his short treatise of 1816. It was largely a response to the contemporary – and short-lived – vogue of the jew's harp on the European concert stage. Scheibler himself was one of its more accomplished practitioners, and published some of his own compositions and arrangments for the instrument in his treatise.

Scheibler's aura consisted of two identical star-shaped frames made from sheet metal or horn, and joined in the centre by a handle with a screw. Mounted into the frames were two sets of five jew's harps, each held in place by the screw of the handle so that their steel reeds pointed inward. The handle of each frame was grasped between the thumb and index finger and the reed was struck with a downward motion of the fourth finger. The harps in the right-hand frame were tuned *f–g–a–bb–d′*, and those in the left-hand frame *c–d–eb–e–f*. To make tuning easier, Scheibler affixed balls of sealing wax to the tips of the reeds. A performer could alternate among the jew's harps quite rapidly, simply by rotating the frames. Scheibler marked the jew's harps in the left-hand frame with red dots, and those in the right-hand frame with vertical bars or note names; he also incorporated these markings into his scores so that performers would know exactly which jew's harp to use for any particular passage.

To extend the range of the instrument, jew's harps tuned to higher or lower fundamentals could be added. W.L. Schmidt (1840) described one consisting of 12 jew's harps, six to a frame, and another consisting of 20 jew's harps, ten to a frame, which both Schmidt and Scheibler believed to be a practical limit; additional jew's harps would make the aura too cumbersome and difficult to learn. In spite of their efforts to promote the instrument, it was all but forgotten by the middle of the 19th century.

Schmidt used the terms 'aura' and 'mouth-harmonica' synonymously, believing the timbre of the instrument was comparable to that of a harmonica. His usage is a little confusing and lingers in some of the literature; the aura invented by Scheibler is not a harmonica, and Scheibler did not follow Schmidt's usage.

See also JEW'S HARP.

BIBLIOGRAPHY

J.H. Scheibler: 'Die Aura', *AMZ*, xviii (1816), 505–12

W.L. Schmidt: *The Aura or Mouth-Harmonica Presented as a Musical Instrument* (Quedlinburg and Leipzig, 1840)

L. Fox, ed.: *The Jew's Harp: A Comprehensive Anthology* (Lewisburg, PA, 1988) [incl. Eng. trans. of Scheibler's treatise]

KEVIN MOONEY

Aureli, Aurelio (*b* Murano, Venice; *fl* 1652–1708). Italian librettist. He wrote some 50 librettos, including a few adaptations. Until 1687 he seems to have lived mainly in Venice (except for a brief sojourn in 1659 at the Viennese court), where he was a member of the Accademia Delfica and the Accademia degli Imperfetti, both of them probably offshoots of the famous Accademia degli Incogniti, among whose members there were many librettists. From 1688 to 1694 he was employed by the Duke of Parma; during this period he produced about a dozen dramatic works, all set by the court composer Bernardo Sabadini. Most of his subsequent librettos were written for Venice and other cities of the Venetian republic. He occasionally revised texts of other librettists, including Moniglia and Morselli. His works are whimsical and at times bizarre transformations of the most disparate historical and mythological source material. They reflect the evolution of Venetian taste (to which he admittedly pandered) from the libretto's first point of stability to the era of Arcadian reform.

BIBLIOGRAPHY

DBI (C. Mutini); *ES* (U. Rolandi); *GroveO* (T. Walker and N. Dubowy) [with list of librettos and further bibliography]; *MGG1* (A.A. Abert)

P. Fabbri: *Il secolo cantante: per una storia del libretto d'opera nel Seicento* (Bologna, 1990)

E. Rosand: *Opera in Seventeenth-Century Venice: the Creation of a Genre* (Berkeley, 1991)

C. Lubini: 'Ideologia e struttura del teatro musicale veneziano nel Seicento: i drammi di Aurelio Aureli', *Ecco mormorar l'onde: la musica nel barocco*, ed. C. De Incontrera and A. Zanini (Monfalcone, 1995), 171–202

THOMAS WALKER (with NORBERT DUBOWY)

Aurelian of Réôme [Aurelianus Reomensis] (*fl* ?840–50). Frankish writer. His only known work, *Musica disciplina*, is generally regarded as the earliest extant medieval treatise on music. It is the sole source of evidence concerning Aurelian and his milieu; no other 9th-century writer mentions the text or quotes from it, and it is not listed in surviving Carolingian library catalogues. Palaeographical studies have enabled the earliest extant manuscript of the *Musica disciplina*, F-VAL 148 (ff.57v–89v), to be dated to the middle third of the 9th century, so providing a *terminus ante quem* for the date of the treatise's composition. The preface gives some indication of the circumstances in which the treatise was written and provides certain clues about its possible date. Aurelian refers to himself as a former member of the monastery of St Jean de Réôme (in the diocese of Langres), but having been dismissed from the abbey and wishing to atone for his offence, he dedicated the treatise to Bernardus, the abbot, whom he also described as a 'future archbishop'. The name Bernardus does in fact appear in a list of the abbots of St Jean de Réôme published in the 17th century, in which he is said to have been abbot in about 846 and subsequently bishop of Autun; but no other record of a Bernardus among the 9th-century bishops of Autun has been traced. Without further evidence concerning Aurelian or Abbot Bernardus, therefore, it is impossible to prove beyond doubt Gushee's suggestion that the *Musica disciplina* was written in the 840s.

Aurelian never referred to himself in the treatise as a monk, but his familiarity with the plainchant repertory, particularly psalmody, strongly suggests that he was a member of a monastic community. That the treatise was written at some monastic centre other than St Jean is likely, maybe at St Amand, which not only possessed many of the books quoted by Aurelian in the *Musica disciplina* but was also where F-VAL 148 was copied.

The importance of the *Musica disciplina* rests mainly on its status as the first known medieval music treatise (other than the brief account of ancient music theory by Isidore of Seville); it provides not only valuable evidence for the repertory and performing practice of Gregorian chant in Francia during the first half of the 9th century – a period from which almost no notated melodies are known – but also an insight into the early development of Carolingian music theory. The question of whether

Aurelian should be regarded as the first medieval theorist, rather than the first whose writings have survived, is not easily resolved. There is no evidence that a tradition of writing about music existed before the reign of Charlemagne (768–814). Interest in music as an intellectual discipline reappeared in the West only during the last decades of the 8th century, when Alcuin, a scholar at the Frankish court, sought to revive the ancient liberal arts – of which music was one – as the basis of ecclesiastical education. The earliest descriptions of the art, from the late 8th and early 9th centuries, show that Carolingian scholars were only just beginning to rediscover the Latin manuals of ancient music theory, especially those by Cassiodorus, Martianus Capella and Boethius, and that they found the contents of such works difficult to understand.

The only surviving account of music thought to have been written before the *Musica disciplina* is the text known as *De octo tonis*, a work that has been ascribed to Alcuin, although his authorship is unlikely. This text amounts to no more than a very brief definition of the eight tones and the terminology associated with them; it exists in several versions, of varying length and detail, and is often found attached to tonaries. Aurelian used *De octo tonis* to form part of chapter 8 of his treatise, and although the earliest manuscript of the *Musica disciplina* predates all the extant versions of *De octo tonis*, it is probable that the most primitive forms of the latter text existed before Aurelian composed his work (see Huglo, 1971).

The *Musica disciplina* falls into two distinct sections: the first is a compilation of quotations from writers on ancient music theory, in particular Boethius, Cassiodorus and Isidore of Seville; and the second fulfils the statement given in the preface that the work is to be concerned with 'certain rules of melody they call *toni* or *tenores*', that is, the system of the eight tones (Aurelian never used the term *modus*), thought to have been adopted by Frankish cantors in the late 8th century from Byzantium (*see* MODE, §II, 1). The treatise concludes with a discussion of various aspects of plainchant, including the origins of particular chants, the importance of music in the Church and the definition and history of certain chant genres; there are also further appeals, in the same manner as the preface, to Abbot Bernardus.

In the first section (chaps.1–7), Aurelian's choice of material includes descriptions of the music of the spheres, the ethical effects of music, its inventors (Jubal, Pythagoras and so on) and its division into the subjects of harmonics, rhythmics and metrics; all these were common in early Carolingian definitions of the musical art. Aurelian's most original contribution was his inclusion of selections from Boethius's treatises *De institutione arithmetica* and *De institutione musica*; the latter in particular is not thought to have been widely read before the second half of the 9th century.

Aurelian assumed that the theory described by Boethius was relevant to the music of Gregorian plainchant, and at a few points in his treatise he attempted to integrate the two traditions. In chapter 2, for example, he displays an understanding of the mathematical proportions of the intervals of the octave (2:1), 4th (4:3), 5th (3:2) and whole tone (9:8) described by Boethius, and demonstrates each interval by citing examples from the chant repertory. This passage in the *Musica disciplina* is the first evidence that

Carolingian scholars were beginning to apply the mathematics of Boethius to the sound of chant and using it to define intervals precisely. Yet at the same time it reveals the gulf that existed between ancient music theory and the practice of Carolingian chant, for Aurelian also attempted to associate each of the four intervals with a different authentic chant tone, stating, for example, that the introit antiphon *Inclina Domine aurem tuam* belongs to the tone of the *authentus protus* because it contains the intervals of an octave; this attempt to unite ancient theory and medieval chant has no musical basis. With the exception of the mathematical measurement of intervals, however, Aurelian's use of Boethian material is limited to the non-technical descriptions of music, such as the division of the art into *Musica mundana*, *humana* and *instrumentalis*, and the difference between the *musicus* and the *cantor*. Later generations of Carolingian scholars improved upon Aurelian's understanding of Boethius as they sought to reconcile ancient music theory with contemporary chant practice.

The second section of the *Musica disciplina* (chaps.8–19) begins with an introduction (8–9) to the eight tones: the etymological meaning of their names is discussed ('De octo tonis') and the characteristic melodies associated with each tone are described using the intonation formulae *noannoeane*, *noeagis* and so on; the treatise is the earliest evidence for the use of such formulae in the West. Aurelian also includes the story of how the emperor Charlemagne ordered the introduction of four additional tones.

In chapters 10–17 each tone is described in turn, focussing particularly on the melodic transitions (*differentiae* or *varietates*) between the recitation formula for the psalm verse and the antiphon in the introit, communion and offertory of the Mass and in the Office responsories and antiphons; chapter 18 is a summary of the numbers of *differentiae* belonging to each tone and within each genre of chant. Over 100 different chants are cited as examples and Aurelian assumes that the whole repertory is subject to the system of the eight tones and that the classification of individual chants to particular tones is fixed (although he was aware that some cantors disagreed with a number of his classifications). Later sources, such as tonaries, generally confirm Aurelian's assignment of chants to tones. Aurelian had no pitch-specific notation or terminology at his disposal to demonstrate the melodies of the various *differentiae*, and so their general characteristics are described verbally; the Boethian mathematical definition of intervals which Aurelian discussed in the first section of the *Musica disciplina* is not used to describe the melodies of the *differentiae*. It is clear, however, that Aurelian used neumatic notation, for in chapter 19, which is an account of the recitation formulae of the psalm verses, musical notation is essential to the discussion, is explicitly referred to throughout and is used in two places in the text; the *Musica disciplina* provides the earliest concrete evidence for the use of notation in the West. The other examples of notation in the earliest manuscript of the treatise, *F-VAL* 148, are of a different type, known as Palaeo-Frankish, and are later additions to the work.

Almost no evidence concerning the use or readership of the *Musica disciplina* survives from the century or so after *F-VAL* 148 was copied. The treatise may have been read fairly widely during the 11th century, when most of the extant versions of the text were written, but Aurelian's name is rarely mentioned by other medieval writers on music, although he was cited by Berno of Reichenau (*d* 1048). It is probable that his work was quickly superseded by later 9th-century theorists who displayed a better understanding of Boethian music theory and how it could be applied to Gregorian chant.

BIBLIOGRAPHY

GerbertS, i, 26–7 [edn of Pseudo-Alcuin, *De octo tonis*]

L. Gushee: *The Musica disciplina of Aurelian of Réôme: a Critical Text and Commentary* (diss., Yale U., 1963)

J. Ponte, trans.: *The Discipline of Music (ca. 843) by Aurelian of Réôme* (Colorado Springs, 1968)

M. Huglo: *Les tonaires: inventaire, analyse, comparaison* (Paris 1971)

L. Gushee: 'Questions of Genre in Medieval Treatises on Music', *Gattungen der Musik in Einzeldarstellung: Gedenkschrift Leo Schrade*, ed. W. Arlt and others (Berne, 1973), 365–433

L. Gushee, ed.: *Aurelianus Reomensis: Musica disciplina*, CSM, xxi (1975)

M. Bernard: 'Textkritisches zu Aurelianus Reomensis', *MD*, xl (1986), 49–61

JANE BELLINGHAM

Aurelius Augustinus. *See* AUGUSTINE OF HIPPO.

Auriacombe, Louis (*b* Pau, 22 Feb 1917; *d* Toulouse, 12 March 1982). French conductor. He attended the Toulouse Conservatoire, where he won first prizes for violin (1931), singing, recitation (1937) and harmony (1939). He studied conducting under Markevich at the International Conductors' Course at Salzburg between 1951 and 1956. It was with the orchestra of the Salzburg Summer Academy that he made his first appearance as a conductor (Linz, 1956). Later he assisted Markevich in his conducting courses in Salzburg and Mexico (1957), Santiago de Compostela (1966), Madrid (1967) and Monte Carlo (1968). In 1953 he founded the Orchestre de Chambre National de Toulouse, an ensemble of 12 strings and harpsichord, which specialized in Baroque music but also played many contemporary works. These included the first performance of *Ombres* by Boucourechliev (1970, Toulouse) and the American première of *Ramifications* by Ligeti (1970, Washington, DC). As musical director of this orchestra, which rapidly acquired an international reputation, Auriacombe made several recordings, some of which won the Grand Prix du Disque. Although his experience was principally with chamber orchestras, he also conducted larger bodies, including the Orchestre du Théâtre du Capitole, the orchestras of Toulouse and Paris radio, and the Paris Conservatoire Orchestra. He retired in 1971 because of illness.

CHRISTIANE SPIETH-WEISSENBACHER/R

Auric, Georges (*b* Lodève, 15 Feb 1899; *d* Paris, 23 July 1983). French composer. He spent his childhood in Montpellier, studying at the local conservatory and receiving piano lessons from Louis Combes who introduced him to the music of Debussy, Ravel and Stravinsky. He independently discovered the music of Satie in the periodical *Musica*. Combes also presented him to Déodat de Séverac and gave him free range of his extensive library of modern French literature. Auric was composing from the age of ten (later destroying most of his earliest works), and in 1913 his parents moved to the capital so that he could enter the Paris Conservatoire. Schmitt and Koechlin took great interest in him, as did Roussel, who in 1914 arranged a performance of his songs *Trois interludes*, a charming work of remarkable maturity.

The young prodigy was regularly invited out, and by the age of 15 Auric was acquainted with Stravinsky, Apollinaire, Cocteau (who dedicated *Le coq et l'arlequin* to him in 1918), Radiguet, Braque and Picasso, and was discussing sociology with Léon Bloy and theology with Jacques Maritain. At the Conservatoire he studied with Georges Caussade and met Honegger, Milhaud and Tailleferre. In 1914 he left the Conservatoire in order to study composition with d'Indy at the Schola Cantorum. A fine pianist, Auric played Satie's piano works in public and wrote an article, 'Erik Satie, musicien humoriste' (*Revue française de musique*, 10 Dec 1913), which led to his becoming acquainted with Satie himself, a close friendship that lasted until Auric wrote a highly critical article on *Relâche* (1924).

By the time he found himself a member of Les Six, the style of his music – brilliant and often acidly aggressive – had become well established, and works such as the *Huit poèmes de Jean Cocteau* (1919) or the foxtrot *Adieu, New York!* (1920) show how he can be considered, along with Poulenc, the group's most typical representative. On hearing his 1922 incidental music for Molière's comédie-ballet *Les fâcheux*, Diaghilev asked him to transform it into a ballet. First performed in Monte Carlo on 19 January 1924, it shows a facility for mood creation and a virtuosity in the manipulation of highly varied material that presages his film music. Other successful ballets followed: *Les matelots* (1924) and *La pastorale* (1925) for Diaghilev, *Les enchantements de la fée d'Alcine* (1928) for Ida Rubinstein, while occasional instrumental works such as the Piano Sonatina (1922) or *Cinq bagatelles* (1925) evince a certain unpretentious charm. Auric was also writing regularly for various music and avant-garde literary revues closely linked with the dadaists and surrealists.

A new expressionism and seriousness of purpose is evident in his Piano Sonata (1930–31), a work that interested Dukas and Cortot, though it did not have the success the composer hoped for. In this sprawling work, Les Six is largely forgotten in favour of Skryabin and a grandiloquence of rhetoric. The 1930s saw a few instrumental pieces (Violin Sonata, 1936; Woodwind Trio, 1938), but were more notable for the start of a long series of scores for films that include some of the classics of French cinema: *A nous la liberté* (dir. R. Clair, 1931), *L'éternel retour* (dir. Cocteau and J. Delannoy, 1943) and *La belle et la bête* (dir. Cocteau and J. Delannoy, 1946).

In the 1940s and 50s Auric composed several ballets and one of his most important works, the Partita (1953–5) for two pianos, although film music increasingly occupied him, his biggest popular success coming with *Moulin Rouge* (dir. J. Huston, 1952).

In the 1960s and 70s Auric's lively and sympathetic interest in the avant garde came to the fore in his own music, in the series of *Imaginées* and *Doubles-jeux*. The flirtation with serialism, the concision, and the play of light and shade are admirably suited to Auric's Protean muse.

In 1954 Auric succeeded Honegger as president of SACEM, becoming its honorary president in 1979. He was elected to the Institut in 1962 and was a vigorous and galvanizing director of the Paris Opéra and the Opéra-Comique from 1962 to 1968.

Much has still to be discovered about Auric, a public figure, but a secretive man and an enigmatic composer

Georges Auric, 1958

who so often seemed to hide his feelings behind a curtain of rhetoric. His best works are probably his most unpretentious. Though he is most at ease in stage and film music, Auric has a delicate sense of poetry that comes out particularly well in his songs and instrumental slow movements.

WORKS
(selective list)

DRAMATIC

Sous le masque (op, L. Laloy), 1927
Ballets: Les mariés de la tour Eiffel (after J. Cocteau), 1920, collab. 'Les Six'; Les fâcheux, 1923 [based on incid music]; Les matelots, 1924; Pastorale, 1925; Les enchantements de la fée d'Alcine, 1928; Rondeau, 1928 [for L'éventail de Jeanne]; La concurrence, 1931; Les imaginaires, 1933; La fontaine de jouvence, 1946; Quadrille, 1946; Le peintre et son modèle (B. Kochno), 1948; Phèdre (Cocteau, after Sophocles), 1949; Chemin de lumière, 1951; La chambre, 1954; Le bal des voleurs (after J. Anouilh), 1960
Incid music: Les fâcheux (Molière), 1922; Marlborough s'en va-t-en guerre (M. Achard), 1924; La femme silencieuse (after B. Jonson), 1925; Le dompteur (A. Savoir, after J. Théry), 1925; Le mariage de monsieur le Trouhadec (J. Romains), 1925; Volpone (after Jonson), 1927; Les oiseaux (after Aristophanes), 1928 [rev. 1966]; Le quatorze juillet (R. Rolland), 1931; Margot (E. Bourdet), 1935
Film scores: Le sang d'un poète (Cocteau), 1930; A nous la liberté (dir. R. Clair), 1931; Lac-aux-dames (dir. M. Allegret), 1934; L'enfer du jeu (dir. J. Delannoy), 1939; L'éternel retour (Cocteau, Delannoy), 1943 La belle et la bête (Cocteau), 1946; La symphonie pastorale (dir. Delannoy), 1946; L'aigle à deux têtes (Cocteau), 1947; Hue and Cry (dir. C. Crichton), 1947; Orphée (Cocteau), 1949; Moulin Rouge (dir. J. Huston, 1952); Lola Montes (dir. M. Ophuls), 1955

INSTRUMENTAL

Orch: Ouverture du 14 juillet, 1921 [from ballet Les mariés de la tour Eiffel]; Ritournelle, 1921 [from Les mariés de la tour Eiffel]; Fanfare, wind band, 1924; La Seine, un matin ..., 1937; Ov., 1938; Phèdre, ballet suite, 1949; Chemin de lumière, ballet suite, 1951; Ecossaise, 1952 [for La guirlande de Campra]; ML (Allegro final), 1956 [Variations sur le nom de Marguerite Long]
Chbr: Suite, 6 insts, 1924 [from Marlborough s'en va-t-en guerre]; Aria, fl, pf, 1927 [rev. 1976]; Sonata, G, vn, pf, 1936; Trio, D, ob, cl, bn, 1938; Impromptu, ob, pf, 1946; Imaginées I, fl, pf, 1968: Imaginées II, vc, pf, 1969; Imaginées III, cl, pf, 1971; Imaginées VI, v/ob, ens, 1976
Pf: L'après-midi dans un parc (Gasparet Zoe), 1914; Prélude, 1919 [for Album des six]; 3 pastorales, 1919–20; Adieu New-York, 1921; Sonatine, G, 1922; 5 Bagatelles, duet, 1925 [from La femme silencieuse and Le dompteur]; Petite suite, 1927; Sonata, F, 1930–31; 3 Morceaux, 1934 [from Lac-aux-dames]; La Seine, un matin ..., 1937 [from A l'exposition, collab. Delannoy, Ibert, Milhaud, Poulenc, Sauguet, Schmitt, Tailleferre]; 3 Impromptus, 1940; 9 Short Pieces, 1941; Danse française, 1946; Impromptu, d, 1946; Valse, 2 pf, 1949; Partita, 2 pf, 1953–5; Double-jeux I–III, 2 pf, 1970–71; Imaginées V, 1976

VOCAL

5 chansons françaises, chorus, 1940
Songs: 3 interludes (R. Chalupt), 1914; 8 poèmes (Cocteau), 1919; Les joues en feu (R. Radiguet), 1920; Alphabet (Radiguet), 1922; 5 poèmes (G. de Nerval), 1925; 2 romances (M. Desbordes-Valmore), 1926; Vocalise, 1926; 3 caprices (T. de Banville), 1927; 4 poèmes (G. Gabory), 1927; 5 chansons (L. Hirtz), 1929; Printemps (P. de Ronsard), 1935 [from Margot]; 3 poèmes (L.P. Fargue), 1940; 3 poèmes (L. de Vilmorin), 1940; 6 poèmes (P. Eluard), 1940–41; 4 chants de la France malheureuse (L. Aragon, Eluard, J. Supervielle), Mez, orch, 1943; 3 poèmes (M. Jacob), 1945–6; 2 poèmes (H. de Montherlant), 1965; Imaginées IV (onomatopeia), v, pf, 1975; Imaginées VI, v/ob, ens, 1976

Principal publishers: Chant du monde, Durand, Eschig, Heugel, Leduc, Noël, Salabert, Schott

WRITINGS

Témoignages, Monaco (Paris, 1966)
Quand j'étais là . . . (Paris, 1979)

BIBLIOGRAPHY

A. Schaeffner: *Georges Auric* (Paris, 1928)
J. Bruyer: *L'écran des musiciens* (Paris, 1930)
A. Goléa: *Georges Auric* (Paris, 1958)

JEREMY DRAKE

Aurisicchio [Euresicchio, Eurisechio, Orisicchio], **Antonio** (*b* Naples, *c*1710; *d* Rome, 3/4 Sept 1781). Italian composer. He studied in Rome, according to Giazotto, and supported himself by playing the organ in various Roman churches. Then, like so many southern Italian composers of his generation, he made his professional début in Naples with a comic opera in the Teatro dei Fiorentini, in 1734. To judge from his operatic production he was back in Rome again by the early 1740s, where the librettos of his works call him *maestro di cappella napoletano* – a conventional honorific which may or may not be taken at face value. In 1747 he became a member of the Congregazione dei musici di S Cecilia, to which all professional Roman musicians belonged. By 1751 he was working as assistant to Francesco Ciampi, *maestro di cappella* of S Giacomo degli Spagnoli and, after Ciampi's death, succeeded him as chief director on 30 November 1756, a position he held until at least 1766.

A libretto of 1754 names Aurisicchio as 'Virtuoso di Camera' of Cardinal Domenico Orsini d'Aragona. On 28 November 1776 he was appointed *maestro di cappella* of the Congregazione dei musici di S Cecilia, remaining in this important position until 15 April 1779. Aurisicchio's death in September 1781 was of sufficient public interest for his funeral service in S Maria in Via to be reported in the Roman news journals. The legend that Aurisicchio died young, reported by earlier historians, seems to have been started by Burney who, having visited Rome in 1770, ought to have known better.

A hint about Aurisicchio's personality may be found in an account written to Padre Giovanni Battista Martini in 1755 by Prospero Marmiroli of a social gathering in Rome at which Aurisicchio boasted of the praise he had had from Martini for his own works; Marmiroli dismissed him as a knave and a fool ('gran birbo è quell'Asino Regnicolo'). However, it should be remembered that Martini had in fact earlier found Aurisicchio's music worth serious technical consideration, as the letter dated 12 August 1747 from another Roman correspondent, Girolamo Chiti, shows. Whether or not Aurisicchio was a braggart, he was capable of generosity: in 1778 he warmly and successfully recommended the young composer Giuseppe Pedota – not, apparently, one of his own students – for the position of *maestro di cappella* at the cathedral in Orvieto. Both Grétry, after studying in Rome in 1760, and Burney, after his visit there ten years later, expressed admiration for Aurisicchio's work and attested to his popularity with the Roman musical public.

Aurisicchio's reputation now must rest, as it did during his own time, on his church music. Although he obviously did not disdain the quick income brought by an occasional opera commission, it should be observed that many of these commissions were for a species of operatic hack work: for intermezzos (or 'farsette', as they had come to be called in Rome, where the genre maintained a vigorous life long after going out of fashion elsewhere in Italy, transformed in style and shape into miniature *opere buffe*) or for the revision of works by other composers. Though an aria by Aurisicchio was sufficiently admired to be included in the pasticcio *Attalo* for London in 1758 (and subsequently printed by John Walsh in his Favourite Songs edition), it was, Burney said, his 'only air that was ever sung on our stage'. Again in Burney's account, so high did Aurisicchio rank among Roman composers for the church, that 'upon any festival wherever he is *Maestro di Capella*, and has composed a mass, there is sure to be a very great crowd'.

In Ziino's opinion Aurisicchio demonstrated his talents most impressively in large-scale polyphonic sacred pieces, where skilful fugues contrast with sections in highly decorated solo style. Otherwise, his aria and instrumental styles are characteristic of the period, exhibiting simply constructed but appealing melodic surfaces over essentially tonic–dominant harmonic foundations.

WORKS
SACRED

Surviving church music includes: 2 masses, 3 short masses (Ky, Gl), several mass sections; at least 26 motets; 3 Lezioni for different days; Mag; cants., incl. La morte di Gesù, Già sento fremere le fauci orribili, Dunque fia vera; TeD; Dixit Dominus, 5 settings; Beatus vir, 4 settings; sacred songs, hymns, ps settings, miscellaneous liturgical pieces; Oratio Jeremie prophete; Studi sopra il canto fermo del Benedicamus solenne. MSS mainly in *D-Bsb, MÜd, MÜu*; Archivio della Chiesa Nazionale Spagnola, Rome; Archivio Capitolare, Rieti; also *B-Bc; F-Pn; GB-Cfm; I-Rsc, Rvat*

STAGE

Chi dell'altrui si veste presto si spoglia (commedia, T. Mariani), Naples, dei Fiorentini, wint. 1734
L'inganno deluso (int a 4), Rome, Argentina, carn. 1743
Il cicisbeo consolato (farsetta a 4, C. Mazzarelli), Rome, della Pace, carn. 1748
Chi la fà l'aspetta (int a 3), Rome, della Pace, carn. 1752
Andromaca (os, A. Salvi/A.G. Pampani), Rome, Argentina, carn. 1753; 6 arias in *GB-Lbl*
Eumene (os, G. Pizzi), Rome, Argentina, carn. 1754; *P-La*
Lo sposalizio all'usanza (farsetta a 3), Rome, Valle, carn. 1757
Arias in Didone abbandonata, 1745; Alessandro dell'Indie, *I-FZc*

MISCELLANEOUS

Componimento drammatico … per solennizare gli augustissimi nomi … di Francesco I … e di Maria Teresa, 1747
3 other componimenti, Rome, 1747; Rome, 1760; Florence, 1762
Betulia liberata, Rome, S Girolamo della Carità, 1756
Il furo Camillo, cant., Rome, Collegio Calasanzio delle Scuole Pie, 1760
Giunone placata (componimento drammatico, for the marriage of Filippo Bernualdo Orsini and Teresa Caracciolo), Rome, carn. 1762
Ester, orat
Symphony, 3 movts, *I-Rdp*
Numerous scattered arias, *B-Bc; D-Bsb, Dl* (but the 88 arias, *EitnerQ*, were lost during World War II), *SWl; GB-Lbl; I-Gl; P-La*

BIBLIOGRAPHY

BurneyFl; BurneyH; DBI (D. Di Palma); *ES* (R. Giazotto); *MGG1* (A. Ziino) [with detailed lists of surviving works and archival references on biographical information]
Diario ordinario (8 Sept 1781), 9
C. Goldoni: *Mémoires* (Paris, 1787; Eng. trans., 1814); ed. G. Ortolani in *Tutte le opere di Carlo Goldoni* (Milan, 1935–56), i, 404–5
M. Grétry: *Mémoires, ou essai sur la musique* (Paris, 1789), 85–6
D. Corri: 'Life of Domenico Corri': foreword to *The Singers Preceptor* (London, 1810)
Catalogo dei maestri compositori, dei professori di musica e dei socii di onore della Congregazione ed accademia di Santa Cecilia di Roma (Rome, 1845), 99
G.B. Martini: *Carteggio inedito del P. Giambattista Martini coi più celebri musicisti del suo tempo*, ed. F. Parisini (Bologna, 1888/R), 293, 398
U. Rolandi: 'Giuseppe Pedota, musicista altamurano (1754–1831)', *NA*, xiv (1937), 226–43, esp. 228

JAMES L. JACKMAN/ENRICO CARERI

Ausdrucksvoll (Ger.: 'with expression'). A direction for expressive playing found particularly in German music of the generations after Beethoven. Brahms marked the opening of his *German Requiem* '*ziemlich langsam und mit Ausdruck*' ('quite slow and with expression').

See also TEMPO AND EXPRESSION MARKS.   □

Ausfaltung (Ger.). *See* UNFOLDING.

Ausführung (Ger.). A term used in Schenkerian analysis. *See* LAYER.

Auskomponierung (Ger.). In Schenkerian analysis (*see* ANALYSIS, §II, 4–6), the elaboration of a given contrapuntal-harmonic plan. The term is often rendered in English as 'composing-out', but 'elaboration' is a common alternative. The process of *Auskomponierung* begins with the tonic triad; its initial elaboration produces the URSATZ comprising a conjunct descending URLINIE supported by a I–V–I bass ARPEGGIATION. At subsequent structural levels (*see* LAYER), various techniques of PROLONGATION are applied.

'Composing-out' is sometimes used more generally, in a non-Schenkerian context, to mean the working-out of the implications of some special feature of a piece; for example the C♯ in the seventh bar of Beethoven's 'Eroica' Symphony may be said to be 'composed-out' when it is interpreted as D♭ in the recapitulation of the first movement.

WILLIAM DRABKIN

Auslösung (Ger.). *See* ESCAPEMENT.

Ausm Thal, Alexander. *See* UTENDAL, ALEXANDER.

Aussensatz (Ger.: 'outer part'). The outer parts of a polyphonic structure. *See also* PART (ii).

Aussig (Ger.). *See* ÚSTÍ NAD LABEM.

Austbö, Haakon (*b* Kongsberg, 22 Oct 1948). Norwegian pianist. He gave his first recital in Oslo at the age of 15 and later studied in Paris, New York, Munich and London. In 1970 he became the first non-French pianist to win the Concours National de la Guilde Française des Artistes Solistes in Paris, and he gained international attention in 1971 when he won the Olivier Messiaen Competition for contemporary music. Austbö's repertory is large and exceptionally wide-ranging, but he has won particular renown for his playing of Skryabin and Messiaen both in concert and on disc. A gifted and dedicated teacher, he joined the piano faculty at the Hogeschool voor de Kunsten Utrecht in 1980, and that of the Sweelinck Conservatory, Amsterdam, in 1994. His playing combines a broad tonal palette with an acute and flexible rhythmic profile and is notable alike for its emotional range and its penetrating intellectual command.

JEREMY SIEPMANN

Austin. American city, capital of Texas. The first settlers (1835) were predominantly of German descent. The city was incorporated in 1839. The Austin Lyceum was established in 1841 to promote the study of the arts. It was disbanded the following year. Evening concerts were given in the grounds of the capitol from 1846. In the late 19th century the city, whose population numbered about 15,000, had three opera houses, giving performances by local artists and later visited by touring companies, and a number of vocal and instrumental ensembles that performed regularly. The Austin SO, founded in 1911 and conducted by Hans Harthan, was a loosely organized amateur group that performed sporadically until 1938 when it hired its first paid conductor, Hendrik Buytendorp. In 1948 the players joined the American Federation of Musicians and hired Ezra Rachlin, who conducted until 1969. Other conductors have included Akira Endo (1975–80), Sung Kwak (1982–96) and Peter Bay (1998–). The orchestra gives eight pairs of subscription concerts and numerous 'pops' concerts annually, and has an active community outreach programme. The annual 4th of July Concert on the banks of the Town Lake attracts an audience of 60,000.

The Austin Civic Opera Company was active from 1927 to 1931. The Austin Lyric Opera was founded in 1983 with Walter Ducloux as musical director (retired 1996) and Joseph McClain as stage director; its first production was *Die Zauberflöte* (1987). The company mounts three productions each year at the University in the Performing Arts Center or the Paramount Theater (an old opera house), and engages internationally known and mostly American singers as well as local performers. Highlights have included the American première of Rossini's *La pietra del paragone* (1992).

The community supports several choral organizations (including Austin Choral Artists, Austin Civic Chorus, Austin Vocal Arts Ensemble, Capital City Men's Chorus, New Texas Conspirare Choir) and instrumental ensembles (Austin Chamber Ensemble, Chamber Soloists of Austin, La Follia, Austin Chamber Music Center, Austin Wind Ensemble, Austin Symphonic Band and others). In addition to the productions of the Austin Lyric Opera and the University of Texas, operas are also staged by the Austin Gilbert and Sullivan Society. In 1993 the New Texas Festival was founded. It was renamed New Texas Music Works in 1999.

Austin is the site of the University of Texas, which created a school of music in 1919. The music department sponsors more than 400 performances each year by student and faculty soloists and ensembles, as well as performances, masterclasses and lecture-recitals by visiting musicians. University ensembles include the University of Texas Opera Theatre, directed by Robert Desimone, and the University of Texas SO. The choral programme is headed by Craig Hella Johnson. The Bates Recital Hall (700 seats) houses one of the world's largest tracker organs (Rowland-Visser). The faculty has included the composers Paul Pisk and Kent Kennan, the performers Gerard Souzay, Charles Rosen and Jess Walters, and the musicologists Gilbert Chase and Gerard Béhague. The Grand Concert Hall of the Performing Arts Center seats 3000, and the Opera Theater 400. The university maintains the Lomax folk music archives. Included among the musical holdings of the Harry Ransom Humanities Research Center Library are manuscripts of compositions by Stravinsky, Berlioz, Debussy, Ravel, Copland, Fauré and Dukas. The centre houses the largest institutional collection of music and music-related materials by Paul Bowles and Nicolas Nabokov.

Austin is also noted for its active popular music community, particularly in the areas of country, blues and blues-influenced rock and roll, and identifies itself as the 'Live Music Capital of the World'. Each spring there is a South by Southwest music festival and conference, the largest of its kind, with performances by hundreds of popular musicians from around the world. The Austin community supports a full-time non-profit radio station devoted solely to classical music (KMFA).

BIBLIOGRAPHY

GroveA (H.C. Sparks)

L.M. Spell: *Music in Texas* (Austin, 1936/R)

M.O. James-Reed: *Music in Austin, 1900–1956* (Austin, 1957)

M.S. Barkley: *History of Travis County and Austin, 1839–1899* (Waco, TX, 1963/R)

J. Reid: *The Improbable Rise of Redneck Rock* (Austin, 1974/R)

B.C. Malone: *Southern Music, American Music* (Lexington, KY, 1979)

H.C. Sparks: *Stylistic Development and Compositional Processes of Selected Solo Singer/Songwriters in Austin, Texas* (diss., U. of Texas, Austin, 1984)

HUGH CULLEN SPARKS/JERRY YOUNG

Austin, Elizabeth (*b* Leicester, *c*1800; *d* after 1835). English singer. Performances in Dublin in 1821 led to engagements at the Theatre Royal, Drury Lane (début on 23 November 1822), and the English Opera House. On 10 December 1827 she made her American début at the Chestnut Street Theatre, Philadelphia, in Arne's *Love in a Village*; her New York début was at the Park Theatre on 2 January 1828. For the next six years, managed by F.H.F. Berkeley, she was America's reigning prima donna, performing principally in New York, Boston, Providence, Philadelphia, Baltimore and Washington. Her repertory ranged from *The Beggar's Opera* to *Der Freischütz*; she was most closely identified, however, with Rossini's *Cenerentola* (adapted by M.R. Lacy), which she introduced to the USA. She had a high, sweet and flexible voice, but was only a mediocre actress. Her prestige began to decline after the arrival in the USA of Mary Anne Paton Wood in late 1833; in May 1835 she returned to England and retired from the stage.

BIBLIOGRAPHY

'Mrs. Austin', *American Musical Journal* (1835), April, 114–15

F.C. Wemyss: *Twenty-Six Years of the Life of an Actor and Manager* (New York, 1847)

K.K. Preston: *Opera on the Road* (Urbana, 1993)

WILLIAM BROOKS, KATHERINE K. PRESTON

Austin, John (*b* Craigton, nr Glasgow, 17 April 1752; *d* ? Glasgow, 1830). Scottish manufacturer and inventor of musical devices, noted for his creation of steam-powered looms and other improvements in weaving machinery. He was apprenticed to William and Walter Tait, merchants in Glasgow, and became a burgess and guild brother on 18 January 1776.

His musical inventions are preserved in his *Tonometer* (London, *c*1800) and *A System of Stenographic Music* (London, *c*1802). The former explains the use of moveable brass wheels, which Austin invented as a mechanical aid for transposition and tuning; the latter explains the use of a new musical stenography, in which Austin attempted to represent music in its most 'simple form' by reducing notation to one line and six characters. According to a review in the *Scots Magazine* (lxv, 1803, p.165) the *System* was taught for a time in several Edinburgh boarding schools and in Herriot and Watson's Hospital.

BIBLIOGRAPHY

H. Paton, ed.: *A Series of Original Portraits and Caricature Etchings, by the Late John Kay* (Edinburgh, 1842)

H.T. Wood: *A History of the Royal Society of Arts* (London, 1913)

J.C. Kassler: *The Science of Music in Britain, 1714–1830* (New York 1979), i, 28–30

JAMIE C. KASSLER

Austin, Larry (Don) (*b* Duncan, OK, 12 Sept 1930). American composer. He studied with Violet Archer (North Texas State University), Milhaud (Mills College) and Imbrie (University of California, Berkeley). In the 1960s he also formed associations with Cage, Stockhausen and David Tudor. While a member of the faculty at the University of California, Davis, he co-founded, edited and published the journal *SOURCE: Music of the Avant Garde*. He first gained recognition as a composer through a TV broadcast of his *Improvisations for Orchestra and Jazz Soloists* (1961), performed by Leonard Bernstein and the New York PO. Since that time, Austin's works have been performed and recorded by the Boston SO, the National SO and many other North American and European ensembles. He founded and directed computer music facilities at the University of South Florida (1972–

8) and the University of North Texas (1978–96), and co-founded and served as president of the Consortium to Distribute Computer Music. He has also served as president of the International Computer Music Association (1990–94).

Austin's works from the 1960s are written in an 'open style' that reflects an interest in group improvisation. Later compositions incorporate both live and recorded sound, often employing a combination of acoustic and electronic sources. Several of his works, including *Life Pulse Prelude* (1974–84), are based on studies of Ives's compositional sketches. His complete realization of Ives's *Universe Symphony* (1911–51) was recorded in 1994. In 1996 Austin was the first American to be awarded the Magistère title at the International Electroacoustic Music Competition, Bourges, an honour bestowed for his composition *BluesAx* (1995) and for his 30 years of leadership in electro-acoustic music.

WORKS
(*selective list*)

STAGE

Roma, improvisation ens, tape, 1965; Bass, db, tape, film, 1966; The Maze, perc, dancers, machines, film, 1966; Accidents, elec prep pf, tape, film, 1967; Prelude and Postlude to Plastic Surgery, pf, tape, film, 1971; Tableaux vivants, 4–6 pfmrs, tape, slide projections, 1973, rev. 1981, collab. C. Ringness; Catalogo voce (miniature op), B-Bar, tape, slide projections, 1978; Euphonia: a Tale of the Future (op, 2, T. Holliday, after H. Berlioz), 1982; Beachcombers (dance music, M. Cunningham), 4 pfmrs, live elec, tape, 1983; Ludus fractalis (video), 1984

TRADITIONAL MEDIA

Inst: Fantasy on a Theme by Berg, jazz orch, 1960; Pf Variations, 1960; Improvisations, jazz soloists, orch, 1961; A Broken Consort, fl, cl, hn, db, perc, pf, 1962; Continuum: Open Style, 7 inst 1964; Current, cl, pf, 1964; In Memoriam JFK, wind ens, 1964; Pf Set in Open Style, 1964; Qt in Open Style, str, 1964; Open Style, pf, orch, 1965; Agape Set, jazz orch, 1971; Life Pulse Prelude, perc orch, 1974–84; Universe Sym., 1974–93 [from Ives's sketches, 1911–51]; Charlie's Cornet, cornet, pf, 1976; Art is Self-Alteration is Cage is ..., db qt, 1982; Tango violento, pf, 1984; Clarini!, tpt choir, 1985; Violet's Invention, pf, 1988

Vocal: Homecoming (cant.), S, jazz qnt, 1959; Ceremony, S/T, org, 1980

ELECTRO-ACOUSTIC

Tape: Caritas, 1969; Qt no.3, 1971; Qt no.4, 1971; Primal Hybrid, 1972; Quadrants, 1972; Nineteen Seventy-Six, 1973; Phoenix, 1974; Stars, 1982; SoundPoem Set: PaulineOliveros/JerryHunt/MortonSubotnick/DavidTudor, 1991; Rompido!, 1993; Shin-Edo: CityscapeSet, 1996; Djuro's Tree, 1997

Tape and insts: Changes: Open Style, trbn, tape, 1965; Catharsis: Open Style, large ens, small improvisation ens, tape, 1972; Quadrants: Event/Complex nos.3–4, 6–11, various, 1972–7; Fantasies on Ives's Universe Symphony: 1 The Earth, nar, double brass qnt, tape, 1975; 2 The Heavens, cl, va, perc, kbds, tape, 1976; Catalogo sonoro 'Narcisso', va, tape, 1978; Sonata concertante, pf, tape, 1984; Montage: Themes and Variations, vn, tape, 1985; Sinfonia concertante: A Mozartean Episode, nar, chbr orch, tape, 1986; BluesAx, sax, tape, 1995; Taragato, 1998

Tape and voices: Quadrants: Event/Complex no.2, chorus, tape, 1972; Euphonia 2344: an Intermezzo in 5 Scenes, 4vv, tape, 1988; Transmission Two: The Great Excursion, chorus, vc, perc, pf, tape, 1990; La Barbara: The Name/The Sounds/The Music, 1v, tape, 1991; Variations ... beyond Pierrot, S, 5 insts, elec/tape, 1995; Singing!, Bar, tape, 1998

Cptr: Protoforms: Fractals, cptr, 1980; Canadian Coastlines: Canonic Fractals, 8 pfmrs, cptr, 1981; Protoforms: Fractals, vc chorus, cptr, 1981; AccidentsTwo: Sound Projection, pf, cptr, 1992

Recorded interviews in *US-NHoh*

Principal publishers: Composer Performer (Source), MJQ, Peer-Southern, Larry Austin Music

BIBLIOGRAPHY

CC (T. Clark); *EwenD; VintonD*

A. Kennedy: 'Sound-Script Relations and the New Notation', *Artforum*, xii/1 (1973), 38–44

D. Ernst: *The Evolution of Electronic Music* (New York, 1976)

W. Zimmermann: *Desert Plants: Conversations with 23 American Musicians* (Vancouver, 1976)

T. Clark: 'Duality of Process and Drama', *PNM*, xxiii/1 (1984), 112–25

L. Austin and T. Clark: *Learning to Compose: Modes, Materials, and Models of Musical Invention* (Dubuque, IA, 1989)

T. Clark: 'Coasts: on the Creative Edge', *Computer Music Journal*, xiii/1 (1989), 21–35

THOMAS CLARK

Austin, William W(eaver) (*b* Lawton, OK, 18 Jan 1920, *d* Ithaca, NY, 15 March 2000). American musicologist. He was educated at Harvard University, where he received the BA in 1939, the MA in 1940 and the PhD in 1951; his professors included Walter Piston, Archibald T. Davison and A. Tillman Merritt. Austin began his teaching career at the University of Virginia (1945–7). He taught at Cornell University from 1947 until his retirement in 1990; in 1969 he was elected a Fellow of the American Academy of Arts and Sciences. He was a visiting professor at Princeton University during the academic year 1957–8. In 1970 he became a member of the Gesellschaft für Musikforschung.

Austin specializes in the music of Russia and the USA in the 19th century, and in the history of 20th-century music. With *Music in the 20th Century* he contributed a broad yet comprehensive survey of music from 1900 to 1950. The book deals with stylistic and technical developments, aesthetic trends and music as a facet of cultural history. The author's evaluations may be debated: Debussy is the subject of a lengthy chapter and the discussion of Schoenberg has been criticized by reviewers. But Austin avoided the use of 'isms' and similar labelling often used by writers attempting to come to grips with the musical developments of the past 75 years, and his scholarship produced a valuable body of factual material for the student of 20th-century music.

WRITINGS

Harmonic Rhythm in Twentieth-Century Music (diss., Harvard U., 1951)

'Bartók's *Concerto for Orchestra*', *MR*, xviii (1957), 21–47

'Satie Before and After Cocteau', *MQ*, xlviii (1962), 216–33

'Quelques connaissances et opinions de Schoenberg et Webern sur Debussy', *Debussy et l'évolution de la musique au XXe siècle: Paris 1962*, 319–29

Music in the 20th Century (New York, 1966)

ed.: *New Looks at Italian Opera: Essays in Honor of Donald J. Grout* (Ithaca, NY, 1968)

'Music in Paris around 1920', *IMSCR X: Ljubljana 1967* 216–21

Claude Debussy: Prelude to 'The Afternoon of a Faun' (New York, 1970) [Norton Critical Score]

'Ives and Histories', *GfMKB: Bonn 1970*, 299–302

'Neue Musik', *Epochen der Musikgeschichte in Einzeldarstellungen* (Kassel, 1974), 386–461

'*Susanna', 'Jeanie', and 'The Old Folks at Home': the Songs of Stephen C. Foster from His Time to Ours* (New York, 1975, 2/1987/R)

'Copland, Aaron', *Grove6*

PAULA MORGAN

Austin Organs. American organ building firm. It was founded by John Turnell Austin (*b* Poddington, Beds., 16 May 1869; *d* Hartford, CT, 17 Sept 1948). The son of gentleman farmer and amateur organ builder Jonathan Austin, he emigrated to America in 1889. He first worked for Farrand & Votey of Detroit, rapidly advancing to become foreman. There he first conceived the idea of a radically different system of organ construction called the 'universal wind-chest' system; this consisted of an individual-valve chest, the lower portion of which was a walk-in air chamber with regulator. Pipe valves were operated by a thin wooden trace attached to a motor bellows for each note. Stop action was first achieved by sliders; later a pivoting fulcrum affecting the valves was used. Although Farrand & Votey allowed Austin to experiment, they showed no interest in his ideas, and in 1893 he left them for Clough & Warren of Detroit, who in the same year built their first small organ based on Austin's system. In 1898 Clough & Warren were closed by fire, and Austin moved to Boston. A year later he was persuaded by some Hartford businessmen to move to their city, and with their backing he opened a factory there in collaboration with his brother, Basil George Austin (1874–1958), who came to the US in 1893. He obtained patents for an all-electric console in 1913, and for a self-player mechanism in 1914; an improved version of the latter, called the 'Quadruplex', was made in 1924. Another innovation was the steel plate diamond-shaped hollow swell shade. Austin's mechanical ingenuity was not limited to organ mechanisms; he also designed many labour-saving machines for his factory. In 1937 he retired, and the firm reorganized under the name of Austin Organs Inc., with his nephew, Frederic B. Austin (1903–90), as president. Richard J. Piper (1904–78) joined the company in 1949, becoming vice-president and tonal director. He was succeeded in the latter position by David A.J. Broome (*b* 1932); in 1998 Bruce Q. Buchanan, formerly with J.W. Walker, succeeded him. Donald B. Austin (*b* 1933), the son of F.B. Austin, became president in 1973 and his daughter, Kimberlee J. Austin (*b* 1960) became vice-president in 1994. Noteworthy Austin organs include those in the City Hall Auditorium, Portland, Maine (1912), San Francisco Civic Auditorium (1915), the University of Pennsylvania (1926), St Joseph's Cathedral (1962) and Trinity College (1972), both in Hartford, Holy Family Cathedral, Tulsa (1984), the Shrine of Our Lady of Czestochowa, Doylestown, Pennsylvania (1991) and St John's Church, W. Hartford (1996). As of 1997 the firm has built 2774 organs.

BIBLIOGRAPHY

C.H. Heaton: *A History of Austin Organs, Inc.* (thesis, Union Theological Seminary, 1952)

'Science Aids Art', *Connecticut Industry*, xxxviii/5 (1960), 6–8

W.H. Barnes: *The Contemporary American Organ* (Glen Rock, NJ, 8/1964)

R.E. Coleberd: 'John Turnell Austin, Mechanical Genius of the Pipe Organ', *American Organist*, xlix/9 (1966), 14–19

O. Ochse: *The History of the Organ in the United States* (Bloomington, IN, 1975)

'Austin Organs Inc. 100 Year Anniversary', *American Organist*, xxvii/11 (1993), 40–47

R. Smith: *The Aeolian Pipe Organ and its Music* (Richmond, VA, 1998)

O. Ochse: *Austin Organs* (forthcoming)

BARBARA OWEN

Austral [Fawaz, Wilson], **Florence** (*b* Melbourne, 26 April 1894; *d* Newcastle, NSW, 15 or 16 May 1968). Australian soprano. Her real name was Wilson, but she was also known by that of her stepfather, Fawaz, before she adopted her familiar professional name. Having studied at Melbourne University Conservatorium and with Sibella in New York, she is said to have been offered a contract with the Metropolitan Opera, but preferred to make her career in England. In 1923 she appeared at Covent Garden with the British National Opera Company as Brünnhilde in the complete *Ring* cycle, and this role was to remain her most famous; she was also successful as Isolde and Aida. Less forceful and more lyrical than many Wagnerian dramatic sopranos, she maintained a consistent beauty and evenness of tone through these arduous parts, which she also sang in the international Covent Garden seasons of 1924 and later. She married the flautist John Amadio, and toured widely with him in Australia and America. Her many admirable recordings for HMV include the pioneer late-acoustic English-language series of excerpts from the *Ring*; in the early-electric German-language series, as at Covent Garden, she shared the role with Frida Leider.

BIBLIOGRAPHY
D. White: 'Florence Austral', *Record Collector*, xiv (1961–2), 4–29, 168–9, [with discography by W. Hogarth and D. White]

DESMOND SHAWE-TAYLOR

Australasian Performing Right Association [APRA]. *See* COPYRIGHT, §IV, 1.

Australia. Country and island continent. It is located between the Indian and Pacific oceans south of South-east Asia and is the only continent to comprise a single nation-state. The Australian Aborigines arrived *c*40,000 years ago and developed a highly stable society with complex cultural traditions, aspects of which survived colonization by the British from the 18th century. Of a total population of 18·84 million (est. 2000), *c*355,000 people are Aborigine. Since World War II Australia has played an increasing role in Asia and the Pacific, and in the last decades of the 20th century the influence of Asian immigrants has become important.

I. Aboriginal music. II. Western art music. III. Popular immigrant musics.

I. Aboriginal music

Aboriginal people in Australia live in a variety of environments, including communities with predominantly Aboriginal populations and small settlements (out stations) on traditional land, as well as in country towns and cities with mixed Aboriginal and non-Aboriginal populations. Exchange of songs and dances between groups has historically been a feature of Aboriginal culture, particularly at ceremonial occasions. Songs and dances indigenous to one area were frequently adopted by people in neighbouring areas. In recent decades access to modern transportation and the electronic media has increased the interchange of cultural property between geographically distant Aboriginal populations and has led to increased participation of Aboriginal musicians and dancers in national and global culture. Symptomatic of this trend is the dissemination of the didjeridu; traditionally a northern Australian instrument – to other areas of Australia, where it has been adopted as a pan-Australian symbol of Aboriginal identity, and the immense popularity of the didjeridu within world music and New Age markets (Neuenfeldt, 1997). Popular music genres such as country, rock and reggae have become popular among Aboriginal people and are frequently combined with elements of traditional music by the many Aboriginal bands (some of which now sustain international reputations) that have

sprung up in the communities, towns and cities of northern Australia.

1. Northern Aboriginal music: (i) Kimberley region (ii) Daly region (iii) Arnhem Land (iv) Gulf country (v) Cape York Peninsula. 2. Central Aboriginal music: (i) General (ii) Songs for ages and stages (iii) Ceremonies, ritual knowledge and responsibilities (iv) Musical structures (v) Dance and design (vi) Change over time. 3. Southeastern Aboriginal music: (i) Historical background and collections (ii) Corroboree and related genres (iii) Musical structure in performance (iv) Instruments (v) Modern developments.

1. NORTHERN ABORIGINAL MUSIC. Northern Australia hosts a large variety of Aboriginal languages and musical cultures (fig.1). Research on northern Aboriginal music is uneven: the music and dance of some regions, for example Arnhem Land, have attracted a great deal of attention, while others, most notably the Bathurst and Melville Islands and Cape York Peninsula, have received less, particularly in recent years. The first major surveys of Northern Australian music were carried out by A.P. Elkin and Trevor A. Jones (1958) and by Alice Moyle (1964 and 1974). More recent studies have tended to focus on the musical life of particular communities or on particular public genres.

All traditional Aboriginal performances in northern Australia – singing, dancing, the execution of visual designs and representations – are (or were in the past) associated with religious ritual. Although some are now performed in contexts that are not primarily religious (at official functions or arts festivals, for civil ceremonies and for entertainment), traditional religious ceremonies remain the most potent and significant contexts.

It is generally believed that at the beginning of time, in the period known in English as the Dreaming or Dreamtime, ancestral beings created the world and then deposited their creative power at certain sites. The power they left can be accessed today by correctly reproducing in ceremony the songs and dances originally performed by the ancestors in order to bring the world into being. Such ceremonies are regarded as both powerful and dangerous, and restrictions often apply as to who may perform or witness them. Because of the sensitivity attached to ritual performances of this type, they will not be discussed in detail in this article.

Public songs and dances, performances to which no restrictions apply with regard to who may perform or witness them, occur widely throughout northern Australia. In many cases, these are given to singers by ghosts or ancestral beings in dreams, although some, such as Arnhem Land clan-songs, are said to have existed 'from the beginning'. Public songs are in many cases performed at rituals associated with circumcision and death, in a variety of quasi- or non-ceremonial contexts and for entertainment.

(i) Kimberley region. Located in the north-west corner of Australia, the Kimberley region is bordered to the south by the Great Sandy Desert and to the east by the Victoria River (fig.1). It is linguistically and culturally distinct from the Western Desert cultures to the south (see §2 below) and the Daly and Arnhem Land cultures to the north-east, although there is ongoing cultural exchange with these areas.

As elsewhere in Australia, the most powerful songs and dances are those associated with the creative activities of the Dreaming ancestors, and there are often restrictions as to who may perform or witness them. Some of these

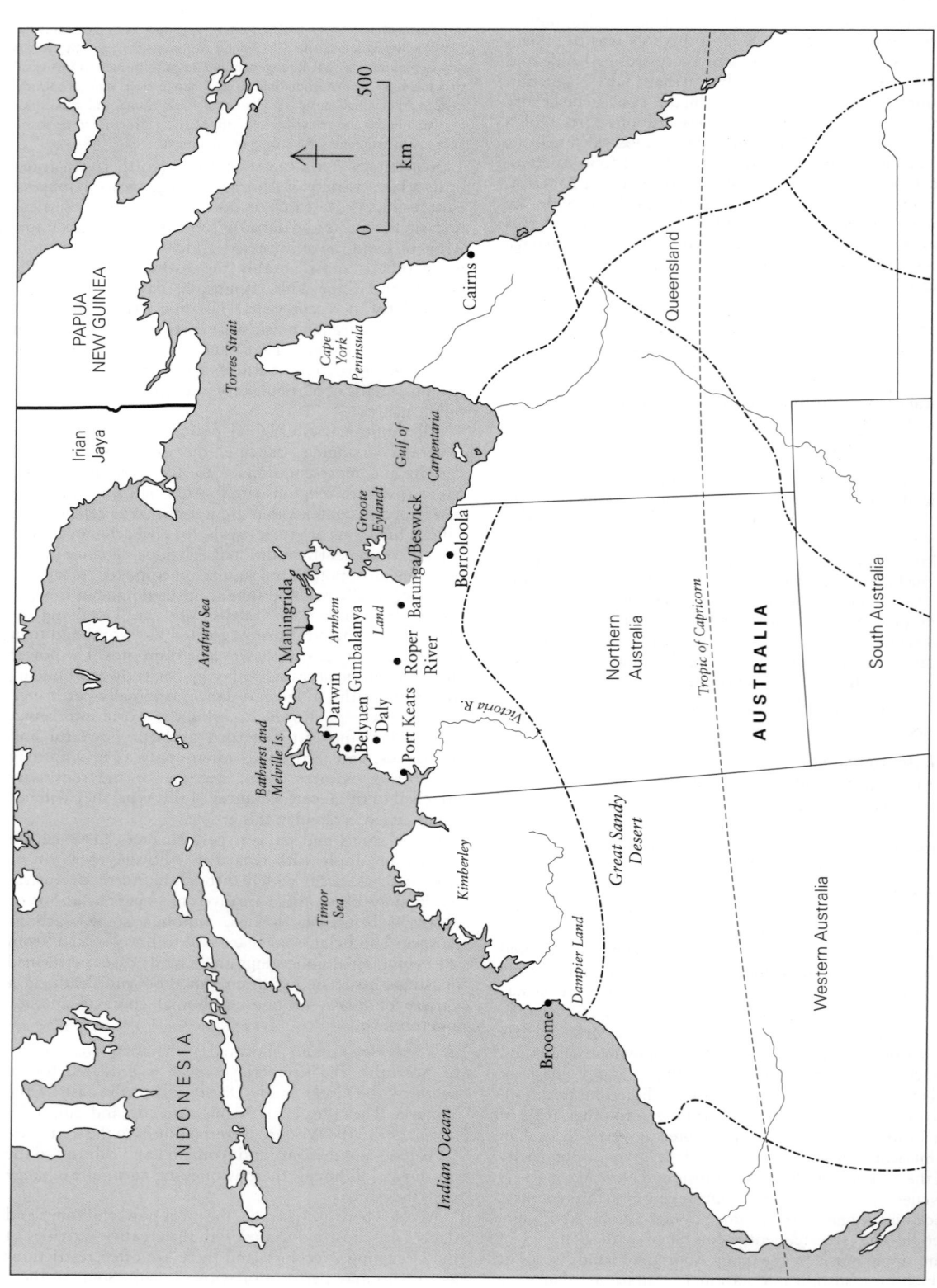

1. Map of northern Australia

ceremonies, such as the *Walungarri* initiation cycles of the Ngarinyin, are indigenous to the area, whereas others have come into the region through ritual exchange with groups to the south and north-east.

The most commonly encountered public performance genre in the Kimberley region is *junba*. There are a number of subgenres distinguished by the Ngarinyin people, which are principally determined by their dance paraphernalia: *jadmi*, performed with long paper bark caps and green leaves at the elbow and knee joints (fig.2); *balga*, performed with string crosses woven from coloured wool; and *galinda*, distinguished by the large painted boards carried on the shoulders of the dancers (fig.3).

While the terms *junba* and *balga* are used widely throughout the region, certain languages have their own names for songs of the *junba* type. These include *nurlu* in the southern Dampier region (Dyabirr Dyabirr, Dyugun, Ngumbarl, Nyigina and Yawuru languages); *ilma* in northern Dampier Land (Baardi and Nyul Nyul); *maru* in the southwest (Garadyarri); *dyudyu* in the south (Mangarla and Walmadyarri) and *dhamba* in the north-east (Murrinhpatha). Within each of these categories there may be a number of different song series, each usually associated with a particular composer. All these genres share important characteristics: they are normally sung by groups that comprise both males and females; their musical organization (which typically comprises isorhythmic texts set to a flexible melodic contour) conforms broadly to Central Australian principles (see §2(iv) below); they are accompanied by sticks or boomerangs and body percussion; they are composed by individuals with the assistance of spirit agents who appear to the singers in dreams and take them on spirit journeys; and

they are accompanied by dance, the style and dance-paraphernalia of which varies from genre to genre.

Other commonly encountered public genres are the didjeridu-accompanied *wangga* and *lirrga*, which in terms of their musical organization, instrumental accompaniment, dance style and other features are stylistically distinct from *junba* and its related genres. *Wangga* and *lirrga* have been imported into the area from the Daly region, but their form and significance is changed in a number of ways in the Kimberley. First, the distinction between *wangga* and *lirrga* is not always recognized, and the meanings of song texts are often not understood; also, *wangga* and *lirrga* are imported to the Kimberley and are rarely, if at all, composed there. Furthermore, their function in ritual is different from that which they have in the Daly region (see §(ii) below). In general, *wangga* and *lirrga* are performed for entertainment and in the public sections of rituals that otherwise have restricted access.

Another public genre, about which less is known, is *lilydyin* (or *ludin*), comprising individually composed and owned songs from northern Dampier Land. These concern contemporary events and are sung by men without dancing. Further south, *dyabi* (or *yabi*) songs, also individually composed and owned, are performed with a rasp unique (within the Australian context) to that genre (Moyle, recordings, 1977, and von Brandenstein, 1969). Rain-making songs addressed to Wandjina, the principal creation Dreamings of the Ngarinyin, Wunambal and Worora people, were recorded by Alice Moyle in 1968 (Moyle, recordings, 1977); it is unclear whether they are still performed.

2. Dicky Tataya and others dance jadmi junba

3. *Dancers from Imintji/Tirralintji displaying painted boards and string crosses, typical of galinda and balga respectively*

A performance from the northern Kimberley of the *jadmi junba* by the Ngarinyin singer-composer Nyalgodi (Scotty) Martin illustrates many musical and dance features typical of the most commonly encountered public genres. *Jadmi* was given to Nyalgodi by the ghost (*agula*) of his grandfather, who appeared to him in a dream in 1973 and took him on a journey to Dulugun, the land of the dead, off the north-western coast of the Kimberley. There he showed Nyalgodi a song series by his deceased relations, which he subsequently shaped into the *jadmi junba* (see also §2(i) below).

Jadmi junba contains some 27 distinct songs, each of which represents a different dream experience. A complete performance is made up of a number of these. Ex.1 shows part of one of these songs. The text 'gurranda wayurlambi/ ngardarri wayurlambi' refers to the ancestral Brogla (*gurranda*), a large estuarine bird with elaborate courting rituals who first taught people how to dance, and to the paper-bark caps (*ngardarri*) of the dancers. Ascertaining the conventions whereby the melody is expanded and contracted to fit texts of different length and structure performed at different tempos is one of the principal tasks of the musical analyst. These conventions have been explicated in detail for a *nurlu* series by Keogh (in Barwick, Marett and Tunstil, 1995) and by Treloyn for *jadmi junba* (recordings, 1999).

Of the many pop bands in the Kimberley, the most well known is the rock-calypso-reggae band Kuckles. Three members of this band (Jimmy Chi, Mick Manolis and Steve Pigram) went on to create the first Aboriginal stage musical, *Bran Nue Dae* in 1990.

(ii) Daly region.   The principal public song genres of the Daly region are the didjeridu-accompanied *wangga* (also *walaka*, *yindiyindi* and *djungguriny*) and *lirrga* (*lirra*). *Wangga* is indigenous to this region, where it is sung by speakers of Batjamalh, Emmi, Marri-tjevin, Marri-ammu, Marri-thiyel and Ngan'gi-tjemerri languages. The genre

has been disseminated outside the Daly region to Barunga (where it is also known as *walaka*), to western Arnhem Land (*djungguriny*) and to the Kimberley. *Lirrga* was imported to the Daly region within living memory from Barunga, Beswick, Gunbalanya and Maningrida, where it is known as *gunborrg*. In the Daly region *lirrga* songs are now composed by speakers of Marri-ngarr and Ngan'gi-wumerri, with the help of local Dreaming ancestors. A number of other public genres are sung by Murrinhpatha speakers, including *dhamba*, which is stylistically related to the public genres of the Kimberley region; *malkarriny*, isorhythmically-organized songs that relate to a prophetic vision of the coming of the first missionaries to Port Keats; and *wurltjerri*, a didjeridu-accompanied genre (fig.4).

Both *wangga* and *lirrga* are performed by one, two or occasionally more singers who accompany themselves on wooden clapsticks and are accompanied by a single didjeridu player. These genres display a variety of formal structures, and it is difficult to distinguish them by musical criteria alone. Both feature spectacular male dancing, which involves a high degree of individual virtuosity, and group women's dancing that emphasizes upper body movement; however, *wangga* dancers perform the stamping movements characteristic of these genres using two legs, whereas *lirrga* dancers stamp only one leg (Marett and Page, in Barwick, Marett and Tunstil, 1995; Page, *GEWM*). The dance movements for *dhamba*, *malkarriny* and *wurltjerri* exhibit the more restrained gestures typical of both Central Australian and Kimberley dance, which are combined with the more flamboyant movements characteristic of the Daly.

Wangga, *lirrga* and *dhamba* are received in dreams by individual songmen from a variety of spirit agents. In some cases, particularly at Port Keats, the song-giving spirits are humanoid Dreaming figures known variously as Walakandha, Ma-yawa and Ginwurri for *wangga*, as

Kanybubi (mermaids) for *lirrga* and as Kunbinyi for *dhamba*. In other places, particularly at Belyuen and Barunga, *wangga* songs are given by the ghosts of deceased songmen. Song texts in some cases comprise the untranslated words sung by song-giving spirits in ghost language; these are heard as meaningless vocables. In other cases the words of the spirit are translated into human language by the singer and are heard as normal language. Meaningful song texts may refer to the song-giving process itself, to particular Dreamings or ghosts, to living people, to contemporary events or to significant places.

The two main ceremonial contexts for all five public genres of this region are ceremonies to make boys into men through circumcision (fig.5) and 'rag-burning' ceremonies performed to assist the spirit of a deceased person to leave the world of the living. In circumcision ceremonies in particular, it is not uncommon for genres from outside the region to be sung. These include Arnhem Land clan-songs (*bunggurl* or *manikay*) as well as ceremonial complexes imported from Central Australia (Stanner, 1966). All five local public genres are also regularly performed in quasi-ceremonial contexts such as building dedications, college graduations and civil ceremonies, as well as for entertainment.

4. Gypsy Jinjarr and Elizabeth Cumaiyi (Karlingkun) sing wurltjerri accompanied by Gerald Longmirr on didjeridu

A song about a man called Benmele, composed by the Belyuen songman Bobby Lambudju Lane, can serve as an illustration of *wangga* style (ex.2). In the first of the two main descents, the text 'Benmele-maka kurraitj-kurraitj

Ex.1 Second verse of *Jadmi junba* (text transcr. L. Barwick, music transcr. S. Treloyn)

Melodic Cycle 1

Sticks:

gur - ran - da   way - ur - lam - bi   gur - ran - da   way - ur - lam - bi   ngar - dar - ri   way - ur - lam - bi

ngar - dar - ri   way - ur - lam - bi   gur - ran - da   way - ur - lam - bi   gur - ran - da   way - ur - lam - bi

ngar - dar - ri   way - ur - lam - bi   ngar - dar - ri   way - ur - lam - bi

Melodic Cycle 2

gur - ran - da   way - ur - lam - bi   gur - ran - da   way - ur - lam - bi   ngar - dar - ri   way - ur - lam - bi

ngar - dar - ri   way - ur - lam - bi   gur - ran - da   way - ur - lam - bi   gur - ran - da   way - ur - lam - bi

Melodic Cycle 3

gur - ran - da   way - ur - lam - bi   gur - ran - da   way - ur - lam - bi

ngar - dar - ri   way - ur - lam - bi   ngar - dar - ri   way - ur - lam - bi   gur - ran - da   way - ur - lam - bi

gur - ran - da   way - ur - lam - bi   ngar - dar - ri   way - ur - lam - bi   ngar - dar - ri   way - ur - lam - bi

x = stick beat; ⊗ = stick beat with body percussion (women beating their thighs with cupped hands)

5. Colin Ferguson, Les Kundjil, Charles Kanggiang and others performing wangga during a circumcision ceremony

kabindje-noeng' ('Benmele, kookuburra, he sang for him') is set isorhythmically. Isorhythm is not, however, the thoroughgoing principle of musical organization that it is in Central Australian song or genres such as *junba* in the Kimberley; it is adopted here as just one of a range of organizational principles that *wangga* composers draw on. Thus it is abandoned in the shorter second descent, which is made up of sustained notes set to the vocable text 'i, a, n'. Before returning to the main descent at the beginning of a second rendition of the song verse, the singer sings a primarily rhythmic passage to the vocables 'e ta' in the lower octave. Even unpatterned, stick-beating is sustained throughout the song; however, many different patterns, implying a range of different metres, may be used in both *wangga* and *lirrga*. Throughout, the didjeridu plays a rhythmic drone on the pitch that is the final of the two main melodic descents. In the Daly region and western Arnhem Land (except in *wurltjerri*) there is seldom any use of the overblown tone of the didjeridu. Expert performers manipulate the upper partials of the didjeridu to produce complex 'chords' that are combined in rhythmic interactions with the vocal part (these are not shown in ex.2).

(iii) Arnhem Land. Here, song ownership is overwhelmingly group-based. Some repertories, most notably those associated with restricted or semi-restricted ceremonies, are owned by one or the other of two patrilineal exogamous moieties, Dhuwa or Yirritja. These include the clapstick- (*bilma*-) accompanied songs for the *Madayin* ceremony, different sets of which are owned by each of the moieties; the Dhuwa-owned *Kunapipi*, *Ngulmarrk* (*Ubar*) and *Djungguwan* ceremonies; and the Yirritja-owned *Yabadurawa*. The exact forms of these ceremonies, which focus on the activities of ancestral Dreaming figures, vary across Arnhem Land.

Ownership of the most commonly performed public songs (termed *manikay* in north-eastern areas of central and eastern Arnhem Land, *bunggurl* in the south-western Barunga/Beswick area and 'clan-song' in English) is invested in exogamous patrilineal clans. Each clan identifies with a set of Dreamings (*wangarr*), some of which

reside on their land and some on the estates of related clans. Didjeridu-accompanied clan-songs, dances, paintings, designs and other ritual property, which are believed to have been handed down unchanged since the creation of the world, make manifest a clan's Dreamings when they are presented in ceremony.

Individually-owned, didjeridu-accompanied songs called *gunborrg* are also composed and performed in western Arnhem Land, particularly among the Maung, Gunwinggu and related language groups. *Gunborrg* are given to individual songmen in dreams and may refer either to topical events or Dreamings. They are widely performed in northern Australia, for example at Barunga and Beswick to the south, in the Daly region (where they are known as *lirrga*) and in the Gulf region (where they are known as *malwa*).

In eastern Arnhem Land yet another form of didjeridu-accompanied song, called *djatpangarri*, is performed by young unmarried men. Often described as 'fun songs', their texts comprise both meaningless vocables and references to everyday topics (Moyle, recordings, 1964, pp.31–2, and 1974). According to Waterman (1971) most *djatpangarri* follow the same melodic pattern. Recently, *djatpangarri* have been incorporated into Western popular music songs by the band Yothu Yindi of Arnhem Land. Other bands, such as Blekbala Mujik from Barunga and Sunrize Band from Maningrida, also mix elements of traditional music with rock, reggae and other popular genres.

Clan-songs (*manikay, bunggurl*) are grouped into series, which are usually owned by more than one clan. In central Arnhem Land these series are known by proper names such as *Murlarra* (Anderson, 1992, and Anderson, in Barwick, Marett and Tunstil, 1995), *Djambidj* (Clunies Ross and Wild, recordings, 1982, and 1984), *Goyulan* (Clunies Ross and Mundrugmundrug, recordings, 1988) or *Baratjarr* (Stanhope, 1991). In eastern Arnhem Land they are referred to by both the name of the owning clans and by the topographical subject matter of the series. While in central Arnhem Land each clan normally (though not exclusively) owns just one series, in eastern Arnhem

Ex.2 Part of a *wangga* by Bobby Lane about Benmele (text transcr. A. Marett, L. Barwick and L. Ford; music transcr. A. Marett)

Land clans own rights to more than one series. Men can sing the songs of their own clans and of their maternal grandmother's clan, or of a clan with which they share song-series.

A song-series comprises a set of clan-songs, each celebrating the activities of one of a number of totemic Dreamings associated with the owning clans. *Djambidj*, for example, is owned by (and binds together) four Burarra-speaking clans as well as a number of clans from other language groups (Hiatt, 1965, p.59). It comprises some 21 song subjects that include various animal or plant species (for example, Crow, White Cockatoo, Green Turtle or Yam), culturally-produced items (Didjeridu and Hollow Log Coffin) and spirit beings (Marrawal).

Clan-songs are sung primarily in three public ritual contexts: mortuary rites, circumcision ceremonies and

ceremonies of ritual diplomacy. They may also be performed in public parts of otherwise secret ceremonies, as well as for entertainment. All ceremonial contexts require singing and dancing with visual representation of Dreamings in several media.

Mortuary ceremonies can be divided into three main stages. The first of these involves the preparation of the body and its burial or exposure on a tree platform. In the second stage, which occurs some months later, after the body has partially decayed, relatives clean the bones and paint them with ochre before handing them to female relatives for safe-keeping. The third stage (which is traditionally the most elaborate) involves crushing the bones of the deceased and placing them in a hollow log-coffin, which is then placed upright and abandoned. In some areas, as a result of Christian influence, the first (burial) stage has become the principal element in the ceremonial complex (see, for example, Dunlop, film, 1979, and Morphy, 1984). In other areas of eastern and central Arnhem Land, the third stage remains the principal one. The film *Waiting for Harry* (McKenzie, film, 1980) documents such a ceremony during which the songs, dances and visual designs of the two song-series *Djambidj* and *Goyulan* are executed.

Mortuary practices in eastern Arnhem Land (including Groote Eylandt) appear to differ in an even more fundamental way from those in other parts of Arnhem Land in that the ceremony is concerned with the journey of the soul of the deceased from the place of death to its spiritual resting place in its clan lands. In a series of ritual episodes made up of a particular set of dances, ritual actions and songs, ancestral events associated with the particular tracts of country through which the soul is travelling are re-enacted in ceremony.

In circumcision ceremonies a boy's connection to his totems, his country and his kin is emphasized by the performance of songs and dances and the painting on his body of emblems associated with his principal totems (Keen, 1994, pp.171–91).

The ceremonies of Marradjirri or Rom have been described as 'rituals of diplomacy' or 'exchange ceremonies'. These involve the presentation of elaborately decorated poles to distant social groups, with attendant singing and dancing of clan-songs (Borsboom, 1978, and Keen, 1994). Rom ceremonies have also been performed to celebrate the relationship between the Anbarra people of central Arnhem Land and the Australian Institute of Aboriginal and Torres Strait Islander Studies in Canberra (fig.6) (For music of Torres Strait aborigines *see* TORRES STRAIT ISLANDS).

The three main musical elements in any performance of clan-songs are a vocal melody carried by one or more specialist male singers, clapstick patterns played by the singers, and a patterned drone played by a single didjeridu, although in eastern Arnhem Land some clan-songs are sung without didjeridu accompaniment. Whereas in central Arnhem Land the pitch of the didjeridu drone is often the same note as the final of the vocal melody, in eastern Arnhem Land there appears to be no attempt to make these two pitches agree (Knopoff, 1992). Women also perform songs (*ngathi manikay*) that follow the same texts, use the same images and carry the same meanings as men's songs. These 'crying-songs' are performed in free

rhythm both during mortuary rituals and in less formal grieving contexts (Magowan, 1994). Songs may or may not be accompanied by dance, with men and women performing independent styles of dancing. Dance forms and gestures may also be regarded as part of the property of clans.

In a typical performance, a particular song subject is sung a number of times followed by the singing of several song items of another song subject and so on (Stubington, 1978, and Anderson, 1992). Song subjects may be sung and danced in a number of styles. In central Arnhem Land, one major distinction is between performances in which there is no fixed metrical relationship between the voice, clapsticks and didjeridu and in which the music of each sound component is unmeasured (termed *ngarkana* in Rembarrnga language); and those in which voice, sticks and didjeridu all conform to the same metre and are aligned to produce complex formal patterning (termed *djalkmi* in Rembarrnga; see Anderson, 1992, and Anderson, in Barwick, Marett and Tunstil, 1995; Clunies Ross and Wild, 1984).

Throughout central and eastern Arnhem Land, 'measured' song items commonly comprise three parts: an introductory section in which the performers rehearse the main musical elements, the song proper and an unaccompanied vocal termination that is typically omitted when a song is danced to. The song proper consists of sung text accompanied by sticks and didjeridu (ex.3). Its beginning is usually marked by the singer or singers leaping to the highest note of the first of a number of vocal descents (marked *A*, *B*, *C* and *D* in ex.3) that form the principal melodic material of the song item. In the course of these descents, singers produce text describing the actions and attributes of the spirit being.

The opening lines of the song proper have the following meanings:

> *wang-gurnga guiya* Cockatoo named Wang-gurnga
> *wnag-gurnga giiya* Cockatoo named Wang-gurnga
> *gulob' arraidja* gorges himself on seeds and grasses and hiccups
> *ngwar-ngwar worria* dances and leaps slowly in the sky calling 'ngwair ngwair'
> *maningala rarei* lives at his waterhole in the upland forest
> (Clunies Ross and Wild, 1982, p.48).

Song texts are performed within a metrical framework articulated by sticks and didjeridu. In ex.3 each of the text lines occupies four beats. Variations in the patterning of sticks and didjeridu also articulate formal subdivisions within the song (see, for example, descent C, in which the stick-beating is varied and the didjeridu introduces overblown 'hoots' about a 10th above the tonic, circled in ex.3). Variant stick-beating and didjeridu hoots also mark the end of this second section.

(iv) Gulf country. South of Arnhem Land lies the Roper River. Several different types of song are recognized in the western Roper, including *lorrgon*, *manggarlagarl* and *gujida*. Lorrgon are associated with mortuary rites, and the other two figure in the initiation of young men. Despite a study of texts of *lorrgon* songs (Merlan, in Clunies Ross, Donaldson and Wild, 1987), little musicological study has been made of songs from this region. Songs of the *wangga* and *gunborrg* genres have also been recorded in this region.

The south-west coast of the Gulf of Carpentaria supports four cultural groups, differentiated primarily by language: Garrawa, Gudanji, Mara and Yanyuwa. Mack-

6. *George Ganjibala dancing bunggurl during a Rom ceremony at the Australian Institute of Aboriginal Studies*

Ex.3 Second section (song proper) of a performance of the song *White Cockatoo (Ngalilag)* from the clan-song series *Djambidj*
(singers: Frank Garramanamana and Frank Malkorda; didjeridu: Sam Gumuyum; transcr. A. Marett)

notes with circled head indicate overblown 'hoot'

inlay (1998, p.44) has suggested that whereas the textual and rhythmical structure of Yanyuwa songs resembles those of Central Australian music, the melodic structures resemble those in parts of north-central and north-eastern Arnhem Land. In Yanyuwa culture, songs are classified according to the origins of the songs. Songs composed by totemic ancestors in the Dreaming are referred to as *kujika*. When performed in ceremony they are often restricted by age or gender (or both). Other restricted repertories include 'love-magic' songs such as men's *djarrada* and women's *yawalyu* (Mackinlay, 1998). These latter two genres are widely encountered in Central Australia as well as in some other areas of northern Australia. *Yalkawarra* and *Kulyukulyu* are sacred public funeral rites which, while incorporating *kujika* songs, are generally not referred to as *kujika*.

Songs may also be composed by humans (*walaba* when composed by men or *a-kurija* when composed by women), in which case they are individually owned. Songs for which there is no generic form may also be received in dreams from spirit beings. West (recordings, 1962) reported that *gunborrg* songs from western Arnhem Land are performed at Borroloola, where they are known as *malwa*. 'Malwa', which was originally the proper name applied to a specific set of *gunborrg* songs, has become a generic term in this area.

A number of song genres are performed by the Lardil of Mornington Island. These include *burdal*, a public danced form given to singers by invisible beings in dream; *kujika* songs that belong to ceremonial complexes associated with Boraloola, *yirrijirr* women's ceremonial song and dance, and *djarrada* love magic songs (Woomera, Aboriginal Corporation, 1999).

(v) Cape York Peninsula. While there has been extensive recording and documentation of the indigenous music and dance of this region (for an account of audio recordings see Moyle, 1968–9, and Koch, in Clunies Ross, Donaldson and Wild, 1987), there have been few detailed musicological studies. Moreover, almost all available studies are based on fieldwork conducted in the 1960s and 70s. The dance styles of western Cape York Peninsula have, on the other hand, been comparatively well studied (von Sturmer, 1978, and von Surmer, in Clunies Ross, Donaldson and Wild, 1987; Arnold, 1991; and Williams, 1988).

Typical of the cultures of western Cape York Peninsula are the Kugu-ngancharra, a subgroup of the Wik people. In the 1970s they possessed a repertory of ceremonial-mythical complexes, songs and dances that comprised a number of different traditions, some restricted and others public: *munka*, *wanam*, *kunalum* or *anytjalam* (turtle), *pucha*, *winychinam*, *nganycha mongkom*, *wungga a'e*, *wungga mangaya*, *panycha pinpanam* (brolga), *thahadjam*, *pidhalam*, *nydyi* and *mapla* or *malgarri*. Of these, the public, boomerang clapstick-accompanied *wanam* is the most vibrant and is seen as both the symbol and the expression of Kugu-ngancharra identity. It is associated with a major initiation ceremony concerning the ancestral Kaha'ungken brothers. There are distinctive schools of *wanam* singing and dancing transmitted from particular individuals. As in north-eastern Arnhem Land, songs are also sung in order to conduct a deceased person's spirit to its final resting site. In creating this journey, songs associated with sites along the route may be chosen from several different traditions.

The traditional country of the Dyirbal lies in the rainforests on eastern Cape York Peninsula, south of Cairns. According to Dixon and Koch (1996, pp.5–6) the last initiation ceremonies were performed in this area in the 1920s, and the last corroborees (public performances of song and dance) were performed in the 1960s. In the past, composition was attributed to spirit intervention. Many surviving songs have been handed down, though some are said to be recently composed without spirit intervention. The surviving body of recordings of Dyirbal song comprises examples of five different genres. The first two, *gama* and *marrga*, are associated with corroborees. They are sung by a man accompanying himself with paired boomerang clapsticks or sticks, and perhaps also accompanied by a woman beating a membrane stretched across her thighs (lap-drum). Most refer to everyday events, although some are concerned with the spirit world, and dances are largely mimetic. By far the most common genre is the boomerang clapstick-accompanied *gama*, songs of which typically have two lines, each of eleven syllables; three-line songs and lines with nine syllables are also found. Meaningless syllables are added in the course of singing. *Marrga* are the corroboree songs of speakers of the Mamu dialect. They are accompanied by sticks and lap-drum and typically consist of four lines, each of eight syllables. The other three song genres (*jangala*, *burran* and *gaynyil*) are all referred to as 'gugulu', from the name of the accompanying stick, which is held vertically and struck with a piece of cane (fig.7). These songs, which often convey personal feelings, are sung by both men and women in private or semi-public contexts. Sometimes a shake-a-leg dance (a dance movement almost ubiquitous in Cape York Peninsula, wherein the feet are spread wide apart and the knees oscillated to and fro) is improvised to the songs. 'Shake-a-leg' is also used as a synonym for corroboree (i.e. a public ceremony), although shake-a-leg movements are also used in initiatory (*bora*) ceremonies.

On Cape York Peninsula, traditional styles of song and dance may be contrasted with more recently introduced forms such as harmonic Pacific island hymn-singing and related dancing. Introduced via the Torres Strait by Christian missionaries, these are now widely performed in public contexts such as sports days and other public festivals or in ceremonies to 'open' houses previously closed by deaths (Black and Koch, 1983, p.159). Unlike

7. Spider Henry strikes his gugulu stick (held vertically) with a piece of lawyer cane

traditional songs, which are received from the spirits of deceased relatives or totemic ancestors, such 'island songs' are composed by individuals. They may be sung by mixed groups of men and women and when danced are typically accompanied by drums and rattles of various sorts.

See also TORRES STRAIT ISLANDS.

2. CENTRAL ABORIGINAL MUSIC. This section covers performances of music and, where possible, aspects of the associated dance, design and ceremonies of Aboriginal people living in the area classified in the *Encyclopedia of Aboriginal Australia* (Horton, 1994) as the desert region, which includes over 40 tribal groups, only a few of which have been studied by ethnomusicologists. This vast area stretches from the desert around Alice Springs south almost to the Great Australian Bight and including the Woomera rocket range, west in places as far as the Western Australian coast, and further north than Tennant Creek. In it there are many common features and two major language groups, each with many dialects there are five Arandic and approximately 40 Pitjantjatjara-related dialects. These two language areas have the best-preserved traditions in the southern parts of the Australian continent.

(i) General. There are a number of stages of acculturation among the central Aboriginal people, more so in the city areas than remote desert locations, although all the latter can now access mass media. In addition to those traditional performers in desert areas who maintain their old song forms, there are others who dream modern songs that can be considered Dreamtime songs that include

reference to modern living; there are performers living in rural areas who introduce many non-traditional musical aspects into their performances; and there are others who, having moved to cities, create and perform majority musics (e.g. rock and Western art musics).

As elsewhere in Australia, the song tradition in this area is based around the travels of Ancestors through the region in the beginning of time. Performers say these songs have been passed from preceding generations since the time of the ancestral activities. Songs and singing have many functions in traditional life, including education, history, law, preservation of the land (for example rain charms and increase rites) and healing.

There are certain elements of desert region music that remain constant throughout the entire area. It is primarily syllabic vocal music based on cyclical structures within the three main structural fields of text, melody and rhythm. Musical instruments are only used for percussive accompaniment or for representation of spiritual beings. These general musical characteristics have also been noted among the *nurlu* of Western Australia, situated at the extreme westerly point of the desert region, although the stories and associated histories appear to have been influenced by styles from Northern Australia (see §1 above). The percussive accompaniment of desert music includes the use of paired sticks beaten together, a single stick or stone beaten on the ground, boomerangs beaten together, hand-clapping, foot-stamping (male) and thigh slapping (exclusively female). Of the instruments that are not percussive (exclusively used by males), both the bullroarer and the *ulbura ilpirra* 'trumpet' have supernatural functions; the former may be regarded as the voice of the sacred ancestor while the latter, a hollow log about 60 cm long and 5 cm in diameter whose sound is produced by singing through the instrument, replaces the bullroarer in some Aranda ceremonies. (The didjeridu is not traditional to this area but is now employed in some performances as an adopted symbol of Aboriginality.)

Song is understood to be a powerful agent in influencing non-musical events. There is a widespread belief that song enables performers to draw on supernatural powers left within the soil by the sacred ancestral people. It is only through the correct presentation, simultaneously, of all the technical features of the song that this power becomes accessible to the performers. Because the power can be used for either good or evil, strict control is maintained over the teaching of these potent songs; a system of exclusion operates, which results in only the oldest and wisest people knowing them.

The first thing children in the Pitjantjatjara (Yankuntjatjara) area learn during a performance is the correct accompaniment to the singing, which includes learning to select a suitable piece of wood for a beating-stick and how to prepare the mound of earth on which to beat the accompaniment; the initial song-instruction occurs through their involvement in the associated dance. There are traditional songs for children, which deliberately obscure the secret information that will be revealed when the same song is learnt later. Teenagers learn the names of special sites associated with the ancestral tracks by singing the songs in the geographical sequence of these Dreamtime journeys. Later, in the gender-segregated secret and sacred songs, the performers' understanding of the principles of song construction, musical coding and geographical identification enables more mature musical

activity. All this learning occurs through observation in a system which does not allow the student to ask questions of the knowledgeable person.

Documentation of the musics in this area often focusses on specific aspects rather than general characteristics; thus a comprehensive statement about the music is difficult. One argument raised in research is that this music lacks creativity, being an exclusively recreative form. General observation, insiders' concepts and analytical research findings contradict this suggestion. In the Alyawarra tradition, the male musical repertory is of fixed size, while the women may dream new songs; among the Warlpiri the process of reorganizing ceremonial life has included the creation of new complexes of songs, designs and dances that are received from the Dreaming through the agency of a spirit (Clunies Ross, Donaldson and Wild, 1987, p.109). Similar processes of accession of songs and ceremonies have been noted by Keogh among the *nurlu* genre in the Kimberleys, in Western Australia. The dreamer's spirit may leave the body during sleep to interact with the *balangan* (spirits of the dead) or *ray* (childlike) spirits, during which time a ceremony may be performed that the dreamer can then bring back to the everyday world. Subjects of these *nurlu* include experiences associated with white people; songs describing the death of soldiers in World War I have also been noted (see Palmer, 1989, p.3). The Pintubi produce songs that are anonymously-composed contemporary accounts of the mythological past, but no traditional explanation is given about how the boundary was crossed between the Dreamtime and historical time in order for mortals to be taught the series.

It has been demonstrated through research that the role of the song leader is crucial in establishing basic patterns from which the desired unison singing can be maintained. Barwick shows, for instance, how the melody can be expanded and contracted to fit the text with a considerable degree of variation. She gives a number of principles that indicate that each act of performance involves constant checking of all levels of rhythmic and melodic construction in the course of making decisions about fitting the text on the melody, and she concludes that this flexibility in the system paradoxically promotes the conservation of what may seem to be very inflexible rhythmic and melodic structures (see Ellis, Barwick and Morais, 1990, pp.69–75). Creativity can also be seen to operate in so far as the traditional concept is reinterpreted with fresh insight in each performance (this can occur only after long immersion in the conventional process). Structural parameters are identified through the systematic interlocking of different structural features, and particular ritual structures are incorporated by a system of cueing, which means that an almost infinite variability in performance detail goes hand in hand with very accurate conservation of the key musical elements of melody, text and rhythm at various hierarchical levels of the cyclical structures in the total performance, including dance.

(ii) Songs for ages and stages. Songs for each age group within the community have their own structures and functions. Songs associated with birth are those used when the life of either mother or child is in danger, or to induce labour. These are not performed for researchers because of their inherent power. The texts of lullabies often stress fear but some simply reiterate, through a repeated rhythmic pattern, a simple phrase such as 'do

not cry'. Songs that children make themselves and pass on to one another have largely disappeared because of contact with European education. Only a few have been recorded, and they all have short rhythmic patterns with only two main accents, most consisting of two widely separated notes (an interval of approximately a 5th or an octave). Melodically they are different from children's songs created by adults, which are diminutive forms of the non-secret sections of adult songs and are made for training boys and girls separately in the musical, textual and dancing techniques and in the expected behaviour and extra-musical effects of songs.

Songs of adults encompass almost the entire field of music-making. The more powerful the song, the more intricate is the overlay of patterning, to a point where error at one level is impossible without disruption of the interlocking process. In general, women's songs have a narrower melodic range and less rhythmic complexity than men's songs. Men's secret songs sometimes deliberately superimpose selected sections of two separate songlines (song series): the ending of one may be performed simultaneously with the start of a related series, the men of each singing group sitting within their own circle with some of each circle sitting back-to-back.

Songs for death are directed to the soul of the departed; they concern totemic affiliation and seek to allow the soul to return to its rightful spiritual home and thus become available for future reincarnation. Other songs performed at the death of a close relative may include, as well as stylized wailing, songs intended to identify the 'murderer'.

(iii) Ceremonies, ritual knowledge and responsibilities. Ancestral history is preserved within a totem-specific, geographically-mapped 'songline' (sometimes referred to by performers as 'history song' and by researchers as a song cycle or song series), which consists of a series of smaller units of composition (verse, text, couplet, item) known among Pitjantjatjara speakers as 'small songs'. Songlines may include hundreds of small songs, each representing one piece of information in relation to the ancestor being commemorated. The small song has an identifying text and accompanying syllabic rhythm, repeated a given number of times to complete the melodic shape of the songline. Tunstill (see Crunies Ross, Donaldson and Wild, 1987, p.65) gives a practical example of the embedded geographical knowledge encoded in such a songline: a group of Pintupi, lost while travelling, sang part of a song series that mapped the way they had come, and by attending to the correct order of the song sequence found out that they had taken an incorrect turn.

The many types of small songs are identified with specific terminology by performers. Named categories of small songs include songs sung when the ground painting is being prepared; when the sacred objects are viewed during performance; to accompany body painting; at the start and at the close of the performance; to accompany specific dances; to represent the 'sonic name' of a sacred place. There are small songs, known as 'carrying' or 'travelling' songs, describing types of scenery (for example dry salt lakes) wherever these recur in ancestral travels. Individual charms may be extracted from songlines for various purposes, including rain-making, attracting a lover, causing injury to an enemy or healing. There are also small songs that link one line from each of two different texts to create a new small song. There are 'true' (sacred) small songs and 'false' ones that are taught to children in preparation for their main learning as adults. Highly secret and sacred small songs may be omitted in some presentations of the appropriate songline.

Each small song will have a section of melody that passes through the essential range of the song, displaying the characteristic melodic shape of its songline. Specific points in the rhythmic pattern fall in predetermined relationship to the melodic shape, and the text may be presented in either of two different positions on the melody. Pitjantjatjara ceremonial performances usually present a selection of songs from the complete set of related songs. Only rarely is the complete set presented by a group of performers or at an occasion: usually its performance is spread out over geographic and social space (according to the mapping and ownership of the song) and through time. Performers regard each of their songs celebrating totemic ancestors as a collection of individual couplets, which may be sung in various traditional sequences since each is a self-contained unit. Among central Australian performers the couplets containing the names of totemic ancestors are the most carefully guarded couplets in all their songs. Among the Pintubi the underlying myth is only sometimes expanded in speech between the singing of small songs, but the explanation or recounting refers directly to the events described in the small songs being performed, not to the whole myth. For them, accurate performance is the essential concept, because without it efficacy is impeded.

Although these accounts of the attitude towards the small song and its aggregation into a songline are from different tribal groups, to a large extent the concepts are common throughout the desert region. There is also a general distinction between aural and visual exposure to performances. The visual aspects of ceremony are vitally important and represent the presence of the ancestor, the design being his identification mark, while the aural aspects contain those words that the ancestor may have been expected to say. Many non-segregated presentations allow women and children to participate in the singing but without seeing the ceremonial acts.

A performance is organized by a manager, whose social and totemic affiliations oblige her or him to control ceremonial activities. The owner of the song and associated ceremony, on the other hand, is the person who leads the singing and without whose consent the performance cannot take place. Not only do owners and managers have different responsibilities dependant on totemic affiliation, but these responsibilities are further graded according to seniority and degree of traditional knowledge. Special duties are fulfilled by the song leader, the group of singers, those in charge of body painting and preparation of ceremonial objects and sites, and the dancers. The knowledgeable singer must be able to carry out all actions, since in different ceremonies the various roles will be the responsibility of different groups and individuals. Many researchers note that ownership of song includes ownership of the country through which that song travels: this has recently been the source of widespread land claims by Aboriginal people. But the relationship between ceremonies and land is not simply that of ownership. Ownership and management of songs entails responsibilities for the economic and healthy survival of the associated land, and ownership rights are transferred at death (or permanent incapacity) from the select group of descendants who know and understand the full significance of their ancestor's song to new owners, previously selected and well-trained.

(iv) Musical structures. Terminology for musical techniques often comes from everyday language, with words taking on specific musical meanings. Although there are differences in terminology between tribal and language groups, the musical-cultural concepts expressed through these terms are widely applicable.

The word for melody in Pitjantjatjara means 'taste' or 'flavour' and in Aranda, 'scent', defining not only melody and rhythm, but also the identity of the totemic ancestor whose life essence is aroused through the performance. McCardell (1976), working in Cundalee, Western Australia, gives further terms for melody: 'tasting the melody', 'one song taste' (a single melody throughout the series), 'another taste' (change of melody within a series). There are other examples of everyday language applied to music: the Pitjantjatjara use the same word for laughter and playing as well as singing; crying is the same word as ritual wailing; 'sighing' also means humming the melody as a reminder prior to singing.

The Pitjantjatjara term *tjunguringanyi*, literally meaning 'coming together as one' or 'meeting', can also refer to singing in unison. Accidental use of harmony is classified as 'noise'. Singers consider their performances to be the product of either the desirable 'big throat' or the unacceptable 'bad throat'. The Pintubi at Balgo define unison as 'singing parallel', 'singing level', 'straight' or 'together', whereas departures from unison are called 'tangled', 'obscured' or 'lacking any melody'. The terms for the beating accompaniment can all be covered by the word 'stick', which may refer to any method of beating and the musical pattern of the beating.

'Singing' also describes the effect of powerful songs on another person during love magic, healing or sorcery. When the power of the song is placed into an object, for example fat used in some healing ceremonies, it is described as 'singing fat' (or other object). The same word may apply to some (but not necessarily all) associated ceremonial objects, each individual song in the series, the singing as a whole and the entire ceremony. The closing song of a series is described in terms of the metamorphosis of the ancestor who may be 'cooled off and metamorphosed to stone'. Strehlow, working with the Aranda people, explains that myths must conclude by relating how the original ancestors passed to their last rest; the Aranda term for this closing small song means 'to push into the ground' (Strehlow, 1971).

Richard Moyle (1979, pp.10–12) argues that the Pintubi have no concept of song composition: they believe that their song series have always existed in the spirit realm. Through activities of human spirits the series are 'found' and 'grabbed' in an act of discovery. A song without words is not a song: music is singing produced by the human voice. The primary verbal mode of explanation is song, because song is the language of the ancestors. 'To name', 'to call by name' and 'to call out one's own name' are Aranda terms for composing the texts for small songs. In ceremonies Walbiri believe they are behaving like the ancestors re-enacting ancestral events.

(a) Text. Of the three main elements in the small song (melody, rhythm and text) it is the text that conveys the sometimes obscured information about the ancestral events being recreated. The syllabic rhythm associated with each text may be the same length, or it may be half or a quarter (and rarely one third) of the length of the text. There is an inextricable connection between text and rhythm, either standing for the other. The text setting in Pintubi song centres around the division of the word group of each small song into repeated rhythmic units, usually three or four. In Pitjantjatjara small songs this division internal to the text occurs only on particular types of songs and is common in children's singing. The melodic contour is apportioned to these units so that movement may not proceed from one unit to the next until all of the text required to be performed therein has been sung. Errors in performance of texts are inexcusable: a process of returning to previous small songs and approaching the incorrect one is used until the text is presented perfectly.

In Aranda songs each couplet generally falls into two halves: the second either reiterates or restates, in slightly different words, a subject already expressed by the first half, or it introduces a new thought or statement, thereby advancing or completing the subject that has been expressed by the first half. Frequently two or more couplets share a common line. Both quantitative and accentual rhythms and repetitive and antithetical expression are used, with many couplets intended to summon forth the ancestors and their magical powers for the benefit of the men who are the guardians of the ceremonial site.

Barwick's work (Ellis and Barwick, 1989), based around Pitjantjatjara songs, examines the interlocking of moveable text structures with fixed melodic structures. She identifies what she terms a 'point of fit' in every small song: it is always marked by a melodic section boundary and by the beginning of the rhythmic-textual cycle or a text line pair, and usually but not always by a breath taken by all performers. A common practice is to place the opposite text line at the start of a small song when it is repeated immediately. This process of text line reversal shifts the interlocking of melody and text.

(b) Melody. There are three separate, closely related aspects of melody: melodic shape, particular melodies and intervallic structure. Melodic shape is normally one of descent followed, after a breath, by a significant rise to further descent. Within this broad framework are the many different melodies used, each repeating different pivotal notes for different lengths of time (fig.8). Usually occurring in pairs, the pivotal tones can be separated by intervals from about a tone to an octave. Each melodic contour can be divided into sections marked by the coincidence of ascents in pitch with significant rhythmic and textual boundaries. There are differing systems for

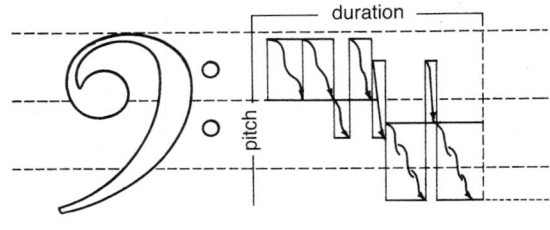

8. *Structure of the melodic movement of a men's song as shown on an enlarged bass staff*

determining the length of time singers spend in any section of the melody: some are governed by the rhythmic unit, some by the duration of the text. It is likely that these systems are used in specific areas and/or for particular functions. The precise shape of the melodic contour depends on a number of factors, including the text type and the duration of the rhythmic pattern. It is the melodic movement towards firmly established pitch frequencies that constitutes the 'flavour' of the ancestor. Any melody can cross tribal and language barriers in tracing the ancestor's travels.

(c) Intervallic system.   As the basis of all melodic movement there are accepted generative intervals forming the series from which the various melodic choices are made. The system being uncovered in the songs is very different from anything reported from other musics throughout the world. Will and Ellis (1994) confirm that the complete tonal space of Pitjantjatjara songs is constituted by a set of consistently recurring frequencies, with some intervals as small as 2–6 Hz. Even common melodic elements such as glides and inflections are well-defined and consistent movements. Interval size does not change with shifts in absolute frequency, the same difference being found in different frequency ranges, while intonational variation in linear terms appears to be constant throughout the range of vocal activity. Small integer ratio intervals (3:4, 4:5 etc.) are only chance occurrences.

There is strong evidence to show that linear construction of melodies operates. For instance, in melodies with a range greater than an octave, the intervals above the octave of the final tone are linear transpositions of the corresponding intervals above this final tone. Again, in transpositions within songlines, groups of intervals around the main frequencies are transposed linearly (maintaining their frequency differences) as far as the non-equidistant tonal space allows. Furthermore, for six different songlines the differences between the final tone and the two adjacent frequencies were about 6 and 9 Hz for all songlines, although the frequency of the final tone changed from 95 to 155 Hz.

Musical practice indicates the existence of a general concept of octave identity: it is a well known and culturally accepted practice that under certain conditions, singers sing the same song or parts of it in octaves, indicating that performers are able to organize frequency production according to the 'octave ratio' of (about) 1:2. However, interval analysis shows that an octave equivalent in a melodic line exists only for the finalis (Will, 1995). All intervals in the upper 'octave' are linear shifts and not octave transpositions of their counterparts in the lower octave. With an average size of 1225·23 cents, however, the octave stretch is considerably larger than in Northern Australian songs accompanied by the didjeridu, or in Western music.

This different interval construction is the single most decisive factor preventing any easy adaptation of traditional desert region music in the face of mass media exposure to various European forms.

(d) Rhythm.   The most conspicuous feature of rhythm (and the one first performed by learners) is the beating song accompaniment. In Pitjantjatjara and Aranda song, regularly spaced beats are separated by three units of the basic pulse; e.g. if the shortest syllable length is notated as a quaver, the beating is in dotted crotchets. There are

several variants (ex.4). Also found are beats separated by two, four or five units of the basic pulse. Beating form

Ex.4 Types of beating accompaniment; rec. and transcr. C. and A. Ellis

(a) Usual beating (irrespective of rhythm of song-line)

(b) 'Slower' beating

(c) Form often used in children's songs

belongs with a particular text and is not varied in repeat performances of that text. Among the Pitjantjatjara, rapid beating produced by rattling a pair of boomerangs is intended to accompany the quivering of the dancers, but among the Pintubi it is used to show the leader's dissatisfaction with the unison singing or accompaniment; occurring during the last few seconds of singing, it indicates the last item in one section of the ceremony. Performers report that they choose tempos by listening to their heartbeats, and stability of speed of beating suggests use of an external measuring device: Morais notes that there is a correlation between dance movements and beating accompaniment patterns (see Ellis, Barwick and Morais, 1990, p.130).

The Pintubi distinguish between beating accompaniment produced directly by the hands (i.e. hand-clapping, chest- and crotch-slapping), and that involving use of hand-held objects (i.e. pairs of boomerangs or sticks, or beating the ground with a single stick). They are considered integral to most song performance and are not found in non-musical situations. Beating also occurs in 'songless sacred performances' that feature occasionally in men's secret rituals, the singers participating by beating a stone or shield on the ground. This beating is understood to be acoustic masking. Another form of acoustic masking results from the accentuation of the sung rhythm, which does not necessarily coincide with the placement of the beat. There is evidence that the two can be deliberately opposed to one another and that only at key points in the rhythmic cycle will the two coincide.

There may be different syllabic rhythmic settings of the one text, for instance, a slow setting using long terminal notes and a fast setting using the same length shorter notes as the slow version, but halving the duration of the longer notes. The text of a small song is given a rhythmic shape different from spoken stresses, which always place the accent on the first syllable of a word in Pitjantjatjara. An example of the spoken form of a children's song text is shown underneath the sung form, which has the main stress on the first note of the bar, in ex.5. The masking of

Ex.5 Typical text with rhythmic setting; rec. and transcr. C. and A. Ellis

[Sung]   tji - tji   tju-ku-tju-ku   pi-lu-ka-ku ya - nai
[Spoken] tjitji   tjukutjuku   pilukaku   yanu

tji - tji   tju-ku-tju-ku   pi-lu-ka-ku ya - nai

The bullocks move away from the small children, leaving many tracks by the water's edge as they go.

verbal information in this way is more deliberate in secret songs.

Text and rhythm are repeated until the melodic shape has been fully presented. Successive small songs in a long songline are interrelated through reference to several primary rhythmic patterns, and sections of the songline may be determined through their relationship to one rhythmic pattern that usually presents important textual information. Indeed, information from some performers indicates that where a language boundary has been crossed in the songline, the performers can decode the information content of the text by its rhythm. This is important considering that texts are often ambiguous or in languages other than that of the performer, and their interpretation is subject to various levels of meaning depending on the knowledge, age, sex and social standing of the recipient. Rhythm therefore serves a fundamental role in the songline, affecting its form, encoding information and assisting in appropriate unison performance.

(v) Dance and design.   The larger scene of a performance encompasses song and ritual and includes an important role for the visual arts. The bodies and faces of actors are painted, and they may wear headdresses and other decorations. Ritual objects are also employed as symbolic expressions of the myth that is being re-enacted. Special songs must be sung during the preparation of the designs, and the power of the ancestor is only fully accessible when all elements of the music, dance and design are correctly and simultaneously presented. It can take many hours to prepare these visual representations, and singing takes place sporadically throughout the process. After the ceremony, any marks left on the ground, whether actual paintings or the tracks of the dancers, are destroyed. This is done both to preserve the secrecy of closed ceremonies and to protect individuals from the power inherent in the designs. Ellis (1985, p.73) supplies terminology related to the various aspects of design.

There are separate types of dance steps for men and women, and it is common for dance calls to occur during performances. Moyle (1979) notes that the pitch of women's dance calls remains constant throughout each woman's individual performance and is directly related to the tonic of the singing, which, for the women, is an octave above the men's. These calls are considered 'speaking' rather than 'singing' and have specific placements within the performance.

Items that include dance in a ceremonial setting may be sung without the dance. When there are dancers present the singing must last for a longer period of time, and the repetition of the entire melody must take place without pause for as long as the dance lasts. In long dances, the singers may pause after three or more repeats of the melody to allow the dancers to rest briefly. At such times the dancers turn their painted designs away from the group of singers until the small song is recommenced.

Morais has done the most extensive work on desert region dance, and in some Andagarinja women's secret ceremonies she identifies dance phrases consisting of repeated leg and arm movements, torso and head movements (or positions) and a locomotive pattern along the ceremonial ground. Dance motives are identified as an unrepeated total body movement and locomotive pattern; a smaller unit is basically a single movement pattern (or position) of the legs, arms or body, synchronized with the beating accompaniment. The smallest units

of movement involve bodily extremities (e.g. fingers), and these too are linked with the smallest musical units. Ellis, Barwick and Morais (1990, pp.111–13) show how locomotion creates given types of tracks on the ceremonial ground and represent diagrammatically (pp.121–89) how the structural features of text, rhythm, melody and dance interlock. They indicate that the dances that occur informally (with the dancers undecorated) and painted closing dances are simpler in structure than the main painted dances. These use fewer body-part and locomotive patterns, few dance phrases, simpler choreographic patterns of sequences and simpler ground patterns.

In the complete performance there is an immense overlap of musical, textual and visual information, which is at times incomprehensible to the outsider. In one performance of a women's secret ceremony (Ellis, 1970, pp.119–200) the dances with designs (each representing specific meanings) occurred in conjunction with rhythmic patterns and song texts that referred to quite different incidents in the myth. Small songs used for accompanying the painting of body designs contained rhythmic references to events in the story other than the events to be presented in the dance for which the design was being prepared, whereas the song text itself merely referred to women dancing. There was constant simultaneous cross-reference: at any one point the rhythmic construction might refer to one segment of the myth, design to another, portrayal of the dance to another and text content to yet another. Multi-dimensional description of a performance shows the intricacy of overlay of design, song text, melodic/intervallic structures and rhythmic pattern, which can only be suggested in fig.9.

(vi) Change over time.   There has been comparatively little research done on innovative Central Aboriginal musical styles. These styles broadly occur in two different ways: the first involves retaining small songs within a larger songline but with the thematic content changed, for example to convey the Christian message; the second is where traditional concepts are maintained, but the songs are in English and use European musical forms, particularly rock music and country and western styles.

Recent events can be encompassed in newly-composed songs of a traditional nature, and in such songs can be found the aurally transmitted history of the past century. Subjects such as cars and aeroplanes are frequent in these songs, and objects such as shoes and tobacco tins have been utilized as beating implements. Intervallic structure of such songs is often recognizably more European, as is melodic movement and rhythm; however, melodic shape and ornamentation preserve some traditional characteristics.

The establishment of the Centre for Aboriginal Studies in Music (CASM) within the University of Adelaide in 1975 occurred at a time when Aboriginal peoples were seeking to get their message across to the Australian public; since then, rock music has been a particularly important vehicle of their protest. CASM students study both Pitjantjatjara music from senior song people and instrumental music and composition. Bands that have emerged through this centre include Coloured Stones, Us Mob and Kuckles, all with connections to the desert region.

The granting of the Northern Territory broadcasting licence to the Central Australian Aboriginal Media Association (CAAMA) enhanced the dissemination of Aboriginal performances, both traditional and contem-

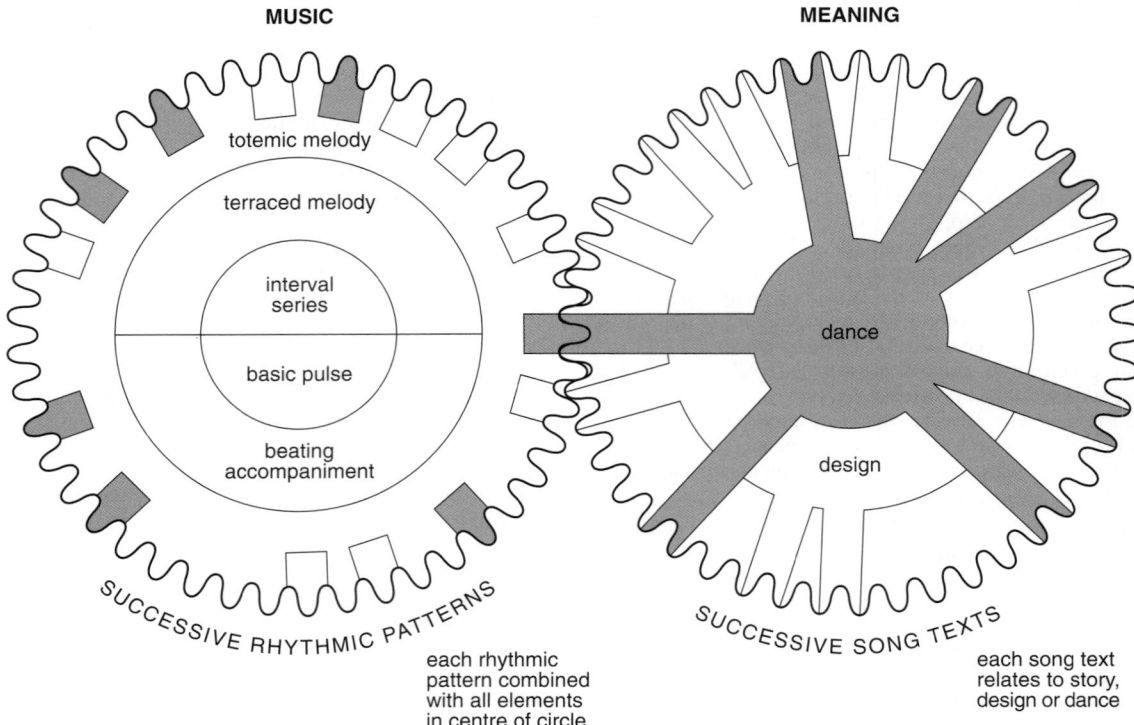

MUSIC

totemic melody

terraced melody

interval series

basic pulse

beating accompaniment

SUCCESSIVE RHYTHMIC PATTERNS

each rhythmic pattern combined with all elements in centre of circle

MEANING

dance

design

SUCCESSIVE SONG TEXTS

each song text relates to story, design or dance

9. Interlocking of structures

porary, through radio, video and television. Other media groups have also contributed to this dissemination.

In 1988 Aboriginal rock musicians established a national Festival of Aboriginal Rock Music. Bands from the desert region who have become well known for their performances include the Warumpi Band, Isaac Yama and the Pitjantjatjara Band, Ayeronga Desert Tigers and Blakbela Mujic.

3. SOUTH-EASTERN ABORIGINAL MUSIC.   The south-eastern region of Australia comprises the southern parts of Queensland, the states of New South Wales (NSW) and Victoria, parts of south-eastern South Australia, and the island state of Tasmania. As this is the area where the most intensive settlement occurred, Aboriginal groups throughout this region have had a long, harsh history of European contact. Of all the Aboriginal peoples of Australia it is those of the south-eastern regions whose culture has been most devastated by that contact.

Throughout this region there are several natural features that traditionally acted as frontiers between Aboriginal groups. The mountains of the Great Dividing Range along the east coast made contact between the coastal and inland groups difficult. Further west, the Darling river can be seen as a boundary between the south-eastern and central regions of the continent. The area west of the Great Dividing Range and east of the Darling river comprises speakers of the related languages Kamilaroi (Gamilaraay) and Wiradjuri. In the south, the Murray river also defines a distinct cultural region comprising speakers of Yorta yorta, Wemba wemba, Yita yita and similar languages.

(i) Historical background and collections. In 1788 British colonization began in the Sydney area. European contact

had a destructive impact on traditional culture, and as early as 1905 ceremonial activity throughout New South Wales was drawing to an end. As a result, by the time recording equipment became available, a large number of songs, rituals and even languages were no longer being regularly practised. Research relies on historical descriptions in conjunction with recordings that were made as part of a salvage operation involving collecting and contextualizing the remaining knowledge of a small number of older Aboriginal people.

There are many descriptions of Aboriginal ceremonies and rituals written by early travellers and explorers. The most notable of these are by A.W. Howitt and R.H. Mathews, who between them documented Aboriginal culture over almost 30 years in the late 19th century. Howitt includes musical notations of three songs from the Melbourne area in Victoria (Howitt, 1904, pp.419–21), whereas Mathews includes six songs associated with the *Bunan* initiation ceremony on the south coast of New South Wales (Mathews, 1907, pp.33–5). In assessing the reliability of these notations it should be borne in mind that they were made from live performance. There are also many drawings of dances and ceremonies that help piece together details concerning body design, headdress, musical instruments and dance in this earlier period (fig.10).

The sound archive of the Australian Institute of Aboriginal and Torres Strait Islander Studies (AIATSIS), situated in Canberra, contains over 1000 traditional songs from south-eastern Australia. (The term 'traditional' is used here to describe songs that are modelled on pre-European forms albeit sometimes with European influences.) In 1899 the Royal Society of Tasmania recorded wax cylinders of songs sung by Fanny Cochrane Smith,

10. Corroboree after initiation ceremony: from C. Hodgkinson, 'Australia, from Port Macquarie to Moreton Bay' (1845)

who was born on Flinders Island. These have been discussed in detail by Alice Moyle (1960 and 1968) and are probably the earliest sound recordings from Australia, together with the Haddon recordings from the Torres Strait Islands. Both Elkin and Tindale made wax cylinder recordings in the 1930s, Elkin at Port Stephens on the central coast, and Tindale at Brewarrina (northern NSW) and Wallaga Lake (south coast of NSW). The remaining recordings were made from the 1950s onwards. Until the 1980s all recording was carried out by non-Aboriginal people, with the exception of Jimmie Barker of Brewarrina, a member of the Murawari group in northern New South Wales, who in the late 1960s and early 70s recorded his own knowledge of language, history-songs and other aspects of his culture. Most of the singers recorded represent one of the very few people in their communities who at the time of recording could still recover old songs, dances and other details from their fading memories of the past. Less than 10% of the recordings involve group singing or dancers. Early films of dance in this region are rare: one newsreel in the National Sound and Film Archive collection dates from 1931 (*Queensland Abos Put on Their War Paint*) and shows performers from Woodenbong singing and dancing; it is only five minutes in length and has been highly edited.

The AIATSIS collection contains few songs whose performance depend on associated ritual contexts, such as initiation songs, healing songs, increase songs and hunting songs. This is not surprising given that such songs have not been performed regularly for their original purpose since the early 1900s. Songs were performed for the specific purpose of recording, and often the singers were understandably diffident about singing. There are

ten songs associated with initiation rites in the collection, of which half of these were recorded by Beckett at Wilcannia in 1957 and performed by George Dutton. Dutton, born in the 1880s, was initiated at 16 years of age; when ceremonial activity ceased in New South Wales he began to travel to Queensland and South Australia to attend the big ceremonies. By the 1930s Dutton was the only surviving ritual leader in New South Wales (Beckett, 1978, p.6). His performances recorded in the 1950s are exceptional, and it is a small number of such performances that represent ritual life in New South Wales in the recording collection.

(ii) Corroboree and related genres. The majority of recorded songs have been described by their performers as 'corroboree songs'. The word 'corroboree' originally comes from the Dharuk language area, which became part of Sydney. It appeared in early word lists as 'ca-rab-ba-ra' ('to dance') and 'car-rib-ber-re' (a mode of dancing), as opposed to 'gnar-ra-mang', the name of a dance in William Dawe's vocabulary list of 1788–91. One of the earliest accounts of a corroboree was written in 1793, when John Hunter described an Aboriginal performance he attended at Port Jackson in 1791, organized by two local Aborigines, Bennelong and Coalby (1793, p.213). Hunter states:

They very frequently, at the conclusion of the dance, would apply to us for our opinions, or rather for marks of our approbation of their performance; which we never failed to give by often repeating the word boojery, which signifies good, or boojery caribberie, a good dance. These signs of pleasure in us seemed to give them great satisfaction, and generally produced more than ordinary exertions from the whole company of performers in the next dance.

Although the word 'corroboree' appears originally to have referred to one specific type of dance, it is often used by Aboriginal and non-Aboriginal people throughout Australia to describe any Aboriginal performance involving song and dance. In the context of the AIATSIS collection the term usually refers to secular, occasional and informal performances.

It is clear that the term corroboree subsumes a number of different genres of song, many of which had specific names. In the Bundjalung area of northern New South Wales one of the generic terms it has replaced is *yawahr*, which originally referred to a specific type of open performance of song and dance in which men, women and children were able to participate. Other Bundjalung performance genres include *burun*, a song performed by men with a dance that involved shaking the chest, and *djangar*, a song and dance often called the 'Leg corroboree' or 'Shake-a-leg'.

This dance is also widespread in northern Queensland and the Cape York region (see §1(v) above). One popular genre of song among the Bundjalung is referred to as 'Sing-You-Down'. These songs were used to control social behaviour in communities, and their stories are concerned with some type of unacceptable behaviour such as drinking and gambling. *Two-Up* is the best-known 'Sing-You-Down' song and was composed by the Bundjalung songman Jack Barron of Woodenbong. The song describes the gambling game 'two-up', in which two pennies are spun in the air and bets are laid on whether they fall heads or tails. This song has been recorded and is still remembered today throughout the Bundjalung area. It has also been recorded on the south coast of New South Wales.

(iii) Musical structure in performance.   The first detailed musicological research in south-eastern Australia was done by the linguist Tamsin Donaldson, who made a comparative study of a single song, the *Lost Boy* song, from the Ngiyampaa (Wangaaypuwan) area of western New South Wales. This song concerns the winter rescue of a lost boy by Aborigines and Europeans in the early 1930s.

Through analysis of several performances of the song, Donaldson concluded that a performance involves repeating sections of the song and hypothesized that the length of a performance might vary depending on the context of the performance. This type of expandable form depends on performers being able to signal their intentions: in the case of the *Lost Boy* song the signal is a melodic cueing pattern. The key word 'thirramakaanhthi' is sung with a descending melodic line if the performer is going to proceed directly from section 1 to section 2. If, however, the singer is going to repeat section 1, the word 'thirramakaanhthi', which appears at the end of the first line, will be sung with an upward leap in pitch (Donaldson, 1987, p.35).

Cueing devices similar to those found in the Ngiyampaa *Lost Boy* song also seem to exist to the north-east, in the Bundjalung area. One song, *Mundala*, a *yawahr* or corroboree song, was sung by men and women and included dance. *Mundala* was originally brought into the Bundjalung area from the Gungari area (near the New England area) by Bessie Comet, a Bundjalung woman who lived at Tabulam in the 1940s and 50s.

In the AIATSIS collection there are ten complete performances of *Mundala* sung by the prolific Bundjalung

singer Dick Donnelly. On several occasions Donnelly stated that this was his favourite song and in 1977 actually taught this song to Willoughby and Oakes, who recorded the session. Analysis of these ten performances show melodic and textual devices that allow expansion and contraction of the song and that are similar to those discovered by Donaldson.

Mundala comprises two sections of text, called *mundala* and *gahmula*. The first section, without the last line, may be repeated any number of times, while the second section is never repeated. The last line of each section begins with a rise in pitch, usually approximately a 7th, and is used by the singer to signal to the dancers that a change in the text is about to occur. Ex.6 is a transcription of a recording made by Malcolm Calley in 1955 in Woodenbong (AIATSIS LA 1178A (9)).

By comparing this recording with others it becomes evident that it is possible to change the way the text is articulated and therefore change the length of the performance. For example, in several recordings of this song the first section is repeated. When the singer is going to repeat this section, the last textual and melodic line is not sung, but once this line has been sung the singer must proceed to the next section. Section 2 is then sung one time only, and every performance returns and ends with section 1. The singing of the last line of each section thus appears to act as a musical cue; this device seems to correspond to the principle of altering the melodic contour of the word 'thirramakaanhthi' in the Ngiyampaa *Lost Boy* song to inform the dancers of the singer's intentions.

From Donnelly's descriptions it is apparent that *Mundala* comprises two different dance steps, which correspond to the two sections of text called *mundala* and *gahmula*. The dance was performed by men, women and children, and in any performance there could be as many as 24 dancers. In several performances, Donnelly stated 'change step now' after the first occurrence of the melodic cue and 'change step again' after its second occurrence, possibly indicating a change of direction.

(iv) Instruments.   Although singing is the predominant form of music in the region, clapsticks and boomerang clapsticks are often used by men (and occasionally by women) as an accompaniment. Throughout this region each language group had a different name for these instruments. In the Bundjalung area the clapsticks were called *murunu* or *mundang* and the boomerang clapsticks, *bargan*.

It is not clear whether, as in other parts of Australia, there were specific occasions during which only boomerangs or clapsticks were used, or if they were interchangeable. It is clear, however, that other objects could be used in place of specific instruments. For example, in 1970 the Bundjalung singer Dick Donnelly left his clapsticks at home and so used a pair of hammer handles during a lecture tour around the New England area. These were so successful that they were used later when Donnelly was recorded; in another recording Donnelly substituted a tin can. This sort of substitution occurs frequently throughout Australia. Body percussion such as foot-stamping and hand-clapping is also commonly used.

The possum skin bundle, drum or pillow was played by women throughout south-eastern Australia, as well as north along the Queensland coast and as far west as Adelaide in South Australia. This was called *bulbing* in the Bundjalung area and comprised an opossum skin

Ex.6 *Mundala*, Bundjalung *yawahr* song; transcr. M. Gummow

turned inside out, stuffed with feathers or rags and struck with the hand or a stick. It was held on the lap and beaten constantly throughout a song. In some regions, such as the Murawari area of western New South Wales, the pillow was made of kangaroo skin and stuffed with possum fur, and several people beat it simultaneously with their hands. The skin pillow was still being used in the early 1990s; later, as it became difficult to obtain possum skins, substitutions such as a rolled up blanket were made. In the Ngarrindjeri area near Adelaide, the pillow was still being used by women in 1951 on Hindmarsh Island during a re-enactment of the journeys of the explorer Charles Stuart (Bell, 1998, p.146). (In 1970 Jimmie Barker, a Murawari elder from northern New South Wales, recorded a performance of the skin drum; it is the only such recording in the AIATSIS archives.) Throughout this region clapsticks were played mainly by men. There were also instruments used specifically in initiation ceremonies and other ritual contexts, described in detail by Mathews (1907).

From the early 20th century onwards it was not uncommon for traditional Aboriginal performers to perform both Aboriginal and European songs and dances. In the early 20th century European dance music such as reels and barn dances were very popular among Aboriginal communities. Aboriginal musicians performed this music on Western instruments such as violins, piano accordions, mandolins and mouth organs. The gumleaf was also played at these dances as well as at corroborees.

(v) Modern developments. Despite the long history of European assaults on traditional cultures throughout this region, there has recently been strong cultural revival activity. There are many cultural revival programmes, including Aboriginal language courses, Aboriginal traditional history, visual and performing arts courses. One such example concerns Bonalbo in the Bundjalung area, where in 1985 a non-Aboriginal teacher organized and arranged for a senior Bundjalung songman both to teach the schoolboys dances and to sing traditional songs while they danced. After some time, due to disagreements, the elder ceased teaching; the boys, however, decided to continue performing without a teacher, creating their own dances while two members of the group learnt the didjeridu, which was used instead of singing. The didjeridu was not traditionally found in this area of Australia, but it is now performed in a variety of contexts and is acknowledged as a symbol of Aboriginal culture and identity. It is in this spirit of revival and identity that many Aboriginal people have begun to document their own culture. For example, the film *Eelemarni* (1988) shows the northern New South Wales elder Millie Boyd discussing traditional stories and singing songs.

In addition to community initiatives focusing on cultural revival, there has also been intense activity in the popular music scene. Recordings of contemporary Aboriginal performers have increased dramatically. Aboriginal performers are active in country and western, rock music and Christian gospel groups. One prolific country and western singer, Dougie Young, composed songs in Wilcannia in the 1950s and is known for his reflections of the country town lives of Aborigines; the songs involved alcohol, encounters with the law and issues concerning Aboriginal identity. Since the 1950s there has been an increase in the popularity of country and western music, and the Tamworth Country Music Festival (the largest music festival of any kind in Australia) is attended by many Aboriginal performers, including Col Hardy, Troy Caser-Daley, Roger Knox and Euraba.

Another prominent singer-songwriter, Essie Coffey, was active in Brewarrina, northern New South Wales, from the 1970s until her death in 1998. She sang blues and rock but is most remembered as a film maker. Her first film, *My Survival as an Aborigine* (1978), featured the people of Dodge City, the Aboriginal community at Brewarrina, and won first prize in the documentary section of the 1979 Sydney Film Festival.

Recently, singers have emerged who perform songs with political themes. Kev Carmody, originally from southern Queensland, is a Sydney-based singer-songwriter who won the 1994 Australian Country Music Golden Awards 'Heritage Song of the Year' for *From Little Things Big Things Grow*, written with non-Aboriginal songwriter Paul Kelly about a protest in the pastoral industry. Another Melbourne-based singer-songwriter, Archie Roach, won the Australian Recording Industry Award (ARIA) for best indigenous album in 1991 for *Charcoal Lane*, which includes one of his best-known

autobiographical songs, *Took the Children Away*, concerning the removal of Aboriginal children from their parents by government welfare officials in the 1960s. Many singers feature themes of cultural identity and reconciliation in their songs. The contemporary music scene in Melbourne has been researched extensively by Robin Ryan (1992 and 1994); for a comprehensive list of recordings by contemporary artists, see Dunbar-Hall (1996).

Within this urban context there are many dance groups, individuals and theatre companies that have developed successful international careers. Some offer training courses to indigenous people. In Sydney the Bangarra Dance Theatre comprises artists from all over Australia and performs unique modern songs and dances that draw on many contemporary Aboriginal traditions. Also in Sydney, the National Aboriginal and Islander Skills Development Association (NAISDA) performs works influenced by indigenous Australian cultures. There are also two major entrepreneurial agencies in Sydney that support and promote Aboriginal music and dance. The Aboriginal Artists Agency was founded in 1976 by the Aboriginal Arts Board of the Australia Council and acts as mediator and negotiator for Aboriginal artists in industries. The National Indigenous Arts Advocacy Association (NIAAA) advocates the recognition and protection of the rights of indigenous artists.

BIBLIOGRAPHY

AND OTHER RESOURCES

NORTHERN ABORIGINAL

GEWM, vii ('Wangga of Northwest Australia', J. Page)

A.P. Elkin and T.A. Jones: *Arnhem Land Music (North Australia)* (Sydney, 1958) [incl. reprs. of articles from *Oceania*, xxiv–xxviii]

A.M. Moyle: 'Bara and Mamariga Songs on Groote Eylandt', *Musicology*, i (1964), 15–24

L.R. Hiatt: *Kinship and Conflict* (Canberra, 1965)

W.E.H. Stanner: *On Aboriginal Religion* (Sydney, 1966)

A. Moyle: 'Aboriginal Music on Cape York', *Musicology*, iii (1968–9), 3–20

C.G. von Brandenstein: 'Tabi Songs of the Aborigines', *Hemisphere*, xiii (1969), 28–31

R. Waterman: 'Music in Australian Aboriginal Culture: some Sociological and Psychological Implications', *Readings in Ethnomusicology*, ed. D. McAllester (New York, 1971)

A. Moyle: *North Australian Music: a Taxonomic Approach to the Study of Aboriginal Song Performances* (diss., Monash U., 1974) [incl. detailed set of maps and lists of aboriginal words connected with instruments]

D.H. Turner: *Tradition and Transformation: a Study of the Groote Eylandt Area Aborigines of Northern Australia* (Canberra, 1974)

A.P. Borsboom: *Maradjiri: a Modern Ritual Complex in Arnhem Land, North Australia* (diss., Bibliotheek Katholieke, U., Nijmegen, 1978)

J. Stubington: *Yolngu Manikay: Modern Performances of Australian Aboriginal Clan Songs* (diss., Monash, U., 1978)

J. von Sturmer: *The Wik Region* (diss., U. of Queensland, 1978)

P. Black and G. Koch: 'Koko-Bera Island Style Music', *Aboriginal History*, v/1–2 (1983), 157–72

A. Grau: 'Sing a Dance-Dance a Song: the Relationship between Two Types of Formalised Movements and Music among the Tiwi of Melville and Bathurst Islands, North Australia', *Dance Research*, i/2 (1983), 32–44

M. Clunies Ross and S. Wild: 'Formal Performance; the Relations of Music, Text and Dance in Arnhem Land Clan Songs', *EthM*, xxviii (1984), 209–35

H. Morphy: *Journey to the Crocodile's Nest: an Accompanying Monograph to the Film 'Mardarrpa Funeral at Gurka'wuy'* (Canberra, 1984)

S.A. Wild, ed.: *Rom: an Aboriginal Ritual of Diplomacy* (Canberra, 1986)

M. Clunies Ross, T. Donaldson and S.A. Wild, eds.: *Songs of Aboriginal Australia* (Sydney, 1987) [incl. G. Koch: 'Dyirbal

Gama Songs of Cape York', 43–62; J. von Sturmer: 'Aboriginal Singing and Notions of Power', 63–76; F. Merlan: 'Catfish and Alligator: Totemic Songs of the Western Roper River, Northern Territory', 142–67; R.M. Berndt: 'Other Creatures in Human Guise and vice versa: a Dilemma of Understanding', 169–91]

D. Williams: 'Homo Nullius: the Status of Aboriginal Dancing in Northern Queensland', *Journal for the Anthropological Study of Human Movement*, vi/3 (1988), 87–111

R.D. Keogh: 'Nurlu Songs from the West Kimberley; an Introduction', *Australian Aboriginal Studies*, i (1989), 2–11

R.D. Keogh: *Nurlu Songs of the Western Kimberley* (diss., U. of Sydney, 1990)

R. Arnold: *A Structural Analysis of Two Dance Idioms: the Wanam (Cape York Peninsula) and Black Jazz Dance (Philadelphia, USA)* (MA thesis, U. of Sydney, 1991)

A.J. Marett: 'Variability and Stability in Wangga Songs of Northwest Australia', *Music and Dance in Aboriginal Australia and the South Pacific: the Effects of Documentation on the Living Tradition*, ed. A.M. Moyle (Sydney, 1991), 194–213

P.T. Stanhope: *Baratjarr: a Preliminary Analysis of a Central Arnhem Land Bunggurl (Clan Song Series)* (BA thesis, U. of Sydney, 1991)

G.D. Anderson: *Murlarra: a Clan Song Series of Central Arnhem Land* (diss., U. of Sydney, 1992)

S. Knopoff: 'Yuta Manikay: Juxtaposition of Ancestral and Contemporary Elements in the Performance of Yolngu Clan Songs', *YTM*, xxiv (1992), 138–53

C.R. Cox: *Mumurrng Exchange Ceremony of the Kunwinjku (Gunwinggu) of North-Central Arnhem Land* (Mmus thesis, U. of New South Wales, 1993)

I. Keen: *Knowledge and Secrecy in an Aboriginal Religion: Yolngu of North-East Arnhem Land* (Oxford, 1994)

F.C. Magowan: *Melodies of Mourning: a Study of Form and Meaning in Yolngu Women's Music and Dance in Traditional and Christian Contexts* (diss., U. of Oxford, 1994)

J. Stubington and P. Dunbar-Hall: 'Yothu Yindi's "Treaty": *Ganma* in Music', *Popular Music* xiii/3 (1994), 243–59

L.M. Barwick, A.J. Marett and G. Tunstill, eds.: *The Essence of Singing and the Substance of Song: an Anthology for Catherine Ellis* (Sydney, 1995) [incl. G.D. Anderson: 'Striking a Balance: Limited Variability in Performances of a Clan Song Series from Central Arnhem Land', 12–25; A.J. Marett and J. Page: 'Interrelationships between Music and Dance in a Wangga from Northwest Australia', 27–38; R.D. Keogh: 'Process Models for the Analysis of Nurlu Songs from the Western Kimberley', 39–51]

R.M.W. Dixon and G. Koch: *Dyirbal Song Poetry* (St Lucia, 1996)

K.W. Neuenfeldt, ed.: *The Didjeridu from Arnhem Land to the Internet* (Sydney, 1997)

E. Mackinlay: *For our Mother's Song we Sing: Yanyuwa Women Performers and Composers of A-nguyulnguyul* (diss., U. of Adelaide, 1998)

A.J. Marett: 'Ghostly Voices: some Observations on Song-Creation, Ceremony and Being in Northwest Australia', *Australian Aboriginal Studies* (forthcoming)

D. Mowaljarlai and T. Redmond: 'David Mowaldjarlai Talks with Tony Redmond about the Origins of Dance and Song in the Ngarinyin World', *Oxford Companion to Aboriginal Art and Culture*, ed. M. Neale and S. Kleinert (Melbourne, forthcoming)

recordings

Arnhem Land: Authentic Australian Aboriginal Songs and Dances, coll. A.P. Elkin, i–ii, OALP 7504–5; iii, OALP 7516 (1957); reissued as Larrikin CD LRH 288 (1993)

Arnhem Land Popular Classics: Aboriginal Dance Songs with Didjeridu Accompaniment, coll. L.M. West, Wattle Ethnic Series 3 (1962) [incl. disc notes by L.M. West]

Songs from the Northern Territory, coll. A. Moyle, i–v, IASM 001–005 (1964); reissued as Australian Institute of Aboriginal Studies AIAS 1–5 CD

The Bora of the Pascoe River, Cape York Peninsula, Northeast Australia, coll. W. Laade, Ethnic Folkways LP FE-4211 (1975)

Songs from North Queensland, coll. A. Moyle, Australian Institute of Aboriginal Studies AIAS 12 (1977) [incl. booklet]

Songs from the Kimberleys, Western Australia, coll. A. Moyle, Australian Institute of Aboriginal Studies AIAS 13 (1977); reissued as AIAS 13 CD [incl. booklet]

Djambidj: An aboriginal Song Series from Northern Australia, Australian Institute of Aboriginal Studies AIAS 16 (1982) [incl. notes by M. Clunies Ross and S.A. Wild]

Song of Aboriginal Australia, coll. S.A. Wild, Australian Institute of Aboriginal Studies AIAS 17 (1987)

Goyulan the Morning Star: an Aboriginal Clan Song Series from North Central Arnhem Land, Australian Institute of Aboriginal Studies AIAS 18 (1988) [incl. notes by M. Clunies Ross and J. Mundrungmundrung]

Bushfire, coll. A. Cummins, Larrikin CDLRF247 (1991)

Bunggridj-bunggridj: Wangga Songs by Alan Maralung, perf. A. Maralung, Smithsonian Folkways CD 40430 (1993) [incl. notes by A. Marett and L. Barwick]

Dyirbal Song Poetry: Traditional Songs of an Australian Rainforest People, coll. R.M.W. Dixon and G. Koch, Larrikin CDLRF 378 (1995)

Jadmi junba, Festival Australia (1999) [incl. notes by L.M. Barwick]

Rak Badjalarr: Wangga Songs by Bobby Lane, coll. A.J. Marett and L. Barwick, Australian Institute of Aboriginal Studies (forthcoming) [incl. notes by A.J. Marett, L. Barwick and L.J. Ford]

films

Dances at Aurukun (Cape York Peninsula), videotape, dir. I. Dunlop, Australian Institute of Aboriginal Studies (Canberra, 1962)

Lockhart Dance Festival, videotape, dir. C. Levy, Australian Institute of Aboriginal Studies (Canberra, 1974)

Madarrpa Funeral at Gurka'wuy, videotape, dir. I. Dunlop, Film Australia (Sydney, 1979)

Waiting for Harry, videotape, dir. K. McKenzie, Australian Institute of Aboriginal Studies (Canberra, 1980)

In Memory of Mawalan, videotape, dir. I. Dunlop, Film Australia (Sydney, 1983)

Bran NueDae, videotape, dir. T. Zubrycki with the Bran Nue Dae Corporation, Ronin Films (Sydney, 1991).

CENTRAL ABORIGINAL

W.D. Ward: 'Subjective Musical Pitch', *JASA*, xxvi (1954), 369–80

C.J. Ellis: 'Pre-Instrumental Scales', *EthM*, ix (1965), 126–44 [126–37 (Ellis); 137–44 (Seymour)]

C.J. Ellis: 'Rhythmic Analysis of Aboriginal Syllabic Songs', *MMA*, iii (Adelaide, 1968), 21–49

C.J. Ellis: 'The Role of the Ethnomusicologist in the Study of Andagarinja Women's Ceremonies', *MMA*, v (1970), 76–206

T.G.H. Strehlow: *Songs of Central Australia* (Sydney, 1971)

R.M. Berndt: 'The Arts of Life: an Introduction', *The Australian Aboriginal Heritage: an Introduction through the Arts*, ed. R.M. Berndt and E.S. Phillips (Sydney, 1973), 31–44

S.A. Wild: *Walbiri Music and Dance in their Social and Cultural Nexus* (diss., Indiana U., 1975)

A. McCardell: *Rhythm and Melody in Australian Aboriginal Songs of the Western Desert* (diss., U. of Western Australia, 1976)

C.J. Ellis and others: 'Classification of Sounds in Pitjantjatjara-Speaking Areas', *Australian Aboriginal Concepts*, ed. L.R. Hiatt (Canberra and New Jersey, 1978), 68–80

H.E. Payne: 'The Integration of Music and Belief in Australian Aboriginal Culture', *Religious Traditions*, i/1 (1978), 8–18

R.M. Moyle: *Songs of the Pintupi: Musical Life in a Central Australian Society* (Canberra, 1979)

R.M. Moyle: 'Jumping to Conclusions', *Problems and Solutions: Occasional Essays in Musicology presented to Alice M. Moyle*, ed. J.C. Kassler and J. Stubington (Sydney, 1984), 51–8

C.J. Ellis: *Aboriginal Music, Education for Living: Cross-Cultural Experiences from South Australia* (Queensland, 1985)

R.M. Moyle: *Alyawarra Music: Songs and Society in a Central Australian Community* (Canberra, 1986)

M. Clunies Ross, T.Donaldson and S.A. Wild, eds.: *Songs of Aboriginal Australia* (Sydney, 1987) [incl. S.A. Wild: 'Recreating the Jukurrpa: Adaptation and Innovation of Songs and Ceremonies in Warlpiri Society', 97–120; G.T. Tunstill: 'Melody and Rhythmic Structure in Pitjantjatjara Song', 121–41]

C.J. Ellis and L.M.Barwick: 'Musical Syntax and the Problem of Meaning in a Central Australian Songline', *Musicology Australia*, x (1987), 41–57

C.J. Ellis and L.M.Barwick: 'Singers, Songs and Knowledge', *MMA*, xv (1988), 284–301

M. Breen, ed.: *Our Place: Our Music* (Canberra, 1989)

C.J. Ellis and L.M.Barwick: 'Time Consciousness of Indigenous Australians', *Introduction to the Performing Arts*, ed. F. Messner (Geelong, 1989), 1–27

K. Palmer, ed.: *Australian Aboriginal Studies* (Canberra, 1989) [incl. R. Keogh: 'Nurlu Songs from the West Kimberley: an Introduction', 2–11; L.M. Barwick: 'Creative (Ir)regularities: the

Intermeshing of Text and Melody in Performance of Central Australian Song', 12–28]

H.E. Payne: 'Rites for Sites or Sites for Rites? The Dynamics of Women's Cultural Life in the Musgraves', *Women, Rites and Sites: Aboriginal Women's Cultural Knowledge*, ed. P. Brock (Sydney, 1989), 41–59

L.M. Barwick: 'Central Australian Women's Ritual Music: Knowing Through Analysis versus Knowing Through Performance', *YTM*, xxii (1990), 60–79

C.J. Ellis, L.Barwick and M. Morais: 'Overlapping Time Structures in a Central Australian Women's Ceremony', *Language and History: Essays in Honour of Luise A. Hercus*, ed. P. Austin and others (Canberra, 1990), 101–36

D. Horton, ed.: *Encyclopedia of Aboriginal Australia* (Canberra, 1994)

U. Will: 'Structure and Frequency Organisation in Central Australian Aboriginal Music', *European Seminar in Ethnomusicology X: Oxford 1994*

U. Will and C.J.Ellis: 'Evidence for Linear Transposition in Australian Western Desert Vocal Music', *Musicology Australia*, xvii (1994), 1–12

U. Will: 'Frequency Performance in Australian Aboriginal Vocal Music With and Without 'Tone' Producing Instruments', *ICTM Conference XXXIII, Musicological Society of Australia: Conference XVII: Canberra, 1995*

U. Will and C.J.Ellis: 'A Re-Analysed Australian Western Desert Song', *EthM*, xl (1996), 187–222

SOUTH-EASTERN ABORIGINAL

W. Dawes: *Vocabulary of the Language of N.S. Wales in the Neighbourhood of Sydney (Native and English but not alphabetical) in MSS Notebooks: "Grammatical Forms and Vocabularies of Languages Spoken in the Neighbourhood of Sydney 1790"* (MS 41645/a-c, Marsden Collection, School of Oriental and African Studies, London, 1788–91)

J. Hunter: *An Historical Journal of the Transactions at Port Jackson and Norfolk Island . . .* (London, 1793)

C. Hodgkinson: *Australia, from Port Macquarie to Moreton Bay* (London, 1845)

A.W. Howitt: *The Native Tribes of South-East Australia* (London, 1904/R)

R.H. Mathews: *Ethnological Notes of the Aboriginal Tribes of New South Wales and Victoria* (Sydney, 1905)

R.H. Mathews: *Notes on the Aborigines of New South Wales* (Sydney, 1907)

A.R. Radcliffe-Brown: 'Notes on Totemism in Eastern Australia', *Journal of the Royal Anthropological Institute of Great Britain and Ireland*, lix (1929), 399–415

K. Kennedy: 'Instruments of Music used by the Australian Aborigines', *Mankind*, no.1 (1933), 147–53

R.M. Berndt: 'Wuradjeri Magic and "Clever Men"', *Oceania*, xvii (1946–7), 327–65; xviii (1947–8), 60–86

J. Beckett: 'Aborigines Make Music', *Quadrant*, ii/4 (1957–8), 32–42

M.J. Longman: 'Songs of the Tasmanian Aborigines as Recorded by Mrs. Fanny Cochrane Smith', *Papers and Proceedings of the Royal Society of Tasmania*, xciv (1960), 79–86

A.M. Moyle: 'Two Native Song-Styles Recorded in Tasmania', *Papers and Proceedings of the Royal Society of Tasmania*, xciv (1960), 73–8

A.M. Moyle: *A Handlist of Field Collections of Recorded Music in Australia and Torres Strait* (Canberra, 1966)

A.M. Moyle: 'Tasmanian Music, an Impasse', *Records of the Queen Victoria Museum, Launceston*, new ser., no.26 (1968) [whole issue]

A. Massola: *The Aborigines of South-Eastern Australia As They Were* (Melbourne, 1971)

J. Mathews: *The Two Worlds of Jimmie Barker* (Canberra, 1977)

J. Beckett: 'George Dutton's Country: Portrait of an Aboriginal Drover', *Aboriginal History*, ii (1978), 3–31

T. Donaldson: 'Translating Oral Literature: Aboriginal Song Texts', *Aboriginal History*, iii (1979), 62–83

T. Pearce: 'Music and the Settled Aboriginal', *Australian Aboriginal Music*, ed. J. Isaacs (Sydney, 1979), 41–8

T. Donaldson: 'Kids That Got Lost: Variation in the Words of Ngiyampaa Songs', *Problems and Solutions: Occasional Essays in Musicology presented to Alice M. Moyle*, ed. J.C. Kassler and J. Stubington (Sydney, 1984), 228–53

T. Donaldson: 'Making a Song (and Dance) in South-Eastern Australia', *Songs of Aboriginal Australia*, ed. M. Clunies Ross, T. Donaldson and S. Wild (Sydney, 1987), 14–42

M.J. Gummow: *Aboriginal Songs from the Bundjalung and Gidabal Areas of South-Eastern Australia* (diss., U. of Sydney, 1992)

R. Ryan: *Koori Sociomusical Practices in Melbourne Since 1988* (thesis, Monash U., 1992)

J. Beckett: '"I Don't Care Who Knows": the Songs of Dougie Young', *Australian Aboriginal Studies* (1993), no.2, pp. 34–8

P. Dunbar-Hall: *Style and Meaning: Signification in Contemporary Aboriginal Popular Music, 1963–1993* (diss., U. of New South Wales, 1994)

M. Gummow: 'The Power of the Past in the Present: Singers and Songs From Northern New South Wales', *World Music*, xxxvi/1 (1994), 42–50

D. Horton, ed.: *The Encyclopaedia of Aboriginal Australia* (Canberra, 1994)

R. Ryan: 'Tracing the Urban Songlines: Contemporary Koori Music in Melbourne', *Perfect Beat*, ii/1 (1994), 20–37

K. Bradley: 'Leaf Music in Australia', *Australian Aboriginal Studies* (1995), no.2, pp.2–14

L. Barwick, A.Marett and G. Tunstill, eds.: *The Essence of Singing and the Substance of Song: Recent Responses to the Aboriginal Performing Arts and other Essays in Honour of Catherine Ellis* (Sydney, 1995) [incl. M. Gummow: 'Songs and Sites/ Moving Mountains: a Study of One Song from Northern NSW', 121–31; T. Donaldson: 'Mixes of English and Ancestral Language Words in Southeastern Australia', 143–58]

P. Dunbar-Hall: *Discography of Aboriginal and Torres Strait Islander Performers* (Sydney, 1996)

National Indigenous Arts Advocacy Association Annual Report 1996 (Sydney, 1997)

K. Neuenfeldt, ed.: *The Didjeridu: from Arnhem Land to Internet* (Sydney, 1997) [incl. K. Carmody: 'Ancient Voice, Contemporary Expression: the Didjeridu (Yidaki) and the Promotion of Aboriginal Rights', 11–19]

D. Bell: *Ngarrindjeri Wurruwarrin: a World that is, Was and Will Be* (Melbourne, 1998)

C. Gibson: '"We Sing Our Home, We Dance Our Land": Indigenous Self-Determination and Contemporary Geopolitics in Australian Popular Music', *Environment and Planning D: Society and Space*, xvi (1998), 163–84

recordings

My Survival as an Aboriginal, Australian Film Institute videotape, dir. E. Coffey (Sydney, 1978)

Eelemarni: the Story of Leo and Leva, prod. L. Mafi-Williams, Australian Film Institute videotape (Sydney, 1988)

Songs of Aboriginal Australia, coll. S. Wild, Australian Institute of Aboriginal Studies AIAS/17 (1988)

Pillars of Society, perf. K. Carmody, Larrikin CDLRF237 (1990)

Charcoal Lane, perf. A. Roach, Hightone Records HCD8037 (1992)

The Songs of Dougie Young, Australian Institute of Aboriginal Studies and the National Library of Australia AIAS/19 (1994)

II. *Western art music*

1. 18th century. 2. 19th century. 3. 20th century.

1. 18TH CENTURY. Aboriginal peoples, with many diverse languages, had, at the arrival of the first European settlers, developed text-driven musical traditions of much complexity and variety. Despite sympathy for Aboriginal identity on the part of the first British colonial governor, Arthur Phillip, and some other officials and earlier European settlers, in the tradition of the 'noble savage' concepts of the later 18th century, the richness of rhythmic and melodic elements in Aboriginal musics inevitably meant little or nothing to Europeans whose own music had tended, during the 17th and 18th centuries, to lose rhythmic and melodic subtlety in its development as a language governed by actual or implied harmonic progressions. Although well-wishing amateur and professional writers, naturalists and musicians showed a sporadic interest in notating (and sometimes harmonizing) Aboriginal songs during the first 50 years of European

settlement, among them Barron Field, John Lhotsky and Isaac Nathan (1790–1864), gold rushes from 1851 onwards decisively ended any ideas that Australia might become either a moated domain for British convicts and their emancipated descendants or, in the view of a small number of idealists, a pastoral community in which indigenous and newly immigrant peoples might live together idyllically.

Anthropologists started using mechanical equipment from early in the 20th century to record and file examples of Aboriginal tribal musics. Ethnomusicologists began to study these examples after World War II and joined the anthropologists in using wire and tape recorders in more systematic attempts at stylistic definition and classification. *Corroboree*, an orchestral ballet score of major ambition and dimensions by John Antill (1904–86), first performed in 1946 in the format of an abbreviated suite, was the most notable attempt in the earlier 20th century to evoke the spirit of Aboriginal ceremonies in Western orchestral terms. Although it used to be said, plausibly, that Australian composers deriving from European and North American traditions had no more in common with Aboriginal music than they had with the music of any other non-European indigenous people, attempts to evoke the mood or memory of Aboriginal music or even to quote it to some degree have been a persistent element in the music of Peter Sculthorpe (*b* 1929), becoming stronger as his career extended, and have engaged the attention of other composers, including such diverse figures as George Dreyfus (*b* 1928) and Colin Bright (*b* 1949), as the movement towards some sort of reconciliation with Aboriginal Australia has gathered strength among non-Aboriginal Australians since the 1970s.

The first European music heard in Australia would have been whatever songs or dance tunes were performed by crews landed temporarily from Dutch ships from the earlier 17th century, from the visit of the British privateer William Dampier in the late 17th century, and from the ships of French and British explorers of the later 18th and early 19th centuries. Most of this music is unnamed, but it is on record that the French song *Malbrouk* was heard frequently at various landfalls in the Pacific at or near the time that the crews of the French explorer La Pérouse and of the First Fleet of Governor Phillip met and fraternized amiably at Botany Bay in January 1788. This tune was apparently learnt quickly by members of an Aboriginal tribe in what is now the Sydney region, showing – something that probably needed to be established at the time – that the musical sensibilities of Aboriginals and Europeans were not incompatible. The element in European music-making found to be inimical and frightening by Aboriginal Australians of that district was, it appears, the noisy beating of drums by naval and military bandsmen to mark the timing of daily routine in the infant colony.

The establishment of a first European settlement at Sydney Cove from 26 January 1788 coincided with the full flowering of the Viennese Classical style, a circumstance which inevitably meant that a settlement struggling to survive inappropriate farming methods and forms of stock mustering unsuited to a vast, unfenced frontier would not discover this music until much later in its history. Mozart's composition of his final trio of symphonies in the summer of 1788 coincided with major concerns in the Sydney community for the straying of the colony's precious cattle well beyond the confines of the existing settlement. It is, however, a matter of record that the surgeon of the flagship of the First Fleet, George Bouchir Worgan, a member of a prominent London musical family, took a fortepiano and a creditably antiquarian enthusiasm for the music of Domenico Scarlatti to the new colony.

A prevalence of fife and drum tunes and other, similar regimental music set a pattern of prominence in Australian colonial history for military ensembles and their bandmasters. Naval and regimental bandsmen, sometimes doubling on string instruments, later played for church services and Sydney's first theatres as well as for all kinds of public ceremonies. Bandmasters wrote patriotic songs (*The Trumpet Sounds Australia's Fame* dates, incongruously, from 1826), arranged popular tunes from opera and ballet as sets of quadrilles and composed waltzes, polkas and other dance music for wider public use until well into the second half of the 19th century. Convicts, forming a majority of the population of the first years of Sydney-based settlement, were sometimes encouraged to sing by humane surgeons and shipmasters during the long, dangerous voyages from Britain on the grounds that it improved their chances of survival. They were involved in 1796 in the first known performance of a late 18th-century English-type opera with spoken dialogue, William Shields's *The Poor Soldier*. But much convict music-making would have consisted of whatever songs they brought in their memories, sometimes taking the form of disrespectful or vengeful parody. *Moreton Bay*, a song commemorating the savagery of life at the penal station of that name (now Brisbane), was set, for example, by an Irish convict to a traditional tune associated with the Irish song *Youghal Harbour*.

2. 19TH CENTURY. Formal music-making, apart from performances provided by bands and the important activity involved in the accompaniment of dances, consisted in early colonial times either of private soirées sponsored by military, governmental or wealthy private sources or of occasional public series of recitals given by non-professional musicians (sometimes described in accounts of the time as Gentlemen and Lady Amateurs) or by ad hoc groupings of professionals, such as the quartet concerts given in Sydney in the mid-1830s by Vincent Wallace (1812–65), the future composer of *Maritana*, and the recitals presented with other members of his family and that of John Phillip Deane (1796–1849).

Concert-giving organizations tended, inevitably, to replicate a structure that formed the backbone of British concert life, that of the choral society. This allowed associations of amateur choristers to keep musical enterprise firmly in their own hands and to assemble or hire orchestral groupings at will. They performed major works by Handel, Haydn, Mendelssohn, Mozart and others, as well as many lesser oratorios and cantatas, and seemed as fond as their counterparts in Britain of championing spuriously attributed works such as the 'Twelfth Mass' printed under Mozart's name or 'Locke's Celebrated Music for Macbeth'. Each of the major centres – Sydney, Hobart, Brisbane, Perth, Melbourne and Adelaide – founded choral societies of this type. Their ethical self-belief existed in symbiosis with the establishment of Mechanics' Institutes and Schools of Arts on the British model from the late 1830s (in Sydney) and with the influx of shiploads of young free settlers in the same decade, many of them zealous for education and self-improvement, under the aegis of a Presbyterian minister, the Rev. John Dunmore Lang. In the colony centred on Adelaide (now South Australia), which drew only on free settlers from its inception, groups of German immigrants, escaping from religious persecution, contributed a disposition to forming male choral groups modelled on the LIEDERTAFEL. The Liedertafel model spread to other colonies and took its place for many years alongside the British-type choral society. A member of the German immigrant community in South Australia, Carl Linger (1810–62), was one of the earliest European composers of professional competence to be active in Australia and won a prize in 1859 for setting words by Caroline Carleton, *Song of Australia*. This setting became a treasured part of South Australian traditions and was a candidate at one time for choice as Australia's national song.

When Isaac Nathan, an ancestor of the Australian conductor Sir Charles Mackerras, arrived in Sydney in 1841 with a reputation preceding him as the musician for whom Byron had written his *Hebrew Melodies* and who had set these verses for the first time, he apparently found more opportunities for professional musical activity in Sydney than in Melbourne. He became choirmaster of St Mary's Roman Catholic Cathedral in Sydney, a busy and expert teacher of singing with, to his credit, a treatise written and published in London on the subject that is increasingly cited as a source of early 19th-century practice and theory. He composed operas on the British model of short airs and spoken dialogue and produced in an opportunistic manner songs and scenas taking note of colonial events, one of them commemorating the presumed loss in the outback of the German-born explorer Ludwig Leichhardt during his first expedition and another Leichhardt's subsequent and unexpected safe arrival after that expedition. Soon after, however, sustainable discoveries of gold in what is now the state of Victoria strongly outweighed those of the original colony of New South Wales. From the 1860s until at least the end of the first third of the 20th century, Melbourne outdistanced Sydney in musical cohesion and organization, financial and political strength and in appetite for concerts, opera and other forms of musical theatre.

It was historically appropriate that the singer known internationally as Melba (Helen Porter Mitchell, 1861–1931) was the daughter of a man who became wealthy through Melbourne's late 19th-century building boom. She received her first instruction in the higher flights of singing from Pietro Cecchi (?1831–1897), a singer whose settlement in Melbourne as a performer and teacher followed his arrival in Melbourne in 1871 as part of a touring quartet of singers and his appearances with the extraordinary Lyster opera company. Melba was the most famous representative of several generations of young Australian musicians whose skills in musical performance were a means of winning international renown in a way directly comparable with the skills exhibited by young Australian sportsmen and women. In each case demonstrable skill and eagerness to succeed allowed these talented performers to bypass the idea that outstanding achievement at an international level rested on the maturation of a long, well-cultivated tradition.

After a vogue for productions of English-style operas or operatic adaptations in Sydney from the 1830s onwards, including the first original short work of ballad opera type (Edward Geoghegan's *The Currency Lass*, Royal Victoria Theatre, Sydney, 1844), the staging of operas now regarded as being in the standard repertory received an enormous boost with the start of the Australian gold rushes. Small touring companies or ensembles of soloists arrived from London or via touring schedules in North and South America. The most significant touring company of the mid-19th century was that formed and subsequently re-formed by an Irish entrepreneur, William Saurin Lyster (1827–80). His productions toured Australian cities for the best part of 20 years between 1861 and 1880, and played impressively extended seasons in Melbourne and to a lesser extent in Sydney. He introduced colonial audiences to a large repertory of new or relatively recent operas, among which Meyerbeer's *Les Huguenots* was one of the two most frequently performed works. In the late 1870s an American-born actor, James Cassius Williamson (1844–1913), began to tour the newest Gilbert and Sullivan operas and eventually became the principal agent of European touring opera companies within a regime (later taken over by the Tait brothers) that lasted under his name until the Sutherland-Williamson company of 1965. Many other entrepreneurs of opera competed in the late 19th and early 20th centuries.

The rapid growth in population and economic activity prompted by the gold rushes coincided with the era of large-scale exhibitions modelled on the Great Exhibition at the Crystal Palace in 1851. Melbourne and Sydney, in particular, advertised their financial and cultural ambitions at a series of intercolonial and international exhibitions. This development reached its peak in the Melbourne Centennial Exhibition of 1888, which celebrated the first centenary of European settlement in Australia and included among its attractions a major series of large-scale concerts directed by the English composer and conductor Frederick Hymen Cowen (1852–1935). German and Italian musicians, such as Cesare Cutolo, Paolo Giorza and August W. Juncker, who arrived in Australia to direct touring operas and other musical theatre pieces, contributed cantatas, anthems, marches and other music to the programme of large-scale colonial exhibitions or to local recital and concert programmes. New pieces of patriotic music were produced for anniversaries of settlement, for developments in Australian city and country life and to mark Australia's involvement in foreign wars. The French music critic and writer Oscar Comettant (1819–98), a musical juror for the 1888 Centennial Exhibition in Melbourne, recorded his belief in his book *Au pays des kangourous et des mines d'or* (Paris, 1890) that Australia had taken the cult of the parlour piano to lengths beyond those evident even in 19th-century Europe, estimating – perhaps wildly – that this newly colonized country contained 700,000 pianos at the time. He found it irksome as a Frenchman that so many of the pianos lodged in modest city and country houses and in isolated cabins and huts were of German manufacture.

The idea that excellence in public music-making belonged exclusively to the traditions of the choral society or the opera company began to change in Australia in the later 19th century, under the influence of the renown enjoyed in Europe and North America by orchestral and chamber music of the Viennese Classical and Austro-German Romantic schools. The decision of a number of young Australian musicians, including Percy Grainger (1882–1961), to study in Germany in the later years of the century was a symptom of this shift of emphasis. Its potency is memorably recorded in a novel of student life and ambition in Germany, *Maurice Guest*, written by a young Australian musician who studied in Leipzig in the late 1880s and published the novel under the pen name of Henry Handel Richardson. A Melbourne-born composer, Alfred Hill (1870–1960), was among the other Leipzig students, playing in the Gewandhaus orchestra under the baton of such musicians as Brahms and Bruch. A talented and impressionable musician, Hill responded to these experiences by composing with the vocabulary of his Leipzig years until halfway through the 20th century, writing (for example) a gypsy finale in a viola concerto that postdated Brahms and Bruch by half a century or more. Grainger, who once shocked his German mentors by proposing to study Chinese music, was one of the most interesting contributors to discussion on what might constitute a distinctively Australian music, suggesting at various times that it might exhibit a deliberate monotony (reflecting the long spans of Australian landscape, in contrast to the segmented nature of European topography and much of its music); become a clearing-house of Pacific, Asian and Aboriginal styles; engage by natural inclination in wistful sentimentality on the model of music in other pioneering countries (cf Stephen Foster in the USA); be democratically equal in its part-writing and happy-go-lucky in its assignment of voices and instruments; or show an affinity, because of its origins in a predominantly warm climate, for broad Italianate dynamic shading and Italianate vocal and instrumental timbres. Henry Tate (1873–1926), a Melbourne musician and writer, suggested in nationalistic pamphlets published in 1917 and 1924 that recognizably Australian music might grow partly from instruction in Aboriginal music in schools, but more instinctively from sensitivity to the riches of melodic inflection and rhythm in Australian birdsong (in which he claimed to distinguish a 'liberty-loving' preference for the major third) and the breeze-induced sighing of the bush.

A local result of the unprecedented prestige of Austro-German orchestral music was a new emphasis on the need to establish symphonic ensembles independent of the orchestral elements in oratorio and opera. Melbourne, typically at this time, took the lead in this movement. Melbourne University's first Ormond professor of music, an English musician named G.W.L. Marshall-Hall (1862–1915), directed a newly assembled orchestra with enormous flair in the 1890s at the same time as he scandalized Melbourne society with the Nietzschean sentiments of his published verses. Sir James Barrett, an enthusiastic associate of Marshall-Hall's orchestral activities, was able to assume with breath-taking narrowness of outlook, in recalling that period from the vantage point of 1940, that the 'history of music in Melbourne really resolves itself into the history of orchestral music, as no great work can be performed satisfactorily without the assistance of a competent orchestra'.

3. 20TH CENTURY.   Similar beliefs were to animate the benevolently despotic centralism of the Australian Broadcasting Commission (now Corporation) in the 1930s when it set about establishing, as part of a policy that might be described as orchestral imperialism, core instrumental ensembles of symphonic ambitions in each of the Australian state capitals on a permanent basis. The choice facing the ABC at the time was whether to bring together, as many competent musicians advised, a national orchestra of unusual merit or to risk the dilution of quality that would probably follow the establishment of permanent orchestras or orchestral nuclei in each of the six State capitals. There is little doubt that the decision to recognize State loyalties and to establish orchestras in all capital cities, however inadequate the musical result in some centres, was the right one. Each capital city developed its own subscription series of professional orchestral concerts and came to see this activity as a continuing part of its musical life rather than an occasional touring treat.

A profusion of choral societies and a marked sense of enterprise in some of them were characteristics of Australian music-making in the first third of the 20th century. Their independent enterprise tended to diminish as soon as the ABC began to take a lead in the programming of choral-orchestral concerts in the mid-1930s and to choose one major choral group in each capital city as the continuing associate of its local orchestra for public and broadcast performances. This was also a period when the ABC followed the example of Reith's BBC in establishing other, supplementary performing groups, including a number of small professional vocal ensembles, a dance band and a military band. The ABC's charter allowed it to go beyond broadcasting music where it felt that creative musical enterprise of its own was required to fill gaps in the nation's musical regime. An ABC triumvirate that took vigorous advantage of this provision consisted of Sir Charles Moses, as ABC general manager, Professor (later Sir) Bernard Heinze (1894–1982) as its initial musical director-general, later musical adviser and principal resident conductor, and W.G. James (1895–1977), a pianist and composer who became the organization's first federal director of music. Heinze successfully proposed and promoted youth concerts, schools concerts and a concerto competition that served as a model for an annual national contest. When the ABC's orchestral network was re-formed after World War II with improved funding from state and municipal sources as well as from the ABC, the identification of public music-making on a large scale with the ABC's subscription concerts was almost complete. Most solo instrumentalists and singers who toured Australia, particularly in the years following World War II, fulfilled an elaborate schedule of ABC appearances and broadcasts, to the point at which singers and instrumentalists who toured for any other organization (unless they were very famous indeed) had some difficulty in not being regarded in the public mind as second-raters. The ABC's subscription concerts rapidly grew multiple series in the larger capitals, particularly in Sydney. Sydney benefited from its position as the headquarters of the ABC and as a capital city now growing faster than Melbourne. Its continuing position as the biggest market for the sale of tickets for orchestral, chamber and solo concerts and (a little later) for opera dates from this period.

Melba took part in several tours of her homeland, including in her enterprises major operatic seasons (1911, 1924, 1928) under the combined banner of the J.C. Williamson organization and the singer herself. The remarkable 1912–13 tours of the company assembled by the Irish promoter Thomas Quinlan (solo singers, chorus of up to 70 members, permanent orchestra of up to 65 players with a reported augmentation to 100 for *Die Meistersinger*, stage and music staff, 365 tons of scenery and costumes) presented, in English, the first Australian stagings of Wagner's later masterpieces, including (in 1913) three cycles of the *Ring*; this initiative was not followed up until a further three complete cycles were presented in Adelaide in 1998, 85 years later. Opera in Australia, with its dependence on sporadic tours, was to take far longer than orchestral concert-giving to find sustainable resident bases. Gertrude Johnson's National Theatre Movement in Melbourne (beginning its work in 1935) and Clarice Lorenz's National Opera of Australia in Sydney (from 1951) were gallant organizations that became important in the years immediately after World War II, incidentally demonstrating that touring opera of any adequacy in Australia was particularly unlikely to survive without subsidy because of the country's vast distances and the related costs of touring. Opera became one of the charges of an inadequately funded Australian Elizabethan Theatre Trust (AETT). The Sydney-based opera company established by the AETT, usually known as the Elizabethan Trust Opera, began annual touring seasons in 1956, occasionally losing continuity during financial crises and dwindling into near-inaudibility during the year (1965) of the Sutherland-Williamson tour, but gradually evolving a viable schedule and drawing back to regular Australian appearances some of the many Australian and New Zealand singers who had made operatic careers abroad, particularly in London. It became independent of the Elizabethan Trust in 1970, retitling itself as the Australian Opera and, more recently, after its absorption of the former Melbourne-based Victorian State Opera, as Opera Australia. Regional opera organizations, usually consisting of administrative and artistic staff who plan seasons and recruit singers on an ad hoc basis, operated with varying degrees of vigour and regularity in all States and increasingly shared production costs through an opera conference.

Jazz achieved considerable popularity in Australia from the 1920s, leading to the formation of large numbers of local groups and, in due course, to sustained and (briefly) international careers for Graeme Bell (1935–75) and his colleagues in traditionally orientated ensembles; to local versions of bop; and to syntheses of several styles by Don Burrows and others. Country ('hillbilly') music, complete in many instances with imitation US accents copied from recorded and broadcast sources, established from the 1930s its own continuing circuit of widely admired performers (among them Tex Morton, Buddy Williams, Smoky Dawson and Slim Dusty) and was accepted by many Australians in rural areas and by many Aboriginal Australians as a completely naturalized form of music. The influence of the British-American blackface minstrel tradition, which had become popular from at least the 1840s onwards and had influenced a number of well-known traditional songs of pastoral life, reasserted its popularity in the years during and after World War I and led to the composition of a large number of songs imitating the conventional nostalgia of wanderers returning to their hometown surroundings with a backdrop suggestive of a southern US milieu and US-style expressions of endearment. Some songs born of this deliberately borrowed idiom, notably Jack O'Hagan's *The Road to Gundagai*, became for a couple of generations more widely accepted as truly Australian than any other music,

including the song *Waltzing Matilda*. Post-World War II rock found its first noted exponent in Johnny O'Keefe and, as in many countries, developed in the course of time local variants which enjoyed international renown in the hands of such groups as AC/DC, Midnight Oil, Dire Straits and INXS (see also §III, 2 below).

One of the many active jazz players in Australia before World War II was a Melbourne musician named Banks, whose jazz-playing son, Don Banks (1923–80), became an accomplished concert-hall and film composer, basing himself in London for much of his career before returning to Australia in the 1970s to take on onerous offical positions, in which he was able to help raise professional standards in composition among a newer generation of young practitioners. Other Australian composers who made careers abroad at a time when Australian society was very inhospitable to any creative ambition in music (beyond the composition of patriotic songs and teaching pieces) included Arthur Benjamin (1893–1960, in London) and Peggy Glanville-Hicks (1912–90, in New York). Composers of notable talent who attempted to pursue their métier in their own country had a difficult path to follow, as the career of Margaret Sutherland (1897–1984) illustrates. John Antill, submerged for much of his career in ABC staff duties, might have been thought likely to become the Australian Copland on the strength of his *Corroboree*, but in much of his other music he sank into a conventionality that had something in common with the practice of his teacher, Alfred Hill.

Dorian Le Gallienne (1915–63), a teacher at Melbourne University Conservatorium and a music critic, was the most convincing symphonist of the years immediately after World War II, despite a long and taxing struggle with ill health. A new generation of Australian composers began to make itself felt in the late 1950s and early 60s, led by Peter Sculthorpe, Richard Meale (*b* 1932), Nigel Butterley (*b* 1935), George Dreyfus, Felix Werder (*b* 1922), Larry Sitsky (*b* 1934) and others, with some temporarily or permanently expatriate figures such as David Lumsdaine (*b* 1931), Keith Humble (1927–95) and Malcolm Williamson (*b* 1931) being added retrospectively to their number. Their activities helped to secure purposeful official funding for composition and an esteem that meant that ambitious and adventurous creativeness in music would be tallied along with comparable activities in writing and visual art among the creditable achievements of Australian society. Women composers, among them Alison Bauld (*b* 1944), Anne Boyd (*b* 1946), the New Zealand-born Gillian Whitehead (*b* 1941), Moya Henderson (*b* 1941), Jennifer Fowler (*b* 1939), Sarah Hopkins (*b* 1958), Elena Kats-Chernin (*b* 1957) and Liza Lim (*b* 1966), have figured prominently among younger generations of Australian musical creators, alongside such colleagues as Brenton Broadstock (*b* 1952), Gerard Brophy (*b* 1953), Barry Conyngham (*b* 1944), Ross Edwards (*b* 1943), Riccardo Formosa (*b* 1954), Elliott Gyger (*b* 1968), Graham Hair (*b* 1943), Brian Howard (*b* 1951), Gordon Kerry (*b* 1961), Graham John Koehne (*b* 1956), Bozidar Kos (*b* 1934 in Slovenia but beginning his formal training and compositional career after his arrival in Australia in 1965), Richard Mills (*b* 1949), Andrew Schultz (*b* 1960), Michael Smetanin (*b* 1958), Carl Vine (*b* 1954), Martin Wesley-Smith (*b* 1945) and Nigel Westlake (*b* 1958). Julian Jing-Jun Yu (*b* 1957, Chinese by birth and earlier musical education), Roger

Smalley and Andrew Ford (*b* 1943 and 1957 respectively, both of them English by birth and training) are among the relatively recent arrivals within a long list of fully equipped creative musicians who have become Australian by choice, enriching their adopted country in the process.

See also ADELAIDE; BRISBANE; CANBERRA; MELBOURNE; PERTH; and SYDNEY.

BIBLIOGRAPHY

H. Tate: *Australian Music Resources: some Suggestions* (Melbourne, 1917)
H. Tate: *Australian Musical Possibilities* (Melbourne, 1924)
I. Moresby: *Australia Makes Music* (Sydney, 1948)
W.A. Orchard: *Music in Australia: More than 150 Years of Development* (Melbourne, 1952)
W.A. Carne: *A Century of Harmony: the Official Centenary History of the Royal Melbourne Philharmonic Society* (Melbourne, 1954)
R. Covell: *Australia's Music: Themes of a New Society* (Melbourne, 1967)
A. McCredie: *Catalogue of 46 Australian Composers* (Canberra, 1969)
A. McCredie: *Musical Composition in Australia* (Canberra, 1969)
J. Murdoch: *Australia's Contemporary Composers* (Melbourne, 1972)
R. Covell, ed.: *E. Geoghegan: the Currency Lass* (Sydney, 1976)
F. Callaway and D.Tunley, eds.: *Australian Composition in the Twentieth Century* (Melbourne, 1978)
H. Love: *The Golden Age of Australian Opera: W.S. Lyster and his Companies, 1861–1880* (Sydney, 1981)
G.A. Baker, ed.: *Australian Made: Gonna Have a Good Time Tonight* (Sydney, 1987)
B. Johnson: *The Oxford Companion to Australian Jazz* (Melbourne, 1987)
C. Spencer and Z.Nowara: *Who's Who of Australian Rock* (Knoxfield, Victoria, 1987, 4/1996)
J. Jenkins: *22 Contemporary Australian Composers* (Melbourne, 1988)
M. Atherton: *Australian Made, Australian Played: Handcrafted Musical Instruments from Didjeridu to Synthesiser* (Sydney, 1990)
A. Gyger: *Opera for the Antipodes . . . 1881–1939* (Sydney, 1990)
B. Broadstock, ed.: *Sound Ideas: Australian Composers Born since 1950* (Sydney, 1995)
N. Brown and others: *One Hand on the Manuscript: Music in Australian Cultural History 1930–1960* (Canberra, 1995)
N. Saintilan, A.Schultz and P. Stanhope: *Biographical Directory of Australian Composers* (Sydney, 1996)
W. Bebbington, ed.: *The Oxford Companion to Australian Music* (Melbourne, 1997)

III. Popular immigrant musics

1. 19th and early 20th centuries. 2. After World War II.

1. 19TH AND EARLY 20TH CENTURIES. The first European settlement group of convicts and their overseers brought with them the rural and urban music cultures of late 18th-century England and Ireland, including ballads and popular theatrical songs. Vernacular performance of this transplanted music continued in informal and domestic settings, along with songs with localized texts in similar styles. Composition and performance of topical ballads by convicts, often on anti-authority themes, was noted from the first decades of settlement. Several songs of the Irish convict Frank Macnamara, written between 1830 and 1850 in Irish prosodic forms with long lines, achieved wide currency and were orally circulated into the mid-20th century, the best known being his convict's lament *Moreton Bay*. Other locally composed songs of colonial experience were printed in early newspapers as verse with a nominated air, which was frequently a popular theatrical air, a traditional melody or songs composed in the style of Irish or Scottish melodies.

Such songs were most often performed as unaccompanied narrative singing and retained their popularity as part of domestic and small-scale community performance into the 20th century, particularly in rural areas with little access to commercial public entertainment. The few contemporary descriptions of early performance practice indicate relatively slow delivery and mannerisms such as the spoken delivery of the last half-line; such features show little variation from parallel British and Irish traditional singing styles. Diatonic and gapped scales and occasional modal pitch ambiguities are sometimes found in melodies collected in the early 20th century. The four-line, 14-syllable 'come-all-ye' song form with its family of *ABBA* tunes (often truncated to a two-line *AB*) was frequently used, particularly for outlaw ballads that continued the convict tradition and were often based on Irish song styles and models.

The population boom of the goldrushes that began from 1853 was accompanied by the opening of many theatres and other entertainment venues on the goldfield settlements and in metropolitan centres. The theatrical entertainer Charles Thatcher wrote and performed many topical goldfield songs to enthusiastic audiences. Minstrel shows toured frequently and provided influential models of popular performance and repertory. In urban centres, music-hall and vaudeville circuits developed. Amateur performance also included the urban middle-class parlour ballad and performance on the upright piano; in a society where rapid social and class transitions were common, these public symbols of musical respectability and competence were broadly spread.

Professional entertainment styles influenced vernacular performance and composition, though older ballad styles continued. The rural, pastoral labour force grew in size and self-confidence in the late 19th century, its shearers and other workers creating many songs that documented and celebrated their life. A selection of these were published by the literary ballad collector A.B. Paterson in *Old Bush Songs* in 1905; other items continued in fairly marginal oral performance, and some were collected in the 1950s. These became the central canon of the Australian folksong revival of the 1950s, including such songs as *The Old Bark Hut*, *The Wild Colonial Boy*, *The Banks of the Condamine* and *Waltzing Matilda*.

Music for social dance has been one of the most important types of vernacular music-making in Australia. The great expansion of public dancing in the 19th century, especially of closed couple dances such as waltzes, polkas, mazurkas and varsoviennes, along with quadrilles, influenced rural and traditional musicians. Solo hornpipe-style step-dancing, often competitive, was also popular. Musicians, particularly in rural regions, usually did not read music and tended to play traditional tunes or modified versions of published music that were learnt orally; the modulation and thematic development found in notated dance music was modified to the simpler alternating binary structures of traditional dance music. Tunes to accompany these dances can still be found among older Australian rural players.

The most popular instruments during this period were the single-action free-reed aerophones: the button accordion, the mouth organ and the Anglo-German concertina. Fiddle players were also common, playing the instrument in styles similar to those of British and American traditional fiddlers, using the first position and open strings. Tone was often thin and light, and ornamentation limited to a few upper grace notes and pitch slides, both up and down. Pianos were also incorporated when available.

Most musical forms were integrated into patterns of community entertainment. For more marginal immigrant groups, the construction of community required entertainment to be linked to more explicitly emblematic music. Cantonese opera troupes (with both overseas and local performers) toured the goldfields from 1858 to 1870, performing exclusively to their compatriots and often meeting with racist opposition from European miners. German emigrants, who constituted about 2% of the population, tended to be concentrated in several regions. In some areas of Southern Queensland their distinctive local dance-music culture survived into the 20th century. The German band, a small brass and reed ensemble favoured by street performers and a common feature of British musical life of the mid-19th century, also had a strong presence in public instrumental music in Australia. In the second half of the 19th century, urban middle-class Germans often formed Liedertafel groups, which were dedicated to organized amateur solo and group singing of German song and later, other music. These were generally suppressed in the anti-German feeling during World War I.

Irish immigrants made up about 25% of settler Australia. They were mainly Catholic, and because of sectarian and cultural prejudices maintained a certain distinctiveness, using music as a means of marking and expressing their identity. Irish language and its songs did not survive in Australia; public performances emphasized bourgeois song forms such as those of Thomas Moore and sentimental songs of exile, some of which were composed and published locally. Step-dancing and its associated music was practised, and with the growth of cultural nationalism in Ireland in the late 19th century, it rose in emblematic status.

By contrast, Scottish immigrants in many cases occupied a dominant place in the economy and had less reason to maintain group cohesion. Nonetheless, pipe bands and Scottish dancing have been widely followed in Australia, supported by the Victorian fashion for tartanry and by the Presbyterian establishment. Pipe bands were frequently associated with public and quasi-military organizations, and a strong branch of the dominion piping movement developed in Australia in the 20th century.

The introduction of sound recording from the beginning of the 20th century, followed by radio in the 1920s, gave Australians greater access to new musical styles and diminished the need for domestic entertainment. It also led to new, commercially disseminated styles influenced by aural and untutored musical practices.

In the 1930s the recordings of American hillbilly performers such as the Carter family, Jimmie Rodgers and singing cowboys such as Wilf Carter seized the imagination of many Australians. Local performers Tex Morton, Buddy Williams and later many others started to perform in this style and to compose local songs with rural and sentimental themes. Based mainly on American styles, these songs also incorporated features of the vernacular ballad, comic song and especially the lyrical themes of the 'bush ballad' poets of the late 19th century such as A.B. Paterson and Henry Lawson. Morton, Williams and others established an indigenous form of country music, emphasizing solo, guitar-accompanied performance, yodelling and localized lyrics. Through

radio, recording and vigorous touring with travelling circuses, rodeos and agricultural shows, such performers established a strong relationship with sections of the Australian rural population.

2. AFTER WORLD WAR II.   The period since 1945 has brought major changes to Australian society and to musical behaviour. American-produced popular culture genres extended their dominance; television was introduced in 1956 and increased its social reach over the next decade; and a vigorous programme of immigration was instituted in the late 1940s, involving Britain, Ireland, other European countries and, in the 1970s, Asian countries, bringing new cultural and musical forms to Australia.

Recordings of popular dance bands and vocalists were popular from the 1930s, and in the 1940s intellectual fans focused on jazz as an alliance of art music and folk music. After the war, performers such as Graham Bell led the popular movement for traditional New Orleans-style jazz involving younger radical fans. This movement and its interpretation was the first manifestation of a distanced, intellectualized engagement with popular culture, which later influenced the reception of traditional music forms in the folk movement. In contrast, country music also grew vigorously in the first decade after the war and developed a rural and urban working-class fan base. Venues for urban performance opened in the outer suburbs of Sydney, and new recording companies formed. Singers such as Slim Dusty toured continuously through rural Australia and gathered a large and durable following for the music.

Popular music was utterly changed by the arrival of rock and roll, television and 45 r.p.m. recording in the mid-1950s. As the new youth popular music market was created, Australian performers in the new rock and popular styles emerged, such as Johnny O'Keefe and Col Joye. Overseas musical models dominated; some styles, such as 'surf music', had a particular attraction for local performers and audiences in the early 1960s.

The Beatles and their immense popularity stimulated a second generation of young popular musicians. Many of the most enthusiastic and successful of these were British post-war migrants who were able to utilize their cultural connections to the new sounds. However, although a group like the Easybeats had short-lived international success, Australian performers in a Euro-American centred music industry could achieve only provincial and marginal status.

In the early 1970s, supported by the new countercultural audiences of a young intelligentsia, rock groups with a more specific local focus rose to prominence alongside independent recording companies (such as Mushroom records). Brash local themes and social styles of performance emerged, often emphasizing youthful bohemian hedonism. As this localized style (comparable with many national rock musics emergent in the 1970s) used an international musical idiom, the existence of a distinctive 'Australian sound' was frequently called into question. Some commentators have signalled the importance of venues and institutions rather than musical techniques in the creation of this music. In 1978 the growing number of new performance venues in large suburban pubs led to the 'pub-rock' or 'oz-rock' movement, predominantly hard rock presented to a male working-class audience, sometimes with localized lyrics, typified by the group Cold Chisel. Experience within this scene was often pointed to as part of the international success of such bands as Men at Work, Australian Crawl and INXS in the 1980s.

Dance music based in recording production rather than on performance became more prominent in the 1980s, and the increased significance of dance-based musical consumption, both collective and individual, devalued the image of pub-rock. Guitar bands, identified as alternative and anti-establishment, typically amateur and performing in smaller pub venues, also reacted against the hyper-masculine, aggressive and aging image of pub-rock.

An Australian folk music movement formed in the 1950s, paralleling similar movements in Britain and America. Radical intellectuals turned to the cultural forms associated with the 1890s to stress the centrality of the 19th-century, male, rural working class in the formation of the national type and ideal. A folk movement formed, collecting and performing the songs identified with this group, recovered from oral tradition and published by collectors such as JOHN MEREDITH and JOHN STREETER MANIFOLD. By the early 1960s this movement was incorporated in the international boom in popular folk music, and a circuit of clubs formed that attracted a young, tentatively bohemian but largely middle-class following. Coffee-lounge folk venues opened, and semi-professional and full-time folksingers performed self-composed, traditional British, American and black American songs alongside songs collected from old Australian rural singers, usually with guitar accompaniment. This movement was strongly tied to the anti-war movement and espoused a liberal cosmopolitanism that supplanted the nationalism of the early part of the revival.

Much of the folk movement's following was eroded by the massive impact of the Beatles-led revolution in popular music, but a core of fans and performers remained. Many folk performers and organizers were British migrants of the 1960s and early 70s, and the model of the British pub-based folk club became dominant. Partly as a reaction to the purist attitude to performance and style in this scene, groups with a less intellectualized style of performing Australian traditional songs developed. These 'bush bands' used a FOLK-ROCK approach, with strongly rhythmic arrangements of Australian vernacular ballads mixed with Irish dance music and its characteristic instrumentation.

From the 1960s the country music movement had included performers espousing images of 'cultural authenticity' popularized by the radical, nationalist folk movement (but emphasizing nostalgia), as well as performers seeking an audience drawn to the styles of American country music. In the 1980s and 90s, perhaps as a reaction to social change and new public and media interests in national identity, performers such as John Williamson and Lee Kernaghan gave explicitly Australian material new popularity. Bush bands, by then less favoured in the folk movement, were welcomed at country music festivals, such as that held annually at Tamworth, New South Wales.

The post-war Australian migration programme brought migrants from northern, then southern and eastern Europe and the Middle East. From the late 1970s South-east Asian refugees began to arrive, followed by other Asian migrants. This has led to the establishment of immigrant communities in Sydney, Melbourne, Perth and a few other cities. Such groups (which in the first stages of southern-European migration included a large proportion of rural migrants) often form social and religious organizations and small entertainment businesses that are culture specific. Music plays a part in many of these community organizations, which often engage immigrant musicians skilled in traditional styles. Genres as diverse as Greek regional dance music, Serbian epic singing and South American harp music have been performed in contexts ranging from individual homes to metropolitan concert halls. Family-based celebrations such as weddings, baptisms and circumcisions, as well as religious calendric events celebrated by regional associations, often provide opportunities for music ensembles, particularly dance bands. Cultural maintenance organizations were formed by communities from the 1960s, promoting nationally sanctioned folkloric styles; regional popular music and especially collective folkdance to second-generation groups. Song composition in some traditional styles also takes place: Parkhill (1983) documents and analyses such items as a Cretan *rizitika* on the subject of the 1975 Australian constitutional crisis and an Arabic *zajal* epic on an Australian football final.

In the mid-1970s Australian national cultural policies shifted from migrant assimilation to cultural pluralism under the rubric of multiculturalism. Under this policy some traditional immigrant musicians and their musical style gained occasional public prominence and access to government assistance. A small network of publicly funded and community-based media outlets for ethnic minorities was developed. Local government-funded community events, as well as larger, nationally orientated cultural showcases promoted representatives of 'multicultural Australia'. Significant numbers of Anglo-Australian musicians were inspired by the existence of these forms in their midst, and some began exploring other styles. In the 1970s and 80s these musicians often collaborated with second-generation minority musicians, many of whom were inspired by overseas developments such as the Latin American *nuevo canción* and Greek retro-rebetika (*see* REBETIKA) movements.

Styles such as Texas swing or Cajun music also became popular in the 1970s, expanding in the 1990s to forms of African pop and Latin American and Balkan styles. The musicians involved and their networks sometimes developed from the folk movement and sometimes from the more intellectual fringes of the rock music scene. The growing numbers of young students from Asian countries in the 1990s often favour their own regional popular musics, forming bands playing Thai pop, *bhangra* or Malay heavy metal, sometimes with deliberate local inflections. These styles are, however, marginal. The Australian Broadcasting Corporation presents many immigrant musics in a number of radio programmes as part of its charter to represent national cultural diversity. It has also strongly fostered Australian country music through its subsidiary, ABC recordings.

BIBLIOGRAPHY

AND OTHER RESOURCES

A.B. Paterson: *Old Bush Songs* (Sydney, 1905, enlarged 2/1957 by D. Stewart and N. Keesing as *Old Bush Songs and Rhymes of Colonial Times*)

J.S. Manifold: *The Penguin Australian Songbook* (Harmondsworth, 1964)

J.S. Manifold: *Who Wrote the Ballads?* (Sydney, 1964)

J. Meredith and H.M.Anderson, eds.: *Folk Songs of Australia and the Men and Women who Sang Them* (Sydney, 1967–87) [score]

H.M. Anderson: *The Story of Australian Folk Song* (Melbourne, 1970 [3rd edn of *Colonial Ballads*])

E. Watson: *Country Music in Australia* (Kensington and Sydney 1975–83)

P. Parkhill: 'Two Folk Epics from Melbourne', *Meanjin*, xlii (1983), 120–39

G. Smith: 'Making Folk Music', *Meanjin*, xliv (1985), 477–90

L. Barwick: 'Italian Traditional Music in Australia', *Australian Folklore*, i (1987), 44–67

M. Breen, ed.: *Missing in Action: Australian Popular Music in Perspective*, i (Melbourne, 1987)

R. Edwards: *200 Years of Australian Folk Song, Index, 1788–1988* (Kuranda, 1988)

L. Zion: 'The Sound of Australian Music', *Constructing a Culture*, ed. V. Burgman and J. Lee (Fitzroy, 1988), 209–23

M. Ryan: 'Australian Ethnic Music: a Reflection of Divergence', *Musicology Australia*, xi–xii (1988–9), 14–22

M. Schuster: 'Persistence versus Assimilation of Ethnic Old-Time Music: a Case Study from the German and Scandinavian Communities in Rural South East Queensland', *Proceedings of the 4th National Folklore Conference: Nov 24–5 1990*, ed. M. Clarke (Canberra, 1991), 97

K. Brisbane, ed.: *Entertaining Australia: an Illustrated History* (Sydney, 1991)

P. Hayward, ed.: *From Pop to Punk to Postmodernism: Popular Music and Australian Culture from the 1960s to the 1990s* (Sydney, 1992) [incl. G. Turner: 'Australian Popular Music and its Contexts', 11–24]

G.B. Davey and G.Seal: *The Oxford Companion to Australian Folklore* (Melbourne, 1993) [incl. E. Waters: 'Folk Song', 153–66; A. Chatzinikolaou and S. Gauntlett: 'Greek-Australian Folk-Song', 202–5; S. Gauntlett: 'Rebetika', 343–5]

G. Smith: 'Australian Country Music and the Hillbilly Yodel', *Popular Music*, xiii (1994), 297–311

G. Smith: 'Irish Meets Folk: the Genesis of the Bush Band', *Music-Cultures in Contact: Convergences and Collisions*, ed. M.J. Kartomi and S. Blum (Basle, 1994), 186–203

W. Bebbington, ed.: *The Oxford Companion to Australian Music* (Melbourne, 1997) [incl. N. Wilmott: 'Liedertafel', 341–3; C. Falk: 'Migrant Music in Australia', 375–81]

J. Stubington: 'The Reconciling of Port Fairy Spirits: the Politics of Aboriginal Reconciliation in an Australian Folk Festival Recording', *Perfect Beat*, iv/1 (1998), 84–105

RECORDINGS

Traditional Singers and Musicians in Victoria, Wattle D4, Archive series no.2 (1960) [incl. notes by E. Waters]

A Garland for Sally, perf. S. Sloane, Larrikin LRF 136 (1983) [incl. notes by W. Fahey]

Cretan Traditional Music in Australia, perf. K. and G. Tsourdalakis, TAR 010 (1984) [incl. booklet by P. Parkhill]

Music Deli in the Can, ABC 512 102–2 (1992)

Folk Songs of Australia, coll. J. Meredith, Carrawobbity WON595–1, 2 (1995)

ALLAN MARETT (I, 1), CATHERINE J. ELLIS (I, 2), MARGARET GUMMOW (I, 3), ROGER COVELL (II), GRAEME SMITH (III)

Australia Ensemble. Australian chamber music group. Founded by Murray Khouri and Roger Covell in 1980 as the University of New South Wales Ensemble, it aimed to present varied chamber music programmes with a substantial commitment to new Australian music. The founding personnel were David Bollard (piano), John Harding (violin), Irina Morozova (viola), David Pereira (cello), David Stanhope (horn/second piano) and Murray Khouri (clarinet). Harding was replaced by Dene Olding in 1982 and the flautist Geoffrey Collins joined the group after the departure of Stanhope in 1983. In 1984, with an expanded international touring programme, the name was changed to the Australia Ensemble, reputedly to avoid confusion with groups from Wales. Donald Westlake took over as clarinettist in 1986, and was succeeded by Nigel Westlake (1987), Alan Vivian (1992) and Catherine McCorkill (1995), while Julian Smiles became

the group's cellist in 1992. The ensemble is noted for its high performing standards, its variety of repertory and its championship of Australian music. It has toured throughout Australia for Musica Viva and internationally to North and South America, Europe, New Zealand, China, India and Japan. The ensemble's recordings range from Mozart and Beethoven to Dallapiccola and the complete string quartets of Peter Sculthorpe. Its numerous commissions, including works by Gordon Kerry, Roger Smalley, Andrew Schultz, Carl Vine, Nigel Westlake and others, have made a significant contribution to contemporary Australian chamber music.

PETER McCALLUM

Austral Islands. *See* POLYNESIA, §II, 3(ii).

Austria (Ger. Österreich). Country in Europe. This article deals with the area of the Republic of Austria, comprising the federated provinces (*Länder*) of Lower Austria, Upper Austria, Burgenland, Carinthia, Salzburg, Styria, Tyrol, Vienna and Vorarlberg. For the remaining successor states to the Danube monarchy, *see* CROATIA, CZECH REPUBLIC, HUNGARY, ITALY, POLAND, SLOVAKIA, SLOVENIA and ROMANIA; *see also* GERMANY for the period up to 1806.

Prehistoric signal pipes, musical instruments and iconographical representations of musical activities from the Hallstatt Period (1000–500 BCE) and the Roman occupation testify to the antiquity of Austrian civilization. The development of a musical culture from the beginning of the Middle Ages has essentially been determined by Austria's geographical position in the centre of Europe, its Alpine terrain, the coming of Christianity and the settlement by Germanic tribes. External influences, especially of the races at its borders – the Latin peoples, the Slavs and the Magyars – further affected the area's cultural evolution. Although each province has a place in Austria's cultural history, the musical centres have always been the cities of Salzburg and Vienna.

I. Art music. II. Folk and traditional music.

I. Art music

1. The early period. 2. Humanism and the Renaissance. 3. The Baroque era. 4. Pre-Classicism and Classicism. 5. Romanticism. 6. The 20th century.

1. THE EARLY PERIOD. Christianity brought plainsong to the country and a *cantor moderatus* is recorded in the 5th century. After the turbulent period of migration, St Rupert built the monastery of St Peter in Salzburg shortly before 700, and Bishop Virgil, a Scot who maintained contact with his homeland throughout his episcopacy, founded the cathedral in 774. Both institutions were at the centre of chant development in Salzburg when it was elevated to an archbishopric in 798 and given the task of converting the *Ostmark* ('Eastern March': Europe east of Austria and Germany). The *cantus romanus*, in the form prescribed by the Carolingian reforms, was disseminated from Salzburg under Archbishop Arno (785–821), a friend of Alcuin, while associations with St Gallen and Metz resulted in the introduction of the types of neumes used there.

The monastery of Kremsmünster was settled in 777 from Mondsee, the oldest Benedictine house in Upper Austria (748), itself a daughter house of Monte Cassino. Numerous other monastic establishments were responsible for the knowledge and dissemination of the chant repertory from the 11th century onwards. Manuscripts using neumes from Austrian monasteries date from the 9th and 10th centuries. Those of importance to liturgical history in the Alpine region include a plenary missal of 1136 from the monastery of St Paul im Lavanttal in Carinthia (*D-Sl*, Cod.bibl.fol.20), copied from a Kremsmünster original, and a 12th-century gradual with Metz neumes from the monastery of Seckau in Styria (*A-Gu* 807), which shows the adaptation of the original Roman version to the German chant tradition. A 13th-century breviary from St Lambrecht (*Gu* 134) contains the oldest version of the Corpus Christi hymn *Pange lingua* with neumes and tonary note names. The ancient *Christ ist erstanden* is the outstanding example of vernacular sacred song; the earliest complete version of the text with neumes dates from 1325 (*KN* 1213). Paraliturgical music includes sacred dramas, such as the Klosterneuburg Easter play and the so-called Erlauer Spiele, six Christmas and Easter plays from Gmünd in Carinthia, the sixth of which shows remarkable similarities to the Donaueschingen *Marienklage*, as well as rhymed Offices and hymns. In addition to the fact that there was practical musical instruction, a number of music treatises of Austrian provenance indicate that *musica theoretica* appeared in the quadrivium in monastic, cathedral and parish schools, and eventually at the University of Vienna (founded 1365). There is, nevertheless, only one well-known medieval Austrian music theorist, Engelbert of Admont.

Minnesang was established principally at the courts of the Babenbergs in Vienna, of Archbishop Eberhard II in Salzburg and of Duke Bernhard von Sponheim in St Veit, Carinthia. Numerous Minnesinger are known by name, the most important of whom are Walther von der Vogelweide, who claimed that he learnt to sing and write poetry in Austria, and the 'courtly village poet' Neidhart von Reuental, who integrated indigenous and popular elements into Minnesang. Only the names and some of the poems survive of most Austrian Minnesinger, for example Ulrich von Liechtenstein. Hugo von Montfort, a late exponent of Minnesang in the Vorarlberg, wrote poems which were set to music by his court musician, Bürk Mangolt. The last important figures in secular medieval monody were the Monk of Salzburg at the court of Archbishop Pilgrim II (1365–96) and the Tyrolean knight, Oswald von Wolkenstein. Both are also responsible for a small body of mensural polyphony and thereby stand at the threshold of an independent German polyphonic style.

Traces of Ars Antiqua and Ars Nova music survive in German manuscripts of the time and seem to have been a strong influence on the growth of indigenous German polyphony: Perotinus's organum *Sederunt* appears in an outdated and mixed notation (*Gu* 756 from the Seckau monastery), motets and a conductus in Franconian notation, also three French chansons (Stiftsbibliothek, Vorau, MSS 23, 380) and the ballade *Fies de moy* (*M* 486). Several French and Italian Ars Nova compositions appear as contrafacta among the works of Oswald von Wolkenstein. The Mondsee-Wiener Liederhandschrift, also known as the Spörlsches Liederbuch, is the source for various forms of secular vernacular polyphony from about 1400 and in particular for that of the Monk of Salzburg. Only when King Friedrich III (later Emperor) summoned Netherlandish and English musicians to his court did polyphony begin to develop rapidly: the Trent Codices (*I-TRmn* 87–92, *TRmd* 93) from the South Tyrol are the most important evidence for the rapid development of polyphony in mid-15th-century Austria. The oldest polyphonic arrangement of *Crist ist erstanden* is by Friedrich's *cantor principalis*, Johannes Brassart, a member of the Kapelle of Friedrich's predecessor, Albrecht II (*d* 1439), the first of an unbroken line of Germanic HABSBURG kings and emperors. The development of music in Austria is inseparably linked with this dynasty.

2. HUMANISM AND THE RENAISSANCE.   Polyphony reached its first peak under Emperor Maximilian I, who ordered the reorganization of the Hofkapelle at Vienna in 1498, under the direction of Georg Slatkonia. The members of the Kapelle included such distinguished composers as Isaac, Senfl and Hofhaimer, whom Maximilian retained from the Innsbruck Kapelle of his predecessor, Archduke Sigismund of the Tyrol. The German Gesellschaftslied, which these composers cultivated alongside their other works, is the earliest significant German contribution to the history of polyphony, and soon became popular outside court circles. A collection of German polyphonic songs and quodlibets was compiled in Vienna (and published in Nuremberg) in 1544 by Wolfgang Schmeltzl, schoolmaster at the Schottenstift. The work of Conradus Celtis led to Vienna becoming a centre of humanism; one of the results in music was to increase the importance of the text in polyphonic song, such as in the homophonic humanist odes performed in imitation of classical style with regard to the textual metre. The earliest example is a chorus from Celtis's festival play *Ludus Dianae* (1501), performed in Linz for Maximilian I; this genre was developed by composers in the circle known as the Sodalitas Litteraria Danubiana (which included Petrus Tritonius, Benedictus Ducis, Wolfgang Grefinger, Hofhaimer and Senfl) and was diffused in the form of school songs. Netherlandish musicians became increasingly prominent when Arnold von Bruck succeeded Heinrich Finck in 1527 as Kapellmeister at the Viennese court of Ferdinand I, a grandson of Maximilian I and the first of the Austrian line of Habsburgs. Other Netherlanders who later held the post included Maessens, Vaet, Monte and Lambert de Sayve; numerous singers, teachers and organists at the imperial court, such as Buus and Luython, also came from the Netherlands.

The contemporaneous flowering of instrumental music for domestic use resulted in intabulations and lute pieces of the kind written by Hans Judenkünig, who spent his last years in Vienna. A mid-16th-century German organ tablature has survived (Landesarchiv, Klagenfurt, Sign.4/3), containing works by Senfl, Josquin, Verdelot and La Rue as well as anonymous pieces. It probably originated in one of the Carinthian monasteries which was dissolved under Joseph II's edict; it is in a neat alphabetic notation and may be the earliest of its kind.

The Flemish influence greatly increased when the Habsburg territories were further divided among the heirs of Ferdinand I (*d* 1564). Thus Innsbruck and Graz again became Habsburg residences, each with its own Kapelle, and developed into cultural centres of the greatest

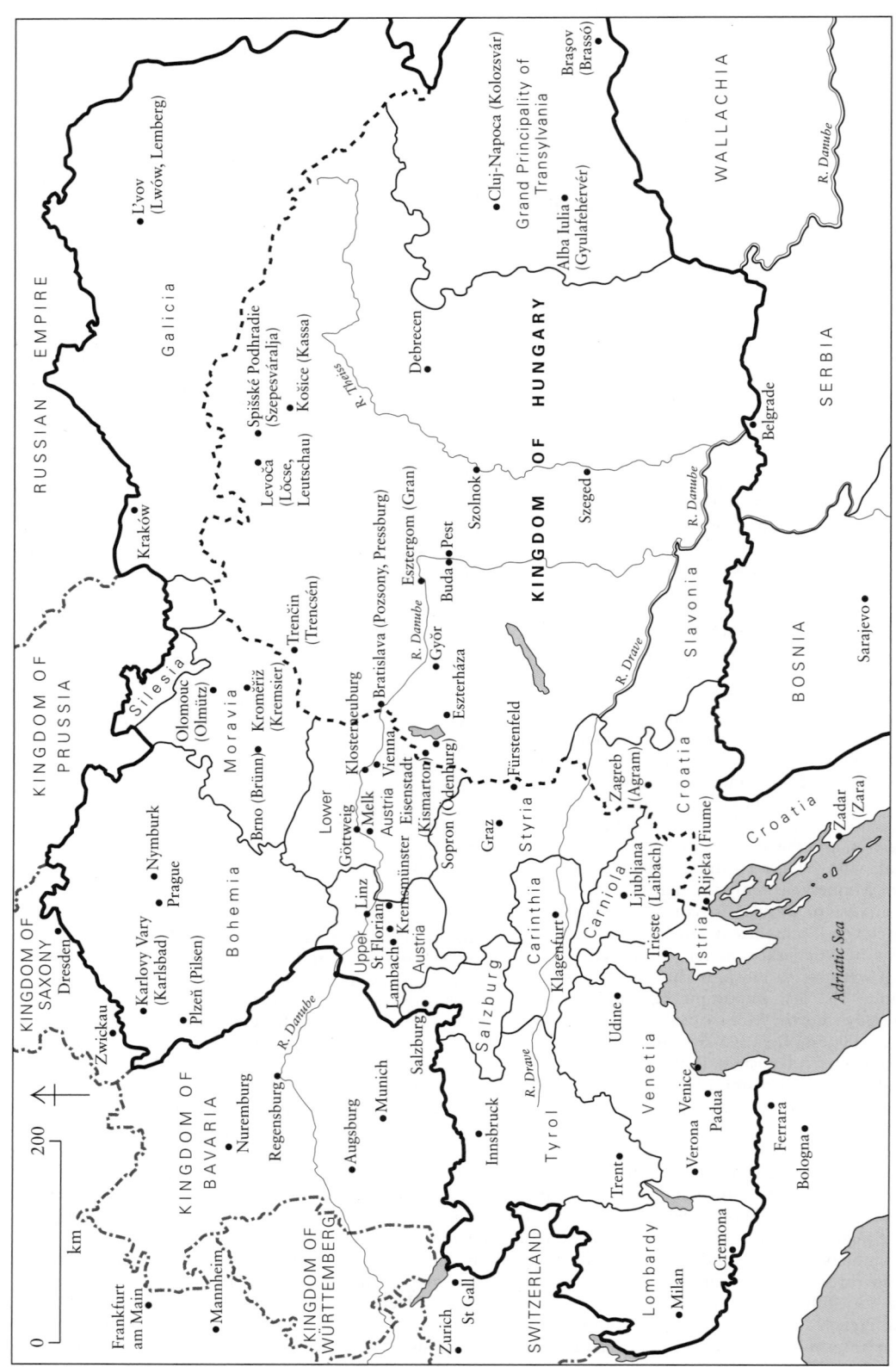

1. Map of the Austro–Hungarian Empire, early to mid-19th century

2. *Pageant car with lutenists and bass viols: woodcut by Hans Burgkmair I from the 'Triumphzug Maximilians', c1516–18*

influence and importance. Outstanding members of the Kapelle of Archduke Ferdinand of the Tyrol (*d* 1595) were Hollander, Regnart and Utendal, while the most distinguished musicians employed by Archduke Karl II in Graz were de Sayve and Cleve, who wrote 20 polyphonic settings of chorale tunes, including some of Protestant origins; they were published in Andre Gigler's *Gesang Postill* (1569 and 1574), the earliest music volume printed in Styria. The sacred works of such composers spread beyond court circles and into the monasteries, as demonstrated by surviving choirbooks and inventories. Archduchess Magdalena's Kapelle at the convent at Hall, Tyrol, was directed by another Netherlander, Franz Sales.

The Graz court, because of its geographical location, was the first to experience the Italian influence that gradually eclipsed that of the Netherlands. Annibale Padovano, an organist at S Marco, Venice, went to Graz in 1565 as principal instrumentalist and succeeded Cleve as Kapellmeister in 1570. On the death of Archduke Karl II in 1590 the Graz Kapelle, then directed by Gatto, was largely made up of Italians, including the organist Rovigo and the singer Zacconi. The process of Italianization continued under Karl II's successor, Archduke Ferdinand of Styria (later emperor), who employed such well-known musicians as Bianco, Giovanni Priuli, Stivori and Giovanni Valentini (i). Ferdinand sent Alessandro Tadei, later court organist at Graz, to study under Giovanni Gabrieli; thus the only surviving Gabrieli autographs came to be in the Styrian Landesarchiv in Graz. Later Netherlandish musicians in Austria also felt the Italian influence, as shown by Monte's madrigals, Regnart's villanellas and the polyphonic sacred works of de Sayve, who wrote exclusively in a Venetian style. The Netherlandish musicians were usually trained as singers, whereas most of the Italians were accomplished instrumentalists. The development of polyphony was not confined to the courts, and even before the Reformation, sacred and secular music in towns was in the hands of schoolmasters and Kantors, assisted by *Türmer* (watchmen) and town musicians. At a celebration of Mass in 1485 at St Daniel, the oldest

church in the Gail Valley (Carinthia), the best singers and instrumentalists took part. The humanist Vadian studied music in Villach, and he taught at the town's thriving Lateinschule between 1506 and 1508. The earliest known guild of musicians in German-speaking lands was the Nicolai-Bruderschaft in Vienna, which was founded in 1288 and survived until 1782 when Joseph II disbanded all such brotherhoods. In some places the post of *Spielgraf* (which also appears to date from the 13th century) was created; for example, in 1464 an imperial court trumpeter, Wolfgang Wetter, held the post for Styria, Carinthia and Carniola (now part of Slovenia). Musicians and bellfounders were already established in Salzburg in the 12th and 13th centuries, and can be traced from the first half of the 15th century in the Carinthian towns of Friesach, Völkermarkt, Klagenfurt, Wolfsberg and St Veit. Noteworthy Austrian and foreign organ builders appeared from the 15th century onwards, including Heinrich Traxdorf from Mainz, who built an organ at St Peter, Salzburg, in 1444, and Hofhaimer, who was associated with Jan Behaim of Dubraw.

From the 15th and 16th centuries sacred and secular instrumental music in towns was often made the responsibility of a *Türmer*, a municipal appointment, while the *Landschaftstrompeter* and *Heerpauker*, who can be traced in Styria from 1527 to 1861, were typically employed by the nobility merely to swell their state; but in the late 16th century some of these musicians also performed polyphony at the Protestant abbey in Graz. The art of Meistergesang left few traces in Austria: *Singschulen* existed in Schwaz (Tyrol) from before 1532, in Steyr (Upper Austria) from 1542, from about 1549 in Wels (Upper Austria), where Hans Sachs had spent a short time in 1513, and from 1604 in Eferding (Upper Austria). The possible existence of *Singschulen* in Waidhofen an der Ybbs and Wiener Neustadt (Lower Austria), Eisenerz (Styria) and Moosburg (Carinthia) is suggested by the histories of individual Meistersinger. Music printing was introduced in Vienna in the early 16th century; music theorists were active chiefly in Vienna (e.g. Simon de

Quercu, Venceslaus Philomathes and Stephan Monetarius) and in Salzburg (Johannes Stomius, an associate of Hofhaimer).

In the 16th and early 17th centuries many people became Protestants. Preachers, schoolmasters and organists arrived from countries with an older Protestant tradition, bringing with them the Lutheran chorale. Better-known Protestant composers included Brassicanus, Hitzler (an editor who transmitted the local hymn repertory and was also a prominent theorist) and Rosthius in Linz; Peuerl in Horn (Lower Austria) and Steyr (Upper Austria); Lagkhner in Loosdorf (Lower Austria); Widmann in Graz and Eisenerz (Styria); Fritzius in Kapfenberg (Styria); Johannes Herold and Posch in Klagenfurt; and Rauch in Hernals and Inzersdorf (both near Vienna). However, the most important composer born in the Tyrol, Lechner, a Protestant convert, worked chiefly in Nuremberg. The Counter-Reformation gradually brought an end to the Protestant music tradition in Austria, which began to decline as early as 1600 and died out after the Battle of the White Mountain in 1620. But the religious schism did not impair cultural development; works of Catholic composers such as Lassus were often used in Protestant services, while organists such as Perini in Graz moved freely between employment in Catholic ducal courts and Protestant churches.

3. THE BAROQUE ERA. When Emperor Matthias died in 1619, his Netherlandish-dominated Hofkapelle was replaced by the Italianized establishment brought from Graz by his heir Archduke Ferdinand of Inner Austria (Ferdinand II), an event which marked the beginning of a Baroque musical style in Vienna and, in spite of the Thirty Years War and the Turkish invasions, the most brilliant period of the imperial Hofkapelle. During the 17th century and the first half of the 18th, the Habsburg emperors, among whom Ferdinand III, Leopold I and Joseph I were themselves reputable composers, brought a large number of notable Italian musicians to the Viennese court: Bertali, Sances, Draghi, Ziani, Bononcini, Caldara, Conti, Porsile, Badia, Palotta and Bonno. Opera was first produced at the court in about 1630 and was firmly established there by the reign of Leopold I. It became a regular part of festive occasions such as namedays, birthdays, births and weddings in the imperial family, princely visits and coronations. A great theatrical event of the 17th century was the performance for Leopold I's wedding in Vienna (1668) of *Il pomo d'oro* by Cesti, who was Kapellmeister in Innsbruck from 1652 and, after the Tyrolean Habsburg line died out, assistant Kapellmeister in Vienna from 1666. Opera became established even earlier in Salzburg, under Archbishop Marcus Sitticus (1612–18), with a performance of an *Orfeo* setting in 1614, followed by an *Andromeda* in 1616. Francesco Rasi, who had links with the Camerata in Florence, presented Archbishop Sitticus with a manuscript collection of his sacred and secular monodies in 1612. Bartolomeo Mutis, Count of Cesana, whose presence at the court of Graz can be traced from 1604, was the first Italian composer working north of the Alps to have secular monodies printed (*Musiche*, Venice, 1613); he moved to Vienna with Ferdinand II. G.B. Bonometti, court tenor in Graz and later in Vienna, dedicated *Parnassus musicus Ferdinandaeus* (Venice, 1615) to the emperor; this comprehensive anthology of motets for one to five voices with figured bass contains chiefly works by

well-known contemporaries, at least nine of them from the Graz court, and it shows the impact of the early Baroque style on sacred music in Austria. Another example is the *Harmonia concertans* (Nuremberg, 1623) by Posch, who was active in Carinthia and Carniola and acknowledged the influence of Viadana.

Instrumental music developed rapidly during the 17th century. G.M. Radino, later organist in Padua, and his son Giulio, whose concertos were published in Venice in 1607, served the Khevenhüllers, a powerful Carinthian noble family. In 1618–19 polyphonic canzonas and sonatas by the Graz Hofkapellmeister Priuli were printed in Venice; motets by Bernardi appeared in Salzburg (1634) and sacred works by Valentini in Vienna (1621). Early variation suites were composed by Peuerl in Steyr and, a little later, by Posch. It was as instrumentalists that Austrians first replaced foreign musicians. Hofhaimer (who was born in Radstadt) was the most important 16th-century organist. Two musicians at the Graz court were outstanding cornett players: Georg Poss, Kapellmeister to Archduke Karl, Bishop of Breslau in 1618, and Giovanni Sansoni, who had connections with Schütz. In 17th-century Vienna, the outstanding keyboard composers were Froberger and Kerll, and, on a lower plane, Ebner and Poglietti. The foundations of the Viennese violin school were laid by Italians such as Buonamente and Bertali. The long succession of Italian imperial Hofkapellmeister was finally broken in 1679–80 by the appointment of J.H. Schmelzer, an Austrian violinist and composer of international reputation. It was principally as a ballet and song composer that he introduced an indigenous element into the Venetian-dominated court music. Biber, a key figure in the development of violin music, was Hofkapellmeister in Salzburg. Muffat was his organist before becoming Kapellmeister at Passau in 1690; he studied in Paris (with Lully) and in Rome (with Corelli) and his conscious fusion of the Italian, French and German musical languages typifies the so-called *vermischter Stil*. The rise of instrumental music encouraged instrument making. Jacob Stainer of Absam founded the Tyrolean school of violin making, and notable organ builders included the families of Egedacher in Salzburg, Schwarz in Graz, and Römer in Vienna, as well as Henke and Sonnholz in Vienna, Gabler (who died during the construction of the organ in St Gallus, Bregenz, in 1771) and Chrismann, who built the organ of St Florian that later was associated with Bruckner.

Austrian taste in church music and opera was conservative; once Italian innovations were adopted, they were retained tenaciously. The Venetian polychoral style in Austria is exemplified by Valentini's *Messa, Magnificat et Jubilate Deo* (Vienna, 1621) for seven choirs, and the anonymous 53-part festival mass with continuo performed in Salzburg Cathedral, probably in 1682; it was still cultivated for its impressive effect in the time of Fux (e.g. his *Missa SS Trinitatis*). The church music of Johann Stadlmayr (d 1648), the best-known Innsbruck composer of the time, is also conservative. A type of oratorio, the *sepolcro*, was created by Viennese opera composers for worshipping the Holy Sepulchre during Holy Week. Baroque music in Austria reached its high point under the musically discerning Emperor Charles VI (1711–40), during whose reign the Turks were finally driven from Austrian territory. The Styrian composer and theorist Fux was imperial Hofkapellmeister from 1715 until his death in 1741. Fux's sacred works, his most significant achievement, became widely known outside the court, especially in other parts of the empire. His music reflects a typical Baroque balance between older and more modern stylistic elements. The operas, oratorios and *sepolcri* of Fux and of his vice-Hofkapellmeister Caldara reflect for the last time the splendour of the imperial court (fig.4).

In the second half of the 17th century, the influence of the composition teaching of Christoph Bernhard (a pupil of Schütz) is evident in treatises by Poglietti, Kerll, Prinner and Samber. Andreas Hofer and Georg Muffat (whose 1699 manuscript treatise contains important elucidation of thoroughbass practice) were teachers of Samber, a Salzburg theorist who published a *Manuductio ad organum* and *Continuatio ad manuductionem organicum* (Salzburg, 1704, 1707), treatises which were succeeded by the frequently reprinted *Fundamenta partiturae* (Salzburg, 1719) of Samber's pupil, Matthäus Gugl. But it was

Fux who became the first Austrian music theorist to achieve a European reputation, with his textbook on strict counterpoint, *Gradus ad Parnassum* (Vienna, 1725). The composer M.S. Biechteler von Greiffenthal was active in Salzburg from 1706; his sacred music was conservative but his instrumental works, notably the trio sonatas, show modern, Neapolitan tendencies.

After the Counter-Reformation monastic culture revived, predominantly under the Jesuits and Benedictines, and continued to flourish until the reforms of Joseph II (reigned 1780–90) struck its death-blow. The close connections between the church and schools gave music education a broad base. The works of numerous church and monastic composers such as J.G. Zechner became widely known.

An official report made in Klagenfurt in 1742 reveals the organization of musical life in towns. For centuries the schoolmaster both directed the church choir and sang

3. *Banquet in the King's Chamber, Vienna, following the Ceremony of Oaths of Allegiance sworn to Charles as Archduke of Austria, 8 November 1705: engraving by Johann Andreas Pfeffel and C. Engelbrecht after Johann Cyriak Hackhofer*

4. *Naval battle during the open-air performance of Fux's opera 'Angelica vincitrice di Alcina' in the gardens of the Favorita, Vienna, 14 September 1716, in celebration of the birth of Prince Leopold: engraving by Elias Schaffhauser after designs by Giuseppe Galli-Bibiena*

bass, and was assisted by an organist, two descant singers (boys), an alto, a tenor and the *Türmer* with his associates, who played the string instruments. These were the usual forces in town churches, where surviving music from Leoben (Styria), Gmünd and elsewhere indicate that polyphony was common in services. In the mid-17th century the parish musicians of Graz joined with the *Türmer* and town violinists to form a musicians' guild. A charter granted by Ferdinand III in 1650 assured them a privileged position in the city's musical life, but also imposed on them the obligation to provide music in the parish churches. Similar conditions, laid down by charters and privileges, also obtained elsewhere until the time of Joseph II.

4. PRE-CLASSICISM AND CLASSICISM. The adoption of popular elements into art music, which were already a feature of the 16th-century German Gesellschaftslied, reached court circles, as exemplified by Prinner's thoroughbass songs for Archduchess Maria Antonia and German vocal music by Leopold I. In instrumental works of the transition period from Baroque to Classicism composers placed increasing emphasis on easily assimilable melody. This can be seen in the works of Gottlieb Muffat (Georg's son and a pupil of Fux), George Reutter (i), Monn and Wagenseil in Vienna; Eberlin, Adlgasser (whose best music is found in his *Schuldramen* and sacred works) and Leopold Mozart (who was most important as a teacher) in Salzburg; Steinbacher and Sgatberoni in Styria; and Haindl and Madlseder in the Tyrol. The divertimento and the string quartet gradually replaced the suite; the south German keyboard concerto took hold, owing much to the Italian violin concerto but independent of the north German keyboard concerto; the symphony became independent of the opera overture; and the *sonata da camera* ultimately led to the modern piano sonata and the genres for chamber ensemble with piano, such as the violin sonata, piano trio and piano quartet.

From the first half of the 18th century, performances outside the court theatres made opera accessible to the general public, in the Vienna Kärntnertortheater (from 1728) and by Italian itinerant troupes such as Pietro and Angelo Mingotti's company. *Opera buffa* rapidly became popular: Mingotti produced Pergolesi's *La serva padrona* in Graz as early as 1739. Soon after the middle of the century, Vienna saw the first example of Gluck's operatic reforms; in this process of renewal numerous minor masters also played their part. The combination of French and Italian stylistic features with German ones created the basis of Viennese Classicism, whose greatest representatives were Haydn, Mozart and Beethoven. This culture, enjoyed by the bourgeoisie as well as by the aristocracy, established Austrian musical pre-eminence.

After the deaths of Charles VI (1740) and Fux (1741), the imperial Hofkapelle forfeited its leading role in musical life. Its later directors included such estimable but historically unimportant composers as Predieri, J.G. Reutter, Gassmann (who instigated the founding of the Vienna Tonkünstler-Societät in 1772), Bonno and Salieri. The many aristocratic Kapellen, of all sizes, were more progressive, especially that of the Esterházys, associated with Haydn. Aristocratic and middle-class amateurs vied with each other in private and public concerts, spreading musical culture and encouraging music publishing, in which Austria had previously lagged behind Italy, England, the Netherlands, France and Germany. Music printing developed rapidly in Vienna from the end of the 18th century, with the establishment of the houses of Artaria, F.A. Hoffmeister, S.A. Steiner, Tobias Haslinger, Anton Diabelli, C.A. Spina and others. Through the reforms of Joseph II, astute at least in their social application, Austria was spared the fate of France at the end of the 18th century. Although Italians continued to play important roles in Austrian musical life well into the 19th century, they had already passed the height of their influence by the 1750s. Joseph II also gave new significance

5. *Music making in a monastic community: drawing by Josef Bergler the younger, c1785 (Kupferstichkabinett, Berlin)*

to the traditional military band (usually two each of oboes, bassoons and horns) by appointing such an ensemble, at a high level of proficiency and supplemented by two clarinets, as the Kaiserliche Kammer-Harmonie, to play *Tafelmusik* in place of the Hofkapelle band. This 'Harmoniemusik' ensemble became popular among the aristocracy of central Europe; Prince Schwarzenberg had such a group and Prince Liechtenstein planned to establish one in 1782. A similar group already existed at the Esterházy court in Eisenstadt. Composers who wrote or transcribed music for such ensembles were, besides Mozart and Haydn, Druschetzky, Gassmann, Joseph Fiala, Karl Kreith, Mysliveček, Rosetti, Salieri, Georg and Josef Triebensee, Johann Went and G.C. Wagenseil. The ensemble was later enlarged with flutes, trumpets, trombones and janissary instruments, and sometimes double bass or double bassoon. In mid-19th century this combination provided the basis of the new Austrian and community wind band movement. (*See* BAND (i), §II, 2(ii), and HARMONIEMUSIK).

The Viennese Singspiel evolved after 1760, influenced by *opera buffa* and *opéra comique*, but with its roots in popular comedy with musical interludes, such as the *Teutsche Comœdie-Arien* (*c*1750) attributed to Haydn. Mozart's *Bastien und Bastienne*, possibly written for performance at Dr Johann Anton Mesmer's house in Vienna, belongs to the new genre, which Joseph II encouraged by establishing a national Singspiel company in the Burgtheater. It opened in 1778 with Ignaz Umlauf's *Die Bergknappen* (fig.7) and reached its zenith with Mozart's *Die Entführung aus dem Serail* (1782). Italian opera provided strong competition and the German opera company soon closed down (which is why Mozart went back to Italian texts); but popular Singspiele by Ditters-

dorf, J.B. Schenk, J.B. Weigl, Haibel (Mozart's brother-in-law), Wenzel Müller and others had numerous performances at non-court theatres and became widely known outside Vienna. The crown of the genre was Mozart's *Die Zauberflöte*, first performed in Vienna in 1791, which had a profound influence on the development of German Romantic opera in the 19th century.

If German opera owed its classic form to Mozart, German oratorio was moulded by Haydn, whose *The Creation* (1798) and *The Seasons* (1801) had their first performances in Prince Schwarzenberg's Vienna palace. Church music too owed its classic profile to Mozart and Haydn, while the latter's brother Michael in Salzburg, Weber's teacher, made a specially large and pervasive contribution to the 19th-century liturgical repertory throughout the empire. The musical heritage of Mozart and Haydn passed to Beethoven, who made Vienna his home. Rejecting the ties of a permanent post which his deafness would have made impossible, he composed independently, though with the support of various noble patrons, notably his talented pupil Archduke Rudolph. Beethoven embodied the ideals of the middle class, which had newly come of age. Through Beethoven, who was no longer writing to commission, absolute music underwent an extraordinary expansion of its expressive potential and its forms, and an imposing legacy was created for future generations of composers.

5. ROMANTICISM. Beethoven's contemporaries and near-contemporaries in Austria include such respected composers as Albrechtsberger (an eminent theorist, with whom Beethoven studied), Eberl, E.A. Förster, Gyrowetz, J.N. Hummel, Leopold Kozeluch, Wölfl, Paul and Anton Wranitzky; and Czerny (a pupil of Beethoven) attracted numerous piano pupils, the most celebrated being Liszt.

Ignaz Schuppanzigh established the Viennese tradition of public quartet recitals; the most prominent violin teachers and performers were Joseph Mayseder and Joseph Bœhm (the teacher of Ernst), Joseph Joachim (born, like Liszt, in the then Hungarian Burgenland) and the elder Georg Hellmesberger. Schubert, a generation younger than Beethoven, reinforced Austria's musical supremacy and established the importance of the lied. Like Beethoven, he wrote many of his works in Vienna or the immediate vicinity, but in 1827 ventured further afield, to Graz, where his old friend and fellow pupil of Salieri, Anselm Hüttenbrenner, the best-known Styrian composer between Fux and Hugo Wolf, came into possession of the 'Unfinished' Symphony. In 1865 he gave it to the Viennese Hofkapellmeister, Johann von Herbeck, for performance, and it finally became the property of the Gesellschaft der Musikfreunde in Vienna. This association of music lovers, led by Joseph Sonnleithner, had been officially founded in 1814 in succession to the Gesellschaft Adeliger Frauen, founded in 1812, and soon became one of the foremost institutions of Viennese concert life and a model for music societies founded by both noble and middle-class amateurs in Innsbruck, Graz (1815), Radkersburg (Styria, 1820), Linz, Klagenfurt (1828), Fürstenfeld (1832) and other towns. In 1819 F.X. Gebauer and Eduard von Lannoy, a native of Brussels, founded the Viennese Concerts Spiri-

tuels, which performed mostly Beethoven. Lannoy also contributed articles on music to Ignaz Jeitteles's *Ästhetisches Lexicon* (Vienna, 1835–7). In Salzburg, public musical life suffered a setback as a result of extreme political instability (it changed rulers four times between 1803 and 1816, when it fell to the Habsburgs) but revived with the foundation in 1841 of the Dommusikverein und Mozarteum, through the initiative of Franz von Hilleprandt. The first Mozart festival took place in 1842, under the direction of Neukomm and with Mozart's two sons participating, on the occasion of the unveiling of the statue by Schwanthaler. In the meantime, Vienna was consolidating its position as a musical capital. Rossini celebrated one triumph after another there, beginning with *Tancredi* in 1816, and Donizetti and Bellini followed soon afterwards. Paganini and Liszt were outstanding among the instrumentalists who dominated public concerts during the first half of the century. The declining standards of the opera and concerts drew sharp criticism from Schumann, who failed to establish himself in Vienna in 1838 but discovered the 'Great' C major Symphony in Schubert's legacy. Orchestras normally consisted of amateurs, reinforced by professional players only on special occasions; standards rose only after the institution of the Philharmonic concerts by Nicolai and his colleagues in 1842; from 1860 they became the centre of Viennese concert life.

6. *Festsaal (now known as the Haydn-saal) in the Esterházy Palace, Eisenstadt, where concerts were held*

The Viennese waltz developed during the Biedermeier era in the hands of Joseph Lanner and Johann Strauss (i), its origins lying in the Upper Austrian ländler, the *Steirer* (from Styria) and the *Deutscher* ('German dances'), which Mozart, Haydn and Schubert admired and composed. Culminating with the composer and conductor Johann Strauss (ii), the waltz conquered the concert halls and ballrooms of the world. *An der schönen blauen Donau* became the most famous Viennese waltz and *Die Fledermaus* (first performed in 1874) marked the high point of the dance-inspired Viennese classical operetta, a genre owing much to Wenzel Müller's earthy and popular incidental music for the plays of Raimund and Nestroy, as well as to Offenbach's tumultuously acclaimed operettas. Josef and Eduard Strauss were also conductors and prolific composers, who helped their brother to sweep the world with Strauss dances. Franz Suppé and Carl Millöcker did the same for operetta, with remarkable interpreters like Marie Geistinger and Alexander Girardi contributing to their success.

A widespread awareness of traditional music, previously transmitted only orally, arose during the Romantic era and led to systematic collections and catalogues. Concert performances, which adapted traditional music to the conventions of art music, were given by the 'Alpensänger' on successful tours abroad. Song inspired by traditional influences also became immensely popular; for example, both *Stille Nacht, heilige Nacht*, written in 1818 in Arnsdorf in the province of Salzburg, with words

by a village priest, Josef Mohr, and music by the schoolmaster and organist F.X. Gruber, and the sentimental song in Carinthian folk style, *Verlassen bin i*, by Thomas Koschat, were translated into many languages. Other forms of popular music which have retained their appeal are the songs associated with the inns in the vineyards of the Viennese suburbs (*Wirtshaus-* and *Heurigenlieder*), *Schrammelmusik*, named after the brothers Johann and Joseph Schrammel, and military marches, evolved from bugle calls as well as from traditional songs and soldiers' songs and mostly composed by regimental bandmasters and bandsmen, notably Philipp Fahrbach (father and son), Julius Fučik, Joseph Gungl, Karel Komzák (father and son), Franz Lehár (father and son), E.N. von Reznicek, Josef and V.H. Zavrtal and C.M. Ziehrer.

Male-voice choral singing, harking back to Michael Haydn, received considerable impetus from the 1848 Revolution. Choral societies were founded in many cities and towns around the middle of the century, including a Männergesangverein in Vienna (1843), in Salzburg (1844) and in Graz (1846), of which one of the first chorus masters was Conradin Kreutzer. A community band movement began to develop in the same period.

Austrian supremacy in instrumental music and song in the second half of the 19th century was maintained by Brahms, Bruckner and Wolf. The development of opera was determined by Wagner, who, despite critical hostility, found rapid public favour, especially in Vienna and Graz,

7. *Catarina Cavalieri as Sophie in a scene from Umlauf's singspiel 'Die Bergknappen', Burgtheater, Vienna, 1778: engraving by J. Adam after Carl Schütz*

8. A musical evening: detail from 'Symphony' by Moritz von Schwind, 1852 (Neue Pinakothek, Munich)

9. Musicians playing clarinet, horn, bassoon and violin: table-sign, oil on tin, from Neuburg, Styria, first half of the 19th century

where *Tannhäuser* was performed in 1854 before its Viennese première. Wagner visited Vienna ten times between 1832 and 1876. Joseph Hellmesberger (i), Hanslick and Julius Epstein introduced Brahms to musical Vienna, which became a second home for him, the heir of the Viennese Classical composers, as it had been for Beethoven. Other Austrian towns associated with Brahms include Bad Ischl, Pörtschach on the Wörther See (Carinthia) and Mürzzuschlag (Styria), where he spent summers. Bruckner lived more than half his life in Upper Austria and is the province's outstanding composer. He was an organist and conductor in St Florian and Linz until 1868, when he became a teacher of theory and the organ at the Vienna Conservatory. Despite Wagner's influence, the organ remained the determining factor for his conception of orchestral sound. The dispute between the supporters of Brahms and Bruckner was aggravated by the influential critic Hanslick and his championship of Brahms. Nevertheless the co-existence of diverse artistic personalities remained a characteristic of Austrian musical culture. Hugo Wolf first studied the piano at Johann Buwa's music school in Graz, one of the most important music academies in Styria. Wolf then studied with the Styrian Robert Fuchs in Vienna, where he spent the rest of his life. There his supporters, including Bruckner's pupil Joseph Schalk, enthusiastically promoted his songs. Noteworthy achievements in popular opera were made by Brüll and Kienzl. Graz was outstanding among the provincial cities in the second half of the 19th century; its opera, where such conductors as Carl Muck, Schalk and, in the early 20th century, Krauss, Oswald Kabasta and Böhm acquainted the public with contemporary as well as classical works, was for performers a springboard to the most famous theatres. The music theorist W.A. Rémy (1831–98), who came to Graz from Prague, taught Busoni, Reznicek, Kienzl, Weingartner and Heuberger. At the same time the Carinthian-born Friedrich von Hausegger worked in Graz as a critic and aesthetician, advocating Wagner's ideas. In Salzburg in 1880 the Internationale Mozart-Stiftung, founded by Carl von Sterneck in 1869–70, united with the Mozarteum (which had severed its links with the Dommusikverein) to form the Internationale Stiftung Mozarteum.

6. THE 20TH CENTURY. In the years around 1890 the culture representative of the Austrian monarchy came face to face with an aggressive modernity. In close relation to literature, architecture and the visual arts (the Vienna Sezession movement was founded in 1897), music experienced a radical renewal, bridging the much debated gulf between Brahms on the one side and Bruckner and Wagner on the other. The first prominent figure in this progressive movement was Mahler (fig.10). The Vienna Hofoper, of which he was director from 1897 to 1907, was at the centre of the intellectual debate; Mahler's adherents included Egon Wellesz, Berg, Webern, Schoenberg, Stefan Zweig, Klimt, Freud and Guido Adler. Until the anti-modern (and anti-Semitic) change of direction in the 1920s, the Musikhistorisches Institut of Vienna University, founded by Adler in 1898, was another refuge for contemporary composers. Its graduates included Karl Weigl, Webern, Wellesz, Hans Gál and Ernst Toch. Weigl, Bruno Walter, Zemlinsky and others worked as Kapellmeister under Mahler and continued his tradition of perfectionism in performance. Zemlinsky was a major figure as both conductor and composer, and his pupils

10. *Gustav Mahler: portrait by Arnold Schoenberg, 1910 (private collection)*

and colleagues included Weigl, Alma Schindler (who married Mahler in 1902), Korngold, Hans Krása, Viktor Ullmann and Webern. The self-taught Schoenberg, in particular, regarded Zemlinsky as the foremost authority on music and a committed campaigner on behalf of musical innovation When Schoenberg set out to dissolve traditional tonality around 1908, he was still working closely with Zemlinsky. However, although Zemlinsky kept abreast of these increasingly experimental procedures, he did not adopt them in his own compositions. Schoenberg himself became the next entral figure of modern music in Austria. His pupils in Vienna included Webern, Berg, Wellesz, Hanns Eisler, Edward Steuermann, Max Deutsch, Hans Erich Apostel and Ullmann.

Even composers who were not close to the Second Viennese School in technique or aesthetic outlook shared the sense of a new departure that it inspired. Josef Mattias Hauer had developed a 12-note system by about 1920, in parallel to Schoenberg, although the musical results were quite different. Franz Schreker, who had studied modern painting and literature as well as the early work of Schoenberg and the music of Zemlinsky and Richard Strauss, became one of the most frequently performed German-language operatic composers of the 1910s and 20s. With the advent after World War I of the Neue Sachlichkeit movement, which originated in Berlin rather than Vienna, Schreker came to be regarded as a late Romantic, although as a teacher of Ernst Krenek, Max Brand and Felix Petyrek he had paved the way for some of the most successful composers of the 1920s.

The central position of Vienna in the final years of the Austro-Hungarian monarchy is perceptible in many crosscurrents: for instance, Mahler had already reorganized the Budapest Opera before he was appointed to Vienna; Lehár settled in Vienna only after spending years in Budapest, Prague and Trieste; and Zemlinsky remained in touch with Vienna during his 16 years as director of the Prague German Theatre. The independent musical life of Graz, Salzburg and Innsbruck, too, was perceptibly influenced by developments in Vienna.

After the collapse of the monarchy, the musical life of the much smaller republic of Austria showed an increasingly anti-modern bias. The departure of Schreker and Schoenberg for Berlin, in 1920 and 1926 respectively, marked a wave of emigration; musicians leaving Vienna for Berlin alone included Karol Rathaus, Krenek, Max Brand (fig.11), Felix Petyrek, Toch and Eisler, as well as many composers of operetta and film music (notably Ralph Benatzky, Robert Stolz, Nico Dostal, Wilhelm Grosz and Hans J. Salter). Those who stayed in Austria, including Joseph Marx (i) and Franz Schmidt, composed mainly in a late Romantic style. Moreover, anti-Semitic, pro-Nazi sentiment was becoming increasingly evident (a Nazi poster campaign was mounted against Krenek's *Jonny spielt auf* in Vienna in 1928). In this fascist climate Austria offered a congenial home only to composers and performers of innocuous light music. For countless musicians the Anschluss of 1938 meant exile or internal emigration, and in some cases arrest and deportation. A cursory glance at the Austrians in Californian exile alone indicates the scale of this exodus: émigrés included Schoenberg, Eisler, Krenek, Walter, Toch, Oscar Straus, Rathaus, Stolz, Eric Zeisl, Korngold, Salter, Max Steiner, Ernest Gold and many others. With the forcible exclusion of a huge number of Jews, Catholics, patriots, socialists and communists, Austria was dominated by an 'Aryanized' adherence to tradition which excluded jazz, Neue Sachlichkeit, Expressionism, dodecaphony and all forms of experimentation.

The situation remained largely unchanged in the years following the war. With the revival of Austrian national awareness, music-making was dominated by the traditional Classical and Romantic repertory. The influential *Österreichische Musikzeitschrift* (ÖMZ) was founded in 1946, and the Vienna Staatsoper, which had been destroyed in the war, was reopened in 1955, the year of the reconstitution of Austria as an independent and democratic country. Little was done, however, to reintegrate the exiles. The post-Romantic composers (Joseph Marx (i), Egon Kornauth, Ernst Ludwig Uray, Otto Siegl) retained their influence and their high reputation, especially in Graz. Meanwhile, neo-classicism, as represented by such composers as Marcel Rubin, Alfred Uhl, Paul Angerer and, to a lesser extent, Gottfried von Einem, was widely regarded as a progressive style; the most influential models for composers up to the 1960s were Hindemith, Stravinsky and Bartók.

A smaller group of composers, notably Robert Schollum, Karl Schiske and Helmut Eder, cultivated a synthesis of tonality and the serial techniques of the Second Viennese School. But in general the implications of the Viennese School still remained as ignored as the experimentation of Neue Sachlichkeit (which was a topic among the young postwar composers, e.g. Paul Kont and Gerhard Rühm). The remaining disciples of the Second Viennese School (Hans Erich Apostel, Hanns Jelinek) came to reject the postwar serialists' interpretation of Webern, and themselves were regarded outside Austria as conservative.

11. Set design by Johannes Schröder for Prologue scene ii (the machine hall) in Max Brand's 'Maschinist Hopkins', Stadttheater, Duisburg, 13 April 1929 (Theatermuseum, University of Cologne)

International recognition among avant-garde composers was achieved first by the Hungarian exile György Ligeti, and later Friedrich Cerha, with their striking post-serial compositions, and by Roman Haubenstock-Ramati, who took his guidelines more from innovations in the visual arts than from the musical avant garde of the postwar period. Pupils of Schiske who took part in the Darmstadt summer courses (Gösta Neuwirth, Erich Urbanner, Kurt Schwertsik, Otto M. Zykan) tended to maintain a sceptical or playful distance from the avant-garde belief in progress. A pointedly detached reaction that emerged after the 1960s was a style of neo-tonality tinged with irony (Schwertsik, Zykan, H.K. Gruber). Since then, more and more composers have cultivated an anti-experimental striving for 'comprehensibility' and 'naturalness' (Iván Eröd and, later, Herbert Willi) or have sought to intermingle 'serious' music, 'light' music and jazz (Gerhard Wimberger, Werner Pirchner and, later, Franz Koglmann and others).

But the diminishing impact of specific schools on compositional techniques or styles in Austria has from the 1980s onward, again paved the way for more determined efforts of composers to be innovative. Even composers of similar aesthetic orientation G.F. Haas, Beat Furrer, Christian Ofenbauer, Wolfram Schurig, Bernhard Lang, Klaus Lang and Olga Neuwirth) have adopted highly individual standpoints. A number of composers draw on extra-musical stimuli, taken from film and video (Neuwirth), literature (Gerhard Rühm, Clemens Gadenstätter), performance art and visual art (Peter Ablinger, Nader Mashayekhi, Hermann Nitsch). In the field of performance this spirit of innovation has been reinforced by internationally renowned ensembles (Die Reihe, founded 1958; Klangforum Wien, founded 1985) and by festivals (the Musikprotokoll at the Styrian Autumn Festival, Graz, from 1968; Wien Modern, founded in 1988).

Electronic music studios were founded at institutions in Salzburg, Vienna and Graz 1965. Since then the cultivation of electronic music in Austria has ranged from 'acousmatics' (Dieter Kaufmann) through computer composition (Karlheinz Essl) and media art (the 'Kunstradio' of Österreichischer Rundfunk) to ambient music and noise music (Christian Fennesz). In addition, jazz (the Vienna Art Orchestra), improvised music (Wolfgang Mitterer, Burkhard Stangl, Werner Dafeldecker, Radu Malfatti, Fritz Novotny) and the 'Austro-pop' initially modelled on American examples have developed as vivid genres. Moreover, the activities of experimental electronic pop labels (mego, Sabotage) in the 1990s are partly a reaction to oligopolistic concentrations in the mass-media industry.

See also GÖTTWEIG; GRAZ; INNSBRUCK; KLOSTERNEUBURG; KREMSMÜNSTER; LAMBACH; LINZ; MELK; ST FLORIAN; SALZBURG; and VIENNA.

BIBLIOGRAPHY

BurneyGN

M. von Millenkovich-Morold: *Die österreichische Tonkunst* (Vienna, 1918)

G. Adler: 'Musik in Österreich', *SMw*, xvi (1928), 3–31

L. Nowak: 'Die Musik in Österreich', *Österreich: Erbe und Sendung im deutschen Raum*, ed. J. Nadler and H. von Srbik (Salzburg, 1936/R), 347–68

R.F. Brauner: *Österreichs neue Musik* (Vienna, 1948)

O. Wessely: 'Die Entwicklung der Musikerziehung in Österreich', *Musikerziehung*, vi (1952–3), 326

O. Wessely: 'Alte Musiklehrbücher aus Österreich', *Musikerziehung*, vii (1953–4), 128–32, 205–9

H.J. Moser: *Die Musik im frühevangelischen Österreich* (Kassel, 1954)

F. Zagiba: *Die ältesten musikalischen Denkmäler zu Ehren des heiligen Leopold, Herzog, und Patron von Österreich: ein Beitrag zur Choralpflege in Österreich am Ausgange des Mittelalters* (Zürich, 1954)

O. Eberstaller: *Orgeln und Orgelbauer in Österreich* (Graz, 1955)

H. Federhofer: 'Die Niederländer an den Habsburgerhöfen in Österreich', *AÖAW*, xciii (1956), 102–20

H. Federhofer: 'Monodie und musica reservata', *DJbM*, ii (1957), 30–36

H. Federhofer: 'Zur handschriftlichen Überlieferung der Musiktheorie in Österreich in der zweiten Hälfte des 17. Jahrhunderts', *Mf*, xi (1958), 264–79

H. Anglès: 'Musikalische Beziehungen zwischen Österreich und Spanien in der Zeit vom 14. bis zum 18. Jahrhundert', *SMw*, xxv (1962), 174–82

W. Suppan: *Steirisches Musiklexikon* (Graz, 1962–6)

Theater in Österreich, Notring Jb 1965(Vienna, 1965)

E. Rameis: *Die österreichische Militärmusik von ihren Anfängen bis zum Jahre 1918*, ed. E. Brixel (Tutzing, 1976)

G. Kars, ed.: *Vie et création musicales* (Rouen, 1977) [incl. essays on 20th-century Austrian music]

R. Schollum: *Das österreichische Lied des 20. Jahrhunderts* (Tutzing, 1977)

R. Flotzinger and G.Gruber, eds.: *Musikgeschichte Österreichs*(Graz, 1977–9, 2/1995)

Musicologica austriaca (1977–) [pubn of the Österreichische Gesellschaft für Musikwissenschaft]

Die süddeutsch-österreichische Orgelmusik im 17. und 18. Jahrhundert: Innsbruck 1979

W. Lipphard: 'Musik in den österreichischen Klöstern der Babenbergerzeit', *Musicologica austriaca*, ii (1979), 48–68

W. Salmen: *Bilder zur Geschichte der Musik in Österreich* (Innsbruck, 1979)

R. Flotzinger, ed.: *Musik in der Steiermark*, Stift Admont, 10 May – 19 Oct 1980 (Graz, 1980) [exhibition catalogue]

W. Pass: *Musik und Musiker am Hof Maximilians II.* (Tutzing, 1980)

R. Flotzinger, ed.: 'Quellen zur österreichischen Musikgeschichte, i: Biographische und topographische Beiträge aus der Allgemeine musikalische Zeitung mit besonderer Rücksicht auf den österreichischen Kaiserstaat (Wien 1817–1824)', *Musicologica austriaca*, iii (1982) [whole issue]

H. Dechant: 'Musikland Österreich', *Welt des Barock*, St Florian Monastery, 25 April – 26 Oct 1986, ed. R. Feuchtmüller and E. Kovacs (Linz, 1986), ii, 162–85 [exhibition catalogue]

S. Lang: *Lexikon österreichischer U-Musik-Komponisten in 20. Jahrhundert* (Vienna, 1986)

L. Kretzenbacher: 'Hiobs-Erinnerungen zwischen Donau und Adria', *Sitzungsberichte der Bayerischen Akademie der Wissenschaften: philosophisch-historische Klasse* (1987), no.1 [whole issue]

J. Trummer: *Kirchenchöre Österreichs* (Graz, 1987)

Österreichische Musiker im Exil: Vienna 1988

R. Flotzinger: *Geschichte der Musik in Österreich: zum Lesen und Nachschlagen* (Graz, 1988)

Musik und Tanz zur Zeit Kaiser Maximilian I.: Innsbruck 1989

O. Kolleritsch, ed.: *Die Wiener Schule und das Hakenkreuz: das Schicksal der Moderne im gesellschaftspolitischen Kontext des 20. Jahrhunderts* (Vienna, 1990)

W. Suppan and J.Janota: *Texte und Melodien der 'Erlauer Spiel'* (Tutzing, 1990)

E. Brixel: 'Zum Signalwesen der Postillione in Österreich-Ungarn', *Musica pannonica*, i (1991), 75–110

W. Suppan: 'Die Harmoniemusik: das private Repräsentations- und Vergnügungsensemble des mitteleuropäischen Adels zwischen Kunst- und gesellschaftlichem Gebrauchswert', *Musica privata . . . Festschrift zum 65. Geburtstag von Walter Salmen*, ed. M. Fink, R. Gstrein and G. Mössmer (Innsbruck, 1991), 151–65

H. Brenner: *Musik als Waffe? Theorie und Praxis der politischen Musikverwendung, dargestellt am Beispiel der Steiermark 1938–1945* (Graz, 1992)

B. Habla, ed.: *Blasmusik und ihre Komponisten im Burgenland* (Eisenstadt, 1993)

H. Zwittkovits: *Die Pflege der zivilen Blasmusik im Burgenland im Spiegel der allgemeinen historischen Entwicklung* (Tutzing, 1993)

K. Blaukopf: *Pioniere empirischer Musikforschung: Österreich und Böhmen als Wiege der modernen Kunstsoziologie* (Vienna, 1995)

F. Stadler and P.Weibel, eds.: *Vortreibung der Vernunft: the Cultural Exodus from Austra*(Vienna and New York, 1995)

D. Wyn Jones, ed.: *Music in Eighteenth Century Austria* (Cambridge, 1996).

II. Folk and traditional music

1. Historical documents (to 1800). 2. Collection and research after 1800. 3. Musical styles.

1. HISTORICAL DOCUMENTS (TO 1800).   Theological and legal writings, iconographic sources and finds of musical instruments provide indirect evidence, from the early Middle Ages onwards, of a wealth of folk music rooted in the pastoral culture of the eastern Alpine area. For instance, an account in the Nonsberger Märtyrerbericht of CE397 gives a detailed description of the function of music and song in the execution of three Christian missionaries: the 'tuba', a kind of bark trumpet, summoned the community to rituals, roused warriors to battle and, like the sound of bells, was supposed to avert misfortune. The singing of the local people was harsh, raucous and appallingly shrill to the ears of a stranger; the 'singers' may, however, have intended to produce such an effect in order to conjure up numinous terrors. This account emphasizes the role of fear and horror in archaic religious ritual and music. The records of the Christian councils at Salzburg and Trent in following centuries refer repeatedly to licentious heathen songs, unbridled pleasure taken in the playing of lutes and pipes, and the clerical Feasts of Fools when musicians and jugglers performed. In particular the church forbade the laments for the departed, described as 'carmina diabolica' (devilish songs), which people used to sing over the dead by night.

Musicians played for dancing, and this was regarded as their principal employment in town and country alike. Many ecclesiastical prohibitions and sermons, condemning secular dancing as a diabolical counterpart of the dance of heaven, show that dancing was widespread and very popular, both in rituals and as entertainment. Historically, musicians practised their art in the region where they lived, for instance in the Tyrol, and in Admont and Aussee in upper Styria. A house in the town of Wels in Upper Austria has pictures of dancing dating from the 15th century, described by Richard Wolfram as the oldest depictions of folkdancing in Austria. Documentation reveals that itinerant and rural musicians played the fife and drum, the fiddle and the bagpipes.

The manuscript tradition which began in 11th-century monasteries provides many references to singing and songs. In the early 14th century, for instance, the Styrian rhyming chronicler Ottokar (from Gaal) not only mentions the 'lotersingarae' and 'muotelsingarae' who used to perform their defamatory songs at the tables of lords and retainers in Vienna, but also gives evidence of the oral transmission of the Nibelungenlied. The early 13th-century Carmina burana manuscripts (*D-Mbs* Clm 4660), made famous by Carl Orff, was compiled in the southern border region of the Bavarian linguistic area, possibly in the Styrian monastery of Seckau or the new foundation at Bressanone in the southern Tyrol.

The invention of printing made it possible to disseminate songs in entirely new ways after the late 15th century. The sacred songs of the Reformation were as much in the spirit of the older, oral tradition as the songs of the Counter-Reformation (Nicolaus Beuttner's *Catholisch Gesang-Buch*, Graz, 1602). Adaptations of folksong for sacred purposes betray their origin when their tunes are specified in handbills and songbooks. As a record of newsworthy events, historical narratives also found their way into the folk tradition, for instance a song about Christian warfare against the Turks printed by Hans Singrener of Vienna in the *Toler melodey* of about 1520–30. Didactic ballads and catechistic legends are found in particular profusion at this time. Examples of the former genre are *Herzog Ernst* (whose tune was used in the early 16th century for the ballad of *Der Ritter aus der Steiermark*), *Tannhäuser*, *Das Schloss in Österreich*, and later ballads of social criticism such as *Die Brombeerbrockerin*, *Ritter Blaubart* (*Halewyn*), *Doktor Faust* and *Der Graf und die Nonne*. An example of the latter genre is *Der Ritter und Martyrer Floriani*, printed in 1705 by Heyinger in Vienna. Handbills very seldom gave musical notation; naming the tune enabled a performer to sing the text. It has been possible to reconstruct many of these tunes, however, from comparative studies of melodies and from recent traditions.

2. COLLECTION AND RESEARCH AFTER 1800.   The concept of the *Volkslied* ('folksong'), formulated by Johann Gottfried Herder in the 1770s, spread in Austria about 1800. The earliest evidence of deliberate folksong collection occurs in the topographical and statistical survey of Neuberg in Styria of 1803, which gives the words and melodies of seven songs, including a *Lulezer* as sung by the dairymaids on the Alpine pastures, in broad melodic construction and without text. The survey was made at the instigation of Archduke Johann and asked for the 'description of the principal popular entertainments and pleasures, rustic games, etc., of the people, with information about the most common folksongs or those peculiar to a certain place, national melodies, with the music if possible, dances, etc., and details of the usual musical instruments'. In this the purpose of early Austrian folksong collections differs from the literary aims of such collectors in Germany as Brentano and Arnim, who edited *Des Knaben Wunderhorn* (1806–8). Probably the most interesting documents from the Archduke Johann collection were those provided by Johann Felix Knaffl, financial administrator of Fohnsdorf. In his 'Attempt at a Statistical Account of the Financial District of Fohnsdorf in the Judenburg Region', he tried to show the difference between the music of rustic performers and the contemporary 'classical' music of such composers as Haydn. He gave a German dance in what he described as its 'botched' version (*verhunzt*,:to his mind, incorrectly harmonized and performed by rustic musicians who could not keep in tune) and also in its 'correct' version (ex.1). The independent Austrian approach to folksong collection at this period is also evident in the appeal for songs to be collected in all parts of the monarchy, made in 1811 by the Viennese Gesellschaft der Musikfreunde.

Also of great documentary value are the first folksong collections to be printed in Austria: Meinert's *Alte teutsche Volkslieder in der Mundart des Kuhländchens* (1817) and Žiška and Schottky's *Oesterreichische Volkslieder* (1819), the former collection without but the latter including musical notation (fig.12: *Drei Wünsche*, from Žiška and Schottky, illustrates the wide-ranging melodic structure found in the Alpine area). Von Spaun's *Lieder, Tänze und Alpenmelodien* (1845) is the first of a series of Austrian literary editions of folksongs. At the same period Alpine

Ex.1 From the Knaffl Manuscript of 1813 (ed. V. von Geramb, 1928): a 'German' dance.

(a) 'botched' version

(b) 'correct' version

Peter Rosegger's suggestion that a 'society for the performance of the old folksong' should be formed (*Bergpredigten*, 1885) led to the founding of the Deutscher Volksgesang-Verein in Wien by Josef Pommer in 1889. This new choral manner of performing folksong, with its national German aspects, spread only slowly in several German-speaking Austrian cities. The journal *Das deutsche Volkslied* began publication in Vienna in 1899, dealt with all activities relating to folksong and continued until 1947. Pommer's name is also connected with the 'production theory', according to which folksongs began as anonymous compositions by the people, who then polished them. Consequently, it was thought, folksongs inherently would be 'of the people', simple, plain, natural, true, heartfelt and national in tone (J. Pommer, 1915, p.155). In 1901 the Viennese publishing firm Universal Edition proposed an independent plan for the collection and publication of Austrian folksongs which was approved by the Minister of Culture. At Pommer's suggestion, this led to the creation in 1904 of a folksong project under the auspices of the Austrian Ministry of Information, whereby a number of experts (linguists, musicologists and folklorists) would coordinate the collection and academic publication of folksongs. However, the outbreak of World War I prevented this plan from being realized. A volume of songs from the Gottschee area, described as being ready for press before 1915, was not completed and published until over 50 years later (in three volumes, 1969–84, ed. Brednich and Suppan). Since the end of World War II, and in changed political circumstances, the Österreichische Volksliedwerk organization has put Pommer's ideas into practice in extracurricular education for young people and adults. Comparative musicological and ethnomusicological work on Austrian folksong was, however, slow to begin.

3. MUSICAL STYLES. The epic and stichic forms of the Gottschee ballad tradition derived from older, medieval styles of song and continued into the 20th century. This tradition was first 'discovered' by German scholars who found relics of the Kudrun epic and the old dialect in the texts, and eventually Walter Wiora pointed out its specific musical character. The people who were moved by the Counts of Ortenberg in the 14th century from the

singers from the Tyrol, Salzburg and Styria toured Europe and America, performing in traditional costume and bringing *Heimatlieder* ('homeland songs') and traditional love songs as well as the *Jodler* (yodel) into concert halls and places of light entertainment. These were the folksong genres to which collectors, publishers and performers turned increasingly, while narrative and historical genres such as the ballad and the legend attracted little attention. Arrangements of folk music were performed in the salons of the aristocracy and the middle classes, for instance Eduard von Lannoy's *Nationale Sang-und Tanzweisen des österreichischen Kaiserstaates: eine Sammlung charakteristischer Rondos für das Pianoforte*, published about 1830 in two volumes, one for Austria and one for Styria, and Bernhard Romberg's *Divertimento über Österreichische-Volkslieder für das Violoncello mit Begleitung des Piano-Forte*. Archduke Johann, who had instigated folksong collection in Austria, was not only the dedicatee of many editions of folksongs and compositions in the folk style, but also frequently featured himself, as 'Prinz Johann', in songs of the folkloristic type.

12. 'Drei Wünsche', from 'Oesterreichische Volkslieder', the first printed Austrian folksong collection, compiled by F. Žiška and J.M. Schottky (Pest, 1819, p.183)

Carinthian area of the east Tyrol to the Gottschee area in southern Krain (now Slovenia) lived in linguistic isolation but not without contact with their south Slav neighbours, and over six centuries they maintained musical practices of the late medieval sung narrative. The typical series of descending, closely graduated lines is well illustrated by the ballad *Der ausgeweidete Jäger* ('The Disembowelled Huntsman'; Brednich and Suppan, 1969, no.9: ex.2).

Ex.2 The Gottschee ballad *Der ausgeweidete Jäger*, text and melody in the 'old style' (from Brednich and Suppan, vol.I, p.48).

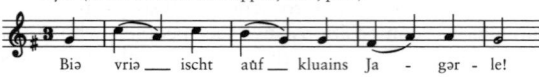

Biə   vriə ____ ischt   aůf ____ kluains Ja —   gər - le!

Biə vriə ischt aůf kluains Jagərle!
Es schteangait schmuaraisch guər vriə aůf,
Es ziəhət ahin in an vinschtrn Bolt;
Pənochtən tet kluains Jagərle.

Another example is the ballad *Der Tod und der Schultheiss* ('Death and the Village Mayor'; Brednich and Suppan, 1969, no.119: ex.3).

Ex.3 The Gotschee ballad *Der Tod und der Schultheiss* (from Brednich and Suppan, vol.I, p.426).

Biə _   vriə ischt aůf nå - rə dar   rai - chə Shůp - pon!

Biə vriə ischt aůf nårə dar raichə Shůppon!
Ar schteanôt schmoarônsch guər vriə aůf når,
Ar kraizigət shi schean, ar drbûgət shi schean,
Ar lêgət shi â guər scheandr uən når,
Ar ziəchət ahin am Bâge proit når,
Ůnd îmon pəgêgnt dar grimmigə Toat.

Epic and stichic forms are found in the Gottschee legends and in the early sacred cries and songs of the *Erlauer Spiele* (ed. Suppan and Janota, 1990).

Alpine vocal forms are marked by wide-ranging melodies in natural notes still played on trumpets made of wood, cowhorns, other animal horns and the more recent alphorn. They include the *Almschrei* (calls for gathering cattle together or summoning people to work) the *Alpsegen* and *Kühreigen*, the *Juchzer* and the *Jodler*. These forms are primarily concerned with acoustic communication: signals between people, between people and animals, or between people and gods. In this context Wiora speaks of 'elementary forms of singing' belonging to a development preceding song itself. The rhythmically free, strongly melismatic movements, without verbal or tonal links, have mainly been recorded in the Salzkammergut area by Konrad Mautner and Hans Gielge. Characteristics of the *Almschrei* are the powerfully sung high note and the descending melodic structure associated with exhaustion. In ex.4, an *Almschrei* from the Salzkam-

Ex.4 *Almschrei* from the Salzkammergut, with untuned alphorn F (×) (Sichardt, 1939, p.48).

1. Hin   ü - wa   d'Rie - d'ln und   her   ü - wa d'Grabn, und ös

lu - sti - g'n   Ålm - mentscha, tuats   nit   da - sta(r)n.

mergut, the uncertain melodic construction, in which the fourth oscillates between F and F♯, indicates the influence of the natural scale (of the alphorn).

Ex.5 Canonic *Jodler* (of the *Nacheinander* type) from Rottenmann (after Sichardt, 1939, p.24).

Sichardt gives an account of the polyphonic *Jodler* of the Austrian Alps, which is stylistically and formally related to Renaissance music in an area always noted for the close links between sacred and rustic musical forms. Both the tenor and the canonic principles occur in the records of oral tradition. Often, as in the songs of the Carinthian *Wildsänger*, the leading voice is in the second tenor, so that the polyphony builds up from the centre, as in vocal polyphony of the 15th and 16th centuries. The terms used also indicate this feature when the high voice is described in folk terminology as the '*Überschlag*' ('superius') (ex.5). Ex.6 is an example of a two-part

Ex.6 Two-part *Jodler* of the *Nacheinander* type from Irdning (after Sichardt, 1939, p.25).

Nacheinander Jochizer, recorded near Irdning in the Ennstal area of Styria.

The pastoral melos survives in a stylized form and has adapted to the major scale in polyphonic sung forms of the yodel, in the instrumental *Ländler* dances of Upper Austria and in Styrian dances, with mannerisms also appearing at times in the melodic and, above all, the rhythmic structure, and in the original and quick 3/4 rhythms of the Salzkammergut *Schleunigen*. Only the main part is fixed; the bass and the accompanying parts are improvised after it has been heard. Accompaniment frequently consists of a flute or clarinet, two fiddles and bass (ex.7). For gradual progressions when there is no

Ex.7 'Styrian' dance from the Salzkammergut (Haager, 1979, p.41).

alternating harmony, the harmonization scheme consists of a series of triads or 6th chords, and the main part is the lowest (ex.8).

Ex.8 Chord progressions in Alpine polyphony (after Haager, 1979, p.40).

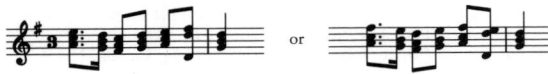

Ländler and Styrian dances are played sometimes on the diatonic or 'Styrian' dulcimer, sometimes on the diatonic or 'Styrian' accordion first made in the 19th century, with the choice of keys limited to tonics, subdominants and dominants.

From the beginning of the 19th century, folksong collection has levelled out and simplified what used to be a primarily oral tradition by writing it down, adapting it to tempered tuning and obliterating characteristic regional performance features relating to techniques of ornamentation and slurring, rhythmic irregularities and individual forms of polyphony. In this way, with a few exceptions, an artistically inert, homogenized kind of Alpine folk music was created from Vorarlberg and the Tyrol to Lower Austria and the Burgenland, a style that could be easily reproduced in its polyphonic triads and 6ths in the major, and could thus be easily trivialized. This was the origin of the 'Upper Krain Sound' in the fashionable light music of the 1970s and 80s, an ensemble for dance and light music consisting of clarinet, trumpet, euphonium, accordion, guitar and percussion, sometimes with song. Austria's most popular television programme, the folkloristic 'Musikantenstadl', took the 'Upper Krain Sound' far beyond Austria itself in the shape of what was known as *Lederhosenmusik*. In the 1990s, hybrid forms mingled techniques of electronically amplified rock music with Alpine folk music traditions (e.g. 'Hubert von Goisern').

The *Kärntnerlied* ('Carinthian song'), on the other hand, has retained some individuality, particularly through the five-part polyphony with a high upper part (ex.9) performed only by men (*Wildsänger*), and especially in its further development as the *Neues Kärtner Volkslied*. Carinthia is notable among the provinces of Austria in that its vocal traditions are stronger than those of instrumental music. Amateur musical activities reflect this fact: Carinthia has more choirs than community wind

Ex.9 Five-part *Kärntnerlied*.

bands, while in the other Austrian provinces wind bands considerably outnumber choirs.

Within the Republic of Austria, a Slovenian minority in Carinthia, and Croatian and Hungarian minorities in the Burgenland maintain the musical traditions of their countries of origin. For both the south Slav groups, the *Tambura* ensembles (*see* CROATIA) have recently become a symbol of their ethnic independence.

BIBLIOGRAPHY

HISTORICAL STUDIES

A. von Spaun: 'Das österreichische Volkslied', *Album aus Österreich ob der Enns* (Linz, 1843, 2/1896)

A. Schlossar: 'Die deutschen Volkslieder in Steiermark', *Österreichische Cultur- und Literaturbilder* (Vienna, 1879), 197–421

E.K. Blümml, ed.: *Quellen und Forschungen zur deutschen Volkskunde* (Vienna, 1908–12)

R. Lach: *Eine Tiroler Liederhandschrift aus dem 18. Jahrhundert* (Vienna, 1923)

V. von Geramb, ed.: *Die Knaffl-Handschrift: eine obersteirische Volkskunde aus dem Jahre 1813* (Berlin and Leipzig, 1928)

A. Kollitsch: *Geschichte des Kärntnerlieds* (Klagenfurt, 1935–6)

H. Commendah: 'Die Gebrauchshandschriften der alten Landlageier', *Zeitschrift für Volkskunde*, xlviii (1939, 181–204

L. Schmidt: 'Die kulturgeschichtlichen Grundlagen des Volksgesanges in Österreich', *Schweizerisches Archiv für Volkskunde*, xlv (1948), 105–29

W. Wiora: *Zur Frühgeschichte der Musik in den Alpenländern* (Basle, 1949)

A. Riedl and K.M.Klier: *Lied-Flugblattdrucke aus dem Burgenland* (Eisenstadt, 1958)

W. Suppan: 'Ein christlich Lied wider die Türken und die Doler Weise', *Jb für Liturgik und Hymnologie*, ix (1964), 152–6

W. Suppan: 'Nikolaus Beuttners Gesangbuch, Graz 1602, und die mündliche Überlieferung', *Innerösterreich 1564–1619*, ed. A. Novotny and B. Sutter, Joannea, iii (Graz, 1968), 261–95

W. Suppan: 'Das steirische Volkslied des 19. Jahrhunderts im Spiegel seiner Forscher, Sammler und Pfleger', *Jb des österreichischen Volksliedwerkes*, xix (1970), 75–95

L. Schmidt: 'Quellenforschungen zum älteren Volkslied', *AÖAW*, cvii (1971), 191–207

W. Suppan: *Deutsches Liedleben zwischen Renaissance und Barock* (Tutzing, 1973)

R.H.P. Helmer: *European Pastoral Calls and their Possible Influence on Western Liturgical Chant* (diss., Columbia U., 1975)

L. Kretzenbacher: *Südost-Überlieferungen zum apokryphen 'Traum Mariens'*, Sitzungsberichte der Bayerischen Akademie der

Wissenschaften: philosophisch-historische Klasse, Jg.1975/1 (Munich, 1975)

W. Suppan: 'Research on Folk Music in Austria since 1800', *YIFMC*, viii (1977), 117–29

W. Suppan: 'Volksmusik seit 1800', *Musikgeschichte Österreichs*, ed. R. Flotzinger and G. Gruber, ii (Graz, 1979), 281–311

W. Suppan: 'Rechtsgeschichte im Volkslied – Rechtsgeschehen um das Volkslied', *Festschrift für Berthold Sutter*, ed. G. Kocher and G.D. Hasiba (Graz, 1983), 353–79

L. Kretzenbacher: *Hiobs-Erinnerungen zwischen Donau und Adria*, Sitzungsberichte der Bayerischen Akademie der Wissenschaften: philosophisch-historische Klasse, Jg. 1987/1 (Munich, 1987)

O. Hafner: *Das grosse Erzherzog Johann-Buch* (Graz, 1992)

L. Kretzenbacher: *Leben und Geschichte des Volksschauspiels in der Steiermark* (Graz, 1992)

W. Salmen, ed.: *Musik und Tanz zur Zeit Kaiser Maximilian I* (Innsbruck, 1992)

W. Suppan: 'Bürgerliches und bäuerliches Musizieren in Mittelalter und früher Neuzeit', *Musikgeschichte Österreichs*, ed. R. Flotzinger, i (Vienna, 1995), 139–67

DANCE

R. Zoder: *Altösterreichische Volkstänze* (Vienna, 1922–8, 2/1946–55)

H. Lager: *Unsere Tänze* (Vienna, 1941)

I. Peter: *Tänze aus Österreich* (Vienna, 1947)

A. Novak: *Steirische Tänze: Volkstänze und Bauernspiele aus Steiermark* (Graz, 1949)

R. Wolfram: *Die Volkstänze in Österreich und verwandte Tänze in Europa* (Salzburg, 1951)

S. Schutte: *Der Ländler* (Strasbourg and Baden-Baden, 1970)

K. Horak: *Tiroler Volkstänze aus alter Überlieferung* (Schwaz, 1971)

W. Deutsch and A.Gschwantler: *Steyerische Tänze* (Vienna, 1994)

GENERAL

Das deutsche Volkslied (1899–1944; contd as *Volkslied, Volkstanz, Volksmusik*, 1947–9; index, 1947)

E.K. Blümml, F.F.Kohl and J. Reiter: *Die Volksliedbewegung in Deutschösterreich* (Vienna, 1910)

C. Rotter: *Der Schnaderhüpfl-Rhythmus* (Berlin, 1912)

J. Pommer: 'Das deutsche Volkslied in Österreich', *Mein Österreich, mein Heimatland*, ed. S. Schneider and B. Imendörffer (Vienna, 2/1915), 152–65

R. Lach: 'Die Tonkunst in den Alpen', *Die österreichischen Alpen*, ed. H. Leitmeier (Leipzig, 1928), 332–80

D. Hummel: 'Bibliographie des weltlichen Volksliedes in Niederösterreich', *Jb für Landeskunde von Niederösterreich*, xxiv (1931), 124–258

W. Sichardt: *Der alpenländische Jodler und der Ursprung des Jodelns* (Berlin, 1939)

K. Horak, ed.: *Burgenländische Volksschauspiele* (Vienna and Leipzig, 1940)

W. Kolneder: *Die vokale Mehrstimmigkeit in der Volksmusik der österreichischen Alpenländer* (diss., U. of Innsbruck, 1949; Winterthur, 1981)

L. Kretzenbacher: *Lebendiges Volksschauspiel in Steiermark* (Vienna, 1951)

Jahrbuch des österreichischen Volksliedwerkes (Vienna, 1952–)

K.M. Klier: *Volkstümliche Musikinstrumente in den Alpen* (Kassel, 1956)

F. Wild, W.Graf and E. Hermann: *Katalog des Phonogrammarchivs der österreichischen Akademie der Wissenschaften* (Vienna, 1960)

K.M. Klier and J.Bitsche, eds.: *Bibliographie des Volksliedes in Vorarlberg* (Montfort, 1964)

K.M. Klier: *Allgemeine Bibliographie des Burgenlandes*, v: *Volkskunde* (Eisenstadt, 1965)

W. Suppan: 'Volksmusik im Bezirk Weiz', *Weizerische Geschichte und Landschaft (in Einzeldarstellungen)*, viii (Weiz, 1967), 19–59

W. Wünsch, ed.: *Beiträge zur österreichischen Volksliedkunde* (Graz, 1967)

L. Schmidt: *Volksgesang und Volkslied: Proben und Probleme* (Berlin, 1970)

R.W. Brednich, L.Röhrich and W. Suppan, eds: *Handbuch des Volksliedes* (Munich, 1973–5)

K. Beitl, ed.: *L. Schmidt Bibliographie* (Vienna, 1977)

M. Haager: *Die instrumentale Volksmusik im Salzkammergut*, Musikethnologische Sammelbände, iii (Graz, 1979)

K. Diemann: *Schrammelmusik* (Graz, 1981)

H. Thiel: 'Totenbrauch und Totenlied in Fladnitz, Schrems und Fladnitzberg (Oststeiermark)', *Jb für Volksliedforschung*, xxvi (1981), 61–74

W. Deutsch and others, eds.: *Volksmusik in Österreich* (Vienna, 1984)

W. Suppan: *Volksmusik im Bezirk Liezen* (Trautenfels, 1984)

H. Brenner: *Stimmt an das Lied: die Geschichte des österreichischen Arbeiterchorwesens* (Graz, 1986)

J. Pöschl: *Das österreichische Jagdhornbläserbuch* (Graz, 1990)

W. Suppan, ed.: *Schladminger Gespräche zum Thema Musik und Tourismus*, Musikethnologische Sammelbände, xii (Tutzing, 1991)

H. Thiel and W.Deutsch: 'Zur Vokalmusik aus "Ebene Reichenau"/Kärnten nach Aufnahmeplatten des "Reichsrundfunks 1942"', *Studien zur Musikwissenschaft*, xli (1992), 245–56

R. Verdel: *Die Entwicklung des Tamburizzawesens in Südkärnten* (thesis, Hochschule für Musik und Darstellende Kunst in Graz, 1992)

W. Deutsch and M.Walcher, eds.: *Sommerakademie Volkskultur* (Vienna, 1992–4)

B. Habla, ed.: *Festschrift zum 60. Geburtstag von Wolfgang Suppan* (Tutzing, 1993)

T. Hochradner and G.Walterskirchen, eds.: *175 Jahre 'Stille Nacht! Heilige Nacht!'* (Salzburg, 1994)

W. Kraxner, ed.: *Das geistliche Lied in Kärnten*, Mageregger Gespräche zur Volkskultur in Kärnten, iv (Klagenfurt, 1994) [incl. W. Suppan: 'Das geistliche Lied in den Ostalpenländern']

W. Deutsch: '90 Jahre Österreichisches Volksliedwerkes', *Jb des österreichischen Volksliedwerkes*, xliv (1995), 12–50

COLLECTIONS

J.G. Meinert: *Alte teutsche Volkslieder in der Mundart des Kuhländchens* (Vienna and Hamburg, 1817, 2/1909)

F. Žiška and J.M. Schottky: *Oesterreichische Volkslieder mit ihren Singweisen* (Pest, 1819/R, rev. 3/1906 by F.S. Krauss)

A. von Spaun: *Lieder, Tänze und Alpenmelodien* (Vienna, 1845)

M.V. Süss: *Salzburgische Volks-Lieder mit ihren Singweisen* (Salzburg, 1865/R)

R. Sztachovics: *Braut-Sprüche und Braut-Lieder auf dem Heideboden* (Vienna, 1867)

P.K. Rosegger and R.Heuberger: *Volkslieder aus Steiermark mit Melodien* (Pest, 1872)

A. Schlossar: *Deutsche Volkslieder aus Steiermark* (Innsbruck, 1881)

W. Pailler: *Weihnachtslieder und Krippenspiele aus Oberösterreich und Tirol* (Innsbruck, 1881–3)

A. Werle: *Almrausch, Almliada aus Steiermark* (Graz, 1884)

J. Gabler: *Geistliche Volkslieder, gesammelt in der Diözese St. Pölten* (Regensburg and Linz, 1890)

H. Neckheim and J.Pommer: *222 echte Kärntnerlieder* (Vienna, 1891–3)

F.F. Kohl: *Echte Tiroler-Lieder* (Vienna, 1899, rev., enlarged 2/1913–15)

J. Pommer: *444 Jodler und Juchezer aus Steiermark* (Vienna, 1902)

E.K. Blümml: *Erotische Volkslieder aus Deutsch-Österreich* (Vienna, 1906, 2/1993)

K. Mautner: *Steyerisches Rasplwerk: Vierzeiler, Lieder und Gasslreime aus Goessl am Grundlsee* (Vienna, 1910)

K. Mautner: *Alte Lieder und Weisen aus dem steyermärkischen Salzkammergute* (Vienna, 1919/R, 2/1925)

R. Wolkan: *Wiener Volkslieder aus fünf Jahrhunderten* (Vienna, 1920)

H. Commenda: *Von der Eisenstrasse* (Vienna, 1926)

H. Pommer: *Volkslieder und Jodler aus Vorarlberg* (Vienna, 1926)

V. Zack: *Volkslieder und Jodler aus dem obersteirischen Murgebiet* (Vienna, 1927)

K. Kronfuss, A. and F.Pöschl: *Niederösterreichische Volkslieder und Jodler aus dem Schneeberggebiet* (Vienna, 1930)

R. Zoder: *Dorfmusik* (Kassel, 1931–7)

R. Zoder and K.M.Klier: *Volkslieder aus Niederösterreich* (Vienna, 1932–4)

O. Eberhard and C.Rotter: *Salzburgische Bauernlieder* (Vienna and Leipzig, 1933)

H. Gielge: *Rund um Aussee* (Vienna, 1935)

V. Korda and K.M.Klier: *Volksmusik aus Niederösterreich* (Vienna, 1937)

K.M. Klier: *Schatz österreichischer Weihnachtslieder* (Klosterneuburg, 1937–8)

G. Kotek: *Volkslieder und Jodler um den Schneeberg und Semmering* (Vienna, 1938, 2/1943)

K.M. Klier: *Volkslieder aus dem Waldviertel* (Vienna, 1942)

R. Maier: *Kärntner Fasten- und Osterlieder* (Klagenfurt, 1953)

A. Anderluh: *Kärntens Volksliedschatz* (Klagenfurt, 1960–93)

A. Quellmalz: *Südtiroler Volkslieder* (Kassel, 1968–76)

R.W. Brednich and W.Suppan, eds.: *Gottscheer Volkslieder* (Mainz, 1969–84)

W. Suppan: *Lieder einer steirischen Gewerkensgattin aus dem 18. Jahrhundert* (Graz, 1970)

N. Wallner: *Deutsche Marienlieder der Enneberger Ladiner (Südtirol)* (Vienna, 1970)

E. Borneman: *Unsere Kinder im Spiegel ihrer Lieder, Reime, Verse und Rätsel* (Olten and Freiburg, 1972–4)

W. Kainz: *Weststeirische Volksdichtung* (Graz, 1976)

J. Künzig and W.Werner-Künzig: *Volkslieder aus Deutsch-Mokra* (Freiburg, 1978) [incl. discs]

C. Bresgen and W.Keller: '. . . *die Liab ist übergross!': Weihnacht im Salzburger Volkslied* (Munich and Salzburg, 1979)

H. Dreo, W.Burian and S. Gmasz: *Ein burgenländisches Volksliederbuch* (Eisenstadt, 1988)

W. Suppan and J.Janota: *Texte und Melodien der 'Erlauer Spiele'* (Tutzing, 1990)

H. Gielge and G.Haid: *Klingende Berge: Juchzer, Rufe und Jodler* (Trautenfels, 1992)

W. Deutsch: *Volksmusik in Niederösterreich* (Vienna, 1993)

L. Steiner: *Lieder des Weihnachtsfestkreises* (Vienna, 1995)

HELLMUT FEDERHOFER/WOLFGANG SUPPAN (I,1–5),
BERNHARD GÜNTHER (I,6), WOLFGANG SUPPAN (II)

Ausweichung (Ger.: 'digression'). A change of key. *See* MODULATION (i).

Auszug (i) (from Ger. *ausziehen*: 'to draw out', 'to extract'). A term used to designate a vocal score (*see* SCORE, §1) of an opera or similar work.

Auszug (ii) (from Ger. *ausziehen*: 'to draw out', 'to extract'). A slide (*see* ZUG (ii)) of a trombone or slide trumpet.

Auteri-Manzocchi, Salvatore (*b* Palermo, 25 Dec 1845; *d* Parma, 21 Feb 1924). Italian composer. He was the son of the mezzo-soprano Almerinda Manzocchi, who in the 1820s and 30s had created a number of roles in operas by Donizetti and others. His most successful opera was *Dolores*, which was widely performed in Italy. Isabella Galletti Gianoli, who sang the title role, included it in her regular repertory and contributed to the opera's popularity. Of his other operas, *Il negriero*, *Stella* and *Il Conte di Gleichen* were well received by Italian critics, but were not so widely performed. Auteri-Manzocchi's style was heavily influenced by Verdi, but also showed some debt to Bellini.

WORKS

Marcellina, op, *c*1870, unperf.; Dolores (os, 4, M. Auteri-Pomar), Florence, Pergola, 23 Feb 1875; Il negriero (os, 2, Auteri-Pomar), Barcelona, Liceo, 27 Nov 1878; Stella (os, 3, S. Interdonato), Piacenza, Municipale, 22 May 1880; Il Conte di Gleichen (os, 4, Auteri-Pomar), Milan, Dal Verme, 16 Oct 1887; Graziella (os, 3, M.C. Cagnuto), Milan, Lirico, 23 Oct 1894; Severo Torelli (os, 4, Auteri-Pomar), Bologna, Duse, 25 April 1903

BIBLIOGRAPHY

ES (E. Zanetti)

T.G. Kaufman: *Verdi and his Major Contemporaries: a Selected Chronology of Performances with Casts* (New York, 1990), 576–7

THOMAS KAUFMAN

Autheman, Nicolas. *See* HOTMAN, NICOLAS.

Authentic cadence. A perfect CADENCE made up of a dominant chord followed by tonic chord (V–I), both normally in root position; the term is contrasted with 'plagal cadence', whose penultimate chord is a subdominant. The term is used mainly in American writings, which sometimes state that the uppermost note in the final chord should be the tonic.

Authenticity. The term 'authenticity' has been used in several senses relating to music. The most common use refers to classes of performance that might synonymously be termed 'historically informed' or 'historically aware', or employing 'period' or 'original' instruments and techniques. A concern with historical performing practices is a by-product of 19th-century historicism and is evidenced, for instance, in the production of critical and Urtext editions, in Mendelssohn's performances of earlier music, in the restoration of plainchant by the monks of Solesmes and in the colourful antiquarianism of Arnold Dolmetsch. However, 'authentic' performance was not to become a central element of Western performance until the 1970s, when it began to prove an extraordinarily successful direction for many performers and groups, encouraged by a buoyant recording industry. (*See also* EARLY MUSIC.)

'Authentic' performance may refer to one or any combination of the following approaches: use of instruments from the composer's own era; use of performing techniques documented in the composer's era; performance based on the implications of the original sources for a particular work; fidelity to the composer's intentions for performance or to the type of performance a composer desired or achieved; an attempt to re-create the context of the original performance; and an attempt to re-create the musical experience of the original audience.

Many critics and scholars have questioned the ideals and aims of the historical performance movement and the term 'authenticity' itself has come in for particularly stern criticism, for example from Joseph Kerman and Richard Taruskin. To Taruskin, 'authenticity' suggests a form of cultural elitism which can imply that any other type of performance is 'inauthentic', as if a forgery or an act of almost purposeful deceit. He further notes that very little in historical performance is truly historical since so many aspects of performance have to be invented or co-opted from existing practices. Moreover, the style of performance and the selection of historical data are conditioned by modern taste and thus represent the hidden musical corollary of high modernism. In an interesting twist of terminology, Taruskin suggests that historical performance is in fact 'authentic' as a true symptom of modernist thought.

Few, however, would dispute that the movement for historical performance has brought with it many advantages. Initially centred on Baroque performing practice, the movement has expanded in all historical directions, even producing period performance of 20th-century music. While the use of the term 'authenticity' has dropped considerably since the early 1990s ('historically informed' or 'period performance' are more common), there is no doubt that it has contributed to the success of the movement. In an age that has experienced both the catastrophic destruction of cultural artefacts and a phenomenal expansion of technological production and reproduction, there is a definite craving for the 'original' and 'authentic' in many areas of Western society. The postwar era has also seen the spectacular growth of interest in 'authentic' restoration and period style in architecture. The cultural theorist Fredric Jameson may be correct in suggesting that the various standardizations of global capitalism and the concomitant expansions of the media and technology towards the end of the 20th century has resulted in a weakening of our historicity. This means that we are no longer so fully aware of our place within human history and are not so able to appreciate ourselves as historically conditioned beings. Thus this period has seen, by way of compensation, a large number of historicist revivals, most notably religious fundamentalism. In these revivals, adherence to details that are assumed to be historically precise and unambiguous may serve to cover the radical difference between the present and the various pre-modern ages. If this analysis is correct, the concept of 'authentic' performance may be a symptom of a postmodern, rather than specifically modern, condition.

Given that the imperative to pursue 'authentic' performance is far greater in our age than ever before, it must respond to a cultural need that was never so crucial. This, in itself, should suggest that the term 'authentic' is dangerous, since it implies some standard of transhistorical truth, to be valid whatever the era. However much we may feel that a particular instrument conditions the playing style, we are still likely to make it sound how we, however subconsciously, want it to sound, even if this directly opposes existing practices. Indeed, a comparison of 'authentic' performers over three decades shows what radical differences might be afforded by increased experience and changes in interpretative fashion. Moreover, it is naive to assume that, were we to hit on exactly the same sounds as those of yesteryear, listeners today would be affected in precisely the same manner as those of the past. Differences in cultural perspective backwards in time are probably as great as, if not greater than, those between different cultures today.

The movement for historically informed performance is, however, one of the most significant developments in performance styles in the 20th century. It has opened up a wide range of possibilities for new ways of performing and hearing and, shorn of its claims to 'authenticity', represents an attitude to performance that, at its best, is both vital and invigorating.

The term 'authenticity' can also be applied, as in the popular art world, to works that are proved to be genuine, demonstrated by the work of a particular composer. However, even this, the simplest use of the term, is by no means unproblematic. Much music, especially before the Renaissance, was not written with the concept of a single, definitive composer in mind. Furthermore, composers, even in the 19th and 20th centuries, may not have had total control over every element of production. Both scribes and publishers might modify a composer's notation to conform to a particular house style and might edit the music at several levels, with or without the composer's consent. Indeed, musical works created within an environment of copyright laws and commercial process almost inevitably involve multiple wills, all conspiring to create a distinctive 'authentic' work.

The 'authenticity' of a work is often seen to be dependent on the 'authenticity' of its sources: if no manuscript or print directly connected with the composer is evident some editors have tended to exclude the work from the official output. Scholars have been reluctant to use issues such as style or quality as ways of authenticating a work; scientific textual study has often unseated the less certifiable assumptions of stylistic criticism. But the absence of evidence is not simply negative evidence for the authenticity of a work.

'Authenticity' is also a prominent term in German philosophy of the 20th century. Although Theodor W. Adorno was highly critical of Heidegger's concept of authenticity (as the state of those who take responsibility for their existential status), he uses a modified form of this concept in his philosophy of music. Authentic musical works are those that conform with Adorno's (negative) dialectical conception of musical truth, works that forge their own internal consistency while acknowledging the historical nature and social function of the material. Such works are necessarily conflicted 'failures', presenting reference to the outside world within autonomous form (and, in the human condition after the Holocaust, this means that the sublimation of suffering completely exhausts the formal possibilities of music).

BIBLIOGRAPHY
J. Kerman: *Musicology* (London, 1985)
Authenticity and Early Music: Oberlin, OH, 1986 and 1987
H. Haskell: *The Early Music Revival: a History* (London, 1988)
P. Kivy: *Authenticities: Philosophical Reflections on Musical Performance* (Ithaca, NY, and London, 1995)
R. Taruskin: *Text and Act: Essays on Music and Performance* (New York, 1995)
JOHN BUTT

Authentic mode (from Gk. *authentos*, Lat. *authenticus* or *authentus*). Any of the church modes whose AMBITUS, or range, includes the octave lying immediately above FINAL. The term is thus applied to the four odd-numbered modes of Gregorian chant (1, 3, 5 and 7), whose Greek-derived names are DORIAN, PHRYGIAN, LYDIAN and MIXOLYDIAN; the ambitus of each of these odd-numbered modes is about a 4th higher than that of its corresponding even-numbered PLAGAL MODE, the term with which 'authentic mode' is contrasted.

The earliest definition of the term is given in Hucbald's *De musica* (?c880; *GerbertS*, i, 116): 'Every authentic tone [i.e. mode] rises from its final up to the 9th [above]. It descends, moreover, to [the tone] next to it, and sometimes to the semitone or to the [minor] 3rd'. Later, the lower limit of the ambitus of an authentic mode was restricted in theory to the subfinal, which lies a tone below the final in the modes where it is available (1st, 3rd and 7th). The contrast between authentic and plagal was extended to the IONIAN and AEOLIAN modes when these (and their corresponding plagals) were added to the original eight church modes in Glarean's *Dodecachordon* (1547).

The word 'authenticus', notwithstanding its Greek derivation, is not reflected in the early Byzantine modal terminology, unlike its counterpart *plagalis*; an 'authentic' Byzantine mode was simply designated *echos* (the later *kyrios* seems to be a back-translation from the Latin system).

HAROLD S. POWERS

Auto (Sp.: 'act', 'judicial proceeding', 'decree'.). A Spanish dramatic work that developed from medieval liturgical drama. The earliest *autos* were religious or allegorical plays with a clear didactic or exemplary purpose, and the term was used in a broader sense in the late 15th century and into the 16th to designate one of many kinds of play, secular or religious in nature. As with the *farsa* and *égloga*, lyric poetry and songs were included in the performance of *autos* by Gil Vicente, Lucas Fernández and Juan del Encina, in very stylized ways. Typically an *auto* or a *farsa* would end with a *villancico*, though some incorporated songs more directly into the drama.

The *auto sacramentale* was an allegorical religious play on the Eucharist performed during or as an adjunct to public, outdoor processions for Corpus Christi from the 16th to 18th centuries. The best known and historically most important examples of this genre are those by Pedro Calderón de la Barca written for performance at the city of Madrid's annual Corpus Christi celebrations. From 1648 until his death in 1681, Calderón supplied the texts (as well as instructions for staging and costumes) for these open-air performances. His *autos* are one-act plays with songs, preceded by a *loa* (prologue) and usually followed by a short comic skit or danced number such as an *entremés* or *baile*. Written in polymetric verse, they are elegant examples of Counter-Reformation religious instruction through very beautiful Baroque poetry, song and spectacle. A number of Calderón's *autos* use classical mythology as the basis for religious allegory. They were performed with elaborate scenery and special effects on special platforms on wheels (*carros*), though they became so popular that many were then performed for weeks on end in the public theatres after the Corpus festival. Around the several performances of the *autos* during the octave of Corpus (usually two autos were performed each year), special danced entertainments were contracted (*danzas de espadas, de cascabeles* etc.) and performed by specialists. Instrumental and vocal music of many sorts (songs, sections of recitative, choruses, instrumental pieces) were brought into the *autos* as important audible props and for the direct expression of special characters. Many of the composers employed by the royal chapels in Madrid, such as Juan Hidalgo, Cristóbal Galán and others, composed songs for the *autos* of Calderón, as did theatrical musicians of the acting troupes such as Juan Serqueira de Lima, Manuel de Villaflor and José Peyró.

Performances of Calderón's *autos sacramentales* continued after his death in 1681, though a few other writers also contributed to the development of the repertory, most notably Francisco de Bances Candamo and Antonio de Zamora in Madrid. The standard form established by Calderón seems to have been continued in the 18th century, although the tradition died out and the genre had outlived its function by about the middle of the century. A royal decree of 1765, which ran counter to the wishes of many in the ecclesiastical community, prohibited the further performances of the *autos sacramentales*; before then they had been widely performed in Spain and in the Hispanic New World, with great acclaim.

BIBLIOGRAPHY

LaborD; RiemannL12

M. Latorre y Badillo: 'Representación de los autos sacramentales en el periodo de su mayor florecimiento (1620–81)', *Revista de archivos, bibliotecas y museos*, xxv (1911), 189–211; xxvi (1912), 235–62

M.N. Hamilton: *Music in Eighteenth Century Spain* (Urbana, IL, 1937/R)

A. Salazar: 'Music in the Primitive Spanish Theatre before Lope de Vega', *PAMS 1938*, 94–108

G. Chase: 'Origins of the Lyric Theater in Spain', *MQ*, xxv (1939), 292–305

M. Bataillon: 'Essai d'explication de l'"auto sacramental"', *Bulletin hispanique*, xlii (1940), 193–212

A.A. Parker: *The Allegorical Drama of Calderón* (Oxford, 1943)

J. Sage: 'Calderón y la música teatral', *Bulletin hispanique*, lviii (1956), 275–300

N.D. Shergold and J.E. Varey: *Los autos sacramentales en Madrid en la época de Calderón, 1637–81* (Madrid, 1961)

J. Díaz and J. Alonso Puga: *Autos de navida en León y Castilla* (León, 1983)

J.M. Díez Borque: 'Teatro y fiesta en el barroco español: el auto sacramental de Calderón y el público, funciones del texto cantado', *Cuadernos hispanoamericanos*, no.386 (1983), 606–42

LOUISE K. STEIN

Autograph. A manuscript written in the hand of a particular person; in normal musical parlance, the manuscript of a work in the hand of its composer. It is thus generally distinguished from 'copy', a manuscript in the hand of another person. There may exist more than one autograph manuscript for a given work: for example, the replacement finale of Beethoven's String Quartet in Bb op.130 survives in two autographs, the writing of the second having been necessitated by the extreme amount of revision and recomposition carried out in the first. In such cases it is usual for the two autographs to be described respectively as *Urschrift* and *Reinschrift*. 'Autograph' may be used adjectivally, for example in referring to 'a copy of the "Eroica" Symphony with Beethoven's autograph corrections'. The term 'holograph' is sometimes used to distinguish a manuscript wholly in the hand of its author or composer (*see* HOLOGRAPH).

For the period before 1600 relatively few manuscripts of works wholly or largely in the hand of the composer can be identified with any certainty (for a discussion of the problems and a list of suggested attributions in the period *c*1450–1600, see Owens, 1997; for earlier cases, see Bent, 1967–8, and Stone, 1994); and in the case of some medieval repertories the distinction between autograph and copy becomes difficult to sustain when a scribe's editorial intervention is such that a significantly different text results from the process of 'copying'. The survival of composers' autographs increases greatly for the period after 1600. And while the advent of computer-based music processing has rendered them theoretically obsolete, preparation of an autograph score remains a normal stage in the process of composition.

See also SKETCH and SOURCES, MS, §I.

BIBLIOGRAPHY

E. Winternitz: *Musical Autographs from Monteverdi to Hindemith* (New York, 1965)

M. Bent: 'Sources of the Old Hall Music', *PRMA*, xciv (1967–8), 19–35

E. Roth, ed.: *Composers' Autographs* (London, 1968) [trans. of W. Gerstenberg and M. Hürlimann, eds.: *Musikerhandschriften*]

C. Wolff, ed.: *The String Quartets of Haydn, Mozart, and Beethoven: Cambridge, MA, 1979*

A. Tyson: *Mozart: Studies of the Autograph Scores* (Cambridge, MA, 1987)

A. Stone: 'Writing Rhythm in Late Medieval Italy: Notation and Musical Style in the Manuscript Modena, Biblioteca Estense, α.M.5.24' (diss., Harvard U., 1994)

J.A. Owens: *Composers at Work: the Craft of Musical Composition, 1450–1600* (New York and Oxford, 1997)

NICHOLAS MARSTON

Autoharp (Ger. Akkordzither: 'chord zither'). A box ZITHER of German origin, popular in the USA from the late 19th century. The player strums the strings with his fingers, a fingerpick or a plectrum; damper bars controlled by buttons damp all the strings except those that sound the required chord. The basis of the instrument is a box, about 30 cm long, 45 cm broad and 3 cm deep (see illustration). Instruments for popular use are factory-made, in the USA and Germany, and are finished with a black lacquer and a soundhole beneath the bars; instruments used for folk music are hand-made in America,

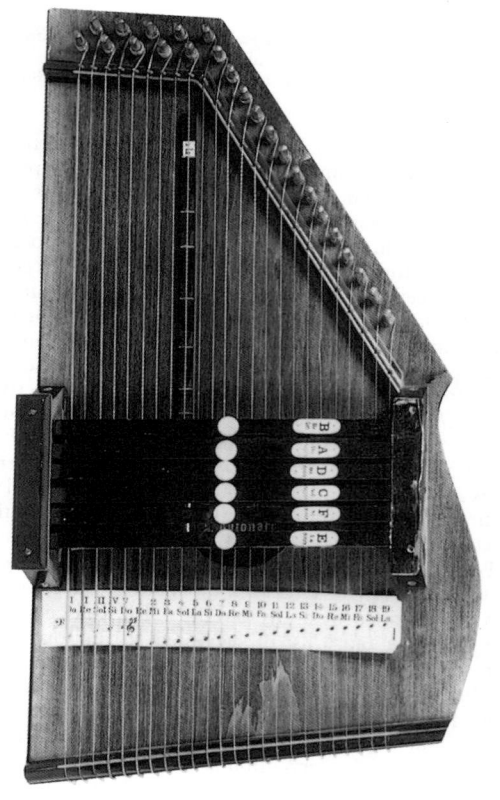

Autoharp with six chord dampers, German, 19th century (Stearns Collection, University of Michigan, Ann Arbor); the fingerboard with frets, beneath the A string, is unusual

lightly varnished with a wood finish and may include marquetry or other decoration. The strings, which are graded in thickness, are attached to wrest-pins; they number between 15 and 50, or even more, and the range is between two and four octaves (C–c'''). Some instruments are diatonic, others partly or fully chromatic. A 15-string instrument is likely to have only three bars, giving the tonic, the subdominant and the dominant 7th of C major. A nine-bar instrument may offer a selection of chords, including these basic chords in two keys and a range of related chords. Autoharps used for folk music may offer fewer chords per key, but a wider range of keys. Some manufacturers supply spare, blank bars for the player to fit as he wishes. The circle of 5ths, normal on other extended diatonic instruments such as the accordion, the zither and the dulcimer, is unusual on the autoharp. Examples of autoharps that are fully chromatic or include frets (see illustration) have also been manufactured.

According to Sachs, the autoharp was invented by C.A. Gütter of Markneukirchen. The first American patent was granted in 1882 to Charles F. Zimmermann, a German who had emigrated to Philadelphia in 1865. He had already devised a new system of musical notation using 'tone numbering' for use with the accordion, and the development of the autoharp was a logical step. He began production in 1885 and sold 50,000 instruments within three years (see Moore, 1963). He offered a wide range

of models, from one with 21 strings and three bars to a 'concert harp' with 49 strings, six bars, slides and levers, enabling it to produce 72 different chords. Zimmermann sold his controlling interest in the company in 1892 to ALFRED DOLGE, who moved the factory to Dolgeville, New York; by the mid-1890s Dolge was manufacturing 3000 autoharps each week, which were sold by door-to-door salesmen and through sale catalogues as well as by local music shops. He produced nearly half a million instruments, but the advent of the gramophone and commercial factors led to the firm's failure in 1898. The instrument was also known in Britain.

Instruction manuals and collections of music for the autoharp (e.g. *Collection of Popular Figure Music for C.F. Zimmermann's Miniature Autoharp*) were commercially distributed as early as 1885 and helped to promote the instrument as a means of providing rhythmic accompaniment to a simple melody or to singing. In this style of playing, the autoharp was laid flat on a table or stand, and a melody plucked with the first finger while chords were strummed with the thumb and first finger. This method required little musical or technical skill and the autoharp thus became known as the 'idiot zither'. A playing style which emphasized the melodic capabilities of the instrument was developed in the mid-1890s and introduced to the public by Aldis Gery, who toured with the Victor Herbert Band. At about the same time, the instrument was introduced to the southern Appalachian mountain region through mail-order catalogues, travelling salesmen and 'home' missionaries.

Around 1910, the autoharp enjoyed a further phase of popularity in the USA, when it came to be used in social gatherings, by travelling preachers, and for therapy by hospital workers. The Pianoharp Company of Boston obtained the right to manufacture autoharps in 1910; in 1926, this company merged with Oscar Schmidt International, of Jersey City. Schmidt's instruments were modelled on Zimmermann's less complex ones. Fretted Industries, of Illinois, bought the firm of Oscar Schmidt in 1978, and continues to manufacture the instruments, as do a number of German firms. The autoharp is still used, especially in schools, for the teaching of rudimentary harmony.

A tradition of using the autoharp for folk music developed, largely independently of the popular tradition, in the Appalachian mountains at the turn of the century. The early style used for folk music was similar to the popular style of the 1880s in that the instrument was laid on the lap or on a table. A noted exponent was Ernest ('Pop') Stoneman, who made the first recording of the instrument in 1924, and developed a style consisting of short strokes in strict rhythm rather than long strokes in free rhythm, bringing forefinger and thumb together in a pinching action; this style allowed for greater agility. The lap playing style was further disseminated in the southern mountain tradition and in early recordings of country music by Sara Carter (of the celebrated Carter family singing group), who used the autoharp for rhythmic accompaniment. Maybelle Carter developed a third style of playing in the 1950s, plucking the strings in the middle instead of close to the hitchpins, and playing erect, holding the instrument vertically against her chest, thus permitting greater flexibility in the use of microphones and in plucking styles. In the popular style, where melodic movement is slow, the player arpeggiates upwards from the bass note, finishing on the melody note; in the folk style, where dance music, fiddle tunes and fastmoving songs may be performed, the arpeggiation is downwards from the melody note (the bass may be provided by a supporting instrument or even omitted). The folksong revival of the 1960s inspired players to use the autoharp for harmonic and rhythmic accompaniment or as a melody instrument. Since then, innovations in tuning, playing styles and repertory have resulted in the expansion of the instrument's versatility and increased its musical potential. Recent techniques include the use of metal or plastic plectra or metal thimbles. The instrument has been used in rhythm-and-blues, folk-rock, Caribbean, flamenco, jazz, Celtic and New Age styles. Electric autoharps have also been made.

In the 1980s a network of autoharp aficionados was developed through magazines and newsletters, including *Autoharpoholic* (1980–), *Autoharp Teachers Digest*, *Autoharp Quarterly* (1989–) and *Autoharp Clearinghouse* (1989–). Competitions, clubs and festivals provide public venues for performance on the autoharp, and there are many workshops on old-time and American folk music where instruction on the instrument is offered.

BIBLIOGRAPHY

C. Sachs: *Real-Lexicon der Musikinstrumente* (Berlin, 1913/R, 2/1964)

M. Seeger: disc notes, *Mountain Music Played on the Autoharp*, Folkways FA 2365 (1962)

A.D. Moore: 'The Autoharp: its Origin and Development from a Popular to a Folk Instrument', *New York Folklore Quarterly*, xix (1963), 261–74

H. Taussig: *Folkstyle Autoharp* (New York, 1967)

B. Blackley: *The Autoharp Book* (Brisbane, CA, 1983)

T. Schroeder: 'In the Beginning: Five Year Review', *Autoharpoholic*, xii (1991), 6

I. Stiles: 'The True History of the Autoharp', *Autoharp Quarterly*, iii (1991), 3–6

DAVID KETTLEWELL/LUCY M. LONG

Autumnus, Johann Andreas. *See* HERBST, JOHANN ANDREAS.

Aux-Cousteaux [Hautcousteaux], **Artus** [Arthur] (*b* ?Amiens, *c*1590; *d* Paris, *c*1656). French composer and singer. Although his birthplace is not known, there were families bearing this name in Amiens; a member of one, a relative of the composer, served as mayor of the town. Aux-Cousteaux studied under Jean de Bournonville at the choir school of the collegiate church at Saint Quentin. From 1613 to 1627 he sang *haute-contre* in Louis XIII's chapel. A period at Noyon followed about which little is known. He succeeded Bournonville as *maître de musique* both at Saint Quentin (1631) and Amiens (*c*1632–4). On 24 June 1634 he relinquished this more lucrative post for that of a 'clerk' *haute-contre* at the Ste Chapelle in Paris. In spite of a recalcitrant and quarrelsome nature ('scandalous, insolent and disrespectful acts committed daily during the Office'), Aux-Cousteaux advanced rapidly and by 1643 was *maître de musique*, secure in the protection of no less a personage than Mathieu Molé, first president of Parlement. He left the Ste Chapelle about 1651 and received a canonry at the church of St Jacques de l'Hôpital, where he remained until his death.

Although esteemed by Gantez for his ability to write both 'agréable' and 'grave' music, Aux-Cousteaux was characterized by Brossard as a 'rank pedant' who 'never wished to hear of adding *Basses-continues* to his works'

(*Catalogue*). In its use of conservative polyphony, Aux-Cousteaux's religious music perpetuates the 'learned' tradition of Du Caurroy and Bournonville. His chansons are models of clear textual declamation but in general lack the melodic grace of Antoine Boësset or Etienne Moulinié. They are closer in spirit to the Le Jeune of the 1612 *Meslanges* than they are to the more progressive *airs de cour*.

In 1656 Le Petit printed Aux-Cousteaux's settings of Godeau's *Paraphrase des psaumes de David* (a first edition of 1654 is lost). At the time of his death, Aux-Cousteaux was working on a new edition of the psalms. Le Petit approached Gobert who agreed to render the melodies 'plus agréables'. The new edition was published in 1659 with Gobert's name substituted for Aux-Cousteau's.

WORKS

SACRED

Missa, 5vv, ad imitationem moduli 'grata sum harmonia' (Paris, 1647)

Missa, 4vv, … secundi toni (Paris, 1726)

Missa quinti toni, 5vv, in *La BordeE*

Missa, 5vv, ad imitationem moduli 'Quelle beauté ô mortels' (Paris, 1651)

4 masses are lost

[21] Psalmi, 4–6vv (Paris, 1631)

Octo cantica Divae Mariae Virginis, 4vv (Paris, 1641)

Noëls et cantiques spirituels, 2vv (Paris, 1644)

Second livre de noëls et cantiques spirituels, 2vv (Paris, 1644)

Canticum Virginis Deiparae (Paris, 1655)

Paraphrase des Psaumes de David, 1v, bc (Paris, 2/1656 [1st edn of 1654, lost]), repr in 1659 attrib. Gobert

SECULAR

Les quatrains de Mr. Mathieu, 3vv (Paris, 1643)

Meslanges de chansons, 3–6vv (Paris, 1644), 32 chansons, 2 madrigals, 1 villageoise, 1 voix de ville

Suite de la première partie des quatrains de Mr. Mathieu, 3vv (Paris, 1652)

BIBLIOGRAPHY

BrenetM

A. Gantez: *L'entretien des musiciens* (Auxerre, 1643); ed. E. Thoinan (Paris, 1878/R)

R. Rebourd: 'Messire Arthus Aux Cousteaux, maître de musique de la Sainte Chapelle du Palais 1590–1654', *Bulletin de la Société d'étude du XVIIe siècle*, xxi–xxii (1954), 403–17

A. Bloch-Michel: 'Les messes d'Aux-Cousteaux', *RMFC*, ii (1961–2), 31–40

A. Bloch-Michel: 'Les meslanges d'Aux-Cousteaux', *RMFC*, iii (1963), 11–19

D. Launay: 'A propos du chant des psaumes en francais au XVIIe siècle: la "Paraphrase des Psaumes" de Godeau et ses musiciens', *RdM*, l (1964), 30–75

E. Schwandt: 'Some 17th-Century French Unica in Canada: notes for RISM', *FAM*, xxvii (1980), 172–4

D. Launay: 'La musique religieuse en France du Concile de Trente à 1804' (Paris, 1993)

JAMES R. ANTHONY

Auxiliary note [neighbour note] (Fr. *broderie*; Ger. *Hilfsnote*). An unaccented NON-HARMONIC NOTE that lies a half step or whole step away from a 'main' note, which it ornaments; the auxiliary note is approached from and returns to the main note directly (e.g. *e–f–e* and *b–a–b* over an E minor chord; *f* and *a* are the auxiliary notes). A similar configuration where the middle note is accented is a form of appoggiatura. In Schenkerian analysis, 'neighbour note' is the preferred term for an auxiliary note prolonging a pitch of the fundamental line.

□

Auxiliary stop. *See* ACCESSORY STOP.

Auza-León, Atiliano (*b* Sucre, 5 Oct 1928). Bolivian composer, violinist and writer. He was a choirboy at Sucre Cathedral and in 1950 graduated as a music teacher from the Escuela Normal in that city. He studied at the La Paz Conservatory (1953–5) with Eisner (counterpoint), Maldonado (violin) and Estenssoro and joined the National SO as a violinist. On returning to Sucre he studied composition with Hochmann and piano with Thorrez. He received a scholarship to the di Tella Institute in Buenos Aires, where his teachers were Ginastera, Gandini, Suarez Urtubey and Davidovsky (1965–6). He taught at the Escuela Normal in Sucre (1971–2) and at the Escuela Normal Simón Bolivar in La Paz (1976), and was composition teacher at the La Paz Conservatory (1976). In 1992 he was elected vice-president of the Bolivian Society of Composers and Authors.

WORKS
(*selective list*)

Trio breve, 1964; Madrigal y cueca, chorus, 1965; Ramillete sonoro, school songs (1965); 6 danzas bolivianas del ciclo Runas, vn, pf (1966); Estructuras, chbr orch, perf. 1970; Melodías y canciones de Tarija (1974); Conc., vn, orch, perf. 1975; Música coral, 8 pieces, chorus (1977); Inkallajta (op, 3, N. Méndez de Paz), 1977–80, 1997; Oda a Moto Méndez (cant.), solo vv, nar, chorus, orch, perf. 1984; Canciones, 1v, pf (1994); Sonata, vn, pf (1996); 3 fantasías, vn, pf; Kipus, 2 pieces, vn, pf; Preludio, invención, passacaglia y postludio; Str Qt; work for str qnt, pf

Principal publisher: Ricordi Americana

WRITINGS

Dinámica musical en Bolivia (La Paz, 1967)
Música contemporánea (La Paz, 1976)
Historia de la música boliviana (La Paz, 1980)
Simbiosis cultural de la música boliviana (La Paz, 1989)
Cantantes líricos bolivianos (Sucre, 1991)

CARLOS SEOANE

Avant garde (Fr.: 'vanguard'). A term derived from French military history where it signified an advance group clearing the way for the main body of troops. The connotations of frontiers, leadership, unknown territory and risk accompanied the term as it was appropriated for and by artists. An early instance of such appropriation was Saint-Simon's proposal that artists might serve as an 'avant garde' in the establishment of his new secular and scientific utopia (*Opinions littéraires, philosophiques et industrielles*, 1829). This is of some significance, as it already suggests that an avant garde might be motivated both by intellectual specialization and by social dissent.

In our own age the term is often used loosely to describe any artists who have made radical departures from tradition, but it has also been freighted with particular meanings, and these have supported a more specific usage referring to art histories of the late 19th and early 20th centuries, the era of cultural history usually labelled 'Modernism'. Here an avant garde would be differentiated from an *ars nova* and from an *ars subtilior*, neither of which need be period-specific. Thus an avant garde shares with an *ars nova* its experimental profile, and with an *ars subtilior* its élitist taste-public, but it carries two additional burdens, both relatable to Saint-Simon's use of the term. First there is a commitment to the idea of continuous progress within a single, notionally unified culture (underlying even its most anarchic manifestations), together with an acknowledgment that such progress is barely compatible with any suggestion of limits or boundaries to our knowledge and experience. Secondly there is an active

engagement – whether critical (as in Adorno's interpretation) or reintegrative (as in Peter Bürger's) – with a social world from which it feels itself separate. In both respects an avant garde is historically contingent, and thus may have a defined end as well as a beginning.

Within the historical period of Modernism we can sharpen the categorical focus of avant-garde music by distinguishing it from two opposing categories. The first is 'classical music', a category that emerged in the 19th century and was institutionalized above all in the public concert. The second is 'popular music', distinguished by its untroubled acceptance of the commodity status inherent in a middle-class 'institution of art' (to use Bürger's phrase). Relative to these repertories, an avant garde began to take on a clear profile in the late 19th century, though it was made up of aesthetically and stylistically contrasted elements. One variety is associated especially with the so-called New German School, notably through the programmes (and rhetoric) of Modernism – a 'music of the future' – proposed by Wagner and the Liszt circle. This prepared the ground of Schoenberg's blatant defiance of the cultural market-place. His Society for Private Musical Performances represented a powerfully symbolic moment in the development of the avant garde, closing off the populace in the interests of preserving musical language from further degeneration.

A considerable pretension attaches to this increasingly specialized 'project of greatness' in art, and that pretension, itself a function of aesthetic autonomy, might be viewed as a prerequisite for the Modernist aesthetic. Music was much more than an object of beauty; it was a mode of cognition, a discourse of ideas whose 'truthfulness' should be protected. It was from this vantage point, predicated on the authority of an avant garde (understood as 'the most advanced stage of the dialectic of expressive needs and technical means', Paddison, 1996), that Adorno surveyed the entire history of Western music. Significantly, he distinguished between the spirit of the early 20th-century avant garde and the New Music of the 1950s and 60s (Boulez, Stockhausen, Berio, Ligeti). This too has been labelled an avant garde, and some of its devices (multiple serialism, electronic composition, aleatory procedures and so on) described, often pejoratively, as 'avant-garde techniques'. Certainly the New Music shared with early Modernism the commitment to a specialized, progressive and 'authentic' art, and to a 'rhetoric of endless innovation' (Williams, 1989). Yet there is also a sense in which it represented an 'official' Modernism, supported by the institutions ('growing old' was Adorno's formulation), and as such it was far removed in tone from the explosive, campaigning and dissenting Modernism of that earlier period, when the bourgeois-romantic project of greatness reached its apotheosis.

A very different face of the avant garde was the subversive, anti-bourgeois protest associated with Dadaism and surrealism, given musical expression by Satie, and further developed in the radical aesthetic promoted by Cage and others in the aftermath of World War II. For Bürger this was the true avant garde, distinguished conceptually from Modernism through its rejection of the 'institution of art' and of aesthetic autonomy (paradoxically it represented for Bürger an attempt at reintegrating the aesthetic and social spheres). Yet from today's perspective Bürger's position seems a development of Adorno's rather than a major departure. More recent critical theory has been compelled to go further, addressing a growing perception (it may be disillusioning or cathartic) that any notion of a single culture, on which modern art was predicated, is no longer viable. Where music is concerned, those explosive tensions between the polarized repertories (avant-garde, classical, commercial) of a unified, albeit increasingly fragmented cultural world have been defused with astonishing ease. Disparate musics can apparently co-exist without antinomies or force fields.

Within critical theory the responses to this 'postmodern condition' have ranged from Andreas Huyssen's cautious welcome of postmodern art, provided its critical potential is acknowledged, to Jürgen Habermas's proposal that Modernism remains an 'incomplete project', now in search of a new communicative pragmatism. Elsewhere, and especially outside the Adornian tradition, postmodernism has been eagerly embraced by cultural theorists such as Jean-François Lyotard, by musicologists such as Lawrence Kramer, and by many composers for whom it seems to offer a cathartic sense of release from the prohibitions of postwar Modernism. In such a climate the fate of an avant garde is clearly open to question. Arguably the concept can have only a narrow, and perhaps a rather emasculated, definition within today's culture, associated with a continuing but now decentred Modernist project. That project is sanctioned rather than dissenting. It occupies a single corner of a plural cultural field. It is neither threatened by, nor threatens, the politics and aesthetics of mass culture.

See also MODERNISM and POSTMODERNISM.

BIBLIOGRAPHY

T.W. Adorno: *Philosophie der neuen Musik* (Tübingen, 1949; Eng. trans., 1973)

S. Rudolf: *Neue Musik* (Göttingen, 1958)

H. Vogt: *Neue Musik seit 1945* (Stuttgart, 1972)

H. Holthusen, ed.: *Avantgarde: Geschichte und Krise einer Idee* (Munich, 1966)

T.W. Adorno: *Ästhetische Theorie* (Frankfurt, 1970; Eng. trans., 1984)

D. Egbert: *Social Radicalism and the Arts* (London, 1970)

Zur Terminologie der Musik des 20. Jahrhunderts: Freiburg 1972

J. Weightman: *The Concept of the Avant-Garde* (London, 1973)

M. Nyman: *Experimental Music: Cage and Beyond* (London, 1974)

P. Bürger: *Theorie der Avantgarde* (Frankfurt, 1974; Eng. trans., 1984)

M. Bradbury and J. McFarlane, eds.: *Modernism 1890–1930* (Harmondsworth, 1976, 2/1986)

S. Buck-Morss: *The Origins of Negative Dialectics: Theodore W. Adorno, Walter Benjamin, and the Frankfurt Institute* (London, 1977)

M. Calinescu: *Faces of Modernity: Avant-Garde, Decadence, Kitsch* (Bloomington, IN, 1977)

C. Butler: *After the Wake: an Essay on the Contemporary Avant Garde* (Oxford, 1980)

P. Griffiths: *Modern Music: the Avant Garde since 1945* (London, 1981, rev. 2/1995 as *Modern Music and After: Directions since 1945*)

T.J. Reiss: *The Discourse of Modernism* (Ithaca, NY, 1982)

J.-F. Lyotard: *The Postmodern Condition: a Report on Knowledge* (Manchester, 1984)

R.J. Bernstein, ed.: *Habermas and Modernity* (Cambridge, 1985)

J. Habermas: 'Modernity – an Incomplete Project', *Postmodern Culture*, ed. H. Foster (London, 1985)

A. Huyssen: *After the Great Divide: Modernism, Mass Culture, Postmodernism* (Bloomington, IN, 1986)

L. Hutcheon: *The Politics of Postmodernism* (London, 1989)

R. Williams: *The Politics of Modernism* (London, 1989)

F. Jameson: *Postmodernism, or the Cultural Logic of Late Capitalism* (London, 1991)

M. Paddison: *Adorno, Modernism and Mass Culture: Essays on Critical Theory and Music* (London, 1996)

A. Williams: *New Music and the Claims of Modernity* (Aldershot, 1997)

JIM SAMSON

Avanzolini, Girolamo (*b* Rimini, *c*1600; *d* Rimini, *c*1678). Italian composer and author. He was a priest and *maestro di cappella* of Rimini Cathedral. From 1649 he was librarian of the Biblioteca Gambalunghiana, Rimini. He wrote literary and historical works; all his music dates from his early years. He had some connection with the pseudonymous composer Accademico Bizzarro Capriccioso, to each of whose opp.1 and 2 (1620–21) he contributed a madrigal, one for two voices, the other for three. As a composer he is known mainly for three volumes of sacred music written mostly in a simple style suited to the needs of a provincial *maestro di cappella*: 14 eight-voice psalms with organ continuo, op.1, a book of four- and five-voice concertato masses, op.2 (incomplete), and four masses and two motets with organ continuo, op.3 (all Venice, 1623). The description 'a tre voci variate' of op.3 refers to an unusual arrangement of partbooks – one each for the highest, middle and lowest voices.

ELEANOR SELFRIDGE-FIELD

Avdeyeva, Larisa (Ivanovna) (*b* Moscow, 21 June 1925). Russian mezzo-soprano. She studied singing and dramatic art at the Stanislavsky Opera Studio (1945–6). From 1947 she was a soloist at the Stanislavsky Music Theatre, Moscow, where she sang Suzuki, La Périchole, Kosova and Varvara (Khrennikov's *V buryu* and *Frol Skobeyev*) and Mistress of the Copper Mountain (Molchanov's *Kamennïy tsvetok* ['The Stone Flower']). In 1952 she moved to the Bol'shoy Theatre, where she sang the leading Rimsky-Korsakov and Musorgsky mezzo roles, Tchaikovsky's Enchantress, Borodin's Konchakovna, Akhrosimova in *War and Peace* and the Commissar (Kholminov's *Optimisticheskaya tragediya*). She married Yevgeny Svetlanov. She toured widely, in the USA, Canada, Japan and Europe, and was made People's Artist of the RSFSR in 1964.

I.M. YAMPOL'SKY/R

Avella, Giovanni d' (*fl* 1657). Italian theorist and ?composer. His treatise *Regole di musica, divise in cinque trattati* (Rome, 1657) indicates that in 1657 he was Predicatore in the Minori Osservanti – an order of strict Franciscans – in the province of Terra Lavoro. In some reference works he is mentioned as a composer of lute music, but there are no known compositions. The *Regole di musica* deals not only with music but with a range of other subjects as well, including astronomy and astrology. However, Avella's theories and views failed to impress his contemporaries and fellow theorists: G.F. Beccatelli, for instance, in his *Annotazioni* (MS, *I-Bc*) on the *Regole*, rightly accused Avella of ignorance of musical history in attributing the Guidonian Hand not only to Boethius but also to Plato and Aristotle, and in making Guido of Arezzo a contemporary of Pope Gregory I.

BIBLIOGRAPHY

J.-H. Lederer: *Lorenzo Penna und seine Kontrapunkttheorie* (diss., U. of Graz, (1970)

E. Apfel: *Geschichte der Kompositionslehre, von den Anfängen bis gegen 1700* (Wilhelmshaven, 1981), ii, 443–6

JOSEF-HORST LEDERER

Ave Maria (Lat.: 'Hail Mary'). A prayer of the Roman rite. It consists of the words of the Archangel Gabriel (*Luke* i.28), the words of Elizabeth (*Luke* i.42) and a formula of petition appended in the 15th century; the present wording was adopted in the 16th century for general liturgical use (*LU*, 1861). The first segment of the text is used as an antiphon for the Feast of the Annunciation with a 10th-century melody (*LU*, 1416). Moreover, as an Offertory antiphon it occurs once with the above-mentioned text and a modern melody (*LU*, 1318) and once with both biblical portions of the text and a medieval melody (*LU*, 355). A considerable number of polyphonic settings, often with textual variants and only loosely based on the chant melody, survive by Renaissance composers, including De Orto, Josquin, Parsons, Willaert and Victoria, and there are *Ave Maria* masses by La Rue, Morales and Palestrina. Giacomo Fogliano set the complete text as a simple four-voice *lauda* (HAM, i, 97). The title is used for Schubert's song after Scott's *Lady of the Lake*. Gounod's celebrated *Ave Maria* consists of a melody superimposed on the C major prelude from the first book of Bach's *Das wohltemperirte Clavier*. For further information See R. Steiner: 'Ave Maria [Antiphon]', *New Catholic Encyclopedia* (New York, 1967).

See also ANTIPHON and MOTET, §II.

□

Avenarius [Habermann], Philipp (*b* Lichtenstein, nr Zwickau, *c*1553; *d* in or after 1610). German composer and organist. He is first heard of as an organist at Amorbach, Odenwald, in 1570 and until February 1571. The dedication of his *Cantiones sacrae* (1572) was written from Falkenau, Bohemia, where his father was working. According to Gerber he was later an organist at Altenburg and then, until 1610, at the Michaeliskirche, Zeitz. He was one of a number of minor composers working in Saxony and Thuringia in the latter half of the 16th century. His output was less varied than, for example, that of Johann Steuerlein, but the pieces in his *Cantiones sacrae* were highly regarded by his contemporaries, as is shown by the praise accorded them by Christoph Schultze. The style of his motets is conservative, as was his preference for Latin texts.

WORKS

Cantiones sacrae, 5vv (Nuremberg, 1572)
Devota acclamatio novis honoribus, 6vv (Jena, 1608)
20 other sacred works D-Bsb, Rp, Z, PL-WRu

BIBLIOGRAPHY

GerberNL
A. Werner: *Städtische und fürstliche Musikpflege in Zeitz bis zum Anfang des 19. Jahrhunderts* (Bückeburg and Leipzig, 1922)
E.F. Schmid: *Die Orgeln der Abtei Amorbach* (Buchen, 1938)
R. Quoika: 'Christoph Harant von Polschitz und seine Zeit', *Mf*, vii (1954), 414–29, esp. 419
R. Quoika: *Die Musik der Deutschen in Böhmen und Mähren* (Berlin, 1956)
G. Pietzsch: 'Orgelbauer, Orgeln und Orgelspiel in Deutschland bis zum Ende des 16. Jahrhunderts', *Mf*, xi (1958), 307–15, esp. 311

AUGUST SCHARNAGL

Avenarius [Habermann], Thomas (*b* Eilenburg, bap. 17 Nov 1584; *d* after 1638). German composer, organist and poet. He enrolled at Leipzig University in 1599 as the son of a schoolmaster, Thomas Habermann, and was later tutor to the von Malnitz family at Berreuth, near Dippoldiswalde. In 1617 he was appointed Kapellmeister at Schloss Weesenstein, near Pirna, and marked Emperor Matthias's visit to Dresden with his *Panegyris Caesarea*, consisting of 1200 verses among which are 20 on the 'pleasant music' conducted by Schütz in a church service on 27 July 1617. In 1621 or 1622 he became organist at the Lambertikirche, Hildesheim, where he was twice

married: on 8 October 1625 to Magdalena Rolzheussen, who died of plague about a year later, and on 29 July 1627 to Anna Dehnen. In 1630 he published his most important work, *Convivium musicale*, which includes 38 dances in four to five parts. He may have played the organ at Celle in 1635; his setting of Psalm cxxxiii is dedicated to Duke August the Elder of Celle. His last three published works consist of canons, some with basso ostinato.

WORKS

Horticello … amorosischer Gesänglein, 4–5vv/insts, pubd 1614, lost [preface (inc.) repr. in *MatthesonGEP*, 12–14]
Convivium musicale, in welchen etzliche newe Tractamenta, als gar schöne und fröhlichen Paduanen, Galliarden, Couranten, Intraden und Balletten … offeriret werden, 4–5 insts (Hildesheim, 1630); 17 dances ed. in Musice varie, ii–iii (Germersheim, 1994)
Adplausus pius et augustus, das ist Christliche Fried und Freuden, Concert (Ps cxxxiii), 5vv, insts (Celle, 1636)
Viridarium musicum, a 3–4 (Hildesheim, 1638)
Fugae musicales inter fugae martiales, 3–4vv/insts (Hildesheim, 1638)
Curae curarum, 3–4vv/insts (?Hildesheim, 1639)

BIBLIOGRAPHY

ADB (J.A. Wagenmann); *EitnerQ*; *FétisB*; *GerberL*; *MatthesonGEP*
H. Müller: 'Thomas Avenarius und Celle', *Celler Chronik* 7, ed. W. Nolte (Celle, 1996), 79–104
H. Müller: 'Der Komponist Thomas Avenarius', *Familienverband Avenarius* (Melle, 1996), 303–11

HARALD MÜLLER

Avenary, Hanoch [Loewenstein, Herbert] (*b* Danzig [now Gdánsk], 25 May 1908; *d* Magen, 16 Sept 1994). Israeli musicologist. He studied musicology, literature and art history at the universities of Leipzig, Munich, Frankfurt and Königsberg (Kaliningrad), where he took the doctorate under Wilhelm Warringer in 1931 with a dissertation on Minnesang. He was prevented from pursuing an academic career in Germany, and turned to publishing Jewish art in Berlin (1932–6). In 1936 he settled as a publisher in Palestine, where research in musicology had barely begun, and he had to carry on his musicological work independently, publishing articles mostly in foreign periodicals. Urged to adapt himself to the demands of a country under war conditions, he developed a chemical production process and worked as a technical manager in industry (1941–8) before joining the Israel Air Force research department. He left the service with the rank of major to take up a research fellowship in musicology at the Hebrew University, Jerusalem (1965–72); in 1966 he became a lecturer, and in 1972 assistant professor in the musicology department of Tel-Aviv University, rising to the rank of Associate Professor. He was also a guest professor in Vienna (1973) and Heidelberg (1982–3). Co-editor of *Orbis musicae* and co-founder of the *Hebrew Quarterly for Music*, he was appointed president of the Israel Musicological Society in 1971. His speciality was sacred music, particularly Jewish music and that of the ancient Near East. In 1994 he received the Israel Prize for his achievements in Jewish music research.

WRITINGS

'Eine pentatonische Bibelweise in der deutschen Synagoge', *ZMw*, xii (1929–30), 513–26
Wort und Ton bei Oswald von Wolkenstein (diss., U. of Königsberg, 1931; Königsberg, 1932)
'Munahei ha–musiqah ba–safrut ha' ivrit shel yemei ha–benayim' [Musical terms in Hebrew medieval literature], *Leshonenu*, xiii (1945), 140
'Abu'l-Salt's Treatise on Music', *MD*, vi (1952), 27–32
'Formal Structure of Psalms and Canticles in Early Jewish and Christian Chant', *MD*, vii (1953), 1–13

'Magic, Symbolism and Allegory of Old Hebrew Sound-Instruments',
  CHM, ii (1956–7), 21–31
'Hieronymus' Epistel über die Musikinstrumente und ihre
  altöstlichen Quellen', *AnM*, xvi (1961), 55–80
Studies in the Hebrew, Syrian and Greek Liturgical Recitative (Tel-
  Aviv, 1963)
'Geniza Fragments of Hebrew Hymns and Prayers Set to Music:
  Early 12th Century', *Journal of Jewish Studies*, xvi (1966), 87–104
'A Geniza Find of Saadya's Psalm-Preface and its Musical Aspects',
  Hebrew Union College Annual, xxxix (1968), 145–62
'The Cantorial Fantasia of the 18th and 19th Centuries', *Yuval*, i
  (1968), 65–85
'Cantos españoles antiguos mencionadas en la literatura hebraea',
  AnM, xxv (1970), 67–79
'The Concept of Mode in European Synagogue Chant', *Yuval*, ii
  (1971), 11–21
*Hebrew Hymn Tunes: the Rise and Development of a Musical
  Tradition* (Tel-Aviv, 1971)
'"Flutes for a Bride or a Dead Man": the Symbolism of the Flute',
  Orbis musicae, i (1971–2), 11–24
'Jewish Music: Post-Biblical History', *Encyclopaedia judaica*, ed. C.
  Roth and G. Wigoder (Jerusalem, 1971–2, 3/1996)
'Die Diskrepanz der ikonographischen und literarischen
  Darstellung altöstlicher Musikinstrumente', *IMSCR XI:
  Copenhagen 1972*, 141–5; Eng. trans. in *Orbis musicae*, ii (Tel-
  Aviv, 1973–4), 121–9
'The Hebrew Version of Abū l-Salt's Treatise on Music', *Yuval*, iii
  (1974), 7–82 [edn, trans. and commentary]
'The Earliest Notation of Ashkenazi Bible Chant', *Journal of Jewish
  Studies*, xxvi (1975), 132–50
'The Northern and Southern Idioms of Early European Music: a New
  Approach to an Old Problem', *AcM*, xlix (1977), 27–49
The Ashkenazi Tradition of Biblical Chant between 1500 and 1900
  (Tel-Aviv, 1978)
'Reflections on the Origins of the Alleluia-Jubilus', *Orbis musicae*, vi
  (1978), 34–42
Encounters of East and West in Music: Selected Writings (Tel-Aviv,
  1979)
'Akten und Briefe als Hilfsmittel Musikalischer Textkritik: Salomon
  Sulzers Schir Zion', *Festschrift Othmar Wessely zum 60.
  Geburtstag* (Tutzing, 1982), 39–54
'Paradigms of Arab Modes in the Genizah Fragment Cambridge T.S.
  N.S. 90, 4', *Yuval*, iv (1982), 11–28
ed.: *Kantor Salomon Sulzer und seine Zeit: ein Dokumentation*
  (Sigmaringen, 1985)
'Persistence and Transformation of a Sephardi Penitential Hymn
  under Changing Environmental Conditions', *Yuval*, v (1986),
  181–237
'The Aspects of Time and Environment in Jewish Traditional Music',
  Israel Studies in Musicology, iv (1987), 93–123

EDITIONS

S. Rossi: *Il primo libro delle canzonette (1589)* (Tel-Aviv, 1975)
S. Rossi: *Il secondo libro di madrigali* (Tel-Aviv, 1989)

WILLIAM Y. ELIAS

Avenpace. *See* IBN BĀJJA.

Aventinus, Johannes [Turmair, Johann; Thurnmaier, John;
Thurnmayer, Jean; Thurinomarus] (*b* Abensberg, 4 July
1477; *d* Regensburg, 9 Jan 1534). German historian and
music theorist. He studied at Ingolstadt University with
Conradus Celtis, at Kraków University, and at Paris
University with Jacobus Faber Stapulensis. After the death
of Albrecht IV, Aventinus was appointed tutor to the
young Duke of Bavaria and his brothers in 1508, and in
1517 became court historian. In this capacity he produced
two of the most important and influential historical works
of his time: *Annales ducum boiariae* and *Bayrischer
Chronicon*.

Aventinus was the author of *Musicae rudimenta*
(Augsburg, 1516; ed. in Keahey) sometimes incorrectly
ascribed to Nicolaus Faber (ii). The treatise, in ten
chapters, was written for the instruction of Ernst, the
youngest of the three dukes. In keeping with the traditional
approach to music as a part of the Quadrivium, the work

deals with speculation about the origins and uses of music,
solmization and the mutation of Guidonian hexachords,
and the Pythagorean division of the monochord. Problems
of current musical practice are only lightly touched on.
Aventinus cited many musical authorities, including Plato,
Aristotle, Aristoxenus, Cleonides, Boethius, Guido of
Arezzo, Ugolino of Orvieto, Johannes de Muris and
Gaffurius. He gave a number of terms and phrases in
German as well as in Latin.

BIBLIOGRAPHY

A. von Dommer: 'Nikolaus Faber', *MMg*, i (1869), 19–23
C. von Halm, ed.: *J. Turmairs sämmtliche Werke* (Munich, 1880–86)
K.W. Niemöller: 'Ist Nicolaus Faber oder Johannes Aventin der
  Verfasser der "Musicae Rudimenta" (Augsburg, 1516)?', *Mf*, xiv
  (1961), 184–5
T.H. Keahey, ed.: *Johann Turmair – Johannes Aventinus: Musicae
  Rudimenta, Augsburg, 1516* (New York, 1971)
E. Dunninger: *Johannes Aventinus: Leben und Werk der bayerische
  Geschichtsschreibers* (Rosenheim, 1977)

T. HERMAN KEAHEY

Ave regina caelorum (Lat.: 'Hail Queen of Heaven'). One
of the four Marian antiphons retained at the Council of
Trent and ordered to be sung at the end of Compline from
the Purification (2 February) until Wednesday in Holy
Week. Its original role in the liturgy appears to have been
to precede and follow the chanting of a psalm. Of the two
melodies in the *Liber usualis* the more elaborate (p.274)
is certainly the older. Pre-tridentine sources have a slightly
different text. Du Fay's four-voice setting, which he
requested be sung at his deathbed, uses the chant melody
as a cantus firmus in the tenor, with sections of the chant
paraphrased in the upper two voices; the traditional text
is troped with a personal supplication for mercy: 'Miserere
tui labentis Du Fay'. Two other settings by Du Fay
survive, both for three voices, and a *Missa 'Ave regina
celorum'*, related to the four-part work. Josquin wrote a
celebrated work setting both this text and that of *Alma
redemptoris mater*, in which all four voices participate in
the paraphrasing of the two chants. Settings by 16th-
century composers include four by Palestrina, an eight-
part setting with organ and a mass by Victoria, and a
five-voice setting by Gesualdo.

A different text, *Ave regina caelorum, mater regis
angelorum*, has a medieval melody (*LU*, 1864) used also
for a number of similar texts including an antiphon for St
Edmund, king and martyr, beginning 'Ave rex gentis
Anglorum'. The Marian text was set, independently of
the chant, by Walter Frye, in a responsorial form in which
lines 3–4 were repeated after lines 5–6 to make an eight-
line text. Jacob Obrecht wrote a four-part setting, taking
Frye's tenor and transposing it from F (major) to D
(minor); he also based his *Missa 'Ave regina celorum'* on
the untransposed tenor of Frye's composition. *Ave rex
gentis Anglorum*, for its part, became the basis of two
14th-century motets in a manuscript from Bury St
Edmunds (Bukofzer, 1950).

See also ANTIPHON and MOTET, §II.

BIBLIOGRAPHY

P. Wagner: *Einführung in die gregorianischen Melodien*, i (Fribourg,
  1895, 3/1911/R; Eng. trans., 1901/R)
M. Bukofzer: *Studies in Medieval and Renaissance Music* (New
  York, 1950)
W. Apel: *Gregorian Chant* (Bloomington, IN, 1958, 3/1966)
R. Steiner: 'Ave regina caelorum', *New Catholic Encyclopedia* (New
  York, 1967)
D. Hiley: *Western Plainchant: a Handbook* (Oxford, 1993)

JOHN CALDWELL

Averroes. *See* IBN RUSHD.

Aversi (Lat.). A term used in the 15th century to describe mass settings in which the number of voices varies from one section to the next. Although the word is found in only one manuscript (*GB-Ob* Can.misc.213), where it is used in the index to describe mass movements by Binchois, Guillaume Legrant and Bartolomeo da Bologna, it is appropriate for describing an important series of works from the first half of the 15th century in which sections marked 'duo' (or 'soli') and 'chorus' alternate.

See also CURSIVA and VIRILAS.

BIBLIOGRAPHY

M.F. Bukofzer: *Studies in Medieval and Renaissance Music* (New York, 1950), 176
H. Schoop: *Entstehung und Verwendung der Handschrift Oxford Bodleian Library, Canonici misc. 213* (Berne, 1971), 49

□

Avery [Burton, Avery] (*b* ?*c*1470; *d* ?*c*1543). English composer. Among the English authorities to whom Thomas Morley referred in preparing his *A Plaine and Easie Introduction to Practicall Musicke* (1597) is one listed simply as 'Averie'. This is undoubtedly the 'Master Averie' who composed an organ *Te Deum* (in *GB-Lbl* Add.29996; ed. in EECM, vi, 1966) and a *Missa 'Ut re mi fa sol la'* (in *Ob* Mus. Sch.E.376–80). In the latter, however, a later hand has added the surname 'Burton' in the bass partbook, and on the strength of this Flood ventured to identify the composer of the two pieces with a number of musicians of similar names to which he found references in his search of the state papers. If these all refer to the same man the following slender biography can be constructed.

On 29 November 1494 Henry VII made a payment 'To Burton for making a Mass, 20s.'. In November 1509 a David Burton was appointed a Gentleman of the Chapel Royal and on 22 February 1511 Davy Burton was issued with livery for the funeral of Prince Henry, the infant son of Henry VIII. On 20 June 1513 the Chapel Royal accompanied the king to France where on 17 September at Tournai a *Te Deum*, attributed without justification to Burton, was performed after Mass. In June 1520 he was again in France with the Chapel Royal attending King Henry's meeting with François I at the Field of the Cloth of Gold, and in July 1527 'Master Avery' was among the Gentlemen of the Chapel who accompanied Cardinal Wolsey to France, an association that may account for the inclusion of his mass in the Forrest-Heyther collection (*GB-Ob*) in second place, after Taverner's *Missa 'Gloria tibi Trinitas'*. In a list of salaries for the year 1526 Avery Burnett, Gentleman of the Chapel, is scheduled to receive 7¼d. a day. During the next 15 years the names Burton and Burnet occur in connection with various payments and grants of leases of land (listed by Flood) in the last of which, dated 25 October 1542, he is described as David Burton, Gentleman of the King's Chapel.

If the composer and the Gentleman of the Chapel Royal are the same person it remains unexplained why both manuscripts should use only the name 'Avery'; though it is perhaps because they do that Avery alone of all the Englishmen listed by Morley is familiarly addressed by his first name. On the other hand, Morley did not use the title 'Master', nor is it clear what that title's significance is. In support of Flood's identification an annotation, presumably by Thomas Tomkins himself in his copy of Morley's treatise (now in the library of Magdalen College,

Oxford), describes a group of names which includes Averie as 'All these of the King's Chapel'.

Avery's *Missa 'Ut re mi fa sol la'*, the only piece of English vocal music on the hexachord, is incomplete, apparently lacking a second bass part, in spite of the fact that it occurs in a complete set of six partbooks. The mass was originally described in the *Tabula* as of 'vi parts' but this was later changed to 'v parts' and it seems quite certain that the sixth part was never copied into Mus. Sch.E.381. The work is available in a modern edition with a reconstructed sixth part (ed. J. Smart, London, 1978).

BIBLIOGRAPHY

BDECM ('Burnett, Avery'; also 'Burton, Davy')
W.H.G. Flood: *Early Tudor Composers* (London, 1925/*R*)
J. Pulver: *A Biographical Dictionary of Old English Music* (London, 1927/*R*)
H. Baillie: 'Les musiciens de la chapelle royale d'Henri VIII au Camp du Drap d'Or', *Fêtes et cérémonies au temps de Charles Quint (Les fêtes de la Renaissance II)* [Brussels, Antwerp, Ghent, Liège 1957], ed. J. Jacquot (Paris, 1960, 2/1976), 147–59
J. Bergsagel: 'The Date and Provenance of the Forrest-Heyther Collection of Tudor Masses', *MD*, xliv (1963), 240–48
L.D. Brothers: 'Avery Burton and his Hexachord Mass', *ML*, xxviii (1974), 153–76
L.D. Brothers: 'New Light on an Early Tudor Mass: Avery Burton's *Missa Ut re mi fa sol la*', *MD*, xxxii (1978), 111–26
P. Phillips: 'A Commentary on Avery Burton's *Mass on the Hexachord*', *EMc*, vii (1979), 218–21 [see also comment by J. Smart and author's reply, p.563]
J. Caldwell: *The Oxford History of English Music*, i (Oxford, 1991)

JOHN BERGSAGEL

Avery, John (*b* ?Avening, 1737/55; *bur*. London, 29 April 1807). English organ builder. Rigby has suggested that the John Avery baptized at Avening, about 5 miles from Stroud, on 3 January 1738 was the organ builder; the record of his burial at Holy Sepulchre without Newgate, London, however, gives his age as 52, making his probable date of birth 1755 (Matthews). Avery's reputation as a craftsman was good: 'an excellent workman … [who] imitated Green a good deal, but was much his superior' (Sutton); 'The general characteristic of Avery's organs was that they combined quantity with quality in every department' (J.C. Bumpus, in Matthews). Major contracts included St Stephen Coleman Street, London (1775); St John the Baptist, Croydon (1794); St Lawrence, Stroud (1798); Winchester Cathedral (1799); St Margaret's, Westminster, London (1804) and Carlisle Cathedral (completed by Elliot in 1808).

Avery's workshop was in the churchyard of St Margaret's, Westminster, but in his final years his address was Queen Street, Westminster. Avery's reputation as an unreliable character – 'generally drunk and often in prison for debt' (Sutton) – is supported by contemporary sources. He died in a debtors' prison.

BIBLIOGRAPHY

J. Sutton: *A Short Account of Organs Built in England from the Reign of Charles the Second to the Present Time* (London, 1847), 86–8
E. Rigby: 'John Avery and Stroud Parish Church', *The Organ*, xlii (1962–3), 125–30
B. Matthews: 'John Avery', *The Organ*, liv (1975–6), 114–23

DAVID C. WICKENS

Avery Fisher Hall. New York concert hall opened in 1962; it was known as the Philharmonic Hall until 1973 and is part of Lincoln Center. *See* NEW YORK, §3.

Avia, Jacob. *See under* JAKOB BANWART.

Avianus, Johannes [Johann] (*b* Tonnedorf, nr Erfurt; *d* Eisenberg, nr Gera, 22 Jan 1617). German writer on music, composer and schoolmaster. In 1579 he was teaching at the Lateinschule at Ronneburg, near Gera, and in 1591 he was Rektor of the Lateinschule at Gera. Later he was a preacher at Bernsdorf, near Torgau, at Munich and at Krossen, near Gera, and from 1614 until his death he was superintendent at Eisenberg. He published *Isagoge in libros musicae poeticae* (Erfurt, 1581), which is typical of the many writings on *musica poetica* of the later 16th century. Another theoretical work survives in manuscript. His only known music is a four-part occasional work, *Delphica & vera pennae literatae nobilitas* (Erfurt, 1595).

Avicenna. *See* IBN SĪNĀ.

Avidom [Mahler-Kalkstein], **Menahem** (*b* Stanislav, 6 Jan 1908; *d* Tel-Aviv, 5 Aug 1995). Israeli composer of Russian birth. His mother was a cousin of Mahler; his adopted surname combines the word 'Avi' ('father of') with the initials of his children's names. He studied at the American University in Beirut and at the Paris Conservatoire, where his teachers included Rabaud. In 1925 he emigrated to Palestine, where, in addition to his work as a composer, he served as a music critic, secretary general of the Israel PO (1945–52), chair of the Israel Composers' League (1958–71) and general director of ACUM, the Israeli performing rights society (1955–80).

In the late 1930s, after writing early works in an Impressionist style, Avidom turned towards atonal composition. While studying in Beirut and during a four-year stay in Egypt, however, he became deeply influenced by Mediterranean and Asian folk music and French culture. These influences found their expression in arrangements for the Yemenite singer Bracha Zefira (1939), the Flute Concerto (1944), Symphony no.1 'Amamit' ('Folk Symphony', 1945), Symphony no.3 'Yam tichonit' ('Mediterranean Sinfonietta', 1951) and other works. A use of modal scales, folk-like dance rhythms, oriental melodic motifs and orchestration influenced by Ravel and Les Six are characteristic of these works. Symphony no.2 'David' (1948–9) depicts the life of the biblical king, while Symphony no.5 'Shirat Eilat' ('The Song of Eilat', 1956–7) is a combination of a conventional symphonic form and a song cycle.

In the early 1960s Israeli music began to move away from regionalism towards international styles and techniques. Influenced by these trends, Avidom turned to 12-note procedures. *Enigma* (1962), a work that imitates electronic effects, displays his interest in sound patterns: the second movement is an inversion of the first, the fourth an inversion of the third and the fifth a recapitulation of the first. The Symphony no.7 (1960–61) features a four-note series (A–B–D–mi) that refers to his name. In 1974, for the first Rubinstein Piano Master Competition, Avidom wrote *ArtHur ruBinStEin*, six inventions based on the series of notes represented in Rubinstein's name (A–H–B–S–E). The last symphony, no.10 (1981), combines 12-note procedures and oriental melodies. *Bachiana* (1984–5), based on B-A-C-H, was written for J.S. Bach's 300th anniversary.

Avidom's first major opera *B'khol dor va'dor* ('In Every Generation', 1953–4) describes events in Jewish history.

Ha'preida ('The Farewell', 1971) creates a strangely unreal atmosphere and a convincing expression of complex psychological situations. His historical opera *Alexandra ha'khashmonait* ('Alexandra the Hasmonean', 1955–6) won the Israel State Prize in 1961.

WORKS
(*selective list*)

Stage: B'khol dor va'dor [In Every Generation] (Spl, L. Goldberg), solo vv, 10 insts, 1953–4; Alexandra ha'khashmonait [Alexandra the Hasmonean] (op, A. Ashman), 1955–6; Haramai [The Crook] (chbr op, E. Kishon), 1966–7; Ha'preida [The Farewell] (radio op, D. Hertz), 1969; Bigdei ha'melekh ha'chadashim [The Emperor's New Clothes] (chbr op, M. Ohad, after H.C. Andersen), 1975; Me'arat Yodfat [The Cave of Jotapata] (dramatic scene, S. Tanai), S, chbr orch, 1978; Sofo shel ha'melekh Og [The End of King Og] (children's op, Tanai), 1979; Ha'chet ha'rishon [The First Sin] (chbr op, A. Meged), 1980–81

Orch: Conc., fl, str, 1944; Sym. no.1 'Amamit' [Folk Sym.], 1945; Sym. no.2 'David', 1948–9; Music for Str, 1949; Sym. no.3 'Yam tichonit' [Mediterranean Sinfonietta], 1951; Sym. no.4, 1954–5; Sym. no.5 'Shirat Eilat' [The Song of Eilat], Mez, orch, 1956–7; Sym. no.6, 1958; Triptyque symphonique, 1960; Sym. no.7 'Philharmonic', 1960–61; Sym. no.8 'Sinfonietta l'moed' [A Festival Sinfonietta], *c*1965; Sym. no.9 (Symphonie variee), chbr orch, 1968; Spring, ov., 1970; Sym. no.10 (Sinfonia brevis), 1981

Vocal: Kantatat t'hilim [Psalm Cant.], chorus, 1955; Yud'bet gueva'ot [Twelve Hills] (cant., R. Freier), Mez, chbr orch, 1976; songs: 1v, pf; 1v, str qt

Chbr and solo inst: Concertino, vn, pf, 1949, orchd 1967; Str Qt no.1, 1954; Str Qt no.2, 1961; Enigma, 5 wind, perc, pf, 1962; Brass Qt, 1969; BACH Suite, ww, str, pf, perc, n.d.; ArtHur ruBinStEin, pf, 1974; Str Qt no.3, 1979; Sonata, va, 1984; Bachiana, pf, 1984–5 [arr. chbr ens]; Sonatina, vc, 1988; Triptiyque, fl, hn, pf, 1988; pf works

MSS in *IL-J*

Principal publishers: Israel Music Institute, Israeli Music

BIBLIOGRAPHY

M. Brod: *Die Musik Israels* (Kassel, 1976)
A. Tischler: *A Descriptive Bibliography of Art Music by Israeli Composers* (Detroit, 1988)
Y. Cohen: *N'imey Zmirot Yisrael* [The heirs of the psalmist] (Tel-Aviv, 1990)

MICHAL BEN-ZUR

Avignon. City in France, capital of the prefecture of the Vaucluse département. Roman chant was introduced to Avignon at the end of the 7th century by the monks of Lérins, who were summoned there by Bishop Agricol. Of the troubadours, only two songs have survived, one by Bertran Folco d'Avigno and one by Raimon d'Avigno. A university was founded in 1303. In 1309 Avignon became the seat of Pope Clement V and the centre of Western Christianity, and also a European trading centre. The 14th century was the richest period in Avignon's musical history. The papal court comprised up to 1000 people employed in up to 500 different capacities. The town became over-populated and phenomenally rich, while the court enjoyed extreme luxury. 'From this impious Babylon from whence all shame has fled, I too have fled to save my life', wrote Petrarch. There were many opulent religious services, and also festivities and secular entertainments to mark official receptions. The writing of music for the services became an excuse to try out the latest methods of composition. Pope John XXII (1316–34) issued a decretal ('Docta sanctorum') on the subject in 1325 which, however, is not the condemnation of polyphony it is sometimes said to be. Moreover, in addition to the *grande chapelle* of 30 or 40 members, Benedict XII, at the beginning of his pontificate in 1334, also established a private chapel, St Etienne, with 12 singers. In Avignon itself no trace remains of the Ordinary repertory, which was most of the time largely improvised on the *super librum*. But two manuscripts, from Ivrea (written after 1350) and from Apt give an idea of the type of music which was fashionable: polyphonic mass fragments for three voices, using Ars Nova techniques; motets, ballades, rondeaux and virelais occasionally written in *ars subtilior* style, which flourished from 1380; and hymns, in which the liturgical melody, in decorated form, appears in the upper voice of the polyphony, anticipating the 15th-century style. Johannes de Muris wrote a motet in honour of John XXII, and Philippe de Vitry stayed in Avignon several times on missions from the French king, and composed an isorhythmic motet in honour of Pope Clement VI (1342–52). The Apt manuscript, on the other hand, contains a Gloria by Baude Cordier which is quite different in feeling and much nearer to 15th-century style. The papal court was receptive to musical novelties, and composers in the service of Clement VII (antipope, 1378–94), and of Benedict XIII (antipope, 1394–1424) included Bosco, Matheus de Sancto Johanne, Hasprois, Haucourt and Philippus de Caserta. In 1372 an organ, one of the first in France, was installed in the Franciscan monastery at Avignon. Jewish music also flourished under the Avignon popes since Clement V protected the Jews from the expulsion orders of King Philip the Fair (1306) and the musical traditions of the synagogue were thus preserved in the four communities of Avignon, Carpentras, Cavaillon and L'Isle sur Sorgue.

The deposition of Benedict XIII at the Synod of Pisa (1409) led to the decline of the chapel choir, but the departure of the popes did not mean the end of all Avignon musical life; in 1449 organs were installed at the cathedral and in 1454 at St Agricol (restored 1489–93). At the end of the 15th century there were two organ makers in Avignon, Barthélémy Prévot and Ramon Vitus. In 1481 Archbishop Giulio della Rovere founded a cathedral choir school for the study of plainchant, and the post of *maître de chant* was created at the university in 1497. The first of many festivities with processions, allegories, music and dancing, characteristic of the Renaissance and clearly influenced by Italy, seems to have been in 1473 for the reception of Cardinal Charles de Bourbon. An early printing industry was briefly established: Etienne Briard, a type founder, cast new characters for music printing, and Jean de Channey published (1533–5) settings of the Mass, Lamentations, *Magnificat* and hymns by Carpentras, who died in Avignon in 1548. But the Avignon printers soon lost their importance to rivals in Lyons. In 1547 Claude Noguyer taught 'letters and musical instruments' to young children. Victor de Montbuisson, an Avignon lutenist at the end of the century, pursued his career in Kassel and The Hague: three of his galliards were included in J.-B. Besard's *Thesaurus harmonicus* (RISM 1603[15]). The late 16th century saw the first substantial collection of Provençal noëls, 130 carols from Notre Dame des Doms (1570–1610). The modern treatment of music in the town's religious ceremonies and secular festivities gave a livelihood to several violin bands, which sometimes included woodwind. A description of the festivities at a reception for Queen Marie de Médicis in November 1600 is in the *Labyrinthe royal de l'Hercule gaulois* (Avignon, 1601); the music for this occasion, by the cathedral organist Antoine Esquirol, was in the Venetian style. In 1622, for the visit of Louis XIII, an exceptional orchestra, 120

strong, was conducted by Sauveur Intermet (*d* 1657), canon and *maître de chapelle* at St Agricol, at that time the main musical centre. Its choir school was reputed to be one of the best in the kingdom and Intermet's reputation spread as far as Paris. When a dramatic performance was mounted in the Jesuit college, Intermet's airs so pleased the king that he asked for a copy of them and next day requested that motets by the canon should be sung during Mass. In 1660, for Louis XIV's visit, another *maître de chapelle*, Béraud (*d* 1687), composed a special motet. The 17th century was the heyday of the Provençal carol; one of the finest collections was of the 57 *Noëls nouveaux* published in seven volumes by Nicolas Saboly between 1669 and 1674. He was responsible for their texts but the music consists of traditional Provençal and French tunes. J.-J. Mouret, the future 'musicien des Graces', was born in Avignon in 1682 and received his musical education there, in the cathedral choir school. During the last years of the century, Pierre Gautier's Marseilles opera company enjoyed great success at Avignon; in 1688 he even staged *Bellérophon* for two private performances in the home of the Marquis de Blauvac. Italian singers and composers were equally successful in Avignon; the repertory of the chapel included works by Carissimi and others.

Nicolas Ranc directed a permanent opera company from 1705, and music lovers remained numerous in the 18th century. Two guilds were formed in the mid-18th century, St Grégoire and Ste Cécile, for 'singing musicians' and 'symphonic musicians' respectively; they acquired a monopoly for giving public concerts, and were able to perform such large-scale choral works as settings of the Psalms by Blanchard and Lalande. But musicians with creative talents tended to leave Avignon to try their luck in Paris. Rameau directed the cathedral choir school, but only from January 1702 to May 1703; three or four years later Mouret left, and Jean-Claude Trial (1732–71), a choirboy in the cathedral choir school, became co-director with Berton of the Paris Opéra from 1767, and Antoine Trial (1737–95), who had the same background, went on to a glorious career as an opera singer in the Théâtre des Italiens in Paris. Pierre Ligon (*b* 1749, known as the abbé Ligon) witnessed the success of his comic opera *Les deux aveugles de Franconville* in Paris; his nephew and pupil, Joseph Agricol Moulet (*b* 1766), after leaving Avignon became a famous harpist. At this point strong regional feeling made itself felt in Provence and Languedoc. At the beginning of the 18th century Mallet, *maître de chapelle* at St Pierre, had composed *Cantates patoises* and an *Impromptu de Nismes*. In the following century Aubanel undertook the reprinting (1803 and 1807) of early regional works, including the carols. The hymn of the *félibres* (modern Provençal writers) 'la coupo santo' was based on a carol by Brother Sérapion, an Avignon monk of the mid-17th century. About 1850 J.S. and M. Crémieu collected together *Chants hébraïques suivant le rite des communautés israélites de l'ancien Comtat Vénaissin*. The lawyer J.V. Avy, at about the same time, became interested in the Apt manuscript. This interest matched that of certain Romantics in the works of the Renaissance and then of the Baroque period. F.J. Séguin, who edited Saboly's carols with piano accompaniment (1856), put on performances of works by Palestrina, Bach and Handel, and composed some *Préludes dans la tonalité grégorienne*. There was also a renewed interest in chamber and symphonic music: for example, Fuzet Imbert composed a quartet and a *Poème symphonique* and in 1897 the Société Avignonnaise de Concerts Symphoniques was formed.

In 1899 Charles Bordes founded the Schola Cantorum of Avignon with the aim of reviving old church music – Gregorian chant and the works of Victoria, Josquin and Palestrina. The Schola Cantorum organized a festival, the Fêtes Musicales d'Avignon, in the first year of its existence. A new Théâtre Municipal was opened in 1825 in the Place de l'Hôtel de Ville for opera and drama. Destroyed by arson in 1846, it was rebuilt within a year, with a seating capacity of 960. Restored in 1900 and again in 1978, the theatre is now the city's opera house. The season runs from October to June with six productions, each of which usually receives three performances. The Opéra d'Avignon has been directed since 1974 by Raymond Duffaut, who since 1982 has also directed the Chorégies d'Orange. The city has a national conservatory. The Festival d'Avignon, although principally devoted to drama, has since 1972 introduced contemporary music theatre works into its programmes, performed in the cloisters in which Avignon abounds. Performances have included premières of works by composers such as Maurice Ohana, Claude Prey, Antoine Duhamel, André Boucourechliev, and Philip Glass (*Einstein on the Beach*, 1976). The holdings of the Bibliothèque Municipale include music and various records of the city's musical activities.

BIBLIOGRAPHY

A. Gastoué: 'Les anciens chants liturgiques des églises d'Apt et du Comtat', *Revue du chant grégorien*, x (1901–2), 152–60, 166–70

A. Gastoué: 'La musique à Avignon et dans le Comtat du XIVe au XVIIIe siècle', *RHCM*, iv (1904), 265–91

J.G. Prod'homme: 'La société Sainte Cécile d'Avignon au XVIIIe siècle', *SIMG*, vi (1904–5), 423–7

J.-B. Ripert: *Musique et musiciens d'Avignon* (Avignon, 1916)

P. Pansier: *Histoire du livre et de l'imprimerie à Avignon du XVIe au XVIe siècle* (Avignon, 1922)

J. Clamon and P.Pansier: *Les noëls provençaux de Notre-Dame des Doms (1570–1610)* (Avignon, 1925)

R. Brun: *Avignon au temps des papes* (Paris, 1928)

N. Pirrotta: 'Il codice estense lat.568 e la musica francese in Italia al principio del '400', *Atti della Reale accademia di scienze, lettere e arti di Palermo*, 4th ser., v/2 (1946), 101–54

F. Lesure: 'Two Documents from Avignon', *GSJ*, vi (1953), 105–6

U. Günther: 'Zur Biographie einiger Komponisten der Ars Subtilior', *AMw*, xxi (1964), 172–99

J. Robert: 'Une famille de "joueurs de violon" avignonais au XVIIe siècle: les de La Pierre', *RMFC*, iv (1964), 54–68

J. Robert: 'Les Ranc d'Avignon, propagateurs de l'opéra à la fin du XVIIe siècle', *RMFC*, vi (1966), 95–115

U. Günther: 'Das Manuskript Modena. Biblioteca Estense α.M.5,24 (olim Lat 568 = Mod)', *MD*, xxiv (1970), 17–67

J.R. Anthony: 'A Source for Secular Vocal Music in 18th-Century Avignon', *AcM*, liv (1982), 261–79

MARCEL FRÉMIOT/CHARLES PITT

Avignone, Bertrand di. *See* FERAGUT, BELTRAME.

Avilez [Avilés, Avilés Lusitano], **Manuel Leitão** [Leitam, Leitán] **de** (*b* Portalegre; *d* Granada, between 13 Sept and 25 Oct 1630). Portuguese composer. He was a choirboy at Portalegre Cathedral, where according to Barbosa Machado he studied with António Ferro. By 1601 he was *maestro de capilla* at Úbeda. Early that year he tried for a similar post at the royal chapel at nearby Granada but did not secure it until two years later; he was inducted on 28 August 1603. He composed copious vernacular festive music (which is now lost), beginning in 1606; on 24 November of that year the royal chapel authorities granted him special leave to compose Christmas *chanzonetas*. The library of João IV of Portugal contained two of his polychoral masses, one, *Salva Theodosium*, in 12 parts, possibly written in 1603, the other the eight-part *Ave Virgo sanctissima*. His surviving music (in *E-GRcr*) includes four penitential motets (*Domine non secundum peccata nostra*, *In jejunio et fletu* and *Adjuva nos* for four voices and *Adjuva nos* for three), two four-part Passions – one for Palm Sunday (St Matthew), the other for Good Friday (St John) – and two incomplete Lamentations verses, *Quomodo sedet sola civitas* and *Non est inventus similis illi*, both for four voices.

BIBLIOGRAPHY

JoãoIL

D. Barbosa Machado: *Bibliotheca lusitana*, iii (Lisbon, 1752/R), 294

J. López Calo: 'El archivo de música de la Capilla Real de Granada', *AnM*, xiii (1958), 103–228, esp. 106, 114; xxvi (1971), 213–35; xxvii (1972), 203–27

R.V. Nery, ed.: *A música no ciclo da 'Bibliotheca lusitana'* (Lisbon, 1984), 49

ROBERT STEVENSON

Avirmed, Baataryn (*b* 1936, Hovd, west Mongolia; *d* Aug 1998). Altai Urianghai Mongol epic bard (*tuul'ch*). Avirmed performed in the deep declamatory *häälah* vocal style and accompanied himself on the two-string plucked lute, TOPSHUUR (see illustration). Although born after the communist revolution in Mongolia, Avirmed inherited this traditional vocal style and associated folk-religious beliefs (*see* MONGOL MUSIC).

At least seven generations of Avirmed's lineage were bards; his grandfather is believed to have been the famous bard Jilker. Included in Jilker's repertory were the epics *Bayan Tsagaan Övgön* ('Rich White Old Man'), *Argil Tsagaan Övgön* ('Snow White Old Man') and *Naran Han Hövgüün* ('The Boy Naran Khan'), all of which were also performed by Avirmed. Other members of Avirmed's family who performed included his father, Baatar, and uncles Buyan, Shirendev and Rinchen.

Avirmed began training seriously at the age of 13 years. His principal teacher was his paternal uncle, Shirendev. After ten years, he gained recognition as a

Baataryn Avirmed of the Altai Urianghai playing the topshuur, Hovd, west Mongolia, 1989

bard by performing throughout two whole nights before Jilker, his pupil Choisüren and Shirendev. He then received the *ulamjlalyn hadag*, a ritual scarf of succession, which was tied to the head of his *topshuur*. He performed in 'modern' theatrical contexts and received a gold medal in Ulaanbaatar for his rendition of *Altain Magtaal* ('Praise-song of the Altai') on the occasion of the 50th anniversary of the communist revolution. With the onset of democracy in Mongolia in 1990, Avirmed began to teach the traditional style to his son Dorjlaln, his nephew Oldoh and his younger brother Seseer.

BIBLIOGRAPHY

AND OTHER RESOURCES

Ts. Damdinsüren: 'Contemporary Mongolian Epic-Singers', *Epensymposium III: Bonn 1980*, Fragen der mongolischen Heldendichtung, ii, ed. W. Heissig (Wiesbaden, 1982), 48–60

Y. Davaasüren: 'Töriin soyorholt tuul'ch' [State prizewinner epic bard], *Ardyn Erh*(1992), 2

Lh. Tuyabaatar: 'Altain Urianhain aldart tuul'chid' [Famous Altai Urianghai bards], *Il Tovchoo*, i/70 (1993), 6–7

C.A. Pegg: 'Ritual, Religion and Magic in West Mongolian (Oirad) Heroic Epic Performance', *British Journal of Ethnomusicology*, iv (1995), 77–99

C.A. Pegg: 'The Power of Performance: West Mongolian Epics', *The Oral Epic: Performance and Music*, ed. K. Reichl (Berlin, 2000), 171–90

C.A. Pegg: *Mongolian Music, Dance and Oral Narrative: Performing Diverse Identities* (Seattle, 2000) [with CD]

RECORDINGS

Mongolie: Musique et Chants de l'Altai, various pfmrs, coll. A. Desjacques, ORSTOM-SELAF Ceto 811 (1986) [notes by A. Desjacques]

CAROLE PEGG

Avison, Charles (*b* Newcastle upon Tyne, bap. 16 Feb 1709; *d* Newcastle upon Tyne, 9/10 May 1770). English composer, conductor, writer on music and organist. He was the most important English concerto composer of the 18th century and an original and influential writer on music.

1. Life. 2. Writings. 3. Compositions.

1. LIFE.   He was the fifth of nine children born to Richard and Ann Avison. Since his father, a Newcastle town wait, was a practising musician, his musical training probably began at home. Later, while in the service of Ralph Jenison, a patron of the arts and MP for Northumberland from 1724 to 1741, he had opportunity for further study. He had additional support in his musical development from Colonel John Blathwayt (or Blaithwaite), formerly a director of the Royal Academy of Music, the operatic organization in London. There is no evidence that, as has been claimed, Avison went to Italy, but William Hayes and Charles Burney wrote that he studied with Geminiani in London.

The earliest known reference to Avison's musical activities is an announcement of a benefit concert on 20 March 1734 in Hickford's Room, London. On 13 October 1735 he was appointed organist of St John's, Newcastle, an appointment that took effect only in June 1736, when a new organ had been installed. On 20 October, on the death of Thomas Powell, he became organist at St Nicholas (now the cathedral) at a yearly salary of £20.

In October 1735 a series of subscription concerts was organized in Newcastle, along the lines of those held in London, Edinburgh and elsewhere, under Avison's direction. In July 1738 Avison was formally appointed musical director, beginning with the fourth season; he retained

the directorship of the Newcastle Musical Society, as well as the post at St Nicholas, until his death. He took part in other musical activities in Newcastle, including concerts at the pleasure gardens and benefit concerts. He also collaborated with John Garth in promoting a series of subscription concerts in Durham, which were held on Tuesdays; theatre productions in Newcastle and Durham were on Wednesdays, the Newcastle concerts on Thursdays, and on Sunday evenings from about 1761 informal concerts were given in a room added for the purpose to the St Nicholas vicarage. Mondays and Fridays were reserved for Avison's private pupils on the harpsichord, violin and flute. Some of the performers in the Avison-Garth concerts included Giardini, Herschel, Shield, and Avison's sons Edward and Charles. Geminiani is believed to have visited Avison in 1760, while travelling between Edinburgh and London, but there is no record of his playing in any concerts. Although Avison was criticized for the anti-Handelian remarks in his writings, Handel's music was well represented in the Newcastle and Durham concerts. In the 1750s Avison and Garth organized a Marcello Society in Newcastle devoted to the performance of choral music and in particular to the edition of Benedetto Marcello's *First Fifty Psalms* which the two men were preparing for publication.

Avison's reputation was not confined to Newcastle. A letter signed 'Marcellinus' in the *Newcastle Journal* (17 March 1759) summarizes some of the opportunities he refused elsewhere: before he was established in Newcastle he had a favourable prospect of establishing himself in London; he was offered the organist's post at York Minster in 1734 (accepted by James Nares), two organists' posts in Dublin on Geminiani's recommendation between 1733 and 1740, a teaching post in Edinburgh with participation in the Musical Society there, and the succession to Pepusch as organist at the Charterhouse, London, in 1753. Burney wrote that Avison was 'an ingenious and polished man, esteemed and respected by all who knew him; and an elegant writer upon his art'.

Avison married Catherine Reynolds on 15 January 1737. Three of their nine children lived to adulthood: Jane (1744–73), Edward (1747–76) and Charles (1751–95). Edward succeeded his father as organist of St Nicholas and musical director of the Newcastle Musical Society, and was a friend of John Wesley; Charles, who held various appointments as organist in Newcastle, including that at St Nicholas from 1789 (succeeding Mathias Hawdon), composed several works and published a hymn collection. The Avison family is buried in the churchyard of St Andrew's, Newgate Street, Newcastle. Robert Browning had a lifelong interest in Avison; his poem *Parleying with Certain People of Importance in their Day: with Charles Avison* was supposedly inspired by a march by Avison in his father's possession.

2. WRITINGS.   Avison's creative output can be divided between writings and musical compositions. Whether he was the author of numerous book reviews and music articles signed 'C.A.' in the local newspapers and magazines during his mature years is conjectural. He often included dedications and substantial, informative and sometimes controversial prefaces ('advertisements') with his published music. His op.3 includes a lengthy preface discussing performing practice in concertos, which was incorporated the next year into his most important literary work, *An Essay on Musical Expression* (which Burney

Charles Avison: portrait attributed to Francis Lindo, c1760 (Laing Art Gallery, Newcastle upon Tyne)

thought to be the first of its kind on musical criticism in England).

The *Essay* is in three parts. Part i contains a brief discussion of the effect of music upon the emotions and character, and a section on the analogies between music and painting. Part ii is a systematic critique of some composers and their styles. Part iii is devoted to remarks on instrumental performance, especially of concertos. The *Essay* was highly controversial, especially in its critical judgments, for example Avison's view that Geminiani and Marcello were superior composers to Handel. William Hayes published (anonymously) a critical review in January 1753 called *Remarks on Mr Avison's Essay*. His criticism, although limited to the first and second parts of the *Essay*, was longer than the total original work, and included several interesting digressions. Avison published *A Reply to the Author of Remarks on the Essay on Musical Expression* on 22 February 1753, and later that year he published the second edition of the *Essay*, which included his *Reply* and also *A Letter to the Author, concerning the Music of the Ancients* by Dr John Jortin. The *Essay* was not all Avison's own work, but, on his own admission, that of a 'junto', never mentioned by name. It could have included Dr John Brown, who along with Avison and several others was a member of a literary club in Newcastle, the poets Thomas Gray of Cambridge and the Rev. William Mason of York (who is known to have contributed some material), Dr John Jortin of London, Joseph Barber, the engraver and printer in Newcastle, and Robert Shaftoe, a brother-in-law of Ralph Jenison.

Avison's bias towards certain composers may have come partly from his musical training with Geminiani. While reviewers felt Hayes was correct in much of his criticism, they also praised Avison's own judicious

observations. The third edition of the *Essay* (1775) consisted of a reprinting of the second edition; in the same year a German translation of the first edition was published in Leipzig.

3. COMPOSITIONS. As a composer Avison is best known for his concerti grossi for strings. His op.2 was revised twice: first, when Walsh published it (along with two additional concertos) as organ concertos in the style made popular by Handel, second when Avison reworked all eight concertos into his op.6. In 1758 he issued his opp.3, 4 and 6 as *Twenty Six Concertos … in Score for the Use of Performers on the Harpsichord*. The idea of a full score came from the publication of Corelli's concertos and sonatas edited by Pepusch (*c*1740) and of Geminiani's opp.2 and 3 (1755). Avison did not always adhere to his original texts in the later full-score versions; there are many revisions as well as movements transposed or substituted without explanation. His op.9 was a versatile and popular work, advertised as being playable several ways: by full string orchestra, as quartets, for harpsichord or organ with accompaniments, or as harpsichord 'sonatas'.

In general, Avison's concertos are modelled on Geminiani's; stylistically there is little difference between the early works and the late ones. If somewhat lightweight in texture and content, Avison's concertos are unusually tuneful; he was a firm believer in the value of 'air' or melody. His op.4 no.4 was very popular in the Concert of Antient Music, where it was much played between 1785 and 1812 along with concertos by Corelli, Geminiani, Sammartini and Handel. During the 19th century the Andante cantabile from op.9 no.5 was set to several religious texts, with numerous arrangements for hymnals and vocal ensembles and transcriptions for various instruments.

Of Avison's chamber music, his op.1 trio sonatas are in a typical Baroque style. However, after he introduced Rameau's *Pièces de clavecin en concerts* (1741) at the Newcastle concerts in the early 1750s, Avison modelled his later sonatas on Rameau's, which are essentially keyboard pieces with accompaniments for other instruments. His opp.5, 7 and 8 were the earliest of their kind to be composed in England. Earlier publications of accompanied keyboard sonatas usually had an accompaniment of a single violin or flute, but Avison's accompaniments were for two violins and cello, with the harpsichord part (in a complex style, closely akin to Geminiani's in his *Pièces de clavecin*) written out with great care and completeness, independent of the string parts, which do little more than provide supporting harmony. These sonatas clearly arose from Avison's objections to the Handelian type of keyboard concerto and the repetitiveness of its ritornello form. In contrast to the relatively conservative concertos, there is evidence here of stylistic change. These works were imitated by a number of composers in north England and the Midlands, most notably John Garth.

Avison's surviving original sacred works are limited to a verse anthem, a hymn and a chant. In collaboration with Giardini he composed a section of an oratorio, *Ruth*, which was first performed at the Lock Hospital, London, on 15 April 1763; it was repeated on 13 February 1765 and 25 May 1768, wholly set by Giardini.

WORKS

printed works published in London unless otherwise stated; for complete thematic index, known library holdings and listing of editions and arrangements, see Stephens

ORCHESTRAL

op.

2   Six Concertos (g, B♭, e, D, B♭, D), 4 vn, va, vc, hpd (Newcastle and London, 1740); rev. with 2 new concs. (D, G) as 8 Concertos, org/hpd (1747) [see op.6]

—   Two Concertos, no.1 (C) a 8, org/hpd, ?str [kbd pt only extant]; no.2, vns in 7 parts (Newcastle, 1742), lost

3   Six Concertos … with General Rules for Playing Instrumental Compositions (D, e, g, B♭, D, G), 4 vn, va, vc, hpd (1751); incl. in 26 Concertos (London, Edinburgh and Newcastle, 1758)

4   Eight Concertos (d, A, D, g, B♭, G, D, c), 4 vn, va, vc, hpd (1755); incl. in 26 Concertos (London, Edinburgh and Newcastle, 1758)

6   Twelve Concertos (g, B♭, e, D, B♭, D, G, G, D, C, D, A), 4 vn, va, vc, hpd (London and Newcastle, 1758); incl. in 26 Concertos (London, Edinburgh and Newcastle, 1758) [incl. rev. of 8 Concertos (1747) plus 4 new concs.]

9   Twelve Concertos, set 1 (G, D, A, g/G, C, e), set 2 (E♭, B♭, c, F, A, D), 2 vn, va, vc (1766); also for org/hpd, or 2 vn, va, vc, org/hpd (1766)

10 Six Concertos (d, F, c, C, E♭, d), 4 vn, va, vc, hpd (1769)

CHAMBER

op.

1   VI Sonatas (chromatic dorian, g, g, dorian, e, D), 2 vn, b (c1737/R)

5   Six Sonatas (G, C, B♭, E♭, G, A), hpd, 2 vn, vc (1756)

7   Six Sonatas (G, g, B♭, d, a, A), hpd, 2 vn, vc (London, Edinburgh and Newcastle, 1760/R)

8   Six Sonatas (A, C, D, B♭, g, G), hpd, 2 vn, vc (London and Edinburgh, 1764)

OTHER WORKS

Hast thou not forsaken us (verse anthem), c1741, GB-DRc

Glory to God (Christmas Hymn/Sanctus), SATB (?c1760)

Ruth (orat), London, Lock Hospital, 15 April 1763, collab. Giardini, ?lost

Ps cvii, chant, SATB, org/pf, ed. T. Ions, *Cantico ecclesiastica* (1849)

EDITIONS AND ARRANGEMENTS

1 Concerto … Done from the Lessons for the Harpsichord Composed by Sig. Domenico Scarlatti, 4 vn, va, vc, hpd (c1743); repr. as pt of no.6 of 12 Concertos (1744)

12 Concertos … Done from 2 Books of Lessons for the Harpsichord Composed by Sig. Domenico Scarlatti, 4 vn, va, vc, hpd (1744/R) [no.6 incl. conc. of c1743]

The First 50 Psalms Set to Music by Benedetto Marcello … and Adapted to the English Version (1757), collab. J. Garth [edn of Marcello's Estro Poetico-Armonico]

A Collection of Psalm Tunes (Newcastle, c1760)

12 [24] Canticles Taken from the Compositions of Sig. Carlo Clari and Adapted to English words Selected from the Psalms, 1769, GB-NTp

Another set of 24 Canticles, dated 1769, arr. from works by Clari, Ouf

ATTRIBUTIONS

Flores musicae, 12 Sonatinas, 2 vn, vc … Taken from the Works of the Best English and Italian Authors by C.A. Esq (London, c1755)

March, D, 2 vn, b (Edinburgh, 1761)

Sae merry as we twa ha' been, a Favourite Scotch Tune with Variations, arr. pf/hpd (c1785)

Grand March, C, in *The Complete and Dramatic Works of Robert Browning* (Boston, 1895)

She's gone, the sweetest flower of May, dirge, S, str, Burghley House, Cambs.

Various works in untitled MS, c1745, GB-NTp

WRITINGS

An Essay on Musical Expression (London, 1752, 2/1753/R, 3/1775)

A Reply to the Author of Remarks on the Essay on Musical Expression (London, 1753)

BIBLIOGRAPHY

BurneyH; HawkinsH

H.M. Schueller: 'Imitation and Expression in British Music Criticism in the Eighteenth Century', *MQ*, xxxiv (1948), 544–66

C.L. Cudworth: 'The English Organ Concerto', *The Score*, no.8 (1953), 51–63

E. Oberti: 'Charles Avison e l'estetica musicale', *Rivista di estetica*, iii (1958), 206–28

J.B. Brocklehurst: *Charles Avison and his Essay on Musical Expression* (diss., U. of Sheffield, 1959)

J.L. Cassingham: *The Twelve Scarlatti-Avison Concertos of 1744* (diss., U. of Missouri, 1968)

N.L. Stephens: *Charles Avison: an Eighteenth-Century English Composer, Musician and Writer* (diss., U. of Pittsburgh, 1968)

C.L. Cudworth: 'Avison of Newcastle, 1709–1770', *MT*, cxi (1970), 480–83

R.R. Kidd: 'The Emergence of Chamber Music with Obligato Keyboard in England', *AcM*, xliv (1972), 122–44

O. Edwards: 'Charles Avison, English Concerto-Writer Extraordinary', *MQ*, lix (1973), 399–410

P.M. Horsley: 'Charles Avison: the Man and his Milieu', *ML*, lv (1974), 5–23

C.M. Eckersley: *Aspects of Structure and Idiom in the Music of Eighteenth-Century England, with Special Reference to the Scarlatti Arrangements of Charles Avison* (diss., U. of Oxford, 1980)

N. de Palézieux: *Die Lehre vom Ausdruck in der englischen Musikästhetik des 18. Jahrhunderts* (diss., U. of Hamburg, 1980)

R.B. Larsson: 'Charles Avison's "Stiles in Musical Expression"', *ML*, lxiii (1982), 261–75

S. McVeigh: 'Music and Lock Hospital in the 18th Century', *MT*, cxxix (1988), 235–40

H.D. Johnstone and R.Fiske, eds.: *The Eighteenth Century* (Oxford, 1990)

A. Longo: 'Charles Avison estetico della Musica', *RIM*, xxvii (1992), 183–204

NORRIS L. STEPHENS

Avison, John (Henry Patrick) (*b* Vancouver, 25 April 1917; *d* Vancouver, 30 Nov 1983). Canadian conductor, broadcaster and accompanist. After studying the piano privately, he took degrees at the universities of British Columbia (1935) and Washington (1936), and subsequently studied at the Juilliard School of Music (1946), Columbia (1946–7) and with Hindemith at Yale (1947). From 1939 to 1980 he was principal conductor of the CBC Vancouver Chamber Orchestra (now the CBC Vancouver Orchestra); there he gave premières of hundreds of works, including music by the Canadian composers Jean Coulthard, Barbara Pentland and Elliott Weisgarber, and earned a citation of merit from the Composers, Authors and Publishers Association of Canada. He was guest conductor with numerous Canadian and European orchestras, conducted at the Aspen Music Festival and taught at the universities of Victoria and British Columbia. He was also accompanist to Maureen Forrester, Lois Marshall and Lauritz Melchior. In 1979 Avison was made a member of the Order of Canada and in 1980 received the medal of the Canadian Music Council.

CHARLES BARBER

Avison Edition. Collection of music issued by the SOCIETY OF BRITISH COMPOSERS.

Avitrano, Giuseppe Antonio (*b* Naples, ?1670; *d* Naples, 19 March 1756). Italian composer and violinist. He came from a musical family and was a member of the Neapolitan court orchestra from the late 1690s until his death. His two sets of *sonate da chiesa* (opp.1 and 2) are notable for their fugal movements, in which the violone shares the counterpoint with the violins, while the continuo remains independent. This principle is systematized in his op.3, which in its instrumentation is based on a model established in Naples at the end of the 17th century by composers such as Pietro Marchitelli and Giancarlo Cailò. In each sonata a brilliant first movement is followed by a three-part fugue, which is separated from a lively closing dance by a short, lyrical movement, usually in 3/2. Avitrano's works show a highly developed sense of tonal effect, particularly his op.3, in which the violins are independent of each other and often complement each other by playing in the same register. Although his violin music does not require technical brilliance from the players, it does demand a sound mastery of the bow, especially in the dance movements. His capacity for invention is limited, particularly in the slow movements, in which the thematic material is often similar to that in other slow movements of his. His harmonic development is conventional but lively. Avitrano's importance lies in his contribution to the four-part sonata, the leading genre in Neapolitan violin music.

WORKS

10 sonate, 2 vn, vle, org, op.1 (Naples, 1697)
10 sonate, 2 vn, vle, org, op.2 (Naples, 1703)
12 sonate, 3 vn, bc, op.3 (Naples, 1713)
7 cants., S, bc, *I-Mc*
Te Mariam laudamus, S, S, A, T, T, B, 2 ob, 3 vn, bc, 1746, *AN*
Missa defunctorum, S, A, bc, 1721, S Gregorio Armeno, Naples

BIBLIOGRAPHY

EitnerQ
U. Prota-Giurleo: 'Breve Storia del Teatro di Corte e della Musica a Napoli', *Il Teatro di Corte del Palazzo Reale di Napoli* (Naples, 1952), 19–125
F. Degrada: 'Appunti critici sui Concerti di Francesco Durante', *Chigiana*, xxiv (1967), 145–65
R. Bossa: 'Le Sonate a Quattro di Giuseppe Antonio Avitrano (1713)', *La musica a Napoli durante il Seicento: Naples 1985*, 307–22
F. Cotticelli and P. Maione: *Le istituzioni musicali a Napoli durante il Viceregno austriaco (1707–1734)* (Naples, 1993)

CHRISTOPH TIMPE

Avitsur, Eitan (*b* Jerusalem, 15 Sept 1941). Israeli composer and conductor. He studied at the Rubin Academy of Music (teacher's diploma 1967, BMus 1972) and at the Salzburg Mozarteum (1976). From 1968 to 1973 he served as the director of Renanot, the Institute of Jewish Music, Jerusalem. In 1971 he joined the music department at Bar-Ilan University, where he founded an electro-acoustic laboratory in 1995. He has conducted numerous concerts in Israel, as well as national television and radio broadcasts. In 1973 he helped establish the Natanya SO, with which he has performed concerts of contemporary Israeli music. An award-winning youth orchestra conductor, he became music director of the Jerusalem Youth Orchestra in 1987.

Avitsur's compositions express a deep commitment to Jewish and Israeli culture. Many of his works are large-scale vocal compositions based on scenes from recent Jewish history. Much of his music, such as the Symphony no.2 'Shirat Hadorot' ('Generations' chanting', 1981), is influenced by traditional melodies and chants. In the *Rhapsody* for wind instruments (1991) traditional tunes and Middle Eastern *māqāmāt* are juxtaposed with a Western idiom. He has also composed Western-style accompaniments for original performances of traditional music. Other compositions, such as the Prelude for nine instruments and electronics (1972) and the Trio for percussion instruments (1992), are innovative in their use of rhythm and tone colour. Some of his concertos and

chamber works show the influence of Mordecai Seter and Alexander Boskovitch. Avitsur himself cites Penderecki as a primary influence.

WORKS
(selective list)
for fuller list see Tischler (1988)

Vocal: Qaddish, vc, chorus, orch, 1971; Yasad Erets [He Established the Earth] (Ps civ), chorus, org, 1974; Eleh ha–banim [These are my Sons] (dramatic orat, I. Shalev, H. Hefer), spkr, Bar, orch, elecs, 1975; Meğillat Ha–esh [The Scroll of Fire] (orat, H.N. Bialik), spkr, S, chbr orch, elecs, 1976; Sym, no.2 'Shirat Ha–dorot' [Generations' Chanting], spkr, Bar, boys' choir, orch, 1981; Shirat Ha–yam [Song of the Sea] (cant.), chorus, orch, 1984; Ha–qhel le–yisra'el [The Community of Israel] (cant.), male vv, orch, 1987; Kinnor David [King David's Harp] (orat), solo vv, chorus, orch, 1996
Orch: Sinfonietta, chbr orch, 1977; Tpt Conc., 1982: Trbn Conc., 1985; Leilot Shabbat [Sabbath Eves], sym., 1986; Rhapsody, wind, 1991; The Israeli Chain, band, 1992; La blanka torre, suite, chbr orch, 1995; Rhapsody, vn, orch [based on Jewish Sephardi romances]; see VOCAL: [Sym. no.2 'Shirat ha–dorot', 1981]
Chbr and solo inst: 3 Pieces, pf, 1968; Str Qt, 1971; Prelude, 9 insts, elecs, 1972; Wind Qnt, 1974; Suite, pf, 1979; Sonatina, gui, 1983; Brass Qnt, 1985; Suite, fl, vc, hp, 1986; Tuga [Grief], tpt, org, 1986; Rhapsody, vc, 1987; Trio, 3 perc, 1992; Duet, fl, db, 1993; Sonata, pf, 1995; Sonata, tpt, trbn, 1998
Other works: incid music for film and TV; arrs. Israeli and Jewish songs, orch/band

Principal recording company: CBS

BIBLIOGRAPHY

A. Tischler: *A Descriptive Bibliography of Art Music by Israeli Composers* (Detroit, 1988), 18–19
Y. Cohen: *Ne'imei zemirot yisra'el* [The heirs of the psalmist], (Tel-Aviv, 1990), 388–9

ELIYAHU SCHLEIFER

Avni, Tsvi [Tzvi] (*b* Saarbrücken, 2 Sept 1927). Israeli composer of German origin. He studied composition with Erlich, Ben-Haim and Seter, and the piano with Pelleg, graduating from the Israel Academy of Music, Tel-Aviv, in 1958. From 1961 to 1975, Avni served intermittently as the director of the AMLI Central Music Library. Between 1962 and 1964 he continued his studies in the USA: at the Columbia–Princeton Electronic Music Center with Ussachevsky and in Tanglewood with Copland and Foss. Avni later taught composition and served as director of the electronic music laboratories at the Jerusalem Rubin Academy of Music and Dance (1971–95); he was appointed head of the department of theory and composition there in 1976. From 1968 to 1982 he also served as editor of *Guitite*, the bi-monthly publication of the Israeli Jeunesses Musicales, and from 1978 to 1980 he was chairman of the Israeli League of Composers. Avni was appointed chairman of the jury of the Arthur Rubinstein International Piano Master Competition in 1989 and 1992. In 1998 he won the Israel Prime Minister's prize for Life achievements as well as the Saarland prize of the Arts.

Avni's early works display eastern folk-like elements such as asymmetric rhythmic patterns while retaining classical forms including sonata and rondo. *Kashtot kayits* ('Summer Strings') (1962), his first string quartet, also reflects the influence of Bartók. Subsequently Avni turned his attention towards electronic music, the *Vocalise* of 1964, for example, integrating a pre-recorded soprano voice with electronic sounds, and *Collage* (1967) merging three sound sources, the human voice (a mezzo-soprano), instruments (flute and percussion) and tape. During the 1960s Avni absorbed other avant-garde elements, in particular an expressionist form of aleatorism. *Hirhurim al Drama* ('Meditations on a Drama') (1965) for chamber orchestra, for instance, comprises contrasting static and dynamic elements, clusters versus melodic development, within a structure that contains aleatory sections; the work won the ACUM Prize (1966). *Five Pantomimes* for eight players of 1968 displays the use of proportional notation and a section written as a 'mobile', the work inspired by paintings by Picasso, Chagall, Kandinsky, Dali and Klee. Of Avni's compositions of the 1970s *Epitaph* (1974–9) is of particular note, an intimate, philosophical piano sonata taking its point of departure from a Jewish legend by Rabbi Nachman of Breslau. The work opens with a recitation on a single note, a prayer-like feature which appears in several other works including *Hirhurim al Drama*. At the start of the 1980s a further development in Avni's style began with signs of a simpler, though still chromatic, language, tending towards neo-tonality in an Impressionist manner. *Ahava Tahat Shemesh Acheret* ('Love under a Different Sun') (1982) – a song cycle based on love poetry from different cultures with music expressing the uniqueness of each – is an example of this change.

WORKS
(*selective list*)

Orch: Hirhurim al drama [Meditations on a Drama], chbr orch, 1966; Dimuyim l'yom chag [Holiday Metaphors], 1970; Al Kef yam mavet ze [On this Cape of Death], chbr orch, 1974; Musica Tochnittit [Programme Music], 1980; Mizmor, santour/xyl/mar, orch, 1982; Desert Scenes, 1990; The Three Legged Monster (H. Yaddor-Avni), nar, orch, pf, 1995; Shaalu Shlom Yerushalayim [Pray for the Peace of Jerusalem], 1997; The Ship of Hours, 1999

Choral: Mizmorei Tehilim [Ps Canticles], chorus, 1967; Yerushlayim shel Ma'la [Jerusalem of the Heavens] (Kabbalah), chorus, orch, 1968; Al harahamim [On Mercy] (Y. Amichai), chorus, 1973; 3 Madrigals (L. Goldberg), chorus, 1978; Deep Calleth unto Deep (pss cxxix, xlii, cxvii), S, chorus, orch/org, 1989; Makhelorka (F. García Lorca), female chorus/children's chorus, 1992; Kol Hazman [The Entire Time] (A. Gilboa), female chorus, pf, 1997; Hodaya [Thanksgiving] (A. Shlonsky), chorus, 1997

Solo vocal: L'yad Umko shel Nahar [By the Depth of a River] (M. Katz), Mez, pf, 1969–75; Leda and the Swan (Avni), S, cl, 1976; Ahava Tahat Shemesh Aheret [Love Under a Different Sun] (song cycle, trad. Middle Eastern and African texts, trans. R. Shani), Mez, fl, vn, vc, 1982; 3 Lyric Songs (P. Celan), Mez, eng hn, hp, 1991; Se Questo è un Uomo (song cycle, P. Levi), S, orch, 1998

Chbr and solo inst: Pastorale and Dance, cl, pf, 1957; Ww Qnt, 1959; Pf Sonata, 1961; Kashtot Kayits [Summer Strings], str qt, 1962; 5 Pantomimes, fl, cl, hn, tpt, va, db, perc, pf, 1968; Mima'amakim [De profundis], str qt/str orch, 1969; Epitaph (Pf Sonata no.2), 1974–9; 2 Pss, ob, str, 1975; Beyond the Curtain, pf qt, 1979; On the Verge of Time (Pf Sonata no.3), 1983; Metamorphoses on a Bach Chorale, orch, 1985; Kaddish, vc, str, 1987; Vitrage, hp, 1990; Triptych, pf, 1994

Tape: Vocalise, 1964; Collage (Amichai), 1v, fl, perc, tape, 1967; Lyric Episodes, ob, tape, 1972; A Monk Observes a Skull (A. Reich), Mez, vc, tape, 1981

MSS in *IL-J*, Tmi

Principal publishers: Culture and Education Centre of the Histadrut, Israel Music Institute, Mills

BIBLIOGRAPHY

W.Y. Elias: *Tsvi Avni* (Tel-Aviv, 1971)
Y. Cohen: 'Tzvi Avni 60', *Das Orchester*, xxxvi (1988), 277–8
A. Tischler: 'Tzvi Avni', *A Descriptive Bibliography of Art Music by Israeli Composers* (Warren, MI, 1988), 21–7
Y. Cohen: 'Tsvi Avni', *Neimey Zmirot Israel* (Tel-Aviv, 1990), 273–83
P. Grandwitz: *The Music of Israel* (Portland, OR, 1996)
R. Fleisher: 'Tzvi Avni', *Twenty Israeli Composers* (Detroit, MI, 1997), 137–61

MIRI GERSTEL

Avoglio [Avolio; née Croumann or Graumann], **Christina Maria** (*b* ? Mainz or Frankfurt; *fl* 1727–46). German soprano. She sang in the Peruzzi company at Brussels, 1727–8, and was at Hamburg in 1729, where she sang Cleopatra in Handel's *Giulio Cesare* and Rodelinda in Telemann's *Flavius Bertaridus*. The same year she was engaged by Fortunato Chelleri as a singer at the court of Kassel. The librettos recording her two appearances at the Sporck theatre in Prague during the 1730–31 operatic season indicate that she was employed at the court of Friedrich I, King of Sweden and Landgrave of Hesse-Kassel, but it is uncertain whether she or her husband, Giuseppe Avoglio (also a musician at the Hesse-Kassel court), ever followed the court chapel to Stockholm. In 1731 she went with her husband to Russia, where she sang for the court opera of Tsarina Anna Ivanovna in Moscow and St Petersburg until 1738. In 1740, after the collapse of G.B. Pescetti's operatic venture in London, she became closely associated with Handel. She is next heard of in Handel's letter of 29 December 1741 to Jennens from Dublin: 'Sig^{ra} Avolio, which I brought with me from London pleases extraordinary'. His leading soprano throughout the Dublin season, she sang the principal soprano part at the first performance of *Messiah* on 13 April 1742; other roles included Rosmene in *Imeneo*. She was a member of Handel's company in the Covent Garden oratorio seasons of 1743 and 1744, singing the Israelite Woman in the first performance of *Samson* and Iris in the first production of *Semele*; in 1744 she created Hecate in Samuel Howard's pantomime *The Amorous Goddess* at Drury Lane. She sang at a benefit concert for herself and two local musicians at the Salisbury Assembly Room on 23 June 1746. Her Handel parts in 1742–3 require a moderate compass (*d'* to *a"*) but considerable flexibility.

BIBLIOGRAPHY

MooserA
C. Engelbrecht: 'Die Hofkapelle des Landgrafen Carl von Hessen-Kassel', *Zeitschrift des Vereins für hessische Geschichte und Landeskunde*, lxviii (1957), 14–173, esp. 157
W. Dean and J.M. Knapp: *Handel's Operas, 1704–1726* (Oxford, 1987, 2/1995)
D. Burrows: *Handel: Messiah* (Cambridge, 1991)
D.E. Freeman: *The Opera Theater of Count Franz Anton von Sporck in Prague* (Stuyvesant, NY, 1992)

WINTON DEAN, DANIEL E. FREEMAN

Avondano, Pedro António (bap. Lisbon, 16 April 1714; *d* Lisbon, 1782). Portuguese composer of Italian ancestry. He studied with his father, Pietro Giorgio Avondano, a Genoese violinist of the Portuguese royal chapel and a composer, and himself became a violinist in the same chapel; others of his family were also members. His duties as a court musician included composing the music for the ballets which accompanied the operas. He also played the violin, and at his own house in the Rua da Cruz promoted balls and concerts mainly for the foreign communities. Three collections of minuets written for these balls were published in London, at the expense of the British community in Lisbon. He was a Knight of the Order of Christ, an honour purchased for 480,000 réis, and he also played an important role in the reorganization after the 1755 earthquake of the Irmandade de S Cecília, the musicians' union of Lisbon. He wrote a *dramma giocoso*, *Il mondo della luna* (1765), and several oratorios and instrumental works.

Other members of the Avondano family, all active in the Real Câmara, include his brother António José (*d*

1783) and his son Joaquim Pedro (*d* 1804), João Francisco (*d* 1794), João Baptista André (*d* 1801), who published a set of *Quattro sonate e due duetti* for two cellos (Paris and Lyons, by 1784) and was a pupil of J.-P. Duport, and Joaquim António (*d* 1828).

WORKS
VOCAL

Le difese d'amore (cant.), Lisbon, 1764, only lib extant
Il mondo della luna (dg, 3, C. Goldoni), Lisbon, Salvaterra, carn. 1765, *P-La*
Il voto di Jefte (dramma sacro, 2, G. Tonioli), Lisbon, 1771, only lib extant
Adamo ed Eva (dramma sacro, 2), Lisbon, Ajuda, 19 March 1772, only lib extant
Gioas, re di Giuda (orat, P. Metastasio), *D-Bsb* (pt 1 only)
La morte d'Abel (orat, Metastasio), *Bsb*
Die Aufopferung Isaacs (orat, after Metastasio), *SWl*
Arias for Lisbon productions of Perez: Dido, 1765, *Bsb*; Majo: Antigono, 1772, *P-Ln*; Galuppi: Il filosofo di campagna, *B-Bc*
Magnificat, 4 vv, 2 vn, 2 hn, vc, org; Psalms cxxi and cxlvii, 4 vv, 2 vn, 2 hn, bc; Ladainha lauretana, 4 vv, 2 vn, org; Tantum ergo, 4 vv, 2 vn, org: *P-EVc* (see Alegria)

INSTRUMENTAL

A Collection of [6] Lisbon Minuets, 2 vn/fl, b (London, 1766)
A Second Sett of 22 Lisbon Minuets, 2 vn, b (London, *c*1770)
Eighteen entire new Lisbon Minuets, 2 vn, b (London, *c*1770)
A Favourite Lesson, hpd (London, 1770)
2 syms., *B-Bc*; 3 vc concs., *D-Bsb*; other inst works in *F-Pn*; ? 2 sonatas, vc, b, *D-Bsb*

BIBLIOGRAPHY

DBP; *MGG1* suppl. (C. Schröder-Auerbach).
J.A. Alegria, ed.: J. Mazza: *Dicionário biográfico de músicos portugueses* (Lisbon, 1945) [orig. pubd in *Ocidente*, xxiii–xxvi (1944–5)]
J. Scherpereel: *A orquestra e os instrumentistas da Real Câmara de Lisboa de 1764 a 1834* (Lisbon, 1985)
M.C. de Brito: *Opera in Portugal in the Eighteenth Century* (Cambridge, 1989)

MANUEL CARLOS DE BRITO

Avosani, Orfeo (*b* Viadana, nr Mantua; *fl* 1641–5). Italian composer and organist. The title-page of his *Compieta concertata a cinque voci* op.1 (Venice, 1641) describes him as organist of S Nicola, Viadana, and he was still there when he published his only other known music, *Messa e salmi a tre voci* op.2 (Venice, 1645).

COLIN TIMMS

Avossa [d'Avossa; Avosa; Avos; d'Anossa], **Giuseppe** (*b* Paola, nr Cosenza, 1708; *d* Naples, 9 Jan 1796). Italian composer. He is often confused with his contemporary Girolamo Abos, several of whose *opere serie* are sometimes attributed to him. The family is reputed to have been of Spanish origin. His father was in the service of Spinelli, Duke of Fuscaldo, and (according to Mondolfi, *MGG1*) the duke used his influence to place the young musician in the Conservatorio dei Poveri di Gesù Cristo in Naples. There he studied with Gaetano Greco and Francesco Durante. He subsequently became *maestro di cappella* of S Maria Verticelli; according to Schmidl he also taught singing in various Neapolitan monasteries and churches. By 1749 Avossa was working in north Italy as *maestro di cappella* in Pesaro and conductor of the municipal theatre orchestra there. He married a Rosa Travi in Naples in 1758.

Although Avossa's principal fame today derives from his highly popular comic opera *La pupilla*, he probably wrote mainly church music. Surviving works have concertato textures of chorus and solo voices, contrapuntal facility, a certain adventurousness in tonal thinking and,

in some cases, an essentially symphonic conception of a whole movement.

WORKS
COMIC OPERAS

Don Saverio (A. Palomba), Venice, S Moisè, aut. 1744
Lo scolaro alla moda, Reggio nell'Emilia, Cittadella, carn. 1748
Il baron gonfianuvoli, Salzburg, carn. 1750
I tutori, Naples, Nuovo, wint. 1757
La pupilla (Palomba), Naples, Fiorentini, carn. 1763, *H-Bn*; in *A-Wn* and *US-Wc* as Il ciarlone; as La pupilla ed il ciarlone, with emendations by G. Scalabrini, Copenhagen, 1769, *DK-Ch*

CHURCH MUSIC

Orats: La nuvoletta d'Elia, Ancona, 1746; La felicità de' tempi, Pesaro, 1749; Il giudizio di Salomone, Pesaro, 1751
3 masses, several mass sections, *I-Nc*; mass, *F-Pn*; 2 Mag, *A-Wn*, *I-Nc*; 2 motets, *GB-Lbl*, *I-Fc*

BIBLIOGRAPHY

DBI (U. Prota-Giurleo); *RosaM*; *SchmidlDS*
M. Scherillo: *L'opera buffa napoletana durante il Settecento: storia letteraria* (Naples, 1883, 2/1916/R), 280, 282
C. Cinelli: 'Memorie cronistoriche del Teatro di Pesaro (1637–1897)', *La cronaca musicale*, ii (1897), 431–2
A. Loewenberg: *The Annals of Opera, 1597–1940* (Cambridge, 1943, 3/1978), i, 268–9
U. Prota-Giurleo: *Ricordi digiacomiani* (Naples, 1956), 10

JAMES L. JACKMAN/DALE E. MONSON

Avotri, Kenneth. *See* KAFUI, KENNETH.

Avraamov, Arseny Mikhaylovich (*b* Malïy Nesvetay, Rostov district, 10/22 April 1886 (elsewhere 10/12 June 1886); *d* Moscow, 19 May 1944). Russian composer and theorist. He studied theory at the music school attached to the Moscow Philharmonic Society with I.N. Protopopov and A.M. Koreshchenko (1908–11) and took private composition lessons with Sergey Taneyev. From 1910 he was active as a music critic under the pseudonym Ars and, having refused to fight in World War I, fled abroad in 1914 and worked, among other occupations, as a stoker and as a circus artist. Returning to Russia in 1917 he was appointed arts commissar of the RSFSR branch of Narkompros (1917–18) and took part in the formation of the Proletkul't organization. 1923 found him working in Dagestan but in 1926 he returned to Moscow where he became involved in a number of activities: he participated in the creation of the first Russian films with sound (1929–34), he led a sound laboratory in the Cinematic Institute of Scientific Research (1932–3) and he lectured at the Moscow Conservatory on the history and theory of sound systems (1934). While living in Nal'chik (1935–41) he collected folk music of the peoples of the north Caucasus and wrote some compositions based on these materials. He later conducted the Russian Folk Chorus (1941–3). During the early Soviet era many artists attempted to integrate technology and creativity; Avraamov's work typifies this trend. He invented a graphic-sonic art which was produced by drawing directly onto magnetic tape. He also sought to overcome equal temperament and tonality by his creation of an 'ultrachromatic' 48-tone system. This method was proposed in a thesis entitled *Universal'naya sistema tonov* ('The Universal System of Tones') and was realized in his demonstrations which took place in 1927 in Berlin, Frankfurt and Stuttgart. He is considered a precursor of the *musique concrète* movement with his *Simfoniya gudkov* ('Symphony of Factory Sirens') which was performed in Azerbaijan in 1923 and later in Moscow. He also wrote a number of compositions for more conventional forces.

WORKS
(selective list)

Simfoniya gudkov [Sym. of Factory Sirens] (text of instructions), several choruses with spectators, cannons, foghorns, Caspian flotilla, 2 batteries of artillery guns, several full infantry regiments incl. machine gun division, hydro-aeroplanes, all of Baku's factory sirens, conductors with pistol shots, central steam whistle machine, noise auto-transports, 1922; Marsh na kabardinskiye temï [March on Kabardin Themes], orch, 1936; Aul Batïr Ov., orch, 1940; Fantasies on Kabardin Themes, orch, 1940; inst works, choral music

WRITINGS

'Puti i sredstva tvorchestva' [Ways and means of creativity], *Muzïka*, no.164 (1914), 39–43; no.172 (1916), 215–17

'Druzhestvennoye otkrïtoye pis'mo kompozitoru N. Roslavtsu' [A friendly open letter on the composer Roslavets], *Muzïka*, no.215 (1915), 192; Ger. trans. in A. Wehrmeyer: *Studien zum russischen Musikdenken um 1920* (Frankfurt, 1991), 326 only

'7–1–13', *Muzïka*, no.232 (1915), 476–9

'Gryadushchaya muzïkal'naya nauka i novaya èra v istorii muzïki' [Music science of the future and a new era in music history], *Muzïkal'niy sovremennik* (1916), no.2, pp.80–103

'"Ul'trakhromatizm" ili "omnitonal'nost'"', *Muzïkal'niy sovremennik* (1916), nos.4–5, pp.157–68 [on Skryabin]

'Jenseits von Temperierung und Tonalität', *Melos*, i (1920), 131–4, 160–66, 184–8

'Klin-klinom' [Like cures like], *Muzïkal'naya kul'tura* (1924), no.1, p.42; Ger. trans. in D. Gojowy: *Neue sowjetische Musik der 20er Jahre* (Laaber, 1980), 443

'Universal'naya sistema tonov (U.T.S.)' [Universal tonal system (U.T.S.)], *Zhizn' iskusstva* (1926), no.12, pp.3–4; no.38, pp.9–10; no.40, pp.6–7

['Vierteltonmusik'], *Muzïka i revolyutsiya* (1927), nos.5–6, p.39; Ger. trans. in *Neue sowjetische Musik der 20er Jahre* (Laaber, 1980), 445–6

'Sinteticheskaya muzïka', *SovM* (1939), no.8, pp.67–75

'The Symphony of Sirens', *Wireless Imagination: Sound, Radio, and the Avant-Garde*, ed. D. Kahn and G. Whitehead (Cambridge, MA, 1992), 245–52 [incl. trans. of instruction text from *Simfoniya gudkov*]

BIBLIOGRAPHY

N. Roslavets: 'Druzhestvennïy otvet Ars. Avraamovu' [A friendly answer to Avraamov], *Muzïka*, no.219 (1915), 256–7; Ger. trans. in A. Wehrmeyer: *Studien zum russischen Musikdenken um 1920* (Frankfurt, 1991), 327–8

L.L. Sabaneyev: 'Pis'ma o muzïke: ul'trakhromaticheskaya polemika' [Letters about music: the ultrachromatic polemic], *Muzïkal'niy sovremennik* (1916), no.6, pp.99–108

D. Gojowy: *Neue sowjetische Musik der 20er Jahre* (Laaber, 1980)

S. Rumyanchev: 'Kommunisticheskiye kolokola' [Communist bells], *SovM* (1984), no.11, pp.54–63 [on Simfoniya gudkov]

A. Wehrmeyer: *Studien zum russichen Musikdenken um 1920* (Frankfurt and New York, 1991)

M. Lobanova: *Nikolay Andreevič Roslavec und die Kultur seiner Zeit* (Frankfurt and New York, 1991)

MARINA LOBANOVA

Avshalomov, Aaron (*b* Nikolayevsk, Siberia, 31 Oct 1894; *d* New York, 26 April 1965). Russian composer, father of JACOB AVSHALOMOV. Self-taught except for one term at the Zürich Conservatory, he spent 30 years in China, where he composed symphonic and dramatic works. Fascinated by Chinese culture, he integrated authentic Chinese thematic material into Western musical styles. In addition to composing, he became head librarian of the Municipal Library of Shanghai (1928–43) and conductor of the Shanghai SO (1943–6). He emigrated to the USA in 1947, joining his son, Jacob Avshalomov. Although he continued to compose, his work never achieved much recognition in the USA, where he became a naturalized citizen. Of his three operas, *Kuan Yin* (*c*1925), *The Twilight Hour of Yan Kuei Fei* (1933) and *The Great Wall* (1945), all composed in China, the last had the most success. First performed in Shanghai in 1945, it was also produced in Nanjing under the sponsorship of both Madame Sun Yat Sen and Madame Chiang Kaishek. In the USA, Leopold Stokowski, Pierre Monteux and Artur Rodzinski conducted his three symphonies, the second of which was commissioned by Koussevitzky in 1949. He also wrote concertos for the piano, violin and flute.

MSS in *US-NYp*

BIBLIOGRAPHY

American Composers Alliance Bulletin, x/2 (1962), 18–19

N. Slonimsky: *Music Since 1900* (New York, 4/1971)

DAVID STABLER

Avshalomov, Jacob (David) (*b* Qingdao, China, 28 March 1919). American composer, son of AARON AVSHALOMOV. After emigrating to the USA in 1937, he studied in Los Angeles with Ernst Toch, at the Eastman School of Music (MA 1942) with Bernard Rogers, among others, and at Tanglewood with Aaron Copland (1947). From 1946 to 1954 he taught at Columbia University, where he conducted the university chorus and orchestra in the American premières of Bruckner's Mass in D minor, Tippett's *A Child of our Time* and Handel's *The Triumph of Time and Truth*. In 1954 he began a 41-year tenure as conductor of the Portland (Oregon) Junior SO (later the Portland Youth PO), the country's first student orchestra. A number of recordings, six international tours, and praise from New York and European audiences followed. In 1968 President Lyndon Johnson appointed him to the National Council of the Humanities. He also served on the committees of the NEA's Music Planning Section (1974–9) and the Pro Musicis Foundation (1986–92). His compositional style embraces Asian sonorities, Renaissance counterpoint and Ivesian allusions to American folk music. He has identified *Inscriptions at the City of Brass* (1957) as his most significant work. His honours include a Guggenheim Fellowship (1951), a New York Music Critic's Circle Award (1953) for *Tom O'Bedlam*, a Naumburg Recording Award (1956) for his Sinfonietta and an Alice M. Ditson Award (1965) for his work with the Portland Youth Philharmonic.

WORKS
(selective list)

Vocal: How Long O Lord (cant.), A, chorus, orch, 1948; Tom O'Bedlam (17th century anon.), SATB, ob, tabor, perc, 1953; Inscriptions at the City of Brass (*1001 Nights*), female nar, chorus, wind, perc, 1957; City Upon a Hill (W. Blake), nar, chorus, bell, orch, 1964; Praises from the Corners of the Earth (J. Donne, Strongwolf, the Qur'an, e.e. cummings), SATB, org, 3 perc, 1964, arr. orch; Doris Songs (D. Avshalomov), 1v, gui, 1994; Glorious th'Assembled Fires (Sym. no.3), chorus, orch, 1994; more than 30 songs, 1v, pf, *c*1943; series of 10 works, chorus, orch, 1952–96

Inst (orch, unless otherwise stated): Sonatine, va/cl, pf, *c*1943; The Taking of T'ung Kuan, 1943; Sinfonietta, 1946; Evocations, cl/va, pf, 1947; Phases of the Great Land, 1958; Sym. 'The Oregon', 1962; Raptures on Madrigals of Gesualdo, 1975; Open Sesame!, 1984; Sym. of Songs, 1992

MSS in *US-NYp*

Principal publishers: E.C. Schirmer, Southern

Principal recording companies: CRI, Albany

BIBLIOGRAPHY

W. Bergsma: 'The Music of Jacob Avshalomov', *American Composers Alliance Bulletin*, iii/3 (1956) [incl. work-list]

C.H. Encell: *Jacob Avshalomov's Works for Chorus and Orchestra: Aspects of Style* (diss., U. of Washington, 1983)

DAVID STABLER

Awang, Khatijah binti (*b* Pasir Mas Kelantan, Malaysia, 13 Aug 1941). Malaysian *ma'yong* (dance theatre) performer. From an early age she developed an interest in singing, dancing and acting, later participating as a singer and dancer in activities organized by both the regional radio and television stations in Kota Baharu and the Kelantan state cultural troupe, as well as in several performances marking national events in Kuala Lumpur. In the mid-1960s she joined the National Cultural Complex under the Ministry of Culture, Arts and Tourism as a dancer.

Although there have been notable performers of *ma'yong*, *main puteri* (shamanic dance) and *silat* (Malay martial art form) on both sides of her family, Awang's involvement in *ma'yong* developed mainly as a response to the Traditional Drama and Music of Southeast Asia conference, held in Kuala Lumpur in August 1969, during which the plight of the genre (then on the verge of extinction) was highlighted. The goal of the 1969 revival, led by Awang, was to save the genre from extinction by making it more visually elaborate; this resulted in the creation of the Seri Temenggung troupe of Kelantan, which Awang has led since its inception in 1970.

Seri Temenggung has become the country's leading troupe, performing extensively within Malaysia as well as overseas, and has been at the forefront of promoting *ma'yong* outside the province of Kelantan in association with various universities and cultural organizations.

Awang herself has become a valuable resource, assisting with research and efforts to preserve and document not only *ma'yong*, but traditional Kelantan performing arts in general. For her efforts in promoting *ma'yong* she has received numerous local awards, as well as the ASEAN Cultural Award. She continues to teach *ma'yong* at the Akademi Seni Kebangsaan (National Arts Academy) in Kuala Lumpur.

See also MALAYSIA, §I, 1(iii).

GHULAM-SARWAR YOUSOF

Aweke, Ashter [Aster] (*b* Gonder, Ethiopia, 1961). Ethiopian singer. Ashter began her singing career in the early 1970s in Addis Ababa, and performed with the band Roha (formerly Shebele Band). Her formative musical years were also shaped by the music of Bezunesh Bekele and the philanthropy of Ali Tango, which provided motivation for the singer. Ashter emigrated to the USA in 1981 after a few cassette releases (such as *Munaya*) in Ethiopia and has since produced important albums for Sony: *Kabu* remained among the top ten of Billboard's world music charts for ten weeks and *Aster Aweke Alive* was recorded at a sold-out concert in London in 1996. Her popularity spread further with the inclusion of her songs on compilation releases involving multiple artists, such as *Afrika*, *Under African Skies* (BBC Videos, vol.2, 1989) and *Fruits of Freedom*. Ashter possesses a unique musical style that fuses indigenous musical and linguistic traditions with influences from singers such as Donna Summer and Aretha Franklin. Along with Angélique Kidjo and Oumou Sangare, Ashter Aweke represents an important African female voice in the popular music industry. She returned to Ethiopia in 1996.

DANIEL AVORGBEDOR

Awshīyāt. Prayers sung by the priest in the Divine Liturgy of the Coptic Orthodox Church. *See* COPTIC CHURCH MUSIC, §4.

Ax, Emanuel (*b* L'viv, 8 June 1949). American pianist of Polish birth. His first teacher was his father, a coach at the L'viv Opera. The family emigrated to Canada in 1959, settling in Winnipeg, then moved to New York in 1961. Ax began seven years of study with Mieczysław Munz at the Juilliard School of Music in 1966 and also attended Columbia University (BA 1970). He had already won honours in the Chopin competition, Warsaw, the Vianna da Motta Competition, Lisbon, and the Queen Elisabeth of Belgium Competition, and had made his New York début (Alice Tully Hall, 1973) when he won the first Artur Rubinstein International Piano Competition in 1974. The next year he received the Young Concert Artists' Michaels Award, and in 1979 he won the Avery Fisher Prize. Ax has performed with many leading orchestras, including the Boston SO, the Philadelphia Orchestra, the New York PO and the LPO. In 1991 he made his début at the Proms in London, performing Brahms's First Piano Concerto. He has taken part in numerous chamber music and recital series, including performances by the Chamber Music Society of Lincoln Center, the Mostly Mozart Festival, and a three-concert series entitled 'Emanuel Ax Invites' at Alice Tully Hall. In 1980 he formed a trio with the violinist Young Uck Kim and the cellist Yo-Yo Ma; he and Ma also play together as a duo, and have made many admired recordings. Other recordings include Haydn sonatas, thoughtful readings of the Beethoven concertos, and the piano concertos of Chopin and Schoenberg.

Ax is in the front rank of his generation of pianists; his often aggressive, dramatic musical inclinations have been increasingly tempered by a maturing musical intelligence and sensibility.

JAMES CHUTE/R

Axman, Emil (*b* Rataje u Kroměříže, 3 June 1887; *d* Prague, 25 Jan 1949). Czech composer, musicologist and archivist. He studied at Prague University under Nejedlý and Hostinský, receiving the PhD in 1912 for a dissertation on Moravian folk opera in the 18th century. He studied composition under Novák (1908–10) and counterpoint under Ostrčil (1920), and he devoted himself to composition while head of the musical archive at the National Museum in Prague (1915). In the 1920s he was an official in the Society for Modern Music. His music was much influenced by the folk music of his native Moravia, but the political and social problems of the World War I period also had a deep effect on him. Passing from late-Romanticism through a transitional period marked by influences from contemporary developments, his music attained a broad lyricism with particularly strong traces of folksong and dance. Most of his works are cast in extended forms. It was in the field of vocal music that he was most successful: there are a number of valuable choral works (principally pieces for male chorus) and his song-cycles and folksong arrangements are notable.

WORKS
(selective list)

Cants.: Moje matka (O. Březina), 1926; Balada o očích topičových [Ballad of the Miner's Eyes] (Wolker), 1927; Ilonka Beniačova (J.V. Rosůlek), 1929; Sobotecký hřbitov [Sobotece Graveyard] (F. Šrámek), 1932; Stabat mater, 1938

Male choruses: Z vojny [From the War], 1916; Měsíčné noci [Moonlit Nights], 1920; Hlas země [Voice of the Earth], 1926; Noc [Night] (K.H. Mácha), 1926; Věčný voják [The Eternal Soldier] (Šrámek), 1933

Mixed choruses: Nenarozenému [To the Unborn Child], 1921; Vánoce chudých [Christmas of the Poor], 1922

Song cycles: Vzpomínání [Reminiscence], 1919; Duha [Rainbow], 1921; Noc [Night], 1928; U plamene [At the Flame], 1930

Syms.: 'Tragická', 1926; 'Giocosa, slovácká' [Moravian Slovak], 1927; 'Jarní' [Spring], 1928; 'Heroická', 1932; 'Dithyrambická', n.d.; 'Vlastenecká' [Patriotic], 1942
Concs. for vn, 1936, pf, 1939, vc, 1942, vn, vc, 1944
Chbr and solo inst: Sonata, vn, pf, 1923; 6 str qts, 1924, 1925, 1930, 1940, 1943, 1946; pf sonatas

WRITINGS

Moravské opery ve století 18. (18th-century Moravian operas] (diss., U. of Prague, 1912) [pubd in *Časopis moravského musea* (1912)]
Morava v české hudbě XIX. století [Moravia in Czech music of the 19th century] (Prague, 1920)

BIBLIOGRAPHY

L. Hovorka: *Sborová tvorba Axmanova* (Prague, 1940)
F. Pala: *E. Axman* (Prague, 1951)

JAN TROJAN

Axt, William L. (*b* New York, 19 April 1888; *d* Ukiah, CA, 13 Feb 1959). American composer and conductor. After private music study in Berlin, he conducted for Oscar Hammerstein's Manhattan Opera Company (which closed in 1910), then for productions on Broadway. By 1921 he had become an assistant conductor at the Capitol Theater, where silent films were presented with full orchestral accompaniment; in 1923, in partnership with David Mendoza, he replaced Erno Rapee as principal conductor. In addition to conducting, he composed incidental film music for the Capitol as needed, including 57 pieces published in the *Capitol Photoplay Series* (New York, 1923–7). From 1925 to 1929 he collaborated with Mendoza in New York on compilation scores for at least 20 MGM films, beginning with *The Big Parade*. Their collaboration continued with the music for *Don Juan* (1926), the first feature film score to be presented using the Vitaphone process, which mechanically synchronized the playback of music recorded on wax discs with the projection of the film. In 1929 or 1930 he moved to Hollywood, where he played a key role in the MGM music department. He continued to work for MGM, providing music for numerous films, until his retirement in the early 1940s.

Neither in the collaborations with Mendoza, nor in the MGM films is a distinctive Axt style easily discernible; his works of the 1920s, however, serve as excellent examples of the compilation score. In the music for *The Big Parade*, principal themes exhibit clear expressive content and undergo simple, skilful transformations; new music is interwoven with arrangements of pre-existent pieces to create a smooth pastiche. The scores of the 1930s are often sparse, consisting mainly of modest mood pieces and source music. Many of these are polished examples of MGM's star-centred style, in which the craftsmanship of the composer was subordinated to the effect of the whole.

WORKS
(selective list)

directors' names in parentheses

Film scores (collab. D. Mendoza): Ben-Hur (F. Niblo), 1925; The Big Parade (K. Vidor), 1925; La Bohème (Vidor), 1926; Don Juan (A. Crosland), 1926; A Woman of Affairs (C. Brown), 1928; Our Dancing Daughters (H. Beaumont), 1928; White Shadows in the South Seas (W.S. Van Dyke), 1928; The Kiss (J. Feyder), 1929; The Single Standard (J.S. Robertson), 1929
Other film scores: Smilin' Through (S. Franklin), 1932; Broadway to Hollywood, 1933; Dinner at Eight (G. Cukor), 1933; The Thin Man (Van Dyke), 1934; Pursuit (E.L. Martin), 1935; Libeled Lady (J. Conway), 1936; The Last of Mrs Cheney (R. Boleslawski), 1937

BIBLIOGRAPHY

GroveA (M. Marks) [incl. further bibliography]
Musical Courier (27 Dec 1923)
E.J. Lewis: 'The Archive Collection of Film Music at the University of Wyoming', *Cue Sheet*, vi/3 (1989), 89–99; vi/4 (1989), 143–60
D. James: 'Performing with Silent Films', *Film Music I*, ed. C. McCarty (1989), 61–79

MARTIN MARKS

Ayala Pérez, Daniel (*b* Abalá, Yucatán, 21 July 1906; *d* Veracruz, 20 June 1975). Mexican conductor and composer. He studied at the Conservatorio Nacional de Música, Mexico City (1927–32), where he was a violin pupil of Revueltas and a composition pupil of Chávez. There he allied himself with Contreras, Galindo Dimas and Moncayo in the 'Group of Four'. From 1931 to 1937 he played second violin in the Mexico SO, and he then directed a chorus in Morelia for two years. Returning to Yucatán in 1940, he quickly took a leading part in all aspects of musical life. He was director of the newly reorganized Mérida SO (inaugural concert 15 November 1944), of the Típica Yukalpetén, of the official state band, of the Yucatán Conservatory (from 1944) and of the Veracruz School of Music (from 1955); later he also worked for the Veracruz Institute of Fine Arts. He composed relatively little after 1944, but his bright picture-postcard pentatonic evocations, usually short danceable pieces with Maya titles or texts, had already established his reputation in Mexico and the USA. *U kayil chaac* was widely broadcast in a CBS concert conducted by Chávez (24 January 1936).

WORKS
(selective list)

Ballets: El hombre maya, 1939; La gruta diabólica, chbr orch, 1940
Orch: Tribu, sym. poem, 1934; Paisaje, suite, 1935; Panoramas de México, suite, 1936; Mi viaje a Norte América, suite, 1947; Pf Concertino, 1974
Vocal: Uchben X'choholte [In an Old Cemetery], S, chbr orch, 1931; El grillo (D. Castañeda), S, cl, vn, pf, rattle, 1933; U kayil chaac [Rain Song] (Maya), S, chbr orch, indigenous perc, 1934; Los Yaquis y los Seris, voice, chbr group, indigenous perc, 1938
Chbr and inst: Radiogramma, pf, 1931; Str Qt, 1933; Vidrios rotos, ob, cl, bn, hn, pf, 1938

BIBLIOGRAPHY

Enciclopedia yucatanense, ed. E. Novelo Torres, iv (Mexico City, 1944), 738, 816ff
Diccionario enciclopédico UTEHA apéndice, i (Mexico City, 1964), 272
Diccionario Porrúa, i (Mexico City, 5/1986), 239
Enciclopedia de México, ed. J.R. Alvarez, ii (Mexico City, 1987), 730 [incl. augmented list of undated compositions]

ROBERT STEVENSON

Ayestarán, Lauro (*b* Montevideo, 9 July 1913; *d* Montevideo, 22 July 1966). Uruguayan musicologist and ethnomusicologist. He studied in Montevideo at the Larrimbe Conservatory and at the school of law and social sciences of the university. In 1937 he was appointed professor of choral music and music history at the teachers' training institute; subsequently he became director of the division of musical research of the Instituto de Estudios Superiores, professor of musicology at the University of Montevideo (1946) and head of the musicology section of the National Historical Museum of Uruguay. He was also active as a music critic for several newspapers and as artistic director of the state broadcasting system, SODRE. Ayestarán was equally interested in music history and ethnomusicology. His first study of Hispano-American Baroque music (1941) dealt with the activities in Argentina of the Italian composer Domenico Zipoli. During the 1940s he did field work for the National Historical Museum, making some 4000 recordings of Uruguayan folk music and publishing his studies of them. He received (among several prizes) the national award Pablo Blanco Acevedo for his major work, *La música en el Uruguay* (1953). He was a corresponding member of several music organizations, including IFMC, the Brazilian Academy of Music, the Argentine Academy of Fine Arts and ISM, and served as vice-president of the Inter-American Music Council (CIDEM).

WRITINGS

Domenico Zipoli, el gran compositor y organista romano del 1700 en el Río de la Plata (Montevideo, 1941)

Crónica de una temporada musical en el Montevideo de 1830 (Montevideo, 1943)

Fuentes para el estudio de la música colonial uruguaya (Montevideo, 1947)

'La música escénica en el Uruguay', *RMC*, no.19 (1947), 17–26

Le música indígena en el Uruguay (Montevideo, 1949)

Un antecedente colonial de la poesía tradicional uruguaya (Montevideo, 1949)

El Minué montonero (Montevideo, 1950)

La primitiva poesía gauchesca en el Uruguay (Montevideo, 1950)

La Misa para Día de Difuntos de Fray Manuel Ubeda, 1802: comentario y reconstrucción (Montevideo, 1952)

La música en el Uruguay (Montevideo, 1953) [only 1 vol. pubd]

Virgilio Scarabelli (Montevideo, 1953)

Luis Sambucetti: vida y obra (Montevideo, 1956)

La primera edición uruguaya del Fausto de Estanislao del Campo (Montevideo, 1959)

Domenico Zipoli: vida y obra (Buenos Aires, 1962)

'Domenico Zipoli y el barroco musical sudamericano', *RMC*, nos.81–2 (1962), 94–124

'Fétis, un precursor del criterio etnomusicológico en 1869', *Conferencia interamericana de etnomusicología I: Cartagena, Colombia, 1963*, 13–37

'El Barroco musical hispano-americano: los manuscritos de la iglesia San Felipe Neri (Sucre, Bolivia) existentes en el Museo Histórico Nacional del Uruguay', *YIAMR*, i (1965), 55–93; rev. in *Revista histórica*, nos.115–17 (1968), 1–43

with F. de M. Rodríguez de Ayestarán and A. Ayestarán: *El tamboril y la comparsa* (Montevideo, 1990)

BIBLIOGRAPHY

G. Chase: 'In memoriam Lauro Ayestarán', *YIAMR*, ii (1966), 161–3

A. Soriano: 'Lauro Ayestarán, 1913–1966', *RMC*, no.101 (1967), 26–35

GERARD BÉHAGUE/R

Ayler, Albert (*b* Cleveland, 13 July 1936; *d* ?New York, between 5 and 25 Nov 1970). American jazz tenor saxophonist and bandleader. He began on the alto saxophone and was playing professionally in black rhythm-and-blues bands by his mid-teens. While serving in army concert bands, he changed over to the tenor saxophone. He occasionally played in Paris clubs while stationed in France in 1960–61. After his discharge, he remained in Europe, leading a bop trio for eight months in Sweden and playing with Cecil Taylor in winter 1962–3 in Copenhagen. In 1963 he moved to New York, where he performed infrequently with Taylor. In summer 1964 he formed a quartet with Don Cherry, Gary Peacock and Sunny Murray which toured Europe later that year.

Ayler was never to find a steady audience for his radical music – his group appeared perhaps only three times in 1965 – and, although his albums were well received by the critics, he remained poor. He made no effort to clarify his music for listeners, actively discouraging musical interpretations of his recordings and instead stressing their social and spiritual issues; the inconsistent and confusing titles to his pieces further obscured his work (see Litweiler). Nevertheless, in studios and New York

clubs (1965–8), at the Newport Jazz Festival (1966), on a brief European tour (November 1966) and for college concerts he was able to assemble faithful sidemen. His groups included his brother, the trumpeter Donald Ayler, one or two double bass players, such as Peacock and Henry Grimes, the drummers Murray, Milford Graves or Beaver Harris, and Cal Cobbs on piano or harpsichord. Only Cobbs remained in Ayler's new rhythm-and-blues groups of 1969–70. On 5 November 1970, shortly after having returned from a tour of Europe with his quintet, Ayler was reported missing in New York; his body was found in the East River on 25 November.

Ayler's extraordinary music of the mid-1960s rejected most of the conventions of the prevailing bop and free-jazz styles. According to Jost (who alone has surveyed his career analytically), Ayler often replaced tempered melody with sweeping flourishes; he combined these 'sound-spans' (Jost) with sudden low-pitched honks and a wide, sentimental vibrato (ex.1). His recordings of 1962–3 in Scandinavia were unsuccessful because of the stylistic gulf between the 'in-tune' bop accompanists and the 'out-of-tune' saxophone. By contrast, Peacock and Murray provided sympathetic accompaniments to Ayler's highly original playing. Their recordings (1964) juxtapose difficult collective improvisation and Ayler's simple, rhythmically square, frequently tonal themes. Sometimes these two factors are interrelated, as in the gradual deformation of the folk-like melody in several versions of *Ghosts* (1964; including one on the album *Spiritual Unity*, ESP). More often, however, the brief themes serve as foils for lengthy, exciting improvisations in which the group, avoiding predictable sounds, achieves remarkably varied textures and rhythms.

Ex.1 From the title track of *Ghosts* (1964, Debut); transcr. B. Kernfeld

Soon after the performance of *Bells* in May 1965, the balance shifted from improvisation to composition. Three tracks on *Spirits Rejoice* (1965, ESP) emphasize thematic material. Later, in a new version of *Ghosts* (1967, on the album *Albert Ayler in Greenwich Village*, Imp.), the players never depart from thematic statements. This striving for simplicity, augmented by pressure from the record company Impulse! to increase his sales, led Ayler to return to rhythm-and-blues in the late 1960s.

Unfortunately, his late rhythm-and-blues songs and his singing were dull, and his last two albums received little attention.

BIBLIOGRAPHY

N. Hentoff: 'The Truth is Marching In', *Down Beat*, xxxiii/23 (1966), 16–18, 40 [interview]

V. Wilmer: 'Albert and Don Ayler', *JazzM*, xii/10 (1966), 11–13

E. Jost: 'Albert Ayler', *Free Jazz* (Graz, 1974/R), 121–32

V. Wilmer: 'Albert Ayler: Spiritual Unity', *As Serious as your Life: the Story of the New Jazz* (London, 1977, 2/1980), 92–111

J. Litweiler: 'Albert Ayler', *Down Beat*, xlix/2 (1982), 45–6

M. Hames: *Albert Ayler, Sunny Murray, Cecil Taylor, Byard Lancaster, and Kenneth Terroade on Disc and Tape* (Ferndown, Dorset, 1983)

BARRY KERNFELD

Ayleward, Richard (*b* Winchester, 1626; *d* Norwich, 15 Oct 1669). English organist and composer. He was a chorister at Winchester Cathedral under Christopher Gibbons from June 1638 to November 1639, his father Richard being a minor canon there. At the Restoration he became Organist and Master of the Choristers at Norwich Cathedral from 12 March 1661 to mid-1664 and again from 5 December 1666 until his death. During at least part of his absence, for some unknown reason Ayleward was at the Assizes. He was buried in the cathedral on 18 October 1669.

Ayleward's output consists mainly of church music, all of which is contained in a set of partbooks formerly belonging to Norwich Cathedral which were later acquired by A.H. Mann. The Service in D major is in the 'short' style of Orlando Gibbons and was probably influenced by the music Ayleward sang at Winchester. The two Evening Services also have predominantly syllabic underlay. The verse anthems range from short pieces with one solo and four chorus parts (*Have pity upon me*) to elaborate settings, whose exceptional length and complexity of design would have made them unsuitable for the choir at Norwich in the early years of the Restoration; *I was glad*, for example, contains a verse for twelve solo voices. The style of the anthems tends towards that of Blow and Locke; *Holy, holy, holy*, one of the longer pieces, is a good example in the new idiom. An unusual feature of some of the anthems is the use of three or four solo voices of the same range; *I will not come*, for example, has a verse for four solo basses and another for four meanes. Many of the anthems have penitential texts and are in the minor mode. In *Hark, methinks I hear* Ayleward's interest in the declamatory style is particularly evident, while *O that I were* has chromatic word-painting of a madrigalian character (at the phrase 'my harp is turn'd'). *I charge you* makes dramatic use of antiphonal passages and also contains two solo sections for the organ, which performs a structural role.

The keyboard suites probably date from before the Restoration. In the D major suite the four movements are given descriptive names, in the manner of the fanciful titles adopted by Giles Farnaby and other Elizabethan and early Stuart virginalists. According to Mann, a manuscript of keyboard music (now lost) contained Ayleward's directions for tuning the harpsichord according to equal temperament. The 'Airs, dance tunes and suites' and a song by 'Mr Aylward' mentioned by Mann are by the later Theodore Aylward.

WORKS

SACRED

all in GB-Ckc

Full Service in D (TeD, Bs, Lit, Re, Cr, Preces, Re, Mag, Nunc), 4vv, Norwich Cathedral library

Evening Service in d, 8/4vv

Triple Evening Service in F, 8/4vv, *NWr*

20 verse anthems: Almighty and everlasting God, for the Purification; Blow the trumpet; Gently, O gently, Father, for the Circumcision; Glory to God; Great God with us, for the Nativity; Hark, methinks I hear; Have pity upon me; Holy, holy, holy (inc.); I charge you; I was glad, *GB-NWr*; I will not come; O how amiable (inc.); O Jerusalem; O Jesu sweet; O that I were; Praise be unto our

God above; Sweet Saviour, what ails this heart?; The King shall rejoice, for the Coronation and Restoration; Who could bring down?, for the Resurrection; Why should this world?

INSTRUMENTAL

Ayre, lyra viol, 1652[7]

2 suites, A, D, kbd, *GB-Llp*

Kbd pieces, *Lcm* [copied from a MS, now lost, formerly belonging to Thomas Taphouse, later acquired by A.H. Mann]

BIBLIOGRAPHY

F. Blomefield [completed by C. Parkin]: *An Essay towards a Topographical History of the County of Norfolk* (Lynn, 1739–75, 2/1805–10)

N. Boston: *The Musical History of Norwich Cathedral* (Norwich, 1963)

A.H. Mann: *Norwich Cathedral Musicians* (MS, GB-NWr)

A.H. Mann: *Old Norwich Cathedral Musicians* (MS of lecture, GB-Ckc)

W. Shaw: *Succession of Organists* (Oxford, 1991)

P. Aston and T. Roast: 'Music in the Cathedral', *Norwich Cathedral: Church, City and Diocese 1096–1996*, ed. I. Atherton and others (London, 1996), 688–704

P.R. GRANGER/PETER ASTON, TOM ROAST

Ayliff [Aylif, Alyff, Ayloff, Ayloffe], **Mrs** (*fl* 1692–6). English soprano and actress. She sang in *The Fairy Queen* at Dorset Garden Theatre in May 1692 and soon became Purcell's leading soprano. In the *Gentleman's Journal* for August 1692 Peter Motteux referred to her performance of Purcell's italianate 'Ah me to many deaths decreed' in Crowne's play *Regulus* as 'divinely sung'. Well over a dozen of Purcell's stage songs and dialogues were published as sung by her and she was a soloist in his *Hail, bright Cecilia* (1692) and *Celebrate this Festival* (1693). In 1695 she went to Lincoln's Inn fields with Betterton's company and there she also acted a little, creating Miss Prue in Congreve's *Love for Love*. Her last recorded appearance was in November 1696 when she sang in *The Loves of Mars and Venus*, a masque with music by Eccles and Finger.

BIBLIOGRAPHY

BDA; *LS*

O. Baldwin and T. Wilson: 'Purcell's Sopranos', *MT*, cxxiii (1982), 602–9

C.A. Price: *Henry Purcell and the London Stage* (Cambridge, 1984)

O. Baldwin and T. Wilson: 'Purcell's Stage Singers', *Performing the Music of Henry Purcell*, ed. M. Burden (Oxford, 1996), 105–29

OLIVE BALDWIN, THELMA WILSON

Aylward, Theodore (*b* ?Chichester, *c*1730; *d* London, 27 Feb 1801). English organist and composer, son of Henry Aylward of Chichester. He may have sung as a boy at Drury Lane Theatre in London. His successive appointments were as organist of Oxford Chapel, London, from about 1760 until 1768; St Lawrence Jewry, 1762–88; St Michael Cornhill, 1768–81; and St George's Chapel, Windsor, 1788 until his death. Meanwhile, from 1771 he was also Gresham Professor of Music, and at the Handel Commemoration of 1784 he was one of the assistant directors. He was elected a member of the Society of Musicians in 1763, and took the Oxford degree of DMus in 1791. About 1780 he directed the Friendly Harmonists, a small glee club whose meetings were held at Anderton's Coffee House in Fleet Street. Most of his compositions were secular, and he won a Catch Club medal in 1769. He also composed for the theatre, and was involved in Garrick's Shakespeare Jubilee Procession in 1769. Harley comments that his *Six Lessons for the Harpsichord, Organ or Piano Forte* (*c*1784) are 'virtually Handelian Suites' and suggests that he was 'indulging in a conscious piece of archaism, inspired by his participation that year … in the Handel Commemoration'. Notwithstanding their strong Handelian orientation, these works at times reflect Aylward's acquaintance with the harpsichord music of Domenico Scarlatti. Elsewhere, there are movements equivalent to contemporary 'cornet voluntaries' for organ, while later lessons demonstrate traits characteristic of music for fortepiano, suggesting the influence of J.C. Bach.

WORKS
printed works published in London unless otherwise stated

VOCAL

Welcome sun and southern show'rs; a New Song (c1750)
Ode on the Dawn of Peace (c1763)
6 Songs in Harlequin's Invasion, Cymbeline, and Midsummer Night's Dream, 1v, hpd (1765)
Come nymphs and fauns, glee, 3vv (c1769)
Oft have I seen at early morn: a Favourite Sonnet (c1785)
8 canzonets, 2vv (c1790)
Elegies and Glees, op.2 (c1790)
Songs pubd in 18th-century anthologies
Morning Services, D, E♭; 5 anthems: GB-WRch

INSTRUMENTAL

6 Lessons, hpd/org/pf, op.1 (c1784)
6 Quartettos, 2 vn, va, vc, op.4 (c1795)

BIBLIOGRAPHY

BDA
J. Foster: *Alumni oxonienses … 1715–1886* (London, 1887–8)
J. Foster: *Alumni oxonienses … 1500–1714* (Oxford and London, 1891–2)
D. Dawe: *Organists of the City of London, 1666–1850* (Padstow, 1983)
W. Shaw: *The Succession of Organists* (Oxford, 1991)
M. Argent, ed: *Recollections of R.J.S. Stevens* (London, 1992)
J. Harley: *British Harpsichord Music* (Aldershot, 1994), ii

WATKINS SHAW/GERALD GIFFORD

Ayo, Felix (*b* Sestao, Bilbao, 1 July 1933). Italian violinist of Spanish birth. When he was 14 he graduated from the Bilbao Conservatory and played Beethoven's concerto with a local orchestra. He then studied in Paris (1949–50, with René Benedetti) and at the Accademia Musicale Chigiana, Siena (1950–51, with Enescu and Principe) before moving to Rome to study under Principe at the Conservatorio di S Cecilia, becoming leader of the chamber orchestra I Musici, with which he first performed in 1952, the year of its formation. He went on many international tours with I Musici until 1968 and with them made numerous recordings, several of which received international awards. In 1968 he formed a piano quartet with Cino Ghedin, viola, Vincenzo Altobelli, cello (both from I Musici), and Marcello Abbado, piano; after Carlo Bruno succeeded Abbado as pianist in 1970 the group was named Quartetto Beethoven and has since toured in many countries. As well as making a number of recordings with the quartet, Ayo has recorded and published an edition of Bach's sonatas and partitas for solo violin. He was appointed to teach at the Rome Conservatory in 1972, becoming professor of violin in 1989.

PIERO RATTALINO

Ayre. *See* AIR.

Ayres (Johnson), Frederic (*b* Binghamton, NY, 17 March 1876; *d* Colorado Springs, CO, 23 Nov 1926). American composer. After studying engineering at Cornell University (1892–3) he worked designing electric motors. He studied composition with Kelley (1897–1901) and Foote

(summer 1899) 'to perfect … what I believed to be my proper work'. Because of ill health (tuberculosis) he moved to Las Cruces, New Mexico (1901), and then to Colorado Springs (1902), where he lived for the rest of his life composing and teaching theory privately. In 1926 he was awarded an honorary doctorate by the Cincinnati Conservatory of Music. His earlier output occasionally drew on thematic material evocative of Amerindian music, but the late works, for instance the Trio in D minor and the Violin Sonata in B minor, discard those influences in favour of a more abstract lyricism.

WORKS
printed works published in New York unless otherwise stated

Songs: 3 Songs (R. Browning, M. Fuller), op.2 (Berlin, 1906); 3 Songs (W. Shakespeare), op.3 (Newton Centre, MA, 1906–7), ed. Lawrence (1970); 2 Songs (Shakespeare), op.4: no.1 (Berlin, 1907), no.2 (Newton Centre, MA, 1907), ed. Lawrence (1970); 2 Songs (anon., Shakespeare), op.5 (1918); 3 Songs (Shakespeare, H. van Dyke, M.T. Ritter) op.6: no.1 (1915), no.2 (Newton Centre, MA, 1911), ed. Lawrence (1970), no.3 (1923); Mother Goose Melodies, op.7 (1919); Sunset Wings (D.G. Rossetti), op.8 (1918); The Seeonee Wolves (song cycle, R. Kipling), op.10, unpubd; 3 Songs (Kipling, H.C. Bunner, W.V. Moody) (1921); My Love in her Attire (anon.) (1924); 2 Songs (Kipling, C. Roberts) (1924); Christmas Eve at Sea (J. Masefield) (1925); Sappho (1927); 19 other unpubd songs
Orch: From the Plains, ov., op.14, unpubd
Chbr: Pf Trio, op.13 (Berlin, 1914); Sonata, op.15, vn, pf (Berlin, 1914); Str Qt, op.16, rev. 1916, unpubd; Pf Trio, d (1925); Elegy, vc, pf, unpubd; Str Qt no.2, unpubd; Sonata, vc, pf, unpubd; Sonata, b, vn, pf, unpubd
Pf solo: 2 Fugues, op.9 (Berlin, 1910); The Open Road, intermezzo, op.11 (1916); 3 Compositions, op.12: no.1 (Newton Centre, MA, 1910), ed. V.B. Lawrence (1970), no.2 (1917), no.3, unpubd; Pf Preludes, b, e♭, unpubd; The West Wind and the Daughter of Nokomis, unpubd

MSS in US-Wc

Principal publishers: G. Schirmer, Stahl (Berlin), Wa-Wan Press

BIBLIOGRAPHY

A.G. Farwell: 'Frederic Ayres', *Wa-Wan Press Monthly*, vi (1907), April; repr. in *The Wa-Wan Press, 1901–1911*, iv, ed. V.B. Lawrence (New York, 1970), 44
W.T. Upton: 'Frederic Ayres', *MQ*, xviii (1932), 39–59 [incl. full list of works]
J.P. Perkins: *An Examination of the Solo Piano Music Published by the Wa-Wan Press* (diss., Boston U., 1969)

BARNEY CHILDS

Ayrton, Edmund (*b* Ripon, bap. 19 Nov 1734; *d* Westminster, London, 22 May 1808). English organist and composer. He was the younger brother of William Ayrton (*b* Ripon, bap. 18 Dec 1726; *d* Ripon, 2 Feb 1799), who was organist of Ripon Cathedral from 7 June 1748 until his death. He was appointed organist, *rector chori* and 'singing-man' (with the additional post of auditor, perhaps merely as an augmentation of stipend) of Southwell Collegiate Church, or Minster (now the cathedral), on 23 October 1755; in April 1756 he was granted leave of absence to study under James Nares for three months. He moved to London on his appointment as Gentleman of the Chapel Royal in 1764. He also became a vicar-choral of St Paul's Cathedral (1767), lay vicar of Westminster Abbey and Master of the Children of the Chapel Royal (1780), holding all these posts simultaneously. He resigned as Master of the Children in 1805, having earlier successfully rebutted charges that he starved the boys. In 1784 he took the Cambridge degree of MusD, and he is stated to have proceeded *ad eundem* at Oxford in 1788, which, despite absence of official record, is not impossible. Samuel Wesley regarded him as 'one of the most egregious blockheads', but that is not the judgment of a well-balanced figure.

Ayrton's chief work is the anthem *Begin unto my God*, a large-scale work which was sung in St Paul's Cathedral at the thanksgiving service for the end of the War of American Independence in 1784. It is a very competent piece in the English tradition of Greene with strong Handelian influences. It goes outside the normal pattern of such anthems by including slightly colourful passages of accompanied recitative.

Edmund Ayrton's many sons included Edward Edmund (*b* London, 26 Jan 1765; *d* Bolton, Lancs., 5 Feb 1811), who was organist of Swansea Parish Church from 1792 to 1809, and WILLIAM AYRTON. Edmund's brother William had sons William Francis Morrall Ayrton (*b* Ripon, bap. 28 July 1778; *d* Chester, 8 Nov 1850) and Nicholas Thomas Dall Ayrton (*b* Ripon, bap. 15 Jan 1782; *d* Ripon, 24 Oct 1822); the former succeeded his father as organist of Ripon Cathedral in 1799, and the latter followed him in 1802 or 1805, retaining the post until his death.

WORKS
printed works published in London

The Prize Carnation (song, C. Smart) (1780)
Begin unto my God with timbrels, anthem of thanksgiving for end of American War of Independence, S, A, T, B, chorus a 4, 2 ob, 2 bn, 2 tpt, timp, str, London, St Paul's Cathedral, 29 June 1784; pubd as An Anthem for Voices and Instruments in Score (1788)
Glory be to the Father, double canon (1790)
An Ode to Harmony (When music with th'inspiring bowl), glee, 4vv (1799)
Thy righteousness, anthem, S, A, T, B, org, 1778, *GB-Lbl*
Short Service, E♭, 29 July 1796, *Lbl*
Service in C, other anthems, canons, catches, glees, songs etc.: all lost

BIBLIOGRAPHY
D. Mannings: 'John Hoppner's Portrait of Dr Edmund Ayrton', *The Burlington Magazine*, cxxxiv (1992), 498–9
C.E. Cooke: *The Life and Works of Edmund Ayrton (1734–1808)* (thesis, U. of Leeds, 1993)
J.H. Thomas: 'Edward Edmund Ayrton: the Swansea Ayrton', *Morgannwg*, xxxix (1995), 30–49
WATKINS SHAW

Ayrton, William (*b* London, 22 Feb 1777; *d* London, 8 May 1858). English editor, critic and impresario, youngest son of EDMUND AYRTON. He was baptized at St Margaret's, Westminster, and probably studied music with his father. In 1794 he was a bass chorus singer at the Ancient Concerts, and by 1803, when he married Marianne Arnold (daughter of Samuel Arnold), a piano teacher. Through the Chapel Royal connections of his father and father-in-law, and the friendship of Frederick Nicolay (Queen Charlotte's music librarian), he had easy access to court circles. But it was his membership in the Society of Antiquaries (1807) that stimulated his serious interest in music history. In 1808 he began collecting materials for a historical music dictionary (never completed), eventually assembling one of the most remarkable music collections of the mid-19th century. Among his circle of acquaintances around this time, mostly journalists and barristers, Henry Crabb Robinson, Martin Burney (the music historian's grandson), Charles Lamb and William Hazlitt were prominent; T.M. Alsager, the *Times*'s financial writer and a notable Beethoven advocate, became a close friend.

Ayrton's social and organizational skills always outshone his musical ones – he was never known as an executant musician or serious composer – though by study and inclination he formed a refined taste, grounded in the Classical style. From 1813 he was at the forefront of English efforts to promote this repertory (in contrast with George III's antiquarian preferences) as well as to encourage music professionalism at a national level. In January that year he helped instigate the Philharmonic Society, and in July, with J.P. Salomon, tried to establish a music academy under its auspices. Successively a concert director and treasurer of the society – and, not incidentally, an honorary music reviewer for the *Morning Chronicle* (1813–26) – he proved himself a dedicated committee man.

By 1816 his administrative skills were being sought by the proprietor of the King's Theatre in the Haymarket, Edmund Waters, who hired Ayrton as managing director of the Italian opera. His success was spectacular. The repertory, including the first complete *Don Giovanni* on an English stage (12 April 1817), strong company (Pasta made her London début), and Ayrton's firm management of day-to-day operations all contributed to his standing as a person of discernment and principle – an impression confirmed when, after Waters interfered with his director's authority over singers, Ayrton resigned and sued the proprietor for damages. In 1821 and 1825 Ayrton again presided over much talked-about seasons (introducing to London, respectively, Rossini's *La gazza ladra* and Meyerbeer's *Il crociato in Egitto*), but again, in each season his authority was undermined by an aristocratic cabal and he withdrew in anger. He finally attempted to lease the King's Theatre himself in mid-1827, but was turned down by the assignors and thenceforward gave up all official connection to the house. He would later recall *Don Giovanni* as the proudest achievement of his career.

Meanwhile, in 1823 his historical interests, collecting habits and desire for influence had found expression in a new job – editor of the *Harmonicon*, the monthly music magazine founded by William Clowes and J.W. Parker. In an accessible style and attractive format, Ayrton offered readers an encyclopaedic range of articles as well as regular sections of news and review. All this was balanced by an equal part of printed music, some specially commissioned and some arranged from the editor's own collections. More important was the journal's critical voice. Knowing and technically specific – if also pedantic and by the end of the 1820s decidedly conservative – it came to be seen as authoritative and influential. The *Harmonicon* was an institution in its own right. When the journal failed financially in 1833, it was revamped as the more practical *Musical Library* (1834–7). Ayrton continued to work for Clowes on this project, and later contributed brief music articles to the *Gallery of Portraits* (1833, 1836), *Penny Cyclopaedia* (1833–46), and from 1835 onwards, the *Pictorial History of England*, *Pictorial Shakespeare*, *George III*, *British Almanac*, *Map of London* and *Standard Bible*. He also compiled and edited Parker's serial music collection, *Sacred Minstrelsy* (1834–5), then, returning to the newspaper press, served as honorary music critic to the *Examiner* (1837–53). As with most of his journalistic work, these later reviews were generally known to be his though published anonymously.

In a period still dominated by amateurism, Ayrton's achievement as a decisive administrator and editor of both music and literature remains extraordinary. His aesthetic values were those of his generation and upbringing; he made no apology for them. With Mozart as paradigm, he consistently looked for what he called clear air and harmony, balance and 'correct expression'. He supported Weber and Mendelssohn (the latter enthusiastically), but was sceptical of much of Beethoven, faulting 'excessive length' or 'unintelligible form'. Though dismissive of Bellini and Donizetti, he was attracted by Rossini's music and could be articulate on its dramatic effects. Purcell's anthems, and what he knew of J.S. Bach, he found uncongenial. Such opinions, stated with the confidence and independence Ayrton invariably displayed, may strike modern readers as naive or imperceptive; what matters is that he gave his reasons, and that he was open to persuasion by effective performance and repeat hearings. He was elected to the Athenaeum in 1824, and the Royal Society in 1837.

BIBLIOGRAPHY

Ayrton Collection (MS, *GB-Lbl* Add.52334–52358); Ayrton Papers (MS, *Lbl* Add.60358–60381); Ayrton Scrapbook (MS, *Lcm* 1163)
J. Ebers: *Seven Years of the King's Theatre* (London, 1828/R)
J.W. Parker, jr: Obituary, *Literary Gazette* (15 May 1858)
Catalogue of the Very Interesting, Rare and Valuable Musical Library of the Late William Ayrton, Esq., F.R.S. (London, 1858)
A. Hyatt King: *Some British Collectors of Music c.1600–1960* (Cambridge, 1963)
L. Langley: *The English Musical Journal in the Early Nineteenth Century* (diss., U. of North Carolina, Chapel Hill, 1983), esp. 284–317, 356–400
L. Langley: 'The Life and Death of *The Harmonicon*: an Analysis', *RMA Research Chronicle*, no.22 (1989), 137–63

LEANNE LANGLEY

Ayton, Fanny (*b* Macclesfield, ?1806; *d* after 1833). English soprano. She studied with Giovanni Liverati in London and with Manielli in Florence, and made her début at the Teatro di S Luca in Venice in Coccia's *Clotilde* in 1825. In 1827 John Ebers engaged her at the King's Theatre in London, where she appeared as Ninetta in Rossini's *La gazza ladra* and as Fiorella in *Il turco in Italia*. The mixed reviews she received were to be repeated throughout her short career: her acting was frequently praised more than her singing. In May 1827 she performed at Drury Lane as Fiorella in an English version of *Il turco* and later as Rosetta in Arne's *Love in a Village*. From December 1827 to January 1828 she performed leading roles with Giuseppe de Begnis's Italian opera company in Edinburgh. In April she again appeared at Drury Lane in *Love in a Village* and subsequently in other English musical works, including a version of *The Taming of the Shrew*, with music by John Braham and Thomas Cooke. She sang at the Birmingham Festival with Malibran in 1828 and 1829, and in 1831 she deputized at the King's Theatre for the indisposed prima donna Verpermann, singing the principal role in *Il barbiere di Siviglia* and later in Rossini's *Ricciardo e Zoraide*. Her last known appearances thereafter were as Isabel in *The Daemon, or The Mystic Branch* (a version of Meyerbeer's *Robert le diable*), opening at Drury Lane on 20 February 1832, when she was hissed on account of her bad intonation. Always overshadowed by foreign singers such as Pasta and British singers such as Mary Anne Wood, in Chorley's words 'she fought up courageously against disappointment and the failure of means for a year or two – and then passed out of public sight'. She married James Wilson Barlow in Liverpool on 12 July 1833.

BIBLIOGRAPHY

J. Ebers: *Seven Years of the King's Theatre* (London, 1828/R), 333–5
R. Edgcumbe, 2nd Earl of Mount Edgcumbe: *Musical Reminiscences of an Old Amateur* (London, 4/1834), 173
H.F. Chorley: *Thirty Years' Musical Recollections* (London, 1862, abridged 2/1926 by E. Newman), i, 240–42
[J.E. Cox:] *Musical Recollections of the Last Half-Century* (London, 1872), i, 148–9, 151

GEORGE BIDDLECOMBE

Azaïs, Hyacinthe (*b* Ladern-sur-Lauquet, nr Carcassonne, 4 April 1741; *d* Toulouse, 30 March 1796). French composer. He began his musical career as a choirboy at Carcassonne Cathedral where he obtained his musical education. He spent most of his life in the south of France. At the age of 15 he became *sous-maître de musique* in the church at Auch; in 1765 he was appointed *maître de musique* at the college in Sorèze (Languedoc). He married Marie Lépine, daughter of the organ builder J.-F. Lépine of Toulouse. After his wife's death, Azaïs spent a year (1770–71) in Paris, where he met Gossec and François Giroust, and had some of his works performed at the Concert Spirituel. His friendship with Abbé Roussier may have helped him obtain the position of *maître et compositeur de musique*, and later director, of the Concert de Marseille, which he assumed in 1771. In 1772 he returned to the college in Sorèze (renamed Ecole Royale Militaire). In 1783 Azaïs left Sorèze for Toulouse, where he established himself as a composer and teacher; he remarried in 1788. At the beginning of the Revolution he fled to Bagnères-de-Bigorre in the Pyrenees; he returned to Toulouse in 1794.

Azaïs was proud of the success he had achieved with the performances of two of his motets, *Cantate Domino* and *Dominus regnavit*, during his stay in Paris. The *Mercure de France* (September 1770) praised his *Cantate Domino*: 'Sa composition a paru d'un bon style, d'une expression juste & d'un effet picquant'. Azaïs described *Dominus regnavit* in the *Méthode de musique* (p.150) as follows: 'j'ai fait entendre ce motet (avec succès) au Concert Spirituel, et plusieurs fois au Concert de Marseille … tous les habiles gens qui frequentent ces Académies, ont été frappés (par l'emploie de l'accord sensible avec fausse quinte, Si, Re♯, Fa, La … une harmonie toute nouvelle)'. Azaïs indicated that the *Mercure de France* had failed to mention his name as the composer, and that he wished it to be known.

Azaïs's six symphonies exemplify the light Italo-French symphonic style of his time fused with some influences from the Mannheim school, evident especially in the dynamics of the Symphony no.1. Usually, however, lyricism prevails (particularly in the Romance of no.1 and in the Andante of no.5); also notable are his use of minor tonalities and the presence of a slow introduction in no.6. The instrumentation comprises first and second violins, viola, bass (figured in nos.1–3), two flutes (replaced by oboes in the slow movements of nos.1–2), and two horns (not used in no.4). All his symphonies have four movements except no.3 which has no minuet. The chamber music is unpretentious and seems to have been designed for amateurs. A rather unusual instrumentation is found in the *Six trios*: violin, cello and horn or clarinet.

Azaïs's fame rested primarily on his role as a teacher. His *Méthode de musique* (dedicated to Abbé Roussier), a large textbook designed for young performers, was praised by many influential musicians at the time of its publication, and later by La Borde (iii, p.567ff) and Gerber.

Azaïs's son, Pierre-Hyacinthe Azaïs (*b* Sorèze, Tarn, 1 March 1766; *d* Paris, 22 Jan 1845), was a philosopher, active in his early years as an organist. According to Fétis, he published a series of letters under the title 'Acoustique fondamentale' in the *Revue musicale*.

WORKS
printed works published in Paris

VOCAL
Motets: Cantate Domino, perf. 1770, Dominus regnavit, perf. 1771, both lost
Ariettes: Le désir de plaire (1771); Le beau jour, 'haute contre', 2 vn, b, and Les douceurs de la vie champêtre, 2vv, 2 vn, b, both in Méthode de musique

OTHER WORKS
6 symphonies, orch (1782) [orig. 1770 edn lost]
Chbr: 6 trio en 4 parties, vn, vc, hn/cl (1776); 12 sonates, vc, bc (1777); 6 duo, 2 vc (*c*1778); 6 trios, 2 vn, b in Méthode de musique; Menuet d'Exaudet varié, vc (n.d.); pièces in Recueil de menuets ... par différent auteurs, 2 vn, pubd Jolivet (*c*1771–9); Pièce en rondeau and 5 sonata movts (from pubd sonatas) pubd in Le violoncelle classique, ed. J. Brizard and H. Classens (Paris, 1963–5)
Pedagogical: Méthode de musique sur un nouveau plan (1776) [incl. *Traité abrégé d'harmonie, Dictionnaire de musique*, vocal, chbr pieces]; Méthode de basse contenant des leçons élémentaires (n.d.) [incl. 12 sonates and 6 duos listed above]; Méthode de violoncelle (n.d.), lost [cited by Lichtenthal, ? = Méthode de basse]

BIBLIOGRAPHY
BrenetC; BrookSF; Choron-FayolleD; FétisB; GerberL; La BordeE
P. Lichtenthal: *Dizionario e bibliografia della musica* (Milan, 1826/R)
M.L. Puech-Milhau: 'Hyacinthe Azaïs', *Revue archistra* (June 1972)
S. Milliot: *Le violoncelle en France au XVIIIe siècle* (Lille, 1981/R)
M. Baude: 'La vie musicale sous la Restauration et la Monarchie de Juillet: le témoignage du journal inédit d'Azaïs', *Revue internationale de musique*, no.10 (1983), 55–86

BARRY S. BROOK, CARL MOSKOVIC

Azanchevsky, Mikhail Pavlovich (von) (*b* Moscow, 24 March/5 April 1839; *d* Moscow, 12/24 Jan 1881). Russian composer and scholar. In 1858 he resigned from the civil service and went to Leipzig, where he studied music theory with Richter and Hauptmann. Later he took lessons from Liszt in Rome. While in Paris in 1886, he bought the extensive collection of music which had belonged to G.E. Anders. On his return to Russia in 1870 he was appointed honorary librarian to the St Petersburg Conservatory, and in the following year became its director. Unlike his predecessor Zaremba, he was favourably disposed towards the New Russian School, and one of his first acts as director was to appoint Rimsky-Korsakov as professor of practical composition and instrumentation. This bold step had a profound effect on the history of composition in Russia, and the conservatory soon became as important in the field of composition as it had already become in producing excellent instrumentalists and singers (one of its graduates during Azanchevsky's time was the great bass Fyodor Stravinsky, whose son Igor later became a pupil of Rimsky-Korsakov). Tchaikovsky referred to him as 'a good and kind person'. Ill-health forced him to resign in 1876. His compositions, which include chamber music, piano pieces, and songs with Russian and German texts, are pleasing rather than profound. He donated his valuable library to the St Petersburg Conservatory.

BIBLIOGRAPHY
V.A. Zhdanov and N.T.Zhegin, eds.: *P.I. Chaikovskiy: perepiska s N.F. fon Mekk* [Correspondence with N.F. von Meck], i: *1876–78*(Moscow, 1934; Eng. trans., 1993)
Yu.A. Kremlyov: *Leningradskaya gosudarstvennaya konservatoriya 1862–1937* (Moscow, 1938)
P.A. Vul'fius, ed.: *Iz istorii Leningradskoy konservatorii: materialï i dokumentï (1862–1917)* [The history of the Leningrad Conservatory: materials and documents 1862–1917] (Leningrad, 1964)

JENNIFER SPENCER/EDWARD GARDEN

Azerbaijan. Country in the Caucasus of Central Asia of 86,600 km², with an estimated population of 7·83 million (2000). Since 1828 Azerbaijan has consisted of two parts; one forms a province of Iran, whilst the other, which was a Soviet socialist republic from 1920 onwards, became independent in 1991.

1. Introduction. 2. Musical categories: (i) *Ashyg* (ii) *Mugam* (iii) Opera, ballet and orchestral music. 3. Instruments.

1. INTRODUCTION.   The varieties of music found in Azerbaijan can be found across an area which extends to Kurdistan in the south and Zanjan and Ghazvin in the east. In terms of ethnicity, culture, religion and politics the Azeri are musically much closer to Iran than Turkey. Their *mugam* music also formed part of the Armenian repertory for a long time. However, there has been a tendency among the Armenians for some decades now to reject this music because of the growth in nationalism on both sides which resulted from the geopolitical division of Transcaucasia in 1917. Moreover, some popular bards (*ashyg*) belong to the Syrian Christian minority in southern Azerbaijan. Although the urban music of Azerbaijan is clearly differentiated from the music found in Central Asia by its characteristically fast rhythms, it has spread in Khiva (Chorasm) and has reached as far as Bukhara and Tashkent.

2. MUSICAL CATEGORIES.   The music which has been described as 'professional' by Soviet musicologists can be divided into two distinct types, namely that of the *ashyg* and that of the musicians who practise the *mugam*. A further variety corresponds to urban music which borrows elements from the *ashyg* and *mugam* traditions as well as from the music of the Middle East and south-western Asia and the West. Finally, as a result of Soviet rule, there came into existence at the beginning of the 20th century an Azeri symphonic repertory, which draws on the *mugam* tradition.

Mugam predominates in the north of the region and in the Karabakh mountain range. It is not common in Azeri Iran, where the musicians prefer the Iranian style (School of Tabriz). The music of the *ashyg* is mainly to be found in the south, above all in the Kirovabad (north-east, Tauus, Kazakh), Karabakh and Nakhcivan (south-west) districts of the Republic of Azerbaijan as well as in Salyany (south-west) and in Azeri Iran in Tabriz, Karadagh, Maraghe, Khoy and as far as Orumïye (Rezaye). In certain regions such as Ganja both traditions exist alongside each other. *Ashyg* tend to perform in rural and provincial regions. *Mugam*, by contrast, has a largely urban audience. Apart from gatherings of experts, the festivities which are organized at weddings (*toj*) are preferred opportunities for performance in both genres.

Mugam and the music of the *ashyg*, which were less shielded from each other in the past, still share common characteristics, which are also found in Iran. These include the initial range, which is restricted to a pentachord (*jins*), readily identifiable modes, melodic lines consisting predominantly of sequential notes, time signatures (4/4, 6/8, 3/4), brevity of compositions, arrangements of dance melodies, tone colour, the dragging of the voice and vocal techniques which are similar to those of popular singing and small instrumental ensembles (three or four musicians).

In addition to these formal similarities, some pieces have their origins in popular music and *mugam* preserves a lasting influence from popular music. *Zarbi-mugam* are compositions which contain instrumental refrains and melismatic vocal parts in non-metrical patterns, and certain songs (*täsnif*) lend themselves to being inserted into the free interpretation of a *mugam*. The instrumental dance forms *reng* or *diringi* represent a further form which is equally likely to be found in the repertory of both *ashyg* and *mugam* groups. Despite these similarities the two genres remain quite distinct from each other.

In the performance of song both male and female voices must be high and powerful. They make use of the technique of yodelling, changing from the chest to the head register with the help of appoggiaturas. This technique is also found in Iran, Kurdistan and some regions of Iraq.

(i) *Ashyg.* The repertory of the *ashyg* consists of short lyric poems on amorous, moral or religious subjects and of long lyrical or epic ballads (*dastan*). The most famous of them are *Koroghlu*, *Asli vä karam* and *Lejli vä mägnun*. The metre is for the most part syllabic (*barmag*, *heja*) and the commonest form is the lyrical poem of the *goshma* variety, made up of four-line verses with 11-syllable lines, or its variants, such as the *bayati* and the *mukhämmäs*. There are also the specific genres of the *ashyg*: the *tajnis* and its variants, the *gärayli*, the *divani* (rare) and the *gazal*. These follow the rules of classical prosody (*aruz*).

Great bards of the past include: Ashyg Gurbani (16th century), Ashyg Abbas Tufarganlu (17th century), the Armenian Sayat-Nova (18th century), Ashyg Äläskär (19th century), Ashyg Talyb (his son, 1877–1979), Ashyg Abbasgul (early 20th century), Ashyg Mirzä Bayramov (1888–1954), Ashyg Islam Yusuf, Ashyg Shämshir and Edälät Nasibov (second half of the 20th century).

The art of the *ashyg* consists of readily identifiable melodic types, which are individually named and collectively known as *ashyg havasi*. It is possible to set different texts to individual melodies. The repertory of an *ashyg* is reckoned to contain about 30 melodic types; there are approximately 100 in all. These melodies are only played on the *saz*, or at the festivities which take place in the open air by ensembles of *zurna*, *nagara* and/or *balaban*. The *ashyg* play pieces known as *hava*, each of which is a melody containing a hierarchical pitch set, a set melodic range, a drone pitch, a preferred tuning and a *forud* or cadential formula (C. Albright-Farr, 1976). Most of the schools use approximately six to eight different modes, most of which are borrowed from the *mugam*. The most important among them are *rast*, *segah*, *shikästeyi fars* and *shur modi*.

Each *hava* consists of two or more separate parts. They are repeated in a specific sequence, nonetheless with considerable scope for variation. Between these sections improvised passages can be inserted. The most common time signatures are 2/4, 4/4, 3/4 and 6/8.

(ii) *Mugam.* The *mugam* music of Azerbaijan draws on the music of the Iranian-Arab-Turkish *maqām*, whose important theoreticians were above all Safi ad-Din al-Urmawi and Abd al-Qadir Ibn Gaibi al-Maragi (14th–15th centuries). They came from Urmiye and Marage in Azerbaijan. However, the music of today differs from that which Ibn Gaibi described, and it is thought that the traditional form of transmission was interrupted in the 18th century. This period, which remains poorly researched, was followed by a revival at the beginning of the 19th century, during which the *mugam* were collected and systematized, above all in collectors' circles such as the one based around Mir Möhsun Nävvab (1833–1918) from Susa, the author of the *Vizuh ul-Aghram*. The names of forms were retained, but due to the influence from other local musics the actual forms described by them sometimes varied from one tradition to another. Older rhythmic cycles (*usul*) were dropped in favour of formulas in 6/8 and 4/4 time. Instruments such as the *'ūd*, *qānūn*, *santūr*, *ney*, *tanbur* and *setär* disappeared in favour of a new lute, the *tar*, which together with the *kamanca* constitutes the main instrument of the contemporary *mugam*. This process of revival also spread to the western centre of Iran as well as Fars and what is now contemporary Azerbaijan. In northern Azerbaijan the focus of musical life around 1880 was the city of Susa in the Karabakh, but it was in Tiflis, the cosmopolitan centre of Transcaucasia, and later in Baku, that Azerbaijani musicians were able to gather a much larger audience.

The modes of Azeri music are always heptatonic and reflect the division of the octave on the fingerboard of the *tar*. The tradition of musical theory handed down by B. Mänsurov (1911–84) and his predecessors distinguishes 13 main *mugam*: *rast*, *mahur-hindi*, *segah-zabol*, *cahar-gah*, *humayun*, *shushtar*, *bayati shiraz*, *shur*, *bayati*, *kurd*, *bajati gajar*, *rähab* and *nava-nishapur*. The following eight *mugam* are regarded as secondary: *dilkesh*, *kurd-shahnaz*, *dogah*, *gata*, *isfahan*, *cupan-bayati* and transpositions or variations of *mahur* and *segah*. Apart from the latter a number of other *mugam* exist, which are generally played in connection with a more important *mugam*: *vilayati*, *khojaste*, *shekästeyi fars*, *mobärrigä*, *ärag*, *pänjgäh*, *rak*, *hissar*, *mukhalif*, *mänsuri*, *saranj*, *ushshag*, *simai shams* and *bästä-nigar*.

All the *mugam* (with the exception of variants or transpositions) can serve as models for compositions such as songs (*täsnif*) and songs for dance accompaniment (*räng*). A *mugam* has a *maye*, a fundamental modal 'substance' as well as individual characteristics (*sho' be*: 'supplementary aspects', *gushe*: 'corners'), which reveal themselves in the course of its exposition. There are approximately 100 of these melodic types (*sho' be* and *gushe*), which do not serve as models for compositions, but which are played during the development of the principal *mugam*. Each of them has a name. Some of them are melodic types, others form interludes set to a certain rhythm in a fast tempo. Each of the 13 main *mugam* contains between ten and 20 of these. Some sequences can appear in other contexts. The important *mugam* are called *dästgah* (modal system), when they combine a certain number of secondary *mugam*, *sho' be* or *gushe*.

The improvised interpretation of the *mugam* requires a precise knowledge of the *gushe* and its particular technique of ornamentation. Nevertheless, this model is by and large so flexible that several levels of improvisation are possible (including the details, the sequence of the musical components, the modulations and the pieces which connect the musical components). In this way the musician can either play the model which he has learnt by heart or distance himself from it and merely retain the modal colouring (*maye*).

Some pieces in canon form should be mentioned in connection with the *mugam*. They are called *zärbi-mugam* ('rhythmic *mugam*') and are fixed compositions for voice and an instrument, which originate from the old repertories of the *ashyg*. They are the *arazbary*, *osmanli* or *mani*, *ovshary*, *herat-kabuli* (an instrumental piece), *ärag-kabuli*, *samai shäms*, *mänsuriyyä*, *heydäri*, *uzzal-zärbi* and *garabag-shikästesi*.

Apart from these, which are essentially non-metrical pieces, there are a very large number of pieces set to a certain rhythm, which do not conform to a strict rendition of a *mugam* and its attendant *gushe*. The main genre is the *täsnif*, a song in one of the most important *mugam* in triple, quadruple or sextuple time and in different tempos. It is divided into two to six sections. *Täsnif* from the *mugam* tradition are written in accordance with the rules of metre (*aruzi*), whilst those which come from other local traditions are structured syllabically. The *sagi-name*, which no longer exists, was a form of the *täsnif* without a percussion accompaniment.

Other pieces are of an instrumental nature and in the performance of a *mugam* form a prelude (*bardast*, *därämad* and *pisro*) or an interlude in dance rhythms (*diringi*, *räng*), likewise in triple, quadruple or sextuple time. These pieces set to a certain rhythm can be accompanied by the *däf* (frame drum, often played by the singer, *khanändä*) and interpreted by a group. Pieces set to certain rhythms, which form sequences known as *chahar-mezrab*, are performed by a solo *tar*. Even if most of the *gushe* from which the *mugam* are composed are not subject to metre, they nonetheless possess a specific rhythm and a phrasing of their own, which in certain cases corresponds to a regular beat or a metrical cycle.

(iii) Opera, ballet and orchestral music. Uzeir Hajibeyov (1885–1948), was the first Azerbaijani composer of symphonies and operas. In his earliest stage works the music was left to the judgment of traditional singers, who drew on the *ta'ziye*, a Shi'a religious music drama. The only instructions concern the *mugam* in which the scenes are to be sung. Later he composed works of his own, whose themes and elements he borrowed from traditional sources. He eventually studied composition in St Petersburg and went on to write operas which only showed traditional influence in their melodic material (*Sheykh Sanan*, 1909; *Rustam i Zohrab*, 1910; *Asli i Kerem*, 1912; *Kor-oglï*, 1937). His first works were performed by an ensemble consisting largely of traditional instruments. Later works were written for a symphony orchestra augmented by Azeri instruments (the *tar* and *kamanca* among others). In 1945 Hajibeyov composed the Azerbaijani national anthem. He attempted the creation of a 'national music' by appropriating elements of the *mugam*, and this 'synthesis' between Western and the Azerbaijani musics was continued by the composers Muslim Makomayev (1895–1937), Asef Zeynally (1909–32), Niyazi Zulfugaroglu (1912–84), Ahmet Hajiev (*b* 1917), Kara Karayev (1918–82), Sultan Hajibeyov (*b* 1919), Jahangir Jahangirov (*b* 1921), Fikret Amirov (1922–84), Suleyman

Äläskärov (*b* 1924), Arif Melikov (*b* 1933), Vasif Adygözälov (*b* 1935) and Agshin Alizadä (*b* 1937).

The introduction of Western music led to the founding of musical institutions: the Akhundov State Academic Theatre of Opera and Ballet (1920), the Hajibeyov symphony orchestra (1938), the Mamedgulizad theatre in Nakhcivan and the Gurbanov Theatre of Musical Comedy in Baku. Musicological research is carried out at the Hajibeyov Institute for Azerbaijani Art at the Academy of Science of Azerbaijan, Baku. The institutionalization of musics led to the use of musical notation by traditional musicians. Nearly all contemporary interpreters of the *mugam* have spent at least a few years studying in an institution and have some knowledge of Western musical notation, even if they never make use of it.

3. INSTRUMENTS.   The *tar* is the principal instrument used in the *mugam* music of Azerbaijan and Iran (fig.1; TĀR). This long-necked lute related to the *rabāb* probably arrived in Iran at the end of the 18th century. Around 1870 Sadyg Jan Asadoghlu gave it its Azerbaijani form and added to the five traditional strings four or six sympathetic strings. The *tar* has an octagonal body made of mulberry wood with rounded corners. The top part of the body is made from two different surfaces, which are

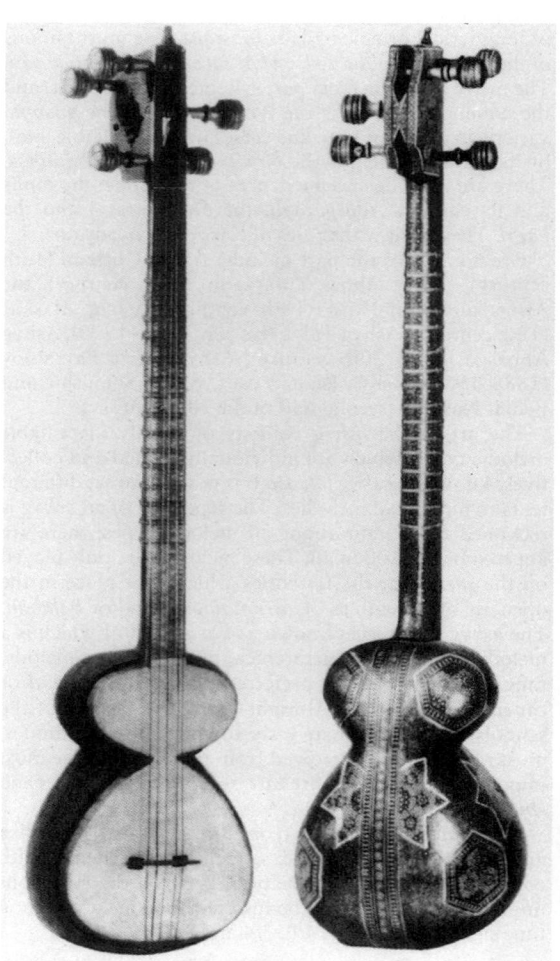

1. Tar (long-necked lute)

2. Two musicians playing the saz (long-necked lute)

covered by the fine skin of a cow's heart. The neck has 22 movable frets, which cover an octave and a fourth. The *kamanca* is a spike fiddle with four steel strings. The body of the instrument, which is turned from a block of walnut-tree wood, is covered with a thin sturgeon skin. The instrument is held upright when played.

The *däf* (or *gaval*) is the most widespread percussion instrument (*see* DAFF). It consists of a circular wooden frame with a diameter of 38 cm, over which the skin of a catfish is stretched. Rings are attached to the inside of the wooden frame which act as jingles. The *tar*, the *kamanca* and the *däf* (the latter is played by the singer) form the traditional range of instruments for the classical music of the Azeri. The double-headed drum *nagara* is played with the fingers in the same way as the *däf* or with sticks. Other drums include the double-headed *käs*, and the *gosha nagara*, a pair of small kettledrums made of clay.

The *cogur* or *saz* is the lute of the *ashyg* (fig.2; SAZ). In its most widespread form it has an overall length of approximately 105 cm, but there are also two other forms, which measure approximately 130 cm and 70 cm respectively. Its pear-shaped body, which is made of mulberry wood, is made up of narrow slats which are glued together. The soundboard is also made from mulberry wood. It is strung with three sets of three steel strings (although in Rezaye it is strung with two sets of three strings), which are tuned according to the mode. The *balaban* is an oboe originating in Central Asia, whose wooden body with a large double reed is 27–38 cm long with eight finger-holes (*see* BĀLĀBĀN). The *saz*, *balaban* and *däf* are most commonly used by *ashyg*, especially in Iran.

The repertory of the *ashyg* and traditional songs can also be played on other instruments without a vocal part, for example on the oboe *zurna* or *gara zurna* and the double clarinet *zammare* (more often found in Iran). Other traditional aerophones include the bagpipes (*tulum*), the recorder (*tutäk*), the transverse flute (*ney*) and a small ocarina with two holes (*tutäk*).

The accordion or bandoneon (*garmon*) is also very popular, as are the clarinet (*klarnet*) and the western oboe (*gaboy*), which are occasionally used to perform *mugam*. Instruments probably introduced by Armenian musicians include the *'ud* and the *qānūn*. It is rare, however, that these instruments are used to perform *mugam*. (*See also* ARMENIA, §I, 2; GEORGIA, §II; IRAN, §III, 1, 3 and 4.)

BIBLIOGRAPHY

Grove6 ('U.S.S.R.§II', Y. Gabay and J. Spector; also 'Iran§II', S. Blum)

T. Mamedov: *Tariel pesni keroglu* [Koroghlu chants] (Baku, 1954)

M. Ismailov: *Zhanry azerbaydzhanskoy narodnoy muzïki* [Popular Azerbaijani music genres] (Baku, 1960)

F. Shushinsky: *Seyyid Shushinsky* (Baku, 1966)

E.G. Abasova: 'Azerbaydzhanskaya muzïka' [Azerbaijani music], *Muzïkal'naya entsiklopediya*, i (Moscow, 1973)

A. Rahmatov: *Azerbaydzhan khalq chalghi alatlari* [Azerbaijani musical instruments] (Baku, 1975)

C. Albright-Farr: 'The Azerbaijani 'Ashiq and his Performance of a Dastan', *Iranian Studies* (1976), 220–47

C. Albright-Farr: *The Music of Professional Musicians of Northwest Iran* (thesis, U. of Washington, 1976)

F. Shushinsky: *Narodnïye pevtsï i muzïkant azerbaydzhana* (Moscow, 1979)

A. Eldarova: 'Azerbayjan ashiq sanati' [The art of bards in Azerbaijan], *Azerbayjan khalq musigisi*, ed. A. Eldarova (Baku, 1981)

A. Eldarova: 'Iskustsvo azerbayzhanski ashugov' [The art of Azerbaijani bards], *Azerbaydzhanskaya narodnaya muzïka* (Baku, 1981)

B. Huseyoli: 'Azerbayjan khalq raqs musiqisi', [Popular dance music of Azerbaijan], *Azerbayjan khalq musiqisi*, ed. A. Eldarova (Baku, 1981), 168–97

A. Isezada: 'Azerbayjan musigi oyrenilmesi tarikbinden', [The history of Azerbaijani music], ibid., 5–29

E. Mänsurov: 'Rast va mabur-hindi mughamlarinin', *Gobustan*, iv (Baku, 1984), 18–20

U. Hajibekov: *Principles of Azerbaijan Folk Music* (Baku, 1985)

F. Shushinsky: *Azerbayjan khalq musiqichileri* [Azerbaijani popular music] (Baku, 1985)

F. Shushinsky: *Jabbar Qaryaghdioghlu* (Baku, 1987)

J. During: *La musique traditionnelle de l'Azerbayjan et la science des muqams* (Baden Baden, 1988)

J. During: 'The Modal System of Azerbaijani Art Music: a Survey', *Maqam, Raga, Zeilenmelodik: Konzeptionen & Prinzipien der Musikproduktion*, ed. J. Elsner (Berlin 1989), 133–45

E. Mänsurov: *Azerbayjan qädim el navallari* [Ancient Azerbaijani airs] (Baku, 1990)

JEAN DURING/R

Azerbayev, Kenen (*b* Maty-Bulak, Semirechye [now Krasnogorsk], 1884; *d* Almata, 1976). Kazakh traditional composer, singer, narrator and *dömbra* player. He was born to the family of a poor herder and lost his mother when he was seven years old. His family was musically talented and Azerbayev gained the nickname *Bala-aqyn* ('Child-singer') early in his life. At the age of ten or 11 he wrote the songs *Ri qoyïm* ('Shoo, my Sheep', a shepherds' cry) and *Boz torgai* ('Sparrow'), which revealed his outstanding talent and became widely popular. Kazakh and Kyrgyz musicians often met in the region of Semirechye, and Azerbayev became famous as a performer of Kyrgyz songs and the *Manas* epic as well as the Kazakh traditional repertory; his songs also became popular in Kyrgyzstan. More than 200 of his works were recorded by the folklorists B. Erzakovich and A. Serikbayeva. Azerbayev's songs are stylistically linked with *aqyn* genres of recitation in their melodic construction, which follow the rhythm and meaning of the verse. He composed many songs in response to important events in Kazakhstan; songs such as *Attan* ('On Horseback') and *Bulbulga* ('To the Nightingale') commemorated the people's liberation movement of 1916, while *Bizdin otan zhenedi* ('Our Country Will Win') concerned World War II. His postwar songs blended elements of traditional and popular Soviet songs. He was also a creator of the modern genre of children's songs. He received the accolade of Honoured Art Worker of Kazakhstan and was awarded several orders and medals of the USSR.

BIBLIOGRAPHY
AND OTHER RESOURCES

Songs of Kenen Azerbayev, Melodiya M30 45419 007

B. Erzakovich: *Kenen Azerbayev* (Moscow, 1961)

A. Zhubanov: *Zamana bylbyldary (Solov'i stoletii: ocherki o zhizni i tvorchestve kazakhskikh narodnïkh kompizitorov-pevtsov)* [The nightingales of the centuries: essays on the life and work of Kazakh folk composer-singers] (Almaty, 1967, 2/1975 in Kazakh), 314–31

ALMA KUNANBAYEVA

Azevedo, Francisco Correa de. *See* CORREA DE ARAUXO, FRANCISCO.

Azevedo, Luiz Heitor Corrêa de [Heitor, Luiz] (*b* Rio de Janeiro, 13 Dec 1905; *d* Paris, 10 Nov 1992). Brazilian musicologist. At the Instituto Nacional de Música he studied the piano with Alfredo Bevilacqua (1924–5) and Charley Lachmund (1926–7) and harmony, counterpoint and fugue with Paulo Silva; initially he was a composer, but by the late 1920s had turned to musicology and music criticism. He became librarian of the Instituto Nacional de Música (1932) and in 1934 founded the *Revista brasileira de música*, which was under his editorship until 1941 and performed a valuable service to nascent Brazilian musicology. While professor of music at the conservatory (1937–47) he held the post of titular professor at the Escola (formerly Instituto) Nacional de Música; he developed there the ethnomusicology curriculum and founded the Centro de Pesquisas Folclóricas, which produced important publications based on fieldwork throughout Brazil. He served as a consultant to the Organization of American States in Washington, DC, for its newly established Music Division (1941–2) and subsequently moved to Paris (1947), where until his retirement (1965) he was the UNESCO music programme specialist and a professor of the Institut des Hautes Etudes de l'Amérique Latine of the University of Paris (1954–68). Besides general studies on Latin American music and history, Azevedo published definitive works on Brazilian 19th- and 20th-century music and musicians and on folk and popular music. He was a founder-member of the Brazilian Academy of Music.

WRITINGS

'Luciano Gallet', *Revista da Associação brasileira de música*, ii/4 (1933), 2–20

'José Maurício Nunes Garcia', *Boletín latino-americano de música*, i (1935), 133–50

'Carlos Gomes e Francisco Manuel: correspondência inédita (1864–1865)', *Revista brasileira de música*, iii (1936), 323–38

'Carlos Gomes folclorista', *Revista brasileira de música*, iii (1936), 177–84

'As primeiras óperas: "A Noite do Castelo" (1861); "Joanna de Flandres" (1863)', *Revista brasileira de música*, iii (1936), 201–45; repr. in *Carlos Gomes, uma obra em foco*, ed. V. Salles (Rio de Janeiro, 1987), 67–88, 91–135

Dois pequenos estudos de folclore musical (Rio de Janeiro, 1938)

Escala, ritmo e melodia na música dos indios brasileiros (Rio de Janeiro, 1938)

Relação das óperas de autores brasileiros (Rio de Janeiro, 1938)

'Introdução ao curso de folclore nacional da Escola nacional de música da Universidade do Brasil', *Revista brasileira de música*, vi (1939), 1–10

'La musique au Brésil', *ReM*, nos.195–6 (1940), 74–81

'Tupynambá melodies in Jean de Léry's "Histoire d'un voyage fait en la terre du Brésil"', *PAMS 1941*, 85–96

'Mário de Andrade e o folclore', *Revista brasileira de música*, ix (1943), 11–14

'La música en el Brasil', *Cuadernos americanos*, no.33 (1947), 250–73

A música brasileira e seus fundamentos (Washington DC, 1948; Eng. trans., 1948)

Música e músicos do Brasil (Rio de Janeiro, 1950)

with C. Person de Matos and M. de Moura Reis: *Bibliografia musical brasileira (1820–1950)* (Rio de Janeiro, 1952)

La musique en Amérique latine (Rio de Janeiro, 1954)

150 anos de música no Brasil (1800–1950) (Rio de Janeiro, 1956)

'Música y cultura en el siglo XVIII', *RMC*, nos.81–2 (1962), 135–52

'Vissungos: Negro Work Songs of the Diamond District in Minas Gerais, Brazil', *Music in the Americas: Bloomington, IN, 1965*, 64–7

'Le chant de la liberté: compositeurs de l'Amérique latine à l'époque des luttes pour l'Indépendance, hymnographie patriotique', *Mélanges à la mémoire de Jean Sarrailh* (Paris, 1966), 259–79

'Music and Society in Imperial Brazil, 1822–1889', *Portugal and Brazil in Transition*, ed. R.S. Sayers (Minneapolis, 1968), 303–9

'La musique à la cour portugaise de Rio de Janeiro, 1808–1821', *Arquivos do Centro cultural português*, i (1969), 335–52

'Arthur Napoléon 1843–1925: un pianiste portugais au Brésil', *Arquivos do Centro cultural português*, iii (Paris, 1971), 572–602

'The Present State and Potential of Music Research in Latin America', *Perspectives in Musicology*, ed. B.S. Brook, E.O.D Downes and S. Van Solkema (New York, 1972), 249–69

'Preliminary Study on the Project of Preparing a Universal History of Music and the Role of the Music of Latin America and the Caribbean in History', *World of Music*, xxii/3 (1980), 56–62

'José Maurício no panorama da música brasileira', *Estudos mauricianos*, ed. J.C. de A. Muricy (Rio de Janeiro, 1983), 35–40

'Etat sommaire de nos connaissances actuelles sur la musique Latino-Américaine et son passé: la contribution européenne', 'Le Nouveau Monde et l'intelligence de la musique européenne au XVIe siècle', *Brussels Museum of Musical Instruments Bulletin*, xvi (1986), 1–11, 41–9

'O compositor latino-americano e o universo sonoro deste fim de século', *Latin American Music Review*, vii/2 (1986), 248–53

'Carlos Gomes: Projeção no exterior', *Carlos Gomes, uma obra em foco*, ed. V. Salles (Rio de Janeiro, 1987), 67–88

'O Villa-Lobos que eu conheci', *Revista do Brasil*, iv/1 (1988), 25–30

BIBLIOGRAFHY

V. Mariz: *Tres musicólogos brasileiros: Mário de Andrade, Renato Almeida, Luiz Heitor Corrêa de Azevedo* (Rio de Janeiro, 1983)

D.M. Lamas, ed.: *Luiz Heitor Corrêa de Azevedo, 80 anos: depoimentos, estudios, ensaios de musicologia* (São Paulo and Rio de Janeiro, 1985) [incl. tributes]

GERARD BÉHAGUE

Azevedo, (António) Sérgio (Arede Torrado Marques) (*b* Coimbra, 23 Aug 1968). Portuguese composer and writer. He studied with Lopes-Graça at the Academia de Amadores de Música and later with Capdeville and Bochmann at the Escola Superior de Música in Lisbon. Since 1993 he has himself taught at the Escola Superior and worked as an editor at Portuguese National Radio.

Azevedo is one of the most representative composers of the younger generation in Portugal. His music has shown many influences ranging from Birtwistle to Pärt but has in recent years settled into a more distinctively personal atonality. With a large number of works for a variety of forces, his style often employs dense textures with clearly structured undercurrents. In many more recent works, whole-tone groups can be seen as a particularly significant characteristic.

WORKS
(*selective list*)

Dramatic: Retábulo de Brecht (morality play, 14 pts, after B. Brecht and W. Gombrowicz), 1998
Orch: Coral I, 1991; Tranquilo, 1997; Festa, 1998; Keep going, 1998
Vocal: 3 or 4 Songs of … e.e. cummings … , S, hn, pf, 1998–9; Conc., 2 pf, chbr orch, 1999–2000
Chbr and solo inst: Trans, 4 cl, 1994; Monodrama, basset hn, 25 cl, 1995; Cl Qnt, 1996; Coda, eng hn, pf, va, db, 1997; Agio, cl, 1998; Aspetto, wind qnt, 1998; Atlas' journey, 15 insts, 1998

WRITINGS

'1958–1998: Forty Years of Contemporary Music in Portugal', *World New Music Magazine*, no.8 (1998)
A invenção dos sons (Lisbon, 1998)

CHRISTOPHER BOCHMANN

Azguime, Miguel (Mascarenhas Pinheiro de Azevedo) (*b* Lisbon, 24 February 1960). Portuguese composer and percussionist. He studied at the Academia de Amadores de Música (1966–76), while also attending the Lisbon Conservatory. From 1975 to 1982 he studied percussion with Catarina Latino and Júlio Campos and founded various groups performing jazz and improvised music. In 1984, with a grant from the German government, he went to Darmstadt, where he studied percussion with James Wood and composition with Horatiu Radulescu, Brian Ferneyhough and Clarence Barlow. He also attended seminars with Emmanuel Nunes, Cristóbal Halffter and Tristan Murail. Between 1985 and 1986 he studied percussion with Gaston Sylvestre in Paris and Nice. On his return to Portugal he founded Miso Records (1985), the Miso Ensemble (in 1985, with the flautist Paula

Azguime), and also the International Festival of Live Music (1992). Azguime's threefold activity as composer, percussionist and poet (besides his work for radio and as a record producer) closely reflects his almost mystical vision of music and art. Some of the titles of his compositions refer directly to his poetic output, while others emerge from the composer's improvisations, reminding us of Azguime's once close association with jazz and improvised music.

WORKS
(*selective list*)

Vocal: Icone II, 1v, perc, 1992; Nónio, S, fl, elecs, 1998
Inst: Ascèse, fl, perc, 1986; Arcano I, II, IV, VI, VII, VIII, fl, perc, 1986–92; Arcano III, V, IX, perc, 1986–92; 1+1=3, fl, perc, 1988; Passing Rooms, fl, perc, 1988; Poemas de 3 sons, perc, 1989; Poemas de 9 sons, perc, 1989; Mandala, mar, 1990; Determinante-Solar, b fl, perc, 1991; Une aile pourvu qu'elle soit du cygne, pf, 1993; Du néant qui le croit, bn, elecs, 1994; Parfaire le bleu, fl, hpd, elecs, 1996; De l'étant qui le nie, pf, elecs, 1997
Tape: Instalações para arquitectura Manuel Vicente, 1989; Déposer la forêt, 1990; Instalação para escultura Bauduin, 1990; Instalação para pintura Jorge Vilaça, 1990; 96 digital bells para arquitectura Nuno Mateus, 1993; Realidade-real, 1993; Terra-Mãe . . . Terra-Pão, 1995; Musica e texturas sonoras para o Pavilhão do Conhecimento dos Mares da EXPO '98, 1997–8

SÉRGIO AZEVEDO

Azione sacra (It.: 'sacred action', 'sacred plot'). One of several terms commonly applied to the SEPOLCRO, composed to texts in Italian for the Habsburg court in Vienna in the second half of the 17th century. The term was also one of many used for the Italian ORATORIO of the 18th century. Both Zeno and Metastasio called their oratorio librettos *azioni sacre*. A 'staged oratorio', or *opera sacra*, of the late 18th and early 19th centuries was also typically called an *azione sacra*. Although oratorio was essentially an unstaged genre, the *sepolcro* was presented with a minimum of staging and action and the *opera sacra* was fully staged and acted in the manner of an opera.

From the 1780s to about 1820, the theatres of Naples often presented staged oratorios during Lent and usually designated them *azione sacra*. Such works differed little from the *opera seria* of the time except for their subject matter, which was that of the traditional oratorio. P.A. Guglielmi's *Debora e Sisara: azione sacra* (1788, Naples) was favoured by numerous performances, both staged and unstaged, throughout Europe, as was Rossini's *Mosè in Egitto*, called *azione tragico-sacra* in the libretto printed at Naples in 1818.

BIBLIOGRAPHY

SmitherHO, i

R. Schnitzler: *The Sacred Dramatic Music of Antonio Draghi* (diss., U. of North Carolina, 1971)

H.E. Smither: 'Oratorio and Sacred Opera, 1700–1825: Terminology and Genre Distinction', *PRMA*, cvi (1979–80), 88–104

M.G. Accorsi: 'Le azioni sacre di Metastasio: il razionalismo cristiano', *Mozart, Padova e la Betulia liberata: Padua 1989*, 3–26

HOWARD E. SMITHER

Azione teatrale (It.: 'theatrical action', 'theatrical plot'). Term coined by Metastasio to denote a species of SERENATA that, unlike many works in this genre, contained a definite plot and envisaged some form of simple staging. The 12 works by Metastasio so described begin with *Endimione* (1721, Naples, set by Sarro) and end with *La corona* (1765, Vienna, set by Gluck); Mozart's setting (1772) of his *Il sogno di Scipione* is one of the last examples of this short-lived subgenre. One of the most celebrated was *L'isola disabitata* (1752), first performed in Madrid with music by Bonno. Gluck's *Orfeo ed Euridice*, to a libretto by Ranieri de' Calzabigi (1762), was originally described as an *azione teatrale*.

MICHAEL TALBOT

Aziz al-Shawān. *See* AL-SHAWĀN, AZIZ.

Azkue (Aberasturi), Resurrección María de (*b* Lequeitio, Biscay, 5 Aug 1864; *d* Bilbao, 9 Nov 1951). Basque composer, ethnomusicologist and philologist. He studied at the seminaries of Vitoria and Salamanca, was ordained priest (1888) and took a doctorate in theology. In addition he studied music with Sáinz Basabe and then at the Paris Schola Cantorum, in Brussels and at the Cologne Conservatory. He was subsequently professor of Basque language at the Instituto de Bilbao for 30 years. In Bilbao he founded a Basque school, the Basque review *Euskalzale* and a Basque opera house, for which he composed works to be performed by pupils of his school. He was a great folklorist: he collected some 2000 folksongs of his native region and published around 1000 of them; he gave numerous lectures and he helped to compile the *Diccionario de la música Labor* (Barcelona, 1954). From 1918 he was president of the Basque Language Academy, and he was a member of the Russian Academy of Sciences and the Real Academia Española de la Lengua.

WORKS
(*selective list*)

Stage: Eguzkie nora [Where Are You Going, Sun] (zar, 2) (1896); Sasi-eskola (zar) (1898); Pasa de Chimbos (zar, 2) (1898); Ortzuri (op, 3), Bilbao, 1911; Urlo (op, 3), Bilbao, 1913; Aitaren bildur [For Fear of the Father] (sainete lírico vasco) (1917); Colonia inglesa (zar, 2); Vizcaytik Bizkaira [From Viscaya to Biskaya] (zar, 3)

Orats: Andra Urraka, Daniel, Lemindano

Church music: Te Deum, 3vv (1933); many other works

EDITIONS

Cancionero popular vasco: canciones selectas harmonizadas (Barcelona, ?1919, 2/1968)

Cancionero popular vasco: edición manual, sin acompañamiento (Barcelona, 1923)

Las mil y una canciones populares vascas (Barcelona, ?1923)

WRITINGS

Música popular baskongada (Bilbao, 1901)

'La música popular Baskongada', *Los baskos en la nación argentina* (Buenos Aires, 1916), 99–104

Música popular vasca: su existencia (Bilbao, 1919)

Aeskera edo Petiribero-inguruetako mintzaera (Bilbao, 1928)

Euskaleriaren yakintza [Literatura popular del país vasco] (Madrid, 1959–71)

Aintzinako ipuinak (Zarauz, 1968)

BIBLIOGRAPHY

L. Villasante: 'Azkue (Aberasturi), Resurrección María de', *Enciclopedia general ilustrada del país vasco*, iii, ed. B. Estomes Lasa (San Sebastián, 1970), 363–5

GUY BOURLIGUEUX

AZ Music [A-Z]. A Sydney-based experimental music organization founded on about 5 February 1970 by DAVID AHERN. For each concert that it held a letter of the alphabet was assigned; its début was concert 'A', a 24-hour concert on 21 February 1970 which included Satie's *Vexations*. Other composers whose works were performed included Ahern, Cardew, Cage, Steve Reich and Terry Riley. Its concerts attracted considerable publicity and in one case provoked a riot (in Sydney Town Hall on 16 February 1971). From the larger AZ contingent Ahern formed Teletopa, an electronic music improvisation

group, which was disbanded after an overseas tour in 1972. A-Z (as the group was called from 1973) held its last concert in August 1975.

BIBLIOGRAPHY

E. Gallagher: 'The State of the Art', *Music Maker* (Oct 1971), 27–8

G. Barnard: *Conversation without Feldman* (Sydney, 1980)

G. Barnard: 'AZ it Was', *New Music Articles*, vii (1989), 17–20

E. Gallagher: 'AZ Music', *New Music Articles*, vii (1989), 9–13

ERNIE GALLAGHER

Aznavour, Charles [Aznavourian, Varenagh] (*b* Paris, 22 May 1924). French singer and songwriter. His parents were Armenian immigrants, and he began acting as a child. In 1941 he wrote the lyrics to the song *J'ai bu*, with music by Pierre Roche, and which brought the songwriting team to the attention of Edith Piaf. Aznavour subsequently wrote songs for Piaf (*Il pleut*, 1949), Gilbert Bécaud (*Donne-moi*, 1952) and Juliette Greco (*Je hais les dimanches*, 1950). As a singer, he toured with Piaf, but major success only came with *Sur ma vie* (1955). Such reflective and romantic songs as *The Old-Fashioned Way* and *She* (1974) brought him international acclaim, while numbers such as *Hier encore* (translated as *Yesterday when I was Young*) typify his introspective and melancholic style. His operetta, *Monsieur Carnaval*, was performed in Paris in 1965, and his film appearances include François Truffaut's *Tirez sur le pianiste* (1960) and *Edith et Marcel* (1982). He also composed the songs for the musical *Lautrec*, based on the life of the French artist, and which was given its London première on 29 March 2000. He has published two volumes of autobiography, *Aznavour on Aznavour* (Paris, 1970) and *Yesterday when I was Young* (London, 1979).

BIBLIOGRAPHY

Y. Salgues: *Charles Aznavour* (Paris, 1964)

A. Aznavour-Garvarentz with D. de La Patellière: *Petit frère* (Paris, 1986)

P. Sakka, ed.: *Un homme et ses chansons* (Paris, 1994) [annotated song texts]

□

Azopardi [Azzopardi], **Francesco** (*b* Rabat, 5 May 1748; *d* Rabat, 6 Feb 1809). Maltese composer, organist and theorist. After early studies with Michel'Angelo Vella, he entered the Conservatorio di S Onofrio a Capuana on 15 Oct 1763 as a *convittore* to study under Carlo Contumacci and the German Joseph Doll. He left in 1767 but stayed on as *maestro di cappella* in Naples and continued to study with Niccolò Piccinni, who is said to have esteemed him greatly. In summer 1774, following an advantageous offer from Mdina Cathedral, he returned permanently to Malta as Cathedral organist with the right to succeed the then *maestro di cappella*, Benigno Zerafa. His growing interest in pedagogy resulted in *Il musico prattico* on the art of the counterpoint, published in the form of French translations and introduced as a textbook in Paris by A.-E.-M. Grétry: Cherubini based the 19th chapter of his treatise *Cours de contrepoint* (1835) on its analysis of imitation. His students included the composers P.P. Bugeja, Nicolò Isouard and Giuseppe Burlon (1772–1856). Owing to Zerafa's failing health, in 1785 Azopardi was appointed as substitute *maestro*, with an increased salary; he inherited the full title in March 1804.

Most of Azopardi's works, written mainly for the cathedral, are extant. Recent revivals have disclosed a gifted composer who fused contemporary Classical techniques with the austere contrapuntal practices of earlier periods. This approach, which shows Piccinni's influence, is most evident in his large-scale 'Kyrie–Gloria' masses. That composed in 1776, for example, for soloists, double chorus and double orchestra, contains an eight-movement Gloria in which the inner sections of virtuoso arias in flexible ternary form and an eight-voice, madrigal-like 'Qui tollis' are framed by double-chorus numbers, with the closing 'Cum sancto spirito' starting homophonically but swelling into a majestic double fugue. The essentially symphonic conception of a whole movement is often dramatic, without however destroying a scrupulous concern for the music's appropriateness to textual spirit and meaning. Azopardi's few instrumental works, though inventive and melodious, are of less significance.

WORKS
(selective list)

MSS, mostly autograph in M-MDca: for SATB, instruments, unless otherwise stated

Masses: 6, 1768–1806, 1 ed. M. Frendo (diss., U. of Malta, 1987); 3 for 8vv, insts, 1775–98; Cr solenne, 1804; San, 1804; 2 requiem settings, 1792, ed. F. Aquilina (diss., U. of Malta, 1993), 1799; Mass propers, vv, insts
Pss, canticles: 4 Dixit Dominus, 1772–90; Domine probasti, 1772; 2 Laudate pueri, S, insts, 1775–6; Confitebor, S, insts, 1776; Confitebor, T, insts, 1780; De profundis, S, insts, 1781; Mag, 1781; Beatus vir, S, SATB, insts, 1783; Confitebor, S, SATB, insts, 1791; Miserere, SATB, 2 va, bc, 1793; Laudate pueri, S, SATB, insts, 1796
Ants, hymns, seqs: Ave maris stella, 1772; TeD, 1776; Sancte Paule, 1780; Veni Creator Spiritus, 1782; Te Joseph celebrant, 1787; Lauda Sion, 1793; TeD, 1798; Vade Anania, T, insts, 1807
Inst: Ov., 2 ob, 2 vn, 2 hn, db, org, 1782; Sinfonia, 2 ob, 2 vn, va, 2 hn, bc, 1797; Sinfonia, ob obbl, ob, 2 vn, 2 hn, bc, 1799
Lost: Malta felice (cant.), 1775; La magica lanterna (ob per Carnevale, 1), 1791; La passione di Cristo (orat, P. Metastasio), 1802

WRITINGS
MSS in M-Vnl

Il musico prattico, Fr. trans. by N.E. Framery (Paris, 1786), by A. Choron (Paris, 1816, 2/1824); ed. and Eng. trans. by O.B. Adams (diss., U. of Texas, 1991); rev. and expanded as Il musico prattico ossia Guida che conduce lo studente nell'arte del contrappunto divisa in quattro libri, after 1786
Dissertazione sulla risoluzione della quinta falsa in 6/4 rivolto dell'armonia di 5/3 [refuting Eximeno's Dell'origine e delle regole della musica]
Dissertazione sulla musica greca

BIBLIOGRAPHY
EitnerO
'Biografia: Francesco Azopardi', L'arte [Malta], i/13 (1863), 3–6
P. Pullicino: Notizia biografica di Francesco Azzopardi (Malta, 1876)
R. Mifsud Bonnici: Mużiċisti Kompożituri Maltin: Maestri di capella tal-Kattidral (Malta, 1950), 11–14
J. Vella Bondin: 'Five Maltese Composers of the 18th Century', Sunday Times [Malta] (25 July 1976)
D. Buhagiar: Il musico prattico by Francesco Azopardi (1748–1809): a Maltese Theorist in the Italian Tradition (diss., U. of Western Ontario, 1987)
F. Bruni: Musica sacra a Malta (Malta, 1993)

JOSEPH VELLA BONDIN

Azpiazú, Don (b Santa Clara, 11 Feb 1893; d Havana, 20 Jan 1943). Cuban pianist and bandleader. As the leader of the Havana Casino Orchestra he is best known for having launched the El manicero ('Peanut Vendor') craze in the United States after his band performed this number at New York's Palace Theater on 26 April 1930. Written by Moises Simon, the song became an instant hit, and within a year popular jazz artists such as Louis Armstrong and Duke Ellington had recorded versions of the tune. Expanding upon the traditional Cuban conjunto (sextet

or septet), Azpiazú's band was a 14-piece dance orchestra with trumpets, saxophones, trombone, tuba, piano, bass and Cuban percussion. Although Latin bands already existed in New York, his was the first group to be successful with the non-Latino public, helping to catalyze the rhumba dance craze that lasted throughout the decade. The Havana Casino Orchestra recorded popular versions of other tunes such as Mama Inéz, Aquellos ojos verdes, Siboney and Amapola, and also appeared in many short and feature-length movies.

Significantly, Azpiazú is remembered for forming the first racially integrated popular dance band in Cuba, also breaking the colour barrier in the United States. After a successful European tour, he went back to Cuba in 1932, returning regularly to New York's ballrooms through the late 1930s and early 40s. A stubborn man who rejected ethnic stereotypes, he reputedly lost a job at the Rainbow Room for playing American tunes and refusing to stick to Cuban numbers. See also J.S Roberts: The Latin Tinge: the Impact of Latin American Music on the United States (New York, 1979).

LISE WAXER

Azpilcueta, Martín de [Navarrus, Martinus] (b Barasoain, c1491; d Rome, 1586). Spanish churchman and jurisconsult. He taught in Salamanca and Coimbra and spent his last 19 years in Rome, revered for his learning and piety. His numerous Latin writings were published throughout Europe in the 16th and early 17th centuries. Forkel, Fétis and others credited him with a musical treatise, De musica et cantu figurato, but no such work apparently exists; reports of it may stem from a misunderstanding of Walther's Musicalisches Lexicon. Azpilcueta's known writings on church music occur in Commentarius de oratione horis canonicis atque aliis divinit officiis (Coimbra, 1561) and the brief Commentarius de silentio in divinis officiis (Rome, 1580; Spanish and Italian translations soon afterwards). He justified music not for God's benefit but man's, as it contributed to man's ability to worship; all excesses and abuses worked against this end. Well-executed plainchant was much to be preferred, but neither polyphonic music nor instruments were inherently improper if they enhanced the attitude of reverence and did not obscure the text. His discussion of specific abuses in the liturgy of his time is of particular interest.

BIBLIOGRAPHY
FétisB; WaltherML
F.J. León Tello: Estudios de historia de la teoría musical (Madrid, 1962, 2/1991)
Estudios sobre el doctor Navarro en el IV centenario de la muerte de Martín de Azpilcueta (Pamplona, 1988)

ALMONTE HOWELL

Aztec music. The Aztecs, a Náhuatl-speaking tribe, were one of the most important Indian groups in pre-Conquest America. According to their own tradition, the Aztecs came into central Mexico from the northern region of Aztlan in the 12th century. Based on a league of three cities, Mexico, Texcoco and Tlacopan, the Aztec empire by the time of the Spanish Conquest (1521) extended as far as present-day Central America. Approximately one million people in Mexico still speak Náhuatl. (For Mexican Indian music, see MEXICO, §II, 3.)

Among the pre-Conquest Aztecs, music had no independent life apart from religious and cult observances. A professionalized caste controlled public musical manifestations and training of an extremely rigid kind was prerequisite to a career in music. Since music was always thought of as a necessary adjunct to ritual, absolutely flawless performances were demanded, such as only the most highly trained singers and players could give. Imperfectly executed rituals were thought to offend rather than to appease the deities, so that errors in the performances of ritual music, such as missed drumbeats, carried the death penalty. Singers and players enjoyed considerable social prestige and in certain cases exemption from tribute payments, because of the important role music played in Aztec life. Despite this prestige, however, the names of musicians have not survived; neither have the names of poets, unless the poet belonged to royalty such as King Nezahualcóyotl (1402–72) of Texcoco.

Music was regarded as essentially a means of communal rather than individual expression, and therefore collectively performed music rather than solo music was the norm. Instrumental performance and singing were always inseparable, as were dance and music, insofar as can be judged from the descriptions of Aztec musical performances bequeathed by Spanish 16th-century chroniclers. Certain instruments were thought to be of divine origin, and the *teponaztli* (slit-drum with two tongues played with mallets) and *huéhuetl* (single-headed upright cylindrical drum open at the bottom, played with bare hands) were held to be gods temporarily forced to endure earthly exile. The *teponaztli* (into which the blood of sacrificed victims was poured at royal accessions) and the *huéhuetl* were therefore often treated as idols. Not only were certain instruments thought to have *mana* (mysterious supernatural powers) but they were also held to represent symbolically such emotional states as joy, delight or sensual pleasure.

Aztec music communicated states of feeling that apparently even the Spaniards could grasp and appreciate, whereas much of the Indian traditional music north of Mexico meant nothing to European ears. In many instances Aztec music seems to have communicated the same emotion to Indian and European listeners alike. Thus a lament, as composed by an Aztec priest-musician, was sad not only in the opinion of the Indians who heard and understood it, but also in the opinion of Spaniards unfamiliar with the Náhuatl language. Every piece of music was composed for a certain time, place and occasion, so that a musician needed a wide repertory if he was to satisfy the demands of the different days in the 260-day religious calendar.

Although the *calmécac* (priest's seminary) at the Aztec capital served as a national conservatory and by 1450 was (according to Diego Durán, *Historia de las Indias de Nueva-España*, Mexico, 1867–80) the model for similar training institutes in surrounding municipalities, the Aztecs themselves lacked any system of music notation; if they had one, it was kept secret from Europeans. Any reconstructions of Mexican pre-Conquest music are therefore largely conjectural, based on the possibilities of surviving instruments in museums, verbal descriptions by Spanish 16th-century chroniclers and the contemporary sounds of Indian traditional music recorded in outlying areas.

Aztec musicians needed prodigious memories. Musicians not only learnt traditional songs but also composed new ones. Creative ability was prized, especially in the households of those powerful *caciques* who were able to employ singers to compose ballads telling of their exploits.

Court music, at least in the Aztec and Tarascan neighbouring kingdoms, differed as much from the music of the *maceualli* (peasant classes) as did court speech from the vernacular Náhuatl and Purépecha spoken by the common people of those kingdoms.

Although Aztec music was predominantly percussive (string instruments were a European importation), the Aztecs had acute pitch sense and tuned with considerable care their various idiophones: *ayacachtli, áyotl, cacalachtli, chichuaztli, chililitli (caililiztli), coyolil, omichicahuaztli, tecomapiloa, teponaztli, tetzilácatl*; aerophones: *atecocoli (atecuculli), chichtli, çoçoloctli, huilacapitztli, quiquiztli, tecciztli (tecziztli, tezizcatli), tepuzquiquiztli, tlapitzalli*; and membranophones: *huéhuetl, tlapanhuéhuetl*. (For descriptions and pictures of these instruments, see Stevenson, 1988.) Bold, assertive qualities such as loudness, clarity and high pitch were preferred by players and singers alike. This crying aloud to their gods served their purpose even when the common people danced (as is still done by indigenous peoples of Mexico) to do penance.

The pre-Conquest Aztecs frequently inscribed their instruments with carvings that tell symbolically the purposes served by their instruments. For instance, the various carvings on the Malinalco *huéhuetl* (see illustration), an upright drum about 90 cm tall, in the Museo de Arqueología, Toluca, show a group of captured warriors being forced to dance to music of their own making just before having their hearts torn out and waved aloft as offerings to the war god Huitzilopochtli. The Aztecs, who burst into the Valley of Mexico to found Tenochtitlan (Mexico City) around 1325, borrowed heavily from the organography of earlier cultures in the extensive territories stretching south to present-day El Salvador, which they conquered during the next two centuries. To the European conquerors, the instruments used by Aztecs, Tarascans, Otomís, Zapotecs, Mixtecs and Mayas greatly resembled each other, with only the names differing in the respective aboriginal languages. In none of these languages do 16th-century lexicographers record a single generic term for music, coming nearest to it in Alonso de Molina's *Arte de la lengua Mexicana* (Mexico, 1571) with *cuica tlamatiliztli* ('knowledge of singing'). Neither did Náhuatl have any single term for 'musician' or 'player' but numerous nouns meaning 'player on the *huéhuetl*', 'player on the *teponaztli*', 'flute player' and 'trumpet player'. The Aztec language also included numerous verbs with such varied specific meanings as 'to sing in praise of someone', 'to sing derisive songs', 'to sing tenderly', or 'to sing in a high voice' (*see also* MEXICO, §II, 1).

The *teponaztli* is still in use among the Náhuatl-speaking people of middle and western Mexico. In the town of Pómaro-Michoacán near the Pacific coast, the Náhuatl-speaking people call this instrument *teponahuastle* (a hollowed tree trunk played in a horizontal position), used to announce Christian ceremonies such as the beginning of the Holy Week pilgrimage and the call to Mass during other Christian festivities. *Teponahuastle* is very often accompanied by a church bell.

The *huéhuetl* is still in use in the valley of Puebla and Tlaxcala among Náhuatl- and Otomí-speaking people to announce the Christian Mass and the beginning of patron saint celebrations. In this region, *huéhuetl* is one of the instruments of an ensemble called *conjunto azteca* which

Aztec huéhuetl from Malinalco (Museo de Arqueología, Toluca)

Malinche, the Amerindian woman who was Hernán Cortés's interpreter. Performed by Náhuatl-speaking people in Acayucan and Pajapan-Veracruz, these dances are accompanied by *jaranas* (small five-string guitars), diatonic harp (12 or 28 strings) and rattles made of thin metal plates. The La Malinche dance is performed in honour of the Virgin of Guadalupe on 12 December and of San Isidro Labrador between 14 and 17 May. Another example is the music to accompany the *cuauileros* dance (the cudgelers' dance) among the Náhuatl-speaking people from Pómaro, Aguila, Coire, Ostula and Maruata in the Pacific Ocean region of Michoacán. The performance of this dance represents a battle between Aztecs and Spaniards and is accompanied by small harps of 28 strings and a violin. Dancers perform with rattles made of thin metal plates and wooden cudgels. *Cuauileros* are performed in honour of St Anthony on 13 June.

BIBLIOGRAPHY

F.W. Galpin: 'Aztec Influence on American Indian Instruments', *SIMG*, iv (1903–4), 661–70

L.M. Spell: 'Music and Instruments of the Aztecs: the Beginning of Musical Education in North America', *Music Teachers National Association: Proceedings*, xxi (1926), 98–105

F.H. Martens: 'Music in the Life of the Aztecs', *MQ*, xiv (1928), 413–37

R. Lach: 'Die musikalischen Konstruktionsprinzipien der altmexikanischen Tempelgesänge', *Musikwissenschaftliche Beiträge: Festschrift für Johannes Wolf*, ed. W. Lott, H. Ostoff and W. Wolffheim (Berlin, 1929/R), 88–96

D. Castañeda: 'Los teponaztlis en las civilizaciones precortesianas'; 'Los percutores precortesianos'; 'Los huehuetls en las civilizaciones precortesianas', *Anales del Museo nacional de arqueología, história y etnología*, viii/1 (1933), 5–80; viii/2 (1933), 275, 287

V.T. Mendoza: 'Supervivencia de la cultura azteca: la canción y el baile del Xochipzahua', *Revista mexicana de sociologia*, iv/4 (1942), 87

G. Chase: *A Guide to Latin American Music* (Washington DC, 1945, enlarged 2/1962 as *A Guide to the Music of Latin America*), 287ff, 304

S. Martí: *Instrumentos musicales precortesianos* (Mexico City, 1955, 2/1968)

L. Schultze Jena, ed. and trans.: *Alt-Aztekische Gesänge* (Stuttgart, 1957)

S. Martí: *Canto, danza y música precortesianos* (Mexico City, 1961)

S. Martí and G.P. Kurath: *Dances of Anáhuac: the Choreography and Music of Precortesian Dances* (New York, 1964)

R. Stevenson: *Music in Aztec & Inca Territory* (Berkeley and London, 1968/R)

S. Martí: *Alt-Amerika: Musik der Indianer in präkolumbischer Zeit* (Leipzig, 1970), 5, 32–111

S. Martí: *La música precortesiana/Music before Cortés* (Mexico City, 1971, rev. 2/1978 by G. Nilsson as *Música precolumbina/Music before Columbus*)

A. Chamorro: *Los instrumentos de percusíon en México* (Zamora, Mexico, 1984)

M. León–Portilla: '¿Una nueva interpretación de los cantares mexicanos?', *Estudios de cultura náhuatl*, xviii (1986), 385–400

R. Stevenson : 'Aztec Organography', *Inter–American Music Review*, ix/2 (1988–9), 1–19

ROBERT STEVENSON/ARTURO CHAMORRO

includes a snare drum and a pair of *chirimías* (double-reed aerophone).

Huéhuetl and *teponaztli* are played together in particular ensembles to accompany *conchero* dances (dances with armadillo-shell guitars and conch shells). The contemporary performance of this dance resembles Aztec dances but with clear syncretism of Christian influences: it takes place on 12 December in honour of the Virgin of Guadalupe in Mexico City, and in some other festivities in Chalma, central Mexico.

The Aztec legacy as regards the use of the *huéhuetl* and *teponaztli* is clear, but there was also a process of acculturation with Spanish musical traditions that began in the early 16th century. This process changed the values and world-view of the Aztec people and transformed their music significantly. New European instruments and concepts of music and Christian cultural values were adopted by emergent musical ensembles among Náhuatl-speaking people in Veracruz and Michoacán. One example is the music for the allegorical dances about La

Azzaiolo, Filippo (*b* Bologna; *fl* 1557–69). Italian composer. He is believed to have been a singer in one of the Bolognese churches, though probably not S Petronio since he is not mentioned in the account books; he may have been connected with members of the Bolognese singing academies as described by Giustiniani. His first two books of villottas were published anonymously and he acknowledged all three only in the third book, after the first two had been sufficiently successful to be reprinted. The value of these collections lies in their preservation of popular texts and melodies arranged in simple four-part homophonic settings following the rhythm of the words, in which the top voice usually carries the melody. The first book contains 20 villottas, together with a 'todesca' by Girardo da Panico and madrigals by Caldarino, Spontone, Ruffo and 'P.H.', whom Vatielli believed to be Pietro de Hostia. Of interest is *Da l'horto se ne vien la vilanella*, which incorporates two 15th-century songs (of which the second, *Torèla mo' vilano*, was set by Verdelot). Also well known are *Chi passa per 'sta strada*, one of the most popular songs of the 16th century, *Ti parti cuor mio* which is found in a three-voice setting in Striggio's *Cicalamento delle donne al bucato* (1569), and *Poi che volse de la mia stella* which appears in Petrucci's first book of frottolas (RISM 1504⁴) where it is ascribed to Tromboncino.

In the second book there are eight compositions by Azzaiolo, including *Girometta, senza te*, which was arranged for 'tromboni, cornetti et cornamuse' and performed in the main square of Bologna, and was also popular among 17th-century composers including Frescobaldi. These works are often set to brisk rhythms with ornamental flourishes that enliven the homophonic textures. Several works freely mix duple and triple metres to accommodate line lengths of text. The third book contains seven pieces by Azzaiolo, of which the most interesting is *E me levai d'una bella mattina*, an eight-voice version of the canzona of the same name from the first book.

WORKS

Il primo libro de villotte alla padoana con alcune napolitane, 4vv (Venice, 1557¹⁸); 13 ed. F. Vatielli: *Villoite del fiore* (Bologna, 1921)

Il secondo libro de villotte del fiore alla padoana con alcune napolitanae e madrigali, 4vv (Venice, 1559¹⁹); ed. in Maestri bolognesi, ii (Bologna, 1953)

Il terzo libro delle villotte del fiore alla padoana con alcune napolitanae e bergamasche, 4vv (Venice, 1569²⁴)

BIBLIOGRAPHY

DBI (R. Nielsen); *EinsteinIM*
C. Spontoni: *Il Bottrigaro* (Venice, 1583)
V. Giustiniani: *Discorso sopra la musica de' suoi tempi* (MS, 1628 *I-La*); pr. in A. Solerti: *Le origini del melodramma* (Turin, 1903/R), 98–128; Eng. trans. in MSD, ix (1962), 63–80
G. Gaspari: *Musicisti bolognesi del XVI secolo* (Imola, 1875), 14ff repr. in *Musica e musicisti a Bologna* (Bologna, 1969), 163ff
F. Vatielli: *Arte e vita musicale a Bologna* (Bologna, 1927/R), 43ff
C. Calcaterra: *Poesia e canto* (Bologna, 1951)
W. Kirkendale: 'Franceschina, Girometta, and their Companions in a Madrigal "a diversi linguaggi" by Luca Marenzio and Orazio Vecchi', *AcM*, xliv (1972), 181–235
E. Apfel: *Aufsätze und Vorträge zur Musikgeschichte und historischen Musiktheorie* (Saarbrücken, 1977)

ANNE SCHNOEBELEN

Azzali, Augusto (*b* Ravenna, 1863; *d* Atlantic City, NJ, July 1907). Italian conductor, composer and impresario. His career was largely spent in touring Latin America and the Caribbean, mostly as the conductor for other impresarios, sometimes as both conductor and impresario of his own company.

His four-act opera *Ermengarda*, to a libretto by P. Martini, had its première at the Teatro Andreani in Mantua on 27 November 1886. Azzali embarked for Colombia in 1891. A six-month season in Bogotá as conductor and musical director for the Zenardo-Lambardi company was followed by an extended tour of the country and another season in the capital in 1893. During that season his *Lhidiak* (2, V. Fontana), based on an Indian legend, the first opera to be written for Colombia, had its première at the Teatro Colón (12 August). In April 1895 he started another tour that included Guatemala City, Quezaltenango, Bogotá and Medellin. In 1896–7 he was in Caracas, during which time *Lhidiak* was repeated. During the next few years his company performed in San José, Kingston, Mexico City and San Francisco, where the company folded in 1900. By 1902 he had his own company again, which travelled to Cuba and Puerto Rico. He then spent much time in Mexico, where he conducted a local première of *Tosca* in Mexico City on 27 July 1901. He died in Atlantic City while trying to save a young chorus member from drowning.

BIBLIOGRAPHY

E. de Olavarria y Ferrari: *Resena historico del teatro en Mexico, 1538–1911* (Mexico City, 3/1961)
J.I. Perdomo Escobar: *La Opera en Colombia* (Bogotá, 1979)

TOM KAUFMAN

Azzolini, Caterina (*fl* 1698–1708). Italian soprano. Sometimes known as 'La Valentina', and probably of Ferrarese birth, her first known appearance was in Crema in 1698. She was employed at the Mantuan court until she entered the service of Ferdinando de' Medici at Pratolino in 1700. A specialist in male roles, she appeared in ten operas there and in Florence, including Handel's *Rodrigo* (1707), in which she played Evanco. She sang in C.F. Pollarolo's *Venceslao* in Venice in 1703. Handel wrote for her within the narrow compass of *f'* to *a"*.

WINTON DEAN

Azzolini, Sergio (*b* Bolzano, 15 Jan 1967). Italian bassoonist and teacher. After studying with Romano Santi in Bolzano from 1978 to 1985, he spent four years in Hanover with Klaus Thunemann. Following success in various international competitions and a brief spell as an orchestral player, he embarked on what has been a spectacular career as soloist, teacher and chamber artist. At the age of 22 he was appointed professor at the Stuttgart Musikhochschule, exchanging this for a similar appointment in Basle in 1998. He has a number of outstanding recordings to his credit. In chamber music, he has been particularly associated with Maurice Bourgue (oboe) and Sabine Mayer (clarinet). As performer on both the modern and Baroque bassoon he is able to communicate with a remarkable degree of intensity and musicality.

WILLIAM WATERHOUSE

B

B. See PITCH NOMENCLATURE.

Ba. The name of the sharpened sixth degree in the (rising) melodic minor scale in TONIC SOL-FA.

Baaren, Kees van (*b* Enschede, 22 Oct 1906; *d* Oegstgeest, 2 Sept 1970). Dutch composer and teacher. The son of a music dealer, he first learned music from his father's stock of scores and recordings, before studying the piano with Rudolph Breithaupt and composition with Friedrich Koch at the Berlin Hochschule (1924–9). Also working as a jazz and cabaret pianist (under the name Billy Barney), and encouraged by his fellow student Boris Blacher, he developed simultaneous enthusiasms for Gershwin and Webern. He returned to the Netherlands in summer 1929, shortly after meeting Pijper in Berlin; some months later he began composition studies with the latter, at the same time destroying all his compositions from before 1930. The study sessions grew progressively less formal, and Pijper remained a friend and mentor until his death in 1947. After several years in Enschede, mostly working with amateur ensembles, van Baaren became director of the Amsterdam Musieklyceum in 1948. In 1953 he was appointed director of the Utrecht Conservatory and in 1958 director of the Royal Conservatory in The Hague. He, like Pijper, became the mentor of younger composers and performers (including Louis Andriessen, Bruins, Reinbert de Leeuw, Misha Mengelberg, Porcelijn, Schat, van Vlijmen and Wisse), who led the Dutch avant garde from the 1970s onwards.

Following public performances of his Piano Concertino (1934) and Trio for winds (1936), which shows Pijper's influence, van Baaren completed nothing more until 1947. His first major work, a striking cantata setting of Eliot's *The Hollow Men*, was written in 1948. While essentially tonal, the harmony grows out of a recurring six-note figure, employed as a series. For a time he wrote simultaneously in an accessible tonal style, largely for students and amateurs (as in the hearty Partita for band, 1953), and in progressively more ambitious applications of serialism. The Settetto (1952), while still reliant on Pijper's germ-cell principle, was his first wholly 12-note work; he became the first major Dutch serialist. Van Baaren's approach was rarely orthodox. Some compositions employ several unrelated rows; others involve exchange of notes within a row. The *Muzikaal zelfportret*, *Variazioni per orchestra*, *Sovraposizioni I* and *II* and the Piano Concerto, and parts of the *Musica per campane*, *Musica per orchestra* and *Musica per organo*, rely on a special formation around a tritone axis, resulting in either an all-interval row or, depending on octave placement, one in which the second half is a strict intervallic retrograde of the first (see ex.1). In portions of the *Musica per campane* and *Musica per organo*, rows of more than one octave appear: 72, 47 and 51 pitches respectively, matching the keys of the instrument.

Van Baaren's close attention to structure is seen in the five *Variazioni per orchestra*, based respectively on isometric pitch series, vertical groupings of notes, intervals, what the composer calls 'variable metres' (actually metres arranged according to interlocking numerical progressions) and groupings of durations. The 'variable metres' are a recurrent feature in the later works and lead to increasingly pointillistic textures. A special case is the sonic collage in the finale of the *Musica per orchestra*, quoting his own music, Latin dance rhythms and eight other composers from Bach to Pijper.

Van Baaren and his music were respected in the Netherlands and he received many prizes. The melodic imagination, sensitivity to instrumental colour and rhythmic vitality in his work overcame the customary resistance of audiences to atonality and won him a dedicated group of supporters at home and abroad. He was awarded the important Sweelinck Prize for his life's work as a composer in January 1970, nine months before his death.

WORKS

Orch: Concertino, pf, orch, 1934; Suite, school orch, 1951; Partita, sym. band, 1953; Sinfonia, orch, 1957; Variazioni per orchestra, 1959; Pf Conc., 1964; Musica per orchestra, 1966, rev. 1968

Vocal: Recueillement (C.P. Baudelaire), Mez, pf, 1947; 3 Poems by Emily Dickinson, female chorus, 1947; The Hollow Men (T.S. Eliot), S, Bar, chorus, chbr orch, 1948, rev. 1955–6; 2 Songs (P. van Ostaijen, H. Marsman), male chorus, 1952

Chbr and solo inst: Kleine étude, pf, 1933; Str Qt no.1, 1933; Trio, fl, cl, bn, 1936; Sonatina, pf, 1948; Settetto, vn, wind qnt, db, 1952; Muzikaal zelfportret, pf, 1954; Canzonetta triste, vn, pf, 1960; Quartetto [no.2] per archi (Sovraposizioni I), 1962; Quintetto a fiati (Sovraposizioni II), 1963; Musica per campane, carillon (72 bells), 1964; Musica per flauto solo, 1964; Musica per campane, 47 bells, 1969; Musica per organo, 1969; Vlug en toch niet langzaam [Quick, yet not Slow], pf, 1969

Arr.: 3 Songs from A. Valerius: Nederlandtsche Gedenck-Clanck, SSAA, 1945

Ex.1 Row from the Piano Concerto (1964)

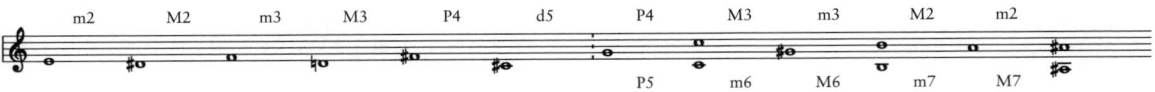

Principal publishers: Alsbach, Broekmans & van Poppel, Donemus

BIBLIOGRAPHY

K. van Baaren: *Het concertwezen in Nederland* [Concert life in the Netherlands] (The Hague,1942)

J. Geraedts: 'Kees van Baaren: variazioni per orchestra', *Sonorum speculum*, vi (1961), 43–5

J. Wouters and A. Jurres, eds.: 'Conversations with Dutch Composers: Kees van Baaren and Hans Henkemans', *Fifteen Years Donemus* (Amsterdam, 1962), 50–59

J. Hill: *The Music of Kees van Baaren* (diss., U. of North Carolina, 1970)

J. Wouters: 'Kees van Baaren', *Dutch Composers' Gallery* (Amsterdam, 1971), 71–87

H. Kien: 'The Composer Kees van Baaren: towards a Revaluation of Sound Material', *Key Notes*, iv (1976), 4–18

E. Vermeulen: 'Kees van Baaren's Antischool', *Key Notes*, xxvi/1 (1992), 14–17

HARRISON RYKER

Baarpijp (Dut.). *See under* ORGAN STOP.

Babadjanian, Aṙno Harutyuni (*b* Yerevan, 22 Jan 1921; *d* Yerevan, 11 Nov 1983). Armenian composer and pianist. He graduated from Talian's composition class at the Yerevan Conservatory in 1947, and in 1948 from Igumnov's piano class at the Moscow Conservatory; his composition studies were continued under Litinsky at the House of Armenian Culture in Moscow (1946–8). He taught the piano at the Yerevan Conservatory (1950–56) and was himself a brilliant pianist. In 1971 he was made a People's Artist of the USSR. His music draws on Khachaturian and Rachmaninoff, but is unmistakably individual, particularly in its scoring. The piano works are in a virtuoso style, liberal in their use of touch, texture, rhythm and register, and with expressive leading parts. This style was formed in the 1940s; later he introduced Prokofiev-like chromaticism, Bartókian rhythm and Schoenbergian dodecaphony into his music, achieving his best work in the Violin Sonata, the Cello Concerto and the *Shest' kartin* ('Six Pictures') for piano. Babadjanian's variation technique, an important feature of his music, springs from folk ornamentation, while peasant music forms the source of his irregular rhythms.

WORKS
(selective list)

Str Qt no.1, 1943; Pf Conc., 1944; Polifonischeskaya sonata, pf, 1947; Str Qt no.2, 1947; Vn Conc., 1949; Haykakan rapsodia [Armenian Rhapsody], 2 pf, 1950; Herosakan Ballad [Heroic Ballad], pf, orch, 1950; Pf Trio, 1952; 4 par [4 Pieces], pf, 1954; Poem-Rhapsody, orch, 1954; Sonata, vn, pf, 1959; Vc Con., 1962; 6 kartin [6 Pictures], pf, 1965; Poem, pf, 1966; Str Qt no.3, 1976; Elegy, pf, 1978; Meditation, pf, 1980; Vocalise, S, orch, 1981; variety songs and film scores

Principal publishers: Sovetakan Grokh; Sovetskiy Kompozitor

WRITINGS

'Tol'ko vliyaniye vremeni' [Only the influence of time], *Sovetaka arvest* (1971), no.6, pp.16–19

'Chcialbym wzruszac serca' [I want to stir hearts], *RM*, xxxii/8 (1988), pp.6–9; repr. in *Arvest* (1991), nos.2–3, pp..14–17

BIBLIOGRAPHY

A. Grigoryan: *Arno Babadzhanyan* (Moscow, 1961)

Y. Yevdokimova: 'Shest' kartin Ar. Babadzhanyana' [Babadjanyan's 6 Pictures], *SovM* (1967) no.2, pp.20–24

Sh. Apoian: *Fortepiannaya muzika sovetskoy Armenii* (Yerevan, 1968), 150–67, 201–09

S. Amatuni: *Arno Badadzhanyan: instrumental'noye tvorchestvo* [Babadjanian: his instrumental work] (Yerevan, 1985)

G. Arakelian, ed.: 'Arno Babadzhanian-75', *Arvest* (1966–7) [special issue]

SVETLANA SARKISYAN

Babaian, Vahram Ohani (*b* Yerevan, 19 Aug 1948). Armenian composer. He began composing at the age of seven, then studied composition with Bagdasarian at the Melikian Music College (1964–8) and later at the Yerevan Conservatory under Yeghiazarian (1968–73). He joined the Armenian Composers' Union in 1973, and as a freelance composer has received numerous prizes and commissions. His works have been performed at festivals of contemporary music in Lithuania, Finland, Georgia, Argentina and Hungary. He is prolific and has written in all genres; his style has evolved from an expressionism which makes use of serial techniques to a Romanticism in which modality and tonality play a major role. He also makes use of impressionist and sonoristic techniques (the ballet *Pygmalion*), heterophony and micropolyphony (Fifth Symphony) and dense textures involving chords and clusters. His preference for clearly defined and logical relationships between form and content has led to unusual assymetrical proportions within works, where the sense of conflict or rhythmic gravitation overrides conventional formal considerations. His symphonies continue the tradition of Mahler and Shostakovich, with outer movements assuming the most significance; his Second Symphony, for example, follows a teleological design which culminates in the finale. Similar formal resolutions can be found in the ballet *Pan*, the opera *Hamlet* and a number of his concertos, lending a sense of coherence to his output as a whole.

WORKS
(selective list)

Stage (all unstaged unless otherwise stated): L'étrange (op, 2, A. Babaian and V. Babaian, after A. Camus), 1970; Pygmalion (ballet, 1, A. Babaian, after Gk. legend), 1975; Die Briefe von Beethoven (chbr op, after letters by L. van Beethoven), 1977; Pan (ballet, 2, A. Babaian, after K. Hamsun), 1977; Hamlet (op, 3, V. Babaian, after W. Shakespeare), 1990; Into the Light (ballet, R. Kharatian), staged Baltimore, Peabody Institute, 7 Dec 1995

9 syms.: no.1, 1964; no.2, 1968; no.3 (A. Isahakian: *Abu-Lala-Mahari*), chorus, orch, 1972; no.4 'Katharsis', 1977; Chbr Sym. no.1, 1979; Chbr Sym. no.2, 1981; no.5, 1981; no.6, 1985; no.7, 1988

Other orch: Pf Conc. [no.1], 1965; Org Conc., 1967; Antuni, sym. poem, 1969; Pf Conc. [no.2], 1969; Utrenniye kokokola [Morning Bells], sym. poem, 1969; Pentimento, chbr orch, 1975; Conc., str qt, orch, 1978; Gisher'e Garnium [A Night in Garni], sym. poem, 1978; Conc., vn, vc, chbr orch, 1981; Conc., sax qt, orch, 1982; Conc., fl, ob, chbr orch, 1983; Requiem, str orch, 1983; Pf Conc. [no.3], 1984; Vc Conc., 1992; Db Conc., 1997

Vocal: 4 zhyoltïye balladï [4 Yellow Ballads] (F. García Lorca), S, pf, 1968; Sonata (García Lorca), S, pf, 1969; Poeti tznund'e [The Birth of the Poet] (E. Charents), S, B, pf, 1977; Ashnanain yerger [Autumn Songs] (Jap. poems), S, pf, 1979; Serenada no.1 (A. Babaian), S, 2 fl, vn, vc, pf, 1985; Ashun'e Kiso lernerum [Autumn in the Kiso Mountains] (M. Basho), S, pf, 1987; Sym.-Requiem 'Armenii skorbyashchey' [For a Grieving Armenia] (V. Batashov), chorus, 1989; Jésus parle (orat, C. Péguy), S, B, chorus, orch, 1992; Serenada no.2, vocalise, S, vn, vc, pf, 1992; From the Life of Christ (orat, Armenian spiritual texts), 4 solo vv, chorus, orch, 1995; Komitasiana suite (trad.), S, Bar, chorus, orch, 1995; Tikhiye pesni [Quiet Songs] (aphorisms by Confucius), S, fl, ob, hn, perc, pf, 1994

Chbr and solo inst: Sonata, vn, vc, 1967; Str Qt [no.1], 1968; Str Qt [no.2], 1969; 6 Fugues, pf, 1970; Sonata, 2 pf, 1970; Sonata, pf, kettle drums, 1970; Str Qt [no.3], 1970; Collages, 2 pf, perc, 1971; Pf Sonata [no.1], 1972; Sonata no.1, vn, pf, 1972; Pf Sonata [no.2], 1973; 2 Pieces, vc, pf, 1973; Sonata no.1, vn, 1975; Sonata no.1, vc, 1975; Pf Sonata [no.3], 1976; 3 Retrospective Pieces, vn, pf, 1977; Pf Sonata [no.4], 1978; Sonata no.2, vn, 1978; Sonata no.2, vc, 1978; Pf Sonata [no.5], 1979; Sonata, ob, pf, 1979; Sonata no.2, vn, pf, 1980; Str Qt [no.4], 1981; Org Sonata, 1982; Sonata, fl, pf, 1982; Mantra, sax, pf, 1983; Str Qt [no.5], 1984; Pf Sonata [no.6], 1985; Sonata, va, pf, 1985; Sonata, cl, pf, 1986;

Wind Qnt, 1986; Conc., fl, cl, vn, vc, pf, 1988; 3 Introspective
Pieces, vn, pf, 1992; Monada, fl, ob, pf, 1995; Sonata, vn, pf,
1995; Pro et contra, pf, 1996

MSS in Armenian Ministry of Culture; Armenian Composers' Union
Principal publishers: Sovetakan Grokh, Sovetskïy Kompozitor, Leduc

BIBLIOGRAPHY
S. Sarkisian: 'O tvorchestve molodïkh kompozitorov Armenii' [On
the work of the young composers of Armenia], *Muzïkal'naya
kul'tura bratskikh respublik SSSR*, ed. G. Kon'kova (Kiev, 1982),
154–60
V. Babaian: 'A Synthesis of New and Old Elements', *Sovetakan
arvest* (1985), no.9, pp.4–5
L. Berger: 'Hasunutyun' [Maturity], *Sovetakan arvest* (1988), no.7,
pp.36–8
G. Tigranov: *Armyanskiy muzïkal'nïy teatr* [The Armenian musical
theatre], iv (1988), 104–9

SVETLANA SARKISYAN

Babán, Gracián (*b* ?Aragon, *c*1620; *d* Valencia, 2 Feb
1675). Spanish composer. In September 1649 he competed
unsuccessfully for the post of *maestro de capilla* of La
Seo, one of the two cathedrals at Zaragoza. In 1653 he
was appointed *maestro de capilla* of Huesca Cathedral
with an annual salary of 120 escudos, which was raised
to 160 escudos on 29 August that year in the expectation
that he would be ordained priest. He asked for more
money on 1 July 1655 but was offered only another 10 or
20 escudos a year for his composition of music for
Christmas and Corpus Christi. On 27 April 1657 he
accepted the post of *maestro de capilla* of Valencia
Cathedral. He was one of the most prolific and respected
Spanish composers of his age. He wrote the *Te Deum* and
two villancicos performed at Valencia Cathedral on 20
May 1659 to celebrate the canonization of St Thomas of
Villanueva, the music commemorating an indult granted
by Pope Alexander VII in 1665 and five villancicos sung
at S Domingo, Valencia, on 8 September 1674 in honour
of the canonization of St Luis Bertrán. The questions he
asked during an examination of six candidates for the
post of music director of the Patriarca, Valencia, reveal
his profound theoretical and contrapuntal expertise (see
Piedra). His music, which includes many polychoral pieces
and numerous works with harp accompaniment, circulated widely and survives in Latin America as well as in
Spain. A painting showing Babán and his singers protected
from the plague by the Virgin Mary was formerly in the
Capilla de Nuestra Señora contra la Peste at Valencia
Cathedral.

WORKS

2 masses, 8vv, 12vv, *E-SEG*
16 masses, 6–14vv, *VAc*
Requiem, 8vv, *SEG*
4 Lamentations, *SEG*
Motet (for the Adoration of the Cross), 4vv, *MA*
3 Passion motets, *SEG*
Psalms, 4, 8vv, *H*, *MA*, *SEG*, *VAc*; 1 ed. in Lira sacro-hispana, i/1
(Madrid, 1869)
Many other vocal works, incl. motets, psalms, hymns, sequences and
villancicos: *CO-B*, *D-Mbs*, *E-Bc*, *E*, *MA*, *SEG*, *VAc*, Guatemala
Cathedral archives; Puebla Cathedral, Mexico; 2 motets ed. in Lira
sacro-hispana, i/1 (Madrid, 1869)

BIBLIOGRAPHY
StevensonRB
M.A. Ortí: *Solemnidad festiva con que en la insigne, leal, noble y
coronada ciudad de Valencia se celebro la feliz nueva de la
canonizacion de su milagroso Arçobispo Santo Tomas de
Villanueva* (Valencia, 1659), 47
F. de la Torre y Sebdil: *Luces de la aurora, dias del sol, en fiestas de la
que es sol de los dias y aurora de las luces Maria santissima*
(Valencia, 1665), 56

J. Alenda y Mira: *Relaciones de solemnidades y fiestas públicas de
España* (Madrid, 1903), 344–5, 382, 393
J. Ruiz de Lihory: *La música en Valencia: diccionario biográfico y
crítico* (Valencia, 1903)
J. Sanchis y Sivera: *La catedral de Valencia* (Valencia, 1909), 456
V. Ripollès: Introduction to *El villancico i la cantata del segle XVIII
a València* (Barcelona, 1935), p.vii
A. Durán Gudiol: 'Los maestros de capilla de la catedral de Huesca',
Argensola, no.38 (1959), 107–31
J. Climent: 'La música en Valencia durante el siglo XVII', *AnM*, xxi
(1966), 211–41, esp. 233, 235, 238
J. Piedra: 'Maestros de Capilla del Real Colegio de Corpus Christi
(Patriarca) (1662–1822)', *AnM*, xxiii (1968), 61–127, esp. 66 and
76
J. Climent: 'La capilla de música de la catedral de Valencia', *AnM*,
xxxvii (1982), 55–69

ROBERT STEVENSON

Babbi. Italian family of musicians.

(1) Gregorio (Lorenzo) Babbi (i) (*b* Cesena, 16 Nov
1708; *d* Cesena, 2 Jan 1768). Italian tenor. Active from
1729 to 1760, he was renowned for his powerful voice
and wide range (*c* to *c''*, full voice; *c''* to *g''*, falsetto), his
dramatic and expressive manner and his mastery of the
improvised bel canto style. Babbi sang in the major
theatres of Italy (notably in Florence, Venice, Rome,
Turin, Padua and Naples) and Portugal (Lisbon), in heroic
opere serie by Hasse, Vivaldi, Albinoni, Galuppi, Porpora,
Jommelli and Perez, among others. He made his début in
Ravenna in 1729 and shortly thereafter was appointed
'virtuoso' to the Grand Duke of Tuscany (*c*1730/31). For
the next two decades Babbi's activities were concentrated
in northern Italy, in Venice particularly, and in the
theatres of his native Romagna. In 1747 he entered the
service of Charles III, King of Naples and the Two Sicilies
and Palermo. Until his retirement in 1759, he performed
almost exclusively for Charles's court in Naples and at
the Teatro S Carlo. In 1759 he received a pension and
returned to Cesena. His last known performance was in
1760 in Faenza when he sang a *Salve regina* composed
for him by the *maestro di cappella* Paolo Alberghi. Babbi
was ranked with the foremost virtuosos of his era and
was included in the illustrious cast assembled for the
production of Perez's *Alessandro nell'Indie* to inaugurate
Lisbon's Casa de Opera in 1755 (the theatre was destroyed
in an earthquake a few months later). De Brosses, who
heard him in his prime in 1741, described him as the
'loveliest high-tenor [haut-taille]' and a good actor, and
compared him with the French tenor Jélyotte. His range
was a 5th higher than most Italian tenors of the time and
equal to Jélyotte's and Amorevoli's ranges. Burney called
him a 'dignified, splendid and powerful performer', with
the 'sweetest, most flexible, and most powerful voice of
its kind, that his country could boast at the time', and
P.L. Ghezzi considered him worthy of a caricature (*I-Rvat*
Cod. Lat. Ottoboniensis 3117, f.161). Babbi's style in his
later years is represented by three arias identified as 'his':
a setting of 'Fra sdegno ed amore' from Latilla's *Siroe*
(1740; in *US-BEm*), and two settings (one incomplete) of
'Vil trofeo d'un alma imbelle' from Galuppi's *Alessandro
nelle Indie* (second version, 1754, Naples; in *I-FZc*). The
latter two arias appear to have been part of a larger
collection of Babbi's favourite arias that was prepared for
use in Faenza. These arias provide a modest suggestion of
the vocal dexterity and virtuosity that earned the singer
unstinting praise from his contemporaries and biographers. Babbi's first wife Giovanna Guaetti [Guaetta,
Guaitti] (*d* before 1767), a soprano, sang in many operas

with him in Venice and Naples. Babbi is not known to have composed; the pieces attributed to him by Schmidl are by his grandson, (3) Gregorio Babbi (ii).

BIBLIOGRAPHY

CroceN; DBI (A. Zapperi); *ES* (E. Zanetti); *FétisB; GerberNL; RicciTB; SchmidlD*

J.J. de Lalande: *Voyage d'un françois en Italie, fait dans les années 1765 & 1766* (Venice and Paris, 1769, enlarged 2/1786), vii, 205ff

C. de Brosses: *Lettres historiques et critiques sur l'Italie* (Paris, 1799); ed. Y. Bezard as *Lettres familières sur l'Italie* (Paris,1931), ii, 344

C. Burney: 'Gregorio Babbi', *Rees's Cyclopaedia*, iii (London, 1819)

N. Trovanelli: 'Due celebri cantanti cesenati del secolo scorso', *Il cittadino* (Cesena, 25 July 1897)

H.-B. Dietz: 'A Chronology of Maestri and Organisti at the Cappella Reale in Naples, 1745–1800', *JAMS*, xxv (1972), 379–406, esp. 390

G. Eive: 'Virtuosi del diciottesimo secolo: la famiglia Babbi', *Studi romagnoli*, xxvii (1976), 287–325

R.L. and N.W. Weaver: *A Chronology of Music in the Florentine Theater, 1590–1750* (Detroit, 1978)

P. Fabbri: *Tre secoli di musica a Ravenna, dalla Controriforma alla caduta dell'Antico Regime* (Ravenna, 1983), 87, 201

F. Dell'Amore: 'Il Settecento musicale a Longiano', *Studi romagnoli*, xxxix (1988), 335–61

P. Fabbri: 'Il teatro per musica a Rimini e in Romagna nel primo Settecento', *Studi in onore di Giuseppe Vecchi*, ed. I. Cavallini (Modena, 1989), 77–93, esp. 78, 85–6

(2) (Pietro Giovanni) Cristoforo (Bartolomeo Gasparre) Babbi

(*b* Cesena, 8 May 1745; *d* Dresden, 19 Nov 1814). Italian violinist and composer, son of (1) Gregorio Babbi. He spent his childhood (1747–59) in Naples, where his parents were employed in the Teatro S Carlo and in the royal chapel. After his family returned to Cesena in 1759 he was sent to Faenza (about 1763 or 1764) to study the violin with Tartini's disciple Paolo Alberghi, who also taught him counterpoint and composition. In Faenza he was *primo violino* for the *festa* of 8 December 1766 and again in 1769, 1770 and 1772. In Rimini he was a violinist in the orchestra for the 1773 opera season, and in the same year he was appointed *primo violino* in the cappella at S Petronio, Bologna, a position which he held until 1781. He became a member of the Bologna Accademia Filarmonica on 4 February 1774. He served as *maestro di cappella* in the Teatro Comunale, Bologna (1775–8), and at the Teatro Zagoni as *primo violino* and *capo d'orchestra* (1776–8).

On 3 March 1781 Babbi was engaged as provisional Konzertmeister in Dresden; after the first year his contract was formalized and extended. Under his direction the Dresden Kapelle was completely reorganized, and the orchestra acquired international renown for its accuracy, precision, discipline and brilliant, full sound. Babbi took part in the selection of musicians (with the elector); although he was officially only in charge of the violins, he actually directed the entire orchestra, and was, in effect, equal in importance to J.G. Naumann, the Kapellmeister. His administrative skills and leadership affected even the soloists and vocal ensembles, raising the level of musicianship in the church and opera choirs and generally improving the discipline and organization. Babbi's musicianship was greatly admired by the Dresden court. He is described as playing with 'fire' and 'exquisite taste', with a tone 'as full and rich as that of a cello and although he could not sustain this tone in passages requiring great agility, yet when he played an Adagio, not an eye was dry' (Mannstein). Although these comments are reminiscent of descriptions of earlier performances of Tartini's pupils including Alberghi, Babbi was incontestably 'mod-

ern' in his approach and achieved his originality through a synthesis of old and new techniques. Tartini's style and aesthetic prinicples, acquired via Alberghi, had been considered old-fashioned even before Babbi's arrival at the Dresden court, yet in his teacher's style, Tartini's 'fire' and unrivalled bowing technique is recognisable in the 'new' orchestral brilliance and precision achieved by Babbi's orchestra.

Babbi served as Konzertmeister until shortly before his death, when he retired with a pension. His compositions included symphonies for the church, the theatre and the Hofkapelle (after 1786), theatre pieces (1786), and entr'acte music performed during spoken dramas (1792–3) and operas (1796), concertos, chamber works and keyboard music for the Hofkapelle (1802–3), and arrangements of concertos and symphonies by other Italian composers. Of these, only one work has survived (keyboard version in *D-Dl*), a cantata *Augusta*, to a text by C.E. Weinlig, written in honour of the Princess Maria Augusta, and given on 21 August 1786. The cantata is scored for small orchestra (strings, wind and horns) and is a modest work consisting of a sinfonia, accompanied recitative, bravura aria and closing *coro*. The introductory sinfonia is in the three-movement cantabile style of contemporary Italian opera overtures and is remarkable for its explicit tempo and dynamic indications: sudden contrasts between *f* and *pp* or *ppp*, crescendos and diminuendos, and even *pianissimo* ritardandos ('mancando poco a poco').

BIBLIOGRAPHY

BurneyGN; DBI (A. Zapperi); *EitnerQ; GerberNL; RicciTB*

Indice de' teatrali spettacoli (Milan, 1780–96)

H. Mannstein [H.F. Steinmann]: *Denkwürdigkeiten der churfürstlichen und königlichen Hofmusik zu Dresden im 18. u. 19. Jahrhundert* (Leipzig, 1863), 45–6

R. Prölss: *Geschichte des Hoftheaters zu Dresden* (Dresden, 1878), 234, 239, 246, 379

R. Engländer: 'Dresdner Musikleben und Dresdner Instrumentalpflege in der Zeit zwischen Hasse und Weber', *ZMw*, xiv (1931–2), 410–20

R. Engländer: *Die Dresdner Instrumentalmusik in der Zeit der Wiener Klassik* (Uppsala, 1956), 28–9, 34, 121, 124–6

P. Fabbri: *Tre secoli di musica a Ravenna, dalla Controriforma alla caduta dell'Antico Regime* (Ravenna, 1963), 87, 201

A. Righetti: *Vita musicale e teatri a Rimini nel Settecento* (diss., U. of Bologna, 1973), 51–9, 219–20

L. Malusi: 'Musica e musicisti a Longiano', *Studi romagnoli*, xxxvi (1985), 217–29

F. Dell'Amore: 'La cappella musicale a Cesena dal 1773 al 1782', *Studi romagnoli*, xxxviii (1987), 265–83, esp. 267–8

O. Gambassi: *La cappella musicale di S Petronio* (Florence, 1987), 199–204

(3) Gregorio Babbi (ii)

(*b* ?Bologna, *c*1770–75; *d* ?Bologna, ? after 1815). Italian bass singer, violinist, composer and organist, son of (2) Cristoforo Babbi. For most of his career Babbi was active in Dresden where he maintained a dual position as supernumerary violinist (from 1788) and bass singer in the Hofkirche. He was granted leave of absence in 1790 and sang in Forlì in 1791. By 1794 he had returned to Dresden, where he continued as bass and violinist in the Hofkirche. In 1805 he was appointed one of the two solo basses in the Hofkirche, although he also retained his former salary as violinist. In the same year he became Musikmeister (as assistant to the Kapellmeister), replacing Frederick Gestewitz. In 1807 he received a pension and returned to Italy, where he served as *primo violino* and orchestra director in Bologna, first at the Teatro Comunale (1807–

8) and then at the Teatro Marsigli-Rossi. His last years were spent in Bologna, where he served as organist in one of the churches.

Babbi's four extant compositions (now in *I-Bc*) were originally written for the Dresden Hofkapelle. The two sinfonias (1804) are the most ambitious of the four works and contain several solo passages, probably a concession to the many virtuosos in the Dresden orchestra; he also wrote an orchestral pastorale (1798). Babbi's harmonic vocabulary is limited and constrained by his short phrases and square rhythms; his melodies are rather unimaginative scale or triad figures, and there is virtually no thematic development. His polacca (1797) is a concert aria in rondo form and was evidently designed to display the technical prowess of its dedicatee, his sister Giovanna Babbi (*b* ?Bologna, *c*1780), an alto who, after making opera débuts in Trieste and Venice (1796–7) and scoring a striking success in Dresden during Carnival 1798–9 (reported in *AMZ*, i, 1799, cols.331–4), permanently damaged her voice in a vain attempt to become a soprano; she left the stage in 1800. Another sister, Teresa Babbi (*fl* 1800–10), was a soprano in the Dresden Hofkapelle from about 1800 to 1806, and received the dedication of Paer's aria *Ti riposa in questo seno*.

BIBLIOGRAPHY

R. Prölss: *Geschichte des Hoftheaters zu Dresden* (Dresden, 1878), 234, 239, 246, 379

R. Engländer: 'Zur Musikgeschichte Dresdens gegen 1800', *ZMw*, iv (1921–2), 199–241

A. Mambelli: *Musica e teatro in Forlì nel secolo XVIIIo* (Forlì, 1933), 205–6

S. Paganelli: 'Repertorio critico degli spettacoli e delle esecuzioni musicali dal 1763 al 1966', *Due secoli di vita musicale: storia del Teatro comunale di Bologna*, ed. L. Trezzini (Bologna, 1966, 2/1987), ii, 15–17

GLORIA EIVE

Babbitt, Milton (Byron) (*b* Philadelphia, PA, 10 May 1916). American composer and theorist. He has contributed extensively to the understanding and extension of 12-note compositional theory and practice and has been one of the most influential composers and teachers in the USA since World War II.

1. Life. 2. Works: (i) Serial theory and practice to 1970 (ii) Electronic works (iii) Later serial developments.

1. LIFE. Brought up in Jackson, Mississippi, he started playing the violin at the age of four and several years later also studied clarinet and saxophone. He graduated from high school in 1931, having already demonstrated considerable skills in jazz ensemble performance and the composition of popular songs. His father's professional involvement with mathematics (as an actuary) was influential in shaping Babbitt's intellectual environment. In 1931 Babbitt entered the University of Pennsylvania with the intention of becoming a mathematician, but he soon transferred to New York University, concentrating on music under Marion Bauer and Philip James. He received the BA in music in 1935. As a student and during the ensuing years, Babbitt immersed himself in the intellectual milieu of New York, encountering influential philosophers such as Sidney Hook and James Wheelright, developing a life-long engagement with analytical philosophy, and reading widely in rapidly emerging and sometimes short-lived journals such as *Symposium* and *Politics*. His early attraction to the music of Varèse and Stravinsky soon gave way to an absorption in that of Schoenberg, Berg and Webern – particularly significant at

a time when 12-note music was unknown to many and viewed with scepticism by others.

After graduation Babbitt studied privately with Sessions, wrote criticism for the *Musical Leader*, and then enrolled for graduate work at Princeton University, where he continued his association with Sessions. In 1938 he joined the Princeton music faculty and in 1942 received one of Princeton's first MFAs in music. His *Composition for String Orchestra*, a straightforward 12-note work, was completed in 1940.

During World War II Babbitt divided his time between Washington, DC, where he was engaged in mathematical research, and Princeton, as a member of the mathematics faculty (1943–5). Musically, these were years of thought and discovery, rather than of actual composition; they resulted in 1946 in a paper entitled *The Function of Set Structure in the Twelve-Tone System*, the first formal and systematic investigation of Schoenberg's compositional method. (The unpublished paper finally gained Babbitt the PhD in 1992.) Between 1946 and 1948, shuttling between Jackson and New York, he again directed his energies to composition, writing some film scores and an unsuccessful Broadway musical.

In 1948 Babbitt rejoined the music faculty at Princeton, eventually becoming Conant Professor of Music (1960); in 1973 he became a member of the composition faculty of the Juilliard School. He has also taught at the Salzburg Seminar in American Studies, the Berkshire Music Center, the New England Conservatory of Music and the Darmstadt summer courses. He has received several honorary doctorates and other honours, including a National Institute of Arts and Letters Award (1959), a Guggenheim Fellowship (1960–61) and membership in the National Institute (1965). He became a fellow of the American Academy of Arts and Sciences in 1974, received a Pulitzer Prize Special Citation in 1982, and in 1986 was elected a member of the American Academy of Arts and Letters (he also received its Gold Medal in Music in 1988). Throughout his career, he has been actively involved in contemporary music organizations, including the ISCM (he was president of the American section, 1951–2), the American Music Center, *Perspectives of New Music* (as a member of its editorial board) and the Columbia-Princeton Electronic Music Center (as director from 1959). A prolific writer of articles and reviews, he has also travelled widely as a lecturer perceptive and adept at logical extemporization: his 1983 Madison lectures are published under the title *Words about Music*. He is also an inveterate follower of popular sports, a raconteur and punster, and an omnivorous reader.

2. WORKS.

(i) Serial theory and practice to 1970. Babbitt's early fascination with 12-note practice, particularly in its formal aspects, developed into a total reconsideration of musical relations. Throughout his compositional career he has been occupied with the extension of techniques related to Schoenberg's (and Webern's) 'combinatorial' sets; with the investigation of sets that have great flexibility and potential for long-range association; and with an exploration of the structuring of nonpitch components 'determined by the operations of the [12-note] system and uniquely analogous to the specific structuring of the pitch components of the individual work, and thus, utterly nonseparable' (Babbitt, 1955, p.61). He has been a pioneer in his ways of talking and thinking about music,

invoking terms from other disciplines, such as philosophy, linguistics, mathematics and the physical sciences.

Babbitt revealed and formalized many of the most salient aspects of 12-note compositional technique in several important essays. In 'Some Aspects of Twelve-Tone Composition' (1955), 'Twelve-Tone Invariants as Compositional Determinants' (1960) and 'Set Structure as a Compositional Determinant' (1961), he systematically investigated the compositional potential of the 12 pitch class set, introducing such terms (derived from mathematics) as 'source set', 'combinatoriality', 'aggregate', 'secondary set', and 'derived set'. These terms facilitate the classification of the various types of pitch class set and contribute to the description of diverse procedures for the compositional projection of such sets. A secondary set, for example, results when a 'new' set of 12 pitch classes emerges from the linear linking of segments of two forms of a 12-note series, as shown in Table 1. Similarly, an 'aggregate can be thought of as a simultaneous statement of … parts [of a 12-note set] … it is not a set, inasmuch as it is not totally ordered, because only the elements within the component parts are ordered, but not the relationship between or among the parts themselves' (Babbitt, 1955, p.57). 12-note sets that yield such aggregate and secondary set formations are called 'combinatorial'. (Further distinctions between various types of combinatorial sets are discussed in the same essay.) The nomenclature that Babbitt has introduced in his prose writings has become widely adopted and is the basis for much theoretical work and composition. Moreover, in his compositions he has demonstrated the efficacy of his theories. Thus Babbitt has extended the notion of compositional creativity to encompass the development of musical systems themselves, as well as specific compositional achievements within such systems. He has also persistently explored the relationships between set transformation and derivation procedures, and virtually all other aspects of musical structure, such as grouping and form, large- and small-scale rhythm, texture and register, instrumentation and timbre.

In 'Twelve-Tone Rhythmic Structure and the Electronic Medium' (1962) Babbitt demonstrates a number of methods for interpreting the structures of pitch class sets in the temporal domain. By positing an analogy between the octave (in pitch structure) and the bar (in rhythmic and metrical structure), and by dividing the bar into 12 equal units (each of which can be musically articulated by individual points of attack), Babbitt provides a basis for mapping pitch class sets onto 'time-point sets'. Thus an uninterpreted set of integers (for example, 0, 11, 6, 7, 5, 1, 10, 2, 9, 3, 4, 8) may be interpreted as a specific instance of a pitch class set (ex.1) or as a specific instance of a time-point set (ex.2). (The time-point of a particular

Ex.1

point of attack is a measure of its position within the bar.) In ex.2 the metrical unit is a demisemiquaver, a 12th of

Ex.2

the whole bar; time-point 0 therefore occurs on the first demisemiquaver of the bar, time-point 1 on the next, and so on. In this example the 12 available points of attack within a bar are ordered according to the numerical set given above.) Exx.1 and 2 each represent only one of the possible interpretations of the numerical set given above; pitch classes may be presented in various registers, just as time-points may be displaced to subsequent bars, as long as the same order of presentation (of pitches or points of articulation) is preserved. Furthermore, a time-point set and a pitch class set determined by the same set of integers may unfold at different speeds: in the first four bars of the second violin part of Babbitt's String Quartet no.3 (1969–70) the first six notes may be understood as a realization in terms of pitch of the first five integers in the set indicated above (ex.3). Also, the three *forte* markings in this passage

Ex.3

pitch-class set: 0 11 6   (6) 7 5

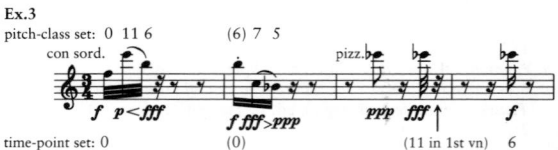

time-point set: 0   (0)   (11 in 1st vn) 6

articulate the time-points that correspond to the first and third entities of the same numerical set (time-point 0 is reiterated in bar 2 before the third time-point, 6, is articulated in bar 4). The second time-point of this set is presented in a different instrumental line, the last note of violin 1 in bar 3 (ex.4). Each of the eight dynamic gradations from *ppp* to *fff* inclusive is employed in the String Quartet no.3 to articulate a particular layer of the time-point structure, and each of these layers is analogous to one of eight layers of pitch class sets simultaneously presented in the work; the eight layers of pitch class sets are differentiated by distinctions of instrumentation, register and mode of sound production (for example, the use of pizzicato and arco) throughout the work. This brief discussion of a musical fragment may serve as an indication of the extraordinary richness of structural relationships that are projected in Babbitt's music.

An earlier example of Babbitt's approach may be seen in his *Three Compositions for Piano* (1947), one of his first consistent attempts to extend Schoenbergian 12-note

TABLE 1

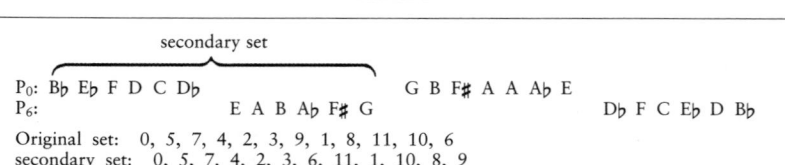

	secondary set	
P₀: B♭ E♭ F D C D♭		G B F♯ A A A♭ E
P₆:	E A B A♭ F♯ G	D♭ F C E♭ D B♭

Original set: 0, 5, 7, 4, 2, 3, 9, 1, 8, 11, 10, 6
secondary set: 0, 5, 7, 4, 2, 3, 6, 11, 1, 10, 8, 9
(B♭ = 0; adapted from *Three Compositions for Piano* no.1)

Ex.4 String Quartet no.3, bars 1–4

procedures. The surface of the music is, in some respects, reminiscent of Schoenberg: registrally dispersed lines alternate with thickly clustered chordal attacks (in the framework of a quasi-ternary structure), yet the absence of expressive indications and the reliance on metronome markings would seem to reveal a Stravinskian concern for a clear, undistracted projection of the temporal domain. Some of the innovative aspects of the work reside in the conjunction of the structuring of pitch and other domains, resulting in an early example of 'totally serialized' music. Points of articulation made by the superimposition of lines and the number of consecutive attacks within a contrapuntal line are determined by a set (whose prime form is 5, 1, 4, 2). In the first four bars of the work, this set is presented twice in its prime form (P), once in retrograde (R) and once in retrograde inversion (RI; ex.5). There is also a correspondence between dynamics and pitch set forms.

Babbitt's *Composition for Four Instruments* and *Composition for Twelve Instruments* (both of which were written in 1948) go a step further towards a structuring of rhythm isomorphic with 12-note pitch structuring. In the 12-instrument work a set of 12 durations emerges and operates throughout. It is transformed by 'classical' serial operations: transposition (addition of a constant to each duration number of the set), inversion (the complementation of the duration numbers), retrogression (the complementation of the order numbers of the set) and retrograde inversion. The ending of each of the three major sections of the work is articulated by the completion of a rhythmic set. The presentation of the rhythmic sets is often complex – various instruments characteristically participate in the presentation of a single rhythmic set, and more than one rhythmic set may be presented simultaneously. Nonetheless, the surface characteristics of the work delineate a simple process. Beginning with sparsely textured single events (which can be considered

an extension of Webern's sound world) and slowly becoming more compact (with regard to aggregate completions), the work concludes with thicker textures and sustained sonorities, unfolding newly shaped but familiar harmonic environments.

Babbitt has been profoundly involved in the clarification and extension of the systematic aspects of 12-note composition, but his music is in no sense rigidly determined by precompositional schemes. Within the constraints of serial techniques, he uses a great range of expressive possibilities and contextually varied structures. A work such as *Partitions* (1957) demonstrates numerous precompositional constraints (such as the projection of an all-interval set, a polyphonic texture in which distinct transformations of 12-note pitch sets are unfolded in each line and aggregates formed by various vertical partitionings of segments of these lines). In the first four bars a hexachord is presented in each of four different registers (ex.6). The hexachords in the lower two registers (E♭ A♭ F♯ F C♯ E; C G A B♭ D B) are complementary and are, respectively, the retrogrades of the hexachords presented in the higher two registers. There are 49 different ways in which the pitches presented in these hexachords might be partitioned to form aggregates. (For example, each hexachord might be divided 3 + 3; or the hexachords might be divided alternately 2 + 4 and 4 + 2 etc.) The actual partitioning of pitches (1 + 5 in the highest register, 3 + 3 in the next highest register, 5 + 1 in the next register, and 3 + 3 in the lowest register) contributes to a rich pattern of interval and pitch associations and echoes. Such partitioning establishes a specific rate of movement through the pitch class sets in each register and also suggests possibilities for hierarchical distinctions among the pitch classes that constitute the sets involved. Each registral line has its own rhythm of movement through its pitch class sets, and these characteristic rhythms are varied contextually throughout the work.

Ex.5 Three Compositions for Piano, no.1, bars 1–4

Ex.6 *Partitions*, bars 1–4

The commitment to systematic precompositional planning is maintained in works with dramatic, poetic or other associative aspects. In *Du* (1951), a song cycle for soprano and piano (which represented the USA at the 1953 ISCM Festival), there is continual interplay between the text and the vocal and piano lines. Phoneme, syllable, word and line are carefully contoured, subtly and imaginatively set to music: the pitch, durational, dynamic and registral schemata, themselves transformed from poem to poem, are allied with the verbal elements and indeed help to project the many delicate nuances of the text. These lyrical, imagist tendencies were most fully realized in *Philomel* (1964) but are also evident in *All Set* (1957), for small jazz ensemble, with its conjunction of 12-note structure (based on an all-combinatorial set) and what Babbitt calls 'jazz-like properties … the use of percussion, the Chicago jazz-like juxtapositions of solos and ensembles recalling certain characteristics of group improvisation'.

Babbitt took a novel serial approach to handling the sonic resources of a large orchestra in *Relata I* (1965). Here timbral 'families' are correlated with set structure, with woodwind instruments as four trios, brass as three quartets, and string instruments as two sextets (one bowed, the other plucked). The work is insistently polyphonic (with as many as 48 instrumental lines), framed at both ends by massive sonorities and filled with constantly changing and recombined textures and colours. While parts of the work are analogous to other parts, there is no simple repetition: all aspects undergo reinterpretation, rearrangement and 'resurfacing'. In the more timbrally homogeneous works of the late 1960s (*Sextets*, *Post-Partitions*, parts of *Correspondences*, the String Quartets nos.3 and 4), the handling of timbre and tone-colour seems even more refined. Sonorously embodied successions of relations are projected in ever varying contexts, producing changes of 'atmosphere' from the most rarefied to the most dense, with every conceivable gradation.

(ii) Electronic works. Another continuing concern of Babbitt's has been electronic sound synthesis. At the time of the first instrumental film soundtrack, in the late 1930s, he had already recognized the enormous compositional potential of such synthesis. Two decades later, in the mid-1950s, when he was invited by RCA to be a composer-consultant, he became the first composer to work with its newly improved and developed synthesizer, the Mark II (see illustration). *Composition for Synthesizer* (1961) was Babbitt's first totally synthesized work. It was followed soon after by *Vision and Prayer* for soprano and synthesizer (1961) and *Ensembles for Synthesizer* (1962–4). His basic compositional attitudes and approaches underwent little change with the new resource; rather,

Milton Babbitt programming the Mark II RCA synthesizer (built early 1950s) at the Columbia-Princeton Electronic Music Center, New York

with the availability and flexibility of the synthesizer's programming control they were now realizable to a degree of precision previously unattainable in live performances of his music. Babbitt's interest in synthesis was not concerned with the invention of new sounds *per se* but with the control of all aspects of events, particularly the timing and rate of change of timbre, texture and intensity. (His Woodwind Quartet (1953) and String Quartet no.2 (1954) had already given some indication of the rapidity of dynamic change he wished to achieve, on both single and consecutive pitches.) The electronic medium allowed him to project time-point sets however he liked, without regard to the demands made on live performers.

Though the lucidity of his conceptual world finally became manifest under the ideal performance conditions provided by sound synthesis, Babbitt nevertheless retained his interest in live performance, and carried over to it several structural procedures from the electronic medium. Perhaps the most appealing work combining live performance with tape is *Philomel*, written in conjunction with the poet John Hollander for the soprano Bethany Beardslee. It is based on Ovid's interpretation of the Greek legend of Philomela, the ravished, speechless maiden who is transformed into a nightingale. New ways of combining musical and verbal expressiveness were devised by composer and poet: music is as articulate as language; language (Philomela's thoughts) is transformed into music (the nightingale's song). The work is an almost inexhaustible repertory of speech-song similitudes and differentiations, and resonant word-music puns (unrealizable without the resources of the synthesizer).

(iii) Later serial developments. Since the 1970s Babbitt has been extraordinarily prolific. The fecundity of his compositional thought has been revealed in such diverse combinations as female chorus, double brass sextet, orchestra and tape, and guitar duo. He has continued to explore the potential, and refine the procedures of, 12-note composition, always discovering new ways of extending and interpreting principles of combinatoriality and correlating the various dimensions of his musical universe.

In works such as *Arie da capo* (1973–4), Babbitt incorporates 'weighted aggregates' – transformations (by inversion) of pitch class arrays (abstract, precompositional designs made up of combinatorially related rows) in which at least one pitch class appears more than once (see Babbitt, 1973–4). *Arie da capo* also employs an 'all-partition array' that systematically uses all the possible partitionings of the structural elements that comprise an aggregate (in this case, all the possible partitionings of 12-note sets into as many as six parts). All-partition arrays are found in much of Babbitt's music after 1960. Each of the sections of *Arie da capo* may be construed as an 'aria' for one of the five instruments; but the conception of the aria is reimagined so that 'the central instrument dominates less quantitatively than relationally, in that its music is the immediate source of, and is complemented and counterpointed by, the music of the "accompanying" instruments'. 'Da capo' repetitions of set forms recur throughout the arias, both on the musical surface and as non-consecutive pitches associated by register, articulation or instrumentation.

A Solo Requiem for soprano and two pianos (1976–7) is Babbitt's most extended composition for voice. This magisterial work (a memorial to the composer Godfrey Winham) incorporates a wide range of vocal techniques and reveals the extraordinary range and sensitivity of Babbitt's response to a variety of dramatic and lyrical poetic texts. In *My Complements to Roger* for solo piano (1978), Babbitt succinctly demonstrates a number of methods for associating pitch and rhythmic structures. The partitioning of metrical units and pitch class sets is correlated in each bar. Often in the piece the grouping of a string of pitches extracted from the abstract pitch class array is articulated on the musical surface by presenting the pitch string within a single beat, subdivided into the same number of parts as there are pitches in the string (see Mead, 1983).

Babbitt has continued to expand the 12-note universe. Since the 1980s he has explored the premise of the 'superarray', the combination of individual arrays to form larger and more intricate 12-note structures. These very large arrays of pitch class structure have inspired ever more inventive musical textures. For example, in *Transfigured Notes* for string orchestra (1986), Babbitt divides each of four instrumental groups (1st and 2nd violins, violas and cellos) into two sub-groups and then distinguishes between three separate registers in each group in order to articulate 24 distinct areas. These instrumental groupings are then recombined to project the structural counterpoint which comprises one interpretation of the abstract superarray.

The world that Babbitt's music evokes is not simple. He has said 'I want a piece of music to be literally as much as possible'. While some critics have felt that such an attitude has resulted in a body of inaccessible music, others have praised his pioneering approach, involving as it has a systematic and comprehensive exploration of the 12-note compositional universe. His emphasis on the relationship between practice and theory, his insistence on the composer's assumption of responsibility for every musical event in a work, and his reinterpretation of the constituent elements of the Western musical tradition have had a vital influence on the thinking and music of numerous younger composers.

WORKS
all published unless otherwise stated

INSTRUMENTAL

Orch: Generatrix, 1935, inc., withdrawn; Composition for Str Orch, 1940, withdrawn; Sym., 1941, inc., withdrawn; Into the Good Ground, film score, 1949, inc., withdrawn; Relata I, 1965; Relata II, 1968; Ars combinatoria, small orch, 1981; Conc. for Pf and Orch, 1985; Transfigured Notes, str orch, 1986; Conc. no.2, pf, orch, 1998

Chbr: Str Trio, 1941, withdrawn; Composition for 4 Insts, fl, cl, vn, vc, 1948; Composition for 12 Insts, wind qnt, tpt, hp, cel, str trio, db, 1948, rev. 1954; Str Qt no.1, 1948, withdrawn; Composition for Va and Pf, 1950; Ww Qt, 1953; Str Qt no.2, 1954; All Set, a sax, t sax, tpt, trbn, db, pf, vib, perc, 1957; Sextets, vn, pf, 1966; Str Qt no.3, 1969–70; Str Qt no.4, 1970; Arie da capo, fl, cl + b cl, pf, vn, vc, 1973–4; Paraphrases, fl, ob + eng hn, cl, b cl, bn, hn, tpt, trbn, tuba, pf, 1979

Dual, vc, pf, 1980; Str Qt no.5, 1982; Groupwise, pic + fl + a fl, vn, va, vc, pf, 1983; Four Play, cl, vn, vc, pf, 1984; The Joy of More Sextets, vn, pf, 1986; Fanfare, 4 hn, 4 tpt, 3 trbn, tuba, 1987; Souper, spkr, fl, cl, vn, vc, pf, 1987; Whirled Series, a sax, pf, 1987; The Crowded Air, fl, ob, cl, bn, pf, mar, gui, vn, va, vc, db, 1988; Consortini, fl, pf, vib, mar, vc, 1989; Soli e Duettini, 2 gui, 1989; Soli e Duettini, fl, gui, 1989; Soli e Duettini, vn, va, 1990

Counterparts, 2 tpt, hn, trbn, tuba, 1992; Septet, but Equal, 2 cl, cl + b cl, vn, va, vc, pf, 1992; Fanfare for All, 2 tpt, hn, trbn, tuba, 1993; Str Qt no.6, 1993; Accompanied Recitative, s sax, pf, 1994; Arrivals and Departures, 2 vn, 1994; Triad, cl, va, pf, 1994; Bicenquinquagenary Fanfare, 2 tpt, hn, trbn, tuba, 1995; Pf Qt,

1995; Qnt, cl, 2 vn, va, vc, 1996; When Shall We Three Meet Again?, fl, cl, vib, 1996

Pf: 3 Compositions for Pf, 1947; Duet, 1956; Semi-Simple Variations, 1956; Partitions, 1957; Post-Partitions, 1966; Tableaux, 1972; Minute Waltz (3/4 ± 1/8), 1977; Playing for Time, 1977; My Complements to Roger, 1978; About Time, 1982; Don, pf 4 hands, 1981; Canonical Form, 1983; Playing for Time, 1983; It Takes Twelve to Tango, 1984; Lagniappe, 1985; Overtime, 1987; In his Own Words, spkr, pf, 1988; Emblems (Ars Emblematica), 1989; Envoi, pf 4 hands, 1990; Preludes, Interludes and Postlude, 1991; Tutte le corde, 1994

Other solo inst: My Ends are my Beginnings, cl, 1978; Melismata, vn, 1982; Sheer Pluck (Composition for Gui), 1984; Homily, snare drum, 1987; Beaten Paths, mar, 1988; Play it Again Sam, va, 1989; None but the Lonely Flute, fl, 1991; Around the Horn, hn, 1993; Manifold Music, org, 1995

VOCAL

Dramatic: Fabulous Voyage (musical, R. Childs, R. Koch, Babbitt), 1946

Choral: Music for the Mass I, SATB, 1940, withdrawn; Music for the Mass II, SATB, 1941, withdrawn; 4 Canons, female chorus, 1968 [after Schoenberg]; More Phonemena, 12vv, 1978; An Elizabethan Sextette, female chorus 6vv, 1979; Glosses, boys' choir, 1988

Solo vocal: Three Theatrical Songs, 1v, pf, 1946 [from musical Fabulous Voyage]; The Widow's Lament in Springtime (W.C. Williams), S, pf, 1950; Du (Stramm), song cycle, S, pf, 1951; Vision and Prayer, S, pf, 1954, unpubd, unperf.; 2 Sonnets (G.M. Hopkins), Bar, cl, va, vc, 1955; Composition for Tenor and 6 Insts, T, fl, ob, vn, va, vc, hpd, 1960; Sounds and Words, S, pf, 1960

Phonemena, S, pf, 1969–70; A Solo Requiem (W. Shakespeare, Hopkins, G. Meredith, Stramm, J. Dryden), S, 2 pf, 1976–7; The Head of the Bed (J. Hollander), S, fl, cl, vn, vc, 1982; The Virginal Book, C, pf, 1988; 4 Cavalier Settings (R. Herrick, T. Carew), T, gui, 1991; Mehr 'Du' (Stramm), Mez, va, pf, 1991; Quatrains, S, 2 cl, 1993; No Longer Very Clear, S, fl, cl, vn, vc, 1994

WORKS WITH TAPE

Composition for Synthesizer, 4-track tape, 1961; Vision and Prayer (D. Thomas), S, 4-track tape, 1961; Ensembles for Synthesizer, 4-track tape, 1962–4; Philomel (Hollander), S, 4-track tape, 1964; Correspondences, str orch, tape, 1967; Occasional Variations, 4-track tape, 1971; Concerti, vn, small orch, tape, 1974–6; Phonemena, S, tape, 1975; Reflections, pf, tape, 1975; Images, sax, tape, 1979

recorded interviews in *US-NHoh*

Principal publishers: Associated, Boelke-Bomart, Peters

WRITINGS
for fuller list see Mead (1994)

The Function of Set Structure in the Twelve-Tone System (unpubd paper, 1946; diss., Princeton U., 1992)

'The String Quartets of Bartók', *MQ*, xxxv (1949), 377–85

'Some Aspects of Twelve-Tone Composition', *The Score*, no.12 (1955), 53–61

'Who Cares if You Listen?', *High Fidelity*, viii/2 (1958), 38–40; repr. in *The American Composer Speaks*, ed. G. Chase (Baton Rouge, LA, 1966), 234–44; repr. in *Contemporary Composers on Contemporary Music*, ed. E. Schwartz and B. Childs (New York, 1967), 243–50

'Electronic Music: the Revolution in Sound', *Columbia University Magazine* (1960), spr., 4–8; rev. as 'The Revolution in Sound: Electronic Music', *Music Journal*, xviii/7 (1965), 34–7

'Twelve-Tone Invariants as Compositional Determinants', *MQ*, xlvi (1960), 246–59; repr. in *Problems of Modern Music*, ed. P.H. Lang (New York, 1960), 108–21

'Past and Present Concepts of the Nature and Limits of Music', *IMSCR VIII: New York 1961*, 398–403; repr. in *Perspectives on Contemporary Music Theory*, ed. B. Boretz and E.T. Cone (New York, 1972), 3–9

'Set Structure as a Compositional Determinant', *JMT*, v (1961), 72–94; repr. in *Perspectives on Contemporary Music Theory*, ed. B. Boretz and E.T. Cone (New York, 1972), 129–47

'Twelve-Tone Rhythmic Structure and the Electronic Medium', *PNM*, i/1 (1962), 49–79; repr. in *Perspectives on Contemporary Music Theory*, ed. B. Boretz and E.T. Cone (New York, 1972), 148–79

'Remarks on the Recent Stravinsky', *PNM*, ii/2 (1963–4), 35–55; repr. in *Perspectives on Schoenberg and Stravinsky*, ed. B. Boretz and E.T. Cone (Princeton, NJ, 1968, 2/1972/R), 165–85

'An Introduction to the RCA Synthesizer', *JMT*, viii (1964), 251–65

'The Synthesis, Perception and Specification of Musical Time', *JIFMC*, xvi (1964), 92–5

'The Use of Computers in Musicological Research', *PNM*, iii/2 (1964–5), 74–83

'The Structure and Functions of Music Theory I', *College Music Symposium*, v (1965), 49–60; repr. in *Perspectives on Contemporary Music Theory*, ed. B. Boretz and E.T. Cone (New York, 1972), 10–21

'Edgard Varèse: a Few Observations of his Music', *PNM*, iv/2 (1965–6), 14–22; repr. in *Perspectives on American Composers*, ed. B. Boretz and E.T. Cone (New York, 1971), 40–48

'Three Essays on Schoenberg', *Perspectives on Schoenberg and Stravinsky*, ed. B. Boretz and E.T. Cone (Princeton, NJ,1968, 2/1972/R), 47–60

'Relata I', *The Orchestral Composer's Point of View*, ed. R.S. Hines (Norman, OK, 1970), 11–38; repr. as 'On Relata I', *PNM*, ix/1 (1970–71), 1–22

'Contemporary Music Composition and Music Theory as Contemporary Intellectual History', *Perspectives in Musicology*, ed. B.S. Brook, E.O.D. Downes and S.J. Van Solkema (New York,1972), 151–84

'Since Schoenberg', *PNM*, xii/1–2 (1973–4), 3–28

'Responses: a First Approximation',*PNM*, xiv/2 (1975–6), 3–23

'The Next Thirty Years', *High Fidelity/Musical America*, xxxi/4 (1981), 51–66

Words about Music, ed. S. Dembski and J.N. Straus (Madison, WI, 1987)

'Stravinsky's Verticals and (Schoenberg's) Diagonals: a Twist of Fate', *Stravinsky Retrospectives*, ed. E. Haimo and P. Johnson (Lincoln, NE, 1988), 15–35

'On Having Been and Still Being an American Composer', *PNM*, xxvii/1 (1989), 106–12

with others: 'Brave New Worlds: Leading Composers Offer their Anniversary Predications and Speculations', *MT*, cxxxv (1994), 330–37

BIBLIOGRAPHY

VintonD (B. Boretz)

'Babbitt, Milton', *CBY 1962*

G. Perle: *Serial Composition and Atonality* (Berkeley, CA, 1962, 6/1991)

R. French: 'Current Chronicle: New York', *MQ*, l (1964), 382–8 [on Philomel]

P. Westergaard: 'Some Problems Raised by the Rhythmic Procedures in Milton Babbitt's *Composition for Twelve Instruments*', *PNM*, iv/1 (1965), 109–18

E. Barkin: 'A Simple Approach to Milton Babbitt's "Semi-Simple Variations"', *MR*, xxviii (1967), 316–22

J. Hollander: 'Notes on the Text of *Philomel*', *PNM*, vi/1 (1967), 134–41

R. Kostelanetz: 'The Two Extremes of Avant-Garde Music', *New York Times Magazine*(15 Jan 1967)

E. Salzman: 'Babbitt and Serialism', *Twentieth-Century Music: an Introduction* (Englewood Cliffs, NJ, 1967, 3/1988), 154–5, 158

'An Interview with Milton Babbitt', *Music Educators Journal*, lv/3 (1968–9), 56 only

S. Arnold and G. Hair: 'Champion of Serialism', *Music and Musicians*, xvii/10 (1969), 46–7

H.W. Hitchcock: 'Systematic Serial Composition', *Music in the United States* (Englewood Cliffs, NJ, 1969, 3/1988), 252–9

P. Lieberson, E. Lundborg and J. Peel: 'Conversation with Milton Babbitt', *Contemporary Music Newsletter*, viii (1974), no.1, pp.2–3; no.2, pp.2–3; no.3, pp.2–4

J. Peel: 'Milton Babbitt: String Quartet no.3', *Contemporary Music Newsletter*, viii/1 (1974), 1–2

PNM, xiv/2–xv/1 (1976) [double issue, 3–23]

B. Benward: 'The Widow's Lament in Springtime', *Music in Theory and Practice*, ii (Dubuque, IA, 1977, 2/1981), 483–96

R. Gauldin: 'A Pedagogical Introduction to Set Theory', *Theory and Practice*, iii/2 (1978), 3–14

H. Wilcox and P. Escot: 'A Musical Set Theory', *Theory and Practice*, iv/2 (1979), 17–37

M. Capalbo: 'Charts', *PNM*, xix/1–2 (1981–2), 310–31

C. Gagne and T. Caras: 'Milton Babbitt', *Soundpieces: Interviews with American Composers* (Metuchen, NJ, 1982), 35–52

A. Mead: 'Detail and the Array in Milton Babbitt's *My Complements to Roger*', *Music Theory Spectrum*, v (1983), 89–109

J. Rockwell: 'The Northeastern Academic Establishment and the Romance of Science', *All American Music: Composition in the Late Twentieth Century* (New York, 1983), 25–36

A. Mead: 'Recent Developments in the Music of Milton Babbitt', *MQ*, lxx (1984), 310–31

P. Lieberson: *Milton Babbitt's 'Post-Partitions'* (diss., Brandeis U., 1985)

P. Swartz: 'Milton Babbitt on Milton Babbitt (Interview with the Composer)', *American Music*, iii/4 (1985), 467–73

S. Blaustein and M.Brody: 'Criteria for Grouping in Milton Babbitt's *Minute Waltz (or) 3/4 ± 1/8*', *PNM*, xxiv/2 (1986), 30–79

W. Lake: 'The Architecture of a Superarray Composition: Milton Babbitt's String Quartet no.5', *PNM*, xxiv/2 (1986), 88–111

J.N. Straus: 'Listening to Babbitt', *PNM*, xxiv/2 (1986), 10–24

R. Taub: 'An Appreciation of Milton Babbitt's Piano Music', *PNM*, xxiv/2 (1986), 26–9

A. Mead: 'About *About Time*'s Time: a Survey of Milton Babbitt's Recent Rhythmic Practice', *PNM*, xxv/1–2 (1987), 182–235

J. Peel and C. Cramer: 'Correspondences and Associations in Milton Babbitt's *Reflections*', *PNM*, xxvi/1 (1988), 144–207

J. Dubiel: 'Three Essays on Milton Babbitt', *PNM*, xxviii/2 (1990), 216–61; *PNM*, xxix/1 (1991), 90–123; *PNM*, xxx/1 (1992), 82–131

A. Mead: *An Introduction to the Music of Milton Babbitt* (Princeton, NJ, 1994) [incl. further bibliography]

M. Brody: '"Music for the Masses": Milton Babbitt's Cold War Music Theory', *MQ*, lxxvii/2 (1993), 161–92

D. Lewin: 'Generalized Interval Systems for Babbitt's Lists and for Schoenberg's String Trio', *Music Theory Spectrum*, xvii/1 (1995), 81–118

Milton Babbitt, videotaped interview, Brandeis University Archive of Electro-Acoustic Music (1997)

Babbitt: Portrait of a Serial Composer, documentary film, dir. R. Hilferty (1998)

ELAINE BARKIN/MARTIN BRODY

Babcock, Alpheus (*b* Dorchester, MA, 11 Sept 1785; *d* Boston, 3 April 1842). American piano maker. He began his career as an apprentice to BENJAMIN CREHORE, as did his brother Lewis (*b* 13 Feb 1779; *d* Milton, MA, 14 Jan 1814); the brothers had their own firm from 1809 to 1811. Alpheus Babcock worked for, supplied pianos for, or was a partner in the following firms: Babcock, Appleton & Babcock (Boston, 1811–14); Hayts, Babcock & Appleton (Boston, 1814–15); J.A. Dickson (Boston); Christopher Hall (Norfolk, Virginia); John, Ruth and G.D. MACKAY (Boston, 1822–9); J.G. Klemm (Philadelphia, 1830–32); William Swift (Philadelphia, 1832–7); and Chickering (Boston, 1837–42). His most significant contribution to the evolution of the piano was his invention of a one-piece cast-iron frame including hitch-pin plate, for which he received a patent on 17 December 1825. This invention is regarded as the basis for subsequent piano frame development. His patents for 'cross-stringing' (24 May 1830), improved action (31 December 1833), and improvement in the jack or 'grasshopper' (31 October 1839) were not of lasting importance. Many historians erroneously credit Babcock with having invented or advocated the overstrung scale. This conclusion undoubtedly results from the equation of overstringing with cross-stringing. Babcock's 'cross-stringing' patent concerns itself with unison double-strung piano strings (formed from a single wire which crosses over itself when looped over either hitch-pin or hook), not with bass strings running diagonally above the others. Babcock's instruments were acclaimed for their superb craftsmanship, and all known examples are of the square variety, patterned after English pianos of the period with a range of either five and a half or six octaves (F′ to c″″ or F′ to f″″). Recent research has shown that stamped numerals on his pianos from the 1820s are probably cumulative serial numbers. Representative instruments are at the Smithsonian Institution, Washington DC (*see* PIANOFORTE, fig.27), Yale University, New Haven, and the Museum of Fine Arts, Boston.

BIBLIOGRAPHY

D. Spillane: *History of the American Pianoforte* (New York, 1890/ R1969, with a new introduction by Rita Benton)

C.M. Ayars: *Contributions to the Art of Music in America by the Music Industries of Boston, 1640 to 1936* (New York, 1937/R)

H.E. Johnson: *Musical Interludes in Boston, 1795–1830* (New York, 1943/R)

K.G. Grafing: *Alpheus Babcock, American Pianoforte Maker (1785–1842): his Life, Instruments, and Patents* (DMA diss., U. of Missouri, Kansas City, 1972)

K.G. Grafing: 'Alpheus Babcock's Cast-Iron Piano Frames', *GSJ*, xxvii (1974), 118–24

KEITH G. GRAFING/DARCY KURONEN

Babell [Babel], **William** (*b* ?London, *c*1690; *d* Islington, London, 23 Sept 1723). English harpsichordist, organist, violinist, composer and arranger. He received his early musical instruction from his father, Charles Babel, a bassoonist in the Drury Lane Theatre orchestra until he was 80, and later from Pepusch and possibly Handel (according to Mattheson, in *Der vollkommene Capell-meister*, 1739, but denied by Hawkins). Babell led an active professional life in London. As a violinist he was said to have played in the private band of George I, while as a harpsichordist, from about 1711, his name frequently appears in London concert notices, usually in conjunction with those of Corbett, Paisible and (later) Dubourg. He was also associated with Lincoln's Inn Fields Theatre. From November 1718 until his death he was organist of All Hallows Bread Street and was succeeded there by John Stanley. Babell was buried at All Hallows.

He acquired an international reputation as a harpsichordist largely through his virtuoso arrangements of fashionable operatic arias and overtures, especially those of Handel. His keyboard style was undoubtedly influenced by his close acquaintance with Handel's playing; it has been proposed that one of the manuscript settings of 'Vo' far guerra' (*GB-Lbl*) is Babell's response to a reworking and development of the material by Handel himself (Pont), but this hypothesis has found no support. These arrangements by Babell, although appearing exceptional, nevertheless give an intriguing insight into early 18th-century practices of keyboard extemporization and ornamentation. Burney commented that Babell:

acquired great celebrity by wire-drawing the favourite songs of the opera of Rinaldo, and others of the same period, into *showy* and brilliant lessons, which by mere rapidity of finger in playing single sounds, without the assistance of taste, expression, harmony or modulation, enabled the performer to astonish ignorance, and acquire the reputation of a great player at a small expence . . . Mr Babel . . . at once gratifies idleness and vanity.

Hawkins, on the other hand, considered that Babell deserved his success; he remarked that Babell's arrangement of favourite arias from Handel's *Rinaldo* 'succeeded so well . . . as to make from it a book of lessons which few could play but himself, and which has long been deservedly celebrated'. Babell's reputation reached France, the Netherlands and Germany, where some of his works were published; Mattheson reported that he was said to have surpassed even Handel as an organist.

The slow movements of Babell's own chamber sonatas, published posthumously, and 'With proper Graces adapted to each Adagio by ye Author', illustrate his approach to non-keyboard-designated ornamentation (ex.1), and offer useful comparative insights. In his preface to the original edition, Walsh described Babell as his 'late lov'd friend' and remarked that 'When the World is so unfortunate [as] to lose and esteem'd Author, the only Consolation we have, is the enjoyment of his Works'. He asked owners of Babell's manuscripts to present them for publication to perpetuate 'that Beautifull and lasting Monument which his genius rais'd to him in his works'. Tilmouth (in the introduction to his edition of the sonatas

Ex.1 Sonata No.2, 3rd movt. (12 solos for a violin, hoboy or German flute, part 2)

in G minor and F minor, London, 1963) wrote that 'many of the sonatas seem best suited to the oboe, an instrument that at the time was played expertly only by a handful of professionals', and suggested that this would have prompted Walsh to prescribe other suitable instruments on the title-pages.

Babell's Concertos in 7 Parts for violins and small flute, or 'sixth' flute (a soprano recorder in D), were also published posthumously (c1726); four are for one sixth flute, one for two sixth flutes and one for two trebles. The string parts exclude viola, but require a solo violin. Although Handelian influence is apparent in these works, Italian inspiration is stronger, particularly that of Vivaldi, both with regard to style and execution. The title-page records that the concertos were 'performed at the theatre with great applause', and several were probably known for a decade or so before they were eventually published. At least one of them was written by December 1714, when the sale catalogue of Thomas Britton's collection included '12 Concertos by Dr Pepusch, young Mr Babel and Vivaldi'.

WORKS
printed; including arrangements; published in London unless otherwise stated

The 3rd Book of the Ladys Entertainment, or Banquet of Musick, hpd/spinet (1709) [arrs. of N.F. Haym (after A. Scarlatti): Pyrrhus and Demetrius (op); Clotilda (pasticcio)]
Marianna's charms wound my heart: a New Song for the Spinnet (c1710)
The 4th Book of the Ladys Entertainment, hpd/spinet (1716) [arrs. of F. Mancini: Hydaspe fedele (op); Almahide (pasticcio)]
Suits of the Most Celebrated Lessons, hpd/spinet (1717) [incl. arrs. of arias in G.F. Handel: Il pastor fido, Rinaldo, Teseo (all ops); G. Bononcini: Etearco (op); Almahide, Antioco, Creso (all pasticcios); arr. in 4 sets, each with prelude by Babell, last set incl. 2 arias by Babell with variations]; as Suits of Harpsichord and Spinnet Lessons (c1718); partly repr. as Pièces de clavecin de Mr Händel, op.8 (Paris, c1745)
The Harpsichord Master Improved . . . with a Choice Collection of Newest and Most Air'y Lessons (1718), incl. 2 items from Suits of the Most Celebrated Lessons

Rigadoon, a (melody only), 6 Dances Composed By Mr. Kellom Tomlinson (1720)
Trios de dieferents autheurs choises & mis en ordre par Mr Babel, livre 1e [2e] (Amsterdam, c1720), probably all arrs.
Would you I the thing discover (L. Theobald), song, in 'Tis well if it takes (play) (c1720)
XII Solos . . . with Proper Graces Adapted to Each Adagio, bk 1, vn/ob, hpd (c1725)
XII Solos . . . with Proper Graces Adapted to Each Adagio, bk 2, vn/ob/fl, hpd (c1725)
Babell's [6] Concertos in 7 Parts, vns, 1/2 fl, op.3 (c1726)
The Milk Maid, song (c1730)
The Musical Pocket Book Containing an Extraordinary Collection of the Newest & Best Lessons of English & Italian Aires . . . Also Some of the Most Celebrated Song Tunes with their Symphonys taken out of the Choicest Operas (c1735), probably incl. reprs. of earlier pieces/arrs.

MSS; including arrangements; all for keyboard solo

5 preludes, G, e, a, d, G, minuet, G, 1714–17, GB-BENcoke*
Lesson (also as Air), E, BENcoke
2 pieces, G, 1 c1714, BENcoke, Lbl*, probably by Babell
Prelude, D, c1714, Lbl*, probably by Babell
Arrs. of arias in Handel: Teseo (op); Clotilda (pasticcio); ov. in Handel: Rinaldo (op); A. Corelli: Sonata, op.5 no.9; Handel: Allegro, d, HWV495b, c1714, Lbl*, probably by Babell
4 versions of the arr. of the aria Vo' far guerra in Handel: Rinaldo (pubd version in Suits, 1717), Ge, Lbl* (c1714), WCr, US-NYp
Arrs. of arias in G.F. Handel: Il pastor fido (op); G. Bononcini: Il trionfo di Camilla (op); Antioco, Arminio, Clotilda, Ernelinda, Thomyris (all pasticcios), 1714-17, GB-BENcoke*
Lost: music for St Cecilia's Day, c1718; conc., ? formerly D-Hs

BIBLIOGRAPHY
BurneyH; HawkinsH

S. Sadie: *British Chamber Music, 1720–1790* (diss., U. of Cambridge, 1958), 161–2
M. Tilmouth: 'A Calendar of References to Music in Newspapers Published in London and the Provinces, 1660–1719', *RMARC*, i (1961), 1–107
A.J.B. Hutchings: *The Baroque Concerto* (London, 1961, 3/1973)
F. Palmer: 'William Babell's Twenty-Four Oboe Sonatas' *Double Reed*, iv/2 (1981), 23 only
D. Dawe: *Organists of the City of London 1666–1850* (Padstow, 1983) [incl. summary of Babell's will]
D. Lasocki: *Professional Recorder Players in England 1540–1740* (diss., U. of Iowa, 1983)
B. Gustafson: 'The Legacy in Instrumental Music of Charles Babel, Prolific Transcriber of Lully's Music', *Jean-Baptiste Lully: Saint-Germain-en-Laye and Heidelberg 1987*, 495–516
J. Harley: *British Harpsichord Music* i: *Sources* (Aldershot, 1992); ii: *History*(Aldershot, 1994)
J.M. Thomson, ed.: *The Cambridge Companion to the Recorder* (Cambridge, 1995)
G. Pont: 'An Early 18th-Century Manuscript of Harpsichord Music: William Babell and Handel's Vo' far guerra', *British Library Journal*, xxi (1996), 176–83

GERALD GIFFORD (with TERENCE BEST)

Babin, Victor (*b* Moscow, 30 Nov/13 Dec 1908; *d* Cleveland, OH, 1 March 1972). American pianist and composer of Russian birth. He studied at Riga, in 1928 moving to Berlin for composition with Franz Schreker and the piano with Schnabel at the Hochschule für Musik. In 1933 he married another of Schnabel's pupils, Vitya (Victoria) Vronsky (1909–92), and his career as a player thereafter was almost exclusively that of a duo-pianist with his wife. Vronsky and Babin quickly established themselves in Europe, then moved to the USA in 1937. Babin taught at the Aspen Music School (where he was director, 1951–4, and member of the Festival Quartet along with Szymon Goldberg, William Primrose and Nikolay Graudan), at the Berkshire Music Center, Tanglewood, at the Cleveland Institute of Music (where he was director from 1961 until his death), and at Case Western Reserve University, also in Cleveland. His compositions, in a conservative, post-Romantic language, include two concertos for two pianos and orchestra, other compositions for one and two pianos, chamber music, and many songs, including a cycle, *Beloved Stranger*, on texts by Witter Bynner.

MICHAEL STEINBERG/R

Babitz, Sol (*b* Brooklyn, NY, 11 Oct 1911; *d* Los Angeles, 18 Feb 1982). American musicologist and violinist. He was largely self-taught after leaving high school. His violin teachers included Carl Flesch and Marcel Chailley; his interest in performing practice was aroused by the writings of Arnold Dolmetsch and encouraged by Igor Stravinsky, whose string parts Babitz edited for many years. From 1933 to 1937 he was a violinist with the Los Angeles PO, then, until 1952, he played with Hollywood studio orchestras. From 1941 to 1962 he was an editor for *International Musician*. In 1948 he was a co-founder of the Early Music Laboratory, an organization which promotes historical accuracy in performance through the publication of bulletins and demonstration tape recordings. Babitz was concerned with a number of aspects of performance which he believed contribute to an accurate 17th- and 18th-century style. These aspects include clear articulation, use of metric accents, rhythmic freedom within the beat and a lighter tone. He also worked for the modernization of violin fingering to facilitate the performance of works by such contemporary composers as Schoenberg and Stravinsky.

WRITINGS

Dance Writing: Preliminary Outline of a Practical System of Movement Notation (Los Angeles, 1939)
'Stravinsky's Symphony in C (1940)', *MQ*, xxvii (1941), 20–25
Principles of Extensions in Violin Fingering (Philadelphia, 1947, enlarged 2/1974 as *Violin Fingering*)
'A Problem of Rhythm in Baroque Music', *MQ*, xxxviii (1952), 533–65
The Violin: Views and Reviews (Urbana, IL, 1955, 3/1980)
'Differences between 18th-Century and Modern Violin Bowing', *The Score*, no.19 (1957), 34–40
ed. and trans.: G. Tartini: *Treatise on the Ornaments of Music* (New York, 1959; practical edn, 1970)
'On Using J.S. Bach's Keyboard Fingerings', *ML*, xliii (1962), 123–8
'Identifying the Renaissance, Baroque and Transition Violins', *The Strad*, lxxvi (1965–6), 9–13
'Notes Inégales: a Communication', *JAMS*, xx (1967), 473–6
'Modern Errors in Mozart Performance', *MJb* 1967, 62–5
'Concerning the Length of Time that Every Note must be Held', *MR*, xxviii (1967), 21–37
'On Using Early Keyboard Fingering', *The Diapason*, lx (1968–9), no.3, pp.15–28; no.4, pp.21–6; no.5, pp.21–4; enlarged, pubd separately, Los Angeles, 1969
The Great Baroque Hoax: a Guide to Baroque Performance for Musicians and Connoisseurs (Los Angeles, 1970, 3/1972)
Commentary on EML Tape-Recording 2 (Los Angeles, 1971)
with G. Pont: *Vocal De-Wagnerization and Other Matters* (Los Angeles, 1973)
Rhythmic Freedom: a Historical Table in the Light of Wind-Instrument Tonguing (Los Angeles, 1975)
Note-Separation in Musical Performance, and Other Matters (Los Angeles, 1976)
How to Restore the Viols and Violins of the Renaissance and Baroque Eras (Los Angeles, 1977)

PAULA MORGAN

Babou, Thomas (*b* Liège, 12 Feb 1656; *d* Liège, *c*1740). French organist and composer. He was organist of the collegiate church of St Jean l'Evangéliste in Liège at least from 1687 to 1704 (the registers preceding and following these dates are missing); from 1703 he was assisted by a young organist, Jean Buston (*d* 1731). The Babou recorded as organist in the accounts from 1726 to 1767 is his son

Jean-François-Pascal (*b* Liège, 10 April 1700; *d* Liège, 13 May 1767), who was a notary from 1726 and secretary to the chapter of St Jean from 1742; he was probably the copyist of a *Livre d'orgue* at the Liège Conservatory containing several pieces attributed to 'Mr. Babou', dated 1709 and 1710, which must be by his father. The pieces (ed. P. Froidebise, Schola Cantorum, Paris, 1959) are in a lively and brilliant italianate manner with little counterpoint, and show the introduction of a secular style into church music.

BIBLIOGRAPHY

AudaM
G. Hansotte: 'Le personnel musical de la collégiale Saint-Jean au XVIIIe siècle', *Leodium*, xxxvi/7–12 (1949), 27–9
J. Quitin: 'Jean Buston et les Babou, organistes de Saint-Jean l'Evangéliste, à Liège', *Bulletin de la Société liégeoise de musicologie*, no.2 (1973)
J. Quitin: *Les musiciens de Saint-Jean l'Evangéliste à Liège de Johannes Ciconia à Monsieur Babou* (Liège, 1982)

JOSÉ QUITIN

Babylonia. *See* MESOPOTAMIA.

Bacarisse (Chinoria), Salvador (*b* Madrid, 12 Sept 1898; *d* Paris, 5 Aug 1963). Spanish composer. Until the outbreak of the Spanish Civil War in 1936, he lived in Madrid where he studied law and philosophy at the university, and music at the Real Conservatorio de Música; his teachers included Manuel Fernández Alberdi (piano) and Conrado del Campo (composition), among others. He was a leading member of the Grupo de los Ocho, whose efforts to combat musical conservatism coincided with the period in which the Second Republic flourished (1931–6). Between 1931 and 1934 he acted as music critic for the republican daily papers *Crisol* and *Luz*. As artistic director of Unión Radio, until the Madrid broadcasting station was closed in 1936, he promoted the performance of contemporary Spanish music both at home and abroad. He also served as a member of the Junta Nacional de Música y Teatros Líricos (founded in 1931) and as deputy chair of the Consejo Central de Música (after 1937), which founded the National Orchestra in 1938. After being appointed to direct the Gran Teatro del Liceo, Barcelona, for the 1938–9 season, he went into exile in Paris (February 1939), escaping reprisals at the end of the Civil War for his republican opinions and his signature on an anti-fascist manifesto published in 1936. From 1945 until his death he worked at RTF as an editor of Spanish-language programmes. His honours include three National Music Prizes (1923, 1931, 1934), RTF's chamber opera prize (1958) and the Jean Vigo Prize (1958).

Bacarisse's works composed in Spain can be assigned to two distinct style periods. The first (1919–23) is notable for its impressionistic, sound-oriented and non-functional compositional technique (*Dos nocturnos*, 1919; *La nave de Ulises*, 1922–3; *Heraldos*, 1923). The second, introduced by *Ofrenda a Debussy* (1926–7), is marked by neoclassical techniques; a transformation of impressionistic methods can be observed in *Tres marchas burlescas* (1928), *La tragedia de doña Ajada* (1929) and Concertino (1929), which resulted in a simplification of the complex harmonic structures characteristic of earlier works. A tendency towards musical parody created by mechanization and deformation (a prominent feature of the music of the Generación de la República to which Grupo de los Ocho belongs) can be perceived in these transitional compositions. Gradually he developed a polyphonic style common to later compositions such as *Tres movimientos concertantes* (1934), in which he used serial techniques for the first time.

Bacarisse's compositional style remained largely unchanged in exile, although a formalization of techniques can be traced back to the moderate neo-classicism of the *Música sinfónica* (1931). Two tendencies can be distinguished: a 'humane' nature, expressed in the adoption of neo-romanticism (Concertino, 1952; *Concierto romántico*, 1954–5) and folk elements (*Fantasía andaluza*, 1948, rev. 1959); and a simplified musical language, 'dehumanized' by an extreme use of mechanical methods (*17 variaciones sobre cinco notas*, 1962). At the same time, an extremely complex style, originating in late neo-classicism and in his own early impressionistic works, emerged in his later operas and songs.

WORKS
(selective list)
for fuller list see Heine (1990)

Dramatic: La tragedia de doña Ajada (M. Abril), 1929, Madrid, 1929; Corrida de feria (ballet, M. Bacarisse), 1930, Barcelona, 1938, orch suite, 1930; Charlot (op, 3, R. Gómez de la Serna), 1932–3; El estudiante de Salamanca (op, 1, E. Enderiz), 1944, radio broadcast, Monte Carlo, 1956; La fausse tante, ou L'amour à Salamanque (ballet, S. Bacarisse), 1949; La sangre de Antígona (op, 3, J. Bergamín, after Sophocles), 1955; Font-aux-cabres (op, 3, J. Camp and J. Cassou, after L. de Vega), 1956, radio broadcast, Paris, 1962; Le trésor de Boabdil (chbr op, 1, A. Camp and F. Puig-Espert), 1958, radio broadcast, Paris, 1958; El retablo de la libertad de Melisendra (incid music, J. Palau, after M. de Cervantes), 1960, Paris, 1960; film scores

Orch: Heraldos, 1923; 3 marchas burlescas, 1928; Concertino, 1929; Música sinfónica, 1931; Pf Conc. no.1, C, 1933, rev. 1945; Impromptu sobre el nombre ARBOS, 1934; 3 movimientos concertantes, str trio, orch, 1934; Balada, pf, orch, 1935; Vc Conc., a, 1935; Fantasía, D, vn, orch, 1937; Pf Conc. no.2, G, 1940; Fantasía andaluza, hp, orch, 1948, rev. 1959; Concertino, a, gui, orch, 1952; Pf Conc. no.3, B, 1952; Pf Conc. no.4, D, 1953; Concertino, pf/hp, orch, 1954; Concierto romántico, G, 2 pf, orch, 1954–5; Hp Conc., 1958; Fantaisie concertante, 2 pf, orch, 1960; Capriccio Concertante, 2 hp, orch, 1961; Clvd Conc., 1961; see also DRAMATIC [La tragedia de doña Ajada, 1929; Corrida de feria, 1930]

Vocal: 2 nocturnos (V. Espinós), T, orch, 1919; La nave de Ulises, SA, orch, 1922–3; Ofrenda a Debussy (F. Villaespesa, J. Ramón Jiménez), 1v, pf, 1926–7; Cantata sinfónica, SATB, orch, 1941; El caballero de Olmedo (de Vega), Bar, SMezATBarB, 1949; Romance de la infanta de Francia, S, T, SATB, 1949; Cantata por la paz y la alegría de los pueblos (R. Alberti), solo vv, SATB, orch, 1950; Mimi Pinson (A. de Muset), SATB, 1950; Amor, no me dexes (J. Alvarez Gato), SATB/(4 S, 2 Mez, 2 A), 1951; Ojos claros, serenos (G. de Cetina), SATB, 1951; Cantata para celebrar el año nuevo (A. Sánchez Rebollo), S, Mez, Bar, orch, 1953; many songs

Chbr and solo inst: Danza de las brujas, vn, pf, 1929; Marcha fúnebre, vn, pf, 1929; Str Qt no.1, 1930; Str Qt no.2, 1932; Berceuse, vn, pf, 1936; Str Qt no.3, 1936; Adagio, vn/vc, pf, 1950; Petite suite, gui, 1950; Romanza, gui, 1953; Balada, gui, 1953; Partita, hp, 1953; Suite impromptu, 4 trbn, 1954; Introducción variaciones y coda, vn/vc, pf, 1956; Para dormir a Estela, hp, 1957; Triptique, vn, vc, hp, 1957; Sonatina, accdn, 1958; Petite suite, gui, 1960; Fantaisie en duo, fl, hp, 1961; Chant de l'orseau-qui-n'existe-pas, 2 fl, 1962; Toccata, vc, pf, 1962

Pf: Heraldos, 1923; Danza de las brujas, 1929; Toccata, 1929; 7 variaciones sobre un tema de las canciones del marqués de Santillana, 1935; Berceuse, 1936; 24 preludios, 1941; Pasodoble, 1943; Preludio, fugueta y rondó, 1950; Tema y variaciones, 1951; Carnaval parisien, 1958; Feuille d'album, 1960; Hommage funèbre, 1960; 17 variaciones sobre cinco notas, 1962

MSS in Fundación Juan March, Madrid

Principal publishers: Consejo Central de Música, Unión Musical Franco-Espagnole, Unión Musical Española, Ediciones Armonices, Schott

BIBLIOGRAPHY
E. Casal Chapí: 'Salvador Bacarisse', *Música*, no.2 (1938), 27–56
C. Heine: *Catálogo de obras de Salvador Bacarisse* (Madrid, 1990)
C. Heine: *Salvador Bacarisse (1898–1963): Die Kriterien seines Stils während der Schaffenszeit in Spanien (bis 1939)* (Frankfurt, 1993)
C. Heine: 'Salvador Bacarisse: su obra de 1926 a 1930: del impresionismo al neoclasicismo', *Nassarre: revista aragonesa de musicología*, xiv (1998), 119–71
C. Heine: 'Salvador Bacarisse (1898–1963) en el centenario de su nacimiento', *Cuadernos de música iberoamericana*, v (1998), 34–75
CHRISTIANE HEINE

Baccaloni, Salvatore (*b* Rome, 14 April 1900; *d* New York, 31 Dec 1969). Italian bass. He studied with Giuseppe Kaschmann and made his début at the Teatro Adriano, Rome, in 1922 as Dr Bartolo. In 1926 he was engaged at La Scala, where he sang regularly until 1940, first in serious roles and then, on Toscanini's advice, specializing in roles like Dulcamara, the two Bartolos and the *buffo* roles in Wolf-Ferrari's operas. During this period he contributed significantly to several complete opera recordings by the La Scala company. He appeared at Covent Garden (1928–9) and at Glyndebourne (1936–9), where his Leporello, Dr Bartolo and especially Don Pasquale set a standard of excellence. He made his North American début in Chicago in 1930 as Melitone and sang at the Teatro Colón (1931–41, 1947). In 1940 he joined the Metropolitan, and sang there regularly until 1962, giving 297 performances, mostly in the Italian *buffo* repertory. He sang Falstaff at San Francisco (1944) and made numerous tours of the USA. Portly in build and good-humoured, Baccaloni had a communicative gift for comedy and was noted for his musicianship; in his early years he displayed a rare vocal quality in his *buffo* roles. (*GV*, R. Celletti; R. Vegeto)

FRANCIS D. PERKINS/ALAN BLYTH

Baccelli, Matteo Pantaleone [Papia Leone] (*b* Lucca, 1690; *d* Lucca, *c*1766). Italian composer. He was a priest, and although he was probably *maestro di musica* at the Seminary of S Giovanni e Reparata in Lucca by 1712, the first certain notice of him there is in 1725, when the seminarians participated in some of the most ambitious music in the city. Between 1717 and 1759 the Lucca confraternity of S Cecilia performed Baccelli's music (for first and second Vespers and Mass, with orchestral accompaniment) on nine different celebrations of the saint's feast; and each year he directed the Requiem Mass for dead members. He was further honoured by election to the society's governing committee (together with Giacomo Puccini) in 1754. In 1756 his oratorio *La concezione* was presented by the Congregazione degli Angeli Custodi, Lucca. In 1758 and 1759 his seminary choir performed as 'secondo coro' for music at S Martino and S Frediano, directed by Puccini. The opera *La donna girandola* has been ascribed to him, but that is unlikely, for it appears from the libretto that its composer was married to one of the singers. Baccelli's sacred music, to judge from his extant antiphon and psalm for Vespers, the *Domine* and *Dixit*, makes great and able use of the *stile concertante*: brilliant, rapid sections alternate with andante, lyrical writing; choruses alternate with solos; counterpoint with homophony; strings, trumpets and occasionally horns combine with continuo to provide rich four- or six-part accompaniment.

Domine ad adiuvandum me, and Dixit Dominus, S, A, T, B, SATB, 2
tpt, 2 hn, 2 vn, va, bc, 1753, *I-Ls*
La concezione (orat), Lucca, 1756, lost
Several vesper settings and masses, all lost

BIBLIOGRAPHY
EitnerQ
G. Puccini: *Libro delle musiche*, Libro C (MS, *I-Li*)
L. Nerici: *Storia della musica in Lucca* (Lucca, 1879/*R*)
E. Maggini: *Lucca, Biblioteca del Seminario* (Milan, 1965)
                                    CAROLYN GIANTURCO

Bacchae. *See* MAENADS.

Bacchetta (It.). A drumstick, or the stick of a BOW or a
conductor's BATON.

Bacchini [Bacchino], **Giovanni Maria** [Fra Teodoro del
Carmine] (*b* Mantua; *fl* 1588–1607). Italian singer,
composer and theorist. Canal erroneously gave his first
name as Girolamo. He was a Carmelite priest. While at
the Mantuan court, he wrote a treatise, *De musica*, now
lost. In 1588 he published a madrigal, *Più che Diana*, in
Alfonso Preti's *L'amoroso caccia* (RISM 1588¹⁴), a
collection consisting of compositions by Mantuan musicians primarily associated with the church. He also
published a book of masses, the *Missarum quinque et sex
vocum, liber primus* (Venice, 1589). In a letter dated 26
November 1594 to the vicar-general of the Carmelite
order, Duke Vincenzo Gonzaga requested that Bacchini,
a 'musico castrato', be exempt from wearing his monk's
habit while singing in the court chamber. In 1594 he
accompanied the duke to the *Reichstag* in Regensburg
and in the following year, along with Monteverdi, G.B.
Marinone, Serafino Terzi and other musicians from the
Gonzaga court, took part in the duke's military expedition
to southern Hungary. A Mantuan court secretary, Fortunato Cardi, described musical performances directed by
Monteverdi, in which Bacchini took part, on the eve of
the Battle of Visegrad. It has been suggested that Bacchini
sang the part of Euridice in the first performances of
Monteverdi's *Orfeo* (1607). The account books of the
Mantuan court mention him in 1595, 1598 and 1605.

BIBLIOGRAPHY
BertolottiM
P. Canal: *Della musica in Mantova* (Venice, 1881/*R*)
V. Errante: 'Forse che sì, forse che no', *Archivio storico lombardo*,
    xlii (1915), 31–2
I. Fenlon: 'Monteverdi's Mantuan Orfeo: Some New
    Documentation', *EMc*, xii (1984), 163–72
                        PIERRE M. TAGMANN/IAIN FENLON

Bacchius [Bakcheios Gerōn] (*fl* ?4th century CE). Greek
writer on music. He was the author of a small musical
catechism preserved under the title *Introduction to the
Art of Music* (*Eisagōgē technēs mousikēs*). The treatise is
usually (though not always) followed in the manuscripts
by a second distinct treatise but with the same title and
author; the second treatise in turn is followed in most
(but not all) manuscripts by this epigram:

> Of music, Bacchius the Elder described
> the *tonoi*, *tropoi*, *mele* and consonances.
> Echoing him, Dionysius writes.
> The all-powerful Emperor Constantine
> he shows to be a wise lover of the works of art.
>
> For one who, of every wise subject of instruction,
> has been seen as discoverer and giver,
> it is most unseemly to be a stranger to music.

The epigram, however, is never found with the first
treatise of Bacchius when it appears alone (the earliest
instance of which is the marginal text in a 13th-century
hand in *I-Vnm* gr.app.cl. VI/3: RISM, B/XI, 270), and
even in its earliest appearance with the second treatise
(*Vnm* gr.app.cl. VI/10: RISM, B/XI, 273), the epigram is
separated from the text by a large space. When it does
appear, the epigram is usually followed by the musical
hymns attributed to Mesomedes (2nd century CE). Nevertheless, the epigram has commonly been taken to refer
to the second treatise, the attribution of which is
accordingly modified (even in some of the manuscripts)
to Dionysius and dated to the reign of Constantine the
Great (*c*283–337 CE). The epigram could, however, be
referring to another emperor of the same name, including
the Byzantine Constantine VII Porphyrogennetus (905–59
CE), known for his support of classical scholarship.
Although Bacchius's *floruit* has been assumed to be
contemporary with Dionysius, this cannot be demonstrated on any grounds. In the end, the epigram is of no
use in dating either treatise.

The first treatise, written as a series of simple questions
and answers, presents a mixture of definitions and theories
that cannot be assigned exclusively to any one school. The
first 88 questions deal with definitions of common
terms and concepts in harmonics; questions 89–101 deal
with definitions in rhythmics. Some of the answers (11,
13–18, 29–34 and 38–42) make use of musical notation,
recognizable from the tables of ALYPIUS. Nothing in the
treatise is completely new, but several of the answers,
especially in the section on rhythmics, provide useful
clarification or confirmation of other sources. The unassuming character and routine content and style of the
treatise suggest a date no earlier than the 4th century CE.
Parts of the first treatise are also preserved in an untitled
anecdoton surviving in seven manuscripts, including one
of the 11th century (*D-HEu* Palat.gr.281: RISM, B/XI,
14).

The second treatise, written in prose, remarks on the
inability of the senses (sight, smell, taste, touch and
hearing) to make consistent quantitative discriminations,
and for this reason musicians must turn to the *canon* for
precise measurements. Most of this appears verbatim, but
without attribution, in Bryennius's *Harmonics* (ii.6). The
second treatise concludes with eight theorems demonstrating the proportions for the consonant octave, 5th, 4th,
12th and 15th; the dissonant 11th; the tone; and the
impossibility of dividing the tone into two equal parts. In
approach, style and content, the second treatise is entirely
different from the first, and its attribution to Bacchius in
some of the manuscripts is simply due to the inadvertent
connection of the end-title of the first treatise with the
beginning of the second.

The treatise of Bacchius was used by later writers,
including Manuel Bryennius, Franchinus Gaffurius, Giorgio Valla, Francisco de Salinas, Girolamo Mei, Marin
Mersenne (who published the first edition in 1623 and a
translation in 1627) and others. Meibom included the
treatise in his collection of 1652, but Jan's editions
presented the first detailed study of the text. The second
treatise was first published (under the name of Bacchius)
by Bellermann.

WRITINGS
M. Meibom, ed. and trans.: 'Bacchii senioris introductio artis
    musicae', *Antiquae musicae auctores septem* (Amsterdam,
    1652/*R*), i [separately paginated; with parallel Lat. trans.]

J.F. Bellermann, ed.: 'Eisagōgē technēs mousikēs Bakcheiou tou gerontos', Anonymi scriptio de musica (Berlin, 1841), 101–8

A.J.H. Vincent, trans.: 'Introduction à l'art musical par Bacchius l'ancien', Notice sur divers manuscrits grecs relatifs à la musique, avec une traduction française et des commentaires (Paris, 1847), 64–72

K. von Jan, ed. and trans.: Die Eisagoge des Bacchius (Strasbourg, 1890–91)

K. von Jan, ed.: 'Bacchii gerontis isagoge', Musici scriptores graeci (Leipzig, 1895/R), 283–316

C.E. Ruelle, trans.: Alypius et Gaudence . . . Bacchius l'Ancien (Paris, 1895)

O. Steinmayer, trans.: 'Bacchius Geron's Introduction to the Art of Music', JMT, xxix (1985), 271–98

L. Zanoncelli, ed. and trans.: 'Bacchio il vecchio: Introduzione all'arte musicale', La manualistica musicale greca (Milan, 1990), 245–304 [incl. commentary]

BIBLIOGRAPHY

J.F. Bellermann, ed.: Die Hymnen des Dionysius und Mesomedes (Berlin, 1840)

G. Hermann: 'De hymnis Dionysii et Mesomedis', Opuscula, viii, ed. T. Fritzsche (Leipzig, 1877/R), 343–52

J. Solomon: 'Ekbole and Eklusis in the Musical Treatise of Bacchius', Symbolae osloenses, lv (1980), 111–26

T.J. Mathiesen: Ancient Greek Music Theory: a Catalogue Raisonné of Manuscripts, RISM, B/XI (1988)

T.J. Mathiesen: Apollo's Lyre: Greek Music and Music Theory in Antiquity and the Middle Ages (Lincoln, NE, 1999), 583–93

THOMAS J. MATHIESEN

Bacchius [Bacchus, Bachus, Bachi, Bachy], **Johannes de** (*d* before 29 Jan 1557). Composer, described by Eitner as French. He became an alto in the Viennese Hofkapelle in March 1554. An Adrianus de Bachy, listed as a singer in the boys' choir of the court, may have been his son. Bacchius's works are typical polyphonic compositions of his time. The motets, most of which appeared in the large anthologies of Berg & Neuber, are in the full-voiced imitative style much favoured in Vienna. The two chansons have their roots in the Parisian style of the earlier part of the century, although they, too, have a higher level of imitative writing.

WORKS

Christus surrexit, 4vv, 1564⁵; Considerate dilectissimi, 5vv, 1559¹; Da Pater omnipotens pacem, 5vv, 1564⁴; Domine Deus caeli, 8vv, 1564¹; Domine Deus qui conteris, 8vv, 1564³; Dum transisset Sabbatum, 5vv, 1564⁴; Ecce Maria genuit, 4vv, 1564⁵; Ego flos campi et lilium, 5vv, 1564⁴

Factum est silentium, 5vv, D-Bsb Z 39, Z 74.1; Fuit homo missus a Deo, 6vv, 1564³; Oculi mei semper ad Dominum, 4vv, Sl 30; Si quis diligit me, 8vv, Brieg Gymnasiumsbibliothek 1 (now in PL-WRu), WRu 1, 3, 5, 18; Surge illuminare Jerusalem, 5vv, 1564⁴; Visitabo in virga, 5vv, 1559¹

Quant je voy son ceur estre mien, 6vv, 1553²⁵; Susanna ung jour, 4vv, 1556¹⁸

BIBLIOGRAPHY

EitnerQ; KöchelKHM; MGG1 suppl. (W. Pass)

O. Wessely: Arnold von Bruck: Leben und Umwelt (Habilitationsschrift, U. of Vienna, 1958), 418ff

VICTOR H. MATTFELD

Bacchus. See DIONYSUS.

Bacchylides [Bakchylidēs] (*b* Iulis [now Tzia], Keos; *fl c*470 BCE). Greek lyric poet. He was a nephew of Simonides and contemporary of Pindar; there are many indications of intense rivalry between the two as composers of victory odes and dithyrambs. Unlike Pindar, Bacchylides had little to say of the power of music; his references are correct but conventional, rendered distinctive only by colourful adjectives. Thus in one of the many victory odes the champion has returned home to the triumphal

accompaniment of auloi 'that delight mortals' and revel-songs 'sweetly breathing' (Edmonds, frag.40.72–3). In another, the sound of the phorminx and 'clear-ringing' choruses are alien to war (Edmonds, frag.41.12–15; liguklangēs is one of many Bacchylidean coinages). Two poems begin with references to the barbitos, 'lyre with many strings' (Edmonds, frags.70, 71); here the term appears to be used with precision.

WRITINGS

F. Blass, ed.: Bacchylides: Carmina cum fragmentis (Leipzig, 1898, rev. 4/1912 by W. Suess, 5/1934 by B. Snell, 10/1970 by H. Maehler)

R.C. Jebb, ed. and trans.: Bacchylides: The Poems and Fragments (Cambridge, 1905/R)

J.M. Edmonds, ed. and trans.: Lyra graeca, iii (London and Cambridge, MA, 1927, 2/1928/R)

R. Fagles, ed. and trans.: Bacchylides: Complete Poems (New Haven, CT, 1961/R)

D.A. Campbell, ed.: Greek Lyric Poetry (London and New York, 1967, 2/1982)

D.A. Campbell, ed. and trans.: Greek Lyric, iv (Cambridge, MA, and London, 1992), 100–317

BIBLIOGRAPHY

O. Crusius: 'Bakchylides, §§2–3', Paulys Real-Encyclopädie der classischen Altertumswissenschaft, ii/A (Stuttgart, 1898/R), 2793–801

A. Körte: 'Bacchylidea', Hermes, lxiii (1918), 113–47

A. Severyns: Bacchylide: essai biographique (Liège and Paris, 1933)

K. Preisendanz: 'Bakchylides', Der kleine Pauly, ed. K. Ziegler and W. Sontheimer, i (Stuttgart, 1964), 810–12

A.P. Burnett: The Art of Bacchylides (Cambridge, MA, and London, 1985)

WARREN ANDERSON/THOMAS J. MATHIESEN

Bacciccia. See RICCIOTTI, CARLO.

Baccio Fiorentino. See BARTOLOMEO DEGLI ORGANI.

Baccusi, Ippolito [Baccusii, Hippolyti] (*b* Mantua, *c*1550; *d* Verona, 1609). Italian composer. Although he was a prolific composer of madrigals and sacred music, the course of his career is not well documented. His earliest position appears to have been that of assistant choir director at S Marco, Venice. That he must have held the post for only a short time can be established from a letter (in I-MAc) dated from Ravenna on 22 April 1570 in which he requested permission to remain another year in Ravenna, since he would be able to complete his degree by the end of a third year of study: he must therefore have left Venice for Ravenna by 1568. On the title-page of his second book of six-part madrigals (1572) he is described as director of music to the 'illustri signori di Spilimbergo', a musical society in Verona. The book is dedicated to the Accademia Filarmonica in Verona, and in the preface Baccusi indicated that he was employed as maestro di cappella at yet another institution there, the church of S Eufemia. The next document concerning his career occurs in the Prattica di musica seconda parte (Venice, 1622/R1967) of Lodovico Zacconi, which states that he went to Mantua in 1583 to study contrappunto alla mente with him and that he was a maestro di cappella there; Zacconi wrote as if Baccusi had held the post for some time, but the exact date of his appointment is not known. In the preface to his fourth book of masses (1593) Baccusi indicated that he was offered the choir directorship at Verona Cathedral in 1592; he accepted and remained in the post until his death.

Stylistically Baccusi belongs to the Venetian school of composers; he early came under the influence of Willaert, Rore and Andrea Gabrieli. He composed two settings of poetic cycles celebrating the Venetian victory over the Turks at Lepanto (in his second books for five and six voices, both 1572). Other works of particular interest are the settings of Petrarch's 11-stanza canzone *Vergine bella* (1605) and of one of the cycles in Francesco Bozza's quaternion *I diporti della villa in ogni stagione* (RISM 1601[7]). Among his contemporaries Baccusi had the reputation of being a fine contrapuntist and a master of improvisation: his works certainly illustrate the first quality. Baccusi was also one of the first composers to acknowledge and recommend the practice of instrumental doubling of vocal parts (see the title-pages of his masses of 1596 and psalms of 1597).

WORKS
published in Venice unless otherwise noted

MASSES
[2] Missarum, 5, 6vv, liber I (1570)
[4] Missarum, 5, 6, 8vv, liber II (1585)
Il primo libro delle [5] messe, 4vv (1588)
Missarum, 5, 6vv, liber III (1589)
[4] Missarum, 5, 9vv, liber IV (1593)
Misse tres tum viva voce, tum omni instrumentorum genere cantatu commodissime, 8vv (1596)

OTHER SACRED
[25] Motectorum, 5, 6, 8vv, liber I (1579)
Psalmi omnes qui in vesperis a romana ecclesia decantantur cum cantico Beatae Virginis, 4vv, liber II (1594)
Psalmorum qui a santa romana ecclesia, ut plurimum in vesperis decantantur, triplici distinctorum ordine, cum cantico Beatae Virginis, 4vv, liber III (Verona, 1594)
Sacrae cantiones psalmi videlicet et omnia quae ad completorium pertinent, 5vv (1596)
Psalmi omnes qui a sancta romana ecclesia in solemnitatibus ad Vesperas decantari solent, cum 2 Magnificat, tum viva voce, tum omni instrumentorum genere, cantatu commodissimi, 8vv (1597)
Psalmi qui diebus festivis a sancta romana ecclesia in Vesperis decantari solent, 5vv (1602)
Single sacred works in 1583[2], 1592[3], 1596[1]

MADRIGALS
Il primo libro de [27] madrigali, 5–8vv (1570)
Il secondo libro de [18] madrigali, con una canzone nella gran vittoria contra i Turchi, 5vv (1572[9])
Il secondo libro de [18] madrigali, con una canzone nella gran vittoria contra i Turchi, 6vv (1572[8])
[21] Madrigali ... libro III, 6vv (1579)
Il quarto libro de [21] madrigali, 6vv (1587)
Il primo libro de [19] madrigali, 3vv (1594[10])
Le vergini ... [11] madrigali, 3vv, libro II (1605[11])
Further madrigals, 4–6, 9vv, 1585[16], 1585[19], 1588[14], 1588[18], 1590[11], 1591[23], 1592[11], 1593[3], 1594[6], 1596[10], 1598[6], 1601[7] (ed. in Collana di Musiche Veneziane Inedite o Rare, i, 1962) 1605[9]
1 French Psalm, 1597[6]; 2 German and 9 Latin contrafacta of madrigals, 1600[5a], 1601[18], 1606[6], 1609[14], 1609[15], 1612[13], 1619[16], 1624[16], Provincial Archives, Torun, Kat.XIV.13a
4 intabulations, 1584[15]; 3 previously pubd, 1587[6], 1588[19], 1588[20]

Various works in MS: *A-Wgm, D-Bsb, Mbs, Z, I-Bc, PL-WRu, Wu*

BIBLIOGRAPHY
BertolottiM
F. Chrysander: 'Lodovico Zacconi als Lehrer des Kunstgesangs', *VMw*, x (1894), 531–67
P.M. Tagmann: *Archivalische Studien zur Musikpflege am Dom von Mantua (1500–1627)* (Berne, 1967)

PATRICIA ANN MYERS/R

Bacewicz, Grażyna (*b* Łódź, 5 Feb 1909; *d* Warsaw, 17 Jan 1969). Polish composer, violinist and pianist. After early instrumental and theory studies in Łódź, she attended the Warsaw Conservatory, where she studied composition with Kazimierz Sikorski, the violin with Józef Jarzębski and the piano with Józef Turczyński (she also studied philosophy at Warsaw University). She graduated in composition and the violin in 1932, furthering her studies in Paris in 1932 and 1933 with Boulanger and the violinist André Touret. After a brief period spent teaching in Łódź, she returned to Paris to study with Carl Flesch in 1934. At the request of the conductor Grzegorz Fitelberg, Bacewicz was principal violinist of the Polish RO (1936–8) and she performed as a soloist in several European countries before returning to Poland two months before World War II. She continued as a concert violinist after the war until the mid-1950s. Her prowess as a pianist should not be ignored: she was, for example, a notable interpreter of her own Second Piano Sonata.

Among her other activities, Bacewicz was an accomplished writer of short stories, novels and autobiographical anecdotes. Among the awards she received for her music were the top prize at the International Chopin Competition for Composers in Warsaw (1949) for her Piano Concerto, first prize at the International Composers' Competition in Liège (1951) for her String Quartet no.4, first prize in the orchestral section at UNESCO's International Rostrum of Composers in Paris (1960) for her *Music for Strings, Trumpets and Percussion* and the Gold Medal at the Queen Elisabeth International Music Competition in Brussels (1965) for her Violin Concerto no.7, as well as various State awards from 1949 onwards.

Bacewicz made her most lasting mark on 20th-century music as a composer rather than as a performer or teacher (she taught composition rarely, but notably at the Warsaw Conservatory during the last three years of her life). She had an uncommonly vibrant yet modest personality and was much admired and loved by her fellow Poles during her lifetime.

Her career as a composer may be seen to divide into three broad spans, of which the first (1932–44) is largely preparatory to the second (1945–59), with the third (1960–69) a more distinct entity. The first period shows the development and refinement of Bacewicz's neo-classical persona. Although only a few of these early works have been published, her music's salient characteristics of clarity, wit and brevity are already evident in the Wind Quintet, a piece in which she seems to be following Szymanowski's example in the incorporation of folk elements. Her works from the time of World War II show a greater muscularity and unrelenting activity, with a daring disregard for traditional classical structures, as in the Sonata no.1 for solo violin. The Overture exemplifies Bacewicz's unerring ability to propel her music towards a final goal.

After the war, Bacewicz's music became increasingly personal, casting off any remaining Parisian *chic* and becoming distinctively resilient. Occasionally she indulged in pastiche (the Sonata da camera), but her stronger music is reminiscent of Szymanowski (the Violin Concerto no.3 and, later, the Piano Sonata no.2 and Violin Concerto no.5). These and other outstanding works such as the String Quartet no.3 and the Concerto for String Orchestra have mostly maintained their place in the international repertory. As with many of her contemporaries, she used folk materials (both directly and indirectly) during the period of intense socialist realism (1949–54), in large forms (the Piano Concerto) and in encore pieces for her recitals. Her output during the height of Stalinist cultural dogma is, however, remarkably free of mass songs or other pieces with a 'message'. The three symphonies are the most grandiose works, though their scoring is at times refreshingly restrained. The chamber music reveals a tougher, more challenging musical idiom, most notably in the fourth and fifth quartets: the former is structurally loose-limbed, while the latter is highly integrated in its motivic design and adventurous for the time in its non-diatonic harmonic language. This innovatory streak in Bacewicz's musical personality is carried through into the Partita, especially in its intermezzo. By the mid-1950s Bacewicz had already moved far from conventional notions of neo-classicism.

In the late 1950s Bacewicz, like her contemporaries, had to recognize the emergence of a new generation of younger composers and an influx of avant-garde influences from abroad. Unlike some, she grasped the nettle, even though it was not always with absolute conviction. In some works, such as the String Quartet no.6, there are passages of outright 12-note writing. But she soon settled down to her own brand of chromaticism and dynamic gestures that veer from the routine (Cello Concerto no.2) to the highly imaginative (*Pensieri notturni*). At times, Bacewicz appears to have experienced some difficulty in putting pen to paper, although in 1965 she composed no fewer than seven large-scale works. The extensive self-borrowings which became evident when discarded works from 1965–7 were published posthumously seem to indicate a degree of uncertainty about the new directions she was taking. Her evident attachment to the Intermezzo from the Partita gave rise to citations from that movement's opening bars in later works (e.g. the Viola Concerto); such quotations form part of a highly successful patchworking technique that Bacewicz developed during the 1960s. There is even the suggestion in the Viola Concerto that Bacewicz, like some of her younger compatriots, was returning to folk material.

Bacewicz's position in Polish postwar music is undeniable: hers was an individual and independent voice; she was more innovative than is generally acknowledged and she carried the torch for the many Polish women composers who followed her example. Even though she may have lost her sure-footedness in the mid-1960s, this should not detract from a musical achievement that is being recognized outside Poland as one of the most remarkable of the mid-20th century.

WORKS
(*selective list*)

STAGE

Z chłopa król [The Peasant King] (ballet, A.M. Swinarski, after P. Baryka), 1953–4, Poznań, 1954
Przygoda króla Artura [The Adventure of King Arthur] (comic op for radio, E. Fischer), 1959, Polish Radio, 1959; televised 1960
Esik w Ostendzie [Esik in Ostend] (comic ballet, L. Terpilowski, after T. Boy-Żeleński), 1964, Poznań, 1964
Pożądanie [Desire] (ballet, 2, M. Bibrowski, after P. Picasso: *Désir attrapé par la queue*), 1968–9, inc.; Warsaw, 1973
Incid music for 7 plays

ORCHESTRAL

Syms.: Sym., 1933, lost; Sym., 1938, lost; Sym. no.1, 1945; Sym., str, 1946; Sym. no.2, 1951; Sym. no.3, 1952; Sym. no.4, 1953
Vn concs.: no.1, 1937; no.2, 1945; no.3, 1948; no.4, 1951; no.5, 1954; no.6, 1957; no.7, 1965
Other concs.: Conc., 1948; Pf Conc., 1949; Vc conc. no.1, 1951; Conc. for Orch, 1962; Vc Conc. no.2, 1963; Conc., 2 pf, 1966; Va Conc., 1968
Other concert works: Sinfonietta, chbr orch, 1929; Suite, str, 1931; 3 karykatury, 1932; Pochód radości [Procession of Joy], 1933; Sinfonietta, str, 1935; Ov., 1943; Introdukcja i kaprys, 1947; Rapsodia polska, vn, orch, 1949; Uwertura polska, 1954; Partita, 1955 [arr. of Partita, vn, pf]; Wariacje, 1957; Music for Str, Tpts

and Perc, 1958; Pensieri notturni, chbr orch, 1961; Divertimento, str, 1965; Musica sinfonica, 1965; Contradizione, chbr orch, 1966; In una parte, 1967
Pieces for radio: Mazur [Mazurka], 1944; Pod strzechą [Under the Thatch], 1945; Suite, str, 1946; Ze starej muzyki [From Old Music], 1946; Polish Dance no.2, 1948; Szkice ludowe [Folk Sketches], 1948; Groteska, 1949; Walc, 1949; Krakowiak, 1950; Serenada, 1950; Suita tańców polskich, 1950; Wiwat, cl, str, 1950; Oberek noworoczny, 1952; others

CHAMBER

Str qts: no.1, 1938; no.2, 1943; no.3, 1947; no.4, 1951; no.5, 1955; no.6, 1960; no.7, 1965
Other works: Wind Qnt, 1932; Trio, ob, vn, vc, 1935; Sonata, ob, pf, 1937; Łatwe utwory [Easy Pieces], cl, pf, 1948; Trio, ob, cl, bn, 1948; Qt, 4 vn, 1949; 2 pf qnts, 1952, 1965; Qt, 4 vc, 1964; Inkrustacje [Incrustations], hn, ens, 1965; Trio, ob, hp, perc, 1965

VIOLIN

With pf: Kaprys no.1, 1932; Witraż [Stained Glass], 1932; Andante i allegro, 1934; Pieśń litewska [Lith. Song], 1934; Theme and Variations, 1934; Legenda, 1945; Concertino, 1945; Sonata no.1 'da camera', 1945, 4th movt (Andante sostenuto) arr. vn/vc, org, 1945; Kaprys, 1946; Łatwe utwory [Easy Pieces], 1946; Sonata, no.2, 1946, no.3, 1948; Taniec polski, 1948; Łatwe utwory, 1949; Melodia, 1949; Oberek no.1, 1949; Sonata, no.4, 1949; Taniec antyczny [Antique Dance], 1950; Sonata no.5, 1951; Taniec mazowiecki, 1951; Oberek no.2, 1951; Kołysanka [Lullaby], 1952; Taniec słowiański, 1952; Humoresque, 1953; Partita, 1955
Solo: Sonata, 1929; Sonata no.1, 1941; Kaprys polski, 1949; Kaprys no.2, 1952; Sonata no.2, 1958; 4 kaprysy, 1968
2 vn: Suite, 1943; Łatwe duety [Easy Duets], 1945

KEYBOARD

Pf: Theme with Variations, 1924; Preludium, 1928; Allegro, 1929; Sonata, 1930; Toccata, 1932; 3 pièces caracteristiques, 1932; Sonatina, 1933; Suita dziecęca [Children's Suite], 1933; Scherzo, 1934; Sonata, 1935; 3 groteski, 1935; 3 preludia, 1941; Krakowiak koncertowy, 1949; Sonata no.1, 1949; Etiuda tercjowa [Study in 3rds], 1952; Sonata no.2, 1953; Sonatina no.2, 1955; 10 etiud koncertowych, 1956; Mały tryptyk [Little Triptych], 1965
Org: Esquisse, 1966

VOCAL

With orch: De profundis, solo vv, chorus, orch, 1932; 3 Songs (10th-century Arabic, trans. L. Staff), T, orch/pf, 1938; Kantata olimpijska (P. Pindar), chorus, orch, 1948; Kantata na 600-lecie Uniwersytetu Jagiellońskiego (S. Wyspiański: *Akropolis*), chorus, orch, 1964
Songs (1v, pf): Róze [Roses] (Arabic, trans. Staff), 1934; Mów do mnie, o miły [Speak to me, Dear] (R. Tagore, trans. J. Kasprowicz), 1936; Oto jest noc [Here is the Night] (K.I. Gałczyński), 1947; Rozstanie [Parting] (Tagore, trans. Kasprowicz), 1949; Smuga cienia [Trail of Shadow] (W. Broniewski), 1949; Usta i pełnia [Lips and Fullness] (Gałczyński), 1949; Boli mnie głowa [My Head Aches] (Bacewicz), 1955; Dzwon i dzwonki [Bells and Little Bells] (A. Mickiewicz), 1955; Nad wodą wielką i czystą [Over the Wide, Clear Water] (Mickiewicz), 1955; Sroczka [Little Magpie] (trad.), 1956

Principal publisher: PWM

BIBLIOGRAPHY

MGG2 (S. Wittig)
A. Malawski: 'Uwertura Bacewiczówny', *RM*, iii/17 (1947), no.17, p.19
J.M. Chomiński: 'Koncert na orkiestrę smyczkową Grażyny Bacewicz', *Muzyka*, vi/5–6 (1955), 20–29; repr. in *Studia muzykologiczne*, v (1956), 385–401
A. Helman: 'Problem stylizacji muzyki dawnej w Sonacie da camera Grażyny Bacewicz', [The problem of early musical idioms in 'Sonata da camera'], ibid., 367–84
M. Gorczycka: '"Pensieri notturni"', *RM*, v/21 (1961), 9–10
T.A. Zieliński: 'Walor szlachetnego rzemiosła (o twórczósca G. Bacewicz)' [The value of noble craftsmanship (in the work of Bacewicz)], *RM*, v/8 (1961), 1–2
S. Kisielewski: *Grażyna Bacewicz i jej czasy* [Bacewicz and her times] (Kraków, 1963)
H. Schiller: 'Ze studiów nad muzyką Grażyny Bacewicz', *Muzyka*, ix/3–4 (1964), 3–15
T. Marek: 'Grażyna Bacewicz', *Polish Music*, iv/1 (1969) 3–8

RM, xiii/7 (1969) [Bacewicz issue]

T.A. Zieliński: 'Ostatnie utwory Grażyny Bacewicz' [Bacewicz's last works], *RM*, xvi/2 (1972), 3–6

J. Rosen: *Grażyna Bacewicz: her Life and Works* (Los Angeles, 1984)

A. Thomas: *Grażyna Bacewicz: Chamber and Orchestral Music* (Los Angeles, 1985)

S.G. Shafer: *The Contribution of Grażyna Bacewicz to Polish Music* (Lewiston, NY, 1992) [on the songs]

M. Szoka, ed.: *Rodzeństwo Bacewiczow* [The Bacewicz siblings] (Łódź, 1996)

S. Wittig: 'Die Kompositionstechnik der letzen Schaffensperiode Grażyny Bacewicz', *Jeder nach seiner Fasson*, ed. U. Liedtke (Saarbrücken, 1997), 65–104

M. Gąsiorowska: *Bacewicz* (Kraków, 1999)

ADRIAN THOMAS

Bacfarc, Valentin. *See* BAKFARK, VALENTIN.

Bach. German family of musicians. From the 16th century to the 19th the extensive Saxon-Thuringian Bach family produced an unparalleled and almost incalculable number of musicians of every kind, from fiddlers and town musicians to organists, Kantors, court musicians and Kapellmeisters. The outstanding figure among them was Johann Sebastian Bach, but a great many other well-known and distinguished musicians were born into earlier, contemporary and later generations of the family.

In the following pages a list of the musical members of the family, in alphabetical order, with brief biographical notes on those who are not discussed separately, precedes an outline of the family history. §III is then devoted to the most important members of the family, in chronological order. The italic numerals *1–53* given in parentheses after the names correspond to the numbers given to members of the family in the genealogy drawn up by J.S. Bach in 1735, the *Ursprung der musicalisch-Bachischen Familie*. The numerals from *54* onwards continue on the same principle. The inadvertent fusion in the *Ursprung* of two family members, Caspar (*b c*1580; *d* 1642–4) and Lips (*c*1590–1626), into a single unnamed individual under the number *3* has been corrected, but in order to facilitate comparison the *3* is retained for them and their descendants along with the new numbers. The arabic numerals preceding the names refer to their individual entries in §III below. Non-musician members of the family are not listed, but some musicians with the surname Bach who did not belong to the main, Wechmar line are included.

I. List of the musicians. II. Family history. III. Individual members.

I. *List of the musicians*

Carl Philipp Emanuel Bach (*46*) (*b* Weimar, 8 March 1714; *d* Hamburg, 14 Dec 1788). Son of Johann Sebastian Bach (*24*); see §III (9) below.

Caspar Bach (*3/a*) (*b c*1580; *d* ?Arnstadt, Sept 1642–1644). Son of Veit (*1*). He is mentioned as a Stadtpfeifer in Gotha in 1619 and as a court and town musician in Arnstadt from 1620; on 23 October 1621 he received the sum of 1 gulden to buy a bassoon ('Dulcian'). As Hausmann (director of the town music) he lived in the so-called Neideckturm (the tower of Schloss Neideck, Arnstadt). In 1633 he left the count's service (as a result of the Thirty Years War the court could no longer afford his salary) and bought a house in the Jacobsgasse. Nothing is known about his subsequent activities.

Caspar Bach (*3/54*) (*b c*1605). Son of Caspar (*3/a*). He was trained as a musician (violinist) at the courts of Bayreuth (1621–3) and Dresden (1623) at the expense of the Count of Schwarzburg-Arnstadt. In 1623 the court paid him 38 gulden for three months' educational and living expenses and for instruments, and on 11 October 1625 he signed a receipt in Arnstadt for the sum of 1 reichsthaler. He is thought to have gone to Italy, and from this point no more is known about him.

Christoph Bach (*5*) (*b* Wechmar, 19 April 1613; *d* Arnstadt, 12 Sept 1661). Son of Johann (*2*) and grandfather of Johann Sebastian Bach (*24*). He was in the princely service and a court musician in Weimar, then from 1642 a town musician in Erfurt and from 1654 court and town musician in Arnstadt. A musical entry by him in the album of Georg Friedrich Reimann, Kantor in Saalfeld, survives (*BJb* 1928, 175).

Ernst Carl Gottfried Bach (*73*) (*b* Ohrdruf, 12 Jan 1738; *d* Ohrdruf, 24 June 1801). Son of Johann Christoph (*42*). He was Kantor in Wechmar, 1765–72, then Kantor at the Michaeliskirche in Ohrdruf.

Ernst Christian Bach (*74*) (*b* Ohrdruf, 26 Sept 1747; *d* Wechmar, 29 Sept 1822). Son of Johann Christoph (*42*). He was Kantor in Wechmar, 1773–1819.

Georg Christoph Bach (*10*) (*b* Erfurt, 6 Sept 1642; *d* Schweinfurt, 27 April 1697). Son of Christoph (*5*). He was trained in music at Arnstadt , and was evidently academically gifted; he attended the Gymnasium Casimi-ranum in Coburg (1663–5) and Leipzig University (1665–6). In 1668 he became Kantor and organist in Themar, and from 1688 he was Kantor at St Johannis in Schweinfurt, where his uncles Johann (*4*) and Heinrich Bach (*6*) had been organists. A vocal concerto by him survives: *Siehe, wie fein und lieblich ist es* for two tenors, bass, violin, three gambas and continuo (ed. in EDM, 1st ser., ii (1935) and in Stuttgarter Bach-Ausgaben, ser. A.4 (Stuttgart, *c*1976)). It was composed on his 47th birthday, evidently for performance with his brothers, the twins Ambrosius (*11*) and Christoph (*12*), probably at some family gathering. A Schweinfurt inventory of 1689 (see Wollny, 1997) lists four other vocal works: *Gott ist unser Zuversicht, Meinen Jesum lass ich nicht, Wie lieblich sind auf den Bergen* and *Wohl her, lasset uns wohl leben*.

Georg Friedrich Bach (*b* Tann, 17 March 1793; *d* Iserlohn, 2 Oct 1860). Not a member of the Wechmar line, he was a son of Johann Michael (see §III (13) below). A flautist, he deserted from Napoleon's army and went to Sweden, where he became music teacher to the crown prince (later Oskar I). On returning to Germany he taught music in Elberfeld and Iserlohn. Several manuscript keyboard compositions and a harmony manual by him survive (*D-EIb*).

Georg Michael Bach (*66*) (*b* Ruhla, 27 Sept 1703; *d* Halle, 18 Feb 1771). Son of Johann Jacob (*3/60*). From 1732 he was Kantor at the Ulrichskirche in Halle, adn from 1747 he taught at the Lutheran Gymnasium.

Gottfried Heinrich Bach (*48*) (*b* Leipzig, 26 Feb 1724; *d* Naumburg, bur. 12 Feb 1763). Eldest son of Johann Sebastian (*24*) and Anna Magdalena Bach. Although he was mentally handicapped, he was evidently a good keyboard player and, according to his half-brother Carl Philipp Emanuel (*46*), showed 'a great genius, which however failed to develop'. From 1750 he lived with his brother-in-law J.C. Altnickol in Naumburg.

Gottlieb Friedrich Bach (*68*) (*b* Meiningen, 10 Sept 1714; *d* Meiningen, 25 Feb 1785). Son of Johann Ludwig (*3/64*). He was court organist and painter (*Kabinetts-maler*) in Meiningen.

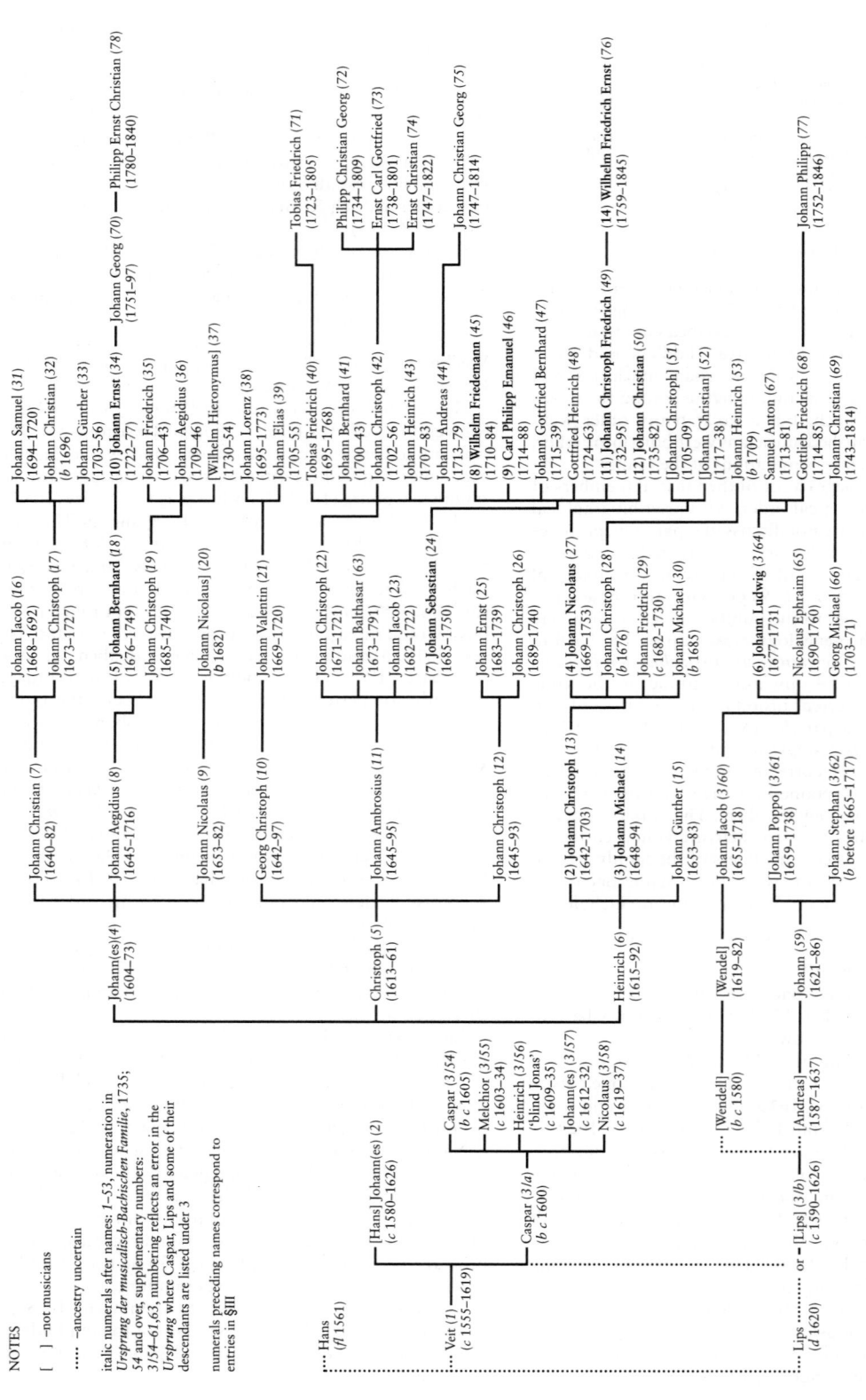

1. The Bach family tree

Hans [Hanns, Johann] Bach (*b* Andelsbuch, Vorarlberg, *c*1555; *d* Nürtingen, 1 Dec 1615). Not a member of the Wechmar line; see §III(1) below.

Hans [Johann(es)] Bach (2) (*b c*1580; *d* Wechmar, 26 Dec 1626). Son of Veit (*1*). In the funeral sermon for his youngest son Heinrich (6) he is described as a 'musician and carpetmaker', and he was the earliest member of the family known to have been a professional musician. According to the *Ursprung*, he trained as a Stadtpfeifer in Gotha and later settled in Wechmar, from where he travelled as a musician to various Thuringian towns, including Gotha, Arnstadt, Erfurt, Eisenach, Schmalkalden and Suhl. He married Anna Schmied of Wechmar in about 1602, and after his father's death took over his business and property. In the Wechmar register of deaths he appears as 'Hanss Bach ein Spielmann'.

Heinrich Bach (*3/56*) (*b* Gotha, *c*1609; *d* Arnstadt, bur. 27 May 1635). Son of Caspar (*3/a*). He is mentioned in the deaths register as blind, and is therefore probably the musician educated in Italy and mentioned in the *Ursprung* as 'blind Jonas' because of his adventurous experiences, in allusion to the biblical figure of Jonah.

Heinrich Bach (6) (*b* Wechmar, 16 Sept 1615; *d* Arnstadt, 10 July 1692). Son of Hans (2). He was taught music by his father and his eldest brother Johann (*4*); his first appointment as town musician and organist of St Johannis in Schweinfurt cannot be dated precisely, but was about 1629–34. In 1636 he went to Erfurt (probably to stay with his eldest brother; there is no evidence that he held any particular appointment there), and in 1641 he became a court and town musician in Arnstadt, where he was also organist of the Liebfrauenkirche. The printed funeral sermon delivered by J.G. Olearius (Arnstadt, 1692; the biographical sections repr. in *BJb 1995*, 101–2) describes him as an 'organist who touched the heart' and a '*musicus practicus* famous for his art', as well as a composer of 'chorales, motets, concertos, fugues and the like'. A vocal concerto, *Ich danke dir, Gott* (1681), for five voices, 2 violins, 2 violas and continuo (EDM, 1st ser., ii (1935)), three organ chorales (ed. D. Hellmann, *Orgelwerke der Familie Bach* (Leipzig, 1967)) and two sonatas for two violins, two violas and continuo (ed. in Stuttgarter Bach Ausgaben, ser. A.3 (Stuttgart, *c*1998)) are extant. The Lüneburg inventory of 1696 lists another vocal work, the ten-part *Als der Tag der Pfingsten erfüllet war*, now lost.

Johann(es) Bach (*3/57*) (*b* Gotha, *c*1612; *d* Arnstadt, bur. 9 Dec 1632). Son of Caspar (*3/a*). He was a town musician in Arnstadt.

Johann(es) Bach (4) (*b* Wechmar, 26 Nov 1604; *d* Erfurt, bur. 13 May 1673). Son of Hans (2). After spending five years as an apprentice and two years as a journeyman to the Stadtpfeifer Johann Christoph Hoffmann in Suhl, he became a town musician in 1633 and from 1634 was organist of St Johannis in Schweinfurt. In 1635 he was appointed town musician in Erfurt and on 16 April 1636 organist of the Predigerkirche there. In 1649, while he was still organist, the church acquired the largest and finest organ in Erfurt, built by Ludwig Compenius. Johann Bach's first wife, Barbara, was the daughter of his master Hoffmann; the marriage was childless and in 1639, after her early death, he married Hedwig Lämmerhirt, daughter of the prosperous and influential Erfurt councillor Valentin Lämmerhirt. Two motets have been ascribed to Johann Bach: *Unser Leben ist ein Schatten* for two sopranos, alto, two tenors and bass, with a three-part echo choir and *Sei nun wieder zufrieden* for double chorus, as well as an aria, *Weint nicht um meinen Tod*, for soprano, alto, tenor, bass and continuo (EDM, 1st ser., i (1935)). See S. Orth: 'Neues über den Stammvater der "Erfurter" Bache, Johann Bach' (*Mf*, ix (1956), 447–50); S. Orth, 'Johann Bach, der Stammvater der Erfurter Bache' (*BJb 1973*, 79–87); and Brück (1990).

Johann Bach (59) (*b* Themar, 1621; *d* Lehnstedt, 12 Sept 1686). Son of Andreas Bach, a councillor in Themar. He was Kantor in Ilmenau and a deacon there from 1668. In 1680 he became a pastor in Lehnstedt.

Johann(es) Bach: see also under Hans Bach above.

Johann Aegidius Bach (8) (*b* Erfurt, bap. 11 Feb 1645; *d* Erfurt, bur. 22 Nov 1716). Son of Johann (4). He was taught music by his father, and in 1671 was a violinist in the Erfurt town music, becoming its director in 1682. From 1674 he also held the post of organist at the Kaufmannskirche in Erfurt, and was appointed organist of the Michaeliskirche in 1690. His pupils, besides his sons and nephews, included J.G. Walther.

Johann Aegidius Bach (36) (*b* Erfurt, bap. 4 Aug 1709; *d* Gross-Monra, nr Kölleda, 17 May 1746). Son of Johann Christoph (*19*). He was Kantor of Gross-Monra.

Johann Ambrosius Bach (11) (*b* Erfurt, 22 Feb 1645; *d* Eisenach, 20 Feb 1695). Son of Christoph (5), twin brother of Johann Christoph (12) and father of Johann Sebastian (24). On 8 April 1668 he married Maria Elisabeth Lämmerhirt (*b* Erfurt, 24 Feb 1644; *d* Eisenach, 1 May 1694), daughter by his second marriage of the late Valentin Lämmerhirt, councillor of Erfurt. She was the half-sister of Hedwig, wife of Johann Bach (4). Ambrosius was first a Stadtpfeifer in Arnstadt, then from 1667 a violinist in the Erfurt town music, and from 1671 court musician and director of the town music in Eisenach. The town chronicler of Eisenach, Georg Dressel, said of this outstanding and versatile musician, 'In 1672 the new *Hausmann* [director of the town music] made music at Easter with organ, violins, voices, trumpets and kettledrums, something no Kantor or director is known to have done before in the history of Eisenach'. When, in 1684, he was offered the post of director of the town music in Erfurt the Duke of Eisenach was unwilling to let him go, and he had to decline the offer. A portrait of Johann Ambrosius in oils, painted after 1671, is extant (*D-Bsb*). See F. Rollberg: 'Johann Ambrosius Bach, Stadtpfeifer zu Eisenach von 1671–1695', *BJb 1927*, 133–52; C. Freyse, 'Das Porträt Ambrosius Bach', *BJb 1959*, 149–55.

Johann Andreas Bach (44) (*b* Ohrdruf, 7 Sept 1713; *d* Ohrdruf, 25 Oct 1779). Son of Johann Christoph (*22*). He was an oboist in the military band in Gotha in 1733. From 1738 he was organist of the Trinitatiskirche in Ohrdruf, and from 1743 of the Michaeliskirche in the same town. He owned the so-called *Andreas Bach Buch* (see Johann Christoph Bach (22) below), one of the main sources for the early organ and keyboard works of Johann Sebastian (24).

Johann Balthasar Bach (63) (*b* Eisenach, 4 March 1673; *d* Eisenach, ?5 April 1691). Son of Johann Ambrosius (*11*). He was apprenticed to his father as a Stadtpfeifer. (Not included in the *Ursprung*.)

Johann Bernhard Bach (18) (*b* Erfurt, bap. 25 Nov 1676; *d* Eisenach, 11 June 1749). Son of Johann Aegidius (8); see §III (5) below.

Johann Bernard Bach (*41*) (*b* Ohrdruf, 24 Nov 1700; *d* Ohrdruf, 12 June 1743). Son of Johann Christoph (*22*). He studied with Johann Sebastian (*24*) in Weimar and Köthen in 1715–19, and was organist of the Michaeliskirche, Ohrdruf, from 1721. Spitta mentions two harpsichord works by him (now lost), a suite in E♭ and a sonata in B♭.

Johann Christian Bach (*7*) (*b* Erfurt, bap. 17 Aug 1640; *d* Erfurt, bur. 1 July 1682). Son of Johann (*4*). He was taught music by his father in Erfurt and by his cousin Johann Christoph (*12*) in Eisenach, and became director of the Erfurt town music in 1666 or 1667.

Johann Christian Bach (*32*) (*b* Erfurt, bap. 31 March 1696). Son of Johann Christoph (*17*). He worked as a musician in Sondershausen.

Johann Christian Bach (*50*) (*b* Leipzig, 5 Sept 1735; *d* London, 1 Jan 1782). Son of Johann Sebastian (*24*); see §III (12) below.

Johann Christian Bach (*69*) (*b* Halle, 23 July 1743; *d* Halle, 20 June 1814). Son of Georg Michael (*66*). He studied in Halle with Wilhelm Friedemann Bach (*45*), who gave him the autograph of Johann Sebastian's *Clavierbüchlein für Wilhelm Friedemann*. He was a teacher at the Pädagogium (preparatory school) in Halle and is known as the 'Clavier-Bach'.

Johann Christoph Bach (*13*) (*b* Arnstadt, bap. 8 Dec 1642; *d* Eisenach, bur. 2 April 1703). Son of Heinrich (*6*); see §III (2) below.

Johann Christoph Bach (*12*) (*b* Erfurt, 22 Feb 1645; *d* Arnstadt, bur. 28 Aug 1693). Son of Christoph (*5*). In 1666 he was a town musician in Erfurt, and from 1671 was a court and town musician (violinist) in Arnstadt.

Johann Christoph Bach (*22*) (*b* Erfurt, 16 June 1671; *d* Ohrdruf, 22 Feb 1721). Son of Johann Ambrosius (*11*). He studied in Erfurt in 1685–8 with Johann Pachelbel, and in 1688 was briefly organist of the Thomaskirche in Erfurt. He then deputized for his sick uncle and godfather Heinrich Bach (*6*) in Arnstadt, was organist of the Michaeliskirche in Ohrdruf from 1690, and from 1700 also taught at the Lyceum there. In 1696 he declined an invitation to succeed Pachelbel as town organist in Gotha, evidently made on Pachelbel's own recommendation. In 1695–1700 Johann Christoph taught his younger brother Johann Sebastian (*24*), who lived at his house in Ohrdruf after his parents' death, and dedicated to him the Capriccio in E BWV993, 'In honorem Johann Christoph Bachii', probably soon after leaving Ohrdruf himself. According to contemporary accounts, Johann Christoph was regarded as an *optimum artifex*, but it is not certain whether his reputation was confined to his practical abilities or whether he was also a composer. His wide-ranging musical interests are evident in two extensive collections of keyboard music compiled by him: the *Andreas Bach Buch* (*D-LEm* Sammlung Becker III.6.4; see Johann Andreas Bach (*44*) above), and the Möller manuscript (*D-Bsb* Mus.ms.40644). As well as being among the most informative keyboard and organ manuscripts of the period around 1700, they are also important sources of J.S. Bach's early works. No compositions are expressly attributed to Johann Christoph, but some keyboard works that have been assigned to Johann Christoph (*13*) could be by Johann Christoph (*22*) instead. See C. Freyse: *Die Ohrdrufer Bache in der Silhouette: Johann Sebastian Bachs ältester Bruder Johann Christoph und seine Nachkommen* (Eisenach, 1957); H.-J. Schulze: 'Johann Christoph Bach (1771–1721), "Organist und Schul Collega in Ohrdruf": Johann Sebastian Bach's erster Lehrer', *BJb* 1985, 55–81; and documents in Bitter, iv, 40–47.

Johann Christoph Bach (*17*) (*b* Erfurt, bap. 13 Jan 1673; *d* Gehren, bur. 30 July 1727). Son of Johann Christian (*7*). After studying music with his father and attending the Erfurt Gymnasium, he became Kantor and organist in Niederzimmern, near Weimar. From 1695 he was Kantor and organist at the Thomaskirche, Erfurt, and from 1698 he pursued a similar career in Gehren. He compiled an organ book that later came into the possession of his son Johann Günther (*33*; see below) and a collection of works by Johann Pachelbel, J.C.F. Fischer and other 17th-century masters, including also some compositions of his own (*US-NH* LM 4983).

Johann Christoph Bach (*28*) (*b* Eisenach, bap. 29 Aug 1676). Son of Johann Christoph (*13*). He was a harpsichordist in Erfurt. In 1702–3 he was in Lübeck (perhaps studying with Buxtehude) and on the death of Johann Christoph (*13*) both he and his brother Johann Nikolaus applied for their father's post as organist in Eisenach. However, their cousin Johann Bernhard Bach (*18*) won the appointment. In 1706 he attended Jena University, and then went to Hamburg, where evidence of him is dated 1708–9 and where he married. He later went to Rotterdam (1717–20) and then to England, and seems never to have returned to Germany. It was evidently from him that the Duke of Chandos bought a harpsichord with two rows of keys in June 1720 for the sum of £572 (W. and M. Eisen, eds.: *Händel-Handbuch*, iv (Leipzig, 1985), p.93). See C. Oefner, 'Neues zur Biographie von Johann Christoph Bach (geb. 1676)', *DJbM*, xiv (1969), 121–3.

Johann Christoph Bach (*19*) (*b* Erfurt, bap. 17 Aug 1685; *d* Erfurt, bur. 15 May 1740). Son of Johann Aegidius (*8*). He was taught music by his father and attended the Ratsgymnasium in Erfurt. He was organist at the Thomaskirche, Erfurt, and from 1705 a member of the town music there, becoming its director in 1716.

Johann Christoph Bach (*26*) (*b* Arnstadt, 12 Sept 1689; *d* Blankenhain, bur. 28 Feb 1740). Son of Johann Christoph (*12*). He was organist in Keula in 1714, and from 1729 an organist, teacher and merchant in Blankenhain.

Johann Christoph Bach (*42*) (*b* Ohrdruf, 12 Nov 1702; *d* Ohrdruf, 2 Nov 1756). Son of Johann Christoph (*22*). He was in the service of the princely court at Sondershausen, and from 1728 was Kantor in Ohrdruf.

Johann Christoph Friedrich Bach (*49*) (*b* Leipzig, 21 June 1732; *d* Bückeburg, 26 Jan 1795. Son of Johann Sebastian (*24*); see §III (11) below.

Johann Christoph Georg Bach (*75*) (*b* Ohrdruf, 8 May 1747; *d* Ohrdruf, 30 Dec 1814). Son of Johann Andreas (*44*). He was organist of the Michaeliskirche in Ohrdruf from 1779.

Johann Elias Bach (*39*) (*b* Schweinfurt, 12 Feb 1705; *d* Schweinfurt, 30 Nov 1755). Son of Johann Valentin (*21*). He studied theology at Jena from 1728 and then in Leipzig from 1738. He lived in the house of Johann Sebastian (*24*), was his pupil and until 1742 acted as his private secretary and tutor to the younger Bach children. In 1743 he went to Schweinfurt as Kantor of the Johanniskirche and inspector of the church boarding-school. See K. Pottgiesser: 'Die Briefentwürfe des Johann Elias Bach', *Die Musik*, xii (1912–13), 3–19; F. Beyschlag: 'Ein Schweinfurter Ableger der thüringischen Musikerfamilie

Bach', *Schweinfurter Heimatblätter*, xi (1925); P. Wollny and E. Odrich: *Die Briefentwürfe des Johann Elias Bach (1705–1755)* (Hildesheim, 2000).

Johann Ernst Bach (*25*) (*b* Arnstadt, 5 Aug 1683; *d* Arnstadt, 21 March 1739). Son of Johann Christoph (*12*). He studied in Hamburg and Frankfurt, and in 1707 became organist of the Neukirche in Arnstadt in succession to Johann Sebastian (*24*), for whom he had already deputized during winter 1705–6 when Johann Sebastian was visiting Buxtehude in Lübeck. From 1728 he was organist of the Liebfrauenkirche in Arnstadt.

Johann Ernst Bach (*34*) (*b* Eisenach, bap. 30 Jan 1722; *d* Eisenach, 1 Sept 1777). Son of Johann Bernhard (*18*); see §III (10) below.

Johann Friedrich Bach (*29*) (*b* Eisenach, *c*1682; *d* Mühlhausen, bur. 8 Feb 1730). Son of Johann Christoph (*13*). He succeeded Johann Sebastian Bach (*24*) in 1708 as organist of the Divi-Blasii-Kirche in Mühlhausen. An organ fugue in G minor by him is extant (*D-Bsb*).

Johann Friedrich Bach (*35*) (*b* Erfurt, bap. 22 Oct 1706; *d* Andisleben, nr Erfurt, bur. 30 May 1743). Son of Johann Christoph (*19*). He attended the Ratsgymnasium in Erfurt and then worked as a schoolmaster, Kantor and organist in Andisleben. From 1739 he deputized for his father as director of the Erfurt town music, returning to Andisleben in 1742.

Johann Georg Bach (*70*) (*b* Eisenach, bap. 2 Oct 1751; *d* Eisenach, 12 April 1797). Son of Johann Ernst (*34*). He succeeded his father in 1777 as court and town organist of Eisenach, titular Kapellmeister, notary and town treasurer.

Johann Georg Bach (*b* ?Güstrow, 1786; *d* Elberfeld, 6 Dec 1874). Not a member of the Wechmar line. He was the son of Johann Michael Bach (see §III (13) below) and taught music in Elberfeld.

Johann Gottfried Bernhard Bach (*47*) (*b* Weimar, 11 May 1715; *d* Jena, 27 May 1739). Son of Johann Sebastian (*24*). He was a pupil of his father, and was organist of the Marienkirche in Mühlhausen, 1735–7. He then became organist of St Jacobi in Sangerhausen (a position for which his father had applied in 1702). He left Sangerhausen in spring 1738, with what intention is not known. In a letter of 26 May 1738 Johann Sebastian complained bitterly of his 'undutiful son', whose character was apparently unstable and who had got into debt. He matriculated as a law student at Jena University on 28 January 1739, but died only a few months later 'of a high fever'.

Johann Günther Bach (*15*) (*b* Arnstadt, bap. 17 July 1653; *d* Arnstadt, bur. 10 April 1683). Son of Heinrich (*6*). From 1682 he was assistant organist to his father in Arnstadt, where he also made keyboard instruments and violins.

Johann Günther Bach (*33*) (*b* Gehren, 4 April 1703; *d* Erfurt, bur. 24 Oct 1756). Son of Johann Christoph (*17*). He was a town musician (a tenor and viola player), and at some time before 1735 became a teacher in Erfurt. The *Günther Bach Buch* in the Lowell Mason Collection (*US-NH*) was compiled by Johann Christoph (*17*; see above).

Johann Heinrich Bach (*43*) (*b* Ohrdruf, 4 Aug 1707; *d* Öhringen, 20 May 1783). Son of Johann Christoph (*22*). He was taught by Johann Sebastian (*24*) and while at the Thomasschule, Leipzig, in 1724–8 was one of his principal copyists (*Hauptkopist* C). He then became assistant to his brother Johann Christoph (*42*) in Ohrdruf, and in 1735 went to Öhringen in Hohenlohe as Kantor and organist.

Johann Heinrich Bach (*53*) (*b* Hamburg, bap. 4 Nov 1709). Son of Johann Christoph (*28*). According to the *Ursprung* he was 'a good keyboard player'.

Johann Jacob Bach (*3/60*) (*b* Wolfsbehringen, 12 Sept 1655; *d* Ruhla, 11 Dec 1718). Son of Wendel (*b* ?Wechmar, 1619; *d* Wolfsbehringen, 18 Dec 1682), a farmer 'who could also sing well', and grandson of Wendel (*b c*1580). He went to school in Eisenach, later became organist in Thal, near Eisenach, and then Kantor in Steinbach (1679–90), Wasungen (1690–94) and Ruhla. The Schweinfurt inventory of 1689 lists a vocal work by him, *Schmücke dich, o liebe Seele*, for four voices and instruments.

Johann Jacob Bach (*16*) (*b* Erfurt, bap. 14 Aug 1668; *d* Eisenach, bur. 29 April 1692). Son of Johann Christian (*7*). He served as apprentice and then journeyman Stadtpfeifer under Johann Ambrosius (*11*) in Eisenach.

Johann Jacob Bach (*23*) (*b* Eisenach, bap. 11 Feb 1682; *d* Stockholm, 16 April 1722). Son of Johann Ambrosius (*11*). He trained as a Stadtpfeifer in Eisenach under Johann Heinrich Halle, his father's successor, joined the Swedish Guard as an oboist about 1704–6 and went to Turkey with the Swedish army under Carl XII. In Constantinople he took flute lessons from Pierre-Gabriel Buffardin, and from 1713 he was a chamber musician with the Stockholm court ensemble. The occasion for the composition by Johann Sebastian (*24*) of his *Capriccio sopra la lontananza del suo fratro dilettissimo* (BWV992) has often, but without plausible grounds, been identified with Johann Jacob's departure from Germany about 1704–6. See C. Wolff. 'The Identity of the "Fratro Dilettissimo" in the Capriccio B-flat Major', *The Harpsichord and its Repertoire: Utrecht 1990*, 145–56.

Johann Lorenz Bach (*38*) (*b* Schweinfurt, 10 Sept 1695; *d* Lahm im Itzgrund, 14 Dec 1773). Son of Johann Valentin (*21*). In 1715–17 he was a pupil of Johann Sebastian (*24*) in Weimar, and from 1718 organist and Kantor in Lahm. A fugue in D by him is extant (ed. D. Hellmann, *Orgelwerke der Familie Bach*, (Leipzig, 1967)), and the existence of other compositions by him is documented (*BJb* 1949–50). See O. Kaul, *Musikgeschichte der ehemaligen Reichstadt Schweinfurt* (Würzburg, 1935).

Johann Ludwig Bach (*3/64*) (*b* Thal, nr Eisenach, 4 Feb 1677; *d* Meiningen, bur. 1 May 1731). Son of Johann Jacob (*3/60*); see §III (6) below.

Johann Michael Bach (*14*) (*b* Arnstadt, bap. 9 Aug 1648; *d* Gehren, 17 May 1694). Son of Heinrich (*6*); see §III (3) below.

Johann Michael Bach (*30*) (*b* Eisenach, bap. 1 Aug 1685). Son of Johann Christoph (*13*). He left Eisenach in 1703 and was later active as an organ builder in Stockholm, but nothing is known for certain about his later life.

Johann Michael Bach (*b* Struth, nr Schmalkalden, 9 Nov 1745; *d* Elberfeld, 1820). Not a member of the Wechmar line, but from a subsidiary Hessian branch of the family; see §III (13) below.

Johann Nicolaus Bach (*9*) (*b* Erfurt, bap. 5 Feb 1653; *d* Erfurt, bur. 28 July 1682). Son of Johann (*4*). He was trained in music by his father and in 1673 became a member of the Erfurt town music as a viol player.

Johann Nicolaus Bach (27) (b Eisenach, 10 Oct 1669; d Jena, 4 Nov 1753). Son of Johann Christoph (13); see §III (4) below.

Johann Philipp Bach (77) (b Meiningen, 5 Aug 1752; d Meiningen, 2 Nov 1846). Son of Gottlieb Friedrich (68). From 1790 he was court organist and painter (Kabinettsmaler) in Meiningen.

Johann Samuel Bach (31) (b Niederzimmern, nr Weimar, 4 June 1694; d Gundersleben, 1 July 1720). Son of Johann Christoph (17). He was a musician and teacher at the princely court of Sondershausen and then a schoolmaster in Gundersleben.

Johann Sebastian Bach (24) (b Eisenach, 21 March 1685; d Leipzig, 28 July 1750). Son of Johann Ambrosius (11); see §III (7) below.

Johann Stephan Bach (3/62) (b Ilmenau, bap. 5 June 1665; d Brunswick, 6 Jan 1717). Son of Johann (59). From 1690 he was Kantor at Brunswick Cathedral (St Blasius). He was also a poet, and there are reports that he wrote sonnets.

Johann Valentin Bach (21) (b Themar, 6 Jan 1669; d Schweinfurt, 12 Aug 1720). Son of Georg Christoph (10). From 1694 he was a town musician and head tower watchman (Obertürmer) in Schweinfurt.

Lips [Philippus] Bach (3/b) (b c1590; d Wechmar, 21 Sept 1626). His relationship with the family of Veit Bach (1) is not clear, but he too was a musician.

Melchior Bach (3/55) (b 1603; d Arnstadt, 7 Sept 1634). Son of Caspar (3/a). He was a town musician in Arnstadt.

Nicolaus Bach (3/58) (b Arnstadt, 6 Dec 1619; d Arnstadt, 1 Oct 1637). Son of Caspar (3/a). He was a town musician in Arnstadt.

Nicolaus Ephraim Bach (65) (b Wasungen, bap. 26 Nov 1690; d Gandersheim, 12 Aug 1760). Son of Johann Jacob (3/60). He was a musician from 1708 and organist from 1719 at the Meiningen Court. In 1724 he became organist in Gandersheim.

Philipp Christian Georg Bach (72) (b Ohrdruf, 6 April 1734; d Wernigshausen, 18 Aug 1809). Son of Johann Christoph (42). In 1759–72 he was Kantor of the Michaeliskirche in Ohrdruf, and from 1772 he was a pastor in Wernigshausen.

Philipp Ernst Christian Bach (78) (b Eisenach, bap. 20 May 1780; d Eisenach, 29 March 1840). Son and pupil of Johann Georg Bach (70). He was an official copyist in Eisenach, and was also active as an organist and an authority on organs. After the death of his father in 1797, and again in 1809, he applied for the post of organist at St Georg and was considered on the grounds that his 'father and forebears . . . have filled this position with credit for almost a century and a half'. However, when the choice was narrowed down he did not get the post. This was probably less to do with the claim made by Kehl, the organist who held the post in 1797–1809, that the organ of St Georg was ruined since Philipp Ernst had played it 'wildly' than because the other candidates had greater practical and theoretical knowledge. With Wilhelm Friedrich Ernst (76) he was the last musical member of the family.

Samuel Anton Bach (67) (b Meiningen, bap. 26 April 1713; d Meiningen, 29 March 1781). Son of Johann Ludwig (3/64). He studied with Johann Sebastian (24) in Leipzig around 1732, and was later organist, and for a time also painter, at the Meiningen court.

Tobias Friedrich Bach (40) (b Ohrdruf, 21 July 1695; d Udestedt, 1 July 1768). Son of Johann Christoph (22). From 1714 he was organist of the Dreifaltigkeitskirche in Ohrdruf. He was appointed court Kantor in Gandersheim in 1717, Kantor in Pferdingsleben in 1720 and Kantor in Udestedt in 1721.

Tobias Friedrich Bach (71) (b Udestedt, bap. 22 Sept 1723; d Erfurt, 18 Jan 1805). Son of Tobias Friedrich (40). In 1747 he became Kantor at the school of the Reglerkirche in Erfurt, and he was appointed Kantor of the Barfüsserkirche there in 1762.

Veit Bach (1) (b Pressburg [now Bratislava], c1555; d Wechmar, nr Gotha, 8 March 1619). As a result of the Counter-Reformation he emigrated from Hungary to Wechmar. The founder of the Wechmar line, he was a miller and baker by trade, and was the first to show musical inclinations and talent in what was to become an extensive family of musicians. Veit Bach had a house in Wechmar, and he and his son Hans (2) are explicitly mentioned as 'musici' in the Wechmar local registry of 1600–10. See §II below.

Wilhelm Friedemann Bach (45) (b Weimar, 22 Nov 1710; d Berlin, 1 July 1784). Son of Johann Sebastian (24); see §III (8) below.

Wilhelm Friedrich Ernst Bach (76) (b Bückeburg, bap. 24 May 1759; d Berlin, 25 Nov 1845). Son of Johann Christoph Friedrich (49); see §III (14) below.

II. Family history

The Bach family lived and worked in central Germany, primarily in Thuringia, with the Ernestine Saxon duchies and principalities of Eisenach, Gotha, Meiningen and Weimar, the county of Schwarzburg-Arnstadt, Ohrdruf in Hohenlohe, and the town of Erfurt in the electorate of Mainz. This area was relatively densely populated at the time, and although bitterly split politically it was denominationally unified. In this economically sound and culturally sophisticated context musical life flourished, encouraged in particular by ambitious displays of magnificence on the part of miniature courts, an awareness of musical tradition in the churches of the area (which apart from the Catholic enclave of Erfurt belonged to the Lutheran heartland), and the desire for prestige of many towns both large and small. The rise and decline of the musical Bach family is closely connected with these social conditions: first with the construction and expansion of musical practice in courts, churches and towns towards the end of the 16th century, then with the gradual decline in importance of such leading musical institutions as court orchestras, church choirs and town bands as the middle-class musical culture of the later 18th century began to develop. Musical life in Thuringia was notable for its wide variety within a small area, but it lacked a major centre (with an opera company, for instance), so that there was nothing to attract really famous musicians to it. In the Bach family itself sound, average competence was the norm. Only a few of its members achieved anything extraordinary, and most of those who did left Thuringia.

The unusual concentration of musical gifts within one family in such a narrow regional context has long interested students of genealogy, heredity and talent. The continual reappearance of musical gifts through the generations, with an increasingly large and then suddenly declining number of prominent family members culminating in the remarkable figure of Johann Sebastian Bach, remains a unique phenomenon. An essential prerequisite for the development of such a dynasty was certainly a general attitude to music as a craft to be learnt, so that the careers of male family members were more or less decided from early childhood. Musical training was usually provided within the family. This was typical even of later generations. For instance, Johann Sebastian, who had himself studied with his brother Johann Christoph (22), is known to have taught six of his nephews – Johann Ernst (34), Johann Lorenz (38), Johann Elias (39), Johann Bernhard (41), Johann Heinrich (43) and Samuel Anton (67) – as well as his own sons. Carl Philipp Emanuel regarded it as quite natural to take his youngest half-brother Johann Christian (50) into his care. Studies or educational tours outside the region were uncommon, although there are instances in the Italian journeys of Caspar Bach's sons (3/54–8; cf the *Ursprung*), of Johann Nicolaus (27) and finally of Johann Christian (50). In these circumstances even Johann Sebastian Bach's journey to Lübeck to study with Buxtehude must be considered decidedly out of the ordinary.

In a self-contained circle of this kind, which was in the nature of a guild, it was natural for relationships with other musical families and intermarriage with them to be frequent. There were other families of musicians in Thuringia, if not as extensive as the Bach family itself. They included the Hoffmann family of Suhl and the Schmidt family of Eisenach. A series of marriages took place with these two families: Johannes (4) and his brother Heinrich (6) both married daughters of the Hoffmann family; Johann Christian (7) and Johann Aegidius (8) married daughters of the Schmidt family. Johann Sebastian himself is a typical example of close relationships between musical families: his first wife was a Bach and his second a descendant of the Wilcke family of musicians from Zerbst.

The family was very close because of its shared social standing and musical interests. Their social status as 'outsiders' (for in the 17th century musicians did not normally have rights of citizenship) and their strict religious views were other important features. Some of the family members even showed a tendency towards sectarianism. Family gatherings were held regularly, and must have resembled small-scale music festivals. A particular speciality of the Bachs was the performance of quodlibets at such gatherings. Drawing on information from J.S. Bach's sons, Forkel wrote in 1802:

The meeting place was usually in Erfurt, Eisenach or Arnstadt. They devoted their time together wholly to making music. Since the company consisted entirely of Kantors, organists and town musicians, all of whom had to do with the church, and in any case it was then still the custom to begin everything on a religious note, the first thing they did on being gathered together was to strike up a chorale. They proceeded from this pious beginning to jests that were often in great contrast. For they now sang folksongs, some of a rather comic and indelicate content, in such a way that the various improvised parts made up a kind of harmony, but the texts for each part were quite different. They called this kind of extempore harmonizing a quodlibet, and not only enjoyed a hearty laugh at it themselves, but provoked equally hearty and irresistible laughter in all who heard them.

The family was well aware that it was maintaining a musical tradition. It is no accident that Johann Sebastian, in a letter of 28 October 1730 to Georg Erdmann, described his children as 'born *musici*', and even the first brief biography of Bach in J.G. Walther's *Musicalisches Lexicon* (1732) and the more extensive account of his career in the obituary of 1754 refer expressly to the great master's background in a remarkable family of musicians.

It was Johann Sebastian himself who systematically investigated the background of the family and its musical heritage. His genealogy of the family, drawn up about 1735, is still the most reliable document on the family history, particularly in its early generations. (The original manuscript of the *Ursprung* is lost, but several copies are extant, including an especially important one with additions by C.P.E. Bach.) Johann Sebastian's estate also contained a collection of compositions by the most important earlier family members, under the title 'Alt-Bachisches Archiv' (the original, containing 20 works, was once owned by the Berlin Singakademie; it was thought lost in World War II, but was rediscovered, along with other Bach manuscripts, in Kiev (Ukraine) in 1999. This collection was probably begun by Johann Ambrosius, as a number of entries in his hand suggest. Johann Sebastian later reordered it, providing new title-pages, and also made practical use of it, preparing some instrumental parts.

The *Ursprung* traces the family tree without a break to Veit (1) in the middle of the 16th century. However, many of the details are unclear up to the generation of Veit's grandsons, the sons of Hans (2), and they cannot be fully clarified for want of insufficient archival documents (for instance, the Wechmar church records do not begin until 1619). Studies of the Bach family have sometimes assumed that Veit Bach was born in Thuringia and merely happened to live in Hungary for some time, or that he was born in Wechmar and was the son of an older Veit who had already emigrated from Hungary in 1545, but these theories are untenable. There is no reason to doubt the data in the *Ursprung*, particularly as Johann Nicolaus Bach (27), in a letter of 24 April 1728, clearly stated that 'The Bachs come from Hungary' (see Schulze, 1989).

It has been shown that other Bachs as well as Veit had settled in the little town of Wechmar, near Gotha, but it has proved impossible to trace the family relationship. For instance, there was a Hans Bach living in Wechmar in 1561, and later a Lips (Philippus) and another Hans Bach. They may have been close relations who had left Hungarian Moravia at some earlier date, and whom Veit then followed, or they may have been more distant relations who had been living in Wechmar for some time. The name of Bach (pronounced with a long 'a', as 'Baach', and often written that way as well) was already common in the Thuringian region, and can be traced there to the 14th century, although there is no evidence of musical activity on the part of these earlier Bachs. Where musicians do occasionally appear (for instance, a trumpeter called Eberhard Heinrich Bach from Rohrborn near Erfurt, who was the son of a Heinrich Bach and went to Indonesia by way of the Netherlands in about 1598), there is no evidence of any concrete family relationship. It seems best to regard the close circle of the musical Bach family as confined to those mentioned in the family genealogy of the *Ursprung*.

Family tradition in that work says of Veit Bach, a baker by trade, that he often amused himself by playing a 'cythringen' (a small cittern). The explicit comment – 'This was, as it were, the beginning of music in his descendants' – seems to indicate that none of Veit's ancestors was a professional musician. Nor indeed was Veit himself. He came from the area of Moravia and Slovakia in what was then the kingdom of Hungary with its capital city of Pressburg, now Bratislava (according to

Korabinsky, Veit's native city), but his date of birth is not known. Nor is it known why and when he emigrated to Thuringia, but at the time of the Schmalkaldian Wars (1545–7) Protestants were being expelled in the wake of the Counter-Reformation, and there were probably restrictions on the practice of Lutheranism in Hungary in the following decades. The mention of Hungary in the *Ursprung* as the Bach family's country of origin should be regarded, in accordance with the terminology of the times, as referring to the central area of the Habsburg possessions in general, including Bohemia and Moravia. There are records of various people surnamed Bach in the 16th and 17th centuries in Moravia and elsewhere in the Habsburg territories, for instance Hans Bach the *Spielmann* (violinist; see §III (1) below).

Veit Bach settled in Wechmar, where he became a householder, and died there on 8 March 1619. Hans Bach (2), his son (probably the eldest) was the first family member to have a thorough musical training; he then practised as a musician, although he was also active in other capacities. His sons were the first of the family to devote themselves entirely to music. Their acceptance of salaried positions shows that they had settled in one place, thus taking the first step towards entering the urban middle classes and breaking with the tradition of the itinerant *Spielmann* or 'beer-fiddler', although their varied activities as instrumentalists point to the *Spielmann* tradition behind them.

Genealogical problems arise with a number of family members who were certainly connected with Veit's main Wechmar line but whose precise origin is unclear. There is a lacuna in the *Ursprung* itself concerning the brother of Hans (2); no name is given under the number (3), only the man's trade (he was a carpet maker), although there is at least brief mention of three of his sons who were musicians. Obviously Johann Sebastian Bach, as author of the *Ursprung*, lacked clear information on this point, and the result was some confusion between two family members. It seems possible that Veit had two sons as well Hans (2) – Johann Sebastian Bach's great-grandfather – and that these sons, Caspar (3/a) and Lips (3/b), have been merged into a single figure in the *Ursprung*. However, it is also possible that Hans Bach and/or Lips Bach of Wechmar were brothers of Veit.

The mention in the *Ursprung* of visits to Italy by the nephews of Hans (2) can in fact refer only to the sons of Caspar (3/a); documents show that the Count of Schwarzburg-Arnstadt encouraged the project. Moreover, Caspar had a son Heinrich (3/56), mentioned in the register of deaths as being blind, who must surely be identical with the 'blind Jonas' of the *Ursprung*; the nickname 'Jonas', deriving from the biblical Jonah, would presumably have referred to his adventures. On the other hand, the forebears of Johann Ludwig Bach (3/64) can go back only to one Wendel Bach, who must have been either a third brother of Hans (2) or, more likely, a son of Lips. This brother could only have been the elder Lips or the elder Hans. In any case, however, the younger Hans (2), Caspar (3/a) Wendel, Lips (3/b) and Andreas must have been closely enough related to each other for family tradition to trace them back to a common origin. The forebears of the Meiningen Bachs were originally farmers, although it is said of the younger Wendel that he could 'also sing very well'. The descent of Andreas Bach in particular is obscure. He was a councillor of Themar, and his son

Johann (59) was first Kantor in Lehnstedt and later a pastor, like several of his descendants. The *Ursprung* expressly mentions that Johann Stephan's brother was a priest. As Georg Michael (66) was present at his funeral in 1738, the Meiningen and Lehnstedt lines must have felt they were closely related, and in that case it can hardly be doubted that they were connected with the main Wechmar line.

In accordance with their origins, nearly all the Bachs were first and foremost instrumentalists. Keyboard instruments headed the list of the instruments they played, but almost all other kinds are also represented. In the true Stadtpfeifer tradition, most of the Bachs learnt several instruments. A number of them were also instrument makers, for instance Johann Christoph (12), Johann Michael (14), Johann Günther (15), Johann Michael (30) and Johann Nicolaus (27), who is credited with the invention of the lute-harpsichord. Johann Sebastian, who was a great expert on the organ, promoted the development of the viola pomposa and criticized Gottfried Silbermann's construction of pianos, clearly shows this aspect of the family's talents. The tendency of most of the Bachs to become instrumentalists made composition a subsidiary pursuit, reserved for those who both had the necessary training and were expected to provide musical works. At least in the 17th century, this meant almost exclusively organists, so it is not surprising that no compositions by Johann Ambrosius (11) are extant. As a court trumpeter, if he composed at all it must have been only as a marginal activity. On the other hand his two organist cousins, Johann Michael and Johann Christoph, were very productive as composers, primarily of works for non-liturgical use (sacred works were the responsibility of the church Kantors). In particular, they wrote funeral motets, no doubt a profitable sideline.

By 1700 the musical Bach family was so widespread in Thuringia that the name 'Bach' was often used as a synonym for 'musician'. In many towns, particularly Erfurt and Arnstadt, they occupied all the key musical positions, and it was typical for a Bach in any post to be succeeded by another Bach. For instance, when Johann Christoph (13) left Arnstadt his younger brother (14) succeeded him, and Johann Sebastian was succeeded in Arnstadt by his cousin Johann Ernst (25) and in Mühlhausen by another cousin, Johann Friedrich (29). The post occupied by Johann Christoph (22) was even passed down through two generations. That of organist at St Georg in Eisenach was held by members of the family for almost 150 years, and it was in the same tradition that C.P.E. Bach applied for his father's position as Thomaskantor in Leipzig.

However, this almost automatic inheritance of musical positions became more difficult when the old institutions, which had enabled musicians to function as a guild, began to break up. It was these institutions that had provided the means of existence for such musical families as the Bachs, who rose gradually from their simple *Spielmann* origins to all positions in the musical hierarchies of the courts, towns and churches. They had been court musicians – Konzertmeisters or Kapellmeisters – Stadtpfeifers, directors of town musical ensembles, organists and Kantors. After the middle of the 18th century at the latest, structural changes were taking place that ran counter to the Bach family's old way of life. Moreover, the family now belonged to the middle class, and its sons had new educational opportunities (almost all the members of the generation of J.S. Bach's sons attended university) fitting them for a number of different professions, whereas previously they had few alternatives to becoming musicians. It is only natural, therefore, that fewer and fewer of them turned to music as a career. Some family members moved into another artistic field, that of painting: the descendants of Johann Ludwig (3/64) were court painters, and the younger Johann Sebastian (1748–78), son of C.P.E. Bach, went to Italy with a high reputation as a gifted painter and died in Rome at the age of 30. In view of the abundance of musical talent in over six generations, it may at first seem surprising, but is understandable if we look back at the circumstances in which they lived and worked, that at the unveiling of the Bach monument donated by Mendelssohn and erected outside the Thomaskirche in Leipzig in 1843 Wilhelm Friedrich Ernst Bach (76) was the last and only representative of a family tradition that had lasted for over 250 years.

BIBLIOGRAPHY

CATALOGUES, BIBLIOGRAPHIES

M. Schneider: 'Thematisches Verzeichnis der musikalischen Werke der Familie Bach (I. Teil)', *BJb* 1907, 103–77 [continuations never appeared]

P. Kast: *Die Bach-Handschriften der Berliner Staatsbibliothek*, (Trossingen, 1958)

J.F. Richter: 'Johann Sebastian Bach und seine Familie in Thüringen', *Deutsches Bachfest*, no.39 (1964), 50–60

K. Beisswenger: *Johann Sebastian Bachs Notenbibliothek* (Kassel, 1992)

H.-J. Schulze and C.Wolff, eds.: *Bach Repertorium* (forthcoming)

SOURCES

'Alt-Bachisches Archive' [MSS of works by older Bach family members], Kiev, Archive for Literature and Art (formerly Berlin Singakademie)

[J.S. Bach]: *Ursprung der musicalisch-Bachischen Familie*, 1735 [orig. MS lost]; ed. M. Schneider, *Bach-Urkunden* (Leipzig, 1917); ed. W. Neumann and H.-J. Schulze, *Bach-Dokumente*, i (Leipzig and Kassel, 1963), no.184; Eng. trans. in H.T. David and A. Mendel, eds., *The Bach Reader* (New York, 1945, rev. and enlarged 3/1998 by C. Wolff as *The New Bach Reader*), 283–94

M. Korabinsky: *Beschreibung der königlichen ungarischen Haupt-Frey- und Krönungsstadt Pressburg*, i (Pressburg, 1784), 110ff

C.S. Terry: *The Origin of the Family of Bach Musicians* (London, 1929)

J. Müller-Blattau: *Genealogie der musikalisch-Bachischen Familie* (Kassel, 1950)

P. Wollny: 'Alte Bach Funde', *BJb* 1998, 137–48

MONOGRAPHS

MGG1 (R. Benecke); *RiemannL12*

C.F.M.: 'Bemerkungen zu dem Stammbaum der Bachischen Familie', *AMZ*, xxv (1823), 187–91

Kawaczynsky: 'Über die Familie Bach: eine genealogische Mitteilung', *AMZ*, xlv (1843), 537–41

P. Spitta: *Johann Sebastian Bach* (Leipzig, 1873–80, 5/1962; Eng. trans., 1884, 2/1889/R), i

A. Lorenz: 'Ein alter Bach-Stammbaum', *NZM*, Jg.82 (1915), 281–2

G. Thiele: 'Die Familie Bach in Mühlhausen', *Mühlhäuser Geschichtsblätter*, xxi (1920–21), 62–84

H. Lämmerhirt: 'Bachs Mutter und ihre Sippe', *BJb* 1925, 101–37

C.S. Terry: *Bach: a Biography* (London, 1928, 2/1933/R)

E. Borkowsky: *Die Musikerfamilie Bach* (Jena, 1930)

H. Helmbold: 'Die Söhne von Johann Christoph und Johann Ambrosius Bach auf der Eisenacher Schule', *BJb* 1930, 49–55

C.S. Terry: 'Has Bach Surviving Descendants?', *MT*, lxxi (1930), 511–13

E. Lux: 'Der Familienstamm Bach in Gräfenroda', *BJb* 1931, 107–11

H. Miesner: 'Urkundliche Nachrichten über die Familie Bach in Berlin', *BJb* 1932, 157–63

H. Lämmerhirt: 'Ein hessischer Bach-Stamm', *BJb* 1936, 53–89

L. Bach: 'Ergänzungen und Berichtigungen zu dem Beitrag "Ein hessischer Bach-Stamm" von Hugo Lämmerhirt', *BJb* 1937, 118–31

K. Fischer: 'Das Freundschaftsbuch des Apothekers Friedrich Thomas Bach: eine Quelle zur Geschichte der Musikerfamilie Bach', *BJb* 1938, 95–102

C.U. von Ulmenstein: 'Die Nachkommen des Bückeburger Bach', *AMf*, iv (1939), 12–20

W.G. Whittaker: 'The Bachs and Eisenach', *Collected Essays* (London, 1940/R)

H. Löffler: '"Bache" bei Bach', *BJb* 1949–50, 106–24

Bach in Thüringen:Gabe der Thüringer Kirche an das Thüringer Volk zum Bach-Gedenkjahr 1950 (Berlin, 1950)

H. Besseler and G.Kraft, eds.: *Johann Sebastian Bach in Thüringen: Festgabe zum Gedenkjahr 1950* (Weimar, 1950)

K. Geiringer: 'Artistic Interrelations of the Bachs', *MQ*, xxxvi (1950), 363–74

W. Rauschenberger: 'Die Familien Bach', *Genealogie und Heraldik*, ii (1949–50), 149–53

E. Wölfer: 'Naumburg und die Musikerfamilie Bach', *Programmheft zu den Bach-Tagen*(Naumburg, 1950), 9–14

C. Schubart: 'Anna Magdalena Bach: neue Beiträge zu ihrer Herkunft und ihren Jugendjahren', *BJb* 1953, 29–50

K. and I. Geiringer: *The Bach Family: Seven Generations of Creative Genius* (London, 1954/R; Ger. trans., enlarged, 1958, 2/1977)

C. Freyse: 'Wieviel Geschwister hatte J.S. Bach?', *BJb* 1955, 103–7

G. Kraft: 'Zur Entstehungsgeschichte des "Hochzeitsquodlibet" (BWV 524)', *BJb* 1956, 140–54

G. von Dadelsen: *Bemerkungen zur Handschrift Johann Sebastian Bachs, seiner Familie und seines Kreises* (Trossingen, 1957)

K. Müller and F.Wiegand: *Arnstädter Bachbuch: Johann Sebastian Bach und seine Verwandten in Arnstadt* (Arnstadt, 1957)

K. Geiringer: 'Unbekannte Werke von Nachkommen J.S. Bachs in amerikanischen Sammlungen', *IMSCR: Cologne 1958*, 110–12

G. Kraft: 'Neue Beiträge zur Bach-Genealogie', *BMw*, i/2 (1959), 29–61

A. Schmiedecke: 'Johann Sebastian Bachs Verwandte in Weissenfels', *Mf*, xiv (1961), 195–200

H.-J. Schulze: 'Marginalien zu einigen Bach-Dokumenten', *BJb* 1961, 79–99

G. Kraft: *Entstehung und Ausbreitung des musikalischen Bach-Geschlechtes in Thüringen: mit besonderer Berücksichtigung des Wechmarer Stammes* (Habilitationsschrift, U. of Halle, 1964)

F. Wiegand: 'Die mütterlichen Verwandten Johann Sebastian Bachs in Erfurt: Ergänzungen und Berichtigungen zur Bachforschung', *BJb* 1967, 5–20

E. Zavarsky: 'Zur angeblichen Pressburger Herkunft der Familie Bach', *BJb*, liii (1967), 21

G. Kraft: 'Das mittelthüringische Siedlungszentrum der Familien Bach und Wölcken', *Musa – mens – musici: im Gedenken an Walther Vetter*(Leipzig, 1969), 153–64

P.M. Young: *The Bachs, 1500–1850* (London, 1970)

I. Lehmann: *Die Wirkungsstätten der Bach-Familie in Thüringen* (Eisenach, 1984)

C. Oefner: *Die Musikerfamilie Bach in Eisenach* (Eisenach, 1984)

H.-J. Schulze: *Studien zur Bach-Überlieferung des 18. Jahrhunderts* (Leipzig, 1984)

R. Hill: *The Möller Manuscript and the Andreas Bach Book: Two Keyboard Anthologies from the Circle of the Young Johann Sebastian Bach* (diss., Harvard U., 1987)

H.-J. Schulze: '"Die Bachen stammen aus Ungarn her": ein unbekannter Brief Johann Nicolaus Bachs aus dem Jahre 1728', *BJb* 1989, 213–20

H. Brück: 'Die Brüder Johann, Christoph und Heinrich Bach und die "Erffurtische musicalische Compagnie"', *BJb* 1990, 71–7

H. Brück: 'Die Andislebener Bache', *BJb* 1991, 199–206

H. Kock: *Genealogisches Lexikon der Familie Bach*, ed. R. Siegel (Wechmar, 1995)

D.R. Melamed: 'The History of the Altbachisches Archiv', *J.S. Bach and the German Motet* (Cambridge, 1995), 161–77

H. Brück: 'Die Erfurter Bach-Familien von 1635 bis 1805', *BJb* 1996, 101–31

III. Individual members

(1) Hans [Johann] Bach (*b* Andelsbuch, Vorarlberg, *c*1555; *d* Nürtingen, 1 Dec 1615). Violinist and court musician. He became a *Spielmann* (violinist) and jester at the Stuttgart court of Duke Ludwig of Württemberg about 1585, and in 1593 he followed the widowed Duchess Ursula to the court of Nürtingen, where he

remained until his death. He apparently often travelled, both alone and in the court entourage. Of his work all that survives is the text of a narrative song of 1614 describing a visit to the town of Weil (*Hanss Baachens Lobspruch zur Weil der Statt*: 'Es ist nun über zwantzig Jahr'); its manner is reminiscent of the late medieval style of Oswald von Wolkenstein. There are two extant portraits of him, an etching of about 1605 and an engraving of 1617. The etching bears the inscription:

Hie siehst du geigen/Hansen Bachen
Wenn du es hörst/so mustu lachen
Er geigt gleichwol/nach seiner Art
Und tregt ein hipschen/Hans Bachen Bart.

Nothing is known of his extraction; he was probably related in some way to Veit Bach (1) of the Wechmar line – Hans was Protestant (no matter of course in the Catholic south) and like Veit he came from Habsburg lands. His portrait of 1617 was in the collection owned by C.P.E. Bach, but since C.P.E. Bach's *Nachlassverzeichnis* of 1790 cited him as 'Bach (Hans), a Gotha musician' his ownership of the picture cannot be taken as confirmation that Hans was a member of the family. He had obviously been confused with the *Spielmann* Hans Bach (2), who trained in Gotha.

BIBLIOGRAPHY

W. Wolffheim: 'Hans Bach der Spielman', *BJb 1910*, 70–85
W. Irtenkauf and H.Maier: 'Gehört der Spielmann Hans Bach zur Musikerfamilie Bach?', *Mf*, ix (1956), 450–52

(2) Johann Christoph Bach (*13*) (*b* Arnstadt, bap. 8 Dec 1642; *d* Eisenach, bur. 2 April 1703). Composer and organist, son of Heinrich Bach. He was probably the most important member of the family before (7) Johann Sebastian (*24*). He received a thorough musical grounding from his father, and on 20 November 1663 was appointed organist of the Arnstadt castle chapel. Two years later he was invited by the Eisenach town council to apply for the post of organist at St Georg, and after an audition on 10 December 1665 he was appointed to that position and also to the post of harpsichordist in the court Kapelle of the Duke of Eisenach. He retained both positions until his death.

Little is known of his work in the court Kapelle. From 1675 the Kapellmeister was Daniel Eberlin, later to become the father-in-law of Telemann, who also conducted the Kapelle on occasion, and for a short while (1677–8) Pachelbel was a member of the Kapelle. During much of his time there Johann Christoph's most important colleague must have been his cousin, the violinist Johann Ambrosius (*11*); Ambrosius often served as his copyist, and their relationship was doubtless a close one. The young Johann Sebastian must also have received his first impressions of organ music from his father's cousin. While Johann Christoph's court position was one of high standing, his tenure of the civic one was marred by a succession of quarrels between him and the town council, for which he was not entirely blameless. It must be said in extenuation that throughout his years in Eisenach he was constantly beset by severe family difficulties, particularly the illnesses of his wife and children. His quarrels with the town council were mostly about his salary and the council's refusal to provide an official residence for him, a deficiency eventually made good by the court. For many years he also battled with the council over the long-overdue restoration (or reconstruction) of the organ at St Georg; he was successful only in 1696, and then did not live to see the completion (by G.C. Stertzing) of the famous instrument in 1707 (his copious, expert notes on the organ's reconstruction are extant; see Freyse). He died in 1703, just ten days after the death of his wife.

Within the family Johann Christoph was highly respected as a composer (a 'profound' one according to the *Ursprung*). In Johann Sebastian's obituary notice of 1754 he is mentioned expressly as one who 'was as good at inventing beautiful thoughts as he was at expressing words. He composed, to the extent that current taste permitted, in a *galant* and *cantabile* style, uncommonly full-textured ... On the organ and the keyboard [he] never played with fewer than five independent parts'. Johann Sebastian performed some of his motets and vocal concertos in Leipzig, as also did C.P.E. Bach later in Hamburg. Although Johann Christoph was primarily an organist and harpsichordist, his extant keyboard works are few, but they show him as a capable composer, stylistically akin to Pachelbel though in general less pedantic. His organ chorales (probably in effect written-down improvisations) demonstrate his mastery of the small form, while the strength of his artistry is developed in his extended harpsichord variations. His vocal works, in particular the motets and concertos, are notable for the variety of their settings. The concertos are characterized by their full instrumental writing, with unusually interesting inner part-writing. While the vocal writing is for the most part technically undemanding (the choral sections were intended for school choirs), the instrumental parts are usually highly elaborate and often call for a virtuoso solo violin (as in the two *lamenti* and the wedding concerto *Meine Freundin, du bist schön*). Johann Sebastian and Carl Philipp Emanuel thought particularly highly of his 22-part concerto for Michaelmas, *Es erhub sich ein Streit*, one of the finest vocal works of the late 17th century. Basically his double-choir motets follow the traditional central German model including both *Spruch* and chorale, with cantabile melodies and often lively alternation of tutti and soloists – a genre which indeed reached its peak in the works of Johann Christoph and his brother (3) Johann Michael (*14*). In both composers' works the older style of writing, with alternating chordal and imitative sections, still predominated, for instance in the motet *Der Gerechte, ob er gleich zu zeitlich stirbt*, which is also a particularly fine example of Johann Christoph's expressive harmony; but the newer style, with its livelier lines (including melismatic semiquaver passages) and looser, more concertante writing, is found in *Sei getreu bis in den Tod* and *Der Mensch, vom Weibe geboren*, obviously later works. The lack of documentation and the small number of the surviving works preclude the establishment of a reliable chronology of Johann Christoph's music.

WORKS
VOCAL

Editions: *Altbachisches Archiv*, i, ed. M. Schneider, EDM, 1st ser., i (1935) [S]
    Johann Christoph Bach: Sämtliche Motetten, ed. E. Franke (Leipzig, 1982) [F]
Arias: Es ist nun aus mit meinem Leben, SATB, bc, S, F; Mit Weinen hebt sichs an, SATB, bc, 1691, S, F
Motets: Der Gerechte, ob er gleich zu zeitlich stirbt, SATTB, bc, 1676, S, F, ed. in Musica sacra, xxxix (Berlin, 1860); Der Mensch, vom Weibe geboren, SSATB, bc, S, F, ed. R. Kubik (Stuttgart, c1984); Fürchte dich nicht, SSATB, bc, F, ed. G. Graulich (Stuttgart, c1992); Herr, nun lässet du deinen Diener, SATB, SATB, bc, F, ed. G. Graulich (Stuttgart, c1980); Herr, wenn ich

nur dich habe, SATB, SATB, bc (anon.), F; Ich weiss, dass mein Erlöser lebt, SATTB, bc, F, ed. G. Graulich (Stuttgart, 1994); Lieber Herr Gott, wecke uns auf, SATB, SATB, bc, 1672, F, ed. G. Graulich (Stuttgart, c1994); Merk auf mein Herz, SATB, SATB, bc, BWV Anh.III.163, ed. P. Wollny (Neuhausen-Stuttgart, 1991); Sei getreu bis in den Tod, SSATB, bc, S, F, ed. R. Kubik (Stuttgart, c1983); Unsers Herzens Freude, SATB, SATB, bc, F; Was kein Aug gesehen hat, SATB, SATB, bc, Bsb (anon.), F

Vocal concertos: Ach, dass ich Wassers gnug hätte (Lamento), A, vn, 3 va, bc, ed. T. Fedtke (Stuttgart, c1976); Die Furcht des Herren, SSATB, SATTB, 2 vn, 2 va, bc, S, ed. H. Bergmann (Stuttgart, c1986); Es erhub sich ein Streit, SATBB, SATBB, 4 tpt, timp, 2 vn, 4 va, bc, ed. D. Krüger (Stuttgart, c1960); Es ist nun aus, SATB, bc Kiev, Archive for Literature and Art (formerly Berlin, Singakademie); Herr, wende dich und sei mir gnädig (Dialogus), SATB, 2 vn, 2 va, bc, ed. H. Bergmann (Stuttgart, c1988); Mein Freundin, du bist schön (Dialogus, wedding piece), SATB, 4 vn, 3 va, bc, S, ed. H. Bergmann (Stuttgart, c1989); Mit Weinen hebt sichs an , SATB, bc , Kiev, Archive for Literature and Art (formerly Berlin, Singakademie); Wie bist du denn o Gott (Lamentation), B, vn, 3 va da gamba, ed. in DTB, x, Jg.vi/1 (1905); attrib. J.P. Krieger), ed. D. Hellmann (Stuttgart, c1976)

Lost: Auf, lasst uns den Herren loben, S, insts, listed in Schweinfurt inventory, 1689; Der Herr ist König, B, insts, listed in Schweinfurt inventory, 1689; Gott schweig doch nicht also, 5vv, insts, listed in Schweinfurt inventory, 1689; Nun gehe ich hin, B, insts, listed in Schweinfurt inventory, 1689; Unsere Tage fahren alle dahin, a 10, listed in Stettin inventory, 1702

INSTRUMENTAL

Aria Eberliniana [15 variations], hpd, 1690, D-Elb (facs. (Leipzig, 1992)); ed. C. Freyse, Veröffentlichungen der Neuen Bachgesellschaft, Jg.xxxix/2 (1940)
Sarabande, G [12 variations], hpd; ed. H. Riemann (Leipzig, n.d.)
Aria, a [15 variations]; ed. G. Birkner (Zürich, 1973)
Praeludium und Fuge, Eb, org, doubtful; ed. D. Hellmann, Orgelwerke der Familie Bach (Leipzig, 1967)
44 chorales with preludes, org, ed. M. Fischer (Kassel, 1936)
4 chorales, org: Ach Herr, mich armen Sünder; Allein Gott in der Höh sei Ehr; An Wasserflüssen Babylon; Wer Gott vertraut, hat wohl gebaut; ed. C. Wolff, appx to Johann Michael Bach: Sämtliche Orgelchoräle (Neuhausen-Stuttgart, 1987)
Lost: 8 chorales, org , listed in GerberNL, i, 209

BIBLIOGRAPHY

MGG1 (R. Benecke)
M. Schneider: 'Thematisches Verzeichnis der musikalischen Werke der Familie Bach', BJb 1907, 103–77
M. Fischer: Die organistische Improvisation im 17. Jahrhundert, dargestellt an den 'Vieruntvierzig Chorälen zum Präambulieren von Johann Christoph Bach (BA 285)(Kassel, 1929)
F. Rollberg: 'Johann Christoph Bach: Organist zu Eisenach 1665–1703', ZMw, xi (1928–9), 549–61
C. Freyse: 'Johann Christoph Bach', BJb 1956, 36–51
P. Wollny: 'Materialen zur Schweinfurter Musikpflege im 17. Jahrhundert: von 1592 bis zum Tod Georg Christoph Bachs (1642–1697)', Schütz Jb 1997, 113–63
H.-J. Schulze and C.Wolff, eds.: Bach Repertorium (forthcoming)

(3) Johann Michael Bach (14) (b Arnstadt, bap. 9 Aug 1648, d Gehren, 17 May 1694). Composer, son of Heinrich Bach (6). He received a sound musical education from his father and the Arnstadt Kantor Jonas de Fletin; the latter's influence may account for his early interest in vocal music. In 1665 he succeeded his brother (2) Johann Christoph (13) as organist of the Arnstadt castle chapel. After an audition on 5 October 1673 he succeeded Johann Effler (who later preceded Johann Sebastian as castle organist in Weimar) as town organist in Gehren. He was also active as an instrument maker there and held the important administrative post of town clerk. On 17 October 1707 his youngest daughter, Maria Barbara (b Gehren, 20 Oct 1684), married her distant cousin (7) Johann Sebastian (24).

A pamphlet issued by the Gehren council refers to Johann Michael as a 'quiet, reserved and artistically experienced subject'; within the family he was considered a 'skilful composer' (Ursprung). As a composer, in fact, he is on almost the same level as his brother Johann Christoph. Especially in the chorale motet, a genre to which he devoted himself with particular intensity, he composed works of real distinction, and his strophic arias, with their parts for obbligato instruments and their resourceful and expressive ritornellos, are also of undisputed value. A notable feature of his music is his varied, natural and convincing treatment of vocal declamation, whether in biblical texts, chorale verses or free poetry. In his motets, as in his brother's, the older, strongly homophonic style predominates; but in such works as Sei lieber Tag willkommen he turned to the freer and more modern style with melismatic passages. His works for double chorus stand firmly in the tradition of Schütz's Psalmen Davids, but go beyond their models. The nine-part funeral motet Unser Leben ist ein Schatten, which has been erroneously attributed to Johann Bach (4), is particularly moving in its illustrative and expressive qualities. His vocal concertos are less extended than those of his brother, but he too favoured a full-textured orchestral palette, which is often quite sophisticated and frequently includes a virtuoso solo violin part.

Almost all the extant keyboard compositions by Johann Michael Bach are organ chorales. They are mainly in the central German tradition of concise, contrapuntal and practical settings, showing a clear relationship to similar works by Johann Pachelbel. Recent discoveries have trebled the number of Johann Michael's extant chorale settings and, although the total remains considerably less than the '72 verschiedene fugirte und figurirte Choralvorspiele' cited by Gerber, these permit a fairer assessment of Bach's merits as an organ composer than was previously possible. The central German organ chorale underwent a slight shift of emphasis in the work of Johann Michael Bach. His four-part figured chorales with the melody in the highest part, as well as others that combine forms more freely, show him to have been a decidedly independent composer, and he must have influenced the young Johann Sebastian in particular. Gerber wrote of him in 1812: 'There is great variety and diversity in the preludes, after the manner of that period, and none is entirely unworthy of the name of Bach'.

WORKS

VOCAL

Edition: Altbachisches Archiv, ed. M. Schneider, EDM, 1st ser., i–ii (1935) [S i–ii]
Arias: Ach, wie sehnlich wart ich der Zeit, S, vn, 3 va da gamba, bc; Auf, lasst uns den Herrn laben, A, vn, 3 va da gamba, bc: ed. in S ii, ed. H. Bergmann (Neuhausen-Stuttgart, c1985)
Motets, SATB, SATB, bc unless otherwise stated: Benedictus, SATTB, ?bc, ed.; Das Blut Jesu Christi, SATTB, bc, ed. in S i, ed. R. Kubik (Neuhausen-Stuttgart, c1981); Dem Menschen ist gesetzt einmal zu sterben, ed. in S i, ed. R. Kubik (Kirchheim, c1985); Ehre sei Gott in der Höhe, ed. in DDT, xlix–l (1915), ed. D. Melamed (Neuhausen-Stuttgart, 1992); Fürchtet euch nicht, ed. in S i, ed. R. Kubik (Neuhausen-Stuttgart, c1980); Halt, was du hast, ed. in S i; Herr, du lässest mich erfahren, ed. in S i; Herr, ich warte auf dein Heil, ed. in S i, ed. R. Kubik (Neuhausen-Stuttgart, c1984); Herr wenn ich nur dich habe, SATTB, bc, ed. in S i, ed. R. Kubik (Neuhausen-Stuttgart, c1984); Ich weiss, dass mein Erlöser lebet, SATTB, bc, ed. in S i; Nun hab ich überwunden, ed. in S i; Nun treten wir ins neue Jahr, ed. D. Melamed (Neuhausen-Stuttgart, 1992); Sei lieber Tag willkommen, SSAATTB, bc, ed. in S i; Sei nun wieder zufrieden, ed. G. Graulich (Stuttgart, 1993); Unser Leben ist ein Schatten, SSAATTB, ATB, bc, ed. in S i (attrib. Johann Bach (4)); Unser Leben währet siebenzig Jahr, SATTB, bc, ed. in S i

Vocal concertos: Ach bleib bei uns, Herr Jesu Christ, SATB, 2 vn, 3 va, bc, ed. in S ii, ed. H. Bergmann (Neuhausen-Stuttgart, c1985); Es ist ein grosser Gewinn, S, 4 vn, bc, ed. in S ii, ed. H. Bergmann (Neuhausen-Stuttgart, c1985); Herr, komm hinab, SATB, 2 vn, 2 va, bc, ed. H.M. Balz (Merseburger, 1995); Liebster Jesu, hör mein Flehen (Dialogus), SATB, 2 vn, 2 va, bc, ed. in S ii, ed. H. Bergmann (Neuhausen-Stuttgart, c1985)

Lost, listed in Ansbach inventory, 1686 (see Schaal): Conditor coeli, a 8; Der Herr is König, a 12; Ich freue mich des, a 15; Lobet, ihr Knechte des Herrn, a 12; Mein Sünd betrüben mich, a 8; Miserere, a 15; Omnipotens Deus, a 12; Pater noster, a 12; Siehe, lobe den Herrn, a 12; Was willtu meine Seele, a 6; Welche ich lieb habe, a 10

Lost, listed in Schweinfurt inventory, 1689 (see Wollny): Auf meinen lieben Gott, SATB, 2 vn, bc (also formerly in Berlin, Singakademie); Benedicat tibi Dominus ex Sion, 5vv, insts; Der Gott Abraham, der Gott Isaac, 5vv, insts; Dies ist der Tag, 6vv, insts; Gott ist mein Heil, 4vv, insts; Herr, lehre uns bedenken, 5vv, insts; Mag, 4vv, insts; Sit nomen Domini benedictum, 5vv, insts; Unser Herr Jesus Christus, B, insts; Wem ein tugendsam Weib, 5vv, insts; Wenn mein Stündlein vorhanden ist, 5vv, insts; Wenn wir in höchsten Nöten sein, 5vv, insts; Wie bin ich doch so herzlich froh, 5vv, insts

Others lost: Ist nicht Ephraim, SATB, 4 va, bc, formerly in Berlin, Singakademie; Wie lieblich sind deine Wohnungen (see Brück); Zion spricht: Der Herr hat mich verlassen, listed in Stettin inventory, c1702

INSTRUMENTAL

Edition: *Johann Michael Bach: Sämtliche Orgelchoräle*, ed. C. Wolff (Neuhausen-Stuttgart, 1987) [W]

Chorales, org, ed. in W: Allein Gott in der Höh sei Ehr; Auf meinen lieben Gott; Der du bist drei in Einigkeit; Derr Herr ist mein getreuer Hirt; Dies sind die heiligen zehn Gebot, also ed. D. Hellmann, *Orgelwerke der Familie Bach* (Leipzig, 1967); Es spricht der Unweisen Mund wohl; Gelobet seist du, Jesu Christ, BWV 723; Gott hat das Evangelium; Gott Vater, der du deine Sohn (anon. in source); Herr Christ, der einig Gottes Sohn; In dich hab ich gehoffet, Herr, also ed. in EDM, 1st ser., ix (1937); In dulci jubilo, BWV 751; Jesus Christus, unser Heiland, der den Tod; Komm, Gott schöpfer, Heiliger Geist (anon. in source); Kommt her zu mir, spricht Gotte Sohn; Mag ich Unglück nicht widerstahn; Meine Seele erhebt den Herren; Nun freut euch lieben Christen gmein; Nun komm, der Heiden Heiland; Nun lasst uns Gott dem Herren; O Herre Gott, Vater in Ewigkeit; Von Gott will ich nicht lassen; Warum betrübst du dich, mein Herz; Wenn mein Stündlein vorhanden ist, also ed. D. Hellmann, *Orgelwerke der Familie Bach* (Leipzig, 1967); Wenn wir in höchsten Nöten sein, also ed. in EDM, 1st ser., ix (1937) and ed. D. Hellmann, *Orgelwerke der Familie Bach* (Leipzig, 1967); Wo Gott der Herr nicht bei uns hält, also ed. in EDM, 1st ser., ix (1937)

Other works: Partita, a, hpd, US-NH; Stark besetzte Sonaten, lost, cited in *GerberL* and *WaltherML*

BIBLIOGRAPHY

GerberL; WaltherML

M. Schneider: 'Thematsiches Verzeichnis der musikalischen Werke der Familie Bach', *BJb* 1907, 103–77, esp. 109

W. Freytag: *Musikgeschichte der Stadt Stettin im 18. Jahrhundert* (Greifswald, 1936), 138–42

R. Schaal: *Die Musikhandschriften des Ansbacher Inventars von 1686* (Wilhelmshaven, 1966)

D. Sackmann: 'Johann Michael, der "Gehrener Bach" (1648–1694)', *Musik und Gottesdienst*, xlviii (1994), 49–57

P. Wollny: 'Materialien zur Schweinfurter Musikpflege im 17. Jahrhundert: von 1592 bis zum Tod Georg Christoph Bachs (1642–1697)', *Schütz Jb* 1997, 113–63

H. Brück: 'Eine "Verordnung der Music" der Kaufmannskirche zu Erfurt von 1671 als Nachweis unbekannter Kompositionen von Johann Michael Bach (1648–1694)', *BJb* 1998, 183–5

H.-J. Schulze and C.Wolff, eds.: *Bach Repertorium* (forthcoming)

(4) Johann Nicolaus Bach (27) (*b* Eisenach, 10 Oct 1669, *d* Jena, 4 Nov 1753). Composer and organist, son of (2) Johann Christoph Bach (13). After his early musical training at home, he entered the University of Jena in 1690, pursuing his musical studies with J.N. Knüpfer (son of Sebastian Knüpfer, Thomaskantor in Leipzig). After a journey to Italy, the purpose and duration of which are not known, he succeeded Knüpfer in 1694 as organist of the town church in Jena. The university authorities were however reluctant to allow him to act in addition as organist at the Kollegienkirche, as Knüpfer had done, and it was not until 1719 that he finally took on the double post of town and university organist. In 1703 he had refused an appointment at St Georg, Eisenach, as successor to his father, primarily, no doubt, because of the better salary in Jena, where he lived in modest prosperity. Presumably he was in contact with his relative Johann Georg Bernhard (47) during the latter's period of study in Jena, 1737–9. From 1745, in consideration of his age, he was provided with an assistant organist. In the *Ursprung* Johann Sebastian called him 'present senior of all the Bachs still living'.

Johann Nicolaus was a skilful composer, but his few extant works – some student music, *Der Jenaische Wein-und Bierrufer* (ed. F. Stein, Leipzig, 1921), and an organ chorale, *Nun freut euch lieben Christen gmein* (D-Bsb) – hardly permit an assessment of his style. There are, however, no noticeable italianate aspects such as might have resulted from his stay in Italy. Apart from being an organist, the leader of the university's collegium musicum and a composer, he was also an instrument maker, particularly of harpsichords. Adlung called him the inventor of the Lautenklavier, and in a letter of 1728 Bach referred explicitly to a 'Lauten Clavier' which he had sold to a Hungarian nobleman in Jena. As an expert on organs he supervised the reconstruction of an instrument with three manuals and 44 stops in the Kollegienkirche, 1704–6. Among his pupils was F.E. Niedt, author of a well-known thoroughbass method, *Musicalische Handleitung* (Hamburg, 1700–17).

BIBLIOGRAPHY

H. Koch: 'Johann Nicolaus, der "Jenaer" Bach', *Mf*, xxi (1968), 290–304

H.-J. Schulze: '"Die Bachen stammen aus Ungarn her": ein unbekannter Brief Johann Nicolaus Bachs aus dem Jahre 1728', *BJb* 1989, 213–20

T. Christensen: 'Johann Nikolaus Bach als Musiktheoretiker', *BJb* 1996, 93–100

H.-J. Schulz and C.Wolff, eds.: *Bach Repertorium* (forthcoming)

(5) Johann Bernhard Bach (18) (*b* Erfurt, bap. 25 Nov 1676; *d* Eisenach, 11 June 1749). Composer and organist, son of Johann Aegidius Bach (8). He studied with his father and about 1695 took up his first post, as organist at the Kaufmannskirche in Erfurt; in 1699 he went to Magdeburg, and in 1703 he replaced his kinsman (2) Johann Christoph (13) as town organist and court harpsichordist in Eisenach, a post which Johann Christoph's son Johann Nicolaus (27) had declined. Repeated rises in salary show the esteem in which he was held, particularly in the court Kapelle, which was directed by Telemann in 1708–12.

His only extant works are instrumental; some of the organ works are in copies made by his pupils in Erfurt, who included J.G. Walther (according to Walther himself). Johann Sebastian Bach evidently valued his orchestral suites, for he had five of them copied (he himself was involved in some of the copying) for his collegium musicum in Leipzig. J.S. Bach's obituary notice of 1754 says that Johann Bernhard 'composed many beautiful overtures in the manner of Telemann', no doubt referring particularly to the forces he employed (*dessus, haute-contre, taille* and continuo) and to the programmatic movement titles ('Les plaisirs', 'La toge') in the French tradition.

WORKS

4 ovs., orch, D-*Bsb*: g, ed. A. Fareanu (Leipzig, 1920); G; e; D, ed. K. Geiringer, *Music of the Bach Family* (Cambridge, Mass., 1955); all ed. H. Bergmann and H. Max (Stuttgart, 1985–8)

Ov., g, lost, listed in C.P.E. Bach's *Nachlassverzeichnis*

Org works: fugue, F, ed. H. Riemann (Leipzig, n.d.); fugue, D, ed. in *FrotscherG*

Org chorales: Du Friedefürst, Herr Jesu Christ; Vom Himmel hoch: both ed. D. Hellmann, *Orgelwerke der Familie Bach* (Leipzig, 1967); Christ lag in Todesbanden; Nun freut euch lieben Christen: both ed. in EDM, 1st ser., ix (1937); Wir glauben all an einen Gott [3 versions]

Chaconne, B♭, hpd

BIBLIOGRAPHY

FrotscherG

H. Kühn: 'Vier Organisten Eisenachs aus bachischem Geschlecht', *Bach in Thüringen: Gabe der Thüringer Kirche* (Berlin, 1950), 103–19

S. Orth: 'Zu den Erfurter Jahren Johann Bernhard Bachs (1676–1749)', *BJb 1971*, 106–11

C. Oefner: *Die Musikerfamilie Bach in Eisenach* (Eisenach, 1984)

H.-J. Schulze and C.Wolff, eds.: *Bach Repertorium* (forthcoming)

(6) Johann Ludwig Bach (*b* Thal, nr Eisenach, 4 Feb 1677; *d* Meiningen, bur. 1 May 1731). Composer, son of Johann Jacob Bach (3/60). Nothing is known of his musical training, but he probably received some early instruction from his father before attending the Gotha Gymnasium in 1688–93. From 1699 he was a court musician at Meiningen, from 1703 Kantor and from 1711 court Kapellmeister. In 1706 he had unsuccessfully applied to succeed A.C. Dedekind as Kantor of St Georg, Eisenach, although he had been interested only in the musical and not the teaching duties of the post. His patron of many years, Duke Ernst Ludwig, died in 1724 and Johann Ludwig wrote the music for his funeral.

Johann Ludwig wrote an imposing number of vocal works. Although orchestral music was probably his principal activity from 1711 onwards, hardly any music at that type is extant. The preservation of the cantatas is due primarily to Johann Sebastian, who performed 18 of them, as well as the two masses, in Leipzig in 1726; some were given again between 1735 and 1750. *Denn du wirst meine Seele* was long considered an early work by Johann Sebastian (BWV15). The cantatas constitute the most important part of Johann Ludwig's work; in contrast with the main corpus of Johann Sebastian's cantatas, they represent the older type of mixed cantata, consisting essentially of biblical text and chorale in the following scheme: text from the Old Testament; recitative; aria; text from the New Testament; aria; recitative; chorus; chorale. The standard scoring is for four-part choir, strings and (usually) two oboes; in one cantata two horns are required, but there are no solo woodwind. These works had at least some small influence on Johann Sebastian, for example in his use of a string ensemble to accompany the words of Jesus.

WORKS

manuscripts in D-Bsb unless otherwise stated

Messe sopra cantilena Allein Gott in der Höh, e, 1716, BWVAnh.III.166 [opening of Gl by J.S. Bach]; ed. K. Hofmann (Stuttgart, 1976)

Mass, G, BWV Anh.III.167

Magnificat, 8vv

23 church cants.: Darum säet euch Gerechtigkeit; Darum will ich auch erwählen; Denn du wirst meine Seele in der Hölle lassen, BWV15, ed. in Johann Sebastian Bachs Werke, ii (Leipzig, 1851/R); Der Gottlosen Arbeit wird fehlen; Der Herr wird ein neues im Land erschaffen; Die mit Tränen säen, ed. H. Hornung and M.G. Schneider (Neuhausen-Stuttgart, 1980); Die Weisheit kommt nicht in eine boshafte Seele; Du sollst lieben Gott, D-Gs; Durch sein Erkenntnis; Er machet uns lebendig; Es ist aus der Angst und Gericht; Es wird des Herrn Tag kommen, F-Pn; Gott ist unser Zuversicht, ed. A.M. Owen (St Louis, n.d.); Ich aber ging für dir über; Ich will meinen Geist in euch geben; Ja, mir hast du Arbeit gemacht, ed. H. Max (Neuhausen-Stuttgart, 1984); Kommt, es ist alles bereit, lost, formerly in Berlin, Singakademie; Küsset den Sohn, dass er nicht zürne (frag.); Mache dich auf, werde Licht, ed. H. Max (Neuhausen-Stuttgart, 1984); Siehe ich will meinen Engel senden; Siehe, ich will viele Fischer aussenden (frag.); Und ich will ihnen einen einigen Hirten erwecken; Wie lieblich sind auf den Bergen

11 motets: Das Blut Jesu Christi; Das ist meine Freude, ed. G. Graulich (Neuhausen-Stuttgart, 1980); Die richtig für sich gewandelt haben; Gedenke meiner, mein Gott; Gott sei mir gnädig; Ich habe dich ein klein Augenblick; Ich will auf den Herrn schauen; Sei nun wieder zufrieden, ed. in Cw, xcix (1964); Unser Trübsal, ed. in Cw, xcix (1964); Uns ist ein Kind geboren, ed. R. Moser (Leipzig, 1930), ed. K. Hofmann (Stuttgart, 1984); Wir wissen so unser irdisches Haus

Klingt vergnügt, secular cant.

Funeral music, 1724, 3 pts; pt 2 ed. K. Geiringer, *Music of the Bach Family* (Cambridge, MA, 1955)

Passion; cant. cycle for 1713, cited in S. Kümmerle: *Enzyklopädie der evangelischen Kirchenmusik*, i (Gütersloh, 1888/R), 67

Suite, G. orch, 1715; ed. K. Hofmann (Neuhausen-Stuttgart, c1984)

BIBLIOGRAPHY

A. Dörffel: 'Verzeichnis der Kirchenkompositionen des Johann Ludwig Bach in Meiningen', Johann Sebastian Bachs Werke, xli (1894), 275–6

A.M. Jaffé: *The Cantatas of Johann Ludwig Bach* (diss., Boston U., 1957)

W.H. Scheide: 'Johann Sebastian Bachs Sammlung von Kantaten seines Vetters Johann Ludwig Bach', *BJb 1959*, 52–94; *BJb 1961*, 5–24; *BJb 1962*, 5–32

W. Blankenburg: 'Eine neue Textquelle zu sieben Kantaten J.M. Bachs und achtzehn Kantaten Johann Ludwig Bachs', *BJb 1977*, 7–25

K. Hofmann: 'Forkel und die "Köthener Trauermusik" Johann Sebastian Bachs', *BJb 1983*, 115–18

K.Küster: 'Meininger Kantatentexte um Johann Ludwig Bach', *BJb 1987*, 159–64

K. Küster: 'Die Frankfurter und Leipziger Überlieferung der Kantaten Johann Ludwig Bachs', *BJb 1989*, 65–106

H.-J. Schulze and C.Wolff, eds.: *Bach Repertorium* (forthcoming)

(7) Johann Sebastian Bach (24) (*b* Eisenach, 21 March 1685, *d* Leipzig; 28 July 1750). Composer and organist. The most important member of the family, his genius combined outstanding performing musicianship with supreme creative powers in which forceful and original inventiveness, technical mastery and intellectual control are perfectly balanced. While it was in the former capacity, as a keyboard virtuoso, that in his lifetime he acquired an almost legendary fame, it is the latter virtues and accomplishments, as a composer, that by the end of the 18th century earned him a unique historical position. His musical language was distinctive and extraordinarily varied, drawing together and surmounting the techniques, the styles and the general achievements of his own and earlier generations and leading on to new perspectives which later ages have received and understood in a great variety of ways.   The first authentic posthumous account of his life, with a summary catalogue of his works, was put together by his son Carl Philipp Emanuel and his pupil J.F. Agricola soon after his death and certainly before March 1751 (published as *Nekrolog*, 1754). J.N. Forkel planned a detailed Bach biography in the early 1770s and carefully collected first-hand information on

Bach, chiefly from his two eldest sons; the book appeared in 1802, by when the BACH REVIVAL had begun and various projected collected editions of Bach's works were under way; it continues to serve, together with the 1754 obituary and the other 18th-century documents, as the foundation of Bach biography.

1. Childhood. 2. Lüneburg. 3. Arnstadt. 4. Mühlhausen. 5. Weimar. 6. Cöthen. 7. Leipzig, 1723–9. 8. Leipzig, 1729–39. 9. Leipzig, 1739–50. 10. Iconography. 11. Sources, repertory. 12. Background, style, influences. 13. Cantatas. 14. Oratorios, Passions, Latin works. 15. Motets, chorales, songs. 16. Organ music. 17. Music for harpsichord, lute etc. 18. Orchestral music. 19. Chamber music. 20. Canons, *Musical Offering*, *Art of Fugue*. 21. Methods of composition.

1. CHILDHOOD.   The parents of Johann Sebastian were Johann Ambrosius Bach (*11*) and Maria Elisabeth Lämmerhirt (1644–94), daughter of a furrier and town councillor in Erfurt, Valentin Lämmerhirt (*d* 1665). Another Lämmerhirt daughter became the mother of Bach's cousin J.G. Walther, suggesting that Lämmerhirt blood was perhaps not unimportant for the musical talents of the Bach family's greatest son. Elisabeth's elder half-sister Hedwig Lämmerhirt was the second wife of Ambrosius Bach's uncle, Johann Bach (*4*), organist of the Predigerkirche in Erfurt. Elisabeth and Ambrosius, who had worked in Eisenach since 1671 as Hausmann and also as a musician at the ducal court of Saxe-Eisenach, were married on 8 April 1668, and had eight children, five of whom survived infancy; as well as Johann Sebastian, the last, these were three sons (nos.*22*, *71* and *23*) and a daughter, Maria Salome. The date of Johann Sebastian's birth, 21 March 1685, was carefully recorded by Walther in his *Lexicon*, by Sebastian himself in the family genealogy, and by his son as the co-author of the obituary. It is supported by the date of baptism (23 March; these dates are old-style) in the register of St Georg. His godfathers were Johann Georg Koch, a forestry official, and Sebastian Nagel, a Gotha Stadtpfeifer. The house of his birth no longer stands; it is not the handsome old structure (Frauenplan 21) acquired by the Neue Bachgesellschaft in 1907 as the 'Bachhaus' and established as a Bach Museum. He would have been born in the house in the Fleischgasse (now the Lutherstrasse) that Ambrosius Bach bought in 1674 after gaining Eisenach citizenship.

After the time of the Reformation all children in Eisenach were obliged to go to school between the ages of five and 12, and (although there is no documentary evidence of it) Sebastian must have entered one of the town's German schools in 1690. From 1692 he attended the Lateinschule (as had Luther, also an Eisenach boy); this offered a sound humanistic and theological education. At Easter 1693 he was 47th in the fifth class, having been absent 96 half-days; in 1694 he lost 59 half-days, but rose to 14th and was promoted; at Easter 1695 he was 23rd in the fourth class, in spite of having lost 103 half-days (perhaps owing to illness, but probably also to the deaths of his parents). He stood one or two places above his brother Jacob, who was three years older and less frequently absent. Nothing more is known about his Eisenach career; but he is said to have been an unusually good treble and probably sang under Kantor A.C. Dedekind at St Georg, where his father made instrumental music before and after the sermon and where his relation (*2*) Johann Christoph Bach (*13*) was organist. His musical education is matter for conjecture; presumably his father

taught him the rudiments of string playing, but (according to Emanuel) he had no formal tuition on keyboard instruments until he went to Ohrdruf. He later described Johann Christoph as 'a profound composer'; no doubt he was impressed by the latter's organ playing as well as by his compositions.

Elisabeth Bach was buried on 3 May 1694, and on 27 November Ambrosius married Barbara Margaretha, née Keul, the daughter of a former mayor of Arnstadt. Aged 35, she had already been twice widowed. Her first husband had been a musician, Johann Günther Bach (*15*), and her second a theologian, Jacobus Bartholomaei (both marriages had taken place in Arnstadt), and she brought to her third marriage two little daughters, Catharina Margareta and Christina Maria, one by each of her earlier husbands. A month before Ambrosius's own second marriage, on 23 October 1694, he and his family had celebrated the wedding of the eldest son, Johann Christoph (*22*) in Ohrdruf. The music on that occasion was by Ambrosius Bach, Johann Pachelbel from nearby Gotha and other friends and family members. This was probably the only occasion on which the then nine-year-old Sebastian met Pachelbel, his brother's teacher. Barely three months after re-marrying, on 20 February 1695, Ambrosius Bach died after a long and serious illness. On 4 March the widow appealed to the town council for help; but she received only her legal due, and the household broke up. Sebastian and Jacob were taken in by their elder brother Johann Christoph, organist at Ohrdruf.

Both were sent to the Lyceum. Jacob left at the age of 14 to be apprenticed to his father's successor at Eisenach; Sebastian stayed on until 1700, when he was nearly 15, and thus came under the influence of an exceptionally enlightened curriculum. Inspired by the educationist Comenius, it embraced religion, reading, writing, arithmetic, singing, history and natural science. Sebastian entered the fourth class probably about March 1695, and was promoted to the third in July: on 20 July 1696 he was first among the seven new boys and fourth in the class; on 19 July 1697 he was first, and was promoted to the second class; on 13 July 1698 he was fifth; on 24 July 1699 second, and promoted to the first class, in which he was fourth when he left the school on 15 March 1700 and went to Lüneburg.

In the obituary Emanuel stated that his father had his first keyboard lessons from Christoph, at Ohrdruf; in 1775, replying to Forkel, he said that Christoph might have trained him simply as an organist, and that Sebastian became 'a pure and strong fuguist' through his own efforts. That is likely enough; Christoph is not known to have been a composer. Several early biographers told the story of how Christoph would not allow his brother to use a certain manuscript; how Sebastian copied it by moonlight; how Christoph took the copy away from him; and how he did not recover it until Christoph died. Emanuel and Forkel assumed that Christoph died in 1700, and that Sebastian, left homeless, went to Lüneburg in desperation. Later authors, knowing that Christoph lived on until 1721, and that the brothers had been on good terms, have tended to reject the story – perhaps unnecessarily, for it may illustrate contemporary attitudes to discipline and restraint. In fact, the story fits in well with the little that is known of the Ohrdruf years, and with the idea that Sebastian taught himself composition by copying. Most probably he recovered his copy when he went to Lüneburg. As for its contents, Forkel implied that it contained works by seven famous composers, three of them northerners. He probably misunderstood Emanuel's reply to another of his questions; according to the obituary, the manuscript was mainly southern (Froberger, Kerll, Pachelbel) – as one would expect, since Johann Christoph had been a Pachelbel pupil. (A good idea of its contents can be obtained from a manuscript collection compiled in 1692 by another of Pachelbel's pupils, J.V. Eckelt.) The larger of the two organs at Ohrdruf was in almost unplayable condition in 1697, and Sebastian no doubt picked up some of his expert knowledge of organ building while helping his brother with repairs.

No documentary evidence exists to establish when Bach started to compose, but it is reasonable to suppose that it was while he lived in Ohrdruf – not least because other contemporaries, and his own sons in due course, began composing original music before reaching the age of 15. The earliest organ chorales in the Neumeister manuscript, as well as such works as bwv749, 750 and 756, provide plausible examples of pieces composed before and around 1700. They are characterized by sound craftsmanship, observance of models provided by Pachelbel (his teacher's teacher) and everywhere the sense of an endeavour to break away from musical conventions and find independent answers.

2. LÜNEBURG.   According to the school register, Sebastian left Ohrdruf 'ob defectum hospitiorum' ('for lack of board and lodging'); clearly Christoph no longer had room for his brother. Since the latter's arrival he had had two children; by March 1700 a third was expected; and (if local tradition can be trusted) his house, now destroyed, was a mere cottage. The brothers' problem seems to have been solved by Elias Herda, Kantor and a master at the Lyceum. He had been educated at Lüneburg, and no doubt it was he who arranged for Sebastian to go north; probably he similarly helped Georg Erdmann, a fellow pupil of Sebastian's, three years older, who left the school just before Bach (for the same reason). According to the obituary they travelled together. They must have reached Lüneburg before the end of March for both were entered in the register of the Mettenchor (Matins choir) by 3 April 1700 and probably sang in it within a matter of days for Holy Week and Easter.

The Michaeliskirche, Lüneburg, had two schools associated with it: a Ritteracademie for young noblemen, and the Michaelisschule for commoners. There were also two choirs: the 'chorus symphoniacus' of about 25 voices was led by the Mettenchor, which numbered about 15, and was limited to poor boys. Members of the Mettenchor received free schooling at the Michaelisschule, up to 1 thaler per month according to seniority, their keep, and a share in fees for weddings and other occasions (Bach's share in 1700 has been put at 14 marks). From the arrangement of the pay-sheets it has been deduced that they were both trebles. Bach was welcomed for his unusually fine voice; but it soon broke, and for eight days he spoke and sang in octaves. After that he may or may not have sung, but no doubt he made himself useful as an accompanist or string player. As the last extant pay-sheet is that for 29 May 1700, no details are known; but it is clear that the school was short of instrumentalists at just this time.

At school, Bach's studies embraced orthodox Lutheranism, logic, rhetoric, Latin and Greek, arithmetic,

history, geography and German poetry. The Kantor was August Braun, whose compositions have disappeared; the organist, F.C. Morhard, was a nonentity. The organ was repaired in 1701 by J.B. Held, who had worked at Hamburg and Lübeck; he lodged in the school, and may have taught Bach something about organ building. There was a fine music library, which had been carefully kept up to date; but whether choirboys were allowed to consult it is uncertain. If Braun made good use of it, Bach must have learnt a good deal from the music he had to perform; but his chief interests probably lay outside the school. At the Nikolaikirche was J.J. Löwe (1629–1703), distinguished but elderly. The Johanniskirche was another matter, for there the organist was Georg Böhm (1661–1733), who is generally agreed to have influenced Bach. It has been argued that the organist of the Johanniskirche would not have been accessible to a scholar of the Michaelisschule, since the two choirs were not on good terms, and that Bach's knowledge of Böhm's music must have come later, through J.G. Walther. But Emanuel Bach stated in writing that his father had studied Böhm's music; and a correction in a note to Forkel shows that his first thought was to say that Böhm had been his father's teacher. This hint is supported by the fact that in 1727 Bach named Böhm as his northern agent for the sale of Partitas nos.2 and 3. That seems to imply that the two were on friendly terms; it is likelier that they became so between 1700 and 1702 than at any later date.

Bach went more than once to Hamburg, some 50 km away; probably he visited his cousin Johann Ernst (25), who was evidently studying there about this time. The suggestion that he went to hear Vincent Lübeck cannot be taken seriously, for Lübeck did not go to Hamburg until August 1702, by which time Bach had almost certainly left the area. He may have visited the Hamburg Opera, then directed by Reinhard Keiser, whose *St Mark Passion* he performed during the early Weimar years and again in 1726; but there is no solid evidence that he was interested in anything but the organ and in particular the organist of St Katharinen, J.A. Reincken, whose influence on the young Bach as both theorist and practitioner it would be difficult to overestimate. Marpurg's familiar anecdote makes the point neatly: how Bach, returning almost penniless to Lüneburg, once rested outside an inn; how someone threw two herring heads out on the rubbish heap; how Bach – a Thuringian, to whom fish were a delicacy – picked them up to see if any portion were edible; how he found that they contained two Danish ducats, and was thus able not only to have a meal, but also 'to undertake another and a more comfortable pilgrimage to Herr Reincken'.

J.A. Reincken (?1623–1722), a pupil of Sweelinck and organist of St Katharinen since 1663, was a father figure of the north German school. Böhm may have advised Bach to hear him; and his showy playing, exploiting all the resources of the organ, must have been a revelation to one brought up in the reticent tradition of the south. As for the organ itself, Bach never forgot it; in later years he described it as excellent in every way, said that the 32′ Principal was the best he had ever heard, and never tired of praising the 16′ reeds. Whether he actually met Reincken before 1720 is uncertain. If he did, Reincken might have given him a copy of his sonatas; Bach's reworkings of them (the keyboard pieces bwv954, 965 and 966) are more likely to have been made soon after

1700 than 20 years later, when Bach no longer needed to teach himself composition.

The market-place in Lüneburg had been graced since the end of the 17th century by a palace used for the visits of the Duke of Celle-Lüneburg and his court; the principal ducal residence and seat of government lay in Celle, some 80 km to the south. The duke, married to Eléonore d'Olbreuse, a Huguenot of noble birth, was a pronounced francophile and maintained an orchestra consisting largely of Frenchmen, which played in both Celle and Lüneburg. Thomas de la Selle, dancing-master at the Ritteracademie next door to Bach's school in Lüneburg, was also a member of the Celle orchestra. Emanuel Bach knew that his father was often able to hear this 'famous orchestra' and thus to become acquainted with French taste. It cannot be ruled out that Bach occasionally helped out as an instrumentalist when the court orchestra played in the ducal residence in Lüneburg.

The date of Bach's departure from Lüneburg is not known, but we may suppose that he completed his final school year after two years and left school at Easter 1702. It seems unlikely that he remained in Lüneburg for any length of time after that, for he left without hearing Buxtehude and took extraordinary pains to do so in winter 1705–6. He probably visited relatives in Thuringia after Easter 1702. All that is definitely known is that he competed successfully for the vacant post of organist at St Jacobi in Sangerhausen (the organist was buried on 9 July), but the Duke of Weissenfels intervened and had J.A. Kobelius, a somewhat older man, appointed in November. Bach is next heard of at Weimar, where he was employed at the court as a musician for the first two quarters of 1703; the court accounts have him down as a lackey, but he described himself as a 'Hofmusikant' (court musician) in the *Ursprung*. This was at the minor Weimar court, that of Duke Johann Ernst, younger brother of the Duke Wilhelm Ernst whom Bach served from 1708 to 1717. Possibly the Duke of Weissenfels, having refused to accept Bach at Sangerhausen, found work for him at Weimar; another possibility is that Bach owed his appointment to a distant relation of his, David Hoffmann, another lackey-musician.

Of the musicians with whom Bach now became associated, three are worth mentioning. G.C. Strattner (c1644–1704), a tenor, became vice-Kapellmeister in 1695, and composed in a post-Schütz style. J.P. von Westhoff (1656–1705) was a fine violinist and had travelled widely, apparently as a diplomat, and is said to have been the first to compose a suite for unaccompanied violin (1683). Johann Effler (c1640–1711) was the court organist: he had held posts at Gehren and Erfurt (where Pachelbel was his successor) before coming in 1678 to Weimar, where about 1690 he moved to the court. He may have been willing to hand over some of his duties to Bach, and probably did something of the kind, for a document of 13 July 1703 at Arnstadt, where Bach next moved, describes Bach as court organist at Weimar – a post that was not officially his until 1708.

3. ARNSTADT.   The Bonifaciuskirche at Arnstadt had burnt down in 1581, and was subsequently rebuilt in 1676–83; it then became known as the Neue Kirche, and so remained until 1935, when it was renamed after Bach. In 1699 J.F. Wender contracted to build an organ, which by the end of 1701 had become usable; on 1 January 1702 Andreas Börner was formally appointed organist.

The organ was complete by June 1703, and was examined before 3 July; there were more examiners than one, but only Bach was named and paid, and it was he who 'played the organ for the first time'. The result was that on 9 August Bach was offered the post over Börner's head; at the same time, 'to prevent any such "collisions" as are to be feared', Börner was given other work. Bach accepted the post 'by handshake' on 14 August 1703. The exact date of his removal to Arnstadt is not known, nor is his address. As his last board and lodging allowance was paid to Feldhaus, he probably spent at least that year in either the Golden Crown or the Steinhaus, both of which belonged to Feldhaus. Considering his age, and local standards, he was well paid; and his duties, as specified in his contract, were light. Normally, he was required at the church only for two hours on Sunday morning, for a service on Monday, and for two hours on Thursday morning; and he had only to accompany hymns. He thus had plenty of time for composition and organ playing, and he took as his models Bruhns, Reincken, Buxtehude (all northerners) and certain good French organists. There is no evidence as to whether he took part in the theatrical and musical entertainments of the court or the town.

Bach was in no position to put on elaborate music at Arnstadt. The Neue Kirche, like the other churches, drew performers from two groups of schoolboys and senior students. Only one of these groups was capable of singing cantatas; it was supposed to go to the Neue Kirche monthly in the summer, but there does not appear to have been a duty roster. The performers naturally tended to go to the churches that had an established tradition and friendly organists; and Bach had no authority to prevent this, for he was not a schoolmaster and was younger than many of the students. Further, he never had much patience with the semi-competent, and was apt to alienate them by making offensive remarks. One result was his scuffle with J.H. Geyersbach (b 1682). On 4 August 1705 he and his cousin Barbara, elder sister (aged 26) to his future wife, fell in with six students who had been to a christening feast; one of these was Geyersbach, who asked why Bach had insulted him (or his bassoon), and struck him in the face with a stick. Bach drew his sword, but another student separated them. Bach complained to the consistory that it would be unsafe for him to go about the streets if Geyersbach were not punished, and an inquiry was held. The consistory told Bach that he ought not to have insulted Geyersbach and should try to live peaceably with the students; further, he was not (as he claimed) responsible only for the chorales but was expected to help with all kinds of music. Bach replied that if a musical director were appointed, he would be willing enough.

Bach, unimpressed, asked for four weeks' leave, and set off for Lübeck – 'what is more, on foot', says the obituary, adding that he had an overwhelming desire to hear Buxtehude. Dates and distance cast some doubts on his straightforwardness. He left Arnstadt about 18 October, and was therefore due to be back, or well on his way back, by about 15 November; he would thus have been unable to hear even the first of Buxtehude's special services, which were given on various dates from 15 November to 20 December. Perhaps, like Mattheson and Handel before him, he went primarily to see if there was any chance of succeeding Buxtehude, and was put off by the prospect of marrying Buxtehude's daughter, aged 30; in any case, by 1705 there was a rival in the field. However that may be, he stayed almost three months at Lübeck, and was absent altogether for about 16 weeks, not returning to Arnstadt until shortly before 7 February 1706, when he communicated.

On 21 February the consistory asked Bach why he had been away for so long; his replies were unsatisfactory and barely civil. They next complained that his accompaniments to chorales were too elaborate for congregational singing, and that he still refused to collaborate with the students in producing cantatas; further, they could not provide a Kapellmeister for him, and if he continued to refuse they would have to find someone more amenable. Bach repeated his demand for a musical director, and was ordered to apologize within eight days. From the next case that the consistory heard that day it seems that there had been actual 'disordres' in the church between Bach and the students. There is no evidence that Bach apologized, and the consistory dropped the matter for eight months. They brought it up again on 11 November, and Bach undertook to answer them in writing. They also accused him of inviting a 'stranger maiden' to make music in the church, but for this he had obtained the parson's permission. The girl in question cannot have been his cousin and future wife, for she had long been resident in Arnstadt and therefore would be unlikely to be described as a stranger.

Neither Bach nor the consistory took further action; no doubt they saw that the problem would soon solve itself. Probably Bach had come back from Lübeck with exalted ideas about church music, requiring facilities that Arnstadt could not provide. His ability was becoming known; on 28 November he helped to examine an organ at Lange-wiesen. Forkel said that various posts were offered to him; and with the death of J.G. Ahle, on 2 December, a sufficiently attractive vacancy seemed to have arisen.

4. MÜHLHAUSEN.   Ahle had been a city councillor of Mühlhausen, organist of St Blasius and a composer of minor rank. Musical standards had fallen during his tenure of office, but the post was a respectable one and various candidates gave trial performances. One was to have been J.G. Walther, the future lexicographer; he sent in two compositions for 27 February 1707 (Sexagesima), but withdrew after being told privately that he had no hope. Bach played at Easter (24 April) and may have performed Cantata no.4. At the city council meeting on 24 May no other name was considered, and on 14 June Bach was interviewed. He asked for the same salary that he was receiving at Arnstadt (some 20 gulden more than Ahle's); the councillors agreed, and an agreement was signed on 15 June. At Arnstadt his success became known; his cousin Johann Ernst (25) and his predecessor Börner applied for the Neue Kirche on 22 and 23 June. He resigned formally on 29 June, and presumably moved to Mühlhausen within a few days. It was perhaps in July that he wrote Cantata no.131; this was clearly intended for a penitential service, perhaps connected with a disastrous fire of 30 May. It was not Bach's own Pastor Frohne who commissioned this cantata, but Pastor Eilmar of the Marienkirche – a fact whose possible significance will be seen later. Bach's responsibilities in Mühlhausen included also the convent of Augustinian nuns where there was an organ by Wender without pedals; his principal duty there was to play for special services.

On 10 August 1707 Tobias Lämmerhirt, Bach's maternal uncle, died at Erfurt. He left Bach 50 gulden, more than half his salary, and thus facilitated his marriage to Maria Barbara (b 20 Oct 1684), daughter of (3) Johann Michael Bach (14) and Catharina Wedemann. The wedding took place on 17 October at Dornheim, a village near Arnstadt; the pastor, J.L. Stauber (1660–1723), was a friend of the family and himself married Regina Wedemann on 5 June 1708. Pupils began to come to Bach at about this time, or perhaps even earlier. J.M. Schubart (1690–1721) is said to have been with him from 1707 to 1717, and J.C. Vogler (1696–1763) to have arrived at the age of ten (at Arnstadt), to have left for a time, and to have returned from about 1710 until 1715. These two were his immediate successors at Weimar; from their time onwards he was never without pupils.

On 4 February 1708 the annual change of council took place, and Cantata no.71 was performed. It must have made an impression, for the council printed not only the libretto, as was usual, but also the music. Bach next drew up a plan for repairing and enlarging the St Blasius organ; the council considered this on 21 February, and decided to act on it. Cantata no.196 may have been written for Stauber's wedding on 5 June. At about this time Bach played before the reigning Duke of Weimar, Wilhelm Ernst, who offered him a post at his court. On 25 June Bach wrote to the council asking them to accept his resignation.

No doubt the larger salary at Weimar was an attraction, particularly as Bach's wife was pregnant. But it is clear, even from his tactful letter to these councillors who had treated him well, that there were other reasons for leaving. He said that he had encouraged 'well-regulated church music' not only in his own church, but also in the surrounding villages, where the harmony was often 'better than that cultivated here' (Spitta found a fragment, BWV223, at nearby Langula). He had also gone to some expense to collect 'the choicest sacred music'. But in all this members of his own congregation had opposed him, and were not likely to stop. Some people no doubt disliked the type of music that he was trying to introduce. Further, Pastor Frohne may have distrusted his organist; an active Pietist, he was at daggers drawn with the orthodox Pastor Eilmar of the Marienkirche – Bach had begun his Mühlhausen career by working with Eilmar, and they had become intimate enough for Eilmar and his daughter to be godparents to Bach's first two children.

The council considered his letter on 26 June and reluctantly let him go, asking him only to supervise the organ building at St Blasius. However badly Bach may have got on with his congregation, he was evidently on good terms with the council. They paid him to come and perform a cantata at the council service in 1709, and possibly also in 1710 (all trace of these works is lost). In 1735 he negotiated on friendly terms with the new council on behalf of his son Johann Gottfried Bernhard (47). He is not known to have been paid for supervising or opening the St Blasius organ, but he may have done so.

5. WEIMAR.   When he announced his resignation from Mühlhausen, Bach said that he had been appointed to the Duke of Weimar's 'Capelle und Kammermusik', and it was long thought that he did not become organist at once. In fact, Weimar documents show that on 14 July 1708, when his 'reception money' was paid over, he was called 'the newly appointed court organist', and that he was almost always so called until March 1714, when he became Konzertmeister as well. Effler, it seems, was

pensioned off on full salary (130 florins); on 24 December 1709 he received a small gift as 'an old sick servant', and he died at Jena on 4 April 1711.

It is said that Bach wrote most of his organ works at Weimar, and that the duke took pleasure in his playing. His salary was from the outset larger than Effler's (150 florins, plus some allowances); it was increased to 200 from Michaelmas 1711, 215 from June 1713, and 250 on his promotion in 1714. On 20 March 1715 it was ordered that his share of casual fees was to be the same as the Kapellmeister's. Moreover, he seems to have had a fair amount of spare time, in which, for instance, to cultivate the acquaintance of Telemann while the latter was at Eisenach (1708–12). Together with the violinist Pisendel he copied a concerto in G of Telemann's (*D-Dl*), probably during Pisendel's visit to Weimar in 1709.

Six of Bach's children were born at Weimar: Catharina (bap. 29 Dec 1708; *d* 14 Jan 1774); (8) Wilhelm Friedemann (*45*) (*b* 22 Nov 1710); twins (*b* 23 Feb 1713; both died in a few days); (9) Carl Philipp Emanuel (*46*) (*b* 8 March 1714); and Johann Gottfried Bernhard (*47*) (*b* 11 May 1715). The various godparents show that Bach and his wife kept in touch with relations and friends from Ohrdruf, Arnstadt and Mühlhausen, besides making fresh contacts at Weimar; it is noteworthy that Telemann was godfather to Emanuel.

On 13 March 1709 Bach, his wife, and one of her sisters (probably the eldest, Friedelena, who died at Leipzig in 1729) were living with Adam Immanuel Weldig, a falsettist and Master of the Pages. They probably stayed there until August 1713, when Weldig gave up his house, having secured a similar post at Weissenfels. Weldig was godfather to Emanuel; Bach (by proxy) to a son of Weldig's in 1714. Weldig's house was destroyed in 1944; where Bach lived before and after the given dates is not known.

Since 29 July 1707, J.G. Walther (the lexicographer) had been organist of the Stadtkirche; he was related to Bach through his mother, a Lämmerhirt, and the two became friendly. On 27 September 1712 Bach stood godfather to Walther's son. Forkel told a story of how Walther played a trick on Bach, to cure him of boasting that there was nothing he could not read at sight. Their relations did not deteriorate, as Spitta supposed; in 1735 Bach negotiated on Walther's behalf with the Leipzig publisher J.G. Krügner, and Walther's references to Bach in his letters to Bokemeyer carry no suggestion of any coolness. From one such letter it seems that during his nine years at Weimar Bach gave Walther some 200 pieces of music, some by Buxtehude, others compositions of his own.

Of Bach's pupils, Schubart and Vogler have already been mentioned. The pupil for whom Bach was paid by Ernst August's account in 1711–12 was not Duke Ernst August himself but a page called Jagemann. J.G. Ziegler (1688–1747) matriculated at the University of Halle on 12 October 1712, but before that he had studied with Bach for a year or so, and had been taught to play chorales 'not just superficially, but according to the sense of the words'; Bach's wife stood godmother to his daughter in 1718, and in 1727 Bach employed him as agent, in Halle, for Partitas nos.2 and 3. P.D. Krauter of Augsburg (1690–1741) set out for Weimar in March 1712, and stayed until about September 1713. Johann Lorenz Bach (*38*) probably arrived in autumn 1713; he

may have left Weimar by July 1717. Johann Tobias Krebs (1690–1762) studied with Walther from 1710, with Bach from about 1714 until 1717. Johann Bernhard Bach (*41*) worked with his uncle from about 1715 until March 1719, alongside Samuel Gmelin (1695–1752), who appears to have left in 1717. C.H. Dretzel of Nuremberg (1697–1775) may have been briefly with Bach. In 1731, when applying for a post, T.C. Gerlach (1694–1768) implied that Bach had been teaching him by correspondence for 14 years, but his confused phraseology should not be taken literally.

The specification of the organ in the castle chapel, published in 1737, has not always been reprinted correctly; in any case, it does not represent the organ that Bach left in 1717. Extensive alterations were made in 1719–30. Still less does the specification represent the organ that Bach was faced with in 1708, for he himself made even more extensive alterations in 1713–14. The organ is said to have been built by Compenius in 1657–8. It was overhauled in 1707–8, and a Sub-Bass added, by J.C. Weishaupt, who carried out further maintenance work in 1712. A contract for alterations had however been signed on 29 June 1712 with H.N. Trebs (1678–1748), who had moved from Mühlhausen to Weimar in 1709. Bach and he had worked together on a new organ at Taubach in 1709–10, opened by Bach on 26 October 1710; in 1711 he gave Trebs a handsome testimonial, and in 1713 he and Walther became godfathers to Trebs's son. Bach and Trebs collaborated again about 1742, over an organ at Bad Berka. Trebs's new organ was usable during 1714; he had done 14 days' tuning by 19 May, and was paid off on 15 September. Of this rebuild nothing is known, except that either Bach or the duke was determined that the instrument include a Glockenspiel; great trouble was taken over obtaining bells from dealers in Nuremberg and Leipzig, and it seems that the original set of 29 (a number hard to account for) had to be replaced because of difficulties over blend and pitch. In 1737 the organ had a Glockenspiel on the *Oberwerk*, but alterations had been made in 1719–20 and it does not follow that the Glockenspiel of 1714 was on a manual.

In December 1709 and February 1710 Bach was paid for repairing harpsichords in the household of the junior duke, Ernst August and Prince Johann Ernst. On 17 January 1711 he was godfather to a daughter of J.C. Becker, a local burgher. In February 1711 Prince Johann Ernst went to the University of Utrecht. From 21 February 1713 Bach was lodged in the castle at Weissenfels. Duke Christian's birthday fell on 23 February, and it is now known that Cantata no.208 was performed in this year, not in 1716. The earlier date is stylistically suitable; moreover, it is compatible both with the watermark of the autograph score and with the fact that in this score Bach contradicted sharps by flats rather than by naturals – an old-fashioned habit that he gave up progressively during 1714.

About May 1713 the young prince returned from Utrecht, apparently with a good deal of music, for in the year from 1 June there were bills for binding, copying and shelving (some of the music came from Halle). In February 1713 he had been in Amsterdam, and may have met the blind organist J.J. de Graff who was in the habit of playing recent Italian concertos as keyboard solos. This may have given rise to the numerous concerto arrangements made by Walther and Bach.

On 7 September 1713 Bach was probably at Ohrdruf, standing godfather to a nephew; and on 6 November he took part in the dedication of the new Jakobskirche at Weimar (there is no evidence that he composed any of the music). On 27 November he was at Weimar, as godfather to Trebs's son. At about this time he seems to have gone to Halle, perhaps to buy music, and to have become accidentally involved with the authorities of the Liebfrauenkirche. The organist there (Zachow, Handel's teacher) had died in 1712, and the organ was being enlarged to a three-manual of 65 stops. The story has to be pieced together from hints in an incomplete correspondence; but it looks as if the pastor, J.M. Heineccius, pressed Bach to apply for the vacant post. Bach may have been involved in planning the enlargement of the organ, when Zachow became incapacitated; at all events, he stayed in Halle from 28 November to 15 December at the church authorities' expense. He also composed and performed a cantata (lost), attended a meeting on 13 December 1713, was offered the post, and let the committee suppose that he had accepted it, although he had not had time to find out what his casual fees would amount to. On 14 December they sent him a formal contract. Bach replied on 14 January 1714, saying cautiously that he had not been released from Weimar, was uneasy about his salary and duties, and would write again within the week. Whether he did so is not known; but on February the committee resolved to tell him that his salary was not likely to be increased. Thus at Halle he could expect a slightly smaller salary than he was already getting; the attraction was the organ, more than twice as large. Bach must then have approached the duke, for on 2 March, 'at his most humble request', he became Konzertmeister (ranking after the vice-Kapellmeister), with a basic salary of 250 florins from 25 February. In finally refusing the Halle post, he probably mentioned that figure, for the committee accused him of having used their offer as a lever to extract more money from the duke. This he denied on 19 March, in a letter so reasonable and so obviously honest that he remained on good terms with Halle and was employed there as an organ examiner in 1716. Gottfried Kirchhoff had meanwhile been appointed organist on 30 July 1714.

Few cantatas (apart from the secular no.208) can be ascribed to these early Weimar years. Nos.18, 54 and 199 appear to date from 1713 and clearly have no specific connection with the cantatas composed with an eye to the church calendar from March 1714 onwards. The work performed at Halle in December 1713 was formerly thought to be no.21 (see F. Chrysander: *G.F. Händel* (Leipzig, 1858–67/R)). The idea that it was no.63 no longer stands up, although the forces required for that work make it extremely unlikely that it was written for the Weimar court; a performance in Halle at Christmas 1715 is conceivable.

On 23 March 1714 it was ordered that cantatas should in future be rehearsed in the chapel, not at home or in lodgings; and on Palm Sunday, 25 March, Bach performed no.182. This was the fourth Sunday after his appointment as Konzertmeister, when he had become responsible for writing a cantata every four weeks. As he evidently hoped to complete an annual cycle in four years, he did not keep strictly to this rule; having written a cantata for Advent Sunday in 1714, he wrote for the last Sunday after Trinity in 1715, and for the second Sunday in Advent in 1716 (in

1717 he was in prison). Apart from such intentional irregularities, there are gaps in the series, and the strange thing is that these gaps became suddenly more numerous after the end of 1715. One of the gaps is accounted for by the death at Frankfurt on 1 August 1715 of the musically gifted Prince Johann Ernst, plunging the duchy into mourning from 11 August to 9 November 1715, when not a note of music might be played. From 1717 there are no cantatas at all. A tentative explanation will be suggested for this; but it is hard to see why Bach's usual allowance of paper was paid for on 16 May 1716 when he is not known to have performed any church cantatas between 19 January and 6 December.

On 4 April 1716 Bach, like the librettist Salomo Franck and 'the book-printer', was paid for 'Carmina', bound in green taffeta, that had been 'presented' on some unspecified occasion – perhaps on 24 January when Duke Ernst August had married Eleonore, sister of the Prince of Cöthen. Ernst's birthday was celebrated in April; two horn players from Weissenfels came to Weimar, possibly brought over for a repeat performance of Cantata no.208. Meanwhile, the new organ at Halle had been making progress, and on 17 April the council resolved that Bach, Kuhnau of Leipzig and Rolle of Quedlinburg should be invited to examine it on 29 April. They all accepted; each was to receive 16 thaler, plus food and travelling expenses. The examination began at 7 a.m., and lasted three days – until some time on 1 May, when the experts wrote their report, a sermon was preached and fine music was performed. On 2 May the organist and the three examiners met the builder to discuss details. The council, who behaved liberally, gave a tremendous banquet, whose date is usually given as 3 May (1 May seems more likely).

On 31 July 1716 Bach and an Arnstadt organ builder signed a testimonial for J.G. Schröter, who had built an organ at Erfurt. In 1717 Bach was mentioned in print for the first time: in the preface to Mattheson's *Das beschützte Orchestre*, dated 21 February, Mattheson referred to Bach as 'the famous Weimar organist' saying that his works, both for the church and for keyboard, led one to rate him highly, and asked for biographical information.

It is against this background that Bach's departure from Weimar has to be considered. In 1703 he had been employed by Duke Johann Ernst; since his return in 1708, by Duke Wilhelm, Johann's elder brother. The brothers had been on bad terms, and when Johann Ernst died in 1707 and his son Ernst came of age in 1709, things became no better. For some time the ducal disagreements do not seem to have affected Bach; perhaps they were kept within bounds by Superintendent Lairitz, and Ernst's younger half-brother (Johann, the composer) may have had some influence. But the latter died in 1715, Lairitz on 4 April 1716, and the new superintendent certainly failed to cope with the 'court difficulties'; like the rest of Wilhelm's household, he was forbidden to associate with Ernst. The musicians, though paid by both households, were threatened with fines of 10 thaler if they served Ernst in any way.

No extant Bach cantata can be securely dated between 19 January and 6 December 1716; it may seem unlikely that this long, continuous gap was due to casual losses. It is tempting to suppose that Bach found his position embarrassing (owing to his early connection with the junior court) and expressed disapproval of Duke Wilhelm's behaviour by evading his own responsibilities. In fact, Bach does not seem to have disapproved of the duke's behaviour until he discovered that a new Kapellmeister was being sought elsewhere. Drese senior died on 1 December 1716; his son, the vice-Kapellmeister, was by all accounts a nonentity. Bach produced Cantatas nos.70a, 186a and 147a for 6, 13 and 20 December (three successive weeks, not months), but there were no more, as far as is known. By Christmas, Bach may have found out that the duke was angling for Telemann. Negotiations with Telemann came to nothing; but apparently Bach now set about looking for a post as Kapellmeister. He was offered one by Prince Leopold of Cöthen, brother-in-law to Duke Ernst (Bach and the prince had probably met at Ernst's wedding in January 1716) and the appointment was confirmed on 5 August 1717. No doubt Bach then asked Duke Wilhelm's permission to leave, and no doubt he was refused – the duke being annoyed because his nephew had obviously had a hand in finding Bach a job that carried more prestige and, at 400 thaler, was better paid.

The duke and Bach must nevertheless have remained on speaking terms for the time being, for at some date hardly earlier than the end of September Bach was in Dresden and free to challenge the French keyboard virtuoso Louis Marchand. Versions of this affair differ, but according to Birnbaum (who wrote in 1739, probably under Bach's supervision), Bach 'found himself' at Dresden, and was not sent for by 'special coach'. Once there, some court official persuaded him to challenge Marchand to a contest at the harpsichord; the idea that they were to compete at the organ seems to have crept in later. Whatever may be the truth about these and other details, it is universally agreed that Marchand ran away.

On his birthday, 30 October 1717, Duke Wilhelm set up an endowment for his court musicians; and the second centenary of the Reformation was celebrated from 31 October to 2 November. Presumably Bach took part in these ceremonies, though there is no evidence that he set any of the librettos that Franck had provided. Emboldened, perhaps, by the Marchand affair, he then demanded his release in such terms that the duke had him imprisoned from 6 November until his dismissal in disgrace on 2 December. The Cöthen court had paid Bach 50 thaler on 7 August. Some have supposed that this was for travelling expenses, and that Bach had his wife and family moved to Cöthen soon after; but it seems unlikely that the duke would have allowed them to move until he had agreed to let Bach go. The younger Drese became Kapellmeister in his father's place and Bach's pupil J.M. Schubart became court organist. The post of Konzertmeister disappeared.

6. CÖTHEN.   Except during the few last months of his Weimar period, Bach had been on good terms with Duke Wilhelm; but his relations with that martinet must always have been official. At Cöthen, until the end of 1721, things were different; Prince Leopold was a young man who, as Bach himself said, loved and understood music. He was born in 1694, of a Calvinist father and a Lutheran mother. The father died in 1704, the mother ruled until Leopold came of age on 10 December 1715. There was no court orchestra until October 1707, when Leopold persuaded his mother to take on three musicians. While studying in Berlin in 1708, he met A.R. Stricker; from the end of 1710 to 1713 he was on the usual grand tour, during which he studied with J.D. Heinichen at Rome. He returned capable of singing bass, and of playing the violin, viola da gamba and harpsichord. The Berlin court orchestra had broken up in 1713, and from July 1714 he employed Stricker as Kapellmeister and his wife as soprano and lutenist; by 1716 he had 18 musicians. In August 1717 Stricker and his wife seem to have resigned, leaving the prince free to appoint Bach.

At Cöthen the St Jakob organ was in poor condition. The court chapel was Calvinist; it had an organist, but no elaborate music was performed there, and the two-manual organ had only 13 or 14 stops, though it may have had a complete chromatic compass to pedal e' and manual e'''. The Lutheran St Agnus had a two-manual organ of 27 stops, again with an exceptional pedal compass. There is not the slightest reason to suppose that Bach wrote any particular work to exploit these pedal compasses, but no doubt he used one or both of the organs for teaching and private practice. He communicated at St Agnus, and took part in the baptisms at the court chapel, but had no official duties in either. He may, however, have been involved in the affair of May 1719, when a cantata was put on for the dedication festival of St Agnus, and 150 copies of (presumably) the libretto were printed. The printer's bill for one thaler and eight groschen was endorsed by the pastor: 'The churchwardens can give him 16 groschen; if he wants more, he must go to those who gave the order'.

Bach's basic salary, 400 thaler, was twice Stricker's, and extra allowances made it up to about 450. Only one court official was paid more, and there is other evidence that Bach was held in high esteem. On 17 November 1718 the last of his children by his first wife (a short-lived son) was named after the prince, who himself was a godfather. Bach's residence in Cöthen is not definitely known, but it seems likely that he began as a tenant in Stiftstrasse 11; in 1721, when that house was bought by the prince's mother for the use of the Lutheran pastor, he moved to Holzmarkt 10. The orchestra needed a room for their weekly rehearsals; the prince supplied it by paying rent to Bach (12 thaler a year from 10 December 1717 to 1722). Presumably there was a suitable room in Bach's first house. Whether he continued to use that room after his move in 1721, and why he was not paid rent after 1722, is not clear.

The date of the first rent payment suggests that Bach and his household moved to Cöthen a day or two after he was released from prison (2 December); and that, after hasty rehearsals, he helped to celebrate the prince's birthday on 10 December. That would normally have been his duty. The court accounts suggest that something connected with the birthday was either printed or bound in 1717, as also in 1719 and 1720 (Anh.7); Bach certainly wrote a cantata in 1722, and Cantatas nos.66a and Anh.5 in 1718. In 1721 there may have been no birthday celebrations, for the prince was married, at Bernburg, the next day. Cantata no.173a was undoubtedly a birthday work, but Bach probably wrote it after he had left Cöthen; 36a, an arrangement of 36c (1725), was performed at Cöthen on 30 November 1726, for the birthday of the prince's second wife.

New Year cantatas also were expected. No.134a dates from 1719, Anh.6 from 1720, Anh.8 from 1723. There is no evidence for 1718, 1721 or 1722; printers' and binders' bills paid on 5 January 1722 may have been for music performed in December 1721. Bach may well have been unable to put on a wedding cantata, but there seems no reason why he should not have offered something for the prince's birthday. Nos.184 and 194 (Leipzig, 1724, and Störmthal, 1723) seem to be arrangements of Cöthen works, and so perhaps are parts of no.120. Whether or not Bach performed a cantata at Cöthen on 10 December 1717, he was at Leipzig on 16 December examining the organ at the university church (the Paulinerkirche). The work had been done by Johann Scheibe, with whose son Bach was later in dispute. Bach is not known to have done any other work of this kind while at Cöthen.

On 9 May 1718 the prince went to drink the waters at Carlsbad for about five weeks, taking with him his harpsichord, Bach and five other musicians. Early in 1719 Bach was in Berlin, negotiating for a new harpsichord. About this time he seems to have been busy composing or buying music, for between July 1719 and May 1720 some 26 thaler were spent on binding. During 1719 Handel visited his mother at Halle, only some 30 km away; it is said that Bach tried, but failed, to make contact with him. Bach also disregarded a renewed request from Mattheson for biographical material.

W.F. Bach was nine in 1719; the title-page of his *Clavier-Büchlein* is dated 22 January 1720. In May Bach again went to Carlsbad with the prince. The date of their return does not seem to have been recorded; but apparently it was after 7 July, for that was the date of Maria Barbara's funeral, and there is no reason to doubt Emanuel's story that his father returned to find her dead and already buried. His wife had been nearly 36. Her death may well have unsettled Bach, and even led him to think of returning to the service of the church; but there was a more practical reason for his taking an interest in St Jacobi at Hamburg. The organist there, Heinrich Friese, died on 12 September 1720; Bach had known Hamburg in his youth, and must have been attracted by the organ, a four-manual Schnitger with 60 stops. There is no evidence that Bach was actually invited to apply for the post; but he may well have made inquiries of his own.

At all events, his name was one of eight being considered on 21 November, and he was in Hamburg at about that time. A competition was arranged for 28 November, but Bach had had to leave for Cöthen five days before. Three candidates did not appear, and the judges were not satisfied with the other four. An approach was made to Bach, and the committee met on 12 December; as Bach's reply had not arrived, they met again a week later, when they found that Bach had refused. Perhaps he was unable, or unwilling, to contribute 4000 marks to the church funds, as the successful candidate actually did.

From the way in which the committee kept the post open for Bach, one may suppose that they had heard his recital at St Katharinen. Exactly how this performance was arranged, no-one knows; but in the obituary Emanuel stated that Bach played before the aged Reincken, the magistracy and other notables; that he played for more than two hours in all; and that he extemporized in different styles on the chorale *An Wasserflüssen Babylon* for almost half an hour, just as the better Hamburg organists had been accustomed to doing at Saturday Vespers. As a fantasia on this chorale was one of Reincken's major works, this may seem a tactless choice; but the obituary makes it clear that the chorale was chosen by 'those present' and not by Bach himself. Reincken is reported to have said, 'I thought this art was dead, but I see it still lives in you', and showed Bach much

courtesy. A later remark of Mattheson's has been taken to imply that Bach also played the G minor Fugue bwv542, but there are good reasons to doubt it.

During 1720 Bach made fair copies of the works for unaccompanied violin, and must have been preparing the Brandenburg Concertos, whose autograph full score was dedicated on 24 March 1721 to the Margrave Christian Ludwig, before whom Bach had played in Berlin while negotiating for the new Cöthen harpsichord, between June 1718 and March 1719. What he played is not known; but he was invited to send in some compositions. As he himself said, he took 'a couple of years' over this commission, and then submitted six works written to exploit the resources of Cöthen. Such resources do not seem to have been available to the Margrave of Brandenburg, and it is not really surprising that he did not thank Bach, send a fee or use the score.

One of Bach's friends at Cöthen was the goldsmith C.H. Bähr; Bach stood godfather to one of Bähr's sons in 1721, and deputized for a godfather to another in 1723. About the beginning of August 1721 he gave a performance of some unspecified kind for Count Heinrich XI Reuss of Schleiz; this may have been arranged by J.S. Koch, the Kantor there, who had held a post at Mühlhausen, though possibly not in Bach's time there. On 15 June 1721 Bach was the 65th communicant at St Agnus; one 'Mar. Magd. Wilken' was the 14th. This may well have been Bach's future wife – the mistake in the first name is an easy one – but Anna Magdalena makes no formal appearance until 25 September, when Bach and she were the first two among the five godparents of a child called Hahn. This baptism is recorded in three registers. In two of them Anna is described as 'court singer', in the third, simply as 'chamber musician' (*Musicantin*). In September Anna was again a godmother, to a child called Palmarius; again the registers differ in describing her occupation. Her name does not appear in court accounts until summer 1722, when she is referred to as the Kapellmeister's wife; her salary (half Bach's) is noted as paid for May and June 1722.

Practically nothing is known of her early years. She was born on 22 September 1701 at Zeitz. Her father, Johann Caspar Wilcke, was a court trumpeter; he worked at Zeitz until about February 1718, when he moved to Weissenfels where he died on 30 November 1731. The surname was variously spelt. Anna's mother (Margaretha Elisabeth Liebe, *d* 7 March 1746) was daughter of an organist and sister of J.S. Liebe who, besides being a trumpeter, was organist of two churches at Zeitz from 1694 until his death in 1742. As a trumpeter's daughter, Anna may well have met the Bachs socially. The stories that she was a public figure, having sung at Cöthen and the other local courts since the age of 15, have been discredited; they are said to have arisen through confusion with her elder brother, a trumpeter. However, she was paid for singing, with her father, in the chapel at Zerbst on some occasion between Easter and midsummer 1721. By September 1721, aged just 20, she was at Cöthen, well acquainted with Bach (aged 36), and ready to marry him on 3 December. The prince saved Bach 10 thaler by giving him permission to be married in his own lodgings. At about this time Bach paid two visits to the city cellars, where he bought first one firkin of Rhine wine, and later two firkins, all at a cut price, 27 instead of 32 groschen per gallon.

2. Autograph MS of Bach's organ chorale 'Der Tag, der ist so freudenreich' BWV605 (completed in new German organ tablature) from the 'Orgel-Büchlein', composed mostly c1713–15 (D-Bsb Mus.ms.Bach P 283, f.9r)

On 11 December 1721 the prince married his cousin Friderica, Princess of Anhalt-Bernburg. The marriage was followed by five weeks of illuminations and other entertainments at Cöthen. This was not however an auspicious event for Bach: he was to leave Cöthen partly because the princess was 'eine Amusa' (someone not interested in the Muses) and broke up the happy relationship between Bach and her husband. Perhaps her unfortunate influence had made itself felt even before she was married.

A legacy from Tobias Lämmerhirt (Bach's maternal uncle) had facilitated Bach's first marriage; Tobias's widow was buried at Erfurt on 12 September 1721, and Bach received something under her will too, though not in time for his second marriage. On 24 January 1722 Bach's sister Maria, together with one of the Lämmerhirts, challenged the will, saying that Bach and his brothers Jacob (in Sweden) and Christoph (at Ohrdruf) agreed with them (Christoph had died in 1721). Bach heard of this only by accident; and on 15 March he wrote to the Erfurt council on behalf of Jacob as well as himself. He objected to his sister's action, and said that he and his absent brother desired no more than was due to them under the will. On 16 April Jacob died; and the matter seems to have been settled on these lines towards the end of the year. Bach's legacy must have amounted to rather more than a year's pay.

In summer 1722 there was no Kapellmeister at the court of Anhalt-Zerbst, and Bach was commissioned to write a birthday cantata for the prince; for this he was paid 10 thaler in April and May. The birthday was in August, and payments made during that month presumably refer to the performance. If so, the work, which seems to have disappeared, was scored for two oboes d'amore and 'other instruments'.

Several didactic works for keyboard belong to the Cöthen period. One is the Clavierbüchlein for Anna Magdalena Bach. 25 leaves are extant, about a third of the original manuscript; there is a kind of title-page, on which Anna Magdalena (probably) wrote the title and the date and Bach (certainly) noted the titles of three theological books. Despite the sceptics, it remains reasonable to suppose that Bach gave the book to his wife early in 1722. It seems to have been filled by 1725. The autograph of Das wohltemperirte Clavier (book 1 of the '48') is dated 1722 on the title-page but 1732 at the end. The writing is uniform in style, and for various reasons it is incredible that he did not finish the manuscript until 1732. This handsome fair copy was preceded by drafts, like those in W.F. Bach's Clavier-Büchlein (begun in 1720); and some of the movements look earlier than that. Presumably Bach brought them together for convenience, partly to serve as the last step in his keyboard course, partly to exhibit the advantages of equal temperament. As in book 2, no doubt Bach transposed some of the pieces to fill gaps in his key scheme; the odd pairing of the prelude in six flats with the fugue in six sharps suggests that the former was originally in E minor, the latter in D minor.

The title-page was almost certainly the only part of the Orgel-Büchlein that Bach wrote while at Cöthen, but as another educational work it is best mentioned here. It was meant to be a collection of chorale preludes, not only for the ordinary church seasons but also for occasions when such subjects as the Lord's Prayer, or Penitence, were being emphasized. The paper is of a kind that Bach used, as far as is known, only in 1714. A few items date from about 1740; in the rest, the writing resembles that of the cantatas of 1715–16. Of the 164 preludes Bach allowed for, he completed fewer than 50. Last in this group of works come the Inventions and Sinfonias, whose autograph fair copy is dated 'Cöthen, 1723'. Its contents had already appeared, in earlier versions and under different titles, in W.F. Bach's Clavier-Büchlein of 1720.

The story of Bach's move to Leipzig begins with the death of Kuhnau, Kantor of the Thomasschule there, on 5 June 1722. Six men applied for the post, among them Telemann, who was still remembered for the good work he had done at Leipzig 20 years before. He had been doing a similar job at Hamburg for about a year, and was probably the most famous of German musicians actually living in Germany. One of the Kantor's duties was to teach Latin. Telemann refused to do that; nevertheless, he was appointed on 13 August. But the Hamburg authorities would not release him, and offered to increase his pay; in November he declined the Leipzig post. At a meeting on 23 November Councillor Platz said that Telemann was no loss; what they needed was a Kantor to teach other subjects besides music. Of the remaining five candidates, three were invited to give trial performances; two dropped out, one because he would not teach Latin. By 21 December two Kapellmeisters had applied, Bach and Graupner. The other candidates were Kauffmann of Merseburg, Schott of the Leipzig Neukirche, and Rolle of Magdeburg. Of the five candidates, Graupner was preferred; he was a reputable musician, and had studied at the Thomasschule. He successfully performed his test (two cantatas) on 17 January 1723. But on 23 March he too withdrew, having been offered more pay at Darmstadt. Meanwhile, Bach had performed his test pieces (Cantatas nos.22 and 23) on 7 February 1723. Rolle and Schott had also been heard, and possibly Kauffmann too. The Princess of Cöthen died on 4 April, too late to affect Bach's decision. On 9 April the council considered Bach, Kauffmann and Schott. Like Telemann, none of them wished to teach Latin. Councillor Platz said that as the best men could not be got, they must make do with the mediocre. The council evidently resolved to approach Bach, for on 13 April he obtained written permission to leave Cöthen. On 19 April he signed a curious document that reads as if he were not yet free from Cöthen, but could be free within a month; he also said he was willing to pay a deputy to teach Latin. On 22 April the council agreed on Bach, one of them hoping that his music would not be theatrical. On 5 May he came in person to sign an agreement; on 8 and 13 May he was interviewed and sworn in by the ecclesiastical authority; on 15 May the first instalment of his salary was paid; and on 16 May he 'took up his duties' at the university church, possibly with Cantata no.59. With family and furniture, he moved in on 22 May, and performed Cantata no.75 at the Nikolaikirche on 30 May. On 1 June, at 8.30 a.m., he was formally presented to the school.

This story has been told in some detail, because it throws light on the circumstances in which Bach worked at Leipzig. To him, the Kantorate was a step downwards in the social scale, and he had little respect for his employers. To the council, Bach was a third-rater, a mediocrity, who would not do what they expected a Kantor to do – teach Latin, as well as organize the city church music. The stage was set for trouble, and in due course trouble came. Councillor Platz on Telemann is curiously echoed by Councillor Stieglitz, ten days after Bach's death: 'The school needs a Kantor, not a Kapellmeister; though certainly he ought to understand music'.

7. LEIPZIG, 1723–9. The position of Kantor at the Thomasschule, held conjointly with that of civic director of music, had been associated with a wealth of tradition since the 16th century. It was one of the most notable positions in German musical life both in this and in the esteem it commanded; and there can be little doubt that the general attractiveness of the position in itself played a part – very likely the decisive part – in Bach's decision to move from Cöthen to Leipzig. His subsequent remark about the social step down from Kapellmeister to Kantor must be seen in the context of his later disagreements with the Leipzig authorities, as indeed the letter in question (to Erdmann, a friend of his youth, on 28 October 1730) makes unequivocally clear. In any event, Bach was not the only Kapellmeister to apply for the post. The duties were incomparably more varied and demanding than those in Cöthen or Weimar (to say nothing of Mühlhausen or Arnstadt) and more or less corresponded to those undertaken by Telemann in Hamburg. It cannot have been mere chance that Bach wanted to tackle a range of duties comparable with those of his friend. Above all he must have preferred the greater economic and political stability of a commercial metropolis governed democratically to the uncertainties of the court of an absolute prince, where personal whim often held sway. The university – the foremost in the German-speaking world at the time – must have been another special attraction in the eyes of a father of growing-up sons.

The 'Cantor zu St. Thomae et Director Musices Lipsiensis' was the most important musician in the town; as such, he was primarily responsible for the music of the four principal Leipzig churches – the Thomaskirche, the Nikolaikirche, the Matthäeikirche (or Neukirche) and the Petrikirche – as well as for any other aspects of the town's musical life controlled by the town council. In carrying out his tasks he could call above all on the pupils of the Thomasschule, the boarding-school attached to the Thomaskirche, whose musical training was his responsibility, as well as the town's professional musicians. Normally the pupils, about 50 to 60 in number, were split up into four choir classes (Kantoreien) for the four churches. The requirements would vary from class to class: polyphonic music was required for the Thomaskirche, Nikolaikirche (the civic church) and Matthäeikirche, with figural music only in the first two; at the Petrikirche only monodic chants were sung. The first choir class, with the best 12 to 16 singers, was directed by the Kantor himself, and sang alternately in the two principal churches, the Nikolaikirche and Thomaskirche; the other classes were in the charge of prefects, appointed by Bach, who would be older and therefore more experienced pupils of the Thomasschule.

Musical aptitude was a decisive factor in the selection of pupils for the Thomasschule, and it was the Kantor's responsibility to assess and train them. This was furthered by the daily singing lessons, mostly given by the Kantor. There was also instrumental instruction for the ablest pupils, which Bach had to provide free of charge but was thus enabled to make good any shortage of instrumentalists for his performances. Indeed, the number of professional musicians employed by the town (four Stadtpfeifer, three fiddlers and one apprentice) was held throughout his period of office at the same level as had obtained during the 17th century. For further instrumentalists Bach drew on the university students. In general the age of the Thomasschule pupils ranged between 12 and 23. Remembering that voices then broke at the age of 17 or 18, it is clear that Bach could count on solo trebles and altos who already had some ten years' practical experience – an ideal situation, impossible in boys' choirs today.

As far as church music was concerned, Bach's duties centred on the principal services on Sundays and church feasts, as well as some of the more important subsidiary services, especially Vespers. In addition, he could be asked for music for weddings and funerals, for which he would receive a special fee. Such additional income was important to Bach, as his salary as Kantor of the Thomaskirche and director of music came to only 87 thaler and 12 groschen (besides allowances for wood and candles, and payments in kind, such as corn and wine). In fact, including payments from endowments and bequests as well as additional income, Bach received annually more than 700 thaler. Further, he had the use of a spacious official residence in the south wing of the Thomasschule, which had been renovated at a cost of more than 100 thaler before he moved in in 1723. Inside the Kantor's residence was the so-called 'Komponirstube' ('composing room'), his professional office containing his personal music library and the school's. The buildings of the old Thomasschule were, scandalously, demolished in 1903 to make room for what is now the senior minister's quarters; it was also then that the west façade of the Thomaskirche was rebuilt in the neo-Gothic style.

During his early Leipzig years, Bach involved himself in church music with particular thoroughness and extreme energy. This activity centred on the 'Hauptmusic' composed for Sundays and church feasts. The performance of a polyphonic cantata, with a text related as a rule to the Gospel for the day, was a tradition inherited from previous Kantors. Even so, Bach engaged on a musical enterprise without parallel in Leipzig's musical history: in a relatively short time he composed five complete (or nearly complete) cycles of cantatas for the Church year, with about 60 cantatas in each, making a repertory of roughly 300 sacred cantatas. The first two cycles were prepared immediately, for 1723–4 and 1724–5; the third took rather longer, being composed between 1725 and 1727. The fourth, to texts by Picander, appears to date from 1728–9, while the fifth once again must have occupied a longer period, possibly extending into the 1740s. The established chronology of Bach's vocal works makes it clear that the main body of the cantatas was in existence by 1729, and that Bach's development of the cantata was effectively complete by 1735. The existence of the fourth and fifth cycles has been questioned, because of their fragmentary survival compared with the almost complete survival of the first, second and third; but until a positive argument for their non-existence can be put forward the number of five cycles, laid down in the obituary of 1754, must stand. Compared with the high proportion of Bach's works of other kinds that are lost (orchestral and chamber music, for instance), the disappearance of about 100 cantatas would not be exceptional. (The preservation of Bach's works is discussed below, §11; see §15 for the correspondence of excess chorales in the Breitkopf collection of 1784–7 to the number of lost cantatas.)

The first cycle begins on the first Sunday after Trinity 1723 with Cantata no.75, which was performed 'mit gutem applausu' at the Nikolaikirche, followed by no.76, for the second Sunday after Trinity, performed at the Thomaskirche. The two largest churches in Leipzig are both Gothic in style, and in Bach's time they contained stone and wooden galleries. The choir lofts were on the west wall of the nave above the council gallery. The organs too were in the choir lofts (the 'Schüler-Chor'): the Nikolaikirche and the Thomaskirche each had a three-manual organ with 36 and 35 stops respectively (*Oberwerk*, *Brustwerk*, *Rückpositiv*, *Pedal*). The Thomaskirche had a second organ, fitted to the east wall as a 'swallow's nest', with 21 stops (*Oberwerk*, *Brustwerk*, *Rückpositiv*, *Pedal*); this fell into dilapidation and was demolished in 1740. The organs were always played before cantata performances, during which they would provide continuo accompaniment; they were played by the respective organists at each church; during Bach's term of office these were Christian Heinrich Gräbner (at the Thomaskirche until 1729), J.G. Görner (at the Nikolaikirche until 1729, then at the Thomaskirche) and Johann Schneider (at the Nikolaikirche from 1729). Bach himself, who had not held a regular appointment as an organist since his time in Weimar, directed the choir and the orchestra, and would not normally be playing the organ. However, he frequently must have directed his church ensemble from the harpsichord, as is documented for the performance of BWV198 in 1727. At any rate, the harpsichord was often, if not regularly, employed as a continuo instrument in addition to the organ.

The cantata was an integral part of the Leipzig Lutheran liturgy. It followed immediately on the reading from the Gospel, preceding the Creed and the sermon (the second part of a two-part cantata would follow the sermon, 'sub communione'). Apart from organ playing and the congregational singing of hymns, selected by the Kantor, the other musical constituent of the liturgy was the introit motet, which would be taken from the *Florilegium Portense* (1618) by Erhard Bodenschatz, a collection mainly drawn from the 16th century (Lassus, Handl etc.), and was performed *a cappella* with harpsichord continuo. Services began at 7 a.m. and lasted three hours; this allowed a mere half-hour for the cantata, and Bach rarely overstepped this duration. The normal performing forces consisted of some 16 singers and 18 instrumentalists; the precise number varied according to the work, but it was rare for the total number of singers and players to fall below 25 or to exceed 40 (the figure required on exceptional occasions, like the *St Matthew Passion*, which demanded two Kantoreien and double the normal number of instrumentalists). Ordinarily the performing forces consisted of four groups: pupils from the Thomasschule (the first Kantorei); the eight salaried town musicians, until 1734 headed by J.G. Reiche and thereafter by J.C. Gentzmer; University students (principally Bach's private pupils); and additional assistants (probably regularly including one or two paid soloists) and guests.

Bach took up his additional duties as musical director to the university, a post traditionally held by the Thomaskantor, in summer 1723, perhaps as early as 16 May, with the performance of Cantata no.59 in the university church, the Paulinerkirche, but in any event by 9 August, when he performed the Latin Ode BWV Anh.20 (now lost) at the university's festivities marking the birthday of Duke Friedrich II of Saxe-Gotha. The major part of his duties for the university comprised the musical provisions for the so-called quarter-day orations and the 'old' services in the Paulinerkirche, employing pupils from the Thomasschule and town musicians on the four major festivals of Christmas Day, Easter Day, Whit Sunday and

Reformation Day; Bach was paid 2 thaler and 6 groschen on each occasion. He carried out the most important of his civic duties for the first time on 30 August 1723, when he introduced Cantata no.119 as part of the annual celebration of the change of town council. The enormous scope of Bach's new responsibilities, as well as his vast workload, may be gauged from the fact that the day before (14th Sunday after Trinity) Cantata no.25 was heard for the first time, and the first performance of no.138 (for the 15th Sunday) was soon to follow.

September 1723 saw the start of Bach's protracted wrangle with the university. In a written request for payment, he laid claim to the traditional right of the Thomaskantor to be responsible for the 'old' services and the quarter-day orations. The university, however, wanted to combine these duties with responsibility for the 'new' services (normal Sundays and holy days), which it had in April 1723 entrusted to J.G. Görner, organist of the Nikolaikirche, together with the title of 'Musikdirektor'. On 28 September Bach's request was turned down, and he was paid only half the fee. He would not give in, and turned to the Elector of Saxony in Dresden with three petitions. Following the intervention of the Dresden court, the university decided to put Görner in charge of the 'new' services only, and awarded Bach his traditional rights with payment as before. Thereafter, as the regular fee payments prove, Bach retained responsibility for the 'old' services and quarter-day orations until 1750.

About 2 November 1723 Bach inaugurated a new organ (which he had previously appraised) in Störmthal, outside Leipzig, with Cantata no.194. Then, from the second Sunday in Advent to the fourth, came his first break in the weekly routine of composing and performing cantatas; in Leipzig, unlike Weimar, this period was a 'tempus clausum', as was Lent up to and including Palm Sunday. On Christmas Day figural music returned, in a particularly splendid manner, with Cantata no.63 and the D major Sanctus BWV238 at the main service and the *Magnificat* BWV243a at Vespers; these were Bach's first large-scale compositions on Latin texts such as were customary in Leipzig on major feast days. At this point in the calendar his duties were unimaginably heavy, yet he carried them out with incomparable creative vigour, producing Cantatas nos.40 and 64 for the feasts of St Stephen and St John the Evangelist, no.190 for New Year, no.153 for the Sunday after New Year (2 January 1724), no.65 for Epiphany (6 January) and no.154 for the following Sunday (9 January); after that, normal weekly services were resumed.

During the next 'tempus clausum' Bach composed his first large-scale choral work for Leipzig, the *St John Passion*, first performed at Vespers in the Nikolaikirche on Good Friday (7 April). This Vespers service had been introduced specially for the performance of a Passion only in 1721; in that year Kuhnau's *St Mark Passion* (now lost) had been performed. Performances alternated annually between the Thomaskirche and the Nikolaikirche, an arrangement to which Bach strictly adhered. There is no documentary evidence of a Passion performance under Bach's direction on Good Friday 1723, from which the older dating of the *St John Passion* derives. The work had several further performances, each time in a greatly altered version (see §14): on 30 March 1725 (in a second version adapted to the annual cycle of cantatas), probably on 11 April 1732 (in a third version) and on 4 April 1749

(fourth version); in about 1739 Bach undertook a revision of the work which remained unfinished.

With the first Sunday after Trinity 1724 (11 June) Bach began his second cycle; these were chorale cantatas. Not least because it included works composed at Weimar, the first cycle had been thoroughly heterogeneous in character, both musically and textually, but Bach gave the new cycle a unifying concept, with all the works based on texts, and their melodies, from the hymnbook. Unfortunately this series of chorale cantatas, beginning with no.20, *O Ewigkeit, du Donnerwort*, and its programmatic overture, was interrupted early in 1725 and Bach did not complete the cycle. On 25 June he was in Gera for the dedication of the organ at the Salvatorkirche. In July he went to Cöthen with Anna Magdalena for a guest appearance as a performer; he had retained the title of Court Kapellmeister there, and it lapsed only on the death of Prince Leopold in 1728. There is evidence of further visits to Cöthen, with Bach performing alongside his wife (who sang as a soprano), in December 1725 and January 1728. During 1725 Bach started to prepare a second *Clavierbüchlein* for Anna Magdalena. On 23 February 1725 he performed Cantata no.249a at the Weissenfels court for the birthday of Duke Christian; this was the original version of the *Easter Oratorio* BWV249, first given at Leipzig the following 1 April. No.249a represents the beginning of a long-standing collaboration with the fluent Leipzig poet Christian Friedrich Henrici (Picander), the chief supplier of texts for Bach's later Leipzig vocal works.

Bach produced congratulatory cantatas for two Leipzig University professors in May and August (nos.36c and 205). On 19–20 September he played on the Silbermann organ at the Dresden Sophienkirche before the local court musicians, thus continuing his practice of giving virtuoso organ performances on concert tours – and undoubtedly in Leipzig, too, although he no longer held a post as organist. His favourite instrument in Leipzig was evidently the great organ of the Paulinerkirche built by Johann Scheibe in 1716, with 53 stops, three manuals (*Hauptwerk*, *Seitenwerk* and *Brustwerk*) and pedals; Bach had been one of its examiners in 1717. Early in 1726 – during the third cycle, which had started in June 1725 – there was an interruption of Bach's production of cantatas, for reasons that remain obscure: between February and September 1726 he performed 18 cantatas by his cousin (6) Johann Ludwig Bach (3/72). In particular, between Purification and the fourth Sunday after Easter, he performed none of his own music at the main Sunday services; even on Good Friday he used a work by another composer, Reinhard Keiser's *St Mark Passion*, which he had performed once before, in Weimar. Difficulties with performers may have been partly responsible; the instrumental forces required in J.L. Bach's cantatas are more modest than those Bach himself normally used. Even apart from this, however, the pattern of Bach's cantata production – as far as can be judged from the available material – changed during the third cycle; there are considerable gaps as early as the period after Trinity Sunday 1725, and it seems that the third cycle, unlike the first two, extended over two years. In the gaps, cantatas by other composers and further performances of Bach's own works were given.

Michaelmas 1726 saw the appearance in print of Partita no.1, under the general title of *Clavier-Übung*: with this

Bach began his activity, later to increase in scope, as a publisher of keyboard music. Partita no.1, published singly, was followed by nos.2 and 3 (1727), no.4 (1728), no.5 (1730) and no.6 (1730 or 1731; no copy is known). Evidently the series was originally planned to comprise seven partitas. There are early versions of nos.3 and 6 in the second book for Anna Magdalena of 1725. Bach sent no.1, with a dedicatory poem, to the Cöthen court as a form of congratulation on the birth of an heir, Prince Emanuel Ludwig (born 12 September 1726). In December 1726, on the installation of Dr Gottlieb Kortte as university professor, Bach produced a more sizable occasional work, the *dramma per musica*, Cantata no.207.

In 1727 Bach composed two extremely important works. The *St Matthew Passion*, for double choir to a libretto by Picander, was performed on Good Friday (11 April; there is evidence that it was repeated in the Thomaskirche in 1729, 1736 and 1742; see §14). The other work was the *Trauer Ode* (Cantata no.198), performed in October at a memorial ceremony, planned by the university, on the death of the Electress Christiane Eberhardine, who had remained a Protestant when her husband, August the Strong of Saxony, converted to Roman Catholicism. For this Bach was commissioned to set a text by the Leipzig professor of poetry, Johann Christoph Gottsched. This became a somewhat controversial affair, as the university director of music, Görner, felt he had been slighted. Bach however retained the commission and performed the two parts of his work, 'composed in the Italian manner', directing it from the harpsichord, in the university church, on 17 October. Between 7 September 1727 and 6 January 1728 there was a period of national mourning, with no other musical performances.

In September 1728 a brief dispute with the church authorities flared up. The sub-deacon, Gaudlitz, demanded that he himself should choose the hymns to be sung before and after the sermon at Vespers; as it was usual for the Kantor to select these hymns, Bach felt that his rights had been encroached upon. The dispute was settled in the sub-deacon's favour. Bach must have seen this as a setback, for once again his grievances had not been met; but his relations with the ecclesiastical authorities were on the whole good throughout his time at Leipzig. His relations with the town council and the head teachers of the Thomasschule went less smoothly, and were to become even more difficult in the 1730s. Documents dealing with the various disputes show Bach to have been a stubborn defender of the prerogatives of his office who frequently reacted with excessive violence and was often to blame if there was a negative outcome. It would be wrong, however, to draw hasty inferences about Bach's personality and his relations with the world about him. It is unfortunate that about a half of Bach's surviving correspondence is concerned with generally trivial but often protracted disputes over rights. This material is extant in public archives, while utterances of kinds not appropriate to archival preservation, which might have complemented this rather austere view of his personality, have survived in only small quantity. From Bach's behaviour during these disputes it can be seen that, under pressure, he would defy bureaucratic regulations in order to preserve his independence and to clear himself an artistic breathing-space. His taking over of the

collegium musicum in 1729, to be directed under his own management, must be seen in this context, as it represents something more than an incidental biographical fact.

Early in 1729 Bach spent some time at the Weissenfels court in connection with the birthday celebrations in February of Duke Christian, with whom he had long been associated. On this occasion the title of court Kapellmeister of Saxe-Weissenfels was conferred on him (his Cöthen title had lately expired); he retained the title until 1736. At the end of March he went to Cöthen to perform the funeral music for his former employer; only the text survives of this large-scale work in four parts (BWV244a), but much of its music can be reconstructed as it consists of parodies of BWV198 and 244. On 15 April (Good Friday) the *St Matthew Passion* was performed again at the Thomaskirche. On the second day of Whit week (6 June), what was probably the last cantata of the Picander cycle was performed, no.174. The manuscript, uniquely for Bach, is dated ('1729'); perhaps this represents some sort of final gesture after a heavy, six-year involvement in cantata composition.

Beside the production of cantatas, Passions and other vocal occasional works, both sacred and secular, instrumental music retreated to the background during Bach's first years in Leipzig. Apart from some keyboard and chamber works (including the sonatas for harpsichord and violin BWV1014–19) there appear to have been only a relatively small number of organ works (preludes and fugues, trio sonatas) which are hard to date individually but will have been primarily connected with Bach's activities as a recitalist.

In June 1729 an invitation to visit Leipzig was delivered to Handel, then in Halle, by Wilhelm Friedemann, in place of his father who was ill at the time; but nothing came of it. Thus Bach's second and last attempt to establish contact with his highly esteemed London colleague met with failure. Significantly, in both cases the initiative was taken by Bach.

8. LEIPZIG, 1729–39. On his appointment as director of the collegium musicum, decisive changes came about in Bach's activities in Leipzig; and at the same time new possibilities were opened up. The collegium had been founded by Telemann in 1702 and had most recently been directed by G.B. Schott (who left to become Kantor at Gotha in March 1729); it was a voluntary association of professional musicians and university students that gave regular weekly (and during the fair season even more frequent) public concerts. Such societies played an important part in the flowering of bourgeois musical culture in the 18th century, and with his highly reputed ensemble, in such an important commercial centre as Leipzig, Bach made his own contribution to this. He took over the direction before the third Sunday after Easter – in other words, by April 1729 – and retained it in the first place until 1737; he resumed it for a few more years in 1739. He must have had strong reasons for wanting to take on this fresh area of work in addition to his other duties. To some extent it is possible to guess those reasons. For six years he had immersed himself in the production of sacred music, and he had created a stock of works sufficient to supply the requirements of his remaining time in office. In his efforts to provide sacred music that was at once fastidious and comprehensive he had met with little appreciation from the authorities, and no additional facilities (for example, much needed professional instru-

mentalists) had been placed at his disposal: it would be understandable if he now felt resigned to the situation. Further, as a former Kapellmeister, he must have been attracted by the prospect of working with a good instrumental ensemble, and another important incentive must have been the thought that, as director of the collegium, he would be able to establish a wholly independent musical praxis, in accordance with his own ideas. It is not known whether the new position brought him some additional income.

Nothing, unfortunately, is known about the programmes of the 'ordinaire' weekly concerts. But the surviving performing parts for such works as the orchestral suites BWV1066–8, the violin concertos BWV1041–3 and the flute sonatas BWV1030 and 1039 demonstrate that Bach performed many of his Cöthen instrumental works (some in revised form) as well as new compositions. The seven harpsichord concertos BWV1052–8, collected together in a Leipzig manuscript, also belong in this context. Bach often performed works by other composers as well, including five orchestral suites by his cousin Johann Ludwig, secular cantatas by Handel and Porpora and the flute quartets that Telemann wrote for Paris. Further, Bach's many musical acquaintances from other places must have made frequent appearances, including his colleagues in the Dresden court orchestra (there is evidence of visits from J.A. Hasse, Georg Benda, S.L. Weiss, C.H. Graun and J.D. Zelenka). C.P.E. Bach's remark that 'it was seldom that a musical master passed through [Leipzig] without getting to know my father and playing for him' must refer to performances of the collegium musicum, which took place on Wednesdays between 4 and 6 p.m. in the coffee-garden 'before the Grimmisches Thor' in the summer and on Fridays between 8 and 10 p.m. in Zimmermann's coffee-house in the winter. In addition, there were 'extraordinaire' concerts, to mark special events; on these occasions, during the 1730s, Bach performed his large-scale secular cantatas. His activities with the collegium must have made heavy demands on him, and the reduction in his production of sacred music is easy to understand.

This does not, however, mean that his interest in sacred music was diminished (as Blume, G1963, claimed, with undue emphasis in the light of the revised dating of his works). Such a view is contradicted not only by the major ecclesiastical works written after 1730 but also by the simple fact that, throughout his period of office, Bach provided performances of his cantatas, a repertory largely completed before 1729, every Sunday at the two main Leipzig churches. His reference to the 'onus' of such undertakings, in connection with the performance of a Passion planned for 1739, might just as well have been made in the 1720s. Admittedly, his difficulties became particularly acute around 1730, as his important memorandum of 23 August 1730, dealing with the state of church music in Leipzig and outlining his remedies, testifies. His letter of 28 October that year, to his old friend Erdmann in Danzig, may be read in the same sense; sheer frustration that the memorandum had proved ineffectual drove him to consider leaving Leipzig. It would seem that his work with the collegium musicum had not yet brought about the intended equilibrium in his activities.

The situation had been aggravated by other, external factors. The old headmaster Johann Heinrich Ernesti had died in 1729 (Bach had performed a motet BWV226 at his funeral in October). During the subsequent interim in the Thomasschule's direction the organization of school life was disturbed. Problems of space appear to have arisen too. It was in this context that complaints were made about Bach's neglect of his school duties (the dropping of singing lessons, absence on journeys without leave); in August 1730 there was even a question of reducing his salary 'because the Kantor is incorrigible'. It would appear that things were put right by J.M. Gesner, who took over the headship of the school in the summer, and who seems soon to have established friendly and familiar relations with Bach.

On Good Friday 1730 Bach apparently performed a *St Luke Passion*, not of his own composition. From 25 to 27 June the bicentenary of the Augsburg Confession was celebrated across Lutheran Germany, and Bach wrote three cantatas for the event (nos.190a, 120b, Anh.4a: all were parody cantatas). They are not untypical of his church compositions of this period, most of which were put together as parodies; and that is true also of the major vocal works like the *St Mark Passion*, the B minor Mass, the small masses and the *Christmas Oratorio*. The only sacred cantatas that Bach composed as entirely new works after 1729 are nos.117 (1728–31), 192 (1730), 112 and 140 (1731), 177 (1732), 97 (1734), 9 and 100 (1732–5) and 14 (1735).

In 1731 a collected edition of the six partitas appeared as op.1, under the title *I.Teil der Clavier-Übung*. From this form of words it is clear that Bach planned further 'parts' in a series of 'keyboard exercises', and these he now proceeded to produce. His new and continuing interest in publishing his own compositions is a clear sign of a new determination with regard to independent and freely creative activity. The first performance of the *St Mark Passion*, predominantly a parody work, took place on Good Friday of that year. At the end of June 1731 Bach and his family had to move to temporary quarters while rebuilding and extension work were being carried out on the Thomasschule. His residence must have become increasingly cramped, for his family was growing. In the early years in Leipzig Anna Magdalena had borne a child almost every year, but few of them survived infancy:

Christiana Sophia Henrietta (*b* spring 1723; *d* 29 June 1726)
Gottfried Heinrich (48)
Christian Gottlieb (bap. 14 April 1725; *d* 21 Sept 1728)
Elisabeth Juliane Friederica (bap. 5 April 1726; *d* Leipzig, 24 Aug 1781)
Ernestus Andreas (bap. 30 Oct 1727; *d* 1 Nov 1727)
Regina Johanna (bap. 10 Oct 1728; *d* 25 April 1733)
Christiana Benedicta (bap. 1 Jan 1730; *d* 4 Jan 1730)
Christiana Dorothea (bap. 18 March 1731; *d* 31 Aug 1732)
Johann Christoph Friedrich (49)
Johann August Abraham (bap. 5 Nov 1733; *d* 6 Nov 1733)
Johann Christian (50)
Johanna Carolina (bap. 30 Oct 1737; *d* Leipzig, 18 Aug 1781)
Regina Susanna (bap. 22 Feb 1742; *d* Leipzig, 14 Dec 1809)

Joy and sorrow were everyday matters. But Bach's family life must have been harmonious in more than one sense; in 1730 he reported, as a proud paterfamilias, that with his family he could form a vocal and instrumental concert ensemble. The family moved back into their refurbished apartment the next April. The school was reconsecrated on 5 June 1732 with a cantata, BWVAnh.18. In September 1731 Bach had been to Dresden for the first performance of Hasse's opera *Cleofide* and to give concerts at the Sophienkirche and at court (there were enthusiastic reports in the newspapers). In September 1732 he went with his wife to Kassel for the examination and inauguration of the organ of the Martinskirche, where he probably played the 'Dorian' Toccata and Fugue in D minor BWV538.

With the death of Elector Friedrich August I of Saxony on 1 February 1733 a five-month period of national mourning began. However, the collegium musicum obtained permission to restart its performances in the middle of June, when a new harpsichord was introduced (possibly in the harpsichord concertos BWV1052–8). During the mourning period Bach composed the D major version of the *Magnificat* BWV243, which was probably first heard in Leipzig when the mourning was ended on 2 July (Visitation). Above all he worked on the Kyrie and the Gloria of the B minor Mass, which, in the hope of obtaining a title at the court Kapelle, he presented to the new Elector Friedrich August II in Dresden, with a note dated 27 July 1733, as a *Missa* in a set of parts. There is evidence to suggest that the *Missa* was performed at this time, perhaps at the Sophienkirche in Dresden, where W.F. Bach had been working as an organist since June 1733. Not until November 1736, however, was the title 'Hofkomponist' conferred on Bach, and even then only through the intervention of his patron Count Keyserlingk after a further letter of application. As a gesture of thanks, Bach paid his respects to the Dresden royal household and an enthusiastic public with a two-hour organ recital on the new Silbermann instrument at the Frauenkirche on 1 December 1736.

After the dedication of the *Missa* in July 1733, Bach kept the Saxon royal family's interests in mind with his 'extraordinaire' concerts of the collegium musicum. On 3 August, the name day of the new elector, Bach began his remarkable series of secular cantatas of congratulation and homage with BWV Anh.12 (music lost), followed by Cantata no.213 (5 September, for the heir to the electorate), no.214 (8 December, for the electress), no.205a (19 February 1734, for the coronation of the elector as King of Poland; music lost), an unknown work (3 August, again for the elector), and no.215 (5 October, also for the elector, who was at the performance). Much of the festive music was performed in the open air with splendid illuminations, and according to newspaper reports the music benefited from a resounding echo. (On the day after the performance of no.215 Bach's virtuoso trumpeter and the leader of the Leipzig Stadtpfeifer, Gottfried Reiche, died as a result of the exertions of his office.) During the following Christmas season Bach gave the people of Leipzig a chance to hear much of the music from his secular festive cantatas in modified form, as the *Christmas Oratorio*, which was heard in six sections between Christmas Day 1734 and Epiphany 1735 (and consisted predominantly of parodies of Cantatas nos.213–15).

On 21 November 1734 the new headmaster of the Thomasschule, Johann August Ernesti, was greeted with a cantata, BWV Anh.19 (Gesner had moved to the newly founded University of Göttingen as its first dean). Bach's dealings with the directors of the school had been untroubled for four years, thanks to his friendly relations with Gesner; but with Ernesti he experienced the most violent controversies of his entire period as Thomaskantor. A dispute flared up in August 1736 over the authority to nominate the choral prefect, in which the interests of the Kantor and the headmaster were diametrically opposed. With his neo-humanist educational ideals, which placed priority on high academic standards, Ernesti showed little appreciation of the musical traditions. The tendency at the Thomasschule, at least from the start of Bach's period of office, had been to restrict musical activities, or at any rate to reduce their proportions; Bach, on the other hand, demanded the best-qualified pupils to assist him, and certainly he must often have overburdened them (with music copying, rehearsals and so on). Against what were to some extent unfair arguments on the headmaster's part, his struggles were doomed to failure. The grievances arising from the nomination of the choir prefect were taken before the courts in Dresden; the affair, which led to Bach's having disciplinary difficulties with his pupils, was settled early in 1738 (the precise outcome is not recorded). The prefect in question, Johann Gottlob Krause, whom Bach refused to acknowledge, had already left the Thomasschule in 1737.

Among the more important events of 1735 was the appearance of the second part of the *Clavier-Übung* at Easter. In the context of Bach's activities as a publisher it should also be mentioned that by 1729 he was also involved in the distribution of musical publications by other authors and kept a stock, including Heinichen's book on figured bass, Walther's *Lexicon* and keyboard works by Hurlebusch, Krebs and his own sons. On 19 May the *Ascension Oratorio* (Cantata no.11) was first performed; probably the *Easter Oratorio* (a revision of Cantata no.249a) was heard on the preceding Easter Sunday. In June he travelled to Mühlhausen, where he had spent part of his early career, to appraise the rebuilt organ in the Marienkirche, where his son Johann Gottfried Bernhard (47) had just been appointed organist. During Advent 1735, when no music was performed, and Lent 1736 Bach was probably engaged on the revision of the *St Matthew Passion* and in making a carefully laid-out fair copy of the new version. In this form, characterized by its writing for double chorus (with two continuo parts), the work was performed in the Thomaskirche on 30 March 1736, with the cantus firmus parts in the opening and closing choruses of part 1 played on the 'swallow's nest' organ. Also at Easter the Schemelli Hymnbook, on whose tunes and figured basses Bach had collaborated, was published.

In summer 1737 Bach temporarily resigned the direction of the collegium musicum. For the last 'extraordinaire' concert on 7 October 1736 he had written the congratulatory Cantata no.206 on the birthday of the elector. Only two further works of homage are known from 1737–8 (BWV30a and Anh.13), which indicates that Bach was occupied primarily with the other things for which he had time after his release from the work associated with the collegium. He now turned to keyboard music, working on the second part of *Das wohltemperirte Clavier*, and on the third part of the *Clavier-Übung*, the largest of his keyboard works. This collection of organ pieces, some freely composed, some based on chorales, with large-scale works for a church organ and small-scale ones for a domestic instrument, appeared at Michaelmas 1739.

Bach obviously also devoted himself more than previously to private teaching in the late 1730s. Between 1738 and 1741, for example, J.P. Kirnberger and J.F. Agricola were studying with him in Leipzig – probably the most

3. Bach's autograph letter of recommendation for his pupil Johann Ludwig Krebs, 24 August 1735 (D-Zsa III Z.40.7, f.36r)

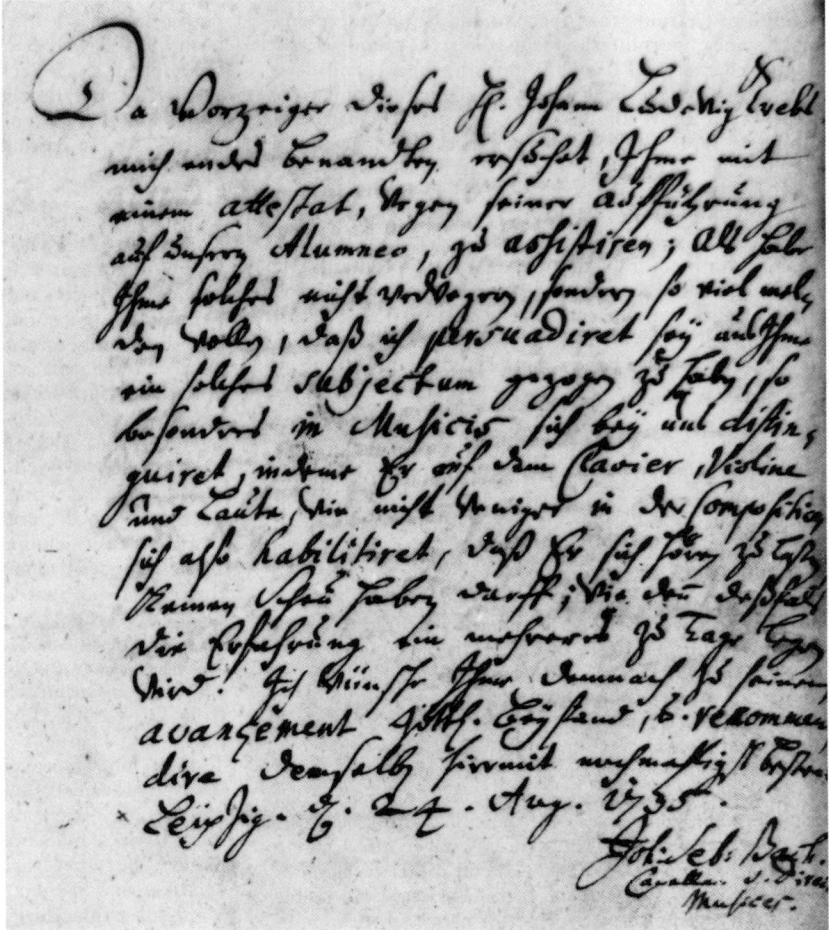

important and influential of all his pupils except for his own sons. Over the years Bach had something like 80 private pupils; among them were C.F. Abel (*c*1743), J.C. Altnickol (1744–8), J.F. Doles (1739–44), G.F. Einicke (1732–7), H.N. Gerber (1724–7), J.C.G. Gerlach (1723–9), J.G. Goldberg (*c*1740), G.A. Homilius (1735–42), J.C. Kittel (1748–50), J.G. Müthel (1750), J.C. Nichelmann (1730–33), J.G. Schübler (after 1740), G.G. Wagner (1723–6) and C.G. Wecker (1723–8).

In October 1737 Bach's nephew Johann Elias (39) came to live with the family, as private secretary and tutor for the younger children; he remained until 1742. The surviving drafts of letters he prepared give a lively picture of Bach's correspondence in these few years – and cause for regret that no other period is similarly documented. At this period Bach gave especially close attention to the study of works by other composers. He was a subscriber to Telemann's Parisian flute quartets of May 1738; but more typical is his preoccupation with Latin polyphonic liturgical compositions. The *stile antico* tradition seems to have held a particular fascination for him. In the first place he owed his knowledge of this repertory, to which he marginally contributed by making transcriptions (works by Palestrina, Caldara, Bassani and others), to his connections at Dresden. His knowledge of Pergolesi's *Stabat mater* of 1736, which he reworked during the 1740s as a setting of Psalm li, *Tilge, Höchster, meine*

Sünden BWV1083 is also surprising; the earliest trace of Pergolesi's work north of the Alps thus leads to Bach – a sign of the latter's remarkable knowledge of the repertory. His interest in Latin liturgical music also relates closely to the composition of the short masses (Kyrie and Gloria) BWV233–6. These may have been written for the Protestant court services in Dresden, but that would not exclude performances in Leipzig.

On 14 May 1737 J.A. Scheibe, in his journal *Der critische Musikus*, published a weighty criticism of Bach's manner of composition. This seems to have come as a severe blow to Bach. Evidently at his urging, the Leipzig lecturer in rhetoric Johann Abraham Birnbaum responded with a defence, printed in January 1738, which Bach distributed among his friends and acquaintances. The affair developed into a public controversy, the literary conduct of which, at least, was suspended only in 1739 after further polemical writings by Scheibe and Birnbaum. Scheibe acknowledged Bach's extraordinary skill as a performer on the organ and the harpsichord, but sharply criticized his compositions, claiming that Bach 'by his bombastic and intricate procedures deprived them of naturalness and obscured their beauty by an excess of art'. Birnbaum's not particularly skilful replies fail to recognize the true problem, which lies in a clash of irreconcilable stylistic ideals. Nevertheless, his discussion of naturalness and artificiality in Bach's style, and his definition of harmony as an accumulation of counterpoint, make some important statements about the premisses and unique character of Bach's compositional art, and Bach himself must have been involved in their formulation. This is clear above all in the way in which 'the nature of music' is represented, with references to biographical details (such as the challenge to Marchand) and express mention of composers and works in Bach's library (Palestrina, Lotti and Grigny). The controversy smouldered on for several more years. Mizler, too, shook a lance, pointing to 'the latest taste' in Bach's cantata style ('so well does our Kapellmeister know how to suit himself to his listeners'). In the end Scheibe climbed down, with a conciliatory review (1745) of the Italian Concerto in which he apologized handsomely ('I did this great man an injustice').

9. LEIPZIG, 1739–50. In October 1739 Bach resumed the direction of the collegium musicum, which had in the meantime been in the charge of C.G. Gerlach (organist at the Neukirche and a pupil of Bach). A composition for the birthday of the elector (7 October; the music is lost) dates from this time, but it would seem that Bach's ambitions and activities in connection with the 'ordinaire' and 'extraordinaire' concerts were considerably diminished. There were few performances of congratulatory cantatas, and these were probably all repeats of earlier works. There are no signs, however, that Bach's interest in instrumental ensemble music slackened; if anything, it underwent a certain revival and he continued to produce chamber music steadily throughout the 1730s.

Bach withdrew from the collegium musicum again in 1741. With the death of the coffee-house owner Gottfried Zimmermann (30 May 1741) the collegium had lost its landlord and organizer, and without him it could not long continue, at least as it had been run hitherto. Signs of reduced activity can be traced until 1744, and it is possible that Bach still presided over performances from time to time until that year. The collegium had made an important contribution to musical life in Leipzig for 40 years, both with and without Bach's leadership, and even its demise was not without consequences for the future. In both its function and its membership it served to prepare the ground for a new focal point in civic musical life, the Grosses Concert, founded in 1743 on the lines of the Parisian Concert Spirituel and destined to be the immediate predecessor of the Gewandhaus concerts.

In August 1741 Bach went to Berlin, probably to visit Carl Philipp Emanuel who in 1738 had been appointed court harpsichord player to Crown Prince Frederick of Prussia (later Frederick the Great). In the two previous years Bach had made brief journeys to Halle (early 1740) and Altenburg (September 1739; he gave a recital on the new Trost organ in the castle church). In November 1741 there was a further journey, this time to Dresden, where he visited Count von Keyserlingk. In the same year, probably in the autumn, the 'Aria with 30 Variations', the so-called Goldberg Variations, appeared in print. Bach's visit to Dresden may lie behind the anecdote related by Forkel, according to which the variations were commissioned by the count as a means of ameliorating sleepless nights, but the lack of any formal dedication in the original edition suggests that the work was not composed to a commission. It is conceivable, on the other hand, that after publication the count received a copy of the work for the use of his young resident harpsichord

player Johann Gottlieb Goldberg, who was a pupil of both J.S. and W.F. Bach. In his own copy (which came to light only in 1975) Bach added a series of 14 enigmatically notated canons on the bass of the Aria (BWV1087) in about 1747–8. They place a special and individual accent on the canonic writing that occupied him so intensively at that period.

On 30 August 1742, on the Kleinzschocher estate near Leipzig, a 'Cantata burlesque' (known as the Peasant Cantata, no.212) was performed in homage to the new lord of the manor, Carl Heinrich von Dieskau; this work is unique in Bach's output for its folklike manner (except perhaps for the quodlibet in the Goldberg Variations). The thoroughly up-to-date characteristics of parts of the work show that Bach was not only intimately acquainted with the musical fashions of the times but also knew how to adapt elements of the younger generation's style for his own purposes (as he also did in the third movement of the trio sonata from the Musical Offering).

Alongside this work, apparently his last secular cantata, Bach's only vocal compositions of the 1740s were isolated sacred works (including Cantatas nos.118, 195, 197 and 200), some new, some refashioned. There is evidence, on the other hand, that he gave numerous performances of works by other composers, some newly arranged or revised. These included a German parody of Pergolesi's Stabat mater (Tilge, Höchster, meine Sünden BWV1083, c1745–7), a Latin parody after the Sanctus and 'Osanna' from J.C. Kerll's Missa superba (Sanctus in D BWV241, c1747–8), Handel's Brockes Passion (c1746–7 and 1748–9) and a pasticcio Passion after C.H. Graun (with inserted movements BWV1088 and 'Der Gerechte kömmt um' BCC 8). Bach also often repeated his own earlier sacred works. Evidence does not exist to form a complete picture, but they included revised versions of the St Matthew and St John Passions; the latter was performed for the last time during Bach's lifetime on Good Friday 1749.

The only new vocal composition of any size was the Credo and following sections of the Mass, which, when added to the Missa of 1773 (BWV232¹), produced the B minor Mass – a continuation of Bach's preoccupation with Latin figural music during the late 1730s. No specific reason for the composition of the B minor Mass, and no evidence of a projected or actual performance, has so far come to light. One of the most plausible hypotheses is that the composition of the work (which is described in C.P.E. Bach's Nachlass as 'the large Catholic Mass') was connected with the consecration of the Catholic Hofkirche in Dresden, planned for the late 1740s and then postponed (building started in 1739). All that is known for certain is that the expansion of the 1733 Missa by the addition of a Credo, a Sanctus (1724) and the movements from 'Osanna' to 'Dona nobis pacem' and the fusing of the various sections to create a unified score (see also §14) were done in the last years of Bach's life – more precisely, between August 1748 and October 1749.

Instrumental music, however, once again came to the fore during the 1740s. Bach had begun to sift through his older organ chorales about 1739–42, probably following completion of Clavier-Übung III. Some of the Weimar pieces were extensively reworked and gathered into a new manuscript collection (the '18', BWV651–68). These revisions may have been undertaken with a view to the subsequent appearance of the chorales in print, as happened with the six chorales on movements from cantatas (the 'Schübler Chorales') about 1748. Apparently Bach was still engaged in work on the chorales in the last months of his life. The copying from dictation of the chorale *Vor deinen Thron* BWV668, later the subject of legend, was in fact probably confined to an improvement of an existing work (the chorale BWV641 from the Weimar *Orgel-Büchlein*).

Bach retained his interest in organ building to the last. In 1746 alone there were two important examinations and inaugurations of organs: on 7 August in Zschortau and on 26–9 September in Naumburg. Bach's appraisal of the large Hildebrandt organ in the Wenzelskirche, Naumburg, was one of his most important. He customarily subjected instruments to the most searching examinations, both of their technical reliability and of their tone quality. He had also taken a critical interest in the pianos that Gottfried Silbermann was building during the 1730s, proposing alterations in the mechanism which Silbermann evidently adopted. At all events, Bach praised Silbermann's later pianos and promoted their sale (a receipt for one sold to Poland, dated 6 May 1749, survives). On his visit to Potsdam in 1747 he played on a range of Silbermann pianos of the newer type which had been purchased by the Prussian court.

The visit to the court of Frederick the Great in May 1747 is one of the most notable biographical events in Bach's otherwise unspectacular life. The invitation probably came about through Count Keyserlingk, who was then in Berlin. Bach's encounter with Frederick began on 7 May at the palace of Potsdam during the chamber music which was a feature of every evening of court life there. Bach's execution on the piano of a remarkable improvisation on a theme supplied by the king met with general applause. The next day Bach gave an organ recital in the Heiliggeistkirche in Potsdam, and during chamber music that evening he improvised a six-part fugue on a theme of his own. He also visited the new Berlin opera house, and possibly went to look at organs in Potsdam and Berlin. On his return to Leipzig, probably in the middle of May, he worked industriously on an 'elaboration of the King of Prussia's fugue theme', beginning with writing down the fugue he had improvised (a three-part ricercare), which, while in Potsdam, he had announced that he would print. But he now decided on a larger project and under the title *Musikalisches Opfer* ('Musical Offering') he prepared a work in several movements dedicated to Frederick the Great; this work was printed in its entirety by the end of September (Michaelmas) 1747. The royal theme serves as the basis for all the movements (two ricercares, in three and six parts, for keyboard; a trio sonata for flute, violin and continuo; and various canons for flute, violin and continuo with harpsichord obbligato).

In June 1747, after some hesitation, Bach joined the Correspondirende Societät der Musicalischen Wissenschaften founded by Lorenz Mizler. It was probably in 1747 that he submitted, as a 'scientific' piece of work, his canonic composition on *Vom Himmel hoch* BWV769. At the same time he sent the members an offprint of the six-part canon from the series on the bass of the Goldberg Variations. He seems, however, to have taken no further interest in the society's affairs as (according to C.P.E. Bach) he thought nothing of the 'dry, mathematical stuff' that Mizler wanted to discuss. Besides his long acquaintance with his pupil Mizler, Bach's most likely reason for

joining the society was that prominent colleagues such as Telemann and Graun were fellow members.

The beginnings of his work on *Die Kunst der Fuge* ('The Art of Fugue') seem to date from around 1740, or before. It is impossible to give an exact date as the original composing score is now lost. However, what must be a first version survives in an autograph fair copy containing 14 movements (12 fugues and two canons) and dating from 1742 at the latest. Thereafter Bach expanded and revised the work in readiness for printing. He himself supervised the printing to a large extent, and the process was probably largely complete by about the end of 1749 (in other words, before his son Johann Christoph Friedrich, who had helped to correct the proofs, left to join the court at Bückeburg in January 1750). But Bach was not to see the entire work (eventually comprising 14 fugues and four canons) in print; his sons, probably C.P.E. in particular, took charge of the publication and the work appeared posthumously in spring 1751. Bach had been unable to complete the fair copy of the last movement, a quadruple fugue, and so the fugal cycle ends with an unfinished movement. The editors decided to mitigate the effect of that by adding the organ chorale BWV668, *Vor deinen Thron tret ich hiermit*, at the end; the revision of this had been the last piece of work to occupy Bach.

In his final years Bach suffered from increasingly severe trouble with his eyes, seriously restricting his ability to work and leading eventually to total blindness. He probably composed nothing after autumn 1749. The last known examples of his handwriting, which give an impression of increasing irregularity, clumsiness and cramping, go up to October 1749 (parts of the score of the B minor Mass). Other documents to which he put his signature date from as late as spring 1750. The cause of the eye disease seems to have lain in untreated (and untreatable) diabetes, which may also have caused neuropathy and degenerative brain disease, evidence of which is found in the dramatic change in his handwriting in manuscripts of 1748–9. He gave a performance of the *St John Passion* on Good Friday 1749 without completing the revision of the work begun in about 1740. His health must have been very poor by spring 1749 at the latest; otherwise the Leipzig town council would surely not have been so tactless as to submit J.G. Harrer, a protégé of the Dresden prime minister Count Brühl, to examination for the post of Kantor on 8 June 1749. Out of consideration for Bach the cantata performance was in a concert hall rather than one of the churches. The town chronicle reported that the authorities expected Bach's death. When his grandson Johann Sebastian Altnickol (his pupil Johann Christoph Altnickol had married Elisabeth Juliane Friederica Bach) was baptized on 6 October 1749 in Naumburg Bach was unable to make the short journey to stand godfather in person.

Bach's state of health and ability to work must have fluctuated during his last year. He appointed Johann Nathanael Bammler, a former choir prefect at the Thomasschule for whom he provided two excellent references in 1749, to deputize for him as occasion warranted. But in spite of everything Bach was not entirely inactive. In spring 1749 he is known to have corresponded with Count Johann Adam vom Questenberg, apparently about a commission or some other project. Although no details are known, this reaffirms Bach's obviously well-established connections with some major noble patrons from the area of Bohemia (Count Sporck of Lissa and Kukus), Moravia (Count Questenberg of Jaroměřice) and Silesia (the Haugwitz family). From May 1749 to June 1750 he was engaged in a controversial correspondence about the Freiberg headmaster Biedermann. In May 1749 Biedermann had violently attacked the cultivation of music schools; Bach immediately felt himself called into battle, and among other things he gave a repeat performance of the satirical cantata about the controversy between Phoebus and Pan, no.201. His involvement is understandable, for he must have seen parallels with the state of affairs at the Thomasschule, where the same tendency fuelled Ernesti's reforms. Bach solicited a rejoinder on the part of C.G. Schröter, a member of Mizler's society, and even Mattheson joined in, from Hamburg. Once again, the affair throws light on the situation in German schools during the early Enlightenment and Bach's last years as Thomaskantor. The integration of academic and musical traditions, which had been an institution for centuries, was in the process of turning into an irreconcilable confrontation.

At the end of March Bach underwent an eye operation, performed by the English eye specialist John Taylor (who was later to perform a similar operation on Handel). It was only partly successful, however, and had to be repeated during the second week of April. The second operation too was ultimately unsuccessful, and indeed Bach's physique was considerably weakened. Yet as late as the beginning of May 1750 Johann Gottfried Müthel could go to Leipzig, stay at Bach's house and become his last pupil. To what extent regular instruction was possible under these circumstances remains uncertain. In the next two months Bach's health had so deteriorated that, on 22 July, he had to take his last Communion at home. He died only six days later, on the evening of 28 July, after a stroke. He was buried two or three days later at the cemetery of the Johanniskirche. It is not known what form the funeral ceremony took or what music was performed.

Bach's wife, Anna Magdalena, who in addition to her domestic tasks was a loyal and industrious collaborator, participating in performances and copying out music, survived him by ten years. She died in abject poverty in 1760. On his death Bach had left a modest estate consisting of securities, cash, silver vessels, instruments – including eight harpsichords, two lute-harpsichords, ten string instruments (among them a valuable Stainer violin), a lute and spinet – and other goods, officially valued at 1122 thaler and 22 groschen; this had to be divided between the widow and the nine surviving children of both marriages. Bach himself had evidently given instructions for the disposition of his musical *Nachlass*, which is ignored in the official valuation. According to Forkel, the eldest son Wilhelm Friedemann 'got most of it' (see §11).

10. ICONOGRAPHY. The oak coffin containing Bach's remains was exhumed in 1894: the detailed anatomical investigation by Professor Wilhelm His confirmed their identity and showed that Bach was of medium build. From a skull impression Carl Seffner, in 1898, modelled a bust, which shows an undoubted similarity with the only likeness of Bach that can be guaranteed as authentic, that of the Leipzig portraitist Elias Gottlob Haussmann. That portrait exists in two versions, one dating from 1746 (Museum für Geschichte der Stadt Leipzig; property of the Thomasschule) and one of 1748 (William H. Scheide

Library, Princeton; see below, fig.4). The earlier, signed 'E.G. Haussmann pinxit 1746', was presented to the Thomasschule in 1809 by the then Thomaskantor, August Eberhard Müller. It is not known whence Müller had obtained the painting, but is quite probable that it had remained in the possession of one of Bach's direct descendants until then. Of these the most likely is Wilhelm Friedemann (unless he had another replica of Haussmann's painting) or Regina Susanna, who lived in Leipzig until her death in 1809. It is often supposed that the Thomasschule portrait is one that members of Mizler's society were required by statute to donate to that institution, but that is highly unlikely: Bach probably did not present a portrait, at least in the form of a painting, to the society. With the passage of time the Thomasschule picture was severely damaged and repeatedly painted over. Thorough restoration in 1912–13 returned it more or less to its original condition, but it remains inferior to the excellently preserved replica of 1748. This has a reasonably secure provenance, out of C.P.E. Bach's estate; it was owned privately for many years by the Jenke family in Silesia and then in England, before being exhibited in public by Hans Raupach in 1950.

The authenticity of an unsigned pastel portrait, probably painted after 1750, allegedly by either Gottlieb Friedrich or Johann Philipp Bach, and handed down in the Meiningen branch of the family, is not altogether certain, and neither is that of a group portrait of musicians, executed around 1733 by Johann Balthasar Denner (now in the Internationale Bachakademie, Stuttgart; a replica, in better condition, is in a private collection in the UK), which shows what may well be Johann Sebastian (with violoncello piccolo) and three of his sons.

Doubt hangs over the authenticity of all the other better-known and much reproduced portraits. The oil by Johann Jacob Ihle, dating from about 1720 and purporting to show Bach as Kapellmeister in Cöthen, comes from the palace at Bayreuth and was identified as a 'picture of Bach' only in 1897. But there is no concrete support for that identification, and the portrait's earlier provenance is obscure; it now hangs in the Bachhaus in Eisenach. The portrait by Johann Ernst Rentsch the elder (now in the Städtisches Museum, Erfurt), allegedly representing Bach at the age of about 30, came to light only in 1907 and has no credible documentation. Many other apocryphal portraits, including the 'portrait in old age' discovered by Fritz Volbach in Mainz in 1903 (now in a private collection in Fort Worth), are of the 'old man with a wig' type and have nothing to do with Bach.

According to *GerberL*, probably authentic portraits that no longer survive were once owned by J.C. Kittel (from the estate of the Countess of Weissenfels) and by J.N. Forkel. A pastel from C.P.E. Bach's collection (not the one referred to above) has not survived. During the 18th and 19th centuries many copies were made of the Haussmann portrait, both in oils and in various types of print; an engraving (1794) by Samuel Gottlieb Kütner, an art student at the Zeichenakademie, Leipzig, along with C.P.E. Bach's son Johann Sebastian (1748–78), was said by Emanuel himself to be 'a fair likeness'. The nearest we can nowadays get to his true physiognomy is probably in the 1748 version of Haussmann's portrait, wherein, as a man in his early 60s, Bach is represented as a learned musician, with a copy of the enigmatic six-part canon BWV1076 in his hand to demonstrate his status (fig.4).

4. Johann Sebastian Bach: portrait by Elias Gottlob Haussmann, 1748, after an original of 1746 (William H. Scheide Library, Princeton, NJ); the composer holds a copy of his six-part canon BWV1076

11. SOURCES, REPERTORY.   The earliest catalogue of Bach's compositions – admittedly a very rough one – was included in the obituary that C.P.E. Bach and J.F. Agricola wrote immediately after Bach's death but did not publish until 1754. It scarcely provides an adequate idea of the extent of Bach's works, but it shows that nearly everything printed during Bach's lifetime has survived to the present day: Cantata no.71, composed for the Mühlhausen town council election in 1708 (but not its counterpart of 1709); the four parts of the *Clavier-Übung*; the Schemelli Hymnbook; the *Musical Offering*; the Canonic Variations BWV769; the Schübler chorales; the *Art of Fugue*; and the canons BWV1074 and 1076. The great majority of Bach's compositions remained unprinted, and most of those survived. The most serious losses occurred among the cantatas: perhaps more than 100, certainly two cycles of church cantatas and several secular occasional works. The funeral music for Prince Leopold of Cöthen (1729) and the *St Mark Passion* (1731) are among large-scale vocal works of which only the texts survive. A greater proportion of the music for organ and other keyboard instruments has probably survived than that in any other category. Losses among the orchestral and chamber works are almost impossible to estimate, but may be regarded (on the evidence of existing transcriptions, for example) as substantial.

On the assumption that Bach managed to keep his music together as far as possible during his lifetime, it seems that major losses occurred only on the division of his legacy in 1750, when the manuscripts, especially of the vocal works, were divided between the eldest sons and Bach's widow. Most of them went to Wilhelm Friedemann, but he, unfortunately, was the least succussful at managing his inheritance; he was compelled for

financial reasons to sell them off item by item, and the material is not simply scattered but for the most part lost. Only a few of the items inherited by Johann Christoph Friedrich and Johann Christian, including a printed copy of the *Musical Offering* and the autograph of the organ Prelude and Fugue in B minor BWV544 (signed with Johann Christian's nickname 'Christel'), can be traced. C.P.E. Bach's and Anna Magdalena's shares were better preserved. Bach's widow gave her portion (the parts of the cycle of chorale cantatas) to the Thomasschule while most of C.P.E. Bach's estate passed through Georg Poelchau's collection into the Berlin Königliche Bibliothek (later the Preussische Staatsbibliothek and now the Staatsbibliothek zu Berlin). This collection forms the basis of the most important collection of Bach archives. During the 19th century this library acquired further, smaller Bach collections, notably those from the Singakademie and the estates of Forkel, Franz Hauser and Count Voss-Buch (in some of which fragments from W.F. Bach's inheritance appear).

Besides the original manuscripts – the autograph scores, and parts prepared for performances under Bach's direction – which, in their essentials, Bach kept by him, many copies were made in the circle of his pupils, particularly of organ and harpsichord music. As many autographs of the keyboard works are lost, this strand is specially significant for the preservation of Bach's works. In particular, important copies have come down through members of Bach's family (including the Möllersche Handschrift and the Andreas-Bach-Buch, both compiled by Sebastian's brother Johann Christoph), through J.G. Walther and through Bach's pupils Krebs and Kittel. After Bach's death Breitkopf in Leipzig became a centre for the dissemination of his music (again, primarily the keyboard music). In Berlin a notable Bach collection was made for Princess Anna Amalia of Prussia, under the direction of Kirnberger, in which all facets of Bach's creative output were represented (now *D-Bsb* Amalien-Bibliothek). These secondary sources have to serve when autograph material is not available – relatively often with the instrumental works (e.g. a large percentage of the organ pieces; the English and French Suites, toccatas, fantasias and fugues for harpsichord; duo and trio sonatas; concertos and orchestral works), more rarely with the vocal ones (e.g. Cantatas nos.106 and 159; motets BWV227–30; and the masses BWV233 and 235).

Research into source materials, notably in conjunction with the Neue Bach-Ausgabe, has proved fruitful. The use of diplomatic research methods has allowed most of the copyists who worked for Bach – and all the important ones – to be identified: 'Hauptkopist A' was J. Andreas Kuhnau (*b* 1703); 'Hauptkopist B' was C.G. Meissner (1707–60); 'Hauptkopist C' was J. Heinrich Bach (1707–83); 'Hauptkopist D' was S.G. Heder (*b* 1713); 'Hauptkopist E' was J.G. Haupt (*b* 1714); 'Hauptkopist F' was J.L. Dietel (1715–73); 'Hauptkopist G' was Rudolph Straube (*b* 1717); and 'Hauptkopist H' was J.N. Bammler (1722–84). Papers, inks and binding have been evaluated for the purposes of identification and dating; but above all Bach's own handwriting, in its various stages of development, has served as the criterion for dating. A far-reaching revision of the chronology of Bach's works (only some 40 of the originals are dated) has been made possible, leading to a substantial revision of previous conceptions, which were based for the most part on

Spitta's work. The new chronology was established in its important details by Dürr and Dadelsen during the 1950s. Since then it has been variously added to, modified and confirmed. For the vocal works it is now essentially complete; sometimes it is precise to the actual day. With the instrumental works the situation is more complicated, because the original manuscripts are often lost; in consequence, results have been less precise since the history of the secondary sources permits of only vague conclusions about composition dates (for example, copies originating from the circle around Krebs and J.G. Walther point to a date in the Weimar period); this makes it unlikely that any complete and exact chronology will be established for the instrumental works, though a relative one is now largely achieved.

Investigations of source material have also led to the solution of crucial questions of authenticity, particularly in connection with the early works but also affecting some of the later ones. For example, Cantata no.15, hitherto regarded as Bach's earliest cantata, has now been identified as by Johann Ludwig Bach; similarly, Cantatas nos.53, 189 and 142 have been excised from the list of his works. Some instrumental works, such as BWV835–8, 969–70, 1024 and 1036–7, have been assigned to other composers. On the other hand, an important early organ work, BWV739, has now been authenticated and its manuscript ranks as probably Bach's earliest extant musical autograph. Completely new finds have been made (BWV1081–120 and Anh.205) and numerous copies by Bach of other composers' works have come to light; these provide additional information about his repertory and its context.

12. BACKGROUND, STYLE, INFLUENCES. Bach's output, unparalleled in its encyclopedic character, embraces practically every musical form of his time except opera. The accepted genres were significantly added to by Bach (notably with the harpsichord concerto and chamber music with obbligato keyboard); further, he opened up new dimensions in virtually every department of creative work to which he turned, in format, density and musical quality, and also in technical demands (works such as the *St Matthew Passion* and the B minor Mass were to remain unique in the history of music for a long time to come). At the same time Bach's creative production was inextricably bound up with the external factors of his places of work and his employers, as was normal in his time. The composition dates of the various repertories thus reflect Bach's priorities in his various professional appointments; for instance, most of the organ works were composed while he was active as an organist at Arnstadt, Mühlhausen and Weimar, whereas most of the vocal works belong to the period of his Kantorate at Leipzig. But Bach's production was by no means wholly dependent on the duties attaching to his office at the time. Thus during his Leipzig period he found time to produce a body of keyboard and chamber music to meet his requirements for concerts, for advertisement, for teaching and other purposes. And his career may be seen as a steady and logical process of development: from organist to Konzertmeister, then to Kapellmeister, and finally to Kantor and director of music – a continual expansion of the scope of his work and responsibilities. This is no matter of chance. Bach chose his appointments, and chose the moment to make each move. If he was unable to accomplish what he required (as was often the case in Leipzig), he was capable

of turning his attention elsewhere in pursuit of his creative aims. Bach was a surprisingly emancipated and self-confident artist for his time.

The uncertainty about the dating of Bach's early works, with so little help in the form of source materials, makes it difficult to reconstruct and assess the beginnings of his work as a composer. It is to be supposed that he started to compose while under the tutelage of his elder brother in Ohrdruf, but although he took no formal lessons with an established composer, as Handel did with Zachow, it would be mistaken to call him self-taught as a composer, for the significance of his belonging to a long-standing family of professional musicians should not be underestimated. Composing was probably overshadowed by instrumental playing in Ambrosius Bach's family; this must to some extent have applied to the young Johann Sebastian, and probably he devoted more attention to developing his skills as an instrumentalist, especially as an organist, than to composition studies. But the art of improvisation – in those days inseparably bound up with practice on the instrument – would at the very least prepare the ground for his work as a composer. This reciprocity between performing and composing is reflected in the unruly virtuoso and improvisatory elements in Bach's early works.

As composers who influenced the young Bach, C.P.E. Bach cited (in 1775, in letters to Forkel) Froberger, Kerll, Pachelbel, Frescobaldi, Fischer, Strungk, certain French composers, Bruhns, Buxtehude, Reincken and Böhm – almost exclusively keyboard composers; C.P.E. Bach also said that Bach formed his style through his own efforts and developed his fugal technique basically through private study and reflection. In his letter of resignation from Mühlhausen Bach himself wrote of having procured a good supply of the very best vocal compositions, suggesting that in vocal music too he was decisively stimulated by the study of other composers' music. Bach came into personal contact with the last three of the composers named by C.P.E.; there was no question of any teacher–pupil relationship. No record survives of what works he collected at Mühlhausen, but they might have included Keiser's *St Mark Passion*, a six-part mass by Peranda and an italianate chamber concerto by Biffi, for his early autograph copies of all these survive, demonstrating the breadth of his knowledge of the repertory. As later influences, C.P.E. Bach named Fux, Caldara, Handel, Keiser, Hasse, the two Grauns, Telemann, Zelenka and Benda. This list, though certainly less representative than the earlier one, suggests that Bach's main interests still lay in his great contemporaries, whose music he not only heard but also studied in transcripts. With them he abandoned his one-sided attention to the organists among older composers, but his interest in the retrospective style represented by Fux and Caldara, complemented by his enthusiasm (mentioned by Birnbaum, 1737) for Palestrina and Lotti, is notable, and is borne out by tendencies in his music from the mid-1730s. Clearly he also became interested in, and ready to follow, more recent stylistic trends, particularly in respect of the music of Hasse, the Graun brothers and Benda (for example in the 'Christe eleison' of what was to become the B minor Mass) and in such works as the Peasant Cantata, the Goldberg Variations and the *Musical Offering*). Mizler, in an article of 1739 on Bach's cantata style, referring to the Scheibe–Birnbaum controversy, mentioned a work (BWV

Anh.13, lost) composed 'perfectly in accordance with the newest taste' ('vollkommen nach dem neuesten Geschmack eingerichtet').

Curiously, C.P.E. Bach's list of the masters his father had 'loved and studied' contains no mention of Vivaldi and the two Marcellos, or of Corelli, Torelli and other late Baroque Italian composers. Forkel compensated for this by his emphasis on the importance of Vivaldi's concertos, without citing any particular source to support his claim. Indeed, it was Vivaldi who exercised what was probably the most lasting and distinctive influence on Bach from about 1712–13, when a wide range of the Italian repertory became available to the Weimar court orchestra. Bach drew from Vivaldi his clear melodic contours, the sharp outlines of his outer parts, his motoric and rhythmic conciseness, his unified motivic treatment and his clearly articulated modulation schemes. His confrontation with Vivaldi's music in 1713–14 provoked what was certainly the strongest single development towards his own personal style. In Forkel's words, Vivaldi 'taught him to think musically'; his musical language acquired its enduring quality and unmistakable identity through his coupling of italianisms with complex counterpoint, marked by busy interweavings of the inner voices as well as harmonic refinement. It is impossible to describe Bach's personal style by means of simple formulae; but the process of adaptation and mutation that can be felt throughout his output seems to have taken a particularly characteristic turn at that point in 1713–14 whose principal landmarks are the *Orgel-Büchlein* and the first Weimar series of cantatas. His adaptation and integration of various contemporary and retrospective styles represent his systematic attempt at shaping and perfecting his personal musical language ('unlike that of any other composer', according to C.P.E. Bach) and expanding its structural possibilities and its expressive powers.

An essential component of Bach's style can be seen in his combination of solid compositional craftsmanship with instrumental and vocal virtuosity. The technical demands made by his music reflect his own prowess as an instrumentalist. Bach's own versatility – his early involvement in singing (it is not known whether he was later active as a singer), and his experience as a keyboard player, violinist and viola player – was partly responsible for the fact that demanding technical standards became the norm for every type of composition he wrote. This led to Scheibe's famous criticism: 'Since he judges according to his own fingers, his pieces are extremely difficult to play; for he demands that singers and instrumentalists should be able to do with their throats and instruments whatever he can play on the keyboard. But this is impossible'. It makes no essential difference at what level these demands are made (for instance between the Inventions and the Goldberg Variations, the four-part chorale and the choral fugue); everywhere Bach's requirements are the antithesis of conventional simplicity. Yet technical virtuosity never predominates; it becomes a functional element within the composition as a whole. Bach's impulse towards integration is also manifested in the typically instrumental idiom in which he cast his vocal parts. He thus produced in his music for voices and instruments a homogeneous language of considerable density. Even so, he differentiated between instrumentally and (less often) vocally dominated types of writing; but even in such vocally dominated pieces as the Credo of the

B minor Mass he maintained both the density and the uncompromising, yet appropriate technical standard. It is of course significant, as regards both matters of technique and the quality of his music in general, that, as far as we know, he wrote almost exclusively for himself, his own ensembles and his own pupils, and never for a broader public (let alone a non-professional one). This partly explains why his music – unlike, say, Telemann's or Handel's – was disseminated within unusually narrow confines.

13. CANTATAS.   About two-fifths of Bach's sacred cantatas must be considered lost; of the secular cantatas, more are lost than survive. Thus it is difficult to draw firm conclusions about the evolution of the cantata in Bach's hands, even though the surviving repertory is considerable and roughly proportional to the number of cantatas composed at each place where he worked.

The earliest surviving cantatas, and probably Bach's first, date from the Mühlhausen and perhaps even the Arnstadt period; they include – as the earliest of all – nos.150, 131, 106 and 196 (c1707). The best, in both form and content, are nos.106 and 71. The latter is especially sumptuous, and its appearance in print bore the young composer's reputation far beyond the boundaries of Mühlhausen. The early vocal works belong almost without exception to the category of 'organist's music', that is they are pieces composed for particular occasions, not regular cantatas for the Sundays and feast days in the church calendar. Nor do they conform to the type established as modern by Neumeister in 1701, but they rely closely on central German tradition. Their texts are mostly taken from the Bible or the chorale repertory; freely conceived poetry is rare (found only in nos.71, 106 and 150). Musically they consist of a succession of different formal types – concerto, motet, (strophic) aria and chorale – adapted and combined to suit the composer's purpose. Bach did not call them cantatas: as a rule he reserved that term for the solo cantata of the Italian type (like nos.211 and 212), calling his sacred cantatas 'Concerto', and in earlier works 'Motetto', sometimes 'Dialogus' (depending on the text) or simply 'Music'.

Bach's early cantatas are distinguished from their central German precursors, which must have been familiar to him from his upbringing, by his tendency to give each movement a unified structure and his development of a broad formal scheme. He found the means to unify movements that for the most part do not function as closed numbers by reducing motivic material (in the solo movements). Reacting against haphazard sequential form, with its danger of formal dissolution, he began to use strictly symmetrical sequences of movements to underpin the overall cyclic structure: for example, chorus–solos–chorus–solos–chorus (no. 106).

During Bach's early Weimar years, organ music must have dominated his output; on the other hand, the letters written in 1712–13 by his pupil at Weimar, Johann Philipp Kräuter, show that Bach encouraged him to write cantatas. 1713 is the date, too, of what seems to be Bach's first secular cantata, the *Jagd-Kantate* no.208, written to a commission from the Weissenfels court (where it had a repeat performance before 1717). The piece shows Bach, obviously newly acquainted with the Italian style, taking up the recitative and the modern kind of aria (for preference the da capo aria), a step which had a decisive effect on the next sacred cantatas, nos.199, 21 and 63 (nos.21 and 63 were probably written in connection with his application to succeed Zachow in Halle in December 1713). With his nomination as court Konzertmeister on 2 March 1714, he started to produce cantatas on the whole regularly from the end of March onwards, in accordance with an agreement 'to perform a piece of his own composition under his own direction, in the chapel of the royal castle, on every fourth Sunday at all seasons'. This was Bach's first opportunity to compose a whole cantata cycle, albeit over a fairly long time-span; however, as things turned out, the number he wrote in Weimar amounted to little more than 20. The principle of the annual cycle is closely bound up with the history of the cantata from Neumeister on; the texts were mostly published in cycles, one for each Sunday and feast day in the church year. Bach, admittedly, never adhered strictly to a single poet (except in the lost Picander cycle of 1728–9), preferring to pick and choose. In Weimar he turned for the first time to librettos by Neumeister (nos.18 and 61) and used texts by G.C. Lehms (1684–1717; nos.199 and 54), but evidently preferred texts by the Weimar court poet Salomo Franck (1659–1725), the author of extremely original and profoundly felt sacred and secular poetic texts, among the best Bach set. Nos.21, 63 and 199 are among cantatas dating from before 1714; regular production began with Cantata no.182 on 25 March 1714. There followed, usually at four-week intervals, in 1714 nos.12, 172, 61, 152; in 1715 nos.18, 54, 31, 165, 185, 163, 132; in 1716 nos.155, 80a, 161, 162, 70a, 186a and 147a. Repeat performances of nos.21, 199, 31, 165 and 185 were slotted into the cycle. Gaps are accounted for by the loss of certain cantatas and in one case by the period of mourning from 11 August to 9 November 1715.

Musically the works are of particular importance for the development they show in Bach's personal style of writing for voices and instruments. The recitatives contain extensive arioso sections to begin with, but these gradually disappear (although the combinatorial element was to remain typical of Bach throughout his life); the arias become longer, in free or (more usually) strict da capo form and occasionally using more complex structures. The choruses embrace a multiplicity of formal principles, among them fugue and canon (no.182), passacaglia (12), concerto (172), motet (21) and French overture (61). Also notable are the overlapping of instrumental and vocal formal schemes (the use of Chor- and VOKALEINBAU) and instrumental quotations of chorale melodies. The extraordinarily colourful instrumentation is especially characteristic: within the smallest of performing ensembles Bach tried out a great variety of combinations, for example recorder, oboe, viola d'amore and viola da gamba in Cantata no.152. Following the Italian ideal, his orchestral writing moved away from the French practice of five-part writing, with two violas, which predominates in the early cantatas towards a more flexible four-part style. Instead of the harmonic weight of the middle voices in five-part writing Bach provided a rhythmically and melodically active viola part that is particularly characteristic.

In Cöthen, corresponding to Bach's official responsibilities, only secular cantatas were composed (with the single exception of BWVAnh.5) and those were mostly written for New Year celebrations or the prince's birthday. Bach's librettist was C.F. Hunold ('Menantes', 1681–1721). Among the Cöthen cantatas, many survive only as verbal

texts (Anh.6–8) or are lost altogether; a substantial part of the music survives only for nos.66a, 134a, 173a, 184a and 194a. These pieces mostly exemplify the 'serenata' type of work, with succinct operatic treatment in dialogues between allegorical figures. It is not surprising that they reflect Bach's study of the instrumental concerto of the period (in part in the solo–tutti differentiation) or that dance characteristics appear, notably in the solo movements. Bach used transverse flutes in Cantata no.173a, evidently for the first time.

At Leipzig the performance of sacred cantatas on Sundays and feast days (some 60 a year) was one of Bach's chief tasks, and he produced a large number of new works. His vast workload meant that within the first cycle, beginning on the first Sunday after Trinity (30 May), he not only had to rely on repeat performances of earlier sacred cantatas but also had to resort to parodies of secular cantatas written at Cöthen. Nevertheless, his first cycle (1723–4) contains the following new compositions: nos.75, 76, 24, 167, 136, 105, 46, 179, 69a, 77, 25, 119, 138, 95, 148, 48, 109, 89, 60, 90, 40, 64, 190, 153, 65, 154, 155, 73, 81, 83, 144, 181, 67, 104, 166, 86, 37 and 44; to these must be added his test works (nos.22 and 23, for Quinquagesima 1723) and no.194, composed for the consecration of the new organ in Störmthal. Apart from no.24 (Neumeister) and nos.64, 69a and 77, the poet or poets of this first cycle remain for the most part unknown. The use of Knauer's Gotha cycle of 1720, which provides two texts for each Sunday and feast day, together with the fact that cantatas in two parts, or two separate cantatas, were sometimes performed (before and after the sermon) – such as nos.75, 76, 21, 24+185, 147, 186, 179+199, 70, 181+18, 31+4, 172+59, 194+165 and 22+23 – indicates that Bach designed his first Leipzig cycle, in part at least, as a double cycle.

Thus in his first year at Leipzig Bach furnished himself with an astonishingly concentrated repertory, and his emphasis on the cantata genre also gave him mastery over an incomparable variety of forms, free from any schematicism. Three favourite groundplans are: biblical text–recitative–aria–recitative–aria–chorale (nos.46, 105, 136 etc.); biblical text–recitative–chorale–aria–recitative–aria–chorale (nos.40, 48, 64 etc.); biblical text–aria–chorale–recitative–aria–chorale (nos.86, 144, 166 etc.). A constant feature, characteristic of the Leipzig cantatas as a whole, is the framework, comprising an introductory choral movement in the grand style (solo pieces appear rarely at the start) and closing four-part chorale, simple but expressive. Compared with the Weimar cantatas, the orchestral forces are larger. From no.75 onwards the brass (mainly trumpets and horns) are more strongly deployed, the flute is brought into play increasingly after 1724, and the oboe d'amore (from no.75) and oboe da caccia (from no.167) are introduced as new instruments, as are the violino piccolo and violoncello piccolo at a later date. Instrumental virtuosity is heightened, and the melismatic quality of the vocal writing is further developed. The 'prelude and fugue' type of movement is frequently used for the introductory chorus (as in no.46).

The second cycle, dating from 1724–5, consists mainly of a series of freshly composed chorale cantatas (i.e. cantatas of which both text and music are based on hymns): nos.20, 2, 7, 135, 10, 93, 107, 178, 94, 101, 113, 33, 78, 99, 8, 130, 114, 96, 5, 180, 38, 115, 139,

5. Autograph MS of Bach's Serenata 'Durchlauchtster Leopold' BWV173a, composed c1722, with the text of the sacred cantata 'Erhöhtes Fleisch und Blut' BWV173 added 1724 (D-Bsb Mus.ms.Bach P 42, f.1r)

26, 116, 62, 91, 121, 133, 122, 41, 123, 3, 111, 92, 125, 126, 127 and 1. From Easter 1725 this series was continued at first with cantatas of the traditional kind, that is with texts related to the prescribed scriptural readings for the day (nos.249, 6, 42 and 85), and then with nine cantatas to texts by Mariane von Ziegler (1695–1760): 103, 108, 87, 128, 183, 74, 68, 175 and 176, in all of which there is a tendency to use forms closer to those of the first cycle. 1724–5 was not only the most productive year for cantatas, as far as is known from the surviving works at least; it also, with the chorale cantata, saw the beginnings of a type that perhaps represents Bach's most important contribution to the history of the genre. What is particularly striking is his endeavour to lay out the introductory movements as large-scale cantus firmus compositions, each adhering to a different structural principle. Cantata no.20, and with it the second cycle, opens with a chorale movement for chorus in the form of a French overture which it is possible to regard as a kind of programmatic statement, whereas the opening

chorus of no.2 takes the retrospective form of a chorale motet. By this means Bach marked out a broad framework, in terms of both musical style and compositional technique, to indicate the conceptual range of the cycle he was starting. Cohesion between the movements within each cantata is guaranteed, at least from the textual point of view, by their relationship to the fundamental chorale (with chorale paraphrases for the solo pieces, as opposed to the procedure in no.4); often it is further emphasized by references to the cantus firmus and by the use of various ways of intermingling cantus firmus and free material. The author of the texts for the chorale cantatas is not known – Pastor Christian Weiss of the Thomaskirche, who used to preach chorale sermons, is a possibility.

With the third cycle, from 1725–7, the continuous, weekly production of cantatas ends, or so the sources indicate. It appears, however, from a surviving printed textbook of 1725 covering the third to the sixth Sunday after Trinity, that this cycle must have suffered substantial losses. When his production was actually interrupted

Bach usually filled the gaps with works by other composers, including no fewer than 18 cantatas by his cousin Johann Ludwig Bach of Meiningen. The cantatas of the third cycle offer no major innovations in the way of musical structure, but they notably include solo (nos.52, 84, 35 etc.) and dialogue cantatas (58, 32, 49 etc.), as well as large-scale works in two parts. There is an absence of overall formal integrity in the planning of this cycle, but Bach reveals a wide variety of ambitions and intentions, among them completing the cycle of chorale cantatas with further works of that type (no.137), reverting to older texts by Neumeister (28), Franck (72), Lehms (110, 57, 151, 16, 32, 13, 170 and 35) or from a Rudolstadt textbook (17, 39, 43, 45, 88, 102 and 187) and experimenting with the use of complementary texts from the Old and New Testaments (the former in the opening movement, the latter in a central one: Rudolstadt texts). One remarkable trait of the cycle is the frequent introduction of older instrumental movements, pre-eminently as sinfonias but sometimes also with choral participation (the reconstruction of the first movement of the Orchestral Suite BWV1069 to open Cantata no.110 is an example of this). A remarkable innovation in summer 1727 was the appearance of obbligato organ parts (nos.34, 146, 169, 49 and 188), found in both sinfonias (recycling instrumental concertos) and arias.

The third cycle was followed by the 1728–9 cycle on texts by Picander, which has disappeared but for a few remnants (1728: nos.149, 188, 197a; 1729: nos.171, 156, 159, Anh.190, 145 and 174). That Bach really did set the whole of Picander's *Cantaten auf die Sonn- und Fest-Tage durch das gantze Jahr* (Leipzig, 1728) as his fourth cycle cannot be accepted without reservation. At the same time, the poet must have been expressing something more than a pious hope when he wrote in the preface 'that any lack of poetic charm may perhaps be compensated for by the gracefulness of the incomparable Herr Kapellmeister Bach and these songs [Lieder] may be performed in the principal churches of prayerful Leipzig'. One of the characteristics of Picander texts is the frequent interpolation of chorale verses in the free poetry, creating attractive opportunities for mingling choruses and arias, which were not wasted on Bach (see nos.156 and 159, or the first movement of the *St Matthew Passion*). The cantatas written after 1729 offer nothing essentially new in formal terms, as far as can be determined from those that survive, but they show signs of a late style beginning to develop, manifested (in no.195 for example) above all in a more refined shaping of the accompanied recitative and a more integral, polyphonic treatment of the final chorale (entailing some modification of the cantus firmus). Some of the later cantatas (nos.117, 192, 112, 177, 97 and 100) show an interesting modification of the chorale type: they relinquish freely composed texts but (unlike the older *per omnes versus* type represented by Cantata no.4) set the central movements as recitatives and arias.

It is impossible to reconstruct a fifth cycle worthy of the name from the surviving works (not even given the large number of unattributed four-part chorales: see §15), but it would have had to be composed over a rather longer period of time, mainly in the 1730s. The mention in the obituary of 'five cycles of church pieces, for every Sunday and holy day' is just a tantalizing hint of how much has been lost.

Besides the cantatas composed in connection with the church year, Bach also wrote sacred cantatas for other occasions, like changes of town council, weddings, funerals, the bicentenary of the Augsburg Confession (1730) and inaugurations of organs; in style these are essentially indistinguishable from the other works. The body of cantatas, for all its variety, has an unusually self-contained character, maintained above all by its consistently high musical quality and its unfailing expressive profundity. The distinctive expressive power of Bach's musical language did not merely evolve in the cantatas, in many respects, but also finds its most characteristic representation in them. His expressive urge, as seen in individual arias and choruses, was not confined to single words as the primary bearers of expression, but was geared to movements and formal sections as a whole, in keeping with Baroque formal models (like the *ABA* of the da capo aria). Only within the context of a movement's structural and expressive unity did he regard the special treatment of single words as possible or meaningful. Among the tools of Bach's craft the traditions of *musica poetica* and musical rhetoric (the theory of musical figures) must certainly be reckoned. They were deeply rooted in him. Yet to reduce Bach's intentions to their rhetorical and figural components, or even to emphasize those components, would be to diminish their true breadth. Over and above this objective of expressive unity, Bach was always primarily concerned with the contrapuntal organization of melodic-rhythmic and harmonic textures to establish coherence. That is a principal reason why his cantata movements lend themselves so readily to parody. The technical prerequisites for producing a parody work – which Bach did so often – are metrical similarity and expressive affinity; the most essential requirement, however, is self-sufficiency of the musical substance, and its flexibility leaves considerable scope for the musical interpretation of a new text.

During his early Leipzig years Bach wrote only isolated secular cantatas, but these became more frequent as time passed. They were produced for various occasions: university ceremonies (nos.36b, 198, 205, 207), celebrations at the Thomasschule (BWV Anh.18, Anh.19, 36c), festivities in the houses of noblemen and prominent citizens (202, 216, 210, 249b, 30a, 210a, 212) and commissions from court (249a, 36a). Most of his large-scale congratulatory and homage cantatas written for the electoral house of Saxony were produced at the collegium musicum. A favourite format was the operatic *dramma per musica*, with a simple plot suited to the specific nature of the occasion being celebrated (nos.213, 206, 214, 207a, 215). The more lyrical cantatas such as no.204, or the two Italian works, nos.203 and 209, would certainly have been performed at the collegium musicum. The Coffee and Peasant Cantatas (nos.211 and 212), to some extent tinged with folk style, are distinguished by their lifelike and humorous characterization. The librettist of most of the works of 1725–42 was the versatile Picander, the only other important poet for Bach's cantatas during this period being J.C. Gottsched (1700–66), the influential Leipzig professor of rhetoric (BWV198, Anh.13, Anh.196). There is concrete evidence of just under 40 secular cantatas composed during the Leipzig years, but in most cases only the texts survive. Their occasional nature is the main reason why so many have been lost: few could have been given a second performance, and then only after alterations to the text. Bach was of course aware that their best chance of survival lay in parody, and he took such opportunities as occurred to save the music, as in the case of the *Christmas Oratorio* (see §14).

14. ORATORIOS, PASSIONS, LATIN WORKS. The three works that Bach called 'oratorios' fall within a very short period: the *Christmas Oratorio* of 1734–5, the *Easter Oratorio* and *Ascension Oratorio* of 1735. The librettists are not known for certain. The place for Bach's oratorios in the Lutheran liturgy was the same as that for the cantata; the only difference between the oratorio and cantata texts is that the former have a self-contained 'plot' or take the form of narration with dialogue. This conforms with the history of the genre, although Bach held the tendency to formal expansiveness firmly in check, in comparison with standard Italian practice. In the *Christmas Oratorio*, especially, the normal character of a single self-contained work is contradicted by its being split into sections for six different services between Christmas Day and Epiphany, and this is further emphasized by Bach in his use of different performing forces for the sections (although these are based on an underlying general scheme, and are grouped round six scenes from the Bible, with certain divergences from the allocation of lessons to be read at the various services). The unusual conception of an oratorio performed over several days is reminiscent of the Lübeck Abendmusiken, and the *Christmas Oratorio* obviously belongs to the oratorio tradition established by Buxtehude. All three of Bach's oratorios are essentially based on parodies of secular cantatas whose music, initially associated with a particular occasion, could reasonably be re-used in this way (the *Christmas Oratorio* from nos.213, 214 and 215 among other works; the *Easter Oratorio* by a reworking of parts of BWV249a; the *Ascension Oratorio* above all from BWV Anh.18). However, there is so much that is new and individual in the *Christmas Oratorio*, especially in the biblical choruses and the chorales, and in the *Ascension Oratorio*, that the works are in no sense subordinate to their originals. The pervasive use of texts from the Gospels, moreover, gives the works a special status, linking them to the Protestant *historia* and thus ultimately to the Passion.

Of the five Passions mentioned in the necrology two survive (*St Matthew* and *St John*), for one the text survives (*St Mark*) and the other two are lost. Judging from the source it seems probable that the anonymous *St Luke Passion* – which is certainly not by Bach – was included among his works in error because the score, dating from about 1730, was copied in his hand and contained additions by him. This means that only one Passion remains to be accounted for. Recent research has shown that various movements in the second version of the *St John Passion* (1725) were taken from a Passion composed for Weimar, most notably the chorus 'O Mensch bewein' and the three arias 'Himmel, reisse', 'Zerschmettert mich' and 'Ach windet euch nicht so'. Curiously enough, Hilgenfeldt (1850) mentioned a Passion by Bach dating from 1717, giving no indication of the source of his information, and Bach gave a guest recital at the Gotha court during the Passion period in 1717, making it conceivable that he put on a Passion performance while the post of Kapellmeister was vacant. Also, he performed Keiser's *St Mark Passion* in Weimar in about 1713, so his interest in the genre is established for the period. The missing fifth Passion must almost certainly, therefore, be

a lost Weimar work, but the traces are too few to allow any conclusions to be drawn about it.

The three known works represent the same type of oratorio Passion, in the tradition of the *historia*, in which the biblical text is retained as a whole (with 'parts' for soloists – Evangelist, Jesus, Pilate etc. – and the turba choruses for disciples, high priests etc.), and is interrupted by contemplative, so-called 'madrigal' pieces set to freely composed verse, as well as by chorales. A special feature of Bach's Passions is the unusual frequency of the chorales, which are set in simple yet extremely expressive four-part writing. The text of the *St John Passion* of 1724, Bach's first large-scale vocal work for Leipzig, is not a unified piece of work. The freely composed parts rely heavily on the famous Passion poem by B.H. Brockes (*Der für die Sünde der Welt gemarterte und sterbende Jesus*, 1712) and on texts by C.H. Postel (*c*1700) and Christian Weise (1675); besides this, the Evangelist's part contains interpolations from St Matthew's Gospel. Unlike any other of Bach's large-scale works, the *St John Passion* underwent substantial changes of every kind in the course of its various performances. For the second performance, in 1725, Bach produced a much altered version adapted conceptually to the cycle of chorale cantatas (see §13) by the incorporation of movements based on a cantus firmus. In a third version (probably of 1732) the interpolations from St Matthew were cut and a new aria and sinfonia added (both lost). Finally a fourth version of 1749 saw the work restored to something much closer to its original form; besides some changes to the text, for his last performance of a Passion in Leipzig Bach greatly enlarged the performing forces (by a part for bassono grosso among other things). It seems that Bach began a thorough-going revision of the work in 1739, but for some reason abandoned the process halfway through movement 10 and did not resume it; furthermore the alterations he made at that time were not adopted in the 1749 performance. For all the modifications made over the 25-year period, the setting of the biblical Passion text remained the work's constant centre, around which the madrigalian movements in particular were fitted in various ways like different settings for a gemstone. Bach skilfully exploited the network of internal textual correspondences which is unique to St John's Gospel, and convincingly translated it into an 'architectural' structure.

The history of the *St Matthew Passion*, with its double chorus, is less complicated, though not entirely straightforward. In this case the date of the first performance seems now to be established (the Thomaskirche, Good Friday 1727), but some details of that occasion remain unclear because of lacunae in the source material (version BWV244b). Furthermore, some ten movements from the *St Matthew Passion* were incorporated into the Cöthen funeral music of 1729 (BWV244a), and the consequences of that for the repeat of the Passion in the same year are not known. On the whole the *St Matthew Passion* is a considerably more unified piece than the *St John*, for which the primary reason is its use of Picander's text. Its greater textual and musical scale allows more space for the arias and 'madrigal' pieces in which the coupling of arioso with aria is an especially characteristic feature. Another special feature is the way the strings provide an accompanying halo in Jesus's recitatives. The pervading cyclical formation of the work (from the interrelating of the chorales, tonal organization and paired movements) is in some respects even more pronounced than in the *St John Passion*, while it lacks the earlier work's 'architectural' centre. After 1729 the *St Matthew Passion* had at least two more performances under Bach's direction. In 1736 he made some important changes, chief among them emphasizing the separation of the two choruses and instrumental ensembles by division of the continuo, exchanging the simple chorale at the end of part i for 'O Mensch bewein' and replacing the lute in 'Komm süsses Kreuz' with bass viol. The additional alterations of about 1742 were mainly a matter of meeting practical performing conditions.

In its main sections, that is in the 'madrigal' pieces, the *St Mark Passion* of 1731 was a parody work whose main sources are the *Trauer Ode* (Cantata no.198) and the Cöthen funeral music (BWV244*a*). While only the text survives, the musical design can in part be deduced from these models, although they scarcely permit it to be reconstructed satisfactorily. The Bach literature includes discussion of parody relationships which go further than this, but they seem to raise more questions than they answer. The most plausible suggestion, made by Smend (1940–48), is that some of the exceptionally large number of chorales in the *St Mark Passion* may have survived in the collections of Bach's four-part chorales.

In Bach's time Latin polyphonic music was still often used in ordinary Lutheran Sunday worship, particularly, in Leipzig, at important church feasts. Further, the concerted *Magnificat* continued to hold its place in Vespers. Bach had been interested in Latin polyphonic music at least since his Weimar period, as his copies of pieces by other composers demonstrate (Peranda, Durante, Pez, Wilderer, Bassani, Caldara, Lotti, Palestrina etc.; catalogue in Wolff, 1968). He also wrote insertions in this style for other composers' works, and made some arrangements (Sanctus BWV241; Credo intonation for a mass by Bassani; 'Suscepit Israel' for a *Magnificat* by Caldara). His earliest surviving work of this type is probably the Kyrie BWV233*a* on the cantus firmus 'Christe, du Lamm Gottes'. Then in his first year at Leipzig came the five-part *Magnificat*, first the E♭ version with four inserted Christmas pieces (BWV243*a*), revised in D major in 1733, without the Christmas pieces, for use on any major feast day (BWV243). Among the various Sanctus settings attributed to Bach, apart from BWV232III, probably only BWV237 and 238 (both 1723) are original compositions. The four short masses (BWV233–6), mostly parody works based on cantata movements, date from about 1738. In the careful selection of models and the subsequent reworking of the musical material, these works, together with the B minor Mass, amount to a valuable anthology of Bach's vocal writing in music of outstandingly high quality. The transposition of German cantata movements into mass settings did more than replace German words, contingent on the time and occasion of their writing, with the timelessness of the Latin (and Greek) texts; it also removed the limitations imposed on the cantatas by their place in the annual church cycle and gave them a more general validity. The longer-term outcome of this was seen soon after 1750, when specifically the Latin sacred music was hailed by connoisseurs like Marpurg, Kirnberger, Hiller and even the south German Prince-Abbot Gerbert as a particularly important sector of Bach's music.

Bach's masterpiece in this genre is of course the work known – though not conceived as a unity – as the B minor Mass. Its genesis stretched over more than two decades. Bach's aim seems originally to have been to bring together a collection of exemplary large-scale mass movements rather than to create a single, cyclical work on an unprecedented scale. In assembling the whole score in 1748–9, however, the composer undoubtedly had the intention of making it a comprehensive work of consistent quality. The oldest section is the Sanctus of 1724. The Kyrie and Gloria come from the 1733 *Missa* dedicated to the Dresden court, while the Credo or 'Symbolum Nicenum' was composed only during Bach's last years. In many respects these two main sections represent Bach's ideals not of Latin polyphonic music alone but of vocal music altogether: in their stylistic multiplicity (the contrast of deliberately archaic and modern styles; the experimentation with the widest variety of instrumental and vocal techniques); their abandonment of the da capo aria and the recitative; and in their formal perfection. The 1733 *Missa* (reminiscent of the *Magnificat* in its five-part writing) emerges as a completely integrated, unified whole, typified by the inner logic of the tonal organization (B minor–D–F♯ minor–D–A–D–G–B minor–D) and the disposition of the vocal and instrumental solos. The Credo is a particularly good example of Bach's many-layered and symmetrical layout (Table 1). The *Missa* and the Credo have a series of parody originals (including movements from Cantatas nos.29, 46, 171, 12 and 120); in the latter the 'Credo', 'Et incarnatus' and 'Confiteor' seem to be the only original compositions.

An earlier version of 'Credo in unum Deum' exists, dating from the early 1740s, while 'Et incarnatus' may be the last vocal composition that Bach completed. However, Bach's reworking of earlier material went much further than usual. In 'Agnus Dei', in particular, nearly half the movement was completely revised, using new thematic material. When the entire work was nearly finished Bach revised it once more, probably in 1749, adding 'Et incarnatus' (the words of which he had originally set as part of the aria 'Et in unum Dominum'). The music of the new 'Et incarnatus' is reminiscent of a movement in Pergolesi's *Stabat mater*, and in its combination of unorthodox polyphony and musically expressive gesture points the way forward to a new stylistic sensibility. It is all the more astonishing that Bach successfully followed it with the earliest music in the mass, the 'Crucifixus' (from the second movement of Cantata no.12) – though he did bring this up to date with a more *empfindsam* style of continuo and more subtle instrumentation of the upper parts.

It was obviously not by chance that Bach turned in his old age to the mass genre. With its centuries-old tradition, by comparison with such modern genres as the cantata and oratorio, the setting of the mass had a natural affinity to the historical and theoretical dimensions of Bach's musical thinking, which also bore fruit in the monothematic instrumental works of his last years.

15. MOTETS, CHORALES, SONGS. In Bach's time motets were sung as introits for services and on certain special occasions. The tradition established at Leipzig was to select introit motets from the *Florilegium Portense* (1603), a classical repertory from the 16th century compiled by Erhard Bodenschatz. For this reason, Bach wrote motets only for special occasions, probably only for burial

services, although in only one case, *Der Geist hilft* (for the funeral of the Thomasschule headmaster Ernesti in 1729), is there documentary evidence of this. Bach's motet texts, following the tradition, are based on biblical quotations and chorales; freely composed poetry is used in only one case, and even this is hymnbook poetry (*Komm, Jesu, komm*, Paul Thymich). On the occasions for which the motets were composed, Bach normally had more than the school choristers at his disposal; he was thus able to use between five- and eight-part writing, as he did in six pieces (BWV225–9 and Anh.159). In line with normal central German practice since the 17th century, it was a rule in the performance of motets at Leipzig, including those from *Florilegium Portense*, that a continuo part should be included – to be precise, organ, harpsichord (in Leipzig the so-called motet harpsichord), lute, with violone, cello, bassoon. In this way the bass of a vocal (choral or polychoral) movement was supported by a larger or smaller continuo depending on the circum-

TABLE 1

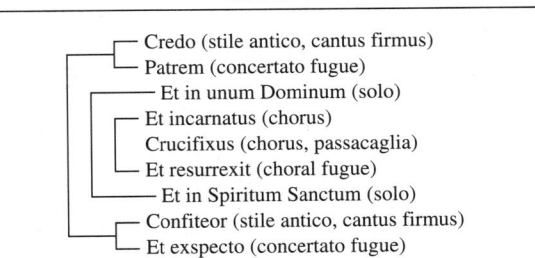

- Credo (stile antico, cantus firmus)
- Patrem (concertato fugue)
- Et in unum Dominum (solo)
- Et incarnatus (chorus)
- Crucifixus (chorus, passacaglia)
- Et resurrexit (choral fugue)
- Et in Spiritum Sanctum (solo)
- Confiteor (stile antico, cantus firmus)
- Et exspecto (concertato fugue)

stances, in the manner of a *basso seguente*. *Colla parte* accompaniment was required only occasionally. The performing parts that have survived for *Der Geist hilft*, with strings (first chorus) and reed instruments (second chorus) doubling the voices, must be connected with the exceptional nature of the occasion and cannot necessarily

6. Autograph MS of the Sinfonia (arranged from the Prelude of the Partita for violin BWV1006) from Bach's cantata 'Wir danken dir, Gott' BWV29, 1731 (D-Bsb Mus.ms.Bach P 166, f.1r)

be taken as applicable to the other motets; similar special cases, with partly obbligato instruments, are BWV118, *O Jesu Christ* (both versions) and *Der Gerechte kömmt um* (not in BWV: BC C 8).

Bach's use of double chorus and his exposition of forms of chorale treatment link the motets with the central German tradition in which he had grown up. That it was part of his direct family inheritance is illustrated by the fact, which can scarcely be coincidental, that motets are particularly well represented in the Alt-Bachisches Archiv. Bach's earliest motet, *Ich lasse dich nicht* BWV Anh.159, long attributed to Johann Christoph Bach of Eisenach, adheres extremely closely to Thuringian models. Composed by 1712 at the latest, the work's foundations in the tradition are typified by the highlighting of upper parts and the largely homophonic conception of the first section, and by the interweaving of a chorale tune in large note values in the second; by contrast, the harmonic intensity of the work (in F minor) and the unified, almost rondo-like, thematic construction of its first section are innovatory. Among later works, Bach's debt to the tradition is best illustrated by the closing section of *Fürchte dich nicht*, in its combination of cantus firmus ('Warum sollt ich mich denn grämen') and freely imitative writing, and the opening section of *Komm, Jesu, komm*, with its chordal writing for double chorus. As a whole, the style of BWV118 too is retrospective, with its archaic instrumentation and its homophonic choral writing.

By contrast, most movements in the motets have a markedly polyphonic vocal manner, dominated by instrumental style and showing unifying motivic work. Another characteristic is the clear formal articulation, with multi-movement works demonstrating different kinds of treatment. Thus *Jesu, meine Freude*, the longest work of this kind, in 11 movements, is the most strictly (that is, symmetrically) conceived: the opening and closing movements are identical, the second to fifth correspond to the seventh and eighth, and the central sixth movement is a fugue. *Der Geist hilft* begins with a concerto-like movement, followed by a double fugue and a simple chorale setting. The form of the instrumental concerto (fast–slow––fast) is used in *Singet dem Herrn*. Precise dating is possible only in the case of *Der Geist hilft* (24 October 1729). *Jesu meine Freude* seems to date from a pre-Leipzig period, although there is no tangible evidence for this; it is possible that an earlier motet, with a text from Romans viii, was expanded into a chorale motet by the addition of stanzas from the hymn *Jesu meine Freude*. The other motets appear to date from the Leipzig years. This is certain in the case of *O Jesu Christ* (c1737): its instrumentation was revised for a repeat performance in the 1740s, with strings, oboes, bassoons and horns; the original had only two *litui*, cornets and three trombones. The authenticity of *Lobet den Herrn* has been questioned, probably groundlessly, but the paucity of material that would permit comparisons weakens the arguments on either side. Bach's arrangement of Pergolesi's *Stabat mater* with the psalm text 'Tilge, Höchster, meine Sünden', dating from 1741–6, should be counted among the motets.

Bach's composition of chorales is most closely associated with his production of cantatas. Four-part chorale style, or *stylus simplex*, was normal for his closing movements, particularly in the Leipzig cantatas; it also often occurred at the ends of subsections in the Passions

and oratorios. Bach's chorale writing is characterized by the 'speaking' quality of the part-writing and the harmonies – meaning that they aim to be a direct interpretation of the text. In its pervasive counterpoint and its expressiveness, Bach's harmonic style stands out from that of his contemporaries, who preferred plain homophonic textures in their chorales. This simpler approach, found in the chorales of such as Graupner or Telemann, with movement mostly in minims, was well suited to congregational singing, but Bach took no account of that in his chorales, which are deliberately more artistic, rhythmically often more lively (written in crotchets) and frequently bolder in their harmonies. The first four-part chorale settings are in the Weimar cantatas (the last movement of no.12, performed on 22 April 1714, is among the earliest examples), and Bach's stylistic development in this type of composition reached a final stage 30 years later in the chorales of the *Christmas Oratorio*, with their elegantly mobile bass lines and their polyphonic refinement of the inner voices. His training as an organist probably contributed to the personal stamp of his style; organ settings such as BWV706 display similar stylistic traits. Chorales such as BWV371, conceived with orchestral forces in mind, act furthermore as reminders that chorales were Bach's favourite medium of instruction. C.P.E. Bach wrote in 1775: 'His pupils had to begin by learning four-part thoroughbass. After that he went on with them to chorales; first he used to write the bass himself, then they had to invent the alto and tenor for themselves … this way of leading up to chorales is indisputably the best way of learning composition, including harmony'.

The posthumously published collections (Birnstiel, 2 vols., 1765, 1769; Breitkopf, 4 vols., 1784–7) contain almost all the chorales known from Bach's vocal works, some under different titles. The Breitkopf edition, prepared by C.P.E. Bach and Kirnberger, contains 371 chorales, among them more than 100 not found in the extant vocal works. This provides an important pointer to the lost vocal music, and though extremely difficult to follow up it has borne some fruits, as in the reconstruction of the *St Mark Passion* or the Picander cycle. It is worth remarking that the number of excess chorales, that is those that cannot be assigned to extant works, more or less corresponds to the number thought to exist in the lost cantatas and Passions.

Under the generic heading of 'sacred songs' come the 69 melodies with figured bass in G.C. Schemelli's *Musicalisches Gesang-Buch* (1736). According to the foreword, Bach edited the figured bass for some of the melodies, while others were entirely new compositions by him. Three are demonstrably his (BWV452, 500 and 505); of the rest at least seven pieces for two voices and ten 'improved' continuo parts can be associated with him. He seems to have been only peripherally occupied with the composition of songs and strophic arias, for which he took texts from religious poetry of the 17th and 18th centuries: that, at least, is the inference to be drawn from the limited surviving repertory, for which the only source is the second *Clavierbüchlein* for Anna Magdalena Bach (1725) containing BWV511–14 and 516 – works which probably have a direct association with the Schemelli *Gesangbuch*. Comparison of BWV512 with 315, and of BWV452 with 299, draws attention to the conceptual association between the composition of chorales for two and for four voices. The collection of four-part chorales which Bach's pupil J.L. Dietel extracted from his teacher's works (Leipzig, *c*1735), like the Schemelli *Gesangbuch* (1736), indicates that Bach was working on chorales rather intensively and systematically at the time, perhaps with a view to a more compendious publication.

Only exceptionally did Bach compose secular songs. A quodlibet for four voices and continuo (BWV542), surviving only in fragmentary form, is unique among his vocal works. It was probably composed for a wedding in Erfurt, at the latest by mid-1708. With its admixture of various melodies and humorous words, the piece forms a link with the musical games played, so tradition relates, when the Bach family got together (see §1 above). Other rarities, from a later period when he was settled in the university town of Leipzig, are the song addressing a pipe of tobacco (BWV515) and the 'Murky' (BWVAnh.40).

16. ORGAN MUSIC.   The obituary written immediately after Bach's death and published in 1754 contains the following statement: 'For as long as there is nought to confute us other than the mere possibility of the existence of better organists and keyboard players, we cannot be reproached if we are bold enough to persist in the claim that our Bach was the most prodigious organist and keyboard player that there has ever been. It may be that this or that famous man has accomplished much in polyphony on these instruments but was he for that reason as expert – with hands and feet together – as Bach was? Whosoever had the pleasure of hearing him and others, being not otherwise disposed by prejudice, will agree that this doubt is not unfounded. And whosoever looks at Bach's pieces for the organ and the keyboard, which he himself, as is universally known, performed with the greatest perfection, will likewise have nothing to say in contradiction of the above statement.' The claim illustrates the well-nigh legendary reputation that Bach enjoyed in his lifetime. His fame had already spread beyond the confines of central Germany by 1717, when he challenged the French virtuoso Louis Marchand to a competition at the court of Dresden and won by default when the Frenchman took flight. 'It would be wrong to conclude from this defeat of Marchand in Dresden that he must have been a poor musician. Did not as great a one as Handel avoid every opportunity of confronting the late Bach ... or of getting involved with him?' (Marpurg).

Keyboard music as a whole occupies a crucial position in Bach's life in many respects, but this is even more true of the works for harpsichord than of those for organ. No other genre occupied Bach so consistently and intensively from the beginning of his career to the end. His life as a professional musician began with learning to play on a keyboard, above all in Ohrdruf in 1695–1700 under the tuition of his elder brother Johann Christoph, and his study of keyboard music by the best composers of the 17th century laid the most important foundations of his training as a composer. The compositions for harpsichord, in particular, provide the opportunity to assess Bach's development at each stage of his creative life.

Bach was bolder than any of his contemporaries: from the first he set no limits to his keyboard skills, and accepted no restrictions to his horizons – from the breadth of the foundations of his style to the comprehensive range of genres in which he composed. The stylistic basis was laid in his youth, and it was undoubtedly important that growing up in the central German environment of his time gave him the opportunity to learn about different stylistic tendencies side by side, without any bias towards one rather than another. As a result his models came from a highly diverse repertory. The north German school, including such masters as Buxtehude, Reincken, Bruhns, Lübeck and Böhm, were ranged alongside central German composers such as Pachelbel's circle and older pupils (J.H. Buttstedt, for example, or A.N. Vetter) and Witt, Krieger, Kuhnau and Zachow, as well as their southern German colleagues J.J. Froberger, J.C. Kerll and J.C.F. Fischer. Italians such as Frescobaldi and Battiferri confronted Frenchmen such as Lully, Marais, Grigny and Raison. Many of these names are to be found in the large manuscript collections (the so-called Andreas-Bach-Buch and Möllersche Handschrift) copied by the Ohrdruf Bach, Johann Christoph. They give a clear picture of the repertory that the younger brother grew up with, and which showed him – like the young Handel, learning his craft in a similar environment – 'the manifold ways of writing and composing of various races, together with each single composer's strengths and weaknesses'. No comparable sphere of influence served to challenge this broadly based group of musicians and exemplars later in Bach's life. There were, of course, individuals who had an effect on him, such as Vivaldi after 1710, or probably Couperin, or his exact contemporary Handel, but no group of musicians of a comparable range or variety.

Bach's dedication to every keyboard genre and form appears equally boundless. The range remains constant throughout his career, from the earliest to the last compositions. All the major types are represented: the freely improvisatory (prelude, toccata, fantasia), the imitative and strict (fugue, fantasia, ricercar, canzona, capriccio, invention), the combinatory (multi-part preludes, prelude and fugue) and multi-movement forms (sonata, suite or partita, overture or sinfonia, chaconne or passacaglia, pastorale, concerto and variations); and then there are the various types and forms of chorale arrangement.

Unlike the vocal music and the chamber and orchestral works, Bach's keyboard output covers his entire creative life. There are quite lengthy periods of heightened activity – organ music before 1717, harpsichord music after that date. As a whole, however, Bach seems to have cultivated the two genres alongside each other. It is thus the more surprising that, right from the beginning, consistently and in defiance of inherited 17th-century tradition, he abandoned the conventional community of repertory between organ and harpsichord, choosing to write specifically for the one or the other. The uncompromising use of obbligato pedals, in particular, is a distinguishing mark of Bach's organ style. Only exceptionally (for example in the chorale partitas and the small chorale arrangements from the third part of the *Clavier-Übung*) do the performing possibilities coincide so that organ and harpsichord become truly interchangeable.

Since most of Bach's keyboard works from the pre-Leipzig years survive in copies (generally made in the circle of Bach's pupils) rather than in autograph scores, it is not possible to establish a precise chronology. Even a relative one is possible only in general terms, with considerations of style and authenticity holding the balance. In the earliest works the influence of Bach's models is pronounced. Pachelbel had taught Johann Christoph Bach, and the master's influence extended to the younger brother, most visibly and prevalently in the earliest of his extant compositions. Besides the little organ chorales which survive individually (BWV749, 750 and 756), regarded by Spitta as Bach's first musical essays, the chorales in the Neumeister collection, which came to light only recently (BWV1090–1120, and BWV714, 719, 737, 742 and 756), are now taken to be among his earliest works. Although the Neumeister manuscript represents neither an integrated body of work nor a unified collection, in its dazzling variety it embodies some contradictory and simultaneously essential traits of Bach's early organ music: imperfect technique alongside daring innovation; reliance on models such as Pachelbel, Johann Michael and Johann Christoph Bach and masters from north, south and central Germany, together with a determination to surpass and dispense with such models; and an entirely unorthodox mixture of free composition and strict polyphony, unconventional harmony and pronounced virtuosity.

A subsequent stage in Bach's development is found in the chorale partitas BWV766–8, mostly wrought in the manner of Böhm (BWV768 was revised and expanded during Bach's Weimar period). The Canzona BWV588, the *Allabreve* BWV589 and the Pastorale BWV590 show south German and Italian characteristics, while the Fantasia in G BWV572 looks to the French style. With their sectional layout, the preludes in E and G minor, BWV566 and 535a, must have been written under Buxtehude's immediate influence.

The extraordinary harmonic boldness and the richness of fermata embellishment in the pieces BWV715, 722 and 732, intended to accompany chorales, imply that they belong to the Arnstadt period when Bach's treatment of chorales caused confusion among the congregation. The fugues after Legrenzi and Corelli, BWV574 and 579, should probably be placed among the early works. Admittedly, the scarcity of autographs, combined with the complicated situation surrounding the other sources, makes it difficult to establish a reliable chronology. It is scarcely possible even to draw definite conclusions about which of the early keyboard works belong within the period of Bach's youth, if that is set at about 1700–07.

The models recede in importance from the Mühlhausen period, at the latest, and Bach's individuality begins to pervade every note of his compositions. This applies particularly to the many extended organ chorale settings probably dating from between 1709 and 1712–13 and already so much in accordance with Bach's later ideals that he found this group of 18 chorales (BWV651–8) worthy of revising in and after about 1740. In his freely composed organ works (toccatas, preludes, fantasias and fugues) Bach tightened up the formal scheme, preparing the way for the two-movement prelude and fugue through an intermediate type in which the fugue was a long, self-contained complex but the prelude was not yet a unified section (such as the first movement of BWV532). Here is an early manifestation of one of the peculiarities of Bach's working methods, encountered later in the '48': fugues attain their final form almost instantaneously, preludes often go through several stages of development. Probably the most important work of these years is the Passacaglia in C minor BWV582.

In about 1713–14 a decisive stylistic change came about, stimulated by Vivaldi's concerto form. Bach's encounter with Vivaldi's music found immediate expression in the concertos after Vivaldi's opp.3 and 7 (BWV593

etc.). Features adapted from Vivaldi include the unifying use of motivic work, the motoric rhythmic character, the modulation schemes and the principle of solo–tutti contrast as means of formal articulation; the influence may be seen in the Toccatas in F and C BWV540 and 564. Apparently Bach experimented for a short while with a free, concerto-like organ form in three movements (fast–slow–fast: cf BWV545 + 529/2 and BWV541 + 528/3) but finally turned to the two-movement form, as in BWV534 and 536. Of comparable importance to the introduction of the concerto element is his tendency towards condensed motivic work, as in the *Orgel-Büchlein*. Bach's conception of this new type of miniature organ chorale, combining rhetorical and expressive musical language with refined counterpoint, probably dates back to a relatively early point, possibly the beginning of the Weimar period, but he cannot have started to collect them systematically in the autograph before 1713–14. Among the earliest entered in the manuscript are, among new compositions, BWV608, 627 and 630, and around 1715–16 Bach added BWV615, 623, 640 and 644 (to cite some typical examples). Some of the pieces, such as BWV601 and 639, are of earlier date. By the end of the Weimar period the *Orgel-Büchlein* was complete in all essentials, although a few isolated pieces were added later, such as BWV620 and 631 (c1730), the fragment O *Traurigkeit* and BWV613 (c1740). The final total of 45 pieces falls considerably short of the 164 originally projected, but Bach had already ceased to work consistently at this major undertaking as early as 1716. The reason for this is unknown; when he took it up again in Leipzig it was only sporadically and apparently in connection with teaching, or so a copy made about 1727–30 suggests.

Bach composed few organ pieces at Cöthen, but among them is undoubtedly the C major Fantasia BWV573 which he added to Anna Magdalena Bach's *Clavier-Büchlein* (1722). In Leipzig, in about 1727, he composed the trio sonatas, a new genre for the organ, which he wrote, according to Forkel, for his eldest son Wilhelm Friedemann. It was probably in conjunction with renewed activity as a recitalist – he is known to have performed in Dresden (1725, 1731 and 1736), Kassel (1732), Altenburg (1739) and Potsdam (1747) – that he returned to the prelude and fugue genre. Now, surely as a consequence of the '48', he always wrote them in two sections, with the preludes as important as the fugues. There was a final flourish of virtuosity (especially in the writing for obbligato pedal) in works such as BWV544 and 548 (both c1730), but always in the context of a clearcut structure (there is a da capo fugue in BWV548).

In 1739, as the third part of the *Clavier-Übung*, Bach published a comprehensive and varied group of organ works. Framed by a Prelude and Fugue in E♭ (BWV552), there are nine chorale arrangements for Mass and 12 for the catechism, followed by four duets. Bach's encyclopedic intentions can be seen in the form of the work – that of a collection of specimen organ pieces for large church instruments and smaller domestic ones (including the harpsichord), symbolized in his invariable coupling of a large piece with a small; they can equally be seen in the variety of his contrapuntal methods, whereby he constantly produced fresh kinds of cantus firmus treatment. At the very end of Bach's output for the organ are such disparate works as the C minor Fantasia and Fugue

BWV562 (1747–8), the 'Schübler' chorales (arrangements after solo movements from cantatas) and the canonic variations on *Vom Himmel hoch* BWV769. The variations, written for Mizler's society in 1747, survive in two original versions, printed and autograph, whose different sequence of movements shows Bach experimenting with symmetrical form and the placing of climaxes.

17. MUSIC FOR HARPSICHORD, LUTE ETC. Just as Bach learnt most about the craft of composition from keyboard music, so too did he use it for preference in teaching others. He was obviously already a sought-after teacher when still in Weimar, but the move to Leipzig brought a decisive expansion of his teaching activities. H.N. Gerber, who studied with him in the early Leipzig years, left an account of Bach's method of introducing the widest variety of composition by gradual stages, along with the technical premisses of their performance. According to Gerber he used to begin with the Inventions and the French and English suites, and conclude the course with the '48'. This canon of characteristic works from the decade 1715–25 constitutes, so to speak, the stylistic core of Bach's music for keyboard and for that reason served later as the yardstick by which to settle questions of authenticity. Nowadays, however, the yardstick's usefulness has become somewhat problematic, since it does not take fully into account either the stylistic breadth of Bach's early output or the unorthodox musical language of the late works.

One of the essential elements of Bach's art as a keyboard composer is the attention he gave, from the first, to the idiomatic qualities of the individual instruments, respecting not only the differences between organ and harpsichord but also those within the family of string keyboard instruments, of which he used at least four types: harpsichord, clavichord, lute-harpsichord and fortepiano. He is specific about the main kinds of harpsichord in the *Clavier-Übung* (the first part is for one-manual harpsichord, the second and fourth for a two-manual instrument). One of the earliest manuscript sources refers to the suitability of the E minor suite BWV996 for the lute-harpsichord ('aufs Lauten Werk'). Bach took an active interest in J.G. Silbermann's experiments in developing the fortepiano during the 1730s and 40s. There is reliable testimony that he improvised on several new Silbermann fortepianos of different types in the presence of Frederick the Great in Potsdam in 1747, which makes it possible to regard the three-part ricercar of the *Musical Offering* as conceived primarily for this new kind of keyboard instrument.

There is an obvious association between Bach's renown as a keyboard virtuoso, together with his work as a teacher, and the fact that his keyboard music is among the most accessible of his entire output, and also that it was the most widely available. Its dissemination shows a marked rising curve during the 18th century, internationally as well as within Germany. Bach's harpsichord works were available in Italy, France, Austria and England by 1750, and in view of this it is not surprising that the young Beethoven was schooled in the '48'. The growing recognition of the significance of this part of his output was reflected in the first complete edition of the works for harpsichord (begun in Leipzig in 1800 by Hoffmeister & Kühnel and continued by C.F. Peters) in which Forkel, among others, was involved.

Bach's early harpsichord compositions are in a similar situation to the early organ works as regards dating and evaluation. None of the very earliest can be dated precisely. The Capriccio BWV992 has been assigned to 1704; there are no biographical data to support this (it is extremely doubtful that it was written for Bach's brother Johann Jakob), but it certainly belongs to the period immediately after 1700. Before 1712–13 there were countless individual pieces like toccatas, preludes and fugues (these last mainly using a 'repercussive' thematic technique like the early organ fugues); variation form is represented by the *Aria variata* BWV989. In the toccatas (BWV910 etc.) Italian, north German and French influences conjoin in equal importance (BWV912 is an interesting counterpart to the organ work BWV532); Bach's penchant for the French style is evident in his abundant use of the *style brisé*. After 1712 the particular influence of concertos by Vivaldi, Marcello and others can be seen in Bach's numerous concerto arrangements (BWV972 etc.).

To the last years in Weimar and the early years in Cöthen belong works such as the so-called English Suites and the Chromatic Fantasia and Fugue BWV903, and also the *Clavier-Büchlein* for Wilhelm Friedemann of 1720, which is predominantly didactic in layout. It is however less important for its instruction in playing technique (the *Applicatio* BWV994 gives fingering and tables of ornaments after D'Anglebert) than as a book of instruction in composition. For Bach himself, the two could not be dissociated: the *Clavier-Büchlein* contains the beginnings of the '48' as well as early versions of the Inventions and Sinfonias, under such titles as 'preambulum' and 'fantasia'. To some extent the 1722 *Clavierbüchlein* for Anna Magdalena is a companion work, though differently laid out.

Then followed, also in 1722, *Das wohltemperirte Clavier* (book 1 of the '48'), with its 24 preludes and fugues in all the major and minor keys, surpassing, in logic, in format and in musical quality, all earlier endeavours of the same kind by other masters, such as J.C.F. Fischer's *Ariadne musica*. The work shows a perfectly balanced contrast between free and strict styles, each represented by several different types of prelude and fugue. Bach's writing in book 1 of the '48' in the most varied fugues – from two- to five-part, in a wide range of styles – represents the culmination of a 20-year process of maturation and stands unparalleled in the history of music. The final version of the two- and three-part Inventions and Sinfonias, also arranged by key and representing a different method of composition whose object (according to Bach's foreword) was 'to teach clear playing in two and three obbligato parts, good inventions [i.e. compositional ideas] and a cantabile manner of playing', dates from 1723.

The first traces of the subsequent great works of the Leipzig period are to be found in the 1725 *Clavierbüchlein* for Anna Magdalena, which in fact anticipates the so-called French Suites BWV812–17 and the Partitas BWV825–30. The Partitas in particular (appearing in print singly from 1726) represent a further culmination in Bach's keyboard output; whereas the '48' shows the prelude and fugue type developed to its most consummate maturity, these present similarly matured specimens of the most popular harpsichord genre of the time, the partita, comprising a suite of dance movements and 'galanteries'. These – the burlesca, capriccio and the like – do not appear in the English or French Suites; as in the English Suites, each partita begins with a large-scale movement, each differently titled and each in a different style. Later, with the collected publication of all six in 1731, Bach inaugurated his series of published works under the general title *Clavier-Übung* (the title was borrowed from a publication by Kuhnau, his predecessor in office). In 1735 appeared the second part, whose contents were intended to be representative of the most prominent and fashionable styles: the Concerto in the Italian Style BWV971 embodies the ultimate stage in the process of transcribing instrumental concertos for keyboard, and stands in contrast to an Overture in the French Manner BWV831 which, more markedly than the partitas, represents what was specifically French in harmony, rhythm, ornamentation and melodic invention. 1741–2 eventually saw the end of the *Clavier-Übung* series with the aria and 30 variations known as the Goldberg Variations. Apparently Bach had not cultivated the variation form since his youth, so that the contrast between the Goldberg Variations and the early works (chorale partitas and the *Aria variata*) is the more marked. This work outshines all others as far as performing technique is concerned (Domenico Scarlatti's influence is unmistakable in places). The large-scale cyclical layout (based on a sequence of 10 x 3 movements, incorporating a series of nine canons, one at every third variation, arranged in order of ascending intervals to move towards a climax, with a final quodlibet) is without precedent. The basis of the composition is a ground bass of 32 bars, developed from the Ruggiero and related bass patterns, first presented in the aria and then subjected to free and canonic elaboration in a wide variety of ways. In their monothematic and emphatically contrapuntal conception, the Goldberg Variations set the scene for Bach's last keyboard works – the *Musical Offering* and *Art of Fugue*.

Besides the harpsichord works published in the 1730s, the only other major work is the second part of *Das wohltemperirte Clavier* (not so titled – the complete autograph does not survive). This companion-piece is less unified than book 1 and was partly assembled from existing preludes and fugues, some of them transposed. The freshly composed pieces probably date chiefly from the late 1730s; the work was complete by 1744 at the latest. Apart from this one major undertaking, Bach appears to have composed very few keyboard works at this period: perhaps the Fantasia 'sur un rondeau' BWV918, certainly the Fantasia in C minor with fragmentary fugue BWV906.

The dates of composition of the seven surviving works for lute – apparently almost his total output for the instrument – cover at least 30 years. The earliest work is the Suite in E minor BWV996, which dates from the Weimar period; it already shows a surprisingly balanced construction. The Prelude in C minor BWV999 shows an affinity with the '48', and may thus belong to the Cöthen or early Leipzig period. All the other lute works were composed in Leipzig, starting with the Fugue in G minor BWV1000, an expanded polyphonic development from the violin fugue (in BWV1001), which (like BWV997) is in a tablature copied by Bach's friend, the Leipzig lawyer and lutenist Christian Weyrauch. The Suite in G minor BWV995 (after 1011, for cello) dates from the period 1727–31 and is dedicated in Bach's autograph to an unidentifiable 'Monsieur Schouster'. The Suite in E

(BWV1006a, after 1006 for violin) also survives in autograph form and is a much less demanding arrangement of its model as compared with BWV1000 and 995. It dates from the second half of the 1730s. Bach must have composed the Suite in C minor BWV997 before 1741; this is an original lute composition and is laid out in a similar virtuoso fashion to the Prelude, Fugue and Allegro in E♭ BWV998 which can be ascribed to the early 1740s. The late works may have been written for the Dresden lutenists S.L. Weiss and Johann Kropffgans, and in any case were probably played by them. There is evidence that Weiss and Kropffgans performed at Bach's house at least once, in 1739. Bach's arrangement for violin and harpsichord of Weiss's lute suite in A major (BWV1025) may have been made in connection with this occasion. His contributions to the repertory of the lute, long past its heyday but enjoying a final flowering in the German-speaking countries, represent, along with the works of Weiss, the culmination of the instrument's 18th-century repertory. They require an instrument with 10 to 14 strings, but in Bach's day were at least occasionally played on the lute-harpsichord, an instrument in whose construction Bach had assisted. The indistinct line between lute and harpsichord music is illustrated by the autograph of BWV998, marked 'pour La Luth ò Cembal'.

18. ORCHESTRAL MUSIC. Many of Bach's orchestral compositions must be presumed lost. The surviving repertory can in any case give only an incomplete idea of his output for larger instrumental ensembles, for he must have written many further works during his years at Cöthen and while he was working with the collegium musicum in Leipzig. Traces of lost concerto movements may be found in numerous cantatas, such as no.42 (first movement), and other large-scale vocal works, such as the *Easter Oratorio* (first two movements); and various of the surviving harpsichord concertos, in particular, invite inferences about lost originals.

In the score bearing the dedication to Margrave Christian Ludwig of Brandenburg, the so-called Brandenburg Concertos are dated 24 March 1721. This is merely a *terminus ante quem*, for the concertos themselves must have been written over a considerable period before being assembled in 1721 as a collection of 'Concerts avec plusieurs instruments' (not as a single work in several parts). It cannot be proved that Bach composed instrumental music in his capacity as Konzertmeister in Weimar; but his position there and his preoccupation with the Italian concerto style during those years make it seem probable that he did. Of the Brandenburg Concertos, no.6 in particular points to the Weimar period, partly because of its indebtedness to the Italian type of concerto (above all in the middle movement) and also because of its unusual instrumentation (the particular combination of low strings is otherwise found only in Weimar cantatas). Other concertos (for instance the conjectural early version of no.1) may also belong to the Weimar period, but it is not possible to draw any firmer conclusion about a Weimar orchestral repertory.

The special significance of the Brandenburg Concertos resides in the fact that, like Vivaldi's, they abandon the standard type of concerto grosso and use a variety of solo combinations. The originality of Bach's ideas extends far beyond Vivaldi's, as do the density of the compositional texture and the level of professional virtuosity. The devising of concise head-motifs, particularly in the first movements, shows a strong Italian influence. Most of Bach's instrumentations are unprecedented. They feature all kinds of combinations, from homogeneous string sound (nos.3 and 6) to the heterogeneous mixing of brass, woodwind, string and keyboard instruments. Just as unusual is Bach's conflation of the group concerto with the solo concerto in nos.2 and 5. No.5 probably represents the latest stage in composition of the set: it was written for the inauguration of the harpsichord he brought back from Berlin early in 1719 (an earlier version survives from about this date). At the same time it marks the beginnings of the keyboard concerto as a form.

For a long time Bach scholars assigned most of his chamber and ensemble music to the Cöthen years. Recent studies based on original sources and style criticism have led to a thorough revision of the chronology affecting this part of his output. It now seems that only the smaller part of the instrumental ensemble music (or at least of what survives of it) belongs to the Cöthen period, while the greater part was composed at Leipzig, and principally for the collegium musicum which Bach was associated with from 1723 and which he directed from 1729 to the early 1740s. Thus the four Orchestral Suites, with their leaning towards French style, were written in Leipzig: no.1 perhaps as early as 1725, nos.3 and 4 in about 1725 and after 1730 respectively and no.2 about 1739. The B minor Suite (no.2), with its hybrid mixture of concerto elements and suite form and the extraordinary virtuosity of its flute writing, is probably Bach's very last orchestral work. The only solo concertos to survive in their original form from this time are the violin concertos in A minor and in E and the two-violin concerto in D minor, which again obviously relate to the collegium musicum. Pointers to lost works that may be supposed to have been composed in Cöthen can be obtained from Leipzig pieces showing clear signs of reworking, above all cantata sinfonias with obbligato organ and the harpsichord concertos. Among the putative originals discernible in later recensions are concertos for oboe d'amore (after BWV1053 and 1055), for violin (after BWV1052 and 1060) and for three violins (after BWV1064). The intended instrumentation of the original cannot always be conclusively determined from the later version, and allowance must also be made for substantial differences between the two versions, so that it is extremely rarely the case that reconstruction of a supposed but lost original is really possible. Bach never proceeded in a mechanical way; rather, he strove to give the arrangement an identity of its own by subjecting the model to further development and exhausting its potential. This often involved the addition of fresh contrapuntal parts, the alteration of detail and structural modification. Of special interest are Bach's adaptations of instrumental works into vocal ones, such as the derivation of the first chorus of Cantata no.110 from BWV1069; also of note is the wresting of the outer movements of an ensemble concerto (BWV1044) out of the Prelude and Fugue in A minor for harpsichord (BWV894).

The most noteworthy of the later concertos composed in the 1730s, with substantial changes to the originals on which they draw, are the Triple Concerto in A minor BWV1044 (sharing several features with Brandenburg Concerto no.5), the seven harpsichord concertos BWV1052–8 and the concertos for two or more harpsichords BWV1060–65, all but one of which were reworkings of earlier works by Bach himself (the exception is BWV1064, an arrangement of Vivaldi's Concerto in B minor for four violins, op.3 no.10). In fact, Bach's alterations and restructurings are sufficiently important – especially the deployment of the left hand of the harpsichord part and the invention of idiomatic harpsichord figuration – for works of this rank to be considered compositions in their own right. They owe their special historical importance to their occurrence at the beginning of the history of the keyboard concerto, a form which was to be taken up above all by Bach's sons so that in Germany, until about 1750, it remained the exclusive preserve of the Bach family. A stimulus for the composition of the harpsichord concertos may have been the new instrument introduced on 17 June 1733 ('a new harpsichord, the like of which no-one here has ever yet heard'), according to the announcement advertising the collegium musicum concert.

19. CHAMBER MUSIC. As with the orchestral music, a great many chamber compositions are thought to be lost. Once again the greatest losses affect the Cöthen period, but the Weimar years also suffer. When the summary worklist in the obituary mentions 'a quantity of other instrumental things, of every kind and for every kind of instrument', it probably refers first and foremost to works for various chamber ensembles.

The unusual flexibility with which Bach manipulated the conventional genres of sonata and suite is comparable to his orchestral output, as regards formal and compositional aspects as much as textures. Particularly important is his emancipation of the harpsichord from its role as continuo instrument and its deployment as a true partner in the sonatas for harpsichord with violin (BWV1014–19), flute (1030–33) and viola da gamba (1027–9). The cycle of six harpsichord and violin sonatas (c1725–6) were the first in a series of works with obbligato keyboard and paved the way for a new musical genre. The traditional trio sonata with continuo still cast its shadow (for example, in the opening movements of BWV1015 and 1019), but yielded by stages to a more integrated three-part style (for example, the opening movements of BWV1014 and 1018). The only genuine trio sonatas to survive, apart from the one in the *Musical Offering*, are BWV1038 and 1039, dating from the 1730s. Bach's arrangement of the gamba sonata BWV1027, after BWV1039 for two flutes and continuo is an illustration of the development of the new type of trio writing from the trio sonata. A similar procedure stood behind his earlier development of the organ sonata. Most movements of the organ sonatas are based on instrumental trios, as the arrangement of the first movement of BWV528 from a trio sonata movement for oboe d'amore, viola da gamba and continuo in Cantata no.76 illustrates. This same movement preserves a trace of the many lost trio sonatas of the Cöthen years. Yet the trio sonatas of the Leipzig period, too, may represent only a small fraction of their original numbers, if the way the genre lingers on in the *Musical Offering* is any guide.

The list of surviving duo sonatas with continuo is also relatively short, and again dominated by works of the Leipzig period: the violin sonatas BWV1021 and 1023 and the flute sonatas BWV1034–5. The Fugue in G minor for violin and continuo BWV1026, from before 1712, is not only Bach's earliest surviving piece of ensemble music, it is also the only chamber-music piece of the pre-Cöthen years to have survived as an independent entity. The only other sources we have for an idea of what kind of chamber music Bach wrote in his early years are the instrumental sonatas and sinfonias of the Weimar cantatas.

Bach's creative powers in the Cöthen years appear in a special light in the sonatas and partitas for solo violin, dating from 1720, and the suites for solo cello, which are probably earlier. The sonata for solo flute (BWV1013) is not likely to have been composed in Cöthen, for the playing technique is much more advanced than, for example, the writing for flute in Brandenburg Concerto no.5. Yet all the works *senza basso* not only demonstrate Bach's intimate knowledge of the typical idioms and performing techniques of each instrument, but also show his ability, even without an accompanying bass part, to bring into effective play dense counterpoint and refined harmony coupled with distinctive rhythms. The special importance of Bach's chamber music was recognized at a very early date. J.F. Reichardt wrote in 1805, reviewing the first edition of the solo violin music, that the pieces represent 'perhaps the greatest example in any art of the freedom and certainty with which a great master can move even when he is in chains'.

20. CANONS, 'MUSICAL OFFERING', 'ART OF FUGUE'. Bach's preoccupation with the canon as the strictest form of counterpoint can be traced back to the Weimar period. In his organ chorales and particularly in the *Orgel-Büchlein* the canonic principle plays a major role. Canonic elements are present also in several of the early vocal works. Here however it is a matter of canonic technique cropping up in a context of complex contrapuntal construction; as a genre in its own right, the canon, in Bach's day, would appear almost exclusively as a theoretical example in composition teaching. It was in this sense that it was often favoured – generally in the form of a circular canon – by musicians for entries in students' albums: such entries were normally notated in enigmatic fashion, setting the would-be solver an intellectual exercise. Bach wrote such canons in albums more than once; for the most part they are probably lost. Except for BWV1076–7, all the surviving individual canons (1072–5, 1078, 1086) were probably dedicatory works of this kind; 1077 was re-used for this purpose. What is probably the earliest of them is dated 2 August 1713 (BWV1073, dedicatee uncertain); the latest is dated 1 March 1749 (BWV1078; dedicatee Benjamin Faber).

A new kind of theoretical canon came into being in connection with the Goldberg Variations, in which the canonic principle played a special part. In his personal copy of the Goldberg Variations Bach wrote in 1747–8 a series of 14 perpetual canons on the first eight bass notes of the aria ground (BWV1087), exploring the most varied canonic possibilities of the subject, subsequently arranging the individual perpetual canons in a progressive order, organized according to their increasing contrapuntal complexity. The types included range from simple, double and triple canons, retrograde canons and stretto canons to a quadruple proportion canon by augmentation and diminution. Nos.11 and 13 of this series are identical with BWV1077 and 1076 (depicted on Haussmann's Bach portrait of 1746).

Closely related to these (and likewise probably dating from the later 1740s) are the *Vom Himmel hoch* variations, where Bach first used a strictly canonic scheme for a monothematic work in several movements of progressive difficulty. The *Musical Offering* (1747) is also plainly influenced by this mode of musical thinking. Here, for a theme incomparably more complex than that of BWV1087, he devised ten canons of differing structural types, notated as puzzle canons in the original printed edition of 1747. The series of canons on the 'royal theme' includes a canonic fugue, providing a bridge between the canons, which are primarily theoretical in conception though also intended for performance, and the two keyboard fugues or ricercares in three and six parts. A further constituent part of the *Musical Offering* is a trio sonata for flute, violin and continuo, also based on the royal theme. In its second slow movement Bach introduced echoes of the fashionable style practised at the Prussian court. The *Musical Offering*, in effect a compendium in three sections, shows Bach elaborating on the theme supplied to him by Frederick the Great in every imaginable way for an ensemble of up to three instruments.

The *Art of Fugue* constitutes the final contribution to this group of monothematically conceived works intended as representative examples of a specific principle. As a didactic keyboard work, the *Art of Fugue* in some ways forms a counterpart to the two books of the '48', with the difference that here it is exclusively the fugue that is in question, and, what is more, the fugues are developed from a single theme. Bach's work on the *Art of Fugue* was accomplished in two stages – from about 1740 to about 1745, and then (in connection with preparing the work for publication) in about 1748–50. The extant autograph score represents the conclusion of the first stage, in which the conception of the work already appears clearly: beginning with simple fugues (Bach avoided this term, speaking of 'contrapunctus'), progressing through 'counter-fugues', double fugues and triple fugues, with interpolated canons, and culminating in a mirror fugue. For the printed version the number of movements was not only increased by four (two canons, a fourth simple fugue and most notably a closing quadruple fugue) but their order was rearranged so as to expound more logically the 'chapter of instruction on fugues'. When Bach died the work may have been more 'complete' than it is in the form in which it has survived. In particular the quadruple fugue had surely been completed in all essentials, since the composition of its combinatorial section must necessarily be an early stage in the composition of a quadruple fugue. Only the three opening sections of the exposition, however, are extant, and these – further abbreviated by the editors, give the *Art of Fugue* the appearance of being a mighty torso.

The *Musical Offering* and the *Art of Fugue* mark both the end and the culmination of Bach's activity as a keyboard composer in the broadest sense. While the two ricercars on the 'royal theme' of the *Musical Offering* represent different fugal styles (forward- and backward-looking) and different textures (three- and six-part polyphony), the *Art of Fugue* explores a notably more intensive monothematic conception. As a didactic keyboard composition in some sense it counterbalances the two parts of the '48', yet with the difference that it concerns itself with fugue alone, in a series of compositions developed out of a single 'principal composition' (theme) – and does so using a technique in which forward- and backward-looking styles operate alongside each other, synoptically as it were. It was probably unintentional, and yet it is hardly by chance, that the initial premiss and the goal of Bach's keyboard art and his musical thinking come together in the *Art of Fugue*.

21. METHODS OF COMPOSITION. Bach's methods of composition can be outlined only roughly: the sources, musical and literary, present no more than a fragmentary picture. 'Methods' here refers to Bach's general procedures of composition, as far as these can be described objectively (without venturing into conjecture about creative psychology) and can be related to certain essential impulses and particularly characteristic approaches.

Bach's vast knowledge of the musical repertory was a decisive factor behind his art. He had an intimate knowledge of the types and styles of composition of his time and in particular of the work of his most important contemporaries; moreover, he had a sound idea of the music of the past, extending back as far as Frescobaldi and Palestrina. The study of works by other masters went hand in hand with experimentation in his own. It is thus characteristic that his acquaintance with the works of Buxtehude and Böhm, with Vivaldi's concertos, with the Passions of Keiser and Handel and with the masses of Lotti and Palestrina should have left an immediate imprint on his compositions in the same genres. It was less a matter of imitation of a model than of an awareness of the possibilities, an expansion of his own manner of writing and a stimulation of his musical ideas. This is confirmed in a contemporary report by T.L. Pitschel on his manner of improvisation, according to which, before beginning his own fantasia, Bach as a rule played from music a work by another master (or perhaps one of his own) which would ignite his imagination. Further, C.P.E. Bach wrote that, in accompanying a trio, his father liked to extemporize a fourth part. This tendency to take compositions by others as a starting-point is paralleled in his late adaptations: in his arrangement of Pergolesi's *Stabat mater* an obbligato viola part is added, replacing the one following the continuo in the original; and his version of the 'Suscepit Israel' from Caldara's *Magnificat* in C expands it from a five-part into a seven-part piece. An important aspect of Bach's procedure of composition is its systematic and encyclopedic nature. He habitually wrote works of one particular type within a relatively limited period: for example the *Orgel-Büchlein*, the '48', the solo violin sonatas and partitas, the canons, the chorale cantatas etc. He was concerned to try out, to develop and to exhaust specific principles of composition. There are practically no completely isolated compositions. Relationships, correspondences and connections with other works can constantly be found. This approach to the procedure of composition is at once deep and yet of great natural simplicity; and it never results in mere repetition. Certainly there is repetition, of a kind, in the case of parodies or transcriptions of existing works. Yet even here it is inappropriate to speak of repetition, since in the process of parodying and transcribing, Bach always modified so that the end-product represents a fresh stage in the development of the original composition.

C.P.E. Bach related that his father did not actually compose at the keyboard – apart from some keyboard works whose material originated in improvisations – but that he often tried out his music on the keyboard afterwards. This procedure may be seen in the few instrumental works of which Bach's autograph draft survives, for example the early versions of the Inventions in the *Clavier-Büchlein* for Wilhelm Friedemann, where

an abundance of inserted corrections are to be found. In the vocal music, where a wealth of source material is available, the main stages of composition can often be reconstructed. In thematically and motivically self-contained movements, like arias and choruses, Bach normally began with the development and formulation of a motif, a phrase or a theme, which would be guided by the prosody of the text; he then added the contrapuntal voices, and continued in the same way, sometimes using 'continuation sketches' to plan the music's progress in advance (see the critical edition of the sketches, Marshall, 1972). In choral fugues he usually began by outlining the thematic entries, and wrote in the accompanying parts afterwards.

The decisive step was the embarkation on the writing of a movement, for progress was in its essentials determined by established models (harmonic-tonal groundplan, modulation patterns, aria schemes) and governed by the principle of unified continuation ('style d'une teneur' and 'Affekteinheitlichkeit' – ensured by a unified motivic organization and interchange, permutation and transposition of component sections). The invention of the central idea was for Bach the critical moment in the process of composition, as the title-page of the Inventions specifies: 'gute inventiones zu bekommen' ('how to achieve good inventions'); and this is borne out by C.P.E. Bach's report that his first requirement of his composition pupils was the invention of ideas. With this the die was cast, down to a work's emotional content. Outlines and sketches relating to this operation can sometimes be found in the original manuscripts; typically, however, Bach hardly required more than one or two attempts before arriving at the definitive form of his principal idea. The further elaboration of the idea – the *dispositio*, *elaboratio* and *decoratio* – required mastery of his craft rather than inspiration.

In composing multi-movement vocal works Bach, understandably, began as a rule with the self-contained movements and only afterwards worked at the recitatives and chorales. In the recitatives he normally first wrote out the text and then added the melody and bass, section by section. In the chorales the bass was added to the melody and the middle parts were inserted later. Then all the movements were revised in detail, and sometimes corrections were made. The appearance of Bach's working drafts is thus unusually clear and neat as a whole, although it is mainly in his fair copies that the particular quality of his handwriting, a quality comparable to that of his music, is expressed. The physical state of the fair copy had to reflect the degree of artistic perfection to which the composer aspired, and the pains taken to achieve neatness and clarity in the copy are not evidence of pedantry. Rather, Bach was aware of the dichotomy between the perfection of the musical idea and that of its representation in performance. For this reason and no other he made the following statement in 1738, through the mouth of his spokesman J.A. Birnbaum: 'One does not judge a composition first and foremost by the impression of its performance. Yet if such judgment, which can be deceptive, is not to be taken into consideration, then I see no other way of forming an opinion about it except by looking at the work as it is set down in notation.'

Ultimately, for Bach, the process of composition was an unending one. Dynamic markings and indications of articulation would be inserted as he looked through the parts; he would revise and improve a work when he was copying it out, and when giving further performances would make fresh alterations and improvements. He also inserted corrections in works already in print. Throughout his life Bach was his own severest critic. Even in works which went through two or three different versions, like the chorale prelude *An Wasserflüssen Babylon* BWV653, the 'final' version does not represent a definitive one but merely a further stage in the search for perfection – the central and ultimate concern of Bach's method of composition.

WORKS

Bach did not always define instruments unambiguously; 'corno' could mean the normal horn of his time, the need for a brass player but not necessarily a trumpeter, or possibly the most suitable brass instrument (horn, cornett, slide-trumpet [tromba da tirarsi] etc.); parts for 'three oboes' at Leipzig may indicate any combination of oboes, oboes d'amore, tailles (tenor oboes in F, with no solo material) or oboes da caccia (a specific local tenor type, designed for obbligato work); four trombones indicate SATB and three ATB (usually below a cornett)

Dates of later copies or performances are given only if modifications are involved

Editions: *J.S. Bach: Werke*, ed. Bach-Gesellschaft. i–xlvii (Leipzig, 1851–99/R) [BG]

J.S. Bach: Neue Ausgabe sämtlicher Werke (Neue Bach-Ausgabe), ed. Johann-Sebastian-Bach-Institut, Göttingen, and Bach-Archiv, Leipzig, ser. I–VIII (Kassel and Basle, 1954–) [vols. in square brackets are in preparation] [NBA; CC = Critical Commentary]

Catalogues: W. Schmieder: *Thematisch-systematisches Verzeichnis der musikalischen Werke Johann Sebastian Bachs: Bach-Werke-Verzeichnis* (Leipzig, 1950, enlarged 2/1990, rev. and abridged 1998 by A. Dürr, Y. Kobayashi and K. Beisswenger as *Bach-Werke-Verzeichnis*) [BWV; A = Anhang]

H.-J. Schulze and C. Wolff: *Bach Compendium: analytisch-bibliographisches Repertorium der Werke Johann Sebastian Bachs* (Leipzig and Frankfurt, 1985–) [BC]

† – *variant versions exist; see* BWV *and* BC

CHURCH CANTATAS

Advent I = 1st Sunday in Advent; Trinity/Easter I = 1st Sunday after Trinity/Easter, etc.; most texts are compilations including at least one chorale; only single text sources given; where the text is entirely or mainly based on that of a chorale, its author's name is given in parentheses

BWV	BC	Title (text/librettist)	Occasion; 1st perf.	Scoring	BG	NBA
1	A 173	Wie schön leuchtet der Morgenstern, chorale (P. Nicolai)	Annunciation; 25 March 1725	S, T, B, 4vv, 2 hn, 2 ob da caccia, str, bc	i, 1	I/xxviii.2, 3
2	A 98	Ach Gott, vom Himmel sieh darein, chorale (M. Luther)	Trinity II; 18 June 1724	A, T, B, 4vv, 4 trbn, 2 ob, str, bc	i, 55	I/xvi, 83
3	A 33	Ach Gott, wie manches Herzeleid, chorale (M. Möller)	Epiphany II; 14 Jan 1725	S, A, T, B, 4vv, hn, trbn, 2 ob d'amore, str, bc	i, 75	I/v, 191
†4	A 54	Christ lag in Todes Banden, chorale (Luther)	Easter; probably by 1708	S, A, T, B, 4vv, cornett, str, bc [3 trbn added 1725]	i, 97	I/ix, 1
5	A 145	Wo soll ich fliehen hin, chorale (J. Heermann)	Trinity XIX; 15 Oct 1724	S, A, T, B, 4vv, tpt da tirarsi, 2 ob, str, bc	i, 127	I/xxiv, 135
6	A 57	Bleib bei uns, denn es will Abend werden	Easter Monday; 2 April 1725	S, A, T, B, 4vv, 2 ob, ob da caccia, vc piccolo, str, bc	i, 153	I/x, 45
7	A 177	Christ unser Herr zum Jordan kam, chorale (Luther)	St John; 24 June 1724	A, T, B, 4vv, 2 ob d'amore, str, bc	i, 179	I/xxix, 27
†8	A 137	Liebster Gott, wenn werd ich sterben?, chorale (C. Neumann)	Trinity XVI; 24 Sept 1724	S, A, T, B, 4vv, hn, fl, 2 ob d'amore, str, bc	i, 213	I/xxiii, 107, 165
9	A 107	Es ist das Heil uns kommen her, chorale (P. Speratus)	Trinity VI; c1732–5	S, A, T, B, 4vv, fl, ob d'amore, str, bc	i, 245	I/xvii/2, 93
10	A 175	Meine Seel erhebt den Herren (*Luke* i.46–55)	Visitation; 2 July 1724	S, A, T, B, 4vv, tpt, 2 ob, str, bc	i, 277	I/xxviii.2, 10
12	A 68	Weinen, Klagen, Sorgen, Zagen (? S. Franck)	Easter III; 22 April 1714	A, T, B, 4vv, tpt, ob, str, bc	ii, 61	I/xi/2, 1
13	A 34	Meine Seufzer, meine Tränen (G.C. Lehms)	Epiphany II; 20 Jan 1726	S, A, T, B, 4vv, 2 rec, ob da caccia, str, bc	ii, 81	I/v, 231
14	A 40	Wär Gott nicht mit uns diese Zeit, chorale (Luther)	Epiphany IV; 30 Jan 1735	S, T, B, 4vv, hn, 2 ob, str, bc	ii, 101	I/vi, 139
16	A 23	Herr Gott, dich loben wir (Lehms)	New Year; 1 Jan 1726	A, T, B, 4vv, hn, 2 ob, ob da caccia, str, bc	ii, 175	I/iv, 105
17	A 131	Wer Dank opfert, der preiset mich	Trinity XIV; 22 Sept 1726	S, A, T, B, 4vv, 2 ob, str, bc	ii, 201	I/xxi, 149

BWV	BC	Title (text/librettist)	Occasion; 1st perf.	Scoring	BG	NBA
†18	A 44	Gleichwie der Regen und Schnee vom Himmel fällt (E. Neumeister)	Sexagesima; ? 24 Feb 1715 or ? 1713–14	S, T, B, 4vv, 4 va, bc [2 fl added 1724]	ii, 229	I/vii, 109
19	A 180	Es erhub sich ein Streit (after Picander)	St Michael; 29 Sept 1726	S, T, B, 4vv, 3 tpt, timp, 2 ob, 2 ob d'amore, taille, str, bc	ii, 255	I/xxx, 57
20	A 95	O Ewigkeit, du Donnerwort, chorale (J. Rist)	Trinity I; 11 June 1724	A, T, B, 4vv, tpt, da tirarsi, 3 ob, str, bc	ii, 293	I/xv, 135
†21	A 99	Ich hatte viel Bekümmernis (?Franck)	Trinity III; 17 June 1714 [part earlier]	S, T, B, 4vv, 3 tpt, timp, ob, str, bc incl. bn [4 trbn added 1723]	v/1, 1	I/xvi, 111
22	A 48	Jesus nahm zu sich die Zwölfe	Quinquagesima; 7 Feb 1723	A, T, B, 4vv, ob, str, bc	v/1, 67	I/viii.1, 3
†23	A 47	Du wahrer Gott und Davids Sohn	Quinquagesima, 7 Feb 1723	S, A, T, 4vv, 2 ob, str, bc [cornett, 3 trbn added 1724]	v/1, 95	I/viii.1, 35, 71
24	A 102	Ein ungefärbt Gemüte (Neumeister)	Trinity IV; 20 June 1723	A, T, B, 4vv, tpt, 2 ob, 2 ob d'amore, str, bc	v/1, 127	I/xvii.1, 49
25	A 129	Es ist nicht Gesundes an meinem Leibe	Trinity XIV; 29 Aug 1723	S, T, B, 4vv, cornett, 3 trbn, 3 rec, 2 ob, str, bc	v/1, 155	I/xxi, 81
26	A 162	Ach wie flüchtig, ach wie nichtig, chorale (M. Franck)	Trinity XXIV; 19 Nov 1724	S, A, T, B, 4vv, hn, fl, 3 ob, str, bc	v/1, 191	I/xxvii, 31
27	A 138	Wer weiss, wie nahe mir mein Ende!	Trinity XVI; 6 Oct 1726	S, A, T, B, 4vv, hn, 2 ob, ob da caccia, org obbl, str, bc	v/1, 219	I/xxiii, 223
28	A 20	Gottlob! nun geht das Jahr zu Ende (Neumeister)	Christmas I; 30 Dec 1725	S, A, T, B, 4vv, cornett, 3 trbn, 2 ob, taille, str, bc	v/1, 247	[I/iii]
29	B 8	Wir danken dir, Gott, wir danken dir	inauguration of town council; 27 Aug 1731	S, A, T, B, 4vv, 3 tpt, timp, 2 ob, org obbl, str, bc	v/1, 275	I/xxxii.2, 3
30	A 178	Freue dich, erlöste Schar (adapted ?Picander from 30a)	St John; 24 June 1738 or later	S, A, T, B, 4vv, 2 fl, 2 ob, ob d'amore, str, bc	v/1, 323	I/xxix, 61
†31	A 55	Der Himmel lacht! die Erde jubilieret (Franck)	Easter; 21 April 1715	S, T, B, 5vv, 3 tpt, timp, 2 ob, str, bc [taille added 1724]	vii, 3	I/ix, 43
32	A 31	Liebster Jesu, mein Verlangen, dialogue (Lehms)	Epiphany I; 13 Jan 1726	S, B, 4vv, ob, str, bc	vii, 55	I/v, 145
33	A 127	Allein zu dir, Herr Jesu Christ, chorale (K. Hubert)	Trinity XIII; 3 Sept 1724	A, T, B, 4vv, 2 ob, str, bc	vii, 83	I/xxi, 25
34	A 84	O ewiges Feuer, O Ursprung der Liebe (adapted from 34a)	Whit Sunday; c1746–7	A, T, B, 4vv, 3 tpt, timp, 2 fl, 2 ob, str, bc	vii, 117	I/xiii, 131
34a	B 13	O ewiges Feuer, O Ursprung der Liebe [partly lost]	?wedding; 1726	S, A, T, B, 4vv, 3 tpt, timp, 2 fl, 2 ob, str, bc	xli, 117	I/xxxiii, 29
35	A 125	Geist und Seele wird verwirret (Lehms) [partly adapted from lost ob conc., cf 1059]	Trinity XII; 8 Sept 1726	A, 2 ob, taille, org obbl, str, bc	vii, 173	I/xx, 217
†36	A 3	Schwingt freudig euch empor (adapted ?Picander from 36c)	Advent I; c1725–30, rev. 2 Dec 1731	S, A, T, B, 4vv, 2 ob d'amore, str, bc	vii, 223	I/i, 19, 43
37	A 75	Wer da gläubet und getauft wird [inc.]	Ascension; 18 May 1724	S, A, T, B, 4vv, 2 ob d'amore, str, bc	vii, 261	I/xii, 81

BWV	BC	Title (text/librettist)	Occasion; 1st perf.	Scoring	BG	NBA
38	A 152	Aus tiefer Not schrei ich zu dir, chorale (Luther)	Trinity XXI; 29 Oct 1724	S, A, T, B, 4vv, 4 trbn, 2 ob, str, bc	vii, 285	I/xxv, 219
39	A 96	Brich dem Hungrigen dein Brot	Trinity I; 23 June 1726	S, A, B, 4vv, 2 rec, 2 ob, str, bc	vii, 303	I/xv, 181
40	A 12	Darzu ist erschienen der Sohn Gottes	2nd day of Christmas; 26 Dec 1723	A, T, B, 4vv, 2 hn, 2 ob, str, bc	vii, 351	[I/iii]
41	A 22	Jesu, nun sei gepreiset, chorale (J. Herman)	New Year; 1 Jan 1725	S, A, T, B, 4vv, 3 tpt, timp, 3 ob, vc piccolo, str, bc	x, 3	I/iv, 39
42	A 63	Am Abend aber desselbigen Sabbats	Easter I; 8 April 1725	S, A, T, B, 4vv, 2 ob, str, bc incl. bn	x, 65	I/xi.1, 63
43	A 77	Gott fähret auf mit Jauchzen (?Helm)	Ascension; 30 May 1726	S, A, T, B, 4vv, 3 tpt, timp, 2 ob, str, bc	x, 95	I/xii, 135
44	A 78	Sie werden euch in den Bann tun	Ascension I; 21 May 1724	S, A, T, B, 4vv, 2 ob, str, bc	x, 129	I/xii, 167
45	A 113	Es ist dir gesagt, Mensch, was gut ist	Trinity VIII; 11 Aug 1726	A, T, B, 4vv, 2 fl, 2 ob, str, bc	x, 153	I/xviii, 199
46	A 117	Schauet doch und sehet	Trinity X; 1 Aug 1723	A, T, B, 4vv, 2 rec, tpt da tirarsi, 2 taille, str, bc	x, 189	I/xix, 111
47	A 141	Wer sich selbst erhöhet (J.F. Helbig)	Trinity XVII; 13 Oct 1726	S, B, 4vv, 2 ob, org obbl, str, bc	x, 241	I/xxiii, 321
48	A 144	Ich elender Mensch, wer wird mich erlösen	Trinity XIX; 3 Oct 1723	A, T, 4vv, tpt, 2 ob, str, bc	x, 277	I/xxiv, 107
49	A 150	Ich geh und suche mit Verlangen, dialogue [sinfonia adapted from lost conc. 1053]	Trinity XX; 3 Nov 1726	S, B, ob d'amore, org obbl, vc piccolo, str, bc	x, 301	I/xxv, 109
50	A 194	Nun ist das Heil und die Kraft (Revelation xii. 10) [movt of inc. or lost cantata]	St Michael	8vv, 3 tpt, timp, 3 ob, str, bc	x, 343	I/xxx, 143
51	A 134	Jauchzet Gott in allen Landen!	Trinity XV; 17 Sept 1730	S, tpt, str, bc [2 tpt, timp added by W.F. Bach]	xii/2, 3	I/xxii, 77
52	A 160	Falsche Welt, dir trau ich nicht	Trinity XXIII; 24 Nov 1726	S, 4vv, 2 hn, 3 ob, bn, str, bc	xii/2, 27	I/xxvi, 133
54	A 51	Widerstehe doch der Sünde (Lehms)	Oculi or Trinity VII; 4 March or 15 July 1714	A, str, bc	xii/2, 61	I/xviii, 3
55	A 157	Ich armer Mensch, ich Sündenknecht	Trinity XXII; 17 Nov 1726	T, 4vv, fl, ob d'amore, str, bc	xii/2, 75	I/xxvi, 57
56	A 146	Ich will den Kreuzstab gerne tragen	Trinity XIX; 27 Oct 1726	B, 4vv, 3 ob, str, bc	xii/2, 89	I/xxiv, 175
57	A 14	Selig ist der Mann, dialogue (Lehms)	2nd day of Christmas; 26 Dec 1725	S, B, 4vv, 3 ob, str, bc	xii/2, 107	[I/iii]
†58	A 26	Ach Gott, wie manches Herzeleid, dialogue	New Year I; 5 Jan 1727	S, B, str, bc [2 ob, taille added 1733–4]	xii/2, 135	I/iv, 219
59	A 82	Wer mich liebet, der wird mein Wort halten (Neumeister)	Whit Sunday; 28 May 1724	S, B, 4vv, 2 tpt, timp, str, bc	xii/2, 153	I/xiii, 67
60	A 161	O Ewigkeit, du Donnerwort, dialogue	Trinity XXIV; 7 Nov 1723	A, T, B, 4vv, hn, 2 ob d'amore, str, bc	xii/2, 171	I/xxvii, 3
61	A 1	Nun komm, der Heiden Heiland (Neumeister)	Advent I; 2 Dec 1714	S, T, B, 4vv, str, bc	xvi, 3	I/i, 3
62	A 2	Nun komm, der Heiden Heiland, chorale (Luther)	Advent I; 3 Dec 1724	S, A, T, B, 4vv, hn, 2 ob, str, bc	xvi, 21	I/i, 77

BWV	BC	Title (text/librettist)	Occasion; 1st perf.	Scoring	BG	NBA
†63	A 8	Christen, ätzet diesen Tag (? N. Heineccius)	Christmas; c1714–15	S, A, T, B, 4vv, 4 tpt, timp, 3 ob, str, bc [org obbl added after c1729]	xvi, 53	I/ii, 3
64	A 15	Sehet, welch eine Leibe (Knauer)	3rd day of Christmas; 27 Dec 1723	S, A, B, 4vv, cornett, 3 trbn, ob d'amore, str, bc	xvi, 113	[I/iii]
65	A 27	Sie werden aus Saba alle kommen	Epiphany; 6 Jan 1724	T, B, 4vv, 2 hn, 2 rec, 2 ob da caccia, str, bc	xvi, 135	I/v, 3
66	A 56	Erfreut euch, ihr Herzen, dialogue [adapted from 66a]	Easter Monday; 10 April 1724	A, T, B, 4vv, tpt, 2 ob, str, bc	xvi, 169	I/x, 3
67	A 62	Halt im Gedächtnis Jesum Christ	Easter I; 16 April 1724	A, T, B, 4vv, hn, fl, 2 ob d'amore, str, bc	xvi, 217	I/xi.1, 1
68	A 86	Also hat Gott die Welt geliebt (M. von Ziegler)	Whit Monday; 21 May 1725	S, B, 4vv, hn, cornett, 3 trbn, 2 ob, taille, vc piccolo, str, bc	xvi, 249	I/xiv, 33
69	B 10	Lobe den Herrn, meine Seele (partly Knauer) [adapted from 69a]	inauguration of town council; 1742–8	S, A, T, B, 4vv, 3 tpt, timp, 3 ob, ob d'amore, str, bc	xvi, 283	I/xxxii.2, 113
69a	A 123	Lobe den Herrn, meine Seele (Knauer)	Trinity XII; 15 Aug 1723	S, A, T, B, 4vv, 3 tpt, timp, rec, 3 ob, ob da caccia, str, bc	xvi, 373 (inc.)	I/xx, 119
70	A 165	Wachet! betet! betet! wachet! (partly Franck) [adapted from 70a]	Trinity XXVI; 21 Nov 1723	S, A, T, B, 4vv, tpt, ob, str, bc	xvi, 329	I/xxvii, 109
70a	A 4	Wachet! betet! betet! wachet! (Franck) [music lost]	Advent II; 6 Dec 1716	—	—	I/i, CC
71	B 1	Gott ist mein König	inauguration of Mühlhausen town council; 4 Feb 1708	S, A, T, B, 4vv; 3 tpt, timp; 2 rec, vc; 2 ob; str, bc incl. org obbl	xviii, 3	I/xxxii.1, 3
72	A 37	Alles nur nach Gottes Willen (Franck)	Epiphany III; 27 Jan 1726	S, A, B, 4vv, 2 ob, str, bc	xviii, 57	I/vi, 59
†73	A 35	Herr, wie du willt, so schick's mit mir	Epiphany III; 23 Jan 1724	S, T, B, 4vv, hn, 2 ob, str, bc [later version, 1730s, with org obbl instead of hn]	xviii, 87	I/vi, 3
74	A 83	Wer mich liebet, der wird mein Wort halten (Ziegler) [partly adapted from 59]	Whit Sunday; 20 May 1725	S, A, T, B, 4vv, 3 tpt, timp, 2 ob, ob da caccia, str, bc	xviii, 107	I/xiii, 85
75	A 94	Die Elenden sollen essen	Trinity I; 30 May 1723	S, A, T, B, 4vv, tpt, 2 ob, ob d'amore, str, bc	xviii, 149	I/xv, 87
†76	A 97, A 185	Die Himmel erzählen die Ehre Gottes	Trinity II; 6 June 1723	S, A, T, B, 4vv, tpt, 2 ob, ob d'amore, va da gamba, str, bc	xviii, 191	I/xvi, 3
77	A 126	Du sollt Gott, deinen Herren, lieben (Knauer)	Trinity XIII; 22 Aug 1723	S, A, T, B, 4vv, tpt da tirarsi, 2 ob, str, bc	xviii, 235	I/xxi, 3
78	A 130	Jesu, der du meine Seele, chorale (Rist)	Trinity XIV; 10 Sept 1724	S, A, T, B, 4vv, hn, fl, 2 ob, str, bc	xviii, 257	I/xxi, 117
79	A 184	Gott der Herr ist Sonn und Schild	Reformation Festival; 31 Oct 1725	S, A, B, 4vv, 2 hn, timp, 2 fl, 2 ob, str, bc	xviii, 289	I/xxxi, 3

BWV	BC	Title (text/librettist)	Occasion; 1st perf.	Scoring	BG	NBA
†80	A 183	Ein feste Burg ist unser Gott (Franck) [adapted from 80a]	Reformation Festival; 1727–31, rev. 1744–7 or earlier	S, A, T, B, 4vv, ob, str, bc [ob d'amore, taille added c1744–7; 3 tpt, timp added by W.F. Bach]	xviii, 319, 381	I/xxxi, 67, 73
80a	A 52	Alles, was von Gott geboren (Franck) [music lost]	Lent III; Oculi, 15 March 1716	—	—	I/viii, CC
81	A 39	Jesus schläft, was soll ich hoffen?	Epiphany IV; 30 Jan 1724	A, T, B, 4vv, 2 rec, 2 ob d'amore, str, bc	xx/1, 3	I/vi, 111
82	A 169	Ich habe genug	Purification; 2 Feb 1727	B, ob, str, bc; other versions for S/A with altered ww	xx/1, 27	I/xxviii.1, 77
83	A 167	Erfreute Zeit im neuen Bunde	Purification; 2 Feb 1724	A, T, B, 4vv, 2 hn, 2 ob, str, bc	xx/1, 53	I/xxviii.1, 3
84	A 43	Ich bin vergnügt mit meinem Glücke (Picander)	Septuagesima; 9 Feb 1727	S, 4vv, ob, str, bc	xx/1, 79	I/vii, 23
85	A 66	Ich bin ein guter Hirt	Easter II; 15 April 1725	S, A, T, B, 4vv, 2 ob, vc piccolo, str, bc	xx/1, 101	I/xi.1, 157
86	A 73	Wahrlich, wahrlich, ich sage euch	Easter V; 14 May 1724	S, A, T, B, 4vv, 2 ob d'amore, str, bc	xx/1, 121	I/xii, 47
87	A 74	Bisher habt ihr nichts gebeten (Ziegler)	Easter V; 6 May 1725	A, T, B, 4vv, 2 ob, 2 ob da caccia, str, bc	xx/1, 137	I/xii, 63
88	A 105	Siehe, ich will viel Fischer aussenden	Trinity V; 21 July 1726	S, A, T, B, 4vv, 2 hn, 2 ob d'amore, taille, str, bc	xx/1, 155	I/xvii.2, 33
89	A 155	Was soll ich aus dir machen, Ephraim?	Trinity XXII; 24 Oct 1723	S, A, B, 4vv, hn, 2 ob, str, bc	xx/1, 181	I/xxvi, 3
90	A 163	Es reisset euch ein schrecklich Ende	Trinity XXV; 14 Nov 1723	A, T, B, 4vv, tpt, str, bc	xx/1, 197	I/xxvii, 61
†91	A 9	Gelobet seist du, Jesu Christ, chorale (Luther)	Christmas; 25 Dec 1724	S, A, T, B, 4vv, 2 hn, timp, 3 ob, str, bc	xxii, 3	I/ii, 133, 164
92	A 42	Ich hab in Gottes Herz und Sinn, chorale (P. Gerhardt)	Septuagesima; 28 Jan 1725	S, A, T, B, 4vv, 2 ob d'amore, str, bc	xxii, 35	I/vii, 43
93	A 104	Wer nur den lieben Gott lässt walten, chorale (G. Neumark)	Trinity V; 9 July 1724	S, A, T, B, 4vv, 2 ob, str, bc	xxii, 71	I/xvii.2, 3
94	A 115	Was frag ich nach der Welt, chorale (B. Kindermann)	Trinity IX; 6 Aug 1724	S, A, T, B, 4vv, fl, 2 ob, ob d'amore, str, bc	xxii, 97	I/xix, 45
95	A 136	Christus, der ist mein Leben, stanzas from 3 chorales	Trinity XVI; 12 Sept 1723	S, T, B, 4vv, hn, 2 ob, ob d'amore, str, bc	xxii, 131	I/xxiii, 67
96	A 142	Herr Christ, der einge Gottessohn, chorale (E. Kreuziger)	Trinity XVIII; 8 Oct 1724	S, A, T, B, 4vv, hn, trbn, fl piccolo, 2 ob, vn piccolo, str, bc	xxii, 157	I/xxiv, 3
97	A 189	In allen meinen Taten, chorale (P. Fleming)	1734	S, A, T, B, 4vv, 2 ob, str, bc	xxii, 187	I/xxxiv, 199
98	A 153	Was Gott tut, das ist wohlgetan	Trinity XXI; 10 Nov 1726	S, A, T, B, 4vv, 2 ob, str, bc	xxii, 233	I/xxv, 243
99	A 133	Was Gott tut, das ist wohlgetan, chorale (P. Rodigast)	Trinity XV; 17 Sept 1724	S, A, T, B, 4vv, hn, fl, ob d'amore, str, bc	xxii, 253	I/xxii, 41
100	A 191	Was Gott tut, das ist wohlgetan, chorale (Rodigast)	c1732–5	S, A, T, B, 4vv, 2 hn, timp, fl, ob d'amore, str, bc	xxii, 279	I/xxxiv, 241

BWV	BC	Title (text/librettist)	Occasion; 1st perf.	Scoring	BG	NBA
101	A 118	Nimm von uns, Herr, du treuer Gott, chorale (Möller)	Trinity X; 13 Aug 1724	S, A, T, B, 4vv, cornett, 3 trbn, fl, 2 ob, ob da caccia, str, bc	xxiii, 3	I/xix, 175
102	A 119	Herr, deine Augen sehen nach dem Glauben	Trinity X; 25 Aug 1726	A, T, B, 4vv, fl, 2 ob, str, bc	xxiii, 35	I/xix, 231
103	A 69	Ihr werdet weinen und heulen (Ziegler)	Easter III; 22 April 1725	A, T, 4vv, tpt, fl piccolo, 2 ob d'amore, str, bc	xxiii, 69	I/xi.2, 25
104	A 65	Du Hirte Israel, höre	Easter II; 23 April 1724	T, B, 4vv, 2 ob, ob da caccia, 2 ob d'amore, str, bc	xxiii, 97	I/xi.1, 113
105	A 114	Herr, gehe nicht ins Gericht	Trinity IX; 25 July 1723	S, A, T, B, 4vv, hn, 2 ob, str, bc	xxiii, 119	I/xix, 3
106	B 18	Gottes Zeit ist die allerbeste Zeit (Actus tragicus)	funeral; ?1707–8	S, A, T, B, 4vv, 2 rec, 2 va da gamba, bc	xxiii, 149	I/xxxiv, 3
107	A 109	Was willst du dich betrüben, chorale (Heermann)	Trinity VII; 23 July 1724	S, T, B, 4vv, hn, 2 fl, 2 ob d'amore, str, bc	xxiii, 181	I/xviii, 57
108	A 72	Es ist euch gut, dass ich hingehe (Ziegler)	Easter IV; 29 April 1725	A, T, B, 4vv, 2 ob d'amore, str, bc	xxiii, 205	I/xii, 19
109	A 151	Ich glaube, lieber Herr, hilf meinem Unglauben	Trinity XXI; 17 Oct 1723	A, T, 4vv, hn, 2 ob, str, bc	xxiii, 233	I/xxv, 159
110	A 10	Unser Mund sei voll Lachens [cf 1069] (Lehms)	Christmas; 25 Dec 1725	S, A, T, B, 4vv, 3 tpt, timp, 2 fl, 3 ob, ob d'amore, ob da caccia, str, bc	xxiii, 265	I/ii, 73
111	A 36	Was mein Gott will, das g'scheh allzeit, chorale (A. von Brandenburg)	Epiphany III; 21 Jan 1725	S, A, T, B, 4vv, 2 ob, str, bc	xxiv, 3	I/vi, 27
112	A 67	Der Herr ist mein getreuer Hirt, chorale (W. Meuslin)	Easter II; 8 April 1731	S, A, T, B, 4vv, 2 hn, 2 ob d'amore, str, bc	xxiv, 31	I/xi.1, 179
113	A 122	Herr Jesu Christ, du höchstes Gut, chorale (B. Ringwaldt)	Trinity XI; 20 Aug 1724	S, A, T, B, 4vv, fl, 2 ob d'amore, str, bc	xxiv, 51	I/xx, 81
114	A 139	Ach, lieben Christen, seid getrost, chorale (J. Gigas)	Trinity XVII; 1 Oct 1724	S, A, T, B, 4vv, hn, fl, 2 ob, str, bc	xxiv, 83	I/xxiii, 289
115	A 156	Mache dich, mein Geist, bereit, chorale (J.B. Freystein)	Trinity XXII; 5 Nov 1724	S, A, T, B, 4vv, hn, fl, ob d'amore, vc piccolo, str, bc	xxiv, 111	I/xxvi, 23
116	A 164	Du Friedefürst, Herr Jesu Christ, chorale (J. Ebert)	Trinity XXV; 26 Nov 1724	S, A, T, B, 4vv, hn, 2 ob d'amore, str, bc	xxiv, 135	I/xxvii, 81
117	A 187	Sei Lob und Ehr dem höchsten Gut, chorale (J.J. Schütz)	c1728–31	A, T, B, 4vv, 2 fl, 2 ob d'amore, str, bc	xxiv, 161	I/xxxiv, 153
119	B 3	Preise, Jerusalem, den Herrn	inauguration of town council; 30 Aug 1723	S, A, T, B, 4vv, 4 tpt, timp, 2 rec, 3 ob, 2 ob da caccia, str, bc	xxiv, 195	I/xxxii.1, 131
120	B 6	Gott, man lobet dich in der Stille	inauguration of town council; ? 29 Aug 1729	S, A, T, B, 4vv, 3 tpt, timp, 2 ob d'amore, str, bc	xxiv, 249	I/xxxii.2, 55
120a	B 15	Herr Gott, Beherrscher aller Dinge [adapted from 120, partly lost]	wedding; ?1729	S, A, T, B, 4vv, 3 tpt, timp, 2 ob, 2 ob d'amore, org obbl, str, bc	xli, 149	I/xxxiii, 77
120b	B 28	Gott, man lobet dich in der Stille (Picander) [adapted from 120, music lost]	2nd day of 200th anniversary of Augsburg Confession, 26 June 1730	—	—	—

BWV	BC	Title (text/librettist)	Occasion; 1st perf.	Scoring	BG	NBA
121	A 13	Christum wir sollen loben schon, chorale (Luther)	2nd day of Christmas; 26 Dec 1724	S, A, T, B, 4vv, cornett, 3 trbn, ob d'amore, str, bc	xxvi, 3	[I/iii]
122	A 19	Das neugeborne Kindelein, chorale (C. Schneegass)	Christmas I; 31 Dec 1724	S, A, T, B, 4vv, 3 rec, 2 ob, taille, str, bc	xxvi, 23	[I/iii]
123	A 28	Liebster Immanuel, Herzog der Frommen, chorale (A. Fritsch)	Epiphany; 6 Jan 1725	A, T, B, 4vv, 2 fl, 2 ob d'amore, str, bc	xxvi, 43	I/v, 49
124	A 30	Meinen Jesum lass ich nicht, chorale (C. Keymann)	Epiphany I; 7 Jan 1725	S, A, T, B, 4vv, hn, ob d'amore, str, bc	xxvi, 63	I/v, 117
125	A 168	Mit Fried und Freud ich fahr dahin, chorale (Luther)	Purification; 2 Feb 1725	A, T, B, 4vv, hn, fl, ob, ob d'amore, str, bc	xxvi, 85	I/xxviii.1, 33
126	A 46	Erhalt uns, Herr, bei deinem Wort, chorale (Luther)	Sexagesima; 4 Feb 1725	A, T, B, 4vv, tpt, 2 ob, str, bc	xxvi, 113	I/vii, 157
127	A 49	Herr Jesu Christ, wahr' Mensch und Gott, chorale (P. Eber)	Quinquagesima; 11 Feb 1725	S, T, B, 4vv, tpt, 2 rec, 2 ob, str, bc	xxvi, 135	I/viii.1, 107
128	A 76	Auf Christi Himmelfahrt allein (Ziegler)	Ascension; 10 May 1725	A, T, B, 4vv, tpt, 2 hn, 2 ob d'amore, taille, str, bc	xxvi, 163	I/xii, 103
129	A 93	Gelobet sei der Herr, mein Gott, chorale (J. Olearius)	Trinity or Reformation; 16 June or 31 Oct 1726	S, A, B, 4vv, 3 tpt, timp, fl, 2 ob, ob d'amore, str, bc	xxvi, 187	I/xv, 39
130	A 179	Herr Gott, dich loben alle wir, chorale (Eber)	St Michael; 29 Sept 1724	S, A, T, B, 4vv, 3 tpt, timp, fl, 3 ob, str, bc	xxvi, 233	I/xxx, 3
131	B 25	Aus der Tiefen rufe ich, Herr, zu dir (? G.C. Eilmar)	1707	S, A, T, B, 4vv, ob, bn, vn, 2 va, bc	xxviii, 3	I/xxxiv, 69
132	A 6	Bereitet die Wege, bereitet die Bahn! (Franck)	Advent IV; 22 Dec 1715	S, A, T, B, 4vv, ob, str, bc	xxviii, 35	I/i, 101
133	A 16	Ich freue mich in dir, chorale (K. Ziegler)	3rd day of Christmas; 27 Dec 1724	S, A, T, B, 4vv, cornett, 2 ob d'amore, str, bc	xxviii, 53	[I/iii]
134	A 59	Ein Herz, das seinen Jesum lebend weiss [adapted from 134a]	Easter Tuesday; 11 April 1724	A, T, 4vv, 2 ob, str, bc	xxviii, 83, 287	I/x, 71
135	A 100	Ach Herr, mich armen Sünder, chorale (Schneegass)	Trinity III; 25 June 1724	A, T, B, 4vv, cornett, trbn, 2 ob, str, bc	xxviii, 121	I/xvi, 199
136	A 111	Erforsche mich, Gott, und erfahre mein Herz	Trinity VIII; 18 June 1723	A, T, B, 4vv, hn, 2 ob d'amore, str, bc	xxviii, 139	I/xviii, 131
137	A 124	Lobe den Herren, den mächtigen König der Ehren, chorale (J. Neander)	Trinity XII; 19 Aug 1725	S, A, T, B, 4vv, 3 tpt, timp, 2 ob, str, bc	xxviii, 167	I/xx, 173
138	A 132	Warum betrübst du dich, mein Herz?, chorale (anon.)	Trinity XV; 5 Sept 1723	S, A, T, B, 4vv, 2 ob d'amore, str, bc	xxviii, 199	I/xxii, 1
139	A 159	Wohl dem, der sich auf seinen Gott, chorale (J.C. Rüben)	Trinity XXIII; 12 Nov 1724	S, A, T, B, 4vv, 2 ob d'amore, str, bc	xxviii, 225	I/xxvi, 99
140	A 166	Wachet auf, ruft uns die Stimme, chorale (Nicolai)	Trinity XXVII; 25 Nov 1731	S, T, B, 4vv, hn, 2 ob, taille, vn piccolo, str, bc	xxviii, 251	I/xxvii, 151
144	A 41	Nimm, was dein ist, und gehe hin	Septuagesima; 6 Feb 1724	S, A, T, 4vv, 2 ob, ob d'amore, str, bc	xxx, 77	I/vii, 3
145	A 60	Ich lebe, mein Herze, zu deinem Ergötzen (Picander)	Easter Tuesday; ?1729	S, T, B, 4vv, tpt, fl, 2 ob d'amore, str, bc	xxx, 95	I/x, 113

BWV	BC	Title (text/librettist)	Occasion; 1st perf.	Scoring	BG	NBA
146	A 70	Wir müssen durch viel Trübsal [partly adapted from lost vn conc.; cf 1052]	Easter III; ? 12 May 1726 or ? 18 April 1728	S, A, T, B, 4vv, fl, 2 ob, 2 ob d'amore, taille, org obbl, str, bc	xxx, 125	I/xi.2, 65
147	A 174	Herz und Mund und Tat und Leben (partly Franck) [adapted from 147a]	Visitation; 2 July 1723	S, A, T, B, 4vv, tpt, 2 ob, ob d'amore, 2 ob da caccia, str, bc	xxx, 193	I/xxviii.2, 65
147a	A 7	Herz und Mund und Tat und Leben (Franck) [music lost]	Advent IV; 20 Dec 1716	—	—	I/i, CC
148	A 140	Bringet dem Herrn Ehre seines Namens (after Picander)	Trinity XVII; ? 19 Sept 1723	A, T, 4vv, tpt, ob, ob d'amore, ob da caccia, str, bc	xxx, 237	I/xxiii, 255
149	A 181	Man singet mit Freuden vom Sieg (Picander)	St Michael; ? 29 Sept 1728 or ? 1729	S, A, T, B, 4vv, 3 tpt, timp, 3 ob, bn, str, bc	xxx, 263	I/xxx, 99
150	B 24	Nach dir, Herr, verlanget mich [? inc.]	? before 1707	S, A, T, B, 4vv, bn, 2 vn, bc	xxx, 303	[I/xli]
151	A 17	Süsser Trost, mein Jesus kömmt (Lehms)	3rd day of Christmas; 27 Dec 1725	S, A, T, B, 4vv, fl, str, bc [ob d'amore added c1727]	xxxii, 3	[I/iii]
152	A 18	Tritt auf die Glaubensbahn (Franck)	Christmas I; 30 Dec 1714	S, B, rec, ob, va d'amore, va da gamba, bc	xxxii, 19	[I/iii]
153	A 25	Schau, lieber Gott, wie meine Feind	New Year I; 2 Jan 1724	A, T, B, 4vv, str, bc	xxxii, 43	I/iv, 201
154	A 29	Mein liebster Jesus ist verloren	Epiphany I; 9 Jan 1724	A, T, B, 4vv, 2 ob d'amore, str, bc	xxxii, 61	I/v, 91
155	A 32	Mein Gott, wie lang, ach lange (Franck)	Epiphany II; 19 Jan 1716	S, A, T, B, 4vv, bn, str, bc	xxxii, 85	I/v, 175
156	A 38	Ich steh mit einem Fuss im Grabe (Picander) [sinfonia adapted from lost ob conc.; cf 1056]	Epiphany III; ? 23 Jan 1729	A, T, B, 4vv, ob, str, bc	xxxii, 99	I/vi, 91
157	A 170, B 20	Ich lasse dich nicht, du segnest mich denn (Picander) [adapted from earlier version as funeral cant.]	Purification; ? 2 Feb 1728 or later	T, B, 4vv, fl, ob d'amore, str, bc	xxxii, 117	I/xxxiv, 43
158	A 61, A 171	Der Friede sei mit dir [? adapted from earlier cant. for Purification] [inc.]	Easter Tuesday; after 1723	B, 4vv, ob, vn, bc	xxxii, 143	I/x, 131
159	A 50	Sehet, wir gehn hinauf gen Jerusalem (Picander)	Quinquagesima; ? 27 Feb 1729	A, T, B, 4vv, ob, str, bc	xxxii, 157	I/viii.1, 159
†161	A 135	Komm, du süsse Todesstunde (Franck)	Trinity XVI; 6 Oct 1715	A, T, 4vv, 2 rec, org obbl, str, bc	xxxiii, 3	I/xxiii, 3, 35
162	A 148	Ach! ich sehe, jetzt, da ich zur Hochzeit gehe (Franck) [inc.]	Trinity XX; 3 Nov 1715	S, A, T, B, 4vv, hn da tirarsi, str, bc	xxxiii, 31	I/xxv, 3, 23
163	A 158	Nur jedem das Seine (Franck)	Trinity XXIII; 24 Nov 1715	S, A, T, B, 4vv, str, bc	xxxiii, 49	I/xxvi, 79
164	A 128	Ihr, die ihr euch von Christo nennet (Franck)	Trinity XIII; 26 Aug 1725	S, A, T, B, 4vv, 2 fl, 2 ob, str, bc	xxxiii, 67	I/xxi, 59
165	A 90	O heilges Geist- und Wasserbad (Franck)	Trinity; 16 June 1715	S, A, T, B, 4vv, str, bc	xxxiii, 91	I/xv, 3
166	A 71	Wo gehest du hin? [inc.]	Easter IV; 7 May 1724	A, T, B, 4vv, ob, str, bc	xxxiii, 107	I/xii, 3
167	A 176	Ihr Menschen, rühmet Gottes Liebe	St John; 24 June 1723	S, A, T, B, 4vv, tpt da tirarsi, ob, ob da caccia, str, bc	xxxiii, 125	I/xxix, 3
168	A 116	Tue Rechnung! Donnerwort (Franck)	Trinity IX; 29 July 1725	S, A, T, B, 4vv, 2 ob d'amore, str, bc	xxxiii, 149	I/xix, 89
169	A 143	Gott soll allein mein Herze haben [partly adapted from lost conc.; cf 1053]	Trinity XVIII; 20 Oct 1726	A, 4vv, 2 ob d'amore, taille, org obbl, str, bc	xxxiii, 169	I/xxiv, 61

BWV	BC	Title (text/librettist)	Occasion; 1st perf.	Scoring	BG	NBA
170	A 106	Vergnügte Ruh', beliebte Seelenlust (Lehms)	Trinity VI; 28 July 1726	A, ob, d'amore, org obbl, str, bc	xxxiii, 195	I/xvii.2, 61
171	A 24	Gott, wie dein Name, so ist auch dein Ruhm (Picander)	New Year; 1 Jan ?1729	S, A, T, B, 4vv, 3 tpt, timp, 2 ob, str, bc	xxxv, 3	I/iv, 133
†172	A 81	Erschallet, ihr Lieder (?Franck)	Whit Sunday; 20 May 1714	S, A, T, B, 4vv, 3 tpt, timp, ob, str, bc	xxxv, 37	I/xiii, 3, 35
173	A 85	Erhöhtes Fleisch und Blut [adapted from 173a]	Whit Monday; ? 29 May 1724	S, A, T, B, 4vv, 2 fl, str, bc	xxxv, 73	I/xiv, 3
174	A 87	Ich liebe den Höchsten von ganzem Gemüte (Picander)	Whit Monday; 6 June 1729	A, T, B, 4vv, 2 hn, 2 ob, taille, str, bc	xxxv, 105	I/xiv, 65
175	A 89	Er rufet seinen Schafen mit Namen (M. von Ziegler)	Whit Tuesday; 22 May 1725	A, T, B, 4vv, 2 tpt, 3 rec, vc piccolo, str, bc	xxxv, 161	I/xiv, 149, 165
176	A 92	Es is ein trotzig, und verzagt Ding (M. von Ziegler)	Trinity; 27 May 1725	S, A, B, 4vv, 2 ob, ob da caccia, str, bc	xxxv, 181	I/xv, 19
177	A 103	Ich ruf zu dir, Herr Jesu Christ, chorale (J. Agricola)	Trinity IV; 6 July 1732	S, A, T, 4vv, 2 ob, taille, bn, str, bc	xxxv, 201	I/xvii.1, 79
178	A 112	Wo Gott der Herr nicht bei uns hält, chorale (J. Jonas)	Trinity VIII; 30 July 1724	A, T, B, 4vv, hn, 2 ob, 2 ob d'amore, str, bc	xxxv, 237; xli, 204	I/xviii, 161
179	A 121	Siehe zu, dass deine Gottesfurcht	Trinity XI; 8 Aug 1723	S, T, B, 4vv, 2 ob, 2 ob da caccia, str, bc	xxxv, 275	I/xx, 57
180	A 149	Schmücke dich, o liebe Seele, chorale (J. Franck)	Trinity XX; 22 Oct 1724	S, A, T, B, 4vv, 2 rec, fl, ob, ob da caccia, vc piccolo, str, bc	xxxv, 295	I/xxv, 43
181	A 45	Leichtgesinnte Flattergeister [? incl. earlier material] [inc.]	Sexagesima; 13 Feb 1724	S, A, T, B, 4vv, tpt, str, bc [fl, ob added later]	xxxvii, 3	I/vii, 135
†182	A 53, A 172	Himmelskönig, sei willkommen (?Franck)	Palm Sunday; 25 March 1714	A, T, B, 4vv, rec, str, bc	xxxvii, 23	I/viii.2, 3, 43
183	A 79	Sie werden euch in den Bann tun (Ziegler)	Ascension I; 13 May 1725	S, A, T, B, 4vv, 2 ob d'amore, 2 ob da caccia, vc piccolo, str, bc	xxxvii, 61	I/xii, 189
184	A 88	Erwünschtes Freudenlicht [adapted from 184a]	Whit Tuesday; 30 May 1724	S, A, T, 4vv, 2 fl, str, bc	xxxvii, 77	I/xiv, 121
185	A 101	Barmherziges Herze der ewigen Liebe (Franck)	Trinity IV; 14 July 1715	S, A, T, B, 4vv, ob, str, bc [later version with tpt da tirarsi instead of ob]	xxxvii, 103	I/xvii.1, 3
†186	A 108	Ärgre dich, o Seele, nicht (partly Franck) [adapted from 186a]	Trinity VII; 11 July 1723	S, A, T, B, 4vv, 2 ob, taille, str, bc	xxxvii, 121	I/xviii, 17
186a	A 5	Ärgre dich, o Seele, nicht (Franck) [music lost]	Advent III; 13 Dec 1716	—	—	I/i, CC
187	A 110	Es wartet alles auf dich	Trinity VII; 4 Aug 1726	S, A, B, 4vv, 2 ob, str, bc	xxxvii, 157	I/xviii, 93
188	A 154	Ich habe meine Zuversicht (Picander) [sinfonia adapted from lost vn conc.; cf 1052]	Trinity XXI; ? 17 Oct 1728	S, A, T, B, 4vv, 2 ob, taille, org obbl, str, bc	xxxvii, 195; xlv/1, 234	I/xxv, 267
190	A 21	Singet dem Herrn ein neues Lied! [partly lost]	New Year; 1 Jan 1724	A, T, B, 4vv, 3 tpt, timp, 3 ob, ob d'amore, bn, str, bc	xxxvii, 229	I/iv, 3
190a	B 27	Singet dem Herrn ein neues Lied! [adapted from 190, lost]	200th anniversary of Augsburg Confession; 25 June 1730	—	—	I/xxxiv, CC

BWV	BC	Title (text/librettist)	Occasion; 1st perf.	Scoring	BG	NBA
192	A 188	Nun danket alle Gott, chorale (M. Rinkart) [partly lost]	1730	S, B, 4vv, 2 fl, 2 ob, str, bc	xli, 67	I/xxxiv, 109
193	B 5	Ihr Tore zu Zion	inauguration of town council; 25 Aug 1727	S, A, 4vv, 2 ob, str, bc	xli, 93	I/xxxii, 203
194	A 91, B 31	Höchsterwünschtes Freudenfest [adapted from 194a]	consecration of Störmthal church and org; 2 Nov 1723	S, T, B, 4vv, 3 ob, str, bc	xxix, 101	I/xxxi, 147
†195	B 14	Dem Gerechten muss das Licht	wedding; 1727–31, rev. c1742 and 1747–8	S, A, T, B, 4vv, 3 tpt, timp, 2 hn, 2 fl, 2 ob, 2 ob d'amore, str, bc	xiii/1, 3	I/xxxiii, 17
196	B 11	Der Herr denket an uns (Ps cxv)	wedding; ?1707–8	S, T, B, 4vv, str, bc	xiii/1, 73	I/xxxiii, 3
197	B 16	Gott ist unsre Zuversicht [partly based on 197a]	wedding; 1736/7	S, A, B, 4vv, 3 tpt, timp, 2 ob, 2 ob d'amore, str, bc	xiii/1, 97	I/xxxiii, 119
197a	A 11	Ehre sei Gott in der Höhe (Picander) [partly lost]	Christmas; 25 Dec ?1728	A, B, 4vv, 2 fl, ob d'amore, vc/bn, str, bc	xli, 109	I/ii, 65
†199	A 120	Mein Herze schwimmt im Blut (Lehms)	Trinity XI; 12 Aug 1714	S, ob, str, bc	xli, 202 (inc.)	I/xx, 3, 25, 46, 48
200	A 192	Bekennen will ich seinen Namen [frag. of lost cantata]	?Epiphany or ?Purification; c1742	A, 2 vn, bc	—	I/xxviii.1, 189

Lost or incomplete

BWV	BC	Title (librettist)	Occasion; 1st perf.	Remarks	BG	NBA, CC
223	A 186	Meine Seele soll Gott loben	—	only incipit of last movt extant	—	I/xxxiv
244a	B 22	Klagt, Kinder, klagt es aller Welt (Picander)	funeral of Prince Leopold of Anhalt-Cöthen; 24 March 1729	music lost, text partly same as St Matthew Passion (244), and Trauer Ode (198)	—	I/xxxiv
1045	A 193	[Sinfonia], from lost cant.	c1743–6	vn, 3 tpt, timp, 2 ob, str, bc	xxi/1, 65	I/xxxiv, 307
1083	—	Tilge, Höchster, meine Sünden (after Ps li) [arr. of Pergolesi: Stabat mater]	c1745–7	S, A, str, bc	—	[I/xli]
A2	A 147	[untexted frag.]	Trinity XIX; 1729	6-bar frag. in autograph of 226	xxxix, p.xxix	I/xxiv
A3	B 7	Gott, gib dein Gerichte dem Könige (Picander)	change of town council; 28 Aug 1730	only text extant	—	I/xxxii.2
A4	B 4	Wünschet Jerusalem Glück (Picander)	change of town council; 26 Aug 1726 or 30 Aug 1728	only text extant	—	I/xxxii.1
A4a	B 29	Wünschet Jerusalem Glück (Picander)	3rd day of 200th anniversary of Augsburg Confession, 27 June 1730	only text extant	—	I/xxxiv
A5	B 30	Lobet den Herrn, alle seine Heerscharen (C.F. Hunold)	birthday of Prince Leopold of Anhalt-Cöthen; 10 Dec 1718	only text extant	—	I/xxxiv
A14	B 12	Sein Segen fliesst daher wie ein Strom	wedding; 12 Feb 1725	only text extant	—	I/xxxiii
A15	B 32	Siehe, der Hüter Israel	degree ceremony, Leipzig; 1723–49	cited in Breitkopf catalogue, 1761; lost	—	I/xxxiv
A17		Mein Gott, nimm die gerechte Seele	funeral	cited in Breitkopf catalogue, 1761; lost	—	I/xxxiv
A193	B 9	Herrscher des Himmels, König der Ehren	change of town council; 29 Aug 1740	last chorus adapted from 208, otherwise lost	—	I/xxxii
A190		Ich bin ein Pilgrim auf der Welt (Picander)	Easter Monday; ? 18 April 1729	only frag. of 4th movt extant	—	I/xxxiii, CC
A192	B 2	[title unknown]	change of Mühlhausen town council; 1709	lost	—	I/xxxii.1

BWV	BC	Title (librettist)	Occasion; 1st perf.	Remarks	BG	NBA, CC
A197		Ihr wallenden Wolken	? New Year	cited in Forkel: *Nachlass-verzeichnis*, 1819, lost	—	I/iv
A64		[title unknown]	Easter I	7-bar sketch in autograph score of 103	xxiii, p.xxxii	I/xi.1
A80		Sie werden euch in den Bann tun	? Ascension I	6-bar sketch in autograph score of 79	—	I/xxxi.1
A182		[title unknown]	St Michael; Sept 1729	14-bar sketch for opening of cant. in autograph score of 201	—	—
—	B 19	Was ist, das wir Leben nennen	dedication service; 2 April 1716	—	—	—
—	B 21	[title unknown]	first funeral music for Prince Leopold of Anhalt-Cöthen; 23 March 1729	music lost	—	—

Doubtful and spurious

BWV	BC	Title (librettist)	Occasion; 1st perf.	Remarks	BG	NBA, CC
15		Denn du wirst meine Seele	Easter	by J.L. Bach	ii, 135	—
53		Schlage doch, gewünschte Stunde (?Franck)	funeral	? by M. Hoffmann	xii/2, 53	—
141		Das ist je gewisslich wahr (Helbig)	Advent III	by G.P. Telemann	xxx, 3	—
142		Uns ist ein Kind geboren (Neumeister)	Christmas		xxx, 19	—
143		Lobe den Herrn, meine Seele	New Year		xxx, 45	I/iv, 167
160		Ich weiss, dass mein Erlöser lebt (Neumeister)	Easter	by Telemann	xxxii, 171	—
189		Meine Seele rühmt und preist	?Visitation	probably by M. Hoffmann	xxxvii, 215	—
217		Gedenke, Herr, wie es uns geht	Epiphany I		xli, 207	—
218		Gott der Hoffnung erfülle euch (Neumeister)	Whit Sunday	by Telemann	xli, 223	—
219		Siehe, es hat überwunden der Löwe	St Michael	by Telemann	xli, 239	—
220		Lobt ihn mit Herz und Munde	St John		xli, 259	—
221		Wer sucht die Pracht, wer wünscht den Glanz	—		—	—
222		Mein Odem ist schwach	—	by (10) J.E. Bach	—	—
224		Reisst euch los, bekränkte Sinnen	c1733	frag., ? by C.P.E. Bach	—	—

SECULAR CANTATAS

BWV	BC	Title (librettist)	Occasion; date	Scoring	BG	NBA
30a	G 31	Angenehmes Wiederau, freue dich (Picander)	for J.C. von Hennicke; 28 Sept 1737	S, A, T, B, 4vv, 3 tpt, timp, 2 fl, 2 ob, ob d'amore, str, bc	v/1, 399; xxxiv, 325	I/xxxix, 53
36a	G 12	Steigt freudig in die Luft (Picander) [music lost; arr. from 36c]	birthday of Princess Charlotte Friedericke Wilhelmine of Anhalt-Cöthen; 30 Nov 1726	—	—	I/xxxv, CC; I/xxxix, CC
36b	G 38	Die Freude reget sich [inc.]	for member of Rivinus family; 1735	S, A, T, 4vv, fl, ob d'amore, str, bc	xxxiv, 41	I/xxxviii, 257
36c	G 35	Schwingt freudig euch empor (?Picander)	birthday; 1725	S, T, B, 4vv, ob d'amore, va d'amore, str, bc	xxxiv, 41	I/xxxix, 3
66a	G 4	Der Himmel dacht auf Anhalts Ruhm und Glück (C.F. Hunold), serenata [music lost]	birthday of Prince Leopold of Anhalt-Cöthen; 10 Dec 1718	2vv, chorus, insts	—	I/xxxv, CC
134a	G 5	Die Zeit, die Tag und Jahre macht (Hunold)	New Year; 1 Jan 1719	S, A, T, B, 4vv, 2 ob, str, bc	xxix, 209 (inc.)	I/xxxv, 51
173a	G 9	Durchlauchster Leopold, serenata	birthday of Prince Leopold of Anhalt-Cöthen; 10 Dec ?1722	S, B, 2 fl, bn, str, bc	xxxiv, 3	I/xxxv, 97

BWV	BC	Title (librettist)	Occasion; date	Scoring	BG	NBA
184a	G 8	[some music preserved in 184, text lost]	? 10 Dec 1720 or 1 Jan 1721	—	—	I/xiv, CC; I/xxxv, CC
193a	G 15	Ihr Häuser des Himmels, ihr scheinenden Lichter (Picander), dramma per musica [music lost]	nameday of August II; 3 Aug 1727	—	—	I/xxxvi, CC
194a	G 11	[some music preserved in 194, text lost]	? for court of Anhalt-Cöthen; before Nov 1723	—	—	I/xxxv, CC
198	G 34	Trauer Ode: Lass, Fürstin, lass noch einen Strahl (J.C. Gottsched)	memorial service for Electress Christiane Eberhardine; 17 Oct 1727	S, A, T, B, 4vv, 2 fl, 2 ob d'amore, 2 va da gamba, 2 lutes, str, bc	xiii/3, 3	I/xxxviii, 181
201	G 46	Der Streit zwischen Phoebus und Pan: Geschwinde, ihr wirbelnden Winde (Picander), dramma per musica	?1729	S, A, T, T, B, B, 6vv, 3 tpt, timp, 2 fl, 2 ob, ob d'amore, str, bc	xi/2, 3	I/xl, 119
202	G 41	Weichet nur, betrübte Schatten	wedding; before 1730	S, ob, str, bc	xi/2, 75	I/xl, 3
203	G 51	Amore traditore [not fully authenticated]	? before 1723	B, hpd obbl	xi/2, 93	[I/xli]
204	G 45	Ich bin in mir vergnügt (Hunold)	1726–7	S, fl, 2 ob, str, bc	xi/2, 105	I/xl, 81
205	G 36	Der zufriedengestellte Äolus: Zerreisset, zerspringet, zertrümmert die Gruft (Picander), dramma per musica	nameday of Dr A.F. Müller; 3 Aug 1725	S, A, T, B, 4vv, 3 tpt, timp, 2 hn, 2 fl, 2 ob, ob d'amore, va d'amore, va da gamba, str, bc	xi/2, 139	I/xxxviii, 3
205a	G 20	Blast Lärmen, ihr Feinde! [adapted from 205; music lost]	? coronation of August III; ? 19 Feb 1734	—	—	I/xxxvii, CC
†206	G 23, G 26	Schleicht, spielende Wellen, dramma per musica	birthday of August III; 7 Oct 1736; 2nd version, nameday of August III; 3 Aug 1740	S, A, T, B, 4vv, 3 tpt, timp, 3 fl, 2 ob, 2 ob d'amore, str, bc	xx/2, 3	I/xxxvi, 159
207	G 37	Vereinigte Zwietracht der wechselnden Saiten, dramma per musica	installation of Professor Gottlieb Kortte; c11 Dec 1726	S, A, T, B, 4vv, 3 tpt, timp, 2 fl, 2 ob d'amore, ob da caccia, str, bc	xx/2, 73	I/xxxviii, 99
207a	G 22	Auf, schmetternde Töne, cant.	nameday of August III; ? 3 Aug 1735	S, A, T, B, 4vv, 3 tpt, timp, 2 fl, 2 ob d'amore, ob da caccia, str, bc	xx/2, 141; xxxiv, 345	I/xxxvii, 3
†208	G 1, G 3	Was mir behagt, ist nur die muntre Jagd! (Franck)	birthday of Duke Christian of Saxe-Weissenfels; 23 Feb ?1713; later versions ?1713–17 or ? after 1738, ?1742	S, S, T, B, 2 hn, 2 rec, 2 ob, ob da caccia, bn, str, bc	xxix, 3	I/xxxv, 3; I/xxxvii, CC
209	G 50	Non sa che sia dolore	departure of scholar (?L. Mizler); after 1729	S, fl, str, bc	xxix, 45	[I/xli]
†210	G 44	O holder Tag, erwünschte Zeit	wedding; ? 1738–41, after earlier version	S, fl, ob d'amore, str, bc	xxix, 69	I/xl, 37
210a	G 29	O angenehme Melodei! [music lost, mostly = 210]	for Joachim Fredrich, Graf von Flemming; before Oct 1740, after earlier version		xxix, 245	I/xxxix, 143
211	G 48	Schweigt stille, plaudert nicht (Coffee Cantata) (Picander)	c1734	S, T, B, fl, str, bc	xxix, 141	I/xl, 195
212	G 32	Mer hahn en neue Oberkeet (Peasant Cantata) (Picander)	manorial accession celebration for C.H. von Dieskau; 30 Aug 1742	S, B, hn, fl, str, bc	xxix, 175	I/xxxix, 153
213	G 18	Hercules auf dem Scheidewege: Lasst uns sorgen, lasst uns wachen (Picander), dramma per musica	birthday of Prince Friedrich Christian; 5 Sept 1733	S, A, A, T, B, 4vv, 2 hn, 2 ob, ob d'amore, str, bc	xxxiv, 121	I/xxxvi, 3
214	G 19	Tönet, ihr Pauken! Erschallet, Trompeten!, dramma per musica	birthday of Electress Maria Josepha; 8 Dec 1733	S, A, T, B, 4vv, 3 tpt, timp, 2 fl, 2 ob, ob d'amore, str, bc	xxxiv, 177	I/xxxvi, 91

BWV	BC	Title (librettist)	Occasion; date	Scoring	BG	NBA
215	G 21	Preise dein Glücke, gesegnetes Sachsen (J.C. Clauder), dramma per musica	anniversary of election of August III as King of Poland; 5 Oct 1734	S, T, B, 8vv, 3 tpt, timp, 2 fl, 2 ob, 2 ob d'amore, str, bc incl. bn	xxxiv, 245	I/xxxvii, 87
216	G 43	Vergnügte Pleissenstadt (Picander) [only vv extant]	wedding; 5 Feb 1728	S, A, insts	—	I/xl, 23
216a	G 47	Erwählte Pleissenstadt [music lost]	for Leipzig city council; after 1728	—	xxxiv, p.xlvi	I/xl, CC
249a	G 2	Entfliehet, verschwindet, entweichet, ihr Sorgen (Picander) [music lost, but most in 249]	birthday of Duke Christian of Saxe-Weissenfels; 23 Feb 1725	S, A, T, B, 3 tpt, timp, 2 rec, fl, 2 ob, ob d'amore, str, bc	—	I/xxxv, CC; II/vii, CC
249b	G 28	Die Feier des Genius: Verjaget, zerstreuet, zerrütet, ihr Sterne (Picander), dramma per musica [music lost]	birthday of Joachim Friedrich, Graf von Flemming; 25 Aug 1726	—	—	I/xxxix, CC

Lost

BWV	BC	Title (librettist)	Occasion; 1st perf.	Remarks	BG	NBA
A5	B 30	Lobet den Herren, alle seine Heerscharen (Hunold)	birthday of Prince Leopold of Anhalt-Cöthen; 10 Dec 1718	only text extant	—	I/xxxv, CC
A6	G 6	Dich loben die lieblichen Strahlen (Hunold)	New Year; 1 Jan 1720	only text extant	—	I/xxxv
A7	G 7	Heut ist gewiss ein guter Tag (Hunold)	birthday of Prince Leopold of Anhalt-Cöthen; 10 Dec ?1720	only text extant	—	I/xxxv, CC
A8	G 10	[title unknown]	New Year; 1 Jan 1723	lost; ? = 184a	—	I/xxxv, CC
A9	G 14	Entfernet euch, ihr heitern Sterne (C.F. Haupt)	birthday visit of August III; 12 May 1727	only text extant	—	I/xxxvi, CC
A10	G 30	So kämpfet nur, ihr muntern Töne (Picander)	birthday of Joachim Friedrich, Graf von Flemming; 25 Aug 1731	only text extant	—	I/xxxix, CC
A11	G 16	Es lebe der König, der Vater im Lande (Picander)	nameday of August II; 3 Aug 1732	only text extant	—	I/xxxvi, CC
A12	G 17	Frohes Volk, vergnügte Sachsen (Picander) [adapted from A18]	nameday of August III; 3 Aug 1733	only text extant	—	I/xxxvi, CC
A13	G 24	Willkommen! Ihr herrschenden Götter (Gottsched)	king's visit and marriage of Princess Maria Amalia; 28 April 1738	only text extant	—	I/xxxvii, CC
A18	G 39	Froher Tag, verlangte Stunden (J.H. Winckler)	opening of Thomasschule after renovation; 5 June 1732	only text extant	xxxiv, p.li	I/xxxix, CC
A19	G 40	Thomana sass annoch betrübt (J.A. Landvoigt)	in honour of new Rektor of Thommasschule J.A. Ernesti; 21 Nov 1734	only text extant	xxxiv, p.lviii	I/xxxix, CC
A20	G 33	Latin ode [title unknown]	birthday of Duke Friedrich II of Saxe-Gotha; 9 Aug 1723	lost	—	I/xxxviii, CC
A196		Auf! süss entzückende Gewalt (Gottsched)	wedding; 27 Nov 1725	only text extant	—	I/xl, 22
A194		[title unknown]	birthday of Johann August of Anhalt-Zerbst; 9 Aug 1722	lost	—	—
—	G 25	[title unknown]	birthday of August III; 7 Oct 1739	lost	—	—
—	G 49	Wo sind meine Wunderwerke	? departure of Rektor J.M. Gesner; 1732–5, ? 4 Oct 1734	frag. of inst parts	—	—

LATIN CHURCH MUSIC

BWV	BC	Title	Remarks	Scoring	BG	NBA
191	E 16	Gloria in excelsis Deo	perf. Christmas 1745; adapted from Mass 232I	S, T, 5vv, 3 tpt, timp, 2 fl, 2 ob, str, bc	xli, 3	I/ii, 173

BWV	BC	Title	Remarks	Scoring	BG	NBA
232	E 1	[Mass in B minor]: Missa (Kyrie, Gloria)	assembled c1747–9 ded. new Elector of Saxony, Friedrich August II, 1733; Gratias agimus from 29, 1731; Qui tollis from 46, 1723	2 S, A, T, B, 5vv, 3 tpt, timp, hn, 2 fl, 2 ob, 2 ob d'amore, 2 bn, str, bc	vi	II/i
		†Symbolum Nicenum (Credo)	added to autograph score c1747–9; Patrem omnipotentem from 171, ?1729; Crucifixus from 12, 1714; Et exspecto from 120, 1728–9; Credo (early version), c1740	S, A, B, 5vv, 3 tpt, timp, 2 fl, 2 ob, 2 ob d'amore, str, bc		
		Sanctus	1st perf. Christmas Day 1724; added to autograph score c1747–9	6vv, 3 tpt, timp, 3 ob, str, bc		
		Osanna, Benedictus, Agnus Dei et Dona nobis pacem	added to autograph score c1747–9; Osanna from A9, 1727, and A11, 1732; Agnus Dei from 11, 1735; Dona nobis pacem from 29, 1731 (cf Gratias agimus, above)	A, T, 8vv, 3 tpt, timp, 2 fl, 2 ob, str, bc		
		4 missae breves:	?1738–9 or later; mostly adaptations of cant. movts			
233	E 6	F	from 11, 40, 102, A18	S, A, B, 4vv, 2 hn, ob, bn, str, bc	viii, 3	II/ii, 199
233a	E 7	Kyrie, F	?1708–17; orig. Kyrie of 233	5vv, bc	xli, 187	II/ii, 287
234	E 3	A	from 67, 79, 136, 179	S, A, B, 4vv, 2 fl, str, bc	viii, 53	II/ii, 3
235	E 5	g	from 72, 102, 187	A, T, B, 4vv, 2 ob, str, bc	viii, 101	II/ii, 129
236	E 4	G	from 17, 79, 138, 179	S, A, T, B, 4vv, 2 ob, str, bc	viii, 157	II/ii, 63
		5 settings of Sanctus:	except 237–8, all probably arrs. of music by other composers			
237	E 10	C	perf. ? 24 June 1723	4vv, 3 tpt, timp, 2 ob, str, bc	xi/1, 69	II/ii, 313
238		D	perf. ? Christmas Day 1723	4vv, cornett, str, bc	xi/1, 81	II/ii, 327
239		d	perf. 1735–46	4vv, str, bc	xi/1, 89	[II/ix]
240		G	perf. 1735–46	4vv, 2 ob, str, bc	xi/1, 95	[II/ix]
241	E 17	D	perf. 1747/8; arr. from piece by J.C. Kerll	8vv, 2 ob d'amore, bn, 2 str, bc	xli, 177	[II/ix]
242	E 8	Christe eleison	inserted in Mass, c, by F. Durante	S, A, bc	xli, 197	II/ii, 306
243a	E 14	Magnificat, E♭	perf. Christmas Day 1723; incl. 4 Christmas texts: Vom Himmel hoch; Freut euch und jubiliert; Gloria in excelsis; Virga Jesse floruit	2 S, A, T, B, 5vv, 3 tpt, timp, 2 rec, 2 ob, str, bc	—	II/iii, 3
243	E 14	Magnificat, D	rev. of above, c1732–5; without Christmas texts	2 S, A, T, B, 5vv, 3 tpt, timp, 2 fl, 2 ob, 2 ob d'amore, str, bc	xi/1, 3	II/iii, 67
1081	E 9	Credo in unum Deum, F	perf. c1747–8; inserted in Mass, F, by G.B. Bassani	4vv, bc	—	II/ii, CC
1082	E 15	Suscepit Israel, e	c1740–42, from Magnificat, C, by Caldara with addl 2 ?vn pts.	4vv, 2 ?vn, bc	—	—

PASSIONS, ORATORIOS

BWV	BC	Title	Remarks	Scoring	BG	NBA
244b		Passio secundum Matthaeum (St Matthew Passion) (Picander)	perf. Good Friday, 11 April 1727 and 15 April 1729	scoring similar to 244, but with only 1 bc group	—	II/va (facs.)

BWV	BC	Title	Remarks	Scoring	BG	NBA
†244	D 3	Passio secundum Matthaeum (S Matthew Passion) (Picander)	perf. Good Friday, 30 March 1736, incl. 2 org; also perf. c1742	S in ripieno; chorus I: S, A, T, B, 4vv, 2 rec, 2 fl, 2 ob, 2 ob d'amore, 2 ob da caccia, va da gamba, str, bc; chorus II: S, A, T, B, 4vv, 2 fl, 2 ob, 2 ob d'amore, va da gamba, str, bc [bc incl. bassono grosso, c1742]	iv, 1	II/v
†245	D 2	Passio secundum Joannem (St John Passion) (anon. compilation from B.H. Brockes and others)	perf. Good Friday, 7 April 1724; 30 March 1725 with 5 nos. replaced (see NBA II/v, suppl. ii); ? 11 April 1732 and 4 April 1749 with further revs.	S, A, T, B, 4vv, 2 fl, 2 ob, 2 ob d'amore, 2 va d'amore, va da gamba, lute/org/hpd, str, bc [bc incl. bassono grosso in late rev., ?1740s]	xii/1, 3	II/iv
247	D 4	Passio secundum Marcum (St Mark Passion) (Picander)	perf. Good Friday, 23 March 1731; lost except for 1 movt ? rev. in 248 and 7 movts in orig. form in 198 and 54; see NBA II/v, CC	—	xx/2, preface	II/v, CC; I/xviii, CC
248	D 7	Oratorium … Die heilige Weynacht (Christmas Oratorio) (?Picander)	in 6 pts. for feast days Christmas to Epiphany 1734–5; pts. of nos.1–5 adapted from secular cants. 213–15, most of no.6 from lost church cant. 248a		v/2	II/vi
		Jauchzet, frohlocket, auf preiset die Tage	perf. Christmas Day 1734	S, A, T, B, 4vv, 3 tpt, timp, 2 fl, 2 ob, 2 ob d'amore, str, bc		
		Und es waren Hirten in derselben Gegend	perf. 26 Dec 1734	S, A, T, B, 4vv, 2 fl, 2 ob d'amore, 2 ob da caccia, str, bc		
		Herrscher des Himmels, erhöre das Lallen	perf. 27 Dec 1734	S, A, T, B, 4vv, 3 tpt, timp, 2 fl, 2 ob, 2 ob d'amore, str, bc		
		Fallt mit Danken, fallt mit Loben	perf. 1 Jan 1735	S, S, T, B, 4vv, 2 hn, 2 ob, str, bc		
		Ehre sei dir, Gott, gesungen	perf. 2 Jan 1735	S, A, T, B, 4vv, 2 ob d'amore, str, bc		
		Herr, wenn die stolzen Feinde schnauben	perf. Epiphany, 6 Jan 1735	S, A, T, B, 4vv, 3 tpt, timp, 2 ob, 2 ob d'amore, str, bc		
249	D 8	Oratorium Festo Paschali: Kommt, eilet und laufet (Easter Oratorio)	perf. Easter, 1 April 1725 as cant.; rev. as orat c1738	S, A, T, B, 4vv, 3 tpt, timp, 2 rec, fl, 2 ob d'amore, str, bc	xxi/3	II/vii
11	D 9	Oratorium Festo Ascensionis Christi: Lobet Gott in seinen Reichen (Ascension Oratorio)	perf. Ascension, 19 May 1735	S, A, T, B, 4vv, 3 tpt, timp, 2 fl, 2 ob, str, bc	ii, 1	II/viii, 3
1088		So heb ich denn mein Auge sehnlich auf	incl. in Passion pasticcio, late Leipzig period; authenticity doubtful	B, insts, bc	—	[II/9]
—	D 1	[Passion]	?1717, lost; some numbers incl. in St John Passion, 1725			II/4, CC
—	†D 5	Addns to R. Keiser: St Mark Passion	c1713; perf. 19 April 1726	S, A, T, 4vv, str, bc	—	—

MOTETS

texts of 225–8 and A159 are compilations, including chorale; other texts and librettist given in parentheses

BWV	BC	Title	Occasion; date	Scoring	BG	NBA
225	C 1	Singet dem Herrn ein neues Lied	1726–7	8vv	xxxix, 5	III/i, 3
226	C 2	Der Geist hilft unser Schwachheit auf	funeral of J.H. Ernesti; 20 Oct 1729	8vv, 2 ob, taille, bn, str, bc	xxxix, 41, 143	III/i, 39
227	C 5	Jesu, meine Freude	before 1735	5vv	xxxix, 61	III/i, 77
228	C 4	Fürchte dich nicht		8vv	xxxix, 87	III/i, 107
229	C 3	Komm, Jesu, Komm! (P. Thymich)	before 1732	8vv	xxxix, 109	III/i, 127
230	C 6	Lobet den Herrn alle Heiden (Ps cxvii)		4vv, org	xxxix, 129	III/i, 149
231	—	Sei Lob und Preis mit Ehren	? after 1 Jan 1725; from 28 and Telemann	8vv	xxix, 167 (inc.)	—
A159	C 9	Ich lasse dich nicht, du segnest mich denn	before Sept 1713	8vv	—	—
†118	B 23	O Jesu Christ, meins Lebens Licht (2 versions), chorale	burial or memorial service; 1st version 1736–7, 2nd version c1746–9	4vv, 2 litui, cornett, 3 trbn; 2nd version 4vv, 2 litui, str, bc (2 ob, ob da caccia and bn, ad lib)	xxiv, 183	III/i, 163, 171
—	C 8	Der Gerechte kommt um (Isaiah lvii.1–2)	? late Leipzig period; reworking of J. Kuhnau: Tristis est anima mea	5vv, 2 ob, str, bc	—	—

CHORALES, SACRED SONGS, ARIAS

BWV	BC		BWV	BC	
		Wedding chorales, 4vv, 2 hn, ob, ob d'amore, str, bc, after 1730; BG 143 xiii/1, 147; NBA III/ii.1, 3	282	F 30.2	Christus, der ist mein Leben
			283	F 31.1	Christus, der uns selig macht
			284	F 32.1	Christus ist erstanden, hat überwunden
250	F 193.3	Was Gott tut das ist wohlgetan	285	F 34.1	Da der Herr Christ zu Tische sass
251	F 59.4	Sei Lob und Ehr' dem höchsten Gut	286	F 183.1	Danket dem Herren
			287	F 119.1	Dank sei Gott in der Höhe
252	F 148.2	Nun danket alle Gott	288	F 36.1	Das alte Jahr vergangen ist
		Chorales, 4vv, from Joh. Seb. Bachs vierstimmige Choralgesänge, ed. J.P. Kirnberger and C.P.E. Bach, i–iv (Leipzig, 1784–7) [excluding those within larger works]; BG xxxix, 177; NBA III/ii.2, 3	289	F 36.2	Das alte Jahr vergangen ist
			290	F 38.1	Das walt' Gott Vater und Gott Sohn
			291	F 39.1	Das walt' mein Gott, Vater, Sohn und heil'ger Geist
			292	F 40.1	Den Vater dort oben
			293	F 41.1	Der du bist drei in Einigkeit
			294	F 43.1	Der Tag, der ist so freudenreich
			295	F 178.1	Des heil'gen Geistes reiche Gnad'
253	F 35.1	Ach bleib bei uns, Herr Jesu Christ	296	F 44.1	Die Nacht ist kommen
254	F 1.1	Ach Gott, erhör' mein Seufzen	297	F 161.1	Die Sonn' hat sich mit ihrem Glanz gewendet
255	F 2.1	Ach Gott und Herr			
256	F 212.1	Ach, lieben Christen, seid getrost	298	F 46.1	Dies sind die heil'gen zehn Gebot'
259	F 5.1	Ach, was soll ich Sünder machen	299	F 47.1	Dir, dir, Jehova, will ich singen
260	F 10.1	Allein Gott in der Höh' sei Ehr'	300	F 51.1	Du grosser Schmerzensmann
261	F 11.1	Allein zu dir, Herr Jesu Christ	301	F 50.1	Du, o schönes Weltgebäude
262	F 8.1	Alle Menschen müssen sterben	302	F 53.1	Ein' feste Burg ist unser Gott
263	F 12.1	Alles ist an Gottes Segen	303	F 53.2	Ein' feste Burg ist unser Gott
264	F 13.1	Als der gütige Gott	304	F 54.1	Eins ist Not! ach Herr, dies Eine
265	F 14.1	Als Jesus Christus in der Nacht	305	F 55.1	Erbarm' dich mein, o Herre Gott
266	F 15.1	Als vierzig Tag nach Ostern war	306	F 58.1	Erstanden ist der heil'ge Christ
267	F 17.1	An Wasserflüssen Babylon	307	F 150.1	Es ist gewisslich an der Zeit
268	F 19.1	Auf, auf, mein Herz, und du, mein ganzer Sinn	308	F 62.1	Es spricht der Unweisen Mund wohl
269	F 21.1	Aus meines Herzens Grunde	309	F 63.1	Es steh'n vor Gottes Throne
270	F 92.1	Befiehl du deine Wege	310	F 64.1	Es wird schier der letzte Tag herkommen
271	F 92.2	Befiehl du deine Wege			
272	F 136.2	Befiehl du deine Wege	311	F 66.1	Es woll' uns Gott genädig sein
273	F 24.1	Christ, der du bist der helle Tag	312	F 66.2	Es woll' uns Gott genädig sein
274	F 27.1	Christe, der du bist Tag und Licht	327	F 105.2	Für deinen Thron tret' ich hiermit
275	F 28.1	Christe, du Beistand deiner Kreuzgemeinde	313	F 68.1	Für Freuden lasst uns springen
			314	F 69.1	Gelobet seist du, Jesu Christ
276	F 25.1	Christ ist erstanden	315	F 70.1	Gib dich zufrieden und sei stille
277	F 26.1	Christ lag in Todes Banden	316	F 71.1	Gott, der du selber bist das Licht
278	F 26.2	Christ lag in Todes Banden	317	F 72.1	Gott, der Vater, wohn' uns bei
279	A 61/4	Christ lag in Todes Banden	318	F 143.1	Gottes Sohn ist kommen
280	F 65.1	Christ, unser Herr, zum Jordan kam	319	F 74.1	Gott hat das Evangelium
281	F 30.1	Christus, der ist mein Leben	320	F 75.1	Gott lebet noch

BWV	BC	
321	F 77.1	Gottlob, es geht nunmehr zu Ende
322	F 76.1	Gott sei gelobet und gebenedeiet
323	F 140.1	Gott sei uns gnädig
325	F 79.1	Heilig, heilig
326	F 105.1	Herr Gott, dich loben alle wir
328	F 83.1	Herr Gott, dich loben wir
329	F 134.1	Herr, ich denk' an jene Zeit
330	F 84.1	Herr, ich habe missgehandelt
331	F 84.2	Herr, ich habe missgehandelt
332	F 85.1	Herr Jesu Christ, dich zu uns wend'
333	F 86.1	Herr Jesu Christ, du hast bereit't
334	F 202.1	Herr Jesu Christ, du höchstes Gut
335	F 170.1	Herr Jesu Christ, mein's Lebens Licht
336	F 88.1	Herr Jesu Christ, wah'r Mensch und Gott
337	F 89.1	Herr, nun lass in Friede
338	F 90.1	Herr, straf mich nicht in deinem Zorn
339	F 23.1	Herr, wie du willst, so schick's mit mir
340	F 91.1	Herzlich lieb hab ich dich, o Herr
341	F 94.1A	Heut' ist, o Mensch, ein grosser Trauertag
342	F 95.1	Heut' triumphieret Gottes Sohn
343	F 96.1	Hilf, Gott, lass mir's gelinge
344	F 97.1	Hilf, Herr Jesu, lass gelingen
345	F 99.1	Ich bin ja, Herr, in deiner Macht
346	F 100.1	Ich dank' dir, Gott für all' Wohltat
347	F 101.1	Ich dank' dir, lieber Herre
348	F 101.2	Ich dank' dir, lieber Herre
349	F 4.1	Ich dank' dir schon durch deinen Sohn
350	F 139.1	Ich danke dir, o Gott, in deinem Throne
351	F 102.1	Ich hab' mein' Sach' Gott heimgestellt
366	F 104.1	Ihr Gestirn', ihr hohlen Lüfte
367	F 107.1	In allen meinen Taten
368	F 110.1	In dulci jubilo
352	F 187.1	Jesu, der du meine Seele
353	F 187.2	Jesu, der du meine Seele
354	F 187.3	Jesu, der du meine Seele
355	F 112.1	Jesu, der du selbsten wohl
356	F 113.1	Jesu, du mein liebstes Leben
357	F 114.1	Jesu, Jesu, du bist mein
358	F 116.1	Jesu, meine Freude
359	F 206.1	Jesu meiner Seelen Wonne
360	F 206.2	Jesu meiner Seelen Wonne
361	F 117.1	Jesu, meines Herzens Freud'
362	F 118.1	Jesu, nun sei gepreiset
363	F 121.1	Jesus Christus, unser Heiland
364	F 120.1	Jesus Christus, unser Heiland
365	F 123.1	Jesus, meine Zuversicht
369	F 124.1	Keinen hat Gott verlassen
370	F 125.1	Komm, Gott Schöpfer, heiliger Geist
371	F 129.1	Kyrie, Gott Vater in Ewigkeit
372	F 82.1	Lass, o Herr, dein Ohr sich neigen
373	F 133.1	Liebster Jesu, wir sind hier
374	F 135.1	Lobet den Herren, denn er ist freundlich
375	F 127.1	Lobt Gott, ihr Christen, allzugleich
376	F 128.1	Lobt Gott, ihr Christen, allzugleich
377	F 137.1	Mach's mit mir, Gott, nach deiner Güt'
378	F 138.1	Meine Augen schliess' ich jetzt
379	F 122.1	Meinen Jesum lass' ich nicht, Jesus
380	F 141.1	Meinen Jesum lass' ich nicht, weil
324	F 140.1	Meine Seele erhebet den Herrn
381	F 142.1	Meines Lebens letzte Zeit

BWV	BC	
382	F 144.1	Mit Fried' und Freud' ich fahr' dahin
383	F 145.1	Mitten wir im Leben sind
384	F 146.1	Nicht so traurig, nicht so sehr
385	F 147.1	Nun bitten wir den heiligen Geist
386	F 148.1	Nun danket alle Gott
387	F 106.1	Nun freut euch, Gottes Kinder all'
388	F 149.1	Nun freut euch, lieben Christen g'mein
389	F 153.1	Nun lob', mein' Seel', den Herren
390	F 153.2	Nun lob', mein' Seel', den Herren
391	F 154.1	Nun preiset alle Gottes Barmherzigkeit
392	F 166.1	Nun ruhen alle Wälder
396	F 155.1	Nun sich der Tag geendet hat
397	F 156.1	O Ewigkeit, du Donnerwort
398	F 45.2b	O Gott, du frommer Gott
399	F 157.1	O Gott, du frommer Gott
400	F 160.1	O Herzensangst, o Bangigkeit und Zagen!
401	F 162.1	O Lamm Gottes, unschuldig
402	F 61.1	O Mensch, bewein' dein' Sünde gross
403	F 163.1	O Mensch, schau Jesum Christum an
404	F 165.1	O Traurigkeit, o Herzeleid!
393	F 166.2	O Welt, sieh hier dein Leben
394	F 166.5	O Welt, sieh hier dein Leben
395	F 166.9	O Welt, sieh hier dein Leben
405	F 167.1	O wie selig seid ihr doch, ihr Frommen
406	F 7.1	O wie selig seid ihr doch, ihr Frommen
407	F 168.1	O wir armen Sünder
408	F 94.1B	Schaut, ihr Sünder!
409	F 173.1	Seelen-Bräutigam
410	F 174.1	Sei gegrüsset, Jesu gütig
411	F 175.1	Singet dem Herrn ein neues Lied
412	F 177.1	So gibst du nun, mein Jesu, gute Nacht
413	F 130.1	Sollt' ich meinem Gott nicht singen
414	F 35.2	Uns ist ein Kindlein heut' gebor'n
415	F 18.1	Valet will ich dir geben
416	F 181.4a	Vater unser im Himmelreich
417	F 185.1	Von Gott will ich nicht lassen
418	F 185.2	Von Gott will ich nicht lassen
419	F 185.3	Von Gott will ich nicht lassen
257	F 212.2	Wär Gott nicht mit uns diese Zeit
420	F 189.1	Warum betrübst du dich, mein Herz
421	F 189.2	Warum betrübst du dich, mein Herz
422	F 190.1	Warum sollt' ich mich denn grämen
423	F 191.1	Was betrübst du dich, mein Herze
424	F 192.1	Was bist du doch, o Seele, so betrübet
425	F 195.1	Was willst du dich, o meine Seele
426	F 197.1	Weltlich Ehr' und zeitlich Gut
427	F 200.1	Wenn ich in Angst und Not
428	F 201.1	Wenn mein Stündlein vorhanden ist
429	F 201.2	Wenn mein Stündlein vorhanden ist
430	F 201.3	Wenn mein Stündlein vorhanden ist
431	F 203.1	Wenn wir in höchsten Nöten sein
432	F 203.2	Wenn wir in höchsten Nöten sein
433	F 204.1	Wer Gott vertraut, hat wohl gebaut
434	F 205.1	Wer nur den lieben Gott lässt walten
435	F 207.1	Wie bist du, Seele, in mir so gar betrübt
436	F 109.1	Wie schön leuchtet der Morgenstern

BWV	BC	
437	F 211.1	Wir glauben all' an einen Gott
258	F 212.3	Wo Gott der Herr nicht bei uns hält
438	F 213.1	Wo Gott zum Haus nicht gibt sein' Gunst
		Sacred songs, 1v, bc, in G.C. Schemelli: Musicalisches Gesang-Buch (Leipzig, 1736) [Bach was involved in the production of Schemelli's hymnal, but research has discredited the methods by which these items were attrib. him; only bc by Bach unless otherwise stated]; BG xxxix, 279; NBA III/ii.1, 104
439	F 274	Ach, dass nicht die letzte Stunde
440	F 229	Auf, auf! die rechte Zeit ist hier [? melody by Bach]
441	F 245	Auf, auf! mein Herz, mit Freuden
442	F 257	Beglückter Stand getreuer Seelen
443	F 265	Beschränkt, ihr Weisen dieser Welt [? melody by Bach]
444	F 242	Brich entzwei, mein armes Herze
445	F 247	Brunnquell aller Güter
446	F 220	Der lieben Sonnen Licht und Pracht
447	F 221	Der Tag ist hin, die Sonne gehet nieder
448	F 222	Der Tag mit seinem Lichte
449	F 249	Dich bet'ich an, mein höchster Gott [? melody by Bach]
450	F 235	Die bittre Leidenszeit beginnet abermal
451	F 219	Die goldne Sonne, voll Freud' und Wonne
452	F 250	Dir, dir Jehovah, will ich singen [melody by Bach]
453	F 225	Eins ist Noth! ach Herr, diess Eine [? melody by Bach]
454	F 230	Ermuntre dich, mein schwacher Geist
455	F 261	Erwürgtes Lamm, das die verwahrten Siegel
456	F 258	Es glänzet der Christen
457	F 275	Es ist nun aus mit meinem Leben
458	F 243	Es ist vollbracht! vergiss ja nicht
459	F 256	Es kostet viel, ein Christ zu sein
460	F 263	Gieb dich zufrieden und sei stille
461	F 255	Gott lebet noch; Seele, was verzagst du doch?
462	F 248	Gott, wie gross ist deine Güte [? melody by Bach]
463	F 223	Herr, nicht schicke deine Rache
464	F 276	Ich bin ja, Herr, in deiner Macht
465	F 231	Ich freue mich in dir
466	F 264	Ich halte treulich still und liebe [? melody by Bach]
467	F 269	Ich lass' dich nicht
468	F 270	Ich liebe Jesum alle Stund' [? melody by Bach]
469	F 232	Ich steh' an deiner Krippen hier [? melody by Bach]
476	F 233	Ihr Gestirn', ihr hohen Lüfte
471	F 228	Jesu, deine Liebeswunden [? melody by Bach]
470	F 271	Jesu, Jesu, du bist mein [? melody by Bach]
472	F 226	Jesu, meines Glaubens Zier
473	F 266	Jesu, meines Herzens Freud'
474	F 251	Jesus ist das schönste Licht
475	F 246	Jesus unser Trost und Leben
477	F 278	Kein Stündlein geht dahin
478	F 277	Komm, süsser Tod, komm, sel'ge Ruh'! [? melody by Bach]
479	F 285	Kommt, Seelen, dieser Tag [? melody by Bach]
480	F 286	Kommt wieder aus der finstern Gruft [? melody by Bach]
481	F 236	Lasset uns mit Jesu ziehen
482	F 252	Liebes Herz, bedenke doch
483	F 279	Liebster Gott, wann werd' ich sterben
484	F 280	Liebster Herr Jesu! wo bleibest du so lange? [? melody by Bach]
485	F 272	Liebster Immanuel, Herzog der Frommen
488	F 281	Meines Lebens letzte Zeit
486	F 227	Mein Jesu, dem die Seraphinen
487	F 237	Mein Jesu! was für Seelenweh [? melody by Bach]
489	F 259	Nicht so traurig, nicht so sehr
490	F 267	Nur mein Jesus ist mein Leben
491	F 238	O du Liebe meine Liebe
492	F 282	O finstre Nacht [? melody by Bach]
493	F 234	O Jesulein süss, o Jesulein mild
494	F 260	O liebe Seele, zieh' die Sinnen [? melody by Bach]
495	F 283	O wie selig seid ihr doch, ihr Frommen
496	F 253	Seelen-Bräutigam, Jesu, Gottes Lamm!
497	F 268	Seelenweide, meine Freude
499	F 240	Sei gegrüsset, Jesu gütig
498	F 239	Selig, wer an Jesum denkt [? melody by Bach]
500	F 241	So gehst du nun, mein Jesu, hin [? melody by Bach]
501	F 244	So giebst du nun, mein Jesu, gute Nacht
502	F 284	So wünsch' ich mir zu guter Letzt
503	F 287	Steh' ich bei meinem Gott
504	F 254	Vergiss mein nicht, dass ich dein nicht
505	F 262	Vergiss mein nicht, vergiss mein nicht [melody by Bach]
506	F 273	Was bist du doch, o Seele, so betrübet
507		Wo ist mein Schäflein, das ich liebe
		Pieces in Clavierbüchlein, ii, for Anna Magdalena Bach; BG xxxix, 289; NBA V/iv, 91:
511	F 214a	Gib dich zufrieden, chorale, g
512	F 214b	Gib dich zufrieden, chorale, e (arr. of 511)
513	F 218	O Ewigkeit, du Donnerwort, chorale [from 397]
514	F 216	Schaffs mit mir, Gott, chorale
516	F 215	Warum betrübst du dich, aria
524	H 1	Quodlibet, SATB, bc, frag., for wedding, Mühlhausen, by mid-1708
A40		Murky: Ihr Schönen, höret an, S, bc, before 1736

Doubtful

		Pieces in Clavierbüchlein, ii, for Anna Magdalena Bach; BG xxxix, 309; NBA V/iv, 102:
508		Bist du bei mir, aria (by G.H. Stölzel)
509		Gedenke doch, mein Geist, aria (anon.)
510		Gib dich zufrieden, chorale, F (anon. bass added)
†515	H 2	So oft ich meine Tobackspfeife, aria (anon., ? by Gottfried Heinrich Bach, ? arr. J.S. Bach)
517		Wie wohl ist mir, o Freund der Seelen (anon.)

BWV	BC		Remarks				BWV	BC	

BWV	BC						BWV	BC	
		Sacred songs, 5 for 1v, bc (probably spurious); NBA [III/iii]:					521		Gott mein Herz dir Dank zusendet
519		Hier lieg' ich nun					522		Meine Seele, lass es gehen
520		Das walt' mein Gott					523		Ich gnüge mich an meinem Stande

ORGAN

independent of chorales

BWV	BC	Title	Remarks	BG	NBA
131a	J 62	Fugue, g	arr. from 131	xxxviii, 217	—
525–30	J 1–6	6 sonatas (E♭, c, d, e, C, G)	c1730; no.3: cf 1044; no.4 arr. from 76	xv, 3–66	IV/vii, 2–76
531	J 9	Prelude and fugue, C	? before 1705	xv, 81	IV/v, 3
†532	J 13, 54, 70	Prelude and fugue, D	? before 1710	xv, 88	IV/v, 58; IV/vi, 95
†533	J 18, 72	Prelude and fugue, e	? before 1705	xv, 100	IV/v, 90; IV/vi, 106
534	J 20	Prelude and fugue, f	? before 1710	xv, 104	IV/v, 130
†535	J 23	Prelude and fugue, g	? before 1705; rev. ?1708–17	xv, 112	IV/v, 157; IV/vi, 109
536	J 24	Prelude and fugue, A	?1708–17	xv, 120	IV/v, 180; IV/vi, 114
537	J 40	Fantasia and fugue, c	? after 1723	xv, 129	IV/v, 47
538	J 38	Toccata and fugue, 'Dorian', d	?1712–17	xv, 136	IV/v, 76
†539	J 15, 71	Prelude and fugue, d	? after 1720; fugue adapted from vn sonata, 1001	xv, 148	IV/v, 70
†540	J 39, 55, 73	Toccata and fugue, F	toccata ? after 1712; fugue before 1731	xv, 154	IV/v, 112
†541	J 22	Prelude and fugue, G	? after 1712; rev. c1724–5	xv, 169	IV/v, 146
†542	J 42, 57, 67	Fantasia and fugue, g	fugue: before 1725; fantasia: c1720	xv, 177	IV/v, 167
†543	J 26	Prelude and fugue, a	after 1715; fugue: cf 944	xv, 189	IV/v, 186; IV/vi, 121
544	J 27	Prelude and fugue, b	1727–31	xv, 199	IV/v, 198
†545	J 10, 51	Prelude and fugue, C	? before 1708; rev. ?1712–17	xv, 212	IV/v, 10; IV/vi, 77
†546	J 12, 53, 69	Prelude and fugue, c	?1723–9	xv, 218	IV/v, 35
547	J 11	Prelude and fugue, C	? by 1725	xv, 228	IV/vi, 20
548	J 19	Prelude and fugue, e	rev. 1727–31	xv, 236	IV/v, 95
†549	J 14	Prelude and fugue, c/d	before 1705; rev. ? after 1723	xxxviii, 3	IV/v, 30; IV/vi, 101
550	J 21	Prelude and fugue, G	? before 1710	xxxviii, 9	IV/v, 138
551	J 25	Prelude and fugue, a	? before 1707	xxxviii, 17	IV/vi, 63
552	J 16	Prelude and fugue, 'St Anne', E♭	in Clavier-Übung, iii, (Leipzig, 1739), see 669–89	iii, 173, 254	IV/vi, 2, 105
553–60	J 28–35	[8 short preludes and fugues] (C, d, e, F, G, g, a, B♭)		xxxviii, 23	[IV/ix]
†562	J 41, 56	Fantasia and fugue, c	fantasia: c1730; fugue (inc.) c1740–45	xxxviii, 64, 209	IV/v, 54, 105
563	J 43	Fantasia, b	before 1708	xxxviii, 59	IV/vi, 68
564	J 36	Toccata, adagio and fugue, C	?c1712	xv, 253	IV/vi, 3
565	J 37	Toccata and fugue, d	? before 1708	xv, 267	IV/vi, 31
†566	J 17	Prelude and fugue, E/C	? before 1708	xv, 276	IV/vi, 40
568	J 47	Prelude, G	? before 1705	xxxviii, 85	IV/vi, 51
569	J 48	Prelude, a	? before 1705	xxxviii, 89	IV/vi, 59
570	J 49	Fantasia, C	? before 1705	xxxviii, 62	IV/vi, 16
571	J 82	Fantasia, G		xxxviii, 67	—
572	J 83	Pièce d'orgue, G	? before 1712	xxxviii, 75	IV/vii, 130, 154, 156
573	J 50	Fantasia, C	c1722; frag. in Clavierbüchlein, i, for Anna Magdalena Bach	xxxviii, 209	IV/vi, 18
†574	J 63	Fugue on theme by Legrenzi, c	? before 1708	xxxviii, 94, 205	IV/vi, 19, 82, 88
575	J 60	Fugue, c	? 1708–17	xxxviii, 101	IV/vi, 26
577	J 61	Fugue, G		xxxviii, 111	—
578	J 66	Fugue, g	? before 1707	xxxviii, 116	IV/vi, 55
579	J 68	Fugue on theme by Corelli, b	? before 1710	xxxviii, 121	IV/vi, 71
†582	J 79	Passacaglia, c	?1708–12	xv, 289	IV/vii, 98, 148
583	J 8	Trio, d	?1723–9	xxxviii, 143	IV/vii, 94
588	J 80	Canzona, d	? before 1705	xxxviii, 126	IV/vii, 118, 150
589	J 64	Alla breve, D		xxxvii, 131	IV/vii, 114
590	J 81	Pastorella, F	? after 1720	xxxviii, 135	IV/vii, 122
591	J 78	Kleine harmonisches Labyrinth		xxxviii, 225	[IV/ix]
		5 concertos:	Weimar, c1714; arrs. of works by other composers		

BWV	BC	Title	Remarks	BG	NBA
†592	J 88, 192	G	arr. of conc. by Prince Johann Ernst of Saxe-Weimar	xxxviii, 149; xlii, 282	IV/viii, 56
593	J 86	a	arr. of Vivaldi op.3 no.8 = RV522	xxxviii, 158	IV/viii
594	J 84	C	arr. of Vivaldi op.7/ii no.5 = RV208	xxxviii, 171	IV/viii, 30
595	J 87	C	arr. of conc. by Prince Johann Ernst of Saxe-Weimar	xxxviii, 196	IV/viii, 65
596	J 85	d	arr. of Vivaldi op.3 no.11 = RV565	—	IV/viii, 3
802–5	J 74–7	4 duettos (e, F, G, a)	in Clavier-Übung, iii (Leipzig, 1739); see also 552, 669–89	iii, 242	IV/vi, 92
1027a		Trio, G	transcr. from last movt of va da gamba sonata, 1027	—	—
A205		Fantasia, c	before 1705	—	—

Doubtful and spurious

BWV	BC	Title	Remarks	BG	NBA
536a		Prelude and fugue, A	variant of 536	—	IV/vi
561		Fantasia and fugue, a	spurious	xxxviii, 48	—
567		Prelude, C	by J.L. Krebs	xxxviii, 84	—
576		Fugue, G	spurious	xxxviii, 106	—
580	J 65	Fugue, D	spurious	xxxviii, 215	—
581		Fugue, G	spurious	—	—
584		Trio, g	probably spurious	—	—
585		Trio, c	by J.F. Fasch	xxxviii, 219	IV/viii, 73
586		Trio, G	after Telemann	—	IV/viii, 78
587		Aria, F	after Couperin: Les nations	xxxviii, 222	IV/viii, 82
597		Concerto, E♭		—	[IV]
598	Q 2	Pedal-Exercitium	? by C.P.E. Bach	xxxviii, 210	[IV/vii]

based on chorales: Orgel-Büchlein

BWV	BC	Title
599–644		Das Orgel-Büchlein, mostly 1713–15; BG xxv/2, 3, 159; NBA IV/i, 3
599	K 28	Nun komm' der Heiden Heiland
600	K 29	Gott, durch deine Güte
†601	K 30	Herr Christ, der ein'ge Gottes-Sohn
602	K 31	Lob sei dem allmächtigen Gott
603	K 32	Puer natus in Bethlehem
604	K 33	Gelobet seist du, Jesu Christ
605	K 34	Der Tag, der ist so freudenreich
606	K 35	Vom Himmel hoch, da komm' ich her
607	K 36	Vom Himmel kam der Engel Schar
608	K 37	In dulci jubilo
609	K 38	Lobt Gott, ihr Christen, allzugleich
610	K 39	Jesu, meine Freude
611	K 40	Christum wir sollen loben schon
612	K 41	Wir Christenleut'
613	K 42	Helft mir Gottes Güte preisen
†614	K 43	Das alte Jahr vergangen ist
615	K 44	In dir ist Freude
616	K 45	Mit Fried' und Freud' ich fahr dahin
617	K 46	Herr Gott, nun schleuss den Himmel auf
618	K 47	O Lamm Gottes unschuldig
619	K 48	Christe, du Lamm Gottes
†620	K 49	Christus, der uns selig macht
621	K 50	Da Jesus an dem Kreuze stund'
622	K 51	O Mensch, bewein' dein' Sünde gross
623	K 52	Wir danken dir, Herr Jesu Christ
624	K 53	Hilf Gott, das mir's gelinge
625	K 55	Christ lag in Todesbanden
626	K 56	Jesus Christus, unser Heiland
627	K 57	Christ ist erstanden
628	K 58	Erstanden ist der heil'ge Christ
629	K 59	Erschienen ist der herrliche Tag
†630	K 60	Heut' triumphieret Gottes Sohn
†631	K 61	Komm, Gott Schöpfer, heilger Geist
632	K 62	Herr Jesu Christ, dich zu uns wend'
634	K 63a	Liebster Jesu, wir sind hier
633	K 63b	Liebster Jesu, wir sind hier
635	K 64	Dies sind die heil'gen zehn Gebot'
636	K 65	Vater unser im Himmelreich
637	K 66	Durch Adam's Fall ist ganz verderbt
†638	K 67	Es ist das Heil uns kommen her
†639	K 68	Ich ruf' zu dir, Herr Jesu Christ
640	K 69	Ich dich hab' ich gehoffet, Herr
641	K 70	Wenn wir in höchsten Nöten sein
642	K 71	Wer nun den lieben Gott lässt walten
643	K 72	Alle Menschen müssen sterben
644	K 73	Ach wie nichtig, ach wie flüchtig
A200	K 54	O Traurigkeit, o Herzeleid (frag.)

based on chorales: other

BWV	BC	Title	Remarks	BG	NBA
		Sechs Choräle ['Schübler' chorales]:	(Zella, 1748–9), transcrs. of cant. movts pubd by Schübler		
645	K 22	Wachet auf, ruft uns die Stimme	from 140, movt 4	xxv/2, 63	IV/i, 86
646	K 23	Wo soll ich fliehen hin	source unknown; cf 694	xxv/2, 66	IV/i, 90
647	K 24	Wer nur den lieben Gott lässt walten	from 93, movt 4	xxv/2, 68	IV/i, 92
648	K 25	Meine Seele erhebt den Herren	from 10, movt 5	xxv/2, 70	IV/i, 94
649	K 26	Ach bleib' bei uns, Herr Jesu Christ	from 6, movt 3	xxv/2, 71	IV/i, 95
650	K 27	Kommst du nun, Jesu, vom Himmel herunter	from 137, movt 2	xxv/2, 74	IV/i, 98
		[17 (18) chorales]:	all probably begun before 1723, and all but 657 also preserved in an early version; 651–65 assembled as an autograph collection, c1735–45, D-Bsb P271; for 2 manuals, pedal		
†651	K 74	Fantasia super Komm, Heiliger Geist	organo pleno; c.f. in pedal; cf 651a	xxv/2, 79	IV/ii, 3, 117
†652	K 75	Komm, Heiliger Geist	alio modo; cf 652a	xxv/2, 86	IV/ii, 13, 121
†653	K 76	An Wasserflüssen Babylon	cf 653a and 653b	xxv/2, 92	IV/ii, 22, 130, 133
†654	K 77	Schmücke dich, o liebe Seele	cf 654a	xxv/2, 95	IV/ii, 26, 136
†655	K 78	Trio super Herr Jesu Christ, dich zu uns wend	cf 655a	xxv/2, 98	IV/ii, 31, 140
†656	K 79	O Lamm Gottes, unschuldig	cf 656a	xxv/2, 102	IV/ii, 38, 146
657	K 80	Nun danket alle Gott	c.f. in soprano; see above	xxv/2, 108	IV/ii, 46
†658	K 81	Von Gott will ich nicht lassen	c.f. in pedal; cf 658a	xxv/2, 112	IV/ii, 51, 154
†659	K 82	Nun komm, der Heiden Heiland	cf 659a	xxv/2, 114	IV/ii, 55, 157
†660	K 83	Trio super Nun komm, der Heiden Heiland	cf 660a and 660b	xxv/2, 116	IV/ii, 59, 160
661	K 84	Nun komm, der Heiden Heiland	organo pleno; c.f. in pedal, cf 661a	xxv/2, 118	IV/ii, 62, 164
†662	K 85	Allein Gott in der Höh sei Ehr	c.f. in soprano; cf 662a	xxv/2, 122	IV/ii, 67, 168
†663	K 86	Allein Gott in der Höh sei Ehr	c.f. in tenor; cf 663a	xxv/2, 125	IV/ii, 72, 172
†664	K 87	Trio super Allein Gott in der Höh sei Ehr	cf 664a	xxv/2, 130	IV/ii, 79, 179
†665	K 88	Jesus Christus, unser Heiland	cf 665; Bach's last autograph entry in Bsb P271	xxv/2, 136	IV/ii, 87, 187
†666	K 89	Jesus Christus, unser Heiland	alio modo; cf 666a; copied into Bsb P271 by J.C. Altnickol, c1744–7	xxv/2, 140	IV/ii, 91, 191
†667	K 90	Komm, Gott, Schöpfer, Heiliger Geist	organo pleno; cf 631; copied into Bsb P271 by Altnickol	xxv/2, 142	IV/ii, 94; IV/i, 58
†668	K 91	Vor deinen Thron tret ich hiermit	partly in Bsb P271, copied ? after 1750; with minor variants, 668a, pubd as Wenn wir in höchsten Nöten sein in 1080; cf 641	xxv/2, 145	IV/ii, 113, 212; IV/i, 71
		Chorale preludes in Clavier-Übung, iii, bestehend in verschiedenen Vorspielen über die Cathechismus- und andere Gesaenge	(Leipzig, 1739); framed by 552; for 2 kbd, pedal unless otherwise stated		
669	K 1	Kyrie, Gott Vater in Ewigkeit	c.f. in soprano	iii, 184	IV/iv, 16
670	K 2	Christe, aller Welt Trost	c.f. in tenor	iii, 186	IV/iv, 18
671	K 3	Kyrie, Gott heiliger Geist	a 5, organo pleno; c.f. in bass	iii, 190	IV/iv, 22
672	K 4	Kyrie, Gott Vater in Ewigkeit	alio modo, manuals only	iii, 194	IV/iv, 27
673	K 5	Christe, aller Welt Trost	manuals only	iii, 194	IV/iv, 28
674	K 6	Kyrie, Gott heiliger Geist	manuals only	iii, 196	IV/iv, 29
675	K 7	Allein Gott in der Höh sei Ehr	a 3; c.f. in alto; manuals only	iii, 197	IV/iv, 33
†676	K 8	Allein Gott in der Höh sei Ehr		iii, 199	IV/iv, 33
677	K 9	Fughetta super Allein Gott in der Höh sei Ehr	manuals only	iii, 205	IV/iv, 41

BWV	BC	Title	Remarks	BG	NBA
678	K 10	Dies sind die heilgen zehen Gebot	c.f. in canon	iii, 206	IV/iv, 42
679	K 11	Fughetta super Dies sind die heiligen zehen Gebot	manuals only	iii, 210	IV/iv, 49
680	K 12	Wir gläuben all an einen Gott	organo pleno	iii, 212	IV/iv, 52
681	K 13	Fughetta super Wir gläuben all an einen Gott	manuals only	iii, 216	IV/iv, 57
682	K 14	Vater unser im Himmelreich	c.f. in canon	iii, 217	IV/iv, 58
683	K 15	Vater unser im Himmelreich	alio modo, manuals only	iii, 223	IV/iv, 66
684	K 16	Christ, unser Herr, zum Jordan kam	c.f. in pedal	iii, 224	IV/iv, 68
685	K 17	Christ, unser Herr, zum Jordan kam	alio modo, manuals only	iii, 228	IV/iv, 73
686	K 18	Aus tiefer Not schrei ich zu dir	a 6, organo pleno, pedal doppio	iii, 229	IV/iv, 74
687	K 19	Aus tiefer Not schrei ich zu dir	a 4, alio modo, manuals only	iii, 232	IV/iv, 78
688	K 20	Jesus Christus, unser Heiland, der von uns den Zorn Gottes wandt	c.f. in pedal	iii, 234	IV/iv, 81
689	K 21	Fuga super Jesus Christus unser Heiland	a 4, manuals only	iii, 239	IV/iv, 89
690	K 127	Wer nur den lieben Gott lässt walten	manuals only; ? before 1705	xl, 3	IV/iii, 98
691	K 99	Wer nur den lieben Gott lässt walten	manuals only; autograph in Clavier-Büchlein for W.F. Bach; c1720–23	xl, 4	IV/iii, 98
694	K 139	Wo soll ich fliehen hin	2 kbd, pedal; before 1708; cf 646	xl, 6	IV/iii, 103
695	K 136	Fantasia super Christ lag in Todes Banden	manuals only; ? before 1708	xl, 10	IV/iii, 20
696	K 142	Christum wir sollen loben schon	fughetta, manuals only; ?1739–42	xl, 13	IV/iii, 23
697	K 147	Gelobet seist du, Jesu Christ	fughetta, manuals only; ?1739–42	xl, 14	IV/iii, 32
698	K 149	Herr Christ, der einig Gottes Sohn	fughetta, manuals only; ?1739–42	xl, 15	IV/iii, 35
699	K 155	Nun komm, der Heiden Heiland	fughetta, manuals only; ?1739–42	xl, 16	IV/iii, 73
700	K 156	Vom Himmel hoch, da komm ich her	before 1708, rev. 1740s	xl, 17	IV/iii, 92
701	K 157	Vom Himmel hoch, da komm ich her	fughetta, manuals only; ?1739–42	xl, 19	IV/iii, 96
702	K 143	Das Jesulein soll doch mein Trost	fughetta	xl, 20	[IV/ix]
703	K 148	Gottes Sohn ist kommen	fughetta, manuals only; ?1739–42	xl, 21	IV/iii, 34
704	K 153	Lob sei dem allmächtigen Gott	fughetta, manuals only; ? 1739–42	xl, 22	IV/iii, 62
705	K 144	Durch Adams Fall ist ganz verderbt		xl, 23	[IV/ix]
706	K 116	Liebster Jesu, wir sind hier	?1708–14; cf 706ii [alio modo]	xl, 25	IV/iii, 59
707	K 137	Ich hab mein Sach Gott heimgestellt		xl, 26	[IV/ix]
708	K 158	Ich hab mein Sach Gott heimgestellt		xl, 30, 152	[IV/ix]
709	K 150	Herr Jesu Christ, dich zu uns wend	2 kbd, pedal; ?Weimar, 1708–17	xl, 30	IV/iii, 43
711	K 140	Allein Gott in der Höh sei Ehr	bicinium; ?1708–17; rev. 1740s	xl, 34	IV/iii, 11
712	K 151	In dich hab ich gehoffet, Herr	manuals only	xl, 36	IV/iii, 48
713	K 138	Fantasia super Jesu, meine Freude	manuals only	xl, 38	IV/iii, 54
714	K 172	Ach Gott und Herr	per canonem	xl, 43	IV/iii, 3
715	K 128	Allein Gott in der Höh sei Ehr		xl, 44	IV/iii, 14
716	K 141	Fuga super Allein Gott in der Höh sei Ehr		xl, 45	[IV/ix]
717	K 106	Allein Gott in der Höh sei Ehr	manuals only	xl, 47	IV/iii, 8
718	K 119	Christ lag in Todes Banden	2 kbd, pedal	xl, 52	IV/iii, 16
719	K 160	Der Tag, der ist so freudenreich		xl, 55	[IV/ix]
720	K 103	Ein feste Burg ist unser Gott		xl, 57	IV/iii, 24
721	K 107	Erbarm dich mein, o Herre Gott	manuals only	xl, 60	IV/iii, 28
†722	K 114	Gelobet seist du, Jesu Christ		xl, 62, 158	IV/iii, 30–31

BWV	BC	Title	Remarks	BG	NBA
724	K 108	Gott, durch deine Güte (Gottes Sohn ist kommen)	before 1705; alternative title in BWV, BG	xl, 65	IV/iii, 33
725	K 199	Herr Gott, dich loben wir	a 5	xl, 66	IV/iii, 36
726	K 130	Herr Jesu Christ, dich zu uns wend		xl, 72	IV/iii, 45
727	K 109	Herzlich tut mich verlangen	2 kbd, pedal	xl, 73	IV/iii, 46
728	K 101	Jesus, meine Zuversicht	manuals only; autograph in Clavierbüchlein, i, for Anna Magdalena Bach	xl, 74	IV/iii, 58
†729	K 115	In dulci jubilo	sketch, 729a	xl, 74, 158	IV/iii, 52, 50
730	K 133	Liebster Jesu, wir sind hier		xl, 76	IV/iii, 60
731	K 134	Liebster Jesu, wir sind hier	2 kbd, pedal	xl, 77	IV/iii, 61
†732	K 117	Lobt Gott, ihr Christen, allzugleich	sketch, 732a	xl, 78, 159	IV/iii, 63–4
733	K 120	Meine Seele erhebet den Herren (Fuge über das Magnificat)	organo pleno	xl, 79	IV/iii, 65
†734	K 125	Nun freut euch, lieben Christen gmein	manuals only; c.f. in tenor; cf 734a	xl, 160	IV/iii, 70
†735	K 104	Fantasia super Valet will ich dir geben	with pedal obbl; Weimar, 1708–17, rev. ? after 1723	xl, 86, 161	IV/iii, 77, 81
736	K 131	Valet will ich dir geben	c.f. in pedal	xl, 90	IV/iii, 84
737	K 112	Vater unser im Himmelreich	manuals only	xl, 96	IV/iii, 90
†738	K 118	Vom Himmel hoch, da komm ich her	sketch, 738a	xl, 97, 159	IV/iii, 94
739	K 97	Wie schön leuchtet der Morgenstern	? before 1705	xl, 99	[IV/x]
741	K 135	Ach Gott vom Himmel sieh darein	organo pleno	xl, 167	IV/iii, 4
742	K 173	Ach Herr, mich armen Sünder		—	[IV/ix]
743	K 121	Ach, was ist doch unser Leben		—	—
744	K 122	Auf meinen lieben Gott		xl, 170	—
747	K 102	Christus, der uns selig macht		—	—
749	K 195	Herr Jesu Christ, dich zu uns wend	? before 1700	—	—
750	K 196	Herr Jesu Christ, meins Lebens Licht	? before 1700	—	—
753	K 124	Jesu, meine Freude	frag.; ? before 1723	xl, 163	V/v
754		Liebster Jesu, wir sind hier		—	—
756	K 197	Nun ruhen alle Wälder	? before 1700	—	—
757	K 126	O Herre Gott, dein göttlichs Wort		—	—
758	K 198	O Vater, allmächtiger Gott		xl, 179	—
762	K 113	Vater unser im Himmelreich		—	—
764	K 98	Wie schön leuchtet uns der Morgenstern	frag.; ? before 1705	xl, 164	[IV/x]
765	K 105	Wir glauben all' an einen Gott		—	—
†1085	K 110, 111	O Lamm Gottes, unschuldig	manuals only	—	IV/iii, 74
A49		Ein feste Burg ist unser Gott		—	—
A50		Erhalt uns, Herr, bei deinem Wort		—	—
A58		Jesu, meine Freude		—	—
A75		Herr Christ, der einig Gottes Sohn		—	—
A76		Jesu, meine Freude		—	—
		Partite diverse:			
766	K 94	Christ, der du bist der helle Tag	c1700	xl, 107	IV/i, 113
767		O Gott, du frommer Gott	K 95	xl, 114	IV/i, 122
†768	K 96	Sei gegrüsset, Jesu gütig	? before 1710, rev. later	xl, 122	IV/i, 132
770	K 93	Ach, was soll ich Sünder machen		xl, 189	—
		Neumeister Chorales	before 1705; in MS belonging to J.G. Neumeister, incl. also 601, 639, 714, 719, 737, 742	—	IV/ix
1090	K 161	Wir Christenleut			
1091	K 162	Das alte Jahr vergangen ist			
1092	K 163	Herr Gott, nun schleuss den Himmel auf			
1093	K 164	Herzliebster, Jesu, was hast du verbrochen			

BWV	BC	Title	Remarks	BG	NBA
1094	K 165	O Jesu, wie ist dein Gestalt			
1095	K 166	O Lamm Gottes unschuldig			
1096	K 167	Christe, der du bist Tag und Licht			
1097	K 168	Ehre sei dir, Christe			
1098	K 169	Wir glauben all an einen Gott			
1099	K 170	Aus tiefer Not schrei ich zu dir			
1100	K 171	Allein zu dir, Herr Jesu Christ			
1101	K 174	Durch Adams Fall ist ganz verderbt			
1102	K 175	Du Friedefürst, Herr Jesu Christ			
1103	K 176	Erhalt uns, Herr, bei deinem Wort			
1104	K 177	Wenn dich Unglück tut greifen an			
1105	K 178	Jesu, meine Freude			
1106	K 179	Gott ist mein Heil, mein Hilf und Trost			
1107	K 180	Jesu, meines Lebens Leben			
†1108	K 181	Als Jesus Christus in der Nacht			
1109	K 182	Ach Gott, tu dich erbarmen			
1110	K 183	O Herre Gott, dein göttlich Wort			
1111	K 184	Nun lasst uns den Leib begraben			
1112	K 185	Christus, der ist mein Leben			
1113	K 186	Ich hab mein Sach Gott heimgestellt			
1114	K 187	Herr Jesu Christ, du höchstes Gut			
1115	K 188	Herzlieblich lieb hab ich dich, o Herr			
1116	K 189	Was Gott tut, das ist wohlgetan			
1117	K 190	Alle Menschen müssen sterben			
957	K 191	Machs mit mir, Gott, nach deiner Güt			
1118	K 192	Werde munter, mein Gemüte			
1119	K 193	Wie nach einer Wasserquelle			
1120	K 194	Christ, der du bist der helle Tag			

		Doubtful and spurious			
691a		Wer nur den lieben Gott lässt walten		xl, 151	[IV/x]
692		Ach Gott und Herr	by J.G. Walther	xl, 4, 152	—
693		Ach Gott und Herr	by J.G. Walther	xl, 5	—
695a		Fantasia super Christ lag in Todes Banden	c.f. in pedal	xl, 153	—
713a		Fantasia super Jesu, meine Freude	c.f. in pedal	xl, 155	—
723		Gelobet seist du, Jesu Christ		xl, 63	[IV/x]
734a		Nun freut euch, lieben Christen gmein	c.f. in pedal; *734; doubtful	xl, 84	—
740		Wir glauben all' an einen Gott, Vater		xl, 103	[IV/x]
745		Aus der Tiefe rufe ich	by C.P.E. Bach	xl, 171	—
746		Christ ist erstanden	by J.C.F. Fischer	xl, 173	—
748		Gott der Vater wohn' uns bei	by J.G. Walther	xl, 177	—
751		In dulci jubilo	by J.M. Bach	—	—
752		Jesu, der du meine Seele		—	—
755		Nun freut euch, lieben Christen		—	—
759		Schmücke dich, o liebe Seele	by G.A. Homilius	xl, 181	—
760		Vater unser im Himmelreich	by G. Böhm	xl, 183	—
761		Vater unser im Himmelreich	by Böhm	xl, 184	—
763		Wie schön leuchtet der Morgenstern		—	—
771		Allein Gott in der Höh sei Ehr'	chorale variations; nos.3, 8 (?all) by A.N. Vetter	xl, 195	—

OTHER KEYBOARD

BWV	BC	Title	Remarks	BG	NBA
†772–86	L 27–41	15 Inventions (C, c, D, d, Eb, E, e, F, f, G, g, A, a, Bb, b)	c1720, rev. 1723	iii, 1; xlv, 213	V/viii; V/v
†787–801	L 42–56	15 Sinfonias (C, c, D, d, Eb, E, e, F, f, G, g, A, a, Bb, b)	c1720, rev. 1723	iii, 19	V/viii; V/v
†806–11	L 13–18	6 [English] Suites (A, a, g, F, e, d)	? before 1720	xlv/1, 3	V/vii
†812–17	L 19–24	6 [French] Suites (d, c, b, Eb, G, E)	c1722–5	xlv/1, 89	V/viii
		Clavier-Übung [i] bestehend in Präludien, Allemanden, Couranten, Sarabanden, Giguen, Menuetten, und anderen Galanterien:	partitas pubd singly (Leipzig, 1726–31) and as op.1 (Leipzig, 1731)	iii, 46	V/i
825–30	L 1–6	6 Partitas (Bb, c, a, D, G, e)			
†831	L 8	Ouvertüre [Partita] nach französischer Art, b	in Clavier-Übung, ii (Leipzig, 1735); see also 971; early version by 1733	iii, 154	V/ii, 20
†846–69	L 80–103	Das wohltemperirte Clavier, oder Praeludia, und Fugen durch alle Tone und Semitonia [i] [The Well-tempered Clavier]: 24 Preludes and fugues (C, c, C♯, c♯, D, d, Eb, eb/d♯, E, e, F, f, F♯, f♯, G, g, Ab, g♯, A, a, Bb, bb, B, b)	1722, rev. later	xiv	V/vi.1
†870–93	L 104–27	[Das wohltemperirte Clavier, ii]: 24 Preludes and fugues (C, c, C♯, c♯, D, d, Eb, eb/d♯, E, e, F, f, F♯, f♯, G, g, Ab, g♯, A, a, Bb, bb, B, b)	c1740; some pieces earlier, rev.	xiv	V/iv.2
971	L 7	Concerto nach italiänischem Gusto [Italian Concerto]	in Clavier-Übung, ii, (Leipzig, 1735)	iii, 139	V/ii, 3
988	L 9	Aria mit [30] verschiedenen Veraenderungen [Goldberg Variations]	Clavier-Übung, [iv] (Nuremberg, 1741)	iii, 263	V/ii, 69
		Miscellaneous suites and suite movts:			
†818	L 25	Suite, a	c1705	xxxvi, 3	V/viii, 129, 146
†819	L 26	Suite, Eb	c1725	xxxvi, 8	V/viii, 136
820	L 173	Ouverture, F	c1705	xxxvi, 14	V/x, 43
821	L 169	Suite, Bb		xlii, 213	[V]
822	L 168	Suite, g	before 1707	—	V/x, 68
823	L 167	Suite, f	frag.; before 1715	xxxvi, 229	V/x, 50
†832	L 174	Partie, A	? before 1708	xlii, 255	V/x, 54
833	L 172	Prelude and partita, F	before 1708	—	V/10, 54
841–3	L 176	3 minuets, G, g, G	c1720; from Clavier-Büchlein for W.F. Bach	xxxvi, 209	V/v, 16
		Miscellaneous preludes, fugues, fantasias, toccatas:			
894	L 130	Prelude and fugue, a	c1715–25; cf 1044	xxxvi, 91	V/ix.2, 40
895	L 129	Prelude and fugue, a	before 1725	xxxvi, 104	V/xii.2, 69
896	L 128	Prelude and fugue, A	before 1710	xxxvi, 157 [fugue only]	V/ix.2, 72
900	L 77	Prelude and fughetta, e	before 1726	xxxvi, 108	[V/ix]
901	L 78	Prelude and fughetta, F	before 1730; fughetta = early version of 886	xxxvi, 112	[V/ix]
†902	L 79	Prelude and fughetta, G	? before 1730; fughetta = early version of 884	xxxvi, 114, 220	[V/ix]
†903	L 134	Chromatic fantasia and fugue, d	before 1723	xxxvi, 71, 219	V/ix.2, 76
904	L 136	Fantasia and fugue, a	Leipzig, c1725	xxxvi, 81	V/ix.2, 100
906	L 133, 138	Fantasia and fugue, c	fugue (c1704) inc.	xxxvi, 145, 238	V/ix.2, 110
910	L 146	Toccata, f♯	c1712	iii, 311	V/ix.2, 3
911	L 142	Toccata, c	before 1714	iii, 322	V/ix.1, 15
†912	L 143	Toccata, D	before 1710	xxxvi, 26, 218	V/ix.1, 28
†913	L 144	Toccata, d	? before 1708	xxxvi, 36	V/ix.1, 52
914	L 145, 163	Toccata, e	?c1710; fugue after ? B. Marcello	xxxvi, 47	V/ix.1, 80
915	L 148	Toccata, g	?c1710	xxxvi, 54	V/ix.1, 89
916	L 147	Toccata, G	before 1714	xxxvi, 63	V/ix.1, 102
917	L 140	Fantasia, g	? before 1710	xxxvi, 143	V/ix.2, 14
918	L 139	Fantasia on a rondo, c	? after 1740	xxxvi, 148	V/ix.2, 18
921	J 44, 52	Prelude (Fantasia), c	before 1714	xxxvi, 136	V/ix.2, 24
922	L 141	Fantasia, a	before 1714	xxxvi, 138	V/ix.2, 27
†923	L 131	Prelude, b	before 1725	xlii, 211	V/ix.2, 116

BWV	BC	Title	Remarks	BG	NBA
†944	L 135, 164	Fantasia and fugue, a	fugue after Torelli	iii, 334	V/ix.2, 133
946	L 160	Fugue on theme by Albinoni, C	? before 1708	xxxvi, 159	V/ix.2, 153
947	L 157	Fugue, a		xxxvi, 161	[V/xii]
948	L 151	Fugue, d	before 1727	xxxvi, 164	V/xii.2, 156
949	L 154	Fugue, A		xxxvi, 169	V/xii.2, 163
950	L 161	Fugue on theme by Albinoni, A	?c1710	xxxvi, 173	V/ix.2, 168
†951	L 162	Fugue on theme by Albinoni, b	c1712; *951a of earlier date	xxxvi, 178, 221	V/ix.2, 118
952	L 150	Fugue, C		xxxvi, 184	V/xii.2, 176
953	L 149	Fugue, C	after 1723 from Clavier-Büchlein for W.F. Bach	xxxvi, 186	V/v, 46
954	L 165	Fugue, B♭	arr. of fugue from J.A. Reincken: Hortus musicus	xlii, 50	V/xi, 200
956	L 152	Fugue, e		xlii, 200	[V/xii]
958	L 155	Fugue, a		xlii, 205	[V/ix]
959	L 156	Fugue, a		xlii, 208	V/ix.2, 178
961	L 158	Fughetta, c		xxxvi, 154	V/xii.2, 182
		Pieces from Clavier-Büchlein for W.F. Bach:	Cöthen, 1720–; incl. also 836–7, 841–3, 924a–5, 931–2, 953, 994; see 691, 753, 772ff, 846ff	xxxvi, 118	V/v
924	L 57	Praeambulum, C			
926	L 58	Prelude, d			
927	L 59	Praeambulum, F			
928	L 60	Prelude, F			
929	L 61	Trio, g	inserted in Partita, g, by G.H. Stölzel		
930	L 62	Praeambulum, g			
		Clavierbüchlein, i, for Anna Magdalena Bach	Cöthen, 1722–5; see 573, 728, 812–16, 841, 991	xliii/2, 3	V/iv, 3
		Clavierbüchlein, ii, for Anna Magdalena Bach	Leipzig, 1725; incl. 82 (recit, aria), 299, 508–18, 691, 812–13, 827, 830, 846 (prelude), 988 (aria); see A183	xliii/2, 6	V/iv, 47
933–8	L 64–9	[6 little preludes] (C, c, d, D, E, e)		xxxvi, 128	V/ix.2, 3
939–43	L 70–74	5 Preludes (C, d, e, a, C)		xxxvi, 119	[V/ix]
		Sonatas, variations, capriccios, etc.:			
963	L 182	Sonata, D	c1704	xxxvi, 19	V/x, 32
964	L 184	Sonata, d	arr. of 1003	xlii, 3	—
965	L 187	Sonata, a	? before 1705; arr. of sonata from J.A. Reincken: Hortus musicus	xlii, 29	V/xi, 173
966	L 186	Sonata, C	? before 1705; arr. of part of sonata from Reincken: Hortus musicus	xlii, 42	V/xi, 188
967	L 183	Sonata, a	c1705; arr. of 1st movt of anon. chamber sonata	xlv/1, 168	—
968	L 185	Sonata, a	arr. of 1005, 1st movt	xlii, 27	—
†989	L 179	Aria variata, a	? before 1710	xxxvi, 203	V/x, 21
990	L 178	Sarabande con partite, C		xlii, 221	[V/xii]
991	L 177	Air with variations, c	frag.; in Clavierbüchlein, i, for Anna Magdalena Bach	xliii/2, 4	V/iv, 40
992	L 181	Capriccio sopra la lontananza del suo fratello dilettissimo [Capriccio on the Departure of his Most Beloved Brother], B♭	? before 1705	xxxvi, 190	V/x, 3
993	L 180	Capriccio, E		xxxvi, 197	V/x, 12
994	Q 1	Applicatio, C	early 1720; 1st entry in Clavier-Büchlein for W.F. Bach	xxxvi, 237	V/v, 4
		16 Concertos:	Weimar, 1713–14; arrs. of works by other composers		
972	L 189	D	after Vivaldi op.3 no.9 = RV230	xlii, 59	V/xi, 3
973	L 191	G	after Vivaldi op.7/ii no.2 = RV299	xlii, 66	V/xi, 12

BWV	BC	Title	Remarks	BG	NBA
974	L 194	d	after ob conc. by A. Marcello	xlii, 73	V/xi, 20
975	L 193	g	after Vivaldi op.4 no.6 = RV316	xlii, 80	V/xi, 30
976	L 188	C	after Vivaldi op.3 no.12 = RV265	xlii, 87	V/xi, 39
977	L 202	C	source unknown (?Vivaldi)	xlii, 96	V/xi, 50
978	L 190	F	after Vivaldi op.3 no.3 = RV310	xlii, 101	V/xi, 56
979	L 196	b	after vn conc. by Torelli	xlii, 108	V/xi, 64
980	L 192	G	after Vivaldi op.4 no.1 = RV381	xlii, 119	V/xi, 79
981	L 195	c	after B. Marcello op.1 no.2	xlii, 127	V/xi, 90
982	L 200	B♭	after conc. by Prince Johann Ernst of Saxe-Weimar	xlii, 135	V/xi, 100
983	L 204	g	source unknown	xlii, 142	V/xi, 110
984	L 197	C	after conc. by Prince Johann Ernst of Saxe-Weimar	xlii, 148	V/xi, 118
985	L 201	g	after vn conc. by Telemann	xlii, 155	V/xi, 128
986	L 203	G	source unknown	xlii, 161	V/xi, 137
987	L 198	d	after conc. by Prince Johann Ernst of Saxe-Weimar	xlii, 165	V/xi, 142

Doubtful and spurious

BWV	BC	Title	Remarks	BG	NBA
824		Suite, A	frag.; by Telemann	xxxvi, 231	—
834		Allemande, c		xlii, 259	[V/xii]
835		Allemande, a	by Kirnberger	xlii, 267	—
836–7		2 allemandes, g (1 inc.)	c1720–22; from Clavier-Büchlein for W.F. Bach; ? by W.F. Bach assisted by J.S. Bach	xlv/1, 214	V/v, 8
838		Allemande and courante, A	by C. Graupner	xlii, 265	[V/xii]
839		Sarabande, g		—	
840		Courante, G	by Telemann	—	—
844		Scherzo, d	? by W.F. Bach	xlii, 220, 281	—
845		Gigue, f		xlii, 263	—
897		Prelude and fugue, a	prelude by C.H. Dretzel	xlii, 173	[V/xii]
898		Prelude and fugue, B♭		—	[V/xii]
899		Prelude and fughetta, d		—	[V/xii]
905		Fantasia and fugue, d		xlii, 179	[V/xii]
907		Fantasia and fughetta, B♭	? by G. Kirchhoff	xlii, 268	[V/xii]
908		Fantasia and fughetta, D	? by G. Kirchhoff	xlii, 272	[V/xii]
909		Concerto and fugue, c		xlii, 190	[V/xii]
919		Fantasia, c	? by J. Bernhard Bach	xxxvi, 152	[V/xii]
920		Fantasia, g		xlii, 183	[V/xii]
945		Fugue, e	spurious	xxxvi, 155	[V/xii]
955		Fugue, B♭	before 1730	xlii, 55	[B/ix]
960		Fugue, e		xlii, 276	[V/xii]
962		Fugato, e	by Albrechtsberger	xlii, 198	—
		Pieces from Clavier-Büchlein for W.F. Bach:	Cöthen, 1720–		
924a		Prelude, C	reworking of 924; ? by W.F. Bach	xxxvi, 221	V/v, 41
925		Prelude, D	? by W.F. Bach	xxxvi, 121	V/v, 42
931		Prelude, a	? by W.F. Bach	xxxvi, 237	V/v, 45
932	L 63	Prelude, e	? by W.F. Bach	xxxvi, 238	V/v, 44
969		Andante, g		xlii, 218	[V/xii]
970		Presto, d	by W.F. Bach	—	[V/xii]
990		Sarabande con partite, C	spurious	xlii, 221	[V/xii]
		Clavierbüchlein, ii, for Anna Magdalena Bach [only anon. pieces listed]:	after 1724; also incl. pieces by C.P.E. Bach (A122–5, 127, 129), J.C. Bach (A131), Böhm (without no.), Couperin (A183), Hasse (A130), Petzoldt (A114–15); remainder anon., ? by members of Bach circle	xliii/2, 25	V/iv, 47

BWV	BC	Title	Remarks	BG	NBA
		Minuet, F (A113); Minuet, G (A116); Polonaise, F (A117a, 117b); Minuet, Bb (A118); †Polonaise, g (A119); Minuet, a (A120); Minuet, c (A121); Musette, D (A126); [Polonaise], d (A128); Polonaise, G (A130); Minuet, d (A132)			

LUTE

BWV	BC	Title	Remarks	BG	NBA
995		Suite, g	c1730; arr. of vc suite 1011	—	V/x, 81
†996	L 166	Suite, e	? after 1712; orig. in d	xlv/1, 149	V/x, 94
997	L 170	Partita, c	c1740	xlv/1, 156	V/x, 102
998	L 132	Prelude, fugue and allegro, Eb	c1740–45	xlv/1, 141	V/x, 114
999	L 175	Prelude, c	c1720	xxxvi, 119	V/x, 122
1000		Fugue, g	after 1720; arr. of fugue from vn sonata 1001	—	V/x, 124
1006a	L 171	Partita, E: see 1006	c1736–7; ? for lute-harpsichord	xlii, 16	V/x, 134

CHAMBER

BWV	Title, scoring	Remarks	BG	NBA
†1001–6	Sonatas and partitas, solo vn: Sonata no.1, g; Partita no.1, b; Sonata no.2, a; Partita no.2, d: Sonata no.3, C; Partita no.3, E	1720; 1006 arr. lute = 1006a	xxvii/1, 3	VI/i, 3
1007–12	6 suites, solo vc (G, d, C, Eb, c, D)	c1720	xxvii/1, 59	VI/ii, 1
1013	Partita, a, fl	after 1723	—	VI/iii, 3
1014–19	6 sonatas, hpd, vn	before 1725, rev. before 1740; earlier version of no.5 (Adagio only) = 1018a (BG ix, 250; NBA VI/i, 195); 1st version of no.6 incl. 1019a (BG ix, 252; NBA VI/i, 197); 3 versions of 1019 [9 movts], 2nd version related to 830	ix, 69	VI/i, 83
	no.1, b; no.2, A; no.3, E; no.4, c; †no.5, f; †no.6, G			
1021	Sonata, G, vn, bc	1732–5	—	VI/i, 65
1023	Sonata, e, vn, bc	after 1723	xliii/1, 31	VI/i, 73
†1025	Suite, A, vn, hpd	c1740; after S.L. Weiss	ix, 43	
1026	Fugue, g, vn, hpd	before 1712	xliii/1, 39	
1027–9	3 sonatas, hpd, va da gamba (G, D, g)	before 1741	ix, 175	VI/iv
†1030	Sonata, b, fl, hpd	c1736; earlier version, g	ix, 3	VI/iii, 33, 89
1031	Sonata, Eb, fl, hpd	1730–34	ix, 22	
1032	Sonata, A, fl, hpd	c1736; 1st movt inc.	ix, 245, 32	VI/iii, 54
1033	Sonata, C, fl, bc	c1736	xliii/1, 3	
1034	Sonata, e, fl, bc	c1724	xliii/1, 9	VI/iii, 11
1035	Sonata, E, fl, bc	c1741	xliii/1, 21	VI/iii, 23
1038	Sonata, G, fl, vn, bc	1732–5	ix, 221	
1039	Sonata, G, 2 fl, bc	c1736–41; cf 1027	ix, 260	VI/iii, 71
1040	Trio, F, vn, ob, bc	movt based on material from Cantata 208, ? perf. with cant.; later used in Cantata 68	xxix, 250	I/xxxv, 47

Doubtful and spurious

BWV	Title, scoring	Remarks	BG	NBA
1020	Sonata, g, hpd, vn	? by C.P.E. Bach	ix, 274	
1022	Sonata, F, vn, hpd	arr. of 1038; ? by one of Bach's sons or pupils	—	
1024	Sonata, c, vn, bc	? by J.G. Pisendel	—	
1036	Sonata, d, 2 vn, hpd	by C.P.E. Bach	—	
1037	Sonata, C, 2 vn, hpd	by J.G. Goldberg	ix, 231	

ORCHESTRAL

where applicable, scoring given as concertino/solo; ripieno

BWV	Title, key	Scoring	Remarks	BG	NBA
1041	Concerto, a	vn; str, bc	c1730; cf 1058	xxi/1, 3	VII/iii, 3
1042	Concerto, E	vn; str, bc	before 1730; cf 1054	xxi/1, 21	VII/iii, 35
1043	Concerto, d	2 vn; str, bc	1730–31; cf 1062	xxi/1, 41	VII/iii, 71
1044	Concerto, a	fl, vn, hpd; str, bc	1729–41; movts adapted from prelude and fugue 894 and trio sonata 527	xvii, 223	VII/iii, 105
	Brandenburg Concertos:		autograph MS ded. Christian Ludwig, Margrave of Brandenburg, 24 March 1721		
1046	no.1, F	2 hn, ob, vn piccolo; 2 ob, bn, str, bc		xix, 3	VII/ii, 3
1046a	Sinfonia, F	2 hn, 3 ob, bn, str, bc	formerly 1071; also used in 52	xxxi/1, 96	VII/ii, 225
1047	no.2, F	tpt, rec, ob, vn; str, bc		xix, 33	VII/ii, 43
1048	no.3, G	3 vn, 3 va, 3 vc, bc		xix, 59	VII/ii, 73
1049	no.4, G	vn, 2 rec; str, bc	cf 1057	xix, 85	VII/ii, 99
1050	no.5, D	fl, vn, hpd; str, bc	*1050a	xix, 127	VII/ii, 145, appx
1051	no.6, B♭	2 va, 2 va da gamba, vc, bc		xix, 167	VII/ii, 197
	Harpsichord concertos:		Leipzig, mostly c1738–9; mostly transcrs. of vn or ob concs; some orig./transcrs. also used in church cants.		
†1052	d	hpd; str, bc	from lost vn conc. reconstructed in NBA VII/vii, 3	xvii, 3	VII/iv, 3
1053	E	hpd; str, bc	from lost ?ob conc; see NBA VII/vii, CC	xvii, 45	VII/iv, 79
1054	D	hpd; str, bc	from 1042	xvii, 81	VII/iv, 127
1055	A	hpd; str, bc	from lost ob d'amore conc. reconstructed in NBA VII/vii, 33	xvii, 109	VII/iv, 161
1056	f	hpd; str, bc	outer movts from lost ob conc. in g reconstructed in NBA VII/vii, 59	xvii, 135	VII/iv, 197
1057	F	hpd, 2 rec; str, bc	from 1049	xvii, 153	VII/iv, 221
1058	g	hpd; str, bc	from 1041	xvii, 199	VII/iv, 283
1059	d	hpd, ob; str, bc	inc., from lost ob conc., see NBA VII/vii, CC	xvii, p.xx	VII/iv, 313
1060	c	2 hpd; str, bc	c1736; from lost ob and vn conc. reconstructed in NBA VII/vii, 75	xxi/2, 3	VII/v, 3
†1061	C	2 hpd; str, bc	1732–5; orig. for 2 hpd, ? without acc.	xxi/2, 39	VII/v, 83, 109
1062	c	2 hpd; str, bc	c1736; from 1043	xxi/2, 83	VII/v, 43
1063	d	3 hpd; str, bc	c1730; source unknown, see NBA VII/vii, CC	xxxi/3, 3	VII/vi, 3
1064	C	3 hpd; str, bc	c1730; from lost 3 vn conc. in D reconstructed in NBA VII/vii, 103	xxxi/3, 53	VII/vi, 57
1065	a	4 hpd; str, bc	c1730; from Vivaldi op.3 no.10 = RV580	xliii/1, 71	VII/vi, 117
	4 orchestral suites:				
1066	C	2 ob, bn, str, bc	before 1725	xxxi/1, 3	VII/i, 3
1067	b	fl; str, bc	c1738–9	xxxi/1, 24	VII/i, 27
1068	D	3 tpt, timp, 2 ob, str, bc	c1731	xxxi/1, 40	VII/i, 49, 119
1069	D	3 tpt, timp, 3 ob, bn, str, bc	c1725; later version 1729–41	xxxi/1, 66	VII/i, 81
1070	Overture, g	str, bc	spurious	xlv/1, 190	—
1071	Sinfonia: see 1046a				

STUDIES IN COUNTERPOINT, CANONS ETC.

BWV	Title, scoring	Remarks	BG	NBA
†769	Einige [5] canonische Veränderungen über das Weynacht-Lied, Vom Himmel hoch da komm ich her, org	written on becoming member of Mizler's Societät der Musicalischen Wissenschaften, June 1747 (Nuremberg, 1748); autograph version 769a, chronology of versions uncertain, several pubd in puzzle form	xl, 137	IV/ii, 197, 98
†1079	Musikalisches Opfer [fl, vn, bc, kbd]	May–July 1747 (Leipzig, 1747); 2 Ricercars, a 3, a 6; 10 canons; sonata, fl, vn, bc; insts not fully specified	xxxi/2	VIII/i, 12
†1080	Die Kunst der Fuge [kbd]	before 1742, rev. c1745 and 1748–9 (Leipzig, 1751, 2/1752)	xxv/1	VIII/ii.1–2
1072	Canon trias harmonica	a 8, in contrary motion; in F.W. Marpurg: Abhandlung von der Fuge, ii (Berlin, 1754)	xlv, 131	VIII/i, 3, 6
1073	Canon a 4 perpetuus	2 Aug 1713	xlv, 132	VIII/i, 3, 6
1074	Canon a 4	1727; ded. L.F. Hudemann; pubd in G.P. Telemann: Der getreue Music-Meister (Hamburg, 1728) and in J. Mattheson:Der volkkommene Capellmeister (Hamburg, 1739/R)	xlv, 134	VIII/i, 3, 7
1075	Canon a 2 perpetuus	10 Jan 1734; ded. ? J.G. Walther (1712–77)	—	VIII/i, 3, 7
†1076	Canon triplex a 6	before 1746; cf 1087	xlv, 138	VIII/i, 3, 8
†1077	Canone doppio sopr'il soggetto	15 Oct 1747; ded. J.G. Fulde; cf 1087	—	VIII/i, 4, 8
1078	Canon super fa mi a 7 post tempus musicum	1 March 1749; ded. ? Benjamin Faber; pubd in F.W. Marpurg: Abhandlung von der Fuge, ii (Berlin, 1754)	xlv, 136	VIII/i, 4, 9
1086	Canon concordia discors	a 2	—	VIII/i, 4, 10
1087	[14] Verschiedene Canones	after 1745; on first 8 notes of aria ground of 988; incl. earlier versions of 1076–7	—	V/ii, 119

BIBLIOGRAPHY

A Bibliographies, research studies. B Catalogues. C Source studies: manuscripts and prints. D Source studies: documents, letters etc. E Iconography. F Biography: life and works. G Biography: special studies. H Works: general. I Works: special studies. J Vocal works. K Instrumental works. L Performing practice.

A: BIBLIOGRAPHIES, RESEARCH STUDIES

M. Schneider: 'Verzeichnis der bis zum Jahre 1851 gedruckten (und der geschrieben im Handel gewesenen) Werke von Johann Sebastian Bach', BJb 1906, 84–113

J. Schreyer: Beiträge zur Bach-Kritik, i (Dresden, 1910); ii (Leipzig, 1912)

W. Blankenburg: 'Zwölf Jahre Bachforschung', AcM, xxxvii (1965), 95–158

W. Blankenburg: 'Die Bachforschung seit etwa 1965: Ergebnisse, Probleme, Aufgaben', AcM, l (1978), 93–154; liv (1982), 162–207; lv (1983), 1–58

R.A. Leaver: Bachs theologische Bibliothek: eine kritische Bibliographie (Neuhausen-Stuttgart, 1983)

C. Wolff, ed.: Bach-Bibliographie: Nachdruck der Verzeichnisse des Schrifttums über Johann Sebastian Bach (Bach-Jahrbuch 1905–1984), mit einem Supplement und Register (Berlin, 1985)

R. Nestle: 'Das Bachschrifttum 1981 bis 1985', BJb 1989, 107–89

R. Nestle: 'Das Bachschrifttum 1986 bis 1990', BJb 1994, 75–162

D.R. Melamed and M.Marissen: An Introduction to Bach Studies(Oxford, 1998)

Bach Bibliography On-Line (Belfast, Queen's University; Y. Tomita) [on-line database]

B: CATALOGUES

W. Schmieder: Thematisch-systematisches Verzeichnis der musikalischen Werke von Johann Sebastian Bach: Bach-Werke-Verzeichnis (Leipzig, 1950, enlarged 2/1990, rev. and abridged 1998 by A. Dürr, Y. Kobayashi and K. Beisswenger as Bach-Werke-Verzeichnis)

P. Kast: Die Bach-Handschriften der Berliner Staatsbibliothek (Trossingen, 1958)

S.W. Kenney, ed.: Catalog of the Emilie and Karl Riemenschneider Memorial Bach Library (New York, 1960)

M. deF. McAll, ed.: Melodic Index to the Works of Johann Sebastian Bach (New York, 1962)

H.-J. Schulze: Katalog der Sammlung Manfred Gorke: Bachiana und andere Handschriften und Drucke des 18. und frühen 19. Jahrhunderts (Leipzig, 1977)

R.W. Wade, ed.: The Catalog of Carl Philipp Emanuel Bach's Estate: a Facsimile of the Edition by Schniebes, Hamburg, 1790 (New York, 1981)

T. Leibnitz, ed.: Katalog der Sammlung Anthony von Hoboken in der Musiksammlung der Österreichischen Nationalbibliothek, i: Johann Sebastian Bach und seine Söhne(Tutzing, 1982)

G. Herz: Bach-Quellen in Amerika/Bach Sources in America (Kassel, 1984)

W. Neumann and C.Fröde: *Die Bach-Handschriften der Thomasschule Leipzig: Katalog* (Leipzig, 1986)

C. Wolff and H.-J.Schulze: *Bach Compendium: analytisch-bibliographisches Repertorium der Werke Johann Sebastian Bachs*(Leipzig and Frankfurt, 1986–)

U. Balestrini: *Catalogo tematico (incipit) delle opere di J.S. Bach: Bach-Werke-Verzeichnis 1–1080*(Milan, 1988)

U. Leisinger: 'Die "Bachsche Auction" von 1789', *BJb 1991*, 97–126

K. Beisswenger: *Johann Sebastian Bachs Notenbibliothek* (Kassel, 1992)

R. Reeder: *The Bach English-Title Index* (Berkeley, 1993)

U. Leisinger and P. Wollny: *Die Bach-Quellen der Bibliotheken in Brüssel: Katalog* (Hildesheim,1997)

C: SOURCE STUDIES: MANUSCRIPTS AND PRINTS

R. Schwartz: 'Die Bach-Handschriften der Musikbibliothek Peters', *JbMP 1919*, 56–73

G. Kinsky: *Die Originalausgaben der Werke Johann Sebastian Bachs* (Vienna, 1937/R)

W. Schmieder: 'Die Handschriften Johann Sebastian Bachs', *Bach-Gedenkschrift*, ed. K. Matthaei (Zürich, 1950), 190–203

G. von Dadelsen: 'Originale Daten auf den Handschriften J.S. Bachs', *Hans Albrecht in memoriam*, ed. W. Brennecke and H. Haase (Kassel, 1962), 116–20

P. Krause, ed.: *Handschriften der Werke Johann Sebastian Bachs in der Musikbibliothek der Stadt Leipzig*(Leipzig, 1964)

H.-J. Schulze: 'Beiträge zur Bach-Quellenforschung', *GfMKB: Leipzig 1966*, 269–75

H. Zietz: *Quellenkritische Untersuchungen an den Bach-Handschriften P 801, P 802 und P 803 aus dem 'Krebs'schen Nachlass' unter besonderer Berücksichtigung der Choralbearbeitungen des jungen J.S. Bach* (Hamburg, 1969)

A. Dürr: 'Zur Chronologie der Handschrift Johann Christoph Altnickols und Johann Friedrich Agricolas', *BJb 1970*, 44–65

K. Engler: *Georg Poelchau und seine Musikaliensammlung: ein Beitrag zur Überlieferung Bachscher Musik im 19. Jahrhundert* (diss., U. of Tübingen, 1970)

P. Krause, ed.: *Originalausgaben und ältere Drucke der Werke Johann Sebastian Bachs in der Musikbibliothek der Stadt Leipzig* (Leipzig, 1970)

Y. Kobayashi: 'Zu einem neu entdeckten Autograph Bachs: Choral Aus der Tiefen', *BJb 1971*, 5–12

W. Hobohm: 'Neue "Texte zur Leipziger Kirchen-Musik"', *BJb 1973*, 5–32

Y. Kobayashi: *Franz Hauser und seine Bach-Handschriftsammlung* (diss., U. of Göttingen, 1973)

'Johann Sebastian Bach: Studies of the Sources', *Studies in Renaissance and Baroque Music in Honor of Arthur Mendel*, ed. R.L. Marshall (Kassel and Hackensack, NJ, 1974), 231–300 [contributions by P. Brainard, A. Dürr, G. Herz, E. May and C. Wolff]

H.-J. Schulze: 'Wie entstand die Bach-Sammlung Mempell-Preller?', *BJb 1974*, 104–22

K.-H. Köhler: 'Die Bach-Sammlung der Deutschen Staatsbibliothek: Überlieferung und Bedeutung', *Bach-Studien*, v (1975), 139–46

Y. Kobayashi: 'Neuerkenntnisse zu einigen Bach-Quellen anhand schriftkundlicher Untersuchungen', *BJb 1978*, 43–60

H.-J. Schulze: 'Das Stück in Goldpapier: Ermittlungen zu einigen Bach-Abschriften der frühen 18. Jahrhunderts', *BJb 1978*, 19–42

Y. Kobayashi: 'Breitkopfs Handel mit Bach-Handschriften', *Beiträge zur Bachforschung*, i (1982), 79–84

H.-J. Schulze: '"150 Stück von den Bachischen Erben": zur Überlieferung der vierstimmigen Choräle Johann Sebastian Bachs', *BJb 1983*, 81–100

A. Dürr: *Johann Sebastian Bach: seine Handschrift; Abbild seines Schaffens* (Wiesbaden, 1984)

H.-J. Schulze: *Studien zur Bach-Überlieferung im 18. Jahrhundert* (Leipzig, 1984)

R. Elvers and H.-G.Klein, eds.: *Die Handschrift Johann Sebastian Bachs*, Musikabteilung der Staatsbibliothek Preussischer Kulturbesitz, Berlin, 22 March – 13 July 1985 (Wiesbaden, 1985) [exhibition catalogue]

H.J. Marx: 'Wiederaufgefundene Autographe von Carl Philipp Emanuel und Johann Sebastian Bach', *Mf*, xli (1988), 150–56

Y. Kobayashi: *Die Notenschrift Johann Sebastian Bachs: Dokumentation ihrer Entwicklung*, NBA, IX (1989)

C. Wolff: 'From Berlin to Lodz: the Spitta Collection Resurfaces', *Notes*, xlvi (1989–90), 311–27

L.A. Federowskaja: 'Bachiana in russischen Bibliotheken und Sammlungen: Autographe, Abschriften, Frühdrucke, Bearbeitungen', *BJb 1990*, 27–36

H.-J. Schulze: 'Bach und Buxtehude: eine wenig beachtete Quelle in der Carnegie Library zu Pittsburgh/PA', *BJb 1991*, 177–82

U. Leisinger: *Die Bach-Quellen der Forschungs- und Landesbibliothek Gotha* (Gotha, 1993)

A. Glöckner: 'Die Teilung des Bachschen Musikaliennachlasses und die Thomana-Stimmen', *BJb 1994*, 41–57

D: SOURCE STUDIES: DOCUMENTS, LETTERS ETC.

J.A. Scheibe: *Der critische Musikus* (Hamburg, 1738–40, 2/1745/R)

L. Mizler: *Neu eröffnete musikalische Bibliothek* (Leipzig, 1739–54/R)

J.F. Agricola and C.P.E.Bach: Obituary in L. Mizler: *Neu eröffnete musikalische Bibliothek*, iv/1 (Leipzig, 1754/R), 158–76; repr. in *BJb 1920*, 11–29

E.H. Müller von Asow: *Johann Sebastian Bach: Gesammelte Briefe* (Regensburg, 1938, rev. 2/1950 with H. Müller von Asow)

H.T. David and A.Mendel, eds.: *The Bach Reader* (New York, 1945, enlarged 3/1998 by C. Wolff as *The New Bach Reader*)

W. Neumann and H.-J.Schulze, eds.: *Schriftstücke von der Hand Johann Sebastian Bachs*, Bach-Dokumente, i (Leipzig, 1963; Fr. trans., 1976)

W. Neumann and H.-J.Schulze, eds.: *Fremdschriftliche und gedruckte Dokumente zur Lebensgeschichte Johann Sebastian Bachs 1685–1750*, Bach-Dokumente, ii (Leipzig, 1969)

A. Dürr: 'Zur Chronologie der Handschrift Johann Christoph Altnickols und Johann Friedrich Agricolas', *BJb 1970*, 44–65

H.-J. Schulze, ed.: *Dokumente zum Nachwirken Johann Sebastian Bachs 1750–1800*, Bach-Dokumente, iii (Leipzig, 1972)

H. Stiehl: 'Taufzettel für Bachs Kinder: ein Dokumentenfund', *BJb 1979*, 7–18

E: ICONOGRAPHY

H. Besseler: *Fünf echte Bildnisse Johann Sebastian Bachs* (Kassel, 1956)

H.O.R. van Tuyll van Serooskerken: *Probleme des Bachporträts* (Bilthoven, 1956)

C. Freyse: *Bachs Antlitz* (Eisenach, 1964)

W. Neumann, ed.: *Bilddokumente zur Lebensgeschichte Johann Sebastian Bachs/Pictorial Documents of the Life of Johann Sebastian Bach*, Bach-Dokumente, iv (Leipzig, 1979)

H. Börsch-Supan: 'Gruppenbild mit Musikern: ein Gemälde von Balthasar Denner und das Problem der Bach-Ikonographie', *Kunst und Antiquitäten*, iii (1982), 22–32

H.-J. Schulze: 'Zur Überlieferung einiger Bach-Porträts', *BJb 1982*, 154–6

H. Raupach: *Das wahre Bildnis des Johann Sebastian Bach: Bericht und Dokumente* (Munich, 1983)

M. Staehelin: 'Zu einer umstrittenen Bach-Porträtzeichnung des 18. Jahrhunderts', *Bachiana et alia musicologica: Festschrift Alfred Dürr*, ed. W. Rehm (Kassel, 1983), 260–66

M. Korth and S.Kuhlmann, eds.: *J.S. Bach: Bilder und Zeugnisse eines Musikerlebens* (Munich, 1985)

G. Wagner: 'Ein unbekanntes Porträt Johann Sebastian Bachs aus dem 18. Jahrhundert?', *BJb 1988*, 231–4

F: BIOGRAPHY: LIFE AND WORKS

J.N. Forkel: *Ueber Johann Sebastian Bachs Leben, Kunst und Kunstwerke* (Leipzig, 1802/R; Eng. trans., 1820/R)

C.L. Hilgenfeldt: *Johann Sebastian Bachs Leben, Wirken und Werke: ein Beitrag zur Kunstgeschichte des achtzehnten Jahrhunderts* (Leipzig, 1850/R)

C.H. Bitter: *Johann Sebastian Bach* (Berlin, 1865, enlarged 2/1881/R; Eng. trans., abridged, 1873)

P. Spitta: *Johann Sebastian Bach* (Leipzig, 1873–80, 5/1962; Eng. trans., 1884)

A. Schweitzer: *J.S. Bach, le musicien-poète* (Paris, 1905; Ger. trans., enlarged, 1908; Eng. trans., 1911/R)

A. Pirro: *J.-S. Bach* (Paris, 1906, rev. 1949; Eng. trans., 1957)

C.H.H. Parry: *Johann Sebastian Bach* (London, 1909, 2/1934/R)

C.S. Terry: *Bach: a Biography* (London, 1928, 2/1933/R)

W. Gurlitt: *Johann Sebastian Bach: der Meister und sein Werk* (Berlin, 1936, enlarged 5/1980; Eng. trans., 1957/R)

W. Neumann: *Auf den Lebenswegen Johann Sebastian Bachs* (Berlin, 1953, 4/1962; Eng. trans., 1957)

W. Neumann: *Bach: eine Bildbiographie* (Munich, 1960, 2/1961; Eng. trans., 1961, rev. 2/1969 as *Bach and his World*)

K. Geiringer: *Johann Sebastian Bach: the Culmination of an Era* (New York, 1966)

B. Schwendowius and W.Dömling, eds.: *Johann Sebastian Bach: Zeit, Leben, Wirken* (Kassel, 1976; Eng. trans., 1978)

A. Basso: *Frau Musika: la vita e le opere di J.S. Bach* (Turin, 1979–83)

M. Boyd: *Bach* (London, 1983, 3/2000)

D. Arnold: *Bach* (Oxford, 1984)

W. Felix: *Johann Sebastian Bach* (Wiesbaden, 1984; Eng. trans., 1985)

P. Buscaroli: *Bach* (Milan, 1985)

M. Geck: *Bach: Leben und Werk* (Reinbek, 2000)

C. Wolff: *Johann Sebastian Bach: the Learned Musician* (New York, 2000)

G: BIOGRAPHY: SPECIAL STUDIES

C. Scherer: 'Joh. Seb. Bachs Aufenthalt in Kassel', *MMg*, xxv (1893), 129–33

B.F. Richter: 'Stadtpfeifer und Alumnen der Thomasschule in Leipzig zu Bachs Zeit', *BJb 1907*, 32–78

C. Freyse, ed.: *Eisenacher Dokumente um Sebastian Bach* (Leipzig, 1933)

G. Herz: 'Bach's Religion', *JRBM*, i (1946), 124–38

G. Fock: *Der junge Bach in Lüneburg 1700 bis 1702* (Hamburg, 1950)

K. Müller and F.Wiegand, eds.: *Arnstädter Bachbuch: Johann Sebastian Bach und seine Verwandten in Arnstadt* (Arnstadt, 1950, 2/1957)

F. Smend: *Bach in Köthen* (Berlin, 1951; Eng. trans., rev. 1985)

H. Löffler: 'Die Schüler Joh. Seb. Bachs', *BJb 1953*, 5–28

K. Geiringer: *The Bach Family: Seven Generations of Creative Genius* (London, 1954/R, Ger. trans., enlarged, 1958, 2/1977)

W. Neumann: 'Das "Bachische Collegium Musicum"', *BJb 1960*, 5–27

F. Blume: 'Outlines of a New Picture of Bach', *ML*, xliv (1963), 214–27

G. Stiller: *Johann Sebastian Bach und das Leipziger gottesdienstliche Leben seiner Zeit* (Kassel, 1970; Eng. trans., 1984)

I. Ahlgrimm: 'Von Reisen, Kirchererbsen und Fischbeinröcken', *Bach-Studien*, v (1975), 155–70

R. Eller: 'Gedanken über Bachs Leipziger Schaffensjahre', ibid., 7–27

W. Schrammek: 'Johann Sebastian Bach, Gottfried Silbermann und die französische Orgelkunst', ibid., 93–107

H.-J. Schulze: 'Johann Sebastian Bach und Georg Gottfried Wagner: neue Dokumente', ibid., 147–54

E. Zavarský: 'J.S. Bachs Entwurf für den Umbau der Orgel in der Kirche Divi Blasii und das Klangideal der Zeit', ibid., 82–93

W. Siegmund-Schultze: 'Über die "unvermeidlichen Lücken" in Bachs Lebensbeschreibung', *Bachforschung und Bachinterpretation heute: Marburg 1978*, 32–42

C. Wolff: 'Bachs Leipziger Kantoratsprobe und die Aufführungsgeschichte der Kantate BWV23', *BJb 1978*, 78–94

C. Wolff: 'Probleme und Neuansätze der Bach-Biographik', *Bachforschung und Bachinterpretation heute: Marburg 1978*, 21–31

W. Frei: 'Bach, das konservative Genie – oder das Schicksal aus seiner Familie', *Musik und Gottesdienst*, xxxiv (1980), 1–6

A. Glöckner: 'Neuerkenntnisse zu Johann Sebastian Bachs Aufführungskalender zwischen 1729 und 1735', *BJb 1981*, 43–76

A. Plichta: 'Johann Sebastian Bach und Johann Adam Graf von Questenberg', ibid., 23–8

U. Siegele: 'Bachs Ort in Orthodoxie und Aufklärung', *Musik und Kirche*, li (1981), 3–14

W. Blankenburg: 'Luther und Bach', *Musik und Kirche*, liii (1983), 233–42

K. von Fischer: *Johann Sebastian Bach: Welt, Umwelt und Frömmigkeit* (Wiesbaden, 1983)

M. Petzoldt: 'Zur Frage nach den Funktion des Kantors Johann Sebastian Bach in Leipzig', *Musik und Kirche*, liii (1983), 167–73

W. Rehm, ed.: *Bachiana et alia musicologica: Festschrift Alfred Dürr* (Kassel, 1983) [incl. W. Felix: 'Johann Sebastian Bach: Leipziger Wirken und Nachwirken', 88–92; H. Heussner: 'Zur Musikpflege im Umkreis des Prinzen Maximilian von Hessen: Pietro Locatelli und Johann Sebastian Bach in Kassel', 108–15; W. Neumann: 'Über die mutmasslichen Beziehungen zwischen dem Leipziger Thomaskantor Bach und dem Leisniger Matthäikantor Stockmar', 201–8; W.H. Scheide: 'Bach vs. Bach: Mühlhausen Dismissal Request vs. Erdmann Letter', 234–42; H.-J. Schulze: '"Monsieur Schouster", ein vergessener Zeitgenosse Johann Sebastian Bachs',

243–50; E. Zavarský: 'Ein Besucher aus der Slowakei bei Johann Sebastian Bach', 363–7]

U. Siegele: 'Bachs Stellung in der Leipziger Kulturpolitik seiner Zeit', *BJb 1983*, 7–50; *1984*, 7–43; *1986*, 33–67

J. Bahns, ed.: *Ex libris Bachianis II: das Weltbild Johann Sebastian Bachs im Spiegel seiner theologischen Bibliothek*, Kurpfälzisches Museum der Stadt Heidelberg, 1 June – 15 July 1985 (Heidelberg, 1985) [exhibition catalogue]

W. Blankenburg: 'Wandlungen und Probleme des Bachbildes', *Musik und Kirche*, lv (1985), 274–84

H.H. Cox: *The Calov Bible of J.S. Bach* (Ann Arbor, 1985)

W. Hildesheimer: *Das ferne Bach: eine Rede* (Frankfurt, 1985)

R.A. Leaver: *J.S. Bach and Scripture: Glosses from the Calov Bible Commentary* (St Louis, 1985)

M. Petzoldt: '"Ut probus & doctus reddar": zum Anteil der Theologie bei der Schulausbildung Johann Sebastian Bachs in Eisenach, Ohrdruf und Lüneburg', *BJb 1985*, 7–42

M. Walter: 'J.S. Bach und die Aufklärung?', *AMw*, xlii (1985), 229–40

J.J. Pelikan: *Bach Among the Theologians* (Philadelphia, 1986)

A. Glöckner: *Die Musikpflege an der Leipziger Neukirche zur Zeit* (Leipzig, 1990)

D. Kranemann: 'Johann Sebastian Bachs Krankheit und Todesursache: Versuch einer Deutung', *BJb 1990*, 53–64

R. Szeskus: 'Bach und die Leipziger Universitätsmusik', *BMw*, xxxii (1990), 161–70

U. Siegele: '"Ich habe fleissig sein müssen …": zur Vermittlung von Bachs sozialem und musikalischem Charakter', *Musik und Kirche*, lxi (1991), 73–8; Eng. trans., *Bach*, xxii/2 (1991), 5–12

P. Wollny: 'Bachs Bewerbung um die Organistenstelle an der Marienkirche zu Halle und ihr Kontext', *BJb 1994*, 25–39

K. Küster: *Der junge Bach* (Stuttgart, 1996)

H: WORKS: GENERAL

A. Pirro: *L'esthétique de Jean-Sébastien Bach* (Paris, 1907)

C.S. Terry: *The Music of Bach: an Introduction* (London, 1933/R)

G. Herz: *Johann Sebastian Bach im Zeitalter des Rationalismus und der Frühromantik* (Kassel, 1935)

A.E.F. Dickinson: *The Art of J.S. Bach* (London, 1936, enlarged 2/1950)

G. Frotscher: *Johann Sebastian Bach und die Musik des siebzehnten Jahrhunderts* (Wädenswil, 1939)

A. Schering: *Johann Sebastian Bach und das Musikleben Leipzigs im 18. Jahrhundert*, Musikgeschichte Leipzigs, iii (Leipzig, 1941)

W. Blankenburg: *Die innere Einheit von Bachs Werk* (diss., U. of Göttingen, 1942)

L. Schrade: 'Bach: the Conflict between the Sacred and the Secular', *Journal of the History of Ideas*, vii (1946), 151–94; pubd separately (New York, 1954/R)

W. Blankenburg: 'Bach geistlich und weltlich', *Musik und Kirche*, xx (1950), 36–46

R. Petzoldt and L.Weinhold, eds.: *Johann Sebastian Bach: das Schaffen des Meisters in Spiegel einer Stadt* (Leipzig, 1950)

H. Besseler: 'Bach und das Mittelalter', *Wissenschaftliche Bachtagung: Leipzig 1950*, 108–30; Eng. trans. in *The Score*, no.9 (1954), 31–42

A.T. Davison: *Bach and Handel: the Consummation of the Baroque in Music* (Cambridge, MA, 1951/R)

P. Hindemith: *Johann Sebastian Bach: Heritage and Obligation* (New Haven, 1952)

H. Besseler: 'Bach als Wegbereiter', *AMw*, xii (1955), 1–39

W. Mellers: *Bach and the Dance of God* (London, 1980)

C. Wolff: '"Die sonderbaren Vollkommenheiten des Herrn Hof Compositeurs": Versuch über die Eigenart der Bachschen Musik', *Bachiana et alia musicologica: Festschrift Alfred Dürr*, ed. W. Rehm (Kassel, 1983), 356–62

A. Dürr: *Bachs Werk vom Einfall bis zur Drucklegung* (Wiesbaden, 1989)

R.L. Marshall: *The Music of Johann Sebastian Bach: the Sources, the Style, the Significance* (New York, 1989)

H.H. Eggebrecht: *Bach – wer ist das?: zum Verständnis der Musik Johann Sebastian Bachs* (Mainz, 1992)

L. Dreyfus: *Bach and the Patterns of Invention* (Cambridge, MA, 1996)

J. Butt, ed.: *The Cambridge Companion to Bach* (New York, 1997)

M. Geck: *Bach und die Stile* (Dortmund, 1999)

I: WORKS: SPECIAL STUDIES

E. Kurth: *Grundlagen des linearen Kontrapunkts: Einführung in Stil und Technik von Bachs melodischer Polyphonie* (Berne, 1917, 5/1956/R)

A. Schering: 'Über Bachs Parodieverfahren', *BJb 1921*, 49–95

K. Geiringer: *Symbolism in the Music of Bach* (Washington DC, 1956); repr. in *Lectures on the History and Art of Music* (New York, 1968), 123ff

A. Dürr: 'Gedanken zu J.S. Bachs Umarbeitungen eigener Werke', *BJb 1956*, 93–104

G. von Dadelsen: *Bemerkungen zur Handschrift Johann Sebastian Bachs, seiner Familie und seines Kreises* (Trossingen, 1957)

G. von Dadelsen: *Beiträge zur Chronologie der Werke Johann Sebastian Bachs* (Trossingen, 1958)

E. Bodky: *The Interpretation of Bach's Keyboard Works* (Cambridge, MA, 1960/R)

A. Mendel: 'Recent Developments in Bach Chronology', *MQ*, xlvi (1960), 283–300

A. Dürr: 'Neues über Bachs Pergolesi-Bearbeitung', *BJb 1968*, 89–100

C. Wolff: *Der stile antico in der Musik Johann Sebastian Bachs* (Wiesbaden, 1968)

R.L. Marshall: 'How J.S. Bach Composed Four-part Chorales', *MQ*, lvi (1970), 198–220

M. Geck: 'Bachs Probestück', *Quellenstudien zur Musik: Wolfgang Schmieder zum 70. Geburtstag*, ed. K. Dorfmüller and G. von Dadelsen (Frankfurt, 1972), 55–68

'Johann Sebastian Bach: Approaches to Analysis and Interpretation', *Studies in Renaissance and Baroque Music in Honor of Arthur Mendel*, ed. R.L. Marshall (Kassel and Hackensack, NJ, 1974), 139–230 [contributions by W. Blankenburg, E.T. Cone, W. Emery, R.L. Marshall, F. Neumann, N. Rubin and W.H. Scheide]

W. Emery: 'A Note on Bach's Use of Triplets', *Bach-Studien*, v (1975), 109–11

H. Eppstein: 'Zum Formproblem bei J.S. Bach', ibid., 29–42

H. Grüss: 'Tempofragen der Bachzeit', ibid., 73–81

R.L. Marshall: 'Bach the Progressive: Observations on his Later Works', *MQ*, lxii (1976), 313–57

U. Meyer: 'Zum Problem der Zahlen in Johann Sebastian Bachs Werk', *Musik und Kirche*, xlix (1979), 58–71

U. Prinz: *Studien zum Instrumentarium J.S. Bachs mit besonderer Berücksichtigung der Kantaten* (Tübingen, 1979)

G.G. Butler: 'Leipziger Stecher in Bachs Originaldrucken', *BJb 1980*, 9–26

L. Prautzsch: *Vor deinen Thron tret ich hiermit: Figuren und Symbole in den letzten Werken Johann Sebastian Bachs* (Neuhausen-Stuttgart, 1980)

K.-J. Sachs: 'Die "Anleitung …, auff allerhand Arth einen Choral durchzuführen" als Paradigma der Lehre und die Satzkunst Johann Sebastian Bachs', *AMw*, xxxvii (1980), 135–54

W. Neumann: *Über das funktionale Wechselverhältnis von Vokalität und Instrumentalität als kompositionstechnisches Grundphänomen, dargestellt am Schaffen Johann Sebastian Bachs* (Berlin, 1982)

G.A. Theill: *Beiträge zur Symbolsprache Johann Sebastian Bachs* (Bonn, 1983–)

Q. Faulkner: *J.S. Bach's Keyboard Technique: a Historical Introduction* (St Louis, MO, 1984)

Bach und die italienische Musik: Venice 1985

M. Dankwardt: *Instrumentale und vokale Kompositionsweise bei Johann Sebastian Bach* (Tutzing, 1985)

M. Petzoldt, ed.: *Bach als Ausleger der Bibel: theologische und musikwissenschaftliche Studien zum Werk Johann Sebastian Bachs* (Göttingen, 1985)

G. Wagner: *Traditionsbezug im musikhistorischen Prozess zwischen 1720 und 1740 am Beispiel von Johann Sebastian und Carl Philipp Emanuel Bach: musikalische Analyse und musikhistorische Bewertung* (Neuhausen-Stuttgart, 1985)

C. Wolff: 'Johann Adam Reinken und Johann Sebastian Bach: zum Kontext des Bachschen Frühwerkes', *BJb 1985*, 99–118; Eng. trans., rev. in *J.S. Bach as Organist*, ed. G. Stauffer and E. May (Bloomington, IN, 1986), 57–80, and in *Bach: Essays on his Life and Music* (Cambridge, MA, 1991), 56–71

G. Stauffer and E. May, eds.: *J.S. Bach as Organist: his Instruments, Music, and Performance Practices* (Bloomington, IN, 1986)

W. Elders: 'Kompositionsverfahren in der Musik der alten Niederländer und die Kunst J.S. Bachs', *Beiträge zur Bachforschung*, vi (1987), 110–34

W.F. Hindermann: '"Seine Einsicht in die Dichtkunst … ": Bachs Rhetorik-Verständnis im Spiegel von Quintilians *Institutio oratoria*', *Musik und Kirche*, lvii (1987), 284–97

H.-J. Schulze: 'The Parody Process in Bach's Music: an Old Problem Reconsidered', *Bach*, xx/3 (1989), 15–33

K. Beisswenger: 'Bachs Eingriffe in Werke fremder Komponisten: Beobachtungen an den Notenhandschriften aus seiner Bibliothek unter besonderer Berücksichtigung der lateinischen Kirchenmusik', *BJb 1991*, 127–58

M. Little and N. Jenne: *Dance and the Music of Bach* (Bloomington, IN, 1991)

R. Tatlow: *Bach and the Riddle of the Number Alphabet* (Cambridge, 1991)

E. Kooiman, G. Weinberger and H.J. Busch: *Zur Interpretation der Orgelmusik Johann Sebastian Bachs* (Kassel, 1995)

J: VOCAL WORKS

BlumeEK

K. Ziebler: *Das Symbol in der Kirchenmusik Joh. Seb. Bachs* (Kassel, 1930)

A. Schering: *Johann Sebastian Bachs Leipziger Kirchenmusik* (Leipzig, 1936)

W. Neumann: *J.S. Bachs Chorfuge* (Leipzig, 1938, 3/1953)

F. Smend: 'Bachs Markus-Passion', *BJb 1940–48*, 1–35

A. Schering: *Über Kantaten Johann Sebastian Bachs* (Leipzig, 1942, 3/1950)

F. Smend: 'Neue Bach-Funde', *AMf*, vii (1942), 1–16; repr. in *Friedrich Smend: Bach-Studien*, ed. C. Wolff (Kassel, 1969), 137–52

A. Mendel: 'On the Keyboard Accompaniments to Bach's Leipzig Church Music', *MQ*, xxxvi (1950), 339–62

A. Dürr: 'Zur Chronologie der Leipziger Vokalwerke J.S. Bachs', *BJb 1957*, 5–162; pubd separately (Berlin, 1958, 2/1976)

W. Neumann: 'Über Ausmass und Wesen des Bachschen Parodieverfahrens', *BJb 1965*, 63–85

R.L. Marshall: *The Compositional Process of J.S. Bach: a Study of the Autograph Scores of the Vocal Works* (Princeton, NJ, 1972)

W. Neumann, ed.: *Sämtliche von Johann Sebastian Bach vertonte Texte* (Leipzig, 1974)

U. Siegele: 'Bachs Endzweck einer regulierten und Entwurf einer wohlbestallten Kirchenmusik', *Festschrift Georg von Dadelsen zum 60. Geburtstag*, ed. T. Kohlhase and V. Scherliess (Neuhausen-Stuttgart, 1978), 313–51

L. Dreyfus: 'J.S. Bach's Experiment in Differentiated Accompaniment: Tacet Indications in Organ Parts', *JAMS*, xxxii (1979), 321–34

J. Rifkin: 'Bach's Chorus: a Preliminary Report', *MT*, cxxiii (1982), 747–54

W. Blankenburg: 'Johann Sebastian Bach und das evangelische Kirchenlied zu seiner Zeit', *Bachiana et alia musicologica: Festschrift Alfred Dürr*, ed. W. Rehm (Kassel, 1983), 31–8

G. von Dadelsen: 'Anmerkungen zu Bachs Parodieverfahren', ibid., 52–7

R. Marshall: 'Bach's Chorus: a Preliminary Reply to Joshua Rifkin', *MT*, cxxiv (1983), 19–22

J. Rifkin: 'Bach's Chorus: a Response to Robert Marshall', ibid., 161–2

G. Wagner: 'Die Chorbesetzung bei J.S. Bach und ihre Vorgeschichte: Anmerkungen zur "hinlänglichen" Besetzung im 17. und 18. Jahrhundert', *AMw*, xliii (1986), 278–304

K. Häfner: *Aspekte des Parodieverfahrens bei Johann Sebastian Bach: Beiträge zur Wiederentdeckung verschollener Vokalwerke* (Laaber, 1987)

S.A. Crist: *Aria Forms in the Vocal Works of J.S. Bach, 1714–24* (diss., Brandeis U., 1988)

H.H. Eggebrecht: 'Sinnbildlichkeit in Text und Musik bei Johann Sebastian Bach', *Musik und Kirche*, lviii (1988), 176–84

E.T. Chafe: *Tonal Allegory in the Vocal Music of J.S. Bach* (Berkeley, 1991)

M. Walter: *Musik-Sprache des Glaubens: zum geistlichen Vokalwerk Johann Sebastian Bachs* (Frankfurt, 1994)

S.A. Crist: 'Bach, Theology, and Harmony: a New Look at the Arias', *Bach*, xxvii/1 (1996), 1–30

D.E. Freeman: 'J.S. Bach's "Concerto" Arias: a Study in the Amalgamation of Eighteenth-Century Genres', *Studi musicali*, xxvii (1998), 123–62

cantatas

R. Wustmann, ed.: *Johann Sebastian Bachs Kantatentexte* (Leipzig, 1913, rev. 2/1967 as *Geistliche und weltliche Kantatentexte*)

C.S. Terry: *Joh. Seb. Bach: Cantata Texts, Sacred and Secular, with a Reconstruction of the Leipzig Liturgy of his Period* (London, 1926/R)

W. Neumann: *Handbuch der Kantaten Johann Sebastian Bachs* (Leipzig, 1947, 5/1984)

F. Smend: *Joh. Seb. Bach: Kirchen-Kantaten* (Berlin, 1947–9, 3/1966)

I. Finlay: *Johann Sebastian Bachs weltliche Kantaten* (Göttingen, 1950)

I. Finlay: 'Bach's Secular Cantata Texts', *ML*, xxxi (1950), 189–95

A. Dürr: *Studien über die frühen Kantaten J.S. Bachs* (Leipzig, 1951, 2/1977)

A. Dürr: 'Zur Echtheit einiger Bach zugeschriebener Kantaten', *BJb 1951–2*, 30–46

K.F. Tagliavini: *Studi sui testi delle cantate sacre di J.S. Bach* (Padua, 1956)

P. Mies: *Die geistlichen Kantaten Johann Sebastian Bachs und der Hörer von heute*, i (Wiesbaden, 1959, 2/1966); ii (1960, 2/1968); iii (1964)

W.H. Scheide: 'Johann Sebastian Bachs Sammlung von Kantaten seines Vetters Johann Ludwig Bach', *BJb 1959*, 52–94; *1961*, 5–24; *1962*, 5–32

W.G. Whittaker: *The Cantatas of Johann Sebastian Bach* (London, 1959)

J. Day: *The Literary Background to Bach's Cantatas* (London, 1961)

P. Mies: *Die weltlichen Kantaten Johann Sebastian Bachs und der Hörer von heute*, i (Wiesbaden, 1966–7)

A. Dürr: *Die Kantaten von Johann Sebastian Bach* (Kassel, 1971, 6/1995)

R. Gerlach: 'Besetzung und Instrumentation der Kirchenkantaten J.S. Bachs und ihre Bedingungen', *BJb 1971*, 53–71

W. Hobohm: 'Neue Texte zur Leipziger Kirchen-Musik', *BJb 1973*, 5–32

A. Dürr: 'Bachs Kantatentexte: Probleme und Aufgaben der Forschung', *Bach-Studien*, v (1975), 63–71

K. Häfner: 'Der Picander-Jahrgang', *BJb 1975*, 70–113

W. Blankenburg: 'Eine neue Textquelle zu sieben Kantaten Johann Sebastian Bachs und achtzehn Kantaten Johann Ludwig Bachs', *BJb 1977*, 7–25

W.H. Scheide: 'Bach und der Picander-Jahrgang', *BJb 1980*, 47–52

K. Häfner: 'Picander, der Textdichter von Bachs viertem Kantatenjahrgang: ein neuer Hinweis', *Mf*, xxxv (1982), 156–62

C. Wolff: 'Wo bleib Bachs fünfter Kantatenjahrgang?', ibid., 151–2

W.H. Scheide: 'Eindeutigkeit und Mehrdeutigkeit in Picanders Kantatenjahrgangs-Vorbemerkung und im Werkverzeichnis des Nekrologs auf Johann Sebastian Bach', *BJb 1983*, 109–14

L. Dreyfus: 'The Metaphorical Soloist: Concerted Organ Parts in Bach's Cantatas', *EMc*, xiii (1985), 237–47

A. Glöckner: 'Zur Chronologie der Weimarer Kantaten Johann Sebastian Bachs', *BJb 1985*, 159–64

A. Dürr: 'Noch einmal: Wo blieb Bachs fünfter Kantatenjahrgang?', *BJb 1986*, 121–2

A. Hirsch: *Die Zahl im Kantatenwerk Johann Sebastian Bachs* (Neuhausen-Stuttgart, 1986)

H.K. Krause-: 'Erdmann Neumeister und die Kantatentexte Johann Sebastian Bachs', *BJb 1986*, 7–31

A. Dürr: 'Merkwürdiges in den Quellen zu Weimarer Kantaten Bachs', *BJb 1987*, 151–7

A. Glöckner: 'Überlegungen zu J.S. Bachs Kantatenschaffen nach 1730', *Beiträge zur Bachforschung*, vi (1987), 54–64

W.M. Young: *The Cantatas of J.S. Bach: an Analytical Guide* (Jefferson, NC, 1989)

H.-J. Schulze: 'Bach's Secular Cantatas: a New Look at the Sources', *Bach*, xxi/1 (1990), 26–41

F. Krummacher: 'Bachs frühe Kantaten im Kontext der Tradition', *Mf*, xliv (1991), 9–32

L. and R. Steiger: *Sehet! Wir gehn hinauf gen Jerusalem: Johann Sebastian Bachs Kantaten auf den Sonntag Estomihi* (Göttingen, 1992)

K. Hofmann: 'Neue Überlegungen zu Bachs Weimarer Kantaten-Kalender', *BJb 1993*, 9–29

D.R. Melamed: 'Mehr zur Chronologie von Bachs Weimarer Kantaten', ibid., 213–16

U. Meyer: '"Flügel her! Flügel her!": gepredigte Sterbekunst als Hintergrund Bachscher Kantatentexte', *Musik und Kirche*, lxiii (1993), 258–65

M. Petzoldt: *Texte zur Leipziger Kirchen-music: zum Verständnis der Kantatentexte Johann Sebastian Bachs* (Wiesbaden, 1993)

R. Steiger: 'So lerne nun die neue Evangelische Sprache: Elemente einer musikalischen Sprache des Trostes in J.S. Bachs Sterbekantaten', *Musik und Kirche*, lxiv (1994), 255–63

F. Krummacher: *Bachs Zyklus der Choralkantaten: Aufgaben und Lösungen* (Göttingen, 1995)

D.L. Smithers: 'The Original Circumstances in the Performance of Bach's Leipzig Church Cantatas, "Wegen seiner sonn- und festtätigen Amts-Verrichtungen"', *Bach*, xxvi/1–2 (1995), 28–47

C. Wolff and T. Koopman, eds.: *De wereld van de Bach-cantates*, i, *Johann Sebastian Bachs geestelijke cantates van Arnstadt tot Köthen* (Abcoude, 1995; Eng. trans., 1997)

Passions and oratorios

SmitherHO, ii

W. Werker: *Die Matthäus-Passion* (Leipzig, 1923)

F. Smend: 'Die Johannes-Passion von Bach', *BJb 1926*, 105–28; repr. in *Friedrich Smend: Bach-Studien*, ed. C. Wolff (Kassel, 1969), 11–23

C.S. Terry: 'The Spurious Bach "Lukas-Passion"', *ML*, xiv (1933), 207–21

A. Schering: 'Zur Markus-Passion und zur "vierten" Passion', *BJb 1939*, 1–32

F. Smend: 'Bachs Markus Passion', *BJb 1940–48*, 1–35; repr. in *Friedrich Smend: Bach-Studien*, ed. C. Wolff (Kassel, 1969), 110–36

A. Dürr: 'Zu den verschollenen Passionen Bachs', *BJb 1949–50*, 81–99

F. Smend: 'Bachs Himmelsfahrts-Oratorium', *Bach-Gedenkschrift*, ed. K. Matthaei (Zürich, 1950), 42–65; repr. in *Friedrich Smend: Bach-Studien*, ed. C. Wolff (Kassel, 1969), 195–211

W. Serauky: 'Die "Johannes-Passion" von Joh. Seb. Bach und ihr Vorbild', *BJb 1954*, 29–39

B. Smallman: *The Background of Passion Music: J.S. Bach and his Predecessors* (London, 1957, enlarged 2/1970)

J. Chailley: *Les Passions de J.-S. Bach* (Paris, 1963, 2/1984)

A. Mendel: 'Traces of the Pre-History of Bach's St John and St Matthew Passions', *Festschrift Otto Erich Deutsch*, ed. W. Gerstenberg, J. LaRue and W. Rehm (Kassel, 1963), 31–48

D. Gojowy: 'Zur Frage der Köthener Trauermusik und der Matthäuspassion', *BJb 1965*, 86–134

P. Brainard: 'Bach's Parody Procedure and the St. Matthew Passion', *JAMS*, xxii (1969), 241–60

A. Glöckner: 'Bach and the Passion Music of his Contemporaries', *MT*, cxvi (1975), 613–16

J. Rifkin: 'The Chronology of Bach's Saint Matthew Passion', *MQ*, lxi (1975), 360–87

E. Axmacher: 'Ein Quellenfund zum Text der Matthäus-Passion', *BJb 1978*, 181–91

G.A. Theill: *Die Markuspassion von Johann Sebastian Bach* (bwv247): *Entstehung, Vergessen, Wiederentdeckung, Rekonstruktion* (Steinfeld, 1978, 2/1981)

P. Steinitz: *Bach's Passions* (London, 1979)

E.T. Chafe: 'Key Structure and Tonal Allegory in the Passions of J.S. Bach: an Introduction', *CMc*, no.31 (1981), 39–54

R. Steiger: 'Die Einheit des *Weinachtsoratoriums* von J.S. Bach', *Musik und Kirche*, li (1981), 273–80; lii (1982), 9–15

W. Blankenburg: *Das Weinachts-Oratorium von Johann Sebastian Bach* (Munich and Kassel, 1982)

E.T. Chafe: 'J.S. Bach's *St. Matthew Passion*; Aspects of Planning, Structure, and Chronology', *JAMS*, xxxv (1982), 49–114

R.A. Leaver: *Music as Preaching: Bach, Passions and Music in Worship* (Oxford, 1982)

E. Axmacher: *'Aus Liebe will mein Heyland sterben': Untersuchungen zum Wandel des Passionverständnisses im frühen 18. Jahrhundert* (Neuhausen-Stuttgart, 1984)

W.F. Hindermann: *Johann Sebastian Bach, Himmelfahrts-Oratorium: Gestalt und Gehalt* (Hofheim am Taunus, 1985)

C. Wolff: 'Bachs Unvollendete: die Johannes-Passion. Mehrbändiges Kompendium erschliesst das monumentale Werk des Komponisten', *Neue Musikzeitung*, xxxvi/2 (1987), 39 only

A. Dürr: *Die Johannes-Passion von Johann Sebastian Bach: Entstehung, Überlieferung, Werkeinführung* (Munich and Kassel, 1988)

C. Wolff: 'Musical Forms and Dramatic Structure in Bach's *Saint Matthew Passion*', *Bach*, xix/1 (1988), 6–20

M. Geck: *Johann Sebastian Bach, Johannespassion* bwv245 (Munich, 1991)

K. Hofmann: 'Zur Tonartenordnung der Johannes-Passion von Johann Sebastian Bach', *Musik und Kirche*, lxi (1991), 78–86

E. Platen: *Die Matthäus-Passion von Johann Sebastian Bach: Entstehung, Werkbeschreibung, Rezeption* (Munich and Kassel, 1991)

W.M. Young: *The Sacred Dramas of J.S. Bach: a Reference and Textual Interpretation* (Jefferson, NC, 1994)

Latin church music, motets and chorales

C.S. Terry: *Bach's Chorals* (Cambridge, 1915–21/R)

A. Schering: 'Die Höhe Messe in h-moll', *BJb 1936*, 1–30

F. Smend: 'Bachs h-moll-Messe: Entstehung, Uberlieferung, Bedeutung', *BJb 1937*, 1–58

W. Blankenburg: *Einführung in Bachs h-moll-Messe* (Kassel, 1950, 3/1974)

R. Bullivant: 'Zum Problem der Begleitung der Bachschen Motetten', *BJb 1966*, 59–68

F. Smend: 'Zu den ältesten Sammlungen der vierstimmigen Choräle J.S. Bachs', ibid., 5–40; repr. in *Friedrich Smend: Bach-Studien*, ed. C. Wolff (Kassel, 1969), 237–69

R. Leavis: 'Bach's Setting of Psalm CXVII (BWV230)', *ML*, lii (1971), 19–26

F. Krummacher: 'Textauslegung und Satzstruktur in J.S. Bachs Motetten', *BJb 1974*, 5–43

M. Geck: 'Zur Datierung, Verwendung und Aufführungspraxis von Bachs Motetten', *Bach-Studien*, v (1975), 63–71

H. Rilling: *Johann Sebastian Bachs h-Moll-Messe* (Neuhausen-Stuttgart, 1979, 2/1986)

G.J. Buelow: 'Symbol and Structure in the "Kyrie" of Bach's B-minor Mass', *Essays on the Music of J.S. Bach and Other Divers Subjects: a Tribute to Gerhard Herz*, ed. R.L. Weaver (Louisville, KY, 1981), 21–41

A. Mann: 'Bach's *A major Mass*; a Nativity Mass?', ibid., 43–7

R.M. Cammarota: 'The Sources of the Christmas Interpolations in J.S. Bach's *Magnificat* in E-flat Major', *CMc*, no.36 (1983), 79–99

H.-J. Schulze: '"150 Stück von den Bachischen Erben": zur Überlieferung der vierstimmigen Choräle Johann Sebastian Bachs', *BJb 1983*, 81–100

G. Wachowski: 'Die vierstimmigen Choräle Johann Sebastian Bachs: Untersuchungen zu den Druckausgaben von 1765 bis 1932 und zur Frage der Authentizität', ibid., 51–79

A. Mann: '*Missa Brevis* and *Historia*: Bach's A Major Mass', *Bach*, xvi/1 (1985), 6–11

Y. Kobayashi: 'Die Universalität in Bachs *h-moll-Messe*: ein Beitrag zum Bach-Bild der Letzten Lebensjahre', *Musik und Kirche*, lvii (1987), 9–24

R.A. Leaver: 'Bach, Kirchenlieder und Gesangbücher', ibid., 169–74

W. Breig: 'Grundzüge einer Geschichte von Bachs vierstimmigen Choralsatz', *AMw*, xlv (1988), 300–19

C. Wolff: 'Bach the Cantor, the *Capellmeister*, and the Musical Scholar: Aspects of the B-Minor Mass', *Bach*, xx/1 (1989), 55–64

R.A. Leaver: 'Parody and Theological Consistency: Notes on Bach's A-major Mass', *Bach*, xxi/3 (1990), 30–43

J. Butt: *Bach: Mass in B Minor* (Cambridge, 1991)

P. Wollny: 'Bachs Sanctus BWV 241 und Kerlls "Missa superba"', *BJb 1991*, 173–6

A. Durr: 'Zur Parodiefrage in Bachs *h-moll-Messe*: eine Bestandsaufnahme', *Mf*, xlv (1992), 117–38

R. Stinson: 'Some Thoughts on Bach's Neumeister Chorales', *JM*, xi (1993), 455–77

P. Wollny: 'Ein Quellenfund zur Enstehungsgeschichte der h-Moll-Messe', *BJb 1994*, 163–9

R.L. Marshall: *Luther, Bach, and the Early Reformation Chorale* (Atlanta, GA, 1995)

D.R. Melamed: *J.S. Bach and the German Motet* (Cambridge, 1995)

K: INSTRUMENTAL WORKS

general

K.A. Rosenthal: 'Über Sonatenvorformen in den Instrumentalmusikwerken Joh. Seb. Bachs', *BJb 1926*, 68–89

C.S. Terry: *Bach's Orchestra* (London, 1932/R)

J.M. Barbour: 'Bach and "The Art of Temperament"', *MQ*, xxxiii (1947), 64–89

A.E.F. Dickinson: *Bach's Fugal Works* (London, 1956/R)

C. Dahlhaus: 'Bach und der "lineare Kontrapunkt"', *BJb 1962*, 58–79

H.-J. Klein: *Der Einfluss der Vivaldischen Konzertform im Instrumentalwerk Johann Sebastian Bachs* (Strasbourg, 1970)

C. Wolff: 'Ordnungsprinzipien in den Originaldrucken Bachscher Werke', *Bach-Interpretationen*, ed. M. Geck (Göttingen, 1969),

144–67; Eng. trans. in *Bach: Essays on his Life and Music* (Cambridge, MA, 1991), 340–58

U. Siegele: *Kompositionsweise und Bearbeitungstechnik in der Instrumentalmusik Johann Sebastian Bachs* (Neuhausen-Stuttgart, 1975)

J.R. Fuchs: *Studien zu Artikulationsangaben in Orgel- und Clavierwerken von Joh. Seb. Bach* (Neuhausen-Stuttgart, 1985)

H.-J. Schulze: 'The French Influence in Bach's Instrumental Music', *EMc*, xiii (1985), 180–84

R. Stinson: 'Toward a Chronology of Bach's Instrumental Music: Observations on Three Keyboard Works', *JM*, vii (1989), 440–70

organ works

FrotscherG

H. Grace: *The Organ Works of Bach* (London and New York, 1922)

F. Dietrich: 'Analogieformen in Bachs Tokkaten und Präludien für die Orgel', *BJb 1931*, 51–71

H. Klotz: *Über die Orgelkunst der Gotik, der Renaissance und des Barock* (Kassel, 1934, 3/1986)

H. Keller: 'Unechte Orgelwerke Bachs', *BJb 1937*, 59–82

S. de B. Taylor: *The Chorale Preludes of J.S. Bach* (London, 1942)

H. Keller: *Die Orgelwerke Bachs: ein Beitrag zu ihrer Geschichte, Form, Deutung und Wiedergabe* (Leipzig, 1948/R; Eng. trans., 1967)

H. Klotz: 'Bachs Orgeln und seine Orgelmusik', *Mf*, iii (1950), 189–203

K. Matthaei: 'Johann Sebastian Bachs Orgel', *Bach-Gedenkschrift*, ed. K. Matthaei (Zürich, 1950), 118–149

P. Aldrich: *Ornamentation in J.S. Bach's Organ Works* (New York, 1950/R)

W. Emery: *Notes on Bach's Organ Works: a Companion to the Revised Novello Edition* (London, 1952–7)

W. Schrammek: 'Die musikgeschichtliche Stellung der Orgeltrio sonaten von Joh. Seb. Bach', *BJb 1954*, 7–28

R. Donington: *Tempo and Rhythm in Bach's Organ Music* (London, 1960)

G. von Dadelsen: 'Zur Entstehung des Bachschen Orgelbüchleins', *Festschrift Friedrich Blume*, ed. A.A. Abert and W. Pfannkuch (Kassel, 1963), 74–9

P.F. Williams: 'J.S. Bach and English Organ Music', *ML*, xliv (1963), 140–51

E.D. May: *Breitkopf's Role in the Transmission of J.S. Bach's Organ Chorales* (diss., Princeton U., 1974)

E. May: 'Eine neue Quelle für J.S. Bachs einzeln überlieferte Orgelchoräle', *BJb 1974*, 98–103

U. Meyer: 'Zur Einordnung von J.S. Bachs einzeln überlieferten Orgelchorälen', *BJb 1977*, 75–89

C. Wolff: 'Bachs Handexemplar der Schübler-Chorale', ibid., 120–29

T.F. Harmon: *The Registration of J.S. Bach's Organ Works* (Buren, 1978)

G.B. Stauffer: *The Organ Preludes of Johann Sebastian Bach* (Ann Arbor, 1980)

P. Williams: *The Organ Music of J.S. Bach* (Cambridge, 1980–84)

P. Williams: 'The Musical Aims of J.S. Bach's "Clavierübung III"', *Source Materials and the Interpretation of Music: a Memorial Volume to Thurston Dart*, ed. I. Bent (London, 1981), 259–78

D. Humphreys: *The Esoteric Structure of Bach's Clavierübung III* (Cardiff, 1983)

D. Kilian: 'Zu einem Bachschen Tabulatorautograph', *Bachiana et alia musicologica: Festschrift Alfred Dürr*, ed. W. Rehm (Kassel, 1983), 161–7

H. Klotz: *Studien zu Bachs Registrierkunst* (Wiesbaden, 1985)

F. Krummacher: 'Bach und die norddeutsche Orgeltoccata: Fragen und Überlegungen', *BJb 1985*, 119–34

R.A. Leaver: 'Bach and Hymnody: the Evidence of the *Orgelbüchlein*', *EMc*, xiii (1985), 227–36

C. Wolff: 'Bach's Organ Music: Studies and Discoveries', *MT*, cxxvi (1985), 149–52

G.B. Stauffer and E.May, eds.: *J.S. Bach as Organist: his Instruments, Music, and Performance Practices* (Bloomington, IN, 1986)

J.-C. Zehnder: 'Georg Böhm und Johann Sebastian Bach: zur Chronologie der Bachschen Stilentwicklung', *BJb 1988*, 73–110

G. Butler: *Bach's Clavier-Übung III: the Making of a Print, with a Companion Study of the Canonic Variations on 'Vom Himmel hoch' BWV 769* (Durham, NC, 1990)

W. Breig: 'Formprobleme in Bachs frühen Orgelfugen', *BJb 1992*, 7–21

G.B. Stauffer: 'Boyvin, Grigny, D'Anglebert, and Bach's Assimilation of French Classical Organ Music', *EMc*, xxi (1993), 83–96

W. Breig: 'Versuch einer Theorie der Bachschen Orgelfuge', *Mf*, xlviii (1995), 14–52

R.D. Claus: *Zur Echtheit von Toccata und Fuge d-moll BWV 565* (Cologne, 1995)

Q. Faulkner: 'Die Registrierung der Orgelwerke J.S. Bachs', *BJb* 1995, 7–30

R. Stinson: *Bach: the Orgelbüchlein* (New York, 1996)

keyboard and lute music

W. Werker: *Studien über die Symmetrie im Bau der Fugen und die motivische Zusammengehörigkeit der Präludien und Fugen des 'Wohltemperierten Klaviers' von Johann Sebastian Bach* (Leipzig, 1922/R)

H. David: 'Die Gestalt von Bachs Chromatischer Fantasie', *BJb* 1926, 2–67

H. Neeman: 'J.S. Bachs Lautenkompositionen', *BJb* 1931, 72–87

H. Keller: *Die Klavierwerke Bachs* (Leipzig, 1950)

J.N. David: *Das wohltemperierte Klavier: der Versuch einer Synopsis* (Göttingen, 1962)

H. Keller: *Das Wohltemperierte Klavier von Johann Sebastian Bach: Werke und Wiedergabe* (Kassel, 1965, 4/1994; Eng. trans., 1976)

W. Breig: 'Bachs Goldberg-Variationen als zyklisches Werk', *AMw*, xxxii (1975), 243–65

H. Eichberg: 'Unechtes unter Johann Sebastian Bachs Klavierwerken', *BJb* 1975, 7–49

H.-J. Schulze: 'Melodiezitate und Mehrtextigkeit in der Bauernkantate und in den Goldberg-Variationen', *BJb* 1976, 58–72

C. Wolff: 'Bach's *Handexemplar* of the Goldberg Variations: a New Source', *JAMS*, xxix (1976), 224–41; repr. in *Bach: Essays on his Life and Music* (Cambridge, MA, 1991), 162–77

A. Burguéte: 'Die Lautenkompositionen Johann Sebastian Bachs', *BJb* 1977, 26–54

J. Barnes: 'Bach's Keyboard Temperament: Internal Evidence from the *Well-Tempered Clavier*', *EMc*, vii (1979), 236–49

C. Wolff: 'Textkritische Bemerkungen zum Originaldruck der Bachschen Partiten', *BJb* 1979, 65–74; Eng. trans. in *Bach: Essays on his Life and Music* (Cambridge, MA, 1991), 214–22

A. Dürr: *Zur Frühgeschichte des Wohltemperierten Klaviers I von Johann Sebastian Bach* (Göttingen, 1984)

P. Williams: 'J.S. Bach's *Well-Tempered Clavier*: a New Approach', *EMc*, xi (1983), 46–52, 332–9

D. Humphreys: 'More on the Cosmological Allegory in Bach's *Goldberg Variations*', *Soundings*, xii (1984–5), 25–45

I. Kaussler: *Die Goldberg-Variationen von J.S. Bach* (Stuttgart, 1985)

R. Dammann: *Johann Sebastian Bachs 'Goldberg-Variationen'* (Mainz, 1986)

A. Street: 'The Rhetorico-Musical Structure of the *Goldberg Variations*: Bach's *Clavier-Übung IV* and the *Institutio oratoria* of Quintilian', *MAn*, vi (1987), 89–131

G. Butler: 'Neues zur Datierung der Goldberg-Variationen', *BJb* 1988, 219–23

D. Schulenberg: *The Keyboard Music of J.S. Bach* (New York, 1992)

Y. Tomita: *J.S. Bach's 'Das Wohltemperierte Clavier II': a Critical Commentary* (Leeds, 1993–5)

orchestral and chamber music

ScheringGIK

N. Carrell: *Bach's Brandenburg Concertos* (London, 1963, 2/1985)

H. Eppstein: *Studien über J.S. Bachs Sonaten für ein Melodieinstrument und obligates Cembalo* (Stockholm, 1966)

H. Eppstein: 'Grundzüge in J.S. Bachs Sonatenschaffen', *BJb* 1969, 5–30

L. Hoffmann-Erbrecht: 'Johann Sebastian Bach als Schöpfer des Klavier Konzerts', *Quellenstudien zur Musik: Wolfgang Schmieder zum 70. Geburtstag*, ed. K. Dorfmüller and G. von Dadelsen (Frankfurt, 1972), 69–77

H.-J. Schulze: 'Johann Sebastian Bachs Konzertbearbeitungen nach Vivaldi und anderen: Studien- oder Auftragswerke?', *DJbM*, xviii (1973–7), 80–100

A. Dürr: 'Zur Entstehungsgeschichte des 5. Brandenburgischen Konzerts', *BJb* 1975, 63–9

W. Breig: 'Bachs Violinkonzert d-moll: Studien zu seiner Gestalt und Entstehungsgeschichte', *BJb* 1976, 7–34

H. Eppstein: 'Chronologieprobleme in Johann Sebastian Bachs Suiten für Soloinstrument', ibid., 35–57

W. Breig: 'Johann Sebastian Bach und die Entstehung des Klavierkonzerts', *AMw*, xxxvi (1979), 21–48

R. Leavis: 'Zur Frage der Authentizität von Bachs Violinkonzert d-Moll', *BJb* 1979, 19–28

R.L. Marshall: 'J.S. Bach's Compositions for Solo Flute: a Reconsideration of their Authenticity and Chronology', *JAMS*, xxxii (1979), 463–98

H.-J. Schulze: 'Ein "Dresdner Menuett" im zweiten Klavierbüchlein der Anna Magdalena Bach, nebst Hinweisen zur Überlieferung einiger Kammermusikwerke Bachs', *BJb* 1979, 45–64

P. Ahnsehl, K.Heller and H.-J. Schulze, eds.: 'Beiträge zum Konzertschaffen J. S. Bachs', *Bach-Studien*, vi (1981)

H. Vogt: *Johann Sebastian Bachs Kammermusik* (Stuttgart, 1981; Eng. trans., 1988)

W. Breig: 'Zur Chronologie von Johann Sebastian Bachs Konzertschaffen: Versuch eines neuen Zugangs', *AMw*, xl (1983), 77–101

L. Dreyfus: 'J.S. Bach's Concerto Ritornellos and the Question of Invention', *MQ*, lxxi (1985), 327–58

C. Wolff: 'Bach's Leipzig Chamber Music', *EMc*, xiii (1985), 165–75; repr. in *Bach: Essays on his Life and Music* (Cambridge, MA, 1991), 223–38

L. Dreyfus: 'J.S. Bach and the Status of Genre: Problems of Style in the G-minor Sonata BWV1029', *JM*, v (1987), 55–78

M. Marissen: 'A Critical Reappraisal of J.S. Bach's A-major Flute Sonata', *JM*, vi (1988), 367–86

C. Berger: 'J.S. Bachs Cembalokonzerte', *AMw*, xlvii (1990), 207–16

E. Lang-Becker: *Johann Sebastian Bach: die Brandenburgischen Konzerte* (Munich, 1990)

M. Boyd: *Bach: the Brandenburg Concertos* (Cambridge, 1993)

J. Swack: 'On the Origins of the "Sonate auf Concertenart"', *JAMS*, xlvi (1993), 369–414

C. Wolff: 'Das Trio A-Dur BWV 1025: eine Lautensonate von Silvius Leopold Weiss, bearbeitet und erweitert von Johann Sebastian Bach', *BJb* 1993, 47–67

M. Geck: 'Köthen oder Leipzig?: zur Datierung der nun in Leipziger Quellen erhaltenen Orchesterwerke Johann Sebastian Bachs', *Mf*, xlvii (1994), 17–24

M. Marissen: *The Social and Religious Designs of J.S. Bach's Brandenburg Concertos* (Princeton, NJ, 1995)

M. Geck: *Bachs Orchesterwerke* (Witten, 1997)

Art of Fugue, Musical Offering, canons

W. Graeser: 'Bachs "Kunst der Fuge"', *BJb* 1924, 1–104

D.F. Tovey: *A Companion to 'The Art of Fugue'* (London, 1931)

H.T. David: *J.S. Bach's Musical Offering: History, Interpretation and Analysis* (New York, 1945/R)

G.M. Leonhardt: *The Art of Fugue, Bach's Last Harpsichord Work: an Argument* (The Hague, 1952)

H.-J. Schulze: 'Johann Sebastian Bachs Kanonwidmungen', *BJb* 1967, 82–92

C. Wolff: 'Der Terminus "Ricercar" in Bachs Musikalischen Opfer', ibid., 70–81

C. Wolff: 'New Research on Bach's *Musical Offering*', *MQ*, lvii (1971), 379–408

C. Wolff: 'Überlegungen zum "Thema Regium"', *BJb* 1973, 33–8

C. Wolff and others: 'Bach's "Art of Fugue": an Examination of the Sources', *CMc*, no.19 (1975), 47–77

N. Kenyon: 'A Newly Discovered Group of Canons by Bach', *MT*, cxvii (1976), 391–3

W. Kolneder: *Die Kunst der Fuge: Mythen des 20. Jahrhunderts* (Wilhelmshaven, 1977, 2/1983)

W. Wiemer: *Die wiederhergestellte Ordnung in Johann Sebastian Bachs Kunst der Fuge: Untersuchungen am Originaldruck* (Wiesbaden, 1977)

U. Kirkendale: 'The Source for Bach's *Musical Offering*: the *Institutio oratoria* of Quintilian', *JAMS*, xxxiii (1980), 88–141

G.G. Butler: 'Ordering Problems in J.S. Bach's *Art of Fugue* Resolved', *MQ*, lxix (1983), 44–61

C. Wolff: 'Zur Chronologie und Kompositionsgeschichte von Bachs "Kunst der Fuge"', *BMw*, xxv (1983), 130–42; Eng. trans. in *Bach: Essays on his Life and Music* (Cambridge, MA, 1991), 265–81

E.T. Chafe: 'Allegorical Music: the Symbolism of Tonal Language in the Bach Canons', *JM*, iii (1984), 340–62

H.H. Eggebrecht: *Bachs Kunst der Fuge: Erscheinung und Deutung* (Munich, 1984; Eng. trans., 1993)

E. Bergel: *Bachs letzte Fuge, die 'Kunst der Fuge', ein zyklisches Werk: Entstehungsgeschichte, Erstausgabe, Ordnungsprinzipien* (Bonn, 1985)

R. Boss: *Die Kunst des Rätselkanons im Musikalischen Opfer* (Wilhelmshaven, 1991)

P. Schleuning: *Johann Sebastian Bachs 'Kunst der Fuge': Ideologien, Entstehung, Analyse* (Munich and Kassel, 1993)

P. Dirksen: *Studien zur Kunst der Fuge von Johann Sebastian Bach: Untersuchungen zur Enstehungsgeschichte, Struktur und Aufführungspraxis* (Wilhelmshaven, 1994)

M. Marissen: 'More Source-Critical Research on Bach's *Musical Offering*', *Bach*, xxv/1 (1994), 11–27

L: PERFORMING PRACTICE

W. Emery: *Bach's Ornaments* (London, 1953)

F. Rothschild: *The Lost Tradition in Music: Rhythm and Tempo in J.S. Bach's Time* (London, 1953/R)

A. Mendel: 'On the Pitches in Use in Bach's Time', *MQ*, xli (1955), 332–54, 466–80

W. Emery: 'Is your Bach Playing Authentic?', *MT*, cxii (1971), 483–8, 697–8, 796–7

H. Grüss: 'Tempofragen der Bachzeit', *Bach-Studien*, v (1975), 73–81

F. Neumann: *Ornamentation in Baroque and Post-Baroque Music with Special Emphasis on J.S. Bach* (Princeton, NJ, 1978)

K. Hochreiter: *Zur Aufführungspraxis der Vokal-Instrumentalwerke Johann Sebastian Bachs* (Berlin, 1983)

R. Kirkpatrick: *Interpreting Bach's Well-tempered Clavier: a Performer's Discourse of Method* (New Haven, CT, 1984)

H. Klotz: *Die Ornamentik der Klavier- und Orgelwerke von Johann Sebastian Bach: Bedeutung der Zeichen, Möglichkeiten der Ausführung* (Kassel, 1984)

A. Newman: *Bach and the Baroque: a Performing Guide to Baroque Music with Special Emphasis on the Music of J.S. Bach* (New York, 1985)

G. Stauffer and E.May, eds.: *J.S. Bach as Organist: his Instruments, Music, and Performance Practices* (Bloomington, IN, 1986)

R. Szeskus and H.Gruss, eds.: *Aufführungspraktische Probleme der Werke Johann Sebastian Bachs* (Leipzig, 1987)

H.-J. Schulze: 'Johann Sebastian Bach's Orchestra: Some Unanswered Questions', *EMc*, xvii (1989), 3–15

P. Badura-Skoda: *Bach-Interpretation: die Klavierwerke Johann Sebastian Bachs* (Laaber, 1990; Eng. trans., 1993)

J. Butt: *Bach Interpretation: Articulation Marks in Primary Sources of J.S. Bach* (Cambridge, 1990)

H.-J. Schulze: *Bach stilgericht aufführen, Wunschbild und Wirklichkeit: einige aufführungspraktische Aspekte von Johann Sebastian Bachs Leipziger Kirchenmusik* (Wiesbaden, 1991)

(8) Wilhelm Friedemann Bach

(8) Wilhelm Friedemann Bach (*45*) (*b* Weimar, 22 Nov 1710; *d* Berlin, 1 July 1784). Composer and organist, eldest son of (7) Johann Sebastian (*24*) and Maria Barbara Bach. Trained by his father and endowed with brilliant gifts, he expressed himself in the genres of his time in a sensitive and highly cultivated musical language.

1. Leipzig, Dresden, 1710–46. 2. Halle, Brunswick, Berlin, 1746–84. 3. Works, reception.

1. LEIPZIG, DRESDEN, 1710–46. He was baptized on 24 November 1710; his godparents were the Weimar chamberlain Wilhelm Ferdinand von Lynker, Anna Dorothea Hagedorn and Friedemann Meckbach, the last two acquaintances of J.S. Bach from Mühlhausen. Friedemann attended the Lutheran Lateinschule in Cöthen (1717–23), and from 14 June 1723 he was a day-boy at the Thomasschule in Leipzig. On 5 March 1729 he matriculated at Leipzig University, where his father had already registered him as a *depositus* on 22 December 1723; he attended lectures on law, philosophy, mathematics and other subjects. His early musical education, provided by his father, is documented in the *Clavier-Büchlein vor W.F. Bach*, begun on 22 January 1720 and containing entries (mainly in the hands of J.S. and W.F. Bach) up to about 1725–6. It is unlikely that this keyboard book reflects his very first systematic music lessons, since even

the earliest entries are technically demanding. More plausibly it may be regarded as instruction in composition. Its repertory consists of works (inventions, sinfonias and preludes) that J.S. Bach probably wrote specifically for educational purposes, as well as several pieces by other authors (Telemann, G.H. Stölzel, J.C. Richter). It also contains fingering instructions, a table of ornaments after D'Anglebert, and Friedemann's own first attempts at composition, written with paternal guidance around 1720 and 1725–6 (two allemandes BWV836–7 and four preludes BWV924*a*, 925, 932 and 931). From Christmas 1724 until August or September 1726 (i.e. while he was a pupil at the Thomasschule) W.F. Bach is known to have copied performing parts for his father, and around 1726 he took violin lessons from J.G. Graun in Merseburg 'to enable him to compose according to the nature of that instrument' (Marpurg).

At this period Friedemann accompanied his father several times to Dresden and thus became familiar with the city where he was later to live and work. He also visited Halle in 1729, when he delivered an invitation from his father to Handel, and on 29 March that year he performed in J.S. Bach's funeral music for Prince Leopold in Cöthen. In December 1732 he stood godfather, in Udestedt, to Dorothea Wilhelmine, the youngest daughter of his cousin Tobias Friedrich Bach (*40*). Little is known about his musical development during his last few years in the parental home. Copies in his hand of organ works by his father (the C major concerto arranged from Vivaldi, BWV594, and the sonatas BWV525–8) suggest that he took a particular interest in organ playing at this period. By about 1730 he must already have acquired a considerable reputation as a virtuoso organist and harpsichordist, since he took over the teaching of Christoph Nichelmann that year, perhaps to lighten his father's workload. Except for the attempts in the *Clavier-Büchlein* mentioned above, there is no certain evidence of any compositions written in Leipzig.

After failing in a competition for a post at Halberstadt in March 1731, Friedemann applied for the post of organist at the Dresden Sophienkirche which had fallen vacant on the death of Christian Petzold; his father wrote the letter of application and signed it in his name. He probably played J.S. Bach's Prelude and Fugue in G BWV541 in the competition for this post. Christoph Schaffrath and Johann Christian Stoy were the other two short-listed candidates. Documents pertaining to the competition state that the deputy Kapellmeister Pantaleon Hebenstreit, who had been invited to adjudicate, praised 'the skill of the younger Bach . . . adding that he was the best of these three well-qualified candidates'. Bach took up his duties on 1 August 1733; he was required only to play the organ for divine service and for the figural music performed on feast days, for which he was paid a modest salary of about 80 reichsthaler. However, the appointment gave him time to pursue other interests. He cultivated the acquaintance of Dresden court musicians such as J.G. Pisendel and S.L. Weiss, and presumably took an active part in the musical life of the court. A glimpse of his activities is provided by his mention of musical evenings at the house of the Electress Maria Antonia Walpurgis of Saxony, recalled in his dedication to her (in 1767) of his Harpsichord Concerto in E minor BRC 12. It seems certain that he made close contacts with music-loving aristocrats, including the Russian ambassador Count von Keyserlingk, to whom Bach dedicated a harpsichord sonata from Halle in 1763, and the *directeur des plaisirs* C.H. von Dieskau, whose wife was godmother to Bach's first son, Wilhelm Adolf, in 1752. At the same time Bach was teaching J.G. Goldberg, and continuing the study of mathematics he had begun in Leipzig under Johann Gottlieb Waltz (later court mathematician and Kommissionsrat). Bach is known to have been in Leipzig for four weeks in summer 1739, accompanied by the lutenists S.L. Weiss and Johann Kropfgans.

In Dresden Bach was also increasingly active as a composer. About 1735 he wrote the harpsichord concertos in A minor and D major (BRC 14 and 9), several sinfonias (BRC 1–6) and trio sonatas (BRB 13–15) and a number of harpsichord sonatas and smaller keyboard works. The compositions of the later part of his Dresden period (*c*1740–46) include such works as the Concerto for two harpsichords in F major BRA 12, the Harpsichord Concerto in F major BRC 13 and the Sinfonia in D minor BRC 7. The Harpsichord Sonata in D major BRA 4 was Friedemann's first work to be printed; it was published in spring 1745 and sold by his father in Leipzig and his brother Emanuel in Berlin. The intention of following it with another five sonatas was abandoned because of poor sales.

2. HALLE, BRUNSWICK, BERLIN, 1746–84. On 16 April 1746, the day that he signed the certificate of his appointment as organist to the Liebfrauenkirche in Halle, W.F. Bach also submitted a letter of resignation to the Dresden city council. He suggested that his father's pupil J.C. Altnickol should replace him in Dresden, but Altnickol was not in fact chosen. For Bach, the move to Halle meant exchanging a city dominated by court life for a middle-class town, and a subordinate position for one of the most important organist posts in central Germany. In Halle he also held the title of *director musices*, and as well as playing the organ his duties included performing figural music on a regular basis, that is on all feast days, but only on every third ordinary Sunday. In his own compositions, Bach therefore concentrated on cantatas for special occasions, since these works could be re-used annually. With the increase in his official duties Bach's income also improved, and indeed was more than doubled, for he now received an annual salary of some 180 reichsthaler. When he officially took up his post on Whit Sunday, 29 May 1746, he performed the cantata *Wer mich liebet* (BRF 13). With its large-scale opening chorus and a virtuoso aria with organ obbligato, it is obviously intended for a grand occasion; the paper used for the autograph manuscript shows that he composed it while still in Dresden.

During his early years in Halle, Friedemann seems to have been in close contact with his father in Leipzig. He accompanied J.S. Bach to Berlin in 1747 on his visit to Frederick the Great, and in 1749–50 he and his father together supported the appointment of the organ builder Heinrich Andreas Contius to Frankfurt an der Oder. Friedemann seems also to have borrowed compositions of his father's for performance in Halle (e.g. BWV31, 34 and 51). He made extensive use of his father's compositions, especially after inheriting many of his cantatas in 1750. According to an (unverifiable) anecdote told by Marpurg, he was suspected of plagiarism on the occasion of a university ceremony in 1749, when he performed parody arias from one of his father's Passions under his own name. Also in 1749, a performance was given in Leipzig of his Advent cantata *Lasset uns ablegen* (BRF 1), perhaps with the purpose of influencing the choice of a successor to J.S. Bach there, a matter under early discussion by the Leipzig city council. Johann Friedrich Wilhelm Sonnenkalb, a pupil at the Thomasschule, mentioned performances by W.F. Bach, both at private concerts in his father's house and publicly in the Grosse Concert.

Bach was embroiled in several conflicts over issues of responsibility and charges of exceeding his authority, including a dispute in 1749 with his Kantor, Johann Gottfried Mittag, who had misappropriated money due to Bach. In 1750 he was reprimanded for overstaying a leave of absence after his father's death; he had gone to Leipzig to settle the estate, and had then escorted his half-brother Johann Christian to the care of Emanuel in Berlin, where he himself stayed for several months. It is difficult to establish the veracity of the many other anecdotes about Bach's neglect of his official duties.

On 25 February 1751 Bach married Dorothea Elisabeth Georgi (1725–91), eldest daughter of the tax collector Johann Gotthilf Georgi. The marriage produced three children, two sons who died in infancy and a daughter, Friederica Sophia (*b* 27 Feb 1757). Bach seems to have had numerous pupils in Halle. As well as his distant relative Johann Christian Bach (77, the so-called 'Halle Clavier-Bach'), who acquired important original sources from Friedemann, and F.W. Rust, whose estate contained invaluable copies of some of Friedemann's keyboard works, they included Daniel Christoph Vahlkamp, J.S. Petri, Samuel Friedrich Brede, Christian Leberecht Zimmermann and Johann Carl Angerstein, who gave an account of W.F. Bach's style of chorale accompaniment in his treatise *Theoretisch-practische Anweisung, Choralgesänge nicht nur richtig sondern auch schön spielen zu lernen* (Stendal, 1800). Bach was also in contact with the Halle printer J.J. Gebauer, who owned a collection of his keyboard works, and with Marpurg, the second part of whose *Abhandlung von der Fuge* (Berlin, 1754), containing 13 canons by Friedemann, is dedicated to the brothers W.F. and C.P.E. Bach. Godparental ties also connected him with the family of the organ builder H.A. Contius, and he seems to have maintained a connection with the court at Cöthen, since the princely couple were godparents to his daughter and Friedemann composed a set of pieces for a grandfather clock mechanism at the castle there (BRA 63–80, previously ascribed to J.S. Bach as BWV Anh.133–50).

Bach's increasing dissatisfaction with his Halle post is evident in his repeated, but unsuccessful, attempts to leave. In 1753 he applied for the post of organist at the Johanniskirche in Zittau, in competition with his brother Emanuel and his father's pupils J.C. Altnickol, J.L. Krebs and Johann Trier; in 1758 and 1759 he applied for the position of Kapellmeister in Frankfurt, with a letter of recommendation from Telemann; and in 1762 he was involved in negotiations with the Landgrave of Hesse for the post of Hofkapellmeister in Darmstadt, which had fallen vacant on the death of Christoph Graupner. He seems to have drawn these negotiations out at some length intentionally, and to have broken them off in the end for unexplained reasons; however, in the dedication of the Harpsichord Concerto in E minor BRC 12 to the Electress of Saxony in 1767 he credits himself with the title of

Hofkapellmeister at Darmstadt, so it seems that the title had at some point been granted to him. After 1756 Bach's attempts to leave Halle may well have been reinforced by the hardships of the Seven Years War, which bore down with particular severity on the city and its inhabitants. The authorities placed Bach in a high tax bracket because of his wife's landed property, so that the taxes regularly levied on account of the war weighed heavily on him, and in about 1759 he was obliged to sell some of the music he had inherited from his father to Johann Georg Nacke, Kantor at Oelsnitz. The tension in Halle led to Bach's leaving his post in May 1764, a decision he took without the security of any other prospective employment. In a letter written at the end of June 1764 he mentioned plans for leaving the city, perhaps in the hope of a position in Fulda. However, he stayed in Halle until at least October 1770, and seems to have supported himself chiefly by private lessons, though his financial situation was obviously deteriorating so drastically in these years that in February 1768 he re-applied (unsuccessfully) for his old post, which had become vacant again after the death of Johann Christoph Rühlmann.

While discharging his duties as organist and music director of the Liebfrauenkirche, Bach also resumed the publication of his keyboard works: in 1748 his Sonata in E flat major BRA 7 appeared with a dedication to Privy Councillor Wilhelm von Happe, and the same piece was published again in November 1763 (not 1739 or 1768, as has variously been claimed), with a dedication to Count von Keyserlingk. In about 1765 Friedemann announced the publication of his 12 polonaises BRA 27–38 and in October 1767 that of the Harpsichord Concerto in E minor BRC 12, but nothing came of these plans. In manuscript both works were dedicated to noble patrons: the first half of the cycle of polonaises to the then director of the Petersburg Academy of Sciences, Vladimir Grigoryevich von Orlov, and the concerto to Maria Antonia Walpurgis, Electress of Saxony. The dedications of BRA 7, 27–38 and C 12 are obviously connected with Bach's search for employment outside Halle. A now lost Abhandlung vom harmonischen Dreyklang, mentioned by Marpurg in 1758 and announced by Friedemann himself in several advertisements in the same year, also remained unpublished. The content and purpose of this treatise is unknown, but it may have dealt with mathematical and philosophical issues.

The rest of Bach's life was a tale of steadily deteriorating circumstances and unsuccessful attempts to obtain permanent employment. In 1770 his wife had to sell part of her property. The family left Halle and moved first to Brunswick, where they lived from about 1771 to the beginning of 1774. In summer 1773 Bach visited J.N. Forkel in Göttingen and in April 1774 he moved to Berlin, where he lived until his death. He applied for posts as organist at the Stadtkirche, Wolfenbüttel, and St Katharina, Brunswick, in 1771, and at the Marienkirche, Berlin, in 1779; documents relating to the Wolfenbüttel and Berlin posts reveal that the reason for his lack of success was his difficult character and unsteady way of life. In 1778 it seems that his efforts to find a permanent post even led him to try ousting J.P. Kirnberger as musician to Princess Anna Amalia of Prussia, whereupon the princess withdrew the financial support she had previously been granting Bach. This intrigue is known to us only from Kirnberger's account of it; his rival Marpurg, in whose house Bach was living during these years, seems to have been involved as well.

In his later years Bach performed in public as an organ virtuoso on many occasions: in Göttingen in summer 1773, Brunswick (22 August 1773) and Berlin (4 May 1774 in the Garnisonkirche, 15 May 1774 in the Nikolaikirche and the Marienkirche, 9 June 1774 in the Marienkirche, and 10 October and 3 December 1776 in the Dreifaltigkeitskirche). These recitals contributed substantially to his reputation as the greatest living organ virtuoso and improviser, but this increase in improvising seems to have gone hand in hand with a decline in his ambitions as a composer. He apparently wrote only a few works in the last years of his life; they include the viola duets BRB 7–9 (in part revisions of earlier works) and two of the six flute duets BRB 1–6, the eight fugues dedicated to Princess Anna Amalia BRA 81–8 (dedicatory copy dated 1778), the harpsichord sonatas in D and G BRA 5, 14 and probably most of the fantasies. In 1778–9 Friedemann was working on an opera, Lausus und Lydie (a later libretto gives the title as Laurus und Lydie), but it was never completed and is now lost. The only pupil he is known for certain to have had in Berlin was Sara Levy, née Itzig, Felix Mendelssohn's great-aunt.

Financial circumstances eventually forced Bach into the piecemeal sale of his music library and those of his father's works he had inherited, as well as compositions of his own. On leaving Brunswick he entrusted the sale by auction of some of his music to J.J. Eschenburg, but whether the auction actually took place is not known; Bach himself did not make inquiries about the proceeds until four years later. It was presumably at this time, and in connection with the sale of manuscripts, that he manipulated the attribution of certain works. For instance, he gave the Vivaldi arrangement BWV596 the misleading inscription, 'di W.F. Bach manu mei patris descriptum', while he conversely ascribed works of his own to his father (e.g. Dienet dem Herrn, BRF 25). During his last years Bach suffered from poor health and became increasingly resigned to retirement from public musical life, but he seems still to have been widely known at the time of his death, as the obituary in Cramer's Magazin der Musik (1784) makes clear: 'In him Germany has lost its foremost organist, and the musical world in general has lost a man who cannot be replaced'. Bach left his wife and daughter in great poverty; a benefit performance of Handel's Messiah was given for them the following year.

3. WORKS, RECEPTION.   Little is known about the extent and location of Bach's musical estate. Part of it was acquired second-hand in Berlin at the beginning of the 19th century by Carl Philipp Heinrich Pistor (1778–1847). Other items found their way into the library of the Berlin Singakademie through Sara Levy and C.F. Zelter, and some music evidently remained in the hands of Bach's daughter and was taken by her descendants to the USA, where it was accidentally destroyed in recent years. The provenance of Georg Poelchau's autograph manuscripts (now in D-Bsb) is still largely unexplained; some seem to have come from the organist Johann Nikolaus Julius Kötschau, others may have been acquired in Berlin in the early 19th century. The early dispersal of his works makes it difficult to assess W.F. Bach's creative achievement satisfactorily. Extensive losses had probably occurred as early as 1800. Evaluations of Bach's work have often

been based on pieces incorrectly attributed (for instance the keyboard pieces in *D-Bsb* Mus.ms.Bach P 883–4).

In Leipzig Bach clearly concentrated more on virtuoso performance than on his career as a composer, perhaps in the depressing realization that he could never attain his father's perfection in all musical genres. His creative energies were therefore expressed more readily in free improvisation, and particularly in his late years the improvisation of fantasies on the organ and harpsichord was very important to him. Only when he became relatively independent from his father in Dresden did Friedemann develop more fully as a composer, especially of keyboard music. Some of his early works (the *Bourlesca* BRA 51, the Clavierstück BRA 54) appear to derive from ideas that came to him while improvising. From the first, his compositions were marked by distinctly virtuoso tendencies; pieces like the harpsichord concertos in A minor and D major (BRC 14, 9) and the Sonata in D major BRA 4 are among the most difficult harpsichord works of their time. The last-named work is unique in its fusion of different stylistic and formal models; only the 'Württemberg' sonatas of C.P.E. Bach can to some extent compare with it. The Dresden compositions in particular employ many technical and stylistic features of J.S. Bach's *Clavier-Übung I*, but even in these early works Friedemann's individual and original style is strongly marked, above all in its characteristic melodic phrasings and a tendency to contrapuntal or imitative development. The capricious style of his ensemble music is obviously modelled on J.D. Zelenka.

In his cantatas, which were all probably written while he was in Halle, Bach employed melodic idioms of the Dresden operatic style, but in many details he followed his father's style of vocal writing. In a series of cantatas probably composed about 1755, for instance, he included instrumental introductory movements, and his large-scale choral movements contain a number of complex fugues. Apart from this, his vocal style must have been strongly influenced by Telemann's cantatas, which formed part of his performance repertory in Halle. Bach's cantata *Ach Gott, vom Himmel sieh darein* (BRF 19) is obviously modelled on Telemann's setting of the same text (TVWV I:14). Bach's vocal works illustrate the great demands he made on the technical abilities of singers and instrumentalists. He was rather conservative in his choice of texts, his favourite sources being Johann Jacob Rambach's *Geistliche Poesien* (Halle, 1720) and Johann Friedrich Möhring's *Gott geheiligtes Beth- und Lob-Opffer der Christen* (Zerbst, 1723).

The late keyboard works follow new stylistic ideals. There is a noticeable tendency towards formal, technical and melodic clarity in the sonatas, while some of the virtuoso fantasias anticipate 19th-century keyboard techniques. At the same time Bach obviously had a predilection for older forms such as the toccata and fugue.

The judgment of posterity on Friedemann Bach was chiefly influenced in the 19th century by the many anecdotes about his personal life that were spread after his death, particularly by Marpurg, J.F. Reichardt and J.F. Rochlitz – an image maintained to this day in A.E. Brachvogel's popular pseudo-biographical novel. Scholarly study of W.F. Bach began with the works by Friedrich Chrysander and C.H. Bitter, although the work of the latter in particular suffers from prejudice, especially in discussion of the works. Martin Falck's dissertation,

published in 1913, is the first comprehensive monograph on the composer's life and work, although many details are in need of revision. Falck's work has been complemented by a series of specialist studies (including those of Braun, Miesner and Schulze) and individual groups of works have been more thoroughly discussed in studies of their genres (by Kelletat, Müller-Blattau and Schleuning).

Only a few of Bach's works were at all widely known in his lifetime, among them the two printed harpsichord sonatas BRA 4 and 7. Even better known were the 12 polonaises BRA 27–38 (*c*1765) and the collection of eight fugues BRA 81–8 (before 1778); more than 20 contemporary manuscript copies of the first collection, and almost 30 copies of the second, are known to have been in circulation. The polonaises were so popular, even at the beginning of the 19th century, that Friedrich Konrad Griepenkerl published them in 1819. Adverse circumstances prevented publication by Hoffmeister & Kühnel of Forkel's planned edition of selected works. Bach's sonatas and fantasies are now available in reliable editions, and a critical edition of the complete works was inaugurated by Carus-Verlag, Stuttgart, in 2000.

Although Friedemann Bach's work is more limited in both quantity and stylistic variety than the music of his brother Emanuel, he must be ranked beside C.P.E. Bach as one of the major composers representing the period between Baroque and Classical composition.

WORKS

Catalogues: M. Falck: 'Thematisches Verzeichnis der Kompositionen Wilhelm Friedemann Bachs', *Wilhelm Friedemann Bach: Sein Leben und seine Werke* (Leipzig, 1913) [Fk; † = addn from Wollny (1993)]

P. Wollny: *Thematisch-systematisches Verzeichnis der Werke Wilhelm Friedemann Bachs*, Bach-Repertorium, ii (in preparation) [BR]

KEYBOARD, ORGAN

Edition: *Wilhelm Friedemann Bach: Orgelwerke*, ed. T. Fedtke (Frankfurt, 1968) [FO]

BR	Fk	
A 1	†200	Sonata (C), *c*1735–40, *D-Bsb*
A 2*a*	1*b*	Sonata (C) (early version), *c*1735–40, *Bsb*; 2nd movt. ed. in NM, clvi (1941)
A 2*b*	1*a*	Sonata (C) (later version), ? after *c*1750, Kiev, Archive for Literature and Art*; ed. in NM, clvi (1941)
A 3	2	Sonata (C), *c*1760–75, Kiev, Archive for Literature and Art*; ed. in NM, clvi (1941)
A 4	3	Sonata (D) (Dresden, 1745); ed. in NM lxxviii (1930)
A 5	4	Sonata (D), *c*1760–75, rev. *c*1778, *Bsb**; ed. in NM, lxxviii (1930)
A 6	11	Sonata (D), 2 hpd, listed in J.C. Westphal catalogue, 1782
A 7	5	Sonata (E♭) (Halle 1748, 1763); ed. in NM, lxxviii (1930)
A 8	†201	Sonata (E♭), *c*1775, Kiev, Archive for Literature and Art*
A 9	†204	Sonata (e), ?*c*1735–40, lost, formerly *RUS-KA*
A 10	†202	Sonata (F), *c*1735, *D-Bsb*
A 11*a*	6*c*	Sonata (F) (1st version), *c*1735–40, *Bsb*; 2nd movt. ed. in NM, clvi (1941)
A 11*b*	6*b*	Sonata (F) (2nd version), *c*1740, *Bsb*; 2nd movt. ed. in NM, clvi (1941)
A 11*c*	6*a*	Sonata (F) (3rd version), ? after 1750, Kiev, Archive for Literature and Art* [Trio from 2nd movt. = BRA 80]; ed. in NM, clvi (1941)
A 12	10	Concerto (F), 2 hpd, *c*1740, *Bsb**; ed. in *J.S. Bach: Werke*, xliii [attrib. J.S. Bach]

BR	Fk	
A 13a–b	40	Concerto (G) (2 versions), c1740, rev. ?c1775, Bsb
A 14	7	Sonata (G), c1775–80, Bsb*; ed. in NM, lxiii (1930)
A 15	8	Sonata (A), c1750–70, Bsb; ed. in NM, lxiii (1930)
A 16	9	Sonata (Bb), ?c1770, Bsb; ed. in NM, lxiii (1930)
A 17	14	Fantasia (C), c1770–75, Bsb; ed. P. Schleuning (Mainz, 1972)
A 18–19	15–16	2 fantasias (c, c), dedic. to G.U. von Behr, c1770–75, Bsb; ed. P. Schleuning (Mainz, 1972)
A 20–22	17–19	3 fantasias (D, d, d), c1770–75, Bsb; ed. P. Schleuning (Mainz, 1972)
A 23	20	Fantasia (e), 1770, Bsb; ed. P. Schleuning (Mainz, 1972)
A 24	21	Fantasia (e), c1770–75, Bsb; ed. P. Schleuning (Mainz, 1972)
A 25	22	Fantasia (G), ?c1750, Bsb [= BRA 63]
A 26	23	Fantasia (a), c1770–75, Bsb; ed. P. Schleuning (Mainz, 1972)
A 27–38	12	12 polonaises (C, c, D, d, Eb, eb, E, e, F, f, G, g), c1765, rev. c1775, F-Pc, PL-Kj*; ed. A. Böhnert (Munich, 1993)
A 39	24	Suite (g), ?c1730 [4th movt. = BRA 48], D-Bsb; ed. A. Böhnert (Munich, 1993)
A 40–41	†205	2 allemandes (g, g), c1725, US-NH* [= BWV836–7]; ed. in NBA, V/5
A 42–43	—	2 minuets (G, g), c1725, US-NH* [=BWV841–2]; ed. in NBA, V/5
A 44–47	†206	4 preludes (C, D, e, a), c1726, US-NH* [=BWV924a, 925, 932, 931]; ed. in NBA, V/5
A 48	25/1	Minuet (g), D-Bsb
A 49a–c	25/2	Presto (Tempo di Menuet) (d), Bsb, US-NH
A 50	†208	Minuet (F), MS lost, formerly RUS-KA [also attrib. C.P.E. Bach]
A 51a–b	26	Bourleska (Imitation de la chasse) (C), c1735, D-Bsb*
A 52	27	Reveille (C), c1735–9, Bsb
A 53a–b	28	Gigue (G), c1735–9, Bsb
A 54	29	Clavierstück (Präludium) (c), c1740, Bsb*
A 55a–b	—	Scherzo (d/e), ?c1730–35 [=BWV844/844a]; ed. in J.S. Bach: Werke, xlii [attrib. J.S. Bach]
A 56	30	March (Eb), ?1770, Bsb
A 57	—	March (F), formerly RUS-KA [=BRA 76]
A 58	13	Polonaise (C), D-Bsb [= Trio from 2nd movt of BRA 11c; = BRA 80]
A 59	—	Ouverture (Eb), Bsb
A 60	†209	Andante (e), ?c1775, GB-Cfm [= 2nd movt. of BRA 13; see also 'Secular vocal', BRH 1]
A 61	†203	Allegro non troppo (G), ?c1775, lost, formerly D-Bhm
A 62	—	Un poco allegro (C), c1775, LEm*
A63–80	†207	18 pieces for musical clock, 1759 [=BWVAnh.133–50]; ed. A. Klughardt [attrib. J.S. Bach] (Leipzig, 1897)
A 81–88	31	8 fugues (C, c, D, d, Eb, e, Bb, f), c1774–8, B-Bc*, D-Bsb; ed. in FO
A89	32	Fugue (c), before 1758, Bsb; ed. in FO
A 90	33	Fugue (F), c1740, Bsb; ed. in FO
A 91	36	Fugue (F), org, Bsb; ed. in FO
A 92	37	Fugue (g), org, US-NH; ed. in FO
A 93–99	38/1	7 chorale preludes, org, D-LEm; ed. in FO
A 100	38/2	Trio on 'Allein Gott in der Höh', org, lost
A 101–104	—	4 chorale preludes, doubtful, MS lost, formerly RUS-KA

CHAMBER

BR	Fk	
B 1–6	54–9	6 duets (e, Eb, Eb, F, f, G), 2 fl, D-Bsb, Kiev, Archive for Literature and Art* (1745–70); ed. G. Braun (Wiesbaden, 1988)
B 7–9	60–62	3 duets (C, G, g), 2 va, c1775, Kiev, Archive for Literature and Art*; ed. Y. Morgan (Winterthur, 1994)
B 10–12	51–3	3 sonatas (F, a, D), fl, bc, lost, cited in Breitkopf catalogues, 1761, 1763
B 13–15	47–9	3 trios (D, D, a), 2 fl, bc, c1740, Kiev, Archive for Literature and Art*
B 16	50	Trio (Bb), vn/fl, vn, bc, before 1762, Kiev, Archive for Literature and Art
—	—	Trio (B), vn, hpd, US-CA, doubtful

ORCHESTRAL

BR	Fk	
C 1–5	63, 67–69, 71	5 sinfonias (C, F, G, G, Bb), str (no.1 with 2 hn, 2 ob ad lib; no.3 with 2 ob, bn), c1735–40, MS lost, formerly D-Bsa
C 6	70	Sinfonia (A), 2 ob, bn, str, c1735–40, Bsb* (frag.)
C 7	65	Sinfonia (d), 2 fl, str, c1740–45, Bsb*; ed. W. Lebermann (Mainz, 1971)
C 8	64	Sinfonia (D), 2 ob/fl, bn, 2 hn, str, c1755, / A-Wn//* [used as introduction to BRF 14 and ? G 1]; ed. W. Lebermann (Mainz, 1971)
C 9	41	Conc. (D), hpd, str, c1735–40, D-Bsb*; ed. in SBA
C 10	42	Conc. (Eb), hpd, str, c1740–45, Bsb* (frag.)
C 11	46	Conc. (Eb), 2 hpd, orch, ?c1745, Bsb, Kiev, Archive for Literature and Art
C 12	43	Conc. (e), hpd, str, c1767, Bsb, Dl; ed. W. Upmeyer (Berlin, 1931)
C 13	44	Conc. (F), hpd, str, c1740–45, Bsb
C 14	45	Conc. (a), hpd, str, c1735–40, Bsb*
—	—	Conc. (D), fl, str, c1775, Kiev, Archive for Literature and Art
—	—	Conc. (g), hpd, str, Bsb, doubtful (? by J.C. Altnickol)

CHURCH CANTATAS

for SATB, instruments and continuo; MSS in D-Bsb unless otherwise stated

BR	Fk	
F 1	80	Lasset uns ablegen (J.F. Möhring), 1749
F 2	92	O Wunder, wer kann dieses fassen? (Möhring)
F 3	93	Ach, daß du den Himmel zerrissest (J.J. Rambach), 1755–60
F 4	†250	Ehre sei Gott in der Höhe, ?1759, F-Pc*; ed. K. Schultz-Hauser (Berlin, 1964)
F 5	73	Der Herr zu deiner Rechten (partly by Möhring), c1755
F 6	74	Wir sind Gottes Werke (Möhring), c1755
F 7	82	Wie schön leuchtet der Morgenstern, ?1764 [partly parody of BRF 6 and 18]
F 8	74a	[cantata for Palm Sunday; parody of BRF 6], lost
F 9	83	Erzittert und fallet, c1750–55; ed. in SBA
F 10	95	Auf, Christen, posaunt, Kiev, Archive for Literature and Art [parody of BRF 24]
F 11	75	Gott fähret auf mit Jauchzen (Rambach), ?c1760–64
F 12	91	Wo geht die Lebensreise hin? (Möhring), c1755
F 13	72	Wer mich liebet, 1746
F 14	85	Dies ist der Tag (Möhring), c1755, F-Pc* [sinfonia = BRC 8]; ed. in SBA
F 15	88	Ertönt, ihr seligen Völker (partly by D. Stoppe), c1755–60 [parody of BRF 19]
F 16	[93]	Ach, daß du den Himmel zerrissest (after Rambach), c1755–60 [parody of BRF 3]
F 17	89	Es ist eine Stimme (Möhring), ?1753
F 18	81	Der Herr wird mit Gerechtigkeit (Möhring), c1750–55
F 19	96	Ach Gott, vom Himmel sieh darein (Stoppe), 1752/3

BR	Fk	
F 20	76	Wohl dem, der den Herrn fürchtet, catechism music, c1750
F 22	86	Der Höchste erhöret das Flehen der Armen, on departure of G.L. Herrnschmidt, 3 Oct 1756 [partly parody of BRF 18]
F 23	87	Verhängnis, dein Wüten entkräftet die Armen, for memorial service for Sophia Dorothea of Prussia, 24 July 1757 [parody of BRF 22], PL-Kj*
F 24	95	Auf, Christen, posaunt, for the peace of Hubertusburg, 1763, Kiev, Archive for Literature and Art

OTHER SACRED

for SATB, instruments and continuo; MSS in D-Bsb unless otherwise stated

E 1	100	Missa (g), formerly D-LEm*
E 2	98	Missa (d)
E 3	78a	Heilig ist Gott, chorus
E 4	98b	Agnus Dei [= BRE 2/5]
E 5	99/1	Amen, chorus, Kiev, Archive for Literature and Art*
E 6	99/2	Halleluja, chorus, Kiev, Archive for Literature and Art*
E 7	78b	Lobet Gott, unsern Herrn Zebaoth, chorus; ed. in SBA
F 21	77	Wie ruhig ist doch meine Seele, recit from catechism music, A, bc, ?c1753 [from pasticcio after BWV170/i and 147/i]
F 25	84	Dienet dem Herrn (Ps c.1–2), 1755, Kiev, Archive for Literature and Art*, US-CA
F 26	89/iii	Der Trost gehöret nur für Kinder (Möhring), aria, S, org, bc [= BRF 17/iii], GB-Lbl*
F 27	94	Zerbrecht, zerreißt, ihr schnöden Banden (Rambach), aria, S, hn, org [? from lost cantata]
F 28	96/iv	Laß dein Wehen in mir spielen (Stoppe), aria, S, Fl, ob, org, bc, ?c1755 [= BR F19/iv]
F 29	79	... Gnaden ein, aria (frag.), B, 2 fl, 2 ob, str, bc, ?c1750

SECULAR VOCAL

G 1	90	O Himmel, schone, for birthday of Frederick the Great, 24 Jan 1756, SSATB, fl, tpt, 2 hn, timp, str, bc [partly parody of BRF 9 and F 24; movts 1 and 7 lost, ? = BRC 8]
G 2	106	Lausus und Lydie (op, C.M. Plümicke), 1778–9, inc., lost
H 1	97	Herz, mein Herz, sei ruhig, S, hpd, ?1780, Kiev, Archive for Literature and Art*

DIDACTIC

I 1	39	canons and contrapuntal sketches, c1735–40, Kiev, Archive for Literature and Art*; some in F.W. Marpurg: *Abhandlung von der Fuge*, ii (Berlin, 1754)
I 2–5	—	4 triple canons a 6; in J.P. Kirnberger: *Die Kunst des reinen Satzes*, ii (Berlin and Königsberg, 1776–9), 226–30
I 6	35	Fugal exposition (C), org, 14 June 1771, D-BS* [for organists' audition at Katharinenkirche, Brunswick]
I 7	—	Fugal exposition on BACH, 25 July 1773, KII* [in album of C.F. Cramer]

THEORETICAL WORKS

I 8	—	*Abhandlung vom harmonischen Dreiklang*, before 1754, announced 1758, unpubd, lost

BIBLIOGRAPHY

F. Chrysander: 'Johann Sebastian Bach und sein Sohn Friedemann Bach in Halle, 1713–1768', *Jb für musikalische Wissenschaften*, ii (1867), 235–48, esp. 241–8

C.H. Bitter: *Carl Philipp Emanuel und Wilhelm Friedemann Bach und deren Brüder* (Berlin, 1868)

W. Nagel: 'W.F. Bach's Berufung nach Darmstadt', *SIMG*, i (1899–1900), 290–94

C. Zehler: 'W.F. Bach und seine hallische Wirksamkeit', *BJb 1910*, 103–32

M. Falck: *Wilhelm Friedemann Bach: sein Leben und seine Werke, mit thematischem Verzeichnis und zwei Bildern* (Leipzig, 1913/R)

P. Epstein: 'W. Fr. Bachs Bewerbung in Frankfurt', *BJb 1925*, 138–9

W. Guericke: *Friedemann Bach in Wolfenbüttel und Braunschweig, 1771–1774* (Brunswick, 1929)

H. Miesner: 'Einige neu entdeckte Notizen über die Familie Friedemann Bachs', *BJb 1931*, 147–8

H. Miesner: 'Urkundliche Nachrichten über die Familie Bach in Berlin', *BJb 1932*, 157–63

H. Kelletat: *Zur Geschichte der deutschen Orgelmusik in der Frühklassik* (Kassel, 1933)

H. Miesner: 'Beziehungen zwischen den Familien Stahl und Bach', *BJb 1933*, 71–6

H. Miesner: 'Graf v. Keyserlingk und Minister v. Happe: zwei Gönner der Familie Bach', *BJb 1934*, 101–15

H. Miesner: 'Portraits aus dem Kreise Philipp Emanuel und Wilhelm Friedemann Bachs', *Musik und Bild: Festschrift Max Seiffert*, ed. H. Besseler (Kassel, 1938), 101–12

W. Serauky: *Musikgeschichte der Stadt Halle*, ii/2 (Halle, 1942/R)

C. Freyse: 'Die Schulhefte Wilhelm Friedemann Bachs', *BJb 1951–2*, 103–19

J. Müller-Blattau: 'Bindung und Freiheit: zu W.F. Bachs Fugen und Polonaisen', *Festschrift Wilhelm Fischer*, ed. H. von Zingerle (Innsbruck, 1956)

G.B. Weston: 'Some Works Falsely Ascribed to Friedemann Bach', *Essays on Music in Honor of Archibald Thompson Davison* (Cambridge, MA, 1957), 247–52

E. Simon: *Mechanische Musikinstrumente früherer Zeiten und ihre Musik* (Wiesbaden, 1960)

W. Strube: 'Ein unbekanntes Probespiel Friedemann Bachs in Halberstadt', *Walcker-Hausmitteilungen*, xxxi (July 1963), 42–3

W. Braun: 'Material zu Wilhelm Friedemann Bachs Kantatenaufführungen in Halle (1746–1764)' *Mf*, xviii (1965), 267–76

P. Schleuning: *Die Freie Fantasie: ein Beitrag zur Erforschung der klassischen Klaviermusik* (Göppingen, 1973)

H.-J. Schulze: 'Ein "Drama per musica" als Kirchenmusik: zu Wilhelm Friedemann Bachs Aufführungen der Huldigungskantate BWV205a', *BJb 1975*, 133–40

E. Borysenko: *The Cantatas of Wilhelm Friedemann Bach* (diss., U. of Rochester, 1981)

H.-J. Schulze: 'Ein dubioses "Menuetto con Trio di J.S. Bach"', *BJb 1982*, 143–50

H.-J. Schulze: *Studien zur Bach-Überlieferung im 18. Jahrhundert* (Leipzig und Dresden, 1984)

C. Henzel: 'Zu Wilhelm Friedemann Bachs Berliner Jahren', *BJb 1992*, 107–12

P. Wollny: *Studies in the Music of Wilhelm Friedemann Bach: Sources and Style* (diss., Harvard U., 1993)

P. Wollny: 'Sara Levy and the Making of Musical Taste in Berlin', *MQ*, lxxvii (1993), 651–88

P. Wollny: 'Ein unbekanntes Autograph von Wilhelm Friedemann Bach', *BJb 1994*, 185–90

P. Wollny: 'Wilhelm Friedemann Bach's Halle Performances of Cantatas by his Father', *Bach Studies 2*, ed. D. Melamed (Cambridge, 1995), 202–28

(9) Carl Philipp Emanuel Bach (46) (b Weimar, 8 March 1714; d Hamburg, 14 Dec 1788). Composer and church musician, second surviving son of (7) Johann Sebastian Bach (24) and his first wife, Maria Barbara. He was the most important composer in Protestant Germany during the second half of the 18th century, and enjoyed unqualified admiration and recognition particularly as a teacher and keyboard composer.

1. Early years. 2. Berlin. 3. Hamburg. 4. Character and temperament. 5. Works: general. 6. Keyboard music. 7. The *Essay*. 8. Chamber music. 9. Orchestral works. 10 Vocal music. 11. Reception.

1. EARLY YEARS.   He was baptized on 10 March 1714, with Telemann as one of his godfathers. In 1717 he moved with the family to Cöthen, where his father had been appointed Kapellmeister. His mother died in 1720, and in spring 1723 the family moved to Leipzig, where Emanuel began attending the Thomasschule as a day-boy on 14 June 1723. J.S. Bach said later that one of his reasons for accepting the post of Kantor at the Thomasschule was that his sons' intellectual development suggested that they would benefit from a university education. Emanuel Bach received his musical training from his father, who gave him keyboard and organ lessons. There may once have been some kind of *Clavierbüchlein für Carl Philipp Emanuel Bach* containing early compositions by Wilhelm Friedemann and works by the young C.P.E. Bach himself, as well as educational pieces by his father. J.F. Reichardt's reference to the difficulty of playing the string parts in Bach's orchestral works may be taken to indicate that he also learnt the violin or viola, but the argument that the difficulties result from his having held the violin incorrectly because he was left-handed is not convincing. From the age of about 15 he took part in his father's musical performances in church and in the collegium musicum. He appears relatively seldom as a copyist, no doubt because, as an able musician himself, he was usually excused such duties. The one large-scale work of sacred music in Leipzig mainly copied by him is the anonymous *St Luke Passion* BWV246, obviously arranged by J.S. Bach to an urgent deadline for Good Friday 1730. On 1 October 1731 Emanuel matriculated at Leipzig University. Following his godfather's example, he studied law, although he was obviously destined for a musical career. His first compositions were probably written about 1730. They consisted mainly of keyboard pieces and chamber music as it was understood in the 18th century (i.e. solos with continuo, concertos and trios).

At the age of 19 Emanuel applied unsuccessfully for the position of organist at St Wenzel in Naumburg (the letter of application, dated 19 August 1733, refers incorrectly to the cathedral of St Peter und Paul). In September 1734 he moved to the university in Frankfurt an der Oder, where he was prominent in musical activities; the Musikalische Akademie mentioned in his autobiography would have been a student collegium musicum. Besides his own compositions, he performed works by his father in Frankfurt, including the Ouverture in D major BWV1068, the Coffee Cantata and the Concerto in D minor BWV1052 in what was probably his own arrangement (BWV1052a). He also wrote occasional pieces for university events and for weddings. The genealogy of the Bach family compiled by J.S. Bach about 1735 makes it clear that C.P.E. Bach was also teaching the keyboard in Frankfurt. In about 1738 he was offered the opportunity to go on an educational tour abroad as companion to Heinrich Christian von Keyserlingk, a son of Reichsgraf Hermann Carl von Keyserlingk, a patron of J.S. and W.F. Bach. However, his appointment to the service of Crown Prince Frederick of Prussia prevented him from accepting.

2. BERLIN.   The background to Bach's entry into the service of the Prussian court is not clear. He says in his autobiography that his appointment became official only after the prince succeeded to the throne (as Frederick II) on 31 May 1740, but he then had the honour of accompanying the 'first flute solo' played by the new king 'alone at the harpsichord'. The first mention of Bach in the court budget is as one of 'those who joined the Kapelle in 1741', so he must initially have been paid from the prince's privy purse. The orchestra consisted of some 40 musicians and was one of the largest in Germany. It had grown out of the crown prince's Kapelle in Ruppin and Rheinsberg, which was regarded as an outstanding ensemble, with Carl Heinrich Graun as Kapellmeister and his brother Johann Gottlieb as leader. Frederick, who took flute lessons from J.J. Quantz and studied composition with J.S. Bach's pupil J.F. Agricola, usually played in the concerts himself. He was an enthusiastic advocate of the new italianate style of the time, and was also interested in Italian opera, which he promoted in the opera house inaugurated on 7 December 1742. As an absolute, though enlightened, monarch, Frederick dictated large areas of the musical life of Berlin and exerted considerable influence on the lively development of music in the city between about 1740 and 1755, but from the beginning of the Seven Years War at the latest his taste ceased to develop, and he eventually contributed to the stultification of musical life at court. The belief that Bach was poorly paid for his services is unfounded. His salary was 300 thalers a year from the time he took up his duties, as much as was paid to any of the other musicians engaged at the same time. Only those above him in the hierarchy – the Kapell- and Konzertmeister and the singers at the opera – were paid a distinctly higher salary.

Unless they were busy with chamber music, which was initially played to Frederick the Great daily, the court musicians took part in the performances of the Berlin Hofoper. Bach's duties were considerably reduced from 1742 at the latest, when Christian Friedrich Schale was appointed second harpsichordist (succeeded by Christoph Nichelmann in 1745); the harpsichordists alternated monthly, and each drew a full salary. This meant that Bach could pursue other activities as a keyboard teacher and composer. His teaching in Berlin inspired the writing of his *Versuch über die wahre Art das Clavier zu spielen* (*Essay on the True Art of Playing Keyboard Instruments*; see §7 below), the most important 18th-century German-language treatise on the subject. However, Bach never won recognition at court as a composer and virtuoso: Frederick would allow only Hasse, the Graun brothers, Quantz and Agricola that status. Even the dedication to him of Bach's first published work, the Prussian Sonatas H24–9 (W48) made no lasting impression on the king.

As early as 1743 an attack of the gout that was to trouble Bach all his life obliged him to visit the Bohemian spa of Teplitz for treatment. Early in 1744 he married Johanna Maria Dannemann, the daughter of a Berlin wine merchant. Of the three children of the marriage who lived to adulthood – Johann Adam (1745–89), Anna Carolina Philippina (1747–1804) and Johann Sebastian, also known as Johann Samuel (1748–78) – only the youngest showed any artistic inclinations. He became a painter, but died at the age of 30 in Rome. On 7 May 1747 the famous meeting between Johann Sebastian Bach and Frederick II, to which we owe the *Musical Offering* BWV1079, took place in Potsdam. However, it brought no improvement in Emanuel Bach's position at court, and his efforts to leave Berlin can be traced from that time.

7. 'Frederick the Great's Flute Concert in Sans Souci': painting by Adolph Menzel, 1852 (Alte Nationalgalerie, Berlin); Frederick plays the flute, Carl Philipp Emanuel Bach is at the keyboard, and Quantz stands on the extreme right

On 25 August he completed an impressive and ornate vocal work, his *Magnificat* H772 (w215), which was intended to pave his way to a post as a church musician and was evidently performed in Leipzig during his father's lifetime, but his applications for the position of Thomaskantor in Leipzig in 1750 and 1755 failed, even though he had Telemann's support, and so did an application for the post of organist at the Johanniskirche in Zittau in 1753. A journey in early summer 1751 took him to Bückeburg, where his younger half-brother Johann Christoph Friedrich had been a court musician since early 1750. The occasion for the visit was the award of the Order of the Great Eagle by Frederick II to his childhood friend Count Wilhelm Friedrich Ernst zu Schaumburg-Lippe, and Bach dedicated his two trios H578–9 (w161) to the art-loving count. He travelled home by way of Halberstadt, Brunswick and Hamburg, where he visited Johann Mattheson on 15 June, and no doubt he also took the opportunity of visiting his godfather Telemann, with whom he regularly corresponded. Three years later, on 21 June 1754, he stood godfather to his cousin Johann Ernst Bach's son Johann Carl Philipp in Eisenach; he combined this private reason for travelling with his professional interests, and gave concerts in Gotha and Kassel.

C.P.E. Bach took part in the première of Graun's *Tod Jesu* on 26 March 1755, playing continuo. Tensions at the Berlin court came to a head that year. In his treatise *Die Melodie, nach ihrem Wesen sowohl, als nach ihren Eigenschaften* (Danzig, 1755) Christoph Nichelmann had criticized Emanuel Bach's style for its affectation; Bach

commissioned a polemical riposte by 'Caspar Dünkelfeind' – in all probability the organist Christoph Gottlieb Schröter of Nordhausen, a friend of the Bach family – and this in turn unleashed a further onslaught from Nichelmann. Early in May 1755, in a memorandum which survives only in extracts, Bach complained to the king about what he regarded as Nichelmann's unwarrantedly preferential financial treatment, and threatened to give notice. Although the details are not known, this dispute finally led to Nichelmann's leaving the service of the court, while Bach's salary was raised by 200 thalers. On 1 February 1756 the young C.F.C. Fasch was appointed second harpsichordist at the standard salary of 300 thalers.

As a result of these quarrels Bach evidently distanced himself still further from court life. He mingled more in the private musical circles of Berlin, although again not many details are known. Some conclusions about the people who were Bach's friends may be drawn from the character pieces in H79–82, 89–98 etc. (w117), most of them portraying prominent characters in the cultural life of the city, and from certain secular occasional compositions such as the aria *La Sophie* H125 (w117.40) and the song *L'Ernestine* H24 (w117.38). Bach was a member of the so-called first Berlin lied school, founded by Christian Gottfried Krause, and played a prominent, but not central, part in it. His songwriting brought him into close touch with F.W. Marpurg, the leading Berlin music critic at the time. Bach assisted Marpurg by providing music examples for his treatises (e.g. the fugues H76 and 99 (w119.1 and 2) and two Allegros H338 (w116.16 and 17)), and he also wrote a short essay on double counterpoint printed in Marpurg's *Historisch-kritische Beyträge*, iii (Berlin, 1757/*R*). His merits were appreciated at this period in the circle around Princess Anna Amalia and Kirnberger. He composed most of the organ sonatas for the princess, and possibly the two organ concertos H444 and 446 (w34 and 35) as well. The importance of these private musical circles increased after 1756, for the outbreak of the Seven Years War meant that Frederick II visited Berlin only occasionally, and on the whole there was no court life. The war brought with it conditions of great austerity for the people of Berlin. Salaries were paid in paper money which had only a fifth of its supposed purchasing power. In view of the military threat, Bach joined the militia, but when Berlin was occupied by the Russian army in 1758 he moved to Zerbst to stay with Carl Fasch's family. He made a brief visit to the court of Mecklenburg in Strelitz in 1762.

The close relationship of the character pieces to the sonatinas for one or two harpsichords and orchestra, written between 1762 and 1764, suggests that they were intended for domestic performance, like some of the keyboard and chamber music works, for example H143 and 507 (w65.33 and w74). Bach composed most of his symphonies at the same time, and probably for the same kind of milieu. He made his name throughout Germany with a quantity of publications in almost all musical genres apart from vocal compositions with orchestral accompaniment. Typically, it was he rather than his brother Wilhelm Friedemann, director of church music in Halle, who was commissioned to write a festive work for trumpets and drums to celebrate in that city the Peace of Hubertusburg in 1763 (the piece is now lost, unless it is identical with the march H621 (w188), which bears the still unexplained epithet 'für die Arche'. After Telemann's death on 25 June 1767 Bach applied to succeed him as music director of the principal churches of Hamburg. His competitors for the post were H.F. Raupach, J.H. Rolle (music director at Magdeburg), and his own half-brother Johann Christoph Friedrich Bach; he narrowly defeated Rolle in the second and deciding ballot. There is no evidence to support the statement in his autobiography of 1773 that he had previously turned down several other offers. Although he was appointed to Hamburg on 6 November 1767, he did not arrive there until March 1768: at first Frederick II refused to release him, and then a particularly hard winter made it impossible for him to leave Berlin any earlier. Meanwhile Georg Michael Telemann, the composer's grandson, acted as interim director of church music in Hamburg. By appointing Bach her honorary Kapellmeister Princess Amalia brought a note of conciliation to the close of his period in Berlin. Johann Christian Schramm (*c*1711–96) from Dresden was appointed his successor in the royal Kapelle.

3. HAMBURG.   Bach took over as director of sacred music in Hamburg on Easter Saturday (2 April) 1768, but he was not officially inaugurated in his new post until 19 April. A festive work written for the occasion by G.M. Telemann exists (in *D-Bsb* Mus.ms.21729), but Bach's inaugural address, *De nobilissimo artis musicae fine*, is lost. His duties in Hamburg were much like his father's in Leipzig. He was on the staff of the Hamburg Lateinschule (still in existence today as the Johanneum) and was responsible for the teaching of music there. However, he claimed one of Telemann's privileges, that of engaging a deputy at his own expense to teach at the school. His main task was the organization of the music in Hamburg's five principal churches, the Michaeliskirche, Jakobikirche, St Katharinen, Nikolaikirche and Petrikirche. According to a report made after Bach's death, the number of musical performances was almost 200 a year – a difficult task for a small choral establishment consisting of pupils from the Johanneum and a few professional singers.

Telemann's 40 years and more in Hamburg and his extraordinary creative powers, which remained with him into old age, had aroused expectations which Bach certainly could not satisfy. He worked relatively slowly, and consequently tried to avoid the pressure of deadlines by planning well ahead. For instance, the Passion music for 1768 was evidently written for the most part while Bach was still in Berlin (and its performance was postponed until 1769 because of his delayed move to Hamburg), and in subsequent years he usually completed his Easter preparations by the previous Christmas. A plan to compose two cantata cycles for the church year, mentioned to G.M. Telemann in 1771, was never realized. Instead, much of the music he performed was by other composers (in particular Georg Benda, G.A. Homilius and G.P. Telemann), which Bach adapted, as was usual at the time, by changing the instrumentation, composing additional movements and, in particular, revising recitatives. Only for the 'Quartalsmusiken' – performed in turn in all the principal churches at the main festivals of Easter, Michaelmas and Christmas – did he write works of his own in appreciable numbers. In line with a tradition dating from the 17th century, Bach annually compiled Passions based on the accounts from the four Gospels in strict rotation, and these were performed in several smaller churches as well as in the principal churches of Hamburg. The official sacred music of the city thus consisted to a great extent of works by other composers and pasticcios, laying Bach open at first to accusations of performing his duties only vicariously. On the other hand, he took great pains with works commissioned for special occasions, such as the inauguration of clerical or administrative officials or mayoral funerals. Twice, in 1780 and 1783, he composed music for the celebrations of the 'Bürgerkapitäne', and in 1770 an Italian festive chorus for a visit by the Crown Prince of Sweden, later King Gustav III. He turned his attention in particular to oratorio, which was performed as often in churches as in concert halls, although obviously not within regular church services, since female singers took part (including Elisabeth Winthem, Klopstock's wife). All three of Bach's sacred oratorios – *Die Israeliten in der Wüste*, *Die Auferstehung und Himmelfahrt Jesu* and the cantata H776 (w233), derived from the first Passion music Bach composed for Hamburg – were performed beyond Hamburg itself; they are among the most important Protestant vocal works of the second half of the 18th century.

Bach's circle of friends during his early years in Hamburg included Gotthold Ephraim Lessing, whom he had known in Berlin, and the syndics Hans Jacob Faber and Jacob Schuback; later, his friends included theologians such as Christoph Christian Strum, the professor of mathematics Johann Georg Büsch, who with Christoph Daniel Ebeling was head of the Handlungsakademie, and the physicians Friedrich Ludwig Christian Cropp, Johann Albert Heinrich Reimarus and Johann August Unzer.

Bach was also a close friend of F.G. Klopstock, living in retirement, and he took care to maintain friendships outside Hamburg: with J.N. Forkel in Göttingen, J.J. Eschenburg in Brunswick, J.G.I. Breitkopf in Leipzig, Johann Friedrich Hering in Berlin, Ewald von Grotthus in Gieddatz (Curland) and Johann Jacob Heinrich Westphal in Schwerin. Bach was regarded as the undisputed leading figure in the musical society of Hamburg, and many musicians, men of letters and other artists visiting the city sought him out. The accounts relating to his early years in Hamburg by Matthias Claudius, Charles Burney and J.F. Reichardt are particularly informative. At this time Bach was much involved in teaching, and his pupils included professional musicians such as J.D. Holland, C.F.G. Schwencke and Nils Schiørring, and the future mayor of Altona, Casper Siegfried Gähler.

Besides performing his official duties as director of church music – a post that (except during a severe illness from February to April 1772) he filled conscientiously until his last years while (unlike Telemann and Schwencke) remaining on good terms with the contentious Hamburg clergy – Bach assumed from the beginning a leading position in the city's concert life. In winter 1768–9 he announced a series of 20 subscription concerts; the following winter there were at least six concerts, and 12 Wednesday concerts were advertised for winter 1771–2. Over the next few years there were considerably fewer concerts in which Bach featured as a keyboard player; as far as is known, he stopped giving public concerts when he was 65. As well as his own oratorios he performed a number of other composers' works in Hamburg, including Graun's *Tod Jesu* and Telemann's *Seliges Erwägen* and the *Donnerode*. Bach brought his public appearances (outside his official duties) to a close with a 'historical' concert on 9 April 1786, consisting of one of his own orchestral symphonies, isolated movements from works by J.S. Bach (the Credo from the Mass in B minor with a newly composed introduction) and Handel's 'I know that my Redeemer liveth' from *Messiah* and his own two most powerful compositions, the *Magnificat* and the *Heilig* for double choir H778 (W217). Bach remained actively creative until the last year of his life, although he was in poor health after summer 1788. The double concerto for keyboard, piano and orchestra W47 (probably commissioned for Sara Levy in Berlin), the three quartets for harpsichord, flute and viola H537–9 (W93–5), preparations for a collection of songs, H700–60 (W200), published by Donatius in Lübeck in 1789, and a pasticcio Passion for 1789 were all written in Bach's last year. He died on 14 December 1788 of a 'chest ailment', and was buried on 19 December in the crypt of the Michaeliskirche (the location of his grave was identified only in 1925). After his death Johanna Maria Bach temporarily administered the office of music director. Proposals for a reorganization of church music in Hamburg meant that a successor to her husband was not appointed until autumn 1789, and it was only in December that year that she handed the post over to C.F.G. Schwencke, who had been elected on 1 October in preference to J.A. Hiller and Bach's own protégé J.N. Forkel.

4. CHARACTER AND TEMPERAMENT. Among his contemporaries Emanuel Bach had the reputation of being a pleasant, sociable man with a gift for wordplay, who was not afraid of making critical remarks even to persons of high rank. He seldom took sides in musical controversies,

but when he did he expressed himself vigorously; some light is shed on his own views by his comment, printed in the *Hamburgischer Unpartheyischer Correspondent* of 20 September 1785, on an English newspaper report claiming that there was tension between him and Haydn: 'It is my belief that every master has his own true worth. Praise and blame can do nothing to alter it. The work alone allots praise or blame to the master, and I therefore take everyone as I find him'. He reacted angrily to criticism of his father and to the publication of unauthorized editions, vehemently attacking Birnstiel's edition of J.S. Bach's chorales and Rellstab's reprints of his own works issued when Rellstab took over the publishing firm of Emanuel's friend G.L. Winter. Nor did he conceal his dislike of the modern Italian music of the time, in particular of such excesses as the intrusion into sacred music of stylistic elements from comic opera. He also had a low opinion of the style developed by Johann Schobert and by his own half-brother Johann Christian.

Bach was a good businessman. Most of his publications were commercially successful, and indeed he preferred not to publish a work if he thought it unlikely to sell, as in the case of his *Auferstehung und Himmelfahrt Jesu* in 1784. His business acumen was sometimes interpreted as avarice, but he was extremely generous to his friends and family, and would give them copies of his printed works and autograph manuscripts that he no longer needed, or let them have copies at cost price to himself. He took his half-brother Johann Christian into his family after their father's death and later did the same for his nephew Wilhelm Friedrich Ernst on the latter's return from England; he also provided regular financial support for his widowed half-sister Elisabeth Juliana Friederica. He was particularly close to his half-brother Johann Christoph Friedrich, exchanging sheet music with him on a regular basis.

Bach would often play for hours to visitors, his favourite instrument being a clavichord built by Gottfried Silbermann which he passed on to his pupil and friend Ewald von Grotthuss in 1781, together with the rondo *Abschied von meinem Silbermannischen Claviere* H272 (W66); Grotthuss responded with thanks in the form of a rondo composed by himself. Writing about rhetoric in his *Essay on the True Art of Playing Keyboard Instruments*, Bach emphasized that the musician must be able to place himself in the same emotional state as he wishes to arouse in his hearers, and warned against mannerisms and exaggerations. When improvising he seemed quite enraptured; his playing as a whole was notable for its clarity and cantabile style, and left a lasting impression on his audience.

Like many other musicians and music lovers of the time, Bach owned a large collection of portraits of musicians, which he was always seeking to extend through purchase and exchange. He even toyed with the idea of publishing a catalogue of his collection, but that project was realized only after his death.

5. WORKS: GENERAL. In a composing career of almost 60 years Emanuel Bach wrote over 1000 separate works, ranging from songs to oratorios and from keyboard dance movements to orchestral symphonies. He must have begun compiling a catalogue of his own works at an early date, and it served as the basis for the *Nachlass-Verzeichnis*, or catalogue of his musical estate, printed in Hamburg in 1790. By about 1770 at the latest Bach had

lists available enabling him to choose works for customers outside Hamburg who gave him details of the compositions they wanted and those they already owned. The *Nachlass-Verzeichnis* lists his works systematically classified into groups, with dates and places of composition. It gives information about published editions, while unpublished works are identified by their titles and the first words of the text where applicable, or by the opening bars in the case of instrumental works. The *Nachlass-Verzeichnis* is probably the earliest catalogue of the works of a single composer that can still satisfy the requirements of scholars today. Its publication served as both a record of Bach's creative activity and part of the provision he made in old age for his wife and children, since it was intended to facilitate the purchase of compositions by interested parties outside Hamburg. The relatively large number of extant copies made in Hamburg around 1790 shows that the opportunity was taken up.

The *Nachlass-Verzeichnis* is our major source for the precise details of Bach's output, and in many cases it gives more information about dates and places of composition than the autograph manuscripts. However, it is reliable only on the works of Bach's prime. In the course of a systematic survey of his music collection made in 1786, he destroyed a number of juvenilia, sketches and rejected versions (the precise details cannot now be determined), as we learn from a letter he wrote to Eschenburg on 21 January 1786. Moreover, certain occasional works, such as the cantatas of his Frankfurt period, may no longer have been available to him at this date.

Bach's musical estate remained intact until about 1797, apart from a few items auctioned in 1789. After Johanna Maria Bach's death, however, the composer's daughter Anna Carolina Philippina began disposing of some items, particularly works by other composers and portraits. After her death what remained of the estate was sold at auction. Much of it came into the hands of such collectors as Casper Siegfried Gähler in Altona and Georg Poelchau in Hamburg, and passed from their collections to Berlin before the great fire of 1842 in Hamburg. At the beginning of the 20th century, consequently, almost all the works were still extant in Bach's autograph or in copies made under his supervision, and were available for modern scholarly evaluation. However, considerable losses, particularly of the occasional works written in Hamburg, were sustained during World War II when sources in the Berlin Singakademie and the library of Königsberg University were removed or destroyed. Those from the Berlin Singakademie were, however, recovered in Kiev in 1999. The next most important collection after Poelchau's was made by the Schwerin organist Johann Jacob Heinrich Westphal (1756–1825). It comprised almost all the instrumental works in original prints and manuscript copies, as well as many vocal compositions. Most of it is now in the library of the Brussels Conservatory, which also acquired original manuscripts of symphonies and chamber works from the Guido Richard Wagener collection; a smaller portion passed with the Fétis collection to the Bibliothèque Royale Albert Ier, also in Brussels. There are also particularly valuable collections in the Library of Congress, Washington (purchased mainly in the Berlin antiquarian market around 1900), the Bibliothèque Nationale, Paris (including autographs from the Charles Malherbe and Auguste Vincent collections), and the Gesellschaft der Musikfreunde, Vienna (domestic copies and autographs from Brahms's estate and gifts from Anthony van Hoboken). In spite of losses the source material is good, and scholars face few problems of authenticity or chronology.

We have no information about Bach's methods of composing. However, the few extant sketches (most of which survive only because he wrote them on blank spaces in manuscripts of other works destined to be kept) suggest that after the 1740s he sketched his compositions extensively before polishing them. Interim sketches of vocal works are usually set out on two systems (voice and bass), with only minimal indication of the text. Instrumental works are usually notated on one system only, though with indications of harmony or important subsidiary parts. Final versions often diverge only slightly from the sketches; however, some sketches do not fit any of the extant works, and we may surmise that the composer quite often noted down ideas which he never developed. There is support for this theory in a comment Bach made, on the composition of keyboard fantasias, in a letter to Forkel of 10 February 1775, saying that he had 'a great many *collectanea* for that purpose', and in the existence of a manuscript entitled *Miscellanea musica* H867 (W121), unfortunately extant only in a copy), only part of which coincides with the *collectanea* mentioned in the letter.

Bach's ornamentation, arrangements and revisions pose considerable musicological problems because of the complex relations between the sources, Bach's own mingling of procedures and the terminological inconsistency that still persists. His ornamentation entailed the writing down of procedures adopted in performance, as he remarked in a letter of 28 April 1784 to Johann Heinrich Grave in Greifswald, accompanying a copy of the Concerto in C minor H441 (W31) of 1753: 'The concerto in C minor used to be one of my showpieces. The recitative is written out very much as I played it'. Prominent among his ornamental devices are the 'varied repeats', probably used for the first time in the third movement of the *Probestück* H74 (W63.5) in the *Essay* and developed further in the six sonatas H126, 136–40 (W50: 1760) dedicated to Princess Anna Amalia of Prussia. In his preface to the collection he described its aesthetic background, commenting that 'variation in repeats is indispensable today'. It is expected to such a degree in performance, he adds, that the clumsiest of variations receive more applause than a faithful note-by-note rendering of the music as set down by the composer. He believed, he said, that ornamentation must suit the emotional affect of the piece, taking harmonic requirements into account, and must have some claim to be at least as good as the original. Here Bach was entering the debate on the variations of musical ideas expressed, for instance, in a series of articles signed 'T.S.' and published in the *Berlinischer Magazin* (reprinted in J.A. Hiller's *Wöchentliche Nachrichten*) and in a contribution by F.W. Riedt to Marpurg's *Historisch-kritische Beyträge* (ii, 1756). G.S. Löhlein's op.2 sonatas (1768) are in direct line of descent from Bach. Except in the 'Short and Easy Keyboard Pieces' H193–203, 228–38 (W113, 1766; W114, 1766), Bach himself continued the practice of varied repeats only occasionally, for instance in the sonatas H240, 83 and 135 (W62.24, 65.29 and 65.32). However, a number of other sonatas and slow movements from concertos were varied and ornamented at dates that cannot now be determined; the Sonata in C major H150 (w51.1) even exists in two different ornamented versions, H157 and 174 (w65.36, 37). It is clear from the section 'Variations and ornaments to certain sonatas and concertos for students' in the *Nachlass-Verzeichnis* (p.53 no.11) that these ornaments were written down for teaching purposes. The original versions remained concurrent with, or were even preferred to, the ornamented versions and circulated in prints and authorized copies to which the ornamented versions represent alternatives. Ornamentation in the wider sense includes the cadenzas H264 (w120), numbering over 70. A striking feature is that several concerto movements are allotted more than one cadenza; a few bear general descriptions such as 'cadenza for the Adagio' and cannot be assigned to any of the surviving works.

Bach's arrangements involve alterations in the scoring of a work. In the simplest cases they are merely alternative versions. Many of the Berlin trio sonatas exist in versions for two melody instruments and continuo or for one melody instrument and obbligato harpsichord; the Sonata in C H515 (w87), a special case, exists also in a version for two harpsichords. The composer's arrangements here are chiefly limited to octave transpositions to suit the chosen instruments. There are variant settings among the concertos too: the Concerto in A minor of 1750 exists in authentic versions for cello (H432; w170), flute (H431; w166) and harpsichord (H430; w26); in all three versions the accompanying parts are the same except for some slight changes to the continuo. It is not always possible to be sure which is the original version. Other arrangements entail the rescoring of works for larger forces, particularly frequent in Bach's symphonies. He also rearranged several songs with keyboard accompaniment for chorus; but it is debatable whether the term 'arrangement' is adequate for such processes of revision as occur in the reworking of *Bitten*, a strophic song with keyboard (H686.9; w194.9), as a four-part through-composed song motet (H826.3; w208.3).

Revision proper differs from the procedures described above in that the composer made substantial changes to the actual musical material and intended the second version to supersede the first. Revisions include newly composed or substitute movements (for example the new version of 'Et misericordia' in the *Magnificat* and that of 'O Petrus, folge nicht' in the Passion cantata), but above all reworkings of existing compositions, chiefly instrumental pieces from the Leipzig and Frankfurt periods, some of which Bach himself marked as 'rewritten' in the *Nachlass-Verzeichnis*. Judging from what can be traced in the sources, Bach cut some passages and extended others, eliminated whole movements, and now and then rewrote older works to adapt them to new compositional styles while retaining their form and thematic substance. Many of his early works, for instance the March BWVAnh.127, exist in three or more different versions. A number of major revisions are not noted in the *Nachlass-Verzeichnis*, including that of H211 (w65.44) the original central movement of which was incorporated in a revised form into the Sonata in B♭ H282 (w59.3) in 1748 and replaced by a few transitional chords in H211 (w65.44), and that of *Auferstehung und Himmelfahrt Jesu* between 1774 and 1778, when Bach added a slow introduction and replaced the *dramatis personae* in the recitatives with a neutral *testo*. Although Emanuel Bach, like his father and his elder brother Wilhelm Friedemann, continued

working on his compositions all his life, adapting them to changing conditions of performance and to different aesthetic requirements, various main phases of revision can be distinguished. Between 1743 and 1747 he revised works written before 1740; in the context of his publishing activities around 1760 he revised many earlier works, for example H171–2, 216 (w116.1, 2, 5) and H77 (w62.14); and during his Hamburg period he added wind parts to many of the orchestral works. A final phase of revision around 1786 was no doubt carried out so as to leave his musical estate in good order for his heirs; it included systematic replacement of the slow movements in the sonatinas H7–12 (w64) in order to remove their outmoded tonal unity with a view to publication. There is no suitable term for Bach's transfer of thematic material to a different musical genre, as occurred with some of the character pieces.

6. KEYBOARD MUSIC.   The keyboard music that Bach composed almost without interruption from about 1730 to the last years of his life lies at the heart of his creative work. The sources suggest that he began by composing separate dance movements, marches, minuets and polonaises. Some of these were entered in his own hand (*c*1732) in the *Clavierbüchlein* for Anna Magdalena Bach. Models were to hand in the first part of J.S. Bach's *Clavier-Übung*; the Partita in G major BWV829 seems to have made the greatest impression on him, as can be seen from the minuet with hand-crossing, H1·5 (w111), and the G major suite (D-Bsb Mus.ms.Bach P 368), which is anonymous but can be shown to be at least partly by C.P.E. Bach. Dance movements could then be put together into cycles, preserving tonal unity; examples may be found in a manuscript volume (D-Hs ND VI 3191), thought until 1991 to have been lost, which contains sources going back to Bach's years in Frankfurt. The composition of suites seems to have been considerably more important to Bach's early creative period than the catalogue in the *Nachlass-Verzeichnis* might suggest. It is noticeable that the young Bach adopted the standard movements of his father's suites only in exceptional cases; only the allemande and gigue are prominent, and feature in some of the keyboard 'sonatas' of the 1730s and 40s. Otherwise the composer showed an early preference for fantasia-like movements, which for all their technical deficiencies display harmonic boldness and a high degree of originality. J.S. Bach's two- and three-part Inventions also provided an important stimulus (as they did later to Emanuel's half-brother Johann Christoph Friedrich), for example in the first movement of H3 (w65.1); three-part invention style occurs chiefly in slow movements, including those of the sonatas H26 (w48.3) and H34 (w49.5).

Two collections of six keyboard sonatas, H24–9 (w48; the 'Prussian' sonatas, printed in 1742) and H30–34, 36 (w49; the 'Württemberg' sonatas, intended for Bach's pupil Carl Eugen of Württemberg and printed in 1744), form a landmark in the history of keyboard music. They indirectly bear out Mattheson's polemical statement in *Der vollkommene Capellmeister* (Hamburg, 1739/R): 'For some years now composers have been writing sonatas for keyboard to great acclaim, but they do not yet have the right form, wishing to be moved rather than to move; that is to say, they aim more at the touch of the fingers than to touch the heart'. J.F. Reichardt claimed with justice in his *Musikalischer Almanach* of 1796 that 'no instrumental music had previously appeared in which as rich and yet well-ordered a harmony was united with such noble song, so much beauty and order with such originality, as in Bach's first two sonata collections engraved in Nuremberg'. In these collections Bach systematically, and for the first time, showed how it was possible to write affecting keyboard music freed from the suite tradition, and he was able to develop his ideas over the following decades; the experimental instrumental recitative that serves as the central movement of the first Prussian sonata, for example, impressively illustrates a style of utterance to be found in the newest instrumental music. Unity of affect is evident in the dense thematic working of the opening movements of H24 (w48.1) and H30 (w49.1). Fantasia-like elements occur more particularly in the sonatas in E minor and B minor, H33, 36 (w49.3, 6), while the closing movement of H29 (w48.6) is particularly full of surprises. The unusual importance ascribed to these collections even by Bach's contemporaries is evident from the fact that the Württemberg sonatas were still being reprinted in Vienna and Pest around 1800. Bach established quite early a basic three-movement sonata pattern in these collections, with fast opening and closing movements and a slow central movement in a related key. Later he also experimented with the use of different keys for all three movements, with transitional passages between movements and – particularly in the last years of his life – very short central movements. Like his father, Emanuel Bach regarded his printed collections as models, and made them as different as possible with a view to their usefulness in teaching.

Nowhere in Bach's work is the distinction so clearly drawn between professional and amateur music-making, and between works written to commission and those for personal development, as in his keyboard compositions. The published works are principally for amateurs, particularly the collections published during the 1760s: the six 'Easy Sonatas' H162–3, 180–83 (w53; Leipzig 1766) and the six sonatas 'à l'usage des dames' H184–5, 204–7 (w54) eschew the daring of the early works. The Württemberg sonatas, with their greater technical and musical demands, constitute an exception among Bach's printed works; unusually for Bach, they present public evidence that the composer was undergoing a personal mental crisis (most of the sonatas were written in Teplitz, where he was taking the waters in 1743, when an acute attack of gout at the age of only 30 seemed to endanger his career as a keyboard virtuoso). Most of the other experimental sonatas of this period were distributed by Bach to his friends only in manuscript copies or were published many years later; this group includes the sonatas H46–7 and 51 (w65.16–17 and 65.20) and the Sonata in F sharp minor H37 (w52.4).

Bach's composition and publication of keyboard works temporarily moved into the background to some extent after 1770. He rounded off his keyboard writing with the six collections of keyboard sonatas 'für Kenner und Liebhaber'; by public demand he included rondos in the second collection and rondos and fantasias in the third and subsequent collections. While the first collection, published in 1779, was a compilation of older compositions (H130 (w55.2) dates from as early as the 1750s), new compositions predominate in the later volumes, which employ a less astringent tonal language than the early keyboard sonatas and earned respect as individual creations fit to stand beside the works of Haydn and Mozart. The rondos were particularly popular, and for a while Bach considered publishing a separate collection of them. The number of subscribers began to fall, however, not necessarily because of any slackening of interest in Bach's works but perhaps because of the competition provided by the soaring number of published keyboard sonatas by composers from north and central Germany and Vienna after about 1780; there was also a change in market conditions, with series sold in bookshops superseding individual subscriptions. From Bach's letters to Breitkopf in May 1788, offering all remaining copies of the *Clavier-Sonaten für Kenner und Liebhaber* at a fixed price (obviously to spare his family the trouble of selling his works after his death), it is clear that at this point over half the entire edition of 6300 copies had been sold, bringing Bach a considerable profit of over 3000 thalers, or 10,000 marks (several times his annual salary).

7. THE 'ESSAY'. Bach's keyboard music cannot be assessed in isolation from his didactic writing. Around the middle of the 18th century amateur music-making assumed proportions scarcely imaginable previously. As a result, there was a growing demand for instruction books and performance manuals, particularly in Berlin, where music-making had been encouraged to an extraordinary degree by the example of the flute-playing King Frederick II. In 1750 Marpurg had published a short manual entitled *Die Kunst das Clavier zu spielen*, which proved so successful that it was reprinted the following year. With his *Essay on the True Art of Playing Keyboard Instruments* Emanuel Bach provided what was to be the leading keyboard tutor for a long period. Together with Quantz's flute tutor of 1752, Leopold Mozart's violin tutor of 1756, and J.F. Agricola's singing manual of 1757 (after P.F. Tosi), it was the most important work of practical musical instruction of the second half of the 18th century.

The first (self-contained) part, which appeared in 1753, sets out the basics of keyboard performance in three sections, tacitly giving precedence to the elements of harmony. The first section deals with fingering, for, says Bach, 'more is lost by incorrect fingering than can be compensated for by all the art and good taste in the world'. Bach encouraged the use of the thumb but recommended avoiding it on black keys, and restricted the crossing of fingers still quite common at the time. Naturally, all his examples show the fingering. The second section deals with ornaments, distinguishing between those indicated by signs (Quantz's 'essential ornaments') and those written out in full ('optional ornaments'). The third section deals with 'good performance', comprising both practical and aesthetic criteria. Bach saw the absence of practical examples in the existing keyboard tutors of the time as a great drawback, and accordingly added 18 *Probestücke* ('sample pieces') as an integral part of the *Essay*, in different keys and in ascending order of difficulty; put together, they form the six three-movement sonatas H70–75 (w63). These pieces could be used either as studies or for performance; the sonata in F minor in particular, with hand-crossing, circulated widely in manuscript copies.

The *Essay* was complemented in 1762 by a second part containing mainly instruction in continuo playing and correct accompaniment. It clearly reflects Bach's own activity at court. In it he moves systematically from simple intervals and their description to 'refinements' and 'necessary precautions' in accompaniment. Together with

Quantz's *Versuch einer Anweisung die Flöte traversiere zu spielen*, Bach's *Essay* is our most important source of information about performing practices and issues of taste prevalent in Berlin in the mid-18th century. Bach's introduction is also of particular interest today, dealing as it does with the choice of instruments and basic questions of accompaniment, and so too is the final chapter on improvisation (with the Fantasia in D H160 (w117.14) as a practical illustration), which was unique in its time. The *Essay* held an undisputed position in the 18th century, and its influence was not confined to north Germany; Haydn bought and studied it as a young man and Christian Gottlieb Neefe introduced Beethoven to it. Both composers continued into the 19th century to use the *Essay* in their own teaching.

The first part was reprinted in 1759, and a revised edition (1787) contained six new single-movement sonatinas that Bach hoped would make up for the excessively rapid increase in difficulty of the *Probestücke*. A new edition of the second part, also with corrections and additions by the author, did not appear until 1797. The two collections of piano pieces with varied repeats, H193–203 (w113) and H228–38 (w114), were also very popular; H193–7 (w113.1–5) were reprinted in rival editions in Berlin, Vienna and Linz until 1800. Bach's immense influence as a keyboard teacher made the 'Bach manner' accepted as a general term for an elegant style of performance throughout the second half of the 18th century.

8. CHAMBER MUSIC.   Next to keyboard writing, chamber music was the most important experimental medium for Bach, particularly that with obbligato keyboard. His compositions in the genre from the 1730s onwards are notable for their originality and variety, and, like the keyboard compositions, they employ the whole spectrum of keys: the compositions for keyboard and violin, for instance, range from A♭ to A major and from C to B minor. The trio in all its forms lies at the heart of his chamber music; solos (sonatas) featured less prominently after the 1740s, and in the last years of his life Bach turned to the quartet.

The early solos have continuo accompaniment, except for the flute solo in A minor H562 (w132), presumably composed for Frederick II. They correspond to the basic three-movement type described by J.A. Scheibe in the *Critische Musikus* (Leipzig, 2/1745, pp.681–3), and are succinctly written. All three movements are in the tonic key. The first is usually the slowest, and is followed by an Allegro (rarely, as in H554 (w127), in fugal style), followed in its turn by either a dance (usually a minuet with variations) or another Allegro. Locatelli's flute sonatas op.2 (Amsterdam, 1732) may be regarded as the model.

Both numerically and in its importance for the history of the genre, the trio takes pre-eminence among Bach's chamber compositions. The term 'trio' refers to the number of obbligato parts, not the number of participants. Trios with obbligato keyboard and those with continuo accompaniment are roughly equal in number; many survive in variant scorings, most of which may be regarded as authentic. While the solos aim at idiomatic treatment of the leading instrument, the upper parts of the trios, with the exception of some works with obbligato keyboard, are treated almost identically. There are contrapuntal trios, such as H567 and 569 (w143 and 145), in which the bass shares in the thematic material, and homophonic works in the Italian style, such as H578 (w161.2), in which the bass serves only as a harmonic foundation. The programmatic trio 'Sanguineus und Melancholicus' H579 (w161.1), published in 1751, made a great sensation.

Trios are found among Bach's earliest compositions; they include a work (now lost) for violin, viola and bass, which according to the *Nachlass-Verzeichnis* (p.65, no.1) was 'prepared together with Johann Sebastian Bach'. These works were revised while Bach was in Berlin; only in the case of H569 (w145) has the original version survived (as BWV1036). Comparison of the two versions shows Bach's outstanding early talent and the tremendous progress he made by the time he produced the later version: the introductory fantasia and closing movement were cut, the two other movements thoroughly revised and a new opening movement added. In the 1740s, then, Bach entirely abandoned the basic four-movement form of the trio, which was initially at least as important to him as the three-movement form.

After the early 1760s figured bass played a less important role in Bach's chamber music. During the process of composing the central movement of the Trio in C minor H514 (w78; 1763) he decided to write out the keyboard accompaniment instead of merely figuring the bass; the Trio in C major H515 (w87; 1766) has a fully written-out keyboard part. The pre-eminence of the keyboard is most in evidence in the three printed collections of keyboard trios, H522–34 (w89–91); the title-page of the English first edition of H525–30 (w89) fails even to mention the accompanying violin and cello parts. The type of rondo used by Bach in his trios and further developed later in his solo keyboard music, with the theme reappearing in different keys and varied, was noticed as a pointer to the future by Forkel (*Musikalisch-kiritische Bibliothek*, ii, 1778, pp.275–300) and was copied in England in particular (by Muzio Clementi and by A.F.C. Kollmann in his *Essay on Practical Musical Composition*, 1799). In his last year Bach composed three quartets (i.e. works with four obbligato parts) for keyboard, flute and viola, H537–9 (w93–5). Publication of these particularly attractive works was abandoned because of the composer's death. During his Hamburg period he also wrote several smaller works for wind instruments; the occasion for their composition is not known. He wrote no chamber music for string instruments without continuo, a genre central to the development of the Classical style.

9. ORCHESTRAL WORKS.   All the known orchestral works by Bach belong to the 'modern' genres of symphony and concerto. A special part was also occupied in the early 1760s by a genre evidently of his own invention, the sonatina for one or two harpsichords and orchestra, which no other composer imitated; Bach's sonatinas differ from the Viennese divertimento for keyboard and strings, which they outwardly resemble and which may have influenced the composer, in the enormous technical demands made on the soloists.

The symphonies of the Berlin period are all in three movements and most of them were conceived as string symphonies; in many cases wind parts were added only during Bach's Hamburg period. The absence of repeat signs in the opening movements is noticeable; slow movements are often not separated from the others, and

8. Autograph MS of the opening of C.P.E. Bach's 'Clavier-Fantasie mit Begleitung einer Violine, C.P.E. Bachs Empfindungen' in F♯ minor, composed 1787 (D-Bsb Mus.ms.Bach P 36i)

in many cases serve as a transition. The famous four-part string symphonies H657–62 (W182) owe their existence to a commission from Baron Gottfried van Swieten, and the composer was subject to no restrictions. J.F. Reichardt wrote an account of the rehearsals of these daring works, admiring their 'great variety and novelty of form and modulation'. Their importance was also recognized by music dealers; manuscript copies made for van Swieten's private use were sold, against Bach's will, by Johann Traeg in Vienna, C.G. Thomas in Leipzig and J.C.

Westphal in Hamburg. There must have been similar interest in the four orchestral symphonies H663–6 (W183), which Bach had published in 1780 with a dedication to Crown Prince Friedrich Wilhelm of Prussia; they show an advanced handling of the wind instruments.

The keyboard concertos, numbering over 50, represent an early peak in the genre, the importance of which has not been fully appreciated. The first ones, like W.F. Bach's early concertos, were written just after 1730. Their relationship to the concertos of J.S. Bach has yet to be studied, but it must be remembered that most of J.S. Bach's harpsichord concertos did not take the shape in which they are familiar today until about 1738–9. C.P.E. Bach remained faithful to the ritornello form, and did not adopt dance, variation or rondo structures. Concertos such as H403, 409, 414, 420–22 and 442 (w1, 6, 11, 17–19 and 32) were widely distributed in their time. The orchestra here has equal importance with the soloist. The opening ritornello is usually on a broad scale, setting disparate musical ideas side by side, and these ideas recur in varying order in subsequent ritornellos. In the solo sections the orchestra continues to share in the thematic development. The uniformity of their overall structure, their consistent thematic development and their wide emotional range made the concertos of Bach's early and middle Berlin period a model for other composers (e.g. J.F. Reichardt, J.W. Hertel and J.G. Müthel) and for the teaching of composition (H.C. Koch). The concertos of his later Berlin years and of his Hamburg period, written in the 1760s, contain more experimental features and are sometimes almost reminiscent of chamber music. With the exception of the six 'easy' concertos H471–6 (w43; Hamburg 1772) Bach prevented their dissemination during his lifetime.

10. VOCAL MUSIC. Emanuel Bach was a member of the first Berlin lied school, although he did not play a leading role in it and took no part in the controversies about the particular merits of French, Italian and German music. He was particularly fond of humorous texts such as those by Lessing and Gleim, and did not set odes (as Karl Wilhelm Ramler and Moses Mendelssohn understood the term) or foreign-language texts. It was also only at the beginning that Bach contributed to the joint publications of the Berlin lied school. In 1762 he published a collection of his own which was reprinted soon after with a new title-page and reissued in 1774. Contemporary song composition distinguished between *Sing-Oden* and *Spiel-Oden*; Bach's songs fall predominantly into the latter category, with keyboard accompaniment an integral component. This does not mean that the keyboard part is entirely obbligato – the songs are notated on two, not three staves – but that its melodic phrases and harmony contribute to the emotional effect. The melodies are not therefore primarily intended to be catchy, and Bach only occasionally composed songs 'in the folk style' (e.g. the drinking-song *Der Wirt und die Gäste*, to a text by Gleim). The vocal compass is large by the criteria of the time and does not exclude extreme registers, particularly in the holding of high notes.

The collection of 54 sacred songs and odes by C.F. Gellert, which Bach set to music immediately after publication of the texts in 1757, was of particular historical importance. By 1784 it had been issued five times in all and influenced many other composers (right up to the time of Beethoven and his Gellert songs op.48). Many of the songs were included in hymnals. During his Hamburg period Bach followed the success of the Gellert settings with a collection of psalm settings (H733; w196) in the translation by the Copenhagen superintendent Johann Andreas Cramer and two collections of sacred songs to texts by his friend the principal pastor of Hamburg, Christian Carl Sturm. Bach's compositions of this type cover the entire contemporary spectrum: the Cramer psalms, for instance, include chorale melodies with bass, songs with continuo and some with a fully

9. *Carl Philipp Emanuel Bach (centre), Christian Carl Sturm (right) and the artist: drawing by Andreas Stöttrup, pen and ink with wash, 1784 (Kunsthalle, Hamburg)*

composed keyboard accompaniment (e.g. the setting of Psalm viii, 'Wer ist so würdig als du', which Bach later arranged as a chorus). In Hamburg he frequently adapted solo songs for choral performance, often giving the separate verses individual form and making song motets of them.

Bach had a hand in the compilation of the Danish psalter of 1778, edited by his pupil N. Schiørring, the Schleswig-Holstein hymnal (Altona 1780 and 1783) and the Hamburg hymnal which in 1787 superseded Telemann's of 1730. His secular songs were much sought after by the editors of the *Musenalmanach* volumes which became fashionable in the 1770s. They met with a good deal of criticism, however, for by comparison with typical *Musenalmanach* works by F.W. Weis, C.G. Neefe, J.F. Reichardt and others Bach's songs seemed sometimes rather contrived and stiff. C.F. Cramer's plan to publish in his *Polyhymnia* the secular songs previously printed elsewhere could not immediately be realized. Bach supervised the preparation of an incomplete edition of his unpublished songs (H700–60 passim; w200) which appeared in Lübeck in 1789.

With the exception of the *Magnificat* of 1749 and the Easter cantata *Gott hat den Herrn auferweckt* (1756; the text, by the Berlin court preacher Leonhard Cochius, was set at the same time by Telemann, TWV1:615), Bach's sacred vocal works date from his Hamburg period. Most of them were composed for particular functions; Bach did not expect them to be widely distributed and in general he restricted his efforts on their preparation to what was essential. The Passions provide an illuminating example: according to Miesner, the six *St Matthew Passions* (most of which perished in World War II) all employed the same biblical framework. Bach composed the recitatives himself, but he usually used the turba choruses from his father's *St Matthew Passion*.

This framework was repeated unchanged every four years, with new arias, choruses and chorales for which Bach again often resorted to works by other composers. Similarly, the *St John Passions* are based on Telemann's printed Passion music for 1745 (*Ein Lämmlein geht und trägt die Schuld*, TWV5:30) and the *St Mark Passions* on a work by G.A. Homilius. The model for the *St Luke Passions* is not known. The Passions are thus pasticcios made up of a biblical framework, Bach's own inserted movements (particularly arias and choruses, and in the 1770s and 80s hymns) and music by other composers. In this way he satisfied the constant demand for new Passion music without having to compose a new work himself each year.

Most of Bach's occasional works are, however, original creations, particularly those for inaugurations of the clergy and the oratorios and serenatas he wrote for the 'civic captains' of Hamburg in 1780 and 1783 (the commission for 1788 came too late for him to meet it). His prime models were G.A. Homilius and Georg Benda. A certain development of the repertory in the inaugural music can be traced: the 1780s saw many repeat performances of older works and on occasion, at the request of the pastors, Bach even resorted to works in his library by Telemann. He distinguished meticulously between the price for composing a piece and that for simply performing or arranging one.

The paucity of contrapuntal movements in Bach's Hamburg church music is striking. An exception is the *Heilig* for double choir (composed in 1776), with its magnificent double fugue, 'Herr, es ist dir keiner gleich', which became an established part of the Michaelmas music and other festive music performed in Hamburg, and came to be regarded as one of the most important sacred vocal works of its time after its publication in 1779.

Bach ascribed particular importance to his oratorios. The score of *Die Israeliten in der Wüste*, composed for the consecration of the Lazarethkirche in 1769, was printed in 1775. *Die Auferstehung und Himmelfahrt Jesu*, probably written in 1774 and revised 1778 at the latest, was offered for subscription in 1784 but did not appear in print until 1787. The third oratorio, the Passion cantata H776 (w233) derived from the composer's first *St Matthew Passion*, was not printed but was nevertheless widely distributed: performances were given during the 18th century in Copenhagen, Berlin, Göttingen, Schwerin and Breslau, as well as in smaller places such as Halberstadt and Colditz. Bach himself owned two copies of the score, one of which he would lend to friends so that they could copy it. Because of the nature of the text, the distribution of the Passion cantata remained limited to Protestant Germany, but *Die Auferstehung* and *Die Israeliten* also reached Catholic parts of southern Germany and were occasionally even performed outside the German-language area (in England and Italy). *Die Israeliten* in particular maintained its place in the repertory as a concert oratorio until well into the 19th century.

11. RECEPTION. Between 1740 and 1775 Bach's many publications ensured a wide distribution for his works, which substantially influenced the development of instrumental music in Germany. With Gluck and later Haydn, he was regarded by his contemporaries as the leading representative of a specifically German musical taste, as

is evident from J.K.F. Triest's description of him after his death as 'a Klopstock using notes instead of words'. His sphere of influence was not confined to northern Germany, where J.C.F. and J.E. Bach, J.F. Reichardt, J.A.P. Schulz, J.W. Hässler and others were directly subject to it; soon after 1760 it spread to south German and Austrian areas as well, particularly through the *Essay* and the printed collections of keyboard works. Although accounts of the esteem in which he was held by Haydn, Mozart and Beethoven are partly anecdotal and cannot be verified in detail, they are a strong indication that the north German master also influenced the Classical Viennese style, not so much formally as in matters of thematic development and the idiomatic treatment of instruments. However, the late keyboard works, the double concerto H479 (w47) and the quartets H537–9 (w93–5) make it clear that C.P.E. Bach should by no means be regarded merely as a precursor of Viennese Classicism, but as a composer who wrote in his own independent style throughout his life. The posthumous publication of his compositions between 1790 and about 1802 in Berlin, Leipzig and Vienna bears witness to his enduring fame.

Developments during the 19th century made Vienna the musical capital of the German-speaking part of Europe, even superseding Leipzig as the centre of the music-publishing industry, and to the extent that J.S. Bach was rediscovered as the 'father' of German keyboard music, so Emanuel Bach's reputation began to fade.

WORKS

Catalogues: J.M. Bach, ed.: *Verzeichniss des musikalischen nachlasses . . . Carl Philipp Emanuel Bach* (Hamburg, 1790/R) [NV]
A. Wotquenne: *Thematisches Verzeichnis der Werke von Carl Philipp Emanuel Bach (1714–1788)* (Leipzig, 1905/R) [W; addns from Kast (1958) shown as n.v.]
E.E. Helm: *Thematic Catalogue of the Works of Carl Philipp Emanuel Bach* (New Haven, CT, 1989) [H]

Principal MS sources: *A-Wgm*, *B-Bc*, *Br*, *D-Bsb*, *F-Pc*, *GB-Lbl*, Kiev, Archive for Literature and Art; for full information see H

composition dates of instrumental works are from NV unless otherwise stated

SOLO KEYBOARD

Editions: Le trésor de pianistes (Paris, 1861–72) [T]
Carl Philipp Emanuel Bach: Die Sechs Sammlungen von Sonaten, freien Fantasien und Rondos für Kenner und Liebhaber, ed. C. Krebs (Leipzig, 1895, rev. 2/1953 by L. Hoffmann-Erbrecht) [K]
Carl Philipp Emanuel Bach: Klavierwerke, ed. H. Schenker (Vienna, 1902–3) [S]
Carl Philipp Emanuel Bach: Ausgewählte Kompositionen, ed. H. Riemann (Leipzig, n.d.) [R]
Carl Philipp Emanuel Bach: Kleine Stücke für Klavier, ed. O. Vrieslander (Hanover, 1930) [VK]
Carl Philipp Emanuel Bach: Vier leichte Sonaten, ed. O. Vrieslander (Hanover, 1932) [VL]
Carl Philipp Emanuel Bach: Sonaten und Stücke, ed. K. Hermann (Leipzig, 1938) [HS]
Carl Philipp Emanuel Bach: Leichte Tänze und Stücke für Klavier, ed. K. Hermann (Hamburg, 1949) [HL]
Carl Philipp Emanuel Bach: Six Sonatas for Keyboard, ed. P. Friedheim (New York, 1967) [F]
Carl Philipp Emanuel Bach 1714–1788: The Collected Works for Solo Keyboard, ed. D. Berg (New York, 1985) [facs.] [B i–vi]
Musikalisches Allerley (Berlin, 1761) [1761]
Musikalisches Mancherley (Berlin 1762–3) [1762]
Clavierstücke verschiedener Art (Berlin, 1765) [1765]
Kurze und leichte Clavierstücke mit veränderten Reprisen, i (Berlin, 1766) [1766¹]
Kurze und leichte Clavierstücke mit veränderten Reprisen, ii (Berlin, 1766) [1766²]
Musikalisches Vielerley, ed. C.P.E. Bach (Hamburg, 1770) [1770]

sonatas: printed collections

H	W	
24–9	48	Sei sonate per cembalo (Prussian sonatas), F, Bb, E, c, C, A, 1740–42 (Nuremberg, 1742/R in B i); ed. R. Steglich (Kassel, c1988), ed. in T, 29 ed. in R
30–31, 33, 32, 34, 36	49	Sei sonate per cembalo (Württemberg sonatas), a, Ab, e, Bb, Eb, b, 1742–3 (Nuremberg, 1744/R in B vi); ed. R. Steglich (Kassel, c1987), ed. in T
136–9, 126, 140	50	Sechs Sonaten für Clavier mit veränderten Reprisen, F, G, a, d, Bb, c, 1758–9 (Berlin, 1760/R in B i); ed. E. Darbellay (Winterthur, 1976), ed. E. Hashimoto (Tokyo, c1984), ed. P. Lescat (Courlay, c1992), 126 ed. in HS
150–51, 127–8 141, 62	51	Fortsetzung von Sechs Sonaten fürs Clavier, C, Bb, c, d, G, g, 1758–60 (Berlin, 1761/R in B i); ed. J.M. Rose (Bryn Mawr, PA, 1973), ed. E. Hashimoto (Tokyo, c1984), 127–8 ed. in HS
50, 142, 158, 37, 161, 129	52	Zweite Fortsetzung von Sechs Sonaten fürs Clavier, Eb, d, g, f♯, E, e, 1744–62 (Berlin, 1763/R in B i); ed. E. Hashimoto (Tokyo, c1984), 50 ed. in SBA, 142 ed. in F, 158 ed. in HS, 37 ed. in R
162, 180–82, 163, 183	53	Sechs leichte Clavier-Sonaten, C, Bb, a, D, C, F, 1762–4 (Leipzig, 1766/R in B i) [see also H 156–7]; 182 ed. in F
204–5, 184, 206, 185, 207	54	Six sonates pour le clavecin à l'usage des dames, F, C, d, Bb, D, A, 1765–6 (Amsterdam, 1770/R in B i); ed. K. Johnen (Frankfurt, 1950)
244, 130, 245, 186, 243, 187	55	Sechs Clavier-Sonaten für Kenner und Liebhaber, i, C, F, b, A, F, G, 1758–74 (Leipzig, 1779/R in B ii); ed. K, S, 130, 186–7, 244 ed. in T
260, 246, 261, 269, 262, 270	56	Clavier-Sonaten nebst einigen Rondos . . . für Kenner und Liebhaber, ii: Rondo, C; Sonata, G; Rondo, D; Sonata, F; Rondo. a; Sonata, A: 1774–80 (Leipzig, 1780/R in B ii); ed. in K, 246, 269–70 ed. in T, 246 ed. in S
265, 247, 271, 208, 266, 173	57	Clavier-Sonaten nebst einigen Rondos . . . für Kenner und Liebhaber, iii: Rondo, E; Sonata, a; Rondo, G; Sonata, d; Rondo, F; Sonata, f: 1763–80 (Leipzig, 1781/R in B ii); ed. in K, 173, 208, 247 ed. in T, S, 173, 165 ed. in R
276, 273–4, 188, 267, 277–8	58	Clavier-Sonaten und freye Fantasien nebst einigen Rondos . . . für Kenner und Liebhaber, iv: Rondo, A; Sonata, G/E; Rondo, E; Sonata, e; Rondo, Bb; Fantasia, Eb; Fantasia, A: 1779–82 (Leipzig, 1783); ed. in K, 267, 274, 276 ed. in T, 188 ed. in S (inc.)
281, 268, 282–3, 279, 284	59	Clavier-Sonaten und freye Fantasien nebst einigen Rondos . . . für Kenner und Liebhaber, v: Sonata, e; Rondo, G; Sonata, Bb; Rondo, c; Fantasia, F; Fantasia, C: 1779–84 (Leipzig, 1785/R in B ii); ed. in K, 282–3 ed. in T, 268, 282 (inc.) ed. in S
288, 286, 289–90, 287, 291	61	Clavier-Sonaten und freye Fantasien nebst einigen Rondos . . . für Kenner und Liebhaber, vi: Rondo, Eb; Sonata, D; Fantasia, Bb; Rondo, d; Sonata, e; Fantasia, C: 1785–6 (Leipzig, 1787/R in B ii); ed. in K, 286 ed. in HS, 291 ed. in R

sonatas printed separately

H	W	
2	62.1	Sonata, Bb, 1731, rev. 1744 (1761/R in B iii); ed. in T
20	62.2	Sonata, G, 1739, in Nebenstunden der berlinischen Musen (Berlin, 1762/R in B vi)
22	62.3	Sonata, D, 1740, in F.W. Marpurg: Clavier-Stücke mit einem practischen Unterricht für Anfänger und Geübtere, iii (Berlin, 1763/R in B vi)
38	62.4	Sonata, d, 1744, in Oeuvres mêlées, iii (Nuremberg, 1757/R in B vi); ed. in T
39	62.5	Sonata, E, 1744, in Oeuvres mêlées, iv (Nuremberg, 1758–9/R in B vi); ed. in T
40	62.6	Sonata, f, 1744 (1761/R in B iii); ed. in T, ed. D. Schulenberg, Carl Philipp Emanuel Bach Edition, I/xviii (Oxford, 1995)
41	62.7	Sonata, C, 1744, in Collection récréative, ii (Nuremberg, 1761/R in B vi); ed. in T
55	62.8	Sonata, F, 1748, in Tonstücke für das Clavier vom Herrn C.P.E. Bach und andern classischen Meistern (Berlin, 1762/R in B vi, 2/1774 as C.P.E. Bachs, Nichelmanns und Händels Sonaten und Fugen); ed. in T
58	62.9	Sonata, F, 1749, in Oeuvres mêlées, i (Nuremberg, 1755/R in B vi); ed. in T
59	62.10	Sonata, C, 1749 (1762/R in B iii); ed. in T
63	62.11	Sonata, G, 1750 (1761/R in B iii)
66	62.12	Sonata, e, 1730s, rev. 1751 (1761/R in B iii), ed. in T
67	62.13	Sonata, D, in Raccolta delle più nuove composizioni (Leipzig, 1756/R in B iii)
70–75	63.1–6	18 Probestücke in 6 Sonaten, C, d, A, b, Eb, f, 1753 [exx. for H868, see 'Theoretical works']; facs. in B i, vi, 71–5 ed. in T, 75 ed. in R
77	62.14	Sonata, G, 1754 (1762/R in B iii)
105	62.15	Sonata, d, in Raccolta delle più nuove composizioni (Leipzig, 1757/R in B iii); ed. in T
116	62.16	Sonata, Bb, 1757, in Oeuvres mêlées, v (Nuremberg, 1759/R in B vi); ed. in T
117	62.17	Sonata, E, 1757, in Oeuvres mêlées, xii (Nuremberg, c1765/R in B vi); ed. in T

H	W	
118–20	62.18–20	3 sonatas, g, G, C, 1757 (1762/*R* in B iii); 118–19 ed. in T, B, 119 ed. in F
131	62.21	Sonata, a, 1758, in Oeuvres mêlées, xi (Nuremberg, 1765/*R* in B vi); ed. in T
132	62.22	Sonata, b, 1758, in Collection récréative, i (Nuremberg, 1760/*R* in B vi); ed. in T
179	112.7	Sonata, d (1765/*R* in B ii); ed. in T
209	60	Sonata, c, 1766, ? rev. later (Leipzig and Dresden, 1785/*R* in B vi)
210	62.23	Sonata, g, 1766 (1770/*R* in B iii)
240	62.24	Sonata, F, 1769 (1770/*R* in B iii)

sonatas: manuscript

H	W	
3–6	65.1–4	4 sonatas, F, a, d, e, 1731–3, rev. 1744; 3–5 facs. in B iii, 6 facs. in B iv, 5 ed. in T
7–12	64	6 sonatas, G, G, a, a, e, D, c, 1734, rev. 1744 and ?*c*1786; facs. in B iii, ed. K. Johnen (Frankfurt, 1952)
13	65.5	Sonata, e, 1735, rev. 1744; facs. in B iii
15–19	65.6–10	5 sonatas, G, E♭, C, B♭, A, 1736–8, rev. 1743–4; facs. in B iii, 15 ed. in T, 18 ed. in F
21	65.11	Sonata, g, 1739, rev. later; facs. in B iii, ed. in T, VL
23	65.12	Sonata, G, 1740, rev. later; facs. in B iii
32·5	65.13	Sonata, b, 1743; facs. in B iii, ed. in T
42–3	65.14–15	2 sonatas, D, G, 1744–5; facs. in B iii, 42 ed. in VL, 43 ed. D. Schulenberg, Carl Philipp Emanuel Bach Edition, I/xviii (Oxford, 1995)
46–8	65.16–18	3 sonatas, C, g, F, 1746; facs. in B iii, ed. D. Schulenberg, Carl Philipp Emanuel Bach Edition, I/xviii (Oxford, 1995), 46 ed. in F, 47 ed. in T
49	65.19	Sonata, F, *c*1786 (1746 acc. NV); facs. in B vi, ed. D. Schulenberg, Carl Philipp Emanuel Bach Edition, I/xviii (Oxford, 1995)
51–2	65.20–21	2 sonatas, B♭, F, 1747; ed. in T, R, 51 facs. in B iii, 51 ed. D. Schulenberg, Carl Philipp Emanuel Bach Edition, I/xviii (Oxford, 1995), 52 facs. in B iv
53	69	Sonata per il cembalo a due tastature, 1749; facs. in B iii
56–7	65.22–3	2 sonatas, G, d, 1748; facs. in B iv, 56 ed in VL, 57 ed. in F
60, 371·5	65.24	Sonata, d [see also 'Organ']; facs. in B iv, ed. in T
61	65.25	Sonata, a, 1749; facs. in B iv
64	65.26	Sonata, G, 1750; facs. in B iv
68	65.27	Sonata, g, 1752; facs. in B iv, ed. in T
78	65.28	Sonata, E♭, 1754; facs. in B iv, ed. in T
83	65.29	Sonata, E, 1755; facs. in B iv
106	65.30	Sonata, e, 1756; facs. in B iv
121	65.31	Sonata, c, 1757; facs. in B vi, ed. in T
135	65.32	Sonata, A, 1758, rev. later [see also 'Organ', H133]; facs. in B vi
143	65.33	Sonata, a, 1759; facs. in B iv, ed. in VL

H	W	
152	65.34	Sonata, B♭, 1760; facs. in B iv
156–7	65.35–6	2 sonatas, C, C, after 1760 [revs. of H162–3]; facs. in B i
174–8	65.37–41	5 sonatas, A, B, e, D, C, 1763; facs. in B iv, 174, 176–8 ed. in T, 176–8 ed. C. Widgery, Carl Philipp Emanuel Bach Edition, I/xxiv (Oxford, 1989)
189	65.42	Sonata, E♭, 1765; facs. in B iv, ed. in T, ed. C. Widgery, Carl Philipp Emanuel Bach Edition, I/xxiv (Oxford, 1989)
192	65.43	Sonata, A, 1765–6; facs. in B iv, ed. in T, ed. C. Widgery, Carl Philipp Emanuel Bach Edition, I/xxiv (Oxford, 1989)
211–13	65.44–6	3 sonatas, B♭, B♭, E, 1766, rev. later; facs. in B iv, ed. in T, ed. C. Widgery, Carl Philipp Emanuel Bach Edition, I/xxiv (Oxford, 1989)
248	65.47	Sonata, C, 1775; facs. in B iv
280	65.48	Sonata für das Bogenklavier, G, 1783; facs. in B iv, ed. in T, HS
298–9	65.49–50	2 sonatas, c, G/a, 1786 [299 based on earlier ww compositions]; facs. in B iv, 298 ed. in T

variations

H	W	
14	118.7	Minuet (from Locatelli's Sonata op.2 no.10, fl, bc) with 18 variations, G, 1735; facs. in B vi
44	118.3	Minuet with 5 variations, C, 1745; facs. in B v
54	118.4	Arioso with 7 variations, F, 1747; facs. in B v, ed. in VK
65	118.5	Allegretto with 6 variations, C, 1750; facs. in B v, ed. in HL
69	181.1	Variations on Ich schlief, da träumte mir, F, 1752, enlarged later; 17 variations (1761), 7 variations (1770); facs. in B v, ed. F. Goebels (Mainz, *c*1986)
155	118.2	?8 variations on an Arietta (? by J.F. Agricola), 1760; contribution to set of 22 variations (collab. C. Fasch, ?J.A. Steffan and others), variations 1–17 (1761), 18–22 (1770); facs. in B v
226	118.6	12 variations on Romance: Colin a peine a seize ans, G, 1766; facs. in B v
259	118.10	Arioso with 20 variations, C, after 1775 [based on H534, see 'Chamber']; facs. in B v
263	118.9	12 variations on La folia d'Espagne, d, 1778; facs. in B v, ed. in HS
275	118.8	Canzonetta (? by Luise Dorothea of Saxe-Gotha) with 6 variations, F, 1781; facs. in B v
351	—	Arioso with 6 variations, A; doubtful, anon. (with 8 variations) in G.S. Löhlein: Clavier-Schule (Leipzig and Züllichau, 1765)
—	—	Arioso with 5 variations, A, 1781; see 'Chamber', H535

H	W	
		miscellaneous
1	—	March, D; Polonoise, g; March, G; Polonoise, g; Marche, E♭; Solo per il cembalo, E♭: 1730s, in Clavierbüchlein, ii, for Anna Magdalena Bach, BWV Anh.122–5, 127, 129; not listed in NV
1·5	111	Menuet pour le clavessin, C (Leipzig, 1731); facs. in B v
75·5	119.7	Fantasia and fugue, c; in F.W. Marpurg: *Abhandlung von der Fuge* (Berlin, 1754); facs. in B v
76	119.1	Fuga a 2, a; in F.W. Marpurg: *Abhandlung von der Fuge* (Berlin, 1754); facs. in B v)
79–82	117.17–18, 26, 37	La Borchward, polonoise, G; La Pott/Lott, tempo di minuet, in Raccolta delle più nuove composizioni (Leipzig, 1756); La Böhmer, murky, D; La Gause, F: c1754–5; facs. in B v
89–91	117.19–21	La Gleim, rondeau, a; La Bergius, B♭; La Prinzette, F: c1754–5, in Raccolta delle più nuove composizioni (Leipzig, 1756); 89, 91 facs. in B v, 90 facs. in B vi, 89–90 ed. in R, 91 ed. in HL
92–5	117.23–5, 27	L'Hermann, g; La Buchholtz, d; La Stahl, d; L'Aly Rupalich, C: c1754–5 (1762/R in B v); 92 ed. in HL, 94–5 ed. in R, 94 ed. in HS
96–8	117.34–5, 39	La Philippine, A; La Gabriel, C; La Caroline, a: c1755; facs. in B v, ed. in HL
99	119.2	Fuga a 2, d, by 1755; in F.W. Marpurg: Fugensammlung, i (Berlin, 1758); facs. in B v
100	119.3	Fuga a 3, F, by 1755; in Tonstücke . . . vom Herrn C.P.E. Bach und andern classischen Meistern (Berlin, 1762, 2/1774 as C.P.E. Bachs, Nichelmanns und Händels Sonaten und Fugen); facs. in B vi
101, 101·5, 102	119.4–6	Fuga a 3, A; Fuga a 3, g; Fuga a 4, E♭: all by 1755; 101 in Raccolta delle più nuove composizioni (Leipzig, 1757), facs. in B v; 102 in F.W. Marpurg: Clavierstücke mit einem practischen Unterricht (Berlin, 176), facs. in B vi; 101·5 (1765)
108	116.18	Andantino, F; in F.W. Marpurg: *Kritische Briefe über die Tonkunst* (Berlin, 1760); facs. in B v
109–13	117.28, 30–33	La complaisante, B♭; Les langueurs tendres, f; L'irréssolué, G; La journalière, c; La capricieuse: e: c1754–5 (1761/R in B v)
114	117.36	La Louise, D, c1755; facs. in B v
122–5	117.22, 29, 38, 40	L'Auguste, polonoise, F, in Raccolta delle più nuove composizioni (Leipzig, 1756); La Xénophon–La Sybille, C♯ (1761); L'Ernestine/La Frédérique, D; La Sophie, B♭: c1754–5; facs. in B v, 122 ed. in HL

H	W	
144–9	112.2, 4, 8, 10, 15, 18	Fantasia, D; Solfeggio, G; Fantasia, B♭; Solfeggio, G; Fantasia, F; Solfeggio, G: (1765/R in B ii), 144, 146, 148–9 ed. in VK, 145, 147 ed. in HL
153–4	116.21–2	Allegro, solfeggio, C; Polonoise, g: 1760; 153 ed. in HS
160	117.14	Fantasia, D [ex. for H870, see 'Theoretical works']; facs. in B v
165–70	112.3, 5, 9, 11, 16–17 [116.9–14]	Minuet, D; Alla polacca, a; Minuet, C; Alla polacca, g; Minuet, A; Alla polacca, D: (1765/R in B ii); 165, 169 ed. in HL, 166, 168, 170 ed. in VK
171–2	116.1–2	Minuet, E♭; Polonoise, E♭: (1762/R in B v)
190	112.1	Conc., C, hpd solo (1765/R in B ii) [orig. intended for kbd, str in D]
191	112.13	Sinfonia, G (1765/R in B ii)
193–203	113	Allegro, G; Arioso, a; Fantasia, d; Minuet, F; Alla polacca, C; Allegretto, d; Alla polacca, D; Allegretto, A; Andante e sostenuto, g; Presto, B♭; Allegro, d: (1766¹/R in B ii); ed. O. Vrieslander, *Kurze und leichte Klavierstücke* (Vienna, 1914), ed. O. Jonas (Vienna, 1962)
214–17, 219	116.3–6, 8	Minuet, D; Alla polacca, C; Minuet, C; Alla polacca, D; Minuet, F; Alla polacca, G: (1762/R in B v); 214–16 ed. in VK
220–22	117.2–4	3 solfeggios, c, E♭, A: (1770/R in B v); 220 ed. in R
223–5	117.11–13	3 fantasias, G, d, g: (1770); 223, 225 facs. in B v, 223–4 ed. in VK
228–38	114	Allegro di molto, d; Andantino e grazioso, B♭; Presto, c; Minuet, G; Alla polacca, D; Alla polacca, E♭; Fantasia, d; Allegro, E; Allegretto, A; Andante, C; Poco allegro, e: (1766²/R in B ii); ed. O. Vrieslander, *Kurze und leichte Klavierstücke* (Vienna, 1914), ed. O. Jonas (Vienna, 1962), 234 ed. in R
241	117.1	Clavierstück für die rechte oder linke Hand allein, A; facs. in B v, ed. in VK
249–54	116.23–8	Sechs leichte Clavierstückgen, C, F, D, G, g, D, 1775 [no.6 also in variant version]; facs. in B v
256–8	n.v.37–9	Allegro, F; Allegretto, D; Menuet, F: c1775
264	120	Cadenzen, 1778 or later, B-Bc, for his own concs. and sonatas
272	66	Rondo: Abschied von meinem Silbermannischen Claviere, e, 1781; facs. in B v
292–7	63.7–12	6 neue Sonatinen, G, E, D, B♭, F, d, 1786 [exx. for H868 (2/1787), see 'Theoretical works']; facs. in B i, ed. in VK, ed. L. Hoffmann-Erbrecht (Leipzig, 1957)
300	67	Fantasia (Carl Philipp Emanuel Bachs Empfindungen), f♯, 1788 [see also 'Chamber', H536]; facs. in B vi, ed. A. Kreutz (Mainz, 1950)

H	W	
301–2	116.19–20	Allegretto, F; Allegro, D; facs. in B v
338	116.16–17	Allegro, A; Allegro, G; in F.W. Marpurg: *Anleitung zum Clavierspielen* (Berlin, 1755); ed. in HS
348	—	Fantasia, E♭, c1748; attrib. erroneously to C. Nichelmann
—	—	Suite, B♭, c1730, *D-Kl*; not listed in NV
—	—	Suite, E♭, c1730, *Hs*; not listed in NV
—	—	Suite, G, c1730, *Hs*; not listed in NV
—	—	Suite, G, ?1730s, *Bsb*; not listed in NV
—	—	Menuet, E♭, 1730s, in Klavierbüchlein attrib. W.A. Mozart; not listed in NV
—	—	March, F, 1730s, *Hs*; not listed in NV
—	—	Murqui pour l'amour, A, 1730s, *Hs*; not listed in NV
—	—	Allemande, A♭, 1730s, *Hs*; not listed in NV

TWO KEYBOARDS

H	W	
610–13	115	4 kleine Duetten, B♭, F, a, E♭, ? after 1768
—	—	Sonata, C, after 1766, *F-Pc** [based on H515, see 'Chamber']

ORGAN

sonatas

H	W	
60, 371·5	65.24	Sonata, d, 1749
133	70.1	Sonata, A, 1758, rev. later [see also 'Keyboard solo', H135]; facs. in B iv
134	70.2	Sonata, B♭, 1758, rev. later, in III sonates . . . par Mrs. C.P.E. Bach (Nuremberg, 1770); facs. in B iv
84–7	70.3–6	4 sonatas, F, a, D, g, 1755; facs. in B iv
107	70.7	Sonata, D, 1755; facs. in B iv

other pieces, mostly doubtful

H	W	
336	—	5 Choräle mit ausgesetzten Mittelstimmen
—	—	Pedal-Exercitium (inc.), g, by 1734 [= BWV598]
—	n.v.66	Adagio, d
—	—	Aus der Tiefe rufe ich, e [= BWV745]
—	—	Ich ruf zu Dir, Herr Jesu Christ, f [= BWV Anh.73 (after BWV639)]

CHAMBER

Edition: *Carl Philipp Emanuel Bach: Complete Sonatas for Flute and Obbligato Keyboard*, ed. U. Leisinger (Monteux, 1993–) [L]

solos

H	W	
548	134	Sonata, G, fl, bc, ? by 1735
549	135	Solo, g, ob, bc, ? by 1735, rev. later
550	123	Sonata, G, fl, bc, 1735
551	124	Sonata, e, fl, bc, 1737
552, 560	125, 130	Sonata, B♭, fl, bc, 1738, rev. 1746
553–5	126–8	3 sonatas, D, G, a, fl, bc, 1738–40
556, 561	129, 131	Sonata, D, fl, bc, 1740, rev. 1747

H	W	
557	138	Solo, g, vc, bc, 1740, rev. 1769, lost
558–9	136–7	2 solos, C, D, va da gamba, bc, 1745–6
562	132	Sonata, a, fl, 1747 (1763); ed. M. Nastasi (Vienna, c1986)
563	139	Solo, G, harp, 1762 (facs. (Utrecht, c1996))
564	133	Sonata, G, fl, bc, 1786

trios, quartets

H	W	
502	71	Sonata, D, kbd, vn, 1731, rev. 1746
503, 596	72	Sonata, d, kbd, vn (or fl, vn, kbd), 1731, rev. 1747
504, 573	73, 149	Sonata, C, kbd, vn/fl (or fl, vn, kbd), 1745
505, 575	83, 151	Sonata, D, kbd, fl (or fl, vn, bc), 1747
506, 580	84, 162	Sonata, E, kbd, fl (or 2 fl, bc), 1749
507, 585	—	Sinfonia, D, kbd, vn (or 2 vn, bc), 1754
508, 581, 157	85, 152	Trio, G, kbd, fl (or fl/vn, vn, bc), 1754; ed. C. Hill (Monteux, c1986)
509, 586	86, 153	Sonata, G, kbd, fl (or fl, vn, bc), 1755; ed. C. Hill (Monteux, c1986)
510, 541	88	Sonata, g, kbd, va/va da gamba, 1759
511	75	Sonata, F, kbd, vn, 1763
512	76	Sonata, b, kbd, vn, 1763
513	77	Sonata, B♭, kbd, vn, 1763
514	78	Sonata, c, kbd, vn, 1763
515	87	Trio, C, kbd, fl, 1766 [also for 2 hpd, *F-Pn*]
516–21	92	6 qts, E♭, E♭, E♭, B♭, E♭, B♭, after 1768
522–4	90	3 sonatas, a, G, C, kbd, vn, vc (Leipzig, 1776)
525–30	89	6 sonatas, e, B♭, C, A, E♭, e, D, kbd, vn, vc (London, 1776; Amsterdam, c1778)
531–4	91	4 sonatas, e, D, F, C, kbd, vn, vc (Leipzig, 1777) [H534 variations]
535	79, n.v.70	Arioso, A, kbd, vn, 1780 [orig. kbd solo]
536	80	Fantasie (C.P.E. Bachs Empfindungen), f♯, kbd, vn, 1787 [orig. kbd solo]
537–9	93–5	3 qts, a–D–G, kbd, fl, va, 1788
542, 570	146	Sonata, A, kbd, vn (or fl, vn, bc), 1731, rev. 1747
566	—	Trio, vn, va, bc, c1731, lost [composed under supervision of J.S. Bach]
567	143	Sonata, b, kbd, vn (or fl, vn, bc), 1731, rev. 1747
568	144	Trio, G, fl, vn, bc, 1731, rev. 1747
569	145	Sonata, d, kbd, vn (or fl, vn, bc), 1731, rev. 1747 [early version = BWV1036]
571	147	Sonata, C, kbd, vn (or fl, vn, bc), 1731, rev. 1747
572	148	Sonata, a, kbd, vn (or fl/vn, vn, bc), 1735, rev. 1747
574	150	Trio, G, fl, vn, bc, 1747
576	154	Sonata, F, fl/vn, vn, bc, 1754
577	155	Sonata, e, 2 vn, bc, 1747
578	161.2	Sonata, B♭, kbd, vn (or fl, vn, kbd), 1748 (Nuremberg, 1751)

H	W	
579	161.1	Trio (Sangineus und Melancholicus), c, kbd, vn (or 2 vn, bc), 1749 (Nuremberg, 1751)
582	156	Sinfonia, a, 2 vn, bc, 1754
584	158	Sonata, B♭, 2 vn, bc, 1754
587, 543	159	Trio, B♭, 2 vn, bc, c1755 [= H588–9]
588–9	163	Trio, F, b fl, va/bn, bc, 1755, rev. later [= H587, 543]
590	160	Sonata, d, 2 vn, bc, 1756, rev. later
600	81	12 kleine Stücke, G g, e, a, D, D, D, B, D, C, F, d, kbd, fl, vn (Berlin, 1758)
628	82	12 . . . kleine Stücke, e, E, G, g, A, a, D, d, C, c, g, B♭, kbd, fl, vn (Hamburg, 1770)

miscellaneous

H	W	
598	140	Duetto, e, fl, vn, *D-Bsb**, in Musikalisches Vielerley (Hamburg, 1770)
599	141	Duetto, d, 2 vn, lost
604–5	190.1, 3	2 polonoise, F, a, 2 cl, 2 vn, bc
607–9, 627	190.2, 4–6	4 polonoise, G, D, C, A, 2 vn, bc (with 2 cl in H608)
614–19	185	6 marches, D, C, F, G, E♭, D, 2 ob, 2 cl, bn, 2 hn
620	186	2 kleine Stücke, a, F, 2 cl, bn, 2 hn, lost
637	187	2 marches, F, D, 2 ob, bn, 2 hn
621	188	Marche für die Arche, C, 3 tpt, timp, after 1767; ed. H.M. Lewis (Monteux, c1988)
629–34	184	6 sonatas, D, F, G, E♭, A, C, 2 fl, 2 cl, bn, 2 hn
635	193	[30] Stücke für Spieluhren auch Drehorgeln
636	142	Duetto, C, 2 cl [= H635, 26–7]
—	—	?Marche, ?3 tpt, timp, 1763, lost (? = H621)
—	—	Marche, E♭, tpt, 2 ob, bn, by 1767

ORCHESTRAL

Editions: *Carl Philipp Emanuel Bach: Six Symphonies*, ed. C.C. Gallagher and E.E. Helm, in The Symphony 1720–1840, ser. C, viii (New York, 1982) [GH]
Carl Philipp Emanuel Bach 1714–1788: The Collected Works for Solo Keyboard, ed. D. Berg (New York, 1985) [facs.] [B i–vi]

solo concertos and sonatinas

H	W	
190	112.1	Conc., C, hpd solo (1765) [see 'Solo keyboard']; facs. in B ii
403	1	Conc., a, hpd, str, 1733, rev. c1740 and 1744
404	2	Conc., E♭, hpd, str, 1734, rev. 1743; early version (Paris, c1761)
405	3	Conc., G, hpd, str, 1737, rev. 1745
406	4	Conc., G, hpd, str, 1738
407	5	Conc., c, hpd, str, 1739, rev. 1762
409	6	Conc., g, hpd, str, 1740, rev. later
410–13	7–10	4 concs., A, A, G, B♭, hpd, str, 1740–42
414	11	Conc., D, hpd, str, 1743 (Nuremberg, 1745)
415–16	12–13	2 concs., F, D, hpd, str, 1744; listed as fl. conc. in Ringmacher catalogue (Berlin, 1773)

H	W	
417	14	Conc., E, hpd, str, 1744 (Berlin, 1760), rev. later; also with 2 hn
418–24	15–21	7 concs., e, G, g, d, D, A, C, a, hpd, str, 1745–7
425, 484·1	22	Conc., d, fl/hpd, str, 1747, rev. later; also with 2 hn
427–8	23–4	2 concs., d, e, hpd, str, 1748
429	25	Conc., B♭, hpd, str, 1749 (Nuremberg, 1752)
430–32	26, 166, 170	Conc., a, vc/fl/hpd, str, 1750; 431 ed. U. Leisinger (Monteux, c1992)
433	27	Conc., D, hpd, 2 hn, str, with 2 fl, 2 ob, 2/?3 tpt/hn, timp ad lib, 1750
434–6	28, 167, 171	Conc., B♭, vc/fl/hpd, str, 1751
437–9	29, 168, 172	Conc., A, vc/fl/hpd, str, 1753
440–43	30–33	4 concs., b, c, g, F, hpd, str, 1753–5
444–5	34, 169	Conc., G, org/hpd/fl, str, 1755
446	35	Conc., E♭, org/hpd, str, 1759; also with 2 hn
447	36	Conc., B♭, hpd, str, 1762
448	37	Conc., c, hpd, 2 hn, str, 1762; ed. E.N. Kulukundis and P.G. Wiley, Carl Philipp Emanuel Bach Edition, II/xv (Oxford, 1989)
449	96	Sonatina, D, hpd, 2 fl, str, 1762, rev. later; also with 2 hn
450–51	97–8	2 sonatinas, G, G, hpd, 2 fl, 2 hn, str, 1762; 451 ed. P.G. Wiley and C. Widgery, Carl Philipp Emanuel Bach Edition, II/xxiii (Oxford, 1992)
452, 485	99	Sonatina, F, hpd, 2 fl, str, 1762 [also with 2 hn]; ed. P.G. Wiley and C. Widgery, Carl Philipp Emanuel Bach Edition, II/xxiii (Oxford, 1992)
454	38	Conc., F, hpd, 2 fl, str, 1763; ed. E.N. Kulukundis and P.G. Wiley, Carl Philipp Emanuel Bach Edition, II/xv (Oxford, 1989)
455	100	Sonatina, E, hpd, 2 fl, 2 hn, str, 1763
456–7	102–3	2 sonatinas, D, C, hpd, 2 fl, 2 hn, str, 1763
458, 460	106, 101	Sonatina, C, hpd, 2 fl, str, 1763 (Berlin, 1764), rev. later; also with 2 hn
461, 463	107, 104	Sonatina, F, hpd, 2 fl, str, 1764 (Berlin, 1764), rev. later; also with 2 hn
462, 464	108, 105	Sonatina, E♭, hpd, 2 fl, str, 1764 (Berlin, 1766), rev. later; also with 2 hn
465–6	39, 164	Conc., B♭, ob/hpd, str, 1765
467–8	40, 165	Conc., E♭, ob/hpd, str, 1765
469	41	Conc., E♭, hpd, 2 fl, 2 hn, str, 1769
470	42	Conc., F, hpd, 2 hn, str, 1770 [also for kbd solo, H242; facs. in B iv]
471–6	43	Sei concerti, F, D, E♭, c, G, C, hpd, 2 fl, 2 hn, str, 1771–2 (Hamburg, 1772)
477–8	44–5	2 concs., G, D, hpd, 2 hn, str, 1778

double concertos and sonatinas

H	W	
408	46	Conc., F, 2 hpd, 2 hn, str, 1740; ed. G. Kiss (Hamburg, c1988)
453	109	Sonatina, D, 2 hpd, 2 fl, 2 ob, bn, 3 tpt, 2 hn, str, 1762; also for 1 hpd, 2 fl, str, H480, 480·5

H	W	
459	110	Sonatina, B♭, 2 hpd, 2 fl, str, 1763; also for 1 hpd, 2 fl, str, *D-LEm*
479	47	Conc., E♭, hpd, pf, 2 fl, 2 hn, str, 1788

symphonies

H	W	
648	173	Sinfonie, G, str, 1741; GH, kbd red., 1745, H45 (W122.1), facs. in B iv
649	174	Sinfonia, C, str, 1755, rev. later; also with 2 fl, 2 hn
650	175	Sinfonia, F, str, 1755, rev. later; also with 2 fl, 2 bn, 2 hn; GH, kbd red., H104 (W122.2), by ? F.W. Marpurg, in Raccolta delle megliore sinfonie (Leipzig, 1761), facs. in B iii
651	176	Sinfonia, D, str, 1756, rev. later; also with 2 fl, 2 ob, 2 hn, 2 tpt, timp; GH
652–3	177–8	2 sinfonias, e, e, str, 1756 (Nuremberg, 1759), rev. later; kbd red. listed as H115 (W122.3), unrealized
654	179	Sinfonia, E♭, str, 1757, rev. later; also with 2 ob, 2 hn; GH
655	180	Sinfonia, G, str, 1758, rev. later, also with 2 ob, 2 hn; GH, kbd red. W122.4 (= H191; W112.13) in Clavierstücke verschiedener Art (Berlin, 1765)
656	181	Sinfonia, F, str, 1758 [not in NV], rev. ?1762, also with 2 fl, 2 hn; GH, kbd red., 1766, H227 (W122.5), in Musikalisches Vielerley (Hamburg, 1770), facs. in B iii
657–62	182	Sei sinfonie, G, B♭, C, A, b, E, str, for G. van Swieten
663–6	183	[4] Orchester-Sinfonien, D, E♭, F, G, 1775–6 (Leipzig, 1780)
667	—	Sinfonia, str, *c*1751, collab. Count Ferdinand of Lobkowitz [cf NV, 65], lost
—	—	Sinfonia, G, str, by 1766, listed in Breitkopf catalogue, 1766, doubtful, lost
—	—	Sinfonia, C, by 1766, *S-Skma*, listed in Breitkopf catalogue, 1766, doubtful
—	—	Sinfonia, F, str, by *c*1766, *D-Bsb*, doubtful

miscellaneous

H	W	
601	192	2 minuets, C, C, 2 fl, 2 bn, 3 tpt, timp, 2 vn, bc, in Musikalisches Mancherley (Berlin, 1762)
602–3	189.1–2	2 minuets, D, D, 2 fl, 2 cl, 2 vn, bc
606	189.8	Minuet, G, 2 fl, 2 cl, 2 vn, bc
622–6	189.3–7	5 minuets, G, G, G, F, D, 2 fl, 2 cl, 2 vn, bc
638	191	2 minuets, D, D, 2 fl, 2 ob, 2 hn, 3 tpt, timp, str

ORATORIOS AND PASSIONS

H	W	
—	—	Ich freue mich des, das mir geredet ist, orat, 2 Dec 1736, for consecration of the Unterkirche, Frankfurt an der Oder, lost
775	238	Die Israeliten in der Wüste (D. Schiebeler), orat, 1 Nov 1769 (Hamburg, 1775)

H	W	
777	240	Die Auferstehung und Himmelfahrt Jesu (C.W. Ramler), orat, 1774, rev. by 1778 (Leipzig, 1787); ed. G. Darvas (Adliswil, *c*1975)
776	233	Du Göttlicher, Passion cant. (A.L. Karsch, C.D. Ebeling and J.J. Eschenburg), 1770, rev. by 1772, rev. later; based on H782; ed. H.-J. Irmen (Vaduz, *c*1982)
782	—	St Matthew Passion, 1769, ?inc.
783	—	St Mark Passion, 1770, inc., based on G.A. Homilius: St Mark Passion
784	—	St Luke Passion, 1771, frag., incl. movt by G. Benda
785	—	St John Passion, 1772
786	—	St Matthew Passion, 1773, frag.
787	—	St Mark Passion, 1774, frag.
788	—	St Luke Passion, 1775, frag.
789	—	St John Passion, 1776, frag.
790	—	St Matthew Passion, 1777, frag.
791	—	St Mark Passion, 1778, frag.
792	—	St Luke Passion, 1779, frag.
793	—	St John Passion, 1780, frag.
794	—	St Matthew Passion, 1781, inc.
795	—	St Mark Passion, 1782, frag.
796	—	St Luke Passion, 1783, frag.
797	—	St John Passion, 1784, frag.
798	—	St Matthew Passion, 1785, frag.
799	—	St Mark Passion, 1786, frag.
800	234	St Luke Passion, 1787, frag.
801	—	St John Passion, 1788, frag.
802	235	St Matthew Passion, 1789
822a–b	—	Hebt an, ihr Chöre der Freude, orat – Der Trommeln Schlag, serenata (C.W. Alers), 7 Sept 1780
822c–d	—	Schallt Jubel, orat – Schlagt die Trommel, wirbelt Freude, serenata (Alers), 4 Sept 1783; music of orat lost

SACRED LATIN

H	W	
772	215	Magnificat, by 25 Aug 1749, rev. later; alternative version of 'Et misericordia', ?*c*1780–82; ed. G. Darvas (Adliswil, *c*1971)
825	207	Veni Sancte Spiritus, S, S, bc, after 1768
839–40	209–10	Antiphonia, 4vv; Amen, 4vv: after 1768, lost
828	219	Sanctus, after 1768
855	220	Veni Sancte Spiritus, after/?by Telemann, TWV3:84

SACRED CANTATAS AND CHORUSES

H	W	
762	231	Er lebt! Ihm tönen unsre Lieder (Freudenlied for F.L.C. Cropp), (P.L. Cropp), 1785
778	217	Heilig, SATB, SATB, 2 ob, bn, 3 tpt, timp, str, bc, 1776 (Hamburg, 1779)
779	239	Morgengesang am Schöpfungsfest (F.G. Klopstock), 1783 (Leipzig, 1784)
803–5, 807	244, 242, 241, 243	4 Oster-Musik: Gott hat den Herrn auferweckt (L. Cochius), Easter 1756, rev. later; Jauchzet, frohlocket [partly from BWV248¹], Easter 1778; Nun danket alle Gott, Easter 178; Anbetung dem Erbarmer, Easter 1784

H	W	
809–10	248, 245	2 Michaelis-Musik: Den Engeln gleich, St Michael 1769; Ich will den Namen des Herrn preisen, St Michael 1772
811	—	?Weihnachts-Musik: Ehre sei Gott in der Höhe, Christmas ?1772 [also for St Michael 1782]
812	247, 212	Michaelis-Musik: Siehe! Ich begehre deiner Gerechtigkeit, St Michael 1775 [incl. aria 'Sing ihm voll Rührung' w212]
814	246	Michaelis-Musik: Der Frevler mag die Wahrheit schmähn, Christmas 1785 [incl. Heilig H778]
815	249	Weihnachts-Musik: Auf schicke dich, Christmas 1775
816	—	4 Weihnachts-Musik: Die Himmel rühmen die Ehre Gottes, Christmas c1770, music lost; 3 others, Christmas 1782, 1784, 1786, lost
821	—	15 inauguration cants., 1769–87, music mostly lost
823	—	Versammelt euch dem Herrn zu Ehren, for completion of the tower of St Michael, 31 Oct 1786 [incl. Heilig H778], lost
824	—	6 celebratory cantatas, 1765–85, lost
829	216	Spiega, Ammonia fortuna, chorus for visit of Gustav III of Sweden, Hamburg, 1770
830	221	Mein Heiland, meine Zuversicht, chorus for Trinity X, 5 Aug 1787
831	222	Wer ist so würdig als du (J.A. Cramer), chorus, Easter 1780, ? used earlier
832	223	Zeige du mir deine Wege (Cramer), chorus for Trinity VIII, 20 July 1777
—	224	Lass mich nicht deinen Zorn empfinden (Cramer), chorus, 1775 [after H733.13; used in St Matthew Passion H798]
833	225	Gott, dem ich lebe, des ich bin (C.C. Sturm), chorus
834–5	226—7	2 choruses: Amen, Lob und Preis und Stärke (Sturm) for Quasimodogeniti, 27 April 1783; Leite mich nach deinem Willen (B. Münter) for Quasimodogeniti, ? 27 April 1783
836	—	Meine Lebenszeit verstreicht, funeral music for M.H. Schele, Dec 1774 [incl. w228], frag.
837	—	Meinen Leib wird man begraben, funeral music for J. Luis, Feb 1788 [incl. w229], frag.
838	n.v.1	Merkt und seht, chorus, ?1780s
—	—	Wedding cant. for J.S. Ungnad and A.E. Thiele, 18 Jan 1736, lost
—	—	Birthday cant. for Crown Prince Friedrich of Prussia, 24 Jan 1737, lost
—	—	Frankfurt, lass in vollen Chören, cant. for visit of Friedrich Wilhelm I and Sophia Dorothea Maria of Prussia, 18 March 1737, music lost
—	—	Entdeckt durch tausend frohe Töne, cant. for visit of Friedrich Wilhelm I, Nov 1737, lost

H	W	
—	—	Vater, deines Sohnes Geist, cant., ? Hamburg, 1770 [perf. with H829]
—	—	Oster-Kantate, Ist Christus nicht auferstanden, Easter 1771, lost
—	—	Freuet euch, ihr Kinder Zions (C.H.E. Müller), inauguration cant. for J.M. Müller and J.A.G. Schetelig, Hamburg, 7 Nov 1773, music lost
—	—	Funeral music for V. Rumpf, March/April 1781 [incl. H833 and movt from H856 (anon.)], frag.
—	—	Funeral music for F. Doormann, 7 Sept 1781, music lost
—	—	Funeral music for A. Schulte, 10 Jan 1786, lost

SECULAR ARIAS AND CANTATAS

H	W	
669	211	3 arias: Edle Freiheit, Götterglück; Himmelstochter, Ruh der Seelen; Reiche bis zum Wolkensitze: T, 2 fl, bc
697	232	Thirsis, willst du mir gefallen (Phillis und Thirsis) (J.E. Schlegel), S, S, 2 fl, bc, 1765 (Berlin, 1766)
723	237	Freude, du Lust der Götter (Der Frühling), cant., T, str, after 1760 [orch version of H688, see 'Songs, motets and chorales']
735	200.22	Als einem Frühlingsabende (Die Grazien) (H.W. von Gerstenberg), cant., S, kbd (Lübeck, 1789)
739	236	Sie liebt, mich liebt die Auserwählte (Selma) (J.H. Voss), S, 2 fl, str, after 1775
761	214	Fürsten sind am Lebensziele, aria, S, str, 1785, lost
767	213	D'amor per te languisco, arietta, S, 2 fl, bc
—	—	Reiss euch los, bekränte Sinnen, aria, S, ?orch, by 1734, frag., doubtful [= BWV224]

SONGS, MOTETS AND CHORALES

songs with keyboard or continuo

H	W	
670–84, 687, 689–92	199	[20] Oden mit Melodien (Berlin, 1762) [incl. 3 in Samlung verschiedener und auserlesener Oden, ii–iv (Halle, 1741–3)]
685	—	La Sophie, by 1768
686	194	[55] Geistliche Oden und Lieder (C.F. Gellert), 1757 (Leipzig, 1758)
688	202/A	Freude, du Lust der Götter und Menschen (C.M. Wieland), in Drey verschiedene Versuche eines einfachen Gesanges für den Hexameters (Berlin, 1760) [also arr. S, orch, see 'Secular arias and cantatas', H723]
693–5	202/B	3 songs: Das Privilegium (N.D. Giseke); Die Landschaft; Belinde (K.W. Müller): in Clavierstücke verschiedener Art (Berlin, 1765)
696	195	Zwölf geistliche Oden und Lieder als ein Anhang zu Gellerts geistliche Oden und Lieder (Leipzig, 1764)

H	W	
698	202/D	Bachus und Venus (H.W. von Gerstenberg), in Musikalisches Vielerley (Hamburg, 1770)
699	201	Der Wirt und die Gäste (J.W.L Gleim) (Berlin, 1766), rev. later
700–08, 734–5, 740–41, 747–8, 755–60	200	[21] Neue Lieder-Melodien nebst einer Cantate (Lübeck, 1789) [incl. Die Grazien H735, see 'Secular arias and cantatas']
709–21	202/C	13 songs in Unterhaltungen (Hamburg, 1768–70)
724–9	202/E	6 songs (B. Münter) in Balthasar Münters 1. Sammlung geistlicher Lieder (Leipzig, 1773)
730	202/O/2	Klagelied eines Bauren (J.M. Miller)
733	196	[42] Psalmen mit Melodien (J.A. Cramer) (Leipzig, 1774)
742	202/O/1	Auf den Flügeln des Morgenrots (C.F. Cramer)
743	202/O/4	Die Trennung (J.J. Eschenburg, after P. Metastasio)
749	197	[30] Geistliche Gesänge mit Melodien (C.C. Sturm) (Hamburg, 1780)
752	198	[30] Geistliche Gesänge mit Melodien, ii (Sturm) (Hamburg, 1781)
763	—	Die Alster (F. von Hagedorn); Harvstehude (von Hagedorn): after 1768, lost
764	202/N	12 songs in Freymaurer-Lieder mit ganz neuen Melodien von der Herren Capellmeister Bach, Naumann und Schulz (Copenhagen and Leipzig, 1788) [also attrib., erroneously, to W.F.E. Bach]
765	202/O/3	Kommt, lasst uns seine Huld besingen (J.A. Cramer)
766	202/O/5	Die Schönste soll bei Sonnenschein
—	—	Allgütiger, gewohnt Gebet zu hören [another version of H700] Also 12 songs in various Musenalmanachs (1775–82): H731–2, 736–8, 739·5, 744, 746, 750–51, 753–4 (w202/F–L)

motets

H	W	
773–4	205–6	2 pss (J.A. Cramer): Warum versammeln sich und dräuen, S, A, T, B; Wenn ich zu dir in meinen Ängsten flehe, S, A, bc
826	208	4 motets: Gedanke, der uns Leben gibt (Gellert), S, A, B, bc; Oft klagt dein Herz, wie schwer es sei (Gellert), S, A, T, B, bc; Gott, deine Güte reicht so weit (Gellert), S, A, bc; Dich bet ich an, Herr Jesu Christ (Sturm), S, A, T, B, bc: arrs. of H686.30, 53, 9, 752.3

chorales

H	W	
337	n.v.18	Wo Gott zum Haus nicht gibt
780, 871	204	Zwey Litaneien aus dem Schleswig-Holsteinischen Gesangbuch, 1785 (Copenhagen, 1786); ed. in SBA

H	W	
781	203	[14] Neue Melodien zu einigen Liedern des neuen Hamburger Gesangbuches (Hamburg, 1787): texts mainly by Gellert; nos.3, 6, 13 also with orch
842	—	[10] Choräle (H.E. zu Stolberg-Wernigerode) (Wernigerode, 1767)
843	—	Naglet til et Kors paa Jorden (B.J. Sporon), in Kirke-Melodierne til den 1778 udgangne Psalmebog (Copenhagen, 1781)
844	—	3 chorales: Erheb, erheb, o meine Seele; Des Ewigen und der Sterblichen Sohn; Von ganzem Herzen rühmen wir: in Vollständige Sammlung der Melodien . . . des neuen allgemeinen Schleswig-Holsteinischen Gesangbuch (Leipzig, 1785)

THEORETICAL WORKS

H	W	
285	—	Fughetta on C-F-E-B-A-C-H, by 1784
867	121	Miscellanea musica, B-Bc [incl. canons in J.P. Kirnberger: Die Kunst des reinen Satzes (Berlin, 1771–4)]
868	254	Versuch über die wahre Art das Clavier zu spielen, i (Berlin, 1753/R, 2/1787); Eng. trans., ed. W.J. Mitchell, as Essay on the True Art of Playing Keyboard Instruments (New York, 1949)
869	257	'Einfall einen doppelten Contrapunct in der Octave . . . zu machen', in F.W. Marpurg, ed.: Historisch-kritische Beyträge zur Aufnahme der Musik, iii (Berlin, 1757/R); Eng. trans in Helm (1966)
870	255	Versuch über die wahre Art das Clavier zu spielen, ii (Berlin, 1762/R, 2/1797); Eng. trans., ed. W.J. Mitchell, as Essay on the True Art of Playing Keyboard Instruments (New York, 1949)
—	—	Fughetta on B-A-C-H, in J.F. Reichardt: Briefe eines aufmerksamen Reisenden (Hamburg, 1774)

ARRANGEMENTS

Various arrs. of vocal and inst works by J.E., J.C., J.C.F, J.S. and W.F. Bach, G. Benda, C.F.C. Fasch, J.G. Goldberg, C.H. Graun, Handel, G.A. Homilius, Telemann and others: for details see H; others in D-Bsb

MISATTRIBUTED WORKS

H	W	
115	122.3	Sinfonia, kbd: planned red. by J.J.H. Westphal of H652, unrealized
159	116.15	Minuet, kbd, C: arr. of H601 by Westphal

H	W	
303–31	116.29–57	29 kbd pieces: arrs. by Westphal of works for mechanical insts or ww (facs. in Carl Philipp Emanuel Bach 1714–1788: The Collected Works for Solo Keyboard, v (New York, 1985))
333	—	La Juliane, F, kbd, A-Wn: doubtful, not autograph
540	—	Largo, e, kbd, melody inst, B-Bc: by C. Schaffrath
874	258	Kurze Anweisung zum Generalbass, B-Br; doubtful, not autograph
—	202/M	2 fantasias: Socrates: Nein, nein die ernste hohe Gestalt; Hamlet: Sein, oder Nichtsein: = H75, 3rd movt, with text underlay by H.W. von Gerstenberg

BIBLIOGRAPHY

A: CATALOGUES, LETTERS, DOCUMENTS

J.M. Bach, ed: Verzeichnis des musikalischen Nachlasses des verstorbenen Capellmeisters Carl Philipp Emanuel Bach (Hamburg, 1790/R1981 with preface and annotations by R.W. Wade)

J.J.H. Westphal: Catalogue thématique des oeuvres de Ch.Ph.Emm. Bach (MS, B-Br, Fétis 5218)

A. Wotquenne, ed.: Thematisches Verzeichnis der Werke von Carl Philipp Emanuel Bach (1714–1788)(Leipzig, 1905/R) [in Ger. and Fr.]

H.-J. Schulze, ed.: Dokumente zum Nachwirken Johann Sebastian Bachs 1750–1800, Bach-Dokumente, iii (Kassel, 1972)

H.-G. Ottenberg, ed: Der Critische Musicus an der Spree: Berliner Musikschrifttum von 1748 bis 1799, eine Dokumentation (Leipzig, 1984)

E. Suchalla: Briefe von Carl Philipp Emanuel Bach an Johann Gottlob Immanuel Breitkopf (Tutzing, 1985)

R. Angermüller: 'Carl Philipp Emanuel Bachiana: Briefe die bei Ernst Suchalla nicht veröffentlicht wurden', JbSIM (1985–6), 9–168

E.E. Helm: Thematic Catalogue of the Works of Carl Philipp Emanuel Bach (New Haven, CT, 1989)

U. Leisinger: 'Die Bachsche Auktion von 1789', BJb 1991, 97–126

W.S. Newman, ed.: Carl Philipp Emanuel Bach: Autobiography, Verzeichniss des musikalischen Nachlasses (Buren, 1991)

E. Suchalla, ed.: Carl Philipp Emanuel Bach im Spiegel seiner Zeit: die Dokumentensammlung Johann Jacob Heinrich Westphals (Hildesheim, 1993)

H.-G. Ottenberg, ed: Carl Philipp Emanuel Bach: Spurensuche: Leben und Werk in Selbstzeugnissen und Dokumenten seiner Zeitgenossen, Carl-Philipp-Emanuel-Bach-Konzepte, Sonderreihe, i (Leipzig, 1994)

E. Suchalla, ed.: Carl Philipp Emanuel Bach: Briefe und Dokumente. Kritische Gesamtausgabe (Göttingen, 1994)

E.N. Kulukundis: 'Die Versteigerung von C.P.E. Bachs musikalischem Nachlass im Jahre 1805', BJb 1995, 145–76

H.-J. Schulze: 'Regesten zu einigen verschollenen Briefen Carl Philipp Emanuel Bachs', BJb 1996, 151–4

P. Wollny: 'Zur Überlieferung der Instrumentalwerke Johann Sebastian Bachs: der Quellenbesitz Carl Philipp Emanuel Bachs', BJb 1996, 7–21

S.L. Clark, ed.: The Letters of C.P.E. Bach (Oxford, 1997)

B. Wiermann: Carl Philipp Emanuel Bach und Hamburg: Dokumente aus der zeitgenössischen Presse bis 1790 (Hildesheim, forthcoming)

B: SOURCES

J. Müller: Die musikalischen Schätze der Koeniglichen- und Universitaets-Bibliothek zu Königsberg in Pr. aus dem Nachlasse Friedrich August Gotthold's (Bonn, 1870)

P. Kast: Die Bach-Handschriften der Berliner Staatsbibliothek (Trossingen, 1958)

K. Hortschansky: Katalog der Kieler Musiksammlungen: die Notendrucke, Handschriften, Libretti und Bücher über Musik aus der Zeit bis 1830 (Kassel, 1963)

T. Aigner: Thematisches Verzeichnis der Werke von Johann Mederitsch detto Gallus (Munich, 1974) [incl. list of copies by Mederitsch in A-Sd, Sm]

R.W. Wade: 'Newly Found Works of C.P.E. Bach', EMc, xvi (1988), 523–32

U. Leisinger: Die Bach-Quellen der Forschungs- und Landesbibliothek Gotha (Gotha, 1993)

U. Leisinger and P.Wollny: Die Bach-Quellen der Bibliotheken in Brüssel: Katalog (Hildesheim, forthcoming)

C: EXHIBITION CATALOGUES, PROGRAMME BOOKS

Carl Philipp Emanuel Bach: Musik und Literatur in Norddeutschland: Ausstellung zum 200. Todestag Bachs, Staats- und Universitätsbibliothek, Hamburg, 23 Sept – 31 Oct 1988; Schleswig-Holsteinische Landesbibliothek, Kiel 16 Nov 1988 – 29 Jan 1989 (Heide in Holstein, 1988) [exhibition catalogue]

Carl Philipp Emanuel Bach 1714–1788, herausgegeben anlässlich der Ausstellung zum 200. Todestag Carl Philipp Emanuel Bachs, Staatliches Institut für Musikforschung Preussischer Kulturbesitz, Berlin, 10 July – 4 Sept 1988 (Berlin, 1988) [exhibition catalogue]

H.-G. Klein, ed.: 'Er ist Original!': Carl Philipp Emanuel Bach: sein musikalisches Werk in Autographen und Erstdrucken aus der Musikabteilung der Staatsbibliothek Preussischer Kulturbesitz Berlin, Staatsbibliothek Preussischer Kulturbesitz, Berlin, 14 Dec 1988 – 11 Feb 1989 (Wiesbaden, 1988) [exhibition catalogue]

K. Maehnert and V.Wolf, ed.: Bach-Tage Hamburg '88 (Hamburg, 1988) [St Michaelis-Chor Hamburg e.V.; programme book]

H.J. Marx, ed.: Der Hamburger Bach und die Neue Musik des 18. Jahrhunderts: eine Veranstaltungsreihe anlässlich des 200. Todesjahres von Carl Philipp Emanuel Bach 1714–1788 (Hamburg, 1988) [programme book]

D: CONGRESS REPORTS, ESSAY COLLECTIONS

Carl Philipp Emanuel Bach und die europäische Musikkultur: Hamburg 1988

S.L. Clark: C.P.E. Bach Studies (Oxford, 1988)

Fragen der Aufführungspraxis und Interpretation von Werken Carl Philipp Emanuel Bachs: Blankenburg, Harz, 1988

Untersuchungen zur Musikkultur des 18. Jahrhunderts: Potsdam 1988

H. Poos, ed: Carl Philipp Emanuel Bach: Beiträge zu Leben und Werk (Mainz, 1993)

Carl Philipp Emanuel Bach: Frankfurt an der Oder 1994

Carl Philipp Emanuel Bach und die Romantik: Frankfurt an der Oder 1996

E: BIOGRAPHY: GENERAL

F. Rochlitz: 'K.Ph.E. Bach', Für Freunde der Tonkunst (Leipzig, 2/1832), iv, 271–316

C.H. Bitter: Carl Philipp Emanuel und Wilhelm Friedemann Bach und deren Brüder (Berlin, 1868/R)

O. Vrieslander: Carl Philipp Emanuel Bach (Munich, 1923)

H. Miesner: Philipp Emanuel Bach in Hamburg: Beiträge zu seiner Biographie und zur Musikgeschichte seiner Zeit (Leipzig, 1929/R)

D. Plamenac: 'New Light on the Last Years of Carl Philipp Emanuel Bach', MQ, xxxv (1949), 565–87

H.-G. Ottenberg: Carl Philipp Emanuel Bach (Leipzig, 1982, 2/1987; Eng. trans., 1987)

F: SPECIAL STUDIES, RELATIONSHIPS, RECEPTION

H. von Hase: 'Carl Philipp Emanuel Bach und Joh.Gottl.Im. Breitkopf', BJb 1911, 86–104

R. Steglich: 'Karl Philipp Emanuel Bach und der Dresdner Kreuzkantor Gottfried August Homilius im Musikleben ihrer Zeit: ein Beitrag zur Geschichte der Stilwandlung im 18. Jahrhundert', BJb 1915, 39–145

H. von Hase: 'Beiträge zur Breitkopfschen Geschäftsgeschichte', ZfMw, ii (1919–20), 454–81

B. Engelke: 'Gerstenberg und die Musik seiner Zeit', Zeitschrift der Gesellschaft für Schleswig-Holsteinische Geschichte, lvi (1927), 417–48

H. Killer: 'Zur Musik des deutschen Ostens im 18. Jahrhundert', Königsberger Beiträge: Festgabe zur vierhundertjährigen Jubelfeier der Staats- und Universitätsbibliothek zu Königsberg Pr. (Königsberg, 1929), 228–43

E. Fritz Schmid: 'Joseph Haydn und Carl Philipp Emanuel Bach', ZfMw, xiv (1931–2), 299–312

H. Miesner: 'Urkundliche Nachrichten über die Familie Bach in Berlin', BJb 1932, 157–63

H. Miesner: 'Aus der Umwelt Philipp Emanuel Bachs', BJb 1937, 132–43

H. Miesner: 'Porträts aus dem Kreise Philipp Emanuel und Wilhelm Friedemann Bachs', *Musik und Bild: Festschrift Max Seiffert zum siebzigsten Geburtstag*, ed. H. Besseler (Kassel, 1938), 101–12

A. Holschneider: 'C.Ph.E. Bachs Kantate "Auferstehung und Himmelfahrt Jesu" und Mozarts Aufführung des Jahres 1788', *MJb 1968–70*, 264–80

M. Terry: 'C.P.E. Bach and J.J.H. Westphal: a Clarification', *JAMS*, xxii (1969), 106–15

A. Glöckner: 'Neuerkenntnisse zu Johann Sebastian Bachs Aufführungskalender zwischen 1729 und 1735', *BJb 1981*, 43–75

E.E. Helm: 'An Honorable Shortcut to the Works of C.P.E. Bach', *Music in the Classic Period: Essays in Honor of Barry S. Brook*, ed. A.W. Atlas (New York, 1985), 85–98

R. von Zahn: 'Johann Maria Bach und das Hamburger Stadtkantorat', *Mf*, xliii (1990), 146–50

R. von Zahn: *Musikpflege in Hamburg um 1800: der Wandel des Konzertwesens und der Kirchenmusik zwischen dem Tode Carl Philipp Emanuel Bachs und dem Tode Christian Friedrich Gottlieb Schwenkes* (Hamburg, 1991)

U. Leisinger: *Joseph Haydn und die Entwicklung des klassischen Klavierstils* (Laaber, 1994)

G: THEORY, AESTHETICS

H. Mersmann: 'Ein Programmtrio K.Ph.E. Bachs', *BJb 1917*, 137–70

O. Vrieslander: 'C.Ph.E. Bach als Theoretiker', *Von Neuer Musik* (Cologne, 1925), 222–79

A. Schering: 'Carl Philipp Emanuel Bach und das "redende Prinzip" in der Musik', *JbMP 1938*, 13–29

N. Fischman: 'Estetika F.E. Bacha', *SovM* (1964), no.8, 59–65

E.E. Helm: 'Six Random Measures of C.P.E. Bach', *JMT*, x (1966), 19–51

C. Dahlhaus: 'Si vis me flere . . .', *Mf*, xxv (1972), 51–2

E.E. Helm: 'The "Hamlet" Fantasy and the Literary Element in C.P.E. Bach's Music', *MQ*, lviii (1972), 277–96

P. Cohen: *Theorie und Praxis der Clavierästhetik Carl Philipp Emanuel Bachs* (Hamburg, 1974)

H. Danuser: 'Das imprévu in der Symphonik: Aspekte einer musikalischen Formkategorie in der Zeit von Carl Philipp Emanuel Bach bis Hector Berlioz', *Musiktheorie*, i (1986), 61–81

H: KEYBOARD MUSIC

I.G. Faisst: 'Beiträge zur Geschichte der Claviersonate von ihrem erstem Auftreten bis auf C.P. Emanuel Bach', *Caecilia*, xxv (1846), 129–58, 201–31; xxvi (1847), 1–28, 73–83; repr. in *NBeJb 1924*, 7–85

H. Schenker: *Ein Beitrag zur Ornamentik als Einführung zu Ph.E. Bachs Klavierwerken* (Vienna and Leipzig, 1908)

H. Uldall: *Das Klavierkonzert der Berliner Schule mit kurzem Überblick über seine allgemeine Entstehungsgeschichte und spätere Entwicklung* (Leipzig, 1928)

S. Clercx: 'La forme du rondo chez Carl Philipp Emanuel Bach', *RdM*, xvi (1935), 148–67

E.H. Beurmann: *Die Klaviersonaten Carl Philipp Emanuel Bachs* (diss., U. of Göttingen, 1952)

K. von Fischer: 'C.Ph.E. Bachs Variationenwerke', *RBM*, vi (1952), 190–218

P. Schleuning: *Die Freie Fantasie: ein Beitrag zur Erforschung der klassischen Klaviermusik* (Göppingen, 1973)

D.M. Berg: *The Keyboard Sonatas of C.P.E. Bach: an Expression of the Mannerist Principle* (diss., SUNY, 1975)

R.W. Wade: *The Keyboard Concertos of Carl Philipp Emanuel Bach* (Ann Arbor, 1981)

G. Wagner: *Traditionsbezug im musikhistorischen Prozess zwischen 1720 und 1740 am Beispiel von Johann Sebastian und Carl Philipp Emanuel Bach* (Neuhausen-Stuttgart, 1985)

A. Edler: 'Zwischen Händel und Carl Philipp Emanuel Bach: zur Situation des Klavierkonzerts im mittleren 18. Jahrhundert', *AcM*, lviii (1986), 180–221

D.M. Berg: 'Carl Philipp Emanuel Bachs Umarbeitungen seiner Claviersonaten', *BJb 1988*, 123–61

W. Horn: *Carl Philipp Emanuel Bach. Frühe Klaviersonaten: eine Studie zur 'Form' der ersten Sätze nebst einer kritischen Untersuchung der Quellen* (Hamburg, 1988)

P. Whitmore: *Unpremeditated Art: the Cadenza in the Classical Concerto* (Oxford, 1991)

D. Schulenberg: 'Carl Philipp Emanuel Bach', *Eighteenth-Century Keyboard Music*, ed. R.L. Marshall (New York, 1994), 191–229

I: VOCAL AND INSTRUMENTAL MUSIC

NewmanSCE

E. Fritz Schmid: *Carl Philipp Emanuel Bach und seine Kammermusik* (Kassel, 1931)

G. Busch: *Busch: Carl Philipp Emanuel Bach und seine Lieder* (Regensburg, 1957)

E. Simon: *Mechanische Musikinstrumente früherer Zeiten und ihre Musik* (Wiesbaden, 1960)

E. Suchalla: *Die Orchestersinfonien Carl Philipp Emanuel Bachs* (Augsburg, 1968)

S.L. Clark: *The Occasional Choral Works of C.P.E. Bach* (diss., Princeton U., 1984)

D. Schulenberg: *The Instrumental Music of Carl Philipp Emanuel Bach* (Ann Arbor, 1984)

S.L. Clark: 'C.P.E. Bach and the Tradition of Passion Music in Hamburg', *EMc*, xvi (1988), 533–41

W. Maertens: *Georg Philipp Telemanns sogenannte Hamburgische Kapitainsmusiken (1723–1765)* (Wilhelmshaven, 1988)

L. Miller: 'Carl Philipp Emanuel Bach's Flute Sonatas', *JM*, xi (1993), 203–49

G. Wagner: *Die Sinfonien Carl Philipp Emanuel Bachs: Werdende Gattung und Originalgenie* (Stuttgart and Weimar, 1994)

A. Nagel: *Studien zur Passionskantate von Carl Philipp Emanuel Bach* (Frankfurt, 1995)

G. Quarg: '"Passions-Cantatte von Ph.E.Bach": zur Kölner Markus-Passion', *Musik und Kirche*, lxv (1995), 62–71

(10) Johann Ernst Bach (*34*) (*b* Eisenach, 28 Jan 1722; *d* Eisenach, 1 Sept 1777). Composer and organist, son of (5) Johann Bernhard Bach (*18*). On 16 January 1737 he entered the Thomasschule in Leipzig and became a pupil of his uncle (7) Johann Sebastian (*24*). After studying law at Leipzig University he returned to Eisenach in 1741 and deputized, without pay, for his ailing father. Plans to go to Frankfurt, Hamburg or Berlin, mentioned in a letter written by his cousin Johann Elias Bach (*39*), were never realized. In 1748 he became his father's official assistant and the next year his successor. He continued to practise as a lawyer as well, and in addition he was appointed Kapellmeister at the Weimar court in 1756 'in view of his well-known skill and musical knowledge'. This entailed regular journeys to Weimar, and during his frequent absences from Eisenach he was permitted to hire a substitute for his organist's duties. When the Hofkapelle was dissolved after the death of Duke Ernst August Constantin in 1758, Johann Ernst returned permanently to Eisenach but retained his Kapellmeister title and salary, for which he had to fulfil certain administrative duties. He wrote the foreword to Adlung's *Anleitung zu der musikalischen Gelahrtheit* (Erfurt, 1758), in which he criticized the current decay of church music and demanded that this be countered by 'artistic and regular manners of composing'; as models of sacred cantatas he praised the 'admirable masterpieces' of J.S. Bach, Telemann and Stölzel. J.E. Bach was apparently in close contact with his cousin (9) Carl Philipp Emanuel (*46*), serving as agent for the first part of the *Versuch* (1753) and the harpsichord concertos w43 (1772). He contributed to the anthology *Musicalisches Vielerley* published by C.P.E. Bach in 1770.

As a composer Johann Ernst was abreast of the stylistic innovations of his time although, like Johann Sebastian's sons, he did not exclude contrapuntal writing. Characteristic of his personal style is the extended use of chromaticism and syncopated rhythms. His vocal works are often highly dramatic and full of effects. In his time he was particularly known for his 'beautiful chorale settings' (*Musicalische Realzeitung*, ii (1789), 179); these represent an important contribution to the genre of the sacred cantata as they form a link between J.S. Bach's chorale cantatas and the chorale settings of the generation of

Doles and Hiller. His songs depend on the older tradition of Görner, Gräfe and Mizler; he wrote *galant* melodies full of expressive word-painting with lively basses and often elaborate accompaniments. His Passion oratorio is influenced by C.H. Graun's well-known *Der Tod Jesu*.

WORKS

VOCAL

O Seele, deren Sehnen (Passion oratorio), 1764, *D-GOa*, ed. in DDT, xlviii (1914); 2 Passions, lost, cited in *GerberNL*

Church cantatas: Ach Herr, strafe mich nicht (Ps vi), *D-DS, US-CA*; Auf und säumt euch nicht, ihr Frommen (Dank-Kantate), *AAu*; Der Herr ist nahe bei denen, for funeral of Duke Ernst August Constantin, 1758, *D-Bsb, US-AAu*; Die Liebe Gottes ist ausgegossen, *D-Bsb*, ed. in SBA; Ein feste Burg ist unser Gott, 1762, *LEb*; Herzlich lieb hab ich dich (Ps xviii), *Bsb, Hs*; Kein Stündlein geht dahin, *Bsb, Bhm, Hs*; Kommt herzu, lasset uns frohlocken (Ps xcv), *LEb*; Lobe den Herrn, meine Seele, lost, cited in Breitkopf catalogue, 1770; Mein Odem ist schwach (= BWV 222), *Bsb, Hs, GB-Lbl*, choral movts also as motet, Unser Wandel ist im Himmel (= BWV Anh. 165); Meine Seele erhebet den Herren (i), *D-Bsb*, ed. in SBA; Meine Seele erhebet den Herren (ii), *MLHb*; Meine Seele erhebet den Herrn (iii), *F-Pn*; Nach dir, Herr, verlanget mich (Ps xxv), private collection; Sei willkommen, mächtiger Herrscher, *D-CR*, doubtful, probably by J.E. Bach; Singet dem Herrn ein neues Lied (Ps cxlix), *BNu, WFmk* (erroneously attrib. C.P.E. Bach); So gehst du nun, mein Jesu, hin, *US-AAu*; Straf mich nicht in deinem Zorn, *D-BNu, GOa*; Wenn Donnerwolken über dir sich türmen (Das Vertrauen der Christen auf Gott), *Bsb* (inc.), *GOa*; Wie der Hirsch schreiet (Ps xlii), lost, cited in Breitkopf catalogue, 1764; Wünschet Jerusalem Glück, *NTRE*; others (?incl. annual cycle, 1766), lost

Mass [Ky–Gl] on Es woll uns Gott gnädig sein, SATB, bc, *D-Bsb*

Motets, SATB: Aus der Tiefen, *GB-Lbl*; Mein Odem ist schwach, in G.P. Weimar: Versuch von kleinen leichten Motetten und Arien (Leipzig, 1785); Unser Wandel ist im Himmel (= BWV Anh. 165), *D-DS*; 11 others, *ARk*, doubtful

Secular cantatas: Gesegneten Auftritt, for birthday of Duke Friedrich of Saxe-Gotha, 1756, lost, mentioned in H. Kretschmar, Preface to DDT, xlii (1910); Wer sagt mir doch, was für Entzücken, lost

Sammlung auserlesener Fabeln, i (Nuremberg, 1749) [pt ii ?unpubd]; ed. in DDT, xlii (1910)

Lächerliche Mammonshüter (An die Geizigen), in C.P.E. Bach: Musicalisches Vielerley (Hamburg, 1770)

INSTRUMENTAL

Sinfonia, B♭, *US-BETm*; other sinfonias mentioned in *GerberNL*

3 Sonaten, kbd, vn, pt i (Eisenach, 1770); no.1 ed. in NM, ii (1927)

3 Sonaten, kbd, vn, pt ii (Eisenach, 1772)

Sonata, A, fl, vn, bc, *D-Bsb*

Sonatas, kbd: G, F, in J.U. Haffner: Oeuvres mêlées, v, vi (Nuremberg, 1759); A, *Bsb*

Org: Fantasia and fugue, d, *Bsb*; Fantasia and fugue, a, *Bsb*, ed. in Mw, xlii (1972); Fantasia and fugue, F, in C.P.E. Bach: Musicalisches Vielerley (Hamburg, 1770), ed. in D. Hellmann: Orgelmusik der Familie Bach (Leipzig, 1985); Chorale, Valet will ich dir geben, *Bsb*, ed. in D. Hellmann: Orgelmusik der Familie Bach (Leipzig, 1985)

BIBLIOGRAPHY

GerberNL

H. Löffler: '"Bache" bei Seb. Bach', *BJb* 1949–50, 106–24

H. Kühn: 'Vier Organisten Eisenachs aus Bachischem Geschlecht', *Bach in Thüringen* (Berlin, 1950), 103–19

C. Oefner: *Die Musikerfamilie Bach in Eisenach* (Eisenach, 1984)

H. Max: 'Verwandtes im Werk Bachs, seiner Schüler und Söhne' *Johann Sebastian Bachs Spätwerk und dessen Umfeld: Duisburg 1986*, 117–47

E. Odrich and P. Wollny: *Die Briefkonzepte des Johann Elias Bach* (Hildesheim, 2000)

(11) Johann Christoph Friedrich Bach (49) (*b* Leipzig, 21 June 1732; *d* Bückeburg, 26 Jan 1795). Composer, son of (7) Johann Sebastian Bach (24) and Anna Magdalena Bach. He is known as the 'Bückeburg Bach'.

1. LIFE. He received his musical education from his father. After leaving the Thomasschule, Leipzig, he is thought to have studied law briefly, but there is no record of his matriculation at Leipzig University. At the express wish of Count Wilhelm of Schaumburg-Lippe he was appointed harpsichordist to the court in Bückeburg, where he may at first have been subordinate to the court organist Ludolf Münchhausen. In June 1751 his brother Carl Philipp Emanuel visited him in the retinue of Frederick the Great when the king awarded the Order of the Great Eagle to Count Wilhelm. At this time the musical life of the court in Bückeburg was dominated by the Konzertmeister Angelo Colonna and the court composer Giovanni Battista Serini; they left Bückeburg in the middle of 1756 for reasons which remain obscure. On 8 January 1755 Bach had married Münchhausen's daughter Lucia Elisabeth, who was trained as a singer by Serini and held a position at court, probably as an alto, with an annual salary of 100 thaler. The Seven Years War imposed considerable restrictions on the court of Bückeburg. Bückeburg itself was occupied by French troops in 1757 and Count Wilhelm, with a few trusted courtiers including Bach, withdrew to his estate of Niensteden on the Elbe, near Pinneberg, from October 1757 to April 1758. Bach took this opportunity to apply, successfully, for the vacant post of organist at the German church in Altona, then under Danish rule, but for unknown reasons he never took it up. On 18 February 1759 he was appointed Konzertmeister of the Bückeburg Hofkapelle, with a rise in his annual salary to 400 thaler (later, temporarily, to 416 thaler), and he also received the usual allowances in kind. However, court life did not return to normal until after the Peace of Hubertusburg, for which Bach wrote a thanksgiving cantata performed on Ascension Day 1763, and the return of Count Wilhelm from his military missions in Portugal in November 1764. The Hofkapelle usually gave concerts twice a week; the ensemble consisted of about 15 musicians, with assistance when necessary from outside performers and military bandsmen. Bach was responsible for the composition or procurement of the works played at these concerts and for rehearsing them, and he adjusted his choices to the taste of Count Wilhelm, who liked secular Italian vocal music and played keyboard instruments and perhaps the flute himself. In the period up to 1770 Bach wrote symphonies, trio sonatas, a number of Italian arias and cantatas (mainly to texts by Metastasio) and perhaps his most important work of this time, the large-scale cantata *Cassandra*. After Count Wilhelm's marriage to Marie Barbara Eleonore zur Lippe-Biesterfeld on 12 November 1765, Protestant sacred music was performed at the Bückeburg court. Perhaps encouraged by his successful application to Altona, Bach applied on 24 June 1767 to succeed the late G.P. Telemann in Hamburg. He was, in fact, one of the short-listed candidates, but his half-brother Carl Philipp Emanuel gained the appointment. Between 1765 and 1773 Johann Christoph Friedrich set the best-known Protestant oratorio texts of his time, *Der Tod Jesu, Die Hirten bei der Krippe Jesu* and *Die Auferstehung und Himmelfahrt Jesu*, all by C.W. Ramler, and *Die Pilgrime auf Golgatha* by F.W. Zachariä. The tendency towards sacred vocal composition increased with the arrival in Bückeburg of J.G. Herder, who was court preacher and superintendent there from 1771 to 1776. His oratorio texts, highly regarded by Countess Marie Barbara, had a lasting effect on the music of the court. In these years Herder and Bach, who later regarded this as the happiest

time of his life, collaborated on the cantata *Michaels Sieg, oder Der Kampf des Guten und des Bösen in der Welt* (1771, not 1775), the 'biblical painting' *Die Kindheit Jesu* (1772, for the birth of Countess Emilie Eleonore Wilhelmine in June 1771), *Die Auferweckung Lazarus* (1773, on the occasion of the death of Countess Marie Barbara's twin brother Ferdinand Benjamin on 23 April 1772) and *Der Fremdling auf Golgatha* (1776), as well as the secular 'scenes with song', *Brutus* and *Philoktetes*, which have not survived.

The death of Countess Marie Barbara in 1776, Herder's appointment to Weimar in the same year and the death of Count Wilhelm in 1777 marked a watershed in the intellectual life of the Bückeburg court. Count Philipp Ernst zu Schaumburg-Lippe-Allverdissen (1723–87) took over the government, holding court partly in Münster and partly in Bückeburg. In spring 1778 Bach asked for three months' leave to visit his brother Johann Christian in London. He took his son Wilhelm Friedrich Ernst on this journey, which began some time between 16 March and 23 May 1778 and ended at the latest in November of the same year; the son was left with Johann Christian for further musical training. A series of string quartets and a set of six keyboard concertos, printed in London with dedications to members of the house of Schaumburg-Lippe, show how rapidly J.C.F. Bach adapted his music to English tastes. He also brought back an English piano from his travels, so his keyboard compositions after 1778 were not necessarily for the harpsichord. In 1780 Count Philipp Ernst took as his second wife Princess Juliane zu Hessen-Philippsthal (1761–99), who was particularly fond of the fine arts. At the Princess's wish, attendance at court concerts was now open to the citizens of Bückeburg and to visitors. Forkel (*Musikalischer Almanach*, 1782) regarded the little Kapelle as one of the finest in Germany. Juliane took lessons in foreign languages and drawing, and studied the keyboard with J.C.F. Bach. Among the better known of his pupils (in addition to his son Wilhelm Friedrich Ernst and C.F. Geyer, later Kantor of Bückeburg) were the future Thomaskantor A.E. Müller and perhaps Adolf, Baron von Knigge. For teaching purposes Bach wrote a number of pedagogically valuable keyboard works, including the *Sechs leichte Clavier-Sonaten* (printed in 1784 with a dedication to Princess Juliane), variations (including a set on 'Ah, vous dirai-je maman'), concertos and sonatas for four hands.

Bach also increased his efforts to get his compositions published. He could not muster enough subscribers for the edition of the large-scale sacred works he had been planning since about 1773, but he did publish the collection *Musikalische Nebenstunden*, containing mainly works by himself but also some songs by W.F.E. Bach and by noble dilettantes from Bückeburg and Minden. A comment in a letter to Breitkopf of 1 October 1788, in which Bach sought subscribers for a collection of three easy keyboard sonatas ('These sonatas are easy, written in the latest style and composed in London, where they were much to the liking of Her Majesty the Queen') may suggest that he paid a second visit to England, though further evidence of this is so far lacking.

The arrival in Bückeburg about 1793 of the brilliant Bohemian musician Franz Neubauer presented Bach with unaccustomed competition in the last years of his life. It inspired him to write new works (including a dozen large-scale symphonies and several double concertos) but it also intensified the latent depression from which he had been suffering since the death of his half-brother Carl Philipp Emanuel and which may have hastened the course of the chest ailment that brought about his death on 26 January 1795. In his obituary his friend Karl Gottlieb Horstig, superintendent at Bückeburg from 1793, described him as an industrious composer, always ready to be of service, and praised his upright character and 'kindness of heart'.

2. WORKS. With his predisposition towards the use of existing models, his extensive revisions and his liking for experimentation, Bach showed in his compositions several apparently contradictory tendencies. His father had given him a thorough grounding in keyboard and organ playing and in the rudiments of composition, but when he moved to Bückeburg he found himself in an entirely different world. As a result he was obliged to adapt to new stylistic principles, studying them on his own with concrete models. His first works in almost all genres, therefore, are stylistic copies: the early piano sonatas are based on models by C.P.E. Bach, the aria 'Luci amate, ah, non piangete' (*c*1760) is an arrangement of a work by Matteo Capranica, and *Der Tod Jesu* (1769) is influenced by C.H. Graun's setting of the same text (1755). However, Bach usually managed to move on rapidly, leaving his models behind, and to find new forms of expression. His secular cantatas from the period around 1773 are particularly noteworthy. They include *Die Amerikanerin* (after H.W. von Gerstenberg's *Lied eines Mohren*) and *Ino* (text by Ramler), which during Bach's lifetime brought him a reputation as one of the major cantata composers in Germany. The oratorios and cantatas written in collaboration with Herder may merit similar interest; they remained unpublished but were circulated and appreciated in aristocratic circles in Rheda, Detmold and Wernigerode. Although Bach preferred a lyrical tone, he had a special feeling for dramatic development, particularly evident in accompagnato scenes. The style of his vocal compositions is close to that of C.H. Graun, Telemann, and (particularly in choral movements) his brother Carl Philipp Emanuel, whom he even surpassed in his solidly constructed but fluent fugues. His keyboard compositions cover a wide range, from simple practice pieces in the style of J.S. Bach's two-part Inventions (in the *Musikalische Nebenstunden*), through dance pieces and 'easy keyboard sonatas' to extremely demanding works written for his own use or for patrons outside Bückeburg. They felicitously unite the modern stylistic features of J.C. Bach with the sound musical construction of Carl Philipp Emanuel. The *Drei leichte Sonaten fürs Klavier oder Piano Forte* (Rinteln, 1789), as well as many of the works surviving only in manuscript, are among the best keyboard compositions of their time.

Bach's compositions after the death of Count Wilhelm are notable for a willingness to experiment, encouraged by the attitude of Princess Juliane, who was always open to innovations, and by his continuing to work with an excellent Kapelle. He was turning to new genres even in the last years of his life, for example in the sonatas for two pianos of 1791, the wind septet of 1794 and two concertos for keyboard and another instrument dating from about 1791. In accordance with Bach's conception of his duties, compositions written for the court and other patrons were exclusively for the use of those who had commissioned them, with the result that most of his music could not be widely disseminated. His reputation was therefore founded mainly on the compositions published during his lifetime. The music collection of the Bückeburg Hofkapelle, left by Prince Adolf in 1917 to the Fürstliches Institut für Musikforschung in Bückeburg which he had founded (in 1935 it became the Staatliches Institut für Musikforschung, Berlin), was destroyed in World War II, apart from a few fragments, making it difficult to evaluate Bach's work as a whole. Almost without exception, the innovative compositions of his last years in particular were extant only in this collection.

WORKS

Catalogues: H. Wohlfarth: 'Neues Verzeichnis der Werke von Johann Christoph Friedrich Bach', *Mf*, xiii (1960), 404–17; repr. in *Johann Christoph Friedrich Bach* (Berne, 1971) [W]
  Bach-Repertorium (forthcoming) [BR; Inc[ertum] = doubtful]
Edition: *Friedrich Bach; Ausgewählte Werke*, ed. G. Schünemann (Bückeburg, 1920–23) [S]
Sources: C.P.E. Bach, ed.: *Musikalisches Vielerley* (Hamburg, 1770) [MV]
  J.C.F. Bach, ed.: *Musikalische Nebenstunden*, i–iv (Rinteln, 1787–8) [MN]

KEYBOARD

Edition: *Le trésor des pianistes*, ed. A. and L. Farrenc, xv (Paris, 1870/R) [F]

BR	W	
A 1–2	XI/1–2	2 sonatas, F, C, MV; ed. in F
A 3–8	XI/3	6 leichte Sonaten, C, F, E, D, A, Eb (Leipzig, 1785); ed. H. Ruf and H. Bemmann (Mainz, 1966), nos.4–5 ed. in F
A 9–12	XI/4–7	3 sonatas, C, G, F, 1 sonatina, MN; sonatas 2–3 ed. in F, sonatina ed. in Stuttgarter Bach-Ausgaben, ser.F, ii (Stuttgart, 1989)
A 13–15	XI/8	3 leichte Sonaten, D, A, E, (Rinteln, 1789); no.2 ed. in S
A 16–21	XI/9 (= BRA 18)	6 'easy' sonatas, D, A, F, B, G, Eb, c1785, D-GOl
A 22–7	—	6 sonatas (nos.1–4 lost, no.5 Eb, no.6 F), c1785, GOl
A 28–34	—	7 sonatas (no.4 D, others lost), by 2 April 1789, HVl*
A 35–7	—	3 sonatas, after 1777, lost, listed in Bückeburg inventory, 1799
A 38–9	—	2 sonatas, by 1789, lost, mentioned in letters from J.C.F. Bach to Breitkopf
A 40	XIII/1	Sonata, A, for 4 hands, 1786, Bsb*
A 41	XIII/2	Sonata, C, for 4 hands, 1791, MS lost, formerly Bim; ed. in S
A 42–3	—	2 sonatas, 2 kbd, by 16 Feb 1791, lost, mentioned in letters from J.C.F. Bach to Breitkopf
A 44	XII/1	Romanza con XII variazioni, A, c1785–90, lost, formerly Bim
A 45	XII/2	Allegretto ['Ah, vous dirai-je maman'] con VXIII variazioni, c1785–90, Bsb*
A 46–50	XII/3–7	5 dance movts, MV
A 51–120	XII/13	70 pieces, MN
A 121–5	XII/8–12	5 dances morts, c1745–9, Bsb
A Inc 1	—	Partia, C, by 1745, WD
A Inc 2–7	—	6 fugues, g, e, C, F, D, C, only no.4 (also attrib. G.P. Telemann) extant; pubd (Erfurt and Leipzig, c1858)
A Inc 8	—	Galanterie-Stücke, lost, listed in Bückeburg inventory, 1799

CHAMBER

B 1	X/3	Solo, A, vc, bc, MV
B 2	X/1	Solo, A, vc, b, c1780–85, D-Bsb*
B 3	VII/1	Trio, A, fl, vn, bc, (or Kbd, fl), MV
B 4	—	Trio, e, fl, va, bc, by 1760, Bsb
B 5–10	—	6 trios, 2 fl, bc, by 1770, lost
B 11–12	VII/2–3	2 trios, A, F, by 1768, US-BETm
B 13	—	Trio, 2 vn, bc, by 1788, lost, mentioned in Verzeichniss des musikalischen Nachlasses . . . Carl Philipp Emanuel Bach (Hamburg, 1790)
B 14	VIII/2	Trio, Eb, kbd, fl/vn, MV
B 15–20	VIII/3	6 Sonaten, d, D, D, C, A, C, kbd, fl/vn (Riga, 1777)
B 21–2	IX/2–3	2 sonatas, G, D, kbd, vn, MN
B 23–4	—	2 trios, kbd, fl, by 1770, lost
B 25	VIII/1	Trio, F, kbd, fl/vn, by 1777, MS lost, formerly D-Bim; ed. W. Hinnenthal (Leipzig, 1937)
B 26–7	—	2 sonatas, F, D, by 1777, RH* (inc.)
B 28	IX/1	Sonata, G, kbd, vn, after 1777, lost, formerly Bim
B 29	VII/4	Sonata, D, kbd, fl/vn, vc, c1780, Bsb*; ed. in S
B 30–35	VII/5–7 (= BRB 31–2, 34)	6 sonatas (no.2 G, no.3 A, no.5 C, others lost), kbd, fl/vn, va, 1770–80, Bsb*, PL-Kj*; nos.2, 5, ed. in S
B 36	X/4	Sonata, A, kbd, vc, 1789, MS lost, formerly D-Bim; arr. J. Smith (Brunswick, 1905)
B 37–42	VI	6 quartetti, D, G, C, A, F, Bb, fl, vn, va, bc (Hamburg, c1768)
B 43–8	—	6 quatuors, Eb, Bb, A, D, G, F, str (London, c1778)
B 49	IV	Septet, Eb, 2 ob, cl, 2 bn, hn, 1794, MS lost, formerly Bim; ed. in S
B 50–53	—	4 marches, after 1777, lost, listed in Bückeburg inventory, 1799
B Inc 1	XX/3	Trio, Bb, 2 vn, bc, Bsb
B Inc 2	—	Trio, C, 2 fl, lost, formerly Berlin, Singakademie
B Inc 3	X/2	Solo, D, vc, bc, lost, formerly ?Bsb (?= BRB 36)
B Inc 4	—	Sonata, kbd, ?vn, by 29 Sept 1789, lost

ORCHESTRAL

symphonies; for 2 oboes, 2 horns and strings unless otherwise stated

C 1	—	Sym., D, MN (kbd red.)
C 2–3	—	2 syms., by 1770, lost
C 4	I/3	Sym., d, str, by 1768, US-WS
C 5–6	I/1–2	2 syms., F, Bb, by 1768, BETm
C 7	I/4	Sym., E, 2 hn, str, by 1768, WS
C 8–10	I/6 (= BRC 10)	3 syms. (no.3 C, others lost), 1770, D-Bsb*
C 11–13	I/7–9	3 syms., D, G, D, ? by 1770, lost, formerly Bim
C 14	I/10	Sym., Eb, c1770–75, BÜC
C 15–17	—	3 syms., ? after 1777, lost, listed in Bückeburg inventory, 1799
C 18–23	I/11–15	6 syms., D, F, D, C, G, nos.2–3 with 2 bn, c1792–3, lost, formerly Bim (= BRC 19–23)
C 24–7	I/18–19, 16–17	4 syms., Eb, Eb, d, C, 1794, lost, formerly Bim
C 28	I/20	Sym., Bb, with fl, 2 cl, bn, 1794, Bsb*

BR	W	
concertos; for keyboard and orchestra (2 oboes/flutes, 2 horns and		
strings) unless otherwise stated		
C 29	—	Conc., E♭, kbd, str (Riga, c1770)
C 30	—	Concerto II, A, kbd, str (Riga, c1772)
C 31–6	—	6 concs., G, F, D, E♭, B♭, C, kbd, vn, bc (London, n.d.)
C 37	II/1	Conc., E, kbd, str, by 1760, D-Bsb*
C 38	—	Conc., kbd, ?str, by 27 Oct 1766, lost
C 39	—	Conc., by 1788, lost, listed in *Verzeichniss des musikalischen Nachlasses . . . Carl Philipp Emanuel Bach* (Hamburg, 1790)
C 40	II/4	Conc., F, 1782, Bsb*
C 41	II/2	Conc., D, c1780–85, Bsb*
C 42	II/3	Conc., A, ?c1785–90, lost, formerly Bim
C 43	II/5	Conc., E♭, 1792, Bsb*
C 44	—	Conc., E♭, va, kbd, orch, c1790, F-Pc*
C 45	III	Conc., E♭, ob, kbd, orch, 1791, lost, formerly D-Bim

ORATORIOS

D 1	—	Die Pilgrime auf Golgotha (F.W. Zachariä), by 1769, D-F, Mbs
D 2	XIV/1	Der Tod Jesu (K.W. Ramler), 1769, rev. c1784, B-Bc*; ed. H. Salzwedel (Bückeburg, 1964)
D 3	XIV/10	Die Auferstehung und Himmelfahrt Jesu (Ramler), by 1772, rev. c1784, D-Bsb* (frag.)
D 4	XIV/9	Die Hirten bei der Krippe Jesu (Ramler), by 1773, lost, formerly Bim
D 5	XIV/2	Die Kindheit Jesu (J.G. Herder), 1773, rev. after 1777, Bsb*; ed. in DDT, lvi (1917/R)
D 6	XIV/3	Die Auferweckung Lazarus' (Herder), 1773, rev. after 1777, Bsb*; ed. in DDT, lvi (1917/R)
D 7	XIV/7	Der Fremdling auf Golgotha (Herder), 1776, music lost, formerly Bim
D 8	XVII/3	Mosis Mutter und ihre Tochter (G.D. Stille), 1787, Bsb* (inc.)

OTHER SACRED VOCAL

in German unless otherwise stated

E 1	—	Miserere (Ps li) [Lat.], by 1770, rev. after 1777, F-Pc, private collection, USA (autograph); ed. in Stuttgarter Bach-Ausgaben, ser.F, i (Stuttgart, 1992)
F 1	XIV/4	Herr, wie lange willst du unser also veressen (J.G. Herder), cant. for Whitsun, c1773, music lost, formerly D-Bim
F 2	—	Sieh, Bückeburg, was Gott an Dir getan (J.H. Cramer), cant. for Ascension, 8 May 1763, music lost
F 3	XIV/8	Gross und mächtig, stark und prächtig, cant. for Ascension, 1776, perf. ?1777, Bsb*
F 4	XIV/5	Wie wird uns werden (Herder), cant. for feast of St Michael, 29 Sept 1771, Bsb

BR	W	
F 5	—	Nun, teures Land, der Herr hat dich erhört, cant. on birth of Countess Emilie Eleonore Wilhelmine, perf. July 1771, music lost
F 6	XIV/11	Singet dem Herrn ein neues Lied, cant. on birth of Count Georg Wilhelm, perf. 6 Feb 1785, music lost, formerly Bim
F 7a–c	XIV/12	Gott wird deinen Fuss nicht gleiten lassen (G.D. Stille), cant. for birthday of Countess Juliane, perf. 8 June 1787, Bsb* [orig. as cant. for Count Philipp Ernst, unperf.]
F Inc 1	—	Funeral music for Count Philipp Ernst, perf. 31 May 1787, lost
F Inc 2	—	Heut ist der Tag des Dankens, ihr Völker, cant., ?1780s, music lost

SECULAR VOCAL

G 1	XVIII/8	Luci amate ah non piangete, aria, S, insts, by 1760, rev. later, D-Bsb*
G 2–11	—	10 It. arias (P. Metastasio and others), by 1766, lost
G 12–17	—	6 It. cants. (Metastasio), by 1766, lost
G 18–44	—	27 cants. (Metastasio), incl. L'inciampo, S, bc (BRG 27, wXVIII/2), Bsb*, others lost
G 45	—	scenes from Il pastor fido (G.B. Guarini), by 27 Sept 1766, lost
G 46	XVIII/1	Cassandra (A. Conti), A, insts, by 1770, B-Bc*
G 47	XVIII/3	Die Amerikanerin (H.W. von Gerstenberg), S, insts (Riga, 1776); ed. G.A. Walter (Berlin, 1919)
G 48	XVIII/4	Ino (K.W. Ramler), S, insts, D-Bsb*, vs (Leipzig, 1786)
G 49	XVIII/6	Prokris und Cephalus (J.E. Schlegel), S, S, insts, vs, MN
G 50	XVIII/5	Pygmalion (Ramler), A/B, insts, by 1772, Bsb
G 51	—	Ariadne auf Naxos (Gerstenberg), by 1773, music lost
G 52	XVII/1	Brutus (J.G. Herder), by 1774, music lost, formerly Bim
G 53	XVII/2	Philoktetes (Herder), by 1775, music lost, formerly Bim
G Inc 1	—	Stimmt an, greift rasch in eure Saiten, cant. on return of Count Wilhelm from Portugal, Nov 1764, music lost
G Inc 2	—	Va crescendo il mio tormento, aria, Mbs, by ?J.C. Bach

SONGS AND MOTETS

songs; for 1 voice and keyboard/continuo unless otherwise stated

H 1–5	XIX/1	5 songs, MV
H 6–10	XVI/1	5 sacred songs (B. Münter) in *D. Balthasar Münters Erste Sammlung geistlicher Lieder* (Leipzig, 1773)
H 11–60	XVI/2	50 sacred songs (Münter) in *J. Balthasar Münters . . . Zweyte Sammlung geistlicher Lieder* (Leipzig, 1774) [BRH 47 also arr. 4vv (=wXV/3), D-Bsb*]
H 61–81	XIX/2	21 songs and arias, MN

BR	W	
H 82	—	Volkslied in *Einige melodienreiche und leichte Klavier- und Singstücke von guten Komponisten unserer Zeit*
H 83	—	Das schlafende Mädchen (H.W. von Gerstenberg) in J.C.F. Rellstab: *Winterblumen am Clavier*, ii (Berlin, 1794)
H 84	—	Feuerfarb (S. Mereau), *c*1794, in K.G. Horstig and C.U. Ulmenstein: *Westfälisches Taschenbuch für das Jahr 1801* (Münster, *c*1800)
H 85–93	—	9 songs by ?1770, lost, listed in *Verzeichniss des musikalischen Nachlasses . . . Carl Philipp Emanuel Bach* (Hamburg, 1790), [? some incl. in BRH 1–5 and/or 61–81]
H 94	—	Klavier-Ode (C. Hölty), by 29 Sept 1789, lost
H 95	—	Berg-Lied, 1790, *BÜC**
H 96	XVIII/7	O wir bringen gerne dir, aria, S, S, bc, *c*1790, *Bsb**

motets; for 4 voices and continuo

BR	W	
H 97–99	XXI/1–3	3 motets after C.P.E. Bach (C.F. Gellert), *Bsb**
H 100	XV/1	Ich lieg und schlaf, 1780, *Bsb**; ed. in S, ed. in Stuttgarter Bach-Ausgaben, ser.F, i (Stuttgart, 1992)
H 101	XV/2	Wachet auf, ruft uns die Stimme (P. Nicolai), *Bsb**; ed. in S, ed. in Stuttgarter Bach-Ausgaben, ser.F, i (Stuttgart, 1992)
H 102	—	Wie sie so sanft ruhn, alle die Seligen (J. Stockmann), *c*1792, lost, mentioned in obituary
H Inc 1	—	Wiegenliedschen, by 1772, *BÜC*
H Inc 2–4	—	3 songs for Georg Wilhelm von Schaumburg-Lippe, after 1784, inc.
H Inc 5	—	Der Unterschied der Künste, after ?1777, lost, listed in Bückeburg inventory, 1799

BIBLIOGRAPHY

EitnerQ; GerberL; GerberNL; MGG1 (R. Benecke); *NewmanSCE*
J.G. Meusel: *Teutsches Künstlerlexikon* (Lemgo, 1778, 2/1808–14)
J.N. Forkel: *Musikalischer Almanach für Deutschland* (Leipzig, 1782–8)
K.G. Horstig: 'Johann Christoph Friedrich Bach', *Nekrolog der Deutschen auf das Jahr 1795*, ed. F. Schlichtegeroll (Gotha, 1797), 269–84; ed. R. Schaal in *Friedrich von Schlichtegroll: Musiker-Nekrologe* (Kassel, 1954)
C.H. Bitter: *Carl Philipp Emanuel und Wilhelm Friedemann Bach und deren Brüder* (Berlin, 1868)
G. Schünemann: 'Johann Christoph Friedrich Bach', *BJb 1914*, 45–165
G. Schünemann: 'Friedrich Bachs Briefwechsel mit Gerstenberg und Breitkopf', *BJb 1916*, 20–35
G. Schünemann: *Thematisches Verzeichnis der Werke von Johann Christoph Friedrich Bach*, DDT, lvi (1917) [ix]–xvii
G. Hey: 'Zur Biographie Johann Friedrich Bachs und seiner Familie', *BJb 1933*, 77–85
J. Domp: *Studien zur Geschichte der Musik an Westfälischen Adelshöfen im XVIII. Jahrhundert* (Regensburg, 1934)
K. Geiringer: *The Bach Family: Seven Generations of Creative Genius* (London, 1954; Ger. trans., enlarged, 1958; enlarged 2/1977)
K. Geiringer: 'Unbeachtete Kompositionen des Bückeburger Bach', *Festschrift Wilhelm Fischer*, ed. H. von Zingerle (Innsbruck, 1956), 99–107

U. Wulfhorst: 'Ein Orgelgutachten von Johann Christoph Friedrich Bach', *Mf*, xiii (1960), 55–7
H.-J. Schulze, 'Frühe Schriftzeugnisse des beiden jüngsten Bach-Söhne', *BJb 1963–4*, 61–9
H. Wohlfahrt: *Johann Christoph Friedrich Bach: ein Komponist im Vorfeld des Klassik* (Berne, 1971) [incl. list of works]
B. Poschmann: *Johann Christoph Friedrich Bach, Schaumburg-Lippischer Capellmeister 1732–1795*, Niedersächsisches Staatsarchiv, 1982 (Bückeburg, 1982) [exhibition catalogue]
L. Salter: 'Which Bach?', *The Consort*, no.42 (1986), 50–60
G. Rötter: 'London gegen Bückeburg: fünf zu drei? Ein Bach-Porträt und zwei Komponisten', *Musica*, xliv (1990), 83–6
B.J. Sing: *Geistliche Vokalkompositionen zwischen Barock und Klassik: Studien zu den Kantatendichtungen Johann Gottfried Herders in den Vertonungen Johann Christoph Friedrich Bachs* (Baden-Baden, 1992)
U. Leisinger: 'Die geistlichen Vokalwerke von Johann Christoph Friedrich Bach: Aspekte der Entstehungs- und Überlieferungsgeschichte', *BJb 1995*, 115–43
U. Leisinger, ed.: *Johann Christoph Friedrich Bach (1732–1795): ein Komponist zwischen Barock und Klassik*, Niedersächsisches Staatsarchiv, 8 June – 11th Aug 1995 (Bückeburg, 1995) [exhibition catalogue, incl. list of works]
H. Tiggemann: 'Graf Wilhelm und Johann Christoph Friedrich Bach im Exil auf Gut Niensteden', *Shaumburg-Lippische Heimat-Blätter*, xlvi (1995), 66–73

(12) Bach, Johann [John] Christian (50) (*b* Leipzig, 5 Sept 1735; *d* London, 1 Jan 1782). Composer, youngest son of (7) Johann Sebastian Bach. As a composer he was the most versatile of J.S. Bach's sons and the only one to write Italian operas. He was an important influence on Mozart and, with C.F. Abel, did much to establish regular public concerts in London.

1. Germany and Italy. 2. London, 1762–72. 3. Mannheim and London, 1772–82. 4. Style and reputation. 5. Church music and oratorio. 6. Operas. 7. Symphonies and concertos. 8. Keyboard and chamber music.

1. GERMANY AND ITALY.   It is likely that J.C. Bach's early musical education was supervised by his father, though some instruction may have been given by Johann Elias Bach (39), who lived in the Leipzig household between 1738 and 1743 and acted as secretary to the elder Bach. Johann Christian himself assumed some secretarial duties in 1749–50, preparing music manuscripts and receipts on his father's behalf. Christian, evidently a favourite child of Sebastian, inherited three of his father's harpsichords. J.S. Bach's keyboard music played an important role in his son's development: the second book of *Das wohltemperirte Clavier* was completed in the early 1740s and probably served as a teaching manual for Christian, as had the first book for his half-brother Wilhelm Friedemann in the 1720s; it is known that J.C. Bach owned a manuscript of the English Suites; a knowledge of the B♭ keyboard Partita must be inferred from Christian's use of a modified version of the opening in his accompanied sonata op.10 no.1; and the earliest datable music manuscript in J.C. Bach's hand, a *Stammbuch* entry dated 23 October 1748, is a keyboard version in D minor of the Polonaise from J.S. Bach's Second Orchestral Suite. None of J.C. Bach's own compositions can be assigned to his Leipzig years except for a march in the second *Clavierbüchlein* of Anna Magdalena Bach (BWV Anh.131) and, possibly, a handful of keyboard dances.

After his father's death in 1750 Christian moved to Berlin, where he studied composition and harpsichord with his half-brother Carl Philipp Emanuel. According to Gerber, the young Bach performed his own works on the harpsichord in Berlin 'with great applause' and composed his first large-scale compositions. Of the '5 harpsichord concertos, 1 cello concerto, 2 trios and 3 arias' listed as Johann Christian's in Emanuel's *Nachlass* (1790), only the harpsichord concertos – large-scale works in the manner of C.P.E. Bach – are known to survive. The authenticity of the first publication attributed to J.C. Bach, the ode *An Aeglen* in a collection of 1755, has been disputed by Warburton (*Thematic Catalogue*, 1999). A similar song, *Mezendore*, printed in a similar collection the following year, is probably by Bach, though J.C.F. Bach's authorship cannot be ruled out. A third song, *Der Weise auf dem Lande*, may be confidently attributed to J.C. Bach's Berlin period; the autograph entry in a *Stammbuch* is dated 16 April 1755.

In late spring or summer 1755 Bach took his first steps towards abandoning the Protestant, Kapellmeister tradition which had nourished the Bach family for two centuries: he left for Italy, possibly in the company of an Italian lady singer, and took up residence in Milan. Little is known about his first months there: three arias attributed to him were evidently inserted in Cocchi's *Emira*, performed in Milan in January 1756. Evidently he was installed in the house of his Milanese patron, Count Agostino Litta, by that time and began having lessons in counterpoint with Padre Martini in Bologna. The main biographical sources for Bach's Italian years are his letters to Martini, beginning in January 1757 and continuing sporadically after Bach settled in London in 1762. These reveal Bach's expanding reputation as a composer, first in Italy and later north of the Alps. His first music written in Italy was mostly liturgical, some of it in the antique contrapuntal style associated with Martini, and performed in churches in Milan and elsewhere. In June 1760 Bach was appointed second organist at Milan Cathedral, and it is probable that he embraced the Roman Catholic faith at this time. Increasingly, the opera house provided a stronger lure for him. After composing arias for pasticcios in Milan and elsewhere, he was commissioned to write an *opera seria* for the Teatro Regio, Turin; *Artaserse* was given its première there on 26 December 1760. In the following year Bach, neglecting his organist's duties in Milan and thereby attracting Litta's displeasure, travelled extensively in Italy, composing his next and most popular early opera, *Catone in Utica*, for the S Carlo, Naples, and *Alessandro nell'Indie* for the same theatre (performed on 20 January 1762; a cantata by Bach for the birthday of Charles III of Spain performed on the same day). *Catone* was revived in Milan in 1762, performed in Pavia, Perugia and Parma in 1763 and again in Naples in 1764 and was heard as late as 1768 in Brunswick. Wider European recognition was achieved with the publication of the overture to *Artaserse* by Venier in Paris in 1761. Bach himself had signalled this recognition in an important letter to Martini dated 14 February 1761: 'for some time past I have almost had to put my studies aside, being every day called upon to write something for concerts – a symphony, concerto, cantata and so forth for Germany or Paris'. The success of his operas attracted the attention of the management of the King's Theatre, London, who commissioned two operas for the 1762–3 season; by accepting he gave up the opportunity of composing a third opera for Naples and one for Venice. Bach sought leave of absence for a year from the Milan Cathedral authorities, and although the post was kept open for him, he never returned. In late June or early July 1762 he made his way to London for the final and decisive stage of his career.

2. LONDON, 1762–72.   During Bach's 20 years in London he lived comfortably at various addresses in Soho, Mayfair and later Richmond and Paddington. He found fame, success and, at least until the late 1770s, financial stability. He enjoyed the acquaintance of the royal family, the patronage of the aristocracy and the friendship of musicians and artists, including Abel, the painter Gainsborough and Charles Burney, and soon established a pre-eminent position in the concert and operatic life of the city. If, as Burney stated, Bach was initially disappointed by the mediocre operatic standards in the city, his future in London was assured by the triumph of his first complete stage work, *Orione* (February 1763; the première was attended by King George III and Queen Charlotte), followed by the less successful *Zanaida* (May 1763), and by his appointment as music master to the queen. It was now unnecessary for him to return to the claustrophobic and restrictive atmosphere of Milan. Bach's court duties involved giving music lessons to the queen and her children, organizing chamber concerts, directing the queen's band and accompanying the flute-playing of the king. Links with the royal family were strengthened with the publication of the keyboard concertos op.1, advertised in March 1763 and dedicated to Queen Charlotte. The finale of the sixth concerto, a set of variations on *God Save the King*, became one of Bach's most popular and oft-published works.

Bach's earliest years in London were those of his most vigorous activity in the opera house. His relationship with the King's Theatre was not without setbacks. The violinist Felice Giardini took over the management for the 1763–4 season, and although he and Bach were later to collaborate professionally there were tensions in their relationship; no operatic work by Bach was staged during Giardini's tenure. Bach was invited to return to Naples, but he evidently preferred to remain north of the Alps. He travelled to Paris in July 1763, establishing an important connection with the city, and was immediately granted a privilege for the publication of his works there; a similar privilege was granted in London on 15 December that year.

In the 1764–5 season Bach returned to the King's Theatre, contributing to two pasticcios and composing *Adriano in Siria*, given on 26 January 1765. The opera received seven performances and met with Burney's disapproval: 'Every one seemed to come out of the theatre disappointed'. Apart from a few arias contributed to pasticcios, Bach had little further to do with the King's Theatre until *Carattaco*, performed on 14 February 1767. Like *Orione*, it is on a grand scale with choruses, but although praised by Burney and others it was never revived. The singer Cecilia Grassi, later Bach's wife, was to have sung in it, but she was indisposed. Bach also contributed arias for the English stage, including music for the pasticcios *The Maid of the Mill* (1765), *The Summer's Tale* (1765) and *Tom Jones* (1769). In addition, he supplied songs, occasionally arranged from operatic arias, for performance at Vauxhall Gardens; four sets of Vauxhall songs were published between 1766 and 1779.

From his earliest days in London Bach took advantage of the flourishing music trade, publishing a whole series of works and establishing a relationship with the printer and publisher Peter Welcker, and later with his son John.

Bach's practice for the most part in the 1760s was to publish a work under his own auspices; Welcker would usually reissue it shortly afterwards under his own imprint. This relationship began about 1765 with the reissue of the concertos op.1 (first published in 1763) and continued with the accompanied sonatas op.2, the first set of symphonies op.3 and the first set of canzonets op.4, all dating from 1765. Most of Bach's works were published a few months later in Paris by Huberty (and later Sieber) and by Hummel in Amsterdam. There is reason to believe that Bach had some arrangement with the continental firms, especially Sieber, who published the first edition of the piano sonatas op.17 (as op.12) in Paris in 1773 or 1774. Bach evidently took great care to protect his interests, and in 1773 he took Longman, Lukey & Co. to court for the unauthorized publication of several pieces.

From early 1764 Bach shared lodgings with Carl Friedrich Abel, the composer and viol da gamba player who had lived in London since 1759 and whose father had served at Cöthen with J.S. Bach. Carl Friedrich himself had studied with Sebastian in Leipzig and therefore may have known Johann Christian as a boy. Their collaboration in the series of concerts later dubbed the Bach-Abel concerts was to have a major impact on London concert life. The first one took place at the Great Room in Spring Gardens on 29 February 1764. In the following year they participated in the subscription series organized by Teresa Cornelys at Carlisle House, Soho Square, giving ten concerts in all that year and increasing to 15 from 1766. Bach and Abel took over the management of the concerts from 1768 when they moved to Almack's Assembly Rooms in King Street, St James's, where they remained until 1774. The concerts were directed alternately by Bach and Abel. Although few details are known, the programmes included the latest symphonies, concertos, chamber and vocal works of Bach, Abel and other fashionable composers. The performers were the best in London, and often of German origin; they included the oboist J.C. Fischer, the violinist Wilhelm Cramer (father of John, the pianist) and later the pianist J.S. Schroeter, one of Bach's pupils.

In April 1764 Leopold Mozart arrived in London with his family. Although there is no evidence that Wolfgang Amadeus appeared at the Bach-Abel concerts, he did perform at court and became a great admirer of J.C. Bach. They are known to have performed duets on the harpsichord together. Mozart had a high regard for the man and his music: in the early 1770s he arranged three of Bach's piano sonatas from op.5 as keyboard concertos, and the symphonies and sonatas from the time of his 15 months in London bear the stamp of both Bach's and Abel's music. The Mozarts evidently left London in 1765 with an autograph manuscript of a piano sonata by Bach (later published in modified form as op.17 no.3) which was kept in Leopold Mozart's library in Salzburg.

Bach's keyboard sonatas op.5, published in 1766, are a landmark in that they are the first published in London to bear the option of the piano on the title-page. Bach's central role in the development of the piano in London is defined by Burney: 'After the arrival of John Chr. Bach in this country, and the establishment of his concert[s] . . . all the harpsichord makers tried their mechanical powers at piano-fortes'. Bach is credited with performing the first solo in public on the piano in 1768 and had dealings with many of the major instrument makers of the day. He is known to have sent pianos to France, to the pianist Madame Brillon and also to the daughter of the Encyclopedist Diderot. A square piano, apparently by Zumpe, survives in a British private collection, bearing Bach's signature on the soundboard.

At the end of the 1760s Bach was well established as the leading composer and musician in London, and as an international figure much in demand as a composer, performer and teacher. He evidently charged high fees as a teacher according to Charles Wesley writing in the late 1770s. Works such as the symphonies opp.3, 6 and 9 and piano concertos op.7 were performed in all (and published in many) of the major music centres of Europe. In the early 1770s this fame was consolidated in London and on the Continent. In 1770 he wrote his last major religious work, the two-act *Gioas re di Giuda*, performed at the King's Theatre and revived the following year. R.J.S. Stevens reports that Bach, persuaded to perform an organ concerto between the acts, was hissed at by the audience and laughed at by the choristers for his style of playing – the first reference, perhaps, to Bach's deteriorating keyboard abilities. In 1770, also for the King's Theatre, Bach and Pietro Guglielmi adapted Gluck's *Orfeo ed Euridice*, adding choruses and supplementary music to bring it to 'a necessary length for an evening's entertainment'. Although it blunted the reform elements in Gluck's opera, this version was a success; it was revived with modifications in 1771 and 1773 and was also given at the Teatro S Carlo in Naples in 1774.

3. MANNHEIM AND LONDON, 1772–82. Apart from the two-act serenata *Endimione* (1772), no new work by Bach was performed at the King's Theatre until 1778. In the meantime he fulfilled operatic commissions abroad. In about 1770 he had befriended Johann Baptist Wendling, first flautist in the electoral orchestra at Mannheim and husband of the singer Dorothea (both were later friends of Mozart). It was perhaps due to Wendling, who had lodged with him during his time in London, that Bach was commissioned to write *Temistocle*, to a libretto adapted from Metastasio by the Mannheim court poet Verazi, for the nameday festivities of the Elector Carl Theodor. The orchestra in the German city was unrivalled in quality, and Bach's sumptuous score exploits the capabilities of the Mannheim orchestra and soloists to the full. Bach was able to experience this at first hand when he travelled to Mannheim in August or September 1772 and remained there for the première on 5 November. The opera was extremely successful and was revived the following year. This elicited a further operatic commission, and the result, *Lucio Silla*, was performed on 5 November 1775. It is not known for certain whether Bach himself attended the performance, but given that he attended all his other operatic premières it is possible that he made the trip. *Lucio Silla* was evidently less successful, although it was valued by Mozart who examined the score in Mannheim in 1777. Mozart himself had set the same text, by Giovanni de Gamerra, for Milan in 1772. Other works by Bach performed at Mannheim include the cantatas *Amor vincitore* (first performed in London in 1774) and *La tempesta* (published in Mannheim in 1778). *Endimione* was revised for a performance there in 1774.

The early 1770s saw a number of new publications: the keyboard concertos op.7 (1770), the flute quartets op.8 (1772) perhaps written with Wendling in mind, three symphonies op.9 (1773), the accompanied sonatas op.10 (1773) and the quintets op.11 (1774) dedicated to the Elector Carl Theodor. Many of these pieces would have been used in Bach's English concerts, which were not restricted to London. In 1773 he visited Blandford and Salisbury, performing there with Cecilia Grassi. Terry and others have suggested that they married later in 1773 or early in 1774, on the evidence that Bach moved to 80 Newman Street, while Abel moved elsewhere. But concert advertisements continued to refer to Cecilia as Signora (or Mrs) Grassi until at least 1776, and so the date of the wedding remains in conjecture.

In 1774 the Bach-Abel concerts moved back to Carlisle House, Soho, now vacated by the bankrupt Mrs Cornelys. But Bach and Abel had more ambitious plans: with Giovanni Andrea Gallini they acquired a property in Hanover Square, on the corner of Hanover Street, and in the garden built a new concert hall, the Hanover Square Rooms, a lavishly appointed building with paintings by Gainsborough. This was the final home of the Bach-Abel concerts, but it also marked the beginning of their decline. Bach's finances were depleted and receipts diminished, especially after 1778. The concerts remained Bach's main forum for new works, including the cantatas *Cefalo e Procri* (1776) and *Rinaldo ed Armida* (1778). It is likely that the final set of keyboard concertos, op.13 (1777), received an airing there, along with his last major set of symphonies (including three for double orchestra) op.18 and the last major chamber works, including a sextet for keyboard, oboe, strings and two horns and quintets and quartets for various combinations of strings, keyboard and woodwind. Probably these chamber works were also performed by the queen's band at Richmond Lodge. Bach had taken a house nearby as early as 1770, and Mrs Papendiek recalled performances there led by Bach and Abel.

In the mid-1770s Padre Martini requested Bach to send him his portrait. Although Gainsborough's celebrated painting (fig.10) was apparently completed by May 1776, Bach waited for over two years before despatching it to Italy. It survives in the Civico Museo Bibliografico Musicale, Bologna, and another version, formerly in the collection of the Earl of Hillingdon, is in the National Portrait Gallery, London.

Bach made a return to the King's Theatre with the revival of *Orione* in 1777 (in a revised version) and in the following year produced his last and finest stage work for London, the opera *La clemenza di Scipione* (4 April 1778). Bach took the trouble to have the full score published (omitting most of the recitatives), a practice almost unknown in London in the 1770s. In 1778 Bach's brother Johann Christoph Friedrich paid a visit to London with his son Wilhelm Friedrich Ernst, who stayed behind after his father had returned to Germany and remained in London until after Johann Christian's death in 1782.

Bach's last complete operatic venture, the *tragédie lyrique Amadis de Gaule* was performed in Paris in 1779. The composer had visited the French capital in August 1778 to audition singers, at the same time renewing his acquaintance with Mozart, who reported to his father his delight in meeting again his former mentor. *Amadis*, an unusual work, clearly written to accord with the current French taste, was a failure. It was withdrawn for revision after only three performances and returned to the stage in January 1780. A manuscript in the Bibliothèque de

10. *Johann Christian Bach: portrait by Thomas Gainsborough, 1776 (Civico Museo Bibliografico Musicale, Bologna)*

l'Opéra, Paris, presumably for the revised version, shows heavy cuts and alterations. In the printed score, which appeared shortly after Bach's death, these cuts are restored. The first issue contains a poignant preface by Bach's widow, in which she states that the published version is not as it was performed in Paris, but is the version preferred by the composer.

The last years of Bach's life show declining fortunes and health. The Bach-Abel concerts continued to lose money; Bach was apparently defrauded of more than £1000 by a servant and his bank account became overdrawn. His pre-eminence in the opera house was usurped by Sacchini and others, and in the concert hall by his pupil Johann Samuel Schroeter; as Mrs Papendiek remarked: 'Bach played occasionally, but Schroeder (*sic*) was the planet'. Ill-health supervened: Cecilia Grassi in the preface to *Amadis* reported on the 'long illness which led him to the tomb'; the last known example of his handwriting, a list of subscribers for a proposed (but unrealized) series of new chamber works, dating from 1780 or 1781, reveals a shakiness of hand far removed from the confident script of Bach's earlier years; and on 14 December 1781 the singer Angelo Morigi sent news to Martini that Bach was suffering from a chest illness. Bach died on 1 January 1782 and was buried in St Pancras churchyard on 6 January, leaving substantial debts which neither the last season of the Bach-Abel concerts, continued by Bach's widow, nor a benefit concert on 27 May 1782 managed to efface completely. Cecilia Bach returned to Italy via Paris in summer 1782 after some of her debts had been repaid with assistance from Queen Charlotte.

Bach's death elicited obituaries particularly in the German magazines. None is as eloquent as the few words of Mozart who, in a letter to his father, described Bach's passing as 'a loss to the musical world'.

4. STYLE AND REPUTATION.   J.C. Bach's music is more cosmopolitan and varied than that of any other of J.S. Bach's sons. Abandoning the restrictive Lutheran sensibility of his brothers, he turned his face towards the south, embracing Catholicism and Italian opera, and his musical style was transformed accordingly. Bach's German works (before mid-1755), notably the keyboard concertos written in Berlin, are strongly influenced by C.P.E. Bach, with their preponderance of minor keys, their severe character, and their solid, lumbering ideas with long melodic lines, wide leaps, sudden interruptions to the rhythmic and melodic flow and syncopations. After the move to Italy, this severe style all but vanished. It is still to be found from time to time, for example in the opening movement of the *Dies irae*, the keyboard Toccata in Bb minor and the Ab Sonata, though in a watered-down manner. The influence of Padre Martini is prominent in the first Italian works, notably in the strict counterpoint and antique pseudo-Palestrina style of the music for the Office of the Dead (1757) and also in the keyboard Sonata op.5 no.6 which, although not published until 1766, recalls Martini's sonatas of the 1730s in its serious prelude, double fugue and gavotte.

The main influence on Bach during his years in Milan was Italian *opera seria*, which he wholeheartedly embraced. It transformed his style, tipping the balance from severity to a lighter, more bland manner: the stiff, terse and long-winded ideas of the Berlin works are softened into smooth, clear, symmetrical phrases composed of short motivic ideas underpinned by simple harmonies, with none of the sudden dramatic surprises of the Berlin concertos and with a marked slowing-down of the harmonic rhythm. The slow movements are often imbued with a sensuality and quiet passion unknown in the earlier works. Most compositions of the Italian years (1755–62) – the three operas, at least one symphonie concertante, church works, accompanied sonatas and operatic overtures – are representative of this new *galant* manner.

It was this 'international' style that Bach brought to London. During his period in England his musical language developed: the short motivic phrases of his Italian works gradually expanded into a more wholeheartedly melodic style, in some cases influenced by British popular songs and folksong. Bach widened his tonal range and structures became more expansive and varied, the binary sonata forms of his earlier works becoming larger and more diverse, often embracing a full recapitulation in the tonic key. Burney remarked that

Bach seems to have been the first composer who observed the law of contrast as a principle. Before his time, contrast there frequently was in the work of others, but it seems to have been accidental. Bach in his symphonies and other incidental pieces as well as in his songs, seldom failed, after a rapid and noisy passage, to introduce one that was slow and soothing.

Burney thus draws attention to Bach's habitual use of contrasting themes in the sonata structures of his London works, and these 'second subject' ideas are a consistent feature of his later style.

Bach's orchestration is often imaginative and felicitous, and occasionally calls for new or unusual instruments to achieve effects – for example clarinets in *Orione*, a pair of 'octave flutes' in the Vauxhall song 'Hither turn thy wand'ring eyes' and obbligato instruments such as the

bassoon in the aria 'Non m'alletta' from *Temistocle*. Perhaps as a result of exposure to the orchestral manner of the Mannheimers, his orchestration became even more adept and imaginative, with greater freedom in the use of woodwind and pizzicato string effects and the use of two orchestras in three of the op.18 symphonies.

In London Bach broadened his range of musical subjects, embracing (in addition to operas and concertos) symphonies, chamber works, popular songs, canzonets, cantatas and various types of keyboard work, including duet sonatas. These are written in a Classical style with italianate thematic material, enlivened by contact with French and British melodies and ideas and allied to German strength and rigour. This synthesis of musical idiom resulted in an essentially popular style geared towards the large, music-loving aristocratic and middle-class audiences of London, which, as Haydn discovered in the 1790s, appreciated new and lavish effects and at the same time enjoyed familiar themes. Bach's use of national songs in concerto finales and his exploitation of the piano and other new instruments, such as the 'voce umana', in the Bach-Abel concerts can be regarded as catering to the taste of the new audience.

Bach's music had considerable influence on contemporary composers in London, namely Schroeter and Mazzinghi (his pupils), J.C. Fischer, W.F.E. Bach and, most notably, Mozart, whose symphonies and sonatas of the mid-1760s reveal the influence of both Bach and Abel. Although commentators have often noted several resemblances, such as that between 'Martern aller Arten' in Mozart's *Die Entführung aus dem Serail* and 'Infelice, in van m'affanno' in Bach's *La clemenza di Scipione*, Bach's influence on Mozart is probably more general and fundamental, notably in the sensual slow movements and in particular in Bach's highly developed sense of musical balance.

It is often stated that Bach's reputation was immediately eclipsed after his death, that his music was no longer performed and his influence died with him. This is not strictly true. Though his reputation continued to decline in the 1780s, an analysis of London concert programmes reveals that Bach's music continued to be performed in London at least until the mid-1790s, when his symphonies were still played alongside those of Haydn. His works, and arrangements of them, were posthumously printed in London and on the Continent, albeit sporadically, until the mid-1790s, and they continued to be available in manuscript until the end of the century and beyond, to judge by the vast number of late copies now in libraries in Italy and elsewhere. It was in the early 19th century that Bach's music virtually ceased to be performed and published. An exception was the extraordinarily late revival (in a thoroughly revised form) of *La clemenza di Scipione* at the King's Theatre in 1805, perhaps due to the advocacy of his pupil Mrs Billington; there were also isolated pockets where Bach's works continued to be played in the 19th century, such as the monastery of Einsiedeln, where his church music was still heard and where 'new' religious works were created by supplying contrafact Latin texts to Italian arias from his operas. The 19th century nevertheless proved to be the nadir of J.C. Bach's popularity. His self-deprecatory remark, 'My brother [C.P.E. Bach] lives to compose, I compose to live', provided the underlying text of much of the critical writing on the composer. It was only in the early years of the 20th century, with the writings of Terry, Schökel and Tutenberg among others, that a more balanced view of J.C. Bach has been achieved and the composer has taken his place among the most gifted and influential musicians of the early Classical period.

5. CHURCH MUSIC AND ORATORIO. Bach's Latin church music comprises large-scale psalm and canticle settings, mass movements, music for the Office and Mass for the Dead (including three lessons, an invitatory, an introit, Kyrie and *Dies irae*), all scored for chorus, soloists and orchestra; and smaller works, such as motets for a single voice and orchestra, including settings of *Attendite mortales* and *Salve regina*. With only two exceptions, the oratorio *Gioas, re di Giuda* and *Let the solemn organs blow*, all the pieces are for Roman Catholic services; by contrast with his father and brothers, there are no Lutheran church works by J.C. Bach. Most of the religious works were composed during his Italian period (1755–62), and most date from 1757–9, that is, surprisingly, from the period before Bach took up his only church post as second organist at Milan Cathedral. The most important sacred composition of his later years is his only oratorio, *Gioas* (1770), to an Italian text by Metastasio.

The earliest church works, notably the introit and Kyrie from the *Messa de' morti*, are in a pseudo-Palestrina contrapuntal style influenced by Padre Martini. For example, the responsory sections of the invitatory *Regem cui omnia vivunt* employ cantus firmus technique in the upper parts. All these apprentice works were shown to Martini for his comments, and though several have the manner of elaborate contrapuntal exercises they were nevertheless performed in churches in Milan. The impressive *Dies irae*, two early *Magnificat* settings and a *Te Deum*, all dating from 1757–8, are similarly somewhat backward-looking in their use of two choirs, often treated antiphonally. In the later church works, with Martini's influence clearly waning, the style is more modern and the choral writing less contrapuntal, often with a simple chordal texture pitted against an active orchestral accompaniment, though the composition is frequently rounded off by a fugue, usually based on a brief, desultory subject treated in business-like fashion. Alongside the choruses, even those in archaic style, are arias and duets influenced by contemporary Italian opera, frequently of a virtuoso kind and sometimes with elaborate instrumental obbligatos (for organ, bassoon etc.). Perhaps the most ambitious of these is the aria 'Intellectus bonus' from *Confitebor*, which requires a chamber accompaniment of six solo instruments. As Bach matured, the number and importance of the arias increased, showing clearly where his true interests lay.

Arias dominate Bach's only oratorio, *Gioas, re di Giuda*, an opera in all but name and a setting of a text by Metastasio. The choral writing is nevertheless composed with English taste in mind and displays the strong influence of Handel.

6. OPERAS. Bach was no innovator in the world of *opera seria*. All ten works written for Italy, London or Mannheim use the Metastasian format of recitative punctuated by long arias. In the Italian works and those written for Mannheim, the da capo aria is frequently used; in the London operas there is more variety in aria forms and the da capo is used less and less (*La clemenza*

di Scipione has none at all). The chorus is more prominent in the London operas, in accordance with British taste, notably in *Orione*, *Zanaida* and *Carattaco*. These three works also are not based on texts by Metastasio and in terms of subject differ from the statuesque classical dramas of the other operas, with their greater emphasis on spectacle and lavish effects.

Bach would have encountered Italian and italianate opera in Berlin. Indeed C.P.E. Bach's *Nachlass* documents '3 Arien' composed by Christian before he went to Italy in 1755. His arrival in Milan allowed him to encounter *opera seria* at source and he immersed himself in the music and style. Three arias attributed to Bach, evidently inserted in Cocchi's *Emira* in January 1756, survive in a contemporary manuscript of Italian provenance in the Bibliothèque Nationale, Paris. Bach contributed arias to other operas elsewhere in the late 1750s, but his first complete score, *Artaserse*, was not composed until 1760 for Turin. In it he severely curtailed the Metastasian recitative and used a variety of aria forms. The da capo principle returned in force in his two works for Naples, *Catone in Utica* (1761) and *Alessandro nell'Indie* (1762). Two arias, 'Confusa, smarrita' from the former and 'Non so d'onde viene' from the latter, achieved great popularity in Bach's lifetime, the second attracting the young Mozart's approbation. Bach made use of them again in pasticcios in London.

Of the five operas for London, only *Adriano in Siria* (1765) is without chorus and is as dominated by arias as Bach's works for Italy. Significantly, it was not a success. Perhaps the finest of the London operas is the last, *La clemenza di Scipione* (1778), in which, with da capo arias banished in favour of a variety of structures and with a more prominent use of the chorus, Bach achieved a greater sense of movement and dramatic flow. He also made an interesting attempt to integrate the overture into the opera: motifs from it appear in the final chorus in Act 3.

For the two operas for Mannheim, *Temistocle* (1772) and *Lucio Silla* (1775), Bach took advantage of the superb orchestral facilities of the electoral court orchestra and produced showpieces of vocal and instrumental virtuosity, with the woodwind in particular gaining especial prominence. Da capo arias predominate in *Temistocle*, but in *Lucio Silla* a greater variety of forms is used.

Bach's most ambitious operatic venture was his only *tragédie lyrique* written for Paris, *Amadis de Gaule* (1779). The libretto, a botched condensation into three acts of Quinault's five-act text written for Lully, is unlike anything Bach had previously set, with its vivid plot set in chivalric times – a tale of love, jealousy and attempted revenge with frequent interventions of the supernatural (ghosts, demons, etc.) and nature (thunder, lightning and enveloping clouds). The chorus, in various guises as prisoners or demons, is a protagonist, and ballets and divertissements are important elements. Bach rose to the challenge magnificently, taking advantage of the large Paris orchestra to create sumptuous and occasionally extraordinary effects. As in *La clemenza*, the overture is integrated into the opera: a dramatic crescendo and diminuendo on a diminished 7th chord scored for trombones, bassoon and woodwind is used again in Acts 2 and 3. The opera had the misfortune to receive its première at the time of the Gluck–Piccinni controversy and suffered accordingly; it was not revived until the 20th century.

7. SYMPHONIES AND CONCERTOS.   It is probably to the symphony and the piano concerto that Bach made his most important contribution. For Bach the symphony was intimately connected with the three-movement (fast–slow–fast) Italian operatic overture and all his mature symphonies follow that plan; indeed Bach regarded the word 'overture' as synonymous with 'symphony'. C.P.E. Bach's *Nachlass* records that Johann Christian composed a symphony and an overture, both in six parts, before he left for Italy. These are almost certainly lost. His first opera overtures written for Turin and Naples appeared in print in Paris and in London in the early 1760s. The first symphonies for concert use, the set of six op.3, appeared in London in 1765. Their publication coincided with the early years of the Bach-Abel concerts and these works were almost certainly performed there. They are fine pieces, with sturdy, sonata-form first movements, contrasting second subjects and practically all-inclusive recapitulations in the tonic key. The opening of the Fifth Symphony is a particularly fine example, with its playful, quasi-Baroque running bass and attractive syncopated melodic material. The central slow movements mine that particular vein of sensual, nocturnal music that Bach made his own and the finales are in dance rhythms – minuets, gigues or bucolic dances as in the earthy horn-calls of the last movement of no.6.

Bach himself published no other set of symphonies in England until 1781. Three sets, opp.6, 8 (containing three works from op.6) and 9, were printed in the Netherlands between 1770 and 1775 and are again, with one exception, concert works. The most extraordinary piece in these collections is op.6 no.6 in G minor, Bach's only gesture in the direction of the 'Sturm und Drang' symphony and a work worthy to be mentioned alongside the early G minor symphonies of Haydn and Mozart. All three movements are, extraordinarily, in the minor key (the slow movement is in C minor) – a noteworthy feature for a composer normally reticent in his use of the minor mode – and they all seem to breathe the air of an earlier sensibility: the presence of C.P.E. Bach and the north German school is not far away. Given that J.C. Bach often recycled earlier material, there is reason to conjecture that much of the material here might have belonged to one of the lost works mentioned in C.P.E. Bach's *Nachlass*.

Bach's crowning achievements in the concert symphony are the three for double orchestra published in the op.18 set (1781). They are large, richly orchestrated works, making much interplay of the two orchestras treated antiphonally and combining different textures, for example violins in four parts. The woodwind instruments, now liberated from merely doubling and reinforcing the strings, are given solos and contrasting passages.

Most of Bach's concertos are for keyboard, although works survive for flute, oboe and bassoon and an early lost composition for cello is listed in his half-brother's *Nachlass*. Also listed there are the five keyboard concertos which survive in Bach's autograph in Berlin. A manuscript of a sixth in F minor also probably dates from those early years. The influence of C.P.E. Bach presides over these works, which adopt the ritornello/solo technique of the elder Bach's Berlin compositions. None of Bach's keyboard concertos can be firmly dated to his Italian period, though it is possible that several of the op.1 set (1763) may have been composed there. This set and opp.7 (1770) and 13 (1777), all first published in London, established

Bach's new, more Classical concerto style, with fewer and pared down ritornellos and a simpler, sparer keyboard style. This became the model for the keyboard concerto in London in the late 18th century.

Most of Bach's mature keyboard concertos are in two movements, without a slow movement; two concertos from each of the three published collections are in three movements. In the later two sets Bach, in line with his maturing style, broadened the musical range, expanded the length of the movements and enriched the melodic content. In a recently discovered, partly autograph manuscript of the solo part of op.7 no.6, is revealed a much more extended version of the concerto, with longer ritornellos and a more technically difficult and extended keyboard part. Bach evidently reduced the scale of the work for publication.

Although no concertos can be ascribed with certainty to Bach's Italian years, he did experiment with the genre of the symphonie concertante. The existence of an autograph manuscript in Regensburg of a work in D major, in his early hand and written on Italian paper, suggests that Bach's earliest essays may date from the early 1760s. In all about 17 works in this or related genres are attributed to Bach. Solo instruments vary from two to nine players; most works are in three movements, though a number, including the earliest, are in two.

8. KEYBOARD AND CHAMBER MUSIC.   As a keyboard performer and teacher Bach composed a large number of works for concert and didactic purposes, including two sets of solo sonatas, accompanied sonatas and chamber works with obbligato keyboard. The composition of keyboard works forms a constant thread throughout all three periods of his creative career. The only such works which can be dated from his German years are a march in the second *Clavierbüchlein* of Anna Magdalena a series of minuets and polonaises, which he may have composed even before he left Leipzig and also an early 'Solo' for keyboard in A minor, his first substantial German harpsichord work. These were followed by sonatas in B♭ and A♭ and an intriguing Toccata in B♭ minor which have been dated to his years in Italy and survive in manuscript in Padre Martini's library (and elsewhere). Bach's lighter, italianate style can be seen in the eight accompanied sonatas in manuscript in Milan. This style was carried over into his first London works in this genre, the accompanied sonatas op.2. As in his other London works, Bach expanded and refined his musical language and forms, and in general the later sets of accompanied sonatas opp.10 (1773), 15 (1778), 16 (1779) and 18 (1780/81) are more accomplished. Opp.15 and 18 also include duet sonatas for keyboard.

The two most important keyboard publications of Bach's London years are the sonatas opp.5 and 17. The earlier set was published in 1766 and was the first publication in London to mention the option of the piano on the title-page, preceding John Burton's *Lessons* by a few months. The six works here are in a variety of styles and one at least – no.6 in C minor, with its imposing prelude, double fugue and gavotte all in the tonic key – may date from Bach's Italian years. The grandiose D major sonata (no.2), with its orchestral sonorities and changes of dynamics, represents Bach's first published attempt at idiomatic piano writing. The second set, commonly known by its London opus number, 17 (1779), was in fact published by Sieber in Paris (*c*1774) as op.12.

Once again these works reveal a wide range of styles, from the vigorous gigue finales of the Second and Sixth Sonatas to the sensuous slow movement of the C minor, one of Bach's greatest achievements.

Outstanding among the many chamber works, trios, quartets and quintets for strings and wind in various combinations are the four late pieces: a sextet, two quintets and a quartet with obbligato keyboard, published posthumously. The Sextet, for the unusual combination of keyboard, oboe, violin, cello and two horns has often been attributed to J.C.F. Bach, but a set of parts in J.C.F. Bach's hand discovered in Kraców (*PL-Kj*) transmits the work, in a slightly different form from that of the published version (1783), with an attribution to 'J.C. Bach'. The Quintet in D for keyboard, flute, oboe, violin and cello is justly one of Bach's most popular compositions. Worthy of note is the highly attractive slow movement with its pathos-filled *minore* central section, as far away from the facile 19th-century view of a 'porcelain' composer as can be imagined.

WORKS
printed works published in London unless otherwise stated
Edition: *The Collected Works of Johann Christian Bach 1735–1782*, ed. E. Warburton, i–xlviii (New York, 1984–99) [CW]
Catalogues: C.S. Terry: *John Christian Bach* (London, rev. 2/1967/R by H.C.R. Landon) [T] [T numbers show the page no./no. of the incipit on the page and are not Terry's numbers; in a group the number of the first incipit only is given; roman numerals denote corrigenda pages]; E. Warburton: *The Collected Works of Johann Christian Bach 1735–1782*, xlviii/1: *Thematic Catalogue* (New York, 1999) [W]

LITURGICAL

W	T	
F2	199/4	Attendite mortales, motet, T, orch, ? after 1767, 1st aria arr. from Carattaco; CW xviii
E17	200/6	Beatus vir (F), S, A, T, B, SATB, orch, 1758; CW xxiii
E16	202/1	Confitebor tibi Domine (Eb), S, A, T, B, SATB, orch, 1759; CW xxiii
E5	202/3	Credo (C), SATB, orch; CW xx
E12	202/4	Dies irae; see [Messa de' morti], below
E15	202/6	Dixit Dominus (D), S, A, T, B, SATB, orch, by March 1758; CW xxiii
E13	203/3	Domine ad adiuvandum (D), S, SATB, orch, 1758; CW xlviii
E14	203/2	Domine ad adiuvandum (G), S, A, SATB, orch, 1760; CW xxii
E3	204/3	Gloria in excelsis (D), S, A, T, B, SATB, orch, 1758/9; CW xix
E4	204/1	Gloria in excelsis (G), S, A, T, B, SATB, orch; CW xx
E2	204/8	Kyrie (D), S, T, SATB, orch; CW xix
F3	205/2	Larvae tremendae (D), motet, S, orch; CW xviii
E18	206/3	Laudate pueri (E), S, orch, Milan, 12 Aug 1758; CW xlviii
E19	206/1	Laudate pueri (G), S, T, orch, 1760; CW xxii
F5	199/1	Let the solemn organs blow (W. Dodd), anthem for Magdalen Chapel, London, c1764; CW xxv

W	T	
E7–9	206/4	[3] Lezioni del officio per gli morti, 1757: Parce mihi, Domine (Bb), S, A, SATB, orch; Taedet animam meam (F), S, A, B, SATB, orch; Manus tuae (C), S, A, T, SATB, orch; CW xxi
E20	207/1	Magnificat (C), SATB, SATB, orch, 1758, inc.; CW xxii
E21	207/2	Magnificat (C), SATB, SATB; CW xxii
E22	207/3	Magnificat (C), S, A, T, B, SATB, orch, 1760; CW xxii
E11–12	208/5, 202/4	[Messa de' morti], 1757: Requiem aeternam (F), Kyrie (F), SSAATTBB, orch; Dies irae (c), S, A, T, B, SSAATTBB, orch; CW xxi
E10	207/5	Miserere (Bb), S, A, T, B, SATB, orch, 1757; CW xxi
F1	—	Pater noster, lost, sent with letter to G.B. Martini, 6 Sept 1757
E6	208/4	Regem cui omnia vivunt (F), invitatory, S, A, T, B, SATB, orch, 1757; CW xxi
E23	209/3	Salve regina (Eb), S, orch; CW xviii
E24	209/3	Salve regina (F), S, orch; CW xviii
F4a and b	209/5	Si nocte tenebrosa (F), motet, S/T, orch (two versions); CW xviii
E25	210/2	Tantum ergo (F), T, orch, 1757; CW xlviii
E26	209/7	Tantum ergo (G), S, A, T, B, SATB, orch, 1759; CW xxiv
E27	210/3	Te Deum (D), 2S, 2A, 2T, 2B, SATB, SATB, orch, 1758, inc.; CW xxiv
E28	210/5	Te Deum (D), S, A, T, B, SATB, orch, 1762; CW xxiv

doubtful

W	T	
YE4	202/7	Domine ad adiuvandum (C), S, SATB, str, *GB-Lbl*
YE7	—	Expugna impugnantes me (d), SSATB, CW xxiv
YE3	—	Gloria solenne (C), S, A, T, B, SATB, orch, inc.; CW xxiv
YE5	—	Laudate pueri (Bb), S, orch; CW xxiv
YE1	204/7	Messa in pastorale (Ky-Gl) (D), SATB, orch, *Lbl* (attrib. F. Durante)
YE2	204/6	Messa a più voci (Ky-Gl) (G), SATB, orch, *Lbl* (attrib. Durante)
YE6	208/6	Salve regina (D), S, S, A, T, B, SSATB, orch, *Lbl*

OPERAS

drammi per musica in 3 acts unless otherwise stated; facsimiles of libretto in CW xliii–xlvii

LCG – *London, Covent Garden*
LKH – *London, King's Theatre in the Haymarket*

W	T	
G1	217[1]	Artaserse (P. Metastasio), Turin, Regio, 26 Dec 1760, CW i
G2	222; xlii, xliii	Catone in Utica (Metastasio), Naples, S Carlo, 4 Nov 1761, CW ii

W	T	
G3	212; xxxii	Alessandro nell'Indie (Metastasio), Naples, S Carlo, 20 Jan 1762, CW iii; staged with his Cantata a tre voci
G4	237; xlvii	Orione, ossia Diana vendicata (drama, 3, G.G. Bottarelli), LKH, 19 Feb 1763, CW iv and xii; rev. LKH, 24 May 1777
G5	241; xlix	Zanaida (Bottarelli), LKH, 7 May 1763, CW iv and xii
G6	211; xxxi	Adriano in Siria (Metastasio), LKH, 26 Jan 1765, CW v
G42	—	The Fairy Favour (masque, 1, T. Hull), LCG, 29 Jan 1767, lib CW xlv, music lost [perf. by children as afterpiece]
G7	221; xli	Carattaco (Bottarelli), LKH, 14 Feb 1767, CW vi
G8	283/3; xlviii	Temistocle (Metastasio, rev. Verazi), Mannheim, Hof, 5 Nov 1772, CW vii
G9	232; xlv	Lucio Silla (G. De Gamerra, rev. Verazi), Mannheim, Hof, 5 Nov 1775, CW viii
G10	229; xliv	La clemenza di Scipione (serious op, 3), LKH, 4 April 1778, CW ix
G39	215; xxxiii	Amadis de Gaule (tragédie lyrique, 3, P. Quinault, rev. A.-D.-M. de Vismes du Valgay), Paris, Opéra, 14 Dec 1779, CW x

insertions in operas and pasticcios

W	T	
G Inc 2	251/4	G. Cocchi: Emira, Milan, Jan 1756: 3 arias; CW xii
G21	252/2	A. Ferradini: Demofoonte, Milan, 26 Dec 1758: 1 aria; CW xii
G23	277/4	F. Gassmann: Gli uccellatori, Turin, Carignano, 1 Sept 1760: ov.; CW xii
G1/3	—	Zenobia, Lucca, aut. 1761: 1 aria
G22	275/3	G.B. Lampugnani and others: La Giulia, Milan, carn. 1761: ov.; CW xii
G24	273/2	Il tutore e la pupilla (pasticcio, Bottarelli), LKH, 13 Nov 1762: ov., from Cantata a tre voci with new 2nd movt; CW ix
G25	273/8; l	Astarto, re di Tiro (pasticcio, Bottarelli), LKH, 4 Dec 1762: ov., from Alessandro nell'Indie, qt, 2 duets (lost), 5 arias (2 lost); CW ix
G26	273/5	La cascina, (pasticcio, Bottarelli), LKH, 8 Jan 1763: ov.; CW ix
G27	272/5	B. Galuppi and others: La calamita de' cuori, LKH, 3 Feb 1763: ov.; CW ix
G2/18	—	Catone in Utica (pasticcio), Turin, carn. 1763: qt, *La*
G1/9b, YG12	—	G.M. Rutini: Gli sposi in maschera, Florence, aut. 1763: 2 arias, *I-Fc*
G21, G1/3	—	J.A. Hasse, rev. Cafaro: L'Issipile, Naples, 26 Dec 1763: 2 arias, *P-La*
G Inc 7	244/1	Menalcas (pastoral, J. Harris), Salisbury, 22/24 Aug 1764: 3 arias 2 choruses; CW xxv

W	T	
G3/19, 22b	225/1; xliii	Ezio (pasticcio, after Metastasio), LKH, 24 Nov 1764: 2 arias from Alessandro nell'Indie; CW ix
G2/16	219/3; xli	Berenice (pasticcio), LKH, 1 Jan 1765: 3 arias (1 from Catone in Utica, others lost); CW ix
G43	245/3	The Maid of the Mill (pasticcio, I. Bickerstaffe), LCG, 31 Jan 1765: 1 aria, 1 duet; CW xxv
—	—	Zophilette (pasticcio, J.-F. Marmontel), Paris, 17 May 1765: 2 ariettes (music lost)
G44	246/1	The Summer's Tale (pasticcio, R. Cumberland), LCG, 6 Dec 1765: 2 arias, 1 duet; CW xxv
G6/20	—	Pharnaces, or The Revenge of Athridates (op, T. Hull), Dublin, Smock Alley, 12 Dec 1765: 1 aria; CW xxv
G2/3, 12; G3/ 18, 21	238/1; xlviii	Sifare (pasticcio), LKH, 5 March 1767: 4 arias; CW ix
G7/24, H24, H27	li	Tom Jones (pasticcio, J. Reed, after A. Poinsinet, after H. Fielding, LCG, 14 Jan 1769: 3 arias; CW xxv
G2/4	231/2	N. Piccinni: Le contadine bizzarre, LKH, 7 Nov 1769: 1 aria; CW ix
G28	231/3	L'olimpiade (pasticcio, after Metastasio), LKH, 11 Nov 1769: 1 aria; CW ix
G28	256/2	F. Tenducci and others: Amintas (op., R. Rolt), LCG, 15 Dec 1769: 1 aria; CW xxv
G29, LG1	234; xlvi	C.W. Gluck and P. Guglielmi: Orfeo ed Euridice, LKH, 7 April 1770: 6 arias (incl. 2 lost), 1 duet (lost), ballet music (lost), chorus (lost), CW ix; 3 arias, added 17 April 1770, ov. T346/8 added 30 April 1771, CW ix; rev. version, Naples, 4 Nov 1774, with new ov., 5 new arias, 5 choruses, ballets, CW xi; draft of discarded scena T251/5, D-Bsb*
LG2	245/2	The Flitch of Bacon (pasticcio, H. Bate), London, New Theatre, Haymarket, 17 Aug 1778: 1 aria; CW xxv
G45	—	The Genius of Nonesense (extravaganza, G. Colman), London, New Theatre, Haymarket, 2 Sept 1780: 1 aria, lost

Doubtful arias etc., incl. T250/5, 251/2–3, 252/1, 252/6–7, 253/2–5, 24 others, *A-Wgm, Wn; B-Bc; CH-A, E; D-Bsb, Dl, Hs, LEb, LÜh, Mbs, MÜu; DK-Kc; GB-Er; I-Gl, MC, Nc, MAav, Tf, Rc; S-Skma; US-AAu, BEm*

ORATORIOS, CANTATAS AND SERENATAS

W	T	
G Inc 6	244/6	Ode on the Auspicious Arrival and Nuptials of . . . Queen Charlotte (Thanks to the God who rules the deep) (J.Lockman), S, SAB, vn, bc; CW xxv
G11	—	Cant. a 3 voci . . . per festeggiare il felicissimo giorno natalizio di sua Maestà cattolica, S, S, T, SATB, orch, Naples, S Carlo, 20 Jan 1762; CW xiii

W	T	
G12	—	La Galatea (serenata, after Metastasio), 3vv, orch, London, Spring Gardens, 29 Feb 1764, music lost, lib in CW xlv
D1	226: xliv	Gioas, re di Giuda (orat., after Metastasio), London, King's, 22 March 1770; CW xvii
G41	243/1	Happy morn, auspicious rise! (? birthday ode for George III), S, S, A, T, SATB, SATB, orch [incl. arrs. from Gioas, re di Giuda]; CW xxv
G15	248/3	Endimione (serenata, after Metastasio), S, S, S, T, SATB, orch, London, King's, 6 April 1772; rev. Mannheim, Hof, 24 July 1773, with scene by N. Jommelli; CW xiv
G16	—	La tempesta (cant., Metastasio), S, orch, ? London, Hickford's Rooms, 17 May 1773, perf. Mannheim, c1776; CW xiii
G18	247/2	Amor vincitore (serenata), S, S, SATB, orch, London, King's, 15 April 1774; CW xv
G19	li	Cefalo e Procri (cant., ? G.G. Bottarelli), S, S, S, orch, London, Hanover Square Rooms, 26 April 1776; recit and aria pubd as Aurora: a Favourite Cantata. T248/1–2; CW xiii
G20	250/2	Rinaldo ed Armida (cant.), 3vv, orch, London, Hanover Square Rooms, 20 May 1778, lost except 1 recit and aria (c1785), A-Wn, B-Bc, D-Bsb, Mbs, F-Pn, GB-Lbl, I-PEsf, Vc
G38	—	Berenice che fai! (scena), S, orch, music lost, lib in CW xlv

OTHER VOCAL

chamber duets

W	T	
H4–11	—	[8] duetti (P. Metastasio), S, S, bc, ? before mid-1762: 1 Io lo so; 2 Trova un sol; 3 Che ciascun per te sospiri; 4 Chi mai di questo core; 5 Ascoltami, o Clori; 6 Lascia ch'io posso; 7 Parlami pur; 8 Eccomi alfin [nos. 3, 5, rev. as op.4 nos.5, 6; others different from opp. 4, 6]; CW xvi
H12–17	259/1	Sei canzonette (Metastasio), S, S, bc, op.4 (1765/R): 1 Già la notte; 2 Ah rammenta oh bella Irene; 3 Pur nel sonno almen talora; 4 T'intendo sí, mio core; 5 Che ciascun per te sospiri; 6 Ascoltami, o Clori; CW xvi
H18–23	260/2	Sei canzonette (Metastasio), S, S, bc, op.6 (1767): 1 Torna in quell'onda; 2 Io lo so; 3 E pur fra le tempeste; 4 Trova un sol; 5 Chi mai di questo core; 6 Se infida tu mi chiami; CW xvi

miscellaneous songs and arias

W	T	
G36a	—	Perchè sì ingrata, S, orch [another version of aria Cara ti lascio; cf G36b]; CW xlviii/3
G36b	—	Ah che gl'istessi numi . . . Cara ti lascio, S, orch [cf G36a]; CW xxi
H2	—	Der Weise auf dem Lande (O Wald! o Schatten grüner Gänge!), 16 April 1755, in Stammbuch of Friedrich Nicolai; CW xlviii/3
LG5	247/1	Infelice . . . Là nei regni, S, kbd 4 hands, pubd as A Favourite Scene and Rondo on the Duke of Nivernois Air (c1783); CW xvi, xlviii/3
H1	—	Mezendore (Herr Nicolaus Klimm erfand) (F. von Hagedorn), in F.W. Marpurg: Neue Lieder zum singen beym Clavier (Berlin, 1756); CW xlviii/3
G7/24	258/1	The London Lass (While Cecilia we admire), S, bc (c1772), based on Non è ver from Carattaco; CW xxv
G17	252/3	O Venere vezzosa (Horace, trans. G.G. Bottarelli), S, orch; CW xvi
LG4	251/1	Sentimi, non partir . . . Al mio bene (récit and rondo, after G. Roccaforte), S, pf, 2 vc, orch, as Rondeau . . . sung by Mr Tenducci at Messrs Bach and Abels Concert (1779); CW xvi
G35	—	Sventurata in van mi lagno, S, orch, after 1772; CW xvi

Doubtful: An Aeglen (Und fehlten dir der Schönheit holde Gaben (?Gemmingen) wYH1, in Oden mit Melodien, ii (Berlin, 1755); Farewell ye green fields, S/T, bc (Edinburgh, n.d.) [version of canzonette Ich schlief, da träumte mir], CW xxv; Ist das Leben nicht ein Traum?, D-LÜh; La sorte spietata T251/6, in B. Mengozzi: Méthode du chant du Conservatoire (Paris, 1803); Luci amate a voi non chiedo wYG15 (1777), CW xxv; Neptune (When an angry woman's breast) T256/3, S/T, bc (c1762), CW xxv; [9] Solfeggi . . . del Sig. Giovanni Bach in Genova wYH7–15, S, bc, I-Gl; So oft ich meine Tobacks-Pfeife, D-Bsb; The World (When launched into life) (J.M. Perrin), S/T, orch (n.d.), CW xxv

music for Vauxhall Gardens

W	T	
H24–7	254/1	A Collection of Favourite Songs sung at Vaux Hall by Mrs Weichsell (1766/R), S, orch: 1 By my sighs; 2 Cruel Strephon; 3 Come Colin; 4 Ah why shou'd love; CW xxv
H28–31	254/5	A Second Collection of Favourite Songs sung at Vaux Hall by Mrs Pinto and Mrs Weichsell (1767/R), S, orch: 1 In this shady blest retreat; 2 Smiling Venus; 3 Tender virgins [arr. from Non è ver from Carattico, rev. as Blest with thee in Tom Jones (pasticcio, 1769)]; Lovely yet ungratefull swain; CW xxv
H32	—	When chilling winter hies away, S, orch, music lost, text pubd (1768)

W	T	
H33–6	255/2	A Third Collection of Favorite Songs sung at Vaux Hall by Miss Cowper (1771/R), S, orch: 1 Midst silent shades; 2 Ah seek to know; 3 Would you a female heart inspire; 4 Cease a while; CW xxv
H38–9	—	A Fourth Collection of Favorite Songs sung at Vauxhall Gardens (1779/R): 1 Oh how blest; 2 Hither turn thy wand'ring eyes; CW xxv
H40	—	Ode to Pleasure, S, S, S, T, chorus, orch, music lost, text in *A Genuine Collection* (London, 1766)
H41	—	Ode to Summer, 4 solo vv, chorus, orch, music lost, text in *A Genuine Collection* (London, 1766)
H42	—	The Pastoral Invitation (Ye nymphs and swains), S, S, T, orch, music lost, text in *Westminster Journal*, 2 July 1768; CW xxv (text only)
H37	257/2	See the kind indulgent gales: a Favourite Song sung by Mrs Weichsell at Vaux Hall Gardens (1777/R), S, orch [Eng. rev. of Se spiegò from Zanaida]; CW xxv

folksong settings

W	T	
LH1	—	Braes of Ballanden (Beneath a green shade) (T. Blacklock), A, ob, vn, va, vc, kbd (1779); CW xxv
LH2	257/3	The Broom of Cowdenknows (How blyth was I each morn), A, 2 fl, 2 vn, bc (c1784); CW xxv
LH3	—	I'll never leave thee (One day I heard Mary say) (R. Crawford), A, 2 fl, 2 vn, bc (c1784); CW xxv
LH4	256	Lochaber (Farewell to Lochaber) (A. Ramsay), A, 2 fl, 2 vn, bc (c1785); CW xxv
LH5	—	The Yellow-Hair'd Laddie, lost, attrib. Bach in S. Storace: Gli equivoci, 1786, A-Wn; arr. in last movt of pf conc. op.13 no.4

transcriptions

W	T	
LG2	250/2	Ebben si vada . . . Io ti lascio (after P. Metastasio), acc. recit and rondo, S, pf, orch, pubd as The Favourite Rondeau sung by Mr Tenducci (c1778); ? from cant. Rinaldo ed Armida; expanded version of Ombra felice . . . Io ti lascio from M. Mortellari: Arsace, 1775; another version, No 'twas neither shape nor feature, in A Flitch of Bacon (1778, London); CW xvi
LG3	251/7	Mi scordo i torti miei . . . Dolce aurette, S, orch, c1778, recit and aria from G. Gazzaniga: Perseo ed Andromeda with new coda by Bach, *D-Bsb*, *WRgs*; CW xvi

W	T	
—	253/6	Wenn nach der Stürme, aria, S, bc, in J.A. Hiller: Deutsche Arien und Duette (Leipzig, 1785), based on Allor che il vincitore from La clemenza di Scipione

SYMPHONIES AND OVERTURES

for 2 oboes, 2 horns and strings unless otherwise stated

W	T	
G4, 27, 1, 24, 26, 25	272/2	Six Favourite Overtures (1763): ovs. to the operas: 1 Orione (D), 2 ob, 2 hn, 2 bn, str; 2 La calamita de' cuori (D); 3 Artaserse (D); 4 Il tutore e la pupilla (C); 5 La cascina (G); 6 Astarto (= Alessandro nell'Indie) (G); no.2 in VI sinfonie a più stromenti composte da vari autori op.13 (Paris, 1762); no.3 in VI sinfonie a più stromenti composte da vari autori op.12 (Paris, 1761); arr. kbd (1763)
G23B	277/4	The Periodical Overture no.1 (D) (1763): ov. to Gli uccellatori
C1–6	262/1	Six simphonies (D, C, E♭, B♭, F, G), 2 ob/fl, 2 hn, str, op.3 (1765), =w C1a–6a, CW xxvi; arr. Bach as Six Overtures Composed and Adapted for the Harpsichord (c1769), =wC1b–6b, T347/2, CW xlii
G22B	275/3	An Overture in 8 parts (D) (1766); corrected version of Periodical Overture no.xv (1766): ov. to La Giulia
C16a	276/3	Symphony (C), as no.46 in Sinfonie a più stromenti composte da vari autori (Paris, 1770/71), CW xxvii; with different 2nd and 3rd movts wC16b, CW xxix
C7–12	264/1	Six simphonies (G, D, E♭, B♭, E♭, g), 2 ob/fl, 2 hn, str, op.6 (Amsterdam, 1770); nos.3–5 in Six simphonies périodiques op.8 nos.1, 5, 6; CW xxvi–xxvii
C9, 13–15, 10–11	266/5	Six simphonies périodiques (E♭, G, D, F, B♭, E♭), 2 ob/fl, 2 hn, str, op.8 (Amsterdam, c1775); nos.1, 5, 6 = op.6 nos.3–5; CW xxvi–xxvii
C17–19	268/3	Trois simphonies (B♭, E♭, B♭), 2 ob/fl, 2 hn, str, op.9 (The Hague, 1773) [also as op.21]; no.1, 2 cl, 2 bn, 2 hn, str, in Six sinfoni . . . par J.C. Bach, Toesky et Stamitz (Paris, 1773); no.2 with addl movt (Paris, ?1776); 2 movts from no.2 arr. kbd in J.A. Hiller: Sammlung kleiner Clavier- und Singstücke (Leipzig, 1774), ed. S. Staral (Graz, 1981); no.1 ed. in EDM, 1st ser., xxx (1956); CW xxvii (nos.1 and 2), iv (no.3)

W	T	
C26, G9, G15, C27, C28, XC1	269/4	Six Grand Overtures (Eb, Bb, D, D, E, D), 2 fl, 2 ob, 2 cl, 2 bn, 2 hn, 2 tpt, timp, str, op.18 (*c*1782); nos.1, 3, 5 for double orch (2 ob, bn, 2 hn, str; 2 fl, str); no.1, *I-Gl* [dated 1779]; no.2 = ov. to Lucio Silla; no.3 = ov. to Endimione; no.4 = no.2 of T271/6, Deux sinfonies op.18, 2nd movt of no.4 = arr. of 2nd movt of ov. to Temistocle; no.6 arr. from Amadis de Gaule; CW xxviii
XC2, C27	271/6	Deux sinfonies à grand orchestre (D, D), 2 fl, 2 ob, 2 bn, 2 hn, str, op.18 (Amsterdam, *c*1785); 1st movt of no.1 = ov. to La clemenza di Scipione, 2nd movt = Andante from ov. to Amadis de Gaule; no.2 = no.4 of T269/4, Six Grand Overtures op.18; CW xxviii
G27*a*	—	Sym. (D) (inc., = ov. to La calamita de' cuori with different finale), CW xxix; Sym. (D), 2 ob/fl, 2 hn, str, CW xxix
G27*b*	—	Sym. (D), 2 ob/fl, 2 hn, str, CW xxix
—	279/4	Sym. (F), CW xxix
C Inc 4	279/7	Sym. (F), 2 ob, 2 hn/tpt, str, *CH-A*, *Bu*, E, *I-MAav*; CW xxix
C Inc 3	282/5	Sym. (Eb), as Divertimento notturno (Paris, before 1775); CW xxvii
C84	361/7	Menuett (F), for Her Majesty's birthday, 1767; CW xxv
C85	361/8	Menuett (C), for Her Majesty's birthday, 1769; CW xxv

Lost, listed in *Verzeichniss des musikalischen Nachlasses . . . Carl Philipp Emanuel Bach* (Hamburg, 1790): Sym. in 6 pts, before 1755; ov. in 6 pts, before 1755
for doubtful and misattributed works see wYC1–83

SYMPHONIES CONCERTANTES

instruments listed as concertante; ripieno

W	T	
C32	284/1	Sinfonia concertante (G), 2 vn, vc; 2 fl, 2 hn, str, ?*c*1760 (Paris, by 1772); CW xxx
C33	284/6	Concert ou symphonie (Eb). 2 vn, ob; 2 fl, cl, bn, 2 hn, str (Paris, 1773); CW xxx [also as pf conc., wC75, T300/8]
C34	284/4	Simphonie concertante (A), vn, vc; 2 ob, 2 hn, str (Paris, by 1775); CW xxx
C36*a*	286/1	Sym. conc. (C), 2 vn, vc; 2 fl, 2 ob, 2 hn, str, CW xlviii/3; rev. version w C36*b*, CW xxx
C45	286/4	Sym. conc. (G), ob, vn, va, vc; 2 fl, 2 hn, str
C Inc 5	—	Sym. conc. (G), fl, 2 vn, vc; fl, 2 hn, str, doubtful; CW xxx
C44	286/8	Sym. conc. (E), fl, 2 vn, vc; 2 ob, 2 hn, str, by 1775; CW xxx
C38	287/2	Sym. conc. (F), ob, bn/vc; ob, 2 hn, str; CW xxx
C46	287/7	Sym. conc. (Bb), vc; 2 cl, bn, 2 hn, str; CW xlviii/3 formerly *D-Bsb* (see White, 1958)
C42	288/4	Sym. conc. (Eb), 2 vn, vc; 2 ob, 2 hn, str; CW xxx [also as bn conc., wC82, T288/4]
C40	288/7	Notturno (Eb), 2 ob, 2 hn/tpt, 2 vn, 2 va, vc; str; CW xxxi
C43	289/4	Sym. conc. (C), fl, ob, vn, vc; 2 fl, 2 cl, 2 bn, 2 hn, str; CW xxxi
C48	289/7	Sym. conc. (Bb), ob, vn, vc, pf; 2 fl, 2 hn, str; CW xxxi
C39	290/2	Sym. conc. (D), 2 fl, 2 vn, vc; 2 hn, str, *c*1760; CW xxxi
C37	290/4	Sym. conc. (Eb), fl, ob, bn; ob, 2 hn, str; CW xxxi
C41	290/9	Sym. conc. (Eb), fl, 2 cl, bn, 2 hn; 1/2 fl, str; CW xxxi
C35	—	Concerto a più istrumenti (D), 2 vn; 2 ob/fl, 2 hn, str, ?doubtful; CW xxx
YC95	—	Sym. (Bb), vn, vc (ad lib); 2 ob (ad lib), 2 hn, str, *I-MAav*, attrib. J.C. Bach in Breitkopf suppl. 1767, doubtful; probably by F.P. Ricci, op.9 no.2 (The Hague, London and Paris, *c*1775)

CONCERTOS

W	T	
C74	—	Conc., hpd, before 1755, lost, listed in *Verzeichniss des musikalischen Nachlasses . . . Carl Philipp Emanuel Bach* (Hamburg, 1790)
C68–72	298/1	5 concs. (Bb, f, d, E, G), kbd, str; CW xxxii
C73	301/4	Conc. (f), hpd, str, CW xxxii
C77	—	Conc, vc, before 1755, lost, listed in *Verzeichniss des musikalischen Nachlasses . . . Carl Philipp Emanuel Bach* (Hamburg, 1790)
C49–54	292/1	Six Concertos (Bb, A, F, G, C, D), hpd, str, op.1 (1763); CW xxxiii
C79	286/7	Conc. (D), fl, 2 hn, str; CW xxxvi
C55–60	293/4	Sei concerti (C, F, D, Bb, Eb, G), hpd/pf, str, op.7 (1770); CW xxxiii–xxxiv [cadenzas for no.5 and expanded solo pt of no.6, private collection, USA]
C62–7	295/1	A Third Sett of Six Concertos (C, D, F, Bb, G, Eb), hpd/pf, str (2 ob, 2 hn ad lib), op.13 (1777); CW xxxv
C75	300/8	Conc. (Eb), kbd, 2 fl, 2 cl, bn, 2 hn, str; CW xxxiv [also as sym. conc., wC42 T284/6]
C61	301/1	Conc. (Eb), hpd/pf, str (2 hn ad lib), as op.14 no.1 (Paris, *c*1776); CW xxxiv
C80	287/4	Conc. (F), ob, 2 hn, str; CW xxxvi [also as fl conc. (G)wC78, private collection, USA]
C81	290/7	Conc. (F), ob, 2 hn, str; CW xxxvi
C83	288/1	Conc., (Bb), bn, 2 ob, 2 hn, str; CW xxxvi
C82	288/4	Conc., (Eb), bn, 2 ob, 2 hn, str; CW xxxvi [also as sym. conc., wC42 T288/4]
C76	—	Conc. (C), vn, 2 ob/fl, 2 hn, str; CW xlviii/3

W	T	
		doubtful
YC90–91	297/1	[2] Concerto (E♭, A), hpd, str (Riga, *c*1776), attrib. 'I.C. Bach', Breitkopf suppl. 1776–7, also attrib. C.P.E. Bach and J.C.F. Bach; no.1 ed. E. Praetorius (1937), no.2 ed. in Antiqua (1935)
YC92	300/1	Conc. (A), hpd, str, *Bsb* [? by C.P.E. Bach; also attrib. Schaffrath and C.H. or J.G. Graun]; ed. A. Hoffmann (Wolfenbüttel, 1963)
C Inc 6	300/4	Conc. (E), hpd, str, *Dl*

WIND MUSIC

see Sadie for information on borrowed material and transcriptions

W	T	
B Inc 7–12	285/3	Sei sinfonie (E♭, B♭, E♭, B♭, E♭, B♭), 2 cl, 2 hn, [2] bn (1782); CW xxxvii
B79–82	—	Military Pieces [Quintette] (E♭, E♭, B♭, B♭), 2 cl, 2 hn, bn (Dublin, *c*1794); CW xxxvii
B83–5	359/3	3 military marches: Marche du régiment de Prince Ernst; Marche du régiment de Braun[schweig]; Marche du régiment de Wür[tte]mb[erg], all in E♭, 2 ob, 2 hn, bn; CW xxxvii [nos.2–3 arr. kbd, *GB-Lbl* (part autograph)]
B88–9	360/1	2 Märsche . . . vom ersten . . . zweiten Batallion Garde-Regiment in Hannover (E♭, E♭) 2 ob, 2 cl, 2 hn, 2 bn, no.2 spurious, by Abel, *Lbl* (part autograph); CW xxxvii
B86–7	360/5	Due marce . . . di cavalleria e d'infanteria (E♭, E♭), 2 ob, 2 cl, 2 hn, bn; CW xxxvii [also arr. kbd, *Lbl* (part autograph)]
B90–93	361/2	4 marches (E♭, E♭, E♭, B♭); CW xxxvii [also arr. kbd, *Lbl* (part autograph)
YB85–6	360/3	Due marce . . . Prince Walles (E♭, E♭), 2 cl, 2 hn, bn; spurious, by C.F. Abel

CHAMBER MUSIC

W	T	
B78	302/1	Sestetto (C), ob, 2 hn, vn, vc, kbd; CW xli [arr. kbd, vn in Three Favorite Quartetts and One Quintett (1785), = T311/3]
B Inc 5	305/1	Quintet (B♭), 2 vn/ob, va, vc/bn, bc; CW xli
B70–75	303/1	Six Quintettos (C, G, F, E♭, A, D), fl, ob, vn, va, bc, op.11 (1774); CW xli
B76–7	304/6	Deux quintetts (D, F), op.22 (1785), fl, ob, vn, vc, kbd; CW xli [arr. kbd, vn in Three Favorite Quartetts and One Quintett (1785) = T311/2, 4]
B51–6	306/1	Six Quartettos (C, D, E♭, F, G, B♭), fl, vn, va, vc, op.8 (1772); CW xl
B57–9	309/1	3 qts (D, C, A), fl/vn, vn, va, bc, nos.1, 3, 5 in Six Quartettos . . . by Messrs Bach, Abel and Giardini (1776); CW xl

W	T	
B60	—	Qt (B♭), 2 vn, va, vc, no.1 in Six Quatuors . . . par J.C. Bach et C.F. Abel, op.14 (Paris, 1776); CW xl [also arr. eng hn, vn, va, vc, *I-Gl*; erroneously attrib. Haydn, HII:B4]
B66	310/9	Quartetto (G), vn, 2 vc, hpd, op.2 (Offenbach, 1783); CW xl [arr. hpd, vn in Three Favorite Quartetts and One Quintett (1785) = T311/5]
B61–4	307/4	Four Quartettos (C, D, G, C), op.19 (1784): nos. 1, 3, for 2 fl, va, vc; no.2 for fl, ob/fl, va, vc; no.4 for 2 fl, vn; CW xl [arr. hpd/pf, vn, fl, vc (*c*1787)]
B30–35	314/5	Six Trios (B♭, A, E♭, G, D, C), 2 vn, va/bc, op.2 (1763), also as op.4 (Amsterdam, 1767), in Breitkopf suppl. 1766 as first 6 of set of 12 (see also T317/5); CW xxxix
B36–41	317/5	6 trios (G, D, E, F, B♭, E♭), 2 vn, bc, in Breitkopf suppl. 1766 as second 6 of set of 12 (see also T314/5); CW xxxix
B43–8	313/1	Six sonates (F, G, D, C, D, E♭), hpd, vn/fl, vc, op.2 (1764); CW xxxix
B42	311/6	Sonata (B♭), 2 vn, vc, no.1 in Six Sonatas . . . by Messrs Bach, Abel and Kammel (1777); CW xxxix
B49–50	323/5	2 sonatas (C, A), hpd/pf, vn, vc, nos.1–2 in Four Sonatas and Two Duetts op.15 (1778); CW xxxix
B Inc 3	330/5	Sonata (B♭), harp, (vn, vc)/hpd, no.6 in Musical Remains, ed. E. Jones (*c*1796) [1st movt based on 1st movt of wB78; CW xxxix
B Inc 2	317/7	Trio sonata (G), 2 fl/vn, bc; CW xxxix
B20–26	332/4	[7] sonatas (F, D, G, A, G, D, F), hpd, vn; CW xxxviii
B27	—	Sonata (A), hpd, vn; CW xxxviii
B2–7	322/1	Six Sonatas (B♭, C, G, A, F, D), hpd/pf, vn, op.10 (1773), also for 2 vn, va, bc, op.17 (Paris, *c*1779); CW xxxviii [nos.1, 3, 5 arr. kbd, va da gamba, private collection, USA]
B8–9	324/2	2 sonatas (D, B♭), hpd/pf, vn, nos.3–4 in Four Sonatas and Two Duetts op.15 (1778); CW xxxviii
B10–15	325/1	Six Sonatas (D, G, C, A, D, F), hpd/pf, vn/fl, op.16 (1779/R); CW xxxviii [other versions of no.6, private collection, USA, and CW xlviii/3]
B16–19	326/3	4 sonatas (C, D, E♭, G), hpd/pf, vn/fl, nos.1–4 in Four Sonatas and Two Duetts op.18 (*c*1781); CW xxxviii
—	—	Sonata (F), hpd, va da gamba, private collection, USA [1st movt from op.10 no.5, 2nd movt from ob conc. wB80, T287/2]

Doubtful: 4 canzonette (F, E♭, G, B♭), 2 vn, T336/6, arr. of Sei canzonette op.6 nos.1, 4, 3, 2; 2 qts (F, C), fl/vn, va, vc, in L'anné musicale (Liège, 1776); Qt (F), fl/vn, va, vc *I-Rdp*; 2 qt (F, D), fl/vn, vn, va, vc, *Gl*; Sonata (C), gui, vn (*c*1770), CW xxxviii; Six Sonatas (C, G, D, A, E♭, B♭), hpd/pf, vn/fl, op.19 (1783), T327/5; Three [= 6] Sonatas [i, ii] (C, D, F, G, A, B♭), hpd/pf, vn, op.20 (*c*1785), T329/1; Trois sonates (E♭, B♭, D), hpd/pf, vn, op.21 (Paris, *c*1784), T344/2; Sonata (F), hpd, fl, *D-Bsb* (2 copies: 1 attrib J.C. Bach, 1 attrib. C.P.E. Bach), *US-Wc* (attrib. 'Sigr. Bach'), also attrib. W.F. Bach, ed. K. Marguerre (Celle, 1960), T332/1; Sonata (D), vn, bc, *D-Bsb*, ?lost, T3323/5; 3 sonatas (D, G, C), fl, vn, *A-Wn*, T337/1; Sonata (C), hpd/of, vn, in The Feast of Apollo (1788), T352/2; Trio sonata (F), 2 vn, bc, lost, formerly *D-Bsb*, T318/8; for others see wYB1–86

KEYBOARD

for harpsichord unless otherwise stated

W	T	
A22	—	Untitled piece [March]BWVAnh.131, in Clavierbüchlein for Anna Magdalena Bach; CW xlviii/3
A23–31	—	6 minuets (c, C, d, g, C, C), 2 polonaises (B♭, E♭), aria (a), *c*1750; CW xlii
A13	358/4	Solo (a), ? before 1755; CW xlii
A14	—	Sonata (A♭), *I-Bc*, *Mc*, *MC*; CW xlii
A16	—	Sonata (B♭); *Bc*; CW xlii
A15	—	Toccata (b♭), *Bc*, *Mc*, *MC* (as Sonata); CW xlii, xlviii/3 (2 versions)
A1–6	338/1	Six Sonatas (B♭, D, G, E♭, E, c), hpd/pf, op.5 (1766/R); CW xlii
C1*b*–6*b*	347/2	Six simphonies (D, C, E♭, B♭, F, G), op.3 (1769); CW xlii [see 'Symphonies and overtures']
A10*b*	—	A New Lesson (G), hpd/pf (1772) [early versions of movts from op.17 nos.4 and 1]
A21, 18	340/5	2 duets (G, C): 1 for 2 hpd/pf, 1 for hpd/pf 4 hands, in Four Sonatas and Two Duetts op.15 (1778); CW xlii
A7–12	341/1	Six Sonatas (G, c, E♭, G, A, B♭), hpd/pf, op.17 (1779/R), previously pubd as op.12 (Paris, 1773/4); CW xlii; other versions of nos.2–3, CW xlviii/3; see also A New Lesson, above
A19–20	343/3	2 duets (A, F), hpd/pf 4 hands, in Four Sonatas and Two Duetts op.18 (1781); CW xlii
—	—	2 marches (A, C), *GB-Lbl* (part autograph)

For doubtful works see wYA1–54

BIBLIOGRAPHY

BrookB; BurneyH; DNB (S.W. Roe); *EitnerQ; FiskeETM; FétisB; GerberNL; LS; MGG1* (H. Wirth); *WalterG*

The Lyric Muse Revived in Europe (London, 1768)

G.J. Vogler: *Betrachtungen der Mannheimer Tonschule* (Mannheim, 1778–81/R)

ABC Dario Musico (Bath, 1780)

C.F. Cramer, ed.: *Magazin der Musik* (Hamburg, 1783–6/R)

H. Angelo: *Reminiscences of Henry Angelo* (London, 1828–30)

Earl of Mount Edgcumbe: *Musical Reminiscences of an Old Amateur* (London, 1824, 4/1834/R)

[T. MacKinley]: *Mrs Cornely's Entertainments at Carlisle House, Soho Square* (Bradford, *c*1840)

Mrs V.D. Broughton, ed.: *Court and Private Life in the Time of Queen Charlotte: being the Journals of Mrs. Papendiek* (London, 1887)

M. Schwarz: *Johann Christian Bach (1735–82): sein Leben und seine Werke* (Leipzig, 1901)

M. Schwarz: 'Johann Christian Bach', *SIMG*, ii (1900–01), 401–54

M. Brenet: 'Un fils du grand Bach à Paris en 1779–1779', *Guide musical*, xlviii (1902), 551–3, 571–3

H. Abert: 'Joh. Christian Bachs italienische Opern und ihr Einfluss auf Mozart', *ZMw*, i (1919), 313–28

G. de Saint-Foix: 'A propos de Jean-Chrétien Bach', *RdM*, vii (1926), 83–91

H.P. Schökel: *Johann Christian Bach und die Instrumentalmusik seiner Zeit* (Wolfenbüttel, 1926)

F. Tutenberg: *Die Sinfonik Johann Christian Bachs* (Wolfenbüttel, 1928)

C.S. Terry: *John Christian Bach* (London, 1929 [review by H. Miesner in *ZMw*, xvi (1934), 182]; rev. 2/1967/R by H.C.R. Landon [review by S. Sadie in *MT*, cviii (1967), 330–31]

A. Wenk: *Beiträge zur Kenntnis des Opernschaffens von J. Christian Bach* (diss., U. of Frankfurt, 1932)

C. Sartori: 'A Milano J.C. Bach in disaccordo con il tesoriere', *La Scala*, no.2 (1950), 29–31

S. Sadie: 'The Wind Music of J.C. Bach', *ML*, xxxvii (1956), 107–17

R. Seebandt: *Arientypen Johann Christian Bachs* (diss., Humboldt U., Berlin, 1956)

E.O.D. Downes: *The Operas of Johann Christian Bach as a Reflection of the Dominant Trends in Opera Seria 1750–1780* (diss., Harvard U., 1958)

J.A. White: *The Concerted Symphonies of John Christian Bach* (diss., U. of Michigan, 1958) [incl. edns of 3 concerted syms.]

E.J. Simon: 'A Royal Manuscript: Ensemble Concertos by J.C. Bach', *JAMS*, xii (1959), 161–77

C.B. Oldman: 'Mozart's Scena for Tenducci', *ML*, xlii (1961), 44–52

H.-J. Schulze: 'Frühe Schriftzeugnisse der beiden jüngsten Bach-Söhne', *BJb* 1963–4, 61–9

S. Kunze: 'Die Vertonungen der Arie "Non sò d'onde viene" von J. Chr. Bach und von W.A. Mozart', *AnMc*, no.2 (1965), 85–111

E. Warburton: 'J.C. Bach's Operas', *PRMA*, xcii (1965–6), 95–106

A. Weinmann: 'Eine "Arie von Bach" für die Storace', *ÖMz*, xxi (1966), 53–61

B. Matthews: 'J.C. Bach in the West Country', *MT*, cviii (1967), 702–4

B.A. Mekota: *The Solo and Ensemble Keyboard Works of Johann Christian Bach* (diss., U. of Michigan, 1969)

M.A.H. Vos: *The Liturgical Choral Works of Johann Christian Bach* (diss., Washington U., 1969)

E. Warburton: *A Study of Johann Christian Bach's Operas* (diss., U. of Oxford, 1969)

P.M. Young: *The Bachs 1500–1850* (London, 1970)

N. Krabbe: 'J.C. Bach's Symphonies and the Breitkopf Thematic Catalogue', *Festskrift Jens Peter Larsen*, ed. N. Schiørring, H. Glahn and C.E. Hatting (Copenhagen, 1972), 233–54

I.S. Baierle: *Die Klavierwerke von Johann Christian Bach* (Graz, 1974)

J. Bolen: *The Five Berlin Cembalo Concertos P390 of Johann Christian Bach: a Critical Edition* (diss., Florida State U., 1974)

B. Matthews: 'The Davies Sisters, J.C. Bach and the Glass Harmonica', *ML*, lvi (1975), 150–69

H.-J. Schulze: 'Die Bach-Überlieferung: Plädoyer für ein notwendiges Buch', *BMw*, xvii (1975), 45–57, esp. 48

H. Brofsky: 'J.C. Bach, G.B. Sammartini, and Padre Martini: a Concorso in Milan in 1762', *A Musical Offering: Essays in Honor of Martin Bernstein*, ed. E.H. Clinkscale and C. Brook (New York, 1977), 63–8

D.J. Keahey: *The Genoa Manuscripts: Recently Rediscovered Trios of J.C. Bach* (diss., U. of Texas at Austin, 1977)

F.C. Petty: *Italian Opera in London 1760–1800* (Ann Arbor, 1980)

D. McCulloch: 'Mrs Papendiek and the London Bach', *MT*, cxxiii (1982), 26–9

R. Maunder: 'J.C. Bach's "Endimione"', ibid., 474–5

S.W. Roe: 'J.C. Bach (1735–1782): Towards a New Biography', ibid., 23–6

E. Warburton: 'J.C. Bach's Latin Church Music', ibid., 781–4

S.W. Roe: 'J.C. Bach's Vauxhall Songs: a New Discovery', *MT*, cxxiv (1983), 675–6

H.-J. Schulze: 'Wann begann die "italienische Reise" des jüngsten Bach-Sohnes?', *BJb* 1983, 119–22

R. Maunder: 'J.C. Bach and the Basset Horn', *GSJ*, xxxvii (1984), 42–7

J. Small: 'J.C. Bach Goes to Law', *MT*, cxxvi (1985), 526–9

S.W. Roe: 'J.C. Bach and "new Music, at a more Reasonable Expence"', ibid., 529–31

E. Warburton: '"Lucio Silla": by Mozart and J.C. Bach', ibid., 726–30

S. Staral: 'Aufführungspraktische Aspekte im Klavierwerk von Johann Christian Bach, dargestellt an den Sonaten Op.V', Mf, ix (1986), 245–53

H.-J. Schulze: 'Noch einmal: Wann begann "die italienische Reise" des jüngsten Bach-Sohnes?', BJb 1988, 235–6

J.R. Stevens: 'Concerto no.6 in F minor: by Johann Christian Bach?', RMARC, no.21 (1988), 53–6

S.W. Roe: The Keyboard Music of J.C. Bach (New York, 1989)

H. Gärtner: Johann Christian Bach, Mozarts Freund und Lehrmeister (Munich, 1989; Eng. trans., 1994)

C. Esch: 'Lucio Silla': vier Opera-seria-Vertonungen aus der Zeit zwischen 1770 und 1780 (diss., U. of Göttingen, 1991)

L. Finscher, ed.: Die Mannheimer Hofkapelle im Zeitalter Carl Theodors (Mannheim, 1991)

R. Maunder: 'J.C. Bach and the Early Piano in London', JRMA, cxvi (1991), 201–10

S. Staral: 'Wolfgang Amadé Mozart, Johann Christian Bach und Mannheim', 176 Tage W.A. Mozarts in Mannheim, ed. K. von Welck and L. Homering (Mannheim, 1991), 164–73 [exhibition catalogue]

C. Esch: 'Michele Mortellari, Johann Christian Bach', MISM, xxxviii (1991), 133–58

M. Sickbert: 'The Mozarts in Milan, February 9–10, 1770: a Funeral Performance of Johann Christian Bach's Dies Irae and Vespers Music?', MJb 1991, 461–7

M. Feldman: 'Mozart and his Elders: Opera-Seria Arias, 1766–1775', ibid., 564–75

K.-J. Sachs: 'Impuls und Ingenium: der Kopfsatz aus Mozarts Haffner-Sinfoni KV 385 vor dem Hintergrund von Johann Christian Bachs "Grand Ouverture" Es-Dur op.19/1', ibid., 844–51

R. Allorto: Gli anni milanesi di Giovanni Cristiano Bach e le sue composizioni sacre (Milan, 1992)

E. Warburton: 'Johann Christian Bach und die Freimaurer-Loge zu den Neun Musen in London', BJb 1992, 113–17

C. Price, J.Milhous and R. Hume: The Impresario's Ten Commandments (London, 1992)

M. Argent, ed.: Recollections of R.J.S. Stevens, an Organist in Georgian London (London, 1992)

U. Leisinger: Die Bach-Quellen der Forschungs- und Landesbibliothek (Gotha, 1993)

S.W. Roe: 'Johann Christian Bach', The Viking Opera Guide, ed. A. Holden (London, 1993), 43–6

D.E. Freeman: 'Johann Christian Bach and the Early Classical Italian Masters', Eighteenth-Century Keyboard Music, ed. R.L. Marshall (New York, 1994), 230–69

C. Price, J.Milhous and E. Hume: Italian Opera in Late Eighteenth-Century London, i: The King's Theatre, Haymarket, 1778–1791 (Oxford, 1995)

Y. Kobayashi: 'Breitkopf Attributions and Research on the Bach Family', J.S. Bach, the Breitkopfs and the Eighteenth-Century Music Trade, Bach Perspectives, ii, ed. G.B. Stauffer (Lincoln, NE, and London, 1996), 53–64

Y. Kobayashi: 'On the Identification of Breitkopf's Manuscripts', ibid., 107–22

R. Charteris: 'The Music Collections of the Staats- und Universitätsbibliothek, Hamburg: a Survey of its British Holdings Prior to the Second World War', RMARC, no.30 (1997), 1–138

C. Eisen: 'The Mozarts' Salzburg Library', Mozart Studies 2 (Oxford, 1997), 85–138

U. Leisinger: '"Berlinischer Oden und Lieder" von Bückeburger, Londoner und Hallischen Bach', JbSIM 1997, 117–21

U. Leisinger and P.Wollny: Die Bach-Quellen der Bibliotheken in Brüssel(Hildesheim, 1997)

B. Robins, ed.: The John Marsh Journals: the Life and Times of a Gentleman Composer (1752–1828) (Stuyvesant, NY, 1998)

S.W. Roe: 'The Sextet in C Major, by J.C. or J.C.F. Bach?', Haydn, Mozart and Beethoven: Studies in the Music of the Classical Period: Essays in Honour of Alan Tyson, ed. S. Brandenburg (Oxford, 1998), 13–19

S.W. Roe: 'Neuerkenntnisse zu einigen autographen Notenhandschriften von Johann Christian Bach', BJb 1999, 179–90

S.W. Roe: 'The Paris Bach' Bunte Blätter: Klaus Mecklenburg zum 23. Februar 2000, ed. R. Elvers and A. Moirandat, (Basle, 2000), 247–54

(13) Johann Michael Bach (b Struth, nr Schmalkalden, 9 Nov 1745; d Elberfeld, 1820). Composer. He was descended from a Hessian line of Bachs that can be traced back to a Caspar Bach (d Struth, c1640) and already had many branches in the 17th century. It is probable, but cannot be proved, that this line was originally connected with the main Wechmar line of the Bach family. Johann Michael evidently went on his travels at an early date, and in about 1767 visited Holland, where he was in touch with the Amsterdam music publisher Hummel; he then went to England and America. On his return he studied law in 1779–80 at the University of Göttingen, where he met J.N. Forkel, and from 1781 at Leipzig University. He was practising as a lawyer in Güstrow, Mecklenburg, in 1790 but composed music at the same time, and in 1793 (or earlier) he was appointed Kantor and organist in Tann. He was then active as a music theorist and composer in Elberfeld, and when he died there he was employed as a music teacher at the Gymnasium.

As well as an early set of piano concertos (the finale of no.6 is a fugue on B–A–C–H), Johann Michael Bach published a treatise in 1780 which had a surprisingly wide distribution in its time. His musical style is reminiscent of that of Johann Christoph Friedrich Bach (49) and rather derivative. Two of his sons were also musicians, Johann Georg and Georg Friedrich (see §I above).

WORKS

6 Klavierkonzerte, C, G, D, F, D, B♭, op.1 (Amsterdam, 1767)
Cants.: Gott fähret auf mit Jauchzen, D-Bsb; Jehova, Vater der Weisen, Bsb; others GOl
Jauchzet dem Herren, motet, GOl
Kurze und systematische Anleitung zum General-Bass und der Tonkunst überhaupt (Kassel, 1780)

BIBLIOGRAPHY

H. Lämmerhirt: 'Ein hessischer Bach-Stamm', BJb 1936, 53–89
H.-J. Schulze and C.Wolff: Bach Repertorium (forthcoming)

(14) Wilhelm Friedrich Ernst Bach (84) (b Bückeburg, 24 May 1759; d Berlin, 25 Dec 1845). Keyboard player and composer, son of (11) Johann Christoph Friedrich Bach. He was baptized on 27 May, with Count Wilhelm von Schaumburg-Lippe standing godfather. W.F.E. Bach was musically educated by his father and Christian Friedrich Geyer, Kantor of the Stadtkirche, Bückeburg. In 1778 he went with his father to London and remained there in the care of his uncle (12) J.C. Bach, making a name for himself as a pianist and keyboard teacher. He appeared at one of the Bach-Abel concerts in Hanover Square as early as 6 December 1778, playing a sonata of his own, and his first keyboard and chamber works were published by leading English firms. Some time after the death of his uncle on 1 January 1782, W.F.E. Bach returned to Germany. His route took him through Paris and the Netherlands, where he met the publisher J.J. Hummel in Amsterdam, and then to north Germany, where he gave concerts in Oldenburg and elsewhere. According to his own account, he stayed for some time with his uncle (9) C.P.E. Bach in Hamburg before settling in 1784 in Minden, near Bückeburg. He seems to have given himself the title of Musikdirektor, since there is no evidence that such a post actually existed. His position, however, allowed him to perform dramatic works and cantatas (probably including compositions by his father). He received particular encouragement from the Kammerpräsident Franz Wilhelm Traugott von Breitenbauch (1739–96), whose daughter Antoinette (b 1766) was probably his pupil. Cantatas in celebration of the royal house of Prussia, performed in 1786 and 1788, secured for Bach a post in Berlin, where he arrived at the end of March or beginning of April 1789. There he succeeded Christian Kalkbrenner (1755–1806) as Kapellmeister to the widowed Queen Elisabeth Christine and he also taught keyboard to Queen Friederike. From 1798 at the latest he was employed as teacher 'to the reigning Queen [Luise] and all the brothers and sisters of the King [Friedrich Wilhelm III]', as he put it in a letter to W.C. Müller on 14 May 1830.

Bach's salary in Berlin was a modest one, and in a letter of 15 October 1809 to the privy councillor and Oberpräsident von Altenstein, now lost, he dwelt on his poverty-stricken situation. It was improved only by a pension of 300 thaler thought to have been granted by Prince Heinrich in 1811 after the death of Queen Luise. Thereupon Bach, who had previously played an active part in Berlin concerts as a keyboard virtuoso and violinist, retired from public life. In 1843 he was present at the ceremonial unveiling of the J.S. Bach monument in Leipzig. He was twice married and had four children. He was survived by his second wife and an unmarried daughter from each marriage, one of them a good soprano and the other an alto.

W.F.E. Bach was a stylish if not outstandingly talented composer. His extant works are varied and substantial, but too many have been lost for a true assessment to be made. Apart from the few that were printed, they remained confined to the courts of Berlin and Bückeburg, which he regularly supplied with compositions until the death of Princess Juliane in 1799. Contrary to previous assumptions, most of the surviving works date from his Berlin period. Those written in London show him as a typical representative of the early London pianoforte school in the tradition of J.C. Bach and Clementi, while of the occasional cantatas written in Minden, only one survives (in vocal score). In Berlin he composed, as well as orchestral works for Queen Christine Elisabeth's Kapelle, a great many pedagogical keyboard pieces for two, four or occasionally even six hands. The keyboard works are typical of early Romantic music, while the vocal compositions in particular are notable for a sense of humour and irony; they include, for instance, a *Concerto buffo*, probably composed for his royal pupils, which employs toy instruments and features a singing Kapellmeister, probably Bach himself. Some of the songs and keyboard pieces which circulated at the turn of the century, either singly or in collections, were very popular. From his Minden period onwards Bach was associated with freemasonry, and wrote several masonic songs. He apparently closed his career as a composer in 1822 with the publication of 12 *grandes variations* on the folksong 'Gestern Abend war Vetter Michel da', bearing in the autograph manuscript the title *Reminiscences, ou XII Grandes variations sur un air allemand populaire*, with a dedication to two of his former royal pupils. However, he is said to have written an overture of rejoicing for Prince Heinrich the year before his death.

The extant compositions do not support claims by Ledebur and others that Bach was an adherent of the strict style and despised modern music; there has probably been some confusion here with Wilhelm Friedemann Bach, who was almost certainly also the composer of the strongly contrapuntal Trio in G major for two flutes and viola, published as W.F.E. Bach's by Rudolf Ermeler.

Bach's modest and unassuming nature was an obstacle to a wide distribution of his compositions, and he was soon forgotten after his retirement in 1811.

WORKS

KEYBOARD

4 Progressive Lessons and 2 Duets (London, 1782) [also attrib. J.C. Bach]

5 Sonatas and 1 Duett (London, c1785) [also attrib. J.C. Bach]

6 sonates (Berlin, ?1796)

16 pieces, in F.F. Franz, ed.: *Musikalisches Journal* (Berlin, 1799–1800)

Tempo di minuetto, with 7 variations, *S-Smf** (Berlin, ?c1800), print lost

2 pieces, in Apollo, v (Stockholm, 1805–6)

12 pieces, in Monatsfrüchte für Klavier (Berlin, n.d.)

XII grandes variations sur un air allemand populaire (Berlin, 1822)

Amusement [Sonata, Andante with variation, Sonatina, Walzer, Sonatina], *D-Bsb**; Das Dreyblatt, pf 6 hands, *GB-Lbl**; Divertimento, *Lbl**; Doppelsonate, by 1805, lost; Variations on God save Frederick our King, doubtful, *Lbl*; Grand Sonata, E♭, 1778, *Lbl**; Grand Walzer, D, *D-Bsb**; Le melancholique, *GB-Lbl**; Minuet, D, *CH-SObo*; Variations, C, *GB-Lbl**; 6 Waltzer, *D-Bsb**, 3 ed. K. Geiringer (Vienna, 1936)

CHAMBER

6 sonates, C, D, B♭, E♭, F, G, pf, vn (Berlin, c1781)

3 sonates, C, B, E♭, pf, vn (Berlin and Amsterdam, c1789)

6 Sonatas, C, D, F, B, E, A, pf, vn, vc (London, n.d.); nos.1, 2 ed. F. Goebels (Wolfenbüttel, 1986)

Divertimento, E♭, cl, 2 hn, vn, va, vc, *GB-Lbl**; Fantasia, E♭, fl, cl, 2 hn, 2 vn, va, vc, *D-Bsb*; Parthie, E♭, 2 fl, 2 ob, 2 cl, 2 bn, 2 hn, *GB-Lbl**; Sestetto, E♭, cl, 2 hn, vn, va, vc, *D-Bsb*, *GB-Lbl**, ed. K. Janetzky (Halle, 1951); Sinfonia, C, *D-Bsb**; Sinfonia, C, *GB-Lbl**

Lost, listed in Bückeburg inventory, 1799: Divertimento, E♭; Qt, ? pf, str

ORCHESTRAL

Ballet-pantomime (ov., 43 dance movts), *GB-Lbl**; Conc., E, 2 kbd, orch, *D-Bsb*; Overture, D, 1793, private collection, USA; Sinfonia, C, private collection, USA; 2 syms., C, G, *GB-Lbl**

Lost: 3 concs., G, E, E♭, kbd, orch, formerly *D-Bsb*; Jubel-Ouverture, 1844, mentioned in obituary; Sinfonia, C, listed in Bückeburg inventory, 1799; 2 intermezzos, C, D, listed in Bückeburg inventory, 1799; Largo, A, kbd, orch, doubtful, formerly *D-Bsb*; 2 ovs., B♭, E♭, doubtful, listed in *EitnerQ*

VOCAL

Stabat mater, ? by 1784, lost, mentioned in Meusel

Colma (Ossian), perf. Minden, 1 May 1785, music lost

Der edelsten Freude geweiht (S.F. Martini), cant. for birthday of Friedrich II of Prussia, perf. Minden, 24 Jan 1786, music lost

Liesst von unsrer Wang herab (Martini), cant. for birthday of Friedrich II of Prussia, perf. Minden, 10 Sept 1786, music lost

Kommt vor sein Angesicht mit Jauchzen (Martini), cant. for installation of Friedrich Wilhelm II of Prussia, perf. Minden, 28 Oct 1786, music lost

Triumph, Triumph, Westphalia (Martini), cant. for visit of Friedrich Wilhelm II, perf. Minden, 5 June 1788, *A-Wn**, vs (Rinteln, 1791)

Wer spricht es aus, was wir verloren haben (Martini), funeral cant. for Pastor Wesselmann, perf. Minden, 6 Feb 1789, music lost

Vater unser (S.A. Mahlmann), T, B. choir, orch, by 1799, *GB-Lbl**; ed. in Stuttgarter Bach-Ausgaben, ser.A, v, suppl. (Stuttgart, c1977)

Der Theaterprinzipal, by 1809, lost, mentioned in *AMZ*, xii (1809–10)

Auf muntere Zecher, T, B, pf, *D-Bsb*

Columbus, oder Die Entdeckung von Amerika (after F. Schiller), T, B, chorus, orch, *GB-Lbl**

Concerto buffo, B, pf, toy insts, **Lbl*

Der Schmerz, der Trost (Erinnerung an Schillers Sterbetag), 4vv, pf, *Lbl**

Der Wechselschlag, lost, listed in estate catalogue of W.H. Cummings (London, 1917)

Durchs Leben führt so mancher Pfad (Der Pfad des Lebens), T, T, B, pf, *D-Bsb*, *GB-Lbl**

L'amour est un bien suprême; Ninfe se liete: S, orch, *Lbl**

Schön o schön ist diese Welt (Die Ruhe des Lebens) – Sie lebt (Der Dichter und der Komponist), T, B, pf, **Lbl*

Wie sehr lieb ich mein Mädchen nicht (Der Vorsatz), 4vv, pf, *Lbl**

Lieder: Auswahl [7] deutscher und [2] französischer Lieder und Arietten (Berlin, c1798); Etwas lieben und entbehren (An Lauren), in Blumenkranz dem neuen Jahrhundert (Berlin, 1800); Berlinade, oder Lindenlied (F. Monti) (Berlin, n.d.); Freude, schöner Götterfunken, ode (F. Schiller) (Berlin, n.d.), lost; Rheinweinlied (C. Müchler) (Berlin, n.d.); Ruf zur Freude, *Lbl**; Seid gegrüsst, ihr grün bemooste Hügel (C.F.D. Schubart), in J.C.F. Bach, ed.: Musikalische Nebenstunden (Rinteln, 1787); 1 other in J.M. Böheim: Auswahl von Maurer-Gesängen, iii (Berlin, 1814)

Cavatines, ?S, orch, lost, listed in Bückeburg inventories, 1799, 1865

6 It. arias (Metastasio and others), S, orch, by ?1799, lost, listed in Bückeburg inventory, 1865, some listed in estate catalogue of J.F. Reichart (Berlin, 1815)

Oue des maux loin de toi, S, orch, by ?1799, lost, listed in Bückeburg inventory, 1865

3 romances, lost, listed in Bückeburg inventories, 1799, 1865

Doubtful: Als einst die Gottheit Völker zu beglücken (Martini), cant. for birthday of Queen Luise of Prussia, ? perf. Berlin/Minden, 10 March 1793/4, music lost; Er segnet Au, er segnet Felder, cant., *D-BO*; 3 Gedichte (Kahlert), T, pf (Leipzig, n.d.), ? by A.W. Bach; Lobsingt dem Gott der Ernte, cant., *BO*; song, in F.F. Hůrka, ed.: Auswahl maurerischer Gesänge (n.p., c1803)

BIBLIOGRAPHY

GerberL; GerberNL

C. von Lederbur: *Tonkünstler-Lexicon* (Berlin, 1861/R)

J.G. Meusel: *Teutsches Künstlerlexikon* (Lemgo, 1778, 2/1808–14)

Neuer Nekrolog der Deutschen, xxiii (Weimar, 1847)

H. Miesner: 'Urkundliche Nachrichten über die Familie Bach in Berlin', *BJb 1932*, 157–63

G. Hey: 'Zur Biographie Johann Friedrich Bachs und seiner Familie', *BJb 1933*, 77–85

K. Geiringer: *The Bach Family: Seven Generations of Creative Genius* (London, 1954; Ger. trans., enlarged, 1958; enlarged 2/1977)

H. Wohlfahrt: 'Wilhelm Friedrich Ernst Bach: Werkverzeichnis', *Schaumburg-Lippische Mitteilungen*, xvi (1964), 27–32

J.K. von Schroeder: 'Verschollene Werke von Wilhelm Friedrich Ernst Bach, Musikdirektor in Minden', *Mindener Mitteilungen 1965*, 171–2

M. Jahrmärker: *Ossian, eine Figur und eine Idee des europäischen Musiktheaters um 1800*(Cologne, 1993)

U. Leisinger: 'Wilhelm Friedrich Ernst Bach, der letzte musikalische Enkel Johann Sebastian Bachs', *Johann Christoph Friedrich Bach (1732–1795): ein Komponist zwischen Barock und Klassik*, Niedersächsisches Staatsarchiv, 8 June – 11 Aug 1995 (Bückeburg, 1995) [exhibition catalogue], 71–82, 127–34 [incl. list of works]

A. Rockstroh: 'Der Hofkapellmeister, Cembalist und Musiklehrer der Königlichen Familie: zum 125. Todestag von Wilhelm Friedrich Ernst Bach, dem letzten musikalischen Enkel Johann Sebastian Bachs', *Neue berlinische Musikzeitung*, x/2 (1995), 97–102

CHRISTOPH WOLFF (I–II; III, 1–6, 7 (§7–21), 13, work-list, bibliography), WALTER EMERY/CHRISTOPH WOLFF (III, 7 (§1–6)), PETER WOLLNY (III, 8, 10), ULRICH LEISINGER (III, 9, 11, 14), STEPHEN ROE (III, 12)

B–A–C–H. In German nomenclature, the letters of Bach's name provide a motif (ex.1) which is frequently found as

Ex.1

B   A   C   H

a germinal idea in musical compositions. It was used by Bach himself in the unfinished Contrapunctus XIV of the *Art of Fugue* (1751), and its possibilities were earlier mentioned in Walther's *Musicalisches Lexikon* (1732/R). Probably because of the context in which Bach used it, later composers have mostly regarded this rather intractable motif as a challenge to their contrapuntal skill. Bach's son, Johann Christian, and his pupil, J.L. Krebs, both wrote organ fugues on it, but its wider popularity follows the 19th-century Bach revival and the development of a harmonic vocabulary which could more easily accommodate its tonal ambiguities. Schumann, whose interest in letter-pitch equations is well known, wrote six

fugues on B–A–C–H (op.60) for organ or pedal piano, and Liszt, Reger and Busoni also used the motif to raise imposing contrapuntal monuments to its originator. Other 19th-century composers who have used it include Rimsky-Korsakov and d'Indy.

The B–A–C–H motif is easily incorporated into a totally chromatic idiom and has been widely used by members and disciples of the Second Viennese School, e.g. by Schoenberg as an incidental theme in his Variations op.31 for orchestra and Third String Quartet, by Webern as the basic set of his String Quartet, and by Humphrey Searle as a motto in his First Symphony. For a list of over 400 B–A–C–H-inspired works see Boyd. The name B–A–C–H has also been expressed as a single note (ex.2).

Ex.2

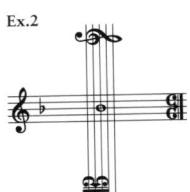

BIBLIOGRAPHY

S.W. Robinson: *The B–A–C–H Motive in German Keyboard Compositions from the Time of J.S. Bach to the Present* (thesis, U. of Illinois, 1972)

U. Prinz, J. Dorfmüller and K. Küster: 'Die Tonfolge B–A–C–H in Kompositionen des 17. bis 20. Jahrhunderts: ein Verzeichnis', *300 Jahre Sebastian Bach* (Tutzing, 1985), 389–419 [exhibition catalogue]

W. Häcker: 'Erberezeption im Sozialismus: das Tonsymbol B–A–C–H im Musikschaffen der DDR', *BMw*, xxxi (1989), 266–78

M. Boyd: 'BACH', *Bach*, Oxford Composer Companions (Oxford, 1999)

MALCOLM BOYD

Bach, August Wilhelm (*b* Berlin, 4/5 Oct 1796; *d* Berlin, 15 April 1869). German organist, teacher and composer. He was not a descendant of J.S. Bach. He received his earliest musical training from his father Gottfried Bach, organist at the Dreifaltigkeitskirche in Berlin, and accompanied services there while still a boy. After completing his secondary education he took a teaching position in a noble household outside Berlin. On his father's death in 1812 he returned to seek the post of organist at the Dreifaltigkeitskirche but did not succeed in obtaining the situation. He received instead an appointment in 1814 at the Gertraudenkirche, a less prominent position. During his two-year term there he studied counterpoint and fugue with Zelter and the piano with Ludwig Berger. He joined the Berlin Singakademie in 1815. He was appointed organist and music director at the important Marienkirche in 1816. In the following years he studied the violin with C.W. Henning and broadened his general education through travel and the study of languages. In 1819 Bach was one of the first members of Berger's 'jüngere Liedertafel'. The next year he became music director and teacher in Stettin. In 1822 he was engaged to teach the organ, harmony and chorale setting at Zelter's new Institut für die Ausbildung von Organisten und Musiklehren, and in 1826 he received a commission to oversee organ building in Prussia; this gave him not only a wide influence on organ building but also the opportunity of travelling throughout Europe. A brief organ textbook by him survives in several manuscript exemplars; it provides valuable information about organ builders and instruments at the time. When Zelter died in 1832 Bach succeeded him as director of the institute. He was elected to the senate of the Royal Academy of the Arts in 1833 and taught theory and composition there. In 1845 he was awarded the medal of the Order of the Red Eagle and in 1858 was granted the title Royal Professor.

As organist Bach not only played for services but also gave important chamber and concert performances, becoming thereby a notable exponent of the works of J.S. Bach. Of his organ students Felix Mendelssohn is the most famous, though many others won local prominence in the mid-19th century. His organ method, *Der praktische Organist* (*c*1840), and his *Choralbuch für das Gesangbuch zum gottesdienstlichen Gebrauch für evangelische Gemeinden*, first published in 1830 and repeatedly revised for use until well after his death, established his reputation. His largest work is the oratorio *Bonifaz, der deutsche Apostel*, not inappropriately described by a contemporary critic as 'a hotchpotch of opera and church' (*NZM*, xiv, 1841, p.61). The style of his compositions, mostly sacred and keyboard music, shows his attempt to accommodate the academic tendencies inherent in his studies and his profession as a teacher to the lyricism and saccharine harmonies popular in his time.

BIBLIOGRAPHY

BlumeEK; FrotscherG, ii; *MGG1* suppl. (T.-M. Langner); *ScheringGO*, 427, 457; *SchillingE*

C. von Ledebur: *Tonkünstler-Lexicon Berlin's* (Berlin, 1861/*R*)

H. Mendel and A.Reissmann, eds.: *Musikalisches Conversations-Lexikon* (Berlin, 1870–80, 3/1890–91/*R*)

D. Siebenkäs: *Ludwig Berger: sein Leben und seine Werke unter besonderer Berücksichtigung seines Liedschaffens* (Berlin, 1963), 25–6, 244

A. Meyer-Hanno: *Georg Abraham Schneider und seine Stellung im Musikleben Berlins* (Berlin, 1965), 139, 141, 160ff

S. Jeans: 'August Wilhelm Bach und seine Lehrbuch für Orgel', *Orgel, Orgelmusik und Orgelspiel: Festschrift Michael Schneider*, ed. C. Wolff (Kassel, 1985), 65–77

C. Albrecht: 'August Wilhelm Bach (1796–1869): ein Berliner Organist, Organologe und Orgelpädagoge des 19. Jahrhunderts', *Studien zur Berliner Musikgeschichte: eine Bestandaufnahme*, ed. H. Seeger and W. Goldhan (Berlin, 1988), 105–16

DOUGLASS SEATON

Bach, Cecilia. See GRASSI, CECILIA.

Bach, Jan (Morris) (*b* Forrest, IL, 11 Dec 1937). American composer. He studied with Kenneth Gaburo and Robert Kelly (University of Illinois, BM 1959, DMA 1971), Donald Martino (Yale University, 1960), Aaron Copland and Roberto Gerhard (Tanglewood, 1961) and Thea Musgrave (Aldeburgh and London, 1974). The recipient of many honours, including a Koussevitzky Award (1961), he taught at the University of Tampa (Florida) (1965–6) before joining the music department at Northern Illinois University.

Bach's accessible style combines traditional and contemporary musical elements. A predominant aspect of his work is his charming and inexhaustible sense of humour. *Four Two-Bit Contraptions* (1964), for example, is a study in musical caricature cast in the form of rags, waltzes and other dances. Later works, such as *Rounds and Dances* (1980), are more eclectic in nature, employing playful and teasing thematic materials, but making more strenuous demands on the performer. His operatic works, the most frequently performed being *The Student from Salamanca*, exhibit an ingenious use of ensembles; contrapuntal textures are a primary feature. In all genres, Bach's works display both structural clarity and a subtle use of instrumental timbre.

WORKS
(*selective list*)

Ops: The System (1, Bach), New York, 5 March 1974; The Student from Salamanca (1, Bach), New York, 9 Oct 1980

Orch: Toccata, 1959; Dionysia, band, 1964; Burgundy Variations, 1968; Pf Conc., 1975; The Eve of St Agnes, band, 1976; Praetorius Suite, band, 1977; Hn Conc., 1983; Escapade, 1984; Dompes and Jompes, str, 1986; Hp Conc., 1986; Conc., tpt, wind, 1987; Euphonium Conc., 1990; Steel Drum Conc., 1994

Vocal: 3 Shakespeare Songs, chorus, 1960; 3 Choral Dances, female vv, 1969; 3 Sonnets on Woman, T, hpd, 1972; Hair Today, chorus, 1977; 5 Sylvan Songs, Bar, str qt, 1981; With Tpt and Drum, 16vv, pf, 1991; People of Note, vv, insts, 1993

Chbr: Str Trio, 1956; Str Qt, 1957; Four Two-Bit Contraptions, fl, hn, 1964; Laudes, brass qnt, 1971; Concert Variations, euphonium, pf, 1977; Qnt, tuba, str, 1978; Rounds and Dances, brass qnt, 1980; 8 Duetudes, fl, bn, 1983; Helix, a sax, fl, cl, bn, hn, tpt, trbn, 2 perc, 1983; Anachronisms, str, 1991

BIBLIOGRAPHY

Anderson2; Baker7

K.E. Shrum: *An Analytical Commentary on the Euphonium and Tuba Music of Jan Bach* (diss., Arizona State U., 1989)

R.H. Kornick: *Recent American Opera: a Production Guide* (New York, 1991), 36–9

JAMES P. CASSARO

Bach, Maria (*b* Vienna, 1 March 1896; *d* Vienna, 26 Feb 1978). Austrian pianist and composer. Her ancestors, Catholic members of the Bach dynasty, came to Austria during Luther's time. Brought up in an artistic milieu, she studied the violin (with Arnold Rosé) and the piano from an early age, presenting her first successful piano recital when she was ten. Although she decided to become a concert pianist, her *Flohtanz* for piano (1917) was so successful that she took up composition seriously, studying with Joseph Marx. In 1962 she received the first prize in the Buenos Aires International Composers' Competition. In her later years she took up painting and writing poetry, composing music for her own poems. Her large output, in the late Romantic tradition, includes much vocal music with orchestra and smaller forces. A full account of her life and works is given in G.M. Eiselmair: *Die männliche Gilde sehe sich vor! Die österreichische Komponistin Maria Bach* (Vienna, 1996).

WORKS
(*selective list*)

Stage: Silhouetten (ballet), orch, 1939

Vocal-orch (all song cycles): 4 Narrenlieder (after J. Bierbaum), Bar/T, orch, 1921; Japanischer Frühling (15 songs, trad. Jap. lyrics), S/T, orch, 1930; 4 Lieder des Hafis (trad. Persian texts), T/S, vc, orch/pf, 1940; 6 Marienlieder (trad. Ger. texts), S, str, 1944, rev. 1v, pf, 1944–5; 3 Orchesterlieder, S, orch, 1944; 2 Orchesterlieder, S, str, 1949; Das Marienleben (R.M. Rilke), S, Bar, str, 1952; 5 Orchesterlieder, S/T, 2 hn, str, 1952

Choral (for SATB): 7 Japanische Lieder (trad. Jap. texts), 1932; Draussen im weiten Krieg (C. Morgenstern), 1945; 4 Volkslieder (trad. Chin. texts), 1952

Other vocal (for 1v, pf): 6 Lieder (A. Wildgans, F. Hebbel, Hartlieb, G. Falke, Bierbaum, F. Werfel), 1925–8; 18 Lieder (Rilke), 1925–6; 5 Sonette (E. Barrett-Browning), 1940; 5 Lieder (song cycle, A. Lambe), 1959

Chbr and solo inst: Flohtanz, pf, 1917; Sonata, vc, 1922; Sonata, vc, pf, 1924; Pf Qnt, 1930; Str Qt no.1, 1935; Str Qnt, 1936; Str Qt no.2, 1937; Wilde Myrte (T. Lanjus), C (cl, vc, pf)/str, 1952; Stücke: Caravelle, Glockenspiel, Holztanz, pf, 1957

ROSARIO MARCIANO/R

Bach, P.D.Q. See *under* SCHICKELE, PETER.

Bach, Vincent [Schrottenbach, Vinzenz] (*b* Baden, nr Vienna, 24 March 1890; *d* New York, 8 Jan 1976).

American brass instrument maker of Austrian birth. He played the violin as a child and studied the trumpet (cornet) with Josef Weiss and Georg Stellwagen. In 1910 he earned a degree in mechanical engineering at the Maschinenbauschule in Wiener Neustadt. After a year as an Austrian navy bandsman, he studied the solo cornet repertory with Fritz Werner in Wiesbaden (1911–12), then toured as a cornet virtuoso in Germany, Denmark, Sweden, Russia, Poland and England, arriving in New York in September 1914. While continuing his solo career in the USA, he played a season as assistant first trumpet with the Boston SO (1914–15) and a season as first trumpet with Dyaghilev's ballet orchestra at the Metropolitan Opera House (1915–16). In 1916–18 he was bandmaster of the 306th Field Artillery Regiment. He became an American citizen in 1925.

On 1 April 1919 Bach set up a shop at 204 East 85th Street in New York, mainly for the purpose of making mouthpieces for his own use. In 1922 he moved to 241 East 41st Street, where he had ten employees; the manufacture of cornets and trumpets was started there in 1924. From 1928 to 1952 he was at 621 East 216th Street, with 50 employees, and began the manufacture of tenor and bass trombones. In 1953 he built a factory in Mount Vernon, New York. He sold his business to the H. & A. Selmer Co. in September 1961; four years later the firm moved to Elkhart, Indiana.

In combining his musical proficiency with his engineering training, Bach succeeded in establishing the most exacting standards of brass instrument design and construction. His point of departure, as with Elden Benge (1904–60), was the French Besson Bb trumpet; unlike Benge, however, who desired more flexible intonation, Bach strove to give his instruments a secure 'feel' for each note in the scale. Bach was also the first to set up a system for duplicating mouthpieces exactly. His instruments, especially trumpets, are employed more widely than any others. They are prized for their full and yet compact tone, with a solid core.

BIBLIOGRAPHY

G. Fladmoe: *The Contributions to Brass Instrument Manufacturing of Vincent Bach, Carl Geyer and Renold Schilke* (diss., U. of Illinois, 1975)

A. Smith: 'The Life and Work of Vincent Bach', *Journal of the International Trumpet Guild*, xix (1994–5), no.2, pp.5–35; no.3, pp.4–34

EDWARD H. TARR

Bach-Abel Concerts. London concert series organized between 1765 and 1781 by J.C. Bach and C.F. Abel; *see* LONDON, §V, 2.

Bacharach, Burt (F.) (*b* Kansas City, MO, 12 May 1928). American composer and pianist. He learnt the cello, drums and piano from an early age and developed a particular interest in jazz. He played as a night club pianist, and then served in the army, touring as a pianist (1950–52). He went on to study music at the Mannes College of Music, New York, the New School of Social Research, McGill University, Montreal and gained a scholarship to the Music Academy of the West, Santa Barbara, California. His composition teachers included Milhaud, Martinů and Cowell. Bacharach became an accompanist for Vic Damone, subsequently working with such performers as Polly Bergen, Steve Lawrence, the Ames Brothers and Paula Stewart, to whom he was married from 1953 to 1958. From 1958 to 1961 he

toured internationally with Marlene Dietrich. Bacharach began writing arrangements and composing songs in the mid-1950s, working at the Brill Building and collaborating with the lyricist Hal David (*b* Brooklyn, NY, 25 May 1921), the brother of the lyricist Mack David, on a large number of popular songs, including *The Story of My Life* (1957), *Magic Moments* (1958), *Anyone Who Had a Heart* (1963), *Walk on by* (1964) and *(There's) Always something there to remind me* (1964). Some 60 of their songs were recorded by their protégée Dionne Warwick and these, along with recordings by Dusty Springfield (notably *I just don't know what to do with myself* and *The Look of Love*), remain among the best interpretations of the Bacharach-David repertory. Such songs, in addition to the Broadway musical *Promises, Promises* (1968), which was also staged to great success in Australia and Europe, made them one of the most successful songwriting teams in American music history.

Bacharach's style, though eclectic, is well defined and accessible; its heterogenous elements include variable metre, irregular phrasing, pandiatonic and jazz harmonies, rhythmic ostinatos from various sources and effects from the black American styles. Many of his melodies – for example, *Do you know the way to San Jose?* – exhibit an internal momentum, created by the repetition of short, syncopated rhythmic patterns, which complements David's clever, colloquial lyrics. Bacharach has written a number of film scores, and won two Academy Awards for *Butch Cassidy and the Sundance Kid* (1969), for best score and best song ('Raindrops keep fallin' on my head'). He has also contributed to other films including the title song to *Alfie* (1966), and collaborated with Carole Bayer Sager on the song 'Arthur's Theme' for *Arthur* (1981) which won an Academy Award. He married Sager in 1982.

A revival of interest in 'lounge' music and easy-listening in the early 1990s brought Bacharach back to international prominence, and his work has since been covered by such groups as REM and Oasis. He has continued to perform regularly in concert, wrote a further song for Dionne Warwick (*Sunny Weather Love*, 1993) and collaborated with Elvis Costello on the song *God give me strength* (1995) and the album *Painted from Memory* (1998).

WORKS
(*selective list*)

lyrics by H. David unless otherwise stated

Stage, writers shown as (lyricist; book authors): Promises, Promises (musical, 2, H. David; N. Simon after B. Wilder and I.A.L. Diamond: *The Apartment*), Schubert, New York, 1 Dec 1968 [incl. I'll never fall in love again; Promises, Promises; Whoever you are I love you]

Film scores and songs: What's New, Pussycat?, 1965 [incl. Here I am, My Little Red Book]; Casino Royale, 1968 [incl. the Look of Love]; Butch Cassidy and the Sundance Kid, 1969 [incl. Raindrops keep fallin' on my head, Come touch the sun]; Lost Horizon (musical), 1973 [incl. Question me an answer, Reflections, The world is a circle]; Night Shift (C.B. Sager), 1982 [incl. That's what friends are for]; Arthur 2: On the Rocks (Sager), 1988 [incl. Love is my decision]

Many popular songs, incl. Magic Moments, 1957; The Story of my Life, 1958; I just don't know what to do with myself, 1962; Make it easy on yourself, 1962; (The Man who Shot) Liberty Valance, 1962; Close to You, 1963; Twenty-Four Hours from Tulsa, 1963; Wishin' and Hopin', 1963; Everyone needs someone to love, 1964; (There's) Always something there to remind me, 1964; Walk on by, 1964; Don't go breaking my heart, 1965; Trains and Boats and Planes, 1965; What the world needs now is love, 1965; Alfie, 1966; Made in Paris, 1966; Do you know the way to San Jose?,

1967; This guy's in love with you, 1968; The Hurtin' Kind, 1970; Arthur's Theme (Sager, C. Cross and P. Allen), 1981; Sunny Weather Love, 1993; God give me strength (E. Costello), 1995

Principal publishers: Blue Seas, Jac, US Songs

BIBLIOGRAPHY

CBY 1970

D. Ewen: *Popular American Composers* (New York, 1972)

B.A. Lohof: 'The Bacharach Phenomenon: a Study of Popular Heroism', *Popular Music and Society*, i (1972), 73–82

R. Prendegast: *A Neglected Art: a Critical Study in Films* (New York, 1978)

J. Fitzgerald: 'When the Brill Building Met Lennon-McCartney: Continuity and Change in the Early Evolution of the Mainstream Pop', *Popular Music and Society*, xix (1995), 59–77

R. Platts: 'Anyone who had a Heart: the Songs of Burt Bacharach and Hal David', *Discoveries* (Dec 1997)

R.L. Doerschuk and H. Kubernik: 'The Harmony of Opposites: Elvis Costello and Burt Bacharach Explore the Art of Unlikely Collaboration on *Painted from Memory*', *Musician*, no.242 (1999), 30–40 [interview]

MICHAEL J. BUDDS/R

Bachauer, Gina (*b* Athens, 21 May 1910; *d* Athens, 22 Aug 1976). Greek pianist. Her father was from an Austrian family which had settled in Greece in 1877, while her mother came from near Trieste. Bachauer studied at the Athens Conservatory under Woldemar Freeman and later at the Ecole Normale, Paris, with Cortot. Freeman introduced her to Rachmaninoff, with whom she also took lessons. Her French solo début took place in the Salle Chopin, Paris, in 1929, and she first played in England in 1932 at the Aeolian Hall, London. In 1933 she won the medal of honour at an international piano competition in Vienna, and in the 1930s played concertos with the Paris SO conducted by Monteux and the Athens SO under Mitropoulos. For several years following her marriage in 1936 to John Christodoulo she lived in Alexandria, giving over 600 concerts for allied troops in various parts of northern Egypt during World War II. In 1946 she made her British orchestral début at the Albert Hall, London, playing Grieg's Piano Concerto with the New London Orchestra under Alec Sherman. Following her American début at New York's Town Hall in 1950, she undertook many coast-to-coast tours of the USA. After the death of her first husband she married Alec Sherman in 1951.

Bachauer was at her most formidable in the 19th- and early 20th-century repertory, impressing with the strength and breadth of her keyboard command and essentially balanced musicianship. Her recordings of concertos by Beethoven, Brahms, Chopin and Grieg, as well as solo works by Debussy, Ravel and Stravinsky, have been re-issued on compact disc.

BIBLIOGRAPHY

G. Wade: *Gina Bachauer: a Pianist's Odyssey* (Leeds, 1999)

GRAHAM WADE

Bach Choir. London amateur choir founded in 1875. *See* LONDON, §VI, 3 (ii).

Bach disposition. A disposition used on many early 20th-century harpsichords (and thus specified in some 20th-century compositions) in imitation of the so-called BACH HARPSICHORD.

Bache. English family of musicians.

(1) Francis Edward Bache (*b* Birmingham, 14 Sept 1833; *d* Birmingham, 24 Aug 1858). Composer and pianist. He was the eldest of the seven children of Samuel

Bache (1804–76), a well-known Unitarian minister who officiated at the New Meeting, Birmingham (1832–59), and his wife Emily Higginson (*d* 1855), from whom Francis inherited his musical gifts. He was educated at his father's school and studied with James Stimpson, city organist of Birmingham, and with Alfred Mellon. He played the violin in the 1846 Birmingham Festival, and in 1849 went to London as a private pupil of Sterndale Bennett, with whom he studied composition for more than three years. In October 1850 he became organist of All Saints, Gordon Square. In this period he composed concertos, overtures, two dramatic pieces, a string quartet and a piano trio, as well as many piano pieces. His first appearance as a concert performer was at Keighley, Yorkshire, on 21 January 1851. When he played the Allegro of an unpublished piano concerto of his own in June 1852, Henry Chorley was moved to remark: 'We have met with no Englishman more likely to give us the English composer for whom we have so long been waiting than Mr Bache'. In November 1851 he went to live with Mellon, by then resident in London, and in 1852 was given a contract by Addison, Hollier and Lucas to write light piano pieces, which he turned out in considerable numbers. Of one of these he wrote, 'I must say that I would *sooner* have written my *Galop di Bravura* than many a Sonata which is only printed to lie on the shelf a dead weight on account of deficiency of anything like idea'.

In October 1853, on Bennett's recommendation, Bache went to Leipzig, where he studied with Moritz Hauptmann, and acquired the conventional prejudices against the music of Berlioz, Liszt and Wagner. He visited Dresden, and returned to England by way of Paris in February 1855. He attended the 1855 Birmingham Festival, writing some of the reviews for the local newspapers, but was then attacked by a severe recurrence of the tuberculosis which had troubled him for several years. Early in 1856 he went to Algiers on medical advice, where he gave a concert on 28 March. He travelled by way of Paris to Leipzig (June 1856), and then, through Dresden and Vienna, to Rome (December 1856). His health again deteriorated and he returned home in June 1857, spending the next winter in Torquay, where he succeeded in giving a concert in February 1858. On his return to Birmingham he gradually declined, and after a farewell concert of his music on 5 August, he died less than three weeks later, at the age of 24.

Bache's piano music has many qualities of his master, Sterndale Bennett, with a pleasant freshness and vitality to compensate for a certain lack of solidity and substance. He was most at ease in the virtuoso concert piece. More remarkable are the Six Songs op.16, which come near to establishing an English analogue of the lied; and the Piano Trio in D minor op.25, which, in spite of obvious gleanings from Mozart, Beethoven, Mendelssohn and Bennett, has a vigour found in few English instrumental compositions of its period (it was revived at a concert given by the Victorian Society at Leighton House on 26 September 1964). Bache's early death deprived Victorian music of one of its most promising talents.

WORKS
(selective list)

printed works published in London unless otherwise stated

Which is Which? (op, A. Mellon), 1851, not perf.

Rubezahl (op, J. Palgrave Simpson), *c*1852, not perf.

Orch: 3 pf concs., 1, E, perf. June 1852; Fl Conc., 1852; Jessie Gray,
  ov., London, Adelphi, Nov 1850; Ov., E, March 1851, *GB-Lam*;
  Polonaise, pf, orch, op.9, pf score (1854), ed. in LPS, xvi (1985)
Chbr: Str Qt, F, July 1851, *Lcm*; Pf Trio, d, op.25 (1852); 2
  romances, pf, vn/vc, op.21 (1859), op.posth.
48 pubd pf pieces, incl. 3 Impromptus, op.1 (1851); 4 Mazurkas de
  salon, op.13 (1855), ed. in LPS, xvi (1985); 5 Characteristic Pieces,
  op.15 (1855–8); [8] Souvenirs d'Italie, op.19 (1857); [5] Souvenirs
  de Torquay, op.26 (1859)
Introduction and Allegro, 2 short voluntaries, org, in Stimpson's
  Organist's Standard Library (London, n.d.), xxi, xxii, xxiv
17 songs, incl. 6 Songs (J.L. Uhland, J.W. von Goethe, H. Heine),
  op.16 (*c*1850); 4 songs, n.d.

(2) **Walter Bache** (*b* Birmingham, 19 June 1842; *d*
London, 26 March 1888). Pianist and conductor, brother
of (1) Francis Edward Bache. Like his elder brother he
attended his father's school and studied with Stimpson.
In August 1858 he too went to Leipzig, but after a short
stay at Milan and Florence he arrived at Rome in the
summer of 1862, where for three years he received regular
lessons from Liszt; this experience gave his life a different
direction. In 1865 he returned to London, and soon began
his lifelong crusade to establish his master's reputation
there: he played a two-piano arrangement of *Les préludes*
with Edward Dannreuther on 4 July 1865. In the summer
of 1867 he and Dannreuther formed a small association
for the promotion of the music of Wagner and Liszt in
England, dubbing themselves 'The Working Men's Society', with Karl Klindworth as a kind of elder statesman.
At first they had to be content with piano arrangements,
but in 1871 Bache began annual orchestral concerts at
which more and more works by Liszt and other controversial composers were introduced to the London public.
In the course of these concerts (1871–86) Bache introduced five of Liszt's symphonic poems, the *Faust* and
Dante symphonies, *Die Legende von der heiligen Elisabeth*, and other major works. In this enterprise he had to
face an almost continuous barrage of opposition and
scorn from other musicians and critics. Joseph Bennett
wrote of him: 'I was content to remain on my own side of
the great gulf which circumstances had fixed between us'.
But, largely through Bache's indomitable perseverance, a
section of the public was gradually brought round. On
Liszt's visit to England in the spring of 1886 Bache gave
a memorable reception at the Grosvenor Gallery on 8
April, followed by a series of concerts in which he and his
master appeared together. Bache was a professor of piano
at the RAM, and was instrumental in founding the Liszt
Scholarship there.

(3) **Constance Bache** (*b* Birmingham, 11 March
1846; *d* Montreux, 28 June 1903). Writer on music, sister
of (1) Francis Edward Bache. She prepared the English
version of Humperdinck's *Hänsel und Gretel* and also
translated La Mara's edition of *Letters of Franz Liszt*
(London, 1894) and *The Early Correspondence of Hans
von Bülow* (London, 1896).

BIBLIOGRAPHY
F.E. Bache: Letters to his parents, 1840–53 (MS, *GB-Lbl* Add.54193)
C. Bache: *Brother Musicians: Reminiscences of Edward and Walter
  Bache* (London, 1901) [with list of F.E. Bache's works]
G. Langley: 'The Pianoforte Works of Francis Edward Bache', *MMR*,
  xxxv (1905), 83–7
J. Bennett: *Forty Years of Music 1865–1905* (London, 1908)

NICHOLAS TEMPERLEY

Bachelbel, Johann. *See* PACHELBEL family, (1).

Bacheler [Bachiler, Batchiler, Batchelar], **Daniel** (bap.
Aston Clinton, Bucks, 16 March 1572; bur. Lee, Kent, 29
Jan 1619). English lutenist and composer. He
was apprenticed at age seven to his uncle Thomas Cardell,
lutenist and dancing master to Queen Elizabeth, suggesting that special talent was already evident. In 1587 his
apprenticeship was transferred to the Queen's principal
secretary, Sir Francis Walsingham, a move that was to
determine the course of Bacheler's career. In that same
year he took part as a page in the funeral procession of
Walsingham's son-in-law Sir Philip Sidney. The earliest
music attributed to Bacheler survives in the Walsingham
consort books whose date, 1588, indicate that the music
was composed and copied when Bacheler was only 15 or
16. His contribution includes seven pieces scored for the
recently developed mixed consort of treble and bass viols,
flute, lute, cittern and bandora.

By October 1594, a year before the stipulated completion of his apprenticeship, he was in the service of the Earl
of Essex at the generous salary of £30 (£20 was normal).
The position may have been secured for him by Lady
Essex (née Walsingham), who was Sir Philip Sidney's
widow. Most likely Bacheler was still servant to Essex in
1599, when he was paid to deliver letters from the Privy
Council to him in Ireland. During the same period
Bacheler set the Earl's bitter sonnet *To plead my faith*,
addressed and almost certainly sung directly to Queen
Elizabeth. The song was printed in Robert Dowland's
Musicall Banquet in 1610.

Bacheler presumably remained as servant to Lady Essex
after the Earl's execution in 1601; he accompanied her to
the court of James I two years later. There, he was
appointed groom of Queen Anne's Privy Chamber at the
extraordinarily high yearly salary of £160. Other grooms
were paid £60 and royal lutenists only £20–£40. Bacheler
was also employed as secretary (a 'thank-you' letter on
behalf of the Queen is preserved in Hatfield House
Library, C.P.118/134), but no doubt his musical skills
were specially valued. The advanced style of some lute
solos suggests that he was still composing in the last years
of his life. He applied for and was granted a coat of arms
in February 1607, confirming his status as 'gentleman'.
He died at age 46 in 1619 and was buried at Lee, close to
Queen Anne's household at Greenwich, and where the
Walsinghams had property.

More than 50 lute solos survive, an output exceeded
only by Dowland and Holborne. Bacheler's divisions are
florid, requiring technical skill, and he was one of the first
lutenists to explore the lower sonorities of the instrument,
occasionally taking a melody down to the fourth and fifth
courses. He wrote divisions on three French popular tunes
and was probably the first English lutenist to play
unmeasured preludes. These last are preserved in the
lutebook of Lord Herbert of Cherbury (*GB-Cfm*) who
may well have introduced Bacheler to French influence
when he visited Queen Anne on his return from Paris in
1609. Many solos survive in unreliable texts with irregular
strain lengths and one galliard exists in two versions
(Long's nos.13b and 29), suggesting that Bacheler improvised more than most lutenists and that scribes such as
Matthew Holmes had difficulty notating his playing.
Because he was employed as groom he probably did not
feel constrained by the expectations placed on professional
lutenists, encouraging a more experimental approach to
composition and playing. He was frequently referred to

as 'Mr Daniell', which has caused confusion with John Danyel, particularly as the same divisions of *Monsieur's Almain* were ascribed to both composers. It is now clear that 'Mr Daniell' refers to Bacheler.

WORKS

Edition: *Daniel Bacheler: Selected Works for Lute*, ed. M. Long (London, 1972) [incl. complete list of works and sources][L]

LUTE SOLO

6 preludes, 1 in L; 1 fantasy, L; 1 pavan and galliard pair, pavan in L; 17 pavans, 2 in L; 15 galliards, 3 in L; 1 almain, L; 3 courantes, 2 in L; 1 volt, L (no.39 as 'courante'); 4 divisions on popular tunes, 1 in L; Daniells Jigge, *GB-Cu* Dd.v.78.3, f.69 (not listed in L)

MIXED CONSORT

Sir Francis Walsingham's Goodnight; Sir Francis Walsingham's Goodmorrow; The Lady Sidney's Felicity: The Lady Walsingham's Conceits; Daniel's Trial; The Widow's Mite; Daniel's Almain; all ed. in MB, xl (1977)

SONG WITH LUTE AND BASE VIOL

To plead my faith (poem by Robert Devereux, Earl of Essex); ed. P. Stroud: *Robert Dowland: A Musicall Banquet* (London, 1968)

BIBLIOGRAPHY

E. Doughtie: 'Sidney, Tessier, Bachelar and *A Musicall Banquet*: Two Notes', *RN*, xviii (1965), 123–5
W. Edwards: 'The Walsingham Consort Books', *ML*, lv (1974), 209–14
A. Batchelor: 'Daniel Bacheler: The Right Perfect Musician', *LSJ*, xxviii (1988), 3–12
A. Batchelor: *A Batchelor's Delight* (Beverley, 1990)

ROBERT SPENCER

Bachelet, Alfred (*b* Paris, 26 Feb 1864; *d* Nancy, 10 Feb 1944). French composer. After studying with Guiraud at the Paris Conservatoire he won the Prix de Rome in 1890. He became chorus master and subsequently conductor at the Paris Opéra and succeeded Ropartz as head of the Conservatoire in Nancy in 1919. In 1929 he replaced Messager on the Académie des Beaux-Arts.

He was from the start drawn towards programmatic works for large orchestra, and extracts from projected works were performed in several concerts around 1900 with some success. He was considered a French Wagnerian by many critics and, apart from the *Ballade* for violin and orchestra, the Nocturne from which enjoyed some celebrity, it is for his operas that he is best remembered. His first, *Scemo*, set in Corsica, was first performed on the eve of World War I; it is an opulent, lengthy score somewhat in the manner of Richard Strauss. Its naturalistic subject matter was not well received by the critics either at the première or at its revival at the Opéra-Comique in 1926, although the music drew praise from Dukas and Hahn among others. The one-act *Quand la cloche sonnera* is set in World War I and concerns a girl who rings the church bell as a signal to soldiers to blow up a bridge, even though she knows her lover is waiting beneath it. His third and last opera, *Un jardin sur l'Oronte*, was widely considered his most successful. It tells of the love between an oriental princess and a Christian invader, and Bachelet uses pastiche of both oriental and medieval music to portray the clash of cultures. Gustave Samazeuilh, one of his most faithful supporters, considered the poème lyrique *Sûryâ* to be one of the finest pieces of French music to be written during World War II. Bachelet was also active as a conductor; his début at the Paris Opéra was with Gounod's *Faust* in 1907.

WORKS

STAGE

Cléopâtre (scene lyrique, F. Beissier), 1890
Scemo (drame lyrique, 3, C. Méré), Paris, Opéra, 6 May 1914, vs (Paris, 1914)
Quand la cloche sonnera (drame musical, 1, Y. de Hansewick and P. de Wattryne), Paris, OC (Favart), 6 Nov 1922 (Paris, 1922)
Un jardin sur l'Oronte (drame lyrique, 4, Franc-Nohain, after M. Barrèn), Paris, Opéra, 3 Nov 1932, vs (Paris, 1932)

VOCAL

Choral: Fiona (légende irlandaise), solo vv, chorus, orch, 1896; L'amour des Ondines, sym. poem, solo vv, chorus, pf, orch, 1903; Sûryâ, Hymne Védique (C.M.R. Leconte de Lisle), solo vv, chorus, orch (1943)
Songs (1v, pf unless otherwise stated): Vocalise-étude (1893); Tendresse (J. Lahor) (1894); Le vent (E. Vollaine) (1894); Le dormeur du val (A. Rimbaud) (1915); Noël (T. Gautier), 2vv, pf (1918); La chanson des trois roses (A. Bausil) (1924); Le vent (Vollaine) (1935); Terre Lorraine (J. Grosdidier de Matons) (1938); Chère nuit (Eugène Adenis); Mélodies: Au bois dormant (L. Durocher), Pâle étoile du soir (A. de Musset), also orchd

INSTRUMENTAL

Orch: Poème, vc, orch, 1890–5 (1952); Ballade, vn, orch (1920); Barcarolle, Nocturne et Petit Histoire, vn, vc, orch, pf (1927); Joie, sym. poem
Chbr and solo inst: 2 impromptus, pf (1894); Fantaisie mélancolique, pf (1895); Morceau de concours, trbn, pf (1902); Chant nuptiale, vn, vc, pf (1905); Dans la montagne, ballade, hn/vn, pf/orch (1907); Lamento, F, vc/hn, pf/orch (1927, 1935); Berceuse, pf (1928); Humoresque, pf (1928); Fantasie et fugue, org (1943); Sérénade

BIBLIOGRAPHY

J. Tiersot: *Un demi-siècle de musique française* (Paris, 1919)
L. Rohozinsky: *Cinquante ans de musique française 1874–1925* (Paris, 1925)
G. Samazeuilh: 'Alfred Bachelet', *Le théâtre lyrique en France* (Paris, 1937–9), iii, 219–28 [pubn of Poste National/Radio Paris]
R. Dumesnil: *La musique en France entre les deux guerres 1919–1939* (Paris, 1946)
P. Bertrand: *Le monde de la musique* (Geneva, 1947)
M. Kelkel: *Naturalisme, vérisme et réalisme dans l'opéra de 1890 à 1930* (Paris, 1984)

RICHARD LANGHAM SMITH

Bachelier, Louis (*b* 1703; *d* Angers, 1782). French composer. He received his musical education in the Angers choir school, which he left in 1723 to become an adult chorister. On 14 November 1724 he was a candidate for the post of *maître de chapelle* to succeed Louis Vigné, and it is likely that he was appointed to the post and occupied it until 1732, the year in which he left Angers. He is next heard of in Orléans and then in Verdun, where a *Te Deum* and motets by him were sung before the king. In 1747 he became *maître de musique* at Clermont-Ferrand, a position he left in 1760 to return to Angers, where he was again *maître de chapelle* until 1768 at the latest, after which he undertook various responsibilities within the chapter. On 8 May 1772 he donated 14 masses (no longer extant) to the chapter.

Three works, dated 1749, by Bachelier have survived (*F-Pn* Vm1 1315–17). They are the grands motets *Deus deorum locutus est* (Psalm xliv), *Nisi Dominus* (Psalm cxxvi) and *Deus misereatur nostri* (Psalm lvi) for soloists, five-part chorus, *symphonie* (violins and oboes) and continuo, composed in the Versailles manner of the time. Certain short passages call for trumpets and a bassoon. (J. Poirier: *La maîtrise de la cathédrale d'Angers: six cents ans d'histoire*, Angers, 1983)

JEAN-CHARLES LÉON

Bach-Gesellschaft. A society founded on the centenary of Bach's death (1850) to publish a complete critical edition of his works. By that time all the principal keyboard works had been printed, but it was obvious that a non-commercial scheme was needed for the vocal works.

The notion of a Bach-Gesellschaft, dating back to the 1830s, can be linked with Mendelssohn's efforts on the composer's behalf. A further stimulus came in 1843 when the English Handel Society was founded in London. In July 1850 Otto Jahn, together with Robert Schumann, C.F. Becker, Mortiz Hauptmann and the Leipzig firm of Breitkopf & Härtel, issued a preliminary announcement which was sent to a number of prospective supporters. By the end of the same month it had gained the support, in various periodicals, of Liszt, Spohr and many others. The society's inaugural meeting took place in Leipzig on 15 December 1850.

As the first German musicological project of such vast scope, the Bach edition encountered many problems over the following years. The main difficulty was in obtaining a comprehensive overview of the composer's surviving output. A catalogue of his works begun in the 1830s by Franz Hauser was a basic source of information on Bach's compositions and the location of autographs and other relevant manuscripts. Individual volumes were delayed because the owners of various sources denied the editors access to important material. For example, the edition of the B minor Mass was deferred several times because Hermann Nägeli would allow no-one to inspect the autograph in his possession; it was not until Friedrich Chrysander had obtained the source that the volume could be completed. There were also differences of opinion among the members of the committee as to how far the edition should cater for the needs of practical music-making; it was debated, for example, whether the scores of the vocal works should be provided with piano reductions. When the idea was rejected, Moscheles, who had championed the cause of the performing musician, resigned from the committee. The first volume of the Bach edition, containing cantatas nos.1–10, appeared in December 1851; it was edited by Hauptmann, who over the next few years shared the responsibility for a number of volumes with Julius Rietz and Wilhelm Rust. From 1859 Rust assumed sole charge, which he finally relinquished in 1882 after disagreements with Philipp Spitta. The later volumes were again supervised by several different editors.

The complete Bach edition initiated a significant change in contemporary attitudes to early music, and paved the way for comparable editions of the works of Handel, Schütz, Palestrina and Lassus. Although it does not match contemporary standards of source criticism, the editors' approach was remarkably scrupulous and scientific for its time. The whole edition is free of editorial accretions. Rust prefaced numerous volumes with forewords discussing the sources and performance practice, and in volume xliv the editors provided a thorough documentation of the composer's handwriting. Only a few of Bach's works are missing, while a few compositions now known to be by other composers were erroneously included.

With the completion of volume lxvi, presented to the committee on 27 January 1900, the Bach-Gesellschaft was dissolved, in accordance with its statutes. On the same day the Neue Bachgesellschaft (NBG) was founded in order to disseminate and research into the composer's works, and from the early years of the century held regular Bach festivals. In its first years, especially, it published a large quantity of music, including collections of arias and arrangements aimed at the needs of performing musicians. Its journal, the *Bach-Jahrbuch*, has appeared almost every year since 1904. In 1906 the society acquired the house in Eisenach where the composer was once thought to have been born, and opened a Bach museum there. Unlike many other German musicological organizations, the NBG survived intact during the period of the country's division.

BIBLIOGRAPHY

'Aufforderung zur Stiftung einer Bach-Gesellschaft', *Signale für die musikalische Welt*, viii (1850), 289–91
H. Kretzschmar: 'Die Bach-Gesellschaft: Bericht im Auftrage des Directoriums', *Johann Sebastian Bach's Werke*, xlvi (Leipzig, 1900), pp.xv–lxi
'Die alte und die neue Bachgesellschaft', *Die Grenzboten: Zeitschrift für Politik, Litteratur und Kunst*, lix (1900), 535–40
Passionsmusiken im Umfeld Johann Sebastian Bachs: Leipzig 1994
L. Klingberg: *Politisch fest in unseren Händen: musikalische und musikwissenschaftliche Gesellschaften in der DDR* (Kassel, 1997), 76–101

BARBARA WIERMANN

Bach Guild. American record label. *See* VANGUARD.

Bach harpsichord [Ger. *Bach-Cembalo, Bach-Flügel*]. A two-manual instrument made after 1700 by the workshop of Harrass in Breitenbach, Thuringia. It was owned by the Voss family of Berlin at the end of the 18th century. The instrument then passed into the hands of the family of the Bach scholar Wilhelm Rust, and in 1890 it was sold by the Leipzig collector Paul de Wit to the newly founded Sammlung Alter Musikinstrumente, now the Musikinstrumenten-Museum des Staatlichen Instituts für Musikforschung Preussischer Kulturbesitz, Berlin (catalogue no.316). During the sales negotiations it was said that the instrument had once belonged to J.S. Bach and had come into the possession of the Voss family by way of W.F. Bach. This claim, which cannot be proved, led to its being regarded from about 1900 to about 1960 as the ideal of the harpsichord, so that it was copied and imitated in all sorts of ways. It has a rather unusual disposition (8' and 16' on the lower manual, 4' and 8' with buff stop and push coupler on the upper manual), which has been followed in instruments produced by Ammer, Dolmetsch, Neupert, Sperrhake and Wittmayer. Recent research has shown that the instrument originally had a three-register disposition (4' and 16' in the lower manual; 8' with buff stop and push coupler in the upper manual) which was expanded to four in the 18th century.

The characteristic four-register disposition of the Bach harpsichord, together with the rapid changes of register made possible by the addition of pedals in the modern instruments, is taken as the norm in many 20th-century compositions for harpsichord. The contrasts of sound made possible cannot be fully achieved with a normal historical disposition of 2 × 8', 1 × 4'. The Bach harpsichord should not be confused with the keyboard instrument known as a BACHKLAVIER.

See also REGISTRATION, §II, 1.

BIBLIOGRAPHY

F. Ernst: *Der Flügel Joh. Seb. Bachs: Ein Beitrag zur Geschichte des Instrumentenbaues im 18. Jahrhundert* (Frankfurt, 1955)
M. Elste: 'Nostalgische Musikmaschinen: Cembali im 20. Jahrhundert', in J.H. van der Meer and others: *Kielklaviere: Cembali, Spinette, Virginale* (Berlin, 1991), 239–77
D. Krickeberg and H.Rase: 'Einige Beobachtungen zur Baugeschichte des "Bach-Cembalos"', *JbSIM 1987–8*, 184–97
Das Berliner 'Bach-Cembalo'. Ein Mythos und seine Folgen (Berlin, 1995) [incl. bibliography]

M. Elste: 'Kompositionen für nostalgische Musikmaschinen: Das Cembalo in der Musik des 20. Jahrhunderts', *JbSIM 1994*, 199–246

M. Elste: *Modern Harpsichord Music: a Discography* (Westport, CT, 1995)

MARTIN ELSTE

Bachiler, Daniel. *See* BACHELER, DANIEL.

Bachklavier. A keyboard instrument of the harpsichord type designed and built by the Munich instrument-making firm of MAENDLER-SCHRAMM in the 1920s. Its mechanism was designed to allow dynamic gradation: a pad was fitted diagonally between the back key lever and the adjustable screw of a specially sprung jack, so that the length of the plectrum could be regulated by touch (patented 25 May 1923). These instruments were advertised as 'harpsichords with a sound capable of modulation in the modern way'. Similar instruments were built by other firms in the first half of the 20th century, but they did not prove popular. The Bachklavier should not be confused with the BACH HARPSICHORD.

MARTIN ELSTE

Bachmann, Carl Ludwig (*b* Berlin, 1748; *d* Berlin, 26 May 1809). German viol player and instrument maker. He was a viol player in the royal chapel from 1765, and in 1770, together with J.F.E. Benda, he established the Berlin Liebhaberkonzerte. With Benda's death in 1785 Bachmann succeeded him as director of the concerts; in the same year he married the noted singer and pianist Charlotte Caroline Wilhelmine Stöwe. Throughout this period he also made instruments in the shop of his father, the violin maker and court violinist Anton Bachmann (1716–1800), and may have been responsible for several innovations, including a screw-tuning mechanism for double basses which he introduced in about 1778, although a similiar mechanism was already known in France, having been developed by Benoît Fleury in 1766. He continued alone in his father's business from 1791, at about which time he passed the directorship of the Liebhaberkonzerte to his younger brother, the court violinist Friedrich Wilhelm Bachmann (1749–1825). Rellstab, though agreeing with the generally held low opinion of Bachmann's musical abilities, found his instruments excellent, a judgment which has been borne out by Henley alone among later commentators.

BIBLIOGRAPHY

J.C.F. Rellstab: *Über die Bemerkungen eines Reisenden* (Berlin, 1789)

C. von Ledebur: *Tonkünstler-Lexicon Berlin's* (Berlin, 1861/R)

W. Henley: *Universal Dictionary of Violin and Bow Makers* (Brighton, 1959–60)

M. Elste: 'Berlin als ein Zentrum des Grossstadtgeigenbaus', *Handwerk im Dienste der Musik: 300 Jahre Berliner Musikinstrumentenbau*, ed. D. Droysen-Reber, M. Elste and G. Haase (Berlin, 1987), 11–27

H. Heyde: *Musikinstrumentenbau in Preussen* (Tutzing, 1994)

EUGENE HELM/MARTIN ELSTE

Bachmann [née Stöwe], **Charlotte Caroline Wilhelmine** [Charlotte Wilhelmine Caroline] (*b* Berlin, 2 Nov 1757; *d* Berlin, 19 Aug 1817). German singer. The daughter of a musician, she received early training in singing and keyboard playing, and at the age of nine sang in the Berlin Liebhaberkonzerte, whose performances she was later to dominate. In 1785 she married the Berlin violist and instrument maker Carl Ludwig Bachmann (1748–1809). She was one of the original 20 members of the Berlin Sing-Akademie (founded in 1791), and was essential in establishing its annual performances of C.H. Graun's *Der Tod Jesu* between 1797 and 1806, the beginning of the cult of that work. Her singing was highly regarded in her native Berlin, though the *Bermerkungen eines Reisenden* (1788) found her voice lacking in natural qualities, and declared her excellent keyboard playing to be her finest attainment. She also composed a few songs, one of which appeared in Rellstab's *Clavier-Magazin* (1787).

BIBLIOGRAPHY

MGG1 suppl. (C. Schröder-Auerbach)

A. Hartung and K.W.Klipfel: *Zur Erinnerung an Charlotte Wilhelmine Karoline Bachmann* (Berlin, 1818)

C. von Ledebur: *Tonkünstler-Lexicon Berlin's* (Berlin, 1861/R)

EUGENE HELM

Bachmann, Sixt [Joseph Siegmund Eugen] (*b* Kettershausen, nr Illertissen, 18 July 1754; *d* Reutlingendorf, nr Ehingen an der Donau, 18 Oct 1825). German composer and keyboard player. A child prodigy, he probably received his earliest instruction in music from his grandfather Franz Joseph Schmöger, choral director and organist in Markt Biberbach. It was there on 5 or 6 November 1766 that the famous organ contest between Bachmann and the ten-year-old Mozart took place, from which both emerged with credit. In 1771 he entered the Premonstratensian monastery in Obermarchtal, where he took his vows in 1773 and was ordained to the priesthood in 1778. There he met the writer Sebastian Sailer (*d* 1777), whose *Schriften im schwäbischen Dialekte* he later edited (Buchau, 1819). In Obermarchtal he taught music and directed choirs, and was professor of theology (from 1800). He was also responsible for the monastery parish of Reutlingendorf (1779, 1789, 1796–9); he then became pastor in Seedorf but returned to Reutlingendorf in 1800. In 1803 the monastery in Obermarchtal was dissolved and he settled in Reutlingendorf.

Bachmann obtained his grounding in composition principally from the study of theoretical works, especially G.J. Vogler's. His output includes piano sonatas characterized by contrapuntal technique and monothematic movements; he also wrote organ works and ecclesiastical music combining (according to Wilss) the new homophonic style with the traditional contrapuntal language of church music. Gerber stated that one of his sonatas was arbitrarily altered by the Viennese publisher Hoffmeister.

WORKS

Pf: 2 sonatas (both Vienna, 1786); pieces in Clavier-Magazin für Kenner und Liebhaber (Berlin, 1787), Sammlung kleiner Clavier Stücke, i (Vienna, *c*1787) and Notenblätter zur musikalischen Korrespondenz (Speyer, 1792); Sonate, op.1 bk 1 (Munich, 1800); Sonatine, 4 hands, *D-Rp*; 6 sonatas, 2 fantasias, variations, further single works in Musikalische Aufsätze, i–ii, 1803–*c*1820, *Rp* [Allegrino from vol.ii in Siegele, 18–19]

Missa solemnis, C, S, A, T, B, double choir, insts, org, *c*1786, ed. in Denkmäler der Musik in Baden-Württemberg, v (Munich, 1997)

Other works, incl. masses, cants., syms., org fugues, str qts, pf sonatas and songs, many cited in *GerberNL* and Christmann

BIBLIOGRAPHY

GerberNL

J.F. Christmann: 'Brief', *Musikalische Korrespondenz der Teutschen Filarmonischen Gesellschaft* (1790), 103–7, 163–6

L. Wilss: *Zur Geschichte der Musik an den oberschwäbischen Klöstern im 18. Jahrhundert* (Stuttgart, 1925)

W. Siegele: 'Musik des oberschwäbischen Barock', *Der Barock, seine Orgeln und seine Musik in Oberschwaben: Ochsenhausen 1951*, 40–58

EBERHARD STIEFEL

Bachofen, Johann Caspar [Hans Kaspar] (*b* Zürich, 26 Dec 1695; *d* Zürich, 23 June 1755). Swiss composer and music pedagogue. The year of his birth has been given incorrectly in some sources as 1697. His father Joseph, originally a tailor and from 1692 a schoolteacher, planned a theological training for Johann Caspar, who was his second son. After study at the cathedral school, the Collegium Humanitatis, and (from 1715) the theology class, Bachofen gained the title V.D.M. (*verbi divini minister*) in 1720. In 1711 he joined the collegium musicum at the chapter house, and in 1715 he became a member of one that met at the German School. In 1720 he became a singing teacher at the lower grammar school. His small income compelled him to seek a secondary source of income, from trading in violin strings. Despite disputes with officials and colleagues, he was appointed, after J.K. Albertin's death in 1742, to the important position of Kantor at the Grossmünster, the most important cathedral in Zürich; at the same time he became director of the chapter house collegium musicum. In 1739 he had also assumed the role of Kapellmeister at the German School, thus combining several of the most important musical posts in Zürich. By 1748, however, he had become ill, and bad health hindered the execution of his duties and overshadowed his final years.

Bachofen's significance in the history of Swiss music lies primarily in the exceptional popularity of some of his works. His music was criticized, even by his contemporaries, for deficiencies of construction, harmonic language and melodic development; but his most important collection of sacred songs, *Musicalisches Hallelujah*, appeared in no less than 11 editions between 1727 and 1803, and became one of the favourite songbooks for popular music-making in the home. In the St Gall district the term 'bachofele' was used well into the 19th century for a gathering of singers for rehearsal. Three of Bachofen's arrangements of sacred songs were reprinted by Goldschmid (1942), and he is represented today in the hymnbook of the Swiss Reformed Church by the hymn *Auf, auf ihr Reichsgenossen*.

As the preface of the *Musicalisches Hallelujah* makes clear, Bachofen's works were specifically intended for domestic use. He broke away from the tradition of four-part writing (in the manner of Goudimel's psalms), and most of his settings are in three voices. The continuo part, presumably to be played on the home organ, also constitutes the vocal bass, and there are two soprano parts which frequently cross. Solo songs with organ are inserted to fill gaps on the printed pages resulting from publication in separate parts, with each three-part song beginning a new page.

Bachofen is also important for his pedagogical work, in particular his expansion of the collegia musica, the centres of the day for German Swiss music and the predecessors of the future concert institutions. He also published a *Musicalisches Noten-Büchlein* (Zürich, n.d.), designed to provide the beginner with a 'theoretical conception of the art of music and song in a short time'.

WORKS
all printed works published in Zürich

Musicalisches Hallelujah: Oder [206] schöne und geistreiche Gesänge, 1–3vv, bc (1727, rev. and enlarged 2/1733 with 570 Gesänge; rev. 3/1739; rev. 4/1743; rev. 5/1750 with 581 Gesänge; rev. and abridged 6/1754 with 380 Gesänge; rev. 11/1803 with 570 Gesänge), examples in A. Nef, Goldschmid (1917, 1942) and Geering

Psalmen Davids, 3vv, bc (1734, rev. 2/1759)
[12] Musicalisch-monatliche Aussgaaben, bestehend in teutschen, geistlichen Arien, 2–3vv, bc (?1729, 2/1732)
Herrn B.H. Brockes … Irdisches Vergnügen in Gott, bestehend in physicalisch und moralischen Gedichten, 1v, bc (1740)
Musicalisch-wöchentliche Aussgaaben, 2vv, bc (1748–50)
Musicalische Ergezungen, bestehende in [17] angenehmen Arien, 1–2vv, bc, vn ad lib (1755)
Der für die Sünden der Welt gemarterte und sterbende Jesus (B.H. Brockes) (1759), with appendix containing short solos
New Year's cantatas for the Musikgesellschaft zur deutscher Schule, 1733–5, 1741
Kantate zum 50. Jubiläum der Musikgesellschaft zur deutschen Schule, 1729; Sonett, dem Obmann Hans Jacob Lavater gewidmet (J.H. Köchli), 1735; Kantate, dem neuen Obmann des Musikkollegiums 'auf dem Musiksaal', J.M. Köchli, gewidmet, 1739; Huldigungstück an den Obmann Junker Landvogt Escher, 1750; Konzert zur Einweihung des neuen Saales der Musikgesellschaft Bischofszell, 14 Nov 1745; all lost

BIBLIOGRAPHY
RefardtHBM
M. Friedlaender: *Das deutsche Lied im 18. Jahrhundert* (Stuttgart and Berlin, 1902/R)
A. Nef: *Das Lied in der deutschen Schweiz Ende des 18. und Anfang des 19. Jahrhunderts* (1909)
T. Goldschmid: *Schweizerische Gesangbücher früherer Zeiten* (Zürich, 1917)
M. Fehr: 'Kantor Joh. Kaspar Bachofen', *Zürcher Wochen-Chronik* (1917), 397, 405, 413
M. Fehr: 'Das alte Musikkollegium Bischofszell', *SMz*, lviii (1918), 185, 194, 202
E.M. Fallet: 'Johann Kaspar Bachofen', *SMz*, lxvi (1926), 363, 379
K. Nef: 'Schweizerische Passionsmusiken', *Schweizerisches Jb für Musikwissenschaft*, v (1931), 113
A.-E. Cherbuliez: *Die Schweiz in der deutschen Musikgeschichte* (Frauenfeld, 1932)
A. Geering: 'Von der Reformation bis zur Romantik', *Schweizer Musikbuch*, i, ed. W. Schuh (Zürich, 1939), 54–130
T. Goldschmid: *Geistliche Sologesänge und Duette … aus alten schweizerischen Gesangbüchern*, ii (Zürich, 1942)
B.D. Arnold: *The Life and Works of Johann Caspar Bachofen* (diss., U. of Southern California, 1956)

PETER ROSS

Báchorek, Milan (*b* Staříč, north-eastern Moravia, 18 Aug 1939). Czech composer. He studied the piano with Milada Šlachtová in Ostrava (1953–60) and composition with Miroslav Klega at the Ostrava Conservatory (until 1967). He began teaching at the Ostrava Conservatory in 1960 and was appointed its director in 1992. He was secretary to the Union of Composers in Ostrava for many years. His early compositions are influenced by 20th-century composers and by the folk music of his native region. *Ritornello* (1969) marked a new period in his composition, in which he evolved a more uncompromisingly modern language. His other pieces include an important series of three vocal works (*Lidice*, *Stereophonietta* and *Hukvaldská poéma*), and the Cello Concerto (awarded a prize by the Czech Composers' Union in 1991). These works are notable for their imaginative exploration of timbre, their melodiousness and their sense of drama.

WORKS
(selective list)

Orch: Dramatická předehra [Dramatic ov.], 1965; Ritornello, 1969; Scény [Scenes], ob, str, 1982; Concerto piccolo, vc, str, 1991; Symčcové rozmanilosti [Miscellaneous Pieces for Str], 1992; Konfrontace [Confrontations], vn, str, hpd, 1998
Vocal: Ztracená milá a Hezký Janek [Lost sweetheart and Sweet Jack] (folk texts), chorus, 1966, 1969; Lidice (K. Šiktanc), solo vv, spkr, male and female chorus, perc, orch, 1973; Balada (folk texts), S, spkr, female chorus, fl, va, pf, 1975; Klasy [Spikes] (J. Wolker), T, spkr, male chorus, vib, bells, 1976; Píseň domova [Song of the Home] (chbr cant., Z. Malý), Bar, chorus, cl, vn, vc, pf, 1976; Stereofonietta (V. Rakovsky), S, Bar, perc, org, 2 orch,

1977; Ke staré Lysé [To old Lysá] (3 choruses, M. Jahn), 1982; Omluvenky pro žáky poškoláky [Apologies from Kept-In Pupils] (L. Dvořák), children's chorus, cel, pf 4 hands, children's toys, 1985; Hukvaldská poéma [Poem of Hukvaldy] (K. Vůjtek), S, T, Bar, children's and female chorus, orch, 1986; Cesta světla [The Way of Light] (L. Romanská), mixed chorus, 1989

Chbr and solo inst: Fantasia da camera, fl, cl, bn, str, 1966; Epigramy [Epigrams], cl, 1970; Dialogy [Dialogues], 2 va, 1970; Hudba pro žesťové kvinteto [Music for Brass Qnt], 1979; Inspirace pro pět [Inspiration for 5], jazz qnt, 1984; 3 věty [3 Movts], cl, pf, 1989

Principal publishers: Czech Music Fund, Panton, Stylton Ostrava

BIBLIOGRAPHY

M. Navrátil: 'Lidice a Stereofonietta Milana Báchorka' [Lidice and Stereophonietta by Milan Báchorek], HRo, 1x (1981), 316–21

V. Gregor and K. Steinmetz, ed.: Hudební kultura na Ostravsku po roce 1945 [Musical life in the Ostrava region after 1945] (Ostrava, 1984)

J. Mazurek: 'Sborová tvorba Milana Báchorka' [Choral works by Milan Báchorek], Slovo v hudbě 20. století (Ostrava, 1990), 56–65

L. Zenkl: 'Jak mi zní hudba M. Báchorka' [What Báchorek's music sounds like to me], OM, xxii (1990), 21–4

B. Cigánková and J. Mazurek: 'Raná tvorba skladatele Milana Báchorka' [Early works by the composer Milan Báchorek], Z hudební topografie severní Moravy a Slezska (Ostrava, 1995), 80–91

KAREL STEINMETZ

Bach Revival. The rediscovery during the first half of the 19th century of Johann Sebastian Bach's music marked the first time that a great composer, after a period of neglect, was accorded his rightful place by a later generation. Palestrina, Lully, Purcell and Handel had never been quite forgotten by the musical public, but Bach was known only to a small circle of pupils and devotees until the Romantic movement stimulated a growing interest in his art. The Bach Revival was an early example of a new historicism which eventually opened all periods of Western music to discovery and performance, and which now constitutes the dominant factor in the musical taste of advanced Western societies. It began at about the same time in Germany, where most of Bach's descendants and pupils, and most of his surviving music, were to be found; and in England, where musical historicism was already well advanced by the end of the 18th century.

See also EARLY MUSIC.

1. Germany and Austria. 2. England.

1. GERMANY AND AUSTRIA.   Bach was always a conservative composer, and in the latter part of his career his style had become outmoded, failing to win for him any reputation as a composer in the fashionable world. His music was attacked by Scheibe in 1737 for 'excess of art' and for its 'turgid and confused style'. In the works of his last few years – the completed Mass in B minor, the Musical Offering, the Art of Fugue and others – he virtually turned his back on what remained of his public, writing for himself and, perhaps, for posterity. At his death public knowledge of his music was at a low ebb. Even at the Leipzig Thomaskirche, his successors only occasionally used his cantatas; the organ works, too, were rarely heard, unless they were played by one of his sons or pupils. Recent research has, however, modified the widespread belief, dating from the late 19th century, that Bach's compositions were largely ignored by his contemporaries and forgotten for more than 50 years after his death. Although few of his works were published during his lifetime, his keyboard music was disseminated widely in manuscript and enormous numbers of copies were made, particularly of Das wohltemperirte Clavier. There is evidence that Bach lent his sacred music to friends and former pupils such as J.W. Koch and C.G. Wecker. Indeed, Bach's large circle of pupils was a major force in the distribution of his works.

In the latter half of the 18th century Bach was remembered as a master of organ playing and of learned counterpoint. The first extended biographical notice of Bach, by J.A. Hiller, his third successor at the Thomaskirche, gave only a superficial and condescending account of his compositions (1784); while Reichardt remarked in 1782: 'Had Bach possessed the high integrity and the deep expressive feeling that inspired Handel, he would have been much greater even than Handel; but as it is he was only more painstaking and technically skilful'. Bach's own sons played a part in the rejection of the artistic principles he stood for, which went far beyond the normal changes in style that are found at other periods. C.P.E. Bach's feelings were ambivalent. During his Hamburg period (1768–88) he used recitatives and choruses from his father's two Passions as a framework for his own Passion music; he also incorporated some of the cantatas in pasticcios and edited the four-part chorales for publication. J.C.F. Bach too included chorale movements by the elder Bach in his cantata Der Tod Jesu and his oratorio Die Auferweckung Lazarus.

It was at Berlin, where C.P.E. Bach was employed until 1767, that the strongest group of Bach disciples was concentrated. They preserved and passed on most of the original manuscripts of Bach's works that have survived. Agricola, Kirnberger, Nichelmann and Marpurg owned large collections of music and published influential treatises which discussed Bach's compositions for various purposes. Increasingly conservative tendencies were manifested in the veneration of Bach by Kirnberger and the circle of Princess Amalia, where Bach was seen as a counterweight to recent developments in musical aesthetics. In Leipzig the cantatas acquired in 1750 from Anna Magdalena Bach's inheritance served as the basis for performance of his music by Gottlob Harrer, Bach's successor at the Thomaskirche, and J.F. Doles. A wish to have some of the large-scale choral works that had left Leipzig with Bach's sons available for performance by the pupils of the Thomasschule accounts for a number of spurious ascriptions (the St Luke Passion, the oratorio Jesu, deine Passion, the Mass in G major), which had a considerable effect on the image of Bach around the turn of the century. There is evidence that Bach's cantatas were performed in Leipzig in the early 19th century as well as in the second half of the 18th.

The Bach revival in Vienna in the late 18th century was instigated and greatly encouraged by such key figures as Baron Gottfried van Swieten and Fanny von Arnstein. The former was familiar with the Bach tradition from his post as ambassador to the Prussian court, and the latter from her origins in the Itzig family of Berlin. These two patrons must have had considerable influence on the regard in which Mozart and Beethoven held Bach. In April 1782 Mozart wrote that 'nothing but Handel and Bach' was played at the Sunday recitals in van Swieten's house. The Austrian government officer Franz Joseph, Reichsritter von Hess, also owned an extensive Bach collection.

A more general appreciation of Bach came only as a result of the Romantic cult of the past. Arising in England, this movement was immensely strengthened in its German phase by patriotic and religious motives. The military and political humiliations of the Napoleonic period generated a desire to recover older German traditions, while a religious revival prompted the search for what was truly and distinctively religious in the cultural heritage. In this Bach was to become the archetypal figure. The influence of J.N. Forkel, organist and music director at Göttingen University, was particularly important. Forkel began planning a biography of Bach in the mid-1770s, and consequently was in touch with Bach's two eldest sons. Through them he became acquainted with many of Bach's compositions, and was able to acquire copies and in some cases original manuscripts. 'This great man', Forkel wrote, 'was a German. Be proud of him, German fatherland, but be worthy of him too. … His works are an invaluable national patrimony with which no other nation has anything to be compared'.

Forkel was joined by Rochlitz in the Leipzig *Allgemeine musikalische Zeitung*, whose first volume (1798) contained a portrait of Bach. Rochlitz was inclined to paint a romantic, saintly picture of the master, comparing him aesthetically and morally with Dürer, Rubens, Newton and Michelangelo. The religious aspect of Bach's art was important to another early convert, C.F. Zelter, a conductor at the Berliner Sing-Akademie, founded in 1791 by C.F.C. Fasch, one of the earliest German institutions to organize historical concerts. He had inherited an extensive collection of Bach's music from Kirnberger and Agricola, and he drew from it in his pioneering revivals of Bach's motets and other sacred works. He rehearsed the Mass in B minor in 1811 and the *St Matthew Passion* in 1815, but did not think it practical to perform them. Through Rochlitz and Zelter, Goethe in his old age came to a profound appreciation of Bach. E.T.A. Hoffmann, another influential literary figure, developed the idealized Romantic conception that Rochlitz had begun to build.

The mounting enthusiasm for Bach culminated in the performance of the *St Matthew Passion* by the Sing-Akademie in 1829, with Mendelssohn conducting. This was the decisive turning-point in Bach's reputation, for it swiftly transformed the revival from a cult of intellectuals into a popular movement. Zelter had allowed a copy of the autograph to be made in 1823; with commendable self-effacement he turned over the honour of conducting the performance to his pupil. Mendelssohn, though at first hesitant, eventually agreed to attempt the formidable task. He made his own arrangement of the music from Zelter's copy; cuts, changes and additions were made (see illustration). After nearly two years of rehearsals, the performance took place on 11 March 1829, and was far more successful than the first performance exactly a century earlier. The audience was deeply moved; Hegel, who was present, later wrote of 'Bach's grand, truly Protestant, robust and erudite genius which we have only recently learnt again to appreciate at its full value'. Two more performances followed, the last conducted by Zelter. Mosewius, who also heard the work at Berlin, conducted it in 1830 at Breslau, an important centre of the Protestant religious revival and the home of Winterfeld. Königsberg was the next city to hear the Passion; it was not performed at Leipzig until 1841. Meanwhile the Berlin Sing-Akademie produced the *St John Passion* in 1833, and a truncated version of the Mass in B minor in 1835 (the Credo had been revived by Schelble at Frankfurt in 1828).

A growing number of the cantatas were added to the choral repertory at this period.

The first half of the 19th century saw extensive efforts to preserve Bach's oeuvre. With the deaths of his sons and pupils, there was a danger that the cultivation of Bach's music, nurtured largely by oral traditions in the 18th century and based on private collections, would gradually fade away. In 1801 the Leipzig firm of Hoffmeister & Kühnel began publishing the keyboard works in a collection entitled *Oeuvres complettes*. It was subsequently supervised by Forkel, and concluded in 1804 with the appearance of the 16th volume. The publication of Forkel's biography of Bach by the same firm in 1802 was influential in advertising this 'complete edition'.

Further selections of Bach's music appeared soon after 1800, published in Leipzig by Breitkopf & Härtel (the motets, a four-volume edition of chorale preludes for organ and the spurious mass BWV Anh.167), by Simrock in Bonn (*Das wohltemperirte Clavier*) and in the series Musikalische Kunstwerke im strengen Style, edited by Hans Georg Nägeli (the sonatas for violin and harpsichord, the Goldberg Variations, *Das wohltemperirte Clavier* and *The Art of Fugue*). These editions emphasized the instrumental works, and with few exceptions paid little attention to Bach's vocal compositions. Significantly, music historians of the Romantic period saw Bach as a composer of instrumental music, and Forkel's biography takes the same line.

The editions mentioned above had a crucial effect on the image of Bach in the first four decades of the 19th century. At the same time there was an increasing demand for a complete edition of Bach's compositions. In many respects the London Handel Society editions, which began in 1843, were regarded as a model for the practicality of the project. The Bach-Gesellschaft was founded in 1850, on the 100th anniversary of Bach's death, to promote the complete edition of his works, and the society devoted itself to the task for the next 50 years. As a result the full range of Bach's achievement, particularly as a composer of vocal music, gradually became apparent to a larger audience. A companion-piece to the edition is Philipp Spitta's monumental Bach biography, published in two volumes in 1873 and 1880, which superseded all previous biographical writings on the composer. Yet while all of Bach's known music became available between 1850 and 1899, there was no immediate increase in the number of performances; indeed, during the 1870s, when the number of subscribers to the Bach-Gesellschaft dropped to little more than 300, it was doubtful for some time whether the edition could be completed. Nevertheless, the volumes, though they varied in scholarly precision, were a remarkable achievement, and established the basic principles for scholarly musical editions that have been followed ever since. They completed the Bach Revival, and made it possible for Bach to take his place in public esteem beside or above other great composers.

2. ENGLAND.   England lacked the group of pupils and descendants who formed the nucleus of the German Bach Revival; but historicism and antiquarianism were more advanced than in Germany. The music of Handel, Corelli, Domenico Scarlatti and other late Baroque composers continued to be popular throughout the 18th century, while such bodies as the Academy of Ancient Music (1710–92), the Madrigal Society (founded 1741) and the Concert of Ancient Music ('Ancient Concerts', 1776–

Page of Mendelssohn's performing edition of Bach's 'St Matthew Passion', showing the end of no.4, with Mendelssohn's tempo, dynamic and phrasing marks in pencil (GB-Ob MS M. Deneke Mendl. 46, p.44)

1848) cultivated a taste for the music of the remoter past. Burney and Hawkins, though they failed to appreciate Bach's importance, gave him due mention in their histories of music – books of a kind that did not yet exist on the Continent.

The earliest extant copies of Bach's music in England come from the collection of Richard Fawcett and probably date from around 1750. According to Forkel, Bach composed his 'English' Suites for an English nobleman, but no documentation for this claim has been found. A note on a now lost manuscript containing excerpts from the Goldberg Variations stated that the copy was presented to the owner 'J.H.' (probably James Hutton) by Bach in 1749. There is evidence that a good deal of Bach's music was circulating in manuscript in England during the last three decades of the 18th century. J.C. Bach probably had little interest in his father's music, but he

may have possessed some copies. Burney received a copy of book 1 of the '48' from C.P.E. Bach in 1772, while Clementi possessed a partly autograph copy of book 2. Queen Charlotte owned a manuscript volume dated 1788, containing the '48', Clavier-Übung, iii, and the Credo from the Mass in B minor. This music may have reached the queen through either of two German musicians recently arrived in London: C.F. Horn (1762–1830), her music teacher from 1782, or A.F.C. Kollmann (1756–1829), organist at the German chapel in the court of St James's from 1784.

Clementi, Horn and Kollmann are the most important early figures in the English Bach Revival. Clementi is said to have practised Bach for hours on end during his time at Peter Beckford's house in the early 1770s. His own music shows early traces of Bach's influence which become much stronger in the late sonatas and the Gradus ad

Parnassum. He incorporated several of the keyboard pieces in his didactic works. He must have passed on his love of Bach to his two most famous pupils, J.B. Cramer, whose studies of 1804 and 1810 show an obvious influence of the '48', and Field, who astonished audiences with his playing of Bach during his European tour of 1802–3 and who taught Bach's music to his Russian pupils. Kollmann consistently stressed the importance of Bach in his theoretical works in English, beginning with the *Essay on Musical Harmony* (1796), which offered a detailed analysis of the F minor fugue from book 2 of the '48'. In 1799 he advertised a plan to issue an analytical edition of the entire '48', but the scheme was anticipated by the three continental editions of 1801, two of which were reissued in London. He published the Chromatic Fantasia in 1806, with 'additions' by himself, analysed 12 Bach fugues in his *Quarterly Musical Register* (1812) and translated excerpts from Forkel's life of Bach into English, possibly assisting in a complete translation of the work (1820). Horn arranged 12 organ fugues for string quartet – with figured bass – and published them in 1807, and later collaborated with Wesley in the first English edition of the '48'. His son, C.E. Horn, another Bach enthusiast, included part of a fugue from the '48' in the overture to his comic opera *Rich and Poor* (1812).

The movement quickly spread to native English musicians. William Shield's *Introduction to Harmony* (1800) gave due place to Bach, and incorporated the D minor prelude from book 1 of the '48'. George Frederick Pinto, a close friend of Field's, tried to imitate Bach in his C minor Fantasia and Sonata (published posthumously, *c*1808), and it was he who first introduced Samuel Wesley to Bach's preludes and fugues, according to Wesley's memoirs. Wesley took up the cause with feverish intensity, shown in his well-known letters to Benjamin Jacob, another English Bach enthusiast. Wesley edited, with Horn, the six organ trios, published (for the first time anywhere) in 1809–10 in instalments, and a 'new and correct edition' of the '48' in 1810–13. In 1808 he began a series of concerts of Bach's music at Surrey Chapel, with Jacob, who was organist there; and soon afterwards he began a similar series at the Portuguese Embassy chapel, where his friend Vincent Novello was organist and soon became a Bach convert. Because of the lack of pedals on most English organs, Wesley often played Bach's organ music as duets with Jacob or Novello assisting him on a second manual (in some cases Dragonetti played the pedal parts on his double bass). He also played fugues from the '48', which he regarded as organ music.

Wesley saw Bach as a superhuman genius, even though there is a touch of whimsy in the nicknames he used for him – 'Saint Sebastian', 'The Man', 'Our Apollo' and so on. He felt that militant propaganda was needed to persuade the English that any musician could be superior to Handel. He found that his brother Charles was an unrepentant Handelian. But he won many converts, including even the aged Burney who at last recanted his earlier criticism of Bach. William Crotch was recruited to the cause, and was the first to play the 'St Anne's' fugue in public (on the piano). Both Wesley and Crotch gave prominence to Bach in lectures on the history of music. In later life Wesley's enthusiasm was unabated, and he converted Henry John Gauntlett and his own son S.S. Wesley, who played the 'St Anne's' fugue as an organ duet at St Stephen's, Coleman Street, in 1827.

As well as the keyboard works, Wesley endeavoured to promote other music of Bach. The motet *Jesu, meine Freude* was sung at his concert in the Hanover Square Rooms on 3 June 1809, and the following year he presented to the Madrigal Society a score of the same work (with text translated into Latin). He played the sonatas for violin and keyboard many times with Jacob, and on 6 June 1814 he played one with Salomon at the latter's benefit. Nevertheless, for many years Bach was known in England more by reputation than by experience. John Sainsbury's *Dictionary of Musicians* (1824) gave twice as much space to J.S. Bach as to all his sons and relatives put together – in itself a surprising fact; yet as late as 1849, at the opening of the Bach Society, he was still called 'this great and comparatively unknown master'. After Wesley's early efforts there was a period when little new progress was made. Mendelssohn's visits of 1829 and 1832 were a fresh stimulus, and his performances of organ works at St Paul's Cathedral, with pedals, and played with a degree of confidence and understanding that no English musician could equal, were undoubtedly a revelation to English audiences. Moscheles also played his part: he performed the D minor keyboard concerto (with additional orchestral parts of his own) at the King's Theatre on 13 May 1836, and the following year included preludes and fugues from the '48' at several concerts. Monck Mason announced Bach's Passion oratorios for the 1832 season of oratorio concerts at the King's Theatre, but nothing came of this. Parts of the *St Matthew Passion*, B minor Mass and *Magnificat* were given at the Birmingham Festival (1837) and at the Ancient Concerts. Prince Albert, after his marriage to Victoria in 1840, introduced music by Bach into concerts at Buckingham Palace and Windsor Castle and at aristocratic musical societies in which he was concerned. Sterndale Bennett was another champion of Bach, performing keyboard and chamber works at many of his concerts and editing some of the music, including the *St Matthew Passion*, for publication. At Cambridge in the 1840s T.A. Walmisley lectured on Bach and taught his students to revere him above all other composers.

The English Bach Revival culminated in the formation of the Bach Society, founded by Sterndale Bennett. The first meeting, on 27 October 1849, at Bennett's house in Russell Place, formulated the objects of the society, which included the collection and promotion, but not publication, of the works of the master (though the society did publish a volume of the motets, with English text added, in 1851). A number of concerts were given, and at last the *St Matthew Passion* had its first English performance (with English words) at the Hanover Square Rooms on 6 April 1854, Bennett conducting. Several other important works were revived before the society disbanded in 1870. The popularization of Bach was completed when his choral masterpieces were accepted alongside Handel's and Mendelssohn's. The *St Matthew Passion* was introduced at the Three Choirs Festival in 1871, and the Bach Choir undertook the regular performance of the larger choral works, beginning with the Mass in B minor in 1876.

BIBLIOGRAPHY

J.F. Reichardt: 'Johann Sebastian Bach', *Musikalisches Kunstmagazin*, iv (1782), 196–7; repr. in H.-J. Schulze, ed.: *Bach Dokumente, iii: Dokumente zum Nachwirken Johann Sebastian Bachs, 1750–1800* (Kassel, 1972), 357–60

J.A. Hiller: 'Bach (Johann Sebastian)', *Lebensbeschreibungen berühmter Musikgelehrten und Tonkünstler neuerer Zeit* (Leipzig, 1784/*R*), i, 9–29; repr. in H.-J. Schulze, ed.: *Bach Dokumente*, iii: *Dokumente zum Nachwirken Johann Sebastian Bachs, 1750–1800* (Kassel, 1972), 395–403

[C.P.E. Bach]: comparison between Bach and Handel, *Allgemeine deutsche Bibliothek*, lxxxi (1788), 295–303; repr. in H.-J. Schulze, ed.: *Bach Dokumente*, iii: *Dokumente zum Nachwirken Johann Sebastian Bachs 1750–1800* (Kassel, 1972), 437–445

J.N. Forkel: *Über Johann Sebastian Bachs Leben, Kunst, und Kunstwerke* (Leipzig, 1802; Eng. trans. in David and Mendel)

A.F.C. Kollman: 'Of John Sebastian Bach and his Works', *QMR*, i (1812), 28–40

M. Mason: Announcement of plans for opera season, *Harmonicon*, x (1832), 29–31

E. Wesley, ed.: *Letters of Samuel Wesley to Mr. Jacobs* (London, 1875)

M. Schneider: 'Verzeichnis der bis zum Jahre 1851 gedruckten (und der geschrieben im Handel gewesenen) Werke von Johann Sebastian Bach', *BJb* (1906), 84–113

J.R. Sterndale Bennett: *The Life of William Sterndale Bennett* (Cambridge, 1907), 202–17, 232–5

H.T. David and A.Mendel, eds.: *The Bach Reader* (New York, 1945, rev.3/1998 as *The New Bach Reader* by C. Wolff)

F. Blume: *Johann Sebastian Bach im Wandel der Geschichte* (Kassel, 1947; Eng. trans., 1950, as *Two Centuries of Bach*)

W. Emery: 'The London Autograph of "The Forty-eight"', *ML*, xxxiv (1953), 106–23, esp. 114

S. Grossman-Vendrey: *Felix Mendelssohn-Bartholdy und die Musik der Vergangenheit* (Regensburg, 1969)

W. Wiora, ed.: *Die Ausbreitung des Historismus über die Musik* (Regensburg, 1969)

L. Plantinga: 'Clementi, Virtuosity, and the "German Manner"', *JAMS*, xxv (1972), 303–30

H.-J. Schulze, ed.: *Bach-Dokumente*, iii: *Dokumente zum Nachwirken Johann Sebastian Bachs 1750–1800*(Kassel, 1972)

H.-J. Schulze: *Studien zur Bach-Überlieferung im 18. Jahrhundert* (Leipzig and Dresden, 1984)

L. Finscher: 'Bach in the Eighteenth Century', *Bach Studies*, ed. D.O. Franklin (Cambridge, 1989), 281–96

G. Stauffer: *The Forkel – Hoffmeister & Kühnel Correspondence: a Document of the Early 19th-Century Bach Revival* (New York, 1990)

C. Wolff: 'On the Recognition of Bach and "the Bach Chorale": Eighteenth-Century Perspectives', *Bach: Essays on his Life and Music* (Cambridge, MA, 1991), 382–90

R. Kaiser: 'Palschaus Bach-Spiel in London: zur Bach-Pflege in England um 1750', *BJb 1993*, 225–9

P. Wollny: 'Wilhelm Friedemann Bach's Halle Performances of Cantatas by his Father', *Bach Studies 2*, ed. D. Melamed (Cambridge, 1995), 202–28

P. Wollny: 'Zur Überlieferung der Instrumentalwerke Johann Sebastian Bachs: der Quellenbesitz Carl Philipp Emanuel Bachs', *BJb 1996*, 7–21

M. Heinemann and H.-J.Hinrichsen, eds.: *Johann Sebastian Bach und die Nachwelt* (Laaber, 1997)

NICHOLAS TEMPERLEY/PETER WOLLNY

Bachschmidt [Bachschmid], **(Johann) Anton (Adam)** (*b* Melk, Lower Austria, 11 Feb 1728; *d* Eichstätt, 29 Dec 1797). German composer and violin virtuoso of Austrian birth. He came from a long line of musicians who emigrated to Melk late in the 17th century from Traunstein, Bavaria. While still a young man he was appointed *Thurnermeister* (director of instrumental music) in Melk, a post which he held from July 1751 to May 1753. He left his native town for travels as a virtuoso and may have been employed briefly at Würzburg (or Wurzbach) before settling in Eichstätt. There he established himself as a versatile musician in the court orchestra of Prince-Bishop Johann Anton II, using steadily in rank from violinist (September 1753) to Konzertmeister (March 1768) and finally to court Kapellmeister (July 1773). Although he developed a reputation primarily as a church composer, Bachschmidt wrote a number of dramatic works for Eichstätt's theatres. His turn from Latin school drama to Italian opera reflects the closing of the Jesuit theatre in Eichstätt in 1773.

WORKS

MSS mainly in CH-E, D-BB, EB, Es, Ew, Mbm, OB, Rtt, WEY, WS

Operas: Erstickter Neid und Eifersucht, 1762, lost; Die Liebe zum Vaterland, 1766, lost; Il re pastore (P. Metastasio), 1774; L'eroe cinese (Metastasio), 1775, lost; La clemenza di Tito (Metastasio), 1776; Demetrio (Metastasio), 1777, lost; Antigono (Metastasio), 1778; Ezio (A. Raimund), 1780, lost

Lat. school dramas, music lost: Constantinus ultimus orientis Caesar, 1761; Jactura fidei, 1764; Pietas in parentem, 1765; S Richardus rex, 1766; Sol ex eclipsi, 1768

Church music: 21 masses, incl. Missa pastoritia, *A-M*; 1 Requiem; 3 Domine; 10 hymns; 29 litanies; 34 offertories; 2 processional songs for Corpus Christi; 9 psalms; 2 Stabat mater; 6 Te Deum; 12 vespers

Inst: 1 orch suite; 1 ov.; 3 vn concs.; Bn Conc.; 24 syms. listed in catalogue of *D-Rtt*; 6 str qts listed in Breitkopf catalogue (1773), lost; Ob Conc., listed in *GerberL*, lost

BIBLIOGRAPHY

BrookB; *EitnerQ*; *LipowskyBL*

R. Schlecht: *Musikgeschichte der Stadt Eichstätt* (MS, 1883, *D-Es*) [with thematic catalogue]

J. Sax: 'Musik und Theater in der fürstbischöflichen Residenzstadt Eichstätt bis zum Jahre 1802', *Jahresbericht des historischen Vereins für Mittelfranken*, xlvi (1898), 6

J. Gmelch: *Die Musikgeschichte Eichstätts* (Eichstätt, 1914)

H. Dennerlein: 'Musik des 18. Jahrhunderts in Franken: die Inventare der Funde von Ebrach, Burgwindheim, Maria Limbach und Iphofen', *Bericht des historischen Vereins für die Pflege der Geschichte des Ehematigen Füstbistums Bamberg*, xcii (1952–3), 273–321

R. Münster and R. Machold: *Thematischer Katalog der Musikhandschriften der ehemaligen Klosterkirchen Weyarn, Tegernsee und Benediktbeuern* (Munich, 1971)

R.N. Freeman: *The Practice of Music at Melk Abbey, based upon the Documents, 1681–1826* (Vienna, 1989)

H. Unverricht: 'Die Eichstätter Hofkapellmeister', *Musik in Bayern*, xlii (1991), 97–109

ROBERT N. FREEMAN

Bach Society. English society founded in 1849 by Sterndale Bennett as part of the English Bach Revival. *See* BACH REVIVAL, §2.

Bach trumpet (Ger. *Bachtrompete*). A misnomer still prevalent in German-speaking countries for any high TRUMPET used in modern performances of Baroque music. Originally, the term was applied to a straight trumpet in A (a 5th higher than the Baroque trumpet in D and a semitone lower than the modern B♭ trumpet) with two valves; such an instrument was first employed by the Berlin trumpeter Julius Kosleck in September 1884 in Eisenach. He also played it on 21 March 1885 in a historic performance of Bach's Mass in B minor at the Royal Albert Hall in London, with Walter Morrow and John Solomon playing the second and third parts on normal instruments. Kosleck's trumpet was described as being in B♭/A and possessing a posthorn (conical) bore. Its mouthpiece was also deeply conical. Morrow and Solomon immediately had such instruments made (they were apparently imported by Silvani & Smith from France), although theirs had the standard cylindro-conical trumpet bore and were played with a normal trumpet mouthpiece. Morrow first employed his at the 1886 Leeds Festival; Solomon's instrument still survives.

The public was misled by journalists to believe that the 'Bach trumpet' was a replica of the valveless trumpet of Bach's day, even though W.F.H. Blandford, with Morrow's support, published an article thoroughly exploding the fallacy. The straight 'Bach trumpet' in B♭/A was, furthermore, discarded as soon as still shorter trumpets in D were made, also in the straight form but with three valves. The first was manufactured by Mahillon in 1892. Even before that, in 1885, Besson of Paris had made a high G trumpet for the Parisian Teste for a performance of Bach's *Magnificat*, and V.C. (not Barthélémy) Mahillon is said to have invented a so-called 'piccolo B flat "Bach" trumpet' a year later. The shorter instruments, with correspondingly greater distance between the notes of the harmonic series in any given register, considerably simplified the problem of accuracy in the high register. Curiously, the term 'Bach trumpet' was used to refer to the shorter instruments as well as to Kosleck's original model.

BIBLIOGRAPHY

W. Menke: *History of the Trumpet of Bach and Handel* (London, 1934/R), 228
W.F.H. Blandford: 'The "Bach Trumpet"', *MMR*, lxv (1935), 49–51, 73–6, 97–100
P. Bate: *The Trumpet and Trombone* (London, 1966, 2/1972), 174–80
H. Heyde: *Das Ventilblasinstrument* (Leipzig, 1987), 199–200
W. Waterhouse: *The New Langwill Index* (London, 1993), 249, 273
R. Dahlqvist and B.Eklund: 'The Bach Renaissance and the Trumpet', *Euro-ITG Newsletter* (1995/1), 12–17
R. Dahlqvist and B.Eklund: 'The Brandenburg Concerto No. 2', *Euro-ITG Newsletter* (1995/2), 4–9

EDWARD H. TARR

Bachus, Johannes de. *See* BACCHIUS, JOHANNES DE.

Bacilieri, Giovanni (*fl* 1607–19). Italian composer. All that is known of his life is that for a time he was a priest at Ferrara. His three published collections are of church music intended for particular liturgical rites: some double-choir psalms and two rather more unusual compilations, for Holy Week and the Office of the Dead, neither of which was commonly set to measured music at this period. The Holy Week collection uses traditional styles, including *falsobordone*, chanting and *alternation* polyphony in five parts. This, together with the pompous Latin titles, suggests a rather conservative style for Ferrara, which on the whole had a progressive musical outlook at this time.

WORKS
all published in Venice

Lamentationes, Benedictus et Evangelia, quae publice in ecclesiis diebus Dominicis Palmarum, et Feriae Sextae leguntur, ad novum musicae concentum, 5vv, redacta, op.1 (1607)
Vesperae 8vv, una cum parte organica concinendae, op.2 (1610)
Totum defunctorum officium ex Pauli V Pont. Max. rituali recentiori modulatione, 5vv, musice redditum, op.3 (1619)

JEROME ROCHE/ELIZABETH ROCHE

Bacilly [Basilly, Bassilly], **Bénigne de** (*b* ?Normandy, ?*c*1625; *d* Paris, 27 Sept 1690). French singing teacher and composer. He may have been a priest. He lived for most of his life in Paris but he was also in the service of Charles of Lorraine, Duke of Elbeuf. Although he was important as a composer and teacher, Bacilly's most valuable legacy is the vocal treatise *Remarques curieuses sur l'art de bien chanter*, which has for long been recognized as one of the most detailed sources of information on French 17th-century vocal practice. However, until the publication of an English translation with the examples included, the application of its precepts to vocal performance had been virtually impossible since the examples Bacilly used to illustrate his teachings were not included in the text (he simply referred instead to specific passages in published volumes of *airs de cour*). The importance of the *Remarques* lies in two main areas: it is one of the earliest volumes to give specific descriptions and applications of the expressive melodic figures (*agréments*) that had been adopted into the musical language of all Europe by the 18th century, and fully half the treatise is devoted to an exhaustive discussion of the meaning, structure, pronunciation and rhythm of French poetry, with detailed instructions as to its amplification through musical ornamentation – ample evidence of the master–servant relationship between poetry and ornamentation. Bacilly took his examples from *airs* whose short, delicate couplets are matched by tender, unobtrusive melodies. In the anthologies of *airs* of Bacilly's time it was the composer's custom to print the melody of the second verse as an elaborate variation of the first. Bacilly referred to those diminutions as written-down improvisations of the singer-composer and analysed their relationship to the poetry. He was himself active as a composer in this genre, but many of his collections of *airs* were published in limited runs of 30 or fewer, and in some cases no copies are extant.

WORKS
all printed works published in Paris

SACRED

Les airs spirituels ... sur les stances chrestiennes de M l'Abbé Testu ... avec basse continue, et les seconds couplets en diminution (1672)
Les airs spirituels ... avec la basse continue, les chiffres pour l'accompagnement, et les seconds couplets en diminution, seconde partie (1677)
Les airs spirituels ... dans un plus grand nombre et une plus grande perfection que dans les précédents éditions, deux parties (1688) [revision of the two collections above; further edns in 1692 and 1693]

SECULAR

Nouveau livre d'airs (1661)
Premier livre d'airs (1662)
XXII livre de chansons pour danser et pour boire à deux parties (1663)
Second livre de chansons pour danser et pour boire à deux parties (1664)
Second livre d'airs à deux parties ... dédié à son Altesse Mademoiselle de Nemours (1664)
III. livre de chansons pour danser et pour boire (1665)
IIII. livre de chansons pour danser et pour boire (1666)
V. livre de chansons pour danser et pour boire (1667)
Capilotade bachique à deux parties contenant les alphabets de fragmens choisis des meilleures chansons à boire (1667)
Les trois livres d'airs ... augmentez de plusieurs airs nouveaux, de chiffres pour le théorbe et d'ornemens pour la méthode de chanter, première partie (1668)
VI. livre de chansons pour danser et pour boire (1668)
Meslanges d'airs à deux parties, d'airs à boire et autres chansons (1671)
II. livre des meslanges, de chansons, airs sérieux et à boire, à 2 et 3 parties (1674)
Second livre d'airs bachiques ... contenant plusieurs récits de basses et autres airs à deux et à trois parties avec une seconde édition du premier recueil corrigée et augmentée (1677)
Recueil des huit livres de chansons pour boire e pour danser (1699)
Songs, sacred and secular, in Airs de différents autheurs à deux parties (1658); IIe livre d'airs de différents autheurs à deux parties (1659); XX recueil de chansons pour danser et pour boire (1661); IVe [–XIIIe] livre d'airs de différents autheurs à deux parties (1661–70); XXI. livre de chansons pour danser et pour boire (1662); Premier livre d'airs à boire ... contre les incommoditez du temps (1673); Recueil de chansonettes de différents autheurs (1675); Mercure galant (1679–90); VIe recueil de Chansonettes de differents autheurs (1680); Nouvelles poésies spirituelles et morales (1737); Airs notez des cantiques sur les points les plus importans de la religion et de la morale chrétienne (1738); Airs et

brunettes à 2 et 3 dessus pour les flûtes traversières tirez des meilleurs autheurs (n.d.); MSS in *F-Pn*

EDITIONS

Recueil des plus beaux vers ... mis en chant, avec le nom des autheurs tant des airs que des paroles (1661)
Recueil des plus beaux vers ... mis en chant. 3me partie (1661)
Suite de la première partie du recueil des plus beaux vers ... (1661)
Recueil des plus beaux vers ... Seconde et novelle partie dans laquelle sont compris les airs de Versailles (1668)
Journal de toutes le nouveautés du chant (?1668), lost
Recueil de tous les plus beaux airs bachiques, avec les noms des autheurs du chant et des paroles (1671)
Le bon mary. Comédie (1678), lost, cited in *Le Mercure galant*
Premier recueil d'airs sérieux et à boire de différents autheurs, à deux et trois parties (1679)
Nouveau recueil des plus beaux vers mis en chant, augmenté de tous les airs les plus nouveaux et de plusieurs grands récits et autres couplets de Mme la Comtesse de la Suze ... (1680)

THEORETICAL WORKS

Remarques curieuses sur l'art de bien chanter (1668/R, 4/1681; Eng. trans., 1968; Eng. trans. of pt 1 in Lorimer)
Traité de la méthode, ou Art de bien chanter par le sieur B.D.B. (1671)
L'art de bien chanter de M de Bacilly, augmenté d'un discours qui sert de réponse à la critique de ce traité (1679)
Traité de la méthode, ou Art de chanter par M de B*** (1681), lost, cited in *FétisB*

BIBLIOGRAPHY

T. Gérold: *L'art du chant en France au XVIIe siècle* (Strasbourg, 1921/R)
H. Prunières: 'Un maître de chant au XVIIe siècle: Bénigne de Bacilly', *RdM*, iv (1923), 156–60
A.B. Caswell: *The Development of Seventeenth-Century French Vocal Ornamentation and its Influence upon Late Baroque Ornamentation Practice* (diss., U. of Minnesota, 1964)
G.K. Ryhming: 'L'art du chant français au XVIIIe siècle selon Bénigne de Bacilly', *Revue musicale de Suisse romande*, xxxv/1 (1982), 10–25
C. Massip: *Michel Lambert (1610–1696): contribution à l'histoire de la monodie en France* (diss., U. of Paris-Sorbonne, 1985)
C. Guinamard: 'Remarques curieuses sur l'art de bien chanter de Bénigne de Bacilly', *Aspects de la musique baroque et classique à Lyon et en France*, ed. D. Paquette (Lyon, 1989), 73–86
C.E. Gordon-Seifert: *The Language of Music in France: Rhetoric as a Basis for Expression in Michel Lambert's 'Les airs de Monsieur Lambert' (1669) and Bénigne de Bacilly's 'Les trois livres d'airs' (1668)* (diss., U. of Michigan, 1994)
P. Lescat: 'Catalogue des ouvrages de Bénigne de Bacilly', *Benigne de Bacilly: Les trois livres d'airs regravez en deux volumes* [facs.] (Courlay, 1996), 4–15
E.M. Lorimer: *An Annotated Translation of the First Part of Bénigne de Bacilly's 'Remarques curieuses sur l'art de bien chanter'* (diss., U. of Oxford, 1998)

AUSTIN B. CASWELL/R

Back [Bagg], Konrad (*b* Haigerloch, 23 June 1749; *d* Ottobeuren, 10 April 1810). South German monastic composer. After studying in Zwiefalten and Ehingen an der Donau, he entered the Benedictine monastery of Ottobeuren in 1771. He was taught music by Ernestus Weinrauch in Zwiefalten and by Franz Schnitzer and Christoph Neubauer in Ottobeuren. He served the monastery as choir leader, music teacher and master of novices. After the suspension of the state endowment to Ottobeuren in 1802, he continued to live there as a pensioner. Back enriched the active musical life of the abbey primarily through his liturgical compositions, of which two masses, dated 1793, survive in the Munich Staatsbibliothek and several smaller works in Ottobeuren. He also wrote at least one cantata for the abbey (*Der Tod Jesu*, manuscript copies in Munich and Salzburg), and some stage works, including a *drama musicum*, *Authore parente servata religio* (1794, autograph in Munich), and

Josephus honoratus, performed at Ottobeuren in 1792 and now lost. His only known printed work is a symphony which appeared in an anthology published in Berlin by Hummel.

BIBLIOGRAPHY

EitnerQ
P.A. Lindner: 'Album Ottoburanum', *Zeitschrift des Historischen Vereins für Schwaben und Neuburg*, xxxi (1904), 1–90, esp. 45 [with list of compositions]
W. Klemm: 'Benediktinisches Barocktheater in Südbayern, insbesondere des Reichsstiftes Ottobeuren', *Studien und Mitteilungen zur Geschichte des Benediktinerordens und seiner Zweige*, liv (1936), 95–184, 397–432; lv (1937), 274–304
W. Pfänder: 'Das Musikleben der Abtei Ottobeuren vom 16. Jahrhundert bis zur Säkularisation', *Ottobeuren 764–1964: Beiträge zur Geschichte der Abtei* (Augsburg, 1964), 58–9
S. Michl: 'Theatermusik Ottobeurer Hauskomponisten im 18. Jahrhundert', *Musik in bayerischen Klöstern*, i, ed. R. Münster (Regensburg, 1986), 189–224

ADOLF LAYER

Back, Oskar (*b* Vienna, 9 June 1879; *d* Brussels, 3 Jan 1963). Dutch violinist and teacher of Hungarian origin. He studied at the conservatories in Vienna and Brussels (with Ysaÿe and César Thomson), and taught at the Brussels Conservatory, 1910–18. In 1919 he settled in Holland and was one of the distinguished violinists who supplemented the Amsterdam Concertgebouw Orchestra under Mengelberg for the historic Mahler Festival of 1920. Back devoted himself chiefly to teaching, first with private lessons and later at the Amsterdam Muzieklyceum and the Rotterdam Conservatory. He taught most of the leading Dutch violinists and orchestral leaders, among whom the best-known are Herman Krebbers, Theo Olof, Willem Noske, Jo Juda, Emmy Verhey and Jean Louis Stuurop; he also taught a number of foreign students, including Alma Moodie. The Oskar Back Foundation was set up after his death to provide assistance for talented young Dutch violinists; it organizes a national violinists' competition, held every other year.

BIBLIOGRAPHY

W. Paap: 'Oskar Back 80 jaar', *Mens en melodie*, xiv (1959), 192–4
W. Noske: 'In memoriam Oskar Back', *Sonorum speculum*, no.15 (1963), 44–8

TRUUS DE LEUR

Bäck, Sven-Erik (*b* Stockholm, 16 Sept 1919; *d* Stockholm, 10 Jan 1994). Swedish composer. He was born into a Protestant family and came into early contact with unpretentious chamber music, jazz and Lutheran church music. He studied the violin with Sven Karpe and then (1938–43) at the Stockholm Music High School with Charles Barkel, in whose quartet he played the viola (1944–53). The decisive influence on him, however, was Rosenberg, who gave him private tuition in composition (1940–45). With other Rosenberg pupils, including Blomdahl and Lidholm, he formed the Monday Group which met, from 1944 for some years, on Mondays at Blomdahl's home to discuss and analyse their own and other music; they also studied Hindemith's *Unterweisung im Tonsatz* and other works. Bäck subsequently took a leading position in Swedish musical life: he was on the boards of the Swedish Royal Academy of Music and of the Theatre and Music Council, and in 1958 he was appointed principal of the Edsberg Music School attached to Swedish radio, where he proved himself a brilliant teacher of interpretation and performance in Renaissance, Baroque and contemporary music. This side of his work dates back to 1948, when he visited the Schola Cantorum in Basle, the orchestra whose style was emulated by the Lilla Kammarorkestern in which Bäck played (1943–8) and by the Kammarorkestern –53, which he led from its creation in 1953 to 1957.

Bäck first developed an individual style in religious works, notably *Ur Johannes 3* (1946) and *Ur Jesaja 9* (1947). The much-performed Solo Flute Sonata (1949) shows how short was the step, in his mind, from vocal to instrumental writing, for its first movement is a direct development of a setting of Psalm xlii. Rosenberg's teaching had stressed melody as an essential element even in polyphonic works, and Bäck introduced quite original melodic ornaments, easily recognized in his music of the 1950s. When, with the other members of the Monday Group, he discovered 12-note composition, he preferred the aphoristic and lyrical qualities of Webern, and this led him to a thoroughly *pointilliste* style best exploited in *A Game around a Game* for orchestra (1959). He often worked with artists in other media, notably in the successful chamber opera *Tranfjädrarna* ('The Crane Feathers', 1956), and extended the collaboration in such works as *Favola* (1962), for which Östen Sjöstrand wrote a poem and Björn Erling Evensen produced a sculpture; Evensen also constructed murals to be seen to the accompaniment of electronic music by Bäck. Towards electronic composition, as practised by Stockhausen and others, Bäck had at first remained sceptical, but from 1969 he worked intensively in the medium, composing some 'electronic motets' that form a sequel to those more conventional motets of his, for mixed choir *a cappella*, which are among the major contemporary contributions to liturgical music.

WORKS
(selective list)

STAGE

Operas: Tranfjädrarna [The Crane Feathers] (chbr op, B. Malmberg, after Kinoshita), 1956, Swedish radio, 1957; Gästabudet [The Banquet] (Ö. Sjöstrand), Stockholm, 1958; Fågeln [The Bird] (A. Obrenovic), 1960, Swedish radio, 1961
Ballets: Svanesång (B. Åkesson), children's chorus, fl, va, timp, 1947; Danssvit (Åkesson), 2 pf, 1951; Nature morte (Åkesson), va, bn, perc, 1955; Ikaros (Åkesson), orch, 1963; Movements (Åkesson), orch, 1965

ORCHESTRAL

Sinfonia, str, 1951; Variationer över en luthersk kyrkovisa, 1954, rev. as Fantasi över 'Dies sind die heilgen zehn Gebot', 1957; Sinfonia da camera, 1955; Vn Conc., 1957; A Game around a Game, 1959; Arkitektur, 2 ww orchs, perc, 1960; Intrada, 1964; Vc Conc., 1965; Movimento II [concert version of ballet Movements], 1966; O altitudo II, 1966; Ruoli, 1966; Serenade/Sumerki, str orch, 1977; Sumerki 90, 1990

VOCAL

Choral: Ur Johannes 3, vv, org ad lib, 1946; Ur Jesaja 9, 1947; Glädje i Gud, cant., solo vv, vv, org, 1948; Dityramb (G. Ekelöf), unison female vv, chbr orch, 1949; Kattresan (Conc. per bambini) (I. Arosenius), cant., children's vv, rec, vn, perc, 1952; Himlaljusens fader, cant., solo vv, vv, str, org, 1952; Sinfonia sacra, vv, orch, 1953; 15 motets for the church year, 1959–81; Uppbrottets mässa (O. Hartman, L. Håkansson), vv, unison vv, org, perc. 1967; Humlan (F. Isaksson), vv, vc, pf, perc, 1968; Behold I am Making all Things New, vv, 1968; Vid havets yttersta gräns (cant., Sjöstrand), solo vv, mixed choir, orch, tape, 1979
Solo vocal: 3 kinesiska sånger, 1v, pf, 1945; Neither nor, S, pf, perc, 1971

CHAMBER, INSTRUMENTAL AND ELECTRONIC

Str qts: 1945, 1947, 1962, 1984
For 3–10 insts: Exercitier, str qnt, 1948; Préambule pour Pierre, str qt, 1949; Str Trio no.1, vn, va, db, 1953; Nuovo su vecchio, old insts, 1962; Postludium, fl, pf, perc, 1967; sentire ..., fl, vc, pf,

1969; Str Trio no.2, 1970; Decet, wind qnt, str qnt, 1972; Signos, perc ens, 1980; Trio (Sentire . . .), vn, vc, pf, 1986; Octet, str, 1988; Stella maris, wind qt, 1988; Sumerki 92, cl, vc, pf, 1992
For 1–2 insts: Sonata, fl, 1949; Elegie, a sax, pf, 1952; Sonata, 2 vc, 1957; Favola, cl, perc, 1962; 5 preludier, fl/vn/va/vc/cl/bn, 1964; O altitudo, org, 1966; For Eliza, org, tape ad lib, 1971; Time Present, 2 vn, elec, 1975
For pf: Expansiva preludier, 1950; Sonata alla ricercare, 1950; Impromptu, 1957; Tollo, 2 pf, 1974
Tape: In principio, 1969; Porten, 1969; Mur och port, 1971; Nox lucebit, 1971; Genom jorden genom havet, 1972; Muri, 1972; Les grands faux-penseurs ..., 1975

Incid music for plays, films

Principal publisher: Hansen

BIBLIOGRAPHY

Nutida musik, x/3–4 (1966–7) [special number]
H. Connor: *Samtal med tonsättare* (Stockholm, 1971)
G. Bergendal: *33 svenska komponister* (Stockholm, 1972)
P.A. Hellquist: 'Bäck, Sven-Erik', *Sohlmans musiklexikon*, i (Stockholm, 2/1975)
G. Aulén: *Sven-Erik Bäcks motetter: en musikalisk teologisk studie* (Stockholm, 1977)
G. Schönfelder: 'Sven-Erik Bäck: "Den stund kommer"', *Prinzip Wahrheit, Prinzip Schönheit* ed. G. Schönfelder and H. Åstrand (Stockholm, 1984), 129–172; Eng. trans. in *Contemporary Swedish Music through the Telescopic Sight* (Stockholm, 1993), 58–109
S.R. Peterson: *A Performance Guide to the Unaccompanied 'Motetter för kyrkoårt' of Sven-Erik Bäck* (Ann Arbor, MI, 1990)
J.L. Höglund, ed.: *Sven-Erik Bäck: en bok om musikern och medmänniskan* (Stockholm, 1999)

PER-ANDERS HELLQUIST, HANS ÅSTRAND

Back check. *See* CHECK.

Backer Grøndahl, Agathe (**Ursula**) (*b* Holmestrand, 1 Dec 1847; *d* Kristiania [now Oslo], 4 June 1907). Norwegian composer and pianist. She married the conductor Olams Andreas Grøndahl in 1875. She first studied the piano in Christiania with Winter-Hjelm and Kjerulf, then in Berlin at Kullak's Neue Akademie der Tonkunst (1865–7) and later (1871–2) with Bülow in Florence and Liszt in Weimar. She also studied theory and composition with L.M. Lindeman in Christiania and R. Wüerst in Berlin. Influential in Norway as both performer and teacher, she also made concert tours in the other Scandinavian countries and in Germany and England, and was recognized as an outstanding pianist by her contemporaries. Her chief significance, however, was as a composer of songs (of which she wrote about 190) and piano pieces (about 120); she also wrote some songs for chorus, and more than 50 Norwegian folksong arrangements; her orchestral compositions are limited to two works from her student days in Berlin.

The best of Backer Grøndahl's songs, such as the cycles *Barnets vårdag* ('The Child's Spring Day') to poems of A. Jynge, and *Ahasverus*, to poems of B.S. Ingemann, belong to the standard Norwegian Romantic song repertory. Their strength lies in the shapely, singable melodies reflecting the moods of the texts. Although the piano generally plays a supporting role, only rarely functioning independently, the accompaniments are nonetheless carefully worked out and sometimes include elements of tone-painting. Most of the songs are in varied strophic form, but there are also simple strophic and through-composed examples. Her piano works are for the most part descriptively titled lyric pieces in simple song forms or, less often, in larger fantasy-like forms. Among the best known are the *Serenade* (op.15 no.1), *Ballade* (op.36 no.5), *Sommervise* ('Summer Song') (op.45 no.3) and the fairytale suite *I blaafjellet* ('In the Blue Mountain') (op.44). The concert studies are among her finest works, and some of them make considerable technical demands on the performer. Although Backer Grøndahl's career was in the heyday of late Romanticism, her style remained conservative and principally modelled on earlier composers, including Schubert, Mendelssohn and Schumann. The specifically folk-influenced Norwegian tradition, which left its stamp on many of her contemporaries, seems to have had only a slight effect on her music; her folksong arrangements show some of the characteristic traits of Norwegian folk music, but do not have the stylistic interest and originality of the arrangements by Grieg and Kjerulf. Her original compositions, however, have a melodic charm that has secured them a lasting place at the heart of the Norwegian Romantic repertory.

WORKS
(selective list)
published in Kristiania unless otherwise stated

SONGS

3 sange (V. Bergsøe, Caralis), op.1, 1868–9 (Copenhagen, 1872); 5 sange, op.2, 1871 (Copenhagen, 1873); 5 sange, op.3, 1870–73 (Copenhagen, 1874); 7 sange, op.4, 1869–74 (Copenhagen, 1875); 4 sånger (Z. Topelius), op.5, 1871–2 (Stockholm, 1875); 6 sange, op.6, 1867–71 (Stockholm, 1879); Sommerliv [Summer Life] (H. Hertz), 4 songs, op.7 (Stockholm 1879); 5 sange (Bergsøe), op.8, 1871–6 (Stockholm, 1879); 6 sange, op.9, 1871–9 (1879); 4 Gesänge, op.10, 1871–5 (1879); 5 sånger (Topelius, Runeberg), op.12, 1879 (Stockholm, 1882); 5 sange, op.13 (1881)

6 deutsche Lieder, op.14 (1881); 6 sange, op.16 (1884); Sange ved havet [Songs at Sea] (H. Drachmann), op.17, 1884 (Copenhagen, 1887); 7 folkeviser og romanser, op.18 (1886); Serenade (E. von der Recke), op.21 (1888); Blomstervignetter, 5 songs, op.23 (1888); 6 sange (Drachmann), op.26 (1890); 6 sange, op.27 (1890); Chant de noces: Bryllupsmorgen (H. Gréville), op.28 (1890); 10 sange (V. Krag), op.29 (1892); 10 sange (Krag), op.31 (1894); Norske folkeviser, arr. S, op.34 (1894); Natten er stille [The Night is Calm] (J. Halmrast), De gamles Vals [Old Folk's Waltz] (H. Lunde), op.40 (1897)

5 sange, op.41 (1897); Barnets vårdag [The Child's Spring Day] (A. Jynge), song cycle, op.42 (1899); 8 kjaempeviser, op.43, 1896–7 (1897); 20 folke- og skjaemteviser, op.43, 1896–7 (1897); 5 sange, op.46, 1897–9 (1899); 2 sange fra havet, op.48 (1899); 3 sange i moll, op.49 (1899); Sommer (Jynge), 8 songs, op.50, 1899 (1900); 12 folkeviser og melodier fra fremmede lande, op.51 (1902); Mor synger [The Mother Sings] (Jynge), 8 songs, op.52 (1900); Sydover (H. Reynolds), 6 songs, op.54, 1900 (1901); Ahasverus (B.S. Ingemann), 6 songs, op.56, 1900 (1902); 6 deutsche Liebeslieder aus der Jugend, op.60, 1869–1900 (1903); Kløvereng [Clover Field] (T. Caspari), op.62, 1901 (1903); 4 sange, op.65, 1901–4 (1904); Endnu et streif kun [One more Glimpse] (Somerset), op.70 (1907)

PIANO SOLO

6 concert-etuder, op.11 (1881); 3 morceaux, op.15 (1882); 4 skizzer, op.19 (1886); Suite, 5 movts, op.20 (1887); 3 études, op.22 (1888); 6 idylles, op.24 (1888); 3 klaverstykker, op.25 (1890); [11] Norske folkeviser og folkedanse, op.30 (1891); 3 études de concert, op.32 (Copenhagen, 1895); [8] Norske folkeviser og folkedanse, op.33 (1894); 3 klaverstykker, op.35 (1894); [10] Fantasistykker, op.36 (1895); Serenade, op.37 (1896); 3 ungarske studier, op.38 (1896); [10] Fantasistykker, op.39 (1896)

I blaafjellet [In the Blue Mountain], fairytale suite, 6 pieces, op.44 (1897); [5] Fantasistykker, op.45 (1897); Etudes de concert, op.47 (Copenhagen, 1901); 3 klaverstykker, op.53 (1900); [12] Smaa fantasistykker, op.55 (1902); Etudes de concert, op.57 (Copenhagen, 1903); Concert-études, op.58 (Copenhagen, 1903); 6 klaverstykker, op.59 (1903); Prélude, op.61 no.1, Grand menuet, op.61 no.2 (Copenhagen, 1904); [5] Lettere fantasistykker, op.63 (Copenhagen, 1904); Danse burlesque, op.64 no.1, Valse caprice, op.64 no.2 (1905); Barnlige Billeder [Children Pictures], 6 fantasias, op.66 (1905); 2 klaverstykker, op.68 (1907); 3 klaverstykker, op.69 (1907)

BIBLIOGRAPHY

I. Hoegsbro: *Biography of the Late Agathe Backer-Gröndahl* (New York, 1913)

W.P. Sommerfeldt: *Boktrykker Christopher Grøndahls efterkommere* (Oslo, 1916)

O.M. Sandvik: *Agathe og O.A. Grøndahl 1847–1947* (Oslo, 1948) [with catalogue of works]

K.M. Ganer: *Agathe Backer Grøndahls klaveretyder* (diss., U. of Oslo, 1968)

B. Kortsen: *Agathe Backer Grøndahl og folketonen* (Bergen, 1970)

N. Grinde: *Norsk musikkhistorie* (Oslo, 1971, 4/1993; Eng trans., 1991)

H.-M. Weydahl: 'Agathe Backer Grøndahl og Erika Nissen', *Norsk musikktidsskrift*, xi (1974), 77–83

G. Risa: *Agathe Backer Grøndahl som romansekomponist: en analyse av et utvalg romanser* (diss., U. of Oslo, 1980)

J.L. Iverson: *Piano Music of Agathe Backer Grøndahl* (diss., U. of Northern Colorado, 1993)

C. Dahm: *Agathe Backer Grøndahl: komponisten og pianisten* (Oslo, 1998)

NILS GRINDE

Backers, Americus (*d* London, Jan 1778). Dutch or German maker of harpsichords and pianos, active in England. He worked at 22 Great Jermyn Street, London, from 1763 to 1778. Writing to the *Gentleman's Magazine* in 1812, James Shudi Broadwood attributed the invention of the English grand-piano action to the 'Dutchman' Backers in 1772. It was not until 90 years later that Henry Fowler Broadwood wrote, in his observations on his father's manuscript notes, that John Broadwood and Robert Stodart had assisted Backers with his invention; since Backers had advertised his 'Original Forte Piano' in the *Public Advertiser* of 1 March 1771, claiming that it was 'no Copy, being entirely his own Invention', Backers must have been primarily responsible. The English grand action was an improvement on the action invented by Cristofori: the intermediary underhammer was removed, allowing the hopper to work directly on the notch in the butt of the hammer, and a regulating button and screw to control the escapement was incorporated. Simple but perfect, it was a direct lever action and became standard as the English grand action. (For illustration *see* PIANOFORTE, fig.12.)

The earliest surviving piano that incorporates the English grand action is owned by the Duke of Wellington, and is on loan to Edinburgh University. Its nameboard reads: 'Americus Backers No. 21 Londini fecit 1772'; it is bichord and has una corda and damper pedals. Its hammers have rolled leather heads, although, according to Broadwood's *1862 International Exhibition: List of the Articles Exhibited*, Backers first planned to fit cork or softwood hammerheads, 'with a view to obtain the Harpsichord tone so much admired at that period'. Burney stated that Backers was German, and that he made trichord pianos costing between £60 and £70. Backers made 59 grand pianos; his only surviving harpsichord, owned by Lord Hylton, is dated 1766. It has a compass of five octaves and its disposition is 2 x 8', 1 x 4', with a lute which was originally operated by a pedal.

BIBLIOGRAPHY

BurneyGN

J.S. Broadwood: *Some Notes made by J.S. Broadwood, 1838, with Observations & Elucidations by H.F. Broadwood, 1862* (London, 1862)

S. Newman and P.Williams: *The Russell Collection and Other Early Keyboard Instruments in Saint Cecilia's Hall, Edinburgh* (Edinburgh, 1968)

W.H. Cole: 'Americus Backers: Original Forte Piano Maker', *English Harpsichord Magazine*, iv/4 (1987), 79–86

A. Ribeiro, ed.: [Letter of 21 Jan 1774 to Thomas Twining], *The Letters of Dr Charles Burney*, i: *1751–1784* (Oxford, 1991), 163–5

M. Cole: *The Pianoforte in the Classical Era* (Oxford, 1998)

MARGARET CRANMER

Backfall (i). A term used to denote a short, descending appoggiatura applied on the beat to conjunct notes or notes a pair apart. The 'forefall' ('beat' or 'half-fall') was a rising appoggiatura. The less common slide or double backfall descended a 3rd onto the main note. *See* ORNAMENTS, §6.

Backfall (ii). A lever in an organ's key action or coupler mechanism, which transfers the key action to the vertical tracker or sticker, which in turn causes the pallet in the wind-chest to open. For illustrations *see* ORGAN, figs.5 and 6.

Backfall [backwell] (iii). A lever in a carillon's mechanism.

Background (Ger. *Hintergrund*). In Schenkerian analysis (*see* ANALYSIS, §II, 4) the first, i.e. fundamental, LAYER that underlies a piece or movement. The background layer of a piece is represented by one of a limited number of basic contrapuntal designs, called the URSATZ of the piece.

Thus many pieces of tonal music have the same background structure. For this reason the word 'background' is sometimes used more loosely by analysts to mean structure itself, in opposition to 'foreground' which connotes the surface of the piece.

WILLIAM DRABKIN

Background music. *See* ENVIRONMENTAL MUSIC.

Backhaus, Wilhelm (*b* Leipzig, 26 March 1884; *d* Villach, 5 July 1969). German pianist. He studied the piano with Alois Reckendorf and composition with Salomon Jadassohn at the Leipzig Conservatory. In 1898–9 he was a pupil of d'Albert, but after the age of 15 he was largely self-taught. In 1900–01 he toured England, substituting

Wilhelm Backhaus

for Ziloti in a performance of Beethoven's Fourth Piano Concerto with the Hallé Orchestra under Hans Richter, and in 1901 he made his Promenade Concerts début with Mendelssohn's G minor Concerto, returning to perform Brahms's Paganini Variations at the Proms later the same season. In 1905 he won the Rubinstein Prize in Paris and commenced an intensive international career. Backhaus made the first of many North American tours in 1912–13, playing Beethoven's 'Emperor' Concerto with Walter Damrosch and giving a Carnegie Hall recital. A New York Town Hall recital given in 1921 drew a tumultuous response. However, between 1926 and 1954 his career was based chiefly in Europe, and in 1931 he became a Swiss citizen. His return to America in 1954 to give a series of Beethoven recitals in Carnegie Hall showed an undiminished authority. He held teaching appointments at the RMCM (1905) and at the Curtis Institute in Philadelphia (1925–6). However, he did not view himself as a teacher, and when questioned about his fabled technique commented drily that it was based on scales, arpeggios and Bach. Backhaus made the first-ever concerto recording (the Grieg A minor Concerto) in 1909, and the first complete recording of the Chopin études in 1928; shortly before his death he was completing a second recorded cycle of Beethoven's 32 sonatas which he had begun in 1964, when he was 80. His mastery in such daunting music as the Chopin études was legendary, although he is chiefly remembered for the ruggedness and integrity of his Beethoven and Brahms. Even in his 80s his command of the Brahms B♭ Concerto (which he played in the Royal Festival Hall, London, with Klemperer and recorded with Böhm) remained unfaltering, a tribute to his formidable technical security.

BIBLIOGRAPHY

A.H. Eichmann: *Wilhelm Backhaus* (Geneva, 1957; Eng. trans., 1958)

F.F. Clough and G.J. Cuming: 'A Backhaus Discography', *Gramophone Record Review*, no.68 (1959), 578

J. Kaiser: *Grosse Pianisten in unserer Zeit* (Munich, 1965, 5/1982; Eng. trans., 1971)

E. Werba: 'Wilhelm Backhaus zum Gedenken', *ÖMz*, xxiv (1969), 462 only

BRYCE MORRISON

Backofen, Johann Georg Heinrich (*b* Durlach, 6 July 1768; *d* Darmstadt, 10 July 1839). German harpist, clarinettist and basset-horn player. With his brothers Ernst (bassoonist) and Gottfried (violinist and clarinettist) he went to Nuremberg in 1780 to study music. The Kapellmeister, G.W. Gruber, taught him composition, and H. Birckman the clarinet. From 1789 Backofen made several tours as a clarinettist. He returned to Nuremberg in 1794 and studied the flute. In 1802 he lived at Gotha, where he taught the harp. In 1806 he was appointed court chamber musician and in the same year saw the marriage in Gotha of his pupil Dorette Scheidler to Spohr. In 1811 Backofen became court musician at Darmstadt, where he manufactured clarinets. He wrote a clarinet and basset-horn method in 1803, but as this became outdated when Müller's inventions appeared he produced a new edition in 1824; this contains much useful information. Backofen also wrote a harp method (1801) and compositions for harp, clarinet, basset-horn and wind band. It was probably his niece who appeared as a singer, and whom Hermstedt engaged for the Sondershausen theatre.

BIBLIOGRAPHY

MGG1 suppl. (H.J. Zingel)

P. Weston: *More Clarinet Virtuosi of the Past* (London, 1977), 29–31

H. Rosenzweig: 'Johann Georg Heinrich Backofen: die deutsche Harfe um 1800', *Historische Harfen: Beiträge zur Theorie und Praxis historischer Harfen* (Dornach, 1991), 80–97

PAMELA WESTON

Backus, John (Graham) (*b* Portland, OR, 29 April 1911; *d* Los Angeles, 28 Oct 1988). American acoustician. After studying at Reed College, Portland (BA 1932), he undertook postgraduate study at the University of California in Berkeley (MA 1936, PhD 1940). His early research work was in nuclear physics, working under the supervision of Ernest Lawrence in the Radiation Laboratory at Berkeley. In 1945 he was appointed professor of physics at the University of Southern California, and he continued in that post until his retirement in 1980. An accomplished performer on the piano and the bassoon, Backus was awarded the degree of MMus in conducting by the University of Southern California in 1959. In the later stages of his research career he made major contributions to the study of the acoustics of woodwind instruments, brass instruments and organ pipes. In 1969 the first edition of *The Acoustical Foundations of Music* was published; this became one of the most popular and successful introductory textbooks in musical acoustics. He was awarded the Silver Medal of the Acoustical Society of America in 1986.

WRITINGS

'Small-Vibration Theory of the Clarinet', *JASA*, xxxv (1963), 305–13

with T.C. Hundley: 'Wall Vibrations in Flue Organ Pipes and their Effect on Tone', *JASA*, xxxix (1966), 936–45

The Acoustical Foundations of Music (New York, 1969, 2/1977)

'Input Impedance Curves for the Reed Woodwind Instruments', *JASA*, lvi (1974), 1266–79

'Input Impedance Curves for the Brass Instruments', *JASA*, lx (1976), 470–80

'The Effect of the Player's Vocal Tract on Woodwind Instrument Tone', *JASA*, lxxviii (1985), 17–20

MURRAY CAMPBELL

Bacon, Ernst (*b* Chicago, IL, 26 May 1898; *d* Orinda, CA, 16 March 1990). American composer and pianist. He studied at Northwestern University (1915–18), the University of Chicago (1919–20) and the University of California (MA 1935). Among his teachers were Alexander Raab and Glenn Dillard Gunn (piano), Weigl and Bloch (composition), and Eugene Goossens (conducting), under whom he was assistant conductor of the Rochester Opera Company. He taught at the Eastman School (1925–8) and the San Francisco Conservatory (1928–30); in 1935 he instituted and conducted the Carmel Bach Festival in California, and the next year he was supervisor of the WPA Federal Music Project in San Francisco and conductor of its orchestra. Subsequent teaching appointments took him to Converse College, Spartanburg, South Carolina, as dean and professor of piano (1938–45), and to Syracuse University, as director of the school of music and professor (1945–63, professor emeritus from 1964). Among the awards he received were a Pulitzer Prize (1932, for the Symphony no.1) and two Guggenheim Fellowships.

As a composer Bacon is best known for his songs, which show unusual sensitivity to the colour and inflection of words and a masterly use of syncopation to give the impression of natural speech. His settings of texts by Emily Dickinson and Walt Whitman are considered by many to be among the finest examples of 20th-century American art song. He made many folksong arrangements, and a number of his works on American subjects, such as the folk opera *A Tree on the Plains* (1942) and the orchestral suite *From these States* (1951), draw on various types of indigenous music, including black American and Appalachian tunes, hymns, spirituals and jazz. His music favours clear melodic contours, vigorous contrapuntal energy and strong rhythms that allude occasionally to ragtime and other dance idioms. Though he made use of non-diatonic scales, such as the octatonic, Bacon's harmony remained fundamentally tonal, with an emphasis on open, diatonic intervals.

In addition to composing, Bacon performed as a pianist in Europe and the USA. His published writings include two books, *Words on Music* (Syracuse, NY, 1960/*R*) and *Notes on the Piano* (Syracuse, NY, 1963/*R*). His article 'Our Musical Idiom', published in *The Monist* in October 1917, represents one of the earliest attempts at a systematic classification of all possible harmonies within the 12-note system.

WORKS

Dramatic: Take your Choice (musical comedy), collab. P. Mathias and R. Stoll, San Francisco, 1936; A Tree on the Plains (musical play, 2, P. Horgan), Spartanburg, SC, 1942; A Drumlin Legend (children's op, H. Carus), New York, 1949; Dr. Franklin (musical play, C. Lengyel), 1976; ballets

Orch: Sym. no.1, d, 1932; Bearwalla, pf, str, 1936; Country Roads, Unpaved, suite, 1936; Sym. no.2, 1937; Ford's Theater, 1946; From these States, suite, 1951; Fables (E. Bacon, J. Edmunds), nar, orch, 1953; Great River (Sym. no.3), 1956; Conc. grosso, 1957; Elegy, ob, str, 1957; Erie Waters, suite, 1961; Riolama (Pf Conc. no.1), 1963; Over the Waters, ov., 1976; Pf Conc. no.2, 1982; Remembering Ansel Adams, cl, str, 1985; band works; songs with orch

Chbr: Buncombe County, vn, pf, 1943; Sonata, vc, pf, 1948; Qnt, str qt, db, 1950; Peterborough, suite, va, pf, perf. 1952; A Life, suite, vc, pf, 1966–81; Old Airs from Many Countries, wind ens, 1968; Pf Trio no.1, 1978; Tumbleweeds, cycle, vn, pf, 1979; Sonata, vn, pf, 1982; Pf Trio no.2, 1986; Sonata, va, pf, 1987; pieces for pf, pf 4 hands and org; other works for various insts

Choral: Ecclesiastes, cant., S, B, SATB, orch, 1936; From Emily's Diary (E. Dickinson), women's chorus, pf/small orch, 1947; By Blue Ontario (W. Whitman), cant., A, B, SATB, orch, 1958; Requiem 'The Last Invocation' (Dickinson, Whitman), B, chorus, orch, 1968–71; orats; choral folksong arrs, hymns, and anthems

Songs, 1v, pf: Songs at Parting (Whitman) (1930); 6 Songs (C. Sandburg, Whitman, Dickinson) (1942); The Erie Canal (Amer.) (1942); 5 Poems (Dickinson) (1943); Along Unpaved Roads (Amer.), 8 songs (1944); Is there such a thing as day? (Dickinson) (1944); Buffalo Gals (Amer.) (1946); The Grass (Dickinson) (1946); O Friend (Dickinson) (1946); 4 Songs (W. Shakespeare, J. Lewis, E. Millay) (1946); The Commonplace (Whitman) (1946); The Red Rose (R. Burns) (1947); Velvet People (Dickinson) (1948); over 200 others

Principal publishers: Associated, Birchard, Broude, Chappell, Lawson-Gould, Leeds, E.B. Marks, Mercury, G. Schirmer, Shawnee, Southern, Syracuse UP, Peters, L. Webster

BIBLIOGRAPHY

EwenD; *VintonD*

J. St. Edmunds: 'The Songs of Ernst Bacon', *Shawnee Review* (Oct 1941)

W. Fleming: 'Ernst Bacon', *Musical America*, lxix/36 (1949), 8, 28

E. Bacon: *Ernst Bacon* (Orinda, CA, ?1974) [incl. bibliography, discography, and P. Horgan: 'A Contemporary Tribute']

R.C. Friedberg: *American Art Song and American Poetry*, i (Metuchen, NJ, 1981)

S. Neff: 'An American Precursor of Non-Tonal Theory: Ernst Bacon', *CMc*, no.48 (1991), 5–26

PHILIP L. MILLER/R

Bacon, Richard Mackenzie (*b* Norwich, 1 May 1776; *d* Cossey [now Costessey], 27 Nov 1844). English journalist and writer on music. He was the only son of Richard Bacon (1745–1812), a grocer and printer from Yarmouth who in 1788 became co-proprietor of the weekly *Norwich Mercury*. R.M. Bacon joined him as manager of the printing department at the age of 18, and by 1804, on his father's retirement, became sole proprietor of the paper, a leading Whig journal with a county-wide circulation. The younger Bacon's musical interests – he had a good baritone voice and studied singing with Samuel Arnold – developed naturally in the convivial atmosphere of late 18th-century Norwich. He participated in cathedral events directed by J.C. Beckwith and vocal concerts given by the Anacreontic Society. He also gained local theatre ties, first through his marriage in 1797 to Louise Noverre (1768–1808), niece of the celebrated dancing-master Jean-Georges Noverre, and then through his share-holding interest in the Theatre Royal, Norwich (1806–12).

Bacon became a freeman of the city in 1798, served as captain (1803), then major (1804) in the Norwich Rifle Volunteers, and worked tirelessly to promote advances in local industry. From about 1805 he helped develop a new printing press using a rotary principle, and about 1807 formed a partnership to modernize the paper mill at nearby Taverham, installing a huge Fourdrinier machine. Neither project was completely successful; the mill speculation was in fact disastrous and Bacon spent several years trying to recover his loss. His idea for a quarterly music review – itself based on the innovatory critical approach of the new *Edinburgh Review* – sprang directly from personal financial need about this time. In 1816 he sold the mill and became salaried editor of the *Mercury*. Now living on the outskirts of Norwich, he and his second wife, Margaret Gilbert Burks, reared six children, and Bacon built a reputation as a cultured and articulate writer on many subjects. Liberal minded and humane, he proved to be one of the most distinguished newspaper editors of the early 19th century. Besides writing essays for the *Quarterly Musical Magazine and Review* (*QMMR*) and leading articles and arts reviews for the *Mercury*, he wrote pamphlets and essays on economic, social and political topics, drama and arts criticism (*Literary Gazette*), essays on music (*London Magazine*, 1820–25; *New Monthly Magazine*, 1833–5), two political biographies, and three books on singing: *The Grace Book, or Guide to the Science and Practice of Vocal Ornament* (London, c1821), *The Elements of Vocal Science, being a Philosophical Enquiry into some of the Principles of Singing* (London, 1824) and *The Art of Improving the Voice and Ear* (London, c1825). His ambitious plan for a two-volume encyclopaedia of music (c1819–22) was never realized.

Bacon's signal achievement in music was the *QMMR* (published by Robert Baldwin, then Hurst & Chance, autumn 1818–spring 1830), the first long-running English journal devoted to music literature. Its concept as both miscellany and serious critical organ, with a high literary-philosophical style, was unprecedented, and all the more extraordinary for originating outside London music circles. As the journal's founder, editor and chief contributor (all anonymously), printer and, probably, co-proprietor – with support from the London music seller Chappell – Bacon had complete control of the journal's content and tone. His goal was not only to establish a viable public forum for the exchange of musical ideas, but also to raise the intellectual respectability of music in Britain,

and encourage mutual understanding among disparate social groups involved with its practise. He printed a mix of essays on theory, performance, musical institutions, vocal style in Italian and English music, social relations between amateurs and professionals, and issues in music education and patronage, as well as substantial reviews of printed music and books. A few articles are signed or initialled by genuine correspondents, many are translated excerpts from foreign music literature, and still more take the form of pseudonymous essay-letters 'To the Editor'. A large proportion of these can be shown to be by Bacon himself, promoting his Handelian tastes, the need for serious, 'all-sung' English opera, the benefits of the provincial festival movement, and the place of music in society. Among his certain collaborators, William Horsley was particularly important, serving as Bacon's most trenchant reviewer and his inside line to the London professional scene. The editor also relied on a wide circle of musical correspondents, British and foreign, for news, opinion, essay contributions and technical information. The *QMMR* eventually failed for lack of purchasers, but not before Bacon's influence had been felt. It was he who, in 1822, first suggested the Norwich Triennial Festival (established 1824) and, about the same time, was personally consulted over the curriculum of the new RAM. Later he was an effective intermediary between nobility and profession in sharing out printed editions from the King's Library, and in engaging singers for the Ancient Concerts.

Bacon's preoccupation with systems of music education, the rudiments of singing, formation of taste and the social status of musicians was at least partly connected with his concerns as a parent. Each of his four oldest children had some musical skill or interest, and helped with the *QMMR* project. Richard Noverre Bacon (1798–1884) played the cello and probably wrote on cadenzas; an authority on Norfolk agriculture, he later became proprietor of the *Norwich Mercury*. Louisa Mary Bacon (1800–85) gave editorial assistance, possibly wrote on Haydn for the journal, and later published several popular-education works for and about children, 1833–51, giving attention to music. She married a local merchant, John Barwell, and raised a family. Jane Margaret Bacon (*fl* 1820–70) studied music theory and singing in London and Paris, and attained some notice as a mezzo-soprano; she sang for RAM and Philharmonic Society concerts as well as for provincial festivals. Her reputation and professional contacts were helpful in securing musical intelligence for *QMMR*. She married George Taylor, a physician of Kingston, Surrey. Mary Anne Bacon (c1805–75) translated and wrote articles for the journal, translated German, French and Italian songs for Norwich festivals and the Concerts of Ancient Music, and later served as organist of a village church. She also wrote verse and prose tales, and reviewed French literature for the *New Monthly Magazine*. Latterly she compiled and annotated Bacon family papers (now in Cambridge University Library), and served as executrix of her father's estate, valued at around £8000.

BIBLIOGRAPHY

Bacon Collection (MS, *GB-Cu* Add.6239-6247)
'The Late Mr. R.M. Bacon', *Norwich Mercury* (7 Dec 1844)
'Norfolk Notes: a Noted Norwich Editor', *Norfolk News and Weekly Press* (9 April 1921)

Rex Stedman: *Vox Populi: the Norfolk Newspaper Press,
  1760–1900* (thesis for Fellowship of the Library Association,
  1971), 92–101
Jamie Croy Kassler: *The Science of Music in Britain, 1714–1830: a
  Catalogue of Writings, Lectures, and Inventions* (New York,
  1979)
Leanne Langley: *The English Musical Journal in the Early
  Nineteenth Century* (diss., U. of North Carolina, 1983), 194–281

LEANNE LANGLEY

Bacon [Baco], **Roger** (*b* nr Ilchester, *c*1214; *d* Oxford,
*c*1292). English theologian and philosopher. He studied
first under Grosseteste in Oxford, then in Paris. In 1247
he gave up his official teaching in Paris, returning some
three years later to Oxford. In about 1255 he entered the
order of friars minor. Guy de Foulques (later Pope
Clement IV), then Archbishop of Narbonne, wrote about
1265 asking him to outline a syllabus for the reform of
learning – a sign of the high esteem in which Bacon and
his teaching were held. Bacon responded by composing
the three summaries known as the *Opus maius*, the *Opus
minor* and the *Opus tertium*, submitting them to the pope
in 1268. Clement died, however, that same year, before
he had had time to study or implement them. During the
next decade Bacon produced further writings on mathematics, science and language, including Greek and
Hebrew grammars and a *Compendium* to the study of
philosophy. His opponents in Paris contrived to have him
formally condemned by the General of his order in 1277
and forced to remain for over ten years in some form of
compulsory retirement. He died shortly after regaining
his freedom.

Bacon brought to its full flowering the school of Oxford
thinkers founded by Grosseteste and developed by Adam
Marsh. He was the first to presume to the authority of
Aristotle, suggesting that results obtained by argument
must always be tested by observation and experiment. He
wrote extensively on music, his thoughts on this subject
being scattered through several of his encyclopedic
treatises. Following Boethius, he divided music into its
three customary categories, *mundana*, *humana* and *instrumentalis*, but questioned whether *musica mundana* (the
'music of the spheres') should be included, since it could
not be perceived by the human ear. With Cassiodorus he
subdivided instrumental music into percussion, strings
and wind, a division still used today. 'Human' music
covered both song and speech, the latter embracing prose,
metre and rhythm. Bacon further discussed music as being
either audible or visible, classifying under this last head
dancing and other gestures of the body. His notion of an
all-embracing aesthetic experience – music as a synthesis
of poetry, dancing and the art of sound – can be traced
back through Gundissalinus and al-Fārābī to Remigius of
Auxerre.

Bacon considered a knowledge of music to be essential
to the study of theology, and *a fortiori* to the practical
exercise of public worship. It contributed to the fostering
of the moral and the spiritual life. He recommended a
systematic study of the effect of music on the temper and
health of men and beasts. An understanding of the art of
dance and gesture was necessary to those who preach.

In discussing the diatonic, chromatic and enharmonic
genera, Bacon asserted, on the authority of Boethius and
the Fathers, that the enharmonic genus was the one best
suited to chant and to the further development of music.
He condemned abuses that had crept into sacred music in
his own day, particularly falsetto singing, and he pointed

the finger at great cathedrals and famous colleges that
indulged in new-fangled and dissolute styles. He deplored
a decline in the quality of hymn writing, attributing this
to insufficient knowledge of metre and rhythm.

In the pursuit of knowledge, Bacon maintained, the
importance of music could not be overestimated. All
beauty, in his opinion, was ultimately derived from
harmony and proportion, which in a final analysis was
based on the science of numbers. Here alone could one
find the absolute certainty of truth, for 'in sola mathematica est certitudo sine dubitatione'.

EDITIONS

Rogeri Bacon opera quaedam hactenus inedita, ed. J.S. Brewer
  (London, 1859/*R*) [incl. *Opus minus*, *Opus tertium* and part of
  Compendium studii philosophiae]
Opus maius, ed. J.H. Bridges, i–ii (Oxford, 1897/*R*); iii (London,
  1900/*R*)
Opera hactenus inedita, ed. R. Steele and others (London and
  Oxford, 1905–40)
Compendium studii theologiae, ed. H. Rashdall (Aberdeen, 1911/*R*)
  [incl. appx by A.G. Little: 'De operibus Rogeri Bacon', with full list
  of writings]
Part of the Opus tertium of Roger Bacon, ed. A.G. Little (Aberdeen,
  1912/*R*)
The Opus maius of Roger Bacon, ed. and trans. R.B. Burke
  (Philadelphia, 1928/*R*)

BIBLIOGRAPHY

J.H. Bridges: *The Life and Work of Roger Bacon: an Introduction to
  the Opus Majus*, ed. H.G. Jones (London, 1914/*R*)
H. Müller: 'Zur Musikauffassung des 13. Jahrhunderts', *AMw*, iv
  (1922), 405–12
E. Hutton: *The Franciscans in England, 1224–1538* (London, 1926)
D.E. Sharp: *Franciscan Philosophy at Oxford in the Thirteenth
  Century* (London, 1930/*R*)
A.G. Little: *Franciscan Papers, Lists and Documents* (Manchester,
  1943)
L. Ellinwood: 'Ars musica', *Speculum*, xx (1945), 290–99
E. de Bruyne: *Etudes d'esthétique médiévale* (Bruges, 1946/*R*)
S.C. Easton: *Roger Bacon and his Search for a Universal Science*
  (Oxford, 1952)
E. Massa: *Ruggero Bacone* (Rome, 1955)
J. Moorman: *A History of the Franciscan Order* (Oxford, 1968)
T. Adank: 'Roger Bacons Auffassung der Musica', *AMw*, xxxv
  (1978), 33–56

MARY BERRY

Bacquier,   Gabriel(-Augustin-Raymond-Théodore-Louis)
(*b* Béziers, 17 May 1924). French baritone. Having gained
a *premier prix* and two opera prizes at the Paris
Conservatoire he began his career in Beckman's Compag-
nie Lyrique (1950–52). After three years at La Monnaie,
Brussels (début as Rossini's Figaro), he joined the Opéra-
Comique (1956) singing Sharpless, Alfio, Albert
(*Werther*), Zurga, Ourrias, Yevgeny Onegin and Gianni
Schicchi. At the Opéra (1958–81) his roles included
Germont, Rigoletto, Valentin, Escamillo, Boris, Boccane-
gra and Leporello; at Aix-en-Provence (1960–89) he sang
Don Giovanni, Don Alfonso, Golaud, Falstaff, Don
Pasquale and the King of Clubs. In 1962 he made his
British début at Glyndebourne as Mozart's Count Alma-
viva and in 1964 sang Riccardo in *I puritani* at Covent
Garden and the High Priest in *Samson et Dalila* at the
Metropolitan, where his later roles (until 1981) included
Melitone, the Hoffmann villains, Massenet's Lescaut, and
Iago. His voice became richer and firmer during the early
1970s, his command of vocal and dramatic nuance
increasingly skilful. His Scarpia was the more formidable
for being sophisticated, his Dr Bartolo the more humorous
for being stripped of buffoonery; his Don Alfonso, if
suave, was also dominating. During the 1980s he sang
Sancho Panza, the Father (*Louise*) and the Viceroy (*La*

Périchole) with great success. In 1990 he returned to Covent Garden as Rossini's Dr Bartolo. Among his many recordings, his Dulcamara, Don Giovanni, William Tell, Iago, Sancho Panza and Golaud vividly reveal his native wit and skilled vocal acting. He was made a Chevalier of the Légion d'Honneur in 1975. (S. Segalini: 'Gabriel Bacquier', *Opera*, xxxiii (1982), 577–81)

ANDRÉ TUBEUF, ELIZABETH FORBES/R

Bacri, Nicolas (*b* Paris, 23 Nov 1961). French composer. After studying music analysis and composition with Françoise Gangloff, Christian Manen and Louis Saguer (from 1979), he entered the Paris Conservatoire (graduated 1983, premier prix for composition), where his teachers were Ballif, Marius Constant, Nigg and Philippot. During a two-year residency at the Académie de France in Rome (1983–5), he met Scelsi, who had a great influence on him. From 1987 he was head of the chamber music department of Radio France, a position he relinquished in 1991 to devote himself entirely to composition. He has also held residencies at the Casa de Velasquez (Spain) and with a number of French orchestras (from 1993). His early works, which culminate with the First Symphony (1983–4, dedicated to Elliott Carter), are rooted in a constructivist post-Webernian aesthetic. Later compositions, beginning with the Cello Concerto (1985–7, dedicated to Dutilleux), draw on the melodic continuity displaced by the predominant aesthetic of the postwar period. This change of style has placed Bacri in the musical aesthetic of his own time, where a spirit of reconciliation prevails. His honours include the grand prize of l'Académie du Disque (1993), and several awards from SACEM and the Académie des Beaux-Arts.

WORKS
(selective list)

Stage: Fleur et le miroir magique (conte lyrique for children, 1, C. Juliet), op.56, 1996–7

Orch: Vn Conc., op.7, 1982–3; Sym. no.1, op.11, 1983–4; Vc Conc., op.17, 1985–7; Capriccio notturno (Cl Conc.), op.20, 1986–7; Sym. no.2 'Sinfonia dolorosa', op.22, 1986–90; 3 canti e finale (Vn Conc. no.2), op.29, 1987–9; Requiem 'Musica notturna nos.1–3', op.23, va/vc, 1987; Folia, op.30, 1990 [arr. as op.30b, va/vc, str orch, 1990]; Musica, op.36b, str, 1991–2; Tpt Conc. 'Episodes', op.39, 1992; Conc., op.51, 2 pf, str orch, 1995–6; Sym. no.4 'Classique Sturm und Drang', op.49, 1995–6; Une prière, op.52, va/vc/vn, orch, 1995–7; Sym. no.5 'Conc. for Orch', op.55, 1996–7; Conc. da camera (Cl Conc. no.2), op.61, 1998; Sym. no.6, op.60, 1998; Fl Conc., op.63, 1999; Tpt Conc., op.65, 2000; other pieces

Vocal: Notturni (E. Cetrangolo), op.14, S, 7 insts, 1985–6; Sinfonia da requiem (Sym. no.3), op.33, Mez, chorus, orch, 1988–94; Fils d'Abraham (3 cants. from Sym. no.3), 1988–94: Vitae abdicatio, op.33/1 (cant., S.A. Madyan), Mez, ob, chbr orch, 1992–4, Vita et mors, op.33/3 (cant., B.I. Paqůda), Mez, vc, chbr orch, 1992–3, Coplas de Don J. Manrique por la muerte de su padre, op.33/2 (cant.), mixed chorus, 1993 [arr. as op.33/2b, female vv, 4 insts, wind/org, 1993–5]; Sonnet 66 (cant., W. Shakespeare), 1v, str orch, 1994–5 [arr. as 44b, 1v, pf, 1994–5]; 5 motets de souffrance et de consolation (W. Raleigh, Psalms, Jeremy), op.59, chorus, 1998

Chbr: Str Qt no.1 'Fantaisie', op.1, 1980; Str Qt no.2 '5 pièces', op.5, 1982; Str Trio '6 Sonatas', op.8, 1982–3; Esquisses pour un tombeau (Str Qt no.3), op.18, 1985–8, rev. 1989; Duo, op.25, vn, vc, 1987–92; Toccata sinfonica, op.34, pf trio, 1987–93; Str Qt no.4 'Omaggio a Beethoven', op.42, 1989–94, rev. 1994–5; Sonata, op.32, vn, pf, 1990–94; Str trio, op.37, 'Divertimento', 1991–2 [arr. as op.37b, cl, str trio, 1991–2]; Sonata, op.40, vn, pf, 1993–4; Im Volkston, op.43, vn, cl, vc, 1994; Pf Trio no.2 'Les contrastes', op.47, 1995; Pf Trio no.3 'Sonata notturna', op.54, 1996; Str Qt no.5 'Elegiaco', op.57, 1997; other pieces

Solo inst: 3 suites, op.31, vc, 1987–94; 2 préludes, op.24, pf, 1988; 3 préludes, op.28, pf, 1989; Prélude no.6, op.33/3b, pf, 1991; 3 préludes, op.46, pf, 1994–5; Sonata breve, op.45, vn, 1994; Suite no.4, op.50, vc, 1994–6; Sonata no.2, op.53, vn, 1996; other pieces

Principal publishers: Durand, Salabert, Peer Musik

PHILIPPE MICHEL

Bactria. Ancient civilization in Central Asia. It flourished in the last three centuries BCE in the area now covered by northern Afghanistan, Uzbekistan, Tajikistan and southern Turkmenistan. See IRAN, §II.

Baculewski, Krzysztof (*b* Warsaw, 26 Dec 1950). Polish composer and writer on music. He studied composition at the Warsaw Academy of Music with Rudziński (1969–74) and in Paris with Messiaen and Schaeffer (1975–6); he took the doctorate at Warsaw University in 1982. Subsequently, he became a lecturer at the Warsaw Academy. His music up to the mid-1970s shares many characteristics with Polish music generally at that time, including a concern with group textures and with focal pedal points. His involvement with extended instrumental techniques, however, came to an abrupt end with *Is-slottet* (1975). He has paid particular attention to musical form, and in several works, including *Vivace e cantilena* and *Ground*, he has developed a bipartite structure (also favoured by Górecki) of a segmented and often aggressive first section resolved in a quiet coda. Like some of his contemporaries in the 1980s and 90s, he found inspiration in 17th- and 18th-century idioms: *The Profane Anthem* is a mildly distorted reflection of the music of Purcell, while *Antitheton I* is based on Baroque musical-rhetorical figures (*tirata*, *aposiopesis* and *circulatio*) and *Antitheton II* incorporates more dislocated references, including overt allusions to the finale of Bach's Brandenburg Concerto no.3.

WORKS
(selective list)

Inst: Perc Sonata, 1972; Epitaphium, brass, perc, str, 1973; Meander, fl, 1973; La terra incompareggiabile, org, 1973; Vivace e cantilena, inst septet, 1974; 3 grâces, org, 1975; Is-slottet, chbr orch, 1975; Pf Concertino, str, 1978; Partita I, a sax, hpd, 1979; Passacaglia, 4 perc, 1979; Ground, orch, 1981; Quartier Latin, tpt, 1981; A la recherche des harmonies perdues, orch, 1981; Sonata wiosenna [Spring Sonata], fl, 1982; Conc. for Orch, 1983; Str Qt no.1, 1984; Suite de cheminée, 2 accdn, 1984; Str Qt no.2, 1985; Str Qt no.3, 1986; The Whole and Broken Consort, period insts, 1986; Concerto armonico, str, 1987; Qt for 12 insts, 4 perc, 1987; Partita II, vn, pf, 1988; Antitheton I, vn, vc, pf, 1989; A Walking Shadow, orch, 1990; Voyage à travers le paysage métaphysique, tpt, 1992; Antitheton II, 2 vn, continuo, b viol, 1996

Vocal: Nowe wyzwolenie [New Deliverance] (op, 1, S.I. Witkiewicz), 1974; La notte (cant., Michelangelo), S, chbr orch, 1975; Sierpniowy relief [August Relief] (cant., T. Gajcy), S, chbr orch, 1985; The Profane Anthem to Anne (cant., J. Donne), 2 S, A, T, B, chorus, 7 period insts, 1993; Christmas motet (trad.), S, A, T, B, chorus, 7 period insts, 1994; Rilke-Lieder, S, B, 2 choruses, 1994; Nox ultima, nox beata (motet, A. Tibullus), chorus, 1995; Tu ne quaesieris (motet, Q.H. Flaccus), male chorus, 1995; Gloria, A, chorus, 1996

Principal publishers: Agencja autorska, PWM

WRITINGS

'In statu nascendi: a New Generation of Composers', *Polish Art Studies*, vii (1986), 139–61

Polska twórczość kompozytorska 1945–84 [Polish composition] (Kraków, 1987)

Współczesność i: 1939-1974 [Contemporary i: 1939-1974] (Warsaw, 1997)

BIBLIOGRAPHY

M. Kominek: 'Wernisaż muzyczny Krzysztofa Baculewskiego' [The musical Vernissage of Baculewski], *RM*, xxv/14 (1980), 8–9

O. Pisarenko: 'Jeszcze raz Witkacy' [Witkacy once more], *RM*, xxxi/14 (1986), 7–8

M. Ługowska: 'Under Pressure of the Avant Garde, in Search of Independence', *Polish Music* (1989), no.2, pp.15–20 [interview]

ADRIAN THOMAS

Baçus Correçarius de Bononia, Johannes. *See* JOHANNES BAÇUS CORREÇARIUS DE BONONIA.

Badajoz, Garci Sánchez de (*b* Ecija, province of Seville, *c*1460; *d* after 1524). Spanish poet, vihuelist and composer. He was one of the leading Castilian poets of the generation of JUAN DEL ENCINA; one of his poems received a response by Pedro de Cartagena, who died in 1485. His poetic style, quick-witted sallies and ingenious conceits were praised long after his death by Lope de Vega and Baltasar Gracián. His poetry is characterized by a desperate amatory vein in which suffering and death are always present. He is supposed to have been imprisoned for some time, owing to a madness brought on by an incestuous passion for a close relation, probably his sister. He is last recorded attending an imperial feast in Toledo in 1525.

The *Cancionero General* (Valencia, 1511/14/*R*, 2/1520/*R*) contains eight poems attributed to 'Badajoz el músico', and there are five villancicos and three canciones ascribed to 'Badajoz' in the *Cancionero Musical de Palacio* (*E-Mp* II-1335, ed. in MME, v, 1947; x, 1951). Resende, reminiscing about the period around 1500, included 'Badajoz' among a group of great musicians. Literary scholars have supposed that the poet-musician was to be identified with João de Badajós, who was listed as a *músico da camera* of João III of Portugal in 1558 (a romance by Badajós was printed with Antonio de Portalegre's *Meditação*, Coimbra, 1547). But Román referred to Garci Sánchez de Badajoz as the best vihuelist from the time of Ferdinand and Isabella, and João de Badajós' dates are a generation too late. Garci Sánchez is therefore much more likely to be the poet and composer referred to in the *Cancionero General* and the *Cancionero Musical de Palacio*; he may well be the composer of eight further villancicos whose poems are ascribed either to Garci Sánchez de Badajoz or to Badajoz el músico (RISM *c*1516[2] [actually two separate publications: Rome, 1518; Venice, 1520], 1576[8]; *F-Peb* Jean Masson 56, *I-Fn* Magl.XIX.107bis, *P-Cmn* 3391, *Em* 11793, *Ln* Ivo Cruz 60; ed. M. Joachim, *O cancioneiro musical e poetico da Biblioteca Pública Hortênsia*, Coimbra, 1940; ed. in G. Haberkamp, *Die weltliche Vokalmusik in Spanien um 1500*, Tutzing, 1968; ed. in PM, xxxi, 1977; PM, xlvii, 1986; CMM, xcviii, 1987). Two villancicos by Garci Sánchez were set by Escobar and one by Peñalosa.

BIBLIOGRAPHY

StevensonSM

G. de Resende: *Crónica de Dom João II e miscelânea* (Lisbon, *c*1532/*R*), 362–3

J. Román y Zamora: *Repúblicas del mundo* (Medina del Campo, 1575, 2/1595), 304

J. Romeu Figueras: *La música en la corte de los reyes católicos*, iv/1, MME, xiv/1 (Barcelona, 1965)

P. Gallagher: *The Life and Works of Garci Sánchez de Badajoz* (London, 1968)

N.G. Round: 'Garci Sánchez de Badajoz and the Revaluation of *cancionero* Poetry', *Forum for Modern Language Studies*, vi (1970), 178–87

J. Castillo: *Cancionero de Garci Sánchez de Badajoz* (Madrid, 1980)

M. Frenk: *Corpus de la antigua lírica popular hispánica* (Madrid, 1987)

B. Dutton: *El cancionero del siglo XV, c.1360–1520*, vii (Salamanca, 1991)

E. Ros-Fábregas: *La obra musical del poeta Garci Sánchez de Badajoz* (Granada, forthcoming)

EMILIO ROS-FÁBREGAS

Badalla, Rosa Giacinta (*b* ?Bergamo, *c*1660; *d* Milan, *c*1710). Italian composer. A Benedictine nun, she took her vows at the musical convent of S Radegonda in Milan about 1678. Her only printed collection, *Motetti a voce sola* (1684), is notable among contemporary Milanese solo motets for its vocal virtuosity, motivic originality and formal experimentation, with frequent use of ostinato figures and some surprising modulations. Of her two surviving secular cantatas (a testimony to the practice of secular music inside S Radegonda's walls), *Vuò cercando* is a succession of short da capo arias interspersed with recitative, while *O fronde care* (for which she also wrote the text) is a more extended piece with short melismas, repetitive bass patterns and instrumental *sinfonie*, probably dating from about 1700.

WORKS

Motetti a voce sola, 1v bc (Venice, 1684): 1 ed. in R.L. Kendrick: *Celestial Sirens: Nuns and their Music in Early Modern Milan* (Oxford, 1996); 1 ed. in S. Glickman and M.F. Schleifer: *Women Composers: Music through the Ages*, ii (New York, 1997)

Vuò cercando, A, bc, *GB-Lbl*; ed. in R.L. Kendrick: '*Le sirene celesti': Generations, Gender and Genres in Seicento Milanese Nuns' Music* (diss., New York U., 1993)

O fronde care, A, 2 vn/tpt, 2 rec, bc, *F-Pn*

ROBERT L. KENDRICK

Bądarzewska-Baranowska, Tekla (*b* Warsaw, 1834; *d* Warsaw, 29 Sept 1861). Polish composer. An amateur, with no musical training, she is known chiefly for her *Modlitwa dziewicy* ('The Maiden's Prayer'). This piece, which won world-wide popularity, was originally published in Warsaw in 1856; later the music appeared as a supplement to the *Revue et gazette musicale* (Paris, 1859), entitled *La prière d'une vierge*, and was issued by more than 80 publishers in France, Germany, Italy, England, Australia and the USA. Arrangements were produced for piano (four or eight hands) and other instruments, and for voice. *The Maiden's Prayer* is of no artistic merit, being a salon composition of a type common in the 19th century. Other works of a similar nature failed to repeat its success, although some of them gained some popularity: they include *Seconde prière d'une vierge*, *Prière exaucée, ou Réponse à la prière d'une vierge*, *Wspomnienie chatki* ('Memories of a Hut'), *Słodkie marzenia* ('Sweet Dreams') and *Pamiątka przyjaźni* ('Memories of a Friendship').

BIBLIOGRAPHY

PadzírekH [incl. complete list of works]; *SMP*

ZOFIA CHECHLIŃSKA

Badea, Christian (*b* Bucharest, 10 Dec 1947). American conductor of Romanian birth. He was a boy chorister at the Budapest Opera, studied the violin at the conservatory and joined the Opera as a répétiteur. After leaving Romania in 1970 he studied further in Brussels and Salzburg and at the Juilliard School. He was music director at the Spoleto Festival of Two Worlds in Italy from 1978 and directed the festivals in both Italy and Charleston, South Carolina, from 1980 to 1986, conducting a variety of operas ranging from Mozart and Verdi to Menotti and Shostakovich. During this time he conducted the first European production of Menotti's *The Hero* (1980) and made his British début in 1983 with Prokofiev's

The Gambler for the ENO. He has worked with the Metropolitan Opera, Canadian Opera, Netherlands Opera and at Verona, and made the first recording (with the Spoleto Festival Orchestra) of Barber's *Antony and Cleopatra* in 1985. He made his début with the Royal Opera at Covent Garden in 1996 with *La Bohème*. Badea is admired for his dramatic vitality and secure command of phrasing and balance, and has also appeared widely as an orchestral conductor. From 1983 to 1991 he was music director of the Columbus SO in Ohio, with whom he recorded works by Sessions and Mennin.

BIBLIOGRAPHY
E. Seckerson: 'Taking a Gamble for a Stunning Impact', *Classical Music* (30 April 1983)

NOËL GOODWIN

Bad Ems. German town. *See under* KOBLENZ.

Baden, (Peter) Conrad (Krohn) (*b* Drammen, 31 Aug 1908; *d* Oslo, 12 June 1989). Norwegian composer and teacher. He graduated as an organist from the Oslo Conservatory in 1931 and then studied in Leipzig (1931–2), with later periods of study with Rivier in Paris (1950) and Hanns Jelinek in Vienna (1965). In 1932 he became an organist in Drammen; he held organ recitals and was also active as a choirmaster, accompanist and music critic for several newspapers. He taught theory and composition at the Oslo Conservatory (1948–73) and continued there until 1978 as a lecturer when the institution became the Norges Musikkhøgskole.

The first public performance of his works in 1946 revealed his thorough knowledge of classical forms allied to a national Romantic style. A strong interest in the polyphony of Palestrina is reflected in the Mass (1949) and other vocal works. In Paris he became acquainted with French neo-classicism, and with Hindemith's compositional technique as his background, Baden composed two symphonies, a concertino for clarinet and orchestra and chamber music that was frequently performed, such as the Wind Trio no.1. In the 1960s he ventured into 12-note technique (seen in his themes and his increasingly bold use of dissonance), and although he only used it extensively in the chamber work *Hymnus* (1967), he retained a certain freedom of approach (e.g. *Fantasia breve*, *Concerto per orchestra* and *Intrada sinfonica*). The form and treatment of dissonance is more free; at the same time greater importance is attached to sound planes and to timbre. In later works, such as the Symphony No.6 ('Sinfonia espressiva', 1982), there can be seen a synthesis of his earlier concentration on variation technique, on motivic-thematic development and on strict counterpoint. The tone is also warm and more lyrical, the form expressive and well-balanced.

WORKS
(selective list)

Divertimento, orch, 1950; Sym. no.1, 1952; Concertino, cl, str, 1953; Toccata, koral og fuge, org, 1956; Sym. no.2, op.42, 1957; Sym. no.3 'Sinfonia piccola', op.48, 1959; Eventyrsuite [Fairy Tale Suite], orch, 1960; Str Qt no.3, 1963; Fantasia breve, orch, 1964; Pezzi concertante, org, 1966; Hymnus, A, fl, ob, va, 1967; Conc. for Orch, 1968; Sym. no.4, op.85, 1970; Sym. no.5 'Sinfonia voluntatis', op.109, 1976; Sym. no.6 'Sinfonia espressiva', op.124, 1980; other chbr works, org, works, solo vocal and choral works

Principal publishers: Lyche, Norsk Musikforlag

BIBLIOGRAPHY
H. Herresthal: 'Kirkemusikeren og komponisten Conrad Baden', *Norsk musikktidsskrift*, viii/2–ix/1 (1971–2), suppl., 1–76 [pubd in 4 instalments]

T.O. Baden: 'Fantasia breve per orchestra og Conrad Badens symfoniske stil', *Studia musicologica norvegica*, v (1979), 9–25

HARALD HERRESTHAL

Baden-Baden. Town in south-west Germany. Before its 19th-century blossoming as a spa town, the town's musical life was unremarkable. The margraves patronized music from the 15th century onwards, most notably Philip II (*d* 1588), and the Jesuit college gave comedies with music until 1771.

Baden-Baden became one of the most famous international spas in Europe in the 19th century, not least because of its casino. It was the artistic 'summer capital' of Europe, and a meeting-place of fashionable society. Such virtuosos as Liszt, Thalbert and Paganini gave concerts there. The newly renovated Konversationshaus opened in 1855 with the première of *Les amoureux de Perrette*, an *opéra comique* by the French composer Louis Clapisson, successor to Halévy at the Académie des Beaux-Arts. Only a year later Clapisson's *opéra comique Le sylphe* also had its première in Baden-Baden. Berlioz conducted the Baden-Baden orchestra in the summer of 1853 and the summers of 1856 to 1863. He composed his last work, the opera *Béatrice et Bénédict*, for the opening of the theatre (Theater der Stadt) in 1862, devising its construction with the director of the casino, Edouard Bénazet. Bénazet also persuaded Gounod to have his opera *La Colombe* given its première in Baden-Baden (1860).

In the 1860s a series of famous musicians visited the spa, including Anton Rubinstein, Hugo Heermann and Aglaja Orgeni. Others settled in the town, among them the pianist Jacob Rosenhain and the singer Pauline Viardot, who opened a popular salon there. Clara Schumann moved into a permanent residence in Baden-Baden in 1863 and regularly performed in the town. Her house became a meeting-place for musicians, among others Joseph Joachim, Julius Stockhausen, Hermann Levi and above all Brahms, who composed and conducted in Baden-Baden during his summer holidays between 1864 and 1872 (the apartment in which he lived is now a museum). Offenbach was another guest in the town, and Bénazet commissioned his *opéra bouffe La princesse de Trébizonde*. Offenbach conducted its première himself at the Kurtheater in 1869 with the Bouffes-Parisiens.

In 1854 the town founded its own orchestra, the Symphonie- und Kurorchester (still extant as the Baden-Baden SO). Its guest conductors included Johann Strauss, Hans von Bülow and Brahms, and later Richard Strauss and Reger. A peak was reached in 1880 with the Tonkünstlerfest des Allgemeinen Musikvereins, in which Liszt, Felix Dessoff and Saint-Saëns took part.

In the 1920s Baden-Baden began to acquire an international reputation for the performance of contemporary music. Particularly important was the move of the Kammermusik-Aufführungen für Zeitgenössische Tonkunst concert series from Donaueschingen to Baden-Baden in 1927–9, where it was known as the Deutsche Kammermusik Baden-Baden. So-called Minutenopern had their premières there in 1927, including Hindemith's *Hin und zurück*, Milhaud's *L'enlèvement d'Europe* and Weill's *Mahagonny* Songspiel (with Lotte Lenya), one of the most notorious premières of the 1920s. For the first time a radio station featured as co-promoter of a musical festival, broadcasting the premières of 'Radiomusiken' – works composed expressly for radio – including *Der*

Lindberghflug by Brecht, Hindemith and Weill in 1929. Another important première was that of Bartók's piano sonata, played by the composer.

After World War II the radio network of south-west Germany, Südwestfunk (SWF), had great influence in Baden-Baden. The Grosses Orchester des SWF was founded in 1946 (renamed SWF SO in 1966 and SWF Orchestra of Baden-Baden in 1990). It immediately attracted guest conductors such as Klemperer and Stravinsky, who made his first post-1945 appearance in Germany here. Conducted by Gotthold Ephraim Lessing (1946–8), Hans Rosbaud (1948–62), Ernest Bour (1964–79), Kazimierz Kord (1980–86) and Michael Gielen (from 1986), the SWF orchestra became one of the leading orchestras of the Federal German Republic, particularly for contemporary music. Boulez performed contemporary works with them for many years, and began his international career in Baden-Baden. In 1998 SWF merged with Süddeutscher Rundfunk Stuttgart (SDR) to form Südwestrundfunk (SWR). The orchestra was renamed SWR Sinfonieorchester Baden-Baden und Freiburg. In 1999 Sylvain Cambreling was appointed chief conductor. In 1955 the 29th international music festival of the ISCM took place in Baden-Baden. The radio orchestra has commissioned works from such composers as Stockhausen, Ligeti, Boulez, Nono, Zimmermann and Rihm. Since the 1950s the orchestra, and the radio station's experimental studio in Freiburg im Breisgau (next to IRCAM in Paris, the most important European studio for the production of live electronic music) have been the major musical institutions involved in the internationally renowned Donaueschinger Musiktage für Neue Musik.

BIBLIOGRAPHY

H. Berl: *Baden-Baden im Zeitalter der Romantik: der literarische und musikalische Romantik des neunzehnten Jahrhunderts* (Baden-Baden, 1936/R)

F. Baser: *Grosse Musiker in Baden-Baden* (Tutzing, 1973)

K. Schultz, ed.: *Badener Musiktage 1927–1929, 1977: Texte, Bilder, Programme* (Baden-Baden, 1977)

P. Martin: *Salon Europas: Baden-Baden im 19. Jahrhundert* (Konstanz, 1983)

U. Reimann and J.Draheim: *Clara und Robert Schumann in Baden-Baden und Carlsruhe* (Baden-Baden, 1994)

FRIEDRICH BASER/THORSTEN LORENZ

Bader. German family of organ builders. Daniel Bader (*b* ?Münster, ?*c*1560; *d* ?1636) may have been a pupil of Arnold Lampeler (who worked in Münster from 1573 to 1579 and from 1585 to 1588); possibly on his recommendation Bader went to Antwerp, where from 1603 to 1604 he worked in the church of St James; he also worked in Liège. In Westphalia he carried out extensive rebuilding in Münster Cathedral (1610–12). His son Hans Heinrich Bader (*fl c*1626–65) worked in Paderborn (1626–7, 1655–60); in Zutphen (1637–43); at the Willibrordikirche, Wesel (1644–50); in Unna (1661–5) and in Hildesheim (1655–64). Arnold, Ernst, Conrad and Tobias Bader (all sons of Daniel Bader) often worked together, both in Westphalia (at Herford and Vreden) and in Friesland (at the residence in Leeuwarden). Johann Gottfried Bader (a grandson of Daniel) worked at Recklinghausen and Coesfeld as well as at Brussels. For their larger instruments Daniel and Hans Heinrich used the Lampeler pattern, which they extended by means of narrow foundation stops and pedal stops. The most important organ workshops in Westphalia followed the Bader family

tradition, and used the Bader principle of the spring-chest until well into the 18th century.

BIBLIOGRAPHY

J.H. Biermann: *Organographia hildesiensis specialis* (Hildesheim, 1738); ed. E. Palandt (Kassel, 1930)

H. Wohnfurter: *Die Orgelbauerfamilie Bader 1600–1742* (Kassel, 1981)

HANS KLOTZ

Badessa, Giovanni Battista. *See* ABATESSA, GIOVANNI BATTISTA.

Badger, Alfred G. (*b* Connecticut, 1815; *d* Brooklyn, NY, 8 Nov 1892). American flute maker. He began to make fifes and recorders at the age of 12, and in 1834 became apprenticed to Ball & Douglass, flute makers, in Utica, New York. In 1838 he went to Buffalo, where he was a partner in the Nickels & Badger music store from 1839 to 1841, making simple system flutes. After leaving Nickels he made flutes and clarinets on his own; these were BADGER/BUFFALO. He moved to Newark, New Jersey, after 1843, had opened a workshop in New York by 1846, and was briefly associated with Tebaldo Monzani in 1858.

Badger, a superb craftsman, stated that he always tried to make each instrument superior to its predecessor; many of his flutes are beautifully engraved. His instruments won silver medals and diplomas at several fairs and exhibitions in Massachusetts and New York. His insistence on excellence, his support of performers, and his widespread publications encouraged the rapid acceptance of the Boehm flute, of which he was the first commercial manufacturer in the USA (1846) and the most important American manufacturer during the mid-19th century. He was also the first musical-instrument manufacturer to use ebonite; he made four flutes in 1851 for Charles Goodyear, who exhibited them in London at the Great Exhibition (1851) and in Paris at the Exposition Universelle of 1855. By 1859 Badger had, at great cost, procured from the patentee of Goodyear's hard rubber the exclusive right to use this material in the construction of the Boehm flute. How long he owned the rights is not known; Theodore Berteling began to use ebonite before 1883. Badger apparently made the first American silver Boehm flute (1886) and the first American Boehm-system alto flute (before 1873). He was the first to use ebonite heads on silver bodies. He also made piccolos, experimental flutes and a combination flute-clarinet. Were it not for the excessively high pitch at which most of Badger's flutes were built (some as high as $a'=452$), his instruments might be played today. The Dayton C. Miller Collection at the Library of Congress has 11 of Badger's flutes, four are in the Yale University Collection, and many others are maintained in public and private collections. Badger's factory continued in operation after his death, and it was purchased by Penzel & Mueller in 1920.

BIBLIOGRAPHY

Waterhouse-LangwillII

A.G. Badger: *An Ilustrated History of the Flute* (New York, 1853, 4/1875)

'India-Rubber Flutes', *Scientific American*, new ser., i (1859), 284

C.R. Anderson and A.H.Starke, eds.: *Sidney Lanier, Centennial Editions* (Baltimore, 1943) [vii–x, 1857–77]

M.J. Simpson: *Alfred G. Badger (1815–1892), Nineteenth-Century Flute-Maker: his Art, Innovations, and Influence on Flute Construction, Performance and Composition, 1845–1895* (diss., U. of Maryland, 1982)

S. Berdahl: *The First Hundred Years of the Boehm Flute in the United States, 1845–1945: a Biographical Dictionary of American Boehm Flutemakers* (diss., U. of Minnesota, 1985)

N. Groce: *Musical Instrument Makers of New York: a Directory of Eighteenth- and Nineteenth-Century Urban Craftsmen* (Stuyvesant, NY, 1991)

MARY JEAN SIMPSON

Badham, Charles (*fl* London, 1698-1716). English church musician and copyist. He was probably a son (or other relation) of John Badham, vicar-choral and organist of Hereford Cathedral, 1660–88. Between 1698 and 1716 he was the seventh minor canon of St Paul's Cathedral, where his anthem *Unto thee will I cry* survives (incomplete). He was a none too reliable copyist of music by Blow, Purcell, Clarke and others. Manuscripts that are wholly or partly in his hand include *GB-Ob* Mus.Sch.B.7, Mus.Sch.C.38–40 and Tenbury 1031 and 1258. (I. Spink: *Restoration Cathedral Music, 1660–1714*, Oxford, 1995)

IAN SPINK

Badḥan (Yid.). A master of ceremonies at Jewish weddings or social festivities. *Badḥanim* often improvised poems and composed and performed their own songs. In eastern Europe they were also known as *marshaliks* or *leyzim* (sing. *leyz*) and performed at the almost obligatory traditional Purim celebrations, singing, dancing and acting in *Aḥashverosh* plays. Thus they were the real forerunners of the Yiddish theatre. These merry-makers, wandering actors and musicians performed in all Jewish towns and congregations. Elyokum Zunser (1840–1913), a *badḥan* from Vilna (now Vilnius), wrote about 600 songs, many of which were very popular and of strong Jewish appeal. Another very popular *badḥan* was Mark Varshavsky (1845–1907), a scholar and lawyer from Kiev; he was much influenced by the Yiddish writer Shalom Aleichem, and notated and published some of his own songs. His *Alefbet* ('Oyfn pripechok') is still sung in Jewish schools and homes, and in Hebrew translation in Israeli schools.

See also JEWISH MUSIC, §IV, 2(iv)(a).

SHLOMO HOFMAN

Badia, Carlo Agostino (*b* ?Venice, 1672; *d* Vienna, 23 Sept 1738). Italian composer. His earliest known work is the oratorio *La sete di Cristo in croce*, a *sepolcro* written for Innsbruck in 1691. At the begining of 1692 he may have lived in Rome, where his earliest secular dramatic works were produced. By spring 1692 he was a court composer at Innsbruck. He gained the enthusiastic patronage of Eleonora Maria (1653–97), widow of both King Michael Wisniowiecki of Poland and Duke Charles of Lorraine, and stepsister of Emperor Leopold I. Besides the 1691 oratorio, Badia composed for Innsbruck two operas in 1692, as well as two *sepolcri* for Holy Week 1693. With the support of Eleonora Maria, who moved to Vienna late in 1693, and with a recommendation from the King of Poland, he was appointed *Musik-Compositeur* at the imperial court on 1 July 1694, receiving an initial monthly salary of 60 florins retroactive to 1 July 1693. Badia thus became the first in a succession of distinguished composers (including Fux, Giovanni Bononcini, P.F. Tosi and Francesco Conti) to hold the title of court composer at Vienna.

After initial successes, Badia was sent by the emperor to Rome, probably in 1695, to complete his musical education, but because of a lack of funds he returned to Vienna before the end of that year. Until 1697 he seems to have composed only oratorios for Vienna. His first opera for the Habsburg court, *Bacco, vincitore dell'India*, was produced during Carnival 1697 and dedicated to Eleonora Maria. During 18 years at the courts of Leopold I (*d* 1705) and Joseph I (*d* 1711), Badia enjoyed a period of remarkable creative activity, producing at least 34 oratorios and 20 secular dramatic works. He also composed more than 50 chamber cantatas and duets. His salary was increased by 30 florins in 1699 and by an additional 30 in 1702, making him one of the highest-paid musicians at the court. He seems to have become a favourite of Leopold I, and was praised by Draghi as a 'guter Virtuoso' and by Draghi's successor Pancotti as 'gar guten Talento und ungeheimer prontezza'.

The date of Badia's marriage to the prima donna Anna Maria Elisabetta (Lisi) Nonetti, who arrived in Vienna in 1700, is unknown. In 1706 he probably accompanied her to Venice, where she appeared at the Teatro S Giovanni Grisostomo. Badia's operas and oratorios continued to be performed in northern Italy, but there is no evidence that he had a direct hand in any of the productions. In 1709 he was commissioned to write the opera *Gli amori di Circe con Ulisse* for Dresden; the performance took place during a visit by the King of Denmark. It seems unlikely that Badia travelled to Dresden for the performance, which was directed by Baron Francesco Ballerini, one of the most famous singers at the imperial court. Badia composed less prolifically during the reign of Joseph I, who favoured the Bononcini brothers, Giovanni and Antonio Maria, but the emperor frequently supplemented Badia's income with secret sums of money that apparently rescued him from persistent debts. After the death of Joseph I, the imperial chapel was reorganized and many musicians were released. But on 1 October 1711 the contracts of both Badias were renewed, and Carlo remained in the employ of the Habsburgs until his death, serving 44 years as court composer.

Under Charles VI (*d* 1740), who preferred the more progressive composers Fux and Caldara, Badia's activity declined sharply. Between 1712 and 1738 he is known to have composed only six oratorios and secular dramatic works. Anna Maria Lisi died on 7 January 1726, and by 1729 he had married Anna Maria Sophia Novelli, his first wife's niece; a son, Antonius Nicolaus, was born in 1729. In his last years Badia was closely associated with G.J. Dornberger, a pupil of Caldara.

Badia was the first of a group of Italian composers (including the Bononcinis, M.A. Ziani and Conti) who introduced the stylistic innovations of the late Baroque era to the Viennese court, long dominated by the conservative Draghi. Badia's style underwent a gradual maturing process (as Wellesz, 1919, showed). The numerous early works are characterized by smooth melodic writing, lyric grace and a lack of contrapuntal complexity. He can be credited with increasing the importance of idiomatic string writing at Vienna. The ritornellos and sinfonias of his operas and oratorios are longer than those of his predecessors, and he also called for more varied instrumental combinations as well as more frequent solo obbligatos. He may have been the first composer at Vienna to use concerto grosso contrasts: in the trio 'Quanti e di grande' from *Le gare dei beni* (1700; also attributed to M.A. Ziani) the composer called for two large opposing groups (he was perhaps influenced by Torelli, who visited Vienna between 1699 and 1700). The overture to one of Badia's best works, *Ercole, vincitore di*

Gerione, is unusual in consisting of four movements, the third a minuet. In his oratorios and his secular dramatic works he made extensive use of vocal ensemble numbers, especially trios. *La concordia della Virtù e della Fortuna* (1702) ends with a trio, a technique that foreshadows the use of ensemble finales in the operas of Fux and Caldara.

Most of Badia's chamber cantatas are for soprano or alto with continuo accompaniment only, but about a dozen require obbligato instruments: lutes, violins, flutes, or larger combinations. Formally, the cantatas consist of the regular alternation of recitative and aria normally found in the late Baroque era; Badia used the da capo aria almost exclusively. The numerous ritornellos are often thematically related to the vocal writing, which includes some large melodic leaps and long virtuoso, sequential patterns. The recitatives are also characteristic of the time with their simple modulations and cadential formulae.

It seems likely that Badia was related to the two other musicians of the name at the Habsburg court: Giuseppe (*b* 1642; *d* Vienna, 30 March 1706), who began his service as an instrumentalist on 26 August 1690, and Giovanni Giuseppe, who was active in Vienna as a singer about the same time. A letter from Parma from a Carlo Francesco Badia to G.A. Perti is preserved (*I-Bc*) and reproduced by Nemeth, who indicates that the author was definitely not C.A. Badia.

WORKS

STAGE

performed in Vienna unless otherwise stated

Amor che vince lo sdegno, ovvero Olimpia placata (A. Aureli), Rome, Capranica, carn. 1692
La Rosaura, ovvero Amore figlio della gratitudine (O. Malvezzi), Innsbruck, April 1692
L'amazone corsara, ovvero L'Alvilda, regina de' Goti (dramma per musica, G.C. Corradi), Innsbruck, aut. 1692, *A-Wn*
La ninfa Apollo (favola pastorale o scherzo scenica, F. de Lemene), Rome and Milan, 1692
Bacco, vincitore dell'India (festa teatrale, D. Cupeda), 14 Feb 1697
La pace tra i numi discordi nella rovina di Troia (serenata, N. Minato), 21 May 1697, *Wn*
L'idea del felice governo (serenata, Cupeda), Laxenburg, 9 June 1698
Lo squittinio dell'eroe (componimento per musica da camera), Neue Favorita, 26 July 1698
Imeneo trionfante (serenata), 28 Feb 1699, *Wn*, for the wedding of Joseph I and Wilhelmine Amalie of Braunschweig-Lüneburg
Il Narciso (favola boschereccia, Lemene), Laxenburg, 9 June 1699, *Wn*
Il commun giubilo del mondo (musica da camera, Cupeda), Neue Favorita, 26 July 1699, *Wn*
Cupido fuggitivo da Venere e ritrovato a' piedi della Sacra Reale Maestà d'Amalia (trattenimento carnevalesco, G. Spedazzi), carn. 1700
Diana rappacificata con Venere e con Amore (trattenimento musicale), Schönbrunn, 28 April 1700, *Wn*
La costanza d'Ulisse (dramma per musica, Cupeda), Neue Favorita, 29 June 1700
Le gare dei beni (applauso poetico per musica), 25 July 1700, *Wn*; also attrib. M.A. Ziani
L'amore vuol somiglianza (dramma per musica, P.A. Bernardoni), 18 Jan 1702
La concordia della Virtù e della Fortuna (poemetto drammatico, Bernardoni), Neue Favorita, 21 April 1702, *Wn*
Enea negli Elisi (poemetto drammatico, Bernardoni), 9 June 1702, *Wn*
L'Arianna (poemetto drammatico, Bernardoni), 21 Feb 1702
La Psiche (poemetto drammatico, Bernardoni), 22 July 1703, *Wn*
Napoli ritornata ai romani (componimento per musica, S. Stampiglia), Neue Favorita, 1 Oct 1707, *Wn*
Ercole, vincitore di Gerione (poemetto drammatico, Bernardoni), 4 Nov 1708, *Wn*
Gli amori di Circe con Ulisse (dramma per musica, G.B. Ancioni), Dresden, 20 June 1709
Il bel genio dell'Austria ed il Fato (dialogo), Nov 1723, *Wn*

ORATORIOS

first performed at Vienna, S Ursula, unless otherwise stated

La sete di Cristo in croce, Innsbruck, Jesuitenkirche, Holy Week 1691, lib *A-Imf*
Il transito de San Giuseppe, Innsbruck, Holy Week 1693, lib *Imf*
L'amor della redentione, Innsbruck, Jesuitenkirche, Good Friday 1693, lib *Imf*
L'innocenza, illesa dal tradimento, descritta in San Carlo (M. Angelico), Vienna, Imperial Chapel, Lent 1694, *Wn*
S Ursula, vergine e martire (R.M. Rossi), 21 Oct 1694, *Wn*
Gesu crocifisso (?A. Catelani), 2 April 1695, lib *I-Vnm*
Sant' Orsola, vergine e martire, 21 Oct 1695, *A-Wn*
La morte del Redentor (P. de Massimi), 21 April 1696, lib *I-Mb*
Il sacrificio d'Abramo (?M. Cavesano), 21 Oct 1696, lib *Vnm*
L'invenzione della croce (Massimi), 6 April 1697, lib *A-Wn*, *I-Vnm*
Il pianto di Maria vergine, e di S Maria Maddalena al S Sepolcro raddolcito dalla consolazione (?G. Spedazzi), 6 April 1697, lib *A-Wn*
Lo sposalizio di S Orsola, vergine e martire (?S. Amerighi), 21 Oct 1697, lib *I-Vnm*
La vicende di Giosafatte, Re di Giuda (?Cupeda), Vienna, Imperial Chapel, Lent 1698, *A-Wn*
La sepoltura di Christo (R.N. Batticassa), 29 March 1698, *Wn*
Il ritorno di Tobia (?G.B. Lampugnani), 21 Oct 1698, *Wn*
La depositione dalla croce, e sepoltura di Gesu, 18 April 1699, lib *I-Mb*, *Vnm*
Il trionfo della bellezza, della grazia e della virtu espresso nelle felicissimie nozze di Ester, la piu degna vergine del popolo eletto, con Assuero, il maggior monarco del mondo (G. Frigimelica Roberti), 21 Oct 1699, lib *Vnm*
Giesu nel pretorio, osia L'innocenza giudicata della malizia (Frigimelica Roberti), 10 April 1700, lib *A-Wn*, *I-Vnm*
La corte, noviziato del chiastre per la beata Caterina da Bologna (Frigimelica Roberti), 21 Oct 1700, *A-Wn*
L'empieta trionfante nella morte di Giesu Cristo, 26 March 1701, lib *I-Vnm*
L'amante innocenza, trionfatrice della perfidia, ovvero S Cecilia, vergine e martire, Vienna, Imperial Chapel, Lent 1702, lib *A-Wn*, *Wst*
La resurrezione di Giesu Cristo, 15 April 1702, lib *Wn*, *I-Mb*
Le promesse nuziali di S Orsola, 21 Oct 1702, lib *A-Wn*, *I-Vnm*
I pensieri divoti (Frigimelica Roberti), Rome, Palazzo Apostolico, Christmas Eve, 1702
La clemenza di Davide (P. Ruggieri), Vienna, Imperial Chapel, Lent 1703, *A-Wn*
La fuga in Egitto dal Patriarca S Giuseppe con Giesu e Maria, 21 Oct 1703, *Wn*
Trattenimento divoto, place of perf. unknown, 1703, lib *I-Vnm*
S Romoaldo, Vienna, Imperial Chapel, Lent 1704, lib *A-Wn*, *I-Vnm*
La Giuditta (?P. Ottoboni), 21 Oct 1704 and 1710, lib *Vnm*
La fuga di S Teresa, 21 Oct 1705, lib *Bc*, *Vnm*
La sepoltura di Cristo (Bernardoni), place of perf. unknown, 1706
S Teresa (?Filippeschi), Vienna, Imperial Chapel and Milan, S Giovanni in Conca, Lent 1706, lib *Wn*, *I-Vnm*
L'innocenza calpestata dal mondo, e proletta da Dio (?Spedazzi), 21 Oct 1706, lib *Vnm*
Il ritorno di Tobia (P.A. del Negro), Vienna, Imperial Chapel, Lent 1707, *A-Wn*
Il martirio di S Susanna (Negro), 1707, lib *I-Vnm*
Il pentimento di Davide (S. Stampiglia), Vienna, Imperial Chapel, Lent 1708, *A-Wn*
Santa Teresa (Bernardoni), 21 Oct 1708, *Wn*
Il martirio de' Maccabei (Stampiglia), Vienna, Imperial Chapel, Lent 1709, *Wn*
La Giuditta (Stampiglia), Vienna, Imperial Chapel, Lent 1710, *Wn*
Santa Geltrude (Filippeschi), Vienna, Imperial Chapel, Lent 1711, *Wn*, *D-MEI*
La esaltazione di Salomone (B. Maddali), place of perf. unknown, ?21 Oct 1716, *Wn*
Ismaele (B. Perfetti), Vienna, Imperial Chapel, 11 March 1717, *Wn*, *D-MEI*
Il profeta Elia (G. Zati), Vienna, Imperial Chapel, 2 March 1730 [?previously perf. Venice, 1720], *A-Wn*

CANTATAS

Tributi armonici, 12 chamber cants. (Nuremberg, *c*1699)
La Pace e Marte, supplicanti avanti al trono della Gloria (Filippeschi), Vienna, 19 March 1701, score *A-Wn*

Il sacrificio di Berenice (P.A. del Negro), Vienna, 28 August 1712, score *Wn*

41 chbr cants., *Wn, D-Bsb, Dl, MEIr, F-Pn, GB-Lgc*; 4 chbr duets, *A-Wn*; facs. of 2 cants. in ICSC, xvi (1985)

BIBLIOGRAPHY

AllacciD; EitnerQ; GerberNL; KöchelKHM; LaMusicaD; SchmidlDS; SennMT; WaltherML

A. von Weilen: *Zur Wiener Theatergeschichte* (Vienna, 1901)

A. Koczirz: 'Exzerpte aus den Hofmusikakten des Wiener Kammerarchivs', *SMw*, i (1913), 278–303

E. Wellesz: 'Die Opern und Oratorien in Wien von 1660–1708', *SMw*, vi (1919), 5–138

L. Ferrari: 'Per la bibliografia del teatro italiano in Vienna', *Studi di bibliografia e di argomento romano in memoria di Luigi de Gregori*, ed. C.A. Barletta (Rome, 1949)

E. Wellesz: *Essays on Opera* (London, 1950)

F. Hadamowsky: 'Barocktheater am Wiener Kaiserhof mit einem Spielplan (1625–1740)', *Jb der Gesellschaft für Wiener Theaterforschung 1951–52* (Vienna, 1955), 7–117; pubd separately (Vienna, 1955)

C. Nemeth: 'Zur Lebensgeschichte von Carlo Agostino Badia (1672–1738)', *AÖAW*, xcii (1955), 224–38

H. Knaus: *Die Musiker im Archivbestand des kaiserlichen Obersthofmeisteramtes (1637–1705)* (Vienna, 1967–9)

O.E. Deutsch: 'Das Repertoire der höfischen Oper, der Hof- und der Staatsoper', *ÖMz*, xxiv (1969), 369–70, 379–421

H. Knaus: 'Die Musiker in den geheimen kaiserlichen Kammerzahlamtsrechnungsbüchern (1669, 1705–1711)', *AÖAW*, cvi (1969), 14–38

H. Seifert: *Die Oper am Wiener Kaiserhof im 17. Jahrhundert* (Tutzing, 1985)

L. Bennett: 'The Italian Cantata in Vienna, 1700–1711: an Overview of Stylistic Traits', *Antonio Caldara: Essays on His Life and Times*, ed. B.W. Pritchard (Aldershot, 1987), 183–211

S. Carter: 'Trombone Obbligatos in Viennese Oratorios of the Baroque', *HBSJ*, ii (1990), 52–77

R. Schnitzler: 'Fux or Badia? The Attribution of *Santa Geltrude* and *Ismaele*', *FAM*, xlii (1995), 205–45

LAWRENCE E. BENNETT

Badía [d'Agustí], **Conchita** [Conxita; Concepción] (*b* Barcelona, 14 Nov 1897; *d* Barcelona, 2 May 1975). Spanish soprano. She studied with Granados, Casals and Falla, and made her début in Barcelona in 1913, giving the first performance of the *Canciones amatorias* of Granados (two of which are dedicated to her) with the composer accompanying. Many other first performances included Falla's *Psyché* (1927), Gerhard's *Cançons populars catalanes* (1928) and the *Cançons* of Casals (1934). She was a frequent oratorio soloist with the Pablo Casals Orchestra, and gave numerous recitals (often of lieder), sometimes to her own accompaniment. Her only important operatic appearance was in the title role of *María del Carmen* (Granados) at the Liceo, Barcelona, in 1935. Although much of her career was spent in her native city, she sang in Paris in 1937 (more than once with Cortot as accompanist) and in 1958, at the 1932 ISCM Festival in Vienna (first performance of the orchestral version of Gerhard's Catalan songs), in London (five BBC broadcasts, 1937), in Belgium and Switzerland. From 1938 to 1947 she lived in Argentina, where she worked closely with Falla during the last years of his life.

Badía was professor of singing at the Barcelona Conservatory and of piano at the Granados Academy. Among her pupils was Montserrat Caballé. As a singer Badía combined intelligence and spontaneity with a keen sense of style and exemplary diction; her voice had a strongly distinctive, personal quality. She recorded a number of discs in the 1960s, including one with De Larrocha.

BIBLIOGRAPHY

J. Alavedra: *Conxita Badia: una vida d'artista* (Barcelona, 1975) [with discography]

RONALD CRICHTON/ALAN BLYTH

Badian, Maya (*b* Bucharest, 18 April 1945). Canadian composer and musicologist of Romanian origin. She began to study the piano from the age of five. Later (1961–8) she attended classes in composition under Tiberiu Olah at the Academy of Music in Bucharest. After graduation, she became an editor at Romanian Radio-Television (1968–72), after which she taught at the George Enescu School for the Arts (1972–86). Between 1972 and 1974 she completed her training in Weimar and at the Francesco Canetti Institute in Vicenza.

In 1987 she emigrated to Canada, settling in Montreal, teaching in the Music department at the University (1990–92), later transferring to the Faculty of Continuing Education at the same University (1992–5). Badian obtained her doctorate in music and composition in Montreal in 1992. She has given lectures about the music of Canada in Germany, Italy and Hungary.

Her compositional style interprets modernism through the 'prism' of Romanian traditional music, enriched by aspects of Canadian folk music which she collected enthusiastically, building a collection of lesser-known material. Through her melodic techniques, she makes these themes her own, with recurring motifs, incantations and outbursts of vitality.

WORKS
(*selective list*)

Orch: Sym. Movt, 1968, rev. 1975; Towards the Pinnacle (A. Blandiana), S, orch, 1971; Images, str orch, 1973; Sinfonietta, 1976, rev. 1982; Sym. Diptych, 1976; Pf Conc., 1978; Sym. Images, 1979; Vn Conc., 1980, rev. 1981; Gui Conc., 1981, rev. 1983; Toccata and Passacaglia, 1982; Conc., 4 timp, tpt, str orch, 1987; Holocaust in memoriam, sym., 1987; Conc., mar, vib, orch, 1988; Conc., 'Accents', vc, str orch, 1992; Conc., 'Laurentian Reflections', cl, sax, orch, 1994; Daily Tumult, str orch, 1994; Children's World, 1997

Chbr and solo inst: Dance, str trio, 1972; Monolog, vn 1972; Monody, ob, 1973; Incantation, cl, 1974; Valachian Dance, vc 1974; Echoes, fl, 1974; Chbr Conc., hn, perc, 1977; Movimente, wind qnt, 1978; Profiles, trbn, 1978; Children's World, 14 pieces, pf, 1988, rev. 1995; Suite on Romanian Themes, mar, vib, pf, 1988; Sonorous Mosaics, tuba, 1990; Cantus planus, ob, org, 1994; Fantasia, pf, 1994; Jeu de tons, 2 fl, pf, 1995

Choral: Canada 125, Cantata profana, 1992

OCTAVIAN COSMA

Badinage, badinerie (Fr.: 'jest', 'piece of fun', 'trifle'). A term applied to suite movements of a playful nature. The titles 'badinage' or 'badinerie' first appeared in the early 18th century; they have no precise musical meaning but rather suggest a mood, jocular, frivolous or bantering.

The only known badinerie is the final movement of J.S. Bach's Suite no.2 in B minor BWV1067. Rhythmically, this movement has much in common with the gavotte: it begins with a half-bar, the first phrase is eight beats long (the crotchet is the beat), with a caesura after the fourth and a point of repose on the eighth; the phrases are later extended. It is in 2/4, faster in tempo than an ordinary gavotte.

Telemann included a badinage in the orchestral suite in his *Musique de table*, iii (1733); the suite includes dances as well as character pieces with French titles. His badinage is based on gavotte rhythms: it is in common time, marked 'très vite'. The piece uses drone basses and alternates with a trio. The third cantata of Montéclair's first book is entitled *La badine*, and opens with an air in 2/4, in gavotte rhythm. The opening words give an idea of the cantata's bantering nature: 'The ever sighing lover makes me sigh with boredom'. Several 18th-century harpsichord collections include pieces entitled 'badinage' or 'badine' (see B. Gustafson and D.R. Fuller: *A Catalogue of French Harpsichord Music, 1699–1780*, Oxford, 1990).

Examples of the badinage in the 19th and 20th centuries are few. Lyadov's *Musical Snuffbox* op.32 is subtitled 'Valse-badinage'. Godowsky, in his Studies on Chopin's Etudes, combined the two G♭ études into a piece he called 'Badinage' – 'a polyphonic joke'. Prokofiev included a badinage or *shutka* ('little joke') in his piano pieces of op.3.

ERICH SCHWANDT

Badings, Henk (*b* Bandung, Java, 17 Jan 1907; *d* Maarheeze, 26 June 1998). Dutch composer.

1. LIFE.   Born of Dutch parents in Java, he went to the Netherlands in 1915 as an orphan. His wish to follow a musical career met with strong opposition from his guardian, who forced him to train at the Technical University in Delft. He graduated with honours in 1931 and was appointed demonstrator in palaeontology and historical geology there. During his student years he had been teaching himself composition and music theory, and in 1930 he sat for an examination set by Pijper. He then studied composition with Pijper for a time, but this contact was not particularly fruitful because of their widely differing views. Pijper did, however, stimulate Badings to write a major symphonic work, his prize winning First Symphony (later withdrawn), whose first performance by the Concertgebouw Orchestra in 1930 aroused the interest of press and public in the then completely unknown composer. In 1933 Eduard van Beinum conducted his Second Symphony and in 1935 his Third was given its première by the Concertgebouw under Mengelberg, followed by the *Symphonic Variations*, and the Second Violin Concerto.

In 1934 Badings was appointed lecturer in composition and theory at the Rotterdam Conservatory, and in 1937 he became co-director of the Amsterdam Muzieklyceum, his special task being the reorganization of the system of instruction. From 1941 to 1945, during the German occupation, he directed the State Conservatory in The Hague; he was subsequently punished for holding the post and banned for some years from public life, though in 1948 the Concertgebouw Orchestra commissioned him to write his Sixth Symphony. Until 1961, Badings mainly lived as a freelance composer. In 1960–61 he directed the electronic music studio at the University of Utrecht and was appointed there in 1961 to teach acoustics (until 1977). From that period his reputation as an outstanding teacher began to spread abroad; he had already achieved international renown as a composer. He was professor of composition at the Staatliche Hochschule für Musik, Stuttgart (1962–72), and gave lectures at the University of Adelaide (1962–3), in addition to numerous lectures in the USA and South Africa.

2. WORKS.   The features of Badings's music for which he became best known are his use of various scales of six, or especially eight notes, systems built on harmonic or subharmonic series and micro-intervals, in particular as part of a 31-note scale. However, Badings also retained a preference for counterpoint, a gift for striking instrumentation and great care for formal integration. The second

of these is evident as early as the first movement of the Second Symphony, a sonata form which is clearly divided into five sections, partly through contrasting orchestration; formal integration is displayed in the work's finale, where the rondo theme functions as a link between numerous ingenious variants developed from the material of the first two movements. There is also evidence here of Bading's predeliction for contrasting motifs, on the one hand lyrical, on the other strongly punctuated, which result in a sort of Beethovenian dialectic propelling the music forward. Further examples of such propulsion are to be found in the other early symphonies and concertos, together with the first four piano sonatas and most of the chamber music.

All Bading's finest works from the 1930s to the 1950s continued to exhibit traditional structures of three or four movements, coupled with the employment of sonata, song or variation forms. Such works include the *Tema con variazioni* for piano (1938), the *Four Sacred Songs* for a cappella choir (1941), the choreographic drama *Orpheus en Euridice* (1941), the *Sinfonischer Prolog* (1942), the Octet (1952) and the Double Concerto no.1 (1954). Stylistically speaking, Badings's music remained during these years mainly Romantic and expressive; nevertheless a predominant Germanic quality gradually gave way during World War II to a greater degree of French-like lightness and brilliance. Badings's Fifth Symphony, written on the occasion of the 60th anniversary of the Concertgebouw Orchestra in 1948, typifies this change. This is a work which also clearly shows his preoccupation with non-diatonic tonalities; there are scales of six, seven and eight notes, which on the one hand suggest a combination of Lydian and Mixolydian modalities, and on the other, as a result of the successions of augmented and minor 2nds in the six-note scales, influence the music towards polytonality.

In the 1950s Badings began to experiment with new scales, micro-intervals and diverse acoustical phenomena. This resulted in the development of the 31-note scale, in conjunction with A.D. Fokker and based on ideas formulated by Christiaan Huygens in the 17th century (*see* MICROTONE). Bading's first compositions with the scale are *Preludium en Fuga I* (1952) and the Suite (1954) written for the 31-note organ Fokker had constructed in the Teylers Museum in Haarlem. The microtonal system (with the *diesis* as the smallest interval) allowed for a finer control of overtones as well as leading to experimentation with different kinds of tuning. Subsequent works which explore the various attributes of the scale include the Sonatas nos.2–5 for two violins, the Fourth String Quartet (1966) and the Fifth Double Concerto for two violins and orchestra (1969).

During the early 1950s Badings also worked in the electronic studio of the Technical University, Delft. This resulted in his first electronic compositions: a fragment of theatre music for *The Countess Cathleen* (1952) and parts of the radiophonic opera *Orestes* (1954). This attracted great international attention – it was awarded the Italia Prize in 1954 – for its skilful use of the manipulative possibilities offered by tape, and by electronic sound generators and filters. For example, Badings achieved a fearsome effect for the Eumenides by using a recording of a male chorus played at accelerated speed, and, in another choral section, a slower speed was used to attain extreme bass notes. Varied speed techniques were also employed with instrumental sounds, as well as reversed recordings of cymbals and tam-tams. Badings's principle throughout was to realize previously unavailable pitches, timbres and rhythms. The ballet *Kain* (1956) was his first completely electronic work: an oscilloscope was used to assist in tuning in pure harmonics up to the 12th, and a 'melody' of timbre was produced by means of a photo-siren. A second radio opera, *Asterion*, was composed in 1957 to a commission from South African radio, and the television opera *Salto mortale* received a prize in the 1959 International Competition of Television Societies in Salzburg. From 1960 Badings used electronic sounds in combination with conventional instruments in many compositions, and his work with electronics influenced his orchestral writing. He was given a second Italia Prize in 1971 for the oratorio *Ballade van die bloeddorstige Jagter*, again commissioned by South African radio.

Electronics came to play a significant role in Badings's music, but of his enormous output – he wrote over 600 compositions – most were acoustic and encompassed all genres, including, particularly in his later career, music for amateurs and for educational purposes. For example he wrote many scores for wind band, eight volumes of *Arcadia* for piano and piano four hands (1945–67), and 16 volumes of *Trois Cosmos* for three violins or three violin groups (1981–2) from beginning to advanced levels. His many choral pieces, e.g. *Trios chansons bretonnes* (1946), *Languentibus in purgatorio* (1959) and *Missa antiphonica* (1985), are still a backbone for amateur and professional choral societies alike.

WORKS
dates are generally of publication

STAGE

Ops: Der nachtwacht (dramatic op, 3, T. Bouws), 1942, Antwerp, Flemish, 13 May 1950; Liefd's listen en lagen [Love's Ruses and Snares] (chbr op), 3 Badings and Bouws), 1945, Radio Hilversum, 6 Jan 1948; Orestes (radio op, Badings and Starink), Florence, 24 Sept, 1954; Asterion (radio op, P.N. van Wijk Louw), Johannesburg, 1957; Salto mortale (TV chbr op, 12 scenes, Badings and Belcampo), Nederlandse Televisie Sichting, 19 June 1959; Martin Korda, DP (dramatic choral op.3, Badings and A. van Eijk), Amsterdam, Stadsschouwburg, 1960

Ballets: Balletto grottesco, 1939; Orpheus en Euridice (choreographic drama), 1941; Balletto serioso, 1955; Kain, tape, 1956; Evolutionen, tape, 1958; Jungle, tape, 1959; Die Frau von Andros, tape, 1959; Genesis, tape, 1968; Ballet notturno, 2 pf, 1975

ORCHESTRAL

Vn Conc. no.1, 1928, unpubd; Vc Conc. no.1, 1930, unpubd; Sym. no.1, 1932; Sym. no.2, 1932; Sym. no.3, 1934; Largo en Allegro, str, 1935; Vn Conc., no.2, 1935; Sym. Variations I, 1936; Ov. I, 1937; Ov. II, 1937; Gedenckclanck, suite, 1938; Pf Conc. no.1, 1939; Concertino, pf trio, chbr orch, 1942; Ov. III, 1942; Sinfonischer Prolog, 1942; Sym. no.4, 1943; Fanfare de Jeanne d'Arc, 1944; Vn Conc. no.3, 1944; Vn Conc. no.4, 1947; Ov. IV, c1948; Aria trista e rondo giocoso, 1948; Divertimento, 1949; Pupazetti azzurri, 1950

Sym. Variations II, 1950; Conc., sax, orch/wind orch, 1951; Org Conc. no.1, 1952; Serenade, 1953; Sinfonisches Scherzo, 1953; Sym. no.6, chorus, orch, 1953; Sym. no.7, 1954; Ov. V, 1954; Vc Conc. no.2, 1954; Double Conc., 2 vn, orch, 1954; Pf Conc. no.2 'Atlantic Dances', 1955; Fl Conc. no.1, 1956; Marcia, 1957; Niederländische Tänze, 1957; Sym. Variations III, 1956; Sym. no.8, 1956; Sym. Variations IV, 1960; Sym. no.9, str, 1960; Sym. no.10, 1961; Ov. VI, 1961; Fl Conc. no.2, 1963

Double Conc., bn, dbn, orch, 1964; Double Conc., 2 pf, orch, 1964; Double Conc., vn, va, orch, 1965; Sym. no.11, 1964; Sym. no.12, 1964; Pittsburgh Conc., 1965; Conc., va, str, 1965; Org Conc. no.2, 1966; Conc., hp, chbr orch/wind orch, 1967; Armageddon, S, orch, 1968; Sym. no.14, 1968; Vn Conc. no.4, 1969; Symphonietta, 1971; Twentse suite, 4 solo insts, 4 groups, 1976; Sym. Variations IV, 1960; Vijf Nederlandse Dansen, 1976; Conc.,

fl, ob, cl, orch, 1981; Conc. for Orch, 1982; Conc., 4 sax, orch, 1984; Serenade, str orch, 1985; Huygens Suite, chbr orch, 1987

Wind orch: Partita, 1960; Sym. no.13, 1966; Conc., 2 hn, wind, tape, 1970; Transitions, 1972; Lieshout en zijn molens, wind/brass band, 1976; Ciacona concertante, 1978; Cl Conc., 1979; Eng Hn Conc., 1979; Epiphany, 1979; Golden Age, 1979; Reflections, 1980; Sinfonietta no.2, 1981; Ciacona, seria, 1982; Sym. no.15 'Conflicts and Confluences', 1983; Images, 1983; Figures sonores, 1984; 3 Apparitions of a Hymn, 1984; Vc Conc., 1985; Trbn Conc., 1986; Introduction, Variation and Indonesian National Anthem, 1986

CHORUS WITH ORCHESTRA

Kantate I 'Festival kantate' (W. Buning), solo vv, chorus, children's chorus, orch, 1936; Kantate II (A. Verwey), S, chbr chorus, chbr orch, 1937; Apocalypse, orat, solo vv, chorus, orch, 1948; Kantate III (Rijnsdorp, Badings), chorus, children's chorus, wind, carillon, 1954; Kantate IV 'Laus pacis' (Erasmus), S, male chorus, wind, 1956; Ps cxlvii, children's chorus, chbr chorus, chorus, orch, 1959; Cantate VI 'Laus stultitiae' (Erasmus), chorus, large, ens, 1961; TeD, male chorus, orch, 1962; Jonah, orat., solo vv, chorus, orch, tape, 1963

Hymnus Ave Maris Stella, female chorus, orch, 1965; 4 Old Dutch Songs, 1967; Genesis, T, Bar, male chorus, perc, tape, 1967; Kantate VII 'Ballade van die bloeddorstige Jagter' (Watermeyer), solo vv, chorus, orch, tape, 1970; Klaagzang; Kantate VIII 'Song of Myself' (W. Whitman), nar, chorus, wind, 1973; Kantate IX (C. Huygens, Badings), S, T, chorus, chbr orch, 1987; see also ORCHESTRAL [Sym. no.6, 1953]

OTHER CHORAL

Mixed chorus: Vechter, 1939; 3 Songs, 1940; 4 Sacred Songs, 1941; Geestelijke liederen, 1942; Missa brevis, 1946; 3 chansons bretonnes, chorus, pf, 1946; Daar was een wuf, 1947; Maria, 14 songs, solo vv, chbr chorus, fl, vc, 1947; Het kwezelke, 1947; Meisjes van Duinkerken, 1947; Pools volkslied, 1947; 6 images, 1950; Contrasten, 1952; Cantamus amici, 1957; Languentibus in purgatorio, 1959; 3 Schwärmereien, 3 songs, chorus, tape, 1965; 5 poèmes chinois, 1973; 2 Chorlieder, 1977; Aus tiefer Not, 1978; Finnigan's Wake, 1978; Notturna triste alla lune, 1978; Requiem, 1978; Vocalizzo burlesco, 1978; Querella pacis, 1979; 3 Serious Songs, 1983; Missa antiphonica, 2 choruses, 1985; An den Mond, A, chorus, 1987; Ave maris stella, 1987; Ballade van de omkransde boot, 1987; Tristis est anima mea, 1987

Male chorus: Jagerslied, 1933; Dat Liet van den rhynscen wyn, 1934; Een weemoedig lied, 1940; Boutensliederen, 1947; 3 geestelijke liederen, 1947; 2 kerstliederen, 1947; 3 chants populaires, 1950; 3 romances, 1950; In memoriam, 1952; 4 geestelijke liederen, 1954; 4 wereldlijke liederen, 1954; Piet Hein, 1963; Carmina stultitiae, 1964; Lucerbertliederen, 3 songs, male chorus, tape, 1964; Folksongs, arr. male chorus, 1967; Ave Regina coelorum, male chorus, 1978; Gebed, male chorus, 1978; Gruselett, male chorus, 1978; Chanson de Bourgogne en rondeau, male chorus, 1982; Jub Deo, male chorus, 1982; Polnischer Winter, male chorus, 1982; Ps xxvii, male chorus, 1982

Female chorus: 3 ballades, 1950; 6 Christmas Songs, 1950; 3 chants populaires, 1953; Stabat mater, 1954; Ave Maria, 1978; Mater cantans filio, 1978; Kyrie eleison, 1979; Ballade van de twee konigskinderen, 1983; 3 chansons d'amour, 1983; 3 Liederen van Minne, 1983; Tria amoris carmina, 1983; Pastorale, 1985; De Zoom, 1985

CHAMBER

3 or more insts: Qnt, fl, str trio, pf, 1928; Wind Qnt, 1929; Sextet, A, fl, cl, vn, va, pf, 1931; Str Qt no.1, 1931; Pf Trio, 1934; Str Qt no.2. 1936; Qnt, fl, str trio, hp, 1936; Trio, ob, cl, bn, 1943; Str Qt no.3, 1944; Trio, 2 vn, va, 1945; Trio, 2 ob, eng hn/3 vn, 1946; Trio, fl, vn, va, 1947; Qt, 2 tpt, hn, trbn, 1947; Wind Qnt, 1948; 3 Dutch Dances, 2 tpt, hn, trbn, 1950; Trio, 2 vn, pf, 1951; Pf Qnt, 1952; Octet, 1952; Trio, 2 vn, va, 1953; Trio, 3 rec, 1955; Trio, fl, va, gui, 1962; Str Qt no.4, 1966; Pf Qt, 1973; Trio, a fl, va, hp, 1977; 7 qts, any insts, 1978; Str Qt no.5, 1980; Trio, 2 vn, archiphone, 1981; Trio Cosmos, i–xvi, 3 vn.3 groups of vns, 1981–2; Qnt, cl, vn, vc, gui, hp, 1985; Trio, cl, eng hn, bn, 1986

1–2 insts: Sonata, vc, pf, 1927; Sonata, vn, vc, 1927; Sonata, vn, va, 1928; Sonata, 2 vn, 1928; Sonata no.1, vc, pf, 1929; Sonata, vn, pf, 1931; Sonata no.1, vn, pf, 1933; Sonata no.2, vc, pf, 1934; Capriccio, fl, pf, 1936; Capriccio, vn, pf, 1936; Canzona, ob, org, 1938; Intermezzo, vn, org, 1938; Sonata no.2, vn, pf, 1939;

Sonata no.1, vn, 1940; Sonata no.1, vc, 1941; Suite no.1, carillon, 1943; Sonata, hp, 1944

Elfenland, 45 easy pieces, vn, pf, 1945; Duets, 2 vn, 1945; Air triste, vn, pf, 1947; La malinconia, a sax, pf, 1949; Sonata no.1, carillon, 1949; Sonata no.2, carillon, 1950; Ballade, fl, hp, 1950; Suite no.1, 2 rec, 1950; Sonata no.2, vc, 1951; Sonata no.2, vn, 1951; Sonata no.3, vn, 1951; Sonata, va, pf, 1951; Suite no.2, carillon 1951; Cavatine, a fl, hp, 1952; Cavatine, a sax, pf, 1952; Cavatine, vn, pf, 1952; Sonata no.3, vn, pf, 1952; Suite no.3, carillon, 1953; Suite no.4, carillon, 1953; Romance, vn, pf, 1957; Blues, harmonica, pf, 1957; Sonata, rec, hpd, 1957

Suite no.3, 2 rec, 1958; Rondino, vn, pf, 1960; 12 preludes, gui, 1961; Sonata no.2, 2 vn, 1963; Canzona, eng hn, org, 1967; Dialogues, fl, org, 1967; It is Dawning in the East, gui, org, 1967; Quempas, vn/va, org, 1967; Sonata no.3, 2 vn, 1967; Toccata, mar, 1973; Sonata no.4, 2 vn, 1975; pf, 1976; Sonata, accdn, 1981; Sonata no.5, 2 vn, 1981; Sonata, fl, hp, 1982; Sonata, fl, gui, 1983; Suite no.5, carillon, 1983; Variations, vn, gui, 1983; Sonata no.6, 2 vn, 1984; Preambolo, aria e postludio, gui, 1985; 3 Etudes, carillon, 1987

KEYBOARD

Org: Toccata, 1929; Preludium, 1938; Preludium en Fuga no.1, 31-note org, 1952; Preludium en Fuga no.2, 1952; Preludium en Fuga no.3, 1953, Preludium en Fuga no.4, 31-note org, 1954; Suite, 1954, 31-note org, 1954; Reihe kleiner Klangstücke, 31-tone org, 1957; Variations on a Medieval Dutch Theme, 1969; Ricercar, 1973; Introduction, Chorale and Finale, 1975; Archifonica, 31-tone org, 1976; Apparizioni, 1977; Passacaglia piccola, 1979; 4 pezzi, 1980; Prelude and arioso, 1983; Preludium on B.A.C.H., org, 1985

Pf: Suite, 1930; Tema con variazioni, 1938; Balletto grotesco, 2 pf, 1939; Reihe kleiner Klavierstücke, 1939; Arcadia, easy pf pieces, i–iii, pf, iv–v, pf duet, 1945; Variations à la manière de ..., 1951; Balletto serioso, pf duet, 1955; Foxtrot, pf duet, 1955; Xenie, pf, 1958; Adagio cantabile, 1967; Arcadia, easy pf pieces, vi–vii, 1967; 5 Pf Pieces, 1967; Balletto notturno, 1975; 4 sonori, 1976; La megicana, pf, 1978; Passacaglia, pf, 1979; Images de Noël, pf, 1982; 5 kleine Klavierstücke, pf, 1983; 6 sonatas, 4 sonatines

SONGS

3 Rilke-Lieder, 1v, pf, 1932; Coplas, 1935; Dullaert-Liederen, T, pf, 1935; Vildraclieder, 1935; 3 Baritonliederen, 1936; 3 Duette, 1936; 4 Wiegeliedjes, 1936; Minnedeuntje, 1937; Chansonnetes, 1941; Chansons orientales, 1942; Ariettes méchantes, 1944; Liederne van de dood, 1946; Meiregen, 10 children's songs, 1946; Liedjes van weemoed, 1948; Morgenstern-lieder, 4vv, pf, 1961; Burying Friends, 1963; 8 Cummings Songs, 1965; 6 Lechler-Lieder, 1966; 3 Oud-Nederlandse Liederen, 1v, fl, hp, 1967; 5 Reich-Lieder, Mez/Bar, pf, 1974; Najaarsnacht (R. Holst), 1976; 5 Rilke-Lieder, 1978; 2 Whale Songs, 1980; Ode aan Aphrodite, 1982; Sextet, S, fl, cl, vn, db, gui, 1987

TAPE

The Countess Cathleen (incid music), 1952; Sonatine, 1955; Variations electroniques, 1957; Capriccio, vn, 2 tapes, elektromagnetische Klangfiguren, 1959; Toccata no.1, 2 tapes, c1960; Toccata no.2, 2 tapes, 1964; Chaconne, tpt, tape, 1965; Conc., pf, 2 tapes, 1967; Kontrapunkte, pf, tape, 1970; Music, org, tape, 1970

Principal publishers: Donemus, Schott (Mainz)

WRITINGS

De hedendaagsche Nederlandsche muziek (Amsterdam, 1936)
'Heilige huisjes', Wereld der muziek, v (1938–9), 273–7
'De ivoren toren van de componist', Wereld der muziek, vii (1940–41), 1–4
'Kompositionen für Kinder', Musik im Unterricht, xliv (1953), 245
'Spezields Gesicht der Funkoper', NZM, Jg.116, nos.10–12 (1955), 15 only
with J.W. de Bruyn: 'Elektronische muziek', Philips technisch tijdschrift, xix/9 (1957), 269–79
'Sur les possibilités et les limitations de la musique électronique', Revue belge de musicologie, xiii (1959), 57–62
'Experiences with Electronic Ballet Music', The Modern Composer and His World: Stratford, ON, 1960, 106–8
'Sonata for Cello Solo', Sonorum speculum, no.7 (1961), 23–4
Over 31-toon stemming (Brussels, 1978)
'Aantekeningen over enige fundamentele elementen in de muziek', Mens en melodie, xli (1986), 380–88, 452–53, 503–09, 547–51

BIBLIOGRAPHY

S. van Ameringen: 'Henk Badings, Profil eines holländischen Komponisten von heute', ÖMz, vii (1952), 297–300
C. MacDaniel: Henk Badings: Musico-Technical Study of his Woodwind Chamber Works (diss., U. of Texas, 1960)
J. Geraedts: 'Symphony for String Orchestra', Sonorum speculum, no.6 (1961), 9–13
J. Wouters: 'Dutch Music in the 20th Century', MQ, li (1965), 103–4
J. Wouters: 'Henk Badings', Sonorum speculum, no.32 (1967), 1–23; repr. in Dutch Composers' Gallery, i: Nine Portraits of Dutch Composers (Amsterdam, 1971), 50–70
J. Ditto: The Four Preludes and Fugues: the Ricercar and the Passacaglia for Timpani and Organ by Henk Badings (diss., U. of Rochester, 1979)
M.K.K. Clardy: Compositional Devices of Willem Pijper (1894–1947) and Henk Badings (b.1907) in Two Selected Works: Pijper's 'Sonata per flauto e pianoforte' (1925) and Badings' 'Concerto for Flute and Wind Symphony Orchestra' (1963) (diss., U. of North Texas, 1980)
L. Samama: Zeventig jaar Nederlandse muziek (1915–1985) (Amsterdam, 1986), 138–48
R. de Beer: 'An Odour of Taboo: Henk Badings, 1907–1987', Key Notes, no.24 (1987), 28–9
P.T. Klemme: Henk Badings, Choral Compositions for Unaccompanied Mixed Chorus with Latin Text: Analysis and Commentary (diss., U. of Washington, 1988)
C. Becx: Henk Badings: Symfonische blaasmuziek/Music for Wind-Orchestra (Utrecht, 1989)
P.T. Klemme: Henk Badings, 1907–87: Catalog of Works (Warren, MI, 1993)
P.T. Klemme: 'The Choral Music of Henk Badings', American Choral Review, xxxv/2 (1993), 2–8

JOS WOUTERS/LEO SAMAMA

Badini, Carlo Francesco (fl 1770–93). Italian librettist and journalist. He was in London by 1769, when he wrote the libretto for Pugnani's comic opera Nanetta e Lubino. Probably supplementing his income by translating and teaching Italian, Badini wrote a few librettos for the King's Theatre during the 1770s, including Le pazzie di Orlando (set by P.A. Guglielmi in 1771), a witty, ambitious work which Nunziato Porta adapted for Haydn as Orlando paladino (1782, Eszterháza). Badini's other works from this period include Il disertore (1770), set by Guglielmi and revived in Lisbon in 1772, and L'ali d'amore (1776), which was set by Venanzio Rauzzini.

An early sign of Badini's individuality is found in the libretto for Bertoni's La governante, a free translation of the English dialogue opera The Duenna by R.B. Sheridan. While Badini retained many of Sheridan's lyrics, he reworked the drama into a typical three-act burletta whose arias, unlike Sheridan's, advance the plot. Another example of Badini's interest in English drama is Il duca d'Atene (set by Bertoni in 1780), the plot of which is partly drawn from The Taming of the Shrew.

Badini kept abreast of new developments in opera, as evidenced in Il trionfo della costanza (set by Anfossi in 1782). Indebted to Sedaine's Le roi et le fermier, this highly melodramatic libretto includes an exceptionally long first-act finale comparable to those of Casti and Da Ponte in its depiction of domestic chaos. Badini later expressed contempt for his fellow Italian librettists in the preface to his libretto L'amore protetto dal cielo, o sia La vestale (1787), an opera seria with music composed and assembled by Rauzzini.

Badini's fortunes fluctuated during his later career. In 1779 he was sued by the King's Theatre manager, Antoine Le Texier; two years later he was sued by the harpsichord maker Jacob Kirkman and sentenced to debtors' prison. Beginning with the 1783–4 season, he was employed by the King's Theatre as one of two house poets, with a salary of £100 which rose to £150 in the following seasons. In 1785 he was appointed principal librettist at the King's and became a close associate of the manager, G.A. Gallini. In 1788 it was reported that he had briefly been editor of the *Morning Post*. With his compatriot Andrea Carnavale, he was accused of writing a libellous pamphlet, the *Case of the Opera-House Disputes* (1784), a vicious attack on the former owner-manager of the King's Theatre, William Taylor, Gallini's arch-enemy. He may also have been a newspaper critic.

In early 1791 Badini was commissioned to write a libretto for Haydn during his first visit to London: this was *L'anima del filosofo* (*Orfeo ed Euridice*), which Haydn did not finish. Badini's brilliant though flawed libretto is one of the most peculiar for an *opera seria*. Taking a completely different approach from Calzabigi and Gluck, Badini reverts to Virgil's violent ending, with Orpheus killed by the Bacchantes. In 1792 Badini was reappointed house poet at the King's Theatre only to be dismissed a year later for unknown reasons. He was replaced by Lorenzo da Ponte, who had arrived in London in 1792.

BIBLIOGRAPHY

BDA; *GroveO* (C. Price) [incl. list of libs]

Documents in *GB-Lpro*: PRIS 10/51; C31/239/203 (Chancery Affidavits); C38/754 (Masters' Reports); C107/201 (Masters' Exhibits); LC 7/3

L. da Ponte: *Memorie* (New York, 1823; Eng. trans., London and Philadelphia, 1929/R)

H.C.R. Landon: *Haydn in England 1791–1795* (London, 1976)

F.C. Petty: *Italian Opera in London 1760–1800* (Ann Arbor, 1980)

C. Price, J. Milhous and R.D. Hume: 'The Rebuilding of the King's Theatre, Haymarket, 1789–1791', *Theatre Journal*, xliii (1991), 421–44

C. Price, J. Milhous and R.D. Hume: *Italian Opera in Late Eighteenth-Century London*, i: *The King's Theatre, Haymarket 1778–1791* (Oxford, 1995)

J. Milhous, G. Dideriksen and R.D. Hume: *Italian Opera in Late Eighteenth-Century London*, ii: *The Pantheon Opera and its Aftermath, 1789–1795* (Oxford, forthcoming)

CURTIS PRICE

Badinski, Nikolai (*b* Sofia, 19 Dec 1937). Bulgarian composer. He graduated from the Sofia Academy of Music in 1961, and from 1962 worked in Halle as a violinist and composer. From 1967 to 1970 he studied composition with Wagner-Régeny and Günter Kochan as a postgraduate at the Akademie der Künste in East Berlin. In 1975 and 1976 he attended courses in Siena given by Dallapiccola and Donatoni, and from 1974 took part in Darmstadt summer courses. In 1976 he moved to West Berlin, where he has since worked as a freelance composer. In 1980 he received a one-year scholarship to the Villa Massimo, Rome, and in 1981–2 and 1985–6 received stipends to live and work in Paris. He was composer-in-residence at the Djerassi Foundation, 1987, and has taught at a number of colleges and universities, notably in Stockholm and Copenhagen. He has won many international awards, for instance in the Viotti, Stockhausen and Trieste competitions, and in 1983 he became a corresponding member of the European Academy of Arts, Sciences and Literature.

In his extensive output (over 130 works) Badinski has a tendency towards a polystylistic means of expression, often in a late Romantic manner, as witnessed by his dense orchestration and the dynamic range of detailed and intricate treatment of individual instruments. His voluminous melodies, full of glissandos, tremolos and melismas, are particularly noticeable in his instrumental concertos. In both his acoustic and his electronically composed music there is often a wave-like or crescendo development of form based on superimposition of different rhythms and instrumental colours. His music alludes to styles ranging from Johann Strauss, Bach and Stravinsky to Bulgarian folk music.

WORKS
(*selective list*)

Inst: Str Qt no.1 'Das Leben – über dem Krieg', 1965; Berlin Divertimento, fl, cl, db, perc, 1968; Moscow Wind Qnt, 1969; Vn Conc. no.1 'Triptychon', vn, perc, str, 1970–71; Vn Conc. no.2, 1971–2; Die Ruinen unter Sofia, cl, bn, hn, 2 vn, va, vc, db, 1972; Dialoghi, va, 1973; Str Qt no.2, 1973; Vn Conc. no.3, 1973; 5–1 Euphonien, db, 1974; Va Conc. 'Col legno', 1977; Cottidianus no.1, vn, 1977; Omaggio a BACH, hpd, fl, ob, cl, bn, 2 vn, va, vc, hpd, 1977; Klavieriada, conc., pf, tape/5 pf, 1977–8; Str Qt no.3 'Hommage à Bela Bartok', 1978; AMEKDIL no.2 (Sym. no.2) 'AaAaN', large orch, 1978; AMEKDIL no.3 (Sym. no.3) 'Situationi mobili', orch, 1981; Connections, vn, pf, orch, 1982–3; Cottidianus no.2, vc, 1987; many pf works

Vocal: AMEKDIL no.1 (Sym. no.1), S, orch, 1967; Sono ancora qui, il sole gira . . . (cant., S. Quasimodo), medium v, cl, vn, va, vc, pf, 1970; Martialphonien (szenische Aktionen, Martial), 12vv, 1975; Wiederspiegelungen der Weisheit, solo vv, chorus, orch, 1983–6; . . . gia addolicito da un po d'aria di mare (P. Pasolini), S, perc, 1984–6

El-ac: Phönixe, 1974; Sevtoplis, 1974; Trio imaginable, cptr, 1980; Fridenpsalm, 1983; Begegnung von Unendlichkeiten, elec modified insts, tape, 1983; Schwebende Berliner Märchen, 1983–6; Gajdi [Bagpipes], 1984; Kukeri-eine Ritus-szene, 1984–5; Venexiana, cptr, 1984–5; Dance elektroakustique, 1985; Ab-stand, Ab-seits: Werste, Weiten . . . , vn, cptr, 1988; 6 Orpheus Gesänge, vn, elecs, 1988–9; Decipio no.6, 12 sax, 1990–91; Decipio no.7, 32hp/(hp, elecs), 1990–91

El-ac material in Institute of Sonology at the Royal Conservatory, The Hague

Principal publishers: Deutscher Verlag, Tonos

Principal recording companies: ABAN, ProVive

BIBLIOGRAPHY

U. Stürzbecker: 'Der Komponist sollte mit Zuhören sprechen: ein Interview mit "multinationalen" Komponisten Nikolai Badinski', *NZM*, Jg.140 (1979), 48

G. Eberle: 'Schütz original, verfremdet und zerstückelt', *NZM*, Jg.146 (1985), 41

G. Eberle: 'Mental-integrales Komponieren: Nikolai Badinski und seine Musik', *NZM*, Jg.148, no.11 (1987), 24–7

MARIA KOSTAKEVA

Badoaro [Badoer, Badoero, Badovero], **Giacomo** [Iacopo] (*b* Venice, 1602; *d* Venice, 1654). Italian librettist. He was a member of the Venetian nobility. He wrote a great deal of verse in Italian and in Venetian dialect and had an extensive poetic exchange with G.F. Busenello. His reputation as a librettist rests on Monteverdi's supposed predilection for his work in his *Il ritorno d'Ulisse in patria* (1640) and *Le nozze d'Enea in Lavinia* (1641). The latter text, however, is by another (unidentified) poet, as its printed scenario makes clear. Badoaro's next libretto, *L'Ulisse errante* (1644, music by Sacrati), also drew on the Odyssey; each of its five acts presents an independent episode of Ulysses' adventure. The deliberate, even selfconscious rejection of Aristotelian unity of action may have been inspired by Giacomo Torelli, who created sets and machinery for the production. Chronicles of Venetian opera also attribute to Badoaro *Helena rapita da Theseo* (1653, music possibly by Cavalli), which is not, contrary to the assertion of Ivanovich, based on a plot by Giovanni Faustini. His works were given only single productions in Venice, except for the Bolognese performance of *Il ritorno* *d'Ulisse* (also 1640), one of several works exported there during the first decade of public opera in Venice. The presence at Vienna of the sole surviving score of *Il ritorno d'Ulisse in patria* has led some scholars to suppose that it was used for a performance there. Like many of the other early Venetian librettists, Badoaro was a member of the cynical and libertine Accademia degli Incogniti; he was financially involved in the Teatro Novissimo at the time of its closure in 1645.

BIBLIOGRAPHY

C. Ivanovich: *Minerva al tavolino* (Venice, 1681, 2/1688)
W. Osthoff: *Das dramatische Spätwerk Claudio Monteverdis* (Tutzing, 1960)
T. Walker: 'Gli errori di "Minerva al tavolino": osservazioni sulla cronologia delle prime opere veneziane', *Venezia e il melodramma nel Seicento: Venice 1972*, 7–20
L. Bianconi and T. Walker: 'Dalla *Finta pazza* alla *Veremonda*: storie di Febiarmonici', *RIM*, x (1975), 379–454
E. Rosand: 'Iro and the Interpretation of *Il ritorno d'Ulisse in patria*', *JM*, vii (1989), 141–64
T. Carter: 'In Love's Harmonius Consort? Penelope and the Interpretation of *Il ritorno d'Ulisse in patria*', *COJ*, v (1993), 1–16
E. Rosand: 'The Bow of Ulysses', *JM*, xii (1994), 376–95

THOMAS WALKER

Bado y Gómez, Juan del. *See* VADO Y GÓMEZ, JUAN DEL.

Badura-Skoda [née Halfar], **Eva** (*b* Munich, 15 Jan 1929). Austrian musicologist, wife of PAUL BADURA-SKODA. She studied the violin, the piano and theory, both privately and at the Vienna Academy. She attended universities in Heidelberg, Regensburg, Vienna and Innsbruck, working with Stäblein and Wilhelm Fischer, and in 1953 received the doctorate from the University of Innsbruck with a dissertation on music teaching in Austria from the 16th century to the 18th. She was on the staff of the International Summer Academy of the Salzburg Mozarteum in 1962 and 1963 and taught at the University of Wisconsin, first as a guest professor in 1964 and then as professor from 1966 to 1974. She has also been a visiting professor at Boston University, Queens University, Ontario, the University of Göttingen and McGill Uiversity, and has lecturered at institutions in Europe, Asia and North America.

Badura-Skoda's research has centred on 18th-century topics, particularly the music of the Scarlattis, Mozart and Haydn, and also on Schubert. She has also written on problems of editing and performing practice, the history of the fortepiano, Viennese music history and the development of various genres of comic opera such as Singspiel, *opera buffa* and *opéra comique*. As co-author with her husband of *Mozart-Interpretation* she has combined her experience as a pianist with her historical studies to give useful insights into the performance of Mozart's keyboard works, particularly the piano sonatas and concertos. She has contributed articles to German and English music dictionaries (including *MGG1* and *Grove6*) and is a member of the Joseph-Haydn-Institut and the Zentralinstitut für Mozart-Forschung. In 1986 she was awarded the Österreichisches Ehrenkreuz für Wissenschaften und Kunst. She and her husband were concerned with the publicity surrounding the 'Haydn' sonatas later found to be forged.

WRITINGS

Beiträge zur Geschichte des Musikunterrichtes in Österreich (diss., U. of Innsbruck, 1953)
with P. Badura-Skoda: *Mozart-Interpretation* (Vienna and Stuttgart, 1957; Eng. trans., 1962/R as *Interpreting Mozart on the Keyboard*)
'Über die Anbringungen von Auszierungen in den Klavierwerken Mozarts', *MJb* 1957, 186–98
'Zur Echtheit von Mozarts Sarti-Variationen KV460', *MJb* 1959, 127–39
'Eine private Briefsammlung', *Festschrift Otto Erich Deutsch*, ed. W. Gerstenberg, J. LaRue and W. Rehm (Kassel, 1963), 280–90
'Textual Problems in Masterpieces of the 18th and 19th Centuries', *MQ*, li (1965), 301–17
'Clementi's "Musical Characteristics" Op.19', *Studies in Eighteenth-Century Music: a Tribute to Karl Geiringer*, ed. H.C.R. Landon and R.E. Chapman (New York, 1970), 53–67
'"Teutsche Comoedie-Arien" und Joseph Haydn', *Der junge Haydn: Graz 1970*, 59–73
'Haydn, Mozart and their Contemporaries', *Keyboard Music*, ed. D. Matthews (London, 1972), 108–66
Wolfgang Amadeus Mozart: Klavierkonzert c-moll, KV491 (Munich, 1972) [monograph]
'The Influence of the Viennese Popular Comedy on Haydn and Mozart', *PRMA*, c (1973–4), 185–99
'Personal Contacts and Mutual Influence in the Field of Opera', *Haydn Studies: Washington DC 1975*, 419–21
'Performance Conventions in Beethoven's Early Works', *Beethoven, Performers, and Critics: Detroit 1977*, 52–75
'Zur Salzburger Erstaufführung von Joseph Haydns Singspiel "Die reisende Ceres"', *ÖMz*, xxxii (1977), 317–24
'Der Bildhauer Anton Dietrich: ein Beitrag zur Ikonographie Beethovens und Schuberts', *Musik, Edition, Interpretation: Gedenkschrift Günter Henle*, ed. M. Bente (Munich, 1980), 30–52
'Giuseppe Scarlatti und seine buffa-Opera', *Musik am Hof Maria Theresias: Graz 1980*, 57–75
'Prolegomena to a History of the Viennese Fortepiano', *Israel Studies in Musicology*, ii (1980), 77–99
ed.: *Joseph Haydn: Vienna 1982*
ed., with P. Branscombe: *Schubert Studies: Problems of Style and Chronology* (Cambridge, 1982)
'"Clavier"-Musik in Wien zwischen 1750 und 1770', *SMw*, xxxv (1984), 65–88
'The Piano Works of Schubert', *Nineteenth-Century Piano Music*, ed. L. Todd (New York, 1990), 97–146
'Komponierte J.S. Bach "Hammerklavier-Konzerte"?', *BJb 1991*, 159–71
'Aspects of Performance Practice', *Eighteenth-Century Keyboard Music*, ed. R.L. Marshall (New York, 1994), 33–67
'Zur Vorgeschichte der Symphonik der Wiener Klassik', *SMw*, xliii (1994), 67–143
'Stringed Keyboard Instruments after 1700: Reconstructions of *Lautenwercke* and a *Hammerpantalone*', *Festa musicologica: Essays in Honor of George J. Buelow*, ed. T.J. Mathiesen and B.V. Rivera (Stuyvesant, NY, 1995), 271–87

EDITIONS

Paul Homberger: Brautgesänge, MAM, vii (1959)
with P. Badura-Skoda: *Wolfgang Amadeus Mozart: Konzerte für ein oder mehrere Klaviere und Orchester mit Kadenzen*, Neue Ausgabe sämtlicher Werke, V: 15/V (Kassel, 1965)
Franz Schubert: Trios für Klavier, Violine and Violoncello (Munich, 1973)
J. Haydn *Die reisende Ceres* (Vienna, 1982) [Singspiel, in Eng. and Ger.]
Carl Ditters von Dittersdorf: Six Symphonies, The Symphony 1720–1840, ser. B, i (New York, 1985)
with A. Mann: *J.J. Fux: Singfundament*, Sämtliche Werke, vii/2 (Graz, 1993)

PAULA MORGAN

Badura-Skoda [Badura], **Paul** (*b* Vienna, 6 Oct 1927). Austrian pianist, husband of EVA BADURA-SKODA. He studied the piano and conducting at the Vienna Conservatory under Viola Thern (1945–8), and then in Lucerne at the masterclasses of Edwin Fischer, who exerted a great influence on him. After winning the Austrian Music Competition in 1947, he made his concert début the following year. He soon became one of the most prominent Austrian pianists, touring throughout the world. From 1966 to 1971 he was artist-in-residence at the University of Wisconsin, USA. His recital programmes have centred on the Viennese Classics, but have also embraced contemporary composers, for instance Frank Martin, whose Second Piano Concerto is dedicated to him. Badura-Skoda has a strong interest in historical keyboard instruments, and his own collection includes instruments by Schantz, Broadwood, Graf and Schneider. With these, and by means of his interpretative and editorial research, he strives to achieve fidelity to the original sources and tone-colours. He has made many recordings on period and modern instruments, including the complete sonatas of Beethoven and Schubert. He also composes and has written numerous cadenzas for concertos of the Viennese Classical period. His editions include three Mozart piano concertos (with his wife, Eva), K453, 456 and 459, for the Neue Mozart-Ausgabe (Kassel, 1965); Beethoven's piano sonatas; Chopin *Etudes* opp.10 and 25 (Vienna, 1973); and piano works by Schubert.

WRITINGS

(*selective list*)

with E. Badura-Skoda: *Mozart-Interpretation*(Vienna and Stuttgart, 1957; Eng. trans., 1962/*R* as *Interpreting Mozart on the Keyboard*)

'Chopin's Influence', *Frederic Chopin: Profiles of the Man and the Musician*, ed. A. Walker (London, 1966, 2/1973 as *The Chopin Companion*), 258–76

with J. Demus: *Die Klaviersonaten von Ludwig van Beethoven* (Wiesbaden, 1970, 2/1974)

'Eine ungedruckte Brahms-Kadenz zu Mozarts D-Moll-Konzert KV 466', *ÖMz*, xxxv (1980), 153–6

'Von der Vieldeutigkeit der musikalischen Notation', *Logos musicae: Festschrift für Albert Palm*, ed. R. Görner (Wiesbaden, 1982), 3–7

'A propos de l'interprétation des oeuvres de Frédéric Chopin', *Sur les traces Frédéric Chopin*, ed. D. Pistone (Paris, 1984), 113–30

Bach-Interpretation: die Klavierwerke Johann Sebastian Bachs (Laaber, 1990; Eng. trans., 1993, as *Interpreting Bach at the Keyboard*)

'Mozart's Trills', *Perspectives on Mozart Performance*, ed. R.L. Todd and P.F. Williams (Cambridge, 1991), 1–26

RUDOLF KLEIN/MARTIN ELSTE

Baehr, Joseph. *See* BEER, JOSEPH.

Baena, Gonzalo de (*b* ?Seville, *c*1476–80; *d* ?Lisbon, after 1540). Spanish composer. A number of musicians by the name of Baena were employed in the Castilian, Aragonese and Portuguese royal chapels in the latter part of the 15th century and first half of the 16th. At least three families or clans can be identified: from Valladolid (the royal singer Alonso de Baena and his son Bernaldino), Segovia (*see* BAENA, LOPE DE) and Seville, Gonzalo's home town. Gonzalo was one of three musical sons born to a different Alonso de Baena who served as a player of the bowed vihuela in the royal household of Isabella from May 1493 until 1499; he died in 1505. Gonzalo and his two brothers, Francisco and Diego, may have served at the queen's court before moving to Portugal some time between 1496 and 1500; a document dated 1508 refers to all three as chamber musicians at the court of Manoel I. Gonzalo himself had a musical son, Antonio, who, together with his father and his uncle Francisco, was also in the service of João III. (Their relationship, if any, with the Afonso de Baena in the service of Don Enrique, the king's brother, at Evora, is not clear.)

In June 1536 Gonzalo applied for a royal licence to print a keyboard manual and four years later he published his *Arte nouamente inuentada pera aprender a tanger* (Lisbon, 1540) with a dedication to João III. This is the earliest surviving book of keyboard music from the Iberian peninsula and its musical repertory includes intabulations of vocal works by Franco-Flemish and Spanish composers from the latter part of the 15th century through to his son's generation of the 1530s. Ockeghem, Compère, Agricola, Févin, Josquin, Peñalosa, Escobar, Anchieta, Basurto and Morales are among the composers represented. Eight items (all of which are sections from Mass movements) are attributed to Gonzalo's son Antonio, while two, a setting of the hymn *Ave maris stella* and a motet *Si dedero*, are by Gonzalo himself. The prologue includes a concise set of instructions on how to read the tablature (an alphabet-based version unique to this source) and how to play the keyboard (the frontispiece depicts an organ but Baena refers to the 'monachordio' or clavichord throughout). The didactic purpose of the collection is thus clear and is reinforced by the grouping of the pieces by the number of voice parts, from two to four; the volume ends with a four-part canon attributed to Antonio de Baena. Gonzalo's own works are conservative in style. His three-voice setting of *Ave maris stella* preserves the chant unadorned and in equal note values in the tenor. The motet, likewise in three voices and on the same text as, and with a similar opening to, the well known version by Agricola (also included in the *Arte*), is more contrapuntally conceived.

BIBLIOGRAPHY

BrownI

V.A. Deslandes: *Documentos para a historia da typographia portugueza nos seculos XVI e XVII* (Lisbon, 1888), 19

G. de Resende: *Miscelânea*, ed. J. Mendes dos Remedios, *Subsidios para o estudo da história da literatura portuguêsa*, xix (Coimbra, 1917), 65

T. Knighton: 'A Newly Discovered Keyboard Source (Gonzalo de Baena's *Arte nouamente inuentada pera aprender a tanger*, Lisbon, 1540): a Preliminary Report', *PMM*, v (1996), 81–112

TESS KNIGHTON

Baena [Vaena], **Lope de** (*b* Segovia; *fl* 1476–*c*1506). Spanish composer. He was appointed 'player [of the organ] and singer of the chapel' of Ferdinand of Aragon on 15 April 1478 and served the king until at least 1482. By 1495 he was being paid as a member of the Castilian household as organist of the royal chapel, but after Isabella's death in 1504 he returned to the service of the king until August 1506 when his name disappears from the pay documents. He may have died shortly afterwards.

Baena's Segovian origins distinguish him from at least two other musical families using the name Baena, one from Valladolid, the other from Seville (*see* BAENA, GONZALO DE). This has led to some confusion as to the identity of Lope: he was praised as a vihuelist and composer by Fray Francisco de Avila in 1508, but he was almost certainly not the organist-composer mentioned by the Portuguese chronicler Garcia de Resende, who was probably referring to Gonzalo.

Since several of the other Baenas are known to have been composers, there may be some doubt as to the authorship of those pieces attributed only to 'Baena' in the sources: all nine extant songs have until now been associated with Lope, but only five of these are firmly ascribed to him. Nevertheless, he remains the strongest candidate as the song composer. With the exception of the canción *Vos mayor, vos mejor*, all the compositions are villancicos. Four of the pieces are sacred and the rest are love songs. The refrain text and melody of *Todos duermen, coraçón* were well known throughout the 16th century. Baena's style is versatile: *Vos mayor, vos mejor* and *Rogad vos, virgen, rogad*, are in a hymnlike, chordal style, whereas the prayer to St Michael, *Arcángel San Miguel*, is in a fluid triple metre with independently moving parts. *Todo quanto yo servi* is exceptional in using F clefs for all the voices. Occasionally brief points of imitation are used to introduce inner phrases.

WORKS

Editions: *La música en la corte de los reyes católicos: Cancionero musical de palacio*, ed. H. Anglès, MME, v, x (1947–51) [A i–ii]
E. Ros-Fàbregas: *The Manuscript Barcelona, Biblioteca de Catalunya, M.454: Study and Edition in the Context of the Iberian and Continental Manuscript Traditions* (diss., CUNY, 1992)
Amor, pues nos das plaçer, 4vv (Lope de Vaena), *E-Bc* 454; Arcángel San Miguel, 3vv (Lope de Baena), A ii, no.409; A repastar mi ganado, 3vv (Vaena), A ii, no.433; ¡Que desgraciada sagala!, 3vv (Baena), A i, no.161; Rogad vos, virgen, rogad, 3vv (Baena), A ii, no.160; Todos duermen, coraçon (Baena), 3vv, A i, no.172; Todo quanto yo servi, 3vv (Lope de Baena), A ii, no.287; Virgen reyna gloriosa, 3vv (Lope de Vaena), *Bc* 454; Vos mayor, vos mejor, 3vv (Lope de Baena), A ii, no.394

BIBLIOGRAPHY

StevensonSM; Vander StraetenMPB, vii
F. Asenjo Barbieri, ed.: *Cancionero musical de los siglos XV y XVI* (Madrid, 1890)
M. Schneider: 'Studien zur Rhythmik im Cancionero de palacio', *Miscelánea en homenaje a Mons. Higinio Anglés* (Barcelona, 1958–61), ii, 833ff
T. Knighton: *Music and Musicians at the Court of Fernando of Aragon, 1474–1516*, i (diss., U. of Cambridge, 1984), 255–7
E. Casares, ed.: *F.A. Barbieri: Biografías y documentos sobre música y músicos españoles* (Madrid, 1986), 54–5
T. Knighton: 'A Newly Discovered Keyboard Source (Gonzalo de Baena's *Arte nouamente inuentada pera aprender a tanger*, Lisbon, 1540): a Preliminary Report', *PMM*, v (1996), 81–112, esp. 89

ISABEL POPE/TESS KNIGHTON

Baer, Johann. *See* BEER, JOHANN.

Baermann. German family of musicians.

(1) Heinrich (Joseph) Baermann (*b* Potsdam, 14 Feb 1784; *d* Munich, 11 June 1847). Clarinettist. He and his brother Carl Baermann (i) (1782–1842), a bassoonist in the Berlin court orchestra, were sent by their soldier father to the School of Military Music in Potsdam. At 14, having first studied the oboe, Heinrich became a bandsman in the Prussian Life Guards and during this time studied the clarinet with Beer. In 1805, under the patronage of Prince Louis Ferdinand, he had lessons with Tausch. He fought at the battles of Saalfeld and Jena and was captured, but escaped and found his way to Munich. Here he obtained a court appointment, which he held until his retirement in 1834.

Baermann toured extensively, first to Switzerland and France in 1808. In 1811, after successful performances at Munich of Weber's newly composed Concertino and concertos, clarinettist and composer toured together through Austria and Germany. At Berlin Baermann's artistry helped to convince the musical public of the composer's worth. In Vienna and Prague in 1813, Italy in 1815–16 and Berlin in 1818, Baermann gave concerts with the Munich prima donna, Helene Harlas (1785–1818); she had four children by him. Paris gave him a phenomenal reception in 1817 and 1838, as did Russia in 1822–3 and 1832. In 1819 Baermann was invited to England, where he played for the Prince Regent at Brighton and, during six months of concerts in London,

performed his own compositions on two occasions for the Philharmonic Society.

Heinrich Baermann was sometimes called the Rubini of the clarinet on account of his expressive playing and his luxurious, velvety tone, in contrast to the shriller style of some earlier players. Weber referred in his diary to the 'welcome homogeneity of tone from top to bottom', and gave great credit to Baermann for the success of his clarinet works. All of these except the Grand Duo were written for Baermann, as were Mendelssohn's concert pieces and Meyerbeer's Quintet and (also for Helene Harlas) his cantata *Gli amori*. His liveliness of mind and his companionable nature made him widely popular, and he became a close friend of these composers, who made frequent reference to him in their correspondence. His own works include quartets, quintets and concertinos for clarinet and various instrumental combinations. His instrument was first a ten-keyed clarinet made by Griesling & Schlott; by 1819 he had one of twelve keys.

(2) Carl Baermann (ii) (*b* Munich, 24 Oct 1810; *d* Munich, 23 May 1885). Clarinettist and basset-horn player, son of (1) Heinrich Baermann and Helene Harlas. He was taught the clarinet by his father and by the age of 14 was occasionally playing in the court orchestra. In 1832 he was officially appointed second clarinettist and in 1834 succeeded his father as principal. Carl accompanied his father on concert tours in 1827, 1832 and 1838, attracting much attention playing the basset-horn. Conscious of his father's superior talent as a soloist, he turned to teaching, making a great success of this as professor at the Königliche Musikschule in Munich. His *Vollständige Clarinett-Schule* (1864–75) remains one of the most used methods. His other compositions, comprising 88 opus numbers in all, were once popular with virtuosos. In 1860, in conjunction with Ottensteiner of Munich, he produced an 18-keyed Müller-type clarinet, which found favour with many players, including Mühlfeld. He was pensioned from the court orchestra in 1880 and retired from teaching in 1882.

(3) Carl Baermann (iii) (*b* Munich, 9 July 1839; *d* Newton, nr Boston, MA, 17 Jan 1913). Pianist, son of (2) Carl Baermann (ii). He studied in Munich with Franz Lachner and Peter Cornelius and later became a pupil and close friend of Liszt. He taught for many years at the Königliche Musikschule in Munich, becoming a professor in 1876. In 1881 he moved to the USA, where he made a successful début as a pianist in Boston and also became highly esteemed as a teacher (Amy Beach and Frederick Converse were among his pupils). His compositions include a *Festival March* for orchestra and a number of piano compositions including a set of 12 *Etüden* op.4 (1877) and a *Polonaise pathétique* (1914).

BIBLIOGRAPHY

NDB (H. Becker)
A. Lewald: 'Heinrich Baermann', *Der Freimüthige*, xxxi (1834), 649–63
A. Lewald: *Panorama von München* (Stuttgart, 1840), 130–48
M.M. von Weber: *Carl Maria von Weber: ein Lebensbild* (London, 1864–6, abridged 2/1912 by R. Pechel; Eng. trans., 1865/R)
M. Zenger: *Geschichte der Münchener Oper*, ed. T. Kroyer (Munich, 1923)
H. Becker, ed.: *Giacomo Meyerbeer: Briefwechsel und Tagebücher* (Berlin, 1960–85)
J. Warrack: *Carl Maria von Weber* (London, 1968, 2/1976)

P. Weston: *Clarinet Virtuosi of the Past* (London, 1971), 114–53

P. Weston: *More Clarinet Virtuosi of the Past* (London, 1977), 35–8

PAMELA WESTON

Baervoets, Raymond (*b* Brussels, 6 Nov 1930; *d* Rome, 19 Aug 1989). Belgian composer. After studying at the Brussels Conservatory, he attended Petrassi's composition course at the Accademia di S Cecilia (1961–2). He received the Belgian Music Critics' Prize (1961), the Koopal Prize (1962) and the prize awarded by the city of Trieste (1965). At Gaudeamus Foundation courses he received instruction from Seiber, van Baaren and Ligeti; in 1966 he joined the group Spectra in Ghent. His classical education led him at first to compose traditional works in a neo-classical style in which he did not venture beyond polytonality. Under the influence of Petrassi his aesthetic outlook changed radically. He followed a path leading towards post-serialism, with some incursions into the aleatory field, and he used quarter-tones in a systematic way. He retained the traditional orchestra, using it to create new sonorities.

WORKS
(selective list)

Gui Conc., 1959; Composizione, orch, 1962; Improvisazioni concertanti, vc, 19 insts, 1962; Musica, 14 insts, 1962; Metamorphoses, orch, 1963; Mag, S, orch, 1962–4; Erosions I, A, 9 insts, 1965; Erosions II (G. Soetens), female chorus, orch, 1965; Espressioni, orch, 1965–6; Constellations, 4 ens, 1966; Les dents de la terre, solo vv, chorus, orch, 1968; Musica '72, chbr orch, 1972; Figures, brass, 1973; Immagini, 14 insts, 1974; Qt, fl, cl, vn, pf, 1974

Principal publishers: CeBeDeM, Ricordi

BIBLIOGRAPHY

CeBeDeM directory

C. Mertens: *Hedendaagse muziek in België* (Brussels, 1967), 54, 63

CORNEEL MERTENS/DIANA VON VOLBORTH-DANYS

Baethen [Batius, Bathenius], **Jacob** (*b* ?Leuven, *c*1525; *d* ?Düsseldorf, after 1557). South Netherlandish printer. His publications are important in the history of music printing in the Low Countries. From 1545 to 1551 he worked at Leuven, probably as a university printer. Besides music, he printed mainly official documents and religious commentaries, of which a number were published by M. Rotaire and PHALÈSE. During this period he printed the first, third, fourth (and perhaps fifth) of *Des chansons reduictz en tablature de lut*, which were Phalèse's first music publications and the first books of lute tablature printed from type in the Low Countries.

By 1554 Baethen was in Maastricht, where his publications included a book of Flemish songs, *Dat ierste boeck vanden nievve Duytsche liedekens*, one of five such anthologies published in the Low Countries during the 16th century. In 1555 he moved to Düsseldorf, where he published three books of motets, 1555–6 (for the heirs of Arnold Byrckmann), and a theory book, *Practicae musicae* (1557). The music type used by Baethen in Maastricht and Düsseldorf is identical with that used by Phalèse at that time so it may be assumed that he took a fount with him when he left Leuven. He is sometimes confused with Johan Baethen (perhaps his brother), who was a printer in Leuven and Cologne from 1552 to 1562, but who printed no music.

BIBLIOGRAPHY

BrownI; GoovaertsH; Vander StraetenMPB, iii

R.B. Lenaerts: *Het Nederlands polifonies lied in de zestiende eeuw* (Mechelen and Amsterdam, 1933)

S. Bain: *Music Printing in the Low Countries in the Sixteenth Century* (diss., U. of Cambridge, 1974)

A. Rouzet: *Dictionnaire des imprimeurs, libraires et éditeurs des XVe et XVIe siècles dans les limites géographiques de la Belgique actuelle* (Nieuwkoop, 1975)

B.J.P. Salemans: 'Jacob Bathen, Printer, Publisher and Bookseller in Louvain, Maastricht and Düsseldorf c.1545 to c.1557', *Quaerendo*, xix (1989), 3–47

SUSAN BAIN

Baetz. *See* BÄTZ firm.

Baeyens, August (*b* Antwerp, 5 June 1895; *d* Antwerp, 17 July 1966). Belgian viola player and composer. He studied at the Antwerp Conservatory and was partly self-taught. Shortly after World War I he became the leader of the Expressionist school in Flemish music, his principal fellow members being Karel Albert and Jef Van Durme. He played the viola in the Antwerp Chamber Music Society, thereby wielding great influence in promoting modern chamber music, especially the works of the Second Viennese School. He was secretary of the Koninklijke Vlaamsche Opera in Antwerp from 1931 to 1944, when he was made director. In 1958 he retired from active musical life to dedicate himself entirely to composition.

In his last orchestral works, concertos for viola (1956) and for trumpet (1965), the Expressionist phrasing yielded to concertante playfulness, and in the late chamber works and songs the musical substance is treated with a remarkable purity of expression. (*CeBeDeM directory*)

WORKS
(selective list)

Stage: De dode dichter (ballet), 1920; De liefde en de kakatoe (op, 1, R. Avermaete), 1928; Coriolanus (radio op, 1, L.A.J. Burgerskijk, after W. Shakespeare), 1940, Antwerp, Vlaamse Opera, 27 Nov 1941; De Ring van Gyges (op, A. Monet), 1943, Antwerp, Vlaamse Opera, 15 Dec 1945

Orat: Lofzang aan de Haven, 1929

Orch: 8 syms., 1923, 1939, 1949, 1952, 1954, 1955, 1958, 1961

Entrata, 1917; Niobe, 1918; 4 Pieces, 1922; Harlekijn (sym.), 1924; De Cyclopen (sym.), 1925; Notturno, 1926; Sinfonia breve, 1927; Arkadia, 1951; Va Conc., 1956; Hn Conc., 1960; Tpt Conc., 1965

Vocal: songs to words by the Flemish poets Paul van Ostayen, Gaston Burssens, Bert de Corte

6 str qts, 1922, 1925, 1927, 1949, 1951, 1962

CORNEEL MERTENS/DIANA VON VOLBORTH-DANYS

Baez, Joan (Chandos) (*b* New York, 9 Jan 1941). American folk singer and songwriter. Her early repertory drew on Child ballads (*Mary Hamilton*), Appalachian songs (*Wildwood Flower*) and a smattering of international material such as *Donna, Donna* and *Plaisir d'Amour*, along with radical songs such as the civil rights anthem *We Shall Overcome* and Earl Robinson's *Ballad of Joe Hill*. The influence of Bob Dylan brought such contemporary songs into her repertory as Dylan's *Farewell Angelina*, *Suzanne* by Leonard Cohen and *There but for Fortune* by Phil Ochs (1965).

By the early 1970s Baez was beginning to compose, the most durable of her songs being *Rider, please pass by* (1972) and *Diamonds and Rust* (1975). She also varied the format of her recordings, choosing to work in Nashville, Tennessee, with a group of country session musicians supervised by producer Norbert Putnam. The most commercially successful of her recordings from this relationship was a version of The Band's stirring Civil War ballad *The Night They Drove Old Dixie Down* (1971). She also increasingly paid tribute to her Latin heritage notably with a 1974 album, *Gracias a la Vida*, which contained songs by the Chilean musicians Violeta Parra and Victor Jara.

From her debut performance at the Newport Folk Festival in 1959, Baez's untrained yet pitch-perfect soprano has set the standard for female singers of folk revival material. Her purity of tone and almost unornamented vocal delivery is perhaps less suited to the singer-songwriter and even rock material which she has also performed and recorded in a prolific career which has included nearly 30 albums and some thousands of concerts. Throughout her career Baez strove to coordinate her professional career with her radical political convictions. In the mid 1960s she financed an Institute for Non Violence and withheld tax payments in protest at nuclear weapons; she has also performed numerous fund-raising concerts and appeared in war zones such as Vietnam and Bosnia.

BIBLIOGRAPHY
J. Cohen: 'Joan Baez', Sing Out!, xiii/3 (1963), 6–8
J. Swanekamp, ed.: Diamonds and Rust: a Bibliography and Discography on Joan Baez (Ann Arbor, 1980)
J. Baez: And A Voice To Sing With: a Memoir (New York, 1987)

DAVE LAING

Baeza [Vaeza] Saavedra, Juan de (*fl* Puebla, 1662–77). Mexican composer. His extant works – three *romances*, a villancico, a *chanzoneta* and a *negrilla* – are in the Jesús Sánchez Garza collection at the Centro Nacional de Investigación, Documentación e Información Musical, Mexico City. They were composed for the Convento de la SS Trinidad, Puebla. The best known is the *negrilla*, *Por celebrar este día* (ed. R. Stevenson, *Christmas Music from Baroque Mexico*, Berkeley and Los Angeles, 1974; ed. F. Ramírez Ramírez, *Trece obras de la colección J. Sánchez Garza*, Mexico City, 1981; ed. in Stevenson, 1984–5); it imitates African American dialect and speech, and is rich in the metrical shifts and cross-rhythms typical of the genre.

BIBLIOGRAPHY
R. Stevenson: Renaissance and Baroque Musical Sources in the Americas (Washington DC, 1970)
R. Stevenson: 'Puebla Chapelmasters and Organists: Sixteenth and Seventeenth Centuries, Part II', Inter-American Music Review, vi/1 (1984–5), 29–139

CRAIG H. RUSSELL

Baffo, Giovanni [Joannes] Antonio (*fl* Venice, 1570–79). Italian harpsichord and virginal maker. Although many antique instruments were fraudulently given Baffo's name, his genuine, signed work comprises only three harpsichords and one virginal. Two further harpsichords and five polygonal virginals may also be identified as his work (see Wraight), one of which is the so-called 'Queen Elizabeth's Virginal' (Victoria and Albert Museum, London; *see* VIRGINAL, fig.3). This virginal and the signed harpsichord of 1574 (*see* HARPSICHORD, fig.3) in the same collection are excellent examples of the highly ornate style of case decoration used in late 16th-century Venetian instruments. Documents record that Baffo also made instruments for the court at Ferrara. Baffo's harpsichords are of considerable interest since they were made for unusual pitches. The Victoria and Albert Museum harpsichord and one of 1579 (which originally had the unusually wide compass C/E–c'''') in the Musée de la Musique, Paris, were both built to be tuned a 4th lower than one of the most common 8' pitches of the time (a' = c467). Another unsigned harpsichord attributed to Baffo

(private collection) is pitched a 4th above a' = c448. It would not be correct to call these 'transposing' instruments (*see* TRANSPOSING KEYBOARD): a wide range of pitch standards were in use in Venice (*see* HARPSICHORD, §2(i)).

BIBLIOGRAPHY
BoalchM
D. Wraight: The Stringing of Italian Keyboard Instruments c1500–c1650 (diss., Queen's U. of Belfast, 1997), i, 235–6; ii, 317–21
D. Wraight: 'The Pitch Relationships of Venetian String Keyboard Instruments', Fiore musicologi: studi in onore di Luigi Ferdinando Tagliavini, ed. F. Seydoux (Bologna, 2000)

DENZIL WRAIGHT

Bafoyev, Mustafa (*b* Ganchkash, Bukhara district, 10 Nov 1946). Uzbek composer. He trained at the Tashkent Conservatory as a performer on Uzbek instruments (1964–9) and as a composer (1972–7), finishing a postgraduate course under Boris Giyenko in 1979. He has taught at the Bukhara Pedagogical Institute (1969–72), has conducted the Uzbek folk instruments orchestra for the Uzbek TV and radio company (1980–86) and in 1986 was appointed artistic director of this folk orchestra. His works have a broad appeal and are heard in festivals and competitions as well as local celebrations; they are rooted in Uzbek folk traditions. Bafoyer has received numerous awards, including the A. Kadïri State Premium (1997) and the title of Meritorious Worker of Arts of Uzbekistan (1995).

WORKS
(*selective list*)

Dramatic: Ettinchi jin [Seventh magician] (musical drama, L. Babakhanov), 1983; Uzilgan torlar [The Ragged Strings] (musical drama, K. Amirov), 1984; Omar Haiyam (op), 1987; Radja (musical drama, after R. Tagor), 1987; Sunmas Alanga (Prometey) (musical drama, M. Martinkyavichyus), 1987; V Tashkente tuman [A Smog in Tashkent] (musical drama), 1988; Buhoroy Sharif [Noble Bukhara] (TV op-dastan), 1993; Sevgi nidosy (musical drama, F. Djurayev), 1994; Ulugbek Burgi (TV ballet, Yu. Ismatova), 1994; Mosyidan Nur (TV ballet), 1995; Ritualï Zaroastriytsev [Rites of Zoroastrianism] (ballet-orat.), chorus, orch, 1995; Velikiy shyolkovïy put' [The Great Silk Road] (ballet), pf, cptr, 1996; Ahmad Al-Farghoni (op, D. Djabbarov), 1998

Other: The Legend of Shirak, sym. Poem, 1974; Conc. Rhapsody, tpt, orch, 1979; Sym. no.1 'Gazel', solo vv, chorus, perc, str, 1979; Pesn'o Tashkente [Song about Tashkent] (orat), 1983; Sym. no.2 'Pamyati Avitsenni', str, 1984; Slyozï Roksanï [Tears of Roksana] (orat), nar, solo vv, chorus, pf, str, 1987; Sym. no.3, pf, str, 1987; Sym. no.4 'Mavranahr', 1991; Sym. no.5 'Holoti Alisher Navoiy', 1991; Hajnoma (orat), nar, solo vv, chorus, orch, 1995; chbr music, choral works, works for Uzbek folk orch

RAZIA SULTANOVA

Bagatelle. A trifle, a short piece of music in light vein. The title implies no specific form. It is first found in François Couperin, who published in 1717 in his tenth *ordre* for harpsichord a rondeau entitled 'Les bagatelles'. It was also used by the French publisher Borvin for a collection of dances (*c*1753), and in 1797 Breitkopf & Härtel published a series called *Musikalische Bagatellen*. The term as a generic title received its accolade with Beethoven's three sets of bagatelles for piano opp.33, 119 and 126. Some of these are trifles (Beethoven called the first six of op.119 by the equivalent German term 'Kleinigkeiten'), but many of the later ones are thoroughly typical of their composer and show affinities with the greater instrumental works written at the same time.

The bagatelle since Beethoven has usually been given a descriptive title, and more often than not composers have published them in sets; Smetana composed a collection of bagatelles and impromptus in 1844, and Saint-Saëns published a set of six as his op.3 in 1856. Sibelius's Six Bagatelles op.97 have titles, including 'Little Waltz' and 'Humorous March'. Other composers of bagatelles are Bartók (14, op.6, 1908; he orchestrated the last one as no.2 of *Two Portraits* op.5), Vítězslav Novák (op.5) and Krenek (Four Bagatelles op.70). The bagatelle is also found in the work of three British composers: Tovey (Bagatelles, 1900), Rawsthorne (Bagatelles, 1938) and Howard Ferguson (Five Bagatelles op.9, 1944).

Bagatelles have almost invariably been written for piano solo, but the four in Dvořák's op.47 (1878) are charmingly scored for two violins, cello and harmonium. Webern's *Sechs Bagatellen* for string quartet op.9 (1911–13) was probably the first in a series of 20th-century ensemble works to use the title; a later example is Nicolaus A. Huber's *Sechs Bagatellen* of 1981.

BIBLIOGRAPHY

MGG2 (H. Schneider)

J. Schumway: *A Comparative Study of Representative Bagatelles for the Piano since Beethoven* (diss., Indiana U., 1981)

B.A.R. Cooper: 'Beethoven's Portfolio of Bagatelles', *JRMA*, cxii (1987), 208–28

MAURICE J.E. BROWN/R

Bagatti [Bagati], Francesco (*fl* 1658–*c*1680). Italian composer and organist. He seems to have spent his whole life in Milan. From Picinelli and from the title-pages of his publications we know that he was organist and *maestro di cappella* of the churches of S Sepolcro, S Vittore al Corpo and S Maria alla Porta between 1658 and 1672. In 1662 he was also organist at the ducal court. In 1669, after the death of M.A. Grancini, he competed for the office of *maestro di cappella* at the Duomo, Milan, but was passed over in favour of G.A. Grossi. As far as we know, Bagatti composed only sacred music. In his concertato compositions he showed a marked preference for expressive solo writing, and he wrote a number of dialogues, for instance between Man, an Angel and the Devil in op.3, and between the Soul and an Angel in op.4.

WORKS

all published in Milan

Il primo libro de sacri concerti, 2–4vv, bc, con una messa, e Letanie della Beata Virgine, op.1 (1658)

Messa e salmi brevi con motetti, Te Deum laudamus, e Letanie della Beata Virgine, 4vv, bc (org), op.2 (1659)

Il secondo libro de concerti ecclesiastici, 2–4vv, bc, op.3 (1662)

Il terzo libro de concerti ecclesiastici, 2–4vv, insts, bc (org), con una messa, 4vv [op.4] (1667)

Motetti, messa, e salmi brevi, e pieni per li vesperi di tutte le solennità dell'anno, e Letanie della madonna, 8vv, bc (org), op.5 (1672)

Il quarto libro de concerti ecclesiastici con una messa, Magnificat, e Letani ... 2–4vv, bc (org), op.6 (1676)

Motet, 1679[1], 1681[1]; antiphon, 1669, *I-Md*

BIBLIOGRAPHY

F. Picinelli: *Ateneo dei letterati milanesi* (Milan, 1670), 199

Annali della fabbrica del duomo di Milano (Milan, 1877–85), appx iii, 143

M. Donà: *La stampa musicale a Milano fino all'anno 1700* (Florence, 1961)

MARIANGELA DONÀ

Bagg, Konrad. *See* BACK, KONRAD.

Bagge [Bach], Baron de [Ennal, Charles-Ernest] (*b* Fockenhof, Kurland, 14 Feb 1722; *d* Paris, 24 March 1791). French dilettante, amateur violinist and composer, patron of the arts and instrument collector. A magnificent and very wealthy nobleman, he both amused and astounded his contemporaries. M. Audinot in his comic opera *La musicomanie* (1779), and possibly E.T.A. Hoffmann in his tale *Die Serapionsbrüder* (1819), attempted to evoke his strange personality, emphasizing its ridiculous nature.

At the death of his father, a landed nobleman, in 1747, Bagge inherited a large fortune which enabled him to study the violin in Italy with Tartini. By 1750 he had settled in Paris; in the following year he was awarded the title *chambellan du Roi de Prusse* (then Frederick II) and married the daughter of the Swiss banker Jacob Maudry. With Maudry's death in 1762 the very large inheritance proved a source of contention to the ill-matched couple and they soon separated. Bagge later attempted to gain possession of the inheritance of Mme Maudry, who had died in 1767, and the resulting lawsuits scandalized Paris until the Parlement decided in his wife's favour in 1773.

After the separation Bagge devoted himself entirely to music, and exercised considerable influence on Parisian musical life as concert organizer, patron, performer, composer and teacher. Every Friday in his hotel in the rue de La Feuillade he held a concert at which his protégés performed; on one of these occasions in 1783 Kreutzer gave the first performance of one of Bagge's violin concertos. He travelled in 1778 to England and in 1784 to Vienna, where he performed before Mozart. In 1790, having left France at the outbreak of the Revolution, he was appointed Kammerherr to Friedrich Wilhelm II in Berlin. His death in the following year was accompanied by rumours that he had been poisoned by his mistress, though several public disclaimers later that year discredit the accusation.

Bagge was a freemason and belonged to two of the Parisian lodges with the most active music programmes: the celebrated Loge Olympique and particularly Les Neuf Soeurs, where he was director of concerts and organized the musical side of Voltaire's initiation. His talent as a violinist and particularly his technical capabilities were perhaps not so negligible as earlier writers have maintained. He showed special skill in performing ascending and descending scales on a single string using only one finger of the left hand. His compositions, though hardly original, reveal sureness of taste and irreproachable workmanship. He was criticized for his nervous twitches and strange attitudes while performing; the *Allgemeine musikalische Zeitung* (iii, 1800, col.841) recalled of his playing that

No Baron can ever have made such horrible grimaces the moment he took violin and bow in hand. His face, his muscles, the whole of his body underwent most painful contortions, and, as his playing increased in animation, the sounds that proceeded could only be likened to the wailing of a cat.

This doubtless gave rise to the ambiguous compliment paid by the Emperor Joseph II ('My dear Baron, I have never heard anyone play the violin quite like you'), and the quatrain under one of his portraits:

Du Dieu de l'harmonie adorateur fidèle,
Son zèle impetueux ne saurait s'arrêter;
Dans l'art du violon il n'a point de modèle
Et personne jamais n'osera l'imiter.

As a patron Bagge was extraordinarily generous. Although he favoured artists who were also freemasons (Kreutzer, Viotti, Duport, Capron and Gossec), or who were closely linked with the order (Gaviniès and Boccherini), he nevertheless helped only deserving musicians. He insisted, however, on giving lessons to the violinists among them, paying them to accept his tuition, and was thus able to boast of himself as leader of the French violin school. His private collection of violins was prodigious, and included instruments by Stradivari, Amati and Gasparo da Salò, which he generously conferred on his 'pupils'. This collection, as well as his large music library which he freely extended to other musicians, reverted at his death to his wife together with the rest of his largely depleted estate, and has since been untraced.

Several portraits of Bagge are known, one of which was engraved by Nicolas Cochin (reproduced in Terry) and another of which portrayed him with a violin 'comme un ménétrier'.

WORKS
all printed works published in Paris

Orch: 3 sinfonie (1788); 4 vn concs., all (n.d.); vn conc., *F-Pn*; 2 symphonies concertantes, *D-Bsb*
Chbr: 6 quatuors concertants, str qt, op.1 (1773); 6 trio, 2 vn, b (n.d.); Airs de Marlborough variés, hpd, vn (n.d.); 2 str qts, 4 str qnts, collab. ?F. Fiorillo, destroyed
Cantata, 1786, for accession of Friedrich Wilhelm II, *D-Bsb*

BIBLIOGRAPHY
FétisB; GerberL
L. Petit de Bachaumont and others: *Mémoires secrets*, xx (London, 1783), 83–4
F. Marpurg: *Legende einiger Musikheiligen* (Cologne [*recte* Breslau], 1786), 224–5, 277ff
P. Smith: 'Les élèves du Baron de Bagge', *RGMP*, xii (1845)
G. Cucuel: 'Le Baron de Bagge et son temps', *Année musicale*, i (1911), 145–86
C.S. Terry: 'Baron Bach', *ML*, xii (1931), 130–39
C.M. Carroll: 'A Beneficent Poseur: Charles Ernest, Baron de Bagge', *RMFC*, xvi (1976), 24–36
R.J.V. Cotte: *Les musiciens franc-maçons à la cour de Versailles et à Paris sous l'ancien régime* (doctorat d'Etat, diss., 1982, *F-Pn*)
R.J.V. Cotte: *La musique maçonnique et ses musiciens* (Paris, 2/1987), 72–4

ROGER J.V. COTTE

Bagge, Selmar (*b* Coburg, 30 June 1823; *d* Basle, 16 July 1896). German critic, teacher and composer. He studied the piano and cello at the Prague Conservatory and moved to Vienna in 1842, where he studied theory with Sechter and was active performing, teaching and composing. He was appointed to the Vienna Conservatory in 1852, but his high standards and outspoken critical stance led to his dismissal in 1855. In 1859 Bagge became the editor of a new journal, the *Deutsche Musik-Zeitung*, which opposed the 'New German' sympathies of Franz Brendel's *Neue Zeitschrift für Musik*. He moved to Leipzig in 1863 to edit the *Allgemeine musikalische Zeitung* (later the *Leipziger allgemeine musikalische Zeitung*); it closely reflected his conviction that composers should strive to imitate music of the past. Bagge's own reviews praise music by such composers as Bargiel, Volkmann, Reinecke and Kirchner. He regarded much of Brahms's music as undisciplined, contributing to a critical climate that may have prompted Brahms to adopt a more classically-oriented style.

In 1868 Bagge became the director of the Musikschule in Basle, and held this post until his death in 1896. From 1876 he lectured at the University of Basle, was granted an honorary doctorate in 1880 and promoted to extraordinarius professor in 1893. Bagge's published compositions include piano music, string quartets and songs. He also wrote choral works, symphonies, overtures and a piano concerto. His music is skilfully crafted and conservative, and its marked dependence upon Beethoven accords well with Bagge's values as a critic.

WRITINGS
Gedanken und Aufsätze über Musik und Musikzustände in einer Reihe gesammelte Aufsätze (Vienna, 1860)
'Robert Schumann's "Szenen aus Göthes Faust"', *Deutsche Musik-Zeitung*, i (1860), 273–8, 281–4
'Die alte Harmonielehre im Streit mit der neuen', *Deutsche Musik-Zeitung*, ii (1861), 177–9, 185–8
'Das moderne Claviertrio und seine Vertreter', *Deutsche Musik-Zeitung*, ii (1861), 369–72, 377–80, 385–8, 393–4
'Unser Programm', *AMZ*, new ser., i (1863), 1–6
'Johannes Brahms', *AMZ*, new ser., i (1863), 461–7
'Über die Stellung und Aufgabe der modernen Tonkünst', *AMZ*, new ser., ii (1864), 3–5, 24–9, 41–6, 57–61
'Der Künstler und das heutige Publicum in ihren gegenseitigen Anforderungen', *Leipziger allgemeine musikalische Zeitung*, ii (1867), 133–6
Lehrbuch der Tonkunst (Leipzig, 1873)
'Robert Schumann und seine Faust-Szenen', *Sammlung musikalischer Vorträge*, ser. I, vol. iv (Leipzig, 1879), 123–40

BIBLIOGRAPHY
E. Refardt: 'Selmar Bagge', *Historisch-Biographisches Musikerlexicon der Schweiz* (Leipzig, 1928), 17–19 [with work-list]
I. Fellinger: 'Das Brahms-Bild der Allgemeinen Musikalischen Zeitung', *Beiträge zur Geschichte der Musikkritik*, ed. H. Becker (Regensburg, 1965), 27–54
H. Oesch: *Die Musik-Akademie der Stadt Basel* (Basle, 1967), 13–17 [with portrait]
A. Horstmann: *Untersuchungen zur Brahms-Rezeption der Jahre 1860–1880* (Hamburg, 1986)
Répertoire International de la Presse Musicale, Deutsche Musik-Zeitung 1860–1862, ed. B.J. Sing (Ann Arbor, 1994), ix–xii
G.S. Bozarth: 'Brahms and the Breitkopf and Härtel Affair', *MR*, lv (1994), 202–13
N. Meurs: *Neue Bahnen? Aspekte der Brahms-Rezeption 1853–1868* (Cologne, 1996)

ROSE MAURO

Baggiani, Guido (*b* Naples, 4 March 1932). Italian composer. He graduated from the Conservatorio di S Cecilia as a pupil of Porena. In 1965 he joined the Rome-based Nuova Consonanza group, serving as one of its directors in 1971–2. He studied with Stockhausen in Cologne in 1966, an experience that decisively influenced him as a composer. The following year he attended Evangelisti's seminars on electronic music in Rome. In 1972, together with Mario Bertoncini, Walter Branchi and Giorgio Nottoli, he formed the Gruppo Team Roma, an ensemble making use of live electronics. Again with Branchi, in 1977, he founded Musica Verticale, an association devoted mainly to electro-acoustic music. He taught composition at the conservatoires of Pesaro (1972–9) and Perugia (1979–95). In 1995 he returned to Rome to teach at the Conservatory.

In the first phase of his output (*Mimesis* and *Metafora*) the elements of the music are rigorously predetermined; later he used forms offering a choice to the performers. After exploring new forms of expression using electroacoustic and instrumental techniques, he has progressively abandoned timbral research in pursuit of more abstract formal possibilities, especially in orchestral works such as *Gongora* and *Labirinti*.

WORKS
(selective list)

Metafora, 11 str, 1968; Memoria, 20 insts, 4 × 2-track/2 × 4-track tape, 1972; Contr-azione, 2 orch, 1975; Double, 2 wind qnt, 2 hn, 2 db, 1977; 4 studi, 2 pf, 1981; Anabasi (A. Rostagno), 4 female vv, 4 winds and ring modulator, 1985; Danza, vn, vc, cl, pf, 1986; Gongora, S, pf, orch, 1989, text by the 17th-century Spanish poet Gongora; A più voci nell'ombra, 2-track tape, 1990; E con il suono per un instante l'eco fa ritorno, orch, 1993; Perso per perso (madrigale drammatico, V. Magrelli), 6vv, 1995; Labirinti, 5 str, 8 wind, 2 perc, 1997; Anelli del tempo, vn, vc, pf, 1998; Kahal (Bible: *Ecclesiastes*), 2 pf, 2 trbn, tape, 2000

BIBLIOGRAPHY
G. Baggiani: 'Le miroir et son double', *Silences*, i (1985), 151–6
F. Galadini: 'Con Guido Baggiani', *La musica: rivista di musica contemporanea*, xxi (1992), 24–6

PIERLUIGI PETROBELLI

Bag-hornpipe. An early type of bagpipe. *See* BAGPIPE, §8 and HORNPIPE (i).

Bagiński, Zbigniew (*b* Szczecin, 19 Jan 1949). Polish composer. From 1967 to 1972 he attended the Warsaw Academy, where his teachers included Paciorkiewicz. He was appointed lecturer at the Academy in 1987, and in 1989 he was elected general secretary of the Union of Polish Composers. Something of a late developer, Bagiński came to the fore as a composer during the mid-1980s. He developed a vein of lighthearted mock antiquity which owed more to pre-war European models than to contemporary postmodernist trends. His referential inclinations adopted a more serious tone in the Piano Quartet (1990) which carried echoes of 19th century music, while the impulse for *Hawaiian Songs* stemmed from a walk along Waikiki Beach. Bagiński's sensitivity to humour in music is balanced by profound, introspective lyricism (as in the two symphonies), supported by his preference for clearly delineated ideas, forward-moving structures and resonant harmony. His music has a simple, unabashed directness which eschews unnecessary clutter.

WORKS
(*selective list*)

Tryptyk, cl, pf, 1968; Refren [Refrain], 2 pf, 1975; Sinfonia notturna, orch, 1984; Solo, Duo, Trio, ob, cl, bn, 1984; Hpd Conc, 1985; O, Sweet Baroque!, suite, str, 1985; Kanony, scherza, epigramaty . . ., 13 pfmrs, 1987; Inventorum rerum (J. Protasowicz), chorus, 1988; Symfonia w 7 odsłonach [Sym. in 7 Scenes], orch, 1988; Blanc et noir, gui, 1990; Pf Qt, 1990; Solo IV, vc, 1991; Hawaiian Songs, 4 perc, 1982, rev. 1991; Str Qt no.3, 1992; Mass, chorus, 1994; Mała symfonia elegijna [Little Elegiac Sym.], orch, 1995; Pf Conc, 1995; Vc Conc., str, 1996

Principal publishers: Agencja Autorska, PWM

ADRIAN THOMAS

Bağlama. Turkish long-necked lute of the TANBŪR family (for illustration *see* KURDISH MUSIC, fig.2). The pear-shaped bowl resonator is carved (*oyma*) or carvel-built (*yapraklı*). The soundtable is of wood, usually coniferous. The neck has a variable number of movable frets. Traditionally these were made of sheepgut or copper wire but nylon line is now used. The instrument's name, dating from the 17th century, derives from these 'tied' frets (*bağ*: 'fret', 'knot'; *bağlamak*: 'to tie, knot'). The movability of the frets allows the setting of scales to include microtones. There are three double courses of metal strings tuned with wooden pegs. The *bağlama* is generally played with a cherry-bark plectrum, though formerly the fingertips were widely used. The melody is commonly played on the first double course of strings, while the remaining courses are struck open as drones. Sometimes, however, the second and third courses are also fingered. The second finger of the plectrum hand is often used to strike the soundtable to add a percussive element to the melody.

The *bağlama* is the most popular and widely played long-necked lute in TURKEY. It is often known as, simply, SAZ ('instrument'). By the 11th century, a long-necked lute similar to the *bağlama*, called *kopuz*, was the favoured instrument of the minstrel poets (*ozan*) of the Oğuz

Turkish tribes of south-west Asia. Their Ottoman descendants, called *saz şairleri* ('*saz* minstrel poets') or *aşıklar* (sing.: *aşık*), use the *bağlama* to accompany the recitation of epics and popular tales (*halk hikayeleri*) as well as their own compositions and repertory of songs by earlier *aşıklar*. The *bağlama* is still played in the dervish ceremonies of some sects, including the Alevi. The instrument itself is viewed as symbolically significant: the body is 'Alī, the neck his sword, and so on; *see* ISLAMIC RELIGIOUS MUSIC §III, 2(i).

The *bağlama* is also the prime melody instrument of entertainment and dance music in both town and country. In this case it is sometimes accompanied by percussion instruments such as *dümbelek* (goblet drum), *parmak zili* and *zilli maşa* (types of cymbal). The *bağlama* is also played in small ensembles with other types of *saz* (long-necked lutes). In the 1970s the addition of a built-in electric pick-up produced a type of instrument known as *elekrosaz*. This is used at rural weddings with voice and *darbuka* (goblet drum). The *bağlama* and *elektrosaz* are important in Turkish music (*see* TURKEY, §§1–4).

The Greek *baylamas* is a miniature version of the *bouzouki*, with three double courses of metal strings, and is used mainly to accompany the *bouzouki* or the smaller *tzouras* (long-necked lutes).

BIBLIOGRAPHY
L. Picken: *Folk Musical Instruments of Turkey* (London, 1975)
M. Stokes: *The Arabesk Debate: Music and Musicians in Modern Turkey* (Oxford, 1992)

R. CONWAY MORRIS

Bagliani, Carlo. *See* BALIANI, CARLO.

Baglioni, Antonio (*fl* 1780s–90s). Italian tenor and singing teacher. He may have been related to Francesco Baglioni. He sang in productions of comic opera, particularly in Venice during the late 1780s and early 90s, and of serious opera. Two of his most important roles were Don Ottavio in the first production of Mozart's *Don Giovanni* (1787, Prague) and Titus in *La clemenza di Tito* (1791, Prague). His range encompassed *e* to b♭′. He was said to have had a well-trained, pure and expressive voice. As a singing teacher, he taught, among others, Giulietta da Ponte, the niece of Mozart's librettist, Lorenzo Da Ponte, who claimed that Baglioni was 'a man of perfect taste and great musical knowledge who had trained the most celebrated singers in Italy'. Baglioni published a set of vocal exercises (Milan, n.d.) and a duet *Sommo ciel* (Venice, n.d.); his only other extant works are an *Ave regina* for three voices and an aria, *Come aboro fu deciso* (MSS in *I-Bc, Fc*).

BIBLIOGRAPHY
DBI (R. Meloncelli); *ES* (E. Zanetti)
A. Capacio: *Poesia e lodi della cattedrale di Cracovia* (Warsaw, 1790)
J.A. Rice: *W.A. Mozart: La clemenza di Tito* (Cambridge, 1991)

SVEN HANSELL/BARBARA D. MACKENZIE

Baglioni, Francesco [Carnace] (*fl* 1729–62). Italian bass and impresario. He was one of the most popular comic opera singers of his day and a particularly important figure in the development and dissemination of the genre in the middle of the century. He performed in at least 100 productions beginning in the late 1720s, when he sang intermezzos in Foligno and Pesaro. He launched his comic opera career in Rome in 1738 with Gaetano Latilla's *La finta cameriera* and *Madama Ciana* and *Rinaldo di*

Capua's *La commedia in commedia*. Productions throughout northern Italy of these operas along with another first performed in Rome, Rinaldo's *La libertà nociva* (1740), dominated Baglioni's career for the next decade. In 1749 he appeared in the *dramma giocoso L'Arcadia in Brenta* in Venice, the first collaboration between Galuppi and Goldoni, and for the remainder of his career he primarily sang texts written by Goldoni, in cities along the axis from Venice to Turin. His range encompassed B♭ to *f'* and music written for him is predominantly syllabic and laden with comic effects. Baglioni sang in the opera troupes of at least three well-known impresarios: Angelo Mingotti, Eustachio Bambini and Girolamo Medebach. Evidence that he worked as an impresario himself include a payment record from 1744 indicating his fee of 155 lire for duties as impresario in Venice's San Cassiano for the autumn and carnival seasons (*I-Vas*). Three of his daughters appeared in productions with him: Giovanna from 1752, Clementina from 1754 (she later created the role of Rosina in Mozart's *La finta semplice*) and Vincenza from 1757. His other children include the singers Costanza, Rosina and perhaps Antonio (who created both Don Ottavio in Mozart's *Don Giovanni* and Tito in Mozart's *La clemenza di Tito*).

BIBLIOGRAPHY

BurneyFI; SartoriL
F.S. Quadrio: *Della storia e della ragione d'ogni poesia* (Bologna and Milan, 1739–52), vii, 251
E.H. Müller von Asow: *Die Mingottischen Opernunternehmungen, 1732–1756* (Dresden, 1915)
'Memorie di G. Zanetti', *Nuovo archivio veneto*, new ser., xxiv (1912), 130, 133–5, 139
D. Heartz: 'The Creation of the Buffo Finale in Italian Opera', *PRMA*, civ (1977–8), 67–78
B.D. Mackenzie: *The Creation of a Genre: Comic Opera's Dissemination in Italy in the 1740s* (diss., U. of Michigan, 1993), 256–67

BARBARA D. MACKENZIE

Baglioni [Ballioni], Girolamo (*b* Milan, *c*1575; *d* Milan, 1608). Italian composer. He was organist of S Maria della Scala, Milan, and was a pupil of Guglielmo Arnone. At the end of his *Liber primus et opus secundum sacrarum cantionum*, published by his father Francesco soon after his death and dedicated in March 1608, the printer Filippo Lomazzo recalled that Baglioni was learned both in Greek and Latin literature and in philosophy. His first published works are two instrumental duos included in a collection of works by Gastoldi and other Milanese composers (RISM 1598[13]), dedicated by the printer to Baglioni's father; they are described as 'the first work by this his son'. This information shows that there was a close relationship between the two Baglionis, the well-educated printers Lomazzo, Tini, Besozzi and Castiglioni, and, through the agency of Arnone and Gastoldi, the musical centre at the Mantuan court. Baglioni's compositions consist solely of sacred music. In the *Sacrae cantiones* he follows the practice, then popular in Milan, of treating the voices in a concertante style above a bass played on the organ. In the instrumental score the vocal lines are combined. One of these, 'Maria Magdalena con una canzon francese in soprano', uses instrumental passages alternating with vocal polyphony. The two instrumental duos of 1598 are skilful fugal pieces.

WORKS

Sacrarum cantionum, liber primus, 1–6vv, op.2 (Milan, 1608)
2 instrumental duos, 1598[13]; 1 antiphon, 6vv, 1612[3]; 1 motet, 1621[2]; 1 motet, 3vv, bc, 1627[1]

MARIANGELA DONÀ

Baglioni, Luigi. *See* BAILLOU, LUIGI DE.

Bagnacavallo, Giuseppe da. *See* TAMBURINI, GIUSEPPE.

Bagni, Benedetto [Bagnius, Benedictus] (*b* ?Ferrara; *fl* 1608). Italian composer and organist. His birthplace is given in *FétisB*. On the title-page of his publication of 1608 he called himself a 'musician to the illustrious city fathers of Bologna'. This statement is confirmed by Banchieri (*Conclusioni del suono dell'organo*, Bologna, 1609/R, 2/1626 as *Armoniche conclusioni nel suono dell'organo*; Eng. trans., 1982, p.25), who referred to him as a distinguished organist in the service of the city of Bologna. His *Motectorum octonis vocibus … una cum basso generalis pro organo liber primus* (Venice, 1608) contains 21 eight-part motets for double choir, organized on the concertato principle and with two continuo parts. Several of the motets in this collection were included in leading German anthologies of the period and are also found intabulated in manuscripts.

JOHANNES GÜNTHER KRANER

Bagniera [Bagnera, Baniera, Bannieri], **Antonio** [Antoine] (*b* ?Rome, 1638; *d* Versailles, 1740). Swiss boy (later castrato) singer, active in France. Son of one of Louis XIV's Swiss guards, Bagniera was a *Page de la Chapelle* (a boy singer in the royal chapel choir) noted for the 'prodigious volume and extreme beauty of his voice' (Bêche). Small stature and physical deformities may have been factors in his decision to persuade his cousin, a surgeon, to castrate him in a (successful) bid to preserve his greatest asset, his voice. When Louis XIV discovered what had taken place, he threatened Bagniera with banishment, but pardoned him after intervention by the Swiss guards who pleaded that his action had only been for the best interests of the king's music. Bagniera continued to sing both in the chapel and in court operatic performances (e.g. Lully's *Alceste* in 1677). He became a naturalized French citizen in 1680. From a year earlier, Louis XIV employed as many as five Italian castrati at any one time, alongside Bagniera, who sang to the age of 77, retiring at the king's death in 1715; he survived to 102.

BIBLIOGRAPHY

M.-F. Bêche: [Mémoires], *F-Pn*, Rés.F.1661, 92–106
M. Benoit: *Versailles et les musiciens du Roi 1661–1733* (Paris, 1971)
L. Sawkins: 'The Brothers Bêche: an Anecdotal History of Court Music', *RMFC*, xxiv (1986), 192–221
L. Sawkins: 'For and against the order of Nature: who sang the Soprano?', *EMc* xv (1987), 315–24

LIONEL SAWKINS

Bagnolesi, Anna Maria Antonia (*fl* 1726–43). Italian contralto. She was a Florentine in the employment of the Grand Duchess of Tuscany, and married to the tenor G.B. Pinacci (1732). She sang in Florence (1725–6), Bologna (1726–8), Livorno (1727), Naples (1727, in operas by Vinci and Hasse) and Milan (1728, 1730). She may have been the Anna Bolognesi who appeared in Venice in 1729, and she sang in Turin in 1731 (Porpora's *Poro*). Engaged by Handel for the London season of 1731–2, she made her début at the King's Theatre as Alcestis in a revival of *Admeto* on 7 December. She sang in the original productions of *Ezio* and *Sosarme*, in revivals of *Giulio Cesare*, *Flavio*, the bilingual *Acis and Galatea* and Ariosti's *Coriolano*, and in the pasticcio *Lucio Papirio dittatore*. The two parts Handel composed for her,

Valentinian in *Ezio* and Erenice in *Sosarme*, are restricted in compass (b♭ to e♭″ in the arias) and of no exceptional technical difficulty, but the scope and quality of the music suggests confidence in her powers of expression; her affected delivery, however, reminded Horace Mann of 'a person talking upon a close stool'. After her return to Italy she sang in Naples in operas by Hasse, Pergolesi and N. Conti (1733–4), Milan (1736–7, 1739), Venice (1739–40) and Florence (1732–3, 1739, 1741–3). She often took male roles. There is a caricature of her by A.M. Zanetti in the Cini collection (*I-Vgc*).

WINTON DEAN

Bagnols, Magister **Leon de.** See GERSONIDES.

Bagpipe (Fr. *cornemuse*; Ger. *Dudelsack, Sackpfeife*; It. *cornamusa, piva, zampogna*; Port. *gaita*; Sp. *cornamusa, gaita, zampoña*). A wind instrument which in its commonest forms consists of a chanter and one or more drones, all supplied with air from the bag, which is compressed under the player's arm to provide a constant pressure. The instrument is classed as a composite reedpipe.

Bagpipes are generally used in the performance of traditional folk musics, and their designs vary in different countries or ethnic regions. The main exceptions to this rule include the occasional adoption of bagpipes by fashionable society and by composers of opera, ballet, concertos and chamber music, most notably in 18th-century France (*see* MUSETTE (i), §§1 and 2), and the case of the Scottish Highland bagpipe, which became widespread in the 19th century and has displaced some local types. Some bagpipe traditions have flourished continuously to the present day, notably in Great Britain and Ireland, in north-western Spain, and in Bulgaria, but by the mid-20th century many regional types had become obsolete. Since the 1960s, however, there has been a considerable revival of interest, and many regional and older types are again being manufactured and played.

1. Structure. 2. General history. 3. Scotland: (i) Highland pipe (pìob mhór) (ii) Other bagpipes. 4. Ireland. 5. England. 6. France, Belgium. 7. Other countries: (i) Spain and Portugal (ii) Northern Europe (iii) Italy (iv) Poland, Czech Republic, Slovakia (v) Hungary, Romania (vi) Yugoslavia, Bulgaria (vii) India. 8. Bag-hornpipes. 9. Music. 10. Present state.

1. STRUCTURE.   The principal variables within the above definition are the type of chanter, either conical- or cylindrical-bored; the number and tuning of the drones; and whether the pipes are blown by mouth or with bellows strapped between the player's arm and waist. Mouth blowing is generally associated with bagpipes intended for outdoor use; bellows with more delicate instruments for indoor playing. Some bagpipes have double chanters, and some have keywork to extend the tonal range.

In many traditions, bags consist of the whole skin of an animal such as a sheep or goat, variously cured or tanned, and with the hair side turned inside. Usually the pipes are tied into the natural neck and forelegs. Almost always the pipes are actually inserted into wooden or bone sockets ('stocks'), so that they can easily be taken out to adjust the reeds. Most modern bagpipes have bags of cured or tanned skin cut to shape and sewn, and this type of bag can be seen in some medieval depictions as well. For a mouth-blown bagpipe it is of course essential that the bag should not only be airtight but should maintain a constant temperature and humidity. The materials that work best depend very much on the local climate; some are mentioned below.

Conical chanters are generally turned from one piece of wood, like a shawm; cylindrical chanters more often have a separable foot joint at the lower end. The foot joint may be formed from an animal horn (*see* HORNPIPE (i)). Drones are cylindrical with one or more sliding joints for tuning. Conical chanters generally have a double reed; cylindrical chanters and drones have a beating reed, but there are exceptions, notably the British varieties of 'small pipe' which have the double reed in a cylindrical chanter, and the French musette and Italian *zampogna* which have double reeds throughout. Reeds are generally made from cane, especially *arundo donax*, grown in southern Europe and supplied to pipe makers' particular requirements, but plastic and metal are coming into use, especially for drone reeds. Double reeds resemble the oboe reed in general design and construction (though they are usually much shorter and broader in the blade). The traditional beating (or 'percussion') is an 'idioglot percussion reed' (*see* REED, and REED INSTRUMENTS, fig. 1). It is formed from a short length of cane, closed at one end and with the pith removed. A transverse cut is made through the skin to form a tongue which is then split back and raised slightly so that it vibrates in the airstream. A waxed string or 'bridle' is tied tightly round the root of the tongue to prevent further splitting (fig.1). In some traditions the reed is cut so that the vibrating end of the tongue is closer to the open end of the reed, in others a greater gap is preferred. In modern bagpipes the chief timbers used for the pipes are ebony, cocus wood and brazil-wood, replacing native woods such as box and fruit woods, though these continue to be used in a few traditions. The ends of the pipes are reinforced with rings or ferrules, made of bone ivory, plastic, metal, or bone. The tone of the instrument depends very much on the nature of the wood, and recent experiments with Scottish bagpipes (Moore, 1991) suggest that it is the density more than any other factor which makes the difference. With the increase in prices of exotic timbers and the general desire to conserve non-renewable materials, synthetic materials are coming more into use.

2. GENERAL HISTORY.   There are a few references to bagpipes in ancient literature (Aristophanes, Suetonius, Martial, Dio Chrysostom; see Baines, 1960) but no surviving instruments, or unambiguous depictions. Popular writings on bagpipes over the last two hundred years have given a different impression about this ambiguity, but on re-examination, such claims may all be discounted, notably the persistent belief that the bagpipe had military use in the Roman army (Askew, 1940; Collinson, 1975).

Closely related to the bagpipe is the hornpipe, consisting of one or two pipes made from natural tubular materials (bone or cane), with beating reeds blown directly by mouth with circular breathing so that the music is continuous, as is that of the bagpipe. Hornpipes with bags also exist and constitute a supposedly primitive type of bagpipe. Although rare, hornpipes are distributed over a very wide area, 'from Atlantic Europe and the Maghrib to the Urals and India' (Baines, 1960), and if bagpipes are viewed as a technical development from the hornpipe this is the strongest reason for supposing that they too have an ancient history.

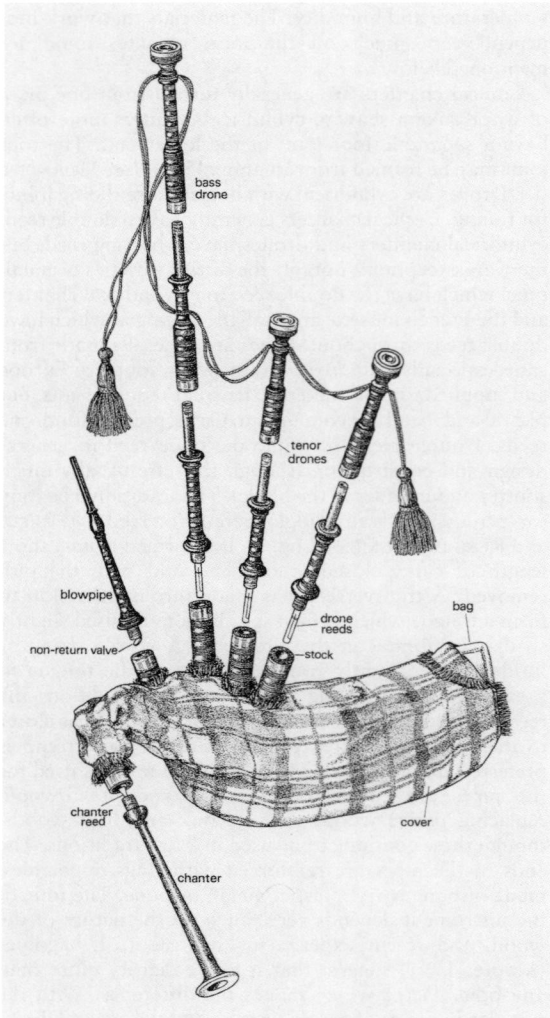

1. Exploded diagram of a Scottish Highland bagpipe

The historical record effectively begins in the early Middle Ages, in Western Europe. The word 'musa' (root of the medieval French word 'muse', meaning 'bagpipe') occurs between 'tibiae' and 'fistula', both pipe names, in the *Epistola de armonica institutione* of Regino of Prüm (*c*842–915). The term ESTIVE, also believed to denote a form of bagpipe, occurs frequently in medieval French poetry and romances, usually in association with 'soft' instruments such as the harp and fiddle, which would indicate that it, too, had a refined and delicate sound. An Anglo Saxon riddle of the 10th century has been considered as referring to a bagpipe (Sutherland, 1967). The independent drone is mentioned in Adam de la Halle's *Jeu de Robin et de Marion* (*c*1283), and a drone pipe of this period has been found at Weoley Castle, Warwickshire, England. Depictions in pictures and carvings become abundant from then on. In the British Isles bagpiping was both a popular and a courtly entertainment at least from the early 14th century (Bullock-Davies, 1978), but began gradually to die out, receding north-wards and westwards from the 16th century onwards

(Cannon, 1971). From the 17th century, mouth-blown bagpipes tended to be displaced by bellows-blown forms for indoor use, and in Ireland and Northumberland these became progressively more elaborate during the 18th and 19th centuries. Historical references to 'Lincolnshire' (16th century) and 'Lancashire' (18th century) bagpipes presumably imply persistent playing traditions; they may or may not refer to distinctive regional types of instrument. The last traces of bagpiping in 19th-century Yorkshire have been carefully researched (Schofield, 1993–4), indicating that the Irish type of 'union pipe' was played.

3. SCOTLAND.

(i) Highland pipe (pìob mhór). The Highland bagpipe (figs.1 and 4*a*) has been a martial instrument at least since the 16th century. It has three drones, two tenor and one bass, the chanter and the blowpipe. The latter is long, thus enabling the bag to be held well under the left arm and the piper's head to be kept erect. Blowpipes in other traditions are shorter, and the bag may be held in front of the body, leading to a crouching attitude unlike the military bearing of the Scots piper. The drones are spread fanwise and held at their distance by ornamental cords, the bass drone resting on the piper's shoulder. Each tenor drone is 40 cm long and is tuned an octave below the six-finger note of the chanter (which is named A, i.e. *a'*, though the actual pitch is closer to *b♭*). The bass drone is 80 cm and is tuned an octave below the tenors. Bagpipes with two tenor drones and no bass drone were customary in some districts in the 18th century, but the three-drone arrangement is now standard.

The chanter is of a wide conical bore, with eight holes and a double vent-hole which is never stopped. The tone is exceedingly loud and penetrating. Highland pipes are made in two sizes; in addition there is a miniature-sized pipe with a practice chanter in place of the normal bagpipe chanter. Scottish bagpipe manufacture is a well-established industry. The instrument is largely standardized in design and construction. The favourite timbers since the early 19th century have been African blackwood

2. Bagpipes without drones: miniature from the 'Cantigas de Santa María', Spanish, c1270–90 (E-E b.I.2, f.235v)

3. Bagpipe with single drone and chanter: marginal illustration from the Luttrell Psalter, English, c1330–40 (GB-Lbl Add.42130, f.176r)

or cocus wood, with ivory or silver reinforcing rings and ferrules. Imitation ivory is now usual, and makers are experimenting with synthetic materials in place of wood. Moulded plastic 'Polypenco' pipe chanters are widely accepted for use by bands. Plastic and metal drone reeds are beginning to replace cane. For the bag, sheepskin, cured but not tanned, is traditional in northern climates, but leather works better in drier conditions; more recently the synthetic material Gore-Tex has become popular.

The scale of the Highland chanter consists of the notes *g'*, *a'*, *b'*, *c♯"*, *d"*, *e"*, *f♯"*, *g"*, *a"*; but they are tuned in a characteristic way, which has given rise to a good deal of speculation and research (early results and discussions are summarized by MacNeill and Lenihan, 1960–61). In the 19th century there was fairly general agreement that the *c♯"* and *f♯"* were appreciably flatter, and the *g'* and *g"* appreciably sharper than in the accepted diatonic scales of the period; in fact most of the 3rds were thought to be intermediate between major and minor 3rds. Baines (1960) pointed out that neutral 3rds are a common characteristic of folk wind instruments, and a general explanation is that pipe makers everywhere have tended to set the holes in the pipe at equal distances so as to lie comfortably under the fingers: some refinement of pitch is then obtained by varying the size of the holes. The first reliable measurements, made by Lenihan and MacNeill in 1954, gave somewhat different results, showing the following intervals, expressed in cents, between *g'* and each successive note: *a'* = 199 cents above *g'*; *b'* = 395 cents; *c♯"* = 582 cents; *d"* = 715 cents; *e"* = 904 cents; *f♯"* = 1086 cents; *g"* = 1220 cents; and *a"* = 1404 cents. The *c♯"* and *f♯"* are close to their values in just intonation while the *d"* is appreciably sharp. Harris and others

(1963) confirmed these intervals, and also reported details of the harmonic structure of the notes of both chanter and drones.

Measurements made by Mackenzie (1995) have used greatly improved techniques, sampling the notes actually played in performance, with the drones sounding, and taking care that the players were themselves satisfied with the sound produced. The results have shown very close agreement between different pipers and instruments, and a strong tendency to tune the chanter notes in consonance with appropriate harmonies of the drones. But no corresponding measurements have been reported for old chanters. What is certain is that all good players are keenly aware of, and strive to attain, what they consider to be the true intonation, different though this may be from the standards adopted by other musicians.

The nine notes are not produced simply by successive opening of the eight finger-holes: as with most bagpipes, the fingering system is such that when middle and upper notes are played, certain of the lower holes must be kept closed. Although in theory cross-fingerings could be used to produce additional chromatic semitones, in practice all the traditional music is restricted to the nine notes listed above. The 19th-century bagpipe maker David Glen published fingering charts showing two notes *g"*, one slightly sharpened, but this innovation was not generally adopted. A considerable number of tunes have been adapted to the bagpipe from other sources and this has led to a number of 'wrong' notes which are now accepted as traditional. Thus, *g"* is accepted as a passing note in place of *g♯"*, in tunes which would otherwise be in the key of A major, and to a lesser extent *c♯"* is accepted where parallel traditions have *c"*. Some tunes exist in minor modes in the song and fiddle traditions but in major modes in the bagpipe tradition, perhaps for a similar reason.

(ii) Other bagpipes. The Lowland bagpipe is a bellows-blown instrument, with three drones all in one stock. They lie across the piper's chest while in use, and the piper is seated. The chanter and drone are slightly smaller than in the Highland pipe, but in musical essentials they are the same (see fig.4b). By the end of the 19th century the Lowland bagpipe had almost ceased to be played (Duncan, 1990), though in the early 20th century some pipe makers offered instead the half-sized Highland bagpipe blown by bellows. In the late 20th century the Lowland pipe has been revived.

Another type of bagpipe made and played in Scotland in the 18th and early 19th centuries is essentially similar to early forms of Irish union pipe (see fig.4c and §4 below). In 20th-century literature it has been called the 'hybrid union pipe'; more recently, the 'pastoral' pipe, following Geoghegan (c1746; see §4 below).

A Scottish form of small-pipe is found in some museum collections. The chanter is cylindrical and gives a nine-note scale. The three drones are set in one stock and tuned as in the Northumbrian pipes (see §5 below), i.e. the smallest in unison with the six-finger note on the chanter, the largest an octave below, and the intermediate drone at the 5th in between. After a long period of disuse, small-pipes are again being played, with a chanter redesigned to accept Highland pipe fingering. It is available in two pitches, one an octave below the Highland pipe (nominally 'in A') with the corresponding scale including *g* and *g'*,

4. *(a) Scottish Highland bagpipe, with blowpipe, chanter and three drones; (b) Scottish Lowland bagpipe, with bellows and three drones; (c) early Irish union pipe, with bellows, plain chanter, three drones and a tenor regulator with four keys (all Pitt Rivers Museum, Oxford); (d) early Northumbrian small-pipe, with bellows, plain chanter and three drones, c1770 (National Bagpipe Museum, Newcastle upon Tyne)*

5. *Piper to the Laird of Grant playing the Scottish Highland bagpipe: painting by Richard Waitt, 1714 (Royal Museum of Scotland, Edinburgh)*

both natural; and the other a 4th higher ('in D'). Both mouth-blown and bellows forms are played.

4. IRELAND. Historical and literary references to the bagpipe in Ireland go back to 1544, and show that it was used for the same purposes as in Gaelic Scotland, notably in battle and for laments at funerals (see Donnelly, 1981). A crudely drawn illustration was given by John Derricke in *Image of Irelande* (London, 1581; fig.6): it depicts a mouthblown instrument with two drones of unequal length set in one stock, and a long chanter with bell; the proportions are grotesque, and the woodcut must be accepted with caution. These references imply a loud instrument, presumably mouth-blown and similar to the Scottish bagpipe of the time, but in the 18th century it died out and little is known about it. It is said that there used to be an example in the Musée de Cluny, Paris (Collinson, 1975).

The Scottish bagpipe began to be used in Ireland in the 19th century, and in time the custom began of using a variant form with a single tenor drone instead of a pair. The two drones are set in separate stocks, with the bass resting on the piper's shoulder. Another pattern of Irish war-pipe was evolved about 1900–10 by Henry Starck of London and named the 'Brian Boru' bagpipe. It had three drones all set in one stock and sounding as follows: tenor, one octave below the key note; bass, one octave below this; baritone, the 5th between. The chanter was made with several differing key arrangements and was capable of sounding a diatonic scale from a 3rd below the key note to a 3rd above. The Brian Boru pipe was used by the

Royal Inniskilling Fusiliers from 1926 to 1968, but all Irish infantry regiments now use the Scottish Highland bagpipe, though their repertories still emphasize Irish tunes.

The Irish uilleann pipe is a bellows pipe, played sitting and with the drones lying across the knees, and is believed to have been introduced in the early 18th century. The name 'uilleann pipe', from the Irish word *uilleann* ('elbow'), has been shown to be spurious (see Carolan, 1981–2) but is now firmly established. The usual term in the 19th century was 'union pipe'. Successive elaborations in its design and musical capabilities can be traced through the earlier published tutors (Geoghegan, O'Farrell, Colclough).

The earliest known form of uilleann pipe was the 'pastoral or new bagpipe' (Geoghegan). It had an open-ended chanter without keywork, giving the six-finger note *d′* and a range of *c′* to *d‴*, the upper register being obtained by overblowing; the two drones were set in one stock and tuned *a* and *A*. Subsequent developments include lowering the drones to *d* and *D*, the extra length of the bass drone being obtained by folding the tube back into the stock (see fig.4c), and the addition of a third, treble, drone (tuned *d′*) and of what is now known as the tenor regulator. This latter is inserted in the same stock as the drones and is of conical bore, stopped at the end and possessing four or five keys. It is fitted with a double reed like that used in the chanter, and the purpose is to enable the piper to provide a variable chord by striking a suitable key with the heel of his hand. Bagpipes of this type are no longer played, but a number survive in museum collections. The chanter is characteristically made in two parts, the main part with the finger-holes, and a removable foot joint with two holes, bored crossways, which determine the pitch of the lowest note, as in the Scottish Highland and Lowland chanters. For

6. *Possible representation of the old Irish war-pipe: woodcut from John Derricke's 'Image of Irelande' (London, 1581)*

this reason the pipes are sometimes called 'hybrid uilleann pipes', on the supposition that they represent a fusion of Irish and Scottish forms. This may not be correct: the alternative view is that these pipes represent the older form, and that the present Irish pipe is a further development.

In the modern Irish uilleann pipe (first described in O'Farrell, c1804, and later in Colclough) the chanter has no foot joint and its range is two octaves (d'–d'''), and it has three drones (D, d, d'). A fourth drone, occasionally found, is tuned to g'. Many drone stocks are fitted with a plug to silence the drones, at the same time allowing the regulators to sound. The bass drone is a simple folded pipe, not re-entering the stock, and the regulators are increased to three, and occasionally four, which together give the piper the ability to sound full chords. Players have been known to silence their chanter on occasion and play the air entirely on the regulator keys, to the plain drone accompaniment, but the general method of using regulators is either to provide an occasional chord or to emphasize the time by a rhythmic 'vamping'. A modern set of regulators is tuned to sound: tenor, f♯', g', a', b', c'; baritone, d', f♯', g', a'; bass, g, a, b, c♯'. Where a double bass is provided, it usually sounds one octave below the baritone. Regulators are tuned by inserting a length of wire or rush pith into the bore. Many of them are very loud and have a tendency to overwhelm the chanter. Some players dispense with them.

Early chanters were made without keys, but at various times these have been added, and now up to nine may be found, the compass of two octaves remaining the same. The chanter, though an open one, is played with the end closed by resting it on a pad of leather on the piper's knee, and raised for certain notes.

The uilleann bagpipe varies considerably in pitch from two whole tones below standard (a' = 440) up to standard pitch itself. For concert-hall work, where greater volume is desired, chanters have been made with a double bore and two reeds, the piper's fingers spanning both sets of holes. Double reeds are used in all chanters and regulators, and beating reeds in the drones. The modern uilleann pipe has become such a complex instrument that it has sometimes been called the 'Irish organ'.

5. ENGLAND.   The Northumbrian half-long pipe may be identified with the Scottish Lowland pipe, having three drones in one stock, and an open chanter sounding nine notes. The drones, however, differ in one respect, for instead of bass, tenor and tenor, the Northumbrian pattern is bass, tenor and treble, the treble being a 5th above the tenor. Apart from this difference in the drones, the instrument is identical to the Lowland variety and, if played sitting, the drones lie across the breast, but if in use for marching they lie on the piper's shoulder. Having died out in the 19th century, this instrument was revived in the 1920s with partial success for the use of Scout troops and other groups, and has been revived again since about 1980. The earlier revival used a different drone tuning with a baritone drone and no treble, but this is now considered erroneous and the later revival uses the tuning described here.

The shuttle pipe, long disused, had barrel drones of the musette type (see fig.7b below) and a chanter of early Northumbrian type, keyless and open-ended. Only two examples are known. One of these is dated 1695 and was formerly in the possession of J. Campbell Noble. The other, of about the same date, was in the collection of W.A. Cocks (now in the Morpeth Chantry Bagpipe Museum).

The Northumbrian small-pipe (see fig.4d) is an indoor instrument and in its early form consisted of a plain open chanter, cylindrically bored, with double reed, giving a scale of nine notes. It had three drones sounding the key note, the octave below and the 5th between, all inserted in one stock. Small-pipe drones lie across the player's chest in all cases. The small-pipe was not standardized, each maker having worked to his own set of measurements. The earliest known small-pipe (now in the Morpeth Chantry Bagpipe Museum) probably dates from the late 17th century. It is of ivory, and has a plain open-ended chanter of narrow cylindrical bore, 16 cm long. The three open-ended drones are 22, 13·5 and 12 cm and sound g, d' and g' respectively. This type was in use until the middle of the 18th century. About that time an unknown pipe maker conceived the idea of closing the end of the chanter, and this has been the rule ever since; it is the only closed chanter found on any type of bagpipe. The closure reduced the compass of the chanter by one note, but, since the fingering method is to open only one hole at a time, it enabled the piper to play staccato and to repeat the same note many times in succession, without having to interpolate grace notes. It added greatly to the crispness and distinctness of the music, and this feature is characteristic of Northumbrian piping.

The small-pipe remained at this stage until about 1805, when John Peacock, one of the town waits of Newcastle upon Tyne, collaborated with John Dunn, pipe maker, also of Newcastle, to add the first four keys to the chanter. This increased the compass from d' to a'', the key note being g'. The later addition of a fifth key, c♯'', enabled the piper to play in the key of D, which necessitated a fourth drone to provide the correct harmony. At the same time stops were fitted to all drones, so that any of them could be silenced at will. The increased possibilities of the keyed small-pipe led other makers, notably Robert Reid of North Shields, to add further keys, and by the time of Reid's death in 1837, at the age of 53, the number of keys had been increased to 14 and the drones to five, fitted with a switch in the drone stock, so that the piper may change over quickly from key G to key D, or vice versa. His son James Reid further increased the keys to 17, giving a full chromatic scale from b to b''.

These multi-keyed chanters are not common, the most usual pattern having seven keys only, with which nearly all the existing pipe music may be played. These seven keys are closed, worked by the little finger of the upper hand or the thumb of the lower, and the holes they cover are the seven plain finger-holes and top thumb-hole. Since the fingering principle is still to open only one hole at once, this gives 15 notes: d', e', f♯', g', a', b', c'', c♯'', d'', d♯'', e'', f♯'', g'', a'', b''. Of the four drones, three can give either of two notes, thus d, g/a, d'/e', g'/a', and by sounding only three drones at any one time, the harmonies g–d'–g', d–a–d', a–e'–a' can be selected. The six-finger note is called G and written g' on the stave, though the actual pitch is usually f''. (For a set of pipes designed to play with other instruments it is precisely f'' at a'' = 440 Hz, but traditionally it was little sharper than this). As regards the intonation, Butler (1987) describes a system in which G, B and D notes of the chanter are designed to be in consonance with the G drones, F♯ and A with the D drones, C♯ and E with the A drones, presumably seeking pure 5th, 4th and major 3rd intervals respectively.

Small-pipes were made mainly from home-grown materials in early days, the woods used including box, walnut and holly; modern pipes are usually of ebony or cocus-wood. Many old instruments were constructed wholly of ivory, with silver mounts and chains; they are exceedingly elegant, but the tone is not so mellow as that from pipes of wood. Small-pipe reeds are made of cane or elderberry, or often entirely of metal.

6. FRANCE, BELGIUM.   The bellows-blown musette is a highly developed bagpipe of great compass and refined musical quality (fig.7). It became fashionable at the French court and in society during the 17th and 18th centuries, and the artistic skill lavished on the adornment of the wood and ivory work was of an exceedingly high order. The bag-covers were of rich silks, often covered with embroidery and bordered with metallic fringe and tassels. These pieces of fine needlework required protection from the grease of the bag by means of padded undercovers, and they frequently had an outer cover in addition. Musettes were often made entirely of ivory (see MUSETTE).

The origin of the musette, which appears to have been the prototype of the bellows bagpipe, is not known with certainty, but it was probably 16th-century, for at the beginning of the 17th century the instrument is found in an advanced state of development. It was described by Praetorius (*Syntagma musicum*, ii) as having a single chanter, a set of barrel drones, and bellows. The chanter was of narrow cylindrical bore and without keys; it was fitted with a double reed.

By 1636–7, the date of Mersenne's *Harmonie universelle*, it had been supplied with the first keys for the production of semitones. Later in the same century Martin

Hotteterre added a second chanter with six keys, which lay parallel to the first and extended the scale upwards. Both chanters were set in a double stock which was in turn inserted into the bag stock. The larger of the two (*grand chalumeau*) sounded the scale from f♯ to a″ by means of eight open holes and seven keys; the smaller (*petit chalumeau*) extended the scale to d‴, all the extra notes being sounded by the six keys, three of which were on the upper- and three on the underside of the chanter. All the musette keys were actuated by the fourth finger of the left hand and the thumb of the right. The chanters remained in this form until the musette became extinct.

The drone barrel was formed of a cylindrical block of wood or ivory, about 15 cm long and 4 cm in diameter, inserted 2·5 cm into the stock. It was pierced longitudinally by parallel bores which were connected in series in twos or more to give the necessary lengths and terminated in slots in the side (fig.7a). These slots were in dovetailed grooves, in which were fitted *layettes* (slides), by means of which the drones were tuned. The *layettes* were the equivalent of the sliding joints on the usual type of bagpipe drone, and they could also be used to silence unwanted drones completely. Lissieu of Lyons was a noted maker of musettes, and a fine specimen by him, in the Morpeth Chantry Bagpipe Museum, is fitted with six drones. Double reeds were fitted throughout the entire instrument. Musette drones were usually tuned in octaves of C and G. Very detailed descriptions and illustrations of all the French bagpipes were given by Mersenne in *Harmonie universelle* and in the *Encyclopédie* of Diderot and D'Alembert (Paris, 1763).

The traditional bagpipe of the Auvergne and Bourbonnais is characterized by a chanter and drone set parallel to each other, either joined (fig.8), or set in a common

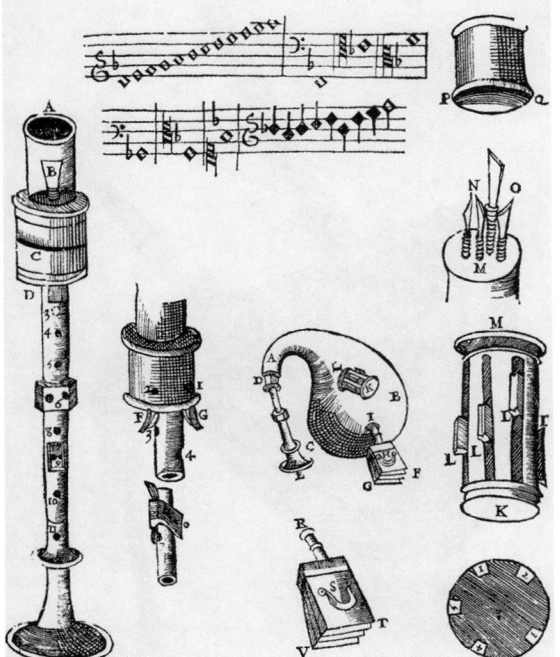

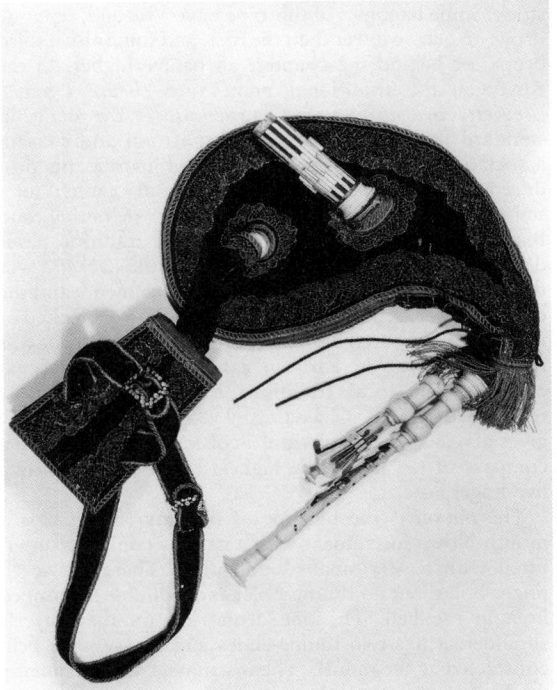

7. Musette: (a) details of the chanter, bellows, barrel drone and drone reeds, from Mersenne's 'Harmonie universelle' (1636–7); (b) musette with bellows, two chanters and barrel drone, French, 18th century (Royal College of Music, London)

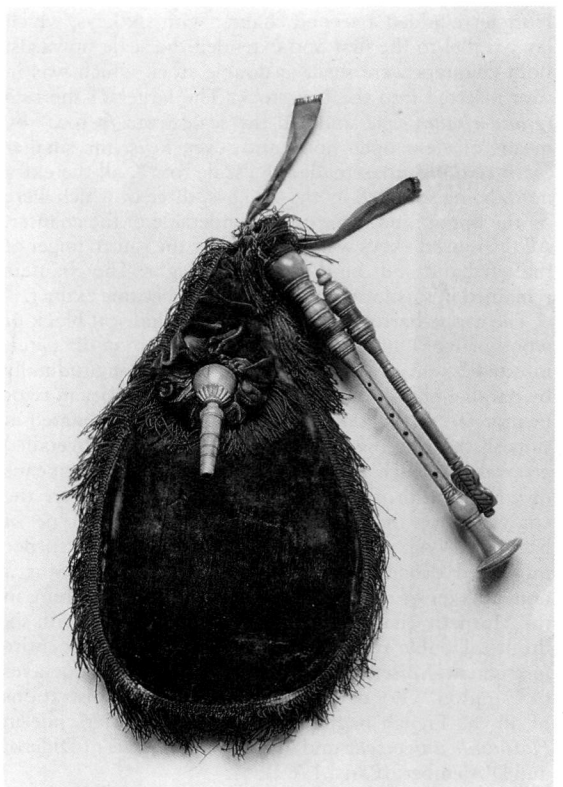

8. Cornemuse with blowpipe, and chanter with side extension carrying a single treble drone, French, 18th century

stock. Some bagpipes of this type have a second, separate drone an octave lower than the first, and some also a third drone set behind the chanter, an octave higher. In the Auvergne the traditional names are *chèvre* ('goat'), *chèvrette* or *cabrette*, but *cornemuse* is the name in standard French. Although it has pastoral and peasant associations, the elaborately decorated instruments produced by several makers in the 19th century catered for a self-consciously rural bourgeois taste (Montbel and Blanchard, 1990). The Auvergne piping tradition never died out, but by the later 19th century the *cabrette* was mainly played in concert with other instruments and the drones had ceased to be used; they were either blocked or replaced by unbored dummy drones. The instrument was regularly played in Paris in cafés with an Auvergnat clientele. The local traditions have been extensively researched by J.F. Chassaing (1982). Ladonne (1987) gives playing instructions and a collection of tunes with a compass of ten notes, the highest being the overblown five-finger note.

The *biniou* is the bagpipe of Brittany (fig.9). It is a mouth-blown instrument with a narrow conical chanter, fitted with a very small double reed. There are seven finger-holes, but no thumb-hole, and a double unstopped hole in the bell. The one drone lies on the player's shoulder; it has two tuning-slides and a very wide bell, contracted at the mouth. The instrument was frequently made of boxwood, without any metal or mountings, but now is generally of blackwood. The bag is of sheepskin and it is held high on the piper's chest in playing. The

instrument is generally played *àcouple*, that is in conjunction with the *bombarde*, which is a separate chanter (without a bag; a type of shawm) of wide conical bore, pitched an octave lower and blown directly from the mouth of a second player (*see* FRANCE, fig.16*d*). Traditionally the two were used at weddings and dances. Since World War II a loud bagpipe, *biniou bras* (actually the Highland bagpipe introduced from Scotland), pitched in the same octave as the *bombarde*, has been introduced and is played in pipe and drum bands along with the *bombarde*. The older instrument is still played, nevertheless, and is enjoying a considerable revival (Bigot, 1991). The *veuze* is a similar instrument to the *biniou*, though larger and sounding an octave lower. It survived until the 19th century in the Nantes region, and has recently been revived.

In Belgium, the early history of the bagpipe was similar to that of the French mouth-blown pipes; the musette was also played. In the 19th century, up to 1900, two types of bagpipe were still played by shepherds in Hainaut and east Flanders. One had a chanter only; the other, the *muse-au-sac*, had two drones of which the smaller lay beside the chanter as in the French *cornemuse*. Examples of the second type are in the Instruments Museum of the Brussels Conservatory (fig.10). A few bagpipe melodies

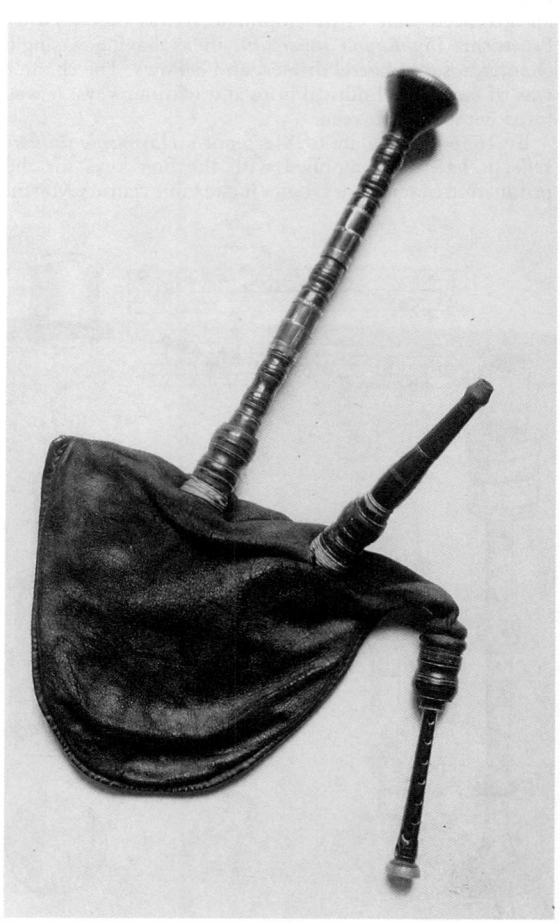

9. Biniou with blowpipe, chanter and single drone, French, 17th century

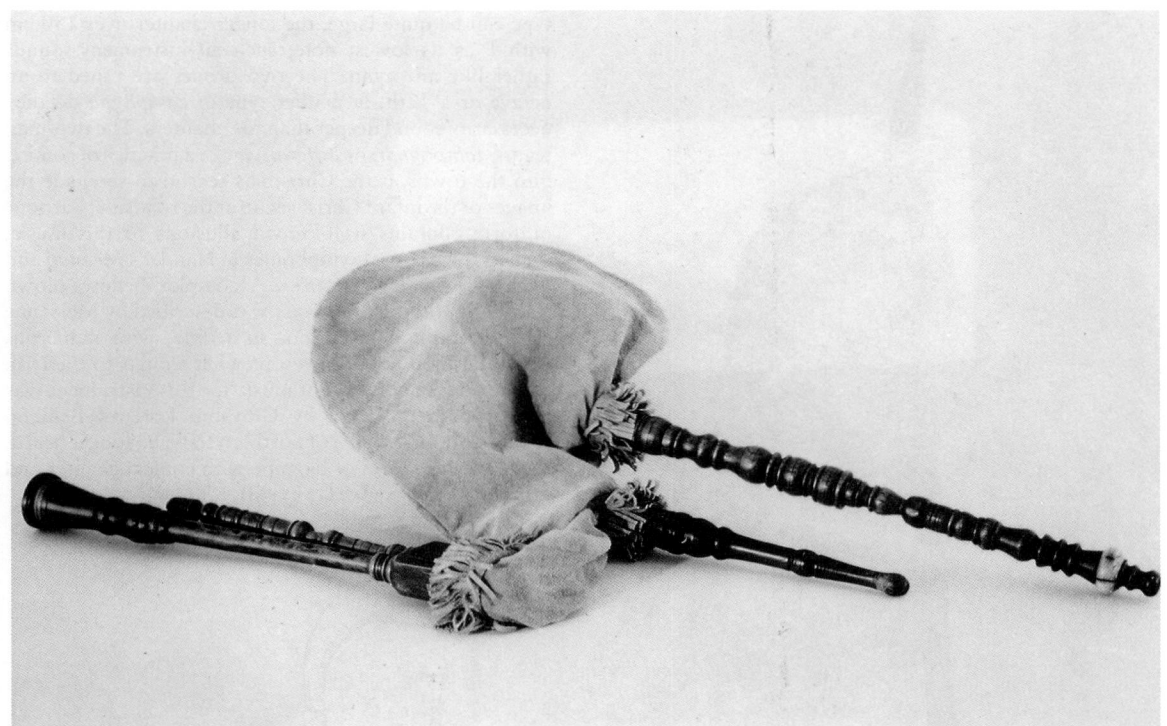

10. *Muse-au-sac from Arc-Ainières, Hainaut (Musée des Instruments de Musique, Brussels)*

from France and Belgium have been published (Boone, 1983).

The *bouha* of the Landes de Gascogne had a double chanter, one bore having melody holes, the other bore a single hole giving alternate tonic and dominant drone, the whole strongly resembling the Hungarian *duda* (see §7(v) below; Dominique, 1987).

7. OTHER COUNTRIES.

(i) Spain and Portugal. In Asturias, Galicia and the Minho across the border the mouth-blown *gaita* (fig.11) continues to flourish. It usually has only one drone. The chanter has a wide conical bore, seven holes and a thumb-hole, three vent-holes lower down, and a double reed. The drone has two tuning-slides; it is fitted with a beating reed, adorned with a heavy silk fringe, and lies on the player's shoulder. The pipes are still often made of boxwood with brass mounts for the drone but blackwood is used for the best quality instruments. Modern bags are made of moulded rubber covered with cloth. The chanter has a C major scale from b' to c''', though Galician pipers can reach f''' or g''' by overblowing. Instruments also exist in Bb and D. Among the many tutors published for the *gaita*, those by Covello (1978), Santiago (1978) and Estévez Vila (1987) may be mentioned.

The Catalan *cornamusa* has been extinct for a century, but the shepherd's *zampoña* of the Balearic Islands is still played. The chanter resembles that of the *gaita* but the drone hangs down in front of the bag, held in a large stock in which are also two small drones, usually blocked up and silent.

(ii) Northern Europe. Praetorius (*Syntagma musicum*, ii) gave the best descriptions and illustrations of old German bagpipes (fig.12). The *Bock*, with deep-sounding horn-belled chanter and drone, was of the western Slav type. It survived in use in the Böhmerwald, where it was recorded by Künzig (1958). The *Schäferpfeife*, called *Sackpfeiff* in Virdung's *Musica getutscht* (1511), was of a kind which in one form or another was widespread over northern Europe up to the 18th century. The chanter was narrowly conical, and the two drones held in one drone-stock were of unequal length and probably tuned to a 5th. Only one bagpipe which fits this description is known to exist in the Kunsthistorisches Museum, Vienna. Its provenance is unknown but it is conjectured to be 18th-century German (Boone, 1983).

The *Hümmelchen* and the *dudy* (a Czech name) were much smaller, again with drones of unequal length, the *dudy* having three. Their chanter bores may have been cylindrical, as in the present Baltic types, but no specimens are known to survive and the nature of the reed is unknown. Praetorius also described a bagpipe that he heard in Magdeburg, with two chanters branching from a single stock (one for each hand and sounding a 5th apart), enabling the piper to play simple two-part melodies; it had a drone-stock with two drones like those of the *Schäferpfeife*.

A simple bagpipe, the *Säckpipa*, survived into the 20th century in the Swedish district of Dalarna. It has a cylindrical chanter 23 cm in length with six holes and a thumb-hole, and a beating reed. Two short drones are held in one stock, but the shorter is a dummy. In certain islands and coastal districts of Estonia the bagpipe consists of a bag made from a seal's stomach, a cylindrical chanter 15 cm long with six holes and beating reed, and two drones tuned to a 5th, branching from a single drone-stock. The drones have cavernous terminations as in

11. *Gaita from Galicia, Spain*

Scotland and Spain. There are (or were) similar instruments to be found in Latvia.

(iii) Italy.   The principal bagpipe is the *zampogna* (fig.13), native to the south and to Sicily (where the name is *cornamusa*) but often heard in the north played by itinerant players. It has a bag usually formed of a whole skin. The four pipes, all held in one large stock, include two conical chanters, one for each hand, and two crudely bored cylindrical drones. All four have double reeds of a characteristic long-bladed pattern. There are two main types of *zampogna*: one is played alone, the other accompanies a conical chanter (*ciaramella*, *cornamusina*, occasionally *piffaro*) which a second player blows directly with his mouth. The holes of the chanters of the first type, five in one, four in the other, give a series of notes a 4th apart whereby the chanters are sounded in 3rds or contrapuntally. The visual effect recalls that of the Roman Phrygian aulos. The chanters of the second type are an octave apart, and the lowest hole of the larger chanter is covered by an open key protected by a wooden barrel as in many Renaissance wind instruments (fig.13a). This

type can be quite large, the longer chanter over 150 cm with *F* as its lowest note; such an instrument sounds rather like an organ. The two drones are tuned to an octave or a 12th; in neither type of *zampogna* do they necessarily sound deeper than the chanters. The two-man teams, *zampognari* or *pifferari*, make a practice of coming into the towns at the Christmas season to serenade the images of the infant Christ set up at the roadside. Baroque oratorio contains well-known allusions to this music, such as the pastoral symphonies in Handel's *Messiah* and Bach's *Christmas Oratorio*. A complex bellows-blown elaboration of the *zampogna* was described by Mersenne as a Neapolitan invention, *sordellina*, with numerous closed keys on the drones somewhat similar to the Irish regulators. A collection of music for this instrument was published in tablature by Giovanni Lorenzo Baldano (1576–1660). The *piva* of northern Italy, no longer heard, was a western form of bagpipe with conical chanter and cylindrical drone. (*See* ITALY, §II, 6.)

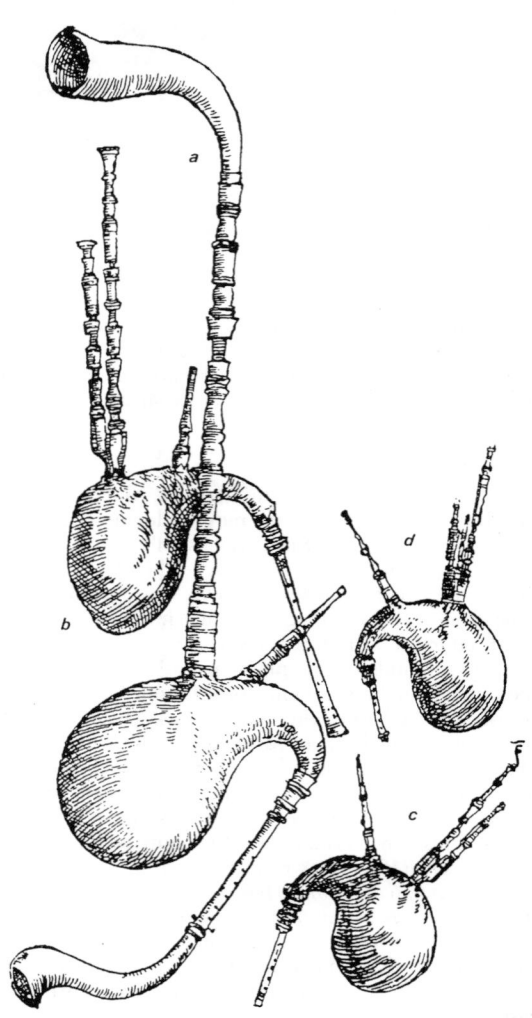

12. *German bagpipe types, (a) Bock, (b) Schäferpfeife, (c) Hümmelchen, (d) dudy: woodcut from Praetorius's 'Theatrum instrumentorum' (1620)*

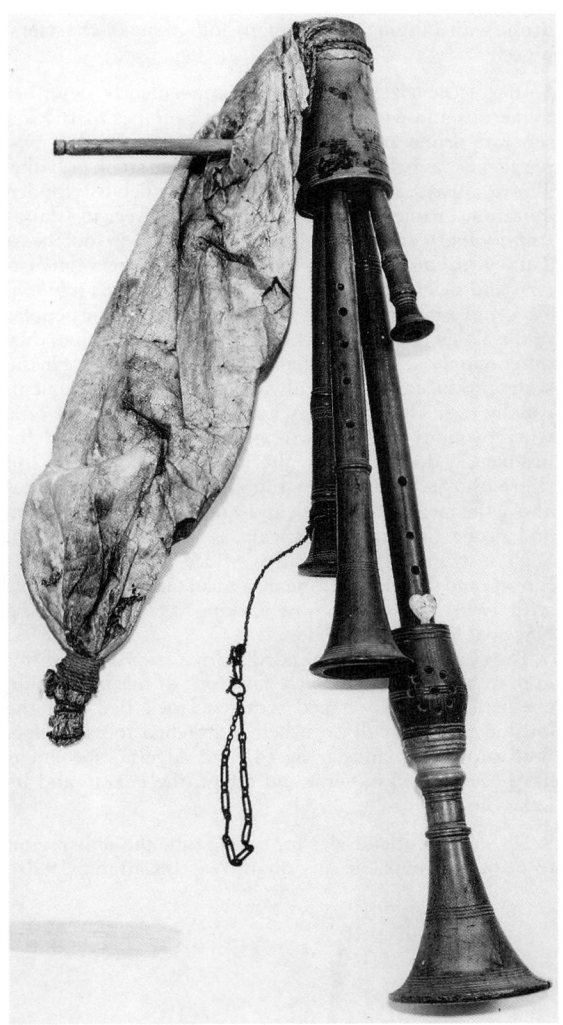 

13. (a) Zampogna with blowpipe, two chanters and two drones, Italian (Pitt Rivers Museum, Oxford); (b) zampogna player: detail from 'The Shepherds', fresco from the cycle 'Life and Glory of the Virgin' by Ludovico Seitz, 1892–1902 (Cappella Tedesca, Santa Casa, Loreto)

See also PHAGOTUM.

(iv) Poland, Czech Republic, Slovakia.   The Polish *dudy* and *kozioł* (*see* POLAND, §II, 5, figs.5 and 6) are bellows-blown, with a cylindrical, beating-reed chanter held in a carved stock. The drone rests on the shoulder and is either straight, or right-angled to hang down behind the player's back. Often the tube is twice doubled back inside a wooden butt joint for compactness. Both chanter and drone have large upturned bells of cowhorn or horn and metal. The *dudy* has six finger-holes and a thumb-hole giving a plagal scale omitting the lower submediant. The *kozioł* includes a seventh hole for the little finger and covers a plagal 11th, the top two notes being overblown. Closed fingering is used in both types, and staccato can be made by closing all holes to interpose the low dominant, which when continually touched in this manner gives the effect of a subsidiary drone. The common name 'wedding pipes' indicates the instruments' traditional association; they can be traced in pictures back to the 14th century. The earliest examples were mouth-blown. The Bohemian *dudy* is similar to the Polish; its beating reeds sometimes

consist of a slip of cane tied over a slot in a short metal or bone tube, on the principle of the clarinet. This *dudy* is much used with fiddle and clarinet. Moravia and Slovakia have bagpipes of this kind or rather smaller (in Slovakia they are called *gajdy* and may be mouth-blown), and a double-bore chanter resembling the Hungarian type. Simplified instruments resembling the single-chanter *dudy* are found in Belarus and the Ukraine (*duda*).

(v) Hungary, Romania.   The Hungarian *duda* (*see* HUNGARY, §II, 6(iv)) is mouth-blown, though bellows-blown versions exist in museums. The goat-head stock holds a chanter carved in rectangular cross-section containing two parallel cylindrical bores. One is the chanter proper, with six holes and a thumb-hole. The highest finger-hole, placed opposite the thumb-hole, is very small (the 'flea hole') and when uncovered raises any note of the scale by approximately a semitone, whereby sharps and modulations are possible. The lowest note sounds through an oblong vent. The other bore, the *kontra*, has one hole controlled by the little finger of the

lower hand. When open it sounds in unison with the bottom note of the melody bore. When closed the note is emitted through a bell extension (often ending with a cowhorn) and sounds a 4th lower. Movement of the little finger provides a drone harmony which pendulates between these two notes, independent of the fingering of the melody bore. A very efficient staccato is possible since the interpolated bottom note of the melody bore is in unison with the open hole note of the *kontra*, effecting a momentary silence in the melody. The instrument has a normal bass drone. Traditional playing died out in the 1960s but was revived in the 1980s, with instruments again being manufactured and music published (Csoóri, 1986). Romania has a similar instrument, the *cimpoi* (see Habenicht, 1972–4).

(vi) Yugoslavia, Bulgaria. The bellows-blown *gajde* of the north-eastern plains and parts of Serbia has a double-bore chanter of oval outer cross-section with large upturned wooden bell. It has only five holes, but the *kontra* bore also has a hole for the little finger, which is used as in Hungary but at a slower speed appropriate to the deeper sound of the pipes; the bass drone may sound as low as G′, the necessary length being obtained with the help of a butt section or a length of rubber hose. The *diple sa mješinom* or *mih* of Dalmatia and Bosnia is a simple mouth-blown instrument with double-bore chanter without bell, and no drone. There are six holes to each bore, spanned by the same finger and sounding a unison except on the low note, where one hole only is covered to produce a major 2nd. In some specimens one bore is a plain drone; in others different arrangements of the holes are found, similar to those among hornpipes. The *diple* is also played without a bag, the cup-like stock being placed directly to the mouth.

The Macedonian *gajde* has a single chanter turned in boxwood and mounted with horn. The lower end is formed in a characteristic obtuse angle carved from horn. There are seven holes and a thumb-hole, the first finger-hole being a 'flea hole' bushed with quill. The drone is also of boxwood and horn-mounted. This bagpipe is also found in Bulgaria, as are other types of *gayda* with conically bored chanters (still with beating reed) and a similar arrangement of holes. Its size and pitch vary according to region. The *gayda* remains strongly associated with weddings and village dance festivities, though mostly it is heard in large ensembles and 'folk orchestras'. Accounts of Bulgarian piping at different periods are given in Katzarova, 1937; Levy, 1985; and Rice, 1994.

The Serbian *gajde* and the *diple* are now rare, but the Macedonian and Bulgarian bagpipes continue to flourish. (*See* BULGARIA, §II.)

(vii) India. The native bagpipe of India (Hindustani *maśak*); also known by other names, e.g. *śruti upaṅga*) has a melody pipe and a drone pipe lashed together, but some examples have one pipe only, with the finger-holes often sealed with wax for sounding a drone to another instrument. It appears in ceremonial and devotional ensembles. The principal bagpipe in use throughout India and the Indian army is, however, the Scottish Highland pipe, which is manufactured commercially in both India and Pakistan. It sometimes is used at wedding ceremonies, especially in the North, where it is known by various local names such as *mashak* and *bīn bājā* (Alter, 1997–8). The Scottish bagpipe may have inspired the fitting of a long

drone with a tuning-slide to many Indian snake-charmers' pipes.

8. BAG-HORNPIPES.   This term conveniently describes numerous and widespread primitive bagpipes that lack a separate drone and possess a chanter composed of two parallel canes held in a cradle-like wooden stock or 'yoke' almost always mounted with a cowhorn bell or wooden imitation of one. Examples occur in the Aegean Islands (*tsambouna*) and Crete (*askomandoura*), in northeast Turkey (*tulum*), Armenia (*parkapzuk*), Georgia (*gudastviri*) and neighbouring regions of the Caucasus (*chiboni* etc.), and among the Mari and other Finno-Ugric peoples of the Volga (*shüvïr* etc.). Like the bagless hornpipes they differ mainly in the arrangement of holes and hence in the scales produced. One pipe always has the full complement, usually five. The other may have five, three, two or one, whereby many kinds of two-part effects are obtained: for instance, a drone rapidly alternating over a major 2nd (Karpathos); decoration by rapidly interposed high notes above the melody (Turkey); and a mixture of 3rds, unison and drone (Russia) so intricate as to defy description. Such instruments once had a wider distribution over Europe and the Mediterranean, and an old Welsh example with twin horn bells, now lacking its bag, is in the National Museum of Wales.

The common species of north Africa (*zukra* etc.) differ in that the two canes, which have four or five holes each, are held in a disc-shaped wooden stock tied into the kidskin bag; a small horn bell is attached to each pipe. Best known in Tunisia (fig.14) and Algeria, specimens have been found in Syria and Egypt, the Fezzan and by Lake Chad.

9. MUSIC.   Scotland was for a long time the only region to print pipe music in any quantity (see Cannon, 1980),

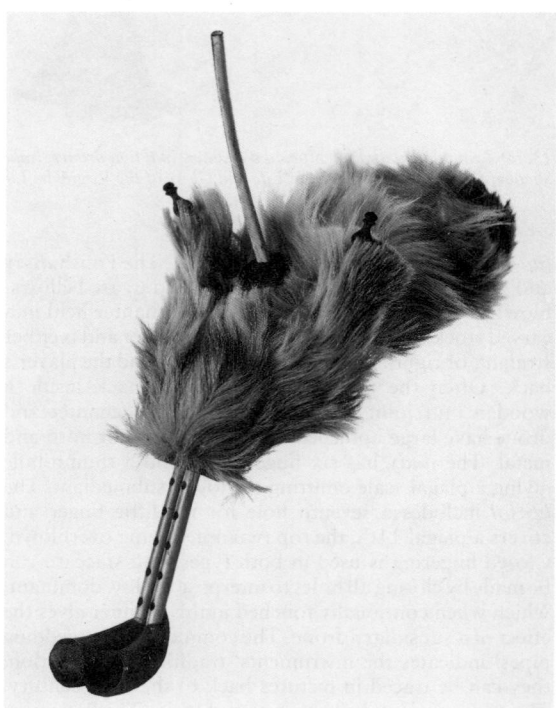

14. Bag-hornpipe, Tunisia (Pitt Rivers Museum, Oxford)

with Ireland, Northumberland and Brittany following far behind; but, along with the revival in playing, other countries have begun to print tutors and anthologies of traditional pipe tunes.

Among the chief characteristics of bagpipe music are the facts that the chanter is never silent, so that there can be no rests or momentary pauses between notes, and that its loudness cannot be varied. These problems are overcome to some extent by the use of grace notes, which at their simplest consist of the momentary uncovering of a hole by one finger, to produce a high-pitched grace note, or momentary covering of one or more holes simultaneously to produce a low-pitched grace note. The actual pitch of the grace note is not usually fully perceived, and the effect is of a bright or dull clicking sound. Grace notes are essential to divide two successive melody notes of the same pitch, and are also commonly played on the downbeat notes of the melody to mark out the rhythm. In many piping traditions grace notes are used sparingly, but Scottish pipers have a large fund of embellishments – 'doublings', 'shakes', 'throws' and 'grips' – which are carefully taught and are written into the music, and an analogous but largely different set in the older PIBROCH repertory. Irish uilleann pipers use multiple grace notes, but to a much lesser extent. The Northumbrian small-pipe chanter, being closed, can be silenced and this makes the use of grace notes unnecessary, though in fact they are played to some extent. On some bagpipes (for instance the Czech *dudy* and Hungarian *duda*; see §7(iv) and (v) above) the same effect is obtained by relying on the illusion of silence when certain chanter notes are sounded.

10. PRESENT STATE. The Scottish Highland pipe continues to dominate the public perception of bagpiping. It is played in ever-increasing numbers, and the standards both of playing and of construction and tuning have risen markedly in the last half of the 20th century. Although the British army maintains fewer pipe bands than before, this decrease is more than offset by the increase in civilian pipe bands throughout the world, and not only in countries of obvious British influence. Solo piping continues at virtuoso level including the traditional *piobaireachd*, with pipers from the USA, Brittany and elsewhere regularly taking prizes in competitions. But throughout Europe, there has also been a revival of interest in other bagpipes, fostered usually by young players who have relearnt the craft of pipe making by copying instruments from museum collections, and playing technique from old recordings or, when possible, directly from the remaining traditional players. There have also been attempts to reconstruct medieval and later bagpipes from purely iconographic evidence; among these may be mentioned the English Great Pipe by Jon Swayne, and impressive reconstructions of the large peasant bagpipes shown in paintings by Breughel and others. In the British Isles these activities have been generally encouraged by the foundation of the Lowland and Border Pipers' Society (1983) and the Bagpipe Society (1985), as well as the longer-established Northumbrian Pipers' Society (1928) and Na Píobairí Uilleann (1963). These and similar groups in other countries publish periodicals, maintain websites, organize concerts and instrument making workshops, and provide a market for the sale of pipes. International gatherings of makers and players take place regularly at St Chartier, France, and Strakonice, Czech Republic. The publication of bagpipe music, arranged from old sources

or from diverse piping traditions, has increased. The bagpipes of the revival tend to follow traditional models closely in general construction and playing technique, but entirely new or remodelled instruments are also being developed (Goodacre, 1992; Swayne, 1995; Moore, 1999). These are designed to play together with each other and with other instruments, and in public performance they may be heard as part of a line-up of instruments in many folk or folk-rock groups. Some of these groups have achieved international reputations, such as the pioneering Whistlebinkies (Scotland), Blowzabella (England), Battlefield Band (Scotland) and Run Rig (Gaelic, folk-rock). If the question is asked, whether some essential element of bagpiping is being lost in these new formats, it can be answered at least in part by noticing how, in many cases, it is still the bagpipe that dominates the sound and is perhaps the chief attraction to the listening public.

BIBLIOGRAPHY

GENERAL, EARLY HISTORY

MersenneHU; PraetoriusSM; PraetoriusTI

G.H. Askew: 'The Bag-Pipe in Early Britain', *Proceedings of the Society of Antiquaries of Newcastle-upon-Tyne*, 4th ser., ix (1940), 171

A. Baines: *Bagpipes* (Oxford, 1960, 3/1995)

J.H. van der Meer: 'Typologie der Sackpfeife', *Anzeiger des Germanischen Nationalmuseums* (1964), 123–46

R. Sutherland: 'The Bagpipe in Old English Literature', *Piping Times*, xix/4 (1967), 18–19

F. Crane: *Extant Medieval Musical Instruments: a Provisional Catalogue by Types* (Iowa City, IA, 1972)

F. Collinson: *The Bagpipe* (London, 1975)

C. Page: 'Biblical Instruments in Medieval Manuscript Illustration', *EMc*, v (1977), 299–309

C. Bullock-Davies: *Menestrellorum Multitudo: Minstrels at a Royal Feast* (Cardiff, 1978)

D. Macmillan: 'The Mysterious Cornamuse', *EMc*, vi (1978), 75–8

G. and J. Montagu: 'Beverley Minster reconsidered', *EMc*, vi (1978), 401–15

R.D. Cannon: *A Bibliography of Bagpipe Music* (Edinburgh, 1980)

J. Rimmer: 'An Archaeo-Organological survey of the Netherlands', *World Archaeology*, xii (1981), 232–45

D. Stephens: 'History at the margins: Bagpipers in Medieval Manuscripts', *History Today*, xxxix/Aug (1989), 42–8

REGIONAL BAGPIPES

B. Bartók: *Volksmusik der Rumänen von Maramures* (Munich, 1923); repr. in *Ethnomusikologische Schriften*, ii, ed. D. Dille (Budapest, 1966)

W.A. Cocks: *The Northumbrian Bagpipes* (Newcastle upon Tyne, 1933, 2/1967)

R.D. Katzarova: 'Koprishki gaydi i gaydari', *Vjesnik etnografskog muzeja u Zagrebu*, iii (1937), 14–22

M. Rehnberg: *Säckpipan i Sverige* (Stockholm, 1943)

Bretagne, art populaire, Musée national des arts et traditions populaires, Paris, 23 June – 23 Sept 1951 (Paris, 1951), 101 [exhibition catalogue]

J.M.A. Lenihan and S. MacNeill: 'An Acoustical Study of the Highland Bagpipe', *Acustica*, iv (1954), 231–2

F. Dobrovolný: *Lidové hudebni nástroje na Morava* [Folk musical instruments in Moravia], i (Prague, 1958)

J. Künzig: *Ehe sie verklingen* (Freiberg, 1958)

S. MacNeill and J.M.A. Lenihan: 'The Scale of the Highland Bagpipe', *Piping Times*, xiii (1960–61), no.2, pp.6–10; no.3, pp.6–10; no.4, pp.8–11; no.5, pp.8–11; no.6, pp.6–10; no.7, pp.8–10

C.M. Harris, M. Eisenstadt and M.R. Weiss: 'Sounds of the Highland Bagpipe', *JASA*, xxxv (1963), 1321–7

L. Bonnaud: 'Essai sur une chronologie de la cornemuse', *Bulletin de la Société archéologique et historique du Limousin*, xciv (1967), 207–29

L. Leng: *Slovenské ľudové hudobné nástroje* [Slovak folk-music instruments] (Bratislava, 1967)

I. Macák: 'Typologie der slowakischen Sackpfeifen', *Studia instrumentorum musicae popularis I: Brno 1967*, 113–27

J. Markl: 'Typologie der tschechischen Sackpfeifen', *Studia instrumentorum musicae popularis I: Brno 1967*, 128–33

B. Sárosi: *Die Volksmusikinstrumente Ungarns* (Leipzig, 1967)

R.D. Cannon: 'The Bagpipe in Northern England', *Folk Music Journal*, ii/2 (1971), 127–47

R.D. Cannon: 'English Bagpipe Music', *Folk Music Journal*, ii/3 (1972), 176–219

G. Habenicht: 'Un cimpoier bănăţean' [A bagpiper from Bănăţ], *Revista de etnografie şi folclor*, xvii (1972), 261–97

G. Habenicht: 'Cimpoiul hunedorean' [The bagpipe of Hunedoara], *Revista de etnografie şi folclor*, xviii (1973), 365–408

C. Ahrens: 'Polyphony in *touloum* playing by the Pontic Greeks', *YIFMC*, v (1973), 122–31

F.J. de Hen: 'Folk Instruments in Belgium: Part II', *GSJ*, xxvi (1973), 86–129

G. Habenicht: 'Die rumänischen Sackpfeifen', *Jb für Volksliedforschung*, xix (1974), 117–50

J.K. Partridge and F. Jeal: 'The Maltese *zaqq*', *GSJ*, xxx (1977), 112–44

M. Bröckner: 'Die Sackpfeifen Italiens', *Brussels Museum of Musical Instruments Bulletin*, viii (1978), 16–52

B. Sárosi: 'The Hungarian Bagpipe', *Brussels Museum of Musical Instruments Bulletin*, viii (1978), 1–15

R. Le Moigne: *Quelques éléments sur la tradition populaire de la veuze dans le pays nantais* (Nantes, 1979)

N. Carolan: 'Shakespeare's Uilleann Pipes', *Ceol*, v (1981–2), 4–9

S. Donnelly: 'The Warpipes in Ireland', *Ceol*, v (1981–2), 19–24, 55–9; vi (1983), 19–23

J.F. Chassaing: *La tradition de cornemuse en Basse-Auvergne et Sud-Bourbonnais* (Moulins, 1982)

R. Hollinger: *Les musiques à bourdons, vielles à roue et cornemuses* (Paris, 1982)

H. Boone: *La cornemuse* (Brussels, 1983)

H. Cheape: 'The Making of Bagpipes in Scotland', *From the Stone Age to the 'Forty Five': Studies Presented to R.B.K. Stevenson*, ed. D.V. Clarke and A. O'Connor (Edinburgh, 1983), 596–615

S. Donnelly: 'Lord Edward Fitzgerald's Pipes', *Ceol*, vi (1983), 7–11

M. Levy: *The Bagpipe in the Rhodope Mountains of Bulgaria* (diss., UCLA, 1985)

L. Mabru: *La cornemuse des Landes de Gascogne* (Bazas, 1986)

I. MacInnes: 'Who Paid the Pipers?', *Common Stock*, iii (1986), 18–27

L.-C. Dominique: *Musique populaire en Pays d'Oc* (Garonne, 1987)

R. Butler: *Handbook for the Northumbrian Small Pipes* (Rothbury, 1987)

H. Cheape: 'The Black Chanter of Clan Chattan', *Scottish Pipe Band Monthly*, no.8 (1988), 12–14, 18, 24 only

A. Ricci and R. Tucci: 'Folk Musical Instruments in Calabria', *GSJ*, xli (1988), 36–58

R.D. Cannon: 'Bagpipes in English Works of Art', *GSJ*, xlii (1989), 10–31

P.-U. Allmo: *Säckpipan i Norden* (Stockholm, 1990)

J. Duncan: 'A Man of Marrow', *Common Stock*, v (1990), 21–5

H. Cheape: '"The Bagpiper" [painting] by Sir David Wilkie, 1812–1814: Caricature, Character Study, or Historical Document?' *Common Stock*, vi (1991), 10–15

E. Montbel and J. Blanchard, eds.: *Cornemuses: souffles infinis, souffles continus* (Vouillé, 1991) [incl. L. Bigot: 'Quand on entend le bruit de biniou', 94–7]

D. Moore: 'Bagpipe Woods', *Proceedings of the Piobaireachd Society Conference*, xviii (1991) [unpaginated]

R.A. Schofield: 'Piping in Yorkshire', *Chanter* (1993–4), 59–66

T. Rice: *May it Fill your Soul: Experiencing Bulgarian Music* (Chicago, 1994)

H. Cheape: 'The Piper to the Laird of Grant', *Proceedings of the Society of Antiquaries of Scotland*, cxxv (1995), 1163–73

A.C. Mackenzie: 'Some Recent Measurements on the Scale of the Great Highland Bagpipe', *Proceedings of the Piobaireachd Society Conference*, xxii (1995) [unpaginated]

D. Campbell: 'Eastern Bagpipes: Origins, Construction and Playing Techniques', *Chanter* (1995–6), 8–20

A. Alter: 'Garhwali Bagpipes: Syncretic Processes in a North Indian Regional Musical Tradition', *Asian Music*, xxix/1 (1997–8), 1–16

H. Moore: Interview, *Common Stock*, xiv (1999), 10–21

BAGPIPE MUSIC

G.L. Baldano: *Libro per scriver l'intavolatura per sonare sopra le sordelline* (Savona, 1600); ed. M. Tarrini, G. Farris and J.H. van der Meer (Savona, 1995) [incl. facs.]

C.-E. Borjon: *Traité de la musette* (Lyons, 1672, 2/1678/R)

J. Hotteterre: *Méthode pour la musette* (Paris, 1737/R)

J. Geoghegan: *The Compleat Tutor for the Pastoral or New Bagpipe* (London, c1746)

J. MacDonald: *A Compleat Theory of the Scots Highland Bagpipe* (Edinburgh, 1803/R), ed. R.D. Cannon (Glasgow, 1994)

P. O'Farrell: *O'Farrell's Collection of National Irish Music for the Union Pipes* (London, c1804)

S.T. Colclough: *New and Complete Instructions for the Union Pipes* (Dublin, c1819)

D. MacDonald: *A Collection of the Ancient Martial Music of Caledonia, called Piobaireachd* (Edinburgh, 1822/R)

D. MacDonald: *A Collection of Quicksteps, Strathspeys, Reels and Jigs, arranged for the Highland Bagpipe* (Edinburgh, 1828)

A. MacKay: *A Collection of Ancient Piobaireachd* (Edinburgh, 1838/R)

J.C. Bruce and J. Stokoe: *Northumbrian Minstrelsy* (Newcastle upon Tyne, 1882, rev. 2/1965 with introduction by A.L. Lloyd)

L. Rowsome: *Tutor for the Uillean Pipes* (Dublin, 1936)

A. Campbell: *The Kilberry Book of Ceol Mor* (Glasgow, 1948) [incl. important historical introduction]

Scots Guards Standard Settings of Pipe Music (London, 1954) [incl. history of regimental pipes]

L. Vargyas: 'Die Wirkung des Dudelsacks auf die Ungarische Volkstanzmusik', *Studia memoriae Bélae Bartók sacra*, ed. B. Rajeczky and L. Vargyas (Budapest, 1956, 2/1957; Eng. trans., 1959), 503–40

P. Monjarret: *Waraok, kit! Toniou evit ar bagadou* (Rennes, n.d.)

S. Karakazi: *Ellinika mousika organa* (Athens, 1970)

B. Breathnach: *Ceol Rince na héireann* [Folk music and dances of Ireland] (Dublin, 1971)

A. Janiszewski: *Wielkopolskie dudy, kosioł weselny, kosioł słubny* (Poznań, 1971)

M. Sarisonen: *Kaval, tulum, cifte* (Ankara, n.d.)

The Royal Irish Rangers Standard Settings of Pipe Music (London, 1976) [incl. history of Irish regimental pipes]

J. Mariano Barrenechea: *Alboka: entorno folklórico* (Lecaroz, 1976)

E.O. Covelo: *Leccións de Gaita* (Vigo, 1978)

M. de Santiago: *Metodo de Gaita por cifra y música* (Santiago de Compostela, 1978)

S. Csoóri: *Dudanóták gyüjteménye (énekelt dallamok)* [A collection of bagpipe songs] (Budapest, 1986)

P. James: *Encyclopaedia Blowzabellica: the Blowzabella Tune and Dance Book* (Blyth, 1987)

P. Ladonne: *Méthode de Cabrette* (Riom, 1987)

X. Estévez Vila: *A gaita no eido música* (Vigo, 1987)

B. Sárosi: 'Sackpfeife und Sackpfeifenmusik in Ungarn', *Österreiche Musik Zeitschrift*, xliii/9 (1988), 474–5

K. Govil-Willers and F. Capelle: *Sackpfeifers Notenbuch* (Brensbach, 1992)

J. Goodacre: *Toodle Oodle Bagpipes* (Ashby Parva, 1992)

J. Swayne: *Moebius Music for Three Bagpipes* (Blyth, 1995)

WILLIAM A. COCKS/ANTHONY C. BAINES, RODERICK D. CANNON

Bags. MILT JACKSON. *See also* MODERN JAZZ QUARTET.

Baguala [joi-joi, tonada, vidalita, vidala coya]. A lyric song form of Paraguay and northern Argentina. The *baguala* is characterized by melodies that use only the three pitches of a single major triad. Accompanied by the *caja* (frame drum) and *tambor* (bass drum), it is typically performed in Carnival season by men, women and children, grouped in a circle and singing choruses in unison and in octaves, while a leader uses falsetto and *kenko* (appoggiatura and vocal ornamentation) in the rendition of the main text. *Bagualas* are often sung as part of the music performed at the ritual marking of animals in the Argentine pampa and northern provinces, the *señalada*, accompanied by the *erkencho* (single reed concussion aerophone) and snare drum.

WILLIAM GRADANTE/R

Baguer, Carles [Carlos] (*b* Barcelona, ?13 March 1768; *d* Barcelona, 29 Feb 1808). Catalan composer and organist. He was known affectionately as 'Carlets' to his Catalan contemporaries. Having studied under his uncle Francesc Mariner, in 1786 he succeeded him as organist of Barcelona Cathedral, where he remained until his death. He played an active part in the city's musical life, was much admired for his organ improvisations and attracted many pupils, such as Francisco Andreví y Castellar, Ramón Carnicer and Mateo Ferrer. He was a prolific composer and his work was unusually widely disseminated for a Catalan composer of the day.

Baguer's sacred works testify to a clear Italian influence and he only occasionally used the learned style. His oratorios consist chiefly of four-part homophonic choruses alternating with arias (often with coloratura) and recitative interspersed with arioso passages. His sinfonías fall into two patterns: a single sonata-form movement with a slow introduction, or four movements. In the latter case the second movements take the form of theme and variations and the third are minuets. His style shows a desire to emulate that of Haydn, especially in his use of musical form and his melodic patterns. But in tonal range, thematic treatment, textures and harmonic progressions Baguer's style is simpler and more restrained. His keyboard works, for organ or piano and probably written for his own and his pupils' use, span a broad variety of styles and forms. Some pieces recall the Spanish polyphonic organ tradition. Others in the modern pianistic style combine Italian and Austrian influences with a traditional local style. On the whole, his output bears witness to this singular mixture of influences that affected Catalan music at the time. Baguer's works, however, remain the only surviving examples of a movement of unprecedented diffusion within this geographical area.

WORKS
all MS, principally E-MO and Bc, also Bu, E, SU, TAc and various other Catalan archives

VOCAL
La Principessa filosofa, o sea El desdén con el desdén (op), Barcelona, S Creu, 4 Nov 1797
14 dramas sacros (orats), mostly for S Felip Neri, Barcelona: El santo Job, 1804; La adoración del Niño Dios por los ángeles y pastores, 1805; La partida del hijo pródigo, 1806; La resurrección de Lázaro, 1806; El regreso a Barcelona su patria de Dr Josef Oriol, 1807; El regreso del hijo pródigo, 1807; Cavatina, recitativo y polaca, 1808; Aplaude festivo el mundo; Conozco de tu mano; Coro y aria de tenor; Dios supremo; Grande Dios tu fuerte diestra; La bondad y tierno amor; La mística Raquel: all E-Bc, OL or Manresa, S Maria de la Seu
Secular arias (for bass): Quel amabile sembiante; T'amerò benché tirana
Sacred arias: Al rigor de adversa suerte, A, orch; Bello infante, S, orch; Este nuevo esplendor, A, orch; El dolor, B, orch; Hasta que el cruel, T, orch; Hasta que mi contrario, B, orch; La dulce memoria, T, orch; La tranquilidad, S, orch; Si el arca; Varón perfecto
8 masses, 3–4vv, orch; requiem, 4vv, orch; motets, psalms, lamentations, other sacred works, 3–8vv, orch

INSTRUMENTAL
Orch: Conc., 2 bn, orch; 19 sinfonías, 8 ed. J.M. Vilar (Barcelona, 1996–7), many arr. by Baguer for solo kbd, 3 ed. M.A. Ester-Sala (Madrid, 1984); Pastorela, D
8 duos, 2 fl
Kbd: 7 sonatas, ed. M.A. Ester-Sala (Madrid, 1976); rondos, sinfonías, minuets, contredances, preludes, fugues, versos, other pieces

BIBLIOGRAPHY
B. Saldoni: *Diccionario biográfico-bibliográfico de efemérides de músicos españoles*, i (Madrid, 1868/R)
F. Pedrell: *Catàlech de la Biblioteca musical de la Diputació de Barcelona*, i (Barcelona, 1908)

M.A. Ester-Sala: 'Algunos datos biográficos de Carlos Baguer (1768–1808), organista de la catedral de Barcelona', *RdMc*, vi/1 (1983), 223–51
M.A. Ester-Sala and J.M.Vilar: 'Una aproximació als fons de manuscrits musicals a Catalunya', *AnM*, xlii (1987), 229–44; xliv (1989), 155–66; xlvi (1991), 295–320
J.M. Vilar: 'The Symphony in Catalonia c1760–1808', *Music in Spain during the Eighteenth Century: Cardiff 1993*
J.M. Vilar: *Les simfonies de Carles Baguer: fonts, context i estil* (diss., Autonomous U. of Barcelona, 1994)

JOSEP M. VILAR TORRENS

Baguette (Fr.). A drumstick (as *baguette de tambour*), the stick of a BOW, or a conductor's BATON.

Bahatïrow [Bogatïryov], **Anatol' Vasil'yevich** (*b* Vitebsk, 31 July/13 Aug 1913). Belarusian composer. He graduated from the Conservatory of Belarus' in 1937 where he studied under Zolotaryov. He was chairman of the board of the Belarusian Union of Composers (1938–41 and 1942–9) and pro-rector of the Sverdlovsk Conservatory (1941–3). From 1948 he taught composition at the National Conservatory, Minsk (rector 1948–62, professor 1960, head of department 1962) where his pupils included Hlebaw, Luchanok, Mdivani and Smol'sky. He was awarded many honours including the USSR State Prize (1941). Bahatïrow is one of the founders and leading representatives of the Belarusian school; he composed one of the first national operas – *U pushchakh Palessya* ('In the Virgin Forests of the Poles'ye') – while his contribution to the development of the genres of cantata, oratorio, a cappella chorus and the romance has been considerable. Whether vocal or instrumental, his works are arresting for the richness of their melodies and for their polyphonic textures. Remaining true to traditional tonal thinking, Bahatïrow enriched his style by unique use of natural modal systems and by the employment of rhythmic characteristics of Belarusian folk music.

WORKS
(selective list)

Ops: V pushchakh Palessya [In the Virgin Forests of the Poles'ye] (Ye. Romanovich, after Ya. Kolas: *Drïgva* [Quagmire]), 1939, Minsk, 28 Aug 1939; Nadezhda Durova (I. Keller), 1946, Minsk, 22 Dec 1956
Vocal: Skaz o medvedikhe [The Tale about the She-Bear] (cant., A.S. Pushkin), 1937; Leningradtsï [The Citizens of Leningrad] (cant., Dzhambul), 1942; Belaruskim partïzanam [To the Belarusian Partisans] (cant., Ya. Kupala), 1943; Belarus' (cant., P. Brovka, P. Trus, Kupala), 1949; Belaruskiya pesni [Belarusian Songs] (cant., trad., N. Gilevich), 1967; Yubileynaya kantata [Jubilee Cant.] (Kolas), 1973; Bitva za Belarus' [The Battle for Belarus'] (orat, G. Buravkin, N. Gilevich, A. Kuleshov), 1985; Malyunki rodnaga krayu [Drawings of our Native Land] (cant., trad., Gilevich), chorus, Belarusian folk orch, 1987; choruses, romances, song cycles (A. Akhmatova and others), folk song arrs.
Inst: Pf Trio, 1943; Sonata, trbn, 1946; Sonata, vn, 1946; Sym. [no.1], orch, 1946; Sym. [no.2], orch, 1947; Sonata, vc, 1950; Pf Sonata, 1958; Vc Conc., 1962; Db Conc., 1964; Sonata, db, 1965; 12 Preludes, pf, 1995
Orthodox Church music, incid music, film scores

Principal publishers: Belgiz, Muzgiz, Muzïka, Sovetskiy kompozitor

BIBLIOGRAPHY
T. Dubkova: *Anatol' Bahatïrow* (Minsk, 1972)
T. Dubkova: 'Simfonii Bahatïrowa', *Belaruskaya simfoniya* (Minsk, 1974), 150–61
T. Leshchenya: *O putyakh rasshireniya narodnoy diatoniki v garmonicheskom yazïke kantatï A. Bogatïreva 'Belaruskiya pesni'* [On the ways that Bahatïrow extends folk diatonicism in the harmonic language of his cantata 'Belarusian songs'], *Voprosï teorii i istorii muzïki*, ed. K. Stepantsevich (Minsk, 1976), 36–53

YELENA SOLOMAKHA

Baher, Joseph. *See* BEER, JOSEPH.

Bahia. Brazilian state. *See* SALVADOR.

Bahr [Bähr], **Johann** (*b* ?Schleswig, *c*1610; *d* Visby, Gotland, 3 June 1670). Swedish organist and composer of German birth. He went to Visby, on the Swedish island of Gotland, about 1630 as a poor music student in search of his brother. In 1633 he was appointed assistant organist to David Herlicius at the cathedral there, and at Herlicius's death in 1638 he became organist and registrar. He retained these posts until his death. On his arrival at Visby he had in his possession an organ tablature (now in *S-VIl*) copied in 1611 by Berendt Petri, who was probably a pupil of Jacob Praetorius (ii) in Hamburg. On the inside cover (now missing) he wrote 'Johann Bahr organ m.m.: Anno 1638', and for this reason the book is often misleadingly referred to as the Johann Bahr Tablature Book. His ownership of it suggests that he studied with Praetorius or Petri. The book contains compositions by Praetorius and his father, Hieronymus, as well as many anonymous pieces, possibly by the latter. On pages left blank by Petri, Bahr wrote out two organ pieces and two vocal concertos of his own composition (all ed. in Kite-Powell). The *Magnificat a 4 voci octavi toni* has three verses and is markedly influenced by the style of the pieces in the tablature; *O lux beata Trinitas*, dated 20 March 1655, is in the manner of a chorale fantasia consisting principally of passages using echo devices. The four-part concerto *So ziehet hin* is for two discants (instrumental or vocal), tenor, bass and continuo, and the solo concerto *Befiehle dem Herrn deine Wege*, dated 15 October 1666, is for discant or tenor and continuo (both ed. A. Sjögren, Slite, 1970). All four works are written in the new German organ tablature notation. The alto parts of two other vocal pieces by Bahr, *Adora me in die* and *Die nobis Maria*, are in the Källunge book (*VIl*).

BIBLIOGRAPHY

ApelG

B. Anrep-Nordin: *Johan Bahr: en gotländsk kompositör och organist* (Stockholm, 1914) [orig. pubd in *Musiktidningen* xvi (1914)]

A. Sjögren: 'Johann Bahr: gotländsk tonsättare', *Hundra kyrkornas ö*, xlviii (1970)

J.T. Kite-Powell: *The Visby (Petri) Organ Tablature: Investigation and Critical Edition* (Wilhelmshaven, 1979–80)

JEFFERY T. KITE-POWELL

Bähr, Johann. *See* BEER, JOHANN.

Bähr, (Franz) Josef (*b* 19 Feb 1770; *d* Vienna, 7 Aug 1819). Austrian clarinettist. He was employed as a clarinettist from 1787 to 1794 in the Hofkapelle of Prince Kraft Ernst of Oettingen-Wallerstein. The prince sent him to Würzburg to study with the clarinet virtuoso Philipp Meissner, and in 1794 Bähr left on a concert tour to Potsdam and Ludwigslust. In 1796 he went to Vienna on a tour accompanied by the composer Friedrich Witt. About 1797 he resigned his position and entered the service of Count Johann Joseph Liechtenstein, who had brought his orchestra to Vienna for the season. The Liechtenstein family was associated with Beethoven, and it is quite possible that all of Beethoven's solo clarinet parts composed between 1796 and 1802 were written for Bähr. Reviews of his playing were quite complimentary.

Bähr has often been confused with the better-known virtuoso Josef Beer because of the similarity of names. When both of these clarinettists performed in the same city Bähr received the greater praise for his playing.

BIBLIOGRAPHY

GerberNL

L. Schiedermair: 'Die Blütezeit der Öttingen-Wallerstein'schen Hofkapelle', *SIMG*, ix (1907–8), 83–130

P. Weston: *Clarinet Virtuosi of the Past* (London, 1971)

M. Jacob: *Die Klarinettenkonzerte von Carl Stamitz* (Wiesbaden, 1991)

ALBERT R. RICE

Bähr, Joseph. *See* BEER, JOSEPH.

Bahrain (Arab. Dawlat al Bahrayn). An independent state, consisting of an archipelago of islands, in the ARABIAN GULF.

Bahr-Mildenburg [née Mildenburg von Bellschau], **Anna** (*b* Vienna, 29 Nov 1872; *d* Vienna, 27 Jan 1947). Austrian soprano. Having studied with Rosa Papier, she sang in 1895 to the Hamburg impresario Pollini, including in a formidable audition programme Bellini's 'Casta diva', Weber's 'Ozean, du Ungeheuer', Ortrud's curse, Brünnhilde's battle-cry and arias of Donna Anna and the Queen of Night. Pollini immediately engaged her, and presented her as Brünnhilde in *Die Walküre* on 12 September 1895 in a performance conducted by Mahler.

Anna Bahr-Mildenburg as Clytemnestra in Richard Strauss's 'Elektra'

This was the beginning of a relationship between the young singer and Mahler which was personally emotional and somewhat tempestuous, but artistically harmonious and fruitful. Though greatly admired in Hamburg, she soon followed Mahler to Vienna, where she remained a much valued member of the company from 1898 until 1916, returning as a guest in 1920 and 1921. She excelled in all the great Wagner roles (including Kundry, which she often sang at Bayreuth between 1897 and 1914) and as the heroines of *Fidelio*, *Oberon* and *Don Giovanni* (Donna Anna); she also appeared successfully as Norma and in other Italian parts. In 1906 she was seen at Covent Garden as Isolde and Elisabeth; she made a still greater impression in the Beecham seasons of spring and winter 1910, and in 1913, especially for her masterly study of Strauss's Clytemnestra (see illustration). With such demands placed on it, her voice began to show signs of deterioration, and she gradually relinquished the heavier roles in favour of less vocally strenuous parts. As an intimate friend of the Wagner family, she assisted Cosima in her work at Bayreuth and later undertook similar duties with the Munich Opera. In 1922 and 1925 she appeared as an actress at the Salzburg Festival, and in 1927 gave an operatic recital there at the Mozarteum. Her one recording, made in 1904, is of the recitative only of Weber's 'Ozean' aria, and gives a good, though tantalizing, impression of her brilliant voice and commanding style. In 1909 she married the Viennese author Hermann Bahr (1863–1934).

WRITINGS

with H. Bahr: *Bayreuth und das Wagner-Theater* (Leipzig, 1912; Eng. trans., 1913)
Erinnerungen (Vienna and Berlin, 1921)

BIBLIOGRAPHY
P. Stefan: *Anna Bahr-Mildenburg* (Vienna, 1922)
H.-L. de La Grange: *Mahler*, i (New York, 1973)

DESMOND SHAWE-TAYLOR

Bai, Tommaso. *See* BAJ, TOMMASO.

Baiczka, Franz Xaver. *See* WOSCHITKA, FRANZ XAVER.

Baïf, Jean-Antoine de (*b* Venice, 19 Feb 1532; *d* Paris, 19 Sept 1589). French poet. He was the illegitimate son of Lazare de Baïf (*c*1496–1547), a humanist and translator who served as François I's ambassador to Venice between 1529 and 1534. He studied Latin and Greek under Charles Estienne and Jacques Toussaint (1540–44). Like Ronsard, he continued his studies with Jean Dorat at the Collège de Cocqueret (1547–50) and became associated with the young literary group known as the Brigade and subsequently as the Pléiade. His first significant collection of 42 Petrarchan sonnets with 32 sensual 'baisers' and 'chansons' (based mainly on Latin or neo-Latin elegiac or erotic models) was published in 1552 as *Les amours de J.-A. de B.* and republished in the *Euvres* of 1573 as *Les amours de Méline*. In 1554 he accompanied Jacques Tahureau to Poitiers, where he fell in love with Françoise de Gennes, to whom he dedicated the Italianate sonnets and voluptuous chansons of his *Quatre livres de l'amour de Francine* (1555). Having received the tonsure, he enjoyed four church livings as well as a pension, first granted by François II and subsequently continued by Charles IX, whom he served as secretary. Much of the occasional and official verse which he wrote for the court appeared collectively in the *Euvres* of 1573, as did his neo-classical tragedy *Antigone*, his comedy *Le brave*

(adapted from Plautus and staged in January 1567) and his eclogues.

Important as his innovations in drama and bucolic verse (eclogues) were, Baïf's most radical work dates from 1567, when he experimented with a new poetic style, the *vers mesurés à l'antique*, in order to achieve a closer union of verse and music. Here he made use of the quantitative metres of classical poetry in an attempt to revive the fabled moral and spiritual 'effects' of the ancients. Collaborating with the musician Joachim Thibault de Courville, he founded the Académie de Poésie et de Musique, the statutes of which were confirmed by letters patent from Charles IX. The Académie met regularly at Baïf's Paris home in the Fossés-St-Victor from May 1571 until 1576. It comprised 'musiciens' (poets, singers and instrumentalists) and 'auditeurs' (subscribers) and promoted the composition and performance of *musique mesurée* as well as intellectual, artistic and physical disciplines of many kinds. Henri III changed the enterprise to the Académie du Palais, holding meetings at the Louvre and indulging, under the guidance of Guy du Faur de Pibrac, in more philosophical debate and oratory.

Although the first Académie guarded the art of measured verse and music as secret, Baïf devised a new phonetic orthography in order to fix the pronunciation and thereby to determine the value of syllables and to regulate the laws of prosody. His first extended work in measured verse was a translation of the Psalter, which he began in 1567 (see Groth). He completed a second metrical translation by 1573 and a third, in rhymed verse, by 1587 (see Le Hir); manuscript copies of these, with three books of measured 'chansonnettes', survive (*F-Pn* fr.19140). In 1623 Mersenne referred to another measured version of the *Psalms* in Latin as being set to music by Le Jeune and Mauduit: this is now lost. Some of the psalms were printed, as were settings of *chansonnettes mesurées* (many not in the Paris manuscript) by Courville, Beaulieu and Caietain (1576), Lassus (1576), Le Blanc (1578), La Grotte (1583), Le Jeune (1583–1603), Mauduit (1586) and Du Caurroy (1610). The only collection published by the poet himself was the *Etrénes* (1574), which included official odes and translations of Greek gnomics but which betrayed the basic principles of measured verse by appearing without music.

Baïf reverted to rhymed verse with the Latin *Carminum* (1577) and the three editions of *Mimes, enseignemens et proverbes* (1576, 1587 and 1597), which reflect the new vogue for sententious poetry instigated by Pibrac's *Quatrains* (1574). His last works (*Epitafes de feu M. Anne de Joieuse* and *Prières*) are characterized by religious lyricism. On 1 November 1589 his friend Mauduit rescued his unpublished manuscripts from his home in the suburbs of Paris during the invasion of Henri IV's troops.

Baïf stressed rhythm rather than harmony as the prime element in lyric verse: an innovator in versification and prosody, he helped to establish the Alexandrine (12-syllable line), invented the 15-syllable *vers baïfin* and displayed great diversity of strophic forms and metrical patterns in his odes, chansons, chansonnettes and psalms. The weakness of measured verse was the arbitrary element in quantifying vowels by the 2:1 ratio in a language with accentual rhythm; by establishing fixed rules (he insisted for instance that all vowels followed by two consonants be long) he confused accent and quantity, counting stressed syllables as long and unstressed as short, and thus in many cases ignoring the effects of tonic accent. Yet his experiment had important results for music, liberating the rhythm of the new *air* from the chanson's conventional octosyllabic and decasyllabic lines, creating novel syncopations and fluctuating metres. In this he worked closely with Courville, Guy du Faur de Pibrac, Le Jeune and Mauduit, whom he praised in his poetry. Some of his earlier sonnets and chansons were set by Janequin (RISM 1556[14]), Arcadelt (1557[15]), François Roussel (1559[13]) and Clereau (1559).

Contemporary bibliographies by Antione Du Verdier (1587) and Philippe Maréchal (1598) refer to a collection of 12 *chansons spirituelles* by Baïf set for four voices by Adrian Le Roy in 1562; La Borde's *Essai sur la musique* (1780, iv, p.11) even suggests that the poet wrote both its words and music. Baïf dedicated a sonnet to Adrian Le Roy in Janequin's *Verger de musique* (1559) and in the *Euvres* (1573) there is an epitaph to Alberto da Ripa and an *estrene* to Costeley.

Baïf's measured verse made an immediate impact in England and is reflected in the work of Spenser, Harvey, Sidney, Webbe, Fraunce, Ascham and Campion.

BIBLIOGRAPHY

MersenneHU
M. Mersenne: *Quaestiones celeberrimae in Genesim* (Paris, 1623)
C. Marty-Laveaux, ed.: *Euvres en rime de Jean Antoine de Baïf* (Paris, 1881–90/R)
E.J. Groth. ed.: *Jean Antoine de Baïfs Psaultier* (Heilbronn, 1888)
M. Augé-Chiquet: *La vie, les idées et l'oeuvre de Jean-Antoine de Baïf* (Paris, 1909/R)
H. Chamard: *Histoire de la Pléiade* (Paris, 1939–40/R)
D.P. Walker: 'Musical Humanism in the 16th and Early 17th Centuries', *MR*, ii (1941), 1–13, 111–21, 220–27, 288–303; iii (1942), 55–71; Ger. trans. pubd separately as *Der musikalische Humanismus im 16. und frühen 17. Jahrhundert* (Kassel, 1949)
D.P. Walker: 'The Aims of Baïf's *Académie de poésie et de musique*', *JRBM*, i (1946–7), 91–100
F.A. Yates: *The French Academies of the Sixteenth Century* (London, 1947/R)
D.P. Walker: 'The Influence of *musique mesurée à l'antique*, particularly on the *airs de cour* of the Early Seventeenth Century', *MD*, ii (1948), 141–63
D.P. Walker: 'Some Aspects and Problems of *musique mesurée à l'antique*: the Rhythm and Notation of *musique mesurée*', *MD*, iv (1950), 163–86
Y. Le Hir, ed.: J.-A. de Baïf: *Le psautier de 1587* (Paris, 1963)
G.C. Bird, ed.: *Jean Antoine de Baïf: Chansonnettes* (Vancouver, 1964)
R.J. Sealy: *The Palace Academy of Henry III* (Geneva, 1981)
P. Bonniffet: *Un ballet démasqué: l'union de la musique au verbe dans 'Le Printans' de Jean-Antoine de Baïf et Claude Le Jeune* (Paris and Geneva, 1988)
J. Vignes: *Jean-Antoine de Baïf* (Paris, 1999)

FRANK DOBBINS

Baij, Tommaso. *See* BAJ, TOMMASO.

Baildon, Joseph (*b* c1727; *d* London, bur. 2 May 1774). English composer and singer. He was for some time a lay clerk in Westminster Abbey and in 1754, 1758 and 1759 took part in the Foundling Hospital performances of *Messiah* under Handel. He was described in the subsequent list of Boyce's *Cathedral Music* (1760) as organist of St Luke's, Old Street, and All Saints, Fulham. Baildon's best songs rival those of T.A. Arne and his music for 'When is it best', with which he won the Catch Club prize in 1763, was occasionally borrowed for the theatre by Arne and Stephen Storace (ii).

In accordance with the spirit of the age Baildon sometimes parodied Handel, as for example with the extravagant figuration in 'A Complaint'. The songs in the final version of *The Laurel* almost constitute a song cycle.

His brother Thomas Baildon (*d* London, 1 Oct 1762) was a member of the choirs of St Paul's Cathedral, Westminster Abbey and the Chapel Royal; he sang in the Foundling Hospital performances mentioned above and was also in demand as a soloist. He composed some songs in *Clio and Euterpe* (London, 1758–9).

WORKS
printed works published in London

Sacred: St Luke's, St Luke's New, Fulham, hymn tunes in *Parochial Harmony*, ed. W. Riley (1762); Behold how joyful a thing it is, anthem, in *Harmonia Sacra*, ed. J. Page, ii (1800); Behold how good, anthem, *GB-Lbl*; Melodies for the Psalms … according to the version of Christopher Smart (c1760); single and double chants in *Divine Harmony*, ed. T. Vandermant (1770)

Song collections: A New Favourite Cantata and 2 Songs … sung by Mr Lowe at Vauxhall (1750); The Laurel: a New Collection of English Songs sung by Mr Lowe and Miss Faulkner at Marybone-Gardens (1750–57, enlarged as The Laurel: a Collection of English Songs sung by Miss Stevenson and Mr Beard, c1784); A Collection of New Songs sung … at Ranelagh (1760); A Collection of New Songs, sung by Mr Beard, Miss Stevenson and Miss Formantel (1765); A Collection of Glees and Catches (1768)

Many solo and partsongs pubd singly and in 18th-century anthologies

BIBLIOGRAPHY
Gentleman's Magazine, xxxii (1762), 504 only
W.A. Barrett: *English Glees and Part-Songs* (London, 1886)

PERCY M. YOUNG

Baile. A Spanish term with a wide variety of connotations, all relating to dance. It can refer simply to an occasion for social dancing (thus as an equivalent of the English 'ball'), or to a specific dance type like the waltz or the minuet, or it can be used as the Spanish equivalent of 'ballet'. Some 17th-century writers (e.g. Rodrigo Caro and Gonzalo de Salas) distinguished between 'baile' and the nearly synonymous 'danza', saying that 'danza' referred to a courtly, ceremonious dance using grave and measured steps and little or no arm movement, while 'baile' referred to an energetic dance involving arm gestures, especially if performed in the theatre. Thus pavans were considered 'danzas' while *zarabandas* and *ciacconas* were 'bailes'.

During the 17th and 18th centuries the term 'baile' was used for a specific literary form, a combination of poetry, music and dance performed between the second and third acts of a play (thus resembling the intermezzo; *see* INTERMEZZO (ii)). These *bailes* consisted of rhymed poetry recited by one or more actors to a usually simple musical accompaniment. Despite the dance connotations of the term, not all theatrical *bailes* actually included dancing, although most at least had dance-songs (e.g. sung *minués*). The *bailes* included in the plays of Lope de Vega are considered unusual for their dominance of dance over poetry. *See also* SPAIN, §II, 4.

In Central America 'baile' refers to a genre of music-dramatic spectacle performed at religious festivals that combine Christian and pre-Christian imagery.

BIBLIOGRAPHY
F.A. Barbieri: 'Danzas y bailes en España en los siglos XVI y XVII', *La ilustración española y americana*, xliii–xliv (1887), 330
F. Pedrell: *Teatro lírico español anterior al siglo XIX* (La Coruña, 1897)

E. Cotarelo y Mori: *Colección de entremese, loas, bailes, jácara y mojigangas desde fines del siglo XVI à mediados del XVIII* (Madrid, 1911)

M.N. Hamilton: *Music in 18th-Century Spain* (Urbana, 1937)

☐

Bailecito [bailecito de tierra]. A couple-dance common to the indigenous peoples of Bolivia and northern Argentina, featuring *zapateo* (foot-stamping), handkerchief-waving and other circular movements. Melodies are frequently pentatonic and performed in parallel 3rds to melancholy *seguidilla* verses. A common trait is the contrast between the 3/4 melodies of the voices, violin, harp and accordion, and the syncopated 6/8 accompaniment of the *caja* (frame drum), *bombo* (bass drum), guitar and *charango*.

WILLIAM GRADANTE

Bailey [née Rinker], **Mildred** (*b* Tekoa, WA, 27 Feb 1907; *d* Poughkeepsie, NY, 12 Dec 1951). American jazz singer. She was educated in Spokane, Washington, and began her career on the West Coast as a cinema pianist and radio performer. In 1929 she made her first recording (with Eddie Lang), and from then until 1933 sang with the band led by Paul Whiteman, to whom she was introduced by her brother, Al Rinker, a member of the vocal trio Whiteman's Rhythm Boys. On radio, she sang for the shows of George Jessel and Willard Robison (1934–5) and with Benny Goodman (1939). From 1936 to 1939 Bailey performed Eddie Sauter's arrangements in Red Norvo's band. During the 1930s she was known as the 'Rockin' Chair Lady' because of her renditions of Hoagy Carmichael's song *Rockin' Chair* (1932, Vic.). Despite recurrent illness after 1940, Bailey continued to perform.

Bailey was the first white singer to absorb and master the jazz-flavoured phrasing, enunciation, embellishments, improvisatory fervour and swinging rhythm of her black contemporaries, notably Ethel Waters, Bessie Smith and Billie Holiday. She was essentially a jazz musician and at her best when inspired by a band of the finest players; she often used her voice as if it were the lead instrument, and was a skilled scat singer.

BIBLIOGRAPHY

B. Esposito: 'That Rockin' Chair Lady', *JJ*, xxv/2 (1972), 2–3

S. Dance: *The World of Swing* (New York, 1974), 391–5

H. Pleasants: 'Mildred Bailey', *The Great American Popular Singers*(London, 1974), 143–56

M. Pinfold: 'Dead, but not Remembered', *JJ*, xxx/12 (1977), 12–13, 20 only

D. Chamberlain and R.Wilson, eds.: *The Otis Ferguson Reader*(Highland Park, IL, *c*1982)

L. Gourse: 'Tales of Big-Band-Era Singers', *Louis' Children: American Jazz Singers* (New York, 1984), 100–05

RAYMONDE S. KRAMLICH/R, HENRY PLEASANTS

Bailey, Norman (Stanley) (*b* Birmingham, 23 March 1933). English baritone. He studied at Rhodes University, South Africa, and at the Vienna Music Academy, making his début with the Vienna Chamber Opera as Tobias Mill in Rossini's *La cambiale di matrimonio* in 1959. He sang at Linz (1960–63) and in Germany (1963–7), where his roles included Rigoletto, Boccanegra, Nabucco and Renato. He joined the Sadler's Wells Opera (later the ENO) in 1967, making his British début in Manchester as Mozart's Count Almaviva; he celebrated his 25th anniversary with the company in 1992 as Sharpless. His London début, as Hans Sachs under Goodall (1968), established him as a Wagnerian of more than local importance, and he later undertook the role at Covent Garden, in Hamburg, Brussels and Munich, and at Bayreuth. He was an equally impressive Wotan (in a new production of the *Ring* at the London Coliseum, 1970–73), while at Bayreuth (Gunther, Amfortas) and elsewhere he expanded his Heldenbariton repertory. In 1972, starting with Luna at the Coliseum, he resumed the big Italian roles of his early days in Germany. At the Coliseum Bailey sang Pizarro, Kutuzov (*War and Peace*), the Forester and Prince Gremin. His La Scala début was in 1967 as Dallapiccola's Job. In 1975 he sang Hans Sachs with the New York City Opera and in 1976 made his début with the Metropolitan in the same role. In 1985 at Duisburg he created Johann Matthys in Goehr's *Behold the Sun*. Later roles included Oroveso (1993) and Landgrave Herrmann in *Tannhäuser* (1997) for Opera North. In 1996 he made his Glyndebourne début, as Schigolch (*Lulu*). He was made a CBE in 1977. His timbre was definite, individual, firm, not rich or romantic in an italianate manner. Clarity, incisiveness and high musical intelligence distinguished his interpretations, as can be heard in his authoritative recordings of Wotan and Hans Sachs. His command of musical gesture, his vivid projection and his 'three-dimensional' presentation of a character have given his performances at once romance and uncommon dramatic power. (E. Forbes: 'Norman Bailey', *Opera*, xxiv, 1973, 774–80)

ANDREW PORTER

Bailey, Robert (*b* Flint, MI, 21 June 1937). American musicologist. He received the BA from Dartmouth College in 1959. Following a year of study at the Staatliche Hochschule für Musik in Munich, he began graduate work in musicology at Princeton University. He studied piano with Eduard Steuermann during this time, and his Princeton professors included Oliver Strunk and Milton Babbitt; he received the MFA from Princeton in 1962 and the PhD in 1969. Bailey taught at Yale University from 1964 to 1977. He was on the faculty of the Eastman School of Music, first as associate professor (1977–85) and then as professor (1985–6); in 1986 he was appointed Carroll and Milton Petrie Professor of Music at New York University and a member of the graduate faculty of the Juilliard School.

In his research, Bailey has concentrated on German music of the 19th and 20th centuries, particularly Wagner, Brahms and Mahler, and on 19th-century musical autographs. In addition to his more strictly academic activities, he has lectured on Wagner at the Bayreuth Festival (1990 and 1992) and at the Seattle Opera (1991).

WRITINGS

'Wagner's Musical Sketches for *Siegfrieds Tod*', *Studies in Music History: Essays for Oliver Strunk*, ed. H.S. Powers (Princeton, NJ, 1968), 459–94; repr. in *The Garland Library of the History of Western Music*, ed. E. Rosand, xii (New York, 1985), 91–126

The Genesis of 'Tristan und Isolde', and a Study of Wagner's Sketches and Drafts for the First Act (diss., Princeton U., 1969)

'The Evolution of Wagner's Compositional Procedure after *Lohengrin*', *IMSCR XI: Copenhagen 1972*, 240–46

'The Structure of the Ring and its Evolution', *19CM*, i (1977–8), 48–61

'Visual and Musical Symbolism in German Romantic Opera', *IMSCR XII: Berkeley 1977*, 436–44

'The Method of Composition', *The Wagner Companion*, ed. P. Burbidge and R. Sutton (London, 1979), 269–338

'Musical Language and Structure in the Third Symphony', *Brahms Studies: Washington DC 1983*, 405–22

'Musical Language and Formal Design in the Symphonies of Kurt Weill', *A Stranger Here Myself: Kurt Weill Studien*, ed. K.H. Kowalke and H. Edler (Hildesheim, 1993), 207–15

PAULA MORGAN

Bailleux, Antoine (*b c*1720; *d* Paris, *c*1798). French publisher, composer and teacher. On 27 April 1765 he took over the music publishing house known as A la Règle d'Or, which comprised businesses once owned by Boivin, Ballard and Bayard. During some 30 years he issued many works by both French and foreign composers, the latter including not only early masters like Corelli and Vivaldi, but also some of those who were influential in the development of the emerging Classical school: Carl Stamitz, Haydn, Piccinni, Paisiello, Cimarosa, Boccherini and Clementi. French composers included Gossec, Davaux, Monsigny and Brassac, and some of the earlier generation, Lully, Lalande and Campra. One of his major publications was the *Journal d'ariettes des plus célèbres compositeurs*, comprising 240 works issued in 63 volumes (scores and parts) from 1779 to 1788. Bailleux's adoption of the royal privilege granted to the Ballard family led to his imprisonment during the Terror. He was released after the coup d'état of 9 Thermidor (27 July 1794). His publishing house was taken over by Erard between 1798 and 1801.

Although it was probably as a publisher that Bailleux exerted his greatest influence on French music, his compositions, especially the symphonies, must also be reckoned as interesting contributions to the music of their day. The stimulus of mid-century Italianism in France (after the 1752 performance of Pergolesi's *La serva padrona*, a work which Bailleux was to publish) can clearly be seen in his music. For his first published compositions, *Sei sinfonie a quatro* published by Bayard *c*1758, he even styled himself Antonio Bailleux; in a considerably later work, the *cantatille Pigmalion* (1770), the music is described as being in 'le goût italien' and stands in striking contrast to the Baroque texture of the earlier, more characteristic French cantata. As a teacher Bailleux's qualities may be gauged from his *Méthode raisonée pour apprendre à jouer du violon* cited by La Laurencie as an important contribution to the pedagogy of the subject.

WORKS
all published in Paris

VOCAL

6 cantatilles: Le bouquet de l'amitié, 1v, orch (1758), Borée et Orithie (1760), Le prix de la beauté, 1v, bc (*c*1760), La vengeance de l'Amour, 1v, orch (1761), L'Hymne à Bacchus (1761), Pigmalion (1770)
Ariettes: Le berger malheureux (1758); La timidité (1765); Le ruisselet, with insts (1766); L'amour bravé, with insts (1771); Recueil d'ariettes choisis dans les meilleurs opéra-comiques (1773)
Duos: Duo français (1761); La constance couronnée, S, T, insts (1761)
Les petits concerts de Paris, airs, 1–3vv, some with hpd/hp, vn/fl acc. (1768)
Ode patriotique sur la prise de Toulon par les Français, et 2 romances, pf acc. (1794)

INSTRUMENTAL

6 sinfonia a quatro, 2 vn, va, b (1756–8)
6 symphonies à grande orchestre, op.11 (*c*1767)

PEDAGOGICAL WORKS

Méthode de chant (Paris, 1760)
Méthode pour apprendre facilement la musique vocale et instrumentale . . . et 100 leçons dans le goût nouveau à 1 et 2 parties (Paris, 1770, 3/1770 as Solfèges)
Méthode de guitare par musique et tablature (Paris, 1773/R)

Nouveaux solfèges d'Italie avec la basse . . . suite aux Solfèges (Paris, 1783)
Méthode raisonnée pour apprendre à jouer du violon . . . précédé des principes de musique (Paris, 1798)

BIBLIOGRAPHY

BrookSF; DEMF, i; *FétisB; HopkinsonD; JohanssonFMP; La LaurencieEF*
J.P. Larsen: 'Der musikalische Stilwandel um 1750 im Spiegel der zeitgenössischen Pariser Verlagskataloge', *Musik und Verlag: Karl Vötterle zum 65. Geburtstag*, ed. R. Baum and W. Rehm (Kassel, 1968), 410–23
D. Tunley: *The Eighteenth-Century French Cantata* (London, 1974, 2/1997)

DAVID TUNLEY

Baillie, Alexander (*b* Stockport, 6 Jan 1956). English cellist. He studied with Joan Dickson and Anna Shuttleworth at the RCM (1972–5), with Navarra at the Hochschule für Musik in Vienna (1975–8) and also with Fournier, Pleeth, Rostropovich and du Pré. He was a prizewinner in the ARD Competition in Munich (1978) and the Casals Competition in Budapest (1982). He made his recital début at the Wigmore Hall in 1978 and his orchestral début playing Dutilleux's *Toute un monde lointain* with the BBC SO under Mark Elder in 1981. From 1978 to 1980 he was a member of the Fires of London. Baillie also plays in the Villiers Piano Quartet, and in recital with the pianists Piers Lane and Kathron Sturrock. Several composers have dedicated works to him, including Colin Matthews (First Concerto and *Three Enigmas*), Gordon Crosse (*Wavesongs*), Mark-Anthony Turnage (*Sleep On*) and Richard Rodney Bennett (Sonata). He has also given the premières of Takemitsu's *Orion and Pleiades*, Schnittke's Cello Sonata and Lutosławski's *Grave*. His recordings include Britten's Sonata and suites for solo cello as well as contemporary British works. He was appointed visiting professor at the RCM in 1994 and professor at the Hochschule für Künste in Bremen in 1995.

BIBLIOGRAPHY

M. Campbell: 'Alexander Baillie: a Profile', *The Strad*, xciii (1982–3), 480–84

MARGARET CAMPBELL

Baillie, Dame Isobel (*b* Hawick, Roxburghshire, 9 March 1895; *d* Manchester, 24 Sept 1983). Scottish soprano. She was brought up in Manchester and studied there before going to Milan. She made her London début in 1923 and was for more than 30 years one of Britain's leading oratorio sopranos, particularly renowned for her singing in *Messiah*, *Elijah* and Brahms's *German Requiem*. She sang at Covent Garden in Gluck's *Orphée* in 1937, but did not consider opera her true métier. She was also an engaging recitalist, continuing to sing until well into her seventies. Her voice had a treble-like purity; 'angelic' was sometimes applied to it to suggest the effect, 'not so much personal as brightly and serenely spiritual, made by her soaring and equable tones' (R. Capell, *Grove5*). Her many recordings, particularly her early ones, give a fair idea of her attributes. An autobiography, *Never Sing Louder than Lovely*, was published in London in 1982. She was made a DBE in 1978.

ALAN BLYTH

Baillion [Ballioni, Baillon], **Luigi de**. See BAILLOU, LUIGI DE.

Baillot, Pierre (Marie François de Sales) (*b* Passy, nr Paris, 1 Oct 1771; *d* Paris, 15 Sept 1842). French violinist and composer. He showed remarkable talent when very young and, according to Fétis, was taught first by the Florentine Polidori and then by Sainte-Marie. When his father died in 1783 Baillot was placed under the care of M. de Boucheporn, a high government official, who sent him with his own children to Rome. There he was placed under the tuition of Nardini's pupil Pollani. Between 1791 and 1795 he had a varied life in Paris, first as a violinist in the orchestra of the Théâtre Feydeau (an appointment gained thanks to Viotti, and one that led to a close friendship with Rode), then in the ministry of finance and afterwards in military service. However, his main enthusiasm was for music; when he was ten Viotti's violin playing had fired his imagination. He applied himself with renewed zest to the study of the Classical violin composers and took lessons in composition from Catel, Reicha and Cherubini. After a successful public performance of a Viotti concerto he was appointed professor at the recently opened Conservatoire on 22 December 1795, at first temporarily as Rode's replacement, and then officially on 21 March 1799. In 1802 he joined Napoleon's private orchestra to lead the second violins, and between 1805 and 1808 he toured Russia with brilliant success.

Baillot's excellence as a chamber music player was firmly established when he led a series of concerts in Paris beginning in 1814 – both Mendelssohn and Spohr praised him enthusiastically – and his fame spread to Holland, Belgium and England where he toured in 1815–16. From 1821 to 1831 he was the leader of the orchestra of the Paris Opéra; from 1825 he occupied the same position in the orchestra of the Chapelle Royale, where he was officially appointed in 1827. In 1833 he made a final tour through Switzerland and Italy.

Baillot was the last representative of the Classical Paris school of violinists. A remarkable virtuoso, his playing was distinguished by a noble, powerful tone, neatness of execution and a pure, elevated style. It is said that he hid his face when Paganini played harmonies, left-hand pizzicatos or staccato passages. The founder in France of the first chamber music group of professional musicians, he made a major contribution to the diffusion of a hitherto unknown repertory (principally the quartets and quintets of Boccherini and Mozart and the quartets of Hadyn and Beethoven) as a result of his 154 concerts, organised between 12 December 1814 and 4 April 1840 and attended by an appreciative public; he also scheduled concerts of his own works (notably his 'airs variés') and those of his contemporaries (Cherubini, Onslow and Mendelssohn, but also Kreutzer, Rode, Romberg and Viotti among others). Respectful of the tradition he had inherited, he was responsible for a rediscovery of old music: J.S. Bach, Barbella, Corelli, Germiniani, Handel and Tartini.

A renowned and influential pedagogue, Baillot had numerous pupils, including Mazas, Sauzay, and Charles and Léopold Dancla. A prolific and talented composer, besides nine concertos and a symphonie concertante for two violins, he wrote 'airs' and 'thèmes variés', caprices and études, duos, trios, string quartets and a sonata for piano and violin. Although his compositions are almost entirely forgotten, *L'art du violon* (1834) still holds its place as a standard work. He took a prominent part with Viotti's other two greatest pupils, Rode and Kreutzer, in compiling and editing the *Méthode de violon* and a similar

work for the cello. His obituary notices of Grétry (Paris, 1814) and Viotti (Paris, 1825) and other occasional writings show remarkable critical power and elegance of style. He left an abundance of correspondence.

WORKS
published in Paris unless otherwise stated

ORCHESTRA WITH VIOLIN SOLO

Symphonie concertante, 2 vn, op.38, 1816 (Lyons)
9 concertos: no.1, op.3, 1802; no.2, op.6, c1804; no.3, op.7, c1804; no.4, op.10, c1805; no.5, op.13, 1807; no.6, op.18, 1811; no.7, op.21, 1809; no.8, op.22, 1809; no.9, op.30, c1820
Air russe, op.14, 1808; Thème varié, op.17, 1807; Air russe, op.24, 1807; Air 'Vive Henri IV' varié, op.27; Andante, op.29, 1817; Menuet favori de Pugnani varié, op.36, 1817 (Lyons)

CHAMBER AND SOLO VIOLIN MUSIC

Vn solo, 2 vn, va, b: Air russe varié, op.11, 1810; 3 airs français variés, op.15, 1807; Air russe varié, op.37, c1825
2vn, va, b: 3 airs russes variés, op.20, 1810; Romance variée et air russe, op.23, 1813; Charmante Gabrielle, air varié, op.25, 1814; 3 quatuors, op.34, 1805
2vn, b: 6 trios, op.1, 1800; 3 trios, op.4, 1803; 2 airs variés en trio, op.5, 1803; 3 trios, op.9, 1805; Air varié en trio de Paisiello, op.19, 1810; Air de Grétry varié en trio, op.33, 1815; 3 trios ou sonates, op.39, c1831; 2 trios, unpubd
Vn, pf: 3 airs variés, op.31, 1818; Sonate, op.32, 1820; 3 nocturnes op.35, 1821 (Lyons); Caprice, unpubd
2vn: 3 duos, op.8, 1804; 6 airs russes variés, op.12, 1806 [2nd vn acc.]; 3 duos, op.16, 1811; 24 études, op. posth. (1851) [2nd vn acc.]
Vn, b: 12 caprices, op.2, 1802; Andante, op.26, 1814; Air de la famille Suisse varié, op.28, 1815; Adagio et rondo, op.40; various unpubd pieces

PEDAGOGICAL WORKS

Méthode de violon (with Rode and Kreutzer) (1803/R)
Méthode de violoncelle (with Levasseur, Catel, Baudiot) (1804/R)
L'art du violon: nouvelle méthode (1834)

BIBLIOGRAPHY

BerliozM; EitnerQ; FétisB
L. Spohr: *Selbstbiographie*, ii (Kassel, 1860–61; Eng. trans., 1865/R, 2/1878/R); ed. E. Schmitz (1954–5), 129f
J. Tiersot, ed.: *Lettres de musiciens écrites en français*, i (Turin, 1924); ii (Paris, 1936)
P. Soccane: 'Quelques documents inédits sur P. Baillot', *RdM*, xx (1939), 71–8; xxii (1943), 15 only
B.François-Sappey: 'Pierre Marie François de Sales Baillot (1771–1842) par lui-même: étude de sociologie musicale', *RMFC*, xviii (1978), 126–211
J.-M. Fauquet: 'La musique de chambre à Paris dans les années 1830', *Music in Paris in the Eighteen-Thirties: Northampton, MA, 1982*, 299–326
J. Mongrédien: *La musique en France, des lumières au romantisme: 1789–1830* (Paris, 1986; Eng. trans., 1996)

PAUL DAVID/MANOUG PARIKIAN/MICHELLE GARNIER–BUTE

Baillou [Baylou, Ballion, Baillon, Baglioni], **(Pietro) Luigi** [Louis] **(Francesco) de** (*b* Milan, 27 July 1936; *d* Milan, 14 March 1804). Italian violinist and composer. Burney's erroneous alliance of Baillou with the famous 18th-century family of opera singers – the Baglioni – has led nearly every later writer to distinguish Luigi Baglioni the Stuttgart court violinist from the Milanese Luigi (Louis) de Baillou; but a programme for the ballet *Le premier âge de l'innocence* (in *I-Ma*) clearly states that the music was by 'Monsieur Bailou, formerly in the service of the Most Serene Duke of Württemberg', and a libretto for a Roman production of one of his ballets (Teatro Argentina, Carnival 1789) names the composer 'Sig. Baglioni, *primo viol. del ducal Teatro La Scala di Milano*'.

Grigolato has shown that Baillou was born in Milan, not Paris, as Fétis and others have claimed; this is now confirmed by the discovery of his baptismal certificate in

Milan Cathedral (under the metropolitan parish of S Tecla). There is documentation (in the archives of S Maria presso S Satiro) of the Baillou family's presence in Milan from the second half of the 18th century onwards, although there is no information covering the years Baillou spent there before his appointment at Stuttgart (28 Jan 1762). Baillou may have studied in Paris with the virtuoso violinist Nicolas Capron, as Fétis reported, although no records of any Parisian orchestras of the late 1750s or early 1760s include his name. One of many foreign musicians at Stuttgart, Baillou advanced through the ranks to become first orchestral violin of the ducal orchestra by 1771. Little is known about his activities as a composer there however since the few works attributed to him are of doubtful authenticity. On 19 July 1774 he was dismissed along with all other remaining foreign musicians, and by the succeeding winter he had re-established himself in Milan where he remained until his death.

Between 1 February 1775 and 1 January 1777 Baillou composed scores for six ballets, four of them choreo-graphed by the controversial Noverre, who had been at Stuttgart during Baillou's tenure there. Baillou's name does not appear again in Milanese productions until the inauguration of the Teatro alla Scala one and a half years later; during this period he wrote two ballets for Florence and possibly an opera for Stuttgart. The return to Milan of the choreographer Gasparo Angiolini coincided with Baillou's elevation to the post of opera orchestra director at La Scala (1779), a prestigious position which he held for 23 years. Because Angiolini wrote his own ballet music, Baillou composed for the dance only during the choreographer's sojourn at St Petersburg (1783–8), writ-ing at least seven more ballets for La Scala. Also from 1783 Baillou was principal violinist and occasional spokesman for the newly founded Pio Istituto de' Professori di Musica, an organization which provided employment for musicians and concerts for the city between the carnival and autumn opera seasons.

In January 1797 Bailiou contributed the 'republican' ballet Lucio Giunio Bruto for the first carnival season of Napoleon's occupation of Milan. His last ballet; La disfatta di Abderamo written in collaboration with Capuci, was staged posthumously at the La Scala during the 1809 season. The registration of Baillou's death on 14 March 1804, is held at the church of S Babila, Milan.

In the absence of Baillou's ballet scores and of contemporary evaluations of them, little can be said about the quality of his efforts in his most important genre. His collaborations with Noverre were poorly received by Milanese audiences, but the cause lay with the choreog-rapher, none of whose grandiose ballets succeeded there; indeed, Baillou continued to be called upon as a ballet composer for La Scala and his music was performed in Naples, Rome and elsewhere.

Baillou's orchestral output, which includes five symphonies and an overture, reveals a brilliant, fluent, but not particularly inspired, composer: his themes are based on simple melodic ideas that are often repeated without modification; the harmony is fairly simple as is his orchestration. His pedagogic works include an Arpegio a 4 corde and Solfeggi; his duet for two violins and five trios were also probably composed for teaching purposes as they present only elementary difficulties.

Recent archive acquisitions (in I-Mt) reveal that several of Baillou's children and grandchildren were also musi-cians. These include his son Francesco (b Ludwigsburg, 1772; d Milan (1842), first violin at La Scala and composer of two symphonies (I-Mc); His grandson Giuseppe (b Milan 1796; d Milan, 1739), a violinist at La Scala; and his granddaughter Felicita de Baillou Hillaret (b Milan 1804; d Milan 1871) a mezzo-soprano who sang leading roles at La Scala between 1831 and 1843.

WORKS

BALLETS

all performed as entr'actes; music lost

Rinaldo ed Armida (ballo eroico, 5, J.-G. Noverre), Milan, Regio Ducal, Feb 1775, in C. Monza's Alessandro nell'Indie

Festa di villaggio (Noverre), Milan, Regio Ducal, 1 Feb 1775, in Monza's Alessandro nell'Indie

Le premier âge de l'innocence, ou La rosière de Salency (ballet pantomime, 12 scenes, Noverre), Milan, Regio Ducal, Aug 1775, in Paisiello's La Frascatana

La nuova sposa persiana (3 scenes, Noverre), Milan, Regio Ducal, 27 Jan 1776, in Traetta's La Merope

Il disertor francese (ballo pantomimo, 5, D. Ricciardi), Milan, Interinale, 8 Oct 1776, in Antossi's L'avaro

Andromaca e Pirro (ballo tragico pantomimo, 4, Ricciardi), Milan, Interinale, 1 Jan 1777, in Bertoni's Artaserse

Il Tancredi, Florence, della Pergola, 13 Sept 1777, in Sarti's Medonte, rè di Epiro

La guinguette allemande, Florence, della Pergola, 13 Sept 1777, in Sarti's Medonte, rè di Epiro

Apollo placato (azione teatrale pantomimica, 3 scenes, G. Canziani), Milan, La Scala, 3 Aug 1778, in Salieri's Europa riconosciuta; with recit, aria, chorus by Salieri

Mirza (V. Monari), Milan, La Scala, 9 Aug 1783, in Guglielmi's I fratelli pappamosca

La guinguetta inglese (Monari), Milan, La Scala, 9 Aug 1783, in Guglielmi's I fratelli pappamosca

La zingara riconosciuta (ballo comico pantomimo, 5, Monari), Milan, La Scala, aut. 1783, in Paisiello's Il Socrate immaginario

Giulio Sabino (ballo eroico pantomimo, 5, P. Franchi), Milan, La Scala, 27 Dec 1783, in Tarchi's Ademira

Ludovico il Moro (ballo eroico pantomimo, 5, S. Gallet), Milan, La Scala, 26 Dec 1785, in Rispoli's Ipermestra

Il Vologeso (Gallet), Milan, La Scala, Jan 1786, in Tarchi's Ariarate

Guatimozin, ossia La conquista del Messico (ballo eroico tragico pantomimo, 5, Franchi), Milan, La Scala, Jan 1787, in Zingarelli's Ifigenia in Aulide

Bellezza e onestà, Osia Una cosa rara (ballo eroicomico, F. Beretti), Rome, Argentina, carn. 1789, collab. V. Martín y Soler

Lucio Giunio Bruto (ballo eroico tragico pantomimo, 5, Franchi), Milan, La Scala, Jan 1797, in Zingarelli's Meleagro

Die beiden Nebenbuhlerinnen (Die allzustrenge Probe) (P. Angiolini), Vienna, Kärntnertor, 20 Jan 1809

La disfatta di Abderamo, ossia Consalvo di Cordova (ballo serio, 5, De Rossy), Milan, La Scala, 9 April 1809, collab. A. Capuci, in Weigl's L'uniforme

OTHER WORKS

Aria in Gli avventurieri (op), I-Tf

4 syms., C, Eb, D, d; Ov., C, obbl insts; Padedù e Alemande, A, carn. 1796: Duet, G, 2 vn; Solfeggi, vn, b; Arpegio a 4 corde, vn: all Mc

Sinfonia, A, arr. hpd, IBborromeo; 5 trios, C, Eb, G, F, Bb 2vn, va, OS; Divertimento, Eb, CH-Zz; Marcia, f, F-Pn

DOUBTFUL WORKS

Tancredi (op), Stuttgart Hof, 1770 or 1777, probably identical to ballet of same title

Il casino di campagna (comic op), Stuttgart, Hof, 1777

L'amante generosa (ballet, G. Canziani), Milan, Interinale, aut. 1777

Raimira ed Attida (ballet, L. Bardelli), Pavia, Associati, carn. 1792

BIBLIOGRAPHY

BurneyGN; FétisB; MGG1 (G. Grigolato); SartoriL; StiegerO

G. Chiappari: Serie cronologica delle rappresentazioni drammatico-pantomimiche poste sulle scene dei principali teatri di Milano dall' autunno 1776 sino all'intero autunno 1818 (Milan, 1818–25)

J. Sittard: *Zur Geschichte der Musik und des Theaters am württembergischen Hofe*, ii (Stuttgart, 1891/R), 73, 144, 175–7, 194–7, 203–8, 211ff

R. Krauss: 'Das Theater', *Herzog Karl Eugen von Württemberg und seine Zeit*, i (Esslingen, 1907), 485–554, esp. 507, 530

E. Greppi and others, eds.: *Carteggio di Pietro e di Alessandro Verri* [Oct 1766–Sept 1782] (Milan, 1923), vii, viii, xi

D. Lynham: *The Chevalier Noverre: Father of Modern Ballet* (London, and New York 1950/R), 152

W. Pfeilsticker: *Neues Württembergisches Dienerbuch* (Stuttgart, 1957), i, §885

G. Barblan: 'La musica strumentale e cameristica a Milano nel '700', *Storia di Milano*, xvi (Milan, 1962), 619–60 esp. 654–6 [pubn of the Fondazione Treccani degli Alfieri per la storia di Milano]

G. Barblan: 'L'Ottocento e gli inizi del secolo XX', *Storia di Milano*, xvi (Milan, 1962), 668 [pubn of the Fondazione Treccani degli Alfieri per la storia di Milano]

C. Gatti: *Il Teatro alla Scala nella storia e nell'arte 1778–1963* (Milan, 1964), ii, 147, 149–50, 156, 164

KATHLEEN KUZMICK HANSELL/CARLO BELLORA

Bailly, Henry du [de]. *See* LE BAILLY, HENRY.

Bails, Benito (*b* San Adrián de Besós, nr Barcelona, 4 Feb 1730/31; *d* Madrid, 1797). Spanish mathematician. He attended university in France, at Toulouse and Perpignan. By 1755 he was in Paris, where he was acquainted with d'Alembert and became involved with work on the *Encyclopédie*. He returned to Spain in 1761 and in 1767 was appointed professor of mathematics at the Real Academia de Bellas Artes de S Fernando. He translated numerous foreign scientific writings, publishing them in the ten-volume *Elementos de matemáticos* (1772–83); the eighth volume contains a translation of d'Alembert's *Eléments de musique théorique et pratique*, first published in 1752. An enthusiastic amateur musician, he prepared a Spanish version of Bemetzrieder and Diderot's *Leçons de clavecin, et principes d'harmonie* (Paris, 1771) under the title *Lecciones de clave y principios de harmonia* (Madrid, 1775). In the dedication he described his frustration in endeavouring to learn keyboard improvisation until a friend showed him this work, which proved to be 'the philosopher's stone'. He was helped in preparing the translation by the royal organist Juan Sessé. Bails's version is more a paraphrase than a translation; by suppressing the dialogue form and social small talk of the original, and by rearranging material, he achieved a clearer and more systematic though less entertaining approach to the subject. The modern harmonic concepts, wide-ranging modulations and advanced chord structures illustrated in the work were in striking contrast to the general conservatism of contemporary Spanish music pedagogy.

BIBLIOGRAPHY

SubiráHME

F.J. León Tello: *La teoria española de la música en los siglos XVII y XVIII* (Madrid, 1974)

A. Martín Moreno: *Historia de la música española*, iv: *Siglo XVIII* (Madrid, 1985), 434

F.A. Barbieri: *Biografías y documentos sobre música y músicos españoles*, i, ed. E. Casares (Madrid, 1986), 55

F.J. León Tello: 'D'Alembert en España: los elementos de música especulativa de Benito Bails', *Nassarre*, xi/1–2 (1995), 275–98

ALMONTE HOWELL/ALMA ESPINOSA

Baily, Anselm. *See* BAYLY, ANSELM.

Bainbridge, Simon (Jeremy) (*b* London, 30 Aug 1952). English composer. Son of the painter John Bainbridge, he studied with Lambert (composition) and Sidney Fell (clarinet) at the RCM (1969–72) and with Schuller at Tanglewood (1973–4). He was Forman Fellow in Composition at the University of Edinburgh (1976–8), holder of a USA bicentennial fellowship (1978–9) and composer-in-residence at Southern Arts (1983–5). Subsequently he taught composition at the RCM (1988–2000), the GSM (1990–99), the University of Cardiff (1992) and the University of Louisville (1998-2000); in 1999 he was appointed head of composition at the RAM. His awards include the 1987 Gemini Fellowship, for which he wrote *Cantus contra cantum* for orchestra (1989), and the 1997 Grawemeyer Prize for *Ad ora incerta* (1994), four songs from Primo Levi for mezzo-soprano, bassoon and orchestra.

Bainbridge came to public attention with *Spirogyra* (1970), which already displays a characteristic luminous textural tracery and sensuous melodic nuance. In the works which followed, sonorous surfaces were moulded into gradually unfolding linear structures – in the 1970s exemplified by the expressive sweep of the Viola Concerto (1976), written for Walter Trampler, and the patterned continuities of *Music for Mel and Nora* for oboe and piano (1979, rewritten in 1983 as the *Concertante in moto perpetuo* for oboe and small ensemble). The use of close repetition in the latter work was in part a response to American minimalism, which Bainbridge had experienced during his fellowship year in the USA. But the unpredictability of harmonic change and tension between stasis and directedness gives the music a quality quite its own. The interplay of 'solid' patternings and organic fluidity has remained a fundamental aspect: from the spaced, hypnotic recurrences of the low flute in *The Path to Othona* (1982) and the antiphonally pulsating, long-breathed harmonies at the start of the *Fantasia* for double orchestra (1983–4, rev. 1989); to the variation principle behind the beautifully understated *For Miles* (1994) – a homage to Miles Davis and to be-bop harmony – and the heterophonic *Chant* (1999). The last of these exemplifies Bainbridge's continuing passion for elaborate textures, not least in the intricate relationship of foreground to background layers. It is something which he has explored in a number of other pieces, including *Metamorphosis*, a chamber concerto for 13 players (1988), and the orchestral *Toccata* (1992), in which a long-limbed melody expands spiral-fashion against a polyrhythmic panoply of secondary lines. Though Bainbridge's music has often been built upon abstract ideas, this has rarely been at the expense of an expressive dimension. During the 1990s, a new expressivity emerged, exemplified by the searing melodic richness, at times reminiscent of Berg, of *Ad ora incerta*.

WORKS

Orch: Va Conc., 1976; Fantasia, double orch, 1983–4, rev, 1989; Cantus contra cantum, 1989; Double Conc., ob, cl, orch, 1990; Toccata, 1992; 3 Pieces, 1998

Large ens: 3 Pieces: Spirogyra, 1970, Flugal, 1973, the Path to Othona, 1982; Voicings, 1982; Concertante in moto perpetuo, ob, ens, 1983 [from Music for Mel and Nora, ob, pf, 1979]; Ceremony and Fanfare, 11 brass, 3 perc, 1985; Trace, dance work, 1987; Metamorphosis, 1988; Landscape and Memory, hn, large ens, 1995; Gui Conc., gui, large ens, 1998; Towards the Bridge, 1999

Vocal: People of the Dawn (Navajo Indian text), S, cl + sop sax, 2 cl, perc, pf + cel, 1975; Landscapes and Magic Words, S, ens, 1981; A capella, 6 solo vv, 1985; The Devil's Punchbowl, children's vv, chbr orch, 1987; Folksong, S, 1988; A Song from Michelangelo, S, 2 cl, va, vc, db, 1989; Caliban Fragments and Aria (W. Shakespeare), Mez, chbr orch, 1991; A Song from Tagore, children's vv, ens, va, vc; From an English Folksong, S, 2 cl, va, vc,

1992; Herbsttag (R.M. Rilke), 2 SATB, 1993; Ad ora incerta (P. Levi), Mez, bn, orch, 1994; 4 Primo Levi Settings, Mez, cl, va, pf, 1996; 'Tis Time I Think (A.E. Housman), S, str qt, 1996; Éicha (Bible: *Lamentations*), Mez, SATB, wind ens, 1997; Chant, 12 amp vv, large ens, 1999

Chbr and solo inst: Ww Qnt, 1970–71, rev. 1974; Str Qt, 1972; Ww Qt, 1974; Music for Mel and Nora, ob, pf, 1979; Three Players, vc, b cl, pf, 1985; Path to Othona, hn, 1987; Marimolin Inventions, vn, mar, 1990; Mobile, eng hn, pf, 1991, version for solo va, fl, 2 cl, hp, 1994; Kinneret Pulses, 1992, viol consort; Cl Qnt, 1993; Henry's Mobile, viol consort, 1995; Henry's Rondeau, fl, ob, cl, tpt, pf, 1995 [after Purcell: Suite from Abdelazar]; 60 Seconds for Elliott, cl; Dances for Moon Animals, gui, 1999

Principal publishers: Chester Music, United Music Publishers

BIBLIOGRAPHY

P. Griffiths: 'Simon Bainbridge', *New Sounds, New Personalities: British Composers of the 1980s in Conversation* (London, 1985), 39–45 [interview]

D.C.F. Wright: 'An Introduction to Bainbridge', *MT*, cxxix (1988), 294–7

G. Thomas: 'L'emploi du temps', *MT*, cxxxvi (1995), 585–8

MICHAEL ZEV GORDON

Bainbridge, William (*d c*1831). English woodwind instrument inventor, maker and player and music publisher. Having originally trained as a turner, he began his career playing oboe, flute and flageolet at two London theatres. As maker, his first patent was in 1803 for a new model of 'English flageolet', which, by changing the fingering of the tonic from six to three fingers, led in about 1805 to the development of his double flageolet model in collaboration with John Parry (ii) (1776–1851). Between 1808 and 1821 he was in partnership with John Wood as Bainbridge & Wood, writing and publishing tutors and music for his instruments. From *c*1830 to 1835 the business was continued by Bainbridge's widow Harriet, and thereafter until 1855 by his successor, Hastrick, whose mark usually included the words 'late Bainbridge, inventor'.

The firm's speciality was the 'English flute' or 'English flageolet' – not to be confused with the French or the 'quadrille' flageolet – in its single, double and occasionally triple form. In addition they made single and double concert flutes with flageolet-type heads to be held transversely. These instruments, designed for amateurs of both sexes, enjoued enormous popularity, the double flageolet being much plagiarised (in spite of two unsuccessful legal actions) by rival makers both at home and abroad. Bainbridge was perhaps the earliest wind-instrument maker with the all-round abilities required to launch such projects successfully, combining single-handedly as he did the diverse skills of inventor, performer, teacher, manufacturer, author and publisher.

WRITINGS

Observations on the cause of imperfections in Wind Instruments, particularly of German Flutes … also remarks on Oboe, Clarionet, & Bassoon Reeds (London, 1823)

BIBLIOGRAPHY

Waterhouse-LangwillI

W.R. Waterhouse: 'Das Doppelflageolett: "Made in England"', *Flöten, Oboen und Fagotte des 17. und 18. Jahrhunderts [I]: Blankenburg 1991*, 42–6; repr. in *Tibia*, xx (1995), 337–43; Eng. trans., rev., in *GSJ*, lii (1999), 171–82

PHILIP BATE/WILLIAM WATERHOUSE

Baines, Anthony C(uthbert) (*b* London, 6 Oct 1912; *d* Farnham, Surrey, 2 Feb 1997). English musicologist, conductor and instrumentalist, brother of the double-bass player and composer FRANCIS BAINES. During his educa-

tion at Westminster School (King's Scholar, 1925–30), his musical talents became evident, encouraged by the school director of music, C. Thornton Lofthouse. In 1930 he went to Christ Church, Oxford, where he studied natural sciences and graduated with honours in chemistry in 1933. The award of an open scholarship to the RCM changed the direction of his career, and after two years' study devoted mainly to the bassoon he joined the LPO as third bassoon and double bassoon in 1935. This appointment (interrupted by six years' army service) continued until 1948 and led to his election as assistant conductor in 1949. The following year he became associate conductor to the International Ballet Company, but remained a regular conductor of the LPO Schools Concerts. Between 1955 and 1965, as teacher of wind instruments at Uppingham School and later Dean Close, Baines devoted himself to the training of young musicians. During this period his musicological activities expanded greatly, and he travelled extensively in Europe studying both folk and art instruments and taking part in international conferences. From 1970 to 1980 he was a lecturer in music at Oxford University and curator of the Bate Collection of wind instruments there. By his retirement in 1982 he had enlarged its scope and content and created a unique resource centre for the practical study of musical instruments of all periods. A founder-member of the Galpin Society, he edited its journal from 1956 to 1963, and again from 1970 to 1984. His writings are chiefly concerned with instruments, particularly wind instruments, and their history, however, as a man of many parts, his career emcompassed several diverse fields. As an organologist of world rank, his writings are informed by a rare combination of enthusiasm, with and authority, backed by an unrivalled range of practical experience and research. Some of his books are now standard texts, and many have also appeared in German and Italian. The American Musical Instrument Society presented the Curt Sachs Award to him in 1985 for his contribution to a 'fuller understanding of the parallels and interactions between folk and art traditions'. Elected Ordinary Fellow of the British Academy in 1980, he received the degree of D. Litt. from Oxford University in 1977, and of D. Mus. from Edinburgh University in 1994. He is survived by his wife Patricia, née Stammers, whom he married in 1960.

WRITINGS

'James Talbot's Manuscript, I: Wind Instruments', *GSJ*, i (1948), 9–26

'Fifteenth-Century Instruments in Tinctoris's *De inventione et usu musicae*', *GSJ*, iii (1950), 19–26

'Two Cassel Inventories', *GSJ*, iv (1951), 30–38

'Shawms of the Sandana Coblas', *GSJ*, v (1952), 9–16

'Two Curious Instruments at Verona', *GSJ*, vi (1953), 98–9

Woodwind Instruments and their History (London, 1957, 3/1967)

Bagpipes (Oxford, 1960, 3/1995) [on the Pitt Rivers Museum collection]

ed.: *Musical Instruments through the Ages* (Harmondsworth, 1961, 2/1966/R)

European and American Musical Instruments (London, 1966)

Catalogue of Musical Instruments, ii: *Non-Keyboard Instruments* (London, 1968) [on the Victoria and Albert Museum collection]

'The Evolution of Trumpet Music up to Fantini', *PRMA*, ci (1974–5), 1–9

ed.: *The Bate Collection of Historical Wind Instruments: Catalogue* (Oxford, 1976)

ed.: *Brass Instruments: their History and Development* (London, 1976)

ed.: *The Oxford Companion to Musical Instruments* (Oxford, 1992)

BIBLIOGRAPHY
J. Montagu: 'Anthony Baines, 1912–97', *EMc*, xxv (1997), 345–6
J. Rimmer: 'Anthony Cuthbert Baines (1912–1997): a Biographical Memoir', *GSJ*, lii (1999), 11–26

PHILIP BATE

Baines, Francis (Athelstan) (*b* Oxford, 11 April 1917; *d* Ballydehob, Cork, 4 April 1999). English double bass player, viol player and teacher, brother of ANTHONY C. BAINES. He studied at the RCM, London (including composition with Herbert Howells), and became principal double bass of the Boyd Neel Orchestra and, later, the Philomusica, performing on an instrument by Nicolas Amati. In the 1970s he played with the newly formed period-instrument orchestras such as the Academy of Ancient Music. In 1959, with his wife June, he founded the JAYE CONSORT OF VIOLS, which gave over 70 broadcasts. To popularize the Jaye Consort in its early days, Baines would also perform medieval music on medieval bagpipes, harp, pipe and tabor, and shawm. The Baines's sweet and lyrical treble-viol playing, modelled on the English choral tradition, heralded a new approach to the instrument. However, Baines's greatest legacy is perhaps as a teacher. He had an intuitive feel for period instruments which made them come to life for a generation of students, notably those studying at the RCM where he founded and directed the (conductorless) Baroque orchestra. The debt felt to him by the early music fraternity was demonstrated by the 'Concert to remember Francis and June Baines' on 20 June 1999 in which many of the most distinguished British players performed, among them Alison Bury, Monica Huggett, Annette Isserlis, Catherine Mackintosh and Andrew Parrott. Baines also composed three symphonies, two overtures, a violin concerto and many chamber works.

WRITINGS
'Life with the viol: Francis Baines talks about the Jaye Consort and the revival of a tradition', *EMc*, vi/1 (1978), 45–6

BIBLIOGRAPHY
P. Holman and others: 'Obituary: Francis and June Baines', *EMc*, xxvii/3 (1999), 508–9

LUCY ROBINSON

Baines, William (*b* Horbury, Yorks., 26 March 1899; *d* York, 6 Nov 1922). English composer and pianist. Although he came from a musical background (his father was a chapel organist and cinema pianist), his only training in composition came through lessons at the Yorkshire Training College of Music in Leeds and advice from the pianist Frederick Dawson. After a productive year in 1917, which saw many new compositions and his first solo recital, he was called up for military service in 1918. On his return to York in 1919 he worked as a relief pianist for his father at the Fossgate Cinema. His local concert recitals featured the works of Debussy, Ravel, Bridge and Scriabin in addition to his own compositions. Ill-health, exacerbated by influenza contracted in 1918 while in the army, led to his early death.

Baines was primarily a composer of impressionistic piano miniatures. The full spectrum of his style is encapsulated in the *Seven Preludes* (1919), whose characteristics range from virtuoso brilliance to rhapsodic contemplation, and from a lush Romanticism to sparse textures and acrid harmonies. A love of nature, frequently expressed in his diaries, is revealed in works such as *Paradise Gardens* and *Tides*. His fascination with light inspired a number of his later piano pieces, including the evocative 'Glancing Sunlight' from *A Last Sheaf*. Baines was an inveterate reviser, and works such as the F♯ minor Piano Sonata underwent a number of metamorphoses. His other notable composition is a symphony, which, despite its individuality and original orchestration, was not performed until 1991.

WORKS
(selective list)

PIANO

3 Slumber Songs, op.6, 1917; 4 Miniature Tone Pictures, 1917, withdrawn 1922; Impression from Cherry Ripe, 1917, withdrawn 1922; 5 Pieces, op.8a, 1917; 3 Impressions, op.9, 1917; 2 Elegies, op.11, 1917; 3 Playtime Sketches, op.12a, 1917; Sonata no.2, a, op.13, 1917; 6 Pieces, op.14, 1917; Rococo, 1917; Passion of Destiny, 1917, unfinished; 4 Sketches, 1917–18; 6 Dream Impressions, op.16, 1918; Sonata, f♯, op.4, 1918, rev. 1919 and 1921; Poem, B, op.6/2, 1918; Introduction and Valse Caprice, op.3/1, 1918; Concert Study, a, op.6/3, 1918; The Island of the Fay, 1918–19; Paradise Gardens, 1918–19; 7 Preludes, 1919; Dead Heart Flower, 1919
The Little Wavelets, 1919 [from Sonata no.2]; February Pastoral, 1919; Vale of Memories, 1919; 4 Poems, 1919–20; Coloured Leaves, 4 pieces, 1919–20; 3 Concert Studies, 1919–20; Milestones, 3 pieces, 1920; Prelude, D♭, 1920; Cyril Scott Fragment, 1920; Silverpoints, 4 pieces, 1920–21; Tides, 2 pieces, 1920–21; Pictures of Light, 3 pieces, 1920–22; 7 Preludes, set 2, 1920–22; Prelude and 7 Diversions, 2 pf, 1921; Twilight Pieces, 3 pieces, 1921; Poème de concert, 1921 [from final movt of Sonata, 1919]; Idyll (Nocturne), 1921, rev. 1922; Prelude-Filigree, 1921; A Last Sheaf, 4 pieces, 1921–2

OTHER WORKS

Orch: Sym., c, op.10, 1917; Andante, a, 1918–19; Island of the Fay, 1918–19 [arr. of pf work]; Prelude to a Doll's Ballet, str, 1920; Thought Drift, 1921 [arr. of no.3 of Twilight Pieces]; Poem [from Poème de concert], pf, orch, 1921
Chbr: Pf Trio, d, op.5/2, 1917, rev. 1 movt, 1918; Aubade, op.8b, str qt, 1917; Sonata, G, vn, pf, 1917, rev. 1919; Str Qt, E, op.2, 1917–18; 2 Pieces, vc, pf, 1918; Romance, F, vc, pf, 1918; Rain Splash, vc, pf, 1919, unfinished; Marionettes, vn, pf, 1919; Piece, C, str qt, 1919; Rhapsody, f♯, str qt, 1920; Dream Temple, vn, pf, 1920; 2 Fragments, str qt, 1920–21; Andante, str qt, 1922
Songs: 2 Songs, op.12b, 1917; Nights of Music, 1919; 5 Songs, 1919

MSS in *GB-Lbl*
Principal publishers: Augener, Elkin

BIBLIOGRAPHY
P.J. Pirie: 'William Baines', *Music and Musicians*, xxi/3 (1972–3), 36–40
R. Carpenter: *Goodnight to Flamboro': the Life and Music of William Baines* (Rickmansworth, 1977)
F. Richards: 'William Baines and his Circle', *MT*, cxxx (1989), 460–63

FIONA RICHARDS

Baini, Giuseppe (Giacobbe Baldassarre) (*b* Rome, 21 Oct 1775; *d* Rome, 21 May 1844). Italian musicologist and composer. At 13 he entered the Seminario Romano and studied there under Stefano Silveyra. In 1795 he was accepted as a member of the choir of the papal chapel, even though he was not yet a priest (he became one in 1798). He studied singing with a bass from the choir, Saverio Bianchini, and, from 1802, counterpoint with Giuseppe Jannacconi. He was probably also a pupil of the organist G.B. Batti and of his uncle, the composer Lorenzo Baini. In 1814 he was entrusted with the reorganization of the archives of the papal chapel and in 1819 became *camerlengo* (general administrator) of the college of papal singers, an elective office which he held until his death. In 1825 he was made an examiner at the Congregazione di S Cecilia, although he was not a member of it. His efforts to persuade the pope to found a school of singing and a conservatory were unsuccessful. A member of many European academies and the teacher of numerous composers and musicologists, among them Cartoni, La Fage, Nicolai, Proske and Hiller, he spent the last part of his life in extreme seclusion.

Baini was most important as a Palestrina scholar. It is to him – and to Alfieri, who continued his work after his death – that one owes the publication of a large number of Palestrina's works in the seven volumes of the Raccolta di Musica Sacra (Rome, 1841–6). The *Memorie storico-critiche*, in spite of its many failings in historical and philological method and its inaccuracies of fact, was the first attempt to provide a full and systematic view, biographical and musicological, of Palestrina. It contains much information on previously unknown composers. Baini also planned and gathered material for a history of the papal chapel, which was never written.

Baini demonstrated his devotion to the Roman tradition also on the political level, as a defender of the Catholic Church in its conflict with the Napoleonic empire. This resulted in some polemical works and in his refusing in 1811 the leadership of the ecclesiastical part of the reform of the Church within the empire. In 1838 he refused Spontini his support for a reform of sacred music because of his mistrust of the Prussian Protestant culture which Spontini at that time served. This aloofness and conservatism also influenced his own music, which aimed at an anachronistic and impossible reinstatement of the past, represented by Palestrinian polyphony. For the same reasons Baini did not understand the music of his own time, particularly instrumental music, to which he was strongly averse.

WRITINGS
all MSS in I-Rc

Dissertazione sopra i tuoni del canto gregoriano con l'aggiunta in fine delle regole per gli istromenti ebdomadarj: scritta a maggior chiarezza per interrogazioni e risposte ad uso de' cappelani-cantori pontificj (MS)

Regole circa il modo di cantare le Lezioni, le Lamentazioni ed i Capitoli, e di intuonare il canto gregoriano secondo lo stile osservato dai cappellani-cantori della Cappella pontificia: epilogate da uno de' cappellani suddetti l'anno 1806 (MS)

Breve notizia istorica e regole del contrappunto solito farsi da' Cantori pontificj nel cantare il canto gregoriano; e per incidenza, si tratta la questione se i cantori della Cappella giulia nella Basilica vaticana siano più antichi o almeno fosse immutato il loro corpo per formare a parte li cappellani-cantori pontificj (MS)

Mottetto a quattro cori del sig. maestro D. Marco Santucci premiato dall'Accademia Napoleone in Lucca, l'anno 1806 (n.p., 1807)

Difesa del solfeggiamento regolato dalla variazione de' tuoni, contro i partigiani delle mutazioni, del setticlave e dell'unica lettura (MS, 1808)

Dimostrazione della preminenza del solfeggio con dodici monosillabi, sopra tutti gli altri sistemi di solfeggio (MS, 1808)

L'artificio e le regole da osservarsi nel comporre sorte di canoni: 1° monotoni ne' quali la guida sia una sola parte; 2° monotoni ne' quali la guida sia in quattro parti; 3° sopra una sola riga (MS, 1808)

Controversia musicale fra Giuseppe Baini, cappello-cantore pontificio ed i sig. esaminatori della vener. Congregazione de' musici di S. Cecilia di Roma insorta per il pubblico concorso delli 2 maggio 1809, in cui fu rimesso a nuoo esame il giovinetto Giuseppe Giovannini, alunno nella vener. pia Chiesa degli orfani (MS, 1809)

Seconda Lettera ... ai venerat. sig. Maestri esaminatori della Congregazione di S. Cecilia, sullo stesso soggetto (MS)

Trattato della fuga sul canto fermo (MS)

Risposta di Giuseppe Baini, cappellano-cantore pontificio all'opuscolo del sig. Maestro Giuseppe Rossi, impresso in Terni nel 1809, col titolo 'Alli intendenti di contropunto': opuscolo dove oltre la principal questione circa gli accordi da darsi alla scala, si dilucidano alcuni punti quanto interessanti altretanto oscuri della scienza musica (MS, 1810)

Saggio sopra l'identità de' ritmi musicale e poetico (Florence, 1820)

Tentamen renovationis musicae harmonicae syllabico-rhythmicae, super cantu gregoriano, saeculo primo in ecclesia pervulgatae (MS)

Memorie storico-critiche della vita e delle opere di Giovanni Pierluigi da Palestrina, cappellano-cantore, e quindi compositore della cappella pontificia, maestro di cappella delle basiliche Vaticana, Lateranense e Liberiana, detto il principe della musica (Rome, 1828/R); 1st 6 chaps. ed. A. Cametti: *La critica musica* (1918–23)

Disquisizione sopra le note di canto delle sei sequenze o ritmi di Pietro Abelardo detti 'Pianti' (MS)

Risposta ai dubbj proposti al sig. Maestro Basily dal Maestro Catrufo con lettera dei 29 septembre 1843, da Londra (MS)

Intorno alla creazione di una scuola di musica nella pia casa di lavoro detta 'Delle terme Diocleziame' (MS)

BIBLIOGRAPHY

DBI (R. Meloncelli)

A.M. Carcano: 'Cenni biografici intorno a Monsignor D. Giuseppe Baini', *Diario di Roma* (3 Sept 1844)

A. de La Fage: *Miscellanées musicales* (Paris, 1844/R)

G. De Ferrari: 'Biografia di Monsignor D. Giuseppe Baini', *Giornale arcadico di scienze, lettere ed arti*, cxxxi (1850), 328–92

P. Alfieri: 'Biografia di Monsignor Giuseppe Baini', *Gazzetta musicale di Milano*, xiv (1856), 153–267

A. de La Fage: 'Notice sur la vie et les ouvrages de Joseph Baini', *Essais de diphthérographie musicale* (Paris, 1864/R), 17–60 [includes description of MSS in *I-Rc*]

F.X. Haberl: 'Zum 50. Todesjahre von Joseph Baini: eine biographische Skizze', *KJb*, ix (1894), 77–85

G. Stanghetti: 'Nota biografica su Giuseppe Baini', *NA*, i (1924), 290 only

O. Ursprung: 'Palestrina und Deutschland', *Festschrift Peter Wagner* (Leipzig, 1926), 190–221

K.G. Fellerer: 'Verzeichnis der kirchenmusikalischen Werke der Santinischen Bibliothek', *KJb*, xxvi (1931), 126–7

J.M. Llorens: *Cappellae sixtinae codices musicis notis instructi* (Vatican City, 1960)

A. Della Corte: *La critica musicale e i critici* (Turin, 1961)

R. Giazotto: 'La Congrégation de Sainte-Cécile et le retour à la culture classique dans la Rome musicale du début du XIXième siècle', *RBM*, xxvi–xxvii (1972–3), 7–13

S.L. Balthazar: 'The Rhythm of Text and Music in Ottocento Melody: an Empirical Reassessment in Light of Contemporary Treatises', *CMc*, no.49 (1992), 5–28

R. Boursy: *Historicism and Composition: Giuseppe Baini, the Sistine Chapel Choir, and Stile Antico Music in the First Half of the 19th Century* (diss., Yale U., 1994)

SERGIO LATTES

Bainton, Edgar (Leslie) (*b* London, 14 Feb 1880; *d* Sydney, 8 Dec 1956). English composer, pianist and teacher. He studied at the RCM under Stanford and Franklin Taylor. In 1901 he was appointed to teach the piano and composition at the Newcastle Conservatory of which he became principal a few years later. He was on the Continent at the outbreak of World War I and was interned at Ruhleben. On his return to Newcastle he resumed his activities as teacher, pianist, conductor and composer until the end of 1933, when he was appointed director of the New South Wales State Conservatorium, Sydney. Immediately before his departure he was elected an FRCM and awarded an honorary DMus by the University of Durham. In Sydney he exercised a strong influence on the development of musical life, particularly through his fine conducting. His symphony 'Before Sunrise' won a Carnegie Award in 1917. Bainton was less affected by the modality of English folksong than were many contemporaries, although much of his work has a pastoral tone. He was drawn to late-Romantic harmony, yet even his richest writing never obscures the direct lyrical impulse. His works have clarity of form and show a high degree of craftsmanship. One of his major works, *The Pearl Tree*, was produced with great success in Sydney in 1944.

WORKS
(selective list)

Ops: Oithona, 1906, lost; Walookie the Bear (children's operetta, R. Buckley), 1912; The Crier by Night (G. Bottomley), 1919, unpubd; The Pearl Tree (R.C. Trevelyan), 1927, unpubd

Vocal orchestral: The Blessed Damozel, 1907, Sym. 'Before Sunrise', 1907; Sunset at Sea, 1910; The Making of Viola (cant.), 1913; The Vindictive Staircase, 1913; A Song of Freedom and Joy, 1920; The Tower, 1923; The Dancing Seal, 1926; Hymn to God the Father, 1926; 5 unpubd works incl. An English Idyll, 1946

Orch: Conc. fantasia, pf, orch, 1920; Pavane, Idyll and Bacchanal, str, 1924; 14 unpubd works incl. 3 Pieces, 1920; Epithalamion, 1929; Sym. no.2, 1940; Sym. no.3, 1956

Other works: Str Qt, A, 1915, rev. 1920; Sonata, va, pf, 1922; Sonata, vc, pf, 1924; 2 other chbr pieces; Fantasia on 'Vexilla regis', org, 1925; 32 pf works; over 100 songs, over 100 unison and partsongs

Principal publishers: Boosey & Hawkes, Novello, OUP, Stainer & Bell

BIBLIOGRAPHY
H. Bainton: *Remembered on Waking* (Sydney, 1960)
D.E. Tunley: 'Thoughts on the Music of Edgar Bainton', *Westerly* (1963), no.2, p.55–7
M. Jones: 'Edgar Bainton: Musical and Spiritual Traveller', *Journal of the British Music Society*, xii (1990), 19–40
DAVID TUNLEY/MICHAEL JONES

Bainville, François (*b* Chartres, 1 April 1725; *d* Chartres, 26 Sept 1788). French organist and composer. He began his musical training as a choirboy in Chartres Cathedral. In September 1741 he received permission to play the organ there, provided he was properly supervised, and he was soon substituting for the cathedral organist J.-P. Dumail. He later played the organ at the Benedictine abbey of St Père-en-Vallée (now the parish church of St Pierre, Chartres). In 1751 he married Marie-Claude Renault, an organist in the parish of Ste Marguerite, Paris, and they moved to Paris in about 1754. In 1763 he was appointed organist of the Cathedral of St Maurice in Angers. Four years later his only known published work, *Nouvelles pieces d'orgue, composées sur différens tons*, appeared in Paris and Angers. Bainville retired from his post at Angers in 1782 and, having been granted a pension on full pay by the cathedral chapter, returned to Chartres. According to Port, Bainville had a son (name not given) who served as organist of St Pierre (? at Angers) and who 'soon departed for Paris'.

BIBLIOGRAPHY
EitnerQ; FétisB; GerberL
Mercure de France (April 1767), ii, 145 only
C. Port: *Dictionnaire historique, géographique et biographique de Maine-et-Loire* (Paris, 1874–8, 2/1965)
L. Merlet: *Bibliothèque chartraine antérieure au XIXe siècle* (Orléans, 1882)
J.A. Clerval: *L'ancienne maîtrise de Notre-Dame de Chartres du Ve siècle à la Révolution* (Chartres, 1898/R)
M. Jusselin: *Les orgues de Saint-Pierre de Chartres depuis leur origine, 1592–1922* (Chartres, 1922)
KENNETH LANGEVIN

Baiocchi, Regina Harris (*b* Chicago, 16 July 1956). American composer and writer. She studied at Roosevelt and De Paul universities, where her teachers included Robert Lombard and George Flynn. She has also studied jazz piano with Alan Swain and composition with Hale Smith. Her music reveals an eclectic mixture of idioms and techniques, from serialism to black American folk music. Jazz is seldom far from the surface in *Sketches* (1992) and *Gbeldahoven: No One's Child* (1996), an opera based on the lives of Harlem Renaissance writers Zora Neale Hurston and Langston Hughes that includes numbers inspired by African chant, spirituals, blues, jazz, gospel, work songs and rap music. The aria 'How It Feels to Be Colored Me' shares motivic material with the final movement of the brass quintet *QFX* (1993); both are based on a 12-note series she describes as her 'stand-by tone row', as well as on black American harmonies and rhythms. Her African heritage also provides sounds for *African Hands* (1997), a concerto for African drummer and orchestra. Works showing a strong influence of jazz include *Miles Per Hour* for trumpet (1990), which recalls the style of Miles Davis, and *Friday Night* (1995) for jazz singer and ensemble.

WORKS
(selective list)

Op: Gbeldahoven: No One's Child, 1996

Inst: Equipoise by Intersection, pf, 1978; Miles Per Hour, tpt, 1990; Orch Suite, 1992; Sketches, vn, vc, pf, 1992; QFX, brass qnt, 1993; After the Rain, sax, pf, perc, 1994; Deborah, pf, perc, 1994; Liszten, My Husband Is Not a Hat, pf, 1994; Kidstuff, chbr ens, 1995; African Hands, african drummer, orch, 1997; Message to My Muse, pf, 1997

Vocal: Black Voices, rap singers, perc, 1992; Best Friends, S, B, pf, 1993; Friday Night, 1v, jazz ens, 1995

MSS in Center for Black Music Research, Chicago

BIBLIOGRAPHY
S. Honaker: 'A Musical Fete for Kids', *Chicago Tribune* (1 Oct 1995)
H. Walker-Hill: *Music by Black Women Composers* (Chicago, 1995)
B. Herguth: 'First Opera is a Dream Come True', *Chicago Sun Times* (6 Oct 1996)
KARIN PENDLE

Baird, Tadeusz (*b* Grodzisk Mazowiecki, 26 July 1928; *d* Warsaw, 2 Sept 1981). Polish composer. He first studied composition in Warsaw during World War II with Woytowicz and Kazimierz Sikorski. He was taken prisoner by the Germans in 1944 after the Warsaw Uprising, and after liberation underwent treatment for spinal tuberculosis in Cologne before returning to Poland to train with Rytel and Perkowski at the Warsaw Academy of Music (1947–51). During this period he also studied piano with Tadeusz Wituski and musicology at Warsaw University.

In 1949, in response to the imposition of socialist realism as the only acceptable basis for composition, Baird formed Group 49 with Serocki and Krenz, their aim being the composition of anti-elitist music without abandoning contemporary techniques. Baird's works of these years were generally traditional in form (e.g. Sinfonietta, Concerto for Orchestra, First Symphony and the sonatinas for piano) and sometimes archaic in style (e.g. the *Colas Breugnon* suite based on 16th-century French dances), an approach he continued in later, post-socialist-realist works such as *Cztery sonety miłosne* ('Four Love Sonnets', 1956) and *Pieśni truwerów* ('Trouvère Songs', 1963). The slightly more permissive attitude of the authorities in the post-Stalinist era enabled Baird to collaborate with Serocki in the foundation of the Warsaw Festival of Contemporary Music (the 'Warsaw Autumn') in 1956 and, after becoming familiar with some of Alban Berg's works, to experiment with serialism, first evident in *Cassazione per orchestra* (1956).

Baird adopted an exceptionally free, essentially lyrical approach to serialism, introducing material unrelated to the original row, emphasizing specific intervals within the row (which becomes a freely exploitable fund of source material) and permitting tonal references to emerge. His encounter with Berg's work also resulted in greater intensity of expression, evident in the String Quartet

(1957) and *Cztery eseje* ('Four Essays', 1958), in which the orchestra is frequently treated in a chamber style. Sonata-schemes were abandoned in favour of freely-evolving structures, and by the late 1960s Baird regularly introduced static colouristic textures within his orchestral works. Such passages perhaps indicate the influence of Lutosławski's aleatory technique, but Baird always maintained strict control over their progress in that the pulse is not relaxed and they are usually composed of short, rapid figurations, the general effect of which is consistent from one performance to another.

Baird is often regarded as a late Romantic lyricist and successor not only to Berg, but Mahler and Szymanowski. Melody was of prime importance in his work, and especially in his later music there was an increasing reliance upon the voice or some underlying programmatic concept in an attempt to transmit concrete, unambivalent matter to his listeners. At the same time there was a perceptible darkening in tone, first apparent in 1966 with the opera *Jutro* ('Tomorrow'), based on a short story by Conrad, and culminating in his final work, *Głosy z oddali* ('Voices from afar'), a song cycle for baritone and orchestra to words by Jarosław Iwaszkiewicz dealing with death and personal extinction, its musical symbolism incorporating both the *Dies irae* and references to the sound world of 'Der Abschied' from Mahler's *Das Lied von der Erde*. Baird admitted that the more direct style of his later works arose from an attempt to portray bitterness in the face of reality, most notably in the orchestral pieces *Psychodrama* (1972), in his opinion the most brutal of all his works, and *Elegeia* (1973), which reveals a continuing affinity with the music of Berg.

Throughout his career Baird played an active part in Polish musical life. He continued to be involved in the organization of the Warsaw Autumn until 1969, and from 1974 taught at the Academy of Music in Warsaw, becoming director of the composition department in 1977. His numerous honours included several awards from the Polish government, the Cologne Music Prize (1963), the Koussevitzky Prize (1968), the Alfred Jurzykowski Foundation of New York Prize (1971), the Arthur Honegger Prize (1974), and three first prizes at the UNESCO International Rostrum of Composers (1959, 1963, 1966).

WORKS
(selective list)

DRAMATIC AND ORCHESTRAL

Stage: Jutro [Tomorrow] (music drama, 1, J.S. Sito, after J. Conrad) 1964–6; Warsaw, Wielki, 18 Sept 1966
Other dramatic works: 62 incid scores; 26 film and TV scores
Orch: Conc. grosso w dawnym stylu [In the Old Style], small orch, 1949; Pf Conc., 1949; Sinfonietta, 1949; Sym. no.1, 1950; Uwertura w dawnym stylu [Ov. in the Old Style], small orch, 1950; Colas Breugnon, suite, fl, str, 1951; Giocosa uwertura, 1952; Sym. no.2, 1952; Conc. for Orch, 1953; Cassazione, 1956; 4 eseje [4 Essays], 1958; Espressioni varianti, vn, orch, 1959; Wariacje bez tematu [Variations without a Theme], 1962; Muzyka epifaniczna, 1963; 4 dialogi, ob, chbr orch, 1964; 4 nowele [4 Novels], chbr orch, 1967; Sinfonia breve, 1968; Sym. no.3, 1969; Psychodrama, 1972; Elegeia, 1973; Ob Conc., 1973; Conc. lugubre, va, orch, 1975; Sceny, vc, hp, orch, 1977; Canzona, 1981

CHORAL AND SOLO VOCAL

Suita liryczna (J. Tuwim), S, orch, 1953; 2 Choral Songs (trad.), 1953; Ballada o żolnierskim kubku [Ballad about a Soldier's Cup] (S. Strumph-Wojtkiewicza) (cant.), 1954; 5 Children's Songs (J. Czechowicz), female v, pf; 4 sonety miłosne [4 Love Sonnets] (W. Shakespeare), Bar, chbr orch, 1956; Egzorta (old Hebrew) reciter, chorus, orch, 1960; Erotyki (M. Hillar), S, orch, 1961

Etiuda, vocal orch, perc, pf, 1961; Pieśni truwerów [Trouvère Songs], A, 2 fl, vc, 1963; 4 pieśni (V. Parun), Mez, chbr orch, 1966; 5 pieśni (H. Poświatowska), Mez, 16 insts, 1968; Listy Goethego [Goethe Letters], Bar, chorus, orch, 1970; Głosy z oddali [Voices from Afar] (J. Iwaszkiewicz), Bar, orch, 1981

CHAMBER AND SOLO INSTRUMENTAL

2 sonatinas, pf, 1949, 1952; Mała suita dziecięca [Little suite for children], pf, 1953; 2 kaprysy, cl, pf, 1953; 4 preludia, bn, pf, 1954; Divertimento, fl, ob, cl, bn, 1956; Str Qt, 1957; Play, str qt, 1971; Wariacje w formie ronda [Variations in Rondo Form], str qt, 1978

Principal publisher: PWM, Litolff/Peters

BIBLIOGRAPHY

EMuz (B. Pociej); *KdG* (Z. Helman)
S. Jarociński: 'Nowe wybitne dzieło na orkiestrę' [An outstanding new orchestral work], *Przegląd kulturalny* (1954), no.21 [on the Conc. for Orch]
Z. Lissa: '"Ballada o żolnierskim kubku" T. Bairda', *Muzyka*, vi/1–2 (1955), 42–54
M. Gorczycka: '"Cztery eseje" Tadeusza Bairda', *Ruch muzyczny*, iv/15 (1960), 5–6
T.A. Zieliński: 'Wokół problematyki ekspresji', *Ruch muzyczny*, v/3 (1961), 5–6
A. Prosnak: 'Cztery eseje Bairda i perspektywy techniki serialnej', *Muzyka*, ix/3–4 (1964), 26–43 [Ger. trans., abridged, 134–7]
J. Kański: 'Dramat muzyczny Tadeusza Bairda', *Ruch muzyczny*, x/23 (1966), 4–5 [on Jutro]
T.A. Zieliński: *Tadeusz Baird* (Kraków, 1966)
M. Kotyńska: 'Pieśni Tadeusza Bairda' [Baird's songs], *Ruch muzyczny*, xii/23 (1968), 9–10
K. Tarnawska-Kaczorowska: *Świat liryki wokalno-instrumentalnej Tadeusza Bairda* [The world of Baird's vocal-instrumental lyricism] (Kraków, 1982)
Muzyka xxix/1–2 (1984) [Baird issue; incl. articles on style and technique, analyses, catalogue of works, writings and bibliography]

ALISTAIR WIGHTMAN

Bairstow, Sir **Edward C(uthbert)** (*b* Huddersfield, 22 Aug 1874; *d* York, 1 May 1946). English organist, composer and conductor. He studied with John Farmer of Balliol College, Oxford, and was articled to Frederick Bridge at Westminster Abbey, where he received organ tuition from the assistant organist Walter Alcock. In 1893 Bairstow became organist of All Saints, Norfolk Square, and in 1899 of Wigan parish church. In Wigan he built up a teaching practice, concentrating particularly on singing, and successfully directed the town's Philharmonic and other choral societies. On being appointed to Leeds parish church in 1907, he became organist to the Leeds Festival of that year and of 1910 and, later, conductor of the Leeds Philharmonic Society (from 1917 until his death). In 1913 he was appointed organist at York Minster, and from then until 1939 he directed the York Musical Society. His conducting engagements took him further afield; his appearances in London included a notable concert with the Royal Choral Society, in 1927, celebrating the 50th anniversary of the first English performance of Bach's B minor Mass. In 1929 he was appointed professor of music at Durham, then a non-resident post that enabled him to continue his duties at York; he had taken the DMus degree at the same university in 1901. He was knighted in 1932, and received honorary degrees of DLitt (Leeds, 1936) and DMus (Oxford, 1945). An accomplished performer and accompanist, he was also in frequent demand as a lecturer and guest speaker, proving an avid supporter in particular of the competitive festival movement. Above all, he was aware of his own special aptitude as a teacher.

Bairstow's compositions, published principally by OUP and Novello, are mainly for the church. Of his 29 anthems

Blessed City (1914), *Let all mortal flesh keep silence* (1925) and *Save us, O Lord* (1902) are well known. As with most of his other compositions, they are possessed of a deeply felt sentiment and enduring quality. Both his settings of the Morning, Communion and Evening services – in D and E♭ – and the late Evening in G are widely used and contrasted in style. Of his 13 organ pieces the *Evening Song* quickly gained popularity, but his finest is undoubtedly the Sonata in E♭ (1937), a late Romantic work displaying consummate craftsmanship and inspiration. Equally inspired are the Variations on an Original Theme for two pianos (1908) and the unjustly neglected Six Variations on an Original Theme for violin and piano (1916). The choral works *The Prodigal Son* (1939) and *Five Poems of the Spirit*, published posthumously in 1954, were composed during his later years.

WRITINGS
Handel's Oratorio 'The Messiah' (London, 1928)
Counterpoint and Harmony (London, 1937)
The Evolution of Musical Form (London, 1943)
with H.P. Greene: *Singing Learned from Speech* (London, 1945)

BIBLIOGRAPHY
E. Bradbury: 'Sir Edward Bairstow: a Birthday Tribute', *MT*, lxxxv (1944), 233–6
S. Lindley: 'Bairstow: the Leeds Legacy', *Church Music Quarterly*, no.133 (1996), 21–3
F. Jackson: *Blessed City: the Life and Works of Edward C. Bairstow, 1874–1946* (York, 1996)

FRANCIS JACKSON

Baitz. See BÄTZ.

Baj [Bai, Baij], **Tommaso** (*b* Crevalcuore, nr Bologna, *c*1650; *d* Rome, 22 Dec 1714). Italian composer and singer. He is first heard of on 20 October 1670 as an alto in the Cappella Giulia at S Pietro, Rome, which he served for the rest of his life. The account books from 1696 to 1713 list him as a tenor; he may have become a tenor shortly before this, but the account books for 1693–5 are missing. His long experience as a singer under such renowned directors as Benevoli, Ercole Bernabei, Masini and Lorenzani stimulated him to compose, and it may have been because of this that on 19 November 1713, shortly before Lorenzani died, he was himself appointed *maestro di cappella*, a post that he held for the 13 months until his own death. He was best known for his famous nine-part *Miserere* in falsobordone style. Except in 1768 and 1777 it has been sung regularly, together with Allegri's *Miserere*, by the papal choir during Holy Week (in 1821 Baini's *Miserere* was added). He was an adherent of the severe *stile antico*, but he also adopted an expressive manner more typical of his own day (as in the *Miserere*): the two styles are in apposition in his work, which includes choral parlando writing. Some of his works are for double choir.

WORKS
2 masses, 4, 5vv, *A-Wn*, *D-Bsb*, *Mbs*, *Mm*, *Rp*; Christe eleison, 4vv, *MÜs*
3 Miserere, 5vv, 8vv (1700), 9vv (1713, 1st chorus by Gregorio Allegri), *A-Wn*, *D-AÖhk*, *Bsb*, *HEms*, *LÜh*, *Mbs*, *Mf*, *Mk*, *Mm*, *MÜs*, *OB*, *Po*, *Rp*, *TRb*, *I-Bc*, *Nc*, *Rf*, *Rvat*; 1 ed. C. Burney, *La musica che si canta annualmente* (London, 1771)
c20 motets, *D-Mbs*, *Mk*, *Mm*, *MÜs*, *Rp*, *TRb*, *I-Md*; 3 ed. K. Proske, *Musica divina*, ii (Regensburg, 1854)

BIBLIOGRAPHY
DBI (L. Pannella)
P. Alfieri: *Giudizi e osservazioni sui due Miserere di Gregorio Allegri e Tommaso Baj, riveduti e ristampati da Pietro Alfieri* (MS, *c*1740, *I-Rvat* Capp. Sistina 658, ff.42–50)

G. Baini: *Memorie storico-critiche della vita e delle opere di Giovanni Pierluigi da Palestrina* (Rome, 1828/*R*), ii

SIEGFRIED GMEINWIESER

Bajamonti, Julije [Giulio] (*b* Split, 4 Aug 1744; *d* Split, 12 Nov 1800). Croatian composer. He studied medicine in Parma and between 1785 and 1790 practised in Hvar, on the island of the same name, where he was also the organist at the cathedral. In 1789 he moved to Split in the hope of becoming the town physician but was rejected because he was a musician. In Split he again performed the duties of cathedral organist. Of about 140 surviving works, over 120 are church music. Most of his music is simple in harmonic structure, with an obvious bias towards the development of melody. Italian operatic style exercised a strong influence on his sacred works.

WORKS
La traslazione di S Doimo, orat, Split, 1770
17 masses for choir and orchestra; 2 requiem masses; 2 Passions; 2 Stabat mater; 3 TeD; 8 Tantum ergo; Miserere; Magnificat; 54 motets, a cappella and for choir and orchestra
10 syms.; Str Qt, F (attrib. Bajamonti); Org Sonata, C, 1776
Non temo, aria buffa for bass, 1776
MSS in *HR-Sk*, *Zha*

BIBLIOGRAPHY
J. Andreis: *Music in Croatia* (Zagreb, rev.2/1982), 90–94
I. Bošković: 'Veze Julija Bajamontija s Lukom i Antunom Sorkočevićem' [Bajamonti's contacts with Antun and Luka Sorkočević], *Luka i Antun Sorkočević*, ed. S. Tuksar (Zagreb, 1983), 117–29
I. Frangeš, ed.: *Splitski polihistor Julije Bajamonti* (Split, 1995)
M. Grgić: *Glazbena kultura u splitskoj katedrali 1750–1940* [Music in Split Cathedral 1750–1940] (Zagreb, 1997)

BOJAN BUJIĆ

Bajete [Bajón] (Sp.). *See under* ORGAN STOP.

Bajić, Isidor (*b* Kula, 10 Aug 1878; *d* Novi Sad, 15 Sept 1915). Serbian composer. He was a pupil of Koessler in Budapest and later became an organizer of musical life in Novi Sad. From 1901 until his death he taught at the high school there and was also the school's principal conductor. He was editor of the magazine *Srpski muzički list* in 1903 as well as a series of music by Serbian composers (1903–4); he also founded a music school in 1909.

His Romantic style of composition, while rich in melodic invention, displays a lack of technical proficiency. His national opera *Knez Ivo od Semberije* ('Prince Ivo of Semberia', 1911), heavily influenced by folk music, is notable for its musical differentiation between Serbian and Turkish characters as well as its incidental music; some of its set pieces, such as the song *Jesen stiže dunjo moja* ('Autumn is Coming, my Dear') and the dance *Srpkinja* are more commonly thought of as folk pieces. His best works are those outside the folk tradition, such as *Pesme ljubavi* ('Songs of love') and the piano pieces with their Liszt-like virtuosity and romanticism akin to Tchaikovsky.

WORKS
(selective list)
Stage: Ksenije i Ksenija (operetta), 1909; Knez Ivo od Semberije [Prince Ivo of Semberia] (op, B. Nušić), perf. 1911; Žrtva ljubavi [The Victim of Love] (operetta); incid music, incl. Seoska loia [The Village Good-for-Nothing], Čučuk Stana [Little Stana], Šaran [The Carp]
Orch: Miloš Obrenović, sym., 1902, lost; Mẹna, ov., 1902
Choral: Iz srpske gradine [From the Serbian Garden]; Srpski zvuci [Serbian Sounds]; Guslareva smrt [Guslar's Death]
Other vocal: Božestvena liturgija, chorus, 1906; Pesme ljubavi [Songs of Love], 1v, pf, 1912

Pf: Album kompozicija, 1908; Srpska fantazija [Serbian Phantasy], 4 hands; Srpsko cveće [Serbian Flowers]; other pf works

BIBLIOGRAPHY

V. Peričić: *Muzički stvaraoci u Srbiji* [Musical Creators in Serbia] (Belgrade, 1969)

S. Đurić-Klajn: *A Survey of Serbian Music through the Ages* (Belgrade, 1972)

R. Pejović: *Kritike, članci i posebne publikacije u srpskoj muzičkoj prošlosti* [Critiques, articles and other publications of the Serbian musical past] (Belgrade, 1994)

ROKSANDA PEJOVIĆ

Bajón (Sp.). *See under* ORGAN STOP (*Bajete*).

Bajoras, Feliksas Romualdas (*b* Alytus, Lithuania, 7 Oct 1934). Lithuanian composer and violinist. He grew up in Kaunas, where he received his first musical education. He then studied the violin with Aleksandras Livontas (1952–7), and composition with Juzeliūnas at the Vilnius Conservatory (1959–63). He worked as a violinist in the Vilnius Philharmonic Orchestra (1959–63), and also in the Lithuanian Radio Orchestra (1958–63). He was music director of the youth theatre from 1965 to 1984 and then spent four years in the USA. He then served as music director of the Academic Drama Theatre in Vilnius (1991–4) and since 1991 has been active in the Vilnius Music Academy, teaching music theory and rhythm to actors and theatrical and cinema directors. He was appointed to a lectureship in 1994. He has received 13 prizes for theatrical music, and was awarded the Lithuanian State Prize in 1981, the Balys-Dvarionas prize in 1989, the J. Švedas Prize in 1990 and the Lithuanian Art Prize in 1998.

Bajoras employs various techniques in his works. In the years from 1968 to 1979 he developed his own style, principally moulded by folk music. Characteristics of this style, which can be traced to Lithuanian folksong, are tonal variability, irregularity of structure and phrasing, traditional techniques of articulation, and rhetorical figures corresponding to these features. The theatre has had a strong influence on Bajoras, and his music indeed resembles a drama staged by performers (for instance in the Violin Sonata). He regards a musical work not primarily as a structure but as a conversation or incident, and consequently extra-musical factors are of great importance to him; in this he could be said to be continuing the Romantic tradition. From around 1980 he began to simplify his style: expressive, rhetorical and theatrical elements and those taken directly from folksong became less prominent, but his tendency towards polyphony and asymmetrical rhythms continued. The opera *Dievo avinėlis* ('Lamb of God', 1982) is regarded as his most important work. It is a psychological drama which, with its unique synthesis of contemporary techniques and folk music, represents a milestone in the history of Lithuanian opera.

WORKS
(*selective list*)

Stage: Dievo avinėlis [Lamb of God] (op, 3, R. Šavelis), 1982, Vilnius, 1991

Vocal: Sakmių siuita [Legend Suite], T/S, pf, 1968; Kodėl? [Why?], cycle, S, pf, 1977; Žiemužė-balta eglužė [The White Fir Tree in Winter] (L. Gutauskas), cycle, B, pf, 1977; Karo dainos [War Song], cycle, S, str orch, 1978; Varpo kėlimas [The Raising of the Bells] (orat, J. Strielkūnas), solo vv, chorus, orch, 1980; Dzūkų dainos [Dzuku Songs], cycle, S, fl, ob, vn, vc, pf, 1981; Paslaptis [A Secret] (Gutauskas), diptych, chorus, 1984; Mišių giemės [Songs of the Mass] (lit. texts), chorus, org, 1989; Missa in musica, S,

trbn, db, pf, 1993, rev. 1996; 3 sonetai [3 Sonnets] (R. Dambrauskaitė), S, org/db, 1995

Orch: Padavimai [Legends], sym. poem, 1962, rev. 1965, 1969; Sym. no.1, 1964, rev. 1970; Intermezzo, str, 1966; Veiksmažodžių siuita, str, 1966; Sym. no.2 'Stalaktitai' [Stalactites], 1970; Sym. no.3, 1972, rev. 1976, 1978; Rondo, 1976, rev. 1977; Diptychon, 1984, rev. 1993; Exodus I, 1995; Exodus II, 1996; Vn Conc., 1999

Chbr and solo inst: Variation Cycles, pf (1959–75); Sonatina, vn, pf, 1960; Trio, ob, vn, org, 1968; 4 Sketches, str qt, 1968; Variations, db, str qt, 1968; Elegija, ob, 1974; Muzika septyniems [Music for Seven], Lithuanian folk insts, cl, pf, elec org, 1975; Vilniaus kvartetas [Vilnius Quartet], str qt, 1975; Rauda [Complaints], pf, 1976; Prabege metai [Bygone Years], Sonata, vn, pf, 1979; Alias, accordion, 1980; Pulvis fiat, db, perc, 1997; Suokos [Chirping], str qt, 1998; more than 20 solo and duet works

Other: Film music, incid music, electro-acoustic works

BIBLIOGRAPHY

H. Gerlach: 'Feliksas Bajoras', *50 sowjetische komponisten* (Leipzig and Dresden, 1984), 27–33

D. Kalavinskaitė: 'Felikso Bajoro muzikos darybos bruožai' [Features of Bajoras's music], *Menotyra*, ii (1997), 21–30

M. Janicka-Słysz: '"Muzyka dla Sandomierza" F.B.', *W kręgu muzyki litewskiej*, ed. K. Droba (Cracow, 1997), 35–46

based on *MGG2* (ii, 38–9), by permission of Bärenreiter

DANUTE KALAVINSKAITĖ

Bakala, Břetislav (*b* Fryšták, nr Holešov, 12 Feb 1897; *d* Brno, 1 April 1958). Czech conductor. At Brno he studied composition with Janáček (1912–15), conducting with Neumann (1919–20) and the piano with Vilém Kurz. He was engaged as a répétiteur and conductor in the Brno Opera in 1920, making his début with Gluck's *Orfeo*, and in 1925 gave the première of Martinů's ballet *Who is the Most Powerful in the World?*, which drew him towards new music. During the 1925–6 season he was an organist and accompanist in Philadelphia. He then worked in Czechoslovak Radio, where he conducted the (abridged) première of Janáček's *Fate* in 1934, and in 1937 became chief conductor of the Brno RSO, that year touring the USSR and Latvia. From 1929 to 1931 he was conductor of Brno Opera, where in 1930 he gave the première of Janáček's posthumous *From the House of the Dead*, completing the score with Osvald Chlubna. He was conductor of Vach's Choir of Moravian Women Teachers from 1936 and from 1956 chief conductor of the Brno State PO. He also taught at the Janáček Academy (JAMU) from 1951.

Musical life in Brno owes much to Bakala's development of the Brno RSO, with which he promoted many new works. One of the finest Janáček experts, he performed nearly all his compositions, and left exemplary recordings of the *Glagolitic Mass*, *Taras Bulba* and the Sinfonietta. His repertory also included the main works of Novák, with whom he had close ties, and of Suk and contemporary Moravian composers (he conducted Novák's *De profundis* at the International Music Festival in Copenhagen in 1947). An intellectual conductor, of sparse gesture, he precisely displayed the internal structure of a work through his firm rhythmic control and careful balance. Among his compositions were popular folksong arrangements for choir. He orchestrated the second movement of Janáček's Piano Sonata and made piano reductions of several of his major works.

BIBLIOGRAPHY

ČSHS

F. Hrabal: 'Břetislav Bakala', *Sborník JAMU*, ii (Brno, 1960), 105–25

J. Trojan: 'Břetislav Bakala-janáčkovský interpret' [Bakala: a Janáček interpreter], *Sborník JAMU*, v (Brno, 1965), 91–9

B. Štědroň: 'Břetislav Bakala, člověk a umělec' [Bakala: man and artist], *Sborník Státní filharmonie Brno 1956–1966* (Brno, 1965),

10–25 [with a reproduction of Bakala's MS 'From my musical life' and discography]
J. Racek: 'Břetislav Bakala a VSMU' [Bakala and VSMU (Vach's Choir of Moravian Women Teachers)], *50 let VSMU* (Brno, 1963), 45–50
'Břetislav Bakala', *OHM* (1977) [special issue, incl. bibliography]
E. Dufková and B. Srba, eds.: *Postavy brněnského jeviště* [Personalities of the Brno stage], i (Brno, 1984–9), 71–72

ALENA NĚMCOVÁ

Bakcheios Gerōn. *See* BACCHIUS.

Bakchos. *See* DIONYSUS.

Bakchylidēs. *See* BACCHYLIDES.

Bake, Arnold Adriaan (*b* Hilversum, 19 May 1899; *d* London, 8 Oct 1963). Dutch scholar of Indian music. He studied oriental languages at the University of Leiden and in 1930 took the DLitt at Utrecht University with a translation of a Sanskrit musical treatise. With his wife Cornelia he spent over 15 years in India. He studied music and language at Tagore's school in Santiniketan, and Bengal became one of his main areas of interest; subsequently he did fieldwork from Ceylon to Nepal, largely on folk and tribal traditions (financed by a fellowship from Brasenose College, Oxford, 1937–44). During the war he served as music adviser to the All India Radio in Delhi and as director of European music at the Calcutta Broadcasting Station. In 1948 he was appointed lecturer (later reader) in Sanskrit and Indian music at the School of Oriental and African Studies, London; he also gave many lectures and recitals (accompanied by his wife) in Europe, India and North America. During his final visit to the Indian subcontinent (1955–6) he again collected invaluable material on music and dance, primarily from Nepal. In the summer of 1958 he and his wife were involved in a street accident in Leiden, from which he never fully recovered. Most of his recordings, which include folk, tribal, devotional and classical music of India (on cylinders, discs and a film-recording device), as well as his many photographs and films, are divided between the School of Oriental and African Studies, University of London, the Research Centre for Ethnomusicology, New Delhi, and the Institute for Ethnomusicology Archive, UCLA.

Bake's publications (which include articles for *MGG1*, *NOHM* and *Grove's Dictionary*, 5th edn) scarcely indicate his vast knowledge of his subject; at his death he was working on a survey of Indian music commissioned by the Oxford University Press. He was a tireless scholar, continually discovering new material and recasting his lectures, which ranged far beyond the usual discussions of north and south Indian classical music and its theory. They included such diverse elements as Vedic chant, ancient music theory, the philosophical and aesthetic basis of Indian music, folk and tribal music and dance of India, music of the devotional and mystic groups, and the music of Tagore. With the help of his recordings, photographs and films, as well as his personal reminiscences and performances as a singer, he succeeded in conveying a real feeling for India in the throes of the industrial revolution.

WRITINGS

Bydrage tot de kennis der Voor-Indische muziek(diss., U. of Utrecht, 1930; Paris, 1930) [Damodara's *Saṅgītadarpana*, chap.i–ii, Sanskrit text with Eng. trans.]
'Indian Music and Rabindranath Tagore', *Indian Art and Letters*, new ser., v (1931), 81–102

'Dr. A. Bake's Researches in Indian Music and Folklore: Short Report on the Work Done in 1931–1933', *Indian Art and Letters*, new ser., vii (1933), 10–13
'The Practice of Sāmaveda', *7th All-India Oriental Conference: Baroda 1933* (Baroda, 1935), 143–55
with P. Stern: Introduction to *Chansons de Rabindranath Tagore* (Paris, 1935) [with transcrs. and trans.]
'Indian Folk Music', *PMA*, lxiii (1936–7), 65–77
'Kīrtan in Bengal', *Indian Art and Letters*, new ser., xxi (1947), 34–40
'Indian Folk Dances', *JIFMC*, i (1949), 47–54
'Some Aspects of the Development of Indian Music', *PRMA*, lxxvi (1949–50), 23–34
'The Impact of Western Music on the Indian Musical System', *JIFMC*, v (1953), 57–64
'Bharata's Experiment with the two Vīnās', *Bulletin of the School of Oriental and African Studies*, xx (1957), 61–7
'Folk Traditions in Nepal: Continuity and Change', *Folk-lore*, lxix–lxx (1958–9), 313–22
'Quelques éléments religieux dans le théâtre indien', *Les théâtres d'Asie: CNRS Royaumont 1959*, 41–8
'La musique indienne', *Histoire de la musique*, ed. Roland-Manuel, i (Paris, 1960), 319–42
'Tagore and Western Music', *Rabindranath Tagore: a Centenary Volume* (New Delhi, 1961), 88–95
'Charlemagne in Malabar', *Folk-lore*, lxxiii–lxxiv (1962–3), 450–59
'Stick Dances', *YIFMC*, ii (1970), 56–62

BIBLIOGRAPHY

C.S. Mundy: 'Obituary, Dr. Arnold Bake', *Folk-lore*, lxxiv (1963), 498–501
J. Gonda: 'Herdenking von Arnold Adriaan Bake', *Jaarboek der Koninklijke nederlandse akademie van wetenschappen* (1963–4), 429–35
J. Brough: 'Obituary, Arnold Adriaan Bake', *Bulletin of the School of Oriental and African Studies*, xxvii (1964), 246–61 [incl. list of writings by J.R. and W. Marr, 262–4]
N.A. Jairazbhoy: 'Arnold Bake and the First Restudy of his Fieldwork, 1984', *Comparative Musicology and Anthropology of Music*, ed. B. Nettl and P.V. Bohlman (Chicago, 1990)
Bake Restudy 1984, videotape, dir. N.A. Jairazbhoy and A. Catlin, Aspara Media (Van Nuys, CA, 1991) [incl. monograph]

NAZIR A. JAIRAZBHOY

Bakels, Kees (*b* Amsterdam, 14 Jan 1945). Dutch conductor. He studied at the Amsterdam Conservatory and began his career as a violinist, later working with Franco Ferrara and Bruno Rigacci at the Accademia Musicale Chigiana in Siena, and also with Kiril Kondrashin. His first conducting appointments were with the Amsterdam PO as associate conductor and the Netherlands CO as principal guest conductor. He has toured extensively in Europe and the USA, and in Britain with the BBC PO and BBC Welsh SO. His ENO début was in 1986 with *Aida*, and he returned for *Fidelio* in 1988; he has also conducted several productions for the WNO. He has a regular association as principal guest conductor with the Bournemouth SO and became principal conductor of the Netherlands RSO in 1993. He has also appeared frequently with the Netherlands Opera, and has conducted operatic performances in San Diego and Vancouver. His conducting is direct and unfussy, although singers have sometimes been disconcerted by his erratic tempos. Among his recordings are Mascagni's *Nerone* and *Il piccolo Marat*, and a series of Vaughan Williams symphonies with the Bournemouth SO.

NOËL GOODWIN

Baker, Arthur. American record producer. A club DJ in Boston, he ventured into dance music production by borrowing money from relatives. After producing a number of obscure dance singles he moved to New York in 1979, the year in which the first rap records were released. A meeting with Tom Silverman led to Baker's engineering and producing Silverman's second release on his new Tommy Boy label, *Jazzy Sensation* by the Jazzy Five. The next single, *Planet Rock* by Afrika Bambaataa and Soul Sonic Force, was influenced by the electronic music of Kraftwerk, Yellow Magic Orchestra and Gary Numan and changed the sound of hip hop. Released in 1982, *Planet Rock* was produced by Baker, along with the ideas of Silverman and Bambaataa and the musicianship of John Robie. Baker's association with futuristic dance music, known as electro, led to production work for New Order and Freeze, along with further Afrika Bambaataa releases such as *Looking For the Perfect Beat* and *Renegades of Funk*. Launching a label, Streetwise, he released New Editions *ABC*. The trend of remixing artists for the dance market led to Baker's producing dance mixes of Bruce Springsteen's *Dancing In the Dark*. Later production and remix work included singles or albums by Hall & Oates, Bob Dylan, the Stylistics, Al Green and Diana Ross. After some years working in the mainstream, Baker returned to producing dance records, for clubs in New York, London and Miami.

DAVID TOOP

Baker, Chet [Chesney Henry] (*b* Yale, OK, 23 Dec 1929; *d* Amsterdam, 13 May 1988). American jazz trumpeter and singer. He first encountered jazz while playing in army bands, and by the time of his discharge in 1951 his distinctive, reticent style was fully developed. In 1952 he played briefly with Charlie Parker before beginning an important association with Gerry Mulligan in the latter's celebrated 'pianoless' quartet. His performances with the group, particularly his ballad rendition of *My Funny Valentine* (1952, Fan.), brought him instant fame; his clear tone and subdued, lyrical manner – he rarely played louder than *mezzo-forte* and sometimes restricted his melodic span to less than an octave – immediately became hallmarks of West Coast cool jazz, and were widely imitated. After leaving Mulligan in 1953 Baker rejoined Parker briefly and then led his own groups. He continued to dominate domestic and international jazz opinion polls for the next few years. Thereafter, owing largely to the effects of drug addiction, his career became erratic, being interrupted at one point by a prison sentence in Italy for drug-related offences (1960–61). Between 1964 and 1970 he played the flugelhorn after his trumpet was stolen. In the 1970s he resumed playing the trumpet regularly, particularly in ensembles without piano or drums, and by the mid-1980s he was again much in demand for club performances and recording dates. In 1989 he was the subject of Bruce Weber's celebrated film documentary *Let's Get Lost*.

BIBLIOGRAPHY

H.H. Lerfeldt and T. Sjøgren: *Chet: the Discography of Chesney Henry Baker* (Copenhagen, 1985, 2/1993, as *Chet: the Music of Chesney Henry Baker*)
B. Borgström and C. Landergren: *Chet Baker* (Stockholm, 1990)
L. Lewein: *Chet Baker: Blue Notes* (Vienna, 1991)
G. Rouy: *Chet Baker* (Paris, 1992)
W. Claxton: *Chet Baker* (Munich, 1993)
I. Wolff: *Chet Baker in Europe, 1975–1988* (Kiel, 1993)

J. BRADFORD ROBINSON

Baker, Israel (*b* Chicago, 11 Feb 1921). American violinist. He studied first at the American Conservatory, Chicago, and made his début at Orchestra Hall in Chicago at the age of six. After further periods of study with Louis Persinger at the Juilliard School and with Jacques Gordon

and Bronisław Huberman, he developed a considerable reputation as a chamber musician, orchestral leader and soloist. Much of Baker's career was spent in California, where he was the regular second violinist in the Heifetz-Piatigorsky Chamber Concerts and leader in the long series of recordings by Stravinsky and by Bruno Walter. As a soloist he had particular success with such works as Schoenberg's Concerto and Phantasy and Berg's Chamber Concerto; his recordings of those pieces combine stylistic acumen with the advantages of a thorough grounding in the Viennese Romantic tradition. Both as a soloist and as a member of the Pacific Art Trio, Baker performed and recorded works by Antheil, Ives, Korngold, Vernon Duke and Gail Kubik.

BERNARD JACOBSON

Baker, Dame Janet (Abbott) (*b* Hatfield, Yorks., 21 Aug 1933). English mezzo-soprano. She studied in London with Helene Isepp and Meriel St Clair, making her début in 1956 as Miss Róza in *The Secret* (Oxford University Opera Club). In 1959 she sang Eduige in the Handel Opera Society's *Rodelinda*; other Handel roles included Ariodante (1964) and Orlando (1966), which she sang to great acclaim at the Barber Institute, Birmingham. With the English Opera Group at Aldeburgh she sang Purcell's Dido (1962), Polly (Britten's version of *The Beggar's Opera*) and Lucretia. At Glyndebourne she appeared again as Dido (1966) and as Diana/Jupiter (*Calisto*) and Penelope (*Il ritorno d'Ulisse*). For Scottish Opera she sang Dorabella, Dido (*Les Troyens*), Octavian, the Composer and Gluck's Orpheus. At Covent Garden she made her début in 1966 as Hermia, and later sang Berlioz's Dido, Kate in *Owen Wingrave* (the role she created in its original television version in 1971), Mozart's Vitellia (see illustration) and Idamantes, Walton's Cressida and Gluck's Alcestis (1981). For the ENO she sang Poppaea,

Janet Baker as Vitellia in Mozart's 'La clemenza di Tito', Covent Garden, London, 1974

Mary Stuart, Charlotte (*Werther*) and Julius Caesar. In 1982 she retired from opera, after singing Mary Stuart at the ENO and Gluck's Orpheus at Glyndebourne. She described her final opera season and her career in *Full Circle* (London, 1982). Complete emotional identification with her roles, many of which she recorded, and a rich, expressive and flexible voice enabled her to excel in florid as well as dramatic music.

Baker divided her time between the stage and the concert platform. Perhaps her greatest single success as a song recitalist was at her début in Town Hall, New York, on 2 December 1966; on that occasion her personal magnetism and sense of communication won her an entirely new audience. In her recital programmes she penetrated far beyond the normal confines of Schubert lieder, becoming a devoted exponent of French and English song. She gave the première (1975, Minneapolis) of Dominick Argento's song cycle *From the Diary of Virginia Woolf*, which won the Pulitzer Prize. Britten wrote his dramatic cantata *Phaedra* for her in 1975 (first performance, Aldeburgh Festival, 1976). She was also a noble interpreter of Mahler (all the great song cycles) and Elgar, and a Bach singer of peculiar eloquence and technical accomplishment. Everything she sang was imbued with an innate feeling for the meaning and emotional import of the text. Many discs document fully all facets of her career. Numerous honours have been awarded her, including the Hamburg Shakespeare Prize (1971), and honorary degrees from the universities of London, Birmingham and Oxford. She was made a CBE in 1970 and a DBE in 1976.

WRITINGS

'The Singer and the Art of Communication', *RSA Journal*, no. 5468 (1996), 53–60

BIBLIOGRAPHY

A. Blyth: *Janet Baker* (London, 1973) [with discography by M. Walker]

J.B. Steane: *The Grand Tradition* (London, 1974), 500ff

ALAN BLYTH

Baker, Josephine (*b* St Louis, 3 June 1906; *d* Paris, 12 April 1975). American singer and actress. She became a professional street musician at the age of 13, and toured with the Dixie Steppers vaudeville troupe. Following her success as end-girl in the chorus line on tour with the musical *Shuffle Along* (1921), she was featured in its sequel, *Chocolate Dandies* (1924), and in a New York nightclub revue. In 1925 she moved to Paris to star in *La revue nègre* at the Théâtre des Champs-Elysées, in which she indulged in frenzied dancing and exaggerated mimicry; the show concluded with a nude savage dance duet. Baker then appeared in the Folies-Bergère (1925), where she made her entrance clad in three bracelets and a girdle of rhinestone-studded bananas. Her combination of the erotic and comic made her one of the most celebrated performers in France: she became a darling of society, portrayed by such artists as Picasso and Calder (see illustration), and acclaimed as an inspiration to American blacks.

In the 1930s she ran nightclubs, appeared in films, toured, and played the leading role in a production of Offenbach's *La créole* (1934). During this period her image became more cultured and she included more songs in her act; her theme song was Vincent Scotto's *J'ai deux amours*. After World War II, during which she assisted the French Resistance and entertained troops, for which

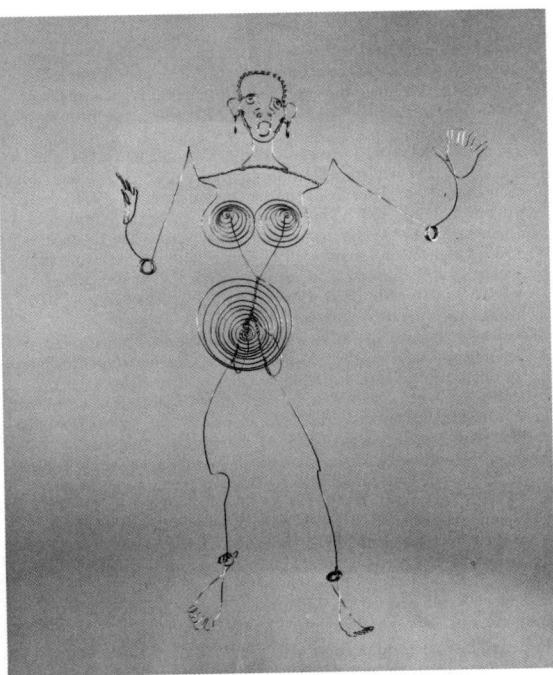

Josephine Baker: iron-wire construction by Alexander Calder, 1927–9 (Museum of Modern Art, New York)

she was made a Chevalier of the Légion d'Honneur, she devoted much of her time to civil rights struggles and her 12 adopted children of different nationalities, her 'Rainbow Tribe'. Although her popularity fluctuated after the 1940s, as a consequence of civil rights confrontations, controversial political alliances and fewer successful performances, she continued performing until four days before her death.

BIBLIOGRAPHY

SouthernB

'Baker, Josephine', *CBY 1974*

J. Baker and J. Bouillon: *Josephine* (New York, 1977)

L. Haney: *Naked at the Feast: a Biography of Josephine Baker* (New York, 1981)

B. Hammond and P.O'Connor: *Jazz Cleopatra: Josephine Baker in her Time* (London, 1987)

SAMUEL S. BRYLAWSKI

Baker, Michael Conway (*b* West Palm Beach, FL, 13 Mar 1937). Canadian composer of American birth. He completed a BMus at the University of British Columbia (1966) and an MA at Western Washington University in Bellingham (1971); he also studied privately with Lennox Berkeley in London (1974–5). Baker's compositional activities have been divided between concert and film music. His style is generally tonal, strongly grounded in lyrical melodic writing and particularly noted for its rich orchestration. These features make his music generally accessible, and have contributed to its popular success. He has received awards for his concert works as well as for his film and television scores. Baker has resided in Vancouver, British Columbia, since 1958. In 1997 he was appointed to the Order of British Columbia for his contribution to the province. A number of his works have been recorded by CBC and Summit records.

WORKS

Dramatic: Washington Square (ballet), orch, 1978; The Grey Fox (film score), 1982; Maggie (film score), 1982; A Midsummer Night's Dream (incid music), 1989; Cinderella: Frozen in Time, 1993 [for D. Hamill's 'Ice Capades']; *c*10 other stage and film scores

Orch: Counterplay, va, str orch, 1971, arr. va, pf, 1973; Fl Conc., fl, str, 1974; A Struggle for Dominion, pf, orch, 1975; Pf Conc., pf, chbr orch, 1976; Duo Concertante, vn, va, str orch, 1976; Sym. no.1 'Highland', 1977; Fanfare for Expo 86, 1983; Symphonia concertante, 1984; Capriccio, solo insts, orch, 1986; Joyeuse, 1987; Celebration Canada, 1993; The Flight of Aphrodite, vn, orch/pf, 1993; Summit Concerto, tpt, orch, 1994; Vancouver Variations, ob, chbr orch, 1996; *c*10 other works for orch, *c*10 other works for orch with solo inst

Chbr and solo inst: Sonata, fl, pf, 1963; Capriccio, 2 pf, 1964; 5 Epigrams, ww Trio, 1965; Concert Piece, org, pf, timp, 1969; Str Qt no.1, 1969; Music for 6 Players, fl, ob, str trio, hpd, 1973; Dance Sequences, vc, 1975; Sonata, pf, 1975; Rainforest Suite, pf, 1987; Star Warriors, synth, 1989; Capriccio, bn, str qt, 1991; To Play with Angels, vn, vc, 1995

Vocal: 5 Canadian Folksongs, 1v, pf, 1973; 6 Songs (Sappho), Mez, pf, 1975; The Unattainable (A.C. Bourne), song cycle, 1v, pf, 1978; A Hymn to Life (Baker), SATB, org, 1983; Rita Joe, tone poem, S, orch, 1983; Seven Wonders, song cycles, S, pf, 1983; Eve of the Garden, S, orch, 1985; Come Make the Music (P.A. Baker), chorus, org, pf, bells, 1988; Fanfare and Chorale (A Better Way) (P.A. Baker), chorus, brass band, 1991; Take Each New Day (P.A. Baker), S, tpt, org, 1992; Eridanus (A Tribute to Malcolm Lowry), fl, rec, ob, a sax, vn, pf, synth, db, perc, nar, 1993

Principal Publisher: Evocation

JOAN BACKUS

Baker, Peter. *See* MEYER, ERNST HERMANN.

Baker, Theodore (*b* New York, 3 June 1851; *d* Dresden, 13 Oct 1934). American music scholar and lexicographer. Trained as a young man for a business career, he decided rather on music. For a time he was an organist in Concord, Massachusetts. He went to Germany to study in 1874 and took the doctorate at Leipzig in 1882 with a dissertation based on field studies among the Seneca Indians in New York state. This, the first serious work on American Indian music, was shown to MacDowell by Henry Gilbert, and provided themes for MacDowell's Second ('Indian') Suite for orchestra. Baker returned to the USA in 1891 and became literary editor and translator for the music publishing firm of Schirmer, Inc. (1892), a post he held until his retirement in 1926, when he returned to Germany. Besides making many translations into English of books, librettos and articles (the last especially for the *Musical Quarterly*, published by Schirmer), Baker compiled a useful dictionary of musical terms (1895) and a biographical dictionary (1900), the work for which he is best known.

WRITINGS

Über die Musik der nordamerikanischen Wilden (diss., U. of Leipzig, 1882; Leipzig, 1882/R1976 with Eng. trans.)
Dictionary of Musical Terms (New York, 1895/R, 23/1923/R)
[Baker's] Biographical Dictionary of Musicians (New York, 1900, 2/1905, rev., enlarged 3/1919 by A. Remy, rev. 4/1940 by C. Engel, rev. 5/1958 by N. Slonimsky, suppl. 1971, rev. 6/1978, 7/1984, 8/1992 by N. Slonimsky)
A Pronouncing Pocket Manual of Musical Terms (New York, 1905, 2/1947)
Beethoven: a Critical Biography (New York, 1913/R) [trans. of V. d'Indy: *Beethoven*, Paris, 1911]
ed.: *The Musician's Calendar and Birthday Book* (New York, 1915–17)

H. WILEY HITCHCOCK

Baker, William (*d* 1685). English violin maker. He worked in Oxford at the end of the 17th century. The baptismal record of his first child in 1672 refers to him as 'Mr Baker the fidell maker', possibly the earliest reference to the profession in England. A cello attributed to the same year is thought to be the earliest surviving English cello, and in addition a small viola still in virtually original condition, once in the possession of the Oxford Music School and bearing a facsimile label of 1685, the year of his death, tells us much about the working practices of early English violin makers. The form of the instruments reflects Brescian patterns of more than 50 years earlier, with full archings and occasionally double purfling, but is probably derived more directly from the work of the Tyrolean-born violin maker Jacob Rayman, who worked in London from 1620 to 1650. Two other Bakers are recorded as viol makers; Francis Baker was contemporary with William and worked in St Paul's Churchyard in London, and John Baker worked in Oxford in the early 18th century. Neither has been proved to be related to William, although it would seem likely.

JOHN DILWORTH

Bakfark [Bacfarc, Bakfarc, Bakfarkh, Bakffark] [Greff alias Bakfark, Greff Bakfark], **Valentin** (*b* Brassó [Kronstadt], Transylvania [now Braşov, Romania], ?1526–30; *d* Padua, 22 Aug 1576). Hungarian lutenist and composer. His biography, formerly founded on inadequate documentation and misconstruction of available facts, has been badly distorted; more recently discovered evidence and reinterpretation of received data allow a far more accurate story to be given. Bakfark's family belonged to the German minority in Transylvania; the Hungarian form 'Bálint' for his Christian name, common in modern scholarship, is not found in contemporaneous sources. From 1565 he preferred the form 'Greff alias Bakfark' for his surname, which has also undergone variation in spelling in modern scholarship beyond what occurred during his lifetime. Bakfark's father Thomas was a lutenist, and so were his brother Michael (probably) and Michael's son Johannes (two dances ed. in *Valentini Bakfark opera omnia*, iii, appx 1–2). Valentin Bakfark's date of birth was formerly believed to be 1507 (or 1506/7) on the evidence of his epitaph in S Lorenzo, Padua, according to which he died in 1576 at the age of 69. Other documents make it probable that he was born between 1526 and 1530.

Information from Bakfark himself, presented in a deed of János Zsigmond, Prince of Transylvania, in 1570, asserts that as a young boy he showed musical talent and was taught as a music apprentice at the court of the Hungarian King János I Szapolyai (ruled 1526–40). A Kronstadt document of 1536 tells of a lutenist being sent with his son (probably Bakfark and his father) to the king. According to the 1570 deed, Bakfark's master was a learned court musician of János I. Although the exact identity of this person is obscure, some characteristics of Bakfark's works suggest an Italian teacher. In the preface to his Kraków publication of 1565 Bakfark referred to the excellent musicians of Pope Leo X whom he followed in his youth; this is probably an allusion to Mathias Marigliano of Milan (formerly *musico segreto* to Leo X), in Hungarian royal service between around 1538 and 1544.

Although it has been assumed that after the death of János I (22 July 1540) Bakfark left Hungary and went to France or possibly to Italy, the deed of 1570 states that from 1540 Bakfark 'served laudably many years' the king's widow, Queen Isabella Jagiełło (who resided in

Transylvania from 1542). Bakfark left her court in 1549 and went to Poland to seek employment. In Kraków on 14 May he was rewarded for his playing by King Zygmunt II August (brother of the widowed queen of Hungary), and from 8 June 1549 he appeared among the Polish court musicians. On 15 June he was officially admitted as an instrumentalist ('fistulator'). Before the summer of 1551 he married Katharina Narbutowna, a widow from Vilna (now Vilnius, Lithuania).

In autumn 1551 the king was visited in Vilna by his uncle Albrecht of Brandenburg, Duke of Prussia, and it was probably on this occasion that Bakfark became acquainted with the duke, an influential patron until at least 1562 or 1563. Bakfark appeared later in Königsberg (now Kaliningrad), Albrecht's city of residence, and also met the duke during his visits to Poland. He did not, however, act as an agent of the duke, as has been assumed owing to a misunderstanding of a letter from Bakfark to Albrecht of 1552. With Albrecht's support, Bakfark left the Polish court in February 1552 and travelled to Italy by way of Germany. In Nuremberg he (probably by chance) encountered Philipp Melanchthon, who recommended him to the Fugger family in Augsburg. However, military actions in southern Germany forced him to return to Poland. In September, after some months at the court, he left Zygmunt August's retinue in Königsberg and went to France (perhaps through Italy).

While in Lyons Bakfark published his first lutebook, which he dedicated on 23 January 1553 to Cardinal François Tournon, Archbishop of Lyons. According to a letter from Duke Albrecht (1554), Bakfark appeared at the French court – he probably accompanied Cardinal Tournon there in May – and also in Rome at the papal court. He returned to Königsberg about spring 1554 and rejoined the Polish king's court in May. Royal accounts and other documents show that from this time he stayed with the court continuously, leaving it only for short periods. (His frequent travels in Poland and Lithuania have been misunderstood: they were not separate journeys of his own, but part of the court itinerary.) Soon after his return in 1554, on Albrecht's recommendation, the king increased Bakfark's salary, making him one of the best-paid musicians of the Polish court; he continually received rises as well as gifts.

Within ten years of service Bakfark had amassed considerable wealth: he bought a house in Vilna in 1559; in the same year Duke Albrecht intervened on his behalf in a letter to Zygmunt August, which mentions some property given to Bakfark by the king; in a document of 1566 Bakfark referred to his estates (*bona*) in Vilna and its environs. His social status, fame and popularity increased immensely during his Polish years. While in Poland in 1552–6, János Zsigmond, son of Bakfark's Hungarian royal patrons, ennobled Bakfark and presumably his brother Michael.

Bakfark's actual service in Poland lasted until May or June 1565. About this time he travelled to Vienna to request a privilege (obtained on 16 July) for his second lutebook from the Emperor Maximilian II. Bakfark then returned to Kraków to take part in the process of publication. Although he dedicated the work to Zygmunt August on 15 October, he did not present it to the king in person. He remained in Kraków, but by the end of 1565 he had decided to transfer into Maximilian's service. His motive for the sudden change is not known (there is no

evidence for his political activity, as has been suggested). He left Poland in June 1566. In the meantime his possessions had been plundered by Polish soldiers, possibly in revenge by the king for his disloyalty.

On 1 July Bakfark joined Maximilian's court, where his position was similar to the one he had left behind. He received the second highest (briefly the highest) salary among the musicians, comparable to that he had enjoyed in Poland. During his service at the Habsburg court he followed the emperor in his retinue to Hungary and Bohemia. His second marriage, to Juliana Taxear of Innsbruck, occurred most likely in 1567 or 1568. In 1569 Bakfark was accused of involvement in a rebellion against the emperor. After some hesitation he returned to Maxmilian in early October. He was arrested, but seems to have been released very quickly, since he left for Padua early in December.

Immediately thereafter, Bakfark entered into the service of János Zsigmond Szapolyai, Prince of Transylvania. In 1570 the prince rewarded the lutenist with the estate of a whole village close to his own residence in Gyulafehérvár (now Alba Iulia, Romania). In late summer or autumn 1571, some months after the death of the prince, Bakfark left Transylvania for Padua where his family had remained. He settled there close to the university and probably had pupils among the foreign students; his contact with them is well documented. Bakfark, his wife and their children (one daughter and three sons) all died during the plague of 1576. He was buried in S Lorenzo, Padua, on 23 August.

The Bakfarks' neighbour and executor of Bakfark's wife's will, the famous lute maker Wendelin Tieffenbrucker, compiled an inventory of their goods, which proves that Bakfark did not destroy his manuscripts as legend had it. The inventory records, besides printed editions of Josquin, Palestrina and Pietro Joanelli Bakfark's own Kraków lutebook and three tablatures in folio, two of them described as manuscripts. In 1578 Tieffenbrucker, together with the 'natio germanica' at the university, erected a memorial for Bakfark in S Lorenzo.

Bakfark's fame caused his name and Polish sobriquet 'Węgrzynek' ('the little Hungarian') to become a part of Polish speech. The Polish proverb concerning those who 'pick up the lute after [or in the presence of] Bakfark' first appeared in print in 1566. Bakfark's name was mentioned in Polish literature into the late 17th century, becoming a figure of legend. He was celebrated by poets, among them the famous Jan Kochanowsky (1530–84). In the next century the poet Andrzej Morsztyn wrote that he 'never wanted to be Bakfark or [Antoine] Gallot'. Foreigners also praised Bakfark: Melanchthon called him an enchanting musician (1552), and the papal nuncio found him excellent (1560). The Hungarian Bishop A. Dudith, sent by Maximilian II as ambassador to Poland, characterized him as a marvellous and unique master of his art (1566), which mirrors Duke Albrecht's statement in his letter to Zygmunt Augustus of 1559: 'one rarely finds anyone comparable in his art, and hardly a king has such a musician'. The Paduan lutenist Giulio Cesare Barbetta commemorated Bakfark in his 1582 lutebook with a *Passo'e mezo … detto il bachffart*, based on a popular German dance-tune (ed. in *Valentini Bakfark opera omnia*, iii, appx 3).

Bakfark's extant works, all for solo lute, date from his Polish years. More than three-quarters are strictly faithful intabulations of motets, chansons and madrigals by Arcadelt, Gombert, Clemens non Papa, Josquin and others. Bakfark's nine fantasias are composed in a dense three- or four-part contrapuntal texture with consistent use of points of imitation. They show the influence of the vocal works of Gombert, Clemens and Willaert, and probably more immediately of the instrumental ensemble ricercares that appeared in Italy during the 1530s and 40s. The 'recercati' of Bakfark's 1553 Lyons publication are among the first such compositions for the lute. They are a clear departure from the less contrapuntal and formally looser fantasias of Bakfark's predecessors Francesco da Milano, Alberto da Ripa, Luis de Narváez and others. All Bakfark's compositions are ornamented with remarkable taste and variety. The frequent use of stereotyped formulae, typical of many contemporaneous lutenists, is absent from his output (with the exception of cadences). Bakfark's works are notably difficult; high left-hand positions and barré fingerings occur frequently.

WORKS

all for lute

Edition: *Valentini Bakfark opera omnia*, ed. I. Homolya and D. Benkő (Budapest, 1976–82) [HB]

Intabulatura Valentini Bacfarc transilvani coronensis liber primus (Lyons, 1553); ed. HB, i [1553]

Valentini Greffi Bacfarci pannonii harmoniarum musicarum in usum testudinis factarum tomus primus (Kraków, 1565); ed. HB, ii [1565]

9 fantasias: 4 in 1553 (HB, i, nos.1–4), 3 in 1565 (HB, ii, nos.21–3), 2 others (HB, iii, nos.34–5); arr. of no.4, HB, i, appx; HB, iii, no.33 is not a fantasia but an intabulation; HB, iii, no.35 is a parody of Clemens non Papa, Rossignolet

32 intabulations (14 motets, 10 chansons, 7 madrigals, 1 ?Pol. song): 16 in 1553 (HB, i, nos.5–20), 9 in 1565 (HB, ii, nos.24–32), 7 others (HB, iii, nos.33, 36–41); arr. of HB, i, no.11, 1573²⁷, *PL-Kj* Mus.ms.40598; arr. of HB, i, no.18, 1573²⁷; arr. of HB, i, no.19, *Kj* Mus.ms.40598; HB, iii, no.33 intabulates Arcadelt, De mes ennuys; HB, iii, no.41 intabulates Sandrin, Doulce mémoire

DOUBTFUL WORKS

'Fantasia V.B.', *D-DEl* Anhaltsche Landesbücherei BB 12150

Non dite mai, galliard (?intabulation), HB, iii, no.42; arr. in 1556³², 1573²⁷, *UA-LV* 1400/1

Passamezo vom Ungern, 'Gagliarda V.B.'*CH-Bu* IX.70

Pass'emeso detto L'ongaro, 'Valentim Bachsen', Italy, Castelfranco Cathedral

BIBLIOGRAPHY

H. Opieński: 'Bekwark lutnista', *Biblioteka warszawska*, ii (1906), 464–85

A. Koczirz: *Österreichische Lautenmusik im XVI. Jahrhundert*, DTÖ, xxxvii, Jg.xviii/2 (1911), pp.xxxii–xvl

H. Opieński: *Beiträge zu Valentin Bakfark's Leben und Werk* (diss., U. of Leipzig, 1914)

E. Haraszti: 'Un grand luthiste du XVIe siècle: Valentin Bakfark', *RdM*, x (1929), 159–76

H.-P. Kosack: *Geschichte der Laute und Lautenmusik in Preussen* (Kassel, 1935), 13–19, 99

O. Gombosi: *Bakfark Bálint élete és művei (1507–1576)/Der Lautenist Valentin Bakfark: Leben und Werke (1507–1576)* (Budapest, 1935/*R*1967 in Ger. only with further bibliography)

D. Benkő: 'Bakfark Problems I. (Lasso-Bakfark "Veni in hortum meum")', *SM*, xvii (1975), 297–313

G. Nussbächer: 'Zur Biographie von Valentin Greff-Bakfark', *Forschungen zur Volks- und Landeskunde*, xxv/1–2 (1982), 103–5

I. Homolya: *Bakfark* (Budapest, 1984)

G. Nussbächer: 'Precizări cu privire la biografia lui Valentin Greff-Bakfark' [Corrections concerning the biography of Bakfark], *Studii de muzicologie*, xiii (1984), 139–48

I. Szabó: 'Bakfark Bálint VIII. fantáziájának zenei mintája' [The musical model of Bakfark's Fantasia VIII], *Magyar zene*, xxvi (1985), 398–9

P. Király: 'Újabb adatok és néhány korrekció Bakfark Bálint lengyelországi működésével kapcsolatban' [New data and some corrections about Bakfark's work in Poland], *Magyar zene*, xxvi (1985), 406–30

P. Király: 'Bakfark Bálint adománylevele' [Bakfark's deed], *Magyar zene*, xxviii (1987), 88–100

P. Király: 'Mikor született Bakfark?' [When was Bakfark born?], *Magyar zene*, xxx (1989), 41–54

P. Király: 'Adalékok Bakfark Bálint életéhez és munkásságához' [Materials for Bakfark's life and work], *Magyar zene*, xxxi (1991), 339–46

P. Király: 'Bakfark hagyatékának inventáriuma' [The inventory of Bakfark's estate], *Muzsika*, xxxv/12 (1992), 25–7

P. Király: 'Bakfark Padovai végrendelete és hagyatéka' [Bakfark's testament and estate in Padova], *Muzsika*, xxxviii/6 (1995), 18–20

P. Király: *A lantjáték Magyarországon a XV. századtól a XVII. század közepéig* [Lute playing in Hungary from the 15th century to the mid-17th] (Budapest, 1995), 103–10, 179–91

E. Deák: '"Albo Juss Dalej", ein Chanson von Sandrin in Bakfarks Transcription', *Die Laute*, i (1998), 18–23

PETER KIRÁLY

Bakhor, Firuz (*b* Dushanbe, 19 Nov 1942). Tajik composer. Born into a family with a strong operatic tradition, he received his first training as a pianist, firstly with Rafael' Danilovich Ayrapetyants (1959–63) and then at the Gnesin Institute in Moscow (1963–6) where he started to show an interest in composition. He studied privately with Khagagortian and Ter-Osipov before transferring to the composition department of the Tashkent Conservatory in 1966. He worked in the Mirzo Tursun-zade Institute of Art (1971–6 and 1993–6) before settling in Germany. Although he has experimented with serial, aleatory and sonoristic techniques, these have always been subordinated to the national traditions which lie at the roots of his work. The six vocal and instrumental *shashmakom* which form the basis of Tajik folk music all constitute the main building blocks of Bakhor's compositions; they can be recognized not only by their modal properties, melodic contours and rhythmic or metrical characteristics of the works, but also by their instrumentation, methods of development, architecture and artistic imagery.

WORKS

(selective list)

Ballets: Prekrasnaya Duvalroni [The Fair Duvalroni] (ballet), 1980; Makom lyubvi [The Makom of Love] (ballet), 1988

Inst: Marakanda, sym. poem, orch, 1970; Sym. no.1, orch, 1974–84; Sym. no.2, orch, 1976; Al'bom dlya Zukhrï [Album for Zukhra], pf, 1979; Sym. no.3, orch, 1980–85; Indiyskaya syuita [Indian Suite], 2 pf, 1984; Sym. no.4 'Buzurg velikiy' [The Great 'Buzurg'], orch, 1984; Risunki po sholku [Drawings on Silk], preludes and fugues, pf, 1985; Irok, makom, orch, 1988

Film scores, incid music, choral and vocal-orch works

LARISA ALEXANDROVNA NAZAROVA

Bäkker, Dietrich. *See* BECKER, DIETRICH.

Baklanov [Bakkis], Georgy (Andreyevich) (*b* Riga, 23 Dec 1880/4 Jan 1881; *d* Basle, 6 Dec 1938). Russian baritone of Latvian birth. He studied with Pets in Kiev, Pryanishnikov in St Petersburg and Vanza in Milan. He made his début (1903, Kiev) as Rubinstein's Demon, sang with the Zimin Private Opera in Moscow and was engaged in 1905 by the Bol'shoy, creating the Baron in Rachmaninoff's *The Miserly Knight* (1906) and remaining until 1909, when he sang Barnaba (*La Gioconda*) at the inaugural performance of the Boston Opera House. At Covent Garden he appeared as Rigoletto (début, 1910), Scarpia and Amonasro, repeating the first two roles at the Komische Oper, Berlin in 1911. He sang in Boston (1915–

18), then with Chicago Opera (1917–26), and in New York, where he later became a mainstay of the Russian Opera Company. Baklanov's repertory included Yevgeny Onegin, Hamlet, Boris, Méphistophélès (*Faust*), the Father (*Louise*), Golaud (*Pelléas et Mélisande*), Telramund and Wotan. He was greatly admired for his dramatic talents, and his voice was rich and vibrant, particularly in the middle and upper registers. Between 1910 and 1930 he made a number of recordings. Further notes on his career can be found in M. Scott: *The Record of Singing*, ii (London, 1979), 12–14.

HAROLD BARNES, KATHERINE K. PRESTON

Bakshi, Aleksandr Moyseyevich (*b* Sukhumi, 12 March 1951). Russian composer. He graduated in 1977 from the Musical Pedagogical Institute of Rostov (now the Rachmaninoff State Conservatory), and later moved to Moscow. He became a member of the Union of Composers in 1983, and was a laureate of the State Prize of Russia in 1994.

Bakshi has been concerned with the concept of synthesis of music and theatre since he wrote *Drama* for piano, violin and cello as a student. Among his works there are almost no purely orchestral or choral pieces. They do not usually involve collective music-making in the usual sense. His attitude to musical material could be likened to that of a theatre producer; he lines up his sonic mise en scènes, and interprets each instrumental or vocal line as an independent musical or stage role. Thus, his poem-play *Ya–poèt . . .* ('I am a poet . . .'), set to verse by Aleksandr Blok and Vladimir Mayakovsky, is a tragifarce for 13 people: two singers and 11 instrumentalists.

Sidur-misteriya (The Sidur-Mystery), inspired by themes drawn from the sculptures of Vadim Sidur (1991) and *Igrï v installyatsiyakh* (Games in Installations) (1993) – both for voice and percussion – were the first works performed in Russia which were wholly built on the principles of instrumental theatre. Collaboration with performers has acquired a particular importance for the composer; a regular participant in Bakshi's instrumental theatre is the soprano L. Bakshi. Besides the works already mentioned, the play in one act *23/6* (1989), and *Prevrashcheniye* (Metamorphosis) for voice, an ensemble of exotic instruments, string trio, and piano (1995) were the result of collaborations with M. Pekarsky and his ensemble. The Pekarsky Ensemble has taken part in productions of *Rokovïye yaytsa* (The Fateful Eggs) and *Kaligula* (Caligula), for which Bakshi wrote incidental music; both were staged at the Yermolova Theatre. Bakshi wrote *Zima v Moskve. Gololyod* (Winter in Moscow. Icy Pavements) (1994), and *Stsena dlya Tat'yanï Gridenko i skripki* (Scene for Tat'yana Gridenko and a Violin) (1995) for the Academy of Ancient Music Ensemble, directed by Gridenko.

Starting from *Numer v gostinitse goroda NN* (A Room in a Hotel in the Town of NN), Bakshi has worked in collaboration exclusively with the producer Valery Fokin. In particular, works such as *Poslednyaya noch' poslednego tsarya* (The Last Night of the Last Tsar), and *Karamazovï i ad* (The Karamazovs and Hell) are based on the interaction of instrumental theatre and realistic psychological drama. *Installyatsii* (Installations) by Bakshi and Fokin was performed with great success at international festivals in France, Germany, Great Britain, Italy and the USA.

WORKS
(*selective list*)

Drama, pf trio, 1977; Ya – poèt . . . [I am a Poet . . .] (poetry play, A. Blok, V. Mayakovsky), 2vv, 11 insts, 1982; Vospominaniye o Gruzii [Recollections about Georgia], sonata, prep pf, 1988; Sonata, 1v, pf, 1988; 23/6, play in one act for the Pekarsky Ensemble, 1989; Sidur-misteriya, S, perc, 1992; Igrï v installyatsiyakh [Games in Installations], musical production, 1v, perc, 1993; Numer v gostinitse goroda NN [A Room in a Hotel in the Town of NN], musical production, 8 perc, kbd insts, S vv, 1994; Zima v Moskve. Gololyod [Winter in Moscow. Icy Pavements], vn, vc, str ens, 1994; Prevrashcheniya [Metamorphosis] (musical production, after F. Kafka), 1v, ens of exotic insts, str trio, pf, 1995; Karamazovï i ad [The Karamazovs and Hell] (musical production, after F. Dostoyevsky), Ct, vocal ens, perc, 1996; Poslednaya noch' poslednego tsarya [The Last Night of the Last Tsar], musical production after Ye. Radzinsky, unacc. vn, str qt, perc, vv, 1996

Chbr and vocal works
Incid music for theatre and film

WRITINGS

A. Bakshi: ' Opït vnutrennego dialoga' [An experiment in an inner dialogue], *MAk* (1995), no.3, pp.13–16

BIBLIOGRAPHY

L. Gurevich: 'Grob-art, zovushchiy k svetu. Fil'm o Vadime Sidure' [Tomb-Art calling out to the light. A film about Vadim Sidur], *Ėkran i stsena* (1991), no.3
L. Semyonova: 'Sidur-Misteriya' [The Sidur Mystery], *Ėkran i stsena* (1993), nos.14–15
V. Sellier: 'Synthese von Musik und Theater: Alexander Bakschi', *Theater am Neumarkt . . . 1992–1993* (Zürich, 1993)
L. Bakshi: 'Sidur-Misteriya: syuzhet rozhdeniya teatra' [Sidur Mystery: the subject of the birth of theatre], *MAk* (1994), no.1, pp.63–5
G. Zaslavsky: 'Sil'nodeystvuyushcheye . . .' [A virulent . . .], *Ogonyok* (1995), no.17, 44–5
Yu. Sidur: 'Pastoral' na gryaznoy vode: povest'' [A pastorale on muddy water: a tale], *Oktyabr'* (1996), no.4, pp.41–108 [see also no.5]

ALLA VLADIMIROVNA GRIGOR'YEVA

Bakuradze, Teimuraz (*b* Kutaisi, 17 April 1943). Georgian composer. In 1967 Bakuradze completed his musical education at the Tbilisi State Conservatory studying composition with Andria Balanchivadze. He lives and works in Tbilisi, composing on a freelance basis. Because of the originality and independence of his approach Bakuradze occupies a special place in Georgian music: having rejected prevailing norms and official aesthetic criteria from the start, he was the first Georgian composer to be interested in experimental instrumental theatre, 'happenings' and also the radical reinterpretation of traditional genres. His style is marked by the use of an array of techniques ranging from atonality and serialism to collage, minimalism, *musique concrète* along with aleatory and sonoristic methods. Most of his pieces contain extra-musical elements: some scores bear witness to his interest in mystical philosophy and Christian symbolism, which is organically combined with provocative wit and a touch of surrealism. In his first significant compositions (dating from the early 1970s), such as the String Quartet and *Praeludium* for soloists, orchestra and tape, instrumentalists are faced with problems concerning freely dramatic characterization, while he seeks to reorientate the role of the listener who is obliged to participate in the performance process. By means of spatial arrangement of musicians, he has achieved acoustical effects which belie minimum numbers of performers. Later works – such as the *Vespers* and *Two Books for Quintet* – are characterized by further stylistic developments which lend greater depth and conceptuality, and incorporate static and meditative elements in addition to tonal episodes of a nostalgic nature. This minimalist, though highly expressive, music is defined by particular temporal relations, and is repetitive in not only thematic, but also textural, timbral, dynamic and rhythmical terms. The repeated elements are always of the utmost simplicity; the task of this sound-meditation is to transform the psyche of the listener, to propel him towards a state of 'abstract consciousness'. Such penetration into the unconscious is of particular significance to Bakuradze, who is one of the most radical representatives of post-avant-garde music and the leader of the young generation of Georgian composers.

WORKS
(selective list)

Stage: Praeludium (happening, 2, after Vazha-Pshavela), solo vv, orch, tape, 1974, Tbilisi, 17 April 1977
Vocal-orch: Lyric verses (cant., after Sh. Rustaveli: *Vepkhis tkaosani* [The Knight in the Tigerskin]), solo vv, chorus, ens, 1963; John Reed (orat, after G. Tabidze), solo v, chorus, orch, 1970; Sym.-cant. (after D. Agmashenebeli), chorus, orch, 1971
Chbr: Sextet, cl, perc, str qt, 1963; Dialogues, cl, bn, vc, 1968; Str Qt 'Pshauri Natirilebi' (after G. Tabidze), 1970; Mtsukhri [Vespers], str, 1978; Two Books for Qnt, pf qnt, 1992 [after anon. 9th-century Georgian author and Bible: *Ecclesiastes*]
Incid music

Principal publisher: Muzfond Gruzii

BIBLIOGRAPHY
N. Mamisashvili: 'Pshauri Natirilebi', *Sabchota Khelovneba* (1975), no.1, pp.69–71 [on Bakuradze's String Quartet]
E. Sanadze: 'Teimuraz Bakuradze', *Muzika republik Zakavkaz'ya*, ed. G. Orjonikidze (Tbilisi, 1975), 152–5

LEAH DOLIDZE

Bālābān [balaman, yasti balaman, duduk]. (1) Cylindrical oboe of the Caucasus (particularly Azerbaijan), northern Iran and north-east Iraq. In northern Iran the *bālābān* is also known by its older Turkish name *nerme ney* or *mey*. It has a cylindrical wooden pipe, a broad reed and eight finger-holes, giving the scale E♭ (with an A♮). The warm, full tone of the *bālābān* is often used with the *choghur* (lute) and *qāvāl* (frame drum) to accompany the singing of an *'āshiq* (poet-singer); it is also played solo, and in pairs with one instrument providing a drone.

The Azerbaijani *balaban* is 28 to 31 cm long and made of mulberry or apricot wood. The reed is 9 to 11 cm long and is inserted into the globular head. The older *balaban* had five to seven finger-holes, while contemporary instruments have eight finger-holes and one thumb-hole. Sometimes an additional hole is made in the lower end of the tube at the back.

The *balaban* produces a diatonic scale with a range of a 9th or 11th. Chromatic notes are produced by partly covering the finger-holes. The *balaban* has a soft, velvety sound rich in dynamic nuances. Primarily an ensemble instrument, it is often played in duet (see IRAN, §III, 3); such instruments as the *nagara* (drum) or *daf* (frame drum) are played with the *balaban* duet for songs, dances and purely instrumental pieces. A *balaban* player also accompanies an *ashug* (poet-singer). The *balaban* is used in folk orchestras and played in larger professional or amateur ensembles belonging to urban and rural clubs.

The *bālābān* or *qarnāta* of the Turkmen and Kurds of north-east Iraq is made from a straight tube about 30 cm long, with seven finger-holes and one thumb-hole. The broad rectangular double reed (*pīk, qamīsh*) is 10 cm long and fitted with ring-shaped regulators. The instrument sometimes replaces the *zurna* at festivals, accompanied by a *ṭabl* (double-headed cylindrical drum). It accompanies the songs of the Turkmen and Kurds in the towns of Arbīl, Sulaymānīyah, Kirkīk and Tuz Khurmātū, either alone or with a single-headed drum. It is similar to the *duduk* of Armenia and Georgia.

(2) The *balaban* of the Uzbek and Tajik peoples of Central Asia is a clarinet. The instrument is called *balaman* by the neighbouring Qārāqalpaks and consists of a narrow cylindrical wooden bore, about 30 cm long, with a single reed inserted into the head. It has seven finger-holes and one thumb-hole.

BIBLIOGRAPHY
Grovel ('Duduk', (i); R. At'ayan)
C. Farr: *The Music of Professional Musicians of Northern Iran (Azerbaijan)* (diss., U. of Washington, 1976)
J. Jenkins and P.R. Olsen: *Music and Musical Instruments in the World of Islam* (London, 1976)
S. Qassim Hassan: *Les instruments de musique en Irak et leur rôle dans la société traditionelle* (Paris, 1980)

JEAN DURING, JOHANNA SPECTOR, SCHEHERAZADE QASSIM
HASSAN, MARK SLOBIN

Balachander, S. (*b* Madras [Chennai], Tamil Nadu, 18 Jan 1927; *d* Bhilai, Madhya Pradesh, 13 April 1990). South Indian *vīnā* player. S. Balachander was one of the greatest and most influential Karnatak musicians of the 20th century. From the age of five he showed a great interest in music and at six he appeared on the concert platform for the first time, as a *kañjīrā* accompanist to vocalists. He also learnt other instruments including the *tabla*, *mṛdaṅgam* and *sitār*. He was a concert artist on the *sitār* between 12 and 16 years of age. From the age of 15 for three years he was a staff artist at the Madras station of All India Radio, playing various instruments, as a soloist, accompanist and as part of an ensemble.

He took up the *vīnā* at age 16 and, self-taught, evolved a highly influential and original style which owed a great deal to the techniques of vocal music. This style is now known as the Balachander *bāni*. The features of the style are largely derived from the technique of deflecting the string across the fret to produce various phrases (*sangatis*) with a single pluck.

S. Balachander is credited with popularizing the *vīnā* in the concert hall (previously it had been thought of as a chamber instrument) and he contributed to a growing awareness of Karnatak music with his numerous tours in India and abroad. His extensive discography includes recordings in all the 72 *melakartas*. He was the recipient of numerous honours and awards, including the Padma Bhushan.

SHANTHA BALACHANDER and S.B.S. RAMAN

Balada, Leonardo (*b* Barcelona, 22 Sept 1933). American composer of Spanish birth. After studying at the Barcelona conservatory, he won a scholarship (1956) to study at the New York College of Music; he graduated from the Juilliard School in 1960. His composition teachers included Aaron Copland, Alexandre Tansman and Vincent Persichetti. He taught at the United Nations International School (1963–70) and at Carnegie-Mellon University, where he became a professor in 1975.

Many of Balada's melodies have a Spanish flavour; although his works are primarily based on triadic harmonies, they are freely coloured by tone clusters, dense overlapping textures and other constructionist features. From around 1966 his experimentation with these techniques dominated his music, almost to the exclusion of melody (*Cuatris*, 1969; *Cumbres*, 1971). The two orchestral *Homages* (1975), to Casals and Sarasate, marked a return to a nationalistic melodic style. Bright colours and aggressive rhythms are characteristic. Whether scored for the piano, tuned percussion, pizzicato strings or staccato brass, hard-edged tones are typical. In the early stage works (*Maria Sabina*, 1969; *No-Res*, 1974) human speech is also treated percussively. Later operatic ventures, beginning with *Hangman! Hangman!* (1982), a satire set in America's Old West, make liberal use of folk melodies. A more traditionally operatic vocal style is used in *Zapata* (1982–4) and especially in *Cristóbal Colón* (1989), composed for the 500th anniversary of Columbus's voyage to America, which also incorporates folk music and dissonant orchestral colours. Balada has cited the influence of Salvador Dali, with whom he collaborated; his presentation of familiar melodies in distorted surroundings often recalls Ives.

WORKS

Stage: Maria Sabina (C.J. Cela), nars, chorus, orch, 1969; No-Res (J. Paris), nars, chorus, orch, 1974, rev. 1997; Hangman! Hangman! (chbr op, 1, Balada), 1982; Zapata (op, 2, T. Capobianco and G. Roepke), 1982–4; Cristóbal Colón (grand op, 2, A. Gala), 1989; Thunderous Scenes (Balada), cant., 1v, chorus, orch, 1992; Thunderous Scenes (cant., solo vv, chorus, orch, 1992; Death of Columbus (op, 2, Balada), 1996; The Town of Greed (chbr op, 1, Balada), 1997

Orch: Musica tranquila, str, 1960; Pf Conc. no.1, 1964; Gui Conc. no.1, 1965; Guernica, 1966; Sinfonia en negro: Homage to Martin Luther King, 1968; Bandoneon Conc., 1970; Cumbres, band, 1972; Persistencies (Sinfonia concertante), gui, orch, 1972; Steel Sym., 1972; Auroris, 1973; Ponce de Leon, nar, orch, 1973; Conc. no.2, pf, wind, perc, 1974; Homage to Casals, 1975; Homage to Sarasate, 1975; Conc., 4 gui, orch, 1976; 3 Anecdotes, castanets/wood perc, orch, 1977; Sardana: Dance of Catalonia, 1979; Quasi un pasodoble, 1981; Quasi Adelita, wind band, 1982; Vn Conc., 1982; Zapata: Images for Orch, 1987; Fantasias sonoras, 1987; Alegrias, 1987; Divertimentos, str, 1991; Columbus: Images for Orch, 1991; Celebration, 1992; Sym. no.4 'Lausanne', chbr orch, 1992; Song and Dance, wind ens, 1992; Music for Ob and Orch (Lament from the Cradle of Earth), 1993; Union of the Oceans, band, 1993; Morning Music, fl, orch, 1994; Concierto magico (Conc. no.2), gui, orch, 1997; Folk Dreams, suite, 1995–8; Shadows, Line and Thunder, Echoes; Reflejos, fo, str, 1999 [from chbr work]; Pf Conc. no.3, 1999; Passacaglia, 2000; Music for Fl and Orch, 2000

Vocal: 4 canciones de la Provincia de Madrid, song cycle, 1v, pf, 1962; 3 Cervantinas, song cycle, 1v, pf, 1967; 3 epitafios de Quevedo, song cycle, 1v, pf, 1967; Las moradas (S. Teresa de Avila), chorus, 7 insts, 1970; Voices no.1, 1972; Torquemada (Balada), B/Bar, 14 insts, chorus, 1980; En la era, song cycle, 1v, pf, 1989

Chbr and solo inst: Musica en 4 tiempos, pf, 1959; Sonata, vn, pf, 1960; Conc., vc, 9 insts, 1962; The Seven Last Words, org, 1963; Geometrias: no.1, fl, ob, cl, bn, tpt, perc, 1966; no.2, str qt, 1967; no.3, bandoneon, 1968; Cuatris, 4 insts, 1969; Minis, bandoneon, 1969; End and beginning, rock ens, 1970; Mosaico, brass qnt, 1970; Elementalis, org, 1972; Tresis, fl/vn, gui, vc, 1973; 3 Transparencies of a Bach Prelude, vc, pf, 1976; Transparency of Chopin's First Ballade, pf, 1977; Persistencies, pf, 1978; Preludis obstinats, pf, 1979; Sonata, 10 wind, 1980; Reflejos, fl, str, insts, 1987; Diary of Dreams, vn, vc, pf, 1995

Gui: Lento with Variation, 1960; Suite no.1, 1961; 3 Divagaciones, 1962; Analogias, 1967; Apuntes (Sketches), 4 gui, 1974; Minis, 1975; 4 Catalan Melodies, 1978; Persistencies, 1979

Principal publishers: Belwin-Mills, Beteca Music, General, G. Schirmer

BIBLIOGRAPHY

Leonardo Balada (Pittsburgh, 1982) [brochure of Carnegie-Mellon University]

P.E. Stone: 'He Writes for the Audience, but on his own Terms', *New York Times* (21 Nov 1982)

P.E. Stone: 'Leonardo Balada's First Half Century', *Symphony*, xxxiv/3 (1983), 85

DAVID WRIGHT

Balaguer, Juan de Sessé y. *See* SESSÉ Y BALAGUER, JUAN DE.

Balakauskas, Osvaldas (*b* Miliūnai, Ukmerge district, Lithuania). Lithuanian composer. In 1961 he concluded his studies at the Vilnius Pedagogic Institute, and then went to study at the Kiev Conservatory with Lyatoshyns'ky (1964–8) and Skoryk (1969). He then worked as an editor with the music publishers Muzychna Ukraïna (1968–72), and was adviser to the Lithuanian Composers' Union (1972–85). In 1985 he was appointed to teach at the Lithuanian Music Academy (chair in composition 1988, full professor 1995). From 1992 to 1994 Balakauskas served as Lithuania's ambassador to France. He received the Lithuanian National Prize in 1996.

Since 1965 Balakauskas has used a serial technique of his own which is distinct from Schoenberg's. His series does not necessarily consist of 12 tones, but of 12 (or fewer) melodic or harmonic sequences, sometimes complete phrases, which are treated in the same way as the separate tones in serialism. The composer's overall aim is to control tensions and avoid extreme dissonances. As a fundamental idea this procedure could be described as a serialism of consonances. Many of his compositions are based on various diatonic systems with eight or more tones, each of which is distinguished by its own logic, colour, and functional possibilities. He set out the theory behind this system in his study *Dodekatonik* (1977). The metre of his works is influenced by jazz and the variable metres of Blacher.

Another typical feature of Balakauskas's his work is the combination of elements usually remote from one other, for instance his 'harmonization' of folk tunes with clusters (*Studi sonori*), his use of classical cadences as a serial element (in the second String Quartet), the combination of the medieval organum with jazz elements on a serial basis (*Erasmus*), and so on. However, he does not use these sources in a postmodern polystylistic sense, but brings them together to create a synthesis which gives rise to a style that is both integrated and individual.

WORKS

Stage: Macbeth (ballet, J. Smoriginas, after W. Shakespeare), 1988

Orch: Šokių siuita [Dance Suite], str, 1964; Concertino, pf, str, 1966; Ludus modorum, vc, chbr orch, 1972; Sym. no.1, 1973; Kalnų sonata [Mountain Sonata], cl, orch, 1975; . . . ad astra, 1976; Sym. no.2, 1979; Passio strumentale, str qt, orch, 1980; Conc., ob, hpd, str, 1981; Sinfonia concertante, vn, pf, orch, 1982; Spengla-Ūla, 16 str; Das bachjahr, fl, hpd, str, 1985; Opera strumentale, 1987; Sym. no.3 'Ostrobotnia', str, 1989; Polilogas, conc., a sax, str, 1991; Meridionale, Hommage à Witold Lutosławski, chbr orch, 1994; Concerto RK, vn, chbr orch, 1997; Sym. no.4, 1999

Vocal: Prie mėlynos gėlės [To the Blue Flowers] (L. Gutkauskas), cycle, chorus, fl, ob, vn, va, vc, pf, 1976; Daugybė pravirų šulinių [Many Half-Open Springs] (Gutkauskas), cycle, S, trbn/vc, pf, 1979; Dada-Conc. (Gutkauskas), S, T, 2 B, insts, 1982; Chopin-Hauer (Schopenhauer), S, T, choruses, 2 pf, va, tape, 1990; Requiem in memoriam Stasys Lozoraitis, Mez, chorus, str, synth, 1995

Chbr: Impresonata, fl, pf, 1964; Sonata, vn, pf, 1969; Quartetto concertante, fl, vn, vc, pf, 1970; Str qts nos.1–2, 1971; Retrospective, vc, pf/pf trio, 1974; Neun Quellen, ob, hpd/pf trio, 1974; Medis ir paukštė [The Tree and the Bird], va, pf, 1976; Albertiana, fl, vn, vc, pf, 1981; Claqua, cl, str qt, 1984; Veda-sekabudi, perc, 1990; Lietus Krokuvai [Cracow Rain], vn, pf, 1991; Betsafta, vc, pf, str qt, 1995; Str Qt no.3, 1998; Tristan, gui, fl, pf, 1998

Solo inst: 10 Pieces, pf, 1964; Org Sonata no.1, 1965; Kaskados I, pf, 1967; Studi sonori, 2 pf, 1972; Eneatonika (Org Sonata no.2), 1980; Movimenti, 2 pf, 1981; Kaskados II, 1986; La Valse, vn, 1997

BIBLIOGRAPHY

R. Mikėnaitė: 'O. Balakausko kompozicinės technikos principai'
[The principles of Balakauskas's compositional technique],
Muzika, ii (1980), 19–23

J. di Vanni: 'Une quête exigeante', *Aspects de la musique soviétique:
la musique en Lithuanie* (Paris, 1986), 119–133

R. Lampsatis: *The Composer Balakausakas* (Peine, 1988)

based on *MGG2* (ii, 58–60), by permission of Bärenreiter

RŪTA GAIDAMAVIČIŪTĖ

Balakirev, Mily Alekseyevich (*b* Nizhniy Novgorod, 21 Dec 1836/2 Jan 1837; *d* St Petersburg, 16/29 May 1910). Russian composer, conductor, teacher and pianist.

1. Life: up to 1866. 2. 1866–72. 3. 1872–1910. 4. Works and influence.

1. LIFE: UP TO 1866.   Balakirev was the son of a minor government official. His musical education began with his mother's piano tuition and proceeded to a course of summer lessons in Moscow with Aleksandr Dubuque. At that time the leading musical figure and patron in Nizhniy Novgorod (and author of books on Mozart and Beethoven) was Aleksandr Ulïbïshev, and it was through his household pianist and musical organizer Karl Eisrich that Balakirev's induction to music, embracing the crucial discoveries of Chopin and Glinka, continued. Eisrich and Ulïbïshev provided Balakirev with further opportunities to play, read and listen to music, and to rehearse other musicians in orchestral and choral works, including, when he was 14, Mozart's Requiem. His first surviving compositions date from the age of 15. Balakirev's formal education began at the Gymnasium in Nizhniy Novgorod and continued after his mother's death in 1847 at the Aleksandrovsky Institute there. In 1853 he became an unmatriculated student of mathematics at the University of Kazan', still spending holidays in Nizhniy Novgorod or on Ulïbïshev's estate. While in Kazan' he met the composer-pianist Ivan Laskovsky and the pianist Antoni Kątski, from whom he thought of taking piano lessons in St Petersburg.

Through Ulïbïshev, Balakirev met Glinka in St Petersburg in the late autumn of 1855. This acquaintance was marked by discussions, by Glinka handing on several Spanish musical themes, and entrusting the musical education of his four-year-old niece to Balakirev. Concert appearances as pianist were made at Kronstadt (December 1855) and St Petersburg (on 12/24 February 1856 at a university concert, Balakirev playing the solo part in the first movement of his projected Piano Concerto; and on 22 March/3 April in a concert of his piano and chamber compositions). Also in 1856 Balakirev made the acquaintance of other important figures, including Cui, the Stasov brothers, Serov, Aleksey L'vov, Dargomïzhsky, Prince Vladimir Odoyevsky and Count Michał Wielhorski [Viyel'gorsky]. In February 1858 he played the solo part in the 'Emperor' Concerto before the Tsar. His first compositions to be published (12 songs) appeared in 1858–9. The deaths of Glinka (in 1857) and Ulïbïshev (in 1858) deprived Balakirev of influential supporters, but in the meantime he was forming a circle of his own, which included Vladimir Stasov and the young composers much of whose early work he was to superintend. He met Musorgsky in 1858, Rimsky-Korsakov in November 1861 and Borodin in November or December 1862; for these three musical amateurs Balakirev was an instructor of magnetic personality capable of inspiring them to improbable heights of creativity. Of projected music for

Korol' Lir ('King Lear'), only the Overture was completed in 1859 and performed on 15/27 November 1859; the other incidental music was finished in 1861, revised from 1902 and the whole work published only thereafter.

The early part of the reign of Aleksandr II (1855–81), especially the first half of the 1860s, saw a new political climate favourable to reform and innovation. In music, the principal developments were the establishment of the Russian Musical Society in 1859 and the opening of its conservatories in St Petersburg (1862) and Moscow (1866). While the new institutions had powerful champions, especially among the social élite, they also found eloquent detractors fearful of the consequences of introducing to Russia alien (i.e. German) musical precepts and teachers. Balakirev's closest contacts (and sympathies) were with the latter group, and he frequently had derogatory comments to make about German musical 'routine', which, he considered, circumscribed a composer's originality. (Ridenour gives a good outline of how matters of personal rivalry, social and political outlook and musical taste were interwoven in the relationships of Russia's most prominent musicians in the 1860s.) Balakirev's piecemeal musical education made him an improbable candidate to play a part in the new institutions, though an invitation to join the staff of the Moscow Conservatory was extended to him twice during the 1870s. The anti-Conservatory group found a focus in the opening (on 18/30 March 1862) of the Free School of Music, whose tasks included providing musical education free of charge (that is the meaning of 'free' in the title, contrasted with the expensiveness of the Conservatory's provision), with an emphasis on singing and in particular on choral singing to meet the demands of the Orthodox Church. The initial idea for the School was Balakirev's, though it made sense for Gavriil Lomakin, an esteemed choirmaster, to be appointed director rather than Balaki-

1. *Mily Alekseyevich Balakirev*

rev. While the director conducted the School's choral concerts, his assistant, Balakirev, directed the orchestral ones, and his programmes favoured music by Russian composers and by Western composers of more advanced musical idiom, thereby forming a contrast with the more staid, 'classical' programmes of the Russian Musical Society concerts. On Lomakin's resignation Balakirev was appointed director on 28 January/9 February 1868, retaining the post until the spring of 1874, though latterly only nominally.

2. 1866–72. In 1866 Glinka's sister Lyudmila Shestakova asked Balakirev to take charge of performances of her brother's operas in Prague; devoted as he was to Glinka, Balakirev accepted. After delays caused by the Austro-Prussian War, he conducted *Ruslan and Lyudmila* there on 4/16, 5/17 and 7/19 February 1867 and *A Life for the Tsar* on 10/22 February. Balakirev was never easy to get on with if disagreement was involved, and this visit gave rise to some antagonism, with bad relations between Balakirev and Smetana; it seems likely that competing ambitions and some national rivalry came into play. On 12/24 May 1867 Balakirev conducted a concert for visitors attending a Slav conference, for which Stasov in his review coined the term *moguchaya kuchka*('mighty handful'). He was referring to the group of Russian composers, belonging to several generations and schools, whose works were now available for performance; it was only subsequently that the phrase was applied to the group more helpfully known as 'the Balakirev circle' (the composers Balakirev, Musorgsky, Rimsky-Korsakov and Borodin plus Cui – more as critic than as composer – and Stasov). The second expression is more helpful in that it describes with greater precision a group of friends who met regularly, with Balakirev as the presiding musician, to listen, play and speak about music, its objectives and methods, and in whose midst were forged ideas which exerted some influence on the course of Russian musical history. In the summer of 1867 Balakirev was also appointed conductor of the Russian Musical Society concerts in St Petersburg. This enabled him to present to the public even more of the music he admired, and he was responsible for inviting Berlioz to conduct a number of the concerts. For these two seasons (1867–8 and 1868–9) Balakirev was at the pinnacle of his career, having won recognition as Russia's leading conductor in charge of the repertory and performing standard of the capital city's two principal series of orchestral concerts. His dismissal from the Russian Musical Society conductorship in the spring of 1869 was the result of his determination to perform the modern and Russian music he liked, rather than offer a wider range of repertory with broader appeal. The arts of diplomacy and consensus passed Balakirev by.

The 1860s were a time of heroic activity, as conductor, teacher and composer. Balakirev encouraged to completion the first symphonies of Rimsky-Korsakov and Borodin, whose premières he conducted on 19/31 December 1865 and 4/16 January 1869 respectively. He also conducted for the first time Musorgsky's *The Destruction of Sennacherib* (6/18 March 1867) and the Polonaise from his *Boris Godunov* (3/15 April 1872). 1866 saw the publication of his *Sbornik russkikh narodnïkh pesen* ('Collection of Russian Folksongs'), which showed a new level of insight into the rhythm, harmony and types of song, even if the choice of key signatures and the elaborate

piano textures disclosed Balakirev as the arranger. Caucasian holidays in 1862, 1863 and 1868 opened Balakirev's ears to the folk music of that region, which was to be an important source for his own compositions (not least *Islamey*, completed in 1869, second version 1902; fig.2) as well as deepening his love for the poetry and prose of Mikhail Lermontov, much of which also has a Caucasian background. The musical idiom known as 'oriental' and found, for example, in the 'oriental fantasy' *Islamey* looms large in Balakirev's music, even though it first surfaced before his 1862 holiday. Nikolay Rubinstein, the work's dedicatee, gave the first performance in St Petersburg on 30 November/12 December 1869. This dedication and its acceptance is one sign that the Moscow Rubinstein's Russian aspirations were stronger than those of his brother in St Petersburg. Tchaikovsky too settled in Moscow, and for a time his music had ideas in common with that of Balakirev. Thus, the Fantasy Overture *Romeo and Juliet* was composed with the same kind of prompting and intervention which Musorgsky, Rimsky-Korsakov and Borodin had experienced. Tchaikovsky was a graduate of the St Petersburg Conservatory and neither a dilettante nor an autodidact, and was therefore unlikely to tolerate much of Balakirev's dictatorship in musical matters. Nonetheless, Tchaikovsky dedicated to Balakirev *Fatum* ('Fate', of which Balakirev conducted the St Petersburg première on 17/29 March 1869), *Romeo and Juliet* and *Manfred*; the last-named project originated with a proposal from Stasov to Balakirev in the 1860s, which Balakirev first passed to Berlioz; the idea was eventually given to Tchaikovsky in a letter of 28 September/10 October 1882, followed in further correspondence by Stasov's programme, Balakirev's recommendations for keys, and a list of compositions (by Chopin, Berlioz, Liszt and Tchaikovsky himself) which Balakirev considered might have some bearing on the new work.

On 3/15 June 1869 Balakirev's father died in Klin, the town where he found his last job, bringing his son responsibility for winding up the estate and for the welfare of his younger sisters.

In the early 1870s, aware that the musical development of his pupils Musorgsky, Rimsky-Korsakov and Borodin was leading them away from him (not least in their interest in composing operas, an interest fostered by Dargomïzhsky and Cui), having lost ground as a conductor, forever struggling to make ends meet both for the Free School and himself (a good part of his life was spent giving piano lessons), and drained by his earlier efforts, Balakirev suffered some kind of breakdown. The earliest hint of the crisis may be traced to early 1871, when rumours about his mental state circulated. He sought consolation in rigorous observance of the prescriptions of the Orthodox Church (he dated his conversion to the anniversary of his mother's death, 9/21 March 1871) and gradually withdrew from the world of music and his friends there. He found clerical employment with a railway company, starting work on 6/18 July 1872.

3. 1872–1910. Balakirev later made a progressive return to musical activity, but never with the intensity of former years, and now with the narrower horizons which his changed religious and political outlook brought; if he had previously been a free thinker and radical, he was now a dogmatic Christian and reactionary. In 1876 Shestakova helped to draw him back into editing Glinka's works for

2. *Autograph manuscript of the opening of the second version of Balakirev's oriental fantasy for piano 'Islamey', composed 1902 (RUS-Psc)*

publication, and the score of *Ruslan and Lyudmila* was issued by Jürgenson on 10/22 November 1878; *A Life for the Tsar* came out in 1881, followed by other works. It was also in 1876 that Balakirev returned to the symphonic poem *Tamara*, started in 1867, all but finished in 1879, and actually completed on 14/26 September 1882; it was performed, with the composer conducting, on 7/19 March 1883. In 1881, after turning down the offer of the directorship of the Moscow Conservatory with the conductorship of the Moscow Russian Musical Society concerts (out of apprehension about the administrative workload and wiser after previous experience of the society), Balakirev accepted the invitation to resume the directorship of the Free School of Music. On 3/15 February 1883 he took up the appointment of musical director at the Court Kapella, a post in which his assistant was Rimsky-Korsakov. The two men worked in tandem, some disagreements notwithstanding, until 1894, thus serving for almost the whole of the reign of Aleksandr III. The Kapella's men and boys sang at court church services and on some other occasions. The institution furnished boys with a general and musical education and played a

role in editing and publishing music for use in the worship of the Russian Orthodox Church. Caring for his charges' welfare was congenial to Balakirev, though the small number of church music compositions which he produced during his time at the Kapella have not generally been well thought of; however the work was well rewarded financially.

Rather than Balakirev, it was the Maecenas with the deep pocket, M.P. Belyayev [Belaïeff], who attracted the notice of the young composers of the 1880s and 90s. Musical gatherings *chez* Balakirev on Tuesdays were no match for Belyayev's convivial Fridays. Belyayev's musical advisers were from the St Petersburg Conservatory and included Rimsky-Korsakov and later Glazunov and Lyadov. Commissions more or less guaranteeing performance and publication were more appealing than anything the Free School could offer. In spite of his own problems in negotiating acceptable arrangements for his own compositions with music publishers, Balakirev did not use the services which Belyayev provided in that line (except when the latter acquired by purchase the rights in Balakirev's 1866 folksong collection after the death of the original publisher). One of several reasons for the composer's antipathy was his idea that Belyayev's generosity gave artificial support to compositions which were unworthy, and thus contributed to lowering the quality of Russian music. It was only in 1899 that Balakirev encountered the music publisher J.H. Zimmermann whose firm was based in St Petersburg, and the latter's persistence yielded him the scores of Balakirev's symphonies (among other works), which he published in 1899 and 1908 respectively.

With the exception of Sergey Lyapunov, Balakirev was neglected by the younger generation of composers. Lyapunov came to him as a Moscow Conservatory graduate in 1884, and remained his faithful disciple and champion until his own death in 1924. Also from 1884 Balakirev enjoyed the friendship of Aleksandr Olenin, who composed, took an interest in folksong and accompanied his sister, the singer Mariya Olenina d'Alheim. Balakirev found stimulation and encouragement in a group gathered around the distinguished philologist, ethnographer and historian A.N. Pïpin and his family. Their musical evenings began in the mid-1880s, and the participants were known as the 'Weimar circle' after an evening when Balakirev had arranged a private concert in memory of Liszt in 1886. There Balakirev was once more the undisputed musical leader.

It is emblematic of Balakirev's outlook that he should have contributed to commemorating the work of the two Slav composers Glinka and Chopin. He raised money to erect a monument to the former in his home town of Smolensk, something which was achieved in 1885. He also worked towards marking Chopin's birthplace at Żelazowa Wola, which witnessed Balakirev's final appearance as a pianist, playing Chopin's B flat minor Sonata on 5/17 October 1894. In 1897 he became a member of the Folksong Commission of the Imperial Russian Geographical Society, and on their behalf harmonized 30 songs taken from the collection made in 1886 by G.O. Dütsch [Dyutsh] and F.M. Istomin in the Arkhangel and Olonets governments. These arrangements were published in about 1899, anticipated by Balakirev's own piano duet versions of them in 1898.

In his final period Balakirev was in the odd position of attending performances of compositions begun long ago but only recently completed. One instance was the First Symphony, which he started to write in 1864 and finished only in 1897; the composer directed the first performance on 11/23 April 1898, his last appearance as a conductor. The Second Symphony was largely composed in the 1900s, though it made use of some earlier material, and first performed on 10/23 April 1909, Lyapunov conducting. It is often the case that musical ideas associated with Rimsky-Korsakov or Borodin prove to have been prefigured in works by Balakirev, yet because of his slowness in bringing works before the public he has been denied credit for his inventiveness. On the other hand, works which if completed and performed in the 1860s or 70s would have enjoyed immense success, when heard for the first time towards the end of the composer's life made a much smaller impact, overtaken by the newer languages forged by younger composers of several nationalities. The late writings of Stasov (d 1906) and especially Cui (d 1918) often reveal minds fixed in an era of heroic struggle (the 1860s), unable to adapt to a world which long since came to terms with their points of view and moved ahead to new controversies. The same may be said of Balakirev's last years in composition.

4. WORKS AND INFLUENCE.   Balakirev's first musical experience was as a pianist, and composers for his own instrument left their mark on the repertory and style of his compositions. All the genres developed by Chopin (except the Ballade) were cultivated by Balakirev, the largest number of whose solo piano works date from after the crisis of the early 1870s. Chopin's textures and musical idioms, to say nothing of the primacy of soloist over orchestra, are clearly audible in the single movement of the Piano Concerto in F♯ minor composed in 1855–6. The long line of nocturnes, scherzos, mazurkas, waltzes and kindred pieces, evoking a mood or derived from a dance, continue to recall the Polish composer, often with a comparable charm and grace, though on occasion without his sense of a satisfactory formal scheme, especially in later compositions where the spark of musical inspiration can seem weaker. Harmonic and emotional restraint seem also to relate these works to an early 19th-century style, of the kind which Balakirev himself met in studying Hummel, for instance; his powerful musical inheritance from Glinka may have strengthened the same characteristic. Noteworthy works for solo piano (besides the Lisztian *Islamey*) include the B♭ minor Sonata, the Second Scherzo, the Berceuse, the first two waltzes, the Dumka and the Tyrolienne. Balakirev's proficiency at the keyboard may have contributed to his strong predilection for certain keys. D♭ major, with its comfortable mixture of white and black keys, is a grateful tonality in which to play. At any rate, key signatures of two sharps and five flats occur with extraordinary frequency in Balakirev's compositions, and sometimes in works influenced by him, of which *Romeo and Juliet* is a striking example.

The other keyboard composer who strongly influenced Balakirev was Liszt. It was only after Schumann and Berlioz had long featured in Balakirev's orchestral programmes that Liszt began to appear there too, but some of the piano works show Lisztian technical bravura and small signs of compositional influence (for instance, in short passages of music linking two principal sections of a composition). *Islamey* demonstrates both aspects, and it is hardly surprising that the work appealed so greatly to Liszt, even without its 'oriental' vitality and languor. The same influence is clear in Balakirev's piano transcriptions of others' compositions, and in his own Fantasia on themes from *Zhizn' za tsarya* ('A Life for the Tsar') (or, at least, from its second form). While Liszt as inventor of the symphonic poem has some claim on *Tamara*, credit for the orchestral compositions which are based on folk themes belongs properly with Glinka and Balakirev himself. On the other hand, Balakirev's sympathy with Liszt's ideals accounts in part for the introduction into Russian music of a number of symphonic poems whether described as 'musical pictures' (*Sadko* and *In Central Asia*) or 'fantasy overture' (*Romeo and Juliet*).

The example of Glinka is felt most strongly when Balakirev deals with folk material. The starting-point is indicated when Balakirev began with the Spanish themes bequeathed to him by Glinka, rather than with Russian material. It is there, in the Fandango-étude (of 1856, revised as the *Sérénade espagnole* in 1902) for piano and the orchestral *Uvertyura na temu ispanskogo marsha* ('Overture on a Spanish March Theme', 1857) that we see the 'Glinka variations', also known as 'variations with changing backgrounds' – without any trace of Russian 'nationalist' inclination. It is only later that explicit native ambitions manifest themselves, once the feeling of Russian distinctness from Europe had grown stronger. Like Glinka's *Kamarinskaya* of 1848, the *Uvertyura na temï tryokh russkikh pesen* ('Overture on the Themes of Three Russian Songs'), whether in its 1858 or 1881 versions, is an abstract work exploring musical relationships among folksong themes. What is most remarkable is the advance which Balakirev makes in handling material. Both the Overture and *Kamarinskaya* demonstrate how it is possible to construct a sustained musical argument employing folk musical resources. Neither composer, whether in his title or anywhere else, gives the slightest hint of any extra-musical narrative associated with his work. Balakirev goes further than Glinka, however, in reconciling the idiomatic treatment of folksong with the standard practices of art music: motivic fragmentation, contrapuntal combination, and a structure exploiting key relationships which also manages to draw on aspects typical of folk usage, such as ostinato, pedal, and harmonic practices foreign to most 19th-century art music. Between the two Overtures on Russian Themes came Balakirev's involvement with folksong collecting and arrangement, which fell largely between 1860 and 1865. That work alerted him to the frequency of the Dorian mode, the tendency of many melodies to swing between a major key and its relative minor or its flat 7th key, and the tendency to accentuate notes not consistent with dominant harmony. These essential qualities were authentically mirrored in Balakirev's harmonizations, and were recognized as significant new perceptions about the character of Russian folksongs. This activity finds reflection in his own subsequent handling of Russian folksong.

The second overture on Russian themes (first published in 1869 as *1000 let*, '1000 Years') is yet more sophisticated in compositional technique and more complex in the implications of its various titles. It shows the composer even more expert in deriving – Beethoven-like – short motifs from longer themes such that the motifs can be sewn together in a convincing contrapuntal fabric. This is a supreme example of how folk material may be reconciled with modern symphonic thinking, technique and structure. It can stand on its own as a specimen of abstract motivic-thematic working, yet since it employs folksongs it could also be represented as making a statement about nationality. It seems that it was first connected in Balakirev's mind (in 1863–4) with Herzen's campaign for political reform in Russia, then in its 1869 publication with the ideas evoked by its composer-given title *1000 Years*, tied to the millennium of the Russian state founded in 862 CE, and finally with the less specific ancient 'Rus'' (as the final version of it was known in Russian, despite the published title, *Russia*) – a form of the title upon which Balakirev insisted, wishing to avoid the modern term *Rossiya*. The changing subtitles, from 'Overture' in 1863–4, to 'musical picture' in 1869 and 'symphonic poem' in 1890 and 1907, tell the same story in a different way. As Richard Taruskin has argued (1983), this work thus illustrates its composer's evolution from a 'progressive', a 'man of the sixties', to the Slavophile obscurantist of his final years; increasing directness in claiming the work for the nationalist cause is underlined by the progression in the subtitles. It was these works of Balakirev, together with his *Uvertyura na tri cheskiye*

temï ('Overture on Czech Themes', 1867), published in 1906 as *V Čechách* ('In Bohemia'), which served as models when Rimsky-Korsakov and Borodin came to write equivalent pieces. The finale of Tchaikovsky's Second Symphony, written in 1872 when the composer's interest in Balakirev's principles was at its height, demonstrates another way of creating a large-scale symphonic movement out of material which includes one folksong.

Balakirev's techniques of developing folk material contrapuntally are evident in his own symphonies, of which the first is by far the finer, being a compelling series of contrasted but uniformly strong movements; as with other late compositions, the second, in spite of some strengths (especially the Scherzo alla Cosacca), too often seems to be retracing familiar paths. Economical and ingenious development of motifs, with not a few harmonic *trouvailles*, are features of the finale of the first symphony.

In 1861–2 Balakirev gave much thought to a Piano Concerto in E♭ major, to the point where he was able to perform it all to Rimsky-Korsakov. Nothing beyond the first movement was written down then, and the composer returned to it only in 1906, even then leaving it unfinished on his death. In Lyapunov's completion the work adds something to our knowledge of the composer chiefly through its references to Russian church music.

The 'oriental' idiom cultivated in parts of *Ruslan and Lyudmila* was developed and made into a more consistent style by Balakirev. It appears in the *Georgian Song* (1863), *Islamey* and *Tamara* as well as occurring in (for example) the Polovtsian Dances, parts of *Sheherazade*, and the Dance of the Persian Slavegirls in *Khovanshchina*. Its ingredients comprise slow sinuous melody with decoration, often scored for clarinet or english horn, slow-moving harmonic progressions, often involving pedal with a movement between the fifth and sixth degrees via the raised 5th, and a drumlike accompanimental figure; the counterpart to that languorous vein is the ecstatic one, marked by a perpetuum mobile at a very fast tempo, with rapid melodic contours over not so rapid harmonic change with immensely colourful instrumentation. As the examples above suggest, this idiom was a somewhat anomalous matter. On the one hand, it served to evoke the mystery of the distant, or at least the exotic, 'east' with which Russia had not very direct contact; on the other hand, it could also be used to refer to recently colonized areas of the Russian Empire. It served to conjure up both the exotic and the local, both the 'self' and the 'other', and precisely which depended on non-musical elements. For Western listeners, on the other hand, the style suggested only the exotic, only the 'other', so that the exceptionally strong representation of this strand in the music of Russian composers, with suggestive costumes (often by Bakst) in Diaghilev's early seasons of opera and ballet in Paris, created a distorted image of Russian music in the minds of its new devotees. *Tamara* may reasonably be thought to be Balakirev's masterpiece. Inspired by Lermontov's poem and its beloved setting in the mountains and gorges of the Caucasus, Balakirev produced a wonderful evocation of the landscape and atmosphere in which the angelic and devilish seductive power of Tamara work their effect before the latest passing lover is discarded. The plot implies a wide musical range, and the composer supplies it with great subtlety within a satisfying structure.

Berlioz's lucid writing for the orchestra, and his magical scherzos (especially that associated with Queen Mab in *Roméo et Juliette*) made their way into Russian music through Balakirev's championship. In the case of orchestration, it was not surprising, since clarity was also a distinguishing aspect of Glinka's scoring – traceable to Weber and again, perhaps, to Berlioz. That quality remained in a great deal of Russian orchestral composition until the influences of Schumann and later Wagner prompted a more experimental blending of diverse sonorities. Several of the symphonic scherzos of Rimsky-Korsakov and Borodin confirm the influence of *Queen Mab*. Like Berlioz (and, for that matter, Schumann), Balakirev turned to Shakespeare for one of his compositions, supplying sensitive treatments of English songs communicated by Stasov for some of his incidental music for *King Lear*. Incidental music for a play was a tradition likewise inherited from Glinka, even if he composed for Kukol'nik's tragedy *Prince Kholmsky* rather than for Shakespearean drama.

Songs occur in both early and late periods of Balakirev's output – again with a tendency for the earlier works to be more strikingly original while the later ones compensate for lower creative temperature with greater craftsmanship. Of some 45 songs, 11 have texts by Lermontov, 8 by Kol'tsov and 5 by Khomyakov, with such lyric poets on permanent standby for composers as Fet or Mey set twice each and Maykov once; Musorgsky's friend Count Golenishchev-Kutuzov makes one appearance. Balakirev's songs are marked by consistency of texture and elegance of vocal line. The piano parts are sometimes demanding; several songs also exist with orchestral accompaniments. All the songs have high ambitions: they are not for the middle-brow market. Sometimes a Russian folklore strand is obvious: *Prologue* (1903) is an excellent example. At other times the 'oriental' pattern is to the fore, as in *Pesnya Selima* ('Song of Selim', 1858) or

Gruzinskaya pesnya ('Georgian Song') – Balakirev's single song setting of Pushkin. *Kolïbel'naya pesnya* ('Cradle Song', 1858) demonstrates the composer's skill in devising a beautifully simple but memorable specimen of a standard genre. *Pesnya zolotoy rïbki* ('Song of the Golden Fish', 1860) is wonderfully suggestive of the enticing mermaid amid the waves and of the escapes from reality afforded by love and dreams; the composer generates an ecstatic atmosphere by means of expert control of technical resources.

Balakirev was a crucial figure in Russian music. He extended and developed the fusion which Glinka had accomplished between on the one hand the common-practice music of his day and on the other some musical elements of Russian character and others of a boldly experimental nature. Balakirev established patterns which could be used to express overtly national feeling in music. In his own compositions he demonstrated how this could be done, laying the basis for a rich repertory spanning all the contemporary genres. By taking amateur musicians of prescribed musical education but enormous potential, he made of Musorgsky, Rimsky-Korsakov and Borodin composers of national and eventually international rank, whose music represented Russia through its history, literature and traditions to the world beyond the Empire's frontiers. In doing so Balakirev imparted what he had himself concluded, so that a great deal of his thinking underlies the music of his pupils. Balakirev's compositions began to find their way abroad with *Islamey*. Thereafter *Tamara* and some other works became known in the wake of compositions by Borodin, Rimsky-Korsakov and Tchaikovsky – partly on account of delay in completing works likely to be found attractive in other countries. When Sibelius, Debussy, Ravel and Falla learnt from their Russian predecessors, they were absorbing Balakirev's discoveries and inventions, whether at first hand or through compositions by his pupils.

WORKS

THEATRICAL

Title	Description	Composed	Publication/MS
Korol' Lir [King Lear]	incid music to Shakespeare's tragedy		
1st version		1858–61	*USSR Lsc*
2nd version		1902–5	Leipzig, 1902–6
Zhar-ptitsa [The Firebird]	op, frags. only	1864	*Lsc*

CHORAL

unaccompanied unless otherwise stated

Title	Translation	Forces	Text	Composed	Publication/MS; remarks
Pesnya: Zholtïy list	Song: The yellow leaf trembles	3-vv chorus	M. Lermontov	*c*1860–70	*Lsc*, sketches only; arr. 1v, pf, 1903–4 (Leipzig, 1904)
6 anthems		mixed chorus	biblical	*c*1880–90	Pubd as Dukhovno-muzïkal'nïye perelozheniya i sochineniya M. Balakireva [Sacred Music Arrangements and Compositions by M. Balakirev], Moscow, 1900

1	Kheruvimskaya pesn'	Song of the Cherubim
2	Da molchit vsyakaya plot'	All flesh is silent
3	Dostoyno	It is worthy
4	Svïshe prorotsï	From heaven the prophets

Title	Translation	Forces	Text	Composed	Publication/MS; remarks
5 Da vozraduyetsya dusha tvoya	Thy soul is regenerated				
6 So svyatimi upokoy	Rest with the holy ones				St Petersburg, 1888
Khristos voskrese	Christ is risen	female or children's vv	biblical	1883	Moscow, 1906; arr. mixed chorus (Moscow, 1906)
Gimn v chest' v.k. Georgiya Vsevolodovicha	Hymn in honour of the Grand Duke Georgy Vsevolodovich	mixed chorus	V. Likhachov	1889	St Petersburg, 1904
Umchalos' vremya zolotoye: pros-chal'naya pesn' vipusknïkh vospitannits Polotskogo zhenskogo uchilishcha dukhovnogo vedomstva	The golden time has flown away; leaving song of the pupils of the Polotsky Ecclesiastical Girls' College	4 female vv	A. Yasherova	1891	St Petersburg, 1891
Gimn v chest' avgusteyshey pokrovitel'nitsï Polotskogo zhenskogo uchilishcha, imperatritsï Marii Fyodorovnï	Hymn in honour of the most august patroness of Polotsky Girls' College, the Empress Mariya Fyodorovna	4 female vv, pf	A. Yasherova	1898	Lsc
Pod sen'yu shchedroy blagostïni: gimn dlya zhenskogo khora	Beneath the shadow of Thy overflowing mercy: hymn for women's chorus	female vv	Likhachov	1899	St Petersburg, 1899
Molitva russkikh, Gimn russkomu tsaryu: gimn dlya zhenskogo khora	The prayer of the Russians, hymn to the Russian tsar: for women's chorus	female vv	A. Pushkin	1899	Moscow, 1899; arr. mixed chorus (Moscow, 1899)
Gimn Khvala vsederzhitelyu bogu	Hymn: Praise to Almighty God	4 female vv	M. Samochernova	1902	Lil
Tebe mï gimn poyem, o shkola dorogaya: shkol'nïy gimn dlya zhenskogo ili detskogo khora	We sing you a hymn, o dear school: school hymn for women's or children's chorus	female or children's vv	P. Lebedinsky	1902	St Petersburg, 1902
Kantata na otkrïtiye pamyatnika M.I. Glinke v Peterburge	Cantata for the unveiling of the memorial to M.I. Glinka in St Petersburg	S, chorus, orch	V. Glebov	1902–4	Leipzig, 1904
Proschchay navsegda, nash priyut nezabvennïy: 2-ya proshchal'naya pesn' vospitannits Polotskogo zhenskogo uchilishcha dukhovnogo vedomstva	Farewell for ever, our unforgettable haven: second leaving song of the pupils of the Polotsky Ecclesiastical Girls' College	3 female vv	N. Zabelina-Bekarevich	1908	St Petersburg, 1908
Angel vopiyashe (valaamskogo rospeva)	The angel cried out (Valaam chant)	male vv			St Petersburg, 1912
Ust tvoikh (Tropar' Ioannu Zlatoustu, valaamskogo rospeva)	From Thy Lips (Troparion to St. John Chrysostom, Valaam chant)	SATB			St Petersburg, 1912

ORCHESTRAL

op.	Title	Composed	Publication/MS	Remarks
4	Grande fantaisie on Russian folksongs, pf, orch	1852	Lsc	arr. 2 pf (Moscow, 1954)
1	Concerto, f♯, pf, orch	1855–6	Lil	1 movt only; score pubd (Moscow, 1952); arr. 2 pf (Moscow, 1954)
—	Uvertyura na temu ispanskogo marsha [Overture on a Spanish March Theme]			
	1st version	1857	Lsc	–
	2nd version	1886	St Petersburg, 1887	–
—	Polonaise-fantaisie	1857	Lsc	unfinished
—	Uvertyura na temï tryokh russkikh pesen [Overture on the themes of three Russian songs]			
	1st version	1858	Lil, Lsc	–
	2nd version	1881	Moscow, 1882	Balakirev's arr. pf 4 hands (Moscow, 1882)
—	Concerto, E♭, pf, orch	1861–2, 1906–9	Leipzig, 1911	unfinished; completed by Lyapunov
—	Second Overture on Russian themes			
	1st version	1863–4	St Petersburg, 1869	Pubd as musical picture 1000 let [1000 Years]
	2nd version	1884	St Petersburg, 1890	Pubd as Russia: poème symphonique pour orchestre; repubd with minor alterations (Leipzig, 1907); known in Russian as Rus'

op.	Title	Composed	Publication/MS	Remarks
—	Symphony no.1, C	1864–6, 1893–7	Leipzig, 1899	Balakirev's arr. 2 pf (Leipzig, 1899)
—	Uvertyura na tri cheshkiye temï [Overture on Czech themes]			
	1st version	1867	Lil,Lk	–
	2nd version	1905	Leipzig 1906	Pubd as V Chechii [In Bohemia]
—	Tamara, sym. poem	1867–82	Moscow, 1884	Balakirev's arr. 2 pf 4-hands (Moscow, 1908)
—	Symphony no.2, d	1900–08	Leipzig, 1908	Scherzo sketched c1864, orig. intended for Sym. no.1; Balakirev's arr. 2 pf (Leipzig, 1908)
—	Suite, b: Préambule, Quasi valse, Tarantella	1901–8	Lil,Lsc	unfinished; completed by Lyapunov
—	Suite on pieces by Chopin: Préambule, Mazurka, Intermezzo, Finale	1909	Leipzig, 1909	based on Chopin's Etude, d, Mazurka, B♭, Nocturne, g, Scherzo, d

CHAMBER

op.	Title	Composed	Publication/MS	Remarks
—	Septet, fl, cl, 2 vn, va, vc, pf	1852	–	lost
2	String quartet (Quatuor original russe)	1854–6	Lsc	unfinished
3	Octet, fl, ob, hn, vn, va, vc, db, pf	1855–6	Moscow, 1959	1st movt and frags. of scherzo only, perhaps rev. of Septet; scherzo adapted for Scherzo no.2, pf, 1900
—	Romance, vc, pf	1856	Leipzig, 1911; Lsc	completed by Lyapunov

PIANO

Edition: *M.A. Balakirev: polnoye sobraniye sochineniy dlya fortepiano*, ed. K.S. Sorokin (Moscow, 1951–4) [B]

for solo pf unless otherwise stated

Title	Composed	Publications/MS	Remarks	B
Fantasia on themes from Glinka's Zhizn′ za tsarya				
1st version	1854–6	Lsc	–	–
2nd version	1899	Leipzig, 1899	as Réminiscences de l'opéra 'La vie pour le czar'	iii/1, 6
Sonata no.1, b♭, op.5	1855–6	Moscow, 1949	3 movts only, adapted from an early Bol'shaya sonata, op.3; pt. of 1st movt used later in Scherzo no.2, 1900, 2nd movt rev. as 2nd movt of Sonata, 1900–05, and as Mazurka no.5, 1900	i/2, 93
Nocturne no.1, b♭				
1st version g♯	1856	Lsc	–	–
2nd version b♭	1898	Moscow, 1898	–	ii, 117
Fandango-étude	1856	Lsc	rev. as Ispanskaya serenada, 1902	–
Scherzo no.1, b	1856	St Petersburg, 1863	–	ii, 3
Polka, f♯	1859	St Petersburg, 1859	–	i/1, 30
Impromptu, f	c1850–60	Lsc	–	–
Mazurka no.1, A♭				
1st version	1861	St Petersburg, 1861	–	ii, 240
2nd version	1884–5	Moscow, 1885	–	ii, 55
Mazurka no.2				
1st version, b	1861	St Petersburg, 1861	–	ii, 248
2nd version, c♯	1884	Moscow, 1885	–	ii, 62
Na Volge [On the Volga], pf 4-hands	c1863	Moscow, 1949	–	iii/1, 288
Zhavoronok [The Lark]			based on Glinka's song	
1st version	c1864	Mainz, 1872		–
2nd version	1900	Mainz, 1900		iii/1, 58
Islamey, oriental fantasy				
1st version	1869	Moscow, 1870	–	
2nd version	1902	Hamburg, 1902	–	i/1, 3
Au jardin, D♭	1884	Moscow, 1885	–	i/1, 36
Mazurka no.3, b	1886	Moscow, 1886	–	ii, 64
Mazurka no.4, G♭	1886	Moscow, 1886	–	ii, 73
Pustïnya [The Wilderness]	1898	Leipzig, 1898	arr. of no.2 of Balakirev's 10 songs, 1895–6	iii/1, 3
30 russkikh narodnïkh pesen [30 Russian Folksongs], pf 4-hands	1898	St Petersburg and Leipzig, 1898	arr. of Balakirev's 2nd collection, 1898	iii/1, 169

Title	Composed	Publications/MS	Remarks	B
Dumka, e♭	1900	Leipzig, 1900	–	i/1, 43
Mazurka no.5, D	1900	Leipzig, 1900	used in Sonata, 1900–05	ii, 82
Scherzo no.2, b♭	1900	Leipzig, 1900	uses pt. of inc. scherzo for Octet, 1855–6, and pt. of 1st movt of Sonata op.5, 1855–6	ii, 21
Valse di bravura no.1, G	1900	Leipzig, 1900	–	ii, 141
Valse mélancholique no.2, f	1900	Leipzig, 1900	–	ii, 161
Sonata, b♭	1900–05	Leipzig, 1905	2nd movt adapted from 2nd movt of Sonata op.5, 1855–6, and also pubd separately as Mazurka no.5, 1900	i/2, 3
Berceuse, D♭	1901	Leipzig, 1901	–	i/1, 58
Gondellied, a	1901	Leipzig, 1901	–	i/1, 49
Nocturne no.2, b	1901	Leipzig, 1901	–	ii, 124
Scherzo no.3, F♯	1901	Leipzig, 1901	–	ii, 39
Valse-impromptu no.3, D	1901	Leipzig, 1901	–	ii, 170
Tarantella, B	1901	Leipzig, 1901	–	i/1, 65
Capriccio, D	1902	Leipzig, 1902	–	i/1, 83
Mélodie espagnole	1902	Leipzig, 1902	–	iii/1, 30
Sérénade espagnole	1902	Leipzig, 1902	rev. of Fandango-étude, 1856	iii/1, 37
Mazurka no.6, A♭	1902	Leipzig, 1902	–	ii, 94
Nocturne no.3, d	1902	Leipzig, 1902	–	i/1, 132
Toccata, c♯	1902	Leipzig, 1902	–	i/1, 106
Tyrolienne, F♯	1902	Leipzig, 1902	–	i/1, 118
Waltz no.4, B♭	1902	Leipzig 1902	–	ii, 180
Chant du pêcheur, b	1903	Leipzig, 1903	–	i/1, 129
Humoresque, D	1903	Leipzig 1903	–	i/1, 134
Phantasiestück, D♭	1903	Leipzig, 1903	–	i/1, 159
Rêverie, F	1903	Leipzig, 1903	–	i/1, 149
Waltz no.5, D♭	1903	Leipzig, 1903	–	ii, 197
Waltz no.6, f♯	1903	Leipzig, 1903	–	ii, 213
La fileuse, b♭	1906	Leipzig, 1906	–	i/2, 69
Mazurka no.7, e♭	1906	Leipzig, 1906	–	ii, 106
Novelette, A	1906	Leipzig, 1906	–	i/2, 57
Waltz no.7, g♯	1906	Leipzig, 1906	–	ii, 223
Impromptu	1907	Leipzig, 1907	based on Chopin's Preludes, e♭ and B	iii/1, 47
Esquisses (Sonatina), G	1909	Leipzig, 1910	–	i/2, 81
Suite, pf 4-hands: Polonaise, Chansonette sans paroles, Scherzo	1909	Leipzig, 1909	orig. sketches c1850–60, Lsc	iii/1, 246

SONGS

all for 1 voice with piano accompaniment; published in St Petersburg unless otherwise stated

Title	English version	Text	Composed	Publication; remarks
Tri zabïtïkh romansa [Three Forgotten Songs]:			1855	Leipzig, 1908
1 Tï plenitel'noy negi polna	Thou art so captivating	A. Golovinsky		
2 Zveno	The Link	V. Tumansky		
3 Ispanskaya pesnya	Spanish song	M. Mikhaylov		
20 songs:				
1 Pesnya razboynika	Brigand's song	A. Kol'tsov	1858	1858
2 Oboymi, potseluy	Embrace, Kiss	Kol'tsov	1858	1858
3 Barkarola	Barcarolle	A. Arsen'yev, after H. Heine	1858	1858
4 Kolïbel'naya pesnya	Cradle song	Arsen'yev	1858	1858; arr. chorus, orch/pf, 1898
5 Vzoshol na nebo mesyats yasnïy	The Bright Moon	M. Yatsevich	1858	1859
6 Kogda bezzabotno, ditya, tï rezvish'sya	When thou Playest, Carefree Child	K. Vil'de	1858	1859
7 Rïtsar'	The Knight	Vil'de	1858	1859
8 Mne li, molodtsu razudalomu	I'm a fine fellow	Kol'tsov	1858	1859
9 Tak i rvetsya dusha	My heart is torn	Kol'tsov	1858	1859
10 Pridi ko mne	Come to me	Kol'tsov	1858	1859
11 Pesnya Selima	Song of Selim	M. Lermontov	1858	1859
12 Vvedi menya, o noch', taykom	Lead me, o night	A. Maykov	1859	1859
13 Evreyskaya melodiya	Hebrew melody	Lermontov, after Byron	1859	1861
14 Isstupleniye	Rapture	Kol'tsov	1859	1861
15 Otchego	Why	Lermontov	1860	1861

Title	English version	Text	Composed	Publication; remarks
16 Pesnya zolotoy rïbki	Song of the Golden Fish	Lermontov	1860	1861
17 Pesnya starika	Old Man's song	Kol'tsov	1865	1865
18 Slïshu li golos tvoy	When I Hear thy Voice	Lermontov	1863	1865
19 Gruzinskaya pesnya	Georgian song	A. Pushkin	1863	1865; orchd c1860–70 (Moscow, 1885)
20 Son	The Dream	Mikhaylov, after Heine	1864	1865; orchd 1906 (Moscow, 1907)
10 songs:			1895–6	Moscow, 1896
1 Nad ozerom	Over the Lake	A. Golenishchev-Kutuzov		–
2 Pustïnya	The Wilderness	A. Zhemchuzhnikov		arr. pf, 1898
3 Ne penitsya more	The sea does not foam	A.K. Tolstoy		–
4 Kogda volnuyetsya zhelteyushchaya niva	When the Yellow Cornfield Waves	Lermontov		–
5 Ya lyubila ego	I loved him	Kol'tsov		–
6 Sosna	The Pine Tree	Lermontov		orig. sketches, 1861, Lil
7 Nachtstück	–	A. Khomyakov		–
8 Kak naladili: durak	The Putting-Right	L. Mey		–
9 Sredi tsvetov porï osenney	'Mid Autumn Flowers	I. Aksakov		–
10 Dogorayet rumyanïy zakat	The rosy sunset fades	V. Kul'chinsky		–
10 songs:			1903–4	Leipzig, 1904
1 Zapevka	Prologue	Mey		orchd 1906, Leipzig, 1911
2 Son	The Dream	Lermontov		–
3 Bezzvezdnaya polnoch'	Starless midnight coldly breathed	Khomyakov		–
4 7 noyabrya	7th November	Khomyakov		–
5 Ya prishol k tebe s privetom	I came to thee with greeting	A. Fet		–
6 Vzglyani, moy drug	Look, my friend	V. Krasov		–
7 Shepot, robkoye dïkhan'ye	A Whisper, a Timid Breath	Fet		–
8 Pesnya: Zholtïy list	Song: The yellow leaf trembles	Lermontov		orig. sketches for 3-vv chorus, c1860–70, Lsc
9 Iz-pod tainstvennoy kholodnoy polumaski	Under the Mysterious Cold Half-Mask	Lermontov		–
10 Spi!	Sleep!	Khomyakov		
Zarya	Dawn	Khomyakov	1909	Leipzig, 1911
Utyos	The Rock	Lermontov	1909	Leipzig, 1911

CHORAL TRANSCRIPTIONS

all unaccompanied unless otherwise stated

Title	Text	Forces	Transcribed	Publication/MS	Remarks
Kolïbel'naya pesnya [Cradle song]	N. Kukolnik	SAATTBB	c1887	Moscow, 1900	arr. of Glinka's song
Mazurka	A. Khomyakov	SATTBB	c1887	Moscow, 1898	arr. of Chopin's Mazurkas op.6 no.4, e♭ and op.11 no.4, A♭
Venetsianskaya noch' [Venetian Night]	I. Kozlov	SATB	c1887	Moscow, 1897	arr. of Glinka's song
Kolïbel'naya pesnya	A. Arsen'yev	2 female or children's vv, orch/pf	1898	Moscow, 1898	arr. of no.4 of Balakirev's 20 songs; arr. mixed chorus, orch/pf c1880–90, Lsc
Dve bïlini [Two Legends]: 1 Nikita Romanovich 2 Korolevichi iz Krakova [The King's Sons from Kraków]	Folksongs	SATB	1902	Moscow, 1902	nos.6 and 8 in Balakirev's 30 russkikh narodnïkh pesen [30 Russian folksongs]
Eko serdtse [Oh! My Heart]	Folksong	SATB	?1902	Lil	No.27 in Balakirev's 30 russkikh narodnïkh pesen

PIANO TRANSCRIPTIONS

Edition: *M.A. Balakirev: polnoye sobraniye sochineniy dlya fortepiano*, ed. K.S. Sorokin (Moscow, 1951–4) [B]
for solo piano unless otherwise stated

Beethoven: Cavatina from Str Qt, op.130, 1859 (St Petersburg, 1859), B iii/1, 150

Beethoven: Allegretto from Str Qt, op.59 no.2, 1862 (Moscow, 1954), B iii/1, 153

Beethoven: Str Qt, op.95, 2 pf, 1862 (St Petersburg, 1875), B iii/2, 165

Berlioz: Introduction to La fuite en Egypte, 1864 (St Petersburg, 1864), B iii/1, 142

Berlioz: Harold en Italie, pf 4 hands, 1876 (Paris, 1879)

Chopin: Romance from Pf Conc. op.11, 1905 (Leipzig, 1905), B iii/1, 158

Dargomïzhsky: 2 excerpts from Rogdana, pf 4 hands, 1908 (St Petersburg, 1908)

Glinka: Kamarinskaya, pf 4 hands, 1863 (St Petersburg, 1863); 2nd version, solo pf, 1902 (Moscow, 1902), B iii/1, 87

Glinka: Jota aragonesa, solo pf and pf 4 hands, 1863–4 (St Petersburg, 1864), B iii/1, 291; rev. 1900 (Mainz, 1900), B iii/1, 64

Glinka: Knyaz′ Kholmsky [Prince Kholmsky], pf 4 hands, 1864 (St Petersburg, ?1864)

Glinka: Noch′ v Madride [Night in Madrid], solo pf and pf 4 hands, 1864 (St Petersburg, ?1864)

Glinka: Quartet, F, pf 4 hands, 1877 (Moscow, 1878)

Glinka: Chernomor's march from Ruslan i Lyudmila, collab. Liszt, 1890 (Moscow 1890)

Glinka: Ne govori [Do not speak], 1903 (Leipzig, 1903), B iii/1, 102

L′vov: Ov. to Undina, pf 4 hands, 1900 (Leipzig, 1901)

Paganini: Vn Caprice op.1 no.3, c1872, Lsc

A.S. Taneyev: 2 Valse-caprices, A♭, C♭, 1900 (Leipzig, 1900), B iii/1, 121, 131

Zapol′sky: Rêverie, ?1890s (St Petersburg, c1900), B iii/1, 110

OTHER ARRANGEMENTS

Chopin: Mazurka op.7 no.7, arr. str orch, ?1885 (Leipzig, 1904)

Chopin: Pf Conc. op.11, orchd and partly rewritten, 1910 (Leipzig, 1910)

Dargomïzhsky: Paladin [The Knight-Errant], arr. 1v, orch, c1860–70, Lil

Dargomïzhsty: 2 excerpts from Rogdana, arr. 1v, pf, c1870–72 (St Petersburg, 1872)

Glinka: Bolero: O deva chudnaya moya [O my beautiful maid], arr. 1v, orch, c1860–70, Lil

Glinka: Nochnoy smotr [Midnight review], arr. 1v, orch, 1860 (Moscow, 1906)

Glinka: Oriental dances from Ruslan i Lyudmila, arr. 1 orch, 1868 (Leipzig, 1878)

L′vov: Ov. to Undina, orchd 1900 (Leipzig, 1901)

Orchestrations of other short works and parts of works by Cui, Dargomïzhsky, Glinka, Gussakovsky and Liszt

FOLKSONG COLLECTIONS

Sbornik russkikh narodnïkh pesen [Collection of Russian Folksongs], 1865–6 (St Petersburg, 1866); ed. Ye. Gippius (Moscow, 4/1957)

30 pesen russkogo naroda [30 Russian Folksongs], 1898 (Leipzig, 1899); arr. pf 4 hands, 1898 (Moscow, 1898), nos.6, 8 and 27 also arr. chorus, 1902

EDITIONS

F. Chopin: Sonate pour piano et violoncelle, op.65 (Leipzig, 1907)

F. Chopin: Premier trio pour pianoforte, violon et violoncelle, op.8 (Leipzig, 1908)

I. Laskovsky: Oeuvres complètes pour piano (St Petersburg, 1858–9)

V. Odoyevsky: Berceuse (Moscow, 1895)

M. Wielhorski and F. Liszt: Lyubila ya [Loved I him] (Moscow, 1887)

Balakirev assisted with the preparation of Berlioz's Te Deum for publication (Leipzig, 1901), edited a selection of Tausig's piano compositions (Leipzig, 1903–4, 1907) and also produced editions of many of Glinka's works, a list of which is contained in Garden (1967), 339ff.

BIBLIOGRAPHY

G.I. Timofeyev: 'M.A. Balakirev v Prage: iz yego perepiski' [Balakirev in Prague: from his correspondence], *Sovremennïy mir* (1911), no.6, pp.147–86

S.M. Lyapunov, ed.: *Perepiska M.A. Balakireva s P.I. Chaykovskim* [Balakirev's correspondence with Tchaikovsky] (St Petersburg, 1912)

B. de Schloezer: 'Balakireff et l'Ecole Nationale Russe', *ReM*, iv/10 (1922–3), 11–19

G. Abraham: 'Balakirev's Symphonies', *ML*, xiv (1933), 355–63; repr. in *On Russian Music* (London, 1939), 179–92

G. Abraham: 'Balakirev: a Flawed Genius', *Studies in Russian Music* (London, 1935), 311–33

M.D. Calvocoressi: 'Mily Balakiref', *Masters of Russian Music*, ed. M.D. Calvocoressi and G. Abraham (London, 1936), 97–146

G. Abraham: 'Balakirev's Music to *King Lear*', 'Balakirev's Piano Sonata', *On Russian Music* (London, 1939), 193–204, 205–15

A. Kandinsky: *Simfonicheskiye proizvedeniya M. Balakireva* [Balakirev's symphonic compositions] (Moscow and Leningrad, 1950, Moscow, 2/1960)

A.S. Lyapunova: 'Glinka i Balakirev', *SovM* (1953), no.2, pp.75–81

M. Montagu-Nathan, ed.: 'Balakirev's Letters to Calvocoressi', *ML*, xxxv (1954), 347–60

V.A. Kiselyov, ed.: *M.A. Balakirev: perepiska s N.G. Rubinshteynom i s M.P. Belyayevïm* [Balakirev's correspondence with N. Rubinstein and Belyayev] (Moscow, 1956)

V.A. Kiselyov and A.S.Lyapunova, eds.: *M.A. Balakirev: perepiska s notoizdatel′stvom P. Yurgenson* [Balakirev's correspondence with Jürgenson's publishing house] (Moscow, 1958)

V.A. Kiselyov: *Avtografï M.A. Balakireva i materialï, svyazannïye s yego deyatel′nost′yu v fondakh gosudarstvennogo tsentral′nogo muzeya muzïkal′noy kul′turï imeni M.I. Glinki* [Balakirev's autographs and other materials connected with his activities, contained in the archives of the Glinka Central Museum of Musical Culture, Moscow] (Moscow, 1959)

E.L. Frid: 'Dva pis′ma M. Balakireva k Éduardu Reysu' [Two letters of Balakirev to Eduard Reiss], *SovM* (1960), no.5, pp.68–71

A.S. Lyapunova: *Tvorcheskoye naslediye M.A. Balakireva: katalog proizvedeniy* [The creative heritage of Balakirev: catalogue of works] (Leningrad, 1960)

D. Brown: 'Balakirev, Tchaikovsky and Nationalism', *ML*, xlii (1961), 227–41

Yu.A. Kremlyov and others, eds.: *Miliy Alekseyevich Balakirev: issledovaniya i stat′i* [Research and articles] (Leningrad, 1961) [incl. articles on an autograph song for *The Firebird*, the symphonic works, an unrealized opera project, Balakirev's journeys to Warsaw, the piano music, the creative relationship between Balakirev and Lyapunov, the choral works and the ballads and songs]

Yu.A. Kremlyov and others, eds.: *Miliy Alekseyevich Balakirev: vospominaniya i pis′ma* [Reminiscences and letters] (Leningrad, 1962) [incl. letters to his father, Filippov, Timofeyev, Chernov, Zhemchuzhnikov, Bulich, Tchaikovsky, Bourgault-Ducoudray; list of pubd letters, reminiscences by Kul′chinsky, Lalayeva and others]

A.S. Lyapunova, ed.: 'Perepiska M.A. Balakireva i N.A. Rimskogo-Korsakova' [Correspondence between Balakirev and Rimsky-Korsakov], *N. Rimsky-Korsakov: literaturnïye proizvedeniya i perepiska*, v (Moscow, 1963), 17–210

R. Davis: 'Henselt, Balakirev and the Piano', *MR*, xxviii (1967), 173–208

E. Garden: *Balakirev: a Critical Study of his Life and Music* (London, 1967)

I. Kunin: *Miliy Alekseyevich Balakirev: zhizn′ i tvorchestvo v pis′makh i dokumentakh* [Life and works in letters and documents] (Moscow, 1967)

A.S. Lyapunova and E.E.Yazovitskaya: *Miliy Alekseyevich Balakirev: letopis′ zhizni i tvorchestva* [Chronicle of his life and works] (Leningrad, 1967)

E. Garden: 'Balakirev's Personality', *PRMA*, xcvi (1969–70), 43–55

A.S. Lyapunova, ed.: *M.A. Balakirev – V.V. Stasov: perepiska, i 1858–80, ii 1881–1906* [Correspondence] (Moscow, 1970–71)

V. Gregor: 'Neznámé kapitoly z česko-ruských hudebních styků' [An unknown chapter in Czech-Russian musical relations], *HRo*, xxviii/10 (1975), 466–9

M.K. Černý: 'Smetana a Balakirev (k interpretaci kulturně politických souvislostí ve Smetanově díle)' [Smetana and Balakirev (concerning the interpretation of the cultural-political dimension in Smetana's works)], *HV*, xiii/3 (1976), 239–56

B. Dobrokhotov, ed.: *Muzïkal′noye nasledstvo* [Musical heritage], iv (Moscow, 1976) [contains correspondence between Balakirev and Glazunov]

E. Garden: 'The influence of Balakirev on Tchaikovsky', *PRMA*, cvii (1981), 86–100

A. Lischké: 'Un complément inédit à la correspondance de Balakirev: trente-quatre lettres à Alexandre Bernardi', *RdM*, lxvii (1981), 35–60 [incl. bibl. of pubd letters by Balakirev]

R.C. Ridenour: *Nationalism, Modernism and Personal Rivalry in Nineteenth-Century Russian Music* (Ann Arbor, 1981)

E. Garden: 'Balakirev's Influence on Musorgsky', *Musorgsky in Memoriam 1881–1981*, ed. M.H. Brown (Ann Arbor, 1982), 11–27

R. Taruskin: 'How the Acorn took Root: a Tale of Russia', *19CM*, vi (1982–3), 189–212; repr. in R. Taruskin: *Defining Russia Musically: Historical and Hermeneutical Essays* (Princeton, 1997), 113–51

E. Garden: 'Russian Folksong and Balakirev's 1866 Collection', *Soundings*, xi (1983–4), 52–9

E. Garden: 'Balakirev: the Years of Crisis (1867–1876)', *Russian and Soviet Music: Essays for Boris Schwarz*, ed. M.H. Brown (Ann Arbor, 1984), 147–55

E. Garden: 'Sibelius and Balakirev', *Slavonic and Western Music: Essays for Gerald Abraham*, ed. M.H. Brown and R.J. Wiley (Ann Arbor and Oxford, 1985), 215–18

S. Slonimsky: 'Balakirev – pedagog' [Balakirev as teacher], *SovM* (1990), no.3, pp.7–12

T. Zaytseva: 'Balakirev i Lyadov: uchitel' i uchenik' [Balakirev and Lyadov: teacher and pupil], *Iz proshlogo i nastoyashchego otechestvennoy muzïkal'noy kul'turï* [From the past and present of the Fatherland's musical culture], ed. Ye.B. Dolinskaya (Moscow, 1993), 84–95

Yu.V. Keldïsh: 'M.A. Balakirev', *Istoriya russkoy muzïki* [History of Russian music], vii: *70–80e godï XIX veka* [The 70s and 80s of the nineteenth century] (Moscow, 1994), 127–72

C.C. Ritchie: *The Russian Court Chapel Choir: 1796–1917* (diss., U. of Glasgow, 1994) [considers Balakirev's contribution as administrator, composer and teacher to the Kapella]

STUART CAMPBELL

Russian balalaika (long-necked lute)

Balalaika. A long-necked chordophone with a triangular body and three strings. The soundboard is usually constructed from four strips of Russian spruce or silver fir and the slightly arched belly of seven pieces of maple. The instrument has a small soundhole, a fretted neck and strings of gut or steel. The balalaika is related to the *dömbra*, a variant of the long-necked lute played by peoples of Central Asia. The earliest mention in literature appeared in 1688 and Peter the Great used balalaikas in his grand orchestral procession of 1715. The instrument may have been a new arrival or a natural development of the 17th-century *domra*. The *skomorokhis* (minstrels) gave it a primary role in accompanying dance.

A public performance in 1886 began the balalaika's elevation from a peasant's instrument to one of artistic stature. The success of the balalaika is attributed to VASILY VASIL'YEVICH ANDREYEV (1861–1918) who, assisted by the instrument makers V. Ivanov, F. Paserbsky and S. Nalimov, produced a metal-fretted chromatic version in a family of sizes: prime ($e'-e'-a'$), second ($a'-a'-d'$), alto ($e'-e'-a$), bass ($E-A-d$) and double bass ($E'-A'-D$). Piccolo and descant sizes were developed but discarded. Andreyev's Society of Lovers of Balalaika Playing gave its first public performance in Russia in 1888 and in 1889 the Society performed at the Paris Exposition Universelle. The sound so impressed composers of art music that they began to include balalaikas in their orchestration. Tchaikovsky eulogized: 'How lovely is the balalaika. How striking the effect it makes in the orchestra. Timbrally – this is an indispensable instrument'.

By 1896 Andreyev had reorganized his instrumentalists as the Grand Russian Orchestra, which between 1909 and 1912 toured Europe and America (1910–11). Balalaika orchestras were soon formed in Britain (the first was the Royal Balalaika Orchestra, formed at royal request by the balalaika player Prince Tschagadaeff), and the USA (formed largely by Russian emigrants and their descendants). The St Louis Russian Balalaika Orchestra was founded in 1911 by Lewis Spindler and balalaika orchestras were formed in New York City in 1912 by A. Ivanoff and A. Kirilloff. The Balalaika and Domra Society was founded in 1961 and in 1974 John Garvey organized a student balalaika orchestra at the University of Illinois. Many film soundtracks incorporated the instrument and Charlie Chaplin, an afficionado, often performed on the violin or mandolin alongside it. The resurgence of balalaika music, after the McCarthyite suppression of all things Russian in the 1950s, came with the success of the motion picture *Dr Zhivago* in 1969.

BIBLIOGRAPHY

A. Rose: 'The Balalaïka', *PMA*, xxvii (1900–01), 73–84

F.V. Sokolov: *Russkaya narodnaya balalaïka* (Moscow, 1962)

K. Vertkov, G. Blagodatov and E. Yazovitskaya: *Atlas of Musical Instruments of the Peoples Inhabiting the USSR* (Moscow, 1963/R)

M. Kiszko: 'The Balalaika: a Reappraisal', *GSJ*, xlviii (1995), 130–55

MARTIN KISZKO

Bălan, George (*b* Turnu-Măgurele, 11 March 1929). Romanian musicologist. He studied at the Bucharest Conservatory (1950–55) and took the doctorate at Moscow University in 1963 with a dissertation on the philosophic content of music. In 1960 he was appointed professor in musical aesthetics at the Bucharest Conservatory, and has focussed his attention on problems of aesthetics and philosophy. He was music critic for the Bucharest *Contemporanul* (1951–7, 1961–3) and has contributed criticism to numerous Romanian journals.

Much of his recent writing has concerned his new listening method, Musicosophia.

WRITINGS

Innoirile muzicii [The renewals of music] (Bucharest, 1960)
George Enescu: mesajul-estetica (Bucharest, 1962)
O filosofskom soderzhanii muzïki [The philosophical content in music] (diss., U. of Moscow, 1963)
George Enescu: viaţa (Bucharest, 1963)
Gustav Mahler, sau cum exprimă muzica idei [Mahler, or how music expresses ideas] (Bucharest, 1964)
Eu, Richard Wagner: o autobiografie (Bucharest, 1966)
Noi şi clasicii, sau, De la muzica spre 'autimuzica'? O istorie mai neobisnuita a muzicii (Bucharest, 1967)
Arta de a înţelege muzica [The art of understanding music] (Bucharest, 1970)
Meditaţii beethoveniene: lupta cu singuăratatea [Meditations concerning Beethoven: the struggle with solitude] (Bucharest, 1970)
Cazul Schœnberg (Bucharest, 1974)
Cu muzica prin veacuri [With music through the centuries] (Bucharest, 1974)
Muzica şi lumea ideilor [Music and the world of ideas] (Bucharest, 1973)
Mică filosofie a muzicii (Bucharest, 1975) [summaries in Fr., Ger.]
O istorie a muzicii europene (Bucharest, 1975)
Musicosophia (Neustadt, 1981–)
Von der Konservenmusik zur Sphärenmusik: eine Philosophie der Schalplatte (Bad Heilbrunn, 1982)
Nebănuitul Eminescu (Munich, 1984)
Manuale mozartiano di saggezza (St Peter, nr Freiburg, 1994)
Rätselhafter Bruckner (St Peter, nr Freiburg, 1996)

BIBLIOGRAPHY

V. Cosma: *Muzicieni români* (Bucharest, 1970), 56–7
E.M. Cioran: *George Bălan: în dialog* (Bucharest, 1996)

VIOREL COSMA

Balanced action (Fr. *mécanique à balanciers/bascules*; Ger. *balancierte Traktur*; It. *meccanica/trasmissione a bilancia-/bilanciere*). A form of mechanical (or tracker) action used in organ construction since the 17th century, in which the key-shanks are pivoted near their centres, the upwards motion of the rear end of the keys being transmitted to open the pallet by an action in which pairs of squares or at least one backfall are essential. *See* ORGAN, §II, 5.

Balancement (Fr.: 'wavering'; Ger. *Bebung*; It. *tremolo*). A term used mainly for the tremolo obtainable on a clavichord, and also for the vibrato in vocal and string music. *See* ORNAMENTS, §7(ii)(a). *See also* BEBUNG; and VIBRATO.

Balanchine, George. *See* BALANCHIVADZE family, (2).

Balanchivadze. Georgian family of musicians.

(1) **Meliton Balanchivadze** (*b* Banoja, nr Kutaisi, 12/24 Dec 1862; *d* Kutaisi, 21 Nov 1937). Composer. One of the pioneers of Georgian professional music, he is the father of the composer Andria Balanchivadze and the ballet master, George Balanchine. He studied music at the Tbilisi Spiritual Seminary (1877–9), then singing in the choir of, and later taking solo roles at the Tbilisi Opera House. In 1882 he set up a folk choir of 12 singers; it was from this date that his musical and public duties began as a promulgator and a collector of Georgian folk songs. It was also during this period that he wrote his first compositions – the romances *Rodesats gitsker* ('When I Look at You'), *Shen ghetrpi marad* ('I am Eternally Drawn to You') and *Nana* ('Lullaby') – which were early and successful examples of the genre in Georgian music.

In 1889 Balanchivadze enrolled at the St Petersburg Conservatory as a singer, but in 1891 he turned to the serious study of composition, and entered Rimsky-Korsakov's class. Here Balanchivadze started work on his principal composition, the opera *Tamar tsbieri* ('Tamara the Cunning'), fragments of which were heard in St Petersburg in 1897. While living in Russia he organized and appeared with choral groups which performed Georgian folk songs in many towns. In 1906 he was a jury member of the First All-Russian Exhibition of musical instruments and in 1907 he financed the publication of Glinka's letters.

In 1917 Balanchivadze returned to Georgia. There he was actively engaged in musical and public duties, resolving matters of musical education and collecting and studying Georgian folk music. In 1918 he founded a music school (now bearing his name) in Kutaisi, the second largest town in Georgia, and at various times he was the director of the Kutaisi (1935), and Batumi (1929–31) music schools, as well as Chairman of the Board of the Georgian Music Society (1928). He completed *Tamara the Cunning* in 1926 and it was immediately staged in Tbilisi. Sometimes called the first Georgian opera (since it was partially composed and performed at the end of the 19th century) it is written on an historical subject in which patriotic and psychological dramatic lines are interwoven. In terms of its music, however, the opera is entirely sustained on a lyrical, small-scale level, and only acquires a dramatic colouring in places. Among the solo numbers of the opera, the following should be noted: King Georgi's aria, the Jester's Couplets, Tsira's Lullaby, and especially Gocha's aria.

WORKS
(*selective list*)

Op: Tamar tsbieri [Tamara the Cunning], extracts perf. 1897; rev. as Darejan tsbieri (V. Velichko, K. Potskhverashvili, after A. Tsereteli), 1937
Cantata: Dideba ZAHESs [Glory to ZAHES], for opening of first hydro-electric power station in the Caucasus
Songs, choral works, folksong arrs. etc.

Principal publishers: Muzgiz, Muzfond Gruzii (Tbilisi), Muzïka (Moscow and Leningrad)

BIBLIOGRAPHY

P. Khuchua: *M. Balanchivadze* (Tbilisi, 1950) [in Georgian]
P. Khuchua: *M. Balanchivadze* (Tbilisi, 1964) [in Russ.]
S. Ginzburg: 'M. Balanchivadze', *Muzïkal'naya literatura narodov SSSR* [The musical literature of the peoples of the USSR] (Moscow, 1970)
V. Donadze: 'M. Balanchivadze', in G. Toradze, ed.: *Istoriya gruzinskoy muzïki* [History of Georgian muisc] (Tbilisi, 1998)

(2) **George Balanchine** [Balanchivadze] (*b* St Petersburg, 10/22 Jan 1904; *d* New York, 30 April 1983). Georgian, later American, choreographer. *See* BALLET, §3(ii).

(3) **Andria Balanchivadze** [Andrey] (*b* St Petersburg, 19 May/1 June 1906; *d* Tbilisi, 28 April 1992). Composer and teacher. He was the son of the composer Meliton Balanchivadze, and brother of the ballet-master George Balanchine. He graduated in 1927 from the Tbilisi Conservatory where he studied composition with Ippolitov-Ivanov, and the piano with I. Aysberg, later continuing his education in the Leningrad Conservatory with Zhitomirsky (composition) and Mariya Yudina (piano). From

1931 he lived in Tbilisi, being for a time artistic director of the Georgian State SO (1941–8). An outstanding teacher, he was on the staff of Tbilisi Conservatory from 1935, was appointed professor in 1942, and later headed the composition department (1962–8). He was secretary of the Georgian Composers' Union more than once (1953–62 and 1968–73), and frequently appeared in performances of his own works as conductor and pianist. Balanchivadze was one of the founders of the modern Georgian school of composition both in terms of creative endeavour and through his teaching work. His most significant contributions lie in the fields of ballet, orchestral music and piano literature. His most successful works are distinguished by an individual musical language, an ability to translate into music the characteristics of the Georgian people and their national traditions, an optimistic attitude, a combination of the lyrical and the poetic with the manly and the epic, and an elegance in his use of form. His name became widely known in 1938 after the performance of his ballet *Mtebis guli* ('The Heart of the Mountains') (in its first version of 1936 as *Mzechabuki*) in Leningrad. It was staged by the great dancer V. Chabukiani who also took the leading role. *Mtebis guli* laid the foundations of Georgian ballet. Using folk material in the score, he blended the Georgian folk dancing tradition with the rigours of classical choreography. Lyrical, poetic and heroic themes predominate and the score is suffused with rich local colour. *Mtebis guli* was staged at many theatres of the former USSR.

Another important stage for Balanchivadze in becoming established as a composer, and indeed, one might say for the establishment of Georgian symphonic music as a whole, was his First Symphony (1944), in which he reacted to the terrible events of the war, recording the thoughts and feelings of his contemporaries. Whilst adhering to a Georgian style, Balanchivadze adopted and gave new life to classical traditions and to the Russian symphonism of that time. Another high point in his output is the Third Piano Concerto (1952), a popular work notable for its radiant lyricism, buoyancy, melodiousness and elegance of form. The work has established itself firmly in both pedagogical and professional repertories. Only the Second and Third Symphonies, the orchestral picture *Ritsis tba* ('Lake Ritsa'), and the Fourth Piano Concerto come close to this in popularity.

WORKS
(selective list)

Ops: Mzia (3, V. Pataraia), Tbilisi, 1949; Okros kortsili [Golden Wedding] (3), Tbilisi, 1969 Ganga (after Indian epic poetry), 1990
Ballets: Mzechabuki, Tbilisi, 1936, rev. as Mtebis guli [The Heart of the Mountains] (3, V. Chabukiani, G. Leonidze, N. Volkov), Leningrad, 1938; Stranitsï zhizni [Pages of Life], (2, L. Lavrovsky), Moscow, 1961; Mtsïri (after M.Yu. Lermontov), Tbilisi, 1964
6 syms.: 1944; 1959; 1979; 1984 'Lesnaya' [Forest]; 1988 'Yunost'' [Youth]; 1990
5 pf concs.: 1934, 1946, 1952, 1967, 1977
Other orch: Ritsis tba [Lake Ritsa], sym. picture, 1939; Krtsanisis brdzola [The Battle of Krtsanisi], sym. picture, 1943; Zgva [The Sea], 1952; Dnepr, 1955; Poéma, vn, orch, 1976
Pf pieces, incidental music, over 20 film scores etc.

Principal publishers: Muzgiz, Muzfond Gruzii, Muzïka, Sovetskii Kompozitor (Moscow and Leningrad)

BIBLIOGRAPHY

P. Khuchua: 'Sovetskaya opera i balet', *Gruzinskaya muzïkal'naya kul'tura* (Moscow, 1957)
A. Tsulukidze: 'Puti razvitiya simfonizma' [Paths of development of symphonism], *Gruzinskaya muzïkal'naya kul'tura* (Moscow, 1957)
G. Orjonikidze: 'A. Balanchivadzis pirveli simfoniya' [Balanchivadze's First Symphony], *Sabchota khelovneba* (1958), no.1
G. Orjonikidze: 'Pirveli kartuli baleti' [The first Georgian ballet], *Sabchota khelovneba* (1958), no.7
G. Orjonikidze: *Andrey Balanchivadze* (Moscow, 1959)
E. Balanchivadze: 'Akhali kartul baletshi' [Something new in Georgian ballet], *Sabchota khelovneba* (1965), no.5
G. Orjonikidze: 'Kartuli simfoniya "gazapkhulidan" "gazapkhulamde"' [The Georgian symphony from one 'spring' to another], *Sabchota khelovneba* (1965), no.5
G. Orjonikidze: *Andrey Balanchivadze* (Tbilisi, 1967)
V. Donadze: *Ocherki po istorii gruzinskoy sovetskoy muzïki* [Outline of the history of Soviet Georgian music] (Tbilisi, 1975)
Andrey Balanchivadze: sbornik [A collection] (Tbilisi, 1979)
'A. Balanchivadze' in G. Toradze, ed.: *Istoriya gruzinskoy muzïki* [History of Georgian music] (Tbilisi, 1998)

GULBAT TORADZE

Balasios [Balasios the Priest and Nomophylax; Balasēs ho Hiereūs kai Nomophylax] (*b* Constantinople, ?1615; *d* ?1700). Romaic (Greek) composer and patriarchal official. Born into a family of Peloponnesian origin, he received his general education at the Patriarchal Academy under Theophilos Korydalleus. Together with Kosmas Makedonos he was taught Byzantine chant by GERMANOS OF NEW PATRAS, for whom he composed an acclamation. In a pre-1660 manuscript Balasios refers to himself as a *domestikos*, which therefore places him among the musicians of the patriarchal cathedral at the time PANAGIOTES THE NEW CHRYSAPHES was *prōtopsaltēs*. After ordination to the priesthood he continued to serve the Ecumenical Patriarchate in an impressive series of liturgical and administrative posts (*c*1663–1700), but in musical manuscripts he is customarily described as 'nomophylax', a patriarchal title that he appears to have held from about 1680.

As a composer Balasios continued the renewal of the received medieval chant repertories pursued by Panagiotes and Germanos, complementing their 'beautified' sticheraria with a new edition of the Heirmologion and a complete series of 8 modally ordered Great Doxologies, the first such set ever written. Other chants for the Divine Office include a modally ordered series of eight *kekragaria* (Psalm cxl.1–2) for Hesperinos, and, for Orthros, eight *Magnificat* verses for the 9th ode of the kanon. He composed numerous works for the Byzantine eucharistic liturgies, including two sets of eight Cherubic Hymns, modally ordered series of 8 communion verses for Sundays, and two *dynamis* (codas to the Trisagia) for the feasts of the Holy Cross and of the Lord (the latter ed. Phōkaeus, 1834). He also contributed to the post-Byzantine repertories of kalophonic *heirmoi* and other paraliturgical chants. A number of his chants, transcribed by Gregorios the Protopsaltes, appear in Chrysanthine editions (see bibliography). A Turkish song attributed to Balasios in *GR-ATSiviron* 999 (f.389r) places him at the head of a distinguished series of Romaic church musicians who participated in the 'external' tradition of Ottoman secular music. (For a fuller list of works see Stathēs, 1995.)

Balasios was the first to produce realizations (*exēgēseis*) of pre-existing chants, featuring the transcription into intervallic neumes of melismas hitherto notated in short-hand with stereotyped melodic formulae (*theseis*). These *exēgēseis*, which mark the beginnings of a movement towards notational precision in florid repertories, also attest the existence in the late 17th century of a stenographic interpretation for Byzantine neumes. Arvanitis, however, has argued persuasively for a comparatively literal realization of Balasios's Heirmologion, an influential volume that remained in use until its replacement by that of Petros Peloponnesios.

BIBLIOGRAPHY

CHRYSANTHINE MUSIC EDITIONS

T. Phōkaeus, ed.: *Tameion anthologias* [Treasury of an anthology] (Constantinople, 1834), ii, 124–6 [transcr. Gregorios the Protopsaltes]

T. Phōkaeus: , ed. *Heirmologion kalophōnikon* (Constantinople, 1835), 3–18, 51–2, 59–64, 79–81, 109–10, 124–6, 141–2, 159–66 [transcr. Gregorios the Protopsaltes]

I. Lampadarios and Stephanos the First Domestikos, eds.: *Pandektē* (Constantinople, 1850–51), i, 149–83; iii, 21–33, 107–18, 152–77, 229–43, 283–93, 306–40; iv, 50–52 [transcr. Gregorios the Protopsaltes]

STUDIES

S.I. Karas: 'Hē orthē hermēneia kai metagraphē tōn byzantinōn mousikōn cheirographōn' [The correct interpretation and transcription of Byzantine musical MSS], *Hellēnika*, ix (1955), 140–49 [repr., with an afterword, Athens, 1990]

G.T. Stathēs: *Ta cheirographa byzantinēs mousikēs: Hagion Oros* [The MSS of Byzantine Music: Holy Mountain] (Athens, 1975–93)

G.T. Stathēs: *Hē dekapentasyllabos hymnographia en tē byzantinē melopoiïa* [15-syllable hymnography in Byzantine composition] (Athens, 1977) [with Fr. summary]

M. Chatzēgiakoumēs: *Cheirographa ekklēsiastikēs mousikēs (1453–1820)* [MSS of ecclesiastical music] (Athens, 1980)

G.T. Stathis: 'The "Abridgements" of Byzantine and Post-Byzantine Compositions', *Cahiers de l'Institut du Moyen-Age grec et latin*, no.44 (1983), 16–38

A. Şirli: *The Anastasimatarion: the Thematic Repertory of Byzantine and Post-Byzantine Musical Manuscripts (the 14th-19th centuries)*, i (Bucharest, 1986)

D. Conomos: 'Sacred Music in the Post-Byzantine Era', *The Byzantine Legacy in Eastern Europe*, ed. L. Clucas (Boulder, CO, 1988), 83–105 [based on Chatzēgiakoumēs 1980]

I. Arvanitis: 'A Way to the Transcription of Byzantine Chant by Means of Written and Oral Tradition', *Byzantine Chant: Athens 1993*, 123–41

G.T. Stathēs: 'Balasēs hiereūs kai nomophylax' [Balasios the Priest and Nomophylax], *Melourgoi tou iz aiōna* [Composers of the 17th century], ed. E. Spanopoulou (Athens, 1995), 33–41

SOUND RECORDING

Polychronismos to the Ecumenical Patriarch by Balasios the Priest, Greek Byzantine Choir, dir. L. Angelopoulos, CD ELBUC 33 (1997)

ALEXANDER LINGAS

Balasanyan, Sergey Artem'yevich (*b* Ashkhabad, 13/26 Aug 1902; *d* Moscow, 3 June 1982). Russian composer of Armenian extraction. After graduating from Kabalevsky's composition class at the Moscow Conservatory (1935), he worked in Stalinabad (now Dushanbe) and took a large part in the development of professional music in the republics of central Asia. He made a serious study of Tajik folk music, recording and arranging a great number of songs. This work assisted him in creating the first Tajik works for the musical stage, among them the opera *Vosstaniye Vose* ('Vose's Uprising', 1939), which relates the story of a peasant revolt at the end of the 19th century and which uses many Tajik melodies in symphonic development. Balasanyan's music gradually grew more complex as his technical mastery became sharper. The ballet *Leyli i Medzhnun*, which achieved particular renown, is based on a widely known eastern legend; its subtle lyricism, vividly characterized images and symphonic growth established it in the Soviet repertory, and a successful film version was produced. Balasanyan has also drawn on other folk musics: Armenian, Afghan, Indian and Latin American. Of his expressive and colourful orchestral works the most notable is the suite 7 *armyanskikh pesen* ('7 Armenian Songs'). His chamber pieces show him as a delicate lyricist and a master of small forms. From 1948 he taught at the Moscow Conservatory, heading the composition department there for many years. He was awarded the titles People's Artist of the Tajik SSR (1970) and Honoured Art Worker of the RSFSR (1964), and he was winner of the State Prize.

WORKS
(selective list)

STAGE

Vosstaniye Vose [Vose's Uprising] (op, 4, A. Dekhoti and M. Tursunzade), 1939, Stalinabad, Tajik Musical, 16 Oct 1939; rev. 1958, Stalinabad, Tajik Ayni, 13 Jan 1959

Kuznets Kova [Kova the Smith] (op, 4, A. Lakhuti, after A.K. Firdousi: *Shakh-name*); Moscow, Tajik Theatre, 15 April 1941, collab. Sh.N. Bobokalonov

Leyli i Medzhnun (ballet, S.A. Tsenin); Stalinabad, 1947, rev. 1964

Bakhtiyor i Nisso [Bakhtiyor and Niso] (op, 4, Tsenin, after P.N. Luknitsky: *Nisso*); Stalinabad, Tajik Ayni, 25 Oct 1954

Shakuntala (ballet, B. Sdanevich, after Kolidasa); Riga, 1963, rev. 1978

OTHER

Orch: Afganskaya syuita; Tadzhikskaya syuita, 1943; Pamir, suite, 1944; Baletnaya syuita, 1946; 7 armyanskikh pesen [7 Armenian Songs], 1955; Ostrova Indonezii [The Islands of Indonesia], 1960; Rapsodiya na temï Rabindranata Tagora, 1961; 8 p'yes na armyanskiye narodnïye temï [8 Pieces on Armenian Themes], str, 1971; Sym., str, 1974; other pieces

Vocal: Moy kray [My Land] (Ye. Yondo), B, pf, 1962, orchd 1966; Sym. (E. Mezhelaytis), unacc. chorus, 1968; 10 rubayaitt Omara Khayyama [10 Ruba'i of Omar Khayyam], Bar, pf, 1974; Ametist [Amethyst], poem, Bar, chbr ens, 1977; Privet tebe, radost' [Greetings to you, my Joy] (G. Ermin), song cycle, 1v, pf, 1979; Polifonicheskiy kontsert [Polyphonic Conc.], unacc. chorus, 1980; Ayreni [Ayrens] (A. Uchak), song cycle, 1v, pf, 1981; arrs., incl. Pesni Armenii [Songs of Armenia], 100 Armenian folksongs from Komitas's collection, 1969

Other inst: Sonatina, vn, pf, 1947; 2 pf sonatinas, 1947, 1948; Sonata, vc, 1976; P. Armenii [Around Armenia], 4 novellas, 2 pf, 1978; Sonata, cl, 1979

BIBLIOGRAPHY

A. Nikolayev: *Leyli i Medzhnun Sergeya Balasanyana* (Moscow, 1959)

V. Blok: 'Afganskiye simfonicheskiye tsiklï S. Balasanyana', *SovM* (1960), no.8, pp.73–6

V. Vinogradov: 'Shakuntala', *SovM* (1964), no.4, pp.41–4

Yu. Butsko: ' Zasluzhennoye priznaniye' [Deserved recognition], *SovM* (1972), no.9, pp.23–7

N. Shakhanazarova and G. Golovinsky: *S. Balasanyan* (Moscow, 1972)

V. Lobanov: ' O S.A. Balasanyane' [About Balasanyan], *SovM* (1977), no.10, pp.40–43

Obituary, *SovM* (1982), no.9, pp.34–8

GALINA GRIGOR'YEVA

Balasaraswati, Thanjavur (*b* Thanjavur, Tamil Nadu, 13 May 1918; *d* ? Madras, 1984). South Indian dancer and musician. Her family included many distinguished dancers and musicians since the 18th century; during the 19th century some of her forebears studied with Subbaraya Śāstri. Her formal training as a dancer started when she was four under the noted teacher Kandappan Pillai (1899–1942), himself the inheritor of a great tradition, and her mother taught her music. When she was seven her *araṇkerram* (formal début) took place at the Kāmākṣi Ammaṇ temple, Kanchipuram, and her professional début was two years later in Madras. As a girl she was already an accomplished and mature dancer with a very large repertory, but she continued to study, notably the basis of *abhinaya* (dramatic expression) and its improvisation. She became a musician in her own right and a leading exponent of forms such as *padam* and *jāvali*.

She toured extensively throughout India and internationally. She also taught in the USA, notably at Wesleyan University with her brothers T. Viswanathan and T. Ranganathan. In 1973 she was the first dancer to preside over the annual conference of the Madras Academy of Music, and the first dancer to receive the title Sangita Kalanidhi. With Venkatarama Raghavan she wrote a book, *Bharata nātya* (1959). She received the presidential award for dancing and the Padma Vibhushan.

BIBLIOGRAPHY

T. Balasaraswati and V. Raghavan: *Bharata nātya* (1959)
V. Raghavan: 'Her Infinite Variety', *Journal of the Music Academy, Madras*, xxxiv (1963), 124–31
J.B. Higgins: 'Padams and Balasaraswati', *The Music Academy Madras: Forty Seventh Conference 1973* [no page numbers] 1973

NARAYANA MENON/R

Balassa, Sándor (*b* Budapest, 20 Jan 1935). Hungarian composer. He was brought up in the country until 1951 when he returned to Budapest to work as a factory mechanic. His first experience of art music there made him decide to study at the Budapest Conservatory (1952–6), and after spending four further years teaching himself, he attended the Liszt Academy of Music (1960–65) as a composition pupil of Szervánszky. From 1964 to 1980 he was music director at Hungarian Radio. Awards made to him include the Erkel (1972), Kossuth (1983) and Bartók-Pásztory (1988, 1999) prizes. Also in 1972 his Requiem was voted the most distinguished composition of the year at the International Rostrum of Composers. In 1989 he was created Outstanding Artist of the Hungarian Republic.

Balassa's early compositions are freely dodecaphonic, generally without a strict application of serial principles (his only thoroughly serial work is the *Intermezzo*). His melodic invention is predominantly vocal in character, although *Antinomia* (1968) is an exception to this, and his use of instruments is formally functional, sometimes dramatic. He is particularly fond of writing for a solo voice embedded in an orchestral texture, or for chorus, and it is in his choral music that the influence of the Kodály school may be detected. Each of the major instrumental works (opp.20, 22, 24 and 25) follows the same fundamental form: a slow, lyrical introduction leading to a scherzo-like section which reaches a climax, with sometimes a gradual lowering of intensity to conclude the piece. Such a plan may be presented in several movements (*Xenia*, *Lupercalia*, *Tabulae*) or in a single one (*Iris*), and sometimes sections are recapitulated or varied later in the work. Above all, Balassa's work is lyrical: his vocal music reveals a strong feeling for the voice and a sensitive susceptibility to poetry.

In later works Balassa's freely dodecaphonic idiom developed strong leanings towards diatonicism as a consequence of drawing upon other musical sources. *Glarusi ének* ('Chant of Glarus', 1978), commissioned by the Koussevitzky Foundation, marked the beginnings of this change. Distancing himself from the stylistic aspirations of the first half of the 20th century, Balassa has sought inspiration from European classicism and the Hungarian folk tradition. With a new sense of freedom he has shaped the characteristics of his music with each new work. A return to tonality and recreating direct links with his audience and with the art of interpretation have become his priorities. Such goals were successfully realized in his three-act opera *Karl és Anna* (1987–92).

WORKS
(*selective list*)

STAGE

Az ajtón kívül [The Man Outside] (op, 5 scenes, G. Fodor, after W. Borchert), op.27, 1986, Budapest, State Opera, 20 Oct 1978
A harmadik bolygó [The Third Planet] (op, 1, Balassa), op.39, 1987, unpubd, concert perf., Budapest, 1989
Karl és Anna (op, 3, Fodor, after L. Frank), op.41, 1987–92, Budapest, State Opera, 20 May 1995

INSTRUMENTAL

Orch: Vn Conc., op.3, 1964, unpubd; Irisz, op.22, 1971; Glarusi ének [Chant of Glarus], op.29, 1978; Az örök ifjúság szigete [The Island of Everlasting Youth], ov., op.32, 1979; Hívások és kiáltások [Calls and Cries], op.33, 1981; Egy álmodozó naplója [A Daydreamer's Diary], orch/chbr orch, op.35, 1983; 3 fantázia, op.36, 1984; Szőlőcske és halacska [Little Grape, Little Fish], op.40, 1987, unpubd; Tündér Ilona [Fairy Helen], op.45, 1992, unpubd; Bölcskei concerto, op.49, str, 1993, unpubd; Csaba királyfi [Prince Csaba], op.46, str, 1993, unpubd; Mucsai táncok [Dances from Mucsa], op.50, 1994, unpubd; A nap fiai [The Sons of the Sun], op.54, 1995, unpubd; 4 arckép [4 Portraits], op.56, 1996, unpubd; 301-es parcella [The 301st Plot], op.58, 1996, unpubd; Pécsi concerto, op.61, ob, bn, vn, vc, hp, str, 1998, unpubd
Chbr: Divertimento, op.6, 2 cimb, 1961, unpubd; Kvartett, op.18, perc, 1969; Xenia, op.20, fl, cl, bn, pf, hp, perc, str trio, 1970; Lupercalia, op.24, wind, brass, 1971–2; Tabulae, op.25, chbr ens, 1972; Quintetto d'ottoni, brass, op.31, 1979; Fűzérke [Little Garland], op.51, fl, va, hp, 1994, unpubd; 3 intermezzo, op.23/1, fl, pf, 1996, unpubd; Nyírbátori harangok [The Bells of Nyírbátor], op.57, 12 brass, 1996, unpubd
Solo inst: Sonatina, op.23/5, pf, unpubd; Az utolsó pásztor [The Last Shepherd], op.30, vc, 1978; Hajta virágai [The Flowers of Hajta], op.38, cimb, 1984; Sonatina, op.47, hp, 1993, unpubd; Jánosnapi muzsika [Music for St John's Day], op.52, vn, 1994; Prelude and Fantasia, op.59, org, 1997, unpubd

VOCAL

Choral: Kelet népe [The People of Orient] (Balassa, after trad.), op.44, children's chorus, 1966–92, unpubd; 5 gyermekkar [5 Children's Choruses] (S. Weöres, Balassa), op.11, 1967; Legenda, op.12, 1968; Requiem Kassák Lajosért, op.15, S, T, Bar, chorus, orch, 1969; Kyrie, op.34, female chorus, 1981; Bánatomtól szabadulnék [I would be free from my sorrow] (Balassa), op.42, female chorus, 1988; Madaras énekek [Songs of Birds] (Balassa), op.37, children's chorus, 1988, unpubd; Oldott kéve [Loosened Sheaf] (Balassa), op.43, 1991, unpubd; Damjanich imája [The Prayer of Damjanich], op.48, 1993, unpubd; Az árvák éneke [The Song of Orphans] (I. Bella, I. Sinka), op.55, 1995, unpubd; Magyar ének [Hungarian Song] (Balassa), op.54a, 1995, unpubd; Tavaszi dal – Őszi dal [Song of Spring – Song of Autumn] (M. Simai, Balassa), op.60, female chorus, 1997, unpubd; Favágó [The Woodman] (A. József), op.62, male chorus, 1998, unpubd
1v (acc.): Dalok a Rottenbiller utcából [Songs from Rottenbiller Street] (Balassa), op.1, S, Mez, pf, 1954–7, unpubd; 2 dal [2 songs] (D. Kosztolányi), op.16, S, pf, 1957; 2 dal (A. József), op.7, Mez, pf, unpubd; Antinomia (I. Leckius, J. Dsida), op.14, S, cl, vc, 1968; Cantata Y (Z. Beney), op.21, S, orch, 1970

BIBLIOGRAPHY

M. Pándi: *Hangversenykalauz* [Concert guide] (Budapest, 1972)
G. Kroó: 'Sándor Balassa', *New Hungarian Quarterly*, no.50 (1973), 215–21
A. Boros: *Harminc év magyar operái 1948–1978* [30 years of Hungarian opera] (Budapest, 1979)
B.A. Varga, ed.: *Contemporary Hungarian Composers* (Budapest, 1970, 5/1989)
A. Horváth: 'Draussen vor der Tür: Oper in fünf Sätzen von S. Balassa und G. Fodor', *Oper heute*, vi (1983), 247–68
G. Staud, ed.: *A budapesti operaház 100 éve* [100 years of Hungarian opera] (Budapest, 1984)
S. Balassa: 'Gondolatok a természet és az ember kapcsolatáról' [Thoughts on the connection of man and nature], *Műhely*, no.1 (1990), 14–16
E. Terényi: 'Hajta virágai: arcképvázlat Balassa Sándor zeneszerzőről' [The flowers of Hajta: a portrait of the composer Balassa] (Budapest, 1995)

S. Balassa: 'Gondolatok a nemzeti zenéről' [Thoughts on national music], *Névjegy a Magyar Művészeti Akadémia kincsestára életrajzok, dokumentumok, 1992–1994*, ed. M. Berlász (Budapest, 1995), 12–16

GYÖRGY KROÓ/MELINDA BERLÁSZ

Balatka, Hans (*b* Hoffnungsthal, nr Olmütz [now Olomouc, Czech Republic], ?26 Feb 1825; *d* Chicago, 17 April 1899). Moravian conductor and composer, active in the USA. He studied music at Hoffnungsthal and later at the gymnasium and university in Olomouc, where he was a choirboy at the cathedral. From 1845 he studied music (under Sechter and Proch) and law at the University of Vienna, where he worked as a music copyist and a tutor. During the 1848 revolution he sided with the Academic Legion, and following its defeat he fled Europe. He arrived in New York in 1849 and went via Chicago to Milwaukee, where he organized a male chorus (1849) and a string quartet (1850). From 1850 to 1860 he was musical director of the Milwaukee Musical Society (Musikverein) and conducted its first concert (May 1850) and its first oratorio, Haydn's *The Creation* (July 1851, in German), and directed and sang in its first opera, Lortzing's *Zar und Zimmermann* (April 1853). He also founded a singing school and served as musical director of the German theatre (1855–60). Because of his reputation with the Milwaukee Musical Society he was asked to conduct music festivals in Cleveland, Cincinnati, Detroit and Chicago. His performance of Mozart's Requiem for the Northwest Sängerfest (Chicago, 1860) led to his appointment as director of the Chicago Philharmonic Society (1860–69). His first concert on 19 November included Beethoven's second symphony and a chorus from *Tannhäuser*. While in Chicago he also conducted the Musical Union, the Oratorio Society and other singing groups. In 1871–2 he again conducted the Milwaukee Musical Society, but returned in 1876 to Chicago where he remained except for a short stay in St Louis (1877). In 1879 he founded the Balatka Academy of Musical Art, which was important to music education in Chicago in the late 19th and early 20th centuries. During his later residence in Chicago he directed the Mozart Club and the Germania Society. He was also active as a journalist and regularly contributed columns on music to the Chicago newspaper *Daheim*.

Balatka wrote several orchestral fantasies, a piano quartet and other piano music; his vocal works include about 30 songs, pieces for chorus such as *The Power of Song* (1856) for double male chorus, and a *Festival Cantata* (1869) for soprano and orchestra. Balatka's significance nevertheless was in his conducting and educationist activities, and he was one of the first important figures for the development of music in the American Midwest.

BIBLIOGRAPHY

The National Cyclopedia of American Biography, x (New York, 1900), 197

J.J. Schlicher: 'Hans Balatka and the Milwaukee Musical Society', *Wisconsin Magazine of History*, xxvii (1943–4), 40–55

J.J. Schlicher: 'The Milwaukee Musical Society in Times of Stress', *Wisconsin Magazine of History*, xxvii (1943–4), 178–93

Dictionary of Wisconsin Biography (Madison, 1960), 23

T.H. Schleis: *Opera in Milwaukee: 1850–1900* (diss., U. of Wisconsin, 1974)

J. Deaville: 'The Origins of Music Journalism in Chicago: Criticism as a Reflection of Musical Life', *American Musical Life in Context and Practice to 1865*, ed. J.R. Heintze (New York, 1994), 301–66

THOMAS H. SCHLEIS

Balbastre [Balbâtre], **Claude-Bénigne** (*b* Dijon, 22 Jan 1727; *d* Paris, 9 May 1799). French organist and composer. He probably received his first organ lessons from his father Bénigne Balbastre (*d* 1737), organist at St Médard, Dijon, from 1691 to 1705 and then at St Etienne until his death. Claude-Bénigne knew Claude Rameau (brother of Jean-Philippe) and may have studied with him; the extent of his other musical studies in Dijon is unknown, but by 1748 he had composed some rather insignificant fugues and other pieces for the harpsichord there.

At the age of 23 Balbastre went to Paris, arriving, according to La Borde, on 16 October 1750. There he befriended Jean-Philippe Rameau and studied composition with him, also receiving organ lessons from the organist Pierre Février. He returned briefly to Dijon, but established permanent residence in Paris. In March 1755 he performed an organ concerto of his own composition at the Concert Spirituel; his playing earned the praise of an anonymous reviewer in the *Mercure de France* (May 1755, pp.180–81):

M. Balbatre played an organ concerto of his own composition, that surprised and charmed the entire assemblage; his brilliant playing made this instrument sound in an authoritative manner and made the impression that he alone has the right to lead all others. One cannot praise too highly … the singular talent of M. Balbatre.

Thereafter he appeared frequently at the Concert Spirituel until 1782, usually playing his own concertos (none of which survives) or transcriptions of overtures and airs from current operas by Rameau or Mondonville (*F-Pn* Vm⁷ 2108). On 26 March 1756 he obtained the post of organist at St Roch, and on 1 October 1760 he was also engaged as organist at Notre Dame for three months a year. In 1776 he was appointed organist to Monsieur (brother of the king, later Louis XVIII), a position he retained until the Revolution. While employed at court, he taught the harpsichord to Marie-Antoinette and the Duke of Chartres and served as organist of the royal chapel. As organist of the Panthémont, he taught the daughters of prominent French and foreign dignitaries, including Thomas Jefferson. With the fall of the royalty, he lived in poverty for the rest of his life. One of his last performances was his own arrangement of the Marseillaise, played on the organ of the deconsecrated Notre Dame.

Balbastre's performances were exceedingly popular, and his reputation was international. When he played his own *noëls en variations* at St Roch every year at Midnight Mass, the performance attracted such a crowd that in 1762 the archbishop finally forbade him to play. Rameau praised his performance of a transcription of the overture to *Pygmalion* at La Pouplinière's home in Passy. Charles Burney, eager to meet Balbastre, went to hear him at St Roch in 1770 and entered a long account of the performance in his *Present State of Music in France and Italy*:

He performed in all styles in accompanying the choir. When the *Magnificat* was sung, he played likewise between each verse several minuets, fugues, imitations, and every species of music, even to hunting pieces and jigs, without surprising or offending the congregation, as far as I was able to discover.

Burney also visited Balbastre at home and described the instruments he saw there, including a large organ and

a fine Rucker harpsichord which he has had painted inside and out with as much delicacy as the finest coach or snuff-box I ever saw at Paris. … On the outside is the birth of Venus; and on the inside of the cover the story of Rameau's most famous opera, *Castor and Pollux*;

earth, hell and elysium are there represented; in elysium, sitting on a bank, with a lyre in his hand, is that celebrated composer himself [i.e. Rameau]; ... The tone of this instrument is more delicate than powerful; one of the unisons is of buff, but very sweet and agreeable; the touch is very light, owing to the quilling, which in France is always weak.

The decoration Burney described survives, although it has been enlarged to serve as the lid for a 19th-century piano now in the private collection of Barbara Johnson in New Jersey. It includes details of scenery and costumes for two scenes of Rameau's opera, probably taken from the 1764 production. The unison of buff (or *peau de buffle*) so casually mentioned by Burney was, according to La Borde, a new invention of Balbastre's. Balbastre is also credited with the invention of the 'fortepiano organisé', a combination of the piano and organ at a single keyboard (*F-Pn* Vm⁷1941). An anonymous portrait (miniature on ivory, in the Dijon Museum), formerly thought to be of Balbastre, is of the singer Pierre de Jélyotte.

Balbastre's keyboard pieces are extremely varied in character. Most of the best pieces in the 1759 book follow the grand tradition of François Couperin ('La d'Héricourt') or Rameau ('La Lamarck'), though with a certain individuality. Others are more modern, such as the outstanding Scarlattian gigue 'La Lugeac', or the more simple-minded 'La Courteille' and 'La Malesherbe'. His *Quatuors* (1779), a volume of quite charming keyboard sonatas accompanied by two violins and cello with two *cors de chasse* ad lib, seem to have been an unsuccessful effort to combat the competition of 'les allemands', such as Honauer and Schobert, the latter of whom, according to Grimm (Ière lettre, December 1765), 'has completely destroyed the reputation of [A.-L.] Couperin, du Phly [Duphly], [and] Balbastre'. However, a *romance* from this collection became very popular, was parodied and has been 'recorded' (a remarkable example of contemporary performing practice) on the barrel organ. Another favourite composition must have been his Pastorale in A (*F-Pn*Vm⁷ 2108), for he had it painted on the nameboard of his harpsichord, where it is dated 6 August 1767. Among his other surviving compositions is an unmeasured prelude which must either be one of the last written for the harpsichord or the first (and possibly last) for the piano.

WORKS

Mes souvenirs, 1v, acc., Etrennes lyriques anacréontiques (Paris, 1786)
Chbr: Sonates en quatuor, hpd/pf, acc. 2 vn, b, 2 hn ad lib, op.3 (Paris, 1779); Sonates en quatuor, 1 movt, *F-Pn*
Kbd: Pièces de clavecin, 1er livre (Paris, 1759); Recueil de noëls formant 4 suittes, hpd/pf (Paris, 1770), nos.1–3 ed. in L'organiste liturgique, xlviii, lii, lv–lvi (Paris, 1968–9); Marche des marseillais et l'air Ça ira, arr. pf (Paris, 1793); pièces and fugues, by 1748, *Pn*; pièces, unmeasured prelude, La canonade, 1777, *Pn*; pièces, 1787, *Pn*; La d'Esclignac, pièce, hpd, 1787, *Pc*; Romance, *Pa*, *Pn*; 5 pièces, *US-CHua*: Marche guerrier, La canonade, Symphonie, La De Villiers, Rondo; other pieces and arrs. of operatic airs, *F-Pn*; parodies of airs in *Amusements d'un convalescent dédiés à ses amis* (1761) and *Mercure de France* (Sept 1767); parody of pastorale, *Pn*; org concs., ?lost

BIBLIOGRAPHY

BrenetC; BurneyFI; FétisB; La BordeE; MGG1 (M. Frécot); PierreH
Mercure de France (May 1755, May 1772, Feb 1779)
F. Bédos de Celles: *L'art du facteur d'orgues*, iv (Paris, 1778/R; Eng. trans., 1977); ed. C. Mahrenholz (Kassel, 1936, 2/1966)
M. Brenet: 'La librairie musicale en France de 1653 à 1790 d'après les registres de privilèges', *SIMG*, viii (1906–7), 401–66
J. Gardien: *L'orgue et les organistes en Bourgogne et en Franche-Comté au dix-huitième siècle* (Paris, 1943)
M. Frécot: *La vie et l'oeuvre de Claude-Bénigne Balbastre (1727–1799)* (diss., U. of Paris, Sorbonne, c1950)
H. Cripe: *Thomas Jefferson and Music* (Charlottesville, VA, 1974)
D. Fuller: 'Accompanied Keyboard Music', *MQ*, lx (1974), 222–45
D. Paquette and P.-M. Gueritey: 'Etude de deux manuscrits de Mr Balbastre de Saint-Jean-de-Losne, 1770', *Revue international de musique française*, xxiii (1987), 99–126
J. Erdman: 'Romance de Mr Balbastre', *Pisma teoretyczne wydzialu kompozycji, dyrygentury i teorii muzyki* [Theoretical papers of the composition, conducting and music theory department], i (Warsaw, 1992), 40–125
J. Erdman: 'Romance de Mr Balbastre: niektóre kwestie zwiazane z tekstem muzycznym' [Romance de Mr Balbastre: some problems regarding the musical text], *Pisma teoretyczne wydzialu kompozycji, dyrygentury i teorii muzyki*, ii (Warsaw, 1995), 15–53

ALAN CURTIS, MARY CYR

Balbi, Giovan Battista [Giambattista; 'il Tasquino'] (*fl* 1636–57). Italian choreographer, dancer, stage designer and impresario. He was involved with Venetian opera from its inception. Cited as 'Veneziano Ballarino celebre' in the libretto for Francesco Manelli's *L'Andromeda* (1637), he continued to provide choreography for operas at Venice for the next seven years. Beginning in 1645, his affiliation with the travelling Febiarmonici introduced Venetian opera to other Italian cities. They produced Francesco Sacrati's *La finta pazza* in Florence in 1645 and Cavalli's *La Deidamia* (first performed Venice, 1644) there in 1650. In December 1652 Balbi and the Febiarmonici produced *Veremonda l'Amazzone d'Aragona* (?Cavalli) in Naples. *Veremonda* and *La finta pazza*, presented earlier that year, served to introduce Neapolitan audiences to the innovations of the Venetian stage machinery and dance. During Carnival 1653 Balbi created the set designs and choreography for the anonymous *Le magie amorose* and for Provenzale's *Il Ciro* in Naples.

Balbi also played an important role in the introduction of Venetian opera to northern Europe. While in Florence in 1645, he was summoned to Paris by Anne of Austria. There he and Giacomo Torelli collaborated on a celebrated production of *La finta pazza* (14 December 1645). In 1647 Balbi created the choreography for the French production of Luigi Rossi's *Orfeo* and the following year he was called to Brussels. For the wedding of Philip IV and Maria Anna of Austria he created *Le balet du monde*, a grand 'balet a entrées' presented in Brussels on 24 February 1650, with Gioseffo Zamponi's *Ulisse nell'isola di Circe*. By carnival 1651 he was once again in Venice, providing choreography and stage designs for Cesti's *Alessandro vincitor di se stesso*. The following year he brought *Ciro* to Venice with new music by Cavalli; in the libretto Balbi noted that the opera had been adapted for Venetian taste. This libretto was reprinted in Palermo in 1657, and there is no further documentation of Balbi's activities.

Balbi's fanciful ballets incorporated animals and other 'exotica'. His descriptions, with engravings by Valerio Spada, were published as *Balletti d'invenzione nella Finta Pazza di Giovanbatta Balbi* (n.p., c1658).

BIBLIOGRAPHY

DBI (F. Marotti); ES (E. Povoledo); OG (I. Alm, incl. illustration)
H. Prunières: *L'opera italien en France avant Lulli* (Paris, 1913)
G. Morelli and T. Walker: 'Tre controversie intorno al San Cassiano', *Venezia e il melodramma nel seicento: Venice 1972*, 97–120
L. Bianconi and T. Walker: 'Dalla *Finta pazza* alla *Veremonda*: storie di Febiarmonici', *RIM*, x (1975), 379–454
R.L. and N.W. Weaver: *A Chronology of Music in the Florentine Theater, 1590–1750* (Detroit, 1978)

G. Donato: 'Su alcuni aspetti della vita musicale in Sicilia nel
   Seicento', *La musica a Napoli durante il Seicento: Naples 1985*,
   567–623
I. Alm: *Theatrical Dance in Seventeenth-Century Venetian Opera*
   (Chicago, forthcoming)
IRENE ALM

Balbi, Ignazio (*fl* 1720–73). Italian composer. The earliest
documentation of him is the score of the *Oratorio della
Madonna de' sette dolori*; this bears a dedication to
Emperor Charles VI, in whose service he already was at
the time, signed 'Ignatio Balbi Dilettante' and dated
'Milan, 24 February 1720'. In 1724–5 Balbi contributed
four arias to two oratorios performed in Milan, and
according to Quadrio he also contributed to one given
there in 1726; this was possibly *Il martirio di S Giovanni
Nepomuceno*, whose published libretto does not bear any
composer's name. The librettos of three other works
performed in Milan name Balbi as composer: *La verità
confessatasi da un'anima dannata* (1729), *La Passione*
(1735) and *Ritornando il giorno trentesimo d'agosto
l'anno MDCCLII* (1752). In the libretto of the last of
these he is described as 'Virtuoso Dilettante Signor Don
Ignazio Balbi Milanese, Segretario di S[ua] M[aestà]
I[mperial] R[egia]'. The title 'Regio Segretario Imperiale'
also appears in some of Balbi's letters, including one dated
2 August 1752 sent to Gasparo Francesconi (now lost;
see Succi), who took the title role in his opera *Lucio
Papirio* at Turin. That *Ciro in Armenia* (1753), an opera
hitherto attributed to Maria Teresa Agnesi, was also by
Balbi is suggested in his letter to Padre Martini dated 11
November 1753, while a relationship between Balbi and
J.C. Bach is documented in three letters written by Bach
to Martini in 1757. Balbi's last surviving letter to Martini
(*I-Bc*) is dated 14 April 1773 (not 1775, as previously
thought). He has been erroneously confused with the
tenor Gregorio Babbi.

WORKS
ORATORIOS

Oratorio della Madonna de' sette dolori, 1720, *A-Wn*
La verità confessatasi da un' anima dannata, Milan, S Francesco, 21
   June 1729, music lost, lib *I-Bc*, *Vnm* (see F.X. Haberl, *KJb*, xvi
   (1901), 45–64)
La Passione (componimento drammatico, G. Riviera), Milan, Teatini
   di S Antonio, 7 March 1735, music lost, lib *Mb*
Music in: La calunnia delusa, Milan, S Maria della Scala, 23 May
   1724, music lost, lib *Mb*, *Vnm*; La necessità socorsa dal glorioso
   Santo di Padoa, Milan, S Francesco, 20 June 1725, music lost, lib
   Mb; Il martirio di S Giovanni Nepomuceno, Milan, 1726,
   doubtful, music lost, lib *Mb*

SECULAR DRAMATIC

Ritornando il giorno trentesimo d'agosto l'anno MDCCLII
   (componimento per musica, A. Perotti), Milan, Casa Litta, 30 Aug
   1752, music lost, lib *I-Mb*
Lucio Papirio (3, ? A. Zeno), Turin, Regio, 26 Dec 1752, Act 1
   Bborromeo, arrs. of ov. and excerpts *Rsc*, 1 aria *D-ROu*, 1 aria
   US-NYp, lib *Wc*
Ciro in Armenia (3), Milan, Regio Ducal, 26 Dec 1753, excerpts *F-
   Pn*, 1 aria *US-BEm*, lib *I-Mb*

OTHER WORKS

Vocal: duet, *I-Bc*; aria, *F-Pn*
Inst: ov., D, 1769, *CZ-Pnm*, *D-Bsb*, *S-Skma* (2 copies); 6 trios, 2 vn,
   b, *A-Wgm*; 14 trios, 2vn, b, *I-CMbc*

BIBLIOGRAPHY

MGG2 (H. Seifert); *SartoriL*; *StiegerO*
F.S. Quadrio: *Della storia e della ragione d'ogni poesia*, iii/2 (Milan,
   1744)
E.F. Succi: *Catalogo con brevi cenni biografici e succinte descrizioni
   degli autografi e documenti di celebri o distinti musicisti posseduti
da Emilia Succi accademica filarmonica di Bologna* (Bologna,
   1888)
M.-T. Bouquet: *Storia del Teatro Regio di Torino, Il teatro di corte
   dalle origini al 1788* (Turin, 1976)
R. Allorto: *Gli anni milanesi di Giovanni Cristiano Bach e le sue
   composizioni sacre* (Milan, 1992)
M. Brusa and A. Rossi: 'Sammartini e il suo tempo: fonti manoscritte
   e stampate della musica a Milano nel Settecento', *Fonti musicali
   italiane*, i (1996), suppl.
MARCO BRUSA, HERBERT SEIFERT

Balbi, Lodovico [Ludovico] (*b* Venice, *c*1545; *d* Venice,
before 15 Dec 1604). Italian composer and friar. He
entered the monastery of S Maria Gloriosa dei Frari,
Venice, as a member of the order of Minor Conventuals.
From 1565 to 1567 he was a pupil in Padua of Costanzo
Porta, who belonged to the same religious order. From
1570 to 1578 he was a singer at S Marco, Venice, at the
time when Zarlino was *maestro di cappella* there, and at
Verona Cathedral. In 1578 he was appointed *maestro di
cappella* of S Maria Gloriosa dei Frari, an appointment
he probably held for four or five years. A document (in *I-
Ma*, reproduced in Garbellotto) shows that in 1579 and
again in 1582 Porta made great efforts to persuade
Cardinal Borromeo, Archbishop of Milan, to accept Balbi
as *maestro di cappella* of Milan Cathedral. At first no
decision came from Milan and only in 1582 did the
officials of the cathedral chapter decide to call Balbi, who,
however, declined to accept, for reasons which are not
recorded. On 7 November 1580 he participated unsuccessfully in a competition for the directorship of the choir
of Padua Cathedral. On 18 May 1585 he was appointed
maestro di cappella of the Cappella Antoniana in Padua,
a post he held for over six years. On 28 November 1591
he obtained exemption from his duties, and from 13 July
1593 held a similar post at Feltre Cathedral. He remained
there until 5 August 1597 when he left to take the post of
maestro di cappella at Treviso Cathedral. On 10 June
1596 the chapter of his religious order named him,
together with Porta and Gerolamo Vespa, *maestro
dell'ordine*, an honorary degree denoting particular skill
exercised over a long period. He left Treviso in 1598 and
returned to S Maria Gloriosa, Venice, where he died.

   Balbi had a thorough mastery of contrapuntal writing,
though unequal in artistry to his teacher Porta. The *Psalmi
ad vesperas* (1596, *I-FELc*), in the usual homophonic and
homorhythmic style, show simple melodic and rhythmic
invention. The *Musicale essercitio*, in which Balbi added
four voice parts of his own under the superius parts of
well-known madrigals, is a curious piece of academicism.
His output has yet to be studied fully, however, and
perhaps the two books of madrigals for four voices may
yield greater musical interest.

WORKS
all published in Venice

SACRED

Ecclesiasticarum cantionum, 4vv (1578)
4 masses: 'Ecce mitto angelum meum', 'Fuggite il sonno', Missa
   duodecim toni, Missa alternatim canenda: 5vv (1580)
Ecclesiasticarum cantionum in sacris totius anni sanctorum
   sollemnitatibus, 4vv (1587)
Graduale et antiphonarium juxta ritum missalis et breviarii novi
   (1587) [collab. G. Gabrieli, Orazio Vecchi]
Missa defunctorum, 5vv (1595) [pubd with repr. of 1580 masses]
Messe et motetti con il Te Deum laudamus, 8vv (1605); bc pubd
   separately (1605)
1 psalm, 5vv, 1590[7]; 9 falsobordoni, 1601[1]; 2 motets, 7, 8vv, 1611[1];
   3 motets, 8vv, 1612[3]; 5 motets, 6–8vv, 1613[2]; 1 motet, 6vv, 1617[1];
   4 concerti ecclesiastici, 1622[2]

Several motets, psalms, *D-Z*, *I-Bc*, FELc, *PL-WRu*, Legnica, Biblioteca Rudofina

SECULAR

Il primo libro de madrigali, 4vv (1570)
Il secondo libro de madrigali, 4vv (1576)
I capricci, 6vv (1586)
Musicale essercitio, 5vv (1589)
1 madrigal, 6vv, 1592[11]; 1 madrigal, 6vv, 1594[6]; 1 madrigal, 5vv, 1598[6]; 1 madrigal, 4vv, 1598[9]

BIBLIOGRAPHY

CaffiS; *EinsteinIM*; *FétisB*; *GaspariC*; *SchmidlD*
E.A. Cicogna: *Delle inscrizioni veneziane*, iii (Venice, 1830/R), 17ff
L. Busi: *Il Padre G.B. Martini* (Bologna, 1891/R)
G. Tebaldini: *L'archivio musicale della Cappella Antoniana in Padova* (Padua, 1895)
P.S. Mattei: 'Serie dei maestri di cappilla Minori Conventuali', *Miscellanea Francescana*, xxi (1920)
D. Sporacio: 'Municisti Minori Conventuali', *Miscellanea Francescana*, xxv (1925)
R. Casimiri: 'Musicisti dell'ordine francescano dei minori conventuali dei secoli XVI–XVIII', *NA*, xvi (1939), 186–99, 238–50, 274–5
R. Casimiri: 'Musica e musicisti nella cattedrale di Padova nei secoli XIV, XV e XVI', *NA*, xviii (1941), 1–31, 101–214; xix (1942), 49–92; pubd separately (Rome, 1942)
Cenni cronistorici intorno agli organi e organisti della Cattedrale di Feltre (Feltre, 1943)
G. d'Alessi: *La cappella musicale del duomo di Treviso (1300–1633)* (Vedelago, 1954), 138–9
A. Garbelotto: *Il Padre Costanzo Porta da Cremona* (Rome, 1955), 35ff
F. Degrada: 'Dante e la musica nel Cinquecento', *Chigiana*, new ser., ii (1965), 257–75
L. Bianconi: Preface to P.M. Marsolo: *Secondo libro dei madrigali*, *MRS*, iv (1973)
A. Sartori: *Documenti per la storia della musica al santo e nel Veneto* (Vicenza, 1977)
R. Spanò: *Il Musicale essercitio (1589) di Ludovico Balbi: trascrizione della stampa e confronto* (thesis, U. of Padua, 1991–2)

GIANCARLO ROSTIROLLA

Balbi, Luigi [Alviso, Alciso, Aluigi, Aloysius] (*b* ?Venice; *fl* 1585–1621). Italian composer, organist and friar, nephew and pupil of Lodovico Balbi. He followed the same religious career as his uncle in the order of the Minor Conventuals. He was at first a singer in the choir of S Marco, Venice (1585), and in August 1585 entered the Cappella del Santo at the basilica of S Antonio, Padua. On 20 June 1586 he succeeded Bartolomeo Formenton as organist there. On 27 November 1587 he was appointed *maestro di cappella* at the church of the Carità in Venice. In 1590 he was in Zara, directing the local choir, after which he returned to Venice to serve in the choir of the Ca' Grande. In April 1606 he competed, at first unsuccessfully, for the directorship of the Cappella del Santo, Padua, a post he obtained on 4 August 1615. He remained there until August 1621, with some interruptions owing to the temporary suppression of the choir because of the lack of discipline among the singers.

WORKS

Ecclesiastici concentus … liber primus (Venice, 1606)
Completorium, 12vv (Venice, 1609)
Motets, sacri concerti and other pieces, 1590[7], 1615[3], 1622[2], 1623[2], 1627[1], 1627[2]

For bibliography see BALBI, LODOVICO.

GIANCARLO ROSTIROLLA

Balbiani-Vegezzi-Bossi. *See* BOSSI family.

Balbun, Noel [Noe]. *See* BAULDEWEYN, NOEL.

Baldan, Angelo (*b* Venice, 1753; *d* Venice, 23 April 1803). Italian composer. He studied with G.F. Brusa, was a singer at S Marco and became director of music at the churches of S Leonardo, S Marcuola and at the convent of S Maria Celeste in Venice. Some of his scores are dated and marked for use at other Venetian churches (S Rocco, S Pietro di Castello and S Geremia). *Assalone*, performed in 1789 in the oratory of S Filippo Neri, Venice, was his only dramatic work; he did, however, write arias to be used in performances of operas by other composers.

Aristocratic families employed Baldan as teacher. At soirées in the Venier palace he performed with his pupil Teresa Venier, née Ventura (known before her marriage as a singer at the Ospizio di S Lazzaro dei Mendicanti), his ballettos, sonatas and ricercares for harpsichord and his songs. Some of these canzoni with Venetian dialect texts became popular in the 19th century and were mistaken for folksongs (e.g. *Nina xe qua el to Nane*, *Per carità Bettina* and *Nella stagion dei boccoli*). At Baldan's funeral in S Geremia his Requiem for chorus and orchestra (1789) was performed.

WORKS
MSS in I-Vc, Vnm, Vs, Vsmc, Nc

Requiem, chorus, orch, 1789; 5 masses, 2–8vv; 12 mass movts, 2–5vv; 2 Mag, 3vv, 4vv; 2 TeD, 3vv, 4vv; 5 motets, S, orch; 26 ants, psalms etc.: mostly T, B, or 2T, B, with bc/orch
Assalone (orat), Venice, 1789
5 arie, 5 ariette, 5 canzoni, 11 duettini; mostly S, bc
Sei sinfonie, ob, hn, 2 vn, va, b (Venice, *c*1785)
Conc., hpd, orch; 6 ricercari, hpd; 7 sonate, hpd; numerous ballettos, hpd; 1 sonata, wind, 1795
Istruzione d'accompagnamento, 2 sets, *Vnm* [incl. 42 arias, B, bc]

BIBLIOGRAPHY

DBI (S. Simonetti)
G.A. Moschini: *Della letteratura veneziana del secolo XVIII*, iii (Venice, 1806), 212
F. Caffi: *Materiali e carteggi per la storia della musica teatrale* (MS, *I-Vnm*)
G. Fantoni: 'Angelo Baldan veneto musicista del passato secolo', *Ateneo veneto: rivista mensile di scienze, lettere ed arti*, 9th ser., i (1885), 449–59
D. and E. Arnold: *The Oratorio in Venice* (London, 1986), 83

SVEN HANSELL

Baldassari, Benedetto [Benedetti] (*fl* 1708–25). Italian soprano castrato. He was in the service of the Elector Palatine at Düsseldorf (*c*1708–14), where he sang a female part in Steffani's *Tassilone* in 1709. In 1710–11 he was at the Berlin court as the agent of the elector and Steffani in an attempt to convert the King and Queen of Prussia to Catholicism. In 1712 he went to London and sang in revivals of Mancini's *Idaspe fedele* and Gasparini's *Antioco* at the Queen's Theatre, playing a female part in the latter, and in the pasticcio *Ercole*. He was much applauded, again in a female role, in Gasparini's *Lucio Papirio* in Rome in 1714, and sang in operas by C.F. Pollarolo and Orlandini in Venice in 1718. Returning to London in 1719, he sang as an original member of the Royal Academy company, in Porta's *Numitore*, Handel's *Radamisto* (where he demanded to be elevated from a captain of the guard to a princely lover) and Roseingrave's adaptation of Domenico Scarlatti's *Narciso* in 1720, and in original productions of Handel's *Floridante* (1721) and Giovanni Bononcini's *Crispo* and *Griselda* (1722). In the autumn of 1725 he was singing in Dublin.

The two parts Handel wrote for him, Fraarte in *Radamisto* and Timante in *Floridante*, show that he was a high soprano with a compass from *e'* to *a"* but the two leading male roles in *Radamisto* were allotted to women, implying that Handel did not rate him as a front-rank castrato. His portrait was painted by Beluzzi and engraved by Vertue.

WINTON DEAN

Baldassari [Baldassare, Baldasari], **Pietro** (*b* ?Brescia, *c*1683; *d* after 1768). Italian composer. Early historians name Rome as his birthplace, but some contemporary documents describe him as being from Brescia, where Baldassari was quite a common name. From his works it can be assumed that he was in Brescia in 1709, and in librettos he is named *maestro di cappella* of the Oratorio di S Filippo Neri (Congregazione della Pace) in Brescia. He held this post from 1714 until at least 1768 and until 1754 he was also *maestro di cappella* of S Clemente, Brescia. In December 1717 he competed, unsuccessfully, for the same post at the basilica of S Maria Maggiore, Bergamo. He took holy orders.

Apart from the *componimento per musica, Il giudizio di Paride*, written to celebrate the name day of the Empress Amalia Wilhelmina, little of Baldassari's music has survived. From that which has survived, his musical language can be said to bear traces of the canonic writing practised by members of the Accademia Filarmonica of Bologna. A letter to Padre Martini dated 21 February 1768 (*I-Bc*) reveals his intention to dedicate a collection of 12 psalms to Farinelli.

WORKS

Il giudizio di Paride (componimento per musica, L.N. Cyni), Vienna, 10 July 1707, *A-Wn*
Oratorios, all lost, libs in *I-Bc*: Applausi eterni dell'amore, Brescia, 1709; La vera idea del ben chiedere mercede, Pavia, 1714; La fuga in Egitto, Bologna, 1721; Le sagre contese dell'amore e dell'umiltà, Bologna, 1721; La santità riconciliata col mondo, Bologna, 1722; S Maria Maddalena de'Pazzi, Bologna, 1723; L'umiltà coronata alla Santità di N.S. Benedetto XIII (G. Bianchi), Bologna, 6 Feb 1725; Per il novello Oratorio (F. Cappello), Brescia, 1747
Benedictus, 4vv, inst, *BRs*
Cantatas, all lost, libs in *Mb*, *BRq*: Cantata nella nascita di N. Signor Gesù Cristo, Brescia, Oratorio di S Filippo Neri, 1715; I Trionfi della Fede in Brescia, Brescia, 1715; Componimento musicale per la creazione di N.S. Benedetto XIII, Brescia, 1724
2 sonatas, cornett, str, bc, *A-Wkm*
1 sonata, hpd, in Raccolta musicale, i (Nuremberg, 1756)

BIBLIOGRAPHY

MGG1 (H. Seifert); *RicciTB*
F. Vatielli: 'L'oratorio a Bologna negli ultimi decenni del Seicento', *NA*, xv (1938), 26–35, 77–87
A. Schnoebelen: *Padre Martini's Collections of Letters in the Civico Museo Bibliographico Musicale in Bologna: an Annotated Index* (New York, 1979), 40
E. Citati: 'La musica presso la congregazione di Santa Maria della Pace in Brescia, con riferimento all'attività esercitata dal compositore Pietro Baldassarri', *La cappella musicale nell'Italia della Controriforma*, ed. O. Mischiati and P. Russo (Florence, 1993), 353–60
M. Bizzarini: 'Una solenne accademia con musica nella chiesa di S. Pietro in Oliveto', *Civiltà Bresciana*, ii/2 (1993), 39–40
E. Citati: 'Alla ricerca di un nome: Pietro Baldassarri compositore italiano', *Civiltà Bresciana*, ii/3 (1993), 56–8
P. Palermo: 'La musica a S. Maria Maggiore nell'infanzia di Locatelli', *Intorno a Locatelli*, ed. A. Dunning (Lucca, 1995), 653–748, esp. 727
R. Del Silenzio: 'Celebrazioni per la festa annuale della Beata Vergine del Santo Rosario nella chiesa di S. Clemente in Brescia', *Civiltà Bresciana*, iv/2 (1995), 69–72

JAMES L. JACKMAN/MARCO BIZZARINI

Baldi, Antonio (*fl* 1714–35). Italian alto castrato. He came from Cortona and may have sung in three operas at Palermo in 1714–16. He appeared in 13 operas in Venice (1722–4, 1729 and 1733–5), including works by Gasparini, Orlandini, Giacomelli, Hasse and Leo, in Genoa

(1723 and 1730), Milan (1723 and 1725), Florence and Turin (1730–31) and Rome (1731). He was engaged for three seasons (1725–8) by the Royal Academy in London, making his début in a revival of the Vinci-Orlandini *Elpidia*. He sang in ten operas by Handel (four of them revivals), the pasticcio *Elisa*, Ariosti's *Lucio Vero* and *Teuzzone* and Giovanni Bononcini's *Astianatte*. The six parts Handel composed for him, Scipio in *Scipione*, Taxiles in *Alessandro*, Trasimede in *Admeto*, Oronte in *Riccardo Primo*, Medarse in *Siroe* and Alessandro in *Tolomeo*, indicate a narrow compass (*a* to *d*″) and a tessitura similar to Senesino's but with far less brilliance. Owen Swiney described him in 1725 as a tolerable actor and neither a good nor a bad singer. Burney called him 'a singer of no great abilities' and suggested, of one of his arias in *Siroe*, that Handel assigned 'the chief part of the business to the instruments, which, so employed, were better worth hearing than the voice'; but Burney can never have heard Baldi sing. There is a caricature of him by A.M. Zanetti in the Cini collection (*I-Vgc*).

WINTON DEAN

Baldi, João José (*b* Lisbon, 1770; *d* Lisbon, 18 May 1816). Portuguese composer. The son of Carlo Baldi (*d* Lisbon, 1779), a favoured court musician who had immigrated from Italy, he was admitted on 10 January 1781 to the Lisbon Seminário Patriarcal, where his music teachers were Sousa Carvalho, the Lima brothers and José Joaquim dos Santos. In September 1789, having completed his studies, he was named *mestre de capela* of Guarda Cathedral. From this year date his earliest surviving works, two orchestral masses. In 1794 he moved from Guarda to Faro Cathedral and in 1800 returned to Lisbon as second *mestre de capela* of the royal chapel of Bemposta.

From 1805 he wrote a series of spectacular polychoral masses, Vespers and Matins for the royal basilica at Mafra, celebrated for its six widely spaced organs and choirs in its four corners. As late as 1825 his Mafra music produced 'a stupendous and admirable effect'. In 1801 he published his first *modinha* and in 1803 wrote the Grand Mass dedicated to the Conde de Borba that made him famous. In 1805 he began composing for the theatre and in 1806 became first *mestre* of Bemposta and of Lisbon Cathedral. In 1812, while a captain in the militia raised by Beresford, he wrote the music for a patriotic hymn dedicated to Wellington.

An extremely versatile artist who wrote in the reigning Italian manner, he composed a great amount of church music, piano works, songs and stage music, the latter for the Rua dos Condes and Salitre theatres. He ranks with Portugal and Moreira as one of the three best Portuguese composers of his generation.

WORKS

SACRED

For 4vv, orch/org: masses: *P-La*, *Em*, 5 in *EVc*; 2, 1789, *Lf*; 1801, *La*; 1801, *BR-Rem**; 1803, ded. Conde de Borba; 2 Mag, *P-EVcn*; Responsories: St Michael's Matins, 1806, Sacred Heart Matins, 1808, Christmas Matins, 1811, Dec 8 Matins, all *P-La*, 52 in *EVc*; 2 TeD, 1808, 1811, *La*; 7 vesper ps, *La*; 7 vesper ps, *EVc*
Polychoral (male vv, acc. 4–6 org; all at *MP*): 4 masses, separate Credo, Mag, 1807; Matins, 1805; Vespers, 1806; 8 vesper ps

OTHER WORKS

Toccata, kbd, *Ln*; Sym., orch, *La*; songs, incl. modinha in *Jornal de modinhas novas* (1801); hymn ded. Wellington, 1803

BIBLIOGRAPHY

DBP

M.A. Machado Santos, ed.: *Biblioteca da Ajuda: catálogo de música manuscrita*, i (Lisbon, 1958), 43–50; vii (Lisbon, 1964), 22–3

J.A. Alegria: *Arquivo das músicas da Sé de Évora: catálogo* (Lisbon, 1973), 19, 24–5, 29, 43–4, 57, 68, 82

J.M.B. Azevedo: *Biblioteca do Palacio nacional de Mafra: catálogo dos Fundos Musicais* (Lisbon, 1985), 10, 57–67, 187–8

ROBERT STEVENSON

Baldini, Vittorio (*b* Venice; *d* Ferrara, 21 Feb 1618). Italian printer and engraver. He began to publish literary texts in 1578, setting up his printing works opposite the Castello Estense at Ferrara. He seems to have started music publishing in 1582 with a collection of madrigals for five voices by various authors entitled *Il lauro secco*, in which a representative group of madrigalists from Ferrara and other Italian cities paid homage to the beauty and virtuosity of Laura Peverara, a singer from Mantua and lady-in-waiting to the Duchess of Ferrara. Baldini probably acquired the edition from the heirs of Francesco Rossi and Paolo Tortorino. He later printed many collections of madrigals, canzonettas, psalms and motets by such leading composers as Lodovico Agostini, Girolamo Belli and Bonfilio. Between 1594 and 1597 he published several of the most significant works of the *seconda pratica* madrigalists (Luzzaschi, Gesualdo, Fontanelli and Macque).

Baldini also published a number of books on the theory and art of music and the theatre, including F. Patrizi's *La deca istoriale* (1586) and *La deca disputata* (1586); G.B. Aleotti's *Gli artifitiosi et curiosi moti spiritali di Herrone* (1589, the Italian translation, with illustrations, of a basic handbook for stage machinists; see illustration); M.A. Ingegneri's *Della poesia rappresentativa* (1598); and Ercole Bottrigari's *Il melone* (1602/R, Monteverdi's reply in his own defence to the attacks of Artusi). Among the most important poetic and theatrical texts that he printed are the descriptive scenarios for intermezzos, tournaments and mock battles staged in melodramatic style at Ferrara from 1600 onwards, for example Guidobaldo Bonarelli della Rovere's *Filli di Sciro* (1607, with scenery and costumes by G.B. Aleotti, engraved by F. Vallegio) and Battista Guarini's *Intermezzi* (various editions, with alterations, 1610, 1612 and 1614).

In contrast to contemporary Venetian publications, Baldini's works show a deeply cultivated and élitist tendency through the beauty of their graphic lettering, engraved decorations and superb title-pages. He used both wood and metal on fine, azure-coloured paper; his musical publications are among the most interesting of the late 16th century as they include both text and music. Baldini used several different imprints: Ducal Printer until 1597, when the Este family lost the Duchy of Ferrara, thereafter Episcopal or State Printer and Printer to the Academy of the Intrepidi. He used a large number of typographical signs including a bell, a flying Daedalus (see illustration) and the sun. After his death, his daughter Vittoria carried on the printing works until 1622, under the imprint of 'the heirs of Vittorio Baldini'.

BIBLIOGRAPHY

SartoriD

G.D. Cucchetti: *La pazzia, favola pastorale* (Ferrara, 1581, later edns to 1623)

ADRIANO CAVICCHI

Baldoni, Tomaso. *See* BOLDON, TOMASO.

Baldovino, Amadeo (*b* Alexandria, 5 Feb 1916). Italian cellist. He spent two three-year periods at the conservatory in Bologna: from 1927 he studied the cello with Camillo Oblach, graduating in 1930, and he returned in 1937 as a composition pupil of Cesare Nordio. His début recital took place in Milan in 1930, and he started a series of international tours the following year with a concerto performance in Berlin: he was welcomed as a sensitive young artist as well as an accomplished technician. His international solo career expanded greatly after World War II, but he later devoted more time to chamber music. He was a founder-member in 1957 of the Italian String Trio; he left in 1962 to replace Libero Lana in the Trio di Trieste. Following Mainardi, he was from 1969 to 1972 professor of the master cello course at the Accademia di S Cecilia, Rome, and subsequently continued to teach there. He played on the 1711 'Mara' Stradivari, formerly the property of John Crosdill and Alessandro Pezze. (*CampbellGC*)

PIERO RATTALINO

Baldrati [Baldradi], **Bartolomeo** (*b* Rimini, *c*1645). Italian ?composer. A Franciscan friar, he was *maestro di cappella* of S Francesco, Rimini, when *Messe a 4 voci a capella* op.1 (Bologna, 1678, 2/1694) was published under his name. A copy (in *I-Bc*) of the first edition, however, bears a manuscript note stating that this music is by Giuseppe da Bagnacavallo (*see* GIUSEPPE TAMBURINI). According to Eitner (*Quellen-Lexikon*) two masses by Baldrati (one for 24 voices) and a few five- and six-part motets survive (in *F-Pn*).

Balducci, Francesco (*b* Palermo, bap. 1 April 1579; *d* Rome, 20 Nov – 31 Dec 1642). Italian poet. Having received a relatively limited education in Palermo, he went before he was 20 to Naples, where he found patronage for his poetry among the aristocracy. He also went to Rome and in 1601 was among the papal troops who opposed the Turks in Hungary. After the campaign he returned to Rome, where he began his period of most intensive literary activity: he worked under the protection of Giovanni Antonio and Paolo Girolamo II Orsini, Cardinals Ludovisi, Scipione Borghese, Orsi, and Antonio

Daedalus, one of the typographical devices used by Vittorio Baldini: from the 'Registro' (last page) of the second part of G.B. Aleotti's 'Gli artifitiosi et curiosi moti spiritali di Herrone' (Ferrara: Baldini, 1589), 104

and Maffeo Barberini, among others. He travelled widely in Italy and became a member of various literary academies in Rome, Perugia, Bologna and Palermo. A man of restless and impulsive temperament, he lived an irregular life, which seems to have alternated between extremes of luxury and misery and included a prison term for insolvency. He took holy orders late in life and became a chaplain in the Roman hospital of S Sisto.

During his lifetime one volume of his *Rime* was published (Rome, 1630), and that and another volume of *Rime* appeared posthumously (Rome, 1645–6). Two oratorio texts, *La fede* and *Il trionfo*, were included in the second volume of *Rime* (edns of both in Alaleona: *Storia*, pp.289ff, and of *La fede* only in Pasquetti, 2/1914, pp.207ff, and Schering, appx, pp.viiff). These are the earliest printed works, either literary or musical, in which the term 'oratorio' is used to designate a genre. A modified version of *Il trionfo* was set to music, possibly by Carissimi, as *Oratorio della Santissima Vergine* (ed. in PIISM, 3rd ser., *Oratori*, viii). His many canzonettas, set to music by Orazio Michi and others, played a crucial role in the origins of the chamber cantata.

BIBLIOGRAPHY

DBI (E.N. Girardi); ScheringGO; SmitherHO, i
G. Pasquetti: *L'oratorio musicale in Italia* (Florence, 1906, 2/1914)
D. Alaleona: *Studi su la storia dell'oratorio musicale in Italia* (Turin, 1908, 2/1945 as *Storia dell'oratorio musicale in Italia*)
R. Holzer: *Music and Poetry in Seventeenth-Century Rome* (diss., U. of Pennsylvania, 1990)
J.W. Hill: *Roman Monody, Cantata and Opera from the Circles around Cardinal Montalto* (Oxford, 1997)

HOWARD E. SMITHER/R

Balducci, Giuseppe (Antonio Luigi Angelo) (*b* Iesi, 2 May 1796; *d* Malaga, 1845). Italian composer. He received the best training available in the Marches, and at the age of 17 formed his own operatic troupe. He was, however, forced to flee after killing the nephew of the Papal Governor of Iesi in a duel. Reaching Naples, he became music master to the three daughters of a retired field marshal, Raimondo Capece Minutolo, and spent the rest of his life as a member of their household. He died on a business trip to Malaga in 1845.

As an operatic composer, Balducci made his début, after further training in Naples with Zingarelli, with *Il sospetto funesto* (Lent 1820, Fondo), an *opera semiseria* with, unusually, a tragic ending. He followed this with further works, but when *Tazia* (15 January 1826, S Carlo) was sabotaged by a disaffected orchestra for unknown reasons, he retired from the theatre. His only subsequent work performed in public was *Bianca Turenga* (11 August 1838, S Carlo). However he also composed five salon operas, beginning with *Boabdil re di Granata* (1827) and ending with *Il conte di Marsico* (26 February 1839) for the Capece Minutolo daughters and their friends. Unique in Italian opera, these works were composed for women's voices only, generally with accompaniments for six hands at two pianos.

Though Balducci may have lacked the melodic gifts of Donizetti and Bellini, his music is well crafted. Whereas other composers complained of the difficulty of finding new ideas for cabalettas, his final movements are nearly always fresh, spontaneous and effective. The stage revival of his works has so far been confined to New Zealand, where Opera Waikato has staged *I gelosi* (1993), *Il noce di Benevento* (1995) and *Scherzo* (1996).

WORKS

OPERAS
first performed in Naples and autograph MSS at I-Nc unless otherwise stated

For public perf.: Il sospetto funesto (? P. Giannone, ? A.L. Tottola), Fondo, Lent 1820; L'amante virtuoso (G. Schmidt), Fondo, 1 April 1823; Le nozze di Don Desiderio, Nuovo, 8 Nov 1823, no autograph, copy at Nc; Riccardo l'intrepido (J. Ferretti), Valle, Rome, 9 Sept 1824; Tazia (L. Ricciuti), S Carlo, 15 Jan 1826; Bianca Turenga (G. Bidera), S Carlo, 11 Aug 1838
For private perf.: Boabdil re di Granata, acc. 2 pf 4 hands, March 1827; I gelosi (G. Tarantino), acc. 2 pf 6 hands, April 1834; Il noce di Benevento, acc. 2 pf 6 hands, male chorus, 5-inst orchestrino in finale, 14 March 1837; Il conte di Marsico (A. Balducci, V. Salvagnoli), acc. 2 pf 6 hands, 26 Feb 1839 (Naples, n.d.), no autograph

OTHER WORKS
Vocal: L'Adamo (orat), inc.; Andromaca (cant.), I-Nc; Mass for 6 vv, Nc; Mass and Credo, D, Nc; Funeral Mass, Nc; Miserere, 4 vv, str, 1825, Nc; Salve regina a voci sole, Nc*; Gira, gira molinello, chorus, orch, Nc*; songs, duets, other pieces, Nc
Inst: 2 qts, hp, pf, hn, vc, Nc; Sonatina, G, hp, pf, Nc; 8 variations for pf on 'Là ci darem la mano' from Mozart's Don Giovanni, Nc*; other pieces

BIBLIOGRAPHY
C. Capece Minutolo: Diary, 1855–9 (MS, I-Nc) [incl. account of her family and her early life in Naples]
J. Commons: 'On Rediscovering a Forgotten Composer: Giuseppe Balducci', *Early Music New Zealand*, ii/1 (1986), 3–9; enlarged, *About the House*, vii/7 (1986), 44–7
J. Commons: 'Giuseppe Balducci: Tazia', *A Hundred Years of Italian Opera (1820–30)*, ORCH 104 (1995) [disc notes]

JEREMY COMMONS

Balduin, Noel [Noe]. *See* BAULDEWEYN, NOEL.

Baldwin. American firm of instrument makers, predominantly of pianos and organs. It was founded in Cincinnati in 1862 by Dwight Hamilton Baldwin (1821–99). He attended the preparatory department of Oberlin College (1840–42) and was then a minister and school singing teacher in Kentucky and Ohio. Moving to Cincinnati in 1857 to teach music in schools, he also became in 1862 or 1863 a retailer of pianos and organs. D.H. Baldwin & Co. was formed in June 1873 when Lucien Wulsin (1845–1912), a clerk in Baldwin's firm since 1866, became partner. Robert A. Johnson (1838–84) opened a Louisville branch in 1877 and became a partner in 1880. Three more partners joined in 1884: Albert A. van Buren, George W. Armstrong jr (1857–1932), and Clarence Wulsin (1855–97), who ran an Indianapolis branch. Until the late 1880s the firm was one of the largest dealers in keyboard instruments in the Midwest as agent for such makers as Decker, Estey, J. & C. Fischer and Steinway.

In 1889, a subsidiary, the Hamilton Organ Co., Chicago, began to manufacture reed organs, and by 1891 the Baldwin Piano Co., a subsidiary in Cincinnati, was making upright pianos. The company acquired the Ellington Piano Co. (1893) and the Valley Gem (originally the Ohio Valley) Piano Co., founded in 1871 in Ripley, Ohio. John Warren Macy led in the early manufacture, developing a piano that won the Grand Prix at the Paris Exhibition in 1900. Baldwin's death caused some upheaval, ultimately solved when Lucien Wulsin and George Armstrong bought control in July 1903. Wulsin was president until 1912, Armstrong from 1912 to 1926, and Lucien Wulsin jr (1889–1964) from 1926 to 1964.

In the late 1920s, in collaboration with the physics department of the University of Cincinnati, the company began a research programme in electronics that resulted in the introduction of an electronic organ in 1947 (see BALDWIN ORGAN). Baldwin's director of electronic research, Dr Winston E. Kock, designed the original models, some of which were intended for use in churches. Most Baldwin organs are smaller instruments for the home, many of them 'spinet' organs with two staggered manuals.

In 1965 the firm introduced the model SD-10, a concert grand piano newly designed by Harold Conklin. By the 1970s the parent company, by then under the chairmanship of the founding partner's grandson, Lucien Wulsin (b 1916), had expanded into Baldwin United, a large corporation. The music subsidiary, Baldwin Piano & Organ Co., continued to manufacture pianos and electronic organs at factories in Mississippi and Arkansas. In 1963 Baldwin bought Bechstein of Berlin, which retained its own identity and continued to make pianos in its own style.

An experimental concert grand piano with electronically enhanced sound served as a prototype for later, more successful electronic and computerized instruments. After 1960 the company extended its range of electronic instruments to harpsichords, guitars and pianos. Several manufacturing operations, including Gretsch (guitars, drums and amplifiers) and Ode (banjos), were sold in 1980 to Charles Roy of Nashville, Tennessee.

In 1983 Baldwin United filed for bankruptcy after sustaining heavy losses in its insurance business. Baldwin Piano & Organ Co. was bought the following year by some of the company's executives, including Harold Smith, who became president, and R.S. Harrison, who became chairman. Baldwin sold Bechstein in 1987 and in the following year purchased the Wurlitzer Company, which owned the Chickering name. Baldwin's mid-range grands are now named Chickering, and the lower-priced instruments are named Wurlitzer. Most recently, the company has produced a digital reproducing player system, the ConcertMaster, housed in a grand piano, which has multimedia capacities and can download from the Internet. Baldwin is now the largest producer of pianos in the USA, producing 20,000 instruments annually.

CYNTHIA ADAMS HOOVER/EDWIN M. GOOD

Baldwin, Dalton (b Summit, NY, 19 Dec 1931). American pianist. He began his formal musical training at the Juilliard School of Music, but gained the BM from the Oberlin College Conservatory. He continued his studies in Paris with Boulanger and Madeleine Lipatti and in 1954 began his long and successful partnership with the baritone Gérard Souzay. Concentrating primarily on the song repertory, Baldwin was coached by such composers as Poulenc, Sibelius, Martin and Barber. He has participated in a number of first performances (notably of Rorem's *War Scenes* in 1969, with Souzay as soloist) and has accompanied such other eminent singers as Elly Ameling, Jessye Norman, Arleen Augér, Marilyn Horne and Frederica Von Stade. Perhaps his finest achievements have been his recordings of the complete songs of Debussy, Fauré, Poulenc, Ravel and Roussel. Baldwin's playing is characterized by a softness of touch and superb legato, which allow him to phrase with the singer; he is supportive without being too subdued.

RICHARD LESUEUR

Baldwin [Baldwine, Baldwyn, Baudewyn, Bawdwine], **John** (b before 1560; d London, 28 Aug 1615). English singer, composer and music copyist. He was appointed a tenor lay clerk at St George's Chapel, Windsor, in 1575. He became a Gentleman of the Chapel Royal on 20 August 1598, and appears to have left Windsor by 1600. He sang in the Chapel Royal at the funeral of Elizabeth I, the coronation of James I and the funeral of Prince Henry.

Baldwin was the copyist of several important music manuscripts. He preserved much pre-Reformation English church music in the partbooks *GB-Och* 979–83, copied about 1575–81 with later additions (the Tenor part is lacking). His so-called Commonplace Book (*Lbl* R.M.24.d.2; facs. in RMF, viii, 1987), begun about 1586 and largely complete by 25 July 1591 (with additions up to c1606), contains a wide variety of music. Baldwin had access to Marenzio's *Madrigali a quattro, cinque e sei voci* (1588) no later than 1591, scoring 13 works from the collection; he also copied a number of three-voice sections from pre-Reformation antiphons as well as complex proportion and hexachord exercises, some of which he ascribed to the 15th-century composer Bedyngham and may well be authentic. Baldwin completed *My Ladye Nevells Booke*, a carefully arranged collection of Byrd's keyboard music, on 11 September 1591, when he was resident in Windsor and Byrd lived nearby in Harlington. The manuscript was probably copied for Rachel, the wife of Sir Edward Nevell, MP for Windsor in 1588–9; it remains in the Neville family, in the collection of the Marquis of Abergavenny. Baldwin also recopied the damaged final section of the Sextus part of the Forrest-Heyther partbooks (*Ob* Arch.F.e.19–24, formerly Mus.Sch.e.376–81) and copied two pieces into Robert Dow's partbooks (*Och* 984–8).

Baldwin's 23 compositions are of indifferent quality, though his nine proportion exercises are of intellectual interest – one presents 28 proportional signatures. His consort music includes two In Nomines (one canonic) and a Browning, which presents the tune successively beginning on B$\flat$, F, C, G and D (twice in canon). His song *In the merry month of May*, dated 1591 in his Commonplace Book, is probably the 'pleasant song of Coridon and Phyllida, made in three parts of purpose' for the visit of Elizabeth I to the Earl of Hertford at Elvetham on 22 September 1591.

BIBLIOGRAPHY

BDECM

E. Brennecke: 'A Singing Man of Windsor', *ML*, xxxiii (1952), 33–40

A. Brown: ' "My Lady Nevell's Book" as a Source of Byrd's Keyboard Music', *PRMA*, xcv (1968–9), 29–39

R. Bray: 'The Part-Books Oxford, Christ Church MSS. 979–83: an Index and Commentary', *MD*, xxv (1971), 179–97

R. Bray: 'British Museum MS Royal 24.d.2 (John Baldwin's Commonplace Book): an Index and Commentary', *RMARC*, no.12 (1974), 137–51

R. Bray: 'John Baldwin', *ML*, lvi (1975), 55–9

H. Gaskin: 'Baldwin and the Nevell Hand', *Byrd Studies*, ed. A. Brown and R. Turbet (Cambridge, 1992), 159–73

D. Hunter: 'My Lady Nevells Booke and the Art of Gracing', ibid., 174–93

ROGER BRAY

Baldwin organ. An electronic organ, many models of which have been manufactured by the Baldwin Piano & Organ Co. since 1946. The original models were designed by Dr Winston E. Kock (1909–82), the company's director of electronic research from 1936. Baldwin organs normally have two manuals and pedals; the earlier models were mostly church, cinema and concert organs, but the company has subsequently manufactured a wide range of instruments, including many for home use, especially 'spinet' organs in which two shorter manuals are staggered by one octave. Advances in electronic technology around 1970 made possible several new devices that are now widespread: rhythm and 'walking bass' units, arpeggiators, memories and a choice of chord systems. Baldwin introduced microcomputer organs around 1981; current models, like Baldwin's Pianovelle digital pianos, are based on sampled timbres.

HUGH DAVIES

Baldwyn, ?John (*fl c*1450–80). English composer. Two four-voice *Magnificat* settings, each with a compass of 22 notes, are attributed to 'Baldwyn' in the index of the Eton Choirbook (*GB-WRec* 178) and a even-voice *Gaude* by 'M. Bawldwyn' was copied at the College of the Holy Trinity, Tattershall in 1498–9, none of these works survive. A *Dominus* John Baudwyn was made BMus at Cambridge in 1470–71. A John Baldwyn of Cheshunt was scholar at Eton College (*c*1448–1452) and was admitted to King's College, Cambridge, on 7 December 1452, where he was a fellow in the later 1450s. Either or both of these may have been the composer, given the prevalence of compositions by old Etonians in the Eton Choirbook, and given the importance to Eton College of Cambridge as a source of polyphony. The composer may also have been the Sir John Baldwyn who was vicar-choral and chantrist at Wells Cathedral between *c*1486 and *c*1500.

BIBLIOGRAPHY
HarrisonMMB
F.W. Weaver, ed.: *Somerset Medieval Wills (1383–1500)* (London, 1901), 297
W.P. Baildon, ed.: *Calendar of the Manuscripts of the Dean and Chapter of Wells* (London, 1914), ii, 101–27, 158, 694
A.B. Emden: *A Biographical Register of the University of Cambridge to AD 1500* (Cambridge, 1963), 33, 45
A. Wathey: 'Lost Books of Polyphony in England: a List to 1500', *RMARC*, no.21 (1988), 1–19, esp.11

MAGNUS WILLIAMSON

Bâle (Fr.). *See* BASLE.

Balestra, Reimundo. *See* BALLESTRA, REIMUNDO.

Balestrieri, Thomas (*fl* Mantua, *c*1750–80). Italian violin maker. On his labels he called himself a Cremonese, but the surviving instruments were made in Mantua. The pattern and style of the best of his work draws much more from Cremona than from Mantua, and he may well have been trained in the first city before setting up on his own in the second. Some of his instruments show the influence of Camillus Camilli, his contemporary in Mantua. His best violins are of a flat Stradivarian model, giving a powerful sound that makes them sought after as solo instruments. He made a large number of violins and an occasional cello, but few, if any, violas. His varnish was often a dull red-brown colour and wore off easily, though sometimes he used an orange varnish of fine quality. (*LütgendorffGL; VannesE*)

CHARLES BEARE

Baley, Virko (*b* Radekhov, 21 Oct 1938). Americn composer and conductor of Ukrainian birth. He studied at the Los Angeles Conservatory of Music and Art (BA 1960, MM 1962; later the California Institute of the Arts), where his teachers included Earle Voorhies and

Morris Ruger; he also studied the piano with Rosina Lhevine and composition with Donald Erb and Mario Davidovsky. He joined the music department at the University of Nevada, Las Vegas in 1970. He has also served as founder-conductor of the Nevada SO (1980–95), music director of the Las Vegas Opera Company (1983–8) and principal guest conductor and music advisor of the Kiev Camerata (from 1995). His scholarly work has established him as an authority on Soviet music.

Although Baley's music frequently refers to Ukrainian sources, his style became increasingly Americanized after 1980. The First Violin Concerto (1987) includes Ukrainian folk elements and exhibits a European polish and mood, but its unusual orchestral textures, rippling with celeste, vibraphone and harpsichord, seem American, as does the energetic drumming of the second movement 'Dies irae' and the muted jazz trumpet of the final 'Agon'. His gradual move away from a mournful, Eastern European, somewhat neo-classical idiom climaxed in *Dreamtime* (1993–5), which includes a Ukrainian *kolo-miyka* dance, but reflects new world styles in its ensemble unisons, tuned water goblets and dream-like suspension of time.

WORKS

Op: Hunger (1, B. Boychuk), 1985–97
Orch: Woodcuts, str, 1971, rev. 1997; Duma, soliloquy, 1985, rev. 1988; Sym. no.1 'Sacred Monuments', 1985, rev. 1997–9; Vn Conc. no.1 'Quasi una fantasia', 1987, arr. vn, chbr orch; Vn Conc. no.2 'Favola in musica', 1988, rev. 1989; Pf Conc. no.1, 1990–93; Adam's Apple, prelude, 1991, arr. wind qnt, 1989, arr. str qt, 1997; Orpheus Singing, ob, str, 1994, arr. ob, pf/str qt; Partita, concerto grosso, tpt, trbn, violect [5-str elec vn], orch, elecs, 1995
Vocal: 2 Songs in Olden Style (W. Wordsworth, J. Joyce), S, pf, 1960; Edge (S. Plath), Mez, fl + a fl, tpt, vc, pf + synth, elecs, 1977, rev. 1997; Treny, S, 2 vc, 1996–7; Klytemnestra (O. Zabuzhko), Mez, cl, pf trio, 1998; A Journey after Loves (Boychuk), Bar, pf, 1999
Chbr and solo inst: Partita no.1, 3 trbn, 3 pf, 1970–76; Duo-Concertante, vc, pf, 1971, rev. 1990; Sculptured Birds, cl, pf, 1978–84; ... Figments (Etudes tableaux, bk I), vn, 10 vn/tape, 1981–92; Partita no.2, bn, pf, 1991–2, rev. 1997; Dreamtime Suite no.1, cl, vn, pf, 1993–4; Dreamtime (masque), fl, cl, vn, vc, kbd, 2 perc, 1993–5; Stamping Dance, b cl, 1995 [from Dreamtime]; Dreamtime Suite no.2, vn, vc, pf, 1996; Lament I, bn, 1996 [from Treny]; Lament Ia, dbn, 1996 [from Treny]; Shadows, fl, pf, 1996; Persona I, ob, 1997; ... à trois, ob, bn, pf, 1998; Persona II, cl, 1999
Pf: Nocturnal no.1 'Mirrors', 1958; 2 Dumas, 1959; Nocturnal no.2 'Tears', 1960; Nocturnal no.3, 3 pf, 1970; Nocturnal no.4, 1971–87; Nocturnal no.5, 1980; Nocturnal no.6, 1988

Principal publisher: Troppe Note (ASCAP)

KYLE GANN

Balfe, Michael William (*b* Dublin, 15 May 1808; *d* Rowney Abbey, Herts., 20 Oct 1870). Irish composer and singer. The most successful composer of English operas in the 19th century, and the only one whose fame spread throughout Europe, he gained wide international recognition with *The Bohemian Girl*.

1. LIFE. Balfe received his earliest musical instruction from his father, a dancing-master and violinist, and the composer William Rooke. When his father died in January 1823, Balfe went to London and became the articled pupil of C.F. Horn, earning a living as deputy leader of the Drury Lane orchestra. He developed a fine baritone voice and made his stage début at Norwich as Caspar in a bowdlerized version of *Der Freischütz*. In 1825 he went to Rome, where he studied composition with Paer, and then to Milan to study counterpoint with Francesco

Federici and singing with Filippo Galli. That autumn his first stage work, *Il naufragio di La Pérouse*, a *ballo pantomimo serio* designed by Alessandro Sanquirico, was given there at the Teatro della Cannobiana.

During the next four years Balfe pursued his career as an opera singer. He returned to Paris where Cherubini, whose good opinion he had already won en route to Rome, introduced him to Rossini. On hearing Balfe sing 'Largo al factotum', Rossini promised to recommend him to the Théâtre des Italiens, if he would first study for a year with Giulio Bordogni. Balfe agreed, and made his Paris début as Figaro in *Il barbiere di Siviglia* at the Théâtre des Italiens in 1827. After two seasons there he returned to Italy, appearing as Valdeburgo in Bellini's *La straniera* at the Teatro Carolino, Palermo, on 1 January 1830. Towards the end of the carnival season, a dispute between the chorus and the management resulted in his being commissioned to compose a short opera without chorus, *I rivali di se stessi*, which was written and produced in about 20 days. His singing engagements took him next to Piacenza and to Bergamo, where he met and shortly afterwards married the Hungarian singer Lina Roser.

In spring 1831 he was invited to write an opera for the Teatro Fraschini, Pavia, the *farsa giocosa Un avvertimento ai gelosi*. His third opera, the more ambitious *Enrico Quarto al passo della Marna*, was given at the Teatro Carcano, Milan (not La Scala, as is often stated) on 19 February 1833, with himself and his wife in leading roles. Later that year Balfe renewed his friendship with Maria Malibran, whom he had known in Paris. She persuaded the management at La Scala to engage him to sing there with her, and recommended that he return to England, which he did in 1835.

Balfe's position as the most popular native composer in Britain was established overnight in London by the triumph of *The Siege of Rochelle* (1835, Drury Lane) which ran for 73 performances during its first season. Almost equal success attended *The Maid of Artois* (1836, Drury Lane), written for Malibran. Balfe continued his career as a singer, playing Papageno in the first English performance of *Die Zauberflöte* at Drury Lane on 10 March 1838. Later that year he was honoured by a commission for the Italian Opera at Her Majesty's Theatre, which resulted in *Falstaff*, one of his best scores; it was sung there by a star cast which included Giulia Grisi, Emma Albertazzi, Giovanni Rubini, Antonio Tamburini and Luigi Lablache. After this he successfully toured Ireland and the west of England.

Balfe was now determined to become his own manager with a view to establishing English opera on a permanent footing. Even though his backers included Queen Victoria and the Prince Consort, his venture was doomed to failure. He leased the Lyceum Theatre (English Opera House) and brought out his latest work, *Këolanthé* (1841), with his wife making her London début in the title role. This was successful, but receipts dwindled when subsequent works were performed, and eventually he was forced to abandon the project. He informed the audience that he would never again appear before them in the capacity of a manager, and he kept his word.

Disheartened by this reverse, Balfe decided to try his luck in Paris. He had nearly completed *Elfrida* for the Théâtre des Italiens when Grisi, who was to have taken a leading role, announced that she was pregnant and unable

Michael William Balfe: drawing by Daniel Maclise, pencil (National Gallery of Ireland, Dublin)

to take part. Balfe's plans appear to have been frustrated, therefore, for the opera was never finished; but fortunately the librettist Scribe, who attended a concert of his works, offered to collaborate with him on a comic opera, *Le puits d'amour* (1843, Opéra-Comique), which was an instantaneous success. In the meantime Alfred Bunn, who had managed Balfe's earlier successes at Drury Lane, had extricated himself from bankruptcy, and *The Bohemian Girl*, on which Balfe had been working for some years, was produced at Drury Lane on 27 November 1843 with Elizabeth Rainforth and William Harrison in the main roles. It was the greatest triumph of his career, and the only 19th-century British opera to enjoy a genuine international reputation. At Drury Lane it ran for over 100 nights, brought in vast profits for the management and produced a furore which J.W. Davison's harsh review in the *Musical World* did nothing to mitigate.

In 1845 *L'étoile de Séville* was given at the Paris Opéra, where it ran for 15 performances. In 1846 Balfe took over from Michael Costa as conductor of the Italian Opera at Her Majesty's Theatre, remaining until the theatre closed in 1852. During the 1850s he toured extensively abroad, visiting Berlin, Vienna (where Johann Strauss hailed him as the 'King of Melody'), St Petersburg and Trieste (where his opera *Pittore e duca* was unsuccessfully produced in 1854). In 1857 the inception of the Pyne-Harrison Opera Company at the Lyceum provided the impetus for a final period of remarkable creativity. *The Rose of Castille* was the first of a series of operas produced for the company between 1857 and 1863, and probably the most popular, after which the company moved to Covent Garden.

In 1864 Balfe decided to retire to the country, and bought a small estate in Hertfordshire, Rowney Abbey, which his wife succeeded in running profitably. His congenital acute spasmodic asthma troubled him increasingly. He was unable to complete his last opera, *The Knight of the Leopard* (based on Scott's novel *The*

Talisman), on which he bestowed extraordinary care; it was produced posthumously by Costa as *Il talismano* at Drury Lane in 1874. Towards the end of the summer of 1870 he caught cold and his condition gradually deteriorated until he died on 20 October.

2. WORKS.   When attempting to evaluate Balfe's works, it should be remembered that two distinct traditions of British opera existed during his lifetime, of which he was only too well aware. The English ballad opera was viewed by the public simply as entertainment, a genre set apart from the more elevated style of 'highbrow' opera. Of Balfe's operas, only *Falstaff* and *Il talismano* belong to the latter category, though it is also notable that he took more trouble over the works for Paris and Italy than for those written for production in London. Throughout his life, Rossini was his mentor to an extent that has hitherto been underestimated: both men possessed the same shrewdness of artistic judgment, the same inexhaustible musical facility, and the same chameleon-like ability to adapt themselves to the situation in hand. In musical terms, the Rossinian influence is most pronounced in the early Italian works, in *Falstaff* and in the English operas written up to 1852. The second most prevalent idiom is French; derived principally from Auber, it finds its most natural expression in *Le puits d'amour*, *Les quatre fils Aymon* and *L'étoile de Séville*, though in this last work, as in some of the later Pyne-Harrison scores, a Meyerbeerian influence is present. Yet the music that made Balfe famous – the ballads which no one surpassed – remains indisputably his own. His operas, and his livelihood, relied on these 'hit' numbers in a manner similar to the 20th-century musical.

Balfe, however, was never less than thoroughly musically literate: the unusual key relationship between the appearances of the second subject in *The Bohemian Girl* overture demonstrates that. His feeling for local colour is especially remarkable in *The Siege of Rochelle*, *The Sicilian Bride* and *The Rose of Castille*. His knowledge of the voice was exceptional: the pyrotechnics of Elvira's Scherzo in *The Rose of Castille* are the work of a composer who understood every aspect of vocal art. His music is never dull, if only because of its rhythmic vitality; when this quality is wedded to striking musical ideas the effect is intoxicating, as, for example, in the quintet 'C'est dit, c'est entendu' from *Les quatre fils Aymon*. The critic Henry Chorley considered this opera to be Balfe's masterpiece, and he was right: of all Balfe's unknown works, it most merits revival. The later operas, such as *Bianca* (1860) and *The Puritan's Daughter* (1861), are more homogeneous in style, but although they are more through-composed, they lack the freshness of inspiration that characterizes their predecessors. In *Il talismano*, Balfe updated his vocabulary to reach a par with middle-period Verdi, but the price paid for stylistic consistency is melodic weakness.

Balfe was no master of characterization, and in his English operas he frequently abused the natural verbal accentuation of his texts, partly, no doubt, because of the speed at which he worked (*Satanella*, for instance, was written in seven weeks). But in his songs it was a different matter: although not averse to altering a poem's shape and design in order to create an effective musical structure (as in Tennyson's *Come into the garden, Maud*, 1857) he treated the words themselves with almost unfailing sensitivity. His melodic genius guaranteed a consistently high level of achievement in his prolific song output: few of his contemporaries could match the finely sculptured vocal line of *Killarney* (1864) or the gentle rhythmic enchantment of *The Sands of Dee* (1859). Best of all are the *Seven Poems by Longfellow* (*c*1855); here, as in the remarkably symphonic late Piano Trio in A major (a work of substance and integrity), he deliberately responded to his critics and proved himself far more than a mere entertainer.

Balfe's music bespeaks his personality: he was the most honest, genial and charming of men. William Harrison recalled that when asked if he ever borrowed from other men's works, he admitted, astonishingly, to stealing snatches of Beethoven: '"Ye can't do better", he said with a beaming face, "than to go to the fountain-head, and come away with a cupful! There are two composers I've never scrupled to borrow from – one's Beethoven, the other's meself!"' (C. Harrison: *Stray Records*, i, London, 1892, p.108).

WORKS
unless otherwise stated, printed works published in London

STAGE
unless otherwise stated, first performed in London, autograph MSS in GB-Lbl and printed works published in vocal score

LDL – *Drury Lane Theatre*
LCG – *Covent Garden Theatre*

Il naufragio di La Pérouse (ballet pantomimo serio), Milan, Cannobiana, aut. 1825)

Atala (after F.R. de Chateaubriand), Paris, between 1826 and 1828, unfinished, lost

I rivali di se stessi (2, A. Alcazar, after C.A.G. Pigault-Lebrun: *Les rivaux d'eux-mêmes*), Palermo, Carolino, ?Feb 1830, lost

Un avvertimento ai gelosi (farsa giocosa, 1, G. Foppa), Pavia, Fraschini, spr. 1831, excerpts (Milan, n.d.), MS lost

Enrico Quarto al passo della Marna (op, 1), Milan, Carcano, 19 Feb 1833, excerpts (Milan, n.d.), MS lost

The Siege of Rochelle (grand op, 2, E. Fitzball, after Comtesse de Genlis:*Le siège de La Rochelle*), LDL, 29 Oct 1835 (1836)

The Maid of Artois (grand serious op, 3, A. Bunn, after A.-F. Prévost:*L'histoire du Chevalier des Grieux et de Manon Lescaut*), LDL, 27 May 1836 (1837)

Adelwina, between 1836 and 1843, inc.

Catherine Grey (grand op, 3, G. Linley), LDL, 27 May 1837 (1837)

Caractacus (historical play, J.R. Planché), LDL, 6 Nov 1837, lost

Joan of Arc (grand op, 3, Fitzball, after R. Southey), LDL, 30 Nov 1837 (1839)

Diadesté, or The Veiled Lady (opéra bouffe, 2, Fitzball, after L. Pillet and Marquis de St Hilaire), LDL, 17 May 1838, 1 song (1838)

Falstaff (ob, 2, S.M. Maggioni), Her Majesty's, 19 July 1838 (?1845)

Elfrida, (Maggioni) begun 1840, inc.

Këolanthé, or The Unearthly Bride (romantic op, 2, Fitzball), 1840, English Opera House, 9 March 1841, selections (1840), MS lost

Le puits d'amour (oc, 3, E. Scribe and A. de Leuven), Paris, OC (Favart), 20 April 1843 (Paris, 1843); as Geraldine, or The Lover's Well (G. Soane), Princess's, 14 Aug 1843, selections (1843)

The Bohemian Girl (grand op, 3, Bunn, after J.-H. Vernoy de Saint-Georges:*La gypsy*, from M. de Cervantes: *La gitanilla*), 1840–43, LDL, 27 Nov 1843 (1844); as La bohèmienne, Paris, 1869

Les quatre fils Aymon (oc, 3, de Leuven and Brunswick [L. Lhérie]), Paris, OC (Favart), 15 July 1844 (Paris, 1844); as The Castle of Aymon, or The Four Brothers (Fitzball), Princess's, 20 Nov 1844

The Daughter of St Mark (grand serious op, 3, Bunn, after Saint-Georges:*La reine de Chypre*), LDL, 27 Nov 1844 (1845)

The Enchantress (grand op, 3, Bunn, after Saint-Georges), LDL, 4 May 1845 (1845)

L'étoile de Séville (grand op, 4, H. Lucas, after F. Lope de Vega: *La estrella de Sevilla*), Paris, Opéra, 17 Dec 1845 (Paris, 1846), MS lost

Le jour de Noël (Scribe), Paris, ?1845, lost

The Bondman (grand op, 3, Bunn, after Mélesville [A.-H.-J. Duveyrier]: *Le chevalier de Saint-George*), LDL, 11 Dec 1846 (1847)

The Maid of Honour (grand op, 3, Fitzball), LDL, 20 Dec 1847 (1848)

[Le roi s'amuse], untitled (after V. Hugo: *Le roi s'amuse*), begun 1848, unfinished, lost

The Sicilian Bride (4, Bunn, after Saint-Georges), LDL, 6 March 1852, selections (1852)

The Devil's in it (comic op, prol, 3, Bunn, after C. Coffey: *The Devil to Pay*), Surrey, 26 July 1852; as Letty, the Basket-Maker (prol, 3, J.P. Simpson), Gaiety, 14 June 1871 (1873)

Pittore e duca (op, prol, 3, F.M. Piave), Trieste, Comunale, 21 Nov 1854, lost; as Moro, or The Painter of Antwerp (grand op, prol, 3, W.A. Barrett), Her Majesty's, 28 Jan 1882 (1882), MS lost

Lo scudiero (Piave), 1854, unperf., lost

The Rose of Castille (op, 3, A.G. Harris and E. Falconer, after A.P. d'Ennery and Clairville: *Le muletier de Tolède*), Lyceum, 29 Oct 1857 (1858)

Satanella, or The Power of Love (romantic op, 4, Harris and Falconer, after A.R. Lesage: *Le diable boiteux*), LCG, 20 Dec 1858 (1876)

Bianca, or The Bravo's Bride (4, Simpson, after M.G. Lewis: *Rugantino*), LCG, 6 Dec 1860

The Puritan's Daughter (op, 3, J.V. Bridgeman), LCG, 30 Nov 1861 (1861)

Blanche de Nevers (op, 4, J. Brougham, from his *The Duke's Motto*, after M. Feval: *Le bossu*), LCG, 21 Nov 1862 (1864)

The Armourer of Nantes (grand romantic op, 3, Bridgeman, after Hugo: *Marie Tudor*), LCG, 12 Feb 1863 (1863)

The Sleeping Queen (operetta, 1, H.B. Farnie), Gallery of Illustration, 31 Aug 1864 (1874); 2-act version (1868)

The Knight of the Leopard (op, 3, A. Matthison, after W. Scott: *The Talisman*), inc.; arr. M. Costa as Il talismano (G. Zaffira), LDL, 11 June 1874 (1874); as The Talisman, New York, 10 Feb 1875; MS as The Talisman

Miscellaneous opera sketches

Addl nos. for Zingarelli: Giulietta e Romeo, between 1826 and 1828, lost

It. recits for Beethoven: Fidelio, 1851, lost

SACRED

3 Sacred Pieces, 1846: Gratias ago, B; Kyrie eleison, 2 B; Sanctus, S, 2 B

Save me, O God (from Pss), motet, 1846; arr. SATB, org by W.A. Barrett (1882) [? from 3 Sacred Pieces]

SECULAR CHORAL, PARTSONGS

International Ode, 1851, lost [for the Great Exhibition]

Cants.: Now doth the spring, soloists, 5vv, pf, before 1837; Mazeppa (J. Rankin), S, G, T, Bar, SATB, orch, vs (1862); sketches, 6 solo vv, c1842–3, GB-Lbl; 3 others, lost

Partsongs: Thou art with me everywhere (Rankin), SATB (1858); Hark! 'Tis the hunter's jovial horn

OTHER VOCAL ENSEMBLE

Go not, happy day (A. Tennyson), S, A, T, B, pf (?1889)

Trios (probably for high vv, unless otherwise stated; all with pf acc.): Where the fairies hold their revel (1868); Autumn leaves are falling (1871); Hark! From the distant convent towers (1871); Now lightly we fays (1871); Sleep on, sleep on (1871); The Zingari (1872); Through the grassy fields (1872); Fairy May-Bells, ? S, S, C (1876); Haste thee boatman, ? S, S, C (1877); Through the golden valley, ? S, S, C (1877); The Gipsy's Home, ? S, S, C (1878); The Breeze from the Moor (C.J. Rowe), high vv (1881); She came to the village church (Tennyson), S, Mez, C (?1889)

Duets (all with pf acc.): Three Duets (S. Rogers), S, C (?1845): 1 Twilight's soft dews, 2 The beauteous maid, 3 Oh! she was good as she was fair; M'offrian cittadi e popli (M. Janetti), recit and duet, S, T (1847); The Alhambra (W.H. Bellamy), high vv (1853); Trust her not (H.W. Longfellow), 2 Mez (?1855), see also SONGS [(?1855): Seven Poems by Longfellow]; Excelsior (Longfellow), T, Bar (1857); Will spring return (W. Scott), S, C (1862); I leave thee mine own (A. Matthison), S, T (1863); The Shell Duet (Tennyson), S, C (1865); Folding Time (F. Enoch), S, C (1870); The sailor sighs, ? 2 female vv (1871); O'er shepherd pipe and rustic dell (E. Fitzball), 2 female vv/Mez, T (c1875); Brief is life's bright summer morn, ? S, C (1878); Come where sleeps the dewy violet, ? S, C (1878); Sweetheart (A. Greville), S, C (1902)

See also ARRANGEMENTS

SONGS
for 1 voice and piano unless otherwise stated

208 pubd singly, unless otherwise stated; † – conjectural date within inclusive years

(1824): Young Fanny, composed 1817, rev. as The Lover's Mistake (T.H. Bayly) (pubd Dublin)

(1825): Oh do not look so bright and blest (T. Moore)

(?1835): Io sentii tremar (F. Romani), aria; The Blighted Flower (J. Hazlett) (pubd Dublin); Oh! suoni un di soavi … Ahi! che Alfredo in questo loco (Count Pepoli), recit and aria

(1837): They bind with costly pearls my brow (E. Fitzball) [for L. Ricci's Un'avventura di Scaramuccia, 1834]

(?1840): A Home in the Heart (E. Cook); A Simple Rose (T.H. Bayly); Come, come from thy sparry cave; Despair (W.H. Bellamy); Il postiglione (Pepoli), with obbl hn; Kathleen dear, forget me not (Fitzball) (pubd Dublin); La speranza (N. di Santo Mango), aria; Le crépuscule (A. de Lamartine) (pubd Paris); Oh! shall we go a-sailing? (Bellamy); Oh! think what joy in roaming (Moore); Six Arietts, Romances, etc.: 1 Gondolier (S.M. Maggioni), 2 Pauvre Lucas (C. Pellecat), 3 La Monaca (Maggioni), 4 Non scordar le notte (Pepoli), 5 La Farfalla (Maggioni), 6 Bel mestier del gondoliere (Maggioni); The Fairy (Bellamy); There's one heart unchanging (Moore); They tell me thou'rt the favoured guest (Moore); Una donna più felice, cavatina

(1842–5): I'll do thy bidding, mother dear (D. Boucicault); In the Sweet May Time (G. Linley); List thy troubadour (Linley); Now hush thee (E. Pickering)†; The Beautiful Nun (Linley); The echoes of the heart (R. Taylor)†; To the land of my birth (Linley); When I am dead (Linley)

(1846–9): Ahi forse in tal momento (M. Janetti), scena and aria: He'll be here tomorrow (Fitzball); Lord be my guide, sacred song; Maureen (B. Cornwall); My dwelling is no lordly hall (Pickering); Qual fior novello (Janetti); Sing, maiden, sing (Cornwall); The Prayer of the Nation (Hoy); When along the light ripple (R. Monckton Milnes); Zillah (Linley)

(1850): If I sing my love at morning (F.W.N. Bayley)†; I'm a merry Zingara (Fitzball), cavatina brillante†; My gentle child (F. Hemans)†; My heart returns to thee (Linley); The joy of tears (Fitzball); The Lonely Rose (Fitzball)†; 'Tis I that love her best (C. Hall); Un pensiero d'amore (G. Torre), arietta

(1851–4): Ah! would that I could love thee less (M.J. Andrews); Hopeful heart should banish care (A. Waymark); I once was happy (F. Judd); Oh I love the early morn; Oh smile again (Judd); Old Friends (Andrews); Poor Nelly (H.S.); Raise a song to the Lord (Linley), sacred song; The Canteeneer (Bellamy)

(?1855): How at night's calm silent noon (H.J. St. Leger); Seven Poems by Longfellow: 1 The Reaper and the Flowers, 2 Good night! Good night! Beloved, 3 The green trees whispered low, 4 Annie of Tharaw, 5 This is the place, 6 The day is done, 7 Trust her not (duet)

(1856): By the rivulet side (W. Crossman); Five months ago, the stream did flow (E.B. Browning); I'll wander when the twilight breaks (T. Newman); Lost and found (P. Simpson); Merry May (H.F. Chorley); On the banks of my own sunny river; Sweet words of Love (Fitzball); The arrow and the song (H.W. Longfellow); The First Kiss (D. Ryan); The Happiest Land (Longfellow); There is a name I never breathe (J.E. Carpenter); The Tomb of the Islander's Daughter (Newman)

(1857): A merry little Savoyard; As the sunshine to the flower (J. Rankin); Come into the garden, Maud (A. Tennyson); Hark to the wind (W.M. Thackeray); Oh! boatman, haste (G.P. Morris); Once more (G. Hodder); Stars of the summer night (Longfellow); The Cymbalier (Bellamy); The Deserted Bride (Morris); The Lady Blanche (A. Smith); The Merry Little Gipsy (Fitzball); The Noble Foe (Hodder); The Rainy Day (Longfellow); The rose that opes at morn (Pickering); The Two Locks of Hair (Longfellow); The Village Blacksmith (Longfellow); Women's Love (Newman)

(1858): Don't let the roses listen (Rankin); I'm not in love (Rankin); Let me whisper in thine ear (Rankin); Norah darling, don't believe them (Rankin); Oh take me to thy heart again (Rankin); The Angel of Prayer (Bellamy); The Ballroom Belle (Morris); The Heroes of the Ranks (A. Matthison); The Scenes of Home (Morris); We'll meet again (Rankin)

(1859): Daybreak (Longfellow); Fail me not (V.P. Willis); I'm leavin' hame, my Willie (Rankin); My old Song (J. Oxenford); Nelly Gray (Oxenford), with chorus; One smile from thee (Mrs H.J. St. Leger); So long as my darling loves (H. Fry); Sunset (J. Ellison); The light from loving eyes (Hodder); The Sands of Dee (C. Kingsley); The Spirit of Light (Ellison); The Sweet Guitar (C.W. Chapman); Threads of Gold (S.E. Young)

(1860): Fresh as a rose (Rankin); If I could change (Rankin); I love you (Morris)†; Margaretta (Morris)†; Merry and free (Carpenter)†; My fairest child I have no song (Kingsley); The Rose on the Heath (A. Baskerville, after J.W. von Goethe); Two little years ago (Carpenter)

(1861): Bird of the twilight (? Rankin or Carpenter); Mary (Morris); Mary don't forget me (Rankin); Oh send me back to dreamland (Rankin); Sweetheart come back to me (Rankin); The Banner of St George (J. Brougham); Victoria and England for Ever (L.L. Ternan)

(1862): A pale, pale cheek (C. Swain); Flowers! Sweet flowers (Rankin); Music and Song; Sleep, my pretty one (Tennyson); The angels call me (? after J.L. Uhland); The Maid and her Moorish Knight (R. McMurray); The old house by the lindens (Longfellow); The Queen of the Spring (Carpenter); The sea hath its pearls (Longfellow, after H. Heine); Why should thy voice still follow me? (Swain)

(1863–9): Falling river; Fortune and her Wheel (Tennyson); Kathleen Machree; Killarney (E. Falconer); Lady Hildred; Maid of Athens (Byron); Mary mavourneen (A. Greville); Over mount, over lea (Linley); Rest, wand'rer rest (W. Sotheby)†; Si tu savais; The bard that on his harp expired (H. Costley); The Bells (E.A. Poe)†; The evening chime is sounding (Matthison); The Song of Love and Death (Tennyson)†; The Tender Time of May (L.H.F. du Terraux); Though age be like December (C. Clarke); Trust me not at all (Tennyson)†; Watching and Waiting (Swain)

(1870): Hidden Voices (Kingsley); I hear a voice you cannot hear (T. Tickell)†; I'll go and gather flowers (F. Enoch); I love thee (O. Meredith); Phoebe the Fair (Rankin); She stood in the sunshine (Rankin); Sweet nightingale, oh! teach me; Three Ballads (Du Terraux): 1 The Underworld, 2 O Daisy pet, 3 That last light of sundown; When woman plights her troth (McMurray)

(1871–9): Eileen bawn (H.J. St. Leger); Farewell, dear home (Bellamy); Long Ago (J.P. Douglas); Long Live the Queen (C. Sheard); My native valley (W. Guernsey); Ognor costante t'amerò [for Donizetti's Don Pasquale]; Oh! sing again that simple lay (Guernsey); Ruth and I; The Bride's Father (Swain) (pubd Leeds); The Gipsy Queen; The Mariner's Bride; The Rowan Tree (J.F. Waller); The Spanish Serenade (S. Lover)

(1881–1901): I saw a love (F.S. Clark); My love far away (M.X. Hayes)†; The Blind Girl's Goodnight; The Dove and the Raven (H. Farnie); The Gipsy Band (A.J. Foxwell) [? for unison male vv]; There is a shadow

(pubn dates unknown): Anabel Lee; Beneath a Portrait; Bridal Ballad; Christmas comes but once a year (Oxenford); Come with the gipsy bride (Bunn); Go, lovely rose (A. Cowley); Maggie's Ransom; Riflemen, form!; The moon is up (Peabody); Three Fishers (Kingsley); Wake, maiden, wake; What does little birdie say? (Tennyson)

unpubd, GB-Lbl: Bel'amie, or The Lay of the Troubadour, 1837; O'er the blue wave, 1838; Dodici fantasie, Bar, 1842, ded. in Paris; Let us haste (W.A. Barrett), 1847; 16 other songs, 1836–43

See also ARRANGEMENTS

INSTRUMENTAL

Polacca, regimental band, 1815, lost

Orch: Country-Dance, Waltzes, Galop and Dance, F, 1836–43, GB-Lbl; Ov., G, 23 April – 8 May 1840, Lbl

Chbr: La curiosita, air and variation, fl, pf (1844); Pf Trio, A (?1875); Sonata, A♭, vc, pf (c1880)

Pf: Waltz, for Mrs Stone's album, c1836, Lbl; Tendresse maternelle, nocturne (1864); Valse, E♭, c1869, Lbl

ARRANGEMENTS

Irish melody arr. as song: Talk not of pleasure (J.R. Planché) (1855)

Moore's Irish Melodies, with new symphonies and accompaniments for the pianoforte, 1v, pf (1859)

Moore's Irish Melodies: a Selection of Fifty, SATB, pf (1859)

The Young May Moon (Moore: Irish Melodies), high vv/SSAA (1889)

PEDAGOGICAL WORKS

The Italian School of Singing (3/?1850)

Indispensable Studies for a Soprano Voice (1851)

Indispensable Studies for a Bass Voice (1851)

A New Universal Method of Singing, without the use of Solfeggi (1857)

BIBLIOGRAPHY

GroveO ('Bohemian Girl, The', 'Siege of Rochelle, The'; N. Burton)

Musical World, xviii (1843), 395 only [on The Bohemian Girl]; xxiii (1848), 209–11

E. Fitzball: Thirty-five Years of a Dramatic Author's Life (London, 1859)

H. Phillips: Musical and Personal Recollections during Half a Century (London, 1864)

H. St Leger: Reminiscences of Balfe (London, 1871)

J.E. Cox: Musical Recollections of the Last Half-Century (London, 1872)

C.L. Kenney: A Memoir of Michael William Balfe (London, 1875/R)

W.A. Barrett: Balfe: his Life and Work (London, 1882)

C. Harrison: Stray Records (London, 1892, 2/1893), i, 95–108

E.W. White: The Rise of English Opera (London, 1951/R)

M.W. Disher: Victorian Song (London, 1955), 95–8, 100, 117

D. Arundell: The Critic at the Opera (London, 1957/R), 324, 326–8

B. Carr: 'The First All-Sung English 19th-century Opera', MT, cxv (1974), 125–6

N. Temperley, ed.: Music in Britain: the Romantic Age, 1800–1914 (London, 1981/R)

E.W. White: A History of English Opera (London, 1983)

NIGEL BURTON (with IAN D. HALLIGAN)

Bali (i). See INDONESIA, §§I–II and SOUTH-EAST ASIA, §§I and II, 1–3 and 4(iii).

Bali (ii). A dance form. See SRI LANKA.

Baliani [Bagliani, Balliani, Basiliani], **Carlo** (b ?Milan, c1680; d Milan, 16 Feb 1747). Italian composer. A Milan Cathedral document of 1714 discloses that he was 34 years old at the time and that he had served for an unspecified period as maestro di cappella of S Maria della Passione, Milan. His selection by the cathedral chapter followed a written examination on 7 April 1714 in which he competed against Francesco Scarlatti (Alessandro's brother), A.F. de Messi, a Milanese musician, and G.A. Costa, a Paduan priest active in Rome (whom the cathedral was pressed to appoint by the Austrian court); accepting the recommendations of seven judges (including A.M. Bononcini and G.A. Perti), the chapter appointed Baliani maestro di cappella on 13 December 1714.

Except for a single cantata (Solitudine amata) and an act of an opera (Ambletto, 1719), no secular music by Baliani has come to light. He wrote a considerable quantity of music for the Ambrosian liturgy during his 33 years at Milan Cathedral, now in the cathedral archive (I-Md). Most of it is for the Mass or vesper services (including lucernarium, hymn, post-hymn, psalm, Magnificat, psallenda and completorium settings). While the vesper services are often in the concertato style (with orchestral accompaniment), the music for the Mass is generally marked 'pieno' (for choir with organ); Baliani's a cappella movements recall the conservative contrapuntal style of contemporaries like Lotti. He avoided the theatrical vocal style.

In a letter of 26 July 1724 to Benedetto Marcello, Baliani praised the contrapuntal art displayed in Marcello's psalm settings, 'in which besides the nobility of the singular ideas by which the music is rendered more lovely, one sees the finest motifs, subjects, answers, imitations and inversions in madrigal style, as well as closing sections and duets both highly tasteful and impressive', devices abundant in Baliani's own music.

Baliani was ill in the summer of 1742 and asked that the cathedral authorities grant him retirement with pay and lodging. Later, however, he resumed his duties as maestro, and at the end of 1743 he helped judge new singers for S Maria presso S Celso, a church for which he composed (music in I-Md). Although his successor at the cathedral, G.A. Fioroni, favoured more florid solo singing, Baliani's music continued to be performed, and as late as

1783 Francesco Bianchi prepared copies of his works for the choir's use.

WORKS

MSS in I-Md unless otherwise stated

La calunnia delusa (orat, G. Machio), Milan, Chiesa Scala, 23 May 1724, 2 arias extant

Masses: 9 for 4vv, mostly a cappella; 4 for 8vv; 8 copied 1731, vv; 1 for 5vv, orch, *D-Dl* according to Eitner; Requiem, 8vv, orch

Gls: 23 for 8vv, mostly concertata; 3 for 8vv, *F-Pc*

Crs: 1 for 8vv a cappella; 1 for 8vv, org; 1 for 8vv, 2 org; 1 for 8vv, *Pc*

5 Cr–Sanctus, 8vv, mostly with org; 1 Cr–Sanctus, *Pc*; 1 Sanctus–Benedictus, 8vv, org

*c*12 ints, 4vv, some with Post Epistolam and Confractorium; 59 short ints, 8vv, org

*c*10 ants, 4/8vv, 1 for double choir

23 hymns, 1 with lucernarium and post-hymn; 16 hymns, 4vv; 15 hymns, 8vv; 2 hymns, 5vv; 9 hymns, double choir

32 pss, some with Ecce nunc; 42 pss, 8vv, 1 ps, 4vv, most with org; 10 Ecce nunc, 2 for 1v, 5 for 2vv, 1 for 4vv, 2 for 8vv

60 motets: 1 for 1v, 30 for 2vv, 9 for 3vv, 3 for 4vv, 17 for 8vv

4 Lits, 4/8vv; 2 Pater noster, 8vv; 15 Mag, 8vv; miscellaneous Psallenda, Completorium and other vesper items for 2 choirs

Sacred duet, Celorum eia Spiritus, dialogo tra S Michele e Lucifero, S, B

SECULAR VOCAL

Ambleto [Act 2] (op, 3, A. Zeno and P. Pariati), Milan, Regio Ducal, 28 Aug 1719 [Act 1 by G. Vignati, Act 3 by G. Cozzi]

Solitudine amata (cant.), S, bc, *A-Wgm*

BIBLIOGRAPHY

EitnerQ

D. Muoni: *Gli Antignati organari insigni e serie dei maestri di cappella del duomo di Milano* (Milan, 1883/R)

G. Barblan: 'Il teatro musicale in Milan nel secoli XVII e XVIII', *Storia di Milano*, xii (Milan, 1959), 949–96, esp. 972 [pubn of the Fondazione Treccani degli Alfieri per la storia di Milano]

C. Sartori: 'Giovanni Battista Sammartini e la sua corte', *Musica d'oggi*, new ser., iii (1960), 106–21

F. Mompellio: 'La cappella del duomo dal 1714 ai primi decenni del '900', *Storia di Milano*, xvi (Milan, 1962), 553–88 [pubn of the Fondazione Treccani degli Alfieri per la storia di Milano]

G. Ciliberti: 'Il "mito" di Amleto nei libretti d'opera italiani del Settecento', *Europäische Mythen der Neuzeit: Faust und Don Juan*, ed. P. Csobádi and others (Anif-Salzburg, 1993), 713–22

SVEN HANSELL

Baline, Israel. *See* BERLIN, IRVING.

Balino. *See* FABRI, ANNIBALE PIO.

Balissat, Jean (*b* Lausanne, 15 May 1936). Swiss composer and conductor. He attended Lausanne Conservatoire, where he studied harmony and counterpoint (Hans Haug), the piano (Denise Bidal) and the horn (Robert Faller); he also studied at the Geneva Conservatoire (composition and orchestration, André-François Marescotti; conducting, Samuel Baud-Bovy; percussion, Charles Peschier). He has taught composition and orchestration at the conservatories of Fribourg (1972–83), Lausanne (since 1979) and Geneva (since 1986), and between 1960 and 1983 he directed several wind ensembles, including La Landwehr, Fribourg (1972–83). In 1986–90 he was chairman of the Swiss Composers' Union.

His own work as a composer is deeply rooted in the tradition of western Switzerland: central to his output is the type of wind and brass music very popular in the Waadtland area, particularly with amateur performers. Balissat became known to a wider public through his choral and orchestral work *Fête des vignerons* (given its première in Vevey in 1977), which was written for a traditional winegrowers' festival. He is fundamentally opposed to experimentation and avant-garde trends; a

number of different, traditional stylistic elements are ranged side by side or confront each other in his orchestral and chamber music, merging in the course of a clearly perceived, often polytonal musical structure. He was awarded the composition prize of the Lausanne Festival in 1982.

WORKS

(selective list)

Choral: Pour un dix août, cant., 2 spkrs, T, Bar, choir, orch, 1971; Fête des vignerons, choir, orch, 1975–7

Orch: Sym., 1955; Ballade, 1958; Sym., 1959; Sinfonietta, str, 1960; Variations concertantes, 3 perc, orch, 1969; Rikblick, vn, orch, 1980; Bioméros, chbr orch, 1982; Intermezzo, chbr orch, 1987; Vn Conc., 1989; Ob Conc., 1990; Cantabile, cl, chbr orch, 1991

Chbr: 7 Variations, cl, hn, bn, str qnt, 1971; Statterostrob, pf, 1983; Rhapsodie, B♭-cl, 2 basset-hn, b cl, 1984; Les sept pohés capitaux, cl, bn, flugelhn, trbn, vn, db, perc, 1994; L'or perdu, str qt, spkr ad lib, 1995

Wind and brass: AGE, 1978; Incantation et sacrifice, 1981; Le premier jour, 1985; Ouverture, 1992; Saisons, 1993; Sym., 1994; Gli elementi, 1997

BIBLIOGRAPHY

J. Perrin: 'Les variations concertantes de Jean Balissat', *Revue musicale de Suisse romande*, xxxii (1979)

J. Stenzl: 'Une affaire jadis clasée – à propos de "Statterostrob" de Jean Balissat', *Dissonanz/Dissonance*, no.8 (1986), 12–19

PATRICK MÜLLER

Balius y Vila, Jaime (*d* Córdoba, 3 Nov 1822). Spanish composer. He studied music as a choirboy in the Escolanía of Montserrat Abbey and was *maestro de capilla* of Urgel Cathedral by 1780, when he competed unsuccessfully for the same post at Toledo. In October that year he was offered the post of *maestro de capilla* at Burgo de Osma Cathedral; he did not however take it up, as in February 1781 he was appointed *maestro de capilla* in Gerona (possibly his native town), and in 1785 in Córdoba, after a public competition. In 1787 he obtained the same post at the Convento de la Encarnación in Madrid (one of the highest appointments to which a Spanish musician could then aspire), but in 1789 he returned to Córdoba, still as *maestro de capilla*, where he remained until his death.

Balius was one of the leading Spanish composers of his period; his works, comprising masses, psalms, motets, Lamentations, villancicos and other sacred pieces (principal sources: *E-ALB, Bc, C, G, GRc, MA*), although lacking in imitative counterpoint, are sound in construction and show elegant melody and interesting harmony. Two of his works have been edited by Paulino Capdepón in *La música en el Real Monasterio de la Encarnación en el siglo XVIII* (Madrid, 1997).

BIBLIOGRAPHY

LaborD

F. Civil Castellví: 'La capilla de música de la catedral de Gerona (siglo XVIII)', *Anales del Instituto de estudios gerundenses*, xix (1968–9), 131–88

JOSÉ LÓPEZ-CALO

Ball. *See* BALLO (1).

Ball, Ernest R. (*b* Cleveland, 21 July 1878; *d* Santa Ana, CA, 3 May 1927). American composer and singer. After studying at the Cleveland School of Music he went to New York, where he became a pianist in vaudeville theatres, and later staff pianist and composer for Witmark. His first success was the ballad *Will you love me in December as you do in May?*, written in 1905 to lyrics by Jimmy Walker. Many of his most popular songs thereafter were composed for the Irish tenors John McCormack and

Chauncey Olcott, with whom he also collaborated. Ball composed some 400 songs, including such standards as *Mother Machree* (1910), *When Irish Eyes are Smiling* (1913), and *A Little Bit of Heaven* (1914). Much of the last decade of his life was spent performing in vaudeville. His work is discussed in J. Burton: 'Honor Roll of Popular Songwriters: Ernest R. Ball', *The Billboard* (14 May 1949).

DALE COCKRELL

Ball, George Thalben. *See* THALBEN-BALL, GEORGE.

Ball, James (*b* 1770; bur. London, 7 Oct 1833). English piano maker, music seller, publisher, printer and organ builder. He worked in Duke Street, Grosvenor Square, London, from 1787 until his death. Domenico Motta joined him briefly to form Motta & Ball about 1794; in 1818 the Post Office London Directory lists the firm as J. Ball and Son. The son must be the Edward Ball who is listed as a piano maker at Duke Street in an 1824 jury roll preserved at Westminster City Archives. James Ball is listed in the 1827 Post Office London Directory as 'Grand cabinet & square Piano Forte maker to his Majesty'. Ball's early five-octave square pianos with the English single action had two hand stops, one for raising the dampers and the other a 'lute' stop. He is best known for his square pianos, but also made cabinet pianos and grands, some of them for the Prince Regent. In 1790 he patented (no.1784) improvements for the square piano including a new under damper, an individual regulating screw for each key and a new music desk, as well as improvements to the English grand action in which the hammers could be removed singly by means of screws. None of these devices was generally adopted, but a five-and-a-half-octave square piano, serial number 120, with a beautifully painted case and a stand, has a most unusual damper mechanism. From 1789 he sometimes printed and sold publications for TEBALDO MONZANI. He died intestate and his estate was administered by his sister. In 1834 it was valued at £5000 but in 1836 his estate was resworn to be under £7000, a large sum.

MARGARET CRANMER

Ball, Michael (*b* Stratford-upon-Avon, 27 June 1963). English popular singer. He studied at the Guildford School of Acting before touring in *Godspell*, later gaining a leading role in the Manchester production of *The New Pirates of Penzance*. He created the role of Marius in the long-running *Les misérables* (1985) in London, introducing the song 'Empty Chairs at Empty Tables', and took over Raoul in *The Phantom of the Opera*. He played Alex in Lloyd Webber's *Aspects of Love* in London (1989) and on Broadway (1990), and so introduced 'Love changes everything', which was arranged to demonstrate Ball's full-bodied top range. The popular success of the number enabled his expansion into the popular field and into concert tours. In 1991 he released his first solo album and the following year represented the UK in the Eurovision song contest with *One Step Out of Time*. His concert repertory has become increasingly wide, and he performed on his 1994 television series with such disparate singers as Tony Bennett, James Brown and Montserrat Caballé. He also played Giorgio in the first London production of Sondheim's *Passion* (1996).

Ballabene [Bellabene], **Gregorio** (*b* Rome, 1720; *d* Rome, *c*1803). Italian composer. In 1746 he was a member of the

Congregazione di S Cecilia, and assistant to the *maestro di cappella* Luigi Besci at the church of the Madonna dei Monti. In 1754 he became a member of the Bologna Accademia Filarmonica, having written a five-part fugue on *Generatio haec* as his test piece (in *I-Baf*). In September 1755 he was at Macerata, where he applied for a post. In the libretto to the oratorio *S Francesco di Sales* (1760) he is described as *maestro di cappella* at Gubbio.

As a composer Ballabene followed the tradition of Roman church music in the Palestrina style, differentiating between concertato and *pieno* styles. His fame rests on his mass for 12 four-part choruses, composed in 1774. This work brought him into correspondence with Martini (in *I-Bc*), who praised its contrapuntal mastery, supported its formal approval by the Accademia Filarmonica, and published a *Descrizione e approvazione dei Chirie e Gloria a 48 voci* (Bologna, 1774). It was also praised in a *Lettera di Giuseppe Heiberger … ad una composizione musicale a 48 voci del Signor Gregorio Ballabene* (Rome, 1774). However, according to Martini, when the mass was performed in Rome in 1777, it was ridiculed by some progressive Roman musicians, who seem to have regarded its colossal construction as outmoded. In 1778 Ballabene, who in these years had Cardinal Albani as his patron, was an unsuccessful candidate for the post of *maestro di cappella* at S Pietro, and in 1779 at Milan Cathedral and S Antonio in Padua. In 1780 he was an examiner of *maestri di cappella* for the Congregazione dei Musici.

WORKS

Masses: Ky, Gl, Cr, 5vv, org, 1769, *D-MÜs*; Ky, Gl, 48vv, org, 1774, *Bsb*, *I-Bc*, *BGc*, *Fc*, *Rsc*; 5vv, *Rvat*
Dixit Dominus: 8vv, org, 1777, *D-MÜs*; 16vv, *GB-Ob*
Orats: S Francesco di Sales, Gubbio, 1760
Other works: Il Marchese del Bisogno, Rome, 1752; Pastorale, Macerata, 1753; Generatio haec, fuga, 5vv, 1754, *I-Baf*; Catone in Utica (op, P. Metastasio), Macerata, 1755; L'eroe cinese (op, Metastasio), Fabriano, 1757; Cum invocarem, compline, 4vv, org, 1762, *Bc**; Mag, 16vv, 1778, *GB-Lcm**; Caro mea, 5vv, org, 1781, *D-MÜs*; Poesia per musica in onore di S Ubaldo, Gubbio, 1784; Le mie pene (cant.), 3vv, *I-Bsf*; Amen, 4vv, org, insts, *D-MÜs*; Ave Maria, 2vv, org, *Bsb*; Lit, 4vv, org, *MÜs*; Lumen mundi, seq, 4vv, org, *MÜs*; Oculi omnium, *I-Rvat*; Tantum ergo, 4vv, *Rvat*; Quartetti, *Rc*; Ov., 2 vn, va, db, *D-Dl*

BIBLIOGRAPHY

DBI (R. Meloncelli) [with detailed bibliography]; *FellererP*; *FétisB*; *GerberNL*
G. Heiberger: *Lettera … ad una composizione musicale a 48 voci del Signor G.B. maestro di Cappella romano* (Rome, 1774) [incl. G.B. Martini: *Descrizione e approvazione dei Chirie e Gloria a 48 voci* (Bologna, 1774)]
G. Baini: *Memorie storico-critiche della vita e della opere di Giovanni Pierluigi Palestrina* (Rome, 1828/R), ii, 65 n.513; 316 n.636
P. Alfieri: *Brevi notizie storiche sulla Congregazione ed Accademia de' maestri e professori di musica di Roma, sotto l'invocazione di Santa Cecilia* (Rome, 1845), 22
G. Tebaldini: *L'archivio musicale della Cappella Antoniana in Padova*(Padua, 1895)
L. Torri: 'Una lettera inedita del Padre Giambattista Martini', *RMI*, ii (1895), 262–86
J. Killing: *Kirchenmusikalische Schätze der Bibliothek des Abbate Fortunato Santini* (Düsseldorf, 1910), 167, 475

SIEGFRIED GMEINWIESER

Ballabile (It.: 'danceable', 'apt for dancing'). A movement, usually in an opera, intended for dancing. In Act 3 of *Macbeth* Verdi termed the song and dance of the witches *ballabile*; the 'Galop con cori' that opens Act 2 of his *Ernani* is a *coro ballabile*; dance divertissements in Meyerbeer's operas are titled 1°, 2° *ballabile* etc. The term is also used for instrumental pieces of a dance character; the dances in Hans von Bülow's *Carnevale di Milano* are headed 'Ballabili'.

ANDREW PORTER

Ballad (from Lat. *ballare*: 'to dance'). Term used for a short popular song that may contain a narrative element. Scholars take it to signify a relatively concise composition known throughout Europe since the late Middle Ages: it combines narrative, dramatic dialogue and lyrical passages in stanzaic form sung to a rounded tune, and often includes a recurrent refrain. Originally the word referred to dance-songs such as the *carole*, but by the 14th century it had lost that connotation in English and had become a distinctive song type with a narrative core. The word has sometimes been used, mistakenly, as a translation for the medieval French *forme fixe* ballade (*see* BALLADE (i)), and for the 18th- and 19th-century German ballade (see §II below); the latter was partly influenced by the narrative strophic folksong tradition of Britain and Scandinavia (*see also* BALLADE (ii) for instrumental pieces bearing this often confused title, and EPICS for a discussion of longer narrative song forms).

The 'ballad opera', a satirical form of theatrical entertainment based on spoken dialogue and popular tunes of the day, was fashionable for several decades during the early to mid-18th century. Literary ballads which imitated the traditional ballad marked a significant phase of influence during the Romantic period. In the 19th century 'ballad' came to denote a sentimental song cultivated by the middle classes in Britain and North America, while in 20th-century popular culture it has come to refer to a slow, personalized love song or one, such as the 'blues ballad' in North America, in which the narrative element is slender and subordinated to a lyrical mood.

I. Folk and popular balladry. II. The 19th- and 20th-century art form.

I. Folk and popular balladry

1. Concepts. 2. Origin and subject matter. 3. International aspects. 4. Narrative form and style. 5. Tunes. 6. Singers and contexts. 7. Broadside ballads.

1. CONCEPTS. Traditional ballads are studied by a variety of disciplines: area studies, ethnomusicology, folkloristics, anthropology, comparative literature and semiotics. Each of these has to some extent imposed its own modern perspective on the ballad which, as a heterogenous type of song with diverse origins and purpose, has seemed of interest and relevance to their field. Literary scholars have sought comparisons between the traditional, orally transmitted ballad and literary creation, or have traced its influence on individual poems (such as the pastiches by Coleridge, Keats, Wilde or Wordsworth). Folklorists and anthropologists have looked in balladry for signs of 'primitive' thought and communal practice, and semiologists for partially submerged cultural markers. Folk-music scholars and ethnomusicologists have dissected ballad tunes to understand the nature of popular song creation, or studied latterday traditional singers to gauge the role of memory, oral transmission, innovation and context in the performance and communication of ballads.

Generally speaking, the nature and structure of the genre have been the focus of literary analysis since the great 19th-century canonical compilations of traditional texts: scholars such as F.J. Child (1882–98) and Svend

Grundtvig (1853–1920) were much preoccupied with identifying ballads by plot type and ordering them in terms of chronology and diffusion. Older ballads such as those they identified have few characters and concentrate on a single incident; they are cast in stanzas with or without a refrain and are sung to a repeated melody that corresponds to the strophic structure. The mood in these ballads is generally stoic and impersonal; the plot may be tragic, romantic, otherworldly, heroic or humorous, while in newer ballads and broadsides the tone becomes personal, partisan or polemical. They are occasionally based on historical events, though the incidents portrayed are often not verifiable. The tune, which raises and intensifies the communicative level of the song, influences the poetics of the line and stanza, as Bronson (1977) has shown, while the refrain, when present, suggests links to dance and, even in modern times, to audience participation.

In the 18th century, when the urban broadside type (which often couched sensational events of the day in ballad stanzas) was coming into its own, scholars began to adopt a new conception of the ballad. Although broadsheets had been a feature of urban life since the 16th century, they and the antiquarian enthusiasm for rural custom had by this time begun to influence scholarly notions of the ballad's social or political purpose. The idea of the ballad crystallized in writings of this period, and the stylistic reworking of ballads by editors and enthusiasts marked an important development in conceptions of the form. This was followed by the great compilations of the 19th century, from those by Walter Scott and William Motherwell to those by Grundtvig and Child, focussing on ballad poetry, while in the 20th century attention shifted to ballad tunes, singers and performance. In one sense this last phase marked a reaction against the idealism with which ballad study was often invested: scholars such as Child were strongly influenced by the idea of the 'popular' as conceived by Herder in the late 18th century, but Child, with some hindsight, saw the ballad evolving from a communal past into a more individualistic genre.

Theories of balladry thus depend to some extent on the collector's conception of the society that produced them. Bishop Percy's wholesale revisions of his manuscript sources, and Scott's and Peter Buchan's reworkings of ballads are familar examples of 'adaptation'. The society from which they were culled was often seen, mistakenly, as rural and homogeneous; ballads did emerge from such a background, but they were also the result of urban poetasters and hacks cobbling together older and newer verse material (usually with the tag 'to the tune of . . .') in salesworthy 'black-letter' (*c*1550–*c*1700) or, later, 'white-letter' broadsheets that had woodcut illustrations and contained news of the day. This material found its way into rural districts through singers, broadsides and chapbooks, in turn influencing these communities. To later singers, though, these ballads were nothing more than the 'old songs' preferred by their community; the term 'ballad', when it signified anything, usually meant a commercial ballad sheet (or 'ballet').

After centuries of disputes over authorship and style, scholars today are less inclined to speculate on the origin, evolution or function of ballads without hard evidence. This caution has also made them less eager to classify definitive 'ballad types' in terms of plot or theme and more inclined to concentrate on elucidating topics that arise in the course of stanzaic narrative song, whether 'ballads' or not. From a musical point of view, the singing of ballads is a primary feature of the genre: folk-music scholars such as Cecil Sharp devoted much time and effort in pointing to melodic links between British ballad tunes and their counterparts in North America. The idea of 'ballad performance' in newer contexts, such as that of the Folk Revival, has broadened the concept of the genre and its uses still further, and assured it of cultural vitality in the contemporary world (*see also* FOLK MUSIC).

2. ORIGIN AND SUBJECT MATTER.   The term 'ballad' has been used in the European literary tradition to refer to the popular or traditional song type that appeared from around the end of the 13th century and was at its height during the 16th and 17th centuries, when ballad singers plied their trade in cities and around village fairs. The ballad originated in the late Middle Ages, when epic and heroic songs served as entertainment, and appears to have flourished initially in conjunction with the rise of a merchant class and the decline of feudalism. Shorter narrative songs were also extant during the feudal period, but the appearance of the ballad as a genre seems to have been closely associated with a fashion for the French CAROLE, both courtly and popular, a dance that flourished from the mid-12th century to the mid-14th. The ballad's connection with dance is suggested by the Latin root *ballare*, and some traditions even today manifest a close association between dance and narrative song, as in the Faeroes or parts of Spain.

The ballad probably emerged as a narrative genre with a dramatic plot from France and the Low Countries at about the same time, spreading in different directions and taking on local characteristics as it evolved. The earliest surviving manuscript version of an English-language ballad is that of *Judas* (Child no.23), which dates from before 1300. There are analogues and parallels to many of the story lines in sagas, romances, lays and wonder tales, but the parallels are not always close or exact. The 'singing bone' motif, for example, is one that has generated both tales and songs in eastern and western Europe. Stanzaic songs probably fulfilled many functions, but became a primary vehicle for celebrating lapidary events such as bloody battles, legendary exploits, family confrontations and tragic love affairs, usually among the upper classes or yeoman class. With the growth of cities after 1500, the minstrel composer of the late medieval period and Renaissance, who entertained in both castle and lowly hostelry, was replaced by the ballad seller, broadside printer and street singer.

The features that mark out the 'classic' ballad – the impersonality of narrative, incremental repetition and recurrence of commonplaces – were noted by Motherwell in 1827. His observations influenced Grundtvig who, in turn, corresponded with Child on the subject matter of traditional ballads and how they might be arranged in an authoritative compilation that would 'close the account' of a genre they considered to be exhausted. Child eventually selected and published 305 ballads, taken mainly from earlier 18th- and 19th-century collections rather than from broadsides, ordered by plot type and printed with multiple variants in chronological sequence. His headnote to each ballad type (e.g. *Edward*, Child no.13) traces the origins and evolution of the song across cultural boundaries. Bronson followed this general scheme

in his compendium of ballad airs (1959–72), but ordered the tunes by melodic type. Earlier, Child had gradually arrived at an awareness of the importance of the tunes, and included an appendix of tunes in his compilation.

Much debate has surrounded the Child corpus, and he was later attacked for his criteria of selection and exclusion. Nevertheless, *The English and Scottish Popular Ballads* is still regarded as a central representation of older English-language ballad subject matter: apocryphal legends (*Judas, St Stephen and Herod, The Cherry-Tree Carol, The Carnal and the Crane, Dives and Lazarus, The Maid and the Palmer*), miracles (*Brown Robyn's Confession, Sir Hugh*), outlaw exploits (*Robin Hood, Adam Bell, Rob Roy*), folk history (*Queen Eleanor's Confession, The Battle of Otterburn, The Battle of Harlaw, The Death of Queen Jane, Mary Hamilton*), the feuds of Scottish clans (*Edom o Gordon, The Bonny Earl of Murray, The Bonnie House of Airlie, The Death of Parcy Reed, The Baron of Brackley*), border raids (*Dick o the Cow, Jock o the Side*), encounters at sea (*Patrick Spens, John Dory, The Sweet Trinity, Henry Martin, Captain Ward and the Rainbow*) and humorous domestic strife (*Our Goodman, The Wife Wrapped in Wether's Skin, Get Up and Bar the Door*). Love, death and sexual relationships predominate in these ballad stories, with a few exceptions such as *Child Waters*, which ends happily. Ballad plots deal frequently with elopement, bride-stealing, adultery and incest but never with homosexual love. Loyalty to a partner often transcends suffering and death, and the symbolic 'rose and briar' motif uniting the lovers in their grave (well known in the Middle Ages) appears in a number of ballads. Riddles, spells and the supernatural are common in the ballad narrative, and humans consort with otherwordly beings (*Thomas Rhymer, Tam Lin, Hind Etin, Clerk Colvill, The Great Silkie of Sule Skerry, The Queen of Elfland's Nourice*) or revenants (*Sweet William's Ghost, The Unquiet Grave, Clerk Saunders, The Grey Cock, The Wife of Usher's Well*). In these encounters, which tend to be more frequent in northern Europe than elsewhere, the ballad imagination is at its most evocative.

In the more pedestrian broadside ballads and later urban tradition, subject matter tends toward the political, satirical and personal. A long tradition, from the 17th century, of composing socially critical ballads exists in Britain and Ireland, and singers were frequently arrested for singing rebel songs. With emigration in the mid-19th century the Irish tradition found its way to the United States with ballads like *Molly Bawn*, in which the heroine, who transforms herself into a swan each evening, is mistakenly shot by her hunter-lover; these supernatural elements tend to be rationalized in North American variants. The 'come-all-ye' type of ballad grew in prominence around this time. Broadsides proliferated in the United States and were at their height between about 1840 and 1880, and these extended the range of topics to include sensational crime (*Naomi Wise, Fuller and Warren, Pearl Bryan, Frankie and Johnny*), criminals' farewells (*Tom Dooley, Charles Guiteau*), historical events (*Brave Wolfe, Paul Jones, The Chesapeake and the Shannon*), disasters (*The Avondale Mine Disaster, Casey Jones, The Wreck of the Old 97, The Ballet of the Boll Weevil, The Titanic*), heroes and outlaws (*Brennan on the Moor, Captain Kidd, The Wild Colonial Boy, Sam Bass, Jesse James, John Henry, John Hardy*) and cowboy topics (*The Streets of Laredo*, *Joe Bowers*, *The Arkansas Traveller*, *The Dying Stockman*). The Australian ballad tradition likewise tells of personal hardship through sentencing to transportation or outlawry (*Jim Jones*, *Van Diemen's Land*, *The Convict Maid*, *Botany Bay*, *The Death of Ned Kelly*).

3. INTERNATIONAL ASPECTS. The ballad has been known by different names outside the English-speaking world, such as the Scandinavian *vise* and the Hispanic *romance* (ballad) or *romancero* (balladry). In Gaelic-speaking regions of Britain and Ireland the equivalent narrative song tradition was the *laoidh* ('lay'), which usually celebrated the exploits of the legendary Fianna (Fenian warriors) and their leader, Fionn Mac Cumhaill (*see* BARD and OSSIAN). Examples of Fenian lays, which lack the refrain common in other native song genres and did not accompany dance, have been recorded in recent times, mainly from Hebridean singers. With the plantation of Ireland, British ballads found their way there and a number of texts were translated into Gaelic equivalents (e.g. *An Tighearna Randal*). At another, broader remove, it has been suggested that Irish vision poetry (the *aisling*) influenced North American balladry, in part as a result of the huge emigration from Ireland to the United States in the mid-19th century.

The ballad corpus in France and Germany is markedly lyrical, and has links to the pastourelle and the Romanze respectively. The Danish ballad tradition, which flourished in the later Middle Ages and was written down from the 16th century, often parallels British balladry in subject matter. Northern European ballads in general tend to share elements such as supernatural lovers, whereas central European traditions such as that in Hungary rarely deal with magical practices or such topics as shape-shifting. Scholars (e.g. Liestøl, Nygard, Vargyas) have nevertheless posited generic and thematic links not only among British, Scandinavian and French balladry but also between Hungarian and French ballads, and suggested a further connection between Hungarian ballads, for example, and Siberian heroic epic. The roots of some ballad traditions thus lie far beyond western Europe. And while ballads and epics are constructed on quite different structural principles, there is clear thematic borrowing in many ballad traditions, especially in the Balkans and Spain.

Some ballad plots are widespread: the Low Countries ballad of *Heer Halewijn*, thought by some to derive ultimately from the tale of Judith and Holofernes, is known in English-language tradition as *Lady Isabel and the Elf-Knight* (Child no.4) and in Hungary, for example, as *Anna Molnár*; and the Scottish ballad of *Clerk Colvill* (Child no.42), which recounts the hero's luckless encounter with a mermaid, is rather rare in English-language tradition but the basic story appears in other countries under the titles *Elveskud*, *Riddar Olaf*, *Seigneur Nann*, *Le roi renaud* or *La muerte occultada* ('Death concealed'). The last of these shows an unusual side of the Spanish *romance* tradition, which normally contains few fantastic elements and deals with concrete events with relatively little supernatural interference. Its main concerns are historical or quasi-historical: conflicts between Moors and Christians, for example, or the legendary exploits of warriors such as el Cid. Whether these analogous plots and motifs are direct borrowings or independent compositions has been the object of much research; while some

paths of diffusion can be traced, scholars are now concerned less with the historical and geographical origins of ballads and more with their content, function and meaning.

Throughout the Mediterranean countries the division between elaborative epic style and concentrated ballad is normally well defined: the ballad flourishes mainly in northern Italy, for example, while in the south the *cantastorie* tradition, rather like epic singing in the Balkans, expands details of dress, armoury or battles and embellishes these into whole episodes. The dispersal of the Sephardim has resulted in a rich Judeo-Hispanic ballad tradition now found in widely separated areas of the Diaspora. In eastern Europe, the subject matter of Slavic ballad traditions combines fantastic and realistic elements. Pan-Slavic themes sometimes emerge, such as the ballad of the bird-daughter: a mother marries off her daughter but she returns as a bird to tell of her misfortune in marriage. As in other east and south-east European traditions, the ballads of Russia and Ukraine should be distinguished from epic songs (*bilini*, *dumy*) on the one hand and historical songs on the other. In the subject matter of these ballads, as throughout the Slavic world, the individual is pitted against severe social constraints: the maltreated wife never kills her abusive spouse, for example, and matricide would be an impossible act of revenge. The fundamental conflict, as in most balladry, lies in the individual's choice between conforming to social norms or protesting and thereby suffering. The Ukrainian ballad tradition, like several European counterparts in the New World, has found change and renewal among Ukrainian emigrants in Canada.

The Spanish and Portuguese *romance* has similarly found its way through outposts such as the Azores or the Canary Islands to Latin America and as far as south-east Asia. The ballad of Hispanic tradition known as *El raptor pordiosero* ('The begging abductor'), for instance, has become *O Cego* ('The blind man') in Brazil through Portuguese versions. A knock on the door provokes the question 'Who is there?'; the knocker replies that he is a blind man, whereupon the unidentified speaker tells a woman to fetch him bread and wine, which the blind man refuses; all he wants is for the woman to show him the way, whereupon he reveals to her that he is not blind, and has disguised himself in order to abduct and marry her. Ballads with such themes spread widely and stimulated newer types of narrative song, occasionally under different names: the *indita* in New Mexico, for example, the *corrido* in Mexico, and the *korido* in the Philippines, which was transmitted from Spain and Mexico during the colonial period (1521–1898). The *indita* ('little Indian girl' or 'song') of the later 19th century in New Mexico is a narrative song on historical, burlesque or even spiritual topics. The *corrido*, found in both the USA and Mexico, has been a productive form for social and historical commentary in the 20th century.

4. NARRATIVE FORM AND STYLE. The older traditional ballads are marked by an essential distillation of plot, character and action or dialogue. Often no more than two people are involved, although a third or others may impinge fatefully on their relationship. Apart from battles or conflict between males the focus is usually on a man and a woman, with dialogue leading to decisive action. As a rule the story is not elaborated through explicit motivation or the description of personae or objects;

rather, the singing pushes the story along relentlessly, leaping or lingering, sketching the story line economically and using the device of incremental repetition as, for example, in *Lady Maisry* (Child no.65B): 'The first horse that he rode upon, He was a raven black ... The next horse that he rode upon/He was a bonny brown ... The next horse that he rode upon/He as the milk was white ...' and so on. The action and dialogue between them bring the ballad drama to a climax. Some ballads consist entirely of dialogue, such as *Edward*, *Lord Randal* and *The Maid Freed from the Gallows*. The impersonality of the narration is offset, to some extent, by the refrains, which underscore not only the archaisms of the form but its participatory nature.

Individual ballad plots are sometimes obliquely related, as in the case of *Edward* (Child no.13), *The Twa Brothers* (Child no.49) and *Lizzie Wan* (Child no.51), though this is rare. Characters are broadly imagined and without complexity. Often they engage each other through confrontation, accusation or challenge of some kind. They are deftly sketched to establish their place in the drama, and any motive is discernible only by means of their speech or actions. They are normally described in commonplaces, such as 'fair lady', 'bonny bride', 'lady gay' or 'false truelove', and their attributes are likewise couched in stereotyped phrases: 'lilywhite breast', 'yellow hair', 'gay gold ring', 'a broad letter'. These commonplaces are not simply fillers, however, since they help to establish the mood and pace of the drama and to stabilize the rhythm and emphasis of the verse line. The verse patterns, usually iambic or trochaic, are also decisively influenced by the shape and rhythm of the tune.

Hispanic ballads are sung in 16-syllable assonant lines divided into hemistichs and Slavic ballads draw on the decasyllabic line, while 'ballad' or 'common' metre in English-language tradition consists of a quatrain of alternating four-stress and three-stress lines (8.6.8.6), the second and fourth having end-rhymes. The stanza may be extended to five, six or eight lines, but it is unusual to find fewer than four lines. The stanza with four-stress lines throughout is also unusual since, in singing, the three-stress lines are lengthened by holding the final syllable as long as a fourth stress so that, melodically, at least, all ballad stanzas consist of four-beat lines. Each line corresponds to a distinct musical phrase. A ballad stanza usually comprises a single unit of meaning, thereby matching a complete statement of the tune. This self-contained structure is important, for syntax and melody combine to discourage the natural emphasis of the words when they are spoken rather than sung. Singing obliterates the accent and subordinates the nominal and adjectival to a broader, more universal telling of the ballad story. A profound ambiguity in the relationship of narrative direction and the singing of the ballad text thus results from the structural tension that emerges in performance.

5. TUNES. Ballads are usually sung solo, though instruments (e.g. fiddle, harp, guitar, banjo or dulcimer) have also been used to accompany singers. The ballad tune, with just one or two notes to a syllable, helps to shape the versification though not the mood of the ballad text. The tune's character, in fact, is sometimes at variance with the tragic tone as in, for example, the lilting 6/8 rhythm and major mode of *Lord Lovel* (Child no.75; ex.1); this ballad has given rise to parodies in the USA where Abraham Lincoln takes the place of Lovel and is

Ex.1 *Lord Lovell* (Child no.75) from D. Scarborough: *A Song Catcher in the Southern Mountains* (New York, 1937)

mocked for his military reverses. In general, though, the tune has a key role to play in the overall rhythm and style of the sung ballad. The main cadence points are at the end of the second and fourth lines, where the normal rhyme of the ballad stanza occurs, and these cadences often (though not always) correspond to a melodic shift from the tonic to the fifth above, as in an English tune for *Barbara Allen* (Child no.84; ex.2), the most widely sung of the British ballads. Some tunes of modal cast, however, are content to repeat the first two phrases, sometimes slightly modified, as in a Scottish tune version for *The Lass of Roch Royal* (Child no.76; ex.3).

The most common phrasal four-line pattern in British ballad tunes is *ABCD*, a non-recurrent form that provides not only the greatest variety of phrase but also the widest space between repetitions. This type accounts for almost half of the 3450 tunes analysed by Bronson (1969, p.153). Its closest rival, *ABCDE*, is not nearly as frequent. In a long ballad the scheme *ABAB* doubles not only the number of repetitions but also their frequency when sung.

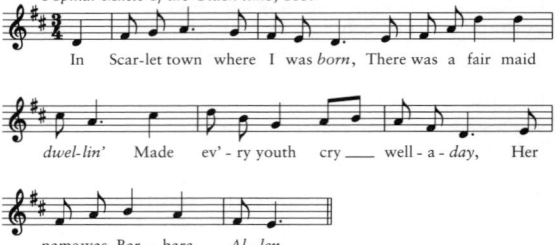

Ex.2 *Barbara Allen* (Child no.84), from W. Chappell: *Popular Music of the Olden time*, 1859

In Scar-let town where I was *born*, There was a fair maid dwel-lin' Made ev'-ry youth cry — well-a-*day*, Her name was Bar - bara Al-len.

ABCA, on the other hand, returns to the opening phrase in cyclical fashion. The 'come-all-ye' type of tune, *ABBA*, juxtaposes inner as well as outer identities. Of tunes with a repeated phrase the pattern *ABAC* is the most often found. Refrains (e.g. 'savoury, sage, rosemary and thyme', 'down a downe, hey downe') force narrative to give way to melody; refrains can consist of a fifth repetitive line, a

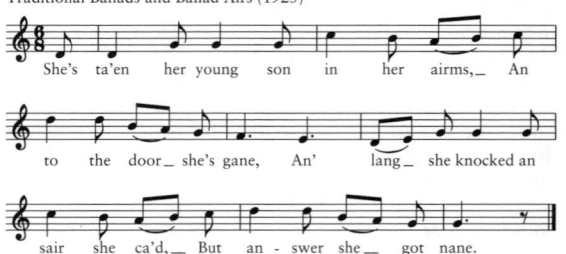

Ex.3 *The Lass of Roch Royal* (Child no.76), from G.Grieg: *Last Leaves of Traditional Ballads and Ballad Airs* (1925)

She's ta'en her young son in her airms,— An to the door— she's gane, An' lang— she knocked an sair she ca'd,— But an - swer she— got nane.

burden between stanzas, or intercalated lines within the stanza.

Because of the skill needed to notate music ballad melodies have been taken down relatively recently; no tune for a Child ballad exists before the 17th century, and a large proportion of notated melodies, whether recorded by phonograph or magnetic tape or transcribed from performance, date from the beginning of the 20th century. Like the editors of texts, 'improving' musical editors have sometimes, like William Christie (1881), tampered with tunes. But ballad tunes are often sturdy enough to have survived in outline for centuries. Some tunes fall into what some have called 'tune families' – that is, groups of tunes that are structurally analogous (e.g. the *Dives and Lazarus* family; see Bayard, 1950; Jackson, 1952; Bronson, 1969). These tunes are 'related' only in the sense of having a comparable tonal structure and not necessarily through direct transmission or borrowing. Although the overall shape of the tune is retained in variant realization, such relationships are based on melodic rather than rhythmic identity.

The modality of ballad tunes is a striking feature of their character since they often rely on structures from before the advent of common-practice harmony in the 17th century. Pentatonic and hexatonic modes are as frequent as heptatonic; the Appalachian and Scottish ballad tunes show a preference for the 'gapped' (pentatonic or hexatonic) forms, while English tradition inclines to the heptatonic forms with a sharp or flattened third and a flattened leading note (Bronson, 1969, pp.155–6). Metre can be two- or three-beat types: in England and Scotland 4/4 predominates, with 6/8 much more common in England, perhaps as a fitting counterpart for iambic metre. But the singer does not always stick rigidly to an isometric formula, and tunes can fall into patterns such as 5/4, or even irregular barring such as 3/2, 9/4, 3/2, 5/4, 4/4. The range of the tunes is usually an octave, but can sometimes extend to a 12th.

6. SINGERS AND CONTEXTS.   Ballad singers have been the object of both scorn and admiration since at least the 17th century, when the diarist Samuel Pepys 'in perfect pleasure' heard Mrs Knipp sing 'her little Scotch song of "Barbary Allen"'. Later, James Hogg's mother berated Scott for printing, in his *Minstrelsy of the Scottish Border* (1802–3), the texts of ballads that she stressed were meant to be sung. Antiquarians had already shown interest in singers such as Anna Brown (1747–1810), a minister's wife from Aberdeen who from 1783 compiled traditional ballads, some of them with variant texts. The interpretation of these texts has been a matter of controversy, but it seems likely that Mrs Brown did not improvise variants each time she sang them but in fact had learned different versions of the same ballad from her mother and her aunt. Evidence of textual improvisation (as opposed to re-creation) is extremely rare, although examples of ballad tunes sung with free melodic variation have been found: Henry Larcombe, described by Sharp, and the Irish traveller John Reilly (c1926–69) both sang in this way.

The matter of ballad singing and repertory was broached in Motherwell's famous study (1827) of Agnes Lyle, a weaver's daughter from Kilbarchan in Ayrshire. While Mrs Brown preferred ballads of magic and romance, Agnes Lyle chose to sing tragic ballads with which she felt a strong sympathy (e.g. *Sheath and Knife*, Child no.16), and would sometimes weep while singing

them. It can thus be difficult to separate a singer's choice of repertory or singing of particular ballad stories from their lived experience. In general, women have cultivated ballad singing to a greater degree than men because of their domestic situation. Ballads can overlap with other genres such as work songs, lullabies or laments; in Hungary, for example, women sang ballads in the context of collective weaving and spinning (see LAMENT and LULLABY. Ballads have also been a means for women to highlight their often subjugated role in society.

As a result of changes in the 20th century brought about mainly by technological developments, ballad singers and the ballad genre have again become a focus of interest. The advent of the phonograph in the late 19th century and of the magnetic tape recorder after World War II allowed scholars such as Percy Grainger to record the flowing graces and decorations in ballad singing: Grainger's transcriptions of English singers (1908) capture the nuances of performance. Since 1950, the performance of ballads has increasingly occurred in the context of folk clubs and folk festivals. New ballads continue to be composed and old ones to be reworked. The publication of ballad collections and of sound recordings made by outstanding singers since World War II has led to a fresh appreciation not only of the ballad form but also of the ballad singer's art.

7. BROADSIDE BALLADS.   A special category of ballad was the 'broadside' or 'broadside ballad', originating in the 16th century and so called because in England the texts were customarily printed and circulated on large folio sheets called broadsides. The broadsheet, as a means of conveying news publicly, was also familiar on the continent, as the *Flugblatt* in Germany, *skillingtryck* (shilling print) in Sweden, *marktlied* in the Low Countries and *pliego suelto* in Hispanic countries. Some ballads were published in pamphlets of two or more leaves; these later became known as 'chapbooks'. The European street singer (*Bänkelsänger* in Germany) set up a stall to sell broadsheets relating sensational events, sentimental relationships or socially important matters.

Except for a few years in the 1680s, music was hardly ever printed on a broadside along with a text; sometimes when it was, it was only a decorative pretence, like the notes sprinkled on some Christmas cards, without musical significance. At best, the printed notation served to jog the purchaser's memory, enabling him to select from a body of tunes known principally through the oral tradition. Tunes would be adapted from popular usage of the day, or remodelled to fit newer verses. Ballad singers might have as many as 100 different melodies in their repertory. Familiar tunes could be harnessed for a ballad text by a broadside printer or a street singer; the evidence suggests, too, that the broadside ballad writer may have had a specific tune in mind as he framed his stanza pattern. Many of those tunes have survived only through this tradition or in notated instrumental music (as airs on which sets of variations were written, for example). Others were included in tutors and in such contemporary sources as Playford's *The English Dancing Master* (1651; numerous subsequent editions as *The Dancing Master* in the late 17th and early 18th centuries) and *A Choice Collection of 180 Loyal Songs* (1685). *Wit and Mirth, or Pills to Purge Melancholy* (1699–1700), an anthology by Thomas D'Urfey that grew to six volumes in its final edition (1719–20), contains the words and music to about

1000 songs, many of them also printed as broadsides. Some of the tunes are by identifiable composers, while others are of earlier, anonymous and traditional. These tunes existed in England and parts of the USA in an oral tradition on which the authors of new topical broadside texts could draw. Other broadside tunes came from abroad, for isntance *Chi passa*, The Spanish Pavan and Farinel's Ground.

Around the end of the 17th century the broadside ballad began to face competition in Britain from the single-sheet song, which contained an air engraved with a bass line, a version of the tune in a key suitable for recorder or flute, and a reduced song text. As a result, reprints of ballads no longer included directions of the tune, and new pieces did not specify a tune to which they should be sung. Since the late 18th century such ballads have been an important, if often unrecognized, element in American popular music. Although there is a quite sizable literature on the broadside as a printed literary form, close connecting musical documentation is mostly lacking.

See also POPULAR MUSIC, §I.

BIBLIOGRAPHY
COLLECTIONS, COMPILATIONS, REFERENCE WORKS

T. D'Urfey, ed.: *Wit and Mirth, or Pills to Purge Melancholy* (London, 1719–20/R)

A. Ramsay: *The Tea-Table Miscellany* (London, 1724–7, many other edns)

W. Thomson: *Orpheus Caledonius* (London, 1725, 2/1733/R)

T. Percy: *Reliques of Ancient English Poetry* (London, 1765, many other edns)

D. Herd, ed.: *Ancient and Modern Scottish Songs, Heroic Ballads* (Edinburgh, 1769, 2/1776/R)

J. Ritson: *A Select Collection of English Songs with their Original Airs* (London, 1783, 2/1813)

J. Johnson: *The Scots Musical Museum* (Edinburgh, 1787–1803, rev. 3/1853/R by W. Stenhouse and D. Laing)

W. Scott: *Minstrelsy of the Scottish Border* (Edinburgh, 1802–3; edn with tunes, 1833)

R. Jamieson: *Popular Ballads and Songs: from Tradition, Manuscripts and Scarce Editions* (Edinburgh, 1806)

E.G. Geijer and A.A.Afzelius, eds.: *Svenska folkvisor* [Swedish folksongs] (Stockholm, 1814–17, 3/1957–60)

G.R. Kinloch: *Ancient Scottish Ballads, Recovered from Tradition* (London, 1827/R)

W. Motherwell: *Minstrelsy, Ancient and Modern* (Glasgow, 1827/R)

P. Buchan: *Ancient Ballads and Songs of the North of Scotland* (Edinburgh, 1828/R)

S. Grundtvig and A.Olrik: *Danmarks gamle folkeviser* (Copenhagen, 1853–1920; completed by H.G. Nielsen, K.-I. Hildeman, E. Dal, I. Piø, T. Knudsen, S. Nielsen and N. Schiørring, 1920–76/R)

W. Christie: *Traditional Ballad Airs* (Edinburgh, 1876–81)

J.C. Bruce and J.Stokoe: *Northumbrian Minstrelsy* (Newcastle, 1882/R)

F.J. Child: *English and Scottish Popular Ballads* (Cambridge, MA, 1882–98)

C. Nigra: *Canti popolari del Piemonte* (Turin, 1888, 2/1957)

F. Kidson, ed.: *Traditional Tunes: a Collection of Ballad Airs* (Oxford, 1891/R)

L. Erk and F.M.Böhme: *Deutscher Liederhort* (Leipzig, 1893/R)

C.J. Sharp and others, eds.: *Songs of the West* (London, 1905/R)

T. Braga: *Romanceiro geral portuguez* (Lisbon, 2/1906–9/R)

J.H. Combs: *Folk-Songs du Midi des Etats-Unis* (Paris, 1925; Eng. trans., 1967)

G. Greig and J.B. Duncan: *Last Leaves of Traditional Ballads and Ballad Airs*, ed. A. Keith (Aberdeen, 1925)

P. Barry, F.H. Eckstorm and M.W. Smyth, eds.: *British Ballads from Maine* (New Haven, CT, 1929) [musical transcrs. by G. Herzog]

A.K. Davis: *Traditional Ballads of Virginia* (Cambridge, MA, 1929)

C.J. Sharp and M.Karpeles, eds.: *English Folk Songs from the Southern Appalachians* (London, 1932/R, 2/1952/R)

J. Meier and others: *Deutsche Volkslieder, mit ihren Melodien* (Berlin, 1935–96)

D. Castañeda: *El corrido mexicano: su técnica literaria y musical* (Mexico City, 1943)

G.G. Korson: *Pennsylvania Songs and Legends* (Philadelphia, 1949/R)

T.P. Coffin: *The British Traditional Ballad in North America* (Philadelphia, 1950, enlarged 3/1977)

J. Canteloube: *Anthologie des chants populaires français, groupés et présentés par pays ou provinces* (Paris, 1951)

H.M. Belden and A.P. Hudson, eds.: *Folk Ballads from North Carolina*, The Frank C. Brown Collection of North Carolina Folklore, ii (Durham, NC, 1952)

I. Csanádi and L.Vargyas, eds.: *Röpülj páva röpülj: magyar népballadák és balladás dalok* [Fly peacock fly: Hungarian ballads and ballad tunes] (Budapest, 1954)

A.B. Friedman, ed.: *The Viking Book of Folk Ballads of the English-Speaking World* (New York, 1956/R)

J.P. Schinhan, ed.: *The Music of the Ballads*, The Frank C. Brown Collection of North Carolina Folklore, iv (Durham, NC, 1957)

N.I. White and others, eds.: *The Frank C. Brown Collection of North Carolina Folklore*, iv: *The Music of the Ballads* (Durham, NC, 1957)

J. Künzig: *Ehe sie verklingen . . . Alte deutsche Volksweisen vom Böhmerwald bis zur Wolga* (Freiberg, 1958)

B.H. Bronson: *The Traditional Tunes of the Child Ballads with their Texts according to the Extant Records of Great Britain and America* (Princeton, NJ, 1959–72)

A.K. Davis: *More Traditional Ballads of Virginia* (Chapel Hill, NC, 1960)

M. Barbeau: *Le rossignol y chante* (Ottawa, 1962)

M.E. Simmons: *A Bibliography of the Romance and Related Forms in Spanish America* (Bloomington, IN, 1963)

A.I. Amzulescu, ed.: *Balade populare românești* (Bucharest, 1967)

E. Seemann, D. Stromback and B.R. Jonsson, eds.: *European Folk Ballads* (Copenhagen, 1967)

R.W. Brednich and W.Suppan: *Gottscheer Volkslieder*, i (Mainz, 1969)

Jahresbibliographie der Volksballadenforschung(Ljubljana, 1970–90)

J. Jagamas and J.Faragó: *Romániai magyar népdalok*[Hungarian folksongs from Romania] (Bucharest, 1974)

M. Karpeles, ed.: *Cecil Sharp's Collection of English Folksongs* (London, 1974)

E.B. Lyle, ed.: *Andrew Crawfurd's Collection of Ballads and Songs*, i (Edinburgh, 1975)

R.L. Wright, ed.: *Irish Emigrant Ballads and Songs* (Bowling Green, OH, 1975)

P. Shuldham-Shaw and others, eds.: *The Greig-Duncan Folk Song Collection* (Aberdeen and Edinburgh, 1976–99)

B.H. Bronson: *The Singing Tradition of Child's Popular Ballads* (Princeton, NJ, 1977)

E. MacColl and P. Seeger, eds.: *Travellers' Songs from England and Scotland* (London and Knoxville, TN, 1977)

S.G. Armistead: 'A Critical Bibliography of the Hispanic Ballad in Oral Tradition (1971–9)', *El romancero hoy: historia, comparatismo, bibliografía critica*, ed. S.G. Armistead, A.S. Romeralo and D. Catalán (Madrid, 1979), 199–310

R. Palmer, ed.: *Everyman's Book of British Ballads* (London, 1980/R)

A.S. Romeralo, S.G. Armistead and S.H. Petersen, eds.: *Bibliografía del romancero oral* (Madrid, 1980–)

H. Shields: *Shamrock, Rose, and Thistle: Folk Singing in North Derry* (Belfast, 1981)

W.G. Day, ed.: *The Pepys Ballads* (Cambridge, 1987)

J. Porter: *The Traditional Music of Britain and Ireland* (New York, 1989)

G. Huntington, ed.: *Sam Henry's Songs of the People* (Athens, GA, 1990)

N. Cohen: *Traditional Anglo-American Folk Music: an Annotated Discography of Published Sound Recordings* (New York, 1994)

STUDIES: BRITISH, NORTH AMERICAN

W. Chappell: *Popular Music of the Olden Time* (London, 1855–9/R as *The Ballad Literature and Popular Music of the Olden Time*, rev. 2/1893/R by H.E. Wooldridge as *Old English Popular Music*)

F.B. Gummere: *The Popular Ballad* (Cambridge, MA, 1907/R)

C.J. Sharp: *English Folk-Song: some Conclusions* (London, 1907, rev. 4/1965 by M. Karpeles)

P. Grainger: 'Collecting with the Phonograph', *JFFS*, iii (1908), 147–242

L. Pound: *Poetic Origins and the Ballad* (New York, 1921/R)

L.C. Wimberly: *Folklore in the English and Scottish Ballads* (Chicago, 1928)

A.G. Gilchrist: 'A Note on the "Herb" and Other Refrains of Certain British Ballads', *JFFS*, viii (1930), 237–50

A. Taylor: *'Edward' and 'Sven i Rosengård': a Study in the Dissemination of a Ballad* (Chicago, 1931)

G.H. Gerould: *The Ballad of Tradition* (Oxford, 1932/R)

R.S. Lamson: *English Broadside Ballad Tunes, 1550–1700* (diss., Harvard U., 1935)

A.J. Walker: *Popular Songs and Broadsides in the English Drama 1559–1642* (Cambridge, MA, 1935)

J.W. Hendren: *A Study of Ballad Rhythm, with Special Reference to Ballad Music* (Princeton, NJ, 1936/R)

W.J. Entwistle: *European Balladry* (Oxford, 1939/R)

R. Harvey: 'The Unquiet Grave', *JEFDSS*, iv (1941), 49–66

S.P. Bayard: 'Prolegomena to a Study of the Principal Melodic Families of British-American Folk Song', *Journal of American Folk-Lore*, lxiii (1950), 1–44

T.P. Coffin: *The British Traditional Ballad in North America* (Philadelphia, 1950, enlarged, 3/1977)

M.J.C. Hodgart: *The Ballads* (London, 1950, 2/1962)

G.M. Laws: *Native American Balladry* (Philadelphia, 1950/R)

G.P. Jackson, ed.: *Another Sheaf of White Spirituals* (Gainesville, FL, 1952/R)

G.M. Laws: *American Balladry from British Broadsides* (Philadelphia, 1957)

A. Paredes: *'With His Pistol in His Hand': a Border Ballad and its Hero* (Austin, 1958)

D.K. Wilgus: *Anglo-American Folksong Scholarship Since 1898* (New Brunswick, NJ, 1959/R)

A.B. Friedman: *The Ballad Revival: Studies in the Influence of Popular on Sophisticated Poetry* (Chicago, 1961)

J.H. Jones: 'Commonplace and Memorization in the Oral Tradition of the English and Scottish Ballads', *Journal of American Folklore*, lxxiv (1961), 97–112

MacE. Leach and T.P.Coffin: *The Critics & the Ballad*(Carbondale, IL, 1961) [incl. P. Barry: 'The Part of the Folk Singer in the Making of Folk Balladry', 59–76]

G.M. Laws: *Anglo-Irish Balladry in North America* (Philadelphia, 1962)

L. Shepard: *The Broadside Ballad: a Study in Origins and Meaning* (London, 1962)

C.M. Simpson: *The British Broadside Ballad and its Music* (New Brunswick, NJ, 1966)

A.L. Lloyd: *Folk Song in England* (London and New York, 1967)

J.B. Toelken: 'An Oral Canon for the Child Ballads: Construction and Application', *Journal of the Folklore Institute*, iv (1967), 75–101

J.Q. Wolf: 'Folk Singers and the Re-Creation of Folksong', *Western Folklore*, xxvi (1967), 101–11

B.H. Bronson: *The Ballad as Song* (Berkeley, 1969)

H. Glassie, E.D.Ives and J.F. Szwed: *Folksongs and their Makers* (Bowling Green, OH, 1970)

A. Munro: 'Lizzie Higgins and the Oral Transmission of Ten Child Ballads', *Scottish Studies*, xiv (1970), 155–88

A. Riddle: *A Singer and Her Songs*, ed. R.D. Abrahams (Baton Rouge, LA, 1970)

A.E. Green: '"McCaffery": a Study in the Variation and Function of a Ballad', *Lore and Language*, i (1970–71), no.3, pp.4–9; no.4, pp.3–12; no.5, pp.6–11

D. Buchan: *The Ballad and the Folk* (London, 1972)

H. Shields: 'Old British Ballads in Ireland', *Folk Life*, x (1972), 68–103

E. Long: 'Ballad Singers, Ballad Makers, and Ballad Etiology', *Western Folklore*, xxxii (1973), 225–36

J. Maguire: *Come Day, Go Day, God Send Sunday*, ed. R. Morton (London, 1973)

S. Smith: *A Study of Lizzie Higgins as a Transitional Figure in the Oral Tradition of Northeast Scotland* (diss., U. of Edinburgh, 1975)

A. Bruford: 'The Grey Selkie', *Ballad Studies*, ed. E.B. Lyle (Cambridge, 1976), 41–65

A. Gardner-Medwin: 'Miss Reburn's Ballads: a Nineteenth Century Repertoire from England', *Ballad Studies*, ed. E.B. Lyle (Cambridge, 1976), 93–116

A. Munro: '"Abbotsford Collection of Border Ballads": Sophia Scott's Manuscript Book with Airs', *Scottish Studies*, xx (1976), 91–108

J. Porter: 'Jeannie Robertson's "My Son David": a Conceptual Performance Model', *Journal of American Folklore*, lxxxix (1976), 7–26

H.O. Nygard: 'Mrs Brown's Recollected Ballads', *Ballad and Ballad Research: Seattle 1977*, 68–87

C. Seeger: 'Versions and Variants of "Barbara Allen"', *Studies in Musicology 1935–1975* (Berkeley, 1977), 273–320

T.G. and A.L. Burton: *Some Ballad Folks* (Johnson City, 1978)

F.G. Andersen and T. Pettitt: 'Mrs Brown of Falkland: a Singer of Tales?', *Journal of American Folklore*, xcii (1979), 1–24

R. Palmer: *A Ballad History of England* (London, 1979)

R. Wehse: *Schwanklied und Flugblatt in Grossbritannien* (Frankfurt, 1979)

G. Dunn: *The Fellowship of Song: Popular Singing Traditions in East Suffolk* (London, 1980)

L. Doucette and C.Quigley: 'The Child Ballad in Canada: a Survey', *Canadian Folk Music Journal*, ix (1981), 3–19

D.K. Wilgus: 'Andrew Jenkins, Folk Composer: an Overview', *Lore and Language*, iii (1981), 109–28

N. Würzbach: *Die englische Strassenballade 1550–1660* (Munich, 1981; Eng. trans., 1990, as *The Rise of the English Street Ballad*)

G. Boyes: 'Performance and Context: an Examination of the Effects of the English Folksong Revival on Song Repertoire and Style', *The Ballad Today: Sheffield 1982*, 43–52

K.S. Goldstein: 'The Impact of Recording Technology on the British Folksong Revival', *Folk Music and Modern Sound*, ed. W. Ferris and M.L. Hart (Jackson, MS, 1982), 3–13

A. Bennett: 'Sources of Popular Song in Early Nineteenth-Century Britain: Problems and Methods of Research', *Popular Music*, ii (1983), 63–89

J. Porter, ed.: *The Ballad Image: Essays Presented to Bertrand Harris Bronson* (Los Angeles, 1983)

M. Pickering: 'Popular Song at Juniper Hill', *Folk Music Journal*, iv (1984), 481–503

F.G. Andersen: *Commonplace and Creativity: the Role of Formulaic Diction in Anglo-Scottish Traditional Balladry* (Odense, 1985)

A. Bruford: 'The Singing of Fenian and Similar Lays in Scotland', *Ballad Research: Dublin 1985*, 55–70

D. Harker: *Fakesong: the Manufacture of British 'Folksong' 1700 to the Present Day*(Philadelphia, 1985)

D.K. Wilgus: 'The "Aisling" and the Cowboy: some Unnoticed Influences of Irish Vision Poetry on Anglo-American Balladry', *Western Folklore*, xliv (1985), 255–300

D.K. Wilgus and E.R. Long: 'The Blues Ballad and the Genesis of Style in Traditional Narrative Song', *Narrative Folksong: New Directions: Essays in Appreciation of W. Edson Richmond*, ed. C.L. Edwards and K.E.B. Manley (Boulder, CO, 1985), 435–82

L.J. Williamson: *Narrative Singing Among the Scots Travellers: a Study of Strophic Variation in Ballad Performance* (diss., U. of Edinburgh, 1985)

E. MacColl and P.Seeger: *Till Doomsday in the Afternoon: the Folklore of Scots Travellers, the Stewarts of Blairgowrie* (Manchester, 1986)

J. Porter: 'Ballad Explanations, Ballad Reality, and the Singer's Epistemics', *Western Folklore*, xlv (1986), 110–25

D.K. Wilgus and B.Toelken: *The Ballad and the Scholars: Approaches to Ballad Study* (Los Angeles, 1986)

M.J. Bell: '"No Borders to the Ballad Maker's Art": Francis James Child and the Politics of the People', *Western Folklore*, xlvii (1988), 285–307

D. Dugaw: *Warrior Women and Popular Balladry, 1650–1850* (Cambridge, 1989, 2/1996)

J. Porter: *The Traditional Music of Britain and Ireland* (New York, 1989)

W.B. McCarthy: *The Ballad Matrix: Personality, Milieu, and the Oral Tradition* (Bloomington, IA, 1990)

H. Shields: 'The History of "The Lass of Aughrim"', *Musicology in Ireland*, ed. G. Gillen and H. White (Blackrock, 1990), 58–73

C.C. Livingston: *British Broadside Ballads of the Sixteenth-Century: a Catalogue of the Extant Sheets and an Essay* (London and New York, 1991)

Ballads and Boundaries: Los Angeles 1993 [incl. S. Douglas: 'Ballad Singing and Boundaries', 289–95; T. Mitsui: 'How was "Judas" Sung?', 241–50]

G. Boyes: *The Imagined Village: Culture, Ideology and the English Folk Revival* (Manchester, 1993)

G. Porter: 'Airs and Graces: Interpretation Based on the Musical Record', *ARV: Scandinavian Yearbook of Folklore*, xlix (1993), 205–14

S. Rieuwerts: 'Field-Collecting of English and Scottish Ballads: a Researcher's Point of View', *ARV: Scandinavian Yearbook of Folklore*, xlix (1993), 237–46

H. Shields: *Narrative Singing in Ireland: Lays, Ballads, Come-All-Yes and Other Songs* (Dublin, 1993)

S. Smith: 'The Categorization and Performance Aesthetics of Narrative Song among Scottish Folk Revival Singers', *ARV: Scandinavian Yearbook of Folklore*, xlix (1993), 225–36

H. Shields: 'The Words and Music of Ballads in Nineteenth-Century Irish Fieldwork', *Visions & Identities: Tórshavn 1994*, 131–8

D. Dugaw, ed.: *The Anglo-American Ballad: a Folklore Casebook* (New York, 1995)

J. Porter and H.Gower: *Jeannie Robertson: Emergent Singer, Transformative Voice* (Knoxville, TN, 1995)

J.C. Bishop: '"The Most Valuable Collection of Child Ballads with Tunes Ever Published": the Unfinished Works of James Madison Carpenter', *Ballads into Books: the Legacies of Francis James Child*, ed. T. Cheesman and S. Rieuwerts (Berne, 1997), 81–94

D. Dugaw: 'The Politics of Culture: John Gay and Popular Ballads', *Ballads into Books: the Legacies of Francis James Child*, ed. T. Cheesman and S. Rieuwerts (Berne, 1997), 189–98

B.N. Smith: *Jane Hicks Gentry: a Singer Among Singers* (Lexington, KY, 1998)

P. Kinney: 'Welsh Ballad Tunes', *Ballads in Wales*, ed. M.-A. Constantine (London, 1999), 19–24

Broadside Index (London, Vaughan Williams Memorial Library Cecil Sharp House; S. Roud) [database on 3 computer disks]

STUDIES: EUROPEAN, COMPARATIVE

A. Duran: *Romancero general* (Madrid, 1849–51, 2/1854)

G. Doncieux and J. Tiersot: *Le romancéro populaire de la France* (Paris, 1904)

R. Menéndez Pidal: *Poesía popular y poesía tradicional en la léteratura española* (Oxford, 1922)

S.B. Hustvedt: *Ballad Books and Ballad Men: Raids and Rescues in Britain, America and the Scandinavian North Since 1800* (Cambridge, MA, 1930/R)

W. Danckert: *Das europäische Volkslied* (Berlin, 1939, 2/1970)

V.T. Mendoza: *El romance español y el corrido mexicano* (Mexico City, 1939, 2/1997)

K. Liestøl: *Scottish and Norwegian Ballads* (Oslo, 1946)

R. Menéndez Pidal: *Romancero hispánico* (Madrid, 1953, 2/1968)

E. Comisel: 'The Rumanian Popular Ballad', *Studia Memoriae Belae Bartók Sacra*, ed. B. Rajeczky and L. Vargyas (Budapest, 1956, 3/1958), 31–54

H.O. Nygard: *The Ballad of 'Heer Halewijn': its Forms and Variations in Western Europe* (Helsinki, 1958)

P.V. Lintur: *Narodnye ballady Zakarpattja i ix zapadnoslavjanskie svjazi* [The Carpathian-Ukrainian folk ballad corpus and West Slavic tradition] (Kiev, 1963)

E. Gerson-Kiwi: 'On the Musical Sources of the Judaeo-Hispanic "Romance"', *MQ*, l (1964), 31–43

L. Vargyas: 'Rapports internationaux de la ballade populaire hongroise', *Littérature hongroise, littérature européenne: Budapest 1964*, 69–104

B.N. Putilov: *Slavjanskaja istoriceskaja ballada* [The Slavic historical ballad] (Leningrad, 1965)

I.I. Zemtsovsky: 'Ballads', *Sovetskaya muzyka*, iv (1966), 89–95

N. Leader: *Hungarian Classical Ballads and their Folklore* (Cambridge, 1967)

P. Bénichou: *Romancero judeo-español de Marruecos* (Madrid, 1968)

R. Barros and M.Dannemann: *El romancero chileno* (Santiago, 1970)

M. Kosová: 'Katálog evrópskych balád', *Slovenský národopis*, xviii (1970), 647–61

H.A. Nud'ha: *Ukrajins'ka balada (Z teoriji ta istoriji žanru)* [The Ukrainian ballad (theory and history of the genre)] (Kyjov, 1970)

I.J. Katz: *Judeo-Spanish Traditional Ballads from Jerusalem: an Ethnomusicological Study* (Brooklyn, NY, 1972–5)

L. Röhrich: 'Rätsellied', *Handbuch des Volksliedes*, ed. R.W. Brednich, L. Rohrich and W. Suppan, i (Munich, 1973), 101–56

W.H. Anders: *Balladensänger und mundliche Komposition: Untersuchungen zur englischen Traditionsballade* (Munich, 1974)

R.B. Klymasz and J. Porter: 'Traditional Ukrainian Balladry in Canada', *Western Folklore*, xxxiii (1974), 89–132

L. Vargyas: *Magyar népballada es Europa* [Hungarian ballads and the European ballad tradition] (Budapest, 1976; Eng. trans., 1983)

Ballads and Ballad Research: Seattle 1977

J. Faragó: *Balladák földjén* [Transylvanian ballads] (Bucharest, 1977)

S.G. Armistead and I.J.Katz: 'The New Edition of "Danmarks gamle Folkeviser"', *YIFMC*, ix (1978), 89–95

R. Benmayor: 'A Greek tragoúdi in the Repertoire of a Judeo-Spanish Ballad Singer', *Hispanic Review*, xlvi (1978), 475–9

P. Burke: *Popular Culture in Early Modern Europe* (London and New York, 1978/R)

R. Benmayor: *Romances judeo-españoles de Oriente* (Madrid, 1979)

I.J. Katz: 'The Musical Legacy of the Judeo-Spanish "Romancero"', *Hispania Judaica*, ed. J.M. Sola-Solé, S.G. Armistead and J.H. Silverman, ii (Barcelona, 1980–84), 45–58

Aspects of the European Broadside Ballad: Belgium 1981

J. Etzion: 'The Polyphonic Ballad in 16th-Century Vihuela Publications', *MD*, xxxv (1981), 179–97

Z. Kumer: 'Singers' Repertories as a Consequence of their Biographies', *Lore and Language*, iii (1981), 49–54

F.G. Andersen, O. Holzapfel and T. Pettitt: *The Ballad as Narrative: Studies in the Ballad Traditions of England, Scotland, Germany and Denmark* (Odense, 1982)

C. Jaremko: 'Baltic Ballads of the "Singing Bone": Prototype and Oicotype', *The Ballad Today: Sheffield 1982*, 66–71

The Concept of Tradition in Ballad Research: Odense 1984

C. Merill-Mirsky: *Judeo-Spanish Song from the Island of Rhodes: a Musical Tradition in Los Angeles* (diss., UCLA, 1984)

A. Doornbosch: 'Twentieth-Century "Halewijn" Recordings in the Netherlands: a Matter of Survival and Persistence', *Ballad Research: Dublin 1985*, 287–97

S.G. Armistead and J.H. Silverman: *Judeo-Spanish Ballads from Oral Tradition* (Berkeley, 1986) [musical transcriptions, commentary by I.J. Katz]

J. Etzion and S.Weich-Shahak: 'The Spanish and the Sephardic Romances: Musical Links', *EthM*, xxxii (1988), 1–37

D. Colbert: *The Birth of the Ballad: the Scandinavian Medieval Genre* (Stockholm, 1989)

J. Seeger: 'The Living Ballad in Brazil: Two Performances', *Hispanic Balladry Today*, ed. R.H. Webber (New York, 1989), 175–217

A. Valenciano: 'Survival of the Traditional "Romancero": Field Expeditions', *Hispanic Balladry Today*, ed. R.H. Webber (New York, 1989), 26–52

R.H. Webber, ed.: *Hispanic Balladry Today* (New York, 1989)

M. Herrera-Sobek: *The Mexican Corrido: a Feminist Analysis* (Bloomington, IN, 1990/R)

J. Seeger: *Count Claros: Study of a Ballad Tradition* (New York, 1990)

G. Nagy: 'Song and Dance: Reflections on a Comparison of Faroese Ballad with Greek Choral Lyric', *The Ballad and Oral Literature*, ed. J. Harris (Cambridge, MA, 1991), 214–32

A. Caufriez: 'The Ballad in Northeast Portugal', *Ballads and Boundaries: Los Angeles 1993*, 251–64

J. Cohen: 'Romancing the "Romance": Perceptions (and Boundaries) of the Judeo-Spanish Ballad', *Ballads and Boundaries: Los Angeles 1993*, 209–17

A.-M. Häggmann: 'Ballad Singing in an Ostrobothnian Village', *ARV: Scandinavian Yearbook of Folklore*, xlix (1993), 215–23

T. Cheesman: 'Bänkelsang: Seeing, Hearing, Telling and Singing in the German Ballad Picture Show', *Lore and Language*, xii (1994), 41–57

M. da Costa Fontes: *O romanceiro portugês e brasileiro: indice temático e bibliográfico* (Madison, WI, 1997) [incl. mus. exx. and commentary by I.J. Katz]

II. The 19th- and 20th-century art form

1. German song. 2. The English sentimental ballad. 3. The ballad in opera.

1. GERMAN SONG. Like the lied, the ballad in German song in its most sophisticated form was the result of changes and developments in literature. The poetic form goes back to the tradition of *Bänkelsang*, in which narrative ditties with primitive accompaniment were performed in public places from a wooden bench as a makeshift podium. The public could buy and take home with them crudely printed versions of the rhymed tales of crime or catastrophe. This vulgar tradition played little or no part in the lofty writings of the Enlightenment, but by the middle of the 18th century poets like Johann Gleim, Ludwig Hölty, the brothers Christian and Friedrich von Stollberg, and G.A. Bürger adopted a popular ballad-like tone in some of their poetry as an alternative to the

dry literary conventions of the time. Usually ballad texts were secular or legendary (on national or supernatural themes); their tone was often tragic, and they tended to idealize primitive life and feeling.

English poetry and the English ballad tradition also played an important part in the development of the German ballad. Thomas Percy's *Reliques of Ancient English Poetry* (1765), which received immediate critical attention in Germany, came to the notice of J.G. Herder in 1771. By 1779 he had published two volumes of *Stimmen der Völker*, which included 24 translations from Percy as well as Goethe's *Der Fischer* and *Heidenröslein*. Schubert later made famous settings of both these poems. Other ballads from the collection which were given musical immortality were *Herr Oluf* (Loewe) and *Edward* (Loewe, Schubert and Brahms). Herder's work was also to influence Bettina and Clemens Brentano, whose *Des Knaben Wunderhorn* was a treasure-trove of ballad material for a later generation of composers. Also of great importance was the influence of one of the greatest British literary controversies of the 18th century. The poeticized prose of 'Ossian' (James Macpherson), often ostensibly translated from Gaelic epic, and published between 1760 and 1765, was similarly disseminated in Germany. The two strains, traditional and literary, blended in the indigenous art ballads of Goethe and Schiller, which are elevated in style and verse form, moral or didactic in tone and have subjects freely derived from classical, oriental or medieval legends.

Although both J.F. Reichardt and C.F. Zelter of the so-called Second Berlin School were to compose extended cantatas for voice and piano, by far the most industrious and influential of ballad composers before Schubert was J.R. Zumsteeg of Stuttgart, who had been a schoolfriend of Schiller. His first published ballad was a setting of Bürger's *Des Pfarrers Tochter von Taubenhain* (1791), issued by Breitkopf & Härtel; a setting of the celebrated ballad *Lenore* followed in 1798. The publisher, no doubt conscious of the fact that Zumsteeg had captured an aspect of the Zeitgeist and cornered the market, encouraged the composer to explore the medium further: seven volumes of *Kleine Balladen und Lieder* (1800–05) consolidated a reputation which remained unassailable until the 1830s. Zumsteeg's achievement was to find a means of freely alternating between recitative and melody so as to heighten the dramatic narrative (often with cunning tempo and key changes) at the same time as giving the conception a sweep and unity that kept the listener's attention over a relatively long time span. The piano writing was imaginative and often gripping by the standards of the contemporary accompanied song. Even more adventurous piano writing was to be found in the work of the Bohemian Václav Tomášek, an important ballad composer who set a number of the Goethe poems later immortalized by Schubert's music; but his *Lenore* (1805), with its 210-bar piano introduction (which can almost stand alone as a piano piece), is his most impressive achievement in the field of the ballad.

Schubert's friend Josef von Spaun related in his memoirs of the composer (1858) that Schubert had 'wanted to modernize Zumsteeg's song form, which appealed very much to him' and that the young Schubert could 'revel in these songs for days on end'. Like an apprentice painter who copies the work of a master, Schubert re-composed a number of Zumsteeg ballads (the first was *Hagars*

Klage, 1811), clearly with the older man's music in front of him. Such details as tonality, prosody and even general melodic shape are often similar, but the hand of genius showed itself at every turn, and Schubert out-composed his model to such an extent that the unjust effect of his well-meant homage was to consign Zumsteeg to a footnote in song history. Not that the ballads of Schubert have been sufficiently understood and valued for the remarkable works they often are; while it is true, for example, that the longest of them, *Adelwold und Emma* (1815), suffers from an intolerable text (and consequent musical weak patches), there are many highly imaginative and moving moments in these works. They show that the true nature of Schubert's dramatic gift depended on a scenario with lightning changes of location and dramatic ellipses to be found only in the (as yet uninvented) realm of cinema, or the (as yet undeveloped) lied. The freedom of the best of these ballads suggests Brahms's later image of Schubert as a young god playing with thunderbolts on Mount Olympus. They show how frustrating Schubert must have found it to labour within the conventions of opera; his mind is quicksilver, and when constrained by the discipline of the unities and the proscenium it becomes sluggish. This also suggests that the narrator of a ballad fulfils the same function as a film camera: impartial, ubiquitous, wide-ranging and responsible for the picture as a whole, unlike the personally involved lieder narrator, whose emotions are filtered and focussed in quite another way. It seems that in composing ballads Schubert enjoyed playing the somewhat distanced role of camera operator (also responsible for lighting, costumes and crowd scenes) as opposed to leading man, as in his own lieder productions (where the poet is of course co-director). In whatever style, Schubert is at his best with texts of high quality; in this case it is the Schiller settings that produce much of abiding interest – *Der Taucher* (1812), *Die Bürgschaft* (1815), *Klage der Ceres* (1815–1816) and *Ritter Toggenburg* (1816). Einstein (in *Schubert*, 1951, pp.49–51) was the first to notice that 'the sheer boldness' of the harmonic progressions in *Der Taucher* were far in advance of [Schubert's] time. There is nothing like them until we reach the Wagner of *Tristan* and the *Ring*'. The linking of Schubert's name with Wagner's in this context seems all the more tenable in view of the fact that the ballads were mostly published as part of the *Nachlass* between 1830 and 1850, just at the time when Wagner was forming his mature style. He was himself a ballad composer, both in song (a French setting of Heine's *Die Grenadiere*, 1840) and in opera (e.g. Senta's ballad in *Der fliegende Holländer*), and time and again can be heard in Schubert's music a prophecy of the Wagnerian narrative line – always on the point of flowering into melody, but rarely doing so in the interests of dramatic continuity. This is neither recitative nor aria, but arioso, poised between the two, which carries the story forward to its next highpoint and creates a genuine sense of tension and release. In this sense, the Wagner operas, some of them based in part on ancient ballad poetry, are perhaps the greatest manifestations of the German ballad tradition. If we hear in Wolf's songs many of Wagner's procedures without the longueurs, the same is surprisingly true of Schubert's ballad writing (as well as a work like the oratorio *Lazarus*), which sometimes sounds at least 50 years ahead of its time. It is also certain that Schubert could never have written a late masterpiece like the Heine setting *Der Doppelgänger* (1828) without his many hours of ballad apprenticeship earlier in his career, much less earlier works in quasi-ballad style like the through-composed songs *Erlkönig* (1815) and *Der Zwerg* (1822/3).

Also influenced by Zumsteeg was Carl Loewe, who consciously modelled his work on that of the older master. Loewe, one of the very few composers to sing to a professional standard, remains the German ballad composer *pur sang*. Highly educated (he was a Goethe scholar and gifted astronomer), he was less fertile than Schubert by far in terms of musical invention, but was brimming with energy of a simpler, almost more physical kind. That he both sang and played the piano seems an apt combination of talents for this greatest of all-round balladeers. He achieved a highly workable synthesis of Zumsteeg's two styles – either simply strophic and repetitive, or more complex scene- and mood-painting with recitative and arioso sections; this avoids overemphasis whether of verbal repetition or musical depiction. The story is related in direct melody and graphically, if naively, illustrated on the keyboard often with effective use of the higher register. (Despite a certain forthright quality, the piano writing is among the most demanding in the song repertory.) Loewe used what he learnt from Zumsteeg not only to set the poets known to the older composer (Goethe, Herder), but also for the next two generations of ballad poets, Ludwig Uhland, Friedrich Rückert and August von Platen, and their successors, Ferdinand Freiligrath and Theodor Fontane. Most of Loewe's work was published between 1821 and 1868; it is a measure of both the power of his winning formula as a composer, and his limitations as an artist, that there is little sign of change or development in his work during the 50 or so years of his creative life (*see also* Song Cycle, §3).

After Loewe the term 'ballad' seems to be far more loosely defined. Because Schubert had absorbed the ballad into the bloodstream of his lieder output, taking what he needed from it to create a hybrid form, later song composers felt able to regard as ballads a number of their lieder that would not have been counted so by singers of Loewe's generation. For example, Schumann composed four sets of *Romanzen und Balladen* without making it clear which songs he considered ballads, and which romances (Brahms later used the same title with similar ambiguity). Of course works like Schumann's *Die Löwenbraut* op.31 no.1 and *Belsatzar* op.57 have many of the characteristics of the true ballad; one is a fantastical animal tale, and the other an elaboration of a biblical story, both familiar areas for ballad poetry. But Schumann, as well as Brahms in songs like *Verrat* op.105 no.5, seems to have lost that element of objectivity and camera-like observation, the *'erzählender Ton'* (narrative tone) that is at the heart of the true ballad. Instead the listener is invited to share in the composer's reaction as if the latter were hearing the ballad for the first time, rather than presenting it as a story he already knows well. In terms of the resulting quality of the music, this may well be having the best of both worlds, but it represented the death of the real ballad tradition; indeed, Schilling (*Encyklopädie*) dates the demise of the form as early as 1835.

Those extended and complex narrative songs of Hugo Wolf which it might be tempting to call ballads *(Der Feuerreiter, Die Geister am Mummelsee*, both Mörike, and *Ritter Kurts Brautfahrt*, Goethe) show an encyclopedic knowledge of song history and styles; they bow to the shade of the composer's predecessors – Loewe particularly, to whom Wolf listened with 'höchster Begeisterung' (greatest enthusiasm) – with a conscious sense of amused and ironic reverence. Loewe had included in *Walpurgisnacht*(1821) a quotation from Spohr's *Faust*; in similar fashion, Wolf, in *Ritter Kurts Brautfahrt* (1888), quotes from the music of Karl Goldmark and Adalbert von Goldschmidt in a much less genial spirit of allusion and cross-cultural nodding and winking. One of the dangers of the ballad, with its historical connotations and connections with the ultra-German tradition of the Minnesinger, was that it should come to suggest a type of music-making that was somehow pan-Germanic because free of neurotic or introverted feeling, music-making to exclude foreigners and those from other backgrounds. Something of this revivalist spirit pervades the ballads of the now largely forgotten Martin Plüddemann, whose work was centred in Graz and who attempted to re-establish the hegemony of the ballad in the 1880s and 90s. This mirrored the rise of a new wave of patriotic ballad poetry in the 1890s which was not of the highest quality. Of more lasting significance were the two large ballads for (respectively) baritone and bass, and orchestra (*Herr Oluf*, 1891, and *Die Heinzelmännchen*) of Pfitzner. These looked back to Schumann's cantatas on ballad texts by Uhland and Geibel (*Des Sängers Fluch* and *Vom Pagen und der Königstochter*, both 1852). For better or worse the genre had become orchestral and remained so in the last 19th-century examples (*see* Ballade (ii)). As a hopeful antidote to the 'entartete Musik' reviled by the Third Reich, there were continuing echoes of an aggressive unification of bad music and poetry to bring the grand old form of the ballad into disrepute; in the 1930s ballad singing was considered by the Nazi regime to be a manly and culturally sound occupation for German baritones (tenors seemed excused largely because Loewe's tessituras favour the lower voices). The critic H.J. Moser at the time was confident of a renascence of German ballad composition which did not come about. But ballad evenings, particularly featuring the works of Loewe, were regularly to be found as a part of music-making in Germany at the end of the 20th century.

2. The English sentimental ballad.   Towards the end of the 18th century English composers began to characterize certain songs (whether published separately or as parts of operas) as 'ballads': they were generally strophic and narrative, like folk ballads, and were inclined to be nostalgic. One of the earliest so named, 'I was, d'ye see, a waterman', was from Charles Dibdin's *The Waterman* (1774). Ballads of this type were a feature of English opera for over a century and can still be traced in Sullivan's Savoy operas. Their form is often stereotyped: each stanza has an introduction giving the first few bars of the main tune, and the tune is then sung, returning near the end of the stanza after an episode in a related key. A ballad was often the most popular number in an opera and was composed with a view to subsequent sale for domestic use; hence the derogatory terms '(music-)shop ballad' and 'drawing-room ballad' came into use. Sometimes ballads were inserted into operas with which they had no connection, as when Mme Vestris introduced C.E. Horn's ballad 'I've been roaming' into an English

adaptation of *Le nozze di Figaro* at Covent Garden in 1828.

In the Victorian period the word began to be used far more loosely to describe almost any kind of sentimental popular song, and a great commercial development of the ballad took place in Britain and the USA. Publishers paid large sums, not to the author or composer of the song (who usually received only a small fee) but to the well-known performer who agreed to sing it at every public appearance for a specified period (hence the term 'royalty ballad'). The singer's name dwarfed the composer's on the garish title-page. The 'ballad concert' became a common form of entertainment: the first was given by Mme Sainton-Dolby on 3 January 1867. The popularity of the ballad stretched far into the 20th century, and the BBC in its early years broadcast ballad concerts. There were many ballads whose sales went into millions, but none perhaps equalled the popularity of 'Home, Sweet Home', composed by Bishop for his opera *Clari* (1823) and publicized by Jenny Lind from 1850 onwards. Many of Stephen Foster's songs belong to the ballad genre.

Since World War II, the word 'ballad' has been used to refer to pop songs with sentimental or narrative texts and (usually) a slow tempo.

3. THE BALLAD IN OPERA.   In opera the interpolation of a ballad recounting events that have taken place beyond the action on stage was sometimes used as a means of clarifying the plot. The dramatic impetus afforded by this device drew an enthusiastic response from 19th-century librettists, who used it increasingly as a means of broadening their palette. Unlike the purely narrative *romance* as developed by Rousseau, the operatic ballad often contains an element of the supernatural – a sea monster in Nélusko's 'Adamastor, roi des vagues profondes' (*L'Africaine*), a faery in Mercutio's Queen Mab ballad (Gounod's *Roméo et Juliette*). The significance of its melodramatic content for the development of German romantic opera has not yet been fully charted, but it seems likely to owe much to what Manicke (preface to EDM, xlv, 1970) has called the 'demonic spectre' of Bürger's *Lenore*. The best-known opera ballad is Senta's in *Der fliegende Holländer*, in which Wagner claimed to have encapsulated unconsciously the thematic germ of the whole opera. Other notable examples are Raimbaut's ballad (*Robert le diable*), Finn's ballad (*Ruslan and Lyudmila*), Mrs Page's 'Vom Jäger Herne' (*Die lustigen Weiber von Windsor*) and Varlaam's ballad (*Boris Godunov*).

BIBLIOGRAPHY

A. Bach: *The Art Ballad* (Edinburgh and London, 1890, 3/1897)

P. Spitta: 'Ballade', *Musikgeschichtliche Aufsätze* (Berlin, 1894), 403–61

A. König: *Die Ballade in der Musik* (Langensalza, 1904)

H. Simpson: *A Century of Ballads 1810–1910* (London, 1910)

H.J. Moser: *Die Ballade* (Berlin, 1930)

G.H. Gerould: *The Ballad of Tradition* (Oxford, 1932/R)

W.J. Entwistle: *European Balladry* (Oxford, 1939/R)

S. Northcote: *The Ballad in Music* (London, 1942/R)

M.J.C. Hodgart: *The Ballads* (London, 1950, 2/1962)

M.W. Disher: *Victorian Song, from Dive to Drawing Room* (London, 1955)

D.C. Ossenkop: *The Earliest Settings of German Ballads for Voice and Clavier* (diss., Columbia U., 1968)

M.R. Turner, ed.: *The Parlour Song Book* (London, 1972) [incl. preface]

J.S. Bratton: *The Victorian Popular Ballad* (London and Totowa, NJ, 1975)

H. Laufhütte: *Die deutsche Kunstballade: Grundlegung einer Gattungsgeschichte* (Heidelberg, 1979)

C. Dahlhaus, ed.: *Die Musik des 19. Jahrhunderts* (Wiesbaden and Laaber, 1980)

N. Temperley: 'The Ballad', *Music in Britain: the Romantic Age 1800–1914*, ed. N. Temperley (London, 1981/R), 121–34

W. Dürr: *Das deutsche Sololied im 19. Jahrhundert* (Wilhelmshaven, 1984)

C. Dahlhaus, ed.: *Die Musik des 18. Jahrhunderts* (Laaber, 1985)

JAMES PORTER (I, 1–6), JAMES PORTER, JEREMY BARLOW (I, 7), GRAHAM JOHNSON (with ERIC SAMS) (II, 1), NICHOLAS TEMPERLEY (II, 2)

Ballad, religious. A type of 19th-century American revivalist music; *see* SHAPE-NOTE HYMNODY and SPIRITUAL, §I.

Ballade (i). One of the three *formes fixes* (the others are the rondeau and the virelai) that dominated French song and poetry in the 14th and 15th centuries. In its standard late medieval shape the ballade text falls into three stanzas, sharing the same metrical and rhyme scheme and ending with the same refrain. The music for each stanza follows the overall pattern I–I–II. Approximations to this form can be found in monophonic song in the 12th and 13th centuries, when the distinction between the ballade and the virelai in particular was not completely clear. Indeed, even in the 14th century, Machaut called his virelais 'chansons baladées'.

The word 'ballade' is derived from Provençal *ballada*, from *balar*, to dance; the ballade, rondeau and virelai were in their earliest phase songs for dancing, the most common dances being the *carole* and the *tresche*. One of the most attractive of the few surviving examples in Provençal is the spring song *A l'entrada del temps clar* (ex.1) contained in the 13th-century Chansonnier de St Germain-des-Prés (*F-Pn* fr.20050; *see* SOURCES, MS, fig.25), though it is more likely to be a learned imitation than a genuine piece of folksong. There are five stanzas altogether, each with the characteristic repetition of the first musical section including varied endings for the first- and second-time bars, followed by the second musical section (here occupied entirely by the refrain, though later this normally took up only the last line or so). The musical

Ex.1

form I–I–II, it should be noted, is the commonest form underlying the most important of early medieval song types, the Provençal *canso* and French *chanson d'amour*. These, however, normally had five or more stanzas, no refrain and a final envoi of a few extra lines; they persisted into the 14th and 15th centuries as the *chant royal*, and during that period poets using the ballade form without musical setting frequently borrowed the envoi to close their piece.

The 13th-century French *chanson à refrain* is sometimes close to the ballade, and a few examples with three stanzas only are known, such as *Li louseignolés avrillouz* by the Arras trouvère Guillaume le Vinier, though the versification here is uncharacteristically complex. One source (*GB-Ob* Douce 308) gives 188 examples described as *ballettes*, though sadly they are divorced from their presumed musical setting. These display great flexibility in structure as regards the placing of the refrain, metre, rhyme and the number of stanzas. It is to be noted that the 14th-century Italian BALLATA is akin to the 14th-century virelai in form, not to the ballade. The flexible *ballette* gave way, at the very close of the 13th century, to a more rigid classification, in which ballades retained refrains in the final position, whereas virelais placed them in the initial position.

The earliest known polyphonic settings, composed by Adam de la Halle in the late 13th century, reflect the *ballette* stage. Of his 16 *rondes*, as the sources call them, 14 are clearly in rondeau form, which had taken on its definitive shape much earlier; but two approximate either to the later ballade or to the virelai: no.4, *Fines amouretes ai*, and no.16, *Dieus soit en cheste maison*. If we ignore the initial refrain (C_7–C_7) of this latter piece, it then has ballade-like proportions, though there are only two stanzas. Starting at line 3, it can be represented thus: I(a_5–b_7) I(a_5–b_7) II(b_7–c_5–C_7–C_7).

With the Parisian Jehannot de l'Escurel (*d* 1304) we find that all three forms, ballade, virelai and rondeau, are completely distinct from one another. Jehannot left 32 settings of lyrics of which 15 are ballades, all monophonic. *Amours, que vous ai meffait* is fairly typical in its style and structure: I(a_7–b_7) I(a_7–b_7) II(b_7–c_7–B_7–C_7). The first musical section has the characteristic first-time (OUVERT) and second-time (*clos*) cadences, and the whole melody shows a greater rhythmic freedom than in the work of Adam de la Halle. This was largely due to the greater refinement of a notational system that already had many of the features of Ars Nova notation. Jehannot's ballades display a flexible approach within the general framework. In some stanzas only one line takes up the whole of the first musical section; in others shorter lines come at almost any point in the setting; in others the refrain is two or more lines long. The early 14th-century taste for eight and three syllables to the line was superseded towards the middle of the century by a preference for ten and seven syllables, though many exceptions can be found.

In Guillaume de Machaut's ballades the refrain is normally one line long; and the short line of text, if any, normally opens the second musical section, as in a typical example, *De toutes flours* (bars 1–8, ex.2): I(a_{10}–b_{10}) I(a_{10}–b_{10}) II(c_7–c_{10}–d_{10}–D_{10}). In this piece a number of important developments appear. The most notable are: elaborate melismas, especially on final syllables; frequent use of syncopation; setting for solo voice with accompanying parts that are clearly instrumental; and extension of the

Ex.2

second musical section to give the refrain greater prominence, preceded and closed by a cadence and reiterating material from the finish of the first musical section. Machaut's contribution was above all to standardize the *formes fixes* and to make them popular; however, among the 42 ballades that he set to music are a number that show a continued interest in experimentation. One of these, *Dous amis, oy mon complaint*, has a fairly elaborate metrical structure of a type more often found in the virelai: I(a_7–a_4–a_3–b_7) I(a_7–a_4–a_3–b_7) II(b_4–b_3–a_7) II(b_4–b_3–A_7). The most striking feature here is the repetition of the second musical section as well as of the first; this extension of the normal form is to be found in a number of 14th-century examples, sometimes described as *baladelle*. Machaut's 'double ballade', *Quant Theseus/Ne quier veoir*, is notable for its application to ballade setting of the 13th- and 14th-century motet polytextual technique; here two voices simultaneously sing different texts, though

Ex.3

Ex.4

Char - le gen - til. c'on dit _____

Char - le gen - til.

Char - le gen - til.

_____ de Ma - le - tes _____

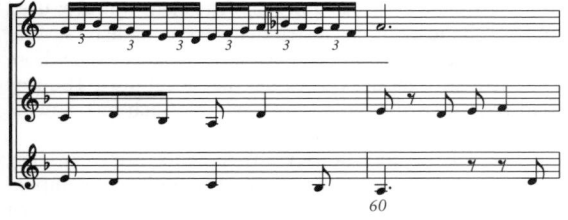

on the same subject, with the same metre and the same refrain. This idea, too, was taken up in a number of 14th- and 15th-century settings of virelais and rondeaux as well.

The Ars Subtilior of the late 14th century brought no structural advance to the composition of the ballade. But

the highly inventive poet-musicians who were fostered in the southern courts of Orthez, Navarre, Barcelona and Avignon – such as Cuvelier, Anthonello de Caserta, Philippus de Caserta, Senleches, Trebor, Solage, Vaillant and Matteo da Perugia – as well as composers in Cyprus, introduced very intricate and subtle rhythmic ideas and often permitted passages of extreme dissonance, while maintaining the setting for the basic forces of voice (mostly in the tenor or countertenor range) and two or three accompanying instruments. Ex.3, bars 15–20 of Philippus de Caserta's *En remirant vo douce pourtraiture*, is typical.

Late 14th-century ballade texts are often in praise of patrons or in celebration of historical events; in the main, however, the ballade was throughout its history the preferred form for the serious love song. Machaut wrote nearly 200 ballades contained in his *La louange des dames* with no musical setting, nearly all on the theme of courtly love. The increasing complexity of musical composition must have been the main contributing factor to the subsequent divorce between poets and musicians; after Machaut no major French poet set his own verses to music, though many, such as Froissart, Deschamps, Christine de Pisan, Chartier, Charles d'Orléans and Villon, continued to use the *formes fixes*, in particular the ballade and the rondeau. In the musical context the ballade receded from favour in the early 15th century when the rondeau became extremely popular. (For a more detailed discussion of the relative popularity of the three principal forms in the 14th and 15th centuries *see* VIRELAI.)

15th-century Burgundian composers nevertheless produced a number of pieces in ballade form. The main innovation, apart from the relative simplicity in style, which was itself a reaction against previous excesses, is the frequent use of a purely instrumental introduction before the entry of the singer(s). Composers such as

Woman singing to a harp, with the opening of the three-voice ballade 'De ce que fol pense' by Phillippe des Molins (Chancellor to the Duke of Berry in 1368): detail of an Arras tapestry, 1420 (Musée des Arts Décoratifs, Paris)

Binchois and Du Fay were able to put their individual stamp on the ballade, as is amply demonstrated by the striking passage in ex.4, from Du Fay's *Resvelliés vous*. This type of song was popular in Italy and was emulated in England, for instance by Walter Frye or Johannes Bedyngham. Later in the 15th century, Dutch and German examples are found, often in Florentine songbooks. Attempts to combine texts and melodies of different national origins generally resulted, however, in the breakdown of the traditional *formes fixes*.

For bibliography *see* CHANSON.

NIGEL WILKINS

Ballade (ii). A term applied to an instrumental (normally piano) piece in a narrative style. It was first used by Chopin (Ballade in G minor op.23, published in 1836 but begun in 1831). He composed four ballades, whose common features are compound metre (6/4 or 6/8) and a structure that is based on thematic metamorphosis governed not so much by formal musical procedures as by a programmatic or literary intention. Full of melodic beauty, harmonic richness and powerful climaxes, they are among his finest achievements. They were said to have been inspired by the ballad poetry of his compatriot Adam Mickiewicz, particularly by his *Świteź* and *Świtezianka*, poems concerning a lake near Nowogródek and a nymph of the lake; but Chopin himself provided no evidence whatever for that belief and probably had no specific ballad or story in mind.

Franck's Ballade op.9 (1844) and Liszt's in D♭ (1845–8) and B minor (1853) follow Chopin's in not being associated with particular literary sources. The earliest such association is in the first of Brahms's Four Ballades op.10 (1854), which bears the heading 'After the Scottish ballad "Edward" in Herder's "Stimmen der Völker"' (Herder's translation of *Edward* had previously been set to music by Loewe and Schubert); but, as Mies suggested, Brahms may have originally planned it as a vocal work in strophic form and converted it into a piano piece while he composed it. Brahms's ballades, attractive examples of his early manner, are distinguishable from Chopin's by their clearer form – usually three-part song form. A strophic form, that most naturally implied by the literary ballad, underlies Grieg's *Ballade in Form von Variationen über eine norwegische Melodie* op.24 (1875–6).

Although instrumental ballades are usually for the piano, among those for other media are Vieuxtemps' Ballade and Polonaise op.38 (c1860), for violin with orchestra or piano, Fauré's Ballade op.19 (1881), for piano and orchestra, and several examples, both chamber and orchestral, by Frank Martin. Orchestral ballades (some designated 'ballad') have usually been inspired by literary sources, often well-known poems, for example Dukas' *L'apprenti sorcier* (based on Goethe's *Der Zauberlehrling*), Somervell's *Helen of Kirkconnell* and Mac-Cunn's *The Ship o' the Fiend*. With the orchestral ballade in particular, the distinction between the ballade and its related forms, the rhapsody and the symphonic poem, appears slight.

BIBLIOGRAPHY

P. Mies: 'Herders Edvard-Ballade bei Joh. Brahms', *ZMw*, ii (1919–20), 225–32

G. Axel: *Die Klavier-Ballade* (diss., U. of Vienna, 1934)

C. Engelbrecht: 'Zur Vorgeschichte der Chopinschen Klavierballade', *Chopin Congress: Warsaw 1960*, 519–21

G. Wagner: *Die Klavierballade um die Mitte des 19. Jahrhunderts* (Munich, 1976)

P.V. Turrill: *The Piano Ballade in the Romantic Era* (diss., U. of Southern California, 1977)

D. Witten: 'Ballads and Ballades', *Piano Quarterly*, xxix/1 (1981), 33–7

J. Parakilas: *Ballads without Words: Chopin and the Tradition of the Instrumental Ballade* (Portland, OR, 1992)

MAURICE J.E. BROWN

Ballad horn. A tenor brass instrument with three valves, circular in shape and pitched in *c* (TRUMPET family). It has a conical bore and a bell about 18 cm in diameter. An amateur's instrument, it was designed to play from songsheets or piano music without transposition.

The ballad horn was introduced by the London maker Henry Distin about 1856. Distin's instruments were made in 'bell-down' (french horn) form (see illustration), but Boosey & Co., who took over the Distin firm in 1868, added a 'bell-up' version and a version pitched an octave higher, which they called the liedhorn. Mouthpieces were funnel-shaped with an 18 mm inner rim diameter. Boosey supplied B♭ crooks with their ballad horns to allow them to be played with other brass instruments in B♭ and E♭, but there is no evidence that the instrument was ever used in brass bands. Similar instruments were made by several other makers, most notably Rudall, Carte & Co., whose 'bell-forward' model was called the 'vocal horn' (Boosey had registered the ballad horn name). Such instruments were very popular and many examples survive.

The Distin and Boosey instruments are very easy blowing and remarkably in tune, even with non-compensating valves. Their tone lies somewhere between that of the french horn and that of the baritone of the brass band, soft and flexible, mellow and lyrical. The last ballad horns were made in the mid-1920s, but their use was revived in the late 20th century in small ensembles of 19th-century brass instruments. Only a single piece published for the instrument has so far come to light: the *Fantaisie originale* (London, 1876) by Carnaud the younger, specified for euphonium, bassoon or ballad horn, with piano. An *Instruction Book for the Concert or Vocal Horn* by G. Tamplini was published c1882.

BIBLIOGRAPHY

J. Webb: 'Notes on the Ballad Horn', *GSJ*, xxxvii (1984), 57–61

JOHN WEBB

Ballad horn by Distin, c1860 (private collection)

Ballad opera. A distinctively English form in which spoken dialogue alternates with songs set to traditional or popular melodies and sung by the actors themselves. A vogue for the form was sparked by the enormous popularity of John Gay's *The Beggar's Opera* (January 1728) but faded out by the mid-1730s. Some 80 such works were written in these years, but only a handful remained in the repertory. The genre was invented by Gay as a complex vehicle for both harsh and subtle satire; for most of his successors it quickly became little more than a way of padding out farces with popular music.

1. Terminology. 2. Origins, *The Beggar's Opera*. 3. Successors.

1. TERMINOLOGY. The term 'ballad opera' is a misnomer. The works so described are plays (almost always comic, usually farcical) into which a variety of songs have been worked. Fewer than half the songs are actually popular ballads: the sources of the music vary widely, ranging from D'Urfey's *Wit and Mirth, or Pills to Purge Melancholy* to arias from Handel's operas and movements of Italian concertos. Sources have been found in *The English Dancing Master* (1651 and its derivatives), traditional favourites such as *Lilliburlero* and *Tweedside*, and most of the popular composers of the time. Among the acknowledged sources are Thomas Arne, Giovanni Bononcini, Henry Carey, Corelli, Francesco Gasparini, Francesco Geminiani, J.B. Grano, Leveridge and Pepusch; among those identified by later scholars are Blow, Jeremiah Clarke, Giovanni Battista Draghi, John Eccles, Galliard, J.F. Lampe, Locke, Henry Purcell and Weldon. In every instance, however, the music is fitted with new words, and the songs are integrated into the dramatic structure of the play, not simply interpolated as variety or entr'acte entertainment.

2. ORIGINS, 'THE BEGGAR'S OPERA'. The sudden appearance of ballad opera in 1728 remains one of the mysteries of 18th-century theatre history. Late 17th-century English plays were heavily laden with music, and many works included integral songs sung by the actors themselves. But these roles were confined to a few specialists, such as Thomas Doggett and Anne Bracegirdle, and the music was freshly written by mainstream composers. Gay's innovation was twofold: to have all the characters sing as much as they speak, and to use tunes well known to everyone. Such generic precursors as can be found are surprisingly remote in both date and kind – Thomas Duffett's musical travesties of the 1670s and Richard Estcourt's musical farce *Prunella* (1708), a crude satire on Giovanni Bononcini's Italian opera *Camilla* (London première, 1706). Whether Gay was familiar with any of these works is uncertain. He may have known contemporaneous plays of the Théâtre Italien and the Théâtres de la Foire in Paris, which included popular tunes fitted with new verses. The immediate inspiration for *The Beggar's Opera* seems to have been provided by Jonathan Swift, who suggested that Gay write 'a Newgate [prison] Pastoral, among the Whores and Thieves there'. None of this detracts from Gay's originality, for *The Beggar's Opera* was radically new: 'instead of cardboard heroes of antiquity, Gay offered very real modern Londoners; instead of noble sentiments, every crime in the calendar' (Fiske). Today *The Beggar's Opera* is usually performed as a charming period piece, but in 1728 it provoked denunciations for incitement to immorality. More to the point, it confronted the audience with an ironic exaltation of criminals and prostitutes that was in radical contrast to the usual decorum of the 18th-century theatre. This was an innovation in which Gay was not followed by his successors.

As Gay conceived it, ballad opera is a fast-moving satirical drama of low-life characters in which the actors frequently break into song. *The Beggar's Opera* contains 69 songs; they are rarely separated by more than a page of spoken dialogue. The familiarity of the music renders it rich in extra-textual references which could either enhance the emotional impact of the dramatic situation or (more often) render it delightfully preposterous. Gay's snide incongruities between his new words and the old ones are a particular pleasure of the piece. For example, in Act 1 scene ix, Peachum's rather lame attack on the legal profession, 'A fox may steal your hens, sir', was set to Eccles's 'A soldier and a sailor' (from Congreve's *Love for Love*), whose notoriously rude original verses would have added an unspoken barb to Gay's message. By no means all the songs in ballad operas were satirical; for sentimental scenes, Gay often chose similarly sentimental music. Many of his less gifted imitators were insensitive to musical reference and simply searched through the popular collections, especially the volumes of Scotch airs, for any tune that would suit a particular verse, regardless of the character of the music itself.

The Beggar's Opera has often been said to be a savage satire on Italian opera as Handel was producing it at the King's Theatre, Haymarket, in the 1720s; it has even been credited with the demise of the Royal Academy of Music in 1728. Neither claim is true. Gay certainly satirized some of the conventions of *opera seria* and its squabbling performers, but he was by no means hostile to Handel, and the troubles of the Italian opera were not caused by competition from popular English fare. Nonetheless, Gay's allusions probably tickled opera fanciers. In the introduction to *The Beggar's Opera*, the Beggar clearly alludes to the rivalry between the sopranos Faustina and Cuzzoni, for whom Handel in *Alessandro* (1726) had written parts of almost exactly equal weight. Gay's improbable happy ending is also a parody of the perfunctory *lieto fine* of Italian opera. But not all reference was satirical. Macheath's brilliantly dramatic soliloquy in 'the Condemn'd Hold' (Act 3 scene xiii), an unbroken chain of ten airs or snatches of tunes, while ultimately modelled on the mad-song concatenations of Purcell or Eccles, is remarkably similar in style to some of Handel's big accompanied recitatives and uncannily anticipates the mad scene in *Orlando* (1733).

The Beggar's Opera was originally produced at Lincoln's Inn Fields by John Rich after it was refused at Drury Lane. In its first partial season it ran for 62 performances, a total far surpassing any play in the recorded history of the London theatre. As early as summer 1728 it was pirated at the Little Haymarket, and the rival Drury Lane company naturally hastened to commission and produce ballad operas. At first these were, like Gay's original, ambitious three-act 'mainpieces': Charles Johnson's *The Village Opera* (Drury Lane, 1729 – ultimately the basis for Isaac Bickerstaff's pasticcio comic opera, *Love in a Village*, 1762), Ebenezer Forrest's *Momus Turn'd Fabulist* (Lincoln's Inn Fields, 1729), James Ralph's *The Fashionable Lady, or Harlequin's Opera* (Goodman's Fields, 1730), Joseph Mitchell's *Highland Fair* and *The Jovial Crew* (both Drury Lane,

'The Stage Medley': satirical engraving aimed at the taste of the town and its admiration for John Gay's 'The Beggar's Opera' (music arranged by J.C. Pepusch), first performed at Lincoln's Inn Fields Theatre, 29 January 1728; top left are portraits of Lavinia Fenton and Thomas Walker, the first Polly Peachum and Macheath

1731). None of these expensive experiments entered the repertory. *Polly*, Gay's sequel to *The Beggar's Opera*, was suppressed by the Lord Chamberlain in December 1728: Sir Robert Walpole did not fancy having himself impersonated as a pirate who meets a richly deserved end on the gallows and kept it off the boards, although Gay made a small fortune by publishing this rather heavy-handed satire.

3. SUCCESSORS.   An enormous variety of ballad operas were produced between 1728 and about 1735. Historical subjects were tried, as in the anonymous *Robin Hood* (1730) and Walter Aston's *The Restauration of King Charles II* (suppressed in 1732 on suspicion of Jacobite implications). John Mottley and Thomas Cooke's *Penelope* (Little Haymarket, 1728) is a delightful little classical spoof: Sergeant Ulysses, who went off to Marlborough's wars, is now living with Circe in Rotterdam, drinking gin; his faithful wife Penelope keeps a London pub and finds herself courted by the local tinker, tailor and butcher. Another such satire is John Breval's *The Rape of Helen* (1733). The best known of this 'classical' group is Gay's posthumous *Achilles* (1733), a rather sodden reprise of the hero-in-petticoats story. Gay never came close to recapturing the charm and bite of his first effort.

With the exception of *The Beggar's Opera*, ballad operas which entered the repertory were all afterpieces, including some which started out as full-length main-pieces. Colley Cibber's *Love in a Riddle* (Drury Lane, 1729) was probably the victim of audience hostility to the author; cut down as *Damon and Phillida*, and produced anonymously at the Little Haymarket the same year, it was long popular. It is a good example of the form's penchant for sentimentalized country low-life and im-probable romance plots. Charles Coffey's *The Devil to Pay* (1731) had a disastrous first night in the off season; the songs were cut from 48 to 16 by Theophilus Cibber and the piece became one of the century's most enduring entertainments. Ballad operas of the early 1730s could be as chastely pastoral and moral as George Lillo's *Sylvia* (Lincoln's Inn Fields, 1730) or as essentially lower-class sentimental as Carey's *The Honest Yorkshireman* (Little Haymarket, 1735), but most tend towards the farcical.

The most important practitioner of ballad opera after Gay was Henry Fielding, now remembered largely as a novelist (*Tom Jones*). Yet Fielding was the foremost English dramatist of his time, and among his 30 plays are about ten that can be plausibly classified as ballad opera, though they vary considerably in the amount of music employed. Fielding's first attempt at the form was *The Author's Farce* (Little Haymarket, 1730, radically revised in 1734) a boisterous spoof on Grub Street life and a brazen attack on theatre managers at Drury Lane and Lincoln's Inn Fields. *The Welsh Opera* (Little Haymarket, 1731) is an impudent political allegory that helped get the theatre suppressed: Fielding exhibits King George II, Queen Caroline, the Prince of Wales, Walpole and Pulteney as master, mistress, not-so-hopeful heir and principal servants in the disorganized household of Squire Ap-Shinken, an amiable Welshman whose only wish is peace and quiet in which to smoke and drink. Fielding expanded the work as *The Grub-Street Opera* (a much more dangerous satire), but the authorities closed the Little Haymarket and appear to have bribed Fielding to withdraw the play, although it received a pirate printing. *Don Quixote in England* (written 1728; staged at Drury

Lane, 1734) was a failure, a scrappy farce with incidental music. *Deborah, or A Wife for you All* (Drury Lane, March 1733) survived just one night and was not printed. It appears to have been a satire on Handel's oratorio *Deborah*.

Several of Fielding's most lastingly successful plays were part of the series of ballad-opera farces concocted for the popular singer-actress Kitty Clive at Drury Lane: *The Lottery* (1732), *The Mock Doctor* (1732), *The Intriguing Chambermaid* (1734), *An Old Man Taught Wisdom* (1735, usually performed as *The Virgin Un-mask'd*), *Eurydice* (1737) and *Miss Lucy in Town* (1742). Except for the last two, all remained theatrical staples throughout the 18th century. *The Lottery* and *The Intriguing Chambermaid* are lightweight musical farce – the latter adapted from Jean François Regnard's *Le retour imprévu* (1700), turning the clever valet into the maid Lettice as a vehicle for Clive. *The Mock Doctor* is a free translation of Molière with just nine songs worked in. *The Virgin Unmask'd* exemplifies Fielding's comic skills: Old Goodwill decides to marry off his silly 15-year-old daughter; she listens to proposals from five boobies (an apothecary, a dancing-master, an Oxford student, a singing-master and a lawyer), accepts three of them – and then elopes with a footman whose fine clothes and elegant *coiffure* have gone to her head. The work offers more ridicule than satire, and Fielding quickly reduced his original 20 songs to 12. It was designed solely to display the talents of Kitty Clive, and both she and her successors found that it worked to perfection.

Fielding's most interesting and ambitious ballad operas are his last two, both of which burlesque Italian opera. Unfortunately the music is lost and the arrangers are unknown. *Eurydice* died in one night, ruined by a footmen's riot at Drury Lane. The piece travesties Orpheus (Stoppelaer) and Eurydice (Clive) as society wastrels from London. Pluto is henpecked; Eurydice tricks Orpheus in order to remain in hell; Orpheus becomes a swipe at Farinelli, the reigning castrato star of the Opera of the Nobility. Nine airs and a 'Grand Dance' and 'Chorus' are included, the airs preceded by 'Recitativo' in English. *Miss Lucy in Town* is a sequel to *The Virgin Unmask'd*. Lord Bawble satirizes Lord Middlesex as director of the opera. Horace Walpole wrote to a friend that 'Mrs Clive mimics the Muscovita [Lord Middlesex's mistress] admirably, and Beard Amorevoli intolerably'. The piece proved quite popular for a season.

Ballad opera was short-lived. *The Beggar's Opera* proved that there was a large, untapped audience in London, and contributed to the establishment of Goodman's Fields Theatre, the increasing use of the Little Haymarket, and the construction of Covent Garden in 1732. Among Gay's successors only Fielding really understood how to use the form to good advantage in several sorts of plays, and in the operatic travesties we find him moving into what must have been newly composed pieces that take us into the realm of burletta. A handful of influential ballad operas continued to be performed throughout the rest of the 18th century, but the later burlettas and English operas of Arne, Dibdin, Storace, the Linleys and others, though often including ballad tunes, bear little resemblance to true ballad opera.

One reason for the relatively brief popularity of the original form is that the quality of the musical perform-ances cannot have been very high. Most of the actors were not trained singers, although the demands of the genre helped to produce a new generation of actors who possessed the necessary musical skills. The extent to which the singers were accompanied is unknown. The arrangements provided by Pepusch, Carey and Seedo are often crude in the extreme, even eschewing the original (and easily obtainable) basses of the pieces they were arranging. Nor was much care taken to preserve the integrity of 'composed' melodies of Purcell, Handel and others. Nevertheless, the theatres which produced ballad operas maintained fairly large orchestras (a dozen or so, mostly strings), and paylists show that the instrumentalists attended every night. Given the presence of the orchestra, we must presume that it was used.

Only *The Beggar's Opera* is now performed, and just a handful of other ballad operas retain even much historical interest. The form is important, however, for its contribution to the musicalization of the British theatre which is one of its most conspicuous features in the second half of the 18th century.

BIBLIOGRAPHY

FiskeETM; NicollH

W.B. Squire: 'An Index of Tunes in the Ballad Operas', *MA*, ii (1910–11), 1–17

F. Kidson: *The Beggar's Opera: its Predecessors and Successors* (Cambridge, 1922/R)

W.E. Schultz: *Gay's Beggar's Opera: its Content, History, & Influence* (New Haven, CT, 1923/R)

E.McA. Gagey: *Ballad Opera* (New York, 1937/R)

W.H. Rubsamen: 'The Ballad Burlesques and Extravaganzas', *MQ*, xxxvi (1950), 551–61

E.V. Roberts: 'Eighteenth-Century Ballad Opera: the Contribution of Henry Fielding', *Drama Survey*, i (1961–2), 77–85

E.V. Roberts: 'Mr Seedo's London Career and his Work with Henry Fielding', *Philological Quarterly*, xlv (1966), 179–90

H. Moss: *Ballad-Opera Songs: a Record of the Ideas Set to Music, 1728–1733* (diss., U. of Michigan, 1970)

L.J. Morrissey: 'Henry Fielding and the Ballad Opera', *Eighteenth-Century Studies*, iv (1971), 386–402

W.H. Rubsamen, ed.: *The Ballad Opera: a Collection of 171 Original Texts of Musical Plays Printed in Photo-Facsimile* (New York, 1974)

R.D. Hume: *Henry Fielding and the London Theatre, 1728–1737* (Oxford, 1988)

CURTIS PRICE, ROBERT D. HUME

Ballantine, Edward (*b* Oberlin, OH, 6 Aug 1886; *d* Oak Bluffs, MA, 2 July 1971). American composer. He studied at Harvard University (BA 1907) with Walter Spalding and Frederick Converse, then went to Berlin, where he was a student of Artur Schnabel, Rudolf Ganz and Philippe Rüfer (1907–9). In 1912 he was appointed to the music faculty of Harvard, and remained there until his retirement in 1947. His music, cast in a post-Romantic, tonal and accessible style, is often marked by humour, occasionally by a satirical eclecticism. These traits are most apparent in his best-known pieces, sets of piano variations on *Mary had a little lamb* (1924, 1943), in which each variation is in the style of a different composer, and in the *Four Lyrical Satires* for voice and piano.

WORKS
(selective list)

Stage: The Lotus Eaters (masque, D.W. Streeter), 1907

Orch: Prelude to 'The Delectable Forest', 1914; The Eve of St Agnes, 1917; By a Lake in Russia, 1922; From the Garden of Hellas, 1923

Chbr and solo inst: Morning, pf, 1913; Sonata, vn, pf; Mary Had a Little Lamb, variations, pf: ser. 1, 1924; ser. 2, 1943

Vocal: Retrospect (Ballantine), 1913; Four Lyrical Satires, v, pf; Song for a Future (T. Spencer), mixed vv (New York, 1945); Lake Werna's Water (E. Bronte), SSAA (New York, 1946); other choruses and songs

Principal publishers: O. Ditson, G. Schirmer, A.P. Schmidt

BIBLIOGRAPHY

S. Arzuni: 'An American Jester', *Keyboard Classics*, xiv/5 (1994), 54–6

H. WILEY HITCHCOCK/MICHAEL MECKNA

Ballard. French family of music printers and composers. They were important for over 200 years.

(1) Robert Ballard (i) (*b* Montreuil-sur-Mer, ?1525–30; *d* Paris, bur. 8 July 1588). The son of Michel Ballard and Colassé Le Roy, he was the founder, along with his cousin Adrian Le Roy, of the printing firm of Le Roy & Ballard. The first document showing their association, by which Le Roy and Ballard received a privilege for printing music from Henri II, is dated 14 August 1551. On 16 February 1553 the partners received the title of music printers to the king (the title held by Attaingnant until his death in late 1551 or 1552). It was reaffirmed in 1568 under Charles IX and in 1594 under Henri IV and was to continue for other members of the family until the mid-18th century.

On 30 October 1559 Ballard married Lucrèce Dugué, who brought him and the firm valuable connections with the musical and political life of the court. Her father Jean Dugué was organist to the king, and Dugué's nephew Pierre was attached to the retinue of the king's brother. Through her mother Perrette Edinthon she was related to Charles Edinthon, lutenist in the king's chamber from 1542 to 1572, and to Jacques Edinthon, lutenist and *valet de chambre* to the king from 1575 to 1590. Since Le Roy also had important connections with court circles and even with Charles IX himself, the influence of the firm at court was assured.

Le Roy, a composer and lutenist of note, was the artistic director of the firm while Ballard seems to have assumed the role of business manager. The two partners worked well together; most transactions, such as the buying of considerable properties outside Paris or contracting for shop repairs, were undertaken jointly. There was nevertheless some independence; for example, one of the rare non-musical works, *Le siège et prinse de Thionville* (1558), bears the name of Ballard alone.

After a three-year break in the firm's production on Ballard's death, Le Roy took up printing again in association with Ballard's widow Lucrèce until his own death in 1598. Le Roy, whose wife had died some time before 1570, was childless, and he left all his share of the property to the widow and heirs of Ballard. Lucrèce carried on the business after Le Roy's death with her son Pierre until 1607, when Pierre began publishing in his own name. Lucrèce was still living in 1611, when a document shows her to have been engaged in settling Le Roy's legacy for her six children.

Its important connections at court, the knowledgeable choice of repertory, the skill in printing and the beauty of its editions gave Le Roy & Ballard a virtual monopoly on music printing in France during the second half of the 16th century. Other printers in Lyons and Paris (including Fezandat, Gorlier and Granjon) issued only occasional musical editions. The firm's most important rival was Nicolas Du Chemin of Paris, who had begun to print music in 1549. Du Chemin was not a musician himself and depended on others to choose and edit the music that he printed. After his editor Claude Goudimel resigned in 1555, he was not able to maintain the brilliant pace

Two facing pages from 'Cinquiesme livre de guiterre' (Paris: Le Roy & Ballard, 1554), showing the voice and guitar parts of Le Roy's 'L'esté chault bouilloit'

Au lict me posay
Pour freschement estre,
Et me reposay
Pour mon aise croistre:
Tant fut la fenestre
Propre à mon desir,
Qu'on n'eust sceu congnoistre
S'il fut iour ou nuict.

Fermée à demy,
A demy ouuerte,
Melloit nuict parmy
Clarté descouuerte:
La forest couuerte
De fueillage frais
Monstroit l'herbe verte
En tel ombre espais.

Voicy arriuer
Celye tant blanche,
Qu'on voit en yuer
Neige dessus branche:
Sa vesture franche
Sa ceinture ouuroit
Vne ferme hanche,
Qui rien ne couuroit,

Son poil long doré
Iusqu'à la racine
Pendoit esgaré
Dessus sa poictrine:
Luy faisant crespine
D'or, au blanc tetin,
Plus poignant qu'espine,
Plus lis que satin.

D'elle m'aprochay
Sous amoureus signe,
Et luy arrachay
Sa chemise fine:
Elle d'une mine
Honteuse à l'ouurir,
Sa beauté diuine
S'efforçoit couurir.

Mais en debatant
Comme ia batue
Fut du combatant
Bien tost abatue,
Qui la serra nue
Dans douce prison,
Aisement vaincue
Par ma trahison.

Mon dieu quelle lors
Espaule touchay-ie,
Quels bras beaus & forts
Vey-ie & empongnay-ie:
Quel tetin cachay-ie
Tout dedans ma main.
Quelle blanche neige
Vey-ie sur son sein.

Quel ventre arondi
Que ride ne plisse,
Quel bas rebondi,
Quelle ronde cuisse,
Quelle hanche propice,
Quel ferme costé,
Pour courir en lice
Du dieu de beauté.

Mais qu'est il besoing
Que pour vn ie compte,
Ie vey son tout loing
De blasme & de honte:
Et pour fin du compte
La pressoye si fort,
Qu'elle me surmonte
D'un semblable effort.

Que diray-ie plus,
Chacun peult entendre
Quel fut le surplus
De ce debat tendre:
Contraint fus de me rendre
Lassé du combat,
Or dieu me doint prendre
Souuent tel esbat.

A iij

established earlier. By about 1560 he was no longer a serious rival.

Between 1551 and 1598 Le Roy & Ballard published more than 3000 works in about 350 known editions. Tablature books for lute and guitar were prominent in the first few years of the firm's production, where Le Roy's expertise was undoubtedly a major asset. But secular vocal music accounts for most of his output, with some 1500 chansons printed and reprinted in a series of 25 *Livres de chansons* between 1552 and 1585 as well as in other collections, and a further 500 or so strophic *airs* (*de cour*) increasingly supplanting the chanson in more than 20 prints between 1571 and 1598. About 650 motets and 500 psalms and other sacred songs appeared in

various collections from 1555 onwards, with 52 masses concentrated especially in the years 1557 to 1559. There were 17 books of instrumental music for lute, cistre, mandora and guitar, including four instruction books for these instruments by Le Roy; they contain music by Le Roy himself (see illustration), Pierre Brunet, Gregor Brayssing of Augsburg, Alberto da Ripa and Bálint Bakfark. Two treatises on music theory were published, one in 1582 written by Jean Yssandon and one in 1583 by Le Roy.

The firm also helped to disseminate Italian music in France, with over 200 Italian and some Spanish pieces mostly printed in the last two decades of the century. Many of these were by Lassus, who was a friend of Le

Roy, and was the composer most frequently published by the firm. Le Roy & Ballard played an important part in disseminating his newest works in France and in Europe generally. Others frequently represented in the firm's output were Arcadelt, Certon, Costeley, Goudimel, Janequin, Le Jeune, Maillard and Claudin de Sermisy.

The typographical material was particularly fine. The elaborate woodcut borders on the title-pages, the printer's marks and the 'lettres grises' or historiated woodcut initials in several sizes in the style of Jean Cousin are superb examples of French Renaissance graphic art. At least three sets of punches of music were made by the famous typecutter Guillaume Le Bé (i). Autograph notes of Le Bé cite in 1554–5 a 'musique grosse', in 1559 a 'petite tablature d'épinette sur la moyenne musique' and at an unspecified date in the 1550s a 'grosse tablature d'épinette pour imprimer à deux foys' sold to Le Roy & Ballard (for illustration see GANDO). One of the sets of punches for spinet tablature was a sample, according to the notes. No book of spinet music by Le Roy & Ballard is extant, nor is there any mention of any in contemporary sources. (4) Christophe Ballard used the small set in 1678 to print a book of Airs à 2 et 3 parties de feu monsieur le Camus, so Le Bé's punches did not go to waste. Robert Granjon cut a set of type for lute tablature for some books he published himself in 1551 and 1552, and then it became the property of Le Roy & Ballard. Both the music types and the 'lettres grises' continued in use unchanged past the mid-18th century.

(2) Pierre Ballard (b Paris, ?1575–80; d Paris, 4 Oct 1639). Music printer, son of (1) Robert Ballard (i). In partnership with his mother he carried on the business after the death of Le Roy. On 25 March 1607 letters-patent from Henri IV officially made him music printer to the king, and henceforth the editions appeared under his name alone. The privilege was renewed by Louis XIII in 1611 and 1633.

An example of one of the many challenges to the power of the house of Ballard over the years occurred after the musician NICOLAS MÉTRU had received a privilege to print music in 1633. Pierre Ballard brought a suit to stop him, and in 1635 the court removed Métru's privilege in exchange for a commitment from Ballard to publish Métru's compositions. On 29 April 1637 Louis XIII issued a decree praising the beauty of the notes and characters of Ballard, which 'far surpass those made in foreign kingdoms and provinces', confirmed the title of royal music printer and stated that no further privileges to print music would be given without Ballard's consent. According to Fournier, Ballard must have granted his consent at times, because there is a record of his having sold matrices of music type called Cicero to Guillaume Le Bé (ii).

Pierre Ballard concentrated on printing airs de cour and similar small-scale vocal genres (such as psalms or, from 1627, chansons pour dancer et pour boire) by composers associated with the royal court such as Guédron and Antoine (de) Boësset, almost to the exclusion of other forms. He largely ignored instrumental music, such as that of the flourishing school of French lute composers, though he did publish collections by his brother, Robert Ballard (ii), and organ music by Titelouze, as well as providing the music examples for Mersenne's Harmonie universelle in 1636–7.

He had eight or ten children; on 8 January 1639 he officially named his son Robert as his heir, with a royal guarantee that the firm's monopoly of music printing would continue. An inventory dated 30 November 1639, mentioned by Gando in 1766, has not been found.

(3) Robert Ballard (ii) (b ?Paris, c1575; d after 1649). Lutenist and composer, son of (1) Robert Ballard (i). He apparently never took part in the family business. His father's partner Adrian Le Roy was probably his first lute teacher; after Le Roy's death in 1598 he became a lutenist of some distinction, and by 1600 he was teaching the lute to his landlord's son in lieu of part of his rent. In 1611 he published his first lutebook, and in the following year the regent, Maria de' Medici, employed him as her maître de luth; in this capacity he became responsible in September 1612 for the tuition of the young King Louis XIII. In 1615 he was still in Maria's service and performed on the lute in the Ballet de Madame; but in the retrenchments of court expenditure of 1618 his salaried position was terminated and he was henceforth paid only as required. Under this arrangement he continued for 16 years to bear the title 'musicien ordinaire du roi' and, although a notarial act of 1640 mentioned him only as 'joueur de luth', he was again designated 'musicien du Roy' in 1650. After that date nothing further is known of him.

Most of his works are ballet music arranged for lute and, apart from their musical value, are important as the only extant portions of several court ballets. His sequences of two or three chants in the ballets of 1611 may be seen as early moves in the direction of suite formation, and employ a number of technical effects later to be particularly associated with the sarabande. Partly because he was in a position to ensure that his music survived in a form of which he approved, Robert Ballard may be seen as the outstanding French lutenist at the end of the Renaissance tradition, before the onset of the new style associated with René Mesangeau in the 1620s. His works are almost all in vieil ton tuning, with the robust four-part texture and clearly defined melodic contours of dance music. But, particularly in the doubles of his courantes, he exploits the low tessitura and unpredictably broken texture of the style brisé. His works are the defining model for this phase of French lute music, and the seven pieces published by his brother Pierre in the Tablature de luth de differents autheurs (Paris, 1631), among works by younger contemporaries, have a rather old-fashioned appearance in spite of being in a new tuning.

WORKS
all for lute

[Premier livre de luth] (Paris, 1611/R) [lacks title-page], ed. A. Souris, S. Spycket and M. Rollin (Paris, 1963, 2/1976)
Diverses piesces mises sur le luth (Paris, 1614), ed. A. Souris and others, Deuxième livre (1614), et pièces diverses (Paris, 1964, 2/1976)
Some works in 1603¹⁵, 1610²³, 1631⁶, L. de Moy: Le petit bouquet de frise orientale (n.p., 1631), M. Mersenne: Harmonie universelle (Paris, 1636–7/R; Eng. trans., 1957)

Other works, CZ-Pu, D-Bsb, Ngm, W, GB-Cfm

(4) Robert Ballard (iii) (b Paris, c1610; d Paris, before May 1673). Music printer, son of (2) Pierre Ballard. He received a privilege from Louis XIII dated 24 October 1639 naming him sole printer to the king for music, the first of the Ballards to have exclusivity specified in the title. Independently of his father he had started in business as a bookseller but apparently was not successful, since a

judgment of 16 April 1638 allowed him to postpone paying his creditors for three years. The inheritance from his father immediately relieved him of his financial troubles, and the printing business continued to thrive under his direction.

Early in 1639 the two Jacques de Senlecque, father and son, received a privilege for a new method of printing plainsong. Like his father, Robert continued to guard the firm's music printing monopoly: on 11 February 1640 Robert Ballard brought a suit to prevent them from printing, but the Parlement ruled against him. Robert took the matter up with the king's council, since he did not consider himself, as a member of the king's household, bound by the decisions of the Parlement. A clear decision was never reached, possibly because Louis XIII died in 1643, leaving France to be governed by a regency for the five-year-old Louis XIV. When the younger de Senlecque died in 1660 Ballard offered to buy his punches and matrices from his widow, but the price she set was too high.

Ballard continued to favour secular vocal forms. He abandoned songs with tablature accompaniments after 1643, noting that they did not sell, and published the first French collection of songs with an exclusively continuo accompaniment, Constantijn Huygen's *Pathodia sacra* of 1647. He continued his father's series of *chansons pour dancer et pour boire*, and in 1658 initiated a series of *Livres d'airs de differents autheurs à deux parties* that continued for 30 years. He also expanded the firm's publication of masses, motets and music treatises. Composers prominent in his collections include Henri Du Mont, Bénigne de Bacilly, Mace, Parisot and Lully.

In 1664 the business maintained three presses and engaged three helpers. In 1666 Robert brought in his eldest son (5) Christophe Ballard as helper. On Robert's death the composer Estienne Droüaux wrote a five-voice *De profundis* and a six-voice *Miserere* in his memory.

(5) **Christophe Ballard**   (*b* Paris, 12 April 1641; *d* Paris, before 28 May 1715). Music printer, eldest son of (4) Robert Ballard (iii). On 11 May 1673 he was named sole music printer to the king. In anticipation of his own death his father had obtained letters-patent from the king dated 25 October 1672 to assure Christophe's succeeding him in the title. Like his father, he had started independently in business as a bookseller, besides working as a helper in the family firm. His only brother Pierre (ii) (*d* 1703) also printed music for some time, but a court edict of 8 August 1696 ordered him to turn over his supply of music type to Christophe and denied Pierre or his widow the right to print any more music.

A highpoint in the firm's success, equal to that of the 16th century, was reached in about 1700, when the house maintained four presses and employed nine helpers and two apprentices. Almost all the music of the time was printed by Ballard, including the works of Lully, Brossard, Campra, Charpentier, Collasse, the Couperins, Dandrieu, Hotteterre, Lalande, Lebègue, Marais and Montéclair. The *Airs* appeared in a new form as *Airs sérieux et à boire* with basso continuo, issued monthly up to 1715, and Christophe revised some of the firm's earlier *chansons pour dancer et pour boire* as a series of *brunetes*, adapted for contemporary tastes. For the first time since the 16th century the Ballard firm also began to print Italian songs in a series of *Recueils des meilleurs airs italiens* between 1699 and 1708.

The firm had to undergo many expensive suits in this period, among them one against Lully's son, who had tried to reprint his father's music without Ballard's permission. But a more serious threat was the new method of printing music from engraved plates which had come increasingly into use since the last half of the 17th century. The Ballards continued to use the old movable type method invented in the 16th century and the antiquated lozenge-shaped notes that had been cast for Le Roy & Ballard in the 1550s, rarely investing in any new typographical material. In 1713 Leclair and several other musicians obtained privileges to print music from engraved plates. Ballard entered a suit against them but lost; he was considered to have the exclusive right only to print music in the old method.

(6) **Jean-Baptiste-Christophe Ballard**   (*b* Paris, *c*1663; *d* Paris, May 1750). Music printer, son of (5) Christophe Ballard and Marie Lamielle. He was established as a master printer and bookseller in the rue Frementelle on 6 June 1694. On his father's death he moved to the Ballard shop in the rue Saint-Jean-de-Beauvais and received his father's title as royal printer for music. He continued the monthly *Airs sérieux et à boire* and flooded the market with various 'Tendresses', 'Parodies', 'Amusements' and 'Menuets chantants', in an attempt to capture a wider audience. He produced monumental editions of the works of Lully, Destouches and Campra and was the publisher of Rameau's *Traité* (1722) and *Nouveau système* (1726). During his later years, as more and more engraved music was issued by others, the prestige and influence of the house of Ballard began to decline.

(7) **Christophe-Jean-François Ballard**   (*b* Paris, *c*1701; *d* Paris, 5 Sept 1765). Music printer, son of (6) Jean-Baptiste-Christophe Ballard. He received the royal privilege on the death of his father. He had been active as a bookseller since 1741 and as a printer since 1742. With him the fame and success of the firm ended. A police report described him as 'lazy and untalented'. In the 18th century printing privileges had become less a matter of royal approval than a means to add to the royal treasury. In 1762 a royal decree restricted their period to 15 years and in 1790 they were abolished. The Ballards, equipped with increasingly meaningless privileges, still using lozenge-shaped notes and old-fashioned initial letters from the 16th century, were unwilling or unable to change with the times. A report from a Parlement commission in 1764 said 'the public has been disgusted for a long time with the music of Sieur Ballard'.

After his death, his widow and then his son Pierre-Robert-Christophe (*d* 23 Nov 1812) carried on after a fashion, frequently moving to new locations. In 1800 Ballard was 'printer to the theatres of the Republic and of the arts'. The last of the Ballards was Christophe-Jean-François' grandson, Christophe-Jean-François Ballard (ii) (*d* 16 Oct 1825).

Over the years the Ballard family received many of the royal favours of the *ancien régime*, its members serving as syndics of the booksellers' guild, royal councillors, commercial judges, administrators of charity hospitals and commissioners of artillery. As a special perquisite the Ballard servants were allowed to wear royal livery. Until the declining years of the firm the care in music printing and the beauty of the results were universally praised. The music books of the house of Ballard constitute in themselves a history of French musical taste over 200 years and with its tight control on the publication of music, the firm played no small part in regulating that taste.

BIBLIOGRAPHY

BrownI; MGG1 (V. Fédorov)

P.-S. Fournier: *Traité historique et critique sur l'origine et les progrès des caractères de fonte pour l'impression de la musique* (Berne, 1765/R)

N. and F. Gando: *Observations sur le Traité historique et critique de Monsieur Fournier le Jeune* (Paris, 1766/R)

M. Brenet: 'La librairie musicale en France de 1653 à 1790, d'après les registres de privilèges', *SIMG*, viii (1906–7), 401–66

F. Lesure and G. Thibault: *Bibliographie des éditions d'Adrian le Roy et Robert Ballard (1551–1598)* (Paris, 1955); suppl., *RdM*, xl (1957), 166–72

D. Heartz: 'Parisian Music Publishing under Henry II', *MQ*, xlvi (1960), 448–67

M. Jurgens: *Documents du minutier central concernant l'histoire de la musique 1600–1650*, i (Paris, 1967), 853–5

J. Cain and P. Marot: *Imprimeurs et libraires parisiens du XVIe siècle, d'après les manuscrits de Ph. Renouard*, ii (Paris, 1969)

D. Heartz: *Pierre Attaingnant, Royal Printer of Music* (Berkeley, 1969)

E. Poole: *The Sources for Christophe Ballard's 'Brunetes ou petits airs tendres' and the Tradition of Seventeenth-Century French Song* (diss., U. of Victoria, BC, 1984)

D. Ledbetter: *Harpsichord and Lute Music in 17th-Century France* (London, 1987)

G. Durosoir: *L'air de cour en France 1571–1665* (Liège, 1991)

C. Massip: 'Airs français et italiens dans l'édition française (1643–1710)', *RdM*, lxxvii (1991), 179–85

§3 based on *MGG1* (xv, 438–9) by permission of Bärenreiter

SAMUEL F. POGUE/ JONATHAN LE COCQ (1, 2, 4–7), MONIQUE ROLLIN/DAVID LEDBETTER (3)

Ballard, Louis W(ayne) [Honganózhe] (*b* Devil's Promenade, OK, 8 July 1931). American composer and music educator of Cherokee Indian, Quapaw Indian, French and Scottish descent. (Honganózhe is a Quapaw name that means 'Grand Eagle'.) He studied at the University of Tulsa (BME 1954, BFA 1954, MM 1962) and had private composition lessons with Milhaud, Castelnuovo-Tedesco, Surinach and Labunski. After teaching in Oklahoma (1954–8), he was appointed director of music and performing arts at the Institute of American Indian Arts, Santa Fe (1962–9). Subsequently, as music programme director for the Bureau of Indian Affairs (1969–79), he developed a bicultural music education programme that earned him a Distinguished Service Award from the Central Office of Education and a citation in the Congressional Record (1975). Ballard has held numerous university appointments and has appeared internationally as a guest conductor and lecturer. Among his honours are National Indian Achievement Awards (1972, 1973, 1976), an honorary doctorate from the College of Santa Fe (1973), the first MacDowell Award for American chamber music (1969), and grants from the Rockefeller Foundation (1969), Ford Foundation (1970) and NEA (1967, 1973, 1977, 1982, 1989). In 1997 he was awarded a Lifetime Musical Achievement Award by First Americans in the Arts.

Ballard's compositional style fuses 20th-century techniques with diverse Amerindian influences. An intimate knowledge of Amerindian culture enables him to create innovative works in many genres that sensitively and respectfully recreate tribal worlds. His compositions have been performed by such prominent organizations as the St Paul Chamber Orchestra, the American Composers Orchestra, the Los Angeles PO, the Tulsa PO and the

Harkness Ballet. In 1989 he became the first American composer to have an entire programme dedicated to his music in the newly constructed Beethovenhalle, Bonn.

WORKS

DRAMATIC

Jijogweh, the WitchWater Gull (ballet, after Iroquois Indian myth), 1960, unperf.

Koshare (ballet, choreog. D. Sadler), 1964, Barcelona, 17 May 1966

The Four Moons (ballet, choreog. G. Skibine, R. Jasinski, M. Terekhov, R. Hightower), 1967, Tulsa, OK, 28 Oct 1967

Sacred Ground (film score, dir. R. Jacobs), 1976

The Maid of the Mist and the Thunderbeings (dance score, choreog. R. Trujillo, L. Smith), 1991, Buffalo, NY, 18 Oct 1991

Moontide (The Man who Hated Money) (rock op, 1, L. Ballard), 1992, Norden, 11 April 1994

INSTRUMENTAL

Orch: Fantasy Aborigine no.1 'Sipapu', 1963; Scenes from Indian Life, 1963, arr. concert band, 1970; Why the Duck has a Short Tail (Ballard, R. Dore), nar, orch, 1968; Devil's Promenade, 1972; Incident at Wounded Knee, chbr orch, opt. perc, 1973; Ishi (America's Last Civilized Man), 1975; Fantasy Aborigine: no.2 'Tsiyako', str, 1976, no.3 'Kokopelli', 1977, no.4 'Xactee'oyan, Companion of Talking God', 1982, no.5 'Naniwaya', 1988, no.6 'Niagara', 1991; Feast Day, sketch, 1994

Band: Siouxiana, ww, 1973; Wamus 77 (Indian Heroes, History and Heritage), marching band, 1977; Nighthawk Keetowah Dances, 1978; Ocotillo Festival Ov., 1978

Chbr: Str Trio, 1959; Perc Ego, perc, pf, 1962; Rhapsody, 4 bn, 1963; Cacega Ayuwipi, 5 perc, 1969; Katcina Dances, vc, pf, 1969; Ritmo Indio, ww qnt, 1969; Desert Trilogy, 8 insts, 1970; Midwinter Fires, Amerindian fl, cl, pf, 1970; Pan Indian Dance Rhythms, 4 perc, 1970; Rio Grande Sonata, vn, pf, 1976; Music for the Earth and the Sky, amp cel, 5 perc, 1986; Bellum atramentum, ob, vn, vc, 1988; Capientur a nullo, va, vc, db, 1988; The Lonely Sentinel, fl, ob, tpt, hn, trbn, tuba, 1993; The Fire Moon, str qt, 1997

Solo: 4 American Indian Pf Preludes, 1963; A City of Silver, pf, 1981; A City of Fire, pf, 1984; A City of Light, pf, 1986; Awakening of Love, org, 1992; Quetzalcoatl's Coattails, gui, 1992

VOCAL

Choral: Espiritu di Santiago (Ballard), SATB, fl, gui, pf, 1963; The Gods will Hear (L.H. New), SATB, (perc, pf)/orch, 1964; Mojave Bird Dance Song, SATB, 1964; Portrait of Will Rogers (Ballard, W. Rogers), nar, SATB, pf/orch, 1971; Thus Spake Abraham (cant., Ballard), solo vv, SATB, pf, 1977; Dialogue differentia (orat, Ballard), chorus, orch, 1989; 4 American Indian Christian Hymns, SATB, pf, 1990; Live on, Heart of My Nation (Ballard, M.C. Fry), nar, SATB, chbr orch/pf, 1990

Solo: The Spider Rock (J. Miami), T, pf, 1966 [composed under pseud. Joe Miami]; Gado Dajvyadvhneli Jisa (trad.), Bar, pf, 1990; Mi Cinski, Hec'ela T'ankalake K'uniyaye (Ballard), Mez, pf, 1997

EDITIONS AND TEACHING MATERIALS

The American Indian Sings (Santa Fe, 1970)

Oklahoma Indian Chants for the Classroom (Santa Fe, 1972)

American Indian Music for the Classroom, Canyon C-3001 to 3004 (1973) [incl. teachers' guide and other materials]

My Music Reaches to the Sky: Native American Indian Instruments (Santa Fe, 1973)

Music of North American Indians (Morristown, NJ, 1975)

Principal publishers: New Southwest, Bourne, Presser

WRITINGS

'Cultural Differences: a Major Theme in Cultural Enrichment', *Indian Historian*, ii/1 (1969), 4–7

'Put American Indian Music in the Classroom', *Music Educators Journal*, lvi/7 (1969–70), 38–44

Native American Music of the Western Hemisphere (Santa Fe, 1974)

'Toward Another (Musical) Aesthetic', *Minority Voices*, i/1 (1977), 29–34

'Two Ogàxpa Sacred Robes Visit Home', *Public Historian*, xviii/4 (1996), 193–7

BIBLIOGRAPHY

J. Katz, ed.: 'Louis Ballard: Quapaw/Cherokee Composer', *This Song Remembers: Self Portraits of Native Americans in the Arts* (Boston, 1980), 132–8

R. Dore: 'Louis Ballard: Music for the Earth and the Sky', *Artspace*, xii/4 (1988), 25–7

R. Luce: 'Louis Ballard, Composer', *Santa Fean Magazine* (1990), Jan–Feb, 24–5

CHARLOTTE J. FRISBIE

Ballarotti, Francesco (*b* Bergamo, 1660; *d* Bergamo, April 1712). Italian composer. The son of Giuseppe 'il Manzino', a violinist and tenor at S Maria Maggiore, Bergamo, from 1656, he attended the school of the Misericordia Maggiore free of charge from 1705. On 4 September 1691 he was appointed *vicemaestro di cappella* of S Maria Maggiore, and on 12 April 1692 *maestro*, replacing Teodoro Reggiani. He was treated with great respect by the *consorzio* of the Misericordia Maggiore, who granted him permission to be absent from service in S Maria Maggiore whenever necessary. The news of his death was reported in the resolutions of 16 April 1712.

As a composer, he was often called on to help with the composition of music to be performed in Turin, Milan and Cremona. In 1692 he was invited by the Governor of Lodi to stage two works, and in 1699 he was summoned by the Serenissimo of Modena to compose *La caduta dei Decemviri*. His moral operetta *Il merito fortunato* was first performed in honour of Agostino Nani, *grande capitano* of Bergamo. When the work was printed in the same year, the following sentence appeared below a list of the performers: 'The defects of the poetry will be less obvious on stage because of the beauty of the music composed by virtue of Sig. Francesco Ballarotti'.

WORKS
STAGE

Enea in Italia (dramma per musica, 3, G.F. Bussani), Milan, Ducale, 1686, 3 arias *I-MOe*, pubd lib *Bc*, collab. C.A. Lonati and P. Magni

Dialogo musicale fra Nettuno e Bergamo, Bergamo, 1688, pubd lib *BGc*

Il merito fortunato (F. Roncalli), Bergamo, 1691

Ottaviano in Sicilia (dramma per musica, 3), Reggio nell'Emilia, 1692, *MOe**

L'Aiace (dramma per musica, 3, P. d'Averara), Milan, Ducale, 1694, *US-Cn*, collab. Lonati and Magni

Ariovisto [part of Act 3] (dramma per musica, 3, d'Averara), Milan, 1699 [Act 1 by A. Perti, Act 2 and part of Act 3 by Magni]

La caduta dei Decemviri (dramma per musica, 3, S. Stampiglia), Reggio nell'Emilia, Comunità, May 1699

Esione (dramma per musica, 3, d'Averara), Turin, Regio, 1699

Alciade, ovvero L'eroico amore [La violenza d'amore; Act 3] (op tragicomica, 3, M.A. Gasparini), Bergamo, 1709 [Act 1 by F. Gasparini, Act 2 by C.F. Pollarolo]

Il cuor del leone, o sia La stella di prima grandezza (serenata, C. Benaglio), Milan, n.d.

OTHER WORKS

Balletti, arie, gighe, corrente, alemande, sarabande, capricci da camera, 2 vn, vle/spinet, op.1 (Milan, 1681) [1st vn only, and vn of Sonate per camera, a 3, presumably same work, *I-Ms*]

3 arias in Ariette a voce sola con e senza instrumenti e basso continuo, *MOe*

1 aria, 1692[1]

Arias for Arione, Milan, 1694; Aetna festivo (introduttione di ballo), Milan, 1696

BIBLIOGRAPHY

EitnerQ

A. Geddo: *Bergamo e la musica* (Bergamo, 1958)

M. Donà: *La stampa musicale a Milano fino all'anno 1700* (Florence, 1961)

F. Testi: *La musica italiana nel Seicento* (Busto Arsizio, 1970–85)

SERGIO LATTES/PAOLA PALERMO

Ballata. Italian dance-song, and poetic and musical form, in use from the second half of the 13th century until the 15th century and beyond.

1. Etymology and form. 2. History.

1. ETYMOLOGY AND FORM. The word, which was synonymous with *danza* in earlier times, refers to the functional origin of the word *ballare* ('to dance'). The first ballata texts survive without music from the second half of the 13th century in the so-called Bolognese *Memoriali*. Dante mentioned the ballata in *De vulgari eloquentia* (II, iii.5, 1304–5), stating that, in contrast to the canzone, it demands a singing dancer. The form is also indicative of the dance-song: it originally consisted of a choral refrain (*ripresa*) and several strophes (*stanze*) performed by a soloist. Moreover, even in the 13th century the oldest ballate were closely linked with the *lauda*. The numerous *laude-contrafacta* of the 14th and 15th centuries are evidence of this link (see Ghisi, 1953). It was in the *lauda*, and in the period of the *dolce stil nuovo*, that the development of the ballata into an artistic lyrical form was completed. The texts are love songs and also often moral aphorisms, in which the choral refrain yields to a solo *ripresa* and the strophes are reduced in length. However, alongside these, popular ballata types survived for a long time (these are still found in Boccaccio and Prudenzani, and are widespread in Quattrocento poetry).

The ballata consists of the following parts: *ripresa*, two (rarely more) symmetrical *piedi* or *mutazioni*, *volta* (equal in length to the *ripresa*) and *ripresa*. The terms 'piedi' and 'volta' were taken over from the canzone. One of the earliest ballate with music (*I-Rvat* 215) is given below. This is a three-strophe ballata piccola (i.e. with a one-line *ripresa* of 11 syllables), and its rhyme scheme is: A (*ripresa*), BB (two *piedi*), A (*volta*), A (*ripresa*):

> Per tropo fede talor se perìgola!
> Non è dolor, nè più mortale spàsemo
> Come sença falir cader in biàsemo
> El ben se tacie e lo mal pur se cìgola.
>
> (Per tropo fede . . .)
>
> Lasso colui che mai si fidò in fèmena,
> Chè l'amor so veneno amaro sèmena,
> Onde la morte speso se ne spìgola.
> (Per tropo fede . . .)
> Oimè, ch'Amor m'à posto in cotal àrcere
> Onde conviene ognor làgreme spàrçere;
> Sì che doglia lo mio cor formìgola.
> Per tropo fede talor se perìgola!

In manuscripts only the *ripresa* and the first *piede* are each notated with music. The text of the second *piede* and the *volta* is distributed between the two musical sections (ex.1), or written below the staves as a *residuum*. The question of whether the *ripresa* is to be repeated after every strophe or only at the end cannot be answered with certainty. In contrast to the madrigal, changes of time signature within the ballata are rare.

Alongside the ballata piccola 14th-century theorists described the ballata minima (one-line *ripresa* with seven syllables), the ballata minore (two-line *ripresa*), the ballata mezzana (three-line *ripresa*) and the ballata grande (four-line *ripresa*). In rare cases both *piedi* of the ballata are provided with musical notation. Even more rarely new music is provided for the *volta*.

2. HISTORY. Only the texts survive from the early history of the ballata. The music was evidently based on oral tradition. With the rise of the ballata to an art form the first monophonic ballate with music appear in a north Italian manuscript (*I-Rvat* 215). Another manuscript

Ex.1

Ripresa: 1.5. Per _____
Volta: 4. El _____

tro-po ___ fe-de ___ ta-lor se _____ pe-rì -
ben se _____ ta-cie e ___ lo mal pur _____ se ___ ci -

Fine

___ go - la!   *Piedi:* 2. Non _____
___ go - la.   3. Co _____

___ è ___ do - lor, ___ nè ___ più mor -
___ me sen - ça ___ fa - lir ca -

Da capo al Fine

- ta - le _____ spà _____ - - se-mo
- der in _____ bià _____ - - se-mo

(*I-Fl* 87) contains five monophonic ballate by Gherardello da Firenze, five by Lorenzo da Firenze and one monophonic piece by Niccolò da Perugia. The first polyphonic ballate appeared in Florence in the 1360s. It is with this development that the form finally reached artistic stature and from that time onward, especially in Florence, but soon also in the Veneto, it remained in the forefront of interest. Jacopo da Bologna's *Nel mio parlar* is the only surviving example of a polyphonic ballata from before 1360; however, judging from its text this piece is a *lauda*. The 141 ballate of Landini (composed between *c*1365 and 1397) offer a good cross-section of the various types of polyphonic ballate: the earlier examples still have many points in common with the madrigal (both voices with text, melismatic style) and the later examples resemble the French chanson (the upper voice only with text, a tendency towards syllabic style, *ouvert* and *clos*, and sometimes identical music at the end of the *ripresa* and *piedi*). The frequent occurrence of ballate with a single strophe of text is an indication of the central role of the music. The aphoristic short ballate of Niccolò da Perugia and Andreas de Florentia are characteristic of Florentine bourgeois culture. In northern Italy, along with the madrigal, the ballata was cultivated by Bartolino da Padova, Ciconia and Zacara da Teramo among others. A particular genre using the ballata's form, the siciliana, flourished in the Veneto at the end of the 14th century (see Pirrotta, 1982, 1984). Works by Du Fay and Arnold de Lantins can be reckoned among the last examples of this specifically Italian form. Only a few ballate by Italian composers from the first half of the 15th century have survived. By the time northern composers settled in Italy the ballata had lost its ancient charm and its distinctive characteristics. While ballate that survive without music can be traced until the end of that century and beyond, pre-eminence in the field of Italian song was passing to the frottola and the *lauda*, both formally related to the ballata.

See also VIRELAI and LAUDA.

EDITIONS

N. Pirrotta, ed.: *The Music of Fourteenth-Century Italy*, CMM, viii (1954–64)

L. Schrade, W.T. Marrocco, M. Bent, A. Hallmark, eds.: *Italian Secular Music*, PMFC, iv–xi (1958–78); xxiv (1985)

THEORETICAL SOURCES

Giovanni del Virgilio: *Diaffonus: Epistola III*, ed. E. Carrara, Atti e Memorie R. Deputaz. St. Patria per le Romagne, xv (1925), 19–21
Dante Alighieri: *De vulgari eloquentia*, ed. P.V. Mengaldo (Padua, 1968/R), 156–60
Francesco da Barberino: *Documenti d'Amore*, ed. F. Egidi I (Rome, 1905–27/R), ii, 260–5, iii, 144–8 [see also O. Antognoni: 'Le glosse ai *Documenti d'Amore* di M. Francesco da Barberino', *Giornale di Filologia Romanza*, viii (1882), 78–98]
Capitulum de vocibus applicatis verbis, ed. S. Debenedetti in 'Un trattatello del secolo XIV sopra la poesia musicale', *Studi medievali*, ii (1906–7), 59–82; repr. in S. Debenedetti: *Il 'Sollazzo': contributi alla storia della novella, della poesia musicale e del costume nel Trecento* (Turin, 1922), 179–84
Antonio da Tempo: *Summa artis rithimici vulgaris dictaminis* (1332), ed. R. Andrews (Bologna, 1977)
Gidino da Sommacampagna: *Trattato dei ritmi volgari* (1381–4), ed. G.B. Giuliari (Bologna, 1870/R); ed. G.P. Caprettini: *Trattato e arte dei rithimi volgari* (Verona, 1993)
F. Baratella: *Compendio dell'arte ritmica* (1447), A. da Tempo: *Delle rime volgari: trattato di Antonio da Tempo . . . 1332*, ed. G. Grion (Bologna, 1869/R), 177–240
Antonii de Tempo ars rithmorum vulgarium, ed. F.A. Gallo: 'Sulla fortuna di Antonio da Tempo: un quarto volgarizzamento', *L'Ars Nova italiana del Trecento*, v, ed. A. Ziino (Palermo, 1985), 149–57

BIBLIOGRAPHY

E. Li Gotti and N. Pirrotta: *Il Sacchetti e la tecnica musicale* (Florence, 1935)
N. Pirrotta: 'Lirica monodica trecentesca', *RaM*, ix (1936), 317–25; repr. in *Poesia e Musica e altri saggi* (Florence, 1994), 35–46
A. Caboni, ed.: *Antiche rime italiane tratte dai Memoriali bolognesi* (Modena, 1941)
F. Ghisi: 'Strambotti e laude nel travestimento spirituale della poesia musicale del Quattrocento', *CHM*, i (1953), 45–78
K. von Fischer: *Studien zur italienischen Musik des Trecento und frühen Quattrocento* (Berne, 1956), 39–73
W.T. Marrocco: 'The Ballata: a Metamorphic Form', *AcM*, xxxi (1959), 32–7
N. Pirrotta: 'Ballate e "soni" secondo un grammatico del Trecento', *Saggi e ricerche in memoria di Ettore Li Gotti*, iii (Palermo, 1962), 42–54; repr. in *Musica tra medioevo e rinascimento* (Turin, 1984), 90–102
A. Roncaglia: 'Nella preistoria della lauda: ballata e strofa zagialesca', *Il movimento dei Disciplinati nel settimo centenario dal suo inizio* (Perugia, 1962), 461–75; repr. in *La metrica*, ed. R. Cremante and M. Pazzaglia (Bologna, 1972), 309–17
F.A. Gallo: 'Ricerche sulla musica a S. Giustina di Padova all'inizio del Quattrocento, ii: due "siciliane" del Trecento', *AnnM*, vii (1964–77), 43–50
N. Pirrotta: 'On Text Forms from Ciconia to Dufay', *Aspects of Medieval and Renaissance Music: a Birthday offering to Gustave Reese* ed. J. LaRue and others (New York, 1966), 673–82
A. Ziino: *Strutture strofiche nel Laudario di Cortona* (Palermo, 1968)
N. Pirrotta: 'Tradizione orale e tradizione scritta nella musica', *L'Ars Nova italiana del Trecento: Convegno II: Certaldo and Florence 1969* [*L'Ars Nova italiana del Trecento*, iii (Certaldo, 1970)], 431–41; repr. in *Musica tra Medioevo e Rinascimento* (Turin, 1984), 177–84; Eng. trans. in *Music and Culture in Italy from the Middle Ages to the Baroque* (Cambridge, MA, 1984), 72–9
G. Reaney: 'The Italian Contribution to the Manuscript Oxford, Bodleian Library, Canonici Misc. 213', *L'Ars Nova italiana del Trecento: Convegno II: Certaldo and Florence 1969* [*L'Ars Nova italiana del Trecento*, iii (Certaldo, 1970)], 443–64
G. Corsi: *Poesie musicali del Trecento* (Bologna, 1970)
N. Pirrotta: 'New Glimpses of an Unwritten Tradition', *Words and Music: the Scholar's View . . . in Honor of A. Tillman Merritt*, ed. L. Berman (Cambridge, MA, 1972), 271–91; repr. in *Music and Culture in Italy from the Middle Ages to the Baroque* (Cambridge, MA, 1984), 51–71
N. Pirrotta: 'Ricercare e variazioni su O rosa bella', *Studi musicali*, i (1972), 59–77; repr. in *Musica tra medioevo e rinascimento* (Turin, 1984), 195–212; Eng. trans. in *Music and Culture in Italy from the Middle Ages to the Baroque* (Cambridge, MA, 1984), 145–58

B.R. Suchla: *Studien zur Provenienz der Trecento-Ballata* (Göttingen, 1976)

D. Baumann: 'Some Extraordinary Forms in the Italian Secular Trecento Repertoire', *La musica al tempo del Boccaccio e i suoi rapporti con la letteratura: Siena and Certaldo 1975 [L'Ars Nova italiana del Trecento*, iv (Certaldo, 1978)], 45–63

G. Capovilla: 'Note sulla tecnica della ballata trecentesca', ibid., 107–47

H.M. Brown: 'Fantasia on a Theme by Boccaccio', *EMc*, v (1977), 324–39

G. Capovilla: 'Le ballate del Petrarca e il codice metrico due-trecentesco', *Giornale storico della letteratura italiana*, cliv (1977), 238–60; repr. in *"Si vario stile": studi sul Canzoniere del Petrarca* (Padua, 1998), 13–46

G. Gorni: 'Note sulla ballata', *Metrica*, i (1978), 219–24; repr. in *Metrica e analisi letteraria* (Bologna, 1993), 243–9

D. Baumann: *Die dreistimmige italienische Lied-Satztechnik im Trecento* (Baden-Baden, 1979)

F.A. Gallo: 'The Musical and Literary Tradition of Fourteenth-Century Poetry set to Music', *Musik und Text in der Mehrstimmigkeit des 14. und 15. Jahrhunderts: Wolfenbüttel 1980*, 55–76

F.A. Gallo: 'Ballata (Trecento)' (1980), *HMT* [Incl. discussion of theoretical sources]

G. Gorni: 'Altre note sulla ballata', *Metrica*, ii (1981), 83–102; repr. in *Metrica e analisi letteraria* (Bologna, 1993), 219–42

N. Pirrotta: 'La siciliana trecentesca', *Schede medievali*, iii (1982), 297–308

M. Fabbri and J. Nádas: 'A Newly Discovered Trecento Fragment', *EMH*, iii (1983), 67–81

N. Pirrotta: 'Rhapsodic Elements in North-Italian Polyphony of the 14th Century', *MD*, xxxvii (1983), 83–99

F.A. D'Accone: 'Una nuova fonte dell'Ars nova italiana: il codice di San Lorenzo, 2211', *Studi musicali*, xiii (1984), 3–31

J. Nádas: 'Manuscript San Lorenzo 2211: some Further Observations', *L'Europa e la musica del Trecento: Congresso IV: Certaldo 1984 [L'Ars Nova italiana del Trecento*, vi (Certaldo, 1992)], 145–68

N. Pirrotta: 'Echi di arie veneziane del primo Quattrocento?', *Interpretazioni veneziane*, ed. D. Rosand (Venice, 1984), 99–108; repr. in *Poesia e musica e altri saggi* (Florence, 1994), 47–64

V. Russo: 'Dante: *Ballata i' voi* (VE II VIII 10–15): Sive cum soni modulatione. . . sive non (VE II VIII 4)', *L'Europa e la musica del Trecento: Congresso IV: Certaldo 1984 [L'Ars Nova italiana del Trecento*, vi (Certaldo, 1992)], 269–86

E. Diederichs: 'Zwei Texte zu einer Ballata von Bartolino da Padova', *L'Ars Nova italiana del Trecento*, v, ed. A. Ziino (Palermo, 1985), 113–22

A. Mazzantini: 'Le ballate di Niccolò da Perugia', ibid., 179–95

B. Brumana and G. Ciliberti: 'Le ballate di Paolo da Firenze nel frammento "Cil"', *Esercizi: arte, musica e spettacolo*, ix (1986), 5–37

A. Ziino: '"Cosa non è ch'a sé tanto mi tiri": una ballata anonima nello stile di Landini', *La Toscana nel secolo XIV: caratteri di una civiltà regionale*, ed. S. Gensini (Pisa, 1988), 519–38

G. Carsaniga: 'I testi di Paolo tenorista', *Studi e problemi di critica testuale*, xl (1991), 5–22

R. Dittrich: 'Textbezüge in den Ballata-Vertonungen von Antonio Zachara da Teramo: drei Beispiele', *Mf*, xliii (1990), 15–30

K. von Fischer: 'Text Underlay in Landini's Ballate for Three Voices', *CMc*, nos. 45–7 (1990) [Festschrift E.H. Sanders, ed. P.M. Lefferts and L.L. Perkins], 179–97

P.G. Beltrami: *La metrica italiana* (Bologna, 1991), 100–01, 248–58

A. Leszczynska: 'Slady trecenta w Poznaniu' [The remnants of the Trecento in Poznan], *Muzyka*, xxxvi/3 (1991), 63–75

N. Pirrotta: Preface to *Il Codice Rossi 215* (Lucca, 1992)

A. Ziino: 'Rime per musica e per danza', *Storia della letteratura italiana*, ii, ed. E. Malato (Rome, 1995), 455–529

G. D'Agostino: 'Le ballate del *Decameron*', *Studi sul Boccaccio*, xxiv (1996), 123–80

L. Pagnotta: *Repertorio metrico della ballata italiana: secoli XIII e XIV* (Milan, 1996)

KURT VON FISCHER/GIANLUCA D'AGOSTINO

Ballestra [Balestra, ?Armbruster], **Reimundo** [Raimundo, Raimundus] (*b* 2nd half of the 16th century; *d* Zabern [now Saverne], Alsace, 11 Oct 1634). Composer, probably German (not Italian, as has sometimes been thought). His name may have been 'Armbruster' (which means 'cross-bow': *balestra* in Italian). Certainly all his surviving writing is in German. He himself said that he received a stipend from the Fuggers, and he studied in Italy and in Germany. He was an instrumentalist at the court of Archduke Ferdinand in Graz from 1602 until 1616, when Archduke Leopold, Bishop of Strasbourg and Passau, a brother of Archduke Ferdinand, appointed him Kapellmeister at his court at Zabern; in 1618 there were 19 singers and instrumentalists under him. He remained in Zabern until his death, although Archduke Leopold became Count of the Tyrol in 1619, took most of his musicians to Innsbruck and in 1625 resigned the see of Strasbourg. In that year Ballestra became organist at the Convent of Our Lady but still spent his last years in financial straits.

All Ballestra's surviving music dates from his years in Graz. He said that his *Sacrae symphoniae* contain 'the musical symphonies [concerted works] and harmonies [choral and polychoral works] composed by me, apart from some *reservata*'. He did not disclose which of his works he thought of as *musica reservata*. Palisca supposed them to be the pieces in which tutti sections are interspersed with solo sections. But since there are also solo parts in his 13-part parody *Magnificat* and in his *Missa con le tronbe*, a likelier candidate is the polytextual eight-part motet *Dux Ferdinandus*, written in homage to Archduke Ferdinand; it is marked as a work 'reserved' for the knowledgeable because of its use of crab canon and series of hexachords recurring ostinato-like in varying rhythms. Ballestra's range embraces Venetian polychoral writing, concertatos for four or fewer solo voices and basso continuo, instrumental canzonas and elaborate counterpoint in the Netherlandish style. His music is sometimes similar in style to that of the Venetian-trained Georg Poss, who was a colleague at Graz.

WORKS

Sacrae symphoniae, liber I, 28 motets, 7, 8, 10, 12vv (Venice, 1611); Magnificat based on Viadana's Judica, Domine, 13vv; 2 canzonas: 1 for 8 insts, 1 for 4 insts ('secondo li Balli tedeschi')

2 motets, solo vv, bc, in Parnassus musicus Ferdinandaeus, 1615[13]

Missa con le tronbe, 16vv, Missa sine nomine, 12vv, 2 Magnificat, 14vv, 20vv, *A-Wn*

BIBLIOGRAPHY

SennMT, 205–6

H. Federhofer: 'Eine neue Quelle der *musica reservata*', *AcM*, xxiv (1952), 32–45

H. Federhofer: 'Graz Court Musicians and their Contributions to the*Parnassus musicus Ferdinandaeus* (1615)', *MD*, ix (1955), 167–244

C.V. Palisca: 'A Clarification of "Musica Reservata" in Jean Taisnier's "Astrologiae", 1559', *AcM*, xxxi (1959), 133–61, esp. 154

H. Federhofer: *Musikpflege und Musiker am Grazer Habsburgerhof der Erzherzöge Karl und Ferdinand von Innerösterreich (1564–1619)* (Mainz, 1967), 145–7

HELLMUT FEDERHOFER

Ballet. A style of theatrical dancing that developed in France during the 17th century, achieved 'classical' status in the 19th century, and today maintains its roots in the past while continuing to evolve. The term also describes a theatrical spectacle, in which use it has a history stretching back to the Middle Ages (*see* DANCE and BALLET DE COUR); as a spectacle, ballet could, in various times and places, include singing as well as dancing. Ballet became institutionalized in Paris in 1672 with the formation of the first permanent professional dance troupe within the newly founded Académie Royale de Musique (known informally as the Opéra), which occurred during a time when the basic movement vocabulary was becoming codified. For much of its history ballet has been closely tied to opera, both in the types of works in which ballet has appeared and because of the institutional structures that supported it; a number of ballet companies are still attached to opera houses. Starting in the 18th century, however, ballet also began gradually to establish itself as an independent art, one through which a narrative could be communicated without sung texts; since the late 18th century 'ballet' as a genre has usually meant a spectacle accompanied by purely instrumental music, although many operas continued to include ballet. The 20th century saw a shift in emphasis away from story ballets set to newly composed scores towards more abstract works set to pre-existing music not necessarily composed for dancing. Although ballet is primarily a Western art, it is now practised in many parts of the world, where it is sometimes absorbed into local dance traditions.

1. 1670–1800: (i) The 17th century in France (ii) The 17th century outside France (iii) 18th century. 2. 19th century: (i) The transition to romantic ballet, 1800-1830 (ii) Romantic ballet and its influence (iii) Ballet in opera (iv) The classical ballet in Russia to 1900 3. 20th century: classical: (i) Diaghilev and the Russian exiles to 1930 (ii) Britain, the USA and elsewhere (iii) The USSR: a continuing tradition (iv) Main trends since 1945. 4. Modern dance.

1. 1670–1800.

(i) The 17th century in France.   The founding of the Académie Royale de Danse by Louis XIV in 1661 marks an important landmark in the professionalization of dance, but the actual contributions made by this élite group of 13 dancing-masters to the development of ballet remain obscure. According to Pierre Rameau (*Le maître à danser*, 1725) it was Pierre Beauchamp, the principal choreographer at both the court and the Opéra, who codified the five positions of the feet and set the standard for the developing art; his tenure as ballet-master at the Académie Royale de Musique from its inception by Jean-Baptiste Lully in 1672 generated widespread admiration. Even François Raguenet, defender of Italian opera, admitted (*Parallèle des Italiens et des François*, 1702):

The Italians themselves will own that no dancers in Europe are equal to ours; the Combatants and Cyclops in *Perseus*, the Tremblers and Smiths in *Isis*, the Unlucky Dreams in *Atys*, and our other entries are originals in their kind, as well as in respect of the *airs* composed by Lully, as of the steps which Beauchamps has adapted to these *airs* . . . No theatre can represent a fight more lively than we see it sometimes expressed in our dances, and, in a word, everything is performed with an unexceptionable nicety.

No employment records survive from the early years of the Opéra's existence, but it is nonetheless known that there was at least some overlap between the professional dancers employed at the court and the members of the dance troupe in Paris, including such notables as Hilaire D'Olivet (who also sometimes choreographed for the Opéra), Louis L'Estang and Jean Favier *l'aîné*. Initially the troupe was entirely male; although a number of professional female dancers had appeared at court over the years, women did not dance on the public stage of the Opéra until 1681 when Lully's ballet *Le triomphe de l'Amour* opened in Paris, after receiving its première at court with a cast that had included both professionals and aristocrats. Even after women began joining the troupe, men continued to dance female roles for a number of years until the increasing number of women made that practice unnecessary. By 1704, the first year for which

there are employment records for the Opéra, there were ten women and 11 men in the troupe, as well as Louis Guillaume Pécour, who had replaced Beauchamp as *compositeur des ballets* following Lully's death in 1687.

Several solo and duet choreographies that Pécour composed for the stage of the Opéra are preserved in Feuillet notation in two published collections (1704, 1713). These dances show that whereas a basic movement style was still shared by both theatrical and social dancers, the gap between the amateurs and the professionals was widening. Theatrical choreographies make use of a very large vocabulary of steps that are recombined in imaginative ways; they tend to involve many leaps and hops ('la danse haute'), and also to use ornamental steps such as *pas battus* or *ronds de jambe*. When men and women danced together, either as a couple or in a group, they almost always performed the same steps in unison; similarly, both wore shoes with heels (whose heights seem to have varied) and made their rising steps onto partial toe. Theatrical choreographies for couples and for solo women are often quite demanding technically (surviving English choreographies for solo women even more so than the French), but the most virtuoso dances were designed for men alone. In the published collections these include *entrées graves* (in a slow duple metre with stately dotted rhythms), sarabandes, canaries, loures and chaconnes, with such virtuoso steps as *entrechats* or *pirouettes* on one foot with multiple beats that are rarely given to women during this period (fig.1). By way of contrast, the few group theatrical dances that have come down to us, most of them in Favier notation (see Harris-Warrick and Marsh, B1994), suggest that their choreographic interest derived less from the steps and more from the varied patterns the dancers traced on the floor. Both choreographic notations and period engravings reveal how symmetrical the dance figures were: when there is an even number of dancers, half are on each side of the stage; with an odd number, one dancer occupies the centre axis while the others are arranged symmetrically on either side (fig.2).

Within the basic technical parameters, different styles emerged by which choreographers characterized the varying types of dancing roles found in operatic divertissements. In Lully's *tragédies en musique*, the dominant genre on the stage of the Opéra in this period, his principal librettist, Phillippe Quinault, took great care to integrate the divertissement that appeared in each of the five acts into the fabric of the drama, a quality for which he was greatly praised by the 18th-century dance reformers Cahusac and Noverre. Although dancers in Quinault's librettos generally represent unnamed minor characters ('un berger' or 'une magicienne') who appear in only one act, they often serve as the moving bodies for the chorus members who, except when making entrances and exits, generally remain motionless around the perimeter of the stage. In this capacity they make visible through their movements the ideas expressed in the vocal numbers with which the instrumental dances are interleaved (fig.3). Even though dancing occurs primarily during instrumental numbers (and in some choruses, most frequently during the instrumental phrases that alternate with the singing), Lully made the connection between dance and sung text explicit by composing back-to-back pairs of dances and songs or choruses that share key, metre, tempo, and rhythmic and melodic figures. The divertissement from Act 2 of *Thésée* has a typical structure: an instrumental *air*, during which 'Theseus appears, accom-

1. *Entrée for two men danced by Piffetau and Cherrier in the Ballet de l'Europe galante: engraving from Louis Guillaume Pécour's 'Recüeil de dances' (Paris, 1704), 164*

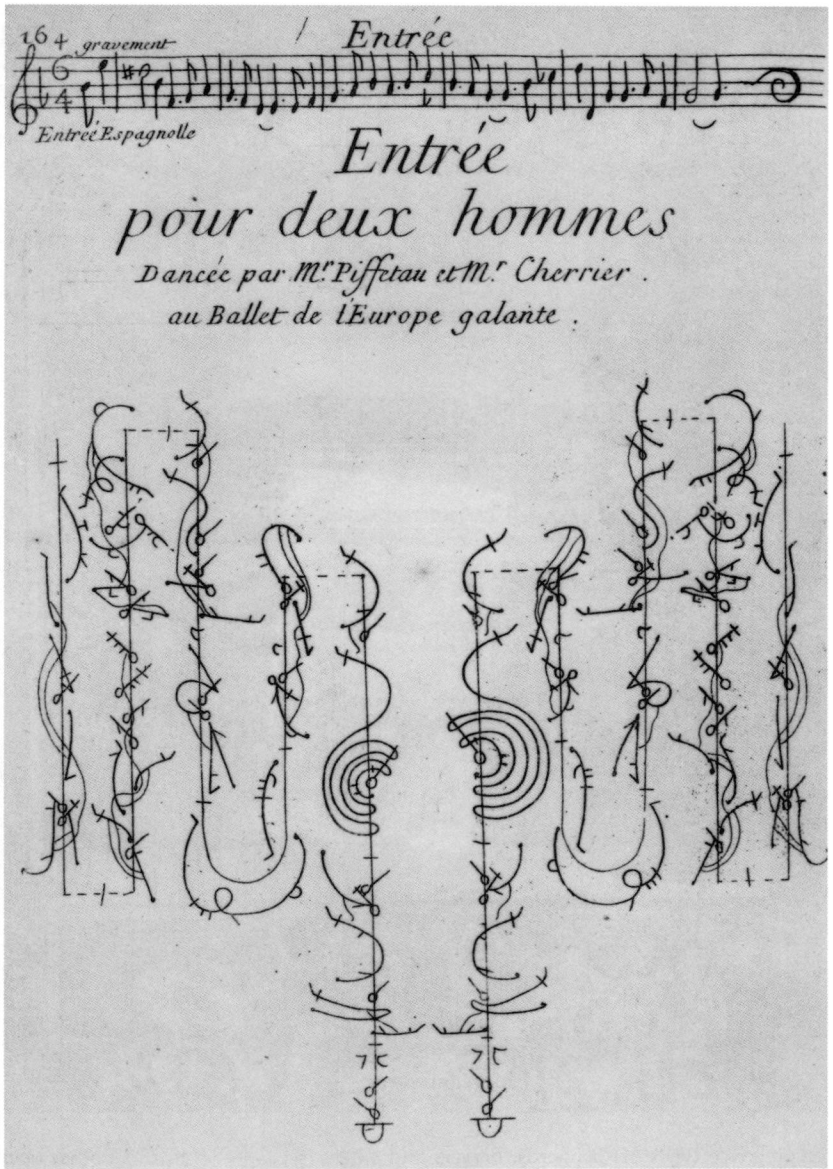

panied by the populace of Athens, celebrating his victory'; a musically related celebratory chorus; an instrumental dance for old men which is heard twice, before each verse of a musically similar duet for *deux vieillards athéniens* ('Pour le peu de bon temps qui nous reste'); and finally a repetition of the celebratory chorus. Thus the audience is invited to view the dancing as one of several media of expression in the service of the divertissement as a whole, which in turn participates fully in the plot of the opera (the old men here serve as irreverent stand-ins for King Aegeus, who sees Theseus as a threat). Very little of the dancing in Lully's operas deserves to be dismissed as merely 'decorative'; on the contrary, it is allied to fundamental concerns within the works.

The implicit connection between text and movement seen in Lully's operas finds support in 17th-century dance theorists such as Michel de Pure (*Idée des spectacles anciens et nouveaux*, 1668), who described ballet as 'a mute representation, in which the gestures and movements signify what could be expressed through words'. Both he and Claude-François Menestrier (*Des ballets anciens et modernes*, 1682) insisted that the movements of the dancers, like the music to which they move, be appropriate to the characters they represent – that dances for shepherds be distinguishable from dances for kings or for sailors. The Abbé Dubos (*Réflexions critiques sur la poésie et sur la peinture*, 1719), who praised Lully for writing well-characterized music, said of choreography that 'years ago, the fauns, shepherds, peasants, cyclops, and tritons danced pretty near in the same manner; but now the dance is divided into several characters. The artists, if I am not mistaken, reckon 16, and each of these characters has its proper steps, attitudes, and figures upon the stage'. Quinault himself even made distinctions as subtle as

2. Scene from Lalande's 'Ballet de la jeunesse', Versailles, 1686: engraving

casting two types of shepherds, *bergers* and *pâtres* (see, for example, *Alceste*, Act 5), the latter probably more rustic and less idealized than the former (a convention found in later ballets as well). Distinctions are also implicit in Quinault's librettos between what Cahusac was later to call 'la danse simple', that is, dance that represents dance (such as in the joyful celebrations that conclude many operas), and Cahusac's 'danse figurée' or 'composée', which mimes an action (the *trembleurs* in *Isis*, the battling warriors in *Cadmus et Hermione*). Both types of dance could occur either on earth or in the realm of the *merveilleux*: demons, for example, could dance for joy or they could frighten people. In either case, choreographies for demons and other transgressive characters seem to have mined a vocabulary of grotesque gestures including false positions of the feet, extravagant leaps and distorted arm positions, whereas distinctions between beneficent character types such as shepherds and sailors seem to have relied on more subtle differences in step vocabulary, arm movements, figures and spatial orientation.

Most of Lully's operatic divertissements contain from one to three instrumental dances, although the prologue may include more. The music generally adheres to one of three structures: binary (the most numerous), rondeau (*ABACA*), or the extended variation forms of chaconne and *passacaille*. Most of his dance pieces make use of the full five-part orchestra, although some are set as trios or contain trio episodes. Wind instruments are often employed to enhance characterization: oboes in pastoral scenes, flutes for sacred rites, and trumpets for battles. The enriched orchestration generally extends to the choruses as well, thus giving the divertissements greater aural sumptuousness than the other portions of the opera, which are primarily accompanied by continuo alone. Although Lully included such titled dances as gavottes, minuets, sarabandes and canaries, many are simply called 'entrée' or 'air', followed by the category of characters dancing (e.g. 'Entrée des bergers'); such pieces may or may not conform to an identifiable dance type. Much of Lully's dance music has irregular phrase structures; even

3. Final scene in Act 5 of Lully's 'Isis', Saint Germain-en-Laye, 1677: engraving by Sébastien Leclerc I; members of the chorus line the sides of the stage, while the dancers surround the altar

dance types such as the minuet may have five- or seven-bar phrases. In fact, four- or eight-bar phrases, while not uncommon, are by no means the norm. Although in some instances the irregularities may be a function of dramatic characterization, they are so endemic to Lully's style in so many different dramatic contexts that they do not support facile generalizations about their restriction to comic or grotesque situations.

(ii) The 17th century outside France. Dance also figured prominently in Italian opera, especially in Venice, although it tended to have a looser connection to the plot than in France. In most mid- or late 17th-century Venetian three-act operas the dances were concentrated at the ends of Acts 1 and 2, where they often functioned in the manner of *intermedi*. Many dances were motivated by joyful occasions or by being set in the realm of the supernatural, although some had only tenuous connections with the sung portions of the opera. Many of the same character types appeared on both the French and the Italian stages – nymphs and shepherds, soldiers, demons, or allegorical characters such as dreams – but Venetian opera allowed for more comic roles such as buffoons, cripples or animals than did the French. (Comic roles had been common in the *ballet de cour* but were abandoned in the *tragédie en musique*.) Although the composer of the vocal music sometimes composed the dances, the practice of entrusting the dance music to the choreographer or to a secondary composer probably originated during this period and had become the norm by the 18th century. Only a few dance types are mentioned in Venetian librettos and scores, such as the *corrento*, *passo e mezzo* and *canario*; more often a dance is simply identified as a 'ballo'. As in France, most of the dances have a binary structure. In the last two decades of the 17th century the French style of dancing began to make inroads into Italy, as can be seen not only from the appearance of dance types such as the minuet or *borèa* (bourrée) in opera scores, but also from the composition

of scenes that interleave dances with musically related vocal pieces on the model of the French *divertissement*, as in *Il pastore d'Anfriso* (1695) by Carlo Francesco Pollarolo. With the introduction of the Arcadian reforms at the turn of the century, however, came an increased separation between danced episodes and vocal music; thereafter dancing was generally independent of the plot of the opera and relegated to appearing between the acts.

Apart from Giovanni Battista Balbi, who between 1636 and 1657 worked not only in Venice but in several European courts (including France; fig.4), few of the choreographers from Venetian theatres are known. No choreographic notations preserve the dances from this period, but Italian dancing is reported to have been more athletic than the French, with greater emphasis on dramatic leaps, speed and lightness and more opportunity for mimetic dancing, particularly (although not exclusively) in comic scenes. Gregorio Lambranzi's *Neue und curieuse theatralische Tantz-Schul* (Nuremberg, 1716), a book showing sequential illustrations from several different theatrical dances (for drunk peasants, *commedia* characters, animated statues and the like; fig.5), provides an idea of the movements – some of them quite acrobatic – available to comic and grotesque dancers. At the same time, the brief descriptions accompanying the engravings show that the French technical vocabulary (*pas de bourrée*, *chassés*, various *contretemps* etc.) had by then become international.

Following the restoration of Charles II to the English throne in 1660, a number of French dancers and musicians made their way across the Channel. Although Robert Cambert's attempt to establish a Royal Academy of Music on the French model failed, his production of two operas, *Ariane* and *Pomone*, as well as several other imported entertainments did expose the English to French dancing. Starting in 1673 Thomas Betterton's blending of Lullian balletic practices with English theatrical traditions produced the new genre of semi-opera in works such as Matthew Locke's *Psyche* (1675), Henry Purcell's *The Fairy Queen* (1692) and *The Island Princess* (1699; music

by R. Leveridge, D. Purcell and J. Clarke). Although semi-opera died out shortly thereafter, dancing continued to figure as entr'acte entertainment in playhouses such as Drury Lane and Lincoln's Inn Fields, where French styles mingled with *commedia dell'arte*-inflected dancing coming from Italy. Prominent English dancers around the turn of the century included John Weaver, Thomas Caverley and Hester Santlow. The publication in 1706 of two translations of Feuillet's *Chorégraphie* (one by Weaver as *Orchesography*, the other by Paul Siris as *The Art of Dancing*) shows that a market had developed in England for French dancing, as does the publication of a substantial number of notated choreographies between the years 1706 and 1735.

French dancing also took root in northern and central European countries, particularly at courts, such as Dresden and Stockholm, that had political connections with France. Even in cities where Italian opera was established, French dancers and choreographers were often employed to embellish theatrical spectacles. In Hamburg Lully's *Acis et Galatée* was performed at the public opera house in 1689; operas composed there in the following decade by Johann Georg Conradi, Johann Sigismund Kusser and Reinhard Keiser reveal Lully's influence.

(iii) The 18th century. Following Lully's death in 1687, French opera began to change in ways that were to expand the place it accorded to ballet. *L'Europe galante* (1697) by Houdar de Lamotte and André Campra inaugurated a new genre, the *opéra-ballet* (called simply 'ballet' at the time), which gave a larger scope to divertissements than did the *tragédie en musique*, although the plots were still communicated through singing. (Related genres, all involving singing, were labelled variously *ballet-héroïque*, *ballet comique* and *acte de ballet*.) The prologue and three or four acts (usually called 'entrées') each had a separate action but were tied together by an overarching theme: *Les fêtes vénitiennes* (Danchet and Campra, 1710), for example, has acts revolving around love intrigues set in contemporary Venice among,

6

4. *Giovanni Battista Balbi's final ballet for 'La finta pazza' (music by Francesco Sacrati) in which Indians release five parrots, Salle du Petit Bourbon, Paris, 14 December 1645: engraving by V. Spada*

5. Scaramouche: engraving from Gregorio Lambranzi's 'Neue und curieuse theatrialische Tantz-Schul' (Nuremberg, 1716)

by turns, gondoliers, gamblers, spectators at the opera, and guests at a ball (the order and inclusion of acts varied from performance to performance). Thus comic dancing characters such as Arlequin or fortune-telling gypsies, who in Lully's day had been restricted to a few pastiche works such as *Le carnaval, mascarade* (1675), began to make regular appearances on the stage of the Opéra.

At the same time that the *opéra-ballet* was expanding both the amount of dramatic time devoted to dance and the range of characters represented, the *tragédies* also began to increase the number of dances within the divertissements. This tendency can be seen not only in newly composed works (where the librettist Lamotte led the way), but even within operas by Lully, which, when they were revived, acquired more and more dance pieces as time went on. The interpolations, whose music was sometimes borrowed from Lully's ballets but more often newly composed, seem primarily aimed at affording solos or pas de deux for the emerging stars of the dance troupe. The enlargement of the divertissement occurred primarily in scenes that represented *fêtes* of various kinds (both on earth and in magical or mythical realms), and that thus favoured dance for dance's sake; the newly written librettos offered many fewer occasions for mimetic dancing than had Quinault's. This shift in emphasis towards more purely decorative kinds of dancing can be observed in the replacement in many librettos of scene descriptions for the divertissements in favour of the laconic 'On danse' or 'Le divertissement commence'. In addition, purely danced works, such as the choreographed 'symphonies' of Jean-Féry Rebel, were sometimes used to round out an evening at the Opéra: in May 1726, for example, Rebel's *Les caractères de la danse* followed a

performance of Lully's *Atys*. The growing profusion of dances did not please all spectators: Campra's *tragédie Achille et Déidamie* (1735) was accused of 'completely drowning the subject in the divertissement', and by 1749 Rémond de Saint-Mard (*Réflexions sur l'opéra*) was complaining that 'too much scope is given to the dances . . . everything is to be danced'.

The number of dancers employed at the Opéra grew to accommodate the demands of the expanded divertissements. By 1738 the troupe included 18 men and 13 women, in 1750 18 men and 24 women. A dance school was established at the Opéra in 1713, with the purpose of training singers and dancers already in the troupe; a school for training children opened in 1779. Early in the century the leading dancers included Jean Balon, Marie-Thérèse Perdou de Subligny, the brothers Dumoulin, Françoise Prévost and Michel Blondi, who also served as choreographer at the Opéra from 1729 until his death in 1739. They were eclipsed in star power (and in salary) by the next generation: Louis Dupré ('le dieu de la danse'), whose long (though interrupted) career at the Opéra spanned the years 1714–51; and two of Prévost's students, Marie Sallé (who made her début at the Opéra in 1727) and Marie-Anne Cupis de Camargo (début in 1726). The two were seen as representing different styles of dance: Sallé was noted for expressivity and finesse (fig.6), Camargo for technical brilliance and agility.

Although no theatrical choreographic notations survive from this period, it appears that ballet technique was growing more virtuoso, especially for women. Because of her adoption of male steps such as *pas battus* and *entrechats*, Voltaire described Camargo as 'the first woman to dance like a man'; her technical innovations drew criticism as well as admiration. The stars of the dance troupe attracted devoted followers who expected to see their favourites prominently featured when they went to the Opéra; that the divertissements favoured solos and pas de deux can often be inferred from the ways the dancers' names and roles are listed in the librettos, although determining which dancers performed in each of the pieces in the score is often difficult. Iconography suggests that couple and group dances retained the symmetrical principles of the previous era, with the dancers doing the same steps in parallel with each other. New dance types – rigaudon, forlane (in Venetian scenes), musette, tambourin, contredanse – appeared on the stage, while traditional ones such as the gavotte, menuet, passepied, sarabande and chaconne remained current; as before, many of the dances simply bear the title of 'entrée' or 'air' in the scores. As dance styles began to crystallize into the three general categories of noble, grotesque and *demi-caractère*, dancers started to specialize; Louis Dupré was seen as the epitome of the *danseur noble*, although he also danced other types of role.

The emphasis on technical brilliance and dance for its own sake found itself at odds throughout this period with a growing desire in some quarters for greater expression, or even for a separation of dance from vocal music. In 1714 in a private performance sponsored by the Duchesse du Maine at her château at Sceaux, two dancers from the Opéra, Balon and Prévost, performed in pantomime the climactic scene from the fourth act of Corneille's tragedy *Les Horaces* in which the Roman Horace kills his sister Camilla. This experiment in representing genuine tragedy through dance remained isolated for many years, but

6. Marie Sallé: engraving by Nicolas de Larmessin III after Nicolas Lancret, 1733

pantomimic dancing had already been a feature of *commedia dell'arte*-inspired performances for some time. Following the example of the Italian comedians working in London, the English dancer and choreographer John Weaver had in 1703 mounted a short pantomimic work, *The Tavern Bilkers*, but in 1717, after having investigated ancient Roman pantomime, he produced at Drury Lane a much more ambitious work, *The Loves of Mars and Venus*. The three principal roles of Mars, Venus and Vulcan were all assigned to dancers – Dupré, Hester Santlow and Weaver himself – and the music (which has not survived) was entirely instrumental. The scenario alternates between two types of scene: those that would have been sung in an opera on the same subject, such as Vulcan's expressions of jealousy (for which Weaver prescribes arm and head gestures appropriate to the reigning emotion), and scenes that resemble operatic divertissements, such as the Pyrrhic dance for the followers of Mars, for which standard dance steps would have been used. Weaver's next such work, *Orpheus and Euridice* (1718), was even more serious, using the version of the myth that ends with Orpheus's dismemberment by the Bacchae, but his last pantomime, *Perseus and Andromeda* (1728), interspersed comic scenes with the mythological ones. Although Weaver's experiments had no immediate imitators in England, Marie Sallé furthered the cause of serious mimetic dancing through two danced entertainments performed in London in 1734, *Bacchus and Ariadne* and *Pygmalion*, in which she attracted notoriety by

wearing only a simple muslin dress in the Greek manner with her hair loose, as she danced the story of the statue coming to life.

The competing demands of a dramatically expressive, wordless ballet on the one hand and the more technically driven dance for its own sake on the other, both find expression in the works of Jean-Philippe Rameau, the composer whose operas and ballets dominated the stage of the Paris Opéra in the middle of the century. The divertissements in his *tragédies lyriques* such as *Hippolyte et Aricie* (c1733) or *Castor et Pollux* (c1737) tend to adhere to the basic outlines of the Lullian model, in which many of the dances are intimately allied to vocal pieces, although several of the divertissements do contain more instrumental dances in a row than would have been found in Lully's works. Some of the *opéras-ballets* (and the shorter *actes de ballet*) include even more extensive danced scenes that approach independence from the surrounding vocal context. In the third entrée ('Les fleurs') of *Les Indes galantes* (c1736), the concluding divertissement is introduced as if it were to be a typical celebratory *fête*, but actually consists of an independent narrative in which the flowers in a garden are buffeted by a storm embodied by the North Wind, Borée, only to be rescued by Zéphire; this scene is built over nine consecutive dance pieces (most simply called 'Airs', but including two gavottes) without a single vocal number intervening. The central role, the personified Rose, was created by Marie Sallé, to great acclaim.

Rameau's openness to a more dramatic role for dance was perhaps promoted by his collaborations with Louis de Cahusac, whose book *La danse ancienne et moderne* (1754) reviewed the history of the art with a goal of promoting greater dramatic expressivity in the dance of his own day. Cahusac saw dance as falling into one of two categories: *la danse simple*, which represents only itself and is motivated by joy, and *la danse composée*, 'which by itself forms continuous action'. He felt frustrated by the outstanding abilities of the dancers of his day, whose talents he saw as being wasted through the overuse of *danse simple*: 'the costumes are different, the intentions are always the same'. Although his definition of *danse composée* seems to call for pantomime, his examples of dances he admired sometimes favour emotional expression over narrative content. In the librettos he wrote for several of Rameau's works (*opéras-ballets*, *pastorales-héroïques* and *tragédies*) Cahusac did not go as far towards integrating the dancing with the plot as his writings suggest he might have liked (he undoubtedly met resistance from the conservative institutional practices of the Opéra), but he did frequently build divertissements around what he called 'ballets figurés', whose movements he briefly described in the scene indications. These sometimes call for no more action than the weaving of garlands around the stage, but others have a narrative function. In Act 1 of the *pastorale-héroïque Naïs* (1749) an athletic contest goes through various stages of competition until an athlete arrives who challenges all the others twice; they refuse both of the times, he dances

7. *Mlle Puvigné as the statue that comes to life in Rameau's 'Pigmalion', Paris Opéra, 1748; costume design by Louis-René Boquet, pen and ink with wash (Bibliothèque et Musée de l'Opéra, Paris)*

triumphantly and Naïs crowns him the victor. The entire scene is set to an extended chaconne that changes character frequently. In other *ballets figurés* Rameau is similarly responsive to the demands of the choreography, but even in the music he composed to accompany standard *fêtes* his inventiveness in characterizing the dancers' roles remains unsurpassed.

During the same period genuine pantomime ballets began to appear in the Parisian theatres that performed lighter works (see PARIS, §IV, 3). According to Desboulmiers (*Histoire du Théâtre de l'Opéra Comique*, 1770), pantomime ballets were mounted at the Opéra-Comique starting in the 1720s, while at the Comédie-Italienne the prolific resident choreographer, Jean-Baptiste François Dehesse, composed not only divertissements for stage works of many types, but more than 50 pantomime ballets between 1738 and 1757 (fig.8). His best-known work, *L'opérateur chinois* (1748, music by Louis-Gabriel Guillemain), features a Chinese seller of patent medicine who has set up shop in the middle of a village fair; a succession of stock characters (an old philosopher, a simpleton with a sore tooth, a ridiculous German baron) involve him in a series of humorous incidents. The libretto, which describes the action scene by scene, divides the cast between dancers, who both mime and dance, and 'performers in the pantomime', who presumably only mime; as in Weaver's works there is a substantial amount of *danse simple* interspersed with the more narrative scenes. The work ends, as was standard in such ballets, with a *contredanse générale*. Dehesse's imaginative choreography was greatly admired in his day, but because he left no theoretical writings his contributions to the development of pantomime ballet have generally been undervalued by historians.

The only known document that preserves theatrical choreographies from this period, the Ferrère Manuscript, dating from 1782 (see Marsh, B1995), mixes various systems for communicating the dances of several comic pantomime ballets: Feuillet notation, sometimes augmented by written commentary; contredanse notation (floor patterns with no notated steps) for the group dances; and sketches with written instructions for the purely pantomimic scenes. The choreography blends dance steps familiar from earlier in the century with more gestural movements and puts rapid changes of movement style to comic effect. Many of Ferrère's solos and duets are technically demanding; the group dances, for six, eight or 12, also require considerable technique. While the ballets are clearly sectional (new movements being signalled by the dancers' entrances and exits as well as by changes in the music), Ferrère also seems interested in sustaining dramatic continuity by keeping the *corps de ballet* on stage when appropriate, and by his fluid transitions from dance to pantomime and back to dance within a movement.

In Italy, the independence of ballet from opera was rarely an issue. Because the already tenuous connections between ballet intermezzos and the acts of the opera that surrounded them had been severed by the start of the 18th century, it was common to find comic dances performed between the acts of an *opera seria*. Although there are isolated instances of Italian operas constructed on a French model, with the dances integrated, usually the ballet and the opera had nothing to do with each other. The separation did not, however, mean that Italian

8. *Dehesse's divertissement-pantomime 'La Guinguette', Comédie-Italienne, Paris, 1750: engraving by Pierre-François Basan after Gabriel de Saint-Aubin*

audiences had any less appreciation for ballet than did their French counterparts; they simply had different ideas about its role. In fact, the use of vocal intermezzos such as Pergolesi's famous *La serva padrona*, according to Hansell (B1988),

constituted but a short-lived historical parenthesis. For notwithstanding the importance according them in most studies of 18th-century Italian opera, the weight of the evidence proves overwhelmingly that they are properly regarded as the exception rather than the rule. The rule for 200 years, even during the period 1710 to 1735, was that entr'acte entertainments with Italian opera consisted of ballet.

Outside Italy, opera in the Italian manner also tended to reserve dancing for entr'actes, although several of Handel's operas for London (e.g. *Admeto*, 1727, and *Ariodante*, 1735) included dance related to the plot within the acts. Well into the middle of the century, Italian entr'acte ballets tended to present dramatically static vignettes that involved character dancing in rustic or exotic settings, such as *Un villaggio nella Germania co' suoi abitatori occupati in varie opere contadinesche* (1758, Milan) or *La celebre Torre di Nanchino nella Cina* (1757, Rome). Such subjects exploited Italian proclivities for mimetic dancing and allowed opportunities for the aerial, acrobatic styles in which Italian dancers excelled. Gennaro Magri's *Trattato teorico-prattico di ballo* (Naples, 1779), which focusses on the highly developed step vocabulary of the *ballarino grottesco*, is the best surviving source for technical information about this style. Magri, like many other Italian dancers of this period, spent a portion of his career abroad; other international stars included Barbara

Campanini, known as 'la Barbarina', whose virtuoso technique and pantomimic abilities created a sensation throughout Europe, and the choreographer Giuseppe Salamoni *père*, generally noted as 'di Vienna' in Italian librettos. At the same time, a look at cast lists shows that a number of French dancers also worked regularly in Italy (Jean-Marie Leclair, ballet-master in Turin before he decided to concentrate on the violin, being one notable example). Before 1740 Italian dance companies tended to have only six or eight dancers, but by the 1760s their numbers increased to around a dozen, and even to 16–18 in Turin. This increase coincided with a shift in interest towards ballets with greater narrative content, such as *La favola di Polifemo con Aci e Galatea* (1748, Milan) or *La scoperta dell'America da Cristoforo Colombo* (1756, Turin). Ballets with mythological plots allowed the fantastic or magical elements that no longer figured in *opera seria* to find a place on Italian stages.

By the mid-century, several choreographers around Europe had become interested in creating pantomime ballets on serious subjects. Vienna, a meeting-ground for artistic trends from Italy, France and central Europe, was an important centre in this regard. Working at both the Burgtheater and the Kärntnertortheater, Franz Hilverding (1710–68) turned away from the 'indecent' comic characters of the Italian theatre first towards 'natural' characters such as Tyroleans or Hungarians and then to mythological subjects. *Psyché* and *Poliphème et Galatée*, both from 1752, may be his earliest independent pantomime ballets. Although Hilverding did not publish scenarios of his ballets (because, Angiolini was to report later, he believed that the dance spoke for itself), eyewitness descriptions of many of them have been preserved. Music by Joseph Starzer survives for several dozen of his ballets (in Turin and Český Krumlov) and follows a general pattern: an opening sinfonia followed by 10 to 25 instrumental dances, mostly binary and usually untitled beyond the occasional tempo marking. Sometimes music is borrowed from other works, for example the chaconne from Rameau's *Castor et Pollux*. The dance pieces are sufficiently gestural as to allow reasonable hypotheses as to how they fit with the story line (see Brown, B1991), although such identifications are far from straightforward. Like Dehesse, Hilverding left no theoretical writings, but his pupil Angiolini later called his teacher 'the true restorer of the pantomimic art' (fig.9).

Gaspero Angiolini (1731–1803), an Italian dancer who had moved to Vienna in 1754 and inherited Hilverding's position at the Burgtheater when the latter accepted a post at the Russian court in St Petersburg in 1758, went further than his teacher by staging 'a complete dramatic action, upon principles handed down by the ancients' (Brown, B1991, p.288). In his role as choreographer for a repertory company he had to produce not only free-standing ballets but also divertissement dances for operas and plays, and whereas many of his pantomime ballets have mythological, pastoral subjects (*Les amours de Flore et Zéphire*, 1759), others are of a lighter variety (*Le tuteur dupé, ou L'amant statue*, 1761). In fact the three works

that he himself saw as landmarks – *Don Juan, ou Le festin de pierre* (1761), *Citera assediata* (1762) and *Sémiramis* (1765) – are no less important for being anomalous in his overall output. (In a pattern that was to become familiar with subsequent pantomime ballets, all three were based on pre-existing works – in this case, two plays and an *opéra comique* that had been performed recently in Vienna; the choreographer could thus count on his audience's familiarity with the stories.) After taking on in *Don Juan* a subject that one spectator characterized as 'extrêmement triste, lugubre et effroyable' (the ballet ends with Don Juan being carried off to the torments of hell by the statue of the murdered Commander), Angiolini decided to move from what he called 'comédie héroïque' to genuine tragedy. 'If there is something of the sublime in dance, it is without doubt a tragic event represented without words and made intelligible through gestures', he wrote in his *Dissertation sur les ballets pantomimes des anciens, pour servir de programme au ballet pantomime tragique de Sémiramis* (Vienna, 1765). After reviewing the precedents in the ancient world for this kind of spectacle, Angiolini turned to practical considerations: for proper effect a tragedy should involve only a few characters, but dancers cannot dance for nearly as long as actors can declaim. Thus a tragic pantomime ballet must be short and to the point; *Sémiramis* should last only 20 minutes. Angiolini did, in fact, reduce the story to its essential elements; although there is a divertissement-like scene in each of the three acts (in Act 3 a group of

9. *Scene from Franz Hilverding's pantomime ballet 'Le turc généreux' (music by Joseph Starzer), Burgtheater, Vienna, 1758: etching after Bernardo Bellotto, 1759*

subjects brings offerings to the queen), the focus remains on Semiramis and her guilty conscience throughout. The balance between *danse simple* and pantomime thus tilts much more heavily towards the latter than in most other ballets.

The composer for all three ballets – and for many others performed in Vienna during this period – was Christoph Willibald Gluck. The collaboration was apparently a happy one: Angiolini said of Gluck's music for *Don Juan*, 'he has perfectly realized the frightful essence of the action. He has undertaken to express the passions that are in play and the terror that governs the catastrophe. Music is essential to pantomimes; it is the music that speaks, we [dancers] only make gestures'. Gluck and other ballet composers did, in fact, find ways to suggest the words missing from pantomime ballets: a sacred procession in *Sémiramis* is set to a 'cantique' that has the simple melody and block chords of a hymn, and a mysterious inscription that appears on a wall is set to instrumental recitative. And although Gluck's scores are divided into separate numbers (*Sémiramis* has 15), many eschew binary or rondo forms in favour of more flexible (sometimes through-composed) structures that respond to the dramatic context through changes in tempo, level of rhythmic activity, and dynamics. Pieces not infrequently end on the dominant, as a means of making the music continuous. Dances in the divertissement sections of the ballets, on the other hand, still tend to adhere to traditional structures. Music for ballets from the court of Mannheim by composers such as Toeschi and Cannabich show a similar balance between the dramatic and the static.

During the same period, Jean-Georges Noverre (1727–1810) was working towards a similar integration of tragedy and ballet. Given the realities of pursuing an international career in the theatre (he had positions at various times in Paris, Lyons, London, Stuttgart, Vienna and Milan), he had to compose many operatic divertissements of the type he was so eloquent to deplore in his famous *Lettres sur la danse* (1760) and thus was unable to pursue what he was to call 'ballet d'action' as assiduously as he would have liked. He staged his first serious pantomime ballet, *Le jugement de Pâris,* in Lyons in 1751, but found a much more supportive working environment for his theories at the Württemberg court at Stuttgart, where he moved in 1760, just after his book had been published. Of the 20 ballets he created there, *Médée et Jason* (with music by the court composer J.J. Rodolphe, first performed after Act 1 of Jommelli's *Didone abbandonata* in 1763) had the greatest success in generating performances abroad; in 1776, in a restaging by Gaetano Vestris, it became the first independent ballet pantomime to appear on the stage of the Paris Opéra.

Noverre argued that, in order to achieve the expressiveness he desired, dancers needed to remove their masks (generally still worn in Paris at that time) so that their faces could augment the expression of their gestures. In a score dating from the Paris revival of 1804 (in *F-Po*), the actions of one highly fraught confrontation between Medea, Jason and Creusa are cued to rapid and dramatic changes in the music, here an extensive *passacaille*: '[Médée et Créuse] se disputent'; '[Jason] s'efforce de leur faire faire la paix'; 'Médée menace'; 'elle montre son poignard' (fig.10). In the absence of choreographies for any of the serious pantomime ballets it is difficult to gauge whether the mimed gestures replaced or supplemented

dance steps. Grimm's reaction to Noverre's ballets (*Correspondance littéraire*, letter of January 1771) is tantalizing but ambiguous: 'There is considerably more walking in them than dancing . . . there is dancing only in great movements of passion, at decisive moments; in the scenes, there is walking in time with the music, but without dancing'. In fact, however, Noverre did allow for dancing by building into his ballet pantomimes typical divertissements (*Médée et Jason* contains dances for the wedding festivities and an infernal scene in which Médée conjures up evil spirits) in which the key roles were assigned to noted soloists. He thus took as his model a structure analogous to sung, not spoken French tragedy – one that, like a *tragédie lyrique*, balanced narrative against moments of visual spectacle.

Noverre's fluency with the written word, demonstrated not only in his *Lettres sur la danse*, which went through several editions, but also in his pamphlet war with Angiolini, helped spread his reformist ideas all over Europe and has given him a place in dance history out of proportion to his actual accomplishments as a choreographer. Although it is true that dancers who had performed in his productions in Stuttgart and Vienna restaged many of his ballets in cities throughout Europe, Noverre was later to complain that these productions did not accurately represent his vision. In fact, he felt at the end of his life that his reach had exceeded his grasp; his most notable failure was in Paris, where his position as *maître de ballet* at the Opéra lasted only three years (1776–9, although his appointment did not officially end until 1781). Parisian audiences found his serious ballets such as *Les Horaces* unsuitable subjects for dancing, although they appreciated such lighter works as *Les fêtes chinoises* and *Les petits riens* (to a score composed partly by Mozart). His successor Maximilien Gardel generally preferred lighthearted subjects, such as *La chercheuse d'esprit* (1777) and *Ninette à la cour* (1778), or sentimental ones such as *Le déserteur* (1788); these three ballets, like many others, were based on well-known *opéras comiques*. Mythological subjects of the pastoral variety also remained in vogue (fig.11), even during the Revolutionary period, as witnessed by the popularity of such works as *Psyché* (1790) and *Le jugement de Pâris*(1794), both of which remained in the repertory of the Opéra for over three decades. (Dancers did participate in politically motivated works such as Gossec's *L'offrande à la liberté* (1792) and *Le triomphe de la République*, 1793.) *La fille mal gardée*, mounted by Jean Dauberval in Bordeaux only days before the fall of the Bastille in 1789, still receives occasional performances.

Whereas some of the music for pantomime ballets was newly composed, in Paris many ballet scores were cobbled together out of a wide variety of pre-existing pieces, both vocal and instrumental. Pierre Gardel's *Télémaque*, which received its première at the Paris Opéra in 1790, contains part of a violin concerto by Giornovichi, passages from Grétry's *opéra comique Richard Coeur-de-Lion*, symphonic excerpts from Haydn, and dances composed by Gossec for Gluck's *Iphigénie en Tauride*, in addition to pieces by Lully, Paisiello, Pleyel, Piccinni and others, all stitched together by the ostensible composer of the score, Ernest Louis Müller. Familiar vocal *airs* were often quoted instrumentally in order to suggest to the audience words otherwise absent from the mute ballet; the opening bars of Gluck's 'Che farò senza Euridice'/'J'ai perdu mon

JASON ET MEDEE   BALLET TRAGIQUE.

10. Scene from Gaetano Vestris's version of Noverre's ballet en action 'Médée et Jason', King's Theatre, London, 1781: etching by Francesco Bartolozzi after ? Nathaniel Dance; the dancers are (from left to right) Giovanna Baccelli, Vestris and Mme Simonet

Euridice' from *Orfeo/Orphée* appear in more than one pantomime ballet score. Furthermore, the surviving musical sources of French pantomime ballets often show radical differences as to what music was performed from one revival to the next, suggesting that the concept of the 'work' may have resided more in the scenario than in the score. Both in pantomime ballets and in ballets within operas from the second half of the century, fewer of the individual pieces bear generic dance designations than had been the case earlier; sometimes a familiar dance type is clearly discernible in the rhythmic and melodic contours, but often a piece is labelled only with a tempo marking because it does not adhere to the traditional binary or rondo structures of earlier dance music. Despite the loss of a substantial amount of the ballet music from the 18th century, a good deal has survived and awaits serious study.

By the last decades of the 18th century, the public's appetite for ballet had resulted in a dramatic growth in the dance troupes: Italian opera houses generally employed 35 to 40 dancers, Stockholm reached a height of 71 in 1786, while the Paris Opéra had 92 dancers in 1770. Dancers tended more and more towards specialized training; Italian librettos even categorized them as *ballerini seri, di mezzo carattere* or *grotteschi*. Despite the persistence of strong local and national traditions (the French and the Italian being the dominant schools), the end of the century saw a growing internationalization of ballet styles. The leading dancers and choreographers pursued their careers across Europe, taking with them not only works and dancing styles, but also theatrical practices borrowed from each other. In St Petersburg the dance troupe which had been led by the Italians Gasparo Angiolini (who had worked many years in Vienna) and Giuseppe Canziani was taken over by the French-trained Charles Le Picq in 1786. The Stockholm opera, like many others around Europe, employed both French and Italian dancers, in addition to locals. Costume reforms initiated in the 1790s by Salvatore Viganò featuring loose neo-classic dress and either open-toe sandals or flat, flexible slippers soon spread throughout Europe and helped open the way for the technical innovations of the 19th century. Even the Paris Opéra was not immune to influences from abroad: although the longstanding French practice of

11. Pastoral pas de trois danced by Jean Dauberval, Marie Allard and Marie-Madeleine Guimard, Paris Opéra, 1779: engraving by Pierre Leleu

integrating dance into the plot of the opera remained in place, individual works sometimes edged towards Italian practices by replacing the traditional internal divertissement with a quasi-independent pantomime ballet at the end of an act. Another point of contact between the two traditions can be observed in the practice of using a long, celebratory *fête* to conclude many operas; in Italy this was the one danced scene that sometimes bore connections to the plot, whereas in France, where celebratory divertissements had traditionally involved both dancing and singing, the final chorus sometimes disappeared in favour of a purely danced conclusion.

Although by the end of the century pantomime ballet was firmly established as an independent genre, ballet still remained a fundamental part of opera, especially, but no means exclusively, in France. *Opéra comique* and other similar genres, not to mention much spoken theatre, routinely incorporated dance. Moreover, the same institutional structures supported both opera and ballet; audiences throughout Europe were to continue to encounter opera and ballet together, in the same houses and on the same evenings, for many decades to come.

2. 19TH CENTURY.   In ballet the terms 'classical' and 'romantic' are chronologically reversed from their musical usage, the romantic style in ballet having preceded the classical.

(i) The transition to romantic ballet, 1800–30. In composing his music for *Die Geschöpfe des Prometheus* (1801) in the form of an overture and 16 numbers, Beethoven wrote for a *ballet en action* derived from Noverre's principles, which in the 18th century had ended the ballet's subservience to opera and made it an independent theatrical art. *Prometheus* was created for the Vienna court theatre (originally as *Gli uomini di Prometeo*) by SALVATORE VIGANÒ (1769–1821), a Neapolitan who often composed the music as well as the scenarios for his ballets; in place of static mime interspersed with dancing, he developed a type of expressive mime-dance based on individual character (fig.12), and

the dramatic use of a *corps de ballet*, especially after he became ballet-master at La Scala in 1811. His achievements paved the way for Carlo Blasis (?1795–1878), whose treatises on the technique of dance (*Traité élémentaire*, 1820; *Code of Terpsichore*, 1828) first codified the methods on which the teaching of classical ballet is still based.

Beethoven's ballet score was an exception to the usual musical practice at this time of a hurriedly assembled

12. Salvatore and Maria Viganò dancing the pas de deux, their first great Viennese success: drawing by Johann Gottfried Schadow, pen and ink with wash, 1793 (Kupferstichkabinett, Berlin)

patchwork by a musician on the theatre staff (those at the Paris Opéra included Rodolphe Kreutzer, the dedicatee of Beethoven's Sonata op.47). It was normal to incorporate melodies from well-known operas or songs whose words would relate to the stage action at a given point; and original music, mostly confined to the set dances, was written in a facile style to fit the choreographer's preconception of rhythm and structure. Similar conditions prevailed in Russia, where Charles-Louis Didelot (1767–1837), a pupil of Dauberval and Noverre, spent two influential periods at St Petersburg, during 1801–12 and 1816–30. However, he is credited with having paid more attention to music than most choreographers of his time, and demanded a corresponding musicality from his dancers; he frequently worked with the composer Catterino Cavos, and Soviet research (by Gozenpud and Rabinovich; see Roslavleva, C1966) suggests that Cavos was musically more successful with his ballets than his operas precisely because they were composed to a preconceived structure supplied to him.

The prevailing situation was engagingly described in memoirs published by V.A. Duvernoy in 1903:

Once the plan of the piece and the dances were arranged, the musician was called in. The ballet-master indicated the rhythms he had laid down, the steps he had arranged, the number of bars which each variation must contain – in short, the music was arranged to fit the dances. And the musician docilely improvised, so to speak, and often in the ballet-master's room, all that was asked of him. You can guess how alert his pen had to be, and how quick his imagination. No sooner was a scene written or a *pas* arranged than they were rehearsed with a violin, a single violin, as the only accompaniment ... Even after having done all the ballet-master required, the composer had to pay heed to the advice of his principal interpreters. So he had to have much talent, or at least great facility, to satisfy so many exigencies, and, I would add, a certain amount of philosophy.

Nevertheless, attempts were made from about 1820 to compose more homogeneous scores for ballet, especially in the work of Jean Schneitzhöffer, the second chorus master at the Paris Opéra, and his superior Hérold, whose score for a new version of *La fille mal gardée* (1828) remains the musical basis for present-day productions. Hérold's successor was Halévy, and his score (1830) for a *Manon Lescaut* ballet by Jean Aumer (1774–1833) is thought to have been the first to use melody to identify character; it earned the grudging admiration of Meyerbeer for its skilled use of musical allusions to suggest period. The function of the scenario writer began to be separated from that of choreographer from about 1827, when Scribe anonymously provided a scenario for Aumer's *La somnambule*, with music by Hérold, while from her début at Vienna in 1822 Marie Taglioni was preparing to bring about the revolution in theatrical dance that became the romantic ballet.

(ii) The romantic ballet and its influence. The ideal embodiment of the romantic image was Marie Taglioni (1804–84), who reflected in her dancing the spirit that infused the literature of Scott and Hugo and the music of Berlioz and Chopin. Her frail physique was schooled relentlessly by her father, the ballet-master Filippo Taglioni (1777–1871), to develop a style distinguished by lightness, grace and modesty, by the use of point-shoes for artistic effect, and by unusual elevation and delicacy on landing. Her freer, more graceful movement, enhanced by a new style of costume with a diaphanous, bell-shaped skirt and fitted bodice, gave a fresh purpose to the art of dance in the theatre (fig.13). It enabled it to become more

13. Marie Taglioni: lithograph by James Henry Lynch after Alfred Edward Chalon, 1830s

poetic and imaginative, an art of illusion rather than illustration. The style was inaugurated by *La sylphide*, staged by Filippo Taglioni for his daughter at the Paris Opéra in 1832. This had a scenario credited to the tenor Adolphe Nourrit, with whom Marie had appeared the year before in Meyerbeer's *Robert le diable*, when she led the ballet of spectral nuns which constituted one of the opera's most novel expressive scenes. (see fig.17 below)

La sylphide reflected the romantic ideal in its theme of a tragically unattainable love, and its combination of the exotic and the supernatural: a Scottish setting and an ethereal being who appears and vanishes with the illusion of flight, which Taglioni was perfectly trained to suggest. Her style of dancing was a creative triumph which has haunted the art of ballet ever since; it not only displaced the male as the dominant figure and established the supremacy of the ballerina for almost a century, but it also required that composers should emphasize the lightness and grace of the ballerina more than the ballet's drama and situation, which is partly why much of the century's ballet music is essentially feminine in character. Taglioni's production of *La sylphide*, with music by Schneitzhöffer, carried the seeds of romantic ballet to Russia when Taglioni first danced there in 1837, but a version choreographed by Auguste Bournonville (1805–79) at Copenhagen in 1836 – the version that survived – had a new score by H.S. Løvenskjold.

The obverse of the romantic image in dance was personified by Fanny Elssler (1810–84), a Viennese of strong dramatic character and virtuoso technique. If Taglioni was a spirit of the air, Elssler was the child of the earth, excelling in colourful character dances in which a theatrical presentation was given to such folkdances as

14. Fanny Elssler dancing the Spanish cachucha: lithograph by Nathaniel T. Currier, 1840

the Spanish *cachucha* (fig.14) and the Polish krakowiak. Elssler first triumphed in Paris in Jean Coralli's (1779–1854) ballet *Le diable boiteux* (1836) with music by Casimir Gide, and while Taglioni continued to suggest ethereal illusion in other ballets by her father, such as *La*

fille du Danube (1836) and *L'ombre* (1839), Elssler dazzled with her virtuosity in *La gypsy* and *La tarentule* (both 1839). From 1840 she toured the USA for two years and achieved an artistic and financial success then unparalleled in American theatrical history, although there European ballet remained a sterile import which failed to stimulate any native dance activity in the theatre until the 20th century.

While Elssler was in the USA and Taglioni was in Russia, the Paris Opéra was conquered by a new ballerina who arrived from Naples by way of Milan: Carlotta Grisi (1819–99), a cousin of the celebrated singers Giuditta and Giulia Grisi. Carlotta was the discovery of Jules Perrot (1810–92), who had partnered Taglioni and turned to choreography when the male dancer became virtually eclipsed. A combination of talents which came together at an opportune moment comprised Perrot and Coralli as choreographers, Théophile Gautier who brought poetry to the writing of a scenario, and Adolphe Adam who extended the expressive character of ballet music: the result was *Giselle*, which had its première at the Opéra in 1841 (fig.15). In its contrast between the realistic peasants of the first act and the disembodied spirits of the second, the need for the ballerina to unite the essential characteristics of each, and the skill of Adam in an incipient use of leitmotifs and musical reminiscence for dramatic effect, *Giselle* represents the romantic ballet at its peak.

Perrot first made London an important centre for ballet during the 1840s, when he worked for six years at Her Majesty's Theatre under Benjamin Lumley's management. Perrot staged *Giselle* for Grisi (whom he had married) and went on to create some of the finest romantic ballets in *Ondine* (1843), *La Esmeralda* (1844), *Catarina* and *Lalla Rookh* (both 1846). These united the dramatic, the supernatural and the exotic in true *ballets d'action* where the choreography created sympathetic characters and carried the narrative forward without superfluous virtuosity, even if the music composed for each of them by Cesare Pugni did little more than embroider the rhythm and reinforce the expressive mood. Perrot also staged

15. Carlotta Grisi and Jules Perrot as Giselle and Albrecht in the first scene of Adam's 'Giselle': engraving, c1842

divertissements to display the finest dancers of the time, culminating in *Pas de quatre* (1845; fig.16), in which Lumley succeeded in presenting four divas simultaneously: Taglioni, Grisi, the Italian Fanny Cerrito (1817–1909) and the Danish Lucile Grahn (1819–1907).

Grahn represented another important centre of romantic ballet in Copenhagen, where Auguste Bournonville returned in 1830 from his studies with Vestris in Paris to direct the Danish Court Ballet (later the Royal Danish Ballet) for the next 47 years. As well as his own version of *La sylphide*, which he staged in 1836 for Grahn on the model of Taglioni's Paris version, Bournonville created more than 50 ballets of different types for his Danish company, which continued independently of theatrical fashion elsewhere; by maintaining the prestige of the male dancer on a par with the ballerina he distinguished the Danish school of ballet from all others in Europe. Bournonville's musical interests (which included the operas of Mozart and Wagner) encouraged native composers to provide original and homogeneous scores for his ballets. Two days before his death in 1879 he witnessed the début of Hans Beck, a dancer who carried the Bournonville ballet style into the mid-20th century with a continuity of tradition unparalleled elsewhere in Europe.

In Russia the foundations laid by Didelot up to 1829 were receptive to the French romantic influences brought first by Taglioni in *La sylphide* to St Petersburg in 1837. She continued to appear there each year to 1842, and Elssler, Grisi, Cerrito and Grahn went there in her wake, dancing the ballets most closely associated with them. These included *Giselle*, which established Yelena Andreyanova (1819–57) as the first Russian romantic ballerina at St Petersburg; her Moscow counterpart was Yekaterina

Sankovskaya (1816–78), who danced *La sylphide* and followed Andreyanova in *Giselle*, Elssler in *La Esmeralda* and Taglioni in *La fille du Danube*. Sankovskaya also choreographed her own production of *Le diable à quatre* in Moscow four years before Perrot staged it in St Petersburg; Perrot went there when London's interest in ballet declined after Jenny Lind's operatic successes, and remained as ballet-master until 1859, when he was succeeded by Arthur Saint-Léon, a virile dancer and Cerrito's husband until they separated in 1851. Saint-Léon had only modest success in Russia except for *The Little Hump-Backed Horse*, one of the first ballets on a specifically Russian folk story which, in spite of the limited musical interest of Pugni's score, supplemented by themes borrowed from Rossini (*Tancredi* in particular), remained in the repertory for many years after its 1864 première (20th-century productions by other choreographers continued to use the Pugni music until a new score was composed by Shchedrin for performance in 1960). The native Russian element in ballet was consolidated by *The Fern* (1867), with choreography by Sergey Sokolov, a pupil of Saint-Léon, and music by Yury Gelber, first violin and conductor of the Bol'shoy Theatre orchestra, and led directly to later balletic triumphs in association with Tchaikovsky.

(iii) Ballet in opera. Throughout the 19th century ballet retained a connection with opera, chiefly when composers incorporated dance scenes to diversify weightier emotional matters. Weber anticipated some elements of *La sylphide* by more than 20 years in his early opera *Silvana* (1810), in which his mostly mute heroine embodies the romantic woodland spirit and expresses herself in dance. Weber evoked a strong flavour of Spanish dance in his music for *Preciosa*; he added a newly composed pas de cinq to *Euryanthe* in 1825 for its Berlin production, to please Friedrich Wilhelm III of Prussia; and *Oberon* has enchanting dances woven into the musical fabric. In Russia, Glinka was an admirer of ballet who took lessons in his youth, and whose knowledge of ballet and folkdance is reflected in dance scenes which grow out of the dramatic action, notably in *A Life for the Tsar* (1836) and *Ruslan and Lyudmila* (1842). By the 1820s ballet had become a necessary element of all productions at the Paris Opéra, where Rossini, after interpolating dance movements from other sources in his earlier operas, provided two extensive dance sequences in *Guillaume Tell* (1829), in which Marie Taglioni first danced the well-known Tyrolean Dance.

Meyerbeer incorporated ballet to more than decorative purpose in *Robert le diable* (1831), his ballet of the spectral nuns serving to tempt the hero from the path of honour (fig.17), but in his later operas such as *Les Huguenots*, *L'étoile du nord* and *L'Africaine* his ballet sequences were more in the nature of divertissements, as were those Donizetti added to *Les martyrs* (the French version of *Poliuto*) or to *La favorite* and *Dom Sébastien*. Verdi's adaptations for the Paris Opéra are particularly interesting in this respect; he added a ballet to *I Lombardi* when it was staged there as *Jérusalem*; he composed a ballet of the Four Seasons as an original element in *Les vêpres siciliennes*; he added Spanish-gypsy dances when *Il trovatore* became *Le trouvère* (including one based on the theme of the Anvil Chorus); he summoned Hecate and the witches to dance in *Macbeth*; and he equipped the Paris production of *Don Carlos* with 'La Pérégrina: ballet de la reine' (fig.18). He resisted blandishments to add a

16. *Marie Taglioni (kneeling) with Lucile Grahn, Fanny Cerrito and Carlotta Grisi in the 'Pas de quatre', Her Majesty's Theatre, London, 1845: lithograph by John Brandard*

17. *The nuns rise from their graves in Act 3 of Meyerbeer's 'Robert le diable': painting by Edgar Degas, 1876 (Victoria and Albert Museum, London); the stage design is still apparently that of the first production at the Paris Opéra in 1831*

18. *'La Pérégrina: ballet de la reine' from Act 3 scene ii of Verdi's 'Don Carlos', Paris Opéra, 1867: engraving from 'L'illustration' (16 March 1867)*

ballet to *Rigoletto*, but in 1894 provided a divertissement for *Otello*, his last music for the theatre.

With the decline of romantic ballet as an artistic entity after about 1850, ballets became more and more an excuse for vulgar display by individual performers or for varying degrees of elaborate spectacle. The entrenched position in Paris within ten years is illustrated by the episode of the ballet Wagner was required to add to *Tannhäuser*: he placed it at the start of Act 1 whereupon part of the audience, having arrived too late to witness it, created a disturbance that wrecked the opera's prospects. French composers such as Berlioz, Gounod and Massenet took care to safeguard themselves by making due provision for ballet in their operas; others alternated between operas and ballets as complementary entertainments. When Grétry's *Zémire et Azor* became a ballet in 1824, Schneitzhöffer retained much of the original music in his transcription, but when Auber turned his *Marco Spada* opera of 1852 into a ballet on the same subject five years later, he constructed a quite different score using themes from *Fra Diavolo* and his other operas.

Adam worked successfully in both genres, as did his pupil Delibes, who was responsible for two scores that raised the standard of ballet music at a time when the art itself was in decline in western Europe. The first of these was *Coppélia* (1870), originally choreographed in Paris by Saint-Léon, in which Delibes extended Adam's device of associating themes with characters. The lack of difference in musical manner between the male and female dances in *Coppélia* is explained by the fact that the male had been so far relegated that his leading role was then, and for many years subsequently, danced by a female *en travestie*. Delibes further developed the leitmotif device in *Sylvia* (1876), and Tchaikovsky came to know and admire the music to fruitful purpose, but none of the original choreography, by Louis Mérante (1828–87), has survived.

(iv) The classical ballet in Russia to 1900. Tchaikovsky once described his music for *Swan Lake* as 'poor stuff compared with *Sylvia*', but it was his score which, by treating ballet as a subject worthy of musical imagination, set new standards for the role of music in classical ballet and achieved one of its enduring masterworks. *Swan Lake* had its origins in a domestic entertainment by the children and friends of Tchaikovsky's sister, performed at their home probably about 1871. It was extended to a four-act ballet on a commission in 1875–6 from the directorate of the Imperial Theatres, and was first performed at the Bol'shoy Theatre, Moscow, in 1877, with Pelagia Karpakova in the dual leading role of Odette-Odile. Nobody was credited with a scenario for *Swan Lake* in the original programme, but the folk story seems to have been given theatrical form by the Bol'shoy Theatre director Vladimir Begichev and the dancer Vasily Heltzor, in collaboration with Tchaikovsky and the ballet-master Julius Reisinger (who was responsible for the first choreography). The ballet achieved a modest success in spite of difficulties presented by the stronger and more organic musical element, and choreography that hardly matched the level of musical invention. A Russian dance at the first performance, and a full-scale pas de deux at the fifth, were added by Tchaikovsky at the request of the ballerinas concerned.

Nikolay Kashkin, who made the first piano transcription of *Swan Lake*, later recalled that the ballet 'held its place on the stage until the scenery was worn out ... Not only the décor became ragged, but the musical score suffered more and more until nearly a third was exchanged with music from other ballets, and not necessarily good ones'. In progressively more mutilated form the ballet continued in the Bol'shoy Theatre repertory through the new choreographic version made by Joseph Hansen in 1880 until it was eventually dropped in 1883. It then remained unperformed until after Tchaikovsky's death when an entirely new version was mounted at St Petersburg in the wake of the greater successes of *The Sleeping Beauty* (1890) and *The Nutcracker* (1892).

Meanwhile in 1869 the Russian imperial ballet had come under the despotic control of Marius Petipa (1818–1910), a French-born ballet-master and choreographer whose brother, Lucien, was *premier danseur* at the Paris Opéra, and whose father, Jean, had taught at the Russian Imperial Academy of Dancing. Building on the existing foundations, Petipa created 46 original ballets in Russia which raised the style to a peak of spectacular grandeur; the best of them continued to influence the course of classical ballet and its teaching throughout the 20th century. Petipa had already toured in France, Spain and the USA; he first went to St Petersburg in 1847 and was *premier danseur* until 1858 when he became second ballet-master under Saint-Léon. In this capacity he staged his first important ballet in 1862, the three-act *Pharaoh's Daughter*, with music by the ubiquitous Pugni, who at that time had the official post of staff ballet composer to the Imperial Theatres. Petipa's mixture of *pas d'action* stemming from Perrot's dramatic principles, with exotic divertissements, fantastic processions and multiple apotheoses, not necessarily germane to the narrative, constituted the first *ballet à grand spectacle*, a type that dominated Russian ballet for the rest of the century. *The Sleeping Beauty* remains the most celebrated example, more of Petipa's choreography having survived from this than from any other, but scenes and pas de deux by him have been handed down from the 1895 revision of *Swan Lake*, from *Don Quixote* (1869) and *La bayadère* (1877) with music by Minkus, and from the 1899 revision of *Le corsaire*.

The composition of *The Sleeping Beauty*, described by Stravinsky as 'the convincing example of Tchaikovsky's great creative power', was brought about by Ivan Vsevolozhsky, director of the Imperial Theatres, who abolished the post of staff ballet composer and engaged composers of more distinction. Vsevolozhsky prepared the scenario and designs, while Petipa mapped out in detail a sequence of dances which, far from being a hindrance to musical composition (as some commentaries have suggested), proved a practical help to Tchaikovsky, whose enthusiastic collaboration resulted in the supreme example of 19th-century classical ballet. It was first performed at the Mariinsky Theatre, St Petersburg, in 1890, and remains a cornerstone of the classical ballet repertory.

Two years later Vsevolozhsky brought Tchaikovsky and Petipa together again for *The Nutcracker*, which was to form part of a double bill with Tchaikovsky's one-act opera *Iolanta*, but Petipa had not progressed very far before illness compelled him to yield the choreography to his assistant, Lev Ivanov (1834–1901), who alone was named on the posters for the first production at St Petersburg in 1892 (fig.19). Ivanov was further responsible for a new version of Act 2 of *Swan Lake*, mounted as

19. *Snowflakes from Tchaikovsky's 'The Nutcracker', Mariinsky Theatre, St Petersburg, 1892*

a memorial to Tchaikovsky after the composer's death in 1893, which led to the full new production in 1895 by Petipa and Ivanov together, from which most later versions of the ballet have stemmed. The scenario for this was modified by Tchaikovsky's brother, Modest, and the alterations made in the musical sequence to meet Petipa's requirements have continued to bedevil most productions of the ballet.

Ivanov worked so much in the shadow of Petipa, mostly revising older ballets, that the transitory nature of unrecorded choreography has denied him much posthumous fame, but he was a talented (though untrained) musician, and the known share of his contribution to *Swan Lake*, still preserved in the familiar Act 2, shows him to have been a much more musical choreographer than Petipa. Besides *The Nutcracker*, Soviet historians also single out Ivanov's original choreography of the Polovtsian Dances in the first production (1890) of Borodin's *Prince Igor*, but at the end of his life Ivanov had to petition the Imperial Theatres for financial assistance, on the strength of 50 years' service, and he died in poverty. Petipa, however, recovered from his illness to collaborate fruitfully in *Raymonda* (1896–7) and *The Seasons* (1899) with Glazunov, whose symphonic aspirations sadly curtailed his evident talent for ballet. A change in the administration of the Imperial Theatres soon after and the failure of Koreschenko's *The Magic Mirror* brought about Petipa's retirement. His legacy was a repertory and a style on which others could build, and

an ensemble of dancers and a school of training which represented an investment for the future; Sergey Diaghilev was one of the first to profit from it.

3. 20TH CENTURY: CLASSICAL.   In balletic usage the term 'classical' continues to define old and new works performed in a style derived from the Franco-Russian *danse de l'école*, in contrast with 'modern dance' (see §4) which commonly refers to the freer style derived in the USA from Isadora Duncan, Ruth St Denis and particularly Martha Graham, and in Europe from Rudolf von Laban, Mary Wigman and Kurt Jooss.

(i) Diaghilev and the Russian exiles to 1930.   Sergey Diaghilev (1872–1929), whose touch of genius changed the face and fortune of classical dance within five years and determined its 20th-century course in the West, could neither choreograph nor compose, but was originally concerned with disseminating Russian art in all its manifestations. He first organized exhibitions of visual art in Paris and then planned a production there of Borodin's *Prince Igor* with a Russian company (1909); financial reasons caused this to be restricted to a presentation of Act 2 only, and consequently the Russian dancers in the scene of the Polovtsian Dances captured as much as if not more attention than the singers. Diaghilev realized that Russian ballet could be even more successful in the West than Russian opera.

His second Paris season (1909) accordingly presented for the first time the 'Ballets Russes de Serge Diaghilev' in

20. Vaclav Nizhinsky (right, also the choreographer) and the nymphs in Debussy's 'L'après-midi d'un faune', designed by Léon Bakst: photograph from the 'Illustrated London News' (22 February 1913)

a repertory almost entirely choreographed by Mikhail Fokine (1880–1942), including the Polovtsian Dances as a separate item. Prompted by what he had seen of the American modern dancer Isadora Duncan, Fokine's other works in this and following years initiated a new trend in the use of pre-existing music, not necessarily composed with dancing in mind. At first he used such music in three different ways: as an anthology of works by one composer, of which the most famous example is the orchestrated Chopin anthology first made in 1909 for *Les sylphides* (originally *Chopiniana*, a title still retained in Russia), which was followed by similar Schumann anthologies for *Le carnaval* (1910) and *Papillons* (1914); a miscellany of works by different composers for the same ballet, as in *Cleopatra* (1909), which used music by Arensky, Glazunov, Glinka, Musorgsky, Rimsky-Korsakov, Taneyev and Tcherepnin; or the association of a new balletic narrative or theme with a single work, as in *Sheherazade* (1910), where Rimsky-Korsakov's music was matched to a story different from that which prompted his composition. Diaghilev soon realized that musical integrity was no less important to dance than choreography and visual character, and the second of these categories was quickly discarded; the others have continued to furnish a wide variety of musical means for dance.

Diaghilev also continued the 19th-century practice of specially written music for dance and engaged composers of true promise or distinction, most notably Stravinsky, whose three pre-1914 Diaghilev commissions, *The Firebird* (1910), *Petrushka* (1911) and *The Rite of Spring* (1913), first brought him international fame. In that

period Diaghilev also engaged Debussy (*L'après-midi d'un faune* and *Jeux*), Ravel (*Daphnis et Chloé*), Florent Schmitt (*La tragédie de Salomé*) and Richard Strauss (*Josephslegende*). From 1917 until Diaghilev's death these were supplemented by Satie (*Parade*), Falla (*El sombrero de tres picos*), Poulenc (*Les biches*), Auric (*Les fâcheux*), Milhaud (*Le train bleu*), Sauguet (*La chatte*), Prokofiev (*The Steel Step* and *The Prodigal Son*) and Constant Lambert (*Romeo and Juliet*), while the production of *Apollon musagète* (1928) initiated the partnership between Balanchine and Stravinsky which had far-reaching consequences for classical dance in the following decades. Diaghilev's policy towards composers confirmed his belief that music could and should have an organic and not merely decorative part in the theatrical conception.

The choreographic interest of Diaghilev's company centred successively on Fokine, Leonid Massine (1896–1979) and George Balanchine (1904–83), and to a lesser extent on the dancer Vaclav Nizhinsky (1888–1950), who was responsible for the first choreography of *L'après-midi d'un faune* (fig.20), *Jeux* and *The Rite of Spring* in versions forgotten until the last named was reconstructed in 1988, and his sister Bronislava Nizhinska (1890–1972) who created, among other works, *The Wedding* and *Les biches*, which continue to be performed in her original choreography. A member of Diaghilev's company at the outset was Anna Pavlova (1881–1931), who broke with him after his first Paris season, formed her own company (mostly English in origin) in 1914 and began the world tours that continued until her death. She spread the interest in classical ballet in many countries where it was a complete novelty, but her inferior taste in music (using that of Aphons Czibulka, Drigo, Paul Lincke and the slighter works of more distinguished names) was also responsible for a widespread and persistent belief that 'ballet music' was confined to works of a trivial nature.

With the sudden death of Diaghilev in 1929 and the disbandment of his company, the conditions became ripe for the establishment of a tradition of classical dance on a more permanent basis in Britain, the USA and elsewhere. Companies calling themselves 'Ballets Russes', or versions of that title, continued to be active and their confused identities are described in detail elsewhere (Lynham, D1947); the first of them, the Ballet Russe de Monte Carlo, produced the so-called 'symphonic ballets' by Massine, of which *Choreartium* (1933), to Brahms's Symphony no.4, occasioned something of a musical scandal but was much admired when revived by Birmingham Royal Ballet in 1991. (It was not, however, the first ballet to make use of a pre-composed symphony; Aleksandr Gorsky (see §iii below) had choreographed Glazunov's Fifth Symphony at the Bol'shoy Theatre in 1915.)

(ii) Britain, the USA and elsewhere.   A direct outcome of the Diaghilev company's activities, and of its first production in the West of Petipa's St Petersburg classic *The Sleeping Beauty* (Alhambra Theatre, London, 1921), was the establishment of classical dance on a regular basis through resident companies in Britain and the USA. Diaghilev had recruited and trained the three women who laid the foundations of classical ballet in Britain: Marie Rambert (1888–1982), Ninette de Valois (*b* 1898) and Alicia Markova (*b* 1910). Marie Rambert began teaching in London in 1920, and in 1926 founded Ballet Rambert, renamed Rambert Dance Company in 1987. Ninette de Valois became associated with Lilian Baylis at the Old Vic from 1926, and from 1931 at Sadler's Wells Theatre, where the Vic-Wells Ballet formed by de Valois was the basis of the Royal Ballet. Alicia Markova was the first British prima ballerina and set the high professional standards that both the Rambert and the Vic-Wells companies aimed at from the outset; she later (1935–8) toured Britain with the Markova-Dolin Ballet.

Operating on Diaghilev's principles as far as she could, de Valois staged classics from the notebooks of the Russian régisseur Nikolay Sergeyev (*Giselle*, *The Nutcracker* and *Swan Lake* in 1934 and *The Sleeping Beauty* in 1939), and supplemented these with works of her own and others by Frederick Ashton (1904–88), who became a resident choreographer in 1935. Where possible, a collaboration was sought with British composers, including Vaughan Williams (*Job*, 1931; fig.21), Walton (*Façade*, 1931), Geoffrey Toye (*The Haunted Ballroom*, 1935), Gavin Gordon (*The Rake's Progress*, 1935), and Bliss (*Checkmate*, 1937), while Constant Lambert as musical director made arrangements of music by such composers as Auber, Liszt and Meyerbeer (for Ashton's *Les rendezvous*, *Apparitions* and *Les patineurs* respec-

21. *Scene from the first production of Vaughan Williams's 'Job', Cambridge Theatre, London, 1931, choreographed by Ninette de Valois, with Anton Dolin (centre) as Satan*

tively), and of Boyce for de Valois' *The Prospect before Us*. The company became known as Sadler's Wells Ballet in the late 1930s, after Markova left in 1935 to form her own company with Anton Dolin; Margot Fonteyn (1919–91) succeeded Markova in the ballerina roles, having begun dancing with the company in 1934. During World War II it was based at the New Theatre, London; it reopened Covent Garden in 1946 with *The Sleeping Beauty* and became the resident company there, receiving the royal charter in 1956. A second company, Sadler's Wells Theatre Ballet (at first Sadler's Wells Opera Ballet), was formed at Sadler's Wells Theatre in 1946, and subsequently became the touring echelon of the Royal Ballet. In 1976 it returned to its former base and was officially renamed Sadler's Wells Royal Ballet. From 1990 it was based in Birmingham (as Birmingham Royal Ballet) with its own director and administration.

Rambert's sphere of operation was more circumscribed, her company never acquiring a regular base for performance, but it complemented that of de Valois by consistently acting as a forcing-house for choreographic talent. Having brought to light Frederick Ashton, whose first ballet, *A Tragedy of Fashion*, to music by Eugene Goossens, inaugurated the Rambert dancers' first appearance (Lyric Theatre, Hammersmith, 1926), Rambert subsequently developed the talents of Antony Tudor (who became a significant influence on classical dance in the USA), Walter Gore, Andrée Howard and Frank Staff, followed in the postwar period by several more, notably Norman Morrice and Christopher Bruce. Rambert encouraged a broad-minded and relatively adventurous approach to music which enabled Tudor to create *The Planets* (to part of Holst's suite, 1934) and *Dark Elegies* (to Mahler's *Kindertotenlieder*, 1937), and which also ranged from Schubert (Howard's *Death and the Maiden*, 1937) to Poulenc, Honegger and Prokofiev before World War II.

Meanwhile Balanchine, who worked in Copenhagen, Paris and London for short periods after the Diaghilev company disbanded, was approached in 1933 with a plan to establish a base for classical dance in New York, to parallel developments in modern dance, and he opened the School of American Ballet there the next year. From it there appeared, as opportunity and funds allowed, a succession of companies including the American Ballet, Ballet Caravan and Ballet Society, and a growing team of dancers trained in Balanchine's style (which he extended to numerous Broadway and film assignments in the 1930s and 40s). These activities brought about American subjects for dance and the participation of American composers; an example is Eugene Loring's *Billy the Kid* with music by Copland, first staged by Ballet Caravan in 1938. Ballet Society, formed in 1946, was in due course invited to make its home at New York City Center, where it became the foundation of the New York City Ballet in 1948 and where it continued to flourish until it was installed at the New York State Theater in Lincoln Center in 1964.

Other major companies to establish the classical tradition in the USA include the San Francisco Ballet (from 1937) and the American Ballet Theatre, originally formed at New York City Center in 1940, with which Tudor became closely associated from the outset, and whose later notable choreographers include Jerome Robbins. From the 1950s classical companies of varying standards proliferated in large cities and regional areas.

In Canada a modest ballet school opened at Winnipeg in 1938, became a professional company from 1949 and received a royal charter in 1953 as the Royal Winnipeg Ballet. It was followed by the National Ballet of Canada based in Toronto (1951) and Les Grands Ballets Canadiens, based in Montreal (1952).

In Europe the once supreme Paris Opéra Ballet declined into the doldrums, from which it was partly lifted by a former Diaghilev principal Serge Lifar (1905–86); it regained much of its old prestige under the direction of Rudolf Nureyev (1938–93). However, the Paris-based company Les Ballets Suédois was influential in experimental work (1920–25), as was Les Ballets des Champs-Elysées in maintaining the Paris Opéra tradition in the period 1945–50. In Copenhagen the Royal Danish Ballet continued on its course undisturbed by the rest of the balletic world and unaffected by Diaghilev (except for brief visits from Fokine in 1925 and Balanchine in 1930), and was rediscovered internationally after 1945 as the repository of the Bournonville style and method, virtually unchanged for a century. More recently, under Flemming Flindt (*b* 1936), the Danish company has sought to maintain a balance between the Bournonville tradition and new developments in classical dance, notably commissioning original music from Maxwell Davies for Flindst's two-act ballets *Salome* (1978) and *Caroline Mathilde* (1991). Flindt left in 1978 to form his own independent company and was succeeded by former principal dancer Hemming Kronstam, and then in 1996 by Maina Gielgud, the first woman to direct the company and the first non-Dane for 180 years. But she found the position untenable and left after one year.

(iii) The USSR: a continuing tradition. Between the retirement of Petipa from St Petersburg in 1903 and the revolution of 1917, the focus of classical ballet moved to Moscow, where Aleksandr Gorsky (1871–1924) was appointed ballet-master at the Bol'shoy Theatre in 1900. He staged new versions of several Petipa ballets, including five progressive versions of *Swan Lake*, making them more dramatic and less formal; he was the first choreographer to make use of a pre-existing symphony for dance (Glazunov's Symphony no.5, 1915); and he introduced *The Nutcracker* to Moscow in 1919. His style of dance-drama was found to accord with the new Soviet aims for classical dance after 1917 when, instead of being swept away as a symbol of imperial decadence (as many activists wanted), it was defended by the first Soviet Commissar of Enlightenment, Anatol Lunacharsky, as a national asset that deserved to be made worthy of the proletariat.

With the classical tradition preserved and nurtured by outstanding teachers such as Agrippina Vaganova in Leningrad and Vasily Tikhomirov in Moscow, the new Soviet ballet passed swiftly through a phase of post-Revolutionary experiment to cultivate a new harvest in the classical tradition. Tikhomirov was the joint choreographer with Lev Lashchilin of the first successful 'socialist ballet', Glier's *The Red Poppy* (1927; fig.22), which established socialist realism as a balletic theme and which is still in the repertory. *The Golden Age* (1930) was a fiercer but more controversial satire on capitalist principles, with music that helped to make Shostakovich more widely known; one of its choreographers, Vasily Vainonen (1898–1964), went on to create in *The Fire of Paris* (to Asaf'yev's pastiche of 18th-century French music, 1932) the emotional human drama against a

22. *Scene from the first production of Glier's 'The Red Poppy', Moscow, 1927, choreographed by Vasily Tikhomirov and Lev Lashchilin*

revolutionary political background which continued to be a prominent theme in Soviet ballet.

Gorsky's naturalistic style of dance-drama reached its peak in the work of Leonid Lavrovsky (1905–67), who began choreography in the 1930s at Leningrad where the former imperial company now took its name from the Kirov Theatre (formerly the Mariinsky Theatre). Lavrovsky's *Romeo and Juliet* in 1940 to Prokofiev's score (the first version was by Vanya Psota at Brno in 1938) was his major achievement; he also choreographed *The Stone Flower* in 1954 to Prokofiev's last ballet score, after the composer's death. Lavrovsky's counterpart and predecessor at Moscow was Rostislav Zakharov (1907–84), whose ballets *The Fountain of Bakhchisaray* (1933, music by Asaf'yev) was the first of several on Pushkin subjects. He also choreographed the first version of *Cinderella* (1945) to Prokofiev's other major ballet score, when the title role was taken by the most celebrated of Vaganova's pupils and the outstanding Soviet ballerina of the mid-20th century, Galina Ulanova (1910–98).

A later version of *Cinderella* in 1964 had choreography by Konstantin Sergeyev (1910–92), another Leningrad dancer who had earlier made the first ballet on race relations in *The Path of Thunder* (1958), with music by Karayev and based on a novel by the South African writer Peter Abrahams. The classic tragedy of *Spartacus*, with music by Khachaturian, has furnished successive ballets by Igor Moyseyev (1958), Leonid Jacobsen (1966) and in 1968 by Yury Grigorovich, who became director of the Bol'shoy Ballet in 1964, remaining in the post until his resignation in 1995. His productions have modified naturalistic dance-drama by reasserting the supremacy of

the classical style, but used with more freedom of imagination, as in his versions of *Swan Lake* and *The Nutcracker*.

The Lavrovsky production of *Romeo and Juliet*, led by Ulanova and Yury Zhdanov, opened the Bol'shoy Ballet's first season at Covent Garden in 1956 and initiated an influence on classical dance in the West which was continued in later tours by the Bol'shoy and Kirov companies (the latter first appeared at Covent Garden in 1961). Ulanova's embodiment of a total commitment to a dramatic role, with musical phrasing to heighten emotional expression, and a technique that was broader in outline and more impassioned in character than that attempted by Western dancers, brought about a new focus of style in classical dance, as did Soviet dancers who left the USSR to settle and work in the West, notably Rudolf Nureyev, Natalia Makarova and Mikhail Barïshnikov. The underlying conservatism of music in Soviet dance, however, has been less fruitful elsewhere.

With the advent of political and economic reform (*perestroika*) promoted from 1985 under the government leadership of Mikhail Gorbachev, leading to the disintegration of the USSR, the major state ballet companies found themselves confronted by artistic and economic problems. Subsidies were reduced, and the greater freedom of the individual allowed more dancers to seek lucrative engagements in the West, chiefly as guest artists for limited seasons. However, some obtained full-time contracts, such as Irek Mukhamedov from the Bol'shoy Ballet who joined London's Royal Ballet as a principal from 1990. A state of flux on the Russian ballet scene left standards in decline, and a season by the Bol'shoy Ballet in London in 1993 was so poorly received and adversely reviewed that a planned return the next year had to be cancelled for lack of public response. The company's artistic director of 30 years, the despotic Yury Nikolaiyevich Grigorovich (*b* 1927), described in some quarters as a 'Soviet fossil', was forced to resign in 1995, and was replaced by Vladimir Victorovich Vasiliyev (*b* 1940), a former dancer and a fierce critic of Grigorovich. From the company's summer season in London in 1999 it appeared that standards were improving, although the repertory and musical character were still stagnant. Similarly in St Petersburg, the Kirov Ballet director of 20 years, Oleg Mikhailovich Vinogradov (*b* 1937) resigned in 1997, and control was taken by the conductor Valery Gergiyev, artistic director of the Kirov Opera, assisted by a committee of ballet advisers including principal dancers.

(iv) Main trends since 1945.   From being concentrated in a few centres and touring companies, classical dance in the latter part of the 20th century became an element of national or civic cultural prestige throughout the world. Whether funded from government, commercial or private sources, full-time companies devoted wholly or mainly to classical dance are active in almost all European countries, Russia and neighbouring republics, the Middle East, North and South America, Cuba, China, Japan, Australasia and South Africa. In many countries two or more companies perform in direct or complementary competition, and it has become a regular practice for tours to be made from one country to another on a continuing basis of cultural exchange, a practice virtually initiated by the successful visit of Sadler's Wells Ballet from Covent Garden to New York in 1949 and repeated for many successive years until costs became prohibitive.

Classical companies involve larger numbers of dancers than their modern-dance counterparts, and their success depends fundamentally on at least one resident choreographer or director whose works give the company a corporate personality, and on schools of ballet where teachers of distinction can provide, year by year, a flow of intensively trained young talent to the professional companies. Basic repertories generally include at least one of the five main 'classics': the three Tchaikovsky ballets, *Giselle* and *Coppélia*, to which a *Romeo and Juliet* (Prokofiev) is often added. These are supplemented by the works of the resident choreographers and others, who may be invited to produce their more successful ballets in other countries. Some choreographers work in peripatetic fashion for any company wishing to engage them, and works from the Diaghilev repertory continue to be revived after more than 50 years. Forms of notation have enabled older works to be re-produced, and new systems of notation ('choreology') can provide a more lasting record of new works, although it is frequently felt that productions staged from notation alone lack the personality their creators would have given them.

The 'dance explosion' of the 1970s and 80s was a world phenomenon, helping in Britain to raise the profile of dance as an art and an entertainment in both professional and community contexts. The fragments of fallout from this explosion of activity have tended to coalesce into numerous small groups, usually of a modern or postmodern character, who come together in performance for a few days, weeks or months, at the behest of any self-styled choreographer who can obtain public funding, commercial sponsors or a mixture of both, and

whose awareness of music is often limited to 'staining the background' with sound, usually on tape and sometimes electro-acoustic.

There are, of course, honourable exceptions, whose choreographic work has reflected an understanding of the creative contribution that music can make to a dance conception and has thus encouraged more composers to realize that new music for dance can bring, as well as artistic fulfilment, more financial reward through repeated performances than much concert work can offer. Financial constraints usually limit new work, whether in the classical or modern category, to single-act length of from 15 to 60 minutes. A large national company may stage four to eight such works a year, unless some special occasion enables the number to be increased; the most memorable example was New York City Ballet's tribute to Stravinsky (1972), when 31 ballets to his music (of which 20 were entirely new works) were staged within a week by Balanchine and six other choreographers.

In postwar economic conditions the full-evening ballet with music specially composed, the most usual kind of work a century earlier, became very rare. The first three-act score by a British composer was Britten's *The Prince of the Pagodas* (1957), created by John Cranko (1927–73) for the Royal Ballet at Covent Garden; others of musical distinction have been Henze's *Undine* (1958) for Ashton and the Royal Ballet, and three ballets by Peter Darrell (1929–87): *Sun into Darkness* (1966; music by Malcolm Williamson) for Western Theatre Ballet; and *Beauty and the Beast* (1969; music by Thea Musgrave) and *Mary, Queen of Scots* (1975; music by John McCabe), both for Scottish Ballet. Original scores for David Bintley's *Hobson's Choice* (Sadler's Wells Royal Ballet, 1989) and *Far from the Madding Crowd* (Birmingham Royal Ballet, 1996) were composed by Paul Reade (1943–97).

Other full-length ballets have been staged to pre-existing music. Some have tried to remodel 19th-century prototypes with new arrangements of the music as well as new choreography, such as *Don Quixote* (Minkus, arranged by Lanchbery), *La fille mal gardée* (Hérold, arranged by Lanchbery; fig.23), and *Beatrix* (Adam, arranged by Horovitz). Various musical compromises have enabled operas and operettas to furnish balletic subjects: Cranko's *Onegin* (1965) for the Stuttgart Ballet and Kenneth MacMillan's *Manon* (1974) for the Royal Ballet use anthologies of smaller works by Tchaikovsky and Massenet respectively, unconnected with the operas of either, but Darrell's *The Tales of Hoffmann* (1972), *Cinderella* (1979) and *Carmen* (1985) for Scottish Ballet, and Ronald Hynd's *The Merry Widow* (1975) for the Australian Ballet, are based on transcriptions of the opera scores by Offenbach, Rossini, Bizet and Lehár. Music may occasionally be derived from more than one composer within the same ballet, as in MacMillan's *Anastasia* (1971), where Martinů is preceded by Tchaikovsky to point up the difference in time between pre- and post-Revolutionary Russia, or the awkward and less justified juxtapositions of Haydn and Joseph Lamb's ragtime in Twyla Tharp's *Push Comes to Shove* (1976), and of Ravel and Christopher Rouse in Lila York's *Sanctum* (1997), both works by American choreographers.

Thus music for classical dance is a flexible matter. Most new ballets use pre-existing music, ranging from a single work to an anthology. Massine's 'symphonic' ballets of the 1930s have had little direct influence, and Roland

23. *Scene from the Royal Ballet's production of 'La fille mal gardée' (Hérold, arranged Lanchbery), Covent Garden, London, 1960, choreographed by Frederick Ashton and designed by Osbert Lancaster, with Alexander Grant as Alain*

Petit's matching of a dramatic narrative to Bach's Passacaglia in C minor (three times repeated) in *Le jeune homme et la mort* (1946) was controversial, but it can reasonably be claimed that Ashton's *Symphonic Variations* (1946, to César Franck) constitutes one of his choreographic masterworks, no less an achievement than his *Enigma Variations* (1968) or MacMillan's *The Song of the Earth* (1965). Narrative associations have tended to become tenuous or have been discarded, not least in the later works of the long and fruitful association of Balanchine and Stravinsky from *Apollon musagète* (1928) to *Duo concertant* (1972); their collaboration includes in *Agon* (1957) and *Movements* (1963) what many regard as the deepest interpenetration of music and dance ever achieved. With or without new music, Stravinsky's dictum holds good: 'Choreography must realize its own form, one independent of the musical form though measured to the musical unit. Its construction will be based on whatever correspondences the choreographer may invent, but it must not seek merely to duplicate the line and beat of the music' (*Memories and Commentaries*).

Where pre-existing music is used, the effect of the resulting ballet is governed by a single crucial principle: that the level of choreographic imagination should never be less than that of the music. A ballet (or a modern dance) can be better than its music, but it can never afford

to be worse. Sometimes a ballet can legitimately and successfully change a musical conception, as was achieved by Fokine with Rimsky-Korsakov in *Sheherazade* (1910) and by Darrell in setting a digest of *Othello* (1973) to the first movement alone of Liszt's *Faust Symphony*. Occasionally a musical work engages the attentions of several different choreographers independently, as happened in the 1960s with Berio's *Sinfonia* and in the early 1970s with George Crumb's *Ancient Voices of Children*.

However, the plethora of small-scale, mostly modern or postmodern dance work found in most European countries and North America, and greatly fostered in Britain by the Arts Councils in a policy of encouraging the wider dissemination of dance in the community, unsupported by either the knowledge or the resources to involve a creative contribution from music, has served mainly to demonstrate the rarity of true choreographic talent. It is a remarkable generation that produces more than two or three new choreographers of distinction anywhere and, while dancers generally are becoming increasingly expert in technical proficiency, choreographers in the 1990s were finding more and more difficulty in keeping pace with them, much less inventing new ways to challenge them and entertain their audiences.

Three factors militate against the more frequent use of specially composed music for dance: the cost of copying, commission fee, extra rehearsal and performing rights; the time taken to compose a score, generally longer than it takes to compose choreography and often longer than production schedules can allow; and the contrasting approaches of the two forms of creative work: the choreographer creates in fragments, discarding and building, while the ballet composer, unlike his 19th-century counterpart, usually begins with a total concept and fills in the detail. Nevertheless, the responsive collaboration of choreographer and composer remains the best means to dance creation, as the ideal 'perfect analogous concord between what we see and what we hear' recommended by Blasis in the early 19th century.

4. MODERN DANCE.   The term 'modern', or 'contemporary', dance is applied to any of the styles and techniques of theatrical dancing, intended for independent presentation, that grew up during the 20th century as an alternative to the strict disciplines of classical ballet. In America its pioneers were Isadora Duncan (1878–1927), who took ancient Greek art as her inspiration, and Ruth St Denis (1877–1968), who modelled her work primarily on Eastern sources. Duncan's influence was worldwide as a result of her many tours, and the impression she made on Fokine during a visit to Russia particularly influenced the course of classical ballet. Her revealing costumes, flimsy draperies and bare feet were regarded as daring, but introduced a valuable reform of dance costumes in general

(for illustration *see* DUNCAN, ISADORA). Musically her great innovation was the use of any score that inspired her; she danced to symphonies by Beethoven, Schubert and Tchaikovsky, and appeared at the Bayreuth Festival in 1904 in some of her interpretations of Wagner's music. Previously dancing had been largely confined to inferior music, and the greater freedom of choice she introduced gave the opportunity for many subsequent developments. Her personal qualities as a performer inspired in many others an interest in dance, but although she devoted much time to founding dance schools for children, the direct influence of her technique remains curiously limited.

In 1915 St Denis and her dance partner Ted Shawn (1891–1972) – a successful propagandist against the misconception that dancing was an effeminate career for men – formed a school, known from 1917 as Denishawn, which produced most of the next generation of American modern dancers. Prominent among them were Doris Humphrey, who devised means of teaching the art of choreography, Charles Weidman, who pioneered specifically American themes, and Martha Graham (1894–1991). It was Graham more than anyone else who successfully devised a technique of modern dance that could be taught as the basis for the dancer's own personal use in different styles. The aim of modern dance has always been expression rather than display, with a consequent emphasis on innovation and a personal style, but the success of the Graham School in New York

24. *Martha Graham and her company in Louis Horst's 'Primitive Mysteries', New York, 1931*

25. London Contemporary Dance Theatre in 'Continuum', London, 1977, choreographed by Micha Bergese (also dancing), with Linda Gibbs, Patrick Harding-Irmer and Sallie Estep

26. Alwin Nikolais Dance Theatre in 'Sanctum', New York, 1964, choreographed and designed by Alwin Nikolais

(founded 1941) prevented the ill-informed charge (analogous to attacks made on modern painters) that modern dancers' style stemmed merely from lack of technique. Graham's own ballets, often based on mythological or psychological subjects, have a theatrical power that established her internationally as the leading modern dancer of her generation and helped to popularize modern dance where it had formerly been resisted (fig.24).

Graham's pupils and partners often went on to form their own companies and soon demonstrated that the technical training they had in common was no bar to strikingly individual development. Among them Merce Cunningham (*b* 1919), in collaboration with his musical director John Cage and artistic directors Robert Rauschenberg and Jasper Johns, had the greatest influence, pioneering a dissociation of music and dance in which, though presented concurrently, each aimed at self-sufficiency instead of the dance taking its rhythms and structure from the music (*see* CAGE, JOHN, fig.2). Cage and some of his fellow musicians greatly affected the course of American modern dance, not only by their collaboration with Cunningham but also by their participation in the many and often completely anarchic dance experiments that took place in Judson Memorial Church, New York. In return, the musicians benefited through their scores having earlier and more frequent performances than if they had waited for concert presentation, and they were heard by an audience in sympathy with radical experiment.

In pre-war Europe modern dance was most successful in Germany, where RUDOLF VON LABAN (1897–1958) and Mary Wigman (1886–1973) were the leading exponents. Laban's pupil Kurt Jooss (1901–79, active in the 1920s in Münster and Essen) created the most successful single work of the German school, *The Green Table* (1932, Paris), with a specially written score for two pianos by F.A. Cohen; because of its perennially relevant theme of anger at political machinations leading to war, this has entered the repertories of several companies, including some based on classical ballet technique. Jooss fled from the Nazis and spent many years in England; he re-founded his school in Essen in 1949, but after the war the slightly heavy style with which he was associated became less popular in central Europe. In Britain it was the success of visiting companies from the USA that revived interest in modern dance and led to the foundation of new companies, of which the London Contemporary Dance Theatre became the most flourishing, under the direction of another of Graham's former partners, Robert Cohan (fig.25).

In spite of increased interest among European dancers and audiences, most innovations in modern dance have continued to come from its American practitioners. Paul Taylor (*b* 1930) developed fresh qualities of humour and lyricism in a form previously tending to be a little dry, and Alwin Nikolais's imaginative use of lighting won much admiration. Nikolais (*b* 1912) also composed his own music, with the aid of a synthesizer, and some other modern-dance choreographers have made their own accompaniments, generally using either percussion or magnetic tape; modern dance has been associated with the full spectrum of contemporary music of all qualities.

The many experimental approaches to both modern and classical dance among the youngest generation of choreographers calls into question the future of both forms. A considerable overlap has developed between the two styles, which at one time regarded each other with hostile caution. The Nederlands Dans Theater pioneered a style combining elements of both forms, and in Britain the established Ballet Rambert was reorganized on similar lines. Some of the best choreographers, led by Glen Tetley (*b* 1926) from the USA, who trained and performed in both styles, now work in a way that could lead to classical and modern dance becoming historical, joint precursors of a new kind of dance combining the brilliance of one, the expressiveness of the other and fresh elements inspired by new developments in theatre and music.

BIBLIOGRAPHY

A General. B 17th and 18th centuries: (i) Contemporary sources (ii) Later studies: France (iii) Later studies: outside France. C 19th century. D 20th century: classical: (i) Individual artists (ii) General studies. E Modern dance: (i) General studies (ii) Individual artists.

A: GENERAL

GroveO ('Dance'; C.B. Schmidt, R.J. Wiley)
Les spectacles à travers les âges: musique, danse (Paris, 1932)
L. Kirstein: *Dance: a Short History of Classic Theatrical Dancing* (New York, 1935/R, 3/1969)
J. Gregor: *Kulturgeschichte des Balletts* (Vienna, 1946)
P. Nettl: *The Story of Dance Music* (New York, 1947/R)
B. Kochno: *Le ballet en France du quinzième siècle à nos jours* (Paris, 1954)
F. Reyna: *Des origines du ballet* (Paris, 1955; Eng. trans., 1965, as *A Concise History of Ballet*)
G.B.L. Wilson: *A Dictionary of Ballet* (Harmondsworth, 1957, 3/1974)
R. Fiske: *Ballet Music* (London, 1958)
H. Searle: *Ballet Music: an Introduction* (London, 1958, 2/1973)
J. Lawson: *A History of Ballet and its Makers* (London, 1964)
P. Brinson: *Background to European Ballet* (Leiden, 1966)
L. Kirstein: *Movement & Metaphor* (New York, 1970, repr. 1984 as *Four Centuries of Ballet: Fifty Masterworks*)
P. Migel: *The Ballerinas: from the Court of Louis XIV to Pavlova* (New York, 1972)
Dictionary Catalog of the Dance Collection of the Performing Arts Research Center of the New York Public Library (Boston, 1974; annual suppls., *Bibliographic Guide to Dance*, 1975–; CD-ROM cumulation, 1994, as *Dance on Disc*; available online <www.catnyp.nypl.org>
S.J. Cohen, ed.: *International Encyclopedia of Dance* (New York, 1998)

B: 17TH AND 18TH CENTURIES
(i) contemporary sources

for dance-specific writings see Schwartz and Schlundt (1987); for notated choreographies see Little and Marsh (1992) and Lancelot (1996)

F. Raguenet: *Paralèle des italiens et des françois* (Paris, 1702; Eng. trans., 1709/R; Eng. trans. also in *MQ*, xxxii (1946), 411–36)
J.L. Le Cerf de la Viéville: *Comparaison de la musique italienne et de la musique françoise* (Brussels, 1704–6/R)
J.B. Dubos: *Réflexions critiques sur la poésie, la peinture et la musique* (Paris, 1719, 6/1755/R; Eng. trans., 1748/R)
L. Riccoboni: *Réflexions historiques et critiques sur les différens théâtres de l'Europe* (Paris, 1738/R; Eng. trans., 1741, 2/1754/R, as *A General History of the Stage, from its Origin*)
C. and F. Parfait: *Histoire de l'Académie royale de musique depuis son établissement jusqu'à présent* (MS, c1740, F-Pn n.a.fr.6532)
A. de Léris: *Dictionnaire portatif des théâtres* (Paris, 1754)
C. and F. Parfait: *Le dictionnaire des théâtres de Paris* (Paris, 1756)
J.B. Durey de Noinville and L. Travenol: *Histoire du théâtre de l'Académie royale de musique en France* (Paris, 2/1757/R)
G. Gallini: *A Treatise on the Art of Dancing* (London, 1762/R)
P.J.B. Nougaret: *De l'art du théâtre* (Paris, 1769/R)

(ii) later studies: France

AnthonyFB
T. de Lajarte: *Bibliothèque musicale du théâtre de l'Opéra: catalogue historique, chronologique, anecdotique* (Paris, 1878)
H. Abert: 'J.G. Noverre und sein Einfluss auf die dramatische Ballettkomposition', *JbMP 1908*, 29–95

P.-M. Masson: 'Les "symphonies" de danse', *L'opéra de Rameau* (Paris, 1930/*R*), 367–422

J.R. Anthony: 'The French Opera-Ballet in the Early 18th Century: Problems of Definition and Classification', *JAMS*, xviii (1965), 197–206

J.R. Anthony: 'Some Uses of the Dance in the French Opéra-Ballet', *RMFC*, ix (1969), 75–90

G. Seefrid: *Die airs de danse in den Bühnenwerken von Jean-Philippe Rameau* (Wiesbaden, 1969, 2/1971)

Jean-Philippe Rameau: Dijon 1983 [incl. G. Sadler: 'The Paris Opéra Dancers in Rameau's Day: a Little-Known Inventory of 1738', 519–31; also 5 articles on dance in Rameau operas]

S. Pitou: *The Paris Opéra: an Encyclopedia of Operas, Ballets, Composers, and Performers*, i–ii (Westport, CT, 1983–5)

N. Lecomte: 'Jean-Baptiste François Dehesse, chorégraphe à la Comédie Italienne', *RMFC*, xxiv (1986), 142–91

J.L. Schwartz and C.L.Schlundt: *French Court Dance and Dance Music: a Guide to Primary Source Writings, 1643–1789*, Dance and Music, i (Stuyvesant, NY, 1987) [incl. sources from across Europe pertaining to dance in the French manner]

J. Chazin-Bennahum: *Dance in the Shadow of the Guillotine* (Carbondale, IL, 1988)

J. de La Gorce: 'Guillaume-Louis Pécour: a Biographical Essay', *Dance Research*, viii/2 (1990), 3–26

M.E. Little and C.G. Marsh: *La danse noble: an Inventory of Dances and Sources* (New York, 1992)

T. Betzwieser: *Exotismus und 'Türkenoper' in der französischen Musik des Ancien Régime*(Laaber, 1993)

R. Harris-Warrick and C.G.Marsh: *Musical Theatre at the Court of Louis XIV: 'Le mariage de la Grosse Cathos'* (Cambridge, 1994)

C.G. Marsh: 'French Theatrical Dance in the Late 18th Century: Gypsies, Cloggers, and Drunken Soldiers', *Border Crossings: Dance and Boundaries in Society, Politics, Gender, Education and Technology: Toronto 1995* (Riverside, CA, 1995), 91–8

S.L. Foster: *Choreography and Narrative: Ballet's Staging of Story and Desire* (Bloomington, IN, 1996)

I. Guest: *The Ballet of the Enlightenment: the Establishment of the Ballet d'Action in France, 1770–1793* (London, 1996)

F. Lancelot: *La belle danse: catalogue raisonné* (Paris, 1996)

R. Legrand: 'Chaconnes et passacailles dansées dans l'opéra français', *Le mouvement en musique à l'époque baroque*, ed. H. Lacombe (Metz, 1996), 157–70

S. McCleave, ed.: *Dance and Music in French Baroque Theatre: Sources and Interpretations* (London, 1998)

M.K. Whaples: 'Early Exoticism Revisited', *The Exotic in Western Music*, ed. J. Bellman (Boston, 1998), 3–25

(iii) later studies: outside France

R. Haas: 'Die Wiener Ballet-Pantomime im 18. Jahrhundert und Glucks Don Juan', *SMw*, x (1923), 6–36

R.-A. Mooser: *Opéras, intermezzos, ballets … joués en Russie durant le XVIIIe siècle* (Geneva, 1945, 3/1964)

G. Croll: 'Ballet und Pantomime um 1750', *IMSCR X: Ljubljana 1967*, 168–71

L. Tozzi: *Il balletto pantomimo del Settecento: Gaspare Angiolini* (L'Aquila, 1972)

M.H. Winter: *The Pre-Romantic Ballet* (London, 1974)

K.K. Hansell: *Opera and Ballet at the Regio Ducal Teatro of Milan, 1771–1776* (diss., U. of California, Berkeley, 1980)

K.K. Hansell: 'Ballet in Stockholm during the Later 18th Century and its Relationship to Contemporary Trends on the Continent', *STMf*, lxvi (1984), 9–42

R. Ralph: *The Life and Works of John Weaver* (New York, 1985)

K.K. Hansell: 'Il ballo teatrale e l'opera italiana', *SOI*, v (1988), 175–306; Eng. trans. in *The History of Italian Opera*, ed. L. Bianconi and G. Pestelli (Chicago, 1998)

B.A. Brown: *Gluck and the French Theatre in Vienna* (Oxford and New York, 1991)

S. Dahms: 'Das Repertoire des "ballet en action": Noverre–Angiolini–Lauchery', *De editione musices: Festschrift Gerhard Croll*, ed. W. Gratzer and A. Lindmayr (Laaber, 1992), 125–42

S. McCleave: *Dance in Handel's Italian Operas* (diss., U. of London, 1993)

I. Alm: 'Pantomime in Seventeenth-Century Venetian Theatrical Dance', *Creature di Prometeo: il ballo teatrale dal divertimento al dramma: studi offerti a Aurel M. Milloss*, ed. G. Morelli (Florence, 1996), 87–102

I. Brainard: 'The Speaking Body: Gaspero Angiolini's *rhétorique muette* and the *ballet d'action* in the Eighteenth Century', *Critica musica: Essays in Honor of Paul Brainard*, ed. J. Knowles (Amsterdam, 1996), 15–56

S. Dahms: 'Das Mannheimer Ballet im Zeichen der Ballettreform des 18. Jahrhunderts', *Mannheimer Hofkapelle im Zeitalter Carl Theodors* (Mannheim, 1992), *Ballet Music from the Mannheim Court*, i, ed. F.K. Grave (Madison, WI, 1996), pp.ix–xxiii

S. Dahms and S.Schroedter, eds.: *Tanz und Bewegung in der barocken Oper: Salzburg 1994* (Innsbruck, 1996)

C. Turocy: 'Reflections on Gilbert Austin's *Chironomia* and Dance Conventions of the Eighteenth Century', *Reflecting our Past, Reflecting our Future: New York 1997*, ed. L.J. Tomko (Riverside, CA, 1997), 311–21

I. Alm: *Theatrical Dance in Seventeenth-Century Venetian Opera* (Chicago, forthcoming)

C: 19TH CENTURY

GroveO ('Bournonville, Auguste', M.N. Costonis; 'Didelot, Charles-Louis', R.J. Wiley; 'Grahn, Lucile', M.N. Costonis; 'Ivanov, Lev Ivanovich', R.J. Wiley; 'Mérante, Louis', I. Guest; 'Taglioni, Filippo', M.N. Costonis [incl. information on Marie Taglioni and illustration])

M. Steuer: Review of M.L. Becker: *Der Tanz* (Leipzig, 1901), *Die Musik*, ii/4 (1902–3), 122–3 [incl. reflections on the history of 19th-century dance]

C.W. Beaumont: *The Romantic Ballet as seen by Théophile Gautier* (London, 1932/*R*) [incl. trans. extracts from Gautier's reviews]

N. Legat: *The Story of the Russian School* (London, 1932)

Yu. Slonimsky: *Mastera baleta* (Leningrad, 1937)

A.L. Haskell: *Ballet* (Harmondsworth, 1938/*R* and later rev. edns)

L. Moore: *Artists of the Dance* (New York, 1938/*R*)

S. Lifar: *Carlotta Grisi* (Paris, 1941; Eng. trans., 1947)

L. Vaillat: *La Taglioni* (Paris, 1942)

C.W. Beaumont: *The Ballet called Giselle* (London, 1944/*R*)

C.W. Beaumont: *The Ballet called Swan Lake* (London, 1952/*R*)

I. Guest: *The Ballet of the Second Empire* (London, 1953–5/*R*)

I. Guest: *The Romantic Ballet in England* (London, 1954/*R*)

I. Guest: *Fanny Cerrito* (London, 1956, 2/1974)

L. Moore, ed.: *Russian Ballet Master: the Memoirs of Marius Petipa* (New York, 1958/*R*)

Yu. Slonimsky: *Didlo: vekhi tvorcheskoy biografii* [Didelot: landmarks in a creative biography] (Leningrad, 1958)

Yu. Slonimsky: *'Lebedinoye ozero' P. Chaykovskogo* [Tchaikovsky's Swan Lake] (Leningrad, 1962)

V. Krasovskaya: *Russkiy baletnïy teatr vtoroy polovinï XIX veka* [Russian ballet theatre from the second half of the 19th century] (Moscow and Leningrad, 1963)

R. Neiiendam: *Lucile Grahn* (Copenhagen, 1963)

I. Guest: *A Gallery of Romantic Ballet* (London, 1965)

I. Guest: *The Romantic Ballet in Paris* (London, 1966, 2/1980)

N. Roslavleva: *Era of the Russian Ballet* (London, 1966)

I. Guest: *Fanny Elssler* (London, 1970)

Teatervidenskab elige studier/Theatre Research Studies, ed. Institute for Theatre Research, U. of Copenhagen, no.2 (1972)

J. Warrack: *Tchaikovsky* (London, 1973)

R.J. Wiley: *Tchaikovsky's Ballets* (London and New York, 1985)

M.E. Smith: *Music for the Ballet-Pantomime at the Paris Opéra, 1825–1850* (diss., Yale U., 1988)

S. Pitou: *The Paris Opéra: an Encyclopedia of Operas, Ballets, Composers, and Performers*, iii (Westport, CT, 1990)

R.J. Wiley, ed. and trans.: *A Century of Russian Ballet: Documents and Eyewitness Accounts, 1810–1910* (London and New York, 1990)

M.E. Smith: *Ballet-Pantomime and its Kinship with Opera in the Age of Giselle* (forthcoming)

D: 20TH CENTURY: CLASSICAL

(i) individual artists

V. Svetloff: *Anna Pavlova* (Paris, 1922/*R*)

T. Karsavina: *Theatre Street* (London, 1930, rev. 1950)

P.D. Magriel, ed.: *Nijinsky, Pavlova, Duncan: Three Lives in Dance* (New York, 1946–7/*R*)

A. Dolin: *Markova: her Life and Art* (London, 1953/*R*)

C. Barnes: *Frederick Ashton and his Ballets* (Brooklyn, NY, 1961)

A.E. Kahn: *Days with Ulanova* (London, 1962)

Yu.I. Slonimsky, ed.: M.Fokine: *Protiv techeniya: vospominaniya baletmeistera* [Against the flow: reminiscences of a ballet-master]

(Leningrad, 1962, 2/1981; Eng. trans., 1961, as *Memoirs of a Ballet Master*)

S. Cohen: *Antony Tudor: the Years in America and After* (Brooklyn, NY, 1963)

J. Percival: *Antony Tudor: the Years in England* (Brooklyn, NY, 1963)

B. Taper: *Balanchine* (New York, 1963, enlarged 1974)

L. Massine: *My Life in Ballet*, ed. P. Hartnoll and R. Rubens (London and New York, 1968)

Z. Dominic and J.S. Gilbert: *Frederick Ashton: a Choreographer and his Ballets* (London, 1971)

J. Percival: *The World of Diaghilev* (London, 1971, rev. 1979)

M. Rambert: *Quicksilver* (London and New York, 1972) [autobiography]

O. Kerensky: *Anna Pavlova* (London, 1973)

K. Money: *Fonteyn: the Making of a Legend* (London, 1973)

M. Fonteyn: *Autobiography* (London, 1975)

J. Percival: *Nureyev: Aspects of the Dancer* (New York, 1975)

D. Vaughan: *Frederick Ashton and his Ballets* (London, 1977)

R. Buckle: *Diaghilev* (London, 1979)

A. Testa: 'Bartók nell'estetica del balletto moderno in generale e nell'opera di Milloss in particolare', *RMI*, xv (1981), 227–40

A. von Milloss: 'Bartóks Bedeutung für die Balletästhetik des 20. Jahrhunderts', *Béla Bartók: zu Leben und Werk*, ed. F. Spangemacher (Bonn, 1982), 27–38

Choreography by George Balanchine: a Catalogue of Works (New York, 1983) [pubn of the Eakins Foundation]

E. Thorpe: *Kenneth MacMillan: the Man and his Ballets* (London, 1985)

(ii) general studies

A. Vaganova: *Osnovi klassicheskogo tantsa* (Leningrad, 1934, 4/1963; Eng. trans., 1946, as *Fundamentals of the Classic Dance*, 2/1969 as *Basic Principles of Classical Ballet*)

C. Lambert: 'Music and Action', *Footnotes to the Ballet*, ed. C. Brahms (London, 1936), 161–74

N. de Valois: *Invitation to the Ballet* (London, 1937/R)

C. Beaumont: *The Diaghilev Ballet in London* (London, 1940, 3/1951)

A. Benois: *Reminiscences of the Russian Ballet* (London, 1941/R)

D. Lynham: *Ballet Then and Now* (London, 1947)

J. Slonimsky and others: *The Soviet Ballet* (New York, 1947/R)

G. Amberg: *Ballet in America: the Emergence of an American Art* (New York, 1949/R)

E. Denby: *Looking at the Dance* (New York, 1949, 1968)

M. Lederman, ed.: *Stravinsky in the Theatre* (New York, 1949/R)

P. Noble, ed.: *British Ballet* (London, 1949)

S.L. Grigor'yev: *The Diaghilev Ballet 1909–29* (London, 1953/R)

M. Clarke: *The Sadler's Wells Ballet: a History and an Appreciation* (London, 1955/R)

Yu. Slonimsky: *The Bolshoi Theatre Ballet* (London, 1956, 2/1960)

W. Terry: *The Dance in America* (New York, 1956, rev. 1971)

N. de Valois: *Come Dance with me: a Memoir, 1898–1956* (London, 1957/R)

P. Brinson, ed.: *The Ballet in Britain* (London, 1962)

M. Clarke: *Dancers of Mercury: the Story of Ballet Rambert* (London, 1962)

H. Read and S.J. Cohen: *Stravinsky and the Dance* (New York, 1962)

E. Denby: *Dancers, Buildings and People in the Streets* (New York, 1965)

N. Roslavleva: *Era of the Russian Ballet* [1770–1965] (London, 1966) [incl. Russ. bibliography]

E.W. White: *Stravinsky: the Composer and his Works* (Berkeley, 1966, 2/1979)

M.G. Swift: *The Art of Dance in the USSR* (Notre Dame, IN, 1968)

O. Kerensky: *Ballet Scene* (London, 1970)

V. Krasovskaya: *Russkiy baletnïy teatr nachala XX veka* [Russian ballet theatre of the early 20th century], i: *Khoreografi* [Choreographers] (Leningrad, 1971); ii: *Tantsovshchiki* [Dancers] (Leningrad, 1972)

L. Kirstein: *The New York City Ballet* (New York, 1973, enlarged 2/1978 as *Thirty Years . . . the New York City Ballet*)

R. Shead: *Constant Lambert* (London, 1973)

N. Goldner, ed.: *The Stravinsky Festival of the New York City Ballet, 1972* (New York, 1974)

A. Croce: *Afterimages* (New York, 1977)

N. de Valois: *Step by Step* (London, 1977)

N. Goodwin: *A Ballet for Scotland* (Edinburgh, 1979)

J. Warrack: *Tchaikovsky Ballet Music* (London, 1979)

P. Brinson and C. Crisp: *Ballet and Dance: a Guide to the Repertory* (Newton Abbot, 1980)

J. Anderson: *The One and Only: the Ballet Russe de Monte Carlo* (London, 1981)

A. Bland: *The Royal Ballet: the First Fifty Years* (London, 1981)

K. Sorley Walker: *De Basil's Ballets Russes* (London, 1982)

L. Garafola: *Diaghilev's Ballet Russes* (Oxford and New York, 1989)

M. Bremser, ed.: *International Dictionary of Ballet* (Detroit and London, 1993)

J. Pritchard, ed.: *Rambert: a Celebration: a Survey of the Company's First Seventy Years* (London, 1996)

R. Taruskin: *Stravinsky and the Russian Traditions* (London, 1996)

E: MODERN DANCE

(i) general studies

J.E. Crawford Flitch: *Modern Dancing and Dancers* (London and Philadelphia, 1913, 3/1921)

H. Brandenburg: *Der moderne Tanz* (Munich, 1917)

E. Blass: *Das Wesen der neuen Tanzkunst* (Weimar, 1921, enlarged 2/1922)

S. Enkelmann: *Tänzer unserer Zeit* (Munich, 1937)

J. Martin: 'Dance as a Means of Communication', *The Dance* (New York, 1946)

M. Lloyd: *The Borzoi Book of Modern Dance* (New York, 1949)

W. Terry: 'Modern Dance', *The Dance Encyclopedia*, ed. A. Chujoy (New York, 1949, 2/1967)

W. Sorell, ed.: *The Dance has Many Faces* (New York, 1951, 3/1992)

D. Humphrey: *The Art of Making Dances*, ed. B. Pollack (New York, 1959)

L. Horst and C. Russell: *Modern Dance Forms in Relation to the Other Modern Arts* (San Francisco, 1961)

A.J. Pischl and S.J. Cohen, eds.: *Composer/Choreographer* (Brooklyn, NY, 1963)

S.J. Cohen, ed.: *The Modern Dance: Seven Statements of Belief* (Middletown, CT, 1966)

J. Martin: 'American Modern Dance', *The Dance Encyclopedia*, ed. A. Chujoy (New York, 2/1967)

W. Sorell: *The Dance through the Ages* (New York, 1967)

J. Percival: *Modern Ballet* (London, 1970, rev. 1980)

D. McDonagh: *The Rise and Fall and Rise of Modern Dance* (New York, 1970, rev. 1990)

J. Percival: *Experimental Dance* (London, 1971)

T. Borek: *The Connecticut College American Dance Festival, 1948–1972* (New York, 1972)

M.B. Siegel: *Watching the Dance go by* (Boston, 1977)

J. Murray: *Dance Now* (Harmondsworth, 1979)

O. Norlyng: 'Ny dans: ny musik', *DMt*, lviii (1983–4), 98–107

A. Robertson and D. Hutera: *The Dance Handbook* (Harlow, 1988)

M. Clarke and C. Crisp: *London Contemporary Dance Theatre: the First 21 Years* (London, 1989)

K. Teck: *Music for the Dance: Reflections on a Collaborative Art* (New York, 1989)

K. Teck: *Movement to Music: Musicians in the Dance Studio* (New York, 1990)

S. Jordan: *Striding Out: Aspects of Contemporary and New Dance in Britain* (London, 1992)

H. Züllig: 'Das Jooss-Ballett im englischen Exil', *Musiktradition im Exil: zurück aus dem Vergessen*, ed. J. Allende-Blin (Cologne, 1993), 205–21

M. Gradinger: 'Bewegungs-freiheit: Ausdruckstanz und Modern Dance: Wege zu einer emanzipierten Weiblichkeit', *NZM*, Jg.155, no.4 (1994), 18–21

(ii) individual artists

M. Allan: *My Life and Dancing* (London, 1908)

L. Fuller: *Quinze ans de ma vie* (Paris, 1908; Eng. trans. 1913/R)

C. Stewart Richardson: *Dancing, Beauty and Games* (London, 1913)

M. Desti: *The Untold Story: the Life of Isadora Duncan 1921–1927* (New York, 1929)

K.S. Dreier: *Shawn the Dancer* (New York, 1933)

R. St Denis: *An Unfinished Life* (New York, 1939)

B. Morgan: *Martha Graham: Sixteen Dances in Photographs* (New York, 1941, rev. 1980)

A.V. Coton: *The New Dance: Kurt Jooss and his Work* (London, 1946)

T. Shawn: *Every Little Movement: a Book about François Delsarte* (Pittsfield, MA, 1954, 2/1963)

W. Terry: *The Legacy of Isadora Duncan and Ruth St Denis* (Brooklyn, NY, 1959)

J.J. Martin: *Days of Divine Indiscipline* (Brooklyn, NY, 1961)

C.L. Schlundt: *The Professional Appearances of Ruth St Denis & Ted Shawn: a Chronology and an Index of Dances 1906–1932* (New York, 1962)

Irma Duncan: *Follow Me!* (Brooklyn, NY, 1965) [autobiography]

C. Tomkins: *The Bride & the Bachelors: the Heretical Courtship in Modern Art* (New York, 1965; London, 1968, as *Ahead of the Game: Four Versions of Avant-Garde*; enlarged 2/1968 as *The Bride and the Bachelors: Five Masters of the Avant-Garde*)

D. Humphrey: *New Dance: an Unfinished Autobiography* (New York, 1966)

L. Leatherman: *Martha Graham: Portrait of the Lady as an Artist* (New York, 1966)

L. Warren and others: *The Dance Theater of Lester Horton* (New York, 1967)

S.J. Cohen, ed.: *Time to Walk in Space: Essays, a Biography and a Chronology about Merce Cunningham* (New York, 1968)

M. Cunningham: *Changes: Notes on Choreography*, ed. F. Starr (New York, 1968)

M.B. Siegel, ed.: *Dancer's Notes* (New York, 1969)

C.L. Schlundt: *Into the Mystic with Miss Ruth* (New York, 1971)

M.B. Siegel, ed.: *Nik: a Documentary* (New York, 1971)

S.J. Cohen, ed.: *Doris Humphrey: an Artist First* (Middletown, CT, 1972)

REBECCA HARRIS-WARRICK (1), NOËL GOODWIN (2, 3), JOHN PERCIVAL (4)

Ballet de cour (Fr.). A type of ballet popular at the French court during the reigns of Henry III, Henry IV, Louis XIII and Louis XIV. It borrowed elements from the earlier *entremets* (pantomimes accompanied by choruses and dances) in vogue at the courts of Burgundy, from the elaborate (though often chaotic) *fêtes* of the Valois kings and from the mascheratas and *intermedi* imported from Italy.

Its components were normally *récits* (see RÉCIT), *vers* (rhymed verses found in the libretto), entrées (*see* ENTRÉE) and a concluding *grand ballet* (a forerunner of the operatic finale) danced by the *grands seigneurs* and, at least once each year, by the king himself. All ballets resulted from the collaboration of a royal patron who determined the subject and the distribution of labour, poets for the *vers* and *récits*, at least two composers responsible for vocal and instrumental music and a machinist. Detailed descriptions of the *mise en scène*, the *vers* (often containing indiscreet references to royal dancers) and the identification of the dancers themselves were published in librettos (*livrets*) distributed to the spectators before the performance.

Early essays in the genre were the *Paradis d'amour* of 1572 (text by Ronsard) and the *Ballet polonais* of 1573 (commissioned from Balthasar de Beaujoyeux by Catherine de' Medici to honour the Polish ambassadors; fig.1), which was described by Brantôme in his memoirs (*Oeuvres Complètes*, Paris, 1823) as 'le plus beau ballet qui fust jamais faict au monde'. More important was *Circé, ou le Balet comique de la Royne*, performed at the Petit Bourbon palace on 15 October 1581 as part of the festivities celebrating the marriage of the Duke of Joyeuse and the queen's sister, Marguerite de Vaudemont. This work has the distinction of being the first *ballet de cour* in which poetry (by La Chesnaye and possibly D'Aubigny), music (by Jacques Salmon and Lambert de Beaulieu), décor (by Jacques Patin) and dance combine to support a single dramatic action: the destruction of the power of the enchantress Circe in order to re-establish harmony, reason and order in the realm. Thus, at its inception, the *ballet de cour* was a political tool of the

1. *'Ballet polonais', devised by Balthasar de Beaujoyeux, Tuileries, Paris, 1573: woodcut from Jean Dorat's 'Magnificentissimi spectaculi' (1573)*

monarchy, a means of domesticating the nobility and of preserving the king's centralized power and control.

By virtue of its dramatic unity, perhaps inspired by the humanistic precepts of Baïf's Académie de Poésie et de Musique, *Circé* has long been considered the first French work to give 'some idea of the musical theatre' (d'Aquin de Château-Lyon). It stands first in the long list of precursors of the *tragédie lyrique*. Beaujoyeux, who had been chosen by Catherine de' Medici to develop the ballet's master plan, wrote in the preface to the Ballard score of 1582 that *Circé* was an 'invention moderne' in which the word 'comique' described a work with the dramatic unity of a comedy.

The structural significance of *Circé* apparently had little effect on the following generation of those responsible for the *ballet de cour*. Their works, based largely on 'mascarades à l'italienne', included unrelated entrées of colourful and grotesque characters. Titles such as *Ballets des foux* (1596), *Ballet des barbiers* (1598), *Ballet des garçons de taverne* (1603), *Ballet des bouteilles et des dames* (1607) and *Ballet des paysans et des grenouilles* (1607) show a preoccupation with burlesque elements at the turn of the century.

Not until 1609 with the *Ballet de la reyne* (*vers* by Malherbe) or 1610 with the *Ballet d'Alcine* was there a return to the unified dramatic action established 29 years before by Beaujoyeux. This type of ballet, labelled 'ballet mélodramatique', remained popular for about a decade.

At its best in such works as the *Ballet de la délivrance de Renaud* (1617), the *Ballet de l'aventure de Tancrède en la forêt enchantée* (1619) and the *Ballet de Psyché* (1619), it was a convincing dramatic spectacle which could have led to French opera long before Lully's *Cadmus*. About 1620 Michel Henry, a violinist of the Chambre du Roi, copied an important collection of ballet music. The music is not extant, but the list enumerates 117 ballets, 96 of which were performed between 1597 and 1618. M.-F. Christout (1992) has identified 392 court ballets performed between 1572 and 1671 by title, year, specific date and place, thereby documenting the popularity of the genre.

In 1621, with the death of the Duc de Luynes, Louis XIII's favourite patron of the ballet, the *ballet mélodramatique* was superseded by the *ballet à entrées* which, under the aegis of the Duke of Nemours, was a choreographic spectacle of many parts, each with its own subject matter and characters, relating in only a general way to a collective idea expressed in the title. In the *Grand bal de la Douairière de Billebahaut* (1626), for example, the four corners of the world each send delegates to the ball (fig.2); each has its own ballet preceded by *récits* and including several *entrées*.

Saint-Hubert classified *ballets de cour* by their length in *La manière de composer et faire réussir les ballets* (1641): a 'ballet royal' ordinarily contained 30 *entrées*, a 'beau ballet' had at least 20 *entrées* and a 'petit ballet' had 10 to 12 *entrées*. The vocal music included choruses and polyphonic *airs*, as well as solo *récits*. These *airs* were provided by the most important composers of the genre, including Pierre Guédron, Antoine Boësset and Etienne Moulinié. Boësset, for example, contributed more than 70 polyphonic *airs* and solo *récits* to 25 different *ballets de cour* (Durosoir, 240–49). From the late 16th century to the death of Lully in 1687, court ballets were performed in Paris at the Grande Salle of the Louvre, the Grand Salon of the Palais des Tuileries, the Palais Royal, the Hôtel de Ville, and, until its destruction in 1660, at the Salle du Petit Bourbon (between the church of St Germain-l'Auxerrois and the Louvre). Outside Paris, performances took place at the royal châteaux at Compiègne, Fontaine-bleau, Chantilly, Vincennes, Saint Germain-en-Laye and Chambord.

Louis XIV danced for the first time as a boy of 13 in the *Ballet de Cassandre* (1651), the ballet in which Isaac de Benserade made his début as a poet of superior literary talents. Two years later the young Florentine Lully found himself on stage dancing next to the king in the *Ballet de la nuit*. It was in the *ballet de cour* that Lully learnt to differentiate between the styles of his native and adopted lands. From 1654 to 1671 he provided music for 16 court ballets. His own private orchestra, the Petits Violons, made its first appearance in the *Ballet de la galantérie du temps* (1656, music lost). In 1657 Lully composed all the instrumental music for the *Ballet de l'amour malade* and in 1658 all the instrumental music and much of the vocal music for the *Ballet d'Alcidiane*. The overture to this ballet bears the classical stamp of all subsequent French overtures. In his dances Lully quickly assimilated the long heritage of French dances and introduced new dances (especially 'airs de vitesse'). By degrees, purely musical features of the ballet began to usurp the position of the dance. The close liaison between the *Ballet des muses* (1666) and the later *tragédie lyrique* was recognized by Brossard, who wrote: 'it is this ballet [*Les muses*] that gave the idea of composing operas in French' (*Catalogue des livres de musique*, 1724). Brossard must have been referring here to the pre-eminence of vocal *airs*, ensembles and choruses in the *Ballet des muses* rather than to any organizational principle, because this ballet best illustrates the improvisatory nature of the *ballet de cour*. From its first performance on 2 December 1666 to its final one on 19 February 1667 it went through six stages of

2. Design for the 'Entrée de Mahomet et ses docteurs' from the 'Grand bal de la Douairière de Billebahaut': pen and ink with colour wash, 1626 (F-Pn)

development. New material was constantly added, seemingly on a trial-and-error basis, to render this ballet 'encore plus agréable'. By 14 February its boundaries had been stretched to include two of Molière's *comédies-ballets*, *La pastorale comique* and *Le Sicilien*.

The *ballet de cour* afforded Lully a ten-year apprenticeship that helped prepare him for the creation of the *tragédie en musique*. According to Le Cerf de la Viéville, Lully modelled his operatic recitative on the intonation of Racine's mistress, the actress Mme Champmeslé, who performed at the Hôtel de Bourgogne. Yet even before her earliest triumphs, Lully had introduced into his court ballets the predominantly anapaestic rhythmic organization and the division of the alexandrine into hemistichs that characterize French recitative (e.g. 'Arreste malheureux', *Ballet des muses*). Although many of the *airs* in Lully's ballets are clearly modelled on the contemporaneous French *airs de cour*, Lully introduced a type of binary *air* that was to assume pride of place in the *tragédie lyrique*. This is the so-called extended binary *air* (*ABB'*) of Italian origin, an early example of which is found in the *Ballet des arts* of 1662 ('Bel art qui retardez').

Lully, who had assimilated the long tradition of French dances, introduced many new 'airs de vitesse' into court ballets. Bourrées and minuets became the most widely used dances; courantes and galliards became rare. The 'Chaconne des Maures', which concludes the *Ballet d'Alcidiane*, already assumed the grand proportions and structural significance of the chaconnes that were to be found in Lully's operas. The choral finale to the prologue of the *Ballet des muses* expresses the same sentiments found in later operatic prologues: 'Rien n'est si doux que de vivre à la cour de Louis, le plus parfait des rois'. The pompous music that Lully wrote for this text consolidated a tradition and remained the supreme gesture of official adoration throughout the *grand siècle*.

The *ballet de cour* suffered an eclipse when Louis XIV ceased dancing (1670) and when Lully moved it closer to opera with his *Triomphe de l'amour* (1681; fig.3) and his *Temple de la paix* (1685). The Parfaict brothers were hard pressed to find a proper category for so mixed a genre as *Le triomphe de l'amour*. In their manuscript *Histoire de l'Académie royale de musique* (*c*1741), they wrote: 'Properly speaking, it is neither an opera nor a ballet but a collection of entrées mixed with *récits*'. The 20 entrées, in fact, contain 16 *récits*, which exceeds by far the number in any other *ballet de cour*. The *Ballet de la jeunesse* (1686) and the *Palais de Flore* (1689), both by Lalande, synthesize opera and ballet and resemble the Lully ballets of the 1680s in this respect.

The *ballet de cour* enjoyed a brief revival in the early 18th century when the young Louis XV and his *seigneurs* danced at the Tuileries in *L'inconnu* (1720, music by Lalande), *Les folies de Cardenio* (1720, music by Lalande) and *Les élémens* (1721, music by Destouches and Lalande) – works that owe as much to opera as the *ballet de cour*. In 1729 the *Ballet du Parnasse* (fragments from Collin de Blamont, Lully, Campra, Destouches and Mouret) was danced at Versailles to celebrate the birth of the dauphin. By 1754, however, Cahusac stated that it was a 'genre which no longer exists' (*La danse ancienne et moderne*). At the Jesuit Collège Louis-le-Grand, its form was maintained up to 1761 (when the Jesuits were expelled from France) as part of the ceremony marking the end of each scholastic year.

3. *Design for an Indian costume for Lully's ballet 'Le triomphe de l'amour', Saint Germain-en-Laye, 1681: engraving by Jacques Le Pautre after Jean Berain I*

BIBLIOGRAPHY

AnthonyFB; *MGG1* (D.P. Walter); *MGG2* (M.M. McGowan, C.J. Schlundt)
Saint-Hubert: *La manière de composer et faire réussir les ballets* (Paris, 1641/R)
C.-F. Ménestrier: 'Remarques pour le conduite de ballet', *L'Autel de Lyon* (Lyons, 1658), 50–56; ed. in Christout (1967)
M. de Pure: *Idée des spectacles anciens et nouveaux* (Paris, 1668/R)
C.-F. Ménestrier: *Les ballets anciens et modernes selon les règles du théâtre* (Paris, 1682/R)
P. Lacroix: *Ballets et mascarades de cour de Henri III à Louis XIV (1581–1652)* (Geneva, 1868–70/R)
H. Prunières: *Le ballet de cour en France avant Benserade et Lully* (Paris, 1914/R)
T. Gérold: *L'art du chant en France au XVIIe siècle* (Strasbourg, 1921/R)
L. de La Laurencie: *Les créateurs de l'opéra français* (Paris, 1921, 2/1930/R)
L. de La Laurencie: 'Un musicien dramatique du XVIIe siècle, Pierre Guédron', *RMI*, xxix (1922), 445–72
H. Prunières: 'Ronsard et les fêtes de cour', *ReM*, v/6 (1923–4), 27–45
W. Storz: *Der Aufbau der Tänze in den Opern und Balletts Lullys vom musikalischen Standpunkte aus betrachtet* (Göttingen, 1928)
C. Silin: *Benserade and his Ballets de cour* (Baltimore, 1940, 2/1970)
F.A. Yates: *The French Academies of the Sixteenth Century* (London, 1947/R)
F. Lesure: 'Le recueil de ballets de Michel Henry', *Les fêtes de la renaissance [I]: Royaumont 1955*, 205–19
J. Rousset: 'L'eau et les tritons dans les fêtes et ballets de cour (1580–1640)', ibid., 235–45
N. Bridgman: 'L'aristocratie française et le ballet de cour', *Cahiers de l'Association internationale des études français*, ix (1957), 9–21
A. Verchaly: 'Les ballets de cour d'après les recueils de musique vocale (1600–1643)', ibid., 198–218

A. Verchaly: 'Airs de cour et ballet de cour', *Histoire de la musique*, i, ed. Roland-Manuel (Paris, 1960), 1529–60

M.M. McGowan: *L'art du ballet de cour en France, 1581–1643* (Paris, 1963)

M.-F. Christout: *Le ballet de cour de Louis XIV, 1643–1672* (Paris, 1967)

H.M. Ellis: *The Dances of J.B. Lully (1632–1687)* (diss., Stanford U., 1967)

J. Jacquot, ed.: *Dramaturgie et société … aux XVIe et XVIIe siècles: Nancy 1967* (Paris, 1968)

M. Ellis: 'Inventory of the Dances of Jean-Baptiste Lully', *RMFC*, ix (1969), 21–55

R.M. Isherwood: *Music in the Service of the King: France in the Seventeenth Century* (Ithaca, NY, and London, 1973)

M.M. McGowan: 'Les Jésuites à Avignon: les fêtes au service de la propagande politique et religieuse', *Les fêtes de la Renaissance III: Tours 1972*, ed. J. Jacquot and E. Konigson (Paris, 1975), 153–71

M.M. McGowan: 'The Origins of French Opera', *NOHM*, v (1975), 169–205, esp. 170–80

D.J. Buch: 'The Influence of the *Ballet de cour* in the Genesis of the French Baroque Dance Suite', *AcM*, lvii (1985), 94–109

J.R. Anthony: 'More Faces than Proteus: Lully's *Ballet des muses*', *EMc*, xv (1987), 336–44

J.R. Anthony: 'Towards a Principal Source for Lully's Court Ballets: Foucault vs Philidor', *RMFC*, xxv (1987), 77–104

M.-F. Christout: *Le ballet de cour au XVIIe siècle* (Geneva, 1987)

D. Launay: 'Les airs italiens et français dans les ballets et les comédies-ballets', *Jean-Baptiste Lully: Saint Germain-en-Laye and Heidelberg 1987*, 31–49

J.L. Schwartz and C.J. Schlundt: *French Court Dance and Dance Music: a Guide to Primary Source Writings* (New York, 1987)

C.G. Marsh and R. Harris-Warrick: 'A New Source for Seventeenth-Century Ballet: *Le mariage de la Grosse Cathos*', *Dance Chronicle*, xi (1988), 398–428

L.E. Auld: 'The Non-Dramatic Art of *Ballet de cour*: Early Theorists', *Beyond the Moon: Festschrift Luther Dittmer*, ed. B. Gillingham and P. Merkley (Ottawa, 1990), 360–93

G. Durosoir: *L'air de cour en France 1571–1655* (Liège, 1991)

M.-F. Christout: 'Ballet de cour', *Dictionaire de la musique en France aux XVIIe et XVIIIe siècles*, ed. M. Benoit (Paris, 1992), 45–9

M. Little and C.G. Marsh: *La danse noble: an Inventory of Dances and Sources* (Williamstown, MA, 1992)

D.J. Buch: *Dance Music from the Ballet de cour 1575–1651* (New York, 1994)

JAMES R. ANTHONY

Ballet du XXème Siècle. Company founded in BRUSSELS in 1960.

Ballet-héroïque (Fr.). A type of French OPÉRA-BALLET during the reign of Louis XV, distinguished by having as its principal characters heroic, noble figures, often from antiquity, classical gods and goddesses, or exotic personages, rather than the comic bourgeois and tender heroines of other *opéras-ballets*. It also differs from the contemporary *tragédie en musique* in that the events portrayed are generally festive and gay, not dramatic and terrifying. While dance, of course, remains prominent, in some works there is greater use of vocal music than in other *opéras-ballets*.

The term is first used in the libretto of Fuzelier's *Les festes grecques et romaines*, set by Collin de Blamont (1723). Among the most famous examples are those by Rameau, beginning with *Les Indes galantes* (1735). The last successful *ballet-héroïque* performed at the Paris Opéra was E.J. Floquet's *L'union de l'Amour et des arts* (1773). The term was occasionally applied to a single entrée in an *opéra-ballet* (for example, to *Euthyme et Lyris* by L.-B. Desormery in 1776).

For bibliography see OPÉRA-BALLET.

M. ELIZABETH C. BARTLET

Ballet Lutebook (*IRL-Dtc* D.1.21/ii). See SOURCES OF LUTE MUSIC, §7.

Ballet(s) Russe(s). Name adopted by various ballet companies in the early 20th century. See BALLET, §3(i).

Ballett. See BALLETTO.

Balletti, Bernardino (*fl* Piacenza, 1554). Italian lutenist and composer. He is known only from his lutebook *Intabolatura de lauto … di varie sorte di balli … libro primo* (Venice, 1554; ed. G. Lefkoff, *Five Sixteenth Century Venetian Lute Books*, Washington DC, 1960). The dedication to Conte Honorio Scotto was signed in Piacenza. Most of the 14 pieces in the volume are familiar Italian dance forms: there are two paduana and saltarello pairs, a work based on the romanesca (*La favorita*), and two pieces on the *bergamasca* harmonic formula (I–IV–V–I). The first of these, *Il sgazzotte*, is an independent work, but the second is a 'represe' for *La moretta* and is a striking piece of more than 50 virtuoso variations. Several dances (*La rocha il fuso*, *Ciel turchino* and *Non ti partir da me*) use popular song melodies; *Non ti partir* appeared later as *Ti parti cor mio caro* in a villotta by Filippo Azzaiola (RISM 1557[18]; both works ed. in L.H. Moe: *Dance Music in Printed Italian Lute Tablatures from 1507 to 1611*, diss., Harvard U., 1956). The pieces form three suites (nos.1–4, 5–9 and 10–14), the third with a short chordal *tocata* to test the tuning of the lute. (*BrownI*)

JEANETTE B. HOLLAND/ARTHUR J. NESS

Balletto (It.; Fr. *ballet*; Eng. ballett). An Italian dance of the 16th and 17th centuries, occasionally called 'bal' or 'ballo'. There seem to be three periods of development, two instrumental and one vocal: for lute during the second half of the 16th century; for voice from 1591 to about 1623; and for chamber ensemble from about 1616 to the end of the 17th century.

The term 'balletto' was also applied at the same time in a more general sense. It was used as early as 1581 by Fabritio Caroso as a heading for some of the choreographies published in *Il ballarino*, and Cesare Negri (*Le gratie d'amore*, 1602) used it alongside the apparently similar 'ballo' and 'brando' as a title for his created social and theatrical dances (see BALLO). In Barbetta's *Intavolatura di liuto* (1585) 'balletto' indicates a dance from a foreign country. Some late 16th-century references use the word 'balletto' for theatrical or dramatic dances that would have been called 'ballets' in France (see A. Solerti: *Gli albori del melodramma*, 1904–5/R, iii, 277ff; the commonest usage in modern Italian is as a translation for the French 'ballet'). In the 17th century the word was sometimes used by musicians to mean simply 'dance', as in Montesardo's *Nuova inventione d'intavolatura per sonare li balletti* (1606). This article, however, is concerned with the instrumental and vocal development of the specific dance called 'balletto' as it originated in Italy and spread to England and Germany.

1. Instrumental. 2. Vocal.

1. INSTRUMENTAL. The Italian instrumental balletto appeared from about 1561 to 1599 (mainly for lute) and from 1616 to 1700 (for chamber ensemble). During the second half of the 16th century, 'bal', 'ballo' or 'balletto' was a generic name in Italy for various foreign dances, such as the *bal boemo*, *ballo francese* and *baletto polaco*. Barbetta in 1585 referred to them collectively as 'baletti de diverse nationi'. The most numerous were those indicating Germanic origin: the *bal todesco* (in the

lutebooks of Gorzanis of 1561, 1563 and 1564), the 'todesca' or 'tedesca' (Mainerio's ensemble collection of 1578), *balo todesco* (Gorzanis, 1579), *baletto todesco* (Barbetta, 1585), *ballo tedesco* (Terzi, 1593) and finally *ballo* or *balletto alemano* (Terzi, 1599). Similar terminology continued in the guitar books of the first half of the 17th century. Some of the earlier chamber examples are also entitled 'balletto alemano' (Biagio Marini, 1617, 1626 and 1655, Farina, 1627, and Gandini, 1655). During the second half of the 17th century such pieces were called simply 'balletto' (or occasionally 'ballo'), and the non-German types (for example, a *balletto francese* of 1692 by Corelli) occurred very rarely.

A *balletto alemano* in Terzi's 1599 book is based on an earlier *baletto todesco* by Barbetta, thus suggesting that the sources from 1561 to 1599, in spite of changing terminology, represent a unified Italian development of the native German dance called 'tantz', 'tanz', or 'dantz' in 16th-century German lute and keyboard tablatures. Furthermore, the three pieces designated 'tedesca' or 'todesca' in Mainerio's volume of 1578 were each called 'almande' in Phalèse's collection of 1583, thus revealing some sort of connection between the Italian balletto and the Franco-Flemish allemande. It is difficult to assess the influence on the Italian instrumental balletto exerted by two other forms using the same name: first the French ballet, which began during the 1570s and later produced lute pieces entitled simply 'ballet' (Besard, 1603 and 1617, Ballard, 1611 and 1614, Vallet and Fuhrmann, 1615); and second, the vocal ballettos beginning with those of Gastoldi, whose 1594 book of three-voice examples also includes intabulations for lute.

Curiously, vocal ballettos seem to have appeared mainly between about 1591 and 1623, thus filling the gap, as it were, between the 16th-century lute and 17th-century chamber developments. Earlier, Mainerio's balli (1578), though without text, were, according to the title-page of the book, 'accommodati per cantar et sonar'. A number of sources from the early 17th century contain both vocal and instrumental examples. Antonio Brunelli's *Scherzi, arie, canzonette, e madrigali, libro terzo* (1616) includes two vocal ballettos that are each followed by 'il medesimo ballo per sonare solo senza cantare', as well as an 'altro ballo per sonare solo senza cantare' for which no vocal version is given. Benedetto Sanseverino, in *Il primo libro d'intavolatura per la chitarra alla spagnuola* (1622), printed four chordal examples, one of which has a text. The *Terzo scherzo delle ariose vaghezze* of Carlo Milanuzzi (1623) contains 12 ballettos for solo voice and continuo, as well as seven for guitar alone. As late as 1639 Martino Pesenti presented 'correnti, gagliarde, & balletti da cantar, & da sonar'.

A few instrumental ballettos appeared for keyboard, by Picchi (1621), Frescobaldi (1627 and 1637), Pesenti (1635, 1639, 1641 and 1645) and Bernardo Storace (1664) and by anonymous composers in manuscript sources (such as the *I-Rvat* Chigi *MSS* ed. in CEKM, xxxii/2 and *US-LAum* manuscripts, formerly 51/1); and for the five-course guitar, by Calvi (1646) and Granata (1646, 1659 and 1680). Most Italian instrumental ballettos of the 17th century, however, occur in some 70 publications for continuo chamber groups. The earliest are the books of Marini (1617, 1620 and 1626), Lorenzo Allegri (1618) and Farina (1626, 1627 and 1628). Marini was the first of them to use the word 'balletti' in the title

of a book (in 1626). In a collection of 1667 G.B. Vitali made a distinction between *balletti per ballare* and *balletti per camera*. In 1666 he entitled a book *Correnti e balletti da camera*; Giuseppe Torelli in 1686 used the title *Concerto da camera*, B.G. Laurenti in 1691 *Sonate per camera*, Giorgio Buoni in 1693 *Allettamenti per camera*. The balletto thus became firmly established in Italy above all as a chamber-music form.

The balletto sometimes occurred, especially before 1675, as a separate dance, either singly or with as many as 12 in succession. It was occasionally coupled with another dance, usually a corrente; Marini in 1626 used the same musical material for each. Although generally the opening dance of a pair, the balletto occasionally appeared as the second movement (Gasparo Zanetti, 1645, and Cazzati, 1651 and 1660). It is associated with two or more dances in suites by Brunelli (1616), Allegri (1618) and Cazzati (1651) and in most sources from 1677 to the end of the century. Usually the balletto is the opening dance of a suite, followed by a corrente, *sarabanda*, *giga* or other dances. In suites from later in the century an introductory movement without dance associations precedes the opening balletto.

The balletto almost always consists of two repeated sections, each with a variable number of bars. Occasionally the initial statement of the music is followed by variations (Fantini, 1638, Marini, 1655, and the keyboard works of Frescobaldi, 1627, and Storace, 1664). Later examples also include a *piano* marking at the end to indicate a *petite reprise*, the exact repetition of several bars of music (Torelli, 1686, and G.B. Brevi, 1693); Domenico Gabrielli's ballettos (1684) sometimes have such a repeat at the end of both sections. The balletto is usually in duple metre but may be in triple metre (as with Fantini, 1638, or Cazzati, 1660). The music has a simple, homophonic, tuneful quality, with short, animated rhythmic motifs, repeated notes and immediately appealing melodic patterns (as in ex.1, a brief ballo that follows an aria).

Tempo markings vary widely. Brunelli in 1616 marked a ballo *grave*; Marini in 1655 indicated *allegro* and Cazzati in 1660 *adagio*. Pirro Albergati (1682) marked two balletto *largo* and three *allegro* or *spiritoso*. Gabrielli (1684) indicated *largo* for five, *allegro* for five, *adagio* for one and *presto* for one. Salvatore Mazzella (1689) included an example in which the opening section is *largo* and the second section *presto* and another such piece which returns to *largo* at the end. Laurenti (1691), Brevi (1693) and Buoni (1693) all indicated *allegro* or *presto*. Italian composers seem to have been far less concerned with uniformity of tempo than the French, for they also subjected other dances to wide tempo variation.

The allemanda, which is likewise *largo* or *presto* in these sources, bears a close relationship to the balletto. Each is in duple metre, and each occupies the position as first dance in a suite. Often, however, both dances appeared in the same collection, usually in different suites (Torelli, Laurenti, Brevi) but sometimes coupled together, as in Gabrielli's balletto with *sua alemanda*. It is difficult to perceive any musical differences between the balletto and the allemanda as they appear in these late 17th-century suites.

Instrumental ballettos also occurred in other countries, especially Germany, where the earliest examples appeared in 1617 in the collections of the Englishmen Thomas

Ex.1 *Maurizio Cazzati: Trattenimenti per camera* (Bologna, 1660)
     Ballo dell'Aria

Simpson and William Brade. These were followed by other examples, usually entitled 'ballet', by composers such as Widmann, Peuerl, Johann Schop (i), Hammerschmidt, Vierdanck, Nicolaus Bleyer, Drese, Rosenmüller, Rubert, J.R. Ahle, Lüder Knop, Hans Hake, Esaias Reusner (ii), Löwe von Eisenach, J.H. Schmelzer, Biber, Pezel, Meister and J.C.F. Fischer. Purely instrumental examples of the form had been preceded earlier in Germany by vocal pieces which, under the influence of Gastoldi, could often be played on instruments as well as sung.

2. VOCAL. Both Morley and Praetorius (*Syntagma musicum*, iii, 1618, pp.18–19) considered the Mantuan composer G.G. Gastoldi to have invented the vocal balletto as a musical genre with his publication in 1591 of the *Balletti a cinque voci con li suoi versi per cantare, sonare, & ballare* (ed. in Le pupitre, x, 1968). These works enjoyed great popularity, being reprinted many times in Italy and northern Europe up to the mid-17th century. In most of his ballettos Gastoldi set strophic texts in a homophonic texture, with sections of nonsense syllables ('fa-la', 'na-na', 'li-rum') interpolated at the ends of couplets or tercets. Nearly all consist of two repeated strains (*AABB*) and the nonsense syllables, sometimes set contrapuntally, act as a refrain at the end of each section. The songs are syllabic and rather repetitious, the strophic form limiting the opportunities to depict the content of the verses, and all are highly rhythmic. It is likely that Gastoldi's songs were originally part of a costumed dance, perhaps performed at the theatrically active Mantuan court or at an academy; the title-page states that they were for 'singing, playing and dancing'. Each has a descriptive title (e.g. *L'innamorato*, *Il premiato*, *Caccia d'Amore*) on which the text (but not the music) elaborates, and several texts suggest the kind of costuming or dance that might have been used (as in *Amor vittorioso*: 'Tutti venite armati, O forti miei soldata, fa-la-la', etc.). The order of texts in the collection suggests that it follows that of a performance, opening with an *Introduttione a i balletti* exhorting the listener to enjoy the delights of the mythical 'Cucagna', 'ove chi più lavora men guadagna' ('where the more one works the less one earns') by dancing, singing and playing, and concluding in the dialogue-like *Concerto de pastori* for eight voices, with a conventional reference to the returning golden age. The six-voice *Mascherata di cacciatori*, more complex than the usual simple form and style of the ballettos, is the only piece that shows any musical reflection of the presumed spectacle.

Gastoldi's later collection, *Balletti a tre voci* (1594), also opens with an exhortation to sing and dance, but it does not seem to represent the music of a particular event as the five-voice collection does. Neither the descriptive titles nor the texts present an obvious performing order. Like the five-voice ballettos, these consist of two or three repeated strains in a simple homophonic texture and a strongly rhythmic style; the phrasing of several immediately suggests particular dance types (e.g. *La Cortegiana*, 'La mia amorosa bella', has the characteristic three- and six-bar phrases of a branle). Only the last balletto in the set uses nonsense syllables, and then only at the end of the second strain.

Vocal ballettos continued to be written in Italy during the 17th century, often in madrigal comedies and particularly by Banchieri and Orazio Vecchi, usually retaining the villanella- or canzonetta-like style of Gastoldi. Some, notably those in Gioseffo Biffi's *Della ricreatione di Posilipo* (1606), Francesco Lambardi's *Canzonette a tre … libro terzo* (1616) and Sigismondo d'India's *Le musiche e balli a quatro* (1621), can be traced to choreographed dances performed at court festivities. D'India's multi-movement ballettos originated as entertainments at the wedding of the Duke of Savoy in 1621, when they were performed by a boy soprano soloist accompanied by 'violino tiorba', 'basso di violone' and 'clavicembalo'. Like the ballettos of Gastoldi and Vecchi, they consist of two repeated strains of chordal, highly rhythmic music cast in regular phrases. Their original conception as music for one voice with instrumental accompaniment may be seen in the rhythmic independence of the upper part, and d'India's habitual concern for detailed text setting occasionally enlivens the otherwise almost utilitarian style. The publication of d'India's solo ballettos with texts to all parts, and with specific indications of passages to be rendered by one voice with instruments, testifies to the continuing Italian use of published ballettos as light vocal household music. His informative description of the appropriate performing practice for his pieces, printed at the end of the book, is justified with the remark that they represented an unusual style in Italy ('si tratta di stile inusitato in Italia'), suggesting, in view of the book's dedication to the Duke of Savoy's mother-in-law, Maria de' Medici, Queen of France, that the spectacle represented by the collection was related to the nascent *ballet de cour*.

Gastoldi's first set of ballettos enjoyed enormous popularity north of the Alps, spawning imitations in Germany (H.L. Hassler's *Lustgarten neuer teutscher Gesäng, Balletti*, 1601) and England, where the ballett as cultivated and transformed by Morley and Weelkes produced a small repertory of enduringly popular vocal music. Morley's *Balletts to Five Voyces* (1595, published

Ex.2

in both English and Italian) deliberately imitated the structure of Gastoldi's five-voice collection, replacing the *Introduttione* with a madrigal and the concluding *Concerto de pastori* with an echo dialogue (the seven-voice *Phillis, I faine wold die now*), the only English work of its kind; each ballet is a free parody of an existing Italian balletto, canzonetta or villanella. Morley's seven parodies of Gastoldi ballettos are fairly close to their models, as a comparison of *Sing wee and chaunt it* with *A lieta vita* clearly shows; the English version is metrically re-arranged and boasts a considerably more sophisticated texture, particularly in the inevitable 'fa-la' sections. More interesting are Morley's adaptations into the ballett form of canzonettas by Croce, Ferretti, Marenzio and Vecchi; by inserting 'fa-la' sections at the ends of the two couplets of Marenzio's *Le rose fronde e fiori*, Morley stretched his model to twice its length and regularized the phrasing, creating a quite new work in *Those dainty daffadillies*. Ex.2 compares the superius of Morley's *Now is the month of maying* with that of its presumed model, a balletto by Vecchi (*So ben mi c'ha bon tempo*, *Selva di varie ricreatione*, 1595), and that accompanying a pavan-derived choreography for the tune published by Cesare Negri (*Le gratie d'amore*, 1602, pp.222–3), revealing how far afield Morley's melodic inventiveness and clear harmonic thinking led him in even so simple a work.

Although Morley knew the tradition of dancing to such songs (to which he referred in *A Plaine and Easie Introduction to Practicall Musicke*), it is now generally assumed that neither his ballets nor those of his English successors were intended for dancing, hence their greater attention to musical and textual refinements. Weelkes's ballets (*Balletts and Madrigals to Five Voyces*, 1598) were clearly influenced more by Morley than by Gastoldi, for the often brilliant counterpoint and expressive text-setting owe little to the Italian form. *Welcome sweet pleasure* and *To shorten winter's sadness* are straightforward enough to have accompanied a dance, but *Hark all ye lovely saints* and *Lady, your eye my love enforceth*, and also *I love, and have my love regarded*, are transformed into vocal chamber music by eliding contrapuntal phrases and, in particular, by madrigalian devices that render both rhythms and phrasing erratic. The six ballets Henry Youll included in his *Canzonets to Three Voyces* (1608) follow Weelkes's and Morley's example to some extent, for example in the use of strict canon in *In the merry month of May* and *Now the country lasses hie them*, but his balletts are more regular in form than those of the better-known composers. Other early 17th-century composers of the English ballett include Greaves, Pilkington, Tomkins and John Hilton (ii).

BIBLIOGRAPHY

BrownI; EinsteinIM; KermanEM; MGG2 ('Ballo, Balletto'; S. Dahms, J. Sutton); *SartoriB; VogelB*

R. Schwartz: 'Hans Leo Hassler unter dem Einfluss der italiänischen Madrigalisten', *VMw*, ix (1893), 1–61

D. Arnold: 'Gastoldi and the English Ballett', *MMR*, lxxxvi (1956), 44–52

R. Rasch: 'The Balletti of Giovanni Giacomo Gastoldi and the Musical History of the Netherlands', *TVNM*, xxiv (1974), 112–45

W.T. Marrocco: *Inventory of 15th-Century Bassedanze, Balli & Balletti in Italian Dance Manuals* (New York, 1981)

R. Hudson: *The Allemande, the Balletto, and the Tanz* (Cambridge, 1986)

D. Harrán: 'Salomone Rossi as a Composer of Theater Music', *Studi musicali*, xvi (1987), 96–131

S. Balestracci: 'Influenze francesi sui balletti di Filippo D'Aglié (con particolare riguardo a *Il gridelino*)', *Studi musicali*, xxv (1996), 329–44

RICHARD HUDSON (1), SUZANNE G. CUSICK/R (2)

Balliani, Carlo. *See* BALIANI, CARLO.

Ballière de Laisement [Delaisement], **(Charles-Louis-)Denis** (*b* Paris, 9 May 1729; *d* Rouen, 8 Nov 1800). French composer and theorist. He combined the surnames of his father (Ballière) and mother (Delaisement) in an aristocratic form. After receiving the maître ès arts from the University of Paris in 1746, he settled in Rouen. A pharmacist and chemist by profession, he took an active scholarly interest in many subjects and was acquainted with Rousseau, Voltaire and other well-known contemporaries. In 1754 he was elected to the Rouen Academy, where he later became vice-president and wrote many works on literature, philology and various sciences. In the 1750s he wrote librettos for several light stage works produced in Rouen and Paris; most of the music (vaudevilles and melodies from serious operas) was unnotated, though the notated *airs* in *Zéphire et Flore* may be his. In his *Théorie de la musique* (Paris, 1764) he developed a system based on the harmonic series of the hunting-horn; a similar system, evidently unknown to him, had been presented by G.A. Sorge in 1741. The *Théorie* had some followers (notably Canon Jamard and Abbé Feytou) and won Rousseau's praise, but was harshly criticized by later theorists, in particular J.-B. de La Borde.

WORKS

unless otherwise stated, all are opéras comiques in 1 act, with libretto by Ballière de Laisement

Les fêtes de l'hymen, ou La rose (A. Piron), ?Rouen, ?c1746
Deucalion et Pyrrha (parodie), ?1751
Le rossignol, Rouen, 8 Oct 1751
Zéphire et Flore, Paris, Opéra-Comique (Foire St Germain), 14 Feb 1754 (Paris, ?1754)
Le retour de printemps (pastorale), Rouen, 13 March 1755
La guirlande, Rouen, 24 March 1757

BIBLIOGRAPHY

DBF (M. Prevost); La BordeE, iii; MGG1 (L. Maurice-Amor)
I. Bent: 'Momigny's "Type de la Musique" and a Treatise in the Making', *Music Theory and the Exploration of the Past*, ed. C. Hatch and D.W. Bernstein (Chicago, 1993), 309–40

Balliett, Whitney (L.) (*b* New York, 17 April 1926). American writer on jazz and broadcaster. After graduating from Cornell University (BA 1951) he joined the staff of the *New Yorker*. For the *Saturday Review* (1953–7) and then for the *New Yorker* he contributed reviews of jazz concerts, recordings and books, as well as interviews with jazz musicians; many of these articles have been reprinted in a continuing series of books. He has also published poetry. In 1957 he conceived the idea and was adviser for a television programme, 'The Sound of Jazz', broadcast live by CBS. Balliett's writings are eloquent and highly stylized. His interviews portray his subjects with dignity, and his reviews often create effects that parallel those of the music being discussed. At his best, in an assessment of style or a description of an improvisation, Balliett has provided insights more penetrating than many formal musical analyses.

WRITINGS

all collections of previously published articles and reviews

The Sound of Surprise (New York, 1959/R)
Dinosaurs in the Morning (Philadelphia, 1962/R)
Such Sweet Thunder (Indianapolis, 1966)
Ecstasy at the Onion (Indianapolis, 1971/R)
Alec Wilder and his Friends (Boston, 1974/R)
American Singers (New York, 1979, enlarged 2/1988)
Jelly Roll, Jabbo and Fats (New York, 1983)
American Musicians (New York, 1986)
Barney, Bradley and Max (New York, 1989)

BARRY KERNFELD

Ballif, Claude (André François) (*b* Paris, 22 May 1924). French composer and theorist. Born into an intellectual family (his uncle, Fr Festugière, was a Greek scholar and a member of the Institut), he decided at the age of 16 to make his career in music and entered the Bordeaux Conservatoire as a pupil of J.-F. Vaubourgoin; later he studied at the Paris Conservatoire with Noël Gallon, Aubin and Messiaen. In 1951 he went to Berlin where, as a pupil of Blacher and Rufer, he became familiar with the music of the Second Viennese School, and where he studied musicology with Stuckenschmidt. Ballif had already made a reputation as the composer of *Cendres*(1946) for percussion when, in 1953, he completed his theoretical work *Introduction à la métatonalité*,

published in 1956 with a foreword by the aesthetician Etienne Souriau. In 1955 Ballif won the first prize for composition at the Geneva International Competition, and he lectured at the French Institutes of Berlin (1955–7) and Hamburg (1957–8). Returning to Paris in 1959, he joined the ORTF Groupe de Recherches Musicales; he was professor of analysis and of the history of music at the Ecole Normale de Musique, Paris (1963–4), and professor of music education, and later of analysis, at the Reims Conservatoire (from 1965). In 1968 he participated in the founding of the University of Paris VIII and directed its music department until the following year. Alongside this teaching activity, he has pursued fundamental research into the philosophy of music: a stimulating book on Berlioz was published in 1968, and a symposium on 'ultrachromatic' music, edited by Ballif, appeared in 1972. Ballif was appointed professor of analysis at the Paris Conservatoire in 1971. His class, which welcomed painters and architects as often as composers, soon grew famous at the same time as his music. A succession of honours and distinctions in the course of a few years underlined his success. He received the Honegger prize in 1974, the Florent Schmitt prize (awarded by the Institut) in 1975, the Grand Prix de la Ville de Paris in 1980. In 1979 his collection of *Voyage de mon oreille*, ten essays summarizing his ideas on the ethics and aesthetics of composition was published. He was appointed professor of composition at the Paris Conservatoire in 1982, and in 1984 the Paris Festival Estival was dedicated to his music. In the same year he was appointed to the Ordre des Arts et des Lettres, on the occasion of the première of his opera *Dracoula*, and he signed an exclusive contract with the publisher Durand. Another book, *Economie musicale*, appeared in 1988: it contains the essence of Ballif's ideas about the education and training of composers, developing a course of lectures he had given ten years earlier at McGill University. He retired in 1990, but further courses of lectures, more music and more honours followed: already an Officer of the Ordre du Mérite, he was appointed Commander in 1994.

The chief characteristic of Ballif's work is his avoidance of conventional musical systems in favour of his own 'metatonality', which he sees as an enlargement of tonality in contrast with the evasion of tonality represented by atonal music. Ballif's metatonality is founded on a scale of 11 notes, and his musical discourse avoids the tonal disorientation of atonality, since the missing pitch suffices to give the music suggestions of tonality, while at the same time implying the presence of the total chromatic. In this way Ballif hopes to have systematized the 'free atonality' of Schoenberg at the period of *Erwartung*. A sense of direction is achieved through the employment of a basic pitch to underpin each large section.

Ballif's metatonal procedures allow an extreme fluidity of detail, a tenuity of structure and great delicacy in the use of timbre. Sometimes the melody is quite simple, as in *Phrases sur le souffle* and *Chapelet*, and Ballif has always preferred straightforward forms, although small-scale dissymmetries may be deployed with subtle finesse (cf *A cor et à cri* and *Ceci et cela*). In the *Imaginaires*, a series of pieces each for seven instruments, the harmony is limited to a single interval within each work; in the vocal music this sobriety is allied with a contained violence, particularly in the slow vocalises or the heavy irregular tread of sound blocks, as at the close of *Phrases sur le souffle*. Although Ballif has allowed the operation of chance into his music, this has not compromised the characteristic directed development: his *Passe-temps* for piano consists of assortable sections, but the use of underlying pitches assures the perception of direction, and the piece has none of the fractured quality of Stockhausen's comparable *Klavierstück XI*.

In Ballif's orchestral works there is an attempt to incorporate the sounds of the environment, an attempt that may be seen as a development from Cage's work of the 1950s and a parallel of the latter's ensemble pieces of the early 1970s (e.g. *Cheap Imitation*), although the means are quite different. The incorporation proceeds through the orchestral mimicking of natural sounds, and these synthetic interruptions are perceived as affecting the progress of the work; the music is no longer opposed to nature but contains, and is illuminated by, the external, just as the experience of an architectural interior is dependent on light from the outside.

In the 1950s Ballif was at least as passionate as Cage in his admiration for Satie and Webern, but not for the same reasons. What fascinated Ballif were Satie's understatement and Webern's economy of means, and he immediately subjected them to analytical study. Taking their different courses, however, Cage and Ballif ran into the same problem: atonality. Ballif conceived metatonality while seeking to dissipate the ambiguities bestowed on atonality by early Schoenberg. In the preface to Michèle Tosi's 1996 monograph on Ballif, the composer Costin Miereanu describes Ballif as the 'first of the pan-serialists'. In fact, like Schoenbergian 'pantonality', metatonality could be considered another name for Lou Harrison's 'proto-tonality', identified by Cage.

Ballif adopted an uncomfortable position as a composer, seeking a style of composition that would allow him to avoid the 'weightlessnesses' linked to the suspension of harmony; he found himself almost alone in the search, somewhere between tonality and atonality but above all not letting himself be deflected by the 'neoserial' current predominant in the France of the time and it took fierce tenacity to stay on course and preserve his independence.

WORKS

STAGE

Mon Faust (incid music, P. Valéry), 1958; Vitrine (incid music), 1960; La musique d'Erich Zahn (incid music, H.P. Lovecraft), 1964; Alice aux pays des merveilles (incid music, L. Carroll), 1965; Les Troyennes (incid music, J.-P. Sartre), 1967; Dracoula (nocturne lyrique, 2, V. Stephan), op.58, 1982–4; Il suffit d'un peu d'air (farce lyrique, 4 tableaux, R. Tremblay), op.65, 1991

ORCHESTRAL

La vie du monde qui vient, sym. mystique, op.11, 8 solo vv, 5 choirs, orch, 1953, rev. 1972–3; Lovecraft, op.13, 1955; Voyage de mon oreille, op.20, 1957; Fantasio, op.21, 1957; Ceci et cela, op.26, 1959, rev. 1965; Fantasio grandioso, op.21a, 1962; A cor et à cri, op.39, 1962; Conc. symphonique no.1, op.49 no.1, cl, orch, 1976; Conc. symphonique no.2, op.49 no.2, vn, orch, 1984; Conc. symphonique no.3 'Le jouet du jeu', ob, orch, 1988; La transfiguration de l'univers, op.67, 1993; Praeludia for la transfiguration de l'univers, 2 Brass Qnt, org, 1997; Conc. symphonique no.4, op.49/4, fl, orch, 1999; Au Clair de la lune bleue, op.75, orch, 1999

CHAMBER AND SOLO INSTRUMENTAL

Cendres, op.1, perc ens, 1946; Trio, op.8, ob, cl, bn, 1952; Brass Qnt, op.9, 1952; Wind Qnt, op.10, 1953; Str Qt no.1, op.12a, 1955; 4 sonates, op.14, org, 1956; Str Trio no.1, op.16, 1956; Sonata, op.17, vn, pf, 1957; Str Qt no.2, op.22, 1958; Sonata, op.23, fl, pf, 1958; Qnt, op.24, fl, ob, str trio, 1958; Mouvements

pour deux, op.27, fl, pf, 1959; Str Trio no.2, op.28, 1959; Str Qt no.3, op.30, 1959; Qnt, op.34, bn, str qt, 1960; Trio, op.35 no.1, fl, bn, hp, 1961; Trio, op.35 no.2, fl, ob, vc, 1961; Trio, op.35, no.3, vn, cl, hn, 1961; Solfeggietto no.1, op.36 no.1, fl, 1961; Solfeggietto no.2, op.36 no.2, eng hn, 1961; Sonata, op.40, vc, pf, 1962; Imaginaire no.1, op.41 no.1, vn, vc, hp, fl, cl, tpt, trbn, 1963; Cahier de violin, 5 pieces, op.42, vn, 1963; Solfeggietto no.3, vn, 1963; Imaginaire no.2, op.41 no.2, pic tpt, tpt, bugle, hn, 2 trbn, tuba, 1967; Solfeggietto no.4, op.36 no.4, ob, 1968; Solfeggietto no.5, op.36 no.5, cl, 1968; Imaginaire no.4, op.41 no.4, org, tpt, b tpt, trbn, bugle, hn, tuba, 1968; Imaginaire no.5, op.41 no.5, 2 pf, fl, ob, cl, cornet, hn, va, db, 1968, rev. 1978; Trio, op.43 no.1, fl, va, hp; Imaginaire no.3, op.41 no.3, 2 va, vc, db, cl, hn, bn, 1969; Str Trio no.3, op.43 no.2, 1969; Imaginaire no.6, op.41 no.6, 11 str, 1974; Qt, op.48, vn, va, vc, perc, 1975; Solfeggietto no.6, op.35 no.6, gui, 1976; Cant de l'innocent, fl, 1977; Chant de charme, ondes martenot, 1977; Timbres et postes, op.51, 6 perc, 1977; Sonata, op.52, cl, pf, 1978; L'habitant du labyrinthe, op.54, 2 perc, 1980; Rêveries, op.55, vn, cl, pf, 1980; Solfeggietto no.7, op.35 no.7, tuba, 1980; Apostrophes et jubilations, op.56, org, 1981; Solfeggietto no.8, op.35 no.8, sax, 1981; Solfeggietto no.9, op.35 no.9, hp, 1982; Solfeggietto no.10, op.35 no.10, hpd, 1982; Solfeggietto no.11, op.35 no.11, bn, 1984; Solfeggietto no.12, op.35 no.12, perc, 1984; Solfeggietto no.13, op.35 no.13, vc, 1985; Solfeggietto no.14, op.35 no.14, tpt, 1986; Un moment de printemps, op.60, fl, cl, vn, vc, pf, 1987; Str Qt no.4, op.61, 1987; Solfeggietto no.15, op.35 no.15, hn, 1988; Str Qt no.5, op.63, 1989; Le taille lyre, op.64, 7 insts, 1990; Str Trio no.4, op.66, 1992; Qnt, op.70, 4 timp, bells, 1994; Chanson d'Anastasio, mar, 1995; La chanson du petit matin, cl, 1995; Sax Qt, op.71, 1995; Solfeggietto no.16, op.35 no.16, mar, 1995; Solfeggietto no.17, op.35 no.17, accdn, 1995; Battez sons pleins, op.73, 4 glock, 1996; Petits refrains de ménestrels, vn, 1996; Solfeggietto no.18, op.35/18, cl, 1997; Solfeggietto no.19, op.35/19, va, 1998

PIANO

Airs comprimés, op.5, 1953; Pièces détachées, op.6, 1953; Diableries, op.12b, pf, 1955; Pf Sonata no.1, op.18, 1957; Pf Sonata no.2, op.19, 1957; Pf Sonata no.3, op.29, 1959; Pf Sonata no.4, op.31, 1960; Pf Sonata no.5, op.32, 1960; Passe-temps, 6 pieces, op.38, 1962; Première ronde nocturne, op.62, 2 pf, 1988; Priamelnen, 8 pieces, op.68, pf 4 hands, 1993; Pf Sonata no.6, op.69, 1994; Notes et menottes, 4 vols, 1951–77, 1995

VOCAL

Le cortège d'Orphée, op.1a, 1v, pf, 1947–8; Apparitions (H. Michaux), op.2, Mez, pf, 1949; Chansons bas (S. Mallarmé), op.3, S, pf, 1949; Minuit pour géants (T. Tzara), op.4, Mez/Bar, pf, 1951; 4 antiennes à la Sainte Vierge, op.7, 6vv, 16 insts, 1952; Musik in Mirabel (G. Trakl), op.15, S, pf, 1956; Phrases sur le souffle, op.25, Mez, chorus, 8 insts, 1958, rev. 1968; Retrouver la parole (cant., R. Giroux), op.33, Ct/S, ens, 1960; Prière à la Sainte Vierge, op.44 no.1, chorus, 1971; Prière au Seigneur, op.45, chorus, tpt, trbn, 1972; Les battements du coeur de Jésus, op.46, chorus, tpt, trbn, 1971; Chapelet, op.44 no.2, chorus, 1972; Fragments d'une ode à la faim, op.47, 12vv, 1974; Poème de la félicité, op.50, 3 female vv, 2 perc, gui, 1977; Un coup de dés, op.53, chorus, 6 insts, elec, 1979; Poèmes lents (A. Brochu), op.57, 1v, pf, 1981; Le livre du serviteur, op.59, T, chorus, orch, 1984; Chansonnette no.1: 5 fables de La Fontaine, op.72, 1995; Moments donnés de mandarins (Li Tai Po), op.74, S, fl, cl, ob, 1998

TAPE

Etudes au ressort, 1961; Points, mouvements, 1962

ARRANGEMENTS

E Satie: Sports et divertissements, orchd 1950; A. Schoenberg: 6 petites pièces pour piano op.19, orchd 1953; G. Gabrieli: Canzone ottavi toni, orchd 1960; H. Berlioz: 'Absence' [Les nuits d'été], orchd 1984

Principal publishers: Durand, Transatlantiques

WRITINGS

Introduction à la métatonalité (Paris, 1956)
Berlioz (Paris, 1968)
'Les trois Russes: Wychnegradsky, Obouhov et Scriabine', *ReM*, nos.290–91 (1972) [whole issue]
Voyage de mon oreille (Paris, 1979)

'Lettre à Daniel Charles', *Digraphe*, no.28 (1982)
Economie musicale (Paris, 1988)
'Les mouvements de l'azur mallarméen', *Six musiciens en quête d'auteurs*, ed. A. Galliari (Paris,1991)

BIBLIOGRAPHY
KdG I.Misch)
'Claude Ballif', *ReM*, no.263 (1968) [whole issue]
'Claude Ballif: carnet critique', *ReM*, no.264 (1968)
D. Charles: 'De Ballif à Mallarmé', *Digraphe*, no.28 (1982)
'Claude Ballif', *ReM*, nos.370–71 (1984) [whole issue]
'Claude Ballif', *Cahiers de CIREM*, nos.20–21 (1991) [whole issue]
S. Bouissou: 'Au-delà de l'imaginaire et de la spéculation: la musique d'orchestre de Claude Ballif', *La musique: de la théorie au politique*, ed. H. Dufourt and J.-M. Fauquet (Paris, 1991), 155–80
A. Galliari: *L'habitant du labyrinthe: entretiens avec Claude Ballif* (Paris, 1992)
M. Tosi: *L'ouverture métatonale* (Paris, 1992)
M. Tosi: *Claude Ballif* (Mercuès, 1996)

DANIEL CHARLES

Balling, Michael (*b* Würzburg-Heidingsfeld, 28 Aug 1866; *d* Darmstadt, 1 Sept 1925). German conductor. He trained as a violist and played in the opera orchestras of Mainz and Schwerin. After touring Australia and New Zealand (1892–5) he went to England in 1895 as musical director of Frank Benson's Shakespearean company. The following year he returned to Germany and played in the orchestra at the Bayreuth Festival. Here his conducting talents were discovered by Felix Mottl and Cosima Wagner and he acted as an assistant for the festivals of 1896, 1899, 1901 and 1902. After posts in Hamburg, Lübeck and Breslau, Balling succeeded Mottl in 1903 as musical director in Karlsruhe. He was a regular conductor at Bayreuth (1904–14, 1924–5), conducting the *Ring*, *Parsifal* and *Tristan*, and in 1905 gave the first performance in Barcelona of *Die Meistersinger*. In 1910 he conducted the first *Ring* performances in Scotland; and in 1911 he succeeded Hans Richter as conductor of the Hallé Orchestra, with which he gave memorable performances of such large-scale works as Berlioz's *Te Deum*, Liszt's *Faust Symphony* and Mahler's First Symphony. He was in Bayreuth at the outbreak of war in August 1914 and never resumed his Manchester post. From 1912 he was editor for Breitkopf & Härtel of a projected critical Wagner edition. His final post was as musical director in Darmstadt (1919–25). In 1908 he married the widow of Hermann Levi.

CHRISTOPHER FIFIELD

Ballioni, Girolamo. *See* BAGLIONI, GIROLAMO.

Ballis, Oliviero (*b* ?Crema; *d* Ceneda, 24 March 1616). Italian composer, singer and priest. He had been appointed priest and contralto singer at Padua Cathedral on 5 May 1577 and he served there for more than 20 years in various capacities. He was an unsuccessful candidate for the post of *maestro di cappella* at the cathedral in 1580, but served as a substitute in the post, being the most senior member of the choir, after Costanzo Porta's dismissal and until the election of G.B. Mosto (from May to December 1595), and again during the latter's absence and after his death until the election of Lelio Bertani (from March 1596 to November 1598). He had various disputes with the new *maestro* in April 1600. The following year, on the recommendation of Bishop Leonardo Mocenigo, he was elected *maestro di cappella* of Ceneda Cathedral, a post which he held, despite new disputes with a local canon, until his death. During these final years he

published his *Sacri hymni*, which are characterized by a solemn antiphonal style.

WORKS

Canzonette amorose spirituali, 3vv, libro primo (Venice, 1607)
Sacri hymni cantiones et litaniae deiparae Virginis Mariae, 8vv (Venice, 1609)
Madrigal: Se Giove, se Pluton, 5vv, in 1598[7]
Musiche, 3, 4vv, lost; see *Mischiati I*
2 masses, 5, 8vv, lost; cited in an inventory of 1602

BIBLIOGRAPHY
Mischiati I
R. Casimiri: 'Musica e musicisti nella cattedrale di Padova nei sec. XIV, XV, XVI: contributo per una storia', *NA*, xviii (1941), 1–31, 101–214; xix (1942), 49–92
E. Casagrande, M. Fontebasso Santorio and A. Ciciliot: *La musica nel Cenedese: ricerche storiche e note musicologiche dal 1300 al 1900* (Vittorio Veneto, 1978), 43, 54
F. Colussi: 'Vita musicale a Valvasone nel secolo di Erasmo', *Erasmo di Valvasone e il suo tempo*, ed. F. Colussi (Pordenone, 1995), 145–93
F. Arpini: 'Oliviero Ballis detto il Crema', *'Scientia musicae' e musicisti a Crema tra '500 e '600* (Crema, 1996), 29–48

LELAND EARL BARTHOLOMEW/FRANCO COLUSSI

Ballo (It.: 'dance', 'ball'; Fr. *bal*; Sp. *baile*; Ger. *Ball, Tanz*). (1) A generic term meaning a social gathering for the purpose of or with the emphasis on dancing.

Although the verb 'ballare', the noun 'ballatio' and related terms can be traced back to classical antiquity (for the complex etymology see Aeppli), the noun 'ballo' did not appear until the late Middle Ages. French narrators and chroniclers of the 12th and 13th centuries used it, together with 'danserie', to indicate a dance activity in the most general sense. Writers of the Italian Renaissance period from Boccaccio to Castiglione reported 'gran balli' for every festive occasion, and this meaning has remained unchanged throughout the history of social dancing at all levels (court, town and country), becoming more specific as time progressed and as distinctions were made according to occasions, places and dress: public dances (*balli pubblici, bals publics*); court balls (*balli di corte, Hof-Ball, Grand bal du Roi*) for invited guests of rank; balls at famous opera houses (Budapest, London, Milan, Paris, Vienna); and masked and costume balls.

(2) A choreography of varying elaborateness invented by a professional dancing-master and performed either at a social gathering or on the stage.

From the 13th century a distinction was made between the ballo (or *bal*) and other types of dance, indicating that the term had a specific choreographic meaning whose precise nature, known to the contemporaries, now eludes scholars (e.g. 'Danses, *baus* et caroles veissiez commencier', *Adenès li Rois: li roumans de Berte aus grans piés*, ed. A. Scheler, Brussels, 1874, p.12, l.302). Andrea da Tempo (*Trattato delle rime volgari*, 1332) testified to the existence of balli in the round ('cantantur in rotunditate choreae sive balli'), while the Italian *trescone* (a rustic dance) ends with a pantomimic sequence called 'il ballo' (Ungarelli, 64ff). All types of entertainers (e.g. jongleurs, *Spielleute*) contributed to the invention and development of these balli, but it was not until the advent of the professional choreographers of the early 15th century that the ballo assumed a definite shape. On the basis of the extensive information given in the dance instruction books of Domenico da Piacenza, Antonio Cornazano and Guglielmo Ebreo da Pesaro, the 15th-century court ballo can be defined. It was a dance piece created by a professional artist for a specified number of performers,

Italian ?ballo: detail from the 'Story of Antiochus and Stratonice' attributed to the Stratonice Master, cassone panel, c1470s (Henry E. Huntington Library and Art Gallery, San Marino, CA)

composed of a sequence of choreographic events (*misure*) based on the four common musical metres (bassadanza, saltarello, quadernaria and piva; *see* SALTARELLO), using all the *movimenti naturali* (particularly the various forms of *salto* – leaps, hops, jumps) and the embellishing *movimenti accidentali*, and ranging from purely ornamental dances to highly dramatic, narrative creations. (The three most explicitly pantomimic choreographies of the known 15th-century repertory are called ballettos; *see* BALLETTO, §1.)

Whether they are for couples, or *alla fila*, or in the round, all balli follow the same structural pattern: they begin with an intrada (usually a saltarello or a piva pattern, occasionally a quadernaria), followed by the ballo proper and ending with either a repeat of the entire dance or a reprise of the intrada during which one set of performers moves out of the centre of the ballroom to make room for the next. (The same sequence, called 'Intrada', 'Figuren', 'Retrajecte', was described by Michael Praetorius, 1618, p.19.) Where musical accompaniment is given, its single melodic line (labelled 'in canto' or 'in canto da sonare') follows and supports the choreographic configurations in the minutest detail.

During the next century of its history, culminating in the choreographic works of Fabritio Caroso (1581) and Cesare Negri (1602), the main characteristics of the social ballo remained essentially the same: it was a performance piece to be danced by well-trained amateurs; it still consisted of sections, although these had grown larger, lending the ballo as a whole a suite-like dimension. Pavans, *pavaniglie* and bassas replaced the old bassadanza and quadernaria metres; *gagliarde*, cascardas, *tordiglioni* and canaries replaced the piva and saltarello. In the 18th century minuets and contredanses were occasionally

called balli (Gennaro Magri, *Trattato del ballo nobile*, 1779), but by this time the specific connotation of the term had been lost.

Outside the repertory for the courtly ballroom the ballo figured prominently in the theatrical entertainments of the 1600s; *intermedi*, early operas and even plays all featured at least one extensive dance-number of this name; Monteverdi's *Ballo delle ingrate* is centred on a large dance-suite. As the professional performer replaced the courtly amateur, the term 'ballo' gradually gave way to 'balletto'; both had been used interchangeably up to about 1600.

(3) A musical composition inspired by or directly related to the art of dancing.

Until the beginning of the 16th century compositions called 'ballo' rarely appeared in purely musical sources. Dance pieces, wherever they did occur, were either given their specific titles (e.g. 'estampie', 'danse royale', 'ballata', 'moresca') or text incipits, depending on whether they came from an instrumental or a vocal tradition. Collections of balli began to appear around 1520 and by the middle of the century most used the term in their title: *Intabolatura nova di varie sorte de balli da sonare per arpichordi* (1551), Bendusi's *Opera nova de balli* (1553), *Intavolatura de liuto di varie sorte di balli* (1554) and Mainerio's *Primo libro de balli* (1578). In all these collections the term 'ballo' covers a variety of fashionable dances: pavans, galliards, branles, saltarellos and canaries for instrumental performance or, less frequently, 'da cantare e sonare' (Bendusi). Balli also occur in more general collections of music such as the organ tablatures of Jakob Paix (1583). Most of these dances are short compositions with evenly balanced phrases, clear rhythmic patterns and comparatively simple harmonies. Frequently sections in contrasting metres were inserted or added at the end, apparently reflecting the suite-like structure of balli in contemporary dance manuals (e.g. those of Caroso and Negri).

Some 17th-century sources contain music for multi-movement balli that were actually presented as court entertainments (Lorenzo Allegri's *Il primo libro delle musiche*, 1618, for example, contains eight complete balli performed at the Medici court between 1608 and 1615); the term 'ballo' was also often applied to the first dance in a group. Such opening dances were formal introductory numbers followed by a series of dances presented in much the same order as they would have had in the ballroom. Thus Antonio Brunelli's 'Balletto a cinque' (in *Scherzi, arie, canzonette, e madrigali, libro terzo*, 1616) presents the dances in the order *ballo grave*, *gagliarda*, corrente; B.G. Laurenti's *12 suonate per camera a violino*, op.1 (1691) in the order *introdutione*, ballo, corrente, *minuetto*; and Cazzati's *Trattenimento per camera* (1660) in the order aria, ballo, corrente. In 18th-century instrumental music the term 'ballo' was used only occasionally to indicate the dance-like character of a composition.

BIBLIOGRAPHY

BrownI; ES (G. Tani); *MGG2* (S. Dahms and J. Sutton; also 'Suite', §II, T. Feilen); *PirrottaDO; PraetoriusSM*, iii; *ReeseMR; SolertiMBD*

G. Ungarelli: *Le vecchie danze italiane* (Rome, 1894/R)

F. Aeppli: *Die wichtigsten Ausdrücke für das Tanzen in den romanischen Sprachen* (Halle, 1925)

F. Blume: *Studien zur Vorgeschichte der Orchestersuite im 15. und 16. Jahrhundert* (Leipzig, 1925/R)

W. Merian: *Der Tanz in den deutschen Tabulaturbüchern* (Leipzig, 1927/R)

C. Sachs: *Eine Weltgeschichte des Tanzes* (Berlin, 1933; Eng. trans., 1937/*R*)

F. Ghisi: 'Ballet Entertainments in Pitti Palace, Florence, 1608–1625', *MQ*, xxxv (1949), 421–36

I. Brainard: *Die Choreographie der Hoftänze in Burgund, Frankreich und Italien im 15. Jahrhundert* (diss., U. of Göttingen, 1956)

L.H. Moe: *Dance Music in Printed Italian Lute Tablatures from 1507 to 1611* (diss., Harvard U., 1956)

H. Spohr: *Studien zur italienischen Tanzkomposition um 1600* (diss., U. of Freiburg, 1956)

D. Heartz: *Sources and Forms of the French Instrumental Dance in the Sixteenth Century* (diss., Harvard U., 1957)

I. Herrmann-Bengen: *Tempobezeichnungen, Ursprung: Wandel im 17. und 18. Jahrhundert* (Tutzing, 1959)

O. Kinkeldey: 'Dance Tunes of the Fifteenth Century', *Instrumental Music*, ed. D.G. Hughes (Cambridge, MA, 1959), 3–30, 89–152

K. Jeppesen: 'Ein altvenetianisches Tanzbuch', *Festschrift Karl Gustav Fellerer zum sechzigsten Geburtstag*, ed. H. Hüschen (Regensburg, 1962), 245–63

K. Jeppesen: Preface to: *Balli antichi veneziani per cembalo* (Copenhagen, 1962)

H. Beck: *Die Suite*, Mw, xxvi (1964; Eng. trans., 1966)

P. Aldrich: *Rhythm in Seventeenth-Century Italian Monody* (New York, 1966), esp. 77ff

D. Heartz: 'A 15th-Century Ballo: *Rôti bouilli Joyeux*', *Aspects of Medieval and Renaissance Music: a Birthday Offering to Gustave Reese*, ed. J. LaRue and others (New York, 1966/*R*), 359–75

I. Brainard: 'Bassedanza, Bassadanza and Ballo in the 15th Century', *Dance History Research: Perspectives from Related Arts and Disciplines*, ed. J.W. Kealiinohamoku (New York, 1970), 64–79

F.A. Gallo: 'Il "Ballare Lombardo" (circa 1435–1475)', *Studi musicali*, viii (1979), 61–84

I. Brainard: *The Art of Courtly Dancing in the Early Renaissance* (West Newton, MA, 1981)

W.T. Marrocco: *Inventory of 15th-Century Bassedanze, Balli & Balletti in Italian Dance Manuals* (New York, 1981)

F.A. Gallo: 'La danza negli spettacoli conviviali del secondo Quattrocento', *Spettacoli conviviali dall'antichità classica alle corti italiane del '400: Viterbo 1982*, 261–7

J.S. Applegate: 'English Cavalier Dance-Songs: Henry Lawes and Robert Herrick', *Proceedings of the Society of Dance History Scholars* (1983), 71–83

I. Brainard: 'The Art of Courtly Dancing in Transition: Nürnberg, Germ. Nat.Mus.MS 8842, a Hitherto Unknown German Dance Source', *Cross-roads of Medieval Civilization: the City of Regensburg and its Intellectual Milieu*, ed. E.E. DuBruck and K.H. Goller (Detroit, 1984), 61–79

B. Sparti: 'Music and Choreography in the Reconstruction of 15th-Century *Balli*: Another Look at Domenico's *Verçepe*', *Fifteenth-Century Studies*, x (1984), 177–94

R. Hudson: *The Allemande, the Balletto, and the Tanz* (Cambridge, MA, 1986)

P. Jones: 'Spectacle in Milan: Cesare Negri's Torch Dances', *EMc*, xiv (1986), 182–96

I. Brainard: 'Pattern, Imagery and Drama in the Choreographic Work of Domenico da Piacenza', *Guglielmo Ebreo da Pesaro e la danza nelle corti italiane del XV secolo: Pesaro 1987*, ed. M. Padovan (Pisa, 1990), 85–96

A. Pontremoli and P. La Rocca: *Il ballare lombardo: teoria e prassi coreutica nella festa di corte del XV secolo* (Milan, 1987)

A. Uguccioni: 'La danza nella pittura di cassone', *Guglielmo Ebreo da Pesaro e la danza nelle corti italiane del XV secolo: Pesaro 1987*, ed. M. Padovan (Pisa, 1990), 235–50

L.M. Brooks: *The Dances of the Processions of Seville in Spain's Golden Age* (Kassel, 1988)

P. Jones: *The Relation between Music and Dance in Cesare Negri's 'Le Gratie d'Amore' (1602)* (diss., U. of London, 1989)

V. Daniels and E. Dombois: 'Die Temporelationen im Ballo des Quattrocento', *Basler Jb für historische Musikpraxis 1990*, 181–247

A. Francalanci: 'The "Copia di Mo Giorgio e del Giudeo di ballare basse danze e balletti" as found in the New York Public Library', ibid., 87–179

Y. Kendall: 'Rhythm, Meter and *Tactus* in 16th-Century Italian Court Dance: Reconstruction from a Theoretical Base', *Dance Research*, viii (1990), 3–27

V. Daniels: 'Tempo Relationships within the Italian *balli* of the XVth Century', *The Marriage of Music & Dance: London 1991* [13 unnumbered pages]

I. Gatiss: 'Realizing the Music in the 15th-Century Italian Dance Manuals', ibid. [9 unnumbered pages]

J. Sutton: 'Musical Forms and Dance Forms in the Dance Manuals of Sixteenth-Century Italy: Plato and the Varieties of Variation', ibid. [25 unnumbered pages]

M. Esses: *Dance and Instrumental 'Diferencias' in Spain During the 17th and Early 18th Centuries*, i, *History and Background, Music and Dance* (Stuyvesant, NY, 1992)

N. Monahin: 'Leaping Nuns? Social Satire in a Fifteenth-Century Court Dance', *Proceedings of the Society of Dance History Scholars* (1993), 171–9

B. Sparti: 'Antiquity as Inspiration in the Renaissance of Dance: the Classical Connection and Fifteenth-Century Italian Dance', *Dance Chronicle*, xvi (1993), 373–90

D.R. Wilson: '"Finita: a larifaccino unaltra uolta dachapo"', *Historical Dance*, iii (1993), 21–6

B. Sparti: Introduction to *Ballo della Gagliarda: Lutio Compasso (1560)* (Freiburg, 1995)

B. Sparti: 'Rûti Bouilli: Take Two "El Gioioso Fiorito"', *Studi Musicali*, xiv (1995), 231–61

For choreographic information *see also* DOMENICO DA PIACENZA; ANTONIO CORNAZANO; GUGLIELMO EBREO DA PESARO; FABRITIO CAROSO; and CESARE NEGRI.

INGRID BRAINARD

Ballou, Esther (Williamson) (*b* Elmira, NY, 17 July 1915; *d* Chichester, England, 12 March 1973). American composer, pianist and educationist. She studied the piano and the organ as a child and graduated from Bennington College, Vermont (1937), Mills College (1938) and the Juilliard School (1943); at Bennington she took composition lessons from Otto Luening, and at Juilliard from Bernard Wagenaar and privately from Wallingford Riegger. While in California she composed ballets for Louise Kloepper and José Limón and toured nationally as a pianist with various dance companies. During the 1940s she taught at Juilliard and from 1955 at the American University, Washington, DC. During her subsequent career as an educationist she put forward experimental methods for theory teaching at college level. Her music, according to her own description, 'tends towards classicism in that it stresses clarity of design and directness of expression'. Among a broad range of compositions are her *Accompaniments for Modern Dance Technique* (1933–7), which were used by such pioneers of the modern dance movement as Martha Hill, Doris Humphrey and Bessie Schoenberg. In 1963 she became the first American woman composer to have a work (the Capriccio for violin and piano) given its first performance at the White House, and in 1964 she received the honorary doctorate from Hood College, Maryland. Her manuscripts, which include a pedagogical text, *Creative Explorations of Musical Elements* (1971), are in the Special Collections Department of the American University Library, Washington, DC.

WORKS
(selective list)

Orch: Suite, chbr orch, 1939; Blues, 1944; Pf Conc. no.1, 1945; Prelude and Allegro, pf, str, 1951; Concertino, ob, str, 1953; Adagio, bn, str, 1960; In memoriam, ob, str, 1960; Gui Conc., 1964; Pf Conc. no.2, 1964

Choral: Bag of Tricks (I. Orgel), SSAA, 1956; The Beatitudes, SATB, org, 1957; A babe is born (15th century), SATB, 1959; May the words of my mouth (Ps xix), SATB, 1965; I will lift up mine eyes (Ps cxxi), S, SATB, org, 1965; O the sun comes up-up-up in the opening sky (e.e. cummings), SSA, 1966; Hear us!, SATB, brass, perc, 1967

Other vocal: 4 Songs (A.E. Housman), S, vc, pf, 1937; What if a much of a which of a wind (Cummings), S, Bar, B, wind qnt, 1959; Street Scenes (H. Champers), S, pf, 1960; 5–4–3 (Cummings), Mez, va, hp, 1966

Chbr: Impertinence, cl, pf, 1936; In Blues Tempo, cl, pf, 1937; Nocturne, str qt, 1937; Pf Trio, 1955, rev. 1957; Divertimento, str qt, 1958; Sonata, vn, pf, 1959; A Passing Word, fl, vc, pf, ob, 1960; Capriccio, vn, pf, 1963; Prism, str trio, 1969; Romanza, vn, pf, 1969

Kbd: Dance Suite, pf, 1937; Sonatina, pf, 1941; Sonata, 2 pf, 1943; Beguine, pf, 8 hands, 1950, arr. 2 pf, 1957, arr. orch, 1960; Music for the Theatre, 2 pf, 1952; Pf Sonata, 1955; Sonata no.2, 2 pf, 1958; Rondino, hpd, 1961; Sonatina [no.2], pf, 1964; Impromptu, org, 1968

Principal publisher: ACA

BIBLIOGRAPHY

E.W. Ballou: 'Theory with a Thrust', *Music Educators Journal*, lv (1968–9), no.1, pp.56–8; no.5, pp.55–7

J.R. Heintze: *Esther Williamson Ballou: a Bio-Bibliography* (New York, 1987)

L.A. Wallace: *The Educational Experiences of American Composer Esther Williamson Ballou* (diss., U. of Wisconsin, Milwaukee, 1995)

JAMES R. HEINTZE

Balmer, Luc (*b* Munich, 13 July 1898; *d* Berne, 1 March 1996). Swiss conductor and composer. Son of the painter Wilhelm Balmer, he studied from 1915 until 1919 at the Basle Conservatory with Hans Huber, Ernst Levy and Egon Petri. From 1921 to 1922 he studied composition with Busoni in Berlin. From 1924 he taught the piano and music theory at the Berne Conservatory. His career as a conductor began at the Lucerne Kursaal (1928–32); then for a short time he was with the Stadttheater in Berne (1934–5). He conducted the Berne symphony concerts (1935–41) and was conductor of the subscription concerts of the Bernische Musikgesellschaft (1941–64). In 1938 he became music advisor to Radio Berne. He was an exceptionally versatile conductor, but his performances of late Romantic works, particularly Bruckner and Reger, were specially notable. His compositions include an opera *Die drei gefoppten Ehemänner* (Berne, 1969), a concertino for piano (1960) and for cello (1962), three string quartets and vocal music.

JÜRG STENZL

Balmer & Weber Music House. American firm of music publishers. Charles Balmer (*b* Mühlhausen, 21 Sept 1817; *d* St Louis, 15 Dec 1892) and Carl Heinrich Weber (*b* Koblenz, 3 March 1819; *d* Denver, 6 Sept 1892) left Germany for the USA in the 1830s; Balmer became an organist and conductor, Weber a cellist, and their early compositions were published in the eastern USA. In 1848 they entered into partnership and opened a shop in St Louis, publishing a variety of popular marches and various piano pieces including Balmer's own arrangements of popular titles. Charles Balmer was so prolific that he adopted a number of pseudonyms, including Charles Remlab, T. van Berg, Alphonse Leduc, Charles Lange, Henry Werner, August Schumann, T. Mayer and F.B. Ryder. Gradually the firm absorbed most of its competitors including Nathaniel Phillips, James & J.R. Phillips, H.A. Sherburne, H. Pilcher & Sons, W.M. Harlow, Cardella & Co. and Compton & Doan; by the end of the century it had an exceptionally large and flourishing business.

After the death of the partners, the business was managed by a company in which the Balmer family predominated. Lack of efficient direction and the rise of Kunkel Brothers, Shattinger and Thiebes-Stierlin caused the business to deteriorate, and in 1907 the catalogue was sold to Leo Feist of New York. He attempted to ship the sheet music to New York down the Mississippi, but the vessel foundered off the coast of New Jersey and its cargo sank.

BIBLIOGRAPHY

E.C. Krohn: *A Century of Missouri Music* (St Louis, 1924); repr. as *Missouri Music* (New York, 1971)

E.C. Krohn: *Music Publishing in the Middle Western States before the Civil War* (Detroit, 1972), 27–8

E.C. Krohn: *Music Publishing in St. Louis* (Warren, MI, 1988), 43

ERNST C. KROHN

Bal'mont, Konstantin Dmitriyevich (*b* Gumnishchi, Ivanov district, 3/15 June 1867; *d* Noisy-le-grand, near Paris, 23 Dec 1942). Russian poet and translator. He was perhaps the most prominent poet of the symbolist movement in Russia. In the late 1890s he made translations into Russian of works by a number of poets, including Shelley, which were later used by many composers in the early years of the next century. For Bal'mont, Symbolism was primarily a poetry of hidden meaning transmitted by allusion, feeling, sound and musical aspects of verse. His works of the early 1900s see him concerned with pantheistic and mystical themes; his interest in theosophy stemmed from reading the writings of Madame Blavatsky, as did that of Skryabin, whose own poetic text which accompanied his *Poème de l'extase* is considered to be very reminiscent of Bal'mont's *Budem kak solntse*. It was probably Bal'mont's friendship with Skryabin which lead many Russian composers to pay attention to his work: the young Stravinsky, for a time infatuated with Skryabin's late works, set Bal'mont's words in his *Zvezdoliki* (Obukhov also used the same poem in 1913), while Rachmaninoff, Prokofiev, Roslavets and Myaskovsky were likewise attracted to Bal'mont's sensuous, exotic and often ecstatic verses. Bal'mont made specific allusion to Skryabin's work in his *Svetozvuk v prirode i svetozvukaya simfoniya Skryabina* ('Light-sound in nature and Skryabin's light-sound symphony') of 1917 in which he ponders the nature of synaesthesia.

BIBLIOGRAPHY

V. Markov: 'Kommentar zu den Dichtungen von K.D. Bal'mont 1890–1909', *Bausteine zur Geschichte der Literatur bei den Slaven*, xxxi/I–II (Vienna and Cologne, 1988, 1992).

A. Pyman: *A History of Russian Symbolism* (Cambridge, 1994), esp. 56–66, 166–71, 385–8

JONATHAN POWELL

Balo [bala, balafou, balafon]. A gourd-resonated frame XYLOPHONE of the Manding peoples of West Africa, found in the Gambia, Senegal, Guinea-Bissau, Guinea, Mali and northern Côte d'Ivoire. Possibly the earliest reference to the instrument is that of Ibn Baṭṭūta, who visited the court of Mali in 1352 and saw an instrument 'made from reeds, and provided with gourds below them'. In 1620, the British gold-prospector Richard Jobson described the *ballards*, the principal instrument of the Gambia, as having 17 keys with gourds suspended beneath them from iron rods. The player used a beater in each hand, the end of which was covered with 'soft stuff', and the instrument was played to accompany dancing. In the 1790s, Mungo Park described the Mandingo *balafou* as having 20 hardwood keys with 'shells of gourds hung underneath to increase the sound'.

The contemporary instrument has 17 to 19 keys strung together on a frame with a gourd resonator beneath each. The keys are from 27·5 to 40 cm long, 2·5 to 4 cm wide and less than 2·5 cm deep; the undersides and ends are thinned for tuning. The instrument is tuned to an apparent

Balo (gourd-resonated xylophone) played by an itinerant musician, Dori, Upper Volta, 1956

equitonal heptatonic scale and has an approximate range of 2·5 octaves. It is played exclusively by professional male musicians and is used to accompany praisesongs; its repertory is almost identical to that of the *kora*, which has largely replaced the *balo* in Senegal and the Gambia (*see* KORA). Players use a rubber-tipped beater in each hand and sometimes have bells strapped to their wrists.

The *balo* may be played on its own or in pairs, in which case one instrument provides the basic melody (*kumbengo*) while the other incorporates melodic variation and ornamentation (*birimintingo*). This is especially common in the Guinea tradition. In Mali the *balo* is considered one of the most prestigious instruments of the professional musician and often accompanies the recitation of epic songs such as *Sunjata*. In the Gambia, the *balo* is played today by only a few families since it was overshadowed by the *kora* early in the 20th century. Nevertheless, much of the *kora* and *konting* repertory, as well as several playing techniques such as damping of notes, derive from the *balo*.

The term *bala* is used by the Kpelle people of Liberia for a free-key log xylophone with four to seven wooden keys resting on banana stems. The instrument is played with beaters of soft wood or raffia midriff and, like the cognate Mano *balau* and Gio *blande*, is used by boys on rice-farms for bird-scaring or signalling. Among the neighbouring Gbunde people it is known as *kipelevelegu* and among the Sapa as *gbwilebo*. The term *balafon*, used for the frame xylophone, was probably introduced by European travellers (from the Greek root 'phono'), since its use is mainly confined to early European literature.

BIBLIOGRAPHY

M. Park: *Travels in the Interior Districts of Africa* (London, 1799)
H.G. Farmer: 'Early References to Music in the Western Sudan', *Journal of the Royal Asiatic Society* (1939), 569–79
G. Schwab: *Tribes of the Liberian Hinterland* (Cambridge, MA, 1947/R)
A.M. Jones: *Africa and Indonesia* (Leiden, 1971)
J.H.K. Nketia: *The Music of Africa* (New York, 1974)
K.A. GOURLAY, LUCY DURÁN

Balox, Johannes (*fl* late 13th century). Theorist. Only the content of his treatise (*CoussemakerS*, i, pp.292–6 and CSM, xxxiv (1987), 11–21) and the character of the manuscript containing it (*F-Pn* lat.15128) point to the late 13th century. 'Gaudent brevitate moderni', the opening sentence, is a common beginning for treatises of the time, and the title *Abbreviatio magistri Franconis a[uctore] Johanne dicto Baloce* indicates a dependence on Franco of Cologne.

Johannes gave Franco's new principles for notating rhythm, elucidating the note symbols and their plicas and the ligatures. Change in the basic duration of each symbol is achieved by its position in the perfection: in this context, Johannes made more of the *divisio modi* for preventing such changes. The rule concerning perfection of a long before a long is stated, although not found in Franco. Franco's five – rather than six – rhythmic modes are reproduced; but unlike Franco, Johannes gave no real examples to illustrate them. Anonymus 2 and 3 (of *CoussemakerS*, i, pp.303–19, 319–27) were virtually identical but appended extra chapters on other topics.

ANDREW HUGHES

Balsach, Llorenç (*b* Sabadell, 16 Apr 1953). Catalan composer. He began his musical education at the Barcelona Conservatory, studying harmony and composition with Carles Guinovart and Josep Soler Sardà, among others. While pursuing a degree in mathematics at the Autonomous University of Barcelona, he experimented with electronic music under the guidance of Brncic. He also attended Petrassi's composition seminars in Italy.

Balsach's musical output comprises two periods. In the first, under the influence of Cage's ideas, he attempted to break down the barrier between musical sounds and noise, explored unconventional means of playing standard instruments, used electronic instruments and mixed taped with live sounds. For example, his *Suite gàstrica* (1979) and *El cant de les artèries* (1979) use traditional instruments to mimic gastrointestinal sounds and the flow of arteries respectively.

Balsach's second creative period relied on more conventional musical procedures, including an unabashedly tonal language. For example, *Visions grotesques* (1992) is a succession of musical images or 'visions' exploring a wide range of orchestral colour, from full orchestra to string quartet. Each 'vision' is an independent and complete piece in itself, but a recurring chromatic motif stated each time by a different instrument creates a sense of prolonged structural unity.

Notwithstanding their variety, Balsach's works are always permeated by a detached, ironic attitude evident in his Satie-like titles, which furnish his music with specific images (visual, tactile and so forth), but privilege above all the concept of 'play'. This playfulness gives his music its postmodern character.

WORKS
(*selective list*)

Stage: Oh! Els bons dies (incid music, S. Beckett), 1980s; L'arlequí (ballet, Perejaume and M. Huerga), 1982; Música-màgica, 1992, magician, fl, cl, vn, vc, pn, perc
Orch: 2 distraccions, pf, perc, str, 1979; Gran Copa especial, 1979, arr. pf 4 hands, 1984, arr. chbr ens, 1983; Poema promiscu, 1981; Visions grotesques, 1992
Vocal: 6 cançons breus, solo v, 1982; Paralàlia de paralaues, Mez, pf, 1992; Música groga, chorus, 1980; 3 palíndroms, chorus, 1990; Cara cosa, chorus, 1991; Olis d'Olímpia, chorus, 1991
Chbr (4 or more insts): 2 contes, 6 perc, 1982; Música vironera, vn, va, vc, gui, pf, perc, 1977; Higiènica . . . ! (Estomacal i marxa), fl, cl, gui, vn, vc, pf, perc, 1978; Rondó, vn, va, vc, fl, ob, cl, tpt, pf, perc, 1983; Música per al llargmetratge (after M. Cussó:

Entreacte), chbr ens, 1989; 4 Dibuixos, gui, str qt/str, 1995; 3
converses, 10 insts, 1997

Chbr (2–3 insts): Marina, fl, pf, 1977; I due ubriachi, vn/fl, vc, 1978;
La negra, lliscosa, cl, pf, 1978; Variacions per a 20 dits, pf 4
hands, 1979; So d'oda, 2 gui, 1981; Ritmes d'ultramar, 2 pf, 1991,
arr. 2 perc, 1993; De Caldetes a Moià, gui, pf, perc, 1978; Str
Trio, 1992

Solo: Escarabat-piano, pf, 1975; Residus, gui, 1976; Peça gomosa,
gui, 1977; Dental, hpd, 1978; Suite gàstrica, pf, 1979; Lleu, fl,
1980; 2 melodies distants, cl, 1982

El-ac: Carota i caramel, tape, 1976; L'assassí Bagliatti, nar, tape,
1977; El cant de les artèries, tape, 1979; Classes de música a la
granja, 1993; El sueño de las olas, 1v, tenora, tape, 1994

Soundscapes: Espais sonors, 1975, exposició sonora, perf. Acadèmia
de Belles Arts de Sabadell, 1975; 14 poemes sonors (after J. Sala
Sanahuja: 14 poemes visuals), gui, slides, 1975

Principal publisher: La Mà de Guido

Principal recording company: EDA

WRITINGS

La convergència harmònica (Barcelona, 1994)

BIBLIOGRAPHY

J. Maderuelo: *Una música para los 80* (Madrid, 1981), 33–69 passim
E. Casares: *14 compositores de hoy* (Oviedo, 1982), 44–386 passim
68 compositors catalans, ed. Associacio Catalana de Compositors
(Barcelona, 1989)
C. Lobo: 'La tonalitat espontània en l'obra de Llorenç Balsach',
Revista musical catalana, no.121 (1994), 44 only
O. Abril: *Els sons trobats: altres músiques natives* (Barcelona, 1995),
46–7

ANTONI PIZÀ

Balsam, Artur (*b* Warsaw, 8 Feb 1906; *d* New York, 1 Sept
1994). American pianist of Polish birth. He studied in
Łódź, where he made his début at the age of 12, and at
the Berlin Hochschule für Musik. He received first prize
in the International Piano Competition in Berlin in 1930,
and then won the Mendelssohn Prize in 1931. He first
toured North America in 1932 with Yehudi Menuhin,
and settled there after Hitler came to power in Germany
in 1933. He gave numerous recitals after 1918 and made
many appearances with orchestras (including a series of
six Mozart concertos for the BBC during the 1956 Mozart
bicentenary); but he was most celebrated as an ensemble
pianist who combined sensibility and a capacity for
listening with strength of personality. Balsam recorded
about 250 works in the solo and chamber literature,
including all Haydn's and Mozart's music for solo piano,
all Mozart's sonatas for violin and piano (with Oscar
Shumsky), and all Beethoven's sonatas with violin and
cello (with Joseph Fuchs and Zara Nelsova). His partners
in concert, and often on recordings, also included
Francescatti, Goldberg, Rostropovich, Szigeti, Totenberg,
Milstein, David Oistrakh and Leonid Kogan. In 1960 he
joined the Albeneri Trio (which then became the Balsam-
Krolf-Helfetz Trio) in place of Erich Itor Kahn. He was a
distinguished teacher at the Eastman School of Music,
Boston University, the Manhattan School of Music and
the Philadelphia Academy of Music; he led summer
courses from 1956 to 1992 at Kneisel Hall in Blue Hill,
Maine. Murray Perahia was one his pupils. Balsam also
edited and composed cadenzas for Mozart's piano
concertos K37, 39–41, 175 and 238.

MICHAEL STEINBERG/R

Balsamino, Simone (*b* Urbino; *fl* 1591–6; *d* ?Venice, ?1607).
Italian composer, poet and instrument inventor. A
connection with Urbino is suggested by the dedications to
the Della Rovere family of his two surviving publications;
his book of madrigals further includes a preface addressed
to 'miei Signori & Patriotti' of Urbino. He was *maestro*

di cappella at Venice Cathedral (S Pietro di Castello) from
1591 until at least 1596. His whereabouts after 1596 are
unknown; a notice in a necrology from S Maria Formosa,
Venice, may refer to his death in 1607.

Balsamino is the author of a tragicomedy, *La perla*
(Venice, 1596), which draws heavily on Tasso's *Aminta*.
He may have intended portions of the drama to be sung:
one scene closes with a parody of the poem *Ancor che col
partir*, famous for its setting by Rore. His only music
publication, a book of six-part madrigals (Venice, 1594;
ed. A. Chegai: *Le 'Novellette a sei voci' di Simone
Balsamino*, Florence, 1993), also owes a debt to Tasso's
Aminta. The book consists of 20 madrigals, 17 of which
are settings of excerpts from Tasso's play. The first 16 are
tonally unified and set a dialogue between Tirsi and
Aminta (2.iii); the remaining, unrelated madrigal sets a
long monologue of Satiro (2.i). These two excerpts are of
different dramatic types, and this is reflected in their
musical treatment: the dialogue divides the six voices into
two three-voice groups, while Satiro's monologue is set in
a chordal recitative style, bearing the indication 'Da
cantarsi senza battute e pause'. In his preface, Balsamino
asserted that his madrigals had been performed, like
certain *commedie armoniche*, in the square in front of the
ducal palace in Urbino. Balsamino's work considerably
influenced the *Aminta musicale* of Erasmo Marotta
(Venice, 1600) which, in fact, includes direct musical
quotations from Balsamino's book.

The preface to the madrigal book also includes a
reference to an instrument of Balsamino's own design: the
'cetarissima', which he claimed combined the virtues of
the lute and guitar in a single instrument.

BIBLIOGRAPHY

DBI (R. Meloncelli); *EinsteinIM*; *VogelB*
A. Einstein: 'Ein Madrigaldialog von 1594', *ZIMG*, xv (1913–14),
202–14
B. Ligi: *La cappella musicale del duomo d'Urbino*, NA, ii (1925), 68,
87
N. Fortune: 'An Italian Arch-Cittern', *GSJ*, v (1952), 43 only
A. Chegai: 'La musica in San Pietro in Castello, Duomo di Venezia,
fra XVI e XVII secolo', *Recercare*, iii (1991), 219–29
A. Chegai: '"La Perla", commedia di Balsamino musico: citazione,
autocitazione, echi musicali', *Medioevo e Rinascimento*, vi (1992),
115–32
A. Chegai: 'Musicalità vs musicabilità: l' "Aminta" fra recezione
madrigalistica e fortuna critica', *Saggiatore musicale*, i (1994),
315–34

LORENZO BIANCONI/ANDREA CHEGAI/R

Balsys, Eduardas (*b* Mykolaïv, Ukraine, 20 Dec 1919; *d*
Drushininkai, Lithuania, 3 Nov 1984). Lithuanian composer. Balsys grew up in Klaipėda (Memel), completing
in 1939 his studies at the Lithuanian Gymnasium, where
he had his first musical education, played in a wind
ensemble, and began composing. He served as a school
teacher in Kretinga (1941–5) and then studied composition at the State Conservatory in Vilnius with Antanas
Račiūnas (1945–50), later studying at the Leningrad
Conservatory in Voloshinov's masterclass (1950–53).
From 1953 until his death Balsys lectured in composition
and orchestration at the Lithuanian State Conservatory,
becoming head of the composition department in 1960
and professor in 1969. He was president of the Lithuanian
Composers' Union (1962–71). His pupils included Ben-
jaminas Gorbulskis, Algirdas Martainaitis and Vidmantas
Bartulis. He was awarded the Lithuanian State Prize in
1960 and 1974.

The style of Balsys is closely linked to the Romantic and folkloristic traditions in Lithuanian music; he was one of the first to extend and deepen these traditions. His work can be divided into three periods. Until 1958 he wrote within the context of the Soviet musical aesthetic of the time, quoting folk music, preferring traditional forms, giving melody a dominant role, and following the harmonic system of major and minor keys. With his Second Violin Concerto (1958), Balsys began to treat traditional material in a different way: motifs were freely reworked, achieving independence from the character of the original model; he attempted to synthesize contemporary means of expression. In harmony, Balsys then went beyond the traditional structure of thirds and used polytonal devices. In his final creative phase (1965–84), his music became polystylistic. Characteristics of the works of this period are expressionistic features and the use of the 12-tone technique; this Balsys often employed freely, sometimes interspersing tonal episodes.

WORKS

Stage: Eglė, žalčių karalienė [Eglė, the Queen of the Snakes] (ballet, 4, after S. Nėris and folk tales), Vilnius, 1960; Kelionė į Tilžę [The Journey to Tilžę] (op, 2, after H. Sudermann), Vilnius, 1980
Vocal: Nelieskite mėlyno gaublio [No Sign of Life on the Blue Globe] (orat, V. Palčinskaitė), solo vv, children's chorus, 2 pf, db, perc, 1969; Saulę nešantis [Sun Bearer] (cant., E. Mieželaitis), S, chorus, org, perc, 1972; 80 choruses; 13 songs, 1v, pf
Chbr and solo inst: Pf Sonata, 1948; Herojinė poema [Heroic Poem], orch, 1953; Str Qt, 1953; 2 vn concs., 1954, 1958; Dramatinės freskos, vn, pf, orch, 1965; Sym.-Conc., org, ww, gui, perc, 1977; Jūros atspindžiai [The Sparkling Sea], str, 1981; Portretai, orch, 1983; Conc., vn, 1984; incid music for 15 films and 10 plays

BIBLIOGRAPHY

O. Narbutinenė: *Eduardas Balsys* (Vilnius, 1971)
H. Gerlach: 'Eduardas Balsys', *50 sowjetische komponisten* (Leipzig and Dresden, 1984)
A. Ruzgaitė: 'Trečioji Eglė baleto scenoje', *Literatūra ir menas* (1995), no.1, p.3

based on *MGG2* (ii, 132–3), by permission of Bärenreiter

ONA NARBUTIENĖ

Baltazar, Johannes. See NINOT LE PETIT.

Baltazarini. See BEAUJOYEUX, BALTHASAR DE.

Baltimore. American city, the largest city in Maryland. Its musical history can be traced to the American Revolutionary period. First settled in 1662, Baltimore became a town in 1730. By 1800 its population of more than 26,000 was larger than that of the state's capital, Annapolis. As early as 1784 concerts in the city were advertised in the press. These early programmes were of great diversity, including works by Bach, Dittersdorf, Haydn, Koczwara, Pleyel, Viotti and Vanhal, as well as by immigrant musicians Alexander Reinagle and Raynor Taylor who were resident in Baltimore.

In 1794, a year after establishing a music shop in Philadelphia, Joseph Carr and his sons Thomas and Benjamin inaugurated a similar enterprise in Baltimore. The first publication of the Star Spangled Banner in sheet music form was by Thomas Carr in November 1814. Following the demise of Thomas Carr's business in 1821, other publications, notably by the firms of Arthur Clifton (fl ?1823), George Willig (1823–1910), John Cole (1821–38), Frederick Benteen (1839–55), Miller and Beecham (1853–73), James Boswell (1835–59), Samuel Carusi (1839–44), W.C. Peters (1844–52) and G. Fred Kranz (1910–c1960), made Baltimore a major centre of music publishing. A significant factor in the success of a number of these firms was the presence in Baltimore of the early American lithography firm of A. Hoen & Co., who supplied illustrated covers for numerous Baltimore imprints. Several of the Baltimore music publishing firms were taken over by the Boston firm of Oliver Ditson in the late 19th century.

1. Orchestras. 2. Educational institutions, libraries. 3. Opera. 4. Concert organizations, halls.

1. ORCHESTRAS. The first orchestra of professional musicians in Baltimore was the Peabody Orchestra in 1866. Under the direction of James Monroe Deems, Lucian Southard and Asger Hamerik the orchestra gave the premières of works by American composers and the American premières of numerous European works, especially those from Hamerik's native Denmark. The Peabody Orchestra ceased in 1896. Ross Jungnickel organized the first Baltimore Symphony Orchestra, which gave its first season in 1890.

Following the demise of Jungnickel's orchestra in 1899, the Florestan Club, an élite group of local musicians and music lovers (including H.L. Mencken), made plans to found the city's first resident orchestra. In 1916 Baltimore became the first city in the USA to found an orchestra on a municipal appropriation. The first conductor of the new Baltimore SO, Gustav Strube, remained in the post until 1930. Subsequent directors of the orchestra were George Siemonn (1930–35), Ernest Schelling (1935–7), Werner Janssen (1937–9) and Howard Barlow (1939–42). This orchestra played its last concert in 1942. The same year Reginald Stewart, also director of the Peabody Conservatory, devised a plan for the reorganization of the Baltimore SO. Stewart attracted superior musicians by offering them faculty appointments at the Peabody Conservatory, an arrangement based on Mendelssohn's direction of the Leipzig Conservatory and the Gewandhaus Orchestra. Although Stewart was the only one to have held both positions, the relationship between the Baltimore SO and the Peabody Conservatory faculty remains strong. Subsequent conductors have included Massimo Freccia (1952–9), Peter Herman Adler (1959–68), Brian Priestman (1968–9), Sergiu Comissiona (1968–84), D.J. Zinman (1985–98) and Yury Temirkanov (since 1999).

Under the inspiration of A. Jack Thomas, the conductors Charles L. Harris and later W. Llewellyn Wilson led the Baltimore Colored SO and Chorus in concerts from 1929 until a bitter musicians' strike in 1939 closed the orchestra. The Baltimore Women's String SO played from 1936 to 1940 under the direction of Stephen Deak and Wolfgang Martin.

2. EDUCATIONAL INSTITUTIONS, LIBRARIES. The Peabody Conservatory, founded on 12 February 1857, is technically the oldest conservatory in the USA, although it did not actually offer instruction until 1868. As part of the Peabody Institute of the City of Baltimore, the conservatory was endowed by George Peabody, one of America's earliest philanthropists. The Institute included provision for an extensive library, well furnished in every department of knowledge, a gallery of art and an Academy of Music (which became the Peabody Conservatory of Music in 1872).

The conservatory's first director was the New England educator Lucian Southard (1868–70) followed by the Danish-born composer and conductor and student of

Berlioz, Asger Hamerik (1871–98), Harold Randolph (1898–1927), Otto Ortmann (1928–41), Reginald Stewart (1941–58), Peter Mennin (1958–62), Charles Kent (1963–7), Richard Franko Goldman (1968–77), Elliot Galkin (1977–82), Robert O. Pierce (1982–95) and Robert Sirota (since 1995). In 1977 the Peabody Conservatory was affiliated with the Johns Hopkins University and in 1983 became a school of the university. It is now known as the Peabody Institute of the Johns Hopkins University.

There are about two dozen other institutions of higher education in Baltimore and its environs. Goucher College, Morgan State University and Towson State University are among those that offer not only music courses but also distinguished concert series. One local body, the Baltimore Chamber Music Society, sponsored a controversial series of concerts consisting almost entirely of 20th-century music. Founded in 1950 by composer Hugo Weisgall and philanthropist Randolph Rothschild, the society has also commissioned a number of important works. Two important adjuncts to Baltimore's musical life are the Arthur Friedheim Library and the archives of the Peabody Institute at the Peabody Conservatory of Music and the Maryland Historical Society. Both collections offer extensive primary source materials for the study of Baltimore's musical life. The Lester S. Levy Collection at Johns Hopkins's Milton S. Eisenhower Library includes one of the most important collections of American sheet music (approximately 40,000 items).

3. OPERA.   Music theatre in Baltimore can trace its beginnings from 1772 with a performance of Milton's *Comus* in a stable by Lewis Hallam's travelling American Company. The first resident theatrical company, Thomas Wall and Adam Lindsay's Maryland Company of Comedians, built Baltimore's first theatre in 1781 and performed there until 1785. A resurgence of Hallam's Old American Company and a series of local companies provided sporadic theatrical, musical and circus entertainment during the 1780s and early 1790s. Thomas Wignell and Alexander Reinagle's Philadelphia Company dominated the last decade of the 18th century, offering substantial seasons of plays, interludes and afterpieces in their newly constructed Holliday Street Theater. From the turn of the century to the Civil War, Baltimore hosted a variety of resident and touring companies in both the Holliday Street Theater and the Front Street Theatre. After the Civil War, a new 'theatre district' sprang up in Baltimore and included the Concordia Opera House (1865–91), Ford's Grand Opera House (1871–1964) and the Academy of Music (1875–1927). All featured a variety of theatrical entertainments, with Ford's hosting at least 24 opera companies performing over 90 different works. With the rise of the New York Theatrical Syndicate around the turn of the century, Baltimore faded as a major stop for touring opera troupes. Local efforts to establish an opera company resulted in the creation of Eugene Martinet's Baltimore Civic Opera Company in 1932. As early as the 1940–41 season, Martinet was able to enlist the help of the soprano Rosa Ponselle, who served as artistic director until 1979. In 1970 the company was renamed the Baltimore Opera Company.

4. CONCERT ORGANIZATIONS, HALLS.   With many inhabitants of British and German extraction, Baltimore has enjoyed a rich choral tradition. 19th-century choral organizations included the Liederkranz (1836–1900), the Germania Männerchor (1856–1929) and the Baltimore Oratorio Society (1881–1900). In the 20th century the Bach Choir, the Handel Society, the Choral Arts Society and the Baltimore Symphony Chorus maintained this tradition. The latter three continue to give distinguished readings of the choral classics, and the Choral Arts Society encourages the creation of new choral works with an annual competition.

Baltimore has six outstanding concert halls, all aesthetically pleasing and acoustically effective. The Lyric, constructed in 1894, is modelled on the Neues Gewandhaus in Leipzig. After extensive renovation in 1980–81, the theatre (cap. 2683) was reopened in 1982. In the same year, the Joseph Meyerhoff Symphony Hall (cap. 2467) was opened as the permanent home of the Baltimore SO. Designed by Pietro Belluschi, the hall is named after one of the city's most generous philanthropists. A second hall named after Meyerhoff, the Joseph and Rebecca Meyerhoff Auditorium (cap. 363), opened in 1982 at the Baltimore Museum of Art and is the home of the Baltimore Chamber Music Society concerts. The Kraushaar Auditorium at Goucher College, again designed by Belluschi, opened in 1962 (cap. 995). The Shriver Hall (cap. 1100) of the Johns Hopkins University is the site of a distinguished chamber music series. Opened in 1866, the Miriam A. Friedberg Concert Hall (cap. 800) at the Peabody Institute is the oldest of the existing halls; it underwent extensive renovation in 1983.

BIBLIOGRAPHY

O.G. Sonneck: *Early Concert-Life in America (1731–1800)* (Leipzig, 1907/R, 3/1959)

S.E. Lafferty: *Names of Music Teachers, Musicians, Music Dealers, Engravers, Printers and Publishers of Music, Conservatories of Music, Music Academies, Manufacturers of Pianos, Organs, and other Musical Instruments appearing in the Baltimore City Directories from 1796–1900* (MS, US-BApi, 1937)

L. Keefer: *Baltimore's Music: the Haven of the American Composer* (Baltimore, 1962)

R.A. Disharoon: *A History of Municipal Music in Baltimore, 1914–1947* (diss., U. of Maryland, 1980)

D. Ritchey, ed.: *A Guide to the Baltimore Stage in the Eighteenth Century* (Westport, CT, 1982)

H. Weems: *The History of the Women's String Symphony Orchestra of Baltimore Inc* (diss., Peabody Conservatory of Music, 1990)

E. Lawrence: *Music at Ford's Grand Opera House, 1871–1894* (diss., Peabody Institute, Johns Hopkins U., 1991)

W. Spencer: *The Baltimore Symphony Orchestra, 1965–1982: the Meyerhoff Years* (Peabody Institute, Johns Hopkins U., 1993)

E. Schaaf and D. Hildebrand: *Music in Maryland* (forthcoming)

ELLIOTT W. GALKIN/N. QUIST

Baltin, Aleksandr Aleksandrovich (*b* Moscow, 2 Jan 1931). Russian composer and pianist. He graduated from the Moscow State Conservatory in 1956 having studied composition under E. Messner and the piano under V. Belov. He was deputy chief editor of the journal *Muzïka* (1963–8), and was president of the council of experts of the Ministry of Culture (1990–92). He is a member of the Composers' Union, and in 1984 he became an Honoured Artist of Russia. He works in a variety of genres. Among his most significant works are the opera *Knyaz' Mïshkin* ('Prince Mïshkin') based on Dostoyevsky's novel *The Idiot*, the oratorio *Spustya stolet'ya* ('Centuries Later') after Michelangelo, a scene from the Gospels entitled *Magdalina* for mezzo soprano and orchestra, four symphonies, numerous concertos (including three for piano), in addition to chamber works and song cycles.

The roots of Baltin's style lie within the Russian tradition; he nonetheless maintains an individual approach to the genre in which he is working. In the oratorio *Spustya stolet'ya* a symphonic breadth is combined with detailed writing reminiscent of chamber music and a laconic mode of expression; within the Romantic framework of the Second Piano Concerto variety is obtained by fusing the principles of cantus firmus, Beethovenian contrast, and monothematism. Baltin is attracted to the concerto as a genre that combines real virtuosity and philosophical profundity. In his works, lyrical and dramatic materials are freely fused with the grotesque and scherzo elements. The composer is particularly restrained in his thematic construction and scoring; Baltin's language – aligned to the so-called new simplicity – is set within a tonal framework.

Baltin's music is heard regularly at the annual Moscow Autumn festival. From the 1950s to the 1970s Baltin regularly appeared as a concert pianist.

WORKS

Op: Knyaz' Mïshkin [Prince Mïshkin] (A. Baltin, after F. Dostoyevsky), 1984

Vocal-orch: Spustya stolet'ya [Centuries Later] (orat., M. Buonarroti), solo vv, chorus, orch, 1975; Magdalina (B. Pasternak), Bar, orch, 1990

4 syms.: Pro éto (V. Mayakovsky), Bar, orch, 1968; 1989; 1993; 1997

Other orch: Hp conc., 1953; Vn conc., 1964; Vc conc., 1971; Conc., Mez, orch, 1973, arr. for a sax, orch., 1982; Letniy den' [Summer Day], poem, va, orch, 1986; Karnaval [Carnival], concert ov., 1992; Bïlina, hp, orch, 1994

3 pf concs.: 1959, 1981, 1991

Chbr: Qnt, fl, ob, cl, bn, hn, 1976; Sonata no.1, vn, pf, 1978; Str qt, 1985; Pf trio, 1986; Zaklikaniya vesnï [The Call of Spring], concertino for fl, ob, bn, hn, 1990; Sonata no.2, vn, pf, 1994; Sonata, vc, pf, 1995

Pf: Sonatina, 1955; Pesenki bez slov [Songs Without Words], 1969; Muzïkal'nïye kartinï [Musical Pictures], 1969; Shkol'naya tetrad' [School Notebook], 1970; Sonata, 1988

Vocal: 4 songs (V. Mayakovsky), Bar, pf, 1962; Songs (A. Akhmatova), C, pf, 1987

BIBLIOGRAPHY

O. Stepanov: 'Znakomstvo obnadezhivayet' [Acquaintance reassures], SovM (1967), no.7

A. Ivashkin: 'Raznoobrazniye resheniya (sochineniya A. Lokshina, K. Volkova, A. Baltina)' [Various solutions: the works of A. Lokshin, K. Volkov and A. Baltin], SovM (1973), no.6, pp.43–7

L. Kokoreva: 'Sozvuchniye sovremennosti' [Consonant contemporaneities], Muzïka Rossii, 5 (1984), 196–211

ALLA VLADIMIROVNA GRIGOR'YEVA

Baltsa, Agnes (*b* Lefkas, 19 Nov 1944). Greek mezzo-soprano. She studied in Athens, Munich and Frankfurt, where she made her début in 1968 as Cherubino. In 1969 she sang Octavian at the Vienna Staatsoper and the following year appeared at the Deutsche Oper, Berlin, and the Salzburg Festival. Baltsa made her American début in 1971 at Houston as Carmen, and first sang at La Scala in 1974 as Dorabella. She made her Covent Garden début in 1976 as Cherubino and first sang at the Metropolitan in 1979 as Octavian, returning as Carmen. Her repertory includes roles by Rossini, Bellini and Donizetti, as well as Orpheus, Sextus, Eboli, Azucena, Dido (*Les Troyens*), Herodias (*Salome*), Delilah and Charlotte. A powerful singing actress, Baltsa has sometimes sacrificed beauty of tone to dramatic effect; but she has brought a rare visceral excitement to a role like Carmen. She is also an admired interpreter of the mezzo part in Verdi's Requiem, which she recorded with both Karajan and Muti.

BIBLIOGRAPHY

N. Goodwin: 'Agnes Baltsa', Opera, xxxvi (1985), 483–8

ELIZABETH FORBES

Baltzar, Thomas (*b* Lübeck, ?1631; *d* London, 27 July 1663). German violinist and composer. He came from a family of Lübeck musicians: his father, David (*d* 1647), his grandfather, Hinrik Thomas, his great-grandfather, Hinrik, and his brothers Joachim and David were all musicians there. According to the English scientist Samuel Hartlib, Baltzar studied with Johann Schop (i), and he is recorded at the Swedish court in 1653. He probably returned home in summer 1654, after Queen Christina's abdication, and was briefly appointed a Lübeck Ratslutenist at the beginning of 1655. He travelled to England later in the year, where he remained until his death.

Baltzar caused a sensation in England. John Evelyn heard him at Roger L'Estrange's London house on 4 March 1656, and wrote that he 'plaid on that single Instrument a full Consort, so as the rest, flung-downe their Instruments, as acknowledging a victory'. Baltzar was in London in September 1656 to play in Davenant's *The Siege of Rhodes*, though Anthony Wood wrote that he spent about two years with Sir Anthony Cope at Hanwell House near Banbury. Presumably he was living there when he made his famous visits to William Ellis's Oxford music meetings in summer 1658. Wood compared him several times with the English violinist Davis Mell, who 'play'd farr sweeter than Baltsar, yet Baltsar's hand was more quick and could run it insensibly to the end of the finger-board'. Mell was also in Oxford in 1658, and their divisions on *John, come kiss me now*, printed in Playford's *The Division Violin* (1684/R), probably record some sort of playing contest. They show that Mell was no match for Baltzar, as a composer as well as a player.

Baltzar probably returned to London at the Restoration, and was given a new place in the King's Private Music by a warrant dated 23 December 1661, back-dated to Michaelmas at the high salary of £110 a year. His appointment brought the number of violins in the group to three, and it was surely for them that he wrote his C major suite, probably the earliest English piece for three violins. A painting at Nostell Priory appears to show him in the company of his Private Music colleagues, including John Banister (i) and the harpist Charles Evans (*d* 1687). According to Burney, Baltzar died on 24 July 1663; he was buried in Westminster Abbey three days later. At first, Wood thought he had died of 'the french pox and other distempers', but subsequently wrote that 'being much admired by all lovers of musick, his company was therefore desired; and company, especially musicall company, delighting in drinking, made him drink more than ordinary which brought him to his grave'.

Unfortunately little of Baltzar's music survives. He introduced English violinists to high positions, elaborate chordal writing, and scordatura. Playford published three unaccompanied pieces in *The Division Violin*, and a number of others apparently by Baltzar are in manuscript (*GB-Ob* Mus. Sch. F.573). Some are arrangements of lyra viol pieces by Jenkins and others, which suggests that he based his chordal idiom on English viol music, rather than on German violin music. His suites for two violins and bass are fine examples of a conservative Anglo–German idiom, though his masterpiece is the grand, extended suite in C major, one of the finest pieces in the three-violin repertory.

WORKS
(for further details see *Dodd I*)

16 pieces, vn, in The Division Violin (London, 1684/*R*), *GB-Lbl*, *Ob*, *Och*

Divisions on John, come kiss me now, G, vn, b, in The Division Violin (London, 1684/*R*)

2 divisions, d, G, b viol, b, *Ob*, *US-NYp*

3 suites, D, c, G, 2 vn, b, *GB-Ob*

Suite, C, 3 vn, b; *Ob*; ed. I. Payne (Hereford, 1999)

Set of sonatas, lyra vn, tr vn, b, lost, listed in T. Britton's sale catalogue (London, 1714)

Solos, vn, b, lost, listed in C. Burney's sale catalogue (London, 1814)

Vn solos, pavans etc., lost, listed in J.B. Cramer's sale catalogue (London, 1816)

BIBLIOGRAPHY

AshbeeR, i, v, viii; *BDA*; *BDECM*; *BoydenH*; *HawkinsH*

C. Stiehl: 'Thomas Baltzar, ein Paganini seiner Zeit', *Mmg*, xx (1888), 1–8

J. Hennings: *Musikgeschichte Lübecks*, i: *Weltliche Musik* (Kassel, 1951)

E.S. de Beer, ed.: *The Diary of John Evelyn* (London, 1955)

J.D. Shute: *Anthony à Wood and his Manuscript Wood D 19(4) at the Bodleian* (diss., International Institute of Advanced Studies, Clayton, MO, 1979)

G. Dodd: 'Matters Arising from Examination of Lyra Viol Manuscripts', *Chelys*, ix (1980), 23–7

P. Holman: 'Thomas Baltzar (?1631–1663), the "Incomperable Lubicer on the Violin"', *Chelys*, xiii (1984), 3–38

P. Walls: 'The Influence of the Italian Violin School in 17th-Century England', *EMc*, xviii (1990), 575–87

P. Holman: *Four and Twenty Fiddlers: the Violin at the English Court 1540–1690* (Oxford, 1993, 2/1995)

PETER HOLMAN

Bal y Gay, Jesús (*b* Lugo, 23 June 1905; *d* Madrid, 3 March 1993). Spanish musicologist and composer. He had private piano lessons in Lugo (under the auspices of the Real Conservatorio of Madrid), and took his degree at the Instituto General y Técnico (Lugo, 1921). He was a founder (1924) of the arts journal *Ronsel* (published in Lugo), for which he wrote his early essays on music and poetry. While serving in the Spanish infantry at Compostela he participated in the Seminario de Estudios Gallegos (1926–8); on his return to Madrid he joined the musicology and folklore section of the Centro de Estudios Históricos under Ramón Menéndez Pidal, and undertook fieldwork in Extremadura and Galicia, the latter with Eduardo Martínez Torner. J.B. Trend invited him to serve as reader in Spanish literature at the University of Cambridge (1935–8), where he also studied privately with Edward Dent and J. Wolff. Owing to his strong Republican sympathies, he began his long voluntary exile in Mexico, where he pursued his own research supported by the Mexican Government (1938–40); he worked at the Casa de México (1940–42), and when it became the Colegio de México (1942) he was appointed lecturer in music there. After working as a freelance journalist, primarily for the British Propaganda Office in Mexico (1943–9), he joined and directed (1949–65) the musicology section of the Instituto Nacional de Bellas Artes under Carlos Chávez. He served as music critic of the daily paper *El universal* (1940–51), taught music appreciation at the Universidad Nacional Autónoma (1958–64), also directing the music section of its radio station (1957–64), and was a founder-member of and a major contributor to *Nuestra música* (1945–50). Upon his return to Spain in 1965, he resumed his lecturing, writing and compositional activities. His published compositions include the Serenade for strings (1949), Clarinet Sonata (1953) and Concerto grosso (1965); his writings include studies and editions of Spanish folksongs.

In 1933 Bal y Gay married the pianist and composer Rosa García Ascot (*b* Madrid, 8 April 1908), a pupil of Granados (1914–16) and Falla (1916–31). Accompanied by Falla, she played the soloist's part in the first performance of the two-piano version of his *Noches en los jardines de España* (1921) at the Salle Gaveaux, Paris. She made a successful career as a concert pianist, specializing in Falla's works in Spain and, after 1935, in England and Mexico. Her compositions include an orchestral suite and numerous chamber works.

WRITINGS

Hacia el ballet gallego (Lugo, 1924)

'España: Bibliographie de la chanson populaire espagnole', *Folklore musical* (Paris, 1929), 64–84

with E. Martínez Torner: 'Folklore musical', *Terre de Melide* (Compostela, 1933), 537–66

'Fuenllana and the Transcription of Spanish Lute-Music', *AcM*, xi (1939), 16–27

'Rodolfo Halffter', *Nuestra música*, i (1946), 141–6

'Las "Escenas de Ballet" de Stravinsky', *Nuestra música*, ii (1947), 199–209

'Manual de Falla', *Nuestra música*, ii (1947), 19–24

'Felix Mendelssohn', *Nuestra música*, iii (1948), 11–25

'Música intramuros (la situación actual de la música en la U.S.S.R.)', *Nuestra música*, iii (1948), 163–87

'Chopin innovador', *Nuestra música*, iv (1949), 267–85

'El nacionalismo y la música mexicana de hoy', *Nuestra música*, iv (1949), 107–13

'"La hija de Colquide" de Carlos Chávez', *Nuestra música*, v (1950), 207–16

'La "Sinfonía de Antigona" de Carlos Chávez', *Nuestra música*, v (1950), 5–17

'La lección de André Gide', *Nuestra música*, vi (1951), 75–99

Chopin (Mexico City, 1959, 2/1974)

Tientos (ensayos de estética musical) (Mexico City, 1960)

Debussy (Mexico City, 1962)

with E. Martinez Torner: *Cancionero gallego* (La Coruña, 1973)

with R. García Ascot: *Nuestros trabajos y nuestros días*, ed. A. Buxán (Madrid, 1990)

EDITIONS

Treinta canciones de Lope de Vega (Madrid, 1935)

Romances y villancicos españoles del siglo XVI (Mexico City, 1939)

Cancionero de Upsala (Mexico City, 1944)

Tesoro de la música polifónica en México (Mexico City, 1952)

BIBLIOGRAPHY

A. Buxán: 'Jesús Bal y Gay: el músico y el hombre', *Abrente*, nos.13–15 (La Coruña, 1986), 203–35

J. Vellisco Amodia: 'Apuntes biográficos sobre los músicos de la "Generación de la República"', *A tempo*, no.40 (1986), 25–32

J.B. Varela de Vega: 'Táboa redonda: Jesús Bal en el recuerdo (i–xiv)', *El progreso* [Lugo] (June 30 – Nov 17, 1993)

X.M. Carreira: 'Jesús Bal y Gay', *RdMc*, xvii (1994), 477–80

ISRAEL J. KATZ

Balyozov, Rumen (*b* Sofia, 6 Sept 1949). Bulgarian composer. He studied at the Bulgarian State Conservatory (1971–6), then worked as a cellist in the Symphony Orchestra of Bulgarian Radio and Television. Balyozov came to prominence as a composer in the 1970s and 80s. Drawing on the aesthetics of Cage and Kagel, he sought to embody the idea of music as the illumination of the intellect in his works, which include elements of self-irony, games, paradoxes and a sense of the absurd. Moral and ethical issues determine the themes of the stage works. In *Kogato kublite ne spyat* ('When Dolls are not Asleep') Balyozov imaginatively evokes the world of fairy tales. In *Zelenata igra* ('The Green Game') contemporary social issues are dealt with alongside more universal human questions; music is the medium by which the text and visual aspects of the work are linked.

WORKS
(*selective list*)

STAGE

Malkiyat Prints [The Little Prince], 1975 (TV op, R. Balyozov, after A. de Saint-Exupéry)
Kogato kuklite ne spyat [When Dolls are not Asleep] (children's op, L. Mileva), Blagoyevgrad, Nov 1980
Zelenata igra [The Green Game] (music theatre, I. Radoyev), Sofia, National Palace of Culture, 13 Oct 1987

OTHER WORKS

Orch: Siluyeti [Silhouette], 1973; Divertimento capriccioso no.1, 1974; Conc. grosso no.1, str qt, orch, 1983; Divertimento capriccioso no.2, 1985; Conc. grosso no.3, mar, str, 1988
Vocal-orch: Sym., S, B, orch, 1979; Starobalgarski stranitsi [Old Bulg. Pages], 1982; Vladeteli, Knizhovniki Yeretiki [Rulers, Writers, Heretics], 1982
Chbr and solo inst: 2 rapsodifeni improvizatsii, vc, 1971–9; Folklorni etyudi, str, perc, 1972; Izmeneniya [Changes], 2 pf, 1972; Pastorali, ob, 1976; Konflikti, fl, vn, hp, pf, tape, 1977; Memorial '78, vc, perc sextet, 1978; Khrabriyat oloven voynik [The Brave Lead Soldier], spkr, brass qt, 1979; Str Qt, 1979; Marsianski tantsi [Martians' Dances], perc sextet, 1981; 3 piesi [3 Pieces], cl, 1981; Str Qt no.2, 1982; Girlyandi [Garlands], wind qnt, 1983; Conc. grosso no.2, cl, pf, perc, str qt, 1987; Bestiarii [Madness], vc, pf, 1988; Divertimento capriccioso no.4, 5–13 insts, 1989; Kontur [Contour], vc, db, 1989; La follia, vn, vc, db, 1992; Da capo, fl, tape, 1994; Kaleyidoskop, 11 insts, 1997; other duos, pf pieces

Principal publishers: Muzika (Sofia)

BIBLIOGRAPHY
M. Manolova: *Opus musicum* (Brno, 1985)
V. Dicheva: 'Rumen Balyozov', *Balgarska muzika*, xl/8 (1989), 10–13

MAGDALENA MANOLOVA

Balzac, Honoré de (*b* Tours, 20 May 1799; *d* Paris, 21 Aug 1850). French writer. Music is one of the subjects treated in *La comédie humaine*, especially in *Gambara* (1837) and *Massimilla Doni* (1839); but although the names of musicians abound in the novels (among them Cimarosa, Pergolesi, Bellini, Rossini, Handel, Bach, Mozart and Beethoven) there are many fewer reflections on music, Balzac having acknowledged his lack of musical competence in the preface to *Massimilla Doni*. Yet music had for him an importance greater than might be supposed, as is evident from his work and his correspondence: to his beloved *étrangère* he wrote 'Beethoven is the only man who has made me feel jealousy. There is in that man a divine power' (*Lettres à l'étrangère*, 14 November 1837). Clearly not only music but certain individual composers had for Balzac a sovereign importance. In distinguishing the sphere of creative sensibility (for a long time uncertain in Balzac) from the sphere of intelligence and culture, it may be suggested that he was less a man who chanced to discover music than a writer who gradually discovered his true way through music.

In Balzac's relationship with music, the period 1833–7 is, after that of his youth, of the greatest importance. It was then that he wrote most about music, in both his correspondence and his musical novels; this was also the period when he acquired, from 1833 onwards through his contact with the 'monde', a certain musical culture. There was the 'loge infernale' at the Opéra and the concerts at the Austrian Embassy or the Conservatoire; there were the personal contacts with Berlioz, Auber, Jakob Strunz, Liszt and Rossini. For the most part, the effect on him seemed small, the attachment light. Beethoven, whose Fifth Symphony he heard on 27 April 1834, at that stage left him cold. Similarly, the Beethovenism of Berlioz and Liszt seems scarcely to have affected him.

Indeed, in his correspondence between 1833 and 1837, Balzac mentioned only Italians, while in his works music is introduced in the form of memoranda prepared by Strunz for use in *Gambara* and *Massimilla Doni*, with the works cited there matching public taste – *Mosè*, *Robert le diable*, *Les Huguenots*, *Il matrimonio segreto*, *I puritani*, Pergolesi's *Stabat mater*. Yet this taste for grand opera, Italian singing and virtuosity was not merely superficial. It is essential to recognize that the feeling for the absolute in Balzac led him to love Italian art in his own way, that Rossini and Mozart were related to a literary project that reached maturity only with his recognition of Beethoven. He took notice of music only to the extent that he found it passionate, what Hegel called the 'symbol of the inward'. This explains his numerous allusions to *Don Giovanni* and his love of the passionate effect of 'Mi manca la voce' in *Mosè*. Rossini was for Balzac 'the composer who has conveyed the greatest human passion in the art of music': Eugénie Grandet and Raphaël (in *La peau de chagrin*, 1831) had Mozart for their confidant and pored over 'les divines pages de Rossini, Cimarosa, Zingarelli'. The missing name is that of Beethoven, whom Balzac saw as his second self, in whom the absolute was wholly accepted and given worthy expression. Around 1834, at the time when Balzac was hesitating between the novel of manners and the philosophical novel, his taste for Rossini and Mozart as 'passionate' composers reflected the tendency of Romanticism to retain its connection with the gaudiness of worldly fashion. Yet in the period 1837–42, when his literary plans became fixed on the concept of the spiritual threatened by the material, and of the social explained by the philosophical, Mozart and Rossini were relegated to a purely decorative role or disappeared altogether in favour of Beethoven, the pure artist *par excellence*.

The concept of the artist plays a key role in his writing. The spirit which possesses the artist is conquered by money: for example, the two musicians Pons and Schmucke are tricked by speculators. These defeats of the spirit, this overthrowing of art by reality, form a kind of obsession with Balzac. His most precise formulation of it is in *Gambara* and *Massimilla Doni*, but it is also to be found in *La peau de chagrin*, *Béatrix* (1839), *Birotteau* (1837) and *Le cousin Pons* (1847), always in some manner connected with music. Balzac's readings of E.T.A. Hoffmann between 1833 and 1839 persuaded him that music was the supreme region of the absolute; this in turn enabled him to discover in Beethoven, above all in the concept of a struggle waged against fate, an artistic project comparable to his own.

It is evident that although Balzac was friendly with musicians, and acquired a veneer of musical culture, these contacts affected him less than his relationship with music itself. The art was to play a revelatory part in his discovery of his own self; these concepts, German, Romantic and musical, played a crucial part in his thought and helped to shape the ideas which inform the entire *Comédie humaine*. Liszt told Balzac: 'I need listeners like you, and in the absence of listeners, in the plural, I need you, in the singular'.

The most important settings of Balzac include five operas: Nouguès, *L'auberge rouge* (1910); Waltershausen, *Oberst Chabert* (or *Le colonel Chabert*) (1912); Levadé, *La peau de chagrin* (1929); Schoeck, *Massimilla Doni* (1937); Françaix, *Apostrophe* (musical comedy,

1940). Shostakovich wrote incidental music to a play based on *La comédie humaine* (1934), Milhaud to *Le faiseur* (1935). Rossini promised to set a poem inspired by Mme Hanska, but seems not to have done so.

BIBLIOGRAPHY

F. Baldensperger: *Orientations étrangères chez Honoré de Balzac* (Paris, 1927)

L. Guichard: *La musique et les lettres au temps du romantisme* (Paris, 1955)

P. Citron: 'Autour de Gambara', *Année balzacienne* (1967), 165

M. Brozska: 'Mahomet et Robert-le-diable: l'esthétique musicale dans Gambara', *Année balzacienne* (1983), 51–78

P. Michot: 'Le spectacle est dans la salle: Balzac et l'opéra', *Littérature et opéra: Cerisy-la-Salle 1985*, 45–54

M. Brozska: 'Mosè und Massimilla: Rossinis Mosè in Egitto und Balzacs politische Deutung', *Oper als Text: romantische Beiträge zur Libretto-Forschung* (Heidelberg, 1986), 125–45

P. Brunel: 'La tentation hoffmannesque chez Balzac', *E.T.A. Hoffmann et la musique*, ed. A. Montandon (Berne, 1987), 315–24

F. Escal: 'Balzac et Beethoven: le théâtre et la 5e symphonie dans César Birotteau', *Contrepoints* (1988), 15–65

J.P. Barricelli: *Balzac and Music: its Place and Meaning in his Life and Works* (New York, 1990)

FRANCIS CLAUDON

Balzano [Balsano], Giuseppe (*b* Valletta, 9 Sept 1616; *d* Mdina, 23 Feb 1700). Maltese composer. Ordained priest in Catania in 1640, he became *maestro di cappella* of Mdina Cathedral in 1661. He held the post until his retirement in 1699 except for two interruptions (1665–9 and 1673–4) when he might have travelled to Naples for further musical studies. His *Beatus Vir* of 1652 is the oldest dated extant composition by a named Maltese composer. He was a prolific composer: an inventory of about 1707 lists 180 sacred vocal compositions, including 18 masses, 64 psalms (some for vespers), 32 hymns, *Responsorii dei morti*, 2 dialogues and 32 motets. Most have parts for basso continuo, some have added violins, and one, unusually, uses timpani. The few works that survive reveal a high degree of technical competence, both in current practices and in 16th-century polyphony. Illustrative melismatic flourishes obtain strong textual images and the virtuoso exploitation of the solo voice reveals dramatic and enriching textures.

Balzano's younger brother, Domenico (*b* Valletta, 24 Sept 1632; *d* Mdina, 9 Dec 1707), succeeded him at Mdina Cathedral, holding the post until his death.

WORKS

all autograph manuscripts preserved at Mdina Cathedral

Beatus Vir, TTB, bc, 1652
Dormi Dormi, TTB, 1652
Da pacem Domine, 2 SATB, bc
Det Tuba Xaverius a otto voci con sinfonia, 2 SATB, 2 vn, va, bc
Ecce Servus Dei, SSAT, 2 vn, bc
Ego Ille a otto con sinfonie, 2 SATB, 2 vn, bc
Jesu Redemptor Omnium, SATB
Te splendor et virtus, SATB, bc
Quis est hic? Dialogo per la Nativita di S. Giovanni Battista, SST, bc
Salmi a otto voci: Domine ad adjuvandum, Dixit Dominus, Magnificat, only bc extant

BIBLIOGRAPHY

J. Azzopardi: 'La cappella musicale della cattedrale di Malta e i suoi rapporti con la Sicilia', *Musica sacra in Sicilia tra rinascimento e barocco*, ed. D. Ficola (Palermo, 1988), 47–67

J. Azzopardi: 'Il-Katidral ta' l-Imdina: Kappella, Mużika u Arkivju Mużikali' [The Mdina Cathedral: chapel, music and music archives], *Oqsma tal-Kultura Maltija*, ed. T. Cortis (Malta, 1991), 101–19

N. Chircop: *Scores Attributable to Giuseppe Balzano: a Critical Analysis* (diss., U. of Malta, 1991)

JOSEPH VELLA BONDIN

Bambaataa, Afrika. *See* AFRIKA BAMBAATAA.

Bamberg. Town in Bavaria, Germany. From the early 11th century to the early 19th the bishop of Bamberg was entitled to the rank of Prince of the Holy Roman Empire. Although vocal music was mentioned in the earliest accounts of the cathedral (founded in 1012), the institution of a song school in 1192 by Bishop Otto II was the beginning of the town's musical significance, as indicated by the extant Bamberg Manuscript, which contains about 100 13th-century motets. A succession of Kantors – the best known being Leopold von Schweinschaupten (*d* 1357) – and chaplains superintended the musical life of the town and surrounding area. The 15th-century composers Heinrich Finck and Johannes Frosch were natives of Bamberg. The music theorist Ulrich Burchard, author of *Hortulus musices* (1514), was a court chaplain there. Conservative principles in church music were maintained during the Reformation and Counter-Reformation through such works as the *Kurtzer Ausszug der Christlichen und Catholischen Geseng* (1575) and the *Catholische Gesangbuch* (1628), and through the teaching in the seminary for priests (founded 1586) and the Jesuit Gymnasium (1613). The most influential musicians in Bamberg during the 17th century (during which the Stadtpfeiferei achieved greater recognition) were Johann Degen, court chaplain, and George Arnold, court organist.

In the 18th century a process of secularization began, encouraged by Prince-Bishop Adam Friedrich von Seinsheim, who ruled Bamberg from 1757 to 1779. He employed as music director Tartini's pupil Fracassini, who reinvigorated the court orchestra, produced operas at the Seehof palace and introduced symphony concerts. Operas and concerts took place from 1788 in the 'Zum schwarzen Adler', where Andreas Bäuml, successor to Fracassini, introduced the public and the court to the operas of Grétry, Paisiello and Mozart, as well as to popular Singspiele. In 1781 the court orchestra comprised 16 strings, two oboes, a bassoon and two horns; it was enlarged to symphonic proportions in 1796. Meanwhile church music had reached a low ebb and worshippers in the cathedral were regaled with symphonies, bravura operatic arias and the occasional *Tusch* (a Bamberg speciality – cheerful music for wind instruments). The subsequent restoration of standards in Catholic church music owed much to the Cecilian movement and the establishment in Bamberg in 1868 of the Allgemeiner Deutscher Cäcilienverein.

Between 1808 and 1813 E.T.A. Hoffmann was active at the theatre (built 1802) in various capacities: as composer of the melodrama *Dirna*, the opera *Der Trunk der Unsterblichkeit* (to a libretto by Count Julius von Soden, director of the theatre) and other works, as music director, and as scenery artist. One of his colleagues was Weber's stepbrother Edmund. Hoffmann's *Aurora*, although composed for Bamberg in 1811, had its first performance there only in 1933. His attempts to control the orchestra were rarely successful, and he made uncomplimentary references to Bamberg in his diaries and in *Kreisleriana*, saying that the time he spent there was 'the worst of all bad times'. He was, nonetheless, commemorated by a statue and his house was preserved.

In 1820 the Bamberger Musikverein was founded, resulting in increased music-making; it was reconstituted in 1872 and still gives chamber music concerts. A number of other societies subsequently grew up including the

Oratorienchor (founded 1835), also still active, and a town music school was established. At the end of the 19th century cathedral music was reorganized by Karl Cohen. After World War II the town's reputation was spread by the Bamberg SO, formed in 1946 from the Prague Deutsche Philharmonie, which had been founded in Prague in 1939 and left there in 1945. The orchestra's permanent conductors have been Keilberth (1940–45, 1949–68), Herbert Albert (1947–8) and G.L. Jochum (1948–9), Eugen Jochum (1968–73), James Loughrun (1978–83), Witold Rowicki (1983–5) and Horst Stein (from 1985). Concerts are frequently given in the cathedral and the Lutheran church of St Stephan. Musica Cantorey Bamberg, founded in 1969 and directed by Gerhard Weinzierl, cultivates the works of Bamberg composers including Georg Arnold (1621–76), Georg Mengel (c1600–67) and Johann Bach (1657–1701).

Among important organ builders in Bamberg were, in the 17th century, Johann Laubinger, in the 18th Johann Wilhelm Hoffmann and in the 19th Justus Karl Hansen, who were all responsible for alterations to the cathedral organ. The Neupert family were active piano and harpsichord makers in Bamberg from 1928.

BIBLIOGRAPHY

E. von Marschalk: *Die Bamberger Hofmusik unter den drei letzten Fürstbischöfen* (Bamberg, 1885)

E.T.A. Hoffmann: *Musikalische Novellen und Aufsätze*, ed. E. Istel (Stuttgart, 1907/R)

T. Leist: *Geschichte des Theaters in Bamberg* (Bamberg, 1908)

E.H. Farrenkopf: *Breviarium Eberhardi cantoris: die mittelalterliche Gottesdienstordnung des Domes zu Bamberg mit einer historischen Einleitung* (Würzburg, 1969)

PERCY M. YOUNG

Bambini, Felice (*b* Bologna, *c*1743; *d* ?after 1787). French composer and harpsichordist of Italian origin. He was the son of the impresario Eustachio Bambini (*b* Pesaro, 1697; *d* Pesaro, 1770). He went to Paris in July 1752 at the same time as the company of Bouffons directed by his father. Jean-Jacques Rousseau mentioned him in the *Lettre sur la musique française*, drawing a favourable comparison between his light manner of playing the continuo (usually in two parts) and the stiff style of the Opéra's harpsichordist. La Borde added that Bambini composed 'several *ariettes* for addition to the *intermèdes* performed at the time'. He stayed in Paris after the departure of the Italian company and studied with André-Jean Rigade. The music of his principal opera, *Nicaise*, is relatively rudimentary and more reminiscent of the Italian intermezzos of the 1740s and 50s than the more elaborate *opéras comiques* of Duni, Monsigny and Philidor. After the failure of *Nicaise* no more of Bambini's works were performed at the Comédie-Italienne, and during the 1780s he had to be content with the modest Théâtre des Beaujolais.

WORKS

all printed works published in Paris

STAGE

all first performed in Paris

Les amans de village (comédie mêlée de musique, 2, A.F. Riccoboni), Comédie-Italienne (Bourgogne), 26 July 1764, 2 airs (1771)

Nicaise (oc, 1, J.-J. Vadé, rev. N.E. Framery, after La Fontaine), Comédie-Italienne (Bourgogne), 15 July 1767, collab. Fridzeri (1767)

Les fourberies de Mathurin (opéra bouffon, l, Davesne), Beaujolais, 5 Aug 1786

L'amour l'emporte (opéra bouffon, 1, Mayeur de Saint-Paul), Beaujolais, 20 Oct 1787

OTHER WORKS

Suzanne (orat)

Symphonie périodique (1764); 6 sinfonie quattro, op.1 (1767); Trii, vn, va, b; 3 bks of sonatas, hpd/pf, vn (1771, 1777, 1788); 6 sonate, hpd, vn obbl, op.4 (*c*1775); 6 sonates, hpd, vn, op.5 (n.d.); 6 sonates, hpd (n.d.); 3 sonates, pf, vn (n.d.); 3 sonatas, hpd, *D-Bsb*; 12 petits airs, hpd/pf, vn (n.d.)

Didactic: Nouvelle méthode pour pianoforte suivie de doigtés, collab. V. Nicolai

BIBLIOGRAPHY

GroveO ('Bambini, Eustachio', E. Cook); *La BordeE*

M. Tourneux, ed.: *Correspondance littéraire, philosophique et critique par Grimm, Diderot, Raynal, Meister, etc.* (Paris, 1877–82), vii, 372

C.D. Brewer: *A Bibliographical List of Plays in the French Language, 1700–1789* (Ann Arbor, 1947)

MICHEL NOIRAY

Bambuco. The national dance of Colombia. It is said to have been the favourite of Símon Bolívar, Colombia's independence leader (1824). Early references identify it with the BUNDE, a dance of African origin. In the 19th century Colombian national composers wrote *bambucos* and *pasillos*, leading popular music into a 'golden age'. Originally a serenading song for the solo voice, the modern *bambuco* is most often sung in duet or parallel 3rds, with strummed accompaniment on *tiple* (small 12-string guitar), guitar and *bandola* (flat-backed lute). A courting or pursuit dance, characterized by delicate toe-dancing by both male and female, it has a specific choreography with variations, involving eight possible basic steps: (i) *invitación*: invitation to the dance; (ii) *ochos*: dancing in a figure-of-eight pattern; (iii) *codos*: dancing with elbows touching; (iv) *coquetos*: 'flirtatious' steps when the man attempts to steal a kiss from the woman; (v) *perseguida*: dancing in a circle, the man pursues the woman; (vi) *pañuelo*: handkerchief waving while dancing; (vii) *arrodillada*: the woman dances in a circle around the kneeling man; (viii) *abrazo*: the man places his right hand on the woman's waist, dances her back to her original starting position. The song texts, often regarded as melancholy, use an octosyllabic *décima* verse or other poetic form, frequently with descending melodies and dramatic modulations through predominantly minor keys, oscillating hemiola rhythms 3/4, 6/8. Texts typically revolve around archetypal subjects often with a gendered chauvinistic viewpoint, including the extolling of a woman's beauty, her desirability, idyllic love, the pain of thwarted love, pride in being Colombian or coming from a particular region. Other texts comment on current events, make philosophical statements about everyday life and the struggles of the peasantry and people. Social change since the late 1940s has inspired certain *bambucos de protesta*. Examination of choreography, song texts, vocal styles, instrumentation and musical function shows a degree of inherent Hispanic influence. The urban *bambuco* has rural counterparts called the *sanjuanero* and the *rajaleña* which exhibit more pronounced African traits. It shares many features with the Chilean *cueca* and the Peruvian *marinera*.

WILLIAM GRADANTE/R

Bamert, Matthias (*b* Ersigen, 5 July 1942). Swiss conductor and composer. He studied the oboe, chamber music and composition at the Conservatoire Nationale Supérieure in Paris, and attended masterclasses by Boulez and Maderna at the Darmstadt summer course in 1965. He was principal oboe in the Salzburg Mozarteum Orchestra (1965–9), and worked as assistant to Szell in Cleveland

(1969–70) and Stokowski at the American SO (1970–71) before spending seven years as resident conductor of the Cleveland Orchestra. He was principal conductor of the Basle RSO (1977–83), principal guest conductor of the Scottish National Orchestra (1985–90) and artistic director of the London Mozart Players (1993–2000). Renowned for his wide repertory and command of contemporary scores, Bamert has conducted world premières of works by Takemitsu, Denisov, Erb, Casken, Rihm, Turnage and others. He has also done much to popularize music by Frank Martin, Parry, Korngold and Gerhard, both in concert and on disc, and with the London Mozart Players has recorded an enterprising series of little-known symphonies by contemporaries of Mozart. As artistic diretor of the Lucerne Festival (1992–8), he strengthened its thematic content while widening its appeal. His compositions, predominantly for orchestra, include a Concertino for english horn, string orchestra and piano (1966), *Septuria Lunaris* (1970), *Rheology* (1970), *Mantrajana* (1971), *Once upon an Orchestra* for narrator, 12 dancers and orchestra (1975), *Ol-Okun* (1976), *Keepsake* (1979) and *Circus Parade* for narrator and orchestra (1979).

ANDREW CLARK

Bamfi [Banfi, Banfo], **Alfonso** (*b* ?Milan; *fl* 1641–55). Italian composer and organist. He may have come from a Milanese family whose members included a lutenist, Giulio Banfi. In 1641 he succeeded G.B. Cima as *maestro di cappella* of Como Cathedral, but he had to leave in 1643, when the cathedral ran into economic difficulties. Later he was *maestro di cappella* and organist of the collegiate church at Domodossola (not at Reggio nell'Emilia as stated by Fétis). He was there when he published his only known music, *Selva de sacri, et ariosi concerti a 1–4 voci con una messa brevissima, Magnificat, Salve regina e Lettanie della BVM con il basso continuo* (Milan, 1655). The *concerti* are concertato motets and are in fact called motets in a note at the end of the volume. They are well-wrought pieces, elaborately ornamented and with numerous time changes.

BIBLIOGRAPHY

GaspariC, ii
Libro mastro (MS, I-COd), ff.151ff
F. Picinelli: *Ateneo de i letterati milanesi* (Milan, 1670), 354
M. Longatti: 'La cappella del duomo di Como nella prima metà del Seicento', *Quadrivium*, xxiii (1982), 41–68

GIUSEPPE VECCHI

Bampton, Rose (Elizabeth) (*b* Lakewood, nr Cleveland, OH, 28 Nov 1908). American mezzo-soprano, later soprano. She studied at the Curtis Institute, made her début in 1929 at Chatauqua as Siébel (*Faust*), and then sang secondary roles with the Philadelphia Grand Opera. She made her Metropolitan début in 1932 as Laura (*La Gioconda*), and sang as a mezzo until 1937, when she made her soprano début as Leonora (*Il trovatore*); other roles included Aida and Amneris (in the same season), Donna Anna, Alcestis, Elisabeth, Elsa, Sieglinde and Kundry. She appeared at Covent Garden (1937) as Amneris; in Chicago (1937–46), where her roles included Maddalena de Coigny; at the Teatro Colón, Buenos Aires (1942–8), where she sang the Marschallin, and Daphne in the South American première of Strauss's opera; and in San Francisco (1949). Bampton had a strong, though not particularly individual, voice, and her sovereign musicianship was admired by Toscanini, for whom she recorded

Leonore in *Fidelio*. Many of her Metropolitan broadcasts are preserved on disc, notably an exciting Donna Anna under Walter in 1942 (see P. Jackson: *Saturday Afternoons at the Old Met*, New York, 1992), as is a performance of *Gurrelieder* with Stokowski.

MAX DE SCHAUENSEE/ALAN BLYTH

Ban, Joan Albert [Bannius, Joannes Albertus] (*b* Haarlem, 1597 or 1598; *d* Haarlem, 27 July 1644). Dutch theorist and composer. He came from a patrician family, entered the priesthood in Haarlem and became a canon in 1628. As a musician he was entirely self-educated. He studied theoretical works from Pythagoras to Zarlino and, dissatisfied, turned to his prominent contemporaries – among them Constantijn Huygens, Mersenne, G.B. Doni and Descartes – for assistance. Although much is made of a song-writing competition between Ban and Antoine Boësset staged by Mersenne in 1640, in which it was a foregone conclusion that Boësset should win, Ban was unaffected by his loss (see Walker). In many of his letters he declared that music must be practised under strict and demonstrable rules and not left to individual arbitrary taste: it must not mask the natural delivery of a text but rather reinforce it. In this light his praise of, and familiarity with, contemporary Italian music is not remarkable; but it is typical of his 'monodic approach' that, although aware of the usefulness of modulation, he recognized neither the musical value nor the expressive power of dissonance.

Ban spent 20 years developing his system of *musica flexanima* ('zielroerende zang': 'soul-moving singing'), wherein the text was expressed musically by means of specific intervals, harmonics and rhythms. The practical application of these theories is found in the ten three-part songs of his *Zangh-bloemzel* (Amsterdam, 1642). He did not complete his theoretical treatise *Zangh-bericht*, though he appended a short summary of it to the *Zangh-bloemzel* and issued a more developed version (*Kort sangh-bericht*) a year later. Ban was also interested in the problem of tuning: he even went so far as to publish a diagram of Mersenne's 18-note clavier, calling it his 'perfect clavier' ('volmaekte klaeuwier'; see illustration). However, neither this keyboard, with its adaption of Mersenne's symbols for the various extra sharps and flats, nor his attempt at a wholly Dutch musical terminology, was accepted by his contemporaries.

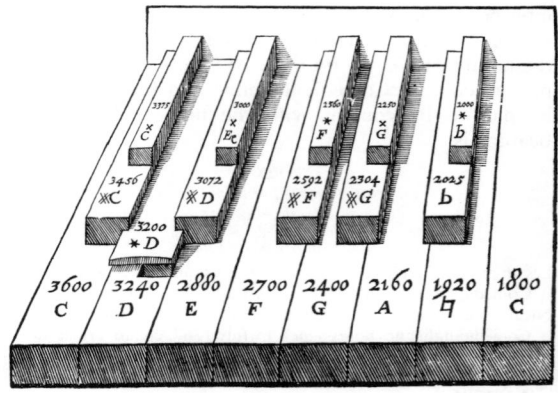

Ban's 'volmaekte klaeuwier': diagram from 'Kort sangh-bericht' (Amsterdam: Matthysz, 1643)

THEORETICAL WORKS

*Joannis Alberti Banni dissertatio epistolica de musicae natura,
origine, progressu* (Leiden, 1637)

Cort beduydsel vant zingen (MS, 1642, *NL-Lu*); ed. in Land

*Kort sangh-bericht van Ioan Albert Ban ... op zyne ziel-roerende
zangen* (Amsterdam, 1643); ed. F. Noske (Amsterdam, 1969)

Zangh-bericht, unfinished, lost

Letters and theoretical fragments, *F-Pn*, *NL-Lu*, many ed. within the
correspondences of G.B. Doni, P.C. Hooft, Huygens and Mersenne

BIBLIOGRAPHY

MersenneHU

J.P.N. Land: 'Joan Albert Ban en de theorie der toonkunst', *TVNM*,
i/2 (1883), 95–111; iii/4 (1891), 204–10

D.P. Walker: 'Joan Albert Ban and Mersenne's Musical Competition
of 1640', *ML*, lvii (1976), 233–55; repr. in *Studies in Musical
Science in the Late Renaissance* (London, 1978), 81–110

R.A. Rasch: 'Ban's Intonation', *TVNM*, xxxiii (1983), 75–99

J.W.N. Valkestijn: 'Een onbekend handschrift van Joan Albert Ban',
Liber amicorum Chris Maas, ed. R. Wegman and E. Vetter
(Amsterdam, 1987), 131–54

RANDALL H. TOLLEFSEN

Banān, Qolāmhoseyn (*b* Tehran, 1911; *d* Tehran, 1986).
Persian singer. He came from an aristocratic background
and was raised in a family circle frequented by literati and
musicians. His father played the *tār* and his mother the
piano; Banān learnt the rudiments of both instruments in
childhood. He had voice lessons from his early teen years
and by his mid-20s he had established a high reputation
as a singer with a marked command of the *radif* and a
sound knowledge of the Persian classical poetry on which
Persian vocal music heavily relies.

In the 1930s Banān was drawn into the circle of
progressive musicians led by Ali Naqi Vaziri, becoming
closely associated with two of Vaziri's leading disciples,
Ruhollāh Khāleqi and Abolhasan Sabā. He participated
in concerts organized by the Vaziri group as the lead
singer, specializing in performances of new *tasnif* compositions. His fame spread after his radio engagements
began in 1942.

By the 1950s Banān was the most highly regarded male
singer in Persia. Recordings of his radio broadcasts and
his published disc recordings are models of refinement in
singing. His versatility in vocal renditions of the classical
repertory of *dastgāh*s and particularly his tasteful presentation of modern compositions in Persian modes have
been admired by connoisseurs and the general public
alike. Contrary to the high vocal register cultivated by
most male singers, Banān had a relatively low-pitched
voice with a graceful, mellow and relaxed tone. He was
also active as a voice teacher at the Conservatory of
National Music in Tehran.

HORMOZ FARHAT

Banaster [Banastir, Banastre], **Gilbert** (*b* ?London, *c*1430;
d London, between 19 Aug and 10 Sept 1487). English
composer. He may have been a choirboy with the Chapel
Royal: his father Henry Banaster, who died in 1456, was
a Yeoman of the Royal Household. He became a
Gentleman of the Chapel Royal in 1468 and Master of
the Choristers in 1478. His will dated 19 August 1487
shows evidence of substantial investment in land and
property. His corrodies were distributed among the
members of the Royal Household on 10 September in
that year. Apart from his musical compositions a poem,
The Miracles of St Thomas, has survived.

Banaster's compositions consist of a setting of the hymn
Exsultet caelum laudibus and a two-voice Mass respond,
Alleluia: Laudate pueri (both in *GB-Cmc* Pepys 1236); a

three-voice carol, *My feerfull dreme* in the Fayrfax
manuscript (*Lbl* Add.5465); and the five-voice antiphon
O Maria et Elizabeth in the Eton Choirbook. The carol is
perhaps the most interesting piece because it displays a
more modern syllabic style with much use of imitation
(its refrain is in *NOHM*, iii, p.346). The syllabic element
is also notable in *O Maria et Elizabeth* (*MB*, xi, no.28)
and was probably used because the text is rather long and
unfamiliar. The antiphon may have been composed to
commemorate the pregnancy of Elizabeth, wife of Henry
VII, who gave birth to Prince Arthur on 10 September
1486.

JOHN CALDWELL/JONATHAN HALL

Banchieri, Adriano [Tomaso] (*b* Bologna, 3 Sept 1568; *d*
Bologna, 1634). Italian composer, organist, theorist and
writer. He was one of the most versatile figures in the
Italian music of his day and is of particular interest as a
theorist.

1. LIFE. Banchieri entered the Olivetan order of Benedictine monks in 1587, officially becoming a novice and
receiving the name Adriano in 1589; he completed his
solemn vows in 1590. He was a pupil of Gioseffo Guami,
under whom he certainly developed much of his skill as
an organist and composer. During his first years as a
monk he worked at various houses of his order: in 1592
he was at the monastery of SS Bartolomeo e Ponziano,
Lucca, in 1593 at S Benedetto, Siena; in 1594 he returned
to the vicinity of Bologna to the monastery of S Michele
in Bosco, where in 1596 he assumed the duties of organist.
From 1600 to 1604 he was organist of S Maria in Regola
at Imola. In 1604 he was sent to the monastery of S Pietro
at Gubbio, where he met Girolamo Diruta and heard one
of the great organs of Italy (built by Quemar Vincenzo),
which he described in his *Conclusioni nel suono
dell'organo* (1609). In 1605 he was at S Elena, Venice,
and in 1606 at S Maria in Organo, Verona. He dedicated
a new organ at Monte Oliveto Maggiore Abbey, the
mother house of the Olivetan order, in 1607. He was in
Milan at the monastery of S Vittore in 1610 during the
celebration of the canonization of S Carlo Borromeo. In
1609 he returned to S Michele in Bosco, where he
remained until just before his death.

In 1615 he helped to found the Accademia dei Floridi,
the first such society in Bologna; his name in it was 'Il
Dissonante'. The academy, which Monteverdi visited in
1620, met at S Michele in Bosco and was the immediate
forerunner of the Accademia dei Filomusi. Banchieri
received the honorary title of Abate Benemerito in 1618.
Because of ill-health he moved to the monastery of S
Bernardo, Bologna, in 1634 and in the same year he died
there of apoplexy.

2. WORKS. Banchieri's sacred music includes psalms for
the Offices (especially Vespers), masses and motets. The
psalms are variously in relatively traditional polyphonic
styles and in the more up-to-date concertato manner. His
12 extant masses all reveal an adherence to the principles
of the Council of Trent. The texts are clearly presented
with rather simple counterpoint and a great deal of
chordal setting. Musically they demonstrate nearly all the
styles of composition used in the early 17th century.
There is some variation among the masses in the formal
divisions of the Ordinary text, with most variety appearing
in the Credo; all but three of the masses substitute a motet
for the Benedictus. Banchieri's other published motets

Adriano Banchieri: engraving, 1609, from his 'Cartella musicale'
(Venice: Vincenti, 1614)

appear not only under that designation but on the title-pages of later volumes in particular as 'concerti', 'pensieri' and 'dialoghi'. They include polyphonic pieces for two four-part choirs (*Concerti ecclesiastici*, 1595, including one of the earliest appearances of a separate instrumental bass part), duets with continuo (*Dialoghi, concerti, sinfonie, e canzoni*) and monodic pieces (*Terzo libro di nuovi pensieri ecclesiastici*, 1613). Organ masses and other liturgical and non-liturgical works for organ are found in various editions of *L'organo suonarino* (1605).

Although there is evidence that some early pieces are lost, Banchieri acknowledged in his own numbering of his works only the 12 secular volumes that survive. He seems to have written most of the texts himself and made some use of dialect in them. These volumes include six books of canzonettas for three voices, each containing some 20 textually related pieces which often employ the plots of the *commedia dell'arte*. Among these is his most famous, widely performed and frequently published work, *La pazzia senile* (1598), based on the amorous adventures of the *commedia dell'arte* character Pantaloon. This is a madrigal comedy in the Vecchi tradition, and two of the other three-voice books belong to this genre, *Il metamorfosi musicale* (1601) and *Prudenza giovenile* (1607) (called *Saviezza giovenile* in its second edition): *see also* MADRIGAL COMEDY. The other six books, which include comparable entertainment works, are basically for five voices (though they contain a few for smaller forces); the individual pieces in the earlier collections are called madrigals. The last three books include a continuo: the music becomes less polyphonic as groups of fewer than five voices are employed in conjunction with the bass, which takes on an individual role and displays melodic

characteristics of its own. The subtitles of these last three books offer some clue to the changing character of the music; as well as vocal pieces *Il virtuoso ritrovo academico* (1626) contains canzonas specifically for violins. The subject matter of these 12 collections, especially those for five voices, also includes the pastoral stories of Greek mythology (*Il zabaione musicale*, 1604) and the presentation of a single idea (in *Vivezze di flora e primavera*, 1622, each madrigal adds to the general idea of nature reawakening in spring). Banchieri was also a pioneer in writing canzonas and fantasias for instrumental ensemble, which are evidently original works for the medium and not arrangements of vocal pieces.

Banchieri's writings about music deal almost exclusively with compositional and performing practice; the *Conclusioni* is exceptional in that it contains extended passages of theoretical speculation. It is also the only text which wholeheartedly embraces the 12- or even 14-mode systems of Glarean and Zarlino; his other writings, notably *L'organo suonarino*, discuss the traditional and more practical 8-mode system. In *Cartella musicale* (1614) Banchieri merged the 8 psalm tones and the 12 modes into a system of 8 'psalm tone keys' that was widely adopted in 17th-century theory and compositions (*see* MODE, §III, 5 (ii)). In *L'organo suonarino* he described the realization of bass figures, gave instruction for accompanying liturgical chant and provided bass parts for many chants: in the second edition he gave specific organ registrations. He was one of the first to expand the solmization system from a hexachord by adding the variable seventh step *ba* (B♭) and *bi* (B♮). This process is outlined in *Cartella musicale*, a large and interesting work in several parts, each of which was evidently published separately, with separate title-pages. The work also includes descriptions of the metrical beat as implied by a bar-line, and of the modern tie (*legatura moderna*): examples of ties are found in the *Terzo libro di nuovi pensieri ecclesiastici*. A short table of vocal ornaments is also given in *Cartella musicale*. Banchieri was one of the first composers to use dynamic marks; an example is found in the concerto *Ego dormio* in the *Terzo libro di nuovi pensieri ecclesiastici*.

Banchieri also wrote extensively outside music, including several popular works that were often reprinted and translated. His earliest such work, *La nobilità dell'asino*, written under the pseudonym Attabalippa dal Peru, appeared in English as *The Nobility of the Ass* (London, 1595) three years after it first appeared in Italy. His usual pseudonym was Camillo Scaliggeri dalla Fratta, under which all his other literary works not identified by his own name appeared. He wrote several books on the dialects found in the vicinity of Bologna and edited and reprinted a book by Giovanni Zanti on the architecture of Bologna.

WORKS

Edition: *A. Banchieri: Opera omnia*, ed. I. Vecchi, AntMI, *Monumenta bononiensa*, xii (1963–) [V]

SACRED
published in Venice unless otherwise stated

Concerti ecclesiastici, 8vv, bc (org) (1595); 2 in V

Salmi … i Vespri di tutte le feste, e solennità dell'anno, e nel fine 2 cantici della BVM, 5vv (1598)

Messa solenne, dentrovi variati concerti all'introito, graduale, offertorio, levatione et comunione, et nel fine l'hinno degli gloriosissimi SS Ambrogio et Agostino … libro III, 8vv (1599); 2 ed. in Wernli

Eclesiastiche sinfonie, dette canzoni in aria francese, per sonare, et
cantare, 4vv, bc (org), op.16 (1607); ed. in Bowman

Gemelli armonici … parto 21, 2vv, bc (org) (1609, enlarged, rev.
2/1622)

Vezzo di perle musicali modernamente conteste alla regia sposa
effigiata nella sacra cantica, 1–2vv/insts, bc (org), op.23 (1610);
ed. M.G. Genesi (Piacenza, 1992)

Secondo libro di nuovi pensieri ecclesiastici, 2vv/insts (Milan, 1611),
lost

Terzo libro di nuovi pensieri ecclesiastici, 1–2vv, bc (hpd/theorbo/
arpichittarone/org), op.35 (Bologna, 1613⁵/R1969 in BMB, xl); 1
ed. in Kirkendale

Salmi da recitarsi à battuta larga, et nel fine 3 variate armonie sopra
il Magnificat, 4vv, bc (org), op.33 (1613)

Due ripieni in applauso musicale, 8vv/insts, bc (org) (Bologna, 1614)

Sacra armonia, 4vv, bc (org), op.41 (1619)

Primo libro delle messe e motetti, 3vv, bc (org) (1620) [incl. inst
pieces]; 1 mass and 1 sonata ed. in Kirkendale

Dialoghi, concerti, sinfonie, e canzoni, 2vv, bc (org), op.48 (1625,
enlarged 2/1629); see Mischiati, 152

Other sacred works, 1616², 1617²⁴, 1620², 1622², 1623², 1624²,
1626², 1626³, 1626⁴, 1627¹, 1627², 1628², 1628³ (according to
Mischiati)

SECULAR

Canzonette, novamente, sotto diversi capricci, composte … Hora
prima di recreatione, 3vv (Venice, 1597); 2 ed. in Wernli

La pazzia senile: ragionamenti vaghi, et dilettevoli … libro II, 3vv
(Venice, 1598, rev. 2/1599); ed. in AMI, iv (n.d.) and in
Capolavori polifonici del secolo XVI, vi (Rome, 1955); 2
intermedii in V

Il studio dilettevole … con vaghi argomenti e spassevoli intermedii
fioriti dal Amfiparnasso … del Horatio Vechi, 3vv (Milan, 1600)
[title taken from 2/1603]

Il metamorfosi musicale: 4° libro delle canzonette … con spassevoli
trattenimenti, diviso in epilogati, e vaghi discorsi, 3vv (Venice,
1601, rev. 2/1606); V

Il zabaione musicale: inventione boscareccia, et 1° libro di madrigali,
5vv (Milan, 1604); ed. P. Mecarelli (Florence, 1987)

Barca di Venetia per Padova … libro II de madrigali, 5vv, op.12
(Venice, 1605, rev. 2/1623 with bc (spinet/chit) ad lib); ed. in
Capolavori polifonici del secolo XVI, ix (Rome, 1969)

Virtuoso ridotto tra signori, e dame … una nuova comedia detta
Prudenza giovenile, 5° libro degli terzetti, op.15 (Milan, 1607, rev.
2/1628 as Saviezza giovenile, 3vv, bc (spinet), op.1); 2/1628 ed. R.
Allorto (Milan, 1956)

Festino nella sera del giovedi grasso avanti cena, genio al 3° libro
madrigalesco, 5vv, op.18 (Venice, 1608); ed. E. Enrico (Norman,
OK, 1981)

Tirsi, Fili e Clori … il 6°, et ultimo libro delle canzonette, 3vv
(Venice, 1614)

Vivezze di flora e primavera, 5vv, bc (spinet/chit), op.44 (Venice,
1622); ed. in Capolavori polifonici del secolo XVI, xii (Rome,
1971)

Il virtuoso ritrovo academico … 1–5vv/insts, bc, op.49 (Venice,
1626) [incl. canzonas, 2 vn]; see Mischiati, 152; 1 ed. in
Kirkendale; 2 ed. in Wernli

Trattenimenti da villa … up to 5vv, bc (chit) (Venice, 1630); 1 ed. in
Kirkendale

Works in 1607²⁰, 1609³³, 1615³; 3 works, 4vv, in A. Banchieri: La
nobilissima anzi asinissima compagnia (Vicenza, 1597), ed. in
Wernli; 4 works, 4vv, in A. Banchieri: Il donativo di 4 asinissimi
personaggi, et insieme 6 servitori d'essi (Milan, 1598); 1 work,
6vv, in A. Banchieri: La nobiltà dell'asino (Venice, 3/1599), ed. in
Wernli

INSTRUMENTAL

Canzoni alla francese, a 4 … in fine una battaglia, 8[vv] e 2 concerti
fatti sopra Lieto godea … libro II (Venice, 1596); V

[21] Fantasie, overo Canzoni alla francese, a 4, bc (org, other insts)
(Venice, 1603); incl. some works from Canzoni (1596); ed. in IIM,
xviii (1995)

Moderna armonia di canzoni alla francese, a 1–2, bc (org/hpd), con
l'aggiunta in fine di 2 fantasie, a 4, et uno Magnificat, 4vv, op.26
(Venice, 1612); 1 ed. in Venetian Instrumental Music c. 1600, xv
(London, 1977)

Other vocal and inst works in A-Wm, B-Br, D-Bsb, Mbs, GB-Lbl, I-
CARcc, PL-GD, WRu (all according to Mischiati)

THEORETICAL WORKS
only those on music

Cartella, overo Regole utilissime à quelli che desiderano imparare il
canto figurato … divise in 2 parti (Venice, 1601; rev. 2/1610; rev.
3/1614 as Cartella musicale, Eng. trans., 1981; rev. 4/1615 as La
cartellina musicale, op.35; rev. 5/1623 as La banchierina, overo
Cartella picciola del canto figurato) [various subdivisions of 1 or
more of the edns are: Brevi documenti musicali; Brevi et primi
documenti musicali; Duo in contrapunto sopra ut, re, mi, fa, sol,
la; Altri documenti musicali nel canto fermo; Duo spartiti al
contrapunto; Canoni musicali, 4vv; Moderna practica musicale,
op.37; Cartelle semplici; Indice delle opere musicali date in luce];
vocal ornaments repr. in Musica practica, sive Instructio pro
Symphoniacis (Nuremberg, 1642); 1 work from rev. 5/1623 repr.
in Synopsis musica, ed. E. Gruber (Regensburg, 1673); 1 work ed.
in Wernli

L'organo suonarino, op.13 (Venice, 1605, Eng. trans., 1970; rev.
2/1611 as op.25; rev. 3/1622 as op.43) [contains music exx.; 9 ed.
in AMI, iii (n.d.); 3 ed. in Venetian Instrumental Music c. 1600, xv
(London, 1977); 1 ed. in Wernli]

Conclusioni nel suono dell'organo, op.20 (Bologna, 1609/R, 2/1626
as Armoniche conclusioni nel suono dell'organo; Eng. trans.,
1982)

La mano, et documenti sicuri prodotti d'autori gravi, et cantici
ecclesiastici, op.25 (Milan, 1611)

Cartellina del canto fermo gregoriano (Bologna, 1614)

Frutto salutifero alli … sacerdoti per prepararsi alla celebrazione
della SS messa privata e cantata (Bologna, 1614)

Prima parte del primo libro al direttorio monastico di canto fermo
per uso particolare della congregatione olivetana (Bologna, 1615,
partial repr. 1616 as Progressi, politici, e christiani)

Cantorino utile a novizzi, e cherici secolari, e regolari, principianti del
canto fermo (Bologna, 1622)

Il principiante fanciullo, che … impara solfizare note e mutationi, e
parole solo, 2vv, op.46 (Venice, 1625) [incl. music exx.]

La sampogna musicale … rappresentata sotto il di 14 novembre
1625 nel virtuoso ridotto (Venice, 1625) [incl. music exx.]

Conclusiones de musica in organo modulanda (Bologna, 1627)

Lettere armoniche (Bologna, 1628, 2/1630 as Lettere scrite a diversi
patroni ed amici)

BIBLIOGRAPHY

M. Scarpini: I monaci benedettini di Monte Oliveo, San Salvatore
Monferrato (Ferrara, 1952), 238ff

H.-J. Wilbert: Die Messen des Adriano Banchieri (diss., Mainz U.,
1969)

C.B. Bowman: The Ecclesiastiche sinfonie (opus 16) of Adriano
Banchieri (1568–1634) (diss., New York U., 1971)

H.-J. Wilbert: 'La messe polifoniche di Adriano Banchieri', Annuario
1965–1970 del Conservatorio di Musica 'G.B. Martini' di Bologna
(Bologna, 1971), 223–7

O. Mischiati: 'Adriano Banchieri (1568–1634): profilo biografico e
bibliografia dell'opere', Annuario 1965–1970 del Conservatorio di
Musica 'G.B. Martini' di Bologna (1971), 38–201

W. Kirkendale: L'Aria di Fiorenza, id est Il ballo di Gran Duca
(Florence, 1972)

W.S. May: Adriano Banchieri: Late Sacred Motets: the 'Seconda
Prattica' in Sacred Music (diss., Tulane U., 1975)

A. Wernli: Studien zum literarischen und musikalischen Werk
Adriano Banchieris (1568–1634) (Berne and Stuttgart, 1981) [incl.
list of Banchieri's lost and non-musical works]

K.G. Fellerer: 'Adriano Banchieri und die kirchliche Orgelmusik',
Orgel, Orgelmusik und Orgelspiel: Festschrift Michael Schneider
zum 75. Geburtstag, ed. Christoph Wolff (Kassel, 1985), 87–96

R. Groth: 'Italienische Musiktheorie im 17. Jahrhundert', Italienische
Musiktheorie im 16. und 17. Jahrhundert: Antikenrezeption und
Satzlehre, ed. F. Zaminer (Darmstadt, 1989), 307–79

M. Farahat: Adriano Banchieri and the Madrigal Comedy (diss., U.
of Chicago, 1991)

WILLIAM S. MAY (with FRANS WIERING)

Banci, Giovanni (*fl* 1619). Italian composer. The only
information about him – that he came from Argenta and
worked in Bologna – appears on the title-page of his one
extant publication: *Il primo libro de sacri concerti . . . et
. . . le litanie della BVM* (Venice, 1619). He was typical
of many modest church composers in northern Italy in
the early 17th century who wrote competently in the new

concertato style for smaller church choirs, using both up-to-date duet and trio textures and also more conventional four- and five-part ones. (J. Roche: *North Italian Church Music in the Age of Monteverdi*, Oxford, 1984)

JEROME ROCHE

Bancquart, Alain (*b* Dieppe, 20 June 1934). French composer and viola player. He studied the viola, chamber music and composition (with Milhaud) at the Paris Conservatoire (1952–9). He became principal viola in the Orchestre National de France (1962–73), where he was later artistic director (1975–6). He was made principal music inspector at the Ministry of Culture and Communication (1977) and became responsible for producing the programmes *Perspectives du XXème siècle* on Radio France (1977–84). He was appointed professor of composition at the Paris Conservatoire in 1984. In 1986 he received the *Grand Prix National de la Musique* and the following year the *Grand Prix de la Musique Symphonique* awarded by SACEM.

From the start he adopted a rigorously serial, atonal language, later (from 1968) making systematic use of quarter tones, defective modes and non-octaves. His lyrical temperament expresses itself above all in chamber and orchestral forms, in concert works and in five symphonies of great breadth. His inspiration frequently comes from poetry, as in *Les cinq dits de Jean-Claude Renard* (1987), and a mystical impression is evident in his work, particularly his vast fifth symphony *Partage de Midi* (1992), after Paul Claudel's play.

WORKS
(*selective list*)

Orch: Sève, 1961; Sym. in 3 movts, 1965; Va Conc., 1965; Passages, 1967; Jeux pour lumière, str trio, orch, 1969; Palimpsestes, 1969; Simple, 1973; Sym. no.1, 1981; Sym. no.2, 1981; Sym. no.3 'Fragments d'Apocalypse', T, 2B, orch, 1983; Sym. no.4, 1987; Ma manière d'arbre 1: De l'étrange circulation de la sève, gui, 24 fl, 1990; Sym. no.5 'Partage du midi' (P. Claudel), Bar, orch, 1992

Chbr: Explosante fixe, hp, str qnt, 1972; Rosace, str qt, 1973; Ma manière d'oiseau, fl, 9 insts, 1978; Chbr Sym., fl, vc, ens, 1980; Sonata, 2 pf, 1985; Nocturne, str trio, 16 wind insts, 1987; Diurne, fl, 11 str, version for fl, str qt, 1988; Ma manière d'arbre 2: Du lent sommeil des feuilles, va, 12 wind insts, 1992; Ricercare 1, str qt, 1992; Livre pour 2 orgues 'Hommage à Olivier Messiaen', 2 org, 1993; Ma manière d'arbre 3: Le grand calcul des arbres, vn, 15 insts, 1993; Ma manière de nuages, wind qnt, 1993

Principal publishers: Jobert, Ricordi

MICHEL RIGONI

Baniera, Antonio. *See* BAGNIERA, ANTONIO.

Band (i) (Fr. *bande*; Ger. *Kapelle*; It., Sp. *banda*). An instrumental ensemble. This article deals exclusively with Western uses of the term 'band'.

I. Introduction. II. History to 1800. III. Mixed wind bands. IV. Brass bands. V. Jazz bands. VI. Rock bands.

I. Introduction

The word 'band' has many applications in music, more or less precise. In a general sense, it may refer to almost any ensemble of instruments. When used without qualification it commonly applies to a group of musicians playing combinations of brass and percussion instruments (a brass band; see §IV below) or woodwind, brass and percussion (e.g. a wind band, a circus band or a symphonic or concert band; see §III below). The '24 violons' of Louis XIV were called 'la grande bande' to distinguish them from Lully's 'petits violons', and Charles II's similar ensemble was known as 'the king's band'. By extension,

'band' came to mean orchestra in colloquial British usage: the two terms can also be used interchangeably. In Europe the wind and percussion band is descended from the 'high' or 'loud' groups (*see* ALTA (i); and see §II (a) below) of the medieval period and from the civic waits or the *Stadtpfeifer*, who generally performed outdoors and therefore used predominantly loud brass and percussion instruments. Bands were often mobile, had a vernacular appeal (they usually performed lighter forms of music, often to a non-paying audience; as such they have also served as useful propaganda tools, or at least assisted in promoting nationalistic or patriotic fervour), and were often associated with specific military or civic duties and were thus uniformed. The ORCHESTRA, on the other hand, is descended from the medieval 'low' or 'soft' instruments (strings and softer wind instruments), and usually plays indoors. It was originally associated with the church or the nobility, and later with formal concerts of more 'serious' and sophisticated music for which audiences paid.

'Band' is often qualified by the dominating instrument or family of instruments, as in brass band, HORN BAND, STEEL BAND, accordion band (piano accordions of various sizes with percussion instruments), banjo band, pipe band (bagpipes and drums), fife and drum band, and flute band (a marching band of flutes and percussion found particularly in Northern Ireland). In a JUG BAND or a WASHBOARD BAND the eponymous instrument plays an integrated part in the musical texture rather than a dominant role.

Bands may also be named according to their function rather than their constitution (although mixed wind bands are often misleadingly described as 'military bands' whether they have a military role or not), as in the dance band, the theatre band (or 'pit band', if it plays in the theatre pit), the marching band and the showband. The stage band is a group of musicians playing either on stage or behind the scenes; a familiar example is the band in Mozart's *Don Giovanni* (1787), and many instances may be found in French and Italian operas by Meyerbeer, Spontini, Verdi and his successors. In Italy it is called 'banda', as is also sometimes the brass section – or the brass and percussion together – of an orchestra.

Bands may also be named according to, or in a way that associates them with, the style of music that they play, as in jazz band and big band (related to the dance band; see §V below), pop, skiffle, rock and folk bands (see §VI below). During the 20th century the words 'band' and 'group' have often been used synonymously in popular culture.

See also MARCH and MILITARY MUSIC.

II. History to 1800

1. Before 1600. 2. 1600–1800: (i) Military music (ii) Harmonie (iii) Civic and church bands.

1. BEFORE 1600.   The earliest wind bands in Europe were well established by the 13th century; they were similar to those of the Near East, consisting of shawms, trumpets and drums (*see* NAQQĀRAKHĀNA). By about 1400 the trumpets and drums had split off into separate ceremonial ensembles (fig.1). Early in the 15th century a slide instrument was added to the shawms, and the ensemble, consisting of three or four musicians (one or two shawms, bombard and trombone), quickly developed (by 1475) a highly sophisticated performance tradition (fig.2). This was the group of choice for dancing, processions, banquets and other secular ritual occasions

1. *Mounted trumpeters and kettledrum players: woodcuts by Hans Burgkmair I from the 'Triumphzug Maximilians', c1516–18*

(*see* ALTA (i)). By the late 15th century it was a preferred ensemble throughout Europe, as every major court and important city patronized one. Courtly ensembles were engaged from the beginning exclusively for their musical capabilities, as was also the case in many German cities where the musicians were known as *Stadtpfeiferei* ('town pipers'; *see* STADTPFEIFER). In many regions, however, city bands initially combined a watchman function with their musical duties, which was reflected in such names as 'waits' in England and *wachters* in the Low Countries (*see* WAIT. The watch function was dropped almost everywhere by the late 15th century, although the bands continued to perform from church and city towers. Soon after 1500 some shawm-based ensembles expanded to six or even eight performers, and at the same time these musicians were expected to command a wider range of instrumental doublings, including cornetti, crumhorns and recorders. Musical demands also expanded, as wind players increasingly joined singers in all manner of performances, including those within church services (*see* PERFORMING PRACTICE, §I, 4). In the early 16th century

the ensemble reached an artistic peak with musicians such as Tromboncino and Susato, whose careers were rooted in the wind band tradition. By about 1550 a new fashion for string instruments (especially the violin) began to mount a challenge, and by late in the 16th century the artistic position of winds began to decline. The decline was gradual, however, and until the early 17th century leading chapel masters and composers (such as Hans Leo Hassler) continued to be associated with wind bands.

See also SHAWM.

2. 1600–1800.

(i) Military music. Musicians in the army of the German Empire were usually supplied by a guild of trumpeters and kettledrummers which had certain privileges. Towards the end of the Thirty Years War (1646) the Brandenburg Dragoon Guards had a band of shawms (two treble and one tenor, with a dulcian for the bass) and drums. Under Louis XIV bands were organized in the French army after the model of those in the German regiments. With the development of the new French *hautbois* (oboe) around the middle of the century, the French bands, probably gradually, adopted the new instrument; by 1665 each company of *Mousquetaires* had three *hautbois*, and the number soon increased to four, including a tenor instrument (possibly at first a *cromorne*, later a *taille de hautbois*; *see* OBOE §I, 2(ii)) and a dulcian or bassoon. Many of the marches and *airs* written for them by Lully, Philidor *l'aîné*, Martin Hotteterre and others are preserved in the manuscripts of the Philidor Collection under the title *Partition de plusieurs marches et batteries de tambour tant françoises qu'étrangères avec les airs de fifre et de hautbois a 3 et 4 parties* (F-Pn Rés. F.671; see ex.1). The use in this period of the word 'hautbois' for both the shawm and the new instrument makes it sometimes difficult to determine which instruments were intended, and it is unclear how long shawms or transitional instruments remained in use in the French

2. *Musicians playing trombones, shawms and trumpets: detail from 'Procession of the True Cross in the Piazza S Marco' by Gentile Bellini, 1496 (Galleria dell'Accademia, Venice)*

Ex.1 *L'assemblée* (*F-Pn*; printed in Kastner, 1848)

army and elsewhere. Many of the pieces in the *Partition de plusieurs marches* could be played by either shawms or oboes. The bassoon appears to have replaced the one-piece dulcian by the end of the century.

The new *hautbois* soon spread, through military and diplomatic contact, across Europe. Johann Philipp Krieger's *Lustige Feld-Music* of 1704 is an early German example of music for the new ensemble of French *hautbois*. Krieger advised certain doublings of the four parts in the open air, and by the end of the 17th century such bands often had six members: a band of six young 'Hautboisten', led by a French musician who trained and directed them, played at Zeitz castle in 1698 and was sent to Vienna at the request of the Habsburg court in 1700. Hans Friedrich von Fleming noted in 1726 that bands of French *hautbois* consisted of six instruments – two trebles, two *tailles* and two bassoons – 'because the [French] *hautbois* were not as loud, but sounded much sweeter, than the shawms' (Fleming, p.181). The combination of three treble *hautbois*, a tenor and two bassoons was also common. By 1720 the tenor instruments had been replaced by horns in many bands in central Europe: such ensembles are depicted in engravings from the period, including one from Leipzig dated 1720 (with three treble *hautbois*, two horns and a bassoon), and music for woodwinds and horns had begun to appear (the earliest dated work is a *Marche* by J.G.C. Störl for pairs of oboes, horns and bassoons, dated 1711). Some bands had a trumpet instead of horns; Fleming considered this combination characteristically English. In Prussia, a trumpet was added to the wind sextet. Bands of *Hautboisten* played for marching; they also played morning and evening before the residence

of the commander and when the commander entertained (then they might sometimes play string instruments). As well, they provided music for processions and other public ceremonies (*see* FESTIVAL, §2). A collection of music assembled between about 1712 and 1725 with pieces scored for two or three oboes, *taille* and bassoon or for three oboes, trumpet and bassoon (most with two bassoon parts) survives as the *Sonsfeldische Musikaliensammlung* (*D-HRD* Fü3741a). The *Douze grands hautbois* of the French court still consisted solely of double-reed instruments in 1722, when they played for the coronation of Louis XV (*see* OBOE, fig.4). Elsewhere in Europe bands had become somewhat larger by the middle of the century with the doubling of the upper parts, and ensembles of eight or ten musicians were not unusual. Also about the middle of the century, clarinets began to be used in place of, or as a supplement to, the oboes. An engraving published in London in 1753 depicts a band of two oboes, two clarinets, two horns and two bassoons preceding a company of grenadiers (fig.3) and in 1762 the Swiss Guards in France were authorized to have a band consisting of four each of oboes, clarinets, horns and bassoons. In 1763 Frederick the Great stipulated that Prussian army bands should consist of two oboes, two clarinets, two horns and two bassoons. However, bands of six players in which the treble instruments were either oboes or clarinets remained common, and many musicians played both. There were also bands of other combinations: the grenadier company in Salzburg had a band of two clarinets, two fifes and two drums in 1766 (*see also* FELDMUSIK).

At the Restoration in England the band of the King's Life Guards consisted of trumpets and kettledrums, but the practice of using the 'hautboy' as a military instrument was soon imported from France: oboes were appointed to the Horse Grenadier Guards in 1678 and to the Foot Guards in 1684–5. The fife, use of which had been discontinued during the period of the Commonwealth, reappeared in the British army in the mid-18th century. The cavalry was still normally restricted to trumpets and kettledrums, although some regiments adopted fifes and drums for unmounted playing. Horns were usual in British army bands by mid-century. Handel wrote marches and other pieces for two oboes, two horns and basso (and also two marches for trumpet, two oboes and basso). His 'Grand Overture of Warlike Instruments', or *Music for the Royal Fireworks* (1749) is scored for an expanded version of the ensemble, with the addition of kettledrums. Clarinets were in general use after the middle of the century; the common scoring for two clarinets, two horns and bassoon is exemplified by J.C. Bach's four *Military Pieces* (the bassoon part may often have been doubled). In 1762 an ensemble was brought from Germany to serve as the 'Royal Artillery Band': it consisted of 'eight men, who must also be capable to play upon the violoncello, bass, violin and flute as other common instruments' and was provided with two trumpets, two horns, two bassoons and 'four hautbois or clarinets' (Farmer, C(i)1904, p.36). A perhaps not uncommon arrangement was described by Richard Hind in *The Discipline of the Light Horse* (London, 1778, pp.206–7): 'in the year 1764 . . . each troop [had] one trumpet, who when they are dismounted, form[ed] a band of music, consisting of two French horns, two clarinetts and two bassoons'.

3. Band of two oboes, two clarinets, two horns and two bassoons: engraving, 1753 (National Army Museum, London)

European musical traditions, including bands, were taken to North America by colonists and military units. Bands took an important role in musical life there and distinct customs soon developed (see §III, 4 below).

An important development during the 18th century was the adoption by European military bands (and orchestras) of 'Turkish' or 'janissary' music (*see* JANISSARY MUSIC). In a miniature from the early 18th century (fig.4) a Turkish *mehter* (military band) is shown playing *boru* (trumpet), *zil* (cymbals), *davul* (cylindrical drum played on one side with a drumstick, on the other with a switch of twigs) and *kös* (large kettledrums). Such ensembles might also include the *zurna* (shawm) and *nakkare* (small kettledrums). The bands of the Sultan of Turkey's elite troops (the janissaries) made a great impression on the European armies during the wars of the 17th century and the first half of the 18th. The Sultan presented a band to Augustus II of Poland (reigned 1697–1733) and an imitation of Turkish music was performed at the Court of Empress Anne of Russia in 1739. A Turkish band had been added to the Austrian Commander Freiherr von Trenck's troop by 1741, and in the War of the Austrian Succession (1740–48) the French Marshal de Saxe's Uhlans adopted this music too. Prussian regiments used janissary instruments and later engaged Turkish musicians to play them. Around the mid-18th century European bands began to add 'Turkish' instruments, first a large bass drum, later cymbals and triangle. The Turkish crescent was added at the end of the century. Some percussionists were Moors or black; they were dressed in an exotic manner and used extravagant gestures. By the 1780s a 'Turkish band' in Europe was usually one of European instruments with added percussion and a piccolo; a band reported in Vienna in 1796 included oboes, bassoons, horns and clarinets, a trumpet, a triangle, a piccolo, a very large drum, an ordinary drum and a pair of cymbals (Schönfeld, *Jahrbuch der Tonkünst in Wien und Prag*, Vienna, 1796, p.98). This band was not engaged in military duties, but rather played outdoor concerts in the summer. British bands often added a

tambourine. The janissary influence remained visible at the end of the 20th century in the tiger- and leopard-skin aprons used by bass drummers and in their elaborate drumstick flourishes, while the shape of the marching band's bell-lyra recalled the Turkish crescent.

Towards the end of the 18th century military bands added more instruments, partly because the increase of percussion under the influence of janissary music made it necessary, for purposes of audibility, to increase the wind as well. More clarinets were added: there were six in the Grenadier Guards in 1794 and in the bands provided from 1795 in France by the Conservatoire Nationale de Musique (founded as the Ecole de Musique de la Garde Nationale by Bernard Sarrette in 1792 to supply the need for military musicians). New instruments came into use: a Divertimento written by Thomas Attwood in collaboration with Pleyel and Storace was scored for pairs of clarinets, basset-horns, horns and bassoons with serpent. An arrangement of J.C. Bach's Overture to *Lucio Silla* copied by Henry Pick in about 1800 includes parts for two flutes, two oboes, three clarinets, two horns, two trumpets, two bassoons, serpent and alto and tenor trombones; some of his other arrangements include parts for side drum. French bands grew larger and more varied during the Revolution. Catel's *Ouverture militaire*, for example, includes parts for two *petites flûtes*, two flutes, two clarinets, two trumpets, two horns, three trombones, two bassoons, serpent and timpani. By about 1810 the larger European military bands had reached their present size (Table 1), having further increased the number of clarinets and added small clarinets and in Germany often basset-horns; the brass instruments regularly included trombones while extra pairs of horns and trumpets made different crookings simultaneously available. In England the serpent was supported by the bass horn and in the German lands by the double bassoon (ex.2). A typical French infantry band of 1809 consisted of piccolo, E♭ clarinet, six to eight B♭ clarinets, two bassoons, two horns, trumpet, two or three trombones, one or two

4. *March of the mehter (military band) with (from left to right) six boru (trumpets), six pairs of zil (cymbals), eight davul (cylindrical drums) and in the background three pairs of kös (kettledrums): miniature from the 'Sūrnūma' ('Book of Festivals') of Ahmed III, c1720 (TR-Itks III.A.3593, f.172r)*

serpents, side drum, bass drum, cymbals and *pavillon chinois* (Turkish crescent).

(ii) Harmonie. From the end of the 17th century bands of *hautbois* often did double duty, playing military music and for outdoor festivals as required, but also playing indoors for court events, either as an independent ensemble or as part of an orchestra. The eight *hautbois* of the *Mousquetaires* played for divertissements, water parties, balls and other events at the French court. Two horn players appointed to the Württemberg court in 1713 were expected to play both in the orchestra and in the regimental band. When the Treaty of Utrecht brought peace in 1713, the band was employed for baptisms, balls,

church services and carnival, and accompanied members of the royal family on their travels. Later in the century, contracts for the wind players hired by the Esterházy court in 1761 indicate that they too performed both military and court duty. It was from such groups that the 'Harmonien' developed; the term was applied both to groups of wind instruments employed by the aristocracy (and others) and to small military bands. The size of *Harmonie* ensembles ranged from two instruments to above 20 (21 were required for a special piece by Georg Druschetzky, performed for the coronation ceremonies for Leopold II in Pressburg in 1790), but most had between five and nine instruments, most commonly in

TABLE 1: European military bands, late 18th century 19th century

	England		France		Austria	
	1794 Grenadier Guards	c1820 Royal Artillery	1795 Corps d'Élite	1825 infantry	1800 Line Regiment	1827 infantry
Piccolo	–	–	–	–	–	1
Flute	1	2	1	2	2	–
Oboe	–	3	–	4	2	–
Clarinet	6	11	6	14	2–4	12
Bassoon	3	3	3	6	2	1
Horn	3	2	2	4	–	4
Trumpet	1	2	1	2	2	7
Keyed trumpet	–	–	–	–	–	2
Keyed bugle	–	3	–	–	–	–
Trombone	–	3	–	–	–	–
Ophicleide	–	1	–	–	–	–
Serpent	2	2	1	–	1[a]	1
Bass–horn	–	2	–	–	–	–
Percussion	1	5	2	–	4	1

[a] or double bassoon

Ex.2 Anon.: *Ungarischer Grenadier Marsch* (Berlin, c1822) three or four groups – horns and bassoons, with either oboes or clarinets or both – and in pairs (sometimes there was a single bassoon part, played by two bassoons). Flutes, english horns and basset-horns were also occasionally used and a double bass or double bassoon was sometimes added (especially towards the end of the 18th century). *Harmonie* bands played at the Concert Spirituel in Paris in the 1760s and 1770s, and Mozart's Serenade in B♭ K361/370*a* for 12 wind instruments and double bass was performed at a public concert in Vienna in 1784. Although *Harmonien* were supported primarily by aristocrats, similar ensembles played in the streets and for less exalted patrons. Mozart's Serenade in E♭ K375 (1781), originally written for an ensemble of clarinets, horns and bassoons, was played in the street (the composer commended the players' performance); it was reworked the following year for pairs of oboes, clarinets, horns and bassoons, perhaps with one of the aristocratic ensembles in mind. The latter combination was popularized by Emperor Joseph II in Vienna in the 1780s. His ensemble was made up of the best wind players of the day, and played a repertory consisting primarily of opera transcriptions. Many *Harmonien* had been disbanded by the end of the 18th century, but some remained active well into the 19th (*see* HARMONIEMUSIK).

(iii) *Civic and church bands.* Bands of musicians continued to form part of the civic establishment throughout the 17th and 18th centuries and into the 19th. They performed civic duties, such as sounding Retreat, and played for celebrations, processions and church services, public and private balls, parties and concerts. To match the wide variety of duties assigned to him the town musician required skill on several instruments (including string instruments: see, for example, the account of a town musician's training in Quantz's *Lebenslauf*) and a wide repertory, including signal pieces, dance pieces, conversation music and, in the 18th century, sinfonias and concertos (*see also* STADTPFEIFER). Some town musicians were retired regimental musicians; others came from families in which the profession was traditional. In their competition with other musical organizations, such as the guild of trumpeters and kettledrummers, the town bands had acquired certain rights and privileges governing, for example, where and when they might play. By the end of the 18th century, however, the social structures that supported this order were disappearing and with them the bands of all-purpose musicians: most bands in Germany had disappeared by the 1790s, and in England many were dissolved at the time of the Napoleonic wars. In France new types of bands sprang up to fill in music the ideals of the new Revolutionary order. Gossec became conductor of the Corps de Musique de la Garde Nationale (with Sarrette) and wrote fervently Revolutionary music for it, beginning with a *Te Deum* performed on 14 July 1790 by a band of over 300 woodwind and brass instruments, serpents and violas, with 300 drums and a chorus of as many as 1000 (violas were not used in subsequent outdoor works). Similar works as well as purely instrumental pieces by Gossec, Méhul and Grétry were performed on state occasions by bands of between 30 and 70 wind players, together with drums.

In Russia a unique type of band was established in 1751 by J.A. Mareš: it consisted of an ensemble of hunting horns ranging from 30 cm to 2 metres in length, each able to play only one or two notes; horn bands of up to 22 players visited Western Europe in 1817 and 1833 and sets of the instruments were exhibited in Vienna as late as 1892 (see HORN BAND). Similar bands of about 13 players were known in Bohemia and Saxony.

In England by about 1740 the singing of the choir had begun to be accompanied in parish churches – which usually had no organ – by an instrument or two, such as a bassoon or bass viol on the bass part and occasionally an oboe to double the melody (the tenor part) an octave higher. By about 1770 'church bands' included singers and two to five or six instrumentalists. Their music was sometimes known as GALLERY MUSIC because they often performed from a specially built gallery. The instrumentalists were an integral part of the ensemble, supporting the vocal lines and leading the singers. Before the turn of the century double reeds predominated (bassoon, oboe and occasionally *vox humana*), but after about 1800 string instruments (bass viol, cello, violin) were more usual, supplemented by clarinets and, later, brass instruments such as keyed bugles, cornopeans and ophicleides. The instrumentation was never standardized, but depended on local resources. Some bands remained active into the 20th century, but most had been replaced by reed organs or barrel organs by the middle of the 19th (*see also* PSALMODY (ii), §I and fig.2).

An ensemble of double-reed instruments, known as the HAUTBOIS D'EGLISE, was used for a similar purpose – to accompany the singing of Lutheran chorales – in Protestant Switzerland between about 1760 and 1810. The instruments included two *dessus de musette*, oboes, recorders or flutes on the upper parts, a *basse de musette* to play the tenor and a *basson d'amour*.

III. Mixed wind bands

1. Terminology. 2. Military bands. 3. Civilian bands. 4. American wind bands. 5. Repertory.

1. TERMINOLOGY. The term 'military band' dates from the late 18th century and denoted at that time a regimental band consisting of woodwind, brass and percussion instruments. During the following century it came to be applied as well to civilian bands of similar constitution. With the growth of civilian wind bands for all sorts of activities (outdoor entertainment, marching etc.) the epithet 'military' became increasingly inappropriate; the more general 'mixed wind band' is accordingly used here to define the whole group of bands, 'military band' being reserved for a mixed wind band maintained by the armed forces. The words used in other languages as equivalents for 'military band' support a more general designation since many of them make no reference to a specific military function: Fr. *bande, harmonie*; Ger. *Blaskapelle, Blasorchester, (Militär-)Musikkorps*; It. *banda, corpo di musica*; Sp. *banda*. A wind ensemble is distinguished from a wind band in having one player to each part.

2. MILITARY BANDS. The band of the Garde Républicaine, among the first of the new, larger bands founded immediately after the French Revolution, set the pattern for the 19th century. A new concept, that of the symphonic wind band, in which groups of like instruments serve in sections analogous to those of the orchestra, began to gain prominence; the new ensemble is apparent in works such as Beethoven's March WOO24 of 1816. The instrumentation of bands evolved separately in different regions, but all came to conform to the new concept (see Table 1). The development of valved brass instruments by both

Stölzel and Blühmel early in the second decade of the 19th century was of overwhelming importance, allowing the entire range of brass instruments to play chromatically.

Infantry bandmasters in Germany and Britain have from the onset of the valve era, out of conservative feeling and practical consideration, generally kept to the well-balanced instrumentation advocated by military journals of the mid-19th century (exemplified in England by C. Boosé's *Military Journal* from *c*1845). As shown in ex.2, this consists of a contemporary orchestral wind and percussion group augmented to fulfil band requirements and filled out with a few extra instruments. Saxophones, invented for the band, were first used in French infantry bands about 1845. The treble is led by cornets, flugelhorns or trumpets and the bass is supplied by valved basses; a string bass is often added in concert performance. The only other instrument foreign to the orchestra is the euphonium, which helps with nearly everything prominent in the tenor and bass registers.

In Austria, the new style of military band, with choirs of woodwind instruments and brass, the clarinets predominating, is mentioned in documents from 1800 onwards. A report of the *Hofkriegsrat* to Emperor Franz I (20 September 1820) draws attention to the large size of some ensembles – 50 to 60 men – and their expensive and 'unmilitary' dress, all due to the officers' desire for prestige and magnificence. Two years later the emperor decreed that infantry bands be limited to 34 men apiece and regimental staff bands to ten. The combination was determined by individual bandmasters. Wind instruments with keys and brass instruments with valves were adopted early in Austria: the *Allgemeine Schule für die Militärmusik*(Vienna, 1845) confirms that trumpets, flugelhorns, horns and even trombones had changed to valves by this time. Table 2 shows the composition of Austrian military bands in 1820 and 1845. The band of Fahrbach's *Organizzazione* is a typical Austrian infantry band, with a large clarinet section, trumpets of different sizes, and the soft-sounding flugelhorns and euphonium. The army Kapellmeister Andreas Leonhardt (1800–66) introduced far-reaching reforms in Austro-Hungarian military music with his *Systemisierung der Militär-Musikbanden* of 1851. The strength of each band was increased to 60 men and the bands of the infantry, cavalry and jäger were made similar. These ensembles remained largely unchanged until World War I. Leonhardt's reforms were influential in the USA and Japan, and above all in Prussia.

In Prussia soon after 1800 different ensembles were assigned to different branches of the military: trumpet corps to the cavalry; horn bands to the jäger; and mixed wind bands to the infantry (ten 'Hoboisten', or military bandsmen), the grenadiers (18 men) and the guards (24 men). In 1816 line regiments were permitted to expand to 30 members, and Prussian bands developed in a similar way to the French and Austrian ensembles, with woodwind and chromatic brass instruments complemented by percussion instruments from janissary music. Wilhelm Wieprecht (1802–72), director of music of the corps of guards from 1838, was in contact with Leonhardt, and reformed the military bands of Prussia after the Austrian model. Wieprecht played a leading role in the development of new valved brass instruments including the *Tenorhorn* (*Bass-Flügelhorn*), the *Tenorbasshorn* in B♭, the *Sopran-* and *Altkornett* and the *Bass-Tuba*. He specialized in large-scale concerts: in Lüneburg in 1843 he conducted

TABLE 2: Austrian military bands, 1820 and 1845

1820 Kriegsarchiv, Vienna	1845 J. Fahrbach, *Organizzazione della musica militare* (Milan, 1846)
	1 piccolo
2 flutes	1 flute
2 oboes	2 oboes
	1 A♭ clarinet
1 F clarinet	
	1 E♭ clarinet
2 C clarinets	
	*c*13 B♭ clarinets
2 B♭ basset-horns	
2 bassoons	2 bassoons
1 double bassoon	1 double bassoon
2 horns	2 E♭ horns
	2 A♭ horns
2 trumpets	1 high B♭ trumpet
	1 obbligato E♭ trumpet
	8 E♭ trumpets
	2 natural trumpets
	2 B♭ bass trumpets
	2 B♭ flugelhorns
	1 bass flugelhorn
	1 euphonium (bombardino or obbligato trombone)
1 tenor trombone	3 trombones
1 bass trombone	
1 C serpent	
1 bass-horn	3 basses (ophicleides and bombardons)
side drum	side drum
bass drum	bass drum
cymbals	2 pairs of cymbals
triangle	
	2 Turkish crescents

the entire musical corps of the 10th Deutsches Bundesarmeekorps, comprising over 1000 bandsmen. Wieprecht's ideal ensemble consisted of two flutes, two oboes, 11 clarinets, two *Tenorhörner*, euphonium, two tenor trombones, bass trombone, four *Bombardons*(tubas), two bassoons and two double bassoons, four trumpets, two soprano and two alto cornets, four horns, drums, cymbals, triangle and Turkish crescent. In Prussia, as elsewhere, military bands undertook a variety of musical and cultural tasks, bringing the army into contact with the civilian population. The repertory included music for military use, original works for military band and transcriptions of the latest music. Table 3 shows the instrumentation of European military bands in the mid-19th century.

The instrumentation of the military bands at a competition at the Paris Exposition of 1867 provides a useful survey of the state of European military bands of the time (Table 4). The Prussian band, however, consisted of the combined musical corps of the Prussian guards; the band of the Garde de Paris was made up of professional musicians recruited from the theatres. The first prize was shared by Austria (band of the 73rd Infantry Regiment), Prussia and the Garde de Paris. Table 5 shows the instruments used in late 19th-century bands.

In 1873 a course to train bandmasters was set up at the Musikhochschule in Berlin. In the following decades Berlin became a centre for the training of military bandmasters, not only for Prussia and other German states, but also for some non-European countries such as Japan. Around 1900 there were some 560 military bands in Germany with 23–40 musicians in each, but after World War I there remained only 140 military bands,

TABLE 3: European military bands, 1838–52

	Prussia		France					England
	1838	1838	1845 11th Light	1845 74th Line	1845 1st Line	1845 62nd Line	1852	1848 Grenadier Guards
	infantry	cavalry					Guides (constituted according to Sax's reform)	
	(reformed by Wieprecht)							
Piccolo	—	—	1	1	1	1	1	— } 2
Flute	2	—	—	—	—	—	1	
Oboe	2	—	—	—	—	—	2	2
Ab clarinet	2	—	—	—	—	—	—	—
Eb clarinet	—	—	1	1	1	1	2	3
Bb clarinet	8	—	12	15	20	12	4	8[a]
Soprano saxophone	—	—	—	—	—	—	1	—
Alto saxophone	—	—	—	—	—	—	1	—
Tenor saxophone	—	—	—	—	—	—	1	—
Bass saxophone	—	—	—	—	—	—	1	—
Bassoon	2	—	—	—	—	—	—	3
Double bassoon	2	—	—	—	—	—	—	—
Horn	4	—	—	—	—	—	2	4
Piccolo cornet	—	1	3	4	—	—	—	—
Eb cornet	4	2	—	—	—	—	} 2	—
Bb cornet	4	4	2	4	2	3		—
Trumpet	4	8	2	1	—	—	4	4[b]
Eb flugelhorn	—	—	—	—	—	—	2	—
Bb flugelhorn	—	—	—	2	—	—	4	—
Eb alto horn	—	—	—	1	1	2	4	1
Baritone	2	2	—	—	—	—	2	1
Euphonium	1	1	—	—	—	—	4	—
Trombone	4	—	4	5	6	3	3	3
Ophicleide	—	—	6	8	6	6	—	2
Tuba	4	3	—	—	—	—	4	1
Percussion	5	—	7	7	6	6	?	5
Timpani	—	—	—	—	—	—	1	—

[a] 1 doubling basset-horn
[b] 1 in Bb, 2 in F, 1 bass trumpet

each with 27–37 members: civil wind music had mostly disappeared also. Military bands frequently played concerts consisting of marches and arrangements by Wieprecht and others of his generation. With the rise of National Socialism military music came to be regarded as an important tool, and many new bands were formed. Between 1935 and 1945 the band of the Luftwaffe occupied a special position: it followed the band of the US Air Force in including a larger woodwind section than usual, and its Inspector of Music Hans-Felix Husadel (1897–1964) commissioned new works from leading German composers. With the founding of the two German states in 1949 there were two separate military music organizations. In the DDR the Ministry of Defense had a band of 72 and each corps had a band for marching and for concerts. The literature was restricted mostly to new works and arrangements of workers' songs. Each corps also had a big band for dancing. The Luftwaffe band became the model for the new Bundeswehr music corps of the Federal Republic of Germany after 1956. From the 1950s there were bands for the border guards (four), the army (13), the air force (four) and the navy (two); at first each band had about 50 members, but the number was increased to 60 in 1958. There were also specialized ensembles, including a ceremonial ensemble (founded 1959) and a big band (founded 1969). In 1998 the military music of Germany consisted of one staff band, 21 bands attached to various army, navy and air force divisions, a training band and a big band.

French military bands in the 19th century included *orchestres d'harmonie* of woodwind, brass and percussion instruments; fanfare bands of brass instruments, saxophones and percussion; and the cavalry trumpet corps of brass instruments and timpani. Instrumentation was strongly influenced by the many new wind instruments developed during the 19th century by makers such as Adolphe Sax. Infantry bands of the 1830s were organized on an extravagant scale: they included full woodwind and the classic brass, strengthened by cornets, keyed bugles, alto ophicleides or clavicors, and bass ophicleides (the first edition of Kastner's *Cours d'instrumentation*, 1839, includes an example in score). The addition of a 'bande turque' made a colourful effect. However, bands were soon 'improved' by the mass of very efficient saxhorns and flugelhorns with which Sax and others smothered the old nucleus, producing a densely homogenous, somewhat bland sonority; saxhorns were widely adopted by French bands following a reorganization in 1845. Leading bands were expanded for concert performance by adding every sort of woodwind instrument, and even in some cases two desks of cellos to warm the lower register. The French model, which grew to enormous proportions, was largely followed in Italy and Spain as well. A peculiarity of French marching music is the *clairon* march, in which horn calls alternate with the band. At the end of the 20th century the Musique de l'Air of Paris was one of the leading professional wind bands in Europe.

A 'military music class' was founded at Kneller Hall in Twickenham in 1857. In 1865 it became the Royal Military School of Music. Its influence on music may be traced in the growth and improvement of the Royal

TABLE 4: European military bands, 1867

	Austria[a]	Baden[b]	Bavaria[c]	Belgium[d]	France[e]	France[f]	Netherlands[g]	Prussia[h]	Russia[i]	Spain[j]
Piccolo	1	1	1	—	2	—	} 4		1	2
Flute	2	2	2	2	2	1	1		1	2
Oboe	—	—	—	2	3	2	2	} 4	2	2
English Horn	—	—	—	—	—	—	—		1	—
A♭ clarinet	2	—	—	—	—	—	—	1	—	1
E♭ clarinet	4	2	4	2	3	4	2	4	2	2
B♭ clarinet	12	15	10	16	12	8	10	16	15	13
Basset-horn	—	—	—	—	—	—	—	—	1	—
Bass clarinet	—	—	1	—	—	—	—	—	1	—
Bassoon	2	2	1	4	—	—	2	6	2	3
Double basson	2 clariofon	—	—	—	—	—	—	4	1	2
Soprano saxophone	—	—	—	}	—	}	}	—	1	—
Contralto saxophone	—	—	—		—			—	—	—
Alto saxophone	—	—	—	} 4	—	} 8	} 4	—	2	—
Tenor saxophone	—	—	—		—			—	2	—
Baritone saxophone	—	—	—		—			—	3	—
Bass saxophone	—	—	—		—			—	—	—
Horn	4	—	5	5	3	2	4	4	8	4
E♭ cornet	—	3	—	—	—	—	—	—	—	1
B♭ cornet	2	1	3	2	4	4	2	4	2	2
E♭ (D) alto cornet	—	—	—	—	—	—	—	4	—	—
B♭ flugelhorn	6	3	3	2	—	—	1	—	—	2
E♭ trumpet	} 12	4	5 in F	} 4	} 3	} 3	} 4	8	8	6 in F
B♭ trumpet		1	3					—	—	—
B♭ tenor cor	—	2	2	—	—	—	—	4	—	—
Alto saxotromba	—	—	} 2	—	2	—	—	—	—	—
Baritone saxotromba	—	—		—	2	—	—	—	—	—
E♭ soprano saxhorn	—	—	—	—	1	1	—	—	—	—
B♭ contralto saxhorn	—	—	—	—	1	2	—	—	—	—
E♭ alto saxhorn	—	—	—	1	—	3	—	—	—	—
B♭ baritone saxhorn	—	—	—	—	—	2	—	—	—	—
C baritone	} 3	1	—	1	—	—	—	—	2 in B♭	2
B♭ euphonium		1	—	—	—	—	—	2		
Alto trombone	} 6	1	—	} 4	} 5	} 5	} 3	} 8	} 6	4
Tenor trombone		1	2							
Bass trombone		2	1							2
B♭ bass saxhorn	—	—	—	—	6	5	2 in C 2 in B♭	—	—	—
E♭ contrabass saxhorn	—	—	—	—	3	2	2	—	—	—
B♭ contrabass saxhorn	—	—	—	—	2	2	—	—	—	—
F tuba	}	2	}	4 in B♭	—	—	—	}	—	2
E♭ tuba		1			—	—	—		3	—
C bombardon	} 8	3	} 3	2	—	—	} 1	6	—	2
F bass	bass	—	bombardon	—	—	—		bass	—	2
C contrabass		—		} 3	—	—		tuba	—	2
B♭ contrabass		—			—	—			3	—
Timpani	—	—	1	—	1	}	1	} 3	1	—
Side drum	2	1	1	—	—		2		1	1
Bass drum	1	1	1	1	—	} 4	1	1	1	1
Cymbal	1	1	1	1	—		1	2	1	—
Triangle	—	—	—	—	—		—	—	1	4
Other	3 bass flugelhorn	E♭ Piston	—	—	—	—	3 double bass	—	—	bass flugel-horn

[a] Austria	Duke of Wurtemberg's Regiment	[f] France	Paris Guards
[b] Baden	Grenadier Guards	[g] Netherlands	Grenadiers and Foot
[c] Bavaria	1st Royal Regiment of Infantry	[h] Prussia	Combined 2nd Regiment, Royal Guard and Grenadier Guards
[d] Belgium	Grenadiers	[i] Russia	Horse Guards
[e] France	Guides of the Imperial Guards	[j] Spain	1st Regiment of Engineers

Artillery Band: in 1857 the band was doubled from 40 to 80 players, and in 1887, at 93 strong, it became the largest band in the service. British army musical directors were often civilians, and mostly foreigners. (It was the proliferation of non-military, foreign bandmasters, together with the need to regulate and standardize British service bands, that stimulated the setting up of Kneller Hall.) From about 1860 bandmasters were ranked as First Class Staff Sergeants and from 1881 they were allowed to be promoted to Warrant Officers; later still they could be commissioned. By 1876 there remained only 35 civilian bandmasters in British army bands.

British military bands were standardized at a conference held at Kneller Hall in 1921: the tenor horn was abandoned and saxophones added, a trend already apparent somewhat earlier in works such as K.J. Alford's march *Colonel Bogey* (1914; ex.3). The instrumentation then established remained in force at the end of the century (for specifications of British bands in the 1980s, see *Grove1*, 'Band (i)', Table 4). The bagpipe tradition has been maintained by the Army School of Piping, founded in 1910. The RAF School of Music, whose first Organizing Director of Music Walford Davies composed the famous *March Past*, was founded in 1918. Bands have long been

TABLE 5: Instrumentation of late 19th-century European bands

France Belgium Holland	England	Italy	Germany	Austria	Switzerland
Db piccolo	Piccolo	Eb piccolo (Db)	Db piccolo	Piccolo	Db piccolo
C flute	Flute	Flute	Db or C flute	Db or C flute	C flute
Oboe	Oboe	Oboe	Oboes		
				Ab clarinet	
Eb clarinet	Eb clarinet	Eb clarinet	Eb clarinet	Eb clarinet	Eb clarinet
Bb clarinets	Bb clarinets	Bb clarinet	Bb clarinets	Bb clarinets	Bb clarinets
	Eb alto clarinet				
		Bb bass clarinet			
Bassoons	Bassoon	Bassoons	Bassoon		
		Double bassoon			
4 saxophones	3–4 saxophones	3 saxophones			4 saxophones
Horns in Eb	Horns in Eb	Horns in Eb	Horns in Eb	Horns in Eb	
Eb (sopranino) flugelhorn (petit bugle)		Eb (sopranino) flugelhorn (pistone)	Eb (sopranino) flugelhorn (Pikkolo-Kornett)		Eb (sopranino) flugelhorn (Pikkolo-Kornett)
Bb Flugelhorns (bugles)	Bb cornets	Bb cornets	Bb cornets	Bb flugelhorns	Bb flugelhorns
Eb (alto) flugelhorns		Eb contralto flicorno (genes)	Eb (alto) cornet		Eb althorns
Eb trumpets	Eb trumpets	Eb trumpets	Bb and Eb trumpets	Bb and Eb trumpets	Bb trumpets
Eb alto saxhorns				Bb bass trumpet (basstrompete)	
Bb baritones	Bb baritones		Bb baritones (Tenorhörner)	Bass flugelhorns	Bb baritones (Tenorhörner)
Bb bass saxhorns	Euphonium	Euphoniums (bombardini)	Euphonium (Baritontuba)	Euphonium	Bb baritone
Trombones	Trombones	Valve trombones	Trombones	Trombones	Trombones
Eb double bass saxhorn	Eb bass tuba	Bombardoni (flicorni basso-gravi)	F bass tuba (baritontuba)	F helicon	Eb bass tuba
Bb double bass tuba	Helicons	Pelittoni (flicorni contrabassi)	Double bass tuba	Bb helicon	Bb double bass tuba
Side drum	Side drum	Side drum	Side drum	Side drum	Side drum
Bass drum	Bass drum	Bass drum	Bass drum	Bass drum	Bass drum
Cymbals	Cymbals	Cymbals	Cymbals	Cymbals	Cymbals
		Triangle	Bell-lyra		

associated with services such as the fire brigade and the police in Britain; the band of the Metropolitan Police was formed in 1927. At the end of the 20th century the United Kingdom supported 16 military staff bands 35–50 musicians strong and 53 regimental bands with 21–35 musicians in each.

The problem of discrepancies in pitch between bands was overcome in Britain by the issue to all regiments in 1858 of a standard Bb tuning fork, which introduced the 'high Philharmonic pitch'. European military bands adopted the recommendations of the Paris conference of tuning standards of 1885 (Habla, C1990).

In Switzerland, where many outstanding municipal bands were initially conducted by German military bandmasters, military music was confined to militia bands and *Rekrutenspiele*. Only with the founding of the *Schweizer Armeespiel* in 1960 did that country acquire a professional military wind band. The Netherlands and Belgium, at first influenced by France and Germany, went their own way from the 1950s and by the end of the century had begun to extend their influence outwards through their excellent music publishing firms (Molenaar, Tierolff, de Haske) and composers. Important bands have included the *Grand orchestre d'harmonie des guides*, founded in 1832 as the Belgian royal musical ensemble;

the Royal Military Band of Belgium; the Marine Band of the Royal Navy of the Netherlands (founded 1864); and the *Kapel van de Koninklijke Luchtmacht* (founded 1945). The *Musique militaire grand ducale* of Luxembourg enjoys a high reputation. In the Irish Republic Wilhelm Fritz Brase, a former German military bandmaster, founded the army music school, serving as its director from 1932 to 1940. At the end of the century there were four military musical ensembles in Ireland with 33–44 musicians each. In Spain, military music in the 19th century was influenced by France; the *Real Cuerpo de Alaberderos* was regarded as the finest military band there between 1875 and 1931. At the end of the 20th century the music corps of the Royal Guard was considered the leading ensemble; like the municipal bands of Madrid, Barcelona and Valencia, it includes cellos and double basses. The Scandinavian countries developed variants on the Prussian, French and English models. Bands there are usually small: the band of the Royal Danish Lifeguards has 35 members and three further Danish bands have 16 members each. The largest band is that of the Norwegian Royal Guard, with 60 members; the staff band has 28 members and the six regional bands have 21 musicians each. The situation is much the same in Sweden (fig.5) and Finland, where there are semi-professional bands of

Ex.3 K.J. Alford: *March: 'Colonel Bogey'* (London, 1914)

national service personnel. Only the band of the Swedish Navy is entirely professional.

An independent Italian development began with Alessandro Vessella (1860–1929), director of the *Banda municipale di Roma* from 1885 to 1924. He standardized the scoring of small, medium and large bands and wrote a treatise on instrumentation, *Studi di strumentazione per*

banda (Milan, 1954). From the 1920s most Italian wind bands followed his model in scoring and repertory.

With the exception of the HORN BAND, military music in 19th-century Russia was influenced by the Prussian model. In 1873 Rimsky-Korsakov was appointed Inspector of Naval Bands and worked to improve standards. After the Revolution of 1917 Russian military music

5. Swedish wind band, Karlskrona, led by drum-major: (from left to right) front row, slide trombone, clarinet, bell-lyra, clarinet, slide trombone; second row, piccolo, clarinet, euphonium, clarinet, valve trombone; third row, alto saxophone, sousaphone, two french horns; fourth row, trumpets; back row, snare drum, cymbals, bass drum

broke away from the Western model. Semyon Aleksandrovich Chernetsky (1881–1950) was appointed Inspector of Music for Soviet bands in 1924; he reorganized the training of military bandsmen and encouraged the composition of new music. In 1935 he established the wind band of the Soviet Ministry of Defence to serve as an example for other military bands; it included tenor horns but had no bassoons or saxophones. Works written for this ensemble include Myaskovsky's Symphony no.19, op.46 (1939) and *Dramatic Overture* (1942), and marches by Prokofiev and Khachaturian. States formerly part of the Soviet Union (e.g. Ukraine, Belarus, Kazakhstan) or in the Soviet orbit paid particular attention to military music in the late 20th century. Poland, Slovakia, the Czech Republic, Hungary, Romania and Bulgaria have preserved their own traditions while the Baltic states and Slovenia were, at the end of the century, striking out on new paths of their own.

In some countries financial concerns resulted in retrenchment during the final decades of the century. In Belgium, for example, a number of bands were decommissioned when it was decided that only a single band for each corps would be supported.

3. CIVILIAN BANDS. The 19th century saw a steady increase in large civic bands in continental Europe. French civilian music was divided into the brass band with saxophones (*fanfare*) and the wind, percussion and brass band (*harmonie*). In 1850 the *Banda Municipal* of Barcelona was dissolved, but later reformed with 40 players associated with the School of Music. The *Banda Communale di Roma*, founded with 40 members in 1871, doubled in size on the appointment of Alessandro Vessella as its director in 1885; it is typical of the 'banda municipale' of a major Italian city, with its brilliant tone colour, excellent players and repertory of orchestral and opera transcriptions. The following list of instruments

specified in a 'transcrizione libera' (1927) of Puccini's *Turandot* illustrates the maximum instrumentation found in such bands:

Ottavino; 2 Flauti; 2 Oboi; Corno inglese; 2 Clarinetti piccoli in Lab; 2 Clarinetti piccoli in Mib; Clarinetti soprani in Sib I.; Clarinetti soprani in Sib II.; Clarinetti contralti in Mib; Clarinetti bassi in Sib; Sarrussofono baritono in Mib; Sarrusofono basso in Sib; Saxofono soprano in Sib; 2 Saxofoni contralti in Mib; Saxofoni tenori in Sib; Saxofono baritono in Mib; Saxofono basso in Sib; Sarrussofono contrabasso; Contrabasso ad ancia; Contrabassi a corda; 4 Corni in Fa; 2 Cornette in Sib; 2 Trombe in Fa; 2 Trombe in Sib basso; 2 Tromboni tenore; Trombone basso in Fa; Trombone contrabasso in Sib; Timpani; Triangolo–Tamburo; G.C. Piatti–Tam-tam; Glockenspiel–Xilofono; Xilofono basso–Gong Chinesi; Celeste; 2 Flicorni sopranini in Mib; 2 Flicorni soprani in Sib; 2 Flicorni contralti in Mib; 2 Flicorni tenori in Sib; 2 Flicorni baritoni in Sib; 2 Flicorni bassi in Sib; 2 Flicorni bassi gravi in Fa-Mib; 2 Flicorni contrabassi in Sib.

(*Contrabasso ad ancia*; a double reed instrument of brass, different from the sarrusophones which in this example replace bassoons; *Flicorni*; generic title covering flugelhorns, alto and tenor horns, baritone and the brass basses; the deeper trombones are valved, sometimes the tenors as well; *G.C. Piatti*: one player, cymbal attached to the bass drum.)

80 players became a common size for municipal bands in southern Europe and Latin America. The Portuguese *Banda da Guarda Nacional* had 60 members by 1901.

In many towns and cities of southern Europe the tendency towards the large ensemble continued. Until 1981 Venice maintained such a band, which played in the Piazza S Marco. Large *bandas municipales* were still thriving in Spain at the end of the 20th century, and in major cities these were made up of professional players; in addition there were many cultural societies that supported bands. An annual contest, which became international in 1982, has been held in Valencia since 1886 during the Gran Feria in July.

In the Benelux countries and Switzerland there are many amateur bands, mostly mixed wind bands, but also brass bands. There are also many in Scandinavia, in Germany, and in central and eastern Europe. Bands have tended not to have fixed instrumentation: Spanish bands often include cellos; in Scandinavia, Belgium and the Benelux countries bands follow the British model sometimes adding trumpets; in Germany and elsewhere in central Europe flugelhorns and *Tenorhörner* (*Bass-Flügelhörner*) are employed; in Italy, Austria and parts of central Europe the small E♭ clarinet is often seen; in Eastern Europe and France saxhorns may be used.

In the final decade of the 20th century national pride in countries newly freed from Soviet domination led to the revival of popular local traditions, including bands. In Lithuania, for example, the Symphonic Wind Band of the Ministry of Internal Affairs, which had been disbanded in 1944, was restored in 1989, and an Association of Lithuanian Wind Instrument Players was formed in 1993 to improve the skills of its members and to promote Lithuanian music.

4. AMERICAN WIND BANDS.   European musical customs and traditions were brought to North America by the colonists. In American military organizations, as in European ones, a distinction was made between 'field music' and the 'band of music'. The former consisted primarily of a snare drum, with a fife, bagpipe or other instrument added wherever available to provide melody. It was used mainly for functional purposes – to set the cadence for marching men and to beat warnings, orders and signals – and normally provided the camp duty calls that regulated the field or garrison. The band of music, on the other hand, served ceremonial and social functions.

The earliest reference to a 'band of musick' in North America is a newspaper account of the celebrations for the accession of George I of England in New York in 1714 where it is stated that the governor and the regular forces marched 'with Hoboys and Trumpets before them'. By the 1750s the term 'band of musick' appears frequently in connection with parades and civic ceremonies. British regimental bands (normally *Harmoniemusik* ensembles) gave concerts in New York, Boston, Philadelphia and Canadian garrison towns before the American Revolution, and residents were quick to form bands of their own. Both British and American regiments supported bands during the Revolutionary War, and performances were frequent. The 3rd and 4th Continental artillery regiments had bands as early as 1777; both served until the end of the Revolution and achieved exceptional reputations. In post-Revolutionary USA, bands welcomed George Washington in almost every village and city that he visited on his grand tour in 1789. Taverns, coffee-houses, theatres, and pleasure gardens all featured bands performing medleys, selections from popular stage works, battle pieces, transcriptions of orchestral works, original compositions, marches and patriotic songs (for examples of the music, see Camus, C(ii)1992).

The Militia Act of 1792, by which every able-bodied adult white male was required to perform military service

6. *Band of the 3rd New Hampshire Regiment at Hiltonhead, South Carolina, 1862*

for at least two 'muster days' each year, greatly promoted the development of bands. A further impetus was supplied by the regular meetings, for drill and ceremonies, of élite organizations. No military, civic, festive or holiday occasion was complete without music, and bands were organized to provide it; these were usually attached to militia units, and, while retaining their civilian status, the bandsmen normally wore uniforms. Tutors such as Timothy Olmstead's *Martial Music* (1807) began to appear in print. Other Revolutionary War bandmasters active into the Federal period included Philip Roth and John Hiwell, the former Inspector of Music in the Continental Army. New leaders, such as Peter von Hagen, James Hewitt and Gottlieb Graupner, came from Europe.

Widespread interest in Turkish (janissary) music in America at the beginning of the 19th century brought the bass drum and cymbals into the band and the field music. Combined performances of the two groups became more frequent, and the snare drum soon became an integral part of the band. Further changes to *Harmoniemusik* in the Federal period included new keys on the woodwind instruments and the addition of the piccolo, bass clarinet, trombone, bass horn and serpent. William Webb's *Grand Military Divertimentos* were published for an ensemble including these newly-added instruments (Table 6, 1828). Another new instrument, the KEYED BUGLE, became popular in New York through the performances of Richard Willis, who within a year of his arrival from Dublin in 1816 became the first teacher of music and leader of the band at the US Military Academy at West Point. Other virtuosos on the keyed bugle included Frank [Francis] Johnson in Philadelphia and Edward [Ned] Kendall in Boston. Keyed bass horns and ophicleides were also added, and bands continued to increase in size. By 1832 US Army infantry regiments had bands consisting of 15 to 24 members, a size emulated by militia bands. In that year, however, infantry bands were limited to ten privates and a chief musician, a drastic reduction that led to the elimination of woodwind instruments in favour of the new and versatile valved brass instruments. Beginning in 1834, many, but not all, bands changed to all-brass combinations (see §IV, ii, below). The 7th Regiment Band, a 42-piece woodwind and brass ensemble led first by Joseph Noll, later by Claudio S. Grafulla, achieved a reputation for excellence surpassed only by that of the all-brass Dodworth Band.

Bands proliferated during the Civil War: Bufkin estimated conservatively that the Union Army had 500 bands and 9000 players besides the two field musicians assigned to each company. These bands provided music for military and civilian ceremonies and entertained the soldiers; bandsmen also served as medical corpsmen during battle. Many civilian and militia bands enlisted as a body in the new volunteer regiments. While most conformed to regulations, some (supported, as in the past, by the officers), exceeded their authorized strength and dressed in elaborate uniforms. The 24th Massachusetts Volunteer Infantry had 20 drummers, 12 buglers, and a 36-piece mixed wind band led by PATRICK S. GILMORE. Other prominent civilian bandmasters who, with their bands, served in the war included Grafulla, Harvey Dodworth, E.B. Flagg, Thomas Coates and Walter Dignam. Gustavus W. Ingalls enlisted a band of 22 men in the 3rd New Hampshire Regiment (fig.6), and their Port Royal Band Books are a primary source for instrumentation and

repertory of the period (Table 6, 1863). Eight members of the Salem (North Carolina) Brass Band enlisted in the 26th North Carolina Regiment, and their story (Hall, C(ii)1963) is typical of the experiences of many bands serving on both sides of the conflict. In 1862 Congress ordered the discharge of the three or four regimental bands per brigade, and authorized instead a brigade band of 16 musicians, with a leader and an assistant.

Due mainly to the influence of Gilmore, brass bands gradually disappeared following the Civil War. Gilmore arrived in the USA from Ireland in 1849 and a few years later became leader of the Salem Brass Band. In 1859 he established Gilmore's Band. He later organized and trained all the bands of the state of Massachusetts and organized the music for large-scale events such as the National Peace Jubilee of 1869, and the even larger World Peace Jubilee of 1872, both in Boston. In 1873 he assumed the leadership of the band of the 22nd New York Regiment, and established it as the finest professional band in the country. A skilled promoter, he attracted large audiences by adept programming and by engaging such outstanding soloists as the cornettists Matthew Arbuckle, Alessandro Liberati, Herman Bellstedt and Jules Levy, the saxophonist E.A. Lefèbre, the trombonist Frederick Neil Innes, the euphonium player Joseph Raffayolo, and the sopranos Emma Thursby, Eugenie Pappenheim and Lillian Nordica. The 22nd Regiment Band normally had a complement of 66 musicians (Table 6, 1878), far exceeding the limits imposed by military regulations at the time. During the 1880s they worked year-round: in summer at Manhattan Beach, in winter at the 22nd Regiment armory and Gilmore's Garden (P.T. Barnum's Hippodrome) in New York, and in autumn and spring on tour. At this time there were only four major professional symphony orchestras in the USA, none of which had a full season; as a result the finest musicians sought employment with Gilmore. His band inspired others to reintroduce the woodwind instruments and to raise their level of performance and improve their repertory. Other bandmasters active at the time included Grafulla, Carlo Cappa, David Wallis Reeves, the former Gilmore's Band soloists Arbuckle, Innes and Liberati, the cornettist R.B. Hall and, in Canada, Ernest Lavigne and Joseph Vézina.

In 1889 *Harper's Weekly* estimated that there were more than 10,000 'military' bands active in the USA. In many western communities the local military post band provided the only music available. Many bands were associated with local militia units but, though uniformed, retained their civilian status. Professional and amateur bands appeared at military and civilian ceremonies and parades, concerts, amusement parks, seaside resorts, county and state fairs, and national and international expositions. Their repertory ranged from the ever popular marches, songs, waltzes and novelties to the classical standards of the day. Many North Americans had their first, and usually only, exposure to the music of Mozart, Beethoven, Rossini, Verdi, Liszt and Wagner through these bands. Opera selections and variations were performed by leading soloists, and even grand operas were staged.

While large bands were conducted, smaller ones were frequently led by their solo cornet player, as in the days of brass bands. Consequently the solo cornet part in printed arrangements usually served as the conductor's

TABLE 6: Comparative band instrumentation

	1777	1828	1846	1853	1863	1878	1900	1918	1926	1944	1946	1948	1952	1960	1986	1994
Flute/piccolo		3		1		4	4	2	1/1/2	3	4	12	3	6	2	3
Oboe/english horn	2					2	2	2	-/1/2	1	2	8	3	3	1	2
Heckelphone												1				
Bassoon	2	2				2	2	2	-/1/2	1	2	6	2	2	1	1
Contrabassoon						1	1					1	1			
Contrabass Sarrusaphone								1	-/-/1							
A♭ clarinet						1										
E♭ clarinet						3	2	1	1/1/2	1	1	1	1	1		
B♭ clarinet	2	3			1	16	16	10	6/8/10	12	19	29	8	18	6	9
Alto clarinet						1	2	2	-/-/2	1		4	1	6		
Bass clarinet						1	2	2	-/-/2	1	1	5	1	3		
Contrabass clarinet												3		2		
Soprano sax						1			-/1/-					1		
Alto saxophone						1	2	1	1/1/1	4	1	3	2	1	2	2
Tenor saxophone						1	2	1	1/1/1	2	1	3	1	1	1	1
Baritone saxophone						1	1	1	1/1/1	1	1	1	1	1	1	1
Bass saxophone												1		1		
E♭ cornet			1	2	2	1										
B♭ cornet				2	2	4	4		2/2/2		4	7	3	3		
E♭ trumpet				2	1											
B♭ trumpet		1				2	2	4	4/4/4	10	3	4	2	3	6	6
B♭ flugelhorn			2			2	2	2				2				
Bugle/posthorn		1	1													
French horn	2	2	2			4	4	4	3/4/4	4	4	9	4	4	3	4
Alto horn				2	2	2										
Alto ophicleide			2													
Tenor horn				2		2										
Trombone		1	3	2		3	4	4	3/3/4	6	6	9	3	4	4	4
Euphonium				1	1	2	2	2	1/2/2	2	2	6	2	3	2	1
Bass ophicleide			2													
Serpent	1															
Bass				2	3	5	4	4	2/3/4	5	4	8	2	3	3	4
Double bass											1	3	1		1	
Electric bass guitar															1	
Percussion				2	2	2	4	3	3	2/2/2	2	3	9	3	5	3	4
Harp											1	2	1		2	1
Keyboard															1	
Guitar															1	
1st Sgt (any inst)															1	
Total	9	13	17	14	16	66	61	48	28/36/48	56	60	136	45	72	40	43

1777: *Harmoniemusik*, Revolutionary period
1828: William Webb, *Grand Military Divertimentos* (Philadelphia: George E. Blake, [c.1828])
1846: E.K. Eaton, *Twelve Pieces of Harmony for Military Brass Bands* (New York: Firth and Hall, 1846)
1853: A. Dodworth, *Dodworth's Brass Band School* (New York: H.B. Dodworth, 1853)
1863: 3rd New Hampshire (Port Royal) band books, 1863–65 (Library of Congress)
1878: Gilmore's 22nd Regiment Band (Goldman, *The Wind Band*, pp.59, 62)
1900: Sousa Band, 1st European Tour, 1900 (Bierley, p.148)
1918: U.S. Army Regimental Band authorization
1926: Instrumentation of 28-, 36-, and 48-piece army bands, 1926 TR 130-5, 1926
1944: US Army Division Band authorization
1946: The Goldman Band (R.F. Goldman, *The Concert Band*, pp.78–79)
1948: The University of Illinois Symphonic Band under Albert Austin Harding
1952: Frederick Fennell, Eastman Wind Ensemble, 1952
1960: College Band Directors National Association 'Ideal Balanced Band'. (R.F. Goldman, *The Wind Band*, 167)
1986: US Army Division and Army Band Table of Organization, 1 Oct 1986
1994: Canadian Regular Force Professional Brass and Reed Band

cue sheet. Carl Fischer of New York was one of the first firms to publish band music with printed parts for each instrument, and to include a two- or three-line conductor's score. The firm engaged many outstanding editors, among them Louis-Philippe Laurendeau, Frank H. Losey, Vincent F. Safranek, Theodore Moses Tobani and Mayhew Lester Lake, many of whose arrangements are still performed. Thomas H. Rollinson prepared many arrangements during his 40 years with Ditson. Later important publishers of band music included Charles L. Barnhouse, John Church, Harry Coleman, Henry Fillmore, George F. Briegel and several bandmasters who issued their own music, such as Jean Missud, Fred Jewell and Karl L. King.

The most important figure in the golden age of American band music was JOHN PHILIP SOUSA, who formed his own band in 1892. An astute showman, a fine composer and an excellent musician, he engaged the finest available players for each position, and attracted such outstanding soloists as the cornet player Herbert L. Clarke, the trombonist Arthur Pryor, euphonium players Simone Mantia and Joseph DeLuca, the violinist Maud Powell and the sopranos Estelle Liebling and Majorie Moody. He experimented with his band's instrumentation and gradually increased its membership (Table 6, 1900). From 1892 until his death in 1932 he made regular tours, including four in Europe (1900, 1901, 1903 and 1905), and a world tour (1910–11; fig.7). A typical Sousa programme listed about nine titles, ranging from his own suites and marches to novelties, solos, orchestral transcriptions and opera selections. After each scheduled work he normally added one or two encores, usually his own marches.

Other major figures of the period included such veterans as Cappa, Missud, Francesco Fanciulli, Thomas Brooke, Monroe Althouse and Victor Herbert; soloists from Sousa's band who went on to form bands of their own (Liberati, Clarke, Bohumir Kryl, Frank Simon, Pryor, Mantia, Herman Bellstedt and Eugene LaBarre); and bandmasters such as Giuseppe Creatore, Patrick Conway, Edwin Franko Goldman, Innes and Canadians Jean-Josaphat Gagnier and Charles O'Neill who organized new professional ensembles. Since women were not admitted to the professional bands except as violin, soprano or harp soloists, they formed bands of their own, such as Helen May Butler's Ladies Brass Band (fig.8).

Besides the professional bands there were thousands of amateur ensembles: civic bands, bands sponsored by fraternal and sororal organizations, industrial bands, the many brass bands of the Salvation Army and, after World War I, Legion and veterans' bands. A town band was a mark of social status: 'a town without its brass band is as much in need of sympathy as a church without a choir. The spirit of a place is recognized in its band' (Dana, C(ii)1878). Many civic bands still in existence date from pre-war times, including the Allentown (Pennsylvania) Band (founded 1828), the Repasz Band (Williamsport, Pennsylvania, 1831) and the Newmarket Band (Ontario, 1843). To train musicians for these bands, many schools were established, such as Hale A. VanderCook's College of Music (Chicago, 1909) and Innes's Correspondence School of Music (Denver, 1921, later Conn National School of Music, Chicago, 1923). There were also bands with specialized styles and repertories such as circus bands (which invariably played everything at much faster 'circus' tempos) and the New Orleans bands, which absorbed

black American and Creole influences. Often associated with benevolent societies, these bands provided music for club functions and funerals. Since at least the 18th century bands traditionally played a solemn march on their way to the cemetery, but a brisk quickstep, usually 'Merry Men Home from the Grave' on their return. The New Orleans musicians began improvising on tunes (such as the spiritual 'When the saints go marching in'), and developed an early form of jazz. There were many permanent black ensembles at the end of the 19th century, including the Excelsior, Onward, Eureka, Tuxedo and St Bernard brass bands, and many leading jazz instrumentalists gained their first experiences in these groups. As bandmaster of the 369th US Infantry Regiment Band serving in France during World War I, James Reese Europe brought jazz to European audiences for the first time.

Although Sousa continued to draw enthusiastic crowds, the popularity of bands declined after World War I, in the face of competition from radio, recordings and motion pictures. After his death in 1932 the focus shifted to education, a side of the movement that had been growing in the background since the second quarter of the 19th century. Music education in the schools in the 19th century had concentrated on vocal music, but there was a school band as early as 1836 in Canada, many in the USA by 1848, and there were bands all over the latter by the end of the century. Harvard and Yale had bands by about 1827, and other universities soon followed their example. After the Civil War there were bands based on the military model and attached to Officers Training Corps at nearly all educational institutions. Military ceremonies, political rallies, parades, dedications, outdoor festivities and sporting events were all enlivened by the music of these bands, which played popular overtures and medleys, spirited marches and school songs.

The participation of bands at sporting events became increasingly important, and by the end of the century pre-game and half-time football performances were common.

7. John Philip Sousa (front row, to the right of the harp) and his band in Johannesburg, while on a world tour, 1911

8. Helen May Butler and her Ladies Brass Band, 1910

With the addition of woodwind instruments, the bands increased in size and were organized more often like professional rather than military ensembles. Professional bandmasters, such as Conway at Cornell University (1895–1908) and Gustav Bruder at Ohio State University (1896–1929), soon replaced student directors. Albert Austin Harding sought to give the University of Illinois Band a symphonic sound by making greater use of woodwind instruments (and in greater variety) and using french horns instead of alto (tenor) horns. Since arrangements for such a band did not exist, he made almost 150 transcriptions of orchestral works for it. The artistic standard of the University of Illinois Band soon equalled that of the best professionals bands, and Harding's work was widely emulated.

World War I brought a renewed interest in military bands, and mobilization fostered an expanded musical instrument industry. American regimental bands compared unfavourably with their European counterparts in size and instrumentation until their membership was increased from 20 to 48 (Table 6, 1918) and greater emphasis placed on thorough musical training. Many members of army bands became band directors in public schools on their return to civilian life, class instruction in band and orchestral instruments having begun to receive support from school officials by the close of the war.

To stimulate demand musical instrument manufacturers organized the first national school band contest, in Chicago in June 1923. Response to such contests was so great that by 1937 the National School Band Association, organized in 1926 to administer the contests, had formed ten regional organizations. By 1941 there were 562 bands (33,398 students) participating, besides the many bands eliminated at district level. Canada had a similar growth, beginning in 1932 when Charles Frederick Thiele founded the Waterloo (Ontario) Band Festival.

Marching bands, now separated from the Officers Training Corps, benefited from the popularity of intercollegiate football. Larger bands were needed to fill the huge stadiums built between the two worlds wars. The University of Illinois Band under Harding is generally credited with being the first to play opening fanfares from the goal line, and to form a block 'I' while marching down the field. Many others soon followed its example and began to form patterns on the field.

During this period measures were taken to raise the musicianship of symphonic and marching bands. As early as 1919 Harding had invited school band directors to observe his rehearsals at the University of Illinois and to discuss specific problems and repertory; in 1930 he began a series of influential band clinics. The American Bandmasters Association was organized in 1929, and the College Band Directors National Association (CBDNA) in 1941. The latter aimed to conduct acoustical and tonal research, improve the musicianship of college band directors, and develop a standard instrumentation (Table

6, 1960), a concept later rejected as too restrictive; it also commissioned original band music. The Canadian Bandmasters Association (later the Canadian Band Directors Association) was founded in 1931.

World War II curtailed the school band movement, but returning veterans inspired its revival in Canada and the USA. Many new works were commissioned by E.F. Goldman (from such composers as Thomson, Piston, Mennin, Persichetti, Creston, Morton Gould and Robert Russell Bennett) and through the League of Composers and the American Bandmasters Association. Marching bands emphasized brass and percussion more and more as football half-time shows developed into elaborate pageants with bands reaching immense proportions and marching with ever higher and faster steps. Symphonic bands also increased in size (Table 6, 1948). In reaction to such developments, Frederick Fennell formed the Eastman Symphonic Wind Ensemble in 1952 (Table 6, 1952). This ensemble originally provided a pool of 45–50 players for composers, and concerts have included works ranging from chamber-sized compositions to large scale works with one player per part, from Renaissance wind music to avant-garde compositions. From 1965 the ensemble was directed by Donald Hunsberger. Symphonic bands and wind ensembles continue to flourish in schools, colleges and universities (fig.9); a 1973 survey counted some 50,000 secondary-school bands in the USA, with 2000 at institutions of higher education. By 1990 Canada had more than 5000 band directors.

Professional bands of the postwar era included the Goldman Band (Table 6, 1946), which remained active until 1980 and commissioned new works from composers such as Bergsma, Giannini and Douglas Moore, and the Detroit Concert Band, founded by Leonard B. Smith in 1946 and still active at the beginning of the 21st century. In 1956 the Ostwald Uniform Company established an award for the best band composition submitted each year to a jury of the American Bandmasters Association; winners have included James Barnes, John Barnes Chance, James Curnow, David Holsinger, Anthony Iannaccone, Robert Jager, Karl Kroeger, Timothy Mahr, Martin Mailman, Ron Nelson, Roger Nixon, Fisher Tull, Clifton Williams and Dana Wilson.

In the military, reductions in the number and size of bands continued. The World War II division band of 56 players (Table 6, 1944) replaced as many as ten regimental bands; the division or post band of the 1980s was a 40-piece multipurpose musical unit (Table 6, 1986). Following reorganization in 1994, Canada maintained four Regular Force Professional Brass & Reed bands (Table 6, 1994) The special bands of the US armed services and the service academies (such as the US Army Band and the US Military Academy Band) may have more than 140 players, choristers and support personnel, and remain the country's leading professional wind ensembles. Community bands enjoyed a revival at the end of the 20th century and some of the 2000 and more adult bands in the USA have achieved a professional level of playing. Many bands have been in existence for more than a century, and some famous names of the past have been revived: the 26th North Carolina and 1st Wisconsin Brigade bands were resurrected in the early 1960s for the Civil War Centennial, and the 3rd and 4th Continental Artillery bands for the Bicentennial in 1976. The American Band of Providence and the Great Western Band of St Paul are only two of the many bands that have taken on new life, and are again entertaining the citizens of their communities in the traditional manner.

5. REPERTORY. Outside the major centres, music in the 19th century was provided to a great extent by local bands, who played an important role in the dissemination of music of all kinds. Besides marches, much of the repertory of both military and civic bands throughout the century consisted of arrangements or transcriptions of overtures, symphonies, operas and oratorios by composers including Beethoven, Weber, Rossini, Liszt, Verdi, Tchaikovsky, Brahms and Bruckner. Arias were performed by solo instruments while the remainder of the band took the part of the orchestra (a style of arrangement used also by *Harmonie* bands of the late 18th century), and each melody was introduced by a cadenza from the instrument about to be heard as a soloist. Composers encouraged the practice of transcription as it helped to disseminate their works: Wagner, for example, appointed Artur Seidel to make wind band arrangements of his latest compositions, and Rossini and Liszt asked bandmasters to arrange their works. Notable works originally composed for band include Mendelssohn's Overture op.24, first written for the spa orchestra at Bad Doberan in 1824 (in 1838 the composer re-set the work for a larger band), Wagner's *Trauermusik* for the funeral of Weber (1844),

9. *Indiana University Symphonic Band, conducted by Ray E. Cramer, 1996*

Meyerbeer's *Fackeltänze* (1842–58), Grieg's *Trauermarsch zum Andenken an Richard Nordaak* (1866, rev. 1878; considered by Goldman to be 'one of the grandest works composed for band'), Saint-Saëns's march *Orient et occident* 1869, and Rimsky-Korsakov's Concerto for trombone and military band (1877), Variations for oboe and military band (1878) and *Conzertstück* for clarinet and military band (1878). In France, celebrations of the anniversary of the Revolution have inspired leading composers to write for the large *orchestre d'harmonie*. Outstanding works have included Reicha's *Musique pour célébrer la mémoire des grandes hommes* (?1809–15), Berlioz's *Grande symphonie funèbre et triomphale* (1840) and Florent Schmitt's *Dionysiaques* (1914–25). Saint-Saëns, Caplet, Ibert, Auric, Milhaud, Roussel, Koechlin, Honegger, Henry Lazarus, Ida Gotkovsky and Désiré Dondeyne have also contributed such works. A special development in Germany and Austria was music for male choir with wind band: works for this combination were written by Schubert, Weber, Mendelssohn (*An die Künstler* op.68, 1846), Schumann, Liszt and Bruckner (see W. Suppan, C(i)1983, and Kinder, C(i)1995). There were also works in more popular styles such as waltzes and novelty pieces. In 1861 Queen Victoria wrote in her diary: 'as we approached the Cavalry, they began to play one of dearest Mama's marches, which they did again in marching past.' The Duchess of Kent was only one of several royal composers of marches.

To meet the growing demand for wind band music specialist publishing houses were founded, including Louis Oertel in Hanover (1861), Bellmann and Thümer in Dresden (1866) and Boosé in London (1845). Their publications began to replace the handwritten music previously used, also helping to standardize the make-up and instrumentation of the bands.

Percy Grainger's *Hill-Song no.2* (1907), *Irish Tune from County Derry* (1917) and *Lincolnshire Posy* (1940), Holst's Suites in E♭ (1909) and F (1911), and Gordon Jacob's *William Byrd Suite* (1924) set new standards in original music for mixed wind band, with Holst, especially, establishing a new idiomatic style of band writing. Much of the music of this 'English group', is marked by the use of melodic material derived from folk songs or inspired by traditional music, and pre-Romantic harmonic structures with polyphonic features. There is a perceptible tendency to give a greater melodic role to the brass instruments, liberating them from their old roles of supporting the woodwind in tutti sections and providing fanfare-like flourishes.

The works of the English group were certainly known to Hindemith when he invited composers to write wind band works for the Donaueschingen Festival of 1926. Hindemith composed his *Konzertmusik* op.41 for this festival and other works included Ernst Pepping's *Kleine Serenade*, Krenek's *Drei lustige Märsche*, Ernst Toch's *Spiel* and Hans Gál's *Promenandenmusik*. While the tonal language of these works is modern, Hindemith's piece is based on a folk song (*Prinz Eugen, der edle Ritter*) and those by Toch and Gál achieve a folk-like effect. Hindemith's idea of *Gebrauchsmusik* (his own term) was not at first successful in central Europe, but the works by Hindemith, Toch and Krenek were taken up in the USA, to where the three composers had emigrated during World War II. After the war these works became popular in Europe as well.

American commissions for works for wind band were received by Schoenberg (Theme and Variations, 1943), Hindemith (Symphony in B♭, 1951) and Krenek (*Dream Sequence*, 1975). Other works popular in the USA have included Stravinsky's Symphonies of Wind Instruments (1920) and Concerto for piano and wind (1924), Martinů's Concertino for cello and wind ensemble (1924), Weill's Concerto for violin and wind band (1924) and Milhaud's *Suite française* (1944).

After World War II American influence made itself felt in Europe in scoring and instrumentation, in serious and light music. The pioneering achievements of Grainger, Holst and Hindemith might thus be said to have returned to Europe by way of the USA. Composers have included Franz Kinzl, Herbert König, Armin Suppan, Sepp Tanzer and Sepp Thaler in Austria; Jacqueline Fonteyn and André Waignein in Belgium; Désiré Dondeyne, Ida Gotkovsky and Serge Lancen in France; Paul Kühmstedt, Edmund Löffler, Albert Loritz, Ernest Majo, Hans Mielenz, Gerbert Mutter, Hermann Regner, Peter Seeger and Willy Schneider in Germany; Adrian Cruft, Joseph Horovitz, Paul Patterson, Philip Wilby and Guy Woolfenden in Great Britain; Jean Balissat, Arpad Balázs, László Dubrovay, Frigyes Hidas, Kamilló Lendvay and Iván Patachich in Hungary; Masaru Kawasaki, Kiyoshige Koyama and Toshiro Mayuzumi in Japan; Hank Badings, Gerard Boedijn, Henk van Lijnschooten, Johan de Meij, Jan van der Roost and Kes Vlak in the Netherlands; Juan Vincente Mas Quiles in Spain; Zdenek Jonák, Jindřich Paveček and Evzen Zámecnîk in Slovakia and the Czech Republic; Georgy Salnikov in Russia; and Albert Benz, Robert Blum, Jean Daetwyler, Albert Haeberling, Paul Huber, Stephan Jaeggi and Franz Königshofer in Switzerland.

IV. Brass bands

1. Introduction. 2. Cavalry bands. 3. The British brass band movement. 4. American brass bands. 5. Other brass bands.

1. INTRODUCTION.   The brass band is an ensemble usually made up exclusively of brass instruments. In Britain the term signifies a specific genre which can be explained in terms of its history, instrumentation, repertory and performance idiom. This British model has been imitated in various parts of the world. A looser usage refers to any ensemble made up primarily of brass instruments, but the term is not synonymous with other commonly used terms such as 'brass quintet' or 'brass ensemble'. Almost always this looser meaning also signifies music making that is amateur and linked with vernacular traditions. So, taking both meanings, it can be said that there are brass bands throughout the world, including many in non-Western countries and cultures. Because all brass bands use valved instruments it follows that none originate – in their present form – earlier than the 19th century.

2. CAVALRY BANDS.   Though cavalry regiments in the 18th century occasionally employed a band of woodwind and horns, they did not forsake the traditional corps of trumpets and kettledrums, which has survived in many countries to this day. It also formed the nucleus of the true cavalry band, instituted in France under Napoleon but cultivated with greater enthusiasm in Germany and Austria. Natural trumpets in E♭ dominated this *Trompetenmusik*, but the introduction of trombone or serpent supplied a diatonic bass and horns enriched the middle

range. The KEYED BUGLE, patented by the Bandmaster of the Cavan Militia, Joseph Haliday, supplied a much-needed brass melody instrument; it became a virtuoso instrument in its own right and was favoured especially in the USA.

Stölzel's valve trumpets and valved *Tenorhorn* and *Basshorn* were regarded specifically as cavalry instruments in Prussia. Under Wilhelm Wieprecht the cavalry band grew into the type of combination illustrated in ex.4: the cornet in B♭ ('Cornett in B') is the Berlin type, almost indistinguishable from the flugelhorn, and 'piccolo cornet' is the smaller size; the cornet in E♭ ('Cornett in Es') is the bell-to-front alto horn and the euphonium (*Tenorbass*) is pitched a 4th lower; the trumpets (*Trombe*), the heart of the band, are all valved; and the basses would have consisted of the new Moritz tubas.

Cavalry bands elsewhere varied the pattern: in Austria, Italy and France trumpets were of special importance (a typical French cavalry band of the First Empire had 16 trumpets, six horns, three trombones and kettledrums); in England the cavalry band was constituted like that of the infantry.

3. THE BRITISH BRASS BAND MOVEMENT. Brass bands, in the form by which they are recognized today, originated in the Victorian period. Some writers have sought to establish a continuous link between them and earlier types of communal, instrumental music making such as waits and church choir bands, but such links are tenuous. Though brass bands existed in Britain from at least the

1830s, most of these very early bands were private or professional. The earliest and most celebrated private brass band is probably the Cyfarthfa Band, which was founded in Merthyr Tydfil, South Wales, by the industrialist R.T. Crawshay, in 1838. Amateur, working-class brass bands became popular from the 1840s. The greater availability of piston-valve instruments was an important factor, and the acquisition of the British franchise for Adolphe Sax's design of instruments by the Distin family in 1844 may have been particularly influential in this respect. Valved instruments were easier to play than keyed instruments, and because of economies gained through the scale of production, the availability of hire-purchase schemes, and other favourable economic circumstances, they were affordable to sectors of the population that would previously have been unable to buy sophisticated musical instruments. By the middle of the century many working-class British people had, for the first time, a modest quantity of free time and some disposable income. They were encouraged to engage in music making activities, which were perceived by their social superiors as respectable, rational recreations.

Brass bands were founded in a number of different ways. Some were the recipients of direct industrial sponsorship, as was the Black Dyke Mills Band which was established in Queenshead (now Queensbury), Yorkshire, in 1855 by the textile manufacturer John Foster. Others were formed by public subscription or through an affiliation with a working-class organization, such as a

Ex.4 J. Gungl: *Parade Marsch* (Berlin, c1850)

etc

mechanics' institute. From 1859 several bands became attached to the Volunteer Movement, but most of these associations were pragmatic rather than patriotic and were seldom permanent.

By the end of the 19th century most brass bands aspired to a single format and style. Magazines such as *The British Bandsman* (founded in 1887 and still the main specialist periodical) disseminated common musical values, and by this time the term 'brass band movement' was widely used. However, it was the proliferation of contests – the central, identifying feature of the movement – that was the most influential element in raising standards and creating a common idiom.

Contests of the modern type originated in the 1840s as professional entertainment promotions. The composer and entrepreneur Enderby Jackson is credited with being the most important figure in establishing these events. An 'Open' contest was held at the Belle Vue Gardens, Manchester, from 1853 and many national, regional and local contests developed. It was the instrumental line-ups favoured by the three most successful contest band conductors of the 19th century – John Gladney, Alexander Owen and Edwin Swift – that led to the adoption of a standard instrumental line-up which is still used today: soprano cornet in E♭, four solo or 1st cornets, repiano cornet, two 2nd cornets, two 3rd cornets, all in B♭; 1st, 2nd and 3rd tenor horns in E♭; 1st and 2nd baritones in B♭; 1st and 2nd euphoniums in B♭; 1st and 2nd tenor trombones; bass trombone; two basses in E♭ and two basses in B♭. Percussion instruments have frequently been used in concerts and for marching but their use in contests has not always been permitted.

From the late 19th century a printed repertory for this instrumentation replaced local, bespoke arrangements made by bandmasters, and the simple, printed music which had been available as subscription 'journals' from the late 1830s. Arrangements and transcriptions have always been a central feature of brass band repertory but many original pieces have been written too. However, very few original works for brass band were written in the 19th century. The earliest surviving substantial work is probably Joseph Parry's *Tydfil Overture* (c1879), written for the Cyfarthfa Band, but other less ambitious pieces such as Enderby Jackson's *Yorkshire Waltzes* (1856) also survive. In the 20th century composers such as Elgar, Holst, Howells, Vaughan Williams, Bantock, Birtwistle and Henze have written for the brass band, but other more specialist composers such as Percy Fletcher, Cyril Jenkins, Eric Ball, Denis Wright, Gilbert Vinter and Edward Gregson have provided the central core of the repertory. Most of the major works for brass bands have either originated as, or become, test-pieces for national contests.

Though brass bands have been particularly strong in the north of England they are found throughout Britain and many receive commercial sponsorship. The most influential figure in the brass band movement in the 20th century was probably Harry Mortimer, a member of a dynasty of brass band musicians, who became a brilliant cornet soloist and an orchestral trumpeter before taking responsibility for the broadcasting of brass bands for the BBC. For the same reason that brass bands were popular with working-class people in the 19th century – the robustness and cheapness of the instruments, the ease with which they could be learned, the fact that when played together they easily produce a homogenous sonority – they have remained a popular and valuable form of music making in schools.

Since the earliest days of its foundation the Salvation Army has used brass bands. The Fry family from Salisbury formed the first Salvationist band in 1878, and since then Salvation Army bands have been formed throughout the world. For almost a century the Salvation Army produced its own instruments and music, but in the mid-1960s the instrument-manufacturing operation was wound up. At that time Salvationist bands, along with brass bands in general, relinquished the characteristic sharp pitch in favour of the standard $a' = 440$.

The high point of the brass band movement, as far as the number of bands and players is concerned, came in the late 19th century. But most of the major developments in the repertory have occurred since then. Despite the many alternative attractions posed by the 20th-century leisure industry, brass bands have retained an important and distinctive place in British musical life. In the 19th century they were an important agency for disseminating instrumental art music to working-class people. In the 20th they have tended to occupy a position somewhere between art and popular music, and some music colleges have incorporated brass band studies into their curricula. Contesting remains a fundamental part of their ethos and many of their musical values and practices are exclusive. It is likely that the vast majority of British professional orchestral brass players in the 20th century had their musical origins in brass bands.

4. AMERICAN BRASS BANDS. In the early 1830s many American bands, among them Thomas Dodworth's City Band of New York (later the Dodworth Band), the Boston Brass Band and the Providence Brass Band, changed to all-brass instrumentation. Such bands included keyed and valved instruments, posthorns, bugles, trombones and ophicleides. Over the next two decades manufacturers such as Thomas D. Paine, John F. Stratton, Isaac Fiske, Samuel Graves, J. Lathrop Allen and E.G. Wright produced a family of conical-bore valved bugles with deep-cupped mouthpieces similar to those developed by Sax in Paris; the new design permitted ease of execution and accurate intonation, and produced an even, mellow timbre throughout the range. This homogeneous brass family soon supplanted mixed woodwind and heterogeneous brass groups. The change to all-brass instrumentation was so swift and complete that by 1856 the editor of *Dwight's Journal of Music* complained that 'all is brass now-a-days – nothing but brass'. The terms used to denote the new instruments were loosely applied; bands using them were called cornet, saxhorn or brass bands. Besides bell-front and bell-upward instruments, a valved over-the-shoulder family was developed. Allen Dodworth claimed that these instruments were first introduced by his family in 1838; he explained that they were intended for military bands 'as they throw all the tone to those who are marching to it', but for general purposes those with their bells upward were 'most convenient'. He also advised that 'care should be taken to have all the bells one way'.

After the reduction of US Army infantry bands to ten privates and a chief musician in 1832 these bands became all-brass. In 1845 the regulations authorized an increase to 16 musicians, and since most civilian bands were associated with militia organizations patterned on army models, this change had a significant impact on the size of these bands as well.

Brass bands flourished in the 1850s: one writer estimated there were some 3000 bands with more than 60,000 members in existence in the years preceding the Civil War (Felts, C(ii)1966–7). While musicianship in amateur groups varied widely, many professional bands performed at the highest level. The Salem (Massachusetts) Brass Band, led in the 1850s by Kendall and later by Patrick S. Gilmore, the Boston Brass Band, led by Eben Flagg (fig.10), and the American Brass Band in Providence led by Joseph C. Greene, were highly reputed. Russel Munger's Great Western Band of St Paul and Christopher Bach's Band of Milwaukee were well known among the many bands organized in the newly settled Midwestern states.

Little printed band music from this period is extant; most bands played from manuscript copies. Published piano music frequently included the statement 'as performed by [some famous band]' to increase sales, and often a note stating that parts for military band – presumably manuscript – were available from the publisher. In 1844 Elias Howe added several brass band arrangements to his collection of dances and other light numbers. In 1846 E.K. Eaton published *Twelve Pieces of Harmony for Military Brass Bands*, an excellent compilation for 17-piece ensemble that demanded advanced technical facility not only from the player of the high E♭

bugle but from the entire group (for instrumentation, see Table 6 above, 1846). To meet the 'increasing demand for such a work, caused by the rapid advancement of the brass bands of our country', Allen Dodworth published his *Brass Band School* in 1853. Besides the rudiments of music, he provided fingering charts, advice on rehearsing and choosing an instrument, and military regulations, tactics and camp duties; he also included 11 popular airs and marches arranged for a band of 12 players, with drums and cymbals (ex.5). The music may be played by as few as six, or, with doubling, as many as 21. In 1854 G.W.E. Friederich published his *Brass Band Journal*, a collection of 24 pieces with similar instrumentation, and in 1859 W.C. Peters & Sons published *Peters' Sax-Horn Journal*. These collections consisted principally of patriotic songs, popular airs, arrangements of songs by Stephen C. Foster, operatic excerpts, waltzes, polkas, schottisches and marches. The music was intended for a large audience and was for this reason not technically difficult. The better professional bands relied on extensive manuscript collections.

At the beginning of the Civil War, infantry regiments were authorized to have bands of 26 musicians (18 for cavalry regiments), but in 1862 in the intersets of economy regimental bands were abolished and brigade bands of 16 musicians authorized. Enforcing regulations in so large an army was difficult, and some regimental, militia and post bands continued to serve until the end of the war.

BOSTON BRASS BAND.

10. *Boston Brass Band, with (from right to left), four soprano saxhorns, four alto (or tenor) saxhorns, cymbals, drums, three over-the-shoulder trombones and three bass saxhorns: engraving from 'Gleason's Pictorial Drawing Room Companion' (9 August 1851)*

Ex.5 Gift Polka from Dodworth's *Brass Band School* (1853)

The band of the 107th US Colored Infantry (fig.11), typical in size and instrumentation of the many brigade bands in service, was a regimental unit.

Civilian brass bands proliferated after the Civil War. At a time when there were few orchestras, a band was seen as a status symbol: 'it is a fact not to be denied that the existence of a good brass band in any town or community is at once an indication of enterprise among its people, and an evidence that a certain spirit of taste and refinement pervades the masses' (Patton, D(i)1875). Some Indian brass bands were formed in British Columbia in the 1880s and 90s. In the USA, however, except for Salvation Army bands, the brass band period gradually drew to a close with the coming of Patrick S. Gilmore who, with the standards and instrumentation set by his mixed wind band, inspired other bands throughout the country to reintroduce the woodwind instruments (see §III, 4, above).

In 1982 Perry Watson spearheaded a movement to introduce British brass bands into North America. The North American Brass Band Association (NABBA) was formed in 1983 to 'foster, promote, and otherwise encourage the establishment, growth, and development of amateur and professional British-style brass bands throughout the United States and Canada'. The NABBA holds yearly graded competitions (Youth through advanced Championship level). In 1996 there were more than 70 member bands in the USA and Canada and more than 1400 individual members. The NABBA publishes a journal-newsletter, *Brass Band Bridge*. Some contemporary American composers who have written for the British brass band are James Curnow, Bruce Broughton, Joseph Turrin and Stephen Bulla.

5. OTHER BRASS BANDS. The British brass band idiom is imitated most strongly in those parts of the world, such

as Australasia, where British colonization was strong in the 19th century. Many European countries have brass band traditions, and some have cloned the British model. In general, the instrumentation of other European bands is not predictable; they are sometimes less serious in their quest for virtuosity, less motivated by a contesting ethos, and individual bands tend to relate more to their own communities than to a broad national movement as in Britain. This does not, however, mean that these traditions are less robust, or less important in the musical life of their countries. Brass bands in central Europe, particularly Bulgaria, are extremely strong and well organized, and their repertories often expose strong ties with other forms of vernacular music. The brass bands of some Scandinavian countries have a strong tradition. This is especially true in Finland, where the form known as *Torviseitsikko* can be reliably traced to the 1870s. *Torviseitsikko* is, in its classic form, a brass septet made up of three cornets, tenor horn, baritone, euphonium and tuba.

In many countries brass bands have tended to reflect an alchemy of vernacular traditions and aspects of the received art music values imported with colonizing powers. In several Asian, African and Pacific regions instrumental line-ups are often similar to those of British bands, and marches, transcriptions and other music from the Western repertory may be performed. But Western playing styles are not always imitated. Often these bands have developed their own distinctive sound-aesthetic, and some include percussion instruments to provide accompanying rhythmic figurations that owe more to local traditions and customs than to a colonial inheritance. Brass bands are particularly popular in South Asia, though many of these include clarinets and saxophones. Indian bands – sometimes known locally as 'band parties' – are owned and run by entrepreneurs called *māliks*. They

11. Band of the 107th US Colored Infantry at Fort Corcoran, Arlington, Virginia, November 1865

are employed for various functions, particularly weddings, and it has been estimated that there are 500,000–800,000 people in India involved in such bands. Here, as in other parts of the world, the use of Western brass instruments does not obscure more indigenous musical traditions and functions. Repertory in South Asia is almost entirely indigenous, often deriving from film music (*see* INDIA, §VIII, 1(v)).

V. Jazz bands

Each successive style of jazz has produced its own characteristic instrumental formations to suit its musical demands. Hence there is no such thing as a standard jazz band, but rather a historical chain of different combinations with certain classical groupings emerging as paramount. However different their instrumentation, all these groupings have one common principle: the distinction between the rhythm section (consisting of piano, drums, bass and optional guitar or banjo), and the melody section (including not only the brass and reed instruments, but also the vibraphone, electric guitar, etc.). Despite the many changes in instrumentation over the years, and although the capability of 'rhythm' players to improvise full-scale solos has increased, this basic distinction between rhythm and melody sections is still valid. Since about 1935 a distinction has also been made between a 'combo' and a 'band'. A combo is a small formation of

up to seven or eight players (though usually no more than five), whereas the term 'band' is generally reserved for larger groups. (For further discussion and illustration, *see* JAZZ.

1. The New Orleans or Dixieland band. 2. Big band. 3. Swing and bop combos. 4. Cool and West Coast ensembles. 5. Free jazz. 6. Fusion groupings. 7. Summary.

1. THE NEW ORLEANS OR DIXIELAND BAND.   Recent research has discovered many regional variants and corresponding differences of instrumentation in early jazz. Jazz instrumentation was to a large extent dependent on the social circumstances surrounding the performance: violins might be appropriate for the indoor, social occasions of the white or Creole middle classes, but not for outdoor funerals or cane-cutting contests, where black brass bands predominated. By 1917, however, when the first jazz recordings were issued, white New Orleans musicians had settled on a certain standard combination consisting of three melody instruments (trumpet or cornet, clarinet and trombone) and two rhythm instruments (piano and drums). This combination was chosen by the first recorded jazz group, the Original Dixieland Jazz Band; their extraordinary popular success spawned an enormous number of imitators throughout the world, known collectively as 'The Fives'. However, early photo-

graphs and recordings of black New Orleans groups sometimes reveal quite different forces: KING OLIVER's 1923 recordings added a banjo and second cornet to the five-man Dixieland group; Louis Armstrong's *Hot Fives* of 1925 dispensed entirely with drums; and 'Jelly Roll' Morton's widely varying ensembles of the 1920s almost always included a tuba or double bass. Although Morton sometimes called on as many as ten musicians, the polyphonic basis of New Orleans jazz made a small number of melody instruments of differing timbres desirable, and by the time this style was revived in the late 1930s a six-piece combination consisting of trumpet or cornet, clarinet, trombone, piano, drums and double bass had become standard.

2. BIG BAND.   From the mid-1920s to about 1950 the jazz orchestra was continually enlarged. It was necessary to accommodate the many emerging soloists in an ensemble with written, or at least fixed, accompaniment. The number of instrumental combinations attempted were many and varied, but by 1928 both DUKE ELLINGTON and FLETCHER HENDERSON in New York had established identical formations consisting of a four-piece rhythm section, three trumpets, two trombones and a multi-instrument reed section of three players, who could double on the clarinet and any member of the saxophone family. Although it had occasionally been used in New Orleans jazz, the saxophone was the most important permanent new addition to the jazz band. It gradually took over the ensemble function of the clarinet, which was reserved for solos or special colouristic effects; by about 1945 the clarinet had become a rarity in big band arrangements and the saxophone the most favoured instrument of younger jazz musicians.

Both the Ellington and Henderson bands clearly divided the melody instruments into brass and reed sections, and this distinction was even more evident in the South-West and Kansas City groups which began to dominate ensemble jazz from the mid-1930s. By 1935 most large jazz bands consisted of 14 players: a four-man rhythm section (with guitar instead of banjo, and double bass instead of the earlier brass or reed bass instruments), a brass section of three trumpets and three trombones, and a four-piece reed section. The instrumental soloists were drawn from the various sections of the band, and some groups regularly featured vocalists. The 14-piece big band has proved remarkably versatile, as is shown, for example, by the wide range of colours produced by the Ellington-Strayhorn groups. During the 1940s, and particularly in STAN KENTON's 'progressive' bands, the numbers were expanded to five trumpets (one a high-note specialist), four trombones and five saxophones. This combination has served as the basis of most big band jazz ever since, as well as the many 'stage bands' found in North American high schools and colleges. Variations include the addition of horns and tuba to Claude Thornhill's band, the use of bass trombone and tuba in Shorty Rogers's groups and, since the advent of electronic amplification, the appearance of flutes in the 'reed' section. The oboe and bassoon, on the other hand, have never been incorporated comfortably into the big band setting; and although string sections appeared regularly in 'sweet' dance bands of the 1930s, their use in big bands is generally regarded by jazz musicians as a concession to popular taste.

3. SWING AND BOP COMBOS.   As swing-band arrangements of the late 1930s became more commercialized and stereotyped it became customary for jazz musicians to perform in smaller group settings. These groups were generally drawn from larger bands: there are many recordings of COUNT BASIE's sidemen using his celebrated four-piece rhythm section, and similar Ellington sub-groups. BENNY GOODMAN's first chamber ensemble was a trio of piano, clarinet and drums, to which he later added vibraphone, electric guitar and double bass; and Artie Shaw's Gramercy Five sometimes featured a harpsichord instead of a piano. One especially enduring combination was the trio of piano, drums and guitar or double bass explored by NAT 'KING' COLE from 1939; there was also some experimentation with duos, such as the Duke Ellington–Jimmy Blanton partnership in recordings made in 1940.

The bop style developed in the early 1940s from these smaller swing groups; since it was almost entirely an improvised art, there was no need for a large ensemble. Furthermore, the complex rhythmic interaction and harmonic explorations of the players rendered the rhythm guitar obsolete, and it was consequently dropped from the rhythm section, just as the clarinet and trombone largely disappeared from the melody instruments. The classic bop combo consisted of two 'horns' (usually trumpet and tenor or alto saxophone) and a rhythm section of piano, double bass and drums; any instrument might be called on to play solos. Innumerable bop and hard bop groups of the 1940s and 1950s followed this arrangement, and it has become the standard vehicle for jazz instruction at conservatories and universities. Attempts by musicians such as DIZZY GILLESPIE to transfer the bop style to a big band setting were singularly unsuccessful, possibly because a closer rapport between performers is necessary.

4. COOL AND WEST COAST ENSEMBLES.   While bop relied on a standardized small group, the cool and West Coast styles of jazz thrived on unusual combinations of instruments, for example the various nonets and 'tentettes' of GERRY MULLIGAN, MILES DAVIS and TEDDY CHARLES, the chamber groups of JIMMY GIUFFRE, and Mulligan's 'pianoless' quartets, which consisted of baritone saxophone, bass, drums, and trumpet or valve trombone. Perhaps the most important 'cool' arranger for jazz band was GIL EVANS, who made full use of symphonic wind instruments such as the piccolo, tuba, bassoon and bass clarinet, and also employed instruments even more unusual to jazz, such as the harp. Evans's and other cool groups produced music of high artistic value, yet their unusual instrumental combinations were seldom adopted by later musicians.

5. FREE JAZZ.   Free-jazz musicians of the 1960s were largely content to explore further solo possibilities of familiar jazz instruments. In the 1970s and 1980s, however, they systematically expanded jazz instrumentation in several directions at once to include previously untried variants of conventional instruments (e.g. Don Cherry's 'pocket trumpet'), new inventions or personal adaptations (e.g. Roland Kirk's 'stritch' and 'manzello', both modifications of the saxophone) and a vast number of exotic instruments and noise-makers reminiscent of the novelty effects of the 1920s, ranging from kazoos and harmonicas to slide whistles and steer horns. Many of

these were employed as much for theatrical effect as for their acoustical properties. At the same time, there was a large influx of instruments from non-American (especially African) cultures, signifying the increasing internationalization of this music. The size of the groups ranged widely from intimate duos to Sun Ra's twenty-piece ensembles, and a new sub-genre emerged in the saxophone quartet. As a rule, however, free-jazz musicians distinctly avoided electric instruments and electronic distortion, and by the late 1980s they had returned to variants of more familiar combo formats.

6. FUSION GROUPINGS.   New instrumentation was a key feature of the jazz fusion music which arose after 1970, combining elements of jazz and rock. This was apparent in the electronic amplification of the entire ensemble and particularly in the use of electric bass guitar, electric piano or synthesizers, and distortion devices such as wah-wah pedals, fuzz bass and bend bars. Another instance of the influence of rock was the new solo importance accorded to the electric guitar, which supplanted the saxophone to some extent. Additional percussion instruments, especially Latin American instruments such as congas, claves, gourds and berimbaus, were quite frequently added for colouristic effect. The number of players in jazz fusion groups varied widely from the four regular members of WEATHER REPORT to the massed rhythm sections in Miles Davis's groups of the early 1970s, which often called for two electric pianos, two drum kits, electric guitar, electric bass guitar, bass clarinet and much additional percussion to accompany a small number of improvising soloists.

7. SUMMARY.   Today all the styles of jazz history are still being avidly cultivated, and with them their characteristic ensembles: the six-piece New Orleans ensemble among amateurs and semi-professionals, the big band at high school and jazz clinics, the bop combo at jazz clubs and concert circuits, and avant-garde groupings in the loft scene and European festivals. The timbral experiments of the 1970s have left a permanent mark on the jazz drum kit and the use of ancillary percussion, and the electric bass guitar and keyboard have replaced their acoustic counterparts in the big band. At the end of the 20th century, although the eclectic and international character of jazz makes the precise constitution of the modern jazz band difficult to define, offshoots of the standard bop combo, divided into two or three melody instruments and rhythm section, are still very much in evidence.

VI. Rock bands

In structural terms, the foremost aim of a rock band's instrumentation is to enable the occupation of four distinct textural layers. These may identified as: the explicit 'beat' layer, the harmonic 'bass', the 'tune' and the harmonic 'filler'. The first of these is the function of the drums or other unpitched percussion; the second is supplied by the bass guitar (or double bass or, very occasionally, a keyboard instrument); the third may be heard through a solo voice or through a melodic instrument such as a solo guitar, a keyboard, saxophone, violin or flute; while the fourth can be the preserve of one or more guitars or keyboards, sometimes supplemented with or substituted by an orchestration such as a horn or string section, or backing voices. Within this list can be found those instruments which dominate the rock ensemble: electric guitar, electric bass guitar, drum kit and keyboards (organ, piano or synthesizers). Occasionally,

an unusual instrument (in a rock context) can help to define a band's sound, e.g. flute (Jethro Tull), violin (early King Crimson), or organ and piano combined (The Band).

As particular band formations have become established they have remained open to appropriation by other bands, often with very different stylistic goals. This article discusses the instruments that are played by members of rock bands and which are the basis of their sound in live performance. Once a band enters a recording studio there is limitless potential for adding the instruments or voices of session musicians who for economic or aesthetic reasons may not travel with the band on tour, or specially created sounds which, until the advent of sequencers, could not be recreated on stage. A live performance by a rock band and the creation of a recording of the same music by the same group may be approached as two completely different art forms (*see* POP, §II).

The ways that the early rock and roll bands of the 1950s approached the layering in their instrumentation varied according to the influence of the musical tradition from which each band arose. Thus, Chuck Berry inherited the guitar-dominated line-up of Chicago rhythm and blues (solo voice, one or two amplified guitars, double bass, drums, and occasionally piano), making much use of 'call and response' phrases between his voice and his guitar. Fats Domino's New Orleans-rooted style combined a dominant piano (playing a rhythmically articulated 'filler') with a sizable horn section (tenor and baritone saxophones, trumpet), bass and drums. Bill Haley's band, the Comets, which came from the jive and western swing traditions, consisted of guitars, saxophone, double bass and drums. Although in this period the individual identities of sidemen were not considered to be particularly important, certain instrumentalists (such as Scotty Moore, Elvis Presley's guitarist) played a crucial role in defining the singer's sound.

The skiffle bands of mid-1950s Britain emphasized the role of the guitar at the expense of the piano, partly out of a desire to imitate the 'wild' American rock and rollers, and partly out of a need (for aesthetic as well as economic reasons) for instruments that were both cheap and portable. The line-up of their successor, the 'beat combo' (short for 'combination'; by the 1990s the term was used only derogatively), was formalized in the late 50s by the Shadows as two guitars, electric bass, guitar and drums. The roles of the two guitars were distinct: Bruce Welch played rhythm guitar, largely strumming conventional chord shapes with rhythmic definition, while Hank Marvin played lead, exploiting the instrument's upper register and its ability to sustain sound.

Early rock bands in the 1960s tended to organize their sound either around guitars (e.g. the Rolling Stones and the Beatles) or around keyboards (the Animals), depending on their principal American stylistic models. The difference in technique is crucial to the sound of the band: whereas a keyboard player can perform separable lines simultaneously (fulfilling both 'filler' and 'tune' functions) and many varieties of chord voicings, the guitar's strengths lie in picking patterns, repeatable chord 'shapes' and, following developments in amplification in the mid-60s, in the physical control of feedback by the guitarist as an expressive device. From this period onwards, in styles where the influence of rhythm and blues or soul was prominent, for example in the work of Van Morrison, the keyboard-dominated ensemble was supplemented by two to six 'horns' (varicus combinations of trumpets, saxophones and trombones).

In the early music of the Kinks (1965–6), the role of the rhythm guitar dwindled to the point where it simply provided riffs (very short, repeatable melodic ideas which minimally outline the song's harmonies). In the contemporaneous work of the Who the rhythm guitar was dispensed with altogether and Pete Townshend tended to cover both guitar roles, although he did not play many of the florid solos associated with other virtuoso lead guitarists of the day. Indeed, their song *Substitute* (1966) is notable in that the 'guitar solo' was taken by the bass player, John Entwistle. The use of controlled feedback on the guitar enhanced its power to fill out musical space, such that the Who's practice of using a single guitar, bass and drums was developed by the end of the 60s into the so-called 'power trio', defined by bands such as Cream and the Jimi Hendrix Experience, in which one or more of the players also took up the vocal duties. This combination was subsequently employed by the Jam (in the late 1970s) and by Nirvana (in the late 80s), where it connoted a return to the 'no frills' raw essentials of music, allied with an aggressive, confrontational aesthetic. The unavailability of overdubbing facilities in live performance meant that some compromises had to be made: on record, Cream's Eric Clapton would often add a rhythm guitar part in addition to playing lead (hence the differences between the studio and live recordings on the album *Wheels of Fire*, 1969), while Led Zeppelin's bass player John Paul Jones would sometimes move over to the organ in live performance, requiring exceptional power from the drummer John Bonham to cover the lack of the bass layer.

There was a resurgence in the use of the keyboard in rock with the development of PROGRESSIVE ROCK (also in the late 60s), with its stylistic references to European art music, too foreign to the blues-based guitar styles of the time. Keyboard players such as Keith Emerson and Rick Wakeman transplanted the visual spectacle of the guitar virtuosos to the keyboard. A concurrent trend was towards using two lead guitars (e.g. Derek and the Dominos, the Allman Brothers Band, and Wishbone Ash); this has survived as an aspect of 'stadium rock' (Big Country) and also in heavy metal (Saxon).

In the late 70s, a new guitar-based style flourished: PUNK ROCK. Its nihilistic, audience-disdaining stagecraft was an antidote to the lavish spectacle and huge touring forces employed by groups such as Emerson, Lake and Palmer (who were accompanied on tour by three massive trucks, a revolving drum kit and even an entire orchestra of individually microphoned musicians). The second resurgence of the keyboard was due to the new generation of cheap and portable synthesizers and sequencers of the late 1970s, as bands such as the Human League went on stage with everything except the vocals pre-recorded (i.e. sequenced for live playback). Within the next two decades this approach to performance became dominant in the dance music of the nightclub scene.

One aspect of the use of synthesizers and sequencers, particularly since the invention of MIDI, has been the ability to reproduce during live performance a host of sounds originally created in the recording studio. A line-up of keyboard and guitar can be balanced in different ways: equally (early Yes), with the keyboard dominant (Elvis Costello and the Attractions) or with the guitar dominant (early Deep Purple).

The early 1980s tended to be overrun with bands made up entirely of synthesizers and sequencers (e.g. Depeche Mode, Soft Cell and Ultravox). Against this background, a space was left for a new generation of bands who paraded the 'authenticity' of their line-ups to create a sense that their emotional expression was to be trusted. For Bruce Springsteen's seven-piece touring band (including two keyboard players), the song lyrics and Springsteen's emotional intensity were crucial. Bands like U2 or, in the 1990s, the Manic Street Preachers, emphasized the idea that the guitarist is directly, physically in touch with his or her sound-producing source in a way that the synthesizer player is not. A similar desire or perceived need appears to have promoted the occasional return of established artists such as Eric Clapton and Rod Stewart to acoustic-only performances, most famously in MTV's 'unplugged' concert series.

Another line of development, exemplified by British 'indie' bands such as the Smiths in the early 80s and the Inspiral Carpets later in the decade, reinvestigated the classic guitar-led line-ups and used them in new musical contexts. Bands such as the Stone Roses adopted Hendrix-inspired guitar techniques, and guitar-work was prominent in the various waves of BRITPOP in the 1990s (The Verve, Oasis, Suede, etc.). The strong sense of recalling the 1960s has also led to a resurgence of the use of analogue keyboards (Pulp uses a Farfisa organ in its line-up) and even small string sections (Catatonia).

BIBLIOGRAPHY

A: GENERAL

G. Kastner: *Manuel général de musique militaire* (Paris, 1848/R)

A. Vessella: *La banda dalle origini fino ai nostri giorni* (Milan, 1935)

F. Fennell: *Time and the Winds* (Kenosha, WI, 1954)

A. Baines: *Woodwind Instruments and their History* (London, 1957, 3/1967/R)

Journal of Band Research (1964–)

Brass Quarterly (Durnham, NH, 1957/8–1963/4); contd as *Brass and Woodwind Quarterly* (Durnham, NH, 1966/8–1969)

A.G. Wright and S.Newcomb: *Bands of the World* (Evanston, IL, 1970)

W. Suppan: *Lexikon des Blasmusikwesens* (Freiburg, 1973, 4/1994 with A. Suppan)

D. Whitwell: *The History and Literature of the Wind Band and Wind Ensemble* (Northridge, CA, 1982–4)

D. Whitwell: *A Concise History of the Wind Band* (Northridge, CA, 1985)

Journal of the Historic Brass Society (1988–)

A. Hofer: *Blasmusikforschung: eine kritische Einführung* (Darmstadt, 1992)

W. Suppan, ed.: *Internationale Gesellschaft zur Erforschung und Förderung der Blasmusik: Kongress X: Felkirch 1992*

M. Anesa: *Dizionario della Musica Italiana per Banda* (Bergamo, 1993)

F.J. Cipolla and D.Hunsberger, eds.: *The Wind Ensemble and its Repertoire* (Rochester, NY, 1994)

T. Herbert and J.Wallace, eds.: *The Cambridge Companion to Brass Instruments* (Cambridge, 1997)

B: HISTORY BEFORE 1800

H.F. von Fleming: *Der Vollkommene Teutsche Soldat* (Leipzig, 1726)

J.C. Hinrichs: *Entstehung, Fortgang und ietzige Beschaffenheit der russischen Iagdmusik* (St. Petersburg, 1796/R)

E. Bowles: 'Haut and Bas: the Grouping of Musical Instruments in the Middle Ages', *MD*, viii (1954), 115–40

T. Volek: 'Pražké muzikantské cechy, městší hudebníci a trubači v druhé polovině 18. století', [Prague musicians' guilds, town musicians and trumpeter players in the second half of the 18th century], *MMC*, no.6 (1958), 75–93

E. Bowles: 'Musical Instruments in Civic Processions during the Middle Ages', *AcM*, xxxiii (1961), 147–61

R. Rastall: 'The Minstrels in the English Royal Households, 25 Edward I – 1 Henry VIII: an Inventory', *RMARC*, iv (1964), 1–41

K. Polk: 'Municipal Wind Music in Flanders in the Late Middle Ages', *BWQ*, ii (1969), 1–15

W. Salmen, ed.: *Der Sozialstatus des Berufsmusikers vom 17. bis 19. Jahrhundert* (Kassel, 1971); Eng. trans., rev., 1983 as *The Social Status of the Professional Musician from the Middle Ages to the 19th Century* [incl. H.W. Schwab: 'Zur sozialen Stellung des Stadtmusikanten', 9–25]

R. Hellyer: *Harmoniemusik: Music for the Small Wind Band in the Late Eighteenth and Early Nineteenth Centuries* (diss., U. of Oxford, 1973)

S.M.G. Sandman: *Wind Band Music under Louis XIV: the Philidor Collection, Music for the Military and the Court* (diss., Stanford U., 1974)

D. Whitwell: *Band Music of the French Revolution* (Tutzing, 1979)

E. Croft-Murray: 'The Wind-Band in England, 1540–1840', *Music and Civilisation*, ed. T.C. Mitchell (London, 1980), 135–79

W.F. Prizer: 'Bernardino Piffaro e i pifferi e tromboni di Mantova: strumenti a fiato in una corte italiana', *RIM* xvi (1981), 151–84

H.W. Schwab: *Die Anfänge des weltlichen Berufsmuikertums in der mittelalterlichen Stadt* (Kassel, 1982)

W. Salmen: *Der Spielmann im Mittelalter* (Innsbruck, 1983)

R. Hellyer: 'The Wind Ensembles of the Esterházy Princes, 1761–1813', *Haydn Yearbook 1984*, 5–92

M.J. Lomas: *Amateur Brass and Wind Bands in Southern England Between the Late 18th Century and circa 1900* (diss., Open U., 1990)

E. Preinsperger: 'Verzeichnis der Noten für Harmonie-Musik und Blasorchester in der Festetics-Sammlung in Keszthely, Ungarn', *Musica pannonica*, ii (1993), 1–159

S. Owens: *The Württemberg Hofkapelle c.1680–1721* (diss., Victoria U. of Wellington, 1995)

F.A. D'Accone: *The Civic Muse: Music and Musicians in Siena during the Middle Ages and the Renaissance* (Chicago, 1997)

J. Pöschl: *Jagdmusik: Kontinuität und Entwicklung in der europäischen Geschichte*(Tutzing, 1997)

C: MIXED WIND BANDS

(i) General

C. Mandel: *A Treatise on the Instrumentation of Military Bands* (London, 1859)

A. Kalkbrenner: *Wilhelm Wieprecht, Direktor: sein Leben und Wirken nebst einem Auszug seiner Schriften*(Berlin, 1882)

A. Kalkbrenner: *Die Organisation der Militärmusikchöre aller Länder* (Hanover, 1884)

A. Vessella: *Studi di strumentazione per banda* (Milan, 1897)

H.G. Farmer: *Memoires of the Royal Artillery Band* (London, 1904)

G. Miller: *The Miltary Band* (London, 1912)

H.E. Adkins: *Treatise on the Military Band* (London, 1931, 3/1958)

H.G. Farmer: *History of the Royal Artillery Band, 1726–1953* (London, 1954)

R. van Yperen: *De Nederlandse militaire muziek* (Bussum, 1966)

E. Rameis: *Die österreichische Militärmusik von ihren Anfängen bis zum Jahre 1918*, ed. E. Brixel (Tutzing, 1976)

J. Eckhardt: *Zivil-und Militärmusiker im Wilhelminischen Reich* (Regensburg, 1978)

A. Suppan: *Repertorium der Märsche für Blasorchester* (Tutzing, 1982–90)

W. Suppan, ed.: *Bläserklang und Blasinstrumente im Schaffen Richard Wagners: Seggau 1983* [incl. W. Suppan: 'Anton Bruckner und das Blasorchester', 189–219]

B. Habla: *Besetzung und Instrumentation des Blasorchesters seit der Erfindung der Ventile für Blechblasinstrumente bis zum Zweiten Weltkrieg in Österreich und Deutschland* (Tutzing, 1990)

T. Akiyama: *Band Music Index 552* (Tokyo, 1992)

L. Marosi: *Két évszázad katonazenéje Magyarországon, 1741–1945*[Two centuries of military music in Hungary, 1741–1945] (Budapest, 1994)

A. Carlini: 'Le bande musicale nell' Italia dell'ottocento', *RIM*, xxx (1995), 85–133

K.W. Kinder: 'Franz Liszt's Music for Voices and Winds', *Journal of the World Association for Symphonic Bands and Ensembles*, ii (1995) [whole issue]

W. Baethge and W. Suppan: 'Military Musicians in Japan During the Early Meiji-Era (since 1868)', *Journal of the World Association for Symphonic Bands and Ensembles*, iii (1996), 13–32

(ii) North America

EMC2 (H. Kallman and others)

W.H. Dana: *J.W. Pepper's Practical Guide and Study to the Secret of Arranging Band Music* (Philadelphia, 1878)

O. Comettant: *La musique de la Garde republicaine en Amérique* (Paris, 1894)

A.A. Clappé: *The Wind-Band and its Instruments* (New York, 1911/R)

J.P. Sousa: *Marching Along* (Boston, 1928, rev. 2/1994 by P.E. Bierley)

E.F. Goldman: *Band Betterment* (New York, 1934)

R.F. Dvorak: *The Band on Parade* (New York, 1937)

R.F. Goldman: *The Band's Music* (New York, 1938)

R.F. Goldman: *The Concert Band* (New York, 1946)

H.W. Schwartz: *Bands of America* (Garden City, NY, 1957/R)

H. Kallmann: *A History of Music in Canada, 1534–1914* (Toronto, 1960/R)

R.F. Goldman: *The Wind Band* (Boston, 1961/R)

H.H. Hall: *A Johnny Reb Band from Salem: the Pride of Tarheelia* (Raleigh, NC, 1963/R)

J. Felts: 'Some Aspects of the Rise and Development of the Wind Band during the Civil War', *Journal of Band Research*, iii/2 (1966–7), 29–33

C. Bryant: *And the Band Played On, 1776–1976* (Washington DC, 1975)

R.F. Camus: *Military Music of the American Revolution* (Chapel Hill, NC, 1976/R)

F.J. Cipolla: 'Annotated Guide for the Study and Performance of Nineteenth Century Band Music in the United States', *Journal of Band Research*, xiv/1 (1978–9), 22–40

F.J. Cipolla: 'A Bibliography of Dissertations Relative to the Study of Bands and Band Music', *Journal of Band Research*, xv (1979–80), no.1, pp.1–31; xvi (1980–81) no.1, pp.29–36

K.E. Olson: *Music and Musket: Bands and Bandsmen of the American Civil War* (Westport, CT, 1981)

R. Garofalo and M. Elrod: *A Pictorial History of Civil War Era Musical Instruments & Military Bands* (Charleston, WV, 1985)

S.T. Maloney: 'A History of the Wind Band in Canada', *Journal of Band Research*, xxiii/2 (1987–8), 10–29

K. Kreitner: *Discoursing Sweet Music: Town Bands and Community Life in Turn-of-the-Century Pennsylvania* (Urbana, IL, 1990)

W.H. Rehrig: *The Heritage Encyclopedia of Band Music: Composers and Their Music*, ed. P. Bierley (Westerville, OH, 1991–6)

R.F. Camus, ed.: *American Wind and Percussion Music* (Boston, 1992) [incl. 'Index to Three Centuries of American Music']

F. Battisti: *20th Century American Wind Band/Ensemble: History, Development and Literature* (Fort Lauderdale, FL, 1995)

R.F. Camus: 'Die Geschichte der Amerikanischen Blasmusik', *Pannonische Forschungsstelle Oberschützen*, vi (1995), 3–114

A. Suppan: 'Blasmusik-Dissertationen in den USA', *SMH*, xxxvi (1995), 181–226

D: BRASS BANDS

(i) General

G.F. Patton: *A Practial Guide to the Arrangement of Band Music* (Leipzig, 1875/R)

A.S. Rose: *Talks with Bandsmen: a Popular Handbook for Brass Instrumentalists* (London, 1895, rev. 1996 with introduction by A. Myers)

E. Jackson: 'Origin and Promotion of Brass Band Contests', *MO*, xix (1895–6), 392–3, 454–5, 538–9, 673, 814–15; xx (1896–7) (1896–7), 101–3

C.J. Vincent: *The Brass Band and How to Write for it* (London, 1908)

H.C. Hind: *The Brass Band* (London, 1934/R)

J.F. Russell and J.H. Elliott: *The Brass Band Movement* (London, 1936)

F. Wright, ed.: *Brass Today* (London, 1957)

B. Boon: *Play the Music, Play!* (London, 1966/R)

Sounding Brass and the Conductor (1972–80)

Directory of British Brass Bands, ed. British Federation of Brass Bands (York, 1975–)

V. and G. Brand, eds.: *Brass Bands in the 20th Century* (Letchworth, 1979)

A.R. Taylor: *Brass Bands* (London, 1979)

C. Bainbridge: *Brass Triumphant* (London, 1980)

H. Mortimer and A. Lynton: *Harry Mortimer on Brass* (Sherborne, 1981)

A.R. Taylor: *Labour and Love: an Oral History of the Brass Band Movement* (London, 1983)

A. Hailstone: *The British Bandsman Centenary Book: a Social History of Brass Bands* (Baldock, 1987)

D. Russell: *Popular Music in England, 1840–1914: a Social History* (Manchester, 1987, 2/1997)

G.D. Booth: 'Brass Bands: Tradition, Change, and the Mass Media in Indian Wedding Music', *EthM*, xxxiv (1990), 245–62

T. Herbert, ed.: *Bands: the Brass Band Movement in the 19th and 20th Centuries* (Milton, Keynes, 1991)

R.B. Flaes: *Bewogen koper* (Amsterdam, 1993)

K. Karjalainen: *Soumalainen torviseitsikko: Historia ja perinteen jatkuminen* (Tampere, 1995)

T. Herbert, ed.: *The British Brass Band: A Musical and Social History* (Oxford, 2000)

(ii) North America

E. Howe: *First Part of the Musician's Companion* (Boston, 1844)

A. Dodworth: *Dodworth's Brass Band School* (New York, 1853/R)

G.W.E. Friederich: *Brass Band Journal* (New York, 1853–4) [music; some pts repr. as *American Brass Band Journal*]

W.C. Peters & Sons: *Peters' Sax-Horn Journal* (Cincinnati, 1859)

W.J. Schafer and R.B. Allen: *Brass Bands and New Orleans Jazz* (Baton Rouge, LA, 1977)

J. Newsom: 'The American Brass Band Movement', *Quarterly Journal of the Library of Congress*, xxxvi (1979), 114–39

J.P. Watson: *Starting a British Band* (Grand Rapids, MI, 1984)

R.W. Holz: *Heralds of Victory: a History Celebrating the 100th Anniversary of the New York Staff Band & Male Chorus, 1887–1987* (New York, 1986)

P. Watson: *The Care and Feeding of a Community British Brass Band* (Farmingdale, NY 1986)

M.H. and R.M. Hazen: *The Music Men: an Illustrated History of the Brass Bands in America, 1800–1920* (Washington DC, 1987)

N.M. Hosler: *The Brass Band Movement in North America: a Survey of Brass Bands in the United States and Canada* (diss., Ohio State U., 1992)

E: JAZZ AND ROCK BANDS

A. Lange: *Arranging for the Modern Dance Orchestra* (New York, 1926)

G. Miller: *Glen Miller's Method for Orchestral Arranging* (New York, 1943)

L.G. Feather: *The Book of Jazz: a Guide to the Entire Field* (New York, 1957, 2/1965 as *The Book of Jazz from Then till Now: a Guide to the Entire Field*)

W. Russo: *Composing for the Jazz Orchestra* (Chicago, 1961)

W. Russo: *Jazz Composition and Orchestration* (Chicago, 1968/R)

D. Baker: *Arranging and Composing for the Small Ensemble* (Chicago, 1970/R)

W. Russo: *Workbook for Composing for the Jazz Orchestra* (Chicago, 1978)

G. Martin, ed.: *Making Music: the Guide to Writing, Performing & Recording* (New York, 1983)

A.M. Dauer: *Tradition afrikanischer Blasorchester und Entstehung des Jazz* (Graz, 1985)

O. Curth: 'Untersuchungen zu Big Band Arrangements von Thad Jones für das Thad Jones–Mel Lewis Jazz Orchestra', *Jazzforschung*, xxii (1990), 53–117

M. Michaels and J. Braider: *The Billboard Book of Rock Arranging* (New York, 1990)

N. York, ed.: *The Rock File: Making it in the Music Business* (Oxford, 1991)

M. Bayton: *Frock Rock: Women Making Popular Music* (Oxford, 1999)

For further bibliography *see* MILITARY MUSIC and SIGNAL (i).

KEITH POLK (II, 1), JANET K. PAGE (II, 2(i–ii)), JANET K. PAGE, STEPHEN J. WESTON (II, 2(iii)), ARMIN SUPPAN, WOLFGANG SUPPAN (III, 1–3, 5), RAOUL F. CAMUS (III, 4; IV, 4), TREVOR HERBERT (IV, 1, 3, 5), ANTHONY C. BAINES/R (IV, 2), J. BRADFORD ROBINSON (V), ALLAN F. MOORE (VI)

Band (ii) (Ger.). *See* FRET.

Band, the. Canadian rock group. It was led by (James) Robbie Robertson (*b* Toronto, 5 July 1944; guitar); its other members were Levon Helm (*b* Marvell, AR, 26 May 1942; drums), Richard Manuel (*b* Stratford, ON, 3 April 1945; *d* Winter Park, FL, 4 March 1986; keyboards), Rick Danko (*b* Simcoe, ON, 9 Dec 1943; *d* Hurley, NY, 10 Dec 1999; bass guitar, fiddle and mandolin), and Garth Hudson (*b* Eric Hudson; London, ON, 2 Aug 1942; organ, saxophone and euphonium). Except for Hudson, all members of the group also sang. They first played together as part of Ronnie Hawkins' group in the late 1950s and early 1960s.

Having left Hawkins in 1964, they were engaged the following year by Bob Dylan as his backing group; they took part in his world tour in 1965–6. They developed a style of songwriting that combined Dylan's allusive lyrics with their own eclectic, stately and enigmatic brand of rock. They recorded a number of songs that showed an extraordinary attention to detail despite the rough quality of the recording; these were widely issued illegally before their commercial release in 1975 on the album *The Basement Tapes*.

In 1968 the Band recorded *Music from Big Pink*; this album is notable for the freedom with which the vocal lines intertwine and overlap with one another, in contrast to their later recordings. Before returning to live performances the group recorded its second album, *The Band* (1969). At this time they were briefly regarded as a country-rock group, but their arrangements, which were characterized by calm tempos, economical playing by Robertson and Helm, and the use of two keyboard instruments, also suggested hymns, parlour songs, Cajun music, brass bands, blues and other American styles.

Between 1971 and 1977 the Band continued to record original and other people's material in studio and concert performances, and in 1974 they joined Dylan for his album *Planet Waves* and a tour of America. The group gave its final performance in 1976, which included guest appearances by Dylan, Eric Clapton, Joni Mitchell, Muddy Waters, Neil Young and others, and was documented in Scorsese's *The Last Waltz* (1978). During the 1980s the Band reunited a number of times for concert tours without Robertson, and in 1993 Danko, Helm and Hudson recorded the album *Jericho*.

The Band's music drew on the basic vocabulary of rock, blues and country, and its restrained style can be seen as a reaction to the musical excesses of the psychedelic rock era. Their first two albums contain deeply felt, carefully crafted rock, but as Robertson's productivity as a songwriter declined, the group's music became increasingly formulaic and less consistently satisfying.

BIBLIOGRAPHY

G. Marcus: *Mystery Train: Images of America in Rock 'n' Roll Music* (New York, 1975, enlarged 2/1982)

D. Emblidge: 'Down Home with the Band: Country-Western Music and Rock', *EthM*, xx (1976), 541–52

B. Hoskyns: *Across the Great Divide: the Band and America* (New York and London, 1993)

JON PARELES

Banda (It.). *See* MILITARY BAND. Also the brass or brass and percussion section of an orchestra; also the stage band used in 19th-century Italian opera; *see* BAND (i), §I.

Banda turca (It.). *See* JANISSARY MUSIC.

Banderali, Davidde (*b* Lodi, 12 Jan 1789; *d* Paris, 13 June 1849). Italian tenor and singing teacher. He made his début at the Teatro Carcano, Milan, in 1806, but after a few years as a singer, specializing in *buffo* roles, he turned to teaching. In 1814 he became director of the Teatro dei

Filodrammatici, Milan, where in the following year the 18-year-old Giuditta Negri, later to be known as Pasta, made her début in Scappa's *Le tre Eleonore*. In 1817 he sang Marco Orazio in two performances of Cimarosa's *Gli Orazi ed i Curiazi* at La Scala, with Josephina Grassini as Orazia. He taught in Milan from 1821 to 1828, and then for 20 years in Paris. His pupils included Pasta, the sopranos Adelaide Comelli-Rubini and Henriette Méric-Lalande, and the baritone Paolo Barroilhet.

ELIZABETH FORBES

Bandiera, Lodovico (*fl* Rome, 1663). Italian composer. He was a Minorite, a doctor of theology and for a time *maestro di cappella* of the church of SS Apostoli, Rome. He published *Psalmi vespertini dominicales una cum quatuor antiphonis*, for four voices and continuo (Rome, 1663), as a thanksgiving to St Anthony for relief from difficulties. The psalms are concerted pieces in which sections for the full complement of voices alternate with solo episodes. As well as these and the antiphons, the volume contains a *Magnificat*, litanies and a responsory.

GIUSEPPE VECCHI

Bandmaster (Fr. *chef d'harmonie*; Ger. *Kapellmeister*; It. *capobanda*). The master, leader or director of a band (see BAND (i)). Earlier titles included Music Master, Music Major and Leader of the Band. Bandmasters normally hold officer's rank in the armed forces; in the 18th century and the 19th they were often civilians. Army bandsmen in Britain have been formally trained as bandmasters since 1857 at Kneller Hall (Royal Military School of Music); see LONDON, §VIII, 3 (ii). Some eminent bandmasters of the past are: Julius Fučík (1872–1916), Josef Gung'l (1809–89), Andreas Leonhardt (1800–66) and C.M. Ziehrer (1843–1922) in the Austro-Hungarian Empire; Carl Boosé (1815–68), Dan Godfrey (1831–1903), Charles Godfrey (ii) (1839–1919) and Ladislao Zavertal (1849–1942) in Britain; J.J. Gagnier (1885–1949), Charles O'Neill (1882–1964) and Joseph Vézina (1849–1924) in Canada; F.-J. Gossec (1734–1829), H.E. Klosé (1808–80), J.-G. Kastner (1810–67), Jean Paulus (1816–98), Gabriel Parès (1860–1934) and Bernard Sarrette (1765–1858) in France; Wilhelm Wieprecht (1802–72) in Germany; Alessandro Vessella (1860–1929) and Giovanni Orsomando (1895–1989) in Italy; and A.A. Clappé (1850–1920), Herbert L. Clarke (1867–1945), Merle Evans (1894–1987), Henry Fillmore (1881–1956), P.S. Gilmore (1829–92), E.F. Goldman (1878–1956), A.A. Harding (1880–1958), Frank Johnson (1792–1844), K.L. King (1891–1971), Arthur Pryor (1870–1942), W.D. Revelli (1902–94) and J.P. Sousa (1854–1932) in the USA (for information on early British history and many additional eminent bandmasters see *Grove5*; see also MILITARY MUSIC, §3 and for bibliography see BAND (i)).

H.G. FARMER/RAOUL F. CAMUS

Bandola. A flat-backed lute of South and Central America, descended from the BANDURRIA (*see also* MANDORE). The modern *bandola* of Colombia has a tear-drop shape, with a flat or concave back. It has six courses of strings, three steel strings in each of the four upper courses, and two copper-wound strings in each of the two lower courses, tuned *f♯–b–e'–a'–d''–g''*. It is played with a plectrum and, as in mandolin playing, a note may be sustained by a tremolo. In the Colombian Andes it plays in the *murga* ensemble to accompany dancing and the singing of *coplas*;

the *murga* is sometimes augmented by a second *bandola*, the two playing in characteristic parallel 3rds and 6ths. The *bandola* is used in Chilean Andean music, where it accompanies solo shepherd songs, and in the Guatemalan *zarabanda* ensemble (*see* GUATEMALA, §II, 2). There are two types of Venezuelan *bandola*: the first, found in the western plains, has four single strings, tuned *b–e'–b'–f'*; the second, from north-eastern Venezuela, has four double courses, the lower pairs tuned in octaves and the higher strings in unison, as follows: *A/a–e/e'–b'/b'–f♯''/f♯''*.

Bandolim (Port.). *See* MANDOLIN.

Bandolin (Sp.). *See* MANDOLIN.

Bandoneon [bandoneón]. Square-built button accordion or CONCERTINA developed in the 1840s by Heinrich Band of Krefeld, but similar to the 'Chemnitz' concertina of C.F. Uhlig, invented in the previous decade. All early models were diatonic: they produced different notes on the push and pull of the bellows (see illustration). In 1921 a chromatic model was introduced that produced the same note on the push and the pull: this instrument has almost totally eclipsed the diatonic variety. Most bandoneons have two reed banks and no shifts (register changes). Different models may have 64, 88, 104, 106, 128, 154, 176, and even 220 notes; the South American instrument usually has 38 keys or buttons for the high and medium registers and 33 for the lower register. The bandoneon has been used since about 1900 as a solo virtuoso instrument in tango orchestras of Argentina, Uruguay and Brazil. Perhaps its most famous exponent was the Argentine Astor Piazzolla (1921–92). *See also* ACCORDION.

Bandora [pandora] (Fr. *pandore, bandore*; Ger. *Bandoer, Pandora*). A plucked chordophone (classified as a lute) of bass register with metal strings and a scalloped and festooned body outline, said to have been invented in London in 1562. Besides having a considerable solo repertory, it was required to accompany some of the earliest printed English songs, and was one of the six obligatory instruments of the mixed CONSORT. There are many references to its use in the theatre and in court entertainments through the late 16th century and the 17th, but by the 18th it was falling into disuse.

The bandora has a flat or slightly domed back and a flat soundboard into which is set a circular ornamental

Arnold diatonic bandoneon

'rose' soundhole. It is strung with iron and brass wires, the lowest of which are twisted from two or more strands, not overspun like modern ones. Bacon (*Sylva Sylvarum*, 1627) writes of 'a *Wreathed String* such as are in the Base Strings of Bandoraes'. The strings run in double courses from the pegbox, usually 'viol' type with lateral pegs, over the fingerboard and soundboard to the bridge, which is glued in position, as on a lute. The bandora has a special method of string attachment at the bridge, that is, a fret-like strip of brass and a row of hitch-pins along its bottom edge. Although the bandora has been described as a kind of bass cittern, its fixed bridge and the lute-like system of bars under its flat soundboard make it acoustically quite distinct. Whereas the cittern was normally a plectrum instrument, the bandora was played with the fingers (although Roger North reported in the late 17th century that the 'pandora' was 'struck with a quill'). The only features the two instruments have in common are the metal strings and sheet brass frets, secured in tapering slots in the fingerboard by hardwood wedges.

Praetorius (2/1619) stated that the bandora was an English invention, which is confirmed in the sixth edition of John Stowe's *Annales, or a General Chronicle Of England* (1631);

In the fourth yere of Queen Elizabeth John Rose, dwelling in Bridewell, devised and made an instrument with wyer strings, commonly called the Bandora, and left a son, far excelling himselfe in making Bandoraes, Voyall de Gamboes and other instruments.

The undulating outline very probably had an allegorical or symbolical meaning, perhaps connected with the scallop shell (see Wells, 1982); the shape was also used on certain viols, at least one of which is attributed to Rose. The alternative spelling, *pandora*, may be an allusion to the legend of Pandora's box. There seems to be no connection with the Spanish *bandurria* nor with the 'pandora' whose invention Alessandro Piccinini claimed in 1623; this was apparently a lute with extension bass strings and additional short metal strings in the treble, perhaps akin to the English POLIPHANT.

The earliest illustrations of both the bandora and its close relative, the orpharion, are in William Barley's *New Booke of Tabliture* (1596). This was published in parts, containing instructions and music for the lute as well as for these two wire-strung instruments. At first glance, the two illustrations look remarkably similar, though the orpharion is shown with seven pairs of strings and the bandora has only six. Furthermore, whereas the bandora has its bridge and frets placed in the normal way, at right angles to the strings (fig.1), the orpharion has them set obliquely, to give a progressive increase in length from treble to bass (*see* ORPHARION, fig 3). This innovation was probably crucial to the subsequent development of the two instruments, and seems to have taken place only a few years before Barley's book was printed. In a letter from Francis Derrick in Antwerp to a friend in London, dated 9 October 1594, there is a postscript:

I am requested by Throck: to write unto you verie earnestly to buy him a bandora or orphery[n] of the new fashion wch hath the bridge and the stoppes slope and aswell the treble as the oth[er] stringes wyre. The best you can fynde wherin you must use the help of some [who] can skill in that instrument. and also to procure some principall les[sons] for the bandora of Ho[l]bornes makinge or other most conninge men i[n that instru]ment And whatsoever you lay out either for the instrument or the lessons he will repay you wth great thankes ...

(Cecil Papers 28/83)

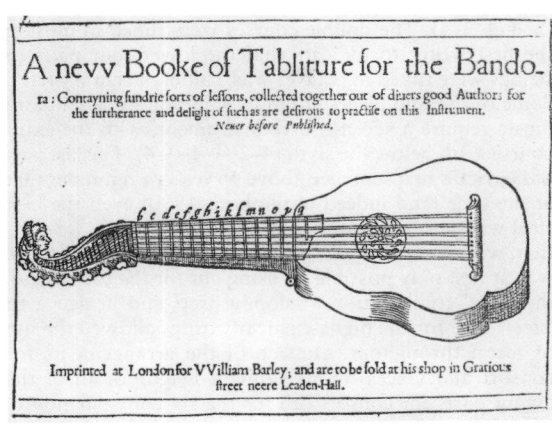

1. Title-page, with woodcut of a bandora, from William Barley's 'A New Booke of Tabliture for the Bandora' (London, 1596)

Subsequent illustrations for the bandora, including those of Fludd (1617), Praetorius (2/1619; fig.2), Mersenne (1636–7), Trichet (*c*1640) and others all show this feature, although some of the engravers have not understood the absurdity of a sloping bridge with straight frets, or vice versa. The measurements recorded by Talbot (*c*1695) also indicated the sloping arrangement.

Barley is the earliest source for the tunings of both bandora and orpharion, which he gives in tablature, indicating the intervals between the courses but not the nominal pitch. For a six-course bandora, starting from the bass, the intervals are 2nd, 4th, 4th, major 3rd, 4th

2. Bandora (1), with an orpharion (3), penorcon (2) and 'Italian' lyra da gamba (4): woodcut from Praetorius's 'Syntagma musicum' (Wolfenbüttel, 2/1619); note that the orpharion and penorcon are wrongly numbered in the illustration

(2–4–4–3–4). The double courses were tuned in unison; the first writer to indicate that the lower four pairs of strings were tuned in octaves was Talbot, a century later. Some of the solo pieces in Barley's anthology of bandora music require a seven-course instrument, with the extra course a 4th below the sixth (4–2–4–4–3–4). The last part of Derrick's first sentence above serves as a reminder that at the time (and indeed until about 1900) even the best steel wire was inferior to gut in tensile strength. It seems that, with parallel bridge and frets, the extension in range was at first only possible by using gut for the top course; the 'new' combination of sloping frets and bridge with 'steel' wire for the highest pair of strings allowed the use of metal throughout. Outside of the arrangements for consort and voices by Sir William Leighton, all of the extant parts for consort call for the six-course bandora. On the other hand, many pieces in the solo literature call for the seventh course.

The question of pitch is still unanswered. Praetorius (2/1619) states that the Bandora was tuned in 'Chorton', a step lower than 'Cammerton'. However, there is reason to believe that, in the consort at least, the bandora was pitched at the higher level (Segerman, 1988). Ian Harwood (1981) has also suggested that there was a high-pitch bandora at a 4th above the larger size. Barley's collection of music included four songs with accompaniment for six-course bandora which give clues to the nominal pitch. However, if the vocal pitch is taken at its face value, the result is somewhat confusing. In two songs the apparent bandora tuning is F–G–c–f–a–d'; in one it is a tone higher, and in another a fourth lower, C–D–G–c–e–a. These variant tunings are most probably a 'transposition of convenience', to avoid the singer's having to read in key signatures that would be most improbable for the time. There are many other examples of this device in the English and continental lute-song repertory. The last of these tunings, with a as the top string, is the only acknowledged tuning for the instrument. It agrees with the nominal pitch of the bandora in the consort lessons of Morley (1599, 1611) and Rosseter (1609), as well as manuscript sources. This tuning is confirmed by writers such as Fludd (1617) and Praetorius (2/1619).

Almost from the date of its invention the bandora was associated with the theatre. In Gascoigne's *Jocasta* (performed in London in 1566), it is named (as 'bandurion') among the instruments used for the dumb-show between the acts. In 1598, Philip Henslowe's inventory of the properties of the Rose Theatre included a bandora among the instruments. On 18 September 1602, the Duke of Stettin-Pomerania wrote in his diary of the music in the indoor Blackfriars Playhouse: 'For a whole hour before the play begins, one listens to a delightful instrumental consort'; he included a bandora in his list of instruments played. The actor Augustine Phillips bequeathed his bass viol, lute, cittern and bandora to two of his apprentices, and Edward Alleyn, actor, manager, and founder of Dulwich College, left a lute, bandora, cittern and six viols to the school in 1626. As Dart commented, 'The pandora positively smells of greasepaint' (*Two Consort Lessons*, London, 1957).

The bandora was by no means confined to the theatre, however. It enjoyed a great vogue in courtly circles, particularly as a member of the mixed consort. The 'consorte of broken musicke' seems to have been first heard at Kenilworth in 1575, during the lavish entertainment given for Queen Elizabeth by the Earl of Leicester; it was later called on to perform at almost every entertainment devised for her famous 'progresses'. During the visit of the queen to Elvetham in Hampshire in 1591 there was a performance by 'an exquisite consort; wherein was the lute, pandora, base violl, citterne, treble viol and flute', the same instruments used in the 'consort lessons' published by Morley and Rosseter. In such music as this, the cittern and bandora play the upper and lower halves of what amounts to a plucked 'continuo' part. However, the bandora part fulfills a second role. It also serves a 16' double bass function as its lowest notes and melodies often sound and double an octave below that of the bass viol. The peculiarly 'binding' quality of the bandora in the mixed consort is most noticeable, and was remarked on by several writers. Trichet (c1640) stated: 'this instrument can be of great use in consorts which are made of several kinds of instruments, for it seems that they become more harmonious by the conjunction and mixture of its sweet temperament'. Later Roger North, in his *Essay, of Musical Ayre*, wrote: 'those pandoras, by way of the thro-base, had a better and more sonorous effect in the mixture, than now may be ascribed to harpsichords'.

The bandora was well known outside England. Trichet's manuscript includes a good drawing of a seven-course example. However, there seems to have been some confusion between bandora and orpharion in continental references; Mersenne (1636–7) described and illustrated a 'pandore', but said that it was tuned like a lute. Other references occur in the inventories of Parisian instrument makers around 1600, including (in 1617) 'une pandore petite', which may have been a bandora at high pitch or simply an orpharion. 17th-century Italian references hearken back ultimately to Mersenne.

The bandora seems to have lasted longest in Germany: the Berlin court orchestra owned one in 1667 and there is another in the frontispiece to Walther's *Lexicon* (1732). It is mentioned as a possible continuo instrument in the *Erster Theil allerhand Oden unnd Lieder*, published by H. Krusen (Sohra, 1642, 1647, 1650, 1651, and 1664). While its North European acceptance as an accompaniment instrument is clear, it is curious that no bandora solo music has been found that distinctly derives from the continent. The sole surviving continental source, the Königsberg manuscript (Ness and Ward, 1989), contains only music of English derivation. The 2–4–4–3–4 tuning survived even longer, being used for the large German MANDORE and gallichone (see COLASCIONE). It is noteworthy that the two orpharions brought to light in the early 1980s are in German collections (see ORPHARION).

Although we have the measured drawings of Praetorius and the dimensions noted by Talbot as well as several drawings, no specimens of early bandoras appear to have survived. Ian Harwood (1981) has suggested that the exquisite *cymbalum decachordon* (for illustration see ROSE, JOHN) made by John Rose in 1580, and belonging to the Tollemache family of Helmingham Hall, Suffolk, is an early high-pitch bandora. Though this speculation has some merit, there has been little other evidence to support this theory. It has been thought to be an orpharion, but it does not match known measurements or string disposition of that instrument either. Several collections contain instruments having bodies with three outcurving lobes that are listed as 'bandora', but they are examples of the later French *pandore-en-luth*, 'Lutherie' section of Diderot and d'Alembert's *Encyclopédie* (Paris, 1751–80). One or two examples are modelled after this illustration in having no soundhole, and may perhaps be later reconstructions.

The main use of the bandora on the Continent seems to have been as a continuo instrument; its solo, consort and song repertory are found in English sources. The printed bandora partbook for Morley's *Consort Lessons* (1599) survives, and there are other consort parts in a number of manuscripts. Also extant is William Leighton's *Teares or Lamentacions* (1614), which includes sacred music for four voices with an accompaniment for the six instruments of the mixed consort. In total, there are 69 of these consort parts currently known. There are also six songs, most predating the publications of the lute 'ayres'.

Although Barley published some of the best known music for the instrument, the greatest share of the bandora repertory is found in manuscripts of lute music, where it is often identifiable only by its different tuning. There are 93 known solo pieces, which include nearly every form of the late 16th and early 17th centuries: fantasias, dances, and settings of popular tunes and grounds. However, the bass quality of the instrument led composers to write more pavans and fantasias, where the sustaining quality of the instrument was put to greatest use. In contrast to the consort parts, which are on the whole technically undemanding, the technique required in the solo music is considerable. With a total of nineteen compositions, Antony Holborne was the most prolific composer (cf Francis Derrick's letter quoted above); Alfonso Ferrabosco (i) composed six pieces, John Dowland five, and John Johnson (i) three. Emanuel Adriaenssen is the only continental composer found in these sources. However, this single piece seems to be an arrangement of a solo lute composition. As the music for solo bandora appears for the most part in manuscripts containing lute music, it is not surprising that there are many concordances between the two genres and it is usually difficult to ascertain whether the bandora version or the lute version is the original. With some of the music of Holborne it seems that the bandora version was the original.

After the second decade of the 17th century we find no more tablature music for this instrument. Judging by the comments of Roger North (see above) we can assume that the bandora was used as a continuo instrument well into the 17th century. However, it was probably gradually replaced in ensembles by the THEORBO, which covered the same range.

BIBLIOGRAPHY

MersenneHU; PraetoriusSM ii

W. Barley: *A New Booke of Tabliture ... to play on Sundry Instruments, as the Lute, Orpharion and Bandora* (London, 1596); ed. W.W. Newcomb as *Lute Music of Shakespeare's Time* (Philadelphia, 1966)

R. Fludd: *Ultriusque cosmi ... metaphysica, physica atque technica hisotories* (Opperheim, 1617–24)

P. Trichet: *Traité des instruments de musique* (MS, *c*1640, *F-Psg* 1070); ed. F. Lesure (Neuilly-sur-Seine, 1957/R; Eng. trans., 1973)

D. Gill: 'An Orpharion by John Rose', *LSJ*, ii (1960), 33–40

D. Gill: 'The Orpharion and Bandora', *GSJ*, xiii (1960), 14–25

D. Gill: 'James Talbot's Manuscript, v: Plucked Strings – the Wire-Strung Fretted Instruments and the Guitar', *GSJ*, xv (1962), 60–69

D. Gill: 'The Sources of English Solo Bandora Music', *LSJ*, iv (1962), 23–7

J. Godwin: 'Instuments in Robert Fludd's *Utriusque cosmi ... historia*", *GSJ*, xxvi (1973), 2–14

J. Godwin: 'Robert Fludd on the Lute and Pandora', *LSJ*, xv (1973), 11–19

D. Gill: *Wire-strung Plucked Instruments Contemporary with the Lute*, Lute Society Booklets, iii (London, 1977)

D. Gill: 'Bandora, Orpharion and Guitar', *GSJ*, xxxi (1978), 144 only

I. Harwood: 'A Case of Double Standards? Instrumental Pitch in England *c*1600', *EMc*, ix (1981), 470–81

R.H. Wells: 'The Orphorion: Symbol of a Humanist Ideal', *EMc*, x (1982), 427–40

E. Segerman: 'On English Lute Sizes and Tunings *c*1600', *FoMRHI Quarterly*, no.51 (1988), 37–8

P. Forrester: 'The Morley Consort Lesson and the English Cittern', *FoMRHI Quarterly*, no.56 (1989), 46–50

A.J. Ness and J.M. Ward: *The Königsberg Manuscript: a Facsimile of Manuscript 285-MF-LXXIX ... Central Library of the Lithuanian Academy of Science, Vilnius* (Columbus, OH, 1989) [with introduction, inventory and index]

L. Nordstrom: *The Bandora: its Music and Sources* (Warren, MI, 1992)

IAN HARWOOD/LYLE NORDSTROM

Band organ. *See* FAIRGROUND ORGAN.

Bandoura. *See* BANDURA.

Bandrowski-Sas [Brandt; Barski], **Aleksander** (*b* Lubaczów, 22 April 1860; *d* Kraków, 28 May 1913). Polish singer. He sang from 1881 in Lwów, Kraków, Łódź and Poznań as a baritone in operetta under the name Aleksander Barski. After studying in Milan and Vienna, he became one of the finest tenors of his time, excelling in Wagner (under the stage name Brandt). From 1887 to 1899 he sang in many of the principal west European houses, including La Scala; he had a permanent contract in Frankfurt (1889–1901). At Dresden in 1901 he created the title role in Paderewski's *Manru*, which he later sang in Lwów, Philadelphia, Boston, Chicago and at the Metropolitan. Bandrowski-Sas wrote three opera librettos: *Stara baśń*, after J.I. Kraszewski (music by W. Żeleński, 1907), *Bolesław Śmiały*, after S. Wyspiański (L. Różycki, 1909) and *Twardowski* (Wallek-Walewski, 1911); he also translated into Polish various excerpts from Wagner's librettos and the whole of *Die Meistersinger*, and published a thematic analysis of the *Ring*, *Rozbiór tematyczny Ryszarda Wagnera trylogii z prologiem* (Lwów, 1907).

BIBLIOGRAPHY

PSB (Z. Jachimecki)

K. Michałowski: *Opery polskie* (Kraków, 1954)

Z. Raszewski, ed.: *Słownik biograficzny teatru polskiego 1765–1965* (Warsaw, 1973)

IRENA PONIATOWSKA

Bandstand (Fr. *kiosque à musique*; Ger. *Musikpavillon*). A small, usually covered building to shelter brass bands, wind bands and military bands giving open-air concerts. It is usually polygonal, less frequently square, round or shell-shaped, and made sometimes of wood but more often of iron or cast iron, or (if built after 1920) of concrete. In form its origin was the Chinese pavilion as introduced into English landscape gardens early in the 18th century (for instance at Stowe and Kew), but in use from the 15th century in Turkey (the French *kiosque* comes from Turkish *köşk*). Its functional origin was in the London pleasure gardens. As a result bandstands were erected in public places (walks and promenades, squares and gardens) full of greenery and intended for relaxation.

Their first purpose was to provide wholesome, free entertainment for social classes with little previous interest in art music. Large family audiences met at the bandstand, made up of people ranging from labourers and artisans, nursemaids and soldiers, to small shopkeepers and the lower middle classes, and consequently it encouraged new kinds of social intercourse and new ways of listening to music; the audience could sit, stand, or continue strolling and talking. The rituals of the middle-class concert were abandoned for the behaviour of natural, everyday life. Another purpose of the bandstand was to educate this new public by inviting it to share the culture of the élite, as a way of breaking down social barriers, and here it had a pioneering role in the tradition of the French Revolution. The omnipresence of military bands shows that the bandstand was also an excellent means of reinforcing social cohesion by stirring up patriotic sentiments. As one of the first mass leisure forms, bandstand concerts may be seen as a concrete manifestation of the great movement towards democratizing music and amateur musical practice, encouraged by the inventions of Adolphe Sax. Consequently the proliferation of bandstands, which were soon being sold in kit form by foundries and metalwork construction companies, went hand in hand with the rise of choral societies in the second half of the 19th century. These societies were an exceptionally useful tool for rising in the social scale, and it is easy to explain their concentration in mining and industrial areas, particularly in the north of England (Lancashire, Yorkshire), France, Belgium, Luxembourg and western Germany. The phenomenon spread rapidly, and at the end of the 19th century almost every village had its bandstand. The fashion reached spas and seaside resorts, where bandstand concerts were popular as daily meeting-places.

In such fashionable towns the music might be played by an instrumental ensemble consisting of strings, a piano and some wind instruments, performing light music or café music, but the usual bandstand repertory was the same as that of wind bands and brass bands. It was tripartite, consisting of military music (marches, galops, quick marches), dance-tunes (quadrilles, polkas, mazurkas, schottisches and waltzes) and extracts from operas in the form of a potpourri or fantasia, with the arias arranged for solo instrumentalists. There were also transcriptions of symphonies (by Mozart, Beethoven, Mendelssohn), overtures (by Mozart, Beethoven, Berlioz), and orchestral suites (by Massenet and Saint-Saëns). Wagner thought bandstands particularly suitable for his music, which was popular in such settings in France before his success at the Paris Opéra. In the 1920s the repertory opened up to include jazz.

In spite of the limitations of transcriptions, bandstands occupy a position central to the mass dissemination of musical culture. They can also be the scene of experimentation: much of the work of Charles Ives and his ventures into polytonality and polyrhythm cannot be understood without reference to them. Bandstands and brass bands play an important part in American festivities, generating a convivial atmosphere especially popular with young people, who can also hear rock music in bandstands. As a formal and cultural model the bandstand has spread far and wide beyond Europe, particularly in former European colonies (cf its social role in Latin America and South America). At present there is a renewal of interest in Europe too; more bandstands are being built, attempts are being made to revive older forms of convivial gatherings, and composers including Berio and Michel Decoust have contributed new works to the repertory.

BIBLIOGRAPHY

Les spectacles, le théâtre et le kiosque à musique, Pavillon du Canada, Expo 67, Montreal (Ottawa, 1967) [exhibition catalogue]
K. De Wolf: 'De kiosk: stenen grammofoonplaat avant la lettre', *Adem*, xxiii/1 (1987), 30–34 [summaries in Eng., Fr.]
M.-C. Le Moigne-Mussat: 'Le kiosque: rôle et pratique d'un espace de diffusion sociale de la musique', *1789–1989: musique, histoire, démocratie: Paris 1989*, 595–604
G. Mott and S. Aall: *Follies and Pleasure Pavilions* (London, 1989)
G.-A. Langlois: *Folies, tivolis et attractions: les premiers parcs de loisirs parisiens* (Paris, 1991)
M.-C. Mussat: *La belle époque des kiosques à musique* (Paris, 1992)
M.-C. Mussat: 'L'exotisme du kiosque à musique', *Les jardins du retour* (Paris, 1994), 65–71
M.-C. Mussat: 'Les kiosques à musique dans les villes d'eau: un mode de vie', *2000 ans de thermalisme: économie, patrimoine, rites et pratiques* (Clermont-Ferrand, 1996), 231–51 [pubn of Institut d'Etudes du Massif Central]

MARIE-CLAIRE MUSSAT

Bandura [bandoura]. A hybrid instrument of the Ukraine combining elements of a lute and box zither, possibly derived from the 10th century Arabic and Persian *pandura* and the *kobuz* of the Kipchak and Polovtsian peoples. It has a short neck, a shallow oval wooden body and a resonating hole on the upper soundboard (seeillustration). There is a varying number of strings; four to eight bass (*bunti*) strings on the neck, plucked by the left hand, and between seven and thirty metal strings (*pidstrunki*, tuned chromatically) across the soundboard, plucked by the right hand. Older examples are tuned diatonically.

The *bandura* (also known as the *kobza* until the end of the 19th century) was widely used by the Cossacks during the 16th and 17th centuries. The performers, called

Ukrainian bandura of the psaltery type (Royal College of Music, London)

banduristï or *kobzari*, were itinerant singer-instrumentalists who used the *bandura* to accompany the epic *dumï*, historical songs, ballads and other forms. The instrument was also adopted by the Polish gentry. The *bandura* was taught by traditional players, who were often blind. The instrument is now taught at state-run institutions and alto, bass and contrabass *banduras* have been developed for ensemble performances of 'folkloric' music.

BIBLIOGRAPHY

A.S. Famintsïn: *Domra i srodnïye yey muzïkal'nïye instrumentï russkogo naroda* [The domra and related musical instruments of the Russian people] (St Petersburg, 1891/R)

A. Baines, ed.: *Musical Instruments through the Ages* (Harmondsworth, 1961/R, 2/1966/R)

A. Gumenyuk: *Ukraïns'ki narodni muzichni instrumenti* [Ukrainian folk instruments] (Kiev, 1967)

A. Buchner: *Folk Music Instruments of the World* (London, 1971)

SOFIA HRYTSA

Bandurichen (Ger.). *See* MANDORE.

Bandurria [mandurria]. A plucked lute. A hybrid of the guitar and cittern families, it is found in Spain and parts of Latin America. It has a small, cittern-shaped body with comparatively deep ribs, flat back, short fretted neck, and large peg-holder with pegs projecting from the rear as on a guitar. The strings pass over a large central soundhole and are usually fixed to a string-holder. In Spain a *púa* (plectrum) is used to pick out melody.

The term 'mandurria' was mentioned in the 14th century by Juan Ruiz in his *Libro de buen amor*. In 1555 Juan Bermudo described the bandurria in his *Comiença el libro llamado declaraciõ de instrumetos* [sic] as a three-string instrument, but he also mentioned other types with four or even five strings. He said that the outer courses were tuned an octave apart, with the middle course either a 5th or a 4th above the lowest. Later, five- and six-course bandurrias were tuned in 4ths throughout, a tuning that is still used (*see* BANDOLA). The bandurria provided music at a child's wake in Jijona, Alicante Province, in the early 1870s (see J.C. Davillier: *L'Espagne*, Paris, 1874, p.409). In Cuba before 1900 the bandurria, with other instruments, accompanied the *zapateo*, a dance derived from the Spanish *zapateado* and introduced by tobacco cultivators from the Canary Islands. It still accompanies Iberian-derived folksong in Cuba and is found also in central and north-eastern Guatemala and in the Andes of Colombia and Chile. The bandurria is said to have flourished about 1800 among the Peruvian blacks. In the early 20th century duos of harp and bandurria performed in Lima (*see* PERU, fig.4), where today the bandurria is still found in ensembles accompanying the popular *vals peruano*, or *vals criollo*.

See also MANDORE.

JOHN M. SCHECHTER

Banerjee, Nikhil Ranjan (*b* Calcutta, 14 Oct 1931; *d* Calcutta, 27 Jan 1986). Indian *sitār* player. He was trained initially by his father Jitendra Nath Banerjee, an amateur *sitār* player, showing such promise that he won the All-Bengal Sitar Competition at the age of nine. He studied briefly with a number of musicians including Jnan Prakash Ghosh (*tablā*, vocal) and Birendra Kishore Roy Choudhury. Choudhury introduced him to Ustad Allauddin Khan, with whom he stayed in Maihar from 1947 to 1954. Later he studied with Allauddin Khan's son Ustad Ali Akbar Khan and daughter Annapurna Devi.

He pursued a highly successful career as a concert and recording artist, touring all over the world. He held a number of teaching posts including professor of music at the Ali Akbar College of Music, Calcutta, and visiting professor of music at the Californian Center for World Music (1970–78), the American Society for Eastern Arts, California (1970–78) and the University of Santiniketan (1977–8). Honours included the Padma Shri (1968) and a Padma Bhushan awarded shortly after his untimely death from a heart attack.

Banerjee was regarded as one of the most accomplished *sitār* players of his time, many connoisseurs judging him the equal of his contemporaries Pandit Ravi Shankar and Ustad Vilayat Khan. The tone of his instrument was quite distinctive, while he excelled in every aspect of the *sitār* player's art; command of *rāg* and *tāl* allied to superb technique, including phenomenal speed as well as the most exquisite control, made him one of the most profoundly affecting performers in the Hindustani tradition.

BIBLIOGRAPHY
AND OTHER RESOURCES

A.D. Sharma: *Musicians of India Past and Present* (Calcutta, 1993)

RECORDINGS

HMV EALP/EASD 1318 (1967) [Raga *Malkauns*, raga *Hem lalit*, *Dhun*]; also released as *The Sitar Genius of Nikhil Banerjee*, Capitol International ST10502 (1967)

Le sitar de Nikhil Banerjee, N. Banerjee, A. Chartejee, R. Mukerjee perfs., Disques Esperance ESP 155 530 (1976) [Raga *Monomanjari*, raga *Manj khamaj*]

N. Banerjee and A.A. Khan perfs., Connoisseur Society CS 2055 (1973); reissued AMMP CD 9405 [Raga *Manj khamaj*, raga *Misra mand*]

Many others for HMV (India), T-Series (India), Sondisc (France), Chhanda Dhara (Germany), Amigo (Sweden), Disques Esperance (France), Audiorec (UK), Oriental (USA), Raga Records (USA)

MARTIN CLAYTON

Banevich, Sergey (*b* Okhansk, 2 Dec 1941). Russian composer. He attended the N.A. Rimsky-Korsakov Music School until 1961 studying composition under Ust-vol'skaya. He graduated from the Leningrad Conservatory in 1966, and went on to complete postgraduate studies with Yevlakhov in 1969. In 1991 he became the organizer and artistic director of an international music festival for children, and in 1995 set up an international competition for children playing piano duets called *Brat'ya i syostrï* ['Brothers and Sisters']. Since 1992 he has been managing director of the music and educational publishers *Severnïy Olen'* ['Reindeer']. Music for children is the main area of Banevich's creative work. Banevich has stated that 'children experience everything that adults do, only far more vividly and acutely'. He writes about children and for them; he also appeals to adults through the prism of a childlike perception of the world. He became an Honoured Representative of the Arts of Russia in 1982.

Banevich writes principally for the stage. He has worked in a variety of genres such as the musical, dramatic operetta, fairy tale operetta, opera-ballet and television opera. His style is lyrically Romantic: the harmony is reminiscent of Puccini and Saint-Saëns, but he also alludes to the language of the American musical, the French chanson and the hits of the Soviet variety stage. Dramatically, he relies on humour of the absurd and free association which he deems appropriate when dealing with children. Banevich is a master of attractive melody, inventive orchestration and operatic ensemble writing, and has the ability to unify material of various styles through the use of developing leitmotifs.

WORKS
(selective list)

Stage: Beleyet parus odinokiy [White is the Lonely Sail] (op, 3, V. Roshchin, after V. Katsev), 1969, Odessa, Opera and Ballet Theatre, 1969

Priklucheniya Toma Soyera [The Adventures of Tom Sawyer] (musical, 2, S. Dimant, N. Slepakova, after M. Twain, 1972, Leningrad, Musical Comedy, 1972

How the Night was Switched On (chbr op, 1, G. Dmitrenko, after R. Bradbury), 1973, Leningrad Radio, 1973

Ferdinand Velikolepnïy [Ferdinand the Magnificent] (op, 3, V. Dreyer, after L. Kern), 1974, Leningrad, Malïy, 1974, film version, 1975

Sud'ba barabanshchika [The Fate of the Drummer] (dramatic operetta, 2, T. Kalinina, after A. Gaydar, 1976, Leningrad, Musical Comedy, 1976

Istoriya Kaya i Gerdï [The Story of Kay and Gerda] (op, 2, with prologue and epilogue, T. Kalinina, after H.C. Andersen, 1979), Leningrad, Kirov, 1979

The Land of Children (musical performance, T. Kalinina), 1984, Leningrad, Bol'shoy kontsertnïy zal 'Oktyabr'skiy', 1984

Stoykiy olovyannïy soldatik [The Steadfast Tin Soldier] (musical fairy play, 2, N. Denisov, after H.C. Andersen), 1984, Leningrad, Leninskiy Komsomol'skiy, 1985

Gorodok v taberkerke [A Small Town in a Snuff Box] (fantastic op, 2, B. Khmel'nitsky after V. Odoyevsky), 1986, Leningrad, Musical Theatre for Children 'Zazerkal'ye', 1986

The Match-Girl (mini-op for children, A. Sokolov, after H.C. Andersen), 1991, collab. D. Smirnov, Łódź, Wielki, 1991

Peterburg [Petersburg] (ballet-fantasia, 2, V. Roshchin, after A. Belïy, choreog. N. Boyarchikov), 1991, St Petersburg, Malïy, 1992

Rusalochka [The Little Water Nymph] (op-ballet, 2, G. Dmitrenko and T. Kalinina, after H.C. Andersen), 1992, Sïktïvkar, Theatre of Opera and Ballet, 1994

Other: The Little Duck Called Grey Neck, fairy-tale suite, after D. Mamin-Sibiryak, chbr ens, 1990; Bless the Beasts and the Children (S. Chyornïy), conc., large children's choir, 1995–6; A Chapter from Buddenbrooks: The Death of Little Hanno, fantasia, vc, pf, 1996

incid music for films, TV

Principal publishers: Sovetskiy Kompozitor (Kompozitor), Severnïy Olen'

BIBLIOGRAPHY
A. Schnittke: ' The Story of Kay and Gerde. A new opera for children', *Knigi i iskusstvo v SSSR*, ii/33 (1982), 44–5

T. Chernova: 'Sergey Banevich: The traits of the master's portrait' (Leningrad, 1986)

R. Neykov: 'Sergey Banevich: "Sowing Seeds of Kindness …"', *Muzikalni horizonti* (Sofia, 1990), no.10, pp.104–5

MARINA NEST'YEVA

Banfi [Banfo], **Alfonso**. *See* BAMFI, ALFONSO.

Banfield, Stephen (David) (*b* Dulwich, 15 July 1951). English musicologist. He studied music at Cambridge (BA 1972) and Oxford (DPhil 1980), studying with Hugh Macdonald both as an undergraduate and postgraduate, and was Frank Knox Fellow at Harvard University, 1975–6. In 1978 he became a lecturer in music at Keele University, becoming senior lecturer in 1988. In 1992 he became Elgar Professor of Music at the University of Birmingham; he was head of the School of Performance Studies, 1992–7, and head of the Department of Music, 1995–9. His main areas of research are British music of the late 19th century to the 20th, and popular musical theatre and vernacular bourgeois music in both Britain and America during the same period.

Banfield's work is characterized by seriousness of intellectual and artistic enquiry combined with a stylish and approachable literary style. His particular interest in music and the literary arts is reflected in his pioneering work on the English art song, which includes a useful catalogue with over 5000 entries. His book on the musicals of Stephen Sondheim uses primary source studies – an approach unprecedented in the literature of Broadway – to trace their compositional development and complex relationship with the European operatic tradition. His monograph on the life and work of Gerald Finzi is the first to assess the achievement of a relatively neglected British composer.

WRITINGS
'The Artist and Society', 'Aesthetics and Criticism', *The Romantic Age, 1800–1914*, ed. N. Temperley (Oxford, 1981), 11–28, 455–73

'A Shropshire Lad in the Making: a Note on the Composition of George Butterworth's Songs', *MR*, xlii (1981), 261–7

Sensibility and English Song: Critical Studies of the Early 20th Century (Cambridge, 1985)

'"Too Much of Albion?": Mrs Coolidge and her British Connections', *American Music*, iv/1 (1986), 59–88

'Housman and the Composers', *Housman Society Journal*, xiii (1987), 14–22

'England, 1918–45', *Modern Times*, ed. R.P. Morgan (Basingstoke, 1993), 180–205

Sondheim's Broadway Musicals (Ann Arbor, 1993)

ed.: *The Twentieth Century* (Oxford, 1995)

'Sondheim and the Art that has no Name', *Approaches to the American Musical*, ed. R. Lawson-Peebles (Exeter, 1996), 137–60

Gerald Finzi: an English Composer (London, 1997)

ROSEMARY WILLIAMSON

Banfield, Volker (*b* Oberaudorf, Bavaria, 9 May 1944). German pianist. At the age of 14 he entered the Nordwestdeutsche Musikakademie in Detmold, later travelling to the USA, where he studied with Adele Marcus at the Juilliard School of Music in New York and Leonard Shure at the University of Texas, from whom he acquired a deep-seated affinity with the Russian school of virtuosity and the German intellectual tradition exemplified by Schnabel. Since his return to Germany he has toured extensively, appearing regularly in the world's major music centres. Banfield's tastes and repertory are wide, but he has tended to focus on music of the later 19th century and the 20th, with special emphasis on Debussy, Skryabin, Rachmaninoff, Prokofiev, Bartók and Messiaen. A number of contemporary composers, most notably Ligeti and Detlev Mueller-Siemens, have dedicated works to him. His playing combines an unflamboyant virtuoso technique with a keen analytical mind, a wide-ranging tonal palette and an emotional spontaneity which serves him particularly well in Schumann, of whom he has become an increasingly ardent champion. Among his recordings are the Schumann sonatas and concertos by Goetz, Busoni and Pfitzner.

JEREMY SIEPMANN

Banister [Bannester]. English family of musicians. (2) John (i) was said by Anthony Wood to have been the 'Son of Banister, one of the musicians or public waits of S. Giles' Parish near London'. He was the father of (3) John (ii), and was probably (1) Jafery Banister's brother. James and Henrietta Banister may have been children of (1) Jafery Banister or (2) John (i). James joined the 24 Violins in May 1676 and served until the end of Charles II's reign, and Henrietta taught Princess Anne the harpsichord between 1679 and 1682. The son of (3) John (ii), also called John (*b* London, 27 Dec 1686), a recorder player, is mentioned in concert announcements between 1702 and 1704 in connection with his father. He was still alive on 5 September 1730, when his father made his will.

(1) Jafery [Jeffrey] Banister (bur. London, 2 Sept 1684). Violinist, music copyist and composer. He was sworn in as an extraordinary member of the 24 Violins on 27 October 1662, and received a salaried place from Michaelmas 1663. The text of Thomas Duffett's masque *Beauty's Triumph* (London, 1676) shows that he and James Hart were running a 'New Boarding-School for Young Ladies and Gentlewomen' in Chelsea. He apparently left royal service in February 1684, when he was given a passport to travel abroad, but died that summer, probably before he could undertake the trip. He seems to have been the copyist of two violin books (*GB-En* 5777, and Scottish Record Office, Edinburgh, GD 45/26/104) that originate respectively from Newbattle Abbey, Midlothian, and Panmure House, Angus, suggesting that he had worked for the Ker and Maule families in Scotland or London. The latter contains a suite signed 'Jafery Bannester'.

(2) John Banister (i) (*b* London, 1624/5; *d* London, 3 Oct 1679). Violinist, flageolet player and composer. He was a member of the ensemble that accompanied Davenant's opera *The Siege of Rhodes* (1656). He joined the 24 Violins at Christmas 1660, and was issued with a passport on 2 December 1661 'to goe into France upon Some speciall Service & returne with all possible expedition'; according to Anthony Wood he went 'to see and learn the way of the French compositions'. On his return he was promoted as an English Lully. On 18 April 1662 he was given the authority to choose 12 violinists to accompany the king to Portsmouth to meet Catherine of Braganza, and the next month they were constituted as a 'Select Band' under his command, doubtless inspired by Lully's *petits violons*. He was also given Davis Mell's place as a violinist in the Private Music; a painting at Nostell Priory near Wakefield seems to show him with other members of the group. He was a leading member of the Corporation of Music in 1663–4.

Banister's prominent court position lasted only until winter 1666–7. Luis Grabu succeeded Nicholas Lanier as Master of the Music in spring 1666, rapidly exerting his authority over the 24 Violins and the Select Band. On 29 March 1667 the 24 Violins sent in a 'remonstrance' against Banister, listing occasions going back to 1663 when he had embezzled money due to them. Without Banister's side of the story it is impossible to judge the case, though it seems that the king bore him ill will for a moment of insubordination. Wood wrote that 'for some saucy words spoken to His Majesty (viz. when he called for the Italian [?French] violins, he made answer that he had better have the English) he was turned out of his place'. Pepys wrote in his diary (20 February 1667) that 'the King's viallin, Bannister, is mad that the King hath a Frenchman come to be chief of some part of the King's music'.

Banister retained his place in the 24 Violins, but turned increasingly to promoting public concerts. According to Pepys, he was already giving concerts in 1660 at the Mitre tavern in Fleet Street, though newspaper advertisements for them exist only from December 1672. He moved them from the George in Whitefriars to Chandos Street in 1675, to Lincoln's Inn Fields in 1676, and to Essex Buildings in 1678. Roger North gave the impression that they were cheap and cheerful, held in 'an obscure room in a publik house' and given by 'most of the shack-performers in towne', though the wordbook *Musick, or A Parley of Instruments* (London, 1676) shows that Banister was able to put on a large-scale semi-dramatic piece with an astonishing array of wind, bowed and plucked instruments, and that his concerts were just one aspect of the activities of a boy's school, the 'Academy in Lincoln's Inn Fields'. According to North, one of the attractions of Banister's concerts was his flageolet playing 'in consort, which was never heard before nor since, unless imitated by the high manner upon the violin'.

He is presumably the John Banister, a widower aged 46 of St Margaret's, Westminster, who married the widow Mary Wood on 14 January 1671. He is listed in 1677 as Princess Anne's music master, and Henrietta Banister received the post in 1679, the year of his death. He and his son John were given a passport to travel abroad on 28 July, but he died on 3 October and was buried in Westminster Abbey the next day.

Banister wrote a good deal of consort music in the genres associated with the 24 Violins, though much of it only survives in fragments. One suite, *The Musick att the Bath* (*GB-Och* Mus.1183), was apparently written for the queen's visit to Bath in September 1663, while another (*En* 5777) seems to come from a 1671 court masque; much of his other dance music was probably written for court balls or other entertainments. The 24 Violins also worked in the London theatres, and Banister wrote the earliest surviving theatre suite, for John Dryden and Sir Robert Howard's play *The Indian Queen* (1664; *US-NYp*). He contributed songs or other music to Sir Samuel Tuke's *The Adventures of Five Hours* (1663), Katherine Phillips's *Pompey* (?1663), Dryden's *Sir Martin Marall* (1667), the Davenant-Dryden version of *The Tempest* (1667), Davenant's *The Man's the Master* (1668), Sir Charles Sedley's *The Mulberry Garden* (1668), Thomas Shadwell's *The Royal Shepherdess* (1669), a revival of Ben Jonson's *The Devil is an Ass* (?1669), Aphra Behn's *The Forc'd Marriage* (1670), part i of Dryden's *The Conquest of Granada* (1670), John Crowne's *Juliana* (1671), William Wycherley's *The Gentleman Dancing Master* (1672), Shadwell's *Epsom Wells* (1672) and Charles Davenant's *Circe* (1677). He also wrote music for Thomas Duffett's masque *Beauty's Triumph* (1676), put on at the Chelsea girl's school run by James Hart and (1) Jafery Banister. It is difficult to reconcile North's judgment that Banister had 'a good theatricall vein, and in composition a lively style peculiar to himself' with the evidence of his shortwinded songs, or the apparently incompetent part-writing of much of his consort music, though the latter may be partly the fault of corrupt sources.

WORKS

Consort suites, dances and grounds, 1662[8], 1677[4], 1678[4], 1678[5] (ed. P.J. Lord, Oxford, 1970), *The Division Violin* (London, 1684), *IRL-Dtc, GB-CDp, Cu, En, Lbl, Lcm, Ob, Och, W, US-NH, NYp* [incl. The Indian Queen, ed. M. Laurie, *Henry Purcell: The Indian Queen*, Purcell Society, xix (London, 1994), appx D]

30 songs, 1667[6], 1673[3], 1673[4], *The Ariels Songs in the Play Call'd the Tempest* (London, 1675), 1675[7], *The Circle, or Conversations on Love and Gallantry* (London, 1675), 1679[7], 1686[4], 1688[6], *GB-Lbl, Och*

Inst and vocal music for *The Slighted Maid* (play, R. Stapylton), 1663, lost

(3) John Banister (ii)   (bap. London, 11 Sept 1662; *d* London, 9 Jan 1736). Violinist, recorder player, publisher and composer, son of (2) John (i). He was admitted to his father's place among the 24 Violins on 6 November 1679 and continued to serve until his death. He has generally been taken to be the 'J.B. gent' who compiled *The Most Pleasant Companion, or Choice New Lessons for the Recorder or Flute* (London, 1681) and signed the preface of the first oboe tutor, *The Sprightly Companion* (RISM 1695¹⁴). In 1686 he and John Carr published from 'his chambers in Essex Street the next door to the Clock' a set of recorder duets by Raphael Couteville (i). The same year he married and then moved to Brownlow Street, off Drury Lane. In 1700 and 1702 he and Robert King were the agents for music by Corelli and Nicola Cosimi. For James Talbot's manuscript he was to have provided material concerning the wait (shawm), kit and treble violin. By 1698 and probably earlier he was promoting concerts at York Buildings and Exeter Change, and by 1702 he was first violin in the Drury Lane Theatre band and regularly played in concerts there and at York Buildings with colleagues such as Jean Baptiste Loeillet (i), James Paisible and Gasparo Visconti. In 1708 he became one of the first violins in the opera orchestra at the Queen's Theatre, Haymarket, remaining there until at least December 1710; about 1715 he was associated with the new Lincoln's Inn Fields Theatre. His violin and recorder playing were praised by contemporaries; Roger North noted his skill at extempore ornamentation and said he was an excellent singing teacher. Hawkins (*History*), perhaps confusing him with Paisible, claimed he was famous 'for playing on two flutes [i.e. recorders] at once'. His few surviving compositions consist of dance movements influenced by both French and Italian styles, and demonstrating some melodic and rhythmic imagination.

WORKS

3 tunes, for vn, 1687⁷, 1691⁵; 12 tunes for 2 rec, 1693⁸, 1694⁷, 1695⁶, 1696⁹
10 dances, 2 tr, t, b, A Collection of Musick in 2 Parts . . . to Which is Added a Sett of Ayres in 4 Parts, bk 1 (London, 1691)
A collection of choice Airs and Symphonys ... out of the Most Celebrated Operas, 2 vn (London, 1717), lost
A Collection of the Most Celebrated Song Tunes, with their Symphonies Taken out of the Choicest Opera's, vn (London, 1717), lost
A Second Collection of the Most Celebrated Song Tunes, with their Symphonies, Taken out of the choicest Opera's, vn (London, 1717), lost

BIBLIOGRAPHY

AshbeeR, i, ii, v, viii; BDA; Day-MurrieESB; SpinkES
J. Wilson: *Roger North on Music* (London, 1959)
M. Tilmouth: *Chamber Music in England, 1675–1720* (diss., U. of Cambridge, 1960)
M. Tilmouth: 'A Calendar of References to Music in Newspapers Published in London and the Provinces (1660–1719)', *RMARC*, i (1961/R)
A.A. Luhring: *The Music of John Banister* (diss., Stanford U., 1966)
C.A. Price: *Music in the Restoration Theater* (Ann Arbor, 1979)
J.D. Shute: *Anthony à Wood and his Manuscript Wood D 19(4) at the Bodleian* (diss., International Institute of Advanced Studies, Clayton, MO, 1979)
D. Lasocki: *Professional Recorder Players in England, 1540–1740* (diss., U. of Iowa, 1983)
P. Daub: *Music at the Court of George II (r. 1727–1760)* (diss., Cornell U., 1985)
C. McCart: 'The Panmure Manuscripts: a New Look at an Old Source of Christopher Simpson's Consort Music', *Chelys*, xviii (1989), 18–29

I. Spink, ed.: *Music in Britain: the Seventeenth Century* (Oxford, 1992)
P. Holman: *Four and Twenty Fiddlers: the Violin at the English Court 1540–1690* (Oxford, 1993, 2/1995)
A. Ashbee and D. Lasocki: *Biographical Dictionary of English Court Musicians, 1485–1714* (Aldershot, 1997)

PETER HOLMAN (1, 2), DAVID LASOCKI (3)

Banister, Henry Charles (*b* London, 13 June 1831; *d* London, 20 Nov 1897). English composer and teacher. His first studies were with his father, H.J. Banister, a well-known cellist in his day. In 1846 he won the King's Scholarship at the Royal Academy of Music, where he studied with Cipriani Potter. He subsequently became a sub-professor at the RAM and, from 1853, professor of harmony. From 1880 he was professor at the Guildhall School of Music and he also taught at the Royal Normal College for the Blind. Banister was a prolific composer of songs, piano pieces and overtures, but most important was his contribution to the mid-19th-century British symphony. Today, however, he is remembered primarily as a theorist.

WRITINGS

Lectures on Musical Analysis (London, 1887, 3/1895)
Musical Art and Study (London, 1887)
George Alexander Macfarren (London, 1891)
The Harmonising of Melodies (London, 1897)
ed. S. Macpherson: *Interludes* (London, 1898) [seven lectures delivered between 1891 and 1897]

J.A. FULLER MAITLAND/JEREMY DIBBLE

Banister, Henry Joshua [John] (*b* London, 1803; *d* Clerkenwell, London, 27 Sept 1847). English cellist. Son of the composer Charles William Banister (1768–1831), he was active in London as an orchestral player and chamber musician, and from 1835 participated frequently in chamber music concerts. His Quartet Parties, given at his residence in Burton Crescent in 1844, were the first West End chamber concerts to exclude vocal items. He wrote a number of didactic works for the cello and made arrangements of operatic overtures for small ensembles. In 1843 the *Musical World* published a series of Bannister's letters, which argued that music lovers among the English aristocracy should patronize music more extensively by employing groups of resident musicians; the correspondence was subsequently published at his own expense as *Domestic Music for the Wealthy, or a Plea for the Art and its Professors* (1843). His brother Joseph Banister (1812–90), a violinist, was a member of the Philharmonic Society and an active chamber musician; his son Henry Charles Banister was a composer and teacher.

BIBLIOGRAPHY

J.D. Brown and S.S. Stratton: *British Musical Biography* (Birmingham, 1897/R)
C. Bashford: *Public Chamber-Music Concerts in London, 1835–50: Aspects of History, Repertory and Reception* (diss., U. of London, 1996)

CHRISTINA BASHFORD

Banjeaurine. A small banjo, pitched a 4th higher than the standard instrument, invented by SAMUEL SWAIN STEWART.

Banjo. A plucked string instrument with a long guitar-like neck and a circular soundtable, usually called the 'head', of tautly stretched parchment or skin (now usually plastic), against which the bridge is pressed by the strings. The banjo and its variants have had long and widespread popularity as folk, parlour and professional entertainers' instruments. The name of the instrument probably derives from the Portuguese or Spanish *bandore*.

1. Structure. 2. History.

1. STRUCTURE.   The modern five-string banjo is normally fitted with raised frets and strung with five steel wire strings, the lowest in pitch being overspun with fine copper alloy wire. It is tuned *g′–c–g–b–d′* (C tuning) or *g′–d–g–b–d′* (G tuning), but many other tuning patterns, e.g. *g′–c–g–c′–d′*, *g′–d–g–c′–d′* and *g′–d–g–a–d′*, are used to facilitate the playing of particular songs. There are usually 24 or more screw-tightening brackets (for adjusting the head tension) attached to the outer side of a tambourine-like rim of laminated wood about 28 cm in diameter. In banjos of high quality the upper edge over which the head is stretched is often of complicated design, as in an early (1920s) 'Mastertone' system of O.H. Gibson (fig.1*a*), which used a tubular metal 'tone tube' resting on spring-supported ball-bearings, or the 'Electric' design of A.C. FAIRBANKS. A pan-shaped wooden 'resonator' is often attached to the lower side of the otherwise open-backed body and serves to reflect outward the sound emitted by the underside of the head. The 'thumb string' (sometimes known in older literature as 'chanterelle'), the

short fifth string (fig.1), is placed adjacent to the lowest-pitched string and secured by a peg inserted into the side of the neck at the fifth fret position.

Until the early 20th century banjos were normally strung with gut strings, and these or nylon strings are still used by 'classical' banjoists. Raised frets were advocated by James Buckley in *Buckley's New Banjo Method* (New York, 1860) but did not become common until the 1880s. George C. Dobson's *'Victor' Banjo Manual* (Boston, 1887) describes frets inlaid flush with the fingerboard as position markers but states that 'the latest and most modern manner … is with raised frets'. Mid-19th-century commercial banjos were larger than modern ones and were tuned to the lower-pitched A tuning of *e′–a–e–g♯–b*. Smaller banjos and higher pitches later became increasingly popular, until by the 1880s most banjos were of modern proportions and commonly tuned to the modern C tuning (which maintains the same interval relationship). By 1890 in the USA the banjo was treated as a transposing instrument pitched in C with music still written in A, a situation that continued until 1909 when the American Guild of Banjoists, Mandolinists, and Guitarists voted to abandon the old A notation and write the music in C or 'English notation'. In England both the written and tuning pitch were fixed at the modern level by the 1880s.

1. Banjos: (a) Mastertone model by the Gibson Co., Kalamazoo, Michigan, c1924; (b) by William Boucher, Baltimore, Maryland, 1846 (both Smithsonian Institution, Washington, DC)

A number of hybrid and specialized banjos were developed during the late 19th and early 20th centuries, including cello and piccolo banjos (tuned an octave below and above the standard banjo); banjeurines; concert and 'ladies' banjos (tuned a whole tone above and below the standard banjo); guitar, mandolin and UKULELE banjos (strung and tuned like their parent instruments); and plectrum banjos (identical to the standard banjo but lacking the fifth string). The tenor banjo (tuned c–g–d'–a') is identical with the standard banjo but has a shorter neck and no fifth string. Like the plectrum banjo it was developed for use in jazz and dance orchestras and is played with a plectrum. It has been widely adopted by players of traditional music in Ireland and England.

In England and Australia banjos with six or more strings were common during the late 19th century, the additional strings serving to extend the compass downwards. Another English type, the 'zither banjo' (distinct from C.L. Steffen's 'banjo zither', invented in Stettin in 1879), had first, second and fifth strings made of wire (the others were gut or wire-covered silk), frets, and geared tuning machines instead of the more usual friction pegs. It had a closed back which reflected the sound outwards through spaces between the head and rim, functioning much like a modern resonator, as do two banjos now in the collection of the Smithsonian Institution, Washington, DC, by the American makers Henry Dobson and George Teed of New York (US Patent 34,913, 8 April 1862).

2. HISTORY.   The development of the modern banjo began in the second quarter of the 19th century as an increasingly commercial adaptation of an instrument used by West African slaves in the New World as early as the 17th century. The earliest known illustration of the instrument is in Sir Hans Sloane's *A Voyage to the Islands of Madeira, Barbados, Nieves, S. Christopher and Jamaica* (London, 1707), written in 1688, which depicts two Jamaican negro 'strum-strumps' with long necks and skin-covered gourd bodies (fig.2). In the French colonies, where the instrument was usually known as the *banza*, it was often associated with the calinda, a dance unsuccessfully suppressed by acts of the Martinique government as early as 1654 and as late as 1772.

In the British colonies the instrument was usually known as *banjer* or *banjar*, pronunciations still common in the southern USA. The Rev. Jonathan Boucher, describing life in Maryland and Virginia before he returned to England in 1775, wrote in *Boucher's Glossary of Archaic and Provincial Words* (London, 1832): 'The favorite and almost only instrument in use among the slaves there was a *bandore*; or, as they pronounced the word, *banjer*. Its body was a large hollow gourd, with a long handle attached to it, strung with catgut, and played on with the fingers'. Thomas Jefferson, in his *Notes on Virginia* (Paris, 1784, and Richmond, Virginia, 1853) stated of the negroes: 'The instrument proper to them is the Banjar, … its chords [strings] being precisely the four lower chords of the guitar'. The common ENGLISH GUITAR of the period was tuned C–e–g–c'–e'–g'; hence the *banjar* would have been tuned C–e–g–c', if by 'lower' Jefferson meant 'lower in pitch', or else g–c'–e'–g', if he meant 'lower in position when held by the player'. The former interpretation gives a traditional tuning pattern still sometimes used for the banjo's four full-length strings; the latter gives the pattern of the modern G tuning.

Although long-necked instruments with skin soundtables are common in North Africa, the Middle East and Asia, the banjo almost certainly derived from one or more of those in Northwest Africa. Coolen (1991) and Conway (1995) favour the Senegalese *xalam* as the closest match in terms of structure and performance style. The *xalam* shares the banjo's characteristic short thumb string, but it and other banjo-like African instruments, such as the *nkoni* of the Manding peoples and *tidinīt* of Mauritania all have round necks. The *banza* probably acquired its flat fingerboard after enslaved musicians in the New World became familiar with European and English plucked string instruments, all of which have flat fingerboards. A similar instrument, the RAMKIE, has existed in South Africa since the early 18th century. Percival Kirby, whose *Musical Instruments of the Native Races of South Africa* (Johannesburg, 1926) includes several *ramkie* illustrations, makes a good case for its being an adaptation of the Portuguese *rabequinha* or *cavaquinho*, possibly introduced by slaves from the Malabar Coast of India, long under Portuguese domination. Even if not directly related to the *ramkie*, the *banza* may have developed in a similar manner since Portuguese slave traders were active in West Africa as early as the 15th century.

The first depiction in the Americas of the modern banjo's distinctive short 'thumb string' appears in J. Stedman's book, *Narrative of a Five-Year's Expedition Against the Revolted Negroes of Surinam from the Year*

2. Two banjos, or 'strum-strumps' (foreground), and a harp-lute: engraving from Hans Sloane's 'A Voyage to the Islands of Madeira, Barbados, Nieves, S. Christopher and Jamaica' (London, 1707)

1772 to 1777 (1796, 2/1806/R). Pl.lxix illustrates a *creole bania*, and a very similar instrument, collected by Stedman about the same time, is now in the Rijksmuseum voor Volkenkunde, Leiden. They both have one short and three long strings and a skin-headed gourd or calabash body. A watercolour entitled *The Old Plantation* (painted between 1777 and about 1800 in South Carolina; fig.3) shows a group of slaves dancing to the music of a gourd-bodied banjo which, like the Stedman instrument, has three full-length strings plus a short thumb string. An inaccurate drawing of this instrument, included in an article by A. Woodward, 'Joel Sweeney and the First Banjo', *Los Angeles County Museum Quarterly*, vii/3, 1949, p.7, omitted the thumb string and contributed to the incorrect popular legend that this feature of the modern banjo was invented by Joel Walker Sweeney (1810–60). Nevertheless, as the first well-known and widely travelled white banjoist, Sweeney played a major role in bringing the banjo to the attention of urban audiences in the USA and England and presumably in popularizing the type of banjo that he played. One owned and said to have been made by him is in the Los Angeles County Museum. Fretless and of light construction, it had screw-tightening brackets (now missing) for adjusting the head tension, four full length strings and a short fifth string. It is also similar to a modern banjo in having a body made of a thin bent-wood rim instead of a gourd, and is thus better suited to commercial mass-production.

Through the influence of Sweeney, Daniel Emmett and many other popular minstrel-show banjoists (for illustration *see* EMMETT, DAN), many of whom had lived near and learned from black banjo players, the banjo was rapidly introduced to white urban culture. By the 1840s and 1850s banjos were being produced by the first commercial maker, William Boucher of Baltimore (see fig.1*b* above), whose banjos were almost identical with Sweeney's, and James Ashburn of Wolcottville, Connecticut. The latter applied an improved tuning-peg to a banjo in 1852 (US Patent 9268).

By the end of the Civil War the banjo had also taken root among traditional white musicians of the rural South, who, like Sweeney, had learned about it from direct contact with black musicians and, also, touring minstrel shows, medicine shows, and circuses. The banjo joined the fiddle to initiate a tradition of what is now called 'old-time string band music,' and was also played as a solo instrument and to accompany songs. The black tradition remained fairly strong in the rural South through the 1930s, but by the 1990s there were few black players (see Conway, 1995). Until the latter decades of the 20th century interplay between the black and white traditions was common.

Two general classes of playing styles, each with many variations, have developed. Apart from numerous accounts from the 17th century to the 19th of the banjo's use by black musicians to accompany singing and dancing, no detailed descriptions or notations are known before the 1850s, when the first minstrel banjo tutors were published. The 'stroke' style they teach produces a sound similar to that described in many of the earlier accounts. It is similar to the earliest style of rural southern white banjo players, today known as 'clawhammer' or 'frailing', in which patterns of downward strikes by the index or middle fingernail are combined with downward strokes of the thumb against the fifth string. More complex patterns may be produced by the thumb dropping further

3. *Banjo accompanying dancing slaves: 'The Old Plantation', watercolour, c1777–1800 (Abby Aldrich Rockefeller Folk Art Center, Williamsburg, VA)*

down to pick individual notes on the full length strings. The other major family of styles, 'finger-picking', combines upward plucking by the first, and sometimes second and third fingers, with downward plucks of the fifth string by the thumb. In both styles the fingers of the left hand pluck, hammer and slide on individual strings to contribute additional notes and rhythmic accents.

Finger-picking is first mentioned by Briggs (1855), as an alternate, guitar-like way to accompany songs, and is more fully described in an 1865 tutor by Frank B. Converse, who credited the Buckley family with being the first to play it. By the 1890s it had become the dominant style on the minstrel, vaudeville and concert stages and for amateur urban musicians, but the down-stroking styles remained popular in many rural areas until well into the 20th century. Finger-style playing became increasingly well-established about 1900 in the rural folk tradition, both black and white, apparently in imitation of classical guitar technique. At first, folk finger styles were primarily two-finger picking (i.e. using thumb and index finger), but a three-finger style (which added the middle finger) was popularized in the 1920s by the North Carolina banjo player Charlie Poole, and somewhat later by Dewitt 'Snuffy' Jenkins and others from the region. In the 1940s it was further developed by Earl Scruggs into 'bluegrass picking', the most widely heard style today.

After the 1850s the banjo was increasingly used in the USA and England as a genteel parlour instrument for the performance of popular music. During the last quarter of the century S.S. STEWART of Philadelphia, and other banjo popularizers, sought to upgrade the instrument's social standing by downplaying its black origins and disparaging the 'old-fashioned' stroke style in favour of the more 'elevated' finger-picking style. Their marketing campaigns were successful and from about 1890 to 1930 there was a vast expansion in the production of banjos and great elaboration in their design and decoration, by makers such as Stewart, the Dobsons (New York and Boston) and A.C. FAIRBANKS (Boston). Besides making regular banjos, these makers (primarily Stewart) created a set of banjo orchestra instruments, all with five strings but of different sizes and pitches. From about 1890 to 1920 there was a craze for banjo, mandolin, and guitar clubs and orchestras; by the turn of the century most good-sized cities and colleges had such organizations. In this period specialized journals and great quantities of marches, rags and transcriptions of popular and light classical music were published for banjo by Stewart, Walter Little of Boston, Clifford Essex of London, and others.

The banjo's important relationship to popular music at that time is well illustrated in the case of RAGTIME. Nathan (1962) finds in some minstrel-show banjo tunes the earliest examples of the kinds of syncopation that later appear in the genre. Banjo pieces such as George Lansing's *The Darkie's Dream* (1887) are among the precursors of ragtime; ragtime itself immediately entered the banjo repertory, and banjo compositions from the mid-1890s onwards were heavily influenced by ragtime. The recorded output of the greatest turn-of-the-century banjo recording artists, VESS L. OSSMAN and Fred Van Eps, includes many rags, and banjo recordings of ragtime (available long before ragtime piano recordings were issued) were influential in increasing its popularity. Other

important concert banjo virtuosos of the time included Parke Hunter, Alfred A. Farland and Fred Bacon.

By the 1920s the popularity of the five-string banjo was rapidly declining among urban players. It was displaced by the four-string tenor and plectrum banjos, which were favoured as rhythm instruments in the jazz and dance orchestras of the day, largely because a pick-played banjo was louder and better suited to the music for the fast, rhythmic new dance steps. The first true tenor banjo was probably the 'banjorine' marketed by J.B. Schall of Chicago in 1907, which was advertised as 'tuned like a mandolin and played with a pick.' Such an instrument found ready acceptance among mandolinists and violinists, whose original instruments did not adapt well to the new music. Regular banjoists converted more easily to the plectrum banjo. Once introduced, these instruments did not long remain as mere accompanying rhythm instruments; solo styles developed, as did virtuoso soloists such as Eddie Peabody and Harry Reser. The 'Jazz Age' created a new society craze for the banjo, this time in its four-string versions. By the 1940s, however, the four-string banjo was being replaced by the guitar, especially the electric guitar, as the rhythm instrument of choice; and by then the five-string banjo had also been abandoned by many rural musicians, either in favour of the guitar, or because of the decline in home music-making.

The five-string banjo regained something of its former popularity after World War II, largely because of the influence of the American banjoists Pete Seeger (*see* SEEGER family, (3)), who popularized traditional rural southern styles among urban players as one aspect of the folksong revival, and Earl Scruggs (*see* FLATT AND SCRUGGS), who became famous as the developer of the 'bluegrass' style of banjo playing (*see* BLUEGRASS MUSIC). It has also regained some popularity as a jazz instrument through the virtuosity of such performers as Bela Fleck (fig.4).

In the southeast USA, many white and a few black traditional country musicians still play banjos, often homemade and fretless; their many tunings, playing techniques and repertory include survivals of 19th-century

4. Bela Fleck

minstrel and black performing practice. The Archive of Folk Culture, Library of Congress, Washington, DC, has a good collection of field recordings of such music, as does the Southern Folk-Life Collection (Wilson Library, University of North Carolina, Chapel Hill, NC). In the USA the American Banjo Fraternity promotes classic banjo playing and holds biannual conventions. Among the few composers to score for the instrument are Weill (*Mahagonny*, 1927), Krenek (*Kleine Sinfonie*, op.58, 1928) and Davies (*The Boy Friend*, 1971).

Public instrument collections possessing banjos include the Smithsonian Institution, Washington, DC; the Metropolitan Museum of Art, New York; the Stearns Collection of Musical Instruments, University of Michigan, Ann Arbor; and the Victoria and Albert Museum, London.

BIBLIOGRAPHY

T.F. Briggs: *Briggs' Banjo Instructor, Containing the Elementary Principles of Music* (Boston, 1855/R)
The Cadenza (1894–1924)
The Crescendo (1908–33)
Pete Seeger: *How to Play the 5-String Banjo* (New York, 1948, 3/1962)
H. Nathan: *Dan Emmet and the Rise of Early Negro Minstrelsy* (Norman, OK, 1962, 2/1977)
D.J. Epstein: 'Slave Music in the United States before 1860: a Survey of Sources', *Notes*, xx (1962–3), 195–212, 377–90
B.C. Malone: *Country Music U.S.A.: a Fifty-Year History* (Austin, TX, 1968, 2/1985)
A. Rosenbaum: *Old-Time Mountain Banjo: an Instruction Method* (New York, 1968)
C.P. Heaton: 'The Five-String Banjo in North Carolina', *Southern Folklore Quarterly*, xxxv (1971), 62–82
T. Adler: 'The Physical Development of the Banjo', *New York Folklore Quarterly*, xxviii (1972), 187–208
D.J. Epstein: 'African Music in British and French America', *MQ*, lix (1973), 61–91
R.C. Toll: *Blacking Up: the Minstrel Show in Nineteenth-Century America* (New York, 1974)
D.J. Epstein: 'The Folk Banjo: a Documentary History', *EthM*, xix (1975/R), 347–71
R.L. Webb: 'Banjos on their Saddle Horns', *American History Illustrated*, xi/2 (1976), 11–20
R.D. Winans: 'The Folk, the Stage, and the Five-String Banjo in the Nineteenth Century', *Journal of American Folklore*, lxxxix (1976), 407–37
D.J. Epstein: *Sinful Tunes and Spirituals: Black Folk Music to the Civil War* (Urbana, IL, 1977)
R.B. Winans: 'The Black Banjo-Playing Tradition in Virginia and West Virginia,' *Journal of the Virginia Folklore Society*, i (1979), 7–30
R.B. Winans: 'Black Instrumental Music Traditions in the Ex-Slave Narratives', *Black Music Research Newsletter*, v/2 (1982), 2–5
S. Cohen: 'Banjo Makers and Manufacturers', *Mugwumps*, vii (1983), 10–16
R.L. Webb: *Ring the Banjar! The Banjo in America from Folklore to Factory* (Cambridge, MA, 1984)
U. Wegner: *Afrikanische Saiteninstrumente* (Berlin, 1984)
R.B. Winans: 'Early Minstrel Show Music, 1843–1852', *Musical Theatre in America*, ed. G. Loney (Westport, CT, 1984), 71–97
N.V. Rosenberg: *Bluegrass: a History* (Urbana, 1985)
G. Kubik: 'The Southern Periphery: Banjo Traditions in Zambia and Malawi', *World of Music*, xxxi/1 (1989), 3–29
R.B. Winans: 'Black Instrumental Music Traditions in the Ex-Slave Narratives', *Black Music Research Journal*, x (1990), 43–53
M.T. Coolen: 'Senegambian Influences on Afro-American Musical Culture', *Black Music Research Journal*, xi (1991), 1–18
M. Hendler: *Altweltiche Wurzeln eines neuweltlichen Musikinstruments: Verschuttete Spuren zur Vor- und Fruhgeschichte der Saiteninstrumente* (Göttingen, 1991)
K.E. Linn: *That Half-Barbaric Twang: the Banjo in American Popular Culture* (Urbana, IL, 1991)
G. Gruhn and W.Carter: *Acoustic Guitars and Other Fretted Instruments: a Photographic History* (San Francisco, 1993)
U. Heier and R.E.Lotz, eds: *The Banjo on Record: a Bio-Discography*(Westport, CT, 1993)
A. Tsumura, *1001 Banjos* (New York, 1993)
P.F. Gura: 'Manufacturing Guitars for the American Parlor: James Ashborn's Wolcottville, Connecticut, Factory, 1851–56', *Journal of the American Antiquarian Society* (1994), 117–56
R.B. Winans and E.Kaufman: 'Minstrel and Classic Banjo: American and English Connections', *American Music* xii/1 (1994), 1–30
C. Conway: *African Banjo Echoes in Appalachia: A Study of Folk Traditions* (Knoxville, TN, 1995)
R.F. Gura and J.F. Bollman: *America's Instrument: the Banjo in the Nineteenth Century* (Chapel Hill, NC, 1999)

JAY SCOTT ODELL, ROBERT B. WINANS

Banjulele [banjo ukulele]. A hybrid instrument combining a banjo body with a UKULELE fingerboard, stringing and tuning.

Bankole, Ayo [Theophilus Ayeola] (*b* Lagos, 1935; *d* Lagos, 6 Nov 1976). Nigerian composer. His parents, both music teachers, and the composers Fela Sowande and T.K. Ekundayo Phillips were his early musical influences. He pursued formal studies in composition, the organ and the piano at the GSM (1957) and read music at Cambridge (BA 1964); he became an FRCO in 1965. Bankole also studied ethnomusicology at UCLA. Although most of his early works do not emphasize African elements, his work at UCLA stimulated Bankole to incorporate traditional Yoruba musical elements into his choral pieces: *Jona* and *Ethnophony* are two works that employ African musical instruments exclusively. As exemplified in *Festac Cantata*, the tonal properties of the Yoruba language became a marked influence on his choral works. He was senior music producer at the Nigerian Broadcasting Corporation (1966–9), and a lecturer in music at the University of Lagos (1969–76).

WORKS
(*selective list*)

Pf: Ya Orule, 1957; Nigerian Suite (1957); Christmas Sonata, 1959; English Winterbirds, 1961; The Passion Sonata (1977); Fugal Dance
Org: Toccata and Fugue (1960); 3 Toccatas, 1967
Choral: Cant. in Yoruba, female chorus, chbr orch, 1958; Choral Fugue, 1962; Ona Ara, solo vv, org, Yoruba insts, orch, 1970; 3-Part Songs, female vv (1975); Festac Cant. no.4, 1976; Jona, chorus, Yoruba insts; Ethnophony, chorus, Yoruba insts
Songs: 10 Yoruba Songs, 1v, pf, 1966; Adura fun Alafia, 1v, pf, 1969; 3 Yoruba Songs, Bar, pf (1977)

MSS in Iwalewa-Haus, U. of Bayreuth

DANIEL AVORGBEDOR

Banks, Benjamin (*b* Salisbury, 14 July 1727; *d* Salisbury, 18 Feb 1795). English violin maker. He lived and worked in Salisbury and, with Forster, did much to raise the standard of English violin-making in the second half of the 18th century. In 1741 he began an apprenticeship under his uncle, William Huttoft. Although it was intended to last seven years, the apprenticeship terminated abruptly on Huttoft's death in 1747. Banks's earliest known instrument is an English guitar branded, signed and dated 1757, and his first advertisement appeared in the *Salisbury and Winchester Journal* on 28 March 1757.

Benjamin Banks has been described as the 'English Amati', and fine examples of his work exist to support this statement. He was the first English maker to recognize the importance of Stradivari's 'long pattern', and his cellos and violins were made to 'Strad' specifications. His violas invariably have a Stainer influence. They are always on the small side, being never more than 39.7 cm along the back. English sycamore and pine were the basic woods

Benjamin Banks: silhouette by Charles Rosenberg, c1790

employed on all Banks instruments, and his varnish is of excellent quality, ranging in colour from brown, through orange-brown and orange-red to deep red. The claim that stain was first laid on as a filler is without foundation. Signatures and initials are to be found in a variety of places, although not all instruments carry labels.

The bows that Banks and most other 18th-century makers sold were made by the Dodd family. In Banks's case they varied in quality and were branded BANKS, sometimes over the Dodd name. This was common practice, and may be assumed to have been carried out with the Dodd family's permission. Banks never made trade instruments, although he did allow his agents, Longman & Broderip, to place their brand over his on the instruments they sold; only a few of these still exist.

Benjamin Banks married Ann Burtt in 1749; they had ten children, including a pair of twins. Their eldest child, Ann (1750–94), married the music publisher Thomas Cahusac (i) in 1780. Benjamin's sixth child, James (*b* Salisbury, 10 Aug 1758; *d* Liverpool, 15 June 1831), was already producing instruments of high quality at the age of 17. His ability and drive have been given less than the notice they deserve by previous writers. Under his direction the string section of the firm blossomed profusely until the business was sold in 1811. His younger brother Henry (*b* Salisbury, 15 Dec 1770; *d* Liverpool, 16 Oct 1830), whose name is always linked with James, served an apprenticeship in the piano department of Longman & Broderip. In 1795 (the year of his father's death), Henry proudly advertised his skills in tuning 'stringed instruments of all kinds' in the *Salisbury and Winchester Journal*. Benjamin Banks's third child, Benjamin (*b* Salisbury, 15 Sept 1754; *d* Liverpool, 22 Jan 1820), also made violins. He worked in London for a short time, but his work tends to be heavy and somewhat clumsy.

In 1785 a fire devastated workshops opposite Banks's house and main workshop in Catherine Street, Salisbury. Although £200 worth of stock was destroyed, it had little effect on production for that year. In 1811 the business was sold to Alexander Lucas, and Henry and James moved to Liverpool. It would seem that the few instruments dated after the move were remaining stock that was brought up from Salisbury and labelled in Liverpool.

BIBLIOGRAPHY

W.M. Morris: *British Violin Makers* (London, 1904, 2/1920)
W. Henley: *Universal Dictionary of Violin and Bow Makers* (Brighton, 1959)
A.W. Cooper: *Benjamin Banks, the Salisbury Violin Maker* (Haslemere, 1989/R)

A.W. COOPER

Banks, Don(ald Oscar) (*b* South Melbourne, 25 Oct 1923; *d* Sydney, 5 Sept 1980). Australian composer. The son of a professional jazz musician, Banks grew up in a house full of musical instruments, and learned to play several. He developed an early interest in jazz, sitting in as trombonist in Roger and Graeme Bell's jazz band. Following wartime service, the army rehabilitation scheme enabled him to undertake musical studies at the University of Melbourne Conservatorium of Music (1947–9), where he studied composition with Nickson and Le Gallienne; his fellow students included the composer Keith Humble, with whom he formed a lifelong friendship. During this period he became the founder and pianist of the Don Banks Boptet which was one of Australia's first bebop groups.

In 1950 Banks went to London, where work as secretary to Edward Clark, the head of music at the BBC and a former Webern pupil, soon brought him into contact with the more progressive circles in London's musical life. He studied composition with Seiber, and later, in 1953, with Dallapiccola in Florence. Neither composer taught 12-note composition *per se* – they were more concerned with broadly applicable disciplines – but the combination of serialism and canonic technique in Dallapiccola's *Goethe Lieder* clearly impressed Banks, and is reflected in the sketches for works from this period. A course given by Babbitt in Salzburg in 1952 had already established Banks's interest in serial thought and this was confirmed by his attendance in 1956 at Nono's seminars in Gravesano, Switzerland.

Initially through Seiber, Banks gained substantial work as a commercial composer, beginning with cartoons and comedy films in the late 1950s, and then moving on to thrillers and horror movies, especially for Hammer Films. This was by no means just a money-spinner: in a musical climate generally hostile to modernism, it gave him instant access to an orchestra, and horror films in particular permitted him to try out all kinds of new resources. In the concert hall, on the other hand, there was a 12-year gap between the Four Pieces which were first performed by the LPO under Boult in 1953, and the fairly consistent stream of orchestral commissions that followed *Divisions* (1964–5). Jazz also proved to be an enduring passion in Banks's life; in London, it led to friendship with John Dankworth and Cleo Laine for whom, in 1966, he wrote the *Settings from Roget*. This was the first of many works espousing the 'third stream' fusion of jazz and contemporary concert music pioneered during the 1950s by Schuller; they include three pieces entitled *Equation*, and reach a peak in *Nexus*.

Following a brief trip to Australia in 1970 while head of music at Goldsmiths' College, University of London (1969–71), a Creative Arts Fellowship at the Australian National University in Canberra took Banks back again in 1972; following this he accepted a composition post at the Canberra School of Music. Ever altruistic, he immediately assumed a central role in the promotion of new music – just as he did in London through the Australian Musical Association, which he co-founded with Margaret Sutherland in the 1950s, and the SPNM – most notably as chair of the Music Board of the Australia Council, and as co-founder of the ACME Ensemble. In 1979 he became head of the school of composition studies at the NSW Conservatorium; by this stage, however, he was already suffering from cancer, compounded by a serious car accident, and he was able to complete only one more work, *An Australian Entertainment*, before his death.

Banks's output covers a wide variety of genres, from major orchestral works to brief choral pieces for school use, and a wide variety of styles. Though essentially a 12-note composer with a preference for tautly argued motivic textures – his finest and most characteristic works are probably the *Sonata da camera*, the concertos for horn and violin, and *Limbo* – he was also fascinated by the more radical musical activities of the 1960s. Witness to this are his graphic score *Form X* and the later *4/5/7*, hastily written on the back of a photocopy of Earle Brown's *December '52*, as well as the orchestral *Assemblies* and *Intersections*, both intended as 'young person's guides' to new music. In England, while at Goldsmiths', he had also taken a keen interest in electronic music, and especially in developments of the synthesizer, though his suspicion of the medium's potential for pretentiousness is reflected in the droll tape part of *Commentary*. In Australia, he was an adviser to Tony Furse in the early development stages of the Fairlight CMI, and a late work like *4 x 2 x 1* suggests that had he lived longer, electroacoustic music would have played an increasingly prominent role in his work. Banks's continual openness and natural curiosity coupled with impeccable traditional craftsmanship was the key to his reputation as a composer and outstanding teacher.

WORKS

Orch: 4 Pieces, 1953; Episode, chbr orch, 1958; Divisions, 1964–5; Hn Conc., 1965; Assemblies, 1966; Vn Conc., 1968; Dramatic Music, youth orch, 1969; Fanfare, 1969; Music for Wind Band, 1971; Nexus, orch, jazz qt/qnt, 1971; Prospects, 1973; Trilogy, 1977: see El-ac [Intersections, 1969]

Vocal: 5 North Country Folk Songs, S/T, pf/str orch, 1954; Ps lxx, S, chbr orch, 1954; 3 North Country Folk Songs, S/T, pf, 1955; Settings from Roget, female jazz vocalist, a sax, pf, drums, db, 1966; Tirade (Porter), Mez/Bar, pf, hp, 3 perc, 1968; Findings Keepings, SATB, drums, db, 1968; 3 Short Songs, 1v, jazz qt, 1971; Aria from Limbo, 1v, pf, 1972; Walkabout, children's vv, insts, 1972; An Australian Entertainment, 6vv, 1979: see El-ac [Limbo, 1971]

Chbr and solo inst: Divertimento, fl, str trio, 1951, rev. 1960; Duo, vn, vc, 1951–2; Sonata, vn, pf, 1953; 3 Studies, vc, pf, 1955; Pezzo dramatico, pf, 1956; Sonata da camera, fl, cl, b cl, pf, perc, str trio, 1961; Trio, hn, vn, pf, 1962; Equation 1, jazz group, ens, 1963–4; Form X, 2–10 players; 3 Episodes, fl, pf, 1964; Sequence, vc, 1967; Prologue, Night Piece and Blues, cl, pf, 1968; Equation 2, jazz group, ens, 1969; 4 Pieces, str qt, 1971; Take Eight, jazz qt, str qt, 1973; Str Qt, 1975; One for Murray, b cl, 1977

El-ac: Intersections, orch, tape, 1969; Commentary, pf, 2-track tape, 1970; Limbo, 3 solo vv, 8 insts, 2-track tape, 1971; Equation 3, jazz group, ens, elecs, 1972; Meeting Place, jazz group, ens, elecs, 1972; Shadows of Space, 4-track tape, 1978; 4 x 2 x 1, b cl, 2-track tape, 1978; Magician's Castle, 2-track tape, 1978

Arr.: Elizabethan Miniatures, lute, b viol, str, 1962

Principal publishers: Chester, Schott

WRITINGS

'Converging Streams', *MT*, cxi (1970), 596–9
'Third-Stream Music', *PRMA*, xcvii (1970–71), 59–67

BIBLIOGRAPHY

W. Mann: 'The Music of Don Banks', *MT*, cix (1968), 719–21
P. Bracanin: 'Don Banks', *Australian Composition in the Twentieth Century*, ed. F. Callaway and D. Tunley (Melbourne, 1978), 97–116

RICHARD TOOP

Bannester. *See* BANISTER family.

Banniera, Antonio. *See* BAGNIERA, ANTONIO.

Bannister, Henry(-Marriott) (*b* Oxford, 18 March 1854; *d* Oxford, 16 Feb 1919). English musical palaeographer. After reading classics and theology at Pembroke College, Oxford (1873–7), he held a number of ecclesiastical appointments before devoting himself to musical palaeography. He travelled extensively and accumulated an encyclopedic knowledge of library collections in his chosen field of the medieval liturgy and its music, in which he published numerous articles (in *Rassegna gregoriana*, *English Historical Review* and the *Journal of Theological Studies*). In 1917 he was appointed acting sub-librarian of the Bodleian Library.

EDITIONS

Analecta hymnica medii aevi, xl, xlii–xliv, xlvi, xlvii, xlix, li–liv (1902–15/R)
Monumenti vaticani di paleografia musicale latina (Leipzig, 1913/R)
Melodiae sequentiarum (MS, *GB-Ob*) [selection in A. Hughes, ed.: *Anglo-French Sequelae, Edited from the Papers of the Late Dr. Henry Marriott Bannister* (London, 1934/R)]

ANSELM HUGHES/MALCOLM TURNER

Bannius, Joannes Albertus. *See* BAN, JOAN ALBERT.

Banse, Juliane (*b* Tettnang, 10 July 1969). German soprano. She studied at the training school of the Zürich Opera, then in Munich with Fassbaender and Daphne Evangelatos. She made her stage début at the Komische Oper, Berlin, in 1989 as Pamina, and followed that role with Ilia and Susanna at the same house. Since then she has appeared as Sophie at the Salzburg Festival, as Zerlina at Glyndebourne (the controversial Warner staging of 1994), at the Deutsche Oper Berlin as Pamina, Sophie and Manon, and at the Vienna Staatsoper as Susanna, Pamina, Marzelline, Sophie and Zdenka. In 1998 she was much praised for her assumption of the title part in the première of Holliger's opera *Schneewittchen* at Zürich. In 1999 she sang Ighino in a new production of *Palestrina* at the Vienna Staatsoper. She has a wide concert repertory ranging from Haydn (she has performed *The Creation* under Rattle with the Berlin PO and under Andrew Davis at the Proms) to Mahler and Berg, and is a leading exponent of lieder. Her recordings of, among others, Mozart, Schumann and Mahler have been much admired for her innate sincerity of purpose allied to a communicative manner, a pleasing timbre and a scrupulous care for the text.

ALAN BLYTH

Banshchikov, Gennady Ivanovich (*b* Kazan', 9 Nov 1943). Russian composer. He studied composition with Balasanian at the Moscow Conservatory (1961–4) and then at the Leningrad Conservatory under Arapov (1965–6) with whom he also undertook postgraduate work (1966–9). He joined the Composers' Union in 1967 and in 1980 was appointed board member of the St Petersburg branch.

He has taught at the St Petersburg Conservatory since 1974, was made senior lecturer in 1983 and professor of orchestration and composition in 1998. Any straightforward definition of Banshchikov's creative personality is precluded by his multifaceted nature: he eschews all aesthetic labels applied to his music. However, while descriptions such as Romantic, lyrical and conservative are in themselves inadequate, taken in aggregate they provide a general representation of his output. He combines the technical suavity, professional restraint and academic approach of the St Petersburg school with a certain impulsiveness and high emotional temperature. He also gives innovation due regard, so his particular link with German Romanticism does not prevent his language from being profoundly contemporary. He combines precise forms with Romantic angst; his kinship with Richard Strauss therefore comes as no surprise – the *Opera o tom, kak possorilsya Ivan Ivanovich s Ivanom Nikiforovichem* ('Opera About how Ivan Ivanovich Quarrelled with Ivan Nikiforovich') is dedicated to that composer's memory. Other works, such as the opera-parody *Lyubov' i Silin*, reveal Banshchikov's wit, sense of irony and comedy. The large scale of his designs is evident not only in his symphonies but also in his chamber and solo instrumental works, among which should be mentioned the first full-scale substantial sonatas for bayan.

WORKS

Stage: Ostalas' legenda [The Legend Remained] (radio op for children, F. Naftul'yev), 1967; Lyubov' i Silin (chbr op, 3, after Koz'ma Prutkov), 1968; Vestris (choreographic composition, L. Yakobson), 1969; Opera o tom, kak possorilsya Ivan Ivanovich s Ivanom Nikiforovichem [Opera About how Ivan Ivanovich Quarrelled with Ivan Nikiforovich] (op, 1, M. Lobodin, after N. Gogol'), 1971, rev. for chbr forces, 1982; Smert' korneta Klyauzova [The Death of Klyauzov's Cornet] (op, 1, A. Kleyman, after A. Chekhov: Shvedskaya spichka [The Swedish Match]), 1976; Gore ot uma [Woe in Wisdom] (op, 2, Banshchikov, after A. Griboyedov), 1979–83; Optimiticheskaya tragediya [An Optimistic Tragedy] (ballet, 2, A. Dement'yev, after V. Vishnevsky), 1985; Dama Pik [Dame Pique] (ballet, 2, A. Polubentsev, after A.S. Pushkin), 1989; Sharman i Venera [The Shaman and Venus] (ballet, 1, A. Raskin, after V. Khlebnikov), 1993

Vocal-orch: Zodchiye [Architecture] (cant., D. Kedrin), B, male chorus, orch, 1964; Pamyati Garsia Lorki [In Memory of García Lorca] (cant., F. García Lorca), chorus, orch, 1965, rev. 1979; Pepel v ladonyakh [Ashes in the Palms] (cant., S. Val'yekho), S, small orch, 1979; Peterburgskiy noktyurn (cant., A. Blok), Mez, small orch, 1985; Oblaka [Clouds] (cant., I. Brodsky), S, small orch, 1995

Orch: Vc Conc. no.1, 1962; Pf Conc., 1963, rev. 1978; Tpt Conc., 1963; Vc Conc. no.2, 1964; Sym. no.1, 1967; Vc Conc. no.5, 1970; Sym. no.2, str, 1977; Vechniy ogon' [Eternal Fire], sym., 1985; Sym. no.3, 1988; Dama Pik, sym. in portraits and scenes, narr, orch, 1990; Shaman i Venera, sym.-dream, 1994

Chbr and solo inst: Chetïre mimoletnosti/4 Visions fugitives, vc, pf, 1963; Muzïka dlya fortepiano [Music for Piano], 1964; Malen'kiy duèt [Little Duet], vn, pf, 1965; Vc Conc. no.3, vc, 1965; Vc Conc. no.4 'Duodetsimet', vc, 11 insts, 1966; 4 p'yesï [4 Pieces], cl, pf, 1968; Pf Sonata no.1, 1968; Sonata, cl, pf, 1972; Trio-Sonata, vn, va, vc, pf, 1972; Pf sonatas nos.2–3, 1973, 1974; Sonata, fl, pf, 1975; Bayan Sonata no.1, 1977; Str Qt, 1982; Bayan Sonata no.2, 1985; Sonata, hp, org, 1987; Bayan Sonata no.3, 1987; Pf Sonata no.4, 1988; Telefonnaya kniga: Kontsert dlya kamernogo orkestra i avtootvetvhika, posvyashchayetsya Rikhardu Shtrausu, moim druzyam i leningradskoy sluzhbe taksi [Telephone Book: A Concerto for Chamber Orchestra and Answering Machine Dedicated to Richard Strauss, my Friends and the Leningrad Taxi Service], 1990; Pf Sonata no.5, 1998

Other: vocal works for 1v, pf; incid music, film scores

WRITINGS

'Orkestr v "Poèma èkstaza" A. Skryabina' [The orchestra in Skryabin's 'Poem of Ecstasy'], *Orkestrovïye stili v russkoy muzïke* (Leningrad, 1987), 73–82

Zakonï funktsional'noy instrumentovki [The Laws of Functional Orchestration], 3 vols. (St Petersburg, 1997)

BIBLIOGRAPHY

M. Rakhmanova: 'Obryashchyonnaya k cheloveku' [Addressed to the man], *SovM* (1968), no.9, pp.42–7

E. Finkel'shteyn: *Gennadiy Banshchikov: monograficheskiy ocherk* (Leningrad, 1983)

L. Raaben: 'Gennadiy Banshchikov', *O dukhovnom renessanse v russkoy muzïke* (St Petersburg, 1997), 131–45

IOSIF GENRIKHOVICH RAYSKIN

Banti, Brigida Giorgi (*b* Monticelli d'Ongina, nr Crema, 1755; *d* Bologna, 18 Feb 1806). Italian soprano. Her father, a street singer and mandolin player, took her to Paris when she was about 20; there she met de Vismes, director of the Opéra, who arranged her début there (1 November 1776) singing a song between the second and third acts of Gluck's *Iphigénie en Aulide*. She had some lessons from Sacchini, and in 1779 went to London, where she met the dancer Zaccaria Banti, whom she married in Amsterdam. She seems at this time to have been a very bad singer with a beautiful voice, and so lazy that she could not be taught. In 1780 she left England and travelled over Europe, singing in Vienna (1780), Venice (1782–3), most of the Italian cities, Warsaw (1789) and Madrid (1793–4) with increasing fame. In 1794 she returned to London, making her début in Bianchi's *Semiramide*, in which she introduced an air with violin obbligato from Guglielmi's *Deborae Sisara*; the song became a favourite with her audiences and was always encored. She was principal soprano at the King's Theatre from 1794 until her retirement in 1802.

Banti's fame was truly international, and she was particularly admired by Mount Edgcumbe, who called her 'far the most delightful singer I ever heard'. He composed *Zenobia* for her in 1800, and wrote in his *Musical Reminiscences*:

Her voice was of most extensive compass, rich and even, and without a fault in its whole range – a true *voce di petto* throughout. In her youth it extended to the highest pitch and was so agile that she excelled most singers in the bravura style; but, losing a few of her upper notes, she modified her manner by practising the cantabile, to which she devoted herself and in which she had no equal. Her acting and recitative were excellent. Her spirits never flagged, nor did her admirers ever grow weary of her. They never wished for another singer.

After her death, Banti's larynx was examined by physiologists, who reported it to be extraordinarily large. Her son, Giuseppe Banti SJ, published a short biography of her in 1869, a copy of which is in the Civico Museo at Bologna.

BIBLIOGRAPHY

FétisB

R. Edgcumbe, 2nd Earl of Mount Edgcumbe: *Musical Reminiscences of an Old Amateur* (London, 1824, 4/1834/R), 43, 79ff

W.T. Parke: *Musical Memoirs* (London, 1830/R), i, 183f, 254, 297–8

C. Lozzi: 'Brigida Banti, regina del teatro lirico nel secolo XVIII', *RMI*, xi (1904), 64–76

A. Kapłon: 'Opera włoska w Warszawie 1784–1793' [Italian opera in Warsaw], *Acta universitatis wratislaviensis*, xx (1979), 13–47

M.G. Genesi: 'Il Teatro Nuovo di Codogno nel Settecento', *Archivio storico lodigiano*, cx (1991), 37–83

M.G. Genesi: *Una primadonna tardosettecentesca: Brigida Giorgi Banti (1755–1806)* (Monticelli d'Ongina, 1991)

M.G. Genesi: '"E non m'involva a sì rea fatalità?" Il repertorio di una soprano d'opera seria Accademica Filarmonica "ad honorem"

– Maria Brigida Giorgi-Banti di Monticelli d'Ongina: per una radiografia della vocalità belcantistica "di maniera" dal 1770 al 1790 circa', *Archivio storico per le province Parmensi*, xliii (1991), 189–213

M.G. Genesi: 'La soprano monticellese Brigida Giorgi-Banti, protagonista a Londra del Galá in onore della vittoria dell'Ammiraglio Howe a Lizard Point', *Strenna piacentina* (1992), 156–65

BRUCE CARR/R

Bantock, Sir **Granville** (*b* London, 7 Aug 1868; *d* London, 16 Oct 1946). English composer. The son of a doctor, and educated for the Indian civil service, which may explain some of his cultural interests, Bantock did not enter the Royal Academy of Music until 1888. There he studied with Corder, a permissive and comparatively progressive teacher who, no doubt, encouraged Bantock's predilection for the music of Wagner and Richard Strauss. Bantock was the first winner of the Macfarren Scholarship, and several of his works were performed at concerts while he was still a student. These tended to be ambitious in scope, and some were inspired by Western concepts of oriental life. In 1890 the overture to his cantata *The Fire Worshippers* was publicly performed, and two years later he came to wider public attention with a concert version of his one-act opera *Caedmar*, already performed at the RAM, which was given at the Crystal Palace (conducted by August Manns), and subsequently produced at the Olympic Theatre. Bantock left the RAM in 1892, and from May of that year until February 1896 he edited the *New Quarterly Musical Review*. With this came an extensive period of conducting, which was useful experience. During 1894–5 he made a world tour with George Edwardes' *A Gaiety Girl* and the latter year he toured England with the more stimulating *Shamus O'Brien* of Stanford.

A characteristic generosity and interest in his fellow English composers early manifested itself. On 15 December 1896 he gave a concert of orchestral music by living English composers, followed in May 1897 by a similar concert of chamber works. He conducted for a while at the Royalty Theatre, and in July of the same year his overture *Saul* was performed at the Chester Festival, shortly before his appointment as musical director of The Tower, New Brighton, in August. At New Brighton the musical fare consisted mainly of dance music played by a military band, and Bantock set about raising the musical standard, firstly by gradually introducing more serious items between the dances, and then by introducing concerts devoted to the works of one composer. The band was gradually increased to a symphony orchestra, and much English music was played, Elgar, Parry and Stanford being among the composers invited to conduct their own works. In 1898 Bantock married Helena von Schweitzer, who wrote verse and provided the texts for many of his numerous songs. The marriage lasted, in spite of some strains. Bantock had a flair for detecting genius in others; he was one of the first outside Finland to encourage Sibelius, and the two composers became firm friends, Sibelius dedicating his Third Symphony to Bantock.

On Elgar's recommendation Bantock was appointed the first full-time salaried principal of the Birmingham and Midland Institute School of Music in 1900, an appointment that was to have a lasting effect on his career and on music in Birmingham. He succeeded Elgar as Peyton Professor at Birmingham University in 1908, and continued there until he left Birmingham in 1934. Bantock's aim at Birmingham was to give his students a complete musical education, with institute and university interacting with each other. To this end he extended the repertory studied to include the music of the Elizabethans, English church music, folksong, and recent works of contemporary composers such as Richard Strauss and Rimsky-Korsakov, in all of which he was showing some interest himself. It was under Bantock's direction that the first English performance of Gluck's *Iphigénie in Aulide* was given, by students, at Birmingham. At this time he developed an interest in large-scale choral composition, an interlude in his lifelong concern with the symphony orchestra. The first fruit of this new interest was his setting of Fitzgerald's very free translation of *Omar Khayyám*, the first part of which was first performed at the Birmingham Festival of 1906, the second at the Cardiff Festival of 1907, and the third at Birmingham in 1909. It was typical of Bantock to go to Fitzgerald rather than to a more authentic source, a tendency also indicated by his youthful plan to compose 24 symphonic scenes based on Southey's *The Curse of Kehama*.

Gradually his interest returned to symphonic music, beginning with revisions of earlier works, among them the symphonic poems *Dante and Beatrice* (1910) and *Fifine at the Fair* (1911). Bantock's output was prodigious, and between this time and his death he poured out, apparently effortlessly, orchestral and choral works, piano and chamber music, compositions for brass band, and hundreds of songs, mainly for children. On his retirement from his Birmingham posts he became associated with Trinity College of Music, for which he was already an examiner; he therefore moved house to London. Although a great home-lover, he also travelled widely, and even in old age his activities, including composition, spoke of inexhaustible energy. Admitted to hospital for a minor operation he fell and broke his femur; pneumonia set in and he died peacefully at the age of 78. He was a

Granville Bantock

prominent figure in the early years of the English musical renaissance, evincing genuine and long-lasting interests in the choral festival and brass band movements. For a while his music was widely performed, and, although offered many honours, apart from his knighthood Bantock refused to accept them. His music has passed out of fashion, for reasons easily understood. He was strongly influenced by Wagner and Richard Strauss, but failed to find a consistently distinctive musical language of his own. He never adopted the advanced harmonic idiom of *Tristan*, let alone *Salome* or *Elektra*. His style, both in orchestration and harmony, suggests rather such works as *Der fliegende Holländer* and *Guntram*. It is based on common chords and diatonic discords; the complex chromatic suspensions of *Tristan* are outside its scope, as is the dissonant counterpoint of Strauss's more advanced works. Bantock's textures are solidly homophonic, and such chromaticisms that appear are usually found in semi-oriental arabesques. His obsession with pseudo-eastern subjects was also a handicap, since it was the theatrical east of magnificent processions, the gigantic and the gaudy that attracted him; and although he travelled to several Asian countries, the subtlety and restraint of oriental thought escaped him. Among his other abiding interests were Greek subjects, Scottish folk music and Celtic legends. More profitable was the Hebridean influence, since Bantock's own attractive melodies to some extent resembled these folktunes even before he met the researches of Marjorie Kennedy-Fraser. He wrote a great many works, both large and small, on Hebridean themes, or using Hebridean melodies. The *Hebridean Symphony* (1915) itself is an evocative and imaginative piece which uses several Hebridean folktunes, as does *The Seal Woman* (1917–24). On the other hand, the *Celtic Symphony* (1940) is musically a much less ambitious work, despite demanding six harps to supplement the string orchestra. A slight French influence, not extending to the more radical complexities of Debussy's harmony, produced *The Pierrot of the Minute* (1908), an atmospheric work which reveals Bantock's orchestration in a more delicate, and less broad style than in some of his other works. The *Pagan Symphony* is a work of greater substance and power, and reveals more facets of his masterful handling of the orchestra.

Bantock felt that orchestral playing should be corporate and anonymous, and for this reason he refused to write concertos, although all other forms are represented in his output. His choral music is headed by the vast *Omar Khayyám* and the choral symphonies *Atlanta in Calydon* (1911) and *The Vanity of Vanities* (1913). These last two, intended ideally for several hundred amateur singers were, together with numerous shorter choral settings, the major outcome of his involvement with choral societies and the competitive festival movement. However, as with many of Bantock's works, the length and the size of forces required is something of an obstacle to performance. Despite its initial success, *The Seal Woman*, too, no longer holds the stage, and, whereas the best of the songs, such as *A Feast of Lanterns* and *The Lament of Isis* have a definite merit, Bantock frequently set inferior verse with a matching banality of musical idiom. Although his music was popular until World War I, it gradually lost public attention, and towards the end of his life, despite a continuing output as well as revision of earlier compositions, relatively few of his new works were published. He

was financially obliged at this time to write simple, often merely atmospheric, piano pieces, which he subsequently orchestrated for gramophone recordings. In addition he made easy piano arrangements of music by Johann Strauss, Chopin and others, sometimes with words provided by his wife. He wrote too much; there are too many works to sift through to separate the good from the mere note-spinners. However, although performances of his larger works are rare, the brass band music, most notably *Prometheus* (1933), and some of the smaller orchestral works are still performed.

WORKS
(*selective list*)

STAGE

Ramses II (incid music, Bantock), 1891
Aegypt, ballet, London, RAM, 1892, orchd 1899
Caedmar (op, 1, F. Corder), 1892, London, Olympic, 25 Oct 1892
The Pearl of Iran (op, 1, Bantock), 1893
Electra (incid music, Sophocles), ?1894, London, Court, 15 July 1909
Eugene Aram (op, 4 after E. Bulwer Lytton and T. Hood), unfinished, 1896
Hippolytus (incid music, Euripides, trans. G. Murray), 1908, Manchester, Gaiety, 6 Oct 1908
The Great God Pan, choral ballet, 1908–14, Glasgow, St. Andrew's Hall, 9 Dec 1919
Music for a Harlequinade (incid music, H.R. Barber: *The Cortege*), 1917, rev. 1920, London, Court, 11 March 1918
Salome (incid music, O. Wilde), 1918, London, Court, 19 April 1918
Judith (incid music, A. Bennet), Eastbourne, Devonshire Park 1919, orchd 1921, 7 April 1919
The Seal Woman (The Celtic folk op, 2, Kennedy-Fraser), 1917–24, Birmingham Repertory, 27 Sept 1924
Macbeth (incid music, W. Shakespeare), 1926, London, Princes, 26 Dec 1926
Fairy Gold (incid music, A.L. Coburn), 1938, Huyton, Liverpool College for Girls, 15 July 1938

VOCAL ORCHESTRAL

The Fire Worshippers (Moore), solo vv, chorus, orch, 1892; Wulstan, v, orch, 1892; The Blessed Damozel (D.G. Rossetti), reciter, orch, 1892; Thorvenda's Dream, reciter, orch, 1892; Christus (Bible) [2 parts of projected 10], solo vv, chorus, orch, 1901; Ferishtah's Fancies, v, orch, 1905; Sappho, v, orch, 1905; Sea Wanderers (H.F. Bantock), chorus, orch, 1906; The Time Spirit (H.F. Bantock), chorus, orch, 1906; Omar Khayyám (E. Fitzgerald), solo vv, chorus, orch, 1906–9
Song of Liberty (H.F. Bantock), chorus, orch, 1914; The March (J. Squire), v, orch, 1919; The Vale of Arden (A. Hayes), v, orch, 1921; The Song of Songs (Bible), solo vv, chorus, orch, 1922; Pagan Chants, v, orch, 1917–26; The Burden of Babylon (Bible), chorus, brass, drums, 1928; The Pilgrim's Progress (J. Bunyan), solo vv, chorus, orch, 1928; King Solomon (Bible), nar, chorus, orch, 1937; The Sphinx, v, orch, 1941; Thomas the Rhymer, v, orch, 1946

ORCHESTRAL

2 Orch Scenes from Southey's The Curse of Kehama, 1894; 3 Dramatic Dances, 1894; Saul, ov., 1897; Elegiac Poem, vc, orch, 1898; Helena Variations, 1899; Russian Scenes, 1899; Tone Poem no.1 'Thalaba the Destroyer', 1899; Tone Poem no.2 'Dante', 1901, rev. as Dante and Beatrice, 1910; Tone Poem no.4 'Hudibras', 1902; Tone Poem no.5 'The Witch of Atlas', 1902; Tone Poem no.6 'Lalla Rookh', 1902
Sapphic Poem, vc, orch, 1906; The Pierrot of the Minute, ov., 1908; Old Eng. Suite, small orch, 1909; Dante and Beatrice [rev. Tone Poem no.2], 1910; Fifine at the Fair, orch drama, 1911; Oedipus Coloneus, ov., 1911; In the Far West, serenade str, 1912 [based on Str Qt, 1900]; Scenes from the Scottish Highlands, suite, str, 1913; Celtic Poem, vc, orch, 1914
Hebridean Symphony, 1915; The Land of the Gael, suite, str, 1915; Coronach, str, hp, org, 1918; Hamabdil, vc, orch, 1919; The Sea Reivers, orch ballad, 1920; Caristiona: Hebridean Seascape, 1920; Pagan Sym., 1923–8; The Bacchae, ov., 1929, rev. 1945; The Frogs, ov., 1935

4 Chin. Landscapes, small orch, 1936; Aphrodite in Cyprus, sym. ode, 1939; Celtic Sym., str, 6 hp, 1940; Macbeth, ov. [arr. of incid music, 1926], 1940; Ov. to a Greek Comedy, 1941; Circus Life, ov., 1941; Dramatic Poem, vc, orch, 1941; 2 Heroic Ballads, 1944: Cuchullin's Lament, Kishmul's Gallery; Hebridean Poem: The Seagull of the Land-Under-Waves, 1944; The Birds, ov., 1946

CHORAL

Mass, B♭, male chorus, 1903; Atlanta in Calydon, choral sym., 1911; Vanity of Vanities, choral sym. 1913; A Pageant of Human Life, choral sym., 1913; Choral Suite from the Chinese, male chorus, 1914; Choral Suite, male chorus, 1926; 7 Burdens from Isaiah, male chorus, 1927; 3 Choruses for male vv, (R. Browning), 1929; 5 Choral Songs and Dances from the Bacchae, female chorus, 1945; many other works for male, female, mixed and children's choruses

CHAMBER

Str Qt, c, 1900, arr. str orch as In the Far West, 1912; Sonata, vc, pf, 1900, rev. 1940; Pibroch, vc, hp, 1917; Sonata, va, pf, 1919; Sonata, vc, 1924; Salve Regina, str trio, 1924; Sonata, vn, pf, 1929; Sonata, vn, pf, 1930; Str Qt 'In a Chinese Mirror', 1933; Sonata, vn, pf, 1940; Sonata, vc, pf, 1945
Over 400 songs incl. 40 song cycles and numerous partsongs, over 100 pf works, works for brass band, several hundred arrs. of own works and of works by others

MSS in *GB-Bu*

Principal publishers: Boosey, Breitkopf, Curwen, Elkin, Novello, Paxton, Swan, Joseph Williams

BIBLIOGRAPHY

H.O. Anderton: *Granville Bantock* (London, 1915)
H. Antcliffe: 'A Brief Survey of the Works of Granville Bantock', *MQ*, iv (1918), 333–46
Granville Bantock, Chester Miniature Essays ser. (London, 1922)
R. Newmarch: *Sibelius* (London, 1944) [incl. Bantock–Sibelius correspondence]
H. Roberton: 'Remembrance: Granville Bantock', *The Lute* (1946) [special issue]; repr. in *Fanfare* [Birmingham], i/4 (1947), 3–5
W. Hayford Morris: 'Thoughts on Granville Bantock', *Fanfare* [Birmingham], i/9 (1948), 10 only
W. Hayford Morris: 'The Choral Work of Granville Bantock', *Fanfare* [Birmingham], iii/1 (1953), 9–12
W. Hayford Morris: 'The Orchestral Works of Granville Bantock', *Fanfare* [Birmingham], iii/4 (1954), 7–10
W. Hayford Morris: 'The Chamber Works of Granville Bantock', *Fanfare* [Birmingham], iii/5 (1955), 4–7
P.J. Pirie: 'Bantock and his Generation', *MT*, xcix (1968), 715–17
M. Bantock: *Granville Bantock: a Personal Portrait* (London, 1972)
T. Bray: *Granville Bantock* (diss., U. of Cambridge, 1972)
T. Bray: *Music in the Midlands Before the First World War* (London, 1973)
Bantock Society Newsletter (1984–7); new ser. *Bantock Society Journal* (1996–)
S. Banfield: *Sensibility and English Song* (Cambridge, 1985) [incl. list of songs]
J.A. O'Neill: *The Symphonies of Granville Bantock* (diss., Colchester Institute, 1986)
H.M. Banton: *Bantock's Settings of Browning's 'Dramatic Lyrics'* (diss., City of Birmingham Polytechnic, 1987)
V. Budd: 'Granville Bantock: the Hebridean Connection', *An Canan* (1996), no.62, p.2; no.63, p.1; rev. in *Bantock Society Journal*, i (1996), 5–18 [available online, Bantock Society homepage]

PETER J. PIRIE/DAVID BROCK

Banwart, Jakob [?Avia, Jacob] (*b* Sigmaringen, 19 May 1609; *d* Konstanz, *c*1657). German composer. He came from a respected middle-class family from Sigmaringen, residence of the Hohenzollerns, and received his first tuition in music from the court organist, Daniel Bollius. From 1629 he studied at Dillingen University, the centre of the south German Counter-Reformation, where he took his master's degree in 1631. He then went to Konstanz, where he was ordained in 1632 and first carried out mostly musical duties at the court of Prince-Bishop John VI, Lord High Steward of Waldburg-Wolfegg. From 1641 until his death he was Kapellmeister of the cathedral.

The musical life of the Hohenzollern court and at the prince-bishop's residences at Konstanz and Meersburg, where Hieronymus Bildstein, an important pioneer of the new music, worked, were equally important for his artistic development. Thus Schmid included him, together with Johann Stadlmayr and Johann Donfrid, among the 'more prominent representatives of the south German church style'. His works were widely performed and are listed in inventories at Freising (1651), Würzburg (1694) and Feldkirch (1699), among others. Brossard praised the masses in his 1657 book as 'graves, harmonieuses et de très bon goût'. The humorous dialogues, quodlibets and other spirited pieces in his secular collection of 1652 are in sharp contrast to these, and if Gerber was right in stating that Banwart had originally published the book in 1650 under a pseudonym, Jacob Avia, it may have been because he felt it would be thought incongruous coming from one hitherto known as a composer of church music. He consciously modelled it on the 'new Italian manner', and, like two works in Kindermann's *Intermedium musico-politicum* (1643), some of the contents are based on pieces by Tarquinio Merula, from the second book of madrigals (1633).

WORKS
published in Konstanz

Liber primus sacrorum concentuum, 2–4vv, 2 vn, bc (1641)
Pars prima missarum brevium cantuque facilium, 4–5vv, 5 insts, chorus 4vv (ad lib), op.3 (1649)
Teutsche mit new componirten Stucken und Couranten gemehrte kurtzweilige Tafel Music von Gesprächen, Dialogen, Quodlibeten, 2–4vv (2/1652; Ulm, 3/1652) [possible earlier edn, 1650]
Pars secunda missarum, 4, 5vv, addita una 10/18vv, bc (org), op.1 posth., alias quintum (1657)
Motetae sacrae, selectae ex Thesauro musico Jacobi Banwart, 3–11vv, chorus 4vv (1661)
Missa unica, alias decima quinta, super motetam Congratulamini, 5vv, 2 vn, bc, chorus 4vv (ad lib) (1662)

BIBLIOGRAPHY

GerberL; MGG1 (E.F. Schmid)
K.G. Fellerer: 'Ein Musikalien-Inventar des fürstbischöflichen Hofes in Freising', *AMw*, vi (1924), 471–83
W. Pass: 'Das Musikalieninventar der Pfarrkirche St. Nikolaus in Feldkirch aus dem Jahre 1699', *Montfort*, xx (1968), 185, 189

WALTER PASS

Baptie, David (*b* Edinburgh, 30 Nov 1822; *d* Glasgow, 26 March 1906). Scottish musical biographer. He was inspired by the first publication of Grove's *Dictionary* (1879) to write a series of musical biographical dictionaries, in order to document glee composers and Scottish composers whom he feared Grove would neglect. Although he was prone to inaccuracy and erratic judgment, his biographies contain much valuable material. A reviewer in the *Scottish Musical Monthly* corrected many errors in *Musical Scotland Past and Present* (1894), nowadays his most used work and in effect the first comprehensive history of Scottish music. Baptie also compiled from 1846 a manuscript catalogue of partsongs, composed glees, and is said to have edited several hymnbooks. His son Charles Robertson Baptie (*b* Glasgow, 29 May 1870) was a successful minor composer whose works include music-hall songs and an operetta for children.

WRITINGS

A Handbook of Musical Biography (London, 1883/R, 2/1887)
Musicians of All Times (London, 1889, rev. 1907 by W.G.W. Woodworth)
Musical Scotland Past and Present (Paisley, 1894/R)
Sketches of the English Glee Composers, Historical, Biographical and Critical, from about 1735–1866 (London, 1896)

A Descriptive Catalogue of upwards of 23,000 Secular Part-songs (MS, 1898, *GB-Lbl*)

BIBLIOGRAPHY

'"Musical Scotland": a Batch of Baptie Blunders', *Scottish Musical Monthly*, i (1893–4), 156–7

T. Driffield Hawkin: 'A Predecessor of Grove', *MO*, lxxiv (1950–51), 637–41

DAVID JOHNSON

Baptista, Johann. *See* SERRANUS, JOHANN BAPTISTA.

Baptist church music. Baptists are an evangelical Christian denomination whose name is derived from the distinctive doctrine of believers' baptism, usually administered by means of total immersion. Traditional Baptist beliefs also include the authority of the Bible, the soul-competency of the individual believer, a symbolic interpretation of the Lord's Supper, and the autonomy of the local church (although churches have often joined together in voluntary associations and conventions). In most other doctrines Baptists are similar to other mainstream evangelical groups. From modest beginnings in the 17th century Baptists have grown into one of the world's largest evangelical Christian denominations; in 1994 their numbers were estimated at over 37 million worldwide (Wardin, 1995, p.8).

1. Great Britain: (i) The 17th century (ii) The 18th century (iii) The 19th and 20th centuries. 2. North America: (i) The 17th and 18th centuries (ii) The 19th and 20th centuries. 3. Other countries: (i) Mexico, Central and South America (ii) Africa (iii) Asia (iv) Europe and Russia (v) Australasia.

1. GREAT BRITAIN.

(i) The 17th century. The earliest English Baptist churches grew out of 17th-century Separatism. In 1607 John Smyth, the pastor of a Separatist congregation at Gainsborough, led his flock to Amsterdam to avoid persecution. Smyth came under the influence of continental Anabaptist ideas and, in about 1609, rebaptized himself and others of his congregation. Smyth died in 1612 and his followers Thomas Helwys and John Murton led many of his congregation back to England, where they formed the first Baptist church on English soil. While in Amsterdam these Baptists had adopted the Arminian belief in general atonement; thus they and their followers became known as General Baptists.

A second Baptist group arose about 1638 when several members of a London Separatist church – called the Jacob-Lathrop-Jessey church after its succession of early pastors – rejected infant baptism and formed their own congregation. The 'mother church' eventually became a 'union' church of mixed Congregationalist and Baptist sentiments. Because of their Calvinistic views of a limited atonement the Baptists originating out of this congregation became known as Particular Baptists. General and Particular Baptists maintained distinct organizational structures until 1891, when they merged to form the Baptist Union of Great Britain and Ireland.

Like most 17th-century Separatists English Baptists rejected the use of choirs and musical instruments in the church, but some went even further and repudiated the practice of congregational song. In *The Differences of the Churches of the Seperation* (sic), published in Amsterdam in 1608, John Smyth claimed that 'singing a psalme is a part of spirituall worship' but that it must proceed from the spirit and not be read from a book. This was amplified in his *Certayne Demaundes from the Auncyent Brethren of the Seperation* (c1608/9), to suggest that 'in a Psalme one onely must speak' and that the use of 'meter, Rithme, and tune' quenched the Holy Spirit. Thus singing was to be allowed only if done by an individual through the direct inspiration of the Holy Spirit without using preset forms. The impracticality of this was evident to Henry Ainsworth, who pointed out that if Smyth and his congregation truly believed that singing is 'an ordinary part of worship', why perform they it not' (*A Defence of the Holy Scriptures*, 1609). Smyth's views, which were further enlarged upon in Thomas Grantham's massive *Christianismus primitivus* (1678), seem to have held sway in most General Baptist churches until well into the 18th century, although there is evidence of singing by a few of these Baptists in the 17th century. In 1684, the General Baptist pastor John Reeve published *Spiritual Hymns upon Solomon's Song* (1684, 2/1693), which he suggested could be 'sung in the ordinary tunes of the singing Psalms'. The matter of singing came before the General Assembly of the General Baptist Churches in England in 1689. At this time some churches were evidently using William Barton's *Book of Psalms in Metre* (1644), but the general conclusion of the body was that the churches should not 'admit to such Carnall formalities' (Whitley, 1909–10). In 1695 the London General Baptist churches in Paul's Alley and Turner's Hall united, agreeing to sing at the conclusion of morning worship and the Lord's Supper. In the following year, Richard Allen, the pastor of the united church, wrote *An Essay to Prove Singing of Psalms with Conjoined Voices a Christian Duty* (1696), perhaps in reaction to criticism for instituting this practice of singing. However, these early singers appear to have had few immediate imitators among the General Baptists.

Particular Baptist views on singing during the 17th century represent a curious blend of conservatism and radical innovation. There is no evidence of singing in Particular Baptist churches before 1650, and some early Particular Baptists wrote against the practice (e.g. Francis Cornwell, Edward Drapes and Thomas Collier). However, by the mid-1650s Particular Baptist writings in support of singing began to appear (William Kaye and Vavasor Powell) and some congregations had evidently adopted the practice. Psalmody was certainly practised early in the history of Bristol's Broadmead Baptist Church, for in 1671 a former sheriff complained that 'he could hear us Sing Psalmes from our meeting-place, at his house in Hallier's Lane'. The pastor of Horselydown church in London, Benjamin Keach (1640–1704), instituted singing about 1673–5 at the conclusion of the Lord's Supper. In 1680 Hercules Collins, a pastor at Wapping, called singing 'a Gospel-Ordinance' (in his *Orthodox Catechism*), thus placing it on the same plane as the other two ordinances generally recognized by Baptists – baptism and the Lord's Supper. By 1691 between 20 and 30 Particular Baptist congregations in London were singing.

This growing acceptance of singing by Particular Baptists was not universally approved, however. In 1690 Isaac Marlow attacked Keach's use of singing by publishing *A Brief Discourse Concerning Singing in the Public Worship of God* in which he reiterated some of the ideas of John Smyth and put forward the Zwinglian notion that 'singing' as used in New Testament passages such as *Colossians* iii:16 did not indicate a vocal utterance but a 'speaking' in the heart. Keach defended his use of singing in *The Breach Repaired in God's Worship* (1691). These publications touched off a pamphlet war between Marlow and the supporters of Keach's position. By 1692 the issue had become so rancorous that the General Assembly of Particular Baptist churches took up the matter and proposed that several of the most vehement books be dropped from circulation; both sides were urged to exhibit more charitable behaviour. This action seems to have created a temporary lull in the controversy, although 22 members of Keach's church withdrew in 1693 and formed the Maze Pond church because of his use of singing. In 1696 Marlow undertook a response to Richard Allen's *An Essay to Prove Singing of Psalms* by publishing *The Controversie of Singing Brought to an End*. The title of Marlow's essay was perhaps wishful thinking, and the pamphlet war was now pursued with renewed vigour on both sides. From 1690 to 1698 at least 19 essays dealing directly with singing were published by Baptist authors. However, by 1699 the controversy was beginning to lose momentum, in part because the large majority of Particular Baptist churches and ministers favoured singing.

Ironically, at a time when some Particular Baptists rejected congregational singing altogether, and most Anglicans and Separatists restricted it to the metrical psalms (*see* PSALMS METRICAL, §III, 1–2), some Particular Baptists approved the use of 'hymns of human composure' and wrote such pieces for use in worship. In 1654 Anna Trapnell, a Fifth Monarchy Baptist, published a collection of prayers and 'spiritual songs', *The Cry of a Stone*, although if the texts were actually used in services they were probably sung as solos rather than congregational hymns. A collection of lyric poetry by Katherine Sutton, *A Christian Womans Experiences of the Glorious Working of God's Free Grace*, was published in Rotterdam in 1663. In the meantime, the Particular Baptist Thomas Tillam had published three hymns in *The Seventh-Day Sabbath* (1657), one each for the Lord's Supper, Pentecost and the Sabbath. Poems that might have been intended or used for congregational singing appeared in scattered sources by Baptist authors during the 1660s, 1670s and 1680s – particularly in children's books by Abraham Cheare, Benjamin Keach and John Bunyan – but the publication of real significance was Keach's *Spiritual Melody* (1691), a collection of 283 texts that probably reflects some of the hymnic repertory used at the compiler's own church. The book included hymns by non-Baptists such as John Patrick, William Barton and John Mason – often in considerably altered form – as well as original contributions by Keach. Keach published three more collections of hymns, but most of his poetry was doggerel, and his hymnals do not seem to have had much influence outside his personal circle. Nevertheless, these collections are significant for being among the earliest English hymnals to provide a well-rounded body of material that was expressly designed for congregational use. If Keach's poetic abilities were limited, the same cannot be said for Joseph Stennett (1663–1713), a Seventh-Day Baptist whose *Hymns in Commemoration of the Sufferings of Our Blessed Saviour Jesus Christ* (1697) and *Hymns Composed for the Celebration of the Holy Ordinance of Baptism* (1712) were written for the two Baptist ordinances.

(ii) The 18th century. Most General Baptist churches were still in a songless state at the dawn of the 18th century. The Virginia Street church in London began singing in 1722. A few other churches must have adopted singing soon after: a meeting of the General Assembly in 1733 agreed that 'singing' churches should not be disfellowshipped for this reason, but admonished such congregations to undertake 'a serious Examination of the Scriptures' on the subject (Whitley, 1909–10). The majority of General Baptist churches remained songless until after the middle of the century. In 1770 the New Connexion of General Baptists was formed under the influence of the Methodist revival and the first officially sanctioned General Baptist hymnal, *Hymns and Spiritual Songs*, was published in London in 1772. This was followed by Samuel Deacon's *A New Composition of Hymns and Poems* (1785, retitled *Barton Hymns* in its second edition of 1797), the General Baptist Association's *Hymns and Spiritual Songs* (1793), and John Deacon's *A New and Large Collection of Hymns and Psalms* (1800).

During the first third of the 18th century the majority of non-singing Particular Baptist churches began to admit the use of congregational song. Even the Maze Pond church introduced singing in 1733 when a prospective pastor insisted upon it as a condition of his acceptance of the post. A number of Baptists were active in the writing and publishing of hymns during the first half of the century; some of these and the dates of their collections were David Cully (1726), Anne Dutton (1734), Daniel Turner (1747), Benjamin Wallin (pastor at Maze Pond, 1750) and Edward Trivett (1755). The hymns of Isaac Watts were also popular among 18th-century English Baptists.

The 'Golden Age' of British Baptist hymnody began with the publication of Anne Steele's two-volume *Poems on Subjects Chiefly Devotional* (1760). Though intended for private rather than congregational use, Steele's texts were widely anthologized in subsequent hymnals. Among the better-known 18th-century English Baptist hymn writers who followed Steele's example were Edmund Jones, Benjamin Beddome, Robert Robinson, John Fawcett, Samuel Stennett, John Ryland, Samuel Medley, Joseph Swain, and the Welshmen David Williams and Benjamin Francis. The 18th-century Particular Baptist hymnals of greatest significance were John Ash and Caleb Evans's *Collection of Hymns* (1769) and John Rippon's *Selection of Hymns* (1787); these were eclectic collections that drew upon the works of both Baptist and non-Baptist authors. Rippon's hymnal, which was intended to be a supplement to Watts, achieved ten editions in 13 years and saw wide distribution in both England and America during the late 18th and early 19th centuries. Rippon additionally published *Psalms and Hymns of Dr. Watts Arranged by Dr. Rippon* (1801), familiarly known as 'Rippon's Watts'.

The 18th century also saw the beginnings of hymn writing and publishing among Welsh and Scottish Baptists. The most significant Welsh Baptist hymnal of this period was Benjamin Francis's *Aleluia*, which had editions in 1774 and 1786. William Sinclair's *Collection of Hymns and Spiritual Songs* (1751) was probably the first Scottish Baptist hymnal. The Scottish Baptist *A Collection of Christian Hymns and Songs*, initially published in 1786, was still in print in an enlarged edition as late as 1841.

All the Baptist hymnals mentioned to this point were words-only collections. The first British Baptist tune book, John Rippon's *A Selection of Psalm and Hymn Tunes* (1791), was important for its systematic provision of expression marks and tempo indications, its role as the largest musical companion to a particular hymnal, and its being one of the best examples of Dissenting psalmody of the period. Furthermore, the book proved to be widely popular, appearing in numerous editions through the early 19th century.

The music of most 18th-century Baptist churches was restricted to *a cappella* congregational singing, but in a few places Baptists formed choirs and instrumental ensembles. At St Mary's Church in Norwich, for example, a singing school was instituted that formed the nucleus of a church choir (1779–88). East Lancashire was the home of the Deighn Layrocks (Larks of Dean), a group of vocal and instrumental musicians and composers from the village of Dean, many of whom became Baptists in 1747. At various times these musicians formed the nucleus of a separate church (at Lumb) or sang in the choir at other churches. The Larks continued to be active until an organ purchased for the Lumb church in 1858 rendered their services unnecessary.

(iii) The 19th and 20th centuries.   By the beginning of the 19th century congregational singing was common in nearly all British Baptist churches. Ironically, the Maze Pond church, which had been formed in the 17th century by those opposed to Benjamin Keach's introduction of singing, was in the mid-19th century 'famed for the excellence of its congregational singing' (Price, 1941, p.205).

The most important 19th-century General Baptist hymnals were *The Hymn-Book of the New Connexion of General Baptists* (1830, a revision of John Deacon's 1800 hymnal), *The New Hymnbook* (1851, ed. J.B. and J.C. Pike) and *The Baptist Hymnal* (1879, ed. W.R. Stevenson). Rippon's *Selection* held sway among Particular Baptists until the 1828 publication of John Haddon's *A New Selection*, which was itself displaced by *Psalms and Hymns* (1858). A 'Psalms and Hymns Trust' was established in 1860 to promote sales of the latter book. C.H. Spurgeon's *Our Own Hymn Book* (1866), a collection issued primarily for use in the compiler's Metropolitan Tabernacle, was also widely used, and many Particular Baptists employed Stevenson's New Connexion *Baptist Hymnal* (1879). Strict Calvinistic Particular Baptists sang from John Stevens's *New Selection of Hymns* (1809), William Gadsby's *Selection of Hymns* (1814) and David Denham's *The Saints' Melody* (1837). The American Methodist I.D. Sankey's *Sacred Songs and Solos* (1873, and later editions) became popular in many English Baptist churches. Special mention must be made of Daniel Sedgwick, a Baptist who was one of the first Englishmen to undertake the systematic collection of material on hymnody for scholarly study.

Significant Welsh Baptist hymnals of the 19th century were Joseph Harris's *Casgliad o hymnau* (1821) and J.H. Roberts's *Llawlyfr moliant* (1880), edited on behalf of the Caernarvonshire Baptist Association by R.M. Jones and Spinther James. Scottish Baptists continued to sing from *A Collection of Christian Hymns and Songs* as well as from Duncan M'Dougall's *Gaelic Hymns* (1841) and Oliver Flett's *Christian Hymnal* (1871).

During the course of the 19th century British Baptist objections to choirs and instruments broke down almost completely. Many churches introduced a choir and bass viol (violoncello) or instrumental ensemble during the first half of the century. East Leake Baptist Church in Nottinghamshire used a bass viol from at least 1823, while at Beeston a bass viol and 'clarionet' accompanied

the singing from 1838 to 1854. Few Baptist churches employed an organ before mid-century; two that did were the Particular Baptist Stone Chapel at Leeds, which was using such an instrument as early as 1817, and the George Street church in Nottingham (installed 1847). During the second half of the century the bass viol and instrumental ensembles began giving way to harmoniums and organs, and by the end of the century it was a rare Baptist church that did not possess a keyboard instrument. At the East Leake church the bass viol was replaced by a harmonium in 1868, while the Beeston congregation purchased a harmonium in 1854. Despite this proliferation of choirs and instruments some churches did not give up the practice of lining-out the congregational songs until quite late (for example, it was not abandoned at Beeston until 1863).

After the formation of The Baptist Union of Great Britain and Ireland in 1891 it was felt that a new hymnbook was needed as an expression of denominational unity. The Psalms and Hymns Trust that had been founded in 1860 was given the exclusive right to publish hymnals for the denomination, the profits of which were to go towards Baptist charitable causes. The Trust issued the *Baptist Church Hymnal* in London in 1900, followed by the *Baptist Church Hymnal: Revised Edition* (1933), and the *Baptist Hymn Book* (1962). Later, the Trust published a supplement of 104 hymns, *Praise for Today* (1974), and a full hymnal *Baptist Praise and Worship* (1991). The Baptist Union of Wales (formed in 1866) published its first hymnal in 1915 under the editorship of H.C. Williams. R.S. Rogers, E.C. Jones and T.E. Jones were responsible for the Union's *Y llawlyfr moliant newydd* (1956).

The music of British Baptist churches in the late 20th century generally followed either a traditional or a more charismatic approach. The traditonal churches have continued to use hymns, hymnals, and the organ; few of these churches maintain choirs, the music being almost entirely congregational and instrumental. Baptist churches that follow a more charismatic style of worship (though usually without the characteristic hallmark of tongue-speaking) employ worship choruses and use the piano as the basic accompanying instrument.

2. NORTH AMERICA.

(i) The 17th and 18th centuries.   The first Baptist church in America was founded in 1639 by Roger Williams at Providence, Rhode Island. In 1644 another church was formed at Newport, Rhode Island, and by 1700 there were 33 Baptist churches in the American colonies. While most British Baptist churches of the time were non-singing, there is evidence that several of the early Baptist churches in the colonies practised psalmody. In some cases singing was apparently abandoned when large numbers of non-singing English Baptists emigrated to the colonies and joined these churches. When objections to singing in Baptist worship began to die out in England during the early 18th century, many non-singing American churches adopted or reintroduced psalmody, while newly formed churches sang from their inception. According to Baptist historian Morgan Edwards, Delaware's Welsh Tract church 'was the principal if not sole means of introducing singing' into the Baptist churches of Middle Atlantic colonies.

British Baptists were not the only members of this communion to settle in the New World. In 1732 a

German, Conrad Beissel, founded the Ephrata community, a Sabbatarian Baptist communal sect, in Lancaster County, Pennsylvania. Unlike some of their British counterparts, the members of Beissel's group had no objections to singing, neither did they have any qualms about singing original hymns. Much of the music sung at Ephrata was written by Beissel himself in a rhythmically free, diatonic, chorale style that sometimes featured multiple choirs and antiphonal effects. The most important published hymnal of the Ephrata community was *Das Gesäng der einsamen und verlassenen Turtel-Taube* (1747).

The psalters and hymnals used by English-speaking Baptists in New England and the Middle Atlantic states during the 18th and early 19th centuries were mostly of British origin. Early Baptists probably used the Ainsworth or Sternhold and Hopkins psalters. After about 1740 many Baptists began singing from Tate and Brady's *New Version of the Psalms*. This was succeeded during the last third of the century by various editions of Isaac Watts's psalms and hymns, often supplemented by Rippon's *Selection of Hymns* (London, 1787, reprinted in New York and Elizabethtown, 1792). Earlier editions of Watts were replaced by 'Rippon's Watts', which was reprinted in Philadelphia in 1820. The ascendancy of Watts among New England Baptists was continued through James Winchell's *An Arrangement of … Watts* (1819). 'Rippon's Watts', continued in use in the Middle Atlantic states until the 1840s.

The earliest Baptist hymnal compiled in America, *Hymns and Spiritual Songs*, was published anonymously at Newport, Rhode Island, in 1766, but does not seem to have met with favour. Baron Stow and S.F. Smith's *The Psalmist* (1843) became the most widely used collection in the North, superseding both 'Winchell's Watts' and 'Rippon's Watts', and marking the turning away of Baptists from 'Watts entire', and from collections that were merely supplementary to Watts. Somewhat outside the mainstream of Baptist hymnody in the North was Joshua Smith's *Divine Hymns* (1791). This early collection of folk hymn texts had little impact on standard northern Baptist hymnals, but it did reach 12 editions. The collections noted above were words-only hymnals, but tunes for Baptist use were published in Morgan Edwards's *The Customs of Primitive Churches* (1768), Samuel Holyoke's *The Christian Harmonist … for the Use of the Baptist Churches* (1804), the anonymous *Boston Collection of Sacred and Devotional Hymns* (1808) and other scattered sources. Several New England psalmodists were associated with the denomination, including Oliver Holden, Oliver Brownson, J.C. Washburn and Oliver Shaw.

(ii) The 19th and 20th centuries. During the 18th century Baptist hymnody appears to have followed much the same course in the North and South. By the turn of the 19th century, however, Baptists of the South had begun to rely increasingly upon the folk hymn. The most popular southern collections – all of which incorporated numerous folk hymn texts – included J. Mercer's *The Cluster* (3/1810), Starke Dupuy's *Hymns and Spiritual Songs* (1811), William Dossey's *The Choice* (1820) and S.S. Burdett's *Baptist Harmony* (1834). Three widely used southern shape-note folk hymn tune collections, William Walker's *Southern Harmony* (1835), B.F. White and E.J. King's *Sacred Harp* (1844) and J.G. McCurry's *Social Harp*

(1855), were compiled by Baptists (*see also* SHAPE-NOTE HYMNODY, §2). Controversies among Baptists caused a division of the denomination into Northern and Southern Baptist Conventions in 1845. A special edition of *The Psalmist* (1847) with a supplement by two Southern Baptist pastors, Richard Fuller and J.B. Jeter, saw some use in the South. The *Baptist Psalmody* (1850) of Basil Manly and Basil Manly jr gained immediate acceptance among Southern Baptists, holding much the same place that *The Psalmist* did among their Northern brethren.

The most important influence on late 19th-century Baptist hymnody was the emergence of the gospel song. Many prominent gospel songwriters were Northern Baptists (e.g. W.B. Bradbury, Robert Lowry and W.H. Doane). A few Northern collections such as E.H. Johnson's *Sursum corda* (1898) attempted to introduce hymnody of the English Oxford Movement. More widely accepted were books such as *The Baptist Hymnal* (1883) that attempted to balance liturgical hymnody with the gospel song. *The New Baptist Hymnal*, produced jointly by Northern and Southern Baptists in 1926, became popular in the North but did not find favour in the South. Two later hymnals of Northern Baptists (renamed the American Baptist Convention in 1950 and the American Baptist Churches in the USA in 1972), *Christian Worship* (1941) and *Hymnbook for Christian Worship* (1970), were jointly compiled with the Disciples of Christ.

Late 19th-century Southern Baptists wholeheartedly embraced the gospel song, which almost entirely replaced the folk hymn as the basis of their congregational singing. This emphasis on the gospel song continued well into the 20th century in such books as R.H. Coleman's *The Modern Hymnal* (1926) and *The American Hymnal* (1933), B.B. McKinney's *The Broadman Hymnal* (1940) and numerous informal songbooks. Later Southern Baptist hymnals, such as *Baptist Hymnal* (1956), *Baptist Hymnal* (1975) and *The Baptist Hymnal* (1991) have drawn from a wider range of hymnic styles and traditions. However, Baptist churches are free to use any hymnal they choose, and some employ collections from independent publishers or no hymnal at all. The strong status of hymnological scholarship among Southern Baptists is evident from the fact that the two most widely used college and seminary hymnology textbooks, W.J. Reynolds's *A Survey of Christian Hymnody* (1963, rev. 4/1999 by D.W. Music and M. Price) and Harry Eskew and H.T. McElrath's *Sing with Understanding* (1980, 2/1995), were written by members of this denomination. Companions for the 1956 and 1975 *Baptist Hymnals* were written by W.J. Reynolds (1964, 2/1967; and 1976), while a *Handbook to The Baptist Hymnal* was compiled by a group of writers and published in 1992.

Early hymnals published by and for Canadian Baptists included John Bowser's *Hymns and Spiritual Songs* (1807), John Buzzell's Free Will Baptist *Psalms, Hymns and Spiritual Songs* (1823), *The Canadian Baptist Hymn Book* (1873) and *The Canadian Baptist Hymnal* (1888). In about 1902 *The [Canadian] Baptist Church Hymnal* ('Canadian' appears on the cover but not on the title page) was published in London; this was a reprint of the 1900 *English Baptist Church Hymnal* with a 'Canadian Supplement' of 26 hymns, a few of which had tunes by Canadian Baptist composers. In 1936 the *Hymnary for Use in Baptist Churches*, a slightly revised edition of the 1930 *Hymnary* of the United Church of Canada, was published in Toronto. Carol M Giesbrecht edited *The Hymnal* for the Baptist Federation of Canada in 1973.

Choirs were generally rejected in Baptist churches of the colonies until after 1770. The earliest record of Baptist choral singing in America dates from the year 1771, when a choir was formed at the First Baptist Church of Boston. Other urban churches in the North soon imitated this practice, and by 1820 most of the larger churches had instituted choirs. A few urban churches in the South formed choirs in the early 19th century, but even as late as 1868 some Southern Baptist churches were struggling with the propriety of admitting such ensembles. Early Baptist choirs were generally composed of volunteers who sat in the balcony facing the pulpit. In the late 19th and early 20th centuries the influence of the English Oxford Movement prompted many Baptist churches to vest their choirs and place them in full view of the congregation. The second half of the 20th century saw a proliferation of children's, youth and senior adult choirs in Baptist churches.

Even more controversial than the use of choirs was the introduction of musical instruments. Despite considerable opposition, the bass viol began appearing in Baptist churches of the North shortly after 1800. In about 1819 an organ was installed in the Baptist church at Pawtucket, Rhode Island, and the older, better-established New England Baptist churches soon began to acquire organs. Lingering objections to instruments prevented most Southern Baptist churches from acquiring organs until after 1850. Many churches made use of the melodeon as their first instrument, since these were generally cheaper to install and maintain than a pipe organ. Except for some conservative groups, most late 20th-century Baptist churches in the USA used some sort of instrument – usually organ and/or piano, sometimes an orchestra or pop ensemble, or sometimes pre-recorded tape or compact disc – in their services.

After World War I a few Baptist churches began to appoint staff members with some responsibility for music. Since the 1950s many of the larger Baptist churches have hired full-time ministers of music who are responsible for a church's entire music programme. The minister of music typically conducts or supervises choirs for different age groups, various types of instrumental ensemble, and the congregational singing. In smaller churches the minister of music is frequently a part-time or volunteer worker with more limited responsibilities.

Two important factors in the development of Southern Baptist church music during the 20th century were the establishment of the Church Music Department of the Baptist Sunday School Board in 1941 and the influence of music schools in several of the seminaries operated by the Southern Baptist Convention. The Church Music Department provides literature, music and training opportunities for church musicians, while the seminaries offer graduate-level instruction in sacred music.

From the 1970s onwards Baptist church music in America has been characterized by great variety. Some churches rely primarily on standard hymnody and choral or instrumental music of an artistic nature. Others, especially in the South, continue to emphasize the gospel song. Still others have dispensed with hymnals, choirs and organs in favour of 'worship' or 'praise' choruses printed on songsheets or displayed by overhead projectors. These are typically led by a 'worship team' of between four and eight singers and accompanied by a rhythm section with occasional participation by other instrumentalists. The worship team also provides 'special music', generally a 'contemporary Christian' song in pop style.

As is true of many denominations since the 1960s, the dichotomy between the 'traditional' and 'contemporary' in Baptist church music of North America, Great Britain and other English-speaking lands has led to much conflict within and between congregations, with those that prefer to remain rooted in traditional musical materials being accused of 'cultural irrelevancy' and those that employ pop music styles in their efforts to win converts being charged with 'cultural accommodationism'. Throughout their history, Baptists have been a populist denomination with a zeal for numerical growth and no authoritative hierarchy to set standards, and they have often relied upon unsophisticated cultural materials (e.g. the gospel song) to carry their evangelistic message. On the other hand, they have also been a largely conservative group – both theologically and in other ways – that typically places little value on change (as evidenced by their continued use of of the gospel song long after it had ceased to be a popular style in the culture as a whole). Many Baptist churches attempt to reconcile this difficulty by blending the traditional and contemporary, with varying degrees of balance and success.

Historically, the American Baptist Churches in the USA and the Southern Baptist Convention have contained the largest numbers of Baptists in America, but there are also numerous smaller bodies. Many of these groups follow essentially the same music patterns as churches that are affiliated with the larger denominational organizations, but a few have maintained distinctive musical practices. Among these are the Primitive Baptists, who originated in the 1830s as a predestinarian reaction against the increasing Arminianism of the major bodies, and some congregations of Regular Baptists, particularly in Appalachia. These Baptists reject the use of choirs and musical instruments, relying exclusively on *a cappella* congregational singing which often consists of folk hymns that are lined-out and sung in the 'old way'. The singing in Primitive Baptist churches typically begins about half an hour before the stated service time, with the songs chosen spontaneously at the time of singing. The two most widely used Primitive hymnals, Benjamin Lloyd's *Primitive Hymns* (1841/R) and D.H. Goble's *Primitive Baptist Hymn Book* (1887), are words-only collections. Some Primitive Baptist churches have adopted books with musical notation, particularly the *Old School Hymnal* (1920, 11/1983), which includes traditional Protestant hymns, tunes of the Mason/Hastings/Bradbury school, folk hymns and gospel songs.

Before the Civil War most black Baptists attended the same churches as whites and presumably sang the same congregational songs. After 1865 the number of African-American Baptist churches grew dramatically. In urban areas black Baptists relied primarily upon Northern Baptist hymnbooks such as *The Baptist Hymnal* (1883), while in rural congregations 'Dr Watts singing' – an unaccompanied style characterized by lining-out, slow tempos, embellishment of the melody and 'surge' singing – held sway. In 1895 black Baptists formed the National Baptist Convention, USA (NBCUSA), which began publishing songbooks in 1897 and issued its first major hymnal, the *National Baptist Hymnal*, in Nashville in

1903. While this contained a few hymns by African-Americans, the book was modelled largely on the 1883 *Baptist Hymnal*. Schisms in the Convention in 1916 and 1961 resulted in the formation of the National Baptist Convention of America (NBCA) and the Progressive National Baptist Convention, respectively. The former immediately began publishing songbooks, one of the most significant being *National Jubilee Melodies* (1916), a major collection of black spirituals. After founding a new publishing board, the NBCUSA issued *Gospel Pearls* (1921) – an important songbook containing a variety of standard hymns, spirituals and gospel songs by both white and black writers – and its first (and only) major hymnal, the *Baptist Standard Hymnal* (1924). The latter collection was reprinted in 1985 and remains in use in many churches. In 1977 the NBCA published the *New National Baptist Hymnal*, the volume now found most often in African-American Baptist churches. The Progressive National Baptist Convention has issued two hymnals, the *Progressive Baptist Hymnal* (1976) and the *New Progressive Baptist Hymnal* (1982), which were 'special editions' of the Southern Baptist *Broadman Hymnal* and NBCA's *New National Baptist Hymnal*, respectively.

By 1906 choirs were such a common feature in African-American Baptist churches that the NBCUSA published a *National Anthem Series* of 14 choral pieces by African-American composers, all of whom were 'choristers' in Baptist churches. Black Baptist churches were heavily influenced by gospel music during the 1920s and 30s and this has continued to be a dominant style for choral and congregational music in the churches. Some rural African-American Baptist churches continue to sing exclusively in 'Dr Watts' style, while 'upscale' urban congregations employ mainly music from the European-American and black spiritual traditions accompanied by pipe organ or piano. Many churches use both of these styles in addition to black gospel music accompanied by Hammond organ and piano or an instrumental ensemble.

3. OTHER COUNTRIES.   English and American Baptists were in the forefront of the modern missions movement. The earliest British Baptist missionary, William Carey (1761–1834), arrived in India in 1793; Adoniram Judson, the first Baptist missionary from America, began work in Burma in 1813. During the 19th century Baptists established congregations and institutions on several continents, particularly Asia, Africa and South America, but most of the numerical and musical growth in these areas has come since World War II.

Throughout much of the history of this missionary activity Baptists, like other denominations, translated Anglo-American hymns and transplanted these and Western musical styles to the lands in which they worked. Since the period of greatest missionary expansion coincided with extensive use of the gospel song in British and American Baptist churches, this type of music became standard for churches in other countries as well. The approach to church music in these countries is often similar to that of Baptist churches in England and the USA, although the musical style may be different: congregations sing hymns and/or choruses; 'special music' is presented by choirs, small ensembles, or soloists; and pianos, organs, guitars or indigenous instruments accompany or play independently. Baptist seminary and combined church choirs in these lands occasionally present larger works of the Western choral repertory such as Handel's *Messiah* and Théodore Dubois' *Les sept paroles du Christ*; these are often seen in the host country as significant cultural events. However, in recent years more emphasis has been placed by missionaries and nationals alike on the cultivation of indigenous church music.

A significant development in Baptist church music in many countries has been the appointment of music missionaries by the Foreign Mission Board (renamed the International Mission Board in 1997) of the Southern Baptist Convention. The first music missionaries, Don and Violet Orr, were sent to Colombia in 1951. Subsequently, music missionaries have been appointed to other Latin American countries, Africa, Asia and Europe. The main responsibility of music missionaries is usually to promote music in the churches or to teach in seminaries, but their work often features a variety of activities, including the formation of choirs and ensembles, giving concerts, leading conferences, and composing, editing and publishing music.

(i) Mexico, Central and South America.   Since Spanish is the dominant language in Mexico, Central and South America, Baptist congregations in these areas often make use of the same hymnals, especially those published by the Spanish Baptist Publishing House in El Paso, Texas, including *Himnos favoritos* (1951), *El nuevo himnario popular* (1955) and *Himnario bautista* (1978). However, many Latin-American Baptist churches cannot afford to purchase a hymnal and rely instead on locally produced words-only collections or no hymnal at all. The publishing house also provides Spanish-language choral music and other resources for use by Latin-American Baptist choirs, instrumentalists and music leaders.

The most important Brazilian Baptist hymnal, *Cantor cristão*, was initially compiled by the missionary Solomon Ginsberg in 1891. This went through 36 editions (the last revision in 1971) and grew from 16 to 581 selections, 387 of which were from I.D. Sankey's *Sacred Songs and Solos*. In 1991 Brazilian Baptists issued a new hymnal, *Hinário para o culto cristão*, under the general editorship of music missionary Joan Sutton. Among the 440 hymns were many adapted from or written in the style of Brazilian folk music. In 1957 a Church Music Department was organized by the Brazilian Baptist Convention under the direction of music missionary W.H. Ichter. One of the first publications of the department was a collection of anthems, *Antemas corais*, for use by Brazilian Baptist church choirs. These and similar publications have generally consisted of English-language works translated into Portuguese.

(ii) Africa.   Baptist churches in Africa use a wide variety of materials, in part because of the many different language groups and the strong social contrasts between city and country dwellers. Urban churches are likely to use 'book music', that is, hymnals containing translations of songs in the Western tradition. Examples of this 'book music' that have been produced by Baptists in Africa are *Nyimbo za chigonjetso* (Lilongwe, Malawi, 1970), *Emo na, eja suine* (Nigeria, n.d.), *Sauti zetu mbinguni* (Nairobi, 1983), and *Baptist asore nnwom* (Kumasi, Ghana, n.d., rev. 1980). These books are usually produced and priced inexpensively and contain words only. In rural areas Baptist congregations are more likely to sing 'body music', which is unwritten and features call and response patterns, hand-clapping, dancing, and accompaniment

by traditional instruments such as the tambourine, kayamba and drum. Even when these congregations sing a Western hymn they are likely to adapt it to indigenous performing practice.

(iii) Asia. The use and publication of hymnals varies considerably in the Baptist churches of Asia. Early Chinese Baptist hymnals were mainly published under the auspices of British Baptist missions. *Gospel Hymns* (Canton, 1903), a words-only collection to which tunes were added in 1907, was reprinted with many variations and minor revisions until 1935. *Hymns of Praise* (Shantung, words 1901, music 1910) was the most important Mandarin hymnal before *Baptist Hymns of Praise* (1932), which in turn gave way to *New Hymns of Praise* (1941). The formation of the People's Republic of China in 1949 closed the mainland to missionary and overtly Christian activity, but Baptist hymnological developments continued in Taiwan, Malaysia and Hong Kong. A significant Chinese Baptist hymnal, *New Songs of Praise*, was issued in Hong Kong in 1973 under the editorship of G. Chi and Southern Baptist music missionary L.G. McKinney. Intended to serve Mandarin, Cantonese and Swatow constituencies, the hymnal was published in an English edition in 1976, a Taiwanese version in 1978, and a combined Chinese-English edition in 1988. The hymnal includes many indigenous productions from Chinese and other Asian sources.

Elsewhere in Asia, Baptist churches often rely on 'union' hymnals, such as the Korean *Chansonggah* (1983), published by a consortium of denominations. A significant Baptist hymnal from Indonesia, *Nyanyian Pujian*, was published at Bandung in 1982.

(iv) Europe and Russia. Although Baptist work began during the 19th century in most countries of Europe, numerical growth has been slow, particularly in areas dominated by the Roman Catholic and Orthodox communions. While almost all churches have traditionally employed instruments, and many of the larger ones have maintained choirs (some of them quite accomplished), hymnody continues to be the most important form of Baptist church music in Europe, as in other areas of the world. Germany – the source for the spread of Baptist principles into many other areas of Europe and the seat of one of the largest Baptist groups on the Continent – may be taken as an example. Early German Baptists sang Lutheran and Moravian chorales, in addition to hymns written by their own people, from collections such as Julius Köbner's *Glaubenstimme* (1849). A German edition of Bliss and Sankey's *Gospel Hymns* translated by the American Walter Rauschenbusch, *Evangeliums-Lieder 1 und 2* (New York, 1897), became very popular and in the late 20th century was still being used in some German-speaking European congregations. An 'official' Baptist hymnal, *Gemeindelieder*, appeared in Wuppertal in 1978, supplemented by a collection of *Neue Gemeindelieder* in 1993.

In the Russian Empire, Baptist work was particularly difficult owing to repression by the tsarist regime. The Revolution of 1917 initially brought about more favourable treatment of Baptists and other evangelical Christians as the government sought to counteract the influence of the Russian Orthodox Church, but during the 1930s the Stalin government closed most of the churches and banished or imprisoned many of their ministers. Overt persecution eased during World War II, and after the war Baptist churches were allowed to exist in the Soviet Union and Eastern bloc countries, although they were subject to various limitations, including the printing of religious literature such as hymnals. Because of the scarcity of such books, congregational song was generally done from memory or with the aid of lining-out. Most churches featured an organ and choir, the latter often singing as many as four or five anthems (sometimes from manuscript) during the two-hour service. Since before the break up of the Soviet Union the typical musical style of Baptists in Russia and other Commonwealth of Independent States countries has been the gospel song accompanied by piano or organ and occasionally guitar; but the churches generally rejected rock-based music and the use of instruments such as saxophones and drums because they were considered to be inappropriate to the seriousness of worship. However, as contact with English-speaking Baptists has increased, Russian Baptist youth have discovered Christian rock, some of which is likely to make its way eventually into the churches.

(v) Australia. Baptists in Australia have typically relied upon British Baptist hymnals such as the *Baptist Church Hymnal: Revised Edition* (1933) and *Baptist Hymn Book* (1962). I.D. Sankey's *Sacred Songs and Solos* was widely used, especially for the more informal evening services. Donald Crowhurst published an Australian *Hymnal* in 1967 which continues to be widely used in the churches. Australian Baptist congregations of the late 20th century have been greatly influenced by musical practices in Britain and America, and their music ranges from vested choirs singing traditional Western choral music with organ/piano accompaniment to pop ensembles leading charismatic-style choruses.

BIBLIOGRAPHY

GENERAL

H.S. Burrage: *Baptist Hymn Writers and their Hymns* (Portland, ME, 1888)

J. Julian: *A Dictionary of Hymnology* (London, 1892, 2/1907/R)

L.F. Benson: *The English Hymn: its Development and Use in Worship* (New York, 1915/R)

R.E. Keighton: 'Baptist Hymnody', *The Chronicle*, x (1947), 75–86, 97–102

W.J. Reynolds: *A Survey of Christian Hymnody* (New York, 1963, rev. 4/1999 by D.W. Music and M. Price)

H. Eskew and H.T.McElrath: *Sing with Understanding* (Nashville, TN, 1980, 2/1995)

A.W. Wardin, ed.: *Baptists Around the World: a Comprehensive Handbook* (Nashville, TN, 1995)

GREAT BRITAIN

T. Crosby: *The History of the English Baptists* (London, 1740/R), iii, 266–71; iv, 298–301

J.J. Goadby: *Bye-Paths in Baptist History* (London, 1871/R), 317–49

J.S. Curwen: *Studies in Worship Music (First Series)* (London, 1880, 2/1888), 93–107, 426–30

W.T. Whitley, ed.: *Minutes of the General Assembly of the General Baptist Churches in England* (London, 1909–10), i, 27; ii, 18

A. Buckley: 'The Deighn Layrocks', *Baptist Quarterly*, iv (1928–9), 43–8

L.F. Benson: *The Hymns of John Bunyan* (New York, 1930)

F.W. Beckwith: 'The Early Church at Leeds', *Baptist Quarterly*, vi (1932–3), 116–24

W.T. Whitley: *Congregational Hymn-Singing* (London, 1933), 119–30

C. Bonner and W.T. Whitley, eds.: *A Handbook to the Baptist Church Hymnal Revised* (London, 1935)

O.A. Mansfield: 'Rippon's Tunes', *Baptist Quarterly*, viii (1936–7), 36–43

C. Bonner: *Some Baptist Hymnists from the Seventeenth Century to Modern Times* (London, 1937)

A.A. Reid: 'The Tercentenary of Benjamin Keach, Baptist Preacher, London, England. I: Benjamin Keach, 1640', *The Chronicle*, iii (1940), 147–60

G.W. Hughes: 'The Tercentenary of Benjamin Keach, Baptist Preacher, London, England, II: He Taught us to Sing: the Story of Benjamin Keach', *The Chronicle*, iii (1940), 160–63

C.B. Jewson: 'St Mary's, Norwich. IV: The Church Takes Root, 1743–1788', *Baptist Quarterly*, x (1941), 282–8

S.J. Price: 'Maze Pond and the Matterhorn', *Baptist Quarterly*, x (1941), 202–8

W.T. Whitley: 'The First Hymnbook in Use', *Baptist Quarterly*, x (1941), 369–75

W.T. Whitley: 'The Tune Book of 1791', *Baptist Quarterly*, x (1941), 434–43

H. Martin, ed.: *A Companion to the Baptist Church Hymnal* [Revised Edition] (London, 1953)

J.O. Barrett: 'Hymns among the Baptists', *Hymn Society of Great Britain and Ireland Bulletin*, iii (1954), 164–6

H. Wamble: 'Benjamin Keach, Churchman', *Quarterly Review: a Survey of Southern Baptist Progress*, xvi/2 (1956), 47–53

E.A. Payne: 'Thomas Tillam', *Baptist Quarterly*, xvii (1957), 61–6

R.H. Young: *The History of Baptist Hymnody in England from 1612 to 1800* (diss., U. of S. California, 1959)

E.P. Winter: 'The Administration of the Lord's Supper among the Baptists of the Seventeenth Century', *Baptist Quarterly*, xviii (1960), 196–204

H. Martin: 'The Baptist Contribution to Early English Hymnody', *Baptist Quarterly*, xix (1962), 195–208

I. Mallard: 'The Hymns of Katherine Sutton', *Baptist Quarterly*, xx (1963), 23–33

H. Martin: 'Daniel Sedgwick: a Baptist Pioneer of Hymnology', *Baptist Quarterly*, xx (1964), 362–4

C.E. Spann: *The Seventeenth Century English Baptist Controversy Concerning Singing* (thesis, Southwestern Baptist Theological Seminary, Fort Worth, TX, 1965)

R.W. Thomson: 'Anne Steele, 1716–1778', *Baptist Quarterly*, xxi (1966), 368–71

K.R. Manley: *John Rippon, D.D. (1751–1836) and the Particular Baptists* (diss., Regents' Park College, London, 1967)

H. Martin, ed.: *The Baptist Hymn Book Companion* (London, 1962, rev. 2/1967 by R.W. Thomson)

H. Martin: 'Benjamin Keach (1640–1704): Pioneer of Congregational Hymn Singing', *Church Musician*, xviii/6 (1967), 8–11; xviii/7 (1967), 8–11

F.M.W. Harrison: 'The Nottinghamshire Baptists: Mission, Worship & Training', *Baptist Quarterly*, xxv (1974), 309–28

R.W. Thomson: 'The Psalms and Hymns Trust and Praise for Today', *Baptist Quarterly*, xxv (1974), 380–83

D.W. Music: 'Psalmody and Hymnody in the Broadmead Baptist Church of Bristol, England', *Quarterly Review: a Survey of Southern Baptist Progress*, xxxvii/4 (1976), 66–71

S.J. Rogal: 'John Bunyan and English Congregational Song', *The Hymn*, xxviii (1977), 118–25

E. Sharpe: 'Bristol Baptist College and the Church's Hymnody', *Baptist Quarterly*, xxviii (1979), 7–16

D.W. Music: 'The Hymns of Benjamin Keach: an Introductory Study', *The Hymn*, xxxiv (1983), 147–54

D.W. Music: 'Congregational Singing in English Baptist Churches of the Seventeenth Century', *Quarterly Review: a Survey of Southern Baptist Progress*, l/1 (1990), 72–8

D.W. Music: 'John Bunyan and Baptist Hymnody', *Baptist History and Heritage*, xxvii/2 (1992), 3–11

N. Clark: 'Baptist Praise and Worship', *Baptist Quarterly*, xxxv (1993), 95–100

J.H.Y. Briggs: *The English Baptists of the Nineteenth Century* (Didcot, 1994), 35–42

P. Westermeyer: 'The Breach Repair'd', *The Hymn*, xlvii/1 (1996), 10–16

NORTH AMERICA

M. Edwards: 'History of the Baptists in Delaware', *Pennsylvania Magazine of History and Biography*, ix (1885), 52

J.F. Sachse: *The Music of the Ephrata Cloister* (Lancaster, PA, 1903/R)

A.L. Stevenson: *The Story of Southern Hymnology* (Salem, VA, 1931/R), 1–15

G.P. Jackson: *White Spirituals in the Southern Uplands* (Chapel Hill, NC, 1933/R)

H.W. Foote: *Three Centuries of American Hymnody* (Cambridge, MA, 1940/R)

G.P. Jackson: *White and Negro Spirituals* (New York, 1943/R)

W. Dinneen: *Music at the Meeting House, 1775–1958* (Providence, RI, 1958)

W.L. Hooper: *Church Music in Transition* (Nashville, TN, 1963), 102–34

'Our Baptist Heritage in Church Music', *Church Musician*, xiv/10 (1963), 14

H. Eskew: 'Hymnody of our Forefathers', *Church Musician*, xv/5 (1964), 5–8

H. Eskew: 'Music of our Forefathers', *Church Musician*, xv/6 (1964), 16–19

W.J. Reynolds: *Hymns of our Faith: a Handbook for the Baptist Hymnal* (Nashville, TN, 1964, 2/1967)

H. Eskew: 'Music in the Baptist Tradition', *Review and Expositor*, lxix (1972), 161–75

W.H. Tallmadge: 'Baptist Monophonic and Heterophonic Hymnody in Southern Appalachia', *Yearbook for Inter-American Musical Research*, xi (1975), 106–36

W.J. Reynolds: 'Our Heritage of Baptist Hymnody in America', *Baptist History and Heritage*, xi (1976), 204–17

W.J. Reynolds: *Companion to Baptist Hymnal* (Nashville, TN, 1976)

P.D. Hartman: 'The Hymn Tradition of the Primitive Baptists', *Music Ministry*, x/3 (1977), 2–5, 27

C.D. Duncan: *A Historical Survey of the Development of the Black Baptist Church in the United States and a Study of Performance Practices Associated with Dr. Watts Hymn Singing: a Source Book for Teachers* (diss., Washington U., 1979)

D.W. Music: 'The Introduction of Musical Instruments into Baptist Churches in America', *Quarterly Review: a Survey of Southern Baptist Progress*, xl/4 (1979), 55–62

H.T. McElrath: 'Hymnody among Southern Baptists', *American Organist*, xiv/5 (1980), 19

E.M. Huntley: 'Hymnody in the National Baptist Convention', *American Organist*, xiv/11 (1980), 20

B. Sutton: 'Shape-Note Tune Books and Primitive Hymns', *EthM*, xxvi (1982), 11–26

C.R. Brewster: *The Cluster of Jesse Mercer* (Macon, GA, 1983)

'Church Music in Baptist History', *Baptist History and Heritage*, xix/1 (1984) [complete issue]

I.H. Murrell: *An Examination of Southern Ante-Bellum Baptist Hymnals and Tunebooks as Indicators of the Congregational Hymn and Tune Repertories of the Period with an Analysis of Representative Tunes* (diss., New Orleans Baptist Theological Seminary, 1984)

J.T. Titon: 'Stance, Role, and Identity in Fieldwork among Folk Baptists and Pentecostals', *American Music*, iii/1 (1985), 16–24

D.C. Measels: *A Catalog of Source Readings in Southern Baptist Music: 1828–1890* (diss., Southern Baptist Theological Seminary, Louisville, KY, 1986)

Y. Robinson: *The Ephrata Cloister and the Lititz Moravian Settlement, 1732–1820, and a Comparative Study of their Musical Cultures* (diss., Juilliard School of Music, New York, 1986)

J.D. Baklanoff: 'The Celebration of a Feast: Music, Dance, and Possession Trance in the Black Primitive Baptist Footwashing Ritual', *EthM*, xxxi (1987), 381–94

D.W. Music: 'Early Baptist Composers and Tunebooks in America', *Quarterly Review: a Survey of Southern Baptist Progress*, xlvii/1 (1987), 68–75

J. Beckwith: 'Tunebooks and Hymnals in Canada, 1801–1939', *American Music*, vi (1988), 193–234

J.T. Titon: *Powerhouse for God: Speech, Chant, and Song in an Appalachian Baptist Church* (Austin, TX, 1988)

R.P. Drummond: *A Portion for the Singers: a History of Music among Primitive Baptists since 1800* (Atwood, TN, 1989)

P.G.A. Griffin-Allwood, G.A.Rawlyk, and J.K. Zeman: *Baptists in Canada, 1760–1990: a Bibliography of Selected Printed Resources in English* (Hantsport, NS, 1989), 208–11

T.J. Studstill: *The Life of Robert H. Coleman and his Influence on Southern Baptist Hymnody* (diss., Southwestern Baptist Theological Seminary, Fort Worth, TX, 1991)

R.W. Rose: *The Psalmist: a Significant Hymnal for Baptists in America during the Nineteenth Century* (diss., Southwestern Baptist Theological Seminary, Fort Worth, TX, 1991)

J.V. Adams, ed.: *Handbook to The Baptist Hymnal* (Nashville, TN, 1992)

J.M. Spencer: *Black Hymnody: a Hymnological History of the African-American Church* (Knoxville, TN, 1992), 74–97

'Shaping Influences on Baptist Church Music', *Baptist History and Heritage*, xxvii/2 (1992) [complete issue]

H. Eskew, D.W.Music and P.A. Richardson: *Singing Baptists: Studies in Baptist Hymnody in America* (Nashville, TN, 1994)

B.B. Patterson: *The Sound of the Dove: Singing in Appalachian Primitive Baptist Churches* (Urbana, IL, 1995)

L.G. Davenport: *Divine Song on the Northeast Frontier: Maine's Sacred Tunebooks, 1800–1830* (Lanham, MD, 1996), 110–11, 115–17, 124

OTHER COUNTRIES

H. Eskew: 'Music in a Mexican Baptist Church', *Church Musician*, xiv/9 (1963), 12–13

K.G. Greenlaw: *Traditions of Protestant Hymnody and the Use of Music in the Methodist and Baptist Churches of Mexico* (diss., U. of S. California, 1967)

J. Nordenhaug: 'A Visit with Russian Baptists', *Baptist World*, xiv/2 (1967), 4–6

M.F. Ellerbe: *The Music Missionary of the Southern Baptist Convention: his Preparation and his Work* (diss., Catholic U. of America, Washington DC, 1970)

T.W. Hunt: 'Music in Missions', *Encyclopedia of Southern Baptists*, iii (Nashville, TN, 1971), 1859–60; iv (1982), 2361–2

N. Corbitt: *The History and Development of Music Used in the Baptist Churches on the Coast of Kenya: the Development of an Indigenous Church Music 1953–1984* (diss., Southwestern Baptist Theological Seminary, Fort Worth, TX, 1985)

I.L. de Paula: *Early Hymnody in Brazilian Baptist Churches: its Sources and Development* (diss., Southwestern Baptist Theological Seminary, Fort Worth, TX, 1985)

J.H. Barker: *The Use of Indigenous Chinese Hymnody in Baptist Churches of Taiwan* (diss., Southwestern Baptist Theological Seminary, Fort Worth, 1992)

A.W. Barrett: *A Study of the Choral Music Tradition in Hungarian Baptist Churches* (diss., U. of Iowa, 1992)

C.E. Spann: 'A Tale of Two Hymnals: the Brazilian Baptist *Cantor cristão* (1891) and *Hinário para o culto cristão* (1991)', *The Hymn*, xliii/4 (1992), 15–21

P.W. Blycker: *A Critical Analysis of Selected Spanish-Language Hymnals Used by Evangelical Churches in Mesoamerica, 1952–1992* (diss., Southwestern Baptist Theological Seminary, Fort Worth, TX, 1997)

DAVID W. MUSIC

Baptiste [Anet, Jean-Jacques-Baptiste] (*b* Paris, 2 Jan 1676; *d* Lunéville, 14 Aug 1755). French violinist and composer. His father was JEAN-BAPTISTE ANET. About 1695–6 he travelled to Rome and studied under Corelli who, according to contemporary reports, was so pleased with Baptiste's performance of his music that he 'embraced him tenderly and made him a present of his bow', and subsequently regarded him as an adopted son. During 1699 and 1700 Baptiste travelled through Germany to Poland. On his return he entered the service of the Duke of Orléans, a position he abandoned after about a year to enter that of the Elector Maximilian Emanuel of Bavaria who, having lost his throne, was living in exile in France.

His début at the French court on 23 October 1701 attracted the notice of the Parisian newspaper *Le mercure galant*:

After his supper, the king heard in his study an exquisite concert of Italian airs, performed by Messrs Forqueray on the viol, Couperin at the harpsichord, and the young Baptiste (who is in the service of the Duke of Orléans) on the violin. The king appeared surprised at the excellence of the latter whom he had not yet heard.

During the first three decades of the 18th century Baptiste appeared frequently in and around Paris – at court, at the homes of the nobility and after 1725 at the Concert Spirituel. During 1709 he was in Schwerin, where he was appointed musical director and concert master of the Hofkapelle; he returned to Paris in 1710. In 1715 Maximilian Emanuel regained his throne and returned to Bavaria; Baptiste left his service and soon entered that of Louis XIV. In 1724 he was granted a *privilège général* to publish 'several sonatas and other pieces of instrumental music'; between 1724 and 1734 he published six volumes. Two of them contain sonatas for violin and continuo, undoubtedly originally for his own use, while the others contain suites for the then popular *musette* (French bagpipes), and were dedicated to his friend, the musette virtuoso Colin Charpentier.

Baptiste's first appearance at the Concert Spirituel was as noteworthy an occasion as had been his first appearance at court. During Easter week 1725, reported *Le mercure de France*, those attending the Concert Spirituel heard:

a species of duel between Messrs Baptiste, Frenchman, and [Jean-Pierre] Guignon, Piedmontese, who are regarded as the two best violinists in the world. They played by turns some instrumental pieces accompanied only by a bassoon and a bass viol, and they were both extraordinarily applauded. Mr Baptiste played without any accompaniment some preludes [i.e. improvisations] which were also extremely applauded.

The two violinists were heard together again in May and June of the same year. Abbé Pluche (1746) described Baptiste's playing:

Mr Baptiste ... does not approve the ambition to devour all sorts of difficulties ... He gives no advantage to a piece whose performance appears prodigious, and he gives his highest esteem to that which pleases the listener surely. He looks for, he often says, not what makes the musician perspire, not what dazzles the apprentice by swiftness or deafens him by noise, but what possesses the ability to touch him, to ravish him ... This point of view requires that the instrumental sound be connected, sustained, mellow, impassioned, and conforming to the human voice, of which it is only the imitation and support ... German, Italian, English – to him it is all the same. If he finds nobility and graciousness there, he plays it and gives its due by the purity of his intonation and the singular energy of his expressiveness. But he constantly refuses his ministrations to all that which has no other merit than to be difficult, bizarre or rough. The freedom and perseverance of his choice have often drawn him reproaches, sometimes as a too obstinate or even capricious man who yields to nothing, sometimes as a musician ignorant of frightening difficulties. He suffered a sort of persecution and exiled himself voluntarily before the honourable retreat which he enjoyed at the court of the King of Poland.

Baptiste left the 24 Violons du Roi in about 1735, undoubtedly for the reasons stated by Pluche but perhaps also due to his rivalry with Guignon, who only a year or so later also drove Leclair from the king's service. The self-exiled violinist remained in Paris until 1737 or 1738, when he became a violinist in the orchestra of Stanislaus Leszczynski, ex-king of Poland, at the court of Lorraine at Lunéville. Here he spent the rest of his days, playing the violin, hunting and fishing, and died poor after a lengthy illness, leaving no heirs.

The two major figures of the French violin school in the first quarter of the 18th century were Baptiste and Senaillé. Contemporary opinion held that the former was the superior performer, the latter the superior composer; this judgment appears to have been just. Baptiste was a moving performer, famed for his abilities as an improviser. He was the best French violinist before Leclair. His music is graceful and often interesting without being original: the first book of sonatas is strongly influenced by Corelli, while the second book is more French in character. The compositions for musette clearly constitute an attempt to please the popular French taste of the time. By the 1730s his style was already old-fashioned, and this may have hastened the decline of his career.

WORKS
all published in Paris

Premier livre de sonates, vn, bc (1724)

Deuxième oeuvre de M. Baptiste, contenant deux suites de pieces à deux musettes, qui conviennent à 2 fl/ob/vn/hurdy-gurdy (1726)

[10] Sonates, vn, bc, op.3 (1729)

Premier oeuvre de musettes (before 1730), same as Deuxième oeuvre, with addl piece in each suite

Second oeuvre de musettes (1730)

3e oeuvre de musettes, vns, fls, hurdy-gurdy (1734)

BIBLIOGRAPHY

LabordeMP; *La LaurencieEF*

J.L. Le Cerf de la Viéville: *Comparaison de la musique italienne et de la musique françoise* (Brussels, 1704–6/*R*)

N.A. Pluche: *Le spectacle de la nature* (Paris, 1732–50; Eng. trans., 1740–48; many later edns)

M. Antoine: 'Naissance et mort de Jean-Baptiste Anet (1676–1755)', *RdM*, xli (1958), 99–102

M. Antoine: 'Note sur les violonistes Anet', *RMFC*, ii (1961–2), 81–93

H. Erdmann: *Schwerin als Stadt der Musik* (Lübeck, 1967)

NEAL ZASLAW

Baptiste, Ludwig Albert Friedrich [Battista, Luigi Alberto Federigo] (*b* Oettingen, 8 Aug 1700; *d* Kassel, *c*1764). German composer, probably of French descent. He was a son of the dancing-master Johann Baptiste, who was at the Darmstadt court from 1703, and was taught dancing by his father. After 1718 he travelled to Paris, Italy and elsewhere in Europe, and in 1726 he was employed as a dancing-master in Kassel. The title-pages of his published works show that he must have been employed after the death of Count Carl (1730) by Carl's son Friedrich, who was at the same time King of Sweden, and his successor, Wilhelm VIII. Baptiste was considered an 'excellent violinist and composer for his instrument'; at the same time he was also praised on his travels as a 'musician and dancer'. Yet, with the exception of 24 minuets, only his chamber works are known. They are typical of the *galant* style around 1735, with uncomplicated melodies, simple counterpoint, and the contrast of major and minor or tonic and relative minor between sonata movements. There is scarcely any specifically virtuoso solo passage-work. Some works are wrongly attributed to Baptiste by Eitner; those in Christ Church, Oxford, are by Jean-Baptiste Lully, as is the *Branle de Mons. Baptiste* (*S-Uu*). Three sonatas in a manuscript belonging to Andreas Düben (ii) in 1692 are also not by him.

WORKS

[6] Sonate da camera, vn, bc/vc, op.1 (Kassel, before 1730), nos.4, 6 for vn/fl: ?MS formerly in *D-Kl* now lost, see Israel

6 sonate da camera, fl/vn, hpd/vc, op.2 (Augsburg, *c*1736)

24 menuets, 2 vn, 2 hn, bc, op.1 (Nuremberg, 1752)

Concerto à 4, fl, 2 vn, hpd, *SWl*

2 pieces, vn, 1728, *ROu*

Lost works: 12 concs., b viol, orch; 6 solos, vc; 6 trios, 2 ob, bc; more than 36 solos, b viol: all cited by Gerber; 12 solos, vn, cited by Lipowsky

Doubtful works: 6 concs., 2 vn, va, bc, *Kl*

BIBLIOGRAPHY

EitnerQ; *FétisB*; *GerberNL*; *LipowskyB*; *MGG1* (C. Bernsdorff-Engelbrecht); *SchillingE*

K. Israel: *Frankfurter Concert-Chronik von 1713–1780* (Frankfurt, 1876, rev. 2/1986 by P. Cahn)

H. Mendel and A. Reissmann: *Musikalisches Conversations-Lexikon* (Berlin, 1870–80, 3/1890–91/*R*)

E. Noack: *Musikgeschichte Darmstadts vom Mittelalter bis zur Goethezeit* (Mainz, 1967)

CHRISTIANE BERNSDORFF-ENGELBRECHT

Baquedano, José de. *See* VAQUEDANO, JOSÉ DE.

Baqueiro Fóster, Gerónimo (*b* Hopelchén, 7 Jan 1898; *d* Mexico City, 29 May 1967). Mexican musicologist and composer. After learning to play the flute and the oboe in Mérida and working in several military and popular bands, he entered the National Conservatory of Music in Mexico City (1922), where he was a pupil of Julián Carrillo. He led the most enthusiastic supporters of Carrillo's microtonal system 'sonido 13', organizing several concerts and giving talks about it. He worked as a music critic until his appointment in 1929 as professor of acoustics, solfège and music history at the National Conservatory, a post he occupied until his retirement in 1965. Concurrently he undertook research on folk music in the states of Veracruz, Nayarit and Yucatán, the isthmus of Tehuantepec, the northern and southern states of Mexico, and the Middle East (Egypt, Israel, Iran, Turkey). In 1938 he founded the Unión Mexicana de Cronistas de Teatro y Música and in 1942 the *Revista musical mexicana*, which he edited until 1946. Besides his numerous pieces of music criticism on Mexican musical life, his most important work deals with the study of Mexican folk music and music history. He owned one of the most extensive and valuable music libraries in the country. Now at CENIDIM, the library contains a significant collection of 19th-century Mexican compositions and writings on music.

WRITINGS

'Los Xtoles: canción al sol de los guerreros mayas', *Mexican Folkways*, viii (1933), 83

Curso completo de solfeo (Mexico City, 1939, 6/1955)

'Aportación musical de México para la formación de la biblioteca americana de Caracas, 1882–1883', *Revista musical mexicana*, ii (1942), 27

'El huapango', *Revista musical mexicana*, i (1942), 174

'El secreto armónico y modal do un antiguo aire maya', *Revista musical mexicana*, i (1942), 11

'Hernández Moncada, el compositor en turno', *Revista musical mexicana*, iii (1942), 87

'Por el mundo de la música: Juan José Castro', *Revista musical mexicana*, i (1942), 157

'Por el mundo de la música: tres directores en el cuarto concierto de la sinfónica de Mexico', *Revista musical mexicana*, ii (1942), 16

'Quinceava temporada, a pesar de todo', *Revista musical mexicana*, i (1942), 243

'Aspectos de la música popular yucateca en tres siglos', *Revista musical mexicana*, iv (1944), 3

'El pasado y el presente del Conservatorio Nacional', *Numen*, i/3 (1946), 11

Antología folklórica y musical de Tabasco (Villahermosa, 1952)

Esencias de la canción popular (Mexico City, 1952)

'La música', *México: cincuenta años de revolución* (Mexico City, 1962), 439

Historia de la música en México, i (Mexico City, 1964)

'La Revolución y sus cantos', *Revista del Conservatorio* (1964), no.8, p.10

'Augusto Novaro, revolucionario mexicano del arte de la violería', *Revista del Conservatorio* (1965), no.9, p.6; no.10, p.6; no.11, p.5

La canción popular de Yucatán (Mexico City, 1970)

BIBLIOGRAPHY

M.C. Taboada: 'Apuntes para la historia de la música en México (selección bibliográfica de Gerónimo Baqueiro Fóster)', *Boletín bibliográfico de la secretaría de hacienda y crédito público*, no.387 (1968), suppl. [pp.2–22]

G. Pareyón: *Diccionario de música en México* (Guadalajara, 1995)

GERARD BÉHAGUE

Bar. In Western notation a vertical line drawn through the staff to mark off metrical units. Hence also the metrical unit thus indicated, which in American usage is called 'measure'. English usage often relies on context alone to make the distinction clear (e.g. 'up to the double bar', 'the end of the bar'), but 'bar-line' is also common.

Vertical lines were occasionally used in early polyphonic music, written in score to help align the voices and text (e.g. *GB-Lbl* 36881; *Cu* Ff.1.17; the Codex Calixtinus,

Ex.1

E-SC; facs. of *E-SC* f.187*v* in Besseler and Gülke). But most of the 'classical' repertories of the 13th (Notre Dame or Parisian, Ars Antiqua), 14th (Ars Nova, Ars Subtilior etc.), 15th and 16th centuries, though written in regular metres, did not use bars. Only the earliest of these repertories, however, regularly used score notation.

The earliest repertories to employ bar-lines at regular metric intervals – keyboard and lute (vihuela) music – were written in TABLATURE. Tablature never used ternary divisions of note values, and was in other respects less ambiguous than staff notation; possibly the fact that it usually represented polyphonic textures made further clarification desirable. Bar-lines are found in, for example, the Faenza Codex (*I-FZc* 117, written 1400–20, facs. in *MD*, xiii–xv, 1959–61), Conrad Paumann's *Fundamentum organisandi* (1452) and the Buxheim Organbook (*D-Mbs* mus.3752, written 1450–70, facs. in *DM*, 2nd ser., i, 1955). In England bars of irregular length are found in keyboard sources as late as the Fitzwilliam Virginal Book (*GB-Cfm* 32.g.29, written 1609–19).

Polyphonic vocal music of the Renaissance was not notated in bars, except when set out in keyboard PARTITURA ('score') at the end of the 16th century. Cipriano de Rore's *Madrigali … a quattro voci spartiti et accommodati per sonar d'ogni sorte d'istromento perfetto*

Ex.2

et per qualunque studioso di contrapunti is the first such score (facs. in *Festschrift Karl Gustav Fellerer*, 1962, p.144). Solo parts and partbooks did not use bars until the beginning of the 17th century. (Besseler and Gülke, p.147, shows an opening from John Dowland's *First Booke of Songes or Ayres of Foure Partes*, 1597: the lute and cantus parts on the one page are barred, but not the other three parts on the opposite page.)

Bar-lines did not always immediately precede the main accented beat; in other words, first beat of the bar and strong beat did not always coincide, particularly in the late 16th and early 17th centuries. This might result in bars of shorter length than would be usual today, in other words with a bar-line after each beat rather than after each bar of modern transcription. There was often a

preference for bars in duple or quadruple rather than ternary metre. Ex.1 shows a passage in *Altri canti di Marte* from Monteverdi's eighth book of madrigals: (*a*) gives the original barring, (*b*) a barring according to accent. Another well-known instance is the beginning of the *Partite sopra l'aria della Romanesca* from Girolamo Frescobaldi's *Toccate … partite … corrente … libro primo* (1637; see illustration). Frescobaldi's barring does not recognize an upbeat, and simply divides the beats into arithmetical groups. Ex.2 gives a barring according to accent. (For many other such examples, from early operas, see H. Riemann: *Handbuch der Musikgeschichte*, ii/2, ed. A. Einstein, 1912, 3/1921, p.195.)

The illustration also shows accidentals repeated later in the bar if other notes intervene, a practice that persisted up to the mid-18th century (it is found in most Bach and Handel autographs). Subsequent practice allowed that an accidental be effective throughout the bar where it appeared, but not after it.

After the mid-17th century it became the rule to precede main beats with bar-lines; Stravinsky's *The Rite of Spring* (1913) is a classic example of a score barred irregularly for this reason.

BIBLIOGRAPHY

J. Wolf: *Handbuch der Notationskunde* (Leipzig, 1913–19)
W. Apel: *The Notation of Polyphonic Music 900–1600* (Cambridge, MA, 1942, 5/1953)
C. Dahlhaus: 'Zur Entstehung des modernen Taktsystems im 17. Jahrhundert', *AMw*, xviii (1961), 223–40
H. Besseler and P. Gülke: *Schriftbild der mehrstimmigen Musik*, Musikgeschichte in Bildern, iii/5 (Leipzig, 1972)

DAVID HILEY

Beginning of 'Partite sopra l'aria della Romanesca' from Frescobaldi's 'Toccate … partite … corrente … libro primo' (1637)

Bär, Joseph. *See* BEER, JOSEPH.

Bär, Olaf (*b* Dresden, 19 Dec 1957). German baritone. At the age of ten he joined the Dresden Kreuzchor and thereafter studied at the Musikhochschule in his native city. After winning the Walter Grüner Lieder Competition in London, he embarked on a career as a recitalist, quickly achieving a reputation for intelligence and sensitivity in his readings of lieder. In 1985 he joined the Dresden Staatsoper, singing Kilian in *Der Freischütz* at the reopening of the Semper Oper. The same year he made his Covent Garden début as Harlequin in *Ariadne auf Naxos*. In 1986 he sang Papageno, probably his best role, at both the Vienna Staatsoper and La Scala, subsequently recording the part with Marriner. Bär made his Glyndebourne début as the Count in *Capriccio* (1987) and returned as Don Giovanni (1991). His US opera début came in 1996, when he sang Papageno in Chicago. As a recitalist he has appeared at all the major festivals in Europe, including Salzburg and Hohenems, and has been a regular visitor to London's Wigmore Hall since the outset of his career. His other recordings include several choral works (notably Brahms's *German Requiem*), the major song cycles of Schubert and Schumann, and many of the songs of Hugo Wolf, all of which reveal his attractive soft-grained tone (occasionally lacking an ideal body) and sympathy for the shaping of music and text.

ALAN BLYTH

Baraka, Amiri [Jones, (Everett) LeRoi] (*b* Newark, NJ, 7 Oct 1934). American writer on music. He studied piano, drums, and trumpet privately and attended Howard University (BA 1954). In the early 1960s he achieved wide recognition for his poetry and plays and for his writings about jazz, which included articles for *Down Beat*, *Jazz* and *Jazz Review*; a selection of his writings, many from *Down Beat*, was published in 1967 as *Black Music*. His book *Blues People* (1963), the first full-length study of jazz by a black writer, is both a sociological enquiry, using blues and jazz as a means of understanding how blacks became assimilated into American culture, and a superb discussion of the cultural context of the music in the USA. Besides his activities as a writer, Baraka has been involved in many black cultural and community projects. He was a founder of the Black Arts Repertory Theater-School, which was in existence from 1964 to 1965, and has also taught African studies at SUNY since 1980.

Baraka has had a profound influence on jazz criticism, ranging beyond its conventional boundaries to examine such topics as the relationship to jazz and the blues of black nationalism and Marxism. In addition to his works on jazz his published writings include more than 20 plays (of which the best-known is *Dutchman*, New York, 1964) and 12 volumes of poetry.

WRITINGS

Blues People: Negro Music in White America (New York, 1963/R)
Black Music (New York, 1967/R)
The Autobiography of Leroi Jones (New York, 1984, 2/1997)
with Amina Baraka: *The Music: Reflections on Jazz and Blues* (New York, 1987)

BIBLIOGRAPHY

K.W. Benston: *Baraka: the Renegade and the Mask* (New Haven, CT, 1976)
K.W. Benston, ed.: *Imamu Amiri Baraka (LeRoi Jones): a Collection of Critical Essays* (Englewood Cliffs, NJ, 1978)
L.W. Brown: *Amiri Baraka* (Boston, 1980)

L. Thomas: 'Ascension: Music and the Black Arts Movement', *Jazz among the Discourses*, ed. K. Gabbard (Durham, NC, 1995), 256

DANIEL ZAGER

Bar-Am, Benjamin [Berman, Bernhardt] (*b* Wiesbaden, 20 July 1923). Israeli critic, composer and musicologist. He moved to Mandatory Palestine in 1936. After studying composition with Paul Ben-Haim, his most influential teacher, Bar-Am attended the Ecole Normale de Paris (1949–51). He studied musicology at Tel-Aviv University (BA 1977), where he became the principal lecturer for courses on Jewish music and Israeli contemporary music (1973–96) and the first director of the Archive of Israeli Music. The secretary general of the Israeli League of Composers (1960–76, 1976–8), he became chair of the organizing committee of the ISCM in Israel in 1980. Though most influential as the music critic of the *Jerusalem Post* between 1958 and 1995, Bar-Am also wrote many essays on Israeli music in Hebrew, English and German, notably 'A Musical Gateway between East and West' (*Jerusalem Post*, 20 April 1988). He ceased composing in the early 1970s but resumed in 1988. His music, mostly songs, song cycles and chamber music with voice, is influenced by the conservative style of Ben-Haim. In his Symphony (1992) he integrates aspects of the 'Mediterranean style' that was in vogue in the 1950s, particularly the evocation of a traditional Jewish melos.

RONIT SETER

Barandello (Old Fr.). *See* FARANDOLE.

Baranović, Krešimir (*b* Šibenik, 25 July 1894; *d* Belgrade, 17 Sept 1975). Croatian composer and conductor. He studied the piano and theory with Kaiser in Zagreb, the horn with Lhotka at the Croatian Institute of Music, and composition at the Vienna Music Academy (1912–14) and in Berlin (1921–2). As conductor (1915–43) and artistic director (1929–40) of the Zagreb Opera, he presided over a notable period in the company's history. He enriched its repertory, with the works to Russian composers especially, and paid particular attention to the performance of modern ballets. As well as the first Croatian performances of Musorgsky's *Boris Godunov* (1918), Shostakovich's *Katerina Izmaylova* (1937) and ballets by Stravinsky, he conducted the first performance of Smetana's *Libuše* outside Czech lands (1933). His tenure at the opera was interrupted when Anna Pavlova engaged him as the conductor for a European tour by her troupe (1927–8). He was also conductor for many years of the Lisinski choir in Zagreb. For three years he lived in Bratislava, first as the conductor of the Radio Orchestra (1943) and then as the artistic director of the opera company (1945–6). On his return to Yugoslavia, he became professor of conducting and orchestration at the Belgrade Academy of Music (1946–64) and from 1951 to 1961 the conductor and artistic director of the Belgrade PO. In 1954 he was elected to the membership of the Academy of Sciences and Arts in Zagreb.

Better than any other Croatian composer of the time, Baranović combined the Slavonic expressionism inherited from Janáček and late 19th-century Russian composers with a more cosmopolitan music style. In his most powerful works – the ballet *Licitarsko srce*, the vocal cycle *Z mojih bregov* and the comic opera *Striženokošeno* – he found inspiration in the folklore of Hrvatsko Zagorje. With his exceptional instrumental skill (*Simfonijski scherzo*, Sinfonietta in E♭), his feeling for refined rhythmic structures, and a particular sense of humour and the grotesque (*Imbrek z nosom*), Baranović avoided neo-classicism, broadening his harmonic language with parallel chords of 4ths and 7ths which support a fundamentally diatonic fabric, often rooted in modality. His works written after 1943 (such as the orchestral songs *Iz osame* and *Oblaci*) were free from dissonant harmonies, and his large-scale vocal-instrumental works from the 1960s and 1970s were marked by greater stylistic simplicity and the aesthetics of realism.

WORKS
(selective list)

Stage: Licitarsko srce [Gingerbread Heart] (ballet, 3 scenes) Zagreb, 17 June 1924; (Cvijeće male Ide [Little Ida's Flowers] (ballet, 3 scenes), Zagreb, 29 March 1925; Striženo-košeno [Shorn-head] (comic op, 3, G. Krklec), Zagreb, 4 May 1932; Imbrek z nosom [Imbrek with the Big Nose] (ballet, 4 scenes), 1934, Zagreb, 19 Jan 1935; Nevjesta od Cetingrada [The Bride from Cetingrad] (comic op, 3, M. Fotez), Belgrade, 12 May 1951; Kineska priča [Chinese Story] (ballet, 5 scenes, D. Parlić, after Klabund), Belgrade, 30 April 1955

Vocal: Z mojih bregov [From my Hills] (F. Galović), Bar, orch, 1927; Moj grad [My Town], 9 (V. Nikolić), female v, orch, 1941; Iz osame [In Loneliness] (Baranović), female v, orch, 1944; Pan (cant., M. Krleža), 1958; Goran (cant., I.G. Kovačić), 1960; Oblaci [The Clouds] (D. Cesarić), female v, orch, 1963; Šume, šume [Forests, forests], 1967; Titov naprijed (cant., V. Nazor), 1971; Balada o Titu (cant., B. Karakaš), 1972; Na moru [At the Sea] (G. Krklec) Bar, orch, 1973; choruses, songs

Orch: Koncertna predigra, ov., 1916; Simfonijski scherzo, 1921; Poème balcanique (1927); Sinfonietta, E♭ (1939); Pjesma guslara [Fiddler's songs], rhapsody, 1945; Conc., hn, orch, 1974

Over 20 Film scores

Principal publisher: IZOD, Hrvatska Akademija Znanosti i Umjetnosti

BIBLIOGRAPHY

K. Kovačević: *Hrvatski kompozitori i njihova djela* [Croatian Composers and their Works] (Zagreb, 1960), 17–31
I. Supičić: 'Estetski pogledi u novijoj hrvatskoj muzici: pregled temeljnih gledanja četrnaestorice kompozitora' [Aesthetic Approaches in Contemporary Croatian Music: a Survey of the Basic Views of 14 Composers], *Arti musices*, i (1969), 23–61
J. Andreis: *Music in Croatia* (Zagreb, 1974); 283–8
K. Kovačević: 'Krešimir Baranović (1894–1975)', *Arti musices*, vii (1976), 5–17
M. Veselinović: *Krešimir Baranović: Stvaralački uspon* [Krešimir Baranović: His Creative Development] (Zagreb, 1979)

EVA SEDAK

Bararipton. Designation attached to a three-voice Gloria in manuscript *F-APT* 16bis; the piece is also transmitted in *I-IV* 115. The Apt manuscript is now thought to contain music from the court of the antipopes at Avignon in the late 14th century. It is not clear whether the word refers to the name of a composer or to something else; it is now known that 'Bararipton' was a mnemonic used in medieval logic for one of the categories of syllogisms. However, any possible musical meaning of the word remains a mystery.

The Gloria seems to be in discant style, with text underlay following the typical French pronunciation of Latin. The lower parts are rhythmically linked and run both in parallel and contrary motion. The preponderance of 8-5 and 5-3 chords is interrupted, sometimes at closing cadences, by 6-3 chords. Likewise, the sequence of 8-5–6-3–8-5 chords often gives way to parallel 5ths between cantus and contratenor. (The Gloria is ed. in PSFM, 1st ser., x, 1936, p.131; CMM, xxix, 1962, p.45 [commentary in MSD, vii, 1962, pp.43–4]; PMFC, xxiii*a*, 1989, p.108 [commentary in PMFC, xxiii*b*, 1991, pp.477–8]).

BIBLIOGRAPHY

A. Tomasello: *Music and Ritual at Papal Avignon 1309–1403* (Ann Arbor, 1983), 123–53
A. Tomasello: 'Notes biographiques sur quelques musiciens?', *Aspects de la musique liturgique au Moyen Age: Royaumont 1986, 1987 and 1988*, 261–79

GIANLUCA D'AGOSTINO

Barat, Jean [Jehan]. *See* BARRA, HOTINET.

Barba, Daniel dal. *See* DAL BARBA, DANIEL.

Bārbad. [Barbad] (*fl* late 6th– early 7th century CE). Persian lutenist, music theorist and composer. He was active during the riegn of Khosrow II (ruled 591–628 CE). *See* IRAN, §§II, 5 and III, 1(i) and fig.11.

Barbaia [Barbaja], **Domenico** (*b* Milan, ?1778; *d* Posillipo, 19 Oct 1841). Italian impresario. He first earned his living as a scullion in local cafés and bars. In 1806 he obtained the lease of the gambling tables in the foyer of La Scala, Milan, and on 7 October 1809 was appointed manager of the royal opera houses in Naples (originally the S Carlo and Nuovo theatres, to which were later added the Fondo and Fiorentini). After the S Carlo burnt down in 1816, he obtained the contract for rebuilding it. Through the Austrian ambassador, Count Gallenberg, he also secured the management of the Viennese Kärntnertortheater and the Theater an der Wien from 1821 to 1828. For several years from 1826 he ran La Scala and the Cannobiana in Milan.

The most famous impresario of his day, Barbaia played an important role in early 19th-century opera. His Neapolitan seasons were of an unparalleled brilliance, with stars such as the tenors Giovanni Davide, Nozzari, García and, later, Rubini; the contralto Benedetta Rosmunda Pisaroni and the soprano Isabella Colbran. His operatic tastes ranged widely. He introduced Spontini's *La vestale* (1811) and Gluck's *Iphigénie en Aulide* (1812), so inaugurating the new tradition of Italian *opera seria* in which all recitative was orchestrally accompanied (early examples include Mayr's *Medea in Corinto* in 1813 and the Rossinian canon beginning with *Elisabetta, regina d'Inghilterra* in 1815). He was among the first to recognize Rossini's genius and in 1815 engaged him at Naples with a six-year contract with the obligation to compose two operas a year and to direct revivals of older works, all for the yearly sum of 12,000 francs and part of the proceeds of the gambling tables. It was to Rossini that Barbaia lost his mistress, Isabella Colbran (later Colbran-Rossini), though relations between the two men remained cordial. In 1822 he produced Rossini in Vienna with great success and the following year mounted Weber's *Euryanthe* at the Kärntnertor. Throughout his life he showed a flair for discovering young talent. Mercadante, Pacini, Carafa and Generali all owed to him many of their earliest opportunities. Through him Bellini first gained a footing at the S Carlo and La Scala. In 1827 Barbaia signed Donizetti to a three-year contract that obliged him to write four operas a year for Naples.

Rough in his manners and poorly educated, Barbaia was held in high esteem by both singers and composers (his word, said Pacini, was as good as a written contract), and his death was mourned throughout Italy. His personality inspired Emil Lucka's novel *Der Impresario* (Vienna, 1937), and he figures as a character in Auber's opera *La sirène* (1844).

BIBLIOGRAPHY

DBI (A. Pironti)

Stendhal: *Rome, Naples et Florence en 1817* (Paris, 1817, 3/1826; Eng. trans., 1959)

P. Fiorentino: *Comédie et comédiens* (Paris, 1866)

G. Monaldi: *Impresari celebri del secolo XIX* (Rocca S Casciano, 1918)

G. Radiciotti: 'Il Barbaia nella leggenda e quello della storia', *L'arte pianistica*, vii/3 (1920), 5–6

A. Curti: 'Impresari d'altri tempi', *Città di Milano*, xl (1943), 17–20

J. Rosselli: *The Opera Industry in Italy from Cimarosa to Verdi* (Cambridge, 1984)

F. Hadamowsky: *Wien: Theater Geschichte* (Vienna, 1988/R)

B. Cagli and S. Ragnieds.: *Gioachino Rossini: lettere e documenti*, i: 1792–1822 (Pesaro, 1992)

JULIAN BUDDEN

Barbaja, Domenico. See BARBAIA, DOMENICO.

Barbandt [Barband, Barbant, Barbault], **Charles** [Stephan Carl Philipp] (bap. Hanover, 30 April 1716; d ?London, after 1775). German composer and instrumentalist. He was the only son and eldest child of Bartholomäus Barbandt (b Hanover, 3 July 1687; d Hanover, 6 May 1764), a musician of the court orchestra at Hanover, and Maria Catharina Barbandt (née Caligari). The first member of the Barbandt family to settle in Hanover seems to have been Joseph, Bartholomäus's father, who, according to records of the parish of St Clemens, Hanover, had come from Modena. Charles followed the example of his grandfather and father and became a member of the Hanoverian court orchestra. Although records do not indicate which instruments he played there, it is likely that he was employed mainly as a woodwind player, as later he often appeared as an oboist, flautist and clarinettist. The exact date of his entry into the orchestra is unknown, but he is listed in its payrolls until 1752 as 'Barbandt junior'. His father remained with the orchestra until his death in 1764, but Charles left for London in the early 1750s.

Barbandt's name first appears in a London concert programme on 14 January 1752, when a benefit concert was given for him at Hickford's Room in Brewer Street. On 4 January 1753 he married Anne Casanova at the Portuguese Embassy chapel and from about the same time appeared as an oboist and flautist in London theatres. In the 1754–5 season he was organist at Covent Garden Theatre and in 1756 embarked on his most ambitious project, a small-scale oratorio series, financed by subscription, at the Little Theatre in the Haymarket. A second series ran during January and February 1761. Barbandt's own concertos and solos were performed during the intervals. *Mr Barbandt's Yearly Subscription of New Music* appeared in monthly instalments between 10 March 1759 and 10 February 1760; it included symphonies (i.e. overtures), chamber music, Italian and English airs and duets, and sonatas. In 1764 he became organist of the Bavarian Embassy chapel in Warwick Street, Golden Square; his *Hymni sacri* was composed for use there. The Bavarian ambassador, Count Haslang, subscribed to some of Barbandt's works – as did a few of the composer's former Hanoverian colleagues – and was godfather to Barbandt's son Franz Xaver Ludwig (b 1753). Later Barbandt was also organist at the Portuguese Embassy chapel, but in 1776 he relinquished this post to a former pupil, Samuel Webbe (i).

According to the playbills, Barbandt's four oratorios each had a bipartite, rather than the more usual Handelian tripartite, structure. Barbandt's surviving works, with their even phrases, simple harmonic progressions and predominance of melodic line, show his awareness of the *galant* idiom, which, even in his sacred works, he preferred to a more solemn, contrapuntal style.

WORKS

ORATORIOS

lost; all first performed London, Little Theatre, Haymarket

Universal Prayer (A. Pope), 13 Feb 1755; 1 air in *Mr Barbandt's Yearly Subscription*, Dec 1759

Paradise Regained (J. Milton), 25 March 1756

On the Divine Veracity (E. Rowe), 9 March 1758

David and Jonathan, 28 Jan 1761

OTHER WORKS

6 Sonatas, 2vn/fl/ob, bc (vc/hpd), op.1 (London, 1752)

6 Sonatas or Duetts, 2 fl/vn, with 6 Lessons, 2 hn, op.2 (n.p., n.d.)

Conc., ?str, cls, hns, timp, lost, perf. in interval of Paradise Regained, 25 March 1756

4 Favourite Italian Songs, 1v, str, fl, ob, with 2 Sonatas, hpd, op.3 (London, ?1760)

Short and Easy Rules for the Thorough Bass, with minuet and 13 variations, hpd, op.4 (London, c1760), minuet also pubd as Lady Powis's Minuet with Variations (London, c1760)

6 Sonatas, hpd, op.5 (London, ?1760)

6 Symphonies, 2 hn, str, bc, op.6 (London, ?1760)

Sonata, hpd (London, 1764) [ded. George III]

Hymni sacri, antiphonae & versiculi, 2–4vv (London, 1766)

Quartetto, 3 vn/fl/ob, bc (vc/hpd) (London, n.d.)

God Save Great George the Third our King, vv, with Sonata, hpd, 1761, GB-Lbl

Miscellaneous works pubd in Mr Barbandt's Yearly Subscription of New Music (London, March 1759–Feb 1760): Sonata, A, hpd (March 1759); The glorious Restoration (Mr Redmond), ode, bound with April 1759 issue but probably later addn; Verra un di che la mia bella fugitiva pastorella, aria, S (April 1759); Sonata, C, 2 vn, 2 ob, 2 fl (May 1759); Lesson, C, cittera/gui (June 1759); Now the bright morning star, recit, Hail, bounteous May, aria, S (June 1759); Sinfonie, D, str, hns, bc (July 1759); Se l'idolo che adoro, S, S (Aug 1759); Sonata, G, hpd, vn/fl (Sept 1759); Occhi vezzosi, aria, S (Oct 1759); Sonata, G, 2 vn, 2 ob, 2 fl, bc (Nov 1759); 2 Lessons, C, gui/cittern (Dec 1759); Teach me to feel, air, S (Dec 1759); Sinfonie, Eb, str, hns, bc (Jan 1760); Per novo amor de lira, S, S (Feb 1760)

BIBLIOGRAPHY

BDA; FétisB; GerberNL; LS

J.R. Parker: *A Musical Biography* (Boston, 1825)

O.E. Deutsch: *Handel: a Documentary Biography* (London, 1955)

J. Gillow: *Literary and Biographical History or Biographical Dictionary of the English Catholics* (New York, 1961)

R. Darby: *The Music of the Roman Catholic Embassy Chapels in London, 1765 to 1825* (thesis, U. of Manchester, 1984)

J.K. Page: 'The Hautboy in London's Musical Life, 1730–1770', *EMc*, xvi (1988), 358–71

E. Zöllner: *English Oratorio after Handel, 1750–1800* (diss., U. of Hamburg, 1998)

EVA ZÖLLNER

Barbarini Lupus, Manfred (b Correggio, nr Reggio Emilia; fl 1557–61). Swiss composer of Italian birth. He was Kantor at Locarno in 1557 and then made a journey to south Germany to visit certain scholars, among them the brothers Johann (Hans) Jakob and Georg Fugger at Augsburg. At Freiburg he probably also met Glarean, and at Augsburg may have met Andreas Schillen, tutor to the Fugger children. In 1561 Abbot Diethelm Blarer commissioned him to make four-part arrangements of chorales for the Wartensee monastery at St Gall, which makes it likely that he was there at that time. He is not heard of again. But he may be identifiable with the Martin Lupus (also known as Lupi or Wolf) from Correggio, who was organist at Chur Cathedral until 1572 and then (though he was a layman) at the convent church of St Leodegar,

Lucerne, until 1576 and who was also an accomplished organ repairer.

The extant works of Barbarini Lupus are in varying styles. While those in the *Symphoniae* unfold through regular, freely imitative five-part polyphony, those in the *Cantiones sacrae* are more discontinuous, now imitative, now homorhythmic, and include short duet and trio sections. The St Gall chorale arrangements are cantus firmus pieces in the old style, in which the chant, mainly in the tenor, moves in regular semibreves and the other three voices, which at times imitate each other, are rather neutral in character. The settings are of interest because they are partly for choir and partly for organ, a layout possibly attributable to the copyist of the manuscripts, the organist Heinrich Keller.

WORKS

Symphoniae, seu insigniores aliquot ... super D. Henrici Glareani panegyrico de Helvetiarum tredecim urbium laudibus, 5vv (Basle, 1558)

Cantiones sacrae, 4vv (Augsburg, 1560)

Antiphonarium, 4vv, incl.: 3 masses, 14 introits, 14 graduals, tract, 15 sequences, 12 offertories, 13 communions, 44 antiphons, Te Deum, motet, 3 Passions, chorale arrangements, *CH-SGs*

BIBLIOGRAPHY

EitnerQ; *FétisB*

R. Schlecht: 'Manfredus Barbarinus Lupus Corregiensis Italus', *MMg*, iii (1871), 12–14, 17–24

O. Marxer: *Zur spätmittelalterlichen Choralgeschichte St. Gallens: der Cod.546 der St. Galler Stiftsbibliothek* (St Gall, 1908), 225ff

G. Eisenring: *Zur Geschichte des mehrstimmigen Proprium Missae bis um 1560* (Düsseldorf, 1912), 188

K. Nef: 'Schweizerische Passionsmusiken', *Schweizerisches Jb für Musikwissenschaft*, v (1931), 113–26

A. Geering: 'Homer Herpol und Manfred Barbarini Lupus', *Festschrift Karl Nef zum 60. Geburtstag* (Zürich and Leipzig, 1933), 48–71

A. Geering: 'Glareans panegyrische Gedichte in den "Symphonien" des Manfred Barbarini Lupus (1558)', in H. Glarean: *Helvetiae descriptio: Panegyrico pro iustissimo Helvetiorum foedere*, ed. and trans. W. Näf (St Gallen, 1948), 99–102

ARNOLD GEERING

Barbarino, Bartolomeo ['Il Pesarino'] (*b* Fabriano, nr Ancona; *d* ?Venice, after 1640). Italian composer. He is first heard of as an alto at the Santa Casa, Loreto, in 1593 and 1594. From then until 1602 he was in the service of Monsignor Giuliano della Rovere at Urbino, and it was probably during these years that he also served the Duke of Urbino, as he mentioned in the dedication of his madrigal book of 1614 (Giuliano was a relative of the duke). He was organist of Pesaro Cathedral – hence his nickname – from 1602 to 1605, when he became a musician of the Bishop of Padua. Between 1608 and 1624 he pursued a freelance career in Venice as a singer, chitarrone player and composer, performing frequently as soloist or member of a hired group in the *cappella* of S Marco and for the feast day celebration at the confraternity of S Rocco. Between 1625 and 1639 nothing is known of his whereabouts, but on 30 May 1639 and 29 Dec 1640 he received payments for performing as an instrumentalist in S Marco, Venice, where his son, Francesco Pesarin, had recently become a member of the *cappella* choir.

Barbarino was one of the first monodists, and one of the most enthusiastic, for nearly everything he wrote, sacred as well as secular, is for solo voice and continuo. Most of his 120 or so secular monodies are madrigals; some respond expressively to the more pathetic type of text, others include a good deal of lighter aria-like writing.

Unusually he named the poets he set, and he wrote some of the poems himself. In his collection of 1617 there are as many monodies as three-part madrigals; many of these multi-part madrigals (and others from a manuscript in *D-W*) exist in similar solo versions by the composer. In addition, Barbarino suggested in the preface to the 1617 collection that each voice be accompanied by its own chitarrone; to this effect he supplied a separate continuo line in each of the partbooks. *Misero e mesto* is a particularly good example of the fragmentary texture used in the trios, the three voices coming together only at cadences; and the very free use of chromatic inflection produces a wayward harmonic sense and abrupt modulations. Some of the canzonettas of 1616 are also wayward, though their tunes are predictably more catchy.

Barbarino's first book of solo motets contains the earliest surviving examples of sacred monodies sung in liturgical contexts: according to the dedication, the composer wrote much of the music in the 1590s and sang it 'at mass, with [his] raucous voice'. The inclusion of numerous Marian motets, especially the four Marian antiphons, in his second book of solo motets suggests the relevance of this collection to his freelance career in Venice, a city particularly noted for its reverence of the Virgin. He was as concerned as any of Giulio Caccini's followers about the quality of ornamentation to be applied to monodic music, and in his second book of solo motets he gave two versions of the vocal line, one simple, one ornamented, from which much can be deduced about contemporary taste in the embellishment of church (and other) music. In a prefatory note he explained how some singers had found difficulty with the divisions in his first book of motets and that the simplified versions were for them, as well as being a basic outline which experienced singers could embellish as they wished. The ornamented versions, he said, were for those who could sing ornaments but could not improvise them. Barbarino used embellishments to strengthen and diversify the melodic outline: he reserved florid passage-work for 4/4 time and lilting melismas and delightful hemiolas for triple time. As well as a fine use of sequence for the building of climaxes, some of his motets show a surer grasp of tonality than do many of his secular songs.

WORKS

SACRED

Il primo libro de mottetti ... da cantarsi da una voce sola, S/T (Venice, 1610)

Il secondo libro delli motetti ... da cantarsi a una voce sola, S/T (Venice, 1614)

7 motets, 1615[13], G. Puliti: Pungenti dardi spirituali (Venice, 1618), 1624[2], 1624[3], 1625[2]

6 sacred Italian pieces, 1613[3]; 1 dialogue ed. in Racek, 246ff

SECULAR

Madrigali, 1–2vv, chit/hpd/other inst (Venice, 1606); ed. in ISS, v (1986)

Il secondo libro de madrigali, 1v, chit/theorbo/hpd/other inst . . . con un dialogo di Anima e Caronte (Venice, 1607)

Il terzo libro de madrigali, 1v, chit/theorbo/hpd/other inst . . . con alcune canzonette nel fine (Venice, 1610)

Il quarto libro de madrigali, 1v, chit/theorbo/hpd/other inst . . . con un dialogo fra Tirsi & Aminta (Venice, 1614)

Canzonette, 1v (S/T), 2vv, chit/other inst (Venice, 1616)

Madrigali, 3vv, chit/hpd, con alcuni madrigali, 1v, chit/hpd (Venice, 1617)

1 madrigal, 1624[11]; 52 madrigals, 1–3vv, *D-W*

BIBLIOGRAPHY

G. Radiciotti: 'Aggiunte e correzioni ai dizionari biografici dei musicisti', *SIMG*, xiv (1912–13), 551–74

E. Schmitz: *Geschichte der weltlichen Solokantate* (Leipzig, 1914, rev. 2/1955)
N. Fortune: *Italian Secular Song from 1600 to 1635: the Origins and Development of Accompanied Monody* (diss., U. of Cambridge, 1954)
J. Racek: *Stilprobleme der italienischen Monodie* (Prague, 1965)
N. Hockley: *I due primi libri monodici di Bartolomeo Barbarino (1606 e 1607)* (diss., U. of Parma, 1969–70) [incl. edns of both books]
N. Hockley: 'Bartolomeo Barbarino e i primordi della monodia', *RIM*, vii (1972), 82–102
D. Arnold: *Giovanni Gabrieli and the Music of the Venetian High Renaissance* (London, 1979)
J.L.A. Roche: *North Italian Church Music in the Age of Monteverdi* (Oxford, 1984)
R. Miller: *The Composers of San Marco and Santo Stefano and the Development of Venetian Monody (to 1630)* (diss., U. of Michigan, 1993)
R. Miller: 'Bartolomeo Barbarino and the Allure of Venice', *Studi musicali*, xxiii (1994), 263–98

JEROME ROCHE/ROARK MILLER

Barbat [barbat]. Sassanian short-necked lute. *See* IRAN, §II, 5.

Barbato, Angelo (*fl* Padua, 1583–7). Italian amateur music editor and composer. He lived at Padua, where the only definite reference to him concerns his loan of a portative organ to the cathedral *cappella* on 6 December 1583. He edited the important anthology *De floridi virtuosi d'Italia* (Venice, 1583[11]), for five voices, which includes works by Marenzio and Giovanni Gabrieli. The dedication, which he addressed to Prince Albert Radziwiłł, provides interesting evidence about musical relations between Italy and Poland. He also published an anthology of pieces by musicians who worked at, or had contact with, Padua, *Canzonette di diversi eccellentissimi musici, libro primo* (Venice, 1587[7]), for three voices. Alongside pieces by G.B. Mosto, Annibale Padovano, M.A. da Pordenon and Giulio Renaldi appear two canzonettas of his own composition, which with their homophonic textures and simple harmony are typical of canzonettas of the period.

BIBLIOGRAPHY
EitnerQ; MGG1 (P. Petrobelli)
R. Casimiri: 'Musica e musicisti nella cattedrale di Padova nei secoli XIV, XV, XVI', *NA*, xviii (1941), 1–31, 101–214; xix (1942), 49–92; repr. in book form (Rome, 1943), 63, 168
F. Piperno: 'Musicisti e mercato editoriale nel 500: le antologie d'ambiente di polifonia profana', *Musica/Realtà*, v/15 (1984), 129–52, esp. 134–5, 145
F. Piperno: *Gli 'eccellentissimi musici della città di Bologna': con uno studio sull'antologia madrigalistica del Cinquecento* (Florence, 1985), 10, 24

PIER PAOLO SCATTOLIN

Barbay, Guillaume. *See* BARBEY, GUILLAUME.

Barbe [Barbé]. Flemish family of musicians.

(1) Antoine [Anthonis] **Barbe (i)** (*d* Antwerp, 2 Dec 1564). Composer. He was *maître de chapelle* of St Jacob, Bruges, before his appointment (1528) as *maître de musique* of the choir school of Antwerp Cathedral, where he remained until 1562. After his wife's death in about 1547 he was ordained; he first officiated as a priest on 11 January 1548. In 1562 he retired and was succeeded in 1563 by Geert van Turnhout. He was buried in the cathedral in 1564. In his mass, a light and mainly imitative parody of the popular late 15th-century chanson *Vecy la danse de Barberie*, he exploited the veiled reference to his own name in his use of the chanson's thematic material. The six-voice chanson *Alligiés moy doulce plaisante*

brunette, attributed to him in a German collection of 1540 (RISM 1540[7]), is ascribed in other sources to Josquin (ed. A. Smijers, *Werken*, v/14), Le Brung and Willaert. His four-voice chanson *On doibt bien aymer le bon vin*, a four-in-one canon for male voices published in Lyons (1540[17]), provides an example of what has been called the 'secret chromatic art of the Netherlands': it requires considerable modulation flatwards for a satisfactory resolution. Another four-voice chanson, *Ung capitaine de Pillars*, is an anecdotal piece in gay syllabic counterpoint. Barbe's two five-voice chansons, like his two-voice motets, were copied in manuscripts owned by Johann Herwart of Augsburg.

WORKS
SACRED
Missa 'Vecy la danse de Barberie', 4vv, 1545[1]
3 motets: Qui sunt isti, 4vv, 1542[7]; Summa regis, Inter spinas, 2vv, D-Mbs 260; ed. in RRMR, xvi–xvii (1974)

SECULAR
Alligiés moy doulce plaisante brunette, 6vv, 1540[7], ed. in Collectio operum musicorum batavorum saeculi XVI, xii (Berlin, 1858); On doibt bien aymer le bon vin, 4vv, 1540[17], ed. in SCC, xxvii (1993); Ung capitaine de Pillars, 4vv, 1544[12], ed. in SCC, xxix (1994)
Och hoort doch ons bediet, 4vv, 1551[18]; ed. in RRMR, cviii (1997)
Ha je ne l'ose dire, J'ay bien cause d'avoir melancolie, 5vv, D-Mbs Mus.ms.1508

(2) Antoine [Anthonis] **Barbe (ii)** (*b* Antwerp, before 1547; *d* Antwerp, 13 Feb 1604). Composer and organist, son of (1) Antoine Barbe (i). He probably studied music with his father and served as a chorister at Antwerp Cathedral. According to Fétis he composed some pavanes and courantes which were included in *Petit trésor des danses et branles à quatre et cinq parties des meilleurs autheurs propres à jouer sur tous les estrumentz* (Leuven, 1573), an anthology of instrumental ensemble music, now lost. In 1601 he was organist at St Walburga, Oudenaard, but he died at Antwerp and was buried in the cathedral.

(3) Antoine [Anthonis] **Barbe (iii)** (*b* Antwerp, after 1573; *d* Antwerp, 10 June 1636). Theorist, organist and teacher, son of (2) Antoine Barbe (ii). On 23 February 1596 he was appointed organist of St Jacobskerk, Antwerp, and later acted as repairer and tuner of organs in other churches in the city. In 1597 he married a teacher in a girls' school where he taught music. His didactic interests are reflected in his treatise *Exemplaire des douze tons de la musique, et de leur nature* (Antwerp, 1599).

BIBLIOGRAPHY
EitnerQ; FétisB
L. de Burbure and L.Theunissens: 'La musique à Anvers aux 14e, 15e et 16e siècles', *Annales de l'Académie royale d'archéalogie de Belgique*, lviii (1906), 159–256, esp. 243
J.A. Stellfeld: *Bronnen tot de geschiedenis der Antwerpsche clavicembel en orgelbouwers in de XVIe en XVIIe eeuwen* (Antwerp, 1942)
F. Dobbins: *The Chanson at Lyons in the Sixteenth Century* (diss., U. of Oxford, 1972)

FRANK DOBBINS

Barbe, Helmut (*b* Halle, 28 Dec 1927). German composer. After studying at the Berlin Akademie für Kirchen- und Schulmusik (1946–52) with Ernst Pepping and Gottfried Grote, among others, he served as Kantor of the St Nikolai-Kirche in Berlin-Spandau (1952–75) and director of church music for West Berlin (1972–85). He founded the Kammerchor Helmut Barbe in 1977. His teaching appointments included posts at the Berlin Kirchenmusik-schule (1955–75) and the Berlin Hochschule der Künste (professor 1975–95). His particular gift lies in his ability to write sacred music that adopts the musical methods of his time (he began to employ 12-note techniques in 1957), while remaining comprehensible to his audience. The expressive intensity of his compositions results from his use of harmonies, rhythms and timbres (often created by highly individual instrumental ensembles) to break up the otherwise static foundations of the music. In *Golgatha* (1972), a characteristic work, dissonant harmonies are combined with 16th-century choral settings, vocalises, glissandos, passages for solo percussion and the spoken word. A tendency towards homophony and transparency in the vocal music ensures the centrality of the text.

WORKS
(selective list)

Choral: Magnificat, 4vv, wind, timp, org, low str, 1956; Canticum Simeonis, T, 4vv, cel, perc, org, str, 1958; Die Auferweckung des Lazarus (cant.), A, T, 8vv, orch, org, 1959; Missa brevis, chorus, 2 fl, ob, eng hn, bn, vc, 1961; Ostergeschichte, A, Bar, 4vv, orch, elec gui, 1961; Chinesische Impressionen (Li Bai [Li Tai Po], trans. Klabund), 6vv, 1964; 2 Choralkonzerte, 2–4vv, org, 1967; Ye shall have a Song (cant.), female 4vv, ob, hn, hp, 1967; Bekenntnis (cant., M. Bollinger), 4vv, ob, str qnt, 1969; Inconstantia (cant., Bollinger), S, 4vv, gui, hpd, str, 1971; Magnalia D (Bible), Bar, chorus, org, tape, 1971; Golgatha, Bar, 3vv, str, perc, 1972; Ursuliner Messe, 4vv, fl, ob, cl, b cl, bn, tpt, 1972; TeD, Bar, 3 choruses, orch, 1976; Laudes 78, Bar, 4vv, org, perc, 1977; 3 Nachtstücke (Li Bai [Li Tai Po], trans. Klabund), 8vv, 1980; Verleih uns Frieden (cant.), 3 choruses, wind, org, perc, 1983; Wir wollen singn ein Lobgesang (cant.), 4vv, 2 tpt, 2 trbn, org, 1985; Magnificat, S, 6vv, 1986; Chorstücke zum 19. Sonntag nach Trinitatis, 1987; Herbst (G. von der Vring), 3 lieder, chorus, hp, 1988; Der du die Zeit in Händen hast (cant.), 2 choruses, congregation, (brass, perc)/org, 1989; Wir sind doch Pilger alle hier, 5 men's vv, 1990; Potsdamer TeD, Mez, 2 choruses, orch, org, 1992; An die Sterne (A. Gryphius), chorus, fl, hp, 1995–6; 1648 (chbr orat, Bible, M. Opitz, Gryphius), Bar, 2 choruses, chbr orch, 1997–8; Lichte Nacht (Gryphius), chorus, str sextet, 1997; Canti di Ungaretti, chorus, hp, accdn, 1998 [after Vivaldi]; motets, psalm settings, folksong arrs., other choral works
Other vocal: Musikantengruss (J. von Eichendorff), lieder, 1v, pf, 1953; Gesang der Abgeschiedenen (G. Trakl), 5 lieder, Bar, pf, 1957; Horoskop gefällig (M. Kaleko), 1v/chorus, cl, gui, db, pf, 1960; Requiem, S, fl, ob, bn, va, vc, db, 1965; Jeruschalajim (C. Heuser), high v, org, 1969; 5 Lieder (M.L. Kaschnitz, von der Vring, R.A. Schröder, P. Ludwig), S, pf, 1969; Ps xlii, high v, org, 1970; Preisungen (M. Buber), S, hp, org, 1974; Gott wohnt in einem Lichte (J. Klepper), T, org, 1992; folksong arrs.
Inst: Org Sonata, 1964; Vn Conc., 1966; Pf Trio, 1969; Hovs Hallar, chbr orch, 1970; Dialog mit J.S.B., org, 1977; 2 pièces, ob, vc, pf, 1979; Suite, 2 trbn, 1979 [after von Eichendorff]; Nordische Bläsersuite, 3 tpt, 2 trbn, 1981; Die vier Jahreszeiten, wind, perc, 1981; Preces, org, 1990; 4 Choralvorspiele, 3 tpt, 3 trbn, 1995; Praeludien/Postludien für die Festzeiten des Kirchenjahres, org, 1995; choral fantasies, org; other org works, incid music

Principal publishers: Hänsler, Strube

BIBLIOGRAPHY
G. Schönian: 'Helmut Barbe', *Gottesdienst und Kirchenmusik* (1960), 85–6
S. Günther: 'Jüngstes kirchenmusikalisches Schaffen: Helmut Barbe', *Gottesdienst und Kirchenmusik* (1962), 87–91
D. Krickeberg: 'Helmut Barbe: Porträt eines Komponisten', *Gottesdienst und Kirchenmusik* (1992), 95–7

DIETER KRICKEBERG

Barbe, Jean-Baptiste (*b* Montferrand, nr Clermont-Ferrand, Oct 1675; *d* Clermont, Aug 1759). French amateur lutenist. He compiled an important late source of French Baroque lute music. During the final decade of the 17th century, following his law studies in Orléans, he was in Paris, where he probably received lute lessons. He was back in Clermont by 1703, the date of his nomination to the Cour des Aydes. Like Vaudry de Saizenay's manuscripts, Barbe's lutebook is a large retrospective anthology containing a wide assortment of 17th-century masterworks. Representative composers include Bocquet, Du But (*père* and *fils*), Du Fault, Hémond, Mouton and Pinel. It was formerly in the possession of Henri Prunières, and is now in the Bibliothèque Nationale, Paris (Rés.Vmb.7; facs. (Geneva, 1985), see Chauvel).

BIBLIOGRAPHY
A. Tessier: 'Quelques sources de l'école française de luth au XVIIe siècle', *IMSCR I: Liège 1930*, 217–24
W.J. Rave: *Some Manuscripts of French Lute Music 1630–1700: an Introductory Study* (diss., U. of Illinois, Urbana-Champaign, 1972)
C. Chauvel: Introduction to *Manuscrit Barbe, pièces de luth de différents auteurs en tablature française* (Geneva, 1985) [facs.]
W.J. Rave: 'Remarks on Gallot Sources: How Tablatures Differ', *JLSA*, xx–xxi (1987–8), 87–107

BRUCE K. BURCHMORE

Barbeau, (Charles) Marius (*b* Ste Marie-de-la-Beauce, PQ, 5 March 1883; *d* Ottawa, 27 Feb 1969). Canadian anthropologist and ethnologist. He studied humanities at the Collège de Ste-Anne-de-la-Procatière (1897–1903) and after completing law studies at Laval University (1907) he won a Rhodes scholarship to Oriel College, Oxford, where he took the BSc in anthropology (1910). Encouraged by M. Marett, M. Mauss and Raoul and Marguerite d'Harcourt, he decided to study the Amerindians. On his return to Canada in 1911 to head the department of anthropology at the National Museum, he began intensive fieldwork among the Huron, Salish, Wyandote, Iroquois and Tsimshian Indians; he became deeply interested in French-Canadian folklore, having encountered much in the oral traditions of Amerindian tribes that was retained from contacts with the early French settlers. His investigation of French-Canadian folksongs superseded the work of Ernest Gagnon.

Barbeau taught at the universities of Ottawa (lecturer 1942), Laval (lecturer 1942–5, professor agrégé from 1945) and Montreal (occasional lecturer). In 1946, with Luc Lacourcière, he established the folklore archives at Laval University. He retired from the National Museum in 1948, but continued to work independently. In 1957 he founded the Canadian Folk Music Society, serving as its president until 1963. He was elected president of the American Folklore Society in 1918 and also served as co-editor of its journal. In 1916 he was elected a fellow of the Royal Society of Canada. Two honorary doctorates were conferred on him by the universities of Montreal (1938) and Oxford (1952). He served as a vice-president of the IFMC (1957–69), and received the Canada Council Medal in 1961.

Barbeau's ethnomusicological contributions lay primarily in the area of field techniques and collecting. His thousands of recorded folksongs and melodies, representing a unique cross-section of Canadian folk traditions, are housed at the Canadian Centre for Folk Culture Studies, National Museum of Man, Ottawa.

WRITINGS
'Les traditions orales français au Canada', *Le bulletin du parler français au Canada*, xv (1917), 300–18
'The Field of European Folklore in America', *Journal of American Folklore*, xxxii (1919), 185–97
with E.Z. Massicotte: 'Chants populaires de Canada', *Journal of American Folklore*, xxxii (1919), 1–89
'French and Indian Motifs in Our Music', *Yearbook of the Arts in Canada, 1928–1929* (Toronto, 1929), 125–32

'Folk Songs of French Canada', *ML*, xiii (1932), 168–82

'Songs of the Northwest', *MQ*, xix (1933), 101–11

'Asiatic Survivals in Indian Songs', *MQ*, xx (1934), 107–16

'How Folk-Songs Travelled', *ML*, xv (1934), 306–23

'La chanson populaire française en Amérique du Nord', *Journal of International Folklore*, v (London, 1936), 318–33; see also *JIFMC*, vi (1954), 7–10

Quebec: where Ancient France Lingers (Quebec and Toronto, 1936)

'French Canadian Folk-Songs', *MQ*, xxix (1943), 122–37

'Modalité dans nos mélodies populaires', *Mémoires de la Société Royale du Canada*, 3rd ser., xxxviii (1944), 15–25

'The Ermatinger Collection of Voyageur Songs', *Journal of American Folklore*, lxvii (1954), 147–61

'Folk Music: Canadian', *Grove5*

'Folk Song', *Music in Canada*, ed. E. Macmillan (Toronto, 1955), 32–54

'How the Folk Songs of French Canada Were Discovered', *Canadian Geographical Journal*, xlix (1954), 58–65

'Folk Songs of French Louisiana', *Canadian Music Journal*, i/2 (1956–7), 10–16

'Indian Songs of the Northwest', *Canadian Music Journal*, ii/1 (1957–8), 16–25

'Buddhist Dirges of the North Pacific Coast', *JIFMC*, xiv (1962), 16–21

En roulant ma boule: deuxième partie du répertoire de la chanson folklorique française au Canada, ed. L. Ouellet (Ottawa, 1982)

FOLKSONG EDITIONS

with E. Sapir: *Folk Songs of French Canada* (New Haven, CT, 1925)

with H. Boulton and A.Somerwell: *Twelve Ancient French Canadian Folk-Songs* (London, 1927)

Folk-Songs of Old Quebec (Ottawa, 1935)

Romancero du Canada (Montreal, 1937)

Chansons populaires du vieux Québec (Paris, 1938)

Jongleur Songs of Old Quebec (New Brunswick, NJ, 1962)

Le rossignol y chante (Ottawa, 1962)

BIBLIOGRAPHY

C. Cardin: 'Bio-bibliographie de Marius Barbeau', *Archives de folklore*, ii (Quebec, 1947), 17–26

E. Fowke: 'Marius Barbeau 1883–1969', *Journal of American Folklore*, lxxxii (1969), 264–7

G. George: 'In Memoriam: Marius Barbeau', *YIFMC*, i (1969), 10–13

I.J. Katz: 'Marius Barbeau 1883–1969', *EthM*, xiv (1970), 129–42

F. Brassard: 'French-Canadian Folk Music Studies: a Survey', *EthM*, xvi (1972), 351–9

ISRAEL J. KATZ

Barbella, Emanuele (*b* Naples, 14 April 1718; *d* Naples, 1 Jan 1777). Italian violinist and composer. His first teacher was his father, Francesco Barbella, composer and *maestro di violino* at the Conservatorio di S Maria di Loreto. He was later instructed by Angelo Zaga and by Pasqualino Bini, a noted pupil of Tartini. In theory and composition he was the pupil of Michele Cabbalone until the latter's death in 1740 and subsequently, until 1744, he studied with Leonardo Leo. The story that Leo thought him stupid resulted from a misinterpretation of Barbella's humorous modesty in the autobiographical sketch he provided for Burney's *History*. In 1753 Barbella became first violinist at the Teatro Nuovo in Naples, and three years later he entered the royal chapel there. From 1761 until his death he was a member of the orchestra at S Carlo. It is possible that he visited England during the 1760s, for his op.1 was printed in London by Oswald 'for the author'.

Although there is no evidence that Barbella ranked among the finest Italian violinists, he was respected as a performer and admired as a teacher and composer. Burney, who became his friend and relied on his knowledge, confessed to some disappointment in his playing, complaining of lack of variety, 'drowsiness of tone', and 'want of animation'. Yet he found much to praise also, especially when hearing Barbella in a small room, and spoke of his 'taste and expression' and of his 'marvellously sweet tone'. Barbella's compositions, which evidently achieved a modest success in London and Paris, reflect his position as a disciple (through Bini) of Tartini. The craftsmanship is sure, but what seemed to Burney as 'a good deal of fancy' appears as no more than graceful imitation of Tartini's style. Occasional harmonic surprises (according to Burney, 'a tincture of not disagreeable madness'), may represent Barbella's interpretation of Tartini's harmonic theories. The humorous side of this attractive musician's personality is sometimes seen in bizarre programmatic titles and unusual tempo indications. His good temper and stable character probably contributed to his effectiveness as a teacher and to the esteem in which he was held by his contemporaries. Ignazio Raimondi was his most famous pupil.

WORKS

Elmira generosa (op, P. Trinchera), Naples, Nuovo, carn. 1753; collab. Logroscino

Tinna nonna, lullaby, vn, b, in *BurneyH*, ii, 452–3

2 concs., *I-Gl*; 12 trios (2 vn, b)/(vn, violetta, b), *US-BEm*; 6 Trios, 2 vn, vc (London, 1772); 6 Solos (vn, b)/2 vn (London, 1765/R); A Second Sett of 6 Solos, vn, b (London, *c*1770)

Duos (for 2 vn, unless otherwise stated): 6 duetti (Paris, *c*1765); 6 for 2 vn/mand, b (va) ad lib (Paris, *c*1770/R); 6 (London, *c*1770), as op.3 (Paris, *c*1774); 6 duos … très faciles, op.1 (Paris, *c*1771); 6 as op.2 (Paris, *c*1773); ?lost; 3, *I-Gl*, *US-Wc*

Sonatas: 6 for 2 vn, vc, bc (hpd), op.1 (London, 1762); 6 for vn, vc, op.4 (Paris, *c*1774); 1 for vn, b, in J.B. Cartier: *L'art du violon* (Paris, 1798); 3 for 2 vn, b, *I-Mc*, *MOe*, *US-BEm*; 7 for vn, b, *I-Gl*, *US-Wc*; 3 for 2 vn, *I-Gl*; 3 for vn, b, *S-Uu*; 6 for vn, b, *I-MOe*; 4 for 2 mand, *S-Uu*; 1 for 2 mand, b, *Uu*

BIBLIOGRAPHY

BurneyFI; *BurneyH*; *FétisB*; *FlorimoN*; *GiacomoC*; *NewmanSCE*

CHAPPELL WHITE

Barber (Donald), Chris(topher) (*b* Welwyn Garden City, 17 April 1930). English jazz trombonist, arranger and bandleader. He studied the trombone and the double bass at the GSM in London, and formed his first traditional jazz band in 1949. In 1953 he helped to organize a band led by Ken Colyer, then the most ardent British propagandist for traditional New Orleans music. The following year Barber took over the band; Colyer was replaced by Pat Halcox, and the ensemble soon became one of the most popular and technically accomplished groups of its kind. From the mid-1950s Barber helped foster British interest in blues by bringing over such American musicians as Muddy Waters, the harmonica player Sonny Terry and the guitarist and singer Brownie McGhee. He made several tours of the USA beginning in 1959, and also recorded two albums with his American Jazz Band, which included Sidney De Paris, Edmond Hall and Hank Duncan. Barber expanded his interests, recording classic rags (scored for his band) long before the popular rediscovery of Scott Joplin, and working with musicians from other areas of jazz (notably the Jamaican saxophonists Bertie King and Joe Harriott). Renewed interest in traditional jazz in the early 1960s brought wide success to Barber and his group, which included as its singer his wife, Ottilie Patterson. After rhythm-and-blues achieved general popularity in the early 1960s he re-formed his group as Chris Barber's Jazz and Blues Band, and, while retaining his roots in New Orleans jazz, engaged rock and blues musicians guitarist John Slaughter and the drummer Pete York. During the 1970s the band toured frequently in Europe. In 1976 Barber made a tour of Britain entitled 'Echoes of Ellington'. In 1981–2 he collaborated with the rock singer and keyboard player Dr John in the show *Take me back to New Orleans*, which was performed widely in Britain, Europe and the USA.

Barber is a skilful trombonist and a highly original arranger, and the identity he has achieved for his band has been imitated throughout Europe

BIBLIOGRAPHY

B. Gladwell: 'Barber Approved', *Jazz Journal*, xii/8 (1959), 25, 36

E. Souchon: 'Chris Barber's Band in New Orleans', *Jazz Journal*, xiii/2 (1960), 1–2

G. Bielderman: *Chris Barber Discography, 1949–1975* (Zwolle, 1976; loose leaf suppl. *c*1978; 2/1992 as *Chris Barber: 40 Years in Music*)

D. Fairweather: 'Barber, Chris', in I. Carr, D. Fairweather and B. Priestley: *Jazz: the Essential Companion* (London, 1987), 25

CHARLES FOX/DIGBY FAIRWEATHER

Barber, Llorenç (*b* Alelo de Malferit, Valencia, 1948). Spanish composer. He studied piano, composition and art history at the universities of Valencia and Madrid, and was in charge of the University of Madrid computer music centre, 1979–84. From 1990 he taught at the Institute of Aesthetics and in 1992 he planned and supervised a series of concerts of 'alternative music' at the Circulo de Bellas Artes.

Since 1980 Barber has been engaged internationally as an improviser on his own personally constructed 'bell towers'. In addition he has fulfilled commissions from all over the world to write 'symphonies of bells', each specifically designed for individual towns and cities; in Spain he has composed one such work for bell towers situated at various points on a mountain range. A performance in Oaxaca, Mexico, in June 1991, was timed to coincide with a total eclipse; another was the closing event of the 1993 ISCM Festival.

A 'symphony of bells' involves making use of all the available bells and bell ringers in any locality, the performance being co-ordinated by stopwatches on each site. Most of these symphonies last 50 minutes and are exact in their contrasts of quiet episodes and great tumults of bell sounds. The same improvisatory and rhythmic processes were utilized to brilliant effect in an outdoor work for multiple school brass bands, *Alberomundo*, played in the Bull Ring at Alicante on 24 September 1995 as part of the annual contemporary music festival there. Barber has also collaborated with the singer Fatima Miranda and with the Fiatus Vocis Trio, exploring new relationships between phonetics and instrumental music; in this he has been influenced by the work of Robert Ashley.

WRITINGS

John Cage (Madrid, 1985)

'Juan Hidalgo', *Ritmo*, no.566 (1986), 112–13

Mauricio Kagel (Madrid, 1987)

'Une musique pneumatique: la linguopharyngocampanologie', *Revue d'esthétique*, nos.13–15 (1987–8), 67–71

'Sobre las ciudades y las campanas españolas', *Ritmo*, no.594 (1988), 140–42

'Bells, a Music from the Space', *Glasba v tehnicnem svetu: Musica ex machina/Die Musik in der technischen Welt* (Ljubljana, 1994), 219–26

'Like an Avalanche: Conlon Nancarrow and Spain', *MusikTexte*, nos.73–4 (1998), 49–50

MEIRION BOWEN

Barber, Robert (i) (*fl* Castleton, Derbys., 1723–53). English psalmodist and ?composer. In 1723 he published the first edition of *A Book of Psalmody* in conjunction with John Barber. A second edition, by Robert Barber alone,

followed in 1733, and a third, entitled *David's Harp Well Tuned*, in 1753. He also published *The Psalm Singer's Choice Companion* in 1727. *A Book of Psalmody* enjoyed a good deal of popularity in the north Midlands. It was similar to other parochial collections, and most of its contents were derivative. The second edition, however, had a remarkable feature: it included, as well as chants for the canticles, a complete musical setting of Morning Prayer, litany and ante-communion on cathedral lines, but for alto, tenor and bass only. Barber made it clear on the title-page that this was designed for 'our Country Churches'. He thus brought to its logical conclusion the trend begun by Henry Playford, who published anthems for parish church use in *The Divine Companion* (1701), and John Chetham, who printed chants in his *Book of Psalmody* (1718). The anthem *By the rivers of Babylon*, attributed to Barber and first printed in his 1723 collection, is one of the finest examples of country church music of the period.

BIBLIOGRAPHY

N. Temperley: *The Music of the English Parish Church* (Cambridge, 1979), i, 193; ii, exx.31, 34

NICHOLAS TEMPERLEY

Barber, Robert (ii) (*b* Newcastle upon Tyne, *c*1750; *d* ?London). English composer and organist. His biography is obscure. He went to Aberdeen in autumn 1774 to take up the post of organist at St Paul's Episcopal Chapel, which he held until autumn 1783, being succeeded (probably at his own wish) by John Ross, also a native of Newcastle. During that time Barber played the harpsichord continuo for the Aberdeen Musical Society's weekly concerts, published several compositions, and performed further unpublished works. After 1783 he seems to have lived in London.

In 1788 Barber's cantata *Thomson's Hymn to the Seasons* was published in London. In about 20 movements, scored for chorus, soloists and large orchestra, on a text adapted from James Thomson, it is his outstanding surviving composition; the choral writing is Handelian, but the arias and *stromentato* recitatives are more modern, and may have been influenced by Gluck. Though written ten years earlier than Haydn's *Seasons*, it contains a duet 'Bleat out afresh' whose theme is identical to that of Haydn's chorus 'Come gentle spring'; it is at least possible that Haydn heard a performance of Barber's work during one of his two visits to London.

WORKS
published in London unless otherwise stated

6 Sonatas, pf/hpd, vn, vc, op.1 (*c*1775)

6 Trios, hpd, vn, vc, op.2 (*c*1780)

A Favorite Sonata, pf/hpd, vn, vc (*c*1780)

A Collection of Songs, Cantatas, Elegies, Catches and Glees, op.3 (1782)

A Favorite Concerto, hpd/pf (*c*1785)

Thomson's Hymn to the Seasons, soloists, chorus, orch, op.4 (1788)

24 Favourite Scots Songs for v, pf (Liverpool, *c*1795)

Org conc., advertised in *Aberdeen Journal* (8 May 1778), lost

BIBLIOGRAPHY

D. Johnson: *Music and Society in Lowland Scotland in the Eighteenth Century* (London, 1972), 55–6

DAVID JOHNSON

Barber, Samuel (Osmond) (*b* West Chester, PA, 9 March 1910; *d* New York, 23 Jan 1981). American composer. One of the most honoured and most frequently performed American composers in Europe and the Americas during the mid-20th century, Barber pursued, throughout his career, a path marked by a vocally inspired lyricism and a commitment to the tonal language and many of the forms of late 19th-century music. Almost all of his published works – including at least one composition in nearly every genre – entered the repertory soon after he wrote them and many continue to be widely performed today.

1. Life. 2. Works and style.

1. LIFE. From the age of seven, he displayed a prodigious talent for composing both vocal and instrumental music, writing an operetta, *The Rose Tree*, when he was ten to a libretto by the family's Irish cook. His musical studies were encouraged by his aunt and uncle – the contralto Louise Homer and the composer Sidney Homer, who, as his nephew's mentor for more than 25 years, profoundly influenced Barber's aesthetic principles. Early piano lessons were with William Hatton Green. At 14 he entered the newly founded Curtis Institute of Music, where he studied the piano with George Boyle and then with Vengerova, singing with Gogorza and composition with Scalero. Also at the institute in 1928, he met Menotti, an encounter which led to a lifelong personal and professional relationship. In 1934, shortly before his graduation, the founder of the Curtis Institute, Mary Curtis Bok, began to take a special interest in Barber; beyond providing financial help, she actively promoted his career.

Early travels and extended stays in Europe, Italy in particular, solidified his affinity with European culture and intensified his Romantic orientation. In Vienna in 1934, he studied conducting and singing with John Braun. After his graduation from Curtis he had a brief career as a baritone, performing on the NBC Music Guild series; in 1935 he won a contract for a series of weekly song broadcasts. His recording of his own setting of Arnold's *Dover Beach* was hailed as having 'singular charm and beauty', 'intelligently sung by a naturally beautiful voice'. First-hand experience as a singer and an intuitive empathy with the voice would find expression in the large legacy of songs that occupy some two-thirds of his output.

Barber gained early recognition as a composer, winning two Bearns awards – for a violin sonata (1928, lost) and for the overture to *The School for Scandal* (1931), his first published large-scale orchestral work. A Rome Prize enabled him to spend two years at the American Academy (1935–7), where he completed the Symphony in One Movement (1936), which received immediate performances in Rome, Cleveland and New York. Rodzinski conducted it at the opening concert of the Salzburg Festival in 1937, the first performance at the festival of a symphonic work by an American composer. His international stature was confirmed in 1938, when Toscanini and the NBC SO broadcast his *Essay* (no.1) and the *Adagio for Strings* (an arrangement of the second movement of the String Quartet). After that point, nearly all of Barber's works were composed on commission for prominent performers or ensembles.

He returned to the Curtis Institute in 1939 where he taught composition until 1942, though he was not really attracted to teaching and did not accept another position. In 1943 Mary Bok enabled Barber and Menotti to purchase 'Capricorn', the house in Mount Kisco, New York, which (until 1972) was the hermitage of Barber's most productive years, as well as a gathering place for many artists and intellectuals. In the same year he completed his Second Symphony, a commission from the

US Army Airforce (in which he served from 1942 to 1945). The work was given its première by the Boston SO, as was the Cello Concerto, written for Garbousova, and the orchestral song *Knoxville: Summer of 1915*, commissioned by the soprano Eleanor Steber. His ballet score *Medea* (1946) was composed for Martha Graham; it was subsequently reworked both as an orchestral suite and as a separate orchestral tone poem, *Medea's Meditation and Dance of Vengeance*. The Piano Sonata (1949), commissioned by Irving Berlin and Richard Rodgers to celebrate the 25th anniversary of the League of Composers, was first performed by Horowitz. Its instant critical success was followed by numerous performances in America and Europe within the first year of its première; it retains a secure place in the repertory.

Barber had studied conducting with Reiner at the Curtis Institute and later with Szell, and in 1951 he was coached by Malko in preparation for the recordings of the Second Symphony, the Cello Concerto and the *Medea* ballet suite. Later that year he also conducted concerts of his Violin Concerto, the Second Symphony and *Medea* in Berlin and Frankfurt. But though he had ambitions as a conductor in the 1950s, these were to be short-lived.

While few think of Barber as a prominent standard-bearer for American music, he was more than once chosen to represent the USA: at an international music festival in Prague in 1946, as vice-president of the International Music Council in 1952, and as the first American composer to attend the biennial Congress of Soviet Composers in Moscow in 1962. He won the first of two Pulitzer Prizes in 1958 for *Vanessa*, staged initially by the Metropolitan Opera (1958) and later that year as the first American opera produced at the Salzburg Festival. Among the many other awards he received were the Henry Hadley Medal (1958) for his exceptional services to American music, nomination to the American Academy of Arts and Letters (1958), and the Gold Medal for Music at the

Samuel Barber

American Academy and Institute of Arts and Letters (1976).

At the peak of his career, Barber was commissioned to write three works for the opening of Lincoln Center: the Piano Concerto, commissioned for the inaugural week of Philharmonic Hall (1962), which won him the Pulitzer Prize; *Andromache's Farewell* (1962), a concert scene for soprano and orchestra based on Euripides; and the opera *Antony and Cleopatra* (1966), written for the opening of the new Metropolitan Opera House. But the third commission, in principle one of the greatest tributes to his work, turned out to be his nemesis. Prompted by a conviction that, in spite of the vitriolic reviews, the opera contained some of his best work, Barber directed much of his energy towards its revision over the following decade.

After 1966 he divided his time between Santa Cristina in Italy and New York. He struggled with depression, alcoholism and creative blocks that profoundly affected his productivity. Yet he continued to concentrate on what had always been for him the gratifying task of writing vocal music in short forms, as well as fulfilling a few commissions for larger works, including the cantata *The Lovers*. From 1978 to the end of his life, Barber was intermittently hospitalized for the treatment of cancer. His last composition, an oboe concerto of which only the second movement was completed, was published posthumously as *Canzone* for oboe and string orchestra.

2. WORKS AND STYLE.   Unlike many of his contemporaries whose careers came to maturity between the two world wars, Barber rarely responded to the experimental trends that infiltrated music in the 1920s and again after World War II. Instead he continued to write expressive, lyrical music, using conventional formal models and the tonal language of the 19th century. Nine years of rigorous training in composition under Scalero, a student of Eusebius Mandyczewski, helped to preserve Barber's connection to the 19th-century tradition. That classical heritage was also reinforced by the personal guidance he received from Sidney Homer, who held up the European masters of the 19th century as role models, while at the same time directing Barber to trust the validity of his 'inner voice'.

Elements of modernism incorporated into his work after 1940 – increased dissonance and chromaticism (*Medea's Meditation and Dance of Vengeance* and the Cello Concerto), tonal ambiguity and a limited use of serialism (movements 1, 2 and 3 of the Piano Sonata, the *Nocturne* and *Prayers of Kierkegaard*) – were only of use in so far as they allowed him to pursue without compromise principles of tonality and lyrical expression. The 12-note rows in the Piano Sonata, for example, are not used as part of a rigid technique of organization. Their presence in melodic lines or accompaniment is rarely in conflict with – indeed often reinforces – the tonal structure. Barber's propensity for writing elegiac, long-lined melodies is exemplified by two of his best-known works, the justifiably admired *Adagio for Strings* and the Violin Concerto. These and such large-scale orchestral works as the three *Essays* from the early, middle and late stages of his career employ a rich orchestral palette and are characterized by well-crafted formal design, fluent counterpoint, and haunting themes – often assigned to solo woodwind instruments – that reflect a strong vocal orientation. The finale of the Violin Concerto and subsequent works from the 1940s, in particular the

Second Symphony, *Medea's Meditation and Dance of Vengeance*, *Capricorn Concerto* (a 20th-century concerto grosso), and the Cello Concerto, show an increasing use of dissonance and syncopated rhythms, displaying some influence of Stravinsky.

A prolific composer of songs that are grateful to the voice as well as the ear, Barber favoured lyrical and nostalgic texts by European, often Celtic, poets. He set Joyce, Stephens, Graves, Spender and Rilke (in French) as well as the American poets Agee, Rothke and Dickinson. Arroyo, Bampton, Fischer-Dieskau and Steber, among others, have introduced his vocal works. *Sure on this shining night* op.13 no.3 – with its long, seamlessly lyrical canonic lines – is one of the most frequently performed of his songs. The cycle *Hermit Songs* op.29, commissioned by Elizabeth Sprague Coolidge and first sung by Leontyne Price, is a major work. The ten songs, based on comments written on the margins of medieval manuscripts by Irish monks, are infused with a modal harmonic language of great stylistic integrity; they led Schuman to hail Barber as an unmatched art-song composer. The intellectually and vocally challenging late cycle *Despite and Still* op.41, written for Price, has profound biographical significance, probing themes of loneliness, lost love and isolation – themes which call for a more dissonant harmonic language characterized by tonal ambiguity, tritones, a frequent use of the complete chromatic, conflicting triads, and whole-tone segments directed towards vivid expression of textual imagery.

Unaccompanied choral works written between 1930 and 1940 include a setting of Emily Dickinson's 'Let down the bars, O Death', a precursor of the sensitivity to textual expression that would come to characterize Barber's later choral compositions. His settings of three poems from *Reincarnations* reflect the exuberance, wit and melancholy of James Stephens's reinterpreted Gaelic texts through a wide variety of musical nuance, ranging from the rapid parlando rhythms of *Mary Hynes* to the chilling dirge *Anthony O'Daly*, its theme intensified by archaic-sounding open 5ths over an E pedal. The large-scale *Prayers of Kierkegaard* (1954), composed at the peak of Barber's maturity, fuses 20th-century, Baroque and medieval musical practice and stands unequivocally as one of the great spiritual works of the contemporary genre.

Barber's long-awaited first opera, *Vanessa* (1956), with a libretto by Menotti inspired by Isak Dinesen's *Seven Gothic Tales*, is in the grand operatic tradition. Eleanor Steber, in one of the great challenges of her career, took the title role. With set-piece arias, love duets, a glimpsed ball scene requiring a waltz, a folkdance ballet (reminiscent of *Yevgeny Onegin*) and a coloratura skating aria (cut from the revised version), it was described by Paul Henry Lang as 'remarkable and second to none on the Salzburg–Milan axis'; Sargeant extolled it as 'by far the finest and most truly "operatic" opera ever written by an American, as well as one of the most impressive things of its sort to appear anywhere since Richard Strauss's more vigorous days'. Predominantly neo-Romantic, the music highlights many of Barber's compositional strengths: metric flexibility that supports the natural rhythms of the text, a fluid use of harmonic colour to underscore the bittersweet poetry, and an abundance of accessible melody.

His second opera, *Antony and Cleopatra*, contains some of Barber's most dramatic vocal writing, but initial appreciation was eclipsed by the inflated Zeffirelli production with its problematic technical apparatus and gaudy costumes, and a press preoccupied with the social glitter of the occasion. Some of the most sensuous and soaring lyrical passages were composed especially with the voice of Price in mind, who created the role of Cleopatra. Revised by Barber and restaged by Menotti, the work subsequently received critical accolade with performances at the American Opera Center at the Juilliard School in New York in 1975 and at the Spoleto festivals in Charleston and Italy in 1984.

While he shared the concern of his generation for writing music accessible to a broadly based audience, unlike Copland, Harris, Blitzstein and Thomson, who searched for a music with national identity, Barber rarely incorporated popular, jazz and folk idioms into his compositions. Of his works that do include native elements, *Knoxville: Summer of 1915* is considered the most American. A reverie of childhood in a small Southern town, on a text by James Agee, it is a palpable evocation of folklore in a quasi-pastoral style, with frequent word-painting, hints of the blues, rich orchestral colour and freely varied metre. Diamond claimed *Knoxville* was 'the pinnacle beyond which many a composer will find it impossible to go'. Barber's few instrumental works that draw on the vernacular include *Excursions* (1941–2), a set of stylized piano pieces based on American idioms (a boogie woogie, a blues, a barn dance and a Latin American popular dance), the Piano Sonata (1949), with its paradigmatic contemporary fugue, and the Piano Concerto (1962), which makes use of motoric jazz rhythms.

Though deemed conservative by contemporary critics, Barber's lasting strength comes precisely from his conservation of a post-Straussian chromaticism along with a typically American directness and simplicity. The international recognition accorded him throughout most of his life and the new significance his works have gained since the arrival of the 'new romanticism' is testimony to the vitality and enduring viability of his extended tonal language and melodic invention.

WORKS
all published unless otherwise stated

STAGE

op.

—	The Rose Tree (op, A.S. Brosius), 1920, inc., unpubd; West Chester, PA
—	One Day of Spring (incid music, M. Kennedy), 1v, str, 1935, lost, upubd; Winter Park, FL, 24 Jan 1935
23	Medea (Serpent Heart) (ballet, M. Graham), 1946, New York, 10 May 1946; rev. as The Cave of the Heart, New York, 27 Feb 1947; arr. as orch suite, 1947, Philadelphia, 5 Dec 1947, Philadelphia Orchestra, cond. E. Ormandy; Medea's Meditation and Dance of Vengeance, op.23a, 1953, New York, 2 Feb 1956, New York PO, cond. D. Mitropoulos
28	Souvenirs (ballet, T. Bolender), 1952, New York, 15 Nov 1955; arr. as suite, pf 4 hands, 1952, NBC TV, July 1952; suite, orch, 1952, Chicago, 12 Nov 1953, Chicago SO, cond. F. Reiner; suite, solo pf, 1954
32	Vanessa (op, 4, G.C. Menotti), 1956–7, New York, Met, 15 Jan 1958, cond. Mitropoulos; rev. 1964
35	A Hand of Bridge (op, 1, Menotti), 4 solo vv, chbr orch, 1953, Spoleto, 17 June 1959
40	Antony and Cleopatra (op, 3, F. Zeffirelli, after W. Shakespeare), 1966, New York, Met, 16 Sept 1966, cond.

T. Schippers; rev. 1974, New York, 6 Feb 1975, cond. Conlon

ORCHESTRAL

5	The School for Scandal, ov., 1931
7	Music for a Scene from Shelley, 1933
9	Symphony no.1, 1936
11	Adagio for Strings, 1936 [arr. of 2nd movt of Str Qt]
12	[First] Essay for Orchestra, 1937
14	Violin Concerto, 1939
17	Second Essay, 1942
—	Funeral March, 1943 [based on Army Air Corps Song], unpubd
—	Commando March, band, 1943
19	Symphony no.2, 1944, rev. 1947; 2nd movt rev. as Night Flight, op.19a, 1964
21	Capricorn Concerto, fl, ob, tpt, str, 1944
22	Cello Concerto, 1945
—	Horizon, c1945, unpubd
—	Adventure, fl, cl, hn, hp, 'exotic' insts, 1954, unpubd
36	Toccata festiva, org, orch, 1960
37	Die natali, chorale preludes for Christmas, 1960
38	Piano Concerto, 1962, 2nd movt transcr., fl, pf, 1961
—	Mutations from Bach, brass choir, timp, 1967
44	Fadograph of a Yestern Scene (after J. Joyce: *Finnegans Wake*), 1971
47	Third Essay, 1978
48 posth.	Canzonetta, ob, str, orchd C. Turner, 1977–8

CHORAL

XIII	Christmas Eve: a Trio with Solos, 2 solo vv, SAA, org, c1924, unpubd
8/1–2	The Virgin Martyrs (Siegebert of Gembloux, trans. H. Waddell), SSAA, 1935; Let down the bars, O Death (E. Dickinson), SATB, 1936
—	God's Grandeur (G.M. Hopkins), SATB, 1938, pubd posth.
—	Motetto (Bible: *Job*), 4vv, 8vv, c1938, unpubd
—	Peggy Mitchell (J. Stephens), 4vv, c1939, unpubd
15	A Stopwatch and an Ordnance Map (S. Spender), male vv, 3 kettle-drums, 1940
16	Reincarnations (Stephens), 4vv, 1937–40: Mary Hynes, Anthony O'Daly, The Coolin
—	Ave Maria (after Josquin Des Prez), 4vv, c1940, unpubd
—	Ad 'bibinem' cum me regaret ad cenam (V. Fortunatus), 4vv unacc., 1943
—	Long Live Louise and Sidney Homer, canon, 1944, unpubd
30	Prayers of Kierkegaard (S. Kierkegaard), S, A ad lib, T ad lib, chorus, orch, 1954
—	Under the Willow Tree, 1v, SATB, pf, 1956 [from Vanessa]
—	Heaven-Haven (A Nun Takes the Veil), SATB/SSAA, 1961 [from op.13 no.1]
—	Sure on this shining night, SATB, pf, 1961 [from op.13, no.3]
—	Chorale for Ascension Day (Easter Chroale) (P. Browning), chorus, brass, timp, org ad lib, 1964
11	Agnus Dei, chorus, org/pf, 1967 [arr. of 2nd movt of Str Qt]
—	The Monk and his Cat, SATB, pf, 1967 [from Hermit Songs op.29]
—	Two Choruses: On the Death of Antony, SSA, pf; On the Death of Cleopatra, SATB, pf, 1968 [from Antony and Cleopatra]
42	Twelfth Night (L. Lee), To be Sung on the Water (L. Bogan), 4vv unacc., 1968
43	The Lovers (P. Neruda), Bar, chorus, orch, 1971

CHAMBER

—	Fantasie, 2 pf, 1924, unpubd
XVI	Sonata in Modern Form, 2 pf, c1925, unpubd
1	Serenade, str qt/str orch, 1928
4	Violin Sonata, f, 1928, lost, unpubd
6	Cello Sonata, 1932
11	String Quartet, 1936 [arrs. for str and chorus, org, see op.11, ORCHESTRAL and CHORAL]
—	Commemorative March, vn, vc, pf, unpubd
31	Summer Music, wind qnt, 1955

38a Canzone (Elegy), fl, pf, 1961 [transcr. of 2nd movt of Pf Conc.]

SOLO INSTRUMENTAL

I/3	Melody in F, pf, 1917, unpubd
—	Sadness, pf, 1917, unpubd
I/4	Largo, pf, 1918, unpubd
I/5	War Song, pf, 1918, unpubd
III/1	At Twilight, pf, 1919, unpubd
III/2	Lullaby, pf, 1919, unpubd
X/2	Themes, pf, c1923, movts 2–3 unpubd [movt 1 = Three Sketches no.3]
—	3 Sketches, pf, 1923–4: Love Song (to Mother), To my Steinway (to Number 220601), Minuet (to Sara) [= Themes: movt 1]
—	[Untitled work] ('Laughingly and briskly'), pf, c1924, unpubd
—	Petite berceuse (to Jean), pf, c1924, unpubd
—	Prelude to a Tragic Drama, pf, 1925, unpubd
—	To Longwood Gardens, org, 1925, unpubd
—	Fresh from West Chester (Some Jazzings): Poison Ivy, a Country Dance, 1925; Let's Sit it out, I'd rather watch (I Sam Barber did it with my little hatchet, a walls [sic]), 1926; unpubd
—	3 Essays, pf, 1926, unpubd
—	4 Chorale Preludes, kbd, 1927, unpubd
—	4 Partitas, kbd, 1927, unpubd
—	Prelude and Fugue, b, org, 1927, unpubd
—	Pieces for Carillon: Round, Allegro, Legend, 1930–31, unpubd
—	Suite for Carillon, 4 pieces, 1932
—	2 Interludes (Intermezzi), pf, 1931–2, no.1 pubd posth., no.2 unpubd
20	Excursions, pf, 1942–4
26	Sonata, pf, 1949
34	Wondrous Love, variations on a shape-note hymn, org, 1958
33	Nocturne (Homage to John Field), pf, 1959
—	Variations on Happy Birthday, 1970, unpubd [to Eugene Ormandy]
46	Ballade, pf, 1977

SONGS
1v, pf, unless otherwise stated

—	Sometime (to Mother), Mez, 1917, unpubd
—	Why Not (K. Parsons), 1917, unpubd
II/3	In the Firelight, 1918, unpubd
II/4	Isabel (J.G. Whittier), 1919, unpubd
—	An Old Song (C. Kingsley), 1921, unpubd
—	Hunting Song (J. Bennett), Bar, pf, cornet, c1921, unpubd
V/2	Thy Will be Done (3 verses from The Wanderer), c1921, unpubd
VII	7 Nursery Songs (to Sara), S, 1920–23, unpubd
—	October Weather (Barber), S, c1923, unpubd
—	Dere Two Fella Joe, high v, 1924, unpubd
—	Minuet, S, A, pf, c1924, unpubd
XIV	My Fairyland (R.T. Kerlin), 1924, unpubd
—	Summer is Coming (after A. Tennyson), 2 solo vv, pf, c1924, unpubd
—	2 Poems of the Wind (F. MacCleod), 1924, unpubd: Little Children of the Wind, Longing
—	A Slumber Song of the Madonna (A. Noyes), 1v, org, 1925, pubd in Ten Early Songs, 1v, pf (1995)
—	Fantasy in Purple (L. Hughes), 1925, unpubd
—	Lady when I Behold the Roses (anon.), 1925 unpubd
—	La nuit (A. Meurath), 1925, unpubd
—	2 Songs of Youth, 1925, unpubd: I Never Thought that Youth would Go (J.B. Rittenhouse), Invocation to Youth (L. Binyon)
—	An Earnest Suit to his Unkind Mistress not to Forsake him (Sir T. Wyatt), 1926, unpubd
—	Ask me to Rest (E.H.S. Terry), 1926, unpubd
—	Au clair de la lune, 1926, unpubd
—	Hey Nonny No (Christ Church MS), 1926, unpubd
—	Man (H. Wolfe), 1926, unpubd
—	Music, when soft voices die (P.B. Shelley), c1926, unpubd
—	Thy Love (E. Browning), 1926, unpubd
—	Watchers (D. Cornwell), 1926, unpubd
—	Dance (J. Stephens), 1927, lost, unpubd

—	Mother I cannot mind my wheel (W.S. Landor), 1927, unpubd
—	Only of Thee and Me (L. Untermeyer), c1927, lost, unpubd
—	Rounds, 3vv, pf, 1927, unpubd: A Lament (Shelley); To Electra (R. Herrick); Dirge: Weep for the World's Wrong; Farewell; Not I (R.L. Stevenson); Of a Rose is al myn Song (anon., 1350); Sunset (Stevenson); The Moon (Shelley); Sun of the Sleepless (Byron); The Throstle (Tennyson); When Day is Gone (R. Burns); Late, Late, so Late (Tennyson: *Guinevere*)
—	There's Nae Lark (A. Swinburne), 1927 [pubd in Ten Early Songs (1995)]
2	3 Songs: The Daisies (Stephens), 1927, With Rue my Heart is Laden (A.E. Housman), 1928, Bessie Bobtail (Stephens), 1934
—	The Shepherd to his Love and the Nymph's Reply, 1928, unpubd
3	Dover Beach (M. Arnold), Mez/Bar, str qt, 1931
—	Addio di Orfeo (C. Monteverdi), 1934, arr. 1v, str, hpd, unpubd
—	Love at the Door (from Meleager, trans. J.A. Symonds), 1934 [pubd in Ten Early Songs (1995)]
—	Serenader (G. Dillon), 1934 [pubd in Ten Early Songs (1995)]
—	Love's Caution (W.H. Davies), 1935 [pubd in Ten Early Songs (1995)]
—	Night Wanderers (Davies), 1935 [pubd in Ten Early Songs (1995)]
—	Of that so sweet imprisonment (J. Joyce), 1935 [pubd in Ten Early Songs (1995)]
—	Peace (from Bhartirihari, trans. P.E. More), 1935 unpubd
—	Stopping by Woods on a Snowy Evening (R. Frost), 1935, unpubd
—	Strings in the earth and air (Joyce), 1935 [pubd in Ten Early Songs (1995)]
10	3 Songs (Joyce: *Chamber Music*), 1936, arr. 1v, orch: Rain has fallen, Sleep now, 1935; I hear an army, 1936
—	The Beggar's Song (Davies), 1936 [pubd in Ten Early Songs (1995)]
—	In the dark pinewood (Joyce), 1937 [pubd in Ten Early Songs (1995)]
13	4 Songs: A Nun Takes the Veil (G.M. Hopkins), 1937, arr. SATB/SSAA; The Secrets of the Old (W.B. Yeats), 1938; Sure on this shining night (J. Agee), 1938, arr. 1v, orch, and chorus, pf; Nocturne (F. Prokosch), 1940, arr. 1v, orch
—	Song for a New House (Shakespeare), 1v, fl, pf, 1940, unpubd
—	Between Dark and Dark (K. Chapin), 1942, lost, unpubd
18	2 Songs: The Queen's Face on a Summery Coin (R. Horan), 1942; Monks and Raisins (J.G. Villa), 1943
24	Knoxville: Summer of 1915 (Agee), high v, orch, 1947, unpubd, rev. 1v, chbr orch, 1950
25	Nuvoletta (from Joyce: *Finnegans Wake*), 1947
27	Mélodies passagères (R.M. Rilke), 1950–51: Puisque tout passe, Un cygne, Tombeau dans un parc, Le clocher chante, Départ
29	Hermit Songs (Irish texts of 8th–13th centuries), 1952–3: At Saint Patrick's Purgatory (trans. S. O'Faolain); Church Bells at Night (trans. H. Mumford Jones); Saint Ita's Vision (trans. C. Kallman); The Heavenly Banquet (trans. O'Faolain); The Crucifixion (anon., from *The Speckled Book*, trans. Mumford Jones); Sea-Snatch (trans. W.H. Auden), arr. SATB, pf (1954); Promiscuity (trans. Auden); The Monk and his Cat (trans. Auden); The Praises of God (trans. Auden); The Desire for Hermitage (trans. O'Faolain)
39	Andromache's Farewell (from Euripides: *The Trojan Women*, trans. J.P. Creagh), S, orch, 1962
41	Despite and Still: A Last Song (R. Graves), My Lizard (T. Rilke), In the Wilderness (Graves), Solitary Hotel (from Joyce: *Ulysses*), Despite and Still (Graves), 1968–9
45	3 Songs, 1972: Now have I fed and eaten up the rose (G. Keller, trans. Joyce), A Green Lowland of Pianos (J. Harsymowicz, trans. C. Milosz), O Boundless, Boundless Evening (G. Heym, trans. C. Middleton)

MSS in *US-Wcg*

Principal publisher: G. Schirmer

BIBLIOGRAPHY

A. Copland: 'From the '20's to the '40's and Beyond', *MM*, xx (1942–3), 78–82

R. Horan: 'Samuel Barber', *MM*, xx (1942–3), 161–9

'Barber, Samuel', *CBY 1944*

N. Broder: 'The Music of Samuel Barber', *MQ*, xxxiv (1948), 325–35

H. Dexter: 'Samuel Barber and his Music', *MO*, lxxii (1948–9), 285–7

N. Broder: 'Current Chronicle: New York', *MQ*, xxxvi (1950), 276–82

H. Tischler: 'Barber's Piano Sonata opus 26', *ML*, xxxiii (1952), 352–4

N. Broder: *Samuel Barber* (New York, 1954/*R*)

R. Friedewald: *A Formal and Stylistic Analysis of the Published Music of Samuel Barber* (diss., U. of Iowa, 1957)

C. Turner: 'The Music of Samuel Barber', *ON*, xxii/13 (1957–8), 7, 32–3

'Classified Chronological Catalog of Works by the United States Composer Samuel Barber', *Inter-American Music Bulletin*, no.13 (1959), 22–8

Compositores de América/Composers of the Americas, v (Washington DC, 1959), 14–21 [pubn of the Pan American Union]

L.S. Wathen: *Dissonance Treatment in the Instrumental Music of Samuel Barber* (diss., Northwestern U., 1960)

B. Rands: 'Samuel Barber: a Belief in Tradition', *MO*, lxxxiv (1960–61), 353 only

J. Briggs: 'Samuel Barber', *International Musician*, lx/6 (1961–2), 20–23

'Barber, Samuel', *CBY 1963*

W.A. Dailey: *Techniques of Composition Used in Contemporary Works for Chorus and Orchestra on Religious Texts as Important Representative Works of the Period from 1952 through 1962* (diss., Catholic U. of America, 1965)

E. Salzman: 'Samuel Barber', *Hi Fi/Stereo Review*, xvii/4 (1966), 77–89

J.E. Albertson: *A Study of Stylistic Elements of Samuel Barber's 'Hermit Songs' and Franz Schubert's 'Die Winterreise'* (DMA diss., U. of Missouri, Kansas City, 1969)

R.L. Larsen: *A Study and Comparison of Samuel Barber's 'Vanessa', Robert Ward's 'The Crucible', and Gunther Schuller's 'The Visitation'* (DMA diss., Indiana U., 1971)

L.L. Rhoades: *Theme and Variation in Twentieth-Century Organ Literature: Analyses of Variations by Alain, Barber, Distler, Dupré, Duruflé, and Sowerby* (diss., Ohio State U., 1973)

S.L. Carter: *The Piano Music of Samuel Barber* (diss., Texas Tech U., 1980)

H. Heinsheimer: 'Samuel Barber: Maverick Composer', *Keynote*, iv/1 (1980), 7

H. Gleason and W. Becker: 'Samuel Barber', *20th-Century American Composers*, Music Literature Outlines, iv (Bloomington, IN, rev. 2/1980) [incl. further bibliography]

J. Sifferman: *Samuel Barber's Works for Solo Piano* (DMA diss., U. of Texas, Austin, 1982)

D.A. Hennessee: *Samuel Barber: a Bio-Bibliography* (Westport, CT, 1985)

J.L. Kreiling: *The Songs of Samuel Barber: a Study in Literary Taste and Text-Setting* (diss., U. of North Carolina, 1986)

B.B Heyman: *Samuel Barber: a Documentary Study of his Works* (diss., CUNY, 1989)

B.B Heyman: 'The Second Time Around: Barber's Antony and Cleopatra', *ON*, lvi/6 (1991–2), 56–7

B.B. Heyman: *Samuel Barber: the Composer and his Music* (New York, 1992)

BARBARA B. HEYMAN

Barberá, José (*b* Barcelona, 27 Jan 1876; *d* Barcelona, 19 Feb 1947). Catalan composer and teacher. In 1887 he entered the Barcelona Conservatory, to study the piano, harmony and composition, and later he was a pupil of Pedrell. He gave much of his time to teaching, collaborating in 1919 with María Montessori in studying music educational methods for primary schoolchildren. In his position at the Conservatory, he taught harmony, counterpoint, composition and orchestration, and was director until March 1938. He instructed many notable musicians, and was one of the driving forces behind Catalan musical life.

WORKS
(selective list)

Orch: Sym., a; Sinfonia sintética; Sinfonietta; Alfeu y Aretusa; Claro de luna; Crepúsculo de invierno; Danza fantástica; Els ballaires; Entierro de la bruja; El fumador de opio; Nenia; Paisaje nevado
Choral: Mass, 4vv
Pf pieces; many songs

Principal publisher: Boileau

BIBLIOGRAPHY

T. Marco: *Historia de la música española: siglo XX* (Madrid, 1983; Eng. trans., 1993)

CARLOS GÓMEZ AMAT

Barberiis, Melchiore de (*fl* Padua, *c*1545–50). Italian priest, composer, lutenist and guitarist. He composed or intabulated books 4, 5, 6, 9 and 10 in Girolamo Scotto's ten volume series of lute tablatures (Venice, 1546–9), which also included tablatures by Francesco da Milano, Rotta, Giovanni Maria da Crema and Borrono. Barberiis's name is absent from lists of prominent Paduan musicians of the time, and only two of his pieces were reprinted in later collections. At best, his five books preserve the practical repertory of a 'sonatore eccellentissimo di lautto' who had little or no formal musical training.

Barberiis's ricercares, fantasias and canzonas, some of which are in two or three sections, are usually constructed from a succession of chords (often drawn from madrigals or dances) filled out and linked by ornamental passage work. One fantasia is a simple gloss upon a composition by Francesco da Milano. Book 4 (1546) is dominated by an intabulation of the entire *Missa 'Ave Maria'* of Antoine de Févin with fantasias (called 'ricercari accomodati sopra il tuono di ditta messa' on the title-page) intended to serve as interludes between sections. Books 5 and 6 (1546) contain intabulations of four-part motets by Josquin, Andreas De Silva, Gombert and others of that generation, and intabulations of madrigals and chansons (one by Leo X). Book 9 (1549), dedicated to Torquato Bembo, son of the poet and papal secretary, consists largely of dances – passamezzos, pavans, saltarellos, galliards and pivas, some loosely grouped in suites in which paired dances share similar thematic material. The last book (1549) includes two lute duets and four short pieces for seven-string (four-course) guitar. The latter pieces, euphemistically called 'fantasias', are notable for their popular character; one uses the *bergamasca* and another employs a drone bass. Several 'discordate' fantasias require the tunings $F–B\flat–f–a–d'–g'$, a tuning also used by Dalza, $G–d–g–a–d'–g'$ and $G–c–f–a–e'–a'$. The canzona *Pas de mi bon compagni* from this volume is based on *Passe tyme with good companye* (in *GB-Lbl* Roy.App.58) attributed to Henry VIII, suggesting that this macaronic text was known in Italy, reversing the usual commerce of lute music from Italy outwards. All of the 1546 volumes contain a detailed instruction for tuning the instrument.

WORKS

Intabulatura di lauto, libro quarto, de la messa di Antonio Fevino sopra Ave Maria (Venice, 1546[22])
Intabulatura de lautto, libro quinto, de madrigali et canzon francese (Venice, 1546)
Intabulatura de lautto, libro sesto, di diversi motetti (Venice, 1546[23])
Intabulatura de lauto, libro nono, intitulato Il Bembo (Venice, 1549); 5 dances ed. in Chilesotti (1902)
Opera intitolata contina ... Intabulatura di lauto ... libro decimo (Venice, 1549[39]); incl. 4 fantasias for guitar, ed. in Koczirz (1921)

BIBLIOGRAPHY

BrownI

O. Chilesotti: 'Note circa alcuni liutisti italiani della prima metà del Cinquecento', *RMI*, ix (1902), 36–61, 233–63, esp. 241–5

A. Koczirz: 'Die Fantasien des Melchior de Barberiis für die siebensaitige Gitarre (1549)', *ZMw*, iv (1921–2), 11–17

J. Ward: 'The Lute Music of MS Royal Appendix 58', *JAMS*, xiii (1960), 117–25

H.C. Slim: *The Keyboard Ricercar and Fantasia in Italy, ca. 1500–1550, with Reference to Parallel Forms in European Lute Music of the Same Period* (diss., Harvard U., 1961)

J.A. Echols: *Melchiore de Barberiis's Lute Intabulations of Sacred Music* (diss., U. of North Carolina, 1973)

C. Wolzien: 'Early Guitar Literature', *Soundboard*, xviii (1991), 69–71

ARTHUR J. NESS

Barberini. Italian family of patrons. Of Tuscan origin, the Barberini gained their fortune in Rome beginning with the ecclesiastical career of Maffeo (1568–1644), who became a cardinal in 1606 and then Pope Urban VIII (1623–44). His literary and musical interests must be traced from dedications in musical scores, settings of his poetry, his participation in the Florentine Accademia degli Alterati and his sponsorship of such figures as the castrato Loreto Vittori and the poet Giovanni Ciampoli. In the spirit of humanistic textual criticism, the pope himself undertook the revision of the Latin hymns of the breviary (Rome, 1629), which engendered new, competing musical settings by A.M. Abbatini, Filippo Vitali and Gregorio Allegri, of which the last gained formal approval.

Urban VIII raised two of his nephews to the purple, Francesco (1597–1679) and Antonio (1607–71); a third nephew, Taddeo (1603–47), headed the line of the princes of Palestrina, followed by his son Maffeo (1631–85) and grandson Urbano (1664–1722). They were all active patrons of opera, oratorio and chamber music. The two cardinals sponsored numerous musical activities in their several ecclesiastical capacities, for celebrations at their titular churches and as protectors at various times of the Collegio Romano, Seminario Vaticano, Collegio Germanico, Collegio Inglese and several other institutions. Francesco also served as archpriest of the basilica of S Pietro from 1633 to 1667 and Antonio as archpriest of S Maria Maggiore and protector of the choir of the Cappella Sistina (from 1638). Taddeo not only sponsored operas at home and perhaps one of the first narrative ballets (in 1638), but as general of the papal armies he occasioned operas and other types of musical entertainments wherever he sojourned, most notably in Ferrara. Jules Mazarin's association with Barberini diplomacy and Cardinal Antonio's exile in Paris (1645–53) prompted the export of Italian opera to France, marked especially by Luigi Rossi's *Orfeo* (1647, Paris). These and other members of the family, including later cardinals, nuns and Barberini princesses married into other noble families after 1722, received dedications of musical prints and opera librettos from the 17th century on. Copying Florentine tradition, the Barberini subsidized publication of commemorative scores of their productions of *Sant'Alessio* (Rome, 1634; music by Stefano Landi), *Erminia sul Giordano* (Rome 1637; music by Michelangelo Rossi) and *La Vita humana* (Rome, 1658; music by Marco Marazzoli), all of which included scenographic engravings. What was significant about their patronage of opera in Rome, however, was its establishment as an annual dramatic entertainment for the carnival season, not tied to specific diplomatic or dynastic occasions. Various members of the family supported subscription opera in Rome, once it became established in the late 17th century. Cardinal Francesco the younger (1662–1738), for example, held a box at the Teatro Tordinona in 1690, while his brother Prince Urbano held one at the Capranica and paid one of his regular *aiutanti di camera*, Giovanni Antonio Haym, to play the violin there that season.

The musicians, poets and librettists that the family supported included one future pope, Clement IX (Rospigliosi) and numerous singers, composers and instrumentalists. Singers who joined the households of Cardinals Francesco and Antonio became virtually family members, often entering as young castratos and being retained well past the age for singing. Angelo Ferrotti, who served Francesco from the late 1620s and retired from the Cappella Sistina in 1654, continued to appear on the cardinal's salary lists in the 1660s.

116 volumes of the family's musical holdings were donated to the Vatican library in 1902, consisting largely of collections of secular vocal music of the 17th century and devotional music in Italian, along with some early works for oratorios and books of lessons for the lute, guitar and keyboard used by the Barberini children. 11 anthologies of Roman and Venetian opera arias bear the arms of Prince Urbano. The additional 200 liturgical volumes have been catalogued (see Salmon).

The first Cardinal Francesco expressed academic as well as practical interest in music. Study of the drama and music of antiquity undertaken by G.B. Doni, one of his secretaries, influenced the first operas that Francesco commissioned, beginning in the 1630s, and also led to the reconstruction of Seneca's *Troades* in 1640 with music by Virgilio Mazzocchi (now lost). Francesco also maintained an interest in music of the immediate past, and under Mazzocchi maintained a viol ensemble to perform Italian madrigals. Theoretical treatises, both printed and manuscript, are included in the Barberini collection, including a 14th-century copy of the *Ars nova* of Philippe de Vitry and a manuscript presentation copy for Urban VIII of Doni's *Lyra Barberina amphichordos* (not published until 1763), seven treatises by Pier Francesco Valentini and the *Antiquae musicae auctores septem* (Amsterdam, 1652) of Marcus Meibom.

BIBLIOGRAPHY

G. Tetio: *Aedes Barberinae* (Rome, 1642)

A.F. Gori, ed.: *De' trattati di musica di Gio. Batista Doni* (Florence, 1763)

L. von Pastor: *Geschichte der Päpste seit dem Ausgang des Mittelalters* (Freiburg, 1886–9); Eng. trans. as *History of the Popes* (London, 1923–53), xxix, chap. 6

P. Salmon: *Les manuscrits liturgiques latins de la Bibliothèque Vaticane* (Vatican City, 1968–72)

M. Fumaroli: 'Cicero pontifex romanus: la tradition rhétorique du Collège Romain et les principes inspirateurs de mécénat des Barberini', *Mélanges de l'École Française de Rome*, xc (1978), 797–835

F. Hammond: 'Girolamo Frescobaldi and a Decade of Music at Casa Barberini, 1634–1643', *AnMc*, no.19 (1979), 94–124

M. Murata: *Operas for the Papal Court, 1631–1668* (Ann Arbor, 1981)

M. Murata: 'Classical Tragedy in the History of Early Opera in Rome', *EMH*, iv (1984), 101–34

F. Hammond: 'More on Music in Casa Barberini', *Studi musicali*, xiv (1985), 235–61

V. Kapp: 'Das Barberini-Theater und die Bedeutung der römischen Kultur unter Urban VIII', *Literaturwissenschaftliches Jb*, new ser., xxvi (1985), 75–100

M. Murata: 'Roman Cantata Scores as Traces of Musical Culture and Signs of its Place in Society', *IMSCR XIV: Bologna 1987*, 272–84

F. Hammond: *Music & Spectacle in Baroque Rome: Barberini Patronage under Urban VIII* (New Haven, CT, 1994) [with full bibliography]

MARGARET MURATA

Barber Institute of Fine Arts. Birmingham arts centre opened in 1939, part of the University of Birmingham. *See* BIRMINGHAM, §2.

Barberis, Mansi (Clemansa) (*b* Iaşi, 12 March 1899; *d* Bucharest, 10 Oct 1986). Romanian composer. She studied music intermittently up to the age of 40 in Iaşi, Berlin, Paris and Vienna. She played the violin and the viola in the George Enescu Orchestra, Iaşi (1918–22), the Filarmonica Moldova, Iaşi (1942–4) and the Femina String Quartet, which she founded in 1944. She was also active as a singer, choral conductor and teacher of singing at the conservatories in Iaşi and Bucharest. She came into conflict with the communist authorities for several years and her activities were restricted for a time. She was later rehabilitated and concentrated her energies on the teaching of singing and composition. Her first composition was the song *La lune blanche* (1916, to a poem by Verlaine), and she followed this with over 100 works, including several for orchestra, of which the First Symphony (1941) and the Piano Concerto (1954) were among the most significant.

The post-Romantic style characteristic of her earlier works was maintained throughout her life, but from the late 1950s she moved away from large-scale instrumental forms and towards the theatre. She composed several full-length operas in the last three decades of her career, beginning with *Apus de soare* ('Sunset') in 1958 and including *Domniţa din depărtări* ('The Maiden from Afar'), first performed on Romanian Television in 1970.

WORKS

Stage: Apus de soare [Sunset] (musical drama, 3, G. Teodorescu after Barbu St Delavrancea), 1958, rev. 1968, Bucharest, Opera Română, 30 Dec 1967; Kera Duduca (op, 3, A. Ionescu Arbore), 1963, rev. 1969, Romanian TV, 26 July 1970; Domniţa din depărtări [The Maiden from Afar] (op 3, after E. Rostand), 1971, Iaşi Opera Română, 9 May 1976; Caruta cu paiate [A Cartful of Clowns] (op, 3, A. Ionesco Arbore after M. Stefănescu), 1981, Iaşi, Opera Română, 10 May 1982
Orch: Viziuni, sym. poem, 1934; Suite no.1 'Pastorală' 1937, Sym. no.1, 1941; Pf Conc., 1954

BIBLIOGRAPHY

D. Popovici: 'Mansi Barberis', *Muzica*, xxvi/6 (1976), 22–3
V. Cosma: *Muzicieni din România* (Bucharest, 1989)

OCTAVIAN COSMA

Barbershop. A style of unaccompanied singing that originated in the USA in the late 19th century. It is characterized by four-part harmony using chords that contain tritones. Dominant and diminished 7th chords, as well as half-diminished 7th and augmented 6th chords, are used, but major 7ths, flattened 9ths and chords of the 13th are considered stylistically inappropriate, as are non-chord notes. The melody is carried by the 'lead' (second) tenor, while the first tenor harmonizes above; the bass provides the foundation, and the baritone completes the harmony, frequently crossing above the melody. Chord progressions

known as 'swipes' often compensate for the lack of instrumental accompaniment (ex.1).

Ex.1 Barbershop *swipes* from the song 'Sweet Adeline', (1903, public domain)

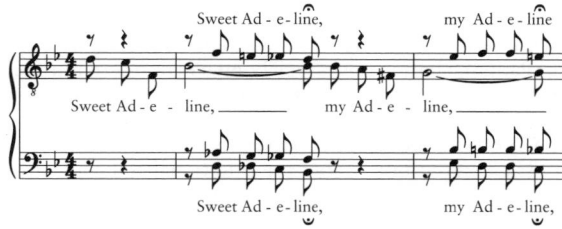

The barbershop quartet movement, which flourished between about 1895 and 1930, was given impetus by the fledgling recording industry. Performances by such professional groups as the Manhansett, Haydn, American and Peerless quartets became widely available and gave rise to the formation of thousands of amateur groups throughout the country during the movement's peak years (1910–25). A fundamental change in the American popular song also contributed to the development of barbershop harmony. Many tunes in the earlier decades of the 19th century were constructed around the tonic octave of the scale, but by about 1895 melodies with a dominant-to-dominant range had evolved. This meant that the bass part was less likely to double low melody notes, and it also allowed the upper tenor part to flow in a smooth line above the lead, mostly in 3rds and 6ths. The words of barbershop songs speak of commonplace ideas: home, spouse, children, love (both joyful and sad) and fond memories of earlier times. Interpretative liberties are taken in performance using rubato, and extended song endings known as tags are also used.

By the late 1920s and early 1930s the increasing popularity of jazz, sound films, records, cars and radio had led to a decline in the number of active quartets. In 1938, however, the Society for the Preservation and Encouragement of Barber Shop Quartet Singing in America was founded. By the end of the 20th century there were affiliated clubs with quartets and choruses in Britain, Scandinavia, Europe, Australia, New Zealand and South Africa. Two organizations for women barbershop singers, Harmony Incorporated and Sweet Adelines, were also formed, both with affiliated societies overseas. From the 1940s on, barbershop harmony was sung either by male or by female quartets and choruses, but in the later 20th century mixed-voice groups gained increasing popularity.

BIBLIOGRAPHY

J.W. Johnson: 'The Origin of the "Barber Chord"', *The Mentor*, xvii/1 (1929), 53
S. Spaeth: *Barbershop Ballads* (Englewood Cliffs, NJ, 1940)
D.K. Antrim: 'The Barbershop Brotherhood', *The Etude*, lxxii/11 (1954), 11
D. Martin: 'Three Eras of Barbershop Harmony', *The Harmonizer*, xv/2 (1955), 20
J.L. McClelland: *Of, By, and For the People: a History of Barbershop Harmony* (thesis, College of Wooster, PA, 1959)
D. Martin: 'The Evolution of Barbershop Harmony', *Music Journal Annual* (1965), 40
V. Hicks, ed.: *Heritage of Harmony* (Kenosha, WI, 1988)

V. HICKS

Barbetta, Giulio Cesare (*b* ?Padua *c*1540; *d* after 1603). Italian lutenist and composer. Title-pages of his publications refer to him as 'Padoano'. Padua was one of the centres of lute building and teaching. Barbetta's surviving lute books are among the most important Italian sources for the old six-course ('second l'uso antico') and new seven-course lute. The dedications of some of his publications to German aristocrats suggests connections with Germany (through German students at the University of Padua). His music was well known in northern Europe: ten gagliardas and two of the passamezzos from his first book (1569) were reprinted in *Theatrum musicum* (RISM 1571[16]) without attribution to Barbetta.

His compositions show the traditional Italian preference for lute fantasias, dance forms of all kinds and vocal intabulations. The first book of intabulations contains only pieces for solo lute: paduanas, gagliardas, passamezzos and fantasias. His 1582 book was issued in two versions, one with a Latin title and German text and another with Italian title and text. The collection contains original lute pieces (preambles, fantasies, dances) and intabulations of vocal works – madrigals and motets by Janequin, Wert, Lassus and Mouton. The *Intavolatura* of 1585 consists entirely of instrumental compositions for solo lute with the exception of six *Arie* – formulae to be used for singing 'Stanze e versi d'ogni sorte, secondo l'uso di Venetia'. The latter are similar to those in the Bottegari Lutebook. In addition to the traditional paduanas and gagliardas, three new dance types are added: the *moresca*, balletto and saltarello 'to be danced *à la gagliarda* in modern style'. Each of the 'Baletti di diverse nationi' has a title, *Baletto Francese*, *Baletto Polaco*, and so on. They are thematically related to the gagliardas.

Barbetta's final volume, printed in 1603, reflects the contemporary vogue for canzonettas, villanellas and *napolitane* for voice with lute accompaniment.

WORKS

Il primo libro dell' intavolatura de liuto (Venice, 1569); 8 pieces ed.
 O. Chilesotti: *Lautenspieler des 16. Jahrhunderts* (Leipzig, 1891/*R*)
Libro secondo, intavolatura de liuto (Venice, 1575), lost
Novae tabulae musicae testudinariae hexachordae et heptachordae (Strasbourg, 1582) [also issued as Il terctio libro de intavolatura de liuto (Strasbourg, 1582/*R*)]
Intavolatura di liuto … si contiene padoane, arie, baletti, pass'e mezi, saltarelli per ballar à la Italiana (Venice, 1585)
Intavolature di liuto delle canzonette, 1v, lute (Venice, 1603)

BIBLIOGRAPHY

T. Zacco: *Cenni biografici di illustri scrittori e compositori di musica padovani* (Padua, 1850)
O. Chilesotti: *Note circa alcuni liustisti italiani della prima metà del Cinquecento* (Turin, 1902)
W. Boetticher: *Studien zur solistischen Lautenpraxis des 16. und 17. Jahrhunderts* (Berlin, 1943)
E. Pohlmann: *Laute, Theorbe, Chitarrone: die Instrumente, ihre Musik und Literatur von 1500 bis zur Gegenwart* (Bremen, 1968, enlarged 5/1982)

CAROL MacCLINTOCK/DINKO FABRIS

Barbey [Barbay, Barbet], **Guillaume** (*fl* Paris, *c*1716–42). French string instrument maker. He was particularly well known as a maker of viols and his instruments are highly valued as examples of French craftsmanship. The viol virtuoso Marin Marais is known to have owned an instrument by him. A lengthy description of his talent and skill survives in the correspondence of Jean-Baptiste Forqueray (1699–1782). Writing in 1767 or 1768, approximately 25 years after Barbey's death, Forqueray praised him as 'the greatest builder we had for the shape, thickness and correct dimensions' of the viol, and also commended his choice of English wood. Forqueray stated

that his father, Antoine, had owned two instruments by Barbey, one for solo playing and the other for accompaniment; he played them for 25 years until his death in 1745, when the younger Forqueray took them over and praised their continuing improvement with age.

At least four bass viols by Barbey survive, all dating from about 1720, two with seven strings and two with six. A six-string pardessus de viole of 1742 is in the Paris Conservatoire.

Another Barbey (first name unknown) was active as a string instrument maker in the second half of the 18th century and may have been Guillaume Barbey's son.

BIBLIOGRAPHY

VannesE
F. Lesure: 'Marin Marais: sa carrière – sa famille', *RBM*, vii (1953), 129–36
F. Lesure: 'Une querelle sur le jeu de la viole en 1688: J. Rousseau contre Demachy', *RdM*, xlvi (1960), 181–99
Y. Gérard: 'Notes sur la fabrication de la viole de gambe et la manière d'en jouer, d'après une correspondance inédite de Jean-Baptiste Forqueray au Prince Frédéric-Guillaume de Prusse', *RMFC*, ii (1961–2), 165–72
H. Bol: *La basse de viole du temps de Marin Marais et d'Antoine Forqueray* (Bilthoven, 1973)
J. Rutledge: 'A Letter of J.B.A. Forqueray', *JVdGSA*, xiii (1976), 12–16
P. Tourin: *Viol List: a Comprehensive Catalogue of Historical Viole da Gamba in Public and Private Collections* (Duxbury, 1979)

MARY CYR

Barbier, Jane (? *b* London, bap. 8 Dec 1695; *d* London, will proved 9 Dec 1757). English contralto. She first appeared in *Almahide* (November 1711) and the *Spectator* commented on her becoming shyness and her 'agreeable Voice, and just Performance'. She had three seasons with the Italian opera, generally taking male roles, singing in Handel's *Rinaldo*, *Il pastor fido* and *Teseo*. She was Telemachus in Galliard's *Calypso and Telemachus*, which had an English libretto by John Hughes, whose poem *The Hue and Cry* described her dark good looks and headstrong nature. She appeared in masques by Pepusch, usually as the heroine, with Margherita de L'Epine as the hero, and from 1717 she sang with John Rich's company in musical afterpieces, pantomimes and English operas. After appearing in Dublin in the winter of 1731–2, she was in two new operas by J.C. Smith and played King Henry in Arne's *Rosamond*. Her career petered out after this; in 1737 the *Gentleman's Magazine* reported the death of 'Mrs Barbier, formerly a Noted Singer in the Opera's', but she sang twice in December 1740, when she was hissed.

BIBLIOGRAPHY

BDA; *BurneyH*; *FiskeETM*; *HawkinsH*; *LS*
W. Dean and J. Knapp: *Handel's Operas 1704–1726* (Oxford, 1987)
B. Boydell: *A Dublin Musical Calender 1700–1760* (Dublin, 1988)

OLIVE BALDWIN, THELMA WILSON

Barbier, René (Auguste Ernest) (*b* Namur, 12 July 1890; *d* Brussels, 24 Dec 1981). Belgian composer and conductor. He studied at the conservatories of Brussels (with Gilson) and Liège (with Sylvain Dupuis) and won the Belgian Prix de Rome with the cantata *La légende de Béatrice* in 1920. A professor of harmony at Liège (1920–49) and Brussels (1949–55), he also directed the Namur Conservatory (1923–55). In 1968 he was elected to the Belgian Royal Academy. He was prepared to tackle any genre, but had a preference for orchestral music, often of a descriptive character. His music is notable for the richness of its orchestration, recalling Dukas and Wagner.

WORKS
(selective list)

Stage: Yvette (comédie lyrique, 2 tableaux, E. Grésini), op.1, 1910, Namur, Royal, 4 Jan 1912; La fête du vieux tilleul (conte lyrique, 2), op.3, 1912, Namur, July, 1913; Les pierres magiques (ballet), op.94, 1957; incid music

Orch: Pièce concertante, op.95, vn/sax, orch, 1959; Gui Conc., op.98, 1960; 3 mouvements symphoniques, op.104, str, 1962; Tableau symphonique, op.105, 1963; Hn Conc., op.106, 1964; Concertino, op.109, ww qt, str, 1964; Sinfonietta, op.111, chbr orch, 1966; Introduction et allegro symphonique, op.112, 1967; Conc., op.113, org, str, timp, 1967; Concertino, op.116, 2 gui, str, 1971; other concertante pieces, 6 sym. poems

Choral: La tour de Babel (orat, M. Henrion), op.39, 1933; Lamentation de la neuvième heure (orat), op.100, 1961; 2 masses, motets

Chbr: Sonata, op.12, hn/va, pf, 1916; Poème, op.14, vc, pf, 1916; Str Qt, op.65, 1939; Hn Qt, op.93, 1956; Sax Qt, op.99, 1961; Divertissement, 4 cl, op.101, 1962; 2 suites, opp.110 and 115, 2 gui, 1965, 1969; Trio, op.117, fl, vc, pf, 1971; Prélude and Barcarolle, op.118, gui, 1973

Pf and org music, songs

Principal publishers: Bosworth (Brussels), CeBeDeM, Metropolis, Schott (Brussels)

MSS in *B-Bcdm*

BIBLIOGRAPHY
CeBeDeM directory
S. Vouillemin: 'Notice sur René Barbier', *Annuaire de l'Académie royale de Belgique*, cxlix (1984), 231–41

HENRI VANHULST

Barbieri, Antonio (*b* Reggio nell'Emilia; *fl* 1720–43). Italian tenor. From 1720 to 1731 (at least) he was in the service of the Landgrave of Hesse-Darmstadt, governor of Mantua, where he made his earliest known appearance, in the première of Vivaldi's *Candace* (1720). The composer seems then to have engaged him for Venice, where he sang in 23 operas from 1720 to 1738. He became well known throughout Italy, appearing in Reggio (1720), Rome (from 1724), Parma and Florence (both 1725 and 1734–5), Naples (1727–9) and Turin (1739–40). In 1731 he sang at Pavia in Vivaldi's *Farnace* alongside his wife, Livia Bassi Barbieri, who also performed at Venice and Florence, 1734–5; it is not known whether he was related to the contralto Santi Barbieri, who appeared in eight operas at Florence from 1730 to 1743. Later he was *maestro di maniera* at the Ospedale dei Mendicanti, Venice, from 1736 until (apparently) 1767 and at the Derelitti, 1741–3.

COLIN TIMMS

Barbieri [de Barbieri], Carlo Emanuele (*b* Genoa, 22 Oct 1822; *d* Pest, 28 Sept 1867). Italian conductor and composer. He received his musical training at the Naples Conservatory, studying singing with Crescentini and composition with Mercadante. Although he wrote operas and vaudevilles and some sacred music, he was known principally as a theatre conductor in central and northern Europe. From 1844 he conducted at the Carltheater in Vienna for two years, also serving as vocal coach at the Kärntnertortheater and composing music for several vaudevilles and pantomimes. He travelled extensively as an opera conductor: to Berlin, for the Königstädtisches Theater, in 1847–8, Dresden in 1849, Hamburg in 1850, Bremen in 1853, and Rio de Janeiro in 1854. From 1856 to 1862 he lived in Vienna, conducting in various Austrian cities, and from 1862 to 1867 he was conductor at the National Theatre in Buda. Barbieri's most important

opera, *Perdita* (1865), is a free adaptation of Shakespeare's *The Winter's Tale*. Its musical structure is continuous (without separable numbers) in the Wagnerian manner but the music itself is old-fashioned: for example, the large orchestra usually accompanies or doubles the voices. The overture is a potpourri of tunes from the opera and the mostly diatonic melodies are frequently in lilting 6/8. The choruses are simple and squarely homophonic.

WORKS
for full list of 16 operas see GroveO (M. Tartak)

La casa dei matti (op, 2), Vienna, Kärntnertor, 16 Sept 1843

Finette, das Gärtnermädchen, oder Mit dem Feuer spielen ist gefährlich (vaudeville, 3, I.F. Castelli, after E. Scribe), Vienna, An der Wien, 15 Feb 1845

Cristoforo Colombo (op, 4, F. Romani), Berlin, Königstädtisches, 20 Dec 1848

Arabella (op, 3, A. de Lauzières), Turin, Angennes, 20 May 1857

Perdita, oder Ein Wintermärchen (op, 4, K. Gross, after W. Shakespeare: *The Winter's Tale*), Prague, Deutsches Theater, 11 Jan 1865

Die Federschlange (operetta, 1, F. Zell), Pest, Deutsches, 16 Feb 1867

10 other operas
Choral works

BIBLIOGRAPHY
DBI (A. Pironti); *GroveO* (M. Tartak) [incl. complete list of operas]

MARVIN TARTAK

Barbieri, Fedora (*b* Trieste, 4 June 1920). Italian mezzo-soprano. She studied at Trieste with Luigi Toffolo and at the school of the Teatro Comunale, Florence, with Giulia Tess. She made her début at Florence in 1940 as Fidalma in Cimarosa's *Il matrimonio segreto*. In 1941 she created Dariola in Alfano's *Don Juan de Mañara* at the Florence Maggio Musicale, and also appeared in Monteverdi revivals. She sang regularly at La Scala from 1942, and at the Metropolitan from 1950 until the 1970s, making her début there as Eboli in *Don Carlos* on the opening night of Sir Rudolf Bing's régime. She first visited England with the Scala company in 1950 when she was heard as Mistress Quickly and in Verdi's Requiem; she returned to Covent Garden in 1957–8 and in 1964. She later appeared in a number of comprimario roles, singing until she was well into her sixties. Her voice, of fine quality and considerable power, was well suited to the dramatic mezzo-soprano parts of Verdi and also capable of majestic calm in the works of Monteverdi, Pergolesi and Gluck. Among many recorded roles, Amneris, Ulrica, Azucena and Mistress Quickly represent her at her appreciate best.

BIBLIOGRAPHY
GV (E. Gara; R. Vegeto)
A. Natan: 'Barbieri, Fedora', *Primadonna: Lob der Stimmen* (Basle, 1962) [incl. LP discography]

DESMOND SHAWE-TAYLOR/ALAN BLYTHE

Barbieri, Francisco Asenjo (*b* Madrid, 3 Aug 1823; *d* Madrid, 17 Feb 1894). Spanish composer, musicologist, conductor and critic. Barbieri's father died in 1823 and the composer used his matronym throughout his life although, in the heated polemic wars of the period, that was sometimes held against him as an Italianate pretence.

1. Life and works. 2. Style.

1. LIFE AND WORKS. Barbieri received his early music training from his maternal grandfather and entered the fledgling Royal Conservatory in 1837, studying the clarinet with Ramón Broca, the piano with Albéniz y Basanta, singing with Saldoni and composition with Carnicer. In 1841 his family moved to Lucena, but

Barbieri remained in Madrid, eking out a living as a clarinettist, pianist, teacher and copyist. His earliest compositions were songs and dances, and a paso doble for a militia band in which he played. He also sang baritone roles in Italian operas at the Conservatory and the Teatro del Circo. He wrote the libretto for a one-act zarzuela but did not complete the music in time for its scheduled première in February 1843. Later that year he was hired as chorus master and prompter by a touring company performing Italian opera and the following year he served as director of a similar company. In April 1845 Barbieri became *maestro de música* at the school of San Eloy in Salamanca and director of the Liceo Salmantino. A manuscript volume of his orchestrations from this period contains his earliest surviving compositions, an orchestral *Introducción y gran vals* and the *Himno a la música* for soloists, chorus and orchestra. He returned to Madrid in July 1846, and in the following year completed a three-act opera buffa, only excerpts of which were performed. He joined a group of progressive musicians agitating for a national opera under the name La España Musical and in the following year joined the Madrid Liceo, for which he sang and composed. He began writing music reviews for *La ilustración* in 1849 and worked as a prompter in Italian operas at the royal palace.

Although his first zarzuela to reach the stage, *Gloria y peluca*, had been completed the previous summer, it opened behind schedule on 9 March 1850, on a typically mixed bill at the Teatro de Variedades. It was a great critical and popular triumph, as was ¡*Tramoya*! in June. These successes secured Barbieri a place as one of the seven founding directors and shareholders of a new company formed in June 1851 to present zarzuelas at the Teatro del Circo. The new society's struggling first season was rescued when Barbieri's *Jugar con fuego* opened in October: the first zarzuela in three acts, it both saved the new theatre company and defined the future path of the genre. Generally the aristocracy had scorned native music theatre, preferring Italian opera, but so great was the popularity of *Jugar con fuego* that the queen mother, María Cristina, asked Barbieri to compose a group of rigadones on its themes for a palace ball. In 1856 the company launched a semi-official house paper, *La zarzuela*, which led its opening issues with an erudite yet skilfully polemical two-part article by Barbieri, defending the genre. Distressed by the excessive rent required for the dilapidated Circo, that year the company also purchased land and built the Teatro de la Zarzuela. It opened on 10 October with a mixed bill that included a large one-movement sinfonía composed by Barbieri on themes from the most popular zarzuelas of the time. In 1859 Barbieri initiated a concert series, featuring a large chorus and orchestra, held at the Teatro de la Zarzuela on the six Fridays of Lent. Nothing like this had been done in recent Spanish history and the concerts were artistic and financial successes. Nonetheless, the personal bickering and none-too-scrupulous insider dealing of the company had become too much for Barbieri and in the December of that year he sold his share to the composer Gaztambide and the baritone Francisco Salas, the only remaining partners of the original seven.

The following decade was dominated by the première of *Pan y toros*, one of the pinnacles of Spanish music theatre, in December 1864. That summer Barbieri became the artistic director of the Campos Eliseos, presenting Madrid's first open-air concerts in the gardens and a season of Italian and French opera in the new theatre there. In 1866 he organized his own orchestral concerts, conducting the first performances of a complete Beethoven symphony in Spain and establishing the durable and influential Sociedad de Conciertos. His only full season as conductor at the Teatro Real was that of 1869–70. Barbieri proved able to ride the ever-changing tides of theatre fashions in Madrid contributing another monument of the zarzuela, *El barberillo de Lavapiés* in 1874. He also composed the most artistically compelling works for the Bufos Madrileños, instituted by Francisco Arderius in imitation of the Parisian model, and for the *género chico* repertory. He continued composing until his death, with his last great success being *El Sr. Luis el tumbón* in 1891. A life-long book collector with a solid classical education, Barbieri published numerous scholarly papers on music and literature, culminating in the groundbreaking *Cancionero musical de los siglos XV y XVI* (1890). His artistic and scholarly honours were legion, including being the first musician seated in the Real Academia Española. The materials he bequeathed the Biblioteca Nacional form the foundation of its music holdings: after his name in the index of the published catalogue is the single word 'passim'.

2. STYLE. The range of Barbieri's scholarly curiosity is apparent in his music. He knew the music of Wagner, Verdi and Gounod intimately, to name only his leading foreign contemporaries in dramatic music, and it was he who established German symphonic compositions in Spain. But more than any other composer of his generation, he was critically and popularly identified with Spanish traditional and ethnic music, and where his harmonic usage differed significantly from that of his coevals in other countries was in the influence of that music. His chord progressions often suggest modality rather than tonal practice, with modulations commonly to 3rd-related keys and often accomplished by a single common tone rather than secondary dominants. He frequently raises or lowers the basic tonal level by a step and changes to minor mode, particularly in switching to the minor subdominant. Harmonic dissonance was usually functional for Barbieri, while melodic dissonance was used for colour. Special compositional techniques or unusual instrumentation were inevitably inspired by the dramatic situation, although occasionally he used imitative counterpoint simply for modulation. Barbieri was a master of combining seemingly disparate melodies to stunning dramatic effect. A justly famous example of this is in Act II of *Pan y toros* (1864), where the five principal protagonists sing a poignant prayer outside the palace of one of the villains, where a dance is taking place. The instrumental gavotte from the palace combines with the vocal supplication outside, and the union of these opposed elements strengthens both dramatically and musically.

His scoring employs important solo obbligatos and cadenzas for many instruments, as well as a predictably wide range of percussion instruments. It is most distinctive, however, in its use of onstage ensembles. Barbieri began his career as a chorister and chorus master, and he made greater and more effective use of the chorus than any other zarzuela composer, ranging from the convincingly antiquarian four-part Pavana of *Juan de Urbina* (1876) to the Seguidillas of *El secreto de una dama* (1862), in which the men's voices imitate the sound of a plucked guitar while the women hum, all accompanying a tenor solo. Whenever resources and libretto permitted, Barbieri used *rondallas* (a traditional group of strolling musicians), consisting of *bandurrias* and guitars in various sizes, onstage throughout his career. He also pioneered the use of actual military bands onstage, some quite large.

For his contemporaries, the use of characteristically Spanish materials was a distinguishing feature of Barbieri's work. His repertory is filled with examples of boleros, *caleseras*, fandangos, habaneras, *jácaras*, *jaleos*, *jotas*, *muñeiras*, paso dobles, seguidillas, sevillanas, tangos, tiranas, villancicos, *vitos* and *zapateados*. Occasionally, motivated by a reference in the libretto, Barbieri might quote traditional thematic material but more often it was the distilled essence of the form that he presented. So definitive was his handling of traditional materials that a piece such as 'Te levaré a Puerto Rico' could be lifted virtually intact from *El hombre es débil* (1871) and reappear, in instrumental form and uncredited, as Sarasate's *Habanera*, op.21 no.2.

In most of his small-scale construction Barbieri relied on stringent, folkloric economy of materials: the repetition, ornamentation, development and expansion of the simplest basic motifs. This can be clearly heard in perhaps his most famous single number, Paloma's now oft-recorded canción from *El barberillo de Lavapié* (1874), but it is also quite apparent in more ostensibly 'art' music, such as the romanza 'Un tiempo fue' from *Jugar con fuego* (1851). In broad outline, Barbieri's ensemble numbers generally begin with an expository section, moving to a cantabile centre and ending with a dramatically important cabaletta. His largest ensemble structures are second-act finales, the point of dramatic crisis in his three-act zarzuelas. The greatest of these is undoubtedly also the most unusual, the second-act finale of *Pan y toros*. Although the structure is much larger than usual and the conflict is a serious political struggle rather than the usual lover's tiff, in gross form and character it seems to conform to Barbieri's conventions. But the exultant cabaletta, with its soaring vocal roulades, does not bring down the curtain; instead, a tense melodrama with the shocking onstage murder of the Santero follows, with the orchestra defining the psychology of the scene through a seething swirl of leitmotifs.

All of Barbieri's theatre works, even the slightest *género chico* pieces, are tightly organized harmonically and motivically, and this organization invariably reflects and enhances the drama. In *Chorizos y polacos* (1876) for example, the feuding theatre claques and the levels of the play-within-a-play action are defined by symmetrical, contrasting blocks of sharp and flat keys. *El barberillo de Lavapiés* is another meticulously planned zarzuela, harmonically closed in G major but with a marked katabasis at the centre of the work. In it, however, motivic relationships, play a more prominent part in unifying the work musically, and in characterization. Barbieri also changes identifying motifs to reflect changes in character, such as the Santero in *Pan y toros*. A hypocritical character, the Santero's identifying music is always at harmonic odds with its musical surroundings, and as the character breaks down, the motif also dissolves into barely coherent stammering.

Barbieri's music has survived both mythologizing adulation and dismissive condescension. In an era when the boundaries between classical and vernacular, national and international art are not as fiercely guarded as they were, the flexible music theatre synthesis that is the zarzuela has found new respect. New editions of Barbieri's writing and music appear regularly, as do fresh productions and recordings, revealing a rare genius for dramatic music of great formal sophistication and emotional immediacy.

WORKS
(selective list)

ZARZUELAS
all first performed and published in Madrid; complete lists in Henken and Casares Rodicio; see also GroveO

Gloria y peluca (1, Villa del Valle), Variedades, 9 March 1850, vs (?1850)

¡Tramoya! (1, J. Olona), Supernumario de la Comedia, 27 June 1850; vs (1850)

Jugar con fuego (3, V. de la Vega), Circo, 6 Oct 1851; vs (?1851), fs ed. E. Cortizo, *MH*, lxiv (1992)

Los diamantes de la corona (3, F. Camprodón, after Scribe), Circo, 15 Sept 1854; vs (?1854)

Los dos ciegos (1, L. Olona), Circo, 25 Oct 1855; vs (?1856)

El vizconde (1, Camprodón), Circo, 1 Dec 1855; vs (?1856)

Un caballero particular (1, Frontaura), Zarzuela, 28 June 1858; vs (?1860)

El niño (1, Pina), Zarzuela, 15 June 1859; vs (?1859)

Entre mi mujer y el negro (2, Olona), Zarzuela, 14 Oct 1859; vs (?1870)

El secreto de una dama (3, L. Rivera), Zarzuela, 20 Dec 1862; vs (?1870)

Pan y toros (3, Picón), Zarzuela, 22 Dec 1864; vs (?1864)

Robinsón Crusoe (3, García Santisteban), Circo, 18 March 1870; vs (?1870)

El hombre es débil (1, Pina), Zarzuela, 14 Oct 1871; vs (?1871)

El tributo de las cien doncellas (3, García Santisteban), Zarzuela, 7 Nov 1872; vs (?1880)

El barberillo de Lavapiés (3, Larra), Zarzuela, 19 Dec 1874; vs (?1874); fs ed. E. Cortizo and R. Sobrino, *MH*, lvii (1994) excerpts, arr. band (1953)

Chorizos y polacos (3, Larra), Circo del Príncipe Alfonso, 24 May 1876; vs (?1876)

Juan de Urbina (3, Larra), Zarzuela, 6 Oct 1876; vs (?1876)

El loro y la lechuza (1, M. Fernández), Español, 23 Dec 1877; vs (?1877)

Los chichones (1, Pina), Comedia, 23 Dec 1879; vs (?1879)

De Getafe al paraíso (2, R. de la Vega), Variedades, 5 Jan 1883; vs (1883)

El Sr. Luis el tumbón (1, R. de la Vega), Apolo, 6 May 1891; vs (?1891)

Contribs. to collaborative zars with Chueca, Gaztambide, Hernando, Inzenga and Oudrid

OTHER WORKS

Vocal: Himno a la música, 5vv, orch, 1845; La jota del Regateo, chorus, band, 1861; La despidida, B, orch, 1874; ¡Visca la pau!, cant., male vv, orch, 1876; Salve Valenciana, solo vv, 4vv, orch, 1882; 3 choral motets; 10 songs

Inst: Pasodoble, band, ?1842; Introdución y gran vals, orch, 1845; Fantasía con variaciones, cornet, orch, 1848; Tarantela, orch, 1848; Ovt, orch, 1848; Sinfonía sobre motivos de zarzs, orch, 1856 (Madrid, 1873); Marcha triunful, band, 1866 (Madrid, ?1866); Marcha funebre, band, 1884; numerous dances for orch and pf

WRITINGS

'Lope de Vega, músico, y algunos músicos españoles de su tiempo', *La gaceta musical barcelonesa*, iii (1863), no.118, p.6; iv (1864), nos.119–29

Contestación al Maestro D. Rafael Hernando (Madrid, 1864)

La música y la mujer: conferencia leída [el] 25 de abril de 1869 (Madrid, 1869)

'Estudio bibliografáfico musical', *Revista de España*, xix (1871), 351–60

ed.: A. Eximeno: *Don Lazarillo Vizcardi* (Madrid, 1872)

La unión de las bellas artes: discurso leído en la Academia de bellas artes de San Fernando . . . para solemnizar la agregación de la sección de música (Madrid, 1874)

Últimos amores de Lope de Vega Carpio (Madrid, 1876)

'Danzas y bailes en España en los siglos XVI y XVII', *La ilustración española y americana*, xxi (1877), nos.44–5, suppl.

El Teatro real y el Teatro de la zarzuela (Madrid, 1877)

Las castañuelas (Madrid, 1878, 2/1879/R)

'Más sobre las danzas y bailes en España en los siglos XVI y XVII', *La ilustración española y americana*, xxii (1878), nos.13–14, suppl.

Preface to L. Carmena y Millan: *Crónica de la ópera italiana en Madrid desde el año 1738 hasta nuestros días* (Madrid, 1878)

El Canto de Ultreja (Madrid, 1883)

'Don Félix Máximo López', *Boletín de la Real Academia de Bellas Artes de San Fernando*, v (1885), 395–408

La zarzuela: carta á D. Pascual Millán (Madrid, 1887)

La música religiosa: discurso leído en la sesión séptima de congreso católico nacional el día 2 de mayo de 1889 (Madrid, 1889)

ed.: *Cancionero musical de los siglos XV y XVI* (Madrid, 1890/R1987 with commentary and inventory by E. Casares Rodicio)

La música de la lengua castellana: discursos leídos ante la Real Academia española en la recepción pública del excmo. Sr. d. F.A.B. el día 13 de marzo de 1892 (Madrid, 1892)

La Zarzuela (Madrid, 1985) [anthology of facsimiles]

E. Casares Rodicio, ed.: *Francisco Asenjo Barbieri: Biografías y documentos sobre música y músicos españoles* (Madrid, 1986)

E. Casares Rodicio, ed.: *Francisco Asenjo Barbieri: Documentos sobre música española y epistolario* (Madrid, 1988)

E. Casares Rodicio, ed.: *Francisco Asenjo Barbieri: Escritos* (Madrid, n.d.)

BIBLIOGRAPHY

A. Peña y Goñi: *La ópera española y la música dramática en el siglo XIX* (Madrid, 1881), 407ff, 529ff; (rev., abridged, 1967 as *España desde la ópera a la zarzuela*)

L. Carmena y Millán: 'Barbieri: en el 5.° aniversario de su muerte', *Cosas del pasado: música, literatura y tauromaquia* (Madrid, 1904), 65 [contains list of writings]

A.S. Salcedo: *Francisco Asenjo Barbieri: su vida y sus obras* (Madrid, 1912/R)

E. Cotarelo y Mori: *Historia de la zarzuela* (Madrid, 1934)

A. Martínez Olmedilla: *El maestro Barbieri y su tiempo* (Madrid, 1941)

J. Subirá: 'Barbieri ante la novísima sección musical de la Academia', *Academia* (1971), 11–48

X. Aviñoa: *El barberillo de Lavapiés: Francisco Asenjo Barbieri, estudio y comentarios* (Barcelona, 1985)

J. López-Calo: 'Barbieri y la Historiografía de la Música Española', *Biografías y documentos sobre música y músicos españoles* (Madrid, 1986), xxi–xxviii

R. Stevenson: 'Francisco Asenjo Barbieri', *Biografías y documentos sobre música y músicos españoles* (Madrid, 1986), vii–xix

J.E. Henken: *Francisco Asenjo Barbieri and the Nineteenth-Century Revival in Spanish National Music* (diss., UCLA, 1987)

R. Sobrino: *El sinfonismo español en el siglo XIX: la sociedad de conciertos de Madrid* (diss., U. of Oviedo, 1992)

M. Encina Cortizo: *La restauración de la zarzuela en el Madrid del XIX* (diss., UCM, 1993)

E. Casares Rodicio: *Francisco Asenjo Barbieri: El hombre y el creador* (Madrid, c1994)

M. Encina Cortizo and R. Sobrino: '*El barberillo de Lavapiés*, cumbre de la zarzuela grande', *El barberillo de Lavapiés*, Auvidis Valois V 4731 (1994) [disc notes]

C. Gómez Amat: 'Letra y música de Madrid', *El barberillo de Lavapiés*, Auvidis Valois V 4731 (1994) [disc notes]

JOHN EDWIN HENKEN

Barbieri, Lucio [Luzio] (*b* Bologna, 24 July 1586; *d* Bologna, mid-Nov 1659). Italian composer, organist and teacher. He was organist at S Giacomo Maggiore, Bologna, where he presumably received his musical training, when, on 6 October 1610, he was appointed organist at Bologna Cathedral, succeeding Manfredi Miglioli. Adriano Banchieri had declined the post. While working at the cathedral he also deputized from April 1612 for the ailing G.B. Mecchi at the second organ of S Petronio. On 16 December 1613, after Mecchi's death, he resigned from the cathedral and took up the S Petronio post permanently, drawing a monthly salary of 17 lire

until November 1649, when he was appointed first organist and received 21 lire. On 26 February 1646, when he had been blind for several years, his salary increased to 30 lire and he obtained P.M. Alessandri as a deputy; on 6 September 1658 Alessandri was replaced by G.P. Colonna, who succeeded Barbieri after his death. In about 1654 Barbieri wrote a petition (now in *I-Bsp*) to the S Petronio authorities to restore a room there to be used for teaching.

Barbieri was known as a teacher of organ and composition; among his pupils was Pietro Paolo Banchieri, Adriano Banchieri's nephew, who in the dedication of his uncle's *La cartellina musicale* described Barbieri as 'virtuosissimo mio maestro in canto figurato e suono dell'organo'. His principal extant work, *Il primo libro de motetti* (Venice, 1620), for five to eight voices and continuo, comprises 21 pieces that show his skill in counterpoint. Some have a narrow vocal range and use a strict polyphonic style, while others, for double choir, have colourful and lively antiphonal scoring. Essential words are often stressed by homophonic declamatory passages or by vigorous, well-measured polyphonic climaxes. Barbieri contributed a concerto for two voices and continuo to Banchieri's *Terzo libro di nuovi pensieri ecclesiastici* (RISM 1613[5]). There is an eight-voice *Dixit Dominus* by him (in *I-Bc*), and a four-voice 'Amen' (also in *Bc*) ascribed to 'Barbieri' may also be by him.

BIBLIOGRAPHY

DBI (O. Mischiati); *EitnerQ*; *GaspariC*, i–ii

A. Banchieri: *Lettere armoniche* (Bologna, 1628/R), 144

G. Gaspari: *Miscellanea musicale* (MS, *I-Bc* UU.12), iv, 91ff, 127–8, 130, 186, 193, 196–7, 200, 211

G. Gaspari: 'Dei musicisti bolognesi al XVII secolo e delle loro opere a stampa', *Atti e memorie delle RR. Deputazione di storia patria per le provincie dell'Emilia*, new ser., iv/1 (1879), 223–43

G. Gasparia: *Musica e musicisti a Bologna* (Bologna, 1969), 411, 493–7 [reprint of various articles pubd between 1858 and 1878]

JUDITH NAGLEY/SUSAN WEISS

Barbieri-Nini, Marianna (*b* Florence, 18 Feb 1818; *d* Florence, 27 Nov 1887). Italian soprano. After study with Luigi Barbieri, Pasta and Vaccai, in 1840 she made a disastrous first appearance at La Scala in Donizetti's *Belisario*. Shortly afterwards she broke her contract with the impresario Merelli and joined Lanari's troupe in Florence. Here she made a second, and this time triumphant, début in Donizetti's *Lucrezia Borgia*. For the next 15 years she sang with great success throughout Italy and in Barcelona, Madrid and Paris. She was a highly dramatic singer with a powerful voice, particularly effective in the title roles of Donizetti's *Anna Bolena* and Rossini's *Semiramide*. She appeared in the first performances of three Verdi operas, singing Lucrezia in *I due Foscari* (1844, Rome), Lady Macbeth (1847, Florence), and Gulnara in *Il corsaro* (1848, Trieste). She retired in 1856.

ELIZABETH FORBES

Barbingant [Barbinguant, Berbigant] (*fl c*1445–60). French composer. Until 1960, he was widely confused with the later composer Jacobus BARBIREAU (see Fox), partly because there is no known documentation for anybody named Barbingant; he may also have been confused in his own time with Bedyngham, whose gently sweet style his work reflects. He must have been active in central France, to judge from the sources of his music and from the musicians who drew on his work. He was twice cited by Tinctoris and was named among groups of distinguished composers by both Eloy d'Amerval and Guillaume Crétin (1497). If *Au travail suis* is by him, as seems likely, he may have been an important influence on Ockeghem, who drew on it in two masses and in his *Ma maistresse*; the song was also paraphrased by Compère. The contrary ascription for *L'omme banny* seems to resolve in favour of Barbingant (rather than Fedé), partly because it was cited as his by Tinctoris, Gaffurius and Giovanni del Lago; it appears in eight surviving sources and was much paraphrased. Strohm has suggested that *Der Pfauensch-wanz* (which is found in six sources, all east European, two ascribed 'Berbigant') may have initiated the genre of German abstract pieces with similar titles; it was used for masses by Martini and Obrecht. Both Barbingant's masses show a sovereign control of large-scale form; that on *Terriblement suis* is perhaps the earliest known example of full parody, considerably expanding the techniques of Bedyngham's Mass *Dueil angoisseux*.

WORKS

Edition: *Jacobi Barbireau: Opera omnia*, ed. B. Meier, CMM, vii/1–2 (1954–7) [M i–ii]

MASSES

Missa sine nomine, 3vv, attrib. in Hamm on the basis of Tinctoris's comment and of style, ed. in L.E. Gottlieb, *The Cyclic Masses of Trent Codex 89* (diss., U. of California, Berkeley, 1958)

Missa 'Terriblement', 3vv (on anon. virelai Terriblement suis fortunée, conceivably also by Barbingant; see Thibault and Fallows), M i

SECULAR

Au travail suis que peu de gens croiroient, rondeau, 3vv (also attrib. Ockeghem), M ii

Der Pfauenschwanz, 4vv, M ii

Esperant que mon bien vendra, rondeau, 3vv, M ii

L'omme banny de sa plaisance, rondeau, 3vv (also attrib. Fedé; text possibly by Meschinot), M ii

BIBLIOGRAPHY

SpataroC; StrohmR

J. Daniskas: 'Een bijdrage tot de geschiedenis der parodie-techniek', *TVNM*, xvii (1948–55), 21–43

C.W. Fox: 'Barbireau and Barbingant: a Review', *JAMS*, xiii (1960), 79–101

C. Hamm: 'Another Barbingant Mass', *Essays in Musicology in Honor of Dragan Plamenac*, ed. G. Reese and R.J. Snow (Pittsburgh, 1969/R), 83–90

L.L. Perkins and H. Garey, eds.: *The Mellon Chansonnier* (New Haven, CT, 1979)

D. Fallows: 'Johannes Ockeghem: the Changing Image, the Songs and a New Source', *EMc*, xii (1984), 218–30

G. Montagna: 'Caron, Hayne, Compère: a Transmission Reassessment', *EMH*, vii (1987), 107–57

G. Thibault and D. Fallows, eds.: *Chansonnier de Jean de Montchenu* (Paris, 1991)

DAVID FALLOWS

Barbion, Eustachius (*d* Kortrijk, before 9 July 1556). South Netherlandish composer and choirmaster. He became *maître de chapelle* at the Onze Lieve Vrouwkerk in Kortrijk (Notre Dame, Courtrai) on 12 April 1543, succeeding Pieter Maessens. Barbion took charge of a musical establishment consisting of a singing school, an organist and a choir of six men and four (later six) choirboys, including for a time his own sons Peter and Wilhelm. Jacobus Vaet studied with Barbion from 1543 to 1546; he paid tribute to his teacher in his parody motet based on Barbion's setting of *Justus germanibit*.

Barbion's surviving compositions include 14 motets and three chansons, which appear in partbooks printed between 1550 and 1570 in Germany and the Low Countries, and in such manuscripts as Codex D of the famous Leiden Choirbooks (*c*1565). The provenance of these sources suggests that Barbion's reputation was confined essentially to northern Europe. His music shows his versatility and skill as a contrapuntist, combining both strict and free imitation within rich, homogeneous textures for five and six voices in the grand northern manner; the multi-voice motets generally reflect the active and some-times dense imitative polyphony that is often found in compositions of the post-Josquin generation. The two compositions for four voices, however, betray a French influence: *Vous avez grace* forces a lightly imitative fabric into the concise formal structure of the Parisian chanson. *Gallis hostibus*, one of a few pieces with Latin text to be included in early editions of Phalèse's *Septiesme livre des chansons*, is a short, homorhythmic composition. A state motet, it may celebrate the heroic fall of Adrien de Croy, a prominent courtier of Emperor Charles V in the war against the forces of Henri II during the 1550s.

WORKS

13 motets, 4–6vv, 1553[11], 1553[13], 1555[4], 1556[6], 1557[3], 1558[4], 1559[1], *A-Wn* 15613, 19189, *D-MÜp* 1525, 2968, *CZ-HKm* 29, 1441 *Sl* Mus.fol.I 2, *NL-L* (olim D); 1 ed. in SCMot, xv (1995), 2 ed. in SCMot, xviii (1997)

State motet, 4vv, 1562[3]

3 chansons, 4–5vv, 1550[13], 1556[17], *GB-Lbl* Add.34071; 1 ed. in SCC, i (1992), 2 ed. in SCC, xxix (1994)

Je prens en gré, a 6, 1589[17] (kbd intabulation by Jakob Paix; vocal model lost)

BIBLIOGRAPHY

J.P.N. Land: 'De koorboeken van de St. Pieterkerk te Leiden', *Bouwsteenen: JVNM*, iii (1874–81), 37–48

G. Caullet: *Musiciens de la collégiale Notre-Dame à Courtrai d'après leurs testaments* (Kortrijk, 1911)

J. Schmidt-Görg: 'Die Acta capitularia der Notre-Dame Kirche zu Kortrijk als musikgeschichtliche Quelle', *Vlaamsch Jb voor muziekgeschiedenis*, i (1939), 21–80

M. Veldhuysen: 'De muziek in de Koorboeken van St. Pieterskerk', *Jb voor geschiedenis en oudheidkunde van Leiden en omstreken*, lvii (1965), 95–9

A. Versprille: 'De geschiedenis van de Leidse Motetboeken', *Jb voor geschiedenis en oudheidkunde van Leiden en omstreken*, lvii (1965), 100–05

A. Dunning: *Die Staatsmotette 1480–1555* (Utrecht, 1970)

LAWRENCE F. BERNSTEIN

Barbireau [Barbirianus], Jacobus (*b* 1455, *d* Antwerp, 7 Aug 1491). South Netherlandish composer. His parents, Johannes Barbireau and Johanna van Saintpol, were both apparently citizens of Antwerp. He must have attended university (probably in the early to mid-1470s), since he is mentioned with the title of Master of Arts in the earliest document to refer to him, dated 1482. He later sought to study with Rudolph Agricola, the famous humanist and musician who had served as organist at the court of Duke Ercole d'Este at Ferrara in 1475. Three letters to Barbireau from Agricola have survived, the third of which, written at Heidelberg, reveals that the addressee was active as a composer by 1484: 'Please send me something of your composition to sing, something composed with care, that you would like to have performed to praise'. Yet Barbireau's musical reputation does not appear to have been widespread at the time, since Agricola continues: 'We have singers here, too, and I often mention your name to them'.

In the end the young composer was unable to study with Agricola, possibly because by 1484 he had succeeded Antoine de Vigne as choirmaster at the church of Our Lady, Antwerp. He was to keep this position until his death seven years later. Records from the church mention

Barbireau's name only in connection with routine duties and payments. There is evidence, however, that he was held in considerable esteem by Maximilian I, King of the Romans, who rewarded him in January 1488 for having housed, maintained and instructed the son of one of his equerries for two years, and had a latter of recommendation written in January 1490 for his visit to the Hungarian court at Buda. During this visit Barbireau was spoken of by his host Queen Beatrix as *musicus prestantissimus* and *familiaris* of Maximilian. The composer's death inspired the humanist Judocus Beyssel to write three epitaphs, in which he is described as *modulator notabilissimus*. Beyssel expressed a sense of tragedy over the death of so gifted a 'youth'; it may well be, however, that Barbireau had never anticipated a long life, perhaps because of poor health, since the earliest surviving document to mention him records financial provisions for daily readings and prayers to be said over his grave – an arrangement established at an age, 27, that was unusual even by the standards of the late 15th century. The composer left a daughter, Jacomyne Barbireau, who survived him by at least 20 years.

Barbireau's oeuvre is small, yet its quality is outstanding. His sacred musical style recalls that of Heinrich Isaac in particular: the material is handled with impressive assurance, and Barbireau shows a degree of contrapuntal polish and melodic-harmonic resourcefulness that puts him firmly on a par with such composers as Isaac and Obrecht. These qualities are evident in the fine Kyrie *Paschale* (of which the top part freely paraphrases the plainchant melody, with occasional imitations in the lower parts), and particularly in the Missa 'Virgo parens Christi' (based on a responsory for the Blessed Virgin), which fully exploits the opportunities for textural variety and sonorous luxuriance offered by its five-part scoring. *Divisi* passages at textual key points suggest that the minimum number of singers required for this mass was 10, distributed from top to bottom as follows: 2–2–1–3–2. The writing here is varied, and rich in alternating textural combinations, motivic filigree around slow-moving parts, imitations, chordal passages and texturally differentiated restatements of two-voice units. Yet these devices are handled with discretion in an effortless flow of counterpoint, in which regular cadences on the final C establish a constant focus of tonal reference.

The four-part Missa 'Faulx perverse' shows the same characteristics, save that the lucid and serene quality of Missa 'Virgo parens Christi' has given way to a much more darkly resonant atmosphere, not only on account of the low scoring (the bass regularly goes down to *D*), but also because the lower parts are more closely spaced, frequently combining to form thirds and triads. Apart from these differences, however, the mass shows the same assurance, resourcefulness and polish of the other works. The model for the mass has not been identified, but patterns of melodic and motivic recurrence suggest that it may have been treated in loose parody fashion. The four-part motet *Osculetur me*, though scored not quite as low as Missa 'Faulx perverse', shares with that mass the persistent exploration of darker sonorities, and seems close to the world of Ockeghem in this respect and in its Phrygian modality. True to the tradition of Song of Songs settings, Barbireau adds light dramatic touches here and there to underline the emotional intensity of the text (general rests, chordal passages, motifs based on the rhythmic scansion of words and phrases), yet these do not diminish the overall lyrical quality of the setting.

Three songs by Barbireau are extant, and it seems significant that all provided cantus firmi for masses by Isaac and Obrecht. In *Gracioulx et biaulx* and *Scoen lief* he developed a penchant for extended sequence in all parts that is not pursued to similar lengths in his sacred music.

WORKS

Edition: *J. Barbireau: Opera omnia*, ed. B. Meier, CMM, vii/1–2 (1954–7) [complete edn]

Missa 'Faulx perverse', 4vv

Missa 'Virgo parens Christi' [Missa de venerabili sacramento], 5vv (c.f. responsory to the BVM)

Kyrie Paschale, 4vv (c.f. Gregorian Kyrie Paschale)

Osculetur me, 4vv

Een vroylic wesen, 3vv (text: incipit only)

Gracuuly et biaulx, 3vv (text: incipit only)

Scon lief, 3vv (text: incipit only)

BIBLIOGRAPHY

J. du Saar: *Het leven en de composities van Jacobus Barbireau* (Utrecht, 1946)

B. Murray: 'Jacob Obrecht's Connection with the Church of Our Lady in Antwerp', *RBM*, xi (1957), 125–33

C.W. Fox: 'Barbireau and Barbingant: a Review', *JAMS*, xiii (1960), 79–101

J. van den Nieuwenhuizen: 'De koralen, de zangers en de zangmeesters van de Antwerpse O.-L.-Vrouwekerk tijdens de 15e eeuw', *Gouden jubileum gedenkboek van de viering van 50 jaar heropgericht Knapenkoor van de Onze-Lieve-Vrouwkatedraal te Antwerpen*, ed. P. Schrooten (Antwerp, 1978), 29–72

P. Kooiman: 'The Letters of Rodolphus Agricola to Jacobus Barbirianus', *Rodolphus Agricola Phrisius 1444–1485* [Groningen 1985], ed. F. Akkerman and A.J. Vanderjagt (Leiden, 1988), 136–46

K.K. Forney: 'Music, Ritual and Patronage at the Church of Our Lady, Antwerp', *EMH*, vii (1987), 1–57

E. Kooiman: 'The Biography of Jacob Barbireau (1455–1491) Reviewed', *TVNM*, xxxviii (1988), 36–58

R.C. Wegman: *Born for the Muses: the Life and Masses of Jacob Obrecht* (Oxford, 1994)

ROB C. WEGMAN

Barbirianus. *See* BARBIREAU, JACOBUS.

Barbirolli, Evelyn. *See* ROTHWELL, EVELYN.

Barbirolli, Sir John [Giovanni Battista] (*b* London, 2 Dec 1899; *d* London, 29 July 1970). English conductor and cellist. He was the son and grandson of Italian musicians settled in London, and his mother was French. As a youth he won scholarships to Trinity College of Music, then to the RAM. In 1916 he became the youngest member of the Queen's Hall Orchestra, and he gave his first solo recital, at the Aeolian Hall, in 1917. The next two years were spent in the army, where he had his first experience of conducting, with a voluntary orchestra. After 1919 he returned to orchestral playing in London, and twice appeared as soloist with the Bournemouth Municipal Orchestra. In 1924 he joined the Music Society (later International) and Kutcher string quartets, and formed a string orchestra, which he often conducted. He was invited to conduct the British National Opera Company on tour and later (1928) in London. From 1929 to 1933 Barbirolli was guest conductor for the Covent Garden international and English seasons. He conducted opera at Sadler's Wells in 1934, and returned to Covent Garden for the coronation season of 1937.

Meanwhile Barbirolli was also active in the concert hall. In 1927 he deputized for Beecham at an LSO concert. Guest appearances with the Scottish Orchestra in 1931

John Barbirolli

led to the permanent conductorship for three seasons. During this period he also took charge of the Northern PO in Leeds, conducted other provincial orchestras including the Hallé and was invited abroad. His growing reputation brought him the offer of ten weeks as guest conductor of the Philharmonic-Symphony Orchestra of New York in the 1936–7 season. Initial success was followed by his appointment for three years as permanent conductor, in succession to Toscanini. The contract was renewed for two years to 1941–2, the orchestra's centenary season, when the conducting was shared with eminent colleagues including Toscanini. In 1942 he made a courageous wartime crossing to Britain for concerts with the LSO, BBC SO and LPO, before resuming work in the USA, and in 1943 he returned to rebuild the Hallé Orchestra. He stayed with the Hallé until 1958 when he became conductor-in-chief with a less onerous schedule. In 1968 he was made conductor laureate for life. From 1961 to 1967 he was also principal conductor of the Houston (Texas) SO and in 1961 he began an association with the Berlin PO, whose guest conductor he was until his death. These last years, crammed with work in spite of deteriorating health, included tours with the Philharmonia (Latin America, 1963), BBC SO (USSR, 1967) and Hallé (Latin America and West Indies, 1968), and numerous guest appearances at home and abroad.

Barbirolli's musical tastes were conventional with a leaning towards the late Romantics. He had little sympathy with contemporary music beyond certain works of Britten, of whose Violin Concerto and *Sinfonia da requiem* he gave the first performances, in New York. He had a passion for Elgar's music, and was a notable interpreter of Delius and of Vaughan Williams, who dedicated his Eighth Symphony to Barbirolli; he became increasingly attached to Mahler and Bruckner. As a technician he understood the orchestra from the inside. As an interpreter he could persuade audiences to share his enthusiasms – sometimes with a loving exhibition of minutely prepared detail that singled out trees at the expense of the wood. The measure of success with which he met the challenge of New York may be disputed, but to survive there for five consecutive seasons, with Toscanini remaining in the city with the NBC SO, and to be invited several times to return as guest conductor, does not look like failure. His subsequent acceptance by an orchestra of equal standing, the Berlin PO, must have

healed any lingering wounds. The musical love of Barbirolli's life, however, was the Hallé Orchestra, which he restored to high excellence; his single-minded devotion to it became a legend.

Up to 1937 Barbirolli had seemed set to become the leading British opera conductor after Beecham, but Beecham became enraged when his junior by 20 years got the job in New York, and did much to undermine Barbirolli's subsequent career. Barbirolli's sole revenge was to keep Beecham away from the postwar Hallé; but he only appeared at Covent Garden, as a guest conductor, for three seasons between 1951 and 1954. In his last years, when he recorded *Madama Butterfly* and *Otello*, and conducted *Aida* in 1969 at the Rome Opera, he appeared to be picking up the threads of his frustrated operatic career. His recording career, on the other hand, extended from the pre-electric days of 1911 to the month of his death and included famous readings of Elgar's symphonies, *The Dream of Gerontius* and the Cello Concerto (with Jacqueline du Pré). His orchestral arrangements include a Suite for Strings from Purcell, an Elizabethan Suite from works of virginal composers, and oboe concertos from Corelli and Pergolesi. Barbirolli was made a Companion of Honour in 1969, was knighted in 1949, and received the Gold Medal of the RPS in 1950 and the Freedom of the City of Manchester in 1958. He was twice married, in 1932 to Marjorie Parry, the singer, and in 1939 to Evelyn Rothwell, the oboist.

BIBLIOGRAPHY

B. Shore: *The Orchestra Speaks* (London, 1938)

M. Kennedy: *The Hallé Tradition* (Manchester, 1960)

D. Bicknell and K. Anderson: 'Sir John Barbirolli, C.H.', *Gramophone*, xlviii (1970–71), 401–02

M. Kennedy: *Barbirolli, Conductor Laureate* (London, 1971) [with discography by M. Walker]

C. Reid: *John Barbirolli* (London, 1971)

M. Kennedy: *The Hallé, 1858–1983: a History of the Orchestra* (Manchester, 1982)

RONALD CRICHTON/JOSÉ BOWEN

Barbitonsoris (*fl* late 14th century). Italian ?composer. One three-voice Sanctus, with a partly isorhythmic tenor, is transmitted with this ascription in the Paduan fragment *GB-Ob* Can.pat.lat.229 ('PadA', f.37v; ed. in PMFC, xii, 1976, p.88). The word may refer to the Greek instrument shaped like a lyre, called a 'barbitos'. That the work comes from northern Italy seems to be confirmed by the additional label 'ambrosius' written next to the second voice.

BIBLIOGRAPHY

H. Besseler: 'Studien zur Musik des Mittelalters', *AMw*, viii (1926), 137–258, esp.235

B.J. Layton: *Italian Music for the Ordinary of the Mass 1300–1450* (diss., Harvard U., 1960), 129ff

F. Facchin: 'Una nuova fonte musicale trecentesca nell' Archivio di Stato di Padova', *Contributi per la storia della musica sacra a Padova*, ed. G. Cattin and A. Lovato (Padua, 1993), 115–39

GIANLUCA D'AGOSTINO

Barbitos (late Gk. *barbiton*). Greek instrument of the LYRE family (a CHORDOPHONE). In Greek literature and vase painting it is generally associated with the Eastern Greek poets (including Terpander, Sappho, Alcaeus and Anacreon) of the Archaic period (7th and 6th centuries BCE), and with drinking parties. The name of the instrument, probably of non-Greek derivation, occurs only once in the fragments of these early poets (in Alcaeus, ed. E.-M. Voigt, *Sappho et Alcaeus: Fragmenta*, 1971, frag.70.4, in the dialect form *barmos*), but it is frequently mentioned by later Greek writers, who attribute the instrument's 'invention' variously to Terpander or Anacreon. The arrival of Anacreon in Athens as a court poet in the late 6th century coincides with the sudden appearance of the barbitos in Athenian vase paintings, many of which show him as a player. As the chief string instrument used to accompany Dionysiac revelry, it is only occasionally depicted in the hands of Muses or of women entertaining themselves at home.

The barbitos is usually portrayed as having a tortoise-shell soundbox, long curved arms (probably made of wood) joined together by a crossbar at the top, and five to seven strings supported by a bridge and sounded with a plectrum attached to the instrument by a cord. The strings are attached at the crossbar by means of tuning devices called *kollopes* (pegs). The arms, which diverge as they leave the soundbox, curve towards each other near the top of the instrument, forming a distinctive shape. Rare profile views indicate that the arms curved forwards as well as outwards. The longer string length as compared to the schoolboy's tortoise-shell lyre suggests a relatively lower pitch.

The barbitos is generally shown held against the body of the player, who is often standing; a sling around the left wrist helps to support the instrument, which is tipped out at an angle of roughly 45 degrees from the vertical (see illustration). The left-hand fingers are probably used both to pluck and to dampen the strings. The right hand strums the strings with the plectrum.

Barbitos player: detail from a skyphos attributed to the Brygos Painter, Attic Red-figure style, c480 BCE (Musée du Louvre, Paris)

After its heyday in Attic vase painting of the late 6th and early 5th centuries, the barbitos was less and less frequently depicted, and was almost never shown after the 5th century. Aristotle condemned it as an instrument inappropriate for education (*Politics*, 1341 a–b), but it continued to be mentioned in Greek literature, especially in drinking songs. In later times the barbitos as a literary symbol remained firmly associated with Lesbos, the homeland of Terpander, Sappho and Alcaeus (see Horace, *Odes*, 1.i.34).

BIBLIOGRAPHY

H. Abert: 'Saiteninstrumente', *Paulys Real-Encyclopädie der classischen Altertumswissenschaft*, 2nd ser., i (Stuttgart, 1920), 1760–67

M. Wegner: *Griechenland*, Musikgeschichte in Bildern, ii/4 (Leipzig, 1963/R)

J. Snyder: 'The *Barbitos* in the Classical Period', *Classical Journal*, lxvii (1972), 331–40

M. Maas and J.M. Snyder: *Stringed Instruments of Ancient Greece* (New Haven, CT, 1987)

JANE McINTOSH SNYDER

Barbizet, Pierre (*b* Arica, Chile, 20 Sept 1922; *d* Marseilles, 18 Jan 1990). French pianist. After early training in Santiago he studied at the Paris Conservatoire, where he won a *premier prix* in 1944 in the class of Armand Ferté. He won first prize in the 1948 international competition at Scheveningen and fifth prize in the 1949 Marguerite Long-Jacques Thibaud Competition. He was director of the Marseilles Conservatoire from 1963 to 1990 and also taught for a time at the Paris Conservatoire; among his students were Hélène Grimaud and Bernard d'Ascoli. He performed frequently as a soloist and chamber musician, especially with the violinist Christian Ferras and the flautist Jean-Pierre Rampal. His recordings with Ferras include notable accounts of the complete sonatas of Beethoven and Brahms, as well as major French works. As a soloist, Barbizet made distinguished recordings of the complete piano works of Chabrier and several sonatas of Beethoven. (C. Timbrell: *French Pianism*, White Plains, NY, and London, 1992, 2/1999)

CHARLES TIMBRELL

Barblan, Guglielmo (*b* Siena, 27 May 1906; *d* Milan, 24 March 1978). Italian musicologist of Swiss origin. He studied law, then the cello with Forino and Becker at Rome Conservatory (diploma 1929) and composition at Bolzano Conservatory (diploma 1932); he also attended lectures on musicology by Liuzzi in Rome and by Sandberger in Munich. While still a student he was music critic of various Rome newspapers (1926–32) and showed particular interest in contemporary musical life (Casella, Pizzetti, jazz, futurism). Subsequently he was music critic of *La provincia di Bolzano* (1932–50), concurrently (until 1949) holding an appointment as professor of cello and music history at the Bolzano Conservatory, and was active as a concert cellist. At the Milan Conservatory he was head librarian (1949) and professor of music history (1965); at the university (where he took the *libera docenza* in 1959) he became professor of music history in 1961. He maintained his involvement in journalism with frequent contributions to *Sicilia del popolo*, *Rassegna dorica* and *Alto adige*, and as foreign correspondent for the *Basler Nachrichten* (1958–62); he was editor of *Verdiana* (1950–51) and of the Milan Conservatory *Annuario* (from 1962), to which he contributed several articles on the library.

Barblan's distinguished career was matched by his catholic interests and thorough research. He was first attracted to the 17th and 18th centuries; his discussion of F.A. Bonporti's life and works, initially published in *Rassegna musicale*, was later enlarged into a book. He next extended his studies to include 19th-century opera and then the Renaissance, his practical musicianship leading him to make editions of the music. His research in the Milan archives and analyses of Milanese music resulted in what many consider his most important works; they were published as independent chapters in *Storia di Milano*, covering several centuries and various musical genres. The discussion of 16th-century musical life at the Sforza court and elsewhere in Milan is based on archival documentation; a complete bibliography, naming instrumentalists and singers and providing analyses of the music and indications of performing practice, is included (vol.ix). A broad but detailed account of chamber music is given for the 17th century, which saw the rise of the violin and its repertory (vol.xvi). Barblan also discussed the Milanese symphonists of the next century, such as Sammartini, and their music (vol.xvi). His survey of opera and other forms of musical theatre discusses works, composers and styles from the 17th century (vol.xii) and continues throughout history to conclude with an assessment of 20th-century musical life in Milan (vol.xvi); these chapters not only describe the city's musical life but are also basic to a study of Italian music in general.

Barblan also contributed numerous articles to music dictionaries (*MGG1* and *Grove5*) and wrote extensively for Italian radio, notably the series 'La cantata dal Barocco all'Arcadia' and 'Bach e il Clavicembalo ben temperato'. In recognition of his singular role in Italian musicology he was elected president of the Società Italiana di Musicologia (1964–8), a member of the Accademia di S Cecilia (1964) and vice-president of the Accademia Musicale Chigiana (1965).

WRITINGS

'Francesco Antonio Bonporti "gentilhuomo di Trento, dilettante di musica"', *RaM*, xii (1939), 313–46, 380–403, 433–57

Un musicista trentino: Bonporti (1672–1749): la vita e le opere (Florence, 1940)

'Francesco Antonio Bonporti', *La scuola veneziana (secoli XVI–XVIII): note e documenti*, Chigiana, iii (1941), 81–5

'L'opera di Giuseppe Verdi e il dramma romantico', *RMI*, xlv (1941), 93–107

Musiche e strumenti musicali dell'Africa orientale italiana (Naples, 1941)

'Quo vadis musice? Appunti sul Festival musicale veneziano', *RMI*, xlviii (1946), 489–98

L'opera di Donizetti nell'età romantica (Bergamo, 1948)

'Di alcuni aspetti del "comico" in Orazio Vecchi', *Orazio Vecchi precursore del melodramma* (Modena, 1950), 105–14

'Strawinski 1951', in A. Casella: *Strawinski* (Brescia, 2/1951, 3/1961), 193–231

'Nel V centenario di un musico umanista: Franchino Gaffurio', *RaM*, xxii (1952), 1–10

'Angelo Mariani e la sua "Scala esatonale"', *CHM*, i (1953), 171–4

'Presagio di gloria e ombre di mestizia ne "La falce" di Alfredo Catalani', *Musicisti toscani*, i, Chigiana, xi (1954), 65–71

'Agostino Agazzari', *Musicisti toscani*, ii, Chigiana, xii (1955), 43–9

'Contributo a una biografia critica di Agostino Agazzari', *CHM*, ii (1956–7), 33–63

ed. with A. Della Corte: *Mozart in Italia: i viaggi e le lettere* (Milan, 1956)

Un prezioso spartito del Falstaff (Milan, 1957)

'Aspetti e figure del Cinquecento musicale veneziano', *La civiltà veneziana del Rinascimento* (Florence, 1958), 59–80

'Sulle tracce di un'espressione musicale "Padana"', 'Sammartini e la scuolo sinfonica milanese', 'Franchino Gaffurio musico-umanista',

Musicisti lombardi ed emiliani, Chigiana, xv (1958), 9–17, 21–40, 41–9

'Il teatro musicale in Milano nei secc. XVII e XVIII', *Storia di Milano*, xii (1958), 947–96 [pubn of the Fondazione Treccani degli Alfieri per la storia di Milano]

'Il termine "Barocco" e la musica', *Miscelánea en homenaje a Monseñor Higinio Anglés* (Barcelona, 1958–61), 93–109

'Ansia preromantica in Gaetano Pugnani', 'Il "Giovedì grasso" e gli svaghi "farsaioli" di Donizetti', *Musicisti piemontesi e liguri*, Chigiana, xvi (1959), 17–26, 109–14

'Boccheriniana', *RaM*, xxix (1959), 123–8, 322–31; xxx (1960), 33–44

'Malipiero e Monteverdi', *Approdo musicale*, iii/9 (1960), 122–33

Guida al 'Clavicembalo ben temperato' di J.S. Bach (Milan, 1961)

'La vita musicale in Milano nella prima metà del Cinquecento', *Storia di Milano*, ix (Milan, 1961), 853–95

'Vita musicale alla corte sforzesca', *Storia di Milano*, ix (Milan, 1961), 787–852

'Contributo alla biografia di G.B. Sammartini alla luce dei documenti', *SMw*, xxv (1962), 15–27

'I "Rognoni" musicisti milanesi tra il 1500 e il 1600', *Anthony van Hoboken: Festschrift*, ed. J. Schmidt-Görg (Mainz, 1962), 19–28

'La musica strumentale e cameristica a Milano dalla seconda metà del '500 alla fine del '700: l'Ottocento e gli inizi del secolo XX', *Storia di Milano*, xvi (Milan, 1962), 589–711

'Un po' di luce sulla prima rappresentazione della "Forza del destino" a Pietroburgo', *Verdi: Bollettino dell'Istituto di studi verdiani*, ii (1964), 831–79

'Spunti rivelatori nella genesi del "Falstaff"', *Situazione e prospettive degli studi verdiani nel mondo: Venice 1966*, 16–21

with C. Gallico and G. Pannain: *Claudio Monteverdi nel quarto centenario della nascita* (Turin, 1967)

'Lettura di un'opera dimenticata "Pia de' Tolomei" di Donizetti (1836)', *Chigiana*, new ser., iv (1967), 221–43

'Claudio Monteverdi: musicista padano fra Rinascimento e Barocco', *L'opera*, iii/6 (1967), 4–10

'Un ignoto "Lamento d'Arianna mantovano"', *RIM*, ii (1967), 217–28

'Sui rapporti italo-tedeschi nella musica strumentale del Settecento', *AnMc*, iv (1967), 1–12

'Donizetti a Napoli', *Rassegna musicale Curci*, xxi (1968), 81–7; Eng. trans. in *Journal of the Donizetti Society*, i (1974), 105–20

'Rossini e il suo tempo', *Chigiana*, new ser., v (1969), 143–80

I quaderni di conversazione di Beethoven (Turin, 1968) [trans. of G. Schünemann: *Ludwig van Beethovens Konversationshefte* (Berlin, 1941–3)]

'Il personaggio dell'Infante nel "Don Carlos" verdiano', *Studi verdiani II: Verona, Parma and Busseto 1969*, 412–29

'Michel' Angelo Grancini a 300 anni dalla morte', *Chigiana*, new ser., vi–vii (1971), 3–34

'Giuseppe Maria Cambini e i suoi scritti sulla musica', *Quadrivium*, xii/2 (1971), 295–310

'Beethoven in Lombardia nell'Ottocento', *NRMI*, vi (1972), 3–63

ed.: *Conservatorio di musica 'Giuseppe Verdi', Milano: catalogo della biblioteca, fondi speciali*, i: *Musiche della cappella di Santa Barbara in Mantova* (Florence, 1972)

'Il sentimento dell'onore nella drammaturgia verdiana (Prolusione)', *Studi verdiani III: Milan 1972*, 2–13

'Un Cimador che divenne Cimarosa', *Quadrivium*, xiv/2 (1973), 197–206

with A. Zecca-Laterza: 'The Tarasconi Codex in the Library of the Milan Conservatory', *MQ*, lx (1974), 195–221

'Maria di Rohan', *Journal of the Donizetti Society*, ii (1975), 14–33

'Gaetano Donizetti mancato direttore dei conservatori di Napoli e di Milano', *Il melodramma italiano dell'Ottocento: studi e ricerche per Massimo Mila*, ed. G. Pestelli (Turin, 1977), 403–11

ed., with A. Basso: *Storia dell'opera*, i–iii (Turin, 1977) [incl. 'Il grande Ottocento', i/2, 169–212]

with B. Zanolini: *Gaetano Donizetti: vita e opere di un musicista romantico* (Florence, 1983)

EDITIONS

F.A. Bonporti: *Concerto in Si bemolle op.XI n.4, per violino, archi e cembalo di ripieno*, Antica musica strumentale italiana, i/7 (Milan, 1959); *Concerto in Si bemolle op.XI n.3, per violino, archi e cembalo di ripieno*, ibid., i/6 (Milan, 1961)

G.G. Cambini: *Concerto in Sol op.XV n.3, per pianoforte e archi*, Antica musica strumentale italiana, i/8 (1959); *Concerto in Si bemolle op.XV n.I, per pianoforte e archi, con oboi e corni ad libitum*, ibid., iii (Milan, 1964)

BIBLIOGRAPHY

'Studi di musicologia in onore di Guglielmo Barblan in occasione del LX compleanno', *CHM*, iv (1966), 1–316 [incl. F. Mompellio: 'Guglielmo Barblan e la musicologia "umana"', 1–6; A. Zecca Laterza: 'Guglielmo Barblan: note bibliografiche', 7–16]

CAROLYN GIANTURCO/TERESA M. GIALDRONI

Barblan, Otto (*b* S-chanf, 22 March 1860; *d* Geneva, 19 Dec 1943). Swiss organist and composer. From 1878 to 1885 he studied the organ, the piano and composition at Stuttgart Conservatory. In 1885 he went to Chur as a music teacher, and in 1887 became organist of St Peter's Cathedral in Geneva, where he stayed until 1942; from 1892 he also taught the organ and composition. As conductor of the Société de Chant Sacré (1892–1938) he introduced to Geneva important works by Bach, Beethoven, Handel, Franck and many other composers. Together with Ernest Ansermet, Barblan had a decisive influence on the musical life of Geneva. He composed in a late Romantic neo-Baroque style, with particular success in his works for organ and choir for patriotic occasions, notably the *Chaconne über B–A–C–H* (1901), *Fantasie* (1907) and *Toccata* (1911) for organ, and *Calvenfeier* (1899) for choir. In 1925 he was made an honorary member of the Swiss Musicians Association, and in 1927 was awarded honorary citizenship of Geneva and an honorary doctorate by Geneva University. He published two articles of reminiscences in *Bündner Monatsblatt* (1929).

BIBLIOGRAPHY

C. Chaix: 'L'oeuvre d'orgue d'Otto Barblan', *Vie musicale* [Lausanne], iv (1910–11), 197

E. Chaponnière: *Otto Barblan: directeur de la Société de chant sacré de Genève* (Geneva, 1917)

E. Perini: 'Das kompositorische Schaffen Otto Barblans', *Bündner Monatsblatt* (1949), 113–34 [with list of compositions]

E. Perini: *Otto Barblan 1860–1943: ed. commemorativa* (Chur, 1960)

C. Tappolet: *La vie musicale à Genève au 20ème siècle*, i: *1918–1968* (Geneva, 1979)

JÜRG STENZL

Barbosa-Lima, Carlos (*b* São Paulo, 17 Dec 1944). Brazilian guitarist and arranger. He began studying the guitar at the age of seven. At nine he began having lessons with Isaias Savio, one of the foremost teachers in South America, who predicted Barbosa-Lima's success. His concert début was in São Paulo in 1957, immediately followed by his début in Rio de Janeiro. At this time, aged 13, he embarked on his first series of recordings. From 1958 he performed regularly on Brazilian television and continued to give concerts throughout Brazil. In 1960 he gave a series of concerts in Montevideo – a major centre for the guitar in South America. His growing international success led many noted composers, among them Guido Santórsola, Francisco Mignone and Alberto Ginastera, to dedicate works to him. In 1967 he made his first US concert tour. On the strength of the tour's success he won a full scholarship from the Spanish and Brazilian governments to participate in Segovia's masterclasses in Santiago de Compostela in 1968, where he received high praise from Segovia. His London début followed in 1971. Barbosa-Lima's numerous guitar arrangements of works by composers as diverse as Scarlatti, Debussy, Gershwin and Scott Joplin are widely known for their fidelity to the original work. A number of his arrangements feature

among his recordings. He has also written articles on guitarists and guitar music.

BIBLIOGRAPHY

W.M. Appleby: 'Carlos Barbosa-Lima', *Guitar News*, no.42 (1958), 45 only; no.48 (1959), 78 only; no.99 (1968), 104 only

P. Danner: 'How I Came to the Guitar', *Soundboard*, xxi/1 (1994), 5–10

RONALD C. PURCELL

Barbosa Machado, Diogo (*b* Lisbon, 31 March 1682; *d* Lisbon, 9 Aug 1772). Portuguese bibliographer. He matriculated in 1708 as a student of canon law at Coimbra University and on 2 July 1724 he was ordained a priest. On 4 November 1728 he became *abad* of the church of S Adrião at Cever in the diocese of Lamego. His life work was a four-volume bibliography of Portuguese authors, *Bibliotheca lusitana, historica, critica, e cronologica* (Lisbon, 1741–59/*R*), which is especially valuable to the music historian because he included 127 composers and theorists. Insofar as he could find them, he listed not only their published works but also their manuscripts, noting in which library they were located. Since he had access to the royal music library before its destruction in the Lisbon earthquake of 1755, he listed numerous works now lost. In vol.iv, pp.593–6, he indexed musicians under 'Musica', thus making it simple for later writers to plagiarize his musical entries. Foreign reference works still copy Vasconcellos's *Os musicos portuguezes* (Oporto, 1870) without recognizing Barbosa Machado's work as the source of everything that he wrote on biographies. Barbosa Machado omitted Ayres Fernandes, Luis Moram, Pedro de Cristo, Pedro Esperança and several others connected with the priory of Santa Cruz at Coimbra. His most substantial error was listing Francisco Guerrero as a native of Beja, a mistake into which he was trapped by a pseudonymously issued forgery of 1734.

Barbosa Machado donated his superb library to King José I. João VI took the bulk of it to Brazil, where it formed the nucleus of the national library; it includes 13 important volumes of villancicos sung at Lisbon between 1640 and 1722. In 1825 Dibdin rightly classed Barbosa Machado's four volumes as 'a work beyond all competition and beyond all praise … the great Oracle', a judgment still valid.

BIBLIOGRAPHY

T.F. Dibdin: *The Library Companion*, i (London, 2/1824), 323f

B.F. Ramiz Galvão: 'Diogo Barbosa Machado', *Annaes da Bibliotheca nacional do Rio de Janeiro*, i (1876–7), 1–43, 248

J. Emerenciano: *Três instrumentos de trabalho (fontes básicas para estudos portuguêses)* (Recife, 1965), 19–67

R.E. Horch: *Vilancicos da Coleção Barbosa Machado* (Rio de Janeiro, 1969)

R.V. Nery, ed.: *A música no ciclo da 'Bibliotheca lusitana'* (Lisbon, 1984)

ROBERT STEVENSON

Barboteu, Georges (*b* Algiers, 1 April 1924). French horn player. He studied with his father in Algeria and with Jean Devémy at the Paris Conservatoire. In 1948 he joined the Orchestre National, and in 1951 won first prize in the international competition in Geneva. He was principal horn for the Concerts Lamoureux and in 1969 became principal of the Orchestre de Paris. Barboteu was the leading French player of his generation, setting a new standard of technical accomplishment and steering the country's school of horn playing away from the continuous vibrato that had dogged it for decades. In this he was influenced by his teacher Devémy, who saw a minimal vibrato as a permissable result of the temperament and sensitivity of the player, but did not deliberately teach it, in contrast to the school headed by Lucien Thévet. Barboteu himself was appointed to the Conservatoire as successor to Devémy in 1969. His recordings include Schumann's *Conzertstück*, which established his international reputation, and the Mozart concertos. He has composed many studies for his instrument and written chamber works, some for the wind quintet Ars Nova which he founded in 1964.

OLIVER BROCKWAY

Barbour, J(ames) Murray (*b* Chambersburg, PA, 31 March 1897; *d* Homestead, PA, 4 Jan 1970). American acoustician, musicologist and composer. He taught himself the piano and the organ and studied at Dickinson College, Pennsylvania (1914–18); after graduating he worked as organist and mathematics teacher at the Haverford School in Pennsylvania (1919–21, 1922–6) while continuing his studies at Dickinson College (MA 1920) and Temple University (MusB 1924). He subsequently taught music theory as assistant professor at Wells College, New York (1926–9), leaving with a fellowship to the universities of Cologne and Berlin. After studies at Cornell University under Kinkeldey (1931–2) he gained the doctorate in 1932 with a dissertation on the history of equal temperament from Ramis de Pareia to Rameau. He taught at Ithaca College, New York (1932–9), while working for the MusD of the University of Toronto (1936). The rest of his career (1939–64) was spent teaching at Michigan State College (later University), as professor from 1954. He was president of the American Musicological Society in 1957–8, and Temple University awarded him an honorary doctorate in 1965.

His book *Tuning and Temperament: a Historical Survey* is widely accepted as the most authoritative study of the history and theory of temperaments, to which he applied his talents as mathematician, historian and musician. His scholarly articles appeared in mathematical as well as musical journals and were marked by precision, clarity and conciseness. With Fritz A. Kuttner he issued three gramophone records concerning the history of tuning systems. His compositions include a Requiem, the symphonic poem *Childe Rowland*, solo and choral songs, works for the organ and piano and some chamber music.

WRITINGS

Equal Temperament: its History from Ramis (1482) to Rameau (1737) (diss., Cornell U., 1932)
'Nierop's Hackebort', *MQ*, xx (1934), 312–19
'Just Intonation Confuted', *ML*, xix (1938), 48–60
'Allgemeine Musikalische Zeitung: Prototype of Contemporary Music Journalism', *Notes*, v (1947–8), 325–37
'Musical Scales and their Classification', *JASA*, xxi (1949), 586–9
Tuning and Temperament: a Historical Survey (East Lansing, MI, 1951/R, 2/1953)
'Franz Krommer and his Writing for Brass', *Brass Quarterly*, i (1957–8), 1–9
'Unusual Brass Notation in the Eighteenth Century', *Brass Quarterly*, ii (1958–9), 139–46
'The Principles of Greek Notation', *JAMS*, xiii (1960), 1–17
The Church Music of William Billings (East Lansing, MI, 1960)
'Pokorny Vindicated', *MQ*, xlix (1963), 38–58
'Missverständnisse über die Stimmung des Javanischen Gamelans', *Mf*, xvi (1963), 315–23
Trumpets, Horns and Music (East Lansing, MI, 1964)
ed.: R. Smith: *Harmonica, or the Philosophy of Musical Sounds (1749)* (New York, 1966)
'The "Unpartheyisches Gesang-Buch"', *Cantors at the Crossroads: Essays on Church Music in Honor of Walter E. Buszin*, ed. J. Riedel (St Louis, 1967), 87–94

BIBLIOGRAPHY

F.A. Kuttner: 'J. Murray Barbour (1897–1970)', *JAMS*, xxiii (1970), 542–3

JON NEWSOM

Barbu, Filaret (*b* Lugoj, 16 April 1903; *d* Timişoara, 31 May 1984). Romanian composer. He started his musical education in his native town with Ioan Vidu, a composer and conductor of works of a folkloristic character. He went on to attend the Vienna Conservatory, where he studied composition with Edmund Eysler (1929–39). As a conductor, he worked with choirs singing music from the Banat region, a part of south-west Romania particularly rich in folk songs and dances. He founded (in 1927) and directed the *Revista Corurilor si Fanfarelor Române* ('The Romanian Choir and Fanfare Magazine'). He served in the Ministry of Arts in Bucharest during the turbulent period from 1947 to 1949. He spent his last years in the town of Timişoara.

Barbu composed choral, orchestral and chamber music, but it was with his operettas that he enjoyed his greatest success. He adapted the conventions of the genre to include Romanian folk music, using plots which are usually of a strongly nationalist character.

WORKS
(selective list)

Stage: Armonii bănăţene [Harmonies from Banat] (operetta, 3, I. Titel), Lugoj, 14 Dec 1933; Ana Lugojana [Anna from Lugoj] (operetta, 3, V. Timuş, P. Andreescu and A. Şahinian), Bucharest, Teatrul de Operetă, 7 Nov 1951; Plutaşul de pe Bistriţa [The Boatman on the Bistrita] (operetta, 3, T. Ianuc and I. Dacian), Bucharest, Teatrul de Operetă, 21 Nov 1958; Târgul de fete [The Maidens' Fair] (operetta, 3, T. Iancu), Bucharest, Teatrul de Operetă, 21 Aug 1964
Choral: Omul [Man] (orat, C.M. Lerca), 1942; Liturghia [Liturgy], mixed chorus
Orch and chbr works

BIBLIOGRAPHY

F. Barbu: *Partitura unei vieţi* [The Score of a Life] (Bucharest, 1976)
V. Cosma: *Muzicieni din România* (Bucharest, 1989)

OCTAVIAN COSMA

Barca, Alessandro (*b* Bergamo, 26 Nov 1741; *d* Bergamo, 13 June 1814). Italian theorist. Having entered the religious order of the Somaschi fathers, in 1761 he was invited to teach philosophy and mathematics in the college of Santa Croce in Padua. There he came into contact with the composer and theorist F.A. Vallotti, to whom he later became technical adviser on the mathematical aspect of harmonic theory; for example, he assisted in the calculations for Vallotti's system of temperament. From 1771 to 1812 he was professor of canon law at the University of Padua; he was also active as a chemist and as a theoretician of architecture. Barca's *Nuova teoria di musica*, a work in six sections (of which only four were published), aimed to explain the harmonic identity between a chord and its inversions; this identity (already established before Rameau by F.A. Calegari) was at the heart of the rules of composition in the Paduan school, which was known as the 'scuola dei rivolti' (because its composers were the first to use certain inverted dissonant chords). Barca made a graduated list of harmonic intervals in order of consonance, according to a mathematical criterion similar in some ways to that put forward by Leonhard Euler in 1739. Much more satisfactory is his explanation of the origin of musical scales, where he concludes that the ascending major scale is the most 'natural', followed by the descending minor scale (50 years later Helmholtz, who did not know Barca's work, confirmed this assertion).

Barca also applied his theory of consonances to the calculation of tempered systems, arriving at the regular temperament which reduced each 5th by 5/29 (roughly $\frac{1}{6}$) of the syntonic comma. He was expert in practical music, and in a *Rapporto sullo stato della musica nel Regno d'Italia* of 1810 (repr. in Alessandri) he pointed to weaknesses of Italian music of the period, wishing to 'stem the tide of German music which was already ruining Italian taste, and threatening ever greater damage'.

WRITINGS
(*selective list*)

further details in Barbieri (1987); MSS in the Biblioteca Mons. G.M. Radini Tedeschi, Bergamo

Nuovi teoremi per la divisione delle ragioni (Bergamo, 1781)

Nuova teoria di musica: [1] 'Introduzione . . . memoria prima', *Saggi scientifici e letterari dell'Accademia di scienze, lettere e arti in Padova*, i (1786), 365–418; [2] 'Introduzione . . . memoria seconda', ibid., ii (1789), 329–62; [3] 'Memoria prima', ibid., iii/2 (1794), 71–87; [4] 'Memoria seconda: de' suoni aggiunti, ossia delle dissonanze e dell'armonia dissonante', *Memorie dell'Accademia di scienze, lettere ed arti di Padova*, iv (1809), 184–221; [5] 'Memoria terza: dei sistemi e delle scale' (MS, *c*1800–05), repr. in Barbieri (1987); [6] 'Memoria sesta: del canto e della modulazione' (MS draft, inc., *c*1810–14), repr. in Barbieri (1987)

Rapporto sulla stato della musica nel Regno d'Italia diretto al Ministero della pubblica istruzione (MS, 1810); repr. in A. Alessandri: *Biografie di scrittori e artisti bergamaschi* (Bergamo, 1875)

BIBLIOGRAPHY

G. Riccati: *Riflessioni sulle Memorie prima e seconda del Ch. P.D. Alessandro Barca che servono d'"introduzione a una nuova Teoria di musica", e si leggono nel tomo i e ii dell'Accademia di Padova* (MS, *c*1786–90); repr. in Barbieri (1990)

P. Barbieri: *Acustica, accordatura e temperamento dell'Illuminismo veneto: con scritti inditi di Alessandro Barca* (Rome, 1987) [incl. complete list of writings]

P. Barbieri: 'Gli armonisti padovani del Santo nel Settecento', *Storia della musica al Santo di Padova*, ed. S. Durante and P. Petrobelli (Vicenza, 1990), 199–221

P. Barbieri: 'La "Nuova teoria di musica" di Alessandro Barca in un inedito esame di Giordano Riccati (1786–90)', *Studi in onore di Giulio Cattin*, ed. F. Luisi (Rome, 1990), 159–76

PATRIZIO BARBIERI

Barcarolle (Fr.; It. *barcarola*). Title given to pieces that imitate or suggest the songs (*barcarole*) sung by Venetian gondoliers as they propel their boats through the water. These songs were already widely known in the 18th century: in *The Present State of Music in France and Italy* (1771), Burney reported that they were 'so celebrated that every musical collector of taste in Europe is well furnished with them'. A basic feature of the barcarolle is the time signature, 6/8, with a marked lilting rhythm depicting the movement of the boat.

The barcarolle has been much used in Romantic opera, where it has a sentimental, even melancholy atmosphere: the most famous example is that by Offenbach in Act 2 of *Les contes d'Hoffmann*. Schubert frequently used the barcarolle lilt in his songs: though neither given the name nor associated with Venice, *Auf dem Wasser zu singen* (D774) and *Des Fischers Liebesglück* (D933) are perfect examples. Schubert also set Mayrhofer's *Der Gondelfahrer*, as a solo song and as a male-voice quartet (D808–9), and both are typical barcarolles of great lyrical beauty.

The most famous example for piano solo is Chopin's superb Barcarolle in F# op.60 (1845–6); it is in 12/8 instead of the customary 6/8. Further examples in Chopin are the early *Souvenir de Paganini* (1829; a barcarolle in A based on the well-known theme *Le carneval de Venise*)

and the Variations in D for piano duet, based on the same theme. There are three pieces entitled *Venetianisches Gondellied* among Mendelssohn's *Lieder ohne Worte*: op.19 no.6 in G minor, op.30 no.6 in F# minor and op.62 no.5 in A minor (he actually composed the first in Venice); he also wrote an isolated *Gondellied* in A in 1837. The most important series of barcarolles, however, are the 13 that Fauré composed between about 1880 and 1921; he also wrote a song called *Barcarolle* (op.7 no.3, 1873). Anton Rubinstein, Balakirev, S.M. Lyapunov, Glazunov, Vítezslav Novák and MacDowell are others who wrote barcarolles for piano.

BIBLIOGRAPHY

MGG2 ('Barkarole'; H. Schneider)

H. Schneider: 'Die Barkarole und Venedig', *L'opera fra Parigi*, ed. M.T. Muraro (Florence, 1988), 11–56

MAURICE J.E. BROWN/KENNETH L. HAMILTON

Barce (Benito), Ramón (*b* Madrid, 16 March 1928). Spanish composer and critic. He studied in Madrid at the conservatory and at the university, where he received the doctorate (1956). Although he followed courses under Messiaen and Ligeti, he is fundamentally a self-taught composer. He was a founder member of the Grupo Nueva Música (1958) and of 'Zaj' (1964–6), a musical theatre group. In 1967 he launched the *Sonda* magazine and the associated series of new music concerts. He was also music critic of the Madrid newspaper *Ya* (1971–8) and deputy director of *Ritmo* (1982–93). He has translated into Spanish numerous books, including works by Reger, Schoenberg, Schenker and Piston. He has been awarded various distinctions, such as the National Prize for Music (1973), the City of Madrid Prize for Musical Creation (1992) and the Gold Medal of Merit in Fine Arts (1996).

His earliest compositions, from the end of the 1950s, dispense with the neo-populist elements fashionable in Spain at that time and show a strong Expressionist leaning. In the early 1960s structural organization and flexible tempo come to the fore. It was during this experimental period that he invented the system of levels, which subsequently shaped his musical production. This involved the construction of chromatic scales in which the higher and lower 5ths (the dominant and subdominant of the traditional system) are suppressed. By avoiding hierarchical functions the harmonies can oscillate between atonal and pseudo-tonal sounds in the same way that tonal music can be tonal to varying degrees within the same work. Barce first used the system in the *Nueve pequeños preludios* (1965). It occurred subsequently in *Períodos en nivel Re* (1967) and received its most systematic exposition in the 48 Preludes for piano (1973–83).

WORKS
(*selective list*)

DRAMATIC AND VOCAL

Op: Los bárbaros (Barce), 1965–73

Music theatre: Abgrund, Hintergrund, 1964; Estudio de impulsos, 1964; Translaciones, 1965; Coral hablado, 1966

Film score: Espectro 7 (Barce, dir. J. Aguirre), 1970

Vocal: Residencias (D. García Bacca), chorus, 1974; 2 aforismos de Juan de Mairena (A. Machado), vocal qt, chorus, 1975; Canciones de la ciudad, S, inst ens, 1961; Tal com'as nubes, S, pf, 1964; Cant. I (E. Andrés), S, inst ens, 1966; Lamentación de Jerusalén (G. Miro), S, pf, 1973; Eterna (Barce), S, cl, pf, perc, 1975; Desierto sibilino (T. Mann), Mez, ob, tpt, 1978; Oleada (melodrama, Barce, after Apollonius of Rhodes: *Argonautica*), S/

Mez, 1982; Hacia mañana, hacia hoy (melodrama, Barce), 1v, cl, pf, 1987

INSTRUMENTAL

Syms.: no.1, 1975; no.2, 1982; no.3, 1983; no.4, 1984; no.5, 1992; no.6, 1998
Other orch: Alfa, str, 1965; Las cuatro estaciones, 1967; Pf Conc., 1974; 4 piezas, 1975

5 or more insts: Quinteto, fl, vn, va, vc, pf, 1960; Objetos sonoros, 1963; Parábola, wind qnt, 1963; Obertura fonética, 1968; Concierto de Lizara I, 1969; Música funébra, 1969; Nuevas polifonías (Libro 1), 1971; Concierto de Lizara III, 1973; Concierto de Lizara IV, 1976; Nuevas polifonías (Libro 2), 1985
4 insts: Str qts: no.1, 1958; no.2, 1965; no.3 'Cuarteto Gauss', 1973; no.4, 1975; no.5, 1978; no.6, 1978; no.7, 1978; no.8, 1983; Serenata, cl, vn, vc, pf, 1978
2–3 insts: Sonata no.1, vn, pf, 1959; Sonata, fl, pf, 1962; Siala, cl, pf, 1964; Canadá-Trio, fl, pf, perc, 1968; Métrica I, vc, pf, 1969; Sonata no.2, vn, pf, 1969; Métrica II, tpt, pf, perc, 1970; Kampa, vn, vc, pf, 1978; Dúo, db, pf, 1980; 12 trios, 2 vn, perc, 1990
Pf: Estudio de sonoridades, 1962; Estudio de densidades, 1965; 9 pequeños preludios, 1965; Estudio de valores, 1967; Períodos en nivel Re, 1967; 48 preludios, 1973–83; Tango para Ivar, 1984

WRITINGS

Fronteras de la música (Madrid, 1985)
'Autoanálisis', 12 compositores espanoles de hoy (Oviedo, 1982), 77–113
'La ópera y la zarzuela en el siglo XIX', España en la música de occidente: Salamanca 1985, 145–53
'Convención e inovación', El pasado en la música de nuestro tiempo (Madrid, 1988)
'Sistema y elección en la composición musical', Composición musical I: Valencia 1988 (Valencia, 1989), 37–50
'L'avangarda i jo', Revista musical catalana, no.59 (1989), 23–6
Boccherini en Madrid: primeros años 1768–1779 (Madrid, 1992)
Tiempo de tinieblas y algunas sonrisas (Madrid, 1992)
'Profilo ideologico de Manuel de Falla', Musica/Realtà, no.42 (1993)
ed.: Actualidad y futuro de la zarzuela (Madrid, 1994)
'Sintesi di folklore professionali in Isaac Albéniz', Musica/Realtà, no.51 (1996)
'Materia sonora y campo simbólico', Revista de Occidente, no.191 (1997), 23–38

BIBLIOGRAPHY

A. Medina: Ramón Barce en la vanguardia musical española (Oviedo, 1983)
A. Medina: 'Intrivista a R. Barce: una voce riflessiva nella musica spagnuola', Musica/Realtà, no.33 (1990), 133–46
A. Charles: 'Ramón Barce, un compositor entre la vanguardia y un lenguaje personalizado', AnM, lii (1997)

TOMÁS MARCO/ANGEL MEDINA

Barcelona. Capital city of Catalonia, Spain. In the 4th century one of its bishops, St Pacian, condemned the citizens' custom of celebrating the New Year with masquerades, music and dance. In 540 the first ecumenical Council of Barcelona, one of whose canons was concerned with regulating the Laudes chant, took place. The earliest known Barcelona composer is St Quiricus (bishop ? 656–66), who wrote a hymn to St Eulalia and possibly another to St Cugat, Barchinone laete Cucufate vernans (E-Tc 35). The rite and chants used in Catalonia at that time were those of the Visigothic Church, based in Toledo. After a short occupation by the Moors, Barcelona became the capital of the Marca Hispánica and transferred its allegiance to the Roman rite. By the mid-12th century the city had become the commercial centre of the Kingdom of Aragón. From the 10th century to the 13th Barcelona's musical life centred on its cathedral, whose first organ was built about 1259. An early 14th century treatise (Bc 23.1) shows that polyphony was well known in the area, as were the latest innovations in mensural notation. The transfer of the papacy to Avignon in 1309 made it easy

for foreign musicians to enter the Kingdom of Aragón, at whose court, based in Barcelona, the most famous Franco-Flemish woodwind players were heard. The royal chapel employed composers of the stature of Steve de Sort and Gacian Reyneau, who contributed to the renewal of the kingdom's musical life. The transfer of the royal residence to Naples in 1433, in the reign of Alfonso V, interrupted this process.

Renaissance composers in Barcelona, some of them active in the cathedral, included the organist Pere Alberch i Ferrament alias Vila and the choirmasters Guillermo de Podio, Pedro Juan Aldomar and Juan Ferrer. In the second half of the 16th century, when the basse danse Barcelonne (B-Br 9085) was composed, the cathedral had 14 choristers. The principal music publisher of the period was Humbert Gotard.

Distinguished 17th-century composers working at the cathedral included Juan Pujol, Marcián Albareda, Luis Vicente Gargallo and the noted theorist Francisco Valls. José Pujol and José Durán, who introduced the Italian style to Catalan religious music, succeeded Valls as maestros de capilla. In the 18th century the principal organist was Carlos Baguer; José Elías was organist at the church of SS Justo y Pastor. The first opera performances, organized for the court, were in 1708–9 and included Caldara's Il più bel nome. At the end of the 1720s zarzuela companies began arriving from Madrid. In 1750 the first Italian opera company was established in the city, based at the Teatro de la S Cruz (Teatre de la S Creu); its repertory was chiefly Neapolitan or Venetian and occasionally Viennese. Works by such Catalans as D.M.B. Terradellas, Josep Durán, Fernando Sor and Baguer were also heard; French opera was unpopular. Later, Rossini met with particular success.

The first Sociedad Filarmónica Barcelonesa began its activities between 1844 and 1854, and promoted a recital by Liszt in the Salón de la Lonja in 1845. It was succeeded from 1866 by the Sociedad de Conciertos de Barcelona, established by Joan Casamitjana, and later by the Sociedad Catalana de Conciertos, founded by Antoni Nicolau in 1892, and the Sociedad Filarmónica, founded in 1897. The Orfeó Català, founded by Lluis Millet in 1891, was successor to the popular movement promoted by the choirs of Anselmo Clavé; the Palau de la Música, still the city's main concert hall, was built between 1905 and 1908 at Millet's initiative (see illustration). The Gran Teatro del Liceo (Gran Teatre del Liceu) opened in April 1847 with Donizetti's Anna Bolena, and from then on was the centre of Barcelona's operatic activities. Lohengrin, performed in 1882 in the Teatro de la S Cruz, was the first Wagner opera to be heard in Barcelona; an Asociación Wagneriana was formed in 1901. The Liceo Filarmoñico Dramático Barcelonés de S.M. Doña Isabel II (later the Conservatorio Superior del Liceo) began its work in 1838, and the Escuela Municipal de Música in 1886; these are still the main centres of musical education.

Among Barcelona composers born at the end of the 19th century, Amadeo Vives is pre-eminent; notable among those with nationalistic tendencies were Frederic Mompou and Eduardo Toldrá, founder in 1912 of the Cuarteto Renacimiento (Quartet Renaixement). In 1944 Toldrá also founded the Orquesta Municipal de Barcelona; this succeeded the Orquesta Pablo Casals, founded in 1919 and active until the Spanish Civil War (1936–9).

Interior of the Palau de la Música, Barcelona, designed by Lluís Domènech i Montaner, opened 1908; the proscenium arch represents the Ride of the Valkyries

The most influential composer and teacher of this generation was Cristòfor Taltabull. The 'Generación del 27', a group of composers born around 1900, formed the Grupo de los Ocho in 1930; its principal representative was Roberto Gerhard, Schoenberg's only Spanish follower. The group disintegrated with the Civil War and traces of its aims are found only in one of Gerhard's disciples, Joaquim Homs. After Spain's post-Civil War isolation, a group of reforming composers, the 'Generación del 51', emerged; notable members are Josep Mestres-Quadreny, Xavier Benguerel, Juan Guinjoán and Josep Soler.

Important 20th-century performers born or trained in Barcelona include the singers Victoria de los Angeles, Montserrat Caballé, Francisco Viñas, Giacomo Aragall and José Carreras, the pianist Alicia de Larrocha and the viol player Jordi Savall, founder and director of Hespèrion XX and the Capella Reial de Catalunya (1987), groups specializing in early music. An early music festival was founded in 1977.

The Instituto Español de Musicología was established in 1943 by Higinio Anglés, who was also director of the music department of the Biblioteca de Catalunya, founded by Felipe Pedrell, which holds the largest collection of music in Barcelona, including manuscripts of works by Catalan composers of the 20th century.

BIBLIOGRAPHY

L. Lamaña: *Barcelona filarmónica* (Barcelona, 1927)
H. Anglès: *La música a Catalunya fins al segle XIII* (Barcelona, 1935/R)
J. Lamote de Grignon: *Musique et musiciens français à Barcelone* (Barcelona, 1935)
F. Baldelló: *La música en Barcelona* (Barcelona, 1943)
F. Baldelló: 'Organos y organeros en Barcelona (siglos XIII–XIX)', *AnM*, i (1946), 195–237
J. Subirá: *La ópera en los teatros de Barcelona* (Barcelona, 1946/R)
J. Madurell: 'Documentos para la historia de maestros de capilla, infantes de coro, maestros de música y danza y ministriles en Barcelona (siglos XIV–XVIII)', *AnM*, iii (1948), 213–34
F. Baldelló: 'La música en la Basílica Parroquial de Santa María del Mar, de Barcelona', *AnM*, xvii (1962), 209–41
M.C. Gómez: *Le música en la casa real catalano-aragonesa durante los años 1336–1432* (Barcelona, 1979)
T. Marco: *Historia de la música española*, vi: *Siglo XX*, ed. P. López de Osaba (Madrid, 1983; Eng. trans., 1993)
X. Aviñoa: *La música i el modernisme* (Barcelona, 1985)
J. Pavía: *La música a la catedral de Barcelona durant el segle XVII* (Barcelona, 1985)
R. Alier: *L'opera a Barcelona* (Barcelona, 1990)
K.R. Kreitner: *Music and Civic Ceremony in Late Fifteenth-Century Barcelona* (diss., Duke U., 1990)
M. Comellas: *L'activitat concertística a Barcelona durant la primera meitat del segle XIX* (diss., Universitat Autònoma de Barcelona, 1997)

MARICARMEN GÓMEZ

Barcelona Mass. A cycle of the ordinary of the Mass belonging to the Avignon school found in the manuscript *E-Bc* M971 (ff.1*r*–8*r*) that almost certainly belonged to the chapel of King Martin I of Aragon (1396–1410). It is made up of five fragments, written, with the exception of the four-part Agnus Dei, for three parts.

The compositional techniques vary from movement to movement. The Kyrie is written in simultaneous style and has no concordances. The Gloria is in discant style and has certain similarities with the melody of a Gloria by Depansis in a contemporary source (*F-APT* 16*bis*, no.12): either one melody provided a model for the other, or both are by the same composer (Stäblein-Harder). There are two other versions of this Gloria (*E-Boc* 2, no.1 and *F-APT* 16*bis*, no.34) which have different countertenors, and another (*F-Sm* 222, no.82) which is lost.

The Credo, in contrast to the Gloria, is in discant style and is less ornamented. Judging from the large number of known concordances (*E-Sa* 109, no.4; *F-APT* 16*bis*, no.46; *F-CA*, no.6; *F-Pn* 23190, no.103 (index); *F-TLm* 94, no.1; *I-CF* 98, no.2; *I-IV*, no.60; *NL-Lu*, 2515, no.3; *US-R* 44, no.3) it is the most famous liturgical fragment of the Ars Nova. Its inclusion in the index of one of these manuscripts (*F-Pn* 23190) suggests that it must have been composed before 1376. The version in the Barcelona manuscript contains notable errors, and the most reliable source is the Apt Codex.

The Sanctus is a motet for three voices with troped text. This fragment has no known concordances, although the Sanctus in the Apt Codex (*F-APT* 16*bis*, no.15) uses the same troped texts. The Agnus Dei is difficult to classify, despite the fact that its basic style is simultaneous. The outer voices are texted, while the inner voices are not. The contra I offers a complementary counterpoint to the quadruplum and tenor, which implies that it was sung. The only known concordance of this composition appears in a wall painting in Notre Dame, Kernascléden, Brittany. Unlike other known 14th-century cycles of the Ordinary of the Mass the Barcelona Mass does not include an Ite missa est or a Benedictus.

The Agnus Dei and the Kyrie are, in a way, related. They are the only fragments of the work written in imperfect time and minor prolation; the other three fragments are in imperfect time and major prolation. They use similar rhythmic motifs, although these are more complex in the Agnus Dei than in the Kyrie. In both movements the highest voice begins with a similar descending motif. The Gloria and Sanctus offer a contrast to the first and the last fragments of the Mass, in terms of their style and mensuration and of their text, which in both cases is troped. Unlike the Kyrie and, partly, the Sanctus, both fragments are related to the Avignon repertory by virtue of their concordances. The Credo is written in the 4th mode, while the others are mainly in the 1st mode. It is also included in the TOULOUSE MASS, where it is integrated into the mass as a whole, whereas in the Barcelona Mass it acts as an element of contrast. It is the only one of the five fragments to mention what may be the name of the composer, Sortes or Sortis. This might be the organist Steve de Sort, who was in the service of the royal chapel of Aragon between 1394 and 1407 (but *see* SORTES). In the Ivrea Codex this composition appears with the subtitle 'de rege'. In general terms, there is less internal cohesion in the Barcelona Mass than in other 14th-century cycles of the Ordinary of the Mass. The mass is edited in PMFC, i (1956), pp.13–64; in CMM, xxix (1962), nos.19, 25, 47, 56, 72; and in M.C. Gómez:

El manuscrito M971 de la Biblioteca de Catalunya (Misa de Barcelona) (Barcelona, 1989).

See also TOURNAI MASS and MASS, §II, 4.

BIBLIOGRAPHY

F. Ludwig, ed.: *Guillaume de Machaut: Musikalische Werke*, ii (Leipzig, 1928/R), 22
H. Anglés: *La música española desde la Edad Media hasta nuestros días* (Barcelona, 1941), 26
H. Harder: 'Die Messe von Toulouse', *MD*, vii (1953), 105–28
L. Schrade: 'The Mass of Toulouse', *RBM*, viii (1954), 84–96
H. Stäblein-Harder: *Fourteenth-Century Mass Music in France*, MSD, vii (1962), nos.19, 25, 47, 56, 72
G. Reaney, ed.: *Manuscripts of Polyphonic Music (c1320–1400)*, RISM, B/IV/2 (1969), 90–92
U. Günther: 'Les anges musiciens et la messe de Kernascléden', *Les sources en musicologie: Paris 1979*, 109–36
M.C. Gómez: 'Quelques remarques sur le répertoire sacré de l'Ars nova provenant de l'ancien royaume d'Aragon', *AcM*, lvii (1985), 166–79
I. Godt: 'The Mass of Barcelona: How many Hands? How much Mass?', *Beyond the Moon: Festschrift Luther Dittmer*, ed. B. Gillingham and P. Merkley (Ottawa,1990), 195–216

MARICARMEN GÓMEZ

Barcewicz, Stanisław (*b* Warsaw, 16 April 1858; *d* Warsaw, 1 Sept 1929). Polish violinist, conductor and teacher. He was a pupil of Apolinary Kątski at the Warsaw Music Institute (*c*1871) and then studied the violin at the Moscow Conservatory with Ferdinand Laub and Jan Hřímalý; on completing his studies in 1876 he was awarded a gold medal. From 1877 he played frequently in Poland and also in England, France, Germany, Denmark, Austria, Sweden, Norway and Russia. He taught the violin and the viola at the Warsaw Music Institute (1886–1918), where he also directed the chamber music class and conducted the student orchestra; he was a member of the governing Pedagogical Council (1888–1901) and later was appointed director (1910–18). He was leader of the Warsaw Opera House orchestra, and from 1886 was conductor there. In 1892 he established his own string quartet. Barcewicz was one of the finest Polish violinists. He won great recognition for his beautiful, deep, full tone, excellent technique and individuality of interpretation. He had a large repertory, comprising chiefly the works of Classical and Romantic composers.

BIBLIOGRAPHY

PSB (M. Gliński); *SMP*
J. Kleczyński: 'Stanisław Barcewicz', *Echo muyczne i teatralne*, i (1883–4), 308–9; x (1894), 598–9

ELŻBIETA DZIĘBOWSKA

Bard. Among the Celts, a composer of praise poetry (and, on occasion, its counterpart of dispraise or satire). The word is almost certainly of Indo-European origin but has no obvious cognates outside the group of Celtic languages: from a common Celtic *bardos* are derived the Gaelic, Manx and Irish *bard*, Welsh *bardd*, Cornish *barth* and Breton *barz*. The basic meaning appears to be 'praise singer', even if the professional and social status of such figures varied from age to age and from culture to culture. In Scots Gaelic 'bard' became the generic term for poet. (The development of 'bard' in English to indicate a poet of lofty imagination, inspired by mysterious powers, is largely a product of Romanticism.)

For an extended use of the term to refer to epic singers of non-Celtic peoples *see* AOIDOS; EPICS; MONGOL MUSIC, §§1(iii–iv), 4(ii), 6(v); and CENTRAL ASIA, §2.

1. Antiquity. 2. Medieval and post-medieval Wales and Cornwall. 3. Medieval and post-medieval Ireland and Scotland. 4. Music and performing practice.

1. ANTIQUITY.   Knowledge of the functions of the bards of ancient Gaul derives from passages in Greek and Roman authors. Some of their most valuable evidence depends on material, now lost, by Posidonius of Apamea (*c*135–*c*51 BCE). Strabo's version may be taken as representative: 'The bards [*bardoi*] are singers and poets, the vates [*ouateis*] interpreters of sacrifice and natural philosophers, while the druids [*druïdai*] in addition to the science of nature study moral philosophy' (*Geography*, iv.4.4). The distinction between these castes may derive from Posidonius, and the idea of a caste system agrees with later Celtic evidence (see below, §§2–3); there is no reason to doubt that the bards were poets whose function included the singing of panegyrics. Tierney has shown, however, that Posidonius's ascription to these groups of philosophical studies cannot be taken at its face value. The ancient authorities – several of them apparently dependent on Posidonius – include, besides Strabo quoted above, Diodorus Siculus (v.31), who mentioned the bards' use of 'instruments similar to lyres', Athenaeus (246c–d), Lucan (*Civil War*, i.442–9) and Caesar (*Gallic War*, vi.13).

Some centuries before the Christian era, the Celts had become dominant in the British Isles: the Goidelic Celts in Ireland, who later colonized Scotland and the Isle of Man, and the Brythonic Celts in England and Wales, who colonized Brittany during the 5th and 6th centuries CE. No contemporary records survive, but the bards of the British Isles before the introduction of Christianity may have been essentially similar to those of the European Continent, and, at the rise of Christianity, may have preserved some of the lore of the druids.

The greater part of what is now England lost some of its Celtic character at the Roman occupation (43–410 CE), although this character persisted in Cornwall until modern times and in Strathclyde (i.e. parts of north-eastern England and southern Scotland) until the 6th century. The bards of antiquity may have used the crwth, a relative of the lyre, said by Venantius Fortunatus (*c*530/40–*c*600) to be played in Britain (F. Leo, ed.: *Venanti Honori Clementiani Fortunati presbyteri italici opera poetica*, MGH, *Auctorum antiquissimorum*, iv/1, 1881/R, 64).

2. MEDIEVAL AND POST-MEDIEVAL WALES AND CORNWALL.   Throughout the British Isles local kings, princes and chieftains maintained bards, bestowing gifts upon them for their services. The bards played the harp and sang elegies and eulogies on famous men, composed proverbs and recited sagas. Monasteries also sometimes maintained bards as historians and genealogists, as at Aberconway and Strata Florida in Wales.

The high esteem in which the class was held is evident in the early legal codes of both Ireland and Wales. The Laws of Hywel Dda (Howel the Good), surviving in Welsh manuscripts from the 12th century but representing in essence a 10th-century codification of customs rather more ancient, distinguish two classes of bard: the *bardd teulu*, who was a permanent official of the king's household, and the *pencerdd* ('chief of song'), or head of the bardic fraternity in the district (this term still survives; for details of original sources, see Gwynn Jones, 1913–14). These classes of resident and itinerant bards, also

found in Ireland and Scotland, are reminiscent of classes found generally among Indo-European ethnic groups, for example, in Anglo-Saxon England, although they cannot be precisely equated with the SCOP and gleeman respectively. These latter, like the Scandinavian *skald* and other poet-musicians of early nations, have sometimes been termed 'bards' in English literature.

During the 12th and 13th centuries in Wales bards no longer came to be appointed to the king's household, and their position changed greatly after the ending of native rule. They increased in number, and just as in France some of the nobility became troubadours and trouvères, so some Welsh princes became bards. (The poetic forms of the troubadours and trouvères, moreover, influenced those of 14th-century Welsh bards.)

The bards were highly organized into various grades and were required to serve a long apprenticeship and to acquire much skill and learning before they were allowed to serve professionally. This is revealed by a Welsh bardic statute, originating in its present form in the 15th century but representing the progressive customs of three centuries or more (for the earliest surviving version, see Parry, 1929). The Laws of Hywel Dda reveal that the bardic instrument was the harp; to this the statute mentioned above adds the CRWTH.

The bards had always encouraged their peoples in the face of hardship, but under the growing influence of the English monarchs their incitements to liberty came to be regarded as incitements to rebellion. In consequence, numerous laws were enacted to put them down. The alleged massacre of Welsh bards by Edward I (whose conquest of Wales virtually brought native rule to an end in 1282) is only a fable; but later laws represented the bards as degenerate (e.g. a statute of Henry IV dated 1402), and a royal proclamation known as the Commission of the Caerwys Eisteddfod, issued by Elizabeth I, complained of 'vagraunt and idle persons naming theim selfes mynstrelles Rithmers and Barthes' who were seditious and went into competition with the skilled bards (see J.G. Evans: *Report on Manuscripts in the Welsh Language*, i/1: *The Welsh Manuscripts of Lord Mostyn, at Mostyn Hall, co. Flint*, HMC, no.48, 1898, pp.291–2). In Cornwall, 'bard' came to mean 'mimic' and 'buffoon'; and in other Celtic areas the loan-word 'bard' in English writings often carried a pejorative meaning. Nevertheless, in all the Celtic countries the household bard continued in function – and often in name – until quite recent times: harpists were still active in some large houses up to the 19th century.

The poet-musician of early times had, however, virtually vanished. Although poetry and music long remained undivided, a partial separation between them occurred at an early period (varying from country to country) and even in the Middle Ages musical and poetical bards were to some extent recognized as separate classes. Latterly, the term 'bard', especially in compound words, occasionally denoted a musician as distinct from a poet, as in the Welsh and Cornish *bardd* (*barth*) *hirgorn*, or trumpet major, found as early as the 18th century. More usually, however, the term has meant a poet alone, not only in the Celtic areas but also in England.

Today the term 'bard' in Wales means the victor at an eisteddfod, whether in poetry or music. Although the bardic rites and customs of the modern Welsh eisteddfod and of the Cornish *gorseth*, established in 1928 with the cultural revival, cannot claim historical continuity with those of the medieval bards, an antiquarian precedent for these customs is not lacking.

Examples of bardic poetry survive, often in critical editions; but the question of bardic music is problematical (see §4 below). The ROBERT AP HUW Manuscript (*GB-Lbl* Add.14905), which was claimed even in the 20th century to contain 'bardic' harp music from about 1100, is an early 17th-century document, part of which appears to be copied from a manuscript of William Penllyn (*fl* 1550–70). The origins of the music can be traced back to named musicians of the 15th century and earlier; the compositional principles are based on the 24 measures of *cerdd dant* ('the craft of the string'), ostensibly formulated in about 1100 according to the document known as the *Cadwedigaeth Cerdd Dannau* ('The Conservation of Cerdd Dant').

See also WALES, §II.

3. MEDIEVAL AND POST–MEDIEVAL IRELAND AND SCOTLAND. In medieval Gaelic society in Ireland and Scotland, professional men of learning were organized in a caste system, under various descriptions: *draoi* (the Gaelic equivalent of 'druid'), *fili*, later *file* (poet-seer), *breitheamh* ('brehon', or lawgiver) and *seanchaidh* (historian-antiquarian). These terms appear to denote various offices, or perhaps duties, of the highest orders in the professional hierarchy.

The *bard* occupied a lower position. Until the Norman Conquest, the *filidh* (plural of *fili*) specialized in a form of poetry called *seanchas* that drew on the high learning, historical and mythological, of the Gaels; and the *filidh* appear to have maintained some vestiges of pagan religion (the word *fili* derives from a root 'to see'). But the *bard*, according to 10th-century Irish juristic tradition, had an honour price only half that of a *fili*; and, according to another medieval juristic tradition, a *bard* might claim nothing on the grounds of his status as a man of learning but should rest satisfied with whatever his native wit might win him.

Both *filidh* and *baird* (plural of *bard*) were divided into classes by the jurists. The two main bardic classes, *sóerbaird* (free, privileged bards) and *dóerbaird* (base bards), were each subdivided into eight further grades. It would seem likely that a general distinction was observed between bards of good family, or of special genius, and others less respected, but the precision of the grades may have been little more than theoretical.

The original function of the bard was to compose eulogy, his craft – *bairdne* (bardic verse) – contrasting with the *filidecht* (*seanchas* poetry) of the *fili*. With the social changes after the Norman invasion of Ireland, however, patronage for the *filidh* disappeared, since there was no longer an audience for the ancient high learning; but bardic praise-poetry, with its obverse of dispraise, continued to exist where Gaelic kings or petty rulers succeeded in saving some part of their ancient lordships from the general ruin. Before this time (the late 12th century), *filidh* had occasionally composed panegyric, but now this seems to have become their primary function.

From about 1200 to 1650, these composers used a highly elaborate and subtle metric system and a standard language (classical Gaelic), perhaps somewhat conservative in pronunciation but very progressive in form. Poets were taught in schools: much didactic material survives – discussions of grammatical and metrical usage – to show that the academic discipline was severe; it is said, but on uncertain evidence, that the period of training was seven years. Much of the poetry survives, particularly from Ireland but also from Scotland (classical Gaelic was common to the two countries); it consists not only of panegyric but also of religious, love and Ossianic verse (*see* OSSIAN). It is known in English as 'bardic' verse, although its composers called themselves *filidh* not *baird*: they knew that the word *bard* had connotations of low rank. To the present day, indeed, the Irish word for 'poet' is not *bard* but *file* (plural *filí*).

The *bard* was mentioned in the context of this poetry in Ireland and Scotland in the 17th century, but in a subordinate role. He might be a kind of literary retainer in the household of a *file*, he might be assigned to recite the poem, or he might also be placed in charge of the musical accompaniment: his exact functions probably varied from place to place. The Irish *Clanricarde Memoirs* (quoted in Bergin, 1913, pp.158–9) relate, in a probably reliable account:

The Action and Pronunciation of the Poem … was perform'd with a great deal of Ceremony in a Consort of Vocal and Instrumental Musick. The Poet himself said nothing, but directed and took care that every body else did his Part right. The Bards having first had the Composition from him, got it well by Heart, and now pronounc'd it orderly, keeping even Pace with a Harp, touch'd upon that Occasion; no other Instrument being allowed for the said Purpose than this alone.

This highly literate tradition of classical Gaelic 'bardic poetry', cultivated by the *filí*, ceased in Ireland in the 17th century; there are fewer survivals in Scotland despite its persistence in that country to the mid-18th century.

With the social changes that followed the introduction of the feudal system to Scotland, during which the court language changed from Gaelic to Norman-French and later to Scots, the classical tradition began to disappear, but the status of the panegyrist *bard* improved, though doubtless not in an identical manner in every place. The

Irish bard and harper: woodcut from John Derricke's 'Image of Irelande' (London, 1581)

Scots Gaelic term for a poet is *bard* to the present day; and by the 17th century, Scottish bardic poetry was dominated not by the strict metres of classical Gaelic but by vernacular Scots Gaelic. Unlike their classical counterparts, the vernacular poets were mostly illiterate until the 18th century, although some earlier bards who recited for poets may have been partially literate. Literacy was unusual, however, until the 19th century, for vernacular Gaelic verse developed in a predominantly oral tradition. Some of these vernacular bards had patrons, some did not; but Gaelic makers of verse have always enjoyed both honour and a kind of diplomatic immunity. From the earliest times the poet (*file* or *bard*) held the power to redress grievances in society and, in popular belief to the present day, to wound or even kill by means of *aer* (later *aoir*), usually translated 'satire'.

The essential rhetorical structure of the poetry derives from panegyric, although its subject matter is very varied. As a result of the 20th-century revival of Scots Gaelic literature, contemporary literary poets may be distinguished from the semi-literate or (now rarely) non-literate 'bards' of the Gaelic-speaking areas of the Highlands and Islands of Scotland. The latter continue to bring traditional attitudes to bear upon topical events at local or national level, with praise, rebuke, humour etc.; they also compose more personal poetry such as love poetry or elegy, and there is a continuing output of religious verse. Like the vast bulk of traditional Gaelic poetry, these compositions are all designed for singing or chanting, and the melodies are drawn from the still considerable mass of orally transmitted traditional song.

4. MUSIC AND PERFORMING PRACTICE. It is impossible to tell with certainty how much or how little of bardic music survives. By the 18th century, when antiquarians in Britain and Ireland became aware of the social function of 'ancient' music (i.e. 'Celtic' music), it was already too late to record in reliable form an authentic bardic style of singing, chanting or reciting poetry to the accompaniment of a harp. It is important, furthermore, to separate the concept of 'bard' from that of 'instrumental musician', for they were distinct in the Middle Ages. The bard would often have with him a harper and a person (*datgeiniaid*) to sing or declaim his songs, but no description of how the songs were performed survives. In Ireland, a parallel class, namely the *recairi*, sang or recited the praises of their leaders, again to the accompaniment provided by a harper. The main part of the verse may have been chanted in a monotone, with cadential melodic inflections as in psalmody, and supported by harp chords; such a method of performance is described in Mayo as late as the 18th century.

The earliest competitive festival in Wales, that held under the patronage of Lord Rhys ap Gruffudd at Cardigan at Christmas 1176, instituted two contests: between the bards and poets, and among harpers, crowthers and pipers. But by the time of the Carmarthen Eisteddfod of 1451, music and poetry were coming into looser association. Later, after 1600, with the decline of patronage, the functions became confused or had merged, although the term lived on: Edward Jones (1752–1824), for example, harper and author of *Musical and Poetical Relicks of the Welsh Bards* (1784), came to be known as 'Bardd y Brenin' (King's Bard), and John Parry of Denbigh (1776–1851), who published Welsh harp music and popularized the term 'penillion singing' (improvised song

with harp accompaniment) in about 1830, was known as 'Bardd Alaw' (Master of Song).

The nine or so Welsh composers represented in the Robert ap Huw harp manuscript (*c*1613), have been dated between approximately 1340 and 1485, and among the compositions are some that suggest accompaniment for sung poems (*caniad*; see ROBERT AP HUW). By the 18th century, however, blind John Parry (*c*1710–82), the Welsh harper, was already being influenced by the Italian Baroque style, as was his counterpart in Ireland, Turlough Carolan (1670–1738), famously described by Goldsmith as 'the last Irish bard'. Carolan composed hundreds of songs in honour of his Irish patrons, singing them to the accompaniment of his harp. By 1792 Edward Bunting was attempting to note down the tunes played at the famous Belfast Harp Festival of that year, and these later formed the basis for his three-volume *The Ancient Music of Ireland* (1796, 1809, 1840). In Scotland the Rev. Patrick Macdonald can be found complaining, in his *Collection of Highland Vocal Airs* (1784), of the foreign influence on clàrsach performance. Carolan's contemporary there, Roderick Morison (*c*1656–1713/14), known as 'An Clarsair Dall' (The Blind Harper), has similarly been termed 'Gaelic Scotland's last minstrel'. Born in Lewis, he completed his musical training in Ireland. Like Carolan, he was itinerant from time to time and dependent on the gentry for his livelihood. Combining the skills of poet, musician and performer, he composed a number of songs to his patrons the MacLeods: for example, his *Féill nan crann* ('Harp-Key Fair'), the words and music of which survive, reflects a satirical, self-mocking strain.

Another noted Highland satirist, Iain Lom (*c*1625–*c*1707) created a famous song, still sung, on the Battle of Inverlochy (1645) in which the MacDonalds overcame the Campbells. The female poet, Sileas na Ceapaich (*c*1660–*c*1729), who possibly used trance-like states induced by starvation as a source for inspiration, left a notable lament for the harper Lachlann Dall, who died in the 1720s. Possibly the last remnants of the bardic profession (in the original sense of that term) to have survived were the MacMhuirich family, hereditary bards to the MacDonalds of Clanranald: the last practising MacMhuirich classical bard was Domhnall (*fl* 1710). A forbear, Niall Mór (*c*1550 – after 1613) may well be the composer of a satire on the bagpipes, which had begun to rival the harp as a basis for extended composition. But although both writing and singing were creative activities among such bards as the MacMhuirichs, there is little evidence of a musical notation. Joseph Walker's *Historical Memoirs of the Irish Bards* (1786, 2/1818) includes airs by Carolan and an essay by William Beauford that purports to prove that a system of musical notation was used in Ireland in the 11th and 12th centuries. In 1980 another scholar put forward the theory of a secret notation contained in the early Irish linear script *ogam*.

Current knowledge of bardic practice in its original environment is largely circumstantial or inadequate to a full description of performing style. The Fenian lays of Ireland and Scotland were composed by bards in the medieval syllabic metres known as *dán*, with a set number of syllables to the line (see OSSIAN). Evidence in the 20th century for the singing style of heroic ballads in modern stressed metres includes a tendency, among the few vernacular singers recorded in South Uist, to regularize the tempo, a fact that may suggest a break with the

Ex.1

1 Laighéa - slain-te throm, throm Air ni-ghean Maigh-re nan còrn fi - al;

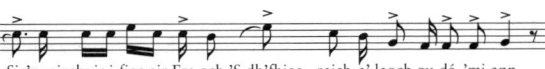

Sin'nuairchuir i fios air Fra och-'S dh'fhios. raich a' laoch gu dé 'mi-ann.

2 Thuirt i ris nach - biodh i   slàn. . .

traditional stress patterns of Gaelic. Certainly, the few examples of heroic lays from the Hebrides and Ireland may, however, also be suggestive of the range and limits of an older style: the melodic shape of an essentially word-orientated style of sung declamation usually falls within the octave, although one notable example (the melody of *Laoidh Fhraoich*) covers the span of a 10th (ex.1).

The term 'bard' has now come, in any case, to mean simply 'poet'. It can have a local connotation in the Highlands and is used in such phrases as *bard baile* ('township poet'), that is, a poet-composer in the Gaelic vernacular idiom. Some of these latterday 'bards' in the Hebrides look to the great songmakers of the 18th century as their ideal if not their actual models for composition: masters such as Alexander MacDonald (*c*1695–*c*1770), a fervent Jacobite who composed his poems to Lowland and English airs, his unschooled friend John MacCodrum (1710–96), family bard to Sir James MacDonald of Sleat, or the untutored Duncan Ban MacIntyre (1724–1812), who, though politically a Hanoverian, forged elaborate songs like *In Praise of Ben Doran*, a composition based on the musical structure of *ceol mor* (i.e. air and variations). In 1789 MacIntyre competed unsuccessfully with Donald Shaw for the post of 'Gaelic Bard' to the Highland and Agricultural Society. More of MacIntyre's songs survive in oral tradition than those of his contemporaries. His reputation, like that of Mary MacLeod (*c*1615–*c*1707), the similarly unschooled Rob Donn Mackay (1714–78), and William Ross (1762–?1791), has carried over, firmly enhanced, into the 20th century and bears testimony to the strength of Gaelic oral tradition.

BIBLIOGRAPHY

TEXTS, EDITIONS

E. Jones: *Musical and Poetical Relicks of the Welsh Bards* (London, 1784/R, enlarged 2/1794; music only, 1800–05, enlarged 3/1808 [as *Musical and Poetical Relicks of the Welsh Bards*, i], 4/1825) [most melodies incl. in *The Welsh Harper*, ed. J. Parry (ii) (London, 1839–48)]

P. MacDonald: *A Collection of Highland Vocal Airs* (Edinburgh, 1784)

E. Jones: *The Bardic Museum* (London, 1802) [as Musical and Poetical Relicks of the Welsh Bards, ii], 2/1825) [most melodies incl. in *The Welsh Harper*, ed. J. Parry (ii), i (London, 1839), ii (London, 1848)]

E. Bunting: *The Ancient Music of Ireland*, iii (Dublin, 1840) [incl. 150 airs and a diss. on the history of music in Ireland]

J.L. Campbell, ed.: *Highland Songs of the Forty-Five* (Edinburgh, 1933/R)

J.C. Watson, ed.: *The Gaelic Songs of Mary MacLeod* (London and Glasgow, 1934/R)

A. MacLeod, ed.: *The Songs of Duncan Ban MacIntyre* (Edinburgh, 1952)

W.J. Watson, ed.: *Bardachd ghaidhlig: Specimens of Gaelic Poetry, 1550–1900* (Stirling, 3/1959)

W.S. Gwynn Williams: *Ceinciau telyn cymru/Harp Tunes of Wales* (Penygroes, 1962)

A.M MacKenzie, ed.: *Orain Iain Luim/Songs of John MacDonald, Bard of Keppoch* (Edinburgh, 1964) [in Gaelic and Eng.]

W. Matheson, ed.: *The Blind Harper (An Clarsair Dall): the Songs of Roderick Morison and his Music* (Edinburgh, 1970)

C.O. Baoill, ed.: Sileas MacDonald: *Poems and Songs* (Edinburgh, 1972) [in Eng. and Gaelic]

STUDIES

antiquity

A. Holder, ed.: *Alt-celtischer Sprachschatz*, i (Leipzig, 1896/R), 347

W. Dinan, ed.: *Monumenta historica celtica*, i (London, 1911), 321–3, 331–3, 345

I. Zwicker, ed.: *Fontes historiae religionis celticae* (Berlin, 1934)

T.G.E. Powell: 'Religion, Celtic', *The Oxford Classical Dictionary* (Oxford, 1948, 2/1970)

J.J. Tierney: 'The Celtic Ethnography of Posidonius', *Proceedings of the Royal Irish Academy*, section C, lx (1960), 189–275

Wales

W.F. Skene: *The Four Ancient Books of Wales* (Edinburgh, 1868), i, 29–32, 522ff; ii, 324

T. Gwynn Jones: 'Bardism and Romance', *Transactions of the Honourable Society of Cymmrodorion* (1913–14), 208–310

T. Roberts: *Gwaith Dafydd ab Edmwnd* (Bangor, 1914)

J. Morris-Jones: 'Taliesin', *Y Cymmrodor*, xxviii (London, 1918)

T. Parry: 'Statud Gruffudd ap Cynan', *Bulletin of the Board of Celtic Studies*, v (1929), 25–33

I. Williams and T.Roberts: *Cywyddau Dafydd ap Gwilym a'i Gyfoeswyr* (Cardiff, 1935)

I. Williams, ed.: *Canu Llywarch Hên* (Cardiff, 1935)

P. Crossley-Holland: 'Secular Homophonic Music in Wales in the Middle Ages', *ML*, xxiii (1942), 135–62; rev. and repr. in *Secular Medieval Music in Wales* (Cardiff, 1942)

I. Williams: *Lectures on Early Welsh Poetry* (Dublin, 1944/R), 9

I. Williams: *Canu Taliesin* (Cardiff, 1960)

T. Parry: *A History of Welsh Literature* (Oxford, 1962/R), 43–66, 69, 84, 128, 133–6, 159

G. Thomas: *The Caerwys Eisteddfodau of 1523 and 1567* (Cardiff, 1968)

I. Williams: *Canu Aneirin* (Cardiff, 1968)

I. Williams: *The Poems of Taliesin* (Dublin, 1975) [incl. Eng. trans. by J.E. Caerwyn Williams]

J.E. Caerwyn Williams: *The Poets of the Welsh Princes* (Cardiff, 1978)

A.O.H. Jarman: *The Cynfeirdd: Early Welsh Poets and Poetry* (Cardiff, 1981)

A.O.H. Jarman, ed. and trans.: *Y Gododdin: Britain's Oldest Heroic Poem* (Llandysul, 1988)

C. Lofmark: *Bards and Heroes* (Felinfach, 1989)

O. Ellis: *The Story of the Harp in Wales* (Cardiff, 1991)

P. Crossley-Holland: *The Composers in the Robert ap Huw Manuscript: the Evidence for Identity, Dating and Locality* (Bangor, 1998)

M. Stephens, ed.: 'Bardic, Order, The', *Companion to the Literature of Wales* (Cardiff, 1998)

Ireland and Scotland

M. Martin: *A Description of the Western Islands of Scotland* (London, 1703, 4/1934)

J.C. Walker: *Historical Memoirs of the Irish Bards* (Dublin and London, 1786/R, 2/1818)

E. O'Curry: *On the Manners and Customs of the Ancient Irish* (London, 1873/R)

G. Sigerson, ed.: *Bards of the Gael and Gall* (London, 1897, 3/1925/R)

P.W. Joyce: *A Social History of Ancient Ireland* (London, 1903, 2/1913/R), i, 417–22, 448–9

O.J. Bergin: 'Bardic Poetry', *Ivernian Journal*, v (1913), 153–203

D. Corkery: *The Hidden Ireland: a Study of Gaelic Munster in the Eighteenth Century* (Dublin, 1925), 58–9, 122–3

E. Curtis: *A History of Ireland* (London, 1936, 6/1950), 113

G. Murphy: 'Bards and Filidh', *Éigse: a Journal of Irish Studies*, ii (1940), 200–07

G. Murphy: *Early Irish Metrics* (Dublin, 1961), 26–7

J.L. Campbell and D.S. Thomson, eds.: *Edward Lhuyd in the Scottish Highlands, 1699–1700* (Oxford, 1963), esp. 33–4

F. Collinson: *The Traditional and National Music of Scotland* (London, 1966), 39, 48, 50–51

E. Knott: 'Irish Classical Poetry', *Early Irish Literature*, ed. E. Knott and G. Murphy (London, 1966), 21–93

D.S. Thomson: 'The MacMhuirich Bardic Family', *Transactions of the Gaelic Society of Inverness*, xliii (1966), 276–304

J. MacInnes: 'The Oral Tradition in Scottish Gaelic Poetry', *Scottish Studies*, xii (1968), 29–43

W. Matheson, ed.: *The Blind Harper (An Clasair Dall): the Songs of Roderick Morison and his Music* (Edinburgh, 1970)

T. Knudsen: 'Calum Ruadh, Bard of Skye', *DFS information*, no.1 (1969)

D.S. Thomson: 'Niall Mór MacMhuirich', *Transactions of the Gaelic Society of Inverness*, xlix (1977) [whole issue]

E. Cregeen and D.W.MacKenzie: *Tiree Bards and their Bardachd: the Poets in a Hebridean Community* (Isle of Coll, 1978)

S.O. Boyle: *Ogam: the Poet's Secret* (Dublin, 1980)

T.P. McCaughey: 'The Performing of Dán', *Eriu*, xxxv (1984), 39–57

A. Bruford: 'The Singing of Fenian and Similar Lays in Scotland', *Ballad Research: Dublin 1985*, 55–70

J. MacInnes: 'Recordings of Scottish Gaelic Heroic Ballads', *The Heroic Process*, ed. B. Almqvist and others (Dun Laoghaire, 1987), 101–30

H. Shields: *Narrative Singing in Ireland* (Dublin, 1993)

T.A. McKean: *Hebridean Song-Maker: Iain MacNeacail of the Isle of Skye* (Edinburgh, 1997) [incl. disc]

RECORDINGS

Gaelic Bards & Minstrels, perf. W. Matheson, Greentrax CTRAX9016D (1993) [2 cassettes, with notes]

PETER CROSSLEY-HOLLAND (1–2), JOHN MACINNES (3), JAMES PORTER (4)

Bardaisan [Bardesanes] (*b* Edessa [now Urfa], 11 July 154; *d* Edessa, 222). Syrian hymnographer, astrologer and philosopher. Born into a pagan priestly family, he was educated by a pagan priest but baptized as a Christian, and in 179 he was ordained deacon and priest. Later denounced as a heretic and excommunicated (*c*216), he fled to Armenia and there taught a kind of astrological fatalism. Bardaisan has been erroneously regarded as a leader of the oriental school of gnosticism founded by Valentinus. His theology, which in fact combined Christian doctrine with astrological and philosophical speculation, is known from the works of later Christian writers such as Eusebius and Ephrem Syrus, who strongly denounced it, and from Bardaisan's own *Dialogue with Antonius concerning Destiny* (or *Book of the Laws of the Lands*), which is the oldest surviving document in Syriac.

Bardaisan wrote many hymns (*madrāshe*) in Syriac, which his disciples translated into Greek. They included 150 psalms in pentasyllabic metre, reportedly modelled on those of David, through which he popularized his heretical doctrines (Bardaisan's son Harmonius is said to have written the tunes). The stanzas of the *madrāshe*, probably sung by soloists, were followed by a fixed choral response; they were constructed on isosyllabic principles, the patterns ranging from the very simple (e.g. five four-syllable lines to each stanza) to the highly complex and diffuse. There is, however, no reason to suppose that in Bardaisan's time isosyllabic poetry was an altogether novel phenomenon. His *madrāshe* were very successful and continued to be sung in Edessa probably until the first half of the 5th century; they earned him the title 'Father of Syriac Poetry'. By way of retribution, Ephrem composed other (orthodox) *madrāshe* based on the same metre and with equivalent verse structure. None of Bardaisan's hymns survives, except for some excerpts cited by Ephrem, although there is a hymn that may be his in the 3rd-century apocryphal *Acts of Thomas* ascribed to circles under Bardaisan's influence. His historical works on India and Armenia are also lost.

BIBLIOGRAPHY

O. Bardenhewer: *Geschichte der altkirchlichen Litteratur* (Freiburg, 1902–32/R), i, 337ff

F.C. Burkitt: *Early Eastern Christianity* (London, 1904), 155–227

H.J.W. Drijvers: *Bardaiṣan of Edessa* (Assen, 1966)

S.P. Brock: 'Syrian and Greek Hymnography: Problems of Origin', *Studia patristica*, xvi (1985), 77–81

DIMITRI CONOMOS

Bardanashvili, Ioseb (*b* Batumi, 23 Nov 1948). Georgian composer. He studied composition with A. Shaverzashvili at the Tbilisi State Conservatory (1968–76) and taught at the College of Batumi Music (1973–95). In 1987 he was awarded the Z. Paliashvili State Prize and in 1995 he emigrated to Israel.

Bardanashvili came to notice in the 1970s when, in his first serious experiments in composition dating from his student years, he set himself complex creative tasks and constantly endeavoured to find uncommon ways of solving them. His creative thinking was formed by a synthesis of national traditions – Georgian and Jewish – and contemporary methods such as dodecaphony, in addition to aleatory and sonoristic techniques, all applied in a non-dogmatic manner.

He seeks to reveal the complex, multi-faceted aspects of the human soul, and the rich spectrum of its emotional world; the varied literary sources of his inspiration include, in particular, Jewish medieval poetry and the work of Marcus Aurelius and Michelangelo. His Symphony (1980) marks an important stage in his artistic career: the dramatic integrity of this three-movement work is achieved by unity in its contemplative material which grows out of the brief sounding of a semitone, an interval generically associated with ancient Jewish melody and which is heard at times in a sharply individualized form (mainly in the wordless voice part), later to dissolve into polylinear, aleatory and sonoristic structures. Depth of thought, vivid emotional response, a fine sense of timbre and clear constructional thinking are all displayed in this work.

Attracted to rock music, Bardanashvili composed one of the first Georgian rock operas in collaboration with R. Sturua and the band '75'; during the 1980s and 90s he has shown an interest in theatrical genres.

WORKS
(selective list)

Stage: Balada kalze [Ballad about a Woman] (ballet, 1, Bardanashvili, after Ye. Yevtushenko: *Ballada o sterve* [Ballad about a Harridan]), 1972; Al'ternativa [The Alternative] (rock op, 2, R. Sturua, after N. Ergemlidze, R. Bardzimashvili), 1976; Mokhetiale varskvlavebi [Comets] (op, 2, J. Ajiashvili, after Sh. Aleichem: *Roman v pis'makh* [A Novel in Letters]), 1982; Mokhetiale suli [A Wandering Soul] (ballet, 2, scenario Bardanashvili, G. Aleksidze), 1991–2

Vocal: Bedistsera [Fate] (I. Ezra), sym. poem, chorus, orch, 1973; Pikrebi [Reflections] (M. Aurelius, I. Gebiroli), sym. mystery-poem, solo vv, chorus, orch, 1975; Mtsukhris lotsvani [Evening Prayers] (cant., Lao-Dzi), chorus, orch, 1986; 2 lotsva [2 Prayers] (Bible: *Psalms 32* and *122*), chorus, chbr orch

Orch: Adamiani da zgra [Man and the Sea], sym. poem, 1971; Vecherniye molitvï [Evening Prayers], chbr orch, 1975; Conc, gui, str, 1978; Sym., 1980; Conc, pf, vc, brass insts, 1981; Serenada-kontserti [Concerto Serenade], vn, str, 1983; Mokhetiale suli, 1994 [suite from ballet]; Conc, pf, str, 1995; Ėlegiya, str

Chbr and solo inst: Pf Qnt, 1973; Pf Sonata no.1, 1974; Poèma-dialogi, 4 hn, pf, gui, vc, 1975; Pf Trio no.1 'Bizes khsovnas' [In Memory of Bizet], 1976; Pf Sonata no.2, 1984; Str Qt no.1, 1984; Pf Trio no.2 'Romantikuli', 1989; Str Qt no.2, 1992

Incid music for films and theatre

BIBLIOGRAPHY

N. Zeyfas: 'Iosif Bardanashvili', *Kompozitorï soyuznïkh respublik* [Composers of the Soviet republics], v (Moscow, 1986)

L. Seturidze: 'Iosif Bardanashvili', *Byulleten' Gruzmuzinforma* (Tbilisi, 1989)

KETEVAN BOLASHVILI

Bardd y Brenin (Welsh: 'The King's Bard'). Title adopted by EDWARD JONES (ii).

Bardella, Il. *See* NALDI, ANTONIO.

Bardi, Giovanni de', Count of Vernio (*b* Florence, 5 Feb 1534; *d* Sept 1612). Italian literary critic, poet, playwright and composer. As host to the CAMERATA and patron of Vincenzo Galilei and Giulio Caccini he gave the main impetus to the movement that led to the first experiments in lyrical and dramatic monody.

1. LIFE. Bardi evidently received a good literary education, since he knew both Greek and Latin. His youth, however, is notable mostly for military exploits. In 1553 he served in the war against Siena under Grand Duke Cosimo I of Tuscany and in 1565 under the command of Chiappino Vitelli in the defence of Malta against the Ottoman Empire. He was one of the captains who commanded the infantry sent by Duke Cosimo to help the Emperor Maximilian II defeat the Turks in Hungary. In 1562 he married Lucrezia Salviati, daughter of Piero Salviati. He enjoyed the favour of Grand Duke Francesco I, who depended on him particularly for the organization of court festivities. But when Francesco's brother became grand duke as Ferdinando I in 1587, Bardi, who had endorsed Francesco's marriage to Bianca Capello (of whom Ferdinando disapproved), was replaced in this role by Cavalieri. He nevertheless remained active at court until he was invited to Rome by Pope Clement VIII to become *maestro di camera* and lieutenant-general of the pontifical guard in 1592. He also maintained cordial links with the court of Duke Alfonso II d'Este in Ferrara, where he was entertained lavishly on several visits in 1583, 1584 and 1590. Bardi's pontifical appointment was renewed by Leo XI, but it was terminated in 1605 by Pope Paul V.

2. WORKS. Bardi began to patronize musicians quite early: in about 1563 he sent Vincenzo Galilei, then a lutenist probably in his employ, to study with Zarlino in Venice. Giulio Caccini also enjoyed his sponsorship at an early age. There is evidence that by 1573 noblemen and musicians were coming to his house to make music and probably to talk about it. According to Bardi's son Pietro, his house was always full of the most celebrated men of Florence, and the youth of the city gathered there to be instructed in poetry, music, astrology and other sciences. Caccini later referred to this group as Bardi's Camerata.

A turning-point in the thinking of this circle was marked by the letters to Galilei and Bardi from Girolamo Mei, who had studied every known source about Greek music and whom Galilei had approached in 1572 for help in solving numerous problems in Greek theory. The letters, besides informing them about Greek music, raised questions about the efficacy of modern polyphonic music that radically changed the aesthetic philosophy of the Bardi group. About 1578 Bardi, stirred by Mei's ideas, addressed to Caccini a discourse on ancient music and singing that probably summed up the group's thinking. The first part of the discourse is a compendium of what he had learnt about Greek music from Mei and Galilei; it explains the 27 tunings, the species of octave and the *tonoi*. With this system and its rich variety he compared the modern modal system of essentially only two species

of octave and no variety of pitch. He was critical of imitative contrapuntal music, not only because it juxtaposed several melodies at once but because it disregarded the rhythms of the texts. He wanted all the parts to sing homorhythmically and counselled Caccini to declaim the words as clearly as he could, never altering the natural length of syllables or including excessive *passaggi*. He urged composers to imitate the Greek poet-singers and limit the range of their melodies to the area of the voice most suitable to an affection and to stay as much as possible around the *mese*.

Galilei dedicated his *Dialogo della musica antica et della moderna* (Florence, 1581) to Bardi and cast him in the role of preceptor in the conversations that are developed in it between him and Piero Strozzi. These imaginary conversations were a vehicle, as Galilei explained later, for instructing the members of Bardi's circle in the theory of music, particularly concerning tuning systems and the Greek *tonoi*, which had been misunderstood by Gaffurius and Glarean. The *Dialogo* went well beyond Bardi's views in its condemnation of polyphony and in the advocacy of monody on the model of the Greeks.

Only a few compositions by Bardi survive: four printed madrigals (one incomplete) and the first soprano part of another in manuscript, though other compositions are mentioned in letters and documents. An oration proposing membership in the Accademia degli Alterati in 1574 testifies that by then he had proved himself in music 'with artful compositions to such a degree that he surpassed many who practise it as their particular profession'. Bardi's characteristic method is one he described in a letter to Duke Alfonso II d'Este: 'keeping the line intact' and 'attending to the expression of the words and the conceit' while limiting text repetition to the minimum. *Miseri habitator del ciec'averno*, in the fourth of the 1589 *intermedi*, is a distinct attempt to build a piece around the Greek *mese* in a blend of the ancient diatonic and chromatic Dorian, as well as to exploit cross-relations for expressive purposes.

More than as a composer Bardi made his mark in Florence as a creator of *intermedi* and other court entertainments. In February 1573 he presented a costly and elaborate work, *Mascherata del Piacere e del Pentimento*, with a text by Antonio degli Albizzi. He also had a share in the *intermedi* for the wedding of Vincenzo Gonzaga and Eleonora de' Medici in 1584 as the composer of a madrigal (which is lost) to a text by Giovanni Battista Strozzi the younger, *Mentre gli acuti dardi*. He was the author of *L'amico fido*, the central play, and the composer of the fifth *intermedio* for the marriage of Virginia, daughter of Cosimo de' Medici, and Cesare d'Este in 1586. He directed and apparently conceived the allegorical theme around the powers of music for the *intermedi* in honour of the marriage of Grand Duke Ferdinando and Christine of Lorraine in May 1589 and even planned the protocol for the ceremony and processions. He also wrote the poetry for the opening song, by Harmony, in the first *intermedio* and for the madrigal *E noi con questa bella nostra diva Anfitrite* in the fifth. A prose comedy in five acts, *L'Idropico*, written for an unknown occasion, also survives. After his return to Florence from Rome he resumed his activities at court: in 1608 he made arrangements for singers and musicians to perform for the entertainments prepared for the wedding of Prince Cosimo de' Medici.

Bardi participated in several academies and their literary debates. In 1574 he was admitted to the Alterati as 'Il Puro', with the motto 'Alterato, io raffino'. He delivered a lecture, *In difesa dell'Ariosto*, in that academy on 24 February 1583, and his *Parere in difesa dell'Ariosto*, which he read at the Alterati on 7 February 1585, prompted Francesco Patrizi to enter the quarrel concerning Ariosto and Tasso. Tasso personally answered Bardi in a *Discorso* (Ferrara, 1595). Bardi was also a member of the Accademia della Crusca; he was admitted on 12 March 1585 and soon became one of its councillors and, on 13 September 1588, the archconsul.

Bardi had at least four sons: Filippo, who became Bishop of Cortona; Cosimo, who became nunzio to Pope Urban VIII and Archbishop of Florence; Alfonso; and Pietro, who addressed a letter to Giovanni Battista Doni in 1634 concerning his father's Camerata and who was four times archconsul of the Accademia della Crusca. In a letter to the Duke of Modena of 24 February 1601 Bardi mentioned a son Fra Anolfo who had then been a friar for 18 years. Another son may have been the Giovanni Bardi who wrote *Eorum quae vehuntur in aquis experimenta* (Rome, 1614), a commentary on Galileo's discourse on floating bodies (Florence, 1612) usually attributed to the Bardi who is the subject of this article; in it the author claimed to have been a pupil of Galileo.

WORKS

1 madrigal each, 1582[5] (ed. *NewcombMF*); 1586[20]; 1591[7] (ed. in D.P. Walker: *Les fêtes du mariage de Ferdinand de Medicis et de Christine de Lorraine: Florence, 1589*, Paris, 1963); Girolamo Montesardo: L'Allegre notti di Fiorenza (Venice, 1608, inc); *I-Rvat* Vat.Mus.11 (inc.)

1 madrigal, text by G.B. Strozzi the younger, and 5th intermedio for marriage of Virginia de' Medici and Cesare d'Este, 1586, lost

WRITINGS

Discourse addressed to G. Caccini (MS, *c*1578, *I-Rvat*; ed. A.F. Gori (with numerous errors) as 'Discorso mandato a Caccini sopra la musica antica e 'l cantar bene' in G.B. Doni: *Lyra Barberina amphichordos* (Florence, 1763), ii, 233–4; ed. and Eng. trans. in Palisca, 1989)

[Discourse on how tragedy should be performed] (MS, *c*1582, anon., in *I-Fn*, VII.398, continued in XIX.42; attrib. Bardi and ed., with Eng. trans., in Palisca, 1989, 132–51)

In difesa dell'Ariosto (lecture to Accademia degli Alterati, 24 Feb 1583), *I-Fn*, VI.168, 50–75*v*

BIBLIOGRAPHY

DBI (R. Cantagalli and L. Pannella); *NewcombMF*; *PirottaDO*

Anon.: [Oration introducing Bardi to the Accademia degli Alterati, *c*1574] (MS, *I-Fl* Ashburnham 559, no.24)

B. de' Rossi: *Descrizione del magnificentissimo apparato e de' maravigliosi intermedi* (Florence, 1585)

B. de' Rossi: *Descrizione dell'apparato, e degl'intermedi fatti per la commedia* (Florence, 1589)

P. de' Bardi: [Letter to G.B. Doni, 16 Dec 1634], ed. in A.M. Bandini: *Commentariorum de vita et scriptis J.B. Doni ... libri quinque* (Florence, 1755), 117–20; repr. in A. Solerti: *Le origini del melodramma* (Turin, 1903/*R*), 143–7; Eng. trans. in *StrunkSR2*, iv, 15–17

N. Pirrotta: 'Temperaments and Tendencies in the Florentine Camerata', *MQ*, xl (1954), 169–89

C.V. Palisca: *Girolamo Mei (1519–1594): Letters on Ancient and Modern Music to Vincenzo Galilei and Giovanni Bardi*, MSD, iii (1960, 2/1977)

C.V. Palisca: 'Musical Asides in the Diplomatic Correspondence of Emilio de' Cavalieri', *MQ*, xlix (1963), 339–55; repr. with prefatory note and orig. It. text in C.V. Palisca *Studies in the History of Italian Music and Music Theory* (Oxford, 1994)

C.V. Palisca: 'The Alterati of Florence, Pioneers in the Theory of Dramatic Music', *New Looks at Italian Opera: Essays in Honor*

of Donald J. Grout, ed. W.W. Austin (Ithaca, NY, 1968), 9–38; repr. in C.V. Palisca: *Studies in the History of Italian Music Theory* (Oxford, 1994)

C.V. Palisca: 'The "Camerata Fiorentina": a Reappraisal', *Studi musicali*, i (1972), 203–36

J.W. Hill: 'Oratory Music in Florence, I: *Recitar Cantando*, 1583–1655', *AcM*, xlv (1979), 108–36

C.V. Palisca: 'The Musical Humanism of Giovanni Bardi', *Poesia e musica nell'estetica del xvi e xvii secolo*, ed. H. Meyvalian (Florence, 1979), 45–72

T. Carter: 'L'Allegre noti di Fiorenza (1608)', *Renaissance Studies in Honor of Craig Hugh Smyth*, ed. A. Morrogh and others (Florence, 1985), 569–79

C.V. Palisca: *Humanism in Italian Renaissance Musical Thought* (New Haven, CT, 1985)

Z. Szweykowski: 'Późny renesans w poszukiwaniu ideału muzycznego', *Muzyka*, xxx/1 (1985), 3–36; appendix, text of Bardi's discourse to Caccini with Polish trans., 1–38

R. Katz: *Divining the Powers of Music: Aesthetic Theory and the Origins of Opera* (New York, 1986)

C.V. Palisca: *The Florentine Camerata: Documentary Studies and Translations* (New Haven, CT, 1989)

W. Kirkendale: *The Court Musicians in Florence during the Principate of the Medici* (Florence, 1993)

CLAUDE V. PALISCA

Bárdos, Kornél (*b* Felsőmindszent, 1 Nov 1921; *d* Budapest, 8 Nov 1993). Hungarian musicologist. Having attended the Zirc Cistercian Theological College (1940–45) he studied at Budapest University (1945–9), where he took the doctorate with a dissertation on Hungarian literature (1948), and at the Liszt Academy of Music with Kodály, Szabolcsi, Bartha and Lajos Bárdos (1946–50). After teaching at the Miskolc State Music School (1951–5) he was professor at the Budapest State Music School (1955–79). In 1979 he became a research fellow at the Institute of Musicology of the Hungarian Academy of Sciences. In 1967 he took the *kandidátus* degree in musicology with a dissertation on Passion singing in Hungary, which he subsequently enlarged (1975) with the results of new research in Transylvania. His main area of research was Hungarian music of the 15th century to the 18th, especially Protestant vernacular settings; he wrote extensively on the 17th- and 18th-century musical life of Transdanubian cities and residences.

WRITINGS

with K. Csomasz Tóth: 'Az Eperjesi Graduál: gregorián kapcsolatok' [The gradual of Eperjes: Gregorian connections], *ZT*, vi (1957), 165–98 [with Ger. summary]

'Die Variation in den ungarischen Passionen des 16.–18. Jahrhunderts', *SMH*, iv (1963), 289–323

Népzenei jellegű variálásmód a 15.–18. századi magyar passiókban [Folklike variation methods in Hungarian Passions of the 15th to 18th centuries] (diss., Hungarian Academy of Sciences, 1967); extracts in 'Harcok a passió éneklése körül Magyarországon' [Difficulties with Passion singing in Hungary], *Theológiai szemle*, xiv (1971), 296–303; Ger. trans., enlarged in *Volksmusikartige Variierungstechnik in den ungarischen Passionen, 15. bis 18. Jahrhundert* (Budapest, 1975)

with K. Csomasz Tóth: 'A magyar protestáns graduálok himnuszai' [The hymns of the Hungarian Protestant graduals], *Népzene és zenetörténet*, ed. L. Vargyas, iii (Budapest, 1976), 134–256

Pécs zenéje a 18. században [The music of Pécs in the 18th century] (Budapest, 1976) [with Ger. summary]

A tatai Esterházyak zenéje 1727–1846 [The music of the Esterházy court in Tata, 1727–1846] (Budapest, 1978)

Győr zenéje a 17.–18. században [The music of Győr in the 17th and 18th centuries] (Budapest, 1980) [with Ger. summary]

Sopron zenéje a 16.–18. században [The music of Sopron from the 16th century to the 18th] (Budapest, 1984) [with Ger. summary]

Eger zenéje 1687–1787 [The music of Eger, 1687–1887] (Budapest, 1987) [with Ger. summary]

ed.: *Magyarország zenetörténete*, ii: *1541–1686* [The history of music in Hungary] (Budapest, 1990)

Székesfehérvár zenéje 1688–1892 [The music of Székesfehérvár, 1688–1892] (Budapest, 1993) [with Ger. summary]

VERA LAMPERT

Bárdos, Lajos (*b* Budapest, 1 Oct 1899; *d* Budapest, 18 Nov 1986). Hungarian composer, musicologist and conductor. Together with Kodály, he laid the foundations of 20th-century Hungarian choral music-making. He studied the violin and the viola as a boy. After a year (1918–19) at the technical university he entered the Budapest Academy of Music, where he studied composition with Siklós and then Kodály (1921–5). In 1925 he was engaged as choral conductor and music teacher in a secondary school and a teacher-training college; from 1928 to 1967 he was a professor at the academy, where he reformed the syllabus, emphasizing the training of choral conductors, the teaching of church music history and instruction in music theory and prosody. In 1931 he co-founded the publishing company Magyar Kórus, and served as editor of the music periodical of that name from then until 1950, when it was banned. From 1934 he organized the Enekio Ifúsag ('Singing Youth') movement for the music education of the young.

Through his work as a conductor Bárdos raised the standards of Hungarian choral singing to an international level within a few decades. He directed the Cecilia (1926–41), the Palestrina Kórus (1929–33), the Budapesti Kórus (1941–7) and the choir of St Mátyás, Budapest (1942–62), as well as encouraging the development of choral activity in remote areas. His repertory was pioneering: he included choral music from before Palestrina, especially that of Josquin, and promoted new music (he introduced, for example, Stravinsky's *Symphony of Psalms* into Hungary). On his tours abroad his purposefulness, vitality and interpretative powers won him considerable acclaim. His compositions, too, were directed towards cultivating Hungarian choral life: they draw on Renaissance polyphony and Hungarian folk music, following in the tradition of Bartók and Kodály. His works, which are models of choral writing, deal sensitively with Hungarian prosody and radiate an inner harmony and vigour.

Bárdos's work as a musicologist began to develop in the 1950s. He had a gift for systematization, which he applied to major studies of Gregorian melody, modal and Romantic harmony, and the analysis of works by Liszt, Bartók and Kodály. Underlying his multifarious activities lay the programme initiated by Bartók and Kodály for the regeneration of Hungarian musical life. In recognition of his work he received the Erkel Prize (1953), the Kossuth Prize (1955), the Bartók-Pásztory Prize (1984) and the titles Merited, and Eminent Artist of the Hungarian People's Republic (1954 and 1970, respectively). He was awarded the Order of the Banner with Laurels in 1984 and the doctorate in musicology in 1985.

WORKS
(selective list)

MYSTERY PLAYS

Nyolc boldogság [The 8 Beatitudes] (V. Dienes), 1926; Hajnalvárás [Waiting for Dawn] (Dienes), 1927; Advent (S. Sík), 1928; Magyar végzet [Hungarian Fate] (Dienes), 1931; Rózsák szentje [The Saint of Roses] (Dienes), 1932; A gyermek útja [The Way of the Child] (Dienes), 1935; Az anya [The Mother] (Dienes), 1937; Szent Imre (Dienes), 1938; Árpádházi Szent Margit [St Margaret of the House of Árpád] (G. Ujházy), 1938; Mi lesz velünk? [What will become of us?] (Dienes), 1938; Alexius (Sík), 1946

CHORAL

With insts: A nyúl éneke [Song of the Rabbit] (F. Jankovich), double chorus, 3 timp, 1946; Körtánc [Roundelay] (E. Rossa), chorus, orch, 1952

Mixed vv: Népdalkórusok [Folk Song Choruses], 4 vols., 1933; Széles a Duna [Wide is the Danube], 1937; Szeged felől [From Szeged], 1938; A földhez [To Earth] (F. Kölcsey), 1951; Tilinkós [The Shepherd's Pipe], 1951; Ungaresca, 1951; 70 év [70 Years] (S. Weöres), 1952; Elmúlt a tél [Winter is Gone] (Weöres), 1953; Kossuth Suite, 1953; Az nem lehet [It Cannot Be] (J. Arany), 1955; Jeremiás siralma [Jeremiah's Lament], 1956

Ének a dalról [Song about Singing] (G. Juhász), 1956; A madár fiaihoz [The Bird to his Sons] (M. Tompa), 1957; A munka [Work] (Juhász), 1962; Tűz-szivárvány [Fire-Rainbow] (L. Nagy), 1963; Óda az igazsághoz [Ode to Justice] (D. Kosztolányi), 1965; Énekeljetek [Sing!] (I. Pákolitz), 1967; Ezekiel látomása [Ezekiel's Vision] (I. Jobbágy), 1967; A dal titka [Secret of Song] (M. Babits), 1972; Zrínyi-ének [Zrínyi's Song], 1972; Bartók (L. Bóka), 1975; Új Vazul éneke [New Vazul Song] (E. Ady), 1975; Az úr érkezése [The Arrival of the Lord] (Ady), 1977; Cantemus (Bárdos, L. Lukin), 1977; Zrínyi harmadik éneke [Zrínyi's 3rd Song] (S. Sík), 1978; Mandulafa [Almond Tree] (J. Pannonius, S. Weöres), 1983; Erkel szózata [Erkel's Hymn] (M. Vörösmarty), 1985

Equal vv: Kicsinyek kórusa [Choruses for Little Ones], i–iii, 1934–52; Megütik a dobot [The Drum is Sounded], 1936; Liszt Ferenchez [To Ferenc Liszt], 1936; Dana-dana [Sing-Song], 1940; Magos a rutafa [The Rue Tree is Full of Seeds], 1941; 20 Choruses, 1963; Négy földrész [4 Continents] (L. Lukin), 1963; Tavunga, 1964; Bartók emlékére [To the Memory of Bartók] (L. Bóka), 1965; Ne félj! [Don't Be Afraid] (S. Weöres), 1967; Nyári vasárnap [Summer Sunday] (M. Radnóti), 1978; Kifehérszik az ég [The Sky Turns White] (É. Finta), 1981; Szeresd hazádat! [Love your Country!] (B. Reviczky), 1985; other choruses, songs, canons, folksong arrs.

Sacred: Missa prima, 1925, Missa secunda, 1934; Missa, 1937, Missa, a, 1938; Missa tertia, 1944; Szent Adalbert miséje Missa quarta, 1962; Magyar Népmise [Hung. Folk Mass], 1985; other works incl. motets and psalms

OTHER WORKS

Str Qt, 1925; pieces for vn, vc, pf etc, songs, folksong arrs., vocal exercises

Principal publishers: Editio Musica, Magyar Kórus

WRITINGS

'Natürliche Tonsysteme', *Studia memoriae Belae Bartók sacra*, ed. B. Rajeczky and L. Vargyas (Budapest, 1956; Eng. trans. 1959), 209–48

Modális harmóniák (Budapest, 1961)

Harminc írás 1929–1969 [30 writings] (Budapest, 1969)

Bartók dallamvilágából [On Bartók's melodic world] (Budapest, 1970)

A Bartók-zene stíluselemei az egyeneműkarok és a Mikrokozmosz alapján [Elements of Bartók's musical style in the choral works for equal voices and Mikrokozmos] (Budapest, 1972)

Tíz ujabb írás 1969–1974 [Ten new writings] (Budapest, 1974)

Liszt Ferenc, a jövő zenésze [Liszt, the renewer of music] (Budapest, 1976)

Zenei prozódia [Musical prosody] (Budapest, 1976)

Bartók-dallamok és a népzene [Bartók's melodies and folk music] (Budapest, 1977)

'Modalen Harmonien in den Werken von Franz Liszt', *Franz Liszt: Beiträge von ungarischen Autoren*, ed. K. Hamburger (Budapest, 1978), 133–66

'Die volkmusikalische Tonleitern bei Liszt', ibid., 168–96

Selected Writings on Music, trans. A. Farkas and K. Ittzés (Budapest, 1984)

Írások népzenénkről [Writings on Hungarian folk music] (Budapest, 1988)

Elemző írások a zenéről I, ed. M. Mohay (Budapest, 1994) [musical analyses]

Other publications, incl. folksong edns.

BIBLIOGRAPHY

I. Sárközy: 'Néhány szó Bárdos Lajos művészetéről' [A few words on Bárdos's music], *Új zenei szemle*, iv/10 (1953), 3–6

Z. Kodály: 'Dreizehn junge Komponisten', *A zene mindenkié*, ed. A. Szőllősy (Budapest, 1956)

I. Fábián: 'Bárdos Lajos, a zenetudós' [Bárdos the musicologist], *Muzsika*, xii/9 (1969), 14 only

J. Mátyás: 'Bárdos Lajos: pályámról, munkámról' [Bárdos: on my career, on my work], *Magyar zene*, xv (1974), 364–72

I. Raics: 'Bárdos Lajos zeneszerzői világa' [The compositions of Bárdos], *Muzsika*, xvii/10 (1974), 1–3

L. Somfai: 'A tudós köszöntése' [Congratulations to the musicologist], *Muzsika*, xvii/10 (1974) 4–6

M. Szabó: 'Bárdos Lajos, a karmester' [Bárdos the conductor], *Muzsika*, xvii/10 (1974), 6–8

Kóta, no.8 (1989) [Bárdos issue]

J. Mátyás, ed.: *Hány színe van az életnek?* [How many colours does life have?] (Budapest, 1996) [interviews with Bárdos]

Bárdos Lajos emlékkonferencia: Budapest 1996 [Bárdos memorial conference],

MELINDA BERLÁSZ

Bareia [bareiai diplai]. Sign used in pairs in Byzantine EKPHONETIC NOTATION.

Barenboim, Daniel (*b* Buenos Aires, 15 Nov 1942). Israeli pianist and conductor. He was first taught by his parents and made his début as a pianist in Buenos Aires when he was seven. In 1951 the family moved to Europe where he played at the Salzburg Mozarteum, and thence to Israel. Back in Salzburg in 1954, he met Edwin Fischer and Furtwängler, both major influences on his future career. Studies at the Accademia di S Cecilia in Rome and with Boulanger completed his education.

Barenboim made his British début as a soloist in 1955 and his American début two years later, and first conducted, in Israel, in 1962. From 1964 he worked for some years with the English Chamber Orchestra as conductor and pianist, recording with them symphonies by Mozart and Haydn, and a series of Mozart piano concertos. Meanwhile he began an international career as a conductor. He directed the South Bank Summer Festival in London (1968–70) in company with a group of musicians that included Zukerman, Perlman and Jacqueline Du Pré, whom he had married in 1967. At this period he played much chamber music and accompanied Janet Baker and Dietrich Fischer-Dieskau (with whom he made many illuminating recordings of Schubert and Wolf). He was chief conductor of the Orchestre de Paris from 1975 to 1989, was appointed music director of the Chicago SO (succeeding Solti) in 1991 and has become a regular guest conductor with the Berlin PO. While concentrating on the central Classical and Romantic repertory, he has also been a firm advocate of new music, giving premières of works by Berio, Boulez, Carter, Goehr and Henze, among others.

Barenboim's experience as an opera conductor began at the Edinburgh Festival in 1973 with *Don Giovanni*, a performance subsequently recorded, followed by *Le nozze di Figaro* there in 1975. In 1978 he undertook *Samson et Dalila* at the Orange Festival, also recording the work. In 1981 he was invited to the Bayeuth Festival for *Tristan und Isolde*, followed by *Parsifal* in 1987. He conducted Harry Kupfer's new staging of the *Ring* in 1988 and continued to conduct at Bayreuth throughout the 1990s. His acclaimed *Ring* there has been recorded live, while studio recordings of *Tristan* and *Parsifal* have been widely praised for their nobility and masterly control of pacing. After his engagement to become music director of the new Opéra Bastille in Paris proved abortive for political reasons, he was appointed director of the Berlin Staatsoper in 1993. In that post he has conducted a wide repertory, most notably of German works, of which his *Wozzeck*, *Elektra* (both recorded), *Doktor Faust* and *Die Zauber-*

flöte have been particularly admired. He conducted the première of Carter's *What Next* in 1999, and of Birtwistle's *The Last Supper* in 2000.

His interpretations of both opera and the orchestral repertory lay emphasis on freedom of expression, allowing for many changes in tempo and a careful disclosure of detail. His conducting of Mozart, eschewing period instruments, is warm and vital, if slightly Romantic by late 20th-century standards. He is a searching, intensely dramatic interpreter of Bruckner, whose later symphonies he has recorded. Barenboim's recordings, as a pianist, of the Mozart and Beethoven concertos (the latter with Klemperer) and the complete Beethoven sonatas, all made when he was young, are distinguished by their flexibility, spontaneity and quick sensitivity, as are more recent discs of the Mozart concertos and the keyboard works of Chopin, Schumann and Brahms. His autobiography, *A Life in Music*, was published in London in 1991. (A. Blyth: 'Daniel Barenboim', *Opera* , xlv (1994), 905–10)

ALAN BLYTH

Barenboym, Lev Aronovich (*b* Odessa, 18/31 Jan 1906; *d* Leningrad, 25 June 1985). Russian musicologist, pianist and teacher. He studied the piano with G.M. Biber and composition with V.A. Zolotaryov at the Odessa Conservatory (1920–25) and mathematics at Odessa University (1922–5). He later completed his musical studies with F. Blumenfel'd at the Moscow Conservatory (1925–30). He taught in a music school in Odessa (1923–5), and worked at the Moscow Central School of Music from 1930 and in the Moscow Music Department of the Commissariat for Public Education (1930–31). Concurrently he was deputy chairman of the piano and methodology section of the State Institute for Musical Sciences in Moscow. From 1931 to 1939 he taught at the Moscow Conservatory, where he ran a class for the piano and the methodology of piano teaching. He was appointed senior scientific officer at the Science Research Institute for Music attached to the Moscow Conservatory in 1933 and was a senior lecturer at the Moscow Institute for Raising the Professional Skills of Teachers (1934–9). In 1940 he gained the *Kandidat* degree with a dissertation entitled *Vospitaniye muzïkanta-ispolnitelya v svete problem, postavlennïkh sistemoy K.S. Stanislavskogo* (The education of the musician-performer in the light of the problems posed by the Stanislavsky system).

During World War II, Barenboym was evacuated to Tashkent with the Leningrad Conservatory (1941), where he worked as head of the education section. After returning to Leningrad in 1944, he continued teaching at the conservatory as senior lecturer and was instrumental in forming a department for the history and theory of piano playing and teaching, of which he was head from 1949 to 1973. He gained the doctorate in 1956 with a dissertation on the life, work and public duties of Anton Rubinstein, and in 1958 was appointed professor at the Leningrad Conservatory.

Barenboym was a major figure in Russian musical culture, a fine musician with a keen and sensitive ear and an erudite scholar. He was one of the founders of the trend in Russian musicology that was devoted to the history and theory of performing. A prolific writer, he worked productively in the area of general musical education and training, piano teaching and methodology, and as a critic of performance practice. His book on piano methodology (1937) and the anthology on the history of

Russian piano music (1949) are important works on these subjects. For decades he regularly published analytical articles and creative portraits of performers in the journal *Sovetskaya muzïka* (many of these are included in collections of Barenboym's articles). He also co-edited a collection of piano pieces for beginners (1969–70), which embodies his teaching principles and has become part of the standard training repertory for children. In addition, with B.S. Dimentman, Barenboym initiated the publication by the Soviet section of the ISME of the series Muzïkal'noye vospitaniye v XX veke (Music education in the 20th century). He also advocated the introduction of the creative methods of Orff and Kodály into Russian music education.

WRITINGS

Fortepiannaya pedagogika [Piano teaching] (Moscow, 1937)

ed., with V.I. Muzalevsky: *Khrestomatiya po istorii fortepiannoi muzïki v Rossii* [An anthology on the history of piano music in Russia] (Moscow and Leningrad, 1949)

ed.: *Anton Grigor'yevich Rubinshteyn: izbrannïye pis'ma* [A.G. Rubinstein: selected letters] (Moscow, 1954)

Anton Grigor'yevich Rubinshteyn: zhizn', artisticheskiy put', tvorchestvo i muzïkal'no-obshchestvennaya deyatel'nost' s 1829 po 1867 g. [A.G. Rubinstein: his life, artistic career, creative work and public duties in music from 1829 to 1867] (diss., 1956; Leningrad, 1957–62)

Fortepianno-pedagogicheskye printsipï F.M. Blumenfel'da [F.M. Blumefel'd's pedagogic principles for the piano] (Moscow, 1964)

Na urokakh Antona Rubinshteyna [At A. Rubinstein's lessons] (Moscow and Leningrad, 1964)

Voprosï fortepiannoy pedagogiki i ispolnitel'stva [Questions of piano teaching and performance] (Leningrad, 1969)

ed., with S.S. Lyakhovitskaya: *Sbornik fortepiannïkh p'yes, ètyudov i ansambley, dlya nachinayushchikh* [Anthology of piano pieces, exercises and harmonies for beginners] (Leningrad, 1969–70)

Put' k muzitsirovaniyu [The path towards making music] (Moscow and Leningrad, 1973, 2/1979)

Muzïkal'naya pedagogika i ispolnitel'stvo [Music teaching and performance] (Leningrad, 1974)

ed.: *Èlementarnoye vospitaniye po sisteme K. Orfa* [Elementary training according to the Orff system] (Moscow, 1978)

ed.: *Muzïkal'noye vospitaniye v SSSR* [Music education in the USSR] (Moscow, 1978–85)

ed., with N.V. Fishman: *L.V. Nikolayev: stat'i i vospominaniya sovremennikov: pis'ma k 100-letiyu so dnya rozhdeniya* [Articles and reminiscences of his contemporaries: letters for the 100th anniversary of his birth] (Leningrad, 1979)

Nikolay Grigor'yevich Rubinshteyn: istoriya zhizni i deyatel'nosti [N.G. Rubinstein: the history of his life and work] (Moscow, 1982)

ed.: *Muzïkal'noye vospitaniye v Vengrii* [Music education in Hungary] (Moscow, 1983)

ed.: *A.G. Rubinshteyn: literaturnoye naslediye v tryokh tomakh* [A.G. Rubinstein: literary heritage] (Moscow, 1983–6)

Èmil' Gilel's: tvorcheskiy portret [Gilels: a creative portrait] (Moscow, 1986, 2/1990)

Za polveka: ocherki, stat'i, materialï [For a half century: essays, articles and materials] (Leningrad, 1989)

BIBLIOGRAPHY

L. Gakkel': :'Muzïkant-uchyonïy' [The musician-scholar], *SovM* (1977), no.4, pp.84–6

'Pamyati ushedshikh (nekrolog)' [To the memory of the departed (obituary)], *SovM* (1985), no.12, pp.132–3

G. Kimelis: 'Pianistu veka – posmertno' [For the pianist of the century – posthumously], *MAk* (1992), no.2, pp.213–14 [review of Barenboym's book about Gilels]

ADA BENEDIKTOVNA SCHNITTKE

Bärenreiter. German firm of music publishers. It was founded in 1924 in Augsburg by Karl Vötterle, a bookshop assistant, then only 21 years old. Vötterle named the firm after the star Alkor ('Bärenreiter' or 'Reiterlein') in the constellation of the Great Bear. The firm's beginnings are closely associated with the musical youth movement then current in Germany. Vötterle's interest in folksong and his collaboration with the folksong researcher and singer Walther Hensel (an alias for Dr Julius Janiczek, 1887–1956), whose *Finkensteiner Blätter* was the firm's first publication, formed the basis of much of Bärenreiter's early work. The first years were characterized by the rapid growth of the *Singbewegung*, organized into the Finkensteiner Bund and developed by Vötterle; the movement was intended to revive musical interest and provide musical education for amateurs. The publication of folksong editions, beginning with the *Finkensteiner Blätter*, and later larger anthologies such as the *Bruder Singer*, characterized the early policy of the young firm. There also appeared song settings by composers such as Dowland, Hans Leo Hassler and Lechner. The firm's first music periodical was *Singgemeinde*, edited by Konrad Ameln. Already at that time Bärenreiter sought an involvement in the revival movement in German musicology, which during the 1920s was closely linked to the youth movement. An annotated edition of J.N. Forkel's 1802 biography, *Ueber Johann Sebastian Bachs Leben, Kunst und Kunstwerke* (1924), was one of the firm's first musicological publications.

An important step forward was made when Wilibald Gurlitt entrusted the firm with the publication of the report on the first Freiburg organ conference in 1926. As a result of this publication and of the association of Christhard Mahrenholz with the firm, Bärenreiter quickly grew to become the leading publisher of the *Orgelbewegung* and a specialist publisher of organ music and research material in the form of books by Klotz, Mahrenholz and others. In 1926, as its first purely musicological enterprise, Bärenreiter took over the publication of the series produced by the Königsberg and Tübingen musical institutes, followed later by those of Erlangen, Greifswald, Heidelberg, Jena and Münster. In 1927 the firm moved to Kassel; at that time its output comprised about 200 publications covering many aspects of music and music literature. The following five years brought further rapid growth and an extension in its publishing activity; in 1929 Vötterle founded the periodical *Musik und Kirche*. The rediscovery by the choirs of the musical youth movement of the works of Heinrich Schütz, with the corresponding new editions published by Bärenreiter, the discussions in *Musik und Kirche*, and the subsequent founding of the active Neue Schütz-Gesellschaft in 1930 by Vötterle, Ludwig, Mahrenholz and H.J. Moser, gave a decisive impetus to the revival of Protestant church music.

In the Nazi period Bärenreiter's development was interrupted as Vötterle and his colleagues were not allowed to follow their original ideals. The Finkensteiner Bund was dissolved in 1933, and in its place Vötterle, together with Richard Baum, founded the Arbeitskreis für Hausmusik. In 1935 the firm was threatened with complete closure when Vötterle was excluded from the Reichspressekammer. As a result all religious printing had to be suspended: it was continued by the Johannes Stauda publishing firm under the direction of Paul Gümbel. Stauda became the publishers of the Evangelische Michaelsbruderschaft, which aimed at a church revival; to the Reichspressekammer church music did not count as religious printing and was therefore able to make relatively undisturbed progress in spite of the anti-Christian tendencies of the time. In 1932 Bärenreiter began to publish works by Hugo Distler, beginning with his op.5. Distler's church music opened up for Bärenreiter the new category of modern church music, which it particularly cultivated in the following years.

In the spheres of secular choral music, songbooks, domestic music and chamber music, the firm's output also increased, with many publications in the period 1933–44. The practical revival of early music led to the reintroduction of early instruments, and Bärenreiter encouraged such developments with literature on the instruments and their technique, sometimes actually making instruments (notably recorders). It also began publishing orchestral and wind music, and an opera section was initiated with some works by early composers, predominantly Handel. Facsimile reprints and works of original research of all kinds appeared. Bärenreiter participated in Reichsdenkmäler, with the series Einstimmige Werke and Mittelalter, and in Landschaftsdenkmäler, devoted to various constituent states of Germany. Complete editions of the works of Gluck, Monteverdi, Pergolesi, Schein, Spohr and Walter, and selected editions of Telemann and Handel were prepared and begun, mostly in collaboration with the Staatliche Institut für Deutsche Musikforschung.

In March 1945 the firm's buildings, all of its departments and nearly all of its stock were destroyed by fire. Vötterle and most of his closer colleagues survived the war, and gradually the firm was reorganized. In 1946 the Arbeitskreis für Hausmusik organized its first postwar Werkwoche. This organization was renamed Arbeitskreis für Haus- und Jugendmusik in 1952 and in 1969 became the Internationaler Arbeitskreis für Musik, which is now responsible for over 70 annual courses of musical instruction and the Kasseler Musiktage (to 1974). Also in 1946 Vötterle opened the Bärenreiter second-hand bookshop which specialized in music and musicology. In 1947 he took part in the founding of the Gesellschaft für Musikforschung, whose works were published by the firm in the periodical Die Musikforschung and in the book series Musikwissenschaftliche Arbeiten. In the same year the periodical Musik und Kirche restarted (with volume xviii), together with the independent Der Kirchenchor and the new Musica, covering all aspects of music. In 1948 appeared Die neue Schau, a cultural family periodical, and Hausmusik. In June 1949 the first fascicle of the encyclopedia Die Musik in Geschichte und Gegenwart (MGG) appeared, edited by Friedrich Blume, having been in preparation since 1942. In 1968 the alphabetical sequence was completed, in 14 volumes, and supplementary fascicles (in two volumes) subsequently appeared up to 1979, followed by an index (1986). A second revised edition, edited by Ludwig Finscher, was begun in 1994.

During the early 1950s the firm began to publish a number of important complete or collected editions, music series and a considerable amount of important musicological literature, notably Acta musicologica and Fontes artis musicae, both from 1954 on. Their postwar publications have included volumes of RISM (series A and C), the series Documenta Musicologica and Catalogus Musicus, complete and collected editions of numerous composers (often in conjunction with various music institutions) including Johann Walter (i), Telemann, Gluck, Bach, Gade, Lechner, Handel, Mozart, Rhau, Berlioz, Berwald, Lassus, Schein, Schubert, Schütz and Janáček. Important series of musical editions include

volumes of Das Erbe Deutscher Musik (1936–), Schweizerische Musikdenkmäler (1955) and Monumenta Monodica Medii Aevi (1956). The firm has also published collections of letters, iconography, yearbooks, congress reports, treatises on instrumental technique and manufacture, as well as works by contemporary composers, including Heinrich Kaminski, Ernst Krenek, Karl Marx, Siegfried Reda, Ernst Pepping and Johannes Driessler. To these may be added members of the younger generation of composers who have been influenced by the Second Viennese School and the avant garde, such as Jean Barraqué, Günter Bialas, Klaus and N.A. Huber, Erhard Karkoschka, Rudolf Kelterborn, Giselher Klebe, George Lopez, Dicter Mack, Matthias Pintscher, Charlotte Seither, Ulrich Streuz, Dimitris Terzakis, Manfred Trojahn, Gerhard Wimberger, Heinz Winbeck and many others. In 1950 the new Protestant hymnbook appeared, after years in preparation, and a new series of early domestic and chamber music, Hortus Musicus, was started. The Nagels Musik-Archiv series was taken over from the Nagel firm and continued in 1952, followed by Chor-Archiv (1953), Flötenmusik (1956), miniature scores (1959), Violoncello (1960), Musica Sacra Nova (1964), Das 19. Jahrhundert (1969), Concerto Vocale (1971), Urtext editions, study scores and a new series of Hausmusik (1986). More recently, pedagogical works have also become an important part of the firm's output.

Today Bärenreiter, following large-scale postwar expansion, is international in organization and repute. It now owns not only Nagel but also, since 1950, the Hinnenthal. The Alkor-Edition was founded in Kassel in 1955, as an offshoot of the Bruckner publishing firm in Wiesbaden; it is now mainly concerned with theatre music publishing, especially opera. Bärenreiter was also the first great German publishing house to produce its own gramophone records (Musicaphon, 1959). Independent affiliates have been set up in Basle (1944), London (1957, independent since 1963; removed to Hitchin, 1977), New York (1957) and Prague (1990).

BIBLIOGRAPHY

K. Vötterle: Haus unterm Stern: ein Verleger erzählt (Kassel, 1949, 4/1969)
Bärenreiter im Bild (Kassel, 2/1968)
R. Baum and W. Rehm, eds.: Musik und Verlag: Karl Vötterle zum 65. Geburtstag (Kassel, 1968)
H.-M. Plesske: 'Bibliographie des Schrifttums zur Geschichte deutscher und österreichischer Musikverlage', Beiträge zur Geschichte des Buchwesens, iii (1968), 135–222
A.M. Gottschick, ed.: Bärenreiter-Chronik: die ersten 50 Jahre, 1923–1973 (Kassel, 1973)
H. Bennwitz and others, eds.: Musikalisches Erbe und Gegenwart: Musiker-Gesamtausgaben in der Bundesrepublik Deutschland (Kassel, 1975)

RICHARD BAUM, DIETRICH BERKE

Barera [Barrera], **Rodiano** [Ahrodiano] (b Cremona, mid 16th century; d Cremona, 25 Sept 1623). Italian composer, active in Cremona. His first known employment was as maestro di cappella in the collegiate church of S Agata, Cremona. In 1592 he became maestro di cappella at Cremona Cathedral, and four years later his duties at the cathedral were extended with his appointment as 'maestro di cappella for the Saturday devotions' or laudi. He remained in these posts until 1622.

Barera's madrigals are characterized by traditional 16th-century procedures, with limited use of innovatory techniques. Particular emphasis is laid on clarity of the text. Settings are syllabic and largely homorhythmic and there is frequent use of antiphonal dialogue between groups of voices. Barera's church music perhaps reflects his specific duties at Cremona cathedral. His *Laudes in honorem B. V. Mariae* were probably conceived for use during the Saturday devotions. The psalms are intended for the principal feasts of the liturgical year; they, too, are essentially syllabic and homorhythmic.

WORKS

Il primo libro de madrigali, 5vv (Venice, 1596)
Laudes in honorem BVM, 8vv, org (Venice, 1620), inc.
Sacra omnium solemnitatum vespertina psalmodia cum BVM cantico, 4vv (Venice, 1622)
Madrigals in 1588[17], ed. H.B. Lincoln, *L'amorosa Ero* (New York, 1968); 1591[12]; 1596[11]

BIBLIOGRAPHY

G. Pontiroli: 'Notizie di musicisti cremonesi dei secoli XVI e XVII', *Bolletino storico cremonese*, xxii (1961–4), 149–92
A. Sgaria: *Rodiano Barera e la vita musicale a Cremona intorno al 1600* (thesis, Scuola di paleografia e filologia musicale, Cremona, 1990–91)
G. Sommi-Picenardi: *Dizionario biografico dei musicisti e fabbricatori di strumenti musicali*, ed. C. Zambelloni (Turnhout, 1997)

SERENA DAL BELIN PERUFFO

Barere [Barer], Simon (*b* Odessa, 20 Aug/1 Sept 1896; *d* New York, 2 April 1951). American pianist of Ukrainian birth. The 11th of 13 children, he received his early musical instruction at the hands of two of his elder brothers and later under the supervision of a neighbour. By the age of 11, after the death of his father, he was able to help support his family by playing for silent films, night-clubs and restaurants.

At 16 he played for Glazunov in St Petersburg and was accepted at the conservatory there, studying first with Anna Yesipova and later with Blumenfeld. Barere graduated in 1919 and was awarded the Rubinstein Prize. The remarkable development of his natural gifts during this period was to lead Glazunov to observe that 'Barere is Franz Liszt in one hand and Anton Rubinstein in the other'. Barere's progress was all the more remarkable in that his personal circumstances (he still supported his family by playing in restaurants) permitted him relatively little time for practice.

After graduation he combined the career of a travelling virtuoso with that of professor of piano at the Kiev Conservatory. The political climate at the time prevented him from touring outside the Soviet Union, and it was not until 1928, when he was sent as a cultural ambassador to the Baltic republics and Scandinavia, that he was able to move to Riga. Four years later he moved with his young son and his wife, fellow St Petersburg student Helen Vlashek whom he had married in 1920, to Berlin. After initial successes the growing persecution of the Jewish community forced him to flee from there to Sweden. Following his successful British début at the Aeolian Hall, London, in 1934, Barere signed a recording contract with HMV, for whom he recorded many of the works with which his name was to become closely associated: Liszt's *Réminiscences de Don Juan* and *Rhapsodie espagnole*, Balakirev's *Islamey*, Blumenfeld's *Etude for the Left Hand* and other virtuoso items by Glazunov, Skryabin, Liszt and Godowsky. As well as demonstrating Barere's astonishing virtuosity, these recordings also testify to his extraordinary delicacy and the consistent tonal beauty of his playing throughout a wide dynamic range. Equally, his playing of works by Chopin evidences breathtaking technical command together with rare poetic nobility.

After an acclaimed American début in November 1936, Barere and his family moved to the USA, which was to remain his base. Tours of Australia, New Zealand and South America, as well as his successes in the USA, served to consolidate his reputation as one of the foremost artists of the day. He died suddenly as a result of a cerebral haemorrhage during his first performance of the Grieg Piano Concerto in a concert at Carnegie Hall.

CHARLES HOPKINS

Baretti, Giuseppe (Marc'Antonio) (*b* Turin, 25 April 1719; *d* Marylebone, London, 5 May 1789). Italian man of letters. His *Fetonte sulle rive del Po* was set by G.A. Giai (1750, Turin). In January 1751 he left Italy, where he had a considerable literary reputation, for an appointment at the Italian Opera in London. Shortly after his arrival he wrote two facetious pamphlets relating to a dispute between the actors and the lessee of the Opera. He adapted selected odes of Horace as a sort of Masonic oratorio. Seeking a composer able to avoid the vocal clichés and long ritornellos of Italian opera and 'to temper alternately the solemnity of church music with the brilliancy of the theatrical', Baretti chose Philidor, with whom he discussed 'every syllable … with respect to the best way of expressing musically the meaning of Horace'. *Carmen saeculare* was performed in London in 1779 and in Paris the year after. Baretti wrote in his copy of Johnson's *Letters* that it 'brought me a hundred and fifty pounds in three nights, and three times as much to Philidor. … It would have benefited us both (if Philidor had not proved a scoundrel) greatly more than those sums'.

WRITINGS

Projet pour avoir un Opéra Italien à Londres dans un goût tout nouveau (London, 1753)
La voix de la discorde, ou La bataille des violons (London, 1753)
Katarinae Aug. Piae Felici Ottomannicae Tauricae Musagetae Q. Horatii Flacci Carmen saeculare lyricis concentibus restitutum A.D. Philidor D.D.D. (London, 1778)
The Introduction to the Carmen Seculare (London, 1779)
MS notes in a copy of H.L. Piozzi, ed.: *Letters to and from the Late Samuel Johnson* (London, 1788), *GB-Lbl*

BIBLIOGRAPHY

DBI (M. Fubini)
L.C. Morley: *Giuseppe Baretti: with an Account of his Literary Friendships and Feuds in Italy and in England in the Days of Dr. Johnson* (London, 1909)
G.C. Rossi: 'Un "don Chisciotte in Venezia" de Giuseppe Baretti', *Anales cervatinos*, xviii (1979–80), 211–17

IAIN FENLON

Bar form (Ger. *Barform*). A term denoting in musicology the three-part form *AAB*. The sections are called first *Stollen* (*pes*; A), second *Stollen* (*pes*; A), together forming the *Aufgesang* (*frons*), and *Abgesang* (cauda; B). German terms are normally retained because the concept of bar form was first introduced into musical terminology through Lorenz's investigations into the form of Wagner's works. It is based on an incorrect use of the word 'Bar' in *Die Meistersinger von Nürnberg*. In Act 3 scene ii Walther von Stolzing sings the first stanza of his Prize Song, which has *AAB* form. Hans Sachs then sings: 'Das nenn' ich mir einen Abgesang! Seht, wie der ganze Bar gelang! … Jetzt richtet mir noch einen zweiten Bar'. *Bar* here means 'a tripartite stanza'. In this Wagner was not in full accord with the terminology of the German Meistersinger of the 15th to 18th centuries from whom the word comes.

In the work of the Meistersinger, a *Bar* is not a single stanza – that was called *Liet* or (from the 16th century) *Gesätz* – but the whole song. The most important formal characteristics of a *Bar* in the Meistersinger tradition were: (1) it always had an uneven number of stanzas, at least three; (2) the stanzas had to be written according to a previously determined model, one of the *Töne* (*see* TON (i)) allowed by the Meistersinger guilds. The *Töne* of the Meistersinger were always constructed, both musically and metrically, according to the *AAB* scheme or some version of this scheme (see below: *see also* MEISTER-GESANG for Hans Folz's *Veilchenweise*). The concepts *Stollen*, *Aufgesang* and *Abgesang* also come from the terminology of the Meistersinger.

The word 'Bar' is probably a shortened form of *Barat*, a word taken from the language of fencing and denoting a skilful thrust. The Meistersinger used the word to designate a particularly artful song. The short form *Bar* (in the sense of *Meisterlied*) was perhaps intended to distinguish the artistry of the Meistersinger from the artless songs of those who were not Meistersinger. The modern concept of bar form is therefore, etymologically considered, an error; but it can scarcely be erased from musicological terminology. Literary historians have not adopted the concept: they normally designate the *AAB* form with the (equally questionable) term 'canzona form' (*Kanzonenform*).

AAB form can exist in various ways. The most important possibilities are as follows: (1) *AA/B*, (2) *ABAB/CB*, (3) *AA/BA*, (4) *AA/BB/A*, (5) *AA/BB/C*, (6) *AA/BB*. These forms are taken from medieval German song, but are also more generally applicable. The following designations may be suggested: (1) *Kanzone* (canzona), (2) *Rundkanzone* (rounded canzona), (3) *Kanzone* with non-repeated bridge and a third *Stollen* (bridge – *Steg* – being the term used by Meistersinger for the section joining the *Aufgesang* either to the repeated *Stollen* at the end of the *Abgesang*, which is in turn called third *Stollen*, or to a new final section), (4) *Kanzone* with repeated bridge and third *Stollen*, (5) *Kanzone* with repeated bridge, (6) *Kanzone* with repeated *Abgesang*.

It can be shown that, in medieval song, forms (2) to (6) are unquestionably variants of the basic *AAB* form. This statement contradicts the (unconvincing) attempt by Gennrich to derive forms (1) and (2) from the hymn, but forms (3) to (6) from the sequence, the lai and the *Leich*. Gennrich thereby arrived at the terms: (1) *Kanzone*, (2) *Rundkanzone* (as above), (3) *reduzierter Strophenlai* (reduced stanzaic lai), (5) *Lai-Ende*, (6) *Lai-Ausschnitt* (lai section). He gave no name to (4). Other names suggested include: for (3) *Reprisenbarform* (bar form with reprise; Gudewill) and da capo form without *Schwellen-repetition* (non-repeated bridge; Pickerodt-Uthleb); for (4) da capo form with *Schwellenrepetition* (repeated bridge; Pickerodt-Uthleb); for (5) *potenzierte Barform* (the *Abgesang* is itself built in bar form; Gudewill); for (6) *Repetitionsform* (repeating form; Pickerodt-Uthleb).

The *AAB* form – one of the most common of all musical form genres – can be documented from the time of the classical Greek ode with its *strophe*, *antistrophe* and *epode*. In the early Middle Ages it can be found in the Gregorian chant repertories and later in many hymns. In a more expanded form it became particularly important in the songs of the Provençal troubadours, the northern French trouvères and the German Minnesinger, *Sang-spruchdichter* and Meistersinger. In Germany it was moreover of paramount importance in the Tenorlied of the 16th century and for the Protestant Kirchenlied. In the more recent history of German song it receded in importance in relation to other form schemes, but saw a significant revival in the songs of Schubert, Schumann and Brahms. The importance of bar form for Wagner has been shown exhaustively by Lorenz.

BIBLIOGRAPHY

MGG2 (K. Gudewill/J. Rettelbach); *HDM3*

A. Lorenz: *Das Geheimnis der Form bei Richard Wagner* (Berlin, 1924–33/R)

F. Gennrich: *Grundriss einer Formenlehre des mittelalterlichen Liedes als Grundlage einer musikalischen Formenlehre des Liedes* (Halle, 1932/R)

C. Petzsch: 'Parat-(Barant-)Weise, Bar und Barform', *AMw*, xxviii (1971), 33–43

H. van der Werf: *The Chansons of the Troubadours and Trouvères: a Study of the Melodies and their Relation to the Poems* (Utrecht, 1972)

H. Brunner: *Die alten Meister: Studien zu Überlieferung und Rezeption der mittelhochdeutschen Sangspruchdichter im Spätmittelalter und in der frühen Neuzeit* (Munich, 1975)

E. Pickerodt-Uthleb: *Die Jenaer Liederhandschrift: metrische und musikalische Untersuchungen* (Göppingen, 1975)

J. Rettelbach: *Variation – Derivation – Imitation: Untersuchungen zu den Tönen der Sangspruchdichter und Meistersinger* (Tübingen, 1993)

HORST BRUNNER

Bargas, Urbán de. *See* VARGAS, URBÁN DE.

Barges [Bargues], **Antonino** [Antonio] (*b* Barges; *fl* 1547–65). Netherlandish composer, active in Italy. In 1550 he was *maestro di cappella* of the Ca' Grande, Venice. About 1555 he moved to Treviso, where he took holy orders and lived at the convent of S Francesco. From 1562 to March 1565 he served as choirmaster at Treviso Cathedral. He was a close friend of Willaert, whom he described as 'the sole inventor of true and good music, who was not only a most diligent teacher but the very best father to me'. He was a witness to Willaert's last will and testament in 1562.

Although said on the title-page to consist mainly of villottas, Barges's publication of 1550 in fact contains only six of them. Two in Paduan dialect are specifically described as *villotte alla padoana*. The remaining four, *La manza mia*, *Facciate alla finestra*, *La canzon della gallina* and *Tanto fui tardo*, all have dance-like passages in triple metre or patter declamation of nonsense syllables. The collection also includes 12 *canzoni villanesche* and four four-part madrigals by Andrea Patricio. In his dedication, to the poet Girolamo Fenarolo, Barges asked him to 'sing these little canzonettas now and then' with colleagues in Domenico Venier's literary academy in Venice. Fenarolo had addressed a sonnet to Barges in 1546, expressing gratitude for a gift of some of the composer's villottas and alluding to his *Canzon della gallina* with its imitation of a cackling hen.

All Barges's *villanesche* are settings of single stanzas in madrigalesque textures: systematic points of imitation built from motives of the borrowed tune and paired voices are hallmarks of his style. When a borrowed tune is quoted literally, it often migrates between the cantus and tenor. Barges's three ricercars are based on plainchant tenors laid out uniformly in semibreves with no rests. The counterpoint is not imitative and bears no relation to the chant.

WORKS

Il primo libro de villotte, 4vv (Venice, 1550), ded. repr. in Feldman
3 ricercares, 3vv, in 1551[16], ed. in IIM, ii (1994)
2 motets, 4vv, 1563[4]
Requiem, 4vv, and Alleluia Concussum est mare, 4vv, *I-TVd*
Various works in *D-Mbs, GB-Lbl, I-Bc, Fm*

BIBLIOGRAPHY

EinsteinIM; Vander StraetenMPB, vi
G. d'Alessi: *La cappella musicale del duomo di Treviso (1300–1633)* (Vedelago, 1954)
R. Giazotto: *Harmonici concenti in aere veneto* (Rome, 1954)
D.G. Cardamone: *The 'Canzone villanesca alla napolitana' and Related Forms, 1537 to 1570* (Ann Arbor, 1981)
M. Feldman: 'The Academy of Domenico Venier, Music's Literary Muse in Mid-Cinquecento Venice', *Renaissance Quarterly*, xliv (1991), 476–512

DONNA G. CARDAMONE

Bargiel, Woldemar (*b* Berlin, 3 Oct 1828; *d* Berlin, 23 Feb 1897). German composer and conductor. He was the son of Adolph Bargiel, a Berlin music teacher, and his wife Mariane (née Tromlitz) Wieck, who had divorced Friedrich Wieck in 1824 and was the mother of Clara Wieck (Schumann). He learnt the piano, violin and harmony from his father, and was a chorister and solo alto of what was later the cathedral choir. From 1846 to 1850 he studied, on the advice of his brother-in-law Schumann, at the Leipzig Conservatory, where his teachers included Moscheles and Plaidy (piano), David and Joachim (violin), Hauptmann, Richter, Rietz and Gade (theory and composition). Returning to Berlin he developed a reputation as a teacher and composer, and in 1859 became teacher of theory at the Cologne Conservatory. He was Kapellmeister and director of the institute of the Maatschappij tot Bevordering der Toonkunst at Rotterdam from 1865 to 1874, when Joachim appointed him teacher of composition at the Berlin Hochschule für Musik. In 1875 he became a senator, and in 1876 professor, of the Akademie der Künste, retaining both positions until his death.

As a composer Bargiel was rather an admirer, but not an epigone or imitator, of Schumann. His works were much performed during his lifetime. His pupils included Ernst Rudorff, Paul Juon, Leo Blech, Leopold Godowsky, Peter Raabe and Johannes Wolf. He served, partly in collaboration with Brahms, on the editorial boards of the first Schumann and Chopin editions, and his eight-volume edition of Bach's chorales *Johann Sebastian Bach's vierstimmige Kirchengesänge* (Berlin, 1891–3) was used well into the 20th century.

WORKS

almost all published, c1850–80

Orch: Sym., C, op.30; Ov. to Prometheus. op.16; Ov. zu einem Trauerspiel (on Romeo and Juliet), op.18; Ov. to Medea, op.22; Intermezzo, op.46; 3 danses allemandes, op.24; Adagio, G, vc, orch, op.38
Chbr: Str Octet, op.15a; 4 str qts, incl. no.3, a, op.15b, no.4, op.47; 3 pf trios, F, op.6, E♭, op.20, B♭, op.37; Sonata, f, vn, pf, op.10; Suite, D, pf, vn, op.17
Choral, with orch unless otherwise stated: Ps xcvi, 8vv, op.33; Ps lxi, Bar, 4vv, 1878, op.43; Ps xiii, 4vv, op.25; Ps xxiii, 3 female vv, op.26; 3 Frühlingslieder, 3 female vv, pf, opp.35, 39
Pf 4 hands: Sonata, G, op.23; Suite, C, op.7; Gigue, op.29
Pf solo: Sonata, C, op.34; 3 fantasies, b♭, op.5, D, op.12, c, op.19; Fantasiestücke, opp.9, 15, 27; 2 suites, opp.21, 31; other characteristic pieces and studies, opp.1–4, 8, 11, 13, 28, 32, 36, 41, 44–5

BIBLIOGRAPHY

H. Deiters: 'Woldemar Bargiel', *AMZ*, new ser., ii (1864), 441–7, 457–65

B. Litzmann: *Clara Schumann: ein Künstlerleben nach Tagebüchern und Briefen* (Leipzig, 1902–8/R; Eng. trans., abridged, 1913/R)
J. Joachim and A. Moser, eds.: *Briefe von und an Joseph Joachim* (Berlin, 1911–13; Eng. trans., abridged, 1913/R)
R. Sietz: 'Bargiel, Woldemar', *Rheinische Musiker*, ii, ed. K.G. Fellerer (Cologne, 1962), 4–7
G. Puchelt: *Verlorene Klänge: Studien zur deutschen Klaviermusik 1830–80* (Berlin, 1969)

EDWARD DANNREUTHER/ELISABETH SCHMIEDEL

Bargielski, Zbigniew (*b* Łomiża, 21 Jan 1937). Polish composer. He studied the piano in Lublin and composition with Szeligowski at the Warsaw Conservatory (1958–62), with Szabelski at the Katowice Conservatory (1963–4) and with Boulanger in Paris (1966–7).

He served for several years as secretary of the Polish Composers' Union. In 1977 he moved to Austria, and was appointed to teach at the music school at Bruck an der Mur. His awards include the Austrian State Prize for Composition (1986) and the UNESCO Prize (1995).

Bargielski's works of the 1960s show the influence of Polish contemporaries such as Lutosławaki and Górecki in their treatment of orchestral sound-masses. Around 1970 he developed his own method of articulating specific pitch centres within a given section of music. These 'focal structures' (*Zentrumsstrukturen*) – which he regards as a means of guiding the listener's perception – can also be created out of intervals, chords or instrumental timbres. He has made a notable contribution to the accordion repertory. (*GroveO*, A. Thomas; *LZMÖ*)

WORKS
(selective list)

Ops (librettos by the composer): Mały książę [The Little Prince] (musical tale, 1, after A. de Saint-Exupéry), 1966, Warsaw, 1970; Alicja w krainie czarów [Alice in Wonderland] (youth op, after L. Carroll), 1971–2, Lublin, 1972; Widma nie kłamia [Phantoms Do Not Lie] (comic op, 3, after S.I. Witkiewicz), 1971–2, rev. 1979 as W małym dworku [In a Little Manor], Wroclaw, 1981
Orch: Sinfonia, 1956; Parady, 1965, rev. as Parady 1970, 1969–70; Conc., perc, orch, 1975; Vn Conc., 1976; Rondo alla polacca, 1983; CHA-ORD, 1990; Requiem für Orchester, 1992; Tpt Conc., 1992; Concertino, pf, chbr orch, 1995; Slapstick, chbr orch, 1997
Works with accdn (solo unless otherwise stated): Nilpferde, 2 accdn, 1979, rev. 1988; Zapferstreich, 3 accdn, perc, 1979, rev. 1988; Traumvogel, accdn, perc, 1980; Gespräch mit einem Schatten, 2 accdn, 1982; Gemalte Wolken, 1982; Abschiednacht, accdn, str qt, 1984, rev. 1995; Schwarzer Spiegel, gui, accdn, 1984; Drei polnische Suiten, 1984; Versunkene Flamme, vn, vc, accdn, 1985; Garten der Leidenschaften, S, b cl/a sax, perc, accdn, 1986; Suite der Tänze und Lieder, 1986; Labyrinth, vc, accdn, 1987; Grazer-Variationen, accdn orch, 1987; Kaleidoskop, 1988; Klangmühle, accdn orch, 1991
Other chbr and solo inst: Neosonatine, vn/va/cl/fl, pf, 1956; Servert, vn/va/vc, pf, perc, 1966; Ein Zimmer, cl, trbn, vc, pf, perc, 1972; Str Qt no.1 'Alpejski', 1976; Schmetterlingskäfig, wind qnt, 1978; Str Qt no.2 'Primaverile', 1980; Vienna G'schichten, 2 pf, 1981; Ikarus, b cl/a sax, perc, 1981; Vier zu eins (Wind Qnt no.2), 1982; Stilleben mit Geschrei (Str Qt no.3), 1985–6; Beethovens Wanderweg zum Fürst Lichnowsky, pf, 1992; Le temps ardent (Str Qt no.4), 1994; Landscape of Remembrance, pf, trio, 1996; Forgotten–Regained, vn, 1996
Vocal: Im Kreis (A. Patey-Grobowska), S, A, Bar, B, Chbr ens, 1969; Es ist noch Nacht, noch ein Laut (abstract text), Mez, orch, 1981; Alptraum (K. Wierzynski), T/Bar, pf, 1982; Sonnelieder (M. Jaroschka), Mez, Bar, B, Chorus, chbr ens, 1983; In Niemansland (orat., Jaroschka, Pss xxiii, cxxxvii), Mez, Bar, mixed chorus, orch, 1989

Principal publisher: Polskie wydawnictwo muzyczne

MIECZYZŁAWA HANUSZEWSKA/R

Bargnani, Ottavio (*b* Brescia, ?*c*1570; *d* Mantua, after 1627). Italian composer and organist. According to a notice in Canale's *Canzoni da sonare a quattro … libro primo* (1600), he was the pupil of Canale, an organist at Brescia. The reference in Canale's publication indicates that Bargnani's first book of instrumental canzoni (now lost) predated the Canale volume, although Bargnani had quoted some of Canale's themes 'to honour in this way the writings of his master'. Bargnani was still in Brescia in 1599 when he signed the dedication to his book of canzonets, arias and madrigals for three and four voices. In this earliest surviving publication, he included two compositions by Luca Marenzio, probably simply in tribute to the great Brescian composer, although it is possible that he met Marenzio when the latter passed through northern Italy on his return from Poland to Rome in 1597 or 1598. Bargnani served as organist at Salò Cathedral, in Treviso (1605–7), and later in the S Barbara chapel in Mantua (1607–27). On 1 May 1611 he dedicated to Duke Vincenzo Gonzaga his second book of instrumental canzoni, on the title-page of which he referred to himself as organist to the duke. He contributed two motets, *Domine ne in furore* and *Domine dominus noster*, to a collection published in 1618 containing works by composers in the duke's service (RISM 1618⁴). On 26 March 1627 he obtained from the duke a pension of 60 scudi.

WORKS

SACRED

Motetti, 1–4vv (Venice, 1597); lost, cited in Cozzando
Motets in 1618⁴, 1622²

SECULAR

Canzonette, 4, 8vv (Venice, 1595); lost, cited in Cozzando
Canzonette, arie et madrigali, 3, 4vv (Venice, 1599¹²)
Il primo libro de madrigali, 5vv (Venice, 1601)
Secondo libro delle canzoni da suonare a 4, 5, 8 (Milan, 1611)

BIBLIOGRAPHY

BertolottiM; SartoriB
L. Cozzando: *Libreria bresciana* (Brescia, 1694)
P. Guerrini: 'La cappella musicale del duomo di Salò', *RMI*, xxix (1922), 81–112

STEVEN LEDBETTER

Bargues, Antonino. *See* BARGES, ANTONINO.

Bargy, Roy F(rederick) (*b* Newaygo, MI, 31 July 1894; *d* Vista, CA, 16 Jan 1974). American composer and pianist. He began to study piano at the age of five in Toledo, Ohio. By the time he was 17 he had discarded his ambitions to become a concert pianist, having become fascinated with ragtime pianists in Toledo's red-light district, including the famous exponent of eastern ragtime Luckey Roberts. After playing professionally in cinemas and organizing a dance band, he was engaged in 1919 by the ragtime composer Charley Straight to edit, play, arrange and compose for Imperial Player Rolls. Bargy's association with Straight led to his acquaintance with the agent Edgar Benson, who assembled a band directed by Bargy to record for Victor. Bargy later joined Isham Jones's orchestra for two years and, in 1928, began a 12-year association with Paul Whiteman's band, for which he is best remembered today. Later he served as conductor and arranger for Larry Ross's radio show, and from 1943 he was music director for Jimmy Durante, a position he held until his retirement 20 years later.

Bargy is noted for his contribution to the ragtime-based style of novelty piano. Like the work of his contemporary Zez Confrey, his compositions may be viewed as advanced rags: he routinely employed 10ths in the bass (a feature more readily associated with early jazz than ragtime), but favoured right-hand patterns found in ragtime of the 1910s, recalling at times the work of Straight and the classic ragtime composer James Scott. Although Bargy's works are not as ambitious or imaginative as Confrey's, they represent a charming recasting of the language of midwestern ragtime in the more vivacious mode of the late 1910s and the 1920s.

WORKS
(selective list)
unless otherwise stated, all are printed works for pf published in Cleveland

Rufenreddy (collab. C. Straight) (1921); Slipova (1921); Knice and Knifty (collab. Straight) (1922); Sunshine Caper (1922); Behave Yourself (1922); Jim Jams (1922); Justin-tyme (1922); Pianoflage (1922); Sweet and Tender (Chicago, 1923); A Blue Streak; Omeomy

BIBLIOGRAPHY

D.A. Jasen: *Recorded Ragtime, 1897–1958* (Hamden, CT, 1973)
D.A. Jasen and T.J. Tichenor: *Rags and Ragtime: a Musical History* (New York, 1978)

DAVID THOMAS ROBERTS

Bari. Main city of the Apulia region in southern Italy. The first records of musical activity there date from the 11th and 12th centuries, when the Cathedral of S Nicola founded its schola cantorum, still active in training choristers and providing music at the services. There are also records of dramatic performances of the Easter sequence during High Mass; *laude* and *sacre rappresentazioni* were performed during the 14th and 15th centuries, following Neapolitan practice and probably imported as a result of the Aragonese domination of the area. The schola cantorum had its finest period between the late 15th century and the early 17th. Music flourished under Isabella of Aragon, who ruled Bari from 1501; she had been brought up at the courts of Aragon and Milan, where music had a prominent place, and she encouraged local musicians, probably also inviting others from Milan and Naples. She was succeeded by her daughter Bona, who ruled until 1557 and offered the city similarly favourable conditions for musical development.

Among prominent *maestri di cappella* at S Nicola were G.G. de Antiquis (*c*1574), Stefano Felis (1585), Giovanni de Marinis (1593) and Giuseppe Colaianni (1603). Antiquis published two volumes of *Villanelle alla napolitana* (Venice, 1574) which contain, besides 13 of his own villanellas, works by 16 other composers employed in Bari, including Felis, Colaianni, Marinis, Simon de Baldis, G.F. Capuano, G.P. Gallo, Pomponio Nenna, C.M. de Pizzolis and Cola Nardo de Monte; the collection testifies to the vitality of the local madrigal school.

At the beginning of the 17th century Bari came under Spanish rule within the jurisdiction of a Neapolitan viceroy; this was detrimental to the musical life of Apulia, and most of the composers born there transferred their activity to the Naples Conservatory, including Giacomo Insanguine, Tommaso Traetta, Niccolò Piccinni, Giacomo Tritto, Giuseppe Millico and Francesco Rossi. Among Apulia's many distinguished performers Caffarelli and Farinelli were prominent; famous 19th-century composers from the region included Saverio Mercadante and Mauro Giuliani.

Although many musicians left Bari, either by choice or from necessity, the city remained musically active, as indicated by the large number of theatres established there from the 17th century onwards; their history, however, is poorly documented. The privately run Teatro del Torrione di S Scolastica became active in the 17th century, performing 'comedies in music and in recitative style'. The Teatro del Sedile (references to which date back to the 15th century) presented opera from the beginning of the 19th century, but was declared unsafe and closed in 1835. A new, larger theatre was planned to replace it; until this was officially inaugurated as the Teatro Comunale Piccinni with a performance of Donizetti's *Poliuto* in 1854, operas were performed in a circus tent, known because of its shape as the Teatro della Zuppiera ('soup tureen theatre'). With Italian unification and the ascendancy of the Teatro S Carlo in Naples, the role of the Teatro Comunale Piccinni diminished; the repertory was traditional and the performers mediocre. Popular demand for a new and larger theatre led to the construction of the Politeama Petruzzelli (cap. 4000), the fourth largest theatre in the country, which was inaugurated in 1903 with Meyerbeer's *Les Huguenots*. After the death of its first impresario, Antonio Quaranta, in 1928, the quality of performances dropped. From the late 1970s, however, the theatre saw some courageous new ventures, especially in dance. In 1986 it gave Piccinni's *Iphigénie en Tauride* and revived the original 1835 version of Bellini's *I puritani*. The following year the company performed a memorable *Aida* in Egypt, at the foot of the pyramids. On 27 October 1991 a fire completely destroyed the Politeama Petruzzelli.

Bari's leading musical associations are the Accademia Polifonica Barese (founded 1926), the Antica e Nuova Musica ensemble, the Fondazione Piccinni and the Conservatorio di Musica Niccolò Piccinni (founded 1925).

BIBLIOGRAPHY

ES (G. Bozzo, V. Raeli); *GroveO* (P. Moliterni); *RicordiE*

G. Petroni: *Del Gran Teatro di Bari* (Bari, 1854)

M.A. Bellucci: 'I musicisti Baresi', *Rassegna pugliese di scienze, lettere ed arti*, ii (1885), 196

I. Ludovisi: *Le accademie di Bari dal secolo 14. al sec. 18.* (Bari, 1903)

A. Vinaccia: 'Il nuovo Politeama Petruzzellis', *Rassegna tecnica pugliese*, ii (1903), 65, 81

Accademia polifonica barese . . . nel 25. annuale della sua fondazione (Bari, 1951)

N. Cosmo: 'Il Liceo Piccinni di Bari', *S. Carlo*, ii/2 (1960), 26

V. Melchiorre and L. Zingarelli: *Il Teatro Piccinni di Bari* (Bari, 1983)

P. Moliterni, V. Attolini and E. Persichella: *Vissi d'arte: gli 80 anni del Petruzzelli: il mito e le vicende* (Bari, 1983)

F. Picca: *Bari 'capitale' a teatro: il Politeama Petruzzelli 1877–1914* (Bari, 1987)

RENATO BOSSA

Baricanor [bariclamans]. *See* BARITONE (i).

Barié, Augustin (Charles) (*b* Paris, 15 Nov 1883; *d* Antony, nr Paris, 22 Aug 1915). French organist and composer. Blind from birth, he studied with Marty at the Institut National des Jeunes Aveugles, with Vierne, and then with Guilmant at the Paris Conservatoire, gaining a *premier prix* in 1906. He became organist at St Germain-des-Prés in Paris and professor of organ at the Institut National des Jeunes Aveugles. He began a brilliant career, and was noted for his virtuosity and talent for free improvisation, but he died of a cerebral haemorrhage at the age of 31. His works, mostly for organ, include a symphony and *Trois pièces*; they show the influence of Guilmant in their counterpoint, and of Vierne in their harmonic refinement.

BIBLIOGRAPHY

N. Dufourcq: *La musique d'orgue française* (Paris, 1941/R)

F. Sabatier: 'Augustin Barié', *Guide de la musique d'orgue*, ed. G. Cantagrel (Paris, 1991)

GILLES CANTAGREL

Bariera. *See* BARRIERA.

Barili, Alfredo (*b* Florence, 2 Aug 1854; *d* Atlanta, GA, 17 Nov 1935). American pianist, conductor and teacher. He was born into one of the leading musical families in 19th-century America, which included Adelina Patti, and made his début as a pianist on 7 April 1865 in New York. His family soon moved to Philadelphia, where he studied the piano with Carl Wolfsohn before embarking for the Cologne Conservatory in 1872. Barili settled in Atlanta in 1880 and became the city's first professional musician, introducing many standard works, including Beethoven sonatas and later Gounod's *Messe solennelle de Sainte Cécile*. In 1883 he planned the first Atlanta Music Festival, which included a chorus of 300 accompanied by Carl Sentz's orchestra from Philadelphia. During that one weekend Barili introduced symphonies by Schubert (no.8), Haydn and Beethoven, as well as a number of Mendelssohn and Verdi overtures. That same year he conducted the chorus for Theodore Thomas and his orchestra. Barili developed a reputation as one of the finest teachers in the South, and many of his pupils achieved successful musical careers. His pioneering work in Atlanta laid the foundation for many of the city's musical institutions.

BIBLIOGRAPHY

N.L. Orr: *Alfredo Barili and the Rise of Classical Music in Atlanta* (Atlanta, GA, 1996)

N. LEE ORR

Baring-Gould, Sabine (*b* Exeter, 28 Jan 1834; *d* Lewtrenchard, Devon, 2 Jan 1924). English clergyman, folksong collector, novelist and writer. He was educated at Cambridge (MA, 1856), ordained in 1864, and on his father's death in 1872 he inherited the family estates at Lewtrenchard, where he became rector in 1881 and served as a Justice of the Peace. He travelled extensively and wrote voluminously on theological and general topics; he was also a pioneer in the collection of English folksong. Between 1888 and 1891 he published 110 examples, transcribed from performances by singers in Devon and Cornwall, as *Songs and Ballads of the West*. The collection was made jointly with the Rev. H.F. Sheppard, sub-dean of the Savoy Chapel, with whom Baring-Gould also collaborated to produce *A Garland of Country Song* (1895) and *English Minstrelsie* (1895–6). Their first joint publications in the field preceded by several years the folksong collections of W.A. Barrett, Frank Kidson, John Stokoe and J.A. Fuller Maitland, and were themselves preceded only by John and Lucy Broadwood's *Sussex Songs* (1843, 1888). Cecil Sharp's revision of *Songs and Ballads of the West* (1905) reflects the influence of Baring-Gould's early work on Sharp's own choice of location. Baring-Gould was the author of the words of many well-known hymns of which the most celebrated is *Onward, Christian Soldiers*, first published in the *Church Times* in 1865 and later popularized by Sullivan's tune. Understandably less well known is the collection in which he deliberately imitated the idiom of Sankey and Moody, *Church Songs* (1884), also produced jointly with H.F. Sheppard.

BIBLIOGRAPHY

G. Boyes: *The Imagined Village: Culture, Ideology and the English Folk Revival* (Manchester, 1993)

H. Orel, ed.: *Gilbert and Sullivan: Interviews and Recollections* (Basingstoke, 1994)

B. Pegg: *Folk: a Portrait of English Traditional Music, Musicians and Customs* (London, 1976)

BERNARR RAINBOW

Bariolage (Fr.: 'odd mixture of colours'). A 19th-century term used in bowed instruments to describe several slightly unorthodox ways of mixing open strings with stopped notes for special effect. This may merely be a matter of using open strings in passages otherwise played in upper positions. In *L'art du violon* (1834) Baillot (who explains the name of the device by saying that it seems 'disordered or bizarre') cites Haydn's fingering indications in the trio of his G major Quartet op.64 no.4 (ex.1). The

Ex.1 Haydn: Quartet in G op.64 no.4, 2nd movt

term is most frequently applied to the special effect in which the same note is played alternately on two strings – one stopped and one open – resulting in the juxtaposition of contrasting tone-colours (a kind of *Klangfarbenmelodie*). *Bariolage* may be produced either by slurred bowing or by individual bowstrokes. Well-known examples occur in the prelude of Bach's Partita in E for solo violin (ex.2).

Ex.2 Bach: Partita in E, Preludio

The device is similar to ONDULÉ or *ondeggiando* (though this does not necessarily involve the use of open strings). See BOW, §II, 2(viii).

DAVID D. BOYDEN/PETER WALLS

Bariolla [Bariola, Barioli, Bariolus], **Ottavio** (*fl* Milan, 1573–96). Italian organist and composer. The archives of Milan Cathedral for 25 June 1573 indicate that the authorities directed 'Octavius Bariolus, organist of the new organ of the aforementioned major church . . . to enter into the first position or accept the second position'. From at least 1588 he was organist at S Maria presso S Celso, Milan. However, it seems unlikely that he continued his activities there beyond 1594; in the following year the chapel organist was Giovanni Paolo Cima. Antegnati ranked Bariolla among the best players and composers of the time and Borsieri praised him particularly for his ensemble canzonas.

Bariolla published at least two collections of instrumental music, *Ricercate per suonar l'organo* and *Capricci overo canzoni a quattro*, both of which survive virtually intact in a 17th-century tablature. Two other pieces appear in collections of the time. The 12 ricercares in four parts make full use of imitation and other conventional

contrapuntal devices; melodic inversion, trills, turns and syncopation occur frequently. The *Capricci* appeared originally in four partbooks; only the two treble parts now survive. In construction they resemble the ricercares and other *canzone alla francese* of the time, but in contrast to the ricercares they employ sprightly, brief subjects in short note values. They exhibit most conventional contrapuntal devices and demonstrate Bariolla's mastery of polyphony.

WORKS

Editions: *Ottavio Bariolla: Keyboard Compositions*, ed. C.W. Young, CEKM, xliv (1986)
Ottavio Bariolla: Canzone prima, ed. W. Young, Early Music Series, xxvi (Oxford, 1976)

Ricercate per suonar l'organo (Milan, 1585); lost, tablature in *I-Tn*
Capricci overo canzoni a quattro . . . libro terzo (Milan, 1594); ed. in IIM, xii (1995)
1 piece, 5vv, 1596[1]; 1, 5vv, 1596[11]

BIBLIOGRAPHY

C. Antegnati: *L'arte organica* (Brescia, 1608/R); ed. R. Lunelli (Mainz, 1938, 2/1958)
P. Morigi: *La nobiltà di Milano* (Milan, 1595, 2/1619), 304
G. Borsieri: *Il supplemento della nobiltà di Milano* (Milan, 1619), 56

CLYDE WILLIAM YOUNG

Baripsaltes [barisonans, baritonans]. *See* BARITONE (i).

Bariton. *See* BARYTON (i).

Baritone (i) (from Gk. *barytonos*: 'deep-sounding'; Fr. *baryton*; Ger. *Bariton*; It. *baritono*). A male voice, usually written for within the compass *A* to *f'*, which may be extended at either end.

1. Early history. 2. 19th century. 3. 20th century.

1. EARLY HISTORY.   The term 'baritonans' was first used in Western music towards the end of the 15th century, principally in French sacred polyphony, where it may signify a voice lower in pitch than the *bassus*. In several five-voice masses of Pierre de La Rue and Nicolas Champion, for example, the voice one from lowest is designated 'bassus' with the 'baritonans' lying lower. Gaffurius (*Practica musice*, 1496) uses the term instead of 'bassus' for the lowest of the four regular voices ('cantus', 'contratenor acutus', 'tenor' and 'baritonans'). In John Dowland's translation (1609) of Ornithoparcus's *Musicae activae micrologus* (1517), the definition 'the *Bassus* (or rather *Basis*) is the lowest part of each Song' is qualified with the statement 'Or it is an Harmony to be sung with a deep voice which is called *Baritonus*'. A partbook in Lodovico Viadana's *Salmi per cantare e concertare* (1612) is marked 'baritono'.

In 17th-century Italy, the term 'baritono' takes up its modern position between the tenor and bass parts. According to Praetorius (*Syntagma musicum*, iii, 1618, p.133), 'by this term the Italians mean the tenor or quintum . . . when the F clef is written on the third line. In one of the earliest references to a solo baritone, Monteverdi, looking for a good bass for his *La finta pazza Licori* (1627, Mantua: lost), gave qualified approval to Don Iacomo Papalino, who, he said, sang with feeling, had a fairly competent *trillo* and *gorgia*, but 'is a baritone and not a bass' (letter to Alessandro Striggio, 1627).

The French counterpart to 'baritono' is BASSE-TAILLE, the lowest of three tenor ranges. Brossard (*Dictionaire de musique*, 1703) defined 'baritono' as 'what we call the *basse-taille* or *concordant*', ranges he distinguished by their lower extension, the *basse-taille* to *B* and the concordant to G. Rousseau (*Dictionnaire*, 1768) placed the *basse-taille* between the tenor and bass and equated the term with both 'baryton' and 'concordant' (he limited the latter to sacred music). Although a separate constituent of the five-part chorus in sacred music, the *basse-taille* had no specific line in the four-part opera chorus; singers in this range joined either with the *tailles* or the basses. Rousseau, however, equated the 'concordant' with the 'part that in Italy is called tenor', not with the bass, but allowed that 'basse-taille' was sometimes used to identify the true bass. Confusion as to whether the baritone is closer to the tenor or the bass has persisted. Walther (*Musicalisches Lexicon*, 1732) split the difference, writing that a baritone 'must have the high range of the tenor as well as some depth in the bass'.

The term did not enter normal operatic parlance until the 19th century, although many 18th-century roles call for what is now considered a baritone. These include the 'bass' parts written by Handel for G.M. Boschi. Lully wrote several important roles, such as Cadmus, Alcides (*Alceste*) and Aegeus (*Thésée*) in the baritone clef (the F clef on the middle line or the C on the top line), but their ranges do not go beyond *G* to *e'* although some have a high tessitura. Rameau's operas include several such roles, extending from *F* or *G* to *f'* or *f♯'*, such as Teucer and Ismenor in *Dardanus* and Jupiter in *Castor et Pollux*. The most notable *basse-taille* of Rameau's day was Claude Chassé, who was admired more for his acting than his singing but was sufficiently versatile to take the *haute-taille* role of Medusa in a revival of Lully's *Persée* in 1738. Gluck's only notable baritone roles are Agamemnon (*Iphigénie en Aulide*) and Orestes (*Iphigénie en Tauride*).

Mozart's leading roles for baritone and bass-baritone derive from the *basso buffo* tradition, in which no clear distinction is drawn between bass and baritone. The first Count Almaviva (*Le nozze di Figaro*), Stefano Mandini, described as a 'primo buffo mezzo carattere', had a voice that would now be considered a baritone. He specialized in *opera buffa* and had earlier played Almaviva in Paisiello's *Il barbiere di Siviglia*. Mozart's first Figaro was the comic bass Francesco Benucci. Luigi Bassi created the title role at the Prague première of *Don Giovanni* (1787); he had sung the Count in *Figaro* shortly before. His range was described in 1800 as lying between tenor and bass. A *basso buffo*, Francesco Albertarelli, sang Don Giovanni at the Vienna première.

2. 19TH CENTURY.   Baritone roles arrived late in opera chiefly because so much emphasis had previously been laid on florid singing, for which the lower male voice was not well suited. The baritone was slow to be accepted for principal roles. Castil-Blaze (*De l'opéra en France*, i, 1820, pp.280ff) explained that 'the Italians dearly love high voices, the French seem to prefer the middle range, and the Germans deep voices'. He found it extraordinary that in *Le nozze di Figaro* and *Don Giovanni* there should be four important roles for 'basses' and that the principal male should be a 'bass' (like others of the time, he did not distinguish between bass and baritone). That Mozart's prominent roles for basses and baritones were found daringly innovatory in England is indicated by Mount Edgcumbe's remark, 'They take the lead in operas with as much propriety as if the double bass were to do so in the orchestra' (*Musical Reminiscences*, 1824).

The acceptance of the baritone voice widened the range of male character types beyond those traditionally asso-ciated with the castrato or the tenor (the hero and the lover) and the bass (the king, the soldier, the high priest, the aged man). The baritone came to be used for new manifestations of virility: the wooer in competition with the lover (Don Carlo, *Ernani*), the trusty friend (Posa, *Don Carlos*), the brother figure (Valentin, *Faust*), the less-than-sage father figure (Germont, *La traviata*), the swashbuckler (Escamillo, *Carmen*), the lascivious villain (Scarpia, *Tosca*), the mature young man (Wolfram, *Tannhäuser*) or the youthful older man (the Flying Dutchman).

Leading Italian baritones of this period include Antonio Tamburini, who created several Donizetti and Bellini roles; Giorgio Ronconi, who sang for Donizetti but scored his greatest triumphs in early Verdi operas; and Felice Varesi, Verdi's first Macbeth, Rigoletto and Germont. Verdi's finest baritone however was the French singer Victor Maurel, a noted interpreter of Posa and Amonasro and creator of Iago and Falstaff as well as Leoncavallo's Tonio (*Pagliacci*). Another outstanding French baritone was Jean-Baptiste Faure, who created Posa, Thomas's Hamlet and several Meyerbeer roles; his successor Jean Lassalle was also admired for the beauty of his timbre. High baritone roles, calling on the head voice, were a French speciality: their leading exponent was Jean-Blaise Martin whose long career at the Opéra-Comique gave rise to the voice-type known as the 'baryton Martin'. In Germany, the heavier 'Heldenbariton' voice, a counter-part to the Verdi baritone, developed, especially with the operas of Wagner, typified by Anton Mitterwurzer, the first Wolfram and Kurwenal. But the principal develop-ment was that of the 'Hoher Bass', the voice-type of Wotan and Hans Sachs (and typified by Franz Betz); this is a bass-baritone rather than a baritone proper.

The burgeoning song and oratorio repertory of the 19th century particularly suited the more lyric type of baritone. Johann Michael Vogl, who began his career in opera performing such roles as Orestes and Count Almaviva and creating Pizarro in the 1814 version of *Fidelio*, is best remembered as the singer Schubert most admired in the performance of his songs. Julius Stockhau-sen, who gave the first public performance of *Die schöne Müllerin*, was one of the first lieder singers to carry the German song repertory abroad; he made his career as a concert artist in such works as Haydn's *Creation*, Beethoven's Ninth Symphony and Mendelssohn's *Elijah*, and Brahms wrote the baritone part in the *German Requiem* for him. Early recordings have captured the voices of a number of concert baritones, including Charles Santley, highly praised by Eduard Hanslick and George Bernard Shaw for his refined singing; George Henschel, who sang in Bach's *St Matthew Passion* under Brahms's direction; and Plunket Greene, who made his début in *Messiah* and for whom Stanford wrote the *Songs of the Fleet*.

Operetta became a strong repertory for light baritones. The comic baritone part, replete with patter song, dates back at least to Mozart and Rossini's characterizations of Figaro; it also became a staple of Gilbert and Sullivan. George Grossmith created the principal comedy baritone roles, including the Major-General (*The Pirates of Penz-ance*), Koko (*The Mikado*) and the Lord Chancellor (*Iolanthe*); his successor, Henry Lytton, also created roles in musical comedies, such as *The Rose of Persia* (1899). In Paris, the Théâtre des Variétés company included a number of baritones. Eugène Grenier and Henri Couder sang in the premières of Offenbach's *La belle Hélène* (1864), *Barbe-bleue* (1866) and *La Grande-Duchesse de Gérolstein* (1867). At the Opéra-Comique, the lyric baritone Alexandre Taskin sang from 1878 to 1894, creating the three villains of *Les contes d'Hoffman* (1881) and also Lescaut in Massenet's *Manon* (1884).

3. 20TH CENTURY.   The early 20th century witnessed an outpouring of new baritone roles in French, Italian and German opera. At the Opéra-Comique in 1902, the two baritones in the première of *Pelléas et Mélisande* were of dissimilar types, Jean Périer (Pelleas) a typical 'baryton Martin' with a comparatively light, high-lying voice, the Belgian Hector Dufranne (Golaud), heavier though still lyrical. In the same year, the baritone Giuseppe De Luca created Michonnet (*Adriana Lecouvreur*) at the Teatro Lirico in Milan; he also sang Sharpless (*Madama Butterfly*, 1904). His repertory ranged from Figaro (Mozart and Rossini) to Rigoletto. Among his contemporaries were Mario Sammarco, a vital singer and actor who created Gérard (*Andrea Chénier*, 1896) and whose roles included Sachs, and Titta Ruffo, a powerful, high baritone, often compared with Caruso, who sang a wide range of other parts including Italian, French and Russian repertory. Strauss's baritone roles began with Kunrad (*Feuersnot*), sung at the Dresden première by Karl Scheidemantel, who also created Faninal in *Der Rosenkavalier* (1911) and sang Amfortas (*Parsifal*) and Hans Sachs at Bayreuth. Karl Perron, the bass-baritone who created John the Baptist (*Salome*, 1905), Orestes (*Elektra*, 1909) and Baron Ochs (*Der Rosenkavalier*), sang Amfortas and Wotan at Bayreuth as well as King Mark and Daland, more usually bass roles. Anton van Rooy, Stockhausen's most famous student, sang in the American première of *Parsifal* (1903) and took all Wagner's leading bass-baritone roles at Bayreuth; he was also a fine lieder singer. The title role of *Wozzeck* was created by Leo Schützendorf, a bass-baritone whose roles also included Ochs, Boris Godunov, Beckmesser, Faninal and Gounod's Mephistopheles; he was one of four brothers, all professional basses or baritones.

Mid-20th-century Wagner baritones include Friedrich Schorr and Rudolf Bockelmann, both especially admired in their performances of Wotan and Sachs between the wars. Hans Hotter, in a career lasting over 60 years, began as a high baritone and progressed through bass-baritone to bass; he created the Comandant in Strauss's *Friedenstag* (1938) and Olivier in *Capriccio* (1942) and during the 1950s became the leading Wagner bass-baritone, unrivalled as Wotan, Kurwenal, Amfortas, Sachs and the Dutchman, and was also a fine singer of lieder. Paul Schöffler began his career, like Hotter, as a lyric baritone before progressing to heavier bass-baritone roles.

An outstanding Verdi baritone was Mariano Stabile, chosen by Toscanini to sing Falstaff at La Scala (1921–2); he also sang the role at Covent Garden, as well as Iago, Rigoletto and Scarpia, and appeared at Glyndebourne. His mantle descended in certain respects on Tito Gobbi, a magnificent comic actor as well as a powerful tragedian. The first Italian Wozzeck, Gobbi had over 100 roles in his repertory, but excelled in Verdi and Puccini; his Posa, Iago, Macbeth, Boccanegra and Falstaff were notable for their dramatic effectiveness, while as Scarpia, opposite Callas's Tosca, he was unrivalled. Noted Verdi interpreters include three distinguished Americans, Lawrence

Tibbett, Leonard Warren and Robert Merrill. Tibbett, a powerful actor, also created roles in several American operas; Warren, larger and more lustrous in voice, concentrated on Verdi, singing Rigoletto, Iago, Amonasro, Luna, Macbeth and Boccanegra; and Merrill, a lyric baritone, was outstanding as Germont (*La traviata*) with a secure technique that enabled him also to sing Rossini, Donizetti and Bellini.

Geraint Evans, the Welsh baritone who often sang Figaro and Leporello to Gobbi's Count and Don Giovanni, became an excellent Falstaff, a role he first sang at Glyndebourne; he created Mr Flint (*Billy Budd*, 1951) and Mountjoy (*Gloriana*, 1953) and also sang Britten's Balstrode, Bottom and Claggart, though his finest 20th-century role was Wozzeck. His natural successor, in the 1990s, was Bryn Terfel, a rich-toned Welsh baritone outstanding in both *buffo* and heroic roles.

Sherril Milnes, the American baritone who succeeded to the Verdi roles once sung by his compatriots Tibbett, Warren and Merrill, was also successful in such French roles as Thomas's Hamlet, Alphonse XI (*La favorite*) and Saint-Saëns's Henry VIII.

In the 1970s and 80s Piero Cappuccilli was regarded as the leading Italian Verdi baritone; other Italians eminent in the Verdi and Donizetti repertories have included Giuseppe Taddei and Renato Bruson. In Britain, Thomas Allen became the most versatile baritone of his generation, especially noted for his Mozart roles (above all Don Giovanni), his accomplishment in Verdi and French music, his sombre Onegin and his stirring Billy Budd. The opening up of central eastern Europe and the former USSR revealed a formidable number of talented Verdi baritones, including Vladimir Chernov.

French operatic roles have been stylishly sung by the Australian John Brownlee, especially Golaud in *Pelléas et Mélisande*, and, more recently, by Russian-born Sergey Leiferkus, whose roles include Escamillo and Zurga (*Les pêcheurs de perles*). An outstanding French lyric baritone was Gérard Souzay, whose French operatic roles ranged from Lully to Poulenc and Ravel; his signature role was Golaud. Souzay's mellifluous voice and subtle musicianship made him also a great singer of French song and German lieder. Other lyric baritones who have excelled in the song repertory include Pierre Bernac, Souzay's teacher, who formed a duo with Poulenc and gave first performances of many of Poulenc's songs.

Important lieder singers from early in the century include the German baritones Heinrich Schlusnus, also well known as a Verdi interpreter, Gerhard Hüsch (admired in such roles as Papageno, Wolfram and Falke) and Herbert Janssen, also a noted Wagnerian.

Two great lieder singers active after World War II were the German baritones Hermann Prey and Dietrich Fischer-Dieskau. Prey, admired in Mozart, sang in a wide range of opera, including works by Verdi, Strauss and Wagner. Fischer-Dieskau, regarded as the most subtle, refined and expressive lieder singer of his era, sang similar operatic roles, but also made the creation of new roles a speciality: Mittenhofer in Henze's *Elegy for Young Lovers* (1961) and the title role of Reimann's *Lear* (1978) were both composed for him. Younger German and Austrian lieder singers include Olaf Bär, Matthias Goerne, Wolfgang Holzman and Stephan Genz.

The warm, relaxed sound of the lyric baritone has continued to make it the most sought-after voice in operetta, musical comedy and popular music. Nelson Eddy, along with soprano Jeanette McDonald, starred in a long series of filmed operetta, including *Rose-Marie*, *Naughty Marietta* and *The Chocolate Soldier*. Two of the great baritones of musical comedy were Alfred Drake (*Kismet*, *Kiss me Kate* and *Oklahoma*) and Robert Goulet (notable as Lancelot in *Camelot*). In popular music and ballads, baritones dominate the field: such singers as Frank Sinatra, Bing Crosby, Nat 'King' Cole, John Raitt and Harry Belafonte indicate the richness of this tradition.

BIBLIOGRAPHY

J.-B. Faure: *La voix et le chant: traité pratique* (Paris, 1866)
M. Kunath: 'Die Charakterologie der stimmlichen Einheiten in der Oper', *ZMw*, viii (1925–6), 403
R. Celletti: 'La voce di baritono', *Musica d'oggi*, new ser., iii (1960), 452
H. Matheopoulos: *Bravo: Today's Great Tenors, Baritones and Basses Discuss their Roles* (London, 1986)
R.M. Knight: *The Development of the Baritone Voice in Operas of Selected Composers from 1750–1830* (DMA diss., Northwestern U., 1988)
J.B. Steane: *Voices: Singers and Critics* (London, 1992)
G. and R. Edwards: *The Verdi Baritone: Studies in the Development of Dramatic Character* (Bloomington, IN, 1994)
J.B. Steane: *Singers of the Century* (London, 1996)

OWEN JANDER, J.B. STEANE, ELIZABETH FORBES/
ELLEN T. HARRIS (with GERALD WALDMAN)

Baritone (ii) [Baritone horn] (Ger. *Tenorhorn*; It. *flicorno tenore, tenore*). A valved brass instrument in B♭, pitched as the trombone, in Britain having a narrower bore than the similarly pitched EUPHONIUM. Two are used in British brass bands to fill the harmony rather than as solo instruments. The usual compass sounds from E to b♭′, and its music is written in the treble clef a 9th higher. The instrument is the final version of Sax's 'saxhorn baryton', known in France as 'baryton en si♭', the euphonium being 'basse en si♭'. In American band music, no consistent musical distinction is made between two B♭ instruments of contrasted bore and timbre, and 'baritone' is the normal term for the valved instrument of this pitch, save insofar as makers offer a variety of bore widths to the customer's choice, and sometimes designate the models of largest bore 'euphonium'. In Germany two B♭ band instruments are distinguished in bore and function as in France and Britain, but have been evolved independently; 'Bariton' describes the large-bore form and 'Tenorhorn' the narrower.

See also SAXHORN; ALTHORN; TENOR HORN.

BIBLIOGRAPHY

Waterhouse-LangwillI
A. Baines: *Brass Instruments: their History and Development* (London, 1976/R)
C. Bevan: *The Tuba Family* (London, 1978)
H. Heyde: *Trompeten, Posaunen, Tuben* (Leipzig, 1980) [museum catalogue]

ANTHONY C. BAINES/TREVOR HERBERT

Baritone oboe. The bass oboe. *See* OBOE, §III, 5(i).

Baritono [flicorno baritono, bombardino] (It.). *See* FLICORNO and EUPHONIUM.

Barizon, Philippe. *See* BASIRON, PHILIPPE.

Bark, Jan (Helge Guttorm) (*b* Härnösand, 19 April 1934). Swedish composer. He studied at the Borgarskolan and at the Musikhögskolan in Stockholm. For 15 years he played jazz trombone, and during the 1960s he was a music teacher and for nine years an instructor of film

Modern baritone in B♭ by Boosey & Hawkes (Besson model), London

editors and cameramen for Swedish broadcasting. Influenced by Varèse and K. Dewey, and more pronouncedly by worldwide folk cultures, his compositions often feature music theatre. In 1963 he co-founded Kulturkvartetten, a group of four trombonists who perform their own theatrical compositions. From the 1960s he has been largely active in collaborative events; a later interest was in films and videotapes attempting to register cultural undercurrents in social change.

WORKS
(*selective list*)

Other inst: Metakronismer, orch, 1961; Pyknos, orch, 1962; Missa bassa, orch, 1964; IRK-ORK 1970, orch, 1970; 2 str qts
Trbn qts: Bolos, 1962, collab. F. Rabe; Polonaise, 1965, collab. F. Rabe; Pipe Lines, 1968, collab. Kulturkvartetten; Zug, 1968, collab. Kulturkvartetten; Crane Step, 1971, collab. Kulturkvartetten; No Hambones on the Moon, 1971, collab. Kulturkvartetten; Narrskeppet [The Fool's Ship], 1983, collab. Nya kulturkvartetten; Fyrbåk [Beacon], 1996, collab. Nya kulturkvartetten
Choral: Nota, 1964; Mansbot, 1965; Thank Heavens for Semantic Veils of Mist, Cried Woe the Fairest Bryde thou hast not Kissed (after A.Z. Robertson), 1968; Light Music, 1969
Tape: Ost funk, 1963; Ach Chamberlain, 1965; Fuzzyfonier, 1967, collab. J.W. Pedersen; Bar, 1971
Semantic music: Kulturen och vi, 1965; The Transparent Egg, 1973
Films and videotapes: Pipa när saven stiger, 1973; … innan örenen faller av (Die Insel der Klänge oder Der unheimliche Ausflug des Audionauten), 1973; Den gamla grottesången, 1974; Härifrån till verkligheten, 1974

Principal publisher: Nordiska musikförlaget

WRITINGS

with F. Rabe: 'Blåsinstrumentens nya möjligheter', *Nutida musik*, v/2 (1961–2), 20–21

'Pyknos', *Nutida musik*, vi/8 (1962–3), 4–12

with F. Rabe: 'Pajasso och Ost funk', *Nutida musik*, vii/4 (1963–4), 18 only

with J.W. Morthenson: 'Två spår', *Rondo: Musiikkelehti* (1964), no.1, p.6

with F. Rabe: 'Bolos', *Nutida musik*, viii (1964–5), 114–15

'Eclaircissement par camouflet', *Nutida musik*, x/2 (1966–7), 16–19

'Musik och bild', *Nutida musik*, x/6–7 (1966–7), 8–14

Musik och bild (Stockholm, 1967)

with F. Rabe: 'Sanning', *Nutida musik*, xi (1967–8), 30–33

with F. Rabe: 'Musikpedagogiskt alternativ', *Tonfallet* (1969), no.17, p.3

BIBLIOGRAPHY

K. Linder: 'Fern unga ton sättare', *Nutida musik*, iv/6 (1960–61), 4–7, esp. 4–5

K.-E. Andersson: 'Jan Barks körverk Nota', *Musiklivet – Vår sång*, xxxviii (1965), 40

T. Åhs: 'Bark-musik är inte bara hambo', *Tonfallet* (1971), no.18, p.1

G. Bergendal: *33 svenska komponister* (Stockholm, 1972)

R. Haglund: 'Bark, Jan', *Sohlmans musiklexikon*, ed. H. Åsh and (Stockholm, 2/1975–9) [incl. worklist]

R. Haglund: 'Kulturkvartetten och Nya Kulturkvartetten', *Nutida musik*, xxix/4 (1985–6) 29–34

ROLF HAGLUND

Barkauskas, Vytautas (*b* Kaunas, 25 March 1931). Lithuanian composer. He studied the piano at the J. Tallat-Kelpša Music College in Vilnius (1949–53), at the same time studying mathematics at the Pedagogic Institute in that city. He then studied with Račiunas at the Lithuanian State Conservatory, graduating in 1959. In 1961, after a brief period as a teacher at the Čiurlionis Art School, Barkauskas began to teach theory at the Lithuanian Music Academy (he was appointed a lecturer in the department of music theory in 1974, and professor of composition in 1989). In 1972 he was awarded the Lithuanian State Prize, and in 1981 he won the title of Honoured Artist of Lithuania. In 1997 he was awarded the State Stipend of Lithuania.

Barkauskas is one of the most productive of modern Lithuanian composers in the field of instrumental music. In his early work (1954–64) he strove to achieve free atonality. The beginning of his second creative period (1964–81) is marked by his interest in the theories of such musicians as Schaeffer and Krenek. In technique, Barkauskas took his guidelines principally from Lutosławski, Penderecki and Ligeti. During the decade from 1965 to 1975, he was one of the most consistent exponents of modern techniques of composition in Lithuania, but at the same time he avoided using them in an orthodox, undiluted manner, instead interpreting them in his own way and seeking natural interactions. This approach is already evident in the composer's first modern works, for instance *Poezija* ('Poetry', 1964, employing a free interpretation of 12-tone technique) and *Intymi kompozicija* ('Intimate Composition', 1968, an interpretation of serialism in terms of aleatory sound). The end of this period in his career is marked by the Viola Concerto (1981), in which the semantic process of confrontations and monologues leads from the clash of soloist and orchestra to a quiet, cathartic culmination. His third creative period, beginning in 1981, which may be described with some qualifications as post avant-garde, is distinguished by more conventional and pluralistic tendencies, a more intuitive method of composition, the

search for natural sonic beauty, and by a certain inner intensity, often expressed within traditional genres and forms. In his work of the 1990s his tonal language was simplified, melody and tone colour are more prominent, and a latent tonality is perceptible. Narrative drama is alien to Barkauskas's compositions, which are more inclined to pursue a concertante course.

WORKS
(*selective list*)

Stage: Legenda apie meilę [The Legend of Love] (op, V. Mikštaitė, after N. Hikmet), 1975

Vocal: Präludium und Fuge, chorus, 1970; La vostra nominanza è color d'erba (after D. Alighieri: *La divina commedia*), mirage-poem, chbr chorus, str qnt, 1970, rev. 1977; Atviri langai [Open Windows] (P. Eluard), 5 essays, Mez, fl, hpd, vn, vc, db, 1978; 7 Omaro Chajamo minatiūros, chbr chorus, 1980; Viltis [The Hope] (orat, J. Mačiulis-Maironis), 2 T, Bar, B, 2 female choruses, org, 1988–90; oratorios, song cycles, choruses

Orch: Trys aspektai [Three Aspects], 1969; Gloria urbi, org conc., 1972; Toccamento, chbr conc., 1978; Sym. no.3, 1978–9; Conc., va, chbr orch, 1981; Sym. no.4, 1984–5; Sym. no.5, 1986; Saule [The Sun], sym. poem, 1986, rev. 1995; Concerto piccolo, chbr orch, 1988, rev. 1995; Pf Conc., 1992; Cia ir dabar [Here and Now], 1998

Chbr and solo inst: Poezija, cycle, pf, 1964; Partita, vn, 1967; Variations, 2 pf, 1967; Intymi kompozicija, ob, 12 str, 1968; Kontrastine muzika, fl, vc, perc, 1969; Pro memoria, 5 perc, fl, b cl, pf, 1970; Str Qt no.1, 1972; Trys legendos apie Čiurlionj [Three Čiurlionis Legends], pf, 1972–93; Sonata subita, vn, pf, 1974; Pf Qnt, 1980; Str Qt no.2, 1983; Sextet, pf, str qt, db, 1985; Sonntagsmusik, 2 pf 8 hands, 1985; Vizija, pf, 1986–8; Trio, vn, cl, pf, 1990; Konzertische Suite, vc, pf, 1993; Allegro brillante, 2 pf, 1996; Modus vivendi, pf trio, 1996; Duo, gui, pf, 1997

BIBLIOGRAPHY

N. Rzavinskaya: 'Kamernaya muzïka V. Barkauskasa' [Barkauskas's Chamber Music], *Kompozitorï soyuznïkh respublik*, ii (Moscow, 1977), 3–34

A. Bajarūnaitė: *Vytauto Barkausko kūrybinio proceso ypatumai* [The Peculiarities of Barkauskas's Creative Process] (diss., Vilnius, 1982)

L. Lesle: 'Vytautas Barkauskas: Trio for violin, clarinet and piano', *Das Orchester* (1998), no.11, p.69

based on *MGG2* (ii, 252–4), by permission of Bärenreiter

GRAŽINA DAUNORAVIČIENĖ

Barker, Charles Spackman (*b* Bath, 10 Oct 1804; *d* Maidstone, 26 Nov 1879). English inventor and organ builder. He was the eldest son of Joseph Barker and nephew of Thomas Barker ('Barker of Bath'), both of whom were artists. Originally an apothecary's assistant in Bath, he worked briefly with an unnamed organ builder in London before returning to Bath about 1830 and setting up on his own account. After seeing a hydraulic press, he became interested in pneumatic actions, an elementary form of which had been used by Joseph Booth in 1827 at Attercliffe near Sheffield. In 1833 he was in correspondence with Matthew Camidge, the organist of York Minster, concerning his experimental apparatus, which at this stage seems to have consisted of a piston working in a small cylinder. He also offered it for use in the large organ at Birmingham Town Hall; it was not adopted (except possibly to operate the Carillon) but the organ builder William Hill assisted Barker to refine his device.

In 1835 David Hamilton used pneumatic action in his organ in St John's Episcopal Church, Edinburgh. Barker meanwhile was in correspondence with Cavaillé-Coll, who invited him to Paris with a view to applying his own pneumatic lever in the construction of the St Denis organ. A French patent was taken out in 1839 and the success of the St Denis organ was followed by the application of

Barker's lever to other large Cavaillé-Coll instruments. After working for a time with Cavaillé-Coll, Barker became manager (*contre-maître*) of Daublaine–Callinet; this firm passed in 1845 to Ducroquet, for whom Barker supervised the building of the prize-winning instrument for the Great Exhibition (1851) and a new organ for St Eustache (1854) following the destruction by fire, accidently started by Barker himself, of the organ reconstructed by Daublaine–Callinet (1844).

Barker exhibited on his own account at the Paris Exposition (1855). Shortly after this the Ducroquet firm was acquired by Merklin, and in 1860 Barker went into partnership with Charles Verschneider (*d* 1865). About this time he became interested in the experiments with electric action performed by Albert Peschard (1836–1903) of Caen. In 1866 Barker completed the first successful electric action at Salon using the system patented by Peschard in 1864. Barker took out his own English patent in 1868 and granted Bryceson a sole concession to use it.

At the outbreak of the Franco–Prussian War in 1870, Barker emigrated to Dublin. There, he was comissioned to build a new organ for the Roman Catholic Cathedral, Marlborough Street, but despite the assistance of the American organ builder, Hilborne Roosevelt, it was not a success, and Barker died in 1879 in reduced circumstances.

BIBLIOGRAPHY

Hopkinson-RimbaultO, 59

W. Pole: *Musical Instruments in the Great Industrial Exhibition of 1851* (London, 1851), 74–7

'The Electric Organ', *Musical Standard* (9 Jan 1869)

C. Pierre: *Les facteurs d'instruments de musique* (Paris, 1893/R), 225

J.W. Hinton: *Story of the Electric Organ* (London, 1909)

R.M. Roberts: 'Charles Spackman Barker', *The Organ*, xiii (1933–4), 186–9

J.I. Wedgwood: 'Was Barker the Inventor of the Pneumatic Lever?', *The Organ*, xiv (1934–5), 49–52

N.J. Thistlethwaite: *The Making of the Victorian Organ* (Cambridge, 1990)

GUY OLDHAM, NICHOLAS THISTLETHWAITE

Barkhudarian, Sarkis [Sergey Vasilyevich] (*b* Tbilisi, Georgia, 26 Aug/8 Sept 1887; *d* Tbilisi, 29 Oct 1972). Georgian composer and teacher. He began his music studies with the pianist Karakhovna in 1898; he then studied the piano with Stakhovsky and Truskovsky, and theory and solfège with Paliashvili at the Tbilisi Music Institute (1900–07). He won by competition a place at the Berlin Hochschule für Musik (1907–9) and later studied with Kalafati, Steinberg and Vītols at the St Petersburg Conservatory (1910–15). Subsequently, as a teacher at the conservatories of Tbilisi (1923–54) and Yerevan (1934–37, professor 1941), he instructed many of the leading composers of Armenia and Georgia including Aleksandr Arutyunian and Muradeli. He also appeared as a pianist in Moscow, Leningrad and Caucasian republics. His honours included the titles People's Artist of the Armenian SSR, Honoured Artist of the Georgian SSR, and the Order of Lenin.

WORKS
(*selective list*)

Dramatic: Narine (ballet, S. Lisitsian), 1938; Strana rodnaya [Native Land] (ballet, V.N. Ajamian), 1941; Keri Kuchi (musical comedy for children, G. Beilerian, after O. Tumanian), 1945; incid music, film scores

Orch: Anush, sym. poem, 1916; Zakfederatsiya, suite, 1930; 1942, ov., 1943, 3 suites from the ballet Narine (1957, 1969)

Vocal: 6 Armenian Folksongs, 1v, pf (1958); songs (A. Isaakian), arrs.

Pf: Vostochniye plyaski [Eastern Dances], 1913; Sonata, 1915; many other pieces

Principal publisher: Sovetskiy Kompozitor

BIBLIOGRAPHY

SKM

M. Ter-Simonian: *Sarkis Barkhudaryan* (Yerevan, 1968)

N. Magakian: *Ocherk o tvorchestve S.V. Barkhudaryana* [A sketch of Barkhudarian's work] (Yerevan, 1973)

DETLEF GOJOWY

Barkin [née Radoff], **Elaine** (*b* Bronx, NY, 15 Dec 1932). American composer, writer and performer. After gaining the BA (1954) from Queens College, CUNY, she studied composition with Fine, Shapero and Arthur Berger at Brandeis University (MFA 1956, PhD 1971) and with Blacher at the Berlin Hochschule für Musik (1956–7). She taught at various colleges and universities before joining the composition and theory faculty at UCLA (1974), where she remained until 1994. For three decades she was a major contributor and adviser to *Perspectives of New Music*; she has also written extensively on 20th-century music for other journals. In her compositions as well as her writings and presentations she has given attention to women and gender issues.

In about 1978 Barkin turned from using 12-note and serial techniques to explore compositional processes involving collaboration, interactive performance and improvisation. In notes written about her 1989 piece for basset-horn and tape, … *out of the air* … , she outlined her aesthetic: 'to foster the potentials of collaborative participation; to enable possibilities for the performer, ranging from the most traditional to the most far-out liberated; to relinquish authority albeit not responsibility; and to minimize my role as proprietary instruction-giver … '. Her search for non-competitive and non-hierarchical socio-musical environments has led to her interest in Javanese and Balinese gamelan. She has been involved with gamelan as a player and composer since 1987 and during four study trips to Bali compiled interviews, led improvisation workshops and produced audio and video tapes about new music in Bali.

Barkin's 'texts' – whether for print medium, live performance or tape collage – often blur the distinction between text and music or between essay and poetry. Some works also merge theoretical commentary with the creative process in the form of poetic-graphic explications of music by other composers. Her compositions invoke extensive verbal and gestural interplay, and later works integrate timbral and conceptual influences from gamelan.

WORKS
(*selective list*)

Stage (incl. text-pieces and tape collages): De amore (chbr mini-op, after A. Capellanus and 12th–20th-century love texts), 8vv, va, gui, hp, db, slide projection, 1980; Media Speak, 9 spkrs, sax, slide projection, 1981; … to piety more prone … , 4 female spkrs, tape collage of spkrs and singers, 1983, rev. 1985; Anonymous was a Woman (tape collage for dancers), 1984; on the way to becoming (tape collage, Barkin), 1985; Past is Part of (tape collage, Barkin), 1985; To whom it may Concern no.2 (tape collage, B. Boretz and others), 1989; (Continuous), minimum 5 players, 1991

Orch: Essay, 1957; Plus ça change, str, 3 perc (incl. mar, vib, xyl), 1971 [also version for tape, arr. S. Beck, 1987]

Chbr and solo inst: Refrains, fl, cl, cel, str trio, 1967; 6 Compositions, pf, 1968; Str Qt, 1969; Inward & Outward Bound, fl + pic, cl + b cl, bn, hn, tpt, trbn, tuba, vn, va, vc, db, 2 perc (incl. vib, mar, timp), 1975; Mixed Modes, b cl, vn, va, vc, pf, 1975; Plein chant, a fl, 1977; … in its surrendering … , tuba, 1980; Rhapsodies, pic + fl, cl + a fl, 1986; [Be]Coming Together Apart, vn, mar, 1987; Encore, Javanese gamelan, 1988; … out of the air … , basset-hn, tape, 1989; Legong Dreams, ob, 1990; exploring the rigors of in between, fl, hn, vn, va, vc, 1991; Gamelange, hp,

mixed gamelan, 1992; touching all bases/di mana-mana, elec db, perc, Balinese gamelan, 1997, collab. I. Nyoman Wenten
Vocal: 2 Dickinson Choruses, SATB, 1977; … the supple suitor … (E. Dickinson), Mez, fl, ob, vc, vib + bells, hpd + pf, 1978; … the sky … (e.e. cummings), SSA, pf, 1978; … for my friends' pleasure … (Sappho and others), S, hp, 1995

Principal publishers: ACA, Association for the Promotion of New Music, Mobart, Open Space

Principal recording companies: CRI, Open Space

BIBLIOGRAPHY

E. Barkin: 'Questionnaire [about being a woman composer in the US]', *PNM*, xix/2 (1980–81), 460–62; continued as 'In Response', xx/2 (1981–2), 288–329
J. Rahn: 'New Research Paradigms', *Music Theory Spectrum*, xi/1 (1989), 84–94
J.M. Edwards: 'North America since 1920', *Women and Music: a History*, ed. K. Pendle (Bloomington, IN, 1991), 211–57, esp. 241
S. McClary: 'A Response to Elaine Barkin', *PNM*, xxx/2 (1992), 234–8
E. Barkin: *e: an anthology: music texts & graphics (1975–1995)* (Red Hook, NY, 1997)
E. Barkin and L. Hannessley, eds.: *Audible Traces: Gender, Identity and Music* (Zürich, forthcoming)

J. MICHELE EDWARDS

Barlaam [Bernard] (*d* 1350). Monk and Bishop of Gerace. Barlaam was his religious name. He was educated in Byzantine monasteries of southern Italy, and visited Constantinople in the 1330s. In 1339 the eastern emperor made him envoy to Pope Benedict XII at Avignon. He taught Greek to Petrarch, and under Petrarch's influence became a convert to Latin Catholicism in 1342. He wrote commentaries on three chapters of Ptolemy's *Harmonics*; these chapters deal with the relation between the simple numbers of the Greek Perfect System and the heavenly spheres, how musical consonances and the movement of the planets are to be found through number, and how the qualities of the spheres agree with those of musical sounds.

BIBLIOGRAPHY

FasquelleE; FétisB
J. Franz: *De musicis graecis commentatio* (Berlin, 1840)
H.D. Hunter: 'Barlaam', *New Catholic Encyclopedia* (New York, 1967)

ANDREW HUGHES

Barley, Willam (*b* ?1565; *d* 1614). English music publisher. His position in the history of music printing in Elizabethan London is a contentious one. In 1596 he produced *The Pathway to Musicke* and *A New Booke of Tabliture*, the latter thought to be the book that John Dowland complained of in his *The First Booke of Songes or Ayres* (1597), declaring that the versions of his lute pieces were 'false and unperfect'. Barley was acquainted with Thomas Morley, and, when Morley acquired a music printing monopoly in 1598, six volumes appeared bearing the imprint 'imprinted at London, in Little St. Helen's by William Barley, the assigne of Thomas Morley'. An examination of these six works, however, makes it clear that they cannot all have been printed by the same man or on the same press. The most significant of this group are Antony Holborne's *Pavans, Galliards, Almains*, the first appearance in print in England of music for instruments rather than voices, and Thomas Morley's *The First Booke of Consort Lessons*, the first appearance in print in England of music for a prescribed instrumentation. Morley's *The First Booke of Ayres* was published with Barley's imprint in 1600, but after that Barley evidently abandoned music publishing for some years. In 1606, however, he laid claim to the same music printing monopoly, which had a further 13 years to run. On Morley's death in 1602 the monopoly had fallen into disuse, but Barley managed to convince the Company of Stationers that, as Morley's business associate, he still possessed certain rights under its terms. Accordingly, Barley was made free of the Company on 25 June 1606, and on that day the Company's court settled an action which Barley had brought against Thomas East concerning copyrights to music books East had registered with the Company. The settlement included the stipulation that East should pay to Barley 20 shillings for each edition of a music book he printed, together with six free copies of the finished volume. In addition, East and other music printers often styled themselves 'the assigne of William Barley' until Barley's death in 1614. A similar dispute with Thomas Adams was settled later.

William Barley's interest in music printing was clearly a pecuniary one. There is no evidence that he was actually a printer who had served the necessary apprenticeship. He owed his membership of the Stationers' Company to a special set of circumstances, and the six volumes published in 1599 show every sign of having been farmed out to different presses. Further, in his *New Booke of Tabliture*, he declared 'I am myself a publisher and seller of books', and it was in this capacity that he kept his shop in Gracechurch Street, London. The exact circumstances of the disposal of his business are not clear, but there is some evidence that his music copyrights were acquired by Thomas Snodham and his partners.

BIBLIOGRAPHY

Humphries-SmithMP; KrummelEMP
R.B. McKerrow, ed.: *A Dictionary of Printers and Booksellers in England, Scotland and Ireland … 1557–1640* (London, 1910/R)
J. Lievsay: 'William Barley, Elizabethan Printer and Bookseller', *Studies in Bibliography*, viii (1956), 218–25
R. Illing: 'Barley's Pocket Edition of Est's "Metrical Psalter"', *ML*, xlix (1968), 219–23
J.A. Lavin: 'William Barley, Draper and Stationer', *Studies in Bibliography*, xxii (1969), 214–23
G.D. Johnson: 'William Barley, "Publisher & Seller of Bookes", 1591–1614', *The Library*, 6th ser., xi (1989), 10–49

MIRIAM MILLER/JEREMY L. SMITH

Bar-line. In Western notation a vertical line drawn through the staff to mark off a metrical unit. *See* BAR.

Barlow, Fred (*b* Mulhouse, 2 Oct 1881; *d* Boulogne, 3 Jan 1951). French composer of English and Alsatian origin. He spent his youth in Switzerland and, though attracted to music from his earliest childhood, gained a diploma in engineering at the Zürich Polytechnic. He soon abandoned this career, however, and in 1908 moved to Paris to complete his musical studies. There he became a pupil of Jean Huré and then of his cousin Koechlin. In 1911 his Violin Sonata and his Cello Sonata were played at the Société Musicale Indépendante, the former by Enescu. He met Les Six, was an acquaintance of Satie and won Ravel's admiration for his *Ave Maria* (1914). An encounter with the actor Pierre Bertin led to the composition of the musical comedy *Sylvie* (1919–21), a sensitive, poetic treatment of juvenile love. A further result of their collaboration was the ballet *La grande Jatte* (1936–8), set in the popular Parisian resort of La Jatte in the 1880s; the score is a masterpiece of delicacy and gaiety suggestive of Chabrier, for whom Barlow felt a special respect. His other notable stage work was *Mam'zelle Prudhomme*, an opérette in the best Messager tradition. Barlow was a conscientious artist, a craftsman who strove to be sincere to himself and to his expressive aims: a recapturing of childhood innocence, and a painful effort towards an ideal beyond human capacity. The fact that he became a Quaker in 1926 had some influence on his music. His work, particularly the instrumental chamber music, is notable both for distinction of thought and formal perfection.

WORKS
(selective list)

Stage: Gladys, ou La légère incartade (ballet, J. de Fleury), 1915–16, Mulhouse, 7 Jan 1956; Sylvie (musical comedy, P. Bertin, after G. de Nerval), 1919–21, Paris, Trianon-Lyrique, 2 March 1923; Mam'zelle Prudhomme, ou Monsieur Pickwick à Paris (opérette, C. Gével), Monte Carlo, Opéra, 22 Dec 1932; La grande Jatte (ballet, Bertin), 1936–8, Paris, Opéra, 12 July 1950

Orch: Menuet, 1910 [orch of pf work]; Capriccioso, pf, orch, 1928 [version of Polichinelle et Colombine, pf]; 5 enfantines, 1948 [orch of pf work, 1927]; Sinfonietta, str orch, timp, 1950 [version of Str Qt 'Les saisons']

Choral: Pater noster, T/S, chorus, org, 1911–12; 4 préludes pour un drame (R. Fauchois), female chorus, orch, 1918

Solo vocal: Rondel (Charles d'Orléans), 1911, unpubd; Ave Maria, S, org/pf, 1914; 3 poèmes chinois, 1915, orchd 1948; Confiance (E. Verhaeren), 1925–7, unpubd; Droite dans la candeur des voiles (T. Derème), 1928, unpubd; 3 chansons du Poitou, 1940, unpubd, 2 orchd 1946; 4 poèmes d'Hortus clausus (H. Michel), 1942–3, orchd twice (orch; str orch)

Chbr: Sonata, vn, pf, 1909; Sonata 'La basilique', vc, pf, 1910, rev. 1943; Str Qt 'Les saisons', 1946–7; Sonatina, 2 vn, pf, 1948, arr. fl, vn, pf, 1950

Pf: Menuet, orchd 1910; 5 enfantines, 1927, orchd 1948; Polichinelle et Colombine, sketch de ballet, 1928 [to a scenario by Barlow]; Sonata, 1940–41, rev. 1950; La flûte de cristal, c1950

Principal publishers: Eschig, Lemoine

BIBLIOGRAPHY

J. Pierné: Hommage à Fred Barlow 1881–1951 (Mulhouse, c1951)
Roland-Manuel and others: Fred Barlow, 1881–1951 (Paris, c1951)
M. Poupet: 'Un compositeur français contemporain trop peu connu: Fred Barlow (1881–1951) I – L'homme', Guitare et musique, new ser., no.8 (1974)

MICHEL POUPET/JEREMY DRAKE

Barlow, Klarenz [Clarence] (b Calcutta, 27 Dec 1945). German composer and theorist of Indian birth. He completed a degree in natural sciences at Calcutta University (1965) and a piano diploma at Trinity College of Music, London (1965). From 1966 to 1968 he taught music theory and directed a madrigal choir and youth orchestra in Calcutta. He went on to study composition and electronic music at the Cologne Musikhochschule (1968–73) and in 1986 founded the Initiative Musik und Informatik Köln (GIMIK). He has taught computer music at the Darmstadt summer courses (1982–94), the Cologne Musikhochschule (from 1984), and the Royal Conservatory, The Hague (from 1994), where he also served as artistic director of the Institute of Sonology (1990–94). His awards include the Kranichstein prize of the Darmstadt summer course (1980) and the Förderpreis of the city of Cologne (1981).

Although Barlow rarely uses digital sounds in his compositions (most works are written for traditional instruments), the computer plays a central role in generating the structures of his works. His comprehensive theory of tonality and metrics, later developed as the basis of computer programmes for the 'real-time' control of musical parameters, was first tested in the piano work Çoğluotobüsişletmesi (1975–9). He has also explored the spectral analysis and instrumental re-synthesis of human speech. A playful treatment of musical traditions and a satirical posture towards the postwar avant garde are also characteristic of Barlow's style.

WORKS
(selective list)

Dramatic: Reidosklopädi? Enzykloskoport? (Hörspiel), 1972–6; Tatsachen, (5 Musiktheaterstücke), 1982

Ens: Verhältnisse, melodic insts, 1974; 1981, vn, va, vc, 1981; Im Januar am Nil, 11 players, 1981–4; 'Spright the Diner' by Nib Wryter, pf trio, 1984–6; Orchideae ordinariae (The Twelfth Root of Truth), orch, 1989

Kbd (pf, unless otherwise stated): Textmusik, 1971; fantasia quasi una sonata con 'Mantra' di Stockhausen, 1973; Ludus ragalis (12 Preludes and Fugues), kbd, 1974; Çoğluotobüsişletmesi, 1975–9; 4 identische Stücke, 1995; 36 skandierte Gesichtspunkte, 1997

El-ac: Sinophonie II, 8-track tape, 1969–72; Fruitti d'amore, vc, elec, 1988; Talkmaster's Choice, cptr installation, spkr, cptr, 1992; Farting Quietly in Church (Vortrag über Haiku), Bar, player pf, elec, 1994

WRITINGS

'Bus Journey to Parametron', Feedback Papers, nos. 21–3 (1980) [whole issue]
'Über die zwei Arten von Computermusik', MusikTexte, no.6 (1984) 27–28
'Two Essays on Theory', Computer Music Journal, xi/1 (1987) 44–60
'On the Spectral Analysis of Speech for Subsequent Resynthesis by Acoustic Instruments', Analyse en musique electroacoustique: Bourges 1996, 276–83

BIBLIOGRAPHY

KdG (P.N. Wilson)
S. Kaske: 'A Conversation with Clarence Barlow', Computer Music Journal, ix/1 (1985), 19–28
M. Supper: '". . . eine Maschine, um die Arbeit abzunehmen . . ."', Positionen, xi (1992), 5–7 [interview]

PETER NIKLAS WILSON

Barlow, Samuel L(atham) M(itchell) (b New York, 1 June 1892; d Wyndmoor, PA, 19 Sept 1982). American composer and administrator. He studied at Harvard University (BA 1914), then in New York with Percy Goetschius and Franklin Robinson, in Paris with Philipp, and in Rome with Respighi (orchestration, 1923). Before World War I, and for two decades thereafter, he was active in New York civic and professional groups formed to promote music, and in liberal political action groups. He was the first chairman of the New York Community Chorus, chairman of the Independent Citizens Committee for the Arts, Sciences, and Professions, governor of the ACA, chairman of the American Committee for the Arts, director of the China Aid Council, and vice-president of the American Committee for Spanish Freedom. In addition, he taught in various settlement schools and was a frequent contributor to Modern Music.

Barlow's opera Mon ami Pierrot, to a libretto by Sacha Guitry on the life of Lully and purporting to show the origin of the French children's song 'Au clair de la lune', was the first by an American to be performed at the Opéra-Comique in Paris (11 January 1935); his 'symphonic concerto for magic lantern', Babar (after Brunoff's picture books), uses slide projections. Despite such novelties, Barlow's style was relatively conservative: he admitted that 'tunes which wouldn't shock Papa Brahms keep sticking their necks out'.

WORKS
(selective list)

Stage: Ballo sardo, ballet, 1928; Mon ami Pierrot (op, S. Guitry), 1934; Amanda, op, 1936; Amphitryon 38 (incid music, J. Giraudoux), 12 orch pieces, 1937

Orch: Vocalise, 1926; Alba, sym. poem, orch/chbr orch, 1927; Circus Ov., 1930; Pf Conc., 1931; Biedermeier Waltzes, 1935; Babar, sym. conc., slide projection, 1936; Leda, 1939; Sousa ad Parnassum, 1939

Chbr and solo inst.: Ballad, Scherzo, str qt, 1933; Spanish Quarter, pf suite, 1933; Conversation with Tchekhov, pf trio, 1940; Jardin de Le Nôtre, pf suite

Vocal: choruses and songs, incl. 3 Songs from the Chinese, T, 7 insts, 1924

Principal publishers: Choudens, Joubert, G. Schirmer

BIBLIOGRAPHY

S.L.M. Barlow: *The Astonished Muse* (New York, 1961) [autobiography]

Obituary, *New York Times* (21 Sept 1982)

M. Lederman: *The Life and Death of a Small Magazine (Modern Music, 1924–1946)* (Brooklyn, NY, 1983)

H. WILEY HITCHCOCK

Barlow, Wayne (Brewster) (*b* Elyria, OH, 6 Sept 1912; *d* Rochester, NY, 17 Dec 1996). American composer and teacher. He studied composition with Edward Royce, Bernard Rogers, and Howard Hanson at the Eastman School (1930–37), where he received the MMus and the PhD degrees, and with Schoenberg at the University of Southern California (1935). In 1937 he joined the faculty of the Eastman School, eventually becoming chairman of the composition department, director of the electronic music studio (1968), and dean of graduate studies (1973); in 1978 he was named professor emeritus. He received two Fulbright scholarships (1955–6, 1964–5) and numerous commissions, and travelled widely as lecturer, guest composer and conductor of his own works. He also served as organist and choirmaster at two churches in Rochester, St Thomas Episcopal (1946–76) and Christ Episcopal (1976–8). He was a prolific composer in an eclectic, tonal, free 12-note style.

WORKS

Dramatic: 3 Moods for Dancing (ballet), 1940

Orch: De Profundis, prelude, 1934; False Faces, ballet suite, 1935; Sinfonietta, C, 1936; The Winter's Passed, rhapsody, ob, str/pf, 1938; Lyrical Piece, cl, str/pf, 1943; Nocturne, chbr orch, 1946; Rondo-Ov., 1947; Sinfonietta, C, 1950; Lento and Allegro, 1955; Night Song, 1957; Intrada, Fugue and Postlude, brass ens, 1959; Rota, chbr orch, 1959; Images, hp, orch, 1961; Sinfonia da Camera, chbr orch, 1962; Vistas, 1963; Conc., sax, band, 1970; Hampton Beach, ov., 1971; Soundscapes, orch, tape, 1972; Divertissement, fl, chbr orch, 1980; Frontiers, band, 1982

Vocal: Zion in Exile (cant.), S, A, T, B, chorus, orch, 1937; Songs from The Silence of Amor, S, orch, 1939; Madrigal for a Bright Morning (J.R. Slater), chorus, 1942; Ps xxiii, chorus, org/orch, 1944; 3 Songs (W. Shakespeare), 1948; Mass, G, chorus, orch, 1951; Poems for Music (R. Hillyer, Shakespeare), S, orch, 1958; Missa Sancti Thomae, chorus, org, 1959; Diversify the Abyss (H. Plutzik), male chorus, 1964; We all Believe in One True God, chorus, brass qt, org, 1965; Wait for the Promise of the Father, T, Bar, chorus, small orch, 1968; Voices of Faith (cant.), spkr, S, chorus, orch, 1974; Voices of Darkness, spkr, pf, perc, tape, 1975; What Wondrous Love, chorus, org, gui, 1976; Out of the Cradle Endlessly Rocking, T, chorus, cl, va, pf, tape, 1978; 7 Seals of Revelation (cant.), S, A, T, B, chorus, orch, 1989

Chbr: Prelude, Air and Variation, bn, str qt, pf, 1949; Pf Qnt, 1951; Triptych, str qt, 1953; Trio, ob, va, pf, 1964; Elegy, va, pf/orch, 1968; Duo, hp, tape, 1969; Vocalise and Canon, tuba, pf, 1976; Intermezzo, va, hp, 1980; Sonatina for 4, fl, cl, vc, hp, 1984

Kbd: Pf Sonata, 1948; Hymn Voluntaries for the Church Year, org, 1963–81; Dynamisms, 2 pf, 1966; 2 Inventions, pf, 1968; 3 Voluntaries, org, 1970; 4 Chorale Voluntaries, org, 1979–80; Pange lingua, org, 1980; Preludes on Darwell's 148th, Gott sei Dank, Knickerbocker, Austria, org, 1983

Tape: Study in Electronic Sound, 1965; Moonflight, 1970; Soundprints in Concrete, 1975

Principal publishers: Concordia, C. Fischer, J. Fischer, Gray, Presser

WRITINGS

'Contemporary Music: an Orientation', *Music Journal*, xi/6 (1953), 26–7, 33–5

Foundations of Music (New York, 1953)

'Crisis!', *Music Journal*, xx/2 (1962), 26–7, 74

'Of Choral Music for the Church', *Choral Journal*, no.6 (1963–4), 13–14

'Electronic Music and Music Education', *Electronic Music Review* (1968), no.6, pp.40–43; repr. as 'Electronic Music: Challenge to Music Education', *Music Educators Journal*, lv/3 (1968), 66–9

W. THOMAS MARROCCO/MARY WALLACE DAVIDSON

Barmen. Town in Germany. It was united with Elberfeld in 1929 to form WUPPERTAL.

Barmherzige Brüder. *See* HOSPITALLERS OF ST JOHN OF GOD.

Bärmig, Johann Gotthilf (*b* Werdau, 13 May 1815; *d* Werdau, 26 Oct 1899). German builder of organs and mechanical organs, and also of physharmonikas and harmoniums. He learnt organ building from Urban Kreutzbach in Borna and afterwards worked as an assistant in Salzburg where he is also said to have first become involved with the physharmonika. In about 1846 he opened a workshop in Werdau, which he ran (possibly at first with Ramming) until 1887 when Emil Müller succeeded him. Bärmig's work extended over the whole of Saxony and east Thuringia. He was awarded a silver medal for the three physharmonikas he displayed at the Leipzig Art and Industry Exhibition in 1854. Favouring classical 18th-century measurements, he built about 50 first-rate one- and two-manual mechanical organs with slider-chests and, usually, chamber bellows, but occasionally concertina bellows. His Great organs have a faultless upper-partial structure, and the large instruments (especially those in Schöneck, Kittlitz and Klingenthal) show a good balance between the two manuals. Terz 1⅗′ and Quint 2⅔′ or Cornet are standard features of the specification; the rich texture of the mixtures is especially attractive. The Pedal, which in Schöneck and Kittlitz includes a 32′ stop, is often enriched by a soft Posaune bass. Solid workmanship and a clear full tone distinguish Bärmig's work, which recalls the splendour of old Saxon organ building. Among his oldest surviving instruments are the organ in the village church at Königswalde bei Werdau (1852) and a beautifully-toned pedal-harmonium in the old school at Gottesgrün bei Greiz. Under the control of Emil Müller, Bärmig's firm developed into the largest harmonium factory in Europe.

BIBLIOGRAPHY

MGG1 (W. Hüttel)

F. Oehme: *Handbuch über ältere und neuere berühmte Orgelwerke im Königreich Sachsen*, i–ii (Dresden, n.d.); iii (Dresden, 1897)

R. Fritzsche: *Werdau und seine Industrie* (Werdau, 1936), 117, 141

W. Hüttel: *Musikgeschichte von Glauchau und Umgebung* (Glauchau, 1995), 95, 105, 107

WALTER HÜTTEL

Barnabei. *See* BERNABEI family.

Barnard [née Pye], **Charlotte Alington** [Claribel] (*b* Louth, Lincs., 23 Dec 1830; *d* Dover, 30 Jan 1869). English ballad composer. She published two volumes of verse and some 100 songs, using the pseudonym 'Claribel'. Forced by her father to break off a long engagement to another, she married Rev. Charles Cary Barnard in 1854; thus her success with such 'jilt songs' as *Won't you tell me why, Robin?* (1861) and *Oh Mother! Take the wheel away* (1865), was ironic. In 1857, moving to London, she studied with the pianist W.H. Holmes and leading singers such as Charlotte Sainton-Dolby, for whom *Janet's Choice* (1859), her first success, was written. Its verse and refrain form contrasted with the more usual strophic settings of that time. Writing her own words allowed formal flexibility. The most commercially successful composer in Boosey's ballad catalogue, she was the first to enjoy a royalty arrangement. Her melodic dexterity is evident in *Five O'Clock in the Morning* (1862), together with an expanding harmonic vocabulary in *Mountain Mabel* (1864), and a growing attention to form in *Come back to Erin* (1866). In 1868, losing £30,000 through her father's fraudulent dealings and bankruptcy, she left for the Continent, but died shortly after returning. Admiration for her songs in North America, especially her waltz song *Take back the heart* (words by Mrs Gifford), equalled British esteem, and her work was well represented in vocal collections long after her death.

BIBLIOGRAPHY

Brown-StrattonBMB [incl. summary list of works]; *DNB* (W.B. Squire); *FétisBS*

D.B. Scott: *The Singing Bourgeois* (Milton Keynes and Philadelphia, 1989), esp. 72–7 [incl. music exx.]

P. Smith and M. Godsmark: *The Story of Claribel (Charlotte Alington Barnard)* (Lincoln, 1965)

DEREK B. SCOTT

Barnard, John (*b* ?1591; *fl c*1641). English music editor and composer. He may well have been the John Barnard who was a lay clerk at Canterbury Cathedral between 1618 and 1622, and whose age at the time of his marriage in 1619 was given as 'about 28'. Barnard, who was a minor canon of St Paul's Cathedral, London, in the early 17th century, was the compiler of *The First Book of Selected Church Musick* (London, 1641/*R*). This anthology of church music by 19 leading composers of the late 16th and early 17th centuries was the only printed collection of English liturgical music to appear between Day's *Certaine notes* (London, 1565) and the Civil War. It comprised ten partbooks – Medius, Primus and Secundus Contratenor, Tenor and Bassus, for each side of the choir, Decani and Cantoris. Only 38 partbooks are now extant, of which 33 are imperfect. No printed organbook exists, and it seems most unlikely that one was ever published, though it may be that the 'Batten' Organbook would have served as a source for one. A much larger collection of English liturgical music which Barnard assembled in manuscript between about 1625 and 1638 has also survived (*GB-Lcm* 1045–51); it consisted originally of ten partbooks. The manuscripts clearly served as printer's copy for some of the pieces which later appeared in Barnard's 1641 publication. The collection contains 174 compositions, of which 50 are otherwise unknown. The settings are by 45 identifiable composers, six of whom (including Barnard himself) are not represented in any other pre-Restoration liturgical source. There are also six anonymous pieces. Barnard's two known compositions (settings of the Preces and of the Responses) are included in this collection. A catch by a 'Mr Barnard' is included in Hilton's *Catch that Catch Can*, published by Playford in 1663. The contents of Barnard's printed collection are listed in *Grove 1–4*.

BIBLIOGRAPHY

Le HurayMR

J.B. Clark: 'Adrian Batten and John Barnard: Colleagues and Collaborators', *MD*, xxii (1968), 207–29

J. Morehen: *The Sources of English Cathedral Music, c.1617–c.1644* (diss., U. of Cambridge, 1969), 244–305

R.T. Daniel and P. le Huray: *The Sources of English Church Music, 1549–1660*, EECM, suppl.i (London, 1972)

JOHN MOREHEN

Barnby, Sir Joseph (*b* York, 12 Aug 1838; *d* London, 28 Jan 1896). English conductor and composer. He was the son of Thomas Barnby, an organist, and became a chorister at York Minster at the age of seven. In 1854 he went to London and entered the RAM. After holding positions as organist at various London and York churches, he received his first important appointment in 1863 as organist of St Andrew's, Wells Street, under its prominent Tractarian rector Benjamin Webb. Responding perhaps to pressure from their affluent and fashionable congregation, Webb and Barnby developed a type of music far removed from the austerity desired by the early Tractarians. A large, paid, surpliced choir adorned the chancel, and performed 'fully choral' services. The music for these services from 1866 onwards included adaptations of Roman Catholic masses and motets, principally those of Gounod, with the words translated by Webb and the music adapted by Barnby. At the performance of Gounod's *Messe solennelle* on 30 November 1866, a harp was for the first time introduced into an Anglican service. These lavish choral services, which were really in the nature of sacred concerts, were continued by Barnby on a still more ambitious scale when he moved to St Anne's, Soho, in 1871. The services at this church soon gained the popular nickname of 'The Sunday Opera'. From 1873 onwards Barnby conducted an annual performance of Bach's *St John Passion* with orchestra in the church.

Meanwhile Barnby had been extremely active elsewhere in the cause of choral music. He had been musical adviser to Novello & Co. since 1861, and in 1867 the company established 'Mr Joseph Barnby's Choir' to perform then little-known works published by Novello, including Handel's *Jephtha*, Beethoven's *Missa solemnis* and Bach's *St Matthew Passion*; Barnby repeated this work at Westminster Abbey on 6 April 1871 with a combined choir from the abbey and other leading churches. This, the first church performance of the work in England, launched it as a profound influence on Victorian society. Barnby was an indefatigable conductor of oratorios and church music for the rest of his life, and was a popular director of provincial festivals. At the end of 1872 he amalgamated his choir with the Royal Albert Hall Choral Society (also under Novello's patronage) and continued to conduct it until his death; in 1888 it became the Royal Choral Society. He performed Dvořák's *Stabat mater* on 10 March 1883, and on 10 November 1884 gave the first performance in England of *Parsifal*. His conducting was accurate and forceful, and he raised choral standards by insisting on greater efforts from the singers; he was progressive in his choice of music, though his interpretations of Handel and Bach were apt to be dull and ponderous.

In 1875 he was appointed precentor of Eton College. Instead of treating this position as largely concerned with the chapel services, he embarked on a programme of choral performances and concerts for the benefit of the boys, becoming Eton's first real director of music. He raised the school's Musical Society to a high standard of precision by means of a quasi-military drill. He also directed a Sunday Evening Musical Society in which masters, boys and chapel choristers sang through the major choral repertory. In 1886 he resigned his position at St Anne's, and in 1892 that at Eton; in the latter year he was knighted, and was also appointed principal of the

Guildhall School of Music. He continued to serve in this position until his death four years later.

As a composer Barnby was very active, writing almost entirely choral and vocal music, in which he was clearly the heir of Gounod. He wrote a large number of cathedral services, anthems, chants and hymn tunes, and one oratorio, *Rebekah* (1870). The services and anthems were popular for many years, especially at St Paul's Cathedral, but they were later singled out by such writers as Walker and Fellowes as particularly deplorable examples of Victorian sentimentality, and are now virtually obsolete. They represented an opposite type of high churchmanship to that of the 'Gregorian' school, in that they adapted for the church whatever methods had recently been found effective in theatre or concert music. Barnby's chants and hymn tunes are still heard: 'Cloisters' in particular, sung to Pusey's hymn *Lord of our life*, has an easy emotionalism and a melodic sweep that has ensured it a long-lived popularity. His tune 'For all the saints' long maintained its hold even against one of the greatest modern hymn tunes, Vaughan Williams's 'Sine nomine'. To many generations of Etonians his music to two of the three school songs has seemed to embody much of their Victorian legacy; while many an amateur choral society has revelled in the blue harmonies of his Tennyson setting *Sweet and Low*. Barnby also edited four hymnbooks, the most important being *The Hymnary* (1872).

BIBLIOGRAPHY

DNB (F.G. Edwards)

J.S. Curwen: 'St Anne's, Soho', *Studies in Worship Music*, i (London,1880, 3/1901), 179–83

D. Baptie: *Sketches of the English Glee Composers* (London, 1896), 199–200

J. Bennett: Obituary, *MT*, xxxvii (1896), 80, 153–5

J.D. Brown and S.S. Stratton: *British Musical Biography*(Birmingham, 1897/R)

M.B. Foster: *Anthems and Anthem Composers* (London, 1901/R), 162–3

A. Mellor: *A Record of the Music and Musicians of Eton College* (Windsor, 1932), 43–8

E.H. Fellowes: *English Cathedral Music* (London, 1941, rev. 5/1969 by J.A. Westrup)

B. Rainbow: *The Choral Revival in the Anglican Church 1839–1872* (London, 1970), 276–82

E. Routley: *The Music of Christian Hymns* (Chicago, 1981), 101–2

W.J. Gatens: 'John Stainer (1840–1901) and Joseph Barnby (1838–96): the High Victorian Idiom', *Victorian Cathedral Music in Theory and Practice* (Cambridge, 1986), 170–201

NICHOLAS TEMPERLEY

Barn dance. (1) Known in the USA in association with celebrations to mark the building of a new barn and derived from the schottische, it became popular in England around the late 1880s originally in conjunction with the tune *Dancing in the Barn* and later with the *Pas de quatre* by Meyer Lutz, and by the 1920s had become a progressive dance. By the 1960s the term had been adopted as a general description of social country dancing which, by this stage, also included elements of the 'old time' dance repertory.

(2) Originally an American rural meeting for dancing, held in a barn or similar large building. After 1920 the term designated variety radio programmes of folk-like entertainment; the first programme so described was broadcast on radio station WBAP in Fort Worth, Texas (1923), though many southern radio stations had presented programmes of country music in previous years. By 1949 some 650 radio stations were broadcasting live performances of country music, the most famous of which were the 'National Barn Dance' (on WLS, Chicago,

1924–70) and the 'Grand Ole Opry' (on WSM, Nashville, 1925–). By the mid-1950s most of these shows had disappeared, although a few, most notably the 'Grand Ole Opry', benefited from the growth of country music as an industry in Nashville.

See also COUNTRY MUSIC, §§1–2 and NASHVILLE SOUND.

BIBLIOGRAPHY

GroveA

G.C. Biggar: 'The WLS National Barn Dance Story: the Early Years', *JEMF Quarterly*, vii/23 (1971), 105–12

T.A. Patterson: 'Hillbilly Music among the Flatlanders: Early Midwestern Radio Barn Dances', *Journal of Country Music*, vi/1 (1975), 12

C. Hagan: *Grand Ole Opry* (New York, 1989)

Barnekow, Christian (*b* Saint Sauveur, Hautes-Pyrénées, 28 July 1837; *d* Frederiksberg, 20 March 1913). Danish composer. He studied with Niels Ravnkilde and Edvard Helsted in Copenhagen and became a skilful pianist and organist. A man of independent means, he had time to contribute to the administration of several Danish musical institutions. He was president of the Society for the Publication of Danish Music from 1871, a committee member of that society from 1880, later chairman of the Music Society, a member of the committee of the Ancker Foundation and founder of a series of subscription concerts in Copenhagen from 1861. He was nominated titular professor in the University of Copenhagen (1891).

Barnekow's compositions are in the romantic style of J.P.E. Hartmann and Gade and include cantatas and choral and solo songs, chamber music and piano works. Many of his hymns are regularly used in the Danish church. As an authority on sacred choral singing, he edited tunes for the Danish hymnbook (1878), which was augmented by a supplement (1892) and several later editions. He also edited collections of spiritual songs by J.A.P. Schulz, F.L.A. Kunzen and Hartmann, and a selection of pieces by Buxtehude, who was almost unknown at that time. Barnekow was an enthusiastic collector of paintings, books and music, and his collections of original editions of Danish music and books now belong to the Musikhistorisk Museum in Copenhagen.

WORKS

printed works published in Copenhagen unless otherwise stated

MSS mainly in DK-Kk

INSTRUMENTAL

Pf trio, f♯, op.1, 1857 (1867); Humoresker, pf 4 hands, op.3 (n.d.); sextet, 2 vn, va, vc, db, pf, 1862, MS; pf qt, D, op.12 (n.d.); qnt, g, 2 vn, va, 2 vc, op.20 (Leipzig, n.d.); sonata, F♯, vn, pf, op.23 (1907); pf sonata, d, op.24 (?1908); Idyller, str orch, op.29 (1910)

VOCAL

Songs (C. Richardt, A. Langsted, B.S. Ingemann), opp.4, 7, 11, 13, 19, 27; Aandelige sange [Spiritual Songs]: i (1863); ii (1870); iii (1874); iv (1903)

Secular cantatas, MS

BIBLIOGRAPHY

DBL (E. Abrahamsen)

G. Lynge: *Danske komponister i det 20. aarhundredes begyndelse* (Århus, 1916/17, 2/1917), 17–27

G. Skjerne: 'Christian Barnekow', *Dansk biografisk haandleksikon*, ed. S. Dahl and P. Engelstoft (Copenhagen, 1920), 92–3

K.A. Bruun: *Dansk musiks histoire fra Holberg-tiden til Carl Nielsen*, ii (Copenhagen, 1969), 204–6

SIGURD BERG/GORM BUSK

Barnes, John (Robert) (*b* Windsor, 11 Oct 1928; *d* Edinburgh, 9 March 1998). English organologist, instrument maker and restorer. He studied physics at the

University of London and began his career with an English firm making sound-recording tape. In 1962 he began to make and restore early keyboard instruments as a full time occupation. His early work included restorations for the Victoria and Albert Museum and the museum of the Royal College of Music, London, as well as building new historically-based instruments. In 1968 he became curator of the Russell Collection of Early Keyboard Instruments at the University of Edinburgh, a position he held until his retirement in 1983.

Through his early work Barnes formulated a number of theories about the stringing and pitch of Italian keyboard instruments; he also wrote an important article about the alterations found in some Italian harpsichords and several important articles about instrument restoration. His restorations were carried out with high technical skill, a solid scientific approach and a respect for the original instruments, resulting in working methods which have set the standard for later restorers. Although his output of instruments was limited, he influenced many modern makers through his work at the Russell Collection, the publication of drawings and a book on traditional spinet construction, and by his association in the mid-1970s with the US firm of instrument kit manufacturers Zuckermann, and with the Early Music Shop, Bradford, in the 1990s. After his retirement from the Russell Collection he continued to build and restore instruments, and to publish research on early keyboard instruments and clavichords in particular. His small collection of instruments includes a number of important harpsichords, a spinet and a clavichord as well as pianos of the English, French and Viennese schools.

G. GRANT O'BRIEN/DARRYL MARTIN

Barnet, Charlie [Daly, Charles] (*b* New York, 26 Oct 1913; *d* San Diego, 4 Sept 1991). American jazz bandleader and saxophonist. He was born into a wealthy family, but rebelled in his teens to become a musician. Although he was never a major jazz improviser, he led a popular dance band during the swing period which was also admired for its jazz playing. Barnet was one of the first white bandleaders to employ black musicians, usually as solo stars, among them Roy Eldridge, Charlie Shavers, Benny Carter and Frankie Newton (who joined the band as early as 1937). Barnet was especially influenced by the Duke Ellington Orchestra, and played many arrangements which frankly imitated Ellington's. In 1939 his hit recording for Bluebird of Billy May's arrangement of *Cherokee* made him one of the most popular swing bandleaders. However, with the decline of the big bands in the late 1940s he was forced to disband his orchestra, which thereafter regrouped only for special occasions. Although at various times he dabbled in music publishing and the restaurant business, Barnet continued to play occasionally into the 1970s.

BIBLIOGRAPHY
E. Edwards, G. Hall and B. Korst: *Charlie Barnet and his Orchestra* (Whittier, CA, 1965, 2/1970) [discography]
J. Burns: 'Charlie Barnet', *Jazz Monthly*, no.183 (1970), 9–12
I. Crosbie: 'Clap Hands, Here Comes Charlie', *Jazz Journal*, xxvi (1973), no.5, 10–12; no.7, 25–8
C. Garrod: *Charlie Barnet and his Orchestra* (Spotswood, NJ, 1973, 2/1984) [discography]
C. Barnet and S. Dance: *Those Swinging Years: the Autobiography of Charlie Barnet* (Baton Rouge, LA, 1984/R) [incl. discography]
Oral history material in *US-NEij*

JAMES LINCOLN COLLIER

Barnett, Alice (Ray) (*b* Lewiston, IL, 26 May 1886; *d* San Diego, 28 Aug 1975). American composer, teacher and patron. She studied with Rudolf Ganz and Felix Borowski at the Chicago Musical College (BM 1906) and with Heniot Levy and Adolf Weidig at the American Conservatory, Chicago; she also studied composition in Chicago with Wilhelm Middleschulte and in Berlin with Hugo Kaun (1909–10). From 1917 to 1926 she taught music at the San Diego High School. A respected and influential leader of musical life in San Diego, she helped to found the San Diego Opera Guild and the San Diego Civic SO (of which she was chairwoman for 14 years). Barnett wrote some 60 art songs, 49 of which were published by G. Schirmer and Summy between 1906 and 1932. They display a lyrical gift, sure tonal sense and, despite her German training, strong French harmonic influence. They are often exotic and colourful, especially *Chanson of the Bells of Oseney* (1924) and the Browning cycle *In a Gondola* (1920), which is also dramatic; others of her songs are *Panels from a Chinese Screen* (1924), *Harbor Lights* (1927) and *Nirvana* (1932). She also wrote instrumental music, including a piano trio (1920) and *Effective Violin Solos* (1924). Although Barnett stopped composing in the late 1930s, she maintained her musical activities in San Diego. Her manuscripts and papers are at the San Diego Historical Society.

BIBLIOGRAPHY
W.T. Upton: 'Some Recent Representative American Song-Composers', *MQ*, xi (1925), 383–417, esp. 398–417
W.T. Upton: *Art-Song in America* (Boston, 1930), 214–24
A.F. Block and C.Neuls-Bates: *Women in American Music: a Bibliography of Music and Literature* (Westport, CT, 1979)
C.K. Smith: *The Art Songs of Alice Barnett* (diss., U. of Northern Colorado, 1996)

ADRIENNE FRIED BLOCK

Barnett, Carol E(dith Anderson) (*b* Dubuque, IA, 23 May 1949). American composer. As a child she studied the piano, the violin and the flute, and performed in various choral and instrumental ensembles. At the University of Minnesota (BA 1972, MA 1976) she studied composition with Dominick Argento and Paul Fetler, the piano with Bernhard Weiser and the flute with Emil Niosi. In 1992 she became composer-in-residence for the Dale Warland Singers. Her works have also been performed by the Minnesota Orchestra and the St Paul Chamber Orchestra.

Barnett's harmonic idiom is flexibly chromatic and freely dissonant within a context that includes references to tonality. She tends to work with small, striking musical ideas, repeating them within various textures and timbres that shift effortlessly from one to the next, as in her *Overture to a Greek Drama* (1994). Her choral cycle *An Elizabethan Garland* (1994) features deftly managed textures that range from imitation and dialogue among the voices to streams of closely positioned chords over a deep bass. Her lyricism is wide-ranging, creating a singing quality in even disjunct melodic lines.

WORKS
(*selective list*)

Vocal (SATB, unless otherwise stated): 5 poemas de Becquer (G.A. Bécquer), 1979; Requiem (liturgical texts), SSA, 1981; Voices (N. Cox), S, gui, 1983; Epigrams, Epitaphs (M. Prior, J. Gay, S. Wesley, H. Walpole, B. Jonson), 1986; Elegy (S. Johnson), 1988; 2 canti meridionali (M. Ferraguti), S, pf, 1989; Valediction (J. Donne), TTBB, vc, pf, 1989; Christmas Eve, Bells, 1989; Let it Go (M. Estok), S, pf, 1992; The King of Yellow Butterflies (V. Lindsay), 1993; An Elizabethan Garland (J. Fletcher, S. Daniel, 2 anon. texts), 1994; Children Songs (E.St.V. Millay, L. Carroll, C.

Sandburg, W. Welles), SA, cl, pf, 1996; Franklin Credo (B. Franklin), 1996; Three Faces of Love, 1996; A Spiritual Journey (trad. spirituals), 1997; The Mystic Trumpeter (W. Whitman), 1997

Orch: Adon Olam Variations, 1976; Hn Conc., 1985; Carnival, 2 pf, orch, 1990; Ov. to a Greek Drama, 1994; Remembering Khachaturian, 1996

Chbr and solo inst: Sonata, hn, pf, 1973; 4 Chorale Meditations, vn, 1982; Str Qt no.1 'Jewish Folk Fantasies', 1986; The Mysterious Brass Band, brass qnt, 1990; Mythical Journeys, fl, gui, 1991

MSS in *US-PHf*

Principal publishers: Plymouth, Boosey & Hawkes, Walton, Thompson

BIBLIOGRAPHY

P. Berg: 'Composer Profile', *Minnesota Women's Press* (28 Dec 1994–10 Jan 1995)

K. Pendle: 'For the Theatre: Opera, Dance and Theatre Piece', *CMR*, xvi (1997), 69–80

KARIN PENDLE

Barnett, Clara Kathleen. *See* ROGERS, CLARA KATHLEEN.

Barnett, John (*b* Bedford, 1/15 July 1802; *d* Leckhampton, 16 April 1890). English composer. E.F. Rimbault (Obituary, *MT*, xxxi, 1890, p.285) is alone in giving his date of birth as 1 July 1802. Barnett's father, Bernhard Beer, was a Prussian diamond merchant of Jewish extraction who is said to have been a cousin of Meyerbeer; on settling in England he changed his surname to Barnett. His mother, a Hungarian, died while he was a child. As a small boy John 'sang like a bird'; in later childhood his fine alto voice attracted much attention. At the age of 11 he was articled to S.J. Arnold, proprietor of the Lyceum Theatre, London, making his first stage appearance in *The Shipwreck* on 22 July 1813, and he continued to sing on the stage until 1818. He studied the piano with Ries, Pérez and Kalkbrenner, and composition with William Horsley and C.E. Horn.

Before 1818 Barnett had already begun his long and immensely prolific career as a composer. His early works include piano sonatas, songs, masses, a sacred cantata, and a grand scena, *The Groves of Pomona*, sung by Braham. Some of these early works were well received by critics, and Barnett was urged to cultivate the higher branches of his art. Between 1826 and 1833, however, much of his energy was spent in providing incidental music for farces, melodramas and burlesques. Though some of these were highly successful, particularly *The Pet of the Petticoats* (1832), and others contained songs that soon became popular favourites, for instance 'Rise, gentle moon' in *Charles XII* (1828), the music in general was not of a high standard. Meanwhile Barnett had opened a music shop in Regent Street (1828) with the dramatist W.T. Moncrieff (1794–1857). In 1832 Lucia Vestris appointed him musical director at the Olympic Theatre.

Barnett's serious interest in music was soon given an unusual opportunity: on 14 July 1834 Arnold reopened the Lyceum Theatre as the English Opera House and began to produce full-length English operas of a kind that had become almost obsolete, the only recent representatives being Bishop's *Aladdin* (1826), Weber's *Oberon* (1826) and Ries's *The Sorceress* (1831). Loder's *Nourjahad* was the first (21 July 1834); Barnett's *The Mountain Sylph* which followed (25 August) went even further than Loder's work in the use of continuous music, with a minimum of spoken dialogue. It was thus one of the first true English operas since Arne's *Artaxerxes* (1762), a work for which Barnett had unbounded admiration. Barnett had written some of the music for a play at the

Victoria Theatre, but he now 'heightened' it into a 'romantic grand opera'. He dedicated the published vocal score to Arnold 'for the spirit, zeal, and enthusiasm which he has shewn in the production of Native Operas, and in cherishing native talent'. However, Arnold's primary effort was towards the establishment of serious opera in the English language; he did not feel that either plot or music need be drawn from English traditions. The story of *The Mountain Sylph* was accordingly taken from French sources, and the music was a good deal less 'English' than most of Bishop's. But its success proved that audiences were now prepared to listen to dramatic music with an English text. It had an initial run of about 100 nights, and held its own on the stage for the rest of the century.

Barnett unfortunately quarrelled with Arnold, and publicly accused him of breaking a financial agreement. He had already been at odds with Alfred Bunn, another leading figure in the world of the theatre; later he was to add Mapleson to his mounting list of theatrical adversaries. His next two serious operas, *Fair Rosamond* and *Farinelli*, were produced at Drury Lane. Neither was through-composed, and both show a tendency to return to the older conception of English opera as a mere string of independent songs and ballads – some of which, however, are of good quality. In 1838 he joined with the dramatist Morris Barnett (unrelated to him) in an effort to set up a permanent English Opera House at St James's Theatre, but it closed after a week. From about this time Barnett's letters to the press were increasingly bitter. He accused theatre managers, concert promoters and the committee of the Philharmonic Society of conspiring to defeat the cause of English music. After one more attempt to establish English opera, this time at the Prince's Theatre (1840), he abandoned the London stage. In 1841 he went to live in Cheltenham, where he became a highly successful singing teacher; soon afterwards he published two books about learning to sing.

He lived nearly 50 years longer but never again attempted to produce an opera, to the disappointment of many admirers. In about 1870 he bought a substantial country house, Cotteswold, Leckhampton, near Cheltenham. He had become an advanced 'free-thinker', supporting evolution and homeopathy, and an inveterate controversialist, constantly writing trenchant letters of protest to *The Times* to put down some musical upstart. In the course of a prolonged attack on the methods of Mainzer and Hullah he produced the astonishing theory that 'singing cannot be taught in classes'. He also engaged in a great battle with Leigh Hunt in the pages of *The Tatler* over the merits of English opera, when he claimed among other things that some of Bishop's music was worthy of Mozart. He continued to compose songs, but many of them remained in manuscript; 'it is much to be regretted', wrote Rimbault in 1876, 'that he has withheld his later works from the public'. His position was an eminent one, but was based largely on one work, *The Mountain Sylph*. Macfarren wrote of this opera that 'its production opened a new period for music in this country, from which is to be dated the establishment of an English dramatic school, which, if not yet accomplished, has made many notable advances'. Barnett's failure to follow up this one great success must be attributed in great part to an irascible disposition verging on paranoia.

with a conventional cabaletta or stretta. There is rather too much dependence on the diminished 7th and other chromatic chords, but the themes used to evoke the supernatural, many of which recur as motifs at various points in the opera, are distinctly original in style (ex.1).

In amorous scenes, such as 'Oh no! 'twas no deceptive spell' and 'Art thou a form?', the disarming warmth and passion of Barnett's music can still move the listener, despite the absurdity of the verses and all the scorn and satire that has been lavished upon sentimental melodrama.

Of the vast quantity of Barnett's songs, many are 'potboilers' (his own term for them), but a proportion have distinction and would bear revival: most of these were originally associated with a dramatic production. His sacred music is sometimes grotesque, but his instrumental music, though it never had wide currency, is not to be despised. A string quartet in C, unashamedly Mozartian in general style, is full of interest and invention and shows a surprising flair for vigorous and witty counterpoint. The other major influence on his musical style is Spohr, as is seen, for instance, in his oratorio *The Omnipresence of the Deity* (1829), a work that clearly foreshadowed Pierson's *Jerusalem*.

Barnett was married on 9 May 1837 at St George's, Hanover Square, to Eliza Emily Lindley (1814–99), youngest daughter of the cellist Robert Lindley. Among their children were two daughters who became well-known singers, Rosamond (Mrs Robert Francillon) and Clara (Mrs Henry Rogers) (1844–1931). Many of Barnett's autographs were acquired by the Boston (Massachusetts) Public Library from Clara Rogers in 1921. A son, Domenico (1846–1911), taught the piano at Cheltenham Ladies' College until his death. One of Barnett's brothers, Joseph (d 1898), was a singing teacher and the father of John Francis Barnett; the other, Zaraeh, was a dramatic writer and provided librettos for some of his operas. There seems to be no connection with James George Barnett (1823–85), a London-born composer and conductor active in Hartford and New Haven, Connecticut, whose papers (including many manuscript compositions) are in *US-NH 58*.

For a further music example *see* CONCERTINA, ex.1.

John Barnett: lithograph by Charles Baugniet, 1845

The importance of *The Mountain Sylph* does not lie in the mere fact of its being largely through-composed; the recitatives are, indeed, quite conventional. What makes it a real opera is the cumulative dramatic effect of the successive musical scenes. The story (to be satirized later in *Iolanthe*) is of a love affair between a mortal, Donald, and a sylph, Aeolia; despite difficulties and stratagems, the pair are eventually united by a special act of the Sylphid Queen. The characters have little human reality and no subtlety, yet Barnett's richly scored music succeeds in creating strong emotion and dramatic tension. Inevitably Weber was his chief inspiration: the fairy choruses recall *Oberon* as much as the invocation scene suggests *Der Freischütz*. But Barnett was the only English composer at the time who could master this new and difficult idiom. He abandoned most traditional forms: there are few strophic songs or rondos, and no binary or sonata form arias; he created forms according to the demands of the various scenes, though he usually concluded each scene

WORKS
all printed works published in London

STAGE
all first performed in London

printed works are vocal scores unless otherwise stated

MS librettos are in GB-Lbl

LCG – *Covent Garden*
LDL – *Drury Lane*
† – *partly adapted*

Before Breakfast (musical farce, R.B. Peake), 31 Aug 1826, *US-Bp*
Two Seconds (operatic farce, Peake), English Opera House, 28 Aug 1827, *GB-Eu*
Rienzi (historical tragedy, 5, M.R. Mitford, after E. Gibbon), LDL, 9 Oct 1828, *US-Bp*, 1 song (1828)
Charles XII, or The Siege of Stralsund (historical drama, 2, J.R. Planché), LDL, 11 Dec 1828, 1 song
Monsieur Mallet, or My Daughter's Letter (burletta, 3, W.T. Moncrieff), Adelphi, 22 Jan 1829, *Bp*, selections (?1830)
The Partizans, or The War of Paris in 1649 (drama, Planché, after Mélesville: *La maison du rempart*), LDL, 21 May 1829, 1 song (Mrs C.B. Wilson) (1830)
†Robert the Devil (musical drama), 1829, LCG, 2 Feb 1830, *Bp* [adapted from Meyerbeer]
The Deuce is in Her (operetta, 1, R.J. Raymond), Adelphi, 28 Aug 1830, 1 song (1830)

Ex.1

(a)

(b)

(c) Presto

(d)

Baron Trenck, or The Fortress of Magdeburg (drama, S.J. Arnold), Surrey, 11 Oct 1830

†The Carnival at Naples (musical play, 5, W. Dimond), LCG, 30 Oct 1830, *Bp*, selections (1830)

Harlequin Pat and Harlequin Bat, or The Giant's Causeway (pantomime, C. Farley), LCG, 27 Dec 1830, *Bp*

Olympic Revels, or Prometheus and Pandora (burlesque, Planché and C. Dance, after G. Colman (ii): *The Sun Poker*), Olympic, 3 Jan 1831

Married Lovers (musical farce, 2, T. Power), LCG, 2 Feb 1831, *Bp*, 1 song (1831)

The Picturesque (operetta, T.H. Bayly), Adelphi, 25 Aug 1831, *Bp*, 1 song (?1840)

Country Quarters (musical farce, I. Pocock), LCG, 6 Dec 1831, *Bp*

The Convent, or The Pet of the Petticoats (operetta, J.B. Buckstone), Sadler's Wells, 9 July 1832, *Bp*

The Court of Queen's Bench (burletta), Olympic, 22 Oct 1832, *Bp*, 1 song (?1840)

The Conquering Game (comedy, W.B. Bernard), Olympic, 28 Nov 1832, 1 song (1833)

Win Her and Wear Her (comic op, 3, S. Beazley, after S. Centlivre: *A Bold Stroke for a Wife*), LDL, 18 Dec 1832, *Bp*

The Paphian Bower, or Venus and Adonis (mythological burletta, 1, Planché and Dance), Olympic, 26 Dec 1832

Nell Gwynne, or The Prologue (comedy, D. Jerrold), LCG, 9 Jan 1833, 2 songs, march, *Bp*

Promotion, or A Morning at Versailles in 1750 (burletta, 1, Planché), Olympic, 18 Feb 1833, *Bp*

A Match in the Dark (farce, Dance), Olympic, 21 Feb 1833, 1 song (Planché) (1833)

The Soldier's Widow, or The Ruins of the Mill (musical drama, E. Fitzball), Adelphi, 4 May 1833, *Bp*

The Mountain Sylph (romantic grand op, 2, J.T. Thackeray), English Opera House, 25 Aug 1834, *Bp* (1834)

Monsieur Jacques (burletta, M. Barnett), St James's, 13 Jan 1836, 1 song (1836)

Fair Rosamond (historical op, 4, C.Z. Barnett, F. Shannon), LDL, 28 Feb 1837, *Bp* (1837)

Blanche of Jersey (musical romance, 2, Peake), English Opera House, 9 Aug 1837, *Bp*, selections (1837–40)

The Little Laundress (musical entertainment, Peake, after Fr.), English Opera House, 21 Aug 1837

Farinelli (serio-comic op, 2, Barnett), LDL, 8 Feb 1839, *Bp*, selections (1839)

Kathleen (op, J.S. Knowles), 1840, *Bp*, unperf.

†The Beggar's Opera, unperf., *Bp* (undated) (c1840) [adapted from Pepusch]

Queen Mab (op), 1841, unperf., *Bp*

Marie (op), 1845, unfinished

SACRED VOCAL

2 Grand Masses, SATB, orch: g, 1823; c, before 1827: *US-Bp*

Abraham on the Altar of his Son (cant.), 1823, *Bp*

The Omnipotence of the Deity (orat, R. Montgomery), *Bp*, vs (1829)

Daniel in the Den of Lions (orat), 1841, *Bp*

12 Collects in Verse (W.H. Bellamy) (1849–51)

2 anthems, 1 sacred duet, 5 sacred songs

SECULAR VOCAL

The Groves of Pomona (F. Thomson: *The Seasons*), grand scena (1820)

70 glees, madrigals and partsongs, incl. 24 listed in Baptie; 9 trios; 48 duets, incl. 6 Vocal Duets (J.E. Carpenter, R. Ryan) (1845)

Songs, said to number 2000, incl. 9 collections: 12 Russian Melodies (H.S. van Dyk) (?1821); 24 Songs in Imitation of the Music of Various Nations (van Dyk, L. Lee) (1824); 12 Songs from Fairyland (Bayly) (1827); Songs of the Minstrels, 2vv (van Dyk) (?1830); Songs of the Slavonians (J. Bowring) (?1830); Lyric Illustrations of the Modern Poets (1834), 2 ed. in MB, xliii (1979); Amusement for Leisure Hours (?1835); Dreams of a Persian Maiden (R.M. Daniel) (1842); 5 Songs (T. Moore) (1885)

INSTRUMENTAL

L'ipocondria, characteristic symphonia, E♭/B♭, 1839, *US-Bp*; 2 ovs.: C, 1826, *Bp*; A, before 1827; Adagio and allegro, brass band, E♭, c1828, *Bp*

Chbr: Fuga per 4 instrumenti: C, c1818, *Bp*; 3 str qts: C, 1835, *Bp*; D, 1836, *Bp*; A, 1837, *GB-Lbl*; Sonata, vn, pf, g, before 1827; Spare Moments, 3 sketches, concertina, pf (1859)

Solo: 2 sonatas, pf: c, c1820, *US-Bp*; E♭, before 1827; Introduction on a Favourite Air from The Beggar's Opera, pf (1824)

EDITIONS

Edns/arrs. for various vv/insts, incl. works by T.A. Arne (Artaxerxes), W.A. Mozart (Don Giovanni), J.L. Dussek (Pf Sonata, E♭, op.18); excerpts from operas by D. Auber, G. Meyerbeer, G. Rossini, C.M. von Weber, P. Winter; songs

WRITINGS

Systems and Singing Masters: an Analytic Comment upon the Wilhem Method … with … Critical Remarks upon Mr. John Hullah's Manual (London, 1842)

School for the Voice (London, ?1845), ed. J.A. Wade: *The Handbook to the Pianoforte* (London, 2/1850)

BIBLIOGRAPHY

*Brown-Stratton*BMB; *DNB*; *Grove1* (E.F. Rimbault); *GroveO* ('Mountain Sylph, The'; N. Burton, N. Temperley); *LoewenbergA*; *NicollH*; *PEM* (N. Temperley); *SainsburyD*; *StieglerO*

'Theatrical Journal', *European Magazine and London Review*, lxiv/ July (1813), 46–7

Monthly Supplement to the Musical Library, i (1834), 70, 84

Musical World, ii (1836), 139–40; iv (1837), 172–3, 188–9; xiv (1840), 349–52, 365–7, 393

A. Bunn: *The Stage* (London, 1840), i, 138–40

G.A. Macfarren: 'Barnett, John', *The Imperial Dictionary of Universal Biography*, ed. J.F. Waller (London, 1857–63)

D. Baptie: *Sketches of the English Glee Composers* (London, 1896), 132

J.F. Barnett: *Musical Reminiscences and Impressions* (London, 1906)

C.K. Rogers: *Memories of a Musical Career* (Boston, 1919)

H.M. Rogers: 'John Barnett, Musician', *Harvard Graduates' Magazine*, xxxiii (1924–5), 595; pubd separately (Cambridge, MA, 1925)

P.A. Scholes, ed.: *The Mirror of Music 1844–1944* (London, 1947/ R), 7–8

A.C. Sprague and B. Shuttleworth, eds.: *Charles Rice: the London Theatre in the Eighteen-Thirties* (London, 1950), 16–17

E.W. White: *The Rise of English Opera* (London, 1951/R)

E.D. Mackerness: 'Leigh Hunt's Musical Journalism', *MMR*, lxxxvi (1956), 212–22, esp. 217

B. Carr: 'The First All-Sung English 19th-Century Opera', *MT*, cxv (1974), 125–6

G. Balanchine and F. Mason: *Balanchine's Complete Stories of the Great Ballets* (New York, 1977), 603–4

N. Temperley, ed.: *Music in Britain: the Romantic Age 1800–1914* (London, 1981/R)

E.W. White: *A History of English Opera* (London, 1983)

E.W. White: *A Register of First Perfomances of English Operas and Semi-Operas* (London, 1983)

NICHOLAS TEMPERLEY, NIGEL BURTON

Barnett, John Francis (*b* London, 16 Oct 1837; *d* London, 24 Nov 1916). English composer and pianist. His father was Joseph Alfred Barnett (*d* 29 April 1898), a professor of music, his uncle the composer John Barnett. Barnett began to study the piano at the age of six with his mother, took lessons from Wylde at 11 and at 13 gained the King's Scholarship at the RAM. In 1853 he made a very successful début with Mendelssohn's D minor Piano Concerto under Spohr at the New Philharmonic Society, and after studying with Hauptmann, Rietz and Moscheles at Leipzig he performed at the Gewandhaus in 1860. On his return to London he played at both the Philharmonic and New Philharmonic Societies with great success. In later years he was better known as a piano teacher. He became a Fellow of the RAM and taught at The National Training School for Music, the RCM and GSM. In 1871 he conducted at the Novello Albert Hall Concerts, and subsequently made occasional appearances as a conductor.

As a composer Barnett first achieved prominence with his Symphony in A (1864), written for the Musical Society of London. It was however as a popular composer of cantatas and oratorios that he achieved some resounding successes, from *The Ancient Mariner* (1867) and *Paradise and the Peri* (1870), both written for the Birmingham Festival, to *The Eve of St Agnes* (1913), produced by the London Choral Society. Although some of the later choral works were considered to be 'modern' and 'Wagnerian', mainly because of Barnett's use of leitmotifs, a critic wrote in the *Musical Times* (1891) that 'The composer's sympathies were always with the clear, refined and gracious art of Mendelssohn, and there they remain'. Barnett devoted much of his time to teaching, but continued to compose and found time to produce several large-scale orchestral works, such as the *Ouverture Symphonique*, the Piano Concerto in D minor and *The Lay of the Last Minstrel*, which won some critical acclaim. Like many of his English contemporaries, however, he never realized where his strength as a composer lay. His talents were essentially those of a miniaturist, for he lacked the originality and consistency of musical thought necessary for success in larger forms. The conservatism of his musical language, which depended principally on the legacy of Mozart and Mendelssohn, is shown by a comparison of his oratorio *The Raising of Lazarus* (1873) with the more vigorous contemporary style of such works as Stanford's *God is our Hope and Strength* (1877) and Parry's *Prometheus Unbound* (1880). Many of Barnett's smaller, descriptive piano pieces, which had a great vogue in 19th-century drawing-rooms (where they provided relief for young ladies from the works of Czerny and Hummel), achieve a simple charm.

In 1883 Barnett completed Schubert's Symphony in E major from autograph sketches in the possession of Sir George Grove (now in *GB-Lcm*). It was performed at the Crystal Palace in the same year.

WORKS
(selective list)

printed works published in London, unless otherwise stated

VOCAL

The Ancient Mariner (cant., S.T. Coleridge), Birmingham Festival, 1867 (1867)
Paradise and the Peri (cant., T. Moore), Birmingham Festival, 1870 (1870)
The Raising of Lazarus (orat), London, 1873, vs (1874)
The Good Shepherd, op.26 (orat, J. Barnett), Brighton Festival, 1876, vs (1876), rev. 1897 (J. Bennett), vs (1897)
The Building of the Ship, op.35 (cant., H.W. Longfellow), Leeds Festival, 1880, vs (1880)
The Golden Gate (scena), A, orch, 1880
The Triumph of Labour (ode), London, Crystal Palace, 1888
The Wishing-bell (cant.), Norwich Festival, 1893, vs (1893)
The Eve of St Agnes (cant., J. Keats), London, 1913, vs (1913)
Tantum ergo, 8vv (1874)
17 partsongs mentioned in Baptie (1895); many separate songs

INSTRUMENTAL

Symphony, a, London, 1864
Ouverture symphonique, London, Philharmonic Society, 1868, rev. 1891
Piano Concerto, d, op.25, 1869, pf part (Leipzig, *c*1885)
Overture, The Winter's Tale, 1873
The Lay of the Last Minstrel, sym. poem (after W. Scott), Liverpool, 1874 (1874)
The Harvest Festival, suite, Norwich, 1881, rev. 1892 as Pastoral Suite
2 Sketches: Ebbing Tide and Elfland, London, Crystal Palace, 1883
2 Sketches: Flowing Tide and Fairyland, London, Crystal Palace, 1891
Liebeslied and Im alten Styl, London, Crystal Palace, 1895
Pensée mélodique and Gavotte, London, 1899 (Leipzig, 1899)
Concerto pastorale, fl, orch

Fantasia, F, org (n.d.); Offertory, G, org (n.d.)
Pf music, chamber music

EDITIONS
F. Schubert: Symphonie (Skizze) in E (Leipzig, 1884) [pf transcr.]

WRITINGS
'Schubert's Unfinished Symphony in E', *Musical Review*, i (1883), 289
'Some Details concerning the Completion and Instrumentation of Schubert's Sketch Symphony ... as performed ... May 5, 1883', *PMA*, xvii (1890–91), 177–90
Musical Reminiscences and Impressions (London, 1906)

BIBLIOGRAPHY
'Philharmonic Society', *MT*, xxxii (1891), 407 [review of Ouverture symphonique]
D. Baptie: *Sketches of the English Glee Composers* (London, 1896), 196f
P.A. Scholes, ed.: *The Mirror of Music 1844–1944* (London, 1947/R)
M.J.E. Brown: *Schubert: a Critical Biography* (London, 1958/R), 110ff
N. Burton: 'Oratorios and Cantatas', *The Romantic Age, 1800–1914*, ed. N. Temperley (London, 1981), 221

JENNIFER SPENCER/JEREMY DIBBLE

Barns, Ethel (*b* 1874; *d* Maidenhead, 31 Dec 1948). English violinist and composer. At the RAM (1887–95) she studied the violin with Prosper Sainton and Emile Sauret, the piano with Frederick Westlake and harmony with Prout. Her first published composition, a Romance for violin and piano, appeared in 1891, and she was soon performing her own works at various concerts in London. In 1899 she married the singer Charles Phillips, with whom she had established the successful Barns-Phillips Chamber Concerts at Bechstein Hall. The series provided an important platform for her own violin music, which began to be taken up by others: Joachim added her Sonata no.2, Sauret her *Fantasie* and Elman her *L'escarpolette* to their repertories. In 1907 she was the soloist in her own *Concertstück* for violin and orchestra at the Promenade Concerts. A highly regarded violinist, Barns served on the first council of the Society of Women Musicians (founded 1911), and accompanied Adelina Patti on her later tours.

Most of Barns's music was written for the violin, ranging from her many short, inventive pieces for violin and piano through the often complex but always violinistic sonatas to her two large-scale works for violin and orchestra. Of the two surviving sonatas, the second (1904) is a richly lyrical work in contrast with the sparser fourth (1910). Her songs can be disappointingly bland but her piano pieces are often dramatic and always well-constructed. (*FullerPG*)

WORKS
(selective list)

Orch: Concertstück, op.19, vn, orch, arr. vn, pf (1908); Conc., d, vn, orch
Chbr (for vn, pf, unless otherwise stated): Romance (1891); Polonaise (1893); Mazurka (1894); Valse caprice (1894); Tarantella (1895); Sonata no.1, d, perf. 1900; Sonata no.2, A, op.9 (1904); Chanson gracieuse (1904); Pf Trio, f, 1904; Sonata no.3, perf. 1906; Chant élégiaque (1907); Danse caracteristique (1907); L'escarpolette (Swing Song) (1907); Hindoo Lament (Chanson indienne) (1907); Légende (1907); Moto perpetuo (1907); Suite, op.21, perf. 1908; Adagio appassionato (1909); Andante for the 4th String (1909); Canzonetta (Scherzo) (1909); Danse nègre (1909); Humoresque (1909); Idylle pastorale (1909); Lullaby (1909); Petite valse (1909); Serenade (1909); 8 Pieces (1910); Sonata no.4, g, op.24, perf. 1910; Andante espressivo (1911); Andante grazioso (1911); Fantasie, op.26, 2 vn, pf (1911); Petite pastorale (1911); Bagatelle (1912); Berceuse (1912); Nachtgesang (Notturno) (1912); 2 Compositions (1913); Crépuscule (Twilight) (1913); Idylle, vc, pf (1913); Aubade (1917); Carina (1917);

Pierette (1917); Sonata no.5, 1927; La Chasse (1928); Poème (1928); A Vision (1928); Pf Trio no.2

Pf: 4 Sketches (1899); 2 Dances (1907); Nocturne, perf. 1908; Prelude (1908); Scherzo, perf. 1908; Toccata, perf. 1908; Valse gracieuse (1908); Humoreske (1910); Scenes villageoises (1911); An Impression (1912); Cri du coeur (1916); Monkey Land (Scherzo) (1916); Landscapes (1919); Petite caprice (c 1919); Valse Slave (c1919)

24 songs, 16 pubd (1892–1918)

MSS in *GB-Lbl*

SOPHIE FULLER

Barnum, P(hineas) T(aylor) (*b* Bethel, CT, 5 July 1810; *d* Bridgeport, CT, 7 April 1891). American impresario. After an early success exhibiting Joyce Heth (advertised as George Washington's 160-year-old nurse), Barnum purchased a moribund collection of curiosities, and by relentless promotion made Barnum's Museum one of New York's central attractions. By 1850 his management of such novelties as the celebrated midget Tom Thumb had established him as America's leading showman, and the lecture hall at the Museum became an early venue for 'family' minstrelsy and variety. In 1844 Barnum capitalized on the enthusiasm for Tyrolean acts by introducing the often parodied 'Swiss Bell Ringers' (who actually came from England). He sponsored the Irish soprano Catherine Hayes on a tour of California (1852), and as president of the New York Crystal Palace he played an important role in Jullien's 'Grand Musical Congress' (1854).

Barnum's greatest triumph, however, was a tour by Jenny Lind (1850–51); under his management she gave 95 concerts in 19 cities, attracting unprecedented receipts of $712,161·34. Barnum travelled with the troupe and, with inspired publicity and an eye for sensation, promoted Lind much like an exhibit; though Lind eventually broke with him, they remained on good terms. This was the first major tour in the USA to be managed by a non-performer, and it marked the rise of a separate class of agents and promoters. Barnum's methods influenced popular entertainers as well as impresarios such as Max Maretzek and the Strakosch brothers; his impact on America's music industry was lasting and profound.

BIBLIOGRAPHY

P.T. Barnum: *The Life of P.T. Barnum, Written by Himself* (New York, 1855; rev. 1869 as *Struggles and Triumphs*); ed. G.S. Bryan as *Struggles and Triumphs, or The Life of P.T. Barnum, Written by Himself* (New York, 1927)
N. Harris: *Humbug: the Art of P.T. Barnum* (Boston, 1973)
W.P. Ware and T.C. Lockard, jr: *P.T. Barnum Presents Jenny Lind: the American Tour of the Swedish Nightingale* (Baton Rouge, LA, 1980)
A.H. Saxon, ed.: *Selected Letters of P.T. Barnum* (New York, 1983)

WILLIAM BROOKS

Barodekar, Hirabai (*b* Miraj, 1905; *d* 1979). Indian singer. She was the daughter of Abdul Karim Khan of the Kirana *gharānā* and studied with her father's cousin, Abdul Wahid Khan. Her first important opportunity as a vocalist came when Vishnu Digambar Paluskar invited her to sing in public in 1923. After the Maharashtrian revival of theatre broke the ban on women appearing on the professional stage in that region, Barodekar performed in plays with mixed casts. When live theatre waned in the face of the new film industry, she joined artists who were introducing art music to the non-court world in North India. In 1949 she performed in Africa, and in 1953 travelled to China under government auspices. In 1965 she received the President's Award for Hindustani Vocal

Music from the Sangeet Natak Akademi, then in 1970 she was awarded the Padma Bhushan by the Government of India. She taught at the Sangeet Research Academy in Calcutta where she trained students in the style of the Kirana *gharānā*.

Barodekar specialized in *vilambit khayāl*, but also sang *tarānā*, *thumrī*, *bhajan* and Marathi songs (*pad*). Typical of the Kirana style, she did not accelerate the speed of the *tāla* counts as the improvisation proceeded; rather, the impression of acceleration was achieved through increasing rhythmic density. Her slow improvisations were punctuated with vocal pauses that permitted brief solos by the *tablā* player; in her fast *khayāls* the role of the drummer was also highlighted.

BIBLIOGRAPHY

Multani, Raga Yaman, perf. H. Barodekar, HMV ECLP2275 (1962)
Hirabai Barodekar: HMV ECLP2356 (1968) *Khyāls* in Ragas Basant Bahar, Chandrakauns (with her sister, Saraswati Rane)
B.C. Wade: *Khyāl: Creativity within North India's Classical Music Tradition* (Cambridge, 1984/R)

BONNIE C. WADE

Baroffio, Bonifacio Giacomo (*b* Novara, 5 Dec 1940). Italian musicologist and liturgist. He studied the violin with Ricciardi (1948–59) and musicology, first in Cologne with Gustav Fellerer, Heinrich Hüschen and Marius Schneider, and later in Erlangen with Bruno Stäblein (1959–63). He obtained the doctorate in 1964 from Cologne University with a dissertation on Offertories in the Ambrosian liturgy. He was a Benedictine monk until 1996 and was Abbot at the Noci Abbey, Bari. He has taught theology in seminaries in Genoa (1976–7) and Novara (1979–80), history of liturgy and codicology at the Institute of Pastoral Liturgy in Padua (1973–81) and Gregorian chant and liturgical codicology at the Pontifical Institute of Sacred Music in Rome (1982–95), where he also became dean in 1988. He teaches the history of liturgy at the School of Musical Palaeography and Philology, University of Pavia, and liturgical codicology at the University of Cassino. His main fields of research are Gregorian chant, palaeography and musical semiology, liturgy and codicology.

WRITINGS

'Il messale di Boccioletto', *Rivista di storia della Chiesa in Italia*, xx (1966), 34–43
'Un antico graduale novarese', *Bollettino storico per la provincia di Novara*, lvii (1967), 45–58
'Die mailändische Überlieferung des Offertoriums Sanctificavit', *Festschrift Bruno Stäblein*, ed. M. Ruhnke (Kassel, 1967), 1–8
'Osservazioni sui versetti degli Offertori ambrosiani', *Ricerche storiche sulla chiesa ambrosiana*, iii (1972), 54–8
'Repertorio bibliografico ambrosiano di studi pubblicati in Germania', *Ricerche storiche sulla chiesa ambrosiana*, iii (1972), 127–43
'Kyriakon: omaggio a J. Quasten', *Rivista liturgica*, lx (1973), 254–74
'L'"Ordo Missae" del vescovo Warmondo d'Ivrea', *Studi medievali*, 3rd ser., xvi (1975), 795–823
'Verso una storia dell'antica eucologia ambrosiana: Judith Frei e l'edizione del Sacramentario di S. Simpliciano', *Ricerche storiche sulla chiesa ambrosiana*, vii (1977), 5–25
ed., with R. Leydi: *Le musiche liturgiche tradizionali* (Venice, 1984) [incl. 'Le origini del canto liturgico nella Chiesa latina e la formazione dei repertori italici']
'I canti per l'assemblea nel repertorio gregoriano', *Christus in ecclesia cantat: Rome 1985*, 202–10
'Liturgia e musica nella vita monastica verso il Mille con particolare riguardo alla Valsusa', *Benedictina*, xxxii (1985), 389–99
'Palestrina e il canto gregoriano: l'innodia', *Studi palestriniani II: Palestrina 1986*, 23–6

with C. Antonelli: 'La passione nella liturgia della chiesa cattolica fino all'epoca di Johann Sebastian Bach', *Ritorno a Bach: dramma e ritualità delle passioni*, ed. E. Povellato (Venice, 1986), 11–33

'Repertori liturgico-musicali nell'Italia meridionale e fonti beneventane', *Tradizione manoscritta e pratica musicale: i codici di Puglia: Bari 1986*, 1–21

with C. Antonelli: 'Impegno liturgico e pedagogico nella vita musicale dei monasteri', *Dall'eremo al cenobio*, ed. G. Pugliese Carratelli (Milan, 1987), 728–40

'I manoscritti liturgici italiani: ricerche, studi, catalogazione', *Le fonti musicali in Italia*, i (1987), 65–126; ii (1988), 89–134; iii (1989), 91–118; v (1991), 7–129

'I manoscritti liturgici: loro individuazione e descrizione', *Documentare il manoscritto: Rome 1987*, 67–85

'Die Musica sacra nach dem II. Vaticanum: aspekte eines noch ungelösten Problems', *Lebendiges Zeugnis*, xli (1987), 69–78

ed., with S. Chierici: *Il canto delle pietre: musiche sacre e spirituali del Medioevo nei monumenti dell'architettura romanica lombarda* (Como, 1988) [incl. 'Musica e drammaturgia nella liturgia pasquale', 13–39]

'L'Ordo Missae del rituale messale vallicelliano E 62', *Traditio et progressio*, ed. G. Farnedi (Rome, 1988), 45–79

'Appunti per un trattato di codicologia liturgica', *Ecclesia orans*, vi (1989), 69–88

'Il canto gregoriano nel secolo VIII', *Lateinische Kultur im VIII. Jahrhundert: Traube-Gedenkschrift*, ed. A. Lhener and W. Berschin (St Ottilien, 1989), 9–23

ed., with V. Jemolo and others: *Guida a una descrizione uniforme dei manoscritti e al loro censimento* (Rome, 1990) [incl. 'I manoscritti liturgici', 143–92]

'San Bernardo e la "lectio divina"', *La Scala*, no.44 (1990), 175–87

'San Bernardo e la musica', *La Scala*, no.44 (1990), 113–16

'La tradizione eucologica nella liturgia delle ore: il Breviario beneventano: Napoli, Biblioteca Nazionale, XVI.A.7', *Ecclesia orans*, vii (1990), 113–30

'I tropi d'introito e i canti pasquali in un graduale italiano del sec. XIII (Monza, Bibl. Capit. K 11)', *Studi in onore di Giulio Cattin*, ed. F. Luisi (Rome, 1990), 3–14

ed., with S. Chierici: *Il canto delle pietre: musiche sacre e spirituali del Medioevo nei monumenti dell'architettura romanica lombarda* (Como, 1991) [incl. 'La musica Medievale tra calcolo Matematico e fantas Simbolica', 15–22]

'I codici liturgici: specchio della cultura italiana nel medioevo: punti fenni, appunti di lettura, spunti di ricerca', *Ecclesia orans*, ix (1992), 233–76

'A proposito di esecuzioni filologiche', *NRMI*, xxvii (1993), 221–6

'The Musical Repertories of the Liturgy of Southern Italy and Beneventan Sources', *Songs of the Dove and the Nightingale: Sacred and Secular music c900–c1600*, ed. O.M. Hair and R.E. Smith (Sydney, 1994), 1–32

TERESA M. GIALDRONI

Baron, Ernst Gottlieb [Theofil] (*b* Breslau, 17 Feb 1696; *d* Berlin, 12 April 1760). German lutenist, composer and writer on music. Neither Baron's life nor his works have as yet been fully explored by scholars. His father Michael was a maker of gold lace and expected his son to follow in his footsteps. The younger Baron showed an inclination towards music in his youth, however, and later made it his profession. He first studied the lute from about 1710 with a Bohemian named Kohott (not to be confused with the later Karl von Kahaut). In Breslau he attended the Elisabeth Gymnasium, and from there went in 1715 to Leipzig, where he studied philosophy and law at the university for four years.

Much of the period from 1719 to 1728 was spent in travels from one small court to another. He first visited Halle for a short period, then in quick succession Cöthen, Schleiz, Saalfeld and Rudolstadt. He arrived in Jena in 1720 and remained for two years. Thereafter he travelled to Kassel, Fulda, Würzburg, Nuremberg and Regensburg, returning in 1727 to Nuremberg where his *Historisch-theoretische und practische Untersuchung des Instruments der Lauten*, the work for which he is principally

remembered, was published the same year. In 1728 he replaced the lutenist Meusel, who had recently died, at Gotha and held the post for four years. With the death of the Duke of Gotha he moved on to Eisenach. In 1737, after visits to Merseburg, Cöthen and Zerbst, Baron joined the musical ensemble of Crown Prince Frederick of Prussia. He was immediately granted permission to go to Dresden to purchase a theorbo, and there met the highly esteemed lutenists S.L. Weiss and Hofer. When Frederick became king in 1740, Baron continued to serve as theorbist in the much expanded royal musical establishment. He remained at this post until his death.

Baron's *Untersuchung* is a valuable though not always reliable source of information about lutenists and lute playing in the late Baroque era, when the instrument was still widely cultivated in solo and ensemble performance in Germany. The work is divided into two main parts. The first deals with the history of the lute, and contains important references to contemporary players. The second is devoted to the practice of the instrument. Baron's other writings, as yet incompletely studied, supplement the *Untersuchung*, and explore several other subjects.

The few accessible examples of Baron's compositions suggest that he cultivated a characteristic late Baroque idiom in his suites, but moved in the direction of the *galant* style in his concertos. The latter are in fact trio sonatas in texture, cast in the three-movement form of the concerto.

WORKS

Suite, D, lute, in G. Telemann: *Der getreue Musikmeister* (Hamburg, 1728)

Fantasie, lute, in F. Seidel: *12 Menuette für die Laute von Herrn F. Seidel, samt einer Fantasie von Herrn Baron* (Leipzig, 1757/*R*1969)

2 concertos, C, lute, vn, bc; duet, G, lute, fl: *B-Bc*

6 partitas, lute; 6 trios, lute, va, vc; sonata, 2 lutes: *D-LEbh*; ed. L. Sayce (n.p., 1998)

Partie, A, lute, *Bsb*

Sonata, 2 lutes, fl, *LEm*

Suite movements, lute, *Dl*, *ROu*, *RUS-KA*

WRITINGS

Historisch-theoretische und practische Untersuchung des Instruments der Lauten (Nuremberg, 1727/*R*; Eng. trans., 1976, as *Study of the Lute*)

'Herrn Barons Fortsetzung seiner in dem Waltherischen Lexico befindlichen Lebensumstände', in F.W. Marpurg: *Historisch-kritische Beyträge zur Aufnahme der Musik*, i (Berlin, 1755/*R*), 544–6

'Herrn Ernst Gottlieb Barons Beytrag zur historisch- theoretisch- und practischen Untersuchung der Laute', ibid., ii (Berlin, 1756/*R*), 65–83

'Herrn Barons Abhandlung von dem Notensystem der Laute und der Theorbe', ibid., 119–23

'Herrn Barons zufällige Gedanken über verschiedene musikalische Materien', ibid., 124–44

Abriss einer Abhandlung von der Melodie: eine Materie der Zeit (Berlin, 1756)

Versuch über das Schöne (Altenburg, 1757) [trans. of Y.M. André: *Essai sur le beau* (1741)]; suppl. *Des Herrn Gresset ... Rede von dem uralten Adel und Nutzen der Musik im Jahr 1751 gehalten* [trans. of Gresset: *Discours sur l'harmonie*], also pubd separately (Berlin, 1757)

BIBLIOGRAPHY

GerberL; *GerberNL*; *MGG1* (Boetticher); *WaltherML*

J. Mattheson: *Der neue göttingische, aber viel schlechter, als die alten lacedämonischen urtheilende Ephorus* (Hamburg, 1727), 109–27

F.W. Marpurg: *Legende einiger Musikheiligen* (Cologne [recte Breslau], 1786), 158–64

A. Koczirz: 'Verschollene neudeutsche Lautenisten', *AMw*, iii (1921), 270–84

H. Neemann: 'Philipp Martin, ein vergessener Lautenist', *ZMw*, ix (1926–7), 545–65

H.-P. Kosack: *Geschichte der Laute und Lautenmusik in Preussen* (Kassel, 1935)

D.A. Smith: 'Baron and Weiss contra Mattheson: in Defence of the Lute', *JLSA*, vi (1973), 48–62

J. Klima: *Ernst Gottlieb Baron, 1696–1760: Partiten aus den verschollenen Handschriften Berlin Mus. ms. 40633 und Königsberg 3026: Themenverzeichnis* (Enzersdorf, 1976)

EDWARD R. REILLY

Baroness, The. See LINDELHEIM, JOANNA MARIA.

Baroni. Italian family of singers and instrumentalists.

(1) **Adriana** [Adreana] **Baroni.** *See* BASILE family, (§3).

(2) **Leonora** [Eleanora, Lionora] **Baroni** (*b* Mantua, Dec 1611; *d* Rome, 6 April 1670). Singer and instrumentalist, daughter of (1) Adriana Baroni; she was sometimes known as 'L'Adrianella' or 'L'Adrianetta'. She spent her childhood at the Gonzaga court at Mantua, where her mother was a leading singer, and was named after the late Duchess of Mantua. She presumably began her musical training with her mother. Gifted with a splendid voice, she specialized as a singer, soon achieved great fame and put even her mother in the shade. She was admired not only for the beauty, artistry and style of her singing but also for her refined manners. She was able to speak several languages and wrote verse as well as music. No compositions attributed to her are known, but the French viol player André Maugars, who knew her in Rome, stated unequivocally that she composed. When still very young she accompanied her mother on her musical journeys, together with her sister (3) Caterina Baroni. At the age of only 16 she received her first enthusiastic acclaim in the aristocratic circles of Naples, where the family resided from 1624 to 1633. In spring 1630, again with her mother, she appeared at Genoa and immediately afterwards at Florence. She was everywhere the object of admiration and gallantries, as is proved by the numerous poems addressed to her by prominent poets such as Fulvio Testi and Francesco Bracciolini, and by influential nobles such as Cardinals Annibale Bentivoglio and Giulio Rospigliosi, and Prince Camillo Colonna, protector of the Accademia degli Umoristi; these were published as *Applausi poetici alle glorie della Signora Leonora Baroni* (ed. F. Ronconi, Bracciano, 1639, 2/1641).

After her family had moved to Rome in 1633, Leonora was declared superior to all other Italian chamber singers of the age. She enjoyed one success after another in the musical entertainments held at her home, accompanying herself on theorbo or viol (both of which she played perfectly according to Maugars) or performing alongside her mother (playing the *lira*) and sister (playing the harp). Milton heard and admired her and in 1639 paid homage to her in three Latin epigrams (*Ad Leonoram Romae canentem*). Her voice, Maugars noted, was 'of a high compass', and 'she mellows it or swells it easily'. On her countenance, he added:

Her [vocal] leaps and her sighs are not at all lascivious, her glances have nothing of lewdness and her gestures have the correctness of a proper young lady. Sometimes, in passing from one note to another, she lets the intervals of the enharmonic and chromatic genera sound with such skill and charm that no one remains unmoved by this beautiful and difficult type of singing.

The only female member of the Accademia degli Umoristi, she frequently attended salons at the Palazzo Barberini, where she was always enthusiastically received in the circle around Cardinal Antonio Barberini. It was there that she met Cardinal Francesco Barberini's secretary, Giulio Cesare Castellani, whom she married on 27 May 1640.

In February 1644, through the mediation of Cardinal Mazarin (who had known her in Rome and was to a great extent indebted to her for the advantageous favour of Cardinal Antonio Barberini), Leonora Baroni was offered by the Queen Regent of France, Anne of Austria, a favourable contract inviting her and her husband to the French court. This she accepted. At first she was not admired in Paris, perhaps because the Italian style of singing did not appeal to French taste. That she nevertheless achieved a measure of success was largely due to the queen regent's benevolent protection. Even so, her stay in Paris was clouded by envy and professional jealousy. She therefore departed for Italy on 10 April 1645, taking with her several precious jewels bestowed on her by the queen regent, who also granted her a large pension for life. She might later have returned to France had not the state of her health prevented it.

In Rome she resumed her active life in the aristocratic society that frequented the salons held at her home. There, even after her husband's death on 4 January 1662, she continued to perform, accompanying herself on the lute or theorbo. She maintained her notable artistic reputation, particularly after the election of Pope Clement IX, who as Cardinal Giulio Rospigliosi had once dedicated one of his best sonnets to her; she enjoyed to the end of her life the patronage and affectionate friendship of the Rospigliosi family. She was buried with her husband in S Maria della Scala.

(3) **Caterina Baroni** (*b* Naples, 1619; *d* ?Rome, *c*1670). Singer, harpist and poet, daughter of (1) Adriana Baroni. She lived in Mantua until 1624, in Naples from 1624 to 1633 and thereafter in Rome, where her family enjoyed the protection of Cardinal Antonio Barberini. Caterina became a singer and harpist and often appeared with her mother and sister (2) Leonora when musical entertainments were held in their house. Maugars heard them in 1639 and reported that their 'three fine voices and three different instruments so took my senses by surprise . . . I forgot my mortality and thought I was already among the angels'. Similarly captivated, Della Valle professed the impossiblity of judging one sister musically superior to the other.

In 1640 her mother retired to Naples and Caterina entered the convent of S Lucia in Selci, although the next year she continued to receive a monthly allowance from Cardinal Barberini. It is thought she probably took the name of Sister Costanza as a tribute to Barberini's mother, who was called Costanza. S Lucia was considered a focal point for intellectual life in Rome, and the music-making of its nuns among the finest in the convents. In 1641 Caterina Baroni was bequeathed three harps by Orazio Michi. She was still at S Lucia in February 1662, when she signed a receipt for a bronze crucifix, a gift from her recently deceased brother-in-law. Of her poetry, only a sonnet in memory of Niccolo Fabri Peresio (*I-Rvat* Barberini lat.1996) is known.

BIBLIOGRAPHY
DBI (L. Pannella); *ES* (E. Zanetti)

A. Maugars: *Response faite à un curieux sur le sentiment de la musique d'Italie, escrite à Rome le premier octobre 1639* (Paris, c1640/R with Eng. trans., Geneva, 1993; ed. E. Thoinan, Paris, 1865/R; Eng. trans. in J.S. Shedlock: 'André Maugars', *Studies in Music*, ed. R. Grey, London, 1901; ed. J. Heuillon, Paris, 1991)

P. Della Valle: *Della musica dell'età nostra* (MS, 1640); pr. in G.B. Doni: *Lyra Barberina amphicordos*, ed. A.F. Gori and G.B. Passeri, ii (Florence, 1763/R); repr. in A. Solerti: *Le origini del melodramma* (Turin, 1903/R), 164–6

A. Ademollo: *La Leonora di Milton e di Clemente IX* (Milan, 1885)

A. Ademollo: *La bell'Adriana ed altre virtuose del suo tempo alla corte di Mantova* (Città di Castello, 1888)

J. Lionnet: 'André Maugars: Risposta data a un curioso sul sentimento della musica d'Italia', *NRMI*, xix (1985), 681–707

S. Parisi: *Ducal Patronage of Music in Mantua, 1587–1627: an Archival Study* (diss., U. of Illinois, 1989)

F. Hammond: *Music & Spectacle in Baroque Rome: Barberini Patronage under Urban VIII* (New Haven, CT, 1994), 86–8, 302

K. Montford: *Music in the Convents of Counter-Reformation Rome* (diss., Rutgers U., 1999)

ARGIA BERTINI/SUSAN PARISI

Baroni, Antonio. *See* BORONI, ANTONIO.

Baroque. A term used generally to designate a period or style of European music covering roughly the years between 1600 and 1750.

1. Etymology and early usage. 2. Chronological limits. 3. Critique of the concept. 4. Technical features of Baroque music.

1. ETYMOLOGY AND EARLY USAGE.   Although used in art and music criticism as far back as the mid-18th century, the term 'Baroque' has only relatively recently been adopted for a historical period. It is derived from the French *baroque*, which comes from the Portuguese *barroco*, meaning a pearl of irregular or bulbous shape. It is often found in texts having to do with the manufacture of jewellery from the 16th century onwards, in Spanish (*berrueco*, *barrueco*), French (*barroque*, *barrocque*, *baroque*) and later Italian (*baroco*, *barocco*).

It has been generally assumed that the word was first applied to the fine arts in reference to architecture. Charles de Brosses in *Lettres familières écrites d'Italie en 1739 et 1740* (Paris, c1755; ed. R. Colomb, Paris, 1855) criticized the architect of a Roman palace for transferring to a large scale the style of baroque ornamentation that better suited small objects like gold cases or dinnerware. But it has been shown that these 'letters' were not drafted until about 1755, long after de Brosses' return to Paris. The earliest application to the fine arts appears to have been, rather, in reference to music. This occurs in a satirical letter prompted by the première of Rameau's *Hippolyte et Aricie* in Paris in October 1733, printed in the *Mercure de France* in May 1734 ('Lettre de M*** à Mlle*** sur l'origine de la musique', pp.868–70). The anonymous author covertly implied that what was new in the opera was 'du baroque' and complained that the music lacked coherent melody, was unsparing in dissonances, constantly changed key and metre, and speedily ran through every compositional device. Rameau was also the target of a poem by J.B. Rousseau (in a letter to Louis Racine, 17 November 1739, in *Lettres sur differents sujets de la littérature*, Geneva, 1750) that called him and his kind 'distillers of baroque chords' (*distillateurs d'accords baroques*).

Noel Antoine Pluche was the most illuminating of the early users of the term. He not only attached it to a category or style of music but he implied an etymology. In *Spectacle de la nature* (vii, Paris, 1746) he maintained that the comparison of French and Italian music no longer divided critics; that the issue now was between the partisans of *musique chantante* (songful or tuneful music)

and *musique baroque* (translated as 'rough' in the English version, *Spectacle de la nature: or Nature Display'd*, London, 1748):

One takes its melody from the natural sounds of our throat and from the accents of the human voice, which speaks to concern others with what touches us, always without grimace, always without effort, almost without art. We shall call this songful music [*la musique chantante*]. The other aims to surprise by the boldness of its sounds and passes for song while pulsating with speed and noise [*veut surprendre par la hardiesse des sons & passer pour chanter en mesurant des vitesses & du bruit*]; we call it Baroque music [*la musique Baroque*].

Pluche had earlier contrasted the concerts directed by Jean-Pierre Guignon (1702–74), who amused and surprised with the admirable lightness and agility of his playing and of the ensembles he directed, and Jean-Baptiste Anet, who did not approve of Guignon's pretence at overcoming all difficulties, of his tendency to 'wrest laboriously from the bottom of the sea some baroque pearls, when diamonds can be found on the surface of the earth' (p.103). To Anet, achieving surprise by brilliant vivacity was a small accomplishment; greatness in art was to please the multitude by sweet and varied emotions. He preferred an instrumental sound 'that was connected, sustained, velvety, passionate, and conforming to the accents of the human voice' (p.104). Pluche's favourite composer was Mondonville, who excelled in both the singing and the Baroque genres. Essentially, however, Baroque music was to Pluche pure instrumental music which, lacking a text, had no significance, not even that which it might acquire through imitating the human voice. For Pluche, as for de Brosses, *baroque* had a pejorative connotation.

Although Guignon was a composer in his own right, Pluche probably thought of him rather as the most famous interpreter of Italian concertos, such as those of Vivaldi and Albinoni, at the Concert Spirituel in the 1720s. Marpurg also contrasted his playing with Anet's: 'Guignon and Battiste were two fine violinists; the first played in the Italian taste, the second in the French taste' (*Historisch-kritische Beyträge zur Aufnahme der Musik*, i, Berlin, 1754, p.238). The brilliant and bold virtuosity that Pluche associated with Guignon probably reflected the music of Vivaldi's 'high Baroque' period and similar works unknown in Paris before the first years of the Concert Spirituel (which began in 1725). Pluche's use of the term 'baroque', while not entirely inconsistent with its present usage, thus had much narrower scope.

Other 18th-century writers tended to call upon the word 'baroque' to evoke impressions of strangeness and distortion. De Brosses, who applied the term to the pseudo-Gothic ornamentation of the Palazzo Doria Pamphili in Rome, was amazed that Italian recitative 'could be at one time so baroque and so monotonous' (*Lettres*, ed. R. Colomb, 4/1885, ii, 330). J.-J. Rousseau ventured a definition in his *Dictionnaire de musique* (Paris, 1768): 'A baroque music is that in which the harmony is confused, charged with modulations and dissonances, the melody is harsh and little natural, the intonation difficult, and the movement constrained'; he thought the term came from the *baroco* of logicians. Rousseau's definition was paraphrased by, among others, Castil-Blaze (*Dictionnaire de musique moderne*, Paris, 1821), Heinrich Koch (*Musikalisches Lexikon*, Frankfurt, 1802), Gustav Schilling (*Encyclopädie der gesammten musikalischen Wissenschaften*, i, Stuttgart, 1835) and

Hermann Mendel (*Musikalisches Conversations-Lexikon*, Berlin, 1870).

Rousseau's etymology, now largely discredited, was vigorously supported by Benedetto Croce (1929) and later René Wellek (1946). *Baroco* was indeed a word coined by medieval logicians along with *Celarent, Baralipton, Darapti, Felapto* etc. as mnemonic aids to recall the various types of syllogism; the fourth mode of the second figure was called *baroco*. The vowel 'a' indicated the universal affirmative character of the major premise, and the two vowels 'o' indicated that the minor premises and conclusion were negative, as in 'Every *A* is *B*; some *C* are not *B*; hence some *C* are not *A*'. *Baroco*, however, was not used in Italy as an art-critical term; when Italians eventually wrote about Baroque qualities in art, the French word was borrowed, and it became *barocco*.

Baroque in the sense of bizarre, irregular and extravagant continued to occur sporadically in criticism of art and music in the rest of the 18th century and most of the 19th without acquiring a more generalized stylistic significance. It was Jacob Burckhardt who gave the post-Michelangelo style this name in his *Der Cicerone* (Leipzig, 2/1839), where he dedicated a substantial chapter to the *Barockstyl*. Whereas for Burckhardt it marked the decadent phase of the high Renaissance, Heinrich Wölfflin (*Renaissance und Barock*, 1888) treated the style and its development in a positive way and suggested the term might also be applied to literature (Tasso) and music

(Palestrina). Cornelius Gurlitt's *Geschichte des Barockstiles in Italien* (Stuttgart, 1887) also accepted the style as a legitimate expression of its time. Wölfflin later expanded the concept of Baroque to include a number of principles that could be applied to any period, though his examples were mainly 17th century (see below; *Kunstgeschichtliche Grundbegriffe*, Munich, 1915).

Meanwhile the concept of Baroque was not immediately adopted by writers on music history. Ambros (1882) mentioned the rampant *barrocco* of painting and architecture in the 17th century (*Geschichte der Musik*, iv, rev. 3/1909, p.286) but not as a musical category. Riemann avoided the term, calling the period 'Generalbass-Zeitalter' (*Handbuch der Musikgeschichte*, ii, 1912), and Guido Adler referred to it simply as the 'Third Style Period' (*Handbuch der Musikgeschichte*, 1924).

Curt Sachs was the first to apply Wölfflin's theory of the Baroque systematically to music. He took the five characteristics that Wölfflin had isolated in the visual arts and explained how each fitted musical developments in this period: (i) the suppression of line in favour of the painterly (*malerisch*) was paralleled by the overwhelming of melody by ornamentation and variation; (ii) the penchant of Baroque painters for placing figures in both foreground and recessed positions as opposed to the single plane of the Renaissance was compared by Sachs to the depth achieved by placing a soprano against a bass and its harmony; and (iii) the drift from the closed form of the

1. *Baroque stage design by Domenico and Gasparo Mauro for the moonlit garden scene (Act 1 scene vii) in Steffani's opera 'Servio Tullio', Opernhaus am Salvatorplatz, Munich, 1686: engraving*

Renaissance to the open form of Baroque art was analogous to the replacement of the rhythmics dominated by arsis and thesis by the natural declamation of speech. Similarly, the tendencies of Baroque art (iv) to replace multiplicity by unity and (v) to obscure rather than make clear were shown to operate also in music.

Sachs's belief in the synchronism of the arts and his rather strained transplantation of Wölfflin's categories were almost immediately challenged. Andrea Della Corte (1933), a follower of Croce, argued that the term 'Baroque' could not transcend its meaning of extravagant, and thus only certain aspects of 17th-century music could be characterized by it – the 'marvellous' monumental polychoral style of Benevoli, which 'Barochized' Renaissance polyphony, the tortuous turns of the late madrigal, or the over-schematization of opera after 1650. Moreover, Della Corte pointed out, Wölfflin's poles for the Renaissance and Baroque could be turned round completely and the concept of linear applied with no strain to monody and that of closed form to the da capo aria.

Robert Haas (1928) saw merits in Wölfflin's principles but doubted whether all five points could be applied to music; he was also less concerned with paralleling the chronology of the visual arts. Whereas art historians pushed the beginnings of the Baroque back to the middle or even the beginning of the 16th century, Haas could not justify a date earlier than 1594, the year Palestrina and Lassus died. He did recognize, however, a certain spiritual unity in the period, and defended it on sociological, intellectual and cultural as well as musical grounds.

It was Lang (1941) and Bukofzer (1940, 1947) who gave the term 'Baroque' currency in English. Lang did not discuss the concept or the word in themselves but elaborated with a wealth of detail the forces at work culturally, intellectually and socially that led to the 'fading' of the Renaissance and rise of the Baroque style in art and music. Bukofzer used the terms 'Renaissance' and 'Baroque' 'as convenient labels for periods which apply equally well to music history and other fields of civilization' (1947, p.2). He recognized the dangers of transposing the terminology of art history to music: 'The concepts of Wölfflin, the linear, closed form, etc., are abstractions distilled from the live development of art, indeed very useful abstractions, but so general in nature that they can be applied to all periods indiscriminately, although they were originally found in the comparison of renaissance and baroque'. For Bukofzer the value of the term lay in the observation that it 'essentially denotes the inner stylistic unity of the period. By technical analysis rather than comparative abstractions it is possible to show that the development of baroque music runs parallel with that of baroque art, but there are undercurrents that do not conform to the "spirit of the time"'.

Independently of Bukofzer, Clercx (1948) arrived at an autonomously musical analysis of the Baroque in music. She too doubted that theories based on the plastic arts and literature could necessarily be adapted to music, 'which has its own laws and its independent development. A study of the Baroque in music, bringing with it new facts, could be of such a nature as to modify the conception that has generally been held of the phenomenon' (p.39). Through a careful analysis of the characteristics of melody, harmony, rhythm and genres of the repertory of the period from the middle of the 16th century, she developed the aesthetic principles on which the variety of works of the period could be said to have been founded. By 'esthétique' Clercx meant not the body of aesthetic philosophy generated by the period itself but the principles that could be induced from an analysis of its products and then be referred back to that period.

Scholars in France and Britain were long reluctant to accept the term 'Baroque' or concepts associated with it. Dufourcq (1961) pointed out that the concept of Baroque as common in German musicology did not fit the development of music and culture in France, where Classicism occupied the first half of the 17th century. Chailley (1958) rejected the term as failing to correspond to any reality. In Britain, Capell (Grove5) found no justification beyond mere convenience for calling such a variety of styles as those of Peri and Bach by the same term. The Histoire de la musique of the Encyclopédie de la Pléiade (Paris, 1960) called the period 'L'ère du style concertant'.

The idea of a Baroque style gained some acceptance in France, however, as shown by the studious attention given to it by V.L. Tapié (1957) and Rémy Stricker (1968). In Britain the term appeared in a book title, The Baroque Concerto (London, 1961) by Arthur Hutchings, although the concept hardly figures in the text, which merely accepts the notion of a Baroque style and period.

2. CHRONOLOGICAL LIMITS. There has been appreciable disagreement concerning the starting date of the period, less about the terminal date. Wölfflin recognized in art history an early phase from 1570, a high phase from 1680, and a late phase extending from about 1700 until the rise of the 'Sturm und Drang'. Haas divided his book into three parts, each covering about half a century, and framing the achievement of the main components of the Baroque style: the conquest over the musical Renaissance (the monodic and concertato style); the melodic structuring of the musical Baroque (the cantata and bel canto style); and the musical high Baroque (the formation of the 'proud' contrapuntal style, kontrapunktischer Prunkstil). Bukofzer distinguished three major periods, though he acknowledged that they did not coincide in different countries: 1580–1630, early Baroque; 1630–80, middle Baroque; 1680–1730, late Baroque. Clercx pushed the beginning of the period back to the middle of the 16th century, where she located a phase of 'primitive Baroque'. The second period, 'full Baroque' (plein baroque), occupied the entire 17th century. Finally after the style was achieved there was a 'tardy Baroque' (baroque tardif), which extended from 1700 to about 1740 or 1765.

3. CRITIQUE OF THE CONCEPT. It is evident that the earliest usages of 'Baroque' in the arts, though suggestive, cannot be a guide to its meaning as a historical category. Nor should the fact that it originally had negative connotations deter us from assigning to it a positive meaning. For, if its pejorative taint stands against it, the critical vocabulary would have to be impoverished by banning also terms such as 'Gothic', 'impressionism', 'mannerism' and 'galant'. But unless the period designated 'Baroque' can be shown to have some stylistic or spiritual unity, the term is ineligible even as a convenient label. The question, therefore, is whether within a sizable period between the Renaissance and the middle of the 18th century a quality or qualities can be identified that strongly dominated musical style.

2. Design by Filippo Juvarra for Act 3 scene xvii of 'Giunio Bruto', the opera (Act 1 by C.F. Cesarini, Act 2 by A. Caldara, Act 3 by A. Scarlatti) intended for performance in Vienna in 1711, but cancelled: watercolour from the presentation copy of the score made for Joseph I (A-Wn Cod.16.682, f.138)

Various traits have been suggested: dynamism, open form, degree of ornamentation, sharp contrast, co-existence of diverse styles, individualism, affective representation and numerous others. Most of these qualities, while they may contrast with the Renaissance, do not hold for any extended period. Although the style of Gesualdo is dynamic and open-formed, that of Alessandro Scarlatti is not. While Caccini's music is ornamented, Corelli's fundamentally is not (although it sometimes invited ornamentation); besides, the style of the 1740s or 1770s was also ornamented. The sharp contrasts observed in the late sacred concertos of Gabrieli are less striking or at least appear normal in an opera of Cesti. Diverse styles have co-existed in many periods, if perhaps less in the

Renaissance. Individualism became even more pronounced in the later 18th century than it was in the 17th. These qualities have served mainly to distinguish from the Renaissance the style that immediately succeeded it. They are less useful to delimit the Baroque or to distinguish it from subsequent styles.

Only one of the general characteristics mentioned survives an analysis of 17th- and 18th-century music and musical thought: the attitude towards affective expression. From the 1540s to at least the 1720s composers in a preponderant share of their music strove for the expression of affective states, whether or not inspired by a text. It is this striving that led to the extravagances that were first deplored as 'Baroque'. Irregularity, amplification, strangeness and grotesqueness, qualities inherent in the word, were often the very products of the search for expression. Anyone who did not understand the motivation behind these manners (like a Frenchman listening to Italian recitative or Vivaldi's violin concertos) could well have found a work embodying them bizarre.

The movement to express the affections was based on the recognition of the existence of distinguishable states of mind or feeling, such as sorrow, admiration, gladness, fear, anger, hope, joy or calm. These were thought to be accompanied by physical conditions that reached a certain stability in the person seized by the passion. This preoccupation with the passions was stimulated by several factors: the revival in the 16th century of the rhetorical treatises of Aristotle, Quintilian and Cicero, which not only described the passions but urged the orator's obligation to stir them; by the renewed reading of the *Poetics* of Aristotle, which emphasized the arousal of pity and fear and the imitation of human actions and passions; and by the general atmosphere of tolerance of the passions, which earlier had been seen as weaknesses of the flesh, and appreciation for the innate value of deep feeling.

Although the urge for expression of the affections persisted throughout the period under consideration, the means by which it was achieved were continually changing. Poets first set the example by paying more attention to emotional expression, and musicians adopted the moving of the passions as their principal objective. This is already evident in the school of Willaert; his own *Musica nova*, compiled in the early 1540s though published in 1559, may be considered the watershed that parts the Renaissance from the beginning of a new stylistic era, the Baroque, if one so wishes to call it. Side by side with works that are exemplary of Renaissance classicism are a few pieces, like *Aspro core*, that point in new directions. Several pupils of Willaert, particularly Cipriano de Rore and Nicola Vicentino, became the fountainheads of the new idiom. Monteverdi gave to the new style a name, *seconda pratica*. Certain more recent critics have called the 16th-century phase 'mannerism', but that term is better reserved for the rhetorical style of for example Marenzio in the madrigal and Lassus in the motet, a style often more concerned with illusionistic images than with affective expression.

Better understanding of physiology, particularly the circulation of the blood and the action of the nerves, spelt the downfall of the affections in the 18th century. At the same time musical artists became disillusioned with the mechanization that the process of affective expression underwent in Italian opera. A new conception of the emotions as fleeting, constantly shifting and conflicting reactions of the mind and body to internal, external and imaginary stimuli, as exemplified by the association psychology of David Hume and David Hartley, took the place of the *Affektenlehre* (see RHETORIC AND MUSIC, §I, 4). The shift is reflected in the practice of Italian composers from about 1730 and can also be documented in the attitudes of critics. Daniel Webb (*Observations in the Correspondence between Poetry and Music*, London, 1769, p.47) observed that the arousal of feelings by music is 'not, as some have imagined, the results of any fixed or permanent condition of the nerves and spirits, but springs from a succession of impressions, and is greatly augmented by sudden or gradual transitions from one kind of strain of vibrations to another'. The music of the 1730s and

1740s by Pergolesi, Hasse and Jommelli, for example, no longer relied on the static passions of the preceding decades but exploited the possibilities of dynamic flux and transition of sentiment. The advent of the sentimental style, which Pluche heralded as the 'musique chantante', marked the end of the period under consideration.

Thus the two centuries between roughly 1540 and 1730 can legitimately be considered an artistic era united by a common ideal, and, if one must find a word for it, 'Baroque' is defensible as a designation. Adoption of the term should not obscure the fact that there is no unity of either idiom or creative directions in this period. Not only do Renaissance practices (and in that sense the Renaissance) continue through much of the 16th century, but the ideals that can be embraced in the concept of Baroque reigned in parts of Europe as late as 1750, while elsewhere a counter-Baroque reaction had set in.

Whether the chronological limits and spirit of the Baroque in music coincide with those in other arts – painting, sculpture, architecture, theatre, literature, dance – can best be determined not by searching for analogies or parallels but by investigating the motivation for certain artistic directions. Perhaps even more important is to recognize the forces that led these arts in common directions. To define these for all the arts is beyond the scope of this article; but some of the forces that shaped Baroque music may be outlined.

The most important stimulus for a new style in the 16th century was HUMANISM. The new knowledge and aspirations that emanated from the revival of ancient learning affected music in numerous ways. The poetry of Petrarch, itself inspired by that of antiquity, became the model for modern poetry and prompted an intense search for new expressive means for setting it to music. The overthrow of the Boethian theory through the fresh insights offered by Ptolemy and Aristoxenus opened up the recognition of chromatic resources and the possibilities of tonal organization outside the modes. Ancient memories of a music that powerfully affected the feelings and morals of men inspired composers to seek similar effects through polyphonic and, later, monodic music, which was thought to correspond more closely to the ancient. Greek tragedy, which by the interpretation of Aristotle's *Poetics* and other recently studied texts could be shown to have been sung throughout, became a model for a style of music that could be sung on the stage for not just certain lyrical moments, as in Renaissance theatre, but for the entire drama.

Experimental science, closely linked with humanism in that it began as a testing of the doctrines found in ancient texts, was another important source of new trends. Discovery of the true cause and nature of sound, pitch and pitch relations liberated musical thought from the numerology that had preserved certain myths (such as the sanctity of the number six as the determinant of consonance). This paved the way for equal temperament and intermodulation among a wide circle of keys. The scientific movement also stimulated Rameau to develop a theory that replaced the purely pragmatic chordal systems of thoroughbass figuring.

The influence of the counter-Reformation on the direction music took in the late 16th century has probably been overestimated. But it surely hastened the secularization of church styles through the introduction of motets for solo or few voices and vernacular oratorios that were essentially in the style of the theatre. These styles eventually spread to the Protestant churches of Germany, England and France.

The patronage of music as an instrument of diplomacy intensified during the second half of the 16th century, particularly among the cardinals in Rome and in the Italian principalities of the Medici, Este and Gonzaga families. Meanwhile in mercantile centres such as Venice, Naples, Hamburg and London, opera theatres that depended upon subscribers or leasers of boxes catered for a new middle class. Taste shifted at these centres from the mythological plots favoured at the princely courts to more realistic or historical subjects. Eventually commercial pressure led to the introduction of comic episodes and eventually comic intermezzos, leading to a counter-Baroque idiom that soon spread to instrumental and sacred genres. The growth of the bourgeois class also led to the establishment of musical academies, such as the Accademia Filarmonica of Verona, or in Germany of cadres of musicians hired by town councils to function both in the church and in the secular community and even in the university through a collegium musicum.

Insofar as these and similar underlying conditions for music-making were part of the intellectual and social substratum of artistic activity in general, music shares with the other arts a common source for stylistic change and continuity. It is not surprising, then, that the music of this period reveals certain superficial features that parallel those of artistic products in other media. The similarity of appearances should not, however, be attributed to a 'spirit of the time' – a Baroque *Zeitgeist* – but rather to the common underlying conditions that sometimes express themselves in uncanny resemblances.

A music historian can contribute more to the understanding of the Baroque as a cultural phenomenon by describing faithfully, as Bukofzer and Clercx have done, the technical features of the music of the period than by pursuing abstractions such as linear versus painterly and picturesque, or closed versus open forms.

4. TECHNICAL FEATURES OF BAROQUE MUSIC. The thoroughbass, which began as a shorthand to indicate the harmony implied by two outer voices, soon became a constructive device, a means of achieving continuity while leaving the upper voice or voices free to express a text or soar in instrumental fantasies. To define the scope of the Baroque period on the basis of the persistence of the thoroughbass has been challenged on the grounds that the basso continuo persists well into the 1770s, by which time a new style had crystallized. This is not a serious objection, however, because by 1722, when Rameau published his *Traité de l'harmonie*, it was evident that a more complex set of considerations ruled the practice of composers than the counterpoint of the outer parts and its chordal filling. A system of relations between triads in a given key and between those and certain supporting triads from outside the key was implicit in the music being written towards the end of the Baroque period. The thoroughbass after the 1740s was an accompaniment convention, and ceased to have much effect on orchestral or choral texture; indeed, it became a sorely inadequate means of notating the accompaniment to solo voices or instruments.

The wish to prolong the rather manneristic and fleeting expressions of particular passions for longer spans than could be achieved through the recitative or even the arioso passages of the early monodies led to the adoption of the strophic variation and of various extended harmonic patterns, such as the aria della romanesca, Ruggiero, ballo del gran duca, the descending tetrachord and similar ostinatos. These permitted both the prolongation of a reigning affection and the constant renewal of melodic invention and ornamentation. That practice too faded out about the 1740s, to be replaced by variations on closed forms, such as minuets, operatic arias and the like, which find their beginnings but not their ultimate flowering in the *doubles* of Baroque dance suites.

A consequence of the thoroughbass practice was to throw the high-pitched voices into relief: and this produced a texture that persisted from the first decade of the 17th century to the 1740s. One or a pair of treble voices elaborated their lines, often through canonic and imitative or other motivic interplay, over a bass that determined or defined the harmonic motion, while other parts or chordal instruments occupied a subordinate filler role. Such a texture may involve non-treble voices, and several such ensembles may be found to proceed simultaneously with more or less interaction.

A specialization of functions resulted from this texture, some instruments fulfilling a function of harmonic 'stuffing' or ripieno, others a solo role. This division of labour, and not the polychoral medium, was the true source of the vocal and instrumental concerto. The 16th-century polychoral idiom and its amplification in the 17th century, which Della Corte identified as a genuine Baroque strain in Italian music, was actually a late survival of the *coro spezzato* technique popular in the Veneto from about 1520. Its true significance for the Baroque is that the polychoral texture served as a model for the earliest attempts at writing church music for few solo voices. The division of ripieno and solo functions together with the antiphonal contrasts inspired by polychoral music produced new combinations of solo and tutti vocal and instrumental ensembles. These combinations result in what is sometimes called the 'concertato style' but is really a concertato medium that lent itself to a variety of styles.

Patterns of stylistic decorum emerged, were consolidated and eventually dissolved during this period. Marco Scacchi recognized that, whereas in the earlier music one style and practice dominated, in his age there were three styles, church, chamber and theatre, and two practices, the ancient and modern, later called strict and free (*Breve discorso sopra la musica moderna*, Warsaw, 1649). Particular styles and practices were thought fitting for particular recreational, entertainment or devotional functions. Stylistic decorum did not prevent the borrowing of styles, however, as when the theatre style was introduced into the chamber or church. But when these styles were borrowed, they were subjected to a process of abstraction and conventionalization that purified them of offensive or distracting connotations, as when recitative or aria was admitted into the church, or dances into a chamber sonata. These distinctions tended to dissolve towards the end of the period, and by the mid-18th century a common style emerged that passed freely from genre to genre and from one social usage to another.

The rhythmic practices of Baroque music reflected the conventions of stylistic decorum. The principal schemes of rhythmic organization were founded on the dance and on speech. To these must be added the *alla breve* of the *stile antico*, continued from an earlier age for the sake of religious propriety. While the rhythm of speech ruled the recitative and arioso, the rhythm of dance governed the aria and chorus. Even keyboard genres and violin sonatas were permeated by this dichotomy. The different dances and their metres became the models for characteristic music that evoked certain affections through association and through mysterious affinities that were perceived between feelings and movement.

Most Baroque composers navigated the uncharted waters of pre-tonality. Some, to be sure, continued to be guided by the church modes, but Vincenzo Galilei was probably more observant than prophetic when he celebrated their demise in 1589 (*Il primo libro della prattica del contrapunto intorno all'uso delle consonanze*, ed. F. Rempp, Cologne, 1980). The dissolution of the modal system was in fact well under way by the 1530s. The return to a key pitch within a discrete piece replaced the unity of mode, and excursions into closely related keys replaced the admissible cadences of modal polyphony. On the other hand, the constraints that tonal writing began to acquire in the middle of the 18th century did not yet hamper composers in the period. The continuous modulation of the recitatives, the innocence with which keys fluctuated in an opera or mass, the inconsistency of modulatory schemes in the concertos: these are evidences of a free exploration of the resources that the new tunings offered.

200 years are a long time in the quickly paced culture of the West. Even the very general characteristics proposed above for the Baroque had to be couched in developmental terms. It is useful, therefore, to divide the period into more homogeneous sub-periods, with the understanding that no border formalities were invoked in passing from one to the other.

The late 16th and early 17th centuries were times of exploration of new resources, such as chromaticism, dissonance, tonality, monody, recitative, and new vocal and instrumental combinations. No consistent approach to composition emerged until about 1640, by which time the new resources were tamed, and a fairly homogeneous style arose in Italy that was to spread everywhere in Europe in the next generation. The period between 1640 and 1690 was a relatively stable one in which genres such as the trio sonata and da capo aria enjoyed a sureness, yet freshness, that has led some to call this a classical phase. From 1690 to 1730 genres such as the aria, concerto and sonata reached an almost overripe elaborateness, and the once spontaneous expression of the affections became formalized, at its worst mechanized. A reaction became inevitable. A new style began to manifest itself in the comic intermezzos to the *opera seria*, more natural in its melody, more varied in its rhythms, simpler yet more moving in its harmonies and, most important, truer to the flow of human sensibilities.

Generalizations of this kind are charged with oversimplifications and admit of abundant exceptions. But there is enough truth to them to make an observer from the vantage point of the 21st century comfortable with the proposition that the period from the late 16th century to 1730 knew some continuity and homogeneity, and that the period might for practical purposes be summed up in a word, 'Baroque'.

BIBLIOGRAPHY

MGG2 (S. Leopold)
C. Sachs: 'Barokmusik', *JbMP 1919*, 7–15

H.J. Moser: 'Die Zeitgrenzen des Musik: Barock', *ZMw*, iv (1921–2), 579–603
E. Wellesz: *Der Beginn des musikalischen Barocks und die Anfänge der Oper in Wien* (Vienna and Leipzig, 1922; Eng. trans. in *Essays on Opera*, London, 1950, pp.13ff)
E. Katz: *Die musikalischen Stilbegriffe des 17. Jahrhunderts* (Berlin, 1926)
T. Kroyer: 'Zwischen Renaissance und Barock', *JbMP 1927*, 45–54
R. Haas: *Die Musik des Barocks* (Potsdam, 1928)
B. Croce: *Storia della età barocca in Italia* (Bari, 1929)
A. Della Corte: 'Il barocco e la musica', *RaM*, vi (1933), 253–66
E. Schenk: 'Über Begriff und Wesen des musikalischen Barock', *ZMw*, xvii (1935), 377–91
M.F. Bukofzer: 'Allegory in Baroque Music', *Journal of the Warburg and Courtauld Institutes*, iii (1940), 1–21
P.H. Lang: 'The Baroque', 'The Late Baroque', *Music in Western Civilization* (New York, 1941/R), 314–429, 430–529
R. Wellek: 'The Concept of Baroque in Literary Scholarship', *Journal of Aesthetics and Art Criticism*, v (1946–7), 77–106; repr. with 'Postscript 1962' in *Concepts of Criticism* (New Haven, 1963), 69–127
M.F. Bukofzer: *Music in the Baroque Era, from Monteverdi to Bach* (New York, 1947)
S. Clercx: *Le Baroque et la musique: essai d'esthétique musicale* (Brussels, 1948/R)
C. Cudworth: 'Baroque, Rococo, Galant, Classic', *MMR*, lxxxiii (1953), 172–81
W. Gerstenberg: 'Die Krise der Barockmusik', *AMw*, x (1953), 81–94
J.H. Mueller: 'Baroque: is it Datum, Hypothesis, or Tautology?', *Journal of Aesthetics and Art Criticism*, xii (1953–4), 421–37
L. Schrade: 'Sulla natura del ritmo barocco', *RMI*, lvi (1954), 3–27
M. Bukofzer: 'The Baroque in Music History', *Journal of Aesthetics and Art Criticism*, xiv (1955), 152–6
R. Stamm, ed.: *Die Kunstformen des Barockzeitalters* (Munich, 1956)
Le 'Baroque' musical: Wégimont IV 1957
H.H. Eggebrecht: 'Barock als musikgeschichtliche Epoche', *Aus der Welt des Barock* (Stuttgart, 1957), 168–91
V.L. Tapié: *Baroque et classicisme* (Paris, 1957, 2/1972; Eng. trans., 1960 as *The Age of Grandeur: Baroque Art and Architecture*)
R.E. Wolf: 'Renaissance, Mannerism, Baroque: Three Styles, Three Periods', *Le 'Baroque' musical: Wégimont IV 1957*, 35–80
G. Barblan: 'Il termine *Barocco* e la musica', *Miscelánea en homenaje a Monseñor Higino Anglés* (Barcelona, 1958–61), i, 93–108
J. Chailley, ed.: *Précis de musicologie* (Paris, 1958, 2/1984)
A. Harman and A. Milner: *Late Renaissance and Baroque Music (c.1525–c.1750)* (London, 1959, 2/1962/R)
L. Ronga: 'La musica', *La civiltà veneziana nell'età barocca: Venice 1958* (Florence, 1959), 123–44
O. Kurtz: 'Barocco: storia di una parola', *Lettere italiane*, xii (1960), 414–44
A. Milner: *The Musical Aesthetic of the Baroque* (Oxford, 1960)
L. Ronga: 'Un problema culturale di moda: il barocco e la musica', *L'esperienza storica della musica* (Bari, 1960), 144–216
F. Blume: 'Begriff und Grenze des Barock in der Musik', *STMf*, xliii (1961), 77–87
N. Dufourcq: 'Terminologia organistica', *L'organo*, ii (1961), 43–52
V.L. Tapié: *Le Baroque* (Paris, 1961)
Manierismo, barocco, rococò: concetti e termini: Rome 1960 (Rome, 1962)
F. Blume: *Renaissance and Baroque Music* (New York, 1967) [Eng. trans. of articles from *MGG1*]
C.V. Palisca: *Baroque Music* (Englewood Cliffs, NJ, 1968, 3/1991)
A. Salop: 'On Stylistic Unity in Renaissance–Baroque Distinctions', *Essays in Musicology: a Birthday Offering for Willi Apel*, ed. H. Tischler (Bloomington, IN, 1968), 107–21
R. Stricker: *Musique du Baroque* (Paris, 1968)
G. Stefani: *Musica e religione nell'Italia barocca* (Palermo, 1975)
G. Cowart: *The Origins of Modern Musical Criticism: French and Italian Music, 1600–1750* (Ann Arbor, 1981)
L. Bianconi: *Il Seicento* (Turin, 1982; Eng. trans. 1987)
R. Donington: *Baroque Music: Style and Performance* (London, 1982)
C. Palisca: 'Barock', *HMT* (1987)
C. Palisca: '"Baroque" as a Music-Critical Term', *French Musical Thought, 1600–1800*, ed. G. Cowart (Ann Arbor, 1989), 7–21
J.A. Sadie, ed.: *Companion to Baroque Music* (London, 1990)
T. Carter: *Music in Late Renaissance and Early Baroque Italy* (London, 1992)

J.H. Baron: *Baroque Music: a Research and Information Guide* (New York, 1993)

N. Anderson: *Baroque Music: from Monteverdi to Handel* (London, 1994)

CLAUDE V. PALISCA

Baroxyton. A bass brass instrument invented by VÁCLAV FRANTIŠEK ČERVENÝ.

Bärpfeife (?Ger., ?Dut.). *See under* ORGAN STOP.

Barra [Barat], **Hotinet** [Hottinet, Houtinet, Hutinet, Jehan, Jean] (*b* ?Montigny-le-Roi; *fl* 1510–23). French composer and singer. Under the name of 'Jehan Barat' he was an haut-contre at the Ste Chapelle, Paris, in 1510–12. As 'Jean Barat dit Hottinet' he was *maître de chapelle* of Langres Cathedral from 1512 to at least July 1514, and as 'Hanotin Barra' he returned to the Ste Chapelle in October 1523. In musical sources he is always 'Hotinet' or 'Hotinet Barra'. Although some of his music is preserved in Italian sources, there is no reason to suppose he travelled to Italy. He must not be confused with Johannes Lomont [Zanin Lumon], called 'Ottinet', a singer from the diocese of Cambrai and member of the ducal chapel in Milan from 1473 until his death in 1493, who applied unsuccessfully for a transfer to the ducal chapel of Ferrara in 1479 and was provost of St Géry, Cambrai, from 1480 to 1489–91, residing there briefly in 1482.

Like many of his French contemporaries, Barra favoured a style built predominantly on short, frequently imitative duets, often overlapped to produce a full-voiced texture. He used fewer melismas and less homophony than Mouton and Févin, his obvious models, but he maintained the clear structural articulation typical of their work. The most widely disseminated composition ascribed to Barra, *Nuptiae factae sunt*, also appears with an ascription to Elimot, a composer known otherwise by a single motet (*Ascendens Christus in altum*, 4vv, *I-Bc* Q20); neither the sources nor stylistic considerations seem to provide adequate grounds for resolving the conflict. Two of Barra's motets published by Attaingnant form part of a Parisian cycle of 'O' antiphon settings (see Wright for the distinctive chant melody employed); *O radix Jesse* in particular is distinguished by its reliance on cantus-firmus construction. The rather widely distributed mass *'Ecce panis angelorum'* paraphrases the plainsong of part of the Corpus Christi sequence *Lauda Sion* in its tenor. Imitation moves motifs of the chant into the other voices, and other chant melodies are quoted from time to time, notably 'Bone pastor' (another section of *Lauda Sion*) and 'O salutaris hostia' (a eucharistic strophe of the hymn *Verbum supernum*).

WORKS
all for 4vv

Edition: *Treize livres de motets parus chez Pierre Attaingnant en 1534 et 1535*, ed. A. Smijers and A.T. Merritt (Paris and Monaco, 1934–64) [S]

Missa 'Ecce panis angelorum', *B-Br* IV.922, *D-Bsb* 40091, *F-CA* 4, *I-Rvat* C.S.26

Missa, *CMac* L(B)

Magnificat secundi toni (i), 1534[7], *Pc*; S v

Magnificat secundi toni (ii), 1534[7], *Pc*, *NL-'sH*; S v

Nuptiae factae sunt, 1521[3], *CH-SGs* 463, ed. in MRM, iv (1968) (attrib. Elimot in *I-Fl* acq.e.doni 666; anon. in 10 other sources); O radix Jesse, 1534[9], S vii; O Rex gentium, 1534[9], S vii; Peccantem me quotidie, *Bc* Q19, ed. in SCMot, vi (19??; Salve regina, 1535[4], S xii; Verbum iniquum et dolosum, 1539[10]

BIBLIOGRAPHY

M. Brenet: *Les musiciens de la Sainte-Chapelle du Palais* (Paris, 1910/*R*)

F. Lesure: 'La maîtrise de Langres au XVIe siècle', *RdM*, lii (1966), 202–3

E.E. Lowinsky: *The Medici Codex of 1518 ... Historical Introduction and Commentary*, MRM, iii (1968)

D. Crawford: *Sixteenth-Century Choirbooks in the Archivio Capitolare at Casale Monferrato*, RMS, ii (1975)

L. Lockwood: *Music in Renaissance Ferrara, 1400–1505* (Oxford, 1984), 174–6

C. Wright: *Music and Ceremony at Notre Dame of Paris, 500–1550* (Cambridge, 1989), 106

L. Matthews: 'Reconstruction of the Personnel of the Ducal Choir in Milan, 1480–1499', *Musica e storia*, vi (1998), 297–311

P. Merkley: 'Trading Lombardy for Picardy: Milanese Ducal Musicians and the Cathedral of Saint-Géry', *Musica e storia*, vi (1998), 313–26

JOSHUA RIFKIN/RICHARD SHERR

Barrachina, Clemente (*b* Teruel, *c*1650; *d* Albarracín, 1727). Spanish composer. He was a choirboy at Teruel Cathedral in 1664 and later studied theology and music in Madrid. In 1675 he succeeded Ortells as *maestro de capilla* of Albarracín Cathedral, where he remained for over 50 years. He composed a large number of polychoral works in five to eight parts for the cathedral services, as well as villancicos (now lost) each year for Christmas and Corpus Christi. The surviving works (all in the archives of Albarracín Cathedral) are mostly for two choirs, contrasting a contrapuntal texture for the first choir (typically in two parts) and a more homophonic style for the fuller second choir. They show an able command of structure and sonority.

WORKS

Edition: *Clemente Barrachina: Opera omnia*, ed. J.M. Muneta (Teruel, 1992–5) [M i–ii]
with instruments unless otherwise stated

Vespers music: Beatus vir, 6vv; Crédidi, 6vv; Deus in adjutorium, 6vv; Dixit Dominus, 6vv; Dixit Dominus, 8vv; Laetatus sum, 7vv; Lauda Jerusalem, 6vv; Laudate Dominum, 6vv; Laudate Dominum, 7vv; Mag, 6vv; Mag, 8vv: all ed. in M i

Other works: Cum invocarem (Ps iv), ST, SATB; Mirabilia (Ps cxviii.9), S, S, SATB; Principes (Ps cxviii.11), ST, SATB; Qui habitat (Ps xc), SS, SATB; Salve regina, S, S, T, B, SATB; Salve regina, S, SATB, 1726; Verbum caro (responsory for Christmas), S, S, SATB, unacc.: all ed. in M ii

Doubtful: Cogitavit Dominus (Lamentation for Maundy Thursday), S, T, SATB; Veni Sancte Spiritus, S, SATB, SATB: both ed. in M ii

BIBLIOGRAPHY

J.M. Muneta: 'Apuntes para la historia de la música en la catedral de Albarracín (Teruel): los maestros de capilla y organistas', *RdMc*, vi (1983), 329–71

J.M. Muneta: *Catálogo del Archivo de música de la catedral de Albarracín* (Teruel, 1984)

JESUS M. MUNETA MARTÍNEZ

Barradas [Pérez-Barradas], **(María del) Carmen** (*b* Montevideo, 18 March 1888; *d* Montevideo, 12 May 1963). Uruguayan composer and pianist. She began composing in her childhood and studied with Antonio Franck. Later she entered the Conservatorio Musical La Lira to study with Aurora, Vicente Pablo and Martín López. In 1914 she settled in Spain and began to develop a new and revolutionary system of musical notation, based on graphic designs similar to those that came in use 50 years later, shocking Spanish and French musicians and critics. Using that system she composed *Fabricación* (1922), a piano work that reproduced the sound of a factory working full blast. This work, *Aserradero*, along with *Taller mecánico*, which she performed in Madrid and Barcelona, established her as a pioneer of modern music, giving her immediate success in Spain and France, where music and art critics, such as André Clavier in Paris and Adolfo Salazar and Eugenio d'Ors in Madrid, praised her works. All her scores have covers featuring the drawings of her brother, the painter Rafael Barradas. In about 1928 she returned to Montevideo, where she began teaching choral singing at the Instituto Normal and continued her career as a composer. She gave her last piano recital in Montevideo in 1934.

WORKS

Chbr: Pf Trio
Vocal: Children songs (several series); Eterno romance (triptych; homage to A. Storni)
Pf: Aserradero; En el molino; Mar Tragédia Misterio, triptych; Procesión; Taller mecánico; Ensayos (cycle), 1919; Fabricación, 1922; Oración a Santos Vega, 1933; Estudios tonales, 1940

BIBLIOGRAPHY

S. Salgado: *Breve historia de la música culta en el Uruguay* (Montevideo, 1971, 2/1980)
M. Ficher, M.Furman Schleifer and J.M. Furman: *Latin American Composers: a Biographical Dictionary* (Lanham, MD, and London, 1996)

SUSANA SALGADO

Barrae, Leonardo. *See* BARRÉ, LEONARDO.

Barraine, Elsa (Jacqueline) (*b* Paris, 13 Feb 1910). French composer. She studied composition at the Paris Conservatoire with Dukas, who instilled in her a strong sense of colour and a classical spirit. She took *premiers prix* in harmony in 1925 and in fugue and accompaniment in 1927. In 1929 she received the Prix de Rome for her sacred trilogy *La vierge guerrière*. She then worked at French Radio, first as a pianist, sound recordist and as head of singing (1936–40) then after the war as a sound mixer. From 1944 to 1947 she was musical director of the recording firm Chant du Monde. In 1953 she became professor of sight-reading and analysis at the Conservatoire, a post she held until 1974.

Barraine's compositions exhibit rigorous technique alongside naturalness and finesse. The work which made her name as a composer, the symphonic variations *Harald Harfagard* (1930), after Heinrich Heine, was the first of many to draw on a literary inspiration: notable later examples include the Eluard settings *Avis* and *L'homme sur terre*. Her works, while disciplined in form, are characterized by expressive intensity as well as a passionate feeling for the human condition and a sensitivity to the social and political disruptions of our time. Her music is essentially tonal, with the exception of the serial *Musique rituelle* (1966–7), inspired by the Tibetan Book of the Dead. Barraine may be considered one of the outstanding French composers of the mid-20th century.

WORKS
(selective list)

Dramatic: Le mur (ballet, R. de Jouvenal), 1947; Pattes blanches (film score, dir. J. Grémillon), 1948; Printemps de la liberté (incid music, J. Grémillon), 1948; La chanson du mal-aimé (ballet, after G. Apollinaire), 1950; Claudine à l'école (ballet, Colette), 1950; Le sabotier du Val de Loire (film score, dir. J. Demy), 1956
Orch: Harald Harfagard, sym. variations after H. Heine, 1930; Sym. [no.1], 1931; Pogromes, 1933; Sym. [no.2], 1938; Suite astrologique, small orch, 1945; Variations sur 'Le fleuve rouge', 1945; Hommage à Prokofiev, hpd, orch, 1953; 3 ridicules, 1955; Les jongleurs, 1959; Les tziganes, 1959
Vocal: Avis (P. Eluard), chorus, orch, 1944; Poésie ininterrompue (cant., Eluard), 3 solo vv, orch, 1948; L'homme sur terre (Eluard), chorus, orch, 1949; La nativité (L. Masson), solo vv, chorus, orch, 1951; Les cinq plaies (M. Manoll), solo vv, chorus, orch, 1952;

Les paysans (A. Frenaud), 4 solo vv, chbr orch, 1958; De premier mai en premier mai (Eluard), 4 mixed vv, chorus, unacc., 1977
Chbr: Wind Qnt, 1931; Improvisation, sax, pf, 1947; Variations, perc, pf, 1950; Atmosphère, ob, 10 str, 1966; Musique rituelle (Bardo Thödol), org, gongs, xylorimba, 1966–7
Kbd: Hommage à Paul Dukas, 1936; Marche du printemps sans amour, 1946; Fantaisie, hpd, 1961
Principal publishers: Costallat, Durand, Salabert, Schott

FRANÇOISE ANDRIEUX/JAMES R. BRISCOE

Barraqué, Jean (Henri Alphonse) (*b* Puteaux, Seine, 17 Jan 1928; *d* Paris, 17 Aug 1973). French composer. His family moved to Paris when he was a small child, but the place that mattered most to him was the Breton coast, where he was taken on visits by his nanny, to stay with her family in Trelevern. In 1940 he entered the Notre Dame choir school, and there underwent a total conversion to music when he heard a recording of Schubert's 'Unfinished' Symphony in a teacher's study. His education continued at the Lycée Condorcet (1943–7), with Langlais (around 1947) and in Messiaen's class (1948–51).

Though he was composing abundantly during this period, he salvaged nothing before three songs of 1950, to words from the Song of Songs, Baudelaire and Rimbaud, out of which *Séquence* emerged in 1955. His intellectual development during the interim – the period also of his Piano Sonata – was powerfully influenced by his relationship with Michel Foucault: *Séquence*, with its texts now from Nietzsche, and the Sonata both embrace a lyrical violence and accept the responsiblity of greatness. No longer guaranteed either by metaphysical or linguistic certainties, for Barráque the musical work had to be a Promethean act of creation from out of the void. Like Boulez, he accepted the inevitability of serialism, but more on philosophical grounds (as a symptom of the abeyance of authority) than as a necessity of musical history, and he departed far from Boulez in his music's dynamism: his published works, numbering only six, are all substantial, continuous and urgent. (The only minor work he produced after 1950 is a study in *musique concrète*, which came out of the time he spent, between 1951 and 1954, in the Groupe de Recherche de Musique Concrète.) In this insistence on forward movement, Beethoven was not merely his model but his ideal, and his high view of the artist's vocation was of a piece with that ideal.

His realization of a Beethovenian dialectic was based on various polarities, in particular between perceptions of notes as either autonomous sounds or elements within the unfolding of a serial form, between freedom and fixity in the registral placing of notes, between pulsed and pulseless rhythm, and between sound and silence. The Piano Sonata exerts itself across all these axes, and across another, which the composer describes in the sonata's preface: the opposition between a 'free style' of motifs and chords in easy flow and a 'strict style' of intensive, quasi-automatic process acknowledging the 'total' serialism of the time. Elements of compulsion are spurs to protest, but protest is compromised by having to be voiced in the same language, based on the same series. Barraqué found this a limitation. In *Séquence* he tried to moderate what he called 'serial tonality' by using two series – separately in the first two songs, together in the last – and in later works he developed a technique of 'proliferating series', similar to Messiaen's practice of rhythmic interversion, but with a quite different intention, to make possible a music of continuous change. However, the musical chains in the Sonata provide it with the means to an artistic success in speaking with the vehemence of despair. The 40-minute work is in two large sections, the first generally fast and the second generally slow, seeming to undermine all that had been promised.

While writing the Sonata and *Séquence*, and for several years thereafter, Barraqué earned a living from educational broadcasts, lectures, programme notes and classes; then from 1961 to 1970 he held a research post at the Centre National des Recherches Scientifiques to do work on Debussy, though he continued to give private classes in analysis and composition. *Séquence* received its first performance at a Domaine Musical concert in 1956, and the recording was released on disc in 1958 with Yvonne Loriod's account of the Sonata. This LP, backed by André Hodeir's acclamation of the composer in his 1961 book, assured Barraqué an international reputation, and his works, starting with *Séquence* in 1963, began to be published by Aldo Bruzzichelli, a Florentine businessman.

By this time Barraqué had embarked on a massive project. At Foucault's instigation he read Hermann Broch's novel *The Death of Virgil* in 1955; almost at once he began making plans to devote the rest of his life to a vast system of musical settings and commentaries. Of these, *Le temps restitué* was drafted in 1956–7 and . . . *au-delà du hasard* completed in 1959 for a Domaine Musical concert early the next year. But copious problems – alcoholism, desperation, a car accident in 1964 – got in the way of composition, and *La mort de Virgile* had to wait until 1966 before receiving its third instalment, *Chant après chant*, which was also its last. In 1968 Barraqué completed two old enterprises, *Le temps restitué* and a concerto he had planned for Hubert Rostaing, the principal clarinettist in the first performance of . . . *au-delà du hasard*. In both cases there was the prompt of an immediate performance, at the Royan Festival in the case of *Le temps restitué* and by the BBC in that of the Concerto. Other parts of *La mort de Virgile* were begun or restarted, but nothing much else was accomplished.

However, the Broch cycle was surely meant to be incomplete and to speak of incompletion. Barraqué based all his endeavours on the second part of the novel, which treats Virgil's night of anguish and hopelessness in the face of what he sees as the failure of his epic; the music is magniloquent, furious and constantly mobile, responding at once to the poetic subject, to the wild Breton sea that Barraqué loved, and to his sense of himself as a descendant not only of Beethoven but of Debussy. In each of the three finished sections of *La mort de Virgile* there is a soprano soloist, but she seems to be speaking directly to the poet rather than of or for him, as if Barraqué had made his works to enter into dialogue with himself as creator. Typical, too, is the cascading of alternative voices, whether from choruses, from solo piano (a main player in all four works in which it appears, though Barraqué himself was not a performer), or from groupings of instruments. Such doubt about the expressive centre is a feature also of the Concerto, in which the clarinet takes some time to arrive (and the secondary vibraphone soloist even longer), and in which the orchestration may be aligned with or against the division of the ensemble into six trios.

Barraqué's final years saw some public successes. He was present at two recordings of the Sonata, by Claude Helffer (1969, for Valois) and Roger Woodward (1972, for EMI), and at one each of *Séquence* and *Chant après chant* (both 1969, again for Valois). He also made a rare appearance to speak at the Royan Festival, just four months before his death. He was buried at Trelevern. His music, after some years of neglect, began to excite conspicuous attention again in the late 1990s, when the complete published works appeared on the CPO label.

WORKS

Séquence (F. Nietzsche, trans. H. Albert), S, vn, vc, hp, pf, cel + glock, xyl + vib, 3 perc, 1950–55
Piano Sonata, 1950–52
Etude, tape, 1954
Le temps restitué (H. Broch, trans. A. Kohn), S, 12-pt chorus, 31 insts, 1956–7, completed 1968
. . . au-delà du hasard (Broch, trans. Kohn; Barraqué), S, SA, 20 insts in 4 groups incl. pf and cl soloists, 1957–9
Concerto, cl, vib, 6 trios, 1962–8
Chant après chant (Broch, trans. Kohn; Barraqué), S, pf, 6 perc, 1966
Unfinished works: Discours, S, A, 5 T, 4 B, pf, orch, 1961; Lysanias, 1966–73; Portiques du feu, 18vv; Hymnes à Plotia, str qt; L'homme couché (op), 1969–72; Affranchi du hasard, chorus, cls, 1970

Principal publishers: Bruzzichelli, Bärenreiter

WRITINGS

'Résonances privilégiées: leur justification', *Cahiers de la Compagnie Renaud-Barrault,* no.3 (1954), 32–45
'Des goûts et des couleurs . . . et où l'on en discute', *Domaine musical,* no.1 (1954), 14–23
'Rythme et développement', *Polyphonie,* no.9–10 (1954), 47–73
Debussy (Paris, 1962/R, 2/1994)
'Debussy ou l'approche d'une organisation autogène de la composition', *Debussy et l'évolution de la musique au XXe siècle: Paris 1962,* 83–95
'Propos impromptu', *Courrier musical de France,* no.26 (1969), 75–80
'*La Mer* de Debussy ou la naissance des formes ouvertes', *Analyse musicale,* no.12 (1988), 15–62

BIBLIOGRAPHY

KdG (H. Henrich)
A. Hodeir: *La musique depuis Debussy* (Paris, 1961; Eng. trans., New York, 1961)
G.W. Hopkins: 'Strasbourg: Barraqué's "Chant après chant"', *MT,* cvii (1966), 701
G.W. Hopkins: 'Jean Barraqué', *MT,* cvii (1966), 952–4
T. Souster: 'Who's Exhausted?', *Tempo,* no.87 (1968–9), 23–6
T. Souster: 'A Composer's Life-Work', *MT,* cx (1969), 66 only [review of *Chant après chant* and . . . *au-delà du hasard*]
G.W. Hopkins: 'Record Guide', *Tempo,* no.95 (1970–71), 37–40 [Sonata, *Séquence, Chant après chant*]
B. Hopkins: 'Barraqué's Piano Sonata', *The Listener* (27 Jan 1972)

Jean Barraqué, 1960

A. Jack: 'Jean Barraqué', *Music and Musicians*, xxi/4 (1972–3), 6–7 [interview]

A. Jack: '"A Contract with Death"', *Music and Musicians*, xxii/2 (1973–4), 6–7

R. Lyon, ed.: 'Portrait de Jean Barraqué', *Courrier musical de France*, no.44 (1973), 130–32

R. Toop: disc notes, Sonata, EMI EMSP 551 (1973)

B. Hopkins: 'Barraqué's Sonata', *Tempo* no.110 (1974), 48–50 [review of Woodward recording]

Dossier Barraqué (Champigny sur Marne, 1974)

R. Black: '". . .and each harmonical has a point of its own ..."', *PNM*, xvii (1978–9), 126–30

B. Hopkins: disc notes, Sonata, Unicorn UNS 263 (1978)

B. Hopkins: 'Barraqué and the Serial Idea', *PRMA*, cv (1978–9), 13–24

R. Black: 'Contemporary Notation and Performance Practice: Three Difficulties', *PNM*, xxii (1983–4), 117–46

A. Riotte: 'From Traditional to Formalized Analysis; in memoriam Jean Barraqué: some Examples Drawn from his Unpublished Analysis of Anton Webern's Piano Variations op.27', *Musical Grammars and Computer Analysis: Modena 1982*, 131–53

Entretemps, no.5 (1987) [Barraqué issue]

A. Poirier: 'L'histoire "toujours recommencée" . . .: introduction à la pensée analytique de Jean Barraqué', *Analyse musicale*, no.12 (1988), 9–13

R.-M. Janzen: 'A Biographical Chronology of Jean Barraqué', *PNM*, xxvii (1989), 234–45

P. Ozzard-Low: 'Barraqué – Broch – Heidegger: a Philosophical Introduction to the Music of Jean Barraqué', *Cahiers d'Etudes Germaniques*, no.16 (1989), 93–106

M. Mesnage and A. Riotte: 'Les Variations pour piano opus 27 d' Anton Webern: approche cellulaire barraquéenne et analyse assistée par ordinateur', *Analyse musicale*, no.14 (1989), 41–67

H. Pfaffenzeller: Review of recording of Concerto and *Le temps restitué*, *NZM*, Jg.152, nos.7–8 (1991), 89 only

Jean Barraqué, Musik-Konzepte, no.82 (1993)

H. Henrich: *Das Werk Jean Barraqués: Genese und Faktur* (Kassel, 1997)

PAUL GRIFFITHS

Barrat, Jean. *See* BARRA, JEHAN DE.

Barraud, Henry (*b* Bordeaux, 23 April 1900; *d* Paris, 28 Dec 1997). French composer. He began to compose at the age of 16 when he was studying harmony and counterpoint in Bordeaux, but his parents intended him for the wine trade, and he trained for this in London. However, he decided on a musical career, and entered the Paris Conservatoire in 1926 to study composition with Dukas, fugue with Caussade and, on the advice of Schmitt, composition and orchestration with Louis Aubert. He was soon expelled from the Conservatoire for having written a string quartet (now lost) that was considered outrageously innovatory. With Rivier he founded the Triton concerts in 1933, and in the same year Monteux conducted a symphonic finale, following this in 1934 with his *Poème*. He helped to organize Resistance broadcasting in occupied France; after the war he was made head of music for Radiodiffusion Française, becoming director of the Programme National in 1948. Besides raising French standards of orchestral playing and choral singing, he gained for French radio a reputation for welcoming music of all types, particularly new music. He continued to compose, but much of his finest work was done after his retirement in 1965.

Barraud combined a reserved demeanour and a critical spirit with deep and imaginative religious conviction and a great sensitivity to people as also to the arts. This dualism is to be found in his music. In some works, felicities of scoring and elegant solutions of formal problems follow too smoothly, adding up to an effect that can seem academic. At the other extreme there are pieces like the *Mystère des Saints Innocents*, the *Te Deum*, the *Trois études* and *Une saison en enfer* (for Barraud, as for Claudel, Rimbaud had a place alongside the Bible and the saints), works that make an immediate and profoundly moving impression. Between these poles there are pieces – such as the concertos for piano and for flute – which delight by continual grace and invention. Barraud was always a seeker, but he refused to employ avant-garde methods for reasons of effect or fashion. His lucid and illuminating book, *Pour comprendre les musiques d'aujourd'hui*, indicates the eagerness and critical alertness with which he followed new developments. In the 1960s he stopped composing for about two years in order 'to weigh the new contributions of the young generation, and see what in them could help me to enrich my own musical language without ceasing to remain faithful to myself'. After this period of reflection, his music took an altogether more adventurous path. His later works such as the *Variations à treize* use a more advanced style, breaking free of the traditional rhythmic and tonal constraints of much of his earlier music, and employ a vast array of percussion including prominent roles for tuned instruments.

WORKS
(selective list)

DRAMATIC

La farce de maître Pathelin (op, 1, G. Cohen, after medieval drama), 1938; Petits métiers (film score), 1942, arr. as sym. suite, 1942; La kermesse (ballet), 1, 1943; L'astrologue dans le puits (ballet, 1), 1948; Rimbaud (radio score), 1950; Numance (op, 2, S. de Madariaga, after Cervantes), 1950–52, ov. and interludes arr. as Symphonie de Numance, 1950; Lavinia (comic op, 3, F. Marceau), 1959; La fée aux miettes (radio score, after C. Nodier), 1968; Le roi Gordogane (chbr op, 3, R. Ivsic), 1974; Tête d'or (tragédie lyrique, 2, after P. Claudel), 1980

ORCHESTRAL

Finale of a Symphony, 1932; Poème, 1933; Conc. da camera, 1934; 4 préludes, str, 1935–7; Suite pour une comédie de Musset, str, 1937; Pf Conc., 1939; Offrande à une ombre, 1942; Images pour un poète maudit, after A. Rimbaud, 1954; Sym., str, 1955–6; Sym. no.3, 1957; Rapsodie cartésienne, 1959; Fl Conc., 1962; Rapsodie dionysienne, 1962; Divertimento, 1962; Sym. concertante, tpt, orch, 1966; 3 études, 1967; Une saison en enfer, after Rimbaud, 1968–9; Conc., str, 1971; Ouverture pour un opéra interdit, 1971

VOCAL

3 poèmes (P. Reverdy), 1v, pf, 1933; 2 choeurs, 2vv, pf/orch, 1933; 3 chansons de Gramedoch (V. Hugo: Cromwell), 1v, orch, 1935; Le feu (Old Testament), chorus, orch, 1937; 3 lettres de Mme de Sévigné, 1v, pf, 1938, orchd 1944; 4 poèmes de Lanza del Vasto, 1v, pf, 1942; Le testament de François Villon, 1v, chorus, hpd, 1945; Le mystère des Saints Innocents (C. Péguy), solo vv, chorus, orch, 1946–7; 8 chantefables pour les enfants sages (R. Desnos), 1v, pf, 1947; Cantate pour l'avènement du prince de Monaco, chorus, 1950; TeD, chorus, 16 winds, 1955; Pange lingua, S, Bar, chorus, orch, 1964; La divine comédie (Dante), 5 solo vv, orch, 1972; Enfance à Combourg (cant. after F.R. de Chateaubriand), children's chorus, 1976

CHAMBER AND SOLO INSTRUMENTAL

Histoires pour enfants, pf, 1933; Premiers pas, pf, 1933; Trio, ob, cl, bn, 1935; Str Trio, 1936, rev. 1943; Str Qt, 1940; Sonatine, vn, pf, 1941; 10 impromptus, pf, 1941; Musiques pour petites mains, pf, 1949; Concertino, pf, fl, cl, bn, hn, 1954; Variations à 13, 1969; Sax Qt, 1972

WRITINGS

Berlioz (Paris, 1955, 2/1966)

La France et la musique occidentale (Paris, 1956)

Pour comprendre les musiques d'aujourd'hui (Paris, 1968)

Les cinq grands opéras (Paris, 1972)

BIBLIOGRAPHY
F.Y. Bril, ed.: *Henry Barraud* (Neuilly-sur-Seine, 1982)
D. Pistone and P. de Prat: 'Henri Barraud et le théâtre lyrique', *Le théâtre lyrique français, 1945–1985*, ed. D. Pistone (Paris, 1987), 203–8

JONATHAN GRIFFIN/RICHARD LANGHAM SMITH

Barre (i) (Fr.). *See* BASS-BAR.

Barre (ii) (Fr.). The stopping of several or all the strings of a fretted string instrument at the same point, by the fingers (*see* BARRÉ) or artificially (*see* CAPO TASTO).

Barré [jeu barré] (Fr.: 'barred', 'stopped'; Ger. *Quergriff*; It. *capo tasto*; Sp. *cejuela*). In the playing of certain fretted plucked string instruments, particularly the lute, guitar and banjo, the term used to describe the technique of stopping all or several of the strings at the same point by holding a finger across them. Although the form of the word is adjectival the term is also used in writings in English as a noun; some English-speaking writers use 'bar' or 'barring', but the French forms *barré* or *jeu barré* are more frequently found. (In the music of the late 17th-century viol masters – particularly that of Marin Marais – the term *doigt couché* is used; *see* FINGERING, §II, 1.) The earliest references to the *barré* seem to date from the second half of the 17th century; Francisco Guerau's introduction to his *Poema harmónico* (1694), for example, advises the player to become accustomed to using the 'cejuela … putting the index finger of the left hand over more or less all the strings, depending on your requirements, which is very necessary in order to play certain passages'.

The essential characteristic of the *barré* is that it is executed with the flat of the finger, whereas the tips of the fingers are used for other fingering. The *barré* is usually executed with the forefinger, but other fingers are also used, particularly by jazz guitarists for the *half-barré* (that is, the stopping of two or more, but not all the strings). The purpose of the *barré* technique is to permit the fingering configurations used on the open strings to be transposed to any position on the fingerboard, the forefinger acting as a moveable nut. The fret at which the *barré* is applied may be indicated in written music: '2ᵉ barré' is a short form of '2ᵉ position barré', and similarly 'C II' stands for 'cejuela 2'; both indicate a *barré* at the second fret. If, for ease of execution, the player wishes to use open-string fingering for an entire piece, the strings may be artificially stopped with a CAPO TASTO (by setting the *capo tasto* across the first fret, the player can finger a piece in C♯ as if it were in C).

Barrè, Antonio (*b* Langres; *fl* Rome, 1551–72). French printer. He was a singer in the Cappella Giulia intermittently from March 1552 until at least the end of 1554, and was also active as a composer: in 1552 his *Madrigali a quattro voci* were printed in Rome by Valerio and Luigi Dorico.

In 1555 he began to print music, publishing a series of collections entitled 'delle muse', Vicentino's *L'antica musica ridotta alla moderna pratica* (1555; in 1551 Barrè had been a witness at the famous debate between Vicentino and Lusitano in Rome) and a few volumes devoted to single composers. His first publication, *Il primo libro delle muse a cinque* (1555), set a high standard, with canzone settings by Barrè himself, Berchem, Vincenzo Ruffo and Arcadelt, including Arcadelt's superb setting of Petrarch's *Chiare, fresch'e dolci acque*.

Barrè's *Primo libro delle muse a quattro voci* (1555) includes his own setting of four stanzas from Ariosto's *Orlando furioso*, in a suitably declamatory and homophonic style. He coined the term 'madrigali ariosi' to describe the pieces in this collection as well as in the second and third books for four voices. It is believed to refer to madrigals in which the upper-voice melody is based on a pattern used by popular singers of stanzas from *Orlando furioso* but it may refer to melodies over bass patterns. The collection was reprinted several times (by Gardano, Rampazetto and Vincenti & Amadino), contributing to the popularity of 'delle muse' collections among Venetian printers; parts of the series remained in print for up to 30 years. The *Secondo libro delle muse a tre voci: canzoni moresche di diversi* (1555) contains the first known examples of *moresche* as partsongs. The *Primo libro … a tre voci* has not survived except as Scotto's *Primo libro delle muse a tre* of 1562, which contains five pieces by Barrè and other works by composers better known in Rome than in Venice.

After 1558 Barrè began printing, or at least publishing, with Blado's music type (e.g., madrigals by Menta, 1560, and by Lasso, 1563), or with Dorico's, as in Brassart's *Primo libro delli soi madrigali a quattro* (1564). A contract of 1564 shows Barrè and Valerio Dorico to have been partners in the publication of Eliseo Ghibel's (or Gibellino's) *De festis introitus missarum* (1565), of which they promised to deliver 30 copies to Ghibel's agent (see Masetti Zannini, 226). This suggests that similar partnerships with Dorico or Blado, or, in Venice, with Scotto or Rampazetto, were behind Barrè's other editions of the 1560s. In 1563 Rampazetto printed *Liber primus musarum cum quattuor vocibus sacrarum cantionum que vulgo mottetta vocantur*, naming Barrè as editor and compiler. Perhaps Barrè had lost his shop and had commissioned other publishers to print his books. Temporary partnerships for one or more books were common in Rome, but most are documented too sketchily to allow confirmation of the exact role of each partner. Barrè also printed a few non-musical books which appear to have been special commissions with Barrè serving only as printer. These include a collection of poems, *Rime … in vita e in morte dell'Ill. Sig. Livia Columna* (1555) and Paolo Giovio's *Dialogo dell'imprese militari et amorose* (1555/R), the first work on *imprese*. No publications by him are known from later than 1565, but documents place him in Rome as late as 1572.

Barrè's music books, some 20 in number (including six or seven presumably commissioned from others), are mostly in oblong quarto format, although two are in upright quarto and a few others are in folio. One of these, the Vincentino treatise, contains the first use of the printed natural sign. These well-executed publications, including first editions of important music by Arcadelt, Palestrina and, notably, Lassus, demonstrate Barrè's taste and initiative as well as his skill. His printer's mark was, appropriately, Apollo surrounded by a chorus of the muses; he also used a device with Orpheus playing a *lira da braccio*. This mark was not used by him after the probable loss of his own music font in 1558.

BIBLIOGRAPHY
DBI (S. Simonetti); *EinsteinIM*; *MGG1* (J. Schmidt-Görg); *PitoniN*; *SartoriD*; *SchmidlD*
C.F. Becker: *Die Tonwerke des XVI. und XVII. Jahrhunderts oder Systematisch-Chronologisch Zusammenstellung der in diesen zwei jahrhunderten gedruckten Musikalien* (Leipzig, 1855/R)

A. Bertolotti: *Artisti belgi et olandesi a Roma nei secoli XVI e XVII* (Florence, 1880)

G. Fumagalli: *Antonio Blado, tipografo romano del secolo XVI: memoria storico-bibliografica* (Milan, 1893)

G. Haydon: 'The First Edition of Kerle's Hymns: 1558 or 1560?', *AcM*, xxxviii (1966), 179–84

H.W. Kaufmann: *The Life and Works of Nicola Vicentino (1511–c.1576)*, MSD, xi (1966), 22–3, 33

G. Rostirolla: 'La Cappella Giulia in S. Pietro negli anni del magistero di Giovanni Pierluigi da Palestrina', *Studi palestriniani [I]: Palestrina 1975*, 101–325

G.L. Masetti Zannini: *Stampatori e librai a Roma nella seconda metà del Cinquecento: documenti inediti* (Rome, 1980), 15, 186, 195, 226

S.G. Cusick: *Valerio Dorico: Music Printer in Sixteenth-Century Rome* (Ann Arbor, 1981)

J. Haar: 'The "Madrigale Arioso": a Mid-Century Development in the Cinquecento Madrigal', *Studi musicali*, xii (1983), 203–19

M. Buja: *Antonio Barrè and Music Printing in Rome in the Mid-Sixteenth Century* (diss., U. of North Carolina, 1996)

THOMAS W. BRIDGES/MAUREEN BUJA

Barré [Barrae, Barri, Barret], **Leonardo** (*b* diocese of Limoges; *fl* Rome, 1537–after 1555). French composer and singer active in Italy. On 13 July 1537 'Leonardus Barre Lemovicensis dioec.' was made a singer of the papal chapel. He remained there until 1555, when, together with Palestrina, he was expelled for being married. He then became *maestro di cappella* of S Lorenzo in Damaso, Rome. Barré was probably unrelated to Antonio Barrè, but he may have been the father of 'Alexandro Bare, sopranus, putto', who served in the Cappella Giulia in 1560 and 1561 and possibly from 1564 to May 1566. His nine surviving madrigals and six published motets appeared in various collections from 1539 to 1544. In a collection of 1540 for five voices he is described as a disciple of Willaert and two of his madrigals, *Oime'l bel viso* and *Lachrime meste*, were attributed to Willaert in the latter's posthumous *Madrigali a quatro voci* (Venice, 1563). If Barré was a pupil of Willaert, it must have been between 1527, when Willaert moved to Venice, and 1537, when Barré joined the Cappella Sistina.

Barré's style is not remarkably different from that of his contemporaries, but his texture is somewhat distinctive in its relative lack of contrast. Clearly defined points of imitation are infrequent, as are passages in chordal style, with uniform declamation in all voices. More often, imitation is masked by the continuous accompaniment of other voices or by the use of paired entries. Word-painting, although not frequent and not very bold, nonetheless enhances the music by providing needed contrast and colour.

Barré's music contains many concealed parallel 5ths and octaves, and too often the rhythmic motion is provided by the voices exchanging tones of the same chord. Nonetheless, his music moves forward smoothly and has many passages of great charm, some enhanced by decorative melismas.

WORKS

Come potro fidarmi di te, 5vv, 1540[18]; Come potro fidarmi, 4vv, 1544[16]; Cosi di ben amar, 5vv, 1542[16]; I sospiri amorosi, 5vv, 1540[18]; Lachrime meste, 4vv, 1544[16]; Oime'l bel viso, 4vv, 1540[20]; Se l'alto duol m'ancide, 5vv, 1540[18]; Se sovra ogn'uso humano, 5vv, 1540[18]; Tengan dunque, 4vv, 1539[24] (attrib. Barré only in 1545[18] ed. in CMM xxxi/5)

4 motets, 4vv, 1543[4]; 2 motets, 5vv, 1544[6]; further motets, *D-Mbs*, *Wa*

BIBLIOGRAPHY

AmbrosGM; EinsteinIM

G. Baini: *Memorie storico-critiche della vita e delle opere di Giovanni Pierluigi da Palestrina* (Rome, 1828/R), i, 52

R. Casimiri: 'I diarii sistini', *NA*, iii (1926), 1–16, esp.10; xiv (1937), 19–33, esp.26

A. Ducrot: 'Histoire de la Cappella Giulia au XVIe siècle depuis sa fondation par Jules II (1513) jusqu'à sa restoration par Grégoire XIII (1578)', *Mélanges d'archéologie et d'histoire*, lxxv (1963), 179–240, 467–599, esp. 227

THOMAS W. BRIDGES

Barrelhouse. A style of piano playing that originated among black American blues musicians in the early 20th century. It was first practised in the makeshift saloons of lumber camps in the South and is related to BOOGIE-WOOGIE, which it may have preceded as a blues piano style (*see* BLUES, §4). Barrelhouse was played in regular 4/4 metre, whereas boogie developed as fast music largely of eight beats to the bar. Ragtime bass figures or the heavy left-hand vamp known as 'stomping' were often employed with occasional walking bass variations. Characteristic early recordings are *Barrel House Man* (1927, Para.) by the Texas pianist Will Ezell, *The Dirty Dozen* by Speckled Red (Rufus Perryman) (1929, Bruns.) and *Soon This Morning* by Charlie Spand (1929, Para.); Perryman and Spand worked in Detroit after leaving the South. *Diggin' My Potatoes* (1939, Bb), by Washboard Sam with Joshua Altheimer on piano, and *Shack Bully Stomp* (1938, Decca), by Peetie Wheatstraw, are examples of the persistence of the style. Many barrelhouse themes became standards, and were played by blues pianists after other styles had superseded the form. The term barrelhouse was also used to mean rough or crude, as in 'Mooch' Richardson's *Low Down Barrel House Blues* (1928, OK), and several blues singers, among them Nolan Welch, Buck McFarland and Bukka White, were known by this nickname.

BIBLIOGRAPHY

S. Calt, J. Epstein and N. Perls: disc notes, *Barrelhouse Blues 1927–1936*, Yazoo 1028 (1971)

E. Kriss: *Barrelhouse and Boogie Piano* (New York, 1974)

P. Oliver: 'Piano Blues and Barrelhouse', *Blues off the Record* (Tunbridge Wells and New York, 1984)

PAUL OLIVER

Barrel organ [hand organ, cylinder organ, box organ, street organ, grinder organ, Low Countries organ] (Fr. *orgue à manivelle, orgue de Barbarie*; Ger. *Drehorgel, Leierkasten, Walzenorgel*; It. *organetto a manovella, organo tedesco*). A mechanical instrument in which the musical programme is represented by projections on the surface of a slowly rotating barrel or cylinder.

In its common form, the barrel organ comprises a small pipe-organ offering 14 notes or more in a non-chromatic scale and represented on between one and four stops or registers controlled by drawstops. To save pipes and space as well as expense, tunes were frequently pinned in only two or three keys, G and D being usual. The music is provided by a pinned wooden barrel arranged horizontally within the organ case and rotated by a worm gear on a cross-shaft extending outside the case and terminating in a crankhandle. This cross-shaft also carries one or (more usually) two offset bearings like a crankshaft and to these are attached reciprocators which pass to the lower part of the organ where a simple air bellows and reservoir is provided. Turning the crankhandle thus fulfils two purposes: it pumps wind into the organ chest and it turns the barrel. As the barrel is rotated, its circumference passes beneath a simple frame containing pivoted metal levers or 'keys'. These keys engage with the barrel pins and are lifted by them. The lifting motion causes the rear end of the key to be depressed, pushing down a slender wooden sticker which enters the wind-chest and controls the pallet to allow wind from the bellows reservoir to enter a particular pipe and produce a sound. In all respects, other than the replacement of a manual keyboard by the mechanical keyframe and the barrel, the barrel organ mechanism is merely a simplification of the conventional pipe organ. Besides pipework, some instruments also included percussion in the form of a drum with two beaters, and a triangle. Rarely, an abbreviated octave of bells would also be added. The mechanism is one of simplicity and extreme effectiveness. That some instruments are still in playing order after 150 or 200 years, with little or no repair work or restoration, is evidence of the practical design and durability of the basic organ component assemblies. The mechanism of the barrel organ is illustrated in fig.1; for the cylinder mechanism itself, *see* MECHANICAL INSTRUMENT, fig.1.

There can be few musical instruments whose nature and construction have given rise to so much confusion in terminology as the barrel organ. The term barrel organ has often been used indiscriminately to describe what is in fact a BARREL PIANO or the small street organ whose music programme is represented on perforated card or paper (*see* ORGANETTE and PLAYER ORGAN). While it is certainly true that small barrel organs were very popular on the streets in the late 18th and early 19th centuries (makers such as Bruder in Germany, White & Langshaw in London and Gavioli in Paris made some extremely fine portable street organs), they were in general replaced by the barrel piano in the mid-19th century.

Although descriptions of automatic and hand-operated water organs go back to the 3rd century BC (*see* HYDRAULIS; ORGAN, §IV, 1; and WATER ORGAN), the first description of an automatic organ using a pinned cylinder appears in the 9th-century Arabic text by the *Banū Mūsā* of Baghdad, which discusses in detail an improvement to the hydraulic flutes originally described by Archimedes (*d c*212 BCE) and Apollonius of Perga (3rd century BCE). These early sources are discussed by Farmer (1931); *see also* MECHANICAL INSTRUMENT, §2.

The oldest surviving barrel organ in playing condition is that built into the wall of the fortress of Hohensalzburg, built by an unknown maker in 1502, restored many times and still played daily. It is currently being restored again

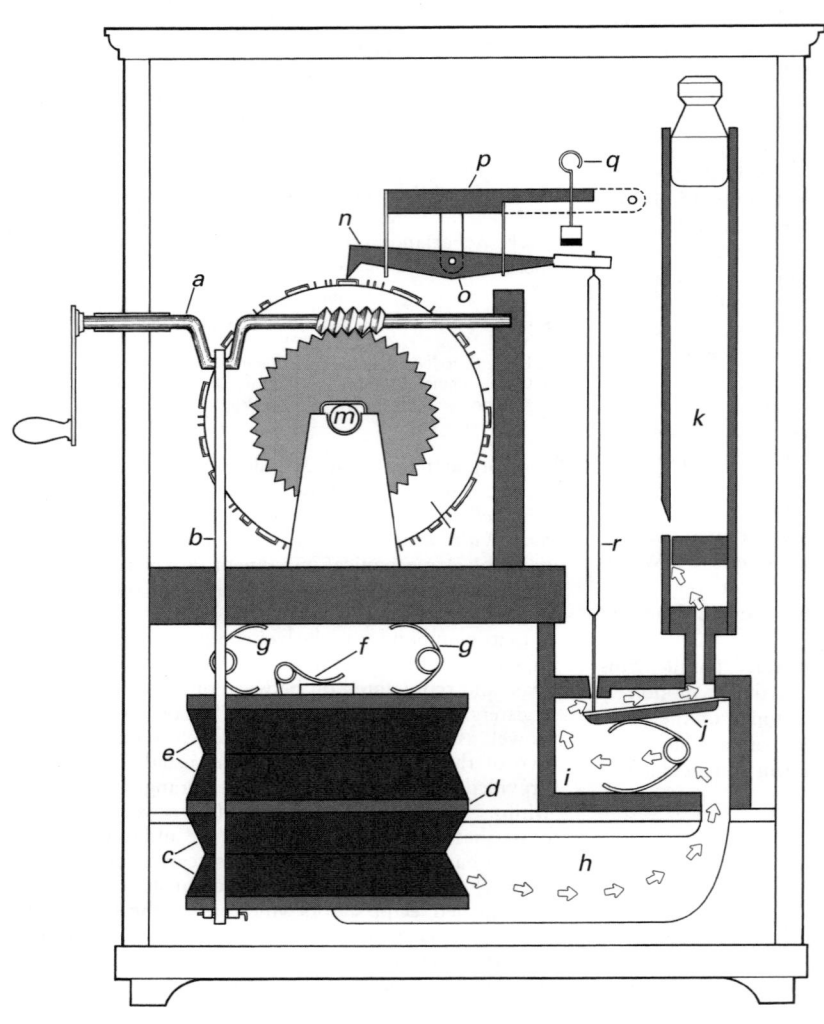

1. Mechanism of the barrel organ

to play its original musical programme. The barrel organ had been perfected by 1597 when the Levant Company, with the approval of Queen Elizabeth I, ordered an elaborate mechanical organ to be sent as a gift to Sultan Mehmed III of Turkey, and Thomas Dallam was entrusted with making and assembling it as well as delivering and erecting it (1599–1600) in the sultan's palace. Dallam's remarkable diary, reproduced by Mayes, gives full details of the organ.

In 1615 Salomon de Caus described and illustrated an instrument in which the barrel was divided into musical bars and each bar into eight beats for the quavers. The whole drum was pierced with holes at the intersecting points so that the pins could be moved and reset to produce another tune. De Caus did not claim to have invented the instrument, only the adaptation of hydraulic power to rotate the drum. He admitted that he had derived inspiration from the writings of Vitruvius (1st century CE) and Hero of Alexandria (1st century CE). The organ was bellows-blown.

Robert Fludd (*Ultriusque cosmi*, 1617–24) depicted very inaccurately a barrel organ activated by hydraulic air compression. Similar drawings and descriptions were given at this period by others including Kircher (1650) and Caspar Schott (1664). In his *Gabinetto armonico* (1722) Filippo Bonanni depicted an 'organo portile': a small barrel organ shown resting on the player's left hip, supported by a sling over the right shoulder; the player turns the handle with his right hand.

In 1752 Leonhard Euler (1707–83) and a Berlin mechanic, Hohlfeld, produced a device, called the Melograph, for recording keyboard performances so that they could be converted into pinned barrels. Similar experiments were made by several other makers (e.g. JOHN JOSEPH MERLIN), but without much success until the invention of the REPRODUCING PIANO at the beginning of the 10th century.

Details of the construction of the barrel organ in the 18th century were given by MARIE DOMINIQUE JOSEPH ENGRAMELLE and by FRANÇOIS BÉDOS DE CELLES. The former's account is of special importance as it describes the method of arranging the music while the latter giving great detail regarding pinning the barrels to give a particular tune.

Instruments were made for both secular and church use and frequently used the same style case; these are referred to as 'church and chamber' barrel organs. Normally each barrel might contain eight or ten tunes, so with four barrels the repertory could be quite large. Secular instruments were often provided with barrels of jigs and reels for dancing and popular airs from the operas and national songs, while for Sundays there would be a barrel of hymn tunes. Such instruments might be 70 cm wide and 180 cm high. The smallest chamber barrel organ was the *serinette* or bird organ (see BIRD INSTRUMENTS, §1), typically measuring some 34 cm wide by 20 cm deep and standing 18 cm high.

While English and French instruments of this type are invariably hand-turned and fully automatic, clockwork-driven instruments were also made, especially in Austria, powered with descending weights. The heavy weight, sometimes in excess of 60 kg, would be wound up to the top of the case using an internal hand-winch. When set to play, the thrust of the descending weight would be regulated by the clockwork mechanism which also turned

the barrel and pumped the bellows. Clockwork barrel organs of a very high quality, both weight-and spring-driven, were also made in southern Germany, Black Forest and Bohemian makers being among the best in the world. Some of these very large instruments were fully chromatic. From them the barrel organ developed in three directions: the miniature barrel organ as used in the MUSICAL CLOCK, the large automatic ORCHESTRION, and the FAIRGROUND ORGAN.

The barrel organ has enjoyed a particularly rich history in England. It has been said that the barrel organ was first introduced into an English church about 1700, that one was installed in that year in the church of King Charles the Martyr, Peak Forest, Derbyshire, and that the instrument was still there in 1870. It has also been asserted that early in the 18th century a certain Wright of London built a barrel organ for All Saints, Fulham. Unfortunately, none of these stories can be corroborated. Instruments were certainly in use around the middle of the 18th century as replacements for church bands or, where churches had ordinary organs for incompetent organists. The peak period of the church barrel organ may be regarded as *c*1760–1840; during that time hundreds were made by over 130 makers, principally in London. Among the earliest makers were John Tax of St Martin's Lane (known to have been active in 1753) and E. Rostrand of Orange Court, Leicester Fields, who made 'all sorts of Chamber-Organs to play with fingers or barrels'. A small chamber barrel organ of his has four stops and two barrels of eight tunes. It is dated 1764 and is still in working order. During the height of the barrel organ's popularity, virtually every organ builder also made mechanical instruments. Such was the skill of these makers and their barrel-pinners that Burney, commenting on the general use of barrel organs, added that, 'the recent improvements of some English Artists have rendered the barrel capable of an effect equal to the fingers of the first-rate performers'.

Chamber barrel organs were often enclosed in very handsome cases which reflect the high standard of cabinet making of the period. Church barrel organs, too, were set in elegant cases but varied greatly in size. Some were placed in a gallery or loft as at Brightling, East Sussex; Hampton Gay, Oxfordshire; Woodrising, Norfolk; Raithby, Lincolnshire; Avington, Hampshire; Sutton, Bedfordshire; and Muchelney, Somerset. Others, usually of small dimensions, stood on the floor of the church. The music played is itself of great interest because an analysis of both the church and secular repertory reveals the popularity of certain tunes. The titles of some 1300 such tunes have been listed by Langwill and Boston.

In the early 19th century several important developments took place. The first was the design of a 'revolver' system to make barrel-changing simpler. Three or more barrels were mounted between circular hoops in a pivoted frame, and the whole mechanism could be unlocked and rotated in a matter of seconds to bring a fresh barrel into play. A large barrel organ with a revolver mechanism for four barrels was built for Northallerton Church by Bishop in 1819. Forster & Andrews of Hull advertised a barrel organ with 'three barrels in a frame' in 1845, and in the following year offered to install improved instruments with three, four or five barrels.

The larger instruments for use in church were also provided with separate mechanisms for blowing and for

2. Barrel organ, built c1800, played by Sidney Armstrong in the parish church of King Charles the Martyr, Shelland, Suffolk

turning the barrel. The bellows were operated either by a blowing lever or by a foot pedal so the player could continue to blow while holding the barrel on a particular note or chord. This improvement allowed 'pointing' for psalm-singing.

For those churches already equipped with an ordinary organ, yet desirous of the benefits of the mechanical player, the 'dumb organist' was introduced in about 1800 to enable a barrel mechanism to be applied to a normal manual organ. It consisted of an oblong box which was fitted on top of the organ keyboard and which contained virtually all of the programme parts of a normal barrel organ save the pipes and bellows. The keyframe stickers projected from the bottom of the box and rested on the keyboard keys so that as the operator turned the crank handle, the stickers moved up and down to play the organ. A number of dumb organists survive.

By the end of the 18th century, barrel mechanisms attached to or built into organs were so common that contemporary records reveal quite specific terminology. Instruments are described variously as 'finger organs' (i.e. played with the fingers) or as 'barrel-and-finger organs'. In the latter the barrel-playing mechanism was built into ordinary organs; this offered the best of both worlds for both home and church. A number of these survive despite the ruthless age when so many such mechanisms were considered redundant and scrapped. The largest barrel-and-finger organ in the world was the APOLLONICON which could reproduce orchestral music: each work in its repertory was represented on a set of three very large wooden barrels.

As the 19th century entered its second half, the barrel organ began losing ground. An indication of the end of the barrel organ period may be gained from the last advertisement of Bates and Son who, in 1864, were selling off secular organs from £2 2s and church organs at £10.

See also REED ORGAN.

BIBLIOGRAPHY

S. de Caus: *Les raisons des forces mouvantes* (Frankfurt, 1615, 2/1624)
A. Kircher: *Musurgia universalis* (Rome, 1650/R)
G. Schott: *Technica curiosa* (Nuremberg, 1664, 2/1687)
F. Bonanni: *Gabinetto armonico* (Rome, 1722/R, rev. and enlarged 2/1776/R by G. Ceruti with plates by A. van Westerhout; Eng. trans., 1969)
V. Trichter: *Curiöses … Tantz … Exercitien-Lexikon* (Leipzig, 1742)
F. Bédos de Celles: *L'art du facteur d'orgues*, iv (Paris, 1766–78/R; Eng. trans., 1977); ed. C. Mahrenholz (Kassel, 1934–6, 2/1963–6)
J. Adlung: *Musica mechanica organoedi*, ed. J.L. Albrecht (Berlin, 1768/R); ed. C. Mahrenholtz (Kassel, 1931)
M.D.J. Engramelle: *La tonotechnie, ou L'art de noter les cylindres … dans les instruments de concerts méchaniques* (Paris, 1775/R)
H. Mendel: *Musikalisches/Conversations-Lexikon* (Berlin, 1878, 3/1890–91/R)
H.G. Farmer: *The Organ of the Ancients from Eastern Sources, Hebrew, Syriac and Arabic* (London, 1931)
A. Protz: *Mechanische Musikinstrumente* (Kassel, 1939)
H.G. Farmer: *The Sources of Arabian Music* (Bearsden, 1940, 2/1965)
S. Mayes: *An Organ for the Sultan* (London, 1956)
A. Buchner: *Hudebni automaty* (Prague, 1959; Eng. trans., 1959)
R. Quoika: *Altösterreichische Hornwerke* (Berlin, 1959)
E. Simon: *Mechanische Musikinstrumente früherer Zeiten und ihre Musik* (Wiesbaden, 1960/R)
L.G. Langwill and N. Boston: *Church and Chamber Barrel-organs, their Origin, Makers, Music and Location: a Chapter in English Church Music* (Edinburgh, 1967, 2/1970)
K. Bormann: *Orgel- und Spieluhrenbau* (Zürich, 1968)
M. Wilson: *The English Chamber Organ: History and Development 1650–1850* (Oxford, 1968) [with biographical notes on makers, incl. many barrel organ makers]
H. Zeraschi: *Das Buch der Drehorgel* (Zürich, 1971)
A.W.J.G. Ord-Hume: *Clockwork Music: an Illustrated Musical History of Mechanical Musical Instruments* (London, 1973)
A.W.J.G. Ord-Hume: *The Mechanics of Mechanical Music: the Arrangement of Music for Automatic Instruments* (London, 1973)
H. Zeraschi: *Drehorgel in der Kirche* (Zürich, 1973)
L. Elvin: *Forster & Andrews, their Barrel, Chamber and Small Church Organs* (Lincoln, 1976)
A.W.J.G. Ord-Hume: *Barrel Organ: the Story of the Mechanical Organ and its Repair* (London, 1978)
A.W.J.G. Ord-Hume: *Joseph Haydn and the Mechanical Organ* (Cardiff, 1982)
W. Malloch: 'The Earl of Bute's Machine Organ: a Touchstone of Taste', *EMc*, xi (1983), 172–83
H. Rambach and O. Wernet: *Waldkircher orgelbauer* (Waldkirch, 1984)
H. Jüttemann: *Schwarzwälder Flötenuhren* (Waldkirch, 1991)

LYNDESAY G. LANGWILL/ARTHUR W.J.G. ORD-HUME

Barrel piano [cylinder piano, self-acting piano, street piano, café piano; sometimes inaccurately called barrel organ or hurdy-gurdy]. A piano played automatically by a pinned barrel or cylinder. In the form made in London by William Rolfe (from 1829) and others, an ordinary piano was augmented by a pinned wooden cylinder placed inside the case under the keyboard. This barrel was provided with a mechanical keyframe and a series of linkages or stickers which extend behind the soundboard to the top of the piano and operate an additional set of hammers which strike the strings through a gap in the soundboard. The barrel is turned by a clockwork motor driven by a heavy weight which is wound up to the top of the case. (For an illustration *see* MECHANICAL INSTRUMENT, fig.4.)

About 1804 John Longman introduced a drawing-room barrel piano with no keyboard which was also weight-driven and included effects such as drum, triangle and buff stop. Around 1860 the Black Forest makers Imhof & Mukle introduced spring-driven clockwork barrel pianos, also for drawing-room use and without

Barrel piano in a London street, c1905

manual keyboard. In other types of barrel piano, the mechanism is operated by turning a hand crank. The domestic automatic piano dispensed with the cumbersome barrel in favour, first, of Debain's *Antiphonel* studded wooden strip piano player, then the perforated roll of the piano player and later the PLAYER PIANO.

The keyboardless hand-turned barrel piano enjoyed one and a half centuries of popularity as a street instrument. The street barrel piano is thought to have emanated from Italy around 1800. By 1805 the Hicks family of Bristol was making small portable barrel pianos, sometimes inaccurately called 'portable dulcimers', which could be carried by itinerant musicians. Joseph Hicks excelled in making these, and George Hicks, who worked for a time in London, took the craft to New York. The large street piano mounted on a handcart was also developed in Italy, and migrant craftsmen took their skills all over Europe and North America. These open-air instruments underwent a variety of improvements; some models, known as 'mandolin' pianos, were made with mechanically driven repeating actions, while others included percussion in the form of drum, triangle and xylophone or wood-block. Some were augmented by a mechanism designed to show advertisements in a travelling picture display built into the vertical fall. Early in the 20th century an instrument with a coin-operated, spring-driven clockwork motor was introduced; these were widely used in public places, particularly public bars. In France and Belgium such instruments developed into large and decorative barrel-playing café pianos, often with elaborately carved cases embellished with mirrors. In the 1950s both Portugal and Spain produced a large number of small novelty barrel pianos on miniature handcarts for performing popular dance music and variety songs. An unusual barrel piano built in the form of a shallow living-room table, the Swedish *pianoharpa*, was invented in 1889 by I.F. Nilsson of Österkorsberga, near Lemnhult,

patented and developed by the brothers Anders Gustaf and Jones Wilhelm Andersson of Näshult, near Vetlanda.

BIBLIOGRAPHY

R.E.M. Harding: *The Piano-Forte: its History Traced to the Great Exhibition of 1851* (Cambridge, 1933/R, 2/1978/R)

A.W.J.G. Ord-Hume: *Player Piano* (London, 1970)

A.W.J.G. Ord-Hume: *The Mechanics of Mechanical Music* (London, 1973)

B. Lindwall: 'The Andersson Pianoharpa', *Music Box*, viii (1977–8), 330–34

A.W.J.G. Ord-Hume: *Pianola: The History of the Self-Playing Piano* (London, 1984)

ARTHUR W.J.G. ORD-HUME

Barrera, Rodiano. *See* BARERA, RODIANO.

Barrera Gómez, Enrique (*b* Valladolid, 26 April 1844; *d* Valladolid, 3 July 1922). Spanish composer. He studied solfège and the piano in Valladolid, learning so rapidly that by the age of nine he was giving piano recitals. He also began to compose salon pieces – waltzes, polkas and mazurkas – and religious music. Some of these compositions are extant, dating from as early as 1854. In 1859 he moved to Madrid to attend the conservatory, where for eight years he studied the piano with José Miró and composition with Hilarión Eslava. At the same time, he made his living by playing the piano in cafés and salons and by giving lessons. Meanwhile he developed an interest in opera and attended performances at the Teatro Real.

On 22 January 1867 Barrera Gómez won by competition the post of choirmaster at Burgos Cathedral, which he held until his death, although in 1897 he was given dispensation from some of his duties because of ill-health. In 1869 the music publisher Antonio Romero announced a national opera competition, which Barrera won with *Atahualpa*, a Spanish opera based on an episode in the conquest of Peru. Another opera, *Saul*, was never staged. Most of his numerous works were written for Burgos Cathedral, and include masses, psalms and motets. (The autograph scores of many of them are extant there.) Of those published, the best is a collection of organ sonatas. Barrera Gómez is one of the best Spanish composers of the second half of the 19th century. His melodies have great elegance and nobility of line. Notable also is the technical aspect of his compositions, the harmony, accompaniments and the richness of his orchestration.

BIBLIOGRAPHY

B. Saldoni: *Diccionario biográfico-bibliográfico de efemérides de músicos españoles*, ii (Madrid, 1880/R), 336–8
'Enrique Barrera', *Ilustración musical hispano-americana*, ii (1888–9), 129–34
J. López-Calo: *La música en la Catedral de Burgos* (Burgos, 1995–7)
J.B. Varela de Vega: 'El vallisoletano Enrique Barrera, maestro de capilla de la metropolitana de Burgos', *Boletín de la Real academia de bellas artes de la Purísma Concepción de Valladolid*, no.30 (1995), 131–50

JOSÉ LÓPEZ-CALO

Barrère, Georges (*b* Bordeaux, 31 Oct 1876; *d* New York, 14 June 1944). French flautist. Trained at the Paris Conservatoire, first with Altès under whom he made slow progress, then under Taffanel, Barrère was one of the most brilliant pupils to win a *premier prix*. His studies completed, he filled a number of important posts leading to the Opéra and Colonne orchestras. In 1895 he formed the Société Moderne des Instruments à Vent which replaced Taffanel's group, disbanded in 1893; during this period Barrère contributed a flute section to Widor's continuation of Berlioz's treatise on orchestration. In 1905 Damrosch invited Barrère to join the New York SO, with which he played, with only one break, for the rest of his life. As an exponent of the French style of flute playing, Barrère's influence was profound, and it is sad to realize that, in spite of his kindly and generous nature, his success led to the eclipse of Carl Wehner, Boehm's pupil and the doyen of flute teachers in New York. In the USA, as in France, Barrère founded small instrumental groups: in 1910 the Barrère Ensemble of Wind Instruments, and in 1915 the Little Symphony chamber orchestra. These activities continued until his death.

PHILIP BATE

Barret, Apollon(-Marie-Rose) (*b* Saint Brieuc, 15 Nov 1804; *d* Paris, 7/8 March 1879). French oboist and oboe designer. In 1823 Barret joined the class of Vogt at the Paris Conservatoire, and the following year was awarded the *premier prix*. His first appointment was with the orchestra of the Théâtre de l'Odéon; in 1827 he transferred to the Opéra-Comique. Two years later he was named first oboist at the Italian Opera in London, a position he held until 1874, concurrent with his activities as principal oboist in the Philharmonic Society and oboe teacher at the Royal Academy of Music.

Barret is known primarily for his improvements to the design of the oboe described in the second edition of his *Complete Method for the Oboe* (1862). His design prioritized simplifying the fingering and perfecting the intonation of trills throughout the range of the oboe. The means by which he achieved these results have had a lasting effect on the physical characteristics and mechanism of the modern French oboe, and in particular the key system still favoured by English players (notably the thumb plate). Despite remaining in England for much of his career, Barret maintained active contact with his homeland, and in particular with Triébert, the Parisian firm of oboe manufacturers who made instruments that incorporate his design features. The list of subscribers printed in the first edition of the *Method* (1850) also

testifies to his international connections. As well as his pedagogic works, Barret composed a considerable array of virtuosic salon music for oboe.

WORKS
(*selective list*)

Ob, pf: Fantasie on La dernière rose d'été, from Flotow's Martha (1873); [3] Fantasies on Donizetti's Lucrezia Borgia (London, 1874); L'absense, romance sans paroles (London, 1874), arr. cornet, orch (London, 1874); Cantilène, romance sans paroles (London, 1874), arr. eng hn, pf (1882); Elégie à la mémoire de Charles Triébert (*c*1870); Mélange sur un motif d'Onslow (n.d.); Air languedocien varié (n.d.)
Pf: Fleur de Marie, valse (London, 1845), arr. military band (1847); La fin du bal, galop (London, 1846); La corbeille fleurie, valse (London, 1850), arr. military band (London, 1850); La fuchsia, valse (London, 1850), arr. military band (London, 1849)
Other: Memory's Tears (Oh! 'tis not easy) (J.W. Lake), song (London, ?1845)

BIBLIOGRAPHY

FétisB; *Waterhouse-LangwillI*
C.D. Lehrer: 'How Barret Accompanied his Forty Progressive Melodies', *Journal* [International Double Reed Society], xxii (1994), 77–85

GEOFFREY BURGESS

Barrett, John (*b c*1676; *d* London, ?Dec 1719). English composer, organist and music master. From about 1686 to 1691 he was a chorister in the Chapel Royal under John Blow. He became organist of St Mary-at-Hill on 25 August 1693 and was appointed music master at Christ's Hospital on 28 September 1697. He held both these posts until his death. He contributed a poem in homage to Blow to *Amphion Anglicus* (London, 1700) and was elected to the Amicable Society of Blues in about 1704. It is possible that he married Mary Saunders on 9 March 1711 in St Mary-at-Hill.

Like many of his contemporaries, such as Jeremiah Clarke, John Eccles and Daniel Purcell, Barrett composed mainly for the theatre, and his many songs, mostly of the double-barrelled art song variety, are both tuneful and attractive, as are the several little keyboard pieces published in the first three books of *The Harpsicord Master* (1697–1702) and various other early 18th-century anthologies. The style is essentially Purcellian, but the use of motto openings in almost all the extended songs reveals an awareness of rather more up-to-date Italian vocal practice, and in one case (*Begone, begone, thou too propitious light*, n.d.) Barrett actually produces what must be one of the very first English recitative–aria–recitative–aria cantatas as such (though the term 'cantata' is not used). His incidental music for Shadwell's *The Lancashire Witches* was popular, and no fewer than 30 performances at Drury Lane between 1713 and 1729 are recorded; like that of several other plays to which he also contributed, however, it is no longer extant.

WORKS
all printed works published in London

INCIDENTAL MUSIC

The Pilgrim (J. Vanbrugh), ?1702 revival, act music in Harmonia Anglicana (1702), song (1702)
All for the Better, or The Infallible Cure (F. Manning), 1703, song (1703)
The Generous Conqueror, or The Timely Discovery (B. Higgons), 1702, act music in Harmonia Anglicana (1702)
Tunbridge Walks, or The Yeoman of Kent (T. Baker), 1703, act music in Harmonia Anglicana (1703)
The Albion Queens, or The Death of Mary, Queen of Scotland (J. Banks), 1704, act music in Harmonia Anglicana (1704)
The Tender Husband, or The Accomplish'd Fools (R. Steele), 1705, music lost, advertised in *The Post Man* (5–8 May 1705)

Hampstead Heath (T. Baker), 1706, music lost, advertised in *The Post Man* (20–22 Dec 1705)

The Fine Lady's Airs, or An Equipage of Lovers (T. Baker), 1708, act music, vns, obs (1709), song (1709)

The Fair Quaker of Deal, or The Humours of the Navy (C. Shadwell), 1710, music, vns, obs, lost, advertised in *The Tatler* (28–30 March 1710)

The City Ramble, or A Playhouse Wedding (E. Settle), 1711, song (1711)

The Wife's Relief, or The Husband's Cure (C. Johnson), 1712, music, vns, obs, lost, advertised in *The Post Man* (11–13 Dec 1711)

The Perplex'd Lovers (S. Centlivre), 1712, music, vns, obs, lost, advertised in *The Post Man* (19–21 Feb 1712)

The Lancashire Witches (T. Shadwell), 1713, music lost

The Wife of Bath (J. Gay), 1713, 3 songs (1713)

The Custom of the Manor (C. Johnson), 1715, 2 songs (1715)

Love's Last Shift, or The Fool in Fashion (C. Cibber), 1696, 7 pieces, *GB-Lcm*, 3 of which, *Cmc*; possibly the act music for The Relapse (Vanbrugh), 1697

Esquire Brainless, or Trick upon Trick, song (n.d.)

OTHER WORKS

O Sing unto the Lord, verse anthem, *GB-Ctc* (org pt only)

An Ode performed at the Anniversary Feast of the Gentlemen ... of Kent, London, Merchant Taylors Hall, 21 Nov 1700, lost

A Psalm of Thanksgiving to be Sung by the Children of Christ's-Hospital ... in Easter Week, 1698 [also (1704), (1706), 1709, 1712, 1713, 1716, 1718], Christ's Hospital Office

Numerous songs pubd singly and in 18th-century anthologies. Several tunes in D'Urfey's Wit and Mirth, or Pills to Purge Melancholy (1719), three of which were included in Gay's The Beggar's Opera, London, 1728

Sonata, tpt, ob, 2 vn, va, bc, *Lbl*; compressed version, as ov. to Tunbridge Walks, str (London, 1703)

2 voluntaries, org, *Ldc*, *Mp*, *J-Tn*

Pieces, hpd, *GB-Cfm*, *Lbl*, *Ob*, *Och*, several pubd in early 18th-century anthologies

BIBLIOGRAPHY

S. Jeans: 'The Easter Psalms of Christ's Hospital', *PRMA*, lxxxviii (1961–2), 45–60

P. Holman: 'The Trumpet Sonata in England', *EMc*, iv (1976), 424–9

C. Price: *Music in the Restoration Theatre* (Ann Arbor, 1979)

D. Dawe: *Organists of the City of London 1666–1850* (Padstow, 1983)

R. Harrison: 'The Magdalene College Partbooks: Origins and Contents', *RMARC*, no.29 (1996), 47–95

CHRISTOPHER POWELL/H. DIACK JOHNSTONE

Barrett, Richard (*b* 7 Nov 1959, Swansea, South Wales). British composer. He only began to study music seriously after graduating in genetics and microbiology at UCL (1980). His principal composition teacher was Wiegold, with whom he studied privately, but under the influence of Xenakis, Hespos and Ferneyhough he became associated with the so-called New Complexity group of British composers, who broadly identified themselves with a radical European aesthetic. He became a member of the Composers' Forum at the Internationale Ferienkurse für Neue Musik, Darmstadt, in 1984, winning the Kranichsteiner Musikpreis there in 1986. He was awarded the Gaudeamus Prize in 1989. From 1989 to 1992, Barrett was composition tutor at Middlesex University, and in 1996 was appointed professor of electronic composition at the Institute of Sonology of the Hague Royal Conservatory. Between 1984 and 1993 he was co-director of Ensemble Exposé; he has also performed improvised music using live electronics, in particular with Paul Obermeyer, with whom he formed the duo Furt in 1987.

Most of Barrett's works are grouped into series with extra-musical connotations. These include the 11 scores collectively entitled *Fictions* – reflecting his long-standing preoccupation with the writings of Beckett, culminating in *Ruin* for six spatially disposed instrumental trios – and

the four works of *After Matta*, inspired by the Mexican painter, Roberto Matta. Other compositions comprise several movements, which can also be performed independently: both *negatives* and *Opening of the Mouth* contain five. The latter was conceived as a performance environment in collaboration with the artist Crow; while the movement titles, which come from the work of Paul Celan, are indicative of Barrett's interest in a wide range of modern poetry. Barrett's creative methods are usually associated with a good deal of mathematical elaboration, often carried out with computer assistance. He has developed a program capable of developing pitch and other material, which is then subjected to a series of selection procedures; he does, however, retain ultimate responsibility for all creative decisions.

WORKS

DRAMATIC

Opening of the Mouth (P. Celan), 2 female vv, insts, tapes, live elecs, 1992–7; incl. knospend-gespaltener, air, CHARON, inward, Von Hinter dem Schmerz, abglanzbeladen/auseinandergeschrieben: see INSTRUMENTAL

Unter Wasser (op, M. Kreidl), Mez, 13 insts, 1995–8

VOCAL

Principia (A.L. Jones, after I. Newton), Bar, pf, 1982–4; Coïgitum, Mez, a, fl, ob d'amore, pf, perc, 1983–5; lieder vom wasser (E. Borchers), S, b, cl, db, perc, 1989–90

INSTRUMENTAL

Orch: Vanity, 1991–4

4 or more insts: Essay in Radiance, pic + b fl, s + t sax, E♭ cl + b cl, elec org/synth, 1 perc, vn + va, vc, 1981–3; I Open and Close, str qt (opt. amp), 1983–8; Illuminer le temps, pic/fl, b cl/ B♭ cl, 1 perc, hp, 2 elec gui, vn, dbn, (amp), 1984–90; Anatomy, fl, eng hn, b cl, bn, hn, perc, 2 vn, va, vc, db, (amp), 1985–6; Ruin, 6 spatially separated inst groups: 2 fl (amp), s sax, cl, b cl, hn, 2 trbn, tuba, 3 perc (amp), 2 vn, va, 2 vc, db, 1985–95; Temptation, a sax + bar sax, cb cl, tpt + pic tpt + cornet + slide tpt, vc, synth, perc, live elecs, 1986; Colloid-E, fl, trbn, mand, db, perc (amp), solo 10 str gui (amp), 1988–92; negatives, 9 players, (amp), 1988–93 (incl. delta, Colloid-E (incorporating Colloid), Archipelago, Basalt-E (incorporating Basalt), Entstellt); Archipelago, b fl + a rec, trbn, perc, 10 str gui, vn, va, vc, db, mand (amp) + retuned mand, 1990–92; Basalt-E, 1 perc, vn, va, vc, db, solo trbn, 1990–92; Delta, a fl, trbn, anklung, sitar (amp), 10 str gui (amp), vn, va, vc, db, 1990–93; Entstellt, pic, trbn, anklung, sitar (amp), 12 str gui (amp), vn, va, vc, db, 1990–93; Trawl, 5 players, 1994–7; Stress, str qt, 1995–7

1–3 insts: Invention VI, pf, 1982; heard, pf (amp), 1985; Ne Songe Plus A Fuir, vc (amp), 1985–6; Alba, bn, live elec, (amp), 1986–7; nothing elsewhere, va, 1987; EARTH, trbn, 1 perc, 1987–8; Dark Ages, vc (2 bows), 1987–90; Reticule, vn, 1988; Colloid, 10 str gui, 1988–91; Another Heavenly Day, E♭ cl, elec gui, db, (amp), 1989–90; Tract, pf, (opt. amp), 1984–96; incl. A Light Gleams an Instant, 1989–96; basalt, trbn, 1990–91; what remains, fl, b cl, pf, 1990–91; Praha, vc (2 bows), 1991; knospend-gespaltener, C cl, 1992–3; abglanzbeladen/auseinandergeschrieben, perc, 1992–6; Von Hinter dem Schmerz, vc (amp), 1992–6

air, vn, 1993; trace, 2 diatonic music boxes, 1994; CHARON, b cl, 1994–5; inward, fl, perc, (amp), 1994–5; transmission, elec gui, live elecs, 1995–7; binary, 2 fl, 1996

ELECTRO-ACOUSTIC
works from 1992 in collaboration with Paul Obermeyer

The Unthinkable, tape, 1988–9; intruders, 1992; The Flesh of Experience, 1992; Hospital of the Soul, 1993; Johannes-Passion, 1993; Terminal V, 1994; Unstern, 1994; modern, 1994–6; the insect class, 1994–6; angel, 1995; irregular, 1996

WORK-SERIES

After Matta: Coïgitum, Le songe plus à fuir, Illuminer le temps, The Unthinkable

Fictions: Anatomy, Temptation, Alba, nothing elsewhere, EARTH, I Open and Close, Another Heavenly Day, Tract, Dark Ages, lieder vom wasser, Ruin

Addenda: What remains, Trawl [in progress]
Hermetica: Transmission [in progress]

WRITINGS

'To answer ...', *Complexity?*, ed. J. Bons (Amsterdam, 1990)
'Beröring som blir till ljud' [Touch Becoming Sound: Notes on Composition/Improvisation], *Nutida musik*, xxxv/2 (1992), 24–5
'Standpoint and Sightlines', *Diskurse zur gegenwärtigen Musikkultur* [Giessen 1994], ed. N. Polaschegg (Regensburg, 1996), 21–32

BIBLIOGRAPHY

R. Toop: 'Four Facets of the "New Complexity"', *Contact*, no.32 (1988), 4–8
'Richard Barrett in Interview', *Sounds Australian*, no.29 (1991), 27–31
K. Cross: 'Sound/Form and the Traditions of Hearing', *Resonance* [London] (Oct 1992), Oct, 1–8
R. Freeman: 'Richard Barrett, compositeur maudit manqué', *Tempo*, no.190 (1994), 41–6
I. Hewitt: 'Fail Worse, Fail Better', *MT*, cxxxv (1994), 148–51
C. Fox: 'Music as Fiction: a Consideration of the Work of Richard Barrett', *Contemporary Music Review*, no.13 (1995), 147–57

JOHN WARNABY

Barrett, Thomas Augustine. See STUART, LESLIE.

Barrett, William Alexander (*b* London, 15 Oct 1834; *d* London, 17 Oct 1891). English church musician, writer and musical educationist. He was trained as a chorister at St Paul's Cathedral between 1846 and 1849, and worked first as a commercial artist and journalist; but in 1859 he became a professional lay clerk, and was appointed to the choir of St Paul's Cathedral in 1866. In the same year he was made music critic of the *Morning Post* and he subsequently became editor of the *Monthly Musical Record* (1877), *The Orchestra* (1881) and the *Musical Times* (1887). Barrett graduated BMus at Oxford in 1871 and was appointed assistant Inspector of Music in the same year, working first with Hullah, then with Stainer, until his death. He was joint editor with Stainer of the *Dictionary of Musical Terms* (1876); and also published *English Glee and Madrigal Writers* (1877), *English Church Composers* (1877), *Balfe: his Life and Work* (1882) and other works, including the collection *English Folksongs* (1890), one of the first products of the revival of interest in English folksong. Barrett's historical interests were supported by his own important collection of madrigals, glees and scarce musical literature. His son F.E.H.J. Barrett later became music editor of the *Morning Post*.

BIBLIOGRAPHY

Obituary, *MT*, xxxii (1891), 659–60
A.H. King: *Some British Collectors of Music* (Cambridge, 1963)

BERNARR RAINBOW

Barri, Leonardo. See BARRÉ, LEONARDO.

Barrientos, Maria (*b* Barcelona, 10 March 1884; *d* Ciboure, Basses-Pyrénées, 8 Aug 1946). Spanish soprano. After a short course of singing lessons at the Barcelona Conservatory, she made her début at the age of 14 at the Teatro Lirico in *La sonnambula*, followed by several other leading roles there and at the Teatro de Novidades. After further studies, she sang at Covent Garden (in *Il barbiere di Siviglia*, 1903), at La Scala (in Meyerbeer's *Dinorah* and in *Barbiere*, 1904–5), and at many leading theatres throughout the world. On 31 January 1916 she made her Metropolitan début in *Lucia di Lammermoor* and she appeared there regularly in the standard coloratura roles during the next four seasons. In later years Barrientos became an admired interpreter of French and Spanish songs, and made a valuable set of records, including Falla's *Siete canciones populares españolas* and *Soneto a Córdoba* with the composer at the piano. These complement many fascinating discs documenting her stage roles and displaying the charm of her airy *soprano leggero*.

BIBLIOGRAPHY

GV (R. Celletti; R. Vegeto)
C. Williams: 'Maria Barrientos', *Record Collector*, xxviii (1983), 71–95 [incl. discography]

DESMOND SHAWE-TAYLOR/R

Barriera [bariera, sbara]. A 16th- and early 17th-century dance found in lute and guitar tablatures. As described in Caroso's dance manuals *Il ballarino* (1581) and *Nobiltà di dame* (1600) and in Cesare Negri's dance treatise *Le gratie d'amore* (1602), it is representative of a battle. The music is based on the second part of Janequin's *La guerre*, which begins 'Fan frere le le lan fan'. This is a parody of a trumpet call, and it may be the trumpet call rather than Janequin's music that recurs so often in the barriera dance. A sbara was performed at the wedding of Francesco de' Medici and Bianca Cappello in 1579 and another at the wedding of Ferdinando de' Medici and Christine of Lorraine in 1589. The guitar tablatures of the early 17th century reduce Janequin's original music to the standard chord-strumming technique of the *rasgueado* style of guitar playing of the period, but, unusually, adding one melodic note.

ELAINE L. BEARER

Barrière, Etienne-Bernard-Joseph (*b* Valenciennes, 7 Oct 1748; *d* ?Paris, 1816 or 1818). French composer and violinist. He went to Paris at the age of 12 (according to Choron), where he studied composition with Philidor and the violin with André-Noël Pagin. At his début at the Concert Spirituel on 20 April 1767 in a concerto for violin, his playing was praised for 'la netteté, la justesse, la délicatesse et la sensibilité' (*Mercure de France*, May 1767). According to Hécart, he soon returned to Valenciennes where he taught the violin, composed more violin concertos, and had his opera *Le baille bienfaisant* (now lost) performed in 1775. The following year he went again to Paris and played at the Concert Spirituel. In 1778 he performed two of his own violin concertos. He is mentioned in the *Almanach musical* as 'Maître de violon', and probably lived in Paris from 1776 to 1782. In 1778 he married Marie Geneviève Dombey. They had four children between 1779 and 1789, during which time they lived in Valenciennes and Paris. In 1801 he played a *symphonie concertante* with Lafont at a concert in the Salle Olympique, and also in 1801 (or 1802), according to Hécart, he was first violinist in Napoleon's chapel, a position which he did not hold long.

WORKS

all printed works published in Paris

op.	
1	Six quatuors concertans, 2 vn, va, b (1776)
2	Deux simphonies concertantes (1776); no.1 for 4 vn, 2 va, 2 b, with 2 ob, 2 hn ad lib, ed. in *The Symphony 1720–1840*, ser. D, v (New York, 1983): no.2 for 2 ob, 4 vn, va, b, with 2 hn ad lib
3	Second oeuvre de six quatuors concertants, 2 vn, va, b (1778)
4	Six airs variés (*c*1777); 3 for 2 vn, 3 for vn, bc
5	Concerto, A, vn, orch (1778)
6	Sei duetti, 2 vn (*c*1780); lost, cited in *GerberNL*
[?7]	Concerto, D, vn, orch (1780)
8	3me oeuvre de six quatuors concertans, 2 vn, va, b (1782)
9	Six duos (?1783); 3 for 2 vn, 3 for vn, va

10	Trois symphonies à 8 parties, 2 fl, 2 hn, 2 vn, va, b (1785); lost, ?identical with 3 symphonies, CH-Bu
12	Trois grands duos concertans, 2 vn (c1790)
14	Premier air varié, vn, orch (?1805)
18	Trois trios concertans, 2 vn, va/b (?1805)
24	Trois grands duos concertans, 2 vn, bk 6 (c1809)

opp.11, 13, 15–17 not known; [?opp.19–23], Grands duos concertans, 2 vn, bks 1–5 (c1805–9), lost; cited in Choron-FayolleD

Rondeau, 2 vn, in Journal de violon dédié aux amateurs (1785), no.9; another piece for 2 vn, ibid. (1786), no.3, lost

Concerto, F, vn, orch, GB-Lbl

Le baille bienfaisant (op, E.T.B. Barrière), Valenciennes, 1775, lost; cited in Hécart, Brenner

BIBLIOGRAPHY

BrookSF; Choron-FayolleD

G.A.J. Hécart: Recherches historiques, bibliographiques, critiques, et littéraires, sur le Théâtre Valenciennes (Paris, 1816)

C.D. Brenner: A Bibliographical List of Plays in the French Language 1700–1789 (Berkeley, 1947, 2/1979)

C. White: From Vivaldi to Viotti: a History of the Early Classical Violin Concerto (Philadelphia, 1992)

MARY CYR

Barrière, Françoise (b Paris, 12 June 1944). French composer. She studied the piano at the Versailles Conservatoire and composition at the Paris Conservatoire; she also studied at the Service de la Recherche of the ORTF and at the Ecole Pratique des Hautes Etudes (ethnomusicology). She is committed to the development and dissemination of electroacoustic music, and to discussion of this music and its place in contemporary artistic creation. In 1970 she founded with Christian Clozier the Groupe de Musique Expérimentale de Bourges (GMEB), which is known for its creation of electroacoustic instruments for broadcasting or performance ('Gmebaphone'), and for beginners ('Gmebogosse'). Her works have been played widely and broadcast since 1970, when her Ode à la terre marine for tape was composed. Barrière writes for both electroacoustic and mixed media. Her music combines technological development, as for example the mixing techniques of Aujourd'hui (1975), which are placed at the service of the compositional process, with a deep humanity, evident in the personal reminiscences of Musique pour le temps de Noël and Par temps calme et ensoleillé. Of Aujourd'hui she wrote that she was inspired by the 'overwhelming solitude of the individual in our modern society'.

WORKS
(selective list)

for tape unless otherwise stated

Ode à la terre marine, 1970; Cordes-ci, cordes-ça, vn, hurdy-gurdy, tape, 1971; Variations hydrophilusiennes, 1971; Java Rosa, 1972; Au paradis des assassins, 1973; Ritratto di Giovane, pf, tape, 1972–3; Aujourd'hui, 1975; Chant à la mémoire des Aurignaciens, 1977; Musique pour le temps de Noël, sax, va, vc, perc, tape, 1979; Mémoires enfuies, 1980

Scènes des voyages d'Ulysse, 1981; Par temps calme et ensoleillé I, pf, tape, 1983; Par temps calme et ensoleillé II, vc, tape, 1985–9; Chant de consonnes, 1987; Le tombeau de Robespierre, 1989; L'envers des mots, 1990; Conversations enfantines, 1991; Nos petits monstres musiciens, child actor-musician, tape, 1992

PIERRE SABY

Barrière, Jean (b Bordeaux, 2 May 1707; d Paris, 6 June 1747). French composer and cellist. He probably lived in Bordeaux since at his death he was cited as a 'négociant de la ville de Bordeaux', and after his death a privilege was granted to a 'Sr Francois Barrière, prestre prébendier de l'église de Bordeaux, pour des Sonates et autres ouvrages de musique instrumentale du feu Jean Barrière'.

In 1730 he lived in Paris as a *Musicien ordinaire de notre Académie Royale de Musique*. In 1733 he was granted a privilege for six years to publish 'plusieurs Sonates et autres ouvrages de musique instrumentale'. According to Fétis, he went to Rome in 1736 to study with the famous Italian cellist Francesco Alborea, called Franciscchello. He remained in Italy for three years, but probably did not study with Franciscchello, who was employed by the court in Vienna from 1726 until his death in 1739. Barrière returned to Paris in 1739 and continued composing for the cello: 'Le Sieur Barrière, de retour d'Italie à Paris, vient de faire graver son troisième livre de Sonates pour le Violoncelle' (*Mercure de France*, November 1739). In 1739 his privilege was renewed for 12 years, and during that time he published his last three books – one each for cello, *pardessus de viole* and harpsichord.

The cello sonatas include a variety of technical problems – passages in double 3rds, arpeggiated chords and multiple stops, and brilliant virtuoso passages extending into the upper range. Each sonata has four or five movements, beginning with a slow movement and ending with a quick one. Several Allegros are titled Allemanda and book 2 no.3 includes a Sarabanda and Minuetto after the Allemande. The final movement of book 2 no.6 is marked 'Giga'. Several sonatas include an 'aria' or simple songlike piece in 6/8 or 6/4 marked either 'amorosa' or 'gratioso'. In the variations on the aria of book 3 no.6 brilliant arpeggios run throughout the entire range (C to a') while the aria melody is heard above (this sonata and possibly others may have been written for the cello piccolo). That the sonatas were meant to be accompanied by a second cello and a keyboard instrument is apparent from the Adagio of book 2 no.4, which includes an independent part for the second cello. Book 3 no.2 is for two cellos throughout with continuo (three cellos in all).

Books 3 and 4, published after Barrière's Italian journey, are technically more advanced and reflect his absorption of the Italian style. Many of the sonatas of book 3 include Italianate suite movements such as Giga and Corrente. These sonatas range from three to five movements, and several have transitional Adagios between movements. Some passages in his work suggest the use of the thumb of the left hand in the upper register (e'' in book 5 no.6), a technique which he probably introduced in France.

The first five sonatas for the *pardessus de viole* (book 5) appear, rewritten with additional ornamentation, elaboration and idiomatic runs, as the first five sonatas in book 6 for the harpsichord. Following the six sonatas are five *pièces*, each named for a musician or acquaintance. Like Duphly and Rameau, Barrière entitled one of his pieces 'La Boucon' for Anne-Jeanne Boucon, who later married Mondonville.

Barrière, like Martin Berteau, was one of the finest cello virtuosos in France during the first half of the 18th century, and the first to write thoroughly idiomatic music for the cello. Although his playing was highly regarded, there are few extant specific descriptions of it. At a Concert Spirituel he played with 'grande précision' (8 September 1738, *Mercure de France*), and P.-L. d'Aquin wrote of him with highest praise: 'Le fameux Barrière, mort depuis peu, possedoit tout ce que l'on peut désirer … il n'y avoit guère d'exécution comme la sienne'.

WORKS

[6] Sonates, vc, bc, bks 1–4 (Paris, 1733–9); bk 3, no.2 for 2 vc, bc; bk 3 and bk 4 nos.1, 2, 4–6 ed. M. Chaigneau and W.M. Rummel as 12 [sic] sonates pour violoncelle et piano, bks 1, 2 (Paris,

1920–25); bks 2, 4 ed. J. Adas: *Mid Eighteenth-Century Cello Sonatas*, xix (New York, 1991)

[6] Sonates, pardessus de viole, bc, bk 5 (Paris, 1739)

[6] Sonates et [5] pièces, hpd, bk 6 (Paris, 1739); sonatas 1–5 same as bk 5, nos.1–5

BIBLIOGRAPHY

FétisB

P.-L. d'Aquin: *Lettres sur les hommes célèbres … sous le règne de Louis XV* (Paris, 1752, 2/1753/R as *Siècle littéraire de Louis XV ou lettres sur les hommes célèbres*

A. Vidal: *Les instruments à archet*, ii (Paris, 1877), 330

M. Brenet: 'La librairie musicale en France de 1653 à 1790 d'après les registres de privilèges', *SIMG*, viii (1906–7), 401–66

J. Adas: 'Le célèbre Berteau', *EMc*, xvii (1989), 368–80

M. Benoit: *Dictionnaire de la musique en France aux XVIIe et XVIIIe siècles* (Paris, 1992)

MARY CYR

Barring (i). The drawing of vertical lines called 'bars' through a staff, system or score, in order to mark off metrical units by their horizontal spacing, and instrumental or vocal groupings by their vertical continuity or discontinuity; *see* BAR and NOTATION, §III, 4(iii). The term is commonly used for the scheme itself whereby such bars are drawn.

IAN HARWOOD

Barring (ii). The system of strips or bars of wood glued under the soundboard (or belly) of many string instruments, such as lute, guitar, violin, cello, harpsichord and piano. Since the number, position, size and method of fixing these bars affect the mode of vibration of the soundboard when excited by the strings, they are crucial to the tone of the instrument, more so, in fact than the materials and method of construction of the soundbox itself (*see* RIBS). The barring does also have a role in strengthening and supporting the belly under stress, but it is most importantly an essentially integral part of the resonating system.

Many modern string instruments are derived from forebears whose resonating surface was made of skin. To vibrate as responsively as skin, wood clearly has to be thin (little more than a millimetre on some lute bellies). Barring differentially loads the vibrating surface: to enhance tonal contrasts transverse bars on lutes are generally heavier towards the bass side of the soundboard, feathering away towards the treble. Soundboards of keyboard instruments are necessarily much heavier, and to optimize responses to low and high frequencies the wood of the board itself can be made thicker towards the bass strings, and thinner towards the treble.

The complexity of barring varies. Violins and cellos have a single BASS-BAR positioned parallel to the lowest string and close to the left foot of the bridge. Lutes characteristically have a number of transverse bars (*see* LUTE, §2). Guitars can have more complex arrays (*see* GUITAR, §1, and especially fig.1), often with radial barring ('fan-strutting') which distributes the energy localized at the bridge, as well as transverse bars. The latter, in order to avoid damping the vibration, may not be attached to the sides, a feature known also in lutes, where bars may be feathered away short of the edges of the belly. Approaches vary not only between different families of instruments, but also between different models of the same instrument, according to the function for which they are designed: thus flamenco guitars require different dynamics to those designed for the solo concert perform-

ance. Individual instruments may even be rebuilt with their barring modified to adjust tonal balance.

IAN MORRISON

Barring (iii). A left-hand technique used by players of many plucked instruments (and a few bowed instruments such as the viol) to facilitate the playing of chords (Fr. *jeu barré*). The first finger is laid flat across all the strings (whole *barré*), or some of them (half *barré*), behind a fret, leaving the other fingers free to stop the remaining notes of the chord (*see* BARRÉ). This technique increases the number of chords that can be played on plucked instruments, particularly those with more than four courses, such as the lute and the guitar.

IAN HARWOOD

Barrington, Daines (*b* London, 1727; *d* London, 14 March 1800). English lawyer and writer on music. The fourth son of John Shute, 1st Viscount Barrington, he was called to the Bar from the Inner Temple and held public offices between 1751 and 1785. His eldest sister, Sarah, married the amateur musician and music theorist Robert Price. Barrington's writings on music are remarkable for their observations on two relatively new topics: child music prodigies and animal communication. The former contains valuable firsthand accounts of five 'infant' musicians (Mozart, Charles and Samuel Wesley, William Crotch and Garret Wesley, 1st Earl of Mornington), and the latter includes an article on birdsong that was cited by Charles Darwin some hundred years later.

WRITINGS

'Account of a Very Remarkable Musician [W.A. Mozart]. In a Letter from the Honourable Daines Barrington, F.R.S. to Mathew Maty, M.D. Sec. R.S.', *Philosophical Transactions of the Royal Society*, lx (1770), 54–64

'Experiments and Observations on the Singing of Birds', *Philosophical Transactions of the Royal Society*, lxiii (1773), 249–58

'Some Account of Two Musical Instruments Used in Wales', *Archaeologia*, iii (1775), 30–34

Miscellanies (London, 1781), 279–325 [contains accounts of William Crotch, Samuel and Charles Wesley and the Earl of Mornington]

BIBLIOGRAPHY

DNB (G.P. Macdonell)

Obituary, *Gentleman's Magazine*, lxx (1800), 291–4

C. Darwin: *The Descent of Man* (London, 1871, 2/1879), 368, 370–71

J.C. Kassler: *The Science of Music in Britain, 1714–1830* (New York, 1979), i, 52–4

JAMIE C. KASSLER

Barrios (Fernandez), Angel (*b* Granada, 4 Jan 1882; *d* Madrid, 17 Nov 1964). Spanish composer, guitarist and violinist. The son of a flamenco guitarist, he studied harmony, the violin and the guitar in Granada, giving most of his attention to the latter instrument. Later he studied in Madrid with del Campo and in Paris with Gédalge. In 1900 he founded the Trio Iberia (lute, bandurria, guitar), for which he wrote many arrangements and with which he toured Europe. Though productive in his youth, he wrote very little after the civil war.

WORKS
(selective list)

Dramatic: La culpa (op, 3, G. Martínez Sierra), Madrid, 1914 [collab. del Campo]; La romería (zar, 2, L.L. Dominguez), Madrid, 1917 [collab. del Campo]; El avapiés (op, 3, T. Borrás), Madrid, Real, 18 March 1919 [collab. del Campo]; Granada mía (sainete granadino, 2, A. López Monís), Madrid, 1919; La suerte (sainete lírico, 1, S. and J. Alvarez Quintero), Madrid, 1926; La Lola se va a los puertos (zar, 32, A. and M. Macado), Madrid, 1951 [also op,

2, G. and R. Fernández Shaw, after A. and M. Machado, perf
Madrid, 1955]; incid music
Orch: Impresiones de Granada (Zambra en el Albaycín), sym. poem,
1917; Una copla en la fuente del Avellano, sym. poem, 1918;
Danzas gitanas, 1923; Copla de soleá
Pf and gui pieces
Principal publisher: Unión Musical Española

BIBLIOGRAPHY
MGG2 (C.Heine)
A. Fernandez-Cid: Cien años de teatro musical en España (Madrid,
1975)
T. Marco: Historia de la música espanõla: siglo XX (Madrid, 1983)
CARLOS GÓMEZ AMAT

Barrios Mangoré, Agustín (Pío) [Barrios, Agustín Pío] (*b*
San Juan Bautista de las Misiones, 5 May 1885; *d* San
Salvador, 7 Aug 1944). Paraguayan guitarist and composer. In his youth in Asunción he studied the guitar with
Gustavo Sosa Escalada and composition with Nicolo
Pellegrini, and practised his compositional skills by
transcribing works by Bach, Beethoven and Chopin. In
1910 he left Paraguay intending to give a week of concerts
in Argentina, but such was his success that he was away
for 14 years, playing in Brazil, Chile and Uruguay (where
he studied with Antonio Giménez Manjón). He found a
patron in the diplomat Tomás Salomini, who arranged
recitals for him in Mexico and Cuba. His first real
successes date from about 1919, when he played for the
President of Brazil. In 1930 he adopted the pseudonym
Mangoré (after a legendary Guaraní chieftain), and in
1934 he went to Europe with Salomini, living in Berlin
and visiting Belgium and Spain. In 1936 he returned to
Latin America, and taught at the conservatory in San
Salvador from 1939 to 1944. Critics compared Barrios
Mangoré with Segovia as an interpreter and with Paganini
as a virtuoso. He was the first Latin-American guitarist of
stature to be heard in Europe, and made numerous
recordings between 1913 and 1929.

Although he lacked a formal musical education, Barrios
Mangoré wrote guitar music of high quality that combined
many of the characteristics of his predecessors, Sor and
Tárrega. He reputedly composed about 300 works for
solo guitar, of which over a third have been located either
in manuscripts or from his recordings. These include *La
catedral*, *Danza paraguaya*, *Un sueño en la floresta*,
Preludio, op.5 no.1, *Julia Florida*, *Una limosna por el
amor de dios*, *Mazurka apasionata*, *Vals*, op.8 nos.3 and
4, and Variations on a Theme of Tárrega, all of which
have become part of the repertory.

BIBLIOGRAPHY
R. Stover: Six Silver Moonbeams: the Life and Times of Agustín
Barrios Mangoré (Clovis, CA, 1992)
PETER SENSIER/RICHARD D. STOVER

Barron, Bebe [née Charlotte Wind] (*b* Minneapolis, 16
June 1927). American composer. She and her husband
Louis Barron were pioneers in the field of electro-acoustic
music. She received the MA in political science from the
University of Minnesota, where she studied composition
with Cordero, and she also spent a year studying
composition at the University of Mexico. In 1947 she
moved to New York and, while working as a researcher
for *Time-Life*, studied composition with Riegger and
Cowell. Married that year, the Barrons began their
experiments with taped electronic sounds; in 1948 in New
York they established one of the earliest electro-acoustic
music studios. It contained both disc and tape equipment

with sine- and square-wave oscillators, mixers and filters,
and four synchronous projectors used for the manipulation of sound on optical tracks. Their experiments led the
Barrons to use and develop characteristics of individual
circuits to create different types of sound events, each of
which was considered a Gestalt, and they eventually
constructed a large collection of cybernetic circuits for
compositional use. When they collaborated on a composition, Louis designed and built the electronic circuits for
sound generation while Bebe searched the taped material
for its musical potential and proposed the application of
particular processing and compositional techniques.

Their first fully realized work was *Heavenly Menagerie*
(1951–2). During 1952 and 1953 their studio was used
by Cage for the preparation of his first tape works. In
1956 they composed the music for *Forbidden Planet*, one
of the first electronic scores written for a commercial film,
and an influential work in the development of electronic
music. In 1962 the Barrons moved to Los Angeles, where,
although divorced in 1970, they continued to collaborate
on compositional projects. Bebe became the first Secretary
of the Society for Electro-Acoustic Music in the United
States in 1985 and also served on the Board of Directors.
In 1997 she was presented with an award from the Society
for Electro-Acoustic Music in the United States for the
Barrons' joint lifetime achievement in electro-acoustic
music.

WORKS
all electro-acoustic, composed with Louis Barron
Dramatic: Legend (American Mime Theatre), 1955; Ballet (P.
Feigay), 1958; incid music for 4 plays, 1957–62
Tape: Heavenly Menagerie, 1951–2; For an Electronic Nervous
System, 1954; Music of Tomorrow, 1960; Spaceboy, 1971; The
Circe Circuit, 1982; Elegy for a Dying Planet, 1982
Film scores: Bells of Atlantis (I. Hugo), 1952; Miramagic (W.
Lewisohn), 1954; Forbidden Planet (F.M. Wilcox), 1956; Jazz of
Lights (Hugo), 1956; Bridges (S. Clarke), 1959; Crystal Growing
(Western Electric), 1959; The Computer Age (IBM), 1968;
Spaceboy (R. Druks), 1973 [arr. of 1971 tape piece]; More than
Human (A. Singer), 1974; Cannabis (Computer Graphics), 1975

BIBLIOGRAPHY
GroveW (B. Schrader) [incl. further bibliography]
L. Barron and B.Barron: 'Forbidden Planet', Film Music, xv/5 (1956),
18
S. Rubin: 'Retrospect: Forbidden Planet', Cinefantastique, iv/1
(1975), 4–13
J. Brockman: 'The First Electronic Filmscore: Forbidden Planet', The
Score, vii/3 (1992), 5–13
V. Vale and A.Juno: Incredibly Strange Music No.2 (San Francisco,
1994), 194–202
M. Burman: 'Making Music for Forbidden Planet', Projections 7, ed.
J. Boorman and W. Donohue (London, 1997), 252–63
BARRY SCHRADER

Barron, Louis (*b* Minneapolis, 23 April 1920; *d* Los
Angeles, 1 Nov 1989). American composer. He and his
wife Bebe wrote pioneering works in the field of electro-
acoustic music. He studied the piano and wrote jazz
criticism while a student at the University of Minnesota.
He then worked for the Gallup organization as a social
psychologist. Married in 1947, the Barrons established
one of the earliest electro-acoustic music studios, in which
Louis's knowledge of electronics allowed him to design
and build so-called behavioural circuits, based on Norbert
Wiener's science of cybernetics.

A fuller discussion of the Barrons' compositional
techniques, with a list of their collaborative works and a
bibliography, can be found under BEBE BARRON.

BARRY SCHRADER

Barrón, Ramón González. *See* GONZÁLEZ BARRÓN, RAMÓN.

Barroso, Ari (Evangelista) (*b* Ubá, 7 Nov 1903; *d* Rio de Janeiro, 9 Feb 1964). Brazilian composer and conductor. In 1920 he moved to Rio de Janeiro where he developed his career, first as a pianist in dance bands and cinemas, then as a composer of pieces for musical theatre, as a radio programmer and announcer, and later as a television programmer. He also composed the sound tracks for various films, especially Walt Disney's *The Three Caballeros* ('Você já foi à Bahia?'), for which he received a diploma from the Hollywood Academy of Cinematographic Sciences and Arts. In 1955, the Brazilian government bestowed upon him, together with Villa-Lobos, the National Order of Merit.

Barroso greatly contributed to the establishment of the classic urban samba in the 1930s. Among the over 160 sambas that he wrote, those of the 1930s and 40s have remained the most popular. Such pieces as *Faceira* (1931), *No tabuleiro da baiana* (1937), *Na Baixa do Sapateiro* (1938), *Morena boca de ouro* (1941), *Os quindins de Iaiá* (1941), among many others, won him prestige and reputation. None, however, had the national and international impact and recognition of his *Aquarela do Brasil*, recorded in the USA as *Brazil*. A 1939 'samba de exaltação', it exalted the beauty and patriotic values of the country in strongly nationalistic terms, and virtually became Brazil's popular 'national anthem'.

BIBLIOGRAPHY
L. Rangel: *Sambistas e chorões* (São Paulo, 1962)
D. Luciana: *Ari Barroso, um turbilhão!* (Rio de Janeiro, 1970)
J. Efegê: *Figuras e coisas da música popular brasileira* (Rio de Janeiro, 1978–80)
M. de Morais: *Recordações de Ary Barroso* (Rio de Janeiro, 1979)
S. Cabral: *No tempo de Ari Barroso* (Rio de Janeiro, *c*1993)
GERARD BÉHAGUE

Barroso Neto, Joaquim Antônio (*b* Rio de Janeiro, 30 Jan 1881; *d* Rio de Janeiro, 1 Sept 1941). Brazilian composer and pianist. He began his piano studies at an early age and later attended the then Instituto Nacional de Música, under Bevilacqua, Braga, Nascimento and Nepomuceno. He was appointed a professor of piano at the same institution in 1906, becoming in a few years one of Brazil's most celebrated piano teachers. For some time he was a member of the Barroso-Milano-Gomes Trio. In the early 1920s he took over the artistic directorship of the Sociedade de Cultura Musical. His consistent interest in choral music resulted in the foundation of the Côro Barroso Neto in 1936. Barroso Neto wrote only piano music, solo songs and choral works. His extensive piano output includes many pieces in a typical Romantic virtuoso style; and others, such as *Minha terra* and *Chôro*, with more national features. He also produced educational piano music, including *Estudos de agilidade*, *Coleção de estudos* and his editions of Clementi, Czerny and Cramer-Bülow. His best-known solo songs are *Canção da felicidade*, *Adeus*, *Olhos tristes* and *Felicidade*.

BIBLIOGRAPHY
T. Gomes: *Barroso Neto* (Rio de Janeiro, 1939)
G. Béhague: *Music in Latin America: an Introduction* (Englewood Cliffs, NJ, 1979)
V. Mariz: *História da música no Brasil* (Rio de Janeiro, 1981, 4/1994)
GERARD BÉHAGUE

Barrta, Josef. *See* BÁRTA, JOSEF.

Barrueco, Manuel (*b* Santiago de Cuba, 16 Dec 1952). American guitarist of Cuban birth. He studied at the Esteban Salas Conservatory in Santiago de Cuba and with Aaron Shearer at the Peabody Conservatory. He won first prize in the Concert Artists Guild Competition in 1974, and that year made his début at Carnegie Hall. In 1986 he gave the first American performance of Takemitsu's concerto *To the Edge of Dream* with the Tulse PO under Bernard Rubenstein. He was also soloist in the world première of Takemitsu's *Spectral Canticle*, a double concerto for guitar, violin and orchestra, with violinist Franz Peter Zimmerman at the Schleswig-Holstein Music Festival, Kiel, in 1995. Barrueco has made several recordings, notably of Albéniz and Granados, and has arranged works for the guitar including transcriptions of J.S. Bach's Three Violin Sonatas. He helped establish the guitar department at the Manhattan School of Music, and also teaches at the Peabody Conservatory.

BIBLIOGRAPHY
S. Cosentino: 'A Conversation with Manuel Barrueco', *Guitar Review*, no.104 (1996), 21–7
J. Ferguson: 'Manuel Barrueco and David Tanenbaum', *Guitar Player*, xxix/6 (1996), 35–9
THOMAS F. HECK

Barry, Gerald (*b* Clarecastle, Co. Clare, 28 April 1952). Irish composer. He graduated from University College, Dublin (BMus 1973) and went to Amsterdam on a Dutch scholarship to study with Piet Kee (organ) and Schat (composition). After returning to University College to complete the MA in 1975, he studied composition in Cologne with Stockhausen and Kagel and in Vienna with Cerha. He worked for a period as a pianist and organist in Cologne before being appointed in 1982 to a lectureship in music at University College, Cork. In 1986, election to Aosdána (the state-sponsored academy of creative artists) and increasing international recognition enabled him to devote himself to full-time composition. His music gained much critical acclaim in the late 1980s with major performances in London: the orchestral *Chevaux-de-frise* was commissioned for the Henry Wood Promenade Concerts in the Royal Albert Hall in 1988 and his opera *The Intelligence Park* was staged at the Almeida Festival in 1990. In 1995 a second opera, *The Triumph of Beauty and Deceit*, was broadcast on Channel 4 TV.

The influence of Kagel is evident in Barry's use of quotation techniques and his predilection for music theatre. Much of his quotation material is derived from sources from the 17th and 18th centuries, in particular Bach and Handel. Handel's sense of theatre and vocal line provides much of the inspiration for the three-act *The Intelligence Park*. Set in Dublin in 1753, it deals with an opera composer whose love for a castrato restores his creativity; it is, in essence, an opera within an opera. *The Triumph of Beauty and Deceit* for five male voices and chamber ensemble is a reworking of Handel's last oratorio, *The Triumph of Time and Truth*, and exemplifies well Barry's preoccupation with melody and linearity. The Baroque influence is also evident in the way in which instrumental colour is rendered subservient to line. Indeed, many of his pieces can be played by any instruments: the graphically entitled '____' for chamber ensemble appears in extended form as *Au milieu* (1981) for piano solo, while "Ø" (1979) for two pianos was arranged for various different instruments as *Sur les pointes*.

Barry's pitch material is often derived by means of aleatory processes from such abstract sources as a chart showing the locations of John Jenkins's manuscripts (as in '____'), the words of the BBC Radio 4 shipping forecast and dissonant harmonies formed by selective use of the passing notes in Bach chorales (as in *The Intelligence Park*), or, in the case of "Ø", by the addition and use of inessential contiguous pitches in the Irish melody *Bonny Kate*. Structurally, his pieces appear to start suddenly in mid-flow and end just as abruptly; elaboration of material is more important than any developmental progression and prolonged pauses can punctuate the course of the music unexpectedly. Episodic sections within pieces shift unpredictably and are accompanied by abrupt dynamic and tempo changes. The momentum generated by the relentless rhythmic energy and extreme virtuoso demands made on the performer results, perhaps, from the fact that he composes at the keyboard and improvises constantly. Barry has withdrawn all his works before 1977; the first work that he acknowledges is the piece of music theatre *Things That Gain By Being Painted* (1977), a setting of *The Pillow Book* by the 10th-century Japanese lady-in-waiting Sei Shonagon.

WORKS
(selective list)

Stage: Things that gain by being painted (music theatre, Sei Shonagon: *The Pillow Book*), 1v, spkr, vc, pf, 1977; The Intelligence Park (op, 3, V. Deane), 1981–8; The Triumph of Beauty and Deceit (op, M. Oakes), 1991–2

Orch: Diner, 1980; Of Queens' Gardens, 1986; Chevaux-de-frise, 1988; Children Aged 10–17, 1989; Flamboys, 1991; Le jalousie taciturne, str, 1996; The Road, 1997

Vocal: Carol, high and low vv, org/pf/hpd, 1986; Water Parted, Ct, pf, 1988 [from op The Intelligence Park, 1982–9]; The Conquest of Ireland (G. Cambrensis), B, orch, 1995; The Ring, SATB, orch, 1996

Chbr and solo inst: '____', chbr ens, 1979, rev. 1987; "Ø", 2 pf, 1979; Au milieu, pf, 1981 [based on '____', 1979]; Handel's Favourite Song, cl, fl, tpt, trbn, pf, gui, db, 1981; Sur les pointes, pf/hpd/org/chbr orch, 1981 [version of "Ø", 1979]; 5 Chorales, 2 pf, 1984 [from op The Intelligence Park, 1982–9]; Swinging tripes and trillibubkins, pf, 1986; Ob Qt, 1988; Bob, cl, cl + b cl, vn, vc, mar, pf, 1989; Triorchic Blues, pf, 1990; Low, cl, pf, 1991; Pf Qt no.1, 1992; Hard D, chbr ens, 1992; Sextet, cl + b cl, tpt, 2 mar, pf, db, 1992–3; Str Qt, 1994; The Chair, org, 1994; Qnt, eng hn, cl + b cl, vc, db, pf, 1995; Octet, 2 cl, vn, vc, pf, mar, 1995; Pf Qt no.2, 1996

Principal publisher: OUP

BIBLIOGRAPHY
CC1 (M. Blake); *KdG* (A. Klein)

V. Deane: 'The Music of Gerald Barry', *Soundpost*, no.2 (1981), 14–17

K. Volans and H. Bracefield: 'A Constant State of Surprise: Gerald Barry and *The Intelligence Park*', *Contact*, no.31 (1987), 9–19

A. Jack: 'Introducing Gerald Barry', *MT*, cxxix (1988), 389–93

A Bye: 'Gay Days Spent in Gladness', *MT*, cxxxiv (1993), 496–500

A. Klein: *Die Musik Irlands im 20. Jahrhundert* (Hildesheim, 1996)

G. Cox: 'The Music of Gerald Barry as an Introduction to Contemporary Irish Art-music', *Explorations*, ed. L. Irwin (Limerick, 1998), 61–72

GARETH COX

Barry, John [Prendergast, John Barry] (*b* York, 3 Nov 1933). English composer. He left school at 15 and gained early film experience as a projectionist in his father's cinemas in York. Through hearing film scores by established Hollywood composers such as Steiner, Korngold, Waxman, Newman and North, he determined upon a career as a film composer. He played the trumpet in a local band, and later in the army during his National Service (1952–5). He studied with Francis Jackson, organist of York Minster, and by correspondence with Joseph Schillinger and William Russo, gaining experience by arranging for several bands. In 1957 he formed John Barry and the Seven (later becoming the John Barry Seven, which toured until early 1966), and was musical director for Adam Faith on several hit songs, including *What do you want* (1959). The Seven's own *Hit and Miss* (1960) was taken up as the theme to the BBC's popular show 'Juke Box Jury'. During this period Barry wrote, performed and recorded pop music, making his first BBC television broadcast (on 'Six-Five Special') in 1957. He then worked in managerial capacities with various record companies, including EMI and the independent Ember International. Following his first jazz inflected rock and roll film score for *Beat Girl* (1959), featuring Adam Faith, he quickly became established, notably for his fusion of rock, pop and jazz in the numerous James Bond films, beginning with his arrangement of the Bond theme for *Dr No* (1962; score composed by Monty Norman) and concluding with his score for *The Living Daylights* (1987).

In between these overtly commercial films he frequently worked with the British director Bryan Forbes, contributing jazz numbers to *The L-Shaped Room* (1962), followed by collaborations on *Séance on a Wet Afternoon* (1964), *King Rat* (1965), *The Wrong Box* (1966), *The Whisperers* (1967) and *Deadfall* (1968), in which Barry himself appears conducting the LPO in a guitar concerto (Romance for guitar and orchestra), written to accompany a robbery sequence. Over many years he has built a song-writing partnership with the lyricist Don Black, with whom he collaborated on the musical *Billy*, after the novel *Billy Liar* by Keith Waterhouse. Its fantasy sequences gave full range to Barry's stylistic versatility and the show ran successfully at Drury Lane from May 1974 with Michael Crawford in the title role. When not orchestrating his own music, Barry has worked with several orchestrators including Bobby Richards, Al Woodbury and Greig McRitchie. He moved to America in 1975, first to Los Angeles and then New York (1980).

His stylistic versatility has enabled him to write for every genre of feature film – adventure, action, comedy, drama, romance and thriller – as well as for television. Although finding many commissions artistically rewarding, he has expressed candid views on some of his work, characterizing the James Bond scores as big-budget 'Mickey-Mouse' music that gives the public what it wants, and, despite being the recipient of two Academy Awards for *Born Free* (1966), admitting that he scored it as a satire on a sentimental Disney picture. Some commentators have identified stylistic fingerprints in whatever Barry writes, citing the recurrent use of typical instrumental textures (for example, xylophone with strings and high flute in his 'Bond' movies), even of individual instruments. His skill, however, equips him to assume specific classical and popular styles, as in his imitation of Duke Ellington for *The Cotton Club* (1984), or the traditional 'western' symphonic score for *Dances with Wolves* (1990). Barry has won five Academy Awards: *Born Free* (1966; Best Score and Best Song), *The Lion in Winter* (1968), *Out of Africa* (1985) and *Dances with Wolves* (1990).

WORKS
FILM AND TELEVISION

Film scores: Beat Girl, 1959; Never Let Go, 1960; Mix Me a Person, 1962; The L-Shaped Room, 1962; The Amorous Prawn, 1962; Dr No, 1962; They All Died Laughing, 1963; The Party's Over, 1963;

From Russia With Love, 1963; Zulu, 1963; Goldfinger, 1964; A Jolly Bad Fellow, 1964; Séance on a Wet Afternoon, 1964; Man in the Middle, 1964; The Ipcress File, 1965; King Rat, 1965; Thunderball, 1965; Mister Moses, 1965; The Knack . . . and How to Get It, 1965; The Quiller Memorandum, 1966; Born Free, 1966; Four in the Morning, 1966; Dutchman, 1966; The Chase, 1966; The Wrong Box, 1966; The Whisperers, 1967; You Only Live Twice, 1967; Petulia, 1968; The Lion in Winter, 1968; Deadfall, 1968; Boom!, 1968; Midnight Cowboy, 1969; On Her Majesty's Secret Service, 1969; The Appointment, 1969

Monte Walsh, 1970; The Last Valley, 1971; Walkabout, 1971; They Might Be Giants, 1971; Murphy's War, 1971; Mary, Queen of Scots, 1971; Alice's Adventures in Wonderland, 1972; Follow Me, 1972; Diamonds Are Forever, 1972; The Tamarind Seed, 1973; A Doll's House, 1973; The Man with the Golden Gun, 1975; The Dove, 1975; The Day of the Locust, 1975; King Kong, 1976; Robin and Marian, 1976; The Deep, 1977; The White Buffalo, 1977; First Love, 1977; The Betsy, 1978; Game of Death, 1978; Moonraker, 1979; The Black Hole, 1979; Starcrash, 1979; Hanover Street, 1979

Raise the Titanic!, 1980; Somewhere in Time, 1980; Night Games, 1980; Murder by Phone, 1980; Inside Moves, 1980; Superman 2, 1980; Touched By Love, 1980; Body Heat, 1981; The Legend of the Lone Ranger, 1981; Hammett, 1982; Frances, 1982; Octopussy, 1983; High Road to China, 1983; The Golden Seal, 1983; Until September, 1984; Mike's Murder, 1984; The Cotton Club, 1984; Jagged Edge, 1985; A View to a Kill, 1985; Out of Africa, 1985; Howard the Duck, 1986; Peggy Sue Got Married, 1986; The Golden Child, 1986; My Sister's Keeper, 1986; The Living Daylights, 1987; Hearts of Fire, 1987; Masquerade, 1988; A Killing Affair, 1988

Dances with Wolves, 1990; John Barry – Moviola, 1992; Chaplin, 1992; Indecent Proposal, 1993; My Life, 1993; Ruby Cairo, 1993; The Specialist, 1994; The Scarlet Letter, 1995; Cry the Beloved Country, 1995; Across the Sea of Time, 1995; Swept from the Sea, 1997; Mercury Rising, 1998

Television scores: Elizabeth Taylor in London, 1963; The Persuaders!, 1971; The Glass Menagerie, 1973; Love Among the Ruins, 1975; Eleanor and Franklin, 1976; Eleanor and Franklin: the White House Years, 1977; The Gathering, 1977; The War Between the Tates, 1977; Young Joe, the Forgotten Kennedy, 1977; Willa, 1979; The Corn is Green, 1979; Svengali, 1983; The Witness, 1992

Other works incl. individual songs for films, television and radio signature tunes, music for television shows, short films and commercials

OTHER WORKS

Stage: Passion Flower Hotel (musical, 2, T. Peacock; W. Mankowitz, after 'Rosalind Erskine'), London, Prince of Wales', 24 Aug 1965; Lolita My Love, 1968; Billy (musical, 2, D. Black; I. La Frenais and D. Clements after K. Waterhouse and W. Hall: Billy Liar), London, Drury Lane, 1 May 1974 [incl. Some of us belong to the stars]

Orch: Americans (1976); The Beyondness of Things (1997) [music from rejected score to The Horse Whisperer, 1998]

BIBLIOGRAPHY

G. Leonard and P. Walker: 'John Barry: the Early Years', From Silents to Satellite, no.15 (1992), 20–40

J. Burlingame: 'John Barry's Television Scores: an Overview', From Silents to Satellite, no.16 (1993), 34–8

R.S. Brown: 'Barry', Overtones and Undertones (Berkeley, 1994), 322–33 [interview]

G. Leonard and P. Walker: 'John Barry: into the Sixties', Music from the Movies, no.5 (1994), 8–12

G. Leonard and P. Walker: 'John Barry: into the Seventies', Music from the Movies, no.6 (1994), 60–62

G. Leonard and P. Walker: 'John Barry: the Seventies Part Two', Music from the Movies, no.8 (1995), 84–6

G. Leonard and P. Walker: 'John Barry: Into the Eighties', Music from the Movies, no.12 (1996), 30–32

G. Leonard and P. Walker: 'The Essential Musical Guide to James Bond', Music from the Movies, no.18 (1997), 42–5

G. Leonard, P. Walker and G. Bramley: John Barry: a Life in Music (Bristol, 1998)

DAVID KERSHAW

Barry, Margaret [Maggie] (b Cork City, Ireland, 1 June 1917; d County Down, N. Ireland, 1989). Irish singer and banjo player. Born into a family of musical semi-settled travellers, Barry left home to become a street singer when she was 15 years old. She began by busking the queues outside Cork's Coliseum cinema, then travelled throughout Ireland by bicycle and horse-drawn bow-top wagon, performing at markets, country fairs, football matches and house ceilidhs. After recording her at Dundalk Fair, Co. Louth, in 1951, the American folk music collector Alan Lomax (see LOMAX, (2)) introduced Barry to London where she performed on the BBC television programme Song Hunter and in Irish public houses. She formed a duo with Sligo fiddler Michael Gorman and played in small dance halls in Ireland and America with him, before returning to London during the 1960s in reduced circumstances. Following Gorman's death, she went home to Ireland and continued as a solo performer. Barry's powerful street-singing vocal style together with her sparse yet appropriate five-string banjo accompaniments captured the imaginations of folk revivalists and guaranteed her a place in the history of traditional Irish music.

BIBLIOGRAPHY
RECORDINGS

Songs of an Irish Tinker Lady, Riverside RLP 12-602 (?1956)

Her Mantle So Green, perf. M. Barry and M. Gorman, Topic CD474 (1994)

I Sang through the Fairs, coll. A. Lomax, Rounder Records 011661–177420 (1998)

DAVE ARTHUR

Barry, Phillips (b Boston, 1880; d Framingham, MA, 1937). American ballad scholar. He studied folklore, theology and classical and medieval literature at Harvard, and was probably self-taught in music. He founded the Folk-Song Society of the North-East and edited its Bulletin from 1930 until his death. His academic training combined with his later fieldwork allowed him to develop a broad yet penetrating view of ballad creation, and he was the first North American scholar to investigate folksong in terms of text, tune, performance and transmission. His idea of 'individual invention plus communal re-creation', which was similar to Cecil Sharp's theory, proposed that a folksong was creatively re-made within the community each time it was sung; this view replaced prevailing theories of a communal origin of the folksong by means of group improvisation. He collected mainly in New England and collaborated with scholars in Vermont and Maine. Through his efforts, research methods used in ballad studies changed from scholarship based on library sources, as in the work of Child and Kittredge, to the study of traditional performers and a more complete analysis of folksong as a genre. His essay 'The Part of the Folksinger' (1961) was particularly influential.

WRITINGS

'Irish Come-All-Ye's', Journal of American Folklore, xxii (1909), 374–88; see also 'Irish Folk-Song', Journal of American Folklore, xxiv (1911), 332–43

'The Origin of Folk-Melodies', 'A Garland of Ballads', Journal of American Folklore, xxiii (1910), 440–45, 446–54

'Some Aspects of Folk-Song', Journal of American Folklore, xxv (1912), 274–83

with F.H. Eckstorm and M.W.Smyth: 'The Music of the Ballads', British Ballads from Maine (New Haven, CT, 1929), xxi–xxxvii

'Notes on the Songs and Music of the Shakers', Bulletin of the Folk-Song Society of the North-East, no.1 (1930), 5–7

'Communal Recreation', Bulletin of the Folk-Song Society of the North-East, no.5 (1933), 4–6; see also 'On the Psychopathology of

'Ballad-Singing', *Bulletin of the Folk-Song Society of the North-East*, no.11 (1936), 16–18
'American Folk Music', *Southern Folklore Quarterly*, i/2 (1937), 29–47
'Notes on the Ways of Folk-Singers with Folk-Tunes', *Bulletin of the Folk-Song Society of the North-East*, no.12 (1937), 2–6
Folk Music in America (New York, 1939)
'The Part of the Folk Singer in the Making of Folk Balladry', *The Critics and the Ballad*, ed. M. Leach and T.P. Coffin (Carbondale, IL, 1961), 59–76

EDITIONS

The Maine Woods Songster: Fifty Songs for Singing (Cambridge, MA, 1939)
with others: *The New Green Mountain Songster* (New Haven, CT, 1939)

BIBLIOGRAPHY

G. Herzog: 'Phillips Barry', *Journal of American Folklore*, li (1938), 439–41
R.G. Alvey: 'Phillips Barry and Anglo-American Folksong Scholarship', *Journal of the Folklore Institute*, x (1973), 67–95

JAMES PORTER

Barsanti, Francesco (*b* Lucca, 1690; *d* London, late 1772). Italian composer. He studied scientific subjects at the University of Padua, and then devoted himself to music. In 1714 he went to London with Francesco Geminiani (also a native of Lucca); there he played the flute and oboe in the orchestra at the Italian opera, and published three sets of solo sonatas. According to Bonaccorsi, he was back in Lucca in 1735, taking part in festivities at S Croce; but that seems unlikely, as by the second half of 1735 he was resident in Edinburgh. He spent eight years in Scotland, where he married a Scots woman, was much patronized by the aristocracy and published his finest compositions, ten concerti grossi (1742) and nine overtures (*c*1743). He also brought out arrangements of 30 Scots songs with continuo in Edinburgh in 1742 (not 1719, as stated by Bonaccorsi and Praetorius).

In 1743 Barsanti returned to London. By this time he had lost his place in London musical society and was forced to take a job as an orchestral viola player. Six Latin motets (*c*1750) were rather wistfully dedicated to a member of the Scottish aristocratic Wemyss family 'in recompense for many obligations'. His daughter Jenny, trained in singing by Charles Burney, later achieved success as a London opera singer and actress.

Barsanti's compositions are accomplished and original. His op.1 recorder sonatas are among the finest in the instrument's repertory. The op.3 concerti grossi have a contrapuntal glitter not unlike those of J.S. Bach; the main movements are constructed in semi-improvised forms, from themes which are stated once and then broken down into smaller imitative units. His Scots-tune arrangements are far more than a foreigner's temporary flirtation with local music-making: Fiske noted Barsanti's sympathetic understanding of Scots-tune structures, and his willingness to end a setting on an 'unfinished' dominant chord if the tune demanded it. Italian virtuosity and Scottish sympathy join forces in the op.4 overtures; the main movement of no.9 introduces the jig *Babbity Bowster* as a fugal countersubject, while the finale of no.2 is a country-dance, suggesting the ringing open strings of Scots fiddling. Much of Barsanti's work still awaits revival.

WORKS

[6] Sonate, rec/vn, b/bc [op.1] (London, 1724 and 1727); nos.3 and 5 ed. W. Bergmann (London, 1949, 1956); nos.1–6 ed. H. Ruf (Kassel, 1965)
6 sonate, fl, b/bc, op.2 (London, 1728) [reprinted as op.3 in 1732]
[10] Concerti grossi, op.3; nos.1–5 2 hn, timp, str; nos.6–10 2 ob, tpt, timp, str (Edinburgh, 1742); nos.4 and 10 ed. E. Praetorius (London, 1953)
9 ov, 2 vn, va, b, op.4 (Edinburgh, *c*1743); no.2 ed. D. Johnson (Mainz, 1978); nos.4 and 6 ed. S. Kirakowska, no.9 ed. D. Johnson, *The Symphony 1720–1840*, E1 (New York, 1984)
6 ant, 5vv, op.5 (London, *c*1750)
6 sonatas, 2 vn, b, op.6 (London, 1769)
Happy is the man that findeth wisdom, canon, 4vv, *GB-Lbl*
12 unknown vn concs. are listed by Praetorius and Bonaccorsi

ARRANGEMENTS

[6] Sonatas, 2 vn, vc, bc (London, *c*1735) [orig. F. Geminiani: Sonate, vn, op.1 nos.7–12]
12 sonate, 2 rec/vn, bc (London, *c*1740) [orig. G. Sammartini]
A Collection of Old Scots Tunes, fl/ob/v, b/bc (Edinburgh, 1742); 1 ed. in Johnson (1984)
[6] Concerti grossi, 2 vn, va, vc soli, 2 vn, bc (London, 1757) [orig. G.B. Sammartini: 6 sonate notturni, op.6]

Some unknown arrs. of Corelli, probably in MS, are listed in the Edinburgh Musical Society's 1765 library catalogue (*GB-Eu* La.III.761)

BIBLIOGRAPHY

E. Praetorius: Forword to *F. Barsanti: Concerto grosso*, op.3 nos.4 and 10 (London, 1953)
W. Bergmann: 'Francesco Barsanti', *The Consort*, no.18 (1961), 67–77
A. Bonaccorsi: *Maestri di Lucca* (Florence, 1967), 44
D. Johnson: *Music and Society in Lowland Scotland in the Eighteenth Century* (London, 1972), 54, 64
R. Fiske: *Scotland in Music* (Cambridge, 1983), 18–20, 191–5
D. Johnson: *Scottish Fiddle Music in the 18th Century* (Edinburgh, 1984), 35–6, 41, 63

DAVID JOHNSON

Barshay [Barshai], Rudol'f (Borisovich) (*b* Krasnodarsk, 1 Oct 1924). Russian viola player and conductor. He studied the violin with Lev Zeitlin and the viola with Borisovsky at the Moscow Conservatory, and began his career in 1946 as an ensemble and solo player, gaining a high reputation and founding the Philharmonic Quartet of Moscow (now the Borodin Quartet) in which he played the viola. He then played in the even more outstanding Tchaikovsky Quartet led by Yulian Sitkovetsky, and took part in some of Leonid Kogan's all-star chamber ensembles. He also studied conducting with Ilya Musin in Leningrad. In 1955 he formed and conducted the Moscow Chamber Orchestra, whose programmes of Classical and contemporary music for small orchestra marked a new development in concerts in the USSR. Under his direction the orchestra became an outstanding ensemble, and toured widely abroad, first appearing in Britain in 1962; their first records in the West were issued in the same year. Barshay's performances were much admired for the exemplary unity of attack and phrasing and the sweetness of tone in the ensemble, but less so for his exaggerated range of dynamics. An outstanding recorded Mozart symphony cycle, the first to observe all the repeats, was free of this fault. A Beethoven cycle was marginally less successful. In 1967 he began to conduct major orchestras in the USSR and in 1969 he conducted the première of Shostakovich's 14th Symphony with Galina Vishnevskaya, Mark Reshetin and the MCO. His numerous transcriptions for small orchestra, notably of Prokofiev's piano suite, *Visions fugitives*, and of Shostakovich's Eighth String Quartet, are highly esteemed. In 1976 Barshay left the USSR and emigrated to Israel, where he directed the Israel Chamber Orchestra until 1981 and the New Israel Orchestra from 1977 to 1979. He served as artistic adviser to the Bournemouth SO (1982–8) and endured an unsuccessful tenure as music director of the Vancouver SO (1985–8), and from 1987–8 was principal guest conductor at the Orchestre Nationale de France. Barshay returned to Russia in 1993, after an absence of 17 years, to conduct Mahler's 9th Symphony with the Russian National Orchestra. He has also appeared as guest conductor with the Moscow Radio Orchestra and the St Petersburg PO.

BIBLIOGRAPHY

'Besedï s masterami: Rudol'f Barshay' [Conversations with the masters], *Muzïkal'naya zhizn'*, no.18 (1968), 10

I.M. YAMPOL'SKY/JOSÉ BOWEN

Barski, Aleksander. *See* BANDROWSKI-SAS, ALEKSANDER.

Barsova, Inna Alekseyevna (*b* Smolensk, 10 Sept 1927). Russian musicologist. She graduated from the Moscow State Conservatory in 1951, and completed her postgraduate studies in 1954, having studied with Igor' Sposobin, Viktor Zuckermann and Vladimir Protopopov. She took the *Kandidat* degree in 1970 with a dissertation on the early symphonies of Mahler, and was awarded the doctorate in 1980 for her monograph *Simfonii Gustava Malera*. She joined the department of orchestration at the Conservatory (1954), rising to senior lecturer (1973) and professor (1981). She was also professor at the conservatories in Nizhniy Novgorod (1979–92) and Minsk (1993–6).

Barsova's main area of research is the music of Mahler, and she has made a comprehensive examination of the creative and epistolatory legacy of the composer. She has addressed Mahler's relationship to Russia, and has written on Mahler and Dostoyevsky, his concert tours to St Petersburg, and the reception history of his music in Russia. She has also studied 20th-century composers such as Skryabin, Hindemith and Kancheli, and written on the Russian avant garde (the music of Mosolov and Shostakovich in the 1920s). Other areas of study include 19th-century Austrian and German music and history, aesthetics and the theory of music and musical analysis. Her work on score notation has approached the subject as a phenomenon of written culture manifesting itself in the context of the spatial discoveries of the Renaissance, along with the upheavals in the natural sciences, mathematics, cartography, architecture and fine art. Her work is characterized by its culturological direction, and its reference to psychological and linguistic data (an attempt has been made to provide an etymological analysis of musical language).

WRITINGS

'Skryabin i russkiy simfonizm' [Skryabin and Russian symphonism], *SovM* (1958), no.5, pp.65–71

Simfonicheskiy orkestr i yego instrumentï [The symphony orchestra and its instruments] (Moscow, 1962)

ed.: *Gustav Maler: pis'ma, vospominaniya* [Mahler: letters, reminiscences] (Moscow, 1964, 2/1968) [incl. 'Gustav Maler: lichnost', mirovozzreniye, tvorchestvo' [Mahler: personality, world outlook, creative work], 3–88]

with Yu.A. Fortunatov: *Prakticheskoye rukovodstvo po chteniyu simfonicheskikh partitur* [A practical guide to reading symphonic scores] (Moscow, 1966)

Kniga ob orkestre [A book on the orchestra] (Moscow, 1969, 2/1978; Ukr. trans., 1981, 2/1988)

'Problema formï v rannikh simfoniyakh Gustava Malera' [The problem of form in the early symphonies of Mahler], *Voprosï muzïkal'noy formï*, ii (1972), 202–60

'Maler v kontekste vremeni' [Mahler in the context of his time], *SovM* (1973) no.3, pp.69–77

'Kamernïy orkestr Paulya Khindemita' [The chamber orchestra of Hindemith], *Muzïka i sovremennost'*, ix (1975), 226–61 [on *Kammermusiken* nos.1–17]

Simfonii Gustava Malera [The symphonies of Mahler] (diss., Moscow Conservatory, 1980; Moscow, 1975)

'Aleksandr Mosolov: dvadtsatïye godï' [Mosolov: the 1920s], *SovM* (1976), no.12, pp.77–87; Cz. trans. in *HRo*, xxx (1977), 509–10, 568–70; xxxi (1978), 85–8

ed., with S.A. Osherov: *Rikhard Vagner: izbrannïye rabotï* [Wagner: selected works] (Moscow, 1978)

'Das Frühwerk von Aleksandr Mosolov', *Jb Peters 1979*, 117–69; repr. in *Aleksandr Skrjabin und die Skrjabinisten*, ii, Musik-Konzepte, nos.39–40 (1984), 122–67; Hung. trans. in *Magyar zene*, xxviii (1987), 244–81

'Mahler und Dostojewski', *Gustav Mahler: Vienna 1979*, 65–75

'Iz istorii partiturnoy notatsii: zvukovaya plotnost' i prostranstvo v mnogokhornoy muzïke XVII veka' [The history of score notation: the density of sound and the space in the 17th century for many choirs], *Istoriya i sovremennost'*, ed. A.I. Klimovitsky, L.G. Kovnatskaya and M.D. Sabinina (Leningrad, 1981), 6–33

'Sto let spustya' [100 years on], *SovM* (1983), no.11, pp.112–20 [on the centenary of Wagner's death]

'Muzïkal'naya dramaturgiya Chetvyortoy simfonii Gii Kancheli' [The dramatic plan of the music of Kancheli's Fourth Symphony], *Muzïkal'nïy sovremennik*, v (1984), 108–34; Georgian trans. in *Sabchota Khelovneba* (1992), 100–07

'Muzïka romantizma' [The music of Romanticism], *Mir romantizma (zhivopis', risunok)* (Moscow, 1985), 7–18 [exhibition catalogue]

'Opït étimologicheskogo analiza: k postanovke voprosa' [An attempt at etymological analysis: formulating the question], *SovM* (1985), no.9, pp.59–66

'Probleme der Mahler-Forschung der achtziger Jahre', *Gustav Mahler: Leipzig 1985*, 130–34; Russ. version in *SovM* (1987), no.2, pp.86–93

'Zum Formproblem bei Gustav Mahler', *Gustav Mahler: Vienna 1985*, 53–7

ed., with N.K. Meshko: *A.V. Mosolov: stat'i i vospominaniya* [Mosolov: articles and reminiscences] (Moscow, 1986) [incl. 'Ranneye tvorchestvo Aleksandra Mosolova' [The early works of Mosolov], 44–122 and a worklist]

'Spetsifika yazïka muzïki v sozdanii khudozhestvennoy kartinï mira' [The specifics of the language of music in creating an artistic picture of the world], *Khudozhestvennoye tvorchestvo: voprosï kompleksnogo izucheniya* (Leningrad, 1986), 98–116

'Mifologicheskaya semantika vertikal'nogo prostranstva v orkestre Rikharda Vagnera' [The mythological significance of the vertical space in Wagner's orchestra], *Problemï muzïkal'nogo romantizma*, ed. A.L. Porfir'yeva (Leningrad, 1987), 59–74

'Inter'yer Sobora Sv. Marka kak prostranstvennïy proobraz mnogokhornïkh kompozitsiy v venetsianskoy i nemetskoy muzïke XVI – nachala XVII vekov' [The interior of S Marco as a spatial prototype for Venetian and German polychoral works of the 16th and early 17th centuries], *Iskusstvo Venetsii i Venetsiya v iskusstve* (Moscow, 1988), 212–39

'Legenda o khudozhnike' [The legend of an artist], *Muzïka – kul'tura – chelovek*, ed. M.L. Muginshteyn (Sverdlovsk, 1988)

'Samopoznaniye i samoopredeleniye istorii muzïki segodnya' [Self-knowledge and self-determination in the history of music today], *SovM* (1988), no.9, pp.66–73

'Iz neopublikovannogo arkhiva A. Mosolova' [From the unpublished papers of Mosolov], *SovM* (1989), no.7, pp.80–92; no.8, pp.69–75

'Das Schaffen Gustav Mahler in Spiegel der russischen Kritik und Musikwissenschaft in der ersten Hälfte des 20. Jahrhunderts', *Gustav Mahler: Hamburg 1989*, 267–77

'Novoye v russkoy maleriane' [New discoveries in Russian studies on Mahler], *SovM* (1990), no.3, pp.98–102

'Russkaya prem'yera Vos'moy simfonii Malera' [The Russian première of Mahler's Eighth Symphony], *SovM* (1990), no.4, pp.55–60

'. . . Samïye pateticheskiye kompozitorï yevropeyskoy muzïki: Chaykovsky i Maler' [Two composers manifesting the greatest pathos in European music: Tchaikovsky and Mahler], *SovM* (1990), no.6, pp.125–32

'Alexander Mosolow: sein Leben und sein Schicksal', *Verfemte Musik: Dresden 1993*, 177–82

'Mahler: ein "Schüler" Čajkovskijs?', *Čajkovskij-Symposium: Tübingen 1993*, 51–6

'Organ v zerkale romanticheskogo orkestra: avstro-nemetskaya traditsiya' [The organ in the mirror of the Romantic orchestra: the Austro-German tradition], *MAk* (1993), no.2, pp.91–7

'Rossiyskaya kar'yera Gustava Franka' [The Russian career of Gustav Franck], *MAk* (1994), no.1, pp.80–92

'Trizhdï lishyonnïy rodinï: arkhetip yevreystva v lichnosti i tvorchestve Gustava Malera' [Thrice deprived of a homeland: the archetype of Jewishness in the personality and creative work of Mahler], *MAk* (1994), no.1, pp.177–81

'Verdrängte Moderne: russische Avangardemusik in den zwanziger Jahren', *Berlin–Moskau, 1920–1950*, ed. I. Antonowa and J. Merkert (Munich, 1995), 167–71 [in Ger., Russ.]

'Mahler und Russland', *Muziek & wetenschap*, v (1995–6), 287–301

'Mezhdu "sotsial'nïm zakazom" i "muzïkoy bol'shikh strastey": 1934–1937 godï v zhizni Dmitriya Shostakovicha' [Between the 'social commission' and the music of 'high passions': the years 1934–7 in the life of Shostakovich], *D.D. Shostakovich: sbornik statey k 90-letiyu so dnya rozhdeniya*, ed. L. Kovnatskaya (St Petersburg, 1996), 121–40

Ocherki po istorii partiturnoy notatsii [Essays on the history of score notation] (Moscow, 1997)

'Svetlïy ruchey: k istorii sozdaniya' [*The Limpid Stream*: on the history of its composition], *MAk* (1997), no.4, pp.51–8

'Sotrudnichestvo i perepiska dvukh izdatel'stv: Universal Edition i Muzsektora Gosizdata v 20–30-e godï: vzglyad iz Venï' [The cooperation and correspondence between two publishing houses: Universal Edition and the State Publishers Music Section in the 1920s and 30s: the view from Vienna], *Muzïkal'noye prinosheniye* (St Petersburg, 1998), 240–58

BIBLIOGRAPHY
A.I. Klimovitsky: 'Muzïkal'nïy tekst, istoricheskiy kontekst i problemï analiza muzïki' [Musical text, the historical context and problems of musical analysis], *SovM* (1984), pp.70–81, esp. 71–4

ABRAHAM I. KLIMOVITSKY

Barsova [née Vladimirova], **Valeriya** (**Vladimirovna**) (*b* Astrakhan', 1/13 June 1892; *d* Sochi, 13 Dec 1967). Russian soprano. She studied with her sister, Mariya Vladimirova, then in Umberto Mazetti's class at the Moscow Conservatory. She made her début with the Zimin Private Opera, Moscow, in 1919, later becoming a soloist at the Bol'shoy (1920–48). She also sang at Stanislavsky's and Nemirovich-Danchenko's opera studios. To a light, silvery tone and an agile technique she added warmth and depth of feeling. She sang Glinka and Rimsky-Korsakov roles; Gilda, Violetta and Leonora (*Il trovatore*); Butterfly and Musetta, Lakmé and Manon. After 1929 she toured in Germany, Britain, Turkey, Poland, Yugoslavia and Bulgaria. (G. Polyanovsky: *V.V. Barsova*, Moscow, 1975)

I.M. YAMPOL'SKY

Barstow, Dame **Josephine** (**Clare**) (*b* Sheffield, 27 Sept 1940). English soprano. She studied in Birmingham and London, then sang with Opera for All. In 1967 she joined Sadler's Wells, singing the Second Lady, Cherubino, Gluck's Eurydice and Violetta, her début role with the WNO, for whom she sang Countess Almaviva, Fiordiligi, Mimì, Amelia (*Boccanegra*), Elisabeth de Valois, Lisa, Jenůfa, Ellen Orford and Tatyana. Having made her Covent Garden début in 1969 as a Niece (*Peter Grimes*), she created Denise in *The Knot Garden* (1970), Young Woman in *We Come to the River* (1976) and Gayle in *The Ice Break* (1977), also singing Mrs Ford, Santuzza, Odabella (*Attila*) and Lady Macbeth, which she recorded on video for Glyndebourne. She has appeared in Paris, Berlin, Munich, San Francisco, Chicago, Boston and at the Metropolitan, where she made her début in 1977 as Musetta. For Sadler's Wells, later the ENO, she created Marguerite in *The Story of Vasco* (1974); she sang Jeanne with them in *The Devils of Loudun* (1973) and Autonoe

with the New Opera Company in *The Bassarids* (1974), both British stage premières. Her repertory at the ENO includes Natasha, Leonore, Salome, Octavian, the Marschallin, Arabella, Leonora (*La forza del destino*), Aida, Sieglinde, Emilia Marty, Katerina Izmaylova, Kostelnička, the Old Prioress (*Dialogues des Carmélites*) and Ellen Orford. Her roles for Opera North include Cherubini's Medea and a much-acclaimed Gloriana. In 1986 at Salzburg she created Benigna in Penderecki's *Schwarze Maske*, then sang Tosca and Amelia (*Ballo in maschera*), recording the latter role with Karajan. An unusually intense actress with a vibrant, flexible voice of highly individual timbre, capable of expressing the strongest emotions, she excels in portraying troubled and distraught characters. She was made a CBE in 1985 and DBE in 1996.

BIBLIOGRAPHY
E. Forbes: 'Josephine Barstow', *Opera*, xxv (1974), 859–64

ALAN BLYTH

Bart [Begleiter], **Lionel** (*b* London, 1 Aug 1930; *d* Hammersmith, 3 April 1999). English composer, lyricist and librettist of Austrian-Jewish descent. He studied at St Martin's School of Art and then became a graphic artist and scene painter. In the mid-1950s, as a member of the skiffle group the Cavemen, he wrote songs for its lead singer Tommy Steele, and also for Cliff Richard and Billy Fury. His subsequent songs for films starring Steele and Richard produced several hit numbers including *Living Doll* and *Little White Bull*. He worked on musicals for Joan Littlewood's Theatre Workshop at Stratford East, from where *Fings Ain't Wot They Used t' Be*, with lyrics inspired by cast improvisations, transferred to become his first West End success. In *Oliver!* (1960) he combined a Jewish modality ('Who will buy?', 'You've got to pick a pocket or two' and 'Reviewing the Situation'), music hall ('Consider Yourself'), overt sentiment ('Where is love?', 'As long as he needs me') and comic word play ('That's your funeral') to produce one of the most successful of all British musicals. The spectacular *Blitz!* (1962) was based on his own experiences in London during World War II, again with Bart's use of contained working-class communities as his main dramatic source. *Twang!!* (1965), which burlesqued the legend of Robin Hood, has become a famous West End disaster, and marked the start of both a personal and artistic decline; his musical *La strada*, after the film by Fellini, survived one performance on Broadway in 1969. His connection with Stratford East continued when he contributed songs to *The Londoners* and *Costa Packet* (both 1972). A resurgence of interest in his work followed the success in 1989 of his award-winning song *Happy Endings*, written for an advertising campaign, and there were major London revivals of *Blitz!* (1990), *Maggie May* (1992) and *Oliver!* (1994). Self-taught, his harmony and word underlay were sometimes idiosyncratic, and he relied on assistants to transcribe his melodies and harmonic indications.

WORKS
(selective list)

unless otherwise stated, music and lyrics by Bart and dates for stage works those of first London performance

Musicals (book authors shown in parentheses): Wally Pone, King of the Underworld (after B. Johnson: *Volpone*), Unity Theatre, 18 July 1958; Fings Ain't Wot They Used t' Be (2, F. Norman), Stratford East, Theatre Royal, 17 Feb 1959; Lock Up Your Daughters (2, B. Miles after H. Fielding: *Rape upon Rape*),

Mermaid, 28 May 1959, music L. Johnson, film 1969; Oliver! (2, Bart after C. Dickens: *Oliver Twist*), New Theatre, orchd E. Rogers, 30 June 1960, film 1968 [incl. Food, Glorious Food; As long as he needs me, Consider Yourself, Where is love?]; Blitz! (2, Bart and J. Maitland), Adelphi, orchd B. Sharples, 8 May 1962 [incl. Who's this geezer Hitler, Mums and Dads, The Day After Tomorrow, Be what you wanna be]; Maggie May (2, A. Owen), Adelphi, orchd R. Jones, 22 Sept 1964 [incl. Maggie, Maggie May; Dey don't do dat t'day, The Ballad of the Liver Bird]; Twang!! (musical, 2, H. Orkin), Shaftesbury, orchd K. Moule, 20 Dec 1965; La strada (musical, 2, after F. Fellini), New York, Lunt-Fontanne, 14 Dec 1969, collab. M. Charnin and E. Elliott

Song contribs. to The Wages of Eve, Unity Theatre, 1953; Turn It Up, Unity Theatre, 1953; The Londoners, Stratford East, Theatre Royal, 27 March 1972; Costa Packet, Stratford East, Theatre Royal, 5 Oct 1972

Film (songs and themes): The Tommy Steele Story, 1957; The Duke Wore Jeans, 1958; In the Nick, 1959; Serious Change, 1959 [incl. Living Doll]; Tommy the Toreador, 1959 [incl. Little White Bull]; Let's Get Married, 1960; From Russia with Love, 1963; Sparrows Can't Sing, 1963; Man in the Middle, 1964; The Optimists of Nine Elms, 1973; Scalawag, 1973

Many pop songs, incl. A Handful of Songs; Rock with the Cavemen; Water, Water

BIBLIOGRAPHY

GänzlBMT; GänzlEMT

S. Morley: *Spread a Little Happiness: the First Hundred Years of the British Musical* (London, 1987)

D. Roper: *Bart* (London, 1994)

JOHN SNELSON

Bárta [Barrta, Bartha, Bartta], **Josef** (*b* Prague, *c*1746; *d* Vienna, 13 June 1787). Czech composer. Before 1772 Bárta was active as organist in two Prague monastic churches. Then he evidently moved to Vienna, where his first Singspiel *La diavolessa* was performed on 18 July 1772 at the court theatre. His last *dramma giocoso*, *Il mercato di Malmantile*, was performed there in 1784. Several years before Mozart's *Die Entführung aus dem Serail* and at the same time as Umlauf, Benda, Ordonez, Asplmayr and others, Bárta contributed his German comic operas to the project of the Viennese National-Singspiel project founded by Emperor Joseph II. The fact that arias from his Singspiele were arranged for instrumental chamber ensembles gives evidence of their popularity.

Of Bárta's instrumental music, the symphonies seem to be most important. An exact chronology cannot be established, but all of them date from his years in Prague, and five are listed as manuscripts in the Breitkopf catalogues of 1774 and 1776–7. For the most part they consist of three movements, Allegro–Andante–Allegro; works in a minor key sometimes have a slow introduction. The first and last movements are generally in sonata form with contrasting theme groups, elaborate development sections and effective modulatory shifts. Slow movements are scored for strings only. The best of Bárta's symphonic output is marked by pregnant and pathetic themes characteristic of the expressive style of the *Sturm und Drang* period in Austria and Germany in the early 1770s.

WORKS
STAGE
all first performed in Vienna

La diavolessa (Spl, 3, C. Goldoni), Burgtheater, 18 July 1772; music and text lost

Da ist nicht gut zu rathen (comische Oper, 2, G. Stephanie), Burgtheater, 8 Aug 1778; inst, arrs., *CZ-Pnm*

Der adeliche Taglöhner (komisches Originalsingspiel, 3, J. Weidmann), Burgtheater, 28 March 1780; 1 scene and duet, *A-Wn*, 3 inst arrs., *CZ-Pnm*

Die donnernde Legion (Originaloratorium, 2, P. Weidmann), Vienna, ?Burgtheater, 1781; H. Federhofer's private collection, Mainz, lib (Vienna, 1781)

Il mercato di Malmantile (dg, 3, F. Bussani, after Goldoni), Burgtheater, 26 Jan 1784; *A-Wn, I-Fc*

Son regina e son amante, aria, S, *A-Wgm*

INSTRUMENTAL

Orch: 13 syms., *CZ-Pnm*, 5 listed in Breitkopf catalogues, 1774–7, 2 ed. in The Symphony 1720–1840, ser. C, xiii (New York, 1984)

Chbr: 6 quartetti, str qt, op.1 (Lyons, *c*1778); 6 sonate, pf/hpd, op.2 (Lyons, *c*1778); Parthia ex C, 2 ob, 2 hn, 2 bn, *Pnm*; 12 str qts, *A-Wgm*; sonata, pf/hpd, *Wgm*; 2 sonatas, pf/hpd, *D-Bsb*

BIBLIOGRAPHY

BrookB; DlabačžKL; SchillingE

G.J. Dlabacz: 'Versuch eines Verzeichnisses der vorzüglichern Tonkünstler in oder aus Böhmen', *Materialen zur alten und neuen Statistik von Böhmen*, ed. J.A. Riegger, vii (Leipzig and Prague, 1788), 133–62, esp. 138

J.G. Meusel: *Teutsches Künstlerlexikon oder Verzeichnis der jetzt lebenden teutschen Künstler*, i (Lemgo, 1778, 2/1808–14/R)

C. Schoenbaum: 'Die böhmischen Musiker in der Musikgeschichte Wiens vom Barock zur Romantik', *SMw*, xxv (1962), 475–95

J. Havlík: *Symfonie Antonína Laubeho a Josefa Bárty* (diss., U. of Prague, 1975)

H. Federhofer: '*Die donnernde Legion* von Joseph Barta', *Beiträge zur Geschichte des Oratoriums seit Händel: Festschrift Günther Massenkeil*, ed. R. Cadenbach and H. Loos (Bonn, 1986), 135–50

MILAN POŠTOLKA

Bárta, Lubor (*b* Lubná, nr Litomyšl, 8 Aug 1928; *d* Prague, 5 Nov 1972). Czech composer. After matriculating in Vysoké Mýto he studied musicology and aesthetics at Prague University (1946–8) and composition at the Prague Academy of Music (1948–52) under Řídký. He then worked as a choral accompanist until about 1956, and was organizing secretary of the Union of Czechoslovak Composers in Prague. Bárta's style developed through three distinct periods. Such works as the Piano Concerto (1959) show an initial indebtedness to Stravinsky and Bartók in their spontaneity, rhythmic vibrancy and use of folk melody, but Bárta later reacted against 20th-century developments, other than those in harmony. In a final phase he brought about a synthesis of his earlier attitudes.

WORKS
(selective list)

Orch: Vn Conc. no.1, 1952; Sym. no.1, 1955; Conc., chbr orch, 1956; Va Conc., 1957; Dramatická suita, 1958; Pf Conc., 1959; Ludi [People], chbr orch, 1964; Sym. no.2, 1969; Vn Conc., no.2, 1970; Musica romantica, str, 1971; Sym. no.3, 1972

Chbr and solo inst: Brass Qnt, 1956; Pf Trio, C, 1956; Str Qt no.2, 1957; Ballad and Burlesque, vc, pf, 1963; Concertino, trbn, pf, 1964; 4 Compositions, ob, cl, pf, 1965; Sonata, fl, pf, 1966; Hpd Sonata, 1967; Str Qt no.3, 1967; Sonata, vn, pf, 1969; Sonata, vc, pf, 1972

Vocal: 3 mužské sbory [Male Choruses] (M. Florian, P. Verlaine, F. Hrubín), 1963; 4 dětské sbory [Children's Choruses] (Z. Kriebl), 1965; 4 písně [Songs], children's chorus, pf, 1965; Rhymes (V. Šiktanc), children's chorus, pf, 1965

Pf: 3 sonatas, 1956, 1961, 1971; 8 Compositions, 1965

Principal publishers: Panton, Supraphon

BIBLIOGRAPHY

I. Štraus: 'Památce Lubora Bárty' [In memory of Lubor Bárta], *HRo*, xxv (1972), 560–62

MILAN KUNA

Bartalani, Orindio. *See* BARTOLINI, ORINDIO.

Bartali, Antonio. *See* BERTALI, ANTONIO.

Bartalus, István (*b* Bálványos-Váralja, 23 Nov 1821; *d* Budapest, 9 Feb 1899). Hungarian musicologist, teacher and composer. He studied theology and law, and the piano, horn, and music theory at the conservatory in

Kolozsvar, starting his musical career in 1846 as a piano teacher in provincial towns. In 1851 he settled in Pest as a teacher and concert pianist, and began to work as a musicologist and journalist (late 1850s); with Kornél Ábrányi and Mihály Mosonyi he was co-editor (1860–63) of the first Hungarian musical weekly, *Zenészeti lapok*. Subsequently he made two study trips to monasteries in Upper Austria and compiled a catalogue of their manuscripts and prints which related to Hungary. In 1869 he was appointed professor of music at the Pest teacher-training college. A member of the Kisfaludy Society of Literature and Science (1867) and a corresponding member of the Hungarian Academy of Sciences (1875), he edited the seven-volume *Magyar népdalok egyetemes gyűjteménye* (1873–96) commissioned by the Kisfaludy Society, the largest such publication of the 19th century. With Mátray, Bartalus was the founder of Hungarian musicology; he was one of the first writers to draw attention to the most significant documents of Hungarian music history, and his extensive collection of Hungarian folksongs, despite its errors and deficiencies, provided the basis for the work of Bartók and Kodály. Although the practical value of his publications has diminished in the light of modern research, his achievements as a pioneer are undisputed.

WRITINGS

A magyar egyházak szertartásos énekei a XVI. és XVII. században [Liturgical song in the Hungarian church of the 16th and 17th centuries] (Pest, 1869)

Jelentés felsőaustriai kolostoroknak Magyarországot illető kézirataíról és nyomtatványairól a Magyar tudományos akadémiához [The Hungarian Academy of Sciences' report on the manuscripts and prints in Upper Austrian monasteries and their connection with Hungary] (Pest, 1870)

A művészet és a nemzetiség [Art and nationalism] (Budapest, 1876)

Emlékbeszéd Mátray Gábor I. tag felett [Memorial address on the corresponding member G. Mátray] (Budapest, 1877)

Vázlatok a zene történelméből [Outline of the history of music] (Budapest, 1877, 2/1889)

Adalékok a magyar zene történelméhez: Bakfark Bálint, lantivirtuóz és zeneköltő és Eszterházy Pál egyházi zeneköltemónyei [Contribution to the history of Hungarian music: the lutenist and composer Bakfark and Pál Esterházy's sacred works] (Budapest, 1882)

Újabb adalékok a magyar zene történelméhez [New contributions to the history of Hungarian music] (Budapest, 1882)

'Musik und Musiker der Ungarn', *Das moderne Ungarn*, ed. A. Neményi (Berlin, 1883), 194–217

'Az egyházi zene' [Church music in Hungary], *Az Osztrák-Magyar monarchia irásban es képben*, iv/3 (Budapest, 1893), 379–91

EDITIONS

101 magyar népdal [101 Hungarian folksongs] (Pest, 1861)

Magyar Orpheus: vegyes tartalmú zenegyűjtemény a XVII.–XIX. századból [Hungarian Orpheus: collection of musical works from the 17th century to the 19th] (Pest, 1869)

Magyar népdalok egyetemes gyűjteménye [Universal collection of Hungarian folksongs] (Budapest, 1873–96)

with I. Gyertyánffy: *Négyesdalok zsebkönyve: férfi énekkarok antológiája* [A pocket anthology of male voice quartets] (Budapest, 1878)

with I. Gyertyánffy: *Női karénekek gyűjteménye: két, három es négyszolamú karénekek nok vagy gyermekek számára* [Collection of 2-, 3- and 4-part choral works for female and children's voices] (Budapest, 1879)

Arany János dalai Petőfi, Amadé és saját verseire [János Arany's songs: settings of Petőfi, Amadé and his own poems] (Budapest, 1884)

Magyar zeneköltők kiállitási albuma [Exhibition album of Hungarian composers] (Budapest, 1885)

BIBLIOGRAPHY

MGG1 (F. Bónis) [incl. list of writings, edns and works]

J. Ságh: 'Bartalus, István', *Magyar zenészeti lexicon* (Budapest, 1879)

J. Szinnyei: 'Bartalus, István', *Magyar irók élete és munkái* [Life and works of Hungarian writers], i (Budapest, 1891)

B. Bartók: *Das ungarische Volkslied* (Berlin and Leipzig, 1925)

P. Gulyás: 'Bartalus, István', *Magyar irók élete és munkái* [Life and works of Hungarian writers], i (Budapest, 1940)

B. Hódossy: 'Bartalus mint népdalgyűjtő' [Bartalus as collector of folksongs], *Zeneközlöny*, xiv (1940), 73–4

B. Szabolcsi: *A XIX. század magyar romantikus zenéje* [Hungarian Romantic music of the 19th century] (Budapest, 1951)

Z. Kodály and Á. Gyulai: *Arany János népdalgyűjteménye* [János Arany's folksong collection] (Budapest, 1952)

F. Bónis: 'A Nagy Iván-féle kézirat' [The Iván Nagy manuscript], *Muzsika*, ii (1959), 42–4

F. Bónis: *Mosonyi Mihály* (Budapest, 1960)

B. Szabolcsi: 'Bertha Sándor levelei Bartalus Istvánhoz' [Sándor Bertha's letters to Bartalus], *Magyar zenetörténeti tanulmányok* (1973), 129

FERENC BÓNIS

Bartay, András (*b* Széplak, 7 April 1799; *d* Mainz, 4 Oct 1854). Hungarian composer, theatre director and collector of folksongs. He came from a Hungarian noble family and embarked on a career in the civil service; it was not until 1829 that he first appeared on the musical scene, when he and Lajos Menner founded and became directors of the first Pest singing school. Bartay was one of the first to publish Hungarian folksongs: in 1833–4 he published a two-volume collection *Eredeti nép-dalok klavir-kísérettel* ('Original folksongs with piano accompaniment'), and in 1834 he brought out one of the earliest Hungarian books on music theory, *Magyar Apollo*.

In 1837 his comic opera *Aurelia, oder Das Weib am Konradstein* had its première at the Pest Town Theatre, and in 1839 his comic opera *Csel* ('Ruse') was first performed at the Pest Hungarian Theatre as Ferenc Erkel's benefit performance (Erkel later composed variations on themes from this opera). Bartay was director of the National Theatre in 1843–5 and it was during this short period that the most popular Hungarian theatrical genre of the 19th century, the so-called 'folk play', including both folksongs and folkdances, began to flourish. Bartay devised a competition to set M. Vörösmarty's poem *Szózat* ('Appeal') to music in 1843, and F. Kölcsey's *Hymnus* ('Anthem') in 1844. The winning work for the latter, composed by Erkel, was subsequently accepted by the Hungarian people as the national anthem. The winner of the first competition was Erkel's librettist Béni Egressy, whose song, used as a second national anthem, was quoted by several composers including Liszt, Erkel, Mosonyi, Dohnányi, Kodály and Járdányi. In 1848 Bartay also composed a patriotic song *Nemzeti dal* ('National song') after S. Petőfi. After the collapse of the Hungarian struggle for independence, in 1849 Bartay emigrated, first to France and then to Germany.

Bartay's significance for the development of Hungarian music did not lie principally in his compositions. His works, which include three operas, two masses, sacred and secular oratorios, a melodrama, songs and piano pieces, show him as a cultivated creator, with good taste but little originality. He did, however, perceive the cultural demands and possibilities of his time and country, and was enterprising as a teacher and organizer, as a collector and publisher of folksongs, as a theatre director and as the author of books on music theory; the initiative which he took in all these fields helped form the basis for progressive musical life in Hungary.

BIBLIOGRAPHY

MGG1 (F. Bónis) [incl. list of works]

G. Mátray: 'A muzsikának közönséges története' [A general history of music], *Tudományos Gyűjtemény*, xii–xvi (Pest, 1828–32)

B. Szabolcsi: *A XIX. század magyar romantikus zenéje* [Hungarian Romantic music of the 19th century] (Budapest, 1951)

G. Papp: 'Die Quellen der "Verbunkos-Musik": ein bibliographischer Versuch', *SM*, xxvi (1984), 59–133

I. Mona: *Magyar zeneműkiadók és tevékenységük 1774–1867* [Hungarian music publishers and their activities, 1774–1867] (Budapest, 1989)

I. Kassai: 'Néhány szó Bartay Endréről' [A few words on A. Bartay], *Magyar zene*, xxxii (1991), 328–32

F. Bónis, ed.: *A Himnusz születése és másfél százada* [Birth of the Hungarian anthem and its 150 years] (Budapest, 1995)

FERENC BÓNIS

Bartay, Ede (*b* Pest, 6 Oct 1825; *d* Budapest, 31 Aug 1901). Hungarian musical administrator, composer and teacher. The fourth son of the composer and theatre director András Bartay, he read law and also studied the piano and music theory with his brother András (*b* ?1822; *d* St Petersburg, 1 July 1846). He worked in the independent Hungarian Ministry of Transport (1848–9) but was forced to earn a living as a piano teacher after the defeat of the Hungarian struggle for independence. About 1850 he completed his musical studies on his own, and a few years later he was a sought-after teacher and a popular composer of piano music. From the 1860s, Bartay played an increasingly important role in Hungarian musical life. He set up an organization to aid musicians living in Hungary (1863), and was its president until his death. As a qualified lawyer, he was responsible for drawing up and presenting to the Hungarian parliament a plan for the organization of the new state music academy (1872). He succeeded Gábor Mátray as director of the National Conservatory in Budapest (1876–1901), and was vice-president (1874–80) and later president (1880–91) of the Hungarian National Choral Society.

In order to uphold the traditions of earlier Hungarian instrumental music Bartay published collections of *verbunkos* and *csárdás* dances. More significant, however, than his own compositions are his editions of these types of dances, which are still important sources for research. Bartay also wrote a symphony, an overture and two symphonic poems for orchestra as well as other pieces for piano.

BIBLIOGRAPHY

MGG1 (F. Bónis) [with selective list of works and editions]

E. Vajdafy: *A Nemzeti Zenede története* [The history of the National Conservatory] (Budapest, 1890)

B. Szabolcsi: *A XIX. század magyar romantikus zenéje* [Hungarian Romantic music of the 19th century] (Budapest, 1951)

FERENC BÓNIS

Bartei, Girolamo (*b* Arezzo, *c*1565; *d* after 1617). Italian composer and organist. He joined the Augustinian order at an early age. On 22 September 1592 he was appointed *maestro di cappella* of Arezzo Cathedral but was dismissed on 23 May 1594. Reinstated on 5 June 1595, he was forced to resign, probably because of his frequent absences, on 24 January 1597. He was reappointed on 18 May 1598 but gave up the post for the last time barely a month later. He probably went to live in Florence, from where he addressed a letter on 23 September 1601. From 4 February 1604 to 4 January 1607 he was *maestro di cappella* of Volterra Cathedral. On 14 June 1608 he was summoned to Rome by the head of the Augustinian order and took up residence at the monastery of S Agostino, of which he became sub-prior. On the title-page of his 1608 book of masses he is described as 'capituli generalis Romae musices moderatoris', which Coradini (1923)

interpreted as meaning that he was director of music at the general chapter held by the Augustinian order in Rome at Whitsuntide 1608. He next held a similar appointment at the church of S Agostino, Rome, and probably remained there until 1610. It is apparent from the dedication of his op.11 (1618), as well as from other documents, that in 1616 he was living in Orvieto at the monastery of S Agostino, where he was sub-prior, organist and a teacher. From 28 April 1617 until some time in 1618 he was at the Augustinian monastery of Marino, near Rome. Dedicating his op.12 (1618) to a citizen of Orvieto, he mentioned his 'absence from the place', presumably meaning that he was away from Orvieto at the time. Nothing is known of him after 1618.

Bartei is considered one of the best musicians of the Augustinian order. His large and varied output, extending to at least op.13, includes sacred, secular and instrumental works and ranges from the richest, most complex polyphony (as in the 1608 masses for double choir), in which he shows his contrapuntal skill, through simpler polyphonic forms (as in the 1609 print and op.11) to some examples of monody. One of these is *Ave gratia plena* in op.11, for soprano, tenor and continuo. This is a true dramatic dialogue (actually headed 'In dialogo'), a setting of the appearance of the angel to Mary in *Luke* i (of which there are also settings in G.F. Capello's op.1, 1610, and in RISM 1618[3]), which shows Bartei's readiness to adopt the new styles and techniques of the early 17th century. There is further evidence for this elsewhere in op.11 and in the 1609 volume, as well as in the two-part ricercares op.12, which break away from the strictly contrapuntal style typical of the form and are notable, as Torchi pointed out, for their freer and more flowing and sinuous movement.

Bartei's nephew Raffaele (*b* Arezzo, 29 June 1592; *d* ?Rome, in or shortly before 1618) became a treble at S Maria della Pieve, Arezzo, on 16 November 1602. He eventually joined his uncle in Rome and on 12 April 1609 was appointed a contralto at S Giovanni in Laterano. He had died by 1618, since a motet composed in his memory appeared in that year in the op.11 of his uncle, who had earlier included two motets by him (not four as stated in *MGG*) in his *Liber primus sacrarum modulationum*.

WORKS

SACRED VOCAL

Responsoria omnia, quintae ac sextae feriae, sabbatique maiores hebdomadae … iuxta breviarij romani formam, una cum Zachariae cantico, ac Davidis psalmo, ipsis ferijs accomodata, equal vv (Venice, 1607)

Missae, liber primus, 8vv (Rome, 1608) [incl. Messa de' morti mentioned as separate work in Pitoni, *c*1690]

Liber primus sacrarum modulationum, 2vv, bc (org) (Rome, 1609[4]) [incl. 2 works by R. Bartei]

Il secondo libro delli concerti, 2vv, bc (org), op.11 (Rome, 1618), ed. M. Giuliani (Trent, 1993)

Litaniarum liber cum motectis nonnullis, ut aiunt concertatis et non concertatis, vv, bc (org), op.13 (Rome, 1618)

2 Mag settings, 4, 5vv, 1600[1]

Salmi, 2vv, lost, cited in Pitoni, *c*1725

SECULAR VOCAL

Il primo libro di madrigali, 5vv (Venice, 1592)

Libro dei madrigali, 6vv (Venice, n.d.)

Balletti, 3vv, lost, cited in Pitoni, *c*1725

INSTRUMENTAL

Il primo libro de ricercari, a 2, op.12 (Rome, 1618), ed. M. Giuliani (Trent, 1995)

BIBLIOGRAPHY

DBI (R. Meloncelli); *EitnerQ*; *MGG1* (A. Ziino); *PitoniN*

G.O. Pitoni: *Guida armonica ... libro primo* (Rome, c1690), 86

G. Baini: *Memorie storico-critiche della vita e delle opere di Giovanni Pierluigi da Palestrina* (Rome, 1828/R), i, 117, n.192

L. Torchi: 'La musica strumentale in Italia nei sècoli XVI, XVII e XVIII', iv, *RMI*, v (1898), 455–89, esp. 482; repr. in book form (Turin, 1901/R)

F. Coradini: *Il musicista aretino P. Girolamo Bartei* (Arezzo, 1923)

S.L. Astengo: *Musici agostiniani anteriori al secolo XIX* (Florence, 1929), 19–20

F. Coradini: 'La cappella musicale del duomo di Arezzo dal secolo XV a tutto il secolo XIX', *NA*, xv (1938), 248–57, esp. 251

E. Hilmar: 'Ergänzungen zu Emil Vogels "Bibliothek der gedruckten weltlichen Vocalmusik Italiens, aus den Jahren 1500–1700"', *AnMc*, no.4 (1967), 154–206, esp. 163–4

H.E. Smither: 'The Latin Dramatic Dialogue and the Nascent Oratorio', *JAMS*, xx (1967), 403–33

G. Dixon: *Liturgical Music in Rome 1605–45* (diss., U. of Durham, 1982), 146–7

G. Dixon: 'Tradition and Progress in Roman Mass Setting after Palestrina', *Studi palestriniani II: Palestrina 1986*, 309–24

AGOSTINO ZIINO (with NOEL O'REGAN)

Bartei, Raffaele. Italian composer and singer, nephew of GIROLAMO BARTEI.

Bartelink, Bernard (Gerard Maria) (*b* Enschede, 24 Nov 1929). Dutch organist. He studied the organ with Albert de Klerk at the Church Music Institute in Urecht (1948–50), and the organ with Anthon van der Horst (1950–54) and composition with Léon Orthel (1952–55) at the Amsterdam Conservatory, where he gained the *prix d'excellence* (1954). In 1961 he won the International Improvisation Competition in Haarlem, and has since served on the jury of this and other competitions. He taught at the Church Music Institute in Haarlem (1965–77) and at the Amsterdam Conservatory (1973–89), and in 1971 was appointed organist of the Roman Catholic St Bavokathedraal, Haarlem. A noted interpreter of the German Baroque and French 19th- and 20th-century repertories and a skilled improviser, Bartelink has performed throughout Europe, toured the USA, Russia, Australia and New Zealand, and given the premières of contemporary works by Daan Manneke, Léon Orthel and Bjorne Sløgedal; he has also keenly promoted the music of Charles Tournemire. His own compositions include church, organ and chamber music, and a cycle of songs for low voice and organ, *De Zaligsprekingen*, commissioned by the city of Amsterdam.

GERT OOST

Barth. Danish family of musicians of German descent.

(1) **Christian Samuel Barth** (*b* Glauchau, Saxony, 11 Jan 1735; *d* Copenhagen, 8 July 1809). Oboist. He was educated at the Thomasschule in Leipzig under J.S. Bach. After serving in court orchestras in Rudolstadt (from 1753), Weimar (1762), Hanover (1768) and Kassel (1769), he was engaged in 1786 as first oboist of the royal orchestra in Copenhagen; Gerber encountered him in Kassel as late as 1785. At this time he was recognized as one of the greatest oboe virtuosos in Europe, particularly for his outstanding tone. He also composed, but because of the frequent misattribution of works among the Barth family the extent of his compositional activity is uncertain. It is likely that a *Potpourri concertant* for piano and oboe or flute (*DK-Kk*) and *Six écossaises* for piano (Copenhagen, n.d.) were by him. He retired in 1797.

(2) **(Frederik) Philip (Carl August) Barth** (*b* Kassel, 21 Oct 1774; *d* Copenhagen, 22 Dec 1804). Oboist and composer, son of (1) Christian Samuel Barth. Though not as eminent a player as his father and his brother (3) Christian Frederik, he was skilful enough to be admitted to the royal orchestra by 1793. Oboe concertos by him (now lost) were performed by his brother with great success in Berlin (1804–5). His other works include concertos for oboe, flute and two horns, a published flute concerto in E minor and two volumes of songs (1793). Barth was also a conductor of the royal Harmonie in Copenhagen (1794–7).

(3) **Christian Frederik Barth** (*b* Copenhagen, 24 Feb 1787; *d* Middelfart, Fyn, 17 July 1861). Oboist and composer, son of (1) Christian Samuel Barth. He was a pupil of his father, and at the age of 15, a year after his début as an oboist, he joined the royal orchestra in Copenhagen. In 1804 a scholarship enabled him to go to Berlin, where he gave concerts with great success. On his return to Copenhagen Barth, then 18 years old, was appointed principal oboist, and on frequent concert tours in Europe soon won international fame as one of the greatest artists on his instrument. In Denmark his oboe technique had lasting influence (his most important pupil was the court oboist Christian Schiemann), but in his own time he also won renown as a composer. Of his published works special mention may be made of the five oboe concertos, the *Rondeau suisse* for oboe and orchestra in E♭, the divertissement for oboe and string quartet, the sonata for oboe and piano, the *Grande sinfonie* for wind instruments, and the overture in E for orchestra. Barth retired from the royal orchestra in 1841 and was not involved with music for the last 20 years of his life. (*DBL* (S.A.E. Hagne); *GerberL*; *MGG1* (W. Hüttel); *SchillingE*)

BO MARSCHNER

Barth, Karl-Heinrich (*b* Pillau [now Baltiysk], nr Königsberg [now Kaliningrad], 12 July 1847; *d* Berlin, 23 Dec 1922). German pianist and teacher. Following early lessons from his father, a music teacher, Barth became a pupil of Ludwig Steinmann in Postdam. He remained with him for six years from 1856. Further teachers were von Bülow, Bronsart von Schellendorf and, for a short time, Tausig. He also took lessons in composition from Adolf Marx and Carl Weitzmann. In 1868 Barth was appointed a teacher at the Stern Conservatory in Berlin; he moved to the Hochschule für Musik in 1871, and was head of the piano department there from 1910 until his retirement in 1921. The Barth Trio, which he formed with Heinrich Karl de Ahna and Robert Hausmann, was highly esteemed. Barth's reputation as a thoughtful pianist with an especially wide repertory is reflected in his early advocacy of Brahms's music. A successful teacher, his pupils included Howard Brockway, Katherine Ruth Heyman, Wilhelm Kempff, Artur Rubinstein and Aline van Barentzen, the latter three of whom were particularly acclaimed as interpreters of Beethoven.

JAMES METHUEN-CAMPBELL

Barth, Richard (*b* Grosswanzleben, Saxony, 5 June 1850; *d* Magdeburg, 25 Dec 1923). German violinist, conductor and composer. He began his violin studies in 1856 with Franz Beck and continued with Joachim in Hanover (1863–7). A childhood accident forced him to bow left-handed. He had a series of appointments as leader of string quartets or orchestras in Münster at J.O. Grimm's invitation (1867), Krefeld (1882) and Marburg, where he was also music director of the university (1887–94). At Marburg he joined the close circle of friends around Brahms, of whom he wrote a two-volume biography. He moved to Hamburg in 1895 as Vernuth's successor to direct the Philharmonic Concerts as well as the Singakademie and, from 1908, the Hamburg Conservatory. Until 1913 he toured frequently with the Hamburg Lehrergesangverein. He appeared at St James's Hall in London on 4 June 1896, playing Beethoven's Kreutzer Sonata and in Brahms's Piano Trio op.87. He was awarded an honorary doctorate from Marburg University in 1905.

WRITINGS

Johannes Brahms und seine Musik (Hamburg, 1904)
ed.: *Johannes Brahms: Briefwechsel*, iv (Berlin, 1908, 2/1915) [correspondence with J.O. Grimm]

BIBLIOGRAPHY

NDB (W. Bollert)
E.T. Deggeller-Engelke: *Zur Brahmsfolge: Richard Barth (1850–1923): Leben, Wirken und Werk* (Marburg, 1949)
H. Engel: *Die Musikpflege der Philipps-Universität zu Marburg seit 1527* (Marburg, 1957)

GAYNOR G. JONES/CHRISTOPHER FIFIELD

Bartha, Dénes (Richard) (*b* Budapest, 2 Oct 1908; *d* Budapest, 7 Sept 1993). Hungarian musicologist. He studied musicology at the University of Berlin (1926–30) with Abert, Wolf, Blume, Schering, Sachs and Hornbostel. His postgraduate years were devoted to medieval and Renaissance topics; he took the doctorate at Berlin in 1930 with a dissertation on Benedictus Ducis and Appenzeller. From 1935 he turned to problems of Hungarian music and folksong. At the same time he worked as a librarian at the music division of the Hungarian National Museum in Budapest (1930–42), and from 1935 was lecturer (later professor) at the Franz Liszt Academy of Music and *Privatdozent* at the University of Budapest. With Szabolcsi he inaugurated a musicology section at the Academy in 1951, responsible for the training of a new generation of Hungarian musicologists. With Szabolcsi, too, he was co-editor of *Magyar zenetudományi tanulmányok* ('Musicological studies') (1953–61) and *Studia musicologica* (1961–). He held teaching appointments at several universities in the USA: Smith College (1964), Harvard (summers of 1964 and 1965), Cornell (1965–6) and Pittsburgh (1966–7) where, from 1969 to 1978, he was A.W. Mellon Professor.

In 1937 Bartha inaugurated a series of recordings of Hungarian folk music; he was also editor of an accompanying volume of transcriptions by Bartók and Kodály, *Magyar népzenei gramofonvételek* (1937). In 1956 he began work on Haydn sources in the Esterházy Archives; his study *Haydn als Opernkapellmeister* (1960) has achieved an international reputation. In his later work he concentrated on structural and source problems in the music of Haydn, Mozart and Beethoven. In recognition of his Haydn research he was awarded the Dent Medal in 1963. In 1969 he was awarded the Erkel National Prize by the Hungarian government.

WRITINGS

Benedictus Ducis und Appenzeller (diss., U. of Berlin, 1930; Berlin, 1930)
'Probleme der Chansongeschichte im 16. Jahrhundert', *ZMw*, xiii (1930–31), 507–30
Szalkai érsek zenei jegyzetei monostor-iskolai diák korából (1490)   Das Musiklehrbuch einer ungarischen Klosterschule aus 1490 (Budapest, 1934)

A Jánoscludai avarkori ketősíp Die avarische Doppelschalmei von Jánoshida (Budapest, 1934)
Erdély zenetörténete [History of Transylvanian music] (Budapest, 1936)
'Studien zum musikalischen Schrifttum des 15. Jahrhunderts', *AMf*, i (1936), 59–82, 176–99
'Neue ungarische Literatur zur vergleichenden Melodieforschung', *AcM*, viii (1936), 38–49
'Untersuchungen zur ungarischen Volksmusik', *AMf*, vi (1941), 1–22, 193–212
with Z. Kodály: *Die ungarische Musik* (Budapest, 1943)
Pelléas és Mélisande (Budapest, 1944, 2/1964)
'Mozart et le folklore musical de l'Europe Centrale', *Les influences étrangères dans l'oeuvre de W.A. Mozart: Paris 1956*, 157–81
Johann Sebastian Bach (Budapest, 1956, 3/1967)
Beethoven kilenc szimfóniája [Beethoven's nine symphonies] (Budapest, 1956, 5/1975)
'A "Sieben Worte" változatainak keletkezése az Esterházy-gyüjtemény kéziratainak tükrében' [The origin of the 'Seven Last Words' as revealed by the Haydn collection in Budapest], *ZT*, viii (1960), 107–46 [with Ger. summary, 146–86]
with L. Somfai: *Haydn als Opernkapellmeister: die Haydn-Dokumente der Eszterházy-Opernsammlung* (Budapest, 1960)
with D. Révész: *Haydn élete dokumentumokban* [Haydn's life in documents] (Budapest, 1961)
'Haydn the Opera Conductor', *MR*, xxiv (1963), 313–21
'Zur Identifikation des "Strassburger Konzerts" bei Mozart', *Festschrift Friedrich Blume*, ed. A.A. Abert and W. Pfannkuch (Kassel, 1963), 30–33
ed.: *Joseph Haydn: Gesammelte Briefe und Aufzeichnungen* (Kassel, 1965)
ed.: *Zenei lexikon* (Budapest, 2/1965–6)
'Volkstanz-Stilisierung in Joseph Haydns Finale-Themen', *Festschrift für Walter Wiora*, ed. L. Finscher and C.-H. Mahling (Kassel, 1967), 375–84
'Haydn's Italian opera Repertoire at Esterháza Palace', *New Looks at Italian Opera: Essays in Honor of Donald J. Grout*, ed. W.W. Austin (Ithaca, NY, 1968), 172–219
'Thematic Profile and Character in the Quartet Finales of Joseph Haydn', *SMH*, xi (1969), 35–62
'On Beethoven's Thematic Structure', *MQ*, lvi (1970), 759–78
'Drei Finale-Themen von Beethoven', *Symbolae historiae musicae: Hellmut Federhofer zum 65. Geburtstag*, ed. F.W. Riedel and H. Unverricht (Mainz, 1971), 210–16
'Liedform-Probleme', *Festskrift Jens Peter Larsen*, ed. N. Schiørring, H. Glahn and C.E. Hatting (Copenhagen, 1972), 317
'Das Quatrain-Modell in Mozarts Perioden- und Liedform-Strukturen', *Mozart und seine Umwelt: Salzburg 1976* [*MJb* 1978–9], 30–44

EDITIONS

A XVIII. század magyar dallamai [Hungarian melodies of the 18th century] (Budapest, 1935)
A zenetörténet antológiája [Historical anthology of music] (Budapest, 1948, 2/1974)
with J. Kiss: *Ötödfélszáz énekek (1813)* [Song collection of Adám Horváth] (Budapest, 1953)
J. Haydn: *La canterina*, Werke, xxv/2 (Munich, 1959); *L'infedeltà delusa*, ibid., xxv/5 (Munich, 1964) [with J. Vécsey]; *Le pescatrici*, ibid., xxv/4 (Munich, 1972) [with J. Vécsey and M. Eckhardt]

MARVIN TARTAK

Bartha [Bartta], Josef. See BÁRTA, JOSEF.

Barthélemon, Cecilia Maria (*b* 1769/70; *d* after 1840). English composer and singer, daughter of François-Hippolyte and Maria Barthélemon. She went with her parents on their continental tour (1776–7) and sang before the King of Naples and Marie Antoinette. She repeated the scena which she had performed for them at her mother's benefit concert in London in March 1778 and continued to appear with her parents as a singer, often in duets with her mother, and later as a pianist. She does not appear to have had an independent performing career or to have composed after her marriage to Captain E.P. Henslowe (not W.H. Henslowe; see the memoir *Francis Barthélemon*, 1896). Haydn was a friend of the

Barthélemons and Cecilia treasured memories of his visits to them during his London years. She dedicated her keyboard sonata op.3 to Haydn and was a subscriber (listed as 'Mrs Ed. Henslow') to *The Creation*.

WORKS
all published in London

Inst: 3 Sonatas, pf/hpd, op.1 (1791), no.2 with vn acc.; 2 Sonatas, pf/hpd, vn/fl, vc acc., op.2 (1792); Sonata, pf/hpd, op.3 (1794); Sonata, pf/hpd, vn acc., op.4 (1795)

Vocal: The Capture of the Cape of Good Hope, pf/hpd, S (1795)

BIBLIOGRAPHY

BurneyH

F.H. Barthélemon: *Jefte in Masfa* [incl. a memoir by C.M. Barthélemon] (London, 1827)

C. Higham: *Francis Barthélemon* (London, 1896)

H.C.R. Landon, ed.: *The Collected Correspondence and London Notebooks of Joseph Haydn* (London, 1959)

H.C.R. Landon: *Haydn in England 1791–1795* (London, 1976)

OLIVE BALDWIN, THELMA WILSON

Barthélemon, François-Hippolyte (*b* Bordeaux, 27 July 1741; *d* Christ Church, Surrey, 20 July 1808). French violinist and composer. He was the oldest of 16 children of the wig-maker Emmanuel Barthélemon and Françoise Laroche. Accounts of his career as a military officer may be apocryphal. He may have studied in Paris, where in 1755 he played the violin in the orchestra of the Comédie-Italienne and where about 1761 he had as patron the Countess of Genlis. He moved to London in 1764, at the instigation of Thomas Alexander Erskine, 6th Earl of Kelly (himself a skilled musical dilettante). One of Barthélemon's earliest appearances in London was on 5 June 1764 'at the Great Room in Spring Garden near St. James's Park' at a benefit concert for the eight-year-old Mozart and his sister. For the next four decades he was a leading figure in London's musical life, appearing as a composer, violin and viola d'amore soloist, and leader of the orchestra – at the King's Theatre, the London playhouses, Marylebone and Vauxhall Gardens, as well as for the Academy of Ancient Music, the New Musical Fund and the Society of French Emigrants. In 1766 he married the outstanding English singer Mary (Polly) Young (a relative of Thomas Arne), and they frequently performed together in plays, operas, oratorios and concerts. After 1778 they were sometimes joined by their daughter Cecilia Maria, a singer, pianist and composer.

Barthélemon's serious opera *Pelopida* was produced at the King's Theatre in 1766 with only moderate success, in spite of the support given to it by J.C. Bach and C.F. Abel. The following year, however, his burletta *Orpheus*, written for insertion into Garrick's farce *A Peep Behind the Curtain*, was warmly received, leading Barthélemon into a series of such works over the ensuing decades. In the same period he visited Paris more than once, appearing with acclaim at the Concert Spirituel on seven occasions between 1767 and 1769, producing an unsuccessful opera, *La fleuve Scamandre*, at the Comédie-Italienne, publishing his op.3, and issuing French editions of two sets of sonatas earlier published in London.

For the Shakespeare Jubilee of 1769 Barthélemon and Charles Dibdin collaborated in writing the music for a theatrical miscellany. This elaborate and costly pageant was a financial failure when mounted at Stratford-on-Avon, but it enjoyed great success when subsequently moved to London. During the winter of 1771–2 the Barthélemons were in Dublin for several months where they had a stage erected in the Rotunda, temporarily transforming it into a burletta theatre.

In the years 1776 and 1777 the couple travelled on the Continent, performing in France, Germany and Italy. They visited Bordeaux, where the ten-year-old *Pelopida* was given in French, one of five of Barthélemon's works that reached the stage of his native city. While in Florence Barthélemon was commissioned by the Grand Duke of Tuscany to compose the music for Semplici's oratorio *Jefte in Masfa*, which was performed then in Florence and Rome, and later in London. Excerpts from this work were published 20 years after Barthélemon's death by his daughter, Cecilia Maria Henslowe, along with an account of her father's life.

Perhaps as a result of his marriage, Barthélemon showed a predilection for English and 'ancient' music; he directed oratorio series at the Haymarket Theatre in 1774, 1779 and 1784 (the last in collaboration with Michael Arne). During the early 1780s he led the ballet orchestra at the King's Theatre, contributing several scores of his own. Increasingly, however, his interest turned to religious matters, and to the newly founded Swedenborg Society in particular. The most important musical fruit of his religious interests was the celebrated morning hymn *Awake my soul*. During Haydn's two visits to London in the 1790s, he and Barthélemon became good friends, and the two men corresponded after Haydn's return to Vienna. It may have been Barthélemon who suggested to Haydn the subject for *The Creation*. After the death of his wife, in 1799 Barthélemon remarried and the couple had two children, George and Angelica. The singer James Bartleman, however, was probably not a child of either of Barthélemon's marriages. Burdened by poor health, Barthélemon spent the final few years of his life in seclusion.

The acclaim which Barthélemon generally received may be judged from a characteristically enthusiastic report from London in the Parisian *Journal de musique*:

On the 19th [May 1770] there was a concert of vocal and instrumental music in the hall of Marylebone Garden. Mr. *Barthélemon* performed a violin concerto of his composition. The exquisite taste, the pleasing sound, and the noble expression of this artist are generally known. One would say that his soul breathes and moves right under his fingers. The charming music that he composes adds further to the pleasure that one has at hearing him. Mr. *Barthélemon* is French: his talents should have been devoted to us, but we do not know how to engage for ourselves the great men whom we know how to produce.

He was clearly one of the best violinists of his time. Burney commented on Barthélemon's 'powerful hand and truly vocal adagio'. He was famed for his interpretations of Corelli's sonatas, and when he died Salomon is said to have exclaimed 'We have lost our Corelli! There is nobody left now to play those sublime solos'.

Barthélemon's compositions exhibit considerable charm, but lack originality or a clearly developed personal style. His songs are perhaps his best efforts. In the longer instrumental movements, despite their undeniable energy, there is a tendency towards incoherence of melodic structure and harmonic direction – a lack of control of the métier about which Grimm had complained as early as 1767. In 1770 Barthélemon was credited by the *Journal de musique* with having introduced to Paris the fashion of rondo finales for concertos. His style never evolved much beyond the mid-century style of which his colleague J.C. Bach was perhaps the most celebrated proponent.

WORKS
STAGE
first performed in London unless otherwise stated

LCG – *Covent Garden*
LDL – *Drury Lane*
LLH – *Little Theatre, Haymarket*
LKH – *King's Theatre, Haymarket*
LMG – *Marylebone Gardens*

Pelopida (op, 3, ? G. Roccaforte), LKH, 22 May 1766, excerpts (London, 1766); as Pélopidas, Bordeaux, Théâtre de Bordeaux, 1776

The Country Girl (incid music, D. Garrick, after Wycherly), LDL, 25 Oct 1766; song (London, 1766)

Love in the City (ballad op, C. Dibdin, I. Bickerstaff), LCG, 21 Feb 1767, incl. music by M. Vento, G. Cocchi, Galuppi, Jommelli, Pergolesi, Piccinni; song (Dublin, n.d.)

Orpheus (burletta, 2, Garrick), LDL, 23 Oct 1767, in A Peep behind the Curtain, or The New Rehearsal (farcical afterpiece), vs (London, 1768)

Oithona (dramatic poem, 3, after J. Macpherson's Ossianic epic), LLH, 3 March 1768 [only 2 acts perf., no further perf.]

The Judgment of Paris (burletta, 2, R. Schomberg), LLH, 24 Aug 1768; as Le jugement de Paris, Bordeaux, Théâtre de Bordeaux, 1768

Le fleuve Scamandre (comic op, J. Renout, after J. de La Fontaine), Paris, Comédie-Italienne, 22 Dec 1768

Shakespeare's Garland (pageant, Garrick), Stratford-on-Avon, 23 April 1769, collab. Dibdin, T.A. Arne, Aylward

The Magic Girdle (burletta, 2 pts, G.S. Carey, after J.B. Rousseau), LMG, 17 July 1770; as La ceinture enchantée, Bordeaux, Théâtre de Bordeaux, 1769

The Noble Pedlar, or The Fortune Hunter (burletta, 2 pts, Carey), LMG, 21 Aug 1770

Le vicende della sorte, or The Turns of Fortune (pasticcio, G. Petrosellini, after Goldoni), LKH, 6 Nov 1770; excerpts (London, 1770); incl. music by Piccinni, Sacchini, T. Giordani

The Portrait (burletta, 2 pts, ? G. Colman), Dublin, Rotunda, c1771 (Dublin, 1772)

A Pasticcio (pasticcio, T.A. Arne), LCG, 19 March 1773, lost, incl. music by Arne, J.C. Bach, Giordani

The Wedding Day (burletta, 2 pts, H. Fielding), LMG, 15 July 1773

La zingara, or The Gipsey (burletta, 2 pts), LMG, 25 Aug 1773

The Heroine of the Cave (incid music, H. Jones, S. Reddish, P. Hiffernan), LDL, 19 March 1774

The Election (musical interlude, 1, M.P. Andrews), LDL, 19 Oct 1774, selections, vs (London, 1774)

The Maid of the Oaks (masque within a comedy, 5, J. Burgoyne, after J.F. Marmontel: *Sylvian*), LDL, 5 Nov 1774, vs (London, c1775); masque in Act 5 incl. music orig. for fête champêtre, Epsom, The Oaks, 9 June 1774; as La fille des chênes, Bordeaux, Théâtre de Bordeaux, 1772

Tit for Tat ('entertainment', ? H. Woodward), Sadler's Wells, 14 Aug 1775, collab. H. Carey

Old City Manners (incid music, C. Lennox, after G. Chapman), LDL, 9 Nov 1775, song (London, 1775)

The Duenna, or The Double Elopement (ballad op, R.B. Sheridan), LCG, 21 Nov 1775 [music partly by Barthélemon], song (London, 1775)

Jefte in Masfa (orat, Abbate Semplici), Florence, Cocomero, aut. 1776, *Us-Wc*, *GB-Lbl*; London, Hanover Square Rooms, 3 May 1782, excerpts (London, 1827)

Belphegor, or The Wishes (comic op afterpiece, 2, Andrews, after J.F. Guichard and N. Castet: *Le bûcheron, ou Les trois souhaits*), LDL, 16 March 1778; vs (London, 1778)

Victory Ode to Admiral Keppel (dramatic cant, W. Tasker), LLH, 17 March 1779

A Sea Storm (dramatic cant.), LLH, 17 March 1779

Les petits riens (ballet, J.G. Noverre), LKH, 11 Dec 1781 [? music partly by Mozart, K299*b*]

The Amours of Alexander and Roxana (ballet, ? C. Lepicq), LKH, 10 April 1783

The Pastimes of Terpsycore (ballet, Dauberval), LKH, 6 Dec 1783

The Slaves of Conquering Bacchus (ballet, Dauberval), LKH, 17 Jan 1784

Le réveil de bonheur (ballet, Dauberval), LKH, 3 Feb 1784

Divertissement (ballet, Dauberval), LKH, 7 Feb 1784

Orpheo (ballet, Dauberval), LKH, 6 March 1784

Le tuteur trompé (ballet, Lepicq), LKH, 1 Jan 1785 [music partly by Barthélemon]

The Deserter (ballet, ?Lepicq), LKH, 11 Jan 1785 [music partly by Barthélemon]

Il convito degli dei (ballet, Lepicq), LKH, 5 Feb 1785

Le jugement de Paris (ballet, Lepicq), LKH, 12 Feb 1785

Le bonheur est d'aimer (ballet, Dauberval), Bordeaux, Grand, 28 Feb 1785

New Divertissement (ballet, Nivelon), LKH, 3 March 1785 [music partly by Barthélemon]

Macbeth (ballet, Lepicq, after W. Shakespeare), LKH, 17 March 1785 [music partly by Barthélemon]

Robin Gray (ballet, ?Lepicq), LKH, 14 April 1785

Psyché (ballet, Dauberval), Bordeaux, Grand, 15 Feb 1788 [music by c15 composers]

The Nativity, or The Birth of the Messiah (orat), per. advertised but postponed, 1803; pt 1, Hanover Square Rooms, 19 June 1807

Doubtful: Ezio (op, P. Metastasio), LKH, 13 Jan 1770, collab. T. Giordani, Sacchini, P. Guglielmi

OTHER WORKS
op.

1	Six Sonatas, 2 vn/fl, bc (London, 1765)
2	Six sonates, vn, bc (London, c1765)
3	Six sinfonies, 2 ob/fl, 2 hn, str, bc (Paris, 1769)
3	Six Concertos, vn, str, bc (London, 1771)
4	Six Duetts, 2 vn (London, 1773)
4	Vn Conc. (Paris, 1775), lost
5	Six Lessons with a Favourite Rondo, hpd/pf, vn ad lib (London, 1773)
6	Six Overtures, 2 ob/fl, 2 hn, str, bc (London, 1773)
8	Six Duettos, 2 for 2 vn, 2 for vn, va, 2 for vn, vc (London, c1778)
9	Six Quartettos, str qt (London, c1783)
10	Six Solos, vn, bc (London, 1784)
11	Six Voluntaries or Easy Sonatas, org (London, 1787)
12	Six Quartetts, 4 for str qt, 1 for orch, 1 for ob, vn, va, vc (London, c1790)

Other inst: numerous single works and groups of works pubd, no op.; many other works in anthologies; additional works extant in MS, *D-Bsb*, *F-Ppincherle*, *GB-Lbl*

Other vocal: many songs, hymns, glees, ballads, canons etc., some pubd

Pedagogical: A New Tutor for the Harpsichord or Pianoforte (London, n.d.); A New Tutor for the Violin (London, n.d.); The Principles of Thorough Bass (London, n.d.); Tutor for the Harp in which are introduced Progressive Examples of Arpeggios and Sonatas with Favourite Airs and Scotch Songs (London, 1787)

BIBLIOGRAPHY
BDA; *FiskeETM*; *La LaurencieEF*; *LS*; *MGG1* (J. Gribenski); *PierreH*

C.M. Henslowe: 'Memoir of the Late F.H. Barthélemon, Esq.', *Selections from the Oratorio of Jefte in Masfa* (London, 1827)

C.F. Pohl: *Mozart und Haydn in London* (Vienna, 1867/R)

M. Pincherle: 'Sur François Barthélemon', *Mélanges de musicologie offerts à M. Lionel de La Laurencie* (Paris, 1933), 235–45

E. Olleson: 'The Origin and Libretto of Haydn's *Creation*', *Haydn Yearbook 1968*, 148–68

H.C.R. Landon: *Haydn: Chronicle and Works*, iii: *Haydn in England 1791–1795*(London, 1976)

S. Lincoln: 'Barthélemon's Setting of Garrick's *Orpheus*', *The Stage and the Page: London's 'Whole Show' in the Eighteenth-Century Theatre*, ed. G.W. Stone (Berkeley, 1981), 148–59

M. Sands: *The Eighteenth-Century Pleasure Gardens of Marylebone 1737–1777* (London, 1987)

S. McVeigh: *The Violinist in London's Concert Life 1750–1784* (New York, 1989)

C. Price, J. Milhous and R.D. Hume: *Italian Opera in Late Eighteenth-Century London*, i: *The King's Theatre, Haymarket, 1778–1791*(Oxford, 1995)

NEAL ZASLAW/SIMON McVEIGH

Barthélemon, Mrs [Maria]. English soprano and composer. *See* YOUNG family, (8).

Barthélemy, Jean-Jacques (*b* Cassis, 20 Jan 1716; *d* Paris, 30 Jan 1795). French archaeologist and man of letters.

Having entered the Lazarists, Barthélemy conceived an early passion for Oriental antiquities. On leaving the seminary he decided not to take holy orders and returned to his family before settling in Paris in June 1744. Gros de Boze, curator of the Médailles du roi, took him on as an assistant in 1745. Barthélemy specialized in the study of medals and succeeded Gros de Boze in 1753. As a protégé of Choiseul-Stainville, whom he accompanied on a long tour of Italy, he was offered the privilege of the *Mercure de France*, which he reassigned to Marmontel. Barthélemy enjoyed the company of such lovers of antiquity and music as Caylus and Chabanon. As a writer who was regularly published in the *Journal des savants*, and the author of dissertations both scholarly and popular, he was elected to the Académie Française in 1789. His *Voyages du jeune anacharsis en Grèce vers le milieu du IVe siècle avant l'ère vulgaire*, an extensive introduction to Greek civilization, had considerable influence on his generation. His comments on Greek music were the subject of a separate publication: *Entretiens sur l'état de la musique grecque, vers le milieu du quatrième siècle, avant l'ère vulgaire* (Amsterdam and Paris, 1777). In this work Barthélemy defends a concept of music comprising melody, rhythm, poetry, dance, gesture, all the sciences and most of the arts. (P. Vendrix: *Aux origines d'une discipline historique: la musique et son histoire en France aux XVIIe et XVIIIe siècles*, Geneva, 1993)

PHILIPPE VENDRIX

Barthélemy, Maurice(-Ghislain-Louis) (*b* Gembloux, 9 April 1925). Belgian musicologist. He studied under Suzanne Clercx-Lejeune in Liège (1946–53), where in 1953 he took the doctorate in the history of art and archaeology; this included a dissertation on Campra. After a year's studies with Dufourcq in Paris (1953–4), he was attached to the Fonds National (Belge) de la Recherche Scientifique (1954–61), investigating Italian influences on late Baroque French music. He became artistic adviser to the fine arts department of the Liège city council (1959), assistant curator of museums (1967) and librarian of the conservatory (1970) and retired in 1990. He has specialized in the history of French music between 1660 and 1760, particularly the relationship of vocal music to literature and the history of ideas.

WRITINGS

Campra et ses contemporains (diss., U. of Liège, 1953)
'Les divertissements de J.J. Mouret pour les comédies de Dancourt', *RBM*, vii (1953), 47–51
'Les opéras de Marin Marais', *RBM*, vii (1953), 136–46
André Campra: sa vie et son oeuvre (1660–1744) (Paris, 1957, 2/1995 as *André Campra (1660–1744): étude biographique et musicologique*)
'Un foyer musical en France au début du XVIIIe siècle: le Palais-Royal', *Cahiers musicaux*, no.14 (1957), 27–35
'La critique et l'actualité musicales dans le "Théâtre italien" de Gherardi', *Revue d'histoire littéraire de la France*, lix (1959), 481–90
'Les cantates de Jean-Baptiste Stuck', *RMFC*, ii (1961–2), 125–37
'Les règlements de 1776 et l'Académie royale de musique', *RMFC*, iv (1964), 239–48
'Essai sur la position de d'Alembert dans la Querelle des Bouffons', *RMFC*, vi (1966), 159–75
'Les deux interventions de Jacques Cazotte dans la "Querelle des Bouffons"', *RMFC*, viii (1968), 191–206
'Marc-Antoine Laugier contre Jean-Jacques Rousseau: un épisode de la Querelle des Bouffons', *Provence historique*, lxxiii (1968), 323–9
'Theobaldo di Gatti et la tragédie en musique *Scylla*', *RMFC*, ix (1969), 56–66

'L'actualité musicale dans les publications périodiques de Pierre-François Guyot Desfontaines (1735–1746)', *RMFC*, x (1970), 107–16
'L'affaire des pages de la Chapelle Royale en 1741', *RMFC*, xiii (1973), 157–61
'Une oeuvre inconnue d'Anne Danican Philidor, au Conservatoire Royal de Musique de Liège', *RMFC*, xv (1975), 91–5
Inventaire général des manuscrits anciens du Conservatoire royal de musique de Liège (Liège, 1977)
De Léopold à Constance: Wolfgang Amadeus (Paris, 1987)
ed.: H. Hamal: *Annales de la musique et du théâtre à Liège de 1738 à 1806* (Liège, 1989)
Métamorphoses de l'opéra français au siècle des Lumières (Paris, 1990)
'Alexis Piron et l'opéra-comique', *Grétry et l'Europe de l'opéra-comique: Liège 1991*, 191–200
Catalogue des imprimés musicaux anciens du Conservatoire royal de musique de Liège (Liège, 1992)
'Les oeuvres de Racine pour Saint-Cyr et le contexte musical contemporain', *Athalie: Racine et la tragédie biblique*, ed. M. Couvreur (Brussels, 1992), 107–16
'L'opéra-comique des origines à la Querelle des Bouffons', *L'opéra-comique en France au XVIIIe siècle*, ed. P. Vendrix (Liège, 1992), 10–78

GUY BOURLIGUEUX

Bartholomaeus Comes. *See* LE CONTE, BARTHOLOMEUS.

Bartholomée, Pierre (*b* Brussels, 5 Aug 1937). Belgian composer and conductor. Drawn to composition at an early age, he studied at the Brussels Conservatory (1953–8), and received further piano tuition from Wilhelm Kempff. While beginning a career as a pianist he taught himself composition, an activity that received special impetus from his encounter with Pousseur in 1961. From 1960 to 1970 he worked as a sound engineer and later producer for the Third Programme on Belgian Radio, then for television; during this period, he wrote a good deal of incidental music, notably for film. A founder-member of the Liège-based Ensemble Musique Nouvelle in 1962, he began his conducting activities with the group in 1964; these became increasingly extensive and in 1977 he was appointed conductor of the Liège PO. From 1972 he taught music analysis at the Brussels Conservatory and from 1984 musical communication at the University of Louvain-la-Neuve. As a conductor he has been responsible for numerous premières (including music by Berio, Boesmans, Messiaen, Pousseur and Xenakis) and for rediscovering works by Lekeu and Tournemire among others. From his earliest works, such as the serial *Chansons* (1964) and *Cantate aux alentours* (1966), his conception of musical form has been based on the variation and repetition of recognizable structural elements (themes, harmonies, instrumental combinations, etc.). From the percussive articulation and chordal writing characteristic of his works of the 1970s, notably the harp piece *Fancy* and the compositions derived from it, he moved in *Mezza Voce* to a more open, heterophonic style, full of characteristic figurations and sonic gestures.

WORKS
(*selective list*)

Orch: Harmonique, 1970; Politophonie, 1984; Pavane pour une ondine du Levant, 1987; Rumeur, 1989; Humoresque, 1994; Fredons et tarabusts, 1997
Vocal: La ténèbre souveraine, 4 vv, 2 choruses, 2 small orch, 1967; Deuxième alentour 'Cueillir', A, perc, pf, 1969–70; Brasier de neige (S. Meurant), Mez, str qt, 1986, enlarged as Le point nocturne, 1993; Accent, 1v, pf, 1992
Chbr: Mouvements, pf, 11 insts, 1963; Tombeau de Marin Marais, baroque vn, 2 b viol, hpd, 1967 [microintervallic piece written in tablature]; Premier alentour, a fl, 2 b viol, 1967; Romance, 1 trad. inst, hp, pf, any insts, 1972; Ricercar, sax qt, 1973; Fancy II, hp,

small orch, 1975; Sonata quasi una fantasia, hp, 4 groups of any insts, 1976; Mezza voce, cl, vn, pf, perc, 1980; Fancy as a ground, 17 pfmrs, 1981; 3 pôles entrelacés (Polyphonie à 7), cl/b cl, bn, eng hn, 2 hn, vn, hp, 1985; Adieu, cl, pf, 1987; Studie, small ens, 1994; Fin de séries, 2 vn, 1995; Presque rien, trbn, vn, 1997

Solo inst: Nocturnes, chromatic hp, 1962; Chanson, vc, 1964; Récit 'Troisième alentour', org, 1970; Mémoires, pf, 1972; Fancy, hp, 1974; Pastorale, diatonic/chromatic hp, 1981; Variations, pf, 1997–8

El-ac: Cantate aux alentours (Bible: *Genesis*, *Revelation*), Mez, B, 4 inst groups, live elecs, 1966; Mémoires d'un gueux (H. Claus), live elec qt, 1987

Principal publishers: Documenta Musicae Novae, Universal

BIBLIOGRAPHY

H. Pousseur: 'Pierre Bartholomée: Le tombeau de Marin Marais', WER 60039 (1970) [disc notes]
H. Sabbe: Introduction to P. Bartholomée: 'Cantate aux alentours', *Documenta musicae novae*, iii (1970–71) [whole issue]
P. Bartholomée: 'Les aventures de "Musique Nouvelle"', *Le centre de recherches musicales de Wallonie* (Brussels, 1976), 39–50
M.-I. Collart: 'Pierre Bartholomée, le temps de l'écriture', *Ars musica 1993*, 160–63
C. Ledoux: 'Pierre Bartholomée, la face cachée du sensible', *Courant d'airs* [Liège], no.87 (1997), 18–21

PASCAL DECROUPET

Bartholomeus, Frater. *See* BARTOLINO DA PADOVA.

Bartholomeus Anglicus (*b* ?before 1200; *d* Saxony, ?1272). English Franciscan theologian. He has been falsely identified with Bartholomeus de Glanvilla (*fl* late 13th century). He studied at Oxford and later at Paris, where he was incepted as a regent master; he joined the Franciscans about 1225. He taught as a *lector* in Magdeburg, and was subsequently elected Provincial in Austria (1247), then Bohemia (*c*1255); he became bishop of Łuków (1257) and was appointed papal legate. Some ten years before his death he was elected minister provincial in Saxony. While at Magdeburg he completed his *De proprietatibus rerum* (*c*1245), of which well over 100 copies in manuscript survive; the editio princeps appeared in Cologne in 1472/3 (see *Bartholomaei Anglici de genuinis rerum . . . proprietatibus*, Frankfurt, 1601/*R*). The text was well known in university circles, and also appeared in several vernacular translations (that of John Trevisa into English, from 1398, is ed. M.C. Seymour and others, Oxford, 1975–88).

Chapters 132–46 of book 19 concern music. Some have questioned Bartholomeus's authorship of this section and, indeed, chapter 132 'De musica sive modulacione cantus' is largely a recapitulation of Isidore of Seville; the final section relies heavily on Boethius. The material drawn from Isidore describes the three kinds of music, *harmoniaca*, *rhythmica* and *metrica*, and the way in which pitches move and sounds are transmitted, as well as the different kinds of voice, such as *clara*, *dura*, *aspera*. As in Isidore, the *vox perfecta* is described as 'alta, suavis, fortis et clara'. The passages from Boethius deal mainly with the mathematical proportions underlying musical intervals.

Chapters 133–46 describe musical instruments and other musical terms, with much quotation from classical authors and attempts at etymology. A large proportion of this material is probably drawn from earlier glossaries – Isidore is quoted frequently – and it is repeated almost verbatim later in the century in the treatise of Egidius de Zamora. Certain descriptions are extremely brief: e.g. '*sambuca* is a kind of delicate wood, whose branches are curved, hollow and even, from which *tibie* and some kinds of *symphonie* are made, as Isidore says'. Instruments themselves are generally described at greater length, and

with some allegorical and symbolic interpretation. The chapters deal with the *tuba*, *buccina*, *tibia*, *calamo*, *sambuca*, *symphonia*, *armonia*, *tympano*, *cithara*, *psalterio*, *lira*, *cymbalis*, *cistro* and *tintinabulo*. Although Bartholomeus's chief aim was biblical exegesis, his work is nonetheless useful for the investigation of 13th-century organology.

BIBLIOGRAPHY

H. Müller: 'Der Musiktraktat in dem Werke des Bartholomaeus Anglicus *De proprietatibus rerum*', *Riemann-Festschrift* (Leipzig, 1909/*R*), 241–55
G.W. Pietzsch: *Die Klassifikation der Musik von Boetius bis Ugolino von Orvieto* (Halle, 1929/*R*)
M.C. Seymour and others: *Bartholomaeus Anglicus and his Encyclopedia* (Aldershot and Brookfield, VT, 1992)

ANDREW HUGHES/RANDALL ROSENFELD

Bartholus (de Florentia) (*fl* Florence, *c*1330–60). Italian composer. In Filippo Villani's chronicle Bartholus (and not Giovanni da Cascia, as given in Galletti; the chronicle is also ed. G. Tanturli, Padua, 1997) is mentioned together with Lorenzo da Firenze. Villani wrote that Bartholus had introduced in Florence Cathedral a Credo which was performed with voices (*vivis vocibus*). This type is perhaps represented by his sole surviving composition, a two-voice Credo in *F-Pn* 568 (no.194; ed. in De Van erroneously under the name of Bartolino da Padora, also ed. in CMM, viii/1, 1954, and in PMFC, xii, 1976) which combines elements of earlier organal style with madrigalesque melismas. Bartholus is not to be confused with Bartolino da Padova.

BIBLIOGRAPHY

F. Villani: *De origine civitatis Florentiae et eiusdem famosis civibus*, ed. G.C. Galletti (Florence, 1847); ed. G. Tanturli (Padua, 1997) [see also E. Li Gotti, *Italica*, xxiv (1947), 196–200]
G. De Van, ed.: *Les monuments de l'Ars Nova* (Paris, 1938), 5ff [under 'Bartolino da Padova']
B.J. Layton: *Italian Music for the Ordinary of the Mass 1300–1450* (diss., Harvard U., 1960), 77ff
K. von Fischer: 'Paolo da Firenze und der Squarcialupi-Kodex (I-Fl 87)', *Quadrivium*, ix (1968), 5–24, esp. 19
K. von Fischer: 'Musica e la societa del Trecento italiano', *L'ars nova italiana del Trecento II: Certaldo and Florence 1969*, 11–28 [*L'ars nova italiana del Trecento*, iii (Certaldo, 1970)]
K. von Fischer: 'The Mass Cycle of the Trecento Manuscript *F-Pn* 568 (Pit)', *Essays on Music for Charles Warren Fox*, ed. J.C. Graue (Rochester, NY, 1979), 1–13

KURT VON FISCHER

Bartleman, James (*b* Westminster, London, 19 Sept 1769; *d* London, 15 April 1821). English bass. Educated under Benjamin Cooke (ii) at Westminster Abbey, he became the leading bass of his generation. In 1788, his name first appears as a chorister at the Concert of Ancient Music, but in 1791 he left to become the first solo bass at the newly established Vocal Concerts at Willis's Rooms. He returned to the Ancient Concerts in 1795 as the principal bass singer, and later he was one of the proprietors and conductors of the Vocal Concerts at the Hanover Square Rooms. Ill health forced him to retire from singing by 1819.

Bartleman was noted for his wide range (*E* to at least *g'*) and his capacity to hold *g'* in chest voice with a tone that did not grate on the ears. William Crotch and John Callcott wrote music which took advantage of his range, but he was best known for his skill in singing Purcell and Handel. He is credited with transforming the heavy, ponderous style of bass singing to one that was polished and graceful. His ability to personify the characters he represented, especially in songs like Handel's 'O ruddier than the cherry' (*Acis and Galatea*) and Purcell's 'Let the dreadful engines' (*King Arthur*), allowed bass singing to become what Bacon described as 'truly theatrical'.

BIBLIOGRAPHY

R. Bacon: 'Mr. Bartleman', *Quarterly Musical Magazine and Review*, i (1818), 325–33
'Memoir of James Bartleman', *The Harmonicon*, viii (1830), 182–3
W. Gardiner: *The Music of Nature* (London, 1832), 109–16

ROBERT TOFT

Bartlet, John (*fl* 1606–10). English composer. Bartlet titled himself 'gentleman', indicating a claim to a coat of arms. He was 'servant' to a noted patron of music, Sir Edward Seymour, Earl of Hertford (1539–1621), accompanying him as musician on his embassy to Brussels in 1605. Hertford is the dedicatee of Bartlet's only publication, the *Booke of Ayres with a Triplicitie of Musicke* (London, 1606/*R*; ed. in EL, 2nd ser., iii, 1925 and in MB, liii, 1987). In September 1609 a 'Mr Bartlet' was employed as a musician in the household of Gilbert Talbot, Earl of Shrewsbury (1553–1616); John Bartlet of Magdalen College, Oxford, was admitted to the BMus degree on 11 July 1610. A 'John Bartlett, gent.' was given 500 marks 'as of his Majesty's free gift' in August 1613.

Despite criticism of his ayres by Warlock and Poulton, many are very effective in performance, though he attempted nothing in Dowland's passionate style. The homophonic settings of *Of all the birds* and *When from my love* work particularly well in the four-voice versions, and the latter has a splendid lute accompaniment sometimes independent of the lower voices.

Bartlet's songs enjoyed widespread popularity, appearing in a number of later manuscripts and prints. A pavan, *The Earl of Hartford's Muse*, exists in both consort and keyboard versions (ed. in CEKM, xliv, 1982). The treble part of another pavan is attributed to 'Joh Bar:' (*US-CLwr*).

BIBLIOGRAPHY

SpinkES
A. Wood: *Athenae Oxonienses* (Oxford, 1691)
P. Warlock: *The English Ayre* (London, 1926)
E.H. Fellowes: *English Madrigal Verse, 1588–1632* (Oxford, 1920, rev., enlarged 3/1967 by F.W. Sternfeld and D. Greer)
E. Doughtie: *Lyrics from English Airs, 1596–1622* (Cambridge, MA, 1970)
D.C. Price: *Patrons and Musicians of the English Renaissance* (Cambridge, 1981)

ROBERT SPENCER

Bartlett, Homer N(ewton) (*b* Olive, NY, 28 Dec 1846; *d* Hoboken, NJ, 3 April 1920). American composer and organist. He studied the piano, the organ and composition in New York, where he began a career as a church organist at the age of 14. He spent 12 years at the Marble Collegiate Church, New York, and over 30 years at the Madison Avenue Baptist Church, retiring in 1912. A founding member of the American Guild of Organists, he was also active in the rival National Association of Organists (president 1910–11) and in the New York Manuscript Society.

Bartlett was a prolific composer: his published opus numbers reached 271. Some of his early salon pieces, for example the *Grande polka de concert* (1867), achieved great popularity and were published in several editions. Other works include *La vallière* (opera, 1887), *Magic Hours* (operetta, 1910), an oratorio, *Samuel*, church music, violin and cello concertos, and the symphonic

poem *Apollo* (1911). He also composed chamber music, organ works, character pieces for piano, over 80 solo songs, and partsongs.

Late in his career Bartlett became fascinated with Japanese themes. The piano pieces *Kuma saka* (1907) and *Dondon-bushi* (1918) display this preoccupation with the 'exotic'; they are not based on any real understanding of Japanese music. His manuscripts are held in the Public Library at Lincoln Center, New York.

BIBLIOGRAPHY

DAB (S. Salter)
R. Hughes: *Contemporary American Composers* (Boston, 1900), 317–23
J. Gillespie: 'Nineteenth-Century American Piano Music', *Sonneck Society Newsletter*, xii/3 (1986), 81–4

WILLIAM OSBORNE

Bartók, Béla (*b* Nagyszentmiklós, Hungary [now Sînnicolau Mare, Romania], 25 March 1881; *d* New York, 26 Sept 1945). Hungarian composer, ethnomusicologist and pianist. Although he earned his living mainly from teaching and playing the piano and was a relentless collector and analyst of folk music, Bartók is recognized today principally as a composer. His mature works were, however, highly influenced by his ethnomusicological studies, particularly those of Hungarian, Romanian and Slovak peasant musics.

Throughout his life Bartók was also receptive to a wide variety of Western musical influences, both contemporary (notably Debussy, Stravinsky, Schoenberg) and historic; he acknowledged a change from a more Beethovenian to a more Bachian aesthetic stance in his works from 1926 onwards. He is now considered, along with Liszt, to be his country's greatest composer, and, with Kodály and Dohnányi, a founding figure of 20th-century Hungarian musical culture.

1. 1881–1903. 2. 1903–8. 3. 1908–14. 4. 1914–26. 5. 1926–34. 6. 1934–40. 7. 1940–45. 8. Legacy. 9. Interpretation and analysis.

1. 1881–1903. At the time of Bartók's birth, Nagyszentmiklós was part of the northern end of the ethnically diverse southern Hungarian province of Torontál. There, his father, also Béla Bartók (1855–88), was headmaster of an agricultural school; his mother, Paula Voit (1857–1939), was a teacher. Both parents were keen amateur musicians, and early encouraged the young Béla's musical development with dance pieces, and then with drumming. By the age of four he was able to play some 40 songs on the piano, and at five he started piano lessons with his mother. Impressions of a summer visit to Radegund, Austria, in 1887 led to one of his first compositions, *Radegundi visszhang* ('Echo of Radegund', 1891). At the age of seven Bartók was tested as having perfect pitch.

The earlier years of Bartók's schooling were unsettled. Not only was he very shy, the supposed result of confinement because of a persistent rash during his first five years, but the premature death of his father in 1888 also caused the family to move frequently in the following six years. Paula Bartók sought teaching positions in provincial towns which were suitably equipped for the broader education of her son and daughter, Elza (1885–1955). A move to Nagyszőllős (now Vinogradov, Ukraine) in 1889 was followed by time in Nagyvárad (now Oradea, Romania) during 1891–2, and in the larger city of Pozsony (now Bratislava, Slovakia) during 1892–3. Finally, after eight months in Beszterce (now Bistriţa,

1. *Béla Bartók aged five, 1886*

Romania), where Bartók attended a German-language grammar school, the family was in April 1894 able to settle in Pozsony.

Despite these many moves and the periodic disruptions to Bartók's general education, his musical talents were rapidly developing. His first compositions, from the early 1890s, were frequently dance pieces – waltzes, ländlers, mazurkas, and, especially, polkas which he often named after friends or family members. Also among his first band of 31 piano compositions (1890–94) were occasional programmatic works, such as the ten-part *A Duna folyása* ('The Course of the Danube', 1890–94) or *A budapesti tornaverseny* ('Gymnastic Contest in Budapest', 1890), and some early attempts in sonatina and theme-and-variation forms. Bartók's pianistic dexterity rapidly increased during the early 1890s, and on 1 May 1892 he made his first public appearance, in Nagyszöllős, presenting a programme of works by Grünfeld, Raff and Beethoven, and his own *The Course of the Danube*.

At the Catholic Gymnasium in Pozsony, Bartók was soon appointed chapel organist, as successor to Ernő Dohnányi, and gained more specialized musical tuition from László Erkel and later Anton Hyrtl. During the school's celebrations of the Hungarian millennium in 1896 Bartók provided the piano accompaniment to Kornél Ábrányi's melodrama *Rákóczi*, and also played the piano in the school orchestra's rendition of the 'Rákóczi' March. In Pozsony he became increasingly involved in the playing and composing of chamber music, with a first attempt, in 1895, at a sonata for violin and piano, in C minor (BB6); a string quartet (now lost) in C minor in 1896; and a piano quintet in C (also lost) in 1897. During these years, as he experienced the city's concerts and occasional operas, his compositional style

and harmonic vocabulary broadened from Classical to early Romantic models. By 1898, with two remarkably mature chamber works, the Piano Quartet in C minor BB13 and String Quartet in F major BB17, the imprints of Brahms and Schumann are strongly felt.

Bartók's health was never robust; a long list of childhood diseases culminated in February 1899 with the start of serious lung problems, which caused him to devote many months to recuperation over the coming two years. During December 1898 and January 1899, nonetheless, he undertook auditions at the Vienna Conservatory and the Budapest Academy of Music, both of which were keen to admit him. Despite his fragile condition, Bartók also managed to matriculate in June 1899 with three excellent results (probably in mathematics, physics, scripture) and four good ones (Hungarian, Latin, Greek, German).

Since the 'Compromise' of 1867, which had established the Austro-Hungarian monarchy, Budapest had grown rapidly. By the turn of the century it had become a vibrant centre of Hungarian culture, and, with a population of three-quarters of a million, the sixth largest city in Europe. In 1875 an Academy of Music had been established there, with Liszt as its first president. Notwithstanding Vienna's illustrious musical reputation, an offered scholarship and Pozsony's proximity to the Austrian capital, Bartók decided to study in Budapest with the same professors who had taught Dohnányi: Thomán, a pupil of Liszt, for piano; Koessler, a pupil of Rheinberger, for composition. On entering the Academy in September 1899, he was granted advanced standing in both subjects.

In Budapest Bartók keenly attended the Opera and the Philharmonic, and started to look beyond chamber music models in his compositions. Earlier in 1899, while still living in Pozsony, he had composed a song for soprano and orchestra, *Tiefblaue Veilchen* BB18. Now, along with his Academy studies in harmony and counterpoint, he engaged in orchestration exercises and wrote short pieces for orchestra. During 1900–1 these included a *Valcer* (BB19/3) and a Scherzo in B♭ (BB19/4). From 1899 until early 1902, however, Bartók's compositional zeal ebbed. He found Koessler a thorough and traditional if uninspiring teacher, who only raised a compositional block in him. Bartók's composition exercises of this time were dutiful but unremarkable, with little suggestion of his later genius. His growing knowledge of the works of Wagner and Liszt did not yet provide a strong stimulus for his own writing.

'From this stagnation I was roused as by a lightning stroke by the first performance in Budapest of *Also sprach Zarathustra* in 1902', Bartók wrote in his autobiography of 1921. Richard Strauss's music offered to Bartók some interim compositional solutions. In 1902 he drafted in piano short score a four-movement Symphony in E♭ (BB25), which merged a Straussian thematic and motivic technique with stylistic gestures of Liszt and popular nationalist rhythmic and melodic turns. He was still dissatisfied with this new amalgam of elements, and only fully orchestrated the third movement, a Scherzo. His only other substantial work of 1902, the Four Songs BB24, set texts of folk-like poetry by Lajos Pósa in a style drawn substantially from the clichés of popular art-song.

While Bartók's compositional development had been sluggish, he had been attracting attention as a pianist. At his first public Academy concert, on 21 October 1901, he performed Liszt's Piano Sonata in B minor. A critic from the *Budapesti Napló* reported that Bartók 'thunders around on the piano like a little Jupiter. In fact, no piano student at the Academy today has a greater chance of following in Dohnányi's tracks than he'. That was, indeed, Bartók's aim. He remained close to his elder townsman through his later years at the Academy, and during the summer of 1903 took masterclasses with Dohnányi in Gmunden. Bartók gained further pianistic notice in late 1902, with private performances of his own piano transcription of Strauss's *Ein Heldenleben*, followed by its successful performance at a Tonkünstlerverein concert in Vienna during January 1903. This encouraged Hanslick to comment: 'So, he must be a genius of a musician at any rate, but it is a pity that he goes in for Strauss', a sentiment echoed by Koessler. Bartók's reputation as a pianist was further enhanced by a brilliant final Academy examination performance of Liszt's *Rhapsodie espagnole* on 25 May 1903.

2. 1903–8. Strauss's *Ein Heldenleben* provided Bartók with both the style and the structure for his next composition, *Kossuth* BB31, a ten-section symphonic poem which glorified Lajos Kossuth, the leader of the abortive Hungarian War of Independence from Austria in 1848–9. Bartók wrote *Kossuth* between April and August 1903, another period of nationalistic fervour concerned with the degree of independence of the Hungarian army. An irony, not lost on Bartók himself, was that this intensely patriotic work relied so heavily upon Strauss's Germanic idiom.

Kossuth and Bartók's rendition of *Ein Heldenleben* were central to the launching of his career as a pianist-composer. Hans Richter, an early promoter also of Dohnányi, scheduled the work with his Hallé Orchestra

2. Béla Bartók, aged 22

in Manchester during February 1904, and provided opportunities for Bartók as a pianist. Meanwhile, during 1903 Bartók had been invited back to Vienna as soloist in Beethoven's 'Emperor' Concerto, while the sizeable audience at Bartók's Berlin début on 14 December 1903, including Busoni and, at rehearsal, Nikisch, owed much to Godowsky's reports of Bartók's performing and compositional feats that year.

From 1903 until 1906 Bartók pursued an itinerant life, following performing or compositional opportunities as they presented themselves. There were substantial residencies in Vienna, Berlin and Pozsony, as well as Budapest, and he spent August and September 1905 in Paris, where he participated unsuccessfully in the Rubinstein competition both as composer (where no award was made) and pianist (where Backhaus gained the prize). However, despite a two-month tour of Spain and Portugal in 1906 with the Hungarian violinist Ferenc Vecsey, Bartók's international performing career had effectively stalled by this point, and it was fortuitous that he was invited to replace Thomán on the piano staff of the Budapest Academy late the same year. He became tenured in 1909 and remained at the Academy (which in 1925 was renamed the Liszt Academy) until 1934. During 1907–9 Bartók all but gave up performing, although he played very occasionally in Academy concerts. One exception was his only appearance as a conductor, with the Berlin PO on 2 January 1909, when he directed a movement of his Second Suite.

Meanwhile, Bartók had begun to develop an enduring interest in peasant music. He realized that his compositional style still lacked originality and unity. His first two opus-numbered works, the Rhapsody for piano and Scherzo for piano and orchestra, for example, are ungainly stylistic and structural amalgams of Brahms, Strauss and Liszt, together with Hungarian identifiers, drawn either from patriotic compositions of Liszt, Mihály Mosonyi and Ferenc Erkel, or from stylized *verbunkos* and *csárdás* dances, popular art-songs or gypsy embellishing figures. Bartók was, however, yearning for a style which was autochthonously Hungarian – to its core, not just in its accoutrements. During May to November 1904 (except for some weeks at Bayreuth) he had stayed at the northern Hungarian resort of Gerlice Puszta (now Ratkó, Slovakia), where he split his time between piano practice and composition, finishing his Piano Quintet BB33, and writing the Rhapsody and Scherzo (originally titled *Burlesque*), both intended as showpieces for his forthcoming concerts. There he heard a Transylvanian-born maid, Lidi Dósa, singing in an adjacent room, and he noted down her songs. He did not yet appreciate the exact boundary between folksong and popular art-song, nor the different classes of Hungarian peasant music, but Dósa's songs had inspired a new direction in Bartók's thinking, as he wrote to his sister in December 1904: 'Now I have a new plan: to collect the finest Hungarian folksongs and to raise them, adding the best possible piano accompaniments, to the level of art-song.' The first, tentative fruits of this intention were his publication in February 1905 of his setting of a Székely (Transylvanian) song, *Piros alma* ('Red Apple') BB34, and a collection of settings of four folksongs (BB37), the second of which Bartók performed as a piano solo in the Rubinstein competition. In these earliest settings Bartók's piano accompaniments still retain many Romantic flourishes, but already show a tendency towards writing in simple block chords and a use of rhythm which shadows rather than complements the melody. Yet Bartók was still some way from appreciating the full potential of folk music for creating a new home-grown style in his compositions. His Suite no.1 op.3 for orchestra (1905), despite his claim regarding its 'Hungarianness', self-consciously uses four-square 'international' thematic material within a five-movement cyclic structure, with frequent resort to Strauss in its orchestration. The Second Suite op.4 for small orchestra (originally Serenade), starts to show a way forward. While its first three movements, written in 1905, cling to national Romantic tenets, with a strong Lisztian influence in the second movement, its fourth and final movement, composed in 1907, commences with a short, pentatonic tune, and unveils a stark, spare texture, which he would develop in succeeding compositions.

On 18 March 1905 Bartók met Kodály, one year his junior, at the Budapest home of Emma Gruber (later Kodály's wife). Like Bartók, Kodály had studied composition under Koessler; he was also taking a teaching diploma, and a year later completed a doctoral dissertation on the stanzaic structure of Hungarian folksong. So began an enduring artistic, scholarly and personal relationship, which sometimes rivalled that of the Schoenberg–Webern–Berg school in intensity but lacked its master-student characteristics. Kodály held the ethnological knowledge, which Bartók for all his enthusiasm then lacked. Bartók had more practical musical skills and phenomenal aural capacities. They soon found themselves teaching colleagues at the Academy of Music, collaborators in many ethnomusicological projects, and the frankest critics of each other's compositions.

In March 1906 Bartók and Kodály issued a joint 'appeal to the Hungarian people' to support 'a complete collection of folksongs, gathered with scholarly exactitude', so setting a goal which remained far from realized even at Kodály's death in 1967. Their appeal warned that the influx of 'light music' and many 'imitation folksongs' would render Hungarian traditional music extinct within a few decades. They called for subscribers to a collection of simple settings for voice and piano of 20 songs (BB42), collected by Béla Vikár and themselves, with the first ten arranged by Bartók and the remainder by Kodály. This collection appeared in December 1906, but drew a scant response from the Hungarian public. Bartók, already feeling alienated from the 'rootless' Germans and Jews so prominent in Budapest's musical life, also now strongly resented the apeing of Western popular culture by the ethnic Hungarian aristocracy and middle class, as well as the undying urban popularity of the gypsy bands. The rural peasants, however, he came to idealize as the conveyors of the pure musical instincts of the nation. Their song was an unauthored 'natural phenomenon', with the potential of reforming the nation's musical life, and also of reforming his own musical approach. While Kodály allowed his attention to encompass broader literary and historical aspects of Hungarian musical folklore, Bartók's interests tended to be more strictly musical and class-related. Hence, he soon found himself becoming interested in the characteristics of the peasant music of the many ethnic minorities living within the Hungarian section of the Empire. As early as 1906 he started to collect Slovak folk music, followed in 1908 by Romanian, and he later collected much smaller numbers

3. Bartók collecting songs from Slovak peasants in the village of Darázs (now Dražovce), 1907

Ex.1 *Romanian Folk Dances* (1915), movt. 3, bars 1-8

of Ruthenian, Serbian and Bulgarian tunes. His interest in the origins of the Hungarians even led him to plan trips further east, to the Csángó people in Moldavia and to the Chuvash and Tartar peoples living along the Volga River, although World War I banished all hope of such trips. He became fascinated not just with the transcription, analysis and classification of the many tunes he collected, but also with the comparisons between these different peasant musics and their dialects.

Ever since hearing Lidi Dósa's singing in 1904 Bartók had wanted to travel to her homeland, Transylvania, the heartland of the Székely people in the far east of the Empire. His collecting trip to the Transylvanian province of Csík during July and August 1907, with a local assistant and two phonographs, proved a revelation. There, among the older people, he found many examples of anhemitonic (lacking semitones) pentatonic tunes and came to realize the pentatonic basis of much of the oldest stratum of Hungarian folk music. As Bartók collected and analyzed more Hungarian tunes he started to distinguish old-style and new-style melodies: the old most characterized by a *parlando, poco rubato* performance style, in ecclesiastical (commonly Aeolian or Dorian) or pentatonic modes, and tending to non-architectonic forms (ABCD, ABBC, for instance); the new performed *tempo giusto*, favouring Aeolian or major modes, and generally with architectonic forms (ABBA, AABA, for instance). Finally, he came to recognize a large class of 'heterogeneous' songs, showing some degree of foreign influence. In a dictionary article on Hungarian music of 1935 (*Révai nagy lexicona*) Bartók determined the percentages of these three classes of Hungarian peasant music as 9% old, 30% new and 61% heterogeneous.

Bartók's Transylvanian tour of 1907 provided him with final proof that the renewal of his own style could be based on folk music. Folk music was not just a fertile field for arrangements, but also introduced a wealth of melodic,

rhythmic, textural and formal models which might creatively be transformed, or transcended, in original composition. While still travelling in Transylvania he worked on the fourth movement of his Second Suite, with its pentatonic melody. Before the year was out he completed settings of three Csík folksongs, *Gyergyóból* ('From Gyergyó') BB45a for recorder and piano, and the first five of his *Nyolc magyar népdal* ('Eight Hungarian Folksongs') BB47 for voice and piano. Of these latter, three are *parlando rubato* with tales of sadness – the betrayed lover, the unhappily married woman, farewell – while the two *tempo giusto* songs are humorous.

When in Transylvania Bartók had also been working upon his own work of love, the Violin Concerto BB48a, written for and about his new infatuation, the violinist Stefi Geyer. Between passionate outpourings to her in a series of intimate letters about the meaning of life, religion and love, he was drafting a work of three movements, with the first depicting the 'idealized Stefi Geyer, celestial and inward', the second as 'cheerful, witty, amusing', and the third as 'indifferent, cool and silent'. One ascending line of 3rds, D–F♯–A–C♯, the so-called 'Geyer' (or 'Stefi') motif, dominates the first movement, while a jagged permutation of descending direction characterizes the second. Bartók decided not to develop the 'hateful' third movement, leaving an unconventional two-movement fantasy-like composition, completed on 5 February 1908, just one week before Geyer terminated the relationship. When she chose not to play it, and other violinists showed little interest, Bartók combined the first movement with an orchestrated version of the last of his *Fourteen Bagatelles*, also based on the 'Geyer' motif, to create the *Két portré* ('Two Portraits') op.5. The two movements were titled 'one ideal' and 'one grotesque'.

3. 1908–14. The many piano pieces of 1908–11 show Bartók's increasing confidence in using folk materials, as well as a growing emphasis upon grotesquerie, often in association with the 'Geyer' motif. Indeed, after this early Violin Concerto none of his works escapes a strong folk influence. In his later lecture 'The Relation between Contemporary Hungarian Art Music and Folk Music' (1941, in *Béla Bartók Essays*, 348–53), Bartók exemplified three types of arrangement: where the folk melody is mounted like a jewel (ex.1), where melody and accompaniment are almost equal in importance, and where the folk melody is a kind of inspirational 'motto' to be creatively developed (ex.2). In original compositions folk elements can be found either in the general spirit of the style, or in specific imitational features; Bartók gave *Este a székelyeknél* ('Evening in Transylvania') from his *Ten*

Ex.2 *Improvisations* op. 20 (1920), movt. 7, bars 29-33

Ex.3 Ten Easy Pieces (1908), *Evening in Transylvania*, bars 30-31

Easy Pieces as an example which uses such imitation (ex.3).

The *Fourteen Bagatelles* op.6 (1908) drew from Busoni the comment 'at last something truly new'. In these short pieces, of varying programmatic and abstract qualities, Bartók pioneered his new style of piano writing, devoid of the unessential embellishments and rippling excesses of late-Romantic piano figuration. The interval of the 7th, first found as a consonance in Bartók's music at the conclusion of the Second Suite's third movement, now assumed a role more equal to the 3rd and 5th, akin to its significance in pentatonic structures. Any sense of functional harmony is persistently undermined by the use of ostinato figures (nos.2, 3, 5, 10, 13), quasi-bitonal writing (nos.1, 13), streams of parallel 5ths and 7ths (no.4), of 4ths (no.11), of tritones (no.8), or of piled-up 3rds (nos.7,

9, 10). In pieces where dominant–tonic relations are invoked, they are soon subverted by dissonance (no.10) or mocked, as in the final Valse 'Ma mie qui danse' (no.14). Two of the pieces directly quote folksongs, an old Hungarian tune (no.4) and a Slovak song (no.5). 'Elle est morte' (no.13), written on the day Bartók received Geyer's letter ending their relationship, mercilessly distorts features of her motif, until near the close it emerges in 'pure' form, at which point Bartók has written in the score 'meghalt' ('she is dead'). The influence of Debussy, about whose works Bartók had recently learnt from Kodály, also lies behind several of the pieces, notably in the use of parallel chords, and in no.3, with its unchanging semitonal ostinato. Some other features, such as the use of 4th chords, could have been spurred either by Bartók's recent folk-music experiences or by his knowledge of the latest trends of his Western contemporaries. As a whole the *Fourteen Bagatelles* laid down a blueprint both for Bartók's new musical language and his new, leaner approach to keyboard writing.

Although Breitkopf & Härtel rejected Busoni's recommendation of Bartók's op.6 for publication, on the grounds that they were 'too difficult and too modern for the public', the pieces were soon accepted by the Budapest firm Károly Rozsnyai, which had already in March 1908 contracted Bartók to provide an educational edition of

4. Bartók's original draft for the first of the 'Fourteen Bagatelles' op.6, 14 April 1908 (Bartók Archives, Budapest)

5. Bartók with Kodály (front right) and the Waldbauer-Kerpely Quartet (from left to right): Jenő Kerpely, Imre Waldbauer, Antal Molnár, János Temesváry

J.S. Bach's *Das wohltemperirte Clavier* – the first of many historic editions which Bartók produced – and agreed to publish his next composition, the *Ten Easy Pieces* BB51 (1908). Rozsnyai also published Bartók's first large collection of folksong arrangements, *Gyermekeknek* ('For Children') BB53 (1908–10), which comprised 42 Slovak and 43 Hungarian tunes. (Two of the Hungarian settings were actually by Emma Gruber, and were omitted, along with four other settings, in Bartók's revision of 1943.) Bartók's aim in the series was to acquaint young pianists with 'the simple and non-Romantic beauties of folk music'. In other piano works of the 1908–11 period, such as the *Két elégia* ('Two Elegies') op.8b, he did sometimes return to the elaboration and stylized emotion of his earlier music. The *Három burleszk* ('Three Burlesques') op.8c unite both old and new aspects of Bartók's piano writing with that capricious programmaticism seen in earlier compositions dedicated to his female friends. For the first *Burlesque*, dedicated to his student and soon-to-be wife Márta Ziegler, he explained in one of its drafts: 'Please choose one of the titles: "Anger because of an interrupted visit" or "*Rondoletto à capriccio*" or "Vengeance is sweet" or "Play it if you can" or "November 27 [1908]"'. Another work dedicated to her, the first of the *Vázlatok* ('Seven Sketches') op.9b, is entitled 'Leányi arckép' ('Portrait of a Girl') and calls again on the 'Geyer' motif. In November 1909 Bartók married Márta Ziegler, and a son, Béla, was born in August 1910. Over the following 15 years she proved his worthy assistant as a copyist, translator and occasional folksong-collecting companion.

The First String Quartet op.7 (1908–9) is an exceptional work of stylistic transition. Although it betrays many disparate influences it is remarkably coherent. The Lento first movement, conceived as a funeral dirge, takes as its main theme the boisterous, jagged transformation of the 'Geyer' motif yet within a contrapuntal, Tristanesque mood of yearning; other late-Romantic influences are evident – those of Reger, about whose works Bartók and Geyer had been enthusiastic, and of Strauss. Yet Bartók's quartet unfolds, in Kodály's words, a 'return to life', with increasingly fast second and finale movements, which are more in keeping with his new, sparer style. The finale establishes the brusque, folk-like style used in the concluding movements of many later chamber works. It twice calls upon pentatonic phrases and in its introduction the cello parodies the opening of a popular Hungarian song, *Csak egy szép lány* ('Just a Fair Girl') by Elemér Szentirmai. The quartet was first performed on 19 March 1910, at one of the earliest concerts of the youthful Waldbauer-Kerpely Quartet, which would also provide the premières of his Second and Fourth Quartets (fig.5).

In the first half of 1910 Bartók's recognition as a composer appeared to be growing, and with it requests for him to perform. At a 'Hungarian festival' concert in Paris on 12 March 1910 he played several of his own works, as well as pieces by Szendy and Kodály. A press comment about these 'young barbarians' from Hungary probably prompted Bartók to write one of his most

6. Autograph MS of the first page of the piano score of 'Bluebeard's Castle', composed 1911; the German translation (unpublished) is in Emma Kodály's handwriting (Bartók Archives, Budapest)

popular piano pieces, the *Allegro barbaro* BB63, in the following year. In other works of 1910–12 French influences are at their most apparent, with Debussy's mark perhaps being too readily identified, notably in the orchestral *Két kép* ('Two Pictures') op.10 and the *Four Orchestral Pieces* op.12. The intervening op.11, the one-act opera *A Kékszakállú herceg vára* ('Bluebeard's Castle') (1911) is, however, a masterful Hungarian emulation of the realism of Debussy's *Pelléas et Mélisande*. Written to an expressionistic libretto by Béla Balázs about the 'mystery of the soul', the action of *Bluebeard's Castle* is negligible, involving just two singing protagonists, Bluebeard and his new wife Judith, who progress through the opening of the eponymous castle's seven doors, drawn by the woman's curiosity. The opera's climactic turning-point comes at the fifth door, to Bluebeard's kingdom, after which Judith's jealousy becomes obsessive, leading to her eventual entombment, along with all Bluebeard's previous wives, and eternal darkness. Bartók's work changed the course of Hungarian opera by successfully developing a fluid form of Hungarian declamation of Balázs's ballad-like text, based largely upon the inflections of *parlando rubato* folksong. He also managed to characterize the protagonists modally: Bluebeard through smooth, pentatonic lines; Judith through more chromatic and angular writing. Bartók's operatic conception owed much to Wagner, particularly in his use of a recurring minor-2nd 'blood' motif, while the orchestration is still indebted to Strauss, whose influence in other compositional respects had waned. The adjudicators of two Budapest opera competitions of 1911–12 nonetheless found little merit in this 'unperformable' work, and it was assigned to Bartók's drawer.

The year 1912 signalled Bartók's withdrawal from public musical life. He was increasingly seen as a radical, out of sympathy with the ruling musical clique led by such figures as the violinist Jenő Hubay. His efforts in 1911 to assist the formation of a New Hungarian Musical Society had, he felt, been futile, and he resigned from it in February 1912. He did not engage in serious composition in 1913, and saw no point in orchestrating his four op.12 pieces until there was some chance of their performance, which only occurred after the war. As a teacher, he was not generating a distinctive 'school', as did Hubay, Szendy or, later, Kodály, for he was fundamentally disinterested in questions of piano technique or didactic method. He did, however, in 1913 contribute nearly 50 easy pieces to the *Zongoraiskola* ('Piano Method') BB66, co-authored with Sándor Reschofsky, from which 18 were later selected for *Kezdők zongoramuzsikája* ('The First Term at the Piano', 1929). In one field, folk music, Bartók's enthusiasms remained undiminished, and he was making reasonable professional progress. These ethnomusicological studies became his life's mainstay during the following six years of isolation.

Since 1906 Bartók had engaged in many folk-music collecting tours, some in collaboration with Kodály, but many undertaken independently. As well as informing his composition – the first Slovak folksong settings (BB46) date from 1907, and the first Romanian-influenced work, *Ket román tánc* ('Two Romanian Dances') BB56 from 1909–10 – these tours had led to Bartók's first ethnomusicological articles in 1908 and 1909. These were simple collections of transcriptions of melodies and texts of Transylvanian (Székely) and Transdanubian ballads. By the immediately pre-war years Bartók had developed more theoretical and speculative interests. His first essay on 'Comparative Musical Folklore' dates from 1912, and his first published book, about Romanian folksongs from the Hungarian county of Bihor (Bihár) which he had collected in 1909–10, appeared from the Romanian Academy in Bucharest in 1913. As a principle of grouping Bartók early came to adopt the system of the Finnish musicologist Ilmari Krohn, which had been endorsed in 1902–3 after a competition of the International Music Society. In Krohn's system all songs were transposed so that their final note was G. Songs were then ordered according to the cadence patterns of each verse. Further differentiation was possible according to cadence types and song ranges. With a growing number of modifications, this strongly structural scheme remained the model for Bartók's many later folk-music editions.

The richness of Romanian folk traditions, which in Bartók's opinion surpassed the Hungarian because of the greater primitivism and isolation of the Romanian population within the Empire, led him in 1913 to collect folk music of the Romanians of the Hungarian province of Máramaros (Maramureş). Bartók's excitement about this Máramaros material rivalled that surrounding his pentatonic discovery of 1907. It concerned his identification of an ancient *cântec lung*, or *horă lungă*. This 'long melody', or 'long dance', which he later identified in Arabic, Ukrainian and Persian musics, was strongly instrumental in character, improvisational, highly ornamented, and of indeterminate structure. Until 1913 virtually all of Bartók's collecting had taken place within Hungary. During June 1913, however, his comparative ethnomusicological interests drew him to north Africa, where among the Berber people around the oasis town of Biskra (now in Algeria) he experienced a folk music strikingly different from that of eastern Europe, in the narrower range and changeability of its scales and the almost constant drumming which accompanied most strict-time melodies. Both his Máramaros and north-African collections were prepared by 1914, but were, because of the war, delayed in publication.

4. 1914–26. Holidaying in France during July 1914, Bartók was almost caught unawares by the rush into World War I. For several months, as the Russians made incursions into the eastern provinces of Hungary, there were fears that even Budapest would be attacked; folk-music collecting became impossible. Bartók himself fearfully undertook several medical examinations, which however confirmed that he was unfit for service. Later, in lieu of military service, Kodály and Bartók were entrusted with the collection of folksongs from soldiers, which in January 1918 resulted in a patriotic concert in Vienna attended by Empress Zita. From Easter 1915, with the military situation stabilized, Bartók again resumed song collecting, mainly in Slovak regions fairly close to the capital, although in 1916 he ventured out into Transylvania on his task with the military. Romania's sudden attack on Transylvania in August 1916 ensured, however, that his further collecting did not venture too far from the Hungarian plain.

Although Bartók hardly performed at all during the war, its years were bounteous in folk-music arrangements. While 1914 had seen the start of work on two Hungarian piano sets – *Tizenöt magyar parasztdal* ('15 Hungarian Peasant Songs') BB79 and *Three Hungarian Folk Tunes* BB80b – both of which were completed in 1918, 1915 was a 'Romanian' year: piano settings of *Romanian Christmas Songs* (*Colinde*) BB67, the Sonatina BB69 (in 1931 transcribed for orchestra as *Erdélyi táncok*, 'Transylvanian Dances'); and one of Bartók's most popular works, the *Román nepi táncok* ('Romanian Folk Dances') BB68. The period 1916–17, by turn, was fruitful with three sets of Slovak folksongs for a variety of vocal resources (BB73, 77, 78).

Bartók's rate of composing original works was not impaired by his wartime conditions. Indeed, his isolation led to a more unified and concentrated compositional approach. With his three-movement Second String Quartet op.17 (1914–17) he maintained something of the nervous introspection of the First Quartet's opening in the outer movements, but for the central Allegro molto capriccioso movement (with which he experienced the most difficulty in composition) he drew on inspiration from north Africa, in the limited range of its harsh tune, in the drumming accompaniment and in the exaggerated embellishments. The Piano Suite op.14 (1916) similarly shows in its third movement a north-African influence, with its urgent ostinato and limited scalar patterns. This suite, originally in five movements with the symmetrical pattern of movement tonalities B♭–F♯–B♭–D–B♭, was later reduced to four movements with the removal of the second-movement Andante, yet still retains a strong interest in pitch symmetries, above all in its Scherzo. In a radio interview of 1944 Bartók described his intention in this work of refining piano technique to achieve 'a style more of bone and muscle'.

Also in 1916 Bartók deviated from his established pattern of vocal settings of folksongs to compose his only mature Lieder: two sets of *Öt dal* ('Five Songs'), opp.15 and 16. The quality of the poetry differs greatly between the works. Op.15 is a setting in *parlando* declamatory style of four love poems by a young woman, Klára Gombossy, with whom Bartók was involved during his 1915–16 collecting tours in Slovakia, with an extra poem by another adolescent friend. Bartók soon realized the folly of his musical (and personal) ways, and ensured that these songs were neither published nor performed during his lifetime. The op.16 songs are settings of poems by Hungary's leading progressive poet, Endre Ady. They exhibit a characteristic melancholy, with autumnal themes of isolation, loss and despair. Bartók's style of setting is less folk-influenced in these songs, but rather reflects a continuation of German Lieder traditions, especially in the complementary rhythmic relationships between voice and piano. This work also pays stylistic homage to the composer Béla Reinitz, well known for his Ady settings, to whom Bartók dedicated the set in 1920.

Most significant professionally among Bartók's wartime compositions was his one-act ballet *A fából faragott királyfi* ('The Wooden Prince') op.17, written to a scenario again by Balázs. The idea of this ballet had grown out of the visit of the Ballets Russes to Budapest in 1912. By March 1913 the Budapest Opera had requested a work from Bartók, but its composition and following orchestration had taken him until early 1917. In the journal *Magyar színpad* at the time of the ballet's production Balázs described how the work reflects 'that very common and profound tragedy when the creation becomes the rival of the creator, and of the pain and glory of the situation in which a woman prefers the poem to the poet, the picture to the painter'. Bartók crafted the work as a symmetrical tripartite symphonic poem, with the final part recalling materials from the first part in reverse order. Its music, as its plot, portrays the constant tension between the ideal prince and the grotesque puppet, who share the same thematic material.

Given Bartók's fatalistic attitude towards his own compositions, he was surprised by the ballet's highly successful première on 12 May 1917 under Egisto Tango (to whom he later dedicated the work). Not only did this success lead to many repeat performances of the work, but it also encouraged the Opera in Budapest to arrange for the première of *Bluebeard's Castle*, which took place on 24 May 1918. Importantly for the future, the enterprising Viennese publisher Universal Edition now contracted to publish Bartók's compositions, an event which he considered his 'greatest success as a composer, so far' and a sure road to greater international exposure. Universal worked hard to clear the backlog of the composer's many unpublished pieces, and, despite Bartók's frequent criticisms, remained his main publisher for the next two decades.

The last years of the 1910s witnessed widespread political and social dislocation in Hungary. Bartók and his family, living at Rákoskeresztúr, some kilometres east of Budapest, found transportation to the city increasingly difficult; food and fuel supplies became scarce; they had no electricity or running water. Medical help had to be brought from Budapest when in October 1918 Bartók succumbed to Spanish influenza during the pandemic. Finally in 1920 he was obliged to move to Budapest, where for two years his family took rooms in the apartment of the banker József Lukács. Meanwhile, the Austro-Hungarian Empire had collapsed. The new national boundaries, based on principles of majority ethnic self-determination and ratified by the Treaty of Trianon in 1920, saw Hungary stripped of those very areas of Transylvania and the northern, Slovak territories which Bartók had found ethnologically most interesting. For some years national tensions in the region ensured the unviability of collecting expeditions. Apart from a brief expedition to Turkey in November 1936 Bartók never again engaged in fieldwork, even within post-Trianon Hungary (as Kodály, for instance, continued to do). The remainder of his life was largely devoted to analyzing and categorizing his existing collection, which by 1918 numbered about 10,000 melodies (including 3,404 Romanian, 3,223 Slovak and 2,771 Hungarian), or to

comparative studies involving knowledge of a large number of mainly eastern European collections.

With the succession of Hungarian governments during 1918–19 Bartók found himself courted for many positions, including director of the Opera, and head of a planned music department at the National Museum, although neither came to pass. In late October 1918 he was appointed by the liberal Károlyi government to be a member of the National Council, and under the short-lived communist government of Béla Kun in 1919 served on its music directorate, along with Kodály, Dohnányi and Reinitz. Bartók bore these rapidly changing events with apparent nonchalance, as he did the establishment of the right-wing rule of Miklós Horthy in the autumn of 1919. Yet he did think of settling abroad, with a first preference for Transylvania (by then part of Romania), followed by Austria or Germany. Of greater day-to-day significance to him was the continuation of sabbatical leave from the Academy of Music and of his attachment to the ethnographic department of the National Museum, both of which ceased in mid-1920. In 1920 he also had to fend off the first of several challenges in the press from the Hungarian right wing that, through his recent folk-music work, he was a supporter of the Romanian national cause and a traitor to Hungary. (This did not stop him in later years being accused by the Romanian authorities of being a Hungarian revisionist.)

Amid this turbulence Bartók succeeded in writing his iconoclastic pantomime *A csodálatos mandarin* ('The Miraculous Mandarin') op.19. He drafted the work in short score to a scenario by Menyhért (Melchior) Lengyel between October 1918 and May 1919, but only orchestrated it in 1924. Lengyel's is a superficially sordid plot about a prostitute, her 'minders' and clients, with a deeper message, conveyed by her last client, the Mandarin, about the powers of human love. The unsavoury aspect of the work caused it to be withdrawn immediately after its November 1926 première in Cologne, and contributed to the continual postponement of its Budapest première until December 1945, after the composer's death. Bartók approached the narrative in a mosaic-like way, using brief intervallically-determined 'tone patches' of variable tonal clarity and density of texture, which parallel the fluctuating sense of tension. *The Miraculous Mandarin* is, however, much more than graphic 'mime music'. Through various revisions up until 1931 Bartók refined a truly symphonic concept based upon his musical symbols of desire and love. It was a continual frustration to him, then, that this work, which he considered one of his finest compositions, so languished, while *The Wooden Prince*, a work he soon came to dislike, was staged more frequently.

With *Mandarin* and its immediate predecessor, the Three Studies op.18 for piano, Bartók launched into his most radical, Expressionist phase (1918–22), during which he believed he was approaching some kind of atonal goal. In his essay 'Das Problem der neuen Musik' (*Melos*, i/5, 1920, pp.107–10) he referred four times to Schoenberg, and recognized the need 'for the equality of rights of the individual 12 tones'; he drew examples of the 'previously undreamt-of wealth of transitory nuances [now] at our disposal' from his own opp.18 and 19. The following *Improvizációk magyar parasztdalokra* ('Improvisations on Hungarian Peasant Songs') op.20 (his last work to receive an opus number) also showed a bold linking of innovative techniques of folksong arrangement and atonal direction. In 'The Relation of Folk-Song to the Development of the Art Music of Our Time' (*The Sackbut*, ii/1, 1921, pp.5–11) Bartók explained that 'the opposition of the two tendencies reveals all the more clearly the individual properties of each, while the effect of the whole becomes all the more powerful'; he further wrote of the peasant tunes saving such works as op.20 from a 'wearying or surfeiting extreme'. Yet towards the end of the 1920s Bartók claimed, in apparent contradiction to such statements, that atonality was incompatible with a style based on (necessarily tonal) folk music. In an interview in 1929 he even suggested that tonality in his early postwar works was not lacking 'but at times is more-or-less veiled either by idiosyncrasies of the harmonic texture or by temporary deviations in the melodic curves'; the Violin Sonatas nos.1 and 2 (BB84 and 85) for example, are, he maintained, in C♯ minor and C respectively. However, though these works of 1921–2 show further merging of folk-derived ideas and atonality, it is difficult to consider them in a key. Moreover, despite their titles, they only pay lip-service to traditional sonata principles. The first movement of the three-movement First Sonata adopts such a strongly variational approach to thematic materials that the point of recapitulation loses its traditional force. The two-movement Second Sonata, with its slower-faster progression is indebted to a rhapsodic model, while in long-term function the tritonal relationship F♯–C is of primary importance.

During the first half of the 1920s Bartók's compositional output slackened, not least because of his intense ethnomusicological work. Already in an essay of January 1918 he had articulated his old–new stylistic distinction in Hungarian folk music; by 1921 Kodály and Bartók had finalized a modest collection of Hungarian folksongs from Transylvania, published two years later; in 1924 Bartók's transcription and analysis of over 320 Hungarian songs was unveiled in his *A magyar népdal*. It appeared in German the following year, and in 1931 in English with the title *Hungarian Folk Music*. Bartók was also engaged during 1921–3 in compiling a two-volume study of some 1,800 Slovak peasant melodies, which he sent for publication in Czechoslovakia. (A third Slovak volume was completed in 1928, although all three remained unpublished during Bartók's lifetime.) He then immediately moved to prepare a volume of Romanian Christmas songs, which occupied much of his time from late 1923 until April 1926. (After many trials, only the musical part of this study appeared in a self-funded edition in 1935.)

The other draw on Bartók's time in the postwar years was his revitalized performing career. Amid the revolutionary atmosphere of 1918–19 he had unexpectedly re-emerged onto the concert platform, after seven years of virtual absence, with a willingness to perform in chamber, orchestral soloist and recitalist roles. One of his first Budapest concerts, on 21 April 1919, introduced his wartime compositions opps.14, 16 and 18 along with one of the earliest performances of the Second Quartet op.17. With the war over and Universal rapidly publishing his scores, Bartók was keen to grasp every opportunity for promoting his works through his own playing. Over the next 12 years he took part in over 300 concerts in 15 different countries. He also quickly took advantage of the promotional, as well as much-needed monetary, opportunities in writing for the international press, for which

during 1920–21 he contributed over 20 scholarly or journalistic essays. Already by February 1920 he had re-established a performing connection with Berlin, where the conductor Hermann Scherchen and the theatrical entrepreneur Max Reinhardt sought to aid his cause. Further Hungarian performances and a concert tour of Romania (Transylvania) in February 1922 preceded a series of major performances during March to May of 1922 in Britain, France and Germany, which culminated in the German premières of *Bluebeard's Castle* and *The Wooden Prince* on 13 May in Frankfurt. Bartók's frequent partner in these concerts and further western European concerts in 1923 was the Hungarian-born violinist Jelly Arányi, to whom he dedicated both violin sonatas. Bartók was impressed by how seriously these sonatas were received, although his avowedly percussive approach to the keyboard was deemed unfortunate by many British critics, brought up on Matthay's views about relaxation and use of weight. The critics also had difficulties comprehending the frequent thematic segregation which exists between the instruments' parts in these two sonatas. Bartók's higher profile soon led to his inclusion in an international chamber music festival in Salzburg in August 1922, after which the International Society for Contemporary Music (ISCM) was founded. He became a staunch supporter of the ISCM; during the 1920s and 30s many of his pieces were performed, some for the first time, at its annual festivals. He served on its first festival jury in 1924, and was nominated to convene the aborted 1940 Budapest Festival.

Despite Bartók's growing opportunities for performing internationally, which extended during 1923–5 to include Czechoslovakia, the Netherlands, Switzerland and Italy, he did not immediately start to compose new works for

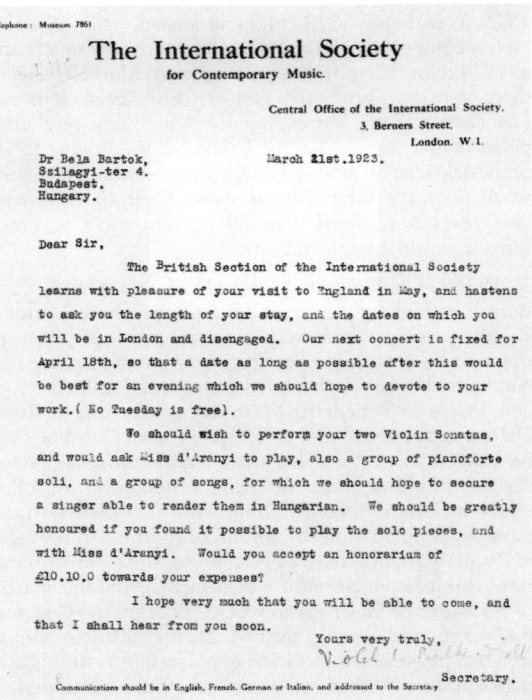

7. *Letter to Bartók from the British Office of the ISCM, inviting him to perform in London, March 1923 (Bartók Archives, Budapest)*

this audience. His only composition of 1923, the orchestral *Táncszvit* ('Dance Suite') BB86a, was commissioned as a companion to Kodály's *Psalmus hungaricus* and Dohnányi's *Ünnepi nyitány* ('Festival Overture') for the celebration of the 50th anniversary of the union of Budapest. The style of the suite marked a retreat from his recent expressive radicality, not least through Bartók's re-acceptance of an accommodating rather than oppositional relationship between tune and accompaniment. It employs idealized peasant musics in its six movements, which are played without a break and connected by a ritornello theme in a serene Hungarian style. Its first movement, for instance, recalls the chromatic 'Arabic' inflections, the second, a brash, minor-3rd-based Hungarian idiom, while the third movement introduces an imitation of Hungarian bagpipe music followed by a section suggesting Romanian folk violins. The later movements reflect a growing stylistic internationalism, culminating in the colourful medley of the sixth movement. Bartók had also drafted a Slovak-styled movement, but omitted this from the final version of the piece. His next composition, *Falun (Dedinské scény)* ('Village Scenes') BB87a was, however, a setting in five movements of old Slovak ceremonial melodies. These mainly Lydian or Mixolydian tunes were given inventive 'motto'-like settings for female voice and piano; in 1926 the final three movements were arranged for female voices and chamber orchestra (BB87b) to a commission from the American League of Composers. The *Village Scenes*, with their themes of love, marriage and babies, are dedicated to Ditta Pásztory, whom Bartók had married in August 1923 following a sudden divorce from Márta Ziegler. Pásztory bore Bartók a son, Péter, in July 1924.

Apart from *Village Scenes* Bartók did not compose between August 1923 and June 1926, and by February 1925, as earlier in 1913–14, he was writing himself off as an 'ex-composer'. Nevertheless, he did devote much time in 1924 to orchestrating *The Miraculous Mandarin*, when there were early hopes of a first performance in Germany. His *Dance Suite*, however, gained a highly publicized performance, under Václav Talich, at the Prague ISCM orchestral festival in May 1925, which catapulted Bartók's work onto the international stage. Over the following two years it received over 60 performances in major European and American centres.

5. 1926–34.   Between March 1925 and March 1926 Bartók visited Italy at least four times. There his long-standing interest in Baroque music, previously centred upon Bach, Domenico Scarlatti, Rameau and Couperin, was roused by the keyboard music of such Italian Baroque composers as Benedetto Marcello, Michelangelo Rossi, Della Ciaia, Frescobaldi and Zipoli. From October 1926 he started to perform his own piano transcriptions of their works and those of their contemporaries, 11 of which he later refined for publication. This new Baroque passion, coupled with the stimuli of rhythmic discoveries in Romanian Christmas songs, the additional performance opportunities which radio now afforded, and the hearing of Stravinsky's latest piano works (notably the Concerto for piano and wind), pushed Bartók into an almost frenzied phase of composition of piano works for his own performance. With these works of 1926 he initiated, in his own analysis, a fundamental creative shift from a Beethovenian ideal of artistic profundity to one more orientated towards the ultimate musical craftsman, Bach.

In compositional process, however, he remained still a composer of essentially Romantic habit, a believer in inspired genius, whose music was 'determined by instinct and sensibility' rather than by theory, and who physically composed, as he explained in a 1925 interview, 'between the desk and the piano'.

While Bartók's international status had grown, his only available work for piano and orchestra remained the 1905 arrangement of the Rhapsody op.1 BB36b. By 1926, it was not only a stylistic anachronism, but also – as with the early Piano Quintet and First Suite – an occasional embarrassment for Bartók, when audiences took a liking to these early works over his more recent and dissonant compositions. From June to November 1926 he set about equipping himself with a new piano repertory: a three-movement Sonata (BB88), two collections of piano pieces, *Szabadban* ('Out of Doors') BB89 and *Kilenc kis zongoradarab* ('Nine Little Piano Pieces') BB90, and for his orchestral engagements the First Piano Concerto BB91. Three further short piano pieces later found a home within the *Mikrokosmos* collection. In these works of Bartók's 'piano year', he provided a preview of so many of the qualities which were to come to fullest maturity in the works of his 'golden age', 1934–40. 'Az éjszaka zenéje' ('The Night's Music') from *Out of Doors*, in depicting the nocturnal sounds of the Hungarian plain, introduced a genre of stylized representation of nature which would be repeatedly invoked up to his Third Piano Concerto of 1945. The 'Menuetto' from BB90 presented a pioneering example of Bartók's principle of expansion and contraction of scalar intervals – in this case notably a major 2nd into a perfect 4th (ex.4) – which would come to its most

Ex.4 *Nine Little Piano Pieces*, Menuetto, 3–4, 9–10

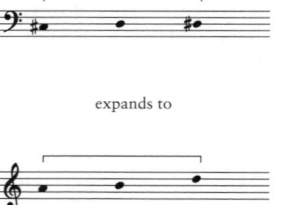

expands to

magisterial expression ten years later in the *Music for Strings, Percussion and Celesta*. The finale of the Sonata revealed Bartók's skilful imitation of traditional styles in the service of his concept of unity through variation. The movement's ritornello theme also provided the basis for the three intervening episodes, the first in imitation of vigorous peasant chanting, the second, of the peasant flute, and the third, of village fiddlers. Bartók drafted another longer episode, which developed a separate life as 'Musettes' (in BB89).

Straddling the borderline between Baroque and barbarism is the hammering rhythmic impulse which underlies the First Piano Concerto. From this impulse spring the main themes of all three movements. In the commencement of the slow, middle movement that impulse also provides the mechanism for the integration of piano and percussion, which Bartók explored further a decade later in the Sonata for two pianos and percussion. The sharp-edged timbral world of Stravinsky's Concerto for piano and wind is often alluded to in Bartók's, but it is especially evident in the middle movement, from which the strings have been banished entirely. Bartók's concerto, played first under Furtwängler at the 1927 ISCM Festival in Frankfurt, proved only moderately successful as a new *carte-de-visite*. Its first edition was so studded with errors that it had to be replaced, and Bartók also confessed in 1939 that 'its writing is a bit difficult – one might even say very difficult! – as much for orchestra as for audience'. Even he found its solo part taxing, and with these experiences in mind he ensured that his Second Piano Concerto was more tuneful and less bristling with difficulties.

Having updated his piano repertory Bartók turned his attention in 1927–8 to chamber music, starting with the Third String Quartet (BB93), composed during the summer of 1927. In this quartet he attained the ultimate compression of his formal, pitch and rhythmic materials. Adorno (1929) wrote: 'What is decisive is the *formative power* of the work; the iron concentration, the wholly original tectonics. The traditional four movements are here fused into a single movement of about 17 minutes' duration. A new colouristic approach to string sonority is displayed, partly inspired by Berg's *Lyrische Suite*, which Bartók had recently heard. The score bristles with 'special effects' – glissando, pizzicato, *col legno*, *sul tasto*, *ponticello*, *martellato*, muted passages, the use of exaggerating vibrato, strumming, and their combinations – all of which give the piece its startling piquancy. In October 1928 it was awarded joint first prize, with Casella's *Serenata*, in a competition of the Musical Fund Society of Philadelphia, where it was given its first performance on 30 December of the same year.

Meanwhile, during the summer of 1928, Bartók had composed his Fourth String Quartet BB95. While taking over the expanded palette of string sonorities of no.3, the Fourth is formally very different. Originally conceived in only four movements, Bartók then added another (the published fourth movement) to provide a symmetrical five-movement structure. The slow, third movement, in a style reminiscent of 'The Night's Music' from *Out of Doors*, is the work's kernel. The second movement's tight thematic material is reflected, in more open guise, in the fourth, entirely pizzicato movement. The first movement's themes are also loosely mirrored in the finale, which ends with a coda that borrows liberally from the first movement's conclusion. Such symmetrical thinking about form had been evident in Bartók's works since the 1910s, but had never been expressed by him as clearly, either in the music or in his own analysis. The pitch relations of the quartet operate at a high level of abstraction, with much interplay between contracted and expanded expressions of short cells, yet in rhythm certain folk models are more apparent. In the first movement, for instance, Bulgarian-type irregular rhythms are used; the third movement involves rhythmic elements of both 'old' Hungarian and Romanian *horă lungă* precedent.

Two further chamber works, the Violin Rhapsodies (BB94, 96), originate from 1928. They were intended for Bartók's many performances with Hungarian violinists, as milder alternatives or adjuncts to his violin sonatas; but he also arranged them for violin and orchestra, as well as the first for cello and piano, on a request from Casals. Both pieces follow the traditional *lassú–friss* (slow–fast) rhapsodic pattern which Bartók knew so well from his scholarly work during the 1910s on Liszt's *Hungarian Rhapsodies* for that composer's complete edition. Bartók's Rhapsodies are cunningly devised con-catenations of predominantly Romanian melodies, although Hungarian and Ruthenian tunes are represented. The First Rhapsody was dedicated to Szigeti, who had recently made a violin and piano arrangement of seven *For Children* pieces, and the Second to Székely (fig.8), who had similarly arranged Bartók's *Romanian Folk Dances*.

The concerts for which Bartók had intended his many compositions of 1926–8 found willing entrepreneurs. The late 1920s were Bartók's heyday as a pianist, with good offerings of concert opportunities, increasing radio work and, from 1928, contracts for producing gramophone records. By this time he often had the chance to specialize in playing his own works. When Bartók was granted a sabbatical from the Budapest Academy for 1927–8 he was finally able to realize a plan he had nurtured ever since graduating, of a concert tour of the USA. Notwithstanding the débâcle of the first two concerts on 22 and 23 December 1928, when the New York PO, under Mengelberg, proved unable to perform the First Piano Concerto and the Rhapsody op.1 had to be substituted at the last minute, Bartók's two-month coast-to-coast tour, with its mixture of small lecture-recitals and large concert events, was a successful musical and promotional undertaking as well as a personally eye-opening experience. In America he performed especially with Szigeti and his former student Reiner, under whose baton the First Piano Concerto did eventually have its American première on 13 February 1928. By 1929 Bartók was starting to live the life of the itinerant performer. During that year's first four months he undertook a three-week tour of the Soviet Union, followed by concerts in Switzerland, Denmark, Britain, Holland, Germany, France, Italy, Austria and

8. *Bartók with Zoltán Székely, to whom he dedicated his second Violin Rhapsody and Violin Concerto 'no.2', 1925 (Bartók Archives, Budapest)*

Hungary, where on 20 March he heard both his recent string quartets in sympathetically received performances from the Waldbauer-Kerpely Quartet. Even the pessimistic Bartók had good reason to be 'relaxed and happy', as his son reported of him on his 48th birthday.

Vocal music absorbed Bartók's compositional energies during 1929–30. Kodály's increasing list of Hungarian folksong arrangements jogged Bartók into contributing one last substantial set of voice and piano arrangements: *Húsz magyar népdal* ('Twenty Hungarian Folksongs') BB98. He grouped these songs thematically – four sad, four dancing, seven diverse and five new-style – but with no intention that they be performed in order. Bartók's settings mostly fall within his creative, 'motto' approach. In publication it was not the music but the German song translations which caused the most acute problems, as had often been the case with previous vocal works, notably his settings of Ady in the Five Songs BB72. Unlike Kodály, Bartók was insistent upon an idiomatic German translation which faithfully maintained the east European musical rhythms but also adhered as far as possible to natural German word accentuation. With *Twenty Hungarian Folksongs* a publishing compromise was finally reached, with both poetic and literal translations being provided for some songs. During early 1930 Bartók also arranged his four-movement *Magyar népdalok* ('Hungarian Folksongs') BB99 for mixed chorus.

For the *Cantata profana* 'A kilenc csodaszarvas' ('The Nine Enchanted Stags') BB100, written during the summer of 1930, Bartók set his own poetic working of an ancient Romanian epic ballad for tenor and baritone soloists, chorus and orchestra. However, before making the score's final copy, he replaced the text with a skilful Hungarian translation, of which he was particularly fond and later independently recorded. A three-movement work running without a break and anchored firmly in D, the cantata marked an important stage in Bartók's long-term reversion to more overtly tonal writing and longer thematic statements. His strengthening interest in symmetries can be clearly illustrated by comparing the mirrored nature of the modes with which the work begins (D–E–F–G–A♭ –B♭–C–D) and ends (D–E–F♯–G♯–A–B–C–D). This latter, Slovak-influenced 'acoustic' form (so-called because of its congruence with the lower degrees of the harmonic series), through its association with the cantata's closing words 'From clear and cooling mountain springs', came to be recognized as Bartók's symbol for the purity of nature. Of all Bartók's compositions, the *Cantata profana* has elicited perhaps the greatest variety of interpretations of its overall musical form – implied four-movement structure (Ujfalussy), 'large sonata form' (Somfai), five-act classical dramatic form (Szabolcsi), to list but three – as well as of its textual message, with its components of initiation–transformation–purification, naturalistic freedom and pantheistic integration. Particularly in its aspects of generational conflict, the cantata has been seen as emblematic of Bartók's response to the rising fascism of its time.

As Bartók approached his 50th birthday he attracted the accolades of international fame, and became more overtly committed to internationalist goals. In late 1930 he received news of awards, namely the French Légion d'Honneur and the Hungarian Corvin wreath. He was honoured again in 1932 with a Romanian cultural award. While his interests in national folk musics remained intense, he was tending to write more generally and more comparatively about folk music, culminating in his study *Népzenénk és a szomszéd népek népzenéje* ('Our [Hungarian] Folk Music and the Folk Music of Neighbouring Peoples') which first appeared in 1934. As a composer Bartók harboured, even into the early 1940s, the aim of adding two or three further 'national' parts to his *Cantata profana*, as a musical tribute to the increasingly tenuous brotherhood of Danube-basin peoples. As a performer, too, he more sought international than national acclaim, having decided in 1930 no longer to perform his own works in unresponsive Budapest. He maintained this ban until late 1936, although he still sometimes played his own works in other Hungarian towns and occasionally other composers' music in the capital. None of Bartók's major works of the 1930s or 1940s received its première in Budapest.

On 13 January 1931 Bartók's internationalism took more concrete form in his acceptance of an invitation to join the Permanent Committee for Literature and the Arts of the League of Nations' Commission for Intellectual Co-operation, where his colleagues included Thomas Mann, Gilbert Murray and Karel Čapek. Over the next five years he occasionally introduced proposals about musical issues requiring international collaboration – gramophone records, Urtext and facsimile editions – but in 1934 also framed a proposal about artistic and scientific freedom. His joining of the Permanent Committee coincided with his much-quoted statement of compositional internationalism, in a letter of 10 January 1931 to the Romanian diplomat and music historian, Octavian Beu. While recognizing the three sources of his creative work as Hungarian, Romanian and Slovak, with the strongest influence being Hungarian, Bartók expressed his belief in

the brotherhood of peoples, brotherhood in spite of all wars and conflicts. I try – to the best of my ability – to serve this idea in my music; therefore I don't reject any influence, be it Slovak, Romanian, Arabic, or from any other source. The source must only be clean, fresh and healthy!

Bartók's consolidation of a more thematic and less rhythmically reiterative style continued in his next major work, the Second Piano Concerto BB101, completed in October 1931. Symmetries abound at many pitch and rhythmic levels, as also in its overall five-part 'bridge' (ABCBA) structure, with the third movement being a free variation of the first, and the second movement of an Adagio–Scherzo–Adagio construction. Stravinsky is again a decided influence upon Bartók's use of instruments – the strings are not used until the second movement – and upon his thematic material, which occasionally alludes to the early Parisian ballets, notably *The Firebird* and *Petrushka*. Apart from this concerto Bartók composed no substantial new works during 1931–4.

During these fallow years, coinciding with the worst years of the Depression, Bartók was occupied with several arrangements of existing compositions and series of miniature 'educational' pieces. His publishers, anxious to counter falling sales by promoting his more popular piano or vocal compositions in new quarters, encouraged him to engage in four orchestral arrangements: of his Sonatina (via Gertler's violin and piano transcription) as *Erdélyi táncok* ('Transylvanian Dances') BB102b in 1931; of five of his piano pieces from 1908–11 in *Magyar képek* ('Hungarian Sketches') BB103 in 1931; of nine of his *Tizenöt magyar parasztdal* ('Fifteen Hungarian Peasant

9. Béla Bartók: caricature from 'Radio Times' (18 May 1934)

eventually found their way into the first volume, comprising the easiest pieces, and nearly half of the sixth volume, the most difficult. Another 20 pieces were added to the collection in 1934, after which Bartók produced only occasional items until a second phase of intense activity in 1937–9.

6. 1934–40.   In the summer of 1934 Bartók achieved a professional goal he had desired for over two decades: a full-time position as an ethnomusicologist. Within weeks of Dohnányi being appointed director of the Budapest Academy of Music Bartók received permission to transfer to the Academy of Sciences, where for the following six years, in conjunction with Kodály, he led a small team of folk-music researchers in an omnibus Hungarian folk-music project. Bartók was overjoyed at the release from institutional teaching, although he still maintained a small number of private piano pupils to supplement his income. The Academy of Sciences' project was based upon a proposal which Bartók and Kodály had originally made to the Kisfaludy Society in 1913 for a 'complete, rigorously critical and exact publication' of Hungarian folk music. The number of items, estimated at nearly 6,000 in 1913, had grown to about 14,000 by the time Bartók closed the collection in 1938. Of these about one fifth had been collected by Bartók himself. By 1940 he had succeeded in refining a complex, closed classification system for the melodies, which paid particular attention to rhythmic characteristics, and his team had transcribed or revised existing transcriptions of the tunes, yet he had managed neither to draft a justificatory introduction nor to address important editorial questions. More seriously, his classification system had diverged considerably from that which Kodály had understood would be used. (Over the years of their acquaintance Bartók and Kodály had come to differ on many fundamental questions on music, for

Songs') BB79 as *Magyar parasztdalok* ('Hungarian Peasant Songs') BB107 in 1933; and, in 1933, of five of his *Húsz magyar népdal* ('Twenty Hungarian Folksongs') (1929) as *Magyar népdalok* ('Hungarian Folksongs') BB108 for voice and orchestra. Bartók did not manage to complete other planned orchestrations of selected pieces from *Out of Doors* and *Nine Little Piano Pieces*; nor did he embark upon a planned 'string symphony' based on the Fourth String Quartet.

Apart from this relatively mechanical work of arrangement, Bartók composed the *Forty-four Duos* BB104 for violins during 1931. These pieces arose through a request from the German violin pedagogue Erich Doflein for permission to set some of Bartók's *For Children* pieces in Doflein's *Geigenschulwerk*. Bartók was excited by Doflein's project and offered to write new pieces which would introduce simple folk music (or, in two numbers, imitations) from a much greater range of cultures: Romanian, Ruthenian, Serbian, Ukrainian and 'Arabic', as well as Slovak and Hungarian. When in 1932 Bartók saw many of these pieces within the context of Doflein's five-volume progressive 'violin school', he formed a broader plan of his own: a series of piano pieces, graded from very easy to recital standard, which he later called *Mikrokosmos* (BB105). During the summer of 1932 he composed some 35 pieces, ranging in difficulty from 'In Dorian Mode' (no.32) to 'Chromatic Invention III' (no.145). When his young son, Péter, began piano lessons with his father in 1933, Bartók had an immediate incentive to compose many simple pieces; the same year he composed a further 30 pieces, including seven which

10. Draft score of Bartók's 'Mikrokosmos' nos.140 and 141, 1933 (Péter Bartók Collection)

11. Bartók with his second wife, Ditta, c1937

instance on the relative melodic versus rhythmic importance in categorization, and even on how differentiated or normalized the ideal transcription should be.) Although both Bartók and Kodály are recognized as the general editors of the Academy's *A magyar népzene tára* series, the first volume of which appeared in 1951, it was neither Bartók's nor Kodály's 'system' of classification which would ultimately prevail, but rather a principally genre-based one to which Pál Járdányi was a principal contributor. The first volume of the re-assembled Bartók system only appeared in 1991.

Bartók's transfer to the Academy of Sciences gave him greater flexibility in engaging his interests in other folk musics. He made final revisions to his Slovak study in 1935–6 and continued to work on his Romanian collections, leading to an expensive, failed attempt at self-publication in 1940. The draft of another study, posthumously published as *Turkish Folk Music from Asia Minor* (Princeton, NJ, 1976), resulted from Bartók's fieldwork in Anatolia during 1936, as part of his assignment to advise the Turkish authorities on the collecting of national folksong and other educational questions. He also further indulged his passion for east European folk music, in which he paid particular attention to south Slavic and Bulgarian musics. The irregular Bulgarian rhythms and metres, awareness of which had caused him considerably to revise his notations of Romanian folk music in the early 1930s, came to exert an important force upon his own compositions, and he developed but did not follow through plans to visit Bulgaria in 1935 to pursue these interests.

As a pianist Bartók started to claw back engagements from the depressed levels of 1932–4, and during 1934–40 he performed approximately equally at home and abroad. Engagements abroad were often hard to secure, due to

the widespread popularity of 'home preference' schemes to assist local artists, to increasing tensions with Romania, and also to lack of opportunities for Bartók in Nazi Germany. Since 1933 German radio stations had not offered him engagements; after two years of negotiations to arrange an orchestral performance in Berlin, he finally in mid-1937 decided no longer to seek engagements in Germany. Accordingly, in the final years of the 1930s he performed more in Hungary, although he also developed some new touring circuits in Switzerland, the Low Countries and Italy, where he gave his last European performances abroad in December 1939. As a soloist during these years Bartók highlighted his Piano Concerto no.2, which was gaining a considerably better press than no.1. As a chamber player he forged an important new partnership, with his wife, Ditta (fig.11). Their concert début took place on 16 January 1938, as the two pianists in the première of Bartók's Sonata for two pianos and percussion. Over the following five years she was his frequent stage companion.

The years 1934–40 constituted, notwithstanding the slide towards war, the pinnacle of Bartók the composer; he produced masterpieces in each of his major genres: chamber, orchestral, vocal and piano music. The few works of his final American years are, despite their concert popularity, probably best seen as compositional addenda to these powerfully integrated creative statements. Apart from an arrangement for piano of several of the *Forty-four Duos*, entitled *Petite suite* (BB113), all pieces of this period are original compositions, nearly all written to commission. They exhibit a greater distance from any models of Bartók's contemporaries than do the works of preceding or following periods, and are also less immediately reflective of his recent folk-music findings than hitherto. Their homogeneity of style is unparalleled in

Bartók's output, and reflects the full flowering of that Bachian aesthetic to which he had been gravitating since 1926. Technically, this achievement was partly the result of the advanced state of evolution of Bartók's contrapuntal and chromatic writing, and also of his handling of variation. In his later Harvard lectures (1943) Bartók identified polymodal chromaticism as a main ingredient of his idiom. By this he meant a kind of chromaticism which draws its elements from strands of different modes based upon a single fundamental note; ex.5 shows a

Ex.5

Lydian

Phrygian

typical, Lydian-Phrygian polymodal construction. From this Bartók further developed a structural (that is, non-embellishing) type of 'melodic new chromaticism' in which earlier modal obligations are dispensed with, even though allegiance to one focal note is retained. The opening 'Arabic' melody in the *Dance Suite* was identified by Bartók as his first 'new chromatic' melody, while he also referred, in his lectures, to examples in a majority of the works of 1934–40, of which the twisting A-based fugal theme in the first movement of the *Music for Strings, Percussion and Celesta* is perhaps the most famous. The 12-note 'row' theme found in the outer movements of the Violin Concerto (BB117) of 1937–8 (Bartók's second concerto for the instrument, though never numbered by the composer) is another instance of such chromaticism, with which, as reported by Yehudi Menuhin, Bartók 'wanted to show Schoenberg that one can use all 12 tones and still remain tonal'.

Bartók's fascination with documenting the ever-changing variants of folk music had by the mid-to-late 1930s also become an ingrained aspect of his compositional strategy. In 1937 he declared to the Belgian scholar Denijs Dille that 'I do not like to repeat a musical thought unchanged, and I never repeat a detail unchanged . . .'. The extreme variety that characterizes our folk music is, at the same time, a manifestation of my own nature'. That variational orientation is seen in Bartók's very occasional theme-and-variation movements, such as the second movement of the Violin Concerto 'no.2'; but much more in his frequent writing of finales as variants of opening movements, his incessant variation (often involving inversion) of exposition material in recapitulations, and his bar-by-bar evolving variation of thematic and motivic materials. It is not by chance that in over 30 statements of Bartók's 12-note theme in the opening movement of the Violin Concerto no two statements are identical.

Most representative of the 1934–40 period, although each is of a very different construction, are four chamber works. Bartók's last two string quartets, the Fifth (BB110) of 1934 and the Sixth (BB119) of 1939, frame the period's output. Written to a commission from Elizabeth Sprague-Coolidge, the Fifth, like its predecessor, has five movements arranged symmetrically around the central, third movement, in this case a Scherzo and Trio in Bulgarian metres. Bartók's variational play is seen nowhere better than in a banal 'barrel-organ' interlude near the end of the finale, which turns out to be an inverted, diatonic relative of that movement's opening chromatic theme. By contrast, the Sixth String Quartet is in four movements, and stylistically retrospective, even nostalgic. Its *mesto*,

solo viola ritornello theme recalls the opening dirge of the First Quartet, while the slow finale looks back to the grim ending of the Quartet no.2. Bartók originally intended to have a fast, dance-like finale, but the brooding ritornello came so to grow through the work – in duration, complexity and instrumental involvement – that it eventually consumed the entire role of finale.

Between these two quartets Bartók composed two chamber works for very different ensembles; in 1937 the Sonata for two pianos and percussion BB115, his only chamber work to involve percussion, and in 1938 *Contrasts* BB116, the only one to involve a wind instrument. The three orchestral works which Bartók had written since 1926 which used piano and percussion had convinced him that one piano could not provide sufficient balance to the sharp sounds of the percussion section – hence the Sonata's instrumentation. Bartók demanded intricate coordination from the two percussionists (although six were used in one early Italian performance), not just in the virtuoso playing of their seven instruments but also in achieving subtle distinctions of sound quality through using different wooden or metal beaters, and even the blade of a pocket-knife. The three-movement structure, as with the immediately preceding *Music for Strings, Percussion and Celesta*, moves from a 'closed', twisting opening chromaticism to the open, 'acoustic' scale forms of the finale. Moreover, the larger and smaller sections of these two works were early identified to have an uncanny sense of proportion, which the Hungarian analyst Ernő Lendvai from the late 1940s onwards claimed as manifestations of golden section principles (*See* FIBONACCI SERIES, and GOLDEN NUMBER). Although Bartók appears not to have known about such proportions, and many of Lendvai's calculations have since been discredited, it is undeniable that a fine sense of proportion and of chromatic–diatonic balance was articulated in these two works. Altogether different in form and intention was Bartók's *Contrasts*, commissioned by Benny Goodman as a light two-movement piece of about six minutes' duration, with each movement to fit on one record side. Bartók, however, exceeded both duration and movement expectations by producing a three-movement work which lasts some 15 minutes. Within the original slow–fast rhapsodic frame, he inserted a 'Relaxation' movement in which the slowly moving clarinet and violin simultaneously mirror each other's lines. In *Contrasts* Bartók formally acknowledged with the first movement's title 'Verbunkos' the resurrection of that kind of stylized national dance which had characterized some of his earliest works, had then been rejected under the sway of peasant music, but had slowly been re-emerging since the violin rhapsodies of the late 1920s.

The most significant of his chamber-orchestral works of the period is *Music for Strings, Percussion and Celesta* BB114, written for Paul Sacher and the Basle Chamber Orchestra during the summer of 1936. The piece shows great originality at all levels of its construction and seamlessly integrates the broadest range of Bartók's folk-music and art-music sources. Formal and pitch symmetries are plentiful, as in the A–C–F♯–A tonal pattern of the four movements, the forward and reverse cycles of 5ths of the opening fugue, and the ABCBA 'bridge' form of the third-movement Adagio. Bartók's variation of materials is constant, with a particularly poignant example in the finale, where, following the model of his Fifth Quartet, a *calmo*, rhythmically uniform version of the movement's snappy opening theme momentarily halts the concluding rush. A sense of monothematicism is achieved through the reintroduction of the opening movement's chromatic fugue theme in each succeeding movement: as a contour model for the second's main subject, as the cement between each block of the third's bridge form, and, using scalar expansion (ex.6), as a grand 'acoustic' transfor-

Ex.6 *Music for Strings, Percussion and Celesta*

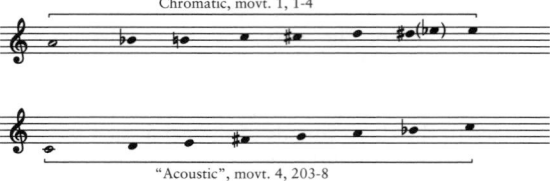

mation at the culmination of the finale. Less technically demanding and profound, but even more in keeping with Bartók's Baroque aesthetic is the *Divertimento* BB118 of 1939, also composed for Sacher, which Bartók described as a cross between a concerto grosso and a concertino.

The only work for full orchestra during the latter 1930s is the three-movement Violin Concerto 'no.2', written to a commission from Zoltán Székely. Not having written a violin concerto in three decades and never having heard a full performance of the earlier one, Bartók was nervous about the balance between soloist and orchestra. However, when he finally heard the work performed, in 1943, he was delighted that 'nothing had to be changed'. The concerto is probably Bartók's most diverse study in variation, not just in the theme and variations of the second movement, which is a virtual catalogue of his techniques, or in the ever-changing forms of his 12-note theme in the outer movements, but also in the way in which the third movement is derived entirely from first-movement material. To Székely, who had requested a traditional concerto, he confided: 'so I managed to outwit you. I wrote variations after all'. Even within the first movement, thematic interrelationships and textural transformations are most ingenious: the placid solo violin melody in the development section, for instance, reveals itself to be a literal quotation of the movement's opening pizzicato bass line. A *verbunkos* character is again present in the concerto's opening, with its suggestion of Transylvanian fiddlers. As in several of Bartók's later compositions, the ending was reworked to give a more expansive peroration in which the solo violin continues playing to the end.

During 1935–6 Bartók composed his last choral pieces, the *Twenty-Seven Two- and Three-part Choruses* BB111 for children's and women's choruses, and *Elmúlt időkből* ('From Olden Times') BB112, three songs for male chorus. Both works present Bartók's own fashionings of folk texts, the short choruses dealing with the domestic world of childhood and adolescence, the longer male chorus songs with the joys and sorrows of peasant life. Kodály, for whose growing choral movement the *Twenty-Seven Choruses* were written, later wrote that Bartók's recent studies of Palestrina might have been a source of inspiration for the heightened polyphonic plasticity and imitational resourcefulness found in these pieces. Despite the quality of Bartók's writing these two works have not gained the level of international attention accorded to

Bartók's late instrumental works, partly because of their educational associations and partly because of the intractably Hungarian nature of their prosody.

At the same time as Bartók was writing this string of masterworks, his collection of *Mikrokosmos* piano pieces continued to grow. Already on 9 February 1937 he had given the public première of 27 of them at an ISCM concert in London, and he continued to unveil such selections in following years. During 1937 he composed ten, mainly more advanced pieces, including five of the 'Six Dances in Bulgarian Rhythm'; these brought what became the sixth volume almost to completion. He added some 50 further pieces in the following two years, including much of the first volume, and also the 33 exercises. In the preface which Bartók sent with the completed collection of 153 pieces to his new publisher, Boosey & Hawkes, in November 1939, he drew attention to the versatility of the series. He had included a second piano part in four pieces, to encourage early ensemble playing, and another four pieces were songs ('All instrumental study or training should really commence with the student singing'). Ten other pieces were recommended for playing on the harpsichord. Bartók stressed that his collection did not present a complete 'progressive method', but rather a base to which works by other composers, such as Bach and Czerny, should be added. In a letter to Boosey & Hawkes of 13 February 1940, he explained that he saw *Mikrokosmos* as a bridge leading from his own 20th-century shore to an older one, either through 'centuries-old folk music' or through such typical devices of older art music as canon and imitation. With the completion of both *Mikrokosmos* and the Sixth String Quartet in November 1939 Bartók entered his longest compositionally unproductive period, which lasted until 1943.

From his vantage point as a committee member of the League of Nations, Bartók was a direct witness to the deterioration in human rights and growing nationalist intolerance which swept so many parts of Europe during the 1930s. His ethnomusicological work was still occasionally attacked by nationalists in both Hungary and Romania, and the publication of his Slovak collection was finally ruled out in early 1939, the victim of other nationalist tensions. Bartók was acutely distressed at Germany's dismemberment of Czechoslovakia in 1938–9, but it was Germany's annexation of Austria in March 1938 which had the most immediate effect upon him. Bartók's then publisher, Universal, was rapidly Nazified, and his main royalty agencies, AKM and Austromechana, were merged with the corresponding German organizations. Bartók quickly sought to secure publication through Boosey & Hawkes, and to join the British PRS. His worries about when Hungary, too, might succumb to Nazi domination caused him in late 1937 to start thinking about a safe haven for his more valuable manuscripts, and in April 1938 to start their despatch, first to Switzerland, and then, via London, to the United States, where they later became the basis of the New York Bartók Archives. In 1988 they entered the private collection of Péter Bartók in Homosassa, Florida. During the first half of 1939 Bartók seriously investigated the possibility of emigrating to Turkey, before deciding that the USA was the most desirable personal refuge. However, on 13 April 1938 Bartók had written 'I have my mother here: shall I abandon her altogether in her last years? – No, I cannot do that!'; and only on her death in December 1939 did he feel morally free to leave. Despite the precarious times – with the period of 'phoney war' drawing to a close – Bartók undertook a successful concert tour of the USA during April–May 1940. Noteworthy were a sonata recital with Szigeti at the Library of Congress in Washington and a Columbia recording session of *Contrasts* in New York with Szigeti and Goodman. His confidence in a move of indefinite duration was immeasurably strengthened when he came to know of a large collection of Serbo-Croat field recordings undertaken by a Harvard professor, Milman Parry, and his associate, Albert B. Lord, in 1933–5.

Back in Budapest by late May of 1940, Bartók started to plan for his permanent return to the USA with his wife in October 1940. Bureaucratic complications associated with indefinitely leaving Hungary before the pensionable age of 60, when he would also become exempt from military service, as well as visa, travel and currency difficulties, were compounded by persistent pains in Bartók's right shoulder, which required daily hydrotherapy. These pains were later interpreted as the first signs of his eventually fatal blood disorders. A final orchestral concert for both husband and wife was held at the Budapest Academy of Music on 8 October 1940, before they travelled to New York, via Lisbon.

7. 1940–45.   Bartók lived in the USA for the remainder of his life. After the trials of the first few months, with the couple's early two-piano concerts gaining less than enthusiastic receptions and insecurities over accommodation, finances, passports and their temporarily mislaid Hungarian luggage, Bartók settled into the familiar routine of regular ethnomusicological work and occasional concert tours. During his American years he declined several offers of composition-teaching positions, although he did privately teach a few students piano or composition. In November 1940 Columbia University awarded him an honorary doctorate, and during 1941–2 he held a research appointment there, working on Parry's Serbo-Croatian collection, which was on loan from Harvard. That work eventually resulted in the volume *Serbo-Croatian Folk Songs* (New York, 1951), of which Bartók completed the musical parts and Lord the textual. Probably Bartók's greatest discovery among this Serbo-Croat material lay with Dalmatian chromatic folk tunes. There he came upon a form of melodic chromaticism very similar to the 'new chromaticism' found in his own compositions since the *Dance Suite*. Moreover, he found that his compositional technique of melodic transformation through expansion or contraction of scalar intervals (exx.4 and 6) occurred naturally among the Dalmatians. Their chromatic melodies were none other than compressed diatonic melodies of surrounding areas. Another Dalmatian effect, which Bartók later compositionally imitated, involved the playing or singing of chromatic tunes in two parallel parts, separated by intervals such as major 2nds or minor 7ths. Mainly in his private time, Bartók also worked on the final forms of his volumes of Romanian instrumental and vocal melodies, which were essentially complete by December 1942, and of Romanian folk texts, which took until late 1944. He also revised and polished his Turkish volume, which was finished in late 1943. Without prospect of publication for either, Bartók deposited them in the music library at Columbia, to be available 'to those few persons (very few indeed) who

may be interested in them'. These Romanian volumes were published in 1967, the Turkish in 1976. A further ethnomusicological appointment, for work on Amerindian music, was periodically offered by the University of Washington, Seattle, but never taken up.

The 'magnificent possibilities' to which Bartók's New York agent had made reference in 1940 soon turned out to be illusory. Twice during 1941 he ventured on tours across the continent, presenting numerous solo or two-piano recitals in universities or colleges. More prestigious engagements were few. His last solo concert performances took place in Chicago on 20 and 21 November 1941, and his last public appearances were with his wife on 21 and 22 January 1943, when Reiner conducted the American première of his Concerto for two pianos, percussion and orchestra BB121, an arrangement of the Sonata for two pianos and percussion. After January 1943 Bartók did still seek performing engagements, and though in January 1945 he played for a New Jersey radio broadcast, for a variety of health and logistical reasons no further public performances followed. As a composer, too, his American output was initially meagre. The orchestral version of the Sonata was made in 1940 and the arrangement of his Second Suite, as the Suite for Two Pianos op.4b BB122, in 1941. But he did not engage in any original composition until the spring of 1942, when some ideas emerged perhaps for a suggested concerto for 'combinations of solo instruments and string orchestra'. From April 1942, however, chronic illness intervened and Bartók put this work aside.

Although suffering more acutely, Bartók decided to go ahead with a visiting appointment at Harvard for the spring semester of 1943. There his duties were to present one recital and two lecture series on recent Hungarian music, principally his own and that of Kodály, and on folksong and ethnomusicological procedure. While Bartók only managed to present three of the first series' lectures and to draft a fourth, these Harvard lectures provide Bartók's most candid and detailed explanation of his compositional techniques. He was then hospitalized, with a tentative diagnosis of blood (polycythemia) and lung (tuberculosis) disorders. The American Society of Composers, Authors and Publishers (ASCAP), of which Bartók was not a member, decided to underwrite the costs of his medical treatment and recuperation. For the following three summers recovery took him to Saranac Lake in New York State, and for the 1943–4 winter to a sanatorium in Asheville, North Carolina. It was while on these rest cures away from New York that Bartók's final compositions were written.

The Concerto for Orchestra BB123 was commissioned by the Koussevitzky Music Foundation in May 1943. Probably drawing on some of his fleeting ideas from 1942, Bartók started in August 1943 to draft the work in five movements, less overtly symmetrical, however, than Bartók's other recent five-movement compositions. The various folk-music and art-music components of its style are also less integrated than in his music of the 1930s. In a programme note Bartók depicted the work's mood as gradually progressing from the 'sternness of the first movement and the lugubrious death-song of the third, to the life-assertion of the last one'. The exception to this progression, as Bartók noted, was the jesting 'game of pairs' second movement, in which he imitated the two-part parallel Dalmatian style found in Parry's collection.

The fourth movement, 'Intermezzo interrotto', is uncharacteristically cheeky in mood, with its parody of a tune from Shostakovich's then-popular Seventh Symphony, and nostalgic quotation of a popular song, *Szep vagy, gyönyörű vagy Magyarország* ('You are lovely, you are beautiful, Hungary') by Zsigmond Vincze. Another strong, nostalgic influence upon the first and third movements is Bartók's own style from the 1908–11 period, in particular that of *Bluebeard's Castle*. The life-asserting finale is, however, a boisterous roll-call of some of Bartók's favourite folk styles. It attempts, if with limited success, to combine aspects of sonata form with the loose 'chain' forms which Bartók had invoked in the second and third movements. First performed in Boston on 1 December 1944, the Concerto for Orchestra proved immediately attractive to the American public, although Bartók was soon persuaded to write a second, less abrupt ending to the finale. Whether, or how much, Bartók's new accessibility betrayed his longer-term creative directions became a frequent point of debate after his death.

During October 1943 Bartók heard excellent multiple performances of his Violin Concerto ('no.2') in the hands of Tossy Spivakovsky, and in November inspired performances of his First Violin Sonata from Menuhin. On Menuhin's suggestion of a commission, Bartók had by 14 March 1944 written the four-movement Sonata for solo violin BB124, a work of overt homage to Bach, in particular Bach's solo Sonata in C, which Bartók had heard Menuhin perform. Of his four major American works this astringent sonata could, however, least be accused of stylistic compromise. Its use of Baroque imitative techniques is sustained in the first movement, marked *Tempo di ciaccona*, and also in the second movement, an ambitious four-voiced fugue whose chromatic subject is characterized by competing major and minor 3rds. The Presto finale is significant in introducing long passages of quarter-tone writing, and some reference to third-tones. However, only Bartók's semitonal alternatives were included in Menuhin's posthumous edition of the work.

While writing the sonata Bartók's health again declined. The first definite signs of leukaemia were detected in the spring of 1944, although through the use of blood transfusions and drugs, including penicillin, Bartók's condition was able to be held reasonably stable until the late summer of 1945. During the summer of 1944 ethnomusicological demands largely took over from composition, but Bartók also regained his enthusiasm for performance, even to the extent of wanting to make new recordings of his own works. His financial circumstances, which had been particularly exacerbated since 1941 because of double taxation on his British-derived royalty income, were now somewhat more secure. The successful premières of his first two American works within a week in late 1944 further reinforced his confidence, and led to several offers of commissions during the first half of 1945.

Bartók's final two substantial compositions were both concertos. While in Saranac during July–August 1945 he worked intensively on the Third Piano Concerto BB127, intended for his wife to perform, in tandem with the Viola Concerto BB128, commissioned by William Primrose. The idea of a new piano concerto grew from Bartók's realization that his wife could not master some of the more challenging sections of his previous one. In the Third, consequently, he wanted something texturally lighter and is reported to have examined Greig's concerto as one possible model for this new lucidity. Bartók's folk-, art- and nature-derived inspirations in the work are relatively undisguised. The second movement, for instance, begins with an extended imitation of Beethoven's 'Heiliger Dankgesang' (from the String Quartet in A minor op.132), while its middle, 'Night Music' section makes explicit reference to the call of the rufous-sided towhee bird, which Bartók had noted down while in North Carolina.

Bartók died in New York on 26 September 1945, after a month-long relapse in health. During his final weeks he managed to complete the Third Piano Concerto, except for the scoring of the final 17 bars, which his colleague Tibor Serly quickly accomplished. His Viola Concerto, however, only remained in sketch, the solo part suggesting a work of comparable ludidity and harmonic restraint to the piano concerto, but with incomplete and less conclusive detail about instrumentation, texture and even the final form. In early August 1945 Bartók had written to Primrose about his concept of a four-movement work with joining ritornello passages, but the evidence of the manuscript suggests only three movements with interconnecting, non-ritornello passages. Since 1945 several attempts have been made to complete the concerto, either for viola or cello. Two of the viola versions have 'authorized' status: that undertaken by Tibor Serly with additional input by Primrose, which was published in 1950 shortly after the première, and a 'revised version' of 1995, which was prepared by Péter Bartók and Nelson Dellamaggiore.

8. LEGACY.   Dying within weeks of the end of World War II, Bartók narrowly missed the wave of popularity which greeted his music in the first postwar decade. A Hungarian diaspora of conductors (Reiner, Doráti), violinists (Székely, Szigeti) and pianists (Kentner, Sándor) energetically spread his music around the world, as did recent commissioners of his works (Sacher, Koussevitzky, Menuhin and Primrose).

His later works, particularly the orchestral and chamber music, gained increasing access to mainstream concerts, sometimes to the chagrin of the postwar avant garde. Within Hungary itself, Bartók's compositions were during the late 1940s and early 1950s subjected to investigation for their socialist-realist qualities, with approval being accorded to his folksong settings, lighter piano works, and such orchestral works as the *Dance Suite*, and disapproval to what one Hungarian critic called 'formalist, modernist works written in an abstract language', such as *The Miraculous Mandarin*, the first two piano concertos, the Fourth String Quartet and the *Cantata profana*. The excesses of this phase passed with the early 1950s, however, and by the mid-1950s Bartók's works were in official favour with the communist authorities, just as his life was now interpreted as a socialist symbol of resistance both to European fascists and to American capitalists. In the 1950s, however, a complex dispute arose concerning the estates which Bartók had left, by different wills, in Hungary and America. Lasting into the 1980s, this dispute perpetuated a 'cold war' attitude of musical and scholarly non-cooperation between the two countries of his residence, and resulted in retarded dissemination of many important primary-source materials as well as distinctly different research traditions and repertory focusses.

Bartók's influence upon other composers certainly lacked the intensity and dogmatic hold of Schoenberg, or the widespread impact of the neo-classical Stravinsky. Always averse to teaching composition, Bartók did not leave behind any loyal 'school'. The composer most directly influenced by Bartók, and Bartók in turn by him, was undoubtedly Kodály. So closely did the two collaborate, especially in their earlier years, that the extent of their interdependence cannot be fully known. Leading composers of following generations on whose works Bartók exerted some measure of direct influence include Messiaen, Lutosławski, Britten, Ginastera, Copland and Crumb. Among Hungarians, György Kroó (in Ránki, B1987) has noted that Bartók provided a powerful model particularly for composers emerging between the late 1950s and mid-1970s, not so much in terms of specific techniques (although there had since 1945 been much superficial imitation of his distinctive string and percussion sounds, and of a narrow band of formal and folksong models) as in the human and professional ideals which he offered, as Hungarian music sought to throw off its postwar isolation and to re-establish a pan-European significance.

For a naturally reluctant teacher Bartók left a surprisingly powerful pedagogic legacy. That legacy lies, to a minor extent, in the students of his Academy and private piano lessons, who included the conductor Fritz Reiner, the pianists Lajos Heimlich (Hernádi), Ernő Balogh, Ditta Pásztory and Andor Földes, the ethnomusicologist Jenő Deutsch, and, briefly, the conductor Georg Solti. More significant, however, for broader musical education were Bartók's publications: the many, early instructive editions of piano 'classics' and studies which he produced between 1907 and the mid-1920s, as well as the Bartók-Reschofsky *Piano Method*, but, above all, his compositions for young pianists (*For Children, Mikrokosmos*), violinists (*Forty-four Duos*) and singers (*Twenty-seven Choruses* and many simpler folksong arrangements). That Bartók produced the most significant of these works in the 1930s, at the height of his maturity, attests to the importance which he placed on educating a new generation in contemporary styles.

As a performer, Bartók's personal legacy was not great. With his dour personality and diffident platform manners he did not manage to thrill the great public; within the Hungarian context he was overshadowed by his better-known contemporary Ernő Dohnányi. An outstanding corner of his pianistic legacy is, nonetheless, the collection of gramophone, piano-roll and live recordings, dating from his last quarter-century. These performances, with their wealth of tonal shadings, tempo fluctuations and occasional deviations from the published scores, remind present-day interpreters of the essentially Romantic underpinning to Bartók's performing art.

The ethnomusicological legacy of Bartók has been varied. Within the international history of that discipline, his stature is more that of a precursor than of a seminal figure. His significance outside Hungary is now largely historic, as an early proponent of transcriptional exactitude rather than as a founder of enduring disciplinary principles. Had he lived to complete his envisaged comparative study of eastern European folk musics his international significance might well have been more profound. Within Hungary his ethnomusicological legacy is perpetuated in the Academy of Sciences' long-term projects for a complete edition of Hungarian folk music and a complete collection of Bartók's own systematization of Hungarian folksong, both of which remain substantially unpublished. The greatest legacy of Bartók's folk-music studies, however, undoubtedly lies in his own compositions. It was exactly those ethnomusicological fascinations with musical detail and subtle observations of variant forms (which have led to periodic accusations from latter-day ethnomusicologists that he was not 'seeing the wood for the trees') which fed his greatest creative strengths. What contemporaries such as Schoenberg or Stravinsky could not well appreciate was that Bartók's folk-music studies provided him with a limitless arsenal for creative transformation. His approach to art-music sources was similarly transformational, as his Romanian colleague Constantin Brăiloiu once observed: 'Impressionism, polytonality, atonality, motorism: Bartók has passionately lived through all these revolutions and reshaped, as it were, for his own use, with his own rich resources, *all* systems' (in Moreux, E1949).

9. INTERPRETATION AND ANALYSIS.   Bartók's highly synthetic process of composition has elicited diverse interpretations of his works. These interpretations have often plotted his achievement as a composer against such generalized coordinates as East and West, Romanticism and Modernism, nationalism and internationalism. More conservative studies of his art have tended to emphasize the first coordinate of these pairs, while more progressive studies, the second. In aesthetic terms Bartók plotted himself as moving along a spectrum from Beethoven (artist and harmonist) towards Bach (craftsman and contrapuntalist), with a decisive point of change around 1926. Between the frequently claimed modernist poles of Schoenberg (Expressionist or emancipator of pitch) and Stravinsky (neoclassicist or emancipator of rhythm), Bartók has sometimes been interpreted as a figure of compromise, and therefore of a lesser creative significance. János Kárpáti (in Crow, B1976), however, views Bartók's position among modernists as one of synthesizing greatness:

in Bartók's art there is not a simple association between these two differing musical conceptions [Schoenberg and Stravinsky] but an organic synthesis of them. Far from wishing to reconcile the two extremes, Bartók merely used them in forming his own creative system ... he found a point upon which the heritage of the past and the revolution of the present – in Adorno's words, restoration and progress – were converging.

Few commentators agree on the precise balance of Bartók's syntheses, for his approach to composition was highly eclectic. He progressed pragmatically through life, ever fascinated by new folk- or art-music experiences and contemptuous of theorizing about music. Most noticeably after his several fallow periods of compositional incubation – 1905–7, 1912–14, 1923–6, 1931–4, 1940–3 – Bartók launched into fresh creative phases with varying degrees of stylistic continuity. The most marked changes in compositional direction could be considered to have taken place in 1907–8 and 1926. Probably the most significant speculative deviation in his output occurred during 1918–22, when, under the influence of both Schoenberg and Stravinsky, Bartók seemed to be approaching an atonal goal. The 1934–40 period, with its many major works in chamber, orchestral, vocal and solo piano genres, shows a more regular transcendence of inspirational sources than does any other; accordingly, these pieces are often deemed his most mature. Bartók himself was indifferent to charges of eclecticism or 'borrowing'. He considered the concept of artistic originality an outworn Romantic-era obsession, and openly acknowledged his liberal attitude to the use of materials by quoting Molière's defence to a charge of plagiarism, 'Je prends mon bien où je le trouve'.

Bartók's transformational approach to such a wide body of sources has generated a huge variety of analyses of his music. Depending upon the sources, theories or dialectical poles from which analyses are initiated, starkly different results can be educed. It is perhaps a measure of greatness that Bartók's music can accommodate so many different approaches yet ultimately defies them all. No one all-embracing theory for his music is, therefore, likely to emerge. Rather, reflecting Bartók's own eclecticism and relatively untheorized attitude to composition, an appropriate range of differing analytical approaches usually produces the best overall understanding of individual works or, indeed, the entire output.

Many analysts of Bartók's music have based their approaches upon the composer's own primary-source materials, as revealed in such documents as essays, analyses, recordings and the very notations of his works. Those interested in the music's pitch, rhythmic or variational components of folk origin have used Bartók's ethnomusicological treatises, with their own detailed analyses, as a profitable starting point (see Kárpáti, G1956; Burlas, E1971; Lenoir, E1986; László, E1995). Analysts of form (such as Hunkemöller, G1982, G1983) have drawn productively on Bartók's work analyses, particularly those of his later chamber pieces with their evidence of large-scale symmetrical thinking. Bartók's descriptions of the phases of his modal and tonal practice, most valuably in his Harvard lectures of 1943, have strongly influenced pitch analyses of his later compositions (see Oramo, F1977, F1980; Kárpáti, G1967, enlarged 1994); his terms 'polymodal chromaticism' and 'new chromaticism' have thereby entered the broader analytical literature. As compositional sketches and drafts have become increasingly available, they have led to notationally-based forms of semiotic analysis (see Gillies, F1989, F1993). Even Bartók's recordings have inspired close observation, not just of his performing style but also of his 'live' variational tendencies (see Somfai in *Documenta bartókiana*, 1977).

Nevertheless, the majority of analytical studies have sought their illumination through approaches less beholden to the composer's own documentary legacy. Among traditional formal analysts, Halsey Stevens (D1953) established enduring conclusions, particularly about the string quartets. Detailed motivic or thematic analyses have proven most analytically fruitful with such later works as the Violin Concerto 'no.2' (see Michael, G1976; Somfai, G1977; Weiss-Aigner, G1993–4), while Schenkerian approaches have been applied to the Fourth String Quartet (Travis, G1970) and the *Mikrokosmos*

pieces (Waldbauer, G1982, G1987). Antokoletz (F1984), through concentration on the interaction of intervallic cells, scalar constructions, interval cycles and axes of symmetries, has demonstrated how Bartók progressively transformed folk-music sources into the more abstract principles of his compositions. Forte's pitch-class set theory has been usefully drawn upon in analyses of both tonal and atonal works (see Cohn, F1988, F1991; Wilson, F1992) while Forte (F1993) has also contributed to the relatively neglected field of analysis of Bartókian rhythm. 'Functional' analyses using aspects of sol-fa solmization have been carried out by several Hungarian scholars, notably Lendvai (F1983) and Bárdos (F1972). Lendvai's contribution to the analysis of proportions, particularly golden sections, in Bartók's music has generated one of the more long-lived debates in the field (see Lendvai, F1971, F1983; Bachmann, F1979; Howat, F1983).

Of increasing importance to Bartók studies during the 1980s and 1990s have been 'genetic' and contextual studies, which investigate the circumstances of the creation of Bartók's works. These studies have included technical documentation of work stages of compositions and resultant analytical conclusions (see Beach, G1988; Vikárius, G1993–4, Móricz, G1995), as well as speculative investigations of specific art-music influences upon Bartók compositions (see Suchoff, 'The Impact of Italian Baroque Music on Bartók's Music', in Ránki, B1987; Gillies, E1992; Schneider, G1997; Vikárius, E1999), or of cultural or natural phenomena believed to have influenced Bartók in composing particular works (Harley, G1994; Leafstedt, G1999).

The history of Bartók analysis has been one of slow changes in trend: from early, postwar concerns with style analysis, mainly in the pitch domain, through to the more structural concerns of the 1950s to 70s. Lendvai, whatever the virtues of his proportional interpretations, was most important during these decades in placing a solid emphasis on non-traditional, large-scale aspects of construction. During the 1980s and 90s, despite an apparently ever-growing divergence of methods, the tendency has again been to concentrate on more 'micro' levels of composition. Over the second half of the 20th century eastern European commentators have been somewhat more concerned with looking to Bartók himself for analytical inspiration, while scholars from elsewhere have been more prominent in other categories of analysis. By the 1990s, with the increasing internationalization of scholarship, these distinctions were becoming tenuous.

Despite the richness and variety of approaches to Bartók's music, only parts of his output have been thoroughly investigated. As with performances and recordings (see Lampert, E1995), Bartók's instrumental music is much more exposed than his vocal. This is more for reasons of language and of score accessibility than for reasons of quality. The range of his vocal music is substantially known only in Hungary; its wider propagation remains a challenge for the 21st century.

WORKS

Catalogues: L. Somfai: 'List of Works and Primary Sources', *Béla Bartók: Composition, Concepts, and Autograph Sources* (Berkeley, 1996), 297–320 [BB]

D. Dille: *Thematisches Verzeichnis der Jugendwerke Béla Bartóks, 1890–1904* (Budapest, 1974) [DD]

Publishers: Boosey & Hawkes [B], Dover [Do], Magyar Kórus [M], Rozsnyai Károly [R], Rószavölgyi [Rv], Universal [U], Zeneműkiadó (Editio Musica) [Z]

Editions [facsimilie]: *Hungarian folksongs*, ed. D. Dille (Budapest, 1970) [BB42]

Andante, ed. L. Somfai (Budapest, 1980) [BB26b, vn, pf]

Zongoraszonáta/Sonata, ed. L. Somfai (Budapest, 1980) [BB88]
Béla Bartók fekete zsebkönyve: vázlatok, 1907–1922/Béla Bartók's Black Pocket-Book: Sketches, 1907–1922, ed. L. Somfai (Budapest, 1987)
Viola Concerto: Facsimilie Edition of the Autograph Draft, ed. L. Somfai and N. Dellamaggiore (Homosassa, FL, 1995) [BB128]

STAGE

BB	op.	Title	Genre (acts, librettist)	Composition	First performance	Original publication; remarks
62	11	A Kékszakállú herceg vára [Bluebeard's Castle]	opera (1, B. Balázs)	1911, rev. 1912, 1917–18	cond. E. Tango, Budapest, Opera, 24 May 1918	vs U 1922; fs U 1922
74	13	A fából faragott Firályfi [The Wooden Prince]	ballet (1, Balázs)	1914–16, orchd 1916–17	cond. E. Tango, Budapest, Opera, 12 May 1917	Pf score U 1921; fs U 1924; suite, small orch, c1925; suite, large orch, 1932; see also ORCHESTRAL
82	19	A csodálatos mandarin [The Miraculous Mandarin]	pantomime (1, M. Lengyel)	1918–19, orchd 1924, rev. 1926–31	cond. E. Szenkár, Cologne, Stadt, 27 Nov 1926	fs U 1924, rev. 1936; pf 4 hands score U 1925; scenes, orch, 1924; rev. as sutie, 1927; see also ORCHESTRAL

ORCHESTRAL

BB	op.	Title, scoring	Composition	First performance	Original publication	Remarks
19/3	–	Valcer	c1900			DD60b; arr. of pf work, DD60a/1–2
19/4	–	Scherzo, B♭	c1901			DD65
25	–	1902, orchd 1903	Scherzo, cond. I. Kerner, Budapest, 29 Feb 1904		DD68; Scherzo, C, orchd; other movts in sketch	
31	–	Kossuth, sym. poem	1903	cond. Kerner, Budapest, 13 Jan 1904	Z 1963	DD75a; tableau 10 arr. pf, DD75b
35	2	Scherzo, pf, orch [orig. titled Burlesque]	1904	E. Tusa, cond. G. Lehel, Budapest, 28 Sept 1961	Z 1961	arr. 2 pf, unpubd
36b	1	Rhapsody, pf, orch	1905	Bartók, cond. C. Chevillard, Paris, early Aug 1905	Rv 1910	arr. of pf work, BB36a
39	3	Suite no.1, full orch	1905, rev. c1920	movts 1, 3–5, Vienna, 29 Nov 1905; complete, cond. J. Hubay, Budapest, 1 Mar 1909	Rv 1912, rev. Z 1956	
40	4	Suite no.2, small orch [orig. titled Serenade]	movts 1–3, 1905, movt 4, 1907; rev. 1920, 1943	movt 2, cond. Bartók, Berlin, 2 Jan 1909; complete, cond. Kerner, Budapest, 22 Nov 1909	Bartók 1907, rev. U 1921, rev. B 1948	freely arr. 2 pf, BB122
48a	–	Violin Concerto (no.1)	1907–8	H.-H. Schneeberger, cond. P. Sacher, Basle, 30 May 1958	B 1959	1st movt rev. as no.1 of BB48b; 2nd movt, arr. vn, pf, 1907–8, unpubd
48b	5	Két portré [Two Portraits]: 1 Egy ideális [One Ideal], 2 Egy torz [One Grotesque]	no.1, 1907; no.2, 1908, orchd 1910	no.1, I. Waldbauer, cond. L. Kun, 12 Feb 1911; complete, E. Baré, cond. I. Strasser, Budapest, 20 April 1616	R 1911	no.1 from 1st movt of Vn Conc., BB48a; no.2, arr. of pf work, BB50/14
59	10	Két kép [Two Pictures]: 1 Virágzás [In Full Flower], 2 A falu tánca [Village Dance]	1910	cond. Kerner, Budapest, 26 Feb 1913	Rv 1912	arr. pf, 1910–11 (Rv 1912)
61	–	Román tánc [Romanian Dance]	1911	cond. Kun, Budapest, 12 Feb 1911	Z 1965	arr. of pf work, BB56/1
64	12	Four Orchestral Pieces: 1 Preludio, 2 Scherzo, 3 Intermezzo, 4 Marcia funebre	1912, orchd 1921	cond. E. Dohnányi, Budapest, 9 Jan 1922	U 1923	
74	13	A fából faragott királyfi [The Wooden Prince], suite, small orch	c1925	cond. Dohnányi, Budapest, 23 Nov 1931	U 1967	3 dances from ballet
74	13	A fából faragott királyfi suite, large orch	1932		U	
76	–	Román népi táncok [Romanian Folk Dances], small orch	1917	cond. E. Lichtenberg, Budapest, 11 Feb 1918	U 1922, rev. edn U 1991	arr. of pf work, BB68

BB	op.	Title, scoring	Composition	First performance	Original publication	Remarks
82	19	A csodálatos mandarin [The Miraculous Mandarin], scenes	1924	cond. F. Reiner, Cincinnati, 1 April 1927	U 1927	From pantomime; rev. as orch suite, 1927
82	19	A csodálatos mandarin, suite	1927	cond. Dohnányi, Budapest, 15 Oct 1928	U 1929	
86a	–	Táncszvit [Dance Suite]	1923	cond. Dohnányi, Budapest, 19 Nov 1923	U 1924	1 no. omitted in draft; arr. pf, BB86b (U 1925)
91	–	Piano Concerto no.1	1926	Bartók, cond. Furtwängler, Frankfurt, 1 July 1927	U 1927	arr. 2 pf (U 1927, rev. edn. U 1992)
94b	–	Rhapsody no.1, vn, orch	1928–9	J. Szigeti, cond. H. Scherchen, Königsberg, 1 Nov 1929	U 1929	arr. of vn, pf work, BB94a
96b	–	Rhapsody no.2, vn, orch	1928, rev. 1935	Z. Székely, cond. Dohnányi, Budapest, 25 Nov. 1929	U 1929, rev. B 1949	arr. of vn, pf work, BB96a
101	–	Piano Concerto no.2	1930–31	Bartók, cond. H. Rosbaud, Frankfurt, 23 Jan 1933	U 1932, rev. edn. U 1994	arr. 2 pf (U 1941, rev. edn U 1993)
102b	–	Erdélyi táncok [Transylvanian Dances]	1931	cond. M. Freccia, Budapest, 25 Jan 1932	Rv 1932	arr. of vn, pf work, BB102a
103	–	Magyar képek [Hungarian Sketches]	1931	nos.1–3, 5, cond. M. Freccia, Budapest, 25 Jan 1932; complete, cond. H. Laber, Budapest, 26 Nov 1934	R-Rv 1932	arr. of pf works, BB51/5, 10, BB58/2, BB55/2, BB53 ii/42
107	–	Magyar parasztdalok [Hungarian Peasant Songs]	1933	cond. G. Baranyi, Szombathely, 18 March 1934	U 1933	arr. of pf works, BB79/6–12, 14, 15
114	–	Music for Strings, Percussion and Celesta	1936	cond. P. Sacher, Basle, 21 Jan 1937	U 1936–7	
117	–	Violin Concerto (no.2)	1937–8	Székely, cond. Mengelberg, Amsterdam, 23 March 1939	B 1946	arr. vn, pf (B 1941)
118	–	Divertimento, str	1939	cond. Sacher, Basle, 11 June 1940	B1940	
121	–	Concerto, 2 pf, perc, orch	1940	L. Kentner, I. Kabos, cond. A. Boult, London, 14 Nov 1942	B 1970	arr. of Sonata, 2 pf, perc, BB115
123	–	Concerto for Orchestra	1943, rev. 1945	cond. S. Koussevitzky, Boston, 1 Dec 1944	B 1946, rev. edn B 1993	arr. pf, 1944, unpubd
127	–	Piano Concerto no.3	1945	G. Sándor, cond. E. Ormandy, Philadelphia, 8 Feb 1946	B 1947, ed. T. Serly and others, rev. edn B 1994	last 17 bars scored by Serly
128	–	Viola Concerto	1945, inc.	W. Primrose, cond. A. Doráti, Minneapolis, 2 Dec 1949	B 1950, ed. T. Serly, rev. edn B 1995	completed from inc. draft by Serly; vc version (B 1956)

VOCAL-ORCHESTRAL

BB	Title	Text	Scoring	Composition	First performance	Original publication, remarks
18	Tiefblaue Veilchen	C. Schoenaich-Carolath	S, orch	1899		DD57
87b	Falun (Tri dedinské scény) [Three Village Scenes]	Slovak trad.	4/8 female vv, chbr orch	1926	cond. S. Koussevitzky, New York, 27 Nov 1926	fs, U 1927; vs, U 1927, rev. edn. U 1996; arr. of songs, BB87a/3–5
100	Cantata profana	Rom. colindă, arr. and Hung. trans. Bartók	T, Bar, double chorus, orch	1930	cond. A. Buesst, London, 25 May 1934	fs and vs, U 1934
108	Magyar népdalok [(Five) Hungarian Folksongs]	Hung. trad.	1v, orch	1933	cond. Dohnányi, Budapest, 23 Oct 1933	arr. of songs, BB98/1, 2, 11, 14, 12

OTHER CHORAL WORKS

BB
30   Est [Evening], DD74 (K. Harsányi), 8 male vv, 1903 (Z 1965)
57   Two Romanian Folksongs, female vv, c1909, completed from draft by B. Suchoff, unpubd: Nu te supăra mireasă [On her wedding day]; Măi badiţă prostule [Fickle lover, silly man]

60   Négy régi magyar népdal [Four Old Hungarian Folksongs], 4 male vv, 1910, rev. 1912, c1926 (U 1928): Rég megmondtam bús gerlice [Long ago I told you]; Jaj Istenem, kire várok [O God, why am I waiting?]; Ángyomasszony

kertje [In my sister-in-law's garden]; Béreslegény, jól megrakd a szekeret [Farmboy, load the cart well]

77   Tót népdalok (Slovácké ludové piesne) [Slovak Folksongs], 4 male vv, 1917 (U 1918): Ej, posluchajte málo [Ah, listen now my comrades]; Ked'ja smutny pojdem [Back to fight]; Kamarádi mojí [War is in our land]; Ej, a ked'mna zabiju [Ah, if I fall in battle]; Ked'som šiou na vojnu [Time went on]

78   Négy tót népdal (Štyri slovenské piesne) [Four Slovak Folksongs], 4vv, pf, c1916 (U 1924): Zadala mamka [Wedding song]; Na holi, na holi [Song of the Hay-Harvesters]; Rada pila, rada jedla [Song from Medzibrod]; Gajdujte, gajdence [Dancing Song]

99   Magyar népdalok [Hungarian Folksongs], mixed vv, 1930 (U 1932): A rab [The Prisoner]; A bujdosó [The Wanderer]; Az eladó lány [Finding a husband]; Dal [Lovesong]

106   Székely népdalok [Székely Folksongs], 6 male vv, 1932 (M 1938): 1 Hej, de sokszor megbántottál [How often I've grieved for you]; 2 Istenem, életem [My God, my life]; 3 Vékony cérna, kemény mag [Slender thread, hard seed]; 4 Kilyénfalvi közeptizbe [In the middle of Kilyénfalva]; 5 Vékony cérna, kemény mag; 6 Járjad pap a táncot [Do a dance, priest]

111   Twenty-seven Two- and Three-Part Choruses (Hung. trad.), children's vv (vols.i–vi), female vv (vols.vii–viii), 1935–6 (M 1937, Z 1953)

vol.i: Tavasz [Spring]; Ne hagyj itt! [Don't leave here!]; Jószág-igéző [Enchanting Song]

vol.ii: Levél az otthoniakhoz [Letter to Those at Home]; Játék [Play Song]; Leánynéző [Courting]; Héjja, héjja, karahéjja! [Hey, you hawk!]

vol.iii: Ne menj el! [Don't leave me!]; Van egy gyűrűm [I have a ring]; Senkim a világon [I've no-one in the world]; Cipósütés [Bread-baking]

vol.iv: Huszárnóta [Hussar]; Resteknek nótája [Loafers' Song]; Bolyongás [Wandering]; Lánycsúfoló [Girls' Teasing Song]

vol.v: Legénycsúfoló [Boys' Teasing Song]; Mihálynapi köszöntő [Michaelmas Greeting]; Leánykérő [Suitor]

vol.vi: Keserves [Grief]; Madárdal [Bird Song]; Csujogató [Jeering]

vol.vii: Bánat [Regret]; Ne láttalak volna! [Had I not seen you!]; Elment a madárka [The bird flew away]

vol.viii: Párnás táncdal [Pillow Dance]; Kánon: Isten veled! [God be with you!]

nos.iv/1, iii/1, iv/2, iv/3, iii/4 arr. with school orch (M 1937); nos.i/2, v/1 arr. with small orch (B 1942)

112   Elmúlt időkből [From Olden Times] (Hung. trad.), 3 male vv, 1935 (M 1937): Nincs boldogtalanabb parasztembernél [No-one's more unhappy than the peasant]; Egy, kettő, három, négy [One, two, three, four]; Nincsen szerencsésebb parasztembernél [No-one is happier than the peasant]

CHAMBER

1/20b	A Duna folyása [The Course of the Danube], DD20b, vn, pf, 1894, pf part lost [arr. of pf work, BB1/20a]
6	Sonata, c, DD37, vn, pf, 1895
7/2–4	Violin pieces, DD39, 1895, lost; 2 fantasias, DD40–41, 1896, lost
7/5	String Quartet no.1, B♭, DD42, 1896, lost
7/6	String Quartet no.2, c, DD43, 1896, lost
9/1	Piano Quintet, C, DD46, 1897, lost
10	Sonata, A, DD49, vn, pf, 1897 [pf part of 2nd movt only sketched]
13	Piano Quartet, c, DD52, 1898
17	String Quartet, F, DD56, 1898
19/1	Scherzo in Sonatenform, f, DD58, str qt, 1899–1900
26a	Duo (Canon), G, DD69, 2 vn, 1902 (in Dille: Thematisches Verzeichnis)
26b	Andante (Albumblatt), A, DD70, vn, pf, 1902 (Z 1980)
28	Sonata, e, DD72, vn, pf, 1903 (Documenta bartókiana, i–ii, 1964–5; Z 1968)
33	Piano Quintet, DD77, 1903–4, rev. to 1920 (Z 1970)
45a	Gyergyóból [From Gyergyó], rec, pf, 1907 (Z 1961); arr. pf, BB45b
52	String Quartet no.1, op.7, 1908–9 (Rv 1909)
75	String Quartet no.2, op.17, 1914–17 (U 1920, rev. edn U 1994)
84	Sonata no.1 [MS: op.21], vn, pf, 1921 (U 1923, rev. edn U 1991)
85	Sonata no.2, vn, pf, 1922 (U 1923, rev. edn U 1997)
93	String Quartet no.3, 1927 (U 1929, rev. edn U 1992)

94a	Rhapsody no.1., vn, pf, 1928, rev. 1929 (U 1929); orchd, BB94b; arr. vc, pf, BB94c
94c	Rhapsody, vc, pf, 1928–9 (U 1930)
95	String Quartet no.4, 1928 (U 1929, rev. edn U 1995)
96a	Rhapsody no.2, vn, pf, 1928 (U 1929), rev. 1945 (B 1947); orchd, BB96b
104	Forty-four Duos, 2 vn, 1931 (32 nos. Schott 1932, complete U 1933, iii–iv rev. edn U 1992)

vol.i: 1 Párosító [Teasing Song]; 2 Kalamajkó [Dance]; 3 Menuetto; 4 Szentivánéji [Midsummer Night Song]; 5 Tót nóta I [Slovak Song I]; 6 Magyar nóta I [Hungarian song I]; 7 Oláh nóta [Romanian Song]; 8 Tót nóta II [Slovak Song II]; 9 Játék [Play]; 10 Rutén nóta [Ruthenian Song]; 11 Gyermekrengetéskor [Lullaby]; 12 Szénagyűjtéskor [Hay-Harvesting Song]; 13 Lakodalmas [Wedding Song]; 14 Párnás-tánc [Cushion Dance]

vol.ii: 15 Katonanóta [Soldier's Song]; 16 Burleszk [Burlesque]; 17 Menetelő nóta I [Marching Song]; 18 Menetelő nóta II; 19 Mese [Fairy Tale]; 20 Dal [Song]; 21 Újévköszöntő I [New Year's Greeting I]; 22 Szúnyogtánc [Mosquito Dance]; 23 Menyasszony-búcsúztató [Wedding Song]; 24 Tréfás nóta [Gay Song]; 25 Magyar nóta II

vol.iii: 26 'Ugyan édes komámasszony ...' [Teasing Song]; 27 Sánta-nóta [Limping Dance]; 28 Bánkódás [Sorrow]; 29 Újévköszöntő II; 30 Újévköszöntő III; 31 Újévköszöntő IV; 32 Máramarosi tánc [Dance from Máramaros]; 33 Aratáskor [Harvest Song]; 34 Számláló nóta [Counting Song]; 35 Rutén kolomejka [Ruthenian kolomejka]; 36 Szól a duda [Bagpipes], with variant form

vol.iv: 37 Preludium és kánon; 38 Forgatós [Romanian Whirling Dance]; 39 Szerb tánc [Serbian Dance]; 40 Oláh tánc [Romanian Dance]; 41 Scherzo; 42 Arab dal [Arabian Song]; 43 Pizzicato; 44 'Erdélyi' tánc ['Transylvanian' Dance]

nos.28, 38, 43, 16, 36, 32 arr. pf, BB113

110	String Quartet no.5, 1934 (U 1936, rev. edn U 1992)
115	Sonata, 2 pf, 2 perc, 1937 (B 1942), arr. 2 pf, perc, orch, BB121
116	Contrasts, vn, cl, pf, 1938 (B 1942)
119	String Quartet no.6, 1939 (B 1941)
124	Sonata, vn, 1944 (ed. Y. Menuhin B 1947, rev. edn with quarter-tone variants B 1994)

PIANO

1/1–31	Walczer, DD1, 1890; Változó darab [Changeable Piece], DD2, 1890; Mazurka, DD3, 1890; A budapesti tornaverseny [Gymnastic Contest in Budapest], DD4, 1890; Sonatina no.1, DD5, 1890; Oláh darab [Wallachian Piece], DD6, 1890; Gyorspolka [Fast Polka], DD7, 1891; 'Béla' polka, DD8, 1891; 'Katinka' polka, DD9, 1891; Tavaszi hangok [Sounds of Spring], DD10, 1891; 'Jolán' polka, DD11, 1891; 'Gabi' polka, DD12, 1891; Nefelejts [Forget-me-not], DD13, 1891; Ländler no.1, DD14, 1891; 'Irma' polka, DD15, 1891; Radegundi visszhang [Echo of Radegund], DD16, 1891; Induló [March], DD17, 1891; Ländler no.2, DD18, 1891; Cirkusz polka, DD19, 1891; A Duna folyása [The Course of the Danube], DD20a, 1890–94, arr. vn, pf, BB1/20b; Sonatina no.2, DD21, 1891; Ländler no.3, DD22, 1892, lost; Tavaszi dal [Song of Spring], DD23, 1892; Szőllősi darab [Piece of (Nagy) szőllős], DD24, 1892, lost; 'Margit' polka, DD25, 1893; 'Ilona' mazurka, DD26, 1893; 'Loli' mazurka, DD27, 1893; 'Lajos' valczer, DD28, 1893; 'Elza' polka, DD29, 1894; Andante con variazioni, DD30, 1894; Allegro, DD31, 1894, lost; all nos. unpubd
2/1	Sonata no.1, g, DD32, 1894, unpubd
2/2	Scherzo, g, DD33, 1894, unpubd
3	Fantasie, a, DD34, 1895, unpubd
4	Sonata no.2, F, DD35, 1895, unpubd
5	Capriccio, b, DD36, 1895, unpubd
7/1	Sonata no.3, C, DD38, 1895, lost
7/7	Andante, Scherzo and Finale, DD44, 1897, lost
8	Drei Klavierstücke, b, C, a♭, DD45, 1897 (no.1 Z 1965)
9/2	Two Pieces, DD47, 1897, lost
9/3	Grosse Fantasie, DD48, 1897, lost
11	Scherzo (Fantasie), B, DD50, 1897 (Z 1965)

12	Sonata, DD51, 1898, lost
14	Drei Klavierstücke, c, g, E, DD53 (nos. 1–2 Z 1965)
16	Scherzo, b, DD55, 1898, unpubd
19/2	Scherzo, b♭, DD59, c1900, unpubd
19/3	Six Dances, DD60a, c1900, facs. of no.1 pubd as Danse orientale (*Pressburger Zeitung*, 1913); nos. 1–2 orchd, DD60b
21	Scherzo, b♭, DD63, 1900, unpubd
22	Változatok [Twelve Variations], DD64, 1900–01 (Z 1965)
23	Tempo di Minuetto, DD66, 1901, unpubd
27	Four Pieces, DD71, 1903 (Bárd, 1904; nos.1–3 B 1950; Z 1956, 1965): Study for the Left Hand; Fantasy I; Fantasy II; Scherzo
31	Marche funèbre, DD75b, 1903 (Budapest, 1905, R 1910) [arr. of Kossuth, tableau 10]
36a	Rhapsody, op.1, 1904 (Adagio mesto Rv 1908; complete Rv 1923), arr. pf, orch, BB36b, arr. 2 pf, 1905 (Rv 1910)
38	Petits morceaux, 1905 (Z 1965) [free arr. of songs BB37/2, BB24/1]
45b	Három Csík megyei népdal [Three Hungarian Folksongs from Csík], 1907 (R 1910) [arr. of rec, pf work, BB45a]: Rubato, L'istesso tempo, Poco vivo
49	Két elégia [Two Elegies], op.8b, 1908–9 (R 1910): Grave, Molto adagio sempre rubato (quasi improvisando)
50	Fourteen Bagatelles, op.6, 1908 (R 1909): 1 Molto sostenuto; 2 Allegro giocoso; 3 Andante; 4 Grave [arr. of folksong Mikor gulyásbojtár voltam]; 5 Vivo [arr. of folksong Ej! po pred naš, po pred naš]; 6 Lento; 7 Allegretto molto capriccioso; 8 Andante sostenuto; 9 Allegretto grazioso; 10 Allegro; 11 Allegretto molto rubato; 12 Rubato; 13 Elle est morte (Lento funèbre); 14 Valse: ma mie qui danse (Presto); no.14 orchd as no.2 of BB48b
51	Tíz könnyű zongoradarab [Ten Easy Pieces], 1908 (R 1908), with Ajánlás [Dedication]: 1 Paraszti nóta [Peasant Song]; 2 Lassú vergődés [Frustration]; 3 Tót legények tánca [Slovak Boys' Dance]; 4 Sostenuto; 5 Este a székelyeknél [Evening in Transylvania (Evening with the Széklers)]; 6 Gödöllei piactéren leesett a hó [Hungarian Folksong]; 7 Hajnal [Dawn]; 8 Azt mondják, nem adnak [Slovakian Folksong]; 9 Ujjgyakorlat [Five-Finger Exercise]; 10 Medvetánc [Bear Dance]; nos.5, 10 orchd, BB103/1–2
53	Gyermekeknek/Pro děti [For Children], 85 pieces, i–iv, 1908–10 (R 1910, R 1912) [i–ii after Hung., iii–iv after Slovak folksongs], rev. 1943, 79 pieces, i–ii (B 1947); orig. ii/42 orchd, BB103/5; orig. i/16 arr. 1v, pf, 1937
54	Vázlatok [Seven Sketches], op.9b, 1908–10 (R 1911): 1 Leányi arckép [Portrait of a Girl]; 2 Hinta palinta [See-Saw, Dickory-Daw]; 3 Lento; 4 Non troppo lento; 5 Román népdal [Romanian Folksong]; 6 Oláhos [In Wallachian Style]; 7 Poco lento
55	Három burleszk [Three Burlesques], op.8c, 1908–11 (Rv 1912): Perpatvar [Quarrel], Kicsit ázottan [A Bit Drunk], Molto vivo capriccioso; no.2 orchd, BB103/4
56	Ket román tánc [Two Romanian Dances], op.8a, 1909–10 (Rv 1910; with rev. no.2, Do 1981): Allegro vivace, Poco allegro; no.1 orchd, BB61
58	Négy siratóének [Four Dirges], op.9a, 1909–10 (Rv 1912): Adagio; Andante; Poco lento; Assai andante; no.2 orchd, BB103/3
63	Allegro barbaro, 1911 (U 1918, rev. edn U 1992)
66	Kezdők zongoramuzsikája [First Term at the Piano], 18 pieces, 1913 (Rv 1929) [from c50 pieces in *Zongoraiskola* [Piano Method] of Bartók and S. Reschofsky (Rv 1913)]
67	Román kolinda-dallamok [Romanian Christmas Songs], 20 pieces in 2 sers., 1915 (U 1918, rev. edn U 1995)
68	Román népi táncok [Romanian Folk Dances], 1915 (U 1918, rev. edn U 1993): 1 Joc cu bâtă [Stick Dance]; 2 Brâul; 3 Pe loc [In One Spot]; 4 Buciumeana [Dance of Buchum]; 5 Poargă românească [Romanian Polka]; 6 Mărunțel [Fast Dance]; orchd, BB76
69	Sonatina, 1915 (Rv 1919), rev. after 1930 (B 1950); authorized arr. vn, pf, by Z. Székely, BB102a; orchd Bartók, BB102b
70	Suite, op.14, 1916 (U 1918, rev. edn U 1992; omitted movt in *Új zenei szemle*, v, 1955)
79	Tizenöt magyar parasztdal [Fifteen Hungarian Peasant Songs], 1914, 1918 (U 1920): 1–4 Négy régi keserves ének

	[Four Old Tunes]; 5 Scherzo; 6 Ballade (Tema con variazioni); 7–15 Régi táncdalok [Old Dance Tunes]; nos.6–12, 14–15 orchd, BB107
80b	Three Hungarian Folk Tunes, 1914, 1918 (no.1 in early version, BB80a, in *Periszkóp* (1925), June–July; complete B 1942): Leszállott a páva [The Peacock]; Jánoshidi vásártéren [At the Jánoshida Fairground]; Fehér liliomszál [White Lily]
81	Etűdök [(Three) Studies], op.18, 1918 (U 1920)
83	Improvizációk magyar parasztdalokra [(Eight) Improvisations on Hungarian Peasant Songs], op.20, 1920 (nos.2, 8 in *Grotesken Album*, ed. C. Seelig, U 1921; complete U 1922)
86b	Táncszvit [Dance Suite], 1925 (U 1925, rev. edn U 1991) [arr. of orch suite BB86a]
88	Sonata, 1926 (U 1927, rev. edn U 1992)
89	Szabadban [Out of Doors], i–ii, 1926 (U 1927 rev. edns U 1990, 1996): i/1 Síppal, dobbal [With Drums and Pipes]; i/2 Barcarolla; i/3 Musettes; ii/4 Az éjszaka zenéje [The Night's Music]; ii/5 Hajsza [The Chase]
90	Kilenc kis zongoradarab [Nine Little Piano Pieces], i–iii, 1926 (U 1927, rev. edn U 1995): i/1–4 Négy párbeszéd [Four Dialogues]; ii/5 Menuetto; ii/6 Dal [Air]; ii/7 Marcia delle bestie; ii/8 Csörgő-tánc [Tambourine]; iii/9 Preludio–All'ungherese
92	Három rondó népi dallamokkal [Three Rondos on (Slovak) Folktunes]: no.1 1916, nos.2–3 1927 (U 1930, rev. edn U 1995)
105	Mikrokosmos, i–vi, 1926, 1932–9 (B 1940, rev. edn B 1987)

vol.i: 1–6 Six Unison Melodies; 7 Dotted Notes; 8 Repetition I; 9 Syncopation I; 10 With Alternate Hands; 11 Parallel Motion; 12 Reflection; 13 Change of Position; 14 Question and Answer; 15 Village Song; 16 Parallel Motion and Change of Position; 17 Contrary Motion I; 18–21 Four Unison Melodies; 22 Imitation and Counterpoint; 23 Imitation and Inversion I; 24 Pastorale; 25 Imitation and Inversion II; 26 Repetition II; 27 Syncopation II; 28 Canon at the Octave; 29 Imitation Reflected; 30 Canon at the Lower Fifth; 31 Dance in Canon Form; 32 In Dorian Mode; 33 Slow Dance; 34 In Phrygian Mode; 35 Chorale; 36 Free Canon; Appendix: Exercises 1–4

vol.ii: 37 In Lydian Mode; 38 Staccato and Legato I; 39 Staccato and Legato (Canon); 40 In Yugoslav Style; 41 Melody with Accompaniment; 42 Accompaniment in Broken Triads; 43 In Hungarian Style, 2 pf; 44 Contrary Motion II, 2 pf; 45 Méditation; 46 Increasing–Diminishing; 47 Country Fair; 48 In Mixolydian Mode; 49 Crescendo–Diminuendo; 50 Minuetto; 51 Waves; 52 Unison Divided; 53 In Transylvanian Style; 54 Chromatics; 55 Triplets in Lydian Mode, 2 pf; 56 Melody in Tenths; 57 Accents; 58 In Oriental Style; 59 Major and Minor; 60 Canon with Sustained Notes; 61 Pentatonic Melody; 62 Minor Sixths in Parallel Motion; 63 Buzzing; 64 Line against Point; 65 Dialogue, 1v, pf; 66 Melody Divided; Appendix: Exercises 5–18

vol.iii: 67 Thirds against a Single Voice; 68 Hungarian Dance, 2 pf; 69 Study in Chords; 70 Melody against Double Notes; 71 Thirds; 72 Dragons' Dance; 73 Sixths and Triads; 74 Hungarian Matchmaking Song, also version for 1v, pf; 75 Triplets; 76 In Three Parts; 77 Little Study; 78 Five-Tone Scale; 79 Hommage à J.S.B.; 80 Hommage à R. Sch.; 81 Wandering; 82 Scherzo; 83 Melody with Interruptions; 84 Merriment; 85 Broken Chords; 86 Two Major Pentachords; 87 Variations; 88 Duet for Pipes; 89 In Four Parts I; 90 In Russian Style; 91 Chromatic Invention I; 92 Chromatic Invention II; 93 In Four Parts II; 94 Once Upon a Time . . .; 95 Fox Song, also version for 1v, pf; 96 Jolts; Appendix: Exercises 19–30

vol.iv: 97 Notturno; 98 Thumbs Under; 99 Hands Crossing; 100 In Folksong Style; 101 Diminished Fifth; 102 Harmonics; 103 Minor and Major; 104 Wandering Through the Keys; 105 Game; 106 Children's Song; 107 Melody in the Mist; 108 Wrestling; 109 From the Island of Bali; 110 And the Sounds Clash and Clang . . .; 111

Intermezzo; 112 Variations on a Folktune; 113 Bulgarian Rhythm I; 114 Theme and Inversion; 115 Bulgarian Rhythm II; 116 Song; 117 Bourrée; 118 Triplets in 9/8 Time; 119 Dance in 3/4 Time; 120 Triads; 121 Two-part Study; Appendix: Exercises 31–3

vol.v: 122 Chords Together and in Opposition; 123 Staccato and Legato II; 124 Staccato; 125 Boating; 126 Change of Time; 127 New Hungarian Folksong, 1v, pf; 128 Stamping Dance; 129 Alternating Thirds; 130 Village Joke; 131 Fourths; 132 Major Seconds Broken and Together; 133 Syncopation III; 134 Three Studies in Double Notes; 135 Perpetuum mobile; 136 Whole-tone Scale; 137 Unison; 138 Bagpipe Music; 139 Jack-in-the-Box

vol.vi: 140 Free Variations; 141 Subject and Reflection; 142 From the Diary of a Fly; 143 Divided Arpeggios; 144 Minor Seconds, Major Sevenths; 145 Chromatic Invention III; 146 Ostinato; 147 March; 148–53 Six Dances in Bulgarian Rhythm

113 Petite suite [arr. of vn duos, BB104/28, 38, 43, 16, 36], 1936 (U 1938, rev. edn 1995); omitted movt [arr. of BB104/32], unpubd
120 Seven Pieces from Mikrokosmos, 2 pf, 1939–40 (B 1947) [arr. of pf pieces BB105/113, 69, 135, 123, 127, 145, 146]
122 Suite, op.4b, 2 pf, 1941 (B 1958) [free arr. of orch work, BB40]

SONGS

15 Drei Lieder, DD54, 1898: Im wunderschönen Monat Mai (H. Heine); Nacht am Rheine (K. Siebel); Die Gletscher leuchten im Mondenlicht
20 Liebeslieder, DD62, 1900 (nos.2, 4 Z 1963): 1 Du meine Liebe, du mein Herz (F. Rückert); 2 Diese Rose pflück ich hier (N. Lenau); 3 Du geleitest mich zum Grabe; 4 Ich fühle deinen Odem (Lenau); 5 Wie herrlich leuchtet (J.W. von Goethe); Herr! der du alles wohl gemacht
24 Four songs (L. Pósa), DD67, 1902 (Bárd 1904): 1 Őszi szellő [Autumn Breeze]; 2 Még azt vetik a szememre [They are accusing me]; 3 Nincs olyan bú [There is no greater sorrow]; 4 Ejnye! ejnye! [Alas! alas!]; no.1 arr. pf, BB38/2
29 Est [Evening] (K. Harsányi), DD73, 1903 (Z 1963)
32 Four Songs, DD76, 1903, lost
34 Székely Folksong: Piros alma leesett a sárba [The red apple has fallen in the mud], DD C8, 1904 (Budapest, 1905)
37 Magyar népdalok [Hungarian Folksongs], planned 1st ser., c1904–5 (no.1 Z 1963), inc.: 1 Lekaszálták már a rétet [They have mowed the pasture already]; 2 Add reám csókodat, el kell mennem [Kiss me, for I have to leave]; 3 Fehér László lovat lopott [László Fehér stole a horse]; 4 Az egri ménes mind szürke [The horses of Eger are all grey]; no.2 arr. pf, BB38/1
41 A kicsi 'tót'-nak [For the Little 'Tót'] (Hung. children's songs), 1905 (no.3 in J. Demény: Bartók Béla: levelek, Budapest, 1948): 1 Álmos vagyok [I am sleepy]; 2 Ejnye, ejnye, nézz csak ide [Oh, oh, look there]; 3 Puha meleg tolla van a kismadárnak [The little bird]; 4 Bim bam zúg a harang [Bim bam, ring the bells]; 5 Esik eső esdegél [The rain is falling]
42 Magyar népdalok [Hungarian Folksongs], 1906 (R 1906), rev. 1938 (Rv 1938): 1 Elindultam szép hazámbul [I left my fair homeland]; 2 Által mennék én a Tiszán ladikon [I would cross the Tisza in a boat]; 3a–b Fehér László lovat lopott [László Fehér stole a horse]; 4a (4 in rev.) A gyulai kert alatt [Behind the garden of Gyula]; 4b (5 in rev.) A kertmegi kert alatt [Behind the garden of Kertmeg]; 5 (not in rev.) Ucca, ucca, ég az ucca [The street is on fire]; 6 Ablakomba, ablakomba, besütött a holdvilág [In my window shone the moonlight]; 7 Száraz ágtól messze virít a rózsa [From the withered branch no rose blooms]; 8 Végigmentem a tárkányi, sej, haj, nagy uccán [I walked to the end of the great street in Tárkány]; 9 Nem messze van ide Kis Margitta [Not far from here is little Margitta]; 10 Szánt a babám [My sweetheart is ploughing]; also nos. 11–20 by Kodály; nos.1, 2, 4, 9, 8 rev. 1928 as Five Hungarian Folksongs, BB97

43 Magyar népdalok [Hungarian Folksongs], 2nd ser., 1906–7 (nos.4, 6, 7, 8, Z 1963): 1 Tiszán innen, Tiszán túl [On this side of the Tisza, on that side of the Tisza]; 2 Erdők, völgyek, szűk ligetek [Woods, valleys, narrow parks]; 3 Olvad a hó [The snow is melting]; 4 Ha bemegyek a csárdába [Down at the tavern]; 5 Fehér László lovat lopott [László Fehér stole a horse]; 6 Megittam a piros bort [My glass is empty]; 7 Ez a kislány gyöngyöt fűz [This maiden threading]; 8 Sej, mikor engem katonának visznek [The young soldier]; 9 Még azt mondják [And they still say]; 10 Kis kece lányom [My dear daughter]; nos.5, 10 arr. pf, BB53/ii/28, 53/i/17
44 Two Hungarian Folksongs, 1907 (no.1 Z 1963, no.2 in Documenta bartókiana, iv, 1970): Édesanyám rózsafája [My mother's rose tree]; Túl vagy rózsám, túl vagy a Málnás erdején [My sweetheart, you are beyond the Málnás woods]
46 Four Slovakian Folksongs (nos.1, 3, 4 Z 1963): 1 V tej bystrickej bráne [Roses in the Fields], 1907; 2 Pod lipko nad lipko, 1907; 3 Pohřebni písen [Dirge], 1907; 4 Pritelel pták [The Message], 1916; no.2 lost
47 Nyolc magyar népdal [Eight Hungarian Folksongs], nos.1–5 1907, nos.6–8 1917 (U 1922): 1 Fekete főd [Black is the earth]; 2 Istenem, Istenem [My God, my God]; 3 Asszonyok, asszonyok, had' legyek társatok [Wives, wives, let me be one of your company]; 4 Annyi bánat [So much sorrow]; 5 Ha kimegyek [If I climb]; 6 Töltik a nagyerdő útját [They are mending the great forest highway]; 7 Eddig való dolgom [Up to now my work]; 8 Olvad a hó [The snow is melting]
65 Nine Romanian Folksongs, c1912 [completed from draft by B. Suchoff, unpubl]: 1 I went off to church one day; 2 Ev'ry lad wants me to perish; 3 Woe is me; 4 See the verdant silken tassel; 5 In the village hall; 6 While I still lived with my mother; 7 You are far away from me; 8 Many thoughts have come into mind; 9 Those who have bad luck
71 Öt dal [Five Songs], op.15, 1916 (U 1961, rev. edn U 1991): 1 Tavasz [Spring] (K. Gombossy); 2 Nyár [Summer] (Gombossy); 3 A vágyak éjjele [Night of Desire] (W. Gleiman); 4 Tél [Winter] (Gombossy); 5 Ősz [Autumn] (Gombossy)
72 Öt dal [Five Songs] (E. Ady), op.16, 1916 (U 1923): 1 Három őszi könnycsepp [Autumn Tears]; 2 Az őszi lárma [Autumn Echoes]; 3 Az ágyam hivogat [Lost Content]; 4 Egyedül a tengerrel [Alone with the Sea]; 5 Nem mehetek hozzád [I cannot come to you]
73 Krutí Tono vretena [Tony Whirls the Spindle], 1916 (Z 1963)
87a Falun (Dedinské scény) [Village Scenes] (Slovak trad.), female v, pf, 1924 (U 1927, rev. edn U 1994): 1 Szénagyűjtéskor (Pri hrabaní) [Haymaking]; 2 A menyasszonynál (Pri neveste) [At the Bride's]; 3 Lakodalom (Svatba) [Wedding]; 4 Bölcsődal (Ukoliebavka) [Lullaby]; 5 Legénytánc (Tanec mládencov) [Lads' Dance]; nos. 3–5 arr. female vv, chbr orch, BB87b
97 Five Hungarian Folksongs, 1928 (Z 1970) [rev. of BB42, nos1, 2, 4, 9, 8]
98 Húsz magyar népdal [Twenty Hungarian Folksongs], i–iv, 1929 (U 1932)

vol.i, Szomorú nóták [Sad Songs]: 1 A tömlöcben [In Prison]; 2 Régi keserves [Old Lament]; 3 Bujdosó ének [The Fugitive]; 4 Pásztornóta [Herdsman's Song]

vol.ii, Táncdalok [Dancing Songs]: 5 Székely lassú [Slow Dance]; 6 Székely friss [Fast Dance]; 7 Kanásztanc [Swineherd's Dance]; 8 'Hatforintos' nóta ['Six-Florin' Dance]

vol.iii, Vegyes dalok [Diverse Songs]: 9 Juhászcsúfoló, [The Shepherd]; 10 Tréfás nóta [Joking Song]; 11 Párosító I [Nuptial Serenade]; 12 Párosító II [Humorous Song]; 13 Pár-ének [Dialogue Song]; 14 Panasz [Complaint]; 15 Bordal [Drinking Song]

vol.iv, Új dalok [New-Style Songs]: 16 (i) Allegro: Hej, édesanyám [Oh, my dear mother]; (ii) Più allegro: Érik a ropogós cseresznye [Ripening Cherries]; (iii) Moderato: Már Dobozon [Long ago at Doboz]; (iv) Allegretto: Sárga kukoricaszár [Yellow Cornstalk]; (v) Allegro non troppo: Búza, búza, búza [Wheat, wheat, wheat] nos.1, 2, 11, 14, 12 orchd, BB108

109   Hungarian Folksong: Debrecennek van egy vize [arr. of pf work, BB53/i/16], ?1937 (in B. Paulini: *Gyöngyösbokréta*, Budapest, 1937, p.10)

125   Ukrainian Folksong: A férj keserve [The Husband's Grief], 1945 (facs. in J. Demény, ed.: *Bartók Béla levelei*, Budapest, 1951)

126   Ukrainian Folksongs, cycle, c1945, inc.: 1 Ta ne sa mam [I was not alone]; 2 Ne budu ja vodu piti [I shall not drink the water]; 3 Če my chlopci nekopalci [Not in a ditch, lads]

See also PIANO [Mikrokosmos, BB105/65, 74b, 95b, 127]

ARRANGEMENTS OF BARTÓK'S WORKS BY OR INVOLVING OTHERS

—   Romanian Folk Dances, vn, pf, arr. Z. Székely, 1925–6 (U 1926) [arr. of pf work BB68]

—   Hungarian Folk Tunes, vn, pf, arr. J. Szigeti with Bartók's advice, 1926–7 (U 1927) [arr. of pf work BB53, orig. nos.ii/28, i/18, i/42, ii/33, i/6, i/13, ii/38]

102a   Sonatina, vn, pf, arr. E. Gertler with Bartók, c1930 (Rv 1931) [arr. of pf work BB69; used by Bartók as basis for orch version BB102b]

109   Magyar népdalok [Hungarian Folksongs], vn, pf, i–ii, arr. T. Országh with Bartók, 1931 (R 1934) [arr. of pf work BB53, orig. nos.ii/34, ii/36, i/17, ii/31, i/16, i/14, i/19, i/8, i/21]

—   Five Pieces from Mikrokosmos, str qt, arr. T. Serly, 1941–2 (B 1942) [arr. of pf pieces BB105/139, 102, 108, 116, 142]

—   Mikrokosmos Suite, orch, arr. T. Serly, c1942 (B 1943) [arr. of pf pieces BB105/139, 137, 117, 142, 102, 151, 153, prefaced by orch of material from piano work BB80b (1942 version)]

EDITIONS AND ARRANGEMENTS BY BARTÓK
CONCERT ARRANGEMENTS FOR PIANO

Italian kbd music, 1–11, BB A4a–k, 1926–8 (New York, 1930): 1 B. Marcello: Sonata, B♭; 2 M. Rossi: Toccata no.1, C; 3 M. Rossi: Toccata no.2, a; 4 M. Rossi: Tre correnti; 5–8 A.B. Della Ciaia: Sonata, G; Toccata, Canzone, Primo tempo, Secondo tempo; 9 G. Frescobaldi: Toccata, G; 10 G. Frescobaldi: Fuga, g [misattrib.; by G. Muffat]; 11 D. Zipoli: Pastorale, C

J.S. Bach: Sonata VI, BWV530, org; BB A5, c1929 (Rv 1930)

H. Purcell: Two Preludes, BB A6, c1929 (Los Angeles, 1947)

EDUCATIONAL EDITIONS OF PIANO WORKS

J.S. Bach: Das wohltemperierte Klavier, i–iv (R 1907–8, rev. i–ii R 1913); 12 Easy Piano Pieces (Rv 1916; rev. with extra no., Rv 1924)

L. van Beethoven: 25 Sonatas (Rv 1909–12; opp.101, 111, unpubd); 7 Bagatelles, op.33; Variations, op.34; 'Eroica' Variations and Fugue, op.35; Polonaise, op.89; 11 neue Bagatellen, op.119 (all R 1910); Ecossaises (Budapest, 1920)

F.F. Chopin: 14 Valses (Budapest, 1920); F. Couperin: 18 Pieces (R 1924); J. Haydn: 19 Sonatas, nos.1–17 (R 1911–13); nos.18–19 (R 1920); W.A. Mozart: 20 Sonatas (R 1910–12); Fantasy K397/K385g (R 1910); D. Scarlatti: 10 Sonatas (R 1921, 1926); F. Schubert: 2 Scherzi (R 1911); R. Schumann: Jugendalbum (R 1911); Studies by J.B. Duvernoy, S. Heller, L. Köhler (Budapest, 1917–20)

CRITICAL EDITIONS

F. Liszt: Hungaria, rev. 1911; in *Musikalische Werke*, i/5 (Leipzig, 1907–36/R)

F. Liszt: Ungarischer Marsch, Ungarischer Sturmmarsch, orch, 1916; in *Musikalische Werke*, i/12 (Leipzig, 1907–36/R)

F. Liszt: Hungarian Rhapsodies, pf, 1911–17, incl. in *Musikalische Werke*, ii/2, ed. P. Raabe (Leipzig, 1926/R)

MISCELLANEA

Cadenza: L. van Beethoven: Pf Conc. no.3, 1st movt, BB A2, 1900, unpubd

Cadenzas: W.A. Mozart: 2 Pf Conc., K365/316a; BB A7, c1939, unpubd

Arr. 'Rákóczi' March, BB A1, pf 4 hands, 1896, unpubd

Arr. L. van Beethoven: Erlkönig, WoO131; BB A3, orchd c1905, unpubd

Unpubd frags., see DD appendices B–E (juvenilia) and main text of BB

WRITINGS
books and collected writings only
for listing of individual articles see Grove6

Cântece poporale româneşti din comitatul Bihor (Ungaria)/Chansons populaires roumaines du département de Bihar (Hongrie) (Bucharest, 1913); repr. as *Ethnomusikologische Schriften*, iii, ed. D. Dille (Budapest, 1967); Eng. trans. of preface in *Béla Bartók Studies in Ethnomusicology*, ed. B. Suchoff (Lincoln, NE, 1997), 1–23

ed., with Z. Kodály: Erdélyi magyar népdalok [Hungarian folksongs from Transylvania] (Budapest, 1923/R); Eng. trans. of preface in *Béla Bartók Studies in Ethnomusicology*, ed. B. Suchoff (Lincoln, NE, 1997), 77–134

Volksmusik der Rumänen von Maramureş (Munich, 1923); repr. as *Ethnomusikologische Schriften*, ii, ed. D. Dille (Budapest, 1966); Eng. edn as *Rumanian Folk Music*, v, ed. B. Suchoff (The Hague, 1975)

A magyar népdal [The Hungarian folksong] (Budapest, 1924); Eng. trans., 1931/R; repr. in Hung. and Ger. in *Ethnomusikologische Schriften*, i, ed. D. Dille (Budapest, 1965–8), 341–432; rev. Hung. version in *Bartók Béla írásai*, v, ed. D. Révész (Budapest, 1990)

Melodien der rumänischen Colinde (Weihnachtslieder) (Vienna, 1935), repr. with unpubd pt. 2 as *Ethnomusikologische Schriften*, iv, ed. D. Dille (Budapest, 1968); Eng. edn as *Rumanian Folk Music*, iv, ed. B. Suchoff (The Hague, 1975)

ed. B. Szabolcsi and A.Szőllősy: Bartók Béla válogatott zenei írásai [Selected musical writings of Béla Bartók] (Budapest, 1948, 2/1956)

with A. Lord: Serbo-Croatian Folk Songs (New York, 1951); repr. as *Yugoslav Folk Music*, i, ed. B. Suchoff (Albany, NY, 1978)

ed., with Z. Kodály: A magyar népzene tára [Corpus of Hungarian music] (Budapest, 1951–)

ed. D. Carpitella: Béla Bartók: scritti sulla musica popolare (Turin, 1955)

ed. Z. Vancea: Béla Bartók: Însemnări asupra cîntecului popular [Béla Bartók: notes on folksong] (Bucharest, 1956)

ed. A. Elscheková, O. Elschek and J. Kresánek: Slovenské ľudové piesne/Slowakische Volkslieder, i, ed. B. Suchoff (Bratislava, 1959); ii (1970), iii (forthcoming); Eng. trans. of preface in *Béla Bartók Studies in Ethnomusicology*, ed. B. Suchoff (Lincoln, NE, 1997)

ed. E. Hykischová: Béla Bartók: Postřehy a názory [Béla Bartók: observations and opinions] (Bratislava, 1965)

ed. D. Dille: Ethnomusikologische Schriften (Budapest, 1965–8)

ed. A. Szőllősy: Bartók Béla összegyűjtött írásai [Collected writings of Béla Bartók], i (Budapest, 1966)

ed. B. Suchoff: Rumanian Folk Music (The Hague, 1967–75)

ed. D. Dille: Documenta bartókiana, iv (Budapest, 1970) [incl. essay drafts and variants]

ed. B. Szabolcsi: Musiksprachen, Aufsätze und Vorträge (Leipzig, 1972)

ed. L. Vikár: Béla Bartók's Folk Music Research in Turkey (Budapest, 1976)

ed. B. Suchoff: Béla Bartók: Turkish Folk Music from Asia Minor (Princeton, NJ, 1976)

ed. B. Suchoff: Béla Bartók Essays (London, 1976)

ed. L. Somfai: Documenta bartókiana, v (1977) [incl. essay drafts and variants]

ed. B. Suchoff: Yugoslav Folk Music (Albany, NY, 1978)

'Bartók és a szavak' [Bartók and words], Arion, no.13 (1982) [whole issue, incl. essay drafts and variants]

ed. T. Tallián: Bartók Béla írásai, i: Bartók Béla önmagáról, műveiről, az új magyar zenéről, műzene és népzene viszonyáról [Béla Bartók's writings, i: on himself, his music, new Hungarian music, and the connection between art and folk music] (Budapest, 1989)

ed. S. Kovács and F.Sebő: Magyar népdalok, egyetemes gyűjtemény, i [Hungarian folksongs, complete collection, i] (Budapest, 1991; Eng. trans., 1993)

ed. B. Suchoff: Béla Bartók Studies in Ethnomusicology (Lincoln, NE, 1997)

RECORDINGS

coll., with Z. Kodály: Magyar népzenei gramofonfelvételek, i [Hungarian Folk-Music Gramophone Recordings, i], rec. 1937

coll., with J. Deutsch and S. Veress: A Magyar rádió és a néprajzi múzeum gyűjteménye [Collection of the Hungarian Radio and Ethnographic Museum], rec. 1937–9; reissued as *Hungarian Folk Music: Gramophone Records with Bartók's Transcriptions*, Hungaroton, LPX 18058–60 (1981) [ed. L. Somfai]

Centenary Edition of Bartók's Records (Complete), i: *Bartók at the Piano, 1920–1945*; ii. *Bartók Record Archives: Bartók Plays and Talks, 1912–1944*, Hungaroton, LPX 12326–38 (1981) [ed. L. Somfai, Z. Kocsis, J. Sebestyén, with notes by L. Somfai] (Budapest, 1981, i: rev. 2/1991, ii: rev. 2/1995)

BIBLIOGRAPHY

A Documents, catalogues and source information. B Symposia, collections of essays. C Periodical issues. D Life and works. E General biographical and critical studies. F General analytical studies. G Individual works and genres. H Ethnomusicological research.

A: DOCUMENTS, CATALOGUES AND SOURCE INFORMATION

J. Demény, ed.: *Bartók Béla levelei* [Letters] (Budapest, 1948–71, enlarged 2/1976; Eng. trans., 1971)

J. Demény: 'Bartók Béla tanuló évei és romantikus korszaka' [Bartók's years of study and his romantic period], *ZT*, ii (1954), 323–487 [documents of 1899–1905]

J. Demény: 'Bartók művészi kibontakozásának évei: találkozás a népzenével' [Bartók's years of artistic development: contact with folk music], *ZT*, iii (1955), 286–459 [documents of 1906–14]

B. Szabolcsi, ed.: *Bartók: sa vie et son oeuvre* (Budapest, 1956, 2/1968)

V. Juhász, ed.: *Bartók Béla amerikai évei* [Bela Bartók's American years] (New York, 1956; Eng. trans., 1981)

F. Bónis, ed.: *Bartók Béla élete képekben* [Béla Bartók's life in pictures] (Budapest, 1956, 2/1958)

J. Ujfalussy, ed.: *Bartók breviárium* (Budapest, 1958, 3/1980) [letters, essays and documents]

W. Reich, ed.: *Béla Bartók: eigene Schriften und Erinnerungen der Freunde* (Basle, 1958)

J. Demény, ed.: 'Bartók Béla megjelenése az európai zeneéletben' [Bartók's appearance in European musical life], *ZT*, vii (1959), 5–425 [documents of 1914–26]

J. Demény, ed.: 'Bartók Béla pályája delelőjén' [The zenith of Bartók's career], *ZT*, x (1962), 189–787 [documents of 1926–40]

V. Bator: *The Béla Bartók Archives: History and Catalogue* (New York, 1963)

F. Bónis: *Béla Bartóks Leben in Bildern* (Budapest, 1964, enlarged 2/1972 in Hung. and Ger.; Eng. trans., 1972, 2/1981)

D. Dille, ed.: *Documenta bartókiana*, i–iv (Budapest, 1964–70)

E. Helm: *Béla Bartók in Selbstzeugnissen und Bilddokumenten* (Hamburg, 1965)

V. Čižik, ed.: *Bartóks Briefe in die Slowakei* (Bratislava, 1971)

D. Dille: *Thematisches Verzeichnis der Jugendwerke Béla Bartóks, 1890–1904* (Kassel, 1974)

F. László, ed.: *99 Bartók-levél* [99 Bartók letters] (Bucharest, 1974)

F. László, ed.: *Béla Bartók scrisori* [Béla Bartók letters] (Bucharest, 1976)

L. Somfai, ed.: *Documenta bartókiana*, v–vi (Budapest, 1977–81)

V. Lampert: *Bartók népdalfeldolgozásainak forrásjegyzéke* [Catalogue of sources of Bartók's folksong arrangements] (Budapest, 1980); Ger. trans. in *Documenta bartókiana*, vi (Budapest, 1981), 15–149

P. Autexier, ed.: *Béla Bartók: musique de la vie* (Paris, 1981)

L. Somfai: 'Manuscript versus Urtext: the Primary Sources of Bartók's Works', *SMH*, xxiii (1981), 2–66

B. Suchoff: 'The New York Bartók Archives', *MT*, cxxii (1981), 156–9

A. Wilheim: 'A Bartók Bibliography, 1970–1980', *SMH*, xxiii (1981), 477–92

B. Bartók, jr and A. Gombocz, eds.: *Bartók Béla családi levelei* [Letters of the Béla Bartók family] (Budapest, 1981)

B. Bartók, jr: *Apám életének krónikája* [Chronicle of my father's life] (Budapest, 1981)

F. Bónis, ed.: *Így láttuk Bartókot: harminchat emlékezés* [So saw we Bartók: thirty-six recollections] (Budapest, 1981, 2/1995)

B. Bartók, jr: *Bartók Béla műhelyében* [In Béla Bartók's workshop] (Budapest, 1982)

L. Somfai: 'The Budapest Bartók Archives', *FAM*, xxix (1982), 59–65

H. Lindlar: *Lübbes Bartók-Lexikon* (Bergisch Gladbach, 1984)

E. Antokoletz: *Béla Bartók: a Guide to Research* (New York, 1988, 2/1997)

T. Tallián: *Bartók fogadtatása Amerikában, 1940–1945* [Bartók's Reception in America, 1940–1945] (Budapest, 1988)

M. Gillies: *Bartók Remembered* (London, 1990)

L. Somfai: 'Problems of the Chronological Organization of the Béla Bartók Thematic Index in Preparation', *SMH*, xxxiv (1992), 345–66

G. Kiss: 'A Bartók Bibliography, 1980–1989', *SMH*, xxxv (1993–4), 435–53

J. Gergely, ed.: *Béla Bartók: eléments d'un autoportrait* (Paris, 1995)

G. Kroó, ed.: *Bartók Béla, 1881–1945* (Budapest, 1995; Eng. trans., 1997) [CD-ROM]

B: SYMPOSIA, COLLECTIONS OF ESSAYS

Béla Bartók: a Memorial Review (New York, 1950)

Musik der Zeit, Ungarische Komponisten, no.9 (1954) [Hungary issue]

Z. Kodály, B. Rajeczky and L. Vargyas, eds.: *Studia memoriae Belae Bartók sacra* (Budapest, 1956)

Liszt–Bartók: Budapest 1961

Conference in Commemoration of Béla Bartók: Budapest 1971

F. László, ed.: *Bartók-dolgozatok* [Bartók studies] (Bucharest, 1974)

T. Crow, ed.: *Bartók Studies* (Detroit, 1976)

F. László: *Bartók Béla: tanulmányok és tanúságok* [Béla Bartók: essays and testimonies] (Bucharest, 1980)

International Music Council Congress: Budapest 1981 [*SMH*, xxiv/3–4 (1982)]

F. László, ed.: *Bartók-dolgozatok, 1981* [Bartók studies, 1981] (Bucharest, 1982)

F. Spangemacher, ed.: *Béla Bartók zu Leben und Werk* (Bonn, 1982)

J. Gergely, ed.: *Béla Bartók vivant* (Paris, 1985)

G. Ránki, ed.: *Bartók and Kodály Revisited* (Budapest, 1987)

M. Gillies, ed.: *The Bartók Companion* (London, 1993)

P. Laki, ed.: *Bartók and his World* (Princeton, NJ, 1995)

Bartók Colloquium: Szombathely 1995 [*SMH*, xxxvi/3–4 (1995); xxxvii/1 (1996)]

C: PERIODICAL ISSUES

Musikblätter des Anbruch, iii/5 (1921)

Musikblätter des Anbruch, viii/5 (1926)

Melos, v–vi (1949)

Új zenei szemle, i/4–5 (1950)

Musik der Zeit, Béla Bartók, no.3 (1953)

Long Player, ii/10 (1953)

ReM, no.224 (1953–4)

ReM, nos.328–35 (1980)

Igaz Szó, xxix/2 (1981)

SMH, xxiii (1981)

SMH, xxiv (1982), suppl.

Musik-Konzepte, no.22 (1981)

Jb Peters, iv (1981–2)

'Bartók és a szavak' [Bartók and words], *Arion*, no.13 (1982)

Melos [Stockholm], nos.12–13 (1995)

D: LIFE AND WORKS

E. Haraszti: *Bartók Béla élete és művei* [Béla Bartók's life and works] (Budapest, 1930; Eng. trans., 1938)

D. Dille: *Béla Bartók* (Antwerp, 1939)

J. Demény: *Bartók élete és művei* [Bartók's life and works] (Budapest, 1948)

A. Molnár: *Bartók művészete, emlékezésekkel a művész életére* [Bartók's art, with recollections of the artist's life] (Budapest, 1948)

H. and J. Geraedts: *Béla Bartók* (Haarlem, 1952, 2/1961)

H. Stevens: *The Life and Music of Béla Bartók* (New York, 1953, rev. 3/1993 by M. Gillies)

I. Martïnov: *Béla Bartók* (Moscow, 1956, 2/1968)

J. Uhde: *Béla Bartók* (Berlin, 1959)

L. Lesznai: *Béla Bartók: sein Leben, seine Werke* (Leipzig, 1961; Eng. trans., 1973)

P. Citron: *Bartók* (Paris, 1963, 3/1994)

G. Berger: *Béla Bartók* (Wolfenbüttel, 1963)

Z. Pálová-Vrbová: *Béla Bartók, 1881–1945: život a dílo* [Béla Bartók: life and works] (Prague, 1963)

J. Ujfalussy: *Bartók Béla* (Budapest, 1965, 3/1976; Eng. trans., 1972)

I. Nest'yev: *Béla Bartók, 1881–1945: zhizn' i tvorchestvo* [Bartók: life and works] (Moscow, 1969)

T. Zieliński: *Bartók* (Kraków, 1969; Ger. trans., 1973)

D. Dille: *Béla Bartók* (Antwerp, 1974)

V. Lampert: *Bartók Béla* (Budapest, 1976)

S. Arvidsson: *Béla Bartók* (Göteborg, 1981)

Y. Quefélec: *Béla Bartók* (Paris, 1981)

T. Tallián: *Bartók Béla* (Budapest, 1981; Eng. trans., 1988)

P. Griffiths: *Bartók* (London, 1984)

J. de Waard: *Bartók* (Haarlem, 1993)

A. Castronuovo: *Bartók* (Sannicandro Garganico, 1995)

K. Chalmers: *Béla Bartók* (London, 1995)

E: GENERAL BIOGRAPHICAL AND CRITICAL STUDIES

A. Cserna: 'Bartók Béla és művei' [Béla Bartók and his works], *Zeneközlöny*, xv (1917)

C. Gray: 'Béla Bartók', *Sackbut*, i (1920), 301–12

E. Wellesz: 'Ungarische Musik, i: Béla Bartók', *Musikblätter des Anbruch*, ii (1920), 225–8

Z. Kodály: 'Béla Bartók', *ReM*, ii/5 (1921), 205–17

M.-D. Calvocoressi: 'Musicisti contemporanei: Béla Bartók', *Il Pianoforte*, iii (1922), 113–17

C. Gray: 'Béla Bartók', *A Survey of Contemporary Music* (London, 1924), 194–209

E. von der Nüll: 'Zur Kompositionstechnik Bartóks', *Anbruch*, x (1928), 278–82

H. Leichtentritt: 'On the Art of Béla Bartók', *MM*, vi/3 (1928–9), 3–11

E. von der Nüll: *Béla Bartók: ein Beitrag zur Morphologie der neuen Musik* (Halle, 1930)

L. Pollatsek: 'Béla Bartók and his Work', *MT*, lxxii (1931), 411–13, 506–10, 600–602, 697–9

H. Leichtentritt: 'Bartók and Hungarian Folksong', *MM*, x (1933), 130–39

E. Ormándy: 'Modern Hungarian Music', *Hungarian Quarterly*, iii (1937), 164–8

E. Blom: 'Bartók's Third Period', *Tempo*, no.5 (1941), 2–4

B. Kiss: *Bartók Béla művészete* [Béla Bartók's art] (Cluj, 1946)

J. Weissmann: 'Béla Bartók: an Estimate', *MR*, vii (1946), 221–41

R. Leibowitz: 'Béla Bartók ou la possibilité de compromis dans la musique contemporaine', *Temps modernes*, iii (1947–8), 705–34

S. Moreux: *Béla Bartók: sa vie, ses oeuvres, son langage* (Paris, 1949; Eng. trans., 1953)

C. Mason: 'Bartók and Folksong', *MR*, xi (1950), 292–302

E. Balogh, 'Bartók's Last Years', *Tempo*, no.36 (1955), 14–16

J. Székely: *Bartók tanár úr* (Pécs, 1957, 2/1978; Ger. rev. 1995)

A. Fassett: *The Naked Face of Genius: Béla Bartók's American Years* (Boston, 1958; R/1970 as *Béla Bartók: the American Years*) [a novel]

F. Fricsay: *Über Mozart und Bartók* (Copenhagen, 1962)

F. Bónis: 'Quotations in Bartók's Music', *SMH*, v (1963), 355–82

W. Rudziński: *Warsztat kompozytorski Béli Bartóka* [Béla Bartók's compositional workshop] (Kraków, 1964)

J. Downey: *La musique populaire dans l'oeuvre de Béla Bartók* (diss., U. of Paris, 1966)

A. Cross: 'Debussy and Bartók', *MT*, cviii (1967), 125–31

J. Demény: *Bartók Béla: a zongoraművész* [Béla Bartók: the pianist] (Budapest, 1968, 2/1973)

G. Kroó: 'Bartók Béla megvalósulatlan kompozíciós terveiről' [Unrealized plans and ideas for projects by Béla Bartók], *Magyar zene*, x (1969), 251–63; Eng. trans., *SMH*, xii (1970), 11–27

A. Benkő: *Bartók Béla romániai hangversenyei, 1922–1936* [Béla Bartók's concerts in Romania, 1922–36] (Bucharest, 1970)

G. Weiss: *Die Frühe Schaffensentwicklung Béla Bartóks im Lichte westlicher und östlicher Traditionen* (diss., U. of Erlangen-Nuremberg, 1970)

G. Kroó: *Bartók kalauz* [A guide to Bartók] (Budapest, 1971; Eng. trans., 1974)

L. Burlas: 'The Influence of Slovakian Folk Music on Bartók's Musical Idiom', *Conference in Commemoration of Béla Bartók: Budapest 1971*, 181–7

E. Lendvai: *Bartók költői világa* [Bartók's poetic world] (Budapest, 1971)

G. Lukács: 'Béla Bartók: on the 25th Anniversary of his Death', *New Hungarian Quarterly*, no.41 (1971), 42–55

O. Nordwall: *Béla Bartók: Traditionalist-Modernist* (Stockholm, 1972)

M. Rogers and Z. Oválry: 'Bartók in the USSR in 1929', *Notes*, xxix (1972–3), 416–25

F. Bónis, ed.: *Magyar zenetörténeti tanulmányok* [Hungarian studies in music history], iii (Budapest, 1973)

W. Fuchss: *Béla Bartók und die Schweiz: eine Dokumentensammlung* (Berne, 1973)

M. Carner: 'Bartók', *NOHM*, x (1974), 274–99

Y. Lenoir: *Vie et oeuvre de Béla Bartók aux Etats-Unis d'Amérique, 1940–1945* (diss., U. of Leuven, 1976)

D. Zoltai: 'Bartók nem alkuszik' [Bartók does not compromise], *Bartók nem alkuszik* (Budapest, 1977)

D. Dille: *Généalogie sommaire de la famille Bartók* (Antwerp, 1977)

J. Breuer: *Bartók és Kodály* (Budapest, 1978)

D. Dille: *Het werk van Béla Bartók* (Antwerp, 1977)

A. Wilheim: 'Bartók találkozása Debussy művészetével' [Bartók's encounter with Debussy's art], *Zenetudományi dolgozatok 1978* (Budapest, 1978), 107–11

T. Tallián: 'Bartók-marginália', *Zenetudományi dolgozatok 1979* (Budapest, 1979), 35–46

B. Bartók, jr: 'Bartók and the Visual Arts', *New Hungarian Quarterly*, no.81 (1981), 44–9

F. Bónis: 'Bartók und Wagner', *ÖMz*, xxxvi (1981), 134–47

J. Breuer: 'Adorno's Image of Bartók', *New Hungarian Quarterly*, no.82 (1981), 29–35

R. Schlötterer-Traimer: 'Béla Bartók und die Tondichtungen von Richard Strauss', *ÖMz*, xxxvi (1981), 311–18

L. Somfai: *Tizennyolc Bartók-tanulmány* [Eighteen Bartók essays] (Budapest, 1981)

B. Bartók, jr: 'Kodály und Bartók', *Kodály Conference: Budapest 1982*, 12–17

J. Takács: *Erinnerungen an Béla Bartók* (Vienna, 1982)

W. Frobenius: 'Bartók und Bach', *AMw*, xli (1984), 54–67

B. Pethő: *Bartók rejtekútja* [Bartók's secret path] (Budapest, 1984)

I. Volly: 'Bartókné Pásztory Ditta', *Életünk*, nos.7–8 (1984), 807–23, 873–84

J. Hunkemöller: 'Bartóks Urteil über den Jazz', *Mf*, xxxviii (1985), 27–36

Y. Lenoir: *Folklore et transcendance dans l'oeuvre américaine de Béla Bartók (1940–1945)* (Louvain-la-Neuve, 1986)

L. Somfai: 'Liszt's Influence on Bartók Reconsidered', *New Hungarian Quarterly*, no.102 (1986), 210–19

B. Suchoff: 'Ethnomusicological Roots of Béla Bartók's Musical Language', *World of Music*, xxix/1 (1987), 43–65

B. Szabolcsi: *Kodályról és Bartókról* [About Kodály and Bartók], ed. F. Bónis (Budapest, 1987)

L. Somfai: 'Bartók Comes Home', *New Hungarian Quarterly*, no.112 (1988), 185–9

J. Frigyesi: *Béla Bartók and Hungarian Nationalism* (diss., U. of Pennsylvania, 1989)

M. Gillies: *Bartók in Britain* (Oxford, 1989)

D. Dille: *Béla Bartók: regard sur le passé*, ed. Y. Lenoir (Namur and Louvain-la-Neuve, 1990)

M. Gillies: 'Bartók as Pedagogue', *SMA*, xxiv (1990), 64–86

F. Bónis: *Hódolat Bartóknak és Kodálynak* [Homage to Bartók and Kodály] (Budapest, 1992)

M. Gillies: 'Stylistic Integrity and Influence in Bartók's Works: the Case of Szymanowski', *International Journal of Musicology*, i (1992), 139–60

A. Surrans: *Bartók és Franciaország/Bartók et la France* (Budapest, 1993)

J. Frigyesi: 'Béla Bartók and the Concept of Nation and Volk in Modern Hungary', *MQ*, lxxviii (1994), 255–87

C. Kenneson: *Székely and Bartók: the Story of a Friendship* (Portland, OR, 1994)

Z. Kocsis: 'Dohnányi and Bartók as Performers', *New Hungarian Quarterly*, no.134 (1994), 149–53

C. Pesavento: *Musik von Béla Bartók als pädagogisches Programm* (Frankfurt, 1994)

J. Bényei, ed.: *A mindenzég zenéje: Magyar költők versei Bartók Béláról* [Music of the universe: Hungarian poetry about Béla Bartók] (Debrecen, 1995)

J. Breuer: 'Bartók and the Third Reich', *New Hungarian Quarterly*, no.140 (1995), 134–40

V. Lampert: 'Bartók's Music on Record: an Index of Popularity', *SMH*, xxxvi (1995), 393–412

F. László: 'Rumänische Stilelemente in Bartóks Musik: Fakten und Deutungen', *SMH*, xxxvi (1995), 413–28

V. Verspeurt: 'Een status quaestionis van het Bartók-onderzoek', *RBM*, xlix (1995), 251–8

L. Somfai: *Béla Bartók: Composition, Concepts, and Autograph Sources* (Berkeley, 1996)

J. Frigyesi: *Béla Bartók and Turn-of-the-Century Budapest* (Berkeley, 1998)

L. Vikárius: *Modell és inspiráció Bartók zenei gondolkodásában* [Model and inspiration in Bartók's musical thought] (Pécs, 1999)

F: GENERAL ANALYTICAL STUDIES

E. Lendvai: *Bartók stílusa* [Bartók's style] (Budapest, 1955)

E. Kapst: *Die 'polymodale Chromatik' Béla Bartóks* (diss., U. of Leipzig, 1969)

L. Somfai: '"Per finire": Some Aspects of the Finale in Bartók's Cyclic Form', *SMH*, xi (1969), 391–408

L. Hartzell: *Contrapuntal-Harmonic Factors in Selected Works of Béla Bartók* (diss., U. of Kansas, 1970)

E. Kapst: 'Stilkriterien der polymodal-kromatischen Gestaltungsweise im Werk Béla Bartóks', *BMw*, xii (1970), 1–28

P. Petersen: *Die Tonalität im Instrumentalschaffen von Béla Bartók* (Hamburg, 1971)

E. Lendvai: *Béla Bartók: an Analysis of his Music* (London, 1971)

L. Somfai: 'A Characteristic Culmination Point in Bartók's Instrumental Forms', *Conference in Commemoration of Béla Bartók: Budapest 1971*, 53–64

L. Bárdos: *A Bartók-zene stílus-elemei* [Style elements of Bartók's music] (Budapest, 1972; Eng. trans., 1984)

J. Breuer: 'Kolinda-ritmika Bartók zenéjében' [Colindă rhythms in Bartók's music], *Zeneelmélet, stíluselemzés* (Budapest, 1977), 84–102

I. Oramo: *Modaalinen symmetria: tutkimus Bartókin kromatiikasta* (Helsinki, 1977)

A. Szentkirályi: 'Some Aspects of Béla Bartók's Compositional Techniques', *SMH*, xx (1978), 157–82

T. and P.J. Bachmann: 'An Analysis of Béla Bartók's Music through Fibonaccian Numbers and the Golden Mean', *MQ*, lxv (1979), 72–82

I. Oramo: 'Modale Symmetrie bei Bartók', *Mf*, xxxiii (1980), 450–64

M. Radice: 'Bartók's Parodies of Beethoven', *MR*, xlii (1981), 252–60

C. Vauclain: 'Bartók: Beyond Bi-Modality', *MR*, xlii (1981), 243–51

E. Antokoletz: 'The Music of Bartók: Some Theoretical Approaches in the USA', *SMH*, xxiv (1982), suppl. pp.67–74

P. Dinkel: 'La tentation atonale de Béla Bartók', *Revue musicale de la Suisse Romande*, xxxv (1982), 119–26

M. Gillies: 'Bartók's Last Works: a Theory of Tonality and Modality', *Musicology*, vii (1982), 120–30

E. Lendvai: *The Workshop of Bartók and Kodály* (Budapest, 1983)

E. Antokoletz: *The Music of Béla Bartók* (Berkeley, 1984)

M. Gillies: 'Bartók's Notation: Tonality and Modality', *Tempo*, no.145 (1983), 4–9

R. Howat: 'Bartók, Lendvai and the Principles of Proportional Analysis', *MAn*, ii (1983), 69–95; see also response by E. Lendvai, *MAn*, iii (1984), 255–64

L. Starr: 'Melody-Accompaniment Textures in the Music of Bartók', *JM*, iv (1985–6), 91–104

J. Bernard: 'Space and Symmetry in Bartók', *JMT*, xxx (1986), 185–201

R. Howat: 'Debussy, Bartók et les formes de la nature', *Revue musicale de la Suisse Romande*, xxxix (1986), 128–41

L. Somfai: 'Nineteenth-Century Ideas Developed in Bartók's Piano Notation in the Years 1907–14', *19CM*, xi (1987–8), 73–91

R. Cohn: 'Inversional Symmetry and Transpositional Combination in Bartók', *Music Theory Spectrum*, x (1988), 19–42

M. Gillies: *Notation and Tonal Structure in Bartók's Later Works* (New York, 1989)

R. Cohn: 'Bartók's Octatonic Strategies: a Motivic Approach', *JAMS*, xliv (1991), 262–300

C. Morrison: 'Fifth Progressions in Bartók: Structural Determinants or Mimicry?', *SMH*, xxxiv (1992), 125–52

P. Wilson: *The Music of Béla Bartók* (New Haven, 1992)

E. Antokoletz: 'Transformations of a Special Non-Diatonic Mode in Twentieth-Century Music: Bartók, Stravinsky, Scriabin and Albrecht', *MAn*, xii (1993), 25–45

A. Forte: 'Foreground Rhythm in Early Twentieth-Century Music', *Models of Musical Analysis: Early Twentieth-Century Music*, ed. J. Dunsby (Oxford, 1993), 133–45

M. Gillies: 'Pitch Notations and Tonality (Bartók)', ibid., 42–55

M. Russ: 'Functions, Scales, Abstract Systems and Contextual Hierarchies in the Music of Bartók', *ML*, lxxv (1994), 401–25

M. Gillies: 'Bartók Analysis and Authenticity', *SMH*, xxxvi (1995), 319–27

D. Schneider: 'Towards Bridging the Gap: the Culmination Point as a Fulcrum between Analysis and Interpretation', *SMH*, xxxvii (1996), 21–36

D. Walker: *Bartók Analysis: a Critical Examination and Application* (diss., McMaster U., 1996)

F. Hentschel: *Funktion und Bedeutung der Symmetrie in den Werken Béla Bartóks* (Lucca, 1997)

D. Cooper: 'The Unfolding of Tonality in the Music of Béla Bartók', *MAn*, xvii (1998), 21–38

G: INDIVIDUAL WORKS AND GENRES

stage

E. von der Nüll: 'Stilelemente in Bartóks Oper *Herzog Blaubarts Burg*', *Melos*, viii (1929), 226–31

G. Kroó: 'Duke Bluebeard's Castle', *SMH*, i (1961), 251–340

B. Szabolcsi: 'Le mandarin miraculeux', *SMH*, i (1961), 341–61

E. Lendvai: 'Der wunderbare Mandarin', *SMH*, i (1961), 363–429

G. Kroó: *Bartók Béla színpadi művei* [Béla Bartók's stage works] (Budapest, 1962)

E. Lendvai: *Bartók dramaturgiája* [Bartók's dramaturgy] (Budapest, 1964/R)

J. Chailley: 'Essai d'analyse du Mandarin merveilleux', *SMH*, viii (1966), 11–39

G. Kroó: 'Data on the Genesis of Duke Bluebeard's Castle', *SMH*, xxiii (1981), 79–123

A. von Wangenheim: *Béla Bartók: 'Der wunderbare Mandarin'* (Overath, 1985)

E. Antokoletz: 'Bartók's *Bluebeard*: the Sources of its "Modernism"', *College Music Symposium*, xxx/1 (1990), 75–95

C. Leafstedt: 'Structure in the Fifth Door Scene of Bartók's *Duke Bluebeard's Castle*: an Alternative Viewpoint', ibid., 96–102

N. John, ed.: *The Stage Works of Béla Bartók* (London, 1991)

C.S. Leafstedt: *Inside Bluebeard's Castle* (New York, 1999)

orchestral

H. Cowell: 'Bartók and his Violin Concerto', *Tempo*, no.8 (1944), 4–6

G. French: 'Continuity and Discontinuity in Bartók's "Concerto for Orchestra"', *MR*, xxviii (1967), 122–34

J. McCabe: *Bartók Orchestral Music* (London, 1974)

T. Serly: 'A Belated Account of the Reconstruction of a 20th-Century Masterpiece', *College Music Symposium*, xv (1975), 7–25 [on Viola Concerto]

D. Dalton: 'The Genesis of Bartók's Viola Concerto', *ML*, lvii (1976), 117–29

F. Michael: *Béla Bartóks Variationstechnik dargestellt im Rahmen einer Analyse seines 2. Violinkonzert* (Regensburg, 1976)

L. Somfai: 'Strategies of Variation in the Second Movement of Bartók's Violin Concerto 1937–8', *SMH*, xix (1977), 161–202

S. Kovács: 'Re-examining the Bartók/Serly Viola Concerto', *SMH*, xxiii (1981), 295–322

E. Lendvai: 'The Quadrophonic Stage of Bartók's Music for Strings, Percussion and Celesta', *New Hungarian Quarterly*, no.84 (1981), 70–85

J. Hunkemöller: *Béla Bartók: Musik für Saiteninstrumente* (Munich, 1982)

J. Hunkemöller: 'Bartók analysiert seine "Musik für Saiteninstrumente, Schlagzeug und Celesta"', *AMw*, xl (1983), 147–63

B. Parker: 'Parallels between Bartók's *Concerto for Orchestra* and Kübler-Ross's Theory about the Dying', *MQ*, lxxiii (1989), 532–56

K. Móricz: *Bartók Béla: Concerto zenekarra* [Béla Bartók: Concerto for Orchestra] (diss., Liszt Academy, Budapest, 1992)

A. Rizzuti: 'Le geometrie imperfette della *Musica per strumenti a corde, percussioni e celesta* di Béla Bartók', *NRMI*, xxvi (1992), 37–51

P. Bartók: 'The Principal Theme of Bartók's Viola Concerto', *SMH*, xxxv (1993–4), 45–50

K. Móricz: 'New Aspects of the Genesis of Béla Bartók's *Concerto for Orchestra*', *SMH*, xxxv (1993–4), 181–219

G. Weiss-Aigner: 'Das zweite Violinkonzert von Béla Bartók im Spektrum der gattungsgeschichtlichen Entwicklung', ibid., 303–39

M.A. Harley: 'Birds in Concert: North-American Birdsong in Bartók's Piano Concerto No. 3', *Tempo*, no.189 (1994), 8–16

K. Móricz: 'Operating on a Fetus: Sketch Studies and their Relevance to the Interpretation of the Finale of Bartók's *Concerto for Orchestra*', *SMH*, xxxvi (1995), 461–76

B. Suchoff: *Bartók: Concerto for Orchestra* (New York, 1995)

P. Bartók: 'Commentary on the Revision of Béla Bartók's Viola Concerto', *Journal of the American Viola Society*, xii/1 (1996), 11–33

D. Cooper: *Bartók: Concerto for Orchestra* (Cambridge, 1996)

D. Maurice and others: 'Panel Discussion: the Bartók Viola Concerto', *Journal of the American Viola Society*, xiv/1 (1998), 15–49

D. Maurice: *Bartók's Viola Concerto: an Investigation of its Genesis, Reconstruction, Reception, Revision and Future Possibilities* (diss., Otago U., 1997)

D. Schneider: *Expression in the Time of Objectivity: Nationality and Modernity in Five Concertos by Béla Bartók* (diss., U. of California, Berkeley, 1997)

chamber

T. Adorno: 'Béla Bartóks Drittes Streichquartett', *Anbruch*, xi/9–10 (1929), 358–60

G. Abraham: 'The Bartók of the Quartets', *ML*, xxvi (1945), 185–94

M. Seiber: *The String Quartets of Béla Bartók* (London, 1945)

M. Babbitt: 'The String Quartets of Bartók', *MQ*, xxxv (1949), 377–85

G. Perle: 'Symmetrical Formations in the String Quartets of Béla Bartók', *MR*, xvi (1955), 300–312

J. Kárpáti: 'Az arab népzene hatásának nyomai Bartók II. vonósnégyesében' [Traces of the influence of Arabic folk music in Bartók's Second String Quartet], *Új Zenei Szemle*, vii (1956), 8–15

R. Traimer: *Béla Bartóks Kompositionstechnik dargestellt an seinen sechs Streichquartetten* (Regensburg, 1956)

C. Mason: 'An Essay in Analysis: Tonality, Symmetry and Latent Serialism in Bartók's Fourth Quartet', *MR*, xviii (1957), 189–201

L. Treitler: 'Harmonic Procedures in the Fourth Quartet of Béla Bartók', *JMT*, iii (1959), 292–8

A. Forte: 'Bartók's Serial Composition', *MQ*, xlvi (1960), 233–45 [on Fourth String Quartet]

J. Kárpáti: *Bartók vonósnégyesei* [Bartók's string quartets] (Budapest, 1967, 2/1976 as *Bartók kamarazenéje* [Bartók's chamber music]); Eng. trans., 1975, enlarged as *Bartók's Chamber Music* (Stuyvesant, NY, 1994)

B. Suchoff: 'Structure and Concept in Bartók's Sixth String Quartet', *Tempo*, no.83 (1967–8), 2–11

K. Stockhausen: 'Bartók's Sonata for Two Pianos and Percussion', *New Hungarian Quarterly*, no.40 (1970), 49–53

R. Travis: 'Tonal Coherence in the First Movement of Bartók's Fourth String Quartet', *Music Forum*, ii (1970), 298–371

V. Lampert: 'Vázlat Bartók II. vonósnégyesének utolsó tételéhez' [Sketch for the last movement of Bartók's Second String Quartet], *Magyar zene*, xiii (1972), 252–63

S. Veress: 'Béla Bartóks 44 Duos für zwei Violinen', *Erich Doflein: Festschrift zum 70. Geburtstag*, ed. L.U. Abraham (Mainz, 1972), 31–57

H. Fladt: *Zur Problematik traditioneller Formtypen in der Musik des frühen zwanzigsten Jahrhunderts, dargestellt an Sonatensätzen in den Streichquartetten Béla Bartóks* (Munich, 1974)

E. Antokoletz: *Principles of Pitch Organization in Bartók's Fourth String Quartet* (diss., City U. of New York, 1975)

G. Perle: 'The String Quartets of Béla Bartók', *A Musical Offering: Essays in Honor of Martin Bernstein*, ed. E.H. Clinkscale and C. Brook (New York, 1977), 193–210

W. Berry: 'Symmetrical Interval Sets and Derivative Pitch Materials in Bartók's Quartet No.3', *PNM*, xviii (1979–80), 287–380

Y. Lenoir: 'Contributions à l'étude de la Sonate pour violon solo de Béla Bartók', *SMH*, xxiii (1981), 209–60

S. Walsh: *Bartók's Chamber Music* (London, 1982)

D. Locke: 'Numerical Aspects of Bartók's String Quartets', *MT*, cxxviii (1987), 322–5

M. Beach: *Bartók's Fifth String Quartet: Studies in Genesis and Structure* (diss., U. of Rochester, 1988)

C. Morrison: 'Prolongation in the Final Movement of Bartók's String Quartet No.4', *Music Theory Spectrum*, xiii (1991), 179–96

P. Petersen: 'Rhythmik und Metrik in Bartóks *Sonate für zwei Klaviere und Schlagzeug* und die Kritik des jungen Stockhausen an Bartók', *Musiktheorie*, ix (1994), 39–48

piano

A. Molnár: *Bartók Két elégiájának elemzése* [An analysis of Bartók's Two Elegies] (Budapest, 1921)

E. Lendvai: 'Bartók: Az éjszaka zenéje' [Bartók: The Night's Music], *Zenei szemle*, i (1947), 216

H.U. Engelmann: *Bela Bartoks Mikrokosmos: Versuch einer Typologie 'Neuer Musik'* (Würzburg, 1953/R)

J. Uhde: *Bartóks Mikrokosmos: Spielanweisungen und Erläuterungen* (Regensburg, 1954, 2/1988)

B. Suchoff: *Guide to Bartók's 'Mikrokosmos'* (London, 1957, 2/1971)

D. Bratuz: *The Folk Element in the Piano Music of Béla Bartók* (diss., Indiana U., 1965)

J. Vinton: 'Toward a Chronology of the Mikrokosmos', *SMH*, viii (1966), 41–69

T. Hundt: *Bartóks Satztechnik in den Klavierwerken* (Regensburg, 1971)

D. Bratuz: 'On Bartók's *Improvisations* and the Pippa Principle', *Studies in Music* [Ontario], ii (1977), 8–14

E. Antokoletz: 'The Musical Language of Bartók's 14 Bagatelles for Piano', *Tempo*, no.137 (1981), 8–16

I. Waldbauer: 'Intellectual Construct and Tonal Direction in Bartók's "Divided Arpeggios"', *SMH*, xxiv (1982), 527–36

K. Agawu: 'Analytical Issues Raised by Bartók's *Improvisations for Piano*, Op.20', *JMR*, v (1984), 131–63

L. Somfai: 'Analytical Notes on Bartók's Piano Year of 1926', *SMH*, xxvi (1984), 5–58

P. Wilson: 'Concepts of Prolongation and Bartók's Opus 20', *Music Theory Spectrum*, vi (1984), 79–89

I. Waldbauer: 'Conflict of Tonal and Non-Tonal Elements in Bartók's "Free Variations"', *Bartók and Kodály Revisited*, ed. G. Ranki (Budapest, 1987), 199–209

D. Yeomans: *Bartók for Piano* (Bloomington, IN, 1988)

V. Fischer: *Béla Bartók's Fourteen Bagatelles op.6: Determining Performance Authenticity* (diss., U. of Texas, Austin, 1989)

I. Waldbauer: 'Polymodal Chromaticism and Tonal Plan in the First of Bartók's *Six Dances in Bulgarian Rhythm*', *SMH*, xxxii (1990), 241–62

L. Somfai: 'The Influence of Peasant Music on the Finale of Bartók's Piano Sonata', *Studies in Musical Sources and Style: Essays in Honor of Jan LaRue*, ed. E. Wolf and E. Roesner (Madison, WI, 1990), 535–55

J. Parakilas: 'Folksong as Musical Wet Nurse: the Prehistory of Bartók's *For Children*', *MQ*, lxxxi (1995), 476–500

vocal

P. Meyer: *Béla Bartóks 'Ady-Lieder' op.16* (Winterthur, 1965)

M. Szabó: *Bartók Béla kórusművei* [Béla Bartók's choral works] (Budapest, 1985)

L. Vikárius: 'Béla Bartók's *Cantata Profana* (1930): a Reading of the Sources', *SMH*, xxxv (1993–4), 249–301

I. Arauco: 'Methods of Translation in Bartók's Twenty Hungarian Folksongs', *JMR*, xii (1992), 189–211

T. Tallián: 'Let this cup pass from me …: the *Cantata Profana* and the *Gospel according to Saint Matthew*', *New Hungarian Quarterly*, no.139 (1995),

H: ETHNOMUSICOLOGICAL RESEARCH

C. Brăiloiu: 'Béla Bartók folkloriste', *SMz*, lxxxviii (1948), 92–4

J. Szegő: *Bartók Béla, a népdalkutató* [Béla Bartók, the folksong researcher] (Bucharest, 1956)

J. Downey: *La musique populaire dans l'oeuvre de Béla Bartók* (diss., U. of Paris, 1966)

J. Kuckertz: *Gestaltvariation in den von Bartók gesammelten rumänischen Colinden* (Regensburg, 1963)

B. Suchoff: 'Bartók and Serbo-Croatian Folk Music', *MQ*, lviii (1972), 557–71

P.P. Domokos: *Bartók Béla kapcsolata a moldvai csángómagyarokkal* [Béla Bartók's connection with the csángós of Moldavia] (Budapest, 1981)

S. Kovács: 'Bartók's System of Folksong Classification', *New Hungarian Quarterly*, no.83 (1981), 71–8

L. Vargyas, 'Bartók and Folk Music Research', *New Hungarian Quarterly*, no.83 (1981), 58–70

S. Erdely: 'Folk-Music Research in Hungary until 1950: the Legacy of Bartók and Kodály', *CMc*, no.43 (1987), 51–61

Y. Lenoir: 'Le destin des recherches ethnomusicologiques de Béla Bartók à la vielle de son séjour aux Etats-Unis', *RBM*, lxii (1988), 273–83

N. Ito: *Barutoku: Minyou o 'hakken' sita henkyou no sakkyoukuka* [Bartók's activities as a folk-music researcher] (Tokyo, 1997)

MALCOLM GILLIES

Bartók Quartet. Hungarian string quartet. It was founded in 1960 by Péter Komlós (*b* Budapest, 25 Oct 1935), Sándor Devich (*b* Szeged, 19 Jan 1935), Géza Németh (*b* Beregszász [now Beregovo, Ukraine], 23 July 1936) and László Mező, all students in Leó Weiner's chamber music class at the Liszt Academy of Music in Budapest. At first they performed as the Komlós Quartet – making their Budapest début in 1958 – and played in orchestras, the leader and viola player as principals of the State Opera Orchestra and the second violinist in the Hungarian State Orchestra. In 1960 Károly Botvay (*b* Sopron, 29 Dec 1932) replaced Mező and in 1963 they were given permission by Bartók's family to use his name. The following year they won the international competition in Liège and commenced the tours which have taken them all over the world. In 1970 they performed in the United Nations General Assembly Hall; in 1973 they gave three concerts in the festival marking the opening of the Sydney Opera House; and in 1981 they were awarded the UNESCO Prize. In 1977 Mező reclaimed the cello chair and in 1982 Devich withdrew, to be replaced first by Bela Bánfalvi and then in 1985 by Géza Hargitai. The ensemble is chiefly famed for performances of the Bartók and Kodály quartets but has championed such contemporary Hungarian composers as Bozay, Durkó, Farkas, Kadosa, Lang, Soproni and Szabó. Its cultured tonal qualities are also heard to advantage in Beethoven, whose late quartets it plays with impressive intensity. Its recordings include works by Haydn, Mozart, Beethoven (a complete cycle), Schubert, Mendelssohn, Brahms (all the chamber music for strings), Dvořák, Debussy, Ravel and Bartók (a complete cycle). Its instruments are a 1736 violin by Giuseppe Guarneri del Gesù, a 1774 violin by Giovanni Baptista Guadagnini, a 1787 viola by Lorenzo Storioni and a 1730 cello by Domenico Montagnana.

TULLY POTTER

Bartoletti, Bruno (*b* Sesto Fiorentino, Florence, 10 June 1926). Italian conductor. He entered the Florence Conservatory, where his studies included the flute with Bruscalupi and the piano with Nardi. After a brief period as flautist in the Maggio Musicale Orchestra he became pianist at the centre for lyric training attached to the Florence Teatro Comunale. He worked as assistant to many leading conductors including Rodzinski, Mitropoulos, Gui and Serafin, who encouraged him to take up conducting. Bartoletti made his conducting début at the Teatro Comunale in December 1953 with a production of *Rigoletto* prepared by Gui; he soon demonstrated the interpretative insight and versatility that enabled him to conduct contemporary works as well as the Italian opera repertory from Rossini to Dallapiccola to which his career has mainly been devoted. He was appointed resident conductor of the Teatro Comunale, 1957–64, and conducted the premières of Rocca's *Antiche iscrizioni* (1955) and Malipiero's *Il figliuol prodigo* and *Venere prigioniera* (1957) at Florence, Mortari's *La scuola delle mogli* (1959) at La Scala, and Ginastera's *Don Rodrigo* (1964) at the Teatro Colón, Buenos Aires. During this time he also introduced Egk's *Der Revisor*, Krenek's *Jonny spielt auf* and Shostakovich's *The Nose* to the Italian stage, and conducted the Italian repertory at the Royal Opera, Copenhagen, 1957–60. He made his American début at the Chicago Lyric Opera in 1956, and was appointed principal conductor there in 1964. He was conductor at the Rome Opera and artistic director of the Teatro Verdi, Pisa, 1965–73. In 1985 he was appointed artistic director at Chicago and musical adviser at the Teatro Comunale and Maggio Musicale in Florence (and subsequently artistic director, 1988–91). In 1992 he became principal guest conductor of the Orchestra della Toscana. He also

teaches conducting at the Accademia Musicale Chigiana in Siena. His recordings include Puccini's *Manon Lescaut* and *Suor Angelica*, and Verdi's *Un ballo in maschera*; the Puccini performances were much admired for their dramatic excitement as well as sympathetic interpretation.

LEONARDO PINZAUTI

Bartoli, Cecilia (*b* Rome, 4 June 1966). Italian mezzosoprano. She sang the Shepherd-Boy in *Tosca* as a child, and studied in Rome at the Accademia di S Cecilia. She made her professional opera début at Verona in 1987 and in 1988 undertook Rosina at Cologne, the Schwetzingen Festival and the Zürich Opera, an interpretation that delighted all who saw it. Following her La Scala début as Isolier (*Le Comte Ory*) in 1991, she quickly acquired a reputation as one of the world's leading Rossini singers, acclaimed both for her vocal accomplishments and her lively, quick-witted stage personality. She has also been admired in several Mozartian roles, including Cherubino (the role of her début at the Opéra Bastille in 1990), Zerlina, Susanna, Dorabella and Despina (the role of her Metropolitan début in 1996). Much of her reputation has, however, been built on her recording career, nurtured by the producer Christopher Raeburn. In addition to notable recitals of Mozart and Rossini arias and Italian and French song, Bartoli has been the central attraction in sets of *Rinaldo*, Haydn's *L'anima del filosofo*, *Il barbiere di Siviglia*, *La Cenerentola* and *Il turco in Italia*. These all reveal her warm, rounded tone, her extreme flexibility in *fioriture* (although she is inclined to aspirate runs) and above all, her infectious zest in projecting character.

Cecilia Bartoli in the title role of Rossini's 'La Cenerentola'

BIBLIOGRAPHY
M. Loppert: 'Cecilia Bartoli', *Opera* , xlviii (1997) 1152–60
K. Chernin and R.Stendhal: Cecilia Bartoli: the Passion of Song
    (London, 1998)
M. Hoelterhoff: *Backstage with Cecilia Bartoli* (London, 1998)
                                                    ALAN BLYTH

Bartoli, Cosimo (*b* Florence, 20 Dec 1503; *d* Florence, 25 Oct 1572). Italian diplomat, philologist, mathematician and humanist. After studies in Rome and Florence he took minor orders and was attached to the baptistery in Florence, where he was also active in the literary academy. In 1560 he became secretary to Cardinal Giovanni de' Medici and two years later became the Venetian diplomatic agent of Duke Cosimo I (Grand Duke from 1569), a post he held until his return to Florence in 1572. Bartoli's importance for music lies in his *Ragionamenti accademici* (Venice, 1567). Although the book is devoted to the criticism of Dante, its third chapter concerns Renaissance musicians living before about 1545. Ockeghem and Josquin are likened to Donatello and Michelangelo, as the originators and perfecters of their respective arts. Bartoli extolled the musicians of the court of Pope Leo X (1513–21). The great number of instrumentalists treated is particularly significant. Francesco da Milano, Alfonso dalla Viola and Alessandro Striggio are a few of the many performers cited. Bartoli's brother Giorgio was also knowledgeable in music, and translated Boethius's *De musica* into Italian (*I-Fn* Magl.XIX.75).

BIBLIOGRAPHY
DBI (R. Cantagalli, N. de Blasi); *EinsteinIM*
G. Benvenuti, ed.: *Andrea e Giovanni Gabrieli e la musica
    strumentale in San Marco*, i, IMii (Milan, 1931), 54ff [incl. chap.3
    of *Ragionamenti accademici*]
D. Kämper: *Studien zur instrumentalen Ensemblemusik des 16.
    Jahrhunderts*, AnMc, no.10 (1970)
J. Haar: 'Cosimo Bartoli on Music', *EMH*, viii (1988), 37–79
                                            CLEMENT A. MILLER

Bartoli, Daniello (*b* Ferrara, 12 Feb 1608; *d* Rome, 13 Jan 1685). Italian scholar. He was a Jesuit and spent much of his later life in Rome (for a summary of his life and works see *DBI*). One of his publications is an extensive work on acoustics, *Del suono, de' tremori armonici e dell'udito* (Rome, 1679, 2/1680).

Bartoli [De Bartolo], Erasmo ['Padre Raimo'] (*b* Gaeta, 1606; *d* Naples, 15 July 1656). Italian composer and singer. His teacher was probably G.B. de Bellis. On 19 December 1626 he joined the royal chapel at Naples as a bass and remained there until 1636. In March of that year he was admitted to the Congregazione dell'Oratorio with a salary for life for himself and his mother. He was music prefect in 1642 and from 1652 to 1656. He played some part in the posthumous publication of Scipione Dentice's *Madrigali spirituali, libro secondo* (Naples, 1640) which he dedicated to Cardinal Buoncompagno. He died of the plague. He was a prolific composer of church music, which the fathers of the oratory valued so highly that in 1713 one of them, Scipione Narni, arranged for the copying of the most often performed works. The motets for four choirs (in *I-Nc* and *Nf*) are mainly homophonic, and the few contrapuntal passages are rather weak.

WORKS
Introit, mass and vespers for S Filippo Neri, 16vv (4 choirs), insts; 2
    masses, 8, 10vv; 2 responsories, vesper hymns, 16vv (4 choirs), vc,
    db, org; litany, 4 choirs; psalms, 2 choirs; cantatas, 4vv; over 30
    motets, 4 choirs; 26 motets, 2 choirs; mottetti pastorali, 4–6vv;

*c*500 other motets; canzoni del P. Raimo; *c*250 other sacred
    works: *GB-Lbl, I-Nc, Nf*
Motets, 4 choirs, *Nc, Nf* (dated 1786)

BIBLIOGRAPHY
C. Franco: Biographical note (in *I-Nc*)
G. Pannain: *Le origini della scuola musicale napoletana* (Naples,
    1914)
U. Prota-Giurleo: 'La musica a Napoli nel Seicento (dal Gesualdo allo
    Scarlatti)', *Samnium*, i/4 (1928), 67–90; ii/2 (1929), 30–49 [incl.
    Franco item above]
                                            RENATO BOSSA

Bartoli, Giovan Battista (*fl* 1617). Italian composer. He is known by one publication, *Il primo libro de madrigali a cinque voci* (Florence, 1617). Dedicated to Lorenzo Bonei, the book opens with a seven-part cycle *O primavera*. This is mostly written in the lighter manner, though its third section, *O dolcezza amarissime*, is a brief if concentrated essay in the pathetic style, making much use of suspensions, dissonances and chromaticism. The printing of the volume, one of Zanobi Pignoni's small number of music editions, is rather rough in appearance.

                                            IAIN FENLON

Bartolini [Bartalani, Bertolini], Orindio (*b* Arcidosso, nr Siena, *c*1580; *d* 1640). Italian composer. He spent most of his working life, from 1609 to 1635, as one of a line of distinguished *maestri di cappella* of Udine Cathedral. For ten years before this he had been a singer at S Marco, Venice. His madrigals are conservative for their date (1606) and handicapped by undistinguished musical ideas and amorphous textures, but his canzonettas and arias are more modern. His three collections of large-scale church music form his main output. Two appeared in the 1630s after the great Venetian plague, which suggests that the choir at Udine was still a fair size if, as must be supposed, they were written for it. The requiem mass and *Te Deum* (both unusual forms) in the 1633 volume may indeed have been composed for the burying of the victims of the plague and thanksgiving for its end. The style of the earlier compline music for double choir (1613) is fairly conservative, but Bartolini shows a fine ear for sonority, a developed sense of form and a varied and imaginative approach to word-setting in the refrain structure of *Regina caeli*.

WORKS
all published in Venice
Il primo libro de madrigali, 5vv (1606)
Canzonette e arie alla romana, 3vv, libro primo (1606)
Compietà con le littanie della B. Vergine, 8vv, bc (org) (1613)
Messe concertate, 8vv, e messa per li morti con un motetto, et il Te
    deum, con bc (org), op.4 (1633)
Messe concertate, 5, 8–9vv, e motetti, 1-3, 8vv, bc (org), op.5 (1634)
1 canzona, 8vv in 1608[24]

BIBLIOGRAPHY
G. Vale: 'La cappella musicale del duomo di Udine', *NA* , vii (1930),
    87–201, esp. 133
J. Roche: 'Musica diversa di Compietà: Compline and its Music in
    Seventeenth-Century Italy', *PRMA*, cix (1982-3), 60–79
J. Roche: *North Italian Church Music in the Age of Monteverdi*
    (Oxford, 1984)
                                            JEROME ROCHE

Bartolino da Padova [Magister Frater Bartolinus de Padua, Frater carmelitus, Frater Bartholomeus; erroneously: Dactalus de Padua] (*fl* Padua and ?Florence, *c*1365–1405). Italian composer, about whom no certain facts are known. As can be seen from *I-MOe* α.M.5.24 (*I bei sembianti*, ascribed to 'Frater carmelitus') and from the portrait of him in *I-Fl* 87 (f.101*v*; see illustration), he

Miniature thought to portray Bartolino da Padova: detail of initial from the Squarcialupi Codex (I-Fl Med.Pal.87, f.101v)

belonged to the Carmelite Order. He is possibly to be identified with one or other of the friars named Bartholomeus who are attested at the Carmelite monastery in Paduain 1376 and 1380 (see Petrobelli, *DBI* and 1968). It has been assumed, from the texts of some works (*Imperial sedendo*, ?1401, for Francesco Novello, *La douce çere*, perhaps also *Quel sole che nutrica*) that probably allude to the Carrara family, lords of Padua, that Bartolino was in their service from 1365 to 1405. It is still an open question whether he lived only in Padua or stayed also in Florence between 1388 and 1390 (as a companion of Francesco Novello who had fled from Padua). However, other pieces seem to contain references to the motto and emblem of the Visconti family (*La fieratesta*; *Alba colomba*, probably for Gian Galeazzo Visconti's entry into Padua, 1388; *Nel sommo grado*; *Quel digno de memoria*; perhaps also *Le aurate chiome*, ?1380), even though some of them could equally well refer to the Carraresi, and be interpreted as directed not in support of but against the campaigns of Gian Galeazzo Visconti in the 1390s. This is probably the case for the poem *La fiera testa*, which was also set to music by Niccolò da Perugia, and was transcribed into the *Novelliere* of Giovanni Sercambi da Lucca (ed. Rossi) in a different reading. It is interesting that a ballata by Paolo da Firenze quotes the same, well known, Visconti motto ('Sofrir m'estuet'), which also appears in poems by Franco Sacchetti and in a piece by Philippus de Caserta.

Evidence for Bartolino's reputation in Tuscany is strengthened by the inclusion of his ballata *Ama chi t'ama* into both the Chronicles and the *Novelliere* of Sercambi, and by the mention of madrigals 'fattia Padova per Frate Bartolino' in Giovanni Gherardi's *Paradiso degli Alberti* (ed. A.Wesselofsky, Bologna, 1867/R, i, 62; iii, 170).

The 38 works that can with certainty be attributed to Bartolino have come down to us complete in the Florentine manuscript *I-Fl 87*; the one exception to this is *Serva çiascuno* (in *I-La* 184). A group of works are also

contained in the Florentine Codex *I-Fl* 2211. In the other Tuscan manuscripts his works occur only in isolation, whilst they are numerous in the northern Italian manuscript *F-Pn* n.a.fr.6771 (26 works) and in *I-La* 184 (12 works). Three pieces are intabulated for a keyboard instrument in *I-FZc* 117. Along with the 'Rondel franceschi', no longer surviving, five or six works are named in Prodenzani's *Liber saporecti*.

Bartolino's style was influenced by Jacopo da Bologna. The monophonic link passages between the lines of his madrigals, and the change in metre which occurs only in the ritornellos of the madrigals (and not always even there), provide evidence of this. It is also striking that Bartolino supplied text for both voices not only in the two-voice madrigals but also in the two-voice ballatas. The Italian tradition is emphasized by the avoidance of *ouvert* and *clos* endings in the ballatas and by the frequent extended melismas– not only in the madrigals – on the first and penultimate syllables of the line. The notation of his works is also strictly Italian. The three-voice pieces *Non cor(r)er troppo*, *Per un verde boschetto* and *I bei sembianti* conform partly with Jacopo's style with two upper voices set against a tenor part; however, elsewhere they show influence from the French style in that countertenor and tenor provide a supporting duet for the upper voice (*El no me giova*, *Sempre, donna*, *Alba colomba* and *La douce çere*). In these last-mentioned pieces, in accordance with the Italian fashion, only the top voice and the tenor are texted; the one exception is no.32 in *I-Fl* 87.

WORKS

Editions: *Der Squarcialupi-Codex Pal.87 der Biblioteca Medicea Laurenziana zuFlorenz*, ed. J. Wolf (Lippstadt, 1955) [W]
Italian Secular Music, ed. W.T. Marrocco, PMFC, ix (1975) [M]

BALLATAS

Ama chi t'ama, 2vv, W 190, M 8 (see Bongi, ii, p.242, and Rossi, ii, p.36)
Amor, che nel pensier, 2vv, W 173, M 10 (text incipit: cf Petrarch's sonnet cxl; same music used for L'invido per lo ben: see Diederichs)
Chi può servir, 2vv, W 181, M 12
Chi tempo à (Matteo Griffoni), 2vv, W 178, M 14
El no me giova (çova), 3vv, W 183, M 18 (in *I-MOe* α.M.5.24, a different Ct, probably by Matteo da Perugia)
Gioia di novi odori, 2vv, W 193, M 20
La sacrosanta carità (Giovanni Dondi dall'Orologio), 2vv, W162, M 34 (Debenedetti, no.29)
L'invido per lo ben, 2vv, W 187, M 38 (see Amor, che nel pensier)
Madonna bench'i' miri, 2vv, W 175, M 40
Miracolosa tua sembianza, 2vv, W 177, M 42
Nel sommo grado, 2vv, W 189, M 44
Non cor(r)er troppo, 2 versions: 2vv, 3vv, W 186, M 46, 48
Perché cançato è il mondo, 2vv, W 184, M 51
Per figura del cielo, 2vv, W 165, M 53
Per subito comando, 2vv, W 163, M 54
Per un verde boschetto, 2 versions: 2vv, 3vv, W 194, M 56, 58 (in *GB-Lbl* Add.29987 wrongly termed a madrigal; Debenedetti, no.25; ?lauda contrafactum, see Ghisi, p.78)
Qual novità cor duro, 2vv, W 176, M 64
Quando necessità, 2vv, W 171, M 70 (text inc.; in W incorrectly treated as a continuation of Le aurate chiome)
Quel digno de memoria, 2vv, W 182, M 72
Recordate de me (Recordati di me), 2vv, W 188, M 77 (Ct in *I-La* 184 may be by another composer)
Sempre, donna, t'amai, 2vv, 3vv, W 179, M 79
Sempre se trova, 2vv, W 162, M 78
Serva chi può, 2vv, W 184, M 86
Serva çiascuno, 2vv, M 88
Strinçe la man, 2vv, W 167, M 89
Tanto de mio cor, 2vv, W 189, M 90
Tuo gentil cortesia, 2vv, W 191, M 92

MADRIGALS

Alba colomba, 2 versions: 2vv, 3vv, W 166, M 1, 5 (Debenedetti, no.29)

Donna liçadra, 2vv, W 172, M 16 (M does not consider the version from *I-La* 184)

I bei sembianti, 3vv, W 160, M 22 (attrib. 'Frater carmelitus' in *I-MOe* α.M.5.24)

Imperial sedendo, 2 versions: 2vv, 3vv, W 174, M 25 (inst version in *I-FZc* 117; Debenedetti, no.25; wrongly attrib. or misspelled Dactalus de Padua in *I-MOe* α.M.5.24; current attribution doubted by Fallows)

La douce çere (çiere), 2 versions: 2vv, 3vv, W 159, M 28 (French text italianized as La dolce cerra in *GB-Lbl* Add.29987; inst version in *I-FZc* 117; Debenedetti, no.25; wrongly attrib. 'Fra Bartolino da Perugia' in *I-Fn* 26)

La fiera testa, 2vv, W 164, M 31 (Italian-Latin-French text, ?Petrarch; see also Rossi, ii, p.203)

Le aurate chiome, 2vv, W 170, M 36 (text inc.; Senhal: 'Catarina'; Debenedetti, no.29)

Qual lege move, 2vv, W 192, M 60 (inst version in *I-FZc* 117)

Quando la terra, 2vv, W 169, M 66, 68 (text inc.)

Quel sole che nutrica, 2vv, W 168, M 74 (Senhal: 'Orsolina')

Se premio de virtù, 2vv, W 180, M 83 (ritornello after stanzas 1 and3; see Corsi, p.243)

DOUBTFUL WORKS

La bianca selva, 2vv, madrigal (see Fischer, 1958–61, p.277)

LOST WORKS

Rondel franceschi (see Debenedetti, no.47)

BIBLIOGRAPHY

DBI (P. Petrobelli)

S. Bongi, ed.: *Le Croniche di Giovanni Sercambi, Lucchese* (Lucca, 1892)

S. Debenedetti, ed.: 'Il "Sollazzo" e il "Saporetto" con altre rime di Simone Prodenzani', *Giornale storico della letteratura italiana*, suppl.xv (Turin, 1913)

D. Plamenac: 'Keyboard Music of the Fourteenth Century in Codex Faenza 117', *JAMS*, iv (1951), 179–201

F. Ghisi: 'Strambottie laude nel travestimento spirituale della poesia musicale del Quattrocento', *CHM*, i (1953), 45–78

K. von Fischer: 'Drei unbekannte Werke von Jacopo da Bologna und Bartolino da Padua?', *Miscelánea en homenaje a Monseñor Higinio Anglés* (Barcelona, 1958–61), 265–81; repr. in *Studi musicali*, xvii (1988), 3–14

N. Goldine: 'Fra Bartolino da Padova, Musicien de Court', *AcM*, xxxiv (1962), 142–55

P. Petrobelli: 'Some Dates for Bartolino da Padova', *Studies in Music History: Essays for Oliver Strunk*, ed. H.S. Powers (Princeton, NJ, 1968/R), 85–112

G. Thibault: 'Emblèmes et devises des Visconti dans les oeuvres musicales du Trecento', *L'Ars Nova italiana del Trecento: Convegno II: Certaldo and Florence 1969 [L'Ars Nova italiana del Trecento*, iii (Certaldo, 1970)], 131–60

G. Corsi, ed.: *Poesie musicali del Trecento* (Bologna, 1970), xliii–xlvii, 239–65

U. Günther: 'Das Manuskript Modena, Biblioteca Estense, α.M.5.24 (olim lat.568 = Mod)', *MD*, xxiv (1970), 17–67, esp. 34

L. Rossi, ed.: *Giovanni Sercambi: Novelliere* (Rome, 1974)

A. Hallock: 'Some Evidence for French Influence in Northern Italy, *c*.1400', *Studies in the Performance of Late Mediaeval Music*, ed. S. Boorman (Cambridge, 1983) 193–225

N. Pirrotta: ' Rhapsodic Elements in North-Italian Polyphony of the 14th Century', *MD*, xxxvii (1983), 83–99, esp. 83

E. Diederichs: 'Zwei Texte zu einer Ballata von Bartolino da Padova', *L'Ars Nova italiana del Trecento*, v, ed. A. Ziino (Palermo, 1985), 113–22

M. Plant: 'Patronage in the Circle of the Carrara Family: Padua, 1337–1405', *Patronage, Art and Society in Renaissance Italy*, ed. F.W. Kent, P. Simons and J.C. Eade (Canberra and Oxford, 1987), 177–99

G. Cattin: ' L'Ars Nova musicale a Padova', *Padua sidus preclarum: I Dondi dall'Orologio e la Padova dei Carraresi*, Padua, July–Nov 1989 (Padua, 1989), 107–22 [exhibition catalogue]

J. Nádas and A.Ziino: Introduction to *The Lucca Codex: Codex Mancini* (Lucca, 1990), 11–99, esp. 40–41

F.A. Gallo: ' La biblioteca dei Visconti', *Musica nel castello: trovatori, libri, oratori nelle corti italiane dal XIII al XV secolo*

(Bologna, 1992), 59–94, esp. 62–3; Eng. trans. (Chicago, 1995), 47–67

F.A. Gallo, ed.: *Il codice Squarcialupi* (Florence, 1992) [incl. J. Nádas: 'The Squarcialupi Codex: an Edition of Trecento Songs, ca. 1410–1415',i, 19–86; K. von Fischer: 'Le biografie', i, 127–44; N. Pirrotta: 'Le musiche del codice Squarcialupi', i, 193–222]

J. Nádas: 'The Lucca Codex and MS San Lorenzo 2211: Some Further Observations', *L'Ars Nova italiana del Trecento*, vi (Certaldo, 1992), 145–68

D. Fallows: 'Ciconia's Late Songs and their Milieu', *Johannes Ciconia: Liège 1998* [forthcoming]

T. Sucato: 'La tradizione notazionale delle opere di Bartolino da Padova e il codice di Lucca (codice Mancini)', *Problemi e metodi della filologia musicale*, ed. S. Campagnolo (Lucca, forthcoming)

KURT VON FISCHER/GIANLUCA D'AGOSTINO

Bartolo, Erasmo de. *See* BARTOLI, ERASMO.

Bartolomeo da Bologna [Bartholomeus de Bononia] (*fl c*1405–27). Italian composer. In the fourth fascicle of *I-MOe* α.M.5.24 (*c*1410), he was described as a Benedictine brother; in the tenth fascicle of *GB-Ob* Can.misc.213 (*c*1425), he was described as 'dominus ... prior'. Pirrotta (in *MGG1*) has suggested that he was the prior of S Nicolò in Ferrara, who was also the cathedral organist in that town in 1407 and present no later than 1405; he is last documented at the cathedral on 5 January 1427 (for further discussion and documentation see Cavicchi, 1975, 1976). In *Que pena maior* Bartolomeo described himself as 'musa resonantem' and took a stand against critics. The Latin ballade *Arte psalentes* was addressed to singers in the papal choir – probably that of John XXIII, elected pope at Bologna in 1410. Both these works are in their formal structure and complex rhythm typical of the Ars Subtilior. In the rondeau *Mersi chiamando* (where the name Galeazzo – probably Malatesta – occurs) and in the two Italian ballate there is word repetition, typical of early 15th century Italian secular works. The rhythm is simpler than in the two earlier works in *I-MOe* α.M.5.24; accidentals (C♯ and G♯) are frequently added to leading notes.

The two mass movements are paired: both employ parody technique, although their modality and style differ, with the Credo set AVERSI. The Gloria incorporates the music of *Vince con lena*, from 'Gracias agimus' to 'deprecacionem', and thus resembles a contrafactum. In the Credo, however, only short sections of *Morir desio* are used, and these not in their original order. This pair of mass movements constitutes an early example of the linking of movements by parody technique; their composition was almost certainly influenced by the mass music of Zacara (who spent some time in the chapel of John XXIII in Bologna in 1412–13). In *GB-Ob* 213 the secular models were copied in juxtaposition with the mass movements based on them – a unique procedure, but nonetheless somewhat reminiscent of the 'parallel' transmission of Zacara's songs and the mass movements based on them.

WORKS
all 3vv

Edition: *Early Fifteenth-Century Music*, ed. G. Reaney, CMM, xi/5 (1975) [complete]

Gloria [parody of *Vince con lena*]

Credo [parody of *Morir desio*]

Arte psalentes (ballade), also ed. in PMFC, xx (1982), p.21

Mersi chiamando (rondeau), also ed. in CMM, xxxvii (1966), p.21

Que pena maior (virelai), also ed. in PMFC, xxi (1987), p.4

Morir desio (ballata)

Vince con lena (ballata)

BIBLIOGRAPHY

MGG1 (N. Pirrotta)

W. Korte: *Studien zur Geschichte der Musik in Italien im ersten Viertel des 15. Jahrhunderts* (Kassel, 1933)

W. Apel: *The Notation of Polyphonic Music, 900–1600* (Cambridge, Mass., 1942, rev. 5/1961; Ger. trans., rev., 1970)

F. Fano: *Le origini e il primo maestro di cappella: Matteo da Perugia, La cappella musicale del duomo di Milano*, ed. G. Cesari, i, IMi, new ser., i (Milan, 1956)

K. von Fischer: 'Kontrafakturen und Parodien italienischer Werke des Trecento und frühen Quattrocento', *AnnM*, v (1957), 43–59

G. Reaney: 'The Italian Contribution to the Manuscript Oxford, Bodleian Library, Canon Misc. 213', *L'Ars Nova italiana del Trecento II: Certaldo and Florence 1969 [L'Ars Nova italiana del Trecento*, iii (Certaldo, 1970)], 443–64

U. Günther: 'Das Manuskript Modena, Biblioteca Estense, α.M.5,24 (olim lat.568 = Mod)', *MD*, xxiv (1970), 17–67

H. Schoop: *Entstehung und Verwendung der Handschrift Oxford, Bodleian Library, Can. misc. 213* (Berne, 1971)

A. Cavicchi: 'Sacro e profano: documenti e note su Bartolomeo da Bologna e gli organisti della cattedrale di Ferrara nel primo quattrocento', *RIM*, x (1975), 46–71

A. Cavicchi: 'Altri documenti per Bartolomeo da Bologna', *RIM*, xi (1976), 178–81

R. Strohm: 'Magister Egardus and other Italo-Flemish Contacts', *L'Europa e la musica del Trecento: Congresso IV: Certaldo 1984 [L'Ars Nova italiana del Trecento*, vi (Certaldo, 1992)], 41–68

D. Fallows: Introduction to *Oxford, Bodleian Library, MS Canon. Misc. 213* (Chicago, 1995)

D. Fallows: *A Catalogue of Polyphonic Songs, 1415–1480* (Oxford, 1999)

HANS SCHOOP/R

Bartolomeo degli Organi [Baccio Fiorentino] (*b* Florence, 24 Dec 1474; *d* Florence, 12 Dec 1539). Italian composer, organist and singer. He acquired the nickname 'degli Organi' because of his profession; it was later adopted by his children. His musical career began shortly after his 13th birthday, when he was appointed a singer at the SS Annunziata. In later life he also sang in the baptistry's chapel, an appointment he received at the behest of Lorenzo de' Medici, Duke of Urbino, in whose personal service he remained for a number of years. He was employed as an organist at several Florentine churches, among them the SS Annunziata and S Maria Novella, before becoming principal organist at the cathedral on 21 December 1509, a position that he held until his death.

Bartolomeo's influence in Florentine musical circles of the time was considerable; one of his contemporaries referred to him as 'the prince of musicians of our city'. Among his pupils were Guido Machiavelli, son of the famous statesman, and the composer Francesco de Layolle. He was a friend of the poets Lorenzo Strozzi, three of whose poems he set to music, and Benedetto Varchi, who wrote a sonnet commemorating his death.

Bartolomeo's extant compositions include ten Italian secular works, four instrumental pieces and a *lauda*. The Italian works (comprising eight ballatas, one *strambotto* and one *canto carnascialesco*) are cast in traditional strophic forms and are characterized by clearly articulated phrases, logical harmonic progression within well-defined key areas and simple rhythms that unfailingly follow the accents of the texts. In several of the ballatas he composed new music for all of the *ripresa* and reduced the amount of repetition within the setting of the strophe. Two ballatas have new music for the entire stanza, a novel feature in Italian music at the time and one which was to be adopted by the earliest madrigal composers. The *lauda*, published in Razzi's 1563 collection, is doubtless an adaptation of a secular work, as is another piece in the same collection which Bartolomeo originally set as a

carnival song. The instrumental pieces share similar motifs with works by Isaac and Agricola, with whom he may have studied in Florence.

Three of Bartolomeo's children became musicians: two of his sons, Antonio and Lorenzo, were organists and served in several of the principal Florentine churches; the youngest, Piero, who was also known as Pierino Fiorentino (*b* Florence, 8 Dec 1523; *d* Rome, 1552), gained fame in the mid-16th century as the outstanding pupil of Francesco da Milano and as a composer in his own right. The musician called 'Baccio degli Organi', who appeared on Medici court rolls as a music teacher in 1574, was probably his grandson.

WORKS

Edition: *Music of the Florentine Renaissance*, ed. F.A. D'Accone, CMM, xxxii/2 (1967) [D]

SACRED

Sguardate il Salvatore (laude), *I-Fd* Musica Vol. 21 (inc.); Signore, soccorr'et aita, 4vv, D 119; S'i' pensassi a' piacer del paradiso [= Donne, per electione]

SECULAR

Amore, paura et sdegnio, 3vv, D 20; Donna, s'i' fu' già degnio, 3vv, D 22; Donne, come redete, *I-Fn* B.R. 337 (inc.); Donne, per electione, 4vv, D 23; Pietà, pietà, 4vv, D 27; Quando e begli occhi, 4vv, D 28; Quell'amor che mi legò, 4vv, D 30; Questo mostrarsi adirata, 4vv, D 31; Questo mostrarsi lieta, 4vv, D 34; Se talor questo o quella, 3vv, D 36; Un di lieto già mai, 3vv, D 37

INSTRUMENTAL

Alles, regres, a 3, *I-Bc* Q17; De tous biens, a 3, *Bc* Q15 (Hayne's T in middle voice); Je vous anpri, *Bc* Q17 [= Meyor d'este non ày]; Je pren congieu de vous mes amours, a 3, *Bc* Q17; Meyor d'este non ày, a 3, D 25

BIBLIOGRAPHY

F.A. D'Accone: 'Alessandro Coppini and Bartolomeo degli Organi: Two Florentine Composers of the Renaissance', *AnMc*, no.4 (1967), 38–76

R. Wexler: 'Newly Identified Works by Bartolomeo degli Organi in the MS Bologna Q 17', *JAMS*, xxiii (1970), 107–18

W. Kirkendale: *The Court Musicians in Florence during the Principate of the Medici* (Florence, 1993), 107

FRANK A. D'ACCONE

Bartolomeus de Bruollis. See BROLLO, BARTOLOMEO.

Bartolotti, Angelo Michele (*b* Bologna, early 17th century; *d* ?Paris, after 1668). Italian composer, guitarist and theorbo player. After publishing two books of his guitar music in Italy, Bartolotti moved to Paris. On the title-page of a treatise on continuo accompaniment for the theorbo, the author is described as 'Angelo Michele Bartolomi Bolognese', but there is little question that 'Bartolomi' is simply a misspelling of Bartolotti. In France Bartolotti was admired principally as a theorbo player: Ouvrard praised him as 'without doubt the most skilful theorbo player in France and Italy', and Constantijn Huygens also mentioned him as a virtuoso on that instrument.

Bartolotti's first book for the five-course guitar contains a cycle of *passacaglias* in all the major and minor keys, combining the *battute* and pizzicato styles seen earlier in the music of Foscarini. His second book shows a more pronounced French influence, with an emphasis on pizzicato textures. These two books are among the most carefully notated Italian guitar tablatures of the period, with indications for various types of strum, arpeggios and left-hand ornaments, and contain some of the most advanced guitar music of the day. Bartolotti's treatise ranks, with those of Fleury (1660) and Delair (1690), among the most noteworthy essays on accompaniment for the theorbo.

WORKS

Libro primo di chitarra spagnola (Florence, 1640/R); 7 ed. in Hudson
Secondo libro di chitarra (Rome, c1655/R with libro primo)
Allemande and Sarabande, by 'Angelo Mikielo', gui, F-Pn Vm⁷ 675
Allemande, by 'Angelus Michiele', lute, A-Wn 17706

Table pour apprendre facilement à toucher le théorbe sur la basse-
continuë (Paris, 1669)

BIBLIOGRAPHY

BenoitMC
R. Ouvrard: Letter to C. Nicaise (16 July 1666), F-Pn fr.9360
A. Rosenthal: 'Two Unknown 17th Century Music Editions by
   Bolognese Composers', CHM, ii (1957), 373–400, esp. 373–8
R. Hudson: The Folia, the Saraband, the Passacaglia, and the
   Chaconne, MSD, xxxv (1982)
G.R. Boye: Giovanni Battista Granata and the Development of
   Printed Guitar Music in Seventeenth-Century Italy (diss., Duke U.,
   1995), 98–9, 140–42
G.R. Boye: 'Performing Seventeenth-Century Italian Guitar Music:
   the Question of an Appropriate Stringing', Performance on Lute,
   Guitar and Vihuela: Historical Practice and Modern
   Interpretation, ed. V.A. Coelho (Cambridge, 1997), 180–94

ROBERT STRIZICH/GARY R. BOYE

Bartolozzi, Bruno (*b* Florence, 8 June 1911; *d* Florence, 12 Dec 1980). Italian composer and violinist. He studied music at the Florence Conservatory, taking his diploma in violin playing with Gino Nucci (1930) and in composition with Paolo Fragapane (1944). His association with Dallapiccola, whom he met at the conservatory, was of enormous importance for his work as a composer. Bartolozzi also studied conducting with Galliera at the Accademia Musicale Chigiana in Siena and from 1964 was himself a lecturer in conducting at the Florence Conservatory. From 1944 to 1965 he played the violin in the orchestra of the Maggio Musicale Fiorentino.

Bartolozzi's first compositions, such as the Concerto for Orchestra (1952), the Divertimento for chamber orchestra (1956) and the Concerto for violin, strings and harpsichord (1957), adhere to 12-note technique, following Dallapiccola's influence. In the 1960s he began to experiment with new woodwind sonorities, thanks to his partnership with the bassoonist Sergio Penazzi, well-known for his dedication to contemporary music. This exploration of materials (microtones, multiphonics, etc.) later described in the volume *New Sounds for Woodwind* (London, New York and Toronto, 1967) had a creative outlet in such works as *Concertazioni* for bassoon, strings and percussion (1963), written for Penazzi, *Concertazioni* for oboe and four instruments (1965), for the oboist Lawrence Singer, and *Concertazioni a quattro* for woodwind quartet (1969). Bartolozzi assimilated other avant-garde compositional techniques of the 1960s, adopting aleatory procedures in the *Collage* pieces – for oboe (1968), bassoon (1969) and clarinet (1973) – and microtonality in *Tres recuerdos del cielo* for soprano and ten instruments (1967).

Bartolozzi's stylistic characteristics attain synthesis in his 'dramatic play' *Tutto ciò che accade ti riguarda* (1965–70). Written to his own libretto after Günter Eich's radio play *Träume*, the work centres on five people on a railway journey, none of whom knows where the train is going. The existential problem facing the characters is emphasized by the anguished, unanswered question posed by the chorus: who will save us? Bartolozzi represents the characters' tragic sense of loneliness and isolation by contrasting electronic and acoustic sounds, and different vocal techniques which, in the case of the chorus, involve not only singing, but also whispering, shouting and speaking. The work thus belongs in a line of avant-garde music-theatre works (which includes Nono's *Intolleranza 1960* and Manzoni's *Atomtod*) concerned with social themes and with the alienation of the individual in the modern industrialized world.

WORKS
(*selective list*)

Stage: Tutto ciò che accade ti riguarda (dramatic play, prol., 1, after
   G. Eich: Traüme), 1965–70, Florence, Teatro della Pergola, 30
   May 1972
Orch: Conc. for Orch, 1952; Divertimento, chbr orch, 1956; Conc.,
   vn, str, hpd, 1957; Concertazioni, bn, str, perc, 1963; Memorie, 3
   gui, orch, 1975; Risonanze, 18 perc, 1978; Vn Conc. no.2, 1979
Vocal: Sentimento del sogno (G. Ungaretti), S, orch, 1952; Immagine
   (R.M. Rilke), S, 17 insts, 1959; 3 recuerdos del cielo (R. Alberti),
   S, 10 insts, 1967
Chbr: Musica a 5, bn, tpt, gui, vn, va, 1953; Serenata, vn, gui, 1955;
   Str Qt no.1, 1960; Concertazioni, ob, gui, perc, va, db, 1965; The
   Hollow Man, any ww, spkr, 1968; Concertazioni a 4, fl, ob, cl, bn,
   1969; Sinaulodia, 4 fl, 1969; Musica per Piero, 2 va, 1971; Auser,
   ob, gui, 1972; Concertazioni, cl, 7 insts, perc, 1973; Repitu, fl, gui,
   perc, va, 1974; The Solitary, eng hn, perc, 1976; Atma, perc ens,
   1978; Str Qt no.2, 1979
Solo inst: 3 Pieces, gui, 1952; 2 studi, vn, 1952; Variations, vn, 1957;
   Estri del fa diesis, pf, 1959; Andamenti, va, 1967; Collage, ob,
   1968; Collage, bn, 1969; Cantilena, a fl, 1970; Omaggio a
   Azzolina, gui, 1971; Collage, cl, 1973; Madrigale di Gesualdo,
   accdn, 1976; Per Olga, fl, 1976; Adles, gui, 1977

Principal publishers: Bruzzichelli, Suvini Zerboni

BIBLIOGRAPHY

R. Smith Brindle: 'Current Chronicle: Italy', MQ, xlix (1963),
   98–101; lii (1966), 106–9
M. Pinzauti: 'Il sogni di Bartolozzi', La nazione (31 May 1972)
F. D'Amico: 'Spogliatevi compagni', L'espresso (11 June 1972)

RAFFAELE POZZI

Bartolozzi, Therese. *See* JANSEN, THERESE.

Bartolucci, Ruffino. *See* RUFFINO D'ASSISI.

Bartolus, Abraham (*b* Meissen, nr Dresden; *fl* 1614). German theorist. He was a teacher at Beuten. His *Musica mathematica* was published at Altenburg in 1614 as the second part (pp.89–175) of Heinrich Zeising's *Theatri machinarum*. Bartolus's treatise is basically speculative in nature. He relied heavily on the horoscope in his interpretation of the effects of music, suggesting that the composer's choice of tonalities, as well as their effect on the listener, could be determined astrologically. Although the monochord tuning which he propounded had been devised by Andreas Reinhard in his *Monochordum* (Leipzig, 1604), Bartolus did suggest an interesting mechanical improvement to the instrument's movable bridge. The monochord also served as the foundation of his earth-centred interpretation of the cosmos.

BIBLIOGRAPHY

C.D. Adkins: The Theory and Practice of the Monochord (diss., U. of
   Iowa, 1963)
R. Dammann: 'Die Musica mathematica von Bartolus (1614)', AMw,
   xxvi (1969), 140–62

CECIL ADKINS

Barton, Marmaduke (Miller) (*b* Manchester, 29 Dec 1865; *d* London, 24 July 1938). English pianist and teacher. Barton was an original scholar (1883) at the RCM. He studied under J.F. Barnett and C.V. Stanford and was the first student ever to play at a pupils' concert (1884). In 1887 he played at Queen Victoria's jubilee concert in Windsor Castle. On leaving the RCM he was granted a further year's study abroad, which he spent at Weimar, under Liszt's pupil Bernhard Stavenhagen. In 1889 he returned to the college to teach. As a student he had been rather impetuous and intolerant, but he fell now under the beneficent influence of another original scholar, Anna Russell, a pupil of Jenny Lind and a devout Catholic. He adopted her faith, and in 1891 they were married. Barton was much in demand for playing concertos with the principal London and provincial orchestras and also for recitals, but teaching, both at the RCM and, from 1911, the GSM, was perhaps his main work. He made recital tours in South Africa (1911) and the Netherlands (1912). Two of his pupils have given complementary summaries of his teaching: '[He was] a stickler for hard work, good manners and punctuality' and 'A great artist who conveyed beauty by deeds, not words'. (G. Warrack: 'Royal College of Music: the First Eighty-Five Years, 1883–1968, and After', typescript, *GB-Lcm*, 203–4)

GUY WARRACK/ROSEMARY WILLIAMSON

Bartoš, František (i) (*b* Mladcová, nr Gottwaldov, 16 March 1837; *d* Mladcová, 11 June 1906). Moravian folksong collector and dialectologist. He was educated at the Gymnasium in Olomouc and at the University of Vienna and became a schoolteacher in Strážnice (1864), Olomouc, Těšín and in 1869 at the first Czech Gymnasium in Brno. From 1888 he directed the second Czech Gymnasium in Old Brno, where he was in contact with Janáček. In collaboration with other schoolteachers and organists, he organized the collecting, categorizing and editing of Moravian folksongs, and through his four published collections and about 4000 other folksongs which appeared in ethnographic monographs he became recognized as the successor to Sušil, the pioneer of Moravian ethnomusicology.

Like many other early scholars in European folk music, Bartoš sometimes changed the song texts, thereby reducing the documentary value of his collections; from a musical point of view, only part of his third collection (1901), a collaboration with Janáček, fulfilled the requirements of modern notational technique. Perhaps of more lasting significance is the comprehensive theoretical treatise written as an introduction to his second collection (1889), in which he worked out a classification of songs according to text and function. He declared that the tunes of some groups of Moravian folksongs follow the metrical, rhythmical and intonational features of the texts, rather than those of instrumental melodies, as is the case, for example, with folksongs from Bohemia. He thus revealed a basic structural feature of the repertory, one which became a subject of great interest to Janáček.

FOLKSONG COLLECTIONS

Nové národní písně moravské s nápěvy do textu vřaděnými [New Moravian folksongs with the tunes fitted to the texts] (Brno, 1882)
Národní písně moravské v nově nasbírané [Newly collected Moravian folksongs] (Brno, 1889)
with L. Janáček: *Kytice z národních písní moravských* [Bouquet of Moravian folksongs] (Telč, 1890, rev. 4/1953 by A. Gregor and B. Štědroň)
with L. Janáček: *Národní písně moravské v nově nasbírané* (Prague, 1901)

BIBLIOGRAPHY

T. Straková, ed.: *František Bartoš a Leoš Janáček: vzájemná korespondence* (Gottwaldov, 1957)
J. Vysloužil: 'Nad folkloristickým dílem Františka Bartoše' [On Bartoš's folkloristic studies], *Ze života a díla Františka Bartoše: sborník studií* [From the life and works of Bartoš: journal of studies] (Gottwaldov, 1957), 71–80

A. Geck: *Das Volksliedmaterial Leoš Janáčeks: Analysen der Struckturen unter Einbeziehung von Janáčeks Randbemerkungen und Volkstudien* (Regensburg, 1975)
J. Ondrusz: 'Frantisek Bartos, 1837–1906: zycie i dzielo' [Life and works], *Z zagadnien polskiej Kultury muzycznej: studia folklorystyczne* [On the problems of Polish music culture: studies of folklore], ed. A. Dygacz and J. Bauman-Szulakowska (Katowice, 1994), 84–92
J. Sehnal and J. Vysloužil: *Hudba na Moravě* [Music in Moravia] (Brno, 2000)

JIŘÍ VYSLOUŽIL

Bartoš, František (ii) (*b* Brněnec, 13 June 1905; *d* Prague, 21 May 1973). Czech composer and writer. He studied composition at the Prague Conservatory under Jirák and Křička (1921–5) and in Foerster's master classes (1925–8). In 1932, together with Bořkovec, Holzknecht, Ježek and Krejčí, he founded in Prague the Mánes group, whose interests focussed on modern French music. Bartoš was a competent critic for the daily press and co-editor of *Tempo* of Prague (1935–8, 1946–8); in later life he gave more of his attention to musicology. As a composer he had begun under the influence of late Romanticism, but subsequently, following the trends of the day, he sought clarity of form, precision and a tender expressivity, qualities which resulted in a cultivated balance, most particularly in the chamber compositions. The suite *Měšťák šlechticem* ('Le bourgeois gentilhomme') for wind quintet, an exquisite piece of neo-classicism, was adapted from Lully's original score. Other works of note include the String Quartet no.2, *Rozhlasová hudba* ('Radio Music') for orchestra (performed at the 1938 ISCM Festival), and the songs and choruses, which indicate his discriminating literary taste. The song cycle *Černý ...* ('Black ... ') is a rare essay on a social theme.

WORKS
(*selective list*)

Orch: Suita, op.6, 1928; Rozhlasová hudba [Radio Music], op.12, 1936; Skizzy ke Gogolovu Revizoru [Sketches for Gogol's Government Inspector], op.17
Choral: Klid [Peace] (A. Sova), op.1b, 1923; Přišel jsem k své milé [I Came to My Beloved] (F. Šrámek), op.3a, 1925; Hudba na náměstí [Music in the Square] (J. Hořejší), op.3b, 1927; 1917, op.9 (J. Hora), 1930; Láska [Love] (K. Toman), op.14, 1939; 2 ženské sbory [2 Female Choruses] (J. Neruda), op.15, 1942
Melodrama: Jaro [Spring] (Šrámek), op.2, 1925
Chbr and solo inst: Str Sextet, op.4, 1926; Str Qt no.1, op.5, 1928; Scherzo, wind qnt, 1932; Str Qt no.2, op.10, 1933–5; Měšťák šlechticem [Le bourgeois gentilhomme], wind qnt, 1934 [from ballet by Lully], Duo, op.13, vn, va, 1937; Polka rusticana, wind trio, 1952; pf pieces
Songs: Bouquet de l'amour (J. Neruda), op.1a, 1923–4; 3 písně [3 Songs] (J. Cocteau, I. Goll, F. Mauriac), op.7, 1928; V. Burlesky (M. Jacob, Nezval), op.11, 1933–4; Deštivé obrazy [Rainy Pictures] (Nezval), op.16, 1945; Černý ... [Black ...] (L. Hughes), 1959
Music for the theatre and cinema, folksong arrs.

Prinicipal publisher: Hudební Matice

WRITINGS

Smetana ve vzpomínkách a dopisech [Smetana in reminiscences and letters] (Prague, 1939, 9/1954; Ger. trans., 1954; Eng. trans., 1955)
Studentské vánoce Bedřicha Smetany [Smetana's student Christmasses] (Prague, 1939)
W.A. *Mozart v dopisech* [Mozart in letters] (Prague, 2/1937, 3/1956)
Bedřich Smetana (Prague, 1940)
with Z. Němec: *Z dopisů Bedřicha Smetany* [From Smetana's letters] (Prague, 1947)
Many articles on Smetana and other Czech composers in *HRo, Rytmus, Tempo*, etc.

BIBLIOGRAPHY

F. Bartoš: 'Skladatelé o sobě' [Composers about themselves], *Rytmus*, vii/3 (1941–2), 29

J. Bachtík: 'Padesát let Františka Bartoše' [Bartoš's 50 years], *HRo*, viii (1955), 538–9

V. Holzknecht: *Hudební skupina Mánesa* [The Mánes music group] (Prague, 1968)

V. Holzknecht: 'In memoriam František Bartoš', *HRo*, xxvi (1973), 329

M. Ladmanová: 'Odešel František Bartoš', *HV*, x (1973), 361

M. Ladmanová: *František Bartoš: svědek čtvrtstoletí* [F. Bartoš: witness of a quarter-century] (Prague, 1980)

JOSEF BEK

Bartoš, Josef (*b* Vysoké Mýto, Bohemia, 4 March 1887; *d* Prague, 27 Oct 1952). Czech musicologist. He studied under Stecker at the Prague Conservatory (1905–7), under Hostinský and Nejedlý at Prague University (1905–9) and for a year at the Sorbonne. On his return he taught French and Czech at training colleges. He translated Bergson, Carrière and Croce into Czech and many of their ideas influenced his own philosophical attitude to music. His articles and books are concerned mainly with Czech music of the 19th and early 20th century, including a valuable study of opera at the Prague Provisional Theatre. For many years he was music critic of the daily papers *Prager Presse*, *Národni práce* and *Právo lidu*.

WRITINGS

Antonín Dvořák: kritické studie (Prague, 1913)

Zdeněk Fibich (Prague, 1914)

Jak naslouchati hudbě [How to listen to music] (Prague, 1916, 2/1920)

Umění: úvod do estetiky [The arts: an introduction to aesthetics] (Prague, 1922)

Josef Bohuslav Foerster (Prague, 1923)

O proudech v soudobé hudbě [Tendencies in contemporary music] (Gdynia, 1924)

'Otakar Jeremiáš', *Tempo* [Prague], viii (1928–9), 4–16

'Stendhal hudebník' [Stendhal as a musician], *Sborník prací k padesátým narozeninám Profesora Dra Zdeňka Nejedlého*, ed. A.J. Patzaková and M. Očadlík (Prague, 1929), 30–68

Karel Burian (Rakovník, 1934)

Dějiny Pražského Hlaholu 1911–36 [History of the Prague Hlahol (Choral society)] (Prague, 1936)

Otakar Ostrčil (Prague, 1936)

Prozatímní divadlo a jeho opera [The Provisional Theatre and its opera] (Prague, 1938)

Z deníku B. Smetany [From Smetana's diary] (Prague, 1938)

ed., with P. Pražák and J. Plavec: *J.B. Foerster: jeho životní pouť a tvorba, 1859–1949* [Foerster: his life and works] (Prague, 1949) [incl. 'Foerstrova životní pouť' [Foerster's journey through life], 39–80; 'Foerstrova píseň' [Foerster's songs], 207–40]

BIBLIOGRAPHY

ČSHS [incl. list of writings]

R. Pečman: 'Umělecká metoda Dvořákova skončila fiaskem: Bartošova syntéza' [Dvořák's artistic method ended in a fiasco: Bartoš's synthesis], *Útok na Antonína Dvořáka* [The attack on Antonín Dvořák] (Brno, 1992), 135–59

JOHN TYRRELL

Bartsch, Franz Xaver. See PARTSCH, FRANZ XAVER.

Bartulis, Vidmantas (*b* Kaunas, Lithuania, 3 April 1954). Lithuanian composer. In 1980 he graduated from the Lithuanian State Conservatory where he had studied with Balsys. From 1980 to 1983 he taught at the J. Gruodis Music College in Kaunas. He has been director of the music department of the Kaunas Theatre since 1983, and a member of the Union of the Arts group since 1990. Bartulis received the Lithuanian National Prize in 1998.

Generically, the music of Bartulis displays extreme polarity, ranging from a mass setting to happenings, from chamber music to electronic works. Typical of his early work are chamber compositions which sound like the manifesto of a new generation of Romantics and which are clearly influenced by oriental philosophy. In later works this minimalist world of Romantic beauty is replaced by the search for a sacred dimension (*Aurora lucis*, the Mass) and the way in which that dimension relates to the present day is taken as a theme (the Requiem). Bartulis later rejected the harmony and transparency of this music and, through experimentation with alternative genres, came to write the only opera of the absurd in Lithuanian musical history, parodying stage conventions.

Confrontation with his musical heritage runs like a guideline through the whole body of Bartulis's work. Sometimes this confrontation is merely a case of allusion, or a few bars resembling quotation (*Hommage à Čiurlionis*), while the group of *I Like ...* works represents his attitude to a particular style. Strict rationality is foreign to Bartulis, who sets particular store by organic elements. However, there is almost always a tragic note concealed behind the playful and ironic quality of his music.

WORKS

Stage: Pamoka [One Hour] (op, Bartulis, E. Ionesco), 1993, Kaunas, 1996; incid music for more than 100 plays

Vocal: Sutemų giesmės [Song of the Twilight] (cant., S. Geda), S, org, 1986; Mass, chorus, org, 1987; Requiem, 3 solo vv, choruses, orch, 1989; Auge der Zeit (P. Celan), 2 B, 2 cl, 2 pf, perc, 1991; Nativitas Domini (cant., R. Mikutavičius), choruses, 2 vn, org 1991; Amen (D. Alighieri, Bartulis, Celan, J. Mekas, G. Patackas), S, trbn, db, pf, tape, 1992; Ant kalno [From the Mountain] (Celan, M. Claudius, H. Heine), 3 elegies, 1v, cl, pf, str qt, 1996; Enfance (P. Handke, A. Rimbaud), 1v, pf, db, trbn, perc, 1996; Aušrinė [A Legend], S, T, chorus, elec keyboard insts, 1998; Kukutis [Idylls] (M. Martinaitis), 1v, pf, trbn, db, perc, 1998; 30 choruses

Orch: Sym. no.1, 1980; Sym. no.2 'Mėlynasis angelas' [The Blue Angel] (S. Geda), chorus, orch, 1985; Pf Conc., 1994; Regensspiele, chbr orch, 1995; I Like F. Chopin (Sonata in B Major), 2 pf, orch, 1997; I Like F. Schubert (Quintet in C, Adagio), str, 1998

Chbr: Vakaryštei dienai [Yesterday], ob, cl, bn, 1981; Ateinanti [The Commands], pf trio, 1982; Keturios paguodos liūdnai violončelei ir daina be žodžiu [Four Words of Comfort for a Mournful Cello and a Song With no Text], vn, vc, 1985; Aurora lucis, 2 vn, org, 1985; De profundis, cl, pf qt, 1988; O, brangioji [Oh, my Love], str qt, 1994; Hommage à Čiurlionis, sax, b cl, elec insts, kanklės, 1995; I Like J.S. Bach (Prelude in C Major), pf, perc, 1995; Reti susitikimai, kuriu metu mes šokame aistringus šokius, mename mirusius draugus ir mus užplūsta sentimentalūs prisiminimai, cl, pf trio, 1997

Other: pf works, org pieces and music for computer, electronics and multimedia

BIBLIOGRAPHY

V. Gerulaitis: 'Tyloje ateinantis' [The Style of the Future], *Nemunas* (1986), no.1, pp.29–32

R. Goštautiene: 'Requiem', *Krantai* (1989), no.10, pp.2–5

R. Gaidamavičiūtė: 'Žvilgsnis j vidmanto Bartulio kūrybą' [An overview of Bartulis's work], *Kultūros barai* (1998), no.11, pp.28–31

based on *MGG2* (ii, 418–20), by permission of Bärenreiter

RŪTA GAIDAMAVIČIŪTĖ

Barvyns'ky, Vasyl' Oleksandrovych (*b* Tarnopol', 8/20 Feb 1888; *d* L'viv, 9 June 1963). Ukrainian composer, musicologist, pianist and teacher. He took piano lessons first at the K. Mikuli Music School (1895–1905) and with W. Kurtz (1905–06) at the conservatory in L'viv. During the same period he studied jurisprudence at Lemberg University, and from 1907, philosophy at the University of Prague. In Prague Barvyns'ky studied musicology with Z. Nejedly and O. Hostinsky, the piano with I. Holfeld and composition with Vítězslav Novák (1908–14), who exerted a powerful influence on him. From 1915 to 1939 Barvyns'ky taught at, and was director of, the Lysenko Music Institute in L'viv, and also taught at the conservatory there (1939–41 and 1944–8). A prolific organizer, he initiated and took part in many musical activities in L'viv and became a member of the editorial board of the journal *Ukraïns'ka muzyka*. In 1934 he helped organize, and later presided over (1936–9) the Union of Ukrainian Professional Musicians, SUPROM. During the purges of 1948, the Soviet authorities sentenced him to ten years' imprisonment in Mordovian labour camps. He was rehabilitated posthumously in 1964. After the period of exile he returned to L'viv and resumed his teaching until his death. In characterizing the L'viv school of composers (and by extension that of Western Ukraine), Barvyns'ky wrote: 'the musical output of the Galician composers, who were brought up in the same Slavic musical centre and in the same cultural atmosphere (Prague), relies to a significant extent on folksong, which inspires each of them in a different way'. Together with Stanislav Lyudkevych, he formed the professional Western Ukrainian school of composition, centered in L'viv. Three major influences formed Barvyns'ky's musical style: the national school as epitomized by Mykola Lysenko, whom he first met in 1967, French Impressionism and the Czech school of Novák. Essentially a traditionalist, Barvyns'ky's talent was lyrical and in essence contrapuntal with a refined harmonic sense influenced by a subtle use of impressionistic techniques (especially in his piano preludes). Barvyns'ky's main contribution was in the area of chamber music, a genre relatively unexplored in Ukrainian music in the early 20th century. His refined ear and an improvisatory manner influenced by folk music and clearly defined structures characterize these works. He was also the first Western Ukrainian composer to write a purely orchestral work, the *Ukrainian Rhapsody* (1911).

WORKS

Vocal: Vecherom v khati [Evening at Home] (B. Lepky), 1v, pf, 1910; V lisi [In the Forest] (Lepky), 1v, pf, 1910; Ukraïns'ke vesillya [Ukrainian Wedding], solo vv, chorus, orch, 1914; Zapovit [Testament] (cant., T. Shevchenko), vv, orch, 1917; Psalom Davyda [Psalm of David] (P. Kulish), 1v, pf, 1918; Pisnya pisen' [Song of Songs] (V. Maslova-Stokiz), S, vn, pf, 1924; Nasha pisnya, nasha tuha [Our Song, our Grief] (M. Cherkasenko), vv, orch, 1933; Nadiya [Hope] (L. Ukraïnka), 1v, pf, 1956

Inst: 8 Preludes, pf, 1908; Pf Sonata, 1910; 2 Pf Trios, 1911; Pisnya, serenada, improvizatsiya [Song, Serenade, Improvisation], pf, 1911; Ukraïns'ka rapsodiya [Ukrainian Rhapsody], orch, 1911; Sextet, variations, 2 vn, va, vc, db, pf, 1915; Ukrainskaya syuita, pf, 1915; Pf Conc., 1917–37, recently discovered; Variations on Ukrainian Folk Themes, vc, pf, 1918; 6 miniatyuri, pf, 1920; Variations and Fughetta on Ukrainian Folk Theme, pf, 1920; Sonata, vc, pf, 1926; Ov.-Poem, orch, 1930, lost; Works on Ukrainian folk themes, vn, pf, 1934–5; 20 Children's Pieces on Ukrainian themes, pf, 1935; Str Qt 'Molodizhniy' [Youth], 1935; Qnt, str qt, pf, 1953–63; Conc., vc, pf, 1956

Songs, choral works, folksong arrs., edns of Ukrainian art music

WRITINGS

Ukraïns'ka narodna pisnya i ukraïns'ki kompozytory [Ukrainian folksong and Ukrainian composers] (Prague, 1914)

Pisni Kholmshchyny i Pidlyassya [Songs of Kholm and Pidlyassya] (Lemberg, 1917)

Tvorchist' V. Novaka [Novak's work] (Lwów, 1930)

Ukraïns'ka muzyka (Lwów, 1936)

Yozef Suk (Lwów, 1936)

'Ohlyad istoriï ukraïns'koï muzyky' [A survey of the history of Ukrainian music], L. Arkhymovych, ed.: *Istoriya ukraïns'koï kultury* (Lwów, 1937)

Viktor Kosenko (Lwów, 1938)

'*Kavkaz' S. Lyudkevycha* [The 'Kavkaz' of Lyudkevych] (Lwów, 1939)

BIBLIOGRAPHY

S. Pavlyshyn: 'Vasyl' Oleksandrovich Barvyns'ky', *Ukraïns'ke muzykoznavstvo*, iii (1968)

L. Mazepa: 'Tahichna dolya mytstya' [Tragic fate of an artist], *Muzyka* [Kiev] (1988), no.5, pp.24–6

M. Kucher: 'Pibtora roku z Vasylem Barvins'kym' [A year and a half with Barvins'ky], *Ukraïna* (1990), no.3

S. Pavlyshyn: *Vasyl' Barvyns'ky* (Kiev, 1990)

S. Pavlyshyn: 'Kompozytor-eksperymentator' [Composer-experimentalist], *Muzyka* [Kiev] (1996), no.3, pp.27–8

VIRKO BALEY

Barwell, Mrs John. *See under* BACON, RICHARD MACKENZIE.

Baryphonus, Henricus [Pipegrop, Pipgrop, Pipgroppe, Heinrich] (*b* Wernigerode, Harz, 17 Sept 1581; *d* Quedlinburg, Saxe-Anhalt, 13 Jan 1655). German theorist and composer. Jacobs established that his German family name was Pipegrop, not Grobstimme as stated in some earlier biographical accounts. He attended the Lateinschule at Wernigerode, where he probably first studied music with the Kantor Johann Krüger as well as with the organist of the Oberpfarrkirche, Paul Becker. He entered the university at Helmstedt in April 1603. In 1605 he went to Quedlinburg as Kantor of St Benedikti and as a teacher at the Gymnasium, whose Subkonrector he became in 1606. He remained in these positions for almost half a century until his death. He seems to have been admired as a composer, but all but two of his pieces are lost, as apparently are all but one of his many treatises. Michael Praetorius, who supported him enthusiastically, announced in the third volume of *Syntagma musicum* (1618) that in the next volume he would publish Baryphonus's *De melopoeia*. He also listed 16 other treatises by him that he expected to finance for publication, but his death both put an end to this project and prevented the continuation of *Syntagma musicum*. His list of Baryphonus's treatises, which also appears in Walther's *Musicalisches Lexicon* (1732), contains only one extant work, *Pleiades musicae*. At least one other treatise not listed by Praetorius may also be lost. Baryphonus is known to have corresponded with Heinrich Schütz and Scheidt: Werckmeister printed a fragment of a letter to Schütz (also in Moser) and Scheidt's reply to a letter from Baryphonus (also in *VMw*, vii, 1891, p.192, and in Serauky). The first edition of *Pleiades musicae* (1615) shows Baryphonus's debt to the theoretical concepts of Zarlino and Calvisius. The second edition (1630), which was significantly expanded, influenced many subsequent theorists, including Werckmeister, J.G. Ahle and Walther (especially in his *Praecepta*). It includes a new section on the triad, which Baryphonus adopted without acknowledgment from Johannes Lippius's *Synopsis musicae novae* (1612). With Lippius, he was the first writer to organize compositional theory on the basis of harmonic rather than contrapuntal principles. Within the concept of the triad, which he called 'triga harmonica', he established a specially influential doctrine of intervals and intervallic progression, though curiously only for consonances, not dissonances. As might be expected from his emphasis on triadic structure, he was an advocate – one of the earliest in Germany – of composing from the bass part, a view that reflected the growing strength of the practice of thoroughbass that had originated in Italy some 30 years earlier.

WORKS

THEORETICAL WORKS

Pleiades musicae, quae in certas sectiones distributae praecipuas quaestiones musicas discutiunt (Halberstadt, 1615, rev. 2/1630 by H. Grimm as *Pleiades musicae, quae fundamenta musicae theoricae ex principiis mathematicis eruta*, together with S. Calvisius: *Melopoeia*)

The following listed by M. Praetorius, *Syntagma musicum*, iii (Wolfenbüttel, 1618, 2/1619/R), 223, 227–8; all lost

De melopoeia, intended for pubn in *Syntagma musicum*, iv

Exercitationes harmonicae, quibus omnia tam ad theoriam, quam ad praxin musicam necessaria per aphorismos, theoremata & problemata nervose & dilucide expediuntur

Diatribe musica artusia, ex tabulis Joan. Mariae Artusii collecta, latine reddita, exemplis illustrata

Dissertatio de modis musicis e veterum & recentiorum tam graecorum quam latinorum & italorum monumentis excerpta

Isagoge musica Euclidis cum notis Henrici Baryphoni; probably identical with *Isagoge musica* (Magdeburg, 1609)

Isagoge musico-theorica ex fundamento mathematico coram ratione & sensu judicium proportione; probably identical with *Institutiones musico-theoricae* (Leipzig, 1620)

Logistica musica, in qua usus proportionum in addendis, subtrahendis, copulandis, comparandis, aequiparandis intervallis synoptice ob oculos ponitur

Arithmologia harmonica, in qua scheseis tam numerorum harmonicorum primorum & radicalium, quam inter se compositorum & secundariorum & tertiariorum tabellares in constituendis intervallis simplicibus, compositis, prohibitis, diminutis & superfluis ob oculos ponuntur

Consonantiarum progressiones, quae ad quosvis animi affectus exprimendos accommodae

Ars canendi, aphorismis succinctis descripta & notis philosophicis, mathematicis, physicis et historicis illustrata (Leipzig, 1620)

Progymnasma melopoëticum in paideian & propaideian tributum

Catalogus musicorum tam priscorum quam recentium

Historia veterum instrumentorum musicorum 25. literis graecis & latinis monumentis atque philosophorum, philologorum, musicorum & historicorum

Exercitationes quatuor: de musica vocali; de musica instrumentali; de musices inventoribus; de musices usu

Monochordi in diatonico, chromatico & enharmonico genere descriptio

Spicilegium musicum, in quo quaestiones musicorum praecipuae per theoremata & problemata succincte & nervose discutiuntur

OTHER

Melos genethliacum oder Weihenacht Gesang: Ein Engel schon vons Himmels Thron, zur neuen Jahrsgabe verehret, 6vv (Magdeburg, 1609); ed. in *VMw*, ix (1893), 383

Wir gläuben an einen Gott, 1v, bc, 1638⁵ and *A-Wn*

BIBLIOGRAPHY

WaltherML

A. Werckmeister: *Cribrum musicum, oder Musicalisches Sieb* (Quedlinburg and Leipzig, 1700/R, 2/1783)

J.G. Walther: *Praecepta der musicalischen Composition* (MS, *D-WRtl*, 1708); ed. P. Benary (Leipzig, 1955)

E. Jacobs: 'Zwei harzische Musiktheoretiker des 16. und 17. Jahrhunderts, ii: Heinrich Baryphonus, 1581–1655', *VMw*, vi (1890), 111–22

E. Jacobs: 'Heinrich Pipegrop (Baryphonus)', *VMw*, vii (1891), 459–63

E. Jacobs: 'Noch einmal Pipegrop–Baryphonus', *VMw*, viii (1892), 145–7

P. Spitta: 'Ein Weihnachts-Gesang des Heinrich Baryphonus', *VMw*, ix (1893), 381–92

D.-R. Moser: *Musikgeschichte der Stadt Quedlinburg von Reformation bis zur Auflösung des Stiftes (1539–1802): Beiträge zu einer Musikgeschichte des Harzraumes* (diss., U. of Göttingen, 1967)

B.V. Rivera: *German Music Theory in the Early 17th Century: the Treatises of Johannes Lippius* (Ann Arbor, 1980)

GEORGE J. BUELOW

Baryton [bariton, barydon, paradon, paridon, pariton, viola di bardone, viola di bordone] (i). A bass string instrument that is simultaneously bowed from above and plucked from behind. (The term 'lyra bastarda' is occasionally – although incorrectly – applied to the baryton.) The baryton is a hybrid instrument based on the Baroque bass viol and incorporating features of the LYRA VIOL and the BANDORA, a metal-strung plucked bass instrument. There are three basic forms: Baroque, Classical and revival. The Baroque baryton was played 'lyra-way' as a solo instrument from tablature. It had six gut bowed strings attached and adjusted like those of a bass viol, but tuned in a range of scordatura tunings (the upper manual), and nine metal bass strings (*C–d*), hitched at the fingerboard nut and tuned by wrest pins in a separate bridge (the lower manual). The metal strings lay parallel to the fingerboard on the bass side and were plucked from behind the neck with the left thumb. They provided the instrument with the capability for self-accompaniment and enhanced the sound by sympathetic resonance (*see* SYMPATHETIC STRINGS).

The number and pitch range of the metal plucked strings was later increased and sometimes a third manual, with gut strings, was added. J.G. Krause, who composed the only known published collection for baryton (*IX Partien, auf die Viola Paradon*, before 1704), suggested 18 strings as the ideal for the lower manual. Daniel Speer (*Grund-richter … Unterricht der musikalischen Kunst*, 1687, p.91) described how a set of gut drone strings might be attached on top, to be plucked by the right little finger; music for such a baryton is found in a German mid-17th-century manuscript (*D-Kl*). Speer's instrument bore six upper, 19 lower and nine drone strings.

The Classical baryton was associated especially with Joseph Haydn and the Esterházy court during the 1760s and 70s. It was a modification of the earlier instrument, with the lower manual tuned to the same pitch range as the upper four strings of the bowed manual (*c–d'*). Other features included a seventh bowed string and either diatonic or chromatic stringing in a lower manual of 15 or more metal strings. Sympathetic (lower manual) strings were now hitched to individual bridges and tuned with pegs from the head of the instrument. At the end of the Esterházy period, which lasted little more than a decade, barytons with up to 44 lower-manual strings were reported; these instruments had both the bass-register strings of the Baroque instrument and the higher-octave strings of the Esterházy tuning. The 1750 instrument by J.J. Stadlmann owned by Prince Nicolaus Esterházy has seven strings on top and ten below (see illustration). The Austrian virtuoso, Andreas Lidl, was said by C.L. Junker (*Musikalischer Almanach*, 1782, p.105) to have played an instrument with 27 underlying strings.

The modern or revival instrument is essentially a reproduction of the Esterházy instrument. Initially a range of heavier modern barytons more appropriately called cellitons was built, but, due to advances in research, light sonorous instruments are now being made again.

Barytons from all periods survive. Important 17th-century instruments may be seen in London (3), Linz (2), Vienna, Berlin and Nuremberg. 14 are known from the 18th century, three from the 19th and at least 30 from the 20th. As befits the 'instrument of kings', almost all barytons are finely decorated with carved heads (painted or plain), purfling, inlay and herring-bone edging, in materials such as ivory, ebony and mother-of-pearl.

From the beginning, the instrument was played as a lyraviol-cum-bandora. While the bowed strings carried

Baryton by Johann Joseph Stadlmann, Vienna, 1750, once in the possession of Prince Nikolaus Esterházy (Hungarian National Museum, Budapest)

the upper and lower sets of strings simultaneously; in fact, they are usually played in alternation, signalling different roles in the musical texture. The most skilled players were renowned for their ability to accompany themselves throughout, following the original baroque practice.

Mersenne (*Cogitata physico-mathematica*, 1644) was one of the first to describe the instrument, but the addition of wire strings to viols for 'bettering the sound' was described in England in the patent application of Edney and Gill in 1608 (Lasocki) and in Germany by Praetorius in 1618 (*Syntagma musicum*). Mersenne's claim that the baryton was much admired by King James I of England (*d* 1625) – and also that Daniel Farrant invented it – remains unsubstantiated. However, the theory that the baryton was introduced to the Continent from England is supported by the reference to Walter Rowe playing the baryton to Peter Mundy in Königsberg in 1641 (Temple). Rowe was an important viol teacher and most probably influential in the creation of the Swan baryton manuscript. That the baryton was little known in France is indicated by Brossard's quaint reference to it (*Dictionaire*, 1703) as a 'viola di bardone' possessing up to 44 strings, and by an article in the *Almanach musical* claiming that it had been heard in Paris for the first time when Lidl toured there in 1775 (Prince Nicolaus Esterházy had, in fact, taken his baryton with him to Paris in 1767). The rest of the instrument's commentators, except for Burney, wrote in German: Majer (*Museum musicum*, 1732), Stoessel and David (*Lexicon*, 1737), Baron (*Abriss*, 1756), L. Mozart (*Versuch*, 1756), F.A. Weber (*Charakteristik der ... Instrumente*, 1788), Albrechtsberger (*Anweisung*, 1790) and Koch (*Lexikon*, 1802).

It was in Austria that the baryton was most beloved and cultivated. Schenk (1972) cited accompanied arias in Ariosto's *Marte placato* (1707) and Fux's *Il fonte della salute, aperto dalla grazia nel Calvario* (1716) as evidence of the occasional use of the baryton in Viennese operas and oratorios. By the middle of the century, however, the Baroque bass viol repertory was decidedly out of fashion; had Prince Nicolaus not taken up the viol and later the baryton, these instruments and their repertories would have suffered neglect earlier. While most of the manuscript music for baryton is in Austrian and German libraries (Dresden and Kassel), some has found its way into the far-flung libraries of St Petersburg, Stockholm, London, Paris, New York and Washington, DC.

Prince Nicolaus may have acquired his first baryton as late as 1765 when, on a trip to Innsbruck, he purchased the Stadlmann. While there he received the first pieces for 'paridon' from his Kapellmeister, Joseph Haydn. His enthusiasm for the baryton continued for more than a decade. Meanwhile, to satisfy the prince's voracious appetite for new chamber music, Haydn was required to compose dozens of trios as well as solos, duos, quintets, octets, concertos and a cantata with obbligato baryton; Haydn also enlisted his colleagues and pupils to compose chamber works using the instrument.

Haydn's own works for baryton were composed between 1765 and 1778. His pupils and colleagues in the Esterházy band, A.L. Tomasini (from 1761, first violinist of the Esterházy Hofkapelle and ultimately Konzertmeister), Joseph Purksteiner (or Burgksteiner; from 1766, a court violinist and violist) and Anton Neumann (Kappelmeister at Olmütz [now Olomouc] Cathedral, who presented the prince with music for the baryton in the

the tune, the plucked strings accompanied. The earliest works – an anonymous collection of dances (Swan baryton MS, *c*1640; now in *RUS-SPan*), manuscripts at Kassel (bearing the dates 1653, 1669 and 1670) and the Krause publication – are notated in modified French lute tablature. Instruction on playing the instrument is best gleaned from Krause's preface (facs. in Liebner) and the music itself. Later, in the 18th century, Haydn and his followers notated their baryton parts in the treble clef, sounding an octave below; the plucked notes were indicated by numbers below the treble staff, the strings numbered from lowest to highest (the reverse of earlier practice). Bass viol solos of the period, for example those by C.F. Abel, were also written in the treble clef. It is rare in the later chamber repertory for the baryton player to be called upon to play hope of gaining special favour) composed trios in a similar style. Tomasini and Purksteiner (1768) each composed at least 24 divertimentos for baryton, violin or viola, and cello, and Neumann composed 24 divertimentos (trios with baryton, 1767), followed by a set of duets (1769). According to the biographies by Griesinger (1809) and Dies (1810), Haydn himself had, in 1769, been upbraided for imprudently surpassing his patron in skill, having secretly learnt to play the baryton. Nevertheless, in that same year the prince sought the professional barytonist Lidl as a member of his band and, more particularly, as a partner for chamber music. Lidl remained until 1774, when he embarked on a tour of France and England. During his time at Eszterháza he composed pieces for the prince; in London he published trios (without baryton) in 1776 and 1778 which are likely to have been conceived with baryton (the Hamburg manuscripts may be compared with the London publications). As a soloist, Lidl was praised for his skill at self-accompaniment. Burney, however, was not impressed, and grumbled that 'it seems with Music as with agriculture, the more barren and ungrateful the soil, the more art is necessary in its cultivation' (*BurneyH*).

In 1769 two Esterházy musicians, both of whom belonged to the coterie of barytonists, resigned their posts: Haydn's friend, the cellist Joseph Weigl, who may have composed music for baryton (see Liebner), and Carl Franz, a virtuoso horn player, barytonist and cellist for whom in 1786 Haydn is said (by Pohl) to have composed the baryton part in his cantata, *Deutschlands Klage auf den Tod Friedrichs des Grossen* (HXXVIb:1). According to Pohl, Franz's playing was at once affectingly melancholic and like 'the sweetness of the pineapple'. Weber dwelt on Franz's superb intonation and the skill with which he provided a plucked accompaniment for his music.

The character of the Esterházy works for baryton was determined by Haydn – a compromise between the idiomatic possibilities of the instrument and the capabilities of its keenest patron. Nicolaus, it must be said, had no pretensions to being a soloist. Judging from the music composed for him, he preferred a few 'safe keys' (D, G and A), related to the instrument's tuning, and a limited use of plucked strings. The only duos for baryton and cello (HXII) accordingly make no use of the underlying strings. Among the trios (HXI:1–126), fewer than half call upon the barytonist to pluck with the left thumb. However, in the duet for two barytons (HXII:4) both parts include plucked notes. Nothing is known of the technical demands of the lost chamber concertos (HXIII:1–3), the lost sonatas for baryton and cello, and the missing baryton part to the Frederick the Great cantata.

Almost all of Haydn's trios were cast in three short movements; this was, perhaps, a reflection of the limited time and attention the prince had to devote to his art. Half of the trios begin with a slow movement; nearly all include a minuet and trio. Variations on the prince's favourite contemporary tunes (mostly from works by Haydn) and fugues frequently make up the remaining movement. Some scholars have seen the fugal movements in particular as experimental essays leading to the op.20 string quartets (see Kirkendale and Wollenberg).

The most common baryton trio texture – baryton, viola and cello – was devised particularly for Nicolaus and, while born of exigency, it proved a stroke of genius. The bowed strings of the baryton blend with the viola and the cello, and the plucked strings provide a contrasting timbre. The overtones produced by the baryton's many strings compensate for the absence of a treble instrument, although Tomasini did compose trios with violin instead of viola. The overall effect mystifies the listener because the individual instruments are often impossible to differentiate. Haydn was, of course, a master of this artful subterfuge, conceding nothing in musical integrity and detail even when composing domestic music. Within the textures of the divertimentos (HX:1–12) – a quartet, quintets and octets – the pair of virtuoso horns is inevitably more prominent than the pair of barytons, making it likely that they were composed for occasions at which the prince was not playing.

The true extent of the repertory, 17th- as well as 18th-century, remains to be determined. A manuscript collection (discovered in the early 1960s, in *A-SCH*) contains further works from the late 18th century: divertimentos for unaccompanied baryton by F.A. Deleschin and the Viennese father and son, Francesco and Giuseppe di Fauner; a sonata for 'viole paridon o viola da gamba', violin and cello by Joseph Fiala, the Czech oboist and viol player who was an intimate of the Mozart family in Salzburg; and a *Parthia per il baritono e violino* by the cathedral musician, J.P. Ziegler (*d* 1767). Similar repositories may exist elsewhere in Austria and Hungary.

Around the turn of the century the baryton still had a few exponents. Vincenz Hauschka, by profession a Viennese court official and member of the board of directors of the Gesellschaft der Musikfreunde, was, according to Pohl, an accomplished player. He contributed two collections of songs with baryton accompaniment (*Cinque notturni* for three solo voices, baryton and guitar, and *Sei canzonetti italiani* for solo voice and baryton); Fétis further attributed five quintets (baryton and string quartet) and five duets for baryton and cello to Hauschka. S.L. Friedl was a cellist, barytonist and composer attached to the Prussian Royal Chapel in Berlin from 1793 to 1826. According to the *Allgemeine musikalische Zeitung*, xiii (1811), he performed a potpourri (after Lefèvre) of his own arrangement on the baryton. He may have left manuscript works for the instrument. During the 1846–7 Paris concert season, Félix Battachon attempted to generate fresh interest in the baryton. The more successful late 20th-century revival was led by players such as José Vázquez, K.M. Schwamberger, A. Lessing, Janos Liebner, Riki Gerardy, John Hsu and Jörg Eggebrecht. Over 20 composers have written new works for baryton since 1960, including Ferenc Farkas and Stephen Dodgson (Gartrell, 1983). All compositions to date in the 20th century have used the Esterházy lower-manual tuning. The International Baryton Society was formed in 1993 to coordinate and promote baryton research and performance.

BIBLIOGRAPHY

L. Greilsamer: 'Le baryton du Prince Esterházy', *Revue musicale mensuelle*, i (1910), 45

R.C. Temple: *The Travels of Peter Mundy, in Europe and Asia, 1608–1667*, Hakluyt Society, 2nd ser., lvi (London, 1925/R), 104–5

W.O. Strunk: 'Haydn's Divertimenti for Baryton, Viola, Bass', *MQ*, xviii (1932), 216–51

B. Csuka: 'Haydn és a baryton', *Zenetudományi tanulmányok*, vi (1957), 669–728

E. Fruchtman: *The Baryton Trios of Tomasini, Burgksteiner, and Neumann* (diss., U. of North Carolina, 1960)

K.M. Schwamberger: 'Das Baryton: ein vergessenes Instrument aus der Barockzeit', *NZM*, 122 (1961), 439–42

E. Fruchtman: 'The Baryton: its History and its Music Re-examined', *AcM*, xxxiv (1962), 2–17

J. Liebner: 'The Baryton', *The Consort*, xxiii (1966), 109–28

H. Walter and M. Härtig: Preface and critical commentary to *J. Haydn: Barytontrios*, Werke, xiv/5 (1968–9)

S. Gerlach: Preface and critical commentary to *J. Haydn: Werke mit Baryton*, Werke, xiii (1969–70)

H. Unverricht: 'Zur Chronologie der Barytontrios', *Symbolae historiae musicae: Hellmut Federhofer zum 60. Geburtstag* (Mainz, 1971), 180–89

A Lessing: 'Zur Geschichte des Barytons', *Beiträge zur Musikgeschichte des 18. Jahrhunderts*, i/2 (1971), 143–53

E. Schenk: Preface to *L. Tomasini: Ausgewählte Instrumentalwerke*, DTÖ, cxxiv (1972)

S. Wollenberg: 'Haydn's Baryton Trios and the "Gradus"', *ML*, liv (1973), 170–78

J. Webster: 'Towards a History of Viennese Chamber Music in the Early Classical Period', *JAMS*, xxvii (1974), 212–47

E. Zimmermann: 'Theorbierte Lauten und die Viola di baritone: frühe Saiteninstrumente von Erich Zimmermann beschrieben', *Instrumentenbau*, xxxi (1977), 366

H.C.R. Landon: *Haydn at Eszterháza, 1766–1790* (London, 1978)

H.C.R. Landon: *Haydn: the Early Years, 1732–1765* (London, 1980)

J. Braun and S. Gerlach: Preface and critical commentary to *J. Haydn: Barytontrios*, Werke, xiv/1 (1980)

S. Gerlach: 'The Reconstructed Original Version of Haydn's Baryton Trio Hob. XI:2', *Haydn Studies* [Washington DC 1975], ed. J.P. Larsen, H. Serwer and J. Webster (New York, 1981), 84–7

C. Gartrell: 'The Origins and Development of the Baryton', *Chelys*, xi (1982), 4–7

C. Gartrell: *The Baryton: its History and Music* (diss., U. of Surrey, 1983)

T. Crawford: 'Constantijn Hughgens and the "Engelsche Viool"', *Chelys*, xviii (1989), 41–61

P. Holman: 'An Addicion of Wyer Stringes Beside the Ordenary Stringes: the Origin of the Baryton?', *Companion to Contemporary Musical Thought*, ii (London, 1992), 1098–1115

T. Crawford and F.-P. Goy, eds.: *The St. Petersburg 'Swan' Manuscript: a Facsimile of Manuscript O No. 124, Library of the St Petersburg Academy of Sciences* (Columbus, OH, 1994)

T.M. Pamplin: 'A Baryton Discography', *International Baryton Society* (London, 1994)

T.M. Pamplin: *The Baryton in the Seventeenth Century, from its Origins at the English Court of James I* (diss., Kingston University, in preparation)

JULIE ANNE SADIE, TERENCE M. PAMPLIN

Baryton (ii) (1) (Fr.). A valved brass instrument in B♭, the same as the English baritone. *See* BARITONE (ii).

(2) (Ger.) The tenor tuba in B♭. *See* TUBA (i) and EUPHONIUM.

Baryton (iii) (Fr.). *See* BARITONE (i).

Barzelletta (It.: 'jest'). Of the different verse forms set by frottola composers, the *barzelletta* appears to have been the most popular, especially in earlier publications (until about 1510). Whereas the term 'frottola' is generic, referring to a variety of prosodic types, in its specific meaning it is usually synonymous with the *barzelletta*, as suggested by Petrucci's fourth book, *Strambotti, ode, frottole* [= *barzellette*], *sonetti* (RISM 1505⁵), or Antico's third book, *Canzoni, sonetti, strambotti et frottole* [= *barzellette*] (1513¹). The *barzelletta* normally scans in trochaic metre, with eight syllables per line (trochaic *ottonario*), and consists of two sections: *ripresa*, four lines that rhyme as *abba* or *abab*; and stanza, six or eight lines in the order of two *mutazioni* or *piedi* (pairs of lines with identical rhymes) and a *volta* (a couplet or quatrain, whose last line generally rhymes with the first of the *ripresa*). A six-line stanza is likely to rhyme as *cdcdda* and an eight-line one as *cdcddeea*. Anticipated in the connect-

ing rhyme or *concatenazione*, the *ripresa* as a whole or, more often, in part (two lines) recurs before successive stanzas (which number anywhere from two to five or more) and after the last one. Some *barzellette* are sung to two musical units (*AB*), others to four (*ABCD*) or more, depending on how many phrases of the *ripresa* are incorporated into the stanza. A two-unit structure may consist of *AB* for the *ripresa*, *AA* for the *piedi*, *B* for the *volta* and *A* for the *ripresa*. When new material appears in the stanza, it may be arranged as *CC* for the *piedi* and *D* for the *volta*. Musical phrases are often equal in length, grouping symmetrically into units of three or four measures. With its trochaic metre, the *barzelletta* tends to be lively and dance-like, with heavy downbeats and accents at the cadence (since Italian usually has stresses on the penultimate, the result is a sequence of strong–weak beats, leading to the so-called 'feminine' cadence, corresponding to a *verso piano*). In this respect it differs from the more languid strambotto, with 11 syllables in iambic verse (and the last syllable falling on a downbeat). The *barzelletta* relates, in prosody, to the ballata (and the French virelai), the *lauda* (of which many examples were *barzellette* supplied with sacred texts) and the Spanish cantiga or villancico. An etymological connection with the bergerette (a monostrophic virelai) may be assumed. *See* FROTTOLA.

DON HARRÁN

Barzin, Leon (Eugene) (*b* Brussels, 27 Nov 1900; *d* Naples, FL, 29 April 1999). American conductor and educator of Belgian birth. Taken to America in 1902 and naturalized in 1924, he studied the violin and viola first with his father, who was principal viola in the Metropolitan Opera Orchestra, and then with Edouard Deru, Pierre Henrotte, Eugène Meergerhin and Eugène Ysaÿe. He also studied composition with Lilienthal before joining the salon orchestra at the Hotel Astor in New York in 1917. By 1919 Barzin had moved to the second violin section of the National SO, shortly before it merged with the New York Philharmonic SO; he became first viola in the New York PO (1925–9). On Toscanini's advice he left this post to become assistant conductor of the American Orchestral Society, which he reorganized in 1930 as the National Orchestral Association with himself as music director (1930–59 and 1969–76). He had other appointments: music director of the Ballet Society, which became the New York City Ballet (1948–58), conductor of the Hartford (Connecticut) SO (1938–40) and guest conductor with the New York PO; however, he was primarily a teacher and a great trainer of young orchestras. His National Orchestral Association was a semi-professional training group for young musicians and he had great success broadcasting with them on local radio stations. The association became the training ground for thousands of musicians who went on to play in professional orchestras. While in Paris conducting the Orchestre Pasdeloup (1958–60), he was also an instructor at the Schola Cantorum and was made a member of the Légion d'Honneur. He also received the Columbia University Ditson Award and the Gold Medal of Lebanon.

JOSÉ BOWEN

Barzun, Jacques (*b* Créteil, 30 Nov 1907). American cultural historian and critic of French origin. He went to the USA in 1920 and was a pupil of Carlton J.H. Hayes at Columbia University (BA 1927), where he took the doctorate in 1932 with a dissertation on the origins of the

French race while working as lecturer (from 1927); he was then appointed assistant professor (1937), professor (1945), Seth Low Professor of History (1955) and university professor (1967). He also served as dean and provost (1955–67) and president of the American Academy of Arts (1972–5; 1977–8), and was made extraordinary Fellow of Cambridge University in 1960.

His writings have been mainly concerned with 19th-century European and 20th-century American culture. His work in music, which represents only part of his entire output, has centred on Berlioz, the subject of his large and exhaustively documented *Berlioz and the Romantic Century* (1950), a pioneering reappraisal of Berlioz's standing and achievement approached from a cultural rather than musicological standpoint. Its influence on postwar Berlioz appreciation has been profound. He has also edited a volume of Berlioz's letters (1954) and translated *Les soirées de l'orchestre* (1956). As a critic Barzun's work is wide-ranging, with a special understanding of the Romantic movement and its belief that music begins to speak at the point where words stop. He has consistently propounded the chief Romantic virtues of energy, sincerity, diversity and imagination as antidotes to the sicknesses of 20th-century society.

WRITINGS

The French Race: Theories of its Origins and their Social and Political Implications Prior to the Revolution (diss., Columbia U., 1932; New York, 1932)
Darwin, Marx and Wagner: Critique of a Heritage (Boston, 1941/R, 2/1958/R)
Berlioz and the Romantic Century (Boston, 1950, rev., abridged 2/1956/R as *Berlioz and his Century*, rev. 3/1969 under orig. title)
ed.: *The Pleasures of Music* (New York, 1951, 2/1977)
Music into Words (Washington DC, 1953); repr. in *Lectures on the History and Art of Music: the Louis Charles Elson Memorial Lectures at the Library of Congress, 1946–1963* (New York, 1968), 65–93
ed. and trans.: *New Letters of Berlioz, 1830–1868* (New York, 1954/R)
Evenings with the Orchestra (New York, 1956) [trans. of H. Berlioz: *Les soirées de l'orchestre* (Paris, 1852)]
Music in American Life (Garden City, NY, 1956)
The Energies of Art (New York, 1956/R)
'Berlioz in 1969: a Fantasia for Friends Overseas', *Adam International Review*, nos.331–3 (1969), 33–108
'Berlioz a Hundred Years After', *MQ*, lvi (1970), 1–13
'Biography and Criticism: a Misalliance Disputed', *Critical Inquiry*, i (1975), 479–96
ed. B. Friedland: *Critical Questions on Music and Letters, Culture and Biography, 1940–1980* (Chicago, 1982)
'Paris in 1830', *Music in Paris in the Eighteen-Thirties*, ed. P. Bloom (Stuyvesant, NY, 1987), 1–22
The Culture We Deserve (Middletown, CT, 1989)
'Overheard at Glimmerglass ("Famous last words")', *Berlioz Studies*, ed. P. Bloom (Cambridge, 1992), 254–71

BIBLIOGRAPHY

D.B. Weiner and W.R. Keylor, eds.: *From Parnassus: Essays in Honor of Jacques Barzun* (New York, 1976) [incl. L. Trilling: 'A Personal Memoir', xv–xxii; B. Clarke: 'The Impact of a Personality', 337–41; C.C. Brown: 'The Scholar as Adminstrator', 342–9; list of writings, 353–76]

HUGH MACDONALD

Baschny, Józef. *See* BASZNY, JÓZEF.

Bas-dessus (Fr.: 'low treble'). Term used, especially in French sources, to denote a female voice below the soprano or *haut-dessus* – in effect a second soprano or MEZZO-SOPRANO. Rousseau (*Dictionnaire*, 1768) specifically identifies these as vocal terms, as opposed to the instrumental first and second treble (*premier dessus* and *second dessus*).

Until the mid-18th century the vocal term was associated only with part-singing. Brossard (*Dictionaire*, 1703) defines it as a second treble part; as early as 1597 Morley describes a bass descant as 'that kinde of descanting, where your sight of taking and using your cordes must be under the plainsong'. However, Rousseau points to the solo use of this voice in Italy and writes that the 'beautiful *bas-dessus*, full and sonorous, is no less esteemed in Italy than the soprano'. Although he says that France pays 'no regard' to these voices, he cites a Mlle Gondré (whose name appears on a 'Second Dessus' part for an 18th-century performance of Lully's *Armide*) for her 'very beautiful *bas-dessus*' that was 'very much applauded' at the Paris Opéra.

Choral writing in French operas from Lully onwards frequently made use of a three-part high-voice *petit choeur*, where the middle part was for *bas-dessus* and the lowest for the male HAUTE-CONTRE. In Rossini's *Guillaume Tell* (1829), both upper voices in four-part choruses were labelled 'dessus', the lower voice corresponding to the *bas-dessus*. Berlioz (*Grande traité d'instrumentation*, 1844) drew attention to Gluck's choruses of priestesses in *Iphigénie en Tauride*, which are for *dessus* and *bas-dessus* only, and observed that 'it cannot be denied that, in France, [Nature] is very sparing of [contraltos]'. *See also* ALTO (i).

BIBLIOGRAPHY

L. Rosow: 'Performing a Choral Dialogue by Lully', *EMc*, xv (1987), 325–35

LIONEL SAWKINS, ELLEN T. HARRIS

Baseggio [Basseggio], Lorenzo (*b c*1660; *d* before 1719). Italian composer. He wrote the opera *L'Adimiro* (text, B. Pisani) for Treviso in 1687 and his oratorio, *Il re pentito* (Padua, 1710), was performed at the home of Count Antonio Alberto De Conti. One of his masses was sung at SS Giovanni e Paolo, Venice, on 29 December 1712 to celebrate the canonization of Pius V. Two of Baseggio's settings of texts by Francesco Passarini also appeared in that year: the *favola boschereccia*, *Gli equivoci del caso* was performed at Dolo, near Venice, in June (*AllacciD*), and *Amor e fortuna* was performed at the Teatro Campagnella, Rovigo, in the autumn. His opera *Laomedonte* (text, G.B. Guizzardi or G.B. Ruperti) was performed at the Teatro S Moisè, Venice, in 1715. Baseggio was a member of the Venetian instrumentalists' guild from at least 1694 to about 1715. A motet, *Pulchra Sum suavis*, for soprano, two violins and continuo, survives (in *D-Bsb*).

BIBLIOGRAPHY

EitnerQ; *FétisB*; *SartoriL*; *SchmidlD*
C. Bonlini: *Le glorie della poesia e della musica* (Venice, 1730)
E. Selfridge-Field: 'Annotated Membership Lists of the Venetian Instrumentalists' Guild, 1672–1727', *RMARC*, no.9 (1971), 1–52; no.12 (1974), 152–5
M. Talbot: *Benedetto Vinaccesi: a Musician in Brescia and Venice in the Age of Corelli* (Oxford, 1994)

THOMAS WALKER/BETH L. GLIXON

Basel (Ger.). *See* BASLE.

Baselli [Boselli, Bosello], Constantino (*fl* Vicenza, 1600–40). Italian composer and singer. He apparently spent his career at Vicenza. He was probably a pupil of Leone Leoni, *maestro di cappella* at Vicenza Cathedral from 1588 to 1607, and certainly had connections at Vicenza by 1600, since his second book of canzonettas, dedicated from there, includes pieces by Leoni and his circle. The dedication of the first to Lorenzo Beccaria suggests that Baselli may have been in his service before 1600. He evidently took holy orders between 1600, when the title-pages of his works refer to him in secular terms, and 8 November 1605, when he is first listed in the *Libri dei processi* of the cathedral as a priest and singer. Eitner claimed that he was *maestro di cappella* there, but this is not supported by the *Libri*, which consistently list him as a singer up to the last reference, on 19 February 1631. Nothing more is known of him until the appearance in 1640 of the *Grati, gratiosi, giocondi, gioiosi et graditi canti*, dedicated to Count G.B. Porta of Vicenza. The forward matter of this publication is unusually elaborate: Porta's coat-of-arms (f.2) is followed by a portrait of Baselli, and the 17 pieces in the book are preceded by verses addressed to Baselli and his letter to the readers. Most of the music is for three voices and one work, *Poi che l'humil capanna*, is strophic.

WORKS
published in Venice

Il primo libro delle canzonette, 3vv (1600)
Il secondo libro delle canzonette, 3vv (1600¹²)
Il primo libro de sacri concerti, 2–4vv, bc (1614), lost, *MischiatiI*
Sacrarum modulationum . . . liber secundus, 2–4vv, bc (1618), lost, *MischiatiI*
Grati, gratiosi, giocondi, gioiosi et graditi canti . . . libro primo, 1–4vv, bc, op.5 (1640)

BIBLIOGRAPHY
EitnerQ; MischiatiI
G. Mantese: *Storia musicale vicentina* (Vicenza, 1956)

IAIN FENLON

Baselt, Bernd (*b* Halle, 13 Sept 1934; *d* Hanover, 18 Oct 1993). German musicologist. He studied with Max Schneider and Walther Siegmund-Schultze at the University of Halle and took the doctorate in 1963 with a dissertation on P.H. Erlebach; he completed the *Habilitation* in 1974 with a thematic catalogue of Handel's stage works. In 1983 he succeeded Siegmund-Schultze as professor at the University and as director of its Musikwissenschaftliches Institut. As a member of the board of the Georg-Friedrich-Händel-Gesellschaft in Halle, Baselt was made a vice-president in 1987, secretary in 1990 and president in 1991, a position he held until his death. In 1991 he also became chief editor of the Hallische Händel-Ausgabe, on whose editorial board he had served for many years; at the same time he took over the editorship of the *Händel-Jahrbuch*.

Baselt was the leading German Handel scholar of his generation: his major contribution to Handel studies is the comprehensive thematic catalogue of the composer's works (HWV) published in three volumes as a supplement to the Hallische Händel-Ausgabe. His achievement is the more remarkable in that the work was done while Baselt was living in the German Democratic Republic, when opportunities for travel to England to consult the sources located there were limited. He played a major part both in raising the standard of the Händel-Ausgabe and introducing authentic performing practice of Handel's works, particularly the operas, to the annual festival in Halle. Although Handel became his main interest, Baselt was also an authority on other music of the Baroque period in Middle Germany; he edited works by Telemann and other composers, and his many writings contributed to a greater understanding of the German background in which Handel was brought up.

WRITINGS
'Friedrich Wilhelm Zachow und die protestantische Kirchenkantate', *Festschrift der II Händelfestspiele Halle (Saale)* (Halle, 1962), 45–54
'Georg Philipp Telemann und die protestantische Kirchenmusik', *Musik und Kirche*, xxxvii (1967), 196–207
Die Bühnenwerke Georg Friedrich Händels: Quellenstudien und thematisches Verzeichnis (Habilitationsschrift, U. of Halle, 1974) [2 vols.]
'Händel und Bach: zur Frage der Passionen', *Johann Sebastian Bach und Georg Friedrich Händel: Halle 1975*, 58–66
'Zum Parodieverfahren in Händels frühen Opern', *Zur Wort-Ton Problematik bei Händel: Halle 1974* [HJb 1975–6], 19–39
ed.: J.A. Hiller: *Anweisung zum musikalisch-zierlichen Gesange* (Leipzig, 1976)
'Miscellanea Haendeliana', *Der Komponist und sein Adressat: Halle 1976*, 60–88 [on Handel and Muffat]
'Georg Philipp Telemann und die Opernlibrettistik seiner Zeit', *Telemann und seine Dichter: Magdeburg 1977*, 31–51
'Georg Philipp Telemanns Serenade *Don Quichotte auf der Hochzeit des Comacho*: Beiträge zur Entstehungsgeschichte', *HJbMw*, iii (1978), 255–269
'Händel auf dem Wege nach Italien', *G.F. Händel und seine italienischen Zeitgenossen: Halle 1978*, 10–21
G.F. Handel: Thematisch-systematisches Verzeichnis, i: *Bühnenwerke*; ii: *Oratorische Werke, vokale Kammermusik, Kirchenmusik*; iii: *Instrumentalmusik, Pasticci und Fragmente*, Händel-Handbuch, i–iii (Leipzig and Kassel, 1978–86)
'Wiederentdeckung von Fragmenten aus Händels verschollenen Hamburger Opern', *HJb 1983*, 7–24
'Muffat and Handel: a Two-Way Exchange', *MT*, cxx (1979), 904–7
'Vorbemekung zum Libretto von Händels verschollener Oper *Der beglückte Florindo*', *HJb 1984*, 21–73 [incl. facs. of libretto]
ed., with W. Siegmund-Schulze: *Händel-Festspiele XXXV: Halle 1986* [HJb 1987] [incl. 'Georg Friedrich Händels Pasticcio Jupiter in Argos und seine quellenmässige Überlieferung,' 57–71]
ed., with S. Flesch: *Aufklärerische Tendenzen in der Musik des 18. Jahrhunderts und ihre Rezeption: Walther Siegmund-Schultze zum 70. Geburtstag* (Halle, 1987) [incl. 'Der spanische Erbfolgekrieg, Italien und Händel', 10–31]
'Handel and his Central German Background', *Handel, Tercentenary Collection: London 1987*, 43–60
ed., with W. Siegmund-Schultze: *Das mitteldeutsche Musikleben vor Händel; Christoph Willibald Gluck: Halle 1988* [incl. 'Die hallesche Musikkultur im Zeitalter des jungen Händel', 58–75]
Georg Friedrich Händel (Leipzig, 1988)
'Georg Friedrich Händels Messias', *Zwischen Bach und Mozart: Stuttgart 1988*, 150–65
'Parodie oder Pasticcio? Zu Händels Schaffensmethode', *Göttinger Händel-Beiträge*, iii (1989), 264–8
ed.: *Musikalisches Füllhorn: Günter Fleischhauer zum 60. Geburtstag* (Halle, 1990) [incl. 'Händels englische Oratorien und ihre Anfänge', 5–11]
'Die Oper um 1700 im mitteldeutschen Raum', *HJb 1990*, 17–31
'Zu einigen gattungstypologischen Besonderheiten in Händels Opern nach antiken Vorlagen', *Gattungskonventionen der Händel-Oper: Karlsruhe 1990 and 1991*, 63–74
'Die frühdeutsche Oper am Schwarzburg-Rudolstädtischen Hofe unter Philipp Heinrich Erlebach (1657–1714)', *Musiktheatralische Formen in kleinen Residenzen: Arolsen 1992*, 32–51
'Brandenburg-Prussia and the Central German Courts', *Man & Music/Music and Society: The Late Baroque Era*, ed. J.G. Buelow (London, 1993), 230–53
'Early German Handel Editions during the Classical Period', *Handel Collections and their History: London 1993*, 238–48
'Händel und die Londoner "Royal Academy of Music"', *Akademie und Musik: Erscheinungsweisen und Wirkungen des Akademiegedankens in Kultur- und Musikgeschichte: Festschrift für Werner Braun*, ed. W. Frobenius and others (Saarbrücken, 1993), 147–56
'Georg Friedrich Händels Gestalt und äusseres Wesen', *HJb 1994–5*, 13–22

EDITIONS
Georg Philipp Telemann: *Musikalische Werke*, xx: *Der geduldige Sokrates* (Kassel, 1967); xxi: *Der neumodische Liebhaber Damon, oder Die Satyrn in Arkadien*, (Kassel, 1969)
C.W. Gluck: *Il Parnasso confuso*, Sämtliche Werke, iii/25 (Kassel, 1970)

G.F. Handel: *Oreste*, Hallische Händel–Ausgabe, ii/suppl.1 (Kassel, 1991)
G.P. Telemann: *Don Qichotte auf der Hochzeit des Comacho*, RRMBA, lxiv–lxv (1991)

BIBLIOGRAPHY
K. Hortschansky and K. Musketa, eds.: *Georg Friedrich Händel: ein Lebensinhalt: Gedenkschrift für Bernd Baselt* (Halle, 1995) [incl. list of writings, 537–49]

TERENCE BEST

Baseo, Francesco Antonio (*b* Lecce; *fl* 1573–82). Italian composer. Of the 28 compositions in his earliest recorded publication, *Il primo libro delle canzoni villanesche alla napolitana a quattro voci* (Venice, 1573[17]), only 18 are by Baseo himself, the rest being the work of seven other composers, unknown except for these pieces, together with some anonymous works. This, together with the tone of the dedication to Baseo's patron Antonio Mettula, suggests that the book represents the activities of a small musical academy that gathered at Mettula's house in Lecce and which included other members of Mettula's family. According to the title-page of the *Primo libro de madrigali a cinque voci, composti da diversi eccell. autori* (Venice, 1573[16]), Baseo had been appointed *maestro di cappella* at Lecce Cathedral by this date. The publication, which was assembled by Baseo, contains five of his own compositions together with pieces by Felis, Le Roy, Monte, Nola, Ortiz and Palestrina.

IAIN FENLON

Basevi, Abramo (*b* Livorno, 29 Nov 1818; *d* Florence, 25 Nov 1885). Italian music critic. Brought up in a wealthy Jewish family, he embarked simultaneously on classical and musical studies. He graduated in medicine from Pisa University and studied composition under Pietro Romani, having an opera performed in Florence in 1840 and another in 1847. Both were unsuccessful with the general public, although praised by some connoisseurs. Giving up composition, he soon became a prominent figure in Florentine cultural life as a critic and organizer. He founded and edited the journal *L'armonia* (1856–9). Through him began the Mattinate Beethoveniane, a series of concerts from which derived the Società del Quartetto di Firenze (1861), whose journal *Boccherini* (1862–82) he also edited, as well as a cycle of concerts of dramatic music (1865) dedicated to classic Italian opera composers such as Sacchini and Spontini, then largely forgotten. In 1861 he instituted an annual competition for string quartet composition and in 1863 organized the Concerti Popolari a Grande Orchestra. He was also from 1855 a member of the Istituto Musicale of the Accademia di Belle Arti, a *consigliere censore* of the Florence Liceo Musicale from its founding in 1859 and a corresponding member of the Brussels Academy of Music.

Basevi was one of the most important and influential figures in Italian criticism in the middle of the 19th century, especially in the movement to reform the Italian musical scene by bringing in new influences. He sought to re-establish a sense of Italy's own musical tradition by creating interest in its older, forgotten composers and collaborated with the publisher G.G. Guidi in bringing out cheap editions of classic Italian works. The concerts he set up were intended to awaken Italians to the German instrumental tradition, then little known. He was an early supporter of Wagner, but did not advocate the wholesale adoption by Italians of the Wagnerian system. Verdi he recognized as a skilful, sometimes inspired, musician, and

his articles on the earlier Verdi operas (up to *Aroldo*), collected into a book in 1859, are still one of the most valuable and perceptive works of Verdi criticism. However, Basevi saw Verdi as one who followed the taste of the time rather than moulding and improving it. For him the most significant contemporary figure was Meyerbeer, whose work, seen as a synthesis of German learning and Italian melody, provided the most appropriate model for Italians to follow.

Basevi published numerous journal articles, some of which are collected in books. In his later years he gave most of his attention to philosophy, on which he also published several works. His valuable library was left to the Istituto Musicale, forming one of its most important holdings.

WRITINGS
Memoria relativa al progetta di riordinamento delle scuole musicali di Firenze (MS, 1855–60, I-Fc)
Studio sulle opere di Giuseppe Verdi (Florence, 1859)
Introduzione ad un nuovo sistema d'armonia (Florence, 1862)
Studi sull'armonia (Florence, 1865)
Compendio della storia della musica (Florence, 1865–6)
Beethoven op.18 con analisi dei sei quartetti (Florence, 1874)

BIBLIOGRAPHY
DBI (A. Pironti); *ES* (E. Zanetti); *FétisB*; *RicordiE*; *SchmidlD*
A. Parenti: 'Il problema della critica verdiana', *RaM*, vi (1933), 197–218
A. Della Corte: *La critica musicale e i critici* (Turin, 1961), 481ff
S. Martinotti: 'Cronache dell'Ottocento sulla musica strumentale in Italia', *Convegno musicale*, i (1964), 211
L. Pinzauti: 'Prospettive per uno studio sulla musica a Firenze nell'Ottocento', *NRMI*, ii (1968), 255–73
B. Friedland: 'Italy's Ottocento: Notes from the Musical Underground', *MQ*, lvi (1970), 27–53
A. Roccatagliati: 'Le forme dell'opera ottocentesca: il caso Basevi', *Le parole della musica: studi sulla lingua della letteratura musicale in onore di Gianfranco Folena*, ed. F. Nicolodi and P. Trovato (Florence, 1994), 311–34
A.M. Trivisonno: 'The Basevi Collection in the Library of Cherubini Conservatory, Florence (Italy)', *FAM*, xxxii (1985), 114–17

LEONARDO PINZAUTI

Baseya, Joan (*b* Mataró, nr Barcelona; *fl* 1679). Spanish composer and organist. As organist and choirmaster of Vich Cathedral he participated in a jury formed in October 1679 to choose an organist for S María del Mar, Barcelona. When the post again became vacant in 1687 one 'Joan Basseya', described as a priest and organist of Ripoll, competed for it without success; he is unlikely to have been the same person as the distinguished organist of Vich, but doubt is cast on the authorship of the surviving compositions. Baseya's reputation rests chiefly on three organ tientos (*E-Bc* 729; ed. H. Anglés, *Antología de organistas españoles del siglo XVII*, ii and iv, Barcelona, 1966 and 1968) which stand out in the 17th-century Spanish keyboard repertory for their sparkling counterpoint and skilful construction: they suggest the variation canzona infused with typically Spanish figuration. Two are for divided register, calling for the Gaitilla or Bagpipe stop in the right hand; the third is for undivided keyboard (*lleno*). A nine-part mass with instruments and two four-part villancicos attributed to Baseya are also extant (in *E-Bc*). José Elías may have studied with him as well as with Cabanilles.

BIBLIOGRAPHY
FrotscherG
F. Pedrell: *Catàlech de la Biblioteca musical de la Diputació de Barcelona*, ii (Barcelona, 1909)

J. Soler i Palet: 'La música a Catalunya: a Santa María del Mar', *Revista musical catalana*, xviii (1921), 19–27

H. Anglés: 'Els organistes i la música d'orgue a Catalunya en els segles XVIIè i XVIIIè', *Revista catalana de música*, i (1923), 29

ALMONTE HOWELL/LOUIS JAMBOU

Bashir, Djamil (*b* Al Mawsil, 1921; *d* Baghdad, 1977). Iraqi *'ūd* and violin player. He was born into a musical family and received his first musical education from his father, who played the *'ūd* and was a famous constructor of the instrument in Al Mawsil. Djamil studied the *'ūd* with al-Sharif Muhieddin Haidar and the violin with the Romanian Sando Albo at the Institute of Fine Arts in Baghdad. He became one of the best representatives of the Baghdad lute school which aimed to give the *'ūd* the status of a solo concert instrument. His musical activities were manifold. He accompanied important singers of the Iraqi *maqām*, thus acquiring knowledge of the Iraqi classical traditions; later he used this material in his *'ūd* and violin improvisations. His training in both European and Arab-Ottoman music helped him to create a new technique and a specific style for violin playing in Iraq. He also produced instrumental arrangements of Iraqi folksongs. He composed more than 20 pieces in various instrumental forms (*bashraf*, *samā'i*, *lunga*), some dance compositions and a concerto for *'ūd*, violin and symphony orchestra. In 1949 he published a collection of national anthems for schoolteachers. He used his knowledge of the Iraqi tradition and the instrumental technique he acquired from al-Sharif Muhieddin to write the first *'ūd* tutor in

Iraq; published in 1961, it contains six levels of exercises based on Ottoman, Arab and Iraqi compositions. Unlike his younger brother MUNIR BASHIR, he was not widely known in the West.

SCHEHERAZADE QASSIM HASSAN

Bashir, Munir (*b* Mosul, 1930; *d* Budapest, 1997). Iraqi *'ūd* player, brother of DJAMIL BASHIR. He studied with al-Sharif Muhieddin Haidar at the Institute of Fine Arts in Baghdad and was also influenced by his elder brother . They both earned a living accompanying singers of the Iraqi *maqām*. From 1966 to 1973 he worked in Beirut as a producer, an arranger of folksongs and a musician in the ensemble of the Lebanese singer Fayrūz. During the 1970s Bashir's career took a new direction; under the influence of the musicologists Simon Jargy and Poul Rovsing Olsen, he limited his playing to solo improvisations (*taqsīm*), which brought him international recognition. In 1973 he became an artistic consultant to the Iraqi government, and was appointed head of the newly constituted Department of Music of the Ministry of Culture and Information. He regrouped the existing musical institutions within the department and centralized the process of making decisions, and also created some official troupes. His position helped to bring him world-wide contacts and the possibility of an international career; he gave recitals in about 50 countries and received numerous honorary positions, degrees and state medals. Bashir's music depends extensively on the melodic mate-

Munir Bashir playing the 'ūd, using the 'baṣm' technique with his right hand while the left hand produces harmonic pitches

rial of the Iraqi *maqām*; by treating this material through improvisations and using the techniques of the Sharif school, he initiated a new trend in '*ūd* playing, achieving al-Sharif Muhieddin's goal of developing a new role for the instrument beyond its use in vocal art. Bashir's music has been diffused through numerous recordings).

SCHEHERAZADE QASSIM HASSAN

Bashkirov, Dmitry (Aleksandrovich) (*b* Tbilisi, 1 Nov 1931). Russian pianist. He was introduced to music by his grandmother and studied with Anastasia Virsaladze at the Tbilisi Conservatory from 1938 to 1949 and subsequently from 1950 to 1955 with Goldenweiser at the Moscow Conservatory, where he began to teach in 1957. Bashkirov's best-known pupils, Dmitry Alekseyev and Nikolay Demidenko, share his intensity of temperament, which borders on wildness. After winning a prize at the 1955 Marguerite Long-Jacques Thibaud Competition in Paris, Bashkirov rapidly developed his performing career both in Russia and the West, making some 30 recordings for Melodiya and, more recently, also recording for Harmonia Mundi and Erato. He formed a well-known trio with violinist Igor' Bezrodny and cellist Mikhail Komnitzer. Between 1980 and 1988 he was forbidden to tour outside the Eastern bloc, and in 1991 he made a second home in Madrid, teaching at the Queen Sofia High School for Music.

WRITINGS

'Tol'ko li étim putyom idti v mastera?' [Is this the only path to artistic perfection?], *SovM* (1983), no.9, pp.61–3
'Bezgranichnost' oshchushcheniya muzïki' [The infinitude of musical awareness], *SovM* (1985), no.6, pp.41–2
'Bït' dostoynïm pamyati uchitelya' [To be worthy of the memory of a teacher], *SovM*, (1990), no.1, pp.80–84

BIBLIOGRAPHY

V. Yuzefovich: 'Besedï s masterami' [Conversations with the masters], *SovM* (1981), no.3, pp.61–9 [interview with Bashkirov]
M. Zilberquit: *Russia's Great Modern Pianists* (Neptune, NJ, 1983), 441–73 [interview with Bashkirov]
G. Tsïpin: *Portretï sovetskikh pianistov* (Moscow, 1990), 198–208
D. Elder: 'Great Russian Pianists', *Clavier*, xxxi (1991/2), 34–6

DAVID FANNING

Bashmakov, Leonid (*b* Terijoki [now Zelengorsk, Russia], 1 April 1927). Finnish composer and conductor. He studied the piano, orchestral conducting and composition (with Merikanto) at the Sibelius Academy in Helsinki (1947–54). He taught at the music college in Kotka before being appointed theory teacher at the Tampere Conservatory in 1959, and rector in 1979. He was conductor of the TTT-Theatre of Tampere between 1960 and 1984.

As a composer his stylistic roots lie in neo-classicism. In his works of the 1960s in particular, his use of melodies based on 2nds and 4ths, and his handling of rhythm and the orchestra, point to Bartók and to his teacher Merikanto. Bashmakov abandoned 12-note technique after his First Symphony (1963) in favour of free chromatic tonality and motivic techniques. The Stravinskian characteristics typical of Bashmakov's generation do not, however, emerge until his ballet *Tumma* ('Dark', 1976) and the closely related Fourth Symphony and Passacaglia. These are dramatically and colourfully orchestrated works marked by the sharp contrasting of characters. The textures are for the most part linear and contrapuntal in construction, and occasionally fugal. His Cello Concerto (1972) is typical in that the most expressive melodies are entrusted to the tenor register. He is a predominantly instrumental composer, with even his *Canzona I* (for mixed choir and orchestra) and *Canzona II* (for soprano and orchestra) being in effect instrumental vocalises. Major exceptions in this respect are *Jumalan elektronit* ('The Electrons of God') and the Requiem to texts by Lassi Nummi.

WORKS
(*selective list*)

Stage: Tumma [Dark] (ballet, H. Värtsi and Bashmakov, after poem by E. Leino), 1976; incid music for several plays
Syms.: 1963, 1965, 1977, 1979, 1982
Other orch: Vn Conc., 1966; Etappeja [Stages], wind orch, 1968; Conc. for Orch, 1969; Divertimento no.1, ob, str, 1971; Sinfonietta, 1971; Vc Conc., 1972; Prelude and Scherzo, wind orch, 1973; Divertimento no.2, 3 wind, str, 1974; Fl Conc., 1974; Org Conc., 1975; Ballata, 1976; Passacaglia, 1977; Vn Conc., 1983; Cl Conc., 1990; Aubades and Serenades, 1991; Conc., pic, tpt, str, 1992; Bn Conc., 1993; The Three Tolls, 1993
Chbr: 7 Duos, 2 vn, 1969; Octet, 1970; Sonata, perc, 1970; Sonata, va, vc, pf, 1971; 4 Bagatelles, fl, perc, 1971; Dialogues, org, perc, 1971; Conc. da camera no.1, fl, str qt, 1972; Str Qt, 1972; Sonatina, vc, pf, 1973; Str Qt, 1974; Visions and Revelations, wind qnt, perc, 1977; 5 Improvisations, vn, pf, 1977, rev. 1985; Conc. da camera no.2, hp, str qt, 1978; Sonatina, a fl, pf, 1979; 7 Inventions, accdn, hpd, 1985; Qt, kantele, str trio, 1988; Kolminpeli, 2 accdn, perc, 1990; Conc., hpd, 2 str qt, perc, 1991; Nelinpeli, 4 kantele, 1991; Sonata, tpt, pf, 1992; Reflections, 3 bn, 1992; Impetuoso e tenero, vc, accdn, 1993; Terpsikhoren jalanjäljillä [In the Footsteps of Terpsichor], 2 tpt, 2 trbn, 1993; Die Offenbarung des Johannes, cl, vn, vc, pf, 1994; Sestetto, chbr ens, 1994
Solo inst: Fantasia, fl, 1972; 6 Preludes, pf, 1974; Cassazione, tuba, 1976; Sonata, bn, 1976; La parade des insectes, mar, 1979; 6 études, kantele, 1986
Vocal: Canzona I, mixed chorus, orch, 1969; Canzona II, S, orch, 1971; Tiitiäisen lauluja [Bird Songs] (K. Kunnas), female vv, 1979; Jumalan elektronit [The Electrons of God] (cant., L. Nummi), 1981; Muutamat kevään päivät [A Few Spring Days] (Nummi), male vv, 1985; Requiem (Nummi), 1988

Principal publishers: Jasemusiikki, Fazer

BIBLIOGRAPHY

E. Salmenhaara, ed.: *Suomalaisia säveltäjiä* [Finnish composers] (Helsinki, 1994)
M. Heiniö: *Aikamme musiikki* [Contemporary music], Suomen musiikin historia [The history of Finnish music], iv (Helsinki, 1995)
K. Korhonen: *Finnish Orchestral Music* (Jyväskylä, 1995)
K. Korhonen: *Finnish Concertos* (Jyväskylä, 1995)
K. Aho and others: *Finnish Music* (Helsinki, 1996)

MIKKO HEINIÖ

Bashmet, Yuri (Abramovich) (*b* Rostov-na-Donu, 24 Jan 1953). Ukrainian viola player. He grew up in L'viv and played the piano as a boy but at eight took up the violin under the tutelage of Zoya Zertsalova, who remained his teacher when he changed to the viola at 14; in his teens he also played the guitar and the piano in a rock band. At 18 he entered the Moscow Conservatory to study with Vadim Borisovsky and then – after Borisovsky's death – with Fedor Druzhinin. He was also influenced by the playing of David Oistrakh, Viktor Tretyakov, Vladimir Spivakov, Gidon Kremer, Natalya Gutman and Rostropovich. In 1976 he won the Munich International Competition but for a decade his international appearances were strictly rationed by the Soviet authorities; he was usually allowed out only to play Mozart's Sinfonia concertante with Spivakov. However his recordings alerted many in the West to his qualities. Meanwhile he formed close ties with such colleagues as Richter, Oleg Kagan, Gutman and Alexey Lyubimov. In 1986 he founded the Moscow Soloists Chamber Orchestra and began to tour more frequently. That year he also gave the première of the concerto by Schnittke, one of the best works written for the viola in the 20th century, and since then he has enjoyed an international career. In 1988 he founded an annual festival in the Rhineland. In 1995 he took part (with Kremer and Rostropovich) in the first performance of Schnittke's Concerto for Three. Although as a virtuoso he is not quite in the class of Michael Kugel – who defeated him in the 1975 Budapest International Competition – Bashmet has a formidable technique, and in the right repertory is as charismatic a performer as any today. His performances of Shostakovich's Sonata with Mikhail Muntyan, his regular piano partner, have generally been spellbinding, as have his interpretations of works by Hindemith and Britten. However he has been criticized for cancelling engagements, changing programmes arbitrarily and arriving ill-prepared for important premières. The Danish State RSO took the unprecedented step of announcing that it would not book him again, after he had gone to Copenhagen to receive an award and give the first performance of the concerto by Poul Ruders. In 1992 he came into conflict with the members of his orchestra, by then based at Montpellier in France, and was forced to form a new group with the same name.

Bashmet remains the most powerful advocate of his underrated instrument. He has taught for many years at the Accademia Musicale Chigiana in Siena, he is president of the Lionel Tertis International Viola Competition on the Isle of Man and he runs his own competition in Moscow, where he has established a foundation to present an annual prize in memory of Shostakovich. In addition to the two concertos, Schnittke dedicated *Monologue* to him; and works introduced by him include concertos by Edison Denisov and Allan Pettersson, *Vom Winde beweint* by Giya Kancheli and pieces by Andrey Tchaikovsky, Aleksandr Raskatov and Andrey Golovin. His recordings include two each of Berlioz's *Harold en Italie*, Britten's *Lachrymae* and the concertos by Schnittke and Walton, as well as Schnittke's Concerto for Three and *Monologue*, Bruch's Double Concerto (with Tretyakov), Mozart's Sinfonia concertante (with Spivakov), Reger's G minor Suite (in both solo form and an orchestral arrangement), Druzhinin's solo Sonata and much chamber music. He plays a 1790 Carlo Giuseppe Testore viola of only moderate size but produces a virile, opulent and flexible tone from it.

BIBLIOGRAPHY
T. Potter: 'Rock Solid', *The Strad*, c (1989), 42–5

TULLY POTTER

Basie, Count [Bill; William] (*b* Red Bank, NJ, 21 Aug 1904; *d* Hollywood, CA, 26 April 1984). American jazz bandleader and pianist. He was a leading figure of the swing era in jazz and, alongside Duke Ellington, an outstanding representative of big-band style.

1. Life. 2. Ensemble style. 3. Solo style.

1. LIFE.   After studying the piano with his mother, as a young man he went to New York, where he met James P. Johnson, Fats Waller (with whom he studied informally) and other black pianists of the Harlem stride school. Before he was 20 he toured extensively on the Keith and Theatre Owners' Booking Association vaudeville circuits as a solo pianist, accompanist and musical director for blues singers, dancers and comedians, an early training which was to prove significant in his later career. From 1923 to 1926 he performed with various bands in New York. Stranded in Kansas City in 1927 while accompanying a touring group, he remained there, playing in silent-film theatres. In July 1928 he joined Walter Page's Blue Devils which, in addition to Page, included Jimmy Rushing; both later figured prominently in Basie's own band. Basie left the Blue Devils early in 1929; later that year he joined Benny Moten's Kansas City Orchestra, as did the other key members of the Blue Devils shortly afterwards. He led members of Moten's band, independent of Moten, from 1933 to 1935, then rejoined Moten. When Moten died suddenly in 1935, the band continued under Buster Moten, but Basie left soon thereafter. The same year, with Buster Smith and several other former members of Moten's orchestra, Basie organized a new, smaller group of nine musicians, which included Jo Jones and Lester Young; as the Barons of Rhythm it began a long engagement at the Reno Club in Kansas City. The group's radio broadcasts led in 1936 to contracts with a national booking agency and the Decca Record Company; it expanded and within a year the Count Basie Orchestra, as it had become known, was one of the leading big bands of the swing era. By the end of the 1930s the band had acquired international fame with such pieces as *One o'Clock Jump* (1937, Decca), *Jumpin' at the Woodside* (1938, Decca) and *Taxi War Dance* (1939, Voc.), but gradual recourse to written arrangements began to lead it towards stylization and conformity, and to subdue its personality to the personalities of its arrangers.

In 1950 financial considerations forced Basie to disband, and for the next two years he led a six- to nine-piece group. After reorganizing a big band in 1952, he undertook a long series of tours and recording sessions that eventually led to his becoming an elder statesman of jazz, while his band was established as a permanent jazz institution and training ground for young musicians. He made the first of many tours of Europe in 1954, visited Japan in 1963, and issued a large number of recordings both under his own name and under the leadership of various singers, most notably Frank Sinatra. In the mid-1970s a serious illness hampered his career, and in the 1980s he sometimes had to perform from a wheelchair; he devoted time increasingly to his autobiography. After Basie's death, the band continued under the direction of Thad Jones (1985–6) and Frank Foster (from 1986).

2. ENSEMBLE STYLE.   Like all bands in the Kansas City tradition, the Count Basie Orchestra was organized about its rhythm section, which supported the interplay of brass and reeds and served as a backdrop for the unfolding of solos. Using an elliptical style of melodic leads and cues, Basie was able to control his band firmly from the keyboard while blending perfectly with his rhythm section. This celebrated group, consisting of Basie, Page, Jones and, from 1937, Freddie Green, altered the ideal of jazz accompaniment, making it more supple and responsive to the wind instruments and helping to establish four-beat jazz (with four almost identically stressed beats to a bar) as the norm for jazz performance. Of particularly far-reaching significance was Jones's technique of placing the constant pulse on the hi-hat cymbal instead of the bass drum, thereby immeasurably lightening the timbre of jazz drumming. Another important factor was the accuracy and solidity of Page's walking bass technique, which obviated the need for left-hand patterns in the piano and imparted a buoyant swing to the ensemble.

Basie's rhythm section was supreme in its day, and its innovations served as models for the even more spare and flexible rhythm sections of the bop school.

During the band's heyday in the late 1930s Basie preferred light, readily expandable arrangements which were particularly notable for their use of riffs, a legacy of the Moten band and of Southwest ensemble jazz generally. Ex.1 shows a typical riff pattern, which might easily have

Ex.1 Riff from *Shout and Feel It* (air-shot recording, first issued on *Shout and Feel It*, 1937, Alamac); transcr. J. B. Robinson

been developed in rehearsal and played from memory. This simple approach to ensemble accompaniment, which contrasts with the more elaborate group writing of Duke Ellington, Don Redman and Sy Oliver, gave full freedom to Basie's outstanding soloists. These included the trumpeters Harry 'Sweets' Edison and Buck Clayton, the trombonists Dicky Wells and Benny Morton, the singer Jimmy Rushing, and two excellent tenor saxophonists, Herschel Evans and Lester Young, whose widely differing styles and artistic personalities gave added breadth and tension to the group's performances. All of these soloists are prominently featured on the band's recordings between 1937 and 1941. Basie also recorded masterpieces with his band's rhythm section and soloists (notably Young), for example, *Lady Be Good* (1936, Voc.) and *Lester Leaps in* (1939, Voc.).

In his bands of the 1950s and 60s Basie retained his swing-style rhythm section but chose soloists with more modern learnings, particularly the trumpeter Thad Jones and the saxophonists Eddie 'Lockjaw' Davis, Frank Foster and Frank Wess. Although the band's sound tended to change with its current arrangers (most notably Neal Hefti, Benny Carter, Quincy Jones and Thad Jones), it was unequalled for its relaxed precision and control of dynamics, as may be heard on the album *April in Paris* (1955–6, Verve). Basie's later bands, though musically less satisfying, never lost their large popular following. In the end, the Count Basie Orchestra proved the most long-lived and enduring in jazz.

3. SOLO STYLE. Basie's eminence as a bandleader tended to overshadow his considerable achievements as a jazz pianist. Early recordings with Moten, such as the introduction to *Moten Swing* (1932, Vic.), reveal his mastery of the ragtime and stride idioms. By the mid-1930s, however, Basie had adopted a highly personal, laconic, blues-orientated style, compounded of short melodic phrases – often nothing more than jazz clichés – expertly placed and accented with wit and ingenuity. These seemingly fragmentary and disjunct solos, of which ex.2 is typical, were nevertheless capable of generating great forward momentum and cumulative energy, and of leading into the next soloist, a gift for which Basie was justly famed. Although sometimes wrongly attributed to laziness, Basie's 'minimal' style, with its avoidance of the ornate mannerisms to which other pianists of the time were prone, was in fact deliberately abstracted from the more elaborate jazz piano styles of his day to meet the demands of large-ensemble improvisation. It was of seminal importance to John Lewis and the cool pianists of the West Coast school in the early 1950s. Jazz pianists

Ex.2 Solo from *One o'Clock Jump* (air-shot recording, first issued on *Shout and Feel It*, 1937, Alamac); transcr. J. B. Robinson

as diverse as Oscar Peterson and Mary Lou Williams have freely acknowledged their debt to Basie.

BIBLIOGRAPHY

B. Harding: *Count Basie's Boogie Woogie Styles* (New York, 1944)
J. Hammond: 'Count Basie Marks 20th Anniversary', *Down Beat*, xxii/22 (1955), 11–12; repr. in *Eddie Condon's Treasury of Jazz*, ed. E. Condon and R. Gehman (New York, 1956/R), 266–73
R. Horricks: *Count Basie and his Orchestra: its Music and its Musicians* (London, 1957)
N. Shapiro: 'William "Count" Basie', *The Jazz Makers*, ed. N. Shapiro and N. Hentoff (New York, 1957/R), 232–43
E. Towler: 'Vintage Basie', *Jazz Monthly*, iii/6 (1957), 2
N. Hentoff: 'Count Basie', *The Jazz Life* (New York, 1961/R), 143–56
B. Schiozzi: *Count Basie* (Milan, 1961)
R. Russell: *Jazz Style in Kansas City and the Southwest* (Berkeley, 1971/R, 2/1973)
A. McCarthy: *Big Band Jazz* (London, 1974)
S. Dance: *The World of Count Basie* (New York, 1980) [collection of previously pubd interviews]
A. Morgan: *Count Basie* (Tunbridge Wells, 1984)
C. Basie and A. Murray: *Good Morning Blues: the Autobiography of Count Basie* (New York, 1985)
B. Clayton and N.M. Elliott: *Buck Clayton's Jazz World* (London, 1986)
C. Sheridan: *Count Basie: a Bio-discography* (Westport, CT, 1986)
G. Schuller: 'The Quintessence of Swing: Count Basie', *The Swing Era: the Development of Jazz, 1930–1945* (New York, 1989), 222–62

Oral history material in *US-KCm* and *US-NEij*

J. BRADFORD ROBINSON

Basile. Italian family of poets and musicians.

(1) **Giovanni Battista** [Giambattista] **Basile** (*b* Giugliano, nr Naples, 25 Feb 1566; *d* Giugliano, 23 Feb 1632). Poet, writer and librettist. He was educated in Naples but left at an early age, travelling around Italy until he arrived in Venice in 1604. He became a soldier and was deployed with the Venetian army to defend Crete, where he joined the literary Accademia degli Stravaganti, taking the name 'Il Pigro' ('the lazy one'). In 1608 he abandoned his military career and returned to Naples, where he began work as a writer and published his first poetry in Neapolitan dialect. He became a member of the Accademia degli Oziosi in 1608 and of the Accademia degli Incauti in 1621. The support of his famous sister, (3) Adriana Basile, no doubt helped his career: after she moved to the Gonzaga court, Mantua, in 1610, Giovanni Battista joined her for a year and was awarded the titles

of *Cavaliere* and *Conte palatino*. He returned to Naples in 1613, where he married Flora Santora and entered the entourage of Prince Caracciolo di Avellino, in whose service he was appointed to various administrative posts as governor of Montemarano, Zungoli, Lagonegro, Aversa (1626) and finally Giugliano (1631), where he died of a contagious disease.

Basile's patron in Naples was Luigi Carafa, Prince of Stigliano, in whose service (3) Adriana already worked. Basile dedicated his first dramatic works in pastoral style to Carafa, including *Le avventurose disavventure* (1611), set in Carafa's villa in Posillipo, and the five-act *dramma per musica Venere addolorata* (1612), probably the first libretto used in a Neapolitan opera. In October 1630, for a visit by the Queen of Hungary, Maria of Austria, Basile carried out his first major assignment as theatre manager and librettist at the viceroy's court. However, only Basile's libretto and descriptions of the elaborate dances of the masquerade entitled *Monte Parnaso* (set to music by Giacinto Lambardi) have survived. Basile was able to display his considerable prowess in the musical dramas of his time, which can be seen in the last of nine eclogues in Neapolitan dialect making up *Le muse napolitane* (Naples, 1635). It was in his dialect works, which were undeniably superior to those in literary Italian, that he found himself as a writer. His masterpiece is *Lo cunto delli cunti*, a collection of 50 popular tales written in Neapolitan dialect under the anagrammatical pseudonym Gian Alesio Abbattutis (Naples, 1634–6) and subsequently translated into Italian and other languages. 15 of his villanellas were edited and set to music by his brother Donato and published in his *Primo libro di Villanelle* (Naples, 1610, dedicated to Prince Carafa). Two villanellas by their older brother (2) Lelio Basile also appear in the collection. Seven Spanish canzonettas by Giovanni Battista appear in a Neapolitan guitar manuscript (*I-Nn*, dated 1622–9), which may have belonged to (3) Adriana. Two poems on the eruption of Vesuvius at the end of 1631 were the last of Basile's works to be set to music. One of these, *Mentre d'ampia voragine tonante*, was set by Michelangelo Rossi. After Basile's death, (3) Adriana moved permanently to Rome where she oversaw a posthumous edition of all his work.

BIBLIOGRAPHY

A. Ademollo: *I Basile alla corte di Mantova* (Genoa, 1885)

M. Petrini: 'La musa napoletana di Giambattista Basile', *Belfagor*, xvii (1962), 405–31

E. Ferrari Barassi: 'Costume e pratica musicale in Napoli al tempo di Giambattista Basile', *RIM*, ii (1967), 74–110

M. Rak: *La maschera della fortuna: letture del Basile 'toscano'* (Naples, 1975)

G. Fulco: 'Verifiche per il Basile', *Filologia e critica*, x (1985)

M. Rak: *Napoli città gentile* (Bologna, 1995)

(2) Lelio Basile   (*b* Naples, ?1575–85; *d* ?Mantua, after 1623). Composer and poet, brother of (1) Giovanni Battista Basile. In May and June 1610 he accompanied (3) Adriana Basile to Rome and Florence en route for Mantua, where Duke Vincenzo Gonzaga took him into his service, making him governor of several territories. He probably also accompanied Adriana to Milan in August 1611. On 30 June 1615 Duke Ferdinando Gonzaga assigned to him an income derived from the sale of silk and wheat. He had now been assigned the rank of nobleman. He published *Il primo libro de madrigali a cinque voci* (Venice, 1619), of which only the alto part now survives. The 22 madrigals in this volume include

settings of texts by Petrarch, Guarini, Marino and Rinuccini. The penultimate madrigal, *Canto in un tempo e piango*, is canonic (possibly in all five voices), as probably is the final madrigal, *Se lontana voi sete*. There are several poems by Lelio Basile in the volume of poems dedicated to Adriana Basile, *Il teatro delle glorie* (Venice, 1623).

BIBLIOGRAPHY

A. Ademollo: *La bell'Adriana ed altre virtuose del suo tempo alla corte di Mantova* (Città di Castello, 1888), 121, 178, 213

E. Hilmar: 'Ergänzungen zu Emil Vogels "Bibliothek der gedruckten weltlichen Vocalmusik Italiens, aus den Jahren 1500–1700"', *AnMc*, no.4 (1967), 154–206, esp. 165

(3) Adriana [Andreana] **Basile** [Baroni]   (*b* Posillipo, nr Naples, *c*1580–83; *d* probably Naples, after 1642). Italian singer and instrumentalist, sister of (1) Giovanni Battista Basile and (2) Lelio Basile. She was the mother of Leonora Baroni (*see* BARONI family, (2)). Little is known about her early life. She may have been the singer in the household of Luigi Carafa; Duke of Traetto, whom Cardinal Montalto considered trying to obtain for his sister, the Duchess of Bracciano, in 1590. Between 1609 and 1610, when Duke Vincenzo Gonzaga and his wife negotiated to bring her to Mantua, her husband, Mutio Baroni, a nobleman, was in Carafa's service and she was in the employ of Carafa's wife, Isabella Gonzaga. Adriana and her family travelled to Mantua via Rome, Bracciano, Bagnaia (the country residence of Cardinal Montalto) and Florence, where her singing won her considerable acclaim (she was lodged in the house of Giulio Caccini and performed with Jacopo Peri, among others). Adriana worked from June 1610 at the Mantuan court with other members of her family: Giovanni Battista and Lelio; her sisters Margherita and Vittoria, both singers; and her husband and their children Camillo, Leonora and Caterina. It was reported that Adriana's repertory comprised over 300 songs in Italian and Spanish, which she sang from memory, accompanying herself on the harp or guitar. Within a few months of her arrival, poets were sending verses to her and Monteverdi had declared her more gifted than Cardinal Montalto's singer Ippolita Recupito and the Medici singer Francesca Caccini. She and her husband were awarded a barony by Duke Vincenzo Gonzaga and the family enjoyed further privileges under his son Ferdinando. She visited Florence, Rome, Naples and Modena between 1618 and 1620, performing at court and in cardinals' residences. In Mantua in March 1621 she performed in Alessandro Guarini's *Licori, ovvero L'incanto d'amore*, and she probably also had a role in Monteverdi's *intermedi* to *Le tre costanti*, staged the following January for the marriage of Duke Ferdinando's sister Eleonora to Emperor Ferdinand II. In May 1623 Adriana accompanied Duke Ferdinando and Duchess Caterina to Venice. Six months later she took part in musical gatherings in Rome, where she sang the *Lamento d'Arianna* to harpsichord accompaniment and on another evening improvised musical settings to stanzas from Marino's *L'Adone* (an exercise Marino also requested of Francesca Caccini in a separate audience). Having been granted a leave of absence from Mantua, Adriana and her husband continued on to Naples to settle personal affairs. In the succeeding period she found favour with the Viceroy of Naples and contemplated, then decided against, entering the service of King Sigismund III of Poland, who had also tried to recruit Monteverdi. Preparing to return to Mantua in 1626 after an absence of more than two years, she found that the Gonzagas no longer wanted her.

The next few years were spent mainly in Naples, where Adriana continued to be favoured by Don Alvarez de Toledo, Duke of Alba and Viceroy of Naples. In May 1630 she visited Florence and Genoa. Then, in 1633, the Baroni family settled in Rome, where Adriana and her daughters Leonora and Caterina gave musical performances in their house and enjoyed generous support from Cardinal Antonio Barberini (see BARONI family). She was still performing in October 1639 when André Maugars reported hearing the trio sing, Adriana accompanying on the lira, Leonora on theorbo and Caterina on harp. Until recently it was thought that Adriana died in Rome a short while later, but documents show that she left for Naples in November 1640 and was still living there in August 1642.

Adriana also composed: in 1616 Monteverdi recommended that she and her sisters write solos for the parts they were to sing in a dramatic entertainment. Her singing was extolled by several poets in *Teatro della glorie della signora Adriana Basile* (1623, 2/1628) and *L'idea della veglia* (1640), by Francesco Rasi in *La cetra di sette corde* (1619), and by Marino in *L'Adone*, canto vii (1623) and *Rime*, ii (edn. of 1629).

Her sister Margherita (d after 1639) was at Mantua from 1615 and in 1617 sang in Santi Orlandi's *Gli amori di Aci e Galatea*, staged for Ferdinando Gonzaga's marriage; she became the principal singer at the court in the 1620s. In 1630 she was among several Mantuan musicians in Vienna, and by January 1631 until apparently at least 1639 she held a position at the Imperial court. However, she may have returned provisionally to Mantua: she is listed on the Mantuan court roster of 1632 and four years later she was the recipient of a gift of land there. Margherita accompanied one of Emperor Ferdinand II's daughters to Poland in 1637.

BIBLIOGRAPHY

DBI (L. Pannella); *SolertiMBD*

P. Della Valle: *Della musica dell'età nostra* (1640), in A. Solerti: *Le origini del melodramma* (Turin, 1903/R), 164–5

A. Ademollo: *La bell'Adriana ed altre virtuose del suo tempo alla corte di Mantova* (Città di Castello, 1888)

J. Lionnet: 'André Maugars: risposta data a un curioso sul sentimento della musica d'Italia', *NRMI*, xix (1985), 697–9

S. Parisi: '*Licenza alla Mantovana*: Frescobaldi and the Recruitment of Musicians for Mantua, 1612–15', *Frescobaldi Studies*, ed. A. Silbiger (Durham, NC, 1987), 55–91

S. Parisi: *Ducal Patronage of Music in Mantua, 1587–1627: an Archival Study* (diss., U. of Illinois, 1989)

J. Whenham: 'The Gonzagas visit Venice', *EMc*, xxi (1993), 525–8

S. Parisi: 'Musicians at the Court of Mantua during Monteverdi's Time: evidence from the Payrolls', *Musicologia Humana: Studies in Honor of Warren and Ursula Kirkendale*, ed. S. Gmeinwieser, D. Hiley and J. Riedlbauer (Florence, 1994), 200–7

S. Saunders: *Cross, Sword, and Lyre: Sacred Music at the Imperial Court of Ferdinand II of Habsburg (1619–1637)* (Oxford, 1995), 181–2

B. Glixon: 'Scenes from the Life of Silvia Gailarti Manni, a Seventeenth-Century *Virtuosa*', *EMH*, xv (1996), 97–146, esp. 102–3

J.W. Hill: *Roman Monody, Cantata, and Opera from the Circles around Cardinal Montalto* (Oxford, 1997), 42–3

S. Parisi: 'New Documents concerning Monteverdi's Relations with the Gonzagas', *Monteverdi: studi e prospettive*, ed. P. Besutti, T. Gialdroni and R. Baroncini (Florence, 1998), 501–7

D. Fabris: *Mecenati e musicisti: documenti sul patronato artistico dei Bentivoglio di Ferrara nell'epoca di Monteverdi (1585–1645)* (Lucca, 1999)

ARGIA BERTINI/DINKO FABRIS (1), KEITH A. LARSON (2), SUSAN PARISI (3)

Basili. Italian family of composers.

(1) Andrea Basili (*b* Città della Pieve, Perugia, 16 Dec 1705; *d* Loreto, 28 Aug 1777). Composer and theorist. After taking minor orders he studied in Rome with Bernardo Caffi. From May to December 1729 he was *maestro di cappella* of Tivoli Cathedral; in 1732 he was a member of the chapter musicians, described as a 'trombonist-organist'. In 1738 he was listed as a member of the Roman Congregazione di S Cecilia. From 10 March 1740 until his death from apoplexy he was *maestro di cappella* of the Santa Casa of Loreto. Among his contemporaries Basili had the reputation of a skilled contrapuntist and learned theorist. Several of his letters are among Padre Martini's surviving correspondence (*I-Bc*).

WORKS

VOCAL

Il martirio di S Sinforosa e dei sette santi suoi figliuoli nobili Tiburtini (orat, Lisippo Imacheo [F.A. Lolli]), Tivoli, 1737, music lost, lib pubd (Rome, 1737)

La Passione di Gesù Cristo (orat), Recanati, 1743, lost

Psalms with Italian paraphrased text (n.p., n.d.), copy in *I-Nc* [no title-page]

Christus factus est, 4vv; Christus factus est, 5vv; 3 Miserere, 8vv; Miserere, 10vv; Missa breve, 4vv: all *A-Wn*

In omnem terram, formerly in the Staatsbibliothek Preussischer Kulturbesitz, Berlin

Beatus vir, 4vv; Confitebor, 4vv; Laetatus, 4vv; Nisi Dominus, 4vv: all lost, formerly *Dl*

Ave Maria, 4vv; Iustorum animae, 5vv; Ky-Gl, 4vv; Salve regina, 4vv: all *GB-Lbl*

Fuga in ottava tono plagale … sopra l'antifono Veni Sponsa Christi, 1740, 8vv; Iustorum animae, 5vv [? identical to that in *Lbl*]: both *I-Bc*

Litanie, 3vv; Miserere, double chorus a 8: both *Mc*

*c*150 other sacred works, many autograph, in *LT* (complete list in Tebaldini, 1921), *Rvat*, cathedral archives, Città della Pieve

Liberty regain'd (ode), to Daphne, imitated from ye Italian (London, *c*1750)

INSTRUMENTAL AND DIDACTIC

Musica universale armonico-pratica … opera utile per i studiosi di contrapunto e per i suonatori di grave cembalo ed organo esposta in 24 esercizi (Venice, 1776)

Sonata, fugina di culcano, hpd, *A-Wgm*

Canon ad unisonum 16 vocibus; canone a 2, 3 e 4 parti; Fuga in ottavo tono plagale; 15 fughe, org/hpd; Solfeggi, B, 1761, S, 1772 [autograph]: all *I-Bc*

WRITINGS

La musica è un'arte di ben modulare (MS, 1748, lost, formerly in the Staatsbibliothek Preussischer Kulturbesitz, Berlin)

BIBLIOGRAPHY

DBI (A. Pironti)

G. Tebaldini: *L'archivio musicale della Cappella Lauretana* (Loreto, 1921)

A. Cametti: *I musici di Campidoglio ossia il concerto di tromboni e cornetti del senato e inclinato popolo romano (1524–1818)* (Rome, 1925)

MICHAEL TALBOT/ENRICO CARERI

(2) Francesco Basili (*b* Loreto, 31 Jan 1767; *d* Rome, 25 March 1850). Composer and conductor, son of (1) Andrea Basili. He studied music first with his father, then with Giovanni Battista Borghi and finally with Giuseppe Jannaconi at the Accademia di S Cecilia in Rome. After successfully passing his examinations in 1783 he was accepted as a member of the academy (16 October), and for the next 30 years worked as *maestro di cappella* at

Foligno (1786–9), Macerata (1789–1803) and Loreto (1809–27); during this time his 13 operas, of which *Gl'Illinesi* (Milan, 1819) was the most successful, were composed and produced. He turned down the nomination for *maestro di cappella* at S Maria Maggiore in Rome to become censor of the Milan Conservatory in 1827, where he was responsible for Verdi's failure to be admitted to the conservatory (1832). Basili succeeded Fioravanti as *maestro di cappella* of St Pietro in Rome in 1837, a post which he held until his death. Inspired by Spontini, he and Giuseppe Baini sought to raise the musical standards of St Pietro, but their efforts were in vain.

Although now forgotten, Basili was well known in his day, particularly for his church music. The last decades of his life were devoted primarily to revising earlier works, especially sacred pieces. His style is similar to Spontini's, and is characterized by march-like rhythms and by melodies that are reminiscent of the Viennese Classical composers and of Schubert. In his earliest works, however, he anticipated Rossini, and in that respect his style contrasts markedly with that of his contemporaries.

WORKS

OPERAS

La bella incognita (farce, 2), Rome, Valle, Feb 1788
La locandiera (farce, 2), Rome, Capranica, carn. 1789
Achille all'assedio di Troia (dramma, 2), Florence, Pergola, 26 Dec 1797
Il ritorno di Ulisse (dramma, 3, G.B. Moniglia), Florence, Pergola, 1 Sept 1798
Antigona (dramma serio, 2, G. Rossi), Venice, Fenice, 5 Dec 1799
Conviene adattarsi (farce, 1), Venice, S Moisè, Nov 1801
L'unione mal pensata (dramma, 1), Venice, S Benedetto, 27 Dec 1801
Lo stravagante e il dissipatore (dg, 2, G.M. Foppa), Venice, Fenice, 25 May 1805
L'ira di Achille (dramma serio, 3, P. Pola), Venice, Fenice, 30 Jan 1817
L'orfana egiziana (dramma, 3), Venice, Fenice, 28 Jan 1818
Gl'Illinesi (melodramma, 2, F. Romani), Milan, Scala, 26 Jan 1819
Il califfo e la schiava (melodramma, 2, F. Romani), Milan, Scala, 21 Aug 1819
Isaura e Ricciardo (os, 2, C. Sterbini), Rome, Valle, 29 Jan 1820

OTHER WORKS

Arianna e Teseo (cant.), c1787; Il Sansone in Tamnata (orat, A.L. Tottola), 1824; La sconfitta degli Assiri (orat), *D-Dlb*
Sacred choral (most with org acc.): 25 masses, 4 requiems, 6 Mag, 36 ps, 9 hymns, 3 litanies, 9 motets, 14 grads, 31 responsories, 19 antiphons, 31 offs, 27 settings of Tantum ergo
Instrumental: syms., pf conc., str qts, pf sonatas, other works

BIBLIOGRAPHY

FétisB; *GaspariC*, i, 151; ii, 36, 175, 377; iii, 8; iv, 4; *MGG1* (R. Meloncelli)
Opera manoscritte autografe di musica di chiesa, di teatro, e di camera del celebre Francesco Basili Romano (Rome, n.d.) [list of works]
G. Tebaldini: *L'archivio musicale della Cappella lauretana* (Loreto, 1921)
F. Abbiati: *Giuseppe Verdi*, i (Milan, 1959)
M. Marx-Weber: 'Römische Vertonungen des Psalms "Miserere" im 18. und früher 19. Jahrhundert', *HJbMw*, viii (1985), 7–43

LEOPOLD M. KANTNER/R

(3) **Basilio Basili** (*b* Macerata, 1803; *d* ?New York, ?c1895). Composer, active in Spain, son of (2) Francesco Basili. He started his career as an operatic tenor but turned to composition soon after arriving in Spain in 1827. In a musical climate monopolized by Italian opera, he tried to revitalize the tradition of Spanish musical theatre, composing several stage works in Spanish, with spoken dialogue. The dichotomy between Spanish and Italian music is presented allegorically in *El novio y el concierto*, in which the young hero's choice of bride symbolizes a choice between Italian opera and Spanish folksong. Basili conducted several seasons of Italian opera in Madrid during the late 1840s. In 1847 Basili, Hilarión Eslava and others formed España Musical, a group that promoted the cause of national music. Though none of Basili's dramatic works gained lasting fame, they paved the way for the successful revival of the zarzuela around 1849.

BIBLIOGRAPHY

GroveO (R.J. Vázquez) [incl. list of stage works]
E. Cotarelo y Mori: *Ensayo histórico sobre la zarzuela* (Madrid, 1937)
R.J. Vázquez: *The Quest for National Opera and the Re-invention of the Zarzuela in Nineteenth-Century Spain* (diss., Cornell U., 1992)

ROLAND J. VÁZQUEZ

Basiliani, Carlo. *See* BALIANI, CARLO.

Basilicus, Ciprianus. *See* BAZYLIK, CYPRIAN.

Basilides, Mária (*b* Jolsva, 11 Nov 1886; *d* Budapest, 26 Sept 1946). Hungarian contralto. She studied at the Budapest Academy of Music under József Sík. In 1911, at the opening of the Budapest City Theatre, she made her début in Jean Nouguès's *Quo vadis?*, and until 1915 played there in such roles as Azucena, Mignon, Carmen and Ulrica. She then joined the Royal Hungarian Opera, appearing there until her death. Her repertory was wide: specially admired in Verdi and Wagner, she also sang Gluck's Orpheus and Clytemnestra and Sylvia in Monteverdi's *Orfeo*; she created the Housewife in Kodály's *The Spinning Room*. She made frequent guest appearances abroad. An innate musicality, a voice of velvety beauty (at its peak), and avoidance of vocal artifice endeared her to Budapest audiences. In addition she was one of Hungary's most eminent concert singers and an enthusiastic supporter of Bartók and Kodály, whose folksong arrangements she recorded (with Bartók at the piano). The second and eighth books of Kodály's *Magyar népzene* were dedicated to her.

BIBLIOGRAPHY

J.A. Molnár: *Basilides Mária* (Budapest, 1967)

PÉTER P. VÁRNAI

Basilj [Basily], Andrea. *See* BASILI, ANDREA.

Basilly, Bénigne de. *See* BACILLY, BÉNIGNE DE.

Basin, Adrien (*d* after 1498). Franco-Flemish composer. In 1457 he was in the household chapel of Isabelle de Bourbon, wife of Charles the Bold (*F-Pn* fr.5904, f.32). When Charles became Duke of Burgundy in 1467, Basin was listed together with Busnoys and Hayne van Ghizeghem as 'chantre et valet de chambre' (Brussels, Archives générales du royaume, CC 1923, f.69*v*); he was still there in 1475 and 1476 (CC 1796, f.99). He seems thereafter to have been resident in Bruges, where he was involved in diplomatic activity in 1482 and 1488 (Strohm, 1979, p.35), later acting as heir to his brother, Pierre, in December 1498 (Wegman, p.154).

Basin's unusually short three-voice rondeau *Nos amys vous vous abusés* (ascribed 'A. Basin' in the Mellon Chansonnier) had considerable success: apart from its five musical sources, it was used for at least three masses (including a lost mass by Tinctoris) and cited as far away as Portugal and Poland; it seems moreover to have been the central piece in a group of songs with similar titles and similar musical materials composed in the court of Charles the Bold shortly before he became duke. The other two songs, *Ma dame faytes moy savoir* and *Vien'avante morte dolente*, are both ascribed simply 'Basin' (in *I-Rc* 2856). Both have contrary ascriptions elsewhere: for *Ma dame faytes moy* the other ascription is cropped and unreadable, but its music is very much that of the Burgundian court; for *Vien'avante*, which must have begun life with a French rondeau cinquain text, the other ascription is implausibly to Robert Morton. All three songs are edited in *StrohmM*.

These last two pieces may possibly be by Adrien's brother, Pierre (or Pierquin) Basin (*d* Bruges, 19 April 1497), who was a singer and, according to his tombstone (now destroyed), councillor to the Duke of Burgundy. He sang in the chapel of Queen Marie d'Anjou from 1455 to June 1460 (Perkins); at St Donatian, Bruges, from 1460, becoming succentor in 1465–6; and in the Burgundian ducal chapel from 1467 to 1485. He held the 14th prebend at St Donatian from 1467 until his death and was briefly succentor again in 1491 after the sudden dismissal of Obrecht. He seems also to have endowed Obrecht's *Missa de Sancto Martino* on 14 March 1486 (using the profits from properties in Ghent), and, along with Gilles Joye, auditioned candidates for the position of organist at St Donatian in 1482. Given that *Ma dame faytes moy* was quoted in Obrecht's *Missa Plurimorum carminum I*, there seems a good chance that it was indeed by Pierre, who had such close contacts with the younger composer.

A third brother, Jean, is documented from 1460 in Bruges, where he became dean of the barbers' guild and in 1488 endowed an altar at the church of Our Lady.

Simon Basin, also known as Fassion, was a minstrel in the household of the Dauphin Louis, Duke of Guyenne, 1414–16. The basse danse *La Basine* (Michel de Toulouse, *c*1490) may possibly be connected with him, just as another dance, *La Verdelete*, is normally connected with his colleague Jean Boisard, known as Verdelet. Three minstrels named Jehan Facien (or Fassion) are recorded in the years 1415–40. Some or all of the Basins and Faciens may be related.

BIBLIOGRAPHY

StrohmM

G. van Doorslaer: 'La chapelle musicale de Philippe le Beau', *Revue belge d'archéologie et d'histoire de l'art*, iv (1934), 21–57, 139–65

J. Marix: *Histoire de la musique et des musiciens de la cour de Bourgogne sous le règne de Philippe le Bon (1420–1467)* (Strasbourg, 1939/R)

D. Fallows: *Robert Morton's Songs: a Study of Styles in the Mid-Fifteenth Century* (diss., U. of California, Berkeley, 1978), chaps. 10–11

L.L. Perkins and H. Garey, eds.: *The Mellon Chansonnier* (New Haven, CT, 1979)

R. Strohm: 'Die Missa super "Nos amis" von Johannes Tinctoris', *Mf*, xxxii (1979), 34–51

L.L. Perkins: 'Musical Patronage at the Royal Court of France under Charles VII and Louis XI (1422–83)', *JAMS*, lxxvii (1984), 507–66, esp. 548

P. Higgins: '*In hydraulis* Revisited: New Light on the Career of Antoine Busnois', *JAMS*, xxxix (1986), 36–86, esp. 47

R.C. Wegman: *Born for the Muses: the Life and Masses of Jacob Obrecht* (Oxford, 1994)

DAVID FALLOWS

Basiola, Mario (*b* Annico, nr Cremona, 12 July 1892; *d* Annico, 3 Jan 1965). Italian baritone. He studied with Antonio Cotogni in Rome, where he made his début in 1918. Appearances in Florence and Barcelona led to an engagement with the S Carlo company which toured America in 1923, and this in turn brought him to the Metropolitan in 1925. His roles there included Amonasro, Escamillo and Count di Luna. In 1930 he appeared in the American première of Felice Lattuada's *Le preziose ridicole* and in that of Montemezzi's *La notte di Zoraima* the following year. He was also the Venetian in the first Metropolitan production of *Sadko* (1930). In 1933 he returned to Italy where for many years he was a leading baritone in Milan and Rome. The enthusiastic reports of his work there were not entirely borne out when, after a serious illness, he came to Covent Garden (as Iago, Amonasro and Germont) in 1939; nor are they well supported by the recordings he made of *Pagliacci* and *Madama Butterfly* with Gigli. In 1946 he joined a company touring Australia, and in 1951 he returned there as a teacher. His earlier recordings show the full-bodied tone and flowing style which earned him a high reputation among the singers of his time. His son, Mario Basiola jr (*b* Highland Park, IL, 1 Sept 1935), was also a successful baritone, singing in many leading houses including La Scala and the Vienna Staatsoper; his repertory included the title role in *Wozzeck*.

J.B. STEANE

Basiron [Barizon, Baziron, Bazison], **Philippe** [Philippon, Phelippon] (*b* ?Bourges, *c*1449; *d* ?Bourges, shortly before 31 May 1491). French composer. He entered the Ste Chapelle of the royal palace in Bourges as a chorister in October 1458. He demonstrated exceptional musical ability: a clavichord was purchased for his use in late 1462 or early 1463 (when Guillaume Faugues was briefly Master of the Children), and in May 1464 he was deputed to 'instruct the other boys in singing and in the art of music'. He passed to the status of a vicar-choral between 1466 and 1467. On 5 February 1469 he was elected Master of the Children; his successor was appointed on 11 January 1474, when Basiron left the Ste Chapelle. Documents from Bourges are lacking from 1476 to 1486, and his return cannot be dated precisely, but about 1490 he is recorded as vicar of an altar in a church in Bourges under the jurisdiction of the Ste Chapelle, and on 31 May 1491 this benefice, last held by 'deffunctus magister Philippus Barizon clericus dicte capelle' was requested for 'Johannes Barizon', probably a brother (see Higgins).

Brief laudatory references by Crétin, Eloy d'Amerval and Moulu, and citations by Gaffurius and Spataro, show that Basiron was highly regarded by his contemporaries. His works were copied as far afield as Spain and Bohemia and reprinted as late as 1520. He was a precocious composer: the four three-voice chansons, which display a distinctive personal style, were composed before Basiron was out of his teens. Most of the surviving works probably date from before he left the Ste Chapelle in 1474 (Ercole d'Este's reference to the *Missa 'L'homme armé'* as 'new' in 1484 means no more than that the mass was new to Ercole). Though his style more resembles that of Busnoys and Ockeghem than of contemporaries Josquin and Obrecht, he was remarkably innovatory in technique. Long chains of repetitions or sequences were a favourite device of his that was much refined by Josquin. His *Regina celi* is by far the earliest composition in which pervasive imitation in all voices is the sole structural technique. The peculiar method of partitioning the plainchant melody into points of imitation, otherwise unique, links this motet with an anonymous setting of *O sacrum convivium* which was recopied in the early 1530s. The *Messa de Franza*, the most widely distributed of Basiron's works, uses a kaleidoscopic technique of chaining together freely composed sections in many different textures to create long movements. This distinctive procedure is shared with an anonymous *Missa 'D'ung aultre amer'*. In all his texted music, Basiron showed an attention to his words that is similar to Ockeghem's (an evident preoccupation with the chanson *D'ung aultre amer* may point to an association with the older composer). He was a master of pacing, who could effortlessly control wide spans of time.

Vanneus lists 'Johannes Basiron' in the company of much younger musicians headed by Willaert, Festa and Conseil. 'Johannes' may be a mistake for 'Philippus', or may refer to the Jean Basiron who inherited Philippe's benefice and who died in 1495. Another brother, Pierre, entered the Ste Chapelle at the same time as Philippe and lived until 1529. Jean or Pierre may be the composer of *Mary de par sa mère*, which seems to have been composed after 1491.

WORKS

Edition in preparation by J. Dean
Messa de Franza, 4vv, CZ-HKm II.A.7, I-Rvat C.S.51, Sc K.I.2 (inc.), 1509[1]; extract ed. in OHM, ii (1905, 2/1932), 194
Missa 'L'homme armé, 4vv, Rvat C.S.35; ed. in Monumenta Polyphoniae Liturgicae Sanctae Ecclesiae Romanae, 1st ser., i (Rome, 1948)
Missa 'Regina celi', 4vv, Rvat C.S.51, VEcap DCCLXI
Missa tetradi plagis [sic], lost, attested by F. Gaffurius, Tractatus practicabilium proportionum (MS, c1480, Bc A69), f.22
Inviolata, integra et casta es, 4vv, 1505[2]; Rvat C.S.15 (with added 5th v)
Regina celi, 4vv, Rvat C.S.42
Salve regina, 4vv, Rvat C.S.46, 1520[1]; ed. in MRM, viii (1987)
De m'esjouir, 3vv, D-W 287 extrav., I-Fr 2794, US-Wc M2.1 L25 Case [Laborde]; ed. M. Gutiérrez-Denhoff, Der Wolfenbütteler Chansonnier (Mainz, 1988)
D'ung aultre amer, 4vv, textless, I-Bc Q17
D'ung aultre amer/L'homme armé, 4vv, textless, Bc Q17, Rvat C.G.XIII.27; ed. A. Smijers, Van Ockeghem tot Sweelinck, i (Amsterdam, 1939)
Je le sçay bien, 3vv, D-W 287 extrav., US-Wc Laborde; ed. Gutiérrez-Denhoff, Der Wolfenbütteler Chansonnier
Nul ne l'a telle, 3vv, D-W 287 extrav., DK-Kk Thott 291 8°, US-Wc Laborde; D-Bkk Kupferstichkabinett 78.B.17 [Rohan] (text only); ed. K. Jeppesen, Der Kopenhagener Chansonnier (Copenhagen, 1927, 2/1965), Gutiérrez-Denhoff, Der Wolfenbütteler Chansonnier
Tant fort me tarde, 3vv, F-Pn n.a.fr.4379/IV, I-Rc 2856, US-Wc Laborde

POSSIBLE WORKS (ANON. IN SOURCES)

Missa 'D'ung aultre amer', 4vv, I-Rvat C.S.51, San Pietro B80, VEcap DCCLV; excerpts ed. in Wegman
O sacrum convivium, 4vv, Rvat C.S.42, Pal.lat.1976–9

DOUBTFUL WORKS

Mary de par sa mère, 4vv, textless, CH-SGs 461, D-Rp C120, F-Pn fr.1597 (attrib. 'Basseron' in D-Rp C120 only; style probably too late for Philippe Basiron, too early for Johannes Bonnevin alias Beausseron; perhaps by Jean or Pierre Basiron); ed. F.J. Giesbert, Ein altes Spielbuch: Liber Fridolini Sichery (Mainz, 1936), 80–81
Rose playsante, 3vv, attrib. 'Philippon' in 1504[3] (with added 4th v), 'Caron' in I-Fn B.R.229, 'Jo. Dusart' in Rc 2856 (3-v orig. probably not by Basiron); ed. in MRM, vii (1983)

BIBLIOGRAPHY

LockwoodMRF
F. Gaffurius: Practica musice (Milan, 1496), sig. gg 3v
G. Crétin: Déploration sur le trepas de Jean Ockeghem (MS, 1497); ed. E. Thoinan (Paris, 1864/R), 33
E. d'Amerval: Livre de la Déablerie (Paris, 1508); ed. C.F. Ward (Iowa City, 1923), f.225v
P. Moulu: motet Mater floreat (?1517), ed. in MRM, iv (1968), 125–32
S. Vanneus: Recanetum de musica aurea (Rome, 1531), f.93
G. Spataro: Tractato di musica (Venice, 1531), sigs. c7v-dr
A. Atlas: The Cappella Giulia Chansonnier: Rome, Biblioteca Apostolica Vaticana, C.G. XIII.27 (Brooklyn, NY, 1976–7), i, 218–21
P. Higgins: 'Tracing the Careers of Late Medieval Composers: the Case of Philippe Basiron of Bourges', AcM, lxii (1990), 1–28
R.C. Wegman: 'The Anonymous Mass D'ung aultre amer: a Late Fifteenth-Century Experiment', MQ, lxxiv (1990), 566–94

JEFFREY DEAN

Basis (Gk.). In the late Renaissance, a name sometimes given to the bass part (*see* PART (ii)) of a polyphonic composition; in some theoretical writings, including Glarean's *Dodecachordon* (1547) and Zarlino's *Le istitutioni harmoniche* (1558), a designation for the bass line of a passage, and even the bass note of a chord. By a humanistic conceit, the four human voice ranges were compared with the four elements, the *basis* being appropriately likened to the element of earth. □

Basle (Ger. Basel; Fr. Bâle). City in Switzerland. Its musical life probably differed little from that of other episcopal sees during the Middle Ages, but with the Great Council (1431–49), the foundation of the university (1460), the establishment of printing houses and the emergence of humanism, the city, located on the Rhine in northern Switzerland, developed an active cultural life. Sacred polyphony was performed, and instrument makers established workshops in the city. Those that took up residence in Basle included Erasmus and his student Glarean. Bourgeois families (among them the Ammerbachs, Iselins and Hagenbachs) cultivated domestic music-making and composing, collected instruments and commissioned portraits and paintings with music as the subject matter. The surviving tablatures show that intabulations were worked out both from written models and from popular tunes. Partbooks reveal a repertory of polyphonic secular music following the latest international trends. The printer Michael Furter published Virdung's *Musica getutscht* in 1511; Johann Froben brought out works of Glarean, including his *Isagoge in musicen*. Glarean's *Dodecachordon* was published in Basle in 1547 by Heinrich Petri. In contrast to the rest of Protestant Switzerland, which came under the reforms of Ulrich Zwingli, Basle was reformed by Johannes Oekolampadius (Husschyn), who had ties with Lutherans in nearby cities. As a consequence the organs were not destroyed, and playing them was soon allowed again. However, plainsong remained predominant, despite the printing of a four-part psalter (1606) by Samuel Mareschall, who taught at the university; only in 1854 did a four-part hymnbook, published jointly by the city and region of Basle for use in all parishes, gain acceptance.

The tradition of drumming and fifing, particularly common among the Swiss mercenary armies but once also widespread in Europe, has continued in Basle since the 15th century, and is maintained by many groups. Since the 19th century the repertory has included foreign marches, and new compositions have been added since the 1960s. In 1692 the collegium musicum was founded, a small group of aristocratic amateurs who played together once a week. A choir of Gymnasium pupils and other students was attached to them, and the combined forces were directed by the university or cathedral organist, who was also the head music teacher. The collegium musicum received subsidies, performed at church and university functions and advised on such matters as musical education and the appointment of organists. Towards the mid-18th century it developed into a concert society, with a board of directors composed of performing members fulfilling their former advisory role, and a circle of subscribers. The latter, necessary for financial reasons, prepared the way for concerts open to the general public. There was also a private Kapelle in the house of the wealthy merchant Lucas Sarasin. His music catalogue and a third of his collection have survived, and show a lively interest in the instrumental repertory of such centres as Paris, Mannheim, Vienna and northern Italy.

As the number of cultured citizens in Basle increased in the 19th century, the cultivation of music also spread. Under German musical directors, especially Ernst Reiter (1839–75) and Alfred Volkland (1875–1905), the orchestra expanded and improved. In 1876 the concert society and the orchestra formed the Allgemeine Musikgesellschaft (AMG). Programmes included relatively early performances of Bach and Handel, as well as contemporary works. Spohr, Weber, Mendelssohn, Robert and Clara Schumann, Liszt, Bülow, Brahms and Joachim often gave concerts in Basle, and also frequented private musical circles. Choral singing also became widespread in the 19th century. The largest choir was the Basler Gesangverein, founded in 1824–5 and followed in 1852 by a male-voice choir, the Basler Liedertafel; both remain active. In 1867 the Musikschule was set up by a charitable society, the Gesellschaft zur Beförderung des Guten und Gemeinnützigen in Basel (founded 1777). The school was later supported mainly by the state, and its director was often also the conductor of the concert societies.

Theatrical and operatic performances took place in a ballroom until 1834, when the Theater auf dem Blömlein was built by Melchior Berri. In 1875 it was replaced by the Theater am Steinenberg, whose architect, Johann Jacob Staehelin, also designed the adjacent Casino with its three concert halls (still extant). The theatre burnt down and was reconstructed in 1909 as the Stadttheater.

About 1900 the musical life of Basle became dominated by native Swiss performers, who were often also accomplished teachers and composers. Under Hans Huber a conservatory affiliated to the Musikschule was founded (1905), and the teaching curriculum was extended to cover a number of academic disciplines. In concert life contemporary music assumed a new importance under the leadership of Hermann Suter, and greater attention was paid to pre-Classical music. Another influential figure was the musicologist Karl Nef, the first lecturer in the general history of music in Switzerland and the organizer of the international musicological congresses in Basle in 1906 and 1924. In recognition of his services, Basle was chosen as the headquarters of the International Musicological Society in 1927.

After World War I musical life expanded further. The Busch Quartet took up residence, followed in the 1950s by the Vegh Quartet. The AMG gave up its chamber music concerts and established itself as an organization separate from its orchestra, which from then on formed its own state-subsidized society, the Basler Orchester Gesellschaft. This development and the appointment of Weingartner, a conductor who specialized in the Classical and Romantic repertory, led to a number of new organizations. The Walter Sterk'sche Privatchor (1920)

was active in promoting both early and contemporary music, and the local section of the International Society for Contemporary Music was founded in 1928. One of the most fruitful contributions to Basle's musical life was made by the patron and conductor Paul Sacher. With his Basler Kammerorchester (founded 1926) he commissioned and performed many works of Swiss and non-Swiss composers, including Bartók's Music for Strings, Percussion and Celesta and Divertimento for Strings; Stravinsky's Concerto in D and *A Sermon, a Narrative and a Prayer*; and important works of Conrad Beck, Willy Burkhard, Fortner, Honegger, Frank Martin, Martinů, Moeschinger and others. With so much emphasis on contemporary music, the city attracted many Swiss composers, including Beck, Robert Suter, Wildberger, Klaus Huber, Kelterborn, Wyttenbach, H.U. Lehmann and Holliger.

In the early 1930s Sacher intensified the efforts of his predecessors to revive early music, not only with the Kammerorchester but by setting up a private teaching and research institute, the Schola Cantorum Basiliensis. From 1934 August Wenzinger and his concert group, the Freunde Alter Musik in Basel, earned the institute a worldwide reputation. After World War II the institute was combined with the conservatory and the Musikschule to form the Musikakademie (directed by Friedhelm Döhl, 1974–82, and Kelterborn, 1983–94). Martin Linde, Eugen M. Dombois, Jaap Schröder, Thomas Binkley with his Studio der Frühen Musik, Dominique Vellard, René Jacobs and others took up residence there, the curriculum was expanded and a journal founded (*Basler Jahrbuch für historische Musikpraxis*). In the 1970s the conservatory established studios for electronic music and musical theatre, and courses in non-Western music.

In 1909 Karl Nef established musicology at the university. It reached prominence under Jacques Handschin (1930–55) and Leo Schrade (1958–64). Hans Oesch became the institute's director in 1967; he was succeeded by Wulf Arlt.

In 1964 the Radio Corporation of German-speaking Switzerland made Basle its centre for music programming; Kelterborn was its director in the 1970s. Premières of contemporary music, as well as the early music concerts of the Schola Cantorum, were broadcast. In 1975 the old Stadttheater, long considered inadequate, was replaced by a new building with two stages designed by Schwarz & Gutmann, where about six new productions and two revivals are produced each season. During the 1960s, 70s and 80s the Stadttheater was well known for its ballet productions, choreographed by Wazlaw Orlikowsky and his student Heinz Spoerli and based on a wide range of music from Orazio Vecchi's *Amfiparnaso* to works by Luigi Nono and Philip Glass.

The largest music collection, going back 800 years, is in the University Library. The Paul Sacher Stiftung research centre holds important 20th-century works. The city owns two notable collections of musical instruments, both begun in the 19th century. That of the Historische Museum contains more than 800 items (mostly European, including a few folk instruments), while the Museum für Völkerkunde holds more than 2000, most gathered from fieldwork in South-east Asia, New Guinea, Oceania and Africa.

BIBLIOGRAPHY

MGG2 (J. Kmetz)

C.J. Riggenbach: *Der Kirchengesang in Basel seit der Reformation* (Basle, 1870)

K. Nef: 'Die Musik in Basel von den Anfängen im 9. Jahrhundert bis zur Mitte im 19. Jahrhunderts', 'Die Stadtpfeifereien und die Instrumentalmusiker in Basel (1385–1814)', *SIMG*, x (1908–9), 532–63, 395–9

W. Merian: *Basels Musikleben im XIX. Jahrhundert* (Basle, 1920)

E. Refardt: 'Biographische Beiträge zur Basler Musikgeschichte', *Basler Jb*, i (1920), 57; ii (1921), 144; iii (1922), 52

W. Mörikofer: *Die Konzerte der Allgemeinen Musikgesellschaft Basel* (Basle, 1926)

M.F. Schneider: *Alte Musik in der bildenden Kunst Basels* (Basle, 1941)

M.F. Schneider: *Musik der Neuzeit in der bildenden Kunst Basels* (Basle, 1944)

Alte und neue Musik: das Basler Kammerorchester 1926–1976 (Zürich, 1952–77)

P.H Boerlin: 'Die Orgelflügel-Entwürfe von Hans Holbein d. Ä', *Jahresberichte der Öffentlichen Kunstsammlung Basel* (1959–60), 141–64

M. Jenny: *Geschichte des deutsch-schweizerischen evangelischen Gesangbuchs im 16. Jahrhundert* (Basle, 1962)

H. Oesch: *Die Musikakademie der Stadt Basel* (Basle, 1967)

Stadttheater einst und jetzt 1807–1975 (Berne, 1975)

T. Seebass, ed.: *Musikhandschriften in Basel aus verschiedenen Sammlungen*, Basle Kunstmuseum, 31 May – 13 July 1975 (Basle, 1975) [exhibition catalogue]

E. Lichtenhahn and T. Seebass, eds.: *Musikhandschriften aus der Sammlung Paul Sacher: Festschrift zu Paul Sachers 70. Geburtstag* (Basle, 1976)

T. Seebass: *Die Allgemeine Musikgesellschaft Basel 1876–1976* (Basle, 1976)

T. Seebass: 'Some Remarks about 16th-Century Music Book Illustration', *RIdIM Newsletter*, iv/2 (1979), 2–3

P. Reidemeister: '50 Jahre Schola Cantorum Basiliensis', *Basler Jb für historische Musikpraxis*, vii (1983), 7–18

Komponisten des 20. Jahrhunderts in der Paul Sacher Stiftung, Basle Kunstmuseum, 25 April – 20 June 1986 (Basle, 1986) [exhibition catalogue]

Mitteilungen der Paul Sacher Stiftung (Basle, 1988–)

I. Fenlon: 'Heinrich Glarean's Books', *Music in the German Renaissance*, ed. J. Kmetz (Cambridge, 1994), 74–102

J. Kmetz: 'The Piperinus-Amerbach Partbooks: Six Months of Music Lessons in Renaissance Basle', *Music in the German Renaissance*, ed. J. Kmetz (Cambridge, 1994), 215–34

TILMAN SEEBASS

Basner, Veniamin Yefimovich (*b* Yaroslavl', 1 Jan 1925; *d* Repino, St Petersburg province, 3 March 1996). Russian composer. His musical gifts – absolute pitch and a phenomenal memory – became apparent from an early age. He studied the violin at the music school in Yaroslavl'; it was here that he became interested in the work of Schoenberg. It was also in Yaroslavl' that in 1938, he heard Shostakovich's Fifth Symphony, an event which became greatly significant to his creative development. Upon leaving the music school in 1942 he was invited to join the Yaroslavl' Philharmonia and also the Estonian State Philharmonia, evacuated to the town. Called up in 1943, he was transferred to a musicians' section where he mastered wind and brass instruments and acquired arranging skills. He entered the Leningrad Conservatory in 1944, studying the violin with Belyakov; after graduating in 1949 he worked both as soloist and orchestral player. He became a board member of the Leningrad section of the Composers' Union in 1955 and also directed its youth commission which auditioned works by would-be members of the organization. In 1994 he fulfilled a lifelong ambition by setting up and opening a Jewish music theatre in St Petersburg; called *Simkha* ('Joy'); the theatre functioned until his death in 1996. Throughout his career he received a number of awards and honours including People's Artist of the RSFSR (1982) and the Order of Friendship (1994).

Basner's relationship with Shostakovich both as composer and individual was crucial to his his own creative personality. While Basner worshipped Shostakovich, the latter regarded Basner as one of his most dependable friends and had high regard for his compositions; the two friends frequently met to show each other their latest work. Basner's symphony *Katerina Izmaylova* is a tribute to his idol, constructed from material found in the notorious opera. He shared with Shostakovich an admiration for Mahler and also Jewish music, even though for Basner the latter originated from personal recollection from his childhood. In his musical *Yevreyskoye schast'ye* ('Jewish Happiness') Basner played the extensive and symbolic solo violin part at its production at the *Simkha* theatre.

Basner was invited to work as a composer of film music on Shostakovich's recommendation; each of his scores contain a song which subsequently had an independent existence. *Na bezïmyannoy vïsote* ('In the Nameless Heights') from *Tishina* ('Silence') of 1946 and *S chego nachinayetsya rodina?* ('From What Does the Homeland Originate') from *Shchit i mech'* ('The Shield and the Sword') of 1968 both enjoyed popularity throughout Russia, as did his songs about World War II. Although in these and many other songs Basner conveyed the feelings of a wide spectrum of society through the lyrical use of everyday turns of phrase, in the same songs he made use of complex intervallic relationships which bear comparison with those of Mahler.

WORKS
(*selective list*)

STAGE

Ops: Veshniye vodï [Spring Waters] (Ye. Gal'perina, after I. Turgenev), 1975; Otel' Tanatos [Hotel Tanatos] (A. Pochikovsky, after A. Maurois), 1991, unfinished

Ballet: Tri mushketyora [The Three Musketeers] (A. Vanin, after A. Dumas), 1964

Operettas and musicals: Polyarnaya zvezda [The Polar Star] (Gal'perina and Yu. Annenkov), 1966; Trebuyetsya geroinya [A Heroine is Needed] (Gal'perina and Annenkov), 1968; Yuzhnïy krest [The Southern Cross] (Gal'perina and Annenkov), 1971; God golubogo zaytsa/Belïy tanets [The Year of the Blue Hare/The White Dance] (Gal'perina), 1978; Mezhdu nebom i zemlyoy [Between Heaven and Earth] (V. Konstantinov and B. Ratser), 1980; Blistayushchiye oblaka [Glittering Clouds] (N. Denisov and È. Nakhamis), 1982; Moya khata s krayu [It's No Business of Mine] (Gal'perina and Annenkov), 1985; Mï iz Odessï, zdras'te! [We're from Odessa, Hello!] (A. Belinsky, after È. Bagritsky), 1988, unfinished; Tï: velikaya aktrisa [You are a Great Actress] (Gal'perina and Annenkov, after Maurois), 1990; Yevreyskoye schast'ye [Jewish Happiness] (Ratser, after D. Friedman), 1994

OTHER WORKS

Vocal: Parabola (A. Voznesensky), Bar, pf, 1962; Vesna, pesni, volneniya [Spring, Songs, Excitement] (L. Martïnov), solo vv, chorus, orch, 1963; Goya (monologue, Voznesensky), B, eng hn, bn, pf, 1965; Vechnïy ogon' [Eternal Flame] (M. Matusovsky and Gal'perina), B, children's chorus, orch, 1971; 8 Poems (A. Akhmatova), Mez, gui/pf, 1977; 5 stikhotvoreniy M.Yu. Lermontova [5 Lermontov Settings], B, orch, 1979, also version for B, pf, 1979; In Memory of Vladimir Vïsotsky, 6 ballads, 1v, inst ens, 1981; Suite (O. Mandel'shtam and others), B, ob, eng hn, 2 bn, pf, 1983; Sym. no.2 'Blokada' [The Blockade] (Matusovsky), B, chorus, orch, 1983; Sym. no.3 'Lyubov'' [Love] (E. Verhaeren), T, orch, 1988; many romances and songs (A.S. Pushkin and others), 1948–90

Inst: Str Qt no.1, 1948; Str Qt no.2, 1953; Poèma ob osazhdyonnom Leningrade [A Poem about Leningrad in the Blockade], orch, 1957; Sym. no.1, orch, 1958; Str Qt no.3, 1960; Vn Conc., 1966; Vc Conc. 'Tsar' David' [King David], 1967–80; Str Qt no.4, 1969;

Sinfonietta, fl, str, 1972; Str Qt no.5, 1975; Sonata, vn, pf, 1982;
Katerina Izmaylova, sym., orch, 1993 [after op. by Shostakovich]
Over 100 film scores

WRITINGS

'Moskovskiye prem'yerï leningradtsev' [Premières in Moscow by
Leningraders], *SovM* (1971), no.6, pp.18–20
'Prazdnik otkrïtiy: avtorskiy vecher A. Petrova' [A festival of
discoveries: an evening of works by Petrov], *Muzïkal'naya zhizn'*
(1986), no.10, p.10 only
'Kak otrazit' mgnoveniye muzïki' [How to reflect a moment of
music], *Sovetskiy ëkran* (1987), no.4, p.16 only
'Schast'ye tvorcheskogo obshcheniya' [The joy of a creative exchange
of views], in A. Yansons: *Vospominaniya o muzïkante i cheloveke*
(St Petersburg, 1994), 102–6
'Yaroslavskiye rebyata v pesne ochen' khoroshi' [The lads from
Yaroslavl' are very good in song], *Rossiya* (18–24 Jan 1995)
[conversation with Yu. Svetov]
'Yesli ne verish' v budushcheye: stoit li zhit'?' [If you cannot believe
in the future is it worth living?], *MAK* (1995), nos.4–5, pp.57–60
'V mire Shostakovicha' [In the world of Shostakovich], *Zapis' besed
o kompozitore*, ed. S.M. Khentova (Moscow, 1996), 189–192
[conversation with D. Shostakovich]
'Pomogaya molodyozhi' [Helping young people], in V.P. Solov'yov-
Sedoy: *Vospominaniya, stat'i, materialï* (St Petersburg, 1998),
158–60

BIBLIOGRAPHY

S. Ziv: 'Zametki o strunnom kvartete Basnera' [A note about
Basner's string quartet], *SovM* (1955), no.11, pp.72–5
A. Sokhor: 'Vtoroy kvartet Basnera' [Basner's second quartet],
Sovetskaya muzïka, i (Moscow, 1956), 255–7; repr. in A. Sokhor:
Stat'i o sovetskoy muzïke (Leningrad, 1972), 162–4
G. Golovinsky: 'O muzïke v kino' [On music in the cinema], *SovM*
(1958), no.7, pp.49–58
A. Leman: 'Zhizn': istochnik khudozhestvennoy pravdï' [Life is the
source of artistic truth], *SovM* (1959), no.3, pp.65–70
S. Katonova: 'Dva tsikla: dva resheniya' [Two song cycles: two
solutions], *SovM* (1965), no.2, pp.10–13 [on Parabola]
I.V. Beletsky: *Veniamin Basner: monografcheskiy ocherk* [Basner: an
essay in monograph form] (Leningrad and Moscow, 1972)
T. Kopïlova: 'Vstrechi s novoy muzïkoy' [Encounters with recent
music], *SovM* (1978), no.9, pp.28–30
B. Tishchenko: 'Veniamin Yefimovich Basner', *Muzïkal'noye
obozreniye* (1996), no.9, p.141 only

LYUDMILA KOVNATSKAYA

Basque, André de. See KETÈLBEY, ALBERT W(ILLIAM).

Basque music. If the term 'Basque music' exists today, it is
because it enables us to describe various forms of musical
performance. The provinces inhabited by the Basque
people are divided politically in a stateless nation between
north-eastern Spain and southern France. The sections
that follow will outline what has been and what still is
signified by the term. Basque music emerged in the 19th
century at a time when Europe was being formed into
large national entities, and the very idea of a Basque or
Euskarian society assumed significance. Basque music
assumes a position alongside the Basque language and
Basque customs which constitute the identity of one of
the oldest European communities.

1. Principal characteristics. 2. Instruments. 3. Recent developments.

1. PRINCIPAL CHARACTERISTICS.   In northern Basque
country, at Izturitz in Laburdi, a 22,000-year-old three-
hole flute made from the bone of a bird was discovered; it
is regarded as an ancestor of the modern *txirula* or *txistu*
duct flutes. In the south, at Atxeta near Guernica in
Biscay, José Miguel de Barandiaran found a trumpet
dating from the Azilian period, suggesting that musical
performance goes a long way back in this mountainous
area. The studies of Resurreccion Maria de Azkue,
Francisco Madina, José Antonio de Donostia and José
Antonio Arana Martija attempt to trace Basque music's

line of descent. Latin books of plainchant show that there
was undoubtedly ritual performance of ecclesiastical
chant in the Middle Ages, and the *Linguae vasconum
primitiae*, published by B. Dechepare in 1545, as well as
older songs such as *Alostorrea*, *Urtsoak zazpi leio* and
Bereterretxen kantoria show that poems intended to be
sung existed. However, people at that time did not
consider them 'Basque music'. The outlines of a form of
Basque music can be traced during the 19th century. A
multiplicity of diffracted practices defined as Basque
occurred at the very moment the consolidation of the
European states threatened these practices, thus legitimiz-
ing preservation campaigns such as the publication in
1826 of Juan Ignacio de Iztueta's *Euscaldun anciña
anciñaco*. Basque music was paradoxically born as a
result of such partimonial efforts.

Iztueta intended his collection as a monument, in that
future generations 'must receive the inheritance of their
ancestors intact, and must act to preserve the inviolability
of their country' (preface, p.i). Documenting a repertory
fixes it, thus constructing an inheritance. In Iztueta's
collection as in others that were to follow, song texts are
given without systematic musical transcription. It was not
until 1870, when J.D.J. Sallaberry published his *Chants
populaires du pays basque*, that words, music and
harmonization are given.

With developments in printing, an enthusiastic desire
to publish seized Basque musicians. José Manterola
published his *Cancionero vasco*, a nine-volume series,
beginning in 1877. Between 1883 and 1898 the Lasserre
publishing house of Bayonne printed four successive
editions of A. Goyeneche's *Eskualdun kantaria*. In 1894
Iztueta's *Euscaldun ancina ancinaco* was reissued in
Bordeaux, and Basque institutions soon followed the lead
of collectors.

In 1912, a few years before the Euskaltzaindia (the
Academy of the Basque Language) was established in
Bilbao in 1918, the four districts of southern Basque
country organized a competition with the aim of awarding
prizes to collections of traditional Basque songs. Two
eminent musicologists took part, Don Resureccion Maria
de Azkue and Father Donostia, who published, respectively, a *Vox populi* containing 1810 vocal and instrumental tunes (edited as *Cancionero popular vasco*, 1920)
and a *Gure abendaren ereserkiak* (in *Obras completas*,
1983) containing 523 melodies. These two collections
mark the climax of a dynamic effort of writing and
publication which allowed Basque music to be recorded
and made available to a general public. Basque music
came to be defined by four criteria: melodic scale, metre,
formal structure and song.

The majority of the documented melodies are tonal,
most of them in a major key, less frequently in a minor
key. Nearly 25% of them, however, are modal. Although
defective modes are seldom used, we can at least conclude
that the Basques were familiar with modal scales. Most
of the melodies are transcribed in single metres. As result,
these transcriptions cannot take account of the constant
displacement of agogic accent. However, no metres are
mentioned in transcriptions of the wordless songs from
the province of Soule. Why not extend that principle to
the repertory as a whole? This unresolved methodological
difficulty is evidence of the complexity of Basque rhythmical structures, as in the *zortziko*.

Zortziko refers to the eight steps of the dances to which the *zortziko* provides an accompaniment. This rhythm is in a double compound metre, the result of combining two single heterogeneous metres: binary (ex.1*a*) and ternary

Ex.1 Zortziko rhythms

(ex.1*b*). The asymmetry of the two basic durations makes this ostinato an irregular bichrome measure, which Constantin Brăiloiu would have classified as an *aksak* rhythm. The *zortziko* is regarded as peculiarly Basque. The Basque national anthem, *Gernikako arbola* (1853), composed by Iparraguirre, is sung to a *zortziko*.

The third characteristic of Basque music is that the strophic form of the melodies adheres to a tripartite structure, *ABA*, often transmuted to *AABA*. On the other hand, although the couplet-refrain form is common in France and Spain, it remains rare in the Basque country. The isomorphic syllabic character of the songs with one note of the melody corresponding to each syllable of the text, makes a great deal of borrowing possible. The same text can be sung to different tunes, and the same melody may be adjusted to fit different texts. Such an adaptation of a new text in rhyming verse to a tune that already exists may even take the form of an improvised poem, the special province of the *bertsulari*.

The *bertsulari* may improvise alone or, more often, contests are held in which *bertsulari* dispute among themselves. The process involves four formal structures, depending on whether the strophes consist of four or five lines (eight half-lines in the *zortziko*, ten in the *hammareko*), and on whether the lines consist of 13 or 18 syllables. There is the *ttiki* (small) form for 13-syllable lines (7/6), and the *haundi* (large) form for 18-syllable lines (10/8). The *bederatzi puntuko* for is also common with nine monorhymed and non-isometric lines: (7/6), 12 (7/5), 13 (7/6), 13 (7/6), 6, 6, 6, 6, and 12 (7/5). Subtle mnemonic devices are worked out for improvising on these tunes. The *bertsulari* value the art of sung improvisation, and they like to improvise on complex existing tunes.

This long-practised improvisatory art became especially popular in 1935 when Manuel de Lekuona published his *Aozko literatura*, the first work devoted to the art of the *bertsulari*, and Aitzol organized the first Basque *bertsulari* championship. The plan was for the competition to be held annually, but Aitzol was shot by Francoist soldiers in 1936 after extracting only a short-lived statute of independence from Spain, still Republican at that time. The Basque language, Euskara, was forbidden, and with it all Basque culture. The performance of Basque music thus became synonymous with resistance. The choral group Eresoinka sang all over the world; at home, the Dindirri dancers defied the cultural ban, and the singer Xabier Lete, among others, challenged censorship. During 24 years of silence, the *bertsulari* continued improvising in secret in remote villages. It was not until 1960 that a third championship was held. The *bertsulari* phenomenon thus surfaced again in the context of fervent claims for a Basque identity. Championships were held in 1962, 1965

and 1967. In 1968 the first violent confrontations between the Spanish Civil Guard and ETA (*Euskadi ta Askatasuna*, the Basque Country and Liberty), led to severe repression, and for another 13 years there was silence from the *bertsulari* who were unable to organize a national competition. From 1980 onwards, the championship has been held every four years. The final round at Anoeta in Gipuzkoa receives wide media coverage, and gives the audience of 12,000 a symbolic satisfaction to counterbalance the feeling that they are not free.

2. INSTRUMENTS. The *txistu* is a three-hole flute made of ebony or other wood (and today sometimes of plastic), encircled by rings and with a metal mouthpiece. Usually in F, the *txistu* is played with the left hand by the *txistulari*, while the right hand beats a drum hanging from the elbow, using a stick. The *txistulari* plays dance music solo; *txistularis* also play in ensembles. In Soule, the *txirula* (*txülüla*)–*ttun-ttun* duo is regarded as a predecessor of the *txistu* and drum ensemble. The *txirula* is a small wooden flute in C, with a very shrill tessitura, and the *ttun-ttun* is a carved wooden box over which are stretched six strings that vibrate when struck with a wooden stick. Today, *trikititxa* ensembles, consisting of diatonic accordion, Basque drum and singer, are extraordinarily popular throughout the country. Such ensembles are used to accompany dances such as *jotas*, fandangos and *arin arin* danced in street parades.

The *gaita* of Arab origin is still found in Alaba in Navarre, and is played together with a drum. It is in the shawm family, with a double reed and eight holes; the *txanbela* is an additional variant from Soule. The *alboka* played in Biscay is an unusual instrument consisting of a double wooden pipe that connects two ends made of horn. One of the horns has two tongues, in the manner of a bagpipe, so that the instrumentalist can play using the continuous breathing technique. The *albokari* is usually accompanied by a *pandero*, a Basque drum. Finally, the *txalaparta* is a percussion instrument consisting of three wooden boards approximately 1·5 metres long. They are arranged horizontally and are struck by two instrumentalists using wooden sticks held vertically.

3. RECENT DEVELOPMENTS. Like the *bertsulari* tradition, which has its own training colleges where the best improvisers teach, the playing of traditional instruments is well on the way to becoming a professional occupation. Traditional instruments are taught more and more in conservatories, but their performance is still the province of associations, grouped into federations, which organize

Dulziana (shawm) players from Navarre, accompanied by a drum

annual competitions to choose a champion and promote social mobilization. Youth championships are also a great attraction. A *Trikitilari gazteen txapelketa* ['Young *trikitilari* championship'], for instance, brings young players of the *trikititxa* together, and hundreds of children hear each other singing on the occasion of the *Haur kantu txapelketa* ['Children's song championship'] festival.

Traditional musicians are in great demand to play at carnivals, masquerades, *pastorales* and village festivals. *Joaldunak*, symbolic carnival figures of Ituren and Zubieta (in Navarre) that are dressed in sheepskins sewn with bells that ring in time to their steps, now figure in many street parades. Traditional instruments are played at the annual demonstration in support of Basque independence. These instruments are also featured in demonstrations supporting the Basque language and the schools that teach it. The *bertsulari* regularly pay tribute to Basque political prisoners held in French and Spanish jails. The *gaita* is played in the Baigorri valley at the funerals of any militant belonging to Iparretarrak (the armed separatist movement operating inside France), and the *txalaparta* is played at the funerals of ETA militants.

The Basque choral movement is one of the strongest in Europe. It includes a unique *oxote* ensemble, consisting of eight male voices singing *a cappella*. In Gipuzkoa in Biscay there are a number of wind bands with a great many instrumentalists. In Soule, a different village every year works on the production of a *pastorale*, a play in the tradition of medieval mystery plays, rendered in a declamatory style to the accompaniment of singing and dancing; it can be traced back to the 16th century. Nearly 5000 people go to the narrow valleys of Soule in summer to watch these open-air performances, which last for over three hours.

The enormous expansion of the modern distribution network for recordings allows singers such as Peio Serbielle and Benat Achiary, or groups like Oskorri, to draw on the traditional repertory. The same network also distributes the hard rock, trash, funk or ragamuffin music of groups such as Negu Gorriak and Ertzainak, which frequently quote traditional music. For instance, the *Bersto hop* performed by Negu Gorriak, takes up a *bertsu* improvised at a championship contest, one which everyone will remember, while some pairs of *trikititxa* players make use of a synthesizer in their performances. The widespread use of imitative forms continues to nourish Basque music, keeping it in an ongoing state of development. Basque music exists in multiple situations involving moments when, at a given moment and in an emotional context, a musician interprets a musical sequence for an audience who can identify it. Basque music is created in the complicity of this partnership, where shared knowledge fashions a common culture.

BIBLIOGRAPHY
AND OTHER RESOURCES

FasquelleE

B. Dechepare: *Linguae vasconum primitiae* (Bilbao, 1545, 2/1980)
J.I. de Iztueta: *Guipuzcoaco dantza gogoangarrien condaira edo historia* (San Sebastián, 1824, 3/1968 in Basque and Sp.) [texts]; (San Sebastián, 1826, 3/1973) [melodies]
J.I. de Iztueta: *Euscaldun anciña anciñaco* (San Sebastián, 1826)
J.A. Santesteban: *Colección de aires vascongados para canto y piano* (San Sebastián, 1862–70)
J.D.J. Sallaberry: *Chants populaires du pays basque* (Bayonne, 1870/R, 2/1930)
J. Manterola, ed.: *Cancionero vasco* (San Sebastián, 1877–80)
A. Goyeneche: *Eskualdun kantaria* (Bayonne, 1883)

C. Bordes: *Cent chansons populaires basques* (Paris, 1894)
C. Bordes: *Douze noëls basques anciens* (Paris, 1897)
La tradition au pays-basque (Paris, 1899/R) [pubn of the Société d'ethnographie nationale et d'art populaire]
C. Bordes: *Douze chansons amoureuses du pays basque française* (Paris, 1910)
F. Gáscue: *Origen de la música popular vascongada* (Paris, 1913)
F. Gáscue: *El aurresku en Guipúzcoa a finales del sigio XVIII según Iztueta* (San Sebastian, 1916)
F. Gáscue: *Materiales para el estudio del folklore músico vasco* (San Sebastián, 1917)
R.M. de Azkue: *Musica popular vasca: conferencias* (Bilbao, 1919)
R.M. de Azkue, ed.: *Cancionero popular vasco* (Barcelona, 1920/R)
G. Hérelle: 'Les charivaris nocturnes dans le pays basque français', *Revista internacional de los estudios vascos*, xv (1924), 505
G. de [W. von] Humboldt: 'Bocetos de un viaje a través del país vasco', *Revista internacional de los estudios vascos*, xv (1924), 448
H. Olazarán de Estella: *Mutil dantza del Baztán* [Dance of the young men of the Baztán valley] (Pamplona, 1925)
M. van Eys: 'Second voyage au pays basque, 1868', *Revista internacional de los estudios vascos*, xviii (1927), 527
R.A. Gallop: *Vingt-cinq chansons populaires d'Eskual-herria* (Bayonne, 1928)
B. Estornés Lasa: 'De arte popular', *Revista internacional de los estudios vascos*, xxi (1930), 206
W. Giese: 'Txiribita = violin', *Revista internacional de los estudios vascos*, xxiv (1933), 616
W. Giese: 'Vasc. bilarrausi', *Revista internacional de los estudios vascos*, xxiv (1933), 71
M. de Lekuona: *Aozko literatura* [Oral poetry] (Tolosa, 1935; 1978 in Basque and Sp.)
J.A. de Donostia and F.de Madina: *De música vasca* (Buenos Aires, 1943)
I. Fagoaga: *La musique représentative basque* (Bayonne, 1944)
L. de Hoyos Sáinz and N. de Hoyos Sancho: *Manual de folklore* (Madrid, 1947)
H. Olazarán de Estella: *Danzas de Baztán* (Viña del Mar, 1957)
J.A. de Donostia: *Obras musicales del padre Donostia*, ed. J. de Riezu (Navarra, 1960–75)
M. García Matos: disc notes, *Antología del folklore musical de España*, Hispavox HH 10 107 to 110 (1960)
A. Zavala: *Auspoa* (Tolosa, 1961–) [Basque folksongs]
G. de Barandiaran: *Danzas de Euskalerri*, i–iii (San Sebastián, 1963–9)
G. de Barandiaran: 'Gizon-dantza: liturgia y sentido' [Men's dance: ritual and significance], *Revue de l'association des danseurs du pays basque* (1968), no.11, p.13; no.12, p.3
J.L. de Echevarría: *Danzas de Vizcaya* (Bilbao, 1969)
J. Orúe Matia, ed.: *Cancionero del país vasco* (Madrid, 1970, 2/1971)
F. Escudero: 'El txistu y el silbote', *Estudios de deusto* (Bilbao, 1972), no.45, p.37
F. Escudero: 'Peculiaridades morfológicas de la canción popular y de la música vasca', *Txistulari*, lxix (1972), 34
H. Olazarán de Estella: *Tratado de txistu y gaita* (Pamplona, 1972)
M.A. Sagaseta: 'Estudio de los bailes de Valcarlos', *Cuadernos de etnología y etnografía de Navarra*, vii/20 (Pamplona, 1975)
J.M. Barrenechea: *Alboka: entorno folklórico* (Lecároz, 1976)
X. Amuriza: *Zu ere bertsulari* (Donostia, 1982)
J.A. de Donostia: *Obras completas, 1917–56* (Bilbao, 1983)
J.-M. Guilcher: *La tradition de danse en Béarn et pays basque français* (Paris, 1984)
J. Haritschelhar, ed.: *Etre basque* (Toulouse, 1984)
J.A. Arana Martija: *Musica vasca* (Bilbao, 1985)
Euskal herriko folklorea, Ikerfolk ELK 142 to 143 (1987); ELK 200 to 201 (1989) [incl. disc notes]
J. Bagües Erriondo: *La musica en la Real Sociedad Bascongada de los Amigos del País* (Donostia, 1990)
J. Goyheneche: *Les basques et leur histoire: mythes et réalités* (Donostia, 1993)
A. Artal, I. Zunzunegui and I. Zorrilla: *Bizkaiko dultzaina* (Bilbao, 1994)
G. Aulestia: *Improvisational Poetry from the Basque Country* (Reno, NV, 1995)
J. Garmendia Azzuabarrena: *Juan Ignacio Iztueta* (Zaldibia, 1995)
J.L. Antsonrema Mizanda: *Txistua eta txistulariak* (San Sebastián, 1996)
D. Laborde, ed.: *Tout un monde de musiques* (Paris, 1996)

E. López Aguirre: *Del txitu a la telecaster: crónica del rock vasco* (Oñati, 1996)

D. Laborde: *Musiques à l'école* (Paris, 1998)

C. Sánchez Equiza: *Del danbolin al silbo: txistu tambozil y danza vasca en la época de la Ilustración* (Pamplona, 1999)

DENIS LABORDE

Bass (i) (Fr. *basse*; Ger. *Bass*; It. *basso*). The lower part of the musical system, as distinguished from the treble, specifically: that part or voice in a composition executed by the lowest-range performers ('bass part'); the lowest pitch in a sonority; hence the succession of lowest notes in a passage or composition ('bass line'); the lowest segment of an instrument's range, or the lowest octave or octaves articulated in a composition ('bass register'); and those notes which 'support' the other parts, which determine the harmonic identity of sonorities and which are in the main responsible for harmonic progressions, cadences, modulations and large-scale tonal relationships ('harmonic', 'functional' or 'musical' bass). These distinct but overlapping meanings are all usually simply called 'bass'. They share the original modifying sense 'low', as in BASS (ii) and (iii); 'bass' is cognate with the adjective 'base' ('low', 'unrefined'), both deriving from Late Latin 'bassus' ('low', 'thick', 'fat').

The term first appeared in music about the middle of the 15th century: in expanding from three- to four-part texture, composers wrote two contratenor parts, the lower of which was distinguished by the title 'contratenor bassus'. By 1500 'Bassus' alone was used as a noun, meaning the lowest part in a composition. In this new sense it rapidly acquired two cognates, one material, the other figurative: the nouns 'base' ('lowest or supporting part') and 'basis' ('main constituent', 'fundamental principle'). Thus Glarean's confusion in the *Dodecachordon* of 1547 (MSD, vi, 1965): 'The lowest voice is called 'bass' (*Basis*) . . . because all voices lean on it as a support' (i, 122); 'From this the common name 'bass' (*Bassus*) has by chance come into use' (ii, 247). Soon afterwards the term acquired philosophical legitimacy through the humanistic conceit of comparing the four human voice ranges with the four elements, as in Zarlino's *Le istitutioni harmoniche* of 1558 (trans. Marco and Palisca, 179):

As the earth is the foundation of the other elements, the bass (*Basso*) . . . is the foundation of the harmony, . . . as if to say the base (*Basa*) and sustenance of the other parts. If . . . the element of earth were lacking, what ruin and waste would result! Similarly a composition without a bass would be full of confusion and dissonance.

These conflated meanings 'bass', 'base' and 'basis' have persisted to the present. Zarlino's usage 'foundation' became more common in the Baroque era, where the basso continuo assumed 'fundamental' importance. The continuo instruments were often called 'foundation instruments', and 'Fundamento' was a common title on bass parts. Thus Walther in the *Musicalisches Lexicon* (1732), 268: "'Fundamento' is, in general, any bass part; in particular, a basso continuo; also the harmony which the latter expresses'. Although 'Fundamento' rarely occurred after 1750, the generic term 'Basso' designated the bass in soloistic chamber music as late as Haydn's string quartets op.20 (1772), and in orchestral music and informal chamber music until 1800. Haydn discussed scorings of the bass part in a letter of 1768 as follows: 'I prefer just three basses [*Bässe*] – that is, one cello, one bassoon, and one double bass'; here 'bass' is still the generic term for any and all bass instruments. The modern practice of identifying every bass instrument by name in musical sources was not fully established until the 19th century.

The history of musical basses forms part of the history of TONALITY. Features that are taken to be characteristic appeared from the 14th century on: movement of the lowest part primarily by leap (Ciconia), articulation of the final at cadences by leap from the 5th above (Du Fay, Binchois), expansion of the tessitura downwards to encompass the full range of the bass voice (Ockeghem, Josquin), and homophonic style 'leaning' on the bass (the frottola). Besseler and Lowinsky argued that these features functioned in Renaissance polyphony as they have in major–minor tonality since 1700. More recently, however, it has been shown that this music was still based on the earlier 'discant theory'. The tenor was still the 'basis'; the 'skeleton' was the note-against-note counterpoint between tenor and soprano, and the bass was an 'added' part not only in compositional practice (as is believed), but in theory. Thus Aaron, in his *Thoscanello de la musica* (1529/R), described ex.1 as a cadence on E, governed by

Ex.1

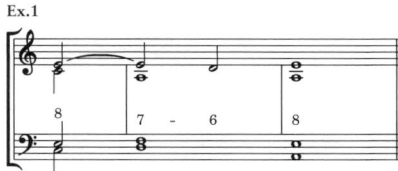

the suspension–resolution configuration 8–7–6–8 (*see also* CADENCE). But in tonality the 'outer parts', that is an expressive melody and a supporting bass, are the 'skeleton' of the music. The distinction is especially clear in early Baroque monody, where these two parts make up the entire notated texture.

Furthermore, Renaissance theorists still thought in terms of intervals. For Zarlino the triad was merely the most complex and perfect collection of intervals; he did not invoke the concept of chordal inversion, which, along with that of root, was first adumbrated just after 1600 in England and especially Germany. The 'basis' of tonality is the triad as a unified entity built on its bass: 'the lowest of the three notes which constitute a triad is called the bass [*Basis*] or fundamental note' (Brossard, *Dictionaire*, 2/1705/R, 169).

Finally, coherence in tonal music depends on the bass, which governs harmonic progressions, cadences (hence phrases and periods) and large-scale tonal relationships (hence form). Especially for large-scale relationships, no 'basis' of this kind has been shown for Renaissance polyphony.

The Baroque basso continuo incorporated every aspect of 'bass', being the bass part 'by definition'. It occupied the lowest register and was virtually always the lowest-sounding part; it was often a true line of melodic and contrapuntal interest; even more often it was the 'basis' of the form, as in the ostinato, the passacaglia and other variations, and numerous dance-related patterns; and it not only supported the other parts but, through the figures supplied, determined the entire harmonic contents. As late as C.P.E. Bach the theory and practice of composition itself were, for most practical purposes, synonymous with mastery of the continuo. Hence Mattheson's apotheosis (in *Der vollkommene Capellmeister*, 1739/R, 104) is less extravagant than may at first appear: 'Musical composition could not exist without the continuo; the one assumes

Ex.2 Bach: Brandenburg Concerto no.2, 2nd movt

the other; and the continuo was born at the same time as harmony itself'. Furthermore the continuo was articulated more strongly than any other part: in performance, by timbral and often by registral doubling between a keyboard instrument (organ, harpsichord, clavichord) and a melody instrument (cello, double bass, viola da gamba, bassoon etc.); in register, by separation from the melodic parts above it, as in solo sonata and trio sonata scoring; and often in musical structure, by its independent musical material and specifically bass-like character and progressions (ex.2). Continuo parts often assumed one of a number of definite types, such as ostinato, figural, walking or stationary basses. Finally, tonality itself was one prerequisite for the rise of autonomous instrumental art music, one of the signal achievements of the Baroque age; but as has been seen, tonality is dependent on the bass.

In the Classical and Romantic periods the hegemony of the continuo was broken in both theory and practice. Rameau's distinction between the 'actual' bass (the lowest pitch) and an 'ideal' bass (the root) once again split 'base' and 'basis' into separate entities. The succession of roots, or FUNDAMENTAL BASS, determined the nature of the harmonies, by its restriction to the 'functions' I, IV and V, and of harmonic progressions, by its preference for movement by 5ths and 3rds. This basis for tonal music lived on in the 'functional harmony' of Riemann and his followers.

Meanwhile a number of independently scored instruments began to share the continuo's old function of 'base'. By late Haydn and Beethoven, there were separate cello, double bass and bassoon parts. Often the horn functioned on its own as the bass; occasionally the timpani and, in

exceptional cases, the contrabassoon and trombone assumed this role. In the 19th century the last two instruments became standard, and tubas, the bass clarinet and bass trumpet were added, as well as other inventions most of which have since disappeared. Each of these bass instruments was now a separate 'part', with its own name, staff in the score and musical substance; each could at any time be the bass, the others resting or playing above it. Hence the musical bass was no longer correlated with any single part; rather it became identified, by and large, with the 'bass line' – the succession of lowest-sounding pitches – the chief denotative sense it retains.

Under these conditions the parts could 'cross' in a meaningful way. Koch noted this new resource, so characteristic of chamber music, as early as 1782 in his *Versuch einer Anleitung zur Composition* (i, 245–6): 'When in a trio or quartet with obbligato cello [as opposed to continuo], the latter has solo passages, and the viola or second violin takes over the bass, . . . there is an exchange of bass function among the participating instruments'; this exchange is illustrated in ex.3. Haydn's basses are

Ex.3 Haydn: String Quartet in C, op.50 no.2, finale

transitional in this respect: in these 'part-crossing' passages the nominal bass often functions as the musical bass, as a continuo would have done. Mozart and Beethoven almost always took the view that the lowest part must be the bass.

The bass retained all its harmonic, tonal and structural importance in Classical and Romantic music. In the hands of composers like Mozart or Chopin, even the much-maligned Alberti, 'murky' and 'oompah' basses were fully compatible with the highest art (see exx.4– 5). Tovey wrote: 'A composer [Schubert] whose basses are magnificent is a great contrapuntist, even if (like Wagner) he never published a fugue in his life' (*Essays and Lectures on Music*, London, 1949, p.112). By the same token Brahms did not return to the 'values' of the Baroque era

Ex.4 Mozart: Piano Trio in G major к496, finale

Ex.5 Chopin: Ballade no.3 in A♭ op. 47

so much as he integrated his basses, at once melodic and structural, into complex textures and widely ranging harmonies.

In the 20th century tonally based art music developed no new general principles in its basses. Composers like Stravinsky, Hindemith and Bartók partly replaced harmonic progressions of the traditional type with repetitive patterns such as the ostinato. In 12-note and other rigorously non-tonal music, it may be doubted whether the bass any longer functions as a 'base' or 'basis' at all. On the other hand, jazz and popular music maintain strongly articulated bass lines as the foundation of their subdominant-orientated tonality.

Schenker's theoretical writings of the 1920s and 30s reinterpreted the bass as a synthesis of harmonic and contrapuntal forces: a line developed by prolongation of the triad in the form I–V–I. At the same time, in conjunction with the Schenkerian *Urlinie*, the bass retained its old importance as one of the two elements of the *Ursatz* or *Aussensatz*, the 'outer parts' in a structural as well as auditory sense. The marriage of bass and tonality remains indissoluble.

BIBLIOGRAPHY

M. Shirlaw: *The Theory of Harmony* (London, 1917/R)

M. Schneider: *Die Anfänge des Basso Continuo und seiner Bezifferung* (Leipzig, 1918/R)

F.T. Arnold: *The Art of Accompaniment from a Thorough-Bass* (London, 1931/R)

F. Oberdörffer: *Der Generalbass in der Instrumentalmusik des ausgehenden 18. Jahrhunderts* (Kassel, 1939)

H. Besseler: *Bourdon und Fauxbourdon* (Leipzig, 1950)

H.H. Eggebrecht: 'Studien zur musikalischen Terminologie' (Mainz, 1955), 62ff.

C. Bär: 'Zum Begriff des "Basso" in Mozarts Serenaden', *MJb 1960–61*, 133–55

E. Lowinsky: *Tonality and Atonality in 16th Century Music* (Berkeley, 1961)

C. Dahlhaus: *Untersuchungen über die Entstehung der harmonischen Tonalität* (Kassel, 1967; Eng. trans., 1990)

E.T. Cone: 'Beyond Analysis', *PNM*, vi (1967–8), 33–51

H. Haack: *Anfänge des Generalbass-Satzes: die 'Cento concerti ecclesiastici' (1602) von Ludovico Viadana* (Tutzing, 1974)

S. Bonta: 'From Violone to Violoncello: a Question of Strings?', *JAMIS*, iii (1977), 64–99

J. Webster: 'The Bass Part in Haydn's Early String Quartets', *MQ*, lxiii (1977), 390–424

R.J. Hoyt: *The Bassline in Atonal Music: its Relationship to Melodic and Harmonic Structure* (diss., U. of Pennsylvania, 1979)

M. Cyr: 'Basses and basse continue in the Orchestra of the Paris Opéra, 1700–1764', *EMc*, x (1982), 155–70

W. Salmen, ed.: *Kontrabass und Bassfunktion* (Innsbruck, 1986)

L. Dreyfus: *Bach's Continuo Group: Players and Practices in his Vocal Works* (Cambridge, MA, 1987)

C.-H. Mahling: 'Con o senza fagotto? Bemerkungen zur Besetzung der "Bassi" (1740 bis ca.1780)', ibid., 197–208

S.A. Edgerton: *The Bass Part in Haydn's Early Symphonies: a Documentary and Analytical Study* (diss., Cornell U., 1989)

J. Lester: *Between Modes and Keys: German Theory, 1592–1802* (Stuyvesant, NY, 1989)

JAMES WEBSTER

Bass (ii). The lowest male voice, normally written for within the range *F* to *e′*, which may be extended at either end, particularly in solo writing. Over time the bass voice has been subdivided into a number of distinct categories: the BASSO PROFONDO or BASSE NOBLE refers to a particularly low bass, the BASSE CHANTANTE (or *basso cantate*) a higher, lyrical voice, and the *basso buffo* a comic bass. By the 19th century the baritone split off from the bass, to be regarded as a separate category, although some overlap (and confusion) remains in the terminological distinction, especially between bass and bass-baritone (*see* BARITONE (i) and BASS-BARITONE).

1. Before 1600. 2. 1600–1800. 3. 19th century. 4. 20th century.

1. BEFORE 1600. Although the bass voice has no doubt existed since time immemorial, Western art music made no specific use of it for centuries, and early writers had therefore little to say about it. Isidore of Seville (*c*559–636) commented that 'in fat voices, as those of men, much breath is emitted at once', and he asserted that 'the perfect voice is high, sweet and loud' (*Etymologiarum sive originum libri xx*). In 9th-century parallel organum, as described in the *Scolica enchiriadis*, several dispositions of the parts called for the addition of apparently quite low voices an octave or 5th below the *vox principalis* 'for the sake of the symphony' (i.e. the sonority; *GS*, i, 186). Resonant bass voices must have created an imposing sound in such a 'symphony'.

Until the second half of the 14th century, upper voice parts in polyphony were composed above a bottom line which, if not always a tenor in function (i.e. holding a cantus firmus), was at any rate written in the tenor range. In the early 15th century TENOR and CONTRATENOR, overlapping in the same range, shared the function of providing a harmonic foundation. After about 1450, however, the role of supporting the harmony was assigned to a single line by the creation of the *contratenor bassus*. Some theorists showed their understanding of the essential function of this line by referring to it not as *bassus* (the medieval Latin word for 'low') but by the Greek word *basis* ('foundation'). The unprecedented sonority created by these low-pitched *contratenor bassus* lines became in itself a source of fascination, as is evident in descriptive terminology of the age that played with the Greek prefix *bari-* ('low'; *see* BARITONE (i)). In the works of such composers as Busnoys, Ockeghem and La Rue there are not only bass lines ranging between *D* and *d* but also two or even three parts in what would now be described as the bass or baritone range. Tinctoris (*De inventione et usu musicae*, 1481–3) singled out Ockeghem as the finest bass he had ever heard. Polyphonic sonorities emphasizing the bass voice, although originating in the chapels of the Burgundian and French courts, soon spread elsewhere.

During the 16th century composers became increasingly sensitive to the bass's function of defining the harmony. Nicola Vicentino (*L'antica musica ridotta alla moderna prattica*; 1555, *f.55v*) remarked that 'it is the bass which governs, and gives the grace of beautiful progressions and

Ex.1 Palestrina: *In festo Sanctae Trinitatis*

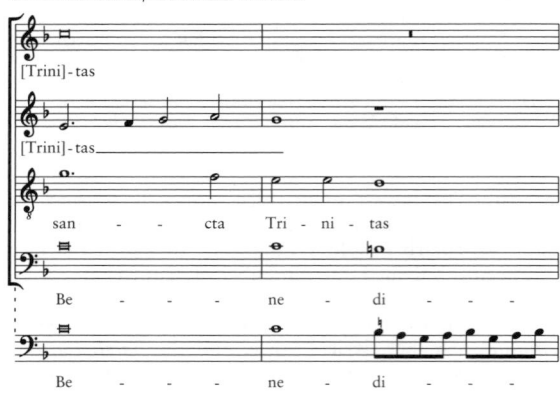

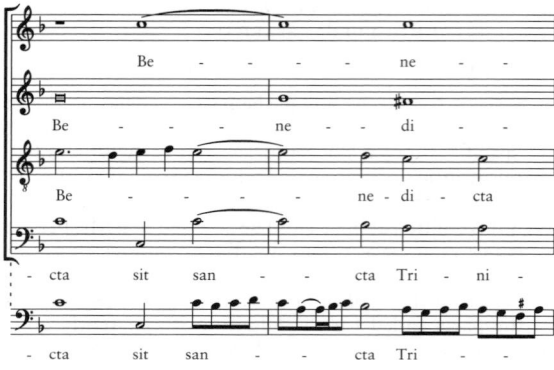

Ex.2 Wert: *Se tal erger*

variety of harmony to all the parts'. In this period there developed a tendency for bass lines to use wide intervals more than other voices did, to be more angular, and to span a wider range in general. Despite the relative angularity of bass lines, bass singers, like those with high voices, became increasingly preoccupied with the art of improvised ornamentation during the 16th century. Giovanni Bassano (*Ricercate, passaggi et cadentie*, 1585) illustrated how the bass part of a Palestrina motet might be sumptuously ornamented (ex.1), but such elaborate ornamentation of bass parts was attacked by Pietro Cerone (*El melopeo y maestro*, 1613), who complained that through such practice the whole fabric of polyphony 'falls to the ground'.

In spite of such resistance, virtuoso basses attracted much attention in the period 1575–1625 and were in great demand. The Neapolitan bass Giulio Cesare Brancaccio was the highest paid singer in the élite corps of virtuosos assembled in Ferrara by Alfonso d'Este, and the availability of such skilled basses was essential to the development of the luxuriant style of madrigal composition cultivated at Ferrara by Giaches de Wert and others, in whose works the bass line is often as florid as any of the upper voices (ex.2).

2. 1600–1800.   The Italian fashion for highly ornate bass music was extended into the monodies of the first

Ex.3 Landi: *Superbe colli*

decades of the 17th century, as can be seen in ex.3 from Stefano Landi's madrigal *Superbe colli* (*Aria a una voce*, 1620). Giulio Caccini, similarly, wrote virtuoso bass arias for Melchior Palontrotti and published one aria, 'Muove si dolce', in his *Le nuove musiche* (1601–2) with the divisions Palontrotti sang. In Italian opera during the 17th century, ornate writing for the bass voice was, in contrast, quite rare. In the surviving operas of Monteverdi the bass already appears in some of its most important historical role types: as a god (particularly the god of the underworld: Pluto in *Orfeo*, Neptune in *Il ritorno d'Ulisse*) or as a sepulchral figure (Charon in *Orfeo*). His most impressive use of the bass was in the tragic role of Seneca in *L'incoronazione di Poppea* (1643).

The comic potential of the bass voice was best realized in the tradition of the *basso buffo*, whose spiritual ancestor was the *commedia dell'arte* character Pantalone. Already in late Renaissance madrigal comedies (e.g. Orazzio Vecchi's *L'Amfiparnaso*, 1597, and Banchieri's *La pazzia senile*, 1598), the blustering, the stammering and the bathetic self-pitying of the classic old fool were given eloquent musical depiction. In the early history of opera similar comic male characters, usually basses, appeared occasionally on the fringe of plots (e.g. Penelope's wooer, Antinous, in Monteverdi's *Il ritorno d'Ulisse*, 1640) and were called upon to perform exaggeratedly wide-spanning phrases that plummet to the depths of the singer's range. In 17th-century Italian opera, the *basso buffo* was frequently aligned with the comic contralto role (see CONTRALTO). As a central figure, the comic bass began to appear only in the last quarter of the century (e.g. in Stradella's *Il Trespolo tutore*, 1679).

The diminishing importance of the bass voice in *opera seria* is reflected in the cantata: of Alessandro Scarlatti's solo cantatas, more than 600 are for soprano and five are for bass. However, the earlier tradition of the virtuoso bass continued to find expression in serenatas which include numerous representations of such characters as Belisarius, Nero and Seneca, usually in a mood of defiance or rage. These vehement emotions are expressed in angular, wide-leaping lines that show the influence of instrumental styles in the developing concerto. Handel inherited this tradition through such predecessors as Stradella and Scarlatti and during his Italian years wrote remarkable parts for bass in his Italian oratorios, serenatas and cantatas, such as Lucifer (*La resurrezione*), Polyphemus (*Aci, Galatea e Polifemo*), and in the cantata *Nell'africane selve*. Vivaldi's vocal music for the Venetian *ospedali* is normally written so that the bass parts can be performed an octave higher by the girls when bass singers were unavailable (Talbot, 1994); as a result the bass is rarely highlighted.

Most Handel operas include a role for bass who, though usually a secondary character, is of sufficient importance to be assigned an aria in each of the three acts. These roles are most often kings or generals, whose noble arias declare pride in rank; sometimes a villain (Achillas in *Giulio Cesare*, 1724, or Garibaldo in *Rodelinda*, 1725, for example) may be cast as a bass. A favourite type of aria is that of rage or defiance, often with huge leaps; James Miller wrote of Handel's Royal Academy bass G.M. Boschi, 'And Boschi-like, be always in a rage'. Boschi's parts are high-lying, in what would now be called a baritone range; some of Handel's finest bass parts were for Montagnana, who sang down to *F* in the remarkable role of the magician Zoroastro in *Orlando* (1733). The 'rage aria' was cultivated even in the oratorio; the most famous of all is 'Why do the nations so furiously rage together?' in *Messiah*.

In French opera, with no castratos for male roles, the bass retained more importance than it did in *opera seria*. Cavalli's only opera for Paris, *Ercole amante* (1662), has a bass title role. The importance of the bass in French opera was remarked on in François Raguenet's *Paralèle des italiens et des françois* (1702; Eng. trans., 1709): 'When the Persons of Gods or Kings, a *Jupiter*, *Neptune*, *Priam*, or *Agamemnon*, are brought on the Stage, our Actors, with their deep Voices, give 'em an air of Majesty, quite different from that of the feign'd *Bases* among the *Italians*, which have neither Depth nor Strength'. Lully's bass roles are often gods (Jupiter in *Cadmus et Hermione*, 1673, and *Isis*, 1677), especially those of the underworld (Pluto in *Alceste*, 1674, and *Proserpine*, 1680; Neptune in *Isis* and *Acis et Galatée*, 1686), but also include roles with comic elements (Charon in *Alceste*, Polyphemus in *Acis*). Only in *Roland* (1685) did he use the bass voice in a title role. Some of the most imposing roles for the bass voice in French Baroque opera are by Rameau, for example Theseus in *Hippolyte et Aricie* (1733) and Pollux in *Castor et Pollux* (1737), both were first sung by C.L.D. de Chassé (1699–1786). This French tradition is further evident in the late operas that Gluck wrote for Paris, which include such roles as Calchas in *Iphigénie en Aulide* (1774), Hercules in *Alceste* (1776) and Thoas in *Iphigénie en Tauride* (1779).

In Germany, the bass was prized for depicting seriousness and wisdom, both in opera and sacred music. In Buxtehude's cantata *Jesu, meine Freude*, for example, the bass sings 'Trotz dem alten Drachen' in which the lowest range of the bass (down to *D*) is explored for the word 'abyss'. J.S. Bach's works are full of remarkable solo parts for bass. In *Jesu, der du meine Seele* (BWV78, 1724), the bass (*G–d'*) represents the dying soul expressing trust in the Lord in an elaborate concerto aria ('Nun, du wirst mein Gewissen stillen'). In the *St Matthew Passion*, the bass arias towards the end are among the most beautiful and affecting in the entire work (especially 'Mache dich, mein Herze, rein'). In his secular music, Bach used the bass for Aeolus, god of the wind, in *Der Streit zwischen Phoebus und Pan* and the old, conservative father in the Coffee Cantata. Extensive passage-work in the music written for bass in Germany demanded a virtuoso technique, but J.F. Agricola (*Anleitung zur Singekunst*, 1757) complained that many German basses, by inserting a 'ga, ga, ga' before each note and gulping for breath every half-bar, created an unpleasing effect.

In England, following the Italian tradition of virtuoso basses, Purcell wrote remarkable arias for John Gostling ('They that go down to the sea in ships') and Richard Leveridge ('Ye twice ten hundred deities'), who had deep and agile bass voices with very wide ranges. Leveridge went on to perform in opera but made his name in such parts as Charon, Merlin and Pluto in the English theatrical pantomime, notably the witch Hecate in *Macbeth*.

In 1781 Mozart expressed a wish to recast *Idomeneo* 'in the French style' and change the title role from tenor to bass: 'I would have altered Idomeneus's role completely and made it a bass part for [Ludwig] Fischer'. Mozart's typical bass roles are more characteristic: Osmin, the comically savage overseer in *Die Entführung* (1782, written for Fischer) and Sarastro, a high priest, in *Die Zauberflöte* (1791, sung by Franz Gerl). Most of his roles nominally for bass in his mature Italian operas are now regarded equally as baritone roles. Figaro and Leporello are often sung by basses and are essentially *basso buffo* roles, the former designed for (and both sung by) the outstanding Viennese exponent Francesco Benucci; another such role is Bartolo in *Figaro*. The tradition to which these and many other roles belong is in fact the hallmark of *opera buffa*; it goes back to the 17th century, appears in numerous intermezzo-type works, such as Pergolesi's *La serva padrona* (1733), is central to the entire repertory of operas to Goldoni's librettos and the principal works of Paisiello and Cimarosa, and continues in the operas of Rossini and Donizetti.

3. 19TH CENTURY.   Rossini expected his basses to have voices as flexible as the tenors, or indeed the sopranos and mezzos. Nicola de Grecis, a comic bass who had sung in operas by Guglielmi and others, was the first to inspire Rossini's *basso buffo* roles; he created roles in *La scala di seta* (1812) and *Signor Bruschino* (1813). Rossini wrote eight roles, serious and comic, for Filippo Galli, among them Mustafa in *L'italiana in Algeri* (1813), the title role of *Maometto II* (1820) and Assur in *Semiramide* (1823); Galli's noble, flexible voice later inspired Donizetti to write the part of Henry VIII in *Anna Bolena* (1830). Michele Benedetti, a more dramatic singer, created bass roles in seven of Rossini's serious operas for Naples, including Elmiro in *Otello* (1816) and the title role of *Mosè in Egitto* (1818).

The illustrious Neapolitan bass Luigi Lablache, who made his début as Dandini (Rossini's *La Cenerentola*), created roles in seven Donizetti operas in Naples (1826–32) and later sang the title roles in two Donizetti premières in Paris, *Marino Faliero* (1835) and *Don Pasquale* (1843). Also in Paris, he created Giorgio in Bellini's *I puritani*, and in London his performance of the title role in Balfe's *Falstaff* (1838) drew the remark that he was 'such a protagonist as would have made Shakespeare's heart leap for joy' (H.F. Chorley). At the Paris Opéra, Henri-Etienne Dérivis, a singer in the classical French tradition with an excellent coloratura technique, created roles in three Spontini operas; he also created Mahomet II in Rossini's *Le siège de Corinthe* (1826). His successor at the Opéra, Nicholas Levasseur, who had a voice of enormous range, sang Don Alvaro in Rossini's *Il viaggio a Reims* at the Théâtre-Italien (1825) and created many roles at the Opéra, including Walter Furst in *Guillaume Tell* (1829) and Zacharie in Meyerbeer's *Le prophète* (1849).

With the rise of the 'Verdi baritone', the bass voice played a smaller role in Italian opera of the second half of the century. Among the singers of Verdi's early bass roles, Lablache created Massimiliano (*I masnadieri*, 1847). Both Jean Procida (*Les vêpres siciliennes*, 1855) and Philip II (*Don Carlos*, 1867) were created by the French bass Louis-Henri Obin. With the role of Jacopo Fiesco (*Simon Boccanegra*, 1857), Verdi largely turned to a style of writing that allowed for a marked distinction between his baritone and bass roles. Based on the talents of the Italian bass Giuseppe Etcheverria, this style, found in practically all his main bass roles after 1860, generally avoided lyrical phrases (Philip II is an exception here), emphasized declamation and made full use of the lowest register (Budden, 1994–5). Verdi's bass roles, adhering to tradition, are chiefly old men, including priests, counts, squires and the like, villains and servants; he also contributed to the tradition of ghosts as basses, with Banquo (*Macbeth*, 1847), like Nino's ghost in Rossini's *Semiramide* and the Commendatore in *Don Giovanni*.

Among Wagnerian basses, Carl Risse created Daland (*Der fliegende Holländer*, 1843) and Wilhelm Dettmer sang the Landgrave (*Tannhäuser*, 1845). Ludwig Zottmayr, the first King Mark in *Tristan und Isolde* (1865), was probably a bass-baritone: his roles in Munich included Count di Luna and Hans Heiling. Kaspar Bausewein – Pogner in *Die Meistersinger* (1868), Fafner in *Das Rheingold* (1869) and Hunding in *Die Walküre* (1870) – was a true bass who also sang Leporello, Caspar and Rossini's Don Basilio. Hagen (*Götterdämmerung*) was created at Bayreuth (1876) by Gustav Siehr, who later alternated as Gurnemanz in *Parsifal* with Emil Scaria, the bass who created the role (1882); Scaria, Escamillo at Vienna in the first performance of *Carmen* outside France, sang Wotan in the first complete Vienna, Berlin and London *Ring* cycles.

Some of the finest basses in German opera were French. Léon Gresse, who created Phanuel in *Hérodiade* (1881) at the Théâtre de la Monnaie, Brussels, was the first Hunding in *Die Walküre* at the Paris Opéra. Pol Plançon, an effective actor as well as a most stylish singer, created Massenet's Count of Gormas in *Le Cid* at the Opéra (1885) and Garrido in *La Navarraise* at Covent Garden (1894). One of the greatest 19th-century basses, he made numerous recordings. Don Diègue in *Le Cid* was created by the Polish-born Edouard de Reszke, an equally fine interpreter of Italian, French and German opera. His prowess as a Wagner singer was legendary: at Covent Garden and the Metropolitan he excelled as King Henry, King Mark, Pogner, the Wanderer and Hunding.

From its beginnings in works by Verstovsky and Glinka, 19th-century Russian opera included important bass roles. The title role in Glinka's *A Life for the Tsar* (1836) was entrusted to Osip Petrov, who went on to create bass roles in many operas by Glinka, Rimsky-Korsakov and Tchaikovsky. Fyodor Stravinsky, father of the composer, who created many bass roles in Tchaikovsky's operas, was equally gifted in comic and dramatic roles. Ivan Mel'nikov created several bass roles in operas by Borodin, Rimsky-Korsakov, Musorgsky (including the title role in *Boris Godunov*, 1874) and others. Later, Fyodor Chaliapin virtually took over the role of Boris and transformed the role of the bass voice in opera by making it the equal in dramatic power (and market value) of the higher voices. His interpretations are as legendary for their vital characterization as for the beauty of his tone and the clarity of his declamation. His roles included Ivan the Terrible (Rimsky-Korsakov's *The Maid of Pskov*), Dosifey (Musorgsky's *Khovanshchina*), and both Prince Galitsky and Khan Konchak in *Prince Igor*, as well as Boito's Mefistofeles, Philip II and Don Basilio.

Outside opera, basses found significant parts in sacred music and oratorio. From Beethoven's Ninth Symphony (1824) to many requiems, including the collaborative mass for Rossini (1869) and works by Brahms (1868), Verdi (1874) and Dvořák (1890), most concerted choral music included important bass or bass-baritone solos, often sung by opera singers. Ormondo Maini, the bass in the première of Verdi's Requiem, was esteemed not only for his Mephistopheles (both Boito and Gounod, in *Faust*) and Ramfis (*Aida*) but also for his Leporello and Don Basilio.

In operetta, the bass rarely played as important a role as the leading tenor or baritone. August Zschiesche, however, engaged for 50 years at the Berlin Hofoper, created Falstaff in Nicolai's *Die lustigen Weiber von Windsor* (1849); a genuine bass, he also sang Rocco (*Fidelio*), Osmin and Bertram (*Robert le diable*, 1831). Karl Formes, Plunkett in the première of Flotow's *Martha* (1847), also sang for many years at Covent Garden, notably as Tsar Peter. In Gilbert and Sullivan opera, the leading bass was Richard Temple, who had made his début as Rodolfo (*La sonnambula*); he was particularly praised for his Mikado.

The bass best known for his performance of song at the turn of the century was Chaliapin, who not only performed works by Glinka, Dargomïzhsky, Rimsky-Korsakov and Rubinstein but was highly esteemed as a singer of Schubert and Schumann lieder. He was renowned for his performances of Musorgsky's *Song of the Flea* and Russian folksongs. Songs written specifically for low voice include Rubinstein's op.72 (1864, for alto or bass and piano) and Wolf's Michelangelo settings (1898, for bass).

4. 20TH CENTURY. The bass roles in Puccini's operas are mainly character parts. Adam Didur, the Polish-born bass who sang for 25 seasons at the Metropolitan, created Ashby (*La fanciulla del West*, 1910) and sang several central roles in Russian operas. French opera, however, continued to contain important roles for bass. Félix Vieuille was the original Arkel in *Pelléas et Mélisande* (1902) and also created roles in Charpentier's *Louise* (1900) and Dukas' *Ariane et Barbe-bleue* (1907). In Strauss's operas, the role of Baron Ochs (*Der Rosenkavalier*, 1911), with its sustained low *E* at the end of Act 2, has always been cherished by basses although its first exponent was a baritone, Karl Perron. A famous early exponent of the role was Richard Mayr, who sang the role at the Viennese première; he also sang Figaro, Leporello and Sarastro at Salzburg and Hagen and Gurnemanz at Bayreuth. In Strauss he was unrivalled: he created Barak in *Die Frau ohne Schatten* (1919) and sang Count Waldner in the Viennese première of *Arabella*.

Strong basses have flourished in Wagner roles. Alexander Kipnis sang Gurnemanz, King Mark and Pogner at Bayreuth, as well as Sarastro at Salzburg and Glyndebourne. After World War II, Ludwig Weber, the finest Gurnemanz of his generation, was also admired as Rocco, Ochs and Barak. Gottlob Frick, a superb Hagen, was another notable Gurnemanz. Kurt Böhme, who sang Pogner, Fafner and Titurel at Bayreuth, was best known

as Ochs. Martti Talvela brought a large, resonant voice to such roles as Fasolt, King Mark and Daland, and was an impressive Sarastro. At the end of the century Wagner's bass roles were sung by the British bass John Tomlinson (an admired Wotan at Bayreuth), the Americans James Morris (notable as Wotan and the Dutchman), and Paul Plishka (also renowned for his interpretations of Mozart and Verdi and of Boris Godunov) and the German Hans Sotin, voluminous of voice not only in Wagner but also Beethoven (Ninth Symphony) and Mozart (Sarastro).

Outside Wagner roles, Boris Godunov and Philip II (*Don Carlos*) provide particular challenges, realized in different ways by several distinguished basses: the Bulgarian Boris Christoff, a voluminous, intensely dramatic artist; Nicolai Ghiaurov, also Bulgarian, with a voice of great depth; Cesare Siepi, a noted Don Giovanni, a more introspective Philip; and Ruggero Raimondi, also an admired Don Giovanni, whose Philip belongs among a gallery of powerful Verdi characterizations.

Britten's operas contain many rewarding bass roles. Owen Brannigan, who created Swallow in *Peter Grimes* (1945), Collatinus in *The Rape of Lucretia* (1946), Noye in *Noye's Fludde* (1958) and Bottom in *A Midsummer Night's Dream* (1960), was a comic actor of great charm. Frederick Dalberg, creator of the evil Claggart in *Billy Budd* (1951) and Raleigh in *Gloriana* (1953), was darker in voice and a more forbidding personality. Michael Langdon, who took lesser roles but created the He-Ancient in Tippett's *The Midsummer Marriage* (1955), was also a stylish Ochs and a sound Wagnerian. Forbes Robinson, who created the title role of Tippett's *King Priam* (1962) and was a powerfully evil Claggart, sang Moses in the British stage première of Schoenberg's *Moses und Aron*.

The Rossini revival has called for basses with agile voices and a good coloratura technique; Justino Díaz, who created Antony in Barber's *Antony and Cleopatra* (which inaugurated the new Metropolitan opera in 1966), sang Mahomet in *Le siège de Corinthe*. Samuel Ramey has also sung Mahomet, as well as Moses, Mustafà, the Podestà (*La gazza ladra*) and Douglas (*La donna del lago*); his flexible but powerful voice can encompass a repertory that runs from Handel roles such as Garibaldo in *Rodelinda* and the Rossini roles written for Galli or Beneditti to Gounod's and Boito's Mephistopheles, Attila and the four villains in *Les contes d'Hoffmann*.

The early music revival has required voices that are not only flexible but light in tone. The English bass David Thomas has sung with distinction a 17th-and 18th-century repertory ranging from Monteverdi to Mozart; he has specialized in Handel (notably Polyphemus) and recorded arias written for Montagnana. The American Simon Estes has also made early music repertory a speciality, singing for example Jupiter in Cavalli's *Calisto* at Glyndebourne, but has also sung the title roles in Verdi's *Oberto* and Wagner's *Der fliegende Holländer* as well as presenting much contemporary music (such as the American première of Shostakovich's Symphony no.14).

Relatively few basses have excelled in the song repertory. Kipnis's unusually wide repertory included Mozart and Wagner operas, as well as Russian songs and lieder; he was a particularly fine interpreter of Brahms and Schubert. Christoff was a fine interpretator of Musorgsky's songs. The Belgian bass-baritone José Van Dam is a notable lieder singer with an operatic and concert repertory covering a broad range both chronologically and vocally, from Mozart to Wagner and Stravinsky, with an emphasis on French music.

Classical basses who have crossed over into the popular repertory include Ezio Pinza, whose enormous repertory was chiefly in Italian (including such Wagner roles as Pogner, King Mark and Gurnemanz); he created roles in Pizzetti's *Debora e Jaele* (1922) and Boito's *Nerone* (1924). At the Metropolitan this velvet-toned bass dominated the stage dramatically and vocally for 22 seasons; late in his career he made a stunning success in musical theatre, creating Emile de Becque in Rodgers and Hammerstein's *South Pacific* (1949). No discussion of the bass voice would be complete without mention of Paul Robeson, the great black actor and singer who gave up the legal profession for the stage, where he was particularly esteemed for his performance of Shakespeare's *Othello*. In musical theatre he created the role of Crown in *Porgy and Bess* and Joe in *Show Boat*, whose song 'Ol' man river' became Robeson's signature piece.

BIBLIOGRAPHY

M. Kuhn: *Die Verzierungs-Kunst in der Gesangs-Musik des 16.–17. Jahrhunderts, 1535–1650* (Leipzig, 1902/R)
M. Kunath: 'Die Charakterologie der stimmlichen Einheiten in der Oper', *ZMw*, viii (1925–6), 403
R. Celletti: 'Il buffo e la tradizione melodrammatica', *Musica d'oggi*, new ser., ii (1959), 61
H. Pleasants: *The Great Singers* (New York, 1966)
H. Matheopoulos: *Bravo: Today's Great Tenors, Baritones and Basses Discuss their Roles* (London, 1986)
O. Termini: 'From a God to a Servant: the Bass Voice in Seventeenth-Century Venetian Opera', *CMc*, no.44 (1990), 38–60
J.B. Steane: *Voices: Singers and Critics* (London, 1992)
M. Talbot: 'Tenors and Basses at the Venetian *ospedali*', *AcM*, lxvi (1994), 123–38
J. Budden: 'The Vocal and Dramatic Characterisation of Jacopo Fiesco', *Studi verdiani*, x (1994–5), 67–75
J.B. Steane: *Singers of the Century* (London, 1996)

OWEN JANDER, LIONEL SAWKINS, J.B. STEANE, ELIZABETH FORBES/ELLEN T. HARRIS (with GERALD WALDMAN)

Bass (iii) (Fr. *contrebasse*; Ger. *Bass* [E♭], *Kontrabass* [B♭]). In military and brass bands, the valved instrument in E♭ or low B♭ corresponding to the orchestral tuba.

The term is also used with other instruments, e.g. bass flute.

Bass (iv). A contraction of DOUBLE BASS or ELECTRIC BASS GUITAR.

Bassadanza. *See* BASSE DANSE.

Bassanelli. A family of late 16th century double-reed, conically bored wind instruments, softer in tone than shawms or curtals. No example survives, although *bassanelli* were described and illustrated by Praetorius (2/1619). They had seven finger-holes, the lowest controlled by a key, the lower part of which was covered by an elaborate *fontanelle*. A reed was fitted to a bassoon-like crook. Uniquely among Renaissance wind instruments *bassanelli* possessed a remarkable amount of decorative turnery. It has been suggested (Foster, 1992) that the *bassanelli* illustrated by Praetorius were of five-part jointed construction, the joints being strengthened and disguised with bulbous collars or bracelets; by extending or contracting these joints, a tuning variation of a semitone may have been obtainable. Praetorius listed three sizes capable of playing a range of about an octave and a 4th above C (bass), G (tenor/alto) and d (cantus).

Although Praetorius attributed the invention of the instrument to Giovanni Bassano, it seems most likely that the inventor was his father, Santo Bassano, who was awarded a patent for a new instrument on 13 June 1582 (Ongaro, p.412). Others have argued that the inventor was Jeronimo Bassano (i), perhaps in 1503 (Ruffatti). Instruments identifiable as *bassanelli* appear in three published inventories: Graz, between 1577 and 1590 (Schlosser, p.20); Verona, 1593 (Castellani, p.16); and Cassel, 1613 (Baines, p.30).

BIBLIOGRAPHY

PraetoriusSM
J. von Schlosser: *Die Sammlung alter Musikinstrumente* (Vienna, 1920/R)
A. Baines: 'Two Cassel Inventories', *GSJ*, iv (1951), 30–38
M. Castellani: 'A 1593 Veronese Inventory', *GSJ*, xxvi (1973), 15–24
G.M. Ongaro: 'New Documents on the Bassano Family', *EMc*, xx (1992), 409–13
C. Foster: 'The Bassanelli Reconstructed: a Radical Solution to an Enigma', *EMc*, xx (1992), 417–25
A. Ruffatti: 'La famiglia Piva-Bassano nei documenti degli archivi di Bassano del Grappa', *Musica e storia*, vi (1998), 349–67

CHARLES FOSTER

Bassani. *See* BASSANO family.

Bassani, Giovanni Battista (*b* Padua, *c*1650; *d* Bergamo, 1 Oct 1716). Italian composer, violinist and organist. He is traditionally said to have studied in Venice with Daniele Castrovillari and in Ferrara with Giovanni Legrenzi, *maestro di cappella* of the Accademia dello Spirito Santo there from 1657 to 1670. The suggestion made by Hawkins, Burney and others that Bassani was Corelli's violin teacher is without foundation although he is likely to have been in touch with Bolognese musicians between early 1675 and 1677. From 1667 he was associated with the Accademia della Morte, Ferrara, where he acted as organist and composed his first oratorios. The libretto of *L'Esaltazione di S Croce*, performed at the academy on 7 April 1675, refers to him as 'già organista della medesima Chiesa', suggesting that he had already left the position of organist by then. On 3 June 1677 he became a member of the Accademia Filarmonica at Bologna and in the same year he published his op.1, in which he is called 'maestro di musica e organista' of the Confraternità della Morte in Finale Emilia, near Modena. In 1680 he was *maestro di cappella* at the court of Duke Alessandro II della Mirandola, a position he probably accepted shortly after the performance of his oratorio *L'Amore ingeniero* in S Maria Maddalena there in 1678. On 9 April 1682 he was elected *principe* of the Accademia Filarmonica, Bologna. Also in 1682 he started participating in the annual celebration of the Accademia Filarmonica in S Giovanni in Monte, contributing several compositions up to 1694. At the end of 1683, probably his most productive year as a composer, he was elected *maestro di cappella* of the Accademia della Morte, Ferrara, succeeding G.F. Tosi. In 1686 he was appointed *maestro di cappella* of Ferrara Cathedral; because of his contribution to the musical life of that city he became known as 'Bassani of Ferrara'. Between 1710 and 1712 he composed 76 services in several cycles for use at Ferrara Cathedral. On 9 May 1712 he was called to Bergamo to direct the music at S Maria Maggiore. He also taught at the music school of the Congregazione di Carità, Bergamo, and continued in both posts until his death.

Bassani's music was prominent in the middle Baroque period in Italy, when the concertato style predominated.

His sacred works in this style are typical of those of the Bolognese school of composers in the last quarter of the 17th century, such as G.P. Colonna, G.B. Vitali and G.A. Perti. Perhaps above all he should be recognized for his solo cantatas, both sacred and secular. Yet although he was a prolific composer of other types of vocal music too, his fame has rested chiefly on his trio sonatas for strings. During his lifetime he was celebrated as a violinist. Some even considered his playing superior to Corelli's, a reputation probably enhanced by Burney, who also claimed that no one before him had written quite so idiomatically for the violin.

A sharp contrast between chamber and church sonatas, previously made by Legrenzi, is maintained by Bassani in his two known sets of trio sonatas. His op.1 contains 12 chamber sonatas, in each of which the four dance movements announced on the title-page follow the order given there. However, the number and character of the movements in the 12 church sonatas of op.5 are variable, and they often have polyphonic textures. According to Newman, Bassani's sonatas differ somewhat from Corelli's in that he preferred long unfolding lines to short balanced phrases, and the overall form, especially of the church sonatas, is less well integrated.

Of 13 known oratorios by Bassani to Italian texts the music of only four has survived, and his 13 operas seem to be entirely lost except for 10 arias from *Gli amori alla moda*. The secular solo cantatas are normally accompanied only by continuo and present a variety of structures, with a preference for da capo and *AAB* forms. Most of the solo motets are 'concerted' with the addition of two violins except in the recitatives, and each begins with a sinfonia. In his masses and psalm settings Bassani was an important exponent of the *stile concertato*; he worked in the style of Cazzati and Vitali (e.g. the latter's *Salmi concertati* op.6, 1677).

Bassani often designed sections and movements on a larger time scale than did his immediate predecessors but was less able than Corelli to build convincing forms. His harmonic range, well within the conventions of his time, is narrow, and he seems to have been unable in his use of clichés to avoid a certain monotony, which is accentuated by a lack of strong harmonic drive towards cadences. His choruses, in four or five parts, combine homophony and simple, weighty polyphonic writing that frequently includes telling use of suspensions; as in his sonatas the orchestral accompaniments to these movements display his natural feeling for the violin. The figurations are based on, but emancipated from, the vocal lines, as in similar works by G.P. Colonna, and the voices are thus given a sonorous halo without the competition of counter-melodies. The writing for solo voices in these works is characteristic of the 'instrumental' approach of the period: the precise mechanical patterns, usually in semiquavers, demand vocal agility and brilliance but lack the elegant contours found in, for example, Neapolitan opera.

WORKS

OPERAS

dm – *drama per musica*

L'amorosa preda di Paride (dm, 3), Bologna, Publico, 1683
Falarido tiranno d'Agrigento (dm, 3, A. Morselli), Venice, S Angelo, 1685
L'Alarico Rè de' Goti (dm, 3), Ferrara, Conte Pinamonte Bonacossi, Feb 1685
Vitige [Rè de'Vandali] (dm, 3), Ferrara, Feb 1686
Agrippina in Baia (scherzo drammatico, G. Contri), Ferrara, 1687

Gli amori alla moda (scherzo melodrammatico, 3), Ferrara, Bonacossi, 1688, 10 arias in *I-MOe*
Il trionfo di Venere in Ida (melodramma), Ferrara, 1688
La Ginerva, infanta di Scozia (dm, 3, G.C. Grazzini, after L. Ariosto), Ferrara, Bonacossi, 1690
Le vicende di Cocceio Nerva (dm, 3), Ferrara, Bonacossi, 1691
Gl'amori tra gl'odii, o sia Il Ramiro in Norvegia (dm, 3, M.A. Rimena), Verona, 1693
Roderico, Ferrara, 1696
L'Alarico (F. Silvani), Padua, 1709
Armida al campo, Ferrara, 1711

ORATORIOS

L'Esaltazione di S Croce (F. Berni), Ferrara, 7 April 1675
L'Epulone, Modena, 1675
La tromba della divina misericordia (G.B. Rosselli), 4 solo vv, chorus 4vv, insts, Modena, 1676; *MOe* Mus.G.14
L'amore ingeniero, Mirandola, 1678
Il mistico Roveto (L. Lotti), Mirandola, 1681
Il Davide punito overo La pestilente strage d'Israele (G.V. Snodelli), Bologna, 10 Dec 1682
La morte delusa dal pietoso suffragio (A. Ambrosini), 5 solo vv, chorus 4vv, insts, Ferrara, 1686; *MOe*; perf. as Nella luna eclissata dal Cristiano valore, Codigoro, 1687, and as La Pietà trionfante della morte, Ferrara 1692 and 1697
Il Giona (Ambrosini), 5vv, vns, va ad lib, Modena, 1689; *MOe*
Mosè risorto dalle acque, Ferrara, 1694; *FEc* Cl.I.n.675 (1696 version)
Il conte di Bacheville (F. Frosini), Pistoia, 1696
Susanna, Ferrara, 1697
Gl'impegni del divino amore nel transito della Beata Caterina Vegri detta di Bologna, Ferrara, 1703
Il trionfo della Fede, Ferrara, 1704

La morte delusa, ?orat, Milan, 1703; collab. G.B. Brevi, G.A. Perti, G. Bononcini, A. Scarlatti

MASSES

op.	
18	[3] Messe concertate, 5 solo vv, chorus 5vv, 2 vn, vle/ theorbo, org (Bologna, 1698)
20	Messa per li defonti concertata, 4 solo vv, chorus 4vv, 2 va, vle/ theorbo, org (Bologna, 1698)
—	Acroama missale, 4 solo vv, chorus 4vv, 2 vn, va, 3 trbn, org, bc (Augsburg, 1709); 6 masses, 3 of these in op.32 without trbn pts.
32	[4] Messe concertate, 4 solo vv, chorus 4vv, 2 vn, va, org, bc (Bologna, 1710)
—	4 other masses and fragments, *GB-Lcm*; *D-Bsb*, *Dmb*, listed in *EitnerQ*

OTHER SACRED WORKS

—	Il trionfo dell'amor divino (Rosselli), sacra rappresentazione, Bologna, 1682 [same lib as the orat La tromba della divina misericordia]
8	Metri sacri resi armonici, in [12] motetti, 1v, 2 vn, bc (Bologna, 1690)
9	Armonici entusiasmi di Davide overo salmi concertati, 4 solo vv, chorus 4vv, 2 vn, va, bc (org) (Venice, 1690)
10	[6] Salmi di compieta, 4 solo vv, chorus 4vv, 2 vn, va/vle, bc (org) (Venice, 1691)
11	Concerti sacri, [12] motetti, 1–4vv, 2 vn, vle/theorbo, bc (org) (Bologna, 1692)
12	[12] Motetti, 1v, 2 vn ad lib, bc (org) (Venice, 1692)
13	Armonie festive o siano [6] motetti, 1v, 2 vn, vle/theorbo, bc (org) (Bologna, 1693)
—	Motetti per concerti ecclesiastici, 5–12vv (Venice, 1698); listed by Eitner
21	Salmi concertati, 3–5 solo vv, chorus 3–5vv, 2 vn, bc (org) (Bologna, 1699)
22	Lagrime armoniche ò sià Il Vespro de defonti, 4 solo vv, chorus 4vv, 2 vn, va/vle, bc (org) (Venice, 1699)
23	Le note lugubri, Concertate ne Responsorij dell'Ufficio de Morti, 4 solo vv, chorus 4vv, 2 va, va/vle, bc (org) (Venice, 1700)
24	Davidde armonico, espresso ne' [6] salmi, 2–4vv, 2 vn, bc (org) (Venice, 1700)
25	[8] Completorij concenti, 4 solo vv, chorus 4vv, 2 vn, vle/ theorbo, bc (org) (Bologna, 1701)
26	[4] Antifone sacre … e 2 Tantum ergo, 1v, 2 vn, vle/ theorbo, bc (org) (Bologna, 1701)

27	[8] Motetti sacri, 1v, 2 vn, vle/theorbo, bc (org) (Bologna, 1701)
30	Salmi per tutti l'anno, 8vv, vle/theorbo, 2 org (Bologna, 1704)
—	Cantata pastorale (F. della Volpe), 2 vv, insts, Imola ?(Ferrara, 1707)
—	76 services, most 4 solo vv, chorus 4vv, bc (vle), some with 4 vn, va, 1710–12, *I-FEd* (8 vols., 3 lost); listed in Cavicchi
—	Several sacred works in *Bc*, *MOe*, *PAc*, *US-Wc*

SECULAR VOCAL

2	L'armonia delle sirene, [10] cantate amorose, 1v, bc (Bologna, 1680)
3	Il cigno canoro, [10] cantate amorose, 1v, bc (Bologna, 1682)
—	Promoteo liberato (introduzione alla Festa popolare, G.A. Bergamori), Bologna, 24 Aug 1683
4	La moralità armonica, [12] cantate, 2–3vv, vle, bc (Bologna, 1683)
6	Affetti canori, [6] cantate et [6] ariette, 1v, bc (Bologna, 1684)
—	Tributi dell'Eridano, cant, 4vv, insts, Ferrara, 1687
7	Eco armonica delle muse, [12] cantate amorose, 1v, bc (Bologna, 1688)
—	Tributi de Parnaso (macchina musicale, G.C. Grazzini), Ferrara, 1688
—	L'Immortalità trionfante, et il Tevere inconsolabile (intramezzo musicale, A.F. Antonini), Ferrara, 1689
14	Amorosi sentimenti, 1v, bc (Venice, 1693)
15	Armoniche fantasie di [6] cantate amorose, 1v, bc (Venice, 1694)
16	La musa armonica, 1v, bc (Bologna, 1695)
17	La sirena amorosa, 1v, 2 vn, vle, bc (org) (Venice, 1699)
19	Languidezze amorose, [12] cantate, 1v, bc (Bologna, 1698)
28	Cantate amorose, 1v, bc (Bologna, 1701)
29	Corona di fiori musicali, tessuta d' [24] ariette, 1v, 2 vn, vc (Bologna, 1702)
31	[12] Cantate et arie amorose, 1v, 2 vn, bc (Bologna, 1703)

INSTRUMENTAL

1	[12] Balletti, correnti, gighe e sarabande, vn, vn ad lib, vle/spinet (Bologna, 1677)
5	[12] Sinfonie, 2 vn, vc, bc (org) (Bologna, 1683), autograph score in *US-Wc*
—	Sonata, 2 vn, bc (org) 1680[7]
—	Several sonatas and organ works in later anthologies listed in Haselbach and *DBI* (A. Cavicchi)

BIBLIOGRAPHY

BurneyH; *DBI* (A. Cavicchi); *EitnerQ*; *FétisB*; *HawkinsH*; *MGG1* (H. Engel); *NewmanSBE*; *RicciTB*; *SartoriB*; *SchmidlD*
Documents and letters, *I-Bc*, FEc, FEd, FEanotarile
G.B. Martini: 'Serie cronologica de'principi dell'Accademia de' filarmonici di Bologna', *Diario bolognese* (Bologna, 1776)
F. Pasini: 'Notes sur la vie de Giovanni Battista Bassani', *SIMG*, vii (1905–6), 581–6
U. Rolandi: 'Opere e oratori di G.B. Bassani', *La scuola veneziana (secoli XVI–XVIII): noti e documenti*, Chigiana, iii (1941), 32–4
R. Haselbach: *Giovanni Battista Bassani* (Kassel, 1955)
A. Cavicchi: 'L'attività ferrarese di Giovanni Battista Bassani', *Chigiana*, xxiii, new ser. iii (1966), 43–58
P. Allsop: *The Italian 'Trio' Sonata From its Origins Until Corelli* (Oxford, 1992), 15, 52
V. Crowther: *The Oratorio in Modena* (Oxford, 1992)
J. Riepe: 'Überlegungen zur Funktion des italienischen Oratoriums im letzten drittel des 17. Jahrhunderts am Beispiel von Giovanni Legrenzis *Sedecia* und *La caduta di Gerusalemme* von Giovanni Paolo Colonna', *Atti del convegno internazionale di studi su G. Legrenzi* [Venice and Clusone 1990], ed. F. Passadore and F. Rossi (Florence, 1994), 605–42

PETER SMITH/MARC VANSCHEEUWIJCK

Bassani, Orazio [Orazio della Viola] (*b* Cento, *c*1550; *d* 8 Nov 1615). Italian instrumentalist and composer. Bassani was a renowned virtuoso of the *viola bastarda*. He entered the service of the Farnese court at Parma as a viola player on 1 November 1574. His service was interrupted by a brief period with Cardinal Farnese in Rome in 1583. During the 1580s and '90s the courts of Mantua and Ferrara tried vigorously but unsuccessfully to lure Bassani to their own music establishments. On the death of Ottario Farnese in October 1586, Bassani was called to serve Alessandro Farnese in Brussels, with an annual pension of 300 gold scudi. On the death of Alessandro Farnese in 1592, he returned to Parma and the service of Duke Ranuccio Farnese, who commissioned Agostino Caracci to paint his portrait (now in the Museo nazionale di Capodimonte in Naples). After returning to Rome again in 1599, Bassani returned a final time to Parma, where he remained until his death. A brother, Cesare, and a nephew, Francesco Maria, were also musicians in Parma. Bassani, a charter member of the Accademia degli Intrepidi at Ferrara (founded in 1601), was particularly admired for his ornamented versions of famous madrigals for solo *viola bastarda*. His place in the history of late 16th-century diminution, and particularly his relationship to Merulo, Luzzaschi and Monteverdi (who came to Mantua as a viol player), may be significant.

WORKS

Several pieces, va bastarda, 1626[14]; authorship questionable, attrib. in Sartori
Madrigal, 5vv, 1591[10], 1605[9]
Arr. madrigals, toccatas, *GB-Lbl*, *I-Bc*

BIBLIOGRAPHY

DBI (A. Cavicchi); *GaspariC*; *NewcombMF*; *SartoriB*
E.T. Ferand: *Die Improvisation in Beispielen aus neun Jahrhunderten abendländischer Musik*(Cologne, 1956, 2/1961; Eng. trans., 1961)
V. Gutmann: 'Viola bastarda: Instrument oder Diminutionspraxis?', *AMw*, xxxv (1978), 178–209
J. Paras: *The Music for Viola Bastarda* (Bloomington, IN, 1986)
O. Fabris: *Andrea Falconieri napoletano* (Rome, 1987)

ANTHONY NEWCOMB

Bassano [Bassani, Piva]. Italian family of musicians, instrument makers and composers, active in England. The family (see illustration) originated in Bassano del Grappa, about 65 km north-west of Venice, where they were known as Piva. Jeronimo [Gieronymo, Hieronymus] (i) (*d* ?Venice, ?1546–50), the founder of the musical dynasty, is first recorded in a contract of his father's dated 24 March 1481; in February 1502 he and his eldest son Jacomo [Jacopo] (*b* ? Bassano, before 1488; *d* Venice, 1559–66) were engaged to tune the organs in the churches of Bassano. They seem to have made the move from Bassano to Venice shortly afterwards. Jeronimo was apparently the 'Ser Jheronimo trombon' who worked in the *trombe e piffari* of the Doge of Venice around 1506–12. Numerous documents call him 'maestro', probably indicating the leader of an ensemble or an instrument maker. Lorenzo Marucini (1577) described him as 'inventor of a new bass wind instrument' and 'most excellent *pifaro*'. Strong circumstantial evidence suggests that Jeronimo was a Jew. Although he and his descendants passed for Christians, they retained some Jewish consciousness into the early 17th century and may well have been practising Judaism in secret. The family coat of arms, on which are displayed three silkworm moths and a mulberry tree, implies that the family had at some time been engaged in silk farming, a trade which the Jews introduced into Italy.

Jeronimo had six sons. At least five were wind players; most or all were also instrument makers. Alvise (*d* London, 15–31 Aug 1554) worked for the Scuola di San Marco, Venice, in 1515, and the Concerto Palatino in Bologna between 1519 and 1521. He and his brothers

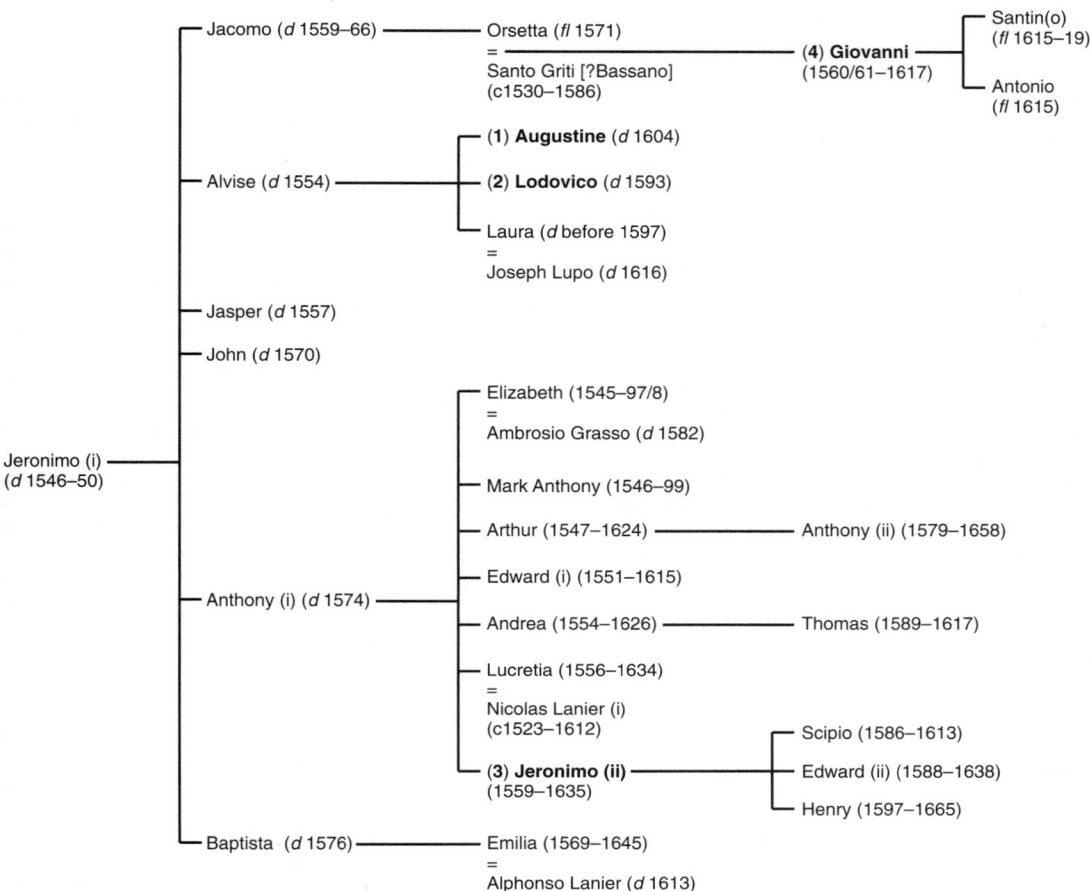

The Bassano family tree

Jasper [Gasparo] (bur. London, 8 May 1577), John [Zuane] (*d* Venice, Sept–Dec 1570) and Anthony [Antonio] (i) (bur. London, 19 Oct 1574) served in the sackbut consort at the English court in 1531 but soon went back to Venice. Anthony returned to England in 1538 and was appointed 'maker of divers instruments' to the court. His brother Jacomo came with him but was not appointed to the court and apparently went back to Venice between 1542 and 1545. His descendants formed the Venetian branch of the family; (4) Giovanni Bassano was his grandson. Alvise, Jasper and John emigrated to England in 1539–40 with Baptista (bur. London, 11 April 1576); they and Anthony were appointed 'brothers in the art or science of music' to the court, and Anthony gave up his position as instrument maker. In 1531 the brothers had used the surname 'de Jeronimo'; on their return to England they adopted Bassani or Bassano, and later generations used Bassano exclusively.

The five brothers in England formed a consort of 'recorders', which may have played other instruments including an early version of the mixed consort of Elizabethan times. Seven of their descendants also served in the recorder consort: Alvise's sons (1) Augustine and (2) Lodovico, Anthony's sons Arthur (*b* London, 31 Oct 1547; bur. London, 10 Sept 1624), Edward (i) (*b* London, 19 Oct 1551; bur. London, 25 May 1615) and (3) Jeronimo (ii), Arthur's son Anthony (ii) (*b* London, 15 Oct

1579; bur. London, 22 Apr 1658) and Jeronimo (ii)'s son Henry (bap. London, 8 April 1597; bur. London, 29 Aug 1665). Henry also served in the sackbut consort, as did three other Bassanos: Anthony (i)'s sons Mark Anthony (*b* London, 10 Jan 1546/7; *d* London, 11 Sep 1599) and Andrea (*b* London, 12 Aug 1554; bur. Horne, Surrey, 3 Aug 1626) and Jeronimo (ii)'s son Edward (ii) (bap. London, 28 Dec 1588; *d* London, 22 Oct 1638). Andrea's probable son Thomas (?bap. London, 27 Feb 1589; bur. London, 29 Sept 1617) apparently served in the flute consort, and Anthony (ii) deputized in it. Jeronimo (ii)'s son Scipio (bap. London, 11 Dec 1586; *d* London, 26 Nov 1613) probably served in the viol consort.

Besides Anthony (i), Alvise also made instruments, and John had a 'fraterna Compagnia' (brotherly company) with his instrument-making brother Jacomo in Venice and perhaps Anthony and Jasper. An inventory made about 1571 by Johann Jakob Fugger, superintendent of the music at the Bavarian court, of a chest of 'beautiful and good' instruments 'made by the Bassani brothers' in London lists 45 wind instruments: six unidentified (perhaps bombards, quiet shawms or bassanelli), seven *Pfeiffen* (perhaps flutes), ten cornetts and a fife considered as a set, twelve crumhorns and nine recorders, all tuned to organ pitch; an accompanying letter mentions a chest of six large viols and a chest of three lutes. The Bassanos presumably also made some of the instruments in the inventories of Henry VIII's collection (1542 and 1547). Edward Seymour, the Lord Protector, bought shawms from Anthony in 1539. Another Fugger, Raimund, an Augsburg banker, listed a case of 27 recorders 'made in England', presumably by the Bassanos, in 1566.

The making, and particularly the repairing, of instruments was continued by the next generation. It was probably Arthur, who bequeathed instruments and tools to Anthony (ii) in his will, who sold 'rare wind instruments' (apparently cornetts) to Brussels. Andrea jointly held (with Robert Henlake, then Edward Norgate) the office of keeper and repairer of keyboard and wind instruments at the court from 1603 until his death in 1626. Only Anthony (ii) of the succeeding generation seems to have made instruments. It was probably he who made the famous large recorders depicted in Marin Mersenne's *Harmonie universelle* (1636) which 'have been sent from England to one of our kings'; Mersenne also apparently knew the Bassanos' crumhorns.

Jacomo's daughter Orsetta married a wind-instrument maker named Santo Griti; Ongaro (1985, 1992) plausibly speculates that he changed his name to Santo Bassano (*d* Venice, 3 Dec 1586). Santo and Jacomo entered into a business partnership with three musicians of the Doge in 1559, in which the latter became in effect their salesmen in return for a large loan; the agreement mentions cornetts, crumhorns, curtals, flutes, recorders and shawms. Santo took out a patent in 1582 to make and sell a new wind instrument, almost certainly the BASSANELLI (although it may well have been invented by Jeronimo (i).

The maker's mark of the Bassanos has been the subject of much speculation. Lasocki (1983, 1985, 1995) surmised that it was what has hitherto been called the 'rabbit's foot' mark found on more than 120 surviving woodwind instruments (cornetts, crumhorns, curtals, flutes, recorders and shawms), and that this mark in fact represents silkworm moths, as found on the family coat of arms. Kirk, building on this theory, suggests that the single mark was used by Jeronimo (i), the double mark by his Venetian descendants (Jacomo and Santo), and the triple mark by the English branch, especially Arthur and Anthony (ii). The HIER.S mark, found on 31 instruments may also belong to the family.

Through instrument-making and business connections the English branch kept up with Venice and made several documented visits there, presumably acting as one of the conduits through which Italian music came to England. Bassano daughters married other court musicians: Ambrosio Grasso, Joseph Lupo, Alphonso Lanier and Nicholas Lanier (i). There is no evidence that the family was related to the Venetian painter Jacopo Bassano (also known as Jacopo or Giacomo da Ponte).

(1) Augustine [Agustino] **Bassano** (bur. London, 24 Oct 1604). Wind player and composer. He was appointed to the recorder consort on 18 April 1551 with effect from 25 March 1550. He became a denizen of England on 17 March 1545, presumably having been born in Venice before 1530. In his will he made a bequest of four lutes, but the evidence that he played the instrument at court, as some authors have suggested, is equivocal. A pavan and galliard, probably written as consort music as early as 1550, survive in arrangements for keyboard (*GB-Rro*, Trumbull Add.6), bandora (*Cu* Dd.2.11) and lute (*Lbl* Add.29485). Some other pieces are in the style of the third quarter of the 16th century: two six-part pavans by 'A.B.',

probably Augustine (*US-NH* Filmer A16/a–c, *GB-Cfm* 734); and two pavans and two galliards for five-part consort as well as a 'galliard' (more likely a corant) headed 'Aug Bassano set by P.P.', presumably arranged by Peter Philips from a lute piece (*Lbl* Eg.3665). Three allmandes for six-part consort by 'A.B.' (*Cfm* 734) are probably late works of Augustine's.

(2) Lodovico [Lodouick] **Bassano** [Bassany]   (bur. London, 18 July 1593). Wind player and composer, brother of (1) Augustine Bassano. He was appointed to the recorder consort on 22 July 1569 with effect from the previous 29 September, although he had been serving unofficially since his father's death in August 1554. He married 'Elizabeth Damon' (probably a daughter of William Daman) on 13 November 1592. Lodovico may be the composer of three surviving lute pieces. A 'Pavan Helena. Lo[dovico?]' is found in *Cu* Dd.2.11. 'A pavan ... mr Lodwick' is in *Lbl* Add.31392 and also anonymously in *Lbl* Add.38539 and in *Cu* Dd.2.11 with the instruction '4 leaves turn back for the galliard'. In the plague year 1593 he died of 'a thought', apparently serious depression.

(3) Jeronimo [Jerome] **Bassano (ii)**   (*b* London, 11 March 1559; bur. Waltham Abbey, Essex, 22 Aug 1635). Wind and viol player and composer, cousin of (1) Augustine Bassano and (2) Lodovico Bassano. He was appointed to the recorder consort on 29 January 1579 with effect from the previous 25 March. He served actively until at least 1630, when he was described as 'the ancientist musition the King hath'. In 1609–13 he also received three payments (one as 'Musycon for the vyoll de Gambo') for viol strings provided for court service; therefore he was probably serving unofficially in the newly developed viol consort. He acquired considerable property – enough to merit the title 'Esquire' – in Hoxton and Waltham Abbey, Essex. Two six-part galliards (*US-NH* Filmer A16/a-c), four skilful five-part fantasias (*GB-Och* 716–720, *Lcm* 1145), and a six-part fantasia and two wordless madrigals (*Cfm* 734) probably all date from the third quarter of the 16th century. Three six-part almandes by 'J.B.' (*Cfm* 734) are probably Jeronimo's works from around 1600.

(4) Giovanni [Zanetto, Zuane] **Bassano** [Bassani]   (*b* ?Venice, 1560/61; *d* Venice, 16 Aug 1617). Wind player and composer, second cousin of (3) Jeronimo Bassano (ii). In May 1576 he was appointed one of the six 'pifferi del doge', a group of instrumentalists placed directly under the authority of the Venetian doge; he was then 'a very young man' of 15 or 16, which explains his appearance under the diminutive 'Zanetto' in the earliest documents. Indeed, he may well have been the Zanetto who was appointed a boy chorister at S Marco in early 1572; this would help explain his appointment in 1583 as singing teacher to the seminary of S Marco, a post normally reserved for singers. He published his manual of ornamentation two years later. In 1586 he was nominated by the Augustinian friars of S Stefano to provide instrumentalists when required for the convent church. He succeeded GIROLAMO DALLA CASA as head of the instrumental ensemble at the basilica in 1601; he remained in this post until his death. He was mentioned in 1612 as leader of one of the many companies of instrumentalists who were periodically engaged to play during major festivities in the various parish and monastic churches of Venice. His age at the time of his death (in the parish of S Maurizio) is stated in the necrology as 56.

Bassano is today largely known for his instruction book (1585) and for his examples of embellished motets, madrigals and chansons by Willaert, Clemens non Papa, Crecquillon, Lasso, Rore, Striggio, Palestrina and Marenzio (1591), several examples of which are published in Erig. His method was to decorate continuously a contrapuntal line, which thus stands out from its fellows to form an unequal relationship, obviously akin to that of solo and accompaniment. The actual ornaments are, however, much more rigid than those of the monodists of the following decades, since the music must still obey the criteria of polyphony, and the rhythms of the various figures are thus quite regular. Although Bassano's collections contain no compositions by his Venetian contemporaries, the similarities between his embellishments and the highly florid works later published by Giovanni Gabrieli suggest that the latter was applying a practice well known in virtuoso circles since the 1580s and probably earlier. Gabrieli's *Canzona in echo* (*Sacrae symphoniae*, i, 1597), probably written for Bassano to play, shows the application of his virtuoso ornamental lines to concertante music in a most forward-looking manner.

Bassano was also a composer of some talent. Some of his charming canzonettas were known (probably through his London cousins) to Morley, who printed them in his *Canzonets or Little Short Songs to Foure Voyces* (London, 1597). The first volume of his motets was dedicated to the governing body of S Marco, and the music doubtless partly reflects his activities there, but it is also likely that some of the motets were conceived for performance on the major feast days in the other churches of Venice. The works are for *cori spezzati*, less intense than those of Giovanni Gabrieli but brighter in sonority in the manner of Giovanni Croce and Andrea Gabrieli. *Dic, Maria, nobis* (1599) is especially attractive with strong rhythms and lively use of the upper voices, much as in the early works of Schütz (who probably knew his music).

WORKS

all published in Venice

SACRED

Motetti per concerti ecclesiastici, 5–8, 12vv (1598; b (org) pubd separately, 1599)

Concerti ecclesiastici, libro secondo, 5–8, 12vv (1599)

SECULAR

Fantasie per cantar et sonar con ogni sorte d'istrumenti (1585)

Canzonette, 4vv (1587)

Il fiore dei capricci musicali per sonar con ogni sorte di stromenti, 4vv (1588)

Madrigali et canzonette concertate per potersi cantare con il basso & soprano nel liuto & istrumento da pena, con passaggi a ciascuna parte … libro primo (1602)

INSTRUCTION MANUAL AND ARRANGEMENTS

Ricercate, passaggi et cadentie per potersi esercitar nel diminuir terminatamente con ogni sorte d'istrumento (1585)

Motetti, madrigali et canzone francese di diversi eccellenti autori, 4–6vv (1591)

BIBLIOGRAPHY

AshbeeR, iii, iv, vi–viii; *BDECM*

M. Kuhn: *Die Verzierungs-Kunst in der Gesangs-Musik des 16.–17. Jahrhunderts (1535–1650)* (Leipzig, 1902)

B. Wallner: 'Ein Instrumentenverzeichnis aus dem 16. Jh.', *Festschrift zum 50. Geburtstag Adolf Sandberger* (Munich, 1918), 275–86

I. Horsley: 'Improvised Embellishments in the Performance of Renaissance Polyphonic Music', *JAMS*, iv (1951), 3–19

T. Dart: 'The Repertory of the Royal Wind Music', *GSJ*, xi (1958), 70–77

J. Izon: 'Italian Musicians at the Tudor Court', *MQ*, xliv (1958), 329–37

H.M. Brown: *Embellishing Sixteenth-Century Music* (London, 1975)

E. Selfridge-Field: 'Bassano and the Orchestra of St Mark's', *EMc*, iv (1976), 152–8

R. Erig: *Italienische Diminutionen* (Zürich, 1979)

J. Glixon: *Music at the Venetian 'Scuole Grandi', 1440–1540* (diss., Princeton U., 1979)

E. Selfridge-Field: 'Venetian Instrumentalists in England: a Bassano Chronicle', *Studi musicali*, viii (1979), 173–221

D. Bryant: *Liturgy, Ceremonial and Sacred Music in Venice at the Time of the Counter-Reformation* (diss., U. of London, 1981)

D. Lasocki: *Professional Recorder Players in England, 1540–1740* (diss., U. of Iowa, 1983)

R. Prior: 'Jewish Musicians in Tudor England', *MQ*, lxix (1983), 253–65

D. Lasocki: 'The Anglo-Venetian Bassano Family as Instrument Makers and Repairers', *GSJ*, xxxviii (1985), 112–32

G. Ongaro: '16th-Century Venetian Wind Instrument Makers and their Clients', *EMc*, xiii (1985), 391–7

D. Kirk: 'Cornetti and Renaissance Pitch Standards in Italy and Germany', *Journal de musique ancienne*, x/4 (1989), 16–22

G. Ongaro: 'Gli inizi della musica strumentale a San Marco', *Giovanni Legrenzi e la cappella ducale di San Marco: Venice and Clusone 1990*, 215–26

G. Ongaro: 'New Documents on the Bassano Family', *EMc*, xx (1992), 409–13

D. Lasocki with R.Prior: *The Bassanos: Venetian Musicians and Instrument Makers in England, 1531–1665* (Aldershot, 1995)

E. Quaranta: *Oltre San Marco: organizzazione e prassi della musica nelle chiese di Venezia nel Rinascimento* (Florence, 1998), 83, 179, 382

A. Ruffatti: 'La famiglia Piva-Bassano nei documenti degli archivi di Bassano del Grappa', *Musica e storia*, vi (1998), 349–67

DAVID LASOCKI (introduction, 1–3); DENIS ARNOLD/FABIO FERRACCIOLI (4)

Bassany, Lodovico. *See* BASSANO family, (2).

Bass-bar (Fr. *barre*; Ger. *Bassbalken*; It. *catena*). In bowed string instruments, a strip of wood glued to the underside of the belly beneath the bass foot of the bridge. It is of vital importance to the acoustical function of the instrument, and is complemented by the soundpost which is placed close to the treble bridge-foot.

In modern practice, the bass-bar runs for three-quarters of the length of the belly, and is made from spruce carefully matched to that of the belly. It is fitted slightly within the outer edge of the bridge foot, and set at a slight angle to the centre line of the instrument, determined by the proportions of the upper and lower bouts. It is deepest at the centre, generally about 12 mm in a violin, and tapers towards the ends, being on average 265 mm long and 6 mm wide. The glued surface is fitted to the curves of the belly, although some luthiers shape it to a slightly tighter radius than the belly itself, known as 'springing', providing a certain amount of stress within the structure when glued in place. An undersized or badly positioned bar cannot provide sufficient stiffness to the front of the instrument and results in a dull, unfocussed sound (particularly in the bass register) and, in extreme cases, deformation and eventual collapse of the arching. Conversely, an oversized bar can stifle the sound, making the instrument unresponsive.

The bass-bar developed as a way of making bowed instruments more responsive by allowing the belly to be made thinner yet still be strong enough where it is needed to withstand the downward pressure of the strings. A painting by Raphael (*Allegory of St Cecilia*, c1514–16; *see* VIOL, fig.7) shows an early viol with an enormously thick belly, which would presumably have had a rather limited sound. Early instruments were made with the bass-bar carved integrally with the belly rather than glued in separately, often in a central position. This practice continued in some areas outside the classical Italian tradition well into the 18th century, although with the bar closer to the modern position near the bass foot of the bridge. At what point the bass-bar migrated away from the centre is not clear. A bass viol from the late 16th century with a central bar is in the Ashmolean Museum, Oxford, ascribed to Gasparo da Salò of Brescia, but the earliest violin bass-bar recorded is from 1621, made by the brothers Antonio and Girolamo Amati in Cremona, and was separately fitted in the offset position.

Early bass-bars were fairly small. The 1621 example is some 5 mm lower than modern practice and 1·5 mm narrower, although it is slightly longer than a modern bar. Bass-bars from early 18th-century violins are shorter than the 1621 model, but with the same height and width and are generally flat along the length. By the late 18th century the bar acquired more mass and a 'hump-backed' shape, and this tendency continued into the 20th century, following the increased demands for projection and depth of sound in modern concert performance.

BIBLIOGRAPHY

W.H., A.F., and A.E. Hill: *Antonio Stradivari: His Life and Work* (London, 1902/R, 2/1909/R)

D.D. Boyden: *Catalogue of the Hill Collection of Musical Instruments in the Ashmolean Museum* (Oxford, 1969)

J. Beamont: *The Violin Explained: Components, Mechanism, Sound* (Oxford, 1997)

JOHN DILWORTH

Bass-baritone (Ger. *Bassbariton, Hoher Bass*). A male voice combining the compass and attributes of the bass and the baritone (*see* BASS (ii) and BARITONE (i)). The term follows the German *Bassbariton*, and the voice itself is particularly associated with the German 19th-century upward development of the bass range. Wagner called the bass-baritone 'Hoher Bass' and first used the term to designate the roles of Wotan, Alberich, Donner and Fasolt in *Das Rheingold* and *Die Walküre*. These, as well as Hans Sachs (*Die Meistersinger*) and the Dutchman, require a powerful upper register for phrases in the baritone range *e* to *f♯'*, but also numerous phrases in the range *A* to *a* requiring the resonance of a bass. The special attribute of this voice type, however, lies less in its range than in the full and powerful sound required at the extremes of the tessitura. Basses with even wider ranges are well known from much earlier periods (for example, JOHN GOSTLING and ANTONIO MONTAGNANA), but these used falsetto in the highest registers. Although associated primarily with Wagnerian and later roles, earlier operatic precedents with similar demands include Mozart's *Figaro* and *Don Giovanni*, Pizarro in *Fidelio* and Caspar in *Der Freischütz*. Another bass-baritone part is that of Elijah in Mendelssohn's oratorio.

OWEN JANDER/ELLEN T. HARRIS

Bassbrechung (Ger.). In Schenkerian analysis, the ARPEGGIATION (ii) of the bass; the lower part of the URSATZ.

Bass clarinet (Fr. *clarinette basse*; Ger. *Bassklarinette*; It. *clarone*). A member of the clarinet family (*see* CLARINET), generally pitched in B♭, an octave below the soprano clarinet (it is classified as an AEROPHONE). Its range is usually extended to E♭ (usually written *e♭*; sounding D♭)

on French and English instruments, D (written *d*; sounding C) on German instruments, and there is a growing tendency to use instruments extended to C (written *c*; sounding B♭') in the manner of the basset-horn. The upward extension of the range is even less well standardized; the composers who established the instrument's position in the modern orchestra were more interested in exploiting its full and fruity chalumeau register than in its upper reaches.

Many late 19th-century orchestral parts use only about two and a half octaves of the range; many bass clarinets are constructed on the premise that this limited range is expected. However, as a solo instrument the bass clarinet has as great a range as the soprano; many of the compositions dedicated to the Czech virtuoso Josef Horák cover four octaves or more.

Technically, the instrument has similar characteristics to the soprano clarinet. In the lower register, the attack is not so effective, for which reason its use in combination with the harp, favoured by the Second Viennese School (as at the opening of Berg's Violin Concerto), is very successful. Particularly striking is the ease with which a wide dynamic range is achieved; in Tchaikovsky's Sixth Symphony (the end of the exposition of the first movement, bar 160) a passage for the bassoon, marked *pppppp* (following a downward clarinet arpeggio), is in practice often given over to the bass clarinet, which achieves this dynamic with ease.

1. History. 2. Notation. 3. Mechanism.

1. HISTORY.   Apart from the instruments discussed under CHALUMEAU, the earliest extant bass clarinet is probably that by Anton and Michael Mayrhofer of Passau (Musikinstrumentenmuseum in Münchner Stadtmuseum, Munich, 52.50; see Young (1980), pl.244). This remarkable instrument is curved in the manner of the better known basset-horns by the same makers, but with an additional 360° section at the lower end. Like contemporary basset-horns, it possesses a key for *c* (sounding B♭'), but not for *d* (sounding C). It seems possible that the 360° section at the bottom, which carries the lowest tone hole, was replaceable by a shorter section to give *d* (sounding C) instead.

Better known is the bass clarinet by Heinrich Grenser, dated 1793 (see illustration) and the similar example dated 1795 by his uncle August Grenser (i) (Darmstadt, Kg 67:133). These finely made instruments are pitched in B♭, with nine keys, and descend to written B♭ (sounding A♭'). The keywork is diatonic from *e* down and there are two thumb-holes, in the manner of the bassoon of that period. It seems not unlikely that the instrument was intended to replace the bassoon in military bands. Several other 19th-century bass clarinets may have been devised for the same purpose: some, like the Grenser example, were built in a doubled-up form like the bassoon, and several had a compass to *c* or B♭. Among the early models were the straight bass clarinet of Desfontanelles of Lisieux (Musée de la Musique, Paris, no.1136); the *basse guerrière* of Dumas, Paris, 1807; the *basse-orgue* of Sautermeister, Lyons, 1812; the bassoon-shaped 'patent clarion' by George Catlin of Hartford, Connecticut, *c*1810; the bass clarinet of J.H.G. Streitwolf, Göttingen, 1828; and the bassoon-shaped *Glicibarifono* of Catterini, Padua. The modern instrument owes a great deal both to Adolphe Sax and to Buffet *jeune* (*see* CLARINET, §II, 4(iii)). Musically, the history of the bass clarinet may be said to

Bass clarinets: (a) by Heinrich Grenser, Dresden, 1793 (Statens Musiksamlingar Musikonmuseet, Stockholm); (b) American, probably made in Hartford, Connecticut, c1815; (c) in B♭, by A. Nechwalsky, Vienna, mid-19th century (both Smithsonian Institution, Washington, DC); (d) in A, by Wilhelm Heckel, Biebrich, modern (private collection)

start with the important part assigned to it in Meyerbeer's opera *Les Huguenots* (1836); the Act 5 solo employs a range from *e* to *g'''*. In the same year Neukomm composed a setting of verses from Psalm lxx for 'a counter-tenor-Lady's voice, with the bass clarionet concertant'. The part for bass clarinet in C, which descends to written *c*, was played in its first performance by Thomas Lindsay Willman, very likely on an instrument by George Wood; although no specimen of Wood's bass clarinet is known, his published fingering chart for the instrument shows it to have been a bassoon-shaped model with a claimed chromatic range of four octaves and a whole tone.

From the later 19th century the bass clarinet figured frequently in orchestral scores; Mahler, Wagner, Schoenberg and Stravinsky used it regularly. In smaller combinations it was used particularly extensively by Webern, in preference to the bassoon. Occasionally two were specified (Stravinsky, *The Rite of Spring*).

2. NOTATION.   Many of the early bass clarinets were pitched in C, as they were intended as replacements for

bassoons rather than as additional members of the wind section. With the instrument's increased acceptance in the orchestra, bass clarinets in B♭ and A became more popular, although instruments in C were made into the 20th century. Many 19th-century composers assumed that the bass clarinet player would alternate between instruments in B♭ and A according to the key of the music. The long bass clarinet solo in Bartók's Suite for Orchestra op.4 was originally scored for an instrument pitched in A. With the widespread lowering of pitch standards to *a'* = 440, very few players or opera houses saw the need to retain the instrument in A, which may now be said to be extinct along with its companion in C.

There are several current conventions regarding notation for the bass clarinet. The so-called 'French system' is generally preferred by players: in this the part is written entirely in the treble clef, to sound a 9th lower than written. As players are accustomed to handling a number of different-sized clarinets with similar key layout (Mahler, in his Fifth Symphony, expects one player to play six different instruments), this system is the most convenient, as no adjustment of fingering relative to notation is needed.

The so-called 'German system' (used by Wagner and Janáček, for example) uses both clefs, but mainly the bass clef, the notes sounding (for the B♭ instrument) a whole tone lower than written. In the treble clef this runs counter to the player's instincts; in an attempt to avoid confusion, some composers change to a 9th transposition when using the treble clef. This may be compared with Mozart's practice (e.g. ᴋ91/516c and ᴋ581) of writing for the lower notes of the basset clarinet in the bass clef, to sound a 7th above the written notes, and with his notation for the horn and basset-horn. Schoenberg notated a few bass clarinet parts in C, perhaps feeling that to specify an instrument in B♭ (or A) carried undesirable implications of tonality. More recently this practice has been revived, possibly because of the chromaticism of present-day music, or simply to avoid the trouble and expense of copying parts in the proper manner.

3. MECHANISM. The size of the bass clarinet has always necessitated some difference in keywork from that of its smaller companions. Thus the instrument by Desfontanelles of Lisieux was built with 13 keys in 1807, before the soprano instrument was built with this number. Today the Boehm-system bass clarinet differs in a few respects from the soprano. In part, this is due to the necessity for large tone holes, so that all are covered by plates rather than directly by the fingers, and for a hole spacing wider than can be directly reached by the fingers. In part, it is that the instrument is large enough to accommodate improvements that are applied with less ease to the smaller instrument (and moreover the weight of additional keywork is of little significance since a spike or a sling is always used). Thus several bass clarinets incorporate superior venting in the lower joint. Possibly the most ingenious attempt to apply to a clarinet Boehm's principles of perfect venting for every note is the bass clarinet by Buffet-Crampon (Galpin Exhibition, Edinburgh, 1968, no.201; Bate Collection, Oxford) which incorporates keywork similar to the Dorus key of the flute, on both the c♯'/g♯" key and the a♭/e♭" key.

The third and most noticeable distinction in bass clarinet keywork concerns the speaker key. The compromise represented by this key, which is required both to define the speaking length of the tube for b♭' and to remain open for all higher notes in the instrument's range, becomes more and more unsatisfactory in lower-pitched instruments. It was Sax who first lessened the compromise by providing two speaker keys. One opens a larger hole lower down the instrument, giving a good b♭' and being satisfactory for several notes above; the second is smaller and closer to the mouthpiece, and serves for all higher notes. Today most bass and alto clarinets, some bassethorns and very few soprano clarinets incorporate this feature. Because of the inconvenience of moving the thumb rapidly from one key to the other while continuing to cover a hole at the same time, various mechanisms have been devised whereby only one touchpiece is used. When the touchpiece is depressed, one hole or another is opened, as determined by some other key. For example, one popular model is so designed that if either the a' key is opened, or the plate controlled by the right-hand third finger is depressed, the lower hole is opened, controlling the notes from b♭' to e♭". The slightly more complex mechanism required by automatic speaker keys is regarded with mistrust by a few players, so that some bass clarinets are still made with two separate touchpieces.

BIBLIOGRAPHY

R.E. Eliason: 'George Catlin, Hartford Musical Instrument Maker II', *JAMIS*, ix (1983), 21–52

J.H. van der Meer: 'The Typology and History of the Bass Clarinet', *JAMIS*, xiii (1987), 65–88

For further bibliography see CLARINET.

NICHOLAS SHACKLETON

Bass drum. *See* DRUM, §II, 1.

Basse (Fr.). *See* BASS (ii). *See also* EUPHONIUM.

Basse chantante (Fr.: 'singing bass'). In the Baroque era a term used to distinguish a vocal bass from an instrumental bass or basso continuo (Brossard, 1703; Walther, 1732; Rousseau, 1768). In the 19th century it came to mean a bass singer with a particularly high or light voice as distinct from a deeper, heavier bass (*see* BASSO PROFONDO and BASSE NOBLE). Operatic roles demanding this voice type include Max in Adam's *Le chalet* (1834), Lothario in Thomas's *Mignon* (1866) and Escamillo in Bizet's *Carmen* (1875). The Italian equivalent of this later usage is BASSO CANTANTE; *see also* BARITONE (i) and BASS (ii).

OWEN JANDER/ELLEN T. HARRIS

Basse chiffrée (Fr.). *See* FIGURED BASS.

Basse-contre (Fr.). A term derived from the Latin 'contratenor bassus' (*see* CONTRATENOR ALTUS), found in 16th-century French sources for the lowest-pitched member of the viol family. In this sense it is synonymous with 'contrebasse' and equivalent to the English DOUBLE BASS. The term has been used also for a bass voice of exceptionally low tessitura.

Basse danse (Fr.; It. *bassadanza*). The principal court dance during the late Middle Ages and Renaissance. It reached a height of cultivation during the 15th century and disappeared after the middle of the 16th century. The musical practice that grew up around it served as a proving ground for many early instrumental techniques such as improvisations over a ground, variations and the forming of suite-like combinations.

1. Choreography. 2. Mensuration. 3. Musical realization.

1. CHOREOGRAPHY. While no pre-15th-century documents describing steps and music have been found, the name of the dance was cited as early as 1340 by the troubadour Raimond de Cornet, who wrote of 'cansos e bassas dansas'. In a poem of about 1415 Alain Chartier described

> Ses fais comme la dance basse,
> Puis va avant, et puis rapasse,
> Puis retourne, puis oultrepasse.

The character of the dance is implicit in its name, which betokened a dance low to the ground, generally lacking the more rapid movements and leaps characteristic of the 'alta dansa' or 'saltarello'. Combination of these two types to form a varied pair can be documented throughout Europe during the late Middle Ages. The classic phase of the form corresponds to the heyday of the Burgundian court under Philip the Good and Charles the Bold. The main source preserving the Burgundian repertory is the Brussels Basse Danse manuscript (*B-Br 9085*), an anonymous treatise with steps and music copied in the late 15th century as a retrospect of several decades. Closely related to it is another version of the same treatise, containing many of the same dances, printed at Paris by Michel de Toulouse in or before 1496 and surviving now by the thread of a single copy in the Royal College of Physicians, London. As presented in these and other French, English and Spanish sources, the dance was performed by couples and employed only five different step-units: R (révérence); b (branle); s (simple, usually found in pairs); d (double) and r (reprise or des marche). These five steps were combined into codified patterns called *mesures*. Several *mesures* made up a complete dance, some dances being of six *mesures* (a total of 62 step-units, as in *Le doulz espoir*). A typical choreographical structure involved alternation of one *mesure* with another of different length. The Italian variety, called 'bassadanza', was recorded by Italian dancing-masters such as DOMENICO DA PIACENZA, GUGLIELMO EBREO DA PESARO and ANTONIO CORNAZANO. Their choreographies allowed more freedom in the variety and sequence of steps, and in the number of participants. In these respects the bassadanza approached a still freer form, the ballo, in which various steps and metres were combined (*see* BALLO, (2)). All sources, northern and southern, laid great stress on lightness and grace of motion, a quality achieved particularly by raising and lowering the body. The resulting effect was wavelike, described by Cornazano as 'ondegiarre'. During the 16th century the variety of step sequences disappeared from published and manuscript versions of the dance. The choreography gradually ossified into a single pattern with no more than 20 step sequences, called the *basse danse commune*, to which could be added a final 12 step sequences, called 'moitié' by Antonius de Arena, 'retour' by Thoinot Arbeau, and 'recoupe' in a musical source, Attaignant's *Dixhuit basses dances* of 1530. The French afterdance most commonly appended to the basse danse during the 16th century was called 'tourdion', and was characterized by quicker motions such as little leaps.

2. MENSURATION.   Only three 15th-century Italian bassadanza 'tunes' have been found in the extant treatises, although bassadanza sections exist in many balli. The lack of mensural sigla in the three Italian treatises and in the more than 50 15th-century Burgundian basse danse 'tunes' with dance steps generated considerable controversy among musicologists in the first half of the 20th century. Many dance historians have chosen to perform basse danses and bassadanzas in a triple (6/2) metre, using the 'tune' as a tenor, around which other musical parts are improvised (see Bukofzer, 1950); this can, however, cause an interesting hemiola effect when the number of dance movements in a step sequence does not correspond with the 6/2 metrical pulses. For example, if the accompaniment consists of six beats, divided usually into 3 + 3, the dancers would have to move in two against the music's three, a rhythmic skill that may help explain the quaint speech in Domenico's treatise: 'I am the bassadanza, queen of measures, and I deserve to wear the crown; few succeed in my employ and those who dance or play me well must perforce be gifted of heaven'. The advent of the *basse danse commune* brought an end to more than one challenging feature. The sextuple division of the long was changed to a quadruple one, i.e. from six semibreves to four dotted ones. The 15th-century afterdance, called 'pas de Brabant' in the north, stood in the relationship of

Basse danse: miniature from Jean de Waurin's 'Recueil des croniques et anchiennes istoires de la Grant Bretgaigne', c1471 (A-Wn 2534, f.17)

diminution by one half to the main dance, i.e. from 6/1 to 3/1 = 6/2. Cornazano explained the proportions in reverse, saying that the saltarello had three beats, while in the bassadanza 'every note is doubled, and the three are worth six and the six, twelve'. Italian theory taught two other diminutions: *quaternaria* in 4/1, called also 'saltarello tedesco' and said by Cornazano to be 'used more by Germans'; and piva, an expression meaning bagpipe, in 12/4 = 6/4 + 6/4. The latter was little used at court, to believe its speech in Domenico's treatise: 'I am called piva, and am the saddest of the measures because the peasants employ me'. Cornazano described it as 'low and vulgar, unsuitable for magnificent persons and dancers of good standing'. Yet it must have had its proponents even so. J.A. Dalza's variation suites for lute printed at Venice by Petrucci in 1508 consisted of *pavana*–saltarello–piva. They testify to the practical consequences of the old measure-theory even as the original dance, the 'queen of the measures', was passing out of existence in Italy.

Marrocco (1981), however, claimed that the *nota senza valore* was purposeful, encouraging the dancers and/or musicians to choose a duple or triple metre at will. To be sure, basse danse music published in the 16th century is predominantly in duple metre, and the 16th-century Italian dancing-masters' choreographies that include 'bassa' in their title begin with duple-metre sections and subsequently include a *sciolta* or *gagliarda* triple-metre afterdance section.

3. MUSICAL REALIZATION.   The cardinal principle of the 15th-century form was that one note of the basse danse tenor corresponded to one complete step-unit. Since every step-unit was of equal duration, lasting three or four seconds in reconstructions by dance historians, there resulted a string of long isometric tones, a cantus firmus constructed to the length of the choreography, which served in performance as the basis for improvised

elaborations. Cornazano included three cantus firmi which he labelled 'Tenori da basse danze et saltarelli': *Re di Spagna* (46 notes in length), *Cançon de' pifari dicto el ferrarese* (46) and *Collinetto* (73). They are notated in semibreves. More than 50 different tenors are preserved in the Brussels manuscript and Toulouse's print ranging in length from 24 to 62 notes. Toulouse contains the sole concordance with Cornazano, its *Casulle la novelle* (46) corresponding to the famous *Spagna* tenor. The northern manner of notation was in breves, the blackening of which hinted at the augmentation to longs that players had to make for the basse danse proper. French chansons were a favourite source from which to fashion dance tenors in both Italy and north Europe. The oldest known example of this is *Je suis pauvre de liesse* (Brussels no.46, 42 notes in length), which was inscribed as a tenor by Noël de Fleurus in some notarial records at Namur dating from 1421–3. The tenors of polyphonic chansons yielded the material for several dance tenors. Much of the vast modern literature on the subject is taken up with such correspondences. Although the source of many dance tenors was in vocal music, their use as dance music was exclusively instrumental. This was made abundantly clear by the Italian masters. Guglielmo counselled the dancers to listen attentively when the instruments begin in order to ascertain which of the two keys, 'B molle' (minor) or 'B quadro' (major), they employ; and the Italians taught that all performances should begin with preparatory upbeats to lead the dancers into the first step. The most popular dances towards the end of the 15th century were *Filles à marier* (32 notes in length) and *Le petit Rouen* (40). This pair inaugurated the Toulouse incunabulum and probably the Brussels manuscript as well, before it was wrongly reassembled in the 19th century. They found their way to England, where their choreographies were written out in the Salisbury Basse Danse manuscript (in Salisbury Cathedral Library) of about 1500 and printed in the Robert Coplande treatise *There followeth the manner of dancing base dances* (London, 1521). *Filles à marier* also reached Spain, while *Le petit Rouen* lived on far into the 16th century as a German Hoftanz. Unlike most tenors in the repertory, these two were built symmetrically in phrases of eight notes. Their periodic nature may provide a clue to their wide dissemination – they were easy to remember. The symmetrical grounds of the 16th-century passamezzo family may be viewed as one offshoot. Signs that the old cantus firmus practice was giving way about 1500 are evident even in the Brussels manuscript. *La franchoise nouvelle* (24), for instance, takes the form of a melody using a variety of rhythmic values, constructed in short phrases of two longs, each with varied repeat; still reminiscent of the past is the notation in a low register and the division of the long into six semibreves. Tuneful melodies in many small sections with abundant repetitions became the normal accompaniment to the 16th-century form. French chansons remained the favourite model for imitation, especially those of Claudin de Sermisy. The final stage is illustrated in Arbeau's treatise of 1588: a *basse danse commune* arranged from Claudin's *Jouyssance vous donneray*.

BIBLIOGRAPHY

MGG2 (I. Brainard)

E. Closson, ed.: *Le manuscrit dit des basses danses de la Bibliothèque de Bourgogne* (Brussels, 1912/R)

O. Kinkeldey: 'A Jewish Dancing Master of the Renaissance (Guglielmo Ebreo)', *Studies in Jewish Bibliography ... in Memory of Abraham Solomon Freidus* (New York, 1929), 329–72 [repr. with suppl., Brooklyn, 1966]

V. Scholderer: Introduction to facs. of *L'art et instruction de bien dancer (Michel Touluoze, Paris)* (London, 1936)

A. Michel: 'The Earliest Dance Manuals', *Medievalia et humanistica*, iii (1945), 117–31

M.F. Bukofzer: 'A Polyphonic Basse Dance of the Renaissance', *Studies in Medieval & Renaissance Music* (New York, 1950), 190–216

O. Gombosi: 'The Cantus Firmus Dances', *Compositione di Meser Vincenzo Capirola* (Neuilly-sur-Seine, 1955), pp.xxxvi–lxiii

I. Brainard: *Die Choreographie der Hoftänze in Burgund, Frankreich und Italien im 15. Jahrhundert* (diss., U. of Göttingen, 1956)

D. Heartz: 'The Basse Dance: its Evolution circa 1450 to 1550', *AnnM*, vi (1958–63), 287–340

O. Kinkeldey: 'Dance Tunes of the Fifteenth Century', *Instrumental Music: Cambridge, MA, 1957*, 3–30, 89–152

E. Southern: 'Some Keyboard Basse Dances of the Fifteenth Century', *AcM*, xxxv (1963), 114–24

D. Heartz: 'Basse Dances', *Preludes, Chansons and Dances for Lute Published by Pierre Attaingnant (1529–1530)* (Neuilly-sur-Seine, 1964), pp.xxxi–lxxxvii

J.L. Jackman, ed.: *Fifteenth Century Basse Dances*, WE, vi (1964)

F. Crane: 'The Derivation of Some Fifteenth-Century Basse-Danse Tunes', *AcM*, xxxvii (1965), 179–88

J.P. Cunningham: *Dancing in the Inns of Court* (London, 1965)

D. Heartz: 'A 15th-Century Ballo: *Rôti bouilli joyeux*', *Aspects of Medieval and Renaissance Music: a Birthday Offering to Gustave Reese*, ed. J. LaRue and others (New York, 1966/R), 359–75

E. Southern: 'Basse-Dance Music in some German Manuscripts of the 15th Century', ibid., 738–55

D. Heartz: 'Hoftanz and Basse Dance', *JAMS*, xix (1966), 13–36

F. Crane: *Materials for the Study of the Fifteenth Century Basse Danse* (New York, 1968) [incl. extensive bibliography]

R. Meylan: *L'énigme de la musique des basses danses du quinzième siècle* (Berne, 1968) [incl. extensive bibliography, classified according to primary and secondary sources]

I. Brainard: *The Art of Courtly Dancing in the Early Renaissance*, ii: *The Practice of Courtly Dancing* (West Newton, MA, 1981)

W. Marrocco: *Inventory of 15th Century Bassedanze, Balli & Balletti in Italian Dance Manuals* (New York, 1981)

Y. Guilcher: 'Les différentes lectures de l'Orchésographie de Thoinot Arbeau', *Le recherche en danse*, i (1982), 39–49

F. Garavini: 'Le traité de danse d'un étudiant provençal autour de 1520: Antonius Arena', *Le recherche en danse*, iii (1984), 5–14

M. Franko: 'Renaissance Conduct Literature and the Basse Danse: the Kinesis of Bonne Grace', *Persons in Groups: Social Behavior as Identity Formation in Medieval and Renaissance Europe*, ed. R.C. Trexler (Binghamton, NY, 1985), 55–66

M. Padovan: 'Da Dante a Leonardo: la danza italiana attraverso le fonti storiche', *La danza italiana*, iii/aut. (1985), 5–37

B. Sparti: 'The 15th-Century Balli Tunes: a New Look', *EMc*, xiv (1986), 346–57

J. Sutton and F.M.Walker, eds.: F. Caroso: *Nobiltà di dame* (Oxford, 1986, 2/1995)

J. Ward: 'The English Measure', *EMc*, xiv (1986), 15–21

A. Pontremoli and P.La Rocca: *Il ballare Lombardo: teoria e prassi coreutica nella festa di corte del XV secolo* (Milan, 1987)

T.J. McGee: *Medieval and Renaissance Music: a Performer's Guide* (Toronto, 1988)

A. Francalanci: 'The "Copia de Mo. Giorgio del guido di ballare basse danze e balletti" as found in the New York Public Library', *Basler Jb für historische Musikpraxis*, xiv (1990), 87–179

M. Padovan, ed.: *Guglielmo Ebreo da Pesaro e la danza nelle corti italiane del XV secolo: Pesaro 1987* (Pisa, 1990)

A. Feves: 'Fabritio Caroso and the Changing Shape of the Dance, 1550–1660', *Dance Chronicle*, xiv (1991), 159–74

D.R. Wilson: 'A Further Look at the Nancy Basse Dances', *Historical Dance*, iii/3 (1994), 24–8 [on the dances in F-Pn fonds fr.5699, formerly 10279]

DANIEL HEARTZ (with PATRICIA RADER)

Basse de Flandre (Fr.). *See* BUMBASS.

Basse de musette. A type of tenor shawm used in Swiss Protestant churches between about 1760 and 1810. *See* HAUTBOIS D'ÉGLISE.

Basse de violon (Fr.). *See* BASS VIOLIN. *See also* VIOLONCELLO.

Basse d'harmonie (Fr.). *See* OPHICLEIDE.

Bassée, Adam de la. *See* ADAM DE LA BASSÉE.

Basse fondamentale. *See* FUNDAMENTAL BASS.

Basseggio, Lorenzo. *See* BASEGGIO, LORENZO.

Bassengius [Bassengo; Passenger], **Aegidius** (*b* Liège; *fl* 1588–94). Flemish composer. In 1588 he was a chorister at Salzburg Cathedral; a year later he was unsuccessful in securing a permanent position in the imperial court chapel in Prague, but was engaged there on a temporary basis and received fees amounting to 65 gulden. His *Motectorum quinque, sex, octo vocum, liber primus* was published in Vienna in 1591. At that time he was Kapellmeister to Archduke Maximilian, as he was until 1594. If Bassengius was identical with 'Eg. Bassange', then he was the town organist of Wiener Neustadt in 1595. (*SennMT*, 187)

JOHN CLAPHAM

Basse noble (Fr.: 'noble bass'). A term first used in the late 19th century as a French equivalent to the Italian BASSO PROFONDO. The higher and more flexible BASSE CHANTANTE is clearly distinguished (in *EMDC*, II/ii, 1926, p.920) from 'the bass without a qualifying adjective [that] is the lowest bass voice, also called *basse taille*, *basse noble*, *basse profonde*'. Although the *basse noble* has been distinguished from the *basso profondo* in terms of its greater flexibility and lighter tone, qualities it shares with the *basse chantante*, comparison of the *basse noble* with the *basse chantante* in range should be avoided.

ELLEN T. HARRIS

Bassere, Jo. (*fl c*1450). ?French composer. He is known through a three-voice mass (in *I-TRmp* 89). Reference to this composition (*EitnerQ*) as a *Missa super Christus surrexit* seems incorrect and apparently arose from a confusion of the work with a mass using *Christus surrexit* which occurs later in the same source. The mass is unified by a head-motif, a pattern of mensurations and the use of F as the cadence pitch of all major sections.

TOM R. WARD

Basse-taille (Fr.: 'low tenor'). In the Baroque, a term for the lowest male tenor voice of three: *haute-taille*, *taille* and *basse-taille*, which correspond to the three *parties intermédiares* of the string orchestra, all played by instruments of the viola type: *haute-contre de violon*, *taille de violon* and *quinte de violon*. Brossard (*Dictionaire de musique*, 1703) uses it to define the Italian word *baritono*, for which he provides the additional synonym *concordans*. However, he distinguishes their ranges, giving the range of the *basse-taille* as B to *f'*, whereas the range of the *concordans* extends to G. Rousseau (*Dictionnaire de musique*, 1768) places the *basse-taille* between the tenor and the bass, but allows that true *basses* are sometimes 'distinguished properly by that name alone, to which custom has given the name *basse-taille*'. This meaning persisted well into the 19th century. Manuel García (*Traité complet de l'art du chant*, 1840–47/R), however, gives *basse-taille* as the lowest male voice and writes that this 'sonorous and powerful' voice extends from E to *d'* with a lower extension to Db and an upper extension to *e'*.

ELLEN T. HARRIS

Basset clarinet. A soprano clarinet (*see* CLARINET, §II, 1) whose range is extended downwards to written *c*, in the manner of the basset-horn (it is classified as an AEROPHONE). The instrument was probably devised by Anton Stadler in collaboration with the Viennese instrument maker T. Lotz. Several of Mozart's compositions were intended for a basset clarinet rather than for an instrument of conventional range: the Concerto K622 and the Quintet K581 required a basset clarinet in A, while the clarinet obbligato in *La clemenza di Tito* required a basset clarinet in Bb. Manuscript cadenzas to a concerto by Leopold Kozeluch [*A-Wn* 5853] are written for a basset clarinet, but little is known of the history of the instrument other than in Stadler's hands. A basset clarinet dating from about 1840 (16 keys) by J.G.K. Bischoff is in the collection at Darmstadt (Kg61:116) and a later 19th-century example (with contemporary 'simple-system' keywork) can be found in the Bate Collection, Oxford (for a list of surviving instruments, see Lawson). The basset clarinet was revived (with modern keywork) in Prague in 1951 by Jiří Kratochvíl in order to perform Mozart's concerto as the composer intended; since that date a number have been made, notably in England by E. Planus. Richard Rodney Bennett (*Crosstalk*, *c*1966) and Anthony Gilbert (*Spell Respell*, 1968) have composed for the instrument.

The term 'basset clarinet' has been preferred for the late 20th-century revival of the historical instrument because the term 'bass clarinet', used originally by Stadler for his extended soprano instrument, is now used to describe the instrument pitched an octave lower.

BIBLIOGRAPHY

(see also CLARINET)
C. Lawson: *Mozart Clarinet Concerto* (Cambridge, 1996)
P.L. Poulin: 'Anton Stadler's Basset Clarinet: Recent Discoveries in Riga', *JAMIS*, xxii (1996), 110–27

NICHOLAS SHACKLETON

Bassetgen (Ger.). *See* BASSETT (i).

Basset-horn (Fr. *cor de basset*; Ger. *Bassetthorn*; It. *corno di bassetto*). Woodwind instrument; a member of the clarinet family (*see* CLARINET, §II, 1, fig.2*f*), normally now pitched in F (it is classified as an AEROPHONE). A distinctive feature is the extension of its compass downwards to written *c* (sounding *F*), a major 3rd below the lowest note of the conventional clarinet. In most early examples, this is achieved without inconvenience by the curious 'book' or 'box' in which the extra length of tube makes three excursions before emerging into a rather flamboyant metal bell. A straight form of basset-horn was invented around the beginning of the 19th century, and a crook for it first appears in the last decade of the 18th (*see* CLARINETTE D'AMOUR).

The origin of the basset-horn, like that of the clarinet itself, is not as clear as is widely believed; it is generally thought to be established by a few instruments (see illustration) which bear on the 'book' the inscription 'ANT et MICH MAYRHOFER INVEN. & ELABOR. PASSAVII', and which are thought to have been made in Passau in the 1760s by the Mayrhofers (similar instruments were made by others). The simplest sickle-shaped basset-horn (which may predate the Mayrhofer instruments) has a mere five keys: thumb-keys for *e* and *c* (no *d* was possible), a fish-tail key for *f/c"* (playable with either hand uppermost) and the two obligatory keys on the

Basset-horns: (a) by Mayrhofer, Passau, c1770 (Oberhaus Museum, Passau); (b) by August Grenser, Dresden, 1795 (Gemeentemuseum, The Hague)

upper joint. Thus the state of development is equivalent to that of the three-key clarinet.

The basset-horn in G, a late 18th-century instrument, is the equivalent in the clarinet family of the C bass chalumeau, the lowest of the three instruments for which the trios for three chalumeaux by Christoph Graupner were written; that is to say, there was probably a direct link from the bass chalumeau to the basset-horn. The question as to whether a lower-pitched clarinet was made and then extended in range by the invention of the 'book', or whether a chalumeau of downwards extended range had already been devised, is certainly not answered by the well-known claim of Mayrhofer, particularly as so many makers have made exaggerated claims as to their innovatory achievements. In short, the history of the lower-pitched clarinets and chalumeaux in relation to the basset-horn is an open question.

Scarcely less secure is the position of higher- and lower-pitched instruments of extended compass. The term BASSET CLARINET is reserved for soprano clarinets of extended range, but the fact that Mozart first drafted the first movement of his concerto K622 for an instrument in G, and then rewrote it for one in A, is a reminder that the line between basset-horn and clarinet is indistinct. The obbligato to *Parto, parto* in *La clemenza di Tito* is for a B♭ instrument of extended range; at the other end of the scale, the distinction between the basset-horn in D specified by Druschetzky and the bass clarinet in C

extended to (written) *c* by means of thumb-keys is again an arbitrary one.

Mozart was especially enamoured of the basset-horn, using it particularly in masonic pieces; when writing for three instruments, he often used the treble clef for the upper two (the instruments sounding a 5th lower than written) and the bass clef for the lowest (sounding a 4th higher than written). The Serenade in B♭ K361/370*a*, the Requiem K626 and four of the notturnos for two sopranos and baritone accompanied by a trio of basset-horns use the basset-horn in F; the notturno K437 (incomplete) specifies a basset-horn in G together with two clarinets in A. It seems that only the instrument in F was made in the 19th century. A number of basset-horns survive, although the fact that many are in good condition suggests that they were never extensively used, as one may also judge from the comparative scarcity of music written for the instrument. Beethoven specified the basset-horn once only (*Prometheus*); Mendelssohn composed (for Heinrich and Carl Baermann) two concert pieces for clarinet, basset-horn and piano. Otherwise, the basset-horn's use was as an alternative recital instrument and in the abundant wind bands of the period.

The manufacture of the instrument diminished greatly during the mid-19th century, although it cannot be said to have become extinct. Henry Lazarus (1815–95) played one, and it was in a sense revived by V.-C. Mahillon at the end of the century. Richard Strauss used it to great effect in several of his operas (e.g. at the opening of *Daphne*) and in his wind Sonatinas AV139 and 143.

It is generally recognized that the particular timbre of the classical basset-horn was due to the fact that its bore was scarcely larger than that of the contemporary clarinet, whereas the alto clarinet in F, which was developed in the early part of the 19th century, had a substantially wider bore. This has left modern makers in something of a quandary as to the ideal towards which they should aim, namely whether a basset-horn can be made to balance the forces of the modern orchestra without losing the special character that distinguishes it.

Some modern examples are made with a clarinet bore, others with a slightly wider bore, and yet others with an alto clarinet bore. The keywork is that of today's clarinet, with the added complexity of an extra four semitones to be coped with. Either control may be exercised entirely by the right thumb, as in all early examples, or the burden may be shared with the already overworked fourth finger of either hand. Most German instruments take the former course, most French the latter. In order to free the thumb, the weight of the instrument is always taken on a sling or a spike. French instruments have an upturned bell like that of the alto and bass clarinets, but many German makers favour a straight wooden bell like that of the soprano clarinet.

BIBLIOGRAPHY

J. Saam: *Das Bassetthorn* (Mainz, 1971)

J.P. Newhill: *The Basset-Horn and its Music* (Sale, Cheshire, 1983, 2/1986)

J. Eppelsheim: 'Bassethorn-Studien', *Studia Organologica: Festschrift für John Henry van der Meer*, ed. F. Hellwig (Tutzing, 1987), 69–125

N. Shackleton: 'The Earliest Basset Horns', *GSJ*, xl (1987), 2–23

For further bibliography see CLARINET, II.

NICHOLAS SHACKLETON

Basset: Nicolo. Term used by Praetorius for a type of wind-cap instrument. *See* CRUMHORN.

Basse-trompette [trombe]. As distinct from *trompette basse* (bass trumpet), a type of upright SERPENT patented by LOUIS ALEXANDRE FRICHOT of Paris in 1810. It was evidently an improvement on the so-called 'English' BASS-HORN which Frichot had invented during the 1790s. The *basse-trompette* was provided with six finger-holes in two groups of three, and four or five keys. Unlike that of the bass-horn, which was sharply mitred and had a large looped crook, the body tube of the *basse-trompette* was bent upon itself three times, forming one large and one smaller loop with a short mouthpipe to carry the mouthpiece. According to the patent specification (see illustration) the lower curve of the smaller loop was formed by interchangeable bows of different length for pitch adjustment (*pièces de rechange*); this idea may have influenced Coëffet's design for his ophimonocleide, which incorporated a double slide (*pompe*) for altering the pitch.

There is a *basse-trompette* in the Musée de la Musique, Paris (no.651). It was described in detail and much praised by Choron (1815), who mentioned that it could be played with a mouthpiece of either serpent or trumpet proportions, yielding different and characteristic tone qualities. However, it is unlikely that a trumpet mouthpiece would be effective on a bass instrument with a large conical bore. Sachs suggested that the *basse-trompette* was the same instrument as Frichot's *basse-cor* of 1806. This view was held by Langwill, who also noted an alternative, later

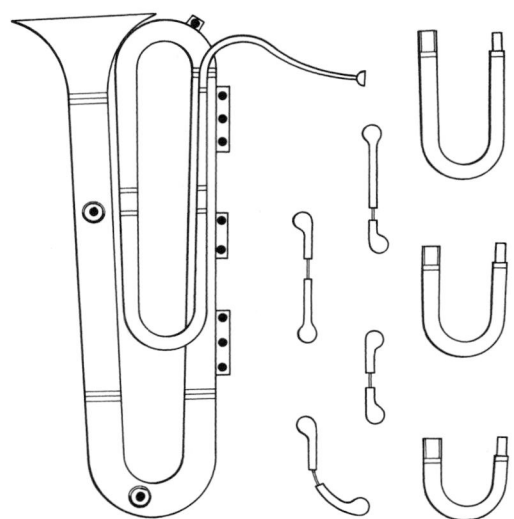

Basse-trompette: arrangement after Frichot's patent specification, 1810

name (*trombe*) and mentioned the announcement of Frichot's invention by the Académie of Beaux-Arts, Paris, in 1812. Pierre (1893) gave the *basse-trompette* as dating from 1806 to 1810, thereby corroborating Sach's opinion. Pierre also referred to the tromba of 1812, but did not associate it with the earlier instrument.

BIBLIOGRAPHY

Waterhouse-LangwillI

Brevet français, no.404 (31 Dec 1810)

L.-J. Francoeur and A.-E. Choron: *Traité général des voix et des instruments d'orchestre et principalement des instruments à vent* (Paris, 1815)

G. Chouquet: *Le musée de Conservatoire national de musique: catalogue raisonné* (Paris, 2/1884)

C. Pierre: *Les facteurs d'instruments de musique* (Paris, 1893/R)

C. Sachs: *Real-Lexicon der Musikinstrumente* (Berlin, 1913/R)

PHILIP BATE/STEPHEN J. WESTON

Bassett [basset] (**i**) (Ger. *Bassett, Bassetgen*; It. *bassetto*). Diminutive of BASS (i). The lowest part of a passage or composition lacking a bass part and which executes the musical bass in higher register. It was defined by Praetorius in the *Syntagma musicum*, iii (1618), 121–2:

the lowest voice in a high-register chorus, which executes the fundament and whose structure resembles a true bass; … any lowest-sounding part in a high register … in both concertos and motets [i.e. in both *stile moderno* and *stile antico*], whether soprano, alto, or tenor, as we see most often in fugues.

This usage, peculiar to the Baroque era, frequently appeared in discussions of basso continuo, where it denoted a passage notated in a C clef or G clef rather than the usual F clef. 'Bassetto' also denoted the lowest part of each separate chorus in a polychoral composition.

BIBLIOGRAPHY

F.T. Arnold: *The Art of Accompaniment from a Thorough-bass* (London, 1931/R), 373ff

JAMES WEBSTER

Bassett (**ii**) (Ger., also *Bassl, Bassetl*). A diminutive of *Bass* in the sense of 'double bass', hence analogous to the Italian *violoncello*, which is a diminutive of VIOLONE. 'Bassetl' was the common designation for the cello in

Austria and south Germany during the 18th century; Leopold Mozart, in his *Violinschule* (1756), wrote: 'The Bassel or Bassette ... also goes under the name *Violoncell*'. The term did not designate a small, short-necked or other type of 'miniature' double bass.

BIBLIOGRAPHY

K. Marx: *Die Entwicklung des Violoncells und seiner Spieltechnik bis J.L. Duport (1520–1820)* (Regensburg, 1963), 62ff

J. Webster: 'Violoncello and Double Bass in the Chamber Music of Haydn and his Viennese Contemporaries, 1750–1780', *JAMS*, xxix (1976), 413–38

JAMES WEBSTER

Bassett (iii). A term specifying instruments in baritone, tenor or alto range, for example the BASSET-HORN and BASSET CLARINET. Praetorius called the tenor shawm 'Bassett' or 'Tenor Pommer', and the lowest (bass) recorder in F 'Bassett'.

Bassett (iv). An organ stop with flue pipes.

Bassett, Leslie (Raymond) (*b* Hanford, CA, 22 Jan 1923). American composer. He studied at the University of Michigan with Finney, by whose teaching he was particularly influenced, and also had lessons with Boulanger and Honegger (1950–51), Gerhard (1960) and Davidovsky (electronic music, 1964). In 1952 he joined the faculty of the University of Michigan, becoming head of the composition department in 1970 and Albert A. Stanley Professor in 1977; he was also a founder-member of the university's electronic studio and directed the Contemporary Directions Performance Project until he retired in 1991. Among the awards he has received are the Rome Prize (which took him to the American Academy in Rome, 1961–3), a Pulitzer Prize (1966, for the Variations for orchestra), Guggenheim Fellowships (1973–4, 1980–81), a Naumburg Foundation recording award for the Sextet for piano and strings (1974) and a Rockefeller Foundation grant (1988); his *Echoes from an Invisible World* was commissioned by the Philadelphia Orchestra for the Bicentennial. In 1976 he was elected a member of the Institute of the American Academy and Institute of Arts and Letters. Bassett's music is carefully structured, its formal processes clear; conventional pitch materials are frequently deployed in an original manner. Even his writing for voices is instrumental in character, a quality he uses to advantage in the choral works, where voices and instruments are cohesively combined.

WORKS

ORCHESTRAL

5 Movts, 1961; Variations, 1963; Designs, Images and Textures, band, 1964; Colloquy, 1969; Forces, vn, vc, pf, orch, 1972; Echoes from an Invisible World, 1975; Conc., 2 pf, orch, 1976; Sounds, Shapes and Symbols, band, 1977; Conc. grosso, brass qnt, wind, perc, 1982; Conc. lirico, trbn, orch, 1983; Colors and Contours, band, 1984; Lullaby, band, 1985; From a Source Evolving, 1985; Fantasy, cl, wind ens, 1986; Conc. for Orch, 1991; Thoughts that Sing, Breathe and Burn, 1995

CHAMBER

Trbn Qt, 1949; Sonata, hn, pf, 1952; Brass Trio, tpt, hn, trbn, 1953; Trio, va, cl, pf, 1953; Qnt, str qt, db, 1954; Sonata, trbn, pf, 1954; Cl Duets, 1955; Sonata, va, pf, 1956; 5 Pieces, str qt, 1957; Suite, trbn, 1957; Ww Qnt, 1958; Sonata, vn, pf, 1959; Vc Duets, 1959; Pf Qnt, 1962; Str Qt no.3, 1962; Music for Vc and Pf, 1966; Nonet, wind qnt, tpt, trbn, tuba, pf, 1967; Music for Sax and Pf, 1968; Sextet, pf, 2 vn, 2 va, vc, 1971

Sounds Remembered, vn, pf, 1972; Music for 4 Hns, 1974; 12 Duos, 2/4 trbn, 1974; Wind Music, fl, ob, cl, a sax, bn, hn, 1975; Soliloquies, cl, 1976; Str Qt no.4, 1978; Sextet, fl, a fl, cl, b cl, vc, db, 1979; Temperaments, gui, 1979–83; A Masque of Bells,

carillon, 1980; Trio, vn, cl, pf, 1980; Conc. da camera, fl, cl, tpt, vn, vc, pf, perc, 1981; Duo Concertante, a sax, pf, 1984; Salute, 5 tpt, 1985; Dialogues, ob, pf, 1987; Duo-Inventions, 2 vc, 1988; Brass Qnt, 1988, Illuminations, fl, pf, 1989; Metamorphoses, bn, 1990; Arias, cl, pf, 1992; Narratives, 4 gui, 1993; Song and Dance, tuba, pf, 1993; 3 Equale, 4 trbn, 1996; Trio-Inventions, 3 vc, 1996

CHORAL

The Lamb (W. Blake), SATB, pf, 1952; Out of the Depths (Ps cxxx), SATB, org, 1957; For City, Nation, World (cant.), T, SATB, children's chorus ad lib, congregation, 4 trbn, org, 1959; Moonrise (D.H. Lawrence), SSA, 9 insts, 1960; Remembrance (H. Rupert), SATB, org, 1960; Eclogue, Encomium and Evocation (Bible: *Song of Solomon*) SSA, pf, hp, 2 perc, 1962; Follow Now that Bright Star (carol), SATB, 1962; Prayers for Divine Service (Lat.), TTBB, org, 1965; Hear my Prayer, O Lord (Ps lxiv), SA, org, 1965; Notes in the Silence (D. Hammarskjöld), SATB, pf, 1966

Collect, SATB, tape, 1969; Moon Canticle, S, amp nar, SATB, vc, 1969; Celebration: in Praise of Earth, amp nar, SATB, orch, 1970; Of Wind and Earth (P.B. Shelley, W.C. Bryant, St Francis), SATB, pf, 1973; A Ring of Emeralds (Irish poets), SATB, pf, 1979; Sing to the Lord (Ps xcv), SATB, org, 1981; Lord, who hast formed me (G. Herbert), SATB, org, 1981; Whoe'er She Be (R. Crashaw), SSA, pf, 1986; Almighty, Eternal (Bassett), SATB, org, 1990; Maker of Our Being (Bassett), SATB, org, 1993

OTHER WORKS

Kbd: 6 Pf Pieces, 1951; Toccata, org, 1955; Voluntaries, org, 1958; Mobile, pf, 1961; 4 Statements, org, 1964; Elaborations, pf, 1966; Liturgies, org, 1980; 7 Preludes, pf, 1984; Configurations, pf, 1987

Solo vocal: 4 Songs (W. Blake, G. Herbert, E.A. Robinson), S, pf, 1953; Easter Triptych (Bible), T, wind ens, 1958; To Music (B. Jonson, R. Herrick, W. Billings), 3 songs, S/T, pf, 1962; The Jade Garden (oriental), S, pf, 1973; Time and Beyond (R.W. Emerson, R. Tagore, M. Van Doren), B, cl, vc, pf, 1973; Love Songs (Gk. anon., W.S. Landor, A. Brodstreet, Emerson, H. Harrington), S, pf, 1975; Pierrot Songs (A. Giraud, Ger. trans. O. Hartleben), S, fl, cl, vn, vc, pf, 1988

Elec: 3 Studies in Elec Sound, 1965; Triform, 1966

*c*20 works now withdrawn, incl. 2 syms., 1949, 1956, 2 str qts, 1949, 1951

Principal publishers: ACA, King, Merion, Peters

BIBLIOGRAPHY

EwenD

A. Brown: 'Leslie Bassett', *Asterisk*, ii/2 (1976), 8–15 [incl. list of works]

E.S. Johnson: *Leslie Bassett: a Bio-Bibliography* (Westport, CT, 1994)

EDITH BORROFF/MICHAEL MECKNA

Bassey, Shirley (*b* Cardiff, 8 Jan 1937). Welsh pop singer. With a booming yet imperious contralto and an arresting stage presence, Shirley Bassey was one of Britain's most popular singers of show tunes and pop ballads during the 1950s and 60s. Her forte was the melodramatic ballad, usually taken from a successful musical play or popular film. Thus, early in her career Bassey made hit recordings of 'As long as he needs me' (from Bart's *Oliver!*) and 'Climb ev'ry mountain' (from Rodgers and Hammerstein's *The Sound of Music*). One of the songs most associated with her was a contrasting showstopper, the brassy, up-tempo 'Big Spender' from Coleman's 1966 musical *Sweet Charity*. In the cinema, Bassey was chosen to perform three of John Barry's themes from the James Bond film series: *Goldfinger* (1964; lyrics by L. Bricusse and A. Newley), *Diamonds Are Forever* (1972; lyrics by D. Black) and *Moonraker* (1979; lyrics by H. David).

Bassey's best-known British recordings were arranged and conducted by Johnny Franz and Norman Newell, but she worked in a more jazz-orientated setting when she recorded the album *Let's Face The Music* in 1962 with leading American bandleader Nelson Riddle. The most unusual of her performances were the collaborations with

Yello on *The Rhythm Divine* (1989) and with the Propellerheads on *History Repeating* (1997). By the early 1990's Bassey was semi-retired and her contribution to British show business was recognised by the award of a CBE in 1993 and a DBE in 2000.

DAVE LAING

Bass flute (i). A term occasionally used to denote the alto flute in G, although more properly reserved for the flute in C an octave below the concert flute. *See* FLUTE, §II, 3(v).

Bass flute (ii). *See under* ORGAN STOP (*Bassflute*).

Bass guitar. *See* ELECTRIC BASS GUITAR.

Bass-horn. An early variety of upright SERPENT invented by LOUIS ALEXANDRE FRICHOT in the 1790s. It is classified as a trumpet. The instrument consists of a conical tube about 230 cm long and generally made of copper. The larger end terminates in a widely flared bell and the smaller in a graceful swan-neck crook, this last accounting for nearly one-third of the instrument's total length. The tube is cut at a distance of about 81 cm from the bell and the two straight sections are set at a very acute angle into a short butt which ensures the continuity of the air column (see illustration).

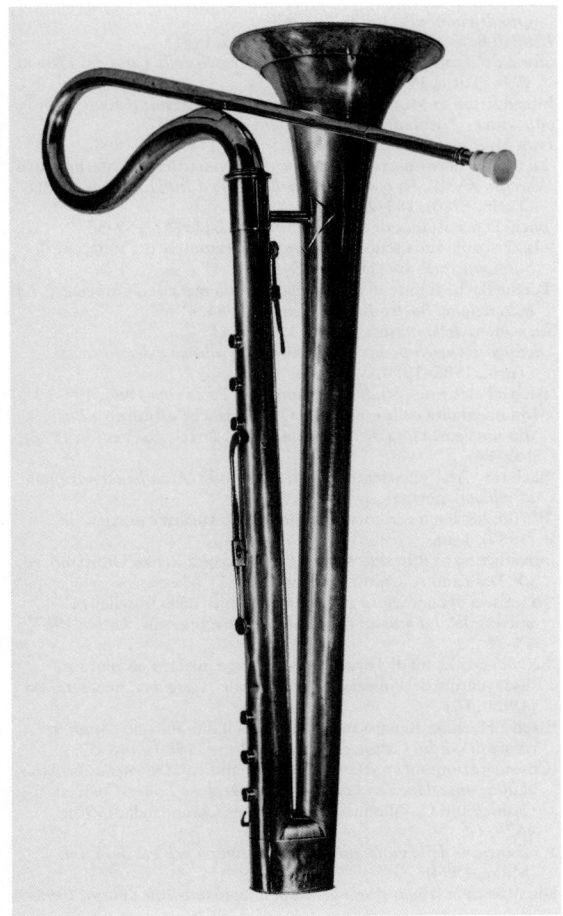

Bass-horn with four keys, maker unknown, c1800 (Spencer Collection, Brighton Museum and Art Gallery)

The bass-horn has six finger-holes and usually either three or four keys. It was always considered to have C as its true fundamental. Compass, fingering and manner of blowing are the same as for the serpent, but its tone was said to be more powerful. With its more convenient playing position, it probably lent itself more readily than the serpent to the display of virtuosity.

The instrument enjoyed considerable popularity in England for more than 30 years but, just as the more conventional types of upright serpent and Russian bassoon never found favour in Britain, so the bass-horn was never taken up on the Continent, though the word is sometimes met in Germany to denote one of these other instruments, as in *russisches Basshorn* (It. *corno di basso*, for Russian bassoon), and Johann Streitwolf's *chromatisches Basshorn* of c1820.

Its natural place was, of course, the wind band, but it was also occasionally found in the large festival orchestras. There were actually four in the orchestras of the 1825 and 1828 York festivals, but by 1835 they had given place to ophicleides with, however, one exception, a sort of contrabass bass-horn called the HIBERNICON. As late as 1840 there was still one London maker who described himself as a 'bass-horn and serpent maker', but by that time the bass-horn had become obsolete. It is likely that the ophicleide part in the overture to Mendelssohn's *Midsummer Night's Dream* was initially played in England on the bass-horn.

There are only two other instruments that can be considered as structurally allied to the bass-horn: Frichot's BASSE-TROMPETTE, a truly remarkable instrument, and Joseph Cotter's hibernicon mentioned above.

REGINALD MORLEY-PEGGE/ANTHONY C. BAINES/R

Bassi, Amedeo (*b* Montespertoli, nr Florence, 29 July 1874; *d* Florence, 15 Jan 1949). Italian tenor. He trained in Florence, making his début at Castelfiorentino in Filippo Marchetti's *Ruy Blas* in 1897. After travelling widely in Italy he sang with great success in South America, where he performed regularly until 1912. He joined the Manhattan Opera Company in 1906 and made his Covent Garden début the following year; he returned in 1911 for the British première of *La fanciulla del West*, in which he also sang at the first performances in Rome and Chicago. At Monte Carlo in 1905 he participated in the première of Mascagni's *Amica* and in Naples the following year that of Frédéric d'Erlanger's *Tess*; he was also in the first American performance of Wolf-Ferrari's *I gioielli della Madonna* (1912). In the 1920s at La Scala he began a second career, as an admired Wagnerian tenor. He taught in Florence where Ferruccio Tagliavini was among his pupils. Early recordings show a powerful voice produced in the typical *verismo* style.

BIBLIOGRAPHY

GV (R. Celletti; R. Vegeto)
M. Scott: *The Record of Singing*, i (London, 1977), 136

J.B. STEANE

Bassi, Luigi (*b* Pesaro, 4 Sept 1766; *d* ?Dresden, 1825). Italian baritone. He studied in Senigallia with Pietro Morandi and appeared on the stage at the age of 13. He completed his studies with Laschi in Florence, where he appeared at the Pergola Theatre. In 1784 he joined Bondini's company in Prague and in 1786 sang Count Almaviva in the first Prague performance of *Le nozze di Figaro*; the next year he created the name part in *Don*

Giovanni (1787). He is said to have asked Mozart to write him another air in place of 'Fin ch'han dal vino' and to have induced Mozart to rewrite 'Là ci darem' five times. In later years he stressed that no two performances were the same and that Mozart had specifically wished that he should improvise as long as he paid attention to the orchestra.

Bassi was praised in the *Gothaer Taschenkalendar* (1793):

This rewarding singer was from the start the ornament of the company and he still is. His voice is as melodious as his acting is masterly. Immediately he comes on, joy and cheerfulness pervade the whole audience and he never leaves the theatre without unequivocal and loud applause.

In 1793 Bassi sang Papageno in Italian at Leipzig. But by 1800 his voice had deteriorated, although his histrionic ability remained unimpaired. According to the *Allgemeine musikalische Zeitung* (1800):

Bassi was an excellent singer before he lost his voice, and he still knows very well how to use what remains. It lies between tenor and bass, and though it sounds somewhat hollow, it is still very flexible, full and pleasant. Herr Bassi is furthermore a very skilled actor in tragedy with no trace of burlesque, and with no vulgarity or tastelessness in comedy. In his truly artful and droll way he can parody the faults of the other singers so subtly that only the audience notices and they themselves are unaware of it. His best roles are Axur, Don Giovanni, Teodoro, the Notary in *La molinara*, the Count in *Figaro* and others.

In 1806 Bassi left Prague because of the war and relied on the patronage of Prince Lobkowitz, making occasional appearances in Vienna. In 1814 he returned to Prague, where Weber consulted him about *Don Giovanni*. In the autumn he was engaged for the Italian company in Dresden; and in 1815 he was made director. He still appeared in Mozart's operas; in 1816 he sang Count Almaviva, although he could no longer encompass the role vocally, but in 1817 he was well received as Guglielmo. He no longer performed Don Giovanni but sang Masetto, for which he was criticized because his figure was unsuited to the part. His contract with the Dresden company continued until his death; in his last years he also appeared in Florence, but only to sing in oratorio.

CHRISTOPHER RAEBURN

Bassilly, Bénigne de. *See* BACILLY, BÉNIGNE DE.

Bassklarinette (Ger.). *See* BASS CLARINET.

Bass line. The succession of the lowest notes in a passage (or composition) which 'support' the other parts and are mainly responsible for the harmonic progression. *See* BASS (i).

Basso (It.). *See* BASS (ii).

Basso, Alberto (*b* Turin, 21 Aug 1931). Italian musicologist. He took a degree in law at Turin University (1956) and though he had no formal training in music he was appointed in 1961 to teach music history at the Turin Conservatory; he became librarian in 1975. For UTET he edited *La musica: enciclopedia storica*, i–iv and *La musica: dizionario*, i–ii (with Gatti), the three-volume *Storia dell'opera* (with Barblan) and the *Dizionario enciclopedico universale della musica e dei musicisti*, all of which are major contributions to Italian musicology. He is also editor of Opera, a series of music guides (1973–5), and director of the editorial committee of Monumenti di Musica Piemontese (1976–), a special series of Monumenti Musicali Italiani. His research interests centre on Bach, organ literature and music in Piedmont. He has been active in various organizations, as vice-president (1968–70) and president (1973–9, 1995–7) of the Società Italiana di Musicologia and co-editor of its *Rivista italiana di musicologia* (1970–74), as an administrative council member of the Teatro Regio, Turin, as a frequent contributor (from 1956) to Italian radio, and as a member (1982) and later vice-president (1996) of the Accademia Nazionale di S Cecilia. In 1984 he was awarded a prize for his monograph, *Frau Musika: la vita e le opere di J.S. Bach*.

WRITINGS

L'Amfiparnaso di O. Vecchi (Turin, 1960)
G. Verdi: autografi esposti per l'esecuzione del Simon Boccanegra (Turin, 1961)
'Il corale organistico di J.S. Bach', *Approdo musicale*, nos.14–15 (1961), 5–263
Autografi di musicisti e stampati di interesse musicale (Turin, 1962)
ed., with G.M. Gatti: *La musica: enciclopedia storica*, i–iv (Turin, 1966)
ed., with G.M. Gatti: *La musica: dizionario*, i–ii (Turin, 1968–71)
Il Conservatorio di musica Giuseppe Verdi di Torino: storia e documenti dalle origini al 1970 (Turin, 1971)
'Repertorio generale dei "Monumenta Musicae", delle antologie, raccolte e pubblicazioni di musica antica sino a tutto il 1970', *RIM*, vi (1971), 1–135
'La rappresentazione a Torino (1804) dell' "Armida" di Haydn', *Quadrivium*, xiv (1973), 235–47
L'età di Bach e di Haendel (Turin, 1976, 2/1991)
Storia del Teatro Regio di Torino, ii: *Il teatro della Città dal 1788 al 1936* (Turin, 1976)
Introduction to Monumenti di Musica Piemontese, i (Milan, 1976)
ed., with G. Barblan: *Storia dell'opera* (Turin, 1977)
Frau Musika: la vita e le opere di J.S. Bach (Turin, 1979–83)
'La musica massonica: rassegna storica con particolare riferimento al secolo XVIII', *La massoneria nella storia d'Italia*, ed. A.A. Mola (Turin, 1980), 183–213
'Bach: la persistance de l'image', *Silences*, ii (1985), 159–65
'Osservazioni sulla scuola strumentale piemontese del Settecento', *Studi musicali*, xiv (1985), 135–56
'Perché Bach? Il mito di Bach nella seconda metà dell'Ottocento', *La trascrizione: Bach e Busoni: Empoli 1985*, 47–57
Sui sentieri della musica (Milan, 1985)
Dizionario enciclopedico universale della musica e dei musicisti (Turin, 1985–1990)
'Bach e Palestrina', *Studi palestriniani II: Palestrina 1986*, 409–19
'Monumentalità delle esecuzioni Ottocentesche', *Ritorno a Bach: dramma e ritualità delle passioni*, ed. E. Povellato (Venice, 1986), 169–84
'Bach tra "Ars" e "Scientia"', *Atti e memorie (Accademia nazionale virgiliana)*, new ser., lv (1987), 53–72
'Il '700: J.S. Bach e la corte di Federico II', *Musica e dossier*, iii (1987), 1–66
Introduction to *Raccolta Mauro Foà, Raccolta Renzo Giordano*, ed. I.F. Data and A. Colturato (Rome, 1987), i–lxxvi
'La musica di concezione massonica e il mito della fratellanza universale', *La musica come linguaggio universale: Latina 1987*, 65–76
'I codici vivaldiani di Torino, ovvero fatti e misfatti, avventure e disavventure del collezionismo musicale', *Chigiana*, new ser., xxi (1989), 161–84
'Bach e Haendel-Renaissance alla luce dell'illuminismo', *Studi in onore di Giulio Cattin*, ed. F. Luisi (Rome, 1990), 145–57
'Considerazioni sul concetto di sacro in musica', *De musica hispana et aliis: miscelánea en honor al Prof. Dr. José López-Calo*, ed. E. Casares and C. Villanueva (Santiago de Compostela, 1990), 467–81
L'invenzione della gioia: musica e massoneria nell'età dei Lumi (Milan, 1994)
ed.: *Musica in scena: storia dello spettacolo musicale* (Turin, 1995–7)

CAROLYN GIANTURCO/TERESA M. GIALDRONI

Bass oboe. *See* OBOE, §III, 5(i).

Basso cantante (It.: 'singing bass'). A light, legato bass voice as distinct from a deeper, more powerful bass (*see* BASSO PROFONDO). Its early meaning sometimes took on a pejorative tone as when the Earl of Mount Edgcumbe referred to 'these new singers [who] are called by the novel appellation of *basso-cantante* (which by-the-bye is a kind of apology, and an acknowledgment that they ought not to sing)' (*Musical Reminiscences*, London, 1824). Although more closely associated with vocal tone than range (*see* BASSE CHANTANTE), the term has also been used in modern commentary to identify the lyrical baritone and bass-baritone roles of the period of Bellini and Donizetti.

ELLEN T. HARRIS

Basso continuo. *See* CONTINUO.

Basson (i) (Fr.). *See* BASSOON.

Basson (ii) (Fr.). *See* ORGAN STOP (*Fagotto*).

Basson d'amour. A type of bassoon with a spherical brass bell, used in Swiss Protestant churches between about 1760 and 1810; *see* HAUTBOIS D'ÉGLISE; *see also* BASSOON, §3.

Basson quinte (Fr.). *See* TENOROON.

Basson russe (Fr.). *See* RUSSIAN BASSOON.

Basso numerato (It.). *See* FIGURED BASS.

Bassoon (Fr. *basson*; Ger. *Fagott*; It. *fagotto*). A wooden conical wind instrument, sounded with a double reed, which forms the tenor and bass to the woodwind section. In the modern orchestra, the family exists in two different sizes: the bassoon and the double bassoon or contrabassoon, sounding one octave lower. Built in four joints, its precursor the dulcian was of one-piece construction. Because of its wide compass and its range of characteristic tone-colours, from richly sonorous at the bottom to expressively plaintive at the top, it is one of the most versatile and useful members of the orchestra. Certain design features are peculiar to it: the doubling back on itself of the bore, like a hairpin; the 'extension bore' beyond the sixth finger-hole; and local wall thickness allowing for finger-hole chimneys. These features give the instrument its essential tone qualities and condition its complex acoustics. The standard compass of the present-day bassoon is from $B\flat'$ to f'' or g''. It is a non-transposing instrument and its music is notated in the bass and tenor clefs; occasionally the treble clef is also used.

In the Hornbostel-Sachs classification it is classified as an oboe.

See also ORGAN STOP.

1. The modern instrument and reed. 2. The dulcian and other precursors. 3. The early bassoon (to 1800). 4. Development of the modern bassoon. 5. The early reed. 6. Charts and tutors. 7. Repertory and use. 8. Performers and teachers. 9. The double bassoon. 10. Other sizes.

1. THE MODERN INSTRUMENT AND REED. The modern bassoon exists in two versions: the German or 'Heckel' system, and the French or 'Buffet' system of differing keywork and slightly modified bore (fig.1). As the German type is more commonly used today, it provides the frame of reference for general statements here about the construction of the modern bassoon.

While early bassoons (like dulcians: see §2) were sometimes made of harder varieties of wood, maple has been the wood traditionally used. Carl Almenraeder (see §4) favoured North American dark maple (*acer nigrum*), considering harder varieties to be unsuitable because they produced a duller tone, while softer varieties, although giving a better tone, were less durable. Most German makers preferred the medium-hard flamed or curly ring maple to the harder and heavier grenadilla or palissander (Brazilian rosewood) more often used by the French. The last serious attempt to make the body out of metal was by Lecomte, and was exhibited in Paris in 1889. However, ebonite has since been used in England for military instruments destined for the tropics. German bassoons today are made of sycamore maple (*acer pseudoplatanus*; Ger. *Bergahorn*). In America they are also made of local sugar maple (*acer saccharum*), though plastics such as polypropylene are successfully used as an alternative to wood. Before World War II the wood was customarily seasoned for up to 12 years, and machined only in gradual stages; now modern drying processes are used and the wood is often impregnated under pressure to stabilize its inner structure.

The machining of the bore and tone holes needs to be done with the utmost precision to achieve a good instrument. Final tuning has to be done by hand and calls for considerable time and skill. The crook is a crucially important element which needs to be carefully matched with its instrument. These factors make the bassoon traditionally more expensive than other wind instruments.

The bassoon stands about 134 cm tall and consists of four wooden joints together with a metal crook and reed (fig.2*a*). The total length of the bore is about 254 cm, flaring from a width of 4 mm at the narrow end of the crook to 39 mm at the bell. The components are:

(*a*) The tenor or wing joint, named after the projecting 'épaule' (a part of the wall thickened to accommodate three obliquely drilled finger-holes); this joint has a protective lining of hard rubber or plastic.

(*b*) The double or butt (boot) joint, which contains two continuously flaring bores connected at the bottom by a metal U-bend bow, which is screwed on to the body and protected by a metal cap. The narrower of these two bores is also lined for protection against water. A 'crutch' or hand rest to support the right hand is usually fitted to this joint.

(*c*) The long joint or bass joint, which lies adjacent to the wing joint.

(*d*) The bell joint, usually with a decorative outer profile and often tipped with an ornamental rim of ivory or plastic. A longer bell for the *A'* was first demanded by Wagner in *Tristan und Isolde* (1865); followed by Liszt, Strauss, Mahler, Delius, Nielsen, Schoenberg and Stravinsky among others. It is generally found to have a detrimental effect on playing characteristics.

(*e*) The crook or bocal which is inserted into the upper end of the wing: a tapering metal tube with a nipple perforated by a pinhole near the wider end; the reed is placed at the other end. The crook is usually bent into a characteristically curved 'S', but this shape is sometimes altered to suit individual players. Crooks are built in different lengths to assist tuning.

When played, the bassoon is held obliquely across the body. Its considerable weight is supported by means of a neck strap or shoulder harness attached to a ring on the

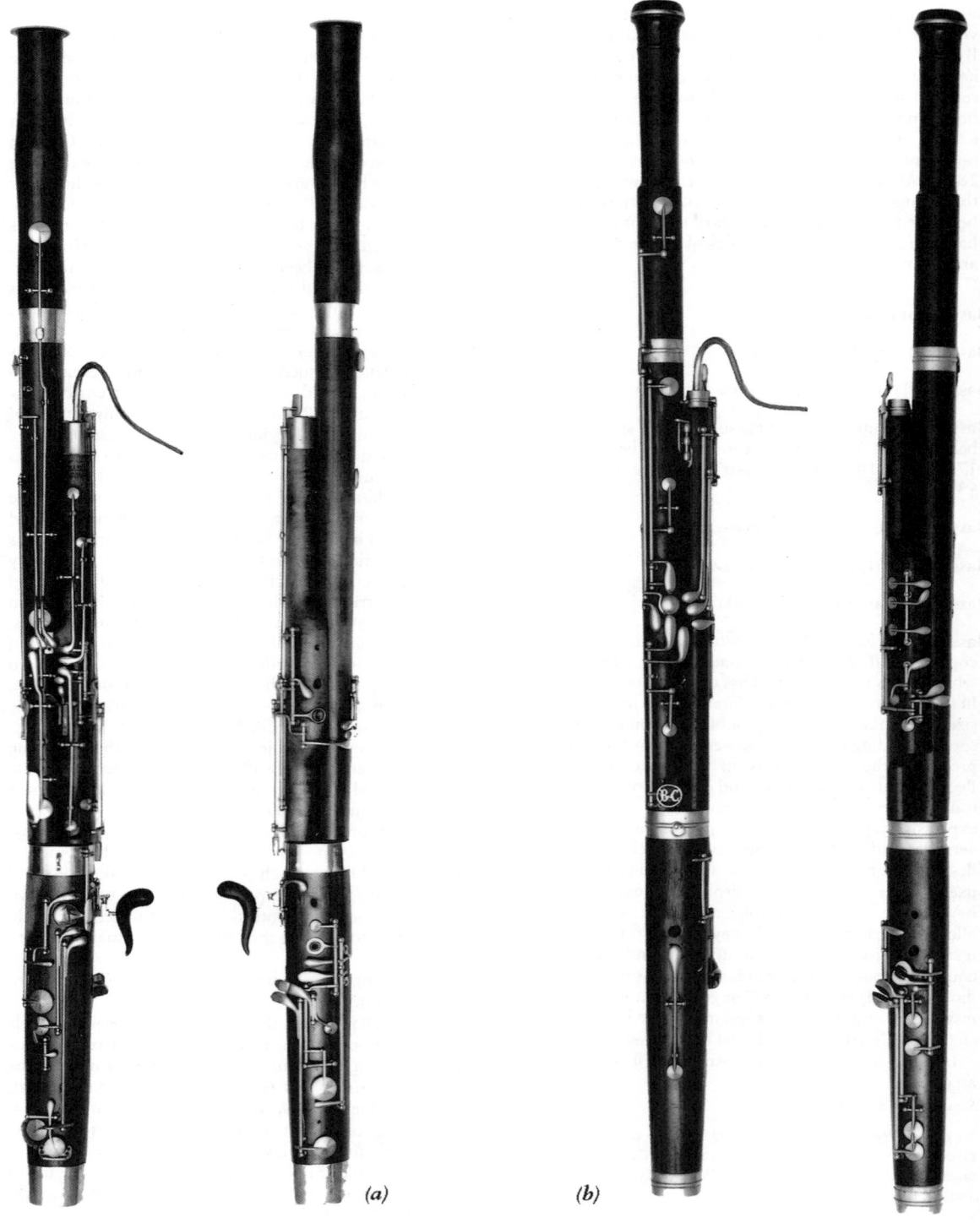

1. Modern bassoons: (a) German system, by Wilhelm Heckel, Biebrich; (b) French system, by Buffet-Crampon, Paris (private collection)

butt, a seat strap or adjustable spike attached to the bottom of the butt, or a leg support fitted to the top of the butt. The left hand is held uppermost: raising the three middle fingers of each hand produces a basic scale of G to *f*. With the help of the crook- and other register-holes these overblow an octave higher. The other fingers control keys which extend the range down to *Bb'*. This considerable extra length of 'resonator' is an important factor in the acoustics of the bassoon, as are the wall thickness, which produces chimneys of significant length on the

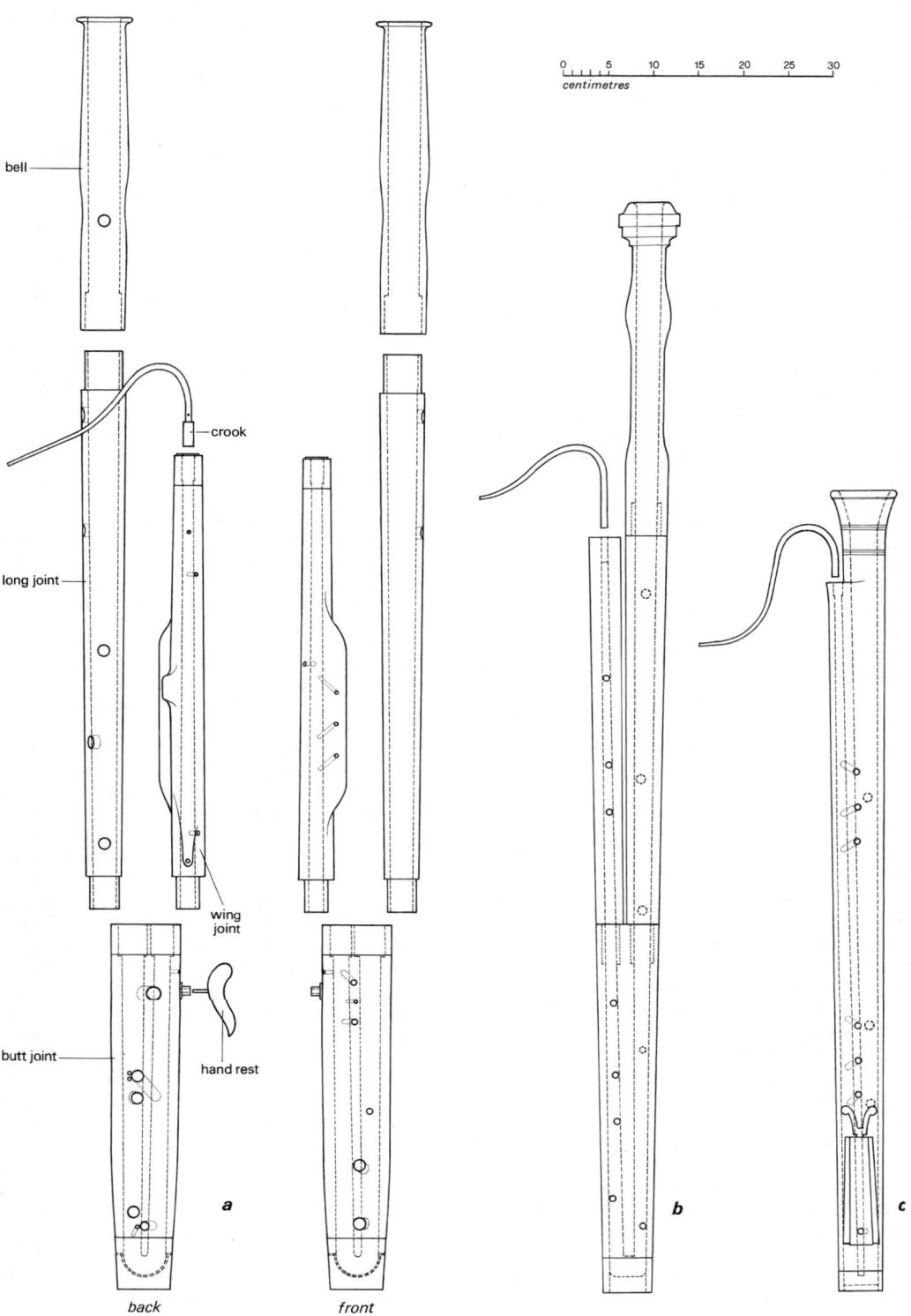

bell

crook

long joint

wing joint

butt joint

hand rest

a

back   front

b

c

0 5 10 15 20 25 30
centimetres

2. *(a) Diagram of a modern German bassoon showing the joints and position of the tone holes in the bore; (b) diagram of the five-key bassoon after an engraving in J.-B. de La Borde's 'Essai sur la musique' (1780); (c) diagram of a dulcian (Choristfagott) after those shown in fig.5 below*

wing joint, and the relatively small size of finger-holes. (For a fuller discussion of acoustics see Benade (1976) and Krüger (*MGG2*); *see also* ACOUSTICS, §IV, 6.)

The fingerings of the upper register are complicated: above *c″* the notes become somewhat more difficult to produce, requiring a progressive increase of wind pressure. While the French instrument with its slightly narrower bore and different layout of tone holes is able to reach *e″* and *f″* without undue difficulty, these notes are less easy on the German bassoon, though extra keys are now available to facilitate them.

Response and intonation is greatly affected by comparatively minute deviations in the conicity of the bore. In recent years makers have devoted great efforts to designing a more evenly-scaled instrument. Luckily the degree of pitch alteration available to the player through regulating air support and embouchure is comparatively great, and players often use individual fingerings to 'humour' certain notes. A new bassoon requires 'playing in' and thus players are hesitant to change their instruments. The problem of playing softly is sometimes assisted by the use of a mute; this can take the form either of a piece of cloth stuffed in the bell (e.g. as demanded by Ligeti) or of a short sleeve-like metal cylinder (*see* MUTE). Many players (especially in the USA) take great pains to seal every trace of porosity in pads and body to facilitate response.

In London there have been two efforts made in the late 20th century to reform the instrument. The 'Logical Bassoon' of Giles Brindley employed an electronic circuit to open and close the tone holes, thereby simplifying the fingering whilst making possible ideal combinations of holes for each note (Brindley, 1968). Edgar Brown's promising experimental bassoon, developed in collaboration with the bassoonist Zoltan Lukacs (1936–91), is built to a design by the distinguished acoustician Arthur Benade (1925–87); in the interests of greater tonal homogeneity, 'the hole proportions are such as to give a uniform tone-holes lattice cut-off frequency' (Brown, 1998).

The French bassoon differs from the German in bore, disposition of tone holes and system of keywork (see fig.1). In general it has retained the basic design of the early bassoon, in contrast to the reformed Almenraeder instrument with its low-register open holes enlarged, increased in number and placed further down the bore. Formerly in common use throughout the non-German-speaking world, it has since the 1930s been replaced by the German model. There is controversy over their respective merits – the light, free tone quality of the French contrasts with the dark homogeneousness of the German. However, much depends on the style of playing and of the reed chosen by the individual player. In general the German instrument may be considered 'safer' and easier to control for the player.

Like the oboe, the bassoon uses a double reed (see fig.11*d* below) made of a type of bamboo cane (*arundo donax*), of which the most suitable quality grows in the Var district of southern France. Cane from Italy, America, southern Russia and China is also used by local players. The modern method of manufacture is as follows: a piece of tube 12 to 14 cm long and about 2·5 cm in diameter is split vertically into three or four pieces and the inside of each planed to the desired thickness by a gouging machine; on the outside the 'bark', except on the top and bottom quarters of the length, is removed to a contoured bevel by

a 'profiler'. The piece is then folded to half its length, cut to size in a metal 'shaper', formed on a mandrel and bound with three wires and thread; lastly the tip of the fold is cut off. The final thinning of the reed blades may be done with a tip profiling machine, or with a file and scraping knife. The reed is very fragile and sensitive (the blade tip is only some 0·1 mm thick) and plays a crucial role in the tone and response of the instrument. Both the quality of the cane and the contour of blade thickness are very important. Recent research by Heinrich (1987), subjecting reed cane to analysis under laboratory conditions, has yielded new insights into the behaviour of what he defines as a *bilâme hydrique* (bilaminate reacting variously to water), and the interaction of the banding wires with cane density. Reeds for the German instrument differ from those traditionally used on the French in the way they are finished; 'French' reeds are usually bevelled evenly like a chisel while the 'German' scrape leaves a thicker spine down the centre. There is considerable divergence of style and scrape between players. Formerly made exclusively by hand, nowadays reed manufacture has become increasingly mechanized. Various experiments have been made with plastic reeds, but so far they have not proved suitable for professional use.

At times the bassoon has been played with a clarinet-type mouthpiece. According to *GerberL* the clarinettist J.W. Hesse attempted to do this in 1786, and in England small bassoon mouthpieces from the early 19th century have survived. They have never been used seriously because of the way they denature the tone, although they were formerly used for tuning instruments. They are still marketed in the USA.

2. THE DULCIAN AND OTHER PRECURSORS. The early history of the bassoon is obscure: few early specimens survive and it is not possible to be sure when and where these were made. Iconographic evidence, though sparse, is more trustworthy than that from written documents, which, because of ambiguities of nomenclature, must be interpreted with caution. In general, two successive versions of the instrument may be distinguished: the earlier, in use up to the beginning of the 18th century (though later in Spain), was essentially in one piece and is best labelled 'dulcian' (fig.2*c*) to distinguish it from the later 'bassoon' proper (i.e. in four joints). Although one early specimen in Vienna (a 16th-century Italian instrument by HIER.S, refurbished during the Baroque era) is inscribed 'DER. DULCIN. BIN. ICH. GENANT ...' the names given to the instrument in early times were, unfortunately, seldom consistent or unambiguous. Derivatives of at least four different names have been in use since early times, 'Fagott' and 'curtal' as well as 'dulcian' and 'bassoon' (also 'tarot' and 'sztort'). Since, of all the derivatives of these names, 'dulcian' has arguably been the least ambiguous, this is the preferred terminology.

The first term originated in 14th-century France as 'fagot', meaning a bundle of sticks, a faggot. While also used as the name of a dance by Phalèse (i) (1549) and Susato (1551), it was first used to denote a musical instrument in the early 16th century in Italy. 'Choristfagott' was an early name for the dulcian, and the name 'Fagott' was applied in the 17th century to the bass pommer as well, in spite of the fact that neither resembled a bundle of sticks. From the mid-18th century onwards *Fagott* and *fagotto* have been respectively the German and Italian names for the bassoon. The name 'dulcian' is commonly used today for the original version of the instrument in one piece (as opposed to the later type in joints). Deriving from the Latin root *dulc* (soft, sweet), it has traditionally been held to refer to the instrument's more subdued tone quality than that of the louder shawms and pommers. However, Klitz (1971) showed that forms like *dulzan* can refer to the pommer as well as to an earlier type of shawm called the 'dolzaina' (*douçaine*). In England the earliest name for the dulcian was 'curtall', which was used well into the 18th century for the bassoon as well, and is related to other wind instrument names such as the French *courtaud* and the German *Kortholt*, which all derive from the Latin *curtus* (short), referring to instruments shortened because of their folded bore. 'Basson' meant originally the bass-register version of an instrument (e.g. *basson de hautbois*, *basson-flûte*). In 18th-century Germany it became the name of the new jointed version of the dulcian, which had been developed in France. In England, Talbot's manuscript made a similar distinction: 'Basson has 4 Joynts, Fagot entire'. Purcell's *Dioclesian* score of 1690 specified 'bassoon' and this anglicized version of the word has been used ever since.

With the rise of instrumental playing in the 16th century, the desire to extend the range of instruments into the lower register caused them to be developed in families: larger versions of the shawm and recorder were made possible by an improved technology which enabled makers to bore longer tubes and to control widely spaced extension holes with the aid of keys. As Kolneder (*MGG1*) showed, there must have been a demand in the 16th century for a deep instrument to form a bass to the wind band that would surpass the trombone in agility, the bass recorder in loudness, and the bass pommer in ease of handling. Early in the 16th century all the constructional elements of the dulcian would have been available: the double reed of the shawm, the curved crook of the bass recorder and bass shawm, and the doubling back on itself of the bore (within a single block of wood) of the phagotus.

The shawm had already been built in large versions which were known as 'bomharten' or 'pommers': it may be assumed that the largest of those made in Nuremberg by Sigmund Schnitzer the elder and described by Johannes Apel in a letter of 1535 as 'vill höher und lenger den ich' (i.e. 'much taller than I') was already like the largest pommer illustrated by Praetorius in 1620. It must have been a cumbersome instrument to manage, especially out of doors.

The first mention of the dulcian in a reference work is in Zacconi's *Prattica di musica* (1592); Virdung (1511), Agricola (1529, 5/1545) and Luscinius (1536) made no reference to it. Zacconi wrote that 'the Fagotto chorista has a range C–b. It is so called because there is another

kind which is not of its pitch but either a little higher or lower'. Sachs derived 'chorista' from the instrument's usual function of supporting the bass in choral music; however this term was applied to other instruments as well to mean a certain register or PITCH level, for example 'Dui corneti, uno di ton chorista, et uno più basso' (Accademia Filarmonica inventory, Verona, 1562).

Of these different types, the *Choristfagott* soon established itself as the most useful member of the family. It consisted of a single shaft of wood (maple or fruit), oval in section, nearly a metre tall, drilled with two bores connected at the bottom so as to form one continuous, conical tube. At the top a curved brass crook was inserted into the narrow end of the bore, and the other end was slightly extended to form a flared bell. This bell sometimes took the form of a perforated cap, thus making the instrument *gedackt* (i.e. covered) as opposed to *offen*, and doubtless affecting both the tone quality and pitch. The thickness of the walls enabled the finger-holes to be drilled obliquely to accommodate the span of the fingers. There were eight finger-holes and two open keys protected by perforated brass boxes: six fingers gave G, and by adding the keys and using the player's thumbs, notes down to C could be played. The basic scale overblew the octave, giving a range up to about g'. The 'swallow-tail' end of the little-finger key allowed the player to hold the instrument on either side of his body with right or left hand uppermost. Sometimes, especially in the larger sizes, the body of the instrument was made in two half-lengths, or even in three sections, which were joined together under an ornamental band, as in figs.4 and 5 below.

Over 50 dulcians of various sizes datable to the 16th and 17th centuries are in museums at Vienna (10); Berlin, Brussels (7); Augsburg, Linz (6); Frankfurt, Nuremberg, Salzburg (4); Brunswick, Leipzig, Merano, Sondershausen (2); Barcelona, Dresden, Hamburg, Paris, Prague (1). Of those in Vienna, eight come from the famous collections of Catajo and Ambras and include several of the earliest dulcians known. The four signed by J.C. Denner (*d* 1707) may be presumed to be among the last non-Spanish examples made. Sachs was the first to dispute the traditional view that the dulcian was a development of the pommer. That the two instruments coexisted for some time is shown in the paintings of a wind band by Alsloot (in the Prado, Madrid; *see* SHAWM, §3, fig.9) and Sallaert (in Galleria Sabauda, Turin). The Nuremberg Stadtpfeifer dropped the pommer in 1643 in favour of the dulcian, but in some places the bass pommer survived into the 18th century.

Where, when and how the dulcian evolved is unknown, there being insufficient evidence to allow tidy conclusions to be drawn. The sparse evidence that is available shows different forms appearing in different places and at different times. Lockwood's researches (1985) into the Ferrara *guardaroba* archives of Willaert's patron Cardinal Ippolito I d'Este reveal that as early as 1516 the musician Gerardo *francese*, in the cardinal's service since 1504, was paid for 'uno faghotto da sonare cum le chiave d'argento' and identified that year as a 'sonator de fagoth'. There is a further reference to payments in 1517 'per fagotto che sona Janes de pre Michele', evidently a colleague. The following year we find the lutenist Giovanni Angelo Testagrossa, in a letter written to Isabella d'Este at Mantua, offering instruments and referring to 'un altro instrumento quale se chiama un fagot' (Bertolotti, 1890).

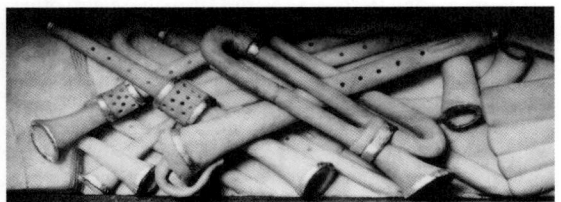

3. Early form of dulcian: detail of an alabaster relief by Antonius von Zerun, from the monument to Moritz, Elector of Saxony, 1563 (Freiberg Cathedral)

4. Dulcian made in two halves, and joined under an ornamental band: detail from the 'Nativity' by Giovanni Benedetto Castiglione, 1645 (S Luca, Genoa)

The phagotum, demonstrated in 1532 at the court of Mantua by its inventor Afranio degli Albonesi and described in 1539 by his nephew Teseo Ambrosio, was traditionally considered to have been the earliest ancestor of the bassoon on the strength of its name; however, with its bellows-blown pair of twin cylindrical bores (each called a *fagoto*) sounded by single metal reeds, it is rather a type of bagpipe. The next earliest Italian citation is from the Verona Accademia Filarmonica *Libro degli atti* of 1546 which mentions 'il 9 maggio furono comperati da Alvise soldato un Fagotto ed una Dolzana'.

Of all the signatures known on early wind instruments, variants of HIER.S (25; *see* HIER.S) and of the so-called 'rabbits foot' (about 143) by far predominate. An attractive theory links both to the Bassano workshop. Significant research by Lasocki and others has revealed much concerning the activities in both Venice and London by members of this remarkable family. He has identified three generations of makers and players descended from Jeronimo (i) (*d* ?1539), a native of Bassano, some 65 km

north-west of Venice. By 1531 four of his sons had visited London in their capacity as sackbut players, where they settled by about 1538. Both they and two subsequent generations were active there and in Venice making and repairing instruments. It is most likely that the eight surviving dulcians signed 'HIER.S' and 'HIERO.S' may be products of the Bassano workshop – the instrument depicted by Castiglione (fig.4) shows a two-section dulcian made in a similar style – as are also the eight others bearing the 'rabbit's foot' mark.

In Germanic countries references appear somewhat later. A Graz inventory of 1577 lists 'a set of old, bad [or plain] fagati, 2 bass, 2 tenor and 1 descant' and '1 good fagat in daily use'; from this, Kolneder deduced that they were at least 40 to 50 years old, setting the time of their introduction in Graz at about 1530. In Augsburg, where a unique set of six (made in Italy) survive (fig.5), they were first listed in 1566.

Nickel argued that in Nuremberg the instrument did not make an appearance until 1575, when a *dulzin* (here

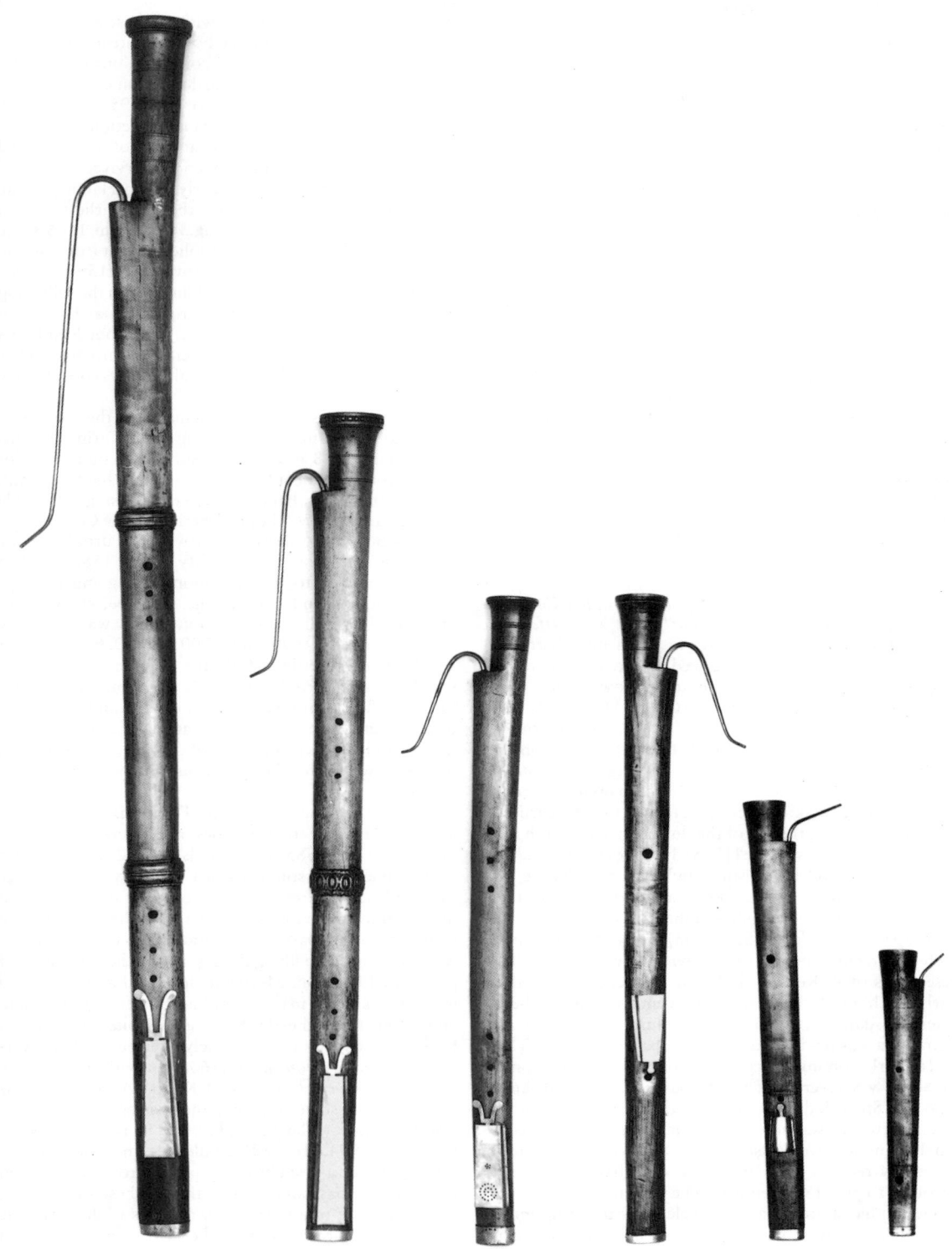

5. Dulcians: (left to right, shown from the front) Oktavbass, Quartbass, Choristfagott (all marked 'Hiero. S'), probably made in Venice, second half of the 16th century; (left to right, shown from the back) Choristfagott (unmarked, probably by the same maker), Tenor and Diskant (both by the same unknown German maker), late 16th century (Maximilianmuseum, Augsburg)

meaning dulcian) was procured from Antwerp: earlier references elsewhere to *dulzana*, *doltzana* and the like refer to the *dolzaina*, an instrument in common use since the 15th century; and the *fagati* of Augsburg and Graz, he suggested, were pommers. Neudörfer (1547) praised the Nuremburg maker Sigmund Schnitzer the younger (*d* 1578) for his ability to turn, tune and perform on large oversized *Pfeiffen*, which Doppelmayr (1730) called *Fagotte*. That this might refer to a *Grossbasspommer*, rather than a dulcian, is supported by the fact that the player Rosenkron who was engraved holding one in 1679 is called *fagotist*. In view of these verbal ambiguities, pictorial sources are more reliable. A relief carved in Antwerp by Antonius von Zerun for the Moritz monument erected in 1563 in Freiberg Cathedral (Lower Saxony) shows a dulcian among a group of wind instruments (see fig.3); the instrument is portrayed again in an engraved frontispiece by Collaert of about 1590 (reproduced in Fraenkel, no.39). These and other sources suggest that it appeared early in Flanders. Venice was also supplying instruments to courts in Germany and Austria in the late 16th century (in 1588 the Munich Hofkapelle acquired 'ein Vagott von Venedig'); in Nuremberg, the leading centre of wind instrument making of the period, the first dulcian was made in 1595.

By the time of Praetorius, the family had reached its maximum extent: in *Syntagma musicum*, ii (2/1619) he described a complete consort of *Fagotten* or *Dolcianen* consisting of eight instruments of varying size – the *Discantfagott* (*g* to *c″*), the *Fagott Piccolo* or *Singel Corthol* (*G* to *g′*), the *Choristfagott* or *Doppel Corthol* (*C* to *g′*), and two varieties of *Doppelfagott*, a *Quartfagott* (*G′* to *a*) and a *Quintfagott* (*F′* to *g*). In his *Theatrum instrumentorum* (1620) he showed in addition an *Altfagott* (presumably *c* to *f′*). A hitherto unknown source was discovered in 1994 in Edinburgh (*GB-Eu* Dc.6.100). The *Instrumentälischer Bettlermantl* by 'A.S.', a south German manuscript datable to the mid-17th century (Campbell, 1995) describes and illustrates four sizes of *Vagött* – Discant, Alt, Tenor and Bass; the accompanying instructions for reed making (see §5 below) are the earliest known. How long the use of the dulcian persisted is hard to ascertain. Eisel's treatise (1738) dismisses the *Teutscher Basson* as outmoded, but still supplies a chart. Its use by the *Pfeifergericht* at the ceremonial opening of the Frankfurt fair persisted well into the 18th century.

In Spain the dulcian (Sp. *bajón*) enjoyed a long and well-documented period of use, which, according to the researches of B. Kenyon de Pascual, extended from the early 16th until the early 20th century. The earliest reference dates from 1530, when Juan de la Rosa of Pamplona was paid two ducats for repairing *bajones*. The 1616 workshop inventory of the court maker Bartolomé de Selma y Salaverde included small and large dulcians. The four Spanish dulcians preserved in Brussels comprise a tenor, two altos, and one descant, indicating that such smaller models were also in use. Surviving music and inventory records show that they were frequently used through to the 18th century. The fact that all known iconographic sources have an ecclesiastical setting indicates that they were primarily played in church, though there is some evidence of secular use. They were still made and played after the jointed bassoon (*fagot*) was introduced; a 1739 Royal Chapel report specified that 'the *fagoto* – which is an instrument of the same family,

though its voice is not so full as that of the *bajón* – will also play'. An early 19th-century listing of 'bajón' with choristers and two 'fagots' with orchestra shows the different functions discharged by each instrument. As late as 1902, a cathedral chapter record mentions a *bajonista*. A painting by the Italian Bernardo Bitti on an organ from a Peruvian convent datable to 1590–95 shows early evidence of a kind of longitudinally sectioned dulcian. Several early 19th-century examples of a five-keyed jointed *bajón* in three or four sections survive.

Evidence for the dulcian's early use in Flanders is the fact that it was there in 1563 that the earliest known representation was carved (see fig.3), while in 1566 some *bajones* were ordered for Valladolid. A print from Philipp Galle's *Encomium musices* (Antwerp, *c*1590) shows another longitudinally sectioned dulcian. In the following century it was portrayed by such painters as Denis van Alsloot, Jan Breughel the younger, Theodoor Rombouts and Anthonis Sallaert, among others. Evidence from other countries (Poland, Denmark etc.) also shows considerable use of the instrument.

In England it is likely that members of the aforementioned Bassano family were making and repairing dulcians from about 1538 onwards. A Suffolk account book of 1574 records payment 'for an instrument called a curtall'. In 1575 the Waits Band of Exeter was using a 'Double Curtall', and in 1597 the chamberlain of the Corporation of London was ordered to provide a curtall for the musicians at the charge of the City. About 1582, Stephen Batman referred to 'the common bleting music in ye Drone, Hobius and Curtall' (i.e. bagpipe, shawm and dulcian). The Talbot manuscript, which was probably written between 1690 and 1700 (*GB-Och* Music MS 1187), while describing fully the 'Basson' (jointed bassoon) still sees fit to describe fully the 'Double Courtaut' (dulcian). The 'Tenor & Treble Courtaut' and 'Fagot' are briefly mentioned; he tells us that the 'Fagot', which is 'entire' and thus evidently also of dulcian construction, is 'unused', while the 'Double Courtaut' is 'not used in Consort'.

Evidence of the dulcian in France is mysteriously lacking. The fact that it does not figure in Cellier's manuscript of *c*1585 (*F-Pn* fonds fr.9152) suggests that at that time it was still unknown. It is however in France that evidence regarding other precursors of the bassoon may be found. Predecessors other than the dulcian, such as the 'fagotted' bass shawm and the sectioned dulcian, were evidently also filling the gap before the emergence of the jointed bassoon. Mersenne described and illustrated instruments which may loosely be considered transitional, and recent researches by Kopp and White have yielded fresh insights. Comparing closely Mersenne's Latin version *Harmonicorum libri* (1635–6) with the French *Harmonie universelle* (1636–7), Kopp (*JAMIS*, 1991) has been able to resolve confusing inconsistencies of nomenclature. White ('The Bass Hautboy in the Seventeenth Century', 1994, 167–82) challenges the conventional assumption of a straight development from bass shawm to dulcian to bassoon, arguing that of these the dulcian, far from being more primitive, requires tooling capable of greater accuracy; none of the instruments illustrated show one-piece construction, but rather two discrete tubes wrapped externally (the illustration of the bass *hautbois de Poitou* showing just such a construction). Mersenne wrote that they were 'different from the preceeding bass [shawm] only in that they break into two parts to be able to be managed and carried more easily; that is why they are called Fagots because they resemble two pieces of wood which are bound and faggotted together'. White surmises: that 'the bassoon may not have evolved directly out of the dulcian, but rather out of an interim "fagotted" version of the bass shawm early in the sixteenth century'; and that the dulcian's simplified 'modern' design allowing for oblique chimneys represented an improvement over the sectioned instrument that must have preceded and then co-existed with it. Trichet appeared to corroborate his contemporary Mersenne in his treatise (c1640) by describing, in addition to a small conventional dulcian, a three-piece 'basson' constructed of two discrete tubes, 'deux tuiaux joincts ensemble', the larger of which 'pour la commodité se peuvent desmonter et se briser en deux parts'. Only one sectioned model of dulcian survives, in the Kunsthistorisches Museum, Vienna (Sammlung Alter Musikinstrumente no.201); unsigned, but of Italian provenance and datable to about 1600, its upper part is divided into two halves.

3. THE EARLY BASSOON (TO 1800).   It is not clear when or where the precursors of the bassoon evolved into the four-jointed instrument of today, descending one extra tone below the C of the dulcian. The gradual abandonment and replacement of the dulcian was doubtless brought about by such factors as the need for an instrument to match the range of the contemporary 'basse de violon' which descended to B♭', and to replace the old high church-pitch instruments that were incompatible with new instruments built at French flat pitch. There was an evident demand for such an instrument with this extended range. Selma y Salaverde had already called for it (see §7 below) and the compass of one of Mersenne's instruments had also been extended to B♭' with the aid of a third key. The impulse for this development can be identified as emanating from Amsterdam, Nuremberg and Paris.

An important early iconographic source for the new bassoon is the Dutch painting Der Fagottspieler in the Suermondt Museum, Aachen. Unsigned, its attribution to Harmen Hals (1611–69) is dubious, White dating it to nearer the end of the century. The instrument has turned mouldings on the upper joints that served both as decoration and mounts for the keys. The wing joint has the characteristic 'épaule' or thickening of the wall necessary to retain the oblique bore of the finger-holes. The extra length afforded by the bell, which has a bulb-like cavity at the end, enabled the range to be extended a whole tone downwards to B♭' with the aid of an extra key, and the longer bore and lighter construction made the instrument more free and flexible in the upper register as well. A well-preserved three-keyed bassoon by Richard Haka (Schlossmuseum, Sondershausen), datable to a terminus ante quem of 1699, provides significant evidence. Its Baroque profile resembles that of the instrument portrayed in Der Fagottspieler. His contemporaries Jan Juriansz van Heerde (fl 1670–91) and Jan Juriansz de Jager (fl c1684–1694) also made bassoons. The additional G♯ key for the right little finger, shown on the trade card of the Amsterdam maker Coenraad Rijkel (c1705), stabilized the position of the player's hands; formerly the swallow-tail design of the F key had permitted interchangeable hand position. Rijkel's contemporaries, Abraham van Aardenberg, Thomas Boekhout, Michiel Parent

and Hendrik Richters, among other notable Dutch woodwind makers, also made bassoons.

The bassoons from J.C. Denner's Nuremberg workshop (fig.6a) resemble Richard Haka's model. It is known that by 1684 Denner was copying the new French recorders and oboes, and his bassoons may have been built to a French pattern. An engraving by Weigel of a bassoon maker – possibly Denner – at work shows both the two-key dulcian and three-key Basson being made (fig.7), but soon the new instrument with its greater potentialities was to dominate. Some 33 three-key bassoons survive.

The traditional view is that the bassoon, along with other Baroque woodwinds, was developed in the time of Louis XIV in France by members of the Hotteterre family, working as wind players and makers in Paris. Nicolas Hotteterre (i) (c1637–1694), a bassoonist for the royal chapel from 1668 and the first identifiable bassoon maker of the family, was possibly foreshadowed by other earlier relations. However, both the dulcian and bassoon are conspicuously absent among the woodwind instruments represented in the Gobelin tapestries of 1669, which show instead the cromorne, which appears to have functioned as bass to the reed group in France at this time (see Haynes, 1997).

Borjon de Scellery's Traité de la musette (1672) mentions the use of musette with 'cromornes, flûtes & bassons'. Haynes concludes that 'since bassoons played with cromornes and musettes, and hautboys did as well, hautboys and bassoons were probably able to play together by 1672. Thus some new model of bassoon would have been in existence by that date'.

By the 1680s there are references to bassoons of the new type, i.e. designed to play at flat pitch like the other new Hotteterre woodwind instruments. In 1680 Lully scored for basson in his opera Proserpine and regularly thereafter (with a range of B♭' to f). In 1686 the Darmstadt court appointed the bassoonist Maillard, presumably from France.

It was in England that the new instrument was first described and illustrated. Here James Talbot gathered detailed information from London professional players, both native and French: White tentatively dates his inquiries to 1685–8. Talbot confirmed that the 'French Basson' in '4 Joynts' had three keys and a compass extending down to B♭'. According to his brass authority William Bull, it had been the 'Fr. Basson' that had replaced the trombone after it had been 'left off' towards the end of the reign of King Charles II (d 1685). Around this time, Randle Holme (before 1688) described and illustrated what he called a 'double curtaile', which however appears to be a three-jointed bassoon. The employment of Jacques Hotteterre, brother of Jean (1648–1732), in London as an oboist is documented in 1675 (Giannini, 1993); doubtless he helped introduce the family products. Both the tenor oboe and bassoon had arrived from France by 1687 (see Lasocki, 1988). This traffic is documented later in a letter of 1711 by Louis Rousselet, another French oboist employed in London, who ordered two bassoons, one right-handed and one left-handed, from the well-known Parisian maker Jean-Jacques Rippert (Giannini, 1987). The earliest French illustration of the new bassoon is on the title page to Marais' Pièces en trio (1692). The plain severity of its bell, free of Baroque turnery, resembles that of Stanesby.

6. Early bassoons: (a) three-key by Johann Christoph Denner, Nuremberg, c1700 (Musikinstrumenten-Museum, Berlin); (b) four-key by Thomas Stanesby (ii), London, 1747; (c) seven-key by Friedrich Kirst, Potsdam, late 18th century (d) Boehm system, with 30 keys, by Triébert-Marzoli-Boehm, Paris, c1855 ((b)–(d) private collection)

Two unique double-reed instruments – the *basse de musette* and *basson d'amour* – built in the 1760s in a French-speaking Swiss valley colonized by Huguenot refugees, were possibly derived from lost French models.

The four-jointed, three-keyed *basson d'amour*, 14 examples of which survive, displays unique features; these include a globular brass bell, which augments the tone like a Helmholtz resonator, and a pirouette at the crook

7. Bassoon maker (possibly Denner) at work on a two-key dulcian, with a three-key 'Basson' to his right: engraving by Christoph Weigel, 1698

end to facilitate playing (see HAUTBOIS D'EGLISE). Designed for church use, many lack the left-hand keys deemed unnecessary for psalm accompaniment (see Staehelin, 1969–70).

The four-key instrument was to remain the model in standard use for the rest of the century. Halle (1764) reported that the best were made of boxwood: examples by J.H. Eichentopf, Poerschmann and Scherer survive. The Baroque mouldings of the upper three joints disappeared, the keys being mounted instead on projecting bosses or on saddles. The bore of the bell was changed to an inverted taper and sometimes a small resonance hole was added. The earliest extra keys to be added were for those low notes for which the standard 'forked' fingerings were less satisfactory: a chart by Hotteterre and Bailleux (c1765) first shows the fifth Eb key for left thumb (later moved by Grenser to left little finger), and a right-thumb key (for a'; also F♯) followed later. A more significant advance was the addition of a 'harmonic key' on the wing joint to obtain high-register notes, sometimes even being added to existing instruments (fig.6c). This was first reported in France in 1787 (according to Ozi, it was 'in almost universal use') and 1786–7 in Germany (a six-keyed instrument, complete with hand rest, is depicted on the seal attached to the will of Franz Anton Pfeiffer, court bassoonist at Ludwigslust). From Ozi (1787) we also learn that French makers had by this time already shifted the G♯ key-hole away from its traditional site on the narrow butt bore to just below the F key-hole; other makers were not to follow suit for at least a generation. Ozi used an instrument by Keller of Strasbourg; the best-known Paris makers of this period were Bizey, Lot, Porthaux and Prudent. In Germany, the Dresden *Fagot* was considered the best; most notable were those made by the Grensers and their contemporaries Grundmann and Floth. A portrait of Felix Rheiner, painted in 1774 by Horemans (fig.8), shows the earliest recorded use of a pinhole in the crook, here operated by a key. Cugnier also advocated the pinhole in 1780, but it was not to come

into general use until the 19th century. Almenraeder considered that it might be dispensed with on a broken-in, but not on a new, instrument. Extra keys of any sort were slow in becoming standard: Koch's lexicon of 1802 describes the five-key instrument with two octave keys 'found on recent instruments'.

In England, bassoons were made in considerable quantities throughout the 18th century; John Ashbury (*fl* London, 1698), Peter Bressan (1663–1731) and Thomas Stanesby (i) are the earliest recorded makers. However, only two English bassoons have survived from before 1750 (one each by Stanesby (i) and (ii); see fig.6b). The Milhouses of Newark and London later became the most notable makers. The bell of these earlier English instruments has a characteristic baluster contour and a pronounced inverted taper. The widespread use of church bands, in some places having up to seven instruments, as well as the demands of professional and military music making, gave work to numerous makers in London and the provinces. The tone-colour of the bassoon became more mellow and expressive throughout the 18th century. In Germany, Mattheson's 'stoltze Basson' (1713) became the 'Instrument der Liebe' of Koch (1802), while French writers stressed its powers of expression, comparing it to the human voice. The early Sonata by Telemann (1728) already makes considerable technical demands, and the works written by Mozart in 1774 (K191/186e and 292/196c) indicate the expressive range expected from the instrument by then.

4. DEVELOPMENT OF THE MODERN BASSOON.   In the 19th century, several factors helped to bring about developments in instrument making. These included the

8. Felix Rheiner: portrait by Peter Jacob Horemans, 1774 (Bayerisches Nationalmuseum, Munich); this is the earliest recorded evidence of a pinhole in the crook of a bassoon, here operated by a key

increasing demands of composers regarding technique, expression and extension of the range upward; the rise of the solo virtuoso-composer; larger orchestras and concert halls demanding louder-toned instruments; international trade exhibitions encouraging competition and experiment; instrument makers who had backgrounds as excellent performers (including Savary *jeune* and Almenraeder); and technical advice from acoustic experts such as Gottfried Weber.

While Cugnier's exceptional chart of 1780 showed fingerings up to *f″* apparently possible on a five-key instrument without octave keys, the gradual introduction of up to three such keys on the wing undoubtedly facilitated notes from *a′* upwards, even if composers were still reluctant to write above *g′* in the orchestra. Simiot of Lyons, an important innovator, provided, in addition to these, closed keys for *B′* and *C♯*, notes hitherto unobtainable except by 'faking'; other refinements included bushing finger-holes with metal tubes against water, and (in 1817) replacing the cork plug with a metal U-bend bow, an improvement later adopted in Germany.

Improvements made by the leading Paris makers Savary *jeune* and Adler included key-rollers (introduced in 1823) and one or two tuning-slides on the wing to obviate the need for several *corps de rechange*. Attempts were made to obtain the greater volume desired for the military band by widening the end of the bore with a broad flaring bell, or even widening the bore of the entire instrument (Winnen's 'Bassonore' of 1834), and by making the instrument in metal. Both Charles-Joseph and Adolphe Sax experimented with brass instruments with covered keys; Sax *fils* patented in 1851 a 24-key metal bassoon with regularly spaced holes which was demonstrated at the London Exhibition that year. The instrument favourably impressed Boehm, who subsequently calculated his 'Schema' of hole dimensions for a bassoon bore which Triébert and Marzoli of Paris used for their model of 1855, together with many of Boehm's innovations for the uniquely intricate keywork (shown in fig.6*d*). Another system comparable to that of Sax was worked out in London by Ward and Tamplini and patented in 1853. However, altering the traditional relationships between size and position of holes and wall thicknesses caused the instrument to lose its characteristic tone quality. The complexity and expense also militated against the 'Boehm bassoon', and it failed to catch on. Meanwhile, however, the efforts of the player and teacher Jancourt, working with Triébert, Gautrot *aîné* and Buffet-Crampon, led to the development in 1879 of the 22-key model which has with minor modifications since established itself as the standard French-system bassoon (fig.1*b*).

In spite of the achievements of the Dresden makers, the bassoon in Germany was still far from satisfactory, especially as compared to the other woodwinds. Fröhlich (1810–11), who praised its qualities – the majesty of its bass and the grace of its middle and high registers – described the situation at this time: to adjust to different pitches, instruments were sold with a set of three wing joints of differing lengths, and with as many crooks. Standard bassoons had six keys, the more recent ones with two extra 'octave' keys on the wing for *a′* and *c″*; but many instruments still had only five or even four keys. Because of the lack of standardization of keywork or bore, no given set of fingerings would suit everyone; different notes were always out of tune, needing correction

with special fingerings. On French bassoons of the period many fingerings were different; those given in the 1805 and 1806 translations of Ozi's 1787 tutor were impracticable on German-built instruments.

This state of affairs was to be remedied by Carl Almenraeder (1786–1843), the 'Boehm of the bassoon' (Sachs, *Reallexikon*, 1913). Though some of his innovations can be traced to others, he nevertheless remains the most important figure in the history of the instrument. With the advantage, like Boehm and Savary, of a virtuoso ability on his instrument, he had experience as bandmaster, teacher, player and composer. In 1817, while playing in the Mainz orchestra, he met Gottfried Weber, who had recently published valuable articles on woodwind acoustics, and started working in the Schott factory at those experiments to improve and reform the bassoon which were to occupy him almost up until his death in 1843. His treatise of 1823 and subsequent articles describe how, by adding certain keys and relocating others, he improved the intonation and response of certain notes, extended the range up to *g″* and facilitated passages in extreme keys. While leaving the bore as far as the fifth finger-hole essentially unaltered, he enlarged the tone holes sounding from A downwards and moved them further down towards the bell. Highly significant too was the replacing of the old resonance hole in the bell with an open key for *B′*. Reports of these improvements appearing in Schott's house journal *Caecilia* attracted the attention of Beethoven, who closely questioned the local Viennese player Mittag about them and even asked Schott (letter of 25 November 1825) to send him one of the new instruments. An important discovery was that the intonation and response of certain notes could be improved by opening a second vent hole into the large bore of the double joint; other innovations included fitting a metal U-bend bow at the end of the butt, using stuffed pads and connecting keys with a pin through the inner wall of the double joint.

Almenraeder's monumental tutor (completed 1836, but not published until 1843) is for his improved 17-key model with a complete chromatic range of four octaves (*B♭′* to *b♭″*), and gives many interesting data on technique, reeds and instrument construction. In 1831 he had founded his own factory in Biebrich with J.A. Heckel (1812–77). After Almenraeder's death in 1843 Heckel (and his descendants for two generations) continued the manufacture and gradual refinement of what has since become known as the *Heckelfagott*, the model gradually adopted by the other German makers. Wagner, who in 1862 was living nearby and took an interest in these developments, persuaded Heckel to build a longer bell to reach *A′*, and later endorsed Wilhelm Heckel's improved double bassoon of 1879, which he subsequently employed in *Parsifal*.

By 1887, when Weissenborn's tutor for the Heckel bassoon appeared, this model of the instrument was starting to predominate throughout Germany and also in Austria, where the traditional 'Wiener Fagott' of Ziegler and Uhlmann (which retained the traditional venting of the bell by having a closed *B′* key like the instruments of the French makers) had hitherto held its own against the reformed instrument. As early as 1825 C.-J. Sax exhibited a model entirely key-operated, while his son Adolphe patented a similar 23-key model in metal in 1851. Elements derived from Boehm's 1832 and 1847 flute models were soon adopted by such makers as Ward-Tamplini, Triébert-Marzoli and Haseneier. The latest and most promising of such 'reform' models was that of F.W. Kruspe (patented 1893), a radical new design that offered logical and simple fingering patterns, though it failed to catch on. Heckel's achievement had been to recapture the good singing qualities of the old Dresden bassoons, which the earlier Almenraeder instruments with their harder tone quality had forfeited, while retaining the technical advantages developed by Almenraeder. Further improvements by Heckel, who in 1898 claimed to have made over 4000 bassoons, included minor alterations to bore and tone-hole placement, especially on the butt; lining the wing, an idea first adopted by Morton (London, c1870), with hard rubber (1889); and fitting a key for the crook-hole (1905).

In England the local production of instruments had dropped considerably by Victorian times owing to the disappearance of the church bands and the preference of professional players, many of them foreigners, for French instruments. Ward's 'Boehm' model, patented in 1853, failed to raise any further interest. The foremost maker, Morton, trained in Vienna, made instruments on the French pattern. From about 1900, while English bassoons remained in military use, the requirements of low-pitch orchestras were met by instruments from abroad.

In the 20th century the use of the German bassoon gradually became more universal. In England the importing by Hans Richter of a pair of Viennese players to Manchester in 1899 subsequently established there a cell of 'German' players which, as Baines related, later spread to London. Cecil James, who retired in about 1980, was the last English protagonist of the 'Buffet' model. In the USA, the takeover occurred even earlier, and Italy and Spain have now followed suit. This process has been brought about by the ever-increasing demands of conductors and record producers for power of sound, homogeneity and balance, but has not always met with approval. In 1934 the English composer and conductor John Foulds remarked that:

it was the common pr*See*actice of Schubert (and his contemporaries) to eke out his two horns with two bassoons in four-part harmony. Now the bassoon is the bass instrument of the oboe family. But so intent have been both players and conductors upon producing instruments capable of fulfilling the duties of deputy horns, so to say, that German bassoons of today, forsaking their true family, have become a sort of wooden horn and have, to really sensitive ears, lost more than they have gained.

He went on to say that 'French, Belgian, and some English bassoons retain the true, slightly more reedy, certainly more sympatheitc quality which allies the instrument to its true double-reed family' (*Music To-Day*, London, 1934). The dying-out of the French instrument would indisputably be a deplorable loss, and there are continuing efforts to improve the instrument and to safeguard its future. At the Paris Conservatoire both systems are currently taught in separate classes.

Among players of German bassoons, the instruments by Heckel maintained a unique status for many years. The production of instruments from other factories, however, has steadily increased. Before World War II the makers Adler, Hüller, Kohlert and Mönnig were notable. Current makers include: Adler-Sonora, Amati, Heckel, Mollenhauer, Mönnig, Moosmann, Püchner, Schreiber, Soulsby, Walter, Wolf (Europe); Bell (Canada); Fox, Linton (USA); and Yamaha (Japan). There are others in China and Brazil. 'Buffet'-model instruments, formerly produced not only in France (Paris and La Couture) but in Belgium (Mahillon) and London (Boosey, Hawkes, Morton), are now made only in Paris (Buffet-Crampon, Selmer). Current makers of replica models include: Olivier Cottet, Laurent, Vergeat (France); Moeck, Rainer Weber, Guntram Wolf (Germany); Matthew Dart, John Hanchet, Graham Lyndon-Jones, Barbara Stanley (UK); Peter de Robinson and Koningh (the Netherlands); Robert Cronin, Robinson and Ross (USA).

5. THE EARLY REED.   In view of the relative importance of the reed, which is continually stressed by the writers on the instrument, it is unfortunate that so little is known about what they were like until comparatively recent times. As an ephemeral accessory in constant need of replacement, surviving specimens (and their reed cases) are relatively rare. Of these, pitifully few can be tentatively assigned to the 18th century.

The earliest iconographic source for a dulcian reed is the painting by Bernardo Bitti in Cuzco, Peru (1590–95);

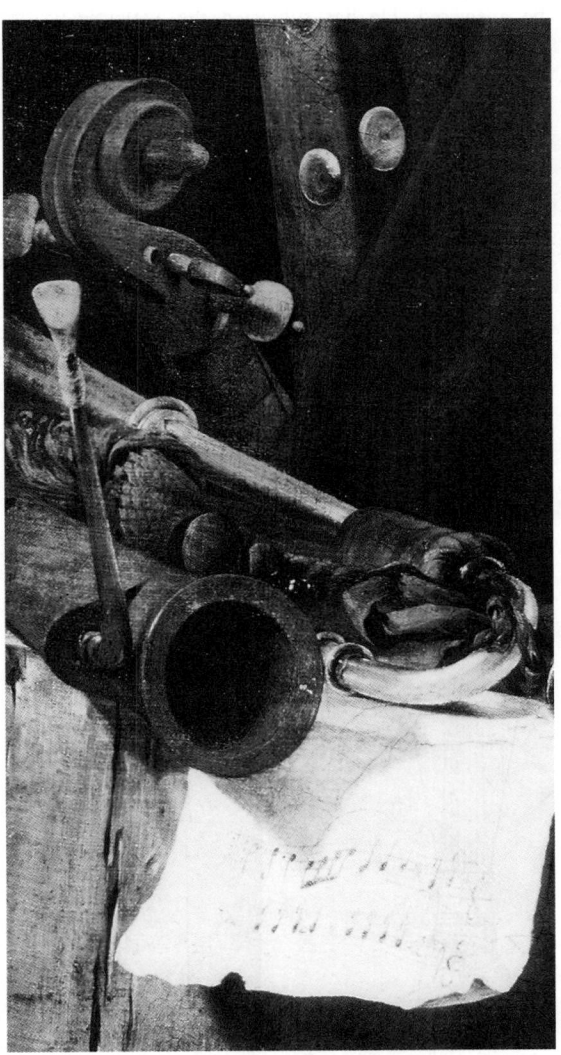

9. *Dulcian reed: detail from 'Portrait of a Musician' by Jan de Reyn, c1670 (Kunsthistorisches Museum, Vienna)*

reeds are also illustrated in Praetorius (1620), Mersenne (1636–7) and by Jan de Reyn (*c*1670; fig.9); all are shaped somewhat like a straight-sided isosceles triangle. A still life by Franz Friedrich Franck (Städtische Kunstsammlungen, Augsburg) shows a dulcian with reed attached of a longer bassoon-like model with a long 'V' scrape extending to the thread wrapping. The earliest reed-making instructions are those in the *Instrumentälischer Bettlermantl* (mid-17th century); though tantalizingly vague, they offer some valuable data – the reed is to be bound with either wire or resined thread – that is not otherwise available at this early date. Otherwise, the sole evidence available is offered by the 21 reeds in Madrid that accompany the late-18th-century *bajones* there (Kenyon de Pascual, 1984; White, 1992). Most are shorter (55–6 mm), flatter and wider (19–20 mm) than bassoon reeds: like these, they are wired.

With regard to the historical bassoon reed, White's ground-breaking research (1992, 1993, 1994) has shed light on many aspects of this hitherto neglected area, while raising many intriguing questions that have yet to be answered. He has subjected the available written sources, together with some 22 reeds for *bajón* and 91 for bassoon, to close scrutiny. His methodology delineates scrape patterns topographically, distinguishing between cane stratae – bark, dermis, dense and broad parenchyme (fig.10). He is able to show that 17th-century reeds were built on staples, were relatively long and narrow, bound with waxed thread rather than metal bands, and scraped to a V or U shape. Several stapled reed-forms co-existed: a conventional oboe-type staple; a cane section inserted into an external staple; or direct reed insertion into a wide-mouthed crook. The transition from stapled to 'cane only' construction occurred towards the end of the era of the four-key bassoon (although persisting locally well into the 19th century). Thread binding was replaced by metal banding. Pre-formed bands were pressed into position to tune the reed, like the rasette (tuning-wire) of an organ reed-pipe, a system persisting longest in England.

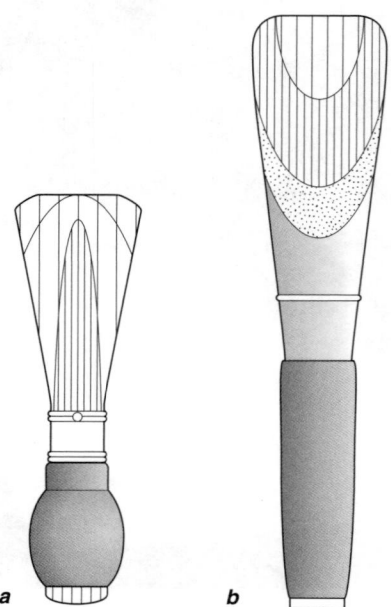

10. Reed scrape patterns: (a) modern reed; (b) early reed

Continental reeds mostly conformed to Ozi and Almenraeder models well into the late 19th century.

The gouge, scrape, banding, size and proportions of early reeds differ markedly from their modern counterparts. Early reeds were hand-gouged, often internally tapered towards the tip, allowing blade material to be of denser cane quality. External scraping was shallow, resulting in a V or U shape stopping well short of the front banding. The adjustment capability of the 'positional' pre-formed band differed both from the continuous support of the earlier thread-wrap and the re-distribution of fulcrum forces through the fixed-position, double-wire banding of today's reed. Tensional difference between these systems may have required compensational alterations in scrape, gouge thickness and embouchure support. White's findings raise uncomfortable questions regarding how certain anachronistic practices employed today relate to 'authenticity'.

Early bassoon reeds were considerably longer than modern ones (fig.11). In *Der Fagottspieler*, the bassoon player's reed is approximately the length of his middle finger and has a wide flare. An engraving (1760) of the virtuoso Felix Rheiner shows him holding a broad reed of similar length with a horseshoe-shaped area of bark removed as in some modern oboe reeds. De Garsault (1761) illustrated a narrow reed 7·5 cm long and 1 cm wide at the tip (fig.11*a*), while Cugnier (1780) recommended a length of 28 or 29 to 32 lignes (6·5–7 cm). Ozi (1803), Fröhlich (1810–11), Neukirchner (1840) and Almenraeder (1843) all gave detailed accounts of reed making which broadly correspond, although Almenraeder's reed is narrower and longer than that of Fröhlich (fig.11*c*). All agree on one significant point: the piece of cane was placed in a wooden mould for gouging by hand with a scoop-shaped chisel in order to leave it thinner at the middle, so that when made up little thinning at the blade was required once the bark was removed. The cane at the tip of the blade was thus of finer texture and more durable: Almenraeder achieved a life of up to two years for a reed in daily use. However, the subsequent universal adoption of the gouging machine (invented by the oboist Henri Brod 1834, later developed by Triébert *c*1845) which gives a rigidly vertical gouge to the piece of cane means that with most modern reeds this rind-wood is removed towards the tip, exposing coarser-grained pithwood. Flament (*Exercises techniques*, op.40, 1919) recommended storing reeds for four years to avoid spongy cane, but still expected them to last only about a week. It cannot be said that modern machinery and precision techniques have done much to alleviate these perennial problems.

6. CHARTS AND TUTORS.   Early fingering charts and tutors constitute a valuable reference source that documents the history and development of every woodwind instrument. With the bassoon, given the virtual non-availablity of surviving historical reeds, authentic matched crooks and even 'uncorrupted' instruments, fingering charts alone are able to offer unimpeachable evidence. White (1990) states that 'by applying these fingering patterns to surviving original bassoons, or modern copies of these instruments, one can determine how close the modern player/maker is coming to an original concept of sound, reed style, temperament, pitch standard, and tuning'. Likewise, guidance on questions of performing practice may be derived from tutors of the period.

Fingering charts are found in many treatises and encyclopedia articles, as well as in tutors and independently published flysheets. They are usually presented in the form of a table: they are especially useful when also accompanied by written annotations regarding individual notes. Apart from the fingerings themselves, other significant information can be gleaned by the way in which they are differentiated, how some distinguish between *d♯′* and *e♭′*, the compass selected, and the illustrations of contemporary models that usually accompany them. Table 1 lists a selection of works containing dulcian and early bassoon charts.

Early tutors can offer information unavailable elsewhere on such significant topics as ornamentation and reed making, as well as playing techniques. The mid-17th-century German treatise *Instrumentälischer Bettlermantl* is an important early source regarding reed making (see §5 above); J.S. Halle's *Werkstätte der heutigen Künste*, iii (*c*1779) also includes brief but significant information on the subject (p.368). The earliest known monograph dedicated to the bassoon is the anonymous *Compleat Instructions for the Bassoon or Fagotto* (London, *c*1770). However the informative 20-page article in La Borde's *Essai* (pp.323–43) by the player Pierre Cugnier constitutes the first real tutor for the instrument. Two significant methods were published by Etienne Ozi: his *Méthode nouvelle et raisonée pour le basson* (1787) has seven pages of material relating to playing position, model of instrument, embouchure, choice of reed and tone production. Ozi's later work, *Nouvelle méthode de basson*, first published in 1803, is the earliest comprehensive tutor for bassoon and has remained in print ever since. It includes information on reed making, with illustrations of tools, and is an entirely different work from his 1787 tutor. The earliest original tutor published in German is Wenzel Neukirchner's *Theoretisch practische Anleitung zum Fagottspiel* (1840); the significant works of Carl Almenraeder have already been discussed (see §4 above). Julius Weissenborn's *Praktische Fagott-Schule* (1887) relates specifically to the Heckel bassoon; it remained in use for a century. More recent examples are by Seltmann and Angerhöfer (based on the German system), Maurice Allard (French system) and Sergio Penazzi (for avant-garde techniques). Additional pedagogical sources are cited in the bibliography.

7. REPERTORY AND USE. While the earliest use of the dulcian was as a strengthening element to the bass, it began in the early 17th century to assume a more independent role; Schütz in his Psalm xxiv (SWV476) used a consort of five dulcians of different pitches (total range A′ to a″) as a self-contained group. The instrument also began to be used with just one or two other instruments and continuo, for example by Mikolai Zielenski (*Fantasia*, 1611), Biagio Marini (*Affetti musicali*, op.1, 1617; *Sonate*, op.8, 1629, ded. 1626), Gabriele Usper (*Compositioni armoniche*, 1619), Giovanni Battisti Riccio (*Terzo libro delle divine lodi musicali*, 1620), Stefano Bernadi (*Madrigaletti*, 1621), Giovanni Picchi (*Canzoni da sonar*, 1625), Dario Castello (*Sonate concertante: libro primo*, 1621, *libro secondo*, 1629), Mathias Spiegler (*Olor Solymaeus nascenti Jesu*, 1631), Giovanni Battista Buonamente (*Sonate et canzoni*, 1636) and Giovanni Battista Fontana (*Sonata*, 1641). (For an extensive listing of 17th-century dulcian music see Wagner, 1976.) The first solo composition was a *Fantasia per fagotto solo* in the

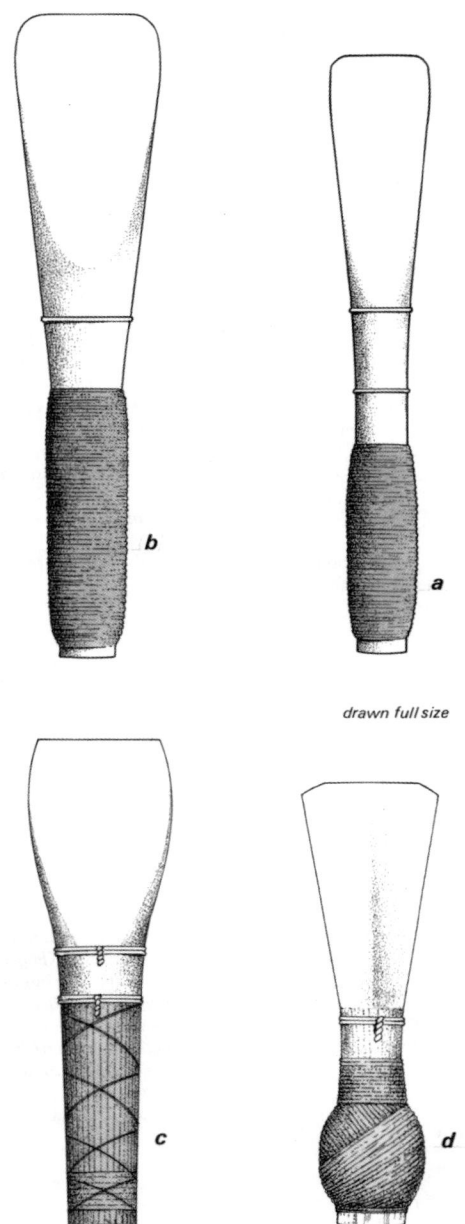

drawn full size

11. Bassoon reeds: (a) French, mid-18th century (after de Garsault, 1761); (b) English, end of the 18th century (Bate Collection, University of Oxford); (c) German, early 19th century (after Fröhlich, 1810–11); (d) modern, by Ludwig, Munich

Canzoni, fantasie et correnti by Selma y Salaverde (Venice, 1638), who was descended from a family of Madrid instrument makers. In a dedicatory sonnet he is praised for his skill on the instrument; exceptionally, the piece descends to B♭′. The nine sonatas comprising the *Compositioni musicali* (1645) by the player Bertoli, the earliest set of sonatas for any one instrument, were written for the two-key dulcian (range C to *d′*), as was the *Sonata sopra La Monica* (from *Sacra partitura*, 1651) by the

TABLE 1

1687	D. Speer	*Grund-richtiger: Unterricht der Musicalischen Kunst*	two-keyed dulcian	C–f′
c1695	J. Talbot	*GB-Och Music MS 1187*	(*basson* or *bass hautbois*)	B♭–F; then 'as flute'
1730	Anon.	*Musica bellicosa*	four-keyed bassoon	B♭–g′
1732	J.F.B.C. Majer	*Museum musicum theoretico practicum*	three-keyed bassoon	B♭–f♯′
1738	J.P. Eisel	*Musicus autodidaktos*	two-keyed dulcian	C–f′ (identical to Speer)
			four-keyed bassoon	B♭–e′f′
1744	J.D. Berlin	*Musikalske elementer*	four-keyed bassoon	B♭–g′
1751	D. Diderot and J. le Rond d'Alembert	*Encyclopédie*	five-keyed bassoon	A′–a′
1756	J. Sadler	*Apollo's Cabinet*	four-keyed bassoon	B♭–g′
c1765	J. Hotteterre	*Méthode pour apprendre à jouer … de la flûte traversière* (incl. fingering charts for cl and bn; repr. of *Principes de la flûte traversière*, 1707)	five-keyed bassoon	B♭–a′
1780	J.-B. de La Borde	*Essai sur la musique ancienne et moderne*	five-keyed bassoon	B♭–f′
1782	L.N. Berg	*Den første prøve*	four-keyed bassoon	B♭–g′
1787	E. Ozi	*Méthode nouvelle et raisonée pour le basson*		
		(a) *Tablature du basson ancien*	five-keyed bassoon (one wing-key)	B♭–d′
		(b) *Tablature du basson moderne*	seven-keyed bassoon (one wing-key)	B♭–d″
1789	J. Verschurere Reynvaan	*Muzijkaal kunst-woordenboek*	two-keyed dulcian (illustration depicts bassoon)	C–f′ (identical to Speer)
			four-keyed bassoon	B♭–c″
			four-keyed bassoon	B♭–g′
			six-keyed bassoon	B♭–c″
1803	E. Ozi	*Nouvelle méthode de basson*	seven-keyed bassoon (one-wing-key)	B♭–d″
1807	S. Holyoke	*The Instrumental Assistant*, ii [chart repr. by Herrick (1807), Shaw (1807), Whiteley (1816) and Goodale (1817)]	six-keyed bassoon	B♭–a♭′
c1810	Anon.		five-keyed bassoon (strongly resembles Ozi, 1803, with so-called F♯-key for right-hand thumb employed merely for b′ and c″, but with neither wing-key nor E♭ key	B♭–d″
1810–11	J. Fröhlich	*Vollständige theoretisch-praktische Musikschule*		
		(a) *Scala für einen Dresd'ner Fagott mit dem hohen A u. C Klappe*	eight-keyed bassoon (two wing-keys)	B♭–b♮′
		(b) *Critik über alle auf dem Fagotte befindlichen Töne*	a critique of the recommended fingerings for each note	
c1819–20	C. Almenraeder	*Traité sur le perfectionement du basson*	15-keyed bassoon	B♭–g′
1822–9	J. Fröhlich	*Systematischer Unterricht* (a)	eight-keyed bassoon	B♭–c″
		(b) *Bemerkungen zu der Fagott-Scala*	a written critique of recommended fingerings for each note	
1823	C.G. Schwarz	letter to unidentified correspondent	six-keyed bassoon (one wing-key); also a critique of recommended fingerings for each note	A′–d″
1836	F. Berr	*Méthode complète de basson*	ten-keyed bassoon	B♭–c″
1840	J. Fahrbach	*Neueste Wiener Fagottschule*		B♭–e″
1840	W. Neukirchner	*Theoretisch practische Anleitung zum Fagottspiel*	17-keyed bassoon	B♭–d♯″
c1842	J.F.B. Cokken	*Méthode de basson: nouvelle édition de la méthode de F. Beer*	22-keyed bassoon (Triébert model)	B♭–c″
1843	C. Almenraeder	*Fagottschule*	17-keyed bassoon	B♭–b♭″
1844	J.B.J.Willent-Bordogny	*Méthode complète pour le basson*	16-keyed bassoon	B♭–e♭″
1847	E. Jancourt	*Méthode théorique et pratique pour le basson*		
		(a) *Tablature du basson ordinaire*	17-keyed bassoon	
		(b) *Tablature du basson perfectionné*	16-keyed bassoon	
1859	G. Tamplini	*Course of Instructions for Military Musical Instruments*	18-keyed bassoon	B♭–g″
		(a) *Ordinarybassoon*		
		(b) *Bassoon*		
1879	E. Jancourt	*Etude du basson perfectionné*	22-keyed bassoon	B♭–f″

Darmstadt *Fagottist* P.F. Böddecker, a tour de force of technical virtuosity for its time. A sonata by 'M.G.' (*c*1686, *I-MOe*) remains unpublished. Daniel Speer's tutor (1687) contains two sonatas for three dulcians designed to exemplify writing for the two-keyed instrument. Its use in ensemble is documented as early as 1589, when *tromboni, cornetti, dolcaina e fagotti* took part in the *intermedi* composed for *La Pellegrina* in Florence by Christofano Malvezzi (Elsner, 1935, p.58). The earliest known use of the instrument in opera is in Cesti's *Il pomo d'oro* (performed 1668), where it is grouped with cornetts and trombones.

The late 17th century was a point of transition when the dulcian still co-existed with the new jointed instrument; therefore it is hard in certain circumstances to know which instrument may have been intended. However, the advent of the new jointed bassoon, with its increased range of tone and expression, gave new impetus to composers, and orchestras increasingly began to include the instrument. In Hamburg, where up to five were available, Keiser's *Atlanta* (1698) and *Octavia* (1705) each included an aria accompanied by five *Fagotte*. With the operas of Lully the instrument assumed a new function of bass to a wind trio consisting of two *hautbois* and *basson*, which are used as a contrasting group to the strings (e.g. *Psyché*, 1678); the same pattern was followed by Purcell in *Dioclesian* (1690). Mattheson (1713) perceived the role of the 'Proud Bassoon' as forming 'the usual bass, *Fundament* or *Accompagnement* to the oboe'. He went on to say that 'it is reckoned easier to play, not calling for the same *Finesse* or ornamenting (but perhaps other skills instead); however anyone wishing to distinguish himself on it in the upper register with delicacy and speed has a considerable task'. In 1728 Telemann published his Sonata in F minor, with its pathetic echo effects and tenor cantilena. Two sonatinas followed in 1731. From this period there are also sonatas by Carlo Besozzi, J.F. Fasch, J.D. Heinichen and Christoph Schaffrath. Vivaldi's 39 concertos for *fagotto* (preserved at *I-Tn*), outnumbering those he wrote for any other instrument save the violin, represent a unique legacy. While RV502 was dedicated to a local player Gioseppino Biancardi, and RV496 to his Bohemian patron Count Wenzel von Morzin, the others were presumably written for the girls of the Pietà orphanage where the composer taught from 1703. Fertonani (1998) dates their composition to between 1720 and 1740. The remarkable solo writing pre-empts many of the characteristics of later bassoon style, including rapid leaping between registers, lyrical tenor passages, and the occasional use of dynamic and expression marks. While the *a'* in RV487 and the *Bb'* in RV495 would appear to demand bassoon, the somewhat restricted compass of *C* to *g'* employed in the other concertos suggests dulcian, raising doubt as to the instrument intended. Other concertos are by J.G. Graun, Graupner, Müthel, J.F. Fasch and J.C. Bach. Chamber works include trio sonatas by Telemann, Handel and C.P.E. Bach and a remarkable set of sonatas with two oboes by Zelenka. J.S. Bach in his cantatas gave the bassoon several important obbligatos; his use of the instrument was limited by the players at his disposal, but for players like Torlle at Cöthen he was able to make considerable demands: movements like the second Bourrée in the fourth suite require fluency in an extreme key, and the 'Quoniam' of the B minor Mass is written up to

a'. C.P.E. Bach gave the bassoon an obbligato in his oratorio *Die Israeliten in der Wüste* (1769), while 'Non m'alletta' from *Temistocle* (1772) by J.C. Bach resembles a concerto in miniature.

In England in 1733 Galliard published his six sonatas, which display characteristic writing for the instrument: no.4 descends to *B'*, a note obtained by 'pinching'. Merci's six sonatas followed in about 1735. The use of the bassoon in English orchestras was also increasing. Galliard's 'New Concerto grosso [for] 24 Bassoons, accompanied by Caporale on the Violoncello', performed on 11 December 1744 in London, has not survived. Concertos with string accompaniment were written by Capel Bond (1766) as well as Henry Hargrave (1762). Boyce's *Solomon* (1743) contains the once well-known aria 'Softly rise' with bassoon obbligato: a reported concerto is lost.

In France Boismortier published, from 1726 onwards, several sets of duets for two bassoons; his were the earliest of a considerable quantity subsequently written for teaching purposes. Corette wrote a charming work, *Le Phénix*, for four bassoons as well as *Les délices de la solitude* (*c*1739) with continuo. In Germany the bassoon was considered indispensable in the orchestra (even if not always given an independent part) as a means of consolidating and clarifying the bass line. Writing in 1784–5, C.F.D. Schubart asserted that the bassoon was able to 'assume every role: accompany martial music with masculine dignity, be heard majestically in church, support the opera, discourse wisely in the concert hall, lend lilt to the dance, and be everything that it wants to be' (*Ideen zu einer Ästhetik der Tonkunst*, Vienna, 1806/*R*). For orchestral playing Quantz in 1789 recommended the proportion of one bassoon to nine strings, two bassoons to 13 strings and three bassoons to 21 strings. A pair were to become the regular complement of the Classical orchestra, although in France two pairs were usual. There was the demand for players was so great that for a period at the end of the century the Conservatoire was employing four professors to teach the bassoon.

Mozart's use of the instrument shows a great understanding of its nature and potentialities; his early Concerto in Bb K191/186*e* (1774) remains the most significant in the bassoonist's repertory. It is not known who commissioned the 18-year-old composer to write it; the amateur Baron Dürnitz, a composer of bassoon music himself for whom the sonata with cello K292/196*c* was probably written, can be discounted. Jahn's supposition that he wrote three further concertos for Dürnitz is unfortunately not supported by any other evidence. A second concerto (KA230/196*d*), first published by Max Seiffert in 1934, was attributed by Hess (*MJb*, 1957) to Devienne, although Montgomery (1975) convincingly disproved this. Chamber works for bassoon and strings, a combination unlikely to entail problems of balance, were written in considerable quantities in the Classical period. G.W. Ritter's lead (1778) was followed by Carl Stamitz, Devienne, Krommer, Danzi, Johann Brandl, Reicha and many others.

Works for bassoon with orchestra from this time fall into two categories. The first consists of concertos written by professional composers, usually with specific players in mind. Among these are notable works by Danzi, David, Michael Haydn (that by Joseph Haydn, *c*1803/4, is lost), J.N. Hummel, J.W. Kalliwoda, Kozeluch and Berwald. Efforts to identify definitively a reported *Concerto da Esperienza* (*c*1845) by Rossini have not so far proved convincing, although more than one work has been proposed. A *Pezzo da Concerto* (1813) for bassoon and horn by Paganini has recently vome to light (as has also his youthful set of three *Duetti concertanti* for violin and bassoon commissioned in 1800 by a Swedish amateur). Weber composed two works of capital importance to the repertory: the concerto written in 1811 for Brandt of Munich, in which the alternation of brilliant passage-work and lyrical melody shows off well the bassoon's capacity for both wit and pathos, and the Andante and Hungarian Rondo, a successful reworking of a piece originally for viola. A recently discovered *Capriccio* by Verdi for bass clef instrument and orchestra, datable to the early 1830s, was probably intended for bassoon. In the second category are works written as display pieces by performers (usually for their own use), for example Gebauer, Jacobi and Almenraeder. According to the fashion of the time, these often took the form of pot-pourris and variations. Among the many concertante symphonies, the one ascribed to Mozart (for oboe, clarinet, horn and bassoon) and that by Haydn (for oboe, bassoon, violin and cello) are notable. Works for two bassoons and orchestra by Dieter, Johnsen, Schacht and Vanhal survive; one by Danzi is lost.

Sonatas with piano were comparatively rare at this period. The substantial sonata by Liste (1807) may be considered the most important for any woodwind instrument prior to Weber. Others were composed by Reicha, Krufft, Amon, Moscheles and Theuss; there are some smaller pieces by Spohr, Christian Rummel and Jacobi. Almenraeder's solo pieces, with their unique exploitation of the highest register up to g′, mark the end of an era in which solo music for wind was fashionable. In France, the virtuoso Jancourt assembled for his repertory a large number of transcriptions as well as his own compositions. Notable examples of 'morceaux de concours' were written by Pierné, Bourdeau and Büsser.

Concerning its role within the orchestra, the bassoon was criticized by 19th-century writers as being 'a weak-sounding instrument that gets lost among loud forces' (Fétis, *Revue musicale*, viii, 1834, pp.148 and 326). Fétis recommended that 'in a well-equipped wind orchestra, there should never be less than eight bassoons'; he even recorded an occasion where he used as many as 30. Berlioz too noted the bassoon's lack of volume and remarked that 'its timbre, totally lacking in *éclat* and nobility, has a propensity for the grotesque which must be borne in mind when giving it prominence'. However, he also said that 'the character of its high notes has about it something painful, complaining, almost wretched, which can sometimes be surprisingly effective in a high register melody or an accompanimental pattern' (*Grand traité d'instrumentation*, 1843).

Among the vast output of the 20th century, the following works are noteworthy: concertos and other concert works by Elgar, Wolf-Ferrari, Villa-Lobos, Jolivet, Françaix, Jacob and Maconchy; recent British works by John Addison, Judith Bingham, Stephen Dodgson, Robin Holloway, John Joubert and Peter Maxwell Davies, and in North America by Elliott Schwartz, Gunther Schuller, John T. Williams and E.T. Zwilich; a concerto by the Russian composer S.A. Gubaydulina (along with two other significant works for bassoon); concertante works by Strauss (clarinet and bassoon) and Hindemith (trumpet and bassoon); sonatas and other works by Tadeusz Baird,

Roger Boutry, Eugène Bozza, Mario Castelnuovo-Tedesco, Dutilleux, Hindemith, Hurlstone, Longo, Nussio, Saint-Saëns, Skalkottas – his Sonata Concertante (1943) is the outstanding sonata of the century – and Tansman (a sonata by Poulenc, 1957, remained unfinished at his death and is lost); unaccompanied solo pieces by Apostel, Arnold, Bruno Bartolozzi, Jørgen Bentzon, Berio, Boulez, Jacob, Stockhausen and Isang Yun; bassoon ensembles by Bozza, Victor Bruns, Alois Hába, Jacob, Prokofiev, William Schuman and Peter Schickele; and bassoon and string works by Kalevi Aho, Bax, Françaix and Jacob. The increased prominence given to the bassoon in many 20th-century orchestral scores is exemplified by the opening of *The Rite of Spring*, a solo in the upper register. During the century various new techniques were demanded of the instrument, among them double- and triple-tonguing, flutter-tonguing, multiphonics, pitch bending, quarter tones, and vocalizing while playing. Many of these are exploited in Bartolozzi's *Concertazioni* for bassoon, strings and percussion and Stockhausen's *Adieu* for wind quintet (see Penazzi, 1982, and Ouzounoff, 1986). More recent is its use with contact microphones and live electronics.

8. PERFORMERS AND TEACHERS. The earliest performers known by name are the composers Bertoli, Selma y Salaverde and Böddecker, whose florid writing indicates the existence of a high level of dulcian technique in the 17th century. Vivaldi's concertos suggest that standards in Italy were particularly high; the playing of Paolo Girolamo Besozzi (1704–78) of Parma was praised by several writers, and the earliest German virtuoso of note, Felix Rheiner (1732–82) of Munich, of whom two interesting portraits survive (see fig.8), was sent to Turin to study with him. His pupil Franz Anton Pfeiffer (1752–87) was praised, among other things, for his double-tonguing; his use of 'three-part harmony' in a solo cadenza was doubtless a multiphonic effect. Georg Wenzel Ritter (1748–1808), 'the finest bassoon player I ever heard' (Kelly, 1826), of Berlin started his career in the Mannheim orchestra, making Mozart's acquaintance there; while in Paris in 1778 he published a pioneering set of bassoon quartets. The bassoon part in the Sinfonia concertante Mozart said he wrote in Paris was for him. Among Ritter's pupils were Carl Baermann (1782–1842), who succeeded him in the Berlin orchestra and became well known as a soloist, and Georg Friedrich Brandt (1773–1836) of Munich, for whom Weber wrote his concerto and Hungarian Rondo. Other German virtuosos included Carl Almenraeder, the Bohemian Carl Wenzel Neukirchner (1805–89) of Stuttgart, who like Almenraeder wrote a tutor and solos as well as attempting practical improvements to his instrument, and Carl Jacobi (1791–1852) of Coburg, who published a number of interesting bravura pieces. Julius Weissenborn (1837–88) of Leipzig and Ludwig Milde (1849–1913) of Prague left teaching material which is still widely used today.

In France the best-known players have traditionally taught and written tutors as well. The treatise of Pierre Cugnier (*b* 1740) appeared in La Borde's *Essai* of 1780; Cugnier wrote that the bassoon 'might imitate the sound of the recorder, were it possible for that instrument to play as low. But its tone must never be denuded of that kind of "bite" (*mordant*) proper to it which lends it the necessary timbre; otherwise it will resemble that of the serpent, which would be disagreeable'. The tutors of

Etienne Ozi (1754–1813), who was appointed to the Conservatoire in 1795, have already been discussed (see §6 above). Tutors were also written by his successors Berr, Willent-Bordogny, Jancourt, Cokken and Bourdeau (see §6 above, esp. Table 1); Eugène Jancourt (1815–1901) had a notable career as a soloist as well, and wrote and arranged an extensive repertory of solo pieces; this corpus of 116 works forms a valuable contribution to the repertory. His tutor includes information on tone vibrato, which was not to be confused with embellishment. Jancourt wrote that 'this is not an ornament dictated by taste, but the result of deep feeling expressed on the instrument' and that it was obtained 'by shaking the right hand over the finger-holes'. Writing over 100 years later, the English bassoonist Archie Camden expressed his opinion that 'the wide, throbbing kind of vibrato – wow-wow, wow-wow – is in bad taste … whether it is vocal or instrumental, and can easily make a bassoon sound like a badly played saxophone'.

In England, early players of note included Kennedy, for whom Galliard in 1733 wrote a set of sonatas; Miller, who was to Burney 'the best Bassoon I can remember'; and James Holmes (d 1820), who played in the première of Haydn's Concertante. John Parry (ii) (1830) wrote of Holmes that his 'tone resembled the most perfect human voice' and that his 'execution was as accurate as rapid'. In the 19th century the renowned James Mackintosh (1767–1844) was followed by the Paris-trained Belgian Friedrich Baumann (1801–56), who was brought over by the conductor Jullien. William Wotton (1832–1912) and his brother Thomas (1852–1918) were succeeded as the leading players by another notable pair, E.F. James (1861–1921), for whom Elgar (himself an amateur bassoonist) wrote his Romance of 1909, and his brother Wilfred (1872–1941). Writing in 1836, George Hogarth noted that 'English performers, in general, use stronger reeds than foreigners, with a corresponding difference in the quality of their tone' (Musical World, iii/38, 1836, p.180). He differentiated between a 'strong, thick reed' which 'produces a great volume of tone; but the pressure of the lips which it requires prevents the attainment of smoothness and flexibility' and a 'weak reed' which 'is easily blown into; but the tone is feeble, and defective in roundness'. Hanslick (Welt Ausstellung: Paris 1867) also observed that the English (along with the French and Belgians) preferred very wide reeds, which in his opinion promoted 'strength of tone at the cost of beauty'. The establishment of the German bassoon in England owes much to Archie Camden (1888–1979), who as a soloist helped popularize the instrument and trained a whole generation of players. Other influential teachers have included Karl Öhlberger (Austria), Karel Pivonka (Czech Republic), Maurice Allard (France), Albert Hennige (Germany), Mordechai Rechtman (Israel), Enzo Muccetti (Italy), Gwydion Brooke (UK), Simon Kovar and Sol Schoenbach (USA), and Roman Terëkhin (Russia).

Notable performers and teachers of the late 20th century include: Milan Turkovic (Austria), Gilbert Audin, Pascal Gallois (France), Sergio Azzolini, Dag Jensen and Klaus Thunemann (Germany), Masahito Tanaka (Japan), Valery Popov (Russia), and Norman Herzberg and Stephen Maxym (USA). 'Period' performers include Danny Bond, Michael McCraw, Milan Turkovic and Marc Vallon. Jazz bassoonists include Paul Hanson and Michael Rabinowitz.

9. THE DOUBLE BASSOON.   The modern double or contrabassoon (fig.12) is basically similar in construction to the bassoon. The normal compass extends from B♭″ to c′. Modern instruments, mostly of the 'compact' model, stand about 122 cm tall with a bore length of 5·5 m. Earlier models have a tall down-turning metal bell, for which a short bassoon-shaped wooden 'C' bell may be substituted when the lowest notes are not required. There are also models descending to A″ (or even A♭″) which require an even taller extension bell. The reed, somewhat larger than that of the bassoon, can vary more than the latter in its dimensions; while some players use inflated bassoon reed dimensions, others alter the ratio of blade to shaft (as required by the model of instrument). The crook fits into a metal shank incorporating a tuning-slide and water-key. The contrabassoon is a transposing instrument, notated one octave higher than it sounds; in a few scores (Wagner, Debussy) its part is written at pitch. As with the bassoon, the crook is crucial as regards response, intonation and tone. The basic problem for the player is to produce a sound of good quality which will nevertheless 'tell' in a tutti passage. While the upper register is weak, it is in the lower register that the contrabassoon sounds at its best, lending a rich organ-like sonority to the full wind section. Brahms specified its use in his Requiem op.45, should no organ be available (letter to Hermann Levi, spring 1869). From the turn of the century, its orchestral role became more independent (works by Ravel, Schoenberg, Berg, Stravinsky, Britten, etc.). Works such as Schoenberg's Kammersymphonie op.9 no.1 and Berg's Kammerkonzert set new standards for the player. Modern scores often demand the player to double between bassoon and contra, a manoeuvre often requiring considerable dexterity. During the era of acoustic recording, the instrument proved an indispensable reinforcement for the string bass. Rarely, a pair is called for; Schoenberg in his Gurrelieder allowed the first player to appear in the unusual role of inner voice. Its use in a solo context is only a recent development. As early as 1922 Ervín Schulhoff scored his Bassnachtigal for unaccompanied double bassoon, partly for extra-musical reasons; more recently concert works have been written by Henk Badings, Victor Bruns, Ruth Gipps, Roger Smalley and Gunther Schuller. There are compositions for double bassoon and piano by Victor Bruns and Vítězslav Novák.

If the folding of 8′ register pommers in the interests of commodity made sense, this was even more the case for 16′ models. Larger members of the bassoon family have existed from the earliest period of its history; Zacconi (1592) referred to more than one size of dulcian and Praetorius (2/1619) listed an entire consort whose deepest members were two 'Doppelfagotte', the Quartfagott (G′ to f, g) and Quintfagott (F′ to e, g). The two larger dulcians in the Vienna collection correspond to the former. Praetorius also referred to a projected Fagotcontra by Hans Schreiber of Berlin which would be pitched one octave below the Choristfagott size of dulcian. The consort of dulcians in Augsburg (see fig.5) contains one such instrument, of Italian origin, dating from the second half of the 16th century (see §2 above). The instrument is constructed of five sections, the glued tenons strengthened with ornamental bands. Of the four keys, the E and D thumb-keys are mounted one over the other. A flush pepper-pot lid similar to that of the gedackt dulcian is

12. Modern double bassoon by Wilhelm Heckel, Biebrich (private collection)

inserted in the bell (see Weber, 1991). Another early period *Oktavbass* instrument is at Dresden (Museum für Kunsthandwerke, Schloss Pillnitz). The other instruments known are two that are slightly later, now in the Schlossmuseum, Sondershausen (one is dated 1681; both are ascribed to Johann Bohlmann) which, aside from detachable bell are of one-piece construction. Four early octave bassoon models survive. One in Leipzig is signed A. Eichentopf, dated 1714. Another in Sondershausen is unsigned but attributed by Heyde to the same maker and tentatively dated to *ante* 1711 (Heyde, 1987). These are like a large version of one of Denner's bassoons and descend to B♭″. An interesting example in the Museum Carolino Augusteum, Salzburg, by the Milanese maker Anciuti, is dated 1732. In England Talbot (*c*1695) mentioned a 'Pedal or Double Basson' descending to *F*′, which would appear to be a jointed version of the 'Quintfagott' of Praetorius. The famous London maker Thomas Stanesby (i) is reported to have made a double bassoon in 1727; a fine specimen in Dublin by his son (dated 1739) descends to B♭″, is built like a large bassoon of the period with four keys, and stands 253 cm high. A contemporary advertisement refers to 'Two Grand or Double Bassoons, made by Mr Stanesby jun. the greatness of whose sound surpasses that of any other Bass Instrument whatsoever'. The double bassoon is not referred to in England for several decades after 1803, and it is unlikely that any other such English instruments were made until the late 19th century.

In Germany the *Quartfagott* was more common than the true *Kontrafagott* pitched one octave below the normal bassoon. Bach used the former in the cantata *Der Himmel lacht! die Erde Jubilieret* BWV31 (1715), and in his *St John Passion* a 'continuo pro Bassono grosso' part is mentioned. Some works (e.g. the cantata *Nach dir, Herr, verlanget mich* BWV150) which contain passages descending to written *A*′ were transposed so as to enable old *Chorton* instruments (bassoon, organ) to play with newer low-pitch woodwinds. *Kontrafagotte* were included in German and Austrian military bands towards the end of the 18th century and were used occasionally in the orchestra when available. Mozart wrote a part for *gran fagotto* descending to *C*′ in his *Maurerische Trauermusik* K 477/479a (however, his Serenade for 13 wind instruments K361/370a specifies *contrabasso*, i.e. string bass). By 1807 the Vienna court orchestra included a double bassoon, and Haydn and Beethoven made use of it in their larger works.

During the 19th century, experiments were made by many different makers to develop a satisfactory double bassoon, mainly to satisfy the need for a powerful contrabass-register instrument in the military band. One type developed was of metal, with a closed key for each note; the earliest maker was Stehle of Vienna, who exhibited his 'Harmonie-Bass' there in 1839. It measured 169 cm and its 15 keys were operated singly like those of the ophicleide giving a range of two and a quarter octaves from E♭″ to *g*. Six of these instruments survive, of which two are in Budapest, and one each in Leipzig, Nuremberg, Paris and Toronto. Later models were more compact: these included Červeny's 'Tritonicon' of 1856 and Moritz's 'Claviatur-Contrafagott', which was fitted with a keyboard like that of a piano-accordion. A version by Mahillon from 1868 was called 'contrebasse à anche', and later on similar instruments of this name (Eng. reed contrabass; Ger. Rohrkontrabass; It. contrabbasso ad ancia) were produced for military bands in France and Italy. The deepest of all was Červený's 'Subkontrafagott' of 1867 which descended to B♭″. Another solution was to widen the bore. Haseneier's wooden 'Contrabassophon' of 1847 had a bore which flared from 6 mm to over 10 cm and tone holes of exceptionally large diameter. It had 19 keys covering all holes and its range extended down to C′. Since the tube was in four sections, the overall length of the instrument was only 140 cm; it was considered a success and was copied by several makers. Some models, such as that of Berthold in 1875, were made in papier-mâché to lessen the weight; W.H. Stone brought one such to England, where it was copied by Morton. However, the open and not easily controlled tone of all these instruments, while acceptable in the military band, was not suitable for the orchestra. The contrabass sarrusophone which later replaced them in France is still found occasionally and appears in some scores by Ravel, Debussy and Delius.

However, it was the achievement of the Heckel factory to bring about the development of the modern instrument. For the preceding years the double bassoons outwardly resembled a large bassoon with a long looped metal crook; their range descended to D′ or C′. In 1875–6 J.A. Heckel redesigned the instrument, retaining its narrow bore but disposing it into three separate wooden tubes; it was held on the left of the player's body and its range descended to C′ (it was patented in 1877 by Heckel's foreman Friedrich Stritter). In 1879 an improved model was made which was held and fingered conventionally; Wagner praised its new-found ability to play smoothly, and subsequently employed it in *Parsifal*. For the first time the instrument was comparable to the bassoon in tone and general response. Later a down-turned metal bell was added, extending the range to B♭″, and after 1900 to A″. All subsequent instruments have been based on these Heckel models, including a version by Buffet-Crampon with French-system keywork introduced in 1906.

10. OTHER SIZES. The family of dulcians as described by Praetorius included three progressively smaller sizes which he called *Diskantfagott*, *Altfagott* and *Fagott Piccolo* or *Singel Corthol*. A set of four small dulcians, of Spanish provenance and listed as *bajoncilli*, is now in Brussels. An early incidence of scoring for such an instrument is by Flaccomio (*Liber primus concentus*, Venice, 1611), marked 'con basoncico alias fagotto piccolo'. Ever since the appearance of the jointed bassoon, smaller-sized instruments have continued to be built by every bassoon maker of note; their survival in surprising numbers is perhaps explained by their lack of serious use. They can be divided into two categories. The more usual type of tenor bassoon pitched in F (a 5th higher than normal) or occasionally in G or E♭, was also known as the 'tenoroon'. This name, presumably a contraction of 'tenor bassoon', appears to have been originally applied to the alto oboe, and Stone in *Grove1* misleadingly confused the two instruments. The French name for this type, *basson quinte*, should not be confused with the *Quintfagott* of Praetorius, the large dulcian which descended to F′. The second type, pitched one octave higher than normal, is named 'octave bassoon' or 'fagottino'. A fine early specimen, 63·6 cm tall, by J.C. Denner, is in Boston.

The only known early works for small bassoon are a mid-18th-century wind parthia by J.G.M. Frost, which includes parts for two *fagotti-octavo* and two *fagotti-quarto*, and a cantata by F.W. Zachow, which includes *bassonetti*. In France a small bassoon was reportedly used about 1833 at the Bordeaux opera to replace the english horn; Larousse (1865), comparing the two instruments, considered that the tone of the *basson quinte* had greater force and penetration. Later it was used occasionally in the military band; Buffet-Crampon exhibited three new models in 1889 and Morton made some in London.

As a solo instrument, the small bassoon had long been used by such recitalists as Eugène Jancourt and E.F. James. In 1992 Guntram Wolf (Kronach) built the first tenor bassoon in modern times for the English player Richard Moore, who subsequently commissioned Victor Bruns to write for it. Another significant use has been as an instrument for young beginners: Almenraeder recommended starting ten-year-olds this way – the age at which Bärmann began his studies with Ritter. The same practice was reported in the Foundling Hospital of London and more recently in the band of a Sicilian orphanage. Since 1992 Wolf, followed by Moosmann and Howarth, has developed successful models for the seven- to ten-year-old age group.

The name 'Caledonica' was given to a modified version of the octave bassoon invented about 1825 by the Scottish bandmaster William Meikle; it had a wider flaring bore and was played with a small clarinet mouthpiece. An improved model was subsequently developed by the London maker George Wood which he called the 'alto fagotto'.

BIBLIOGRAPHY

A Pedagogical. B General. C Early history (to 1800). D Construction and makers. E Repertory and performers.

A: PEDAGOGICAL.

LaBordeE, 323–43
Compleat Instructions for the Bassoon or Fagotto (London, c1770)
E. Ozi: *Méthode nouvelle et raisonnée pour le basson* (Paris, 1787/R)
E. Ozi: *Nouvelle méthode de basson adoptée par le Conservatoire* (Paris, 1803/R)
J. Fröhlich: *Vollständige theoretisch-praktische Musikschule für alle beym Orchester gebräuchliche wichtigere Instrumente* (Bonn, 1810–11)
W. Neukirchner: *Theoretisch practische Anleitung zum Fagottspiel* (Leipzig, 1840)
C. Almenraeder: *Fagottschule/Méthode complète de basson* (Mainz, 1843)
E. Jancourt: *Méthode théorique et pratique de basson* (Paris, 1847/R)
J. Weissenborn: *Praktische Fagott-Schule/Practical Bassoon-School* (Leipzig, 1887, rev. 3/1929/R by C. Schaefer)
J. Satzenhofer: *Neue praktische Fagott-Schule* (Leipzig, 1900)
C. Stadio: *Grand metodo per fagotto* (Naples, 1908)
F. Oubradous: *Enseignement complet du basson*, i–iv (Paris, 1938–44)
M. Allard: *Méthode de basson* (Paris, 1975)
W. Seltmann and G.Angerhöfer: *Das Fagott/The Bassoon*, i–vi (Leipzig, 1976–84)
C.A. Biggers: *The Contra-Bassoon: a Guide to Performance* (Bryn Mawr, PA, 1977)
S. Penazzi: *Il fagotto: altre techniche/The Bassoon: other Techniques* (Milan, 1982)
S.J. Jooste: *The Technique of Bassoon Playing* (Potchefstroom, 1984)
A. Ouzounoff: *Actuellement le basson: traité pratique des nouvelles techniques au basson* (Paris, 1986)
P. Lescat and J. Saint-Arroman, eds.: *Méthodes et traités: France 1600–1800*, iv: *Basson* (Courlay, 1999)

B: GENERAL.

MGG1 (W. Kolneder); *MGG2* (G. Angerhöfer and W. Krüger)

C. Baermann: 'Ueber die Natur und Eigenthümlichkeit des Fagotts', *AMZ*, xxii (1820), 601–7

M. Kelly: *Reminiscences* (London, 1826, 2/1826/R with introduction by A.H. King); ed. R. Fiske (London, 1975)

W. Heckel: *Der Fagott* (Biebrich, 1899, 2/1931)

L. Letellier and E. Flamant: 'Le basson', *EMDC*, II/iii (1927), 1556–96

A. Baines: *Woodwind Instruments and their History* (London, 1957, 3/1967/R)

L.G. Langwill: *The Bassoon and Contrabassoon* (London, 1965)

G.S. Fraenkel, ed.: *Decorative Music Title Pages* (New York, 1968)

C.J. Nederveen: *Acoustical Aspects of Woodwind Instruments* (Amsterdam, 1969, 2/1998)

J. Eppelsheim: 'Das "Subkontrafagott"', *Fachtagung zur Erforschung der Blasmusik I: Graz 1974*, 233–72

W. Voigt: *Untersuchungen zur Formantbildung in Klängen von Fagott und Dulzianen* (Regensburg, 1975) [with Eng. summary]

A.H. Benade: *Fundamentals of Musical Acoustics* (New York, 1976, 2/1990)

J. Kergomard and J. Heinrich: 'Le basson', *Bulletin du Groupe d'acoustique musicale*, nos.82–3 (1976), 116

W. Jansen: *The Bassoon: its History, Construction, Makers, Players and Music* (Buren, 1978–81)

J. Eppelsheim: 'More Facts about the "Subkontrafagott"', *GSJ*, xxxii (1979), 104–14

G. Joppig: *Oboe und Fagott: ihre Geschichte, ihre Nebeninstrumente und ihre Musik* (Berne and Stuttgart, 1981; Eng. trans., 1988)

W.H. Sallagar and M. Nagy, eds: *Fagott Forever: eine Festgabe für Karl Öhlberger* (Wilhering, 1992)

W. Waterhouse: 'Die historische Entwicklung des Fagottklangs', *Festschrift 10 Jahre Berliner Fagottquartett*, ed. U. Liedtke and H. Bartholomäus (Berlin,1996), 29–44

C: EARLY HISTORY (TO 1800)

BertolottiM; *GerberL*; *MersenneHU*; *PraetoriusSM*, ii; *PraetoriusTI*

T. Albonesi: *Introductio in Chaldaicam linguam* (Pavia, 1539)

L. Zacconi: *Prattica di musica* (Venice, 1592/R)

H. de Garsault: *Notionaire* (Paris, 1761)

E. Eslner: *Untersuchung der instrumentalen Besetzungspraxis der weltlichen Musik im 16. Jahrhundert* (diss., U. of Basle, 1935)

F.W. Galpin: 'The Romance of the Phagotum', *PMA*, lxvii (1940–41), 57–72

A. Baines: 'James Talbot's Manuscript, I: Wind Instruments', *GSJ*, i (1948), 9–26

F. Lesure: 'Le traité des instruments de musique de Pierre Trichet: les instruments à vent', *AnnM*, iii (1955), 283–387; pubd separately (Neuilly-sur-Seine, 1957; Eng. trans., 1973)

A. Reimann: *Studien zur Geschichte des Fagotts* (diss., U. of Freiburg, 1956)

E. Halfpenny: 'The Evolution of the Bassoon in England, 1750–1800', *GSJ*, x (1957), 30–39

J. Eppelsheim: *Das Orchester in den Werken Jean-Baptiste Lullys* (Tutzing, 1961)

M. Staehelin: 'Der sogenannte Musettenbass: Forschungen zur schweizerischen Instrumenten- und Musikgeschichte des späten 18. und frühen 19. Jahrhunderts', *Jb des Bernischen historischen Museums in Bern*, xlix–l (Bern,1969–70), 93–121

B. Klitz: 'A Composition for *dolzaina*', *JAMS*, xxiv (1971), 113–18

K. Wagner: *Die Fagott-Instrumente des 17. Jahrhunderts* (diss., U. of Basle, 1976)

B. Kenyon de Pascual: 'A Brief Survey of the Late Spanish Bajón', *GSJ*, xxxvii (1984), 72–9

R. Semmens: 'The Bassoons in Marin Mersenne's *Harmonie universelle* (1636)', *JAMIS*, (1984), 22–31

L. Lockwood: 'Adrian Willaert and Cardinal Ippolito I d'Este', *EMH*, v (1985), 85–112

A. Roberts: *Studien zur Bauweise und zur Spieltechnik des Dulzian* (diss., U. of Köln, 1986)

T. Giannini: 'A Letter from Louis Rousselet, 18th Century French Oboist at the Royal Opera in England', *AMIS Newsletter*, xvi/2 (1987), 10–11

J.-M. Heinrich: *Contribution à l'étude de l'anche du basson* (diss., U. of Paris, 1987)

H. Heyde: 'Contrabassoons in the 17th and early 18th Century', *GSJ*, xl (1987), 24–36

W. Köhler: *Die Blasinstrumente aus der 'Harmonie universelle' des Marin Mersenne* (Celle, 1987)

B. Haynes: 'Lully and the Rise of the Oboe as Seen in Works of Art', *EMc*, xvi (1988), 324–38

D. Lasocki: 'The French Hautboy in England, 1673–1730', *EMc*, xvi (1988), 339–57

W. Waterhouse: 'A Newly Discovered 17th-Century Bassoon by Haka', *EMc*, xvi (1988), 407–10

B. Kenyon de Pascual: 'A Late Sixteenth-Century Portrayal of the Jointed Dulcian', *GSJ*, xliii (1990), 150–53

P. White: 'Early Bassoon Fingering Charts', *GSJ*, xliii (1990), 68–111

J. Kopp: 'Notes on the Bassoon in Seventeenth-Century France', *JAMIS*, xvii (1991), 85–115

R. Weber: 'Kontrabass-Dulciane, die Vorläufer des Kontrafagottes', *Oboe, Klarinette, Fagott*, vi (1991), 97–105

P. White: 'Bajón Reeds', *FoMRHI Quarterly*, no.67 (1992), 10–30

T. Giannini: 'Jacques Hotteterre le Romain and his Father, Martin', *EMc*, xxi (1993), 377–95

P. White: *The Early Bassoon Reed in Relation to the Development of the Bassoon from 1636* (diss., U. of Oxford, 1993)

B. Kenyon de Pascual: 'The Dulcians (Bajón and Bajoncillo) in Spain: an updated Review', *A Time of Questioning: Utrecht 1994*, 25–52

P. White: 'Early Reed Design', *A Time of Questioning: Utrecht 1994*, 189–203

P. White: 'The Bass Hautboy in the Seventeenth Century', *A Time of Questioning: Utrecht 1994*, 167–82

J.P. Campbell: 'Musical Instruments in the *Instrumentälischer Bettlermantl*: a Seventeenth-Century Musical Compendium', *GSJ*, xlviii (1995), 156–67

B. Haynes: 'New Light on Some French Relatives of the Hautboy in the 17th and Early 18th Centuries', *Sine musica nulla vita: Festschrift Hermann Moeck*, ed. N. Delius (Celle, 1997), 257–70

J.B. Kopp: 'The Emergence of the Late-Baroque Bassoon', *Double Reed*, xxii/4 (1999), 73–87

D: CONSTRUCTION AND MAKERS.

Waterhouse-LangwillI

C. Almenraeder: *Abhandlung über die Verbesserung des Fagotts* (Mainz, 1823)

G. Weber: 'Wesentliche Verbesserungen des Fagottes', *Caecilia* [Mainz], ii (1825), 123–40 [incl. illustration]

G. Weber: 'C. Almenräders weitere Fagott-Verbesserung', *Caecilia* [Mainz], ix (1828), 128

C. Almenraeder: 'Bemerkungen über Blasinstrumente mit Tonlöchern, insbesondere die Doppellöcher am Fagott', *Caecilia* [Mainz], xix (1837), 77–87

G. Brindley: 'The Logical Bassoon', *GSJ*, xxi (1968), 152–61

M. Popkin and L.Glickman: *Bassoon Reed Making* (Evanston, IL,1969, 2/1987)

E. Nickel: *Der Holzblasinstrumentenbau in der Freien Reichsstadt Nürnberg* (Munich,1971)

H. Heyde: 'Carl Almenräders Verdienst um das Fagott', *BMw*, xiv (1972), 225–30

J.L. Burton: *Bassoon Bore Dimensions* (diss., U. of Rochester, 1975)

K. Ventzke: 'Boehm-System-Fagotte im 19. Jahrhundert', *Tibia*, i/1 (1976), 13–18

W. Waterhouse: *The Proud Bassoon*, Edinburgh University Collection of Historic Instruments, 17 Aug – 31 Aug 1983 (Edinburgh, 1983) [exhibition catalogue]

G. Joppig: 'Zur Entwicklung des deutschen Fagotts', *Studia organologica: Festschrift John Henry van der Meer*, ed. F. Hellwig (Tutzing, 1987), 253–76

D. Lasocki and R.Prior: *The Bassanos: Venetian Musicians and Instrument Makers in England, 1531–1665* (Aldershot, 1995)

M. Lyndon-Jones: 'Who was HIE.S/HIER.S/HIERO.S?', *FoMRHI Quarterly*, no.83 (1996), 10–18

E. Brown: 'Another Look at the Bassoon', *Double Reed News*, no.42 (1998), 8–10

E: REPERTORY AND PERFORMERS.

E. Hess: 'Ist das Fagottkonzert KV. Anhang 230a von Mozart?', *MJb 1957*, 223–32

W. Montgomery: *The Life and Works of François Devienne, 1759–1803* (diss., Catholic U. of America, 1975)

H.E. Griswold: *Etienne Ozi (1754–1813): Bassoonist, Teacher, and Composer* (diss., Peabody Institute, Johns Hopkins U., 1979)

W.J. Hodges: *A Biographical Dictionary of Bassoonists born berfore 1825* (diss., U. Iowa,1980)

B. Klitz: 'The Bassoon in Chamber Music of the Seventeenth Century', *JAMIS*, ix (1983), 5–20

D.J. Rhodes: 'Franz Anton Pfeiffer and the Bassoon', *GSJ*, xxxvi (1983), 97–103

B. Bulling: *Fagott Bibliographie* (Wilhelmshaven, 1989)

J.P. Beebe: *Music for Unaccompanied Solo Bassoon* (Jefferson, NC, 1990)

H. Bartholomäus: *Das Fagottensemble: kleines Handbuch zur Musikpraxis* (Berlin, 1992)

B. Koenigsbeck: *Basson Bibliography/Bibliographie du basson/Fagott Bibliographie* (Monteux,1994)

C. Fertonani: *La musica strumentale di Antonio Vivaldi* (Firenze, 1998)

WILLIAM WATERHOUSE

Bassoon stop. Name given to a strip of parchment or silk which is made to buzz against the bass strings of the piano by means of a handstop, knee lever or pedal. It was first used towards the end of the 18th century and continued to be popular on the Continent until about 1840.

DAVID ROWLAND

Basso ostinato. *See* GROUND and OSTINATO.

Basso profondo (It.: 'deep bass'). A term first used in the late 19th century to describe a particularly deep, resonant bass voice, often associated with Russian basses and choral singing (*see* BASS (ii)). Earlier identifications of this voice type appear especially in France. Brossard (*Diction-aire de musique*, 1703) writes that this deep voice is called *bassista*, or 'more commonly, *basse-contre*'. Rousseau (*Dictionnaire de musique*, 1768) states that the *basse-contre* 'sings the bass under the bass itself, and should not be confused with the *contre-basse*, which is an instrument'. Raguenet (*Paralèle*, 1702; Eng. trans., 1709) specifically cites the low bass as a particular strength of French opera as opposed to Italian:

> Our operas have a farther advantage over the Italian in respect of the voice, and that is the bass, which is so frequent among us and so rarely to be met with in Italy. For every man that has an ear will witness with me that nothing can be more charming than a good bass; the simple sound of these basses, which sometimes seems to sink into a profound abyss, has something wonderfully charming in it. . .When the persons of gods or kings, a Jupiter, Neptune, Priam, or Agamemnon, are brought on the stage, our actors, with their deep voices, give 'em an air of majesty, quite different from that of the feign'd basses among the Italians, which have neither depth nor strength

In opera, the deep bass solo voice has so often been associated with roles of great authority or majesty that today 'profondo' sometimes is taken to mean 'profound' as well as 'low'. Examples from Mozart operas include Sarastro from *Die Zauberflöte* and Osmin from *Die Entführung aus dem Serail*; later roles include the Grand Inquisitor in Verdi's *Don Carlos* (1867). The Russian school of singers has produced notable deep basses although the most famous exponents (Chaliapin, Regzen) have not been remarkable for their depth and the great Russian roles do not make heavy demands on the lowest register. The *basso profondo* is distinguished from the BASSO CANTANTE by its lower range extension and especially its power (*see also* BASSE NOBLE).

J.B. STEANE, ELLEN T. HARRIS

Basso seguente. A term used by Adriano Banchieri in *Ecclesiastiche sinfonie ... per sonare et cantare et sopra un basso seguente* op.16 (Venice, 1607) to describe the work's CONTINUO bass part, which was drawn from whichever part in the ensemble was the lowest at any one moment. In the third edition of *Cartella* (Venice, 1614 as *Cartella musicale*), Banchieri offered the term *barittono* as an equivalent, thereby pinpointing the wide range of such a bass part. The *Cartella* also suggests that a *basso seguente* part is by definition unbarred (? i.e. unbroken or *seguente*) and therefore less useful to an organist directing

an ensemble than a barred bass part or *bassi continui spartiti*. The use of the term in a restricted sense is essentially a theorist's, and such a composer as G. Piccioni does not appear to have intended any strict distinction between it and *basso continuo* when he published his *Concerti ecclesiastici* for voices *con il suo basso seguito* (Venice, 1610). However, the notion of a 'bass' line played by one or other continuo instrument and incorporating whatever notes or phrases in the ensemble happened to be lowest – for instance, the opening treble theme of a fugue – was one to live well into the second half of the 18th century, especially in Italian and italianate music. Theorists from Praetorius to Quantz and later generally called it the *bassetto* or *bassetgen* part, and it is one of the unsolved questions in figured bass playing – to know when composers no longer expected continuo players to double themes and answers in a fugal exposition.

PETER WILLIAMS/DAVID LEDBETTER

Bass tuba. *See* TUBA (i). The first instrument to be designated 'tuba', introduced in Germany in 1835, was called Bass-Tuba.

Bassus (medieval Lat.: 'low'). The lowest voice in a polyphonic composition. In the second half of the 15th century, as four-part writing became increasingly common, composers invented various designations for the lowest voice: *tenor secundus* (?Du Fay, *Missa 'Caput'*), *theumatenor* (Busnoys, *Regina caeli laetare*), *basistenor* (Busnoys, *Victimae paschali laudes*), *baritonans* (Gaffurius, *Practica musicae*, 1496) and *contratenor bassus* (extremely common in this period). *Basis*, the classical Latin word derived from Greek and meaning 'foundation', was used by various scholars (Glarean, *Dodecachordon*, 1547), while Ornithoparchus (*Musicae activae micrologus*, 1517) used both *basis* and *bassus*. The latter became the generally accepted term in the high Renaissance.

OWEN JANDER

Bass viol. A bowed string instrument. Although in modern usage the term refers to a six- or seven-string instrument of the VIOL family often called VIOLA DA GAMBA, in the 18th and 19th centuries in the USA and occasionally in Britain 'bass viol' meant a four-string instrument tuned in 5ths like a cello. It was probably a shortened version of the term 'bass violin'. Such instruments were of two kinds: the first like a cello except for certain local constructional details, the second of larger body size but with the same string length and fingerboard as a cello, with a short neck (accommodating playing only up to the second position without recourse to thumb positions). Instruments of both kinds were occasionally made with five strings, but no contemporary instruction book refers to the practice or indicates the tuning. The large-sized instruments are called 'church basses'. Certain archaisms in construction reflect earlier European building techniques, the commonest being an f-hole in which small connecting bridges of wood are left at the turns, a groove or channel routed in the wood of the back and belly into which the ribs were fitted and glued, and the use of a foot-like extension of the neck block (almost always integral with the neck itself) projecting into the body and fixed to the wood of the back by a butted glue joint and a screw. A peculiarly American feature is the use of plank-sawn wood in the belly and back, giving the instruments a curious florid appearance; but the best makers used quarter-sawn wood according to traditional European practice.

From the late 18th century up to the mid-19th there was an active American industry in the manufacture of these instruments, probably created partly by the demand for bass instruments to accompany the church choirs which had been relieved of their Puritan obligation to perform unaccompanied. By the 1830s there were makers specializing in the production of bass viols; over 35 are known to have been working in New England in this period. The earliest known maker was Crehore of Boston, who is reported to have made his first bass for a local music master in 1785; he made basses of both sizes. The most prominent and prolific was ABRAHAM PRESCOTT, who made his first instrument in 1809. The popularity of the instrument declined around the time of the Civil War, partly because the pipe or reed organ had superseded it in church music.

BIBLIOGRAPHY

F.R. Selch: 'Some Moravian Makers of Bowed Stringed Instruments', *JAMIS*, xix (1993), 38–64

FREDERICK R. SELCH

Bass violin (Fr. *basse de violon*; It. *basso viola da braccio, violone*). The bass of the violin family in the 16th and 17th centuries. It originally had three gut strings tuned *F–c–g*. By constructing large bass violins with a string length of about 74 cm, it became possible to obtain lower notes, and in the mid-16th century a fourth string was added at the bottom, producing the *Bb'–F–c–g* tuning found in many 16th- and 17th-century treatises. Such instruments were often pictured supported by a stool or resting on the ground. However, bass violins were also made small enough to be played standing or walking, supported, in the words of Jambe de Fer (1556), 'with a little hook in an iron ring, or other thing, which is attached to the back of the said instrument'. They were probably tuned *F–c–g–d'* (*PraetoriusSM*) or *G–d–a–e'* (Banchieri, 1609, 1611, 1628), though Zacconi (*Prattica di musica*, 1592) assigned *F–c–g–d'* to the tenor *viola da braccio* – the origin of the modern notion of the 'tenor violin'. The *violoncino*, called for in collections by G.B. Fontana (1641), Cavalli (*Musiche sacre*, 1656) and others, was presumably also a type of small bass violin, though the lowest notes written for it could only have been obtained by using strings that were thick and unwieldy.

This situation was changed by the invention of thin covered or wire-wound strings dense enough to produce good low notes with a short string length. Bonta has argued that covered strings were first developed in Bologna around 1660, and that they were exploited first on the violoncello, a small variant of the bass violin. Bolognese composers soon developed a solo repertory for the cello, and it rapidly superseded the bass violin in Italy, despite the fact that it lacked the weight of tone of the larger instrument. For this reason, it became necessary to double violoncellos at the octave in orchestras, producing the standard bass scoring of later times.

Italian cellists popularized their instrument in northern Europe in the years around 1700, though the bass violin remained in use in London and Paris until the second decade of the 18th century. According to the *Privilège ... pour l'Académie Royale ... pour l'année 1712–13*, two *basses de violon* were played in the *petit choeur* and eight *basses* in the *grand choeur*, and despite contemporary references describing the *basse de violon* as a crude instrument strung with thick strings that did not speak easily, Saint-Lambert listed it as a continuo string bass. Although the *basse de violon* was probably never used as a solo instrument, Theobaldo di Gatti (*c*1650–1727) became a virtuoso on it. Large bass violins were often subsequently cut down to serve as cellos, and relatively few survive in original condition.

For further discussion of terminology for bass instruments of the violin family *see* VIOLONCELLO and VIOLONE; *see also* VIOL.

BIBLIOGRAPHY

BoydenH

M. Corrette: *Méthode ... pour appendre ... le violoncelle* (Paris, 1741, 2/1783)

D. Boyden: 'The Tenor Violin: Myth, Mystery, or Misnomer?', *Festschrift Otto Erich Deutsch*, ed. W. Gerstenberg, J. La Rue and W. Rehm (Kassel, 1963), 273–9

S. Milliot: 'Réflexions et recherches sur la viole de gambe et le violoncelle en France', *RMFC*, iv (1964), 179–238

D. Abbott and E.Segerman: 'Strings in the 16th and 17th Centuries', *GSJ*, xxvii (1974), 48–73

S. Bonta: 'Further Thoughts on the History of Strings', *The Catgut Acoustical Society Newsletter*, xxvi, Nov (1976), 21–6

S. Bonta: 'From Violone to Violoncello: a Question of Strings?', *JAMIS*, iii (1977), 64–99

S. Bonta: 'Terminology for the Bass Violin in Seventeenth-Century Italy', *JAMIS*, iv (1978), 5–42

M. Cyr: '*Basses* and *Basse Continue* in the Orchestra of the Paris Opéra, 1700–1764', *EMc*, x (1982), 155–70

S. Bonta: 'Corelli's Heritage: the Early Bass Violin in Italy', *Studi Corelliani*, iv (1990), 217–31

J. de La Gorce: 'L'orchestre de l'Opéra et son évolution de Campra à Rameau', *RdM*, lxxvi (1990), 23–43

P. Holman: *Four and Twenty Fiddlers: the Violin at the English Court 1540–1690* (Oxford, 1993, 2/1995)

LUCY ROBINSON, PETER HOLMAN

Bastaini, Vincentio. See BASTINI, VINCENTIO.

Bastard [Bastart], **Jean** (*fl* 1536–52). French composer. He succeeded Jean le Bouteillier as *maître des enfants* at the Ste Chapelle, Bourges, between 1 April 1536 and 13 February 1552. In *Le temple de chasteté* (Paris, 1549, f.6v) François Habert praised him as a musician and a poet. Two of his four-part chansons were printed in anthologies in Paris: *Soyez seur que la repentence* (ed. in RRMR, xxxviii, 1981; RISM 1547[12]) and *Si ton plus grand désir* in 1550 (RISM 1550[7]). The five-voice motet *Ambulans Jesus juxta mare Galileae* was published with ascription to 'Bastart' in a German collection of works by internationally famous composers (RISM 1550[2]).

BIBLIOGRAPHY

F. Lesure: 'Some Minor French Composers of the 16th Century', *Aspects of Medieval and Renaissance Music: a Birthday Offering to Gustave Reese*, ed. J. LaRue and others (New York, 1966/R), 538–44

FRANK DOBBINS

Bastiaans, Johannes Gijsbertus (*b* Wilp, nr Deventer, 31 Oct 1812; *d* Haarlem, 16 Feb 1875). Dutch organist, composer and theorist. After early musical studies in Deventer, he moved in 1832 to Rotterdam as a watch-maker. There he studied counterpoint with C.F. Hommert (1834–6), becoming acquainted with the '48'; in 1836 he attended J.C.F. Schneider's Musikschule in Dessau. In Leipzig in 1837–8 he took composition lessons from Mendelssohn, studied the organ and hymnology with C.F. Becker and played the double bass in the orchestra of the Musikverein Euterpe.

After Bastiaans's return to the Netherlands in 1838, some of his compositions attracted the attention of the Maatschappij tot Bevordering der Toonkunst. He was organist of the Zuiderkerk in Amsterdam (1840–58), and played the double bass in several orchestras. From 1842 to 1844 he also taught singing at the Institute for the Blind. He founded his own music theory school in 1850, adding organ lessons to the curriculum the next year; in 1853 these courses were integrated in the new music school of the Amsterdam section of Toonkunst. In 1858 Bastiaans settled in Haarlem, where he was appointed city organist and carillonneur and played on the celebrated Christian Müller organ of the Grote Kerk until his death. An acknowledged authority on the organ, he was often asked to examine newly built instruments, and in 1867 he studied pneumatic mechanics in Paris. He published several books of harmonized chorales for the Dutch Reformed Church and wrote for the monthly *Caecilia* from 1855. As a hymnologist he was on the board of the Nederlandsche Koraalvereeniging from 1864 and adviser for the Vereeniging voor Nederlandsche Muziekgeschiedenis from 1869.

Bastiaans's main importance lies in his propagation of the music of J.S. Bach in the Netherlands. In 1850 he founded a Bach society in Amsterdam and gave a Bach recital in the Westerkerk. He was a co-founder of the Bach Society in Haarlem (1867) and the national Algemeene Bachvereeniging in Rotterdam (1870). Both Bastiaans and J.A. van Eijken featured Bach's organ works in their programmes, and the Bach societies and Toonkunst began to perform his chamber and vocal music. Bastiaans also set about removing vocal items from organ concerts, evidence of a purist tendency that may be seen in his own four-part chorale harmonizations. These consist almost entirely of simple triads, in his opinion more fitting for church use than the 'worldly' 7th chords, which were best reserved for chorale preludes; in this he was influenced by Renaissance chorale settings, to which Becker had introduced him. He advocated the formation of choirs in the Reformed churches, to perform his chorales in alternation with the congregational singing. His treatise on harmony also stresses the supremacy of the triad in a manner that owes much to the theories of Moritz Hauptmann. Bastiaans's compositions reveal an indebtedness to Bach filtered through the influence of Mendelssohn and A.F. Hesse, though with more chromatic harmony. After 1850 his works became more sober in style.

WORKS
(selective list)

printed works published in Amsterdam unless otherwise stated

most MSS in NL-At

Org: 6 orgelstukken, 1838 (1841), 2 repr. (Hilversum, 1978); Variations on Ps lxxxiv, 1841, ed. (1984); 4 sonatas, 1847–56; Fantasie-sonate Wien Neêrlands bloed, 1849, ed. J. ten Bokum (1967); Variations on Ps xxiv, 1866, ed. (1982); preludes, fughettas, fugues, fantasias

Pf: 6 liederen zonder woorden, op.4, 1839–40 (1843–66); introduction and arr. of ricercare from J.S. Bach: Musikalisches Opfer

Chbr: Harmonie der Spheren, fuga canonica a 4, 1850; Melodisch offer aan den geest van J.S. Bach, vn, vc, hmn, pf

Choral: motet, SATB, 1838; 4 cants., 5 choruses male vv, 10 choruses children's vv, 1845–51

Chorale bks (all SATB): 12 koraalgezangen, acc. pf ad lib., op.6 (1843); Vierstemmig koraalboek, acc. org/pf (Arnhem, 1852); Vierstemmig psalmboek, acc. org/pf (1855); Rhythmische koralen (1869); Vervolgbundel op de Evangelische gezangen, acc. org (Haarlem, 1870), 7 repr. (Hilversum, 1978)

WRITINGS
De zangkunst (Amsterdam, 1864)
Harmonia (Rotterdam, 1867)

BIBLIOGRAPHY
J.G.A. ten Bokum: *Johannes Gijsbertus Bastiaans (1812–1875)* (Utrecht, 1971) [with Eng. summary and full list of works]
H. van Nieuwkoop: *Haarlemse orgelkunst van 1400 tot heden: orgels, organisten en orgelgebruik in de Grote of St.- Bavokerk te Haarlem* (Utrecht, 1988), 244–63, 412–18

JAN TEN BOKUM

Bastianelli, Giannotto (*b* San Domenico di Fiesole, Florence, 20 June 1883; *d* Tunis, 22 Sept 1927). Italian critic, composer and pianist. Largely self-taught, he became music critic of the newspapers *La nazione* (Florence) from 1915 to 1918 and *Il resto del Carlino* (Bologna) during 1919–23. He also taught composition and music history at the Nuova Scuola di Musica, Florence (1917). From 1909 to 1915 he regularly contributed to the influential Florentine cultural periodical *La voce*. His books, notably *La crisi musicale europea* (1912) in which he explored in depth the idea of decadence, are among the most thought-provoking written by any Italian musician of the time; and he had a knowledge and understanding of current trends (Skryabin, Schoenberg, etc.) which was then rare. His ideas exerted an important influence on progressive Italian musical opinion, and particularly on other composers: in 1911 he was the chief spokesman for a short-lived pressure group known as La Lega dei Cinque or 'I "Cinque" Italiani', whose other members were Pizzetti, G. F. Malipiero, Respighi and Renzo Bossi. Bastianelli's propaganda advocated 'the *risorgimento* of Italian music ... which from the end of the golden 18th century till today has been, with very few exceptions, depressed and circumscribed by commercialism and philistinism' (Bastianelli, 1911). Parallels have been drawn between his philosophical ideas and those of some of the literary contributors to *La voce*, who showed a similar spirit of restless search and of a moral commitment more deeply felt than systematic. At the end of his life he turned increasingly towards the ideal of a new classicism, as his posthumous book *Il nuovo dio della musica* reveals clearly. Bastianelli was an imaginative but usually rather undisciplined composer; and he wrote very little music after his early 30s. This was regrettable, for such works as *Sul Bisarno* (1914) seem to presage a new assurance without losing the wayward evocativeness, sometimes strangely Slavonic in character, found in all his best pieces; while *Natura morta* (written in memory of Skryabin and clearly influenced by that composer's later music) and *Umoresca* both show a continuing search for new musical means. He committed suicide.

WORKS
(selective list)

unpublished unless otherwise stated

Stage: La scala (opera, Bastianelli), after 1918, inc., ?lost; ballet, inc., existence uncertain

Chbr: Poema, str qt, *c*1910; Pf Qt, *c*1910; Sonata, vn, pf, 1912 (1914); Sul Bisarno, 2 vn, pf, 1914; Sonata, vc, pf, 1920

Pf: Sonatas nos.1–2, 1907–8 (1910), no.3, begun 1907 (1914), no.4, inc., no.5, formed in 1917 from Umoresca and Natura morta; Piccola suite fiorentina, 1912; Conc., 2 pf, 1912–13; Umoresca (Burlesca), ?*c*1913; Natura morta, ?1915, pubd in *Paragone* (Florence, 1972), no.270, pp.25–37; Suite in omaggio alle maschere italiane, 1920

Self-published works printed by Mignani (in periodical *Dissonanza*, Florence, 1914), Officina Grafica per l'Incisione e Stampa della Musica (Florence)

For fuller lists see De Angelis (1970–71), iii, 153–4 and De Angelis: 'Sintesi …' (1971)

WRITINGS

Pietro Mascagni (Naples, 1910)
'I "cinque" italiani', *Nuova musica*, xvi (Florence, 1911), 71–2
'Per un nuovo risorgimento', *Le Cronache letterarie*, no.63 (1911), 3
La crisi musicale europea (Pistoia, 1912, 2/1976)
Musicisti d'oggi e di ieri (Milan, 1914)
Il Parsifal di Wagner (Florence, 1914)
L'opera e altri saggi di teoria musicale (Florence, 1921)
Il nuovo dio della musica, begun 1925, ed. M. de Angelis (Turin, 1978)
ed. M. Omodeo Donadoni: *La musica pura commentari musicali e altri scritti* (Florence, 1974)

For full list see De Angelis (1970–71), iii, 156–74

BIBLIOGRAPHY

DEUMM (M. de Angelis)
I. Pizzetti: 'La musica di Giannotto Bastianelli', *Nuova musica*, xvii (1912), 36
R. Franchi: 'Giannotto Bastianelli, in memoriam', *Solaria*, ii/7–10 (1927), 35–40
L. Parigi: 'Giannotto Bastianelli', *Il pianoforte*, viii (Turin, 1927), 344–6
D. Petrini: 'L'opera nel pensiero di Giannotto Bastianelli', *RaM*, ii (1929), 137–44
E. Cecchi: 'Fiorentini del primo Novecento', *Nuova antologia*, cc (1955), 439–50
L. Ronga: *L'esperienza storica della musica* (Bari, 1960), 52, 55–7
L. Pestalozza: Introduction, *RaM: antologia* (Milan, 1966)
M. de Angelis: *Giannotto Bastianelli nella vita musicale e nella cultura del suo tempo* (diss., U. of Florence, 1970–71) [incl. fuller bibliography, iii, 175–82]
M. Omodeo Donadoni: 'Scritti inediti di Giannotto Bastianelli', *NRMI*, v (1971), 469–81
Chigiana, xxviii (1971) [special number incl. discussion by M. Mila, F. d'Amico, L. Pinzauti and L. Baldacci chaired by L. Alberti; essays by L. Alberti, G. Prezzolini, M. Omodeo Donadoni and M. de Angelis: 'Introduzione a uno studio critico sul *Nuovo dio della musica*', 105–22 and 'Sintesi cronologica della vita di Giannotto Bastianelli', 123–8; and writings by Bastianelli, ed. M. Omodeo Donadoni]
M. de Angelis: 'Giannotto Bastianelli e la critica italiana nel primo Novecento', *Spettatore musicale*, vii/1 (1972), 28–35
M. de Angelis: 'Componenti metodologiche nella critica italiana del primo Novecento', *Spettatore musicale*, vii/6 (1972), 26
M. Omodeo Donadoni: 'Bastianelli e Scriabin', *Paragone* (Florence, 1972), no.270, pp.4–7
M. de Angelis: 'Contro il "grazioso" in musica: note e documenti sul futurismo fiorentino', *Il ponte*, xxix (Florence, 1973), 109–16
L. Baldacci: 'La mente critica di Giannotto Bastianelli', *Libretti d'opera e altri saggi* (Florence, 1974), 130–47
M. de Angelis: 'Note sul melodramma, la musica pura e l'Europa in Giannotto Bastianelli', *Musica italiana del primo Novecento: Florence 1980*, 261–77
F. Nicolodi: *Musica italiana del primo Novecento: la generazione dell'80*, Palazzo Strozzi, 9 May–14 June 1980 (Florence, 1980) [exhibition catalogue]
M. de Angelis: 'Giannotto Bastianelli, ultimo acto (1925–1927)', *Antologia vieusseux*, nos. 73–4 (Florence, 1984), 22–54
F. Nicolodi: *Musica e musicisti nel ventennio fascista* (Fiesole, 1984), esp. 127–30
M. Donadoni Omedeo: *Giannotto Bastianelli: lettere e documenti editi e inediti (1883–1915)* (Florence, 1989)
M. de Angelis, ed.: *Giannotto Bastianelli: gli scherzi di Saturno, carteggio 1907–1927* (Lucca, 1992)

JOHN C.G. WATERHOUSE

Bastianini, Ettore (*b* Siena, 24 Sept 1922; *d* Sirmione, 25 Jan 1967). Italian baritone. He studied with Flamio Contini in Florence and made his début in 1945, as a bass, singing Colline at Ravenna. He also sang Tiresias (*Oedipus rex*) at La Scala in 1948. After further study he made a second début in 1951, as a baritone, at Bologna as Germont. In 1953 he sang Andrey in the Western première of *War and Peace* at Florence and made his Metropolitan début as Germont, later singing Gérard, Marcello, Posa, Enrico Ashton, Scarpia and Amonasro. He returned to La Scala in 1954 as Yevgeny Onegin and continued to sing there until 1964. His only Covent Garden appearance was in 1962 as Renato. He was specially distinguished in Verdi roles, many of which he recorded; he sang Posa and Luna in Vienna and Salzburg under Karajan. At the peak of his short career his voice was rich and warm, his phrasing both musical and aristocratic.

BIBLIOGRAPHY
GV (F. Serpa; R. Vegeto)

HAROLD ROSENTHAL/R

Bastin, Jules (*b* Brussels, 18 March 1933; *d* Brussels, 2 Dec 1996). Belgian bass. He studied in Brussels, making his début there at La Monnaie in 1960 as Charon in Monteverdi's *Orfeo*. He sang throughout Europe and in North and South America, in a repertory ranging from Rameau's *Hippolyte et Aricie*, through Mozart (notably Osmin and Dr Bartolo) and Rossini, to roles such as Titurel, Varlaam, Graumann (*Der ferne Klang*), Würfl (*The Excursions of Mr Brouček*), the King of Clubs and the Cook (*The Love for Three Oranges*) and the Theatre Director and the Banker (*Lulu*). In 1993 he took part in the first performance of Debussy's *Rodrigue et Chimène* at Lyons.

Bastin's ample, sonorous voice, jovial presence and gift for comedy made him a memorable Baron Ochs; but he was perhaps at his finest in French repertory, as can be heard in his vivid recordings of such roles as Méphistophélès (*La damnation de Faust*), Balducci (*Benvenuto Cellini*), Somarone (*Béatrice et Bénédict*) and Pandolfe (*Cendrillon*).

ELIZABETH FORBES

Bastini [Bastaini], **Vincentio** [Vincenzo di Pasquino] (*b* Lucca, *c*1529; *d* Lucca, 1591). Italian cornettist and composer. He appears to have spent his entire life in Lucca, employed by the city as a cornettist; many other members of his family were similarly employed in the 16th and 17th centuries. His service began on 27 December 1543, when he was engaged at a monthly salary of three scudi. At the same time four other players were taken on at much higher salaries: Bastini was probably paid less because he was both young and local (the accounts show a consistent tendency to pay more to musicians from outside Lucca). He published two books of madrigals, the *Primo libro de madrigali a cinque et a sei voci* (Venice, 1567) and *Secondo libro de madrigali a cinque et a sei voci* (Venice, 1578, inc.). They contain respectively 29 and 34 pieces; the first volume also includes four- and seven-part pieces, the second an eight-part dialogue for two four-part choirs, as well as pieces for four voices. In his choice of texts Bastini exhibited a highly developed taste for Petrarch: the first book includes a complete setting of the sestina *L'aer gravato*, the second book the 11-stanza canzone *Vergine bella*, likewise set complete.

BIBLIOGRAPHY
*Einstein*IM; *Nerici*S
D.A. Cerù: *Cenni storici dell'insegnamento della musica in Lucca* (Lucca, 1871), 103

PATRICIA ANN MYERS

Baston, John (*fl* 1708–39). English composer, recorder player and cellist. From 1708 to 1714 he and his brother Thomas (*fl* 1708–27), a violinist and probably also a recorder player, played in concerts at Stationers' Hall and Coachmakers' Hall, London, and at Greenwich. When the Lincoln's Inn Fields Theatre opened in 1714, they probably became members of its orchestra; they performed there regularly in the interval 'entertainments', often in Baston's own recorder concertos, which have prominent solo violin parts. By 1722 he had moved to the rival Drury Lane Theatre, where he played in the interval music (and occasionally within the plays) until 1733, always in a concerto or solo for the 'little flute' (recorder); the concertos are twice named in advertisements as being by Dieupart and Robert Woodcock. In 1727 he (cello) and his brother (violin) were among the orchestra that played in the Lord Mayor's Day Royal Entertainments. Baston was one of the original subscribers to the Society of Musicians in 1739.

His *Six Concertos in Six Parts for Violins and Flutes, viz. a Fifth, Sixth and Consort Flute* (London, 1729) are all showpieces for the soloist, who in nos.1 and 3 has a part for the normal treble recorder, in nos.2, 4 and 5 for the sixth flute (descant recorder in d″), and in no.6 for a fifth flute (descant recorder). Years of theatre experience showed Baston how to write lively, robust opening themes by balancing short phrases; they are, however, melodically undistinguished. The fast movements mostly provide busy chord-pattern work for the solo line, the simple harmonic style being unrelieved by any contrapuntal interest. Nos.3 and 6 (fast–slow) and 4 (slow–fast) have only two movements each; the others follow the Venetian three-movement model.

BIBLIOGRAPHY

BDA; HawkinsH; LS

D. Lasocki: *Professional Recorder Players in England, 1540–1740* (diss., U. of Iowa, 1983)

D. Burrows: 'Handel's London Theatre Orchestra', *EMc*, xiii (1985), 349–57

OWAIN EDWARDS/DAVID LASOCKI

Baston, Josquin (*fl* 1542–63). ?Netherlandish composer. He probably worked in the Netherlands, as some of his earliest works were published by Phalèse and Susato, and some of his songs have Dutch texts. An elegy for Johannes Lupi was attributed to him, apparently without grounds, by Van Maldeghem (Trésor musical, *Musique profane*, xii, Brussels, 1876); if the ascription is correct it may indicate that he was Lupi's pupil. He may be the musician named Johann (or Josquin) Baston (Basten or Paston) who was active at the courts of Austria, Denmark, Poland, Saxony and Sweden in the mid-16th century. He used a wide range of contrapuntal techniques in his chansons; his motets show features of the declamatory style that came into fashion in the mid-16th century.

WORKS

12 Lat. motets, 4–6vv, 1542[7], 1545[2], 1549[8], 1553[10], 1553[12], 1553[15], 1555[5], 1556[6], 1557[3], 1563[3], Novi prorus et elegantis libri musici in quo continentur ... motecta ... latinae, 4–6vv (Düsseldorf, 1561), lost

29 chansons, 3–6vv, 1543[15], 1543[16], 1544[12], 1544[13], 1545[16], 1549[29], 1550[13], 1552[8], 1552[10], 1552[12], 1552[13], 1552[14], 1552[15], 1553[24], 1553[25], 1554[22], 1556[17], 1562[3]

6 Dutch songs, 4vv, 1551[18], 1551[19]

3 motets; chanson, 3vv: *B-LVu, D-Mbs, NL-Lml*

BIBLIOGRAPHY

BNB (C.L. de Burbure); *EitnerQ*; *FétisB*; *MGG1* (A. Dunning)

D. von Bartha: 'Probleme der Chansongeschichte im 16. Jahrhundert', *ZMw*, xiii (1930–31), 507–30

R.B. Lenaerts: Foreword to *Het Nederlands polifonies lied in de zestiende eeuw* (Mechelen and Amsterdam, 1933)

U. Meissner: *Der Antwerpener Notendrucker Tylman Susato* (Berlin, 1967)

E. Zwolinska: 'Joannes Baston: flämischer *compositor cantus* am Hofe des Jagiellonen-Königs Zygmunt August', *From Ciconia to Sweelinck: donum natalicium Willem Elders*, ed. A. Clement and E. Jas (Amsterdam, 1994), 215–19

ALBERT DUNNING

Bastos, Rafael José de Menezes (*b* Salvador, Bahia, 26 Dec 1945). Brazilian ethnomusicologist. He took the BA in music (1968) and the MA in social anthropology (1976) at the University of Brasília, and completed the doctorate in human sciences (social anthropology) at the University of São Paulo (1990). His research work for his graduate studies was carried out in the High Xingu Indian reservation and dealt with the musical culture of the Kamayurá Indians. His doctoral dissertation, *A festa da Jaguatirica: uma partitura crítico-interpretativa*, deals with the complex relationship of Kamayurá music and ritual. He has been an adjunct professor of anthropology at the Federal University of Santa Catarina, teaching and researching the ethnology and ethnomusicology of South American lowland Indian cultures. He is a researcher for the Federal National Council for Research, coordinating various projects on music, culture and society, and a member of the Committee on Indigenous Affairs of the Brazilian Anthropological Association. From 1992 to 1994 he was a post-doctoral visiting scholar in anthropology at MIT, working on the project Musical Cognition and Structure: the Case of the Yawari of the Kamayurá Indians of Central Brazil, and he also worked at the Smithsonian Institution in 1994 as a research fellow. He has served in various professional national and international organizations, such as the Associação Brasileira de Antropologia, the Centro de Aperfeiçoamento do Pessoal de Nível Superior and the ICTM. Bastos has published extensively in the area of Brazilian Indian ethnomusicology and on Brazilian popular music. His scholarly approach is holistic and integrative.

WRITINGS

'Las músicas tradicionales de Brasil', *RMC*, no.125 (1974), 21–77

'Situación del músico en la sociedad', *América Latina en su música*, ed. I. Aretz (Mexico City, 1977), 103–38

A musicológica Kamayurá: para uma antropologia da comunicação no Alto-Xingu (Brasília, 1978)

'Manipulação étnica e música entre os Indios Kiriri de Mirandela, Estado da Bahia, Brasil', *Portugal e o mundo: Lisbon 1986*, 495–506

'Esboço de uma teoria da música: para além de uma antropologia sem música e de uma musicologia sem homem', *Anuário antropológico*, no.93 (1995), 9–73

'Indagação sobre os Kamayurá, o Alto-Xingu e outros nomes e coisas: uma etnologia da sociedade Xinguara', *Anuário antropológico*, no.94 (1995), 227–69

'A origem do samba como invenção do Brasil: sobre o feitio do oração de Vadico e Noel Rosa (por que as canções têm música?)', *Cadernos de estudo de análise musical*, nos.8–9 (1995–6), 1–29

'Musicalidade e ambientalismo na redescoberta do Eldorado e do Caraíba: uma antropologia do encontro Raoni-Sting', *Revista de antropologia*, xxxix/1 (1996), 145–89

'Música nas Terras Baixas da América do Sul: ensaio a partir da escuta de um disco de Mésica Xikrín', *Anuário antropológico*, no.95 (1996), 251–63

'Ritual music of the Kayapó-Xikrin, Brazil', *Yearbook for Traditional Music*, xxviii (1996), 231–2

'O estrangeiro: em torno da "Farra do Boi"', *Plural*, no.9 (1997), 86–9

'Music in Lowland South America: a Review Essay', *World of Music*, xxxix (1997), 143–51

GERARD BÉHAGUE

Baszny [Baschny], **Józef** (*d* Lemberg [now L'viv], after 1862). Polish composer, teacher and flautist, probably of Czech descent. He was choirmaster at Lemberg Cathedral, and from 1838 to 1844 vice-director of the music society in Lemberg. Later he taught singing and the flute in Kiev. He composed a three-act vaudeville *Skalmierzanki*, to a libretto by J.N. Kamiński (1828, manuscript in *PL-Wn*), and three operas: *Syn i córka* ('Son and Daughter'), *Więzienie Jana Kazimierza we Francji* ('The Imprisonment of Jan Kazimierz in France') and *Twardowski na Krzemionkach*, a five-act comic opera to another libretto by Kamiński. He also wrote sacred music, including a setting of the *Salve regina* (Lemberg, 1858), and some piano works, notably *Collection de polonaises* (1826) and *L'aurora boreale* (Lemberg, 1839).

BIBLIOGRAPHY

SMP
R. Bohdan [K.Estreicher]: 'Raptularzyk podroźny' [Travel diary], *Ruch muzyczny* (1857), 319
K. Estreicher: 'Podróżnik raptowny' [Travel diary], *Ruch muzyczny* (1858), 244
'Towarzystwo muzyczne w Lwowie' [The music society in Lwów], *Ruch muzyczny* (1858), 161
A. Sowiński: *Les musiciens polonais et slaves* (Paris, 1857/*R*; Pol. trans., 1874/*R* as *Słownik muzyków polskich dawnych i nowoczesnych*)
K. Michałowski: *Opery polskie* (Kraków, 1954)

ELŻBIETA DZIĘBOWSKA

Bataille, Gabriel (*b* ?Brie, *c*1575; *d* Paris, 17 Dec 1630). French composer and lutenist. Allusions to Brie in his poetry suggest that he may have come from that province. When he married on 12 February 1600 he was already in Paris. He had not at first been a professional musician: in his marriage contract he stated that he was a clerk to Germain Regnault, a member of parliament. By 1608, however, when Pierre Ballard published the first volume of Bataille's *Airs de différents autheurs, mis en tablature de luth*, he was actively engaged in music. In 1614 he was listed as a *maître de musique*. From 1619 until his death he was a member of the musical establishment of the queen, alternating the directorship each half-year with Antoine Boësset. His close friendship with Ballard, who had launched his career in music, is further shown by his having been a godfather to one of Ballard's children. When he died, both his sons, Gabriel (*c*1614–76) and Pierre, were musicians in the service of the queen.

Bataille's importance lies largely in his arrangements for solo voice and lute of polyphonic *airs de cour* by some of the leading court composers. Between 1608 and 1615, with Ballard's assistance, he published a popular series of six collections of such *airs*, which was later continued by Antoine Boësset, the leading court composer of the next generation. Most of the *airs* were originally composed by Pierre Guédron. Bataille did not change the vocal line and kept the setting very simple. Many of the sacred poems in *La pieuse alouette* (Valenciennes, 1619–21) are to be sung to the music in his collections.

Bataille also wrote his own songs. He set as *musique mesurée* ten psalms of Desportes in *vers mesuré* but mostly composed secular *airs*. A few, such as *Bacchus droit*, are typical *chansons pour boire*. He originally composed others for *ballets de cour* – *Ballet du roi* (*c*1616), *La délivrance de Renaud* (1617), *Ballet de Monseigneur le Prince* (1620), *Ballet des favoris* (*c*1626) and *Ballet des proverbes* (*c*1626) – but he never gained an important enough position at court to be able to compose as often for this major genre as did Guédron and Boësset. The remainder of his songs are simple *airs*, for four voices alone, for one voice accompanied by lute or for one voice unaccompanied. *Depuis que le flambeau* (1618) is unusual in its chromaticism and *C'en est fait ma belle Amarante* (1614) in having several fast ornaments.

WORKS

Edition: *Airs de cour pour voix et luth (1607–43)*, ed. A. Verchaly (Paris, 1961) [incl. *9 airs* by Bataille]

Airs de différents autheurs, mis en tablature de luth par Gabriel Bataille (1608[10], 1609[13], 1611[10], 1613[9], 1614[8], 1615[11]: all *R*); ed. P. Warlock (London, 1926)
15 airs, 4vv, 1613[8]
34 airs, 1v: 21 in 1615[12], 5 in 1617[9], 1 in 1619[10], 3 in 1620[11], 4 in 1626[11]
9 airs, 1v, lute: 5 in 1617[8]/*R*, 1 in 1618[9]/*R*, 3 in 1620[11]/*R*

BIBLIOGRAPHY

LabordeMP
A. Verchaly: 'Gabriel Bataille et son oeuvre personnelle pour chant et luth', *RdM*, xxvi (1947), 1–24, 72–88
M. Jurgens: *Documents du minutier central concernant l'histoire de la musique, 1600–1650* (Paris, 1967–74)
D. Tunley: 'Ballard's Publications *Airs de differents autheurs* (1608–1632): Some Reflections', *MMA*, xv (1988), 100–13

JOHN H. BARON

Batardi, Antonio. *See* PATART, ANTONIO.

Batchelar [Batchilar], **Daniel.** *See* BACHELER, DANIEL.

Bate, Jennifer (*b* London, 11 Nov 1944). English organist. She studied the piano and organ with her father, H.A. Bate, and composition with Eric Thimann, and took a degree in music at Bristol University. She made her professional début in Birmingham Town Hall in 1967, her official London début in Westminster Abbey in 1969 and her Proms début, with music by Liszt, in 1974. In the same period she began to broadcast regularly for the BBC and developed an international career, with performances in several European countries and, in 1974, a tour of Australia, New Zealand and South America. She has subsequently performed frequently in duo recitals with the trumpeters Bram Wiggins and David Mason, and given concerts with the tenor Ian Partridge. Bate made her first recording, of works by Liszt, in 1977, and has since recorded prolifically, including the complete organ works of Messiaen (with whom she often performed), a series of 18th-century British music on organs of the period, and the complete organ music of Lennox Berkeley. She has taken part in many important London or British premières, among them Flor Peeters's Organ Concerto (1973), Fricker's Fifth Symphony (at the 1976 Proms), Panufnik's *Metasinfonia* (1984, making a subsequent première recording) and Messiaen's *Livre du saint sacrement* (1986, again followed by a première recording). In 1985 she gave the world première, in New York, of Peter Dickinson's Blue Rose Variations, a work dedicated to her. Bate has also acted as a consultant in organ restoration and construction, and has composed a number of works for the organ, all of which she has recorded.

RICHARD WIGMORE

Bate, Philip (Argall Turner) (*b* Glasgow, 26 March 1909; *d* London, 3 Nov 1999). British organologist. He was educated in Aberdeen, where his father was museum curator, and where he also took clarinet lessons. At the University of Aberdeen he studied pure science (BSc 1932) and did postgraduate research in geology. His main career was spent in the music department of the BBC, first as a balance and control assistant (1934–7), then as a studio manager and television producer (1937–9, 1946–56) and later (1956–68) in senior training positions. With the encouragement of Galpin he developed his interest in the history and physics of woodwind instruments and assembled an important collection of some 300 wind instruments and associated material which in 1968 he presented to the University of Oxford. The following year the Bate Collection of Historical Instruments was established at the Faculty of Music as a teaching assembly of historic instruments accessible to students. In 1946 he became founder-chairman and, from 1977 until his death, president of the Galpin Society. He was elected Fellow of the Society of Antiquaries in 1979. In 1988 he won the Curt Sachs Award of the American Musical Instrument Society. His main work was a valuable series of monographs on a wide range of wind instruments, together with entries for this dictionary. These have made him an acknowledged authority in the field.

WRITINGS

The Oboe: an Outline of its History, Development and Construction (London, 1956, 3/1975)

The Trumpet and Trombone: an Outline of their History, Development and Construction (London, 1966, 2/1972)

The Flute: a Study of its History, Development and Construction (London, 1969, 2/1979)

ed.: F.G. Rendall: *The Clarinet* (London, 3/1971)

'The Alex Murray Flute', *GSJ*, xxvi (1973), 47–54

'Spurious Marks on Brass', *GSJ*, xxvii (1974), 160

'A Serpent d'Englise I: Notes on Some Structural Details', *GSJ*, xxix (1976), 47–50

'Instruments for the Disabled', *GSJ*, xxix (1976), 124

'Horn Lore', *GSJ*, xxxi (1978), 150–51

'Some Further Notes on Serpent Technology', *GSJ*, xxxii (1979), 124–9

WILLIAM WATERHOUSE

Bate, Stanley (*b* Plymouth, 12 Dec 1911; *d* London, 19 Oct 1959). English composer and pianist. His musical talents were recognized early, and by 1931 he had composed two operas. Between 1932 and 1936 he studied at the RCM with Vaughan Williams, R.O. Morris, Gordon Jacob and Arthur Benjamin, one of his fellow students being Peggy Glanville-Hicks, whom he was later to marry. He won various prizes, went on to study with Boulanger in Paris and Hindemith in Berlin. Bate's Piano Concertino, first performed at the Eastbourne Festival in 1937, brought his name before a wider audience, and he became closely associated with the London stage, writing music for several plays and working as musical director for the ballet company Les Trois Arts at the Lyric Theatre, Hammersmith. As well as composing prolifically, Bate also made his name as a pianist, and in the early 1940s he toured Australia as a lecturer and soloist, before spending a few years in the USA, where his music was well received. He returned to London in 1949. He became depressed at the lack of recognition his music received in the UK, and this led to his suicide.

Performances of Bate's music have been rare since the première of the Third Symphony at the Cheltenham Festival in 1965. Despite its overt indebtedness to Hindemith, Vaughan Williams and Walton, the symphony is his finest work, notable especially for its orchestration. Bate was highly prolific, but his music, with a few exceptions, lacks enduring quality.

WORKS
(selective list)

DRAMATIC

Ops: The Forest Enchanted, 1928, staged Plymouth; All for the Queen, 1929–30, Plymouth, Globe, 30 Nov 1931

Ballets: Eros, 1935; Goyescas, 1937; Juanita (mime-ballet), 1938; Cap over Mill, op.27, 1939; Perseus, op.26, 1939; Dance Variations, op.49, 1944–6; Highland Fling, 1946; Troilus and Cressida, op.60, 1948

Incid music: Electra (Sophocles), 1938; Bodas de Sangre (F. García Lorca), *c*1938; The Cherry Orchard (A.P. Chekhov), *c*1938; Twelfth Night (W. Shakespeare), *c*1938; The White Guard, *c*1938; The Patriots (S. Kingsley), 1944

Music for films: The Fifth Year, 1944; Jean Helion, 1946; The Pleasure Garden, 1952–3; Light through the Ages, 1953

INSTRUMENTAL

Orch: Concertante, op.24, pf, str, 1936–8; Concertino, op.21, pf, chbr orch, 1937; Sym. no.2, op.20, 1937–9; Sinfonietta no.1, op.22, 1938; Pf Conc. no.2, C, op.28, 1940; Sym. no.3, op.29, 1940; Vn Conc. no.2, op.42, 1943; Sinfonietta no.2, op.39, 1944; Va Conc., op.46, 1944–6; Haneen, op.50, fl, gong, str, 1944; Pastorale, op.48a, military band, *c*1946; Vn Conc. no.3, op.58, 1947–50; Pf Conc. no.3, op.66, 1951–2; Conc. grosso, pf, str, 1952; Hpd Conc., 1952–5; Vc Conc., 1953; Sym. no.4, 1954–5; Pf Conc. no.4, *c*1955; Pf Conc. no.5, 1958

Chbr: Sonata, op.11, fl, pf, 1937; 5 Pieces, op.23, str qt, *c*1937; Sonatina, op.12, rec, pf, 1938; Str Qt no.2, op.41, 1942; Sonata no.1, op.47, vn, pf, 1946; Sonata, op.52, ob, pf, 1946; Fantasy, op.56, vc, pf, 1946–7; Recitative, op.52a, vc, pf, 1946–7; Pastorale, op.57, va, pf, *c*1947; Sonata no.2, vn, pf, 1950

Pf: 6 Pieces for an Infant Prodigy, op.13, *c*1938; 2 Sonatinas, op.19, 1939–41; Romance and Toccata, op.25, 1941; Sonatinas nos.3–9, opp.30–6, 1942–3; Ov. to a Russian War Relief Concert, op.37, 2 pf, *c*1943; 3 Pieces, op.38, 2 pf, 1943; Sonata no.1, op.45, 1943; Suite, op.44, 1943; 3 Mazurkas, op.38a, 1944; Sonata no.2, op.59, 1947; Sonata no.3, op.62, 1949; 17 Preludes, op.64, 1949; Prelude, Rondo and Toccata, 1953

VOCAL
for voice and piano unless otherwise stated

Incantations (E. Jolas), op.48, S/T, orch; 4 Songs (A.E. Housman), op.51, 1945; Pomes Penyeach (J. Joyce), op.53, 1946; 3 Songs (C. Day-Lewis, E. Sitwell, Joyce), op.55, 1946; 3 Songs (H. Belloc), op.61, 1947–8; 6 Songs (S. Smith), 1952

MSS in *GB-Lmic*, *Lbl*, *Lcm*

Principal publishers: Lengnick, Schott, AMP

BIBLIOGRAPHY

Obituary, *MT*, c (1959), 680

M. Barlow and R. Barnett: 'Stanley Bate: Forgotten International Composer', *British Music*, xiii (1991), 16–36

MICHAEL BARLOW

Bateman, Robert (*fl* 1609; *d* London, 11 Feb 1618). English composer. The details of his life which are known have all been deduced from his will. He was a member of the Company of Musicians and apparently played the violin and viol. Evidently a man of some means, Bateman bequeathed over £300 to relations and friends, with the residue of his estate going to his wife Joan. It is possible that he was one of the many Englishmen who worked for a time on the Continent, though no direct evidence for this has come to light. Works by him were published in Hamburg in 1609, 1617 and 1621, and it is interesting to note that his 'late servant Valentine Fludd', to whom he bequeathed 'his best treble violyn, his bass viall and his tenor', was engaged at the court of Brandenburg in Berlin in 1627. Bateman left two more violins to his servant

(?apprentice) John Bolles. He was buried in the church of St Alphage on 12 February 1618.

Bateman's music was certainly ideal for the troupes of English comedians and actors to use either at home or abroad; they may have been responsible for taking it to the Continent. All his surviving pieces are short dances, light in style and very attractive. Their concise, simple forms and textures show no originality or personal characteristics beyond a marked fondness for sequential repetition; in any case it cannot be assumed that Bateman was himself responsible for the five-part versions of his pieces published in Germany. A collection of masque music compiled by Sir Nicholas L'Estrange in the 1620s is the principal manuscript source for Bateman's music (*GB-Lbl* Add.10444), though only treble and bass are given.

WORKS

2 galliards, 5 viols/other insts, 1609[30]
Volta, Almain, Näglein Blumen, 5 viols/other insts, 1617[25] [the Almain is attributed to the London wait Stephen Thomas in *GB-Lbl* Add.10444]
Aria I, 4 insts, bc, 1621[19]; Aria 'The Cadua', *Lbl* Add.10444
3 two-part dances: Almain, C, Masque, a, Masque, g, *Lbl* Add.10444; Masque, g ('The Fates Masque') arr. for kbd, *US-NYp* Drexel 5612

ANDREW ASHBEE

Batement (Fr.). *See* ORNAMENTS, §7.

Bates, Django (Leon) (*b* Beckenham, 2 Oct 1960). English composer, keyboard player and tenor horn player. He studied at the RCM (1979) for only two weeks, then worked freelance in the early 1980s in bands led by the saxophonists Tim Whitehead and Dudu Pukwana; he also performed with Bill Bruford's Earthworks. He was a founder member in 1983 of the influential 21-piece big band Loose Tubes, which in 1987 became the first jazz ensemble to appear at the BBC Promenade Concerts. In 1991 he formed the jazz orchestra Delightful Precipice around his quartet Human Chain, initially to provide music for the Snapdragon Circus. In 1997, Human Chain joined with the Swedish vocalist Josefine Crønholm for *Quiet Nights*, commemorating the award to Bates of the Jazzpar Prize, Denmark.

Bates's prodigious talents have been reflected in resourceful reworkings of both contemporary and traditional jazz idioms: his compositions for Loose Tubes and Delightful Precipice, in particular, won acclaim for their unpredictable mixture of elements from sources as diverse as jazz, rock, Caribbean, ethnic and classical music. In the 1990s his output widened to include substantial concert works revealing the influence of pre-serial Stravinsky and American music, and characterized by considerable technical virtuosity, imaginative flair and sardonic humour; representative examples were recorded by the London Sinfonietta (*Good Evening . . . Here is the News*, 1996). The album *Quiet Nights* (1998), by the quintet of the same name, juxtaposed pop and jazz standards by Arlen, Ellington and Jobim with music by Bates featuring a sensitive application of electronic sonorities.

WORKS
(selective list)

Concert works: Tentle Morments, orch, 1989; Candles Still Flicker in Romania's Dark, orch, 1991; Three English Scenes: Good Evening . . . Here is the News, Abandoned Railway Station, Forms of Escape, orch, 1992; Bird Tableau (Feasibility Studies), 3 fl, 1999; Circus Umbilicus, ens, 1999; A Fine Frenzy, dance project, sax qt, 1999; The Gogmagogs (P. Barlow), ens, 1999; They Think It's All Over, kbd conc., 2000

BIBLIOGRAPHY
AND OTHER RESOURCES

GroveJ (D. Fairweather)
R. Cook: 'Django Bates: the Brilliant Spark', *The Wire*, no.32 (1986), 27 only
I. Carr: 'Django Bates', *Jazz: the Rough Guide*, ed. I. Carr and others (London, 1995), 39–40

RECORDINGS
Delightful Precipice (1986, Loose Tubes LTLP003)
Music for the Third Policeman (1988, AH UM003)
Open Letter (1988, Editions EG EGED 55)
summer fruits (and unrest) (1993, jmt 514008-2)
autumn fires (and green shoots) (1994, jmt 514014-2)
winter truce (and homes blaze) (1996, jmt 514023-2)
Like Life (1998, Storeyville 4221)
quiet nights (1998, Screwgun Sc 70007)

MERVYN COOKE

Bates, Joah (*b* Halifax, bap. 19 March 1741; *d* London, 8 June 1799). English organist and concert organizer. He studied music with Hartley, organist at Rochdale, and later, when he was at Manchester Grammar School, with John Wainwright, deputy organist of the collegiate church. A distinguished academic career took him to Eton (1756), where he studied with Edward Webb, and King's College, Cambridge, where he was elected a Fellow in 1770 and later appointed a tutor. He tutored the second son of John Montagu, 4th Earl of Sandwich, and is thought to have written a treatise on harmony about this time. Later he held various civil service posts, as commissioner of the Victualling Office, commissioner of the Customs and as director of various hospitals. He invested the whole of his and his wife's (*see* BATES, SARAH) fortunes in the Albion Mills project, and was nearly ruined when the mills were destroyed by fire in 1791.

Bates was a fierce champion of Baroque music and particularly of Handel's work in the face of strong competition in the form of the *galant* music of J.C. Bach's generation. In this he was inspired by his father, Henry Bates, who presented Handel festivals in Halifax with London singers during the 1760s. Joah Bates's enthusiasm was given substantial support when he was taken on as private secretary by the Earl of Sandwich, 1st Lord of the Admiralty, also an avid Handelian. Sandwich, Bates and Sir Watkin Williams Wynn were prime movers in establishing the Concert of Ancient (Antient) Music in 1776, of which Bates was the energetic director of music until he was succeeded by Greatorex in 1793. In company with Sir Watkin and Lord Fitzwilliam, Bates also planned the Westminster Abbey music festival in London to mark the centenary of Handel's birth. Miscalculation brought it forward a year to 1784, but it was a huge success and the commemoration concerts, which were held under the patronage of George III and involved all the leading singers and instrumentalists who could come (525 performers were named, and Burney gave a total of 828), were directed by Bates playing a harpsichord coupled to an organ by keys extending 'nineteen feet from the body of the organ, and twenty feet seven inches below the perpendicular of the set of keys by which it is usually played'.

BIBLIOGRAPHY

BDA; *BurneyH*; *DNB* (J.A. Fuller Maitland); *SainsburyD*
A Plain and True Narrative of the Differences Between Messrs. B–S and also Members of the Musical Club ... in Halifax (?London, 1767)
C. Burney: *An Account of the Musical Performances ... in Commemoration of Handel* (London, 1785/R)
Obituary, *Gentleman's Magazine*, lxix (London, 1799), 532–3

T. Busby: *Concert Room and Orchestra Anecdotes of Music and Musicians, Ancient and Modern* (London, 1825)

'Mr and Mrs Joah Bates, a Distinguished Amateur and a Notable Singer', *MT*, xlvi (1905), 13–20 [see also 'Batesiana', *MT*, xlvi (1905), 99]

B. Matthews: 'Joah Bates: a Remarkable Amateur', *MT*, cxxvi (1985), 749–51

W. Weber: *The Rise of Musical Classics in Eighteenth-Century England: a Study in Canon, Ritual and Ideology* (Oxford, 1992), 151–5, 169–71

OWAIN EDWARDS, WILLIAM WEBER

Bates [née Harrop], Sarah (*b* Lancs., *c*1755; *d* London, 11 Dec 1811). English singer, wife of JOAH BATES. She came from a poor family and worked in a factory in Halifax. As a girl she sang in choirs, and in 1772 was in the contingent of singers from the north at the Gloucester Music Meeting. She had the good fortune when singing at Halifax to attract the attention of Dr Howard of Leicester who is said to have introduced her to John Montagu, 4th Earl of Sandwich. She was able to devote herself to music in London, studying with Lord Sandwich's private secretary Joah Bates, whom in 1780 she married, and with Antonio Sacchini, then a popular singer. In the four years between her London début (in *Judas Maccabaeus*, Covent Garden, 14 February 1777) and her marriage she came to be in such demand as an oratorio soloist that she reputedly saved a dowry variously estimated between £6000 and £9000 (later lost when the Albion Mills burnt down in 1791). She was admired particularly for her sympathetic interpretation of Handel, and for many years was soloist at the Concert of Ancient Music which her husband directed. She was less apt to add extemporary embellishment than other singers, but her flexibility and control were effectively shown in expressive arias requiring depth of feeling. Some commentators felt they had heard nothing comparable since Mrs Cibber and considered her the finest soprano of her day, comparing her favourably with Mme Mara and Mrs Billington.

BIBLIOGRAPHY

BDA; *DNB* (J.A. Fuller Maitland)

R. Twining, ed.: *Recreations and Studies of a Country Clergyman of the 18th Century* (London, 1882)

'Mr and Mrs Joah Bates, a Distinguished Amateur and a Notable Singer', *MT*, xlvi (1905), 13–20 [see also 'Batesiana', *MT*, xlvi (1905), 99]

W. Weber: *The Rise of Musical Classics in Eighteenth-Century England* (Oxford, 1992)

OWAIN EDWARDS

Bates, Thomas (bur. Westminster, London, 18 Aug 1679). English viol player, teacher and composer. The earliest reference to Bates is by John Playford, who, in his *Musicall Banquet* (1651), listed him among the 'excellent and able Masters' of the voice and viol in London. Bates probably served the royalist cause during the Civil War: as 'Captain' Bates he petitioned unsuccessfully for a place among the vicars-choral at St Paul's Cathedral when the choir was reconstituted in 1660–61, stating that he had formerly been in the choir of St John's College, Oxford. He was sworn as one of Charles II's musicians on 19 June 1660, receiving two posts. One was as viol player and the other as teacher of the royal children, with salaries of £40 and £50 a year respectively. Bates also served as bass viol player in the Chapel Royal; a warrant dated 30 August 1662 orders him to attend on Sundays and holy days. In spite of this potential income, payments were sparse and records show that Bates faced continual financial

difficulties (*AshbeeR*, i, v, viii). He was admitted as a lay-vicar at Westminster Abbey on 23 June 1666, apparently serving until his death. Some time before February 1674 he married a widow, Abigail Hudgebut, perhaps mother of John, the publisher. They lived in the parish of St Margaret's, Westminster. Bates was buried in Westminster Abbey.

Playford included two ayres, three corants, two sarabands, a country dance, an almain and a jig by Bates in *Musick's Recreation on the Viol, Lyra-way* (1669). The manuscript *GB-Mp* MS BrM 832 has a saraband (attributed elsewhere to Simon Ives (ii)) and a corant by 'John Bates'. All these pieces are in tablature. A thematic index of Bates's music can be found in G. Dodd, ed.: *A Thematic Index of Music for Viols* (London, 1980–).

ANDREW ASHBEE

Bates, William [Jack Catch] (*fl* London *c*1750–*c*1780). English composer and singing teacher. In a court case in 1763, he was accused, probably unjustly, of attempting to sell his pupil, the singer Ann Catley, to Sir Francis Blake Delavel for immoral purposes. He wrote much music for the theatres and pleasure gardens of London and was evidently in considerable demand, judging by the number of his publications, though he was not mentioned by any contemporary writer on music. The quality of his works is generally mediocre, with much facile writing in parallel 3rds. They range in style from the Baroque idioms still present in the early Six Sonatas to the deliberate imitation of the Mannheim orchestral style in the overtures to *Pharnaces* and *The Theatrical Candidates*.

WORKS

all first performed and published in London

THEATRICAL

all published in vocal score unless otherwise stated

The Jovial Crew, or The Merry Beggars (revived ballad op, R. Brome), CG, 14 Feb 1760, fs (1760); revived as The Ladies' Frolick (J. Love), Drury Lane, 7 May 1770, collab. T.A. Arne (1770)

Pharnaces (Eng. op, T. Hull, after Lucchini), Drury Lane, 15 Feb 1765 (1765)

Flora, or Hob in the Well (revived ballad op, after J. Hippisley), CG, 25 April 1770 (1770)

The Gamester (burlesque, after E. Moore), Grotto-Gardens, 1771, lost

The Theatrical Candidates (prelude, D. Garrick), Drury Lane, 23 Sept 1775 (1775)

The Device, or The Marriage-Office (afterpiece, Richards), CG, 5 May 1777, lost

Second Thought is Best (afterpiece, J. Hough), Drury Lane, 30 March 1778, lost

1 song each for revivals of Theobald: The Rape of Proserpina (1763) and O'Hara: The Golden Pippin (1773)

VOCAL AND INSTRUMENTAL

Collections of songs for Ranelagh, Vauxhall and the Grotto-Gardens; single songs, glees, catches, canons: see RISM; also *GB-Lbl*, *US-Bp*

6 Sonatas, 2 vn, bc (*c*1750); 6 Concs. in 10 parts, op.2 (*c*1765); 12 Duets, 2 fl/vn (*c*1770); 18 Duettinos, 2 gui/hn/cl (*c*1770); 12 Duettos, 2 hn (*c*1775)

BIBLIOGRAPHY

BDA ('Catley, Ann'); *FiskeETM*; *LS*

Miss Ambross: *The Life and Memoirs of the Late Miss Ann Catley* (London, *c*1790)

PETER WARD JONES

Bateson, Thomas (*b* ?1570–75; *d* Dublin, March 1630). English composer. It is possible that he came from the Wirral of Cheshire; he may well have been born before 1575, since he evidently had a son in 1592. Bateson was appointed organist of Chester Cathedral in 1599, and the various payments made to him between 1601 and 1608 include one for 'mending the organs'. By 24 March 1609 he had moved to Christ Church Cathedral, Dublin, where he was organist and a vicar-choral. In 1612 (some sources give 1615) he received the BMus degree from Trinity College, Dublin, and was admitted MA in 1622. He made his will on 2 March 1630, and died a fortnight before the quarterly rent was due on his house (presumably this would have been payable on 25 March). On 30 April a new lease on his house was granted to his widow. Three of Bateson's children were baptized at Chester between 1603 and 1607.

Of Bateson's church music only one anthem survives. A service by him was sung at Chester until the early years of the 19th century, but this has since disappeared. He composed a madrigal for *The Triumphes of Oriana* (RISM 1601[16]), but it arrived too late for inclusion in that collection, appearing instead at the beginning of Bateson's own first madrigal volume (1604). In his madrigals Bateson shows himself to be an accomplished, if not a faultless, craftsman. His style is rooted in that of Morley, but he also reveals more serious intentions that bring his work closer to that of Wilbye. It may have been from the conclusions of certain of Weelkes's madrigals that Bateson caught the idea of using, in an imitative paragraph, the thematic point in augmentation in the bass as the determinant of the harmonic structure; like Weelkes, he used brief fragmented textures, especially for setting exclamations. Bateson's best madrigals in this first collection are those more elaborately scored ones in which the lyric permits passages of serious expression, and most of his five- and six-voice madrigals are of good quality. Two reset lyrics from Italian madrigal anthologies already published in England, while *Hark, heare you not*, entitled 'Orianaes farewell', is a posthumous tribute to Queen Elizabeth, with the Oriana refrain suitably rephrased.

Although there is a rather larger quantity of more serious verse in Bateson's second madrigal collection (1618), the passages of touching pathos that had provided many of the most striking moments in the earlier volume are in general less arresting than before. One piece, *If floods of teares*, is a viol-accompanied song recalling the pre-madrigalian English tradition. Of the lighter pieces in Bateson's second volume, some are prim and rather lifeless, but others, like *Camilla faire* and *Cupid in a bed of roses*, are admirable. Bateson's second collection confirms the impression given by his earlier volume of a good composer whose best work is distinctive without being in any way original.

WORKS

SACRED

Holie, Lord God allmightie, 7vv, *GB-Lbl, US-NYp*

SECULAR

The First Set of English Madrigales, 3–6vv (London, 1604); ed. in EM, xxi (1922, 2/1958)
The Second Set of Madrigales, 3–6vv/viols (London, 1618); ed. in EM, xxii (1922, 2/1960)

BIBLIOGRAPHY

J.C. Bridge: 'The Organists of Chester Cathedral', *Journal of the Chester and North Wales Architectural … Society* [Chester], xix/2 (1913), 63–124
E.H. Fellowes: *English Madrigal Verse, 1588–1632* (Oxford, 1920, enlarged 3/1967 by F.W. Sternfeld and D. Greer)
E.H. Fellowes: *The English Madrigal Composers* (Oxford, 1921, 2/1948/R)

DAVID BROWN

Bath. City in the county of Somerset, south-west England.

1. History. 2. Festival.

1. HISTORY.   The musical history of Bath goes back no further than the early 18th century when from about 1704 the celebrated 'Beau' Nash first established the city as a fashionable resort. Nash soon promoted a subscription for a band of five or six musicians who were paid a guinea a week and who at first played under some large trees in a grove until the physicians persuaded Nash to permit them to play in the Pump Room itself. Eventually the little band was enlarged to seven players whose engagement at two guineas a week covered performances at the Pump Room in the mornings and at balls in the Assembly Rooms in the evenings. As early as 1747 'breakfast' concerts were announced.

It was in Bath that William Croft died in 1727, and shortly before Handel died it was announced that he intended to visit Bath for his health, though in fact he was unable to do so. J.C. Smith, who was the son of Handel's amanuensis and who eventually inherited the greater part of Handel's manuscripts, lived in retirement there from 1774 until his death. The earliest musician of note to work in Bath was Thomas Chilcot, a competent composer and organist of Bath Abbey from 1728; he also organized concerts and introduced the music of Handel to Bath audiences, and he is the reputed teacher of Thomas Linley senior. Linley was the leading professional musician of his day in Bath and responsible for the regular series of subscription concerts until he undertook the London oratorios from 1774. All his six children were born in Bath, including Thomas Linley junior, who as a boy enjoyed the friendship of Mozart, and Elizabeth Ann, the famous singer who married Sheridan. William Herschel was organist of the Octagon Chapel from 1766 to 1782, a time when his astronomical pursuits were beginning to dominate his interests in music. Benjamin Milgrove, from at least the 1760s until his death in 1810, was precentor of the Countess of Huntingdon's Chapel, for which he published 16 hymns in 1769; he was also at one time a member of the Pump Room band. A knowledgeable amateur of music who settled in Bath in the 18th century was Henry Harington, a physician by profession who also enjoyed a reputation as a glee composer. He was associated with the beginnings of the Bath Catch Club and the Harmonic Society of Bath.

The famous male soprano Venanzio Rauzzini settled in Bath in about 1777 and joined with the violinist Franz Lamotte in managing the subscription concerts, which Lamotte appears to have continued in succession to Linley. Rauzzini took over sole responsibility in 1780. W.T. Parke in his *Musical Memoirs* stated that at these concerts he brought forward 'a succession of singers of the first eminence, at a subscription amounting to no more than about two shillings and ninepence per night, being less than a third of those at the concerts in London'. Parke implied that Rauzzini lost money by this, but was defeated by opposition when he sought to increase the subscription. Haydn, on his visit to Bath in 1794, stayed with Rauzzini, in celebration of whose dog 'Turk' he wrote a round. Michael Kelly in his *Reminiscences* described musical evenings in Bath at Rauzzini's private residence. In 1807 Rauzzini engaged the soprano Catalani, who was a favourite in the city during the next 20 years. Following Rauzzini's death in 1810 the flautist Andrew Ashe (*d* 1838) continued the subscription concerts.

Despite the decline of Bath as a fashionable resort in the 19th century, it remained an important treatment centre, and continued to attract international musicians until the end of the century and beyond. The 'Pump Room' orchestra grew slowly until it was disbanded in 1939. From 1822 to 1827 the subscription concerts were administered and conducted by Sir George Smart; his own copies of the programmes for nine of these concerts are now in the British Library. The French conductor Jullien directed many concerts in the city with his Grand Orchestra between 1845 and 1859. Paganini played three times in 1831–2, and the violinist Joachim, the cellist Piatti and Bottesini, the double-bass virtuoso, performed frequently in Bath during the last half of the century. Jenny Lind gave four acclaimed recitals between 1847 and 1862, while the period 1827–65 witnessed many concerts of music from Italian operas given by leading singers of days, including Malibran, Viardot-Garcia, Mario, Grisi, Pasta, Lablache, Tamburini, Rubini and Donzelli. Liszt played three times in Bath in September 1840, Charles Hallé gave frequent piano recitals between 1855 and 1894, Clara Schumann made six appearances between 1867 and 1873 and Hans von Bülow gave four piano recitals in the period 1874–80. Other pianists to appear in the city during the last quarter of the century incuded Anton Rubinstein, Paderewski, Rosenthal, D'Albert and Dohnányi.

John David Loder, writer of the well-known violin tutor, *General and Comprehensive Instruction Book for the Violin* (1814), was for a time (c1820–35) in business as a music publisher in Milsom Street, Bath. Andrew Loder, probably the uncle of John David Loder, published music from 4 Orange Grove, Bath, between about 1820 and 1826. Two distinguished organists were born in Bath – James Kendrick Pyne (*b* 1852, son of J.K. Pyne senior, organist of Bath Abbey, 1840–90) and T. Tertius Noble (*b* 1867).

The earliest Assembly Rooms in Bath, known as 'Simpson's Rooms', on the Terrace Walks, were opened in 1708 and burnt in 1820. In 1728 the New Assembly Rooms ('Wiltshire's Rooms') were opened on the opposite side of the Terrace Walks, and afterwards became the Bath Literary and Scientific Institution. For many years both were used for concerts, but were superseded when the present Assembly Rooms in Bennett Street (known as 'The Upper Rooms') were built in 1771.

2. FESTIVAL.   A series of international classical and jazz concerts, supplemented by occasional opera, dance, world music and non-musical events. It lasts for 17 days in May–June, and is organized by the Bath Festivals Trust with funds from Bath City Council, South West Arts, sponsors, charitable trusts and other donations. The Festivals Trust succeeded the former Festival Society in 1993, and is also responsible for other kinds of festival at different times of the year (literature, film etc.).

The 18th-century architecture of Bath's principal buildings, dating from its social heyday as a spa, has both influenced and circumscribed the nature of the music festival, which seeks to turn its surroundings to artistic advantage. The lack of any large auditorium other than Bath Abbey has led on occasion to additional concerts within the festival scheme in the neighbouring cities of Bristol and Wells.

The festival was instituted in 1948 as 'The Bath Assembly' under the artistic direction of Ian Hunter. It featured musicians of international repute in association with visiting orchestras and ensembles, in programmes almost entirely devoted to music of the 18th century. Thomas Beecham associated himself with the festival in 1955 (and conducted a production of Grétry's rarely heard *Zémire et Azor*), but mounting financial deficits forced a reconsideration of festival policy.

After being suspended in 1956–7, it was resumed on a broader musical basis under the management of Ian Hunter, at whose invitation Yehudi Menuhin became involved and was appointed artistic director from 1959. An orchestra Menuhin had formed in London to conduct for recording purposes became the Bath Festival Orchestra, and served as the nucleus for most of the concerts (it was renamed the Menuhin Festival Orchestra after his and Hunter's connection with Bath ceased in 1968). Michael Tippett was associated in 1969 and was the sole artistic director for five festivals, 1970–74, aiming to change the 18th-century bias to achieve a wider appeal and to focus attention on new music.

Tippett's successor was William Glock (1975–84), who in 1979 obtained Arts Council support to extend the festival from ten to 17 days, introduced more artists of international distinction and obtained festival commissions for new music to balance the concerts of early music he also favoured. William Mann was artistic director in 1984, and brought a strong Hungarian flavour to the programmes; he was succeeded by Amelia Freedman, who in successive years featured music from different European countries and from the USA in turn. She also incorporated jazz (which first appeared in the Menuhin era via John Dankworth) as a regular element in festival programmes.

After a year with two programme directors, Nicholas Kraemer and Jolyon Laycock, Tim Joss was appointed artistic director and chief executive in 1995, pursuing a programme policy that embraces early, 18th- and 19th-century and contemporary music, jazz, world and folk. The commitment to contemporary music and new commissions is being reaffirmed, and an education programme, linked to the main concert programme, has been set up.

BIBLIOGRAPHY

A. Barbeau: *Life and Letters at Bath in the Eighteenth Century* (London, 1904)
L. Melville: *Bath under Beau Nash and after* (London, 1907)
'Dotted Crotchet' [F.G. Edwards]: 'Bath: its Musical Associations', *MT*, xlix (1908), 695–704
C. Black: *The Linleys of Bath* (London, 1911)
WATKINS SHAW/FRANK BROWN (1), NOËL GOODWIN (2)

Bath, Hubert (*b* Barnstaple, 6 Nov 1883; *d* Harefield, 24 April 1945). English conductor and composer. He studied piano and composition at the RAM from 1901, winning the Goring Thomas Scholarship in 1904 for his opera *The Spanish Student*. Much of his work was for film and he is best remembered for *A Cornish Rhapsody*, his miniature piano concerto for the film *Love Story* (1944). For the concert hall he composed rousing marches, light concert suites and single genre movements. He was well known in the theatre and his other works include *The Visions of Hannele*, a symphonic poem based on incidental music for the stage. His operas, after Longfellow, Hardy, Gerald du Maurier and others, were less popular than the patriotic operetta *Young England*, written with Clutsam and Basil Hood, and first produced during World War I.

Bath's cantatas, especially *The Wedding of Shon Maclean* and *The Wake of O'Connor*, were taken up by choral societies all over Britain; mostly early compositions, they are no longer performed. His greatest popularity after *A Cornish Rhapsody* was to be found in his pioneering and original music for brass band contests: *Freedom*, first used in 1922, and *Honour and Glory* are technically testing and still played. Although he composed much of serious intent, it is Bath's lighter music that has endured.

WORKS
(selective list)

STAGE

The Spanish Student (op, after H.W. Longfellow), London, 1904; Young England (operetta, B. Hood), Birmingham, Prince of Wales, 20 Nov 1916 [musical collab. G.H. Clutsam]; Bubbles (op, 1, after A. Gregory: *Spreading the News*), Belfast, 1923; The Sire de Maletroit's Door (op, 1); The Three Strangers (op, 1, after T. Hardy), inc.; Trilby (op, 3, after G. du Maurier)

VOCAL

Cants: The Legend of Nerbudda, dramatic cant. (F.J. Fraser) 1908; The Wedding of Shon Maclean, a Scottish rhapsody (R. Buchanan), 1909 [for the Leeds Festival]; The Wake of O'Connor, an Irish rhapsody (Buchanan), 1913; The Jackdaw of Reims; Look at the Clock; The Men on the Line; Orpheus and the Sirens; Psyche's Departure

Many partsongs, solo songs and recitations with music

INSTRUMENTAL

Music for films, incl. The Thirty-Nine Steps, 1935 [musical collab. J. Beaver]; Rhodes of Africa, 1936; Love Story, 1944 [incl. A Cornish Rhapsody]

Orch: The Visions of Hannele, sym. poem, 1913, rev. 1920; African Suite, 1915; Devonia; Egyptian Suite; Norwegian Suite; Petite suite romantique; Pierrette by the Stream; Scenes from the Prophets; 2 Troubadour suites; Woodland Scenes

Many individual orch. movts., incl. Summer Nights, waltz, 1901; 2 Sea Pictures, 1909; Princess Mary, waltz, 1923; Midshipman Easy, ov.; 2 Japanese Sketches

Marches: Out of the Blue, 1931; Admirals All; Atlantic Charter; Empire Builders; The Nelson Touch

Brass band: Freedom, 1922; Honour and Glory, 1931

Org solos, incl. Toccatina, 1914; Heroic Prelude, 1928

Pf solos, incl. Coquette; Sonatina in F; Song of Autumn

BIBLIOGRAPHY

K. Shenton: 'From A to B: Kenneth Alford and Hubert Bath', *British Music*, xvii (1995), 49–60

P.L. Scowcroft: *British Light Music: a Personal Gallery of Twentieth-Century Composers* (London, 1997)

PHILIP L. SCOWCROFT

Bathe, William (*b* Dublin, 2 April 1564; *d* Madrid, 17 June 1614). Irish teacher and writer. He was the son of Judge John Bathe. Anthony Wood wrote that he studied at Oxford and constructed a 'harp of a new device' which he presented in 1584 to Queen Elizabeth, to whom he taught mnemonics. By January 1585 he was in the service of Sir John Perrott, and shortly afterwards took possession of family estates in Ireland, including Drumcondra Castle. In October 1591 he left England for Spain; in August 1595 he entered the novitiate at Tournai, and studied successively at Saint Omer and Padua, where he was ordained priest in the order of Jesuits in 1599. In 1601 he was attached to the papal nuncio at the Spanish court, and three years later was appointed director of the Irish college in Lisbon. In 1606 he settled in Salamanca, where he published a language tutor, the *Janua linguarum* (1611), which was subsequently translated into many languages.

Bathe's treatise on music is first listed in Maunsell's 1595 catalogue as an 'Introduction to the true arte of Musicke, wherein are set downe, exact and easie rules, with Arguments, and their Solutions, for such as seeke to knowe the reason of the truth, which Rules, be meanes, whereby any by his owne industrie, may shortly, easily, and regularly attaine to all such things, as to this Arte doe belong. by William Bathe, Student in Oxforde, Pr. by Abell Jeffes. 1584'. Arber recorded that in 1597 Jeffes made over the publication rights to Thomas East. No original of this, the first music textbook to appear in the English language, is known to exist, but a 17th-century manuscript copy is held in Aberdeen University; this formed the basis for an edition of the treatise (ed. C. Hill, Colorado Springs, CO, 1979). Bathe later produced a largely rewritten version under the title *A Briefe Introduction to the skill of Song: Concerning the practise, set forth by William Bathe, Gentleman. In which work is set downe X. sundry wayes of 2. parts in one upon the plainesong. Also a Table newly added of the comparisons of Cleves, how one followeth another for the naming of Notes: with other necessarie examples, to further the learner* (ed. B. Rainbow, Kilkenny, 1982). This undated revision, which has survived, is presumably that referred to in the registers of the Stationers' Company for 1596 (see Arber). In it the author roundly criticized current methods of music teaching, with their 'crabbed confused tedious rules', and claimed that using his own method he had 'in a month or less instructed a child about the age of eight years to sing … at the first sight'.

Although Hawkins devoted most of chapter 101 of his *General History* to a discussion of Bathe's two works, he failed to recognize their historic position in English musical literature and the important innovation that they contained. Cursory inspection suggests that both books are wholly traditional; however, more careful reading shows that while the gamut is described, Bathe immediately contrasts its complexities with a more straightforward method of assigning fixed names to the notes of a scale, using the syllables *ut*, *re*, *mi*, *fa*, *sol* and *la*. The system is shown in a simple diagram using the Mixolydian scale, but as Bathe did not elaborate further on his innovation, its essential significance was not emphasized. As a result Hawkins overlooked the books' central feature – the replacement of hexachordal solmization with a system of movable sol-fa – and later writers accepted his inaccurate account without challenge.

BIBLIOGRAPHY

DNB; *HawkinsH*

A. Maunsell: *The Seconde Parte of the Catalogue of English Printed Bookes* (London, 1595/R)

A. Wood: *Athenae oxonienses* (London, 1691–2, rev., enlarged 3/1813–20/R by P. Bliss)

E. Arber, ed.: *A Transcript of the Registers of the Company of Stationers of London, 1554–1640* (London and Birmingham, 1875–94/R)

B. Rainbow: 'Bathe and his Introductions to Musicke', *MT*, cxxiii (1982), 243–7

PETER LE HURAY/BERNARR RAINBOW

Bathenius, Jacob. *See* BAETHEN, JACOB.

Bathori, Jane [Berthier, Jeanne-Marie] (*b* Paris, 14 June 1877; *d* Paris, 25 Jan 1970). French mezzo-soprano and producer. She studied at the Paris Conservatoire with Hortense Parent (piano) and the Belgian tenor Emile Engel, whom she married in 1908, and made her début at Nantes in 1900. Toscanini engaged her for the first La Scala performance of Humperdinck's *Hänsel und Gretel* (1902), and in Brussels she appeared in opera with her husband. Soon, however, she decided to devote herself to concert work. Her sympathetic and authentic interpretations of works by many French composers of her time – Debussy, Ravel, Chabrier, Satie, Roussel, Milhaud and others – was very important. With Ravel's *Shéhérazade* she achieved wide acclaim. She gave the première of his *Histoires naturelles* (dedicated to her) and of his *Chansons madécasses*, both occasions creating a sensation.

During World War I Bathori managed the Théâtre du Vieux Colombier, producing such works as Chabrier's *Une éducation manquée*, Debussy's *La demoiselle élue* and Honegger's *Le dit des jeux du monde*. The Paris group of Les Six owed much to her efforts in promoting their music and, in turn, her work as a singer influenced composers. In recitals she often accompanied herself, achieving a unity of style in a wide range of songs. She made many important recordings, particularly in the 1930s, of works by French and other composers. Her two books on singing are of great interest to interpreters of French song.

In 1926 Bathori visited Argentina on a recital tour. Each year thereafter she visited Buenos Aires, taking part in the first Latin American performances of many important works (e.g. Honegger's *Le roi David* and *Judith*), and even taking some stage roles at the Teatro Colón, where in 1933 she sang Concepción in Ravel's *L'heure espagnole*. In 1935 she was awarded the Croix de la Légion d'Honneur for her services to French music. During World War II she lived and taught in Buenos Aires, and in 1942 she became organizer there of the music section of the French institute of higher studies. At the end of the war she returned to Paris, taught singing, and gave many talks on French radio.

WRITINGS

Conseils sur le chant (Paris, 1928)
Sur l'interprétation des mélodies de Claude Debussy (Paris, 1953)

BIBLIOGRAPHY

G. Jean-Aubry: 'Jane Bathori', *Recorded Sound*, i (1961–2), 102–10 [with biographical note, and discography by H.M. Barnes]

DAVID COX

Bati, Luca (*b* Florence, 1546; *d* Florence, 17 Oct 1608). Italian composer. He was a pupil of Francesco Corteccia. In 1571 he applied unsuccessfully for the post of *maestro di cappella* in the church of the Cavalieri di S Stefano, Pisa. Between November 1579 and June 1582 he was *maestro di cappella* and organist of Amelia Cathedral, Umbria: an inventory of music (1615) at the cathedral lists a *Lamentationi* and *Vesperi*, both for 5 voices and both lost. He was *maestro di cappella* at Pisa Cathedral from 6 March to 15 November 1596 when the post lapsed owing to a fire in the cathedral. On 1 February 1599 he was appointed *maestro di cappella* of the Medici court and of Florence Cathedral, which included overseeing the music for the baptistry of S Giovanni. On 6 May 1600 he was given a benefice as a canon in the Medici church of S Lorenzo with the title 'SS Vitale and Agricola'. He held all these appointments until his death. Towards the end of his life he was probably a member of the Accademia degli Elevati, which was founded by his former pupil Marco da Gagliano in June 1607. Another notable pupil was Jacopo Corsi. An inscription on Bati's portrait, still in the canons' chapter room at S Lorenzo, gives the year of his death and honours him as much for having taught Gagliano as for his positions at the Medici court and S Lorenzo.

In 1589 Bati composed music (now lost) for the *intermedi* of *L'esaltazione della croce* (text by Cecchi), a *sacra rappresentazione* performed by boys of the Compagnia di S Giovanni Evangelista, a lay religious confraternity, for the festivities attendant on the marriage of Grand Duke Ferdinand I and Christine of Lorraine. He also wrote music (also lost) for *Le fiamme d'amore* (text by Gino Ginori), a mascherata presented on 26 February 1595 on a float that toured the streets of Florence during Carnival. He also composed the third and fourth choruses, now also lost, for Caccini's *Il rapimento di Cefalo* (text by Chiabrera) given in Florence on 9 October 1600 as one of the festival entertainments for the wedding of Maria de' Medici and Henri IV of France. His surviving madrigals and sacred works show him to have been a highly skilled composer. Modern features of his style include careful declamation, use of concertato-like contrast, and incorporation of the canzonetta style into a five-part madrigal ensemble. Not involved in the new monodic experiments, his works reveal elements of the polyphonic tradition of the florentine school. Standing between the composers Corteccia and Marcoda Gagliano, Bati's contribution was to sustain and reinforce authorative stylistic dignity.

WORKS

Il primo libro di madrigali, 5vv (Venice, 1594[11])
Il secondo libro di madrigali, 5vv (Venice, 1598[11]), ed. in Gargiulo, 1991
Works in 1601[5], 1602[6], 1602[9], 1604[17], 1605[13], 1605[14], 1606[11]
Sacred works, incl. masses, Mag, TeD, motets, hymns: *I-Fd*, S Lorenzo Archivo del Capitolo, Florence
Intermedi for L'esaltazione della croce (G. Cecchi), sacra rappresentazione, Florence, 1589, lost
Le fiamme d'amore (G. Ginori), mascherata, Florence, 26 Feb 1595, lost
2 choruses for G. Caccini: Il rapimento di Cefalo (Chiabrera), Florence, 9 Oct 1600, lost

BIBLIOGRAPHY

DBI (L. Pannella); *EinsteinIM*; *SolertiMBD*
E. Vogel: 'Marco da Gagliano: zur Geschichte des Florentiner Musiklebens von 1570–1650', *VMw*, v (1889), 396–442, 509–68, esp. 409, 412f, 418, 442
A. Solerti: *Gli albori del melodramma* (Milan, 1904/R), i, 42–3; ii, 56
F. Ghisi: 'Luca Bati maestro della cappella granducale di Firenze', *RBM*, viii (1954), 106–8
F. Testi: *Storia della musica italiana da Sant'Ambrogio a noi* (Milan, 1970), iii, 383, 385
T. Carter: 'Music and Patronage in Late Sixteenth-Century Florence: the Case of Jacopo Corsi (1561–1602)', *I Tatti Studies: Essays in the Renaissance*, i (1985), 57–104, esp. 70
F. D'Accone: 'The Sources of Luca Bati's Sacred Music at the Opera di Santa Maria del Fiore', *Altro Polo: Essays on Italian Music in the Cinquecento*, ed. R. Charteris (Sydney, 1990), 159–77
P. Gargiulo: 'Rinascimento fiorentino e cultura "instrumentalis": le "collectiones" medicee tra committenza, destinazione e pregio artistico', *Transmissione e recezione della forme di cultura musicale*, ed. A. Pompilio, D. Restani, L. Biariconi and F.A. Gallo (Turin, 1990), iii, 745–9
P. Gargiulo: *Luca Bati, madrigalista fiorentino* (Florence, 1991)
P. Gargiulo: '"Così d'arno sul lido": Madrigali e autori fiorentini ospiti nelle sillogi di area medicea (1594–1629)', *Revista de musicologia*, xvi (1993), 2521–30
W. Kirkendale: *The Court Musicians in Florence during the Principate of the Medici* (Florence, 1993), 114, 182, 185–6, 249, 644–6

EDMOND STRAINCHAMPS/PIERO GARGIULO

Batimientos (Sp.). *See* BEATS.

Batius, Jacob. *See* BAETHEN, JACOB.

Bátiz, Enrique (*b* Mexico City, 4 May 1942). Mexican conductor and pianist. He began piano studies in 1950 with Francisco Agea, and continued from 1960 with György Sandor. Bátiz attended the Southern Methodist University in Dallas, but in 1962 moved to the Juilliard School of Music for piano studies with Adele Marcus, graduating there in 1965. In the same year he was a semifinalist in the Marguerite Long Piano Competition. He then moved to Poland where from 1967 to 1970 he studied the piano with Zbigniew Drzewiecke and conducting with Stanisław Wisłocki. In 1969 he made his conducting début with the Orquesta Sinfónica de Xalapa in Mexico. Two years later he made his most important contribution to Mexican music, the founding of the Orquesta Sinfónica Nacional de Mexico, an ensemble he conducted until 1983, and again from 1990. He also served (1983–9) as music director of the Mexico City PO, and from 1984 has been a principal guest conductor with the RPO in London. In these various capacities Bátiz has made more than 150 recordings, including cycles of Beethoven and Tchaikovsky symphonies. He has also appeared as guest conductor with major orchestras in Europe, the Americas and Asia, and is particularly esteemed for his performances of Latin music in which colour and rhythm predominate.

CHARLES BARBER

Baton (Fr. *baguette*; Ger. *Taktstock*; It. *bacchetta*). The stick with which the conductor of an orchestra or similar ensemble beats the time. An approximation of the modern baton, a thin, tapered stick, perhaps half a metre long, was evidently first used in the late 18th century, but the use of a roll of paper or violin bow for this purpose continued into the 19th century. A more distant predecessor of the baton was the precentor's staff mentioned by various writers from the 15th century to the 17th. For further historical information *see* CONDUCTING.

Bâton (Fr.). *See* ENDPIN.

Bâton, Charles [*le jeune*] (*b* Versailles, early 18th century; *d* Paris, after 1754). French composer and virtuoso on the hurdy-gurdy, son of Henri Bâton, who revolutionized the construction of the instrument. The jurist Antoine Terrasson, a contemporary of Bâton *le jeune*, an amateur player of the veille, and author of a history of the vielle, recounted his progress:

Mr Bâton ... had laboured to make the most of his father's work, and having improved himself in performance on the hurdy-gurdy, as in the composition of music, he earned himself a reputation which procured for him the honour of instructing several princesses to play that instrument. Mr Bâton, after having for a long time performed with success music written for the musette and for the hurdy-gurdy, was the first to set about composing pieces expressly for the hurdy-gurdy – that is, pieces wrought in accordance with the hand positions and the characters befitting that instrument. It was in this style that Mr Bâton produced, to begin with, a first volume which he dedicated to the late *Mademoiselle* [the King's niece]; some years after that he produced a second one which he dedicated to *Madame la Duchesse* [of Orleans]; finally, he has just produced a third volume composed of six sonatas which suffice to show that the hurdy-gurdy is capable of all the beauty and of all the expression of the other instruments.

Bâton was considered, along with Danguy, one of the foremost players of his time. His music consists almost exclusively of suites and dance movements and character pieces. These works reveal refinement combined with virtuosity consisting of rapid scales and arpeggios easily executed on the hurdy-gurdy. Many articulation markings provide a useful source for the study of performing practice related to the instrument. The suites for two hurdy-gurdies are constructed on the basis of equality, and establish a dialogue and interchange between the two instruments. His sonatas, while by no means the most technically demanding works for the hurdy-gurdy, fully exploit the capabilities of the instrument. They reveal an awareness for the *galant* style in their harmonic rhythms and melodies. In these works, Bâton sometimes pushes the harmonic limits for the hurdy-gurdy: in the concluding movement of the second sonata, for example, he explores dissonance by introducing neapolitan harmonies (D♭s) against the C–G drones.

Bâton continued the work of his father by searching for ways to improve the hurdy-gurdy to make it more acceptable as an instrument for chamber music. A detailed notice entitled 'Trois touches augmentées à la vielle, & une autre changée de place' appeared in the *Mercure de France* in September 1750. It described Bâton's new design for the hurdy-gurdy, executed by François Feury, which extended the instrument's range and offered a more convenient layout of its keyboard. A second, briefer notice in the *Mercure de France*, June 1752, headed 'Vielle nouvelle', and a lengthy essay entitled 'Memoir sur la vielle en D-la-ré' in the same journal (143–57) in October of that year, revealed that Bâton and Feury had created an instrument with a range of almost three octaves (*d'–c''''*). The introduction of a D–A tuning, as opposed to the standard C–G tuning, made possible the execution of many pieces written for flute or violin. Further, Bâton eliminated the *trompette*, the vibrating bridge which creates a sharp articulation at the beginning of each note, in favour of the articulation which results from the keys themselves when depressed by the fingers of the left hand, resulting in a more legato execution. In conclusion, he says that after Marie Leczynska, Louis XV's queen and an avid player of the hurdy-gurdy, had examined the essay, he gave her a demonstration at Compiègne on 20 July 1752, repeating the demonstration the next day for Madame la Dauphine (Marie-Josèphe) and that they were all pleased with the new instrument. In spite of this initial success the new instrument never received the public approbation for which Bâton had hoped.

In 1753 Bâton entered the Querelle des Bouffons with a pamphlet *Examen de la 'Lettre de M. Rousseau, sur la musique françois' dans lequel on expose le plan d'une musique propre à notre langue* (Paris, 1954). A reviewer wrote: 'here is an adversary who limits himself to talking sense, a man who does not attack M Rousseau because his name is *Jean-Jacques* or because he was born in *Geneva*' (*Journal de trévoux*). In his pamphlet Bâton agreed with Rousseau that the Italian language had advantages over the French for lyric poetry and singability, but disagreed that French music was largely worthless and strongly refuted Rousseau's notion that fugues, counterpoint and complex harmony were (in Rousseau's term) 'une sottise'. Perhaps because the pamphlet was so well written, another disputant accused Diderot of having written it and Bâton of merely having posed as its author, but there is no evidence of that. Later French writers accused Bâton of having pretended to dispute with Rousseau only in order to agree with him; this unjust charge may have arisen from Bâton's reasonableness and his careful avoidance of the polemical tone and character assasination used so freely by many of Rousseau's opponents.

WORKS

all published in Paris

op.

1   [6] Suites, 3 for 2 hurdy-gurdies/musettes/fl/rec/ob, 3 for hurdy-gurdy/musette fl/rec/ob (1733)

–   Recueil de pièces, 2 musettes/hurdy-gurdies/other insts (1733)

2   La vielle amusante: divertissement en 6 suites, 1 hurdy-gurdy/musette/fl/rec/ob, bc (c1734)

3   6 sonates, hurdy-gurdy/musette, bc (1741), 2 for 2 hurdy-gurdies

4   Les amusements d'une heure, 2 suites, 2 hurdy-gurdies/musettes (1748/R)

BIBLIOGRAPHY

BrenetC; FétisB; GerberL

[? A. Terrasson]: *Dissertation historique sur la vielle* (Paris, 1741/R, 2/1768)

M. Brenet: 'La librairie musicale en France de 1653 à 1790', *SIMG*, viii (1906–7), 401–66

E. de Bricqueville: *Notice sur la vielle* (Paris, 2/1911/R)

D. Launay, ed.: *La Querelle des Bouffons* (Geneva, 1973) [a repr., with introduction and index, of 61 pamphlets pubd Paris, 1752–4]

P. Goldstein: 'Charles Bâton's Memoir on the Hurdy-Gurdy in D-a-d', *A Modest Manual for the Hurdy-Gurdy*, ed. J. Ralyea (Chicago, 1981), 17–34

R.A. Green: 'Eighteenth-Century French Chamber Music for Vielle', *EMe*, xv (1987), 469–79

R.A. Green: *The Hurdy-Gurdy in Eighteenth-Century France* (Bloomington, IN, 1995)

NEAL ZASLAW/ROBERT A. GREEN

Bâton, Henri [*l'aîné*] (*b* late 17th century; *d* Versailles, ?1728). French luthier and player on the musette and hurdy-gurdy. As early as 1672 Borjon de Scellery remarked upon the popularity of the musette among the French noblemen and the hurdy-gurdy among noble ladies. Bâton *l'aîné* took advantage of the continuing fashion for rustic instruments, and worked at transforming the musette and hurdy-gurdy from folk instruments into art ones. His younger contemporary Terrasson wrote:

Mr Bâton, luthier at Versailles, was the first who worked at perfecting the hurdy-gurdy [*vielle*]: he had in his place several old guitars which had not been used for a long time. In 1716 the idea struck him to turn them into hurdy-gurdies, and he carried off this invention with such a great success that people wished to have only hurdy-gurdies mounted on the bodies of guitars; and these sorts of hurdy-gurdies effectively have a stronger and at the same time sweeter sound than that of the old hurdy-gurdies. Mr Bâton also added to that instrument's keyboard the low *e*′ and the high *f*‴; he ornamented his hurdy-gurdies with ivory purfling; he gave the neck a form more beautiful and closely resembling the necks of bass viols – so that then all the ladies wished to play the hurdy-gurdy, and soon the preference for this instrument became general…Mr Bâton imagined that, since the hurdy-gurdies mounted on the bodies of guitars had had so much success, that instrument would take on yet more mellow sounds by mounting it on the bodies of lutes and of theorboes. Accordingly, in 1720 he carried out this new idea, and the hurdy-gurdies in the form of a lute had an even greater success than the others. It was then that the hurdy-gurdy began to face up to the other instruments and to be admitted into concerts: Messrs Baptiste [Anet] and Boismortier even composed duets and trios for the hurdy-gurdy and the musette, and all the pieces which had previously been composed for the musette also became hurdy-gurdy pieces.

The success of Bâton's ideas can be gauged in many ways: by the number of paintings and engravings of the period in which members of the nobility were portrayed playing musettes or hurdy-gurdies, by the number of stage works of the period which featured the instrument, by the many title-pages which suggested that their music was suited for these instruments, by the several instruction books published, by the number of makers who turned out these instruments, and by the number of virtuosos on them. The instruments were heard at the Concert Spirituel at Christmas 1731, 1732 and 1733, and were praised by those glad to hear simple tunes but criticized by those who regarded rustic instruments as too primitive.

BIBLIOGRAPHY

BrenetC

[? A. Terrasson]: *Dissertation historique sur la vielle* (Paris, 1741/R, 2/1768)

E. de Bricqueville: 'Les instruments de musique champêtres au XVIIᵉet au XVIIIᵉsiècle', *Un coin de la curiosité: les anciens instruments de musique* (Paris, 1894), 39–51

E. de Bricqueville: *Notice sur la vielle* (Paris, 2/1911/R)

C. Flagel: 'La vielle parisienne sous Louis XV: un modèle pour deux siècles', *Instrumentistes et Luthiers parisiens XVIIᵉ–XIXᵉsiècles*, ed. F. Gétreau (Paris, 1988), 116–33

R.A. Green: *The Hurdy-Gurdy in Eighteenth-Century France* (Bloomington, IN, 1995)

NEAL ZASLAW

Batrachus, Johannes. *See* FROSCH, JOHANNES.

Batsh, 'Umar al- (*b* Aleppo, 1885; *d* Aleppo, 11 Dec 1950). Syrian composer and mūwashshaḥ expert. He learned classical *muwashshaḥ* songs and their accompanying *samah* dances in Aleppo, memorizing thousands of pieces. He quickly excelled in composing new *muwashshaḥ* and extended the individual performer's role. He was extremely knowledgeable about rare modes (*maqāmāt*) in Arab music, and composed *muwashshaḥ* within any given *maqām* to demonstrate its particular modal characteristics. Once he composed a *muwashshaḥ* based on 14 consecutive *maqāmāt*, with the *maqām* names in the lyrics. He also invented the *samah* cross-dance technique (dancers cross paths to different rhythms and melodic sections of the *muwashshaḥ*).

In 1947 he began teaching *muwashshaḥ* and *samah* at the Oriental Musical Institute in Damascus (Al-ma'had al-mūsīqī al-sharqī); he taught many future masters including Ṣabāḥ Fakhrī. He instructed the girls of the Damascus Dawhet al-'adab School in *samah*; their performance at the university theatre was the first instance of socially acceptable public female dance. In 1949 he returned to Aleppo, where he taught at Fu'ād Rajāi's Music Institute and instructed the radio station's male professional chorus.

SAADALLA AGHA AL-KALAA

Battaglia (It.: 'battle'). A piece of music descriptive of a battle. *See* BATTLE MUSIC.

Battaille, Charles (Amable) (*b* Nantes, 30 Sept 1822; *d* Paris, 2 May 1872). French bass. At first he was trained as a doctor, like his father, and subsequently practised as such in Caen, but he moved to Paris and from 1845 to 1847 studied at the Conservatoire with the younger Garcia. He made his début at the Opéra-Comique as Sulpice in *La fille du régiment* (22 June 1848). A versatile actor, capable of florid singing and possessing an extensive range, he was soon entrusted with principal roles in new operas by Halévy, Adam, Thomas and others, one of his best being that of Peter the Great in Meyerbeer's *L'étoile du nord* (16 February 1854). His career was interrupted by a serious throat ailment in 1857, but in 1860 he appeared at the Théâtre Lyrique as Jacques Sincère in Halévy's *Val d'Andorre* (a role he had created 12 years earlier) and in the première of Gounod's *Philémon et Baucis* (2 February). In the following year he sang both at the Théâtre Lyrique and the Opéra-Comique (in a revival of *L'étoile du nord*), but, after a final appearance at the Théâtre Lyrique early in 1863, he retired from the stage. Battaille taught singing at the Conservatoire from 1851, and published work on the pedagogy of singing based on his medical expertise. Between 1865 and 1867 he gave lectures in several large venues in Paris; these included a talk on the French version of Mozart's *Don Giovanni*. Towards the end of his life, he was elected *sous-préfet* of Ancenis (Loire-Inférieure) and, when the area was attacked by smallpox during the Franco-Prussian War, he practised as a doctor again.

WRITINGS

De l'enseignement du chant, i: *Nouvelles recherches sur la phonation: mémoire présenté et lu à l'Académie des sciences le 15 avril 1861* (Paris, 1861); ii: *De la physiologie appliquée à l'étude du mécanisme vocal* (Paris, 1863)
[lecture, title unknown, in] *Conférences de l'Association philotechnique, année 1865* (Paris, 1866)

BIBLIOGRAPHY

FétisB; GSL
Marquis de Granges de Surgères: *Iconographie bretonne* (Rennes and Paris, 1888–9)
J. Joiner: 'The Garcia Legacy: Charles Amable Battaille', *NATS*, xxxix/5 (1982–3), 7–12

PHILIP ROBINSON/CORMAC NEWARK

Battement [batement, battements] (Fr.). A term used to denote particular ornaments. See ORNAMENTS, §7.

Battements (Fr.). *See* BEATS.

Batten. Composer, possibly identifiable with BATTY.

Batten [Battin, Battyn], **Adrian** (*b* Salisbury, bap. 1 March 1591; *d* London, 1637). English composer. According to the registers of St Thomas's, Salisbury, he was one of the seven children of Richard Batten and Elizabeth Nowell. Richard Batten's will, proved in 1619, states that he was a joiner. Evidence of Adrian Batten's early musical training is scanty; a note on the manuscript *GB-Ob* Tenbury 791 f.400 reads: 'These songs of Mr John Holmes were prickt from his own pricking in the year 1635 by Mr Adrian Batten, one of the Vicars Choral of St Paul's in London who some times was his scoller'. John Holmes was a lay vicar of Winchester Cathedral from 1599 to 1622, and it is probable that Batten was a chorister there and stayed on after his voice had changed. The relevant records are unfortunately missing from the cathedral, but on the outside of the east wall of Bishop Gardiner's chantry is carved 'Adrian Battin: 1608:'. Perhaps this marked the end of his time as a chorister. Further evidence of his stay at Winchester can be found in the registers of the church of St Swithun-upon-Kingsgate, for on 14 March 1614, Adrian, son of Adrian 'Battin' was baptized.

In the following month Batten moved to London and became a lay vicar of Westminster Abbey with a yearly salary of £8. While at the abbey he was a parishioner of St Margaret's, Westminster, and the registers there record the baptisms of Thomas Batten, 'son of Adryan' on 5 June 1616, and Richard on 8 September 1621. The death of a daughter Susan is recorded on 22 May 1623, and those of his two sons Thomas and Richard on 16 July and 31 August 1625. The year 1625 also saw the death of James I; Adrian Batten is mentioned in the Lord Chamberlain's accounts as one of the singers at his funeral. During his time at Westminster Abbey Batten occasionally augmented his income by copying music. The abbey muniments record in 1622: 'Item paied to Mr Batten for

pricking Mr Weekes his service and Mr Talles his Magnificat & nunc dimittis as alsoe Mr Tomkins service xxxs'. Batten's name appears in the Westminster Abbey treasurer's accounts as a lay vicar until the end of October 1626. It would therefore seem that in that year, and not 1624 as is usually stated, he moved to St Paul's Cathedral. His name first appears in the indenture book of Dean Donne on 22 December 1628, when he is named as one of the six vicars-choral. His name continues to appear in similar documents up to 3 December 1635, and in that same year he is mentioned as a vicar-choral there in the Bishop of London's Visitation. In the indentures book of Dean Wynyffe on 13 May 1637 only five vicars-choral are named, Batten's name being absent. On 22 July 1637 letters of administration of the estate of Adrian Batten, late of the parish of St Sepulchre, Newgate Street, London, were granted to John Gilbert, a clothier of the city of Salisbury, with the consent of Edward, John and William Batten, his brothers.

Batten composed a large number of services and anthems, but apparently no secular or instrumental music. It is thought, though sometimes questioned, that he was the copyist of the most extensive source for English church music of the period, the so-called 'Batten Organbook' (*GB-Ob* Ten. 791). He was a competent craftsman, writing in a style which was devotional and restrained. Burney said he was 'a good harmonist of the old school, without adding anything to the common stock of ideas, both in melody and harmony, with which the art was furnished long before he was born'. Most of the criticisms which are levelled at Batten could be applied to almost any of his contemporaries, but Batten makes a convenient 'whipping boy'. It is true that he was no innovator; he displayed a certain reluctance to stray from the home key and his melodic invention could not match that of Gibbons and Tomkins, his more distinguished contemporaries. Nevertheless, there is a certain naive charm about much of his work; the verse anthems, *Hear my prayer O Lord*, *Out of the deep* and *O Lord thou hast searched me out* are excellent examples. The last named contains a quaint and not altogether unsuccessful attempt at word-painting. The five-part full anthems *Hear the prayers, O our God* and *We beseech thee* display a depth of feeling which is at least equal to that found in Gibbons's music, and the eight-part *O clap your hands*, while not reaching the heights of Gibbons's setting of the same words, makes telling use of massive homophonic passages alternating with polyphony. His 'Full' service, which is similar in scope to the 'Great' services of Byrd and Tomkins, is worthy of attention, though in general it would be true to say that he was more successful in simpler forms.

WORKS

SERVICES

Full Service (TeD, Jub, Ky, Cr, Mag, Nunc), 7/8vv, *GB-Lcm, Och*
Short Service (otherwise called Dorian Mode Service; Ven, TeD, Jub, Bs, Ky, Cr, San, Gl, Mag, Nunc), 4vv, *DRc, GL, Lbl, Lcm, Lsp, Ob, Och, Ojc, WB, Y*
Short Service for men (Lit, Bte, Ky, Cr, Mag, Nunc), 4vv, *Lcm, Ob*
First Verse Service (Ven, TeD, Jub, Ky, Cr, Mag, Nunc), inc., *DRc, Lcm*
Second Verse Service (Ven, Preces and Psalms, TeD, Jub, Ky, Cr, Mag, Nunc), inc., *DRc, Lbl*
Third Verse Service (Mag, Nunc), 7/8vv, *DRc, GL*
Fourth Verse Service (Mag, Nunc), 5/4vv, *Cp, DRc, GL*
Service in E fa (Ky, Cr, Mag, Nunc), inc., *DRc*
Litany, 4vv, *Cp, Ob*

Preces and Psalms (6 sets), B only extant, *Och*
Creed for men, Ct only extant, *Lbl*

ANTHEMS

Almighty God, which in thy wrath, inc., 5/5vv, *GB-DRc, Lbl, Lcm, Y*
Behold I bring you glad tidings, inc., 2/4vv, *Ob*
Blessed are those, inc., 1/5vv, *Cp, DRc, Lbl, Y* (probably correctly attrib. W. Deane in *Och, US-NYp*)
Christ our Paschal Lamb, 4vv, *GB-Lcm*
Christ rising (2 p. Christ is risen), 7/5vv, *Cp, Y*
Deliver us, O Lord our God, 4vv, *Cp, DRc, Lbl, Lsp, Och, Y, US-BEm*
Godliness is great riches, 5vv, *GB-DRc, Lcm, Ojc, US-BEm*
Haste thee, O God (2p. But let all those), 4vv, 1641⁵
Haste thee, O God (2p. But let all those), 4vv, *GB-Lcm*
Have mercy upon me, O God, inc., 5vv, *Lcm*
Have mercy upon me, O God, inc., 6/5vv, *Cp*
Hear my prayer, O God, 5vv, *Cfm, Lbl, Lcm, Lsp, Ob, Och, WRch, Y, US-BEm*
Hear my prayer, O God, 7/5vv, *GB-Cp, DRc, GL, Lbl, Y*
Hear my prayer, O Lord, 1/4vv, *Cp, Cu, DRc, Lbl, Lcm, Y*
Hear the prayers, O our God, 5vv, *Lcm, Ojc*
Hide not thou thy face, 4vv, 1641⁵
Holy, holy, holy Lord God, 6/5vv, *GB-Cp, DRc, Lbl, Y*
I heard a voice, 6/6vv (short section for double 5-part choir), *Cp, DRc, Lbl, Lcm, Y*
I will always give thanks, inc. verse anthem, B cantoris only extant, *Lcm*
Jesus said unto his disciples, inc. verse anthem, *Cp*
Let my complaint come before thee, 4vv, *Lsp, Y*
Lord, I am not high minded, inc., 5vv, *Lcm*
Lord, we beseech thee, 4vv, 1641⁵
Lord, we beseech thee, 4vv, *Lcm*
Lord, who shall dwell, 6vv, *Lcm, Y, US-BEm, SM*
My soul truly waiteth, 4vv, *GB-DRc, Lsp, Y*
O clap your hands together, 8vv, *DRc, Lcm, Y*
O God, my heart is ready, inc., 1/4vv, *Ob*
O God that art my righteousness, inc. verse anthem, B cantoris only extant, *Lcm*
O God the king of glory, inc. verse anthem, B cantoris only extant, *Lcm*
O how happy a thing it is, inc. verse anthem, chorus parts differ in sources, *Cp, Lcm, Y*
O Lord our governor, inc. verse anthem, *Y*
O Lord, thou hast searched me out, 2/4vv, *Cp, DRc, GL, Lbl, LF, Ob, Och, Y, US-NYp* (also incorrectly attrib. N. Giles)
O praise God in his holiness, inc. verse anthem, B cantoris only extant, *GB-Lcm*
O praise the Lord, 4vv, *Lcm*
O praise the Lord, 4vv, *Lcm*
O praise the Lord, 4vv, 1641⁵
O sing joyfully, 4vv, *Y*
Out of the deep, 1/4vv, 1641⁵
Out of the deep, 2/5vv, *Cp, DRc, Y*
Out of the deep, inc., *DRc, Lbl, Och, US-BEm* (also attrib. Hutchinson)
Ponder my words, O Lord, inc., 6/5vv, *GB-Cp, DRc, Lbl, Y*
Praise the Lord, O my soul, 6vv, *Lcm, Och, US-BEm*
Praise the Lord, O my soul (2p. Praise the Lord, O Jerusalem), inc., 6/5vv, *GB-Cp, DRc, Lbl, Y*
Sing we merrily unto God, inc., 7vv, *Lcm*
Turn thou us, O good Lord, 5/5vv, *Cp, DRc, Lbl, Lcm, Y*
We beseech thee, almighty God, 5vv, *Lcm, Ojc, Y, US-BEm*
When the Lord turned again, 4vv, 1641⁵
Clifford's The Divine Services and Anthems (London, 1664) preserves the texts for the following anthems, though no music survives: Almighty God, which madest Thy blessed Son; Almighty God, whose praise this day; Behold now praise the Lord; Bow down thine ear; I am the resurrection; If ye love me; In Bethlehem town; Not unto us, O Lord; O sing unto the Lord; Save us, good Lord, waking; So God loved the world; The Lord is my shepheard.

The anthem, O Lord let me know mine end, attrib. Batten in *GB-Cp*, is by Solomon Tozer, a lay clerk of Exeter.
The Preces for Trebles in *Lcm* 1045–1051, listed in the Daniel and le Huray catalogue, is by J. Barnard.

BIBLIOGRAPHY

*Le Huray*MR
P. le Huray: 'Towards a Definitive Study of Pre-Restoration Anglican Service Music', *MD*, xiv (1960), 167–95, esp. 172–76
J.B. Clark: 'Adrian Batten and John Barnard: Colleagues and Collaborators', *MD*, xxii (1968), 207–29
J.B. Clark and M. Bevan: 'New Biographical Facts about Adrian Batten', *JAMS*, xxiii (1970), 331–3
R.T. Daniel and P. le Huray: *The Sources of English Church Music, 1549–1660*, EECM, suppl. i (London, 1972)
P. Phillips: *English Sacred Music 1549–1649* (Oxford, 1991), 260–68, 415–16, 433, 450

MAURICE BEVAN

Batterie (i) (Fr.). A signal or short march sounded by drums. *See* SONNERIE, §(i).

Batterie (ii) (Fr.). *See* BATTERY.

Batterie (iii) (Fr.). *See* RASGUEADO.

Batterie (iv) (Fr.). *See* PERCUSSION.

Battery (Fr. *batterie*; Ger. *Brechung*; It. *battimento*). A term used in Baroque music for the practice of arpeggiating passages notated as chords. *See* ORNAMENTS, §6.
See also BOW, §II, 2(ix) and 3(xi).

Batteux, Abbé **Charles** (*b* Alland'huy, Ardennes, 6 May 1713; *d* Paris, 14 July 1780). French aesthetician. He was professor of rhetoric at the universities of Reims and Paris, the Collège de Lisieux and the Collège de Navarre, and then of Greek and Roman philosophy at the Collège Royal, Paris. It was his *Les beaux-arts réduits à un même principe* (Paris, 1746/R; ed. J.-R. Mantion, Paris, 1989) that made him famous, and Diderot drew upon his *Lettres sur l'inversion et sur la traduction* (published in *Cours de belles-lettres distribué par exercices*, Paris, 1747–8) when writing his own *Lettre sur les sourds et muets*. Batteux was elected to the Académie des Inscriptions in 1754 and became a member of the Académie Française in 1761. In 1777 he coordinated the 45 volumes of the *Cours d'études* for the pupils of the Ecole Royale Militaire.

His works on aesthetics, the most important being *Les beaux-arts* and *Principes de la littérature* (Paris, 1764; Eng. trans., 1761) are principally devoted to the exposition and elucidation of the classical doctrines of which he was a late exponent. His aesthetics are based on the theory of imitation, which he connects with the concept of the beauty of nature: art does not reproduce nature as it is, but seeks to attain an invisible truth by picking out 'characteristics' and 'features' and recombining them into a fictive entity which is truer than reality. While poetry sets out to imitate actions, 'the principal object of music and dance must be to imitate sentiments and passions'. He rejects the idea that its combinations of sound make music sufficient unto itself; it must always be linked to meaning and 'make up a picture'. This very classical concept, in which music is subjected to a significant model, depends largely on a frequently mentioned analogy with painting, the separation of colour (a material with calculable relationships) from design (which gives painting life and meaning), and had already formed the basis of arguments levelled against Rameau at the time of the *Querelle des Lullystes* in 1733. Rousseau was to take the theme up again in his *Essai sur l'origine des langues*, but giving it a different direction by propounding the hypothesis of an original, non-articulated language.

On the level of morphological poetics, Batteux adopts the Aristotelian model, modernizing it and making it systematic. There are two important modifications. First, lyric poetry, a subject on which Aristotle says nothing, is introduced into the 'arts of imitation' and justified by the idea of *fiction possible*, whereas its existence had simply been affirmed in earlier theoretical works on poetry. This hypothesis was the subject of a debate with J.A. Schlegel (father of the famous Romantic theorist), the German translator of *Les beaux-arts* (1751), to whom Batteux replied in his *Principes de la littérature*. Secondly, lyric drama (opera) is introduced into the dramatic system, particularly in connection with the concept of the *merveilleux vraisemblable*. On this point Batteux's theory, like that of Gabriel Bonnot de Mably in his *Lettres sur l'opera* of 1741, allots lyric tragedy a position parallel to that of its dramatic homologue (lyric tragedy is conceived of on the model of classical tragedy, the general laws of the latter still applying while the particular rules, objects and methods are modified), thus allowing it full validity in the system of the classical French theatre. In the theories he puts forward for making these innovations, Batteux takes up the structural and transformational spirit of Aristotelian poetics: his system can be represented as a table in which the various positions are articulated with each other, and not merely juxtaposed. He breaks with the strongly normative tone, more anxious to specify advice on production than to provide an explanation of texts through ordered analysis, which had been characteristic of works on poetics from Horace to Nicolas Boileau.

BIBLIOGRAPHY

L. Dupuy: *Eloge de Batteux: mémoires de l'Académie des inscriptions* (Paris, 1780)

R. Naves: 'L'abbé Batteux et la catharsis', *Mélanges*, [Société toulousaine d'études classiques], i (1946), 285–300

F.C. Tubach: 'Die Naturnachahmungstheorie: Batteux und die Berliner Rationalisten', *Germanisch-romanische Monatsschrift*, xiii (1963), 262–80

J.H. Davis: 'Batteux', *Tragic Theory and the Eighteenth-Century French Critics* (Chapel Hill, NC, 1967), 44–50

F. Bollino: *Teoria e sistema delle belle arti: Batteux e gli esthéticiens del sec. XVIII* (Bologna, 1976)

I. von der Lühe: *Natur und Nachahmung in der ästhetischen Theorie zwischen Sturm und Drang: Untersuchungen zur Batteux-Rezeption in Deutschland* (Bonn, 1979)

M. Fontius: 'Batteux's Kodofizierung des Systems der schönen Künste', *Literatur im Epochenumbruch: Funktionen europäischer Literaturen im 18. und beginnenden 19. Jahrhundert*, ed. G. Klotz, W. Schröder and P. Weber (Berlin, 1977)

A. Becq: *Genèse de l'esthétique française moderne: De la raison classique à l'imagination créatrice, 1680–1815* (Pisa, 1984)

F. Torrigiani: *Lo specchio dei sistemi: Batteux e Condillac* (Palermo, 1984)

M. Modica: *Il sistema delle arti: Batteux e Diderot* (Palermo, 1987)

S. Branca-Rosoff: Introduction and notes to C. Batteux: *Le leçon de leture: textes de l'abbé Batteux* (Paris, c1990)

C. Kintzler: *Poétique de l'opéra français de Corneille à Rousseau* (Paris, 1991)

J.-N. Pascal: 'Le statut de l'histoire littéraire dans l'enseignement secondaire à la fin du XVIIIe siècle et au début du XIXe: note sur les abrégés de Batteux et de La Harpe', *L'école des lettres*, lxxxv/7 (1992), 19–26

CATHERINE KINTZLER

Battiferri, Luigi (*b* Sassocorvaro, nr Urbino, 1600–10; *d* 1682 or later). Italian composer and organist. He studied under Frescobaldi and became a priest. He was a leading musician at Ferrara for a number of years and was also prominent at Urbino: he held a succession of posts as *maestro di cappella* at both these places and elsewhere, but he held no official positions as an organist. In 1642 he was at S Angelo in Vado in his native region, and from 5 July 1650 to 5 May 1653 he was at Spoleto Cathedral.

From 1 October 1653 he was employed at Ferrara, first at the Accademia della Morte and then, in 1657–8, at the Accademia dello Spirito Santo. He was at Urbino Cathedral from 1658 until he returned to Ferrara in the summer of 1660, where he served the Accademia della Morte until 1662 and then the Accademia dello Spirito Santo. In 1665 he was *maestro* of Pesaro Cathedral. From 1666 he lived principally at Urbino, though he was for a third time at the Accademia dello Spirito Santo, Ferrara, in 1669 and 1670. He was still living in 1682, when he endowed a chapel in the principal church at his birthplace; he probably died shortly afterwards. All but the first of his five extant volumes of music appeared in a single year, 1669, when he was probably over 60, and he may well have regarded them as representative of the music he had written during his active years as a musician. His impressive ricercares marked the end of the school of organ music associated with Ferrara; they were copied by Fux and Zelenka and were probably known to Bach. The numerous solo motets that form his opp.4–6 are cantata-like pieces and were doubtless composed for performance in the academies at Ferrara with which he was connected.

WORKS

Messa et salmi concertati, 3vv, bc, con motetti, letanie, & Salve regina, 2–3vv, bc, op.2 (Venice, 1642)

Ricercari, a 4–6, org, op.3 (Bologna, 1669); 1 ed. A.G. Ritter: *Zur Geschichte des Orgelspiels, vornehmlich des deutschen* (Leipzig, 1884), 46

Il primo libro de motetti, 1v, bc, op.4 (Bologna, 1669)

Il secondo libro de' motetti, 1v, bc, op.5 (Bologna, 1669)

Il terzo libro di motetti, 1v, bc, op.6 (Bologna, 1669)

BIBLIOGRAPHY

ApelG; DBI (P. Veronese); *MGG1* (A. Cavicchi)

Various documents (archive of the Accademia della Morte, Ferrara)

L. Torchi: 'La musica istrumentale in Italia nei secoli XVI, XVII e XVIII', *RMI*, v (1898), 455–89; pubd separately (Turin, 1901)

B. Ligi: *La cappella musicale del duomo di Urbino, NA*, ii (1925), 1–369, esp. 111

F.W. Riedel: 'Der Einfluss der italienischen Klaviermusik des 17. Jahrhunderts auf die Entwicklung der Musik für Tasteninstrumente in Deutschland während der ersten Hälfte des 18. Jahrhunderts', *AnMc*, no.5 (1968), 18–33

F.W. Riedel: 'Johann Sebastian Bachs *Kunst der Fuge* und die Fugenbücher der italienischen und österreichischen Organisten des 17. und 18. Jahrhunderts', *Von Isaac bis Bach: Festschrift Martin Just*, ed. F. Heidlberger, W. Ostoff and R. Wiesend (Kassel, 1991), 327–33

ADRIANO CAVICCHI

Battimenti (It.). See BEATS.

Battimento (It.). See BATTERY.

Battin, Adrian. See BATTEN, ADRIAN.

Battishill, Jonathan (*b* London, May 1738; *d* Islington, London, 10 Dec 1801). English organist and composer. In 1747 he became a chorister of St Paul's, where he made rapid progress in his musical studies under William Savage, almoner and master of the choristers, whose articled pupil he became after his voice broke. His proficiency on the organ, especially his extempore playing, soon attracted attention, and he acted as William Boyce's deputy at the Chapel Royal for some time. He also developed a fine tenor voice and frequently appeared as a soloist in London concerts, one of his early engagements being in a performance of Handel's *Alexander's Feast* at the Great Room, Dean Street, on 16 March 1756, where he was described as 'Mr Batichel'. About this time he was appointed conductor at Covent Garden, directing from the harpsichord, and he also began to compose songs for Drury Lane Theatre. On 11 June 1758 he became a member of the Madrigal Society, and on 2 August 1761 a member of the Society of Musicians. He was also a 'priviledged member' of the Noblemen's and Gentlemen's Catch Club from c1762, but twice forfeited his membership for non-attendance at meetings. In 1771 he gained the club's gold medal with his glee *Come bind my hair, ye wood nymphs fair*.

In 1764 Battishill was appointed organist of the united parishes of St Clement Eastcheap and St Martin Orgar, and in 1767 of Christ Church, Newgate Street, holding both posts until his death. On 19 December 1765 he married Elizabeth Davies, a singing actress at Covent Garden Theatre and the original Margery in *Love in a Village*. The marriage was not a success, and his wife eventually lived openly with the actor Anthony Webster, with whom she went to Ireland in 1776; she died in Cork in October 1777. From about 1775 Battishill himself apparently lived with a woman who, on his death, called herself Ann Battishill.

From the mid-1770s Battishill's compositional activity declined and he took increasingly to over-indulgence in drink, for which he had always had a propensity. This was undoubtedly a factor in his failure to exploit his talents more fully, and resulted in his not being appointed organist of St Paul's on the death of John Jones in 1796. From childhood he had been a keen reader, and his later years were spent mostly among his books, of which he had amassed some 6000 to 7000 volumes, consisting chiefly of theology and classical authors. In accordance with his own wishes he was buried in St Paul's, near the grave of William Boyce, after a funeral service that included his own anthem *Call to Remembrance*.

Most of Battishill's compositions date from the period 1760–75, and reflect his many-sided activities during this time. His main operatic venture, *Almena*, proved a theatrical failure, but that was attributed to dramatic faults on the part of the librettist Rolt, rather than to deficiencies in the music, composed jointly with Michael Arne. Of his many songs, *Kate of Aberdeen* was highly popular, as was the catch *I Loved Thee Beautiful and Kind*. It was, however, for his seven-part anthem *Call to Remembrance*, with its fine command of the old full style of writing and effective suspensions, that he was most widely admired, and the work long survived in cathedral repertories.

In addition to his extempore playing, his performances of Handel's keyboard works were highly regarded, and his memory, both musical and otherwise, was reputed to have been exceptional, as shown by the occasion on which he played and sang from memory to Samuel Arnold several airs from the latter's oratorio *The Prodigal Son*, which he had not heard for 20 years.

WORKS

all first performed and published in London

STAGE

The Rites of Hecate (pantomime, J. Love), Drury Lane, 26 Dec 1763, collab. J. Potter, *GB-Lbl*

Almena (Eng. op, 3, R. Rolt), Drury Lane, 2 Nov 1764, collab. M. Arne; songs pubd (1765)

2 songs in Garrick's revival of A Midsummer Night's Dream, 23 Nov 1763; 1 song each in Townley's High Life below Stairs, 31 Oct 1759, and revivals of Moore's The Foundling, 3 Oct 1765, and The Gamester (?1771)

SACRED VOCAL

12 Hymns, The Words by Revd. Mr Charles Wesley (c1765)

2 Anthems as they are Sung at St Paul's Cathedral (1767): Call to Remembrance, 3–7vv, org; How long wilt Thou Forget me, 1–5vv, org

Call to Remembrance (Ps xxv.6), 3–7vv, org (1797); rev. by author

6 Anthems and 10 Chants, ed. J. Page (1804); anthems: Behold how Good and Joyful, 1–5vv, org; I Waited Patiently for the Lord, 1–5vv, org; O Lord look down from Heaven, 7vv, org; Save me, O God, 5vv, org; The Heavens Declare the Glory of God, 1–5vv, org; Unto Thee lift I up mine Eyes, 3–4vv, org

5 anthems in Harmonia Sacra, ed. J. Page, i–iii (1800): Behold how Good and Joyful, 1–5vv, org; Call to Remembrance, rev. version, 3–7vv, org; Deliver us, O Lord our God, 5vv, org; How long wilt Thou Forget me, 1–5vv, org; I will Magnify Thee, O God, 3–6vv, org

2 pieces in A Collection of Hymns, ed. J. Page (1804): O Lord, how Beauteous are Thy Courts, sacred ode, SATTB, org, 1764; Jesus Lord we Look to Thee (C. Wesley), hymn, unison vv, org

Hymns and chants pubd in 18th- and 19th-century anthologies, and in *GB-Lbl*

OTHER WORKS

The Shepherd and Shepherdess, a Favourite Cantata (1764)

A Collection of Favourite Songs sung at the Publick Gardens and Theatres (c1765)

A Collection of Songs, 3–4vv, 2 vols. (c1776)

Select Pieces, ed. J. Page, org/pf (c1805)

Songs, glees and catches pubd singly and in 18th-century anthologies; also *GB-Bu, Lbl, US-Cn*

BIBLIOGRAPHY

BDA; FiskeETM; LS

T. Busby: 'Original Memoirs of the late Mr. Jonathan Battishill', *Monthly Magazine*, xiii (1802), 36–9; rev. as preface to *Six Anthems and Ten Chants*, ed. J. Page (London, 1804)

T. Busby: *Concert Room and Orchestra Anecdotes* (London, 1825), iii, 69–76

S. Wesley: *Reminiscences* (MS, c1836, GB-Lbl, Add.27593)

W.A. Barrett: *English Church Composers* (London, 1882/R), 140–43

J.B. Trend: 'Jonathan Battishill', *ML*, xiii (1932), 264–71

E.H. Fellowes: *English Cathedral Music* (London, 1941, rev. 5/1969/R by J.A. Westrup)

G. Pont: 'French Overtures at the Keyboard: "How Handel rendered the Playing of Them"', *Musicology*, vi (1980), 29–50

M.C. Nelson: *The Church Anthems of Jonathan Battishill* (diss., U. of Southern California, 1984)

G. Pont: 'Battishill's Arrangements of Handel's Keyboard Overtures', *Gedenkschrift für Jens Peter Larsen*, ed. H.J. Marx (Kassel, 1989), 139–53

B. Matthews: 'The Rise and Fall of Jonathan Battishill', *MT*, cxxxiii (1992), 477–9

PETER WARD JONES

Battista, Luigi Alberto Federigo. *See* BAPTISTE, LUDWIG ALBERT FRIEDRICH.

Battistelli, Giorgio (*b* Albano Laziale, 25 April 1953). Italian composer. He studied composition with Giancarlo Bizzi at the L'Aquila Conservatory, and in 1974 he co-founded the Gruppo di Ricerca e Sperimentazione Musicale 'Edgard Varèse', and the Gruppo Sperimentale 'Beat 72' in Rome. An invitation from the Deutscher Akademischer Austauschdienst brought him to Berlin (1985–6) and after being appointed artistic director of the Cantiere Internazionale d'Arte in Montepulciano (1993) he took on the artistic direction of the Orchestra Regionale Toscana in 1996. From the outset, his interests have lain principally in theatrical experimentation and formal exploration – aspects which he places above work on the musical material – with some tendency towards minimalism. He has written various works for the stage and since 1987 has also written the texts, which are sometimes inspired by personal responses to films or historical facts; these include the monodrama *Aphrodite* (1983), the chamber fantasy *Jules Verne* (1987), *Le combat d'Hector* *et d'Achille* (1989), a 'representation of bodies and of memory for speaking musicians' entitled *Keplers Traum* (1989–90, and winner of the 1992 SIAE Prize for a world première outside Italy), *Frau Frankenstein* (1992), *Prova d'orchestra* (1995) and *The Cenci* (1997). The sense of drama is implicit in his purely instrumental works, in which various transformations or restatements of motifs, timbres and intervals can be read acoustically as the development of imaginary characters. The very titles of his orchestral and chamber compositions seem to emphasize this connection with symbolic scenarios: *Il racconto di Monsieur B.* (1980), *La fattoria del vento* (1988) and *Tre voci* (1996). In all his work a rhythmic noise element sometimes assumes a central aesthetic position, often verging on mere effect (*Experimentum mundi*, 1981).

WORKS
(*selective list*)

Stage: Experimentum mundi (opera di musica immaginistica, 1, after M.Diderot, J.-J. Rousseau, Voltaire and others: *Encyclopédie*), 1981, Rome, 1981; Aphrodite (monodramma di costumi antichi, P. Louÿs), 1983, Rome, 1988; Jules Verne (fantasia da camera in forma di spettacolo, Battistelli), 1987, Strasbourg, 1987; Le combat d'Hector et d'Achille (représentation de corps et de mémoire, Homer and others), 1989, Strasbourg, 1989; Keplers Traum (chbr op, Battistelli), 1989–90, Linz, 1990; Globe Theatre (ballet), 1990, Bielefeld, 1990; Frau Frankenstein (monodramma del Prometeo moderno, after M.W. Shelley), 1992, Berlin, 1993; Teorema (parabola in musica, 2, after P.P. Pasolini), 1992, Florence, 1992; Prova d'orchestra (6 scene musicali di fine secolo, Battistelli, after F. Fellini), 1995, Strasbourg, 2 Nov 1995; Die Entdeckung der Langsamkeit (music-theatre, 5 scenes, M. Klögl), 1997, Bremen, 1997; The Cenci (music-theatre, Battistelli and N. Ward, after A. Artaud), 1997, London, 11 July 1997

Inst: Comme un opéra fabuleux, perc, 1979; Il racconto di Monsieur B., orch, 1980; Anima, perc, 1988; La fattoria del vento, orch, 1988; Onde a terra se acaba e o mar comeca, orch, 1988; Psychopompos, perc, 1988; Anarca 'Hommage à Ernst Jünger', orch, 1988–9; Album di famiglia, 6 insts, 1992; Heliopolis, perc, 1992; Paz Music 'Omaggio a Octavio Paz', orch, 1993–4; Begleitmusik zu einer Dichtspielszene, 12 insts, 1994; Orazi e Curiazi, perc, 1996; 3 voci (G. van Straten), spkr, str, perc, tape, 1996

Vocal: Il canto del drago (concerto scenico, B. Bassiri), 1v, 2 pf, cel, synth, 3 perc, 1990; Ascolto di Rembrandt (G. Ceronetti), 1v, small orch, tape, 1991

BIBLIOGRAPHY

H. De la Motte-Haber: '"In die Tiefe der Psyche": Magie und Rationalität im Werk von Giorgio Battistelli', *MusikTexte*, no.30 (1989), 17–19

M. Gamba: *Conversazione con Giorgio Battistelli* (Milan, 1992)

I. Stoianova: *All'ascolto dell'esperienza: i 'teatri-globo' di Giorgio Battistelli* (Florence, 1992)

H. De la Motte-Haber: *Die Reise in Innere der Zeit* (Bremen, 1997)

ANGELA IDA DE BENEDICTIS

Battistini. Italian family of musicians. They were active in Novara in the 18th century.

(1) **Giacomo Battistini** (*b* c1665; *d* Novara, 5 Feb 1719). Composer. He was probably born in northern Italy. From 14 April 1694 he was *maestro di cappella* of Novara Cathedral, and provided the cathedral with a completely new and varied repertory; he was also active in the theatre (1694–5). For financial reasons he left the cathedral on 1 April 1706, becoming *maestro di cappella* of S Gaudenzio on 27 June; he held the post for the remainder of his life and reorganized the music there. Battistini's best-known works are the *Motetti sacri* (1698), the *Armonie sagre* (1700) and his pieces in the concertato style; these show a secure technique and a light though expressive style.

WORKS

Motetti sacri, 2–3vv, op.1 (Bologna, 1698)

Armonie sagre, 1–3vv, some with insts, op.2 (Bologna, 1700)

3 missae breves, 8vv, bc; 2 Mag, 8vv; Stabat mater, 4vv, 1704; Regina coeli, 4vv, org; Regina coeli, 8vv, org; Alma Redemptoris mater, 4vv, vn, org; Alma Redemptoris mater, 8vv, vn, org; Ave regina coelorum, 8vv, vn, org; Gaudeamus omnes, 4vv; O sacrum convivium, 4vv; several inc. compositions: all I-NOVg

Quasi rosa in Aprile ridens, motet, S, 2 vn, bc, GB-Lbl

Lost sacred works, incl.: Mass, 4vv, 4vv, 2 org, 2 orch, and 2 vesper settings, all perf. for the transfer of the relics of St Gaudentius, June 1711; Il trionfo della Pietà (orat, M.A. Porta), Novara, Chiesa di S Quirico, 20 Nov 1712; Mosé ricercato figura di S Gaudenzio (orat, G.A. Prina), Novara, n.d.

Lost stage works: Antemio in Roma, act 3 (dramma, 3, A.R.B. Villa), Novara, Nuovo, carn. 1695, collab. A. Besozzi and D. Erba; Antioco (melodramma, 3, N. Minato), Novara, Nuovo, carn. 1698

(2) **Giuseppe Battistini** (*b* Novara, c1695; *d* Novara, 13 April 1747). Organist and composer, son of (1) Giacomo Battistini. He became first organist of S Gaudenzio at an early age, and succeeded his father as *maestro di cappella* on 27 November 1719, remaining there until 1745. None of his compositions is known to survive. His brother Francesco (*b* c1708) was also a musician.

(3) **Gaudenzio [Girolamo Gaudenzio] Battistini** (*b* Novara, 30 June 1722; *d* Novara, 25 Feb 1800). Organist and composer, son of (2) Giuseppe Battistini. After abandoning an ecclesiastical career, he studied music with his father and uncle. In 1747 he succeeded his father as *maestro di cappella* of S Gaudenzio, having substituted for several years. After spending some time in Milan (perhaps 1748) studying harmony and counterpoint, he remained at S Gaudenzio for 53 years. In 1779 he directed Sarti's opera *Medonte re d'Epiro*, which opened the Teatro Nuovo; his engagement as *maestro concertatore* was renewed in 1780, 1783 and 1785. Battistini sometimes incorporated concertato techniques into his basically polyphonic style, but his music maintains an uncommon standard of solidity and dignity.

WORKS
all in I-NOVg

Passio secundum Lucam; Passio secundum Marcum

Ky-Gl, solo vv, chorus, orch, org, 1779; Requiem, 4vv, 1785, with fugal Cum Sancto, 4vv, org, orch

12 Salve regina, 4–8vv; Regina coeli, 4vv, 4vv, str, org; Statuit ei Dominus, 4vv; Dixit, 4vv, orch, org

15 motets, 4vv, vc; collection of grad, off and comm for Advent, Lent and Holy Week; masses, Mag and other liturgical works

BIBLIOGRAPHY

DBI (G. di Genova); *MGG1* (R. Meloncelli)

G. Bustico: *Il teatro antico di Novara (1695–1873)* (Novara, 1922), 2–3, 22, 24

V. Fedeli, ed.: *Le cappelle musicali di Novara dal secolo XVI a' primordi dell'Ottocento*, IMi, iii (1933), 1–79 [incl. music by Battistinis, 91–347]

D. Tunley: *The Eighteenth-Century French Cantata* (London, 1974)

Battistini, Mattia (*b* Rome, 27 Feb 1856; *d* Colle Baccaro, nr Rieti, 7 Nov 1928). Italian baritone. After a brief period of study with Venceslao Persichini and Eugenio Terziana, Battistini seized a sudden chance to sing the leading role of Alfonso XI in Donizetti's *La favorite* at the Teatro Argentina in Rome on 11 December 1878, when his immediate success inaugurated a career of nearly 50 years. His early London appearances, in 1883 and 1887, attracted no special attention; his major English triumphs came at Covent Garden in 1905 and 1906, when he was heard in several of his leading roles, including Rigoletto, Germont, Amonasro and Yevgeny Onegin.

By that time Battistini had established himself throughout Europe, and especially in Russia, as a baritone almost without rival in the older repertory and scarcely less famous in later and widely varied roles. The Russian aristocracy and imperial family treated him as an equal; the tsar loaded him with honours; on one occasion his personal intervention is said to have secured the release of a man condemned to death. In Germany and Austria, Poland and Spain, he was equally idolized; and his adoring compatriots saluted him with such fanciful titles as 'Il re dei baritoni' and 'La gloria d'Italia'. After an early engagement at Buenos Aires he never again visited America, and was doubtless the most important singer of his day to have resisted the pull of the Metropolitan – owing, it is said, to his dread of the Atlantic crossing. His vocal powers were almost undimmed by age. When, after a lapse of 16 years, he made a series of concert appearances at the Queen's Hall, London, in 1922 and the two following years, his unimpaired tone and technique astonished his audiences.

Battistini's voice was an unusually high baritone, verging on the range of a tenor, with some corresponding weakness in the lowest register. The quality was noble: clear, strong, vibrant, capable also of a deliberately 'villainous' harshness when required, even of a kind of scornful snarl that could prove dramatically telling; then suddenly melting into the extremes of tenderness and delicacy. He had fabulous agility and breath control, and could spin out long phrases in the smoothest legato or execute the most flamboyant of flourishes, all with a natural instinct for the grand manner. His Mozart singing, as recorded, seems too wilful for modern taste; but his majestic style is clearly perceptible even in the delivery of a single line of recitative, such as the simple and lapidary 'Povero Lionello!' which precedes Plunkett's 'Il mio Lionel' in Flotow's *Marta*. This is one of the best of some 100 records that he made between 1903 and 1924. Noteworthy, too, is a group of 1907 recordings from

Ernani, including a 'Vieni meco, sol di rose' of surpassing delicacy and a finely modulated 'Eri tu' from *Un ballo in maschera* made during the same recording session.

BIBLIOGRAPHY

GV (R. Celletti; R. Vegeto)
F. Palmegiani: *Mattia Battistini, il re dei baritoni* (Milan, 1949, 2/1977) [with discography by W.R. Moran]
J. Dennis: 'Mattia Battistini', *Record Collector*, viii (1953), 245–65 [with discography]
D. Shawe-Taylor: 'Mattia Battistini', *Opera*, viii (1957), 283–9
A. Kelly, J.F.Perkins and J. Ward: 'Mattia Battistini (1856–1928): a Discography', *Recorded Sound*, no.65 (1977), 652–6

DESMOND SHAWE-TAYLOR/R

Battle, Kathleen (*b* Portsmouth, OH, 13 Aug 1948). American soprano. She studied with Franklin Bens at the Cincinnati College-Conservatory and in the early 1970s was engaged by James Levine for both the Ravinia Festival and the Metropolitan Opera. She made her début in 1976 as Susanna with New York City Opera. In 1977 she sang Oscar at San Francisco, then made her Metropolitan début as the Shepherd in *Tannhäuser*, subsequently singing Rosina, Despina, Zerlina, Blonde, Pamina, Zdenka, Strauss's and Massenet's Sophie and Handel's Cleopatra. She made her British début in 1979 at Glyndebourne as Nerina (Haydn's *La fedeltà premiata*) and sang Adina at Zürich in 1980. At Salzburg she has sung Despina, Susanna and Zerlina. She made her Covent Garden début in 1985 as Zerbinetta, returning as Norina in 1990. In 1993 she sang Marie (*La fille du régiment*) at San Francisco. A notoriously temperamental artist (now banned from appearing at the Metropolitan), Battle is gifted with a high, sweet soprano of considerable charm, which she governs with technical finesse; she also has an attractive and vivacious stage presence, and her work is skilful and stylish, if not always highly individual. Her numerous recordings include Zerlina, Blonde and Zerbinetta, Fauré's Requiem and Brahms's *German Requiem*, and an admired interpretation of Handel's Semele.

RICHARD DYER, ELIZABETH FORBES

Battle music. Compositions descriptive of battles form a minor but distinctive category of 16th-century music, both vocal and instrumental, with a sporadic continuation, mainly instrumental, down to the early 19th century. The Italian term 'battaglia' has sometimes been applied to the whole of this repertory, but the composers themselves generally used titles in their own languages (Fr. *guerre*, *bataille*; Ger. *Schlacht*; Sp. *batalla*). This article deals with musical representations of battles, rather than the music that might have accompanied actual battles (for which *see* MILITARY CALLS). Battle-pieces do, however, incorporate fragments of military music from time to time, such as the 'tan-ta-ra, tan-ta-ra' motif in Byrd's keyboard work *The Battle*; the words are written in the manuscript (My Ladye Nevells Booke, 1591) just before 'the battels be joyned'.

Some of the typical devices of battle music – rallying-cries, imitations of fanfares – are anticipated in 14th-century cacce (see HAM, i, no.52), and in chansons such as the four-part *A l'arme, a l'arme* by Grimace and the three-part *Alla bataglia* in the Pixérécourt Chansonnier (*F-Pn* fr.15123). Isaac's four-part *A la battaglia* (likely to have been performed in 1485) makes modest use of ostinato figures and has several alternations of duple and triple time (a regular feature later). It lacks words in its only complete source but elsewhere is associated with a

Mattia Battistini as Don Carlo in Verdi's 'Ernani'

text exhorting the soldiers of Florence to take arms against the Genoese.

The most famous and influential of 16th-century battle-pieces was Janequin's four-part chanson *La guerre*, written to commemorate the Battle of Marignano (1515), at which François I secured a victory over Swiss mercenaries employed by Duke Ercole Sforza of Milan. First published by Attaingnant in 1528, it was frequently reprinted, once (by Susato in 1545) with an optional fifth voice added by Verdelot. Janequin's own five-part version of the work (1555) is a substantial revision. The *prima pars*, preliminary to the battle itself, is set in fairly straightforward chanson style; the longer *secunda pars* is a vivid portrayal of the course of the battle, with a largely onomatopoeic text, triadic motifs, and lively rhythms set against a relatively static harmonic background. *La guerre* depended for much of its effect upon the text; nevertheless, Francesco Canova da Milano made a lute arrangement of the whole work (1536 and many reprints). No doubt more amenable to instrumentalists was a 'reduced version' in the form of a pavan of four strains, the first three being derived from the *prima pars*; like its model this enjoyed long popularity. What is perhaps the earliest version, for four-part consort, was printed in Jacques Moderne's *Musicque de joye* (c1544). In Hans Neusidler's *Ein new künstlich Lautten Buch* (1544) the pavan is entitled *Sula bataglia* and the fourth strain is separately labelled 'Der hupff auff' (ed. in DTÖ, xxxvii, Jg.xviii/2, 1911/R, p.56). At Castell'Arquato is a keyboard arrangement of the pavan from c1600, followed by a saltarello and *La tedeschina*, the latter based on a single chord (like the lute piece *La guerre* in Attaingnant's *Introduction* of 1529).

One of many pieces written in imitation of the chanson *La guerre* is *La bataglia taliana* by Matthias Hermann Werrecore, a riposte to Janequin's piece in that it describes a victory of Francesco Sforza, most probably the Battle of Pavia (1525), at which François I was taken prisoner. Werrecore set his piece *a* 4 and in the same F Ionian mode as Janequin and, like him, made extensive use of onomatopoeic syllables. The distinctive musical motif at the start of Janequin's *secunda pars*, to the words 'Fan frere le le lan fan fan', is quoted within the first of Werrecore's three *partes*. While *La guerre* had a fragment of German at the end (1528 version: 'toute frelore bigot' – all is lost, by God), *La bataglia taliana* has text in Italian, French, German and Spanish. The work was published in Vienna in 1544 (RISM 1544[19]) and reprinted in Venice in 1549 and 1552 with considerable variant readings. It seems that Neusidler lost little time in making his lute arrangement (1544[23]; ed. in DTÖ, xxxvii, p.46).

The influence of *La guerre* (both text and music) is still apparent in Andrea Gabrieli's eight-part madrigal *Sento un rumor/Alla battaglia*, published posthumously in 1587 (RRMR, li, 1984, nos.10–11). The battle concerned (if there was one) cannot be identified from the text. Gabrieli and Annibale Padovano also each wrote an *Aria della battaglia* for wind instruments in eight parts, published in *Dialoghi musicali* (1590[11]). Banchieri's *La battaglia* (in his *Canzoni alla francese*, 1596; ed. in RRMR, xx, 1975) is once again unspecific as to the event. It is in a single section, within which the same music (with the two four-part choirs reversed) is used to portray trumpets (to the syllables 'Ta ra ra tun ta ra') and drums ('Tra pa ta pa ta pa'). According to the title-page, the music could be either sung or played.

Janequin appears to have been the starting-point too for the substantial repertory of keyboard battle-pieces by 17th-century Spanish and Portuguese composers. Among the earliest examples, Correa de Arauxo's *Tiento de 6° tono* (MME, vi, 1948, no.23; said to be based on the first part of a *batalla* by Morales) and two *Batallas del 6° tono* by José Ximénez (CEKM, xxxi, 1975, nos.14–15) all adopt Janequin's mode and reflect his opening gesture. Later examples by Cabanilles and others were no doubt intended to exploit the trumpets *en chamade* and echo effects of the Iberian organ, but they remain essentially grounded in Renaissance techniques.

Byrd's *The Battle* owes no particular debt to Janequin; the earliest English example of the genre, it still appears in sources of the mid-17th century. Nevertheless, the item that follows it in the Nevell book, *The Barley Break*, with its characteristic battle-piece scenario (the marshalling of forces, the contest, the retreat from the field) is an altogether more engaging work. Other examples for virginals are the strange *A Battle, and No Battle* attributed to Bull and *The Batell of Pavie* set by William Kinloch (*GB-En* 9447); the latter betrays only the most tenuous links with *La bataglia taliana*. English lute sources contain a number of battle-pieces, including one for two lutes (in *GB-Lbl* Eg.2046).

Battle music of the Baroque period is only occasionally linked to recent events. Rather, composers cultivated the genre for its expressive potential, or for dramatic or allegorical purposes. The allegorical usage, already seen in Vecchi's ten-part vocal *Battaglia d'amor e dispetto* of 1587, is evident in Monteverdi's *Il combattimento di Tancredi e Clorinda* (1624) and the other *canti guerrieri* of his eighth book of madrigals (1638). The *stile concitato* developed by Monteverdi proved a valuable resource in opera and in instrumental compositions such as Biber's *Battalia* of 1673 for strings in nine parts and continuo. This employs special effects including rebounding pizzicato in the double basses as well as the expected rapid note repetitions; the suite ends on a subdued note with the descending semitones of *Lamento der vernundten Musquetirer*. A comparable English work (referring to an actual event) is Jenkins's *Newark Siege* (MB, xxvi, 1969, 2/1975, no.23), the minor-key ending reflecting the royalist composer's view of the outcome. Battle music was quite often used as religious allegory. Banchieri, in *L'organo suonarino* (1605), recommended the performance of a *battaglia* at Easter to symbolize Christ's victory over death; and, where his text called for it, Bach drew on the conventions of battle music, most wonderfully perhaps in the *St John Passion* aria 'Es ist vollbracht', at the words 'Der Held aus Juda siegt mit Macht'.

A final spate of battle-pieces describing recent events occurred between about 1780 and 1815. Examples are František Koczwara's *The Battle of Prague*, a sonata for piano or harpsichord with optional violin, cello and drums (c1788), and J.B. Vanhal's programmatic keyboard sonata *Le combat naval de Trafalgar et la mort de Nelson* (c1806). Other conflicts of the Napoleonic era are depicted in Beethoven's *Wellingtons Sieg, oder Die Schlacht bei Vittoria* (op.91, 1813); in Peter Winter's *Schlachtsymphonie* with chorus and J.F. Reichardt's *Schlachtsymphonie* (both 1814); and Weber's cantata *Kampf und Sieg* (1815), celebrating the Battle of Waterloo. But Beethoven's piece caused some embarrassment even among his own circle, and more familiar to modern listeners are the trumpets and drums whose use underlines the prayer for peace in his Mass in D. A musical battle from the Romantic period is Liszt's symphonic poem *Hunnenschlacht* (1857), inspired not directly by the event (which supposedly took place in the year 451) but by a painting by Wilhelm Kaulbach. As far as battle music is concerned, the 20th century has lost its naivety, and unquestioning portrayals in music of military conquests are hardly to be expected. Kodály's *Háry János* suite (1927) includes a movement entitled 'The Battle and Defeat of Napoleon' in which march tunes and trumpet calls are treated in a spirit of caricature. On another plane are the unforgettable evocations of battle sounds in Britten's *War Requiem* (1961), the true nature of what they represent being starkly revealed in the poems of Wilfred Owen.

BIBLIOGRAPHY

BrownI; MGG2 ('Battaglia'; W. Braun); *ReeseMR*

M. Brenet: 'Essai sur les origines de la musique descriptive', *RMI*, xiv (1907), 725–51; xv (1908), 457–87

M.E. Sutton: *A Study of the 17th-Century Iberian Organ Batalla: Historical Development, Musical Characteristics, and Performance Considerations* (diss., U. of Kansas, 1975)

O.W. Neighbour: *The Consort and Keyboard Music of William Byrd* (London, 1978)

T.J. McGee: '"Alla battaglia": Music and Ceremony in Fifteenth-Century Florence', *JAMS*, xxxvi (1983), 287–302

K. Schulin: *Musikalische Schlachtgemälde in der Zeit von 1756–1815* (Tutzing, 1986)

D. Nutter: Preface to *Orazio Vecchi: Battaglia and Mascherata*, RRMR, lxxii (1987)

H.C. Slim: 'Commentary to Keyboard Music at Castell' Arqunto', *CEKM*, xxxvii (1991)

A. Silbiger, ed.: *Keyboard Music before 1700* (New York, 1995)

ALAN BROWN

Batton, Désiré-Alexandre (*b* Paris, 2 Jan 1798; *d* Versailles, 15 Oct 1855). French composer. He was a pupil at the Paris Conservatoire from 1806 to 1817; he won the Prix de Rome in 1817 with the cantata *La mort d'Adonis*. Before he left for Italy his most successful comic opera, *La fenêtre secrète*, was given at the Opéra-Comique on 17 November 1818, and during the following year it was performed at Brussels and Copenhagen. In Rome Batton wrote both sacred and secular vocal music, including an unperformed opera, *Vellèda* (from Chateaubriand's *Les martyrs*). Moving to Germany, he then composed several orchestral works for the Munich concert society.

After his return to Paris his theatrical compositions met with little success, except for his part in the nine-man collaboration opera, *La marquise de Brinvilliers* (1831). Although the music in his other *opéras comiques* often received critical praise, the works suffered from poor librettos; *Le camp du drap d'or* was whistled so loudly that the music could not be heard. The aspects of Batton's music that received criticism (such as exaggerated orchestration and ambitious formal planning) look impressively resourceful today, and in combination with his melodic grace they reveal a gifted composer forced into premature retirement by the lack of musical opportunities in Restoration Paris. In 1851, Batton was made inspector of the branch schools of the Conservatoire. (J.-M. Bailbé and others: *La musique en France à l'Epoque romantique: 1830–1870*, Paris, 1991.)

WORKS

THEATRICAL

opéras comiques, first performed in Paris unless otherwise stated

La fenêtre secrète, ou Une soirée à Madrid (3, Des Essarts d'Ambreville), OC (Feydeau), 17 Nov 1818, selections, vs (Paris, *c*1819)

Vellèda (1, after Chateaubriand: *Les martyrs*), 1820, unperf., *F-Pc*

Ethelwina, ou L'exilé (3, P, de Kock and Mme Lemaignan), OC (Feydeau), 31 March 1827

Le prisonnier d'état (1, Mélesville [A.-H.-J. Duveyrier]), OC (Feydeau), 6 Feb 1828, *F*

Le camp du drap d'or (3, de Kock), OC (Feydeau), 23 Feb 1828, collab. L.V.E. Rifaut and Leborne

La marquise de Brinvilliers (drame lyrique, 3, E. Scribe and Castil-Blaze [F.-H.-J. Blaze]), OC (Ventadour), 31 Oct 1831 (Paris, 1831), collab. Auber, H.-M. Berton, Blangini, A. Boieldieu, Carafa, Cherubini, Hérold and Paer

Le remplaçant (3, Scribe and J. Bayard), OC (Nouveautés), 11 Aug 1837

OTHER WORKS

La mort du Tasse (cant., E. de Jouy), 1816, *F-Pc*

La mort d'Adonis (cant., J.-A. Vinaty), 1817, *Pc*

Berenice (lyric scena), Rome, 1820, *Pc*

Ciro (lyric scena), Rome, *c*1819–23, *Pc*

Triste hiver, 3vv (Paris, 1855)

L'attente, 1v, pf acc., 1839, *Pc*

Overture, D, Munich, 1821, *Pc* (parts)

Symphony, other orch pieces, Munich, 1819–23, lost, mentioned by Fétis

M.C. CARR/MARIE LOUISE PEREYRA/DAVID CHARLTON/BENJAMIN WALTON

Battre, H. (*fl c*1430–40). Composer. Nothing is known of his life, though two of the texts he set provide possible clues to his place of origin or employment: *Gaudens exulta* is in praise of Ciney (a town in the province of Namur (now in south-east Belgium); and *Chomos condrosi* is thought to refer to the region around Ciney known as the Condroz. The exclusive association of his works with a source in which he is the only named composer (the so-called 'Battre fascicle' of *I-TRmp* 87) may indicate that he was its compiler. It seems unlikely on stylistic grounds that he is the later 15th-century composer BATTY (or Batten).

Battre's small yet varied output shows considerable originality; his music often unfolds in unpredictable ways. *Gaude virgo* is especially unusual in that it exploits the effects of contrasted vocal groupings (based on a distinction between 'pueri' and 'mutate voces'), while *Chomos condrosi*, a two-part canon with a freely composed third voice, is remarkable for its setting of a macaronic text (in Latin and Greek) which actually describes the compositional technique being employed. Although this is his only canonic work, several others use imitation as a structural rather than a decorative device. If Battre's music shows a tendency towards complexity of line and texture (with occasionally clumsy results), he is also capable of a simpler, more declamatory style, as can be seen for example in the hymn *Stirps regia*.

WORKS

all unique in I-TRmp 87

Edition: *Sieben Trienter Codices*, ed. R. Ficker, DTÖ, lxxvi, Jg.xl (1933/R) [F]

Gloria, 3vv; ed. in DTÖ, lxi, Jg.xxxi (1924/R)

Agnus Dei, 3vv; ed. in DTÖ, lxi, Jg.xxxi (1924/R)

Chomos condrosi, 3vv, canonic motet; F; also ed. in Loyan

De qua natus, 3vv, motet with text from the Genealogy of Christ; F

Dulcissime frater, 3vv, motet; F

Gaude virgo mater Christi, 3vv, sequence-motet; F

Gaudens exulta, 4vv, motet in praise of Ciney; F

Stirps regia, 3vv, hymn; F

Veni Creator Spiritus, 4vv, hymn; ed. in DTÖ, liii, Jg.xxvii (1920)

BIBLIOGRAPHY

StrohmR

G. Adler and O. Koller, eds.: *Sechs Trienter Codices: geistliche und weltliche Kompositionen des XV. Jahrhunderts*, DTÖ, xiv–xv, Jg.vii (1900/R)

R. Loyan: *Canons in the Trent Codices*, CMM, xxxviii (1967)

R.J. White: *The Battre Fascicle of the Trent Codex 87* (diss., Indiana U., 1975) [includes edns of all Battre's works]

D. Fallows: 'Specific Information on the Ensembles for Composed Polyphony 1400–1474', *Studies in the Performance of Late Medieval Music*, ed. S. Boorman (Cambridge, 1983), 109–59, esp. 122–3

PETER WRIGHT

Battuta (It.: 'beat', 'bar', 'measure'). *A battuta*, like *a tempo*, means a return to the strict beat. In the scherzo of Beethoven's Ninth Symphony *ritmo di tre battute* and *ritmo di quattro battute* designate that the one-in-a-bar beats should be grouped in threes and fours respectively. Vivaldi used the performance instruction *battute* ('beaten') for repeated semiquavers (p410/RV163) and Kolneder (*Aufführungspraxis bei Vivaldi*, Leipzig, 1955) raised the possibility that this was an instruction to play *col legno*.

For bibliography see TEMPO AND EXPRESSION MARKS; *see also* BEAT (i).

DAVID FALLOWS

Battuto [battute] (It.). Term used in the 17th and 18th centuries to describe the technique of strumming the strings of the guitar. See RASGUEADO.

Batty (*fl c*1450–80). Composer. Nothing is known of his life. His only two known compositions (both in *CZ-Ps* D.G.IV.47) are respectively three- and four-voice settings of the compline antiphon *Regina celi*. Both paraphrase the plainchant elaborately in the superius, and both make occasional use of imitation. Batty may be identifiable with Batten, whose sole surviving piece (in *CZ-HKm* II A 7) is a three-voice Sanctus whose superius either paraphrases an unidentified chant or merely cites fragments of plainchant melodies. All three works are indebted to the English idiom.

Both 'Batty' and 'Batten' may be misnomers, and it is not impossible that one or both of these names are central European 'misspellings'; in this case they may perhaps be identifiable with Ludovicus Patier (who was at the Savoy court in 1454–5) or Luisot Patin (documented at Naples in 1480). However, both of the latter could equally well have been homonyms. A connection with the earlier composer H. Battre (represented in *I-TRmp* 87) seems less likely on the grounds of stylistic differences.

BIBLIOGRAPHY

M. Bouquet: 'La cappella musicale dei duchi di Savoia, dal 1450 al 1500', *RIM*, iii (1968), 233–85

R.J. Snow: *The Manuscript Strahov D.G.IV.47* (diss., U. of Illinois, 1968)

A. Atlas: *Music at the Aragonese Court of Naples* (Cambridge, 1985)

BOB MITCHELL

Battyn, Adrian. See BATTEN, ADRIAN.

Bätz [Baetz, Baitz, Beets, Beetz, Betz]. Firm of organ builders of German origin, active in the Netherlands. The first organ builder of the family was Johann Heinrich Hartmann Bätz (*b* Frankenroda, nr Eisenach, 1 January, 1709; *d* Utrecht, 13 December 1770). Having learned cabinet making, Johann Heinrich was apprenticed to the organ builder J.C. Thielemann in Gotha for four years starting in 1729. In 1733 he joined the organ workshop of Christiaan Müller in the Dutch Republic and helped to build the organ in the Bavokerk of Haarlem. In 1739 he settled in Utrecht as an independent organ builder. His work shows many similarities with the work of Müller in its cases, pipes and mechanisms. He built at least 16 new organs, many of them quite large, with two to three manuals. The most significant instruments are: Grote Kerk, Gorinchem (1760; rebuilt by Witte), Evangelische Lutherse Kerk, The Hague (1761–2), Hoorn, Oosterkerk, (1762; only the case is extant), Petruskerk, Woerden (1766–8), Zierikzee (1768–70). This last was his *opus magnum*, having three manuals, pedal and 46 stops, and being similar to Müller's organ in Haarlem, but it was destroyed in a fire in 1832.

Gideon Thomas Bätz (bap. Utrecht, 8 June 1751; *d* Utrecht, 30 Jan 1820) inherited the workshop after his father's death. Although a very able organ builder he was not a good businessman, and initially the firm was run with his younger brother Christoffel (bap. 15 August, 1755; *d* nr Breukelen, 1 May 1800) under the leadership of his uncle Johann Heinrich Wilhelm Bätz. Gideon Thomas took over the leadership at the age of 21. Following a dispute over the inheritance Christoffel left to start his own organ building workshop in 1778. He built the *rugwerk* of the Medemblik organ, as well as the organ of Loenen aan de Vecht. Gideon Thomas and Christoffel built at least 22 new organs. The organs are smaller than those of their father, reflecting the changing musical requirements and the economic situation of the time; many have one manual and several divided stops. However, the external forms and specifications are more varied than those of their father. They also built a number of cabinet organs. The most significant organs by Gideon Thomas were at Heukelum (1779), Breukelen (1787) Lutheran church, Edam, (1809), Vleuten (1812), Franciscus Xavieriuskerk, Amersfoort (1819), and Weesp (1822).

Under the brothers Jonathan (*b* Utrecht, 5 Feb 1787; *d* Utrecht, 18 July 1849) and Johan Martin Willem (bap. Utrecht, 15 March 1789; *d* Utrecht, 19 Nov 1836), sons of Christoffel, great growth took place. Jonathan was the most important of the two, and Aristide Cavaille-Coll paid him a visit on 16–17 October 1844. Johan Martin Willem lived in Amsterdam between 1812 and 1818 and was a piano maker. He returned to Utrecht to work for his brother until 1831. By then Christiaan Gottlieb Friedrich Witte (*b* Rothenburg, nr Hanover, 12 Jan 1802; *d* Utrecht, 1873) had become the star worker of Jonathan's company. Witte had learned his trade with Bethmann in Hannover and joined the Bätz workshop in 1826. He was the foreman during the building of the organ of the Ronde Lutherse Kerk, Amsterdam. In 1839 Witte married a granddaughter of Gideon Thomas Bätz, and took over the business after Jonathan's death. The sons of Johan Martin Willem (Johan Christiaan, Jonathan (ii) and Johan Martin Willem (ii)) remained active in the workshop. Witte's son Johan Frederik (1840–1902) succeeded his father in 1873. With the death of the latter, the Bätz-Witte dynasty came to an end.

Between 1820 and 1849, when Jonathan Bätz had the leadership, 22 new organs were built. Most of them are extant. As well as the charming, small organs in Nieuwenhoorn, Weesp, 's-Gravenland, Harderwijk, Mijdrecht, the Amstelkerk in Amsterdam, the Lutheran church in Woerden, and the Gothic Room of the Palace of King Willem II at The Hague, he built a number of significant larger organs, such as the three-manual organs in the Domkerk, Utrecht (in a neo-Gothic case with many pipes from the 1571 organ by Peter Janszoon De Swart), the Ronde Lutherse Kerk, Amsterdam and the Nieuwe Kerk, Delft. Organs by the Wittes can be found in Gorinchem, Buren, Tiel, Delft (Oude Kerk), Bunschoten, Naarden,

Kapelle, Geervliet, Rijswijk, Utrecht, Oldenzaal, West-Terschelling, De Rijp, Culemborg, Delfshaven, Dordrecht, Ophemert, Puttershoek and Rotterdam. The organs in Naarden and Delft have 16′ Principals in the *rugwerk*. The J.F. Witte organ in St Jacobskerk, The Hague (1882; demolished), was the largest organ built in the Netherlands in the 19th century. A large organ by him in the Oude Lutherse Kerk, Amsterdam (1885), survives.

Bätz organs are distinguished by their traditional Dutch style, having a very solid construction using the best materials, a very musical sound and great reliability. After Jonathan Bätz's death Witte in many ways broke with the 18th-century Bätz tradition in favour of a fuller, more monumental sound. Also, Witte introduced novelties such as three manual-divisions in one case, keyboards to the side of the organ, accentuation of the treble stops, the importance of the treble labial Cornet, and the introduction of tuning expressions. Some of Witte's cases are in neo-Gothic or neo-Romanesque style while others follow the more traditional Bätz look.

BIBLIOGRAPHY

G. Oost: *De orgelmakers Bätz: een eeuw orgelbouw in Nederland (1739–1849)* (Alphen aan den Rijn, 3/1975)

G. Oost, ed.: *Gebroeders Bätz, Orgelmakers Utrecht* (Utrecht, 1975)

J. Jongepier: *Langs Nederlandse orgels: Noord-Holland, Zuid-Holland, Utrecht* (Utrecht, 1977)

J. Jongepier and T. den Toon: 'Orgels van Witte gerestaureerd', *Het Orgel*, lxxxv (1989), 290–305, 329–346, 357, 377–83, 403–13

T. den Toon: *De orgelmakers Witte* (Rotterdam, 1997)

BARBARA OWEN, ADRI DE GROOT

Bauchspiess, Severus. *See* GASTORIUS, SEVERUS.

Bauckholt, Carola (*b* Krefeld, 21 Aug 1959). German composer. She studied at the Cologne Academy of Music (1978–84) with Kagel, among others. After working with the TAM (Theater am Marienplatz) in Krefeld-Fischeln (1976–84), she co-founded the Thürmchen publishing imprint (1985) and Thürmchen Ensemble (1991), both of which specialize in experimental music and music theatre. As a composer, she has taken the process of listening to her immediate surroundings as a point of departure, subtly imitating and transforming the sounds of everyday life in her compositions. Many of her works (until the mid-1980s) incorporate elements of music theatre (i.e. slides, videos, objects, semantic associations etc.). In *In gewohnter Umgebung I–III* (1991–4) and other works, ordinary sounds are imitated by instruments which assume activities connected with the production of these sounds, such as rubbing or striking. *Geräusche* (1992) uses new instrumental sounds to particularly good effect. Later compositions, such as *Doina* (1996) and *Kurbel und Wolke* (1997), link signifiers (gestural, semantic or associative) to vocal and instrumental sound with increasing diversity. Her many honours include prizes from the international competition of WDR (1989), the Carl Maria von Weber Competition, Dresden (1993) and the Gedok Competition (1994), the Swiss Stiftung Boswil Award (1995) and the Dresden Blaue Brücke Award (1996).

WORKS
(selective list)

DRAMATIC

Stage: Like a Rolling Stone, objects, 1978–9; Lau & Tau (H.C. Artmann), 2 spkrs, ocarina, b harmonica, 1980; Eure Zeichen, 6 players, tape, 1981–2; con espressione, 1982–3: allegretto, 5vv; amoroso, 10 light sources, objects (incl. a glass); furioso, tpt, 5 noise makers; calmato, 5 pfmrs, 2 va; grave, S, tape; grave (G. Rühm, Bible: *Matthew*), S, tape, 1982; Im inneren Ohr, pfmr,

tape, 1983; Der sechste Sinn (K. Bayer), 1v, 1 player, insts, 1983; Der gefaltete Blick (scenic cant.), 2vv, vc, 1984; Das klagende Lied, 5 bandoneons, vn, va, vc, db, tuba, tape, 1985; Geräusche, 2 players, 1992; In gewohnter Umgebung II, 5 pfmrs, cl, vc, pf, light, objects, 1993; Lauschangriff, fl, cl, vn, va, 2 vc, db, perc, 1994–5, collab. C.J. Walther, T. Stiegler and S. Walter; Stachel der Empfindlichkeit, Ct, Mez, 3 vc, 4 perc, 1997–8; Es wird sich zeigen, 3vv, str qt, perc, 1998

Other dramatic: erinnern vergessen, fl, bn, vc, db, perc, objects, slide projections, 1990–91 [arr. concert version]; langsamer als ich dachte, vc, perc, slide projections, 1990; In gewohnter Umgebung I, 2 perc, objects, slide projections, 1991; In gewohnter Umgebung III, vc, espérou/prep pf/cymbalon, video, 1994; Pumpe, 1v, accdn, pf, light, 1994; Vertraute Rätsel, fl, cl, vn, va, vc, db, perc, pf, video, 1995–6

OTHER WORKS

Inst: zwei Trichter, fl, bn, tpt, tuba, va, elec gui, 4 perc, 1978–88; Polizeitrieb, 2 perc, 1985; Hornduo, 2 hn, 1986–7; sottovoce, 2 vc, 1988; Trio, 2 vc, pf, 1988–9; Polsch, pf, 1989; Qnt, variable insts, 1989; 3 Sätze, wind qnt, 1989; Balsam, str orch, 1990; mehr oder weniger, fl, ob, cl, vn, va, vc, db, pf, perc, 1991; offen und beweglich, orch, 1992; Zopf, fl, ob, cl, 1992; Luftwurzeln, fl, cl, va, vc, 1993; Maulwurf, 2 bn, dbn, 1993; Str Trio, 1994; Treibstoff, fl, cl, vn, va, vc, db, perc, pf, 1995; Galopp, fl, sax, vc, elec gui, perc, 1996; Kurbel und Wolke, orch, 1997

Vocal: Die heute Vernunft, 2vv, 2 hn, db, 4 perc, 1986–7; Wortanfall, spkr, Ct, 2 hn, xyl, viol, db, hp, timp, 1986; Schraubdichtung, spkr, vc, dbn, perc, 1989–90; Doina, 1v, str orch, 1996

Principal publisher: Thürmchen

BIBLIOGRAPHY

C. Bauckholt: '*Identitätsfetzen*', *Positionen* (1993), no.16, p.16 only

C. Naujocks: '"Aus gewohnter Umgebung": Carola Bauckholts Musik aus Bildern, Licht und Klang', *Positionen*, no.32 (1997), 23–6

F. Hilberg: 'Krümel des Alltags. Carola Bauckholts Musiktheater "Es wird sich zeigen"', *Musik Texte*, no.79 (1999), 54–6

R. Schulz: 'Hellhörig. Porträt der Komponistin Carola Bauckholt', ibid., 42–6

MARTINA HOMMA

Baud-Bovy, Samuel (*b* Geneva, 27 Nov 1906; *d* Geneva, 2 Nov 1986). Swiss musicologist and conductor. In Geneva he took an arts degree at the university and was a violin pupil of Fernand Closset at the conservatory. He then studied conducting with Nilius and music history with Adler in Vienna (1926–7), composition with Dukas and musicology with Pirro in Paris (1928–9) and conducting with Weingartner at Basle and Scherchen at Geneva; in 1936 he took the doctorat ès lettres at Geneva University.

After a visit to Greece (1929–31), where he studied sacred music and folksong, he returned to Geneva Conservatoire as orchestral instructor (1933–73) and conductor (1942–73), also serving as co-principal (1947), principal (1957) and honorary principal (1970). Concurrently at the university he was director of studies (1931), assistant professor (1942) and honorary professor (1958) of modern Greek. In 1938 he became director of the Société de Chant Sacré; he was also president of the Association des Musiciens Suisses (1955–60) and of the International Society for Music Education (1961–3). In 1975 he was awarded the Prix de la Ville de Genève and in 1977 he became a member of the executive board of the International Council for Traditional Music.

Baud-Bovy's main area of research was Greek traditional music, in particular Kleftic ballad from mainland Greece, and the music of Crete and the Dodecanese islands. He was among the first scholars of Greek traditional music to make a systematic collection of the music as well as the texts from one area (the Dodecanese). Consistent aspects of his research were his preoccupation with the 15-syllable text line (its origins, evolution and relationship to the melodic strophe), and the comparison of melodic variants as a means of determining their possible origin. His work constitutes the most substantial contribution by any one author to the study of Greek traditional music.

WRITINGS

La chanson populaire grecque du Dodécanèse (diss., U. of Geneva; Paris, 1936)
'Sur la strophe de la chanson cleftique', Annuaire de l'Institut de philologie et d'histoire orientales et slaves, ii (1950), 53–78
'Sur la chanson grecque antique et moderne', SMz, xciii (1953), 418–23
'La strophe de distiques rimés dans la chanson grecque', Studia memoriae Belae Bartók sacra, ed. B. Rajeczky and L. Varygas (Budapest, 1956; Eng. trans., 1959), 365–83
Etudes sur la chanson cleftique (Athens, 1958)
with others: Jean Jacques Rousseau (Neuchâtel, 1962) [incl. 'Rousseau musicien', 51–66]
'La place des rizitika tragoudia dans la chanson populaire de la Grèce moderne', Kritika chronika, xv–xvi (1963), 97–105
'La systématisation des chansons populaires', IFMC Conference: Budapest 1964 [SMH, vii (1965)], 213–29
'L'accord de la lyre antique et la musique populaire de la Grèce moderne', RdM, liii (1967), 3–20
'Equivalences métriques dans la musique vocale grecque antique et moderne', RdM, liv (1968), 3–15
'L'évolution d'une chanson grecque', JIFMC, xx (1968), 39–47
with B. Bouvier: pref. & epil. to Mousikē ermēneia tōn demotikōn tragoudiōn tes monēs Iberōn [A transcription of the demotic songs of the convent of Ivira], ed. D. Mazaraki (Athens, 1968)
'Chansons d'Epire du nord et du Pont', YIFMC, iii (1971), 120–27
'Sur une chanson de danse balkanique', RdM, lviii (1972), 153–61
'I epikratisi toy dekapentasyllavou sto elliniko dimotiko tragoydi' [The supremacy of the 15-syllable line in popular Greek song], Hellenika, xxvi (1973), 301–13
'Rousseau as a Musician', Times Literary Supplement (20 July 1973)
'Jean-Jacques Rousseau et la musique française', RdM, lx (1974), 212–16
'Les chansons populaires grecques harmonisées par Maurice Ravel', Maurice Ravel au XXe siècle, ed. D. Pistone (Paris, 1975), 24–32
'Rameau, Voltaire et Rousseau', Revue musicale suisse, cxvi (1976), 152–7
'Sur quelques mirologues de Grèce continentale', Neue ethnomusikologische Forschungen: Festschrift Felix Hoerburger, ed. P. Baumann, R.M. Brandl and K. Reinhard (Laaber, 1977), 141–52
'Le dorien etait-il un mode pentatonique?', RdM, lxiv (1978), 153–80
'L'ornementation dans le chant de l'église grecque et la chanson populaire grecque moderne', SMH, xxi (1979), 281–93
'Chansons populaires de la Grèce ancienne', RdM, lxix (1983), 5–20; lxx (1984), 259–60
Essai sur la chanson populaire grecque (Návpilon, 1983)
'Ein lasisches Lied', 'Weine, meine Laute … ': Gedenkschrift Kurt Reinhard, ed. C. Ahrens and others (Laaber, 1984), 47–56
'Sur le chromatisme dans la musique grecque', Musica e liturgia nella cultura mediterranea: Venice 1985, 169–75
'Le "genre enharmonique": a-t-il existé?', RdM, lxxii (1986), 5–21

FOLKSONG EDITIONS

Chansons populaires du Dodécanèse (Athens, 1935–8)
Chansons populaires grecques du Dodécanèse, recueillies et harmonisées pour chant et piano (Geneva, 1946)
Chansons populaires de Crète occidentale (Geneva, 1972)

BIBLIOGRAPHY

H. Gagnebin: 'Hommage à Samuel Baud-Bovy', SMz, cviii (1968), 334–5
G. Amargianakis: 'Hommage à Samuel Baud-Bovy', Revue musicale de Suisse romande, xl/1 (1987), 13–28
J.-J. Eigeldinger: 'Travaux de Samuel Baud-Bovy: essai de bibliographie', Revue musicale de Suisse romande, xl/1 (1987), 31–5
R.M. Brandl and E. Konstantinou, eds.: Griechische Musik und Europa (Aachen, 1988) [memorial volume]

LUCY DURÁN

Baude de Rains [Baude Fresnel] (*b* Reims, mid-14th century; *d* 1397–8). French harpist and organist. He was musician to Philip the Bold of Burgundy and may be identifiable with BAUDE CORDIER.

Baudelaire, Charles (Pierre) (*b* Paris, 9 April 1821; *d* Paris, 31 Aug 1867). French poet. In 1921 Proust could call him the 'greatest poet of 19th century', but during his own lifetime the praise was more reserved. An 1852 caricature by his friend the photographer Nadar lampooned him as a 'nervous, testy and irritable young poet', who was still 'probably the best' of his generation. Ten years later, a condescending Sainte-Beuve would portray the now 41-year-old Baudelaire as a 'nice, refined boy'.

By that time Baudelaire's reputation had been well established not only as a poet and art critic – with important essays on Delacroix and Constantin Guys – but also as a translator of the macabre stories of Edgar Allan Poe. Published continuously over nearly two decades, Baudelaire's Poe translations represented the most stable part of a troubled literary career, becoming so popular that in France the names of the two authors, as Théophile Gautier later remarked, were practically inseparable.

The reputation spawned by his poetry was quite another matter. The publication of *Les Fleurs du mal* in 1857 thrust Baudelaire into the public eye not only as an artist but as the victim of an obscenity trial, leading to the censoring of the edition and the subsequent bankruptcy of his Parisian publisher. While such negative publicity made Baudelaire infamous, he nonetheless managed to win admiration from established poets such as Alfred de Vigny, whom Baudelaire met in 1861 during a misguided attempt to gain entrance into the Académie Française, as well as from the much younger Verlaine and Mallarmé, who wrote enthusiastically about his work in 1865.

It was in fact the generation of Verlaine and Mallarmé that embraced Baudelaire's oeuvre most passionately. In the salons of the Third Republic the heavy scent of his evil flowers was to hang over a whole community of modern artists, affecting writers no less than musicians. Commenting on this influence in 1921, Koechlin went so far as to assert that if Baudelaire had not existed, it would have been necessary for modern French music 'to invent him'. His poems (brought out in complete edition by 1870) were treated to memorable settings by Duparc, Fauré, Chabrier, d'Indy; Debussy completed the extraordinary Cinq poèmes de Baudelaire in 1889 and left among his many unfinished theatre works an opera based on Baudelaire's translation of Poe's *The Fall of the House of Usher*.

Baudelaire's only other contribution to the world of music comes in the form of a long essay on Wagner (published in 1861 after the Paris performance of *Tannhäuser*), in which his attempt to describe the experience of Wagner's music leads him to speculate on the vast system of 'reciprocal analogy' governing all creation. While this theory of correspondence may not transform our understanding of Romantic art, the essay on the whole offers a remarkable opportunity for us to rehear Wagner through the ears of one of the century's most imaginative listeners.

WRITINGS

only those on music

'Richard Wagner et *Tannhäuser* à Paris', L'art romantique, ed. J. Crépet (Paris, 1925), 199–252 [orig. 2 pts, 1st pubd together in

Revue européenne (4 May 1861), suppl.]; Eng. trans. in *The Painter of Modern Life and Other Essays*, ed. J. Mayne (London, 1964), 111–46

SETTINGS

(selective list)

for 1v, pf unless otherwise indicated

R.R. Bennett: Nightpiece, S, tape, 1972 [Les bienfaits de la lune]

A. Berg: Der Wein, S, orch, 1929 [trans. S. George: L'âme du vin, Le vin des amants, Le vin du solitaire]

E. Blackwood: Un voyage à Cythère, S, wind, 1966

E. Bondeville: La cloche fêlée, 1879–88

P. de Bréville: Harmonie du soir, 1879, La cloche fêlée, 1926 [also arr. orch]

H. Büsser: A celle qui est trop gaie, 1943

M. Canal: Bien loin d'ici, Madrigal triste, Recueillement, 1940

A. Caplet: La cloche fêlée, La mort des pauvres, 1922

E. Chabrier: L'invitation au voyage, 1870

G. Charpentier: La cloche fêlée, 1890, L'invitation au voyage, Le jet d'eau [also arr. orch], La mort des amants, Parfum exotique, 1893, La musique, 1894, Les yeux de Berthe, 1895

J. Cras: Correspondances, 1901 [also arr. 1v, str qt]

J. Corigliano: L'invitation au voyage [trans. R. Wilbur], SATB, 1971

C. Debussy: 5 poèmes de Baudelaire: [Le balcon, Harmonie du soir, Le jet d'eau, Recueillement, La mort des amants], 1887–9

E. Denisov: Chant d'automne, S, orch, 1971

A. Diepenbrock: 3 poèmes de Charles Baudelaire [Recueillement [also arr. orch], Les chats [also arr. orch], L'invitation au voyage], 1906–9

H. Duparc: L'invitation au voyage, 1870 [also arr. orch], La vie antérieure, 1884

G. Fauré: Chant d'automne, Hymne, La rançon, 1879

I. Gotkovsky: Poème lyrique: petit opéra, S, B, chbr orch [after Harmonie du soir], 1986

A. Grechaninov: Tsvetïzia [Hymne, L'invitation au voyage, Je t'adore, Harmonie du soir, La mort joyeux], 1909

J. Harvey: Correspondances, 1975

V. d'Indy: L'amour et le crâne, 1884

R. Laparra: La mort joyeux, 1924, Les aveugles, Bien loin d'ici, 1v, fl, pf/hpd, 1902, Maison tranquille [Je n'ai pas oublié], Parfum exotique, Le vin de l'assassin, 1926

C. Loeffler: Harmonie du soir, 1v, va d'amore, pf, *c*1893, La cloche fêlée, 1v, orch, Le flambeau vivant, *c*1902, lost

C. Matthews: Un colloque sentimental [Le jet d'eau], 1971–8

M. Powell: Little Companion Pieces, S, str qt [Méditation], 1980

A. Powers: Souvenirs du voyage [L'invitation au voyage, La vie antérieure, Elévation, Spleen, Recueillement], 1979–80

J.G. Ropartz: Chant d'automne, 1905

N. Rorem: 3 Poems of Baudelaire [trans. Howard: L'invitation au voyage, Le chat, Les litanies de Satan], SATB, 1986

H. Sauguet: Le chat I, II [Dans ma cervelle se promène . . .], 1938

D. de Séverac: Les hiboux, 1898

K. Stockhausen: 3 Lieder, A, orch [trans. Robinson: La rebelle], 1950

L. Vierne: La cloche fêlée, Le flambeau vivant, Les hiboux, Recueillement, Réversibilité, 1919

R. White: Flowers of Evil, musique concrète [trans. White: La cloche fêlée, Harmonie du soir, Le vin des amants, Les hiboux, Brunes et pluies, L'irrémédiable, Le chat, Spleen, Les litanies de Satan], 1969

BIBLIOGRAPHY

Grove6 (L. Beckett); *MGG2* (C. Reynaud))

C. Koechlin: 'Les tendances de la musique moderne française', *EMDC*, II/i (1925), 56–145

L. Maurice-Amour: 'Musiques inspirées par *Les fleurs du mal*', *Revue des sciences humaines* (1958), 167–80

C. Pichois: *Baudelaire* (Paris, 1987; Eng. trans., 1989)

KATHERINE BERGERON

Baudewyn, John. See BALDWIN, JOHN.

Baudiot, (Charles-)Nicolas (*b* Nancy, 29 March 1773; *d* Paris, 26 Sept 1849). French cellist, teacher and composer. He and Lamare joined Baillot in Paris in 1792 to play Boccherini quintets. He was a pupil of the elder Janson and became a cello professor (second class) at the newly founded Paris Conservatoire in 1795. His appointment was suspended in 1802 but he resumed office from 1805 until 1827 when he retired to undertake a number of tours. During the Empire he continued to perform chamber music with Baillot and other faculty members, and joined the Opéra orchestra. He became principal cello in the imperial chapel and retained the post during the Restoration. In 1818 he became a member of the Société Academique des Enfants d'Apollon. Although he was much esteemed in France, the *Allgemeine musikalische Zeitung* of April 1820 described his playing as cold. Fétis, too, inclined to that view, though he praised his pure tone and fine intonation. Baudiot played a Stradivari cello of 1725.

Baudiot's compositions are almost entirely for the cello, including numerous duos, variations and fantasias on popular melodies. He wrote two concertinos and two concertos for the cello, three string quintets and collaborated on works with Pleyel, Herz and Pixis. Late in life he published a number of songs and *romances*. His treatises include a cello method in collaboration with Baillot, Levasseur and Catel (1805/R) and a treatise on transposition (1837–8) with transposition exercises for piano, violin and viola. His *Méthode de violoncelle*, published in two parts (1826 and 1828), continues the tradition of J.L. Duport, but also integrates aspects of B.H. Romberg's technique, including use of the lower strings.

BIBLIOGRAPHY

FétisB; *MGG1* (R. Cotte and F. Cossarte-Cotte)

E. van der Straeten: *History of the Violoncello* (London, 1915/R)

J.-M. Fauquet: *Les sociétés de musique de chambre à Paris de la restauration à 1870* (Paris, 1986)

R. Benton: *Pleyel as Music Publisher: a Documentary Sourcebook of Early 19th-Century Music* (Stuyvesant, NY, 1990) [incl. list of Baudiot's pubd works]

V. Walden: *One Hundred Years of Violoncello: a History of Technique and Performance Practice, 1740–1840* (Cambridge, 1998)

HUGH MACDONALD/VALERIE WALDEN

Baudo, Serge (*b* Marseilles, 16 July 1927). French conductor. He was the son of an oboe teacher and studied at the Paris Conservatoire, winning *premiers prix* in conducting and other subjects, and making his début in 1950 at the Concerts Lamoureux. He conducted frequently in Paris, toured for the Jeunesses Musicales de France until 1958 and in 1959 was appointed conductor of the Nice-Côte d'Azur RO. From 1962 to 1965 he was resident conductor at the Paris Opéra, and he was invited by Karajan to conduct *Pelléas et Mélisande* at La Scala in 1962. He made his début at the Metropolitan in 1971 in *Les contes d'Hoffmann*, returning in the following three seasons. Baudo has conducted many notable premières, including Menotti's *L'ultimo selvaggio* (as *Le dernier sauvage*, 1963, Paris), Milhaud's *La mère coupable* (1966, Geneva), Messiaen's *Et exspecto resurrectionem mortuorum* (1965, Chartres) and *La Transfiguration* (1969, Lisbon) and works by Daniel-Lesur, Dutilleux, Nigg and Ohana. He was appointed principal conductor of the Orchestre de Paris in 1967 and music director of the Lyons Opera, 1969–71. After becoming music director (1971–87) of the Rhône-Alpes PO (from 1972 the Lyons National Orchestra), he founded and directed an annual Berlioz Festival to include the composer's operas, but resigned in 1989 when a curtailment of funds put an end to the operatic performances. Baudo has specialized in French and Russian music, giving performances imbued with subtlety and passion, and has composed a number of works including film scores. Among his most impressive recordings are orchestral works by Debussy, Dutilleux, Ravel and Poulenc, *Pelléas et Mélisande* and the symphonies and choral works of Honegger. He has been created a Chevalier of the Légion d'Honneur and awarded the Ordre National de Mérite and the Ordre des Arts et des Lettres.

BIBLIOGRAPHY

J.L Holmes: *Conductors: a Record Collector's Guide* (London, 1988), 30–31

NOËL GOODWIN

Baudouin des Auteus (*fl* 1st half of the 13th century). Trouvère. The two works attributed to him are both of disputed authorship. Two settings of *M'ame et mon cors doing a celi* (R.1033) are extant, one in *F-Pa* 5198 and related manuscripts, the other in the Chansonnier du Roi and Noailles Chansonnier (*F-Pn* fr.844 and 12615). The latter unexpectedly couples an isometric poem of *pedes-plus-cauda* construction with a non-repetitive melody. The other song attributed to him is *Avril ne mai, froidure ne let tans* (R.283). The early suggestion that this poet was the Baudouin who appears in jeux-partis with Thibaut IV is now regarded with scepticism.

For general bibliography *see* TROUBADOURS, TROUVÈRES.

THEODORE KARP

Baudrexel, Philipp Jakob (*b* Füssen, Swabia, 2 May 1627; *d* Mainz, 23 March 1691). German composer and priest. He studied first with Johann Rudolph von Rechberg, Dean of Eichstätt and a canon of Augsburg Cathedral, who in the early 1640s sent him to Rome, where in 1644 he entered the Collegio Germanico. He studied composition with Carissimi, the director of music there. Baudrexel entered the priesthood in 1651, and three years later became parish priest of Kaufbeuren, Swabia, and a canon and director of the choir at Augsburg Cathedral. He retained these appointments until 1672, when he became court chaplain to Margrave Bernhard Gustav of Baden-Durlach at Fulda. After the margrave's death in 1679 Baudrexel went to Mainz as court chaplain to the Elector Karl Heinrich von Metternich. In the autumn of 1679 the elector died, but Baudrexel stayed in Mainz, first as court Kapellmeister and then from 1684 as director of music at the cathedral. Ill-health made the last two years of his life comparatively inactive.

It was for the choir at Augsburg Cathedral that Baudrexel published two collections of church music, the only publications of his about whose authenticity there can be no doubt. They are *Primitiae Deo et Agno coelestis hierarchiae cantatae* (Innsbruck, 1664) and *Psalmi vespertini de Dominica ... cum hymnis de communi* (Cologne, 1668). They contain settings of the canticles, antiphons and motets for four, five and eight voices (*Te lucis ante terminum* from the second volume in A. Gottron, ed.: *Dreihundert Jahre Mainzer Kirchenmusik*, Mainz, 1943).

It has been suggested that Baudrexel may have been the translator of the German version of Carissimi's *Ars cantandi* that was published as an appendix to a musical tutor in 1692 by J. Koppmayer; unfortunately no copy of the original tutor seems to survive. (The attribution to Baudrexel of some organ pieces in F. Commer, ed.: *Collection des compositions pour l'orgue des XVI, XVII, XVIII siècles*, i, iii, Leipzig, 1866, seems unconvincing.)

BIBLIOGRAPHY

W.C. Printz: *Historische Beschreibung der edelen Sing- und Kling-Kunst* (Dresden, 1690/R)
A. Steinhuber: *Geschichte des Collegium Germanicum-Hungaricum in Rom* (Freiburg im Breisgau, 1895, 2/1906)
J. Sieber: 'Die Pfarrer von St. Martin in Kaufbeuren', *Die Glocken von St. Martin* (Kaufbeuren, 1930)
E.F. Schmid: 'Philipp Jakob Baudrexel, ein Füssener Komponist des 17. Jahrhundert', *Festschrift zum 1200-jährigen Jubiläum des heiligen Magnus* (Füssen, 1950), esp. 89–99
T.D. Culley: *Jesuits and Music*, i: *A Study of the Musicians connected with the German College in Rome during the 17th Century and of their Activities in Northern Europe* (Rome, 1970), esp. 207–8

GWILYM BEECHEY

Baudrier, Yves (Marie) (*b* Paris, 11 Feb 1906; *d* Paris, 9 Nov 1988). French composer. Essentially self-taught, he turned seriously to composition relatively late, having trained for law. Between 1929 and 1933 he took lessons with Georges Loth, organist of the Sacré-Coeur, and he received advice from Messiaen after their meeting in 1935. The next year he was a co-founder with Messiaen, Jolivet and Daniel-Lesur of the group La Jeune France, formed in opposition to the neo-classical tendencies prevailing in French music; he was the author of the group's manifesto. At about this time he had lessons in counterpoint with Daniel-Lesur at the Schola Cantorum. His subsequent career was associated largely with music for the cinema: he taught at the Institut des Hautes Etudes Cinématographiques (1945–60) and composed a number of film scores. In later years persistent ill-health curtailed his composing and other activities.

The association with Messiaen is rather misleading: Baudrier's music has a great deal more in common with that of Honegger. One of his most important works is *Le musicien dans la cité* (1937), an orchestral piece composed for an imaginary film. Its 'scenario' concerns a composer who wanders the streets of Paris at night, encountering 12 situations illustrated in the continuous movements of the suite. The plan has something in common with that of the *Pictures at an Exhibition*, though Baudrier's gift for the picturesque is not so sharp as Musorgsky's, and his orchestration is rather plainer than Ravel's. The score's most distinctive feature is its slightly bitter grotesque quality. In 1964 it was revised to accompany a television film.

WORKS

Dramatic: Treize histoires liées par un fil de flûte (ballet radiophonique, L. Masson), 1967; film scores incl. Bataille du rail (dir. R. Clément), 1945, Les maudits (dir. Clément), 1947, Château de verre (dir. Clément), 1950, Le monde du silence (dir. J.Y. Cousteau and L. Malle), 1956; music for theatre and TV
Orch: Raz de Sein, sym. poem, 1936; Le musicien dans la cité, poème cinématographique, 1937, rev. 1947, rev. 1964; Eleonora, sym. suite, after E.A. Poe, ondes martenot, small orch, 1938; Le grand voilier, sym. poem, 1939; Sym., 1945; Prélude à quelque sortilège, 1953
Other works: Str Qt no.1, 1944; 2 poèmes de Tristan Corbière, Bar, pf, 1944; 2 poèmes de Jean Noir (J. Cassou), 1v, pf/str, 1946; Cantate de la Pentecôte, pt 3, 1952, other pts by M. Constant and M. Rosenthal; Adjuva Domine – credo, solo vv, boys' chorus, chorus, orch, 1960; Str Qt no.2 'Autour de Mallarmé', 1961

Principal publishers: Amphion, Choudens, Editions Françaises de Musique, Eschig

BIBLIOGRAPHY

S. Gut: *Le groupe Jeune France* (Paris, 1977)

PAUL GRIFFITHS

Baudron, Antoine Laurent (*b* Amiens, 15 May 1742; *d* Paris, 1834). French composer and violinist. After attending the Jesuit college in Amiens, he studied violin in Paris with Pierre Gaviniés. He joined the orchestra of the Comédie-Française in 1763 and became its leader and conductor in 1766; in this position he was responsible for the composition (or arrangement) of stage music for both old and new plays. He collaborated with Beaumarchais from 1770 and probably wrote the famous air 'Je suis Lindor' (from *Le barbier de Séville*) which Mozart later used as the theme of his 12 Variations K354/299*a*. At the request of the actor Larive, he composed new music for Rousseau's *Pygmalion* (1780), the Divertissement in *Le roi de Cocagne* (1781) and the *airs* in *Le mariage de Figaro* (1784), with the exception of the final vaudeville, which is Tissier's tune for *La fauvette*. He composed little after the Revolution but was greatly revered at the Comédie-Française and retired in 1822 on a pension equal to his full salary.

WORKS
all printed works published in Paris

STAGE
first performed at Paris, Comédie-Française, unless otherwise stated

Les amazones modernes (3, M.-A. Legrand and L. Fuzelier), 18 Aug 1770, lost
Le barbier de Séville, ou La précaution inutile (4, P.-A. Beaumarchais), 23 Feb 1775 (1775), many arrs. of excerpts pubd
Pygmalion (scène lyrique, J.-J. Rousseau), 11 Sept 1780, lost [with some of Rousseau's original music]
Le roi de Cocagne (3, Legrand), 19 Feb 1781
Pyrame et Thisbé (scène lyrique, Larive), 2 June 1783, lost
La folle journée, ou Le mariage de Figaro (Beaumarchais), 27 April 1784, excerpts pubd (1785), collab. Beaumarchais
Les trois cousins (G.-D.-T. Levrier-Champ-Rion), Paris, République, 18 June 1792 (1792)
Andante, orch introduction to Les deux amis, ou Le négociant de Lyon (5, Beaumarchais), 13 Jan 1770 (1770)
Other stage works, some lost

OTHER WORKS
Vocal: L'amant mécontent (P.-L. Moline), ariette, S, 2 vn, va, bn, bc (1763); Les plaintes inutiles, ariette (1764); Le portrait de Lise, ariette (*c*1770); Vaudeville d'Epiménide à Paris, gui acc. (n.d.); 6 ariettes, 1v, 2 vn, va, bc, ad lib obs, hns, op.5 (1773), lost; other works, many lost
Inst: Symphonie (1765), lost; 3 symphonies, op.1 (1766); 6 trios, 2 vn, b, ?op.2 (1767), lost; 6 quartetti, ?op.3 (1768), lost; 6 duetti, 2 vn, op.4 (1769), lost; 6 duetti, 2 vn (1770), lost; 6 duo d'amateurs (1776), lost; other works, lost

BIBLIOGRAPHY
BrookSF; Choron-FayolleD; FétisB
E.H. Mueller von Asow: 'Der Komponist des "Je suis Lindor"': Themas', *Wiener Figaro*, xii/Aug (1942), 11
F. Lesure: 'A propos de Beaumarchais', *RdM*, liii (1967), 175–8
P. Robinson: *Beaumarchais et la chanson: musique et dramaturgie des comédies de Figaro* (Oxford, 1999)

PHILIP E.J. ROBINSON

Bauer, Harold (*b* Kingston-upon-Thames, 28 April 1873; *d* Miami, 12 March 1951). American pianist of English birth. Born into a musical family, he began to study the violin at the age of six with his father and subsequently with Adolf Politzer, giving his first concerts by the time he was ten. At 15 he appeared in recital playing both the violin and the piano; he was compared unfavourably with Josef Hofmann, who had recently made his London début, and was advised to concentrate on only one instrument. He continued to study the violin and moved to Paris with the intention of establishing himself as a soloist. Again, he found himself at a disadvantage in that both Kreisler and Thibaud had recently made impressive début appearances, and had to turn to mundane accompaniment work to support himself. Having been intro-

duced by the English pianist Graham Moore to Paderewski in London, Bauer renewed his acquaintance and was asked to play the second piano part for him while he was preparing a number of concertos. Paderewski secured other work for him, arranged for him to play in Russia and advised him to study intensively in order to pursue a career as a pianist. Bauer felt that it was too late for him to study in a conventional sense, and accordingly developed a highly personal method based on a quasi-balletic approach in which technical problems were resolved in terms of gestural responses to musical considerations. This method served Bauer so well that he soon became acknowledged as a player of formidable powers. In 1899 he made highly successful appearances in Scandinavia and the Netherlands and played with the Vienna PO under Richter, and in 1900 he made his American début with the Boston SO in the Brahms D minor concerto. Over the following years he became especially associated with the works of Beethoven, Schumann and Brahms, and in addition to his tours of the USA and Europe he also visited Australia and East Asia, becoming highly respected for the seriousness of his approach and his lack of mannerism.

Bauer was also drawn to the music of the French school, giving the Paris première of Debussy's *Children's Corner* suite and introducing Ravel's G major Concerto in New York (he had previously received the dedication of the same composer's *Ondine*). In addition he played virtuoso music by Alkan and Saint-Saëns, and was a champion of the avant garde of the day, featuring the works of Schoenberg, Skryabin, Laparra and others on his programmes. Equally, he maintained an affection for 17th- and early 18th-century keyboard composers. He was also active as a chamber musician, performing in trios with Thibaud and Casals and forming a piano duo partnership with Gabrilowitsch.

In 1917 Bauer took American citizenship, and in 1919 he founded the Beethoven Society of New York. He later became president of the Friends of Music of the Library of Congress and was associated with various educational establishments, most notably the Manhattan School of Music, where he was head of the piano department, continuing on its advisory board until his death. In the intellectuality of his approach and his lack of egocentricity, Bauer represented a more modern outlook than that of many of his contemporaries; yet his self-effacement did not preclude a degree of personal vision, as reflected in his transcriptions and editions of works by Franck, Schumann and Musorgsky. He was also highly inventive in his use of colouristic pedal effects, which he developed through his study of French music. He wrote *Harold Bauer, his Book* (New York, 1948).

CHARLES HOPKINS

Bauer, Joseph Anton (*b* Elbogen [now Loket], Bohemia, 17 June 1725; *d* ?Würzburg, 30 Aug 1808). Bohemian composer, trumpeter and keyboard player. He received his earliest trumpet tuition from his father, a tailor and town musician, and at the age of 23 he became court trumpeter to the Bishop of Augsburg. After further study, and after an impressive performance at the archbishop's court in Würzburg, he was appointed court trumpeter with a handsome salary; he also gained a reputation there as a good keyboard teacher. Bauer was only a dilettante composer. His published works, which appeared between 1770 and 1776, are quartets for keyboard, flute, violin and cello. They all exhibit the same four-movement scheme: fast (sonata allegro)–slow–minuet and trio–fast. The keyboard is treated largely as a solo instrument; the flute is of secondary importance and the strings are almost exclusively handled as accompanimental components of the ensemble.

Bauer's daughter Catharina (*b* Würzburg, 1785), a noted keyboard player and composer in Würzburg, studied with her father and later with F.X. Sterkel; at the age of 13, she published a set of 12 keyboard variations op.1. This was followed by *12 Variationen über 'Wenn Lieschen nur wollt'* (op.2, 1799) and *12 Variationen über 'A Schisserl und a Reindl'* (op.3, *c*1799); Fétis also mentioned two collections of German dances and waltzes by a C. Bauer published in Munich, but these are likely to be by Charlotte Bauer.

BIBLIOGRAPHY

Choron-FayolleD; EitnerQ; FétisB; GerberL; GerberNL; MCL; SchillingE
O. Kaul: *Geschichte der Würzburger Hofmusik im 18. Jahrhundert* (Würzburg, 1924)
J. Saam: *Zur Geschichte des Klavierquartetts bis in die Romantik* (Strasbourg, 1933, 2/1977)

ELLWOOD DERR

Bauer, Marion Eugénie (*b* Walla Walla, WA, 15 Aug 1882; *d* South Hadley, MA, 9 Aug 1955). American composer, teacher and writer on music. She studied in Portland, Oregon, and in Paris and Berlin, her teachers including Boulanger, Gédalge, Huss and Pugno. During twelve Summers between 1919 and 1944 she visited the Mac-Dowell Colony where she produced many of her compositions and met other important women composers including Amy Beach, Mabel Daniels, Miriam Gideon and Ruth Crawford. Bauer taught music history and composition at New York University (1926–51), was affiliated with the Juilliard School of Music from 1940 until her death and lectured widely. Open to various styles, she was a champion of American music and modern composers, as evidenced by her participation in many organizations, e.g. founding member of the American Music Guild (1921), the Society of American Women Composers, the ACA and the AMC. She was secretary for the Society for the Publications of American Music, and a board member for the League of Composers and the ACA. Frequently she was the only woman in a position of leadership in these associations.

Like many women of her generation, she focussed her initial compositional activity on songs and piano solos. Her works of the 1930s and 40s were larger and more significant. Despite brief experiments with 12-note writing in the 1940s and 1950s, her music rarely ventured beyond extended tonality, emphasizing colouristic harmony and diatonic dissonance. Her compositions remained melodic in focus and grounded in 3rd-based harmony and periodic rhythm even when functional tonality was blurred. On occasion energetic rhythm propelled her works. In the 1920s her music had been seen as that of a left-wing modernist, but by the 1940s it was deemed conservative yet well-crafted. During her lifetime her music received many performances, including the 1947 première of *Sun Splendor* by the New York Philharmonic conducted by Stokowski and a 1951 Town Hall concert devoted to her music. Also recognized were her influence as a music critic and her intellectual approach to new music, demonstrated in writings such as *Twentieth Century Music* (New York, 1933, 2/1947). Addressing general readers as well as

music specialists, her writings were widely published in journals; she also wrote a number of other books, and was editor of the *Musical Leader*.

WORKS
(*selective list*)

INSTRUMENTAL

Orch: A Lament on an African Theme, op.20a, str, 1927; Sun Splendor, ?1936; Sym. Suite, op.34, str, 1940; Pf Conc. 'American Youth', op.36, 1943, arr. 2 pf (1946); Sym. no.1, op.45, 1947–50; Prelude and Fugue, op.43, fl, str, 1948, rev. 1949
Chbr: Up the Ocklawaha, op.6, vn, pf (1913); Sonata no.1, op.14, vn, pf, 1921, rev. 1922; Str Qt, op.20, 1925; Fantasia quasi una sonata, op.18, vn, pf, 1925; Suite (Duo), op.25, ob, cl, 1932; Sonata, op.22, va/cl, pf, 1932; Concertino, op.32b, ob, cl, str qt/str orch, 1939, rev. 1943; Trio Sonata no.1, op.40, fl, vc, pf (1944); 5 Pieces (Patterns), op.41, str qt, 1946–9, no.2 arr. double ww qnt, db, 1948; Aquarelle, op.39/2a, double ww qnt, 2 db, 1948; Trio Sonata no.2, op.47, fl, vc, pf, 1951; Ww Qnt, op.48, fl, ob, cl, bn, hn (1956)
Kbd (pf solo unless otherwise stated): From the New Hampshire Woods, op.12, 1921; 3 Preludettes, 1921; 6 Preludes, op.15, 1922; Turbulence, op.17/2, 1924; A Fancy, 1927; Sun Splendor, ?1929, arr. 2 pf, ?1930; 4 Pf Pieces, op.21, 1930; Dance Sonata, op.24, 1932; Moods (3 Moods for Dance), op.46, 1950; Anagrams, op.48, 1950; Meditation and Toccata, org, 1951
Other inst: Prometheus Bound (incid music, Aeschylus), 2 fl, 2 pf, 1930; Pan and Syrinx [choreog. sketch for film], op.31, fl, ob, cl, pf, vn, va, vc (1937)

VOCAL

Choral: Wenn ich rufe an dich, Herr, mein Gott (Ps xxviii), op.3, S, women's chorus, org/pf, 1903; Fair Daffodils (R. Herrick), women's chorus, kbd (1914); Orientale (E. Arnold), S, orch, 1914, orchd 1932, rev. 1934; The Lay of the Four Winds (C.Y. Rice), op.8, male chorus, pf (1915); 3 Noëls (L.I. Guiney, trad.), op.22 nos.1–3, women's chorus, pf (1930); Here at High Morning (M. Lewis), op.27, male chorus, 1931; The Thinker, op.35, mixed chorus, 1938; China (B. Todrin), op.38, mixed chorus, orch/pf, 1943; At the New Year (K. Patchen), op.42, mixed chorus, pf, 1947; Death Spreads his Gentle Wings (E.P. Crain), mixed chorus, 1949, rev. 1951; A Foreigner Comes to Earth on Boston Common (H. Gregory), op.49, S, T, mixed chorus, pf, 1953
Other vocal: Coyote Song (J.S. Reed), Bar, pf (1912); Send Me a Dream (Intuition) (E.F. Bauer), 1v, pf, 1912; The Red Man's Requiem (E.F. Bauer), 1v, pf (1912); Phillis (C.R. Defresny), medium v, pf (1914); By the Indus (Rice), 1v, pf, 1917; My Faun (O. Wilde), 1v, pf, 1919; Night in the Woods (E.R. Sill), medium v, pf (1921); The Epitaph of a Butterfly (T. Walsh), 1v, pf (1921); A Parable (The Blade of Grass) (S. Crane), 1v, pf (1922); 4 Poems (J.G. Fletcher), op.16, high v, pf (1924); Faun Song, A, chbr orch, 1934; 4 Songs (Suite), S, str qt, 1935, rev. 1936; Songs in the Night (M.M.H. Ayers), 1v, pf (1943); The Harp (E.C. Bailey), 1v, pf (1947); Swan (Bailey), 1v, pf (1947)

MSS in *US-NYamc, US-NYgo, US-NYp, US-Wc,* American Composers Alliance, Mount Holyoke College

Principal publishers: Composers Facsimile Edition/ACA, G. Schirmer, A.P. Schmidt

WRITINGS

with E. Peyser: *How Music Grew: from Prehistoric Times to the Present Day* (New York, 1925, rev. 1939)
with E. Peyser: *Music through the Ages: a Narrative for Student and Layman* (New York, 1932, enlarged 3/1967 by E. Rogers as *Music through the Ages: an Introduction to Music History*)
Twentieth Century Music (New York, 1933/R; 2/1947)
Musical Questions and Quizzes: a Digest of Information about Music (New York, 1941)
with E. Peyser: *How Opera Grew: from Ancient Greece to the Present Day* (New York, 1956)

BIBLIOGRAPHY

EwenD; GroveA (B.H. Renton); GroveW (J.M. Edwards)
M. Goss: *Modern Music Makers* (New York, 1952)
Obituaries: *New York Times* (11 August 1955), *Musical Leader*, lxxxvii/9 (September 1955), 14, 18
A.F. Block and C.Neuls-Bates: *Women in American Music: a Bibliography of Music and Literature* (Westport, CT, 1979)

A.F. Block: 'Arthur P. Schmidt, Music Publisher and Champion of American Women Composers', *The Musical Woman: an International Perspective*, ii, ed. J.L. Zaimont and others (New York, 1987)

P.A. Horrocks: *The Solo Vocal Repertoire of Marion Bauer* (diss., U. of Nebraska, 1994)

E.M. Hisama: *Gender, Politics and Modernist Music: Analyses of Five Compositions by Ruth Crawford (1901–1953) and Marion Bauer (1887–1955)* (diss., City U. of New York, 1996)

J.M. Edwards: 'Bauer, Marion Eugénie', *Jewish Women in America: an Historical Encyclopedia*, ed. P.E. Hyman and D.D. Moore (New York, 1997), 128–30

J. MICHELE EDWARDS

Bauer, Ross (*b* Ithaca, NY, 19 Dec 1951). American composer and conductor. He studied at the New England Conservatory (BM 1975) with John Heiss and Ernst Oster and at Brandeis University (PhD 1984) with Martin Boykan, Arthur Berger and Seymour Shifrin. During the summer of 1982 he was a fellow at Tanglewood, where he worked with Berio. He has taught at Brandeis University (1981–5), Stanford University (1986–8), where he directed the ensemble Alea II, and the University of California, Davis (1988–), where he has founded and directed the Empyrean Ensemble. He also served as a founding member and chair of the Griffin Music Ensemble, Boston (1985–92). His honours include the American Academy & Institute of Arts and Letters Walter Hinrichsen Award (1984), a Guggenheim Fellowship (1988), a prize in the ISCM National Composers Competition (1989) and commissions from the Fromm and Koussevitzky foundations (1991, 1994). He was a MacDowell Colony fellow in 1996.

Bauer's music derives its structure, pitch succession and pitch centricity from relationships between hexachords and the collections of intervals and chords they comprise. An inventive and subtle manipulation of timbre is also characteristic of his work.

WORKS
(selective list)

Orch: Pf Conc., 1990; Halcyon Birds, chbr orch, 1993; Romanza, vn, orch, 1996; Icons, bn, orch, 1997

Chbr and solo inst: Hang Time, cl, vn, pf, 1984; Chimera, fl, cl, hn, vn, va, vc, perc, hp, pf, 1987; Chin Music, va, pf, 1989; Birthday Bagatelles, pf, 1990–93; Anaphora, fl, vn, va, vc, pf, 1991; Tributaries, vc, perf, pf, 1992; Aplomb, vn, pf, 1993; Octet, cl, bn, hn, str qt, db, 1994; Stone Soup, fl, cl, vn, vc, pf, 1995; Motion, vn, vc, pf, 1998; Pulse, cl, va, vc, 1999

Vocal: 4 Honig Songs (E. Honig), S, pf, 1989; Eskimo Songs (trans. J. Houston and L. Millman), Mez, fl, vc, pf, 1992–6; Ritual Frags. (Amerindian), S, fl, cl, vn, vc, perc, pf, 1995

Principal publisher: Peters

RICHARD SWIFT

Bäuerl, Paul. *See* PEUERL, PAUL.

Bauernflöte (Ger.). *See under* ORGAN STOP.

Bauernleier (Ger.). *See* HURDY-GURDY.

Baugé, André (*b* Toulouse, 4 Jan 1892; *d* Paris, 22 May 1966). French baritone. His mother was the soprano Anna Tariol-Baugé and his father, Alphonse, was a teacher of singing. His studies with them led to his début with the Opéra-Comique in 1917 as Frédéric in *Lakmé*. Other roles with the company included Don Giovanni and Pelléas, with the Rossini Figaro as his tour de force. At the Opéra in 1925 he sang Germont in *La traviata* and the title role in Rabaud's *Mârouf*. He appeared at Monte Carlo as Escamillo in 1924. His career took a new turn when at the Marigny Theatre in Paris he sang the title role in the French première of Messager's *Monsieur Beaucaire* in 1925, and from then onwards he became increasingly associated with operetta, enjoying a special success in Lehár's *Paganini*. He also appeared in some early French musical films and after World War II taught at the Ecole Normale. His recordings show a light, high baritone, firmly placed if somewhat dry-toned, better suited to Messager than to Rossini.

J.B. STEANE

Bauld, Alison (Margaret) (*b* Sydney, 7 May 1944). Australian composer. After studying at the National Institute of Dramatic Art, Sydney (1961–2) and working as a stage and television actress, she took a music degree at the University of Sydney in 1967. She moved to England in 1969, studying with Lutyens and Hans Keller and taking a PhD at the University of York in 1974. She won first prize at the Paris Rostrum in 1974 and was music director at the Laban Centre, London (1975–8), then composer-in-residence at the NSW State Conservatorium, Sydney, from 1978; since then she has taught at Hollins College, London. Many of her works have been heard in Europe, including at the Aldeburgh, York and Edinburgh Festivals.

Bauld's output focusses on works with a vocal or dramatic element, such as her ballad opera *Nell* (1988) which, like its antecedents, seeks to find a voice for the harshness of life in early colonial Australia. 'I consciously seek literary, aural and visual stimuli,' she has written. 'When the text is complete I know where I am going.' More recently, she has produced a series of keyboard tutors *Play your Way* (3 vols., 1992) and a novel, *Mozart's Sisters* (1997).

WORKS
(selective list)

Vocal and theatrical: On the Afternoon of the Pigsty (Bauld), female spkr, a melodica, pf, perc, 1971; Humpty Dumpty (Bauld), T, fl, gui, 1972; In a Dead Brown Land, S, Bar, SATB, 2 actors, vn, vc, fl, pipe, a melodica, 1972; Dear Emily (Bauld), S, hp/kbd, 1973; Mad Moll (Bauld), S, 1973; One Pearl (Bauld), S/Ct, str qt, 1973; One Pearl II (Bauld), S, a fl, str, 1973–6; Van Diemen's Land (Bauld), SATB, 1976; I Loved Miss Watson, S, pf, tape, 1977; Banquo's Buried (W. Shakespeare), S, pf, 1982; Richard III (after Shakespeare), v, str qt, 1985; Once upon a Time (Bauld), 5vv, 3 opt. children's vv, chbr orch, 1986; Nell (ballad op, Bauld), 1988; Cry, Cock-a-Doodle-Doo, S, pf, 1989; Exult, children's chorus, org, opt. brass qt, 1990; The Witches' Song, S, 1990; Farewell Already (after Shakespeare), S, ens, 1993; In memoriam Uncle Ken, Bar, pf (1997)

Chbr and solo inst: Concert, (pf, tape)/2 pf, 1974; The Busker's Story, a sax, bn, tpt, vn, db, 1978; Monody, fl, 1985, rev. as Copy Cats, vn, vc, pf, 1985; My Own Island, cl, pf, 1989

Principal publisher: Novello

BIBLIOGRAPHY
P. Griffiths: 'Alison Bauld', *MT*, cxvii (1976), 903–4

N. Amadio: 'Alison Bauld: a Modern Woman Composer', *Hi-Fi and Music* (1979), Feb, 72–7

A. Bauld: 'Sounding a Personal Note', *MT*, cxxxix (1988), 339–40

S. Fuller and N. LeFanu: *Reclaiming the Muse, CMR*, xi (1994)

WARREN BEBBINGTON

Bauldeweyn [Balbun, Balduin, Bauldewijn, Baulduin, Baulduvin, Valdovin], **Noel** [Noe, Natalis] (*b c*1480; *fl* 1509–13). Netherlandish composer. His works combine aspects of the obsolete Netherlandish style of the late 15th century and the newer style of Josquin des Prez and his immediate successors. Bauldeweyn succeeded Jean Richafort as *magister cantorum* of St Rombouts, Mechelen, in 1509 and was in turn succeeded in 1513 by Jacques Champion. The position at St Rombouts was a prestigious one, and the church itself was frequently used by the Burgundian court chapel. No further record of his life or career is known; the documents formerly interpreted as showing his activity at Antwerp Cathedral in 1512–17 and his death in 1529/30 have been shown to refer to two entirely different men, the choirmaster Noel Grant (or Brant) and the canon Nicolaus Bauldini (see Forney). The wide dissemination of his music in Bohemian, Spanish, German, Italian and Netherlandish sources dating from about 1510 to about 1575 is indicative of his high reputation. Seven masses are transmitted with ascriptions to Bauldeweyn, and the vihuelist Valderrábano composed a fantasia on 'un Pleni de una Missa de Bauldoin' otherwise unknown. There are 13 motets ascribed to him, though one of these, *Ave caro Christi cara*, has recently been attributed to Josquin. Contrafacta of two sections of *Missa 'En douleur en tristesse'* circulated as motets also. Of the two secular works ascribed to Bauldeweyn, only the chanson *En douleur en tristesse* (also transmitted with German words) is thought to be by him. Whereas most of Bauldeweyn's motets and one song are preserved in printed sources, none of his Masses reached publication with the possible exception of the *Missa 'Da pacem'* which was printed in 1539 as a work of Josquin

Bauldeweyn was a very skilful and individual contrapuntist and canonic writing in the manner of Josquin and his predecessors formed an important textual role in his music. Characteristic of his generation, more than half his compositions are for five or six voices, and much of his music had a strong harmonic sense and rhythmic drive. None of Bauldeweyn's works can be dated precisely, but differences in style make it possible to trace a tentative chronology; many of these differences also reflect Bauldeweyn's response to the character of the various modes. Early works, such as the six-voice *Missa sine nomine* or the Stabat virgo, both in the phrygian mode, show the occasionally harsh dissonance, low ranges and loose relation of text to music characteristic of late 15th and early 16th century northern style. The tendancy towards full scoring and the use of canon in two or three voices throughout most of *Missa sine nomine*, bring to mind the work of Ockeghem and others and, like the early *Missa 'Myn liefkens bruyn oghen'*, it is characterised both by independence in the contrapuntal lines as well as by imitative textures. Characteristic also of Bauldeweyn's early masses, including the four-voice *Missa sine nomine*, thematic repetition and ostinato are frequently employed as devices for structural expansion and coherence; where these occur at the end of sections they perform crucial elements in drivers to the cadence featuring complex sequences of cambiata and other motifs rather similar to that of mature compositions of Obrecht and Isaac, and works by Josquin. Comparable features characterize the later *Missa 'Da pacem'* and the five-voice *Missa Inviolata* which is the only one of his Masses structured on the old-fashioned cantus firmus principle. By way of contrast the *Missa 'En douleur, en tristesse'* which, like his chanson, is almost entirely canonic in conception, is more florid in style, consisting of long interweaving contrapuntal lines. The latest of the masses is probably the *Missa 'Quam pulchra es'*, a work in which dissonance treatment is thoroughly refined and scoring notably varied; the musical texture is frequently divided in antiphonal fashion, with full six-part writing reserved for important cadences. The recently-discovered motet *Sancta Maria virgo virginum*,

in the same mode (Ionian on F) and for the same number of voices, has many features in common with the mass. The psalm motets *Exaltabo te* and *Benedicam Dominum* (possibly by Stoltzer) are also apparently very late works, and these show an interest in correct text declamation and in appropriate musical expression of the mood, reflecting the influence of Josquin and his followers. Bauldeweyn's music as a whole exhibits a strongly personal style and his best works compare favourably with those of his contemporaries.

WORKS

edition in preparation by B. Nelson
for full source information see Sparks, Nelson

Missa 'Da pacem Domine', 4vv (also attrib. Josquin, Mouton); ed. A. Smijers, *Werken van Josquin des Près: Missen*, iv, fasc.34 (Amsterdam, 1953)
Missa 'En douleur en tristesse' ['Ach Gott wem soll ich's klagen'], 5vv, ed. in MMBel, ix (1963) (on his own chanson)
Missa 'Inviolata', 5vv, *D-Ju* 2
Missa 'Myn liefkens bruyn oghen', 4vv, Ky ed. in Mw, xxii (1962; Eng. trans., 1964) (on popular melody)
Missa 'Quam pulchra es', 6vv (on his own motet), *D-Mbs* 6
Missa sine nomine ('a voce mutata'), 4vv, *I-MOd* Mus.x
Missa sine nomine, 6vv, *I-Rvat*
A fantasia on a Pleni sunt caeli from an otherwise unknown mass was intabulated for lute by Valderrábano, ed. in MME, xxiii (1965)
Ad Dominum cum tribularer, ?5vv (Sup only extant), *I-Bc* A27
Benedicam Dominum, 5vv (also attrib. Stoltzer), ed. in EDM, 1st ser., lxvi (1969) Bauldeweyn
Exaltabo te Deus meus, 4vv, 1519³
Gaude Dei genetrix, 4vv, *CZ-HK* II.A.7 (not listed in Sparks)
Gloriosus Dei apostolus Bartholomeus, 4vv, 1519³
Quam pulchra es, 4vv, 1519³
Qui diligitis Dominum [contrafactum of Bs of Missa 'En douleur en tristesse'], 3vv, 1542⁸
Salve regina, 6vv, *D-Mbs* 34 (Sup of Ockeghem's chanson Je n'ay dueil in Sup)
Sancta Maria, Virgo virginum, 6vv, *E-Bc* M.1967 (not listed in Sparks)
Si vos manseritis [contrafactum of Et ascendit from Missa 'En douleur en tristesse'], 2vv, 1545⁷
Art. 401 Stabat Virgo iuxta crucem, 6vv 2, *D-MÜu* (ant Tota pulchra es in T II; quinta vox missing)
Sum tuus in vita, 5vv, 1540⁷
Tu Domine universorum, 6vv, 1545³
En douleur en tristesse [= Ach Gott wem soll ich's klagen], 5vv (also attrib. Grefinger), ed. H.M. Brown, *Theatrical Chansons of the Fifteenth and Early Sixteenth Centuries* (Cambridge, MA, 1963), ed. in DTÖ, lxxii, Jg.xxxvii/2 (1930/R)

DOUBTFUL AND MISATTRIBUTED WORKS

Ach hülff mich layd, 4vv, attrib. Bauldeweyn, Buchner, Josquin, Pirson
Ave caro Christi cara [= Ave Christe immolate], 4vv, Josquin; ed. A. Smijers, *Werken van Josquin des Près: Motetten*, v, fasc.46 (Amsterdam, 1957)

BIBLIOGRAPHY

G. van Doorslaer: 'Noël Baudoin, maître de chapelle-compositeur, 1480 (?)–1529', *Gulden passer*, viii (1930), 167–80
E.H. Sparks: *The Music of Noel Bauldeweyn* (New York, 1972) [incl. investigation of conflicting attributions, list of works and sources]
H.C. Slim: 'Music in and out of Egypt: a Little-Studied Iconographical Tradition', *MD*, xxxvii (1983), 289–326
K. Forney: 'Music, Ritual and Patronage at the Church of Our Lady, Antwerp', *EMH*, vii (1987), 1–57, esp. 44–5
B. Nelson: 'Pie memorie', *MT*, cxxxvi (1995), 338–45 [incl. discussion of new sources]

EDGAR H. SPARKS/BERNADETTE NELSON

Baulduin, Noel. *See* BAULDEWEYN, NOEL.

Bauman, Thomas (Allen) (*b* Marinette, WI, 10 March 1948). American musicologist. He studied under Daniel

Heartz and others at the University of California, Berkeley, gaining the PhD in 1977 with a dissertation on music and drama. He has taught at the University of Pennsylvania (1977–84), Stanford University (1984–9) and the University of Washington, Seattle. He is currently coordinator of the musicology programme in the Northwestern University School of Music. He has also been an Andrew Mellon Faculty Fellow at Harvard University. His research interests include German opera in the late 18th and early 19th centuries, cultural studies and Mahler.

WRITINGS

Music and Drama in Germany: a Traveling Company and its Repertory, 1767–1781 (diss., University of California, Berkeley, 1977)

'The Music Reviews in the *Allgemeine deutsche Bibliothek*', *AcM*, xlix (1977), 69–85

'Benda, the Germans, and Simple Recitative', *JAMS*, xxxiv (1981), 119–31

North German Opera in the Age of Goethe (Cambridge, 1985)

'The Society of La Fenice and its First Impresarios', *JAMS*, xxxix (1986), 332–54

'Alessandro Pepoli's Renewal of the Tragedia per Musica', *I vicini di Mozart: il teatro musicale tra sette e ottocento: Venice 1987*, 211–20

W.A. Mozart: Die Entführung aus dem Serail (Cambridge, 1987)

'Courts and Municipalities in North Germany', *Man and Music: the Classical Era*, ed. N. Zaslaw (London, 1989), 240–67

ed., with contributing essays, D. Heartz: *Mozart's Operas* (Berkeley, CA, 1990)

'Musicians in the Marketplace: the Venetian Guild of Instrumentalists in the Later 18th Century', *EMc*, xix (1991), 344–55

'Requiem, but no Piece', *19CM*, xv (1991), 151–61

'The Three Trials of Don Giovanni', *The Pleasures and Perils of Genius: Mostly Mozart*, ed. P. Ostwald and L.S. Zegans (Madison, CT, 1993), 133–44

ed., with M. McClymonds: *Opera and the Enlightenment* (Cambridge, 1995) [includes 'Moralizing at the Tomb: Poussins' Arcadian Shepherds in Eighteenth-Century England and Germany', 23–42]

PAULA MORGAN

Baumann, Hermann (Rudolf Konrad) (*b* Hamburg, 1 Aug 1934). German horn player. After studying with Fritz Huth in Hamburg, he was appointed first horn in the Dortmund PO (1957–61) and in the Stuttgart RSO (1961–7). He won the ARD Competition in Munich in 1964, and made his début in 1967 in Strauss's Second Horn Concerto with the Vienna SO under Karl Richter. A turning-point in his career was the decision to give up orchestral playing in 1966 to accept a position as a teacher in the Folkwang Hochschule in Essen, where he became a professor in 1969. He remained there until 1996, with an interlude (1980–83) at the Musikhochschule in Stuttgart. Baumann has toured widely as a soloist and made many recordings, most notably the concertos of Mozart, which he was the first to record on the natural horn (1972, under Harnoncourt), and later recorded on modern horn (under Zukerman). He also recorded concertos by Weber, Strauss and Glier. He has given the first performances of Ligeti's Trio for violin, horn and piano, as well as Hans Georg Pflüger's Horn Concerto, dedicated to him.

EDWARD H. TARR

Baumann, Max Georg (*b* Kronach, upper Franconia, 20 Nov 1917; *d* 18 July 1999). German composer. He studied composition and conducting under Noetel, Blacher and Distler at the Berlin Musikhochschule (1939–43), where he returned as lecturer in 1946, remaining there except for a period as Kapellmeister in Stralsund (1947–9). In 1953 he was appointed professor and from

1963 to 1979 he was in charge of the school music department; he also conducted the Collegium Musicum. He received the arts prize of the city of Berlin in 1953. As a composer he continued the line of Reger and Hindemith, though he introduced new techniques and his cantata *Libertas cruciata* (1963), on letters from Resistance fighters, was the first German composition for stereo radio. Sacred music and organ works stand at the centre of his output; the Passion combines dramatic and liturgical forms, with structural austerity and colourful sonorities. A strong dramatic accentuation is present in the ballet *Pelleas und Melisande* and the oratorio *Der Venus süss und herbe Früchte*, which was composed in homage to Lucas Cranach the elder, photographs of whose paintings are projected during the performance.

WORKS
(selective list)

Orch: Conc. grosso no.1, op.22, str, 1950; Variations, op.29; Suite moderne, op.30, no.1, chbr orch; Pf Conc., op.36, 1952; Petite suite, op.38, 1953; Perspektiven 1, op.55, 1957; II, 1967; Sinfonia piccola, op.65, 1960; Conc., org, str, timp, 1964; Crucifixus, Meditation, 1973

Choral: 4 masses, motets (Ger. and Lat.); Passion, op.63, solo vv, chorus, speaking chorus, orch, 1959; Deutsche Vesper, op.64, 1v, spkr, chorus, orch, 1964; Ankunft des Herrn, op.66, 1960; Geburt des Herrn, op.66, no.1, 1966; Libertas cruciata, dramatic cant., S, spkr, chorus, speaking chorus, orch, 1963; Der Venus süss und herbe Früchte (orat, H. Sachs and others), solo vv, spkr, chorus, orch, 1972; Auferstehung, orat, S, Bar, B, spkr, chorus, speaking chorus, orch, 1980

Stage: Pelleas und Melisande, ballet, op.44, 1954; Das Glockenspiel, op.52, school op, 1956; Die Elixire des Teufels (op, 3, after E.T.A. Hoffmann)

Org: Orgelsuite, op.67 no.1; Psalmi, op.67 no.2, 1962; Sonatine, 1963; 3 Pieces, 1965; Fasciculus pro organo, 1967

Music for amateurs

Principal publishers: Heinrichshofen, Merseburger

BIBLIOGRAPHY

A. Tinz: 'Max Baumann', *Musica sacra* [Regensburg], lxxxiii (1963), 327

K. Kremer: 'Max Baumann: Passion op.63', *Musica sacra* [Regensburg], lxxxvii (1967), 203

E. Weber: 'Max Baumann zum 65. Geburtstag', *Musica sacra* [Regensburg], cii (1982), 375 [with list of sacred works]

E. Weber: 'Prof. Max Baumann zum 70. Geburtstag', *Musica sacra* [Regensburg], cvii (1987), 426

WOLFRAM SCHWINGER/KLAUS KIRCHBERG

Baumbach, Friedrich August (*b* Gotha, bap. 12 Sept 1753; *d* Leipzig, 30 Nov 1813). German composer and writer on music. Between 1777 and 1789 he was intermittently active in the Hamburg theatre, first as a singer and later as a violinist and music director. He also visited St Petersburg (*c*1780), was music director of the newly established theatre in Riga in 1782–3 and appeared in Moscow in 1785. In 1790 he moved to Leipzig, where he wrote the articles on music for J.G. Grohmann's *Kurzgefasstes Handwörterbuch über die schönen Künste* (1794). At the beginning of his career he composed mainly instrumental chamber works, but in Leipzig he published many songs and small instrumental pieces for amateurs. His song *Die Forelle* has been cited as a source of inspiration for Schubert's setting. According to Schilling, he was also a respected piano and mandolin player.

WORKS
all published in Leipzig unless otherwise stated

Vocal: Choix d'airs et de chansons (1792); Lyrische Gedichte vermischten Inhalts, kbd acc. (1792); [3] Duetti notturni, i, pf acc. (1798); Gesänge am Clavier oder Pianoforte, i–ii (Gotha, *c*1798); 3 canzonette, pf acc. (Gotha, n.d.); at least 10 pubd songs, duets, ballads; Komm und hülle mich in deine Schatten, 4vv, *D-Bsb*; aria, S, inst acc., *A-Wn*; 4 thanksgiving cants., *D-GÖl* [no 1st name indicated]

Kbd: 6 sonate, acc. vn obbl, vc (1780); 6 sonates, op.1 (Berlin and Amsterdam, 1781); Air des 3 notes par J.J. Rousseau ... et 24 variations, acc. vn obbl, vc (Berlin, 1792); Russisches Volkslied mit [50] Veränderungen (Gotha, 1793); 3 rondeaux (1798); 3 sonates, acc. vn obbl, vc, op.3 (Bonn, 1805); 6 sonatas, acc. vn, vc, *Bsb*; others mentioned in *GerberNL*, *MGG1* suppl., lost

Other inst: 6 sonates, 2 vn (Dessau, ?1782); Variations sur un allegretto, vn, b (Hamburg, 1799); 3 sonates, vn, b, op.22 (Bonn, 1804); works for gui, mentioned in *MGG1* suppl., lost

Several pieces in contemporary anthologies

BIBLIOGRAPHY

EitnerQ; GerberNL; SchillingE

F. Goebels: '"Die Forelle del Sig. Baumbach": eine Anregungsquelle für Schubert?', *Musica*, xxxii (1978), 152–3

B. Rottermund: 'XVIII-wieczne rosyjskie wariacje fortepianowe kompozytorów profesjonalnych' [18th-century Russian fortepiano variations by professional composers], *Zeszyty naukowe: Akademia muzyczna im. Stanisława Moniuszki w Gdańsku*, xxviii (1989), 155–79 [with Eng. summary]

GUNTER HEMPEL

Baumgarten, Alexander Gottlieb (*b* Berlin, 17 June 1714; *d* Frankfurt an der Oder, 26 May 1762). German philosopher. The founder of aesthetics as a subdiscipline of philosophy, he was the son of a military chaplain in Berlin who had been assistant to the Pietist theologian and pedagogue A.H. Francke. He studied first at the Grauen Kloster school in Berlin, but in 1722 was sent to Francke's well-known school for orphans in Halle. In 1730 he entered Halle University as a student of theology and philosophy, but during this period he frequently went to Jena to attend lectures by the celebrated rationalist philosopher J.C. Wolff, who later, together with Leibniz, became the major influences on Baumgarten's own philosophical theories. In 1735 he received a master's degree with his first major work, the thesis *Meditationes philosophicae*. In 1737 he was appointed professor of philosophy and theology at the university of Frankfurt an der Oder. His several Latin works on metaphysics, ethics and practical philosophy widely influenced the teaching of these disciplines in German universities. Kant thought him one of the greatest philosophers of his time.

Baumgarten's most important contributions were the result of a systematic study of what he was the first to call aesthetics, a subject he introduced into the university curriculum as a branch of philosophy. In his usage, aesthetics treated only in part the problems of beauty. Rather, he created aesthetics as an aspect of empirical psychology concerned with the inferior faculty, that is the faculty of sensible knowledge. For him aesthetics together with logic (superior faculty) constituted a science he labelled 'gnoseology', or a theory of knowledge. He was most concerned with poetic aesthetics; and despite his purpose to give all the arts a place in a total scientific scheme of philosophy, he made little application of his new ideas to music and the other fine arts. However, his student and biographer Georg F. Meier developed these relationships in his *Betrachtungen über den ersten Grundsatz aller schönen Künste und Wissenschaften* (1757); this work influenced the growth of music aesthetics at the turn of the 19th century, for example in the philosophy of Moses Mendelssohn and J.G. Sulzer.

WRITINGS

Meditationes philosophicae de nonnullis ad poema pertinentibus (Halle, 1735/R; Eng. trans., 1954, as *Reflections on Poetry*)

Metaphysica (Halle, 1739)

Ethica philosophica (Halle, 1740, 3/1763/R)

Aesthetica (Frankfurt an der Oder, 1750–58/R)

Initia philosophiae practicae primae acroamatice (Halle, 1760)

Acroasis logica, aucta et in systema redacta a Joanne Gottlieb Toellnero (Halle, 1761)

Jus naturae (Halle, 1763)

ed. J.C. Förster: *Sciagraphia encyclopaediae philosophicae* (Halle, 1769)

ed. J.C. Förster: *Philosophia generalis* (Halle, 1770/R)

BIBLIOGRAPHY

A. Riemann: *Die Ästhetik Alexander Gottlieb Baumgartens* (Halle, 1928)

W. Serauky: *Die musikalische Nachahmungsästhetik im Zeitraum von 1700 bis 1850* (Münster, 1929/R)

H.G. Peters: *Die Ästhetik Alexander Gottlieb Baumgarten und ihre Beziehungen zum Ethischen* (Berlin, 1934)

H.J. Kaiser: 'Musikvermittlung als Vermittlung sinnlicher Erkenntnis', *Musikpädagogische Forschung*, ii (1981), 210–32

GEORGE J. BUELOW

Baumgarten, Karl [Carl] **Friedrich** (*b* Lübeck, *c*1740; *d* London, 1824). German composer, violinist and organist, active in England. He had organ lessons with J.P. Kunzen at Lübeck before he settled in London, at about the age of 18, as organist of the Lutheran Chapel in the Savoy. In addition to serving as an organist, he worked as a teacher, composer and violinist. The imputation made by Haydn, who heard him in London in 1792, that his violin playing lacked energy would seem to be contradicted by the fact that he was a well-known orchestral leader, for example at the Haymarket Theatre in 1763, at Dublin the following year, and for a long period at Covent Garden (1780–94); he was also a violinist in the Duke of Cumberland's band. Burney wrote that Baumgarten had been (1789) 'been so long in England that his merit [was] unknown to his countrymen on the Continent'; and Baumgarten had apparently forgotten his continental connections, for when he met Haydn he could hardly converse in German.

His music for the stage was only moderately successful. Burney wrote that Baumgarten deserved notice 'as an instrumental composer and profound harmonist'. Judging by what was published, this was a generous verdict. His chamber music is written in the style current during the late 18th century in England, in imitation of J.C. Bach, but it is undistinguished and technically undemanding. His organ fugues are archaically 'learned' by comparison with his other work, and rather dull. As an extemporizer at the organ, however, Baumgarten was highly admired; he was respected as a knowledgeable musician and a cultured person of wide interests including astronomy and mathematics. He also had an interest in music theory and wrote an unpublished treatise (*GB-Lbl* Add.36681).

WORKS
all printed works published in London unless otherwise stated

STAGE WORKS
all performed in London

William and Nanny, or The Cottagers (comic op), Covent Garden, 1779

Bluebeard, or The Flight of Harlequin (pantomime), Covent Garden, 1791; Grand March, arr. pf (Dublin, *c*1795)

Ov. to works by W. Shield: Harlequin junior, 1784; Robin Hood, 1784

Songs in pasticcios: Netley Abbey (W. Pearce), 1794, favorite songs (1794); Hercules and Omphale, 1794; Mago and Dago, 1794

OTHER VOCAL

Martin Luther's Hymn sung by Mr Incledon, 1v, bc (before 1800)

The Sailor's Ballad sung by Mr Legar in Perseus and Andromeda, 1v, bc (before 1800)

Charity, an Air ... sung by Mr Incledon (M. Prior), 1v, bc (*c*1800)

INSTRUMENTAL

6 Solos, vn, bc (c1778)
Concertante, ob, vn, va, vc, perf. 23 April 1779
Qt, ob d'amore, vn, va, vc, perf. 27 April 1781
6 Quartettos, op.2 (1781); 3 for vn, ob/fl, va, vc; 3 for 2 vn, ob/fl, vc
6 Quartettos, op.3 (1783); 3 for vn, 2 va, vc; 3 for 2 vn, va, vc
A Celebrated Fugue or Voluntary, hpd/org, no.1(–5) (c1784)
A Periodical Quartetto, fl/ob, vn, va, vc, no.1(–6) (c1785); also for vn, 2 va, vc
3 Capricios, pf/hpd (c1790)
A Grand Concerto, ob/fl/cl, 2 vn, 2 va, 2 fl, 2 bn, 2 hn, vc (c1790)
3 Fugues … each of which has an introductory Prelude, org/hpd/pf (c1798)

BIBLIOGRAPHY
BurneyH
W.T. Parke: *Musical Memoirs* (London, 1830/R)

OWAIN EDWARDS

Baumgarten, Samuel Christian [Christopher Frederick] (*b* c1729; *d* London, will proved 3 Aug 1798). English bassoonist and teacher, probably of German birth. He was in England at least as early as 1750, when he was elected a member of the Royal Society of Musicians. In 1754 and 1758 he took part in the Foundling Hospital performances of *Messiah*. He played at the Three Choirs festivals in Gloucester in 1763, Worcester in 1764 and Hereford in 1765 and was among the four principal bassoonists at the Handel Commemoration in Westminster Abbey in 1784 and in subsequent years; he was also bassoonist at the King's Theatre between 1760 and 1785. He appeared in concert at the Pantheon as late as 1790–91. Baumgarten's name occurs for the last time in the membership book of the Royal Society of Musicians in 1792, after which he retired to Hampstead. The fourth of his 12 children, Charlotte, was the mother of Cipriani Potter; there is no evidence that he was related to Karl Friedrich Baumgarten.

PHILIP H. PETER

Baumgartner [Baumgärtner], **Johann Baptist** [Jean Baptiste] (*b* Augsburg, 1723; *d* Eichstätt, 18 May 1782). German cellist and composer. The son of a flautist at the Augsburg court, he worked in the service of the prince-bishop and at the seminary of St Moritz in Augsburg (1742 and 1749). After the prince's death in 1768 he undertook a series of concert tours in England, Holland, Sweden, Denmark and Germany. For some time he lived in Amsterdam, and about 1774 published a cello tutor in The Hague entitled *Instructions de musique, théorique et pratique, à l'usage du violoncelle*. In 1775 he was appointed to the royal orchestra in Stockholm but never took up the post. He was nevertheless elected to the Swedish Academy of Music the following year. He then undertook further concert tours, including one to Hamburg. In 1777 he played with the flautist Ludwig Gering first in Augsburg and then in Salzburg, where he visited Leopold Mozart. He then travelled to Vienna to play before the Imperial Court. In December 1778 he joined the Hofkapelle of the Prince-Bishop of Eichstätt as a chamber musician with the high salary of 400 gilders.

WORKS

Fugue, vc (Vienna, 1797); Lieder für die Guitarre eingerichtet (Mainz, n.d.)
Arrs. of Fr. op airs, 2 vc, *S-Skma*; Capriccio, vc, *Skma*; Fantasies, vc, *A-Wgm*, *D-DO*; 2 sonatas, vc, b, *S-Skma*; 35 cadenzas, vc, *A-HE*
Lost: 4 concs., vc, orch, [cited by Gerber; 1 listed in Breitkopf catalogue for 1773]; Duo, 2 vc; arrs. of arias, vc

BIBLIOGRAPHY
GerberL
R. Schaal: 'Zur Musikpflege im Kollegiatstift St. Moritz zu Augsburg', *Mf*, vii (1954), 14–15
K.W. Littger: 'Die Eichstätter Hofkapelle bis 1802', *Johann Anton Fils: ein Eichstätter Komponist der Mannheimer Klassik (1733–1760)* (Tutzing, 1983), 70–73
H. Unverricht: 'Prolegomena zu einer Geschichte der Eichstätter Hofkapelle im 18. Jahrhundert', *Sammelblatt des Historischen Vereins Eichstätt*, lxxx (1988), 64–6

HERBERT SEIFERT

Baumgartner, Paul (*b* Altstätten, canton of St Gallen, 21 July 1903; *d* Locarno, 19 Oct 1976). Swiss pianist. He studied with Paul Müller in St Gallen, then with Walter Braunfels in Munich and (from 1925) Cologne, and finally with Eduard Erdmann. From 1927 to 1935 he taught in Cologne, and in 1937 was appointed head of the piano department at the Musikakademie in Basle, where in 1960 he started a series of master classes. From 1953 to 1962 he also taught at the Hanover Akademie für Musik und Theater. Baumgartner gave many concert tours, and played chamber music with, among others, Casals, Pierre Fournier and Végh. Although his repertory was based on the 19th century, he remained a champion of contemporary music; his performances of the complete Beethoven sonatas were also much admired. In 1962 he received the St Gallen Prize for Culture. His recordings included works by Beethoven, Mendelssohn and Brahms, and Bach sonatas with Casals.

BIBLIOGRAPHY
MGG1 (H. Lindlar); SML [incl. discography]
J. Kaiser: *Grosse Pianisten in unserer Zeit* (Munich, 1965, 5/1982; Eng. trans., 1971, with enlarged discography), 99

JÜRG STENZL

Baumgartner, Rudolf (*b* Zürich, 14 Sept 1917). Swiss violinist, conductor and teacher. He studied music at Zürich University and under Stefi Geyer and Paul Müller at the conservatory there, and continued his violin studies in Paris with Flesch and in Vienna with Schneiderhan. He then embarked on a concert career that took him to most European countries as a soloist, and in chamber music as a member of the Stefi Geyer Quartet and later of the Zürich String Trio and the Zürich Chamber Trio. He was also leader of various chamber orchestras. In 1956, with Schneiderhan, he founded the Lucerne Festival Strings, an ensemble of soloists which he continued to direct. With it he toured widely and made numerous successful recordings, many in association with leading soloists, including Fournier, Haskil, Holliger and David Oistrakh. He made arrangements for the ensemble of Bach's *Art of Fugue* and *Musical Offering*, among other works, and directed premières of works by Conrad Beck, Françaix, Krenek, Rafael Kubelík, Ligeti, Martin, Martinů, Ohana, Penderecki, Xenakis and others. Baumgartner taught the violin from 1954 at the Lucerne Conservatory, of which he was appointed director in 1960. From 1969 to 1980 he was also artistic director of the Lucerne Festival.

RUDOLF LÜCK

Baumgartner, Wilhelm (*b* Rorschach, 15 Nov 1820; *d* Zürich, 17 March 1867). Swiss pianist, teacher and composer. His father died when he was young, but his exceptional intelligence assured him of a place at his school and the continuing of his education. In 1833 he was adopted by Joseph Waldmann, a clergyman from Messkirch, Baden, who educated him further. At the age of 14 he was composing and giving music lessons. He attended the Gymnasium in Zürich from 1836 to 1838, and then studied at Zürich University. Resolving to become a professional musician, he studied the piano and theory with Alexander Müller, the director of a number of choirs; Baumgartner was occasionally asked to conduct in his master's absence. Having concluded his apprenticeship after three years, he moved in 1842 to St Gallen, where he taught the piano, gave recitals and composed songs. During this period he was in close contact with Friedrich Kücken, with whom he frequently discussed his compositions; he also became interested in German literature and theology.

On 7 October 1844 Baumgartner gave a farewell recital in St Gallen and moved to Berlin. Here he sought out Mendelssohn, who advised him to study the piano and composition with Taubert. At the same time he gained entry into élite artistic circles, and he often accompanied Jenny Lind in song recitals; his activity as a composer diminished somewhat as he became more receptive to new influences. He followed the news of the political struggles in Switzerland with keen interest, and with a sense of patriotism awakening, he decided to return home to devote himself to the idea of freedom in his capacity as a musician. On 26 February 1845 he left Berlin and made his way back to Switzerland, stopping en route in Leipzig, Dresden and Munich; he arrived in Zürich on 26 April and remained there the rest of his life.

In Zürich, Baumgartner occupied himself chiefly with piano teaching. He gave no recitals (he hated virtuosity for its own sake) and played only in small artistic circles. He was also active as a choirmaster, often taking charge of the so-called Müller Choral Society, directing the city choral society (1851–62) and founding and directing his own male chorus (1862–6), which was later named the Zürich Male Chorus. He also directed the choral society of the canton of Zürich, and from 1849 until 1866 he led the student choral society, for which he was named music director of the university. He contracted tuberculosis in 1866 and died a year later.

Baumgartner's compositions are almost exclusively for the voice and the piano. More than half of his 170 vocal works are solo songs with piano accompaniment; about a quarter are for four-part male chorus, the best-known of which are *O mein Heimatland* op.11 no.1 and *Heisst ein Haus zum Schweizerdegen*, both of which are to texts by Gottfried Keller. His best-known solo song is *Mignon*, a setting of Goethe's *Kennst du das Land*. The subjects of his songs are freedom and the fatherland, love, nature and companionship. Expressive of personal moods and experiences, they are wholly Romantic, though not overly refined or sentimental. His compositions for piano solo consist mostly of dance pieces, character-pieces and songs without words.

BIBLIOGRAPHY

C. Widmer: *Wilhelm Baumgartner: ein Lebensbild* (Zürich, 1868)
K. Nef: 'Die Freunde G. Keller und W. Baumgartner', *SMz*, xlv (1905), 1
L. Gross: *Wilhelm Baumgartner: sein Leben und sein Schaffen* (diss., U. of Munich, 1930)
W. Keller, ed.: *Richard Wagner: Briefe an Wilhelm Baumsgartner 1850–1861* (Zürich, 1976)

LUISE MARRETTA-SCHÄR

Bäumker, Wilhelm (*b* Elberfeld, 25 Oct 1842; *d* Rurich, nr Erkelenz, 3 March 1905). German music historian. After studying philosophy and theology at the University of Bonn, he was ordained a Roman Catholic priest. His chief work is *Das katholische deutsche Kirchenlied*, still the basic study of its topic. The second volume of the work (1883) was originally the completion of a work of the same title begun by K.S. Meister, of which only the first volume had been published (1862); in 1886 Bäumker published an edition of Meister's volume so revised and enlarged with fresh material as to make it quite a new work. In addition to discussing both tunes and texts of the hymns, the study includes a full bibliography of the various collections in which they are found. A third, supplementary volume (1891) brings the subject through the 18th century, and a final volume, edited from Bäumker's papers after his death by Joseph Gotzer, extends the coverage as far as 1909. Bäumker's other works include small monographs on Palestrina, Lassus and the Dance of Death, as well as *Zur Geschichte der Tonkunst in Deutschland*, an account of the German medieval theorists, their treatises, and the beginnings of German vernacular church song.

WRITINGS

Palestrina: ein Beitrag zur kirchenmusikalischen Reform des 16. Jahrhunderts (Freiburg, 1877)
Orlandus de Lassus, der letzte grosse Meister der niederländischen Tonschule (Freiburg, 1878)
'Der Todtentanz: Studie', *Frankfurter zeitgemässe Broschüren*, ii (1881), 175–205
Zur Geschichte der Tonkunst in Deutschland von den ersten Anfängen bis zur Reformation: eine Reihe verschiedener Abhandlungen (Freiburg, 1881)
Das katholische deutsche Kirchenlied, i–iv (Freiburg, 1883–1911/R)
'Niederländische geistliche Lieder nebst ihren Singweisen aus Handschriften des 15. Jahrhunderts', *VMw*, iv (1888), 287–350
Ein deutsches geistliches Liederbuch mit Melodien aus dem XV. Jahrhundert nach einer Handschrift des Stiftes Hohenfurt (Leipzig, 1895)

BIBLIOGRAPHY

MGG1 (F. Haberl)
R. von Liliencron: Review of *Das katholische deutsche Kirchenlied*, *VMw*, ix (1893), 333–53
J. Gotzen: Foreword to *Das katholische deutsche Kirchenlied*, iv (Freiburg, 1911/R)

J.R. MILNE/BRUCE CARR

Baur. French family of musicians.

(1) **Jean Baur** (*b* Bouzonville, Moselle, 1719; *d* ?Paris, after 1773). Composer and harpist. He settled in Paris in 1745, four years before Goepfert introduced the pedal harp there. He used the pedal harp in his chamber works, and his sonatas with clavecin or fortepiano accompaniment mark him as the earliest known composer to differentiate between the harp and keyboard instruments. His daughter Marie-Marguerite Baur (*b* Paris, 1748; *d* Paris, after 1790) was also a harpist; she made her début at the Concert Spirituel in 1762.

WORKS
all published in Paris between 1763 and c1773

6 sonates, vc, b, op.1; 6 sonates, avec plusieurs pièces en sons harmoniques, vc, op.2; Sonates, fl/vn, bc, 2 sets (1761); Qt, fl, vn, b, hp (1769); Premier recueil d'ariettes de différents auteurs, acc. hp, op.4; Deuxième recueil d'airs connus, avec quelques préludes et caprices propres à exercer les mains, hp, op.5 (c1770); 4 sonates, 2 for hp, clavecin/pf, 2 for hp, vn ad lib, op.6 (?1773); 4 sonates: 2 for hp, clavecin/pf, 2 for hp, vn ad lib, op.7; 4 sonates: 2 for hp, clavecin/pf, 2 for harp, vn ad lib, op.8; Premier recueil d'airs, ariettes, menuets et gavottes, avec plusieurs caprices, hp; 6 sonates: 4 for 2 vn, 2 for vn, b

(2) **Barthélemy Baur** [*le fils*] (*b* Paris, 1751; *d* Tours, 1823). Harpist and composer, son of (1) Jean Baur. He settled in Tours, where he and his wife taught the harp,

the piano and singing. His two known works, both published in Paris, are a *Recueil d'ouvertures* op.1 (*c*1771) arranged for harp, and *Trois sonates* for harp op.2, both with ad lib accompaniment for violin and cello.

(3) Charles-Alexis Baur (*b* Tours, 1789; *d* London, after 1820).

Harpist, pianist, teacher and composer, son of (2) Barthélemy Baur. From 1805 he studied with his parents and then with F.-J. Naderman in Paris. In 1820 he settled in London as a teacher. His compositions, all for harp, include six sonatas opp.1–2, duets with piano and flute, a collection of *ariettes* and an arrangement of Grétry's *La caravane du Caire*.

BIBLIOGRAPHY

FétisB; HoneggerD; MCL, i; SainsburyD

J.D. Champlin and W.F. Apthorp, eds.: *Cyclopedia of Music and Musicians*, i (New York, 1888), 134

F. Vernillat: 'La littérature de la harpe en France au XVIIIe siècle', *RMFC*, ix (1969), 162–86

H. Charnassé and F. Vernillat: *Les instruments à cordes pincées* (Paris, 1970), 43

ALICE LAWSON ABER-COUNT

Baur, Jürg (*b* Düsseldorf, 11 Nov 1918). German composer and teacher. He rose to prominence at the age of 18 when his first string quartet was given its première by a professional quartet at the Düsseldorf Hindenburg secondary school. Between 1937 and 1948 he attended the Cologne Musikhochschule as a pupil of Jarnach (composition), Karl Hermann Pillney (piano) and Michael Schneider (organ and sacred music), though his studies were interrupted by the war; he later studied musicology at Cologne University (1948–51). In 1946 he was appointed lecturer in music theory at the Düsseldorf Conservatory and from 1952 to 1960 he was choirmaster and organist at St Paulus, also in Düsseldorf. During 1960 Baur held a scholarship from the Federal German government to study at the Villa Massimo in Rome for six months; he returned to Rome for a second stay in 1968 and was guest of honour there in 1980. He was director of the Düsseldorf Conservatory (1965–71) and was appointed professor in 1969. In 1971 he succeeded B.A. Zimmermann as teacher of composition at the Cologne Musikhochschule, remaining there until 1990. Baur's many distinctions include the Recklinghausen Young Generation Prize (1956), the Robert Schumann Prize of the city of Düsseldorf (1957), the Federal Cross of Merit (first class, 1970), and honorary membership of the German Music Council (1988), the North Rhine-Westphalia Service Award and the City of Duisburg Music Prize (1994).

Born in the generation between Blacher and Henze, Baur achieved widespread recognition as a composer fairly late in his career. Under the influence of Jarnach, he had already encountered the music of Bartók, Stravinsky and Hindemith in the late 1930s, but after the war he heeded Jarnach's advice in avoiding the more extreme manifestations of the musical avant garde. The works of the early 1950s maintain Jarnach's principles of economy of means and formal clarity, with Bartók as the most obvious stylistic model. Baur only gradually turned his attention to dodecaphonic techniques, studying the music of Webern with particular intensity. However, although serial structures influenced his musical thinking, especially in the String Quartet no.3 (1952), the *Quintetto sereno* (1958), also notable for its use of aleatory effects, the Sonata for two pianos (1957) and the *Ballata romana*

(1960), Baur's sound world seems far removed from the Expressionism of the Second Viennese School. During the early 1960s Baur strove to achieve an accessible yet modern style that remained independent of the avant garde. His most successful works at this time include the exhilarating *Concerto romano* for oboe and orchestra (1960–61) and *Romeo und Julia* (1962–3), in which the tragic elements of Shakespeare's play are distilled into a powerful and cohesive entity. In accordance with his desire to maintain links with past traditions, Baur then developed a strong predilection for the quotation of earlier music in his work, though without the ironic, dissociative tone of many of the collage compositions of this period. The range of musical inspiration is surprisingly wide, encompassing such composers as Schumann, Dvořák, Bartók, Johann Strauss, Gesualdo, Mozart and Schubert. Primarily a composer of orchestral and instrumental music, Baur has produced some radical works for less mainstream instruments such as the recorder and the accordion. Although he has rarely written for the theatre, his vocal music demonstrates a remarkable sensitivity to poetic texts, the extended choral work *Perchè* (1967–8, after Ungaretti) numbering among his most powerful compositions.

WORKS

ORCHESTRAL

Conc., str, 1941–8; Overture, 1946–50; Partita über 'Wie schön leuchtet der Morgenstern', tpt, str, 1946–91; Carmen Variations, 1947; Va Conc., 1951–2; Musik, str, 1952; Sinfonia montana, 1953; Concertante Music, pf, orch, 1958; Concertino, fl, ob, cl, str, timp, 1959; Conc. romano, ob, orch, 1960–61; Romeo und Julia, 1962–3; Piccolo mondo, 1963; Lo specchio, 2 cycles, 1965–6; Sym. Prologue, 1966; Pentagramm, wind qnt, orch, 1966; Abbreviaturen, 13 str, 1969; Conc. ticino, cl, orch, 1970, arr. a sax, orch, 1995; Giorno per giorno, in memoriam B.A. Zimmermann, 1971; Musik mit Robert Schumann, 1972; 4 Portraits, vc, orch, 1972; Sinfonia breve, 1974; Triton-Sinfonietta, chbr orch, 1974; Conc. da camera 'Auf der Suche nach der verlorenen Zeit', rec, orch, 1975; Conc. no.1 'Ich sage ade', vn, orch, 1976; Conc. no.2, vn, orch, 1978; Sentimento del tempo, wind trio, orch, 1980; Sinfonische Metamorphosen über Gesualdo, 1981; Sinfonie einer Stadt (Patetica), 1983; Fresken, 1984; Konzertante Fantasie, org, str, 1984–5; Sym. no.2 'Aus dem Tagebuch des Alten', 1987; Sinfonietta Sentieri musicali (Auf Mozarts Spuren), 1990; Frammenti-Erinnerungen an Schubert, 1995/6; Sinfonia sine nomine, 1998

INSTRUMENTAL

3 str qts: 1938, 1942–6, 1952

Other chbr: Choralsuite über 'Erhalt uns Herr bei deinen Wort', brass, 1950; Reminiszenen, Ostinato und Trio, wind qnt, 1950–80; Conc. trautonium, str qt, 1955–6, rev. accdn, str qt, 1987; Quintetto sereno, wind qnt, 1958; Metamorphosen, pf, vn, vc, 1959; Kontraste, str trio, 1964; Movimenti, trio, 1969–70; Cinque impressioni, str qt, 1970; Tre studi per quattro, rec qt, 1972; Nonett-Skizzen, 1973; Skizzen, wind qnt, 1974; Kontrapunkte 77 über das Thema des Musikalischen Opfers von J.S. Bach, fl, eng hn, bn, 1978; Pour rien: ostinato senza fine, wind sextet, 1980; Echoi, 2 ob, eng hn, 1980; Festliche Musik, brass, 1982; Ricordi, 3 rec, 1983; Ritratti, perc ens, cel, bass, 1984; Salutio und Jubilus, brass, 1985–6; Cinque fogli, sax qt, 1986; Quintetto pittoresco – passeggiata con M. Ravel, wind qnt, 1986; Passacaglia, 4 tpt, 4 trbn, 1989; Str Qt 'et respice finem', 1992; Petite Suite, 4 fl, 1992; Improvisation und Ostinato, bn qt, 1996

1–2 insts: Erinnerungen, vc, pf, 1941/2, rev. 1985; Sonata in A, vn, pf, 1948; Music, vc, pf, 1950; Fantasy, ob, pf, 1954, rev. eng hn, org, 1994; Suite, hpd, 1956; Ballata romana, cl, pf, 1960, rev. a sax, pf, 1987; Incontri, fl/rec, pf, 1960; Divertimento, hpd, perc, 1961/2, rev. accdn, perc, 1995; Sonata, vn, 1961–2; Dialoge, vc, pf, 1962; Mutazioni, a rec/fl, 1962; 3 Fantasies, gui, 1963; 6 Bagatelles, cl/b cl, 1964; Pezzi uccelli, rec, 1964; Sonata, va, 1969, rev. vc, 1995; Moments musicaux, vn, pf, 1976; 3 Landschaftsbilder, accdn, 1985; 3 Toccatas, accdn, 1985–6; Arabesken, Girlanden, Figuren, double bn, 1990; Marginalien über Mozart, gui, 1991; Reflexionen, gui, org, 1991, arr. gui, accdn, 1992

KEYBOARD

Org: Fantasy B–A–C–H, 1935; 4 Chorale Preludes, 1948; Orgelmusik in E (Toccata, Trio and Passacaglia), 1950; 4 Chorale Preludes, 1954–9; 5 Chorale Preludes, 1959–61; Partita 'Aus tiefer Not', 1965; Choral-Triptychon ('Christ ist erstanden'), 1970; 3 Ricercare über das Thema des Musikalischen Opfers von J.S. Bach, 1977; 2 free org movts and 2 chorale preludes, 1977; Meditazione sopra Gesualdo, 1977; Chorale Prelude 'Verleih uns Frieden gnädiglich', 1980; Fantasia nuova, 1984; 3 Toccatas, 1985/6; Kaleidoskop, 1989; 2 Chorale Preludes on 'Wie schön leuchtet der Morgenstern', 1990; Fragment mit Frescobaldi, 1992

Pf: Ostpreussensuite, 1939; 3 Pieces in the Olden Style, 1941–3; Aphorisms, 1942–6; Sonata, 2 pf, 1952–7; Capriccio, 1953; Variations, 1956; Heptameron, 7 pieces, 1964–5

Hpd: Suite, 1956

VOCAL

Choral (mixed chorus unless otherwise stated): 2 Humoresques (C. Morgenstern, W. Busch), 1948; Triptychon (R.M. Rilke, C.F. Meyer), chorus, orch, 1948–9; 2 Kinderlieder, 1949; 2 Choralsätze, 1950; Wir glauben all an einen Gott, 1950; O süsser Herre Jesu Christ, 1950; 2 Volksliedsätze, 1952; Pfingstmotette 'Wer mich liebt', Bar, chorus, 1955; Abschied, 1955; 2 Männerchöre (Meyer), male chorus, 1957; Du selber bist das Rad (A. Silesius), 1958; Verleih uns Frieden gnädiglich, chorus, insts, 1965, rev. 1980; Perchè (G. Ungaretti), S, T, chorus, orch, 1967–8; Perchè (Ungaretti), 6 Fragments, S, T, chorus, 1969; Die Blume des Scharon, 3 motets, SATB, 1979; Verleih uns Frieden gnädiglich, SATB, 1980

Other vocal: 12 einsame Lieder (various texts), S, pf, 1942–3; Im Waldesschatten, 5 songs (J.F. von Eichendorff), Bar, pf, 1952, rev. Bar, str qt, 1980; Vom tiefinnern Sang, 4 Songs (F.G. Lorca), S, pf, 1957, rev. 1v, cl, str qt, 1989; Herz, stirb oder singe (J.R. Jiménez), 4 songs, S/T, fl, pf, 1960, rev. S, fl, str orch, 1965, rev. S, fl, str qt, 1984; Mit wechselndem Schlüssel, song cycle (P. Celan), Bar, pf, 1967; Senza speranza (M.A. Bustos, Ungaretti), 1v, pf, 1982

INCIDENTAL MUSIC

Anna, Königin für 1000 Tage, 1949; Das Haus der Angst (B. von Heiseler), chorus, orch, 1950; Die Räuber (F. Schiller), 2 songs, 1v, hpd, 1951; Morgen kommt ein neuer Tag (P. Calderón de la Barca), 1952; Audhumla (Segen der Herde), film score, 1952

Principal publishers: Breitkopf & Härtel, Leuckart, Littolf, Peters, Schott, Tonger

WRITINGS

'Wir unterhalten uns über moderne Musik', Der helle Morgen, ed. H. Mentzel (Essen, 1950), 230–39

'Tonsatzlehren auf neuen Wegen', Melos, xx (1953), 43–5

'Anton Weberns Bagatellen für Streichquartett', Neue Wege der musikalischen Analyse, ed. R. Stephan (1967), 62–8

'Das Finale in der Musik des 19. Jahrhunderts: eigenwillige Gedanken zu Wagners "Götterdämmerung"', Götterdämmerung (Düsseldorf, Deutsche Oper am Rhein, 1991), 1–7 [programme notes]

BIBLIOGRAPHY

H. Krellmann: 'Kalkulierte Vision', Musica, xxii (1968), 432–5

H. Krellmann: Ich war nie Avantgardist: Gespräche mit dem Komponisten Jürg Baur (Wiesbaden, 1968)

J. Baur: 'Baur, Jürg', Rheinische Musiker, vi, ed. D. Kämper (Cologne, 1969)

J. Alf: 'Zwischen den Generationen: Jürg Baur', Studien zur Musikgeschichte des Rheinlandes (Cologne, 1978), 55–71

W. Falcke: 'Zum Chorschaffen von Jürg Baur', Lied und Chor, lxxix/8 (1987), 170 only

K. Lang: 'Gespräch mit Jürg Baur', NZfM, cxliv/10 (1983), 18–20

A. Rössler: 'Über die Orgelwerke von Jürg Baur', Kirchenmusiker, xl/1 (1991), 11–18

L.-W. Hesse, A. Klaes and A. Richter, eds.: Jürg Baur: Aspekte seines Schaffens (Wiesbaden, 1993)

ERIK LEVI

Bausewein, Kaspar (b Aub, nr Ochsenfurt, 15 Nov 1838; d Munich, 18 Nov 1903). German bass. He studied in Munich, making his début there in 1854 at the Hofoper, where he was engaged for 46 years. A fine actor, equally gifted for comic and serious opera, he had a wide repertory ranging from Mozart's Figaro and Leporello and Rossini's Don Basilio to Caspar (Der Freischütz) and the three Wagner roles that he created: Pogner in Die Meistersinger (1868), Fafner in Das Rheingold (1869) and Hunding in Die Walküre (1870). He retired in 1900 after a farewell performance as Lord Cockburn in Fra Diavolo.

ELIZABETH FORBES

Baussnern [Bausznern], Waldemar von (b Berlin, 29 Nov 1866; d Potsdam, 20 Aug 1931). German composer. He studied at the Berlin Hochschule für Musik under Friedrich Kiel (1882–5) and completed his studies in Bargiel's masterclass at the Preussische Akademie der Künste, Berlin (1885–8). He briefly served as the conductor of the Mannheim Musikverein in 1891, before becoming conductor of the Mannheim-Ludwigshafen Lehrergesangverein (1891–4). In 1894 he moved to Dresden, where he held the posts of Liedermeister of the Dresdner Liedertafel (until 1901) and director of the Dresdner Bachverein (1896–7). In 1902 he founded the Dresdner Chorverein. He taught composition, instrumentation and score-reading at the Cologne conservatory (1903–8), was the director of the Ducal Orchestral School in Weimar (1908–16), becoming professor there in 1910, and was later director of the Hoch Conservatory in Frankfurt (1916–23). He was appointed Second Permanent Secretary at the Berlin Akademie der Künste in 1923 and combined the post with teaching composition at the Berlin Akademie für Kirchen- und Schulmusik.

True to his classicist teachers, Kiel and Bargiel, Baussnern was committed to the German Classical-Romantic expressive ideal. His works unite contrapuntal formal principles and chromatic polyphony with an exploration of sound characteristic of the New German School. They reveal a particular affinity for the philosophical and suggest a preoccupation with questions surrounding the meaning of existence.

WORKS
(selective list)

OPERAS

Dichter und Welt (J. Petri), 1894, Weimar, 4 June 1897; Dürer in Venedig (3, A. Bartels, after A. Stern), 1897, Weimar, 3 March 1901; Herbort und Hilde (2, E. König), 1901, Mannheim, Hof- und National, 15 Feb 1902; Der Bundschuh (3, O. Erler), 1903, Frankfurt, Stadt, 27 May 1904; Guniöd (P. Cornelius), 1906, Cologne, 15 Dec 1906 [completion of op by Cornelius]; Satyros (2, Baussnern, after J.W. von Goethe), 1922, Basel, 1923

INSTRUMENTAL

Orch: Champagner, ov., 1899; Sym. no.1 'Jugend', 1899; Sym. no.2 'Dem Andenken von Johannes Brahms', 1899; Sym. no.3 'Leben' (Goethe), SATB, orch, 1908; Grussan Wien, waltzes, 1911; Sym. no.4, chbr orch, 1914; Sym. no.6 'Psalm der Liebe' (E.B. Browning, R.M. Rilke), S, orch, 1921; Sym. no.5 'Es ist ein Schnitter, heisst der Tod' (folksong), SATB, orch, 1922; Hymnische Stunden, str, 1925; Sym. no. 7 'Die Ungarische', 1926; Dem Lande meiner Kindheit, 1929; Passacaglia und Fuge, 1930; Sym. no. 8, 1930

Chbr: Str Qt no.1, 1893; Qnt, cl, hn, vn, vc, pf, 1898; Serenade, cl, vn, pf, 1898; Elegie, v/vc, pf, 1911; Dem Lande meiner Kindheit, fl, cl, 3 vn, vc, db, pf, 1914; Sonata, vn, pf, 1917; Str Qt no.2, 1918; Pf Trio 'Weimarer', 1921; Str Qt no.3, 1923; 4 Instrumentalsuiten, 1924: [1] vn, pf, [2] fl, pf, [3] cl, pf, [4] vc, pf, 1924; 6 Choralinventionen, 2 vn, vc, org, 1925; 3 Fantasiestücke, vn, pf, 1925; O bellissima Italia, vn, vc, pf, 1925; Terpsichore, vc, pf, 1925; 3 ernste Stücke, 1927: [1] vn, org, [2] va, org, [3] vc, org

Kbd: Slawische Noveletten, pf, 1895; Sonata eroica, pf, 1906; Thema mit 8 Variationen, 2 pf, 1915; 3 kleine Sonaten, pf, 1916; 2 Präludien und Fugen, pf, 1916; Nächtliche Visionen, pf, 1926;

Duo, 2 pf, 1927; Orgelwerke 1–3, Phantasie, Passacaglia, Sonate, org, 1927; 26 Choralvorspiele, org, 1929

Choral: 3 Lieder für gemischten Chor (R. Hamerling, H. Heine, F. Rückert), 4-part chorus, 1888; Die Geburt Jesu (Bible: *Luke*), Christmotette, S, A, chbr chorus, chbr orch, org, 1911; 2 Chöre (E. von Wildenbruch, Goethe), 4-part chorus, 1911; Das Hohe Lied vom Leben und Sterben (orat, Goethe, F. Hebbel, J. von Eichendorff, F. Schiller, C.F. Meyer, A. Ritter, E. Mörike, Petri, W. von Polenz, F. Nietzsche, M.R. von Stern, G. Keller), S, A, T, B, SATB, orch, 1913; Das Göttliche (Goethe), SATB, orch, 1927; Steigt hinan zu höherm Kreise (Goethe, Arndt, F. von Münchhausen, F. Hölderlin, Meyer, R.G. Binding), 1927; Hafis (cant., Goethe), S, T, B, SATB, orch, org, 1929; 35 men's choruses; folksong and chorale arrs.

Solo vocal: 100 Lieder und Gesange, 1v, pf, 1887; Das klagende Lied (M. Greif), 6 ballads, 1v, pf, 1897; 2 Gesänge (N. Lenau, A. Ritter), S/T, orch, 1900; 3 Gedichte aus Paul Heyses italienischem Liederbuch, v, pf, 1905; Die himmlische Orgel (R. von Volkmann), A/Bar, chbr orch, 1924; 12 Gesänge aus dem Buch der Freundin (Binding), v, pf, 1925; 3 Qnt, female vv; 3 duets, A, Bar; other songs, for 1v, pf; folksong arrs.

Principal publishers: G. Braun, Breitkopf & Härtel, Elwertsche, Gehann, Karl Hochstein, Friedrich Hofmeister, Willy Müller, Ries & Erler, Simrock, Friedrich Vieweg

BIBLIOGRAPHY

H. Keller: 'Waldemar von Baussnern', *AMz*, l (1923), 635–7

F. Ohrmann: 'Waldemar von Baussnern', *Anregungen* [Berlin], special issue no.2 (1926), 1–17

G. Wehle: 'Die Chorkompositionen Waldemar von Baussnerns, *Die Tonkunst*, xxx/31 (1926)

Siebenbürgisches Baussnern-Fest (Hermannstadt, 1926)

P. Bovermann: 'Waldemar von Baussnern als Orgelkomponist', *Zeitschrift für Kirchenmusiker* (1929), 97–100

L. Hess: 'Waldemar von Baussnern als Künstler und Mensch', *Jb der Staatlichen Akademie für Kirchen- und Schulmusik*, v (1931–2), 7–12

G. Wehle: *Waldemar von Baussnerns Orchesterwerke* (Karlsruhe, 1931)

T. Ernst: 'Waldemar von Baussnern und sein Einfluss auf das Musizieren der Jugendbewegung', *Pro musica* (1965), 39–43

G. Wehle: 'Zum 100. Geburtstag Waldemar von Bausznerns', *Musica*, xx (1966), 296

V. Grützner: *Waldemar von Baussnern (1866–1931)* (Potsdam, 1999)

VERA GRÜTZNER

Bautista, Julián (*b* Madrid, 21 April 1901; *d* Buenos Aires, 8 July 1961). Argentine composer of Spanish origin. He started his piano studies very young with Pilar Fernández de la Mora and at the age of 14 began his composition training with the composer Conrado del Campo. Later he taught harmony at the faculty of the Madrid Conservatory. In 1930, together with prominent young composers such as the Halffter brothers, as a member of the Generation of '27, he co-founded in Madrid the Grupo de los ocho (Group of Eight), whose works were characterized by a colourful style with some neo-classical nuances. Bautista's Spanish works (some of which were destroyed when his house was bombarded during the Spanish Civil War) are concise, with diatonic harmony and frequent modulations. The ballet *Juerga* (1921) was first performed in Paris in 1929, and the *Obertura para una ópera grotesca* (1932) won first prize in an international contest sponsored by Union Radio de Madrid. He won two more prizes in 1923 and 1926 with his String Quartets nos.1 and 2 respectively. At the end of the Spanish Civil War he settled in Buenos Aires, his first few years there being largely occupied in the composition of film scores. The output of his Argentine years is low but significant. The *Catro poemas galegos*, which have been compared with Falla's *El retablo* and his Harpsichord

Concerto, present a very simple, archaic and rustic melodic line above pseudo-primitive, harsh harmonies, with great economy of means. This work was performed at the 1948 Amsterdam ISCM Festival. His later style is primarily contrapuntal, using advanced harmonies while maintaining a traditional form. His Second Symphony (1957) is the culmination of his orchestral production. This well constructed cyclical work is based on a melodic cell formed by two minor thirds, one ascending and the other descending, forming a chromatic progression. His last work, the Third String Quartet, represents the culmination of his chamber music. Written in 1958, it was the winner of a chamber music competition in Buenos Aires; formally it is close to Bartók's last quartets and shows the composer in his maturity.

Stage: Interior (drama lírico, 1), 1920, destroyed; Juerga (ballet-pantomima, 1), 1921

Orch: All'antica, suite, 1932; Obertura para una ópera grotesca, 1932; Sinfonía breve, 1956; Sym. no.2 'Ricordiana', 1957

Vocal: Flûte de jade, 1v, pf, 1921; 3 ciudades (F. García-Lorca), S, orch, 1937; Cantar del Mío Cid (cant., R. Alberti, after El Cid Campeador), solo vv, chorus, orch, 1947; 4 poemas galegos (L. Varela), 1v, fl, ob, cl, va, vc, hp, 1948; Romance del Rey Rodrigo, chorus, 1956

Chbr: 3 str qts, 1922–3, 1926, 1958; Sonata concertata a 4 no.2, pf, str, 1938; several gui pieces

Pf: Colores, suite, 1921; 3 preludios japoneses, 1927

BIBLIOGRAPHY

ARS [Buenos Aires] (1961) [Bautista issue]

J. Vinton, ed.: *Dictionary of Contemporary Music* (New York, 1971)

R. García Morillo: *Estudios sobre música argentina* (Buenos Aires, 1984)

M. Ficher, M. Furman Schleifer and J.M. Furman: *Latin American Classical Composers: a Biographical Dictionary* (Lanham, MD, and London, 1996)

SUSANA SALGADO

Bauyn Manuscript (*F-Pn* Vm⁷ 674–5). *See* SOURCES OF KEYBOARD MUSIC TO 1660, §2(ii).

Bawdwine, John. *See* BALDWIN, JOHN.

Bawr, (Alexandrine-)Sophie (Goury de Champgrand), Mme de [Comtesse de Saint-Simon, Baronne de Bawr; M. François] (*b* Paris, 8 Oct 1773; *d* Paris, 31 Dec 1860). French composer and author. Though born out of wedlock to a marquis and an opera singer, she was recognized and reared by both parents. In her early years she took lessons from the singer Pierre Garat and the composers Grétry and Nicolas Roze and sang her own songs in salons (she was also an accomplished pianist). She was encouraged in composition by Adrien Boieldieu and the singer Jean Elleviou and may have been friendly with the singer-composer Sophie Gail. During her long life she published, mainly as Mme de Bawr, a number of touching and harmonically expert songs, wrote history books, novels, stories, one-act plays, *mélodrames*, as well as an opera. Some of her writings were translated into German or Spanish. An early feminist, she argued in her writings that the position of women in the arts needed to be improved.

She was briefly married (1801–2) to the social theorist Claude Henri de Rouvroy, Comte de Saint-Simon (1760–1825); Grétry was a witness at the wedding. She ran a salon for Saint-Simon so that he might meet prominent musicians and writers. She illegally retained the title 'Comtesse' after marrying the young Russian Baron de

Bawr in about 1809; however, de Bawr soon died (in about 1810). Left penniless, Mme de Bawr turned to a more systematic professional musical career that lasted decades. During the Bourbon Restoration, she was granted a pension by Louis XVIII.

For the *Encyclopédie des dames* she wrote an *Histoire de la musique* (Paris, 1823) and she published her memoirs, *Mes souvenirs* (Paris, 1853).

WORKS
(selective list)

Stage: Les chevaliers du lion (mélodrame, 3, Bawr), lib (Paris, 1804), ?music lost; Léon, ou Le château de Montaldi (op, 3, Bawr), Paris, Théâtre de l'Ambigu-Comique, 22 Oct 1811, lost; Un quart d'heure de dépit (oc, 1), 1813–22, music lost, lib in *F-Pan*

Songs (romances, for 1v, pf, hp or gui): D'aimer besoin puissant (Viot), after 1800; J'étais heureux (Paris, after 1800); A la mémoire d'un être chéri (O, toi qui ne peux plus m'entendre) (Bawr), in *Le souvenir des ménestrels*, no.20 (1814), 78–9

BIBLIOGRAPHY

FétisB; FétisBS; DBF; MGG1 suppl. (R. Cotte); *SchmidlD*

C. Gardeton: *Annales de la musique ... pour l'an 1819* (Paris, 1819), 11 only

C. Gardeton: *Bibliographie musicale de la France et de l'étranger* (Paris, 1822)

J.C.F. Hoefer: *Nouvelle biographie générale* (Paris, 1859)

E. Gagne [E. Moreau]: *Mme de Bawr: étude sur sa vie et ses oeuvres* (Paris, 1861)

J. Janin: Obituary, *Journal des débats* (14 Jan 1861)

H. Gougelot: *Catalogue des romances parues sous la Révolution et l'Empire* (Melun, 1937–43), i, 174 only

H. Gougelot: *La romance française sous la Révolution et l'Empire* (Melun, 1938–43), i, 147 only

R.P. Locke: *Music, Musicians, and the Saint-Simonians* (Chicago and London, 1986), 25–6

RALPH P. LOCKE

Bax, Sir Arnold (Edward Trevor) (*b* Streatham, 8 Nov 1883; *d* Cork, 3 Oct 1953). English composer. Recognized between the wars as one of England's leading young symphonic composers, he wrote evocative, sometimes challenging scores that retained the impulse of a Romantic style.

1. Life. 2. Works. 3. Critical and public acceptance.

1. LIFE.   Bax attended the RAM (1900–05), where he studied composition with Corder; he won a Macfarren Scholarship after two years, but did not attract as much recognition as his contemporaries Benjamin Dale and York Bowen. Though he developed a commanding piano technique, he had no inclination to pursue a career as a performer. He did appear from time to time, however, as an accompanist at the London Music Club, where he was heard by Debussy and Schoenberg. It was his brother Clifford, a writer and playwright, who introduced him to poetry and to Ireland. Influenced by W.B. Yeats's poem *The Wanderings of Oisin*, Bax visited the west coast of the country in 1902, an experience he described (1943) with the proclamation: 'the Celt within me stood revealed'. Fortunate to have a private income, he was able to travel extensively as a young man. Ireland was a favourite destination; for many years he returned to the remote Donegal village of Glencolumbkille for weeks at a time. In his autobiography, he also describes extended visits to Dresden in 1906 (during which he heard an early performance of Strauss's *Salome*) and 1907, and to Russia in 1910. Following his marriage to Elsita Sobrino, the daughter of soprano Luisa and pianist Carlos Sobrino, he moved to Dublin, where he and his wife lived until the spring of 1914. In Ireland he adopted the pseudonym Dermot O'Byrne, under which he published poetry, short

stories and three of his four plays, two of which may have been intended as opera librettos.

Between 1911 and the outbreak of World War I, Bax attended all six London seasons of the Ballets Russes. He had already written the Russian ballet score *King Kojata* (1911), which, although never orchestrated, provided musical material for a number of other works. A heart condition made him unfit for military service and although he acted as a special constable at one point, the war seems to have had remarkably little effect on his life or music. A far more profound impact came from the Easter Rising in Dublin in 1916 and the subsequent execution of its leaders, some of whom he knew. He documented these events in his poetry, which, when printed in 1918 as *A Dublin Ballad and Other Poems*, was banned by the British censor.

During the war, Bax had a passionate love affair with the pianist Harriet Cohen and in 1918 he left his wife and two children for her. In the mid-1920s he met Mary Gleaves and for over 20 years maintained relationships with both women. With peace he became one of the leading younger composers of the day, a position reinforced by performances of the significant new works he had written during the war. On the return of the Ballets Russes, he became acquainted with the ballerina Tamara Karsavina, for whom he wrote *The Truth About the Russian Dancers* (1920, rev. 1926), borrowing some of the music from his aborted ballet *King Kojata*. During the 1920s, at the height of his success, he completed his first three symphonies, some choral works, a variety of shorter pieces and chamber music. Although he was briefly considered the leading British symphonist, the première of his Fifth Symphony (15 January 1934) was shortly followed by premières of Vaughan Williams's Fourth Symphony (10 April 1935) and Walton's First Symphony (incomplete, 3 December 1934; complete, 6 November 1935).

In the late 1930s Bax wrote less and less, remarking that he wanted to 'retire, like a grocer'. His knighthood in 1937 came as a surprise to him, as did the post of Master of the King's Music in 1942. At the beginning of World War II he concentrated on his autobiography, *Farewell, My Youth* (London, 1943), a witty sequence of vignettes of people he had met and places he had visited before 1914. He moved to Sussex and for the rest of his life lived in a room above the bar at The White Horse, Storrington. Among his late works are scores for the films *Malta GC* (1942) and *Oliver Twist* (1948), both of which became popular in the concert hall. When Cohen damaged her right hand in 1948, he composed a *Left-Hand Concertante* (1949) for her. By the end of his life much of his earlier music had been forgotten. He was represented to the public by his late and, on the whole, less demanding output, resulting in a somewhat negative critical assessment followed by a long-term neglect of his works after his death. His full output, however, has since been performed and recorded.

2. WORKS.   Bax's early works consist mainly of songs and piano music, but also include the short tone poem *Cathaleen-ni-Hoolihan* (1903–5) and a few other compositions performed while he was a student. Early songs, such as his setting of William Allingham's *The Fairies* (1905), are notable for their complex piano parts, doubtless reflecting his activity as an accompanist at the time. With *The White Peace* ('Fiona Macleod', 1907), one

Arnold Bax, mid-1920s

of his most popular songs, this tendency became less pronounced. Attempts to write an opera on the story of Deirdre produced a five-act libretto and some musical sketches, but these resulted in the tone poems *Into the Twilight* (1908) and *Roscatha* (1910) rather than an operatic work.

Influenced by the orchestral technique of Wagner, Strauss, Glazunov, Sibelius, Debussy, Ravel and Stravinsky, Bax developed a vivid orchestral style. His first popular success came with the impressionistic tone poem *In the Faery Hills* (1909, rev. 1921), conducted by Henry Wood at the 1910 Proms. This succinct and attractive piece is full of characteristic features and its programme, culled from Celtic folklore, indicates the importance of literature in spurring Bax's creativity. Increasingly complex orchestral music followed, not all of which was performed; the technically difficult tone poem *Spring Fire* (1913), for example, was not heard until long after his death. During World War I, Bax wrote the tone poems *The Garden of Fand* (1913–16), *November Woods* (1917) and *Tintagel* (1917–19), all of which sublimate personal emotion in favour of a musical evocation of nature. In the latter two, the sonata matrix which was to dominate many of his symphonic movements can be discerned, but in each case the poetic programme changes the formal emphasis, resulting in individual structures. At first considered challenging and new, these works quickly found a ready public. *Tintagel* remained in the repertory when much of Bax's music was no longer heard. *In memoriam* (1917), on the other hand, written in memory of Patrick Pearse who was executed with the leaders of the Dublin Easter Rising, was not performed until it was recorded by Handley and the BBC PO in 1998.

Irish events are also reflected in a succession of chamber works and in some of Bax's most striking Irish songs. The First String Quartet (1918), which brings a classical clarity of texture and form to its Celtic inspiration, includes a particularly beguiling folksong-like third movement; the Second Quartet (1925), written in a much grittier and more demanding idiom, features some of Bax's most determined contrapuntal writing. The Viola Sonata (1922), the Phantasy Sonata for viola and harp (1927) and the Sonata for Flute and Harp (1928), later arranged as Concerto for Seven Instruments (1936), are typical examples of Bax's tributes to friends such as Lionel Tertis, Raymond Jeremy, May Harrison, Maria Korchinska and Leon Goossens.

Bax produced a romantic Skryabinesque piano sonata as early as 1910. During World War I he wrote a second, an introspective single movement like the first, and in 1921 a third in three movements. The last of these, orchestrated and given a new slow movement that combines eerie stillness with sudden crises, became the First Symphony (1922). The score is both fiercely new, and still romantic in impulse. Contemporary commentators saw the music as Bax's reaction to the war; Bax was ambivalent, however, and it seems more likely that the work reflected his reaction to the Irish events of Easter 1916. This supposition is reinforced by the subjective and passionate Second Symphony (1924, orchestrated 1926), the slow movement of which quotes from and extends the climactic running string motif of *In memoriam*.

During the late 1920s, Bax's attempts to take his orchestral music forward led to a number of false starts. Eventually, after the lightweight *Overture, Elegy and Rondo* (1927), he completed the Third Symphony (1929). This became a pivotal work which, thanks to Wood, enjoyed a short-lived but wide public success. *Winter Legends* (1930) for piano and orchestra followed. Both of these works are in three movements and include extended reflective closing sections ('epilogues'), one of the most distinctive features of Bax's style. During the 1930s Bax wrote four more symphonies, broadly similar in form and language to the first three. In the Fourth (1931), associations between music and nature create a serene emotional character. The Fifth (1932), overtly influenced by Sibelius, includes a popular finale and epilogue in which a grandly reiterated chorale theme builds to a brilliant climax. The Sixth (1934), tautly realized and full of memorable invention and colourful, idiosyncratic orchestration, represents the pinnacle of Bax's symphonic writing. In both the ternary slow movement and tripartite finale, Bax evolves a form that reconciles the competing elements of orchestral tone poem and symphonic development. The final climax and haunting epilogue suggest a passing of worlds; only at the very end of the work is the serenity for which Bax had been searching for 30 years finally achieved.

In the late 1930s Bax worked on the Violin Concerto (1937–8) and the Seventh Symphony (1938–9), both of which are in a more relaxed idiom than the earlier music. In his last years he composed comparatively little, though as Master of the King's Music he wrote *Morning Song* (1946), a short piece for piano and orchestra for Princess Elizabeth's 21st birthday, obligatory fanfares for the 1947 royal wedding and a *Coronation March* (1953).

3. CRITICAL AND PUBLIC ACCEPTANCE. During his lifetime, Bax saw his works widely performed; only a

small proportion of his output achieved popularity, however, and certainly until the 1930s his music was considered new and difficult. Nevertheless, his works were championed by many artists. He began to be promoted for his later music during World War II, and in the late 1940s a limited repertory of relatively undemanding compositions – the Seventh Symphony, the Violin Concerto, the two film scores *Malta GC* and *Oliver Twist*, the *Morning Song* and the *Left-Hand Concertante* – kept his name in the public eye. These works did little to affirm his critical acceptance among a new generation of critics, however. Only *The Garden of Fand* and *Tintagel* remained in circulation from his earlier output.

The BBC broadcast of Bax's symphonies during 1954–5 and Cohen's broadcast of *Winter Legends* in 1954 introduced a new generation to Bax's music. The Third Symphony was recorded under the auspices of the British Council during World War II, and smaller record companies recorded the Fourth in 1964 and the Sixth in 1967. During the 1970s pioneering revivals of Bax's early orchestral music by the Kensington SO under Leslie Head led the BBC to schedule a number of Bax centenary programmes. These in turn led to further recordings, particularly by Chandos, of Bax's music supported by the Arnold Bax Charitable Trust (established 1985).

WORKS

DRAMATIC

King Kojata (Tamara) (ballet), pf, 1911; Between Dusk and Dawn (ballet), 1917; The Frog Skin (ballet), 1918, lost; The Truth about the Russian Dancers (incid music, J.M. Barrie), 1920, rev. 1926; Malta GC (film score), 1942, orch suite, 1943; Golden Eagle (incid music, C. Bax), 1945; Oliver Twist (film score), 1948, orch suite, 1948; Journey into History (film score), 1952

ORCHESTRAL

Tone poems: Cathaleen-ni-Hoolihan, small orch, 1903–5; A Song of Life and Love, 1905, lost; A Song of War and Victory, 1905; Into the Twilight, 1908; In the Faery Hills, 1909, rev. 1921; Roscatha, 1910; Christmas Eve on the Mountains, 1911, rev. *c*1921; Nympholept, 1912–15; The Garden of Fand, 1913–16; The Happy Forest, 1914–21; November Woods, 1917; Tintagel, 1917–19; The Tale the Pine-Trees Knew, 1931; A Legend, 1944

Syms.: Sym., F-f, op.8, 1907 [not orchd]; Spring Fire, sym., 1913; Sym. no.1, E♭, 1922; Sym. no.2, e and C, 1924–6; Sym. no.3, 1929; Sym. no.4, 1931; Sym. no.5, 1932; Sym. no.6, 1934; Sym. no.7, 1938–9

With solo inst(s): Sym. Variations, E, pf, orch, 1918; Phantasy (Conc.), d, va, orch, 1920; Winter Legends, sinfonia concertante, pf, orch, 1930; Vc Conc., 1932; Saga Fragment, tpt, str, pf, perc [arr. of pf qt]; Vn Conc., 1937–8; Concertino, pf, orch, 1939, unfinished; Morning Song (Maytime in Sussex), pf, orch, 1946; Concertante, eng hn, cl, hn, orch, 1948–9; Concertante (Conc.), pf LH, orch, 1949; Variations on the Name Gabriel Fauré, hp, str, 1949 [also for pf]

Other works: Variations (Improvisations), 1904; A Connemara Revel, 1905; An Irish Ov., 1906; Festival Ov., 1911, rev. 1918; Symphonietta, 1911, unfinished; 4 Pieces (4 Sketches, 4 Irish Pieces), 1912–13, rev. as 3 Pieces, 1928 [Prelude to Adonais, 1912, lost; Summer Music, 1917–20, rev. 1932; Sym. Scherzo, 1917, rev. 1933 [arr. of pf work]; Russian Suite, 1919 [arr. of 1912–15 pf works for Diaghilev]; Mediterranean, 1922 [arr. of 1920 pf work]; Cortège, 1925; Romantic Ov., chbr orch, 1926; Northern Ballad no.1, 1927–31; Ov., Elegy and Rondo, 1927; Prelude for a Solemn Occasion (Northen Ballad no.3), 1927–33; Ov. to a Picaresque Comedy, 1930; Sinfonietta, 1932; Northern Ballad no.2, 1933–4; Ov. to Adventure, 1936; Rogue's Comedy Ov., 1936; London Pageant, march and trio, 1937; Paean, 1938 [arr. of 1920 pf work]; Work in Progress, ov., 1943; Victory March, 1945 [based on film score Malta GC]; Coronation March, 1952; 9 fanfares

CHAMBER AND SOLO INSTRUMENTAL

Str Qt, A, 1902; Str Qt, E, 1903; Concert Piece (Fantasy), vn/va, pf, 1904; Trio, vn, va/cl, pf, 1906; Str Qnt, G, 1908; Sonata no.1, vn, pf, 1910, rev. 1915, 1920, 1945; 4 Pieces, fl, pf, 1912 [from ballet

King Kojata]; Legend, vn, pf, 1915; Pf Qnt, g, 1915; Sonata no.2, vn, pf, 1915, rev. 1921; Ballad, vn, pf, 1916; Elegiac Trio, fl, va, hp, 1916; In memoriam, eng hn, hp, str qt, 1917; Str Qt no.1, 1918; Folk Tale, vc, pf, 1918; Hp Qnt, 1919; Lyrical Interlude, str qnt 1922 [arr. of Str Qnt, 1908, slow movt]; Ob Qnt, 1922; Pf Qt, 1922; Sonata, va, pf, 1922; Sonata, E♭, vc, pf, 1923; Str Qt no.2, 1925; Phantasy Sonata, va, hp, 1927; Sonata no.3, vn, pf, 1927; Sonata, fl, hp, 1928; Sonata, F, vn, pf, 1928; Legend, va, pf, 1929; Nonet, fl, ob, cl, hp, str qt, db, 1930 [arr. of Sonata, F, 1928]; Valse, hp, 1931; Sonatina, vc, pf, 1933; Str Qnt, 1933; Octet, hn, pf, str sextet, 1934; Sonata, cl, pf, 1934; Conc., fl, ob, hp, str qt, 1936 [arr. of Fl Sonata, 1928]; Str Qt no.3, 1936; Threnody and Scherzo, bn, hp, str sextet, 1936 [arr. bn, hp, str orch]; Rhapsodic Ballad, vc, 1939; Legend-Sonata, vc, pf, 1943; Pf Trio, B♭, 1946

CHORAL

Fatherland (J.L. Runeberg, trans. C. Bax), T, chorus, orch, 1907, rev. 1934; Enchanted Summer (P.B. Shelley: *Prometheus*), 2 S, chorus, orch, 1910; Of a Rose I Sing a Song (15th century), chorus, hp, vc, db, 1920; Mater ora Filium (Balliol College MS), SSAATTBB, 1921; Now is the Time of Christymas (15th century), male vv, fl, pf, 1921; This Worldes Joie (c1300), chorus, 1922; The Boar's Head (15th century), male chorus, 1923; I sing of a Maiden that is Makeless (15th century), SAATB, 1923; St Patrick's Breastplate, chorus, orch, 1923; To the Name above every Name (R. Crashaw), S, chorus, orch, 1923; Walsinghame (16th century, attrib. W. Raleigh), T, chorus, orch, 1926; Wonder, hymn, 1930; The Morning Watch (H. Vaughan), chorus, orch, 1935; 5 Fantasies on Polish Christmas Carols, unison Tr, str, 1942; 5 Greek Folksongs, chorus, 1942; To Russia (J. Masefield), Bar, chorus, orch, 1944; Gloria, chorus, org, 1945; Nunc dimittis, chorus, org, 1945; Te Deum, chorus, org, 1945; Epithalamium (E. Spenser), chorus, org, 1947; St George, Bar, chorus, org, 1947–8, unfinished; Magnificat, chorus, org; 1948 [arr. of 1906 song]; What is it like to be young and fair (C. Bax), SSAAT, 1953 [composed for A Garland for the Queen]

SONGS

A Celtic Song Cycle (F. Macleod), 1904, rev. 1922: Eilidh my Fawn, Closing Doors, Thy dark eyes to mine, A Celtic Lullaby, At the last; The Fairies (W. Allingham), 1905; Golden Guendolen (W. Morris), 1905; The Song in the Twilight (F. Bax), 1905; When We are Lost (D. O'Byrne [Bax]), 1905; Magnificat (Bible: *Luke*), 1906; A Milking Sean (Macleod), 1907; The Enchanted Fiddle (B. Bax), 1907; The Flute [Ideala] (B. Bjørnson, trans. E. Gosse), 1907; The White Peacock (Macleod), 1907; A Lyke-Wake (Border Ballad), 1908; Shieling Song (Macleod), 1908; A Christmas Carol (15th century), 1909; Lullaby (S. McCarthy), 1910; To Eire (J. Cousins), 1910; Roundel (G. Chaucer), 1914; Parting (A.E.), 1916; The Splendour Falls (A. Tennyson), 1917

Green grow the rashes O! (R. Burns), 1918; I have house and land in Kent (trad.), 1918; The Maid and the Miller (trad.), 1918; O dear! what can the matter be? (trad.), 1918; Variations sur Cadet Rousselle (trad.), 1918 [with Bridge, Goossens and Ireland]; When I was one and twenty (A.E. Housman), 1918; Youth (C. Bax), 1918; Le chant d'Isabeau (Fr. Can. trad.), 1920; Traditional Songs of France, 1920: Sarabande, Langueo d'amours, Me suis mise en danse, Femmes, battez vos marys, La targo; 5 Irish Songs, 1921: The Pigeons (P. Colum), As I came over the grey, grey hills (J. Campbell), I heard a piper piping (Campbell), Across the door (Colum), Beg-Innish (J.M. Synge)

3 Irish Songs (Colum), 1922: Cradle Song, Rann of Exile, Rann of Wandering; The Market Girl (T. Hardy), 1922; I heard a Soldier (H. Trench), 1924; Wild Almond (Trench), 1924; Carrey Clavel (Hardy), 1925; Eternity (R. Herrick), 1925; In the Morning (Housman), 1926; On the Bridge (Hardy), 1926; Out and away (J. Stephens), 1926; Watching the Needleboats (J. Joyce), 1932; Dream Child (V. Newton) (1957); 75 unpubd songs

OTHER VOCAL

Rune of Age (Macleod), 1v, orch, 1905 [orch score lost]; Viking Battle Song (Macleod), 1v, pf, 1905 [orch score lost]; Nocturnes (R. Dehmel, O.E. Hartleben), 1911; 3 Orch Songs, 1914: A Celtic Lullaby (Macleod) [arr. of 1904 song], A Christmas Carol (15th century) [arr. of 1909 song], Slumber-Song (McCarthy) [arr. of 1910 song]; The Bard of the Dimbovitz (Rom. trad.), Mez, orch, 1914, rev. 1946; The Song of the Dagger, Bar, orch, 1914; Glamour (D. O'Byrne [Bax], R. Newton), 1921; 3 Songs, 1v, orch, 1934: A Lyke-Wake [arr. of 1908 song], Wild Almond (Trench) [arr. of 1924 song], The Splendour Falls (Tennyson) [arr. of 1917 song]; Eternity (Herrick), S, orch, 1934 [arr. 1925 song]

PIANO

Fantasia, a, duo, 1900; Concert Valse, Eb, 1910; Sonata no.1, 1910, rev. 1917–21; 2 Russian Tone Pictures, 1912: May Night in the Ukraine, Gopak; Scherzo, 1913; In the Night, 1914; A Mountain Mood, 1915; Apple-Blossom-Time, 1915; In a Vodka Shop, 1915; The Maiden with the Daffodil, 1915; The Princess's Rose Garden, 1915; Sleepy Head, 1915; Winter Waters, 1915; Dream in Exile, 1916; Nereid, 1916; Moy Mell (The Pleasant Plain: an Irish Tone Poem), duo, 1917; A Romance, 1918; On a May Evening, 1918; The Slave Girl, 1919; Sonata no.2, 1919, rev. 1920; What the Minstrel told us, 1919; Whirligig, 1919; A Hill Tune, 1920; Burlesque, 1920; Country-Tune, 1920; Lullaby, 1920; Mediterranean, 1920; Paean, 1920; Lento con molto espressione, 1921; Sonata no.3, 1926; Hardanger, duo, 1927; The Poisoned Fountain, duo, 1928; Ceremonial Dance, 1929; The Devil that Tempted St Anthony, duo, 1929; Serpent Dance, 1929; Sonata, duo, 1929; Water Music, 1929; Red Autumn, duo, 1931; Sonata no.4, 1932; Legend, 1935; O Dame get up and bake your pies, 1945; Suite for Fauré, 1945 [orchd 1949]; 4 Pieces, 1947; 2 Lyrical Pieces, 1948 [from film score Oliver Twist]; juvenilia, incl. 3 sonatas

ARRANGEMENTS

Campion: Jack and Jone, 1v, pf, 1918; Lyadov: Dance Prelude, Lament of the Swan Princesses, orch, 1919, lost; Chopin: Ballad, Ab, orch, 1921, lost; Vivaldi: Conc., RV 540, hp, str qt, 1927; J.S. Bach: Fantasia, BWV572, pf (1932)

Principal publisher: Chappell

Principal recording companies: Chandos, Lyrita, Naxos

BIBLIOGRAPHY

E. Evans: 'Arnold Bax', MT, lx (1919), 103–5, 154–6

J. and W. Chester: Arnold Bax (London, 1921)

E. Evans: 'Arnold Bax', Cobbett's Cyclopedic Survey of Chamber Music (London, 1929–30; enlarged 2/1963/R by C. Mason)

R.H. Hull: A Handbook on Arnold Bax's Symphonies (London, 1932)

R.H. Hull: 'Approach to Bax's Symphonies', ML, xxiii (1942), 101–15

A. Bax: Farewell, my Youth (London, 1943/R) [autobiography]

J. Herbage: 'Sir Arnold Bax', British Music of our Time, ed. A.L. Bacharach (Harmondsworth, 1946, R/1951), 113–29

N. Demuth: 'Arnold Bax', Musical Trends in the 20th Century (London, 1952/R), 155–67

D. Cox: 'Arnold Bax', The Symphony, ii, ed. R. Simpson (Harmondsworth, 2/1972), 153–65

Bax Society Bulletin (London, 1968–73)

R.L.E. Foreman: 'Bibliography of Writings on Arnold Bax', CMc, x (1970), 124–40

L. Foreman: 'The Musical Development of Arnold Bax', ML, lii (1971), 59–68

P.J. Pirie: 'More than a Brazen Romantic', Music and Musicians, xix/5 (1971–2), 32–40

C. Scott-Sutherland: Arnold Bax (London, 1973)

L. Foreman: 'Bax and the Ballet', PRMA, civ (1977–8), 11–19

L. Foreman: Dermot O'Byrne: Poems by Arnold Bax (London, 1979)

D. Puffett: 'In the Garden of Fand: Arnold Bax and the "Celtic Twilight"', Art Nouveau, Jugendstil und Musik, ed. J. Stenzl (Zürich, 1980), 193–210

J.C. Hoffpauir: Three Tone-Poems by Arnold Bax (diss., U. of Missouri, Kansas City, 1981)

J.L. Rivers: Formal Determinants in the Symphonies of Arnold Bax (diss., U. of Arizona, 1982)

L. Foreman: 'Arnold Bax at the RAM', RAM Magazine, no.233 (1983), 11–17

A. Payne: 'Bax: a Centenary Assessment', Tempo, no.180 (1984), 29–32

S. Banfield: 'The Celtic Twilight', Sensibility and English Song, i (Cambridge, 1985), 248–74

L. Foreman: Bax: a Composer and His Times (Aldershot, 2/1988)

C.E. Mayfield: The Structural Function of Motives in the Piano Sonatas of Arnold Bax (diss., U. of Kansas, 1993)

D. Andrews, ed.: Cuchulan Among the Guns (Cumnor, 1998) [letters from Bax to C. Whelen; Whelen's writings on Bax]

G. Parlett: A Catalogue of the Works of Sir Arnold Bax (Oxford, 1999)

LEWIS FOREMAN